**W9-APS-907**

Printed in the U.S.A.

Typeset in *The Sans* from LucasFonts.

## ART CREDITS

### FRONT COVER, TITLE PAGE

*top center* Sea World of California/Corbis; *top right* Odysseus Slaying the Suitors (400's B.C.), Penelope Painter. Attic red figure painting on kylix. Height 20 cm. Inv F 2588. Antikensammlung, Staatliche Museen zu Berlin, Berlin. Photo by Juergen Liepe. © Bildarchiv Preussischer Kulturbesitz/Art Resource, New York; *bottom center* Colin Anderson/Getty Images; *bottom* Portrait of William Shakespeare (about 1610), John Taylor.  Oil on canvas. National Portrait Gallery, London. © Bridgeman Art Library; *background* © Walter Geiersperger/Corbis; *bottom left* Ken Kinzie/HMH Publishers.

### BACK COVER

*top left* © Taro Yamasaki/Time Life Pictures/Getty Images; *center* The Granger Collection, New York; *bottom right* Photo by  Mary Altaffer/AP/Wide World Photos; *bottom left* Detail of Ulysses from the Polyphemos group (second century B.C.), Hagesandroa, Polydoros, and Athenodoros. Sperlonga, Italy. © Araldo de Luca/Corbis.

ISBN  978-0-547-61846-3

10   2331   20 19 18 17

4500671731            B C D E F G

# HOLT McDOUGAL

# Literature

## Grade 9

HOLT McDOUGAL

HOUGHTON MIFFLIN HARCOURT

T2

# Creating *the future today*

*HOLT MCDOUGAL LITERATURE* creates the perfect environment for embracing the Common Core State Standards, making them accessible to every student. Each strand of the standards comes alive with scaffolded instruction, images, and unique technology tools to prepare students for the demands of the future.

# Prepare for the future

The Common Core State Standards in Reading give equal attention to literary and informational texts. The focus on text analysis and critical thinking, including comparing and contrasting texts and mediums, prepares students to be analytical about resources and ideas.

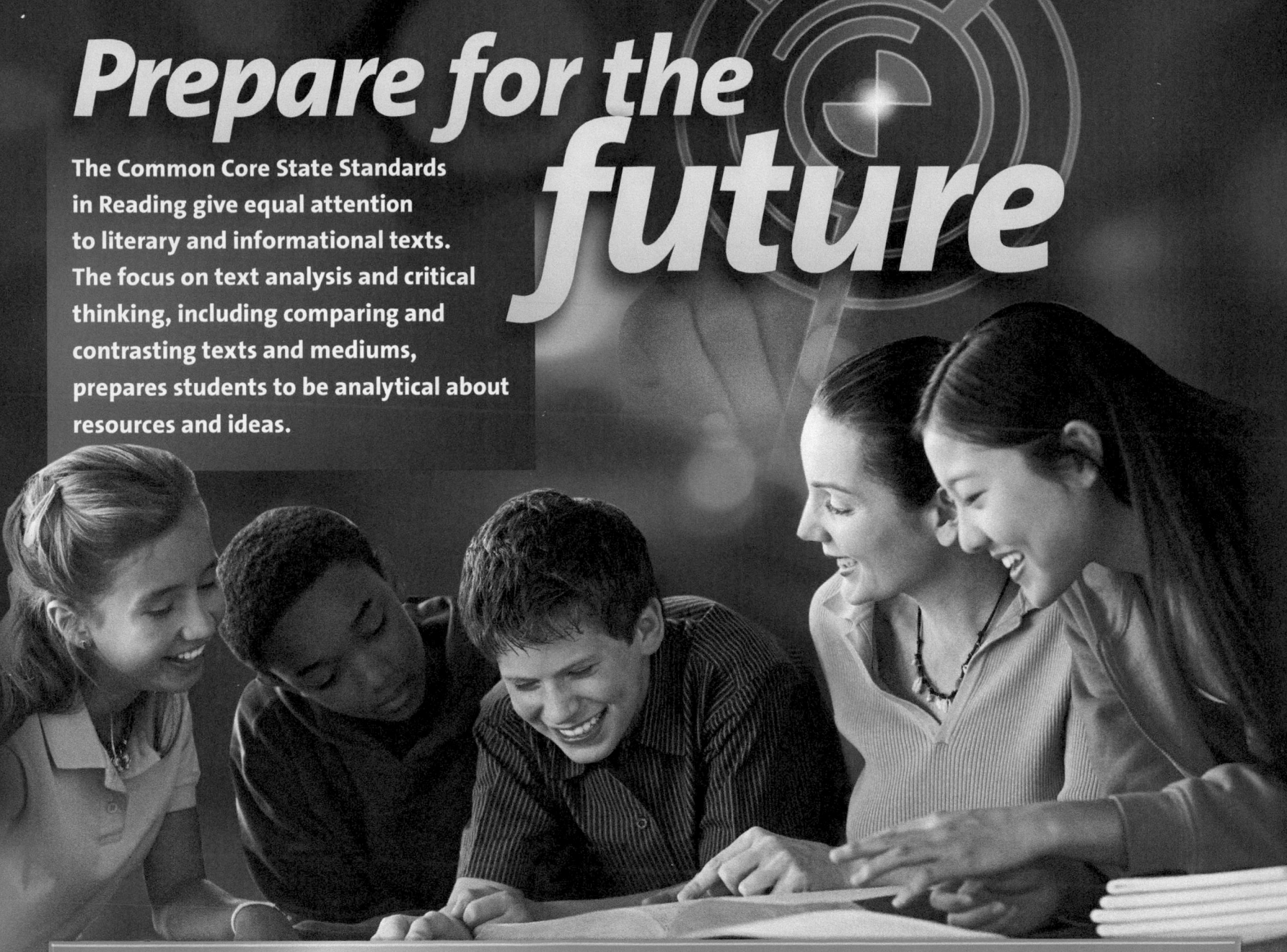

**HOLT MCDOUGAL LITERATURE** is the only resource with **LINE NUMBERS** on every selection, making "citing textual evidence" a natural part of the reading process.

**TEXT ANALYSIS WORKSHOPS** in grades 6–10 begin each unit. Students apply newly learned skills in excerpts of quality text using Close Reading strategies. In grades 11 and 12, the workshops focus on the characteristics of genres in American and British texts.

| ROLE OF SETTING | EXAMPLE SETTING |
|---|---|
| **Setting can influence characters by** <br> • determining the living conditions and jobs available to them <br> • shaping their personalities, their dreams, and their values | A poor, drought-stricken Midwestern farm town in the 1930s <br> Despite months of grueling work, Joe's crops are failing again. Realizing that his life may never improve, he becomes bitter and angry. |
| **Setting can create conflicts by** <br> • exposing the characters to dangerous weather, such as a storm or a drought <br> • making characters endure a difficult time period, such as the Great Depression | The drought has lasted seven years, and most of the farms are failing. People have begun to sell their most prized possessions because they need money. Recently, Mrs. Wilkes sold her wedding band to buy shoes for her daughter. |
| **Setting can serve as a symbol by** <br> • representing an important idea <br> • representing a character's hopes, future, or predicament | Some people have planted a small flower garden in the town square. The garden is a symbol of their hope that their community can still thrive. |

*from*
### Their Eyes Were Watching God
Novel by **Zora Neale Hurston**

It was a spring afternoon in West Florida. Janie had spent most of the day under a blossoming pear tree in the back-yard. She had been spending every minute that she could steal from her chores under that tree for the last three days. That was to say, ever since the first tiny bloom had opened. It had called her to come and gaze on a mystery. From barren brown stems to glistening leaf-buds; from the leaf-buds to snowy virginity of bloom. It stirred her tremendously.

**EXEMPLARY TEXTS** from Common Core State Standards and hundreds of other titles, including your favorite novels, are available to explore different worlds through reading.

**NOVELWISE** offers study guides and PowerPoint® presentations that support reading and discussion of your favorite novels.

**WRITING WORKSHOPS** show students how to craft and support an argument and to explain their ideas.

**INFORMATIONAL TEXT** requires students to apply academic vocabulary in texts with different purposes and structures. Seminal works of American history are important resources for Common Core State Standards.

**CONNECTIONS: NONFICTION FOR COMMON CORE CD-ROM** provides additional informational texts, including seminal or foundational American works, with specific connections to selections in *Holt McDougal Literature*.

Students must think analytically and critically as they **COMPARE TEXTS** that differ in style, genre, medium, and purpose.

# By learning today

The Common Core State Standards are designed for every student. Tools to scaffold learning are seamlessly integrated in *Holt McDougal Literature*.

**INTERACTIVE READERS** contain selections from the Essential Course of Study with close reading support to scaffold and personalize learning.

**ADAPTED INTERACTIVE READERS** provide the same selections in an adapted format with additional vocabulary and comprehension support.

**ENGLISH LANGUAGE LEARNER ADAPTED INTERACTIVE READERS** use the same adapted selections with scaffolded instruction for English Language Learners, including academic vocabulary, language support, and a comprehensive Teacher's Guide.

**AUDIO TUTOR CD** provides an audio version of the adapted selections with the instructional material read in English or Spanish.

***Holt McDougal Literature*** is a comprehensive resource addressing all of the Common Core State Standards for English Language Arts with integrated instruction in Language and Speaking and Listening.

The importance of acquiring academic vocabulary appropriate for college and career readiness is supported with every selection and reinforced with **WORDSHARP: AN INTERACTIVE VOCABULARY TUTOR CD,** which is also online to allow students to expand vocabulary independently.

**GRAMMAR AND STYLE** instruction at point of use within and following each selection reinforces students' command of conventions and supports their learning about language choices and style.

## Language

◆ **GRAMMAR AND STYLE:** Make Effective Word Choices

In the following excerpts, notice how O. Henry uses verbs that help create vivid images for the reader:

> *With a whirl of skirts and with the brilliant sparkle still in her eyes, she fluttered out the door and down the stairs to the street.* (lines 55–57)
>
> *Instead of obeying, Jim tumbled down on the couch....* (line 173)

Now study this model. Notice how the revisions in blue help you to better visualize Jim's trip to the shop. Use similar methods to revise your response to the prompt below.

**COMMON CORE**

**L 3** Make effective choices for meaning or style. **W 3b** Use description to develop characters.

**STUDENT MODEL**

Jim ~~walked~~ *scurried* to the shop; the store would close in just an hour. He reached into his right pocket, ~~took~~ *yanked* out the watch, and ~~held~~ *clasped* it in his hands.

**THE COMMON CORE STATE STANDARDS IN SPEAKING AND LISTENING** prepare students for active participation in their future. **SPEAKING AND LISTENING WORKSHOPS** in many units teach the skills of successful group participation and the formal presentation of ideas in public settings.

# With tools for *tomorrow*

*Holt McDougal Literature's* online platform provides easy access to teacher and student resources at point of use in the selection. HISTORY® film clips and full-length resources provide both motivation and context for texts.

**ONLINE RESOURCES** provide a wealth of instructional support material for Teacher and Student use.

**MEDIASMART DVD** uses movie clips, commercials, political ads, documentaries, and news reports to bring media instruction to life with critical analysis and comparisons to other mediums.

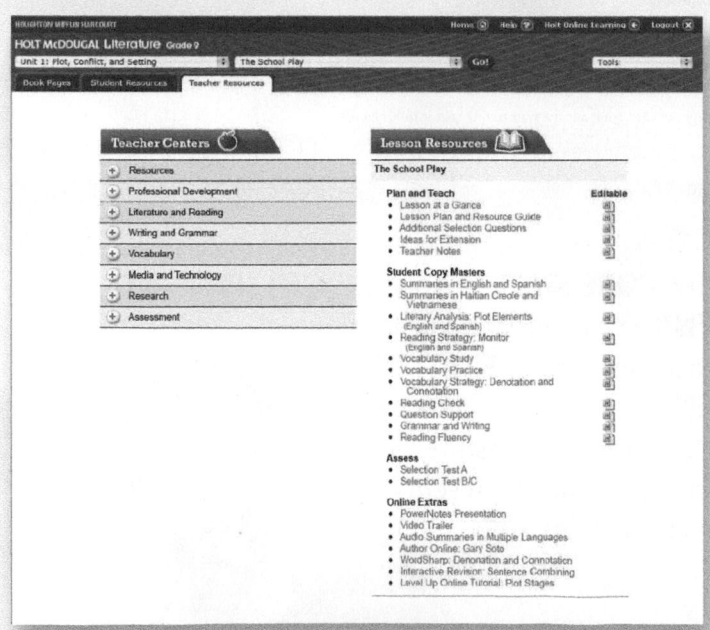

Enhance learning of rigorous standards with **HISTORY®** video streaming and resources at point of use.

**HISTORY**

**WRITESMART CD** (also online) features interactive writing instruction, from prompts to the steps of the process, including editing and revision models. An editable **RUBRIC GENERATOR** allows teachers to customize assessment.

**HOLT MCDOUGAL ONLINE ESSAY SCORING** provides students with the practice and immediate constructive feedback that they need to improve as writers.

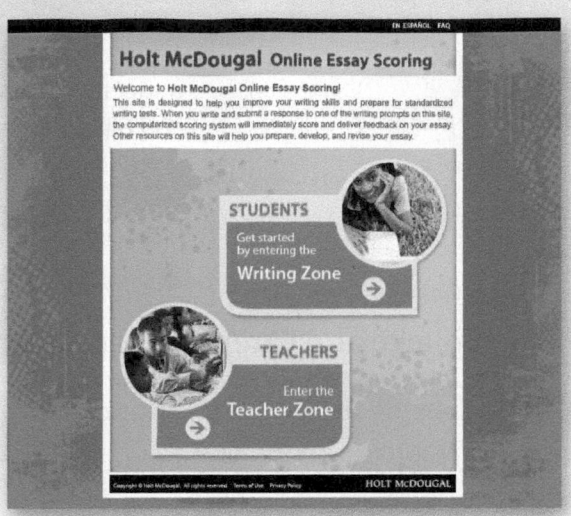

**WHITEBOARD-READY LESSON DEMONSTRATIONS** are available for the most challenging Common Core Standards.

**POWERNOTES DVD** (also online) provides point-of-use images, instructional information, and background knowledge with theater-quality video trailers.

**COMMON CORE**

# English Language Arts Common Core State Standards

The grades 9–10 standards on the following pages define what students should understand and be able to do by the end of grade 10. They correspond to the College and Career Readiness (CCR) anchor standards below by number. The CCR and grade-specific standards are necessary complements—the former providing broad standards, the latter providing additional specificity—that together define the skills and understandings that all students must demonstrate.

## College and Career Readiness Anchor Standards for Reading

**COMMON CORE STATE STANDARD**

### KEY IDEAS AND DETAILS

1. Read closely to determine what the text says explicitly and to make logical inferences from it; cite specific textual evidence when writing or speaking to support conclusions drawn from the text.

2. Determine central ideas or themes of a text and analyze their development; summarize the key supporting details and ideas.

3. Analyze how and why individuals, events, and ideas develop and interact over the course of a text.

### CRAFT AND STRUCTURE

4. Interpret words and phrases as they are used in a text, including determining technical, connotative, and figurative meanings, and analyze how specific word choices shape meaning or tone.

5. Analyze the structure of texts, including how specific sentences, paragraphs, and larger portions of the text (e.g., a section, chapter, scene, or stanza) relate to each other and the whole.

6. Assess how point of view or purpose shapes the content and style of a text.

### INTEGRATION OF KNOWLEDGE AND IDEAS

7. Integrate and evaluate content presented in diverse formats and media, including visually and quantitatively, as well as in words.

8. Delineate and evaluate the argument and specific claims in a text, including the validity of the reasoning as well as the relevance and sufficiency of the evidence.

9. Analyze how two or more texts address similar themes or topics in order to build knowledge or to compare the approaches the authors take.

### RANGE OF READING AND LEVEL OF COMPLEXITY

10. Read and comprehend complex literary and informational texts independently and proficiently.

## Reading Standards for Literature, Grades 9–10 Students

| COMMON CORE STATE STANDARD | STUDENT EDITION |
|---|---|
| **KEY IDEAS AND DETAILS** | |
| **1.** Cite strong and thorough textual evidence to support analysis of what the text says explicitly as well as inferences drawn from the text. | 4, 13, 36–37, 52, 84–85, 97, 100–101, 109, 186, 208–209, 219, 222–223, 234, 286–287, 291, 314, 354–355, 367, 370–371, 381, 424, 440–441, 452, 460–461, 477, 523, 612–613, 619, 724, 748–749, 754, 902, 950–951, 959, 960, 1006, 1178, 1282 |
| **2.** Determine a theme or central idea of a text and analyze in detail its development over the course of the text, including how it emerges and is shaped and refined by specific details; provide an objective summary of the text. | 4, 434, 440–441, 452, 460–461, 477, 500–501, 505, 506–507, 521, 523, 536, 698–699, 708, 724, 792–793, 797, 874–875, 879, 902, 1006, 1026, 1034–1035, 1063, 1087, 1146, 1240–1241, 1267, 1282, R2 |
| **3.** Analyze how complex characters (e.g., those with multiple or conflicting motivations) develop over the course of a text, interact with other characters, and advance the plot or develop the theme. | 84–85, 97, 202, 208–209, 219, 222–223, 234, 240–241, 251, 253, 314, 330, 354–355, 367, 434, 460–461, 477, 479, 506–507, 521, 612–613, 619, 786–787, 791, 792–793, 797, 962–963, 974, 1026, 1027, 1034–1035, 1057, 1063, 1087, 1113, 1129, 1146, 1178, R2 |
| **CRAFT AND STRUCTURE** | |
| **4.** Determine the meaning of words and phrases as they are used in the text, including figurative and connotative meanings; analyze the cumulative impact of specific word choices on meaning and tone (e.g., how the language evokes a sense of time and place; how it sets a formal or informal tone). | 4, 13, 58–59, 81, 84, 88, 90, 144–145, 149, 153, 208, 216, 218, 222, 227, 240, 250, 330, 336–337, 351, 354–355, 367, 370–371, 381, 383, 406–407, 411, 424, 440–441, 451, 477, 478, 500–501, 505, 506, 516, 519, 604–605, 610, 612–613, 740, 748–749, 754, 756–757, 763, 774–775, 779, 780, 784, 786–787, 791, 810, 820, 826–827, 833, 835, 837, 842–843, 847, 868–869, 873, 874–875, 878, 879, 918, 950–951, 959, 960, 982–983, 989, 990–991, 993, 995, 1086, 1087, 1178, 1194, 1202–1203, 1235, 1238, 1240, 1248, R2, R68 |
| **5.** Analyze how an author's choices concerning how to structure a text, order events within it (e.g., parallel plots), and manipulate time (e.g., pacing, flashbacks) create such effects as mystery, tension, or surprise. | 28, 36–37, 52, 58–59, 69, 81, 100–101, 109, 144–145, 152, 153, 154–155, 172, 186, 336, 350, 370, 375, 826–827, 837, 842–843, 847, 1158–1159, 1165, 1194, 1202, 1229, 1240, 1249, 1270–1279 |
| **6.** Analyze a particular point of view or cultural experience reflected in a work of literature from outside the United States, drawing on a wide reading of world literature. | 222–223, 234, 500–501, 505, 604–605, 610, 918, 982–983, 989, 990–991, 995, 1072, 1113, 1158–1159, 1165, 1188, 1194, 1202–1203, 1238 |
| **INTEGRATION OF KNOWLEDGE AND IDEAS** | |
| **7.** Analyze the representation of a subject or a key scene in two different artistic mediums, including what is emphasized or absent in each treatment (e.g., Auden's "Musée des Beaux Arts" and Breughel's *Landscape with the Fall of Icarus*). | 56, 112–115, 292–293, 299, 301, 384–387, 458, 840, 962–963, 974, 980, 1148–1151, 1188 |
| **8.** (Not applicable to literature) | |

## Reading Standards for Literature, Grades 9–10 Students, continued

| COMMON CORE STATE STANDARD | STUDENT EDITION |
|---|---|
| 9. Analyze how an author draws on and transforms source material in a specific work (e.g., how Shakespeare treats a theme or topic from Ovid or the Bible or how a later author draws on a play by Shakespeare). | FM46–FM49, 1026, 1034–1035, 1113, 1158–1159, 1165, 1188, 1267 |
| **RANGE OF READING AND LEVEL OF TEXT COMPLEXITY**<br>10. By the end of grade 9, read and comprehend literature, including stories, dramas, and poems, in the grades 9–10 text complexity band proficiently, with scaffolding as needed at the high end of the range. By the end of grade 10, read and comprehend literature, including stories, dramas, and poems, at the high end of the grades 9–10 text complexity band, independently and proficiently. | 100–101, 109, 144–145, 153, 154–155, 172, 198, 286–287, 291, 326, 406–407, 411, 430, 548, 604–605, 610, 650, 736, 740, 756–757, 763, 764–765, 769, 774–775, 784, 786–787, 791, 792–793, 797, 810, 816, 868–869, 873, 880–881, 889, 914, 962–963, 974, 982–983, 989, 990–991, 995, 1018, 1026, 1034–1035, 1063, 1087, 1129, 1146, 1158–1159, 1165, 1178, 1184, 1194, 1202–1203, 1238, 1282, 1288 |

## Reading Standards for Informational Text, Grades 9–10 Students

| COMMON CORE STATE STANDARD | STUDENT EDITION |
|---|---|
| **KEY IDEAS AND DETAILS**<br>1. Cite strong and thorough textual evidence to support analysis of what the text says explicitly as well as inferences drawn from the text. | 4, 13, 116–117, 118, 123, 138, 143, 186, 282, 285, 314, 400, 401, 405, 480–481, 490, 724, 902, 924–925, 937, 1006 |
| 2. Determine a central idea of a text and analyze its development over the course of the text, including how it emerges and is shaped and refined by specific details; provide an objective summary of the text. | 4, 138, 143, 282, 284, 285, 400, 401, 405, 454, 457, 480–481, 490, 492–493, 498, 536, 568–569, 575, 578–579, 588, 644, 654, 670–671, 677, 698–699, 701, 708, 724, 770, 773, 852–853, 858, 902, 976, 979, 1006, 1152, R2 |
| 3. Analyze how the author unfolds an analysis or series of ideas or events, including the order in which the points are made, how they are introduced and developed, and the connections that are drawn between them. | 116–117, 123, 126–127, 136, 268–269, 280, 314, 454, 457, 480–481, 490, 552, 558–559, 566, 626–627, 631, 644, 680–681, 684, 691, 1152, 1157, R2 |
| **CRAFT AND STRUCTURE**<br>4. Determine the meaning of words and phrases as they are used in a text, including figurative, connotative, and technical meanings; analyze the cumulative impact of specific word choices on meaning and tone (e.g., how the language of a court opinion differs from that of a newspaper). | 13, 116, 121, 138, 142, 268, 279, 280, 388–389, 398, 480, 485, 552, 558–559, 566, 568–569, 575, 590, 595, 620, 622, 626–627, 628, 629, 631, 644, 660, 666, 680–681, 685, 689, 698, 700, 770, 771, 820, 852–853, 858, 860–861, 865, 918, 924, 934, 1006, R2, R68 |

# Reading Standards for Informational Text, Grades 9–10 Students, continued

| COMMON CORE STATE STANDARD | STUDENT EDITION |
|---|---|
| **5.** Analyze in detail how an author's ideas or claims are developed and refined by particular sentences, paragraphs, or larger portions of a text (e.g., a section or chapter). | 186, 254–255, 265, 282, 284–285, 454, 457, 552, 558–559, 566, 568–569, 572, 575, 578–579, 588, 620–621, 625, 644, 654, 670–671, 677, 698–699, 707, 708, 976, 979, R2 |
| **6.** Determine an author's point of view or purpose in a text and analyze how an author uses rhetoric to advance that point of view or purpose. | 126–127, 136, 254–255, 265, 282, 284–285, 388–389, 398, 400, 401, 405, 492–493, 498, 552, 590–591, 598, 620–621, 625, 644, 654, 660–661, 668, 724, 852–853, 858, 918, 924–925, 937, 940–941, 948, 979, 1006 |
| **INTEGRATION OF KNOWLEDGE AND IDEAS** | |
| **7.** Analyze various accounts of a subject told in different mediums (e.g., a person's life story in both print and multimedia), determining which details are emphasized in each account. | 4, 138, 143, 238, 292–293, 299, 301, 600–603, 694–697, 710, 976, 979, 980 |
| **8.** Delineate and evaluate the argument and specific claims in a text, assessing whether the reasoning is valid and the evidence is relevant and sufficient; identify false statements and fallacious reasoning. | 654, 660–661, 668, 670–671, 677, 679, 680–681, 691, 724, 1152, 1157, R2 |
| **9.** Analyze seminal U.S. documents of historical and literary significance (e.g., Washington's Farewell Address, the Gettysburg Address, Roosevelt's Four Freedoms speech, King's "Letter from Birmingham Jail"), including how they address related themes and concepts. | FM50–FM53, 660–661, 666, 668 |
| **RANGE OF READING AND LEVEL OF TEXT COMPLEXITY** | |
| **10.** By the end of grade 9, read and comprehend literary nonfiction in the grades 9–10 text complexity band proficiently, with scaffolding as needed at the high end of the range. <br><br> By the end of grade 10, read and comprehend literary nonfiction at the high end of the grades 9–10 text complexity band independently and proficiently. | 198, 254–255, 265, 326, 548, 650, 736, 816, 860–861, 865, 914, 940–941, 948, 1018, 1022, 1184, 1288 |

# College and Career Readiness Anchor Standards for Writing

**TEXT TYPES AND PURPOSES**

1. Write arguments to support claims in an analysis of substantive topics or texts, using valid reasoning and relevant and sufficient evidence.

2. Write informative/explanatory texts to examine and convey complex ideas and information clearly and accurately through the effective selection, organization, and analysis of content.

3. Write narratives to develop real or imagined experiences or events using effective technique, well-chosen details, and well-structured event sequences.

**PRODUCTION AND DISTRIBUTION OF WRITING**

4. Produce clear and coherent writing in which the development, organization, and style are appropriate to task, purpose, and audience.

5. Develop and strengthen writing as needed by planning, revising, editing, rewriting, or trying a new approach.

6. Use technology, including the Internet, to produce and publish writing and to interact and collaborate with others.

**RESEARCH TO BUILD AND PRESENT KNOWLEDGE**

7. Conduct short as well as more sustained research projects based on focused questions, demonstrating understanding of the subject under investigation.

8. Gather relevant information from multiple print and digital sources, assess the credibility and accuracy of each source, and integrate the information while avoiding plagiarism.

9. Draw evidence from literary or informational texts to support analysis, reflection, and research.

**RANGE OF WRITING**

10. Write routinely over extended time frames (time for research, reflection, and revision) and shorter time frames (a single sitting or a day or two) for a range of tasks, purposes, and audiences.

# Writing Standards, Grades 9–10 Students

| COMMON CORE STATE STANDARD | STUDENT EDITION |
| --- | --- |
| **TEXT TYPES AND PURPOSES** | |
| **1.** Write arguments to support claims in an analysis of substantive topics or texts, using valid reasoning and relevant and sufficient evidence. | 302–311, 712–721, 1166–1175, R28 |
| **a.** Introduce precise claim(s), distinguish the claim(s) from alternate or opposing claims, and create an organization that establishes clear relationships among claim(s), counterclaims, reasons, and evidence. | 302–311, 712–721, 773, 867, R28 |
| **b.** Develop claim(s) and counterclaims fairly, supplying evidence for each while pointing out the strengths and limitations of both in a manner that anticipates the audience's knowledge level and concerns. | 302–311, 712–721, 763, 773, 851, 867, 1166–1175, 1173, R28 |
| **c.** Use words, phrases, and clauses to link the major sections of the text, create cohesion, and clarify the relationships between claim(s) and reasons, between reasons and evidence, and between claim(s) and counterclaims. | 302–311, 712–721, R28 |
| **d.** Establish and maintain a formal style and objective tone while attending to the norms and conventions of the discipline in which they are writing. | 302–311, 307, 712–721, R28 |
| **e.** Provide a concluding statement or section that follows from and supports the argument presented. | 302–311, 309, 712–721, R28 |
| **2.** Write informative/explanatory texts to examine and convey complex ideas, concepts, and information clearly and accurately through the effective selection, organization, and analysis of content. | 524–533, 632–641, 798–807, 890–899, 996–1003, 1001, 1314–1335, R28 |
| **a.** Introduce a topic; organize complex ideas, concepts, and information to make important connections and distinctions; include formatting (e.g., headings), graphics (e.g., figures, tables), and multimedia when useful to aiding comprehension. | 523, 524–533, 632–641, 642–643, 798–807, 890–899, 996–1003, 1314–1335, R28 |
| **b.** Develop the topic with well-chosen, relevant, and sufficient facts, extended definitions, concrete details, quotations, or other information and examples appropriate to the audience's knowledge of the topic. | 267, 405, 523, 524–533, 632–641, 798–807, 890–899, 961, 996–1003, 1314–1335, R28 |

## Writing Standards, Grades 9–10 Students, continued

| COMMON CORE STATE STANDARD | STUDENT EDITION |
|---|---|
| c. Use appropriate and varied transitions to link the major sections of the text, create cohesion, and clarify the relationships among complex ideas and concepts. | 302–311, 524–533, 631, 632–641, 798–807, 890–899, 895, 996–1003, 1314–1335, R28 |
| d. Use precise language and domain-specific vocabulary to manage the complexity of the topic. | 524–533, 632–641, 798–807, 890–899, 996–1003, 1314–1335, R28 |
| e. Establish and maintain a formal style and objective tone while attending to the norms and conventions of the discipline in which they are writing. | 524–533, 632–641, 637, 798–807, 890–899, 996–1003, 1314–1335, R28 |
| f. Provide a concluding statement or section that follows from and supports the information or explanation presented (e.g., articulating implications or the significance of the topic). | 457, 523, 632–641, 798–807, 890–899, 996–1003, 1314–1335, R28 |
| 3. Write narratives to develop real or imagined experiences or events using effective technique, well-chosen details, and well-structured event sequences. | 174–183, 412–421, 1270–1279, R28 |
| a. Engage and orient the reader by setting out a problem, situation, or observation, establishing one or multiple point(s) of view, and introducing a narrator and/or characters; create a smooth progression of experiences or events. | 174–183, 412–421, 1270–1279, R28 |
| b. Use narrative techniques, such as dialogue, pacing, description, reflection, and multiple plot lines, to develop experiences, events, and/or characters. | 54, 111, 174–183, 412–421, 1270–1279, R28 |
| c. Use a variety of techniques to sequence events so that they build on one another to create a coherent whole. | 174–183, 412–421, 1270–1279, R28 |
| d. Use precise words and phrases, telling details, and sensory language to convey a vivid picture of the experiences, events, setting, and/or characters. | 99, 174–183, 412–421, R28 |
| e. Provide a conclusion that follows from and reflects on what is experienced, observed, or resolved over the course of the narrative. | 174–183, 412–421, 1270–1279, R28 |
| **PRODUCTION AND DISTRIBUTION OF WRITING**<br>4. Produce clear and coherent writing in which the development, organization, and style are appropriate to task, purpose, and audience. (Grade-specific expectations for writing types are defined in standards 1–3 above.) | FM57–FM59, 20, 177, 221, 301, 305, 383, 415, 499, 523, 527, 567, 635, 693, 715, 755, 801, 893, 999, 1169, 1273, 1323, R28 |

## Writing Standards, Grades 9–10 Students, continued

| COMMON CORE STATE STANDARD | STUDENT EDITION |
|---|---|
| **5.** Develop and strengthen writing as needed by planning, revising, editing, rewriting, or trying a new approach, focusing on addressing what is most significant for a specific purpose and audience. (Editing for conventions should demonstrate command of Language standards 1–3.) | 20, 125, 174–183, 186, 302–311, 314, 412–421, 424, 523, 524–533, 536, 632–641, 644, 709, 712–721, 724, 769, 798–807, 810, 890–899, 902, 996–1003, 1006, 1166–1175, 1178, 1270–1279, 1282, 1314–1335, R28 |
| **6.** Use technology, including the Internet, to produce, publish, and update individual or shared writing products, taking advantage of technology's capacity to link to other information and to display information flexibly and dynamically. | 422–423, 642–643, 900–901, 996–1003, 1004–1005, 1270–1279, 1336–1337, R28 |
| **RESEARCH TO BUILD AND PRESENT KNOWLEDGE**<br>**7.** Conduct short as well as more sustained research projects to answer a question (including a self-generated question) or solve a problem; narrow or broaden the inquiry when appropriate; synthesize multiple sources on the subject, demonstrating understanding of the subject under investigation. | 632–641, 996–1003, 1292, 1314–1335 |
| **8.** Gather relevant information from multiple authoritative print and digital sources, using advanced searches effectively; assess the usefulness of each source in answering the research question; integrate information into the text selectively to maintain the flow of ideas, avoiding plagiarism and following a standard format for citation. | 999, 1292, 1314–1335 |
| **9.** Draw evidence from literary or informational texts to support analysis, reflection, and research. | 115, 143, 253, 285, 301, 302–311, 387, 499, 527, 603, 668, 697, 763, 801, 979, 999, 1148–1151, 1157, 1165, 1166–1175, 1292, 1314–1335 |
| **a.** Apply *grades 9-10 Reading standards* to literature (e.g., "Analyze how an author draws on and transforms source material in a specific work [e.g., how Shakespeare treats a theme or topic from Ovid or the Bible or how a later author draws on a play by Shakespeare]"). | 115, 253, 285, 301, 302–311, 387, 479, 523, 679, 801, 1165, 1166–1175 |
| **b.** Apply *grades 9-10 Reading standards* to literary nonfiction (e.g., "Delineate and evaluate the argument and specific claims in a text, assessing whether the reasoning is valid and the evidence is relevant and sufficient; identify false statements and fallacious reasoning"). | 143, 285, 527, 603, 668, 697, 979, 999, 1157 |
| **RANGE OF WRITING**<br>**10.** Write routinely over extended time frames (time for research, reflection, and revision) and shorter time frames (a single sitting or a day or two) for a range of tasks, purposes, and audiences. | FM57–FM59, 174–183, 267, 301, 302–311, 412–421, 524–533, 631, 632–641, 712–721, 769, 798–807, 890–899, 1166–1175, 1270–1279 |

# College and Career Readiness Anchor Standards for Speaking and Listening

## COMPREHENSION AND COLLABORATION

1. Prepare for and participate effectively in a range of conversations and collaborations with diverse partners, building on others' ideas and expressing their own clearly and persuasively.

2. Integrate and evaluate information presented in diverse media and formats, including visually, quantitatively, and orally.

3. Evaluate a speaker's point of view, reasoning, and use of evidence and rhetoric.

## PRESENTATION OF KNOWLEDGE AND IDEAS

4. Present information, findings, and supporting evidence such that listeners can follow the line of reasoning and the organization, development, and style are appropriate to task, purpose, and audience.

5. Make strategic use of digital media and visual displays of data to express information and enhance understanding of presentations.

6. Adapt speech to a variety of contexts and communicative tasks, demonstrating command of formal English when indicated or appropriate.

# Speaking and Listening Standards, Grades 9–10 Students

| COMMON CORE STATE STANDARD | STUDENT EDITION |
|---|---|
| **COMPREHENSION AND COLLABORATION** | |
| **1.** Initiate and participate effectively in a range of collaborative discussions (one-on-one, in groups, and teacher-led) with diverse partners *on grades 9–10 topics, texts, and issues,* building on others' ideas and expressing their own clearly and persuasively. | FM61–FM63, 312–313, 534–535, 722–723, R76 |
| **a.** Come to discussions prepared, having read and researched material under study; explicitly draw on that preparation by referring to evidence from texts and other research on the topic or issue to stimulate a thoughtful, well-reasoned exchange of ideas. | FM61, 312–313, 534–535, 722–723, 848–851, 1148–1151, 1280–1281, R76 |
| **b.** Work with peers to set rules for collegial discussions and decision-making (e.g., informal consensus, taking votes on key issues, presentation of alternate views), clear goals and deadlines, and individual roles as needed. | FM61, 312–313, 534–535, 722–723, 1336–1337, R76 |
| **c.** Propel conversations by posing and responding to questions that relate the current discussion to broader themes or larger ideas; actively incorporate others into the discussion; and clarify, verify, or challenge ideas and conclusions. | 20, 312–313, 534–535, 722–723, 1004–1005, 1280–1281, R76 |
| **d.** Respond thoughtfully to diverse perspectives, summarize points of agreement and disagreement, and, when warranted, qualify or justify their own views and understanding and make new connections in light of the evidence and reasoning presented. | 20, 312–313, 534–535, 722–723, R76 |
| **2.** Integrate multiple sources of information presented in diverse media or formats (e.g., visually, quantitatively, orally) evaluating the credibility and accuracy of each source. | 115, 268–269, 280, 387, 422–423, 578, 582, 588, 590–591, 598, 603, 697, 851, 1022, 1036, 1148–1151, 1270–1279, 1336–1337 |
| **3.** Evaluate a speaker's point of view, reasoning, and use of evidence and rhetoric, identifying any fallacious reasoning or exaggerated or distorted evidence. | 312–313, 654, 694–697, 722–723, 1176–1177, R76, R84 |

## Speaking and Listening Standards, Grades 9–10 Students, continued

| COMMON CORE STATE STANDARD | STUDENT EDITION |
|---|---|
| **PRESENTATION OF KNOWLEDGE AND IDEAS** | |
| **4.** Present information, findings, and supporting evidence clearly, concisely, and logically such that listeners can follow the line of reasoning and the organization, development, substance, and style are appropriate to purpose, audience, and task. | 184–185, 312–313, 534–535, 808–809, 851, R76 |
| **5.** Make strategic use of digital media (e.g., textual, graphical, audio, visual, and interactive elements) in presentations to enhance understanding of findings, reasoning, and evidence and to add interest. | 115, 387, 422–423, 603, 900–901, 996–1003, 1004–1005, 1270–1279, 1336–1337 |
| **6.** Adapt speech to a variety of contexts and tasks, demonstrating command of formal English when indicated or appropriate. (See grades 9–10 Language standards 1 and 3 for specific expectations.) | 184–185, 722–723, 808–809 |

## College and Career Readiness Anchor Standards for Language

| COMMON CORE STATE STANDARD |
|---|
| **CONVENTIONS OF STANDARD ENGLISH** |
| **1.** Demonstrate command of the conventions of standard English grammar and usage when writing or speaking. |
| **2.** Demonstrate command of the conventions of standard English capitalization, punctuation, and spelling when writing. |
| **KNOWLEDGE OF LANGUAGE** |
| **3.** Apply knowledge of language to understand how language functions in different contexts, to make effective choices for meaning or style, and to comprehend more fully when reading or listening. |
| **VOCABULARY ACQUISITION AND USE** |
| **4.** Determine or clarify the meaning of unknown and multiple-meaning words and phrases by using context clues, analyzing meaningful word parts, and consulting general and specialized reference materials, as appropriate. |
| **5.** Demonstrate understanding of figurative language, word relationships, and nuances in word meanings. |
| **6.** Acquire and use accurately a range of general academic and domain-specific words and phrases sufficient for reading, writing, speaking, and listening at the college and career readiness level; demonstrate independence in gathering vocabulary knowledge when considering a word or phrase important to comprehension or expression. |

## Language Standards, Grades 9–10 Students

| COMMON CORE STATE STANDARD | STUDENT EDITION |
| --- | --- |
| **CONVENTIONS OF STANDARD ENGLISH** | |
| **1.** Demonstrate command of the conventions of standard English grammar and usage when writing or speaking. | 20, 369, 717, 801, 893, 1173, R46 |
| **a.** Use parallel structure. | 670, 674, 693, 715, 724, 1147, 1178, R46 |
| **b.** Use various types of phrases (noun, verb, adjectival, adverbial, participial, prepositional, absolute) and clauses (independent, dependent; noun, relative, adverbial) to convey specific meanings and add variety and interest to writing or presentations. | 83, 236, 267, 309, 415, 479, 527, 536, 567, 577, 611, 639, 755, 785, 810, 897, 1002, 1006, 1147, 1169, R46 |
| **2.** Demonstrate command of the conventions of standard English capitalization, punctuation, and spelling when writing. | 20, 177, 181, 309, 383, 412–421, 531, 635, 709, 719, 805, 897, 1002, 1323, 1332, R46 |
| **a.** Use a semicolon (and perhaps a conjunctive adverb) to link two or more closely related independent clauses. | 1173, R46 |
| **b.** Use a colon to introduce a list or quotation. | 1332, R46 |
| **c.** Spell correctly. | 181, 419, 531, 639, 719, 803, 805, 1282, R68 |
| **KNOWLEDGE OF LANGUAGE** | |
| **3.** Apply knowledge of language to understand how language functions in different contexts, to make effective choices for meaning or style, and to comprehend more fully when reading or listening. | 16, 54, 99, 111, 125, 173, 179, 221, 253, 353, 369, 383, 499, 679, 715, 820, 826, 834, 837, 839, 867, 961, 1026, 1027, 1034–1035, 1063, 1129, 1178, 1269, R68 |
| **a.** Write and edit work so that it conforms to the guidelines in a style manual (e.g., *MLA Handbook*, Turabian's *Manual for Writers*) appropriate for the discipline and writing type. | 999, 1323, 1332, 1335 |

## Language Standards, Grades 9–10 Students, continued

| COMMON CORE STATE STANDARD | STUDENT EDITION |
|---|---|
| **VOCABULARY ACQUISITION AND USE**<br>**4.** Determine or clarify the meaning of unknown and multiple-meaning words and phrases based on *grades 9-10 reading and content,* choosing flexibly from a range of strategies. | 13, 58, 63, 240, 246, 266, 370, 374, 400, 402, 578, 584, 608, 698, 704, 764, 767, 868, 870, 940, 944, 976, 978, 982, 984, 986, 1084, 1143, 1202, 1209, 1240, 1245, 1252, 1259, 1264, R68 |
|    **a.** Use context (e.g., the overall meaning of a sentence, paragraph, or text; a word's position or function in a sentence) as a clue to the meaning of a word or phrase. | 16, 53, 235, 292, 296, 399, 424, 454, 455, 460, 465, 491, 492, 497, 536, 578, 581, 644, 724, 860, 862, 962, 970, 1062, 1102, 1117, 1152, 1154, 1158–1159, 1164, 1222, 1282, R68 |
|    **b.** Identify and correctly use patterns of word changes that indicate different meanings or parts of speech (e.g., *analyze, analysis, analytical; advocate, advocacy*). | 68, 354, 366, 388, 393, 440, 445, 453, 460, 470, 568, 572, 590–591, 596, 599, 852, 856, 902, 1125, 1227, R68 |
|    **c.** Consult general and specialized reference materials (e.g., dictionaries, glossaries, thesauruses), both print and digital, to find the pronunciation of a word or determine or clarify its precise meaning, its part of speech, or its etymology. | 16, 36, 43, 75, 98, 100, 106, 110, 124, 137, 208–209, 220, 240, 248, 254, 260, 300, 379, 382, 388, 396, 440, 448, 506, 513, 522, 536, 576, 578, 581, 599, 670, 675, 678, 792, 795, 838, 852, 857, 866, 938, 949, 1095, 1107, 1212, 1268, R68 |
|    **d.** Verify the preliminary determination of the meaning of a word or phrase (e.g., by checking the inferred meaning in context or in a dictionary). | 368, 453, 1158–1159, 1164, 1239, R68 |
| **5.** Demonstrate understanding of figurative language, word relationships, and nuances in word meanings. | 16, 480, 489, 740, 868–869, 873 |
|    **a.** Interpret figures of speech (e.g., euphemism, oxymoron) in context and analyze their role in the text. | 292, 298, 612, 616, 618, 669, 740, 842, 846, 975, 1040, 1073, 1087, 1129 |
|    **b.** Analyze nuances in the meaning of words with similar denotations. | 82, 352, 478, 859 |
| **6.** Acquire and use accurately general academic and domain-specific words and phrases, sufficient for reading, writing, speaking, and listening at the college and career readiness level; demonstrate independence in gathering vocabulary knowledge when considering a word or phrase important to comprehension or expression. | FM65–FM66, 16, 186, 252, 281, 314, 536, 589, 644, 692, 1006, 1026, 1282, R68 |

# Essential Course of Study

**ECOS**

**The Essential Course of Study** designates an efficient and effective choice of selections for mastery of the Common Core State Standards.

| STRAND | Reading Literature | Reading Informational Text | Writing | Speaking and Listening | Language |
|---|---|---|---|---|---|
| **UNIT 1** | | | | | |
| *Text Analysis Workshop: Plot and Conflict* | Plot Stages and Conflict RL 5 Sequence and Time RL 5 | | | | |
| *The Most Dangerous Game* | Conflict; Plot Devices RL 5 Visualize RL 4 | | Diary Entry | | Add Descriptive Details L 1b Denotation and Connotation L 5b |
| *The Gift of the Magi* | Irony RL 5, RL 10 Predict RL 1 | | Write a Description W 3b | | Use Precise Verbs L 3 Greek Roots L 4c |
| *Horse of the Century* | | Synthesize Information from Different Texts RI 1, RI 2, RI 7 | Draw Conclusions W 9b (RI 7) | | |
| *The Raven / Incident in a Rose Garden* | Narrative Poetry RL 5 Reading Poetry RL 4, RL 10 | | | | |
| *Writing Workshop: Narrative: Personal Narrative* | | | Write a Personal Narrative W 3a–e, W 4, W 5, W 10 | | Punctuating Dialogue L 2 Compound Sentences L 2 |
| *Speaking and Listening Workshop: Presenting an Informal Speech* | | | | Present an Informal Speech SL 4, SL 6 | |
| **UNIT 2** | | | | | |
| *Text Analysis Workshop: Character and Point of View* | Point of View RL 3 Character Traits and Motivation RL 3 | | | | |
| *The Necklace* | Character Motivation RL 3, RL 6 Make Inferences RL 1 | | Analyze Characters | | Vary Sentence Beginnings L 1b Latin Roots L 4a |
| from *I Know Why the Caged Bird Sings* | | Characterization in Autobiography RI 5, RI 10 Analyze Perspectives RI 6 | Analyze Traits W 2b, W 10 | | Add Descriptive Details L 1b Multiple-Meaning Words L 4 |
| from *Rosa Parks/Rosa* | Characterization Across Genres RL 7 | Characterization Across Genres RI 7 | Writing for Assessment W 4, W 9 (RL 7, RI 7), W 10 | | Paradox L 5a Etymologies L 4c |

| STRAND | Reading Literature | Reading Informational Text | Writing | Speaking and Listening | Language |
|---|---|---|---|---|---|
| **UNIT 2** *continued* | | | | | |
| *Writing Workshop: Argument: Literary Criticism* | | | Write Literary Criticism **W 1a–e, W 4, W 5, W 6, W 9a (RL 1, RL 3), W 10** | | Adjectival and Adverbial Phrases **L 1b, L 2** |
| *Speaking and Listening Workshop: Participating in a Discussion* | | | | Participate in a Discussion **SL 1a–d, SL 3, SL 4, SL 6** | |
| **UNIT 3** | | | | | |
| *Text Analysis Workshop: Setting, Mood, and Imagery* | Setting **RL 3, RL 4** Imagery and Mood **RL 4** | | | | |
| *A Christmas Memory* | Details of Setting **RL 4** Flashback **RL 5** Analyze Imagery **RL 4** | | Rewrite a Scene | | Effective Verb Tense **L 3** Connotation and Denotation **L 5b** |
| *Through the Tunnel* | Setting as Symbol **RL 3** Analyze Details **RL 4** | | Analyze a Character's Actions | | Use Compound Predicates **L 1, L 3** Latin Roots **L 4d** |
| *The Cask of Amontillado* | Mood **RL 4** Irony **RL 5** Paraphrase **RL 1** Use Appropriate Language **RL 4** | | Create a Monologue **W 4** | | Use Appropriate Language **L 2, L 3** Word Families **L 4c** Foreign Words and Phrases **L 4c** |
| *Media Study: from The Cask of Amontillado* | Setting and Mood in Movies **RL 7** | | Compare Film and Written Versions **W 9a (RL 7)** | Compare Film and Written Versions **SL 2, SL 5** | |
| *Linked Selections* from *A Walk in the Woods* | | Setting and Mood **RI 4** Identify Author's Perspective **RI 4, RI 6** | | | Context Clues **L 4a** |
| *Wilderness Letter* | | Read Primary Sources **RI 1, RI 6** Central Idea **RI 1, RI 2, RI 6** | Cite Evidence **W 2b** | | |
| *Writing Workshop: Narrative: Short Story* | | | Write a Short Story **W 3a–e, W 4, W 5, W 10** | | Participles **L 1b** Quotation Marks **L 2** |
| *Technology Workshop: Producing a Story Trailer* | | | Produce a Story Trailer **W 6** | Produce a Story Trailer **SL 2, SL 5** | |

| STRAND | Reading Literature | Reading Informational Text | Writing | Speaking and Listening | Language |
|---|---|---|---|---|---|
| **UNIT 4** | | | | | |
| *Text Analysis Workshop: Theme and Symbol* | Themes in Literature **RL 2** Determine Theme **RL 2, RL 3** | | | | |
| *The Scarlet Ibis* | Symbol **RL 2** Make Inferences About Character **RL 1, RL 3** | | Character Analysis **W 9a (RL 3)** | | Vary Sentence Structure **L 1b** Denotation and Connotation **L 5b** |
| *Poem on Returning to Dwell in the Country / My Heart Leaps Up / The Sun* | Universal Theme **RL 2, RL 6** Reading Poetry for Theme **RL 4** | | | | |
| *Two Kinds/ Rice and Rose Bowl Blues* | Theme Across Genres **RL 2, RL 3** Paradox **RL 4** Set a Purpose for Reading | | Writing for Assessment **W 2a–c, W 2f, W 4, W 5, W 9a (RL 1, RL 2)** | | Word Origins **L 4c** |
| *Writing Workshop: Informative Text: Analysis of Literary Nonfiction* | | | Write an Analysis of Nonfiction **W 2a–f, W 4, W 5, W 9b (RI 1), W 10** | | Relative Clauses **L 1b** Commas with Phrases and Clauses **L 2, L 2c** |
| *Speaking and Listening Workshop: Participating in a Panel Discussion* | | | | Participate in a Panel Discussion **SL 1a–d, SL 4 , SL 6** | |
| **UNIT 5** | | | | | |
| *Text Analysis Workshop: Author's Purpose* | | Author's Purpose and Perspective **RI 4, RI 6** Organization and Format **RI 3, RI 5** | | | |
| *Who Killed the Iceman? / Skeletal Sculptures* | | Text Features **RI 2, RI 5** Take Notes **RI 2, RI 5** | Compare and Contrast | Graphic Sources **SL 2** | Specialized Vocabulary **L 6** |
| *The Lost Boys* | | Author's Purpose **RI 6** Tone **RI 4** | Analyze a Problem | Interpret Graphic Aids **SL 2** | Latin Roots **L 4b–c** |
| *Consumer Documents* | | Consumer Documents **RI 5, RI 6** Adjust Reading Rate | | | |
| *Writing Workshop: Informative Text: Business Letter* | | | Write a Business Letter **W 2a–f, W 4, W 5, W 7, W 10** | | Capitalization **L 2** Complex Sentences **L 1b, L 2** |
| *Technology Workshop: Creating an Online Professional Profile* | | | Create an Online Professional Profile **W 2a, W 6** | | |

| STRAND | Reading Literature | Reading Informational Text | Writing | Speaking and Listening | Language |
|---|---|---|---|---|---|
| **UNIT 6** | | | | | |
| *Text Workshop: Argument and Persuasion* | | The Elements of an Argument  RI 2, RI 5, RI 8<br>The Craft of Persuasion  RI 6, RI 8 | | The Craft of Persuasion  SL 3 | |
| *I Have a Dream* | | Argument  RI 8<br>Understand Rhetorical Devices  RI 6<br>Seminal U.S. Documents  RI 9 | Write an Analysis  W 9b (RI 9) | | Analogies  L 5a |
| *Testimony Before the Senate* | | Persuasive Techniques  RI 5, RI 8<br>Summarize  RI 2 | Write a Memo  W 9a (RI 8) | | Persuasive Techniques  L 1a<br>Imperative Sentences  L 3<br>Using a Dictionary  L 4c |
| *How Private Is Your Private Life?/ The Privacy Debate: One Size Doesn't Fit All* | | Fact and Opinion  RI 4, RI 8<br>Recognize Bias  RI 8<br>Series of Events  RI 3<br>Sarcasm  RI 4 | Write a Critique  W 4 | | Parallelism<br>Specialized Vocabulary  L 6 |
| *Writing Workshop: Argument: Persuasive Essay* | | | Write a Persuasive Essay  W 1a–e, W 4, W 5, W 10 | | Parallelism  L 1a<br>Gerunds  L 2, L 3 |
| *Speaking and Listening Workshop: Debating an Issue* | | | | Debate an Issue  SL 1a–d, SL 3, SL 4, SL 6 | |
| **UNIT 7** | | | | | |
| *Text Analysis Workshop: The Language of Poetry* | Form  RL 10<br>Poetic Elements  RL 4 | | | | Poetic Elements  L 5 |
| *Spring is like a perhaps hand / Elegy for the Giant Tortoises / Today* | Elegy, Diction  RL 4<br>Paraphrase  RL 10 | | Support an Opinion  W 1b, W 9a (RL 10) | | |
| *Writing Workshop: Informative Text: Analysis of a Poem* | | | Write an Analysis of a Poem  W 2a–f, W 4, W 5, W 9a (RL 1, 4), W 10 | | Singular and Plural Possessives  L 1<br>Dashes  L 2 |
| *Speaking and Listening Workshop: Presenting a Literary Analysis* | | | | Present a Literary Analysis  SL 4, SL 6 | |
| **UNIT 8** | | | | | |
| *Text Analysis Workshop: Author's Style and Voice* | What is Style?  RL 4<br>Style and Voice  RL 4 | What is Style?  RI 4<br>Style and Voice  RI 4 | | | Style and Voice  L 3 |
| *Where Have You Gone, Charming Billy? / Tim O'Brien: The Naked Soldier* | Realism  RL 4<br>Analyze Sequence of Events  RL 5 | | Letter | | Passive Voice  L 3<br>Repetition  L 3<br>Prefixes  L 4c |

| STRAND | Reading Literature | Reading Informational Text | Writing | Speaking and Listening | Language |
|---|---|---|---|---|---|
| **UNIT 8** *continued* | | | | | |
| *A Few Words* | | Tone RI 4<br>Paraphrase RI 10 | Express an Opinion W 1a–b | | Vary Sentence Types L 3<br>Homonyms L 4c |
| *The Sneeze* from *The Good Doctor* | Farce RL 10<br>Visualize RL 10 | | | | |
| *Writing Workshop: Informative Text: Analysis of an Author's Style* | | | Write an Analysis of an Author's Style W 2a–f, W 4, W 5, W 10 | | Run-On Sentences L 1b<br>Compound-Complex Sentences L 1b |
| *Technology Workshop: Creating a Podcast* | | | Create a Podcast W 6 | Create a Podcast SL 4, SL 5, SL 6 | |
| **UNIT 9** | | | | | |
| *Text Analysis Workshop: History, Culture, and the Author* | Context Within the Literature RL 4<br>Context Outside the Literature RL 4, RL 6 | Context Within the Literature RI 4<br>Context Outside the Literature RI 4 | | | |
| from *Angela's Ashes* | | Memoir RI 6<br>Use Allusions to Make Inferences RI 1, RI 6<br>Informal Language RI 4 | Argument | | Gerund Phrases L 1b<br>Latin Roots L 4c |
| *American History* | Influence of Author's Background RL 3, RL 10<br>Connect RL 10 | | | | Idioms L 5a |
| *Special Report* | | What's the Connection? RI 7<br>Identify Controlling Idea RI 2, RI 5 | Analyze Author's Style and Purpose W 9b (RI 6) | | Foreign Phrases Used in English L 4 |
| *Writing Workshop: Informative Text: Online Feature Article* | | | Write an Online Feature Article W 2a–f, W 4, W 5, W 6, W 7, W 8, W 9b (RI 1) | | Incorporating Quotations L 3a<br>Participial Phrases L 1b |
| *Technology Workshop: Updating an Online Feature Article* | | | Update an Online Feature Article W 6 | Update an Online Feature Article SL 1c, SL 2, SL 5 | |
| **UNIT 10** | | | | | |
| *Text Analysis Workshop: Shakespearean Drama* | Characteristics of Shakespearean Tragedy RL 3<br>Language of Shakespeare RL 9<br>Reading Shakespearean Drama RL 2 | | | | Characteristics of Shakespearean Tragedy L 6<br>Language of Shakespeare L 3 |
| *The Tragedy of Romeo and Juliet* | Shakespearean Drama RL 3, RL 4, RL 6<br>Reading Shakespearean Drama RL 2, RL 3 | | Blank Verse Poem | | Shakespearean Drama L 3, L 5a<br>Create Rhythm: Parallelism L 1a–b |

| STRAND | Reading Literature | Reading Informational Text | Writing | Speaking and Listening | Language |
|---|---|---|---|---|---|
| **UNIT 10** *continued* | | | | | |
| *Great Movies: Romeo and Juliet* | | Analyze a Critical Review **RI 2, RI 3, RI 8** | Compare and Contrast Views **W 9b (RI 8)** | | |
| *Writing Workshop: Argument: Critical Review* | | | Write a Critical Review **W 1a–e, W 4, W 5, W 9a (RL 7, RL 9), W 10** | | Adverbial Clauses **L 1** Using Semicolons Correctly **L 2a** |
| *Speaking and Listening Workshop: Evaluating a Critical Review* | | | | Evaluate a Critical Review **SL 3** | |
| **UNIT 11** | | | | | |
| *Text Analysis Workshop: The Epic* | Characteristics of the Epic **RL 5** The Language of Homer **RL 4, RL 10** Reading the Epic **RL 4, RL 6** | | | | |
| *The Wanderings of Odysseus* from the *Odyssey* | Epic Hero **RL 5, RL 6** Reading an Epic Poem **RL 4, RL 10** | | | | Prefixes **L 4d** |
| *The Homecoming* from the *Odyssey* | Characteristics of an Epic **RL 2, RL 5** Summarizing **RL 2** | | | | Latin Roots **L 4c** Add Descriptive Details **L 3** |
| *Writing Workshop: Narrative: Video Script* | Write a Video Script **RL 5** | | Write a Video Script **W 3a–c, W 3e, W 4, W 5, W 6, W 10** | Write a Video Script **SL 2, SL 5** | |
| *Speaking and Listening Workshop: Evaluating a Video* | | | | Evaluate a Video **SL 1a, SL 1c** | |
| **UNIT 12** | | | | | |
| *Research Strategies Workshop* | | | Planning and Focusing Research **W 7, W 8, W 9** | Planning and Focusing Research **SL 1a, SL 1c** | |
| *Writing Workshop: Informative Text: Research Paper* | | | Write a Research Paper **W 2a–f, W 4, W 5, W 7, W 8, W 9** | | Punctuating Titles **L 2** Integrating Quotations **L 2b, L 3a** |
| *Technology Workshop: Creating a Wiki* | | | Create a Wiki **W 6** | Create a Wiki **SL 1b, SL 2, SL 5** | |

# HOLT McDOUGAL

# Literature

Grade 9

COMMON CORE

EDITION

Typeset in *The Sans* from LucasFonts.

## ACKNOWLEDGMENTS

### STUDENT GUIDE TO ACADEMIC SUCCESS

**Beacon Press:** "The Sun," from *New and Selected Poems* by Mary Oliver. Copyright © 1992 by Mary Oliver. Reprinted by permission of Beacon Press, Boston.

**Writers House:** "Letter from Birmingham Jail" by Martin Luther King Jr. Copyright 1963 Dr. Martin Luther King Jr.; copyright renewed 1991 Coretta Scott King. Reprinted by arrangement with The Heirs to the Estate of Martin Luther King Jr., c/o Writers House as agent for the proprietor New York, NY.

*Acknowledgments are continued at the back of the book, following the Index of Titles and Authors.*

## ART CREDITS

### COVER, TITLE PAGE

**Front:** (tc) Sea World of California/Corbis; (tr) Odysseus Slaying the Suitors (400's B.C.), Penelope Painter. Attic red figure painting on kylix. Height 20 cm. Inv F 2588. Antikensammlung, Staatliche Museen zu Berlin, Berlin. Photo by Juergen Liepe. © Bildarchiv Preussischer Kulturbesitz/Art Resource, New York; (bc) Colin Anderdson/Getty Images; (b) Portrait of William Shakespeare (about 1610), John Taylor. Oil on canvas. National Portrait Gallery, London. © Bridgeman Art Library; (bkgd) © Walter Geiersperger/Corbis; (bl) Ken Kinzie/HMH Publishers.

*Art Credits are continued at the back of the book, following the Acknowledgments.*

Printed in the U.S.A.

ISBN 978-0-547-61839-5

2 3 4 5 6 7 8 9 10 868 20 19 18 17 16 15 14 13 12 11

4500000000 B C D E F G

# HOLT McDOUGAL

# Literature

## Grade 9

Janet Allen

Arthur N. Applebee

Jim Burke

Douglas Carnine

Yvette Jackson

Carol Jago

Robert T. Jiménez

Judith A. Langer

Robert J. Marzano

Mary Lou McCloskey

Donna M. Ogle

Carol Booth Olson

Lydia Stack

Carol Ann Tomlinson

Special Contributor: Kylene Beers

HOLT McDOUGAL

HOUGHTON MIFFLIN HARCOURT

## SENIOR PROGRAM CONSULTANTS

**JANET ALLEN** Reading and Literacy Specialist; creator of the popular "It's Never Too Late"/"Reading for Life" Institutes. Dr. Allen is an internationally known consultant who specializes in literacy work with at-risk students. Her publications include *Tools for Content Literacy; It's Never Too Late: Leading Adolescents to Lifelong Learning; Yellow Brick Roads: Shared and Guided Paths to Independent Reading; Words, Words, Words: Teaching Vocabulary in Grades 4–12;* and *Testing 1, 2, 3 . . . Bridging Best Practice and High-Stakes Assessments.* Dr. Allen was a high school reading and English teacher for more than 20 years.

**ARTHUR N. APPLEBEE** Leading Professor, School of Education at the University at Albany, State University of New York; Director of the Center on English Learning and Achievement. During his varied career, Dr. Applebee has been both a researcher and a teacher, working in institutional settings with children with severe learning problems, in public schools, as a staff member of the National Council of Teachers of English, and in professional education. He was elected to the International Reading Hall of Fame and has received, among other honors, the David H. Russell Award for Distinguished Research in the Teaching of English.

**JIM BURKE** Lecturer and Author; Teacher of English at Burlingame High School, Burlingame, California. Mr. Burke is a popular presenter at educational conferences across the country and is the author of numerous books for teachers, including *School Smarts: The Four Cs of Academic Success; The English Teacher's Companion; Reading Reminders; Writing Reminders;* and *ACCESSing School: Teaching Struggling Readers to Achieve Academic and Personal Success.* He is the recipient of NCTE's Exemplary English Leadership Award and was inducted into the California Reading Association's Hall of Fame.

**DOUGLAS CARNINE** Professor of Education at the University of Oregon; Director of the Western Region Reading First Technical Assistance Center. Dr. Carnine is nationally known for his focus on research-based practices in education, especially curriculum designs that prepare instructors of K–12 students. He has received the Lifetime Achievement Award from the Council for Exceptional Children and the Ersted Award for outstanding teaching at the University of Oregon. Dr. Carnine frequently consults on educational policy with government groups, businesses, communities, and teacher unions.

**YVETTE JACKSON** Executive Director of the National Urban Alliance for Effective Education. Nationally recognized for her work in assessing the learning potential of underachieving urban students, Dr. Jackson is also a presenter for the Harvard Principal Center and is a member of the Differentiation Faculty of the Association for Supervision and Curriculum Development. Dr. Jackson's research focuses on literacy, gifted education, and cognitive mediation theory. She designed the Comprehensive Education Plan for the New York City Public Schools and has served as their Director of Gifted Programs.

**CAROL JAGO** Teacher of English with thirty-two years of experience at Santa Monica High School in California; Author and nationally known Lecturer; and Past President of the National Council of Teachers of English. With varied experience in standards assessment and secondary education, Ms. Jago is the author of numerous books on education and is active with the California Association of Teachers of English, editing its scholarly journal *California English* since 1996. Ms. Jago also served on the planning committee for the 2009 NAEP Framework and the 2011 NAEP Writing Framework.

**ROBERT T. JIMÉNEZ** Professor of Language, Literacy, and Culture at Vanderbilt University. Dr. Jiménez's research focuses on the language and literacy practices of Latino students. A former bilingual education teacher, he is now conducting research on how written language is thought about and used in contemporary Mexico. Dr. Jiménez has received several research and teaching honors, including two Fulbright awards from the Council for the International Exchange of Scholars and the Albert J. Harris Award from the International Reading Association.

**JUDITH A. LANGER** Distinguished Professor at the University at Albany, State University of New York; Director of the Center on English Learning and Achievement; Director of the Albany Institute for Research in Education. An internationally known scholar in English language arts education, Dr. Langer specializes in developing teaching approaches that can enrich and improve what gets done on a daily basis in classrooms. Her publications include *Getting to Excellent: How to Create Better Schools* and *Effective Literacy Instruction: Building Successful Reading and Writing Programs.*

**ROBERT J. MARZANO** Senior Scholar at Mid-Continent Research for Education and Learning (McREL); Associate Professor at Cardinal Stritch University in Milwaukee, Wisconsin; President of Marzano & Associates. An internationally known researcher, trainer, and speaker, Dr. Marzano has developed programs that translate research and theory into practical tools for K–12 teachers and administrators. He has written extensively on such topics as reading and writing instruction, thinking skills, school effectiveness, assessment, and standards implementation.

**DONNA M. OGLE** Professor of Reading and Language at National-Louis University in Chicago, Illinois; Past President of the International Reading Association. Creator of the well-known KWL strategy, Dr. Ogle has directed many staff development projects translating theory and research into school practice in middle and secondary schools throughout the United States and has served as a consultant on literacy projects worldwide. Her extensive international experience includes coordinating the Reading and Writing for Critical Thinking Project in Eastern Europe, developing integrated curriculum for a USAID Afghan Education Project, and speaking and consulting on projects in several Latin American countries and in Asia.

**CAROL BOOTH OLSON** Senior Lecturer in the Department of Education at the University of California, Irvine; Director of the UCI site of the National Writing Project. Dr. Olson writes and lectures extensively on the reading/writing connection, critical thinking through writing, interactive strategies for teaching writing, and the use of multicultural literature with students of culturally diverse backgrounds. She has received many awards, including the California Association of Teachers of English Award of Merit, the Outstanding California Education Research Award, and the UC Irvine Excellence in Teaching Award.

**CAROL ANN TOMLINSON** Professor of Educational Research, Foundations, and Policy at the University of Virginia; Co-Director of the University's Institutes on Academic Diversity. An internationally known expert on differentiated instruction, Dr. Tomlinson helps teachers and administrators develop effective methods of teaching academically diverse learners. She was a teacher of middle and high school English for 22 years prior to teaching at the University of Virginia. Her books on differentiated instruction have been translated into eight languages.

**SPECIAL CONTRIBUTOR:**

**KYLENE BEERS** Special Consultant; Former Middle School Teacher; nationally known Lecturer and Author on reading and literacy; and former President of the National Council of Teachers of English. Dr. Beers is the nationally known author of *When Kids Can't Read: What Teachers Can Do* and co-editor of *Adolescent Literacy: Turning Promise into Practice,* as well as articles in the *Journal of Adolescent and Adult Literacy.* Former editor of *Voices from the Middle,* she is the 2001 recipient of NCTE's Richard W. Halley Award, given for outstanding contributions to middle-school literacy.

FM5

## ENGLISH LEARNER SPECIALISTS

**MARY LOU McCLOSKEY** Past President of Teachers of English to Speakers of Other Languages (TESOL); Director of Teacher Development and Curriculum Design for Educo in Atlanta, Georgia. Dr. McCloskey is a former teacher in multilingual and multicultural classrooms. She has worked with teachers, teacher educators, and departments of education around the world on teaching English as a second and foreign language. She is author of *On Our Way to English, Voices in Literature, Integrating English,* and *Visions: Language, Literature, Content.* Her awards include the Le Moyne College Ignatian Award for Professional Achievement and the TESOL D. Scott Enright Service Award.

**LYDIA STACK** International ESL consultant. Her areas of expertise are English language teaching strategies, ESL standards for students and teachers, and curriculum writing. Her teaching experience includes 25 years as an elementary and high school ESL teacher. She is a past president of TESOL. Her awards include the James E. Alatis Award for Service to TESOL (2003) and the San Francisco STAR Teacher Award (1989). Her publications include *On Our Way to English; Wordways: Games for Language Learning;* and *Visions: Language, Literature, Content.*

## CURRICULUM SPECIALIST

**WILLIAM L. McBRIDE** Curriculum Specialist. Dr. McBride is a nationally known speaker, educator, and author who now trains teachers in instructional methodologies. A former reading specialist, English teacher, and social studies teacher, he holds a Masters in Reading and a Ph.D. in Curriculum and Instruction from the University of North Carolina at Chapel Hill. Dr. McBride has contributed to the development of textbook series in language arts, social studies, science, and vocabulary. He is also known for his novel *Entertaining an Elephant,* which tells the story of a burned-out teacher who becomes re-inspired with both his profession and his life.

## MEDIA SPECIALISTS

**DAVID M. CONSIDINE** Professor of Instructional Technology and Media Studies at Appalachian State University in North Carolina. Dr. Considine has served as a media literacy consultant to the U.S. government and to the media industry, including Discovery Communications and Cable in the Classroom. He has also conducted media literacy workshops and training for county and state health departments across the United States. Among his many publications are *Visual Messages: Integrating Imagery into Instruction,* and *Imagine That: Developing Critical Viewing and Thinking Through Children's Literature.*

**LARKIN PAULUZZI** Teacher and Media Specialist; trainer for the New Jersey Writing Project. Ms. Pauluzzi puts her extensive classroom experience to use in developing teacher-friendly curriculum materials and workshops in many different areas, including media literacy. She has led media literacy training workshops, guiding teachers in the meaningful and practical uses of media in the classroom. Ms. Pauluzzi has taught students at all levels, from Title I Reading to AP English IV. She also spearheads a technology club at her school, working with students to produce media and technology to serve both the school and the community.

**LISA K. SCHEFFLER** Teacher and Media Specialist. Ms. Scheffler has designed and taught media literacy and video production curriculum, in addition to teaching language arts and speech. Using her knowledge of mass communication theory, coupled with real classroom experience, she has developed ready-to-use materials that help teachers incorporate media literacy into their curricula. She has taught film and television studies at the University of North Texas and has served as a contributing writer for the Texas Education Agency's statewide viewing and representing curriculum.

## TEACHER ADVISORS

These are some of the many educators from across the country who played a crucial role in the development of the tables of contents, the lesson design, and other key components of this program:

**Virginia L. Alford,** MacArthur High School, San Antonio, Texas

**Yvonne L. Allen,** Shaker Heights High School, Shaker Heights, Ohio

**Dave T. Anderson,** Hinsdale South High School, Darien, Illinois

**Kacy Colleen Anglim,** Portland Public Schools District, Portland, Oregon

**Jordana Benone,** North High School, Torrance, California

**Patricia Blood,** Howell High School, Farmingdale, New Jersey

**Marjorie Bloom,** Eau Gallie High School, Melbourne, Florida

**Edward J. Blotzer,** Wilkinsburg Junior/Senior High School, Wilkinsburg, Pennsylvania

**Stephen D. Bournes,** Evanston Township High School, Evanston, Illinois

**Barbara M. Bowling,** Mt. Tabor High School, Winston-Salem, North Carolina

**Kiala Boykin-Givehand,** Duval County Public Schools, Jacksonville, Florida

**Laura L. Brown,** Adlai Stevenson High School, Lincolnshire, Illinois

**Cynthia Burke,** Yavneh Academy, Dallas, Texas

**Hoppy Chandler,** San Diego City Schools, San Diego, California

**Gary Chmielewski,** St. Benedict High School, Chicago, Illinois

**Delorse Cole-Stewart,** Milwaukee Public Schools, Milwaukee, Wisconsin

**Kathy Dahlgren,** Skokie, Illinois

**Diana Dilger,** Rosa Parks Middle School, Dixmoor, Illinois

**L. Calvin Dillon,** Gaither High School, Tampa, Florida

**Dori Dolata,** Rufus King High School, Milwaukee, Wisconsin

**Jon Epstein,** Marietta High School, Marietta, Georgia

**Helen Ervin,** Fort Bend Independent School District, Sugar Land, Texas

**Sue Friedman,** Buffalo Grove High School, Buffalo Grove, Illinois

**Chris Gee,** Bel Air High School, El Paso, Texas

**Paula Grasel,** The Horizon Center, Gainesville, Georgia

**Rochelle L. Greene-Brady,** Kenwood Academy, Chicago, Illinois

**Christopher Guarraia,** Centreville High School, Clifton, Virginia

**Michele M. Hettinger,** Niles West High School, Skokie, Illinois

**Elizabeth Holcomb,** Forest Hill High School, Jackson, Mississippi

**Jim Horan,** Hinsdale Central High School, Hinsdale, Illinois

**James Paul Hunter,** Oak Park-River Forest High School, Oak Park, Illinois

**Susan P. Kelly,** Director of Curriculum, Island Trees School District, Levittown, New York

**Beverley A. Lanier,** Varina High School, Richmond, Virginia

**Pat Laws,** Charlotte-Mecklenburg Schools, Charlotte, North Carolina

**Diana R. Martinez,** Treviño School of Communications & Fine Arts, Laredo, Texas

**Natalie Martinez,** Stephen F. Austin High School, Houston, Texas

**Elizabeth Matarazzo,** Ysleta High School, El Paso, Texas

**Carol M. McDonald,** J. Frank Dobie High School, Houston, Texas

**Amy Millikan,** Consultant, Chicago, Illinois

**Eileen Murphy,** Walter Payton Preparatory High School, Chicago, Illinois

**Lisa Omark,** New Haven Public Schools, New Haven, Connecticut

**Kaine Osburn,** Wheeling High School, Wheeling, Illinois

**Andrea J. Phillips,** Terry Sanford High School, Fayetteville, North Carolina

**Cathy Reilly,** Sayreville Public Schools, Sayreville, New Jersey

**Mark D. Simon,** Neuqua Valley High School, Naperville, Illinois

**Scott Snow,** Seguin High School, Arlington, Texas

**Jane W. Speidel,** Brevard County Schools, Viera, Florida

**Cheryl E. Sullivan,** Lisle Community School District, Lisle, Illinois

**Anita Usmiani,** Hamilton Township Public Schools, Hamilton Square, New Jersey

**Linda Valdez,** Oxnard Union High School District, Oxnard, California

**Nancy Walker,** Longview High School, Longview, Texas

**Kurt Weiler,** New Trier High School, Winnetka, Illinois

**Elizabeth Whittaker,** Larkin High School, Elgin, Illinois

**Linda S. Williams,** Woodlawn High School, Baltimore, Maryland

**John R. Williamson,** Fort Thomas Independent Schools, Fort Thomas, Kentucky

**Anna N. Winters,** Simeon High School, Chicago, Illinois

**Tonora D. Wyckoff,** North Shore Senior High School, Houston, Texas

**Karen Zajac,** Glenbard South High School, Glen Ellyn, Illinois

**Cynthia Zimmerman,** Mose Vines Preparatory High School, Chicago, Illinois

**Lynda Zimmerman,** El Camino High School, South San Francisco, California

**Ruth E. Zurich,** Brown Deer High School, Brown Deer, Wisconsin

COMMON
CORE

# OVERVIEW
## *Student Edition*

- Understanding the English Language Arts Common Core State Standards
- English Language Arts Common Core State Standards
- Spotlight on Common Core State Standards

**LESSONS WITH EMBEDDED COMMON CORE INSTRUCTION**

COMMON CORE  Look for the Common Core symbol throughout the book. It highlights targeted objectives to help you in mastering the knowledge and skills you will need for college or for a career.

© Getty Images.

COMMON CORE CONTENTS

# CONTENTS IN BRIEF

FM10

*Online at*

**Log in to learn more at thinkcentral.com, where you can access most program resources in one convenient location.**

## LITERATURE AND READING CENTER
- Author Biographies
- *PowerNotes* Presentations with Video Trailers
- Professional Audio Recordings of Selections
- Graphic Organizers
- Analysis Frames
- NovelWise

## WRITING AND GRAMMAR CENTER
- Interactive Student Models*
- Interactive Graphic Organizers*
- Interactive Revision Lessons*
- *GrammarNotes* Presentations and Practice

*also available on WriteSmart CD-ROM

## VOCABULARY CENTER
- *WordSharp* Interactive Vocabulary Tutor
- Vocabulary Practice Copy Masters

## MEDIA AND TECHNOLOGY CENTER
- MediaScope: Media Literacy Instruction
- Digital Storytelling
- Speaking and Listening Support

## RESEARCH CENTER
- Writing and Research in a Digital Age
- Citation Guide

### Assessment Center
- Program Assessments
- Level Up Online Tutorials
- Online Essay Scoring

### *MORE TECHNOLOGY*

**Student One Stop**
Access an electronic version of your textbook, complete with selection audio and worksheets.

**Media Smart DVD-ROM**
Sharpen your critical viewing and analysis skills with these in-depth interactive media studies.

# The Plot Thickens
# NARRATIVE STRUCTURE

- FICTION - MEDIA - INFORMATIONAL TEXT - POETRY - DRAMA

*Vocabulary Strategies*

Latin roots: *mal, p. 53*          Greek roots: *chron, p.110*
Denotation and connotation, *p. 82*     Synonyms and antonyms, *p. 124*
Latin prefixes: *in-, p. 98*          Word families: *aud, p. 137*

# COMMON CORE
## UNIT 2

*People Watching*
# CHARACTERIZATION AND POINT OF VIEW

• FICTION • INFORMATIONAL TEXT • POETRY • ACROSS GENRES

*Vocabulary Strategies*

Latin roots: *ben, p. 220*
Latin roots: *spec, p. 235*
Words from Greek culture, *p. 252*

Multiple-meaning words, *p. 266*
Specialized vocabulary, *p. 281*
Etymologies, *p. 300*

## COMMON CORE
# UNIT 3

## A Sense of Place
# SETTING, MOOD, AND IMAGERY

• FICTION • MEDIA • INFORMATIONAL TEXT • POETRY

*Vocabulary Strategies*

Connotation and denotation, *p. 352*　　Word families: *clud, p. 382*
Latin roots: *quest, quer,* and *quisit, p. 368*　　Context clues, *p. 399*

# COMMON CORE
## UNIT 4

# Getting the Message
# THEME AND SYMBOL

• FICTION • INFORMATIONAL TEXT • POETRY • ACROSS GENRES

> ### Vocabulary Strategies
>
> Suffixes: -or, p. 453    Using context clues, p. 491
> Denotation and connotation, p. 478    Word origins, p. 522

## COMMON CORE
### UNIT 5

*Ideas Made Visible*
# AUTHOR'S PURPOSE

• INFORMATIONAL TEXT • MEDIA • FICTION • FUNCTIONAL TEXTS

*Vocabulary Strategies*

Word roots: *gen, p. 576*
Specialized fields: *"ologies," p. 589*

Latin roots: *fract, p. 599*

# COMMON CORE
## UNIT 6

# *Taking Sides*
# ARGUMENT AND PERSUASION

• INFORMATIONAL TEXT • MEDIA • FICTION

FM22

*Vocabulary Strategies*

## *Special Effects*
# THE LANGUAGE OF POETRY

FM24

# COMMON CORE
## UNIT 8

*A Way with Words*
# AUTHOR'S STYLE AND VOICE

• FICTION • MEDIA • INFORMATIONAL TEXT • POETRY • DRAMA

*Vocabulary Strategies*
Prefixes: *in-* , p. 838                          Homonyms, *p. 866*
Appropriate word choice, *p.859*

# *Putting It in Context*
# HISTORY, CULTURE, AND THE AUTHOR

• INFORMATIONAL TEXT • FICTION • POETRY

*Vocabulary Strategies*
Latin roots: *fid, p. 938*          Idioms, *p. 975*
Greek roots: *cosm, p. 949*

# Shakespearean Drama
# THE TRAGEDY OF ROMEO AND JULIET

● DRAMA ● MEDIA ● POETRY

# Epic Poetry
# THE ODYSSEY

**STANDARDS FOCUS**

*Characteristics of the Epic,
The Language of Homer,
Reading an Epic Poem*

Video link at
**thinkcentral.com**

*Epic Hero, Archetypal Character,
Imagery, Figurative Language*

STANDARDS FOCUS

---

*Narrative Techniques in Media*

*Epic, Setting, Theme, Epic Hero*

*Vocabulary Strategies*
Prefixes: *fore-, p. 1239*     Latin roots: *solus, p. 1268*

# Investigation and Discovery
## THE POWER OF RESEARCH

COMMON CORE UNIT 12

FM34

## Student Resource Bank

## Features

**WriteSmart** CD-ROM

**Media Smart** DVD-ROM

### VOCABULARY STRATEGIES

**pages** 53, 82, 98, 110, 124, 137, 220, 235, 252, 266, 281, 300, 352,
368, 382, 399, 453, 478, 491, 522, 576, 589, 599, 669, 678, 692,
838, 859, 866, 938, 949, 975, 1239, 1268

### GRAMMAR AND WRITING

**pages** 54, 83, 99, 111, 125, 173, 221, 236, 253, 267, 353, 369, 383,
479, 499, 567, 577, 611, 679, 693, 709, 755, 785, 839, 867, 939,
961, 1147, 1269

# STUDENT GUIDE TO ACADEMIC SUCCESS

**STUDENT GUIDE**

© Age Fotostock America, Inc.

FM39

# The Common Core for Uncommon Achievement

## Carol Jago

*"If you don't know where you are going,
any road will get you there."* – Lewis Carroll

The Common Core State Standards make clear where students are going. They describe what today's children need to know and be able to do to thrive in post-secondary education and the workplace. By focusing on results — the destination — rather than on the how — the means of transportation — the Common Core allows for a variety of teaching methods and many different classroom approaches. The challenge for teachers is to turn the daily journey towards this destination into an intellectual adventure.

One way to think about the Common Core is as a kind of GPS device to situate curriculum. While some students may choose the road less traveled, the objective is fixed. When students become lost through a wrong turn, teachers recalculate the route, providing a calm and confident voice that guides all students to academic achievement and deep literacy.

### Shared Responsibility for Students' Literacy Development

The Common Core State Standards insist that the responsibility for helping students achieve literacy is not the sole responsibility of the English teacher. The introduction states clearly that, "instruction in reading, writing, speaking, listening, and language (should) be a shared responsibility within the school" (4). Citing NAEP Reading assessment test specification guidelines, the Common Core recommends that 55% of what students read in grade 8 and 70% in grade 12 should be informational text. These percentages are not meant to reflect the balance of reading materials in English class alone but rather the totality of what students should be reading across the curriculum in history/social studies, science, and technical subjects as well as in English. Given the type of reading that will be required of students in college and of graduates in the workplace, this distribution is both relevant and practical.

### Understanding of Other Perspectives and Cultures

The Common Core also makes clear the importance of literature in the education of America's children. "Through reading great classic and contemporary works of literature representative of a variety of periods, cultures, and worldviews, students can vicariously inhabit worlds and have experiences much different from their own" (7). Reading literature demands that readers look inward, examine their beliefs in light of new information, consider the world through different eyes, take time for reflection. Such reading is a key to student learning.

### The Purpose of Exemplar Texts

To describe the quality and complexity of the works students should read at each grade level, the Common Core offers lists of "exemplar texts." While some may choose to treat the texts on these lists as required reading, such usage would represent a misunderstanding of their purpose. "The choices should serve as useful guideposts in helping educators select texts of similar complexity, quality, and range for their own classrooms. They expressly do not represent a partial or complete reading list" (Appendix B, 2). The poems, stories, novels, and nonfiction that appear on the Common Core lists are intended as models for guiding — not dictating — text selection.

### The Difference Between Persuasion and Argument

The Common Core writing standards describe the types and purposes for writing that students need to master. You will find extended definitions of argument, informative/explanatory writing, and narrative writing in Appendix A. Of particular note is the distinction the Common Core draws between persuasion and argument. "When writing to persuade, writers employ a variety of persuasive strategies. One common strategy is an appeal to the credibility, character, or authority of the writer (or speaker). A logical argument, on the other hand, convinces the audience because of the perceived merit and reasonableness of the claims and proofs offered rather than either the emotions the writing evokes in the audience or the character or credentials of the writer" (24). Because of its importance for college and workplace readiness, argument holds a special place in the Common Core writing standards.

> *One way to think about the Common Core is as a kind of GPS device ...*

### Complex Literary and Informational Texts

Throughout the Common Core document you will notice the anchor standard, "Read and comprehend complex literary and informational texts independently and proficiently." It isn't enough for students to read with a teacher by their side. They need to be able, often with a little help from their friends or from the habits of mind they learned from their teachers, to read for themselves. They need to be able, like Huck Finn, to head out for the territory on their own. Such a journey requires confidence in one's ability to navigate uncharted waters and to overcome challenges their teachers can't foresee or even imagine. As we guide students on the academic adventure that is high school, let us never forget that the path we tread is the path to intellectual freedom.

**WORKS CITED**

*Common Core State Standards for English Language Arts and History/Social Studies, Science, & Technical Subjects.* 2010.

*Appendix B. Common Core State Standards for English Language Arts and History/Social Studies, Science, & Technical Subjects.* 2010.

*Carol Jago has taught middle and high school for over 30 years and was a member of the Common Core Initiative feedback team. She serves as Past President of the National Council of Teachers of English.*

# Understanding the Common Core State Standards

## What are the English Language Arts Common Core State Standards?

The Common Core State Standards for English Language Arts indicate what you should know and be able to do by the end of your grade level. These understandings and skills will help you be better prepared for future classes, college courses, and a career. For this reason, the standards for each strand in English Language Arts (such as reading informational text or writing) directly relate to the College and Career Readiness Anchor Standards for each strand. The Anchor Standards broadly outline the understandings and skills you should learn by the end of high school so that you are well-prepared for college or for a career.

## How do I learn the English Language Arts Common Core State Standards?

Your textbook is closely aligned to the English Language Arts Common Core State Standards. Every time you learn a concept or practice a skill, you are working on mastery of one of the standards. Each unit, each selection, and each workshop in your textbook connects to one or more of the standards for English Language Arts listed on the following pages.

The English Language Arts Common Core State Standards are divided into five strands: Reading Literature, Reading Informational Text, Writing, Speaking and Listening, and Language.

### Reading Literature (RL)

This strand concerns the literary texts you will read at this grade level: stories, drama, and poetry. The Common Core State Standards stress that you should read a range of texts of increasing complexity as you progress through high school.

### Reading Informational Text (RI)

Informational text includes a broad range of literary nonfiction, including exposition, argument, and functional text, such as personal essays, speeches, opinion pieces, memoirs, and historical and technical accounts. The Common Core State Standards stress that you will also read a range of informational texts of increasing complexity as you progress from grade to grade.

### Writing (W)

The Writing strand focuses on your generating three types of texts: arguments, informative or explanatory texts, and narratives, as well as using the writing process and technology to develop and share your writing. The Common Core State Standards also emphasize research and specify that you should write routinely for both short and extended time frames.

### Speaking and Listening (SL)

The Common Core State Standards focus on comprehending information presented in a variety of media and formats, on participating in collaborative discussions, and on presenting knowledge and ideas clearly.

### Language (L)

The standards in the Language strand address the conventions of Standard English grammar, usage, and mechanics; knowledge of language; and vocabulary acquisition and use.

---

**COMMON CORE DECODER**

## W 1 a

*Indicates that this standard is from the writing strand.*

*Identifies the standard number and standard subpart for the knowledge or skill.*

*Identifies the specific knowledge or skill for this standard.*

**1.** Write arguments to support claims in an analysis of substantive topics or texts, using valid reasoning and relevant and sufficient evidence.

**a.** Introduce precise claim(s), distinguish the claim(s) from alternate or opposing claims, and create an organization that establishes clear relationships among claim(s), counterclaims, reasons, and evidence.

# English Language Arts
# Common Core State Standards

Listed below are the English Language Arts Common Core State Standards that you are required to master by the end of grade 9. We have provided a summary of the concepts you will learn on your way to mastering each standard. The CCR anchor standards and high school grade-specific standards for each strand work together to define college and career readiness expectations—the former providing broad standards, the latter providing additional specificity.

## College and Career Readiness Anchor Standards for Reading

**COMMON CORE STATE STANDARDS**

**KEY IDEAS AND DETAILS**

1. Read closely to determine what the text says explicitly and to make logical inferences from it; cite specific textual evidence when writing or speaking to support conclusions drawn from the text.

2. Determine central ideas or themes of a text and analyze their development; summarize the key supporting details and ideas.

3. Analyze how and why individuals, events, and ideas develop and interact over the course of a text.

**CRAFT AND STRUCTURE**

4. Interpret words and phrases as they are used in a text, including determining technical, connotative, and figurative meanings, and analyze how specific word choices shape meaning or tone.

5. Analyze the structure of texts, including how specific sentences, paragraphs, and larger portions of the text (e.g., a section, chapter, scene, or stanza) relate to each other and the whole.

6. Assess how point of view or purpose shapes the content and style of a text.

**INTEGRATION OF KNOWLEDGE AND IDEAS**

7. Integrate and evaluate content presented in diverse formats and media, including visually and quantitatively, as well as in words.

8. Delineate and evaluate the argument and specific claims in a text, including the validity of the reasoning as well as the relevance and sufficiency of the evidence.

9. Analyze how two or more texts address similar themes or topics in order to build knowledge or to compare the approaches the authors take.

**RANGE OF READING AND LEVEL OF TEXT COMPLEXITY**

10. Read and comprehend complex literary and informational texts independently and proficiently.

# Reading Standards for Literature, Grades 9–10 Students

The College and Career Readiness Anchor Standards for Reading apply to both literature and informational text.

| COMMON CORE STATE STANDARD | WHAT IT MEANS TO YOU |
|---|---|
| **KEY IDEAS AND DETAILS** | |
| **1.** Cite strong and thorough textual evidence to support analysis of what the text says explicitly as well as inferences drawn from the text. | You will use details and information from the text to support your understanding of its main ideas—both those that are stated directly and those that are suggested. |
| **2.** Determine a theme or central idea of a text and analyze in detail its development over the course of the text, including how it emerges and is shaped and refined by specific details; provide an objective summary of the text. | You will analyze the development of a text's main ideas and themes by showing how they progress throughout the text. You will also summarize the main idea of the text as a whole without adding your own ideas or opinions. |
| **3.** Analyze how complex characters (e.g., those with multiple or conflicting motivations) develop over the course of a text, interact with other characters, and advance the plot or develop the theme. | You will analyze the development of a text's characters and how their actions, thoughts, and words contribute to the story's plot or themes. |
| **CRAFT AND STRUCTURE** | |
| **4.** Determine the meaning of words and phrases as they are used in the text, including figurative and connotative meanings; analyze the cumulative impact of specific word choices on meaning and tone (e.g., how the language evokes a sense of time and place; how it sets a formal or informal tone). | You will analyze specific words and phrases in the text to determine both what they mean individually as well as how they contribute to the text's tone and meaning as a whole. |
| **5.** Analyze how an author's choices concerning how to structure a text, order events within it (e.g., parallel plots), and manipulate time (e.g., pacing, flashbacks) create such effects as mystery, tension, or surprise. | You will analyze the ways in which the author has chosen to structure and order the text and determine how those choices affect the text's mood or tone. |
| **6.** Analyze a particular point of view or cultural experience reflected in a work of literature from outside the United States, drawing on a wide reading of world literature. | You will analyze the point of view or cultural experience of a work of literature from outside the United States. |
| **INTEGRATION OF KNOWLEDGE AND IDEAS** | |
| **7.** Analyze the representation of a subject or a key scene in two different artistic mediums, including what is emphasized or absent in each treatment (e.g., Auden's "Musée des Beaux Arts" and Breughel's Landscape with the Fall of Icarus). | You will compare and contrast how events and information are presented in visual and non-visual texts. |
| **8.** (Not applicable to literature) | |
| **9.** Analyze how an author draws on and transforms source material in a specific work (e.g., how Shakespeare treats a theme or topic from Ovid or the Bible or how a later author draws on a play by Shakespeare). | You will recognize and analyze how an author draws from and uses source material from other texts or other types of sources. |

# COMMON CORE FOCUS

**RL 9** Analyze how an author draws on and transforms source material in a specific work (e.g., how Shakespeare treats a theme or topic from Ovid or the Bible or how a later author draws on a play by Shakespeare).

## Literature: Analyzing Literary Sources

Begin by reviewing some basic terminology related to this standard. Tell students that **source material** is another text from which a writer draws a topic, theme, or idea. Remind them that the **topic** of a work of literature is its subject, or what it is about. The **theme** of a work of literature is its message about the topic.

Point out that in literature, writers sometimes respond to, argue with, or pay tribute to writers who wrote years or even centuries before them. Before they read the poems, point out that although Oliver wrote her poem roughly two hundred years after Wordsworth wrote his, she seems to be echoing his feelings.

## Reading Standards for Literature, Grades 9–10 Students, continued

| COMMON CORE STATE STANDARD | WHAT IT MEANS TO YOU |
|---|---|
| **RANGE OF READING AND LEVEL OF TEXT COMPLEXITY**<br>**10.** By the end of grade 9, read and comprehend literature, including stories, dramas, and poems, in the grades 9–10 text complexity band proficiently, with scaffolding as needed at the high end of the range. | You will demonstrate the ability to read and understand grade-level appropriate literary texts by the end of grade 9. |

## Spotlight on Common Core

**COMMON CORE** — **RL 9** Analyze how an author draws on and transforms source material in a specific work (e.g., how Shakespeare treats a theme or topic from Ovid or the Bible or how a later author draws on a play by Shakespeare).

### Literature: Analyzing Literary Sources

The Common Core State Standards urge readers to make connections across a variety of texts. One type of connection we make is when we notice that an author has drawn **source material**, such as a topic, theme, or idea, from an earlier text. Then, during the writing process, the author transforms this material into something new and original. Study the examples below to see how one reader made this type of connection between two poems.

Although written almost two centuries apart, the poems of William Wordsworth and Mary Oliver speak about nature's beauty, as well as nature's powers of destruction and re-creation. Both poets also find fault with using our energy to obtain the objects of the material world. Wordsworth believed that in contemplating nature a person could gain insight into human experience. In her poems, Oliver often mourns the loss of our innocent delight in nature. As you read, consider how Mary Oliver has drawn on and transformed elements of Wordsworth's work while still echoing his theme.

> ### The World Is Too Much with Us
> #### William Wordsworth
>
> The world is too much with us; late and soon,
> Getting and spending, we lay waste our powers;
> Little we see in Nature that is ours;
> We have given our hearts away, a sordid boon[1]!
> 5 This Sea that bares her bosom to the moon
> The winds that will be howling at all hours,
> And are up-gathered now like sleeping flowers,
> For this, for everything, we are out of tune;
> It moves us not.—Great God! I'd rather be
>
> _____
> **1. sordid boon:** tarnished or selfish gift.

*We spend too much time on material things.*

*We're out-of-touch with nature.*

*We've traded our hearts for selfish material things.*

*We don't feel or see the power and beauty of nature.*

10 A Pagan[2] suckled in a creed outworn;
So might I, standing on this pleasant lea,[3]
Have glimpses that would make me less forlorn;
Have sight of Proteus rising from the sea;
Or hear old Triton blow his wreathèd horn.[4]

> *The speaker praises innocence.*

> *The speaker thinks he would be happier if he were closer to nature and lived more simply.*

2. **Pagan:** someone who is not Christian, Jewish, or Muslim;
   suckled in a creed outworn: raised in an outdated faith or belief system.
3. **lea:** meadow.
4. **Proteus . . . Triton:** sea gods of Greek mythology.

The Sun
Mary Oliver

Have you ever seen
anything
in your life
more wonderful

5 than the way the sun,
every evening,
relaxed and easy,
floats toward the horizon

> *The speaker uses "relaxed and easy" language.*

and into the clouds or the hills,
10 or the rumpled sea,
and is gone—
and how it slides again

out of the blackness,
every morning,
15 on the other side of the world,
like a red flower

> *The speaker describes the sun's daily rising and setting.*

streaming upward on its heavenly oils,
say, on a morning in early summer,
20 at its perfect imperial distance—
and have you ever felt for anything

> *Nature is powerful, "imperial," beautiful.*

such wild love—
do you think there is anywhere, in any language,
a word billowing enough
for the pleasure

> *The speaker loves nature; no word can describe it.*

Ask for a student volunteer to read each poem aloud. Before the readings begin, tell students to listen for similarities and differences between them. Pause after each poem is read to ask:

- What is the topic of this poem?
- What is the theme of this poem?

**FM48** STUDENT GUIDE

25 that fills you,
   as the sun
   reaches out,
   as it warms you

   as you stand there,
30 empty-handed—
   or have you too
   turned from this world—

   or have you too
   gone crazy
35 for power,
   for things?

*The sun's gift of beauty and warmth is free.*

*The speaker asks if we have turned our back on nature.*

*The speaker asks if the reader has also been tempted by power and things.*

**LEARN HOW** Analyzing Literary Sources To **analyze** how the author of one text has drawn on and transformed material from another text, you need to read both texts closely. Then you should cite textual evidence to identify important or memorable elements in each poem, such as poetic diction (or word choice), images, or themes. Finally, you should **compare** and **contrast** these elements in order to analyze the works' similarities and differences.

Study the chart below. By making a chart like this one, you can compare and contrast two texts. In the following chart, the writer cites examples of poetic elements from each text. Then the writer states similarities and differences between the two poems.

| Poetic element | "The World Is Too Much with Us" | "The Sun" |
|---|---|---|
| poetic form | sonnet | free-verse poem |
| diction, or word choice | "Getting and spending, we lay waste our powers"<br><br>"We have given our hearts away, a sordid boon!" | "gone crazy / for power, / for things?"<br><br>"or have you too / turned from this world" |
| tone | tone of emotional excitement | tone of emotional excitement; speaker asks an accusatory question at the end |
| imagery | "This Sea that bares her bosom to the moon"<br><br>"The winds that will be howling at all hours, / and are up-gathered now like sleeping flowers" | "relaxed and easy, / floats toward the horizon"<br><br>"the rumpled sea"<br><br>"and how it slides again / out of the blackness"<br><br>"streaming upward on its heavenly oils" |

**LEARN HOW** Analyzing Literary Sources
Remind students that to **analyze** something means to look at its different parts and how the parts fit together to form the whole. For example, when you analyze a poem you might look at the tone, the theme, and the imagery and how those elements work together to create the meaning of the poem.

Remind students that **textual evidence** means words and phrases from a text that provide clues about the text. To help students understand what it means to cite textual evidence, refer them to the sample chart comparing and contrasting the two poems. Point out that the words and phrases in quotation marks in the chart are textual evidence from the poems that provide clues about the poems.

After the class has read and discussed the sample chart about the similarities and differences between the two poems, ask each student to write a sentence that describes how one writer draws on and transforms the source material. You can give students the following sentence stem to get them started:

*In her poem "The Sun," Mary Oliver draws on and transforms Wordsworth's "The World Is Too Much with Us" by* _____.

*continued*

| theme | We have turned away from nature by chasing power and wealth. In doing so, we've lost our hearts and souls. | The speaker reminds us of the beauty of nature by discussing the sun's rising and setting. The speaker laments that we have turned away from nature in our quest for power and things. |
|---|---|---|

*Differences:* Wordsworth uses the sonnet form, formal language, and references to mythology to explore his theme. Oliver uses the contemporary free-verse form and informal, simple, bold language. Wordsworth begins with "getting and spending, we lay waste our powers," which introduces the poem's theme. Oliver begins with a vivid description of the sun and then concludes by commenting on our separation from nature.

*Similarities:* Wordsworth regrets our lack of closeness with nature and our attention to acquiring material objects and power. Oliver reflects Wordsworth's theme by ending with "or have you too / gone crazy/ for power, / for things?"

By comparing and contrasting two texts in this way, you can clarify an important connection between them. As you read other texts in this book, note how the author of one text draws from and transforms the ideas in another work.

## Reading Standards for Informational Text, Grades 9–10 Students

| COMMON CORE STATE STANDARD | WHAT IT MEANS TO YOU |
|---|---|
| **KEY IDEAS AND DETAILS** | |
| **1.** Cite strong and thorough textual evidence to support analysis of what the text says explicitly as well as inferences drawn from the text. | You will use details and information from the text to support your understanding of its main ideas—both those that are stated directly and those that are suggested. |
| **2.** Determine a central idea of a text and analyze its development over the course of the text, including how it emerges and is shaped and refined by specific details; provide an objective summary of the text. | You will analyze the development of a text's main ideas and themes by showing how they progress throughout the text. You will also summarize the main idea of the text as a whole without adding your own ideas or opinions. |
| **3.** Analyze how the author unfolds an analysis or series of ideas or events, including the order in which the points are made, how they are introduced and developed, and the connections that are drawn between them. | You will analyze the ways in which the author has chosen to structure and order the text and determine how those choices affect the text's central ideas. |
| **CRAFT AND STRUCTURE** | |
| **4.** Determine the meaning of words and phrases as they are used in a text, including figurative, connotative, and technical meanings; analyze the cumulative impact of specific word choices on meaning and tone (e.g., how the language of a court opinion differs from that of a newspaper). | You will analyze specific words and phrases in the text to determine both what they mean individually as well as how they contribute to the text's tone and meaning as a whole. |
| **5.** Analyze in detail how an author's ideas or claims are developed and refined by particular sentences, paragraphs, or larger portions of a text (e.g., a section or chapter). | You will examine specific portions of the text (sentences, paragraphs, or larger sections) to understand how they develop the author's ideas and claims. |

| COMMON CORE STATE STANDARD | WHAT IT MEANS TO YOU |
|---|---|
| 6. Determine an author's point of view or purpose in a text and analyze how an author uses rhetoric to advance that point of view or purpose. | You will understand the author's purpose and analyze how the author uses language to effectively communicate that purpose. |
| **INTEGRATION OF KNOWLEDGE AND IDEAS** | |
| 7. Analyze various accounts of a subject told in different mediums (e.g., a person's life story in both print and multimedia), determining which details are emphasized in each account. | You will compare and contrast the ways in which various media, such as newspapers, television, documentaries, blogs, and the Internet, portray the same events. |
| 8. Delineate and evaluate the argument and specific claims in a text, assessing whether the reasoning is valid and the evidence is relevant and sufficient; identify false statements and fallacious reasoning. | You will evaluate the strength of the author's claims by examining the supporting details and reasoning and identifying any faults or weaknesses in them. |
| 9. Analyze seminal U.S. documents of historical and literary significance (e.g., Washington's Farewell Address, the Gettysburg Address, Roosevelt's Four Freedoms speech, King's "Letter from Birmingham Jail"), including how they address related themes and concepts. | You will read and analyze influential documents and explain how they address important themes related to United States history and culture. |
| **RANGE OF READING AND LEVEL OF TEXT COMPLEXITY** | |
| 10. By the end of grade 9, read and comprehend literary nonfiction in the grades 9–10 text complexity band proficiently, with scaffolding as needed at the high end of the range. | You will demonstrate the ability to read and understand grade-level appropriate literary nonfiction texts by the end of grade 9. |

## COMMON CORE FOCUS

**RI 9** Analyze seminal U.S. documents of historical and literary significance (e.g., Washington's Farewell Address, the Gettysburg Address, Roosevelt's Four Freedoms speech, King's "Letter from Birmingham Jail"), including how they address related themes and concepts.

### Informational Text: Analyzing Seminal U.S. Documents

Ask the class to deduce the meaning of the word *seminal* in the context of the standard. Lead students to conclude that a seminal U.S. document is one from which a change in our nation's laws, society, or ideas about itself grew.

**LEARN HOW** Analyzing and Connecting Seminal U.S. Documents Make sure that students understand that to **analyze** something is to look at its different parts. Explain that they will read excerpts from three documents and then **connect** the ideas they contain.

## Spotlight on Common Core

 **COMMON CORE**

**RI 9** Analyze seminal U.S. documents of historical and literary significance (e.g., Washington's Farewell Address, the Gettysburg Address, Roosevelt's Four Freedoms speech, King's "Letter from Birmingham Jail"), including how they address related themes and concepts.

### Informational Text: Analyzing Seminal U.S. Documents

The Common Core State Standards stress the importance of **analyzing** and **making connections** among significant historical U.S. documents. Reading and comparing themes and concepts among these documents is one of the best ways to understand our history and our national experience. Throughout your reading, you will be asked to analyze and make connections among important historical documents, many also noted for their literary qualities. Use the techniques explained below to read these kinds of texts.

**LEARN HOW** Analyzing and Connecting Seminal U.S. Documents To understand a historical document's importance, you need to know something about its background or **historical context**. Asking questions like the ones below will help you understand its context better.
- Who is the document's author?
- Who was its audience?
- When was it written?
- Where was it written or presented?
- What is the document about?
- Why was it written?

Keep the preceding questions in mind as you read Lincoln's "Gettysburg Address," perhaps the most famous speech in U.S. history. Notice how one reader responded to her reading of this speech.

**Background** The Battle of Gettysburg was fought July 1–3, 1863. The victory for Union forces marked a turning point in the Civil War, but the losses on both sides were staggering: 28,000 Confederate soldiers and 23,000 Union soldiers were killed or wounded. Lincoln delivered his Gettysburg Address on November 19, 1863, at a ceremony to dedicate a national cemetery on the battle site.

> *Lincoln was dedicating a cemetery after a long and bloody battle. Some of the soldiers' families would have been there.*

### The Gettysburg Address
### Abraham Lincoln

> *The speech was written by Abraham Lincoln, president at the time.*

Four score and seven years ago[1] our fathers brought forth on this continent a new nation, conceived in liberty, and dedicated to the proposition that all men are created equal.

> *The war tests our founders' belief that all men are created equal.*

Now we are engaged in a great civil war, testing whether that
5 nation, or any nation so conceived and so dedicated, can long endure. We are met on a great battlefield of that war. We have come to dedicate a portion of that field as a final resting place for those who here gave their lives that that nation might live. It is altogether fitting and proper that we should do this.

> *The speech dedicates a cemetery.*

10 But, in a larger sense, we cannot dedicate—we cannot consecrate—we cannot hallow[2]—this ground. The brave men, living and dead, who struggled here have consecrated it far above our poor power to add or detract. The world will little note nor long remember what we say here, but it can never forget what
15 they did here. It is for us, the living, rather, to be dedicated here to the unfinished work which they who fought here have thus far so nobly advanced. It is rather for us to be here dedicated to the great task remaining before us—that from these honored dead we take increased devotion to that cause for which they gave the
20 last full measure of devotion; that we here highly resolve that these dead shall not have died in vain; that this nation, under God, shall have a new birth of freedom; and that government of the people, by the people, for the people, shall not perish from the earth.

> *The soldiers have done more than we to defend our founders' beliefs.*

> *The living should continue to fight for these beliefs.*

> *...so that the dead will not have died for nothing.*

> *...and democratic government won't disappear.*

---

1. **four score . . . ago:** 87 years ago—that is, in 1776. (*Score* means "a group of 20.")
2. **hallow:** set apart as holy.

Questioning a text often leads to more questions. Further questioning can deepen your understanding of a document's context, meaning, and significance. Consider these examples:

- What do you know about the author's attitudes and beliefs?
- What events or situation probably influenced the author?
- Why do you think the author cared about the topic?
- What do you think the author was trying to achieve?
- Why might the author have chosen to make the points he or she made?

---

**Background** Before students read the Gettysburg Address, make sure that they understand that part of a document's meaning comes from its historical context. To demonstrate this idea, stage a re-creation of the speech. Read the background note to the class. Then ask each student to take on one of these roles as they listen to the speech.

- Union soldier
- Deceased Union soldier's widow or child
- Citizen of Gettysburg whose town was affected by the battle
- News reporter

Next, ask students to imagine that they are standing on the battlefield near a cemetery full of new graves. Finally, choose a student to play the part of Lincoln. Have him or her read the speech to the class. Then discuss as a class how the speech's time, place, and audience might have affected its meaning.

To answer some of these questions, you might have to research the author and the events and attitudes of the day. This helps you build the knowledge and insight necessary for a complete analysis.

Many historically significant documents are also great works of literature. Lincoln's "Gettysburg Address" is read as much for its literary value as for its historical significance. To analyze the literary value of a historic document, ask questions about the way the author expresses his or her ideas. Here are some questions to help you:

- What type of document is this: a letter? article? speech? journal?
- What type of language is used: formal? casual? technical? complex?
- Are there cultural references or references to other texts?
- How suitable is the author's style and tone for its purpose and audience?
- What, if anything, makes the language memorable: phrases? figurative language? symbols? imagery?
- What, if anything, makes the language persuasive: analogy? repetition? parallelism?

Try reading a document once to understand the author's ideas. Then read it again to examine *how* the author expresses these ideas. Multiple readings can help clarify why a document has literary value.

Consider these questions as you read the following excerpt from Martin Luther King Jr's. "Letter from Birmingham Jail." This text is also praised for its literary qualities. Notice how one reader responded to the document's literary and rhetorical qualities.

---

***Background*** In the spring of 1963, Martin Luther King Jr. and the Southern Christian Leadership Conference (SCLC) targeted Birmingham, Alabama, with a series of peaceful demonstrations aimed at ending segregation. The police reacted violently and hundreds of protesters, including King, were jailed. At first, King was criticized for going to Birmingham; eight white clergymen published a letter condemning his actions. King answered them with his own letter, smuggled out of the city jail. The letter was soon published in magazines and newspapers. In it King cited philosophers, religious scholars, and biblical figures to justify his actions.

*letter, audience: supporters, critics, general public*

*from* "Letter from Birmingham Jail"
Martin Luther King Jr.

. . . I am in Birmingham because injustice is here. Just as the prophets of the eighth century B.C. left their villages and carried their "thus saith the Lord" far beyond the boundaries of their home towns, and just as the Apostle Paul left his village of Tarsus and carried the gospel of Jesus Christ to the far corners of the Greco-Roman world, so am I compelled to carry the gospel of freedom beyond my own hometown. Like Paul, I must constantly respond to the Macedonian call for aid.[1]

*references to the early Christian church.*

Moreover, I am cognizant of the interrelatedness of all communities and states. I cannot sit idly by in Atlanta and not be concerned about what happens in Birmingham. Injustice anywhere is a threat to justice everywhere. We are caught in an inescapable network of mutuality, tied in a single garment of destiny. Whatever affects one directly, affects all indirectly. Never again can we afford to live with the narrow,

*"network of mutuality"— memorable*

*parallelism: "affects . . . directly" and "affects . . . indirectly"*

1. **Macedonian call for aid:** According to the Bible (Acts 16), the apostle Paul received a vision calling him to preach in Macedonia, an area north of Greece.

---

***Background*** Before students read the letter, help struggling readers with some difficult vocabulary by writing these words on the board without their definitions:

*compelled:* forced

*cognizant:* aware

*interrelatedness:* state of being connected

*idly:* lazily

*mutuality:* state of having things in common

*garment:* clothing

*destiny:* fate

*provincial:* limited to one's own province, or area

*agitator:* someone who stirs things up

*deplore:* strongly disapprove of

*superficial:* on the surface

*grapple:* struggle

Have students find each word in the letter and examine its context. Ask students to guess what it means. If students cannot guess, work with them to arrive at a definition.

*continued*

provincial "outside agitator" idea. Anyone who lives inside the
United States can never be considered an outsider anywhere within
its bounds.

You deplore the demonstrations taking place in Birmingham. But
your statement, I am sorry to say, fails to express a similar concern for
the conditions that brought about the demonstrations. I am sure that
none of you would want to rest content with the superficial kind of
social analysis that deals merely with effects and does not grapple with
underlying causes. It is unfortunate that demonstrations are taking
place in Birmingham, but it is even more unfortunate that the city's
white power structure left the Negro community with no alternative.

> *tone: polite but determined; persuasive to critics?*

> *rhetorical device: repetition/ parallelism—"It is unfortunate" and "but it is even more unfortunate"*

To deepen your analysis of significant historic documents, consider how they deal with related concepts and themes. You can ask these questions to help you:

- What topics or themes, if any, do these documents share?
- How does each author address them?
- How do the documents differ? Are the differences significant?

Study the following example to see how one student examined related ideas in the two historical documents that you read above.

> *Two historic U.S. documents, spanning 100 years of American history, deal with similar concepts. Writing during the Civil War, Abraham Lincoln said in the Gettysburg Address that the war was a struggle to protect the important ideas of liberty and that "all men are created equal." The battle must be won to preserve America's unique example of "government of the people, by the people, for the people." Like Lincoln, King writes about civil liberties and says that injustice anywhere affects us all because we are part of a "network of mutuality." Reading two important historic documents reveals how different political figures, from different historical periods, have addressed related concepts that have helped shaped our nation: civil liberties, justice, and opportunity.*

> related ideas introduced

> examples, quotations, and summaries develop the topic

> related idea connects to first example

> related idea extended by summarizing

As you study other significant historical documents, consider what they say about the past, what connections exist among them, and what insights they offer us today. Also consider how the language of the texts gives them literary significance as well.

Divide students into groups to answer the questions about connections between the documents. Have one student record their group's answers. Then ask a representative from each group to share their answers with the class.

## College and Career Readiness Anchor Standards for Writing

### TEXT TYPES AND PURPOSES

1. Write arguments to support claims in an analysis of substantive topics or texts, using valid reasoning and relevant and sufficient evidence.

2. Write informative/explanatory texts to examine and convey complex ideas and information clearly and accurately through the effective selection, organization, and analysis of content.

3. Write narratives to develop real or imagined experiences or events using effective technique, well-chosen details, and well-structured event sequences.

### PRODUCTION AND DISTRIBUTION OF WRITING

4. Produce clear and coherent writing in which the development, organization, and style are appropriate to task, purpose, and audience.

5. Develop and strengthen writing as needed by planning, revising, editing, rewriting, or trying a new approach.

6. Use technology, including the Internet, to produce and publish writing and to interact and collaborate with others.

### RESEARCH TO BUILD AND PRESENT KNOWLEDGE

7. Conduct short as well as more sustained research projects based on focused questions, demonstrating understanding of the subject under investigation.

8. Gather relevant information from multiple print and digital sources, assess the credibility and accuracy of each source, and integrate the information while avoiding plagiarism.

9. Draw evidence from literary or informational texts to support analysis, reflection, and research.

### RANGE OF WRITING

10. Write routinely over extended time frames (time for research, reflection, and revision) and shorter time frames (a single sitting or a day or two) for a range of tasks, purposes, and audiences.

# Writing Standards, Grades 9–10 Students

| COMMON CORE STATE STANDARD | WHAT IT MEANS TO YOU |
|---|---|
| **TEXT TYPES AND PURPOSES** | |

**1.** Write arguments to support claims in an analysis of substantive topics or texts, using valid reasoning and relevant and sufficient evidence.

You will write and develop arguments with strong evidence and valid reasoning that include

**a.** Introduce precise claim(s), distinguish the claim(s) from alternate or opposing claims, and create an organization that establishes clear relationships among claim(s), counterclaims, reasons, and evidence.

**a.** a clear organization of precise claims and counterclaims

**b.** Develop claim(s) and counterclaims fairly, supplying evidence for each while pointing out the strengths and limitations of both in a manner that anticipates the audience's knowledge level and concerns.

**b.** relevant and unbiased support for claims

**c.** Use words, phrases, and clauses to link the major sections of the text, create cohesion, and clarify the relationships between claim(s) and reasons, between reasons and evidence, and between claim(s) and counterclaims.

**c.** use of transitional words, phrases, and clauses to link information

**d.** Establish and maintain a formal style and objective tone while attending to the norms and conventions of the discipline in which they are writing.

**d.** a tone and style appropriate to the task

**e.** Provide a concluding statement or section that follows from and supports the argument presented.

**e.** a strong concluding statement or section that summarizes the evidence presented

**2.** Write informative/explanatory texts to examine and convey complex ideas, concepts, and information clearly and accurately through the effective selection, organization, and analysis of content.

You will write clear, well-organized, and thoughtful informative and explanatory texts with

**a.** Introduce a topic; organize complex ideas, concepts, and information to make important connections and distinctions; include formatting (e.g., headings), graphics (e.g., figures, tables), and multimedia when useful to aiding comprehension.

**a.** a clear introduction and organization, including headings and graphic organizers (when appropriate)

**b.** Develop the topic with well-chosen, relevant, and sufficient facts, extended definitions, concrete details, quotations, or other information and examples appropriate to the audience's knowledge of the topic.

**b.** sufficient supporting details and background information

**c.** Use appropriate and varied transitions to link the major sections of the text, create cohesion, and clarify the relationships among complex ideas and concepts.

**c.** appropriate transitions

**d.** Use precise language and domain-specific vocabulary to manage the complexity of the topic.

**d.** precise language and relevant vocabulary

**e.** Establish and maintain a formal style and objective tone while attending to the norms and conventions of the discipline in which they are writing.

**e.** a tone and style appropriate to the task

**f.** Provide a concluding statement or section that follows from and supports the information or explanation presented (e.g., articulating implications or the significance of the topic).

**f.** a strong concluding statement or section that restates the importance or relevance of the topic

## Writing Standards, Grades 9–10 Students, continued

| COMMON CORE STATE STANDARD | WHAT IT MEANS TO YOU |
|---|---|
| **3.** Write narratives to develop real or imagined experiences or events using effective technique, well-chosen details, and well-structured event sequences. | You will write clear, well-structured, detailed narrative texts that |
| **a.** Engage and orient the reader by setting out a problem, situation, or observation, establishing one or multiple point(s) of view, and introducing a narrator and/or characters; create a smooth progression of experiences or events. | **a.** draw your readers in with a clear topic and an interesting progression of events or ideas |
| **b.** Use narrative techniques, such as dialogue, pacing, description, reflection, and multiple plot lines, to develop experiences, events, and/or characters. | **b.** use literary techniques to develop and expand on events and/or characters |
| **c.** Use a variety of techniques to sequence events so that they build on one another to create a coherent whole. | **c.** have a coherent sequence and structure |
| **d.** Use precise words and phrases, telling details, and sensory language to convey a vivid picture of the experiences, events, setting, and/or characters. | **d.** use precise words and sensory details that keep readers interested |
| **e.** Provide a conclusion that follows from and reflects on what is experienced, observed, or resolved over the course of the narrative. | **e.** have a strong conclusion that reflects on the topic |

### PRODUCTION AND DISTRIBUTION OF WRITING

| | |
|---|---|
| **4.** Produce clear and coherent writing in which the development, organization, and style are appropriate to task, purpose, and audience. (Grade-specific expectations for writing types are defined in standards 1–3 above.) | You will produce writing that is appropriate to the task, purpose, and audience for whom you are writing. |
| **5.** Develop and strengthen writing as needed by planning, revising, editing, rewriting, or trying a new approach, focusing on addressing what is most significant for a specific purpose and audience. | You will revise and refine your writing to address what is most important for your purpose and audience. |
| **6.** Use technology, including the Internet, to produce, publish, and update individual or shared writing products, taking advantage of technology's capacity to link to other information and to display information flexibly and dynamically. | You will use technology to share your writing and to provide links to other relevant information. |

### RESEARCH TO BUILD AND PRESENT KNOWLEDGE

| | |
|---|---|
| **7.** Conduct short as well as more sustained research projects to answer a question (including a self-generated question) or solve a problem; narrow or broaden the inquiry when appropriate; synthesize multiple sources on the subject, demonstrating understanding of the subject under investigation. | You will engage in short and more complex research tasks that include answering a question or solving a problem by using multiple sources. The product of your research will demonstrate your understanding of the subject. |

## Writing Standards, Grades 9–10 Students, continued

| COMMON CORE STATE STANDARD | WHAT IT MEANS TO YOU |
|---|---|
| 8. Gather relevant information from multiple authoritative print and digital sources, using advanced searches effectively; assess the usefulness of each source in answering the research question; integrate information into the text selectively to maintain the flow of ideas, avoiding plagiarism and following a standard format for citation. | You will effectively conduct searches to gather information from different sources and assess the relevance of each source, following a standard format for citation. |
| 9. Draw evidence from literary or informational texts to support analysis, reflection, and research.<br><br>a. Apply grades 9–10 Reading standards to literature (e.g., "Analyze how an author draws on and transforms source material in a specific work [e.g., how Shakespeare treats a theme or topic from Ovid or the Bible or how a later author draws on a play by Shakespeare]").<br><br>b. Apply grades 9–10 Reading standards to literary nonfiction (e.g., "Delineate and evaluate the argument and specific claims in a text, assessing whether the reasoning is valid and the evidence is relevant and sufficient; identify false statements and fallacious reasoning"). | You will paraphrase, summarize, quote, and cite primary and secondary sources, using both literary and informational texts, to support your analysis, reflection, and research. |
| **RANGE OF WRITING**<br>10. Write routinely over extended time frames (time for research, reflection, and revision) and shorter time frames (a single sitting or a day or two) for a range of tasks, purposes, and audiences. | You will write for many different purposes and audiences both over short and extended periods of time. |

## Spotlight on Common Core

COMMON
CORE

W 4 Produce clear and coherent writing in which the development, organization, and style are appropriate to task, purpose, and audience.
W 10 Write routinely over extended time frames (time for research, reflection, and revision) and shorter time frames (a single sitting or a day or two) for a range of tasks, purposes, and audiences.

### Writing: Maintaining Clarity and Coherence

The Common Core State Standards remind us that our ability to write clearly and coherently often determines our ability to share what we know with others. Whether writing directions to get to your house or summarizing several months of research, your writing should convey information in a way that readers can follow easily.

**LEARN HOW** Planning Your Writing Before you begin writing, you should know the answers to a few important questions about your project. The answers to these questions will help you determine and plan your writing process. For example, what are you writing? A brief email to a friend normally doesn't require much time or forethought. On the other hand, a research report on a complex topic requires significant time for research and time to plan, draft, revise, edit, and publish the final report. Sometimes you may even need to start over and try a new approach. Thinking about the end product helps you decide how much time and what kind of attention to devote to it.

## COMMON CORE FOCUS

W 4 Produce clear and coherent writing in which the development, organization, and style are appropriate to task, purpose, and audience.
W 10 Write routinely over extended time frames (time for research, reflection, and revision) and shorter time frames (a single sitting or a day or two) for a range of tasks, purposes, and audiences.

### Writing: Maintaining Clarity and Coherence

**LEARN HOW** Planning Your Writing
Students might need to review some basic terminology related to these standards. Remind students that **coherent writing** is writing that readers can follow—the ideas follow one another logically and they all fit together. Then, review the terms *development, organization, style, task, purpose,* and *audience* as needed.

Enhance students' understanding of the material in the chart by asking them to provide their own sample answers to each question. Write their responses on the board, providing guidance as needed. Then ask:

- What other questions do you ask yourself before you begin a writing task?
- What other questions do you think might be helpful?

Students might ask themselves questions such as, *Will I need to do research? What supplies do I need, such a paper, ink cartridges, or access to a computer? Will I write at my kitchen table, in the library, or at the desk in my room? What outcome do I hope for—a good grade, publication, or to change the world?*

Personalizing this process will help students to use it.

**LEARN HOW** Using Writing Strategies
Go through the chart as a class, discussing the strategies in the left-hand column and the examples in the right-hand column. Challenge a student volunteer to restate each strategy in his or her own words.

If necessary, provide definitions for the following terms in chart, and discuss examples.

- **Controlling idea or thesis statement:** the main proposition that a writer attempts to support in a piece of writing. (*The author shows us how Rosa Parks behaved and probably felt when she decided not to give up her seat on the bus.*)

---

Study the chart below. It provides some additional questions that you can ask yourself before you begin writing. Knowing the answers will help you plan your writing process and help you create superior work.

| Planning Your Writing Process | |
|---|---|
| Question | Examples |
| What is my final product? | • *An analytical essay*<br>• *A one-page business letter*<br>• *A research paper for the annual science fair* |
| What is my topic? | • *Similarities and differences between two characters in Romeo and Juliet*<br>• *The malfunctions in my cell phone*<br>• *The effects of pollution on local waters* |
| What is my purpose, or reason, for writing? | • *To better understand and explain two characters in Shakespeare's play*<br>• *To establish an argument for receiving a refund or a replacement cell phone*<br>• *To report on and explain scientific research* |
| Who is my audience? | • *My English class*<br>• *The cell phone manufacturer*<br>• *Science fair judges, including a university teacher and a pollution expert* |
| How much time do I have? Am I writing over a short or extended period of time? | • *Two weeks*<br>• *One day*<br>• *Three months* |

Once you understand your task, purpose, audience, and time constraints, you can plan your writing process. For example, you can decide how much time you should spend researching your topic based on your purpose, audience, due date, and the end product. You might try drafting a schedule, using a calendar and what you already know about how much time to allow for each step in the writing process.

**LEARN HOW** Using Writing Strategies Armed with a writing plan, you can now concentrate on producing clear and coherent writing. The **Writing Workshops** in this book give many strategies to help you write effectively. Study the chart below, which provides examples of some of these strategies. The highlighted text in the right column reflects the bold-faced points in the left column.

| Writing Strategies | |
|---|---|
| **DEVELOPMENT** | **WHAT DOES IT LOOK LIKE?** |
| • Include a memorable introduction and concluding statement or section.<br>• Utilize a **controlling idea or thesis statement.**<br>• Introduce sufficient facts, definitions, **concrete details, quotations,** and other examples that are appropriate to the audience's knowledge of the topic. | *The author shows us how Rosa Parks behaved and probably felt when she decided not to give up her seat on the bus. First the author shows us that Rosa Parks understood the threat she was facing. He writes, "Her heart almost stopped" when the bus driver growled at her, and "The next ten seconds seemed like an eternity," as she waits to see what the angry bus driver will do next.* |

| Writing Strategies | continued |
|---|---|
| **ORGANIZATION** | **WHAT DOES IT LOOK LIKE?** |
| • Establish a **logical organization** that makes sense for the purpose and audience.<br><br>• Provide graphics, use formatting, or other text features to help aid comprehension, if necessary.<br><br>• Use organizational patterns, such as cause-and-effect, definitions, or **compare-contrast** to help readers understand the relationship between ideas.<br><br>• Include words, phrases, and clauses that link sections of text and **create cohesion**, or flow.<br><br>• Introduce a topic, organize complex ideas, concepts, and information to **make important connections and distinctions**. | Some members of the school community argue that students should not bring cell phones to school because they can be used for cheating and can be disruptive during class time. The text message feature can be used for "passing notes" between students.<br><br>On the other hand, other people say that students should be able to bring cell phones in to school because they can help students stay safe, and they can help students and parents communicate directly if somebody's plans change. This reduces phone calls to and from the school office.<br><br>Is there any common ground in this debate? I think there is. |
| **LANGUAGE AND STYLE** | **WHAT DOES IT LOOK LIKE?** |
| • Maintain an appropriate style and tone, such as formal and objective for academic writing.<br><br>• Use **precise language and telling details**.<br><br>• Exhibit a strong command of grammar, usage, capitalization, and punctuation. | I learned that the Georgia O'Keeffe Museum is entirely devoted to this artist and her work. It was built in 1997, and it was designed to blend in with the gently rounded, sandy colored adobe buildings that line the narrow streets of Santa Fe. Inside the museum, I felt welcomed into a quiet, cool sanctuary for art and reflection. In this simple and elegant space O'Keeffe's artwork hangs, set off by inconspicuous picture frames on light gray walls. |

Authors use several strategies to maintain clarity and coherence in their writing. They apply these strategies to texts of varied lengths, purposes, and complexity. Be sure to notice these strategies as you analyze texts throughout this book, and be sure to use them to improve your own writing.

## College and Career Readiness Anchor Standards for Speaking and Listening

**COMMON CORE STATE STANDARDS**

**COMPREHENSION AND COLLABORATION**

1. Prepare for and participate effectively in a range of conversations and collaborations with diverse partners, building on others' ideas and expressing their own clearly and persuasively.

2. Integrate and evaluate information presented in diverse media and formats, including visually, quantitatively, and orally.

3. Evaluate a speaker's point of view, reasoning, and use of evidence and rhetoric.

**PRESENTATION OF KNOWLEDGE AND IDEAS**

4. Present information, findings, and supporting evidence such that listeners can follow the line of reasoning and the organization, development, and style are appropriate to task, purpose, and audience.

5. Make strategic use of digital media and visual displays of data to express information and enhance understanding of presentations.

6. Adapt speech to a variety of contexts and communicative tasks, demonstrating command of formal English when indicated or appropriate.

• **Quotation:** textual evidence quoted from a source or someone's exact words enclosed in quotation marks. (*"Her heart almost stopped" when the bus driver growled at her, and "The next ten seconds seemed like an eternity," as she waits to see what the angry bus driver will do next.*)

• **Cohesion:** coherence, the logical flow from one idea to the next, the sense that ideas are connected; often created by transitional words and phrases, parallel structures, and repeated words. (*on the other hand, help students stay safe, help students and parents communicate directly*)

• **Tone:** the writer's attitude toward the subject or readers, often expressed in the style of language—formal or informal—and the choice of words. (*Inside the museum, I felt welcomed into a quiet, cool sanctuary for art and reflection.*)

## Speaking and Listening Standards, Grades 9–10 Students

| COMMON CORE STATE STANDARD | WHAT IT MEANS TO YOU |
|---|---|
| **COMPREHENSION AND COLLABORATION** | |
| 1. Initiate and participate effectively in a range of collaborative discussions (one-on-one, in groups, and teacher-led) with diverse partners on grades 9–10 topics, texts, and issues, building on others' ideas and expressing their own clearly and persuasively. | You will actively participate in a variety of discussions in which you |
|   a. Come to discussions prepared, having read and researched material under study; explicitly draw on that preparation by referring to evidence from texts and other research on the topic or issue to stimulate a thoughtful, well-reasoned exchange of ideas. |   a. have read any relevant material beforehand and have come to the discussion prepared |
|   b. Work with peers to set rules for collegial discussions and decision-making (e.g., informal consensus, taking votes on key issues, presentation of alternate views), clear goals and deadlines, and individual roles as needed. |   b. work with others to establish goals and processes within the group |
|   c. Propel conversations by posing and responding to questions that relate the current discussion to broader themes or larger ideas; actively incorporate others into the discussion; and clarify, verify, or challenge ideas and conclusions. |   c. initiate dialogue by asking and responding to questions and by relating the current topic to other relevant information |
|   d. Respond thoughtfully to diverse perspectives, summarize points of agreement and disagreement, and, when warranted, qualify or justify their own views and understanding and make new connections in light of the evidence and reasoning presented. |   d. respond to different perspectives and summarize points of agreement or disagreement when needed |
| 2. Integrate multiple sources of information presented in diverse media or formats (e.g., visually, quantitatively, orally) evaluating the credibility and accuracy of each source. | You will integrate multiple sources of information, assessing the credibility and accuracy of each source. |
| 3. Evaluate a speaker's point of view, reasoning, and use of evidence and rhetoric, identifying any fallacious reasoning or exaggerated or distorted evidence. | You will evaluate a speaker's argument and identify any false reasoning or evidence. |
| **PRESENTATION OF KNOWLEDGE AND IDEAS** | |
| 4. Present information, findings, and supporting evidence clearly, concisely, and logically such that listeners can follow the line of reasoning and the organization, development, substance, and style are appropriate to purpose, audience, and task. | You will organize and present information to your listeners in a logical sequence and style that are appropriate to your task and audience. |

## Speaking and Listening Standards, Grades 9–10 Students, continued

| COMMON CORE STATE STANDARD | WHAT IT MEANS TO YOU |
|---|---|
| **5.** Make strategic use of digital media (e.g., textual, graphical, audio, visual, and interactive elements) in presentations to enhance understanding of findings, reasoning, and evidence and to add interest. | ▶ You will use digital media to enhance and add interest to presentations. |
| **6.** Adapt speech to a variety of contexts and tasks, demonstrating command of formal English when indicated or appropriate. | ▶ You will adapt the formality of your speech appropriately, depending on its context and purpose. |

## Spotlight on Common Core

 **COMMON CORE** **SL 1** Initiate and participate effectively in a range of collaborative discussions (one-on-one, in groups, and teacher-led) with diverse partners on grades 9–10 topics, texts, and issues, building on others' ideas and expressing their own clearly and persuasively.

### Speaking and Listening: Participating in Group Discussions

The Common Core State Standards stress the importance of initiating and participating effectively in group discussions. Notice the knowledge and skills that parts b and d of SL 1 require of grade 9 students:

**b.** Work with peers to set rules for collegial discussions and decision-making (e.g., informal consensus, taking votes on key issues, presentation of alternate views), clear goals and deadlines, and individual roles as needed.

**d.** Respond thoughtfully to diverse perspectives, summarize points of agreement and disagreement, and, when warranted, qualify or justify their own views and understanding and make new connections in light of the evidence and reasoning presented.

Remember that effective group discussions are an important part of our democratic process. People may decide to discuss something with others because group discussions often help us to

- answer a question
- build understanding
- solve a problem

A group discussion to address these goals can be as informal as a conversation with a few friends about where to eat, or it can be as formal as a school board meeting involving a few dozen people. A group discussion can be about almost any topic and can involve people of different ages, of different ethnic, cultural, and economic backgrounds—often with very different viewpoints.

As diverse as group discussions are, they are more effective when group members keep the following questions in mind. Here are examples from a student council green-committee meeting.

- What is the purpose of the discussion?
  *Example: to decide how to calculate the school's environmental footprint*

- What roles do group members play during the discussion?
  *Examples: facilitator (runs the meeting), scribe (takes notes), time-keeper*

- Are there any rules the discussion should follow?
  *Example: Only one person speaks at a time; no one speaks for more than four minutes at a time.*

- Is there a deadline or time limit for the discussion?
  *Example: The meeting will last 60 minutes.*

STUDENT GUIDE  **FM61**

## COMMON CORE FOCUS

**SL 1** Initiate and participate effectively in a range of collaborative discussions (one-on-one, in groups, and teacher-led) with diverse partners on *grades 9–10 topics, texts, and issues,* building on others' ideas and expressing their own clearly and persuasively.

### Speaking and Listening: Participating in Group Discussions

Remind students that they participate in group discussions every day—in school, at home, and in social situations. Ask students to give some real-life examples of group discussions they have participated in recently. Then ask:

- Do you participate the same way in all group discussions?

- How does your participation vary according to the topic and members of the group?

- What would you like to change about the way you participate in group discussions?

Discuss as a class the questions to keep in mind and example answers. Ask students if they can think of other questions to keep in mind when initiating or participating in a group discussion. Students might mention questions such as the following:

- What do I hope to accomplish by my participation?

- Do I want the group to agree with my opinions or do I want to build consensus?

Tell students that uncooperative or unproductive behavior includes the following: interrupting; sarcasm; raised voices; disrespectful language; and nonverbal disrespect of other people's ideas, such as eye-rolling.

**LEARN HOW** Participating in Group Discussions Discuss with students each of the behaviors listed in the chart. Expand upon each by telling students the following:

- Listen carefully by remaining quiet, not interrupting, and looking at the person who is speaking.
- When you have the floor, state your own views articulately by speaking slowly and calmly, with enough volume for everyone in the group to hear. Make eye contact with group members as you speak.
- Summarize points of agreement and disagreement by briefly stating the main similarities and differences between two points of view.
- Keep an open mind. Listen for ways that you can agree with others. Try to find the common ground.

Another important factor in group discussions is the behavior of group members. Group discussions are most effective when everyone's contribution is productive. Someone who is argumentative, stubborn, or otherwise unhelpful may negatively affect the outcome and effectiveness of the discussion. This doesn't mean, of course, that everyone must always agree. It means that unproductive or uncooperative behaviors distract the group, preventing the discussion from being effective.

**LEARN HOW** Participating in Group Discussions To help ensure that your group discussions are effective, model the following behaviors:

- Support others' contributions by listening carefully and responding thoughtfully to their views, even if they conflict with your own.
- When it's your turn, state your own views in an articulate, thoughtful way.
- Understand and be able to summarize points of agreement and disagreement.
- As others share new information and views, be willing to justify your views or consider new ones.

The following chart gives an example of each of these behaviors. Consider why these behaviors are effective. Ask yourself how well you model them.

| EFFECTIVE BEHAVIOR | WHAT IT LOOKS LIKE | |
|---|---|---|
| Support others' contributions. | David listens to Mora while she presents her research and views on how to calculate their school's environmental footprint. "I read that article, too," David thinks to himself. "Then I read a more recent article that included a much longer list of considerations than those that were in the first article. I'll make a note about it and let Mora finish." | David realizes that Mora's views are different from his. Instead of interrupting, he listens carefully to make sure he understands her evidence and what she thinks it means. |
| State your own views thoughtfully. | "I read the same article Mora did," David begins, "but I found a more recent and I think more useful article on sustainable building in Architectural Engineering and Construction. It describes how one high school calculated its environmental footprint before building a new addition." | David explains how his research turned up different results. He shows that he has used a reliable source. |
| Summarize agreements and disagreements. | Anh is going to speak next, but rather than silently rehearsing her views, she compares David's views with Mora's: "David listed the same five considerations that Mora did. The only difference between them is how water consumption is calculated." | Anh compares the key points. She notices David and Mora agree except for one point. |
| Justify your views or consider new ones. | Anh points out that Mora's and David's views differ in only one important respect. As David listens to Anh's summary he thinks, "Anh is right. Mora's view and mine are almost the same except for one issue." He makes a mental note of this and continues to listen to Anh for more information and insight. | David sees that he and Mora differ on one point. He can justify his view, but is willing to combine his approach with Mora's and Anh's. |

**Reflect on the Discussion**
- Think of a recent group discussion you participated in. How effective was it? Why?
- What did you contribute to the discussion, and how did the group respond?
- What is one thing you might do differently in your next group discussion?

Throughout this book you will have opportunities to contribute to a variety of group discussions. Be sure to contribute effectively by understanding and modeling effective attitudes and behaviors. When you learn how to contribute effectively to group discussions, your voice is more likely to be heard, and your views are more likely to be understood. And your discussion will accomplish something positive for everyone.

## College and Career Readiness Anchor Standards for Language

### COMMON CORE STATE STANDARDS

**CONVENTIONS OF STANDARD ENGLISH**

1. Demonstrate command of the conventions of standard English grammar and usage when writing or speaking.

2. Demonstrate command of the conventions of standard English capitalization, punctuation, and spelling when writing.

**KNOWLEDGE OF LANGUAGE**

3. Apply knowledge of language to understand how language functions in different contexts, to make effective choices for meaning or style, and to comprehend more fully when reading or listening.

**VOCABULARY ACQUISITION AND USE**

4. Determine or clarify the meaning of unknown and multiple-meaning words and phrases by using context clues, analyzing meaningful word parts, and consulting general and specialized reference materials, as appropriate.

5. Demonstrate understanding of word relationships and nuances in word meanings.

6. Acquire and use accurately a range of general academic and domain-specific words and phrases sufficient for reading, writing, speaking, and listening at the college and career readiness level; demonstrate independence in gathering vocabulary knowledge when considering a word or phrase important to comprehension or expression.

## Language Standards, Grades 9–10 Students

| COMMON CORE STATE STANDARD | WHAT IT MEANS TO YOU |
|---|---|
| **CONVENTIONS OF STANDARD ENGLISH**<br>1. Demonstrate command of the conventions of standard English grammar and usage when writing or speaking.<br>   a. Use parallel structure.<br>   b. Use various types of phrases (noun, verb, adjectival, adverbial, participial, prepositional, absolute) and clauses (independent, dependent; noun, relative, adverbial) to convey specific meanings and add variety and interest to writing or presentations. | You will correctly use the conventions of English grammar and usage, including<br><br>a. parallel structure<br>b. phrases and clauses |

After the class has had a chance to read the entire lesson, hold a group discussion with the topic "group discussions in this class." The purpose of the discussion should be to set ground rules for all future group discussions in the class. Appoint a chairperson, recorder, and timekeeper for this discussion. Afterwards, ask students to reflect on how well the discussion went. Did they successfully establish a set of ground rules for all future discussions?

## Language Standards, Grades 9–10 Students, continued

| COMMON CORE STATE STANDARD | WHAT IT MEANS TO YOU |
|---|---|
| **2.** Demonstrate command of the conventions of standard English capitalization, punctuation, and spelling when writing. | You will correctly use the conventions of English capitalization, punctuation, and spelling, including |
| **a.** Use a semicolon (and perhaps a conjunctive adverb) to link two or more closely related independent clauses. | **a.** semicolons |
| **b.** Use a colon to introduce a list or quotation. | **b.** colons |
| **c.** Spell correctly. | **c.** spelling |

### KNOWLEDGE OF LANGUAGE

| | |
|---|---|
| **3.** Apply knowledge of language to understand how language functions in different contexts, to make effective choices for meaning or style, and to comprehend more fully when reading or listening. | You will apply your knowledge of language in different contexts by |
| **a.** Write and edit work so that it conforms to the guidelines in a style manual (e.g., *MLA Handbook, Turabian's Manual for Writers*) appropriate for the discipline and writing type. | **a.** conforming to a style manual when writing and editing |

### VOCABULARY ACQUISITION AND USE

| | |
|---|---|
| **4.** Determine or clarify the meaning of unknown and multiple-meaning words and phrases based on grades 9–10 reading and content, choosing flexibly from a range of strategies. | You will understand the meaning of grade-level appropriate words and phrases by |
| **a.** Use context (e.g., the overall meaning of a sentence, paragraph, or text; a word's position or function in a sentence) as a clue to the meaning of a word or phrase. | **a.** using context clues |
| **b.** Identify and correctly use patterns of word changes that indicate different meanings or parts of speech (e.g., *analyze, analysis, analytical; advocate, advocacy*). | **b.** recognizing and adapting root words according to meaning or part of speech |
| **c.** Consult general and specialized reference materials (e.g., dictionaries, glossaries, thesauruses), both print and digital, to find the pronunciation of a word or determine or clarify its precise meaning, its part of speech, or its etymology. | **c.** using reference materials |
| **d.** Verify the preliminary determination of the meaning of a word or phrase (e.g., by checking the inferred meaning in context or in a dictionary). | **d.** inferring and verifying the meanings of words in context |
| **5.** Demonstrate understanding of figurative language, word relationships, and nuances in word meanings. | You will understand figurative language, word relationships, and slight differences in word meanings by |
| **a.** Interpret figures of speech (e.g., euphemism, oxymoron) in context and analyze their role in the text. | **a.** interpreting figures of speech in context |
| **b.** Analyze nuances in the meaning of words with similar denotations. | **b.** analyzing slight differences in the meanings of similar words |

## Language Standards, Grades 9–10 Students, continued

| COMMON CORE STATE STANDARD | WHAT IT MEANS TO YOU |
|---|---|
| **6.** Acquire and use accurately general academic and domain-specific words and phrases, sufficient for reading, writing, speaking, and listening at the college and career readiness level; demonstrate independence in gathering vocabulary knowledge when considering a word or phrase important to comprehension or expression. ▶ | You will develop vocabulary knowledge at the college and career readiness level and demonstrate confidence in using it appropriately. |

## Spotlight on Common Core

COMMON CORE

**L 6** Acquire and use accurately general academic and domain-specific words and phrases, sufficient for reading, writing, speaking, and listening at the college and career readiness level; demonstrate independence in gathering vocabulary knowledge when considering a word or phrase important to comprehension or expression.

### Language: Building Useful Vocabularies

The Common Core State Standards stress the importance of building a strong vocabulary made up of domain-specific words and academic vocabulary—words you use in all subject areas. The Standards also emphasize the need to take a skilled and flexible approach to word knowledge and usage.

**LEARN HOW** Building Vocabulary  Most of the words we use every day are words we have heard before and know well. This vocabulary doesn't require much thought about its meaning or use. The Common Core State Standards highlight two other kinds of vocabularies: specialized and academic. By understanding how and when to use each, you dramatically improve your chances for success in school.

**Specialized vocabulary** consists of words about a specific subject-matter or area of study or work. They are usually introduced and studied in a class about a particular subject. Study the following examples from life science:

> chromosome   ecosystem   gene   habitat   mutation   photosynthesis

In each of your classes, you need to understand subject-matter words in order to understand the subject. Fortunately a subject-matter word's definition is usually provided when the word is introduced. You can use the following tools to build these words into your vocabulary.

- flash cards to use on your own or with a partner
- your subject notebooks, in which you can write subject words, definitions, and examples
- word lists from your instructor or from your textbook

Also, look at the subject-matter words and terminology in your textbook. Those that appear in the glossary or have long entries in the index may be important to learn, study, and remember long after they are introduced. For example, the **Glossary of Literary & Nonfiction Terms** (page R102) in this textbook includes definitions of words that relate to the study of literature and nonfiction, such as *figurative language, foreshadowing,* and *autobiography.*

**Academic vocabulary** consists of words about knowledge and learning—words you use in every subject area. Study these examples:

> analyze   conclude   form   interpret   relevant   synthesize

You need to be able to understand and accurately use academic vocabulary because these words are often used to
- assess your understanding of key concepts
- communicate complex or abstract ideas

---

## COMMON CORE FOCUS

**L 6** Acquire and use accurately general academic and domain-specific words and phrases, sufficient for reading, writing, speaking, and listening at the college and career readiness level; demonstrate independence in gathering vocabulary knowledge when considering a word or phrase important to comprehension or expression.

### Language: Building Useful Vocabularies

**LEARN HOW**  Building Vocabulary  To help students understand and relate to the concept of **specialized vocabulary**, have them work in groups of three or four to brainstorm lists of specialized vocabulary related to subjects with which they are familiar, for example, football, knitting, architecture, or astronomy. When groups have finished their lists, have a spokesperson from each group share that group's list.  Discuss as a class whether or not each word fits the definition of specialized vocabulary.

Then, direct students' attention to the list of specialized vocabulary words in their textbooks. Point out that when students encounter unfamiliar specialized vocabulary words, especially words from the sciences, they have a good chance of being able to guess the words' meanings from their word parts—prefixes, suffixes, and roots. Ask student volunteers to identify any word parts they know from the words in this list. (Example: *chromo-* means "color"; *eco-* means "having to do with the environment"; *photo-* means "light.")

To enliven students' study of **academic vocabulary**, hold a scavenger hunt. After students have read the lesson on academic vocabulary, challenge them to locate in this or another textbook each of the academic vocabulary words listed on p. FM 65. Students should note the page numbers on which the words are found. The first student to locate all the words wins a prize, such as a homework pass. After the scavenger hunt is finished, ask for student volunteers to read the sentences in which they located the academic vocabulary words. Discuss as a class the meaning of each word in context.

(For a longer scavenger hunt, add the words *contrast, cite, evaluate, explain, imply, infer,* and *speculate*.)

To help students to demonstrate independence in gathering vocabulary knowledge, make sure they have access to a dictionary and thesaurus in the classroom. Encourage students to consult these references when necessary.

Also, many academic vocabulary words have different shades of meaning, depending on how they are used. You can use references, such as a dictionary or a thesaurus, to research a word if you are not sure of its meaning. You can also use the strategies mentioned above to help you review and use these words. (See also the **Academic Vocabulary Workshop** on page 16 of this book.)

Often academic vocabulary appears on quizzes and tests. If you come across an unfamiliar word on a test, you can use vocabulary strategies, such as using context clues or analyzing word structure, to infer the word's meaning. These techniques are discussed in the **Vocabulary and Spelling Handbook** on page R68 in this text.

You can also create an academic vocabulary notebook that you use for all your classes. To use this type of notebook, read several pages of text or class notes. Then review the text and choose four or five words that you need to learn. Remember, academic vocabulary is not subject-matter specific. Then, create an entry for the word in your notebook. Study the following example for the word *form*:

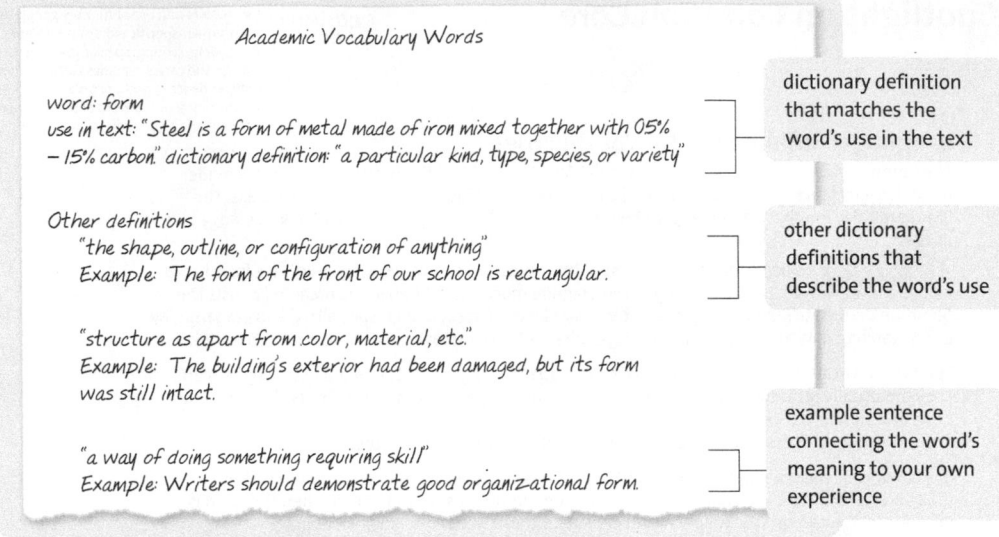

**Academic Vocabulary Words**

word: form
use in text: "Steel is a form of metal made of iron mixed together with 05% – 15% carbon." dictionary definition: "a particular kind, type, species, or variety" — dictionary definition that matches the word's use in the text

Other definitions
"the shape, outline, or configuration of anything"
Example: The form of the front of our school is rectangular. — other dictionary definitions that describe the word's use

"structure as apart from color, material, etc."
Example: The building's exterior had been damaged, but its form was still intact.

"a way of doing something requiring skill"
Example: Writers should demonstrate good organizational form. — example sentence connecting the word's meaning to your own experience

As you read or listen to people, notice when the academic vocabulary word is used. Try to use the word accurately yourself when you write or speak. Also, review your notebook regularly as you add more entries. In all of your classes and in your career you will be expected to use words with fluency, flexibility, and precision.

# The Power of Ideas

For help using this Introductory Unit, see

**R** RESOURCE MANAGER—Introductory Unit
p. I-1

## INTRODUCING THE ESSENTIALS

- Genres Workshop
- Reading Strategies Workshop
- Academic Vocabulary Workshop
- Writing Process Workshop

1

**About the Art** *(Clockwise, from bottom left)*

In 2000, Christopher Myers published the flying boy image in his book *Wings*. See Unit 7, page 777 for more information.

The production still, also shown on page 851 of Unit 8, captures a scene from Alfred Hitchcock's *North by Northwest* (1959).

Daniel Nevins painted *Healing* (bottom right) in 1996; it also appears on page 246. For more information about Nevins, see page 243.

## What Are Life's Big Questions?

The introductory unit provides an overview of the ways in which the anthology engages students in the processes of reading and writing. This unit introduces students to regularly appearing features, such as **Big Questions** and **Close Reads.** Students will preview skills and strategies that they will study in greater depth in later units. Pay attention to side column and bottom channel notes provided to support all students in your classroom.

These two pages will help you introduce students to the concept of **Big Questions** and how readers can use these to explore texts. Begin by having students respond to "The Power of Ideas," the title of this unit. Ask:

- How would you define the word *idea?* ***Possible answer:*** *a thought, concept, or theme*
- How can ideas have power? ***Possible answer:*** *Ideas can expand people's thinking and motivate them to take action.*

Challenge students to think of ideas that have had an impact on history, on society, and on their own lives.

Next, have students read and discuss the introductory paragraph, which presents the idea that literature is a way to explore life's **Big Questions.** Read through the examples of **Big Questions** on pages 2 and 3, and discuss with students their first thoughts about and reactions to each one. Point out that the **Big Questions** on these pages span cultures and time periods.

---

### The Power of Ideas

# What Are Life's Big Questions?

Love and hate, freedom and responsibility, growing up and growing old—these emotions and experiences touch us all, and they are at the heart of the big questions that we ask about the world. This book is all about big questions like the ones shown here. Even though they are challenging to answer, such questions prompt us to think about ideas that affect our lives. Through reading, discussing, and writing about literature, we can unlock the power of these ideas and come closer to understanding ourselves and the world.

## How powerful is LOVE?

In the name of love, Romeo and Juliet risk everything to be together. Similarly, love drives a young wife in O. Henry's "The Gift of the Magi" to chop off her hair. Love is a powerful force, but is it strong enough to overcome all obstacles? You will read works by such writers as William Shakespeare, O. Henry, and Julia Alvarez that explore this age-old question.

## What makes a HERO?

In Homer's epic the *Odyssey,* the hero bravely battles dangerous monsters. In 1955, Rosa Parks refused to give up her bus seat to a white passenger. As a young girl, Maya Angelou admired a more personal hero—the neighborhood woman who introduced her to the power of literature. We can find heroes in ancient stories, recent history, today's movies, and our own lives. What extraordinary qualities set heroes apart?

---

## Introductory Unit Resources

*See resources on the* **Teacher One Stop DVD-ROM** *and on* <u>thinkcentral.com</u>.

**R  RESOURCE MANAGER INTRODUCTORY UNIT**
Lesson at a Glance and Note-Taking, pp. I-1– I-5

**BEST PRACTICES TOOLKIT**
Story Map p. D14
Core Analysis Frame: Poetry p. D34
Reporter's Questions p. C9

**TECHNOLOGY**
⊘ **Teacher One Stop DVD-ROM**
⊘ **Student One Stop DVD-ROM**
⊘ **Write*Smart* CD-ROM**
⊘ **GrammarNotes DVD-ROM**
⊘ **Audio Anthology CD**

Then have students generate other **Big Questions.** Explain that every lesson in this anthology will begin with a Big Question like the ones shown on these pages. Each Big Question will allow students to explore important ideas in depth and to make connections between the literature and their own lives.

## Does good always TRIUMPH?

In Hollywood movies like *The Lord of the Rings,* we expect satisfying endings—ones in which good characters prevail and evil forces are defeated. Literature, like real life, does not always have happily-ever-after endings. Read Edgar Allan Poe's classic spine tingler "The Cask of Amontillado" or Liam O'Flaherty's eye-opening story "The Sniper." Then ask yourself: Does good always triumph?

## What is FAMILY?

Family can mean different things to different people. Relatives, friends, neighbors, and people who share similar cultural and religious backgrounds all can be considered family. You'll explore this idea further in Naomi Shihab Nye's "Hamadi" and in the ripped-from-the-headlines article "The Lost Boys."

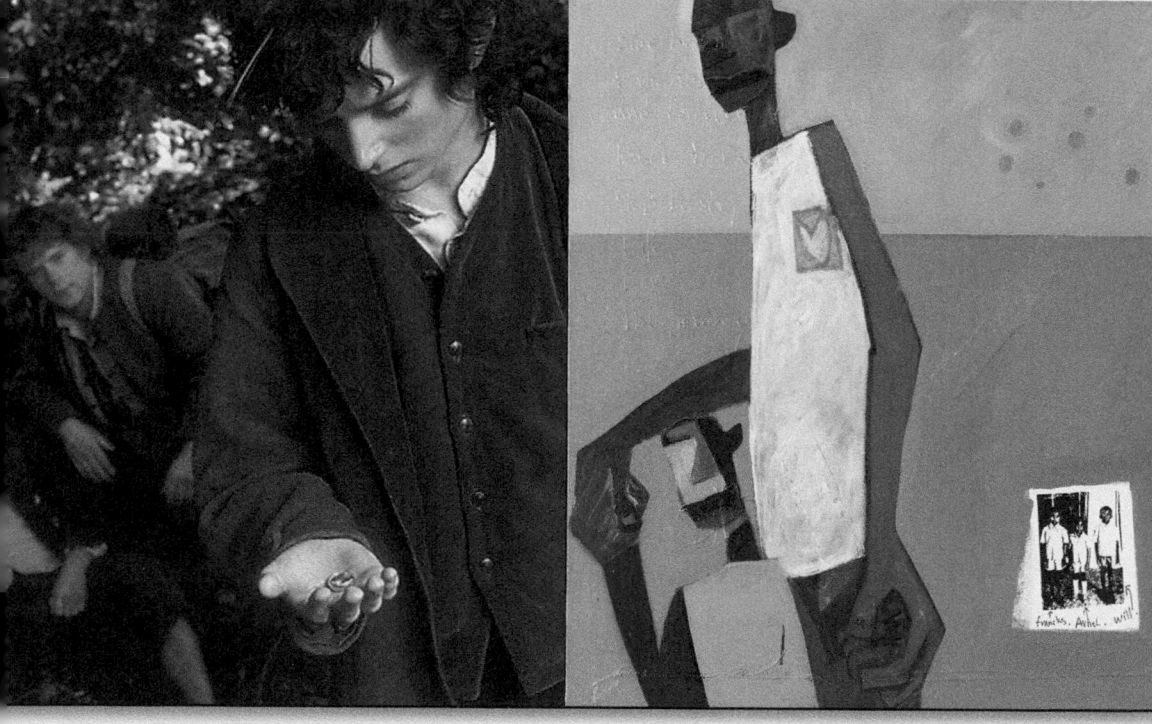

## COMMON CORE FOCUS

**RL 1** Cite strong and thorough textual evidence to support analysis of what the text says explicitly as well as inferences drawn from the text. **RL 2** Determine a theme or central idea of a text and analyze in detail its development over the course of the text. **RL 4** Determine the meaning of words and phrases as they are used in the text; analyze the cumulative impact of specific word choices on meaning and tone. **RI 1** Cite strong and thorough textual evidence to support analysis of what the text says explicitly as well as inferences drawn from the text. **RI 2** Determine the central idea of a text and analyze its development over the course of the text. **RI 7** Analyze various accounts of a subject told in different mediums.

## The Genres

**Determine Readiness** Ask students for possible definitions of each genre listed on the page. Then review the genres, pointing out the definition provided for each one.

**Discuss and Review** Ask students to cite specific examples of each genre that they are familiar with, such as a short story, a lyric poem, a comic play, a news article, or a motion picture.

- Drawing on student examples, point out that different genres allow writers and readers to explore ideas through a variety of approaches and from different perspectives.

- Point out that some texts can combine genre characteristics. For example, a narrative poem might share some characteristics with a story. Similarly, a drama usually incorporates elements of a story, but some dramas also include long passages that would be considered nonfiction speeches if they stood apart from the dramatic context. Invite student questions or comments before moving on to the more detailed genre studies on pages 5–10.

---

## *Genres Workshop*

# Exploring Texts

At some point in your life, you have probably considered big questions like the ones on the preceding pages. For thousands of years, writers have also asked these questions, trying to make sense of the world around them. Many have left a written record of their lives and ideas in literature and other texts—works that are worth reading and understanding both for their ideas and for the forms those ideas take.

## The Genres

**COMMON CORE**
Included in this workshop:
RL 1, RL 2, RL 4, RI 1, RI 2, RI 7

Literature and nonfiction encompass a wide range of text types, or genres. Some are meant to be read; others are meant to be performed by actors on a stage. Informational texts and media may not technically be literature, but they are similarly important to learn about today. Regardless of the genre, good writing allows readers to grapple with important issues and even connect to different cultures.

In this book, you will explore questions and ideas in many genres. An ancient story, a news article, and a poem—despite their differences in form—can all help you explore questions about love or heroism, for example. Before delving into the ideas in texts, familiarize yourself with the genres.

### GENRES AT A GLANCE

**STORIES**
Stories are narrative texts that spring from an author's imagination.
- short stories
- novels
- novellas

**POETRY**
Poetry is the most compact form of literature. Words are chosen and arranged to create powerful effects.
- free-verse poems
- odes
- sonnets
- narrative poems
- lyric poems

**DRAMA**
Drama is meant to be performed. Characters and conflicts are developed through dialogue and action.
- comedies
- tragedies
- farces

**NONFICTION**
Nonfiction is prose writing that deals with real people, events, and places.
- essays
- speeches
- autobiographies
- biographies
- news articles
- opinion pieces

### TYPES OF MEDIA

Media are forms of communication that reach large numbers of people. They include many subgenres, each with its own forms and characteristics.
- feature films
- advertising
- Web sites

---

## *DIFFERENTIATED INSTRUCTION*

### FOR STRUGGLING READERS

**Note Taking** For students who need help with note taking, hand out the note-taking copy master before discussing the genres. Have students read the introductory paragraph silently. As you discuss the main points in the Genres Workshop, have students record them on the copy master.

**R RESOURCE MANAGER—Copy Master**
Note Taking p. I-2

### FOR ENGLISH LANGUAGE LEARNERS

**Vocabulary: Cognates** Many of the genres and examples of genres have names that share linguistic roots with Spanish. Students whose first language is Spanish can use these examples to clarify their understanding:

- English: *story* / Spanish: *historia*
- English: *novel* / Spanish: *novela*
- English: *poetry* / Spanish: *poesía*
- English: *tragedy* / Spanish: *tragedia*
- English: *media* / Spanish: *medios*

## STORIES

At the heart of literature is **narrative,** the telling of a story. Although stories can be inspired by real events and people, they are mainly the product of a writer's imagination. A fiction writer shapes his or her narrative to capture and hold readers' interest, often creating memorable settings and complex characters who face challenging conflicts. Fictional stories can take any of a wide variety of forms, including science fiction, historical fiction, mysteries, and graphic novels. Regardless of the form, a work of fiction usually is one of three types.

- A **short story** often focuses on a single event or incident and usually can be read in one sitting.

- A **novel** is an extended work of fiction. Because it is much longer than a short story, a novel gives a writer space to develop a wider range of characters and a more complex plot.

- A **novella** is longer than a short story but shorter than a novel. Most novellas focus on a limited number of characters and a short time span.

**Read the Model** This excerpt is about an old Cuban fisherman named Santiago. After months at sea, Santiago finally hooks a giant marlin. Can he muster enough strength to reel in the fish as it circles his boat? Notice the elements of fiction that the author uses to hook readers and to explore the idea of strength.

**LITERARY TERMS FOR STORIES**

- plot
- conflict
- character
- setting
- theme
- narrator
- point of view

---

*from*

# THE *Old Man* AND THE *Sea*

Novella by **Ernest Hemingway**

The fish was coming in on his circle now calm and beautiful looking and only his great tail moving. The old man pulled on him all that he could to bring him closer. For just a moment the fish turned a little on his side. Then he straightened himself and began another circle.

5 "I moved him," the old man said. "I moved him then."

He felt faint again now but he held on the great fish all the strain that he could. I moved him, he thought. Maybe this time I can get him over. Pull, hands, he thought. Hold up, legs. Last for me, head. Last for me. You never went. This time I'll pull him over.

10 But when he put all of his effort on, starting it well out before the fish came alongside and pulling with all his strength, the fish pulled part way over and then righted himself and swam away.

"Fish," the old man said. "Fish, you are going to have to die anyway. Do you have to kill me too?"

**Close Read**

1. Using terms from the list above, describe what is happening in this literary text.

2. **Exploring a Big Question** The old man's strength comes from his relentless will to catch the fish. In your opinion, what gives someone strength?

---

## STORIES

Begin by asking students to read the introductory paragraph while you write the **Literary Terms for Stories** on the board. Then ask students to identify favorite stories and to explain why they found each work memorable. As you write their examples on the board, encourage students to use **Literary Terms for Stories,** such as *plot, character,* and *setting,* in their explanations.

### Close Read

Introduce the model by pointing out that it is by Ernest Hemingway, a famous American author noted for the strength of his spare prose. Ask a volunteer to read the model. Then have students answer the **Close Read** questions.

*Possible answers:*

1. *This part of the story's plot focuses on the conflict between two characters: an old fisherman (Santiago) and a large fish (a giant marlin). The setting is the sea, and the story is told from the point of view of a narrator who is not part of the story. This scene suggests a theme of perseverance; it shows the old man's determination to catch a fish that seems determined not to be caught.*

2. *Strength—inner strength, which may manifest itself as physical strength—comes from the belief that one's goals and motivations are meaningful and worthwhile.*

**CHECK UNDERSTANDING** Ask for volunteers to explain the difference between a short story and a novel.

---

### FOR STRUGGLING READERS

**Concept Support** Have students adapt a Story Map by using these terms from the **Literary Terms for Stories:** *plot, conflict, character, setting, theme, narrator.* Then help students complete their story map by identifying these elements for a story they have read.

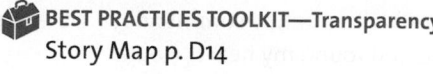 **BEST PRACTICES TOOLKIT—Transparency** Story Map p. D14

### FOR ENGLISH LANGUAGE LEARNERS

**Language: Punctuation and Print Clues** In this passage, Hemingway shows what Santiago says and thinks. Point out that the quotation marks in lines 5 and 13–14 indicate when Santiago speaks aloud (to himself and to the fish). Then direct students to lines 7–9, in which Santiago's thoughts appear as silent dialogue without quotation marks. Note, too, the use of the tags "old man said" (lines 5 and 13) to indicate speech and "he thought" (lines 7 and 8) to indicate thoughts.

## POETRY

Direct students to read the first three paragraphs while you write the **Literary Terms for Poetry** and then this poem on the board:

> My mother told me, "Come and see
> Your newborn baby brother Jack."
> I looked at him, she smiled at me
> Till I said, "Give him back."

Have students explain how the poem illustrates terms from the **Literary Terms for Poetry,** such as *line, stanza, speaker, rhyme, rhythm,* and *meter.*

### Close Read

Read the model, pausing as indicated by the punctuation in the poem. Invite volunteers to read stanzas of their choice. If time permits, also have students listen to the poem on the *Audio Anthology CD.* Then direct students to answer the **Close Read** questions.

#### Possible answers:

1. *The poem consists of three stanzas. The poem has no regular rhythm or rhyme; however, it uses sound devices (such as the /s/ sounds in lines 2 and 4), imagery (such as the description of the couple's clothing in lines 5–7), and figurative language (the comparison of love to dried flowers in lines 16–17) to convey meaning and emotion.*

   **IF STUDENTS NEED HELP . . .** Explain that although many poems have a regular rhythm and rhyme, others do not. Urge students to think about the mental pictures and feelings that "Los ancianos" suggests and the words that Pat Mora uses to express them.

2. *Other qualities of love include patience, respect, compassion, thoughtfulness, and a romantic nature.*

**CHECK UNDERSTANDING** Ask students to identify the line where the first stanza ends.

---

## POETRY

The poet Robert Frost once wrote, "Poetry is a way of taking life by the throat." These words capture the impact of poetry on both writers and readers. In poetry, words and sounds are chosen to convey meaning and emotion.

What you'll most likely notice first about a poem is its **form,** or arrangement on the page. Usually, poems are divided into **lines,** which are arranged into groups called **stanzas.** While some poets follow fixed rules of form, others break with convention and invent unique forms to echo their subjects.

If you have ever read a poem aloud, you know that its impact depends on more than its form. The way a poem sounds—its brash **rhythms** or its predictable **rhymes,** for example—is part of its effect. Language delivers other powerful effects, and **diction,** or word choice, is especially important in poetry. **Imagery,** which consists of language that recreates sensory experiences, helps readers see, hear, and feel what a poem describes.

**Read the Model** Here, the love of an older couple—*los ancianos,* in Spanish— is described in striking detail. As you read, notice the poetic elements that help to paint a moving portrait of the couple. Also, consider what the poet is saying about love.

**LITERARY TERMS FOR POETRY**

- form
- line
- stanza
- speaker
- rhyme
- rhythm
- meter
- sound devices
- diction
- figurative language
- imagery

### Los ancianos    Poem by **Pat Mora**

They hold hands
as they walk with slow steps.
Careful together they cross the plaza
both slightly stooped, bodies returning to the land,
5  he in faded khaki and straw hat,
she wrapped in soft clothes, black
*rebozo*[1] round her head and shoulders.

Tourists in halter tops and shorts
pose by flame trees and fountains,
10  but the old couple walks step by step
on the edge.
Even in the heat, only their wrinkled
hands and faces show. They know
of moving through a crowd at their own pace.

15  I watch him help her
off the curb and I smell love
like dried flowers, old love
of holding hands with one man for fifty years.

---
1. *rebozo* (rĭ-bō'sō) *Spanish:* shawl.

**Close Read**

1. What characteristics immediately signal that this is a poem? Cite specific details.

2. **Exploring a Big Question** The couple in this poem seem compatible and comfortable with each other. What other qualities of a relationship are essential for love to last over the years?

---

## DIFFERENTIATED INSTRUCTION

### FOR STRUGGLING READERS

**Analysis Support: Poetry** To help students apply the **Literary Terms for Poetry** to "Los ancianos" or another poem of your choice, have them work in a group to complete the Core Analysis Frame: Poetry. Monitor their progress, offering assistance as requested or needed.

**BEST PRACTICES TOOLKIT—Transparency** Core Analysis Frame: Poetry pp. D21, D34

### FOR ENGLISH LANGUAGE LEARNERS

**Language: Skill Words** Write these lines on the board, and have students discuss them using one or more terms from the **Literary Terms for Poetry:**

- I adore / That town on the shore. (*rhyme, line, speaker, rhythm*)

- A smile like a sunny summer day / Lit up her face and found my heart. (*sound devices, line, speaker, rhythm, meter, figurative language, imagery*)

## DRAMA

Characters in conflict are at the heart of drama, just as they are in fiction. But since drama is meant to be performed for an audience rather than read, the plot is carried by **dialogue** and **action**—what the characters say and do. Dramas are usually divided into **scenes,** with each scene set in a different time or place. In long plays, scenes are grouped into **acts.**

With their heroes and villains in theatrical settings, staged dramas have been captivating audiences since ancient times. However, dramas also make good reading. To help yourself visualize a drama, you need to consider not only the dialogue but also the **stage directions**—the writer's instructions for the actors, the director, and the other people working on the play. Often printed in italic type, stage directions describe everything from the setting and the props to the characters' movements.

**Read the Model** *The Miracle Worker* dramatizes Helen Keller's relationship with Annie Sullivan, the teacher who taught Helen to use sign language and communicate with others. At this point in the drama, Helen has learned the mechanics of sign language, but she still does not understand the meanings behind the words. Here, Annie expresses her frustration to Helen's mother, Kate. How does Annie's attitude help you understand the power of determination?

> LITERARY TERMS FOR DRAMA
> • plot
> • character
> • act
> • scene
> • stage directions
> • dialogue
> • monologue
> • soliloquy
> • dialect

---

*from*
# The Miracle Worker

Drama by **William Gibson**

### *from* Act Three

**Annie.** . . . We're born to use words, like wings, it has to come.

**Kate.** How?

**Annie** (*another pause, wearily*). All right. I don't know how.
(*She pushes up her glasses to rub her eyes.*)
5 I've done everything I could think of. Whatever she's learned here—keeping herself clean, knitting, stringing beads, meals, setting-up exercises each morning, we climb trees, hunt eggs, yesterday a chick was born in her hands—all of it I spell, everything we do, we never stop spelling. I go to bed with—writer's cramp from talking so much!

10 **Kate.** I worry about you, Miss Annie. You must rest.

**Annie.** Now? She spells back in her *sleep,* her fingers make letters when she doesn't know! In her bones those five fingers know, that hand aches to—speak out, and something in her mind is asleep, how do I—nudge that awake? That's the one question.

### Close Read

1. How do you know that Annie is exhausted? Cite specific details that reveal her state of mind.

2. **Exploring a Big Question** Do you think people can accomplish anything if they are determined enough? Explain your opinion. Then predict how Annie's determination will eventually play out.

---

## DRAMA

Ask students to read the first two paragraphs to themselves and note the boldface words while you list the **Literary Terms for Drama** on the board. Discuss elements that readers might find in both fiction and drama, such as *plot, character, dialogue,* and *dialect.*

### Close Read

Introduce the model by reading the third paragraph aloud. Ask students to read the model silently. Then assign roles to students and ask them to read the model again, this time aloud. Afterward, have students answer the **Close Read** questions.

*Possible answers:*

1. *The stage directions—Annie's weary pause and rubbing of her eyes (lines 3 and 4)—show that she is exhausted, as do the breaks in her words to Kate (indicated by dashes). Kate's comment, "I worry about you, Miss Annie. You must rest" (line 10), indicates that Annie's exhaustion is apparent to others.*

2. *Determination may help people reach some goals, but other goals require more than determination (for example, special skills, education, or funding), and some goals are too unrealistic ever to be reached. Given time and her determination to teach Helen to understand and learn sign language, Annie probably will succeed.*

**CHECK UNDERSTANDING** Have students identify details in the passage that demonstrate Annie's determination.

---

### FOR STRUGGLING READERS

**Analysis Support: Dramatic Character** Have students reread lines 1–4 of the model and identify characters, stage directions, and dialogue. Ask them to use a chart to record lines where these elements appear.

|  | Line Numbers |
|---|---|
| Characters | Annie (lines 1, 3) Kate (line 2) |
| Stage Directions | Lines 3, 4 |
| Dialogue | Lines 1–3 |

## NONFICTION

Read the introductory paragraph and point out the terms *literary works* and *informational texts*. To clarify the distinction, show students a copy or give the title of several specific literary works, such as Bill Bryson's *A Walk in the Woods*. Similarly, show specific examples of informational texts, such as news articles. Invite students to suggest additional examples for each category. Discuss the characteristics of each type of nonfiction listed on the page. Then point out that the **Terms for Nonfiction** refers to terms students will encounter and use in their study of nonfiction.

## NONFICTION

When you see the word *nonfiction*—especially in a literature book—you probably expect to find literary works such as biographies, speeches, and essays. Nonfiction also includes other kinds of **informational texts,** such as news articles and train schedules, which provide factual information. Because you encounter informational texts all the time, you should know what to expect from them.

**TERMS FOR NONFICTION**
- purpose
- organizational patterns
- perspective
- argument
- persuasion

| TYPE OF NONFICTION | CHARACTERISTICS | |
|---|---|---|
| **AUTOBIOGRAPHY/ BIOGRAPHY** The true story of a person's life, told by that person (autobiography) or by another person (biography) | • Provides details that give readers insights into a person's life <br> • Is told from the first-person point of view (autobiography) or from the third-person point of view (biography) <br> • Presents the person's own thoughts about his or her life experiences (autobiography) or information from a variety of sources (biography) |  |
| **ESSAY** A short work that focuses on a single subject. Common types include personal essays and persuasive essays. | • May have the following purposes: to express feelings, to inform, to entertain, to persuade <br> • May be **formal,** with an organized structure and an impersonal style <br> • May be **informal,** with a conversational style |  |
| **SPEECH** An oral presentation of the ideas, beliefs, or proposals of a speaker | • May have the following purposes: to express feelings, to inform, to entertain, to persuade <br> • Achieves its power through effective language, including rhetorical devices and structures, and a compelling delivery |  |
| **NEWS/FEATURE ARTICLES** Informative writing in newspapers and magazines. A news article reports on recent events. A feature article focuses on human-interest topics. | • Are primarily intended to inform or entertain <br> • May use statistics, quotations from sources, examples, and graphic aids to convey information <br> • Usually are objective and balanced |  |
| **FUNCTIONAL TEXTS** Writing that serves a practical purpose. Types include consumer documents, such as instruction manuals, and workplace documents, such as memos and résumés. | • Are written for a specific audience (for example, the user of a product or a potential employer) <br> • May present information in charts or other easy-to-navigate graphic formats <br> • Often include specialized jargon | |

## DIFFERENTIATED INSTRUCTION

### FOR STRUGGLING READERS

**Language: Skill Words** Discuss the meanings of these terms from the chart:

- *point of view:* the perspective from which a text is narrated
- *conversational:* like casual, everyday speech
- *statistics:* numerical facts
- *graphic aids:* charts, diagrams, or other drawings
- *jargon:* specialized words used in a certain profession

**Comprehension: Nonfiction** Have students identify these types of nonfiction:

- An attempt to get readers to support a change of the school mascot (*essay*)
- The story of your life (*autobiography*)
- Details about the city council meeting (*news article*)
- A political leader talking to a group of local voters (*speech*)

## MODEL 1: AUTOBIOGRAPHY

This excerpt is from an autobiography by Monica Sone, a Japanese-American woman who grew up in Seattle during World War II. Here, Sone remembers the moment when she and her brother Henry found out from a classmate about Japan's attack on Pearl Harbor. As you read, consider what the author might be suggesting about the factors that influence a person's identity.

*from*

 Nisei Daughter

Autobiography by **Monica Sone**

With that, Chuck swept out of the room, a swirl of young men following in his wake. Henry was one of them. The rest of us stayed, rooted to our places like a row of marionettes. I felt as if a fist had smashed my pleasant little existence, breaking it into jigsaw puzzle pieces. An old wound opened up again,
5  and I found myself shrinking inwardly from my Japanese blood, the blood of an enemy. I knew instinctively that the fact that I was an American by birthright was not going to help me escape the consequences of this unhappy war.

### Close Read

1. How does Sone react to the news about the attack on Pearl Harbor? Cite details that reveal her feelings.

2. **Exploring a Big Question** Sone feels torn between her American upbringing and her Japanese blood. In your opinion, what forces shape a person's identity?

## MODEL 2: NEWS ARTICLE

This article was published in the *New York Times* on December 8, 1941, one day after the attack on Pearl Harbor.

DECEMBER 8, 1941

# JAPAN MAKES SUDDEN ATTACK

NEWS ARTICLE BY **Frank L. Kluckhohn**

WASHINGTON, Monday, Dec. 8— Sudden and unexpected attacks on Pearl Harbor, Honolulu, and other United States possessions in the
5  Pacific early yesterday by the Japanese air force and navy plunged the United States and Japan into active war.

The initial attack in Hawaii, apparently launched by torpedo-
10  carrying bombers and submarines, caused widespread damage and death.

It was quickly followed by others. There were unconfirmed reports that German raiders participated in the attacks.
15  Guam was assaulted from the air, as were Davao, on the island of Mindanao, and Camp John Hay, in Northern Luzom, both in the Philippines. Lieut. Gen. Douglas MacArthur, commanding
20  the United States Army of the Far East, reported there was little damage, however.

### Close Read

1. How do the details in this article differ from those in Sone's account? Cite evidence from both texts to support your answer.

2. **Exploring a Big Question** Consider other wars you've studied or read about. For what reasons do countries go to war?

9

---

Read the models aloud, explaining that they provide different types of information about the same historical event. Then have students answer the Close Read questions.

## MODEL 1: AUTOBIOGRAPHY

**Close Read**

*Possible answers:*

1. *Sone reacts with shock and fear. She is stunned by the news (lines 3–4), and she worries about what the future will bring her as a Japanese American (lines 4–7).*

2. *The forces that shape a person's identity include heritage, community, family traditions and values, education, and occupations.*

## MODEL 2: NEWS ARTICLE

**Close Read**

*Possible answers:*

1. *Sone's account is a first-person, emotional reflection; she says more about her feelings than about the attack. The article, however, focuses on facts. It gives a third-person, objective account of the attack. Accept all relevant details.*

   **IF STUDENTS NEED HELP . . .** Ask them to think about the difference between a fact and an opinion. Which passage has more facts (names, dates, places)? How would a reader describe the content of the other passage?

2. *Countries sometimes go to war to settle land disputes or political or religious differences, to defend themselves from enemy attacks, or to support allies.*

**CHECK UNDERSTANDING** Have students explain how the two nonfiction models differ in purpose.

---

### FOR STRUGGLING READERS

**Analysis Support: Nonfiction** Model the use of the Reporter's Questions (Who? What? When? Where? Why? How?) as a means of gathering information from and comparing these two nonfiction passages. Answer a few of the questions for the excerpt from *Nisei Daughter;* then have students answer the rest as a group. Allow them to answer the questions about the news article on their own.

BEST PRACTICES TOOLKIT—Transparency
Reporter's Questions p. C9

| Who attacked Pearl Harbor? | Japan |
|---|---|
| What happened? | Bombers and submarines attacked with torpedoes, causing damage and deaths |
| When was the attack? | December 7, 1941 |
| | |
| | |

## TYPES OF MEDIA

Have students read over the introductory paragraph while you write the **Terms for Media** on the board. Then discuss why it is important to develop media literacy. Point out the types of media listed on the page as well as characteristics particular to each type. Then have students compare the purpose and effects of the various types of media. Finally, explain how the **Terms for Media** apply to the types of media listed on the page.

**CHECK UNDERSTANDING** Ask students where examples of news media can be found.

---

## TYPES OF MEDIA

Learning how to "read" media is a key part of being literate in today's world. From screaming headlines at the checkout counter to in-your-face advertising, all media messages have been constructed for a purpose—to grab your attention, entertain you, or influence your decisions. Becoming **media literate** starts with knowing the basics and thinking critically about *all* messages in this media-saturated age.

**TERMS FOR MEDIA**

- medium
- message
- purpose
- tone
- target audience
- technique

| TYPE OF MEDIA | CHARACTERISTICS | |
|---|---|---|
| **FEATURE FILMS** Motion pictures that use narrative elements to tell a story | • Are intended to entertain and make money<br>• Use camera shots, sound effects, music, actors, and sets to tell compelling stories<br>• Are at least 60 minutes in length | 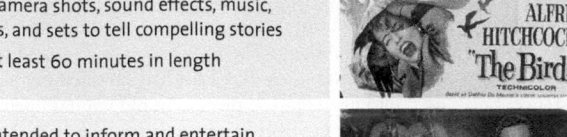 |
| **NEWS MEDIA** Accounts of current events as presented on TV, in newspapers and magazines, on the radio, and on the Web | • Are intended to inform and entertain<br>• Have varying degrees of accuracy and credibility<br>• Medium (TV, radio, print) affects the presentation and delivery of information |  |
| **TV SHOWS** Programs broadcast on television, including dramas, sitcoms, and reality shows | • Are usually intended to inform or entertain<br>• Are financed by sponsors who pay to air ads during the programs<br>• Use visuals and sounds to create programming that will engage viewers<br>• Are typically 30–60 minutes in length | 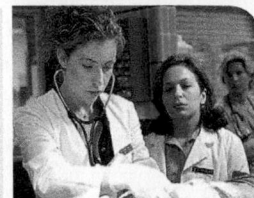 |
| **ADVERTISING** A sponsor's paid use of media to promote products, services, or ideas | • Is intended to persuade a target audience to buy a product or service or to adopt an idea<br>• Uses persuasive techniques, visuals, and sounds to appeal to an audience<br>• Is strategically printed or aired where a target audience is likely to encounter it |  |
| **WEB SITES** Collections of "pages" on the World Wide Web. From a home page, users can explore other pages on a Web site by clicking hyperlinks or menus. | • Can be accessed at any time by anyone with a computer and an Internet connection<br>• Are not always a reliable source of information (because anyone can publish on the Web)<br>• Present content through text, graphics, video, sound, and interactive features |  |

---

## DIFFERENTIATED INSTRUCTION

### FOR STRUGGLING READERS

**Note Taking** Suggest that students use a Three-Column Journal to record key facts from this page. Instruct students to focus on medium, purpose, and methods. (Point out that the messages and target audiences for each medium are practically infinite.) Model the example at right.

 **BEST PRACTICES TOOLKIT—Transparency** Three-Column Journal p. B10

| Medium | Purpose | Methods |
|---|---|---|
| feature films | entertain (and make money) | camera shots, sound effects, music, actors, sets |

### FOR ENGLISH LANGUAGE LEARNERS

**Language: Skill Words** Have students identify the **Terms for Media** that each statement illustrates.

- "Wow—that movie really made me think!" (*message*)
- "A new TV series will be based on that movie." (*medium*)
- "Teens will love this show." (*target audience*)
- "Do we merely want to entertain them, or to teach them?" (*purpose*)

# Literature and Nonfiction Strategies

 Jot your reactions and observations in your **Reader/Writer Notebook**.

## ❶ Ask the Right Questions

An important part of analyzing texts is knowing what questions to ask as you read. What should you be looking for when you are reading a drama? a news article? a classic novel? The following features will help you develop your own instincts for asking the right questions.

| Where to Look | What You'll Find |
|---|---|
| **Text Analysis Workshops** (at the beginning of every unit) ▶ | Interactive practice models and **Close Read** questions |
| Side notes and discussion questions ▶ | Questions (throughout and following each selection) that focus on the analysis of literary and nonfiction elements |
| **Analysis Frames** THINK central Go to **thinkcentral.com**. KEYWORD: HML9-11 ▶ | Guided questions for analyzing different genres |

## ❷ Make Connections

"I can relate to the main character because . . . ," "This writer's view of love is different from . . ."—connections like these are what make the ideas in texts meaningful.

- **Big Questions** Life and literature are both about exploring big questions. Look for opportunities to connect what you read with experiences of your own.

- **Discussion/Journaling** Share your insights with others or jot them down. Consider questions such as:
  - What does this mean to me?
  - Who or what does this remind me of?

## ❸ Record Your Reactions

Writing down your ideas can help you both remember and sort through your reactions and observations. Try a variety of formats.

**GRAPHIC ORGANIZER**

Set up a graphic organizer, such as a cluster diagram.

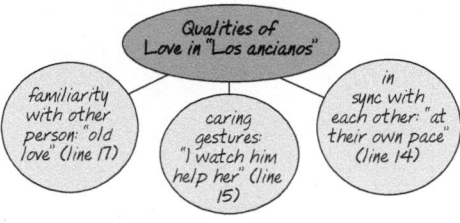

**TWO-COLUMN NOTES**

Divide each page into two columns, one for quotations and information from the text, and the other for your responses.

| "Los ancianos" | My Impressions |
|---|---|
| "I watch him help her off the curb and I smell love" (lines 15–16) | Shows the power of the couple's love; also conveys how moved the speaker is by this sight |

---

# Literature and Nonfiction Strategies

Point out that practically any activity that students may enjoy—sports, art, music, or drama—involves strategies, or ways of helping them become better at that particular activity. Elicit that such activities become more exciting as students' personal involvement with them grows. As you discuss **Literature and Nonfiction Strategies,** emphasize that these strategies can help make reading texts more engaging and exciting.

### 1. Ask the Right Questions
Point out to students that throughout the anthology they will be guided in asking questions that will help them analyze texts. As you discuss the features listed under "Where to Look" and "What You'll Find," explain that students will find these features throughout the anthology.

### 2. Make Connections
Reinforce for students the importance of connecting to text on a personal level. Explain that their ideas and reactions are valid as long as they can support them with examples from the text. As you discuss the explanations of **Big Questions** and **Discussion/Journaling,** encourage students to use these opportunities to connect and respond to the texts in the anthology.

### 3. Record Your Reactions
Emphasize to students the importance of creating a **Reader/Writer Notebook** in which to record their reactions to what they are reading. Encourage them to use the kinds of graphic formats suggested by the text, as well as the questions, reactions, and connections that might occur to them as they read.

---

**Analysis Frames** THINK central

The **Analysis Frames** on **thinkcentral.com** help students learn how to ask the right questions when reading, analyzing, and evaluating:

- stories
- drama
- poetry
- nonfiction
- informational texts
- persuasive writing

---

**FOR STRUGGLING READERS**

**Concept Support** Use these activities to reinforce the teaching in the text:

1. Have students turn to pages 28–35 to see a Text Analysis Workshop. Point out its models and **Close Read** questions. Similarly, have students skim through some of the side notes and discussion questions in "A Sound of Thunder," the first selection in Unit 1. If you have a classroom computer, go to **thinkcentral.com** and show students an example of an analysis frame.

2. Use "A Sound of Thunder" to illustrate **Big Questions.** Then call on volunteers to share positive experiences that they have had with discussion groups and journaling.

3. Have students read the Cluster Diagram and the Two-Column Notes against the text of "Los ancianos" (p. 6). Ask students to suggest how the format could be used to record their reactions to the excerpt from *The Old Man and the Sea* (p. 5).

**RL 1** Cite strong and thorough textual evidence to support analysis of what the text says explicitly as well as inferences drawn from the text.
**RL 4** Determine the meaning of words and phrases as they are used in the text; analyze the cumulative impact of specific word choices on meaning and tone. **RI 1** Cite strong and thorough textual evidence to support analysis of what the text says explicitly as well as inferences drawn from the text.
**RI 4** Determine the meaning of words and phrases as they are used in a text; analyze the cumulative impact of specific word choices on meaning and tone. **L 4** Determine or clarify the meaning of unknown and multiple-meaning words and phrases.

Explain to students that active readers, like explorers discovering new worlds, use a variety of skills and strategies to thoroughly explore a text's contents. Even when they have finished, active readers will continue to share and explore new ideas.

After students have read through the explanation at the top of the page, ask them what strategies they used while exploring this material. For example, did they set a purpose for reading? Did they develop questions to ensure that they understand the material? Encourage students to examine the **SKILLS AND STRATEGIES FOR ACTIVE READING** and to cite those that might also have been useful.

## Reading Strategies Workshop

# Becoming an Active Reader

When you read, you open your mind to new ideas that might be different from anything you've ever imagined. Maybe the world described is one that no longer exists—a world of ravenous dinosaurs or of jousting knights in armor. Maybe the opinions expressed clash with your own. To really explore ideas in texts, you need to fully comprehend what you're reading. Learning how to be an active reader can help you do just that.

### SKILLS AND STRATEGIES FOR ACTIVE READING

**Preview**
Get a sense of a text before you start to read.
- Look for clues in the title, graphics, and subheading.
- Skim the opening paragraphs.

**Set a Purpose**
Decide *why* you are reading a particular text.
- Ask: Am I reading to be entertained, to get information, or for another reason?
- Consider how your purpose might affect the way you approach a text. Take notes or enjoy?

**Connect**
Relate personally to what you are reading.
- Consider whether you've encountered people or situations like the ones described.
- Ask: If I were in this situation, how would I react?

**Use Prior Knowledge**
Bring to mind what you already know about a topic.
- Before reading, jot down what you already know.
- As you read, connect what you know to what you are learning.

**Predict**
Try to guess what will happen next.
- Note details about plot or characters that hint at where the story is heading.
- Keep reading to find out how accurate your prediction was.

**Visualize**
Form sensory images of what is being described.
- Look for descriptive details about characters, settings, and events.
- Use this information to conjure up a vivid scene in your mind's eye.

**Monitor**
Check your own comprehension as you read.
- **Question** what is happening and why.
- **Clarify** your understanding by rereading difficult parts or asking for help.
- **Evaluate** how well you are understanding the text.

**Make Inferences**
Make logical guesses by considering the text and your own experiences.
- Record details about characters and events.
- Ask: How can I combine textual evidence with common sense and my own experiences to help me understand this character or situation?

| Details in "Walter Mitty" | What I Know | My Inference |
|---|---|---|
| Mitty daydreams a lot that he's a hero. | Daydreams are a way to escape real life. | Mitty is probably not content with his real life. |

## DIFFERENTIATED INSTRUCTION

**FOR STRUGGLING READERS**

**Note Taking** For those students who need help, hand out the note-taking copy master for the Reading Strategies Workshop. Read and discuss the introductory paragraph on this page. As students examine the **SKILLS AND STRATEGIES FOR ACTIVE READING,** assist them in completing the copy master as needed.

**R** RESOURCE MANAGER—Copy Master
Note Taking p. I-3

**Concept Support** Remind students that they already use many of the skills and strategies used by active readers. Ask students to recall a movie or TV program they have recently seen. Have them explain and give examples of how they used the **SKILLS AND STRATEGIES FOR ACTIVE READING** when viewing this material.

In this excerpt from James Thurber's classic story, exhilirating daydreams help save Walter Mitty from his own dull existence. As you move between Mitty's imaginary adventures and his ordinary routines, use the **Close Read** questions to practice active reading skills and strategies.

◌ **COMMON CORE**

Included in this workshop:
RL 1, RL 4, RI 1, RI 4, L 4

*from*

# The Secret Life of Walter Mitty

### Short story by **James Thurber**

"We're going through!" The Commander's voice was like thin ice breaking. He wore his full-dress uniform, with the heavily braided white cap pulled down rakishly[1] over one cold gray eye. "We can't make it, sir. It's spoiling for a hurricane, if you ask me." "I'm not asking you, Lieutenant Berg,"
5  said the Commander. "Throw on the power lights! Rev her up to 8,500! We're going through!" The pounding of the cylinders increased: ta-pocketa-pocketa-pocketa-*pocketa-pocketa.* The Commander stared at the ice forming on the pilot window. He walked over and twisted a row of complicated dials. "Switch on No. 8 auxilary!" he shouted. "Switch on No. 8 auxilary!" repeated
10  Lieutenant Berg. "Full strength in No. 3 turret!" shouted the Commander. "Full strength in No. 3 turret!" The crew, bending to their various tasks in the huge, hurtling eight-engined Navy hydroplane, looked at each other and grinned. "The Old Man'll get us through," they said to one another. "The Old Man ain't afraid of Hell!" . . .

15  "Not so fast! You're driving too fast!" said Mrs. Mitty. "What are you driving so fast for?"
"Hmm?" said Walter Mitty. He looked at his wife, in the seat behind him, with shocked astonishment. She seemed grossly unfamiliar, like a strange woman who had yelled at him in a crowd. "You were up to fifty-five," she said.
20  "You know I don't like to go more than forty. You were up to fifty-five." Walter Mitty drove on toward Waterbury in silence, the roaring of the SN202 through the worst storm in twenty years of Navy flying fading in the remote, intimate airways of his mind. "You're tensed up again," said Mrs. Mitty. "It's one of your days. I wish you'd let Dr. Renshaw look you over."
25  Walter Mitty stopped the car in front of the building where his wife went to have her hair done. "Remember to get those overshoes while I'm having my hair done," she said. "I don't need overshoes," said Mitty. She put her mirror back into her bag. "We've been all through that," she said, getting out of the car. "You're not a young man any longer." He raced the engine a little. "Why

---

1. **rakishly:** with a confident, carefree, and dashing look.

**Close Read**

1. **Visualize** Which details in lines 1–14 help you picture the excitement of the scene? Cite details about the setting and the conflict.

2. **Monitor** In the boxed text, the story shifts scenes, from a thrilling adventure to an uneventful car ride. Clarify your understanding by summarizing what is happening.

---

## FOR ENGLISH LANGUAGE LEARNERS

**Vocabulary: Idioms and Sayings** Discuss these idioms and sayings, which appear in the Mittys' conversation (some real, some imagined):

- *going through* (line 1), "proceeding"
- *can't make it* (line 3), "won't succeed"
- *It's spoiling for a hurricane* (lines 3–4), "looks like a hurricane is approaching"
- *Throw on* (line 5) and *Switch on* (line 9), "Put into operation"

- *Rev her up* (line 5), "Increase the speed"
- *What are you driving so fast for?* (lines 15–16), "Why are you driving so fast?"
- *You were up to fifty-five* (line 19), "You increased the speed to fifty-five miles per hour"
- *tensed up* (line 23), "stressed"
- *look you over* (line 24), "examine you"

---

Explain to students that reading the model will provide them with the opportunity to practice the **SKILLS AND STRATEGIES FOR ACTIVE READING.** Ask students to pay attention to the ways in which each strategy provides different information about and insights into the passage.

## MODEL: SHORT STORY

### Close Read

Call on a volunteer to read aloud the introductory paragraph. Point out that students will have to decide which parts of the story present daydreams and which parts present real life. As time permits, also have students listen to the complete story on the *Audio Anthology CD.* Then direct them to answer the **Close Read** questions.

*Possible answers:*

1. *Details that convey excitement include the references to bad weather (lines 3–4 and 7–8), the sound of the engines (lines 6–7), and the many shouted commands. The setting is aboard a "huge, hurtling eight-engined Navy hydroplane" (line 12). The main conflict is between the plane's crew (especially the Commander) and a potentially deadly storm; there also is a brief conflict between the Commander and Lieutenant Berg.*

2. *Mitty has been daydreaming about commanding a Navy hydroplane in a storm when he is snapped back to reality by his wife's command to drive more slowly. As he realizes where he is, the daydream fades, and his wife says that he should see Dr. Renshaw because he is tense.*

**IF STUDENTS NEED HELP . . .** Use the Read Aloud/Think Aloud strategy to model a summary of lines 11–14. Then help students summarize the rest of the boxed text.

▣ **BEST PRACTICES TOOLKIT—Transparency** Read Aloud/Think Aloud p. A34

**Possible answers:**

3. *Unlike the take-charge hero of his day-dreams, the real-life Mitty quietly does what his wife demands of him, even though he seems to want to rebel against her (as evidenced in his racing the engine [line 29] and taking off his gloves as soon as she is out of sight [lines 31–33]). The fact that Mitty's wife dominates the conversation in a very critical way suggests that the Mittys do not have an entirely happy relationship.*

4. *If this daydream is like the previous one, it will be cut short, just before reaching its climax, by words spoken to Mitty in real life.*

**IF STUDENTS NEED HELP . . .** Review what happened in Mitty's previous daydream. In particular, have students reread lines 11–16, noting that (1) Mitty's daydream is interrupted before its story ends and (2) the interruption comes in the form of critical words from Mrs. Mitty.

5. *Accept all reasonable responses. Students may suggest that people dream that they are stars because they want to escape the dullness of their everyday lives or because they admire the wealth, power, attractiveness, confidence, or adoration that they think stars enjoy.*

**CHECK UNDERSTANDING** Ask students how using various reading strategies increased their understanding and enjoyment of Thurber's story.

---

30 don't you wear your gloves? Have you lost your gloves?" Walter Mitty reached in a pocket and brought out the gloves. He put them on, but after she had turned and gone into the building and he had driven on to a red light, he took them off again. "Pick it up, brother!" snapped a cop as the light changed, and Mitty hastily pulled on his gloves and lurched ahead. He drove around the
35 streets aimlessly for a time, and then he drove past the hospital on his way to the parking lot.

. . . "**I**t's the millionaire banker, Wellington McMillan," said the pretty nurse. "Yes?" said Walter Mitty, removing his glasses slowly. "Who has the case?" "Dr. Renshaw and Dr. Benbow, but there are two
40 specialists here, Dr. Remington from New York and Mr. Pritchard-Mitford from London. He flew over." A door opened down a long, cool corridor and Dr. Renshaw came out. He looked distraught and haggard. "Hello, Mitty," he said. "We're having the devil's own time with McMillan, the millionaire banker and close personal friend of Roosevelt. Obstreosis of the ductal tract.[2] Tertiary.
45 Wish you'd take a look at him." "Glad to," said Mitty.

In the operating room there were whispered introductions: "Dr. Remington, Dr. Mitty. Mr. Pritchard-Mitford, Dr. Mitty." "I've read your book on streptothricosis," said Pritchard-Mitford, shaking hands. "A brilliant performance, sir." "Thank you," said Walter Mitty. "Didn't know you were
50 in the States, Mitty," grumbled Remington. "Coals to Newcastle,[3] bringing Mitford and me up here for tertiary." "You are very kind," said Mitty. A huge, complicated machine, connected to the operating table, with many tubes and wires, began at this moment to go pocketa-pocketa-pocketa. "The new anesthetizer is giving way!" shouted an intern. "There is no one in the East
55 who knows how to fix it!" "Quiet, man!" said Mitty, in a low, cool voice. He sprang to the machine, which was now going pocketa-pocketa-queep-pocketa-queep. He began fingering delicately a row of glistening dials. "Give me a fountain pen!" he snapped. Someone handed him a fountain pen. He pulled a faulty piston out of the machine and inserted a pen in its place. "That will
60 hold for ten minutes," he said. "Get on with the operation." A nurse hurried over and whispered to Renshaw, and Mitty saw the man turn pale. "Coreopsis has set in," said Renshaw nervously. "If you would take over, Mitty?" Mitty looked at him and at the craven figure of Benbow, who drank, and at the grave, uncertain faces of the two great specialists. "If you wish," he said. They
65 slipped a white gown on him; he adjusted a mask and drew on thin gloves; nurses handed him shining . . .

"Back it up, Mac! Look out for that Buick!" Walter Mitty jammed on the brakes. "Wrong lane, Mac," said the parking-lot attendant, looking at Mitty closely. "Gee. Yeh," muttered Mitty. . . .

---

2. **Obstreosis of the ductal tract:** Thurber made up this and other terms to sound like—and poke fun at—medical jargon.

3. **Coals to Newcastle:** an unnecessary task. This expression refers to Newcastle, England, which was a major coal-producing city.

3. **Make Inferences** Given Mitty's actions in lines 29–34, what can you infer about his personality and his relationship with his wife?

4. **Predict** Now Mitty pictures himself in an operating room with an important patient. What do you imagine will happen?

5. **Connect** Have you ever been the hero in your own dreams? Explain why you think many people have dreams in which they are stars.

---

## DIFFERENTIATED INSTRUCTION

**FOR STRUGGLING READERS**

**Check Comprehension** Ask pairs of students to create five sentences about events in the story, leaving out key details, as in these examples:

- In Mitty's first daydream, he calls himself "_____," and his crew admiringly calls him "_____." (*the Commander; the Old Man*)

- In real life, his wife criticizes him for _____ and urges him to see _____. (*driving too fast; Dr. Renshaw*)

- As "Dr. Mitty," he is called upon to fix _____ and to operate on _____, who is a _____. (*a failing anesthetizer machine; McMillan; wealthy banker and good friend of Roosevelt*)

Have each pair exchange its sentences for those created by another pair and complete the sentences that they receive.

# Strategies That Work: Reading

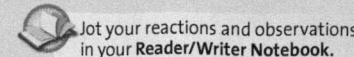 Jot your reactions and observations in your **Reader/Writer Notebook.**

## ❶ Read Independently

The best way to become a better reader is to read as much as you can, every chance you get.

| What Should I Read? | Where Should I Look? |
|---|---|
| **Novels**  | Get Novel Wise **THINK** central Go to thinkcentral.com. KEYWORD: HML9-15 |
| **Magazines Newspapers Web sites**  | Every time you check your favorite Web site or leaf through the daily newspaper, you are reading. Pick up whatever interests you, and keep reading. |

## ❷ Use Graphic Organizers

Graphic organizers can help you track the action in a work of literature, recognize relationships, and understand what is happening. Look for suggested graphic organizers in each lesson.

| Real Mitty | Fantasy Mitty |
|---|---|
| henpecked husband | commander, surgeon |
| boring life | series of adventures |
| meek, confused | courageous, confident |
| often yelled at or admonished | highly respected by many |

## ❸ Build Your Vocabulary

Creating a personal word list in your **Reader/Writer Notebook** can help you better understand not only a specific selection but also other readings throughout your life. Use these tips to get started:

- **List difficult words.** Consider listing vocabulary words from the selections, as well as other challenging terms you encounter.
- **Go beyond the definitions.** To help you remember each word and its meaning, list synonyms and antonyms, or write a sentence using the word. For help finding synonyms and antonyms, consult a thesaurus or dictionary.
- **Try them out.** Using new words in your writing and discussions is one of the best ways to build your vocabulary.

| Word | Meaning |
|---|---|
| **haggard** adj. "The Secret Life of Walter Mitty," line 42 | **Definition:** having a worn appearance **Synonyms:** gaunt; worn **Antonyms:** lively, energetic Months of fierce battle had taken a toll on the haggard soldier. |

## Strategies That Work: Reading

Discuss **Strategies That Work: Reading.** Ask students if they have ever tried any of the strategies listed; invite comments. Explain that these and other features in the anthology will help them develop these strategies and become more engaged, informed, and active readers.

1. **Read Independently**
   Point out that reading independently allows readers to practice reading strategies, increase their reading fluency, and improve their vocabulary. Invite students to share titles and passages from favorite readings, where appropriate, in class.

2. **Use Graphic Organizers**
   Encourage students to use graphic organizers to record their thoughts and reactions while reading as well as to organize questions or useful information. Urge students to record graphic organizers in their **Reader/Writer Notebook.**

3. **Build Your Vocabulary**
   Challenge students to record their personal word lists in their **Reader/Writer Notebook.** Emphasize that a strong vocabulary will help them read and communicate more effectively. Make sure students know where they can access a dictionary and thesaurus.

### NovelWise
 **THINK** central

**NovelWise** is a Web site that helps students choose a novel or other book-length work to read. **NovelWise** also provides

- study guides
- reading strategies and literary elements instruction
- presentations to introduce classic novels
- project ideas

## FOR STRUGGLING READERS

**Concept Support** Use these activities to reinforce the teaching in the text:

1. Have students create a list of fiction and nonfiction readings that they have enjoyed and would recommend to others. Encourage students to try some of the readings during the school year.

2. Point out that graphic organizers have various purposes. For example, the Two-Column Chart is an effective way to record the contrasts in Walter Mitty's world; however, if

there were also similarities between Mitty's daydreams and his real life, a Venn diagram would be more appropriate.

3. Invite students to share tips about learning and using new words. Also explain that each unit in the anthology opens with a feature that includes academic vocabulary—terms relating to the skills and strategies appearing in that unit's lessons. Encourage students to use those terms as they write about and discuss the selections.

**L3** Apply knowledge of language to understand how language functions in different contexts and to comprehend more fully when reading or listening. **L4a** Use context as a clue to the meaning of a word or phrase. **L4c** Consult reference sources to find the pronunciation of a word or determine or clarify its precise meaning, its part of speech, or its etymology. **L5** Demonstrate understanding of figurative language, word relationships, and nuances in word meanings. **L6** Acquire and use accurately academic and domain-specific words and phrases.

Review the Academic Vocabulary word web with students. Starting with the box labeled Language Arts, in the upper right, read the questions aloud and ask for help with answers.

- **Language Arts:** Point out to students that a *tradition* is something passed down from generation to generation. Explain that an *epic* is a long narrative poem that describes the adventures of a great hero. That hero's actions often reflect the ideals and values of a nation.

- **Biology:** Explain that the word *factor* means "an element or condition that contributes to a result." One factor that might affect migration is changing weather conditions. Another could be the different needs of a species at different times. (For example, humpback whales need a warm environment in which to bear and raise their young, but a cooler one for finding food).

- **Other Languages:** Explain that the word *emphasis* means "special stress on something." Tell students that learning the correct syllable to emphasize is especially important when learning a new language.

- **Algebra:** To *evaluate* something means "to judge or determine the worth or quality of." To evaluate the expression on the word web, first plug the number 3 in for *x*. Next, evaluate the operation within the parentheses. (*10*) Then, raise 10 to the 6th power (*1,000,000*) and multiply that number by 2. The answer is 2,000,000. When *describing* steps, a numbered list helps clarify the instructions.

## Academic Vocabulary Workshop

# What Is Academic Vocabulary?

Words travel with you throughout each day—from exchanging greetings with family members to texting friends to reading magazines to writing assignments for school. However, the kinds of words you use change during the day, depending on your purpose and audience. With family and friends, you use informal and conversational vocabulary. In school, though, you rely on **academic vocabulary**, the language you use to talk and write about the subject matter you are studying.

*Affect, interpretation, identify*—you may encounter academic vocabulary words such as these in *all* subject areas, including science, math, social studies, and language arts. Understanding and using these words correctly will help you to be successful in school and on assessments. This web shows examples of academic vocabulary words in different subject areas.

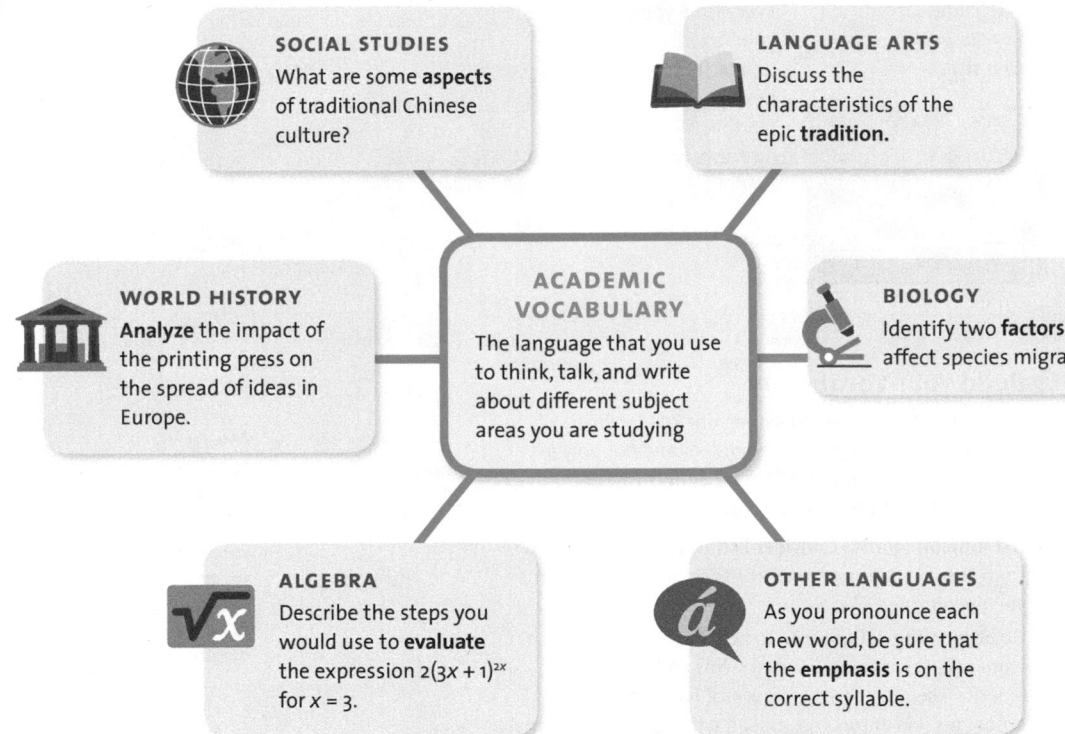

**SOCIAL STUDIES**
What are some **aspects** of traditional Chinese culture?

**LANGUAGE ARTS**
Discuss the characteristics of the epic **tradition.**

**WORLD HISTORY**
**Analyze** the impact of the printing press on the spread of ideas in Europe.

**ACADEMIC VOCABULARY**
The language that you use to think, talk, and write about different subject areas you are studying

**BIOLOGY**
Identify two **factors** that affect species migration.

**ALGEBRA**
Describe the steps you would use to **evaluate** the expression $2(3x + 1)^{2x}$ for $x = 3$.

**OTHER LANGUAGES**
As you pronounce each new word, be sure that the **emphasis** is on the correct syllable.

## DIFFERENTIATED INSTRUCTION

### FOR ENGLISH LANGUAGE LEARNERS

**Language Support** Help students understand that academic vocabulary words often appear on lessons and on tests. Knowing the meaning of these academic vocabulary terms will help English language learners complete their assignments and do better on assessments. Provide students with additional context for some of the terms listed on this page, as follows:

- Who is your hero? What *aspect* of his or her character do you admire the most?

- *Analyze* why the team lost the game. What was one *factor* that affected the outcome?

- On which syllable do you put the *emphasis* in your first name? Last name?

- What are some *traditions* for celebrating Independence Day (July 4th)?

- *Evaluate* yourself. What is your best school subject?

**R** RESOURCE MANAGER—Copy Master
Note Taking p. I-4

Use the following chart to become familiar with some of the Academic Vocabulary terms in this book. As you read, look for the activities labeled "Academic Vocabulary in Writing" and "Academic Vocabulary in Speaking." These activities provide opportunities to use academic language in your writing and discussions.

| Word | Definition | Example |
|---|---|---|
| analyze | to separate or break into parts and examine | **Analyze** how Walt Whitman uses an implied metaphor in "Song of Myself." |
| aspect | a quality, part, or element | Which **aspects** of Madame Loisel's character lead to her financial ruin? |
| coherent | logical, consistent, or connected | Develop a **coherent** argument to support your position on the issue. |
| conclude | to decide or infer by evidence and reasoning | What did you **conclude** was the cause of the revolution? |
| differentiate | to perceive or create a difference between | **Differentiate** between the economic policies and the social policies of the President. |
| emphasis | special stress on something | Which syllable in "predominate" has the most **emphasis?** |
| evaluate | to judge or determine the worth or quality of | **Evaluate** the most suspenseful part of "The Most Dangerous Game." What makes it suspenseful? |
| factor | elements or conditions that create a result | Identify one **factor** that contributes to rising sea levels. |
| incorporate | to join or combine into a single whole | In your paper, **incorporate** details from the story to show how the setting affected the plot. |
| monitor | to check in on, watch, regulate | As you read, pause every few minutes to **monitor** how well you are understanding the story. |
| predominant | most frequent, common, or important | Name the two **predominant** gasses in the Earth's atmosphere. |
| relevant | related or pertinent to the matter at hand | Include **relevant** details to support your opinion on community service. |
| tradition | a practice passed down from generation to generation | Identify one social **tradition** that has been passed down in your family. |

- **World History:** Point out to students that *analyze* means "to separate or break into parts and examine." Explain to students that the invention of the printing press enabled scientists to produce reports of their experiments more easily and quickly, provided more people with access to reading materials, and introduced printing as an art form.
- **Social Studies:** Explain to students that an *aspect* is a feature or characteristic of something. Aspects or qualities of traditional Chinese culture include the practice of Chinese medicine such as acupuncture, the practice of martial arts such as tai chi, and the study of the ancient writings of Confucius.

**FOR STRUGGLING READERS**

**Vocabulary Support** Although this workshop focuses on academic vocabulary, students may need help with some of the other domain-specific terms on this page. Use the following definitions for additional support.

- *climate*: weather patterns
- *expression*: in algebra, any combination of terms representing numbers or quantities, for example (5 + x)

**FOR ADVANCED LEARNERS / PRE—AP**

Challenge advanced learners to come up with other examples of questions using some of the academic vocabulary terms on this page. They should create questions for which they know the answers; for example, they can ask questions about topics they studied in school last year. Groups or individuals can challenge one another to answer the questions they wrote.

## Academic Vocabulary in Action

Review the definition of *tradition* with students. Then, have students complete the chart on their own or in pairs. See the chart below for possible responses.

| Subject Area | Explanation |
|---|---|
| French | Bastille Day is celebrated on July 14 to commemorate the day the Bastille was stormed by French citizens in 1789. |
| Music | Handel's Messiah is traditionally performed at Christmas. |

Have students read the definition of *conclude*. Then ask them to fill out the chart, using a dictionary for help. Possible responses are provided in the chart below.

| Word | Definition | Sentence |
|---|---|---|
| concept | an idea or thought | Behavioral adaptation is a concept we studied in Biology. |
| conclusion | the end or last part | Working with a peer helped me improve the conclusion to my research paper. |
| conference | a formal meeting | Our school holds parent-teacher conferences each semester. |

## Academic Vocabulary in Action

The terms below are academic vocabulary words that can be found in a variety of text types. Knowing the meanings of these terms is essential for completing the activities and lessons in this book as well as mastering test items.

### tradition *(noun)*

*Defining the Word*

The word *tradition* means "a practice passed down from generation to generation." You may learn about cultural traditions in your social studies class. When reading literature, you may learn about literary traditions that were passed along in some cultures.

*Using the Word*

Now that you know the definition of *tradition*, practice using the word.

- Use a chart like the one shown to identify traditions you have learned about in different subject areas.
- Write a brief explanation of each tradition.

| Subject Area | Explanation |
|---|---|
| Language arts: epic tradition | Long poems that praised deeds of heroes were part of the epic tradition. |
| | |
| | |

### conclude *(verb)*

*Defining the Word*

The word *conclude* means "to decide or infer by evidence and reasoning; to bring together ideas or come to an agreement." We may conduct an experiment and conclude that brown eyes are dominant, or we may bring together our main points and conclude our essay. The Latin prefix *con-* means "with" or "together."

*Using the Word*

Once you know the meaning of a prefix, you are able to apply that meaning to other words having that prefix.

- In a chart like this one, make a list of other words you know that begin with the prefix *con-*.
- Look up each word in the dictionary and write down its meaning.
- Write a sentence using each word.

| Word | Definition | Sentence |
|---|---|---|
| conspiracy | a secret plan to act together | Brutus was involved in a conspiracy to kill Caesar. |
| | | |
| | | |

---

## DIFFERENTIATED INSTRUCTION

### FOR ENGLISH LANGUAGE LEARNERS

**Language Support**  Have pairs of students look up and share the meanings of the examples provided, including:

- *the Bastille:* a fortress used as a prison by French rulers
- *Handel's Messiah:* an oratorio written by George Frideric Handel (1685–1759) that describes the life of Jesus

# Strategies That Work: Vocabulary

 Record new vocabulary words in your **Reader/Writer Notebook**.

## ❶ Use Context Clues

The most important part of building your vocabulary is recognizing unfamiliar words as you read. When you encounter an unfamiliar word, look at the **context,** the words, phrases, or sentences that surround that word. Often, the context can give you important clues to the word's meaning, as in the following example:

> **Analyze** the causes of the war. Identify at least three causes and explain how they contributed to the war.

Even if you do not know what *analyze* means, you can figure out from the surrounding context that it means "to separate or break into parts and examine."

## ❷ Clarify Word Definitions

If you cannot rely on a word's context to help you understand its meaning, consult a dictionary. A dictionary entry will provide a word's pronunciation, parts of speech, origin, definitions, and sometimes even connotations—the different shades of meaning and associations taken on by words with similar definitions. When you are reading a textbook or manual, you may find definitions for unfamiliar words in a glossary at the back of the book.

> **totalitarian** (tō-tăl´ĭ-târ´ē-ən) *adj.:* a characteristic of government in which the person or party in charge has absolute control

## ❸ Keep a Word List

List new academic terms in your **Reader/Writer Notebook.** Add to your list each time you take on a new reading assignment. In addition to listing the word and its definition, you might draw a symbol or picture to show you what the word represents or provide examples to remind you of what the word means. Challenge yourself to use words from the list in your writing and discussions. The more frequently you use the words, the easier they will be to remember.

**Interactive Vocabulary**
**THINK** central
Go to **thinkcentral.com.**
KEYWORD: HML9-19

*For a complete list of terms in this book, see the **Glossary of Academic Vocabulary** on pages R121–R122.*

| Word | Examples |
|---|---|
| **tradition**<br>a practice passed down from generation to generation | LANGUAGE ARTS<br>• epic<br>• literary<br><br>SOCIAL STUDIES<br>• religion<br>• culture<br>• older societies |
| **conclude**<br>to decide or infer by evidence and reasoning | |

---

## Strategies That Work: Vocabulary

Share with students that **Strategies That Work: Vocabulary** can be applied not only to Academic Vocabulary terms but also to unfamiliar words or phrases students will find in their reading. Encourage students to use these strategies in their reading both in and out of the classroom.

### 1. Use Context Clues
Ask students to identify the context clues in the example given. Explain that the context of an unfamiliar word may provide clues by way of definition, restatement, or example.

### 2. Clarify Word Definitions
Have students flip to the Glossary of Vocabulary in English and Spanish in the back of this book. Explain that this glossary provides pronunciations, parts of speech, and definitions for the vocabulary words in the selections in this book. Also included are the definitions of these vocabulary words in Spanish. Tell students that a glossary provides less information than a dictionary but may be easier to access and use because of its immediate availability. This textbook also includes a Glossary of Reading and Informational Terms and a Glossary of Literary Terms.

### 3. Keep a Word List
Encourage students to record new academic vocabulary in their **Reader/Writer Notebook.**

Explain that a strong vocabulary will help them read and communicate more effectively. If you have a classroom computer, have students look at Interactive Vocabulary on **thinkcentral.com.**

---

### FOR STRUGGLING READERS

**Concept Support** Use these activities to reinforce the teaching in the text:

1. For more help understanding context clues, have students go to the **Vocabulary and Spelling Handbook** in the back of this book. There they can find specific examples of context clues, including restatement, examples, comparison, contrast, and cause-and-effect relationships.

2. Invite students to share tips about using glossaries and dictionaries. Ask students if they use glossaries in textbooks in other subjects or if they have a particular online dictionary they like to use.

3. Suggest that students form pairs and share their word lists. Have student pairs come up with other examples for some of the unfamiliar terms in their partners' notebooks. Alternatively, have students quiz each other on correct definitions.

---

### WordSharp

**THINK** central

**WordSharp Vocabulary Tutor** provides in-depth instruction in the use of vocabulary development strategies:
- identifying context clues
- applying knowledge of word parts and word origins
- using dictionaries and other resources
- recognizing specialized vocabulary
- studying word derivations

**W 4** Produce clear and coherent writing in which the development, organization, and style are appropriate to task, purpose, and audience. **W 5** Develop and strengthen writing as needed by planning, revising, editing, rewriting, or trying a new approach, focusing on addressing what is most significant for a specific purpose and audience. **SL 1c** Propel conversations by posing and responding to questions that relate the current discussion to broader themes or larger ideas; clarify, verify, or challenge ideas and conclusions. **SL 1d** Respond thoughtfully to diverse perspectives, and qualify or justify views and understanding and make new connections in light of evidence and reasoning presented. **L 1** Demonstrate command of the conventions of standard English grammar and usage. **L 2** Demonstrate command of the conventions of standard English capitalization, punctuation, and spelling when writing.

## Consider Your Options

Draw a triangle on the board and label its corners Purpose, Audience, and Format.

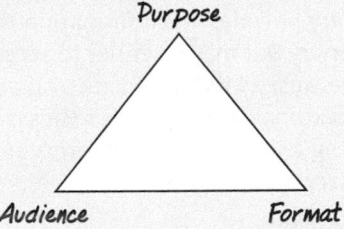

Read the questions that appear beneath these terms in the text, as well as the answers provided. Illustrate how these writing variables affect each other. For example, an explanatory piece on penguins might be presented in these ways:

- in the format of a short story if the audience consists of children
- in the format of a research paper if the audience consists of a teacher
- in the format of a magazine article if the audience consists of adults

Invite students to suggest similar examples.

---

*Writing Process Workshop*

# Expressing Ideas in Writing

Writing is a way of reaching people—of telling them something they didn't know, stirring their emotions, or even persuading them to stand up for a cause. Whether you're writing for the millions (an entry in a blog) or one in a million (a love letter), the act of putting words on paper can have remarkable power.

**COMMON CORE**

Included in this workshop:
W 4, W 5, SL 1c, SL 1d, L 1, L 2

## Consider Your Options

Maybe you want to write a review of a movie, advising other viewers to avoid it at all costs. Maybe you've decided to write an essay on a character in literature whose conflict seems familiar to you. Maybe you're drafting a letter to apply for a job. All kinds of writing start as ideas long before they are transformed into words on a page. Whether you are responding to a prompt or writing in your journal, start by considering **purpose, audience,** and **format.**

| PURPOSE | AUDIENCE | FORMAT |
|---|---|---|
| **Why am I writing?** <br> • to entertain <br> • to inform or explain <br> • to argue or persuade <br> • to describe <br> • to express thoughts and feelings <br> • to inspire | **Who are my readers?** <br> • classmates <br> • teachers <br> • friends <br> • community members <br> • potential employers <br> • Web users | **Which format will best suit my purpose and audience?** <br> • essay   • speech <br> • letter   • research paper <br> • review   • journal entry <br> • script   • Web site <br> • power presentation |

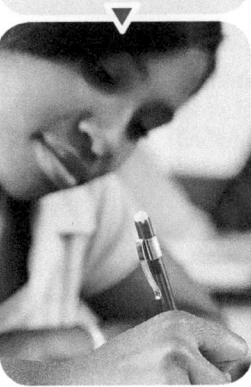

---

## DIFFERENTIATED INSTRUCTION

### FOR STRUGGLING READERS

**Note Taking** An understanding of the writing process will help students communicate effectively—both in class and throughout their lives. If students need help, hand out the note-taking copy master for the Writing Process Workshop. As you discuss the main points on these four pages, have students record them on the copy master.

**R  RESOURCE MANAGER—Copy Master**
Note Taking p. I-5

### FOR ENGLISH LANGUAGE LEARNERS

**Language: Skill Words** Have students identify the term—*purpose, audience,* or *format*—that each of these statements illustrates:

- "I'm writing for the members of the school's Science Club." (*audience*)
- "Should I present a written report, or a speech?" (*format*)
- "I want to share some information about tornadoes." (*purpose*)

# Continue with the Process

Every writer has a different process, and many use different processes at different times. But it's a rare writer who sits down with no plan in mind and types a final draft for publication. The **Writing Workshops** in this book are designed to help you develop and refine your own process for writing. Familiarize yourself with the basic process before you decide what works for you.

## THE WRITING PROCESS

### PLANNING/PREWRITING
Explore your ideas and determine what you want to write about. In addition to considering the questions on the preceding page, try some of these brainstorming strategies: freewriting, clustering, listing. Keep in mind your **purpose** and **audience** as you decide on a topic.

▶ **WHAT DOES IT LOOK LIKE?**

- can be physical or emotional
- can surface unexpectedly
- Strength
- helps people overcome hard times
- not always visible at first glance

### DRAFTING
Turn your prewriting ideas into a first draft without worrying about errors. If you are writing a formal essay, you might **draft from an outline,** such as the one shown. Another option is **drafting to discover**—writing with no set plan, letting the ideas develop as you go.

▶ **WHAT DOES IT LOOK LIKE?**

I. Emotional strength comes from a will to succeed in difficult circumstances.
   A. _The Old Man and the Sea_ (The old man doesn't let fatigue/age stop him.)
   B. _The Miracle Worker_ (Annie Sullivan perseveres in the face of failure.)

### REVISING
Review your draft, making changes to strengthen the development, organization, and style.
- Check your writing against a **rubric,** such as the one on the next page.
- Get suggestions from a **peer reader** or your teacher.

▶ **ASK A PEER READER**

- Is my writing clear and **coherent,** or easy to follow?
- Where do I need to explain my points or cite evidence?
- Which parts are confusing or choppy? Where do I need to add transitions?

### EDITING AND PUBLISHING
Proofread for errors in **grammar, usage, capitalization, punctuation,** and **spelling.** Then let your idea loose on the world. Where you publish, of course, depends on your purpose, audience, and format.

▶ **PROOFREADER'S CHECKLIST**

- ☑ Revise sentence fragments and run-on sentences.
- ☑ Fix errors in subject-verb agreement and pronoun-antecedent agreement.
- ☑ Observe rules for correct capitalization and punctuation marks.

---

## Continue with the Process
Review the stages of the writing process listed in the chart.

**Determine Readiness** Assess students' familiarity with this material by asking them about their experience with each stage. For example, you might ask how students prewrite and draft, what they have gained from working with peer readers, and whether they have ever published their work (and if so, how). Explain that students will learn much more about these stages and ways to apply them to specific kinds of writing in the **Writing Workshops** found throughout the anthology.

---

## FOR STRUGGLING READERS
**Concept Support** Draw a flow chart on the board to help students envision the writing process; write the name of each stage, circle it, and connect it with an arrow to the next stage. Explain that the arrows indicate the natural progression from one stage to the next. Also point out (adding more arrows, if you wish) that the process is recursive; for example, when a writer is revising, he or she may go back and do some prewriting to rework a difficult passage.

## FOR ENGLISH LANGUAGE LEARNERS
**Vocabulary Support** Help students grasp the stages of the writing process by discussing these prefixes and roots:

- *prewriting:* Pre- means "before," so *prewriting* refers to tasks you do before the main writing.

- *drafting:* This word comes from a Middle English word that means "to draw or pull." *Drafting* refers to drawing out your writing ideas.

- *revising: Re-* means "again," and *-vis-* means "to see," so *revising* refers to looking again at what you have written.

- *publishing:* This word comes from a Middle English word that means "to make known publicly." *Publishing* refers to taking your finished writing to the public.

## Scoring Rubric

Briefly discuss the Scoring Rubric, explaining that the rubric is a means by which students can evaluate their writing. (The word *rubric* refers to categorizing—here, categorizing a piece of writing according to its strengths.) Tell students that the best way to understand rubrics is to use them to score an actual piece of writing. Students will have the opportunity to work with a partner to evaluate what they write in the Writing Workshops. Students can score each other's writing using a rubric like the one on this page. They can then write a summary evaluation using the language of the rubric to explain the reasons for the score they gave their partner.

## Scoring Rubric

| Score | COMMON CORE TRAITS |
|---|---|
| 6 | • **Development** Includes a meaningful, engaging introduction; thoroughly develops the topic with well-chosen, relevant, and sufficient evidence; ends powerfully<br>• **Organization** Logically organizes complex ideas, concepts, and information; uses appropriate and varied transitions to create cohesion and clarify relationships among ideas<br>• **Language** Uses precise language in imaginative ways; maintains an appropriate style and tone for the audience and purpose; shows a strong command of conventions |
| 5 | • **Development** Has an engaging introduction; develops the topic with relevant, well-chosen evidence; has an effective concluding section<br>• **Organization** Logically organizes ideas, concepts, and information; uses appropriate transitions to create cohesion and clarify relationships<br>• **Language** Effectively uses precise language; maintains an appropriate style and tone for the audience and purpose; has a few errors in conventions |
| 4 | • **Development** Has an introduction, but it could be more engaging; lacks sufficient support for one or two ideas; has an adequate, though routine, concluding section<br>• **Organization** Is logically organized, with one or two exceptions; could use a few more transitions to clarify the relationships among ideas<br>• **Language** Includes some vague word choices; has one or two lapses in style and tone; includes a few distracting errors in conventions |
| 3 | • **Development** Has both an introduction and conclusion, but they are superficial or uninteresting; includes some unsupported ideas or irrelevant evidence<br>• **Organization** Has some flaws in organization; needs more transitions<br>• **Language** Uses words correctly, though language is unimaginative; has frequent lapses in style and tone; has some critical errors in conventions |
| 2 | • **Development** Has an unfocused, uninteresting introduction; does not develop most ideas; ends abruptly<br>• **Organization** Has an illogical organization; lacks transitions throughout<br>• **Language** Uses vague language and misuses some words; lapses into an inappropriate style and tone in many places; contains many distracting errors in conventions |
| 1 | • **Development** Lacks an introduction, development, and a concluding section<br>• **Organization** Has no discernible organization; lacks transitions or uses inappropriate ones<br>• **Language** Uses many words incorrectly; employs an inappropriate style and tone for the audience and purpose; has major problems with conventions |

## DIFFERENTIATED INSTRUCTION

### FOR ENGLISH LANGUAGE LEARNERS

**Language Support** Have pairs of students look up and share the meanings of skill words such as *cohesion, topic, development,* and *evidence.* Also discuss the contextual meanings of these adjectives in the rubric:

• *meaningful:* with purpose

• *effective:* accomplishing a purpose

• *engaging:* appealing in a way that attracts attention

• *relevant:* connected in a logical way

• *sufficient:* enough, as much as is needed

• *appropriate:* fitting, suited to the situation

• *varied:* mixed

• *precise:* exact or specific

• *superficial:* without depth

# Strategies That Work: Writing

 Jot your writing ideas, plans, and notes in your **Reader/Writer Notebook.**

## ❶ Use Prewriting Strategies

Deciding on a topic and developing ideas can seem like the hardest parts of the process. Try these approaches to jumpstart your process:

- **Freewrite.** Write down anything that comes into your head.
- **Go graphic.** Use cluster diagrams, charts, and other graphic organizers to capture your thoughts.
- **Keep a journal.** Collect quotes, observations, song lyrics, photographs, freewrites, and other possible sources of inspiration.
- **Talk it out.** Brainstorm topics or supporting details with classmates.
- **Write from a prompt.** Consider the idea starters in the **Writing Workshops.**

## ❷ Use Prewriting Strategies

Other writers can help you at any stage of the process, from brainstorming ideas with you to proofreading your final draft. Consider these tips:

| When You're the Writer | When You're the Reader |
|---|---|
| • Tell your readers what kind of feedback you are looking for. Should they focus on content, structure, or both? | • Be honest but kind. Offer positive reactions first. Ask questions if you need clarification from the writer. |
| • Listen to their comments without arguing. | • Be specific. Don't say, "That character was unbelievable" without giving specific details to support your opinion. |
| • Let their suggestions sink in before you decide how you want to proceed. Be open to trying a new approach. | • Let the writer make the final decisions. |

## ❸ Pay Attention to Details

Even minor mistakes—such as errors in grammar, usage, capitalization, punctuation, and spelling—can distract your reader from the ideas you are trying to convey.

Use these spelling tips to make sure your writing is polished and correct.

- Review the spelling rules on pages R72–R74.
- Avoid misusing commonly confused words, such as *allusion* and *illusion*. (See page R75 for some more examples.)
- Use the spell-check feature in your word-processing program, but remember that it won't catch commonly confused words. When in doubt, consult a dictionary.
- Proofread your draft backwards to catch mistakes your eyes might miss when reading the text.

**EXAMPLE**

Shakespeare's works include comedies and ~~tragidies~~ *tragedies* that have influenced writers for generations. One can find ~~illusions~~ *allusions* to Shakespeare in works ranging from modern plays to graphic novels to television sitcoms.

**Writing Online** **THINK** central
Go to **thinkcentral.com.**
KEYWORD: HML9N-23

---

## Strategies That Work: Writing

Share with students that **Strategies That Work: Writing** can open up exciting possibilities for them as writers. Encourage students to make constant use of the strategies to help them with their writing, both in and outside of class.

**1. Use Prewriting Strategies**
Discuss the examples of prewriting strategies. Ask students if they are familiar with these strategies and, if so, which ones they have found helpful and why.

**2. Get Feedback from Peers**
Discuss with students their experiences with peer feedback, both positive and negative. Whatever their experiences have been, remind them that peer feedback, if done responsibly, can be invaluable in learning about themselves and each other as readers and writers. Note that whether they are the writer or the reader in a peer review, they should be as specific as possible. Point out the tips listed for peer readers and writers, emphasizing that readers and writers owe each other respect, sensitivity, and patience.

**3. Pay Attention to Details**
Explain that while details of grammar, capitalization, punctuation, and spelling should not be a priority early in the writing process, it is crucial to address these details before a piece of writing is finalized or published.

---

### FOR STRUGGLING READERS

**Concept Support** Use these activities to reinforce the teaching in the text:

1. Show students what a prompt is by looking with them at the prompt in the first Writing Workshop (page 174). Tell students that as they read various prompts, they will learn how to analyze a prompt for clues about the type of writing being asked for and the audience for whom it is intended.

2. Emphasize that working with peers is not limited to peer readers during the revising and editing stage; peers can help students narrow topics and clarify their plans for a piece of writing.

3. As students read the selections in this anthology, urge them to make notes about topics, style points, and other elements that they would like to attempt in their own writing. Encourage them to experiment with these elements as they develop their individual writing style.

### Writing Online  **THINK** central

The **Writing Center** on **thinkcentral.com** includes Interactive Student Models, which show students how to read and critique others' writing. The **Writing Center** also includes

- Ideas for Writing
- Interactive Graphic Organizers
- Interactive Revision Lessons
- Writing Model Bank

# The Plot Thickens

## NARRATIVE STRUCTURE

- In Fiction
- In Media
- In Nonfiction
- In Poetry
- In Drama

25

**About the Art** Jim Dine (b. 1935) drew *Raven*. For more information, see pages 147 and 150.

## INTRODUCE THE UNIT

When a gravy or sauce thickens, it usually becomes richer, more intense in flavor, and more satisfying. The plot of a piece of writing is said to thicken when surprises and other complications occur and tension rises. Most readers find that such moments make the writing richer, more intense, and more satisfying.

Invite students to consider how the pictures on this page suggest the thickening of a plot. To elicit ideas, ask:

- As you look at each picture, what kind of story do you imagine?
- How might each picture suggest danger? surprise? suspense?
- Which picture does a better job of suggesting that the plot is thickening? Why?

Tell students that as they read the selections in this unit, they will see how a thickening plot fits into the narrative structure of a work. Explain that narrative structure includes the elements found on a story map, such as character, setting, events, climax, and resolution. It also includes elements related to plot, such as conflict, complications, rising action, suspense, and foreshadowing. In this unit, students will discover how the elements combine to thicken a plot and enrich a story.

For help in planning this unit, see

**R** RESOURCE MANAGER UNIT 1
pp. 1–10

# UNIT 1

ECOS

## COMMON CORE

**STRAND**

| | Text Analysis Workshop: Plot and Conflict pp. 28–35 | Comparing Texts **A Sound of Thunder/From Here to There: The Physics of Time Travel/The Time Machine** Short Story/Magazine Article/Movie Poster pp. 36–56 | **The Most Dangerous Game** Short Story pp. 58–83 | **Daughter of Invention** Short Story pp. 84–99 | **The Gift of the Magi** Short Story pp. 100–111 | **Media Study: from The Lord of the Rings** Film Clip pp. 112–115 |
|---|---|---|---|---|---|---|
| | | Lexile: 720 Fry: 6 Dale-Chall: 6.1 | Lexile: 740 Fry: 5 Dale-Chall: 6.3 | Lexile: 980 Fry: 8 Dale-Chall: 6.3 | Lexile: 950 Fry: 7 Dale-Chall: 6.4 | |
| **Reading Literature** | Plot Stages and Conflict pp. 28–29 **RL 5** Sequence and Time pp. 30–31 **RL 5** Analyze the Text pp. 32–35 | Foreshadowing pp. 37, 38, 40, 41, 52 **RL 5** Analyze Sequence pp. 37, 44, 46, 52 **RL 5** Movie Poster p. 56 **RL 7** | Conflict pp. 59, 60, 63, 68, 74, 76, 78, 81 **RL 5** Plot Devices p. 69 **RL 5** Visualize pp. 59, 62–64, 69, 80–81 **RL 4** | Plot and Character pp. 85, 88, 92, 95, 97 **RL 3** Make Inferences pp. 85–86, 90, 93–94, 96–97 **RL 1** Language Coach p. 88, 90 **RL 4** | Irony pp. 101, 104, 108–109 **RL 5, RL 10** Predict pp. 101, 105–107, 109 **RL 1** | Suspense in Movies pp. 113, 114 **RL 7** |
| **Reading Informational Text** | | Magazine Article p. 55 | | | | |
| **Writing** | | Writing Prompt p. 54 **W 3b** | Writing Prompt p. 83 | Writing Prompt p. 99 **W 3d** | Writing Prompt p. 111 **W 3b** | Write or Discuss p. 115 **W 9a (RL 7)** |
| **Speaking and Listening** | | What's the Connection? p. 36 **SL 1** | Discuss p. 58 **SL 1** | Role-Play p. 84 **SL 1** | Discuss p. 100 **SL 1** | Write or Discuss p. 115 **SL 2, SL 5** |
| **Language** | | Use Realistic Dialogue pp. 44, 54 **L 3** Language Coach pp. 43, 47 **L 4c** Latin Root *mal* p. 53 **L 4a** | Language Coach pp. 63, 68, 75 **L 4, L 4b, L 4c** Add Descriptive Details p. 75, 83 **L 1b** Denotation and Connotation p. 82 **L 5b** | Modifiers pp. 88, 99 **L 3** Latin Prefix *in-* p. 98 **L 4c** | Language Coach p. 106 **L 4c** Effective Word Choices pp. 108, 111 **L 3** Greek Root *chron* p. 110 **L 4c** | |

| The Rights to the Streets of Memphis<br>Autobiography<br>pp. 116–125 | Linked Selections | | The Raven/ Incident in a Rose Garden<br>Narrative Poems<br>pp. 144–153 | Sorry, Right Number<br>Teleplay<br>pp. 154–173 | Writing Workshop: Personal Narrative<br>pp. 174–183<br><br>Speaking and Listening Workshop: Presenting an Informal Speech<br>pp. 184–185 |
|---|---|---|---|---|---|
| | from Seabiscuit<br>Biography<br>pp. 126–137 | Horse of the Century<br>Magazine Article, Timeline, Radio Transcript<br>pp. 138–143 | | | |
| Lexile: 930<br>Fry: 8<br>Dale-Chall: 5.3 | Lexile: 850<br>Fry: College<br>Dale-Chall: 7.0 | Lexile: 990/660/N/A<br>Fry: College/3/N/A<br>Dale-Chall: 9.5/5.6/N/A | | | |
| | | | Narrative Poetry pp. 145–146, 148, 150–153 RL 5<br>Reading Poetry pp. 145, 148–150, 152–153 RL 4, RL 5, RL 10<br>Language Coach p. 149 RL 4 | Plot in Drama pp. 155, 160, 165, 172 RL 5<br>Reading a Teleplay pp. 155, 158, 163, 167, 172 RL 10 | |
| Autobiography pp. 117, 120–121, 123 RI 3<br>Identify Cause and Effect pp. 117–118, 122–123 RI 1, RI 3<br>Language Coach p. 121 RI 4 | Suspense in Biography pp. 127, 130, 133, 135, 136 RI 3<br>Identify Author's Purpose pp. 127–128, 132, 136 RI 6 | Synthesize pp. 138–143 RI 1, RI 2, RI 7<br>Language Coach p. 142 RI 4 | | Memoir p. 171 | |
| Writing Prompt p. 125 W 5 | | Writing Prompt p. 143 W 9b (RI 7) | | Quickwrite p. 154<br>Writing Prompt p. 173 | Writing a Personal Narrative pp. 174–183 W 3a–e, W 4, W 5, W 10 |
| Discuss p. 116 SL 1 | Present p. 126 SL 1 | | Discuss p. 144 SL 1 | | Presenting an Informal Speech pp. 184–185 SL 4, SL 6 |
| Emphasize Action pp. 121, 125 L 3<br>Synonyms and Antonyms p. 124 L 4c | Language Coach p. 131<br>The aud Word Family p. 137 L 4c | | | Create Realistic Characters p. 173 L 3 | Drafting p. 177 L 2<br>Revising pp. 178–180 L 3<br>Editing and Publishing p. 181 L 2, L 2c |

To see the complete Essential Course of Study, see pp. T23–T28.

 For additional lesson planning help, see **Teacher One Stop DVD.**

## Instructional Support

**Resource Manager Unit 1**

**UNIT SUPPORT**

Academic Vocabulary, p. 3

Additional Academic Vocabulary, p. 4

Grammar Focus p. 5

Text Analysis Workshop pp. 9–10

Writing Workshop: Personal Narrative
p. 195

**SELECTION SUPPORT\***

**Plan and Teach**

Lesson planning pages

Additional leveled selection questions

Extension activities

**Student Copy Masters**

Selection summaries in four languages

Skills copy masters in English and Spanish

Vocabulary preteaching and support

Reading Check and Question support

Reading Fluency

\*Available for all selections

† Available on **thinkcentral.com**

**Language Handbook**

**Vocabulary Practice**

**Best Practices Toolkit†**

**PowerNotes** DVD-ROM†

**Connections: Nonfiction for the Common Core** CD-ROM†

**Teacher One Stop** DVD-ROM

**Student One Stop** DVD-ROM

**Media*Smart*** DVD-ROM
*from* Lord of the Rings

**Write*Smart*** CD-ROM†

**GrammarNotes** DVD-ROM†

**WordSharp** CD-ROM†

## Differentiated Instruction

| *STRUGGLING READERS AND WRITERS* | *ENGLISH LANGUAGE LEARNERS* | *ADVANCED LEARNERS* |
|---|---|---|
| **Resource Manager Unit 1**<br>Additional Selection Questions<br>Question Support<br>Reading Fluency<br>**Interactive Reader**<br>**Adapted Interactive Reader**<br>**Level Up Online Tutorials**<br>**Audio Anthology**<br>(with Audio summaries)<br>**Diagnostic and Selection Tests**<br>Selection Tests A/B | **Resource Manager Unit 1**<br>Selection Summaries in English, Spanish, Vietnamese and Haitian Creole<br>Skills Copymasters in Spanish<br>**English Language Learner Adapted Interactive Reader Teacher's Guide**<br>**ELL Adapted Interactive Reader**<br>**Audio Tutor**<br>**Guide to English for Newcomers**<br>**Audio Anthology**<br>**Audio Summaries in Multiple Languages**<br>(on **thinkcentral.com**) | **Resource Manager Unit 1**<br>Additional Selection Questions<br>Ideas for Extension<br>**Diagnostic and Selection Tests**<br>Selection Tests B/C |

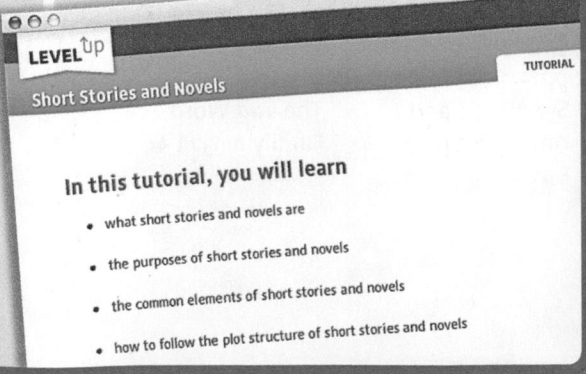

## Assessment and Reteaching

**Diagnostic and Selection Tests**

**Unit and Benchmark Tests**

**ThinkCentral Online Assessment:**
- All program assessments
- Level Up Online Tutorials

**ExamView Test Generator** on the Teacher One Stop DVD-ROM

**Online Essay Scoring** on <u>thinkcentral.com</u>

**ThinkCentral Online Reteaching:**
- Level Up Online Tutorials
- Reteaching Worksheets

Holt McDougal **Online Essay Scoring**

Welcome to Holt McDougal Online Essay Scoring!

This site is designed to help you improve your writing skills and prepare for standardized writing tests. When you write and submit a response to one of the writing prompts on this site, the computerized scoring system will immediately score and deliver feedback on your essay. Other resources on this site will help you prepare, develop, and revise your essay.

STUDENTS

Get started by entering the

Writing Zone →

## Professional Development

**Video Center** Based on interviews with program consultants and other educational experts, these videos feature classroom-ready teaching strategies.

**Teacher Toolkit** Includes a Teacher Handbook as well as a range of articles and handouts by program consultants and other educators.

**Janet Allen**

**Jim Burke**

**Kylene Beers**

**Carol Jago**

# THINK central at a Glance

## One Location, Endless Resources

**Find Resources** Browse all *Holt McDougal Literature* components for the ones that meet your students' needs and match your teaching style.

**Assess Progress and Reteach** Assign electronic versions of program assessments to measure your students' mastery of the Common Core State Standards. On thinkcentral.com, some tests deliver online remediation tutorials to students who have not mastered skills.

 ***Interactive Whiteboard Lessons***

Prepare your students for college and careers by teaching relevant, real-world skills through dynamic, interactive instruction. Go to <u>thinkcentral.com</u> to browse through all white-board lessons or to access the lessons, including the following:

- Citing Textual Evidence
- Plot and Conflict
- Narrative Techniques
- Writing Narratives

 Together Holt McDougal and HISTORY® are revolutionizing the study of English/language arts with video that helps students relive and re-imagine the people, places, and events they are discovering through reading. Look for selections with the HISTORY® icon.

## What makes a
# GREAT STORY?

Read and discuss the introductory paragraph. Point out that the greatness of a story lies partly in what it is about but even more in how it is told. To illustrate, present these sentences:

> Roberto sped toward the finish line, the roar of the crowd numbing his ears.

> "That's the car for me," Emily said, "and I'm buying it right now!"

Ask students which sentence they think would be part of a great story. Elicit that the first sentence captures readers' interest more quickly and evokes more curiosity about the outcome. Note, however, that either sentence has the potential to become part of a great story.

*ACTIVITY* Encourage students to think the story through before summarizing it. When discussing the questions, students should share specific examples. Guide students to conclude that a great story appeals to readers' interests and emotions and has a memorable style.

**CHECK UNDERSTANDING** Have students use their conclusions to create an original definition of the term *great story.*

## What makes a
# GREAT STORY?

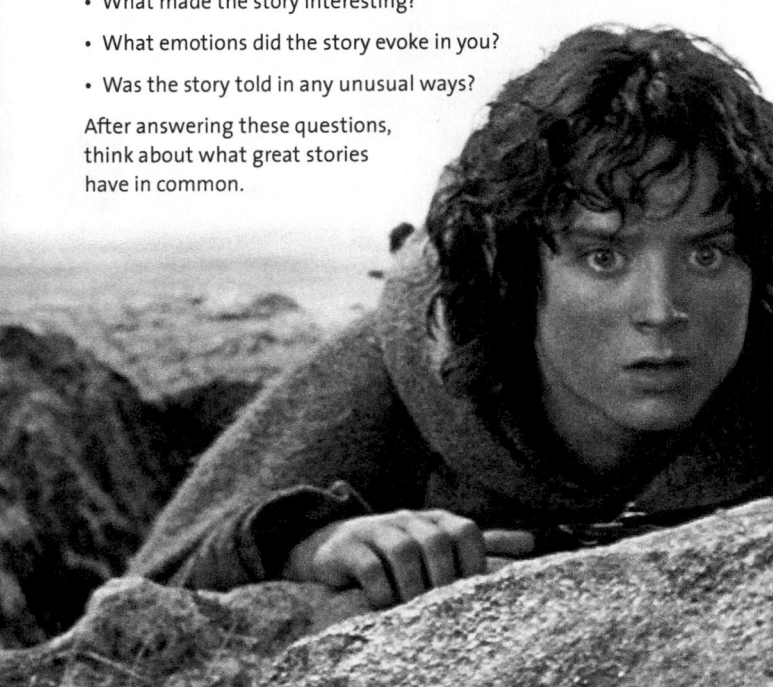

Whether you are riveted by the latest comedy at the local movie theater, caught up in the pages of your favorite novel, or transfixed by your grandparents' tales of growing up, what these great stories have in common is that each is told by someone who can capture your interest, hold your attention, and make you want to know how the story will end.

*ACTIVITY* Think of a story you have read or heard. It can be a powerful true story or a favorite piece of fiction, such as J.R.R. Tolkien's *The Lord of the Rings*. With a partner, share a summary of the story you chose. Then discuss the following questions:

• What made the story interesting?

• What emotions did the story evoke in you?

• Was the story told in any unusual ways?

After answering these questions, think about what great stories have in common.

**Find It Online!**
Go to thinkcentral.com for the interactive version of this unit.

---

## Unit Resources

See resources on the **Teacher One Stop DVD-ROM** and on **thinkcentral.com**.

 **RESOURCE MANAGER UNIT 1**

**UNIT AND BENCHMARK TESTS**

**BEST PRACTICES TOOLKIT**

**INTERACTIVE READER**

**ADAPTED INTERACTIVE READER**

**ELL ADAPTED INTERACTIVE READER**

**LANGUAGE HANDBOOK**

**VOCABULARY PRACTICE**

**TECHNOLOGY**

💿 **Teacher One Stop DVD-ROM**

💿 **Student One Stop DVD-ROM**

💿 **PowerNotes DVD-ROM**

💿 **Write*Smart* CD-ROM**

💿 **Media*Smart* DVD-ROM**

💿 **GrammarNotes DVD-ROM**

💿 **Audio Anthology CD**

💿 **Audio Tutor CD**

**Find It Online!**

The interactive version of this unit on **thinkcentral.com** includes
• video and **PowerNotes** introductions to key selections
• audio support—listen or download
• **ThinkAloud** models
• **WordSharp** vocabulary tutorials
• interactive review and remediation

## Preview Unit Goals

| | |
|---|---|
| **TEXT ANALYSIS** | • Analyze the author's choices on ordering events in a text<br>• Identify stages of plot; analyze plot development<br>• Analyze the effects of narrative techniques, including foreshadowing, irony, and suspense<br>• Identify narrative elements in poetry and drama |
| **READING** | • Cite evidence to make inferences and draw conclusions<br>• Synthesize information from multiple texts |
| **WRITING AND LANGUAGE** | • Write a personal narrative<br>• Use realistic dialogue, descriptive details, and realistic characters to achieve a purpose<br>• Use precise words and phrases to convey meaning |
| **SPEAKING AND LISTENING** | • Present information in an informal speech |
| **VOCABULARY** | • Use word roots to help unlock meaning<br>• Use context as a clue to meaning<br>• Determine figurative and connotative meanings |
| **ACADEMIC VOCABULARY** | • analyze    • element    • infer<br>• sequence    • structure |
| **MEDIA AND VIEWING** | • Identify and evaluate the aesthetic qualities of film<br>• Use media techniques to convey a cohesive story |

## Media Smart DVD-ROM

### Great Stories on Film

Discover how director Peter Jackson creates suspense in an action-packed scene from *The Lord of the Rings*. Page 112

---

### UNIT GOALS

Included in this unit: **RL 1, RL 3-5, RL 7, RL 10, RI 1-7, RI 10, W 3a-e, W 4-5, W 9a-b, W 10, SL 1-2, SL 4-6, L 1b L 2, L 2c, L 3, L 4, L 4b-c, L 5b, L 6**

Complete text of the Common Core State Standards is found in the correlation on p. T 10. Standards covered in this unit are found in the standards overview (pp. 25A–25B) and on the lesson pages where they are taught.

## Preview Unit Goals

This page presents an overview of the skills and strategies covered in this unit. Explain to students that they can get more from their reading by previewing. Then ask them to skim the page to preview the skills that they will learn. Note that each strand or category of skill is color-coded on this page and throughout the unit.

Model the strategy of copying the Academic Vocabulary and writing a preliminary definition for each term. Suggest that students use their **Reader/Writer Notebooks** for this purpose. Encourage them to use the terms in discussions and in writing. Also urge students to revisit each term throughout the unit and to refine its meaning.

---

## DIFFERENTIATED INSTRUCTION

### FOR ENGLISH LANGUAGE LEARNERS

**Academic Vocabulary** Provide students with definitions of each Academic Vocabulary word.

**analyze** (ăn´ə-līz) *v.* to separate or break into parts and examine

**element** (el´ə mənt) *n.* one necessary or basic part of a whole

**infer** (in fər´) *v.* to decide based on evidence or knowledge; to draw a conclusion

**sequence** (sē´kwəns) *n.* the chronological, causal, or logical order in which one thing follows another

**structure** (strŭk´chər) *n.* something constructed or built, such as a building

Use the copy master to help students learn academic words they will use in this unit and on the Assessment Practice.

**R** RESOURCE MANAGER—Copy Masters
Academic Vocabulary p. 3
Additional Academic Vocabulary p. 4

# Focus and Motivate

## COMMON CORE FOCUS

**RL 5** Analyze how an author's choices concerning how to structure a text, order events within it, and manipulate time create such effects as mystery, tension, or surprise.

# Teach

## Part 1: Plot Stages and Conflict

**Conflict** Explain to students that a story may contain several conflicts, but the main conflict is the one that most clearly drives the key events. Use this activity to reinforce the idea of the main conflict driving the key events:

- Brainstorm a list of well-known stories from literature or from the movies.

- For each story, identify one or more struggles that take place between characters, within a character's mind, or between one or more characters and some other force.

- List these conflicts in a chart, labeling each as *internal* or *external*. Once students have completed the exercise, ask them to identify the conflict that is most critical in each story. Be sure to have them defend their choices with specific examples.

### Story Title

| What is the conflict? | Internal | External |
|---|---|---|
| | | |
| | | |

**Stages of Plot** Point out that few stories have plots that neatly match the five stages shown in the plot diagram. Many stories, for example, don't reach their climax until just before the end. Other stories end with a climax. (You might talk about suspense movies that end at the moment of highest tension.) Almost every story, though, begins with an exposition that introduces the characters, setting, and main conflict. In addition, every story has a rising action that introduces events that intensify or complicate the conflict.

**BEST PRACTICES TOOLKIT—Transparency**
Analysis Frame: Plot pp. D21, D28

---

# Plot and Conflict

**Essential Course of Study** ECOS

Every good story is fueled by conflict. Can the hero survive the dangerous journey? Will the star-crossed lovers end up together, despite their feuding families? When a story grabs your interest, it's usually because the conflict is exciting and dramatic. Looking closely at how conflicts develop throughout the stages of a plot is a key part of analyzing a story and understanding *why* it hooks you.

## Part 1: Plot Stages and Conflict

> **COMMON CORE**
>
> Included in this workshop:
> **RL 5** Analyze how an author's choices concerning how to structure a text, order events within it, and manipulate time create such effects as mystery, tension, or surprise.

The series of events in a narrative is called **plot**. At the heart of any plot is a **conflict,** or struggle, between opposing forces. A conflict is internal or external.

- An **internal conflict** is a struggle within a character's mind. The struggle usually centers on a choice or decision the character must make. Should she tell the truth? Can he overcome his jealousy?

- An **external conflict** is a clash between a character and an outside force, such as another character, society, or a force of nature. Will the athlete defeat her bitter rival? Can the soldiers endure the war?

Whether internal or external, a conflict is usually introduced at the beginning of a narrative. As the characters attempt to resolve the conflict, "the plot thickens" at each stage. Will the characters succeed? You keep turning the pages to find out the answer to this question.

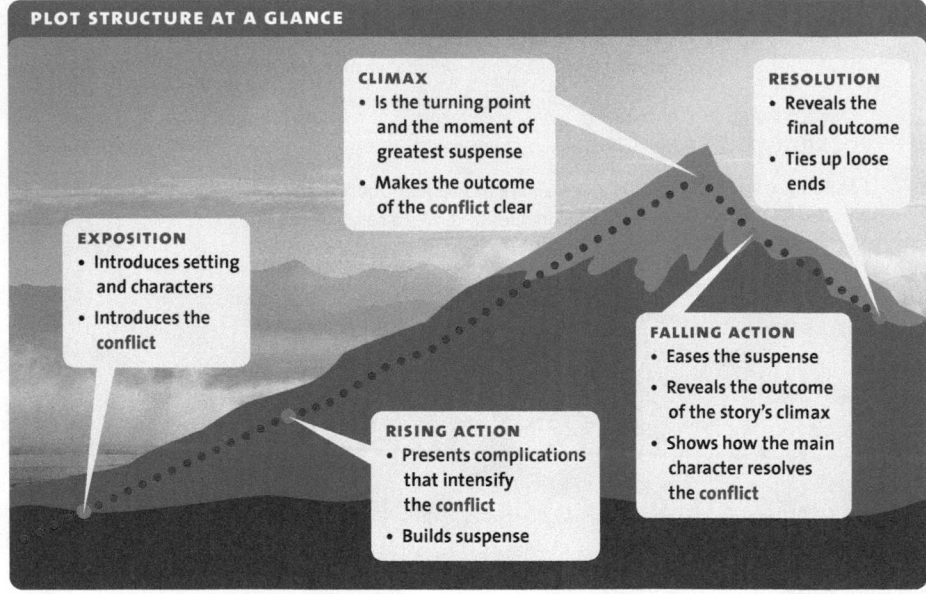

**PLOT STRUCTURE AT A GLANCE**

**CLIMAX**
- Is the turning point and the moment of greatest suspense
- Makes the outcome of the conflict clear

**RESOLUTION**
- Reveals the final outcome
- Ties up loose ends

**EXPOSITION**
- Introduces setting and characters
- Introduces the conflict

**RISING ACTION**
- Presents complications that intensify the conflict
- Builds suspense

**FALLING ACTION**
- Eases the suspense
- Reveals the outcome of the story's climax
- Shows how the main character resolves the conflict

---

## DIFFERENTIATED INSTRUCTION

### FOR ENGLISH LANGUAGE LEARNERS

**Note Taking** Have students work in mixed-ability pairs to practice note taking on plot structure and stages. Hand out the note-taking copy master before discussing the paragraph. Then have students read the first paragraph silently. As you discuss the main points of the paragraph, have students record them on the copy master.

**Illustrate Conflict** Have the student pairs sketch the scene in Model 1 on page 29.

They may use stick figures, lines, dots, X's, or other markings. Have each pair write a caption for its illustration.

 **RESOURCE MANAGER—Copy Master**
Note Taking p. 9-10

## MODEL 1: CONFLICT IN EXPOSITION

In the exposition of this story, a young warrior named Temas is about to face a crucial test of adulthood in Masai culture—killing a lion. What conflicts emerge as Temas prepares for this pivotal moment?

### *from*
# BROTHERS ARE THE SAME
#### Short story by **Beryl Markham**

Yet in his mind Temas now trembled. Fear of battle was a nonexistent thing—but fear of failure could be real, and was. It was real and living—and kept alive by the nearness of an enemy more formidable than any lion—an enemy with the hated name Medoto.

5 He thought of Medoto—of that Medoto who lay not far away in the deep grass watching the same ravine. Of that Medoto who, out of hate and jealousy over a mere girl, now hoped in his heart that Temas would flinch at the moment of his trial. . . .

**Close Read**

1. Review the boxed detail. What does it tell you about the building conflict between Temas and Medoto?

2. In addition to his conflict with Medoto, what internal conflict is plaguing Temas?

## MODEL 2: CONFLICT AT CLIMAX

Later, Temas learns that his rival is actually a friend. Find out how the conflict between Temas and Medoto changes at the story's climax.

*During the test, Temas feels relieved when the lion attacks another hunter. Then Medoto throws a stone, causing the lion to charge Temas. Without hesitation, Temas kills the lion. Later, Medoto explains himself to Temas.*

"If, until now, I have seemed your enemy, it was because I feared you would be braver than I, for when I fought my lion my knees trembled and my heart was white—until that charge was made. No one knew that, and I am called Medoto, the unflinching, but I flinched. I trembled."

5 He stepped closer to Temas. He smiled. "It is no good to lie," he said. "I wanted you to fail, but when I saw you hesitate I could not bear it because I remembered my own hour of fear. It was then I threw the stone—not to shame you, but to save you from shame—for I saw that your fear was not fear of death, but fear of failure—and this I understood. You are a greater warrior than

10 I—than any—for who but the bravest would do what you have done?" Medoto paused and watched a light of wonderment kindle in Temas's eye. The hand of Temas slipped from his sword, his muscles relaxed. Yet, for a moment, he did not speak, and as he looked at Medoto, it was clear to both that the identical thought, the identical vision, had come to each of them. It was the vision that

15 must and always will come to young men everywhere, the vision of a girl.

Now this vision stood between them, and nothing else. But it stood like a barrier, the last barrier.

**Close Read**

1. How has the conflict between Temas and Medoto changed? Support your answer with evidence.

2. What aspect of Medoto's and Temas's conflict still remains unresolved? Explain.

## MODEL 1: CONFLICT IN EXPOSITION
**Close Read**

1. *Possible answer: Medoto and Temas are in conflict over the love of a girl. Temas is afraid of failing in his battle with the lion, since his rival would relish such defeat. Since Medoto is jealous, Temas is probably the preferred suitor but could lose this advantage if he fails.*

2. *Possible answer: Temas is also in conflict over issues related to bravery and manhood. He considers his most frightening enemy to be Medoto (line 3) and not the lion. His defeat would prove Medoto to be the greater warrior and thus more worthy of the girl.*

## MODEL 2: CONFLICT AT CLIMAX
**Close Read**

1. *Possible answer: By this point in the story, Medoto and Temas are no longer in conflict over issues related to bravery and manhood. Medoto acknowledges Temas's greater bravery by saying, in lines 9–10, "'You are a greater warrior than I.'" Temas learns that he can trust Medoto as a man and a warrior. Temas shows this trust when he takes his hand off his sword.*

2. *Possible answer: Medoto and Temas remain in conflict over the girl, shown by lines 13–17: "the identical thought, the identical vision, had come to each of them. . . . the vision of a girl. Now this vision stood between them. . . ."*

---

## FOR STRUGGLING READERS
**Concept Support**

1. Draw two word webs. Label one *External Conflicts* and the other *Internal Conflicts.* Write *main character against* in the center circle of each web.

2. List these terms on the board, clarifying as necessary: *sea, earthquake, brother, friend, personal history, school rules,* and *own values.*

3. Have volunteers write the terms in surrounding circles in the appropriate webs.

## FOR ADVANCED LEARNERS/PRE–AP*
**Analyze Plot Stages** Have students read the workshop independently. Direct students to identify the plot stages in favorite stories or novels by summarizing and labeling the events.

* Pre-AP is a registered trademark of the College Entrance Examination Board. Use of the trademark does not constitute production participation, sponsorship, or endorsement by the College Board.

**Online Remediation**

Are your students struggling with text analysis skills? Consider assigning them one or more **Level Up Online Tutorials** as remediation before beginning this unit. Log in to **thinkcentral.com** to view a list of the skills addressed by **Level Up.**

# Teach

## Part 2: Sequence and Time

**Flashback** After students read the chart, challenge them to develop examples of sentences or phrases that would signal different kinds of flashbacks, such as these:

- I stared at the tattered posters, suddenly remembering my first trip to the circus.
- As Marcus strode into the ballpark for his first major-league game, he thought about the first time his dad had pressed a baseball into his hand.
- Looking at Charla, no one could have imagined the gangly, awkward girl she had once been.

After students generate the sample sentences, have them brainstorm other clue words that might signal flashbacks. (*in the past, when I was ___ years old, the previous winter, years before*)

**Foreshadowing** After students read the chart, explain that the hints or clues of what is to come may be subtle, often appearing in ordinary conversation. In addition to the tips in the chart, suggest that students watch for these clues:

- unusual statements that make a reader wonder, "Why did he or she say that?"
- an ominous or uncertain mood or tone
- warnings that are stated directly or are subtly implied
- heightened tension and suspense
- suggestions that something always or never happens—often a signal that the pattern is about to change
- an unusual setting

You may also wish to elicit from students examples of events or dialogue that foreshadow later developments in favorite movies.

## CHECK UNDERSTANDING

Have students write definitions of *foreshadowing* and *flashback* in their own words.

## Part 2: Sequence and Time

From fairy tales, with their "once upon a time" beginnings and "happily ever after" endings, to modern classics, many great stories feature **chronological order.** The events follow a linear **structure**—that is, they take place one after the other.

Sometimes, however, a writer plays with time by interrupting the chronological order of events. He or she may suddenly focus on an event from the past or hint at future events. A writer may manipulate time for a variety of reasons—for example, to give you a deeper sense of the characters and conflicts or to keep you wondering what will happen next.

**Flashback** and **foreshadowing** are two common devices that writers use to introduce past and future events. By recognizing these devices, you can follow a story more closely and learn how the author manipulates time to create mystery, tension, or surprise.

| FLASHBACK | FORESHADOWING |
|---|---|
| *What is it?* **An account of a conversation, episode, or event that happened before the beginning of the story, or at an earlier point** | *What is it?* **A writer's use of hints or clues in early scenes to suggest events that will occur later** |
|  |  |
| *What does it do?* <br> • Interrupts the main action to describe earlier events <br> • Shows how past events led up to the present situation, sometimes creating mystery or surprise in the process <br> • Provides background information about a character or event | *What does it do?* <br> • Prepares readers for events that come later—often in the climax or the resolution <br> • Creates tension and suspense <br> • Makes readers eager to keep reading |
| *How can I recognize it?* <br> • Look for possible clue words and phrases, such as "that summer," "as a young boy," or "her earliest memories." <br> • Keep track of the chronological order of events so that you will be aware of events that interrupt this order. | *How can I recognize it?* <br> • Pay attention to repeated or emphasized ideas and descriptions. <br> • Notice when characters make important statements or behave in unusual ways. |

**30**   UNIT 1: NARRATIVE STRUCTURE

## DIFFERENTIATED INSTRUCTION

### FOR STRUGGLING READERS

**Note Taking** For those students who need help, hand out the note-taking copy master for this page. Read and discuss the top of the page. Assist students in completing their note-taking copy master as needed.

**R RESOURCE MANAGER—Copy Master**
Note Taking p. 9–10

### FOR ENGLISH LANGUAGE LEARNERS

**Language: Skill Words** On the board, list the vocabulary shown in italics. Then give the examples in random order.

- *chronological order:* After the game, they gathered in the cafeteria.
- *flashback:* As his sister gets off the train, he remembers the summer she was six.
- *foreshadowing:* The tranquil kitten would not stay that way for long.

## MODEL: FLASHBACK

**Flashback**

Moments after meeting the narrator in this story, you are transported to an earlier time in his life. As you read, notice what this flashback reveals about the narrator and his family.

### from Sweet Potato Pie

Short story by **Eugenia Collier**

From up here on the fourteenth floor, my brother Charley looks like an insect scurrying among other insects. A deep feeling of love surges through me. . . .

Because I see Charley so seldom, my thoughts hover over him like hummingbirds. The cheerful, impersonal tidiness of this room is a world away
5  from Charley's walk-up flat in Harlem and a hundred worlds from the bare, noisy shanty where he and the rest of us spent what there was of childhood. I close my eyes, and side by side I see the Charley of my boyhood and the Charley of this afternoon, as clearly as if I were looking at a split TV screen. Another surge of love, seasoned with gratitude, wells up in me.

10    As far as I know, Charley never had any childhood at all. The oldest children of sharecroppers never do. Mama and Pa were shadowy figures whose voices I heard vaguely in the morning when sleep was shallow and whom I glimpsed as they left for the field before I was fully awake or as they trudged wearily into the house at night when my lids were irresistibly heavy.

15    They came into sharp focus only on special occasions. One such occasion was the day when the crops were in and the sharecroppers were paid. In our cabin there was so much excitement in the air that even I, the "baby," responded to it. For weeks we had been running out of things that we could neither grow nor get on credit. On the evening of that day we waited anxiously for our
20  parents' return. Then we would cluster around the rough wooden table—I on Lil's lap or clinging to Charley's neck, little Alberta nervously tugging her plait, Jamie crouched at Mama's elbow, like a panther about to spring, and all seven of us silent for once, waiting. Pa would place the money on the table—gently, for it was made from the sweat of their bodies and from their children's tears.
25  Mama would count it out in little piles, her dark face stern and, I think now, beautiful. Not with the hollow beauty of well-modeled features but with the strong radiance of one who has suffered and never yielded.

"This for store bill," she would mutter, making a little pile. "This for c'llection. This for piece o'gingham . . ." and so on, stretching the money as
30  tight over our collective needs as Jamie's outgrown pants were stretched over my bottom. "Well, that's the crop." She would look up at Pa at last. "It'll do." Pa's face would relax, and a general grin flitted from child to child. We would survive, at least for the present.

**Close Read**

1. Explain what happens before the flashback.

2. At what point does the flashback begin? Explain the words or phrases that helped you identify it.

3. Find three details that describe the narrator's and Charley's family. One has been boxed. What do these details tell you about their childhood?

4. How does the flashback help you understand the narrator's feelings about Charley?

---

### FOR STRUGGLING READERS

**Comprehension: Story Elements** Write these story elements on the board and have students identify them by analyzing the first sentence:

Narrator: *Charley's brother*
Main character: *Charley*
Setting: *fourteenth-floor window*

**Analysis Support: Flashback** Do a choral reading of the second paragraph. Have students snap their fingers when they read phrases that refer to the flashback (*"a world away from," "a hundred worlds from," "I see the Charley of my boyhood"*).

---

## MODEL: FLASHBACK

### BACKGROUND

After the Civil War, former slaves had no land, tools, or places to live and few choices for earning a living. Many of them survived by becoming sharecroppers, farmers who lived and worked on the land of large landowners. In return for the use of the land, the sharecroppers gave a large share of their crops to the landowners. This resulted in a lot of hard work and a meager, often desperate existence.

**Close Read**

1. *Possible answer: The narrator looks lovingly down on Charley from a tidy room on the fourteenth floor.*

2. *Possible answer: The flashback begins with the reference to something "a hundred worlds" away (line 5). A more concrete clue follows: "I close my eyes, and ... I see. ..." A final clue is the reference to the split TV screen (line 8).*

   **IF STUDENTS NEED HELP** . . . Draw a split screen and discuss how it shows two images at once. Help students by labeling the two sides of the split screen "present" and "past," or "Charley now" and "the Charley of my boyhood."

3. *Possible answer: There were five children: the narrator was the youngest and Charley was the oldest (lines 10–11, 17, 20–23); the mother and father were weary from long days of work in the fields (lines 13–14); payday was an exciting time for the family because they desperately needed the money for necessities (lines 15–17, 28–31). These details indicate a childhood of love and closeness as well as poverty.*

4. *Possible answer: Because the narrator and Charley survived tough times together, they have a bond. With the parents away so much, Charley may also have played a nurturing or protective role, for the narrator sometimes clung to his brother's neck.*

## Part 3: Analyze the Text

**Close Read**

1. **Possible answer:** *The setting is Cincinnati. The narrator has just moved there against her will.*

2. **Possible answer:** *The conflict may involve problems relating to the girl falling in love with a bag boy.*

3. **Possible answer:** *The girl is melodramatic (lines 4–5); she finds it hard to leave the past behind (lines 9–11); she likes solitary pursuits (lines 9–11, 16–17); she looks inward (lines 16–17).*

**IF STUDENTS NEED HELP . . .** Ask students to describe what grocery shopping is like for the girl by deciding which term in each of these pairs of opposites describes feelings about shopping: *solitary* or *social, easy* or *challenging, relaxing* or *anxiety provoking.*

## Part 3: Analyze the Text

It seems like a familiar story. Girl meets and falls in love with boy. Boy falls in love with girl. After overcoming a few problems, they live happily ever after. Right? Wrong. This story traces a conflict, but that conflict is not resolved in a predictable way. As you read, use what you've learned about plot structure, conflict, and sequence to analyze the story.

# Checkouts

Short story by **Cynthia Rylant**

Her parents had moved her to Cincinnati, to a large house with beveled glass[1] windows and several porches and the *history* her mother liked to emphasize. You'll love the house, they said. You'll be lonely at first, they admitted, but you're so nice you'll make friends fast. And as an impulse tore at her to lie on the floor,
5 to hold to their ankles and tell them she felt she was dying, to offer anything, anything at all, so they might allow her to finish growing up in the town of her childhood, they firmed their mouths and spoke from their chests and they said, It's decided.

They moved her to Cincinnati, where for a month she spent the greater
10 part of every day in a room full of beveled glass windows, sifting through photographs of the life she'd lived and left behind. But it is difficult work, suffering, and in its own way a kind of art, and finally she didn't have the energy for it anymore, so she emerged from the beautiful house and fell in love with a bag boy at the supermarket. Of course, this didn't happen all at once,
15 just like that, but in the sequence of things that's exactly the way it happened.

She liked to grocery shop. She loved it in the way some people love to drive long country roads, because doing it she could think and relax and wander. Her parents wrote up the list and handed it to her and off she went without

---

1. **beveled glass:** glass whose edges are cut at an angle.

**Close Read**

1. What do you learn about the setting and the main character's situation in the exposition of this story?

2. Reread lines 11–15, which set the stage for the main conflict. What do you think the conflict will be about?

3. Review the boxed details about the girl. What do they reveal about her personality?

---

## DIFFERENTIATED INSTRUCTION

### FOR STRUGGLING READERS

**Vocabulary Support**  Introduce these words from "Checkouts." Have students read the context for each word and suggest a synonym to replace it.

- *emerged* (line 13), "came out of"
- *sacrifice* (line 19), "giving up"
- *lapse* (line 25), "fall"
- *reverie* (line 25), "daydream"
- *bland* (line 44), "mild," "plain"
- *brazen* (line 44), "bold"
- *deftly* (line 54), "skillfully"
- *tattered* (line 57), "shabby"

complaint to perform what they regarded as a great sacrifice of her time and a
20  sign that she was indeed a very nice girl. She had never told them how much
she loved grocery shopping, only that she was "willing" to do it. She had an
intuition which told her that her parents were not safe for sharing such strong,
important facts about herself. Let them think they knew her.

Once inside the supermarket, her hands firmly around the handle of the
25  cart, she would lapse into a kind of reverie and wheel toward the produce.
Like a Tibetan monk² in solitary meditation, she calmed to a point of deep,
deep happiness; this feeling came to her, reliably, if strangely, only in the
supermarket.

**T**hen one day the bag boy dropped her jar of mayonnaise and that is how
30   she fell in love.

He was nervous—first day on the job—and along had come this fascinating
girl, standing in the checkout line with the unfocused stare one often sees in
young children, her face turned enough away that he might take several full
looks at her as he packed sturdy bags full of food and the goods of modern life.
35  She interested him because her hair was red and thick, and in it she had placed
a huge orange bow, nearly the size of a small hat. That was enough to distract
him, and when finally it was her groceries he was packing, she looked at him
and smiled and he could respond only by busting her jar of mayonnaise on the
floor, shards of glass and oozing cream decorating the area around his feet.
40  She loved him at exactly that moment, and if he'd known this perhaps he
wouldn't have fallen into the brown depression he fell into, which lasted the
rest of his shift. He believed he must have looked a fool in her eyes, and he
envied the sureness of everyone around him: the cocky cashier at the register,
the grim and harried store manager, the bland butcher, and the brazen bag
45  boys who smoked in the warehouse on their breaks. He wanted a second
chance. Another chance to be confident and say witty things to her as he threw
tin cans into her bags, persuading her to allow him to help her to her car so
he might learn just a little about her, check out the floor of the car for signs of
hobbies or fetishes and the bumpers for clues as to beliefs and loyalties.
50  But he busted her jar of mayonnaise and nothing else worked out for the
rest of the day.

---

2. **Tibetan monk:** a member of a Buddhist sect in central Asia that practices meditation.

**Close Read**

4. What event on this page sets the rising action in motion?

5. How would you describe the conflict faced by the girl and the bag boy? How does this conflict make the story more interesting?

**Close Read**

4. ***Possible answer:*** *The bag boy drops a jar of mayonnaise (line 29).*

5. ***Possible answer:*** *Each feels attracted to the other, but neither is able to show it (lines 31–42). This builds some suspense. The reader wants to know what will happen next.*

**FOR STRUGGLING READERS**

**Analysis Support: Plot**

1. Have learners copy the graphic and headings from the plot diagram on page 28.

2. Provide these line numbers as clues to the opening plot elements in "Checkouts": lines 9–14 (setting, characters); lines 40–42 (conflict).

3. Have students work in pairs to fill in the details for each plot element.

**6. Possible answer:** *After the boy drops the jar, the girl falls in love. The boy becomes depressed and wishes for a second chance to be confident and talk to the girl. As four weeks pass, they look for each other but do not meet. Suspense develops from understanding the characters' feelings and wondering what will happen when they meet again.*

**7. Possible answer:** *Details include words and phrases like "reason enough to be alive," "hope," "anticipation," and "possibilities of mystery and romance" (lines 70–71, 77).*

**IF STUDENTS NEED HELP . . .** Explain that the word *ecstasy* in line 69 suggests excitement and joy. Have students look for other words and phrases in the paragraph that convey positive emotions.

**8. Possible answer:** *So far, the plot development has been chronological. The events have unfolded in the order in which they occurred.*

---

Strange, how attractive clumsiness can be. She left the supermarket with stars in her eyes, for she had loved the way his long nervous fingers moved from the conveyor belt to the bags, how deftly (until the mayonnaise) they
55 had picked up her items and placed them into her bags. She had loved the way the hair kept falling into his eyes as he leaned over to grab a box or a tin. And the tattered brown shoes he wore with no socks. And the left side of his collar turned in rather than out.

The bag boy seemed a wonderful contrast to the perfectly beautiful house
60 she had been forced to accept as her home, to the *history* she hated, to the loneliness she had become used to, and she couldn't wait to come back for more of his awkwardness and dishevelment.

Incredibly, it was another four weeks before they saw each other again. As fate would have it, her visits to the supermarket never coincided with
65 his schedule to bag. Each time she went to the store, her eyes scanned the checkouts at once, her heart in her mouth. And each hour he worked, the bag boy kept one eye on the door, watching for the red-haired girl with the big orange bow.

Yet in their disappointment these weeks there was a kind of ecstasy. It is
70 reason enough to be alive, the hope you may see again some face which has meant something to you. The anticipation of meeting the bag boy eased the girl's painful transition into her new and jarring life in Cincinnati. It provided for her an anchor amid all that was impersonal and unfamiliar, and she spent less time on thoughts of what she had left behind as she concentrated on what
75 might lie ahead. And for the boy, the long and often tedious hours at the supermarket which provided no challenge other than that of showing up the following workday . . . these hours became possibilities of mystery and romance for him as he watched the electric doors for the girl in the orange bow.

And when finally they did meet up again, neither offered a clue to the other
80 that he, or she, had been the object of obsessive thought for weeks. She spotted him as soon as she came into the store, but she kept her eyes strictly in front of her as she pulled out a cart and wheeled it toward the produce. And he, too, knew the instant she came through the door—though the orange bow was gone, replaced by a small but bright yellow flower instead—and he never

---

6. Review lines 29–68. Summarize the sequence of events that begins with the boy's dropping the jar. How do these events build suspense about what will happen?

7. What details in lines 69–78 tell you that the girl and the boy are enjoying the excitement of the building conflict? One has been boxed.

8. Look for time cues—like the boxed examples in lines 79 and 81—that signal the order of events. Has the structure of this plot been chronological so far? Explain.

---

## DIFFERENTIATED INSTRUCTION

### FOR STRUGGLING READERS

**Analysis Support: Plot**
Have student pairs complete their plot diagrams. Provide these line numbers as clues to the closing plot elements in the story:

Rising Action: lines 63–78
Climax: lines 79–86
Falling Action: lines 87–101
Resolution: lines 102–111

### FOR ENGLISH LANGUAGE LEARNERS

**Vocabulary: Idioms** Help students use context clues to determine the meanings of these idioms in the story: *check out* (line 48), "to examine something"; *stars in her eyes* (line 53), "dazzled by happy dreams"; *As fate would have it* (line 64), "as events of life unfolded"; *heart in her mouth* (line 66), "a feeling of nearly choking from a strong emotion, such as shyness." Then ask volunteers to act out or mime the meanings.

85  once turned his head in her direction but watched her from the corner of his
    vision as he tried to swallow back the fear in his throat.

    It is odd how we sometimes deny ourselves the very pleasure we have longed
    for and which is finally within our reach. For some perverse reason she would
    not have been able to articulate, the girl did not bring her cart up to the bag
90  boy's checkout when her shopping was done. And the bag boy let her leave the
    store, pretending no notice of her.

    This is often the way of children, when they truly want a thing, to pretend
    that they don't. And then they grow angry when no one tries harder to give
    them this thing they so casually rejected, and they soon find themselves in a
95  rage simply because they cannot say yes when they mean yes. Humans are very
    complicated. (And perhaps cats, who have been known to react in the same
    way, though the resulting rage can only be guessed at.)

    The girl hated herself for not checking out at the boy's line, and the
    boy hated himself for not catching her eye and saying hello, and they most
100 sincerely hated each other without having ever exchanged even two minutes
    of conversation.

    Eventually—in fact, within the week—a kind and intelligent boy who lived
    very near her beautiful house asked the girl to a movie and she gave up
    her fancy for the bag boy at the supermarket. And the bag boy himself grew
105 so bored with his job that he made a desperate search for something better
    and ended up in a bookstore where scores of fascinating girls lingered like
    honeybees about a hive. Some months later the bag boy and the girl with the
    orange bow again crossed paths, standing in line with their dates at a movie
    theater, and, glancing toward the other, each smiled slightly, then looked away,
110 as strangers on public buses often do, when one is moving off the bus and the
    other is moving on.

## Close Read

9. Reread lines 79–86, which mark the story's climax. How do the characters resolve the main conflict?

10. In the falling action stage, lines 87–101, the characters reflect on their actions. Are they happy with the way they've handled the conflict? Explain.

11. Reread the resolution in lines 102–111. What are the results of the conflict for each character?

12. Describe the parallel structure of the three encounters between the girl and the boy. How are the meetings similar?

## Close Read

9. ***Possible answer:*** *The characters resolve the conflict by pretending not to notice each other.*

10. ***Possible answer:*** *The characters hate themselves and each other for the way they've handled the situation: "The girl hated herself . . . and the boy hated himself . . . and they most sincerely hated each other. . . ." (lines 98–100).*

    **IF STUDENTS NEED HELP . . .** Write lines 98–101 on the board. Underline the verb *hated* each time it appears. Ask volunteers to identify the object of hatred in each case. Circle their correct answers.

11. ***Possible answer:*** *Each character moves on and finds someone new. In addition, the bag boy gets a better job, and the girl seems to be adjusting to her new home.*

12. ***Possible answer:*** *The three meetings are similar in that the boy and the girl notice each other all three times but do not speak. Instead, they consciously look away from each other.*

## Assess and Reteach

### Assess

Have students summarize "Checkouts" by identifying the exposition, rising action, climax, falling action, and resolution.

### Reteach

For students who are unable to apply the workshop skills to "Checkouts," select from these reteaching options:

1. Review with them the note-taking copy masters for this lesson. Have students
   - read aloud the information recorded about each skill
   - explain one skill to a small group, with each person in the group taking a turn to explain another skill
   - review the note-taking copy master for homework

2. Refer students to a story the class has read recently. Have students name the events associated with the plot, and list them on the board. Define each plot event as you write the events in story order. Annotate the list on the board to help students make an association between terms and events.

## FOR ENGLISH LANGUAGE LEARNERS
### Vocabulary: Multiple-Meaning Words

- Explain that the word *very* is most often used to mean "extremely," as in "very long," or "truly," as in "very nice." In line 87, however, *very* means "exact" or "precise."

- Discuss various meanings of *checkout* and *check out*. Have students tell which meanings the author had in mind when she titled the story. ***Possible answer:*** *to examine someone or something for suitability; an area in a store where goods are paid for*

# Focus and Motivate

## COMMON CORE FOCUS

**RL 1** Cite textual evidence to support analysis of what the text says explicitly as well as inferences drawn from the text. **RL 5** Analyze how an author's choices concerning how to structure a text, order events within it, and manipulate time create tension. **RL 7** Analyze the representation of a subject in two different artistic mediums. **W 3b** Use dialogue to develop experiences, events, and characters. **L 3** Apply knowledge of language to make effective choices for meaning or style. **L 4a, c** Use context as a clue to the meaning of a word; consult reference materials to find the pronunciation of a word.

## SUMMARIES

**"A Sound of Thunder"** describes a safari back to the time of dinosaurs. One hunter's actions result in a future dictatorial government—and in his own death.

**"From Here to There: The Physics of Time Travel"** describes the possibility of time travel and the effects it could have on the world.

**Movie Poster** The poster "The Time Machine" depicts a time traveler in another time period.

## Would you visit the PAST if you could?

Ask students for examples of stories that involve time travel. Were the consequences, or results, of the time travel positive or negative?

## What's the Connection?

Lead students in a discussion about the possibility of time travel.

## Selection Resources

---

**A Sound of Thunder**
Short Story by Ray Bradbury

 Video link at thinkcentral.com

**From Here to There:
The Physics of Time Travel**
Magazine Article by Brad Stone

**The Time Machine**
Movie Poster

# Would you visit the PAST if you could?

### COMMON CORE

**RL 1** Cite textual evidence to support analysis of what the text says explicitly as well as inferences drawn from the text. **RL 5** Analyze how an author's choices concerning how to structure a text, order events within it, and manipulate time create tension. **L 4c** Consult reference materials to find the pronunciation of a word.

Imagine that you could board a time machine and travel into the past. In "A Sound of Thunder," the main character does just that. His journey, however, has unexpected consequences.

## What's the Connection?

You've probably already encountered time machines in books, comics, TV shows, movies, and other media. As you read the selections that follow, you will again ponder the phenomenon of time travel—as both a compelling premise for science fiction stories and a real scientific possibility.

36

---

See resources on the **Teacher One Stop DVD-ROM** and on **thinkcentral.com**.

 Video link at thinkcentral.com

**RESOURCE MANAGER UNIT 1**
Plan and Teach, pp. 11–18
Summary, pp. 19–20†‡*
Text Analysis and Reading
   Skill, pp. 21–22, 23–24†*
Vocabulary, pp. 25–27*
Grammar and Style, p. 30

**DIAGNOSTIC AND SELECTION
   TESTS**
Selection Tests, pp. 23–26

**BEST PRACTICES TOOLKIT**
Two-Column Chart, p. A25
Jigsaw Reading, p. A1
Comparison Matrix, p. A24
New Word Analysis, p. E8
Predicting, p. A10
Timeline, p. B23

**TECHNOLOGY**
- Teacher One Stop DVD-ROM
- Student One Stop DVD-ROM
- Audio Anthology CD
- GrammarNotes DVD-ROM
- ExamView Test Generator
  on the **Teacher One Stop**

---

\* Resources for Differentiation      † Also in Spanish      ‡ In Haitian Creole and Vietnamese

## TEXT ANALYSIS: FORESHADOWING

**Foreshadowing** is a writer's use of clues to hint at events that will happen later in a story. By using this technique Bradbury creates **suspense,** the feeling of tension or excitement that readers experience when they want to know what will happen next. Foreshadowing often occurs when a character makes an unusual statement or issues a strong warning, as in this example:

*"So be careful. Stay on the Path. Never step off!"*

Watch for other examples of foreshadowing as you read Bradbury's story.

*Review:* **Plot**

## READING SKILL: ANALYZE SEQUENCE

A story about time travel presents some interesting challenges. If you were to create a timeline to track the characters' travels, it would go backward and then forward again. Yet the events in the story are presented in the order in which they happen to the characters. As you read the story, keep track of the **sequence** of events by creating a chart like the one shown. Record important events before, during, and after the time safari.

| Before | During | After |
|--------|--------|-------|
| Eckels prepares to travel back in time to hunt dinosaurs. | | |

*Review:* **Make Inferences, Predict**

## ▲ VOCABULARY IN CONTEXT

See which of the following words from the story you already know. Place each word in the appropriate column. Then write a brief definition of each word you're familiar with.

| WORD LIST | annihilate | malfunctioning | subliminal |
|-----------|------------|----------------|------------|
| | correlate | paradox | undulate |
| | expendable | resilient | |
| | infinitesimally | stagnating | |

| Know Well | Think I Know | Don't Know |
|-----------|--------------|------------|
| | | |

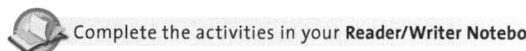 Complete the activities in your **Reader/Writer Notebook.**

---

## Meet the Author

# Ray Bradbury
**born 1920**

### Social Critic for the Future
A major writer in the genres of science fiction and fantasy, Ray Bradbury explores the future, outer space—and the human heart. Over his long career, he has lived to see much science fiction become science fact. His most chilling stories comment on the human consequences of progress and often reflect the ironies of life.

### A Library Education
Bradbury fervently believes in the importance of reading. "I didn't go to college, but when I graduated from high school I went down to the local library," he has said. For ten years Bradbury spent two or three days each week reading in the local public library in Los Angeles, California.

### Not Quite a Technophobe
This master of science fiction writes his stories on a typewriter rather than a computer, scorns the Internet, and has never even driven a car. Still, Bradbury is a strong advocate of space travel because he views it as "life-enhancing."

### BACKGROUND TO THE STORY
**The Fourth Dimension**
Time travel has been a popular idea in science fiction ever since the British author H. G. Wells wrote his short novel *The Time Machine* in 1895. In the novel, Wells suggested that in addition to the three dimensions of length, height, and width, there was a fourth dimension of duration, or time. Wells speculated that if a machine could be invented to move along the fourth dimension, travel backward and forward in time would be possible.

**Author Online** **THINK** central

Go to **thinkcentral.com.**
KEYWORD: HML9-37

37

---

## Teach

**TEXT ANALYSIS** **COMMON CORE** RL 5

● *Model the Skill:* **FORESHADOWING**

To model how to use clues to identify foreshadowing, read aloud this example:

> "People say the shortcut is cursed and that using it will bring serious consequences," Carlos chuckled. "But I don't believe them."

Point out that Carlos's description of the curse suggests that his decision to take the shortcut will have "serious consequences."

**GUIDED PRACTICE** Elicit other examples of foreshadowing from stories or movies.

---

**READING SKILL** **COMMON CORE** RL 5

■ *Model the Skill:* **ANALYZE SEQUENCE**

Help students see that sequence can indicate how one event leads to another. Point out that an author may present events chronologically, moving forward in time (historical novel), or may first describe an occurrence and then show the events that led up to it (detective story).

**GUIDED PRACTICE** Ask students what sequence of events they might see in a story about travel to the past.

**R** RESOURCE MANAGER—Copy Master Analyze Sequence p. 23 (for student use while reading the selection)

---

## VOCABULARY SKILL

**COMMON CORE** L 4

### ▲ VOCABULARY IN CONTEXT

**DIAGNOSE WORD KNOWLEDGE** Have all students complete Vocabulary in Context. Check their definitions against the following.

**annihilate** (ə-nī'ə-lāt') *v.* to destroy completely
**correlate** (kôr'ə-lāt') *v.* to figure out or create a relationship between two items or events
**expendable** (ĭk-spĕn'də-bəl) *adj.* not worth keeping; not essential
**infinitesimally** (ĭn'fĭn-ĭ-tĕs'ə-mə-lē) *adv.* in amounts so small as to be barely measurable

**malfunctioning** (măl-fŭngk'shə-nĭng) *adj.* not working or operating properly **malfunction** *v.*
**paradox** (păr'ə-dŏks') *n.* a statement or an event that sounds impossible but seems to be true
**resilient** (rĭ-zĭl'yənt) *adj.* strong but flexible; able to withstand stress without injury
**stagnating** (stăg'nā'tĭng) *adj.* becoming foul or rotten from lack of movement **stagnate** *v.*
**subliminal** (sŭb-lĭm'ə-nəl) *adj.* below the level of consciousness

**undulate** (ŭn'jə-lāt') *v.* to move in waves or in a smooth, wavelike motion

**PRETEACH VOCABULARY** Use the copy master to help students predict word meanings.

**R** RESOURCE MANAGER—Copy Master Vocabulary Study p. 25

## READ WITH A PURPOSE

*Help students set a purpose for reading. Tell them to read "A Sound of Thunder" to find out about the effects of one person's actions.*

TEXT ANALYSIS
COMMON CORE
RL 5

### Ⓐ FORESHADOWING

**Possible answer:** *The warning foreshadows the possibility of dangerous events during the safari (for there is no guarantee that Eckels will "come back alive"). The mention of a penalty also foreshadows the possibility that someone may "disobey instructions."*

**IF STUDENTS NEED HELP...** Explore the sense of danger by working together to complete a Two-Column Chart like this one:

| When I read ... | I wonder ... |
|---|---|
| "We guarantee nothing" | Why can't you offer a guarantee? |
| "If he says no shooting" | |
| "If you disobey" | |

 **BEST PRACTICES TOOLKIT—Transparency**
Two-Column Chart p. A25

# A SOUND OF THUNDER

### RAY BRADBURY

The sign on the wall seemed to quaver under a film of sliding warm water. Eckels felt his eyelids blink over his stare, and the sign burned in this momentary darkness:

> TIME SAFARI, INC.
> SAFARIS TO ANY YEAR IN THE PAST.
> YOU NAME THE ANIMAL.
> WE TAKE YOU THERE.
> YOU SHOOT IT.

A warm phlegm gathered in Eckels's throat; he swallowed and pushed it
10 down. The muscles around his mouth formed a smile as he put his hand slowly out upon the air, and in that hand waved a check for ten thousand dollars to the man behind the desk.

"Does this safari guarantee I come back alive?"

"We guarantee nothing," said the official, "except the dinosaurs." He turned. "This is Mr. Travis, your Safari Guide in the Past. He'll tell you what and where to shoot. If he says no shooting, no shooting. If you disobey instructions, there's a stiff penalty of another ten thousand dollars, plus possible government action, on your return." Ⓐ

**Analyze Visuals ▶**

Examine this picture. What information can you **infer** about the world it portrays?

**①  Targeted Passage**

**Ⓐ FORESHADOWING**
Reread lines 13–18. What might the man's warning to Eckels foreshadow?

---

## DIFFERENTIATED INSTRUCTION

### FOR ENGLISH LANGUAGE LEARNERS

**Background** This story opens in a travel agency that runs safaris into the past. Explain to students that the first safaris were taken by European hunters in Africa, but that safari travelers today do more sightseeing than hunting. Ask students what they would most like to see if they could travel into the past.

### FOR STRUGGLING READERS

In combination with the *Audio Anthology CD*, use one or more Targeted Passages (pp. 38, 40, 43, 46, 51) to ensure that students focus on key story events, concepts, and skills. Targeted Passages are also good for English learners.

**① Targeted Passage [Lines 4–14]**

This passage introduces the main character, Eckels; the futuristic setting; and the elements of time travel and danger.

## BACKGROUND

***Tyrannosaurus rex*** This safari will take Eckels back in time so that he can shoot a *Tyrannosaurus rex*, "the most incredible monster in history" (lines 46–47). This 40-foot-long, meat-eating dinosaur (whose name literally means "tyrant lizard king") is believed to have lived at least 65 million years ago. Adults could reach a height of about 18 feet and weigh more than 6 tons. These dinosaurs used their powerful jaws, long claws, and 6-inch-long, serrated teeth to tear apart their prey and devour the remains.

## Analyze Visuals

*Possible answer: The lush growth suggests an exotic world, filled with plant and animal life. The abundant growth suggests that the climate is temperate or warm with plenty of sunshine. Since there is no sign of human activity, the region is undeveloped and possibly unexplored.*

**About the Art** Austrian artist Joseph Selleny (1824–1875) is known for his landscape paintings and lithographs. After studying at the Viennese Academy, Selleny traveled by boat around the world and returned with exotic studies that he later turned into paintings, such as the one on this page.

- What does the Time Safari ad promise? (lines 4–8)
- Why does Eckels pay $10,000? (lines 4–8)
- Does the story open in the past, present, or future? (line 5)
- What clue can you find to the dangers of the trip? (line 14)

**FOR ADVANCED LEARNERS/PRE–AP**

**Evaluate Setting** Explain to students that they know this story will partially be set in the past, when dinosaurs lived. Have students discuss in pairs why Bradbury chose this setting and what impact they think it will have on the story. After students have finished reading the story, have pairs discuss whether or not they feel this story could have worked with a different setting.

Eckels glanced across the vast office at a mass and tangle, a snaking and
20 humming of wires and steel boxes, at an aurora[1] that flickered now orange,
now silver, now blue. There was a sound like a gigantic bonfire burning all of
Time, all the years and all the parchment calendars, all the hours piled high
and set aflame.

A touch of the hand and this burning would, on the instant, beautifully
reverse itself. Eckels remembered the wording in the advertisements to the
letter. Out of chars and ashes, out of dust and coals, like golden salamanders,
the old years, the green years, might leap; roses sweeten the air, white hair turn
Irish-black, wrinkles vanish; all, everything fly back to seed, flee death, rush
down to their beginnings, suns rise in western skies and set in glorious easts,
30 moons eat themselves opposite to the custom, all and everything cupping one
in another like Chinese boxes,[2] rabbits into hats, all and everything returning
to the fresh death, the seed death, the green death, to the time before the
beginning. A touch of a hand might do it, the merest touch of a hand.

"Unbelievable." Eckels breathed, the light of the Machine on his thin face.
"A real Time Machine." He shook his head. "Makes you think. If the election
had gone badly yesterday, I might be here now running away from the results.
Thank God Keith won. He'll make a fine President of the United States."

"Yes," said the man behind the desk. "We're lucky. If Deutscher[3] had gotten
in, we'd have the worst kind of dictatorship. There's an anti-everything man
40 for you, a militarist, anti-Christ, anti-human, anti-intellectual. People called us
up, you know, joking but not joking. Said if Deutscher became President they
wanted to go live in 1492. Of course it's not our business to conduct Escapes,
but to form Safaris. Anyway, Keith's President now. All you got to worry
about is—" **B**

"Shooting my dinosaur," Eckels finished it for him.

"A *Tyrannosaurus rex.* The Tyrant Lizard, the most incredible monster in
history. Sign this release. Anything happens to you, we're not responsible.
Those dinosaurs are hungry."

Eckels flushed angrily. "Trying to scare me!"

50 "Frankly, yes. We don't want anyone going who'll panic at the first shot. Six
Safari leaders were killed last year, and a dozen hunters. We're here to give you
the severest thrill a real hunter ever asked for. Traveling you back sixty million
years to bag the biggest game in all of Time. Your personal check's still there.
Tear it up."

Mr. Eckels looked at the check. His fingers twitched. **C**

"Good luck," said the man behind the desk. "Mr. Travis, he's all yours."

They moved silently across the room, taking their guns with them, toward
the Machine, toward the silver metal and the roaring light.

---

1. **aurora** (ə-rôr′ə): a shifting, streaming display of light, like those sometimes seen in the sky in the northern and southern regions of the earth.
2. **Chinese boxes:** a set of boxes, each of which fits neatly inside the next larger one.
3. **Deutscher** (doi′chər).

 **Targeted Passage**

**B FORESHADOWING**
What might the conversation about the election results foreshadow?

**C PLOT**
What have you learned about the characters' situation in the **exposition**?

---

**B FORESHADOWING**

*Possible answer:* *The conversation might foreshadow the frightening possibility that under different circumstances, Deutscher, not Keith, would be the next president. The man's comments (especially the prefix anti- in several of his words) suggest that Deutscher would make the "worst kind" of president.*

**TEXT ANALYSIS:** *Review*                COMMON CORE
                                  RL 5

**C PLOT**

*Possible answer:* *Eckels, a hunter who has signed up to go on a safari back to the time of dinosaurs, meets with an official of Time Safari, Inc., to firm up the plans. After introducing Mr. Travis, who will be the safari guide, the official warns of the great danger in encountering "the most incredible monster in history." He wants to screen out anyone who might panic and jeopardize the safety of others and the success of the trip. Eckels is determined to go, despite his apparent nervousness.*

---

## DIFFERENTIATED INSTRUCTION

### FOR STRUGGLING READERS

 **Targeted Passage [Lines 34–45]**
This passage sets up a crucial story concept: Keith just defeated the evil Deutscher.

- Who just won the election? Who lost? (lines 37–38)
- How do Eckels and the man behind the desk feel about the election results? (lines 37–39)
- The prefix *anti-* means "against." What kinds of things is Deutscher against? (lines 39–40)

### FOR ENGLISH LANGUAGE LEARNERS

**Language: Conversational Patterns** Explain that in line 49 the words *are you* are left out but understood in the dialogue "Trying to scare me!" Have mixed language-ability Jigsaw groups study the dialogue in the rest of the story. Ask each group to fill in missing words in their assigned passages and report back to the class.

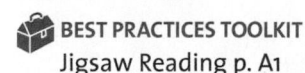 **BEST PRACTICES TOOLKIT**
Jigsaw Reading p. A1

F irst a day and then a night and then a day and then a night, then it was
60 day-night-day-night-day. A week, a month, a year, a decade! A.D. 2055.
A.D. 2019. 1999! 1957! Gone! The Machine roared.

They put on their oxygen helmets and tested the intercoms.

Eckels swayed on the padded seat, his face pale, his jaw stiff. He felt the
trembling in his arms, and he looked down and found his hands tight on the
new rifle. There were four other men in the Machine. Travis, the Safari Leader;
his assistant, Lesperance;[4] and two other hunters, Billings and Kramer. They
sat looking at each other, and the years blazed around them. **D**

"Can these guns get a dinosaur cold?" Eckels felt his mouth saying.

"If you hit them right," said Travis on the helmet radio. "Some dinosaurs
70 have two brains, one in the head, another far down the spinal column. We stay
away from those. That's stretching luck. Put your first two shots into the eyes,
if you can, blind them, and go back into the brain."

The Machine howled. Time was a film run backward. Suns fled, and ten
million moons fled after them. "Think," said Eckels. "Every hunter that ever
lived would envy us today. This makes Africa seem like Illinois."

The Machine slowed; its scream fell to a murmur. The Machine stopped.

The sun stopped in the sky.

The fog that had enveloped the Machine blew away, and they were in an
old time, a very old time indeed, three hunters and two Safari Heads with their
80 blue metal guns across their knees.

"Christ isn't born yet," said Travis. "Moses has not gone to the mountain to
talk with God.[5] The Pyramids are still in the earth, waiting to be cut out and
put up. *Remember* that. Alexander, Caesar, Napoleon, Hitler—none of them
exists."

The man nodded.

"That"—Mr. Travis pointed—"is the jungle of sixty million two thousand
and fifty-five years before President Keith."

He indicated a metal path that struck off into green wilderness, over
streaming swamp, among giant ferns and palms.
90 "And that," he said, "is the Path, laid by Time Safari for your use. It floats
six inches above the earth. Doesn't touch so much as one grass blade, flower,
or tree. It's an antigravity metal.[6] Its purpose is to keep you from touching this
world of the past in any way. Stay on the Path. Don't go off it. I repeat. *Don't
go off*. For *any* reason! If you fall off, there's a penalty. And don't shoot any
animal we don't okay." **E**

"Why?" asked Eckels.

They sat in the ancient wilderness. Far birds' cries blew on a wind, and the
smell of tar and an old salt sea, moist grasses, and flowers the color of blood.

---

4. **Lesperance** (lĕs′pər-äns).
5. **Moses . . . talk with God:** According to the Old Testament, God spoke directly to Moses several times
   in mountainous locations, as when Moses received the Ten Commandments on Mount Sinai.
6. **antigravity metal:** a metal that counteracts the pull of gravity.

A SOUND OF THUNDER **41**

**D MAKE INFERENCES**
On the basis of details
presented so far, what
kind of person is Eckels?

**E FORESHADOWING**
What might Travis's
warning to the hunters
foreshadow? How
does his warning create
**suspense?**

---

---

Would you visit the

# PAST if you could?

**Discuss** In line 99 why does Travis say, "We don't belong here in the Past"? *Possible answer: He understands that altering the past may have undesirable consequences in the future. He also knows that the government disapproves of the company and allows it to operate only because it pays "big graft."*

## Analyze Visuals

**Activity** Ask students how the jungle scene in this painting helps them visualize the setting of the story. *Possible answer: The painting depicts a variety of creatures in a dense jungle, which is similar to the prehistoric jungle setting of the story.*

**About the Art** *Orinoco Jungle Life* is one of many pieces of art from German painter and zoologist Anton Goering (1836–1905). Sponsored by the Zoological Society of London, Goering traveled in Venezuela between 1866 and 1874, detailing its landscapes and collecting specimens of birds. His work made a faraway land—a land that might have seemed as exotic as the prehistoric world seemed to the hunters in Bradbury's story—accessible to many Europeans.

### OWN THE WORD

**annihilate:** Point out that the word *annihilate* comes from the Latin word *annihilare*, meaning "to reduce to nothing." Ask students to find the word *annihilate* in line 109. Then, ask them to explain why *annihilate* is a more appropriate word than *kill* in this context.

*Possible answer: The word* annihilate *is more appropriate because Travis is talking about wiping out a billion mice, not simply killing one mouse.*

---

"We don't want to change the Future. We don't belong here in the Past.
100 The government doesn't *like* us here. We have to pay big graft to keep our franchise.[7] A Time Machine is finicky business. Not knowing it, we might kill an important animal, a small bird, a roach, a flower even, thus destroying an important link in a growing species."

"That's not clear," said Eckels.

"All right," Travis continued, "say we accidentally kill one mouse here. That means all the future families of this one particular mouse are destroyed, right?"

"Right."

"And all the families of the families of the families of that one mouse! With a stamp of your foot, you **annihilate** first one, then a dozen, then a thousand,
110 a million, a *billion* possible mice!"

"So they're dead," said Eckels. "So what?"

"So what?" Travis snorted quietly. "Well, what about the foxes that'll need those mice to survive? For want of ten mice, a fox dies. For want of ten foxes, a lion starves. For want of a lion, all manner of insects, vultures, infinite billions of life forms are thrown into chaos and destruction. Eventually it all boils down to this: fifty-nine million years later, a caveman, one of a dozen on the

**annihilate**
(ə-nī′ə-lāt′) *v.* to destroy completely

---

7. **pay big graft to keep our franchise:** pay large bribes to officials in return for their approval of the business.

## DIFFERENTIATED INSTRUCTION

### FOR STRUGGLING READERS

**Concept Support** After students read lines 112–148, discuss how a very small change can lead to a large change—for example, how one's day can be totally changed by being one minute late for a bus. Help them connect this concept with the evolutionary chain assumed in the story.

### FOR ADVANCED LEARNERS/PRE–AP

**Evaluate** Have students work in pairs to discuss whether Time Safari, Inc., is taking sufficient precautions to protect history. Challenge students to make a list of at least five additional precautions the company might take.

*entire world,* goes hunting wild boar or saber-toothed tiger[8] for food. But you, friend, have *stepped* on all the tigers in that region. By stepping on one single mouse. So the caveman starves. And the caveman, please note, is not just *any*
120 **expendable** man, no! He is an *entire future nation.* From his loins would have sprung ten sons. From *their* loins one hundred sons, and thus onward to a civilization. Destroy this one man, and you destroy a race, a people, an entire history of life. It is comparable to slaying some of Adam's grandchildren. The stomp of your foot, on one mouse, could start an earthquake, the effects of which could shake our earth and destinies down through Time, to their very foundations. With the death of that one caveman, a billion others yet unborn are throttled in the womb. Perhaps Rome never rises on its seven hills. Perhaps Europe is forever a dark forest, and only Asia waxes healthy and teeming. Step on a mouse, and you crush the Pyramids. Step on a mouse, and you leave your
130 print, like a Grand Canyon, across Eternity. Queen Elizabeth might never be born; Washington might not cross the Delaware; there might never be a United States at all. So be careful. Stay on the Path. *Never step off!*"

"I see," said Eckels. "Then it wouldn't pay for us even to touch the *grass?*"

"Correct. Crushing certain plants could add up **infinitesimally.** A little error here would multiply in sixty million years, all out of proportion. Of course maybe our theory is wrong. Maybe Time *can't* be changed by us. Or maybe it can be changed only in little subtle ways. A dead mouse here makes an insect imbalance there, a population disproportion later, a bad harvest further on, a depression, mass starvation, and, finally, a change in *social*
140 temperament in far-flung countries. Something much more subtle, like that. Perhaps only a soft breath, a whisper, a hair, pollen on the air, such a slight, slight change that unless you looked close you wouldn't see it. Who knows? Who really can say he knows? We don't know. We're guessing. But until we do know for certain whether our messing around in Time *can* make a big roar or a little rustle in history, we're being careful. This Machine, this Path, your clothing and bodies, were sterilized, as you know, before the journey. We wear these oxygen helmets so we can't introduce our bacteria into an ancient atmosphere."

"How do we know which animals to shoot?"

150 "They're marked with red paint," said Travis. "Today, before our journey, we sent Lesperance here back with the Machine. He came to this particular era and followed certain animals."

"Studying them?"

"Right," said Lesperance. "I track them through their entire existence, noting which of them lives longest. Very few. How many times they mate. Not often. Life's short. When I find one that's going to die when a tree falls on him, or one that drowns in a tar pit, I note the exact hour, minute, and second. I shoot a paint bomb. It leaves a red patch on his side. We can't miss it. Then I **correlate** our arrival in the Past so that we meet the Monster not more than

---

8. **saber-toothed tiger:** a type of extinct wild cat that lived about 40 million years ago.

---

**expendable**
(ĭk-spĕn′də-bəl)
*adj.* not worth keeping; not essential

**③ Targeted Passage**

**infinitesimally**
(ĭn′fĭn-ĭ-tĕs′ə-mə-lē)
*adv.* in amounts so small as to be barely measurable

**COMMON CORE** L 4c

**Language Coach**

**Oral Fluency** When the letter *b* is followed by a *t*, the *b* is often—though not always—silent, as in the word *subtle* (line 140). Look up the pronunciations of the following words in a dictionary: *doubt, debt, obtain, obtrusive.*

**correlate** (kôr′ə-lāt′)
*v.* to figure out or create a relationship between two items or events

---

**TIERED DISCUSSION PROMPTS**

For lines 105–148, use these prompts to help students understand the dangers of altering the past:

**Connect** Would Travis's explanation of his theory worry you? Why or why not? *Many students will suggest that there is good reason to worry if the theory is correct.*

**Analyze** What might be the effects of introducing the visitors' bacteria into the ancient atmosphere? *Possible answer: No living thing in the ancient time would be immune to the visitors' bacteria. The result might be widespread death and destruction of birds, animals, and plant life.*

**Synthesize** How might the possible "change in *social* temperament" that Travis refers to in lines 139–140 be reflected in a country? *Possible answers: A change in historical circumstances might reshape society's values or its attitudes toward certain groups of people in the society. A change in economic conditions might influence how people feel and think, which in turn affects their choice of leaders and government.*

**VOCABULARY**    **COMMON CORE**
    L 4

**OWN THE WORD**

- **expendable:** Remind students that *expendable* means "not essential"; an antonym is *indispensable.* Have students use both words in sentences.

- **infinitesimally:** Tell students that the word *infinitesimally* is related to the word *infinite.* Both words share a root that means "to be without definable limits." Ask students to identify words and phrases in the surrounding sentences that help them understand the meaning of *infinitesimally.* *Possible answer: multiply; out of proportion; one mouse.*

- **correlate:** Ask students to provide synonyms for *correlate.* *Possible answer: connect, compare, link*

---

**FOR STRUGGLING READERS**

**③ Targeted Passage** [Lines 132–148]

This passage sets up the key cause-effect conflict: If a Safari traveler changes anything in the past, the future may be changed.

- Why is it so important for Safari travelers to stay on the Path? (lines 133–135)

- How might you paraphrase this sentence: "A little error here would multiply in sixty million years, all out of proportion"?

**FOR ENGLISH LANGUAGE LEARNERS**

**Language Coach**    **COMMON CORE**
    L 4c

**Oral Fluency** Tell students that to truly own a word, they need to be comfortable pronouncing it so that they can use it in conversation. Have students work with a partner to practice pronouncing *subtle.* Then, have partners use *subtle* in three additional sentences.

160 two minutes before he would have died anyway. This way, we kill only animals with no future, that are never going to mate again. You see how *careful* we are?"

"But if you came back this morning in Time," said Eckels eagerly, "you must've bumped into *us,* our Safari! How did it turn out? Was it successful? Did all of us get through—alive?"

Travis and Lesperance gave each other a look.

"That'd be a **paradox**," said the latter. "Time doesn't permit that sort of mess—a man meeting himself. When such occasions threaten, Time steps aside. Like an airplane hitting an air pocket. You felt the Machine jump just before we stopped? That was us passing ourselves on the way back to 170 the Future. We saw nothing. There's no way of telling *if* this expedition was a success, *if we* got our monster, or whether all of us—meaning *you,* Mr. Eckels —got out alive."

Eckels smiled palely.

"Cut that," said Travis sharply. "Everyone on his feet!"

They were ready to leave the Machine.

The jungle was high and the jungle was broad and the jungle was the entire world forever and forever. Sounds like music and sounds like flying tents filled the sky, and those were pterodactyls[9] soaring with cavernous gray wings, gigantic bats of delirium and night fever. Eckels, balanced on the narrow Path, 180 aimed his rifle playfully.

"Stop that!" said Travis. "Don't even aim for fun, blast you! If your guns should go off—"

Eckels flushed. "Where's our *Tyrannosaurus?*"

Lesperance checked his wristwatch. "Up ahead. We'll bisect his trail in sixty seconds. Look for the red paint! Don't shoot till we give the word. Stay on the Path. *Stay on the Path!*"

They moved forward in the wind of morning.

"Strange," murmured Eckels. "Up ahead, sixty million years, Election Day over. Keith made President. Everyone celebrating. And here we are, a million 190 years lost, and they don't exist. The things we worried about for months, a lifetime, not even born or thought of yet."

"Safety catches off, everyone!" ordered Travis. "You, first shot, Eckels. Second, Billings. Third, Kramer."

"I've hunted tiger, wild boar, buffalo, elephant, but now, this is it," said Eckels. "I'm shaking like a kid."

"Ah," said Travis.

Everyone stopped.

Travis raised his hand. "Ahead," he whispered. "In the mist. There he is. There's His Royal Majesty now."

200 The jungle was wide and full of twitterings, rustlings, murmurs, and sighs. Suddenly it all ceased, as if someone had shut a door.

Silence.

A sound of thunder.

---

9. **pterodactyls** (tĕr'ə-dăk'təlz): extinct flying reptiles.

**44** UNIT 1: NARRATIVE STRUCTURE

---

## Sidebar (left column)

## Sidebar (right column)

**paradox** (păr'ə-dŏks') *n.* a statement or an event that sounds impossible but seems to be true

**F ANALYZE SEQUENCE**
Up until now, the men have spent most of their time talking and arguing. Now, however, the action begins to pick up. As you read the next sequence of events, pay attention to what happens.

**G GRAMMAR AND STYLE**
Reread lines 188–195. Notice how Bradbury uses **sentence fragments** and **contractions** to create realistic dialogue.

---

Out of the mist, one hundred yards away, came *Tyrannosaurus rex.*

"It," whispered Eckels. "It . . ."

"Sh!"

It came on great oiled, **resilient,** striding legs. It towered thirty feet above
half of the trees, a great evil god, folding its delicate watchmaker's claws close
to its oily reptilian chest. Each lower leg was a piston, a thousand pounds of
210 white bone, sunk in thick ropes of muscle, sheathed over in a gleam of pebbled
skin like the mail of a terrible warrior. Each thigh was a ton of meat, ivory,
and steel mesh. And from the great breathing cage of the upper body those
two delicate arms dangled out front, arms with hands which might pick up
and examine men like toys, while the snake neck coiled. And the head itself, a
ton of sculptured stone, lifted easily upon the sky. Its mouth gaped, exposing a
fence of teeth like daggers. Its eyes rolled, ostrich eggs, empty of all expression
save hunger. It closed its mouth in a death grin. It ran, its pelvic bones
crushing aside trees and bushes, its taloned feet clawing damp earth, leaving
prints six inches deep wherever it settled its weight. It ran with a gliding ballet
220 step, far too poised and balanced for its ten tons. It moved into a sunlit arena
warily, its beautifully reptilian hands feeling the air.

"Why, why," Eckels twitched his mouth. "It could reach up and grab the
moon."

"Sh!" Travis jerked angrily. "He hasn't seen us yet."

"It can't be killed." Eckels pronounced this verdict quietly, as if there could
be no argument. He had weighed the evidence, and this was his considered
opinion. The rifle in his hands seemed a cap gun. "We were fools to come.
This is impossible."

"Shut up!" hissed Travis. **H**

230 "Nightmare."

"Turn around," commanded Travis. "Walk quietly to the Machine. We'll
remit one-half your fee."

"I didn't realize it would be this *big*," said Eckels. "I miscalculated, that's all.
And now I want out."

"It *sees* us!"

"There's the red paint on its chest!"

The Tyrant Lizard raised itself. Its armored flesh glittered like a thousand
green coins. The coins, crusted with slime, steamed. In the slime, tiny insects
wriggled, so that the entire body seemed to twitch and **undulate,** even while
240 the monster itself did not move. It exhaled. The stink of raw flesh blew down
the wilderness.

"Get me out of here," said Eckels. "It was never like this before. I was always
sure I'd come through alive. I had good guides, good safaris, and safety. This
time, I figured wrong. I've met my match and admit it. This is too much for
me to get hold of."

"Don't run," said Lesperance. "Turn around. Hide in the Machine."

"Yes." Eckels seemed to be numb. He looked at his feet as if trying to make
them move. He gave a grunt of helplessness.

**resilient** (rĭ-zĭl´yənt)
*adj.* strong but flexible;
able to withstand stress
without injury

**H** MAKE INFERENCES
Why do you think Travis
is annoyed with Eckels?

**undulate** (ŭn´jə-lāt´)
*v.* to move in waves or in a
smooth, wavelike motion

A SOUND OF THUNDER **45**

---

---

## TIERED DISCUSSION PROMPTS

For lines 257–266, use these prompts to help students understand the dangerous situation:

**Connect** Have you or anyone you know ever panicked to the degree that, even for a moment, you didn't realize what you were doing? Explain. *Accept all reasonable responses.*

**Analyze** How does Bradbury characterize the dinosaur? Cite evidence. ***Possible answer:*** *Bradbury characterizes the dinosaur as awesome in its power. He describes how "trees exploded" (line 261) when the dinosaur swung its tail. He refers to the dinosaur's intent "to twist [the men] in half, to crush them like berries" (line 263).*

**Evaluate** Faced with the charging *Tyrannosaurus*, Eckels, "not knowing it" (line 257), steps off the Path. Should he be held responsible for his actions? *Answers may vary.*

---

**READING SKILL**  COMMON CORE **RL 5**

### ❶ ANALYZE SEQUENCE

***Possible answer:*** *Eckels steps off the Path, which he has been warned repeatedly not to do. Leaving the Path and coming into physical contact with the prehistoric jungle could affect the future in unforeseen ways. He may have killed a species of plant or animal, thus changing the balance of nature.*

"Eckels!"

250 He took a few steps, blinking, shuffling.

"Not *that* way!"

The Monster, at the first motion, lunged forward with a terrible scream. It covered one hundred yards in six seconds. The rifles jerked up and blazed fire. A windstorm from the beast's mouth engulfed them in the stench of slime and old blood. The Monster roared, teeth glittering with sun.

Eckels, not looking back, walked blindly to the edge of the Path, his gun limp in his arms, stepped off the Path, and walked, not knowing it, in the jungle. His feet sank into green moss. His legs moved him, and he felt alone and remote from the events behind. ❶

260 The rifles cracked again. Their sound was lost in shriek and lizard thunder. The great level of the reptile's tail swung up, lashed sideways. Trees exploded in clouds of leaf and branch. The Monster twitched its jeweler's hands down to fondle at the men, to twist them in half, to crush them like berries, to cram them into its teeth and its screaming throat. Its boulder-stone eyes leveled with the men. They saw themselves mirrored. They fired at the metallic eyelids and the blazing black iris.

④ **Targeted Passage**

❶ **ANALYZE SEQUENCE**
Reread lines 252–259. What important event occurs in these lines? What do you think might happen as a result of this event?

**46** UNIT 1: NARRATIVE STRUCTURE

---

## DIFFERENTIATED INSTRUCTION

### FOR STRUGGLING READERS

④ **Targeted Passage [Lines 250–259]**

This passage presents the moment that changes everything: Eckels steps off the Path! The dangers in his action were foreshadowed in the warning in the Targeted Passage on page 43.

- Why does Eckels step off the Path? (lines 252–257)

- Why do Eckels's actions pose a danger for this moment in the past? What might they mean to the future? (lines 256–259)

- What warning foreshadows this moment earlier in the story? (line 132)

◀ **Analyze Visuals**

What qualities of *Tyrannosaurus rex* are emphasized in this illustration? Explain.

**Analyze Visuals**

*Possible answer: The illustration emphasizes the massive size and fearsome appearance of the dinosaur.*

**REVISIT THE BIG QUESTION**

Would you visit the **PAST** if you could?

**Discuss** In lines 267–273, when the dinosaur unexpectedly charged, the hunters had to fire to keep from being killed. What were the consequences of their action? *Possible answer: The falling body of the dinosaur pulled down trees and "wrenched and tore the metal Path," flinging the men backward. The hunters were closer to the animal than they intended to be and were splattered with its blood and body fluids.*

Like a stone idol, like a mountain avalanche, *Tyrannosaurus* fell. Thundering, it clutched trees, pulled them with it. It wrenched and tore the metal Path. The men flung themselves back and away. The body hit, ten 270 tons of cold flesh and stone. The guns fired. The Monster lashed its armored tail, twitched its snake jaws, and lay still. A fount of blood spurted from its throat. Somewhere inside, a sac of fluids burst. Sickening gushes drenched the hunters. They stood, red and glistening.

The thunder faded.

The jungle was silent. After the avalanche, a green peace. After the nightmare, morning.

Billings and Kramer sat on the pathway and threw up. Travis and Lesperance stood with smoking rifles, cursing steadily.

In the Time Machine, on his face, Eckels lay shivering. He had found his 280 way back to the Path, climbed into the Machine.

Travis came walking, glanced at Eckels, took cotton gauze from a metal box, and returned to the others, who were sitting on the Path.

"Clean up."

**Language Coach**

**Frequently Misused Words** The verbs *lie*, meaning "to rest, recline, or stay," and *lay*, meaning "to put (something) in place," are often confused. The past tense of *lie* is *lay* (as in lines 271 and 279), and the past tense of *lay* is *laid*. Write a sentence using the past-tense form *laid*. Remember that the verb *laid* will require an object in your sentence.

**FOR ENGLISH LANGUAGE LEARNERS**

**Language Coach**

**Frequently Misused Words** Have students work in pairs and use *lie*, *lay*, as well as the past tense of *lie*, which is *lay*, in three separate sentences.

**FOR ADVANCED LEARNERS/PRE–AP**

**Analyze Absence of Dialogue** Remind students that although Billings and Kramer are present on the safari, their characters have no dialogue in the story. Have students write a brief essay explaining why Bradbury might have included these silent characters.

**TIERED DISCUSSION PROMPTS**

Use these prompts to help students understand Travis's reaction to Eckels's behavior in lines 310–324:

**Connect** Think about a time when you had to talk to someone who severely disappointed you. How does that experience help you understand Travis's feelings toward Eckels? *Answers should demonstrate an understanding of the anger and fear involved in the confrontation.*

**Analyze** Why does Travis react as he does? *Possible answer: Travis had repeatedly warned Eckels about his behavior (lines 132, 181–182, 206, 224, 229). By disregarding these warnings, Eckels nearly got all of them killed, may have cost the company its license, and may have altered history.*

**Evaluate** Which is Travis more justified in being concerned about—the government's penalties or the possible effects on time and history? *Accept reasonable answers.*

---

**READING STRATEGY:** *Review*    COMMON CORE   RL 1

**J PREDICT**

*Possible answer: The future may be altered.*

**IF STUDENTS NEED HELP . . .** Review lines 105–148 with students and help them use the Predicting chart to speculate about what damage Eckels might have caused by leaving the Path.

 **BEST PRACTICES TOOLKIT—Transparency** Predicting p. A10

---

**VOCABULARY**    COMMON CORE   L 4

**OWN THE WORD**

- **malfunctioning:** Point out that the word *malfunctioning* is usually applied to mechanical objects, not living creatures. Ask students to supply words that have a different connotation. **Possible answer:** *dying, failing, weakening*

- **stagnating:** Point out that the word *stagnant* can be used in many contexts. Ask students to list other things that can be described as *stagnating.* **Possible answer:** *water; air; a country's economy; someone's mind*

---

They wiped the blood from their helmets. They began to curse too. The Monster lay, a hill of solid flesh. Within, you could hear the sighs and murmurs as the furthest chambers of it died, the organs **malfunctioning,** liquids running a final instant from pocket to sac to spleen, everything shutting off, closing up forever. It was like standing by a wrecked locomotive or a steam shovel at quitting time, all valves being released or 290 levered tight. Bones cracked; the tonnage of its own flesh, off balance, dead weight, snapped the delicate forearms, caught underneath. The meat settled, quivering.

Another cracking sound. Overhead, a gigantic tree branch broke from its heavy mooring, fell. It crashed upon the dead beast with finality.

"There." Lesperance checked his watch. "Right on time. That's the giant tree that was scheduled to fall and kill this animal originally." He glanced at the two hunters. "You want the trophy picture?"

"What?"

"We can't take a trophy back to the Future. The body has to stay right here 300 where it would have died originally, so the insects, birds, and bacteria can get at it, as they were intended to. Everything in balance. The body stays. But we *can* take a picture of you standing near it."

The two men tried to think, but gave up, shaking their heads.

They let themselves be led along the metal Path. They sank wearily into the Machine cushions. They gazed back at the ruined Monster, the **stagnating** mound, where already strange reptilian birds and golden insects were busy at the steaming armor.

A sound on the floor of the Time Machine stiffened them. Eckels sat there, shivering.

310 "I'm sorry," he said at last.

"Get up!" cried Travis.

Eckels got up.

"Go out on that Path alone," said Travis. He had his rifle pointed. "You're not coming back in the Machine. We're leaving you here!"

Lesperance seized Travis's arm. "Wait—"

"Stay out of this!" Travis shook his hand away. "This fool nearly killed us. But it isn't *that* so much, no. It's his *shoes!* Look at them! He ran off the Path. That *ruins* us! We'll forfeit! Thousands of dollars of insurance! We guarantee no one leaves the Path. He left it. Oh, the fool! I'll have to report to the 320 government. They might revoke our license to travel. Who knows *what* he's done to Time, to History!" **J**

"Take it easy; all he did was kick up some dirt."

"How do we *know?*" cried Travis. "We don't know anything! It's all a mystery! Get out there, Eckels!"

Eckels fumbled his shirt. "I'll pay anything. A hundred thousand dollars!"

Travis glared at Eckels's checkbook and spat. "Go out there. The Monster's next to the Path. Stick your arms up to your elbows in his mouth. Then you can come back with us."

**malfunctioning** (măl-fŭngk'shə-nĭng) *adj.* not working or operating properly **malfunction** *v.*

**stagnating** (stăg'nā'tĭng) *adj.* becoming foul or rotten from lack of movement **stagnate** *v.*

**J PREDICT** What do you predict might be the consequences of Eckels's action?

---

**DIFFERENTIATED INSTRUCTION**

**FOR ENGLISH LANGUAGE LEARNERS**

**Language: Pronoun Referents** Explain the referents for the pronouns, shown in italics, from line 316: "'Stay out of *this* [the disagreement]!' Travis shook *his* [Lesperance's] hand away." Then have learners work in mixed-language groups to identify referents for the remaining pronouns in Travis's angry speech (lines 316–318).

**FOR ADVANCED LEARNERS/PRE–AP**

**Evaluate** Have students work in small groups to discuss what they think is a reasonable punishment for Eckels. When groups are finished, list their ideas on the board. Have the class vote for the punishment they would choose.

"That's unreasonable!"

330 "The Monster's dead, you idiot. The bullets! The bullets can't be left behind. They don't belong in the Past; they might change anything. Here's my knife. Dig them out!"

The jungle was alive again, full of the old tremorings and bird cries. Eckels turned slowly to regard the primeval garbage dump, that hill of nightmares and terror. After a long time, like a sleepwalker he shuffled out along the Path.

He returned, shuddering, five minutes later, his arms soaked and red to the elbows. He held out his hands. Each held a number of steel bullets. Then he fell. He lay where he fell, not moving.

"You didn't have to make him do that," said Lesperance.

340 "Didn't I? It's too early to tell." Travis nudged the still body. "He'll live. Next time he won't go hunting game like this. Okay." He jerked his thumb wearily at Lesperance. "Switch on. Let's go home."

1492. 1776. 1812.

They cleaned their hands and faces. They changed their caking shirts and pants. Eckels was up and around again, not speaking. Travis glared at him for a full ten minutes.

"Don't look at me," cried Eckels. "I haven't done anything."

"Who can tell?"

"Just ran off the Path, that's all, a little mud on my shoes—what do you 350 want me to do—get down and pray?"

"We might need it. I'm warning you, Eckels, I might kill you yet. I've got my gun ready."

"I'm innocent. I've done nothing!"

1999. 2000. 2055.

The Machine stopped.

"Get out," said Travis.

The room was there as they had left it. But not the same as they had left it. The same man sat behind the same desk. But the same man did not quite sit behind the same desk.

360 Travis looked around swiftly. "Everything okay here?" he snapped.

"Fine. Welcome home!"

Travis did not relax. He seemed to be looking at the very atoms of the air itself, at the way the sun poured through the one high window.

"Okay, Eckels, get out. Don't ever come back."

Eckels could not move.

"You heard me," said Travis. "What're you *staring* at?"

Eckels stood smelling of the air, and there was a thing to the air, a chemical taint so subtle, so slight, that only a faint cry of his **subliminal** senses warned him it was there. The colors, white, gray, blue, orange, in the wall, in the 370 furniture, in the sky beyond the window, were . . . were . . . And there was a *feel*. His flesh twitched. His hands twitched. He stood drinking the oddness with the pores of his body. Somewhere, someone must have been screaming one of those whistles that only a dog can hear. His body screamed silence in return.

**subliminal**
(sŭb-lĭm′ə-nəl) *adj.* below the level of consciousness

---

**REVISIT THE BIG QUESTION**

## Would you visit the
# PAST if you could?

**Discuss** In lines 330–332, why does Travis want Eckels to return to the dinosaur? Is this task really necessary? *Possible answer: Travis wants Eckels to retrieve the bullets because they do not belong in the past. Changing the past in any way might have severe consequences in the future. Most students will agree that it was necessary to retrieve the bullets.*

## TIERED DISCUSSION PROMPTS

In lines 339–352, use these prompts to help students compare the viewpoints of Eckels and Travis:

**Connect** With which character do you identify more—Eckels or Travis? Why? *Students' answers should demonstrate an understanding of the characters' personalities and motives.*

**Analyze** How does Eckels's reaction to what he has done differ from Travis's reaction? *Possible answer: Eckels feels defensive about what happened (line 347) and tries to downplay the whole episode (lines 349–350). He says that he is "innocent" (line 353), and he tries to insist that his actions will have no negative consequences. Travis, on the other hand, is worried about the consequences (lines 340 and 348). Travis remains furious at Eckels and even suggests that he might kill him (lines 351–352).*

**Evaluate** Do you think that Eckels understands the seriousness of the situation? Do you think that Travis is overreacting? Explain your answers. *Students should support their opinions with solid reasons, including details from the story.*

---

**FOR ENGLISH LANGUAGE LEARNERS**

**Comprehension: Transitions** Point out that each of the sentences beginning with "But" (lines 357–358) connects to the previous sentence by telling ways it is no longer true.

**Language: Prefixes** Point out the words *subtle* and *subliminal* in line 368, and remind that their common prefix *sub–* means "under" or "below." Discuss how these words are story clues showing that something *under* the surface is not right.

**FOR RELUCTANT READERS**

**Connect to the Text** "A Sound of Thunder" warns of the unintended consequences that may arise from technology. Ask students to consider the ways in which technology, designed to improve their lives, can have negative effects. Have students brainstorm a list of familiar technological devices, such as the cellular phone and the Internet. Then, have students list some unintended consequences of the use of those technologies.

**VOCABULARY** COMMON CORE
L 4

**OWN THE WORD**

**subliminal:** Point out that the word *subliminal* is made up of the prefix *sub–*, which means "under or below," and the Latin word *limen*, which means "threshold." Have students list other words that use *sub–* as a prefix. *Possible answers: subterranean, subject, submerge*

## Analyze Visuals

**Activity** Ask students how this painting highlights the conclusion of the story. ***Possible answer:*** *The painting relates directly to lines 390–397. It focuses our attention on a single beautiful butterfly, the death of which was enough to alter the future dramatically.*

**About the Art** In his first several years as a painter, Pennsylvania-born artist Martin Johnson Heade (1819–1904) produced rather stiff portraits. When he took an interest in landscapes and still lifes, however, his style matured. On trips to South America, Heade focused on small paintings of the flowers he saw there as well as the animals that could be found in their company. Heade's interest in intimate views of nature and his love for the rainforest setting are both evident in *Blue Morpho Butterfly*.

*Blue Morpho Butterfly* (1864–1865), Martin Johnson Heade. Oil on canvas, 12¼″ × 10″. Anonymous Collection.

## DIFFERENTIATED INSTRUCTION

### FOR STRUGGLING READERS

**Develop Reading Fluency** To give students practice reading dialogue, use the conversation between Eckels and the man behind the desk that begins on line 387. Remind students that prose often mixes dialogue with narration. If students see quotation marks, then they know that a character is speaking. They should use the action occurring at that point in the story to determine the appropriate expression and timing to use while reading the dialogue.

First, read the passage aloud to students. Then, have students work with a partner to take turns reading the passage aloud. Conclude the activity by having several students read the passage aloud to the class.

**R** RESOURCE MANAGER—Copy Masters
Reading Fluency p. 31-32

Beyond this room, beyond this wall, beyond this man who was not quite the same man seated at this desk that was not quite the same desk . . . lay an entire world of streets and people. What sort of world it was now, there was no telling. He could feel them moving there, beyond the walls, almost, like so many chess pieces blown in a dry wind. . . .

But the immediate thing was the sign painted on the office wall, the same
380 sign he had read earlier today on first entering.

Somehow, the sign had changed:

TYME SEFARI INC.

SEFARIS TU ANY YEER EN THE PAST.

YU NAIM THE ANIMALL.

WEE TAEKYUTHAIR.

YU SHOOT ITT.

Eckels felt himself fall into a chair. He fumbled crazily at the thick slime on his boots. He held up a clod of dirt, trembling, "No, it *can't* be. Not a *little* thing like that. No!"

390 Embedded in the mud, glistening green and gold and black, was a butterfly, very beautiful and very dead.

"Not a little thing like *that!* Not a butterfly!" cried Eckels. **K**

It fell to the floor, an exquisite thing, a small thing that could upset balances and knock down a line of small dominoes and then big dominoes and then gigantic dominoes, all down the years across Time. Eckels's mind whirled. It *couldn't* change things. Killing one butterfly couldn't be *that* important! Could it?

His face was cold. His mouth trembled, asking: "Who—who won the presidential election yesterday?"

400 The man behind the desk laughed. "You joking? You know very well. Deutscher, of course! Who else? Not that fool weakling Keith. We got an iron man now, a man with guts!" The official stopped. "What's wrong?"

Eckels moaned. He dropped to his knees. He scrabbled at the golden butterfly with shaking fingers. "Can't we," he pleaded to the world, to himself, to the officials, to the Machine, "can't we take it *back;* can't we *make* it alive again? Can't we start over? Can't we—"

He did not move. Eyes shut, he waited, shivering. He heard Travis breathe loud in the room; he heard Travis shift his rifle, click the safety catch, and raise the weapon.

410 There was a sound of thunder. ❧

**K** MAKE INFERENCES
What important discovery does Eckels make? Why do you think it horrifies him so?

**⑤ Targeted Passage**

---

**K MAKE INFERENCES**

*Possible answer:* Eckels discovers that he unknowingly stepped on and killed a butterfly. His actions in the past apparently set in motion a chain of events that may have significantly changed the future.

**IF STUDENTS NEED HELP . . .** Ask these questions to help students speculate about the possible consequences of killing a butterfly:

- If one butterfly is killed, what happens to that butterfly's future families?
- If the butterfly's future families are eliminated, what might be the effect on the animals that would have eaten them? on the flowers they might have pollinated?
- What effects might these changes have on humans and civilization?

## SELECTION WRAP-UP

**READ WITH A PURPOSE** Now that students have read the selection, ask them to describe the earth-changing events that happen as a result of Eckel's actions. Then have students decide whether the changes are major or minor, positive or negative. *Possible answers: a different president, words spelled differently, different sights and smells; Regarding the importance of the changes, accept any answers that students can justify.*

**★ CRITIQUE** Have students evaluate the ending of the story and explain why they think it is or is not effective. Ask students to suggest other ways in which Bradbury might have ended the story.

### INDEPENDENT READING

Students may also enjoy reading Ray Bradbury's *Fahrenheit 451,* a novel set in a future in which books are banned and burned.

---

### FOR STRUGGLING READERS

**⑤ Targeted Passage [Lines 379–410]**

This passage concludes the story with the consequences of Eckels's action: Deutscher becomes president and Travis shoots Eckels.

- How did the ad in lines 4–8 change? Why is the change significant? (lines 382–386)
- How did Eckels change the past and the future by stepping off the Path? (lines 386–402)

### FOR ADVANCED LEARNERS/PRE–AP

**Synthesize** Tell students to reread lines 400–402 and then go back to read lines 38–44. Have them explain the change in social temperament that results from Eckels's careless actions.

# Practice and Apply

For preliminary support of post-reading questions, use these copy masters:

**R** RESOURCE MANAGER—Copy Masters
Reading Check p. 28
Foreshadowing p. 21
Question Support p. 29

Additional selection questions are provided for teachers on page 15.

**ANSWERS**

## Comprehension

1. *He steps off the Path and kills a butterfly.*
2. *He thinks that there is a different "feel" to this world. The language on the company's sign has changed, and Deutscher, not Keith, has won the presidential election.*
3. *Travis shooting Eckels.*

## Text Analysis

COMMON CORE RL 1, RL 5

***Possible answers:***

4. *Its practices are corrupt; it bribes government officials in order to operate.*
5. *He blames Eckels for altering the future.*
6. ■ **COMMON CORE FOCUS** ***Understand Sequence*** *Before the safari, Eckels had a chance to back out (lines 50–55). During the safari, Eckels could have returned quietly to the Time Machine, as Travis ordered him to do (lines 231–232). Also, Travis could have had someone escort Eckels back to the ship to avoid any problems.*
7. ● **COMMON CORE FOCUS** ***Interpret Foreshadowing***
   ***Foreshadowing:*** *"We're lucky. If Deutscher had gotten in, we'd have the worst kind of dictatorship" (lines 38–39).* ***Outcome:*** *Deutscher wins.*

   ***Foreshadowing:*** *"A little error here would multiply in sixty million years, all out of proportion" (lines 134–135).* ***Outcome:*** *Killing a butterfly changes the future.*

   ***Foreshadowing:*** *"I'm warning you, Eckels, I might kill you yet" (line 351).* ***Outcome:*** *Travis shoots Eckels.*

   *Students may cite a feeling of suspense due to the expectations created by foreshadowing.*
8. ***Believable:*** *Such "scientific" details as the construction of the antigravity Path and the careful marking of specific dinosaurs with red paint add to the believability.* ***Not believable:*** *The paradoxes of time travel (for example, lines 162–172) make the basic premise less believable. Also, the idea that nothing was disturbed on previous safaris is hard to believe.*

## Text Criticism

***Possible answer:***

9. *"Each lower leg was a piston . . . thick ropes of muscle. . . . steel mesh. . . . teeth like daggers. . . . pelvic bones crushing aside trees" (lines 209–218).*

**Would you visit the PAST if you could?** Students might consider the specific event they wish to revisit and consider how a change in that event could affect the present.

---

*After Reading*

## Comprehension

COMMON CORE
**RL 1** Cite textual evidence to support analysis of what the text says explicitly as well as inferences drawn from the text.
**RL 5** Analyze how an author's choices concerning how to structure a text, order events within it, and manipulate time create tension.

1. **Recall** What does Eckels do in the past that has far-reaching consequences?
2. **Summarize** When Eckels returns from the world of dinosaurs, what is different about the present?
3. **Clarify** What is the "sound of thunder" at the end of the story?

## Text Analysis

4. **Make Inferences** How would you characterize the business practices of Time Safari, Inc.? What evidence from the text supports your inference?
5. **Draw Conclusions** Why does Travis kill Eckels? Explain your answer.
6. ■ **Understand Sequence** Look again at the chart you filled out as you read. Determine two points in the story where a character could have taken an action that might have prevented changing the future.
7. ● **Interpret Foreshadowing** Note three or four examples of foreshadowing in the story and the outcome of each example. Make a chart like the one below to record your results. An example has been filled in for you.

| Foreshadowing | Outcome |
|---|---|
| "If you disobey instructions . . ." | Eckels steps off the Path. |

   How did these instances of foreshadowing—or their outcomes—affect your reading experience?
8. **Evaluate Author** "A Sound of Thunder" is a work of science fiction, yet there are realistic aspects to the story. In your opinion, has Bradbury created a believable story? Cite specific examples to support your opinion.

## Text Criticism

9. **Critical Interpretations** In a review of *Dinosaur Tales*, a collection of Bradbury stories that contains "A Sound of Thunder," the critic Andrew Andrews remarked that Bradbury "gets to you—in simple ways he shows you how to marvel over these awesome, startling creatures." Reread Bradbury's description of *Tyrannosaurus rex*. What words and phrases convey its terrifying force?

**Would you visit the PAST if you could?**
What potential consequences might influence your decision?

52 UNIT 1: NARRATIVE STRUCTURE

# Vocabulary in Context

## ▲ VOCABULARY PRACTICE

Answer the questions to show your understanding of the vocabulary words.

1. Which is more **expendable** in a jungle, a book or bug repellent?
2. Which is probably **stagnating**, a weed-filled pond or a flowing stream?
3. If I **correlate** information, do I throw it out or see how it fits together?
4. Would a **malfunctioning** phone never ring or have two choices of ring?
5. If a change happens **infinitesimally,** is it easy or difficult to detect?
6. What makes a person's body more **resilient,** exercising or reading?
7. Which might **annihilate** a bird species, a severe virus or a tasty plant?
8. Is a **subliminal** response an unconscious memory or a prepared speech?
9. Would ocean waves or broken glass be more likely to **undulate?**
10. Which is a **paradox,** a rose's blooming in snow or a tree's budding in spring?

**WORD LIST**

annihilate
correlate
expendable
infinitesimally
malfunctioning
paradox
resilient
stagnating
subliminal
undulate

## ACADEMIC VOCABULARY IN SPEAKING

- analyze - element - infer - sequence - structure

Is it possible to **infer** exactly how Eckels's actions in the past lead to their effects in the present? Discuss your thoughts with a classmate. Use at least one Academic Vocabulary word as you support your opinion.

## VOCABULARY STRATEGY: THE LATIN WORD ROOT *mal*

The vocabulary word *malfunctioning* contains the Latin root *mal,* meaning "bad" or "wrongly." You'll encounter *mal* in many contexts—in terms related to health, for instance, such as *malnourished* and *malady.* When *mal* is used as a prefix with English base words, as in *malnourished,* you can easily figure out meanings. To understand other words containing *mal,* you may need to use context clues in addition to your knowledge of the root.

**PRACTICE** Use the meaning of *mal,* along with context clues, to figure out the meanings of the underlined words.

1. In his speech, the candidate <u>maligned</u> his opponents.
2. She was grateful that the tumor on her spine was not <u>malignant</u>.
3. Anyone who complains as much as he must be a <u>malcontent</u>.
4. We now know that <u>malaria</u> is spread by mosquitoes, not through the air.

**COMMON CORE**

**L 4a** Use context as a clue to the meaning of a word.

**Interactive Vocabulary** THINK central

Go to **thinkcentral.com**.
KEYWORD: HML9-53

A SOUND OF THUNDER  **53**

---

## DIFFERENTIATED INSTRUCTION

### FOR ENGLISH LANGUAGE LEARNERS

**Vocabulary: Cognates** Point out that the Spanish cognate *función* is similar to the English word *function* in the vocabulary word *malfunctioning.* Encourage students who speak Latin-based languages to search for and explain five words in the story similar to those in their language. Have the students compare the similarities in their languages.

### FOR ADVANCED LEARNERS/PRE–AP

**Vocabulary in Writing** Have students use at least three vocabulary words in a paragraph written in the first person from the point of view of one of the characters.

---

## ANSWERS

# Vocabulary in Context

## ▲ VOCABULARY PRACTICE

1. *a book*
2. *a weed-filled pond*
3. *see how it fits together*
4. *never ring*
5. *difficult to detect*
6. *exercising*
7. *a severe virus*
8. *an unconscious memory*
9. *ocean waves*
10. *a rose's blooming in snow*

**R** RESOURCE MANAGER—Copy Master
Vocabulary Practice p. 26

## ACADEMIC VOCABULARY IN SPEAKING

Suggest that students consider how many changes had to have occurred in sixty million years.

🧰 BEST PRACTICES TOOLKIT—Transparency
Timeline p. B23

## VOCABULARY STRATEGY: THE LATIN WORD ROOT *mal*
**COMMON CORE L 4a**

- For each item, help students use their knowledge of the root and context clues to determine word meaning.

- Point out that in item 3, *mal* is used as a pre-fix, just as it is in *malfunction* and *maltreat.* Students will more easily be able to figure out the meaning of the word.

*Possible answers:*
1. *said bad things about; A candidate might say bad things about an opponent.*
2. *harmful; A person would be grateful that a tumor was not harmful.*
3. *an unhappy person; Someone who complains a lot is not happy.*
4. *a disease; Some diseases are spread through the air and others through insect bites.*

**R** RESOURCE MANAGER—Copy Master
Vocabulary Strategy p. 27

**Interactive Vocabulary** THINK central

Keywords direct students to a **WordSharp** tutorial on **thinkcentral.com** or to other types of vocabulary practice and review.

# Language

◆ **GRAMMAR AND STYLE**

- After students examine the student model, list common contractions on the board.

- Write this dialogue on the board. Have students suggest revisions to make the dialogue sound more natural.

> "I ~~cannot~~ can't believe ~~that~~ you did that," cried the man behind the desk. "~~I think that you have~~ You've lost your mind!"
>
> "~~Do not~~ Don't tell anyone what happened," Travis said.
>
> "~~There is no possible way~~ It's impossible to keep something like this quiet. ~~You have~~ You've crossed a line here, Travis."

**R** **RESOURCE MANAGER—Copy Master**
Use Realistic Dialogue p.30

**READING-WRITING CONNECTION**

- Encourage students to reread lines 400–402 to get a feel for the attitude of the man behind the desk. Point out that the other two hunters are also present, though Bradbury has not developed them.

---

**Writing Online** **THINK** central

The following tools are available online at **thinkcentral.com** and on **Write*Smart* CD-ROM**:
- Interactive Graphic Organizers
- Interactive Student Models
- Interactive Revision Lessons

For additional grammar instruction, see **GrammarNotes** on **thinkcentral.com**.

---

# Assess and Reteach

## Assess

**DIAGNOSTIC AND SELECTION TESTS**
    Selection Test A pp. 23–24
    Selection Test B/C pp. 25–26

**Interactive Selection Test on thinkcentral.com**

## Reteach

**Level Up Online Tutorials on thinkcentral.com**

---

# Language

◆ **GRAMMAR AND STYLE: Use Realistic Dialogue**

◯ **COMMON CORE**

**L 3** Apply knowledge of language to make effective choices for meaning or style. **W 3b** Use dialogue to develop experiences, events, and characters.

Review the **Grammar and Style** note on page 44. Bradbury successfully crafts his dialogue by using the following techniques:

1. **Sentence fragments** Although seldom used in formal writing, sentence fragments are common in everyday conversation.

2. **Contractions** Using contractions, like *I've, we'll, hasn't,* and *don't,* makes dialogue sound less formal and more natural. Here is an example from the story:

> "A Tyrannosaurus rex. *The Tyrant Lizard, the most incredible monster in history. Sign this release. Anything happens to you, we're not responsible. Those dinosaurs are hungry."*
>
> *Eckels flushed angrily. "Trying to scare me!"* (lines 46–49)

Notice how the revisions in blue make this dialogue sound realistic. Revise your response to the prompt below by using similar techniques.

---

**STUDENT MODEL**

"Why ~~did~~ you do that? Have you lost your mind?" Lesperance cried.

"~~He was a~~ simpering idiot. ~~He~~ ruined it for all of us. The world ~~is~~ better off without him," Travis shot back.

---

**READING-WRITING CONNECTION**

 Broaden your understanding of "A Sound of Thunder" by responding to this prompt. Then use the **revising tip** to improve your writing.

| **WRITING PROMPT** | **REVISING TIP** |
|---|---|
| **Extended Constructed Response: Dialogue** What might the characters say to one another after the shooting of Eckels? Using Bradbury's style of dialogue as a model, write **one page** of dialogue to show how the characters react to the main incident in the story and its consequences. | Review your response. Did you use informal, conversational language? Consider adding sentence fragments or contractions to make the dialogue more realistic. |

**Interactive Revision** **THINK** central

Go to **thinkcentral.com**.
KEYWORD: HML9-54

---

## DIFFERENTIATED INSTRUCTION

**FOR STRUGGLING WRITERS**

- List the characters that might speak.

- Help students write one sentence in which Travis explains why he shot Eckels.

- Help students write one sentence that would require Travis to make that statement and one sentence that someone would say in response to that statement.

- Suggest that students organize their dialogue in this way:

**Beginning:** Everyone expresses shock and demands an explanation.
**Middle:** Travis defends his action.
**Close:** The others decide what they will do.

## Magazine Article

Will it ever be possible to vacation in the past? And if so, would the fate of a prehistoric butterfly really determine the course of a civilization? Questions like this have been the subject of debate among physicists.

From Here to There:
## The Physics of TIME TRAVEL
Brad Stone

TIME TRAVEL—it's the dream of every science-fiction hack who's ever picked up a pen, and the fantasy of many of the rest of us, too. How wonderful to go back and right the wrongs of the past! But time travel could also let you go back and cause an accident that kills your great-great-grandfather, negating your own existence and provoking a potentially universe-ending paradox. At least that's what armchair temporal theorists worry about. But not Paul Nahin. He's a professor of electrical engineering at the University of New Hampshire and the author of *Time Machines: Time Travel in Physics, Metaphysics, and Science Fiction.* And he's able to translate into plain English an ongoing, esoteric debate between some of the smartest minds in physics over whether time travel is actually possible. "The laws of physics as we know them now don't disallow time travel," explains the 57-year-old Nahin. "Anything that physics doesn't forbid must be considered."

Scientific consideration of time travel has its roots, with much of modern physics, in the genius of Albert Einstein, who married space and time in his theory of relativity. Doing further work on relativity in 1948, mathematician Kurt Gödel declared that it would actually be possible to travel through time under the right conditions. Serious scientists didn't give the matter much thought until the mid-'80s, when Carl Sagan's novel *Contact* sent its heroine on a journey through space-time via a wormhole (a theoretical hyperspace tunnel connecting two points of the universe). That intrigued researchers at Caltech, who three years later released a groundbreaking report on the plausibility of traveling through wormholes.

British physicist Stephen Hawking has been the most prominent skeptic, hypothesizing that any attempt at time travel would lead to a "back reaction," a massive buildup of energy that would rip space apart. His theory is called the Chronology Protection Conjecture, since it would make history safe from explorers who might meddle in important historical events. The best evidence against time travel, according to Hawking's writings, is that "we have not been invaded by hordes of tourists from the future."

Other physicists, hoping to prove that time travel is theoretically possible, have devised on paper four different ways to do it. But all require unrealistic quantities of energy under hugely improbable conditions.

Each proposal has supporters and detractors. But the one thing that physicists don't waste much time on is the paradoxes—like altering the present by killing someone in the past. Nahin says time-travel paradoxes are "manifestations of imperfect understanding." So whatever the resolution of the time-travel debate, rest assured that your great-great-grandpa is safe.

THE PHYSICS OF TIME TRAVEL  **55**

---

## Magazine Article

Lead a discussion with students about the possibility of time travel. Tell students to choose whether they think it will or will not be possible to someday travel through time and why. Have students use the information on time travel from "A Sound of Thunder" in their arguments.

### READING FOR INFORMATION

Point out that "From Here to There: The Physics of Time Travel" is a magazine article.

- Ask students how magazine and newspaper articles are alike and how they differ. ***Possible answer:*** *Both kinds of articles provide facts, but magazine articles are written to entertain as well as to inform. In addition, most newspaper articles are meant to provide the key facts about immediate events, whereas many magazine articles go into greater depth or have a slower pace.*

- After students have read the article, discuss how they can tell that it is more of a "popular science" article than a "hard science" article. ***Possible answer:*** *It is not overly technical; it explains the topic so that a wide range of readers can understand it.*

### TIERED DISCUSSION PROMPTS

Use these prompts to help students consider the feasibility of time travel:

**Connect** How did reading this article affect your appreciation of "A Sound of Thunder"? *Accept all reasonable answers.*

**Analyze** According to this article, what has been the ultimate contribution (so far) to the idea that time travel is possible? Explain. ***Possible answer:*** *So far, the greatest contribution has been the theory of wormholes; if the theory about them is correct, wormholes could provide "tunnels" through which people could travel through time.*

**Synthesize** Suppose that Professor Nahin proved to be correct and that time travel posed no danger of altering events. To what extent would a company such as Time Safari, Inc., benefit from safe time travel? ***Possible answer:*** *Time travel probably would become wildly popular, and such a company would be much in demand. However, competing companies also would spring up as time travel became big business.*

# Practice and Apply

### COMMON CORE FOCUS

**RL 7** Analyze the representation of a subject in two different artistic mediums.

## Movie Poster

Have students study the movie poster and think about where the time traveler might be. Remind students that in "A Sound of Thunder," Eckels changed the present by killing a butterfly. Ask: What change in the past, present, or future might have caused humans to look like the creatures in the movie poster?

### ANALYZE VISUALS    COMMON CORE   RL 7

#### 1. ANALYZE DETAILS

*Possible answer:* *The setting looks like a scary future world in which menacing creatures live underground.*

### ANALYZE VISUALS    COMMON CORE   RL 7

#### 2. INFER

*Possible answer:* *Based on the text and image in the poster, somebody in* The Time Machine *travels into the future. In "A Sound of Thunder," the main character travels into the past.*

### ANALYZE VISUALS    COMMON CORE   RL 7

#### 3. EVALUATE

*Answers will vary.*

---

## Movie Poster

*The Time Machine* by H. G. Wells inspired both fiction writers and scientists to consider the possibility of time travel. This book has also been adapted into feature films, such as the 1960 movie advertised in the poster below. For more on the book *The Time Machine*, see Background to the Story on page 37.

**COMMON CORE**

**RL 7** Analyze the representation of a subject in two different artistic mediums.

1. **ANALYZE DETAILS**
   How would you describe the setting that this movie poster depicts?

2. **INFER**
   Consider both the text and the main image on the poster. In what key way is *The Time Machine* probably different from "A Sound of Thunder"?

3. **EVALUATE**
   Does this poster capture your interest? Would it be effective in persuading you to see *The Time Machine*? Explain.

## Assessment Practice: Short Constructed Response

### LITERARY TEXT: "A SOUND OF THUNDER"

Assessments often require you to form clear, reasonable ideas about a text and support them with evidence. To strengthen your critical-reading skills, answer the **short constructed response** question below. The strategies on the right will help you craft a strong response.

> What theme, or message, is Bradbury conveying through "A Sound of Thunder"? Support your answer with evidence from the story.

◀ **STRATEGIES IN ACTION**

1. A **theme** is a general statement about life that you can **infer** from a literary work. Begin your response with a clear statement of the story's main theme.

2. Evidence can take the form of a direct quotation, a paraphrase, or a specific synopsis. For a question that applies to an entire literary work, consider using a specific **synopsis**, a brief summary of certain events in the story, as evidence.

### NONFICTION TEXT: "FROM HERE TO THERE"

Writers of nonfiction texts use specific organizational patterns, such as cause and effect, problem-solution, and comparison-contrast, to communicate their ideas. Consider a text's organization when drawing conclusions about the text's meaning. The strategies below will help you practice this skill as you answer a **short constructed response** question.

> What is the purpose of "From Here to There: The Physics of Time Travel"? Support your answer with evidence from the article.

◀ **STRATEGIES IN ACTION**

1. Reread the article, and note what the writer is **comparing** and **contrasting**.

2. State the article's major purpose (or purposes) and include relevant evidence to support your statement.

### COMPARING LITERARY AND NONFICTION TEXTS

Tests often require you to synthesize the ideas expressed in multiple texts. Practice this valuable skill by applying the following **short constructed response** question to "A Sound of Thunder" and "From Here to There: The Physics of Time Travel."

> Suppose "A Sound of Thunder" were a true story. Whose theories in the magazine article would its plot contradict? Support your answer with evidence from both texts.

◀ **STRATEGIES IN ACTION**

1. Note that you need to offer evidence from both texts to support your answer.

2. Make sure that the connection between your answer and the evidence you give from each text is clear.

## Assessment Practice: Short Constructed Response

*LITERARY TEXT: "A SOUND OF THUNDER"*
***Possible answer:*** *Bradbury is conveying the theme that small actions can have very large, and sometimes, unforeseen consequences. This theme is shown by the changes in the future caused by the simple, and small, action of killing a butterfly.*

*NONFICTION TEXT: "FROM HERE TO THERE"*
***Possible answer:*** *The purpose of "From Here to There: The Physics of Time Travel" is to present opposing viewpoints on the topic of time travel. The author presents the views of Paul Nahin, who believes time travel is possible, and Stephen Hawking, who is skeptical of time travel.*

*COMPARING LITERARY AND NONFICTION TEXTS* ***Possible answer:*** *The plot of "A Sound of Thunder" would contradict the theories of Stephen Hawking. Hawking believes that traveling through time would build up "energy that would rip space apart." However, this did not happen in the story, as the group of travelers traveled back in time to the past, killed a dinosaur, and then traveled back to the future. The only effect of their visit was caused by the dead butterfly from the past.*

### DIFFERENTIATED INSTRUCTION

#### FOR STRUGGLING WRITERS

**Analyze the Short Constructed Response Question** Explain to students that in order to address the short constructed response question, students must first make a connection between the two selections. Tell students that the question asks students to pick the theories in the magazine article that would contradict with "A Sound of Thunder" if it were a true story. Explain that this means students should look at the theories in the magazine article to see which of them are discussed or used in the story. This will allow students to connect the ideas in the magazine article to the story and subsequently answer the question.

# Focus and Motivate

## COMMON CORE FOCUS

**RL 4** Analyze the cumulative impact of specific word choices on meaning and tone. **RL 5** Analyze how an author's choices concerning how to structure a text, order events within it, and manipulate time create such effects as mystery, tension, or surprise. **L 1b** Use prepositional phrases to convey meanings and add variety and interest to writing. **L 4** Determine the meaning of unknown or multiple-meaning words. **L 5b** Analyze nuances in the meaning of words with similar denotations.

## SUMMARY

Hunter Sanger Rainsford becomes stranded on an island where he seeks the help of General Zaroff. Zaroff forces Rainsford to become his quarry in a hunt to the death.

## What does it take to be a SURVIVOR?

Introduce the question, and discuss the words *survivor* and *survival*. Ask students whether mental or physical strength contributes more to survival. Why? After students complete the *DISCUSS* activity, have them compare their lists and rankings.

---

### Essential Course of Study **ECOS** — The Most Dangerous Game
Short Story by Richard Connell

VIDEO TRAILER **THINK** central   KEYWORD: HML9-58

# What does it take to be a SURVIVOR?

**COMMON CORE**

**RL 4** Analyze the cumulative impact of specific word choices on meaning and tone. **RL 5** Analyze how an author's choices concerning how to structure a text, order events within it, and manipulate time create such effects as mystery, tension, or surprise. **L 4** Determine the meaning of unknown or multiple-meaning words.

In a test of survival, what traits enable a person to succeed? That's the question posed in "The Most Dangerous Game," an adventure story that has thrilled readers since it was first published.

*DISCUSS* Brainstorm in a group to identify a situation that could be a test of survival. This could be as dramatic as a raging flood or as personal as losing a parent. Discuss the qualities and abilities that a person would need to meet the test, and provide reasons for each choice. Then list all the traits you generated and rank the top four, placing them in a diagram like the one shown.

*Traits of a Survivor*

1. resourcefulness   3.

Survivor (a flood)

2. intelligence   4.

58

---

## Selection Resources

*See resources on the **Teacher One Stop DVD-ROM** and on **thinkcentral.com**.*

 **RESOURCE MANAGER UNIT 1**
- Plan and Teach, pp. 35–42
- Summary, pp. 43–44†‡*
- Text Analysis and Reading Skill, pp. 45–48†*
- Vocabulary, pp. 49–51*
- Grammar and Style, p. 54

**DIAGNOSTIC AND SELECTION TESTS**
- Selection Tests, pp. 27–30

 **BEST PRACTICES TOOLKIT**
pp. A10, E6, A13, E8, A25, A35, E10, B6

**INTERACTIVE READER**

**ADAPTED INTERACTIVE READER**

**ELL ADAPTED INTERACTIVE READER**

**TECHNOLOGY**
- Teacher One Stop DVD-ROM
- Student One Stop DVD-ROM
- PowerNotes DVD-ROM
- Audio Anthology CD
- GrammarNotes DVD-ROM
- Audio Tutor CD
- ExamView Test Generator on the Teacher One Stop

 **Video Trailer**

Go to **thinkcentral.com** to preview the **Video Trailer** introducing this selection. Other features that support the selection include
- **PowerNotes** presentation
- **ThinkAloud** models to enhance comprehension
- **WordSharp** vocabulary tutorials
- interactive writing and grammar instruction

---

\* Resources for Differentiation       † Also in Spanish       ‡ In Haitian Creole and Vietnamese

## ● TEXT ANALYSIS: CONFLICT

In the **rising action** of a story, a writer generally introduces one or more **conflicts** that the main character faces. As the rising action unfolds, complications arise that intensify the conflicts and add to the reader's sense of suspense. Plot events, however, are not always as linear—or directly chronological—as this model might suggest. Devices such as foreshadowing, flashbacks, and flash-forwards can further heighten the reader's suspense as the conflict and **tension** build. As you read "The Most Dangerous Game," identify the conflicts the main character faces and note any complications that arise.

## ● READING STRATEGY: VISUALIZE

Good readers constantly **visualize,** or use details in a story to form sensory images of the settings, characters, and events. In this story, for example, Connell's specific word choices help create an image of a dangerous island where strange things happen. As you read, practice the strategy of visualizing. Use a chart like the one shown to record story details that form sensory images for you.

| Details from Story | What I Visualize |
|---|---|
| Dank tropical night … thick warm blackness | The dark, heavy air is almost like a blanket. |

**Review: Predict**

## ▲ VOCABULARY IN CONTEXT

Use the context to help you figure out the meaning of each boldfaced word below.

1. real and **tangible**
2. the hunter's **quarry**
3. put at ease by his **disarming** smile
4. a charming, **cultivated** woman
5. a cruise ship offering every **amenity**
6. **condone** rather than condemn
7. a **droll,** self-mocking grin
8. felt no **scruples** about breaking traffic laws
9. asked **solicitously** about my health
10. recommended but not **imperative**
11. **zealous** support of the mayor's program
12. an **uncanny** coincidence

 Complete the activities in your **Reader/Writer Notebook.**

---

## Meet the Author

# Richard Connell
### 1893–1949

### A Writing Life
Even as a young boy, Richard Connell loved to write. When he was only 10 years old, he covered baseball games for his father's daily newspaper in Poughkeepsie, New York. By 16, Connell was city editor for the same newspaper. After graduating from Harvard and serving in World War I, Connell wrote more than 300 short stories, as well as novels and screenplays. Many of his short stories became successful films. Connell's success enabled him to travel the world and then settle comfortably in Beverly Hills, California, on the opposite side of the country from his previous hometown of Poughkeepsie.

### One-Story Legacy
Although Connell became a prosperous writer during his lifetime, only one of his stories—"The Most Dangerous Game"—is widely read today. It won the O. Henry Memorial Prize in 1924. Because of its action-packed and suspenseful plot, it remains a popular and frequently anthologized work.

### BACKGROUND TO THE STORY
**Big-Game Hunting**
Hunting for big game, such as lions, rhinos, and leopards, was a popular sport among wealthy people in the early 20th century. These people had time and money to spend on travel and on satisfying their thirst for conquest, danger, and excitement. The two main characters in "The Most Dangerous Game" are experienced hunters in search of a greater challenge.

**Author Online**
**THINK** central
Go to **thinkcentral.com.**
KEYWORD: HML9-59

**59**

---

# Teach

TEXT ANALYSIS    COMMON CORE   RL 5

## ● *Model the Skill:* CONFLICT

To model how to identify conflict, read aloud this example:

> The refugee could get on the boat, or she could return to a life of hiding at home. Some people who had taken boats before had been lost at sea.

Point out that the conflict the refugee faces is whether to take the boat or return to hiding. Explain that the complication in this choice is that she faces either death or losing her freedom.

**GUIDED PRACTICE** Ask students to name conflicts in a story or movie.

READING STRATEGY    COMMON CORE   RL 4

## ■ *Model the Skill:* VISUALIZE

Ask students to close their eyes and picture a dangerous tropical island. Have students sketch and describe what they imagine.

**GUIDED PRACTICE** Have students use background details to visualize a scene with wealthy hunters in the early 20th century.

**R** **RESOURCE MANAGER**—Copy Master
Visualize p. 47 (for student use while reading the selection)

---

VOCABULARY SKILL    COMMON CORE   L 4

## ▲ VOCABULARY IN CONTEXT

**DIAGNOSE WORD KNOWLEDGE** Have all students complete Vocabulary in Context. Check their definitions against the following:

**amenity** (ə-mĕn′ĭ-tē) *n.* something that adds to one's comfort or convenience

**condone** (kən-dōn′) *v.* to forgive or overlook

**cultivated** (kŭl′tə-vā′tĭd) *adj.* refined or cultured in manner

**disarming** (dĭs-är′mĭng) *adj.* removing or overcoming suspicion; inspiring confidence

**droll** (drōl) *adj.* amusingly odd or comical

**imperative** (ĭm-pĕr′ə-tĭv) *adj.* absolutely necessary

**quarry** (kwôr′ē) *n.* the object of a hunt; prey

**scruple** (skrōō′pəl) *n.* a feeling of uneasiness that keeps a person from doing something

**solicitously** (sə-lĭs′ĭ-təs-lē) *adv.* in a manner expressing care or concern

**tangible** (tăn′jə-bəl) *adj.* capable of being touched or felt; having actual form and substance

**uncanny** (ŭn-kăn′ē) *adj.* so remarkable as to seem supernatural

**zealous** (zĕl′əs) *adj.* intensely enthusiastic

**PRETEACH VOCABULARY** Use the copy master to help students predict meanings.

**R** **RESOURCE MANAGER**—Copy Master
Vocabulary Study p. 49

**READ WITH A PURPOSE**

*Help students set a purpose for reading. Tell them to read "The Most Dangerous Game" to find out what one hunter thinks is the most dangerous game.*

# The Most Dangerous Game

## Richard Connell

"Off there to the right—somewhere—is a large island," said Whitney. "It's rather a mystery—"

"What island is it?" Rainsford asked.

"The old charts call it 'Ship-Trap Island,'" Whitney replied. "A suggestive name, isn't it? Sailors have a curious dread of the place. I don't know why. Some superstition—"

"Can't see it," remarked Rainsford, trying to peer through the dank tropical night that was palpable as it pressed its thick warm blackness in upon the yacht.

10 "You've good eyes," said Whitney, with a laugh, "and I've seen you pick off a moose moving in the brown fall bush at four hundred yards, but even you can't see four miles or so through a moonless Caribbean night."

"Nor four yards," admitted Rainsford. "Ugh! It's like moist black velvet."

"It will be light enough in Rio,"[1] promised Whitney. "We should make it in a few days. I hope the jaguar guns have come from Purdey's. We should have some good hunting up the Amazon. Great sport, hunting."

"The best sport in the world," agreed Rainsford.

"For the hunter," amended Whitney. "Not for the jaguar."

"Don't talk rot, Whitney," said Rainsford. "You're a big-game hunter, not a philosopher. Who cares how a jaguar feels?"

20 "Perhaps the jaguar does," observed Whitney.

"Bah! They've no understanding." (A)

**Analyze Visuals ▶**

What **mood** does the photo stir in you? Decide which details work to evoke this feeling.

**①** Targeted Passage

**Ⓐ** CONFLICT
Reread lines 16–21. What can you conclude about Rainsford from his conflict with Whitney?

---

1. **Rio:** Rio de Janeiro (rē'ō dā zhə-nâr'ō), a city on the coast of Brazil.

**60** UNIT 1: NARRATIVE STRUCTURE

---

**TEXT ANALYSIS**
COMMON CORE
RL 5

**Ⓐ CONFLICT**

*Possible answer: Rainsford's unfeeling remarks about wildlife reveal his uncaring and arrogant attitude.*

**IF STUDENTS NEED HELP . . .** Have two volunteers read the dialogue aloud, with expression. Then ask these questions:

- How does Rainsford refer to what Whitney has said? *Possible answer: He calls it "rot" (line 18) and says, "Bah!" (line 21).*

- What tone do you hear in Rainsford's voice? *Possible answer: arrogance*

- How sure is Rainsford about his opinions? *Possible answer: quite confident*

**Extend the Discussion** Do you agree with Rainsford that an animal has no feelings or understanding? Explain.

---

## DIFFERENTIATED INSTRUCTION

### FOR ENGLISH LANGUAGE LEARNERS

**Options for Reading** Have students preview the pictures and make predictions about what the story will be about. Then cover the story in sections, asking a question about a half-page or more of text and then having pairs of students scan the section for the answer.

### FOR STRUGGLING READERS

In combination with the *Audio Anthology CD*, use one or more Targeted Passages (pp. 60, 63, 68, 74, 77, 80) to ensure that students focus on key story events, concepts, and skills. Targeted Passages are also good for English learners.

**①** Targeted Passage [Lines 3–21]

This passage introduces several expository details relating to characters, setting, and atmosphere.

**Reading Support**

This selection on **thinkcentral.com** includes embedded **ThinkAloud** models—students "thinking aloud" about the story to model the kinds of questions a good reader would ask about a selection.

## BACKGROUND

**Big-Game Hunting**  In the early years of the 20th century, big-game hunting was a popular sport among the upper classes.  Those who could afford the expense traveled to exotic climes such as Burma (now called Myanmar), Malaysia, India, and various parts of North and South America.  Notice how on page 68, an avid hunter lists a series of particularly popular "trophy" animals—the Cape buffalo, an Amazonian jaguar, an Indian crocodile, an American grizzly bear and an African rhinoceros.  These animals were killed for their coats or skins, or to have their heads preserved as trophies of the hunt.  All of the species mentioned on that page are now endangered, some to near extinction.

## Analyze Visuals

*Possible answer:  Despite the blue sky and the greenery, the island does not seem welcoming. The jagged mountains seem inhospitable to human life, the shore seems too small to permit a safe landing, and a deep shadow falls across much of the island.  These details combine to create a rather forbidding mood that contrasts with the calm blue sea and the puffy white clouds.*

- Which characters are speaking? (lines 1–3)
- Where are they as they talk? (lines 7–8)
- What do sailors call the nearby island?  How do they feel about it? (lines 4–6)
- What is the conflict between the two characters? (lines 13–21)

**FOR ADVANCED LEARNERS/PRE–AP**

Before they read the story, ask students: Is it right to hunt just for sport? Why or why not? Have students write down their answers. Tell them to keep the question in mind as they read the story.  After they have finished reading, ask students if they changed their responses and have them explain why.

**REVISIT THE BIG QUESTION**

## What does it take to be a **SURVIVOR?**

**Discuss**  In lines 15–20, at what point does this conversation introduce the idea of survival?
*Possible answer: When the conversation turns to jaguar hunting, the idea of survival is introduced.  For the hunter, it is a great sport; for the jaguar, it is a matter of life or death.*

## B PREDICT

*Possible answer:* Someone or something on the island will put a visitor in a life-or-death situation.

**IF STUDENTS NEED HELP . . .** Use the Predicting chart to help students list details that create a feeling of evil, such as these:

- the sailors' "curious dread" over a superstition (lines 5)
- the comments about fear, death, and "the hunters and the huntees" (lines 22–26)
- the "Godforsaken" place (line 32)
- the "poisonous" air (line 40)

Work with students to make at least one prediction, based on these details.

**Extend the Discussion** How may Rainsford's skepticism make him more vulnerable to the island's "vibrations of evil" (line 50)?

 **BEST PRACTICES TOOLKIT—Transparency** Predicting p. A10

---

## C VISUALIZE

*Possible answer:* Rainsford's nonchalant mood is reflected in the description of him reclining in a steamer chair and puffing indolently on a pipe. Rainsford is not at all frightened by the possible threat from the nearby island. Instead, he is very relaxed—perhaps too much so for someone who prides himself on his quick hunter's reflexes.

---

### OWN THE WORD

**tangible:** Remind students that *tangible* refers to real, concrete things that can be touched or felt. The opposite is *intangible*—concepts or abstracts that do not have substance or form, such as emotions. Have students create a pair of related statements that show how a *tangible* item can be related to an *intangible* concept.

---

"Even so, I rather think they understand one thing—fear. The fear of pain and the fear of death."

"Nonsense," laughed Rainsford. "This hot weather is making you soft, Whitney. Be a realist. The world is made up of two classes—the hunters and the huntees. Luckily, you and I are hunters. Do you think we've passed that island yet?"

"I can't tell in the dark. I hope so."

"Why?" asked Rainsford.

30 "The place has a reputation—a bad one."

"Cannibals?" suggested Rainsford.

"Hardly. Even cannibals wouldn't live in such a Godforsaken place. But it's gotten into sailor lore, somehow. Didn't you notice that the crew's nerves seemed a bit jumpy today?"

"They were a bit strange, now you mention it. Even Captain Nielsen—"

"Yes, even that tough-minded old Swede, who'd go up to the devil himself and ask him for a light. Those fishy blue eyes held a look I never saw there before. All I could get out of him was: 'This place has an evil name among seafaring men, sir.' Then he said to me, very gravely: 'Don't you feel

40 anything?'—as if the air about us was actually poisonous. Now, you mustn't laugh when I tell you this—I did feel something like a sudden chill. **B**

"There was no breeze. The sea was as flat as a plate-glass window. We were drawing near the island then. What I felt was a—a mental chill; a sort of sudden dread."

"Pure imagination," said Rainsford. "One superstitious sailor can taint the whole ship's company with his fear."

"Maybe. But sometimes I think sailors have an extra sense that tells them when they are in danger. Sometimes I think evil is a **tangible** thing—with wavelengths, just as sound and light have. An evil place can, so to speak,

50 broadcast vibrations of evil. Anyhow, I'm glad we're getting out of this zone. Well, I think I'll turn in now, Rainsford."

"I'm not sleepy," said Rainsford. "I'm going to smoke another pipe up on the afterdeck."

"Good night, then, Rainsford. See you at breakfast."

"Right. Good night, Whitney."

There was no sound in the night as Rainsford sat there but the muffled throb of the engine that drove the yacht swiftly through the darkness, and the swish and ripple of the wash of the propeller.

Rainsford, reclining in a steamer chair, indolently puffed on his favorite

60 brier.[2] The sensuous drowsiness of the night was on him. "It's so dark," he thought, "that I could sleep without closing my eyes; the night would be my eyelids— **C**

---

2. **brier** (brī′ər): a tobacco pipe.

---

**B PREDICT**
Reread lines 30–41. Notice that even a hard-boiled sailor is fearful of the island. What do you predict might happen on the island?

**tangible** (tăn′jə-bəl) *adj.* capable of being touched or felt; having actual form and substance

**C VISUALIZE**
Reread lines 59–62, trying to visualize Rainsford. What does the author's description tell you about Rainsford's mood?

---

## DIFFERENTIATED INSTRUCTION

### FOR ADVANCED LEARNERS/PRE-AP

**Evaluate Author's Choices** At line 54, Whitney leaves the story. After students have finished reading the selection, ask them to think about the impact of his brief appearance. Then have them debate this question in small groups: Did Connell need to include Whitney in this story? In their responses, students should demonstrate an understanding of Whitney's personality and attitudes and how they influence the story's plot and ideas (particularly in regard to the nature of the island and the ethics of hunting).

An abrupt sound startled him. Off to the right he heard it, and his ears, expert in such matters, could not be mistaken. Again he heard the sound, and again. Somewhere, off in the blackness, someone had fired a gun three times.

Rainsford sprang up and moved quickly to the rail, mystified. He strained his eyes in the direction from which the reports had come, but it was like trying to see through a blanket. He leaped upon the rail and balanced himself there, to get greater elevation; his pipe, striking a rope, was knocked from his
70  mouth. He lunged for it; a short, hoarse cry came from his lips as he realized he had reached too far and had lost his balance. The cry was pinched off short as the blood-warm waters of the Caribbean Sea closed over his head.

He struggled up to the surface and tried to cry out, but the wash from the speeding yacht slapped him in the face, and the salt water in his open mouth made him gag and strangle. Desperately he struck out with strong strokes after the receding lights of the yacht, but he stopped before he had swum fifty feet. A certain cool-headedness had come to him; it was not the first time he had been in a tight place. There was a chance that his cries could be heard by someone aboard the yacht, but that chance was slender and grew more slender
80  as the yacht raced on. He wrestled himself out of his clothes and shouted with all his power. The lights of the yacht became faint and ever-vanishing fireflies; then they were blotted out entirely by the night. **D**

Rainsford remembered the shots. They had come from the right, and doggedly he swam in that direction, swimming with slow, deliberate strokes, conserving his strength. For a seemingly endless time he fought the sea. He began to count his strokes; he could do possibly a hundred more and then—

Rainsford heard a sound. It came out of the darkness, a high, screaming sound, the sound of an animal in an extremity of anguish and terror.

He did not recognize the animal that made the sound; he did not try to;
90  with fresh vitality he swam toward the sound. He heard it again; then it was cut short by another noise, crisp, staccato.

"Pistol shot," muttered Rainsford, swimming on.

Ten minutes of determined effort brought another sound to his ears—the most welcome he had ever heard—the muttering and growling of the sea breaking on a rocky shore. He was almost on the rocks before he saw them; on a night less calm he would have been shattered against them. With his remaining strength he dragged himself from the swirling waters. Jagged crags appeared to jut up into the opaqueness; he forced himself upward, hand over hand. Gasping, his hands raw, he reached a flat place at the top. Dense jungle
100  came down to the very edge of the cliffs. What perils that tangle of trees and underbrush might hold for him did not concern Rainsford just then. All he knew was that he was safe from his enemy, the sea, and that utter weariness was on him. He flung himself down at the jungle edge and tumbled headlong into the deepest sleep of his life. **E**

---

**② Targeted Passage**

**D CONFLICT**
Here the author builds **tension** by introducing a complication. What do you think will happen next?

COMMON CORE L 4

**Language Coach**

**Multiple Meaning Words** Many English words are **multiple-meaning words**—words with more than one meaning. What is the meaning of the word *extremity* in line 88?
- a limb on a body
- the farthest point
- extreme danger

**E VISUALIZE**
Reread lines 93–104. Which details in this passage help you visualize the scene?

---

**FOR ENGLISH LANGUAGE LEARNERS**

**Language Coach**    COMMON CORE L 4

**Multiple Meaning Words** *Answer: the farthest point;* Have students work in pairs to discuss the other two meanings of the word *extremity.* Then, have pairs use the word *extremity* in three different sentences, one for each of the three meanings. Have student pairs share their sentences.

**FOR STRATEGIC READERS**

**② Targeted Passage [Lines 63–85]**

This passage presents a pivotal event: an accident that throws the self-assured Rainsford into danger and begins the rising action.

- What sound does Rainsford hear? What might this suggest about the island? (lines 63–65)
- How does Rainsford fall overboard? (lines 68–72)
- How does Rainsford react to his situation?

---

TEXT ANALYSIS     COMMON CORE   RL 5

**D CONFLICT**

***Possible answer:** Rainsford will swim to shore.*

**IF STUDENTS NEED HELP . . .** After students reread lines 77–81, ask what words or phrases suggest that Rainsford is determined to survive and come out the winner in this conflict. ***Possible answers:** "cool-headedness," "not the first time he had been in a tight place," "all his power"*

READING STRATEGY     COMMON CORE   RL 4

**E *Model the Skill:* VISUALIZE**

Model for students how to visualize the setting. Point out that before line 93, students learned that the setting is dark, on the sea, and near an island. Have students read lines 93–104 and then describe what they see as if they were Rainsford. Ask students what Rainsford sees as he climbs to the top of the cliff.

***Possible answer:** The "rocky shore" (line 95) and "swirling waters" (line 97) create an overall visual impression of the scene. The "opaqueness" (line 98) conveys the darkness of the night, while the "jagged crags" (line 97), "dense jungle" (line 99), and "tangle of trees and underbrush" (lines 100–101) present a clear picture of the dangerous terrain.*

**Extend the Discussion** How do the details help you realize that even though Rainsford has escaped the sea, he is far from safe?

## F PREDICT

***Possible answer:*** *The men will be as forbidding as the island and as "snarled" and "ragged" as its jungle.*

**IF STUDENTS NEED HELP...** Have them work in pairs to isolate story details from lines 108–110 (in particular, the pistol shots and the characteristics of the land along the shore). Have students consider what they know about story grammar (plot) and their own knowledge to make predictions.

**REVISIT THE BIG QUESTION**

## What does it take to be a SURVIVOR?

**Discuss** In lines 111–128, how does Rainsford demonstrate that he has survival skills?
***Possible answer:*** *He finds evidence, examines it, makes hypotheses, and successfully finds and follows a trail.*

**COMMON CORE**

**RL 4**

## G VISUALIZE

***Possible answer:*** *a scary castle, something out of Frankenstein; The château is not welcoming. Positioned high on steep cliffs with pointed towers and a "spiked iron gate," it is imposing and frightening.*

**IF STUDENTS NEED HELP...**

• Work with them to list specific details from these lines, such as "lofty structure... gloom.... stone steps... massive door... leering gargoyle."

• Ask them to categorize each detail as warm and inviting, neutral, or cold.

**COMMON CORE**

**L 4**

## OWN THE WORD

**quarry:** Tell students that *quarry* has multiple meanings in English. In this scene, *quarry* means an animal that is hunted. *Quarry* can also mean an open excavation or pit from which natural building materials are obtained.

---

When he opened his eyes, he knew from the position of the sun that it was late in the afternoon. Sleep had given him new vigor; a sharp hunger was picking at him. He looked about him, almost cheerfully.

"Where there are pistol shots, there are men. Where there are men, there is food," he thought. But what kind of men, he wondered, in so forbidding a
110 place? An unbroken front of snarled and ragged jungle fringed the shore. **F**

He saw no sign of a trail through the closely knit web of weeds and trees; it was easier to go along the shore, and Rainsford floundered along by the water. Not far from where he had landed, he stopped.

Some wounded thing, by the evidence a large animal, had thrashed about in the underbrush; the jungle weeds were crushed down, and the moss was lacerated; one patch of weeds was stained crimson. A small, glittering object not far away caught Rainsford's eye, and he picked it up. It was an empty cartridge.

"A twenty-two," he remarked. "That's odd. It must have been a fairly large
120 animal, too. The hunter had his nerve with him to tackle it with a light gun. It's clear that the brute put up a fight. I suppose the first three shots I heard was when the hunter flushed his **quarry** and wounded it. The last shot was when he trailed it here and finished it."

He examined the ground closely and found what he had hoped to find—the print of hunting boots. They pointed along the cliff in the direction he had been going. Eagerly he hurried along, now slipping on a rotten log or a loose stone, but making headway; night was beginning to settle down on the island.

Bleak darkness was blacking out the sea and jungle when Rainsford sighted
130 the lights. He came upon them as he turned a crook in the coastline, and his first thought was that he had come upon a village, for there were many lights. But as he forged along, he saw to his great astonishment that all the lights were in one enormous building—a lofty structure with pointed towers plunging upward into the gloom. His eyes made out the shadowy outlines of a palatial château; it was set on a high bluff, and on three sides of it cliffs dived down to where the sea licked greedy lips in the shadows.

"Mirage," thought Rainsford. But it was no mirage, he found, when he opened the tall spiked iron gate. The stone steps were real enough; the massive door with a leering gargoyle for a knocker was real enough; yet about it all
140 hung an air of unreality. **G**

He lifted the knocker, and it creaked up stiffly as if it had never before been used. He let it fall, and it startled him with its booming loudness. He thought he heard steps within; the door remained closed. Again Rainsford lifted the heavy knocker and let it fall. The door opened then, opened as suddenly as if it were on a spring, and Rainsford stood blinking in the river of glaring gold light that poured out. The first thing Rainsford's eyes discerned was the largest man

**F PREDICT**
Answer Rainsford's question. What kind of men do you think Rainsford will encounter on the island?

**quarry** (kwôr′ē) *n.* the object of a hunt; prey

**G VISUALIZE**
Reread lines 129–140. What sensory image comes to mind when you think of the chateau? Does it seem like a warm and welcoming place? Explain.

---

## DIFFERENTIATED INSTRUCTION

**FOR ENGLISH LANGUAGE LEARNERS**
**Vocabulary: Phrasal Verbs** Use Definition Mapping to teach the meanings of these phrasal verbs from the story:

• *pick off* (line 9), "shoot and kill"
• *pinched off* (line 71), "stopped"
• *picking at* (line 107), "bothering"
• *put up* (line 121), "engaged in [an activity]"
• *get about* (lines 463–464), "move"
• *pressed on* (line 615), "continued"

**BEST PRACTICES TOOLKIT—Transparency**
Definition Mapping p. E6

*Castle at Noon*, William Low. © William Low.

Rainsford had ever seen—a gigantic creature, solidly made and black-bearded to the waist. In his hand the man held a long-barreled revolver, and he was pointing it straight at Rainsford's heart.

150   Out of the snarl of beard two small eyes regarded Rainsford.

"Don't be alarmed," said Rainsford, with a smile which he hoped was **disarming**. "I'm no robber. I fell off a yacht. My name is Sanger Rainsford of New York City."

The menacing look in the eyes did not change. The revolver pointed as rigidly as if the giant were a statue. He gave no sign that he understood Rainsford's words, or that he had even heard them. He was dressed in uniform, a black uniform trimmed with gray astrakhan.[3]

"I'm Sanger Rainsford of New York," Rainsford began again. "I fell off a yacht. I am hungry."

160   The man's only answer was to raise with his thumb the hammer of his revolver. Then Rainsford saw the man's free hand go to his forehead in a military salute, and he saw him click his heels together and stand at attention. Another man was coming down the broad marble steps, an erect, slender man in evening clothes. He advanced to Rainsford and held out his hand.

In a **cultivated** voice marked by a slight accent that gave it added precision and deliberateness, he said: "It is a very great pleasure and honor to welcome Mr. Sanger Rainsford, the celebrated hunter, to my home."

**disarming** (dĭs-är′mĭng) *adj.* removing or overcoming suspicion; inspiring confidence

**cultivated** (kŭl′tə-vā′tĭd) *adj.* refined or cultured in manner

---

3. **astrakhan** (ăs′trə-kăn′): a fur made from the curly, wavy wool of young lambs from Astrakhan (a city of southwest Russia).

## FOR STRUGGLING READERS

**Practice Visualizing** Have students sketch Ivan and make inferences based on the details. Suggest that students complete a Making Inferences chart.

📦 **BEST PRACTICES TOOLKIT—Transparency** Making Inferences p. A13

## FOR ENGLISH LANGUAGE LEARNERS

**Vocabulary Support** Use Definition Mapping to teach these words: *uniform* (line 156), *military* (line 162), *ceased* (line 253), *trace* (line 378), *invariably* (line 400), *inevitable* (line 652).

📦 **BEST PRACTICES TOOLKIT—Transparency** Definition Mapping p. E6

## Analyze Visuals

**Activity** Have students compare and contrast the castle in this painting with the "palatial château" that Rainsford first spies in lines 129–140. *Possible answer: Both the château in the story and the castle in the painting are lofty and immense, with pointed towers (line 133). However, the château is depicted as threatening, with a "spiked iron gate" and a "leering gargoyle" as a door knocker (lines 138–139), while the castle seems mysterious but not ominous.*

**About the Art** In *Castle at Noon*, contemporary painter William Low (b. 1959) shows the eerily amputated midsection of the building. The odd presentation suggests that the viewer does not know the castle's entire story, just as Rainsford does not yet know the entire story of the château where he seeks refuge.

## TIERED DISCUSSION PROMPTS

Use these prompts to help students understand how Connell develops character and builds toward the story's central conflict in lines 150–167:

**Connect** Have you or someone you know ever had to "think on your feet" under adverse circumstances? How does that experience help you to understand Rainsford's predicament in this scene? *Possible answer: It can be difficult to stay calm. Rainsford must have nerves of steel, confidence, and great self-control.*

**Synthesize** What is the purpose of this scene? *Possible answer: It creates suspense (lines 160–161), reminds readers that Rainsford is cool and collected under stress (lines 151–153 and 158–159), and shows similarities between Rainsford and the man in evening clothes (lines 165–167).*

### VOCABULARY
COMMON CORE
L 4

### OWN THE WORD

- **disarming:** Have students list people or situations they could describe as *disarming*. *Possible answers: a dog wagging its tail, a smiling child*

- **cultivated:** Tell students that another meaning for *cultivated* is "land prepared and used for growing crops."

**Activity** This photograph, called *Mounted Animals in a Taxidermy Show Room*, presents a variety of hunting prizes that have been preserved for display. Ask students what they think of such a display; for example, does it reflect pride, accomplishment, wealth, cruelty, love of sport, decorating sense, or other values? *Answers will vary, but students should be able to present a reasonable defense of their view.* What does General Zaroff's similar display tell the reader about him? *Possible answers: He enjoys hunting; he is proud of his skill as a hunter; he is obsessed with killing.*

## REVIST THE BIG QUESTION

## What does it take to be a **SURVIVOR?**

**Discuss** In lines 193–201 Zaroff calls Ivan "a bit of a savage" and a "Cossack." But then Zaroff refers to himself as a Cossack. How does this new information about Ivan and Zaroff raise the question of Rainsford's survival and build suspense? *Possible answer: It suggests that, despite his refined manners, Zaroff, too, may be "a bit of a savage." Rainsford's survival may require confronting people with savage tendencies, adopting savage tendencies, or both. The fact that Zaroff may not be as civilized as he first appeared increases tension about what might happen.*

Automatically Rainsford shook the man's hand.

170  "I've read your book about hunting snow leopards in Tibet,[4] you see," explained the man. "I am General Zaroff."

Rainsford's first impression was that the man was singularly handsome; his second was that there was an original, almost bizarre quality about the general's face. He was a tall man past middle age, 180 for his hair was a vivid white; but his thick eyebrows and pointed military moustache were as black as the night from which Rainsford had come. His eyes, too, were black and very bright. He had high cheekbones, a sharp-cut nose, a spare, dark face, the face of a man used to giving orders, the face of an aristocrat. Turning to the giant 190 in uniform, the general made a sign. The giant put away his pistol, saluted, withdrew.

"Ivan is an incredibly strong fellow," remarked the general, "but he has the misfortune to be deaf and dumb. A simple fellow, but, I'm afraid, like all his race, a bit of a savage."

"Is he Russian?"

200  "He is a Cossack,"[5] said the general, and his smile showed red lips and pointed teeth. "So am I.

"Come," he said, "we shouldn't be chatting here. We can talk later. Now you want clothes, food, rest. You shall have them. This is a most restful spot."

Ivan had reappeared, and the general spoke to him with lips that moved but gave forth no sound.

"Follow Ivan, if you please, Mr. Rainsford," said the general. "I was about to have my dinner when you came. I'll wait for you. You'll find that my clothes will fit you, I think."

4. **Tibet** (tə-bĕt′): a region in central Asia.

5. **Cossack** (kŏs′ăk): a member of a southern Russian people, many of whom served as fierce cavalrymen under the Russian tsars.

## DIFFERENTIATED INSTRUCTION

### FOR ENGLISH LANGUAGE LEARNERS

**Vocabulary: Cognates** Point out that the Spanish word *original* is spelled exactly like the English word *original* (line 177) but that it has a slightly different pronunciation. (Call on Spanish-speaking students to help you demonstrate the difference.) Ask pairs of students who speak the same home language to look for five other English words in the story that are similar to words in their home language. Have students share their findings.

**Media and Language** Use a recorded version of "The Most Dangerous Game" or another suspenseful story. Have students listen to the recording and note any unfamiliar words. Ask students to look up the meaning of each word they noted and use it in a sentence about the story.

It was to a huge, beam-ceilinged bedroom with a canopied bed big enough
210 for six men that Rainsford followed the silent giant. Ivan laid out an evening
suit, and Rainsford, as he put it on, noticed that it came from a London tailor
who ordinarily cut and sewed for none below the rank of duke.

The dining room to which Ivan conducted him was in many ways
remarkable. There was a medieval magnificence about it; it suggested a
baronial hall of feudal times with its oaken panels, its high ceiling, its vast
refectory table where two score men could sit down to eat. About the hall were
the mounted heads of many animals—lions, tigers, elephants, moose, bears;
larger or more perfect specimens Rainsford had never seen. At the great table
the general was sitting, alone.

220 "You'll have a cocktail, Mr. Rainsford," he suggested. The cocktail was
surpassingly good; and, Rainsford noted, the table appointments were of the
finest—the linen, the crystal, the silver, the china.

They were eating *borsch*, the rich red soup with whipped cream so dear to
Russian palates. Half apologetically General Zaroff said: "We do our best to
preserve the **amenities** of civilization here. Please forgive any lapses. We are
well off the beaten track, you know. Do you think the champagne has suffered
from its long ocean trip?"

"Not in the least," declared Rainsford. He was finding the general a most
thoughtful and affable host, a true cosmopolite.[6] But there was one small trait
230 of the general's that made Rainsford uncomfortable. Whenever he looked up
from his plate, he found the general studying him, appraising him narrowly.

"Perhaps," said General Zaroff, "you were surprised that I recognized your
name. You see, I read all books on hunting published in English, French, and
Russian. I have but one passion in my life, Mr. Rainsford, and it is the hunt."

"You have some wonderful heads here," said Rainsford as he ate a
particularly well cooked filet mignon. "That Cape buffalo is the largest I
ever saw."

"Oh, that fellow. Yes, he was a monster."

"Did he charge you?"

240 "Hurled me against a tree," said the general. "Fractured my skull. But I got
the brute."

"I've always thought," said Rainsford, "that the Cape buffalo is the most
dangerous of all big game."

For a moment the general did not reply; he was smiling his curious red-
lipped smile. Then he said slowly: "No. You are wrong, sir. The Cape buffalo is
not the most dangerous big game." He sipped his wine. "Here in my preserve
on this island," he said, in the same slow tone, "I hunt more dangerous game."

Rainsford expressed his surprise. "Is there big game on this island?"

The general nodded. "The biggest."

250 "Really?"

"Oh, it isn't here naturally, of course. I have to stock the island."

---

6. **cosmopolite** (kŏz-mŏp′ə-līt′): a sophisticated person who can handle any situation well.

amenity (ə-měn′ĭ-tē)
*n.* something that adds
to one's comfort or
convenience

---

## TIERED DISCUSSION PROMPTS

For lines 209–237, use these prompts to help
students see that Zaroff and Rainsford are
well-matched opponents for playing the "most
dangerous game":

**Connect** Have you or someone you know
ever dined in a highly formal setting? How
comfortable would you feel dining with
Zaroff? *Possible answer: I would feel intimidated by his sophistication and uncomfortable with his finery.*

**Analyze** In what ways are Zaroff and Rainsford alike, based on details in the passage?
*Possible answer: Both men are sophisticated;
both lead privileged lives in which they are
able to assess the quality of upscale things
like silver and champagne.*

**Evaluate** Why does Connell make these two
characters so alike in some ways? *Possible
answers: He is matching them for the contest
or game that lies ahead; he is making a
statement about hunters or about privileged
people who can afford to play games; the
fact that they are alike makes the contest
more exciting.*

---

**VOCABULARY**                    COMMON
CORE
L 4

## OWN THE WORD

**amenity:** Ask students to complete the
following sentence to show an understanding of the noun *amenity. Amenities
that make my day easier include...*
*Possible answers: the toothbrush,
computer, and cell phone.*

---

## FOR ADVANCED LEARNERS/PRE–AP

**Defend an Interpretation** Offer this statement to students: *Zaroff and Rainsford are
essentially the same, but they wear different
cultural clothing.* Challenge students to find
evidence from the story so far that proves
or disproves this interpretation of these two
characters. Ask them to write one or two
paragraphs supporting or challenging this
interpretation. Let the two sides take turns
sharing their writing with the class.

## Ⓗ CONFLICT

**Possible answer:** *The clues—especially Zaroff's comments about being bored by traditional big game—suggest that Zaroff and Rainsford will become involved in an extremely dangerous hunt for a bizarre type of quarry.*

**IF STUDENTS NEED HELP . . .** Use the Making Inferences chart to help students think about details that may signal future events. You might start with these examples:

| Details from Story | + | What I Know from Reading or Experience | = | My Inference |
|---|---|---|---|---|
| "No thrill left in tigers" (line 254) | + | Tigers' only enemies may be people. | = | He might be thinking of hunting people. |
| "I live for danger" (line 255) | + | Danger-seekers take greater and greater risks. | = | He might involve Rainsford in a weird activity. |

**Extend the Discussion** By now, you probably suspect the nature of the upcoming conflict. Why doesn't Rainsford seem to get it?

 **BEST PRACTICES TOOLKIT**—Transparency Making Inferences p. A13

## CULTURAL CONNECTION

***Cossack Heritage*** Zaroff again refers to his Cossack heritage in lines 274–275. The Cossacks, a privileged class, often were called upon for the toughest jobs in the Russian military. They became known for the daring exploits that mark a warrior culture.

---

"What have you imported, General?" Rainsford asked. "Tigers?"

The general smiled. "No," he said. "Hunting tigers ceased to interest me some years ago. I exhausted their possibilities, you see. No thrill left in tigers, no real danger. I live for danger, Mr. Rainsford."

The general took from his pocket a gold cigarette case and offered his guest a long black cigarette with a silver tip; it was perfumed and gave off a smell like incense.

"We will have some capital hunting, you and I," said the general. "I shall be
260 most glad to have your society."

"But what game—" began Rainsford.

"I'll tell you," said the general. "You will be amused, I know. I think I may say, in all modesty, that I have done a rare thing. I have invented a new sensation. May I pour you another glass of port, Mr. Rainsford?"

"Thank you, General." Ⓗ

The general filled both glasses and said: "God makes some men poets. Some he makes kings, some beggars. Me he made a hunter. My hand was made for the trigger, my father said. He was a very rich man with a quarter of a million acres in the Crimea, and he was an ardent sportsman. When I was only five
270 years old, he gave me a little gun, specially made in Moscow for me, to shoot sparrows with. When I shot some of his prize turkeys with it, he did not punish me; he complimented me on my marksmanship. I killed my first bear in the Caucasus[7] when I was ten. My whole life has been one prolonged hunt. I went into the army—it was expected of noblemen's sons—and for a time commanded a division of Cossack cavalry, but my real interest was always the hunt. I have hunted every kind of game in every land. It would be impossible for me to tell you how many animals I have killed."

The general puffed at his cigarette.

"After the debacle in Russia I left the country, for it was imprudent for
280 an officer of the Tsar[8] to stay there. Many noble Russians lost everything. I, luckily, had invested heavily in American securities, so I shall never have to open a tearoom in Monte Carlo or drive a taxi in Paris. Naturally, I continued to hunt—grizzlies in your Rockies, crocodiles in the Ganges,[9] rhinoceroses in East Africa. It was in Africa that the Cape buffalo hit me and laid me up for six months. As soon as I recovered, I started for the Amazon to hunt jaguars, for I had heard they were unusually cunning. They weren't." The Cossack sighed. "They were no match at all for a hunter with his wits about him, and a high-powered rifle. I was bitterly disappointed. I was lying in my tent with a splitting headache one night when a terrible thought pushed its way into my

---

7. **Crimea** (krī-mē′ə) . . . **Caucasus** (kô′kə-səs): regions in the southern part of the former Russian Empire, near the Black Sea.

8. **debacle in Russia . . . Tsar** (zär): a reference to the 1917 Russian Revolution, in which the emperor, Tsar Nicholas II, was violently overthrown.

9. **Ganges** (găn′jēz′): a river in northern India.

## Ⓗ CONFLICT
Reread lines 228–265. The conversation between Rainsford and Zaroff hints at further plot **complications**. Use clues to predict future events.

### ❸ Targeted Passage

COMMON CORE L 4b

**Language Coach**

**Suffixes** Adding a **suffix** to a word creates a new word. To determine meaning, separate the word's root and suffix. *Marksmanship* (line 272) can be divided as: marksman/ship. Here, the suffix *-ship* indicates skill. What does *marksmanship* mean?

---

## DIFFERENTIATED INSTRUCTION

### FOR ENGLISH LANGUAGE LEARNERS

**Language Coach** 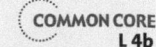 COMMON CORE L 4b

**Suffixes** *Possible answer:*
*skill at being a marksman, or being a good shooter;* Give students the word *craftsmanship*, and have them determine its meaning by separating the word's root and suffix. Then have students work in pairs to think of other words that use the suffix *–ship*. Have pairs share their words with the class.

### FOR STRUGGLING READERS

**❸ Targeted Passage [Lines 266–277]**

By describing Zaroff's background, this passage offers insights into his character and helps set up the conflict that will drive the most important part of the story.

- How old was Zaroff when he was given his first gun? What did he do with it, and what was the result? (lines 269–272)

- What does this passage tell you about how Zaroff views himself?

mind. Hunting was beginning to bore me! And hunting, remember, had been my life. I have heard that in America businessmen often go to pieces when they give up the business that has been their life."

"Yes, that's so," said Rainsford. ▢

The general smiled. "I had no wish to go to pieces," he said. "I must do something. Now, mine is an analytical mind, Mr. Rainsford. Doubtless that is why I enjoy the problems of the chase."

"No doubt, General Zaroff."

"So," continued the general, "I asked myself why the hunt no longer fascinated me. You are much younger than I am, Mr. Rainsford, and have not 300 hunted as much, but you perhaps can guess the answer."

"What was it?"

"Simply this: hunting had ceased to be what you call 'a sporting proposition.' It had become too easy. I always got my quarry. Always. There is no greater bore than perfection."

The general lit a fresh cigarette.

"No animal had a chance with me any more. That is no boast; it is a mathematical certainty. The animal had nothing but his legs and his instinct. Instinct is no match for reason. When I thought of this, it was a tragic moment for me, I can tell you."

310 Rainsford leaned across the table, absorbed in what his host was saying.

"It came to me as an inspiration what I must do," the general went on.

"And that was?"

The general smiled the quiet smile of one who has faced an obstacle and surmounted it with success. "I had to invent a new animal to hunt," he said. ▢

"A new animal? You're joking."

"Not at all," said the general. "I never joke about hunting. I needed a new animal. I found one. So I bought this island, built this house, and here I do my hunting. The island is perfect for my purposes—there are jungles with a maze of trails in them, hills, swamps—"

320 "But the animal, General Zaroff?"

"Oh," said the general, "it supplies me with the most exciting hunting in the world. No other hunting compares with it for an instant. Every day I hunt, and I never grow bored now, for I have a quarry with which I can match my wits."

Rainsford's bewilderment showed in his face.

"I wanted the ideal animal to hunt," explained the general. "So I said: 'What are the attributes of an ideal quarry?' And the answer was, of course: 'It must have courage, cunning, and, above all, it must be able to reason.'"

"But no animal can reason," objected Rainsford.

330 "My dear fellow," said the general, "there is one that can."

"But you can't mean—" gasped Rainsford.

"And why not?"

"I can't believe you are serious, General Zaroff. This is a grisly joke."

THE MOST DANGEROUS GAME 69

▢ **VISUALIZE**
As you read the rest of this page, visualize the expression on Rainsford's face as he listens to General Zaroff. How does his expression change over the course of the conversation?

COMMON CORE RL 5

▢ **PLOT DEVICES**
**Foreshadowing** is when an author gives clues about what might happen next in the story. It increases suspense and makes the reader eager to read on and resolve the mystery. Look back over the last few pages of "The Most Dangerous Game." What clues does the author give you about what animal General Zaroff likes to hunt? What do you think that animal is? Support your answer with evidence.

---

---

**Puritan Ancestors**  In lines 345–346, Zaroff belittles Rainsford by saying that Rainsford must have had "Puritan ancestors." The Puritans, a group of English Protestants who settled parts of New England, were deeply religious. Their strict moral code emphasized hard work. Zaroff is using this comment to suggest that Rainsford is limited by strict standards of right and wrong that are outdated (in Zaroff's view) and that Rainsford lacks the ability to have fun and enjoy life.  Ask students to evaluate Rainford's response.

---

**VOCABULARY**

COMMON CORE

**L 4**

**OWN THE WORD**

- **condone:** Ask students to create a list of actions that would be *condoned* by their school, their parents, and their friends. Have students explain why each of these actions would be *condoned*.

- **droll:** Tell students that *droll* means "amusingly odd or comical." Then have students list synonyms and antonyms for *droll*. **Possible answers:** *synonyms: witty, amusing, funny; antonyms: ordinary, dull, boring*

- **scruple:** Have students complete this sentence: General Zaroff said Rainsford's *scruples* were ill-founded because Zaroff believes that... **Possible answer:** *killing the weak of the world is not murder.*

---

"Why should I not be serious? I am speaking of hunting."

"Hunting? Good God, General Zaroff, what you speak of is murder."

The general laughed with entire good nature. He regarded Rainsford quizzically. "I refuse to believe that so modern and civilized a young man as you seem to be harbors romantic ideas about the value of human life. Surely your experiences in the war—"

340    "Did not make me **condone** cold-blooded murder," finished Rainsford, stiffly.

Laughter shook the general. "How extraordinarily **droll** you are!" he said. "One does not expect nowadays to find a young man of the educated class, even in America, with such a naïve, and, if I may say so, mid-Victorian point of view. It's like finding a snuffbox in a limousine. Ah, well, doubtless you had Puritan ancestors. So many Americans appear to have had. I'll wager you'll forget your notions when you go hunting with me. You've a genuine new thrill in store for you, Mr. Rainsford."

"Thank you, I'm a hunter, not a murderer."

350    "Dear me," said the general, quite unruffled, "again that unpleasant word. But I think I can show you that your **scruples** are quite ill-founded."

"Yes?"

"Life is for the strong, to be lived by the strong, and, if needs be, taken by the strong. The weak of the world were put here to give the strong pleasure. I am strong. Why should I not use my gift? If I wish to hunt, why should I not? I hunt the scum of the earth—sailors from tramp ships—lascars,[10] blacks, Chinese, whites, mongrels—a thoroughbred horse or hound is worth more than a score of them."

"But they are men," said Rainsford, hotly.

360    "Precisely," said the general. "That is why I use them. It gives me pleasure. They can reason, after a fashion. So they are dangerous."

"But where do you get them?"

The general's left eyelid fluttered down in a wink. "This island is called Ship Trap," he answered. "Sometimes an angry god of the high seas sends them to me. Sometimes, when Providence is not so kind, I help Providence a bit. Come to the window with me."

Rainsford went to the window and looked out toward the sea.

"Watch! Out there!" exclaimed the general, pointing into the night. Rainsford's eyes saw only blackness, and then, as the general pressed a button,

370    far out to sea Rainsford saw the flash of lights.

The general chuckled. "They indicate a channel," he said, "where there's none: giant rocks with razor edges crouch like a sea monster with wide-open jaws. They can crush a ship as easily as I crush this nut." He dropped a walnut on the hardwood floor and brought his heel grinding down on it. "Oh, yes," he said, casually, as if in answer to a question, "I have electricity. We try to be civilized here."

---

**condone** (kən-dōn′) *v.* to forgive or overlook

**droll** (drōl) *adj.* amusingly odd or comical

**scruple** (skrōō′pəl) *n.* a feeling of uneasiness that keeps a person from doing something

---

10.   **lascars** (lăs′kərz): sailors from India.

---

**DIFFERENTIATED INSTRUCTION**

**FOR ENGLISH LANGUAGE LEARNERS**

**Culture: Clarify**  In lines 344–345, Zaroff scoffs at Rainsford's "mid-Victorian point of view." Explain that *mid-Victorian* refers to the middle part of the reign of Great Britain's Queen Victoria (1837–1901) and to the culture of that era, known for its strongly conservative moral values. The adjective is often used to mean "old-fashioned."

**FOR ADVANCED LEARNERS/PRE–AP**

**Analyze Reasoning** [small-group option] Note that sometimes even very smart people, like General Zaroff, make errors in their thinking.  Ask students to analyze the thinking behind Zaroff's philosophical statement about the strong and the weak in lines 353–354 and to identify any weaknesses or problems that they find in his thinking. Students may support their responses with details from the story, personal experiences, or both.

Detail of *Downtime*, Dale Kennington. © Dale Kennington/SuperStock.

"Civilized? And you shoot down men?"

A trace of anger was in the general's black eyes, but it was there for but a second, and he said, in his most pleasant manner: "Dear me, what a righteous
380 young man you are! I assure you I do not do the thing you suggest. That would be barbarous. I treat these visitors with every consideration. They get plenty of good food and exercise. They get into splendid physical condition. You shall see for yourself tomorrow."

"What do you mean?"

"We'll visit my training school," smiled the general. "It's in the cellar. I have about a dozen pupils down there now. They're from the Spanish bark *Sanlúcar* that had the bad luck to go on the rocks out there. A very inferior lot, I regret to say. Poor specimens and more accustomed to the deck than to the jungle."

He raised his hand, and Ivan, who served as waiter, brought thick Turkish
390 coffee. Rainsford, with an effort, held his tongue in check.

"It's a game, you see," pursued the general, blandly. "I suggest to one of them that we go hunting. I give him a supply of food and an excellent hunting

Use these prompts to help students follow the story's mounting tension in lines 375–388:

**Connect** How do you react to Zaroff's statement "We try to be civilized here"? *Possible answer:* Zaroff's comment seems ridiculous in view of his hunting game, but I'd be afraid to voice strong objections.

**Analyze** Why does Rainsford's comment anger Zaroff? *Possible answer:* Rainsford is saying that Zaroff is uncivilized, and Zaroff obviously disagrees.

**Synthesize** What comments does Zaroff make to prove that Rainsford is wrong and that he, Zaroff, is civilized? *Possible answer: He tells Rainsford that he treats his "visitors" well (lines 381–383).* What does Zaroff tell Rainsford to contradict his own argument? *Possible answer: He imprisons his "visitors" in the cellar (lines 385–386).*

**FOR ENGLISH LANGUAGE LEARNERS**

**Comprehension: Transitions** Call students' attention to the use of the word *but* (lines 378–379). Explain that the first usage ("<u>but</u> it was there") signals a contrast between this part of the sentence and what has just been stated. The second time *but* is used ("for <u>but</u> a second"), it means "only." Have students work in pairs to find other examples of the use of the word *but* to signal a contrasting idea. Offer examples (lines 193–196 and line 485) to get them started.

knife. I give him three hours' start. I am to follow, armed only with a pistol of the smallest caliber and range. If my quarry eludes me for three whole days, he wins the game. If I find him"—the general smiled—"he loses."

"Suppose he refuses to be hunted?"

"Oh," said the general, "I give him his option, of course. He need not play that game if he doesn't wish to. If he does not wish to hunt, I turn him over to Ivan. Ivan once had the honor of serving as official knouter[11] to the Great
400 White Tsar, and he has his own ideas of sport. Invariably, Mr. Rainsford, invariably they choose the hunt."

"And if they win?"

The smile on the general's face widened.

"To date I have not lost," he said.

Then he added, hastily: "I don't wish you to think me a braggart, Mr. Rainsford. Many of them afford only the most elementary sort of problem. Occasionally I strike a tartar.[12] One almost did win. I eventually had to use the dogs."

"The dogs?"

410 "This way, please. I'll show you."

The general steered Rainsford to a window. The lights from the windows sent a flickering illumination that made grotesque patterns on the courtyard below, and Rainsford could see moving about there a dozen or so huge black shapes; as they turned toward him, their eyes glittered greenly.

"A rather good lot, I think," observed the general. "They are let out at seven every night. If anyone should try to get into my house—or out of it— something extremely regrettable would occur to him." He hummed a snatch of song from the Folies Bergère.[13]

"And now," said the general, "I want to show you my new collection of
420 heads. Will you come with me to the library?" **K**

"I hope," said Rainsford, "that you will excuse me tonight, General Zaroff. I'm really not feeling at all well."

"Ah, indeed?" the general inquired, **solicitously**. "Well, I suppose that's only natural, after your long swim. You need a good, restful night's sleep. Tomorrow you'll feel like a new man, I'll wager. Then we'll hunt, eh? I've one rather promising prospect—"

Rainsford was hurrying from the room.

"Sorry you can't go with me tonight," called the general. "I expect rather fair sport—a big, strong black. He looks resourceful— Well, good night,
430 Mr. Rainsford; I hope you have a good night's rest."

The bed was good, and the pajamas of the softest silk, and he was tired in every fiber of his being, but nevertheless Rainsford could not quiet his brain with the opiate of sleep. He lay, eyes wide open. Once he thought he heard stealthy steps in the corridor outside his room. He sought to throw open the

---

11. **knouter** (nou'tər): a person who whipped criminals in Russia.
12. **strike a tartar**: encounter a fierce opponent.
13. **Folies Bergère** (fô-lē' bĕr-zhĕr'): a music hall in Paris, famous for its variety shows.

**K** PREDICT

***Possible answer:*** *Because this "new collection" is hidden away in the privacy of the library, and because Zaroff has been speaking of a "new animal" to hunt, these may be human heads.*

**IF STUDENTS NEED HELP . . .** Discuss these questions:

• What collection did Rainsford see in Zaroff's dining room? ***Possible answer:*** *He saw the mounted heads of many wild animals in Zaroff's dining hall (lines 216–218).*

• What new quarry has the general been hunting? ***Possible answer:*** *He has been hunting the sailors imprisoned in his cellar.*

**K** PREDICT
Reread lines 419–420. What kind of heads do you think the general is referring to?

**solicitously**
(sə-lĭs'ĭ-təs-lē) *adv.* in a manner expressing care or concern

**OWN THE WORD**

**solicitously:** Have students create a semantic map for *solicitously*. Write the Vocabulary word in a center circle, and add the definition: "in a manner expressing care or concern." Draw spider legs from the center circle, and have students add synonyms to complete the map. ***Possible answers:*** *carefully, anxiously, attentively*

---

*DIFFERENTIATED INSTRUCTION*

**FOR STRUGGLING READERS**
**Evaluate** Work with students to complete a chart evaluating Zaroff. In one column, list details that show Zaroff is civilized, in the other, details that show he is a monster. Have students decide whether he is civilized or a monster, based on this evidence.

📖 **BEST PRACTICES TOOLKIT—Transparency**
Two-Column Chart p. A25

door; it would not open. He went to the window and looked out. His room was high up in one of the towers. The lights of the château were out now, and it was dark and
440 silent, but there was a fragment of sallow moon, and by its wan light he could see, dimly, the courtyard; there, weaving in and out in the pattern of shadow, were black, noiseless forms; the hounds heard him at the window and looked up, expectantly, with their green eyes. Rainsford went back to the bed and lay down. By many methods
450 he tried to put himself to sleep. He had achieved a doze when, just as morning began to come, he heard, far off in the jungle, the faint report of a pistol.

General Zaroff did not appear until luncheon. He was dressed faultlessly in the tweeds of a country squire. He was solicitous about the state of Rainsford's health.

"As for me," sighed the general, "I do not feel so well. I am worried, Mr. Rainsford. Last night I detected traces of my old complaint."

To Rainsford's questioning glance the general said: "Ennui. Boredom."

460 Then, taking a second helping of crêpes suzettes, the general explained: "The hunting was not good last night. The fellow lost his head. He made a straight trail that offered no problems at all. That's the trouble with these sailors; they have dull brains to begin with, and they do not know how to get about in the woods. They do excessively stupid and obvious things. It's most annoying. Will you have another glass of Chablis,[14] Mr. Rainsford?"

"General," said Rainsford, firmly, "I wish to leave this island at once."

The general raised his thickets of eyebrows; he seemed hurt. "But, my dear fellow," the general protested, "you've only just come. You've had no hunting—"

470 "I wish to go today," said Rainsford. He saw the dead black eyes of the general on him, studying him. General Zaroff's face suddenly brightened.

He filled Rainsford's glass with venerable Chablis from a dusty bottle.

"Tonight," said the general, "we will hunt—you and I."

Rainsford shook his head. "No, General," he said. "I will not hunt."

The general shrugged his shoulders and delicately ate a hothouse grape. "As you wish, my friend," he said. "The choice rests entirely with you. But may I not venture to suggest that you will find my idea of sport more diverting than Ivan's?"

---

14. **Chablis** (shă-blē'): a type of white French wine.

## TEXT ANALYSIS

**L CONFLICT**

***Possible answer:*** *The main conflict is between Rainsford and Zaroff—the hunted against the hunter. Rainsford will now have to fight for his life in a battle of brains, skill, strength, and stamina; in other words, "outdoor chess," as Zaroff puts it.*

**Extend the Discussion** What does the expression "worthy of my steel" mean, and how does that term add to the conflict between the main characters?

## Analyze Visuals

**Activity** The title of this photograph is *Person Running at Night*. Ask students how well it fits with the way they visualize Rainsford at this point in the story. ***Possible answer:*** *The photograph shows a figure running through the woods, as if being chased by someone or something. Up to this point, Rainsford has been a strong and fearless character, but Zaroff has just challenged him to a hunt. Rainsford now has a vision—perhaps a vision like that in this image—of what the next few days (and, perhaps, the last few days) of his life will be like.*

---

He nodded toward the corner to where the giant stood, scowling, his thick
480 arms crossed on his hogshead of chest.

"You don't mean—" cried Rainsford.

"My dear fellow," said the general, "have I not told you I always mean what I say about hunting? This is really an inspiration. I drink to a foeman worthy of my steel—at last." **L**

The general raised his glass, but Rainsford sat staring at him.

"You'll find this game worth playing," the general said, enthusiastically. "Your brain against mine. Your woodcraft against mine. Your strength and stamina against mine. Outdoor chess! And the stake is not without value, eh?"

"And if I win—" began Rainsford, huskily.

490 "I'll cheerfully acknowledge myself defeated if I do not find you by midnight of the third day," said General Zaroff. "My sloop will place you on the mainland near a town."

The general read what Rainsford was thinking.

"Oh, you can trust me," said the Cossack. "I will give you my word as a gentleman and a sportsman. Of course, you, in turn, must agree to say nothing of your visit here."

"I'll agree to nothing of the kind," said Rainsford.

**L CONFLICT**
The main conflict in the story has now become clear. What is it?

**4 Targeted Passage**

---

## DIFFERENTIATED INSTRUCTION

**FOR STRUGGLING READERS**

**4 Targeted Passage** [Lines 482–497]
This passage brings the conflict between Rainsford and Zaroff into full focus.

- How is Zaroff feeling about his contest with Rainsford? (lines 493–495)
- How is their contest like "outdoor chess" (line 488)?
- What happens if Rainsford wins the contest? if he loses? (lines 489–492)
- What agreement does Zaroff try to make

with Rainsford? How does Rainsford respond? (lines 494–497)

**FOR ENGLISH LANGUAGE LEARNERS**

**Language: Punctuation and Print Clues**
Several dashes (—) appear in the dialogue on these pages; indeed, they have been part of the story since line 1. To help students understand the purpose of this usage, read aloud lines 479–492 to show that the dashes indicate both a pause and the suggestion that something sinister or dangerous is about to happen.

"Oh," said the general, "in that case— But why discuss that now? Three days hence we can discuss it over a bottle of Veuve Clicquot,[15] unless—"

500 The general sipped his wine.

Then a businesslike air animated him. "Ivan," he said to Rainsford, "will supply you with hunting clothes, food, a knife. I suggest you wear moccasins; they leave a poorer trail. I suggest, too, that you avoid the big swamp in the southeast corner of the island. We call it Death Swamp. There's quicksand there. One foolish fellow tried it. The deplorable part of it was that Lazarus followed him. You can imagine my feelings, Mr. Rainsford. I loved Lazarus; he was the finest hound in my pack. Well, I must beg you to excuse me now. I always take a siesta after lunch. You'll hardly have time for a nap, I fear. You'll want to start, no doubt. I shall not follow till dusk. Hunting at night is so

510 much more exciting than by day, don't you think? Au revoir,[16] Mr. Rainsford, au revoir."

General Zaroff, with a deep, courtly bow, strolled from the room.

From another door came Ivan. Under one arm he carried khaki hunting clothes, a haversack of food, a leather sheath containing a long-bladed hunting knife; his right hand rested on a cocked revolver thrust in the crimson sash about his waist. . . .

Rainsford had fought his way through the bush for two hours. "I must keep my nerve. I must keep my nerve," he said, through tight teeth.

He had not been entirely clear-headed when the château gates snapped shut

520 behind him. His whole idea at first was to put distance between himself and General Zaroff, and, to this end, he had plunged along, spurred on by the sharp rowels of something very like panic. Now he had got a grip on himself, had stopped, and was taking stock of himself and the situation.

He saw that straight flight was futile; inevitably it would bring him face to face with the sea. He was in a picture with a frame of water, and his operations, clearly, must take place within that frame.

"I'll give him a trail to follow," muttered Rainsford, and he struck off from the rude path he had been following into the trackless wilderness. He executed a series of intricate loops; he doubled on his trail again and again, recalling all

530 the lore of the fox hunt, and all the dodges of the fox. Night found him leg-weary, with hands and face lashed by the branches, on a thickly wooded ridge. He knew it would be insane to blunder on through the dark, even if he had the strength. His need for rest was **imperative,** and he thought, "I have played the fox; now I must play the cat of the fable."[17] A big tree with a thick trunk and outspread branches was nearby, and, taking care to leave not the slightest mark, he climbed up into the crotch and, stretching out on one of the broad limbs, after a fashion, rested. Rest brought him new confidence and almost a feeling of security. Even so **zealous** a hunter as General Zaroff could not trace him

---

15. **Veuve Clicquot** (vœv′ klĭ-kō′): a French champagne.

16. **au revoir** (ō′ rə-vwär′): goodbye; farewell till we meet again.

17. **I have played the fox . . . fable:** In Aesop's fable "The Cat and the Fox," the fox brags of knowing many ways to escape an enemy. The cat knows only one, but is successful with it.

THE MOST DANGEROUS GAME    75

COMMON CORE L 4c

**Language Coach**

**Word Origins** The word *moccasins* (line 502) refers to a certain type of soft-soled leather shoe. *Moccasin* comes from the Algonquian (Native American) word *mockasin*. When Europeans first arrived in the Americas, many Native American words entered European languages. In a dictionary, look up the definitions and origins of the following words: *hominy, kayak, opossum, succotash.*

**GRAMMAR AND STYLE**

Reread lines 513–516. Notice how Connell uses multiple **prepositional phrases**—such as "on a cocked revolver" and "in the crimson sash"—to add descriptive details.

**imperative** (ĭm-pĕr′ə-tĭv) *adj.* absolutely necessary

**zealous** (zĕl′əs) *adj.* intensely enthusiastic

---

**GRAMMAR AND STYLE**    COMMON CORE L 1b

**Analyze Descriptive Details** After students read the lines, point out that the descriptive details answer questions (such as "How does Zaroff bid Rainsford farewell?" and "Where is the revolver?"). Ask students how the descriptive details add drama and interest. *Possible answer: The first detail ("with a deep, courtly bow") is a reminder of Zaroff's attempt to appear civilized. The other details help the reader visualize Ivan. In particular, "in the crimson sash" makes Ivan seem even more exotic, for few people in the United States would wear such an item; furthermore, it is the color of blood.* Have students find other prepositional phrases that enliven this part of the story and/or that lend insight into the characters or their conflict.

**VOCABULARY**    COMMON CORE L 4

**OWN THE WORD**

- **imperative:** Tell students that *imperative* comes from the Latin *imperare*, which means "to command." Have students write a sentence explaining the relationship between *imperare* and the adjective *imperative*.

- **zealous:** Ask students to name sports teams that students support so much that they might be considered *zealous* fans. Then have students name current issues that they believe deserve *zealous* support from community leaders.

---

**FOR ADVANCED LEARNERS/PRE–AP**

**Analyze Options** [paired-activity option] Have students come up with options for Rainsford, such as these:

- Go to the swamp, where it would be dangerous for Zaroff and his dogs to follow.

- Turn and fight Zaroff as soon as possible.

- Find a hiding place, and wait for rescue from a passing ship.

- Surrender and accept Zaroff's original offer.

**Language Coach**    COMMON CORE L 4c

*Possible answers: hominy, hulled and dried kernels of corn, Algonquin; kayak, a watertight canoe covered with skins, Canadian Eskimo and Inuit; opossum, a nocturnal, usually arboreal, marsupial, Virginia Algonquin; succotash, a stew of kernels of corn, lima beans, and tomatoes, Narragansett*

*Possible answer: Zaroff may try to kill Rainsford, since that is the point of the hunt.*

**Extend the Discussion** What does Zaroff's ability to find Rainsford's location show about Zaroff? What does it show about Rainsford? How does this detail help you make predictions about the rest of the story?

**TEXT ANALYSIS**

COMMON CORE

RL 5

**◎ CONFLICT**

*Possible answer: Rainsford realizes that Zaroff knew exactly where he was. Zaroff could have killed him then but chose not to do so. Instead, the general prefers to continue his "fun" (and Rainsford's distress). This knowledge adds another layer of tension to Rainsford's already stressful situation.*

**VOCABULARY**

COMMON CORE

L 4

**OWN THE WORD**

**uncanny:** Have students identify context clues in the sentence to help determine the meaning of *uncanny*. *Possible answers: follow a trail at night, follow an extremely difficult trail, only by the merest chance had the Cossack failed to see his quarry*

---

there, he told himself; only the devil himself could follow that complicated
540 trail through the jungle after dark. But perhaps the general was a devil—

An apprehensive night crawled slowly by like a wounded snake, and sleep did not visit Rainsford, although the silence of a dead world was on the jungle. Toward morning, when a dingy gray was varnishing the sky, the cry of some startled bird focused Rainsford's attention in that direction. Something was coming through the bush, coming slowly, carefully, coming by the same winding way Rainsford had come. He flattened himself down on the limb, and through a screen of leaves almost as thick as tapestry, he watched. The thing that was approaching was a man.

It was General Zaroff. He made his way along with his eyes fixed in utmost
550 concentration on the ground before him. He paused, almost beneath the tree, dropped to his knees, and studied the ground. Rainsford's impulse was to hurl himself down like a panther, but he saw that the general's right hand held something metallic—a small automatic pistol.

The hunter shook his head several times, as if he were puzzled. Then he straightened up and took from his case one of his black cigarettes; its pungent, incenselike smoke floated up to Rainsford's nostrils.

Rainsford held his breath. The general's eyes had left the ground and were traveling inch by inch up the tree. Rainsford froze there, every muscle tensed for a spring. But the sharp eyes of the hunter stopped before they reached the
560 limb where Rainsford lay; a smile spread over his brown face. Very deliberately he blew a smoke ring into the air; then he turned his back on the tree and walked carelessly away, back along the trail he had come. The swish of the underbrush against his hunting boots grew fainter and fainter.

The pent-up air burst hotly from Rainsford's lungs. His first thought made him feel sick and numb. The general could follow a trail through the woods at night; he could follow an extremely difficult trail; he must have **uncanny** powers; only by the merest chance had the Cossack failed to see his quarry.

Rainsford's second thought was even more terrible. It sent a shudder of cold horror through his whole being. Why had the general smiled? Why had he
570 turned back?

Rainsford did not want to believe what his reason told him was true, but the truth was as evident as the sun that had by now pushed through the morning mists. The general was playing with him! The general was saving him for another day's sport! The Cossack was the cat; he was the mouse. Then it was that Rainsford knew the full meaning of terror. **◎**

"I will not lose my nerve. I will not."

He slid down from the tree and struck off again into the woods. His face was set, and he forced the machinery of his mind to function. Three hundred yards from his hiding place he stopped where a huge dead tree leaned
580 precariously on a smaller, living one. Throwing off his sack of food, Rainsford took his knife from its sheath and began to work with all his energy.

**N PREDICT**
This is one of the most **suspenseful** moments in the story. What do you think General Zaroff will do to Rainsford? Why?

**uncanny** (ŭn-kăn′ē) *adj.* so remarkable as to seem supernatural

**◎ CONFLICT**
What **complication** is introduced to intensify the conflict and build **suspense?**

---

## DIFFERENTIATED INSTRUCTION

### FOR ADVANCED LEARNERS/PRE–AP

**Evaluate** Have students discuss Connell's effectiveness in building suspense. To what extent does his success depend upon plot, character, or setting? How does foreshadowing contribute to the suspense?

The job was finished at last, and he threw himself down behind a fallen log a hundred feet away. He did not have to wait long. The cat was coming again to play with the mouse.

Following the trail with the sureness of a bloodhound came General Zaroff. Nothing escaped those searching black eyes, no crushed blade of grass, no bent twig, no mark, no matter
590 how faint, in the moss. So intent was the Cossack on his stalking that he was upon the thing Rainsford had made before he saw it. His foot touched the protruding bough[18] that was the trigger. Even as he touched it, the general sensed his danger and leaped back with the agility of an ape. But he was not quite quick enough; the dead tree, delicately adjusted to rest on the cut living one, crashed down and struck the general a glancing blow on the shoulder as it fell; but for his
600 alertness, he must have been smashed beneath it. He staggered, but he did not fall; nor did he drop his revolver. He stood there, rubbing his injured shoulder, and Rainsford, with fear again gripping his heart, heard the general's mocking laugh ring through the jungle.

"Rainsford," called the general, "if you are within sound of my voice, as I suppose you are, let me congratulate you. Not many men know how to make a Malay man-catcher. Luckily for me I,
610 too, have hunted in Malacca.[19] You are proving interesting, Mr. Rainsford. I am going now to have my wound dressed; it's only a slight one. But I shall be back. I shall be back." ⑤ **Targeted Passage**

When the general, nursing his bruised shoulder, had gone, Rainsford took up his flight again. It was flight now, a desperate, hopeless flight, that carried him on for some hours. Dusk came, then darkness, and still he pressed on. The ground grew softer under his moccasins; the vegetation grew ranker, denser; insects bit him savagely. Then, as he stepped forward, his foot sank into the ooze. He tried to wrench it back, but the muck sucked viciously at his foot as if it were a giant leech. With a violent effort he tore his foot loose. He knew
620 where he was now. Death Swamp and its quicksand.

His hands were tight closed as if his nerve were something tangible that someone in the darkness was trying to tear from his grip. The softness of the

---

*Tree Circle* (1992), Peter Schroth. Oil on paper, 7½″ × 8½″.
© Peter Schroth.

18. **protruding bough** (bou): a tree branch that extends or juts out.

19. **Malay** (mə-lā′)...**Malacca** (mə-lăk′ə): The Malays are a people of southeast Asia. Malacca is a region they inhabit, just south of Thailand.

THE MOST DANGEROUS GAME    77

## Analyze Visuals

**Activity** Call students' attention to how the trees in this landscape painting enclose the foreground with their shadows falling like prison bars across the ground. Then have students locate images of imprisonment or entrapment in the story, including details that suggest prison bars (like the shadows in the painting).

**About the Art** This oil painting, *Tree Circle*, by contemporary American landscape painter Peter Schroth does not depict the story's jungle setting, but offers a vision of entrapment that suggests Rainsford's situation.

## TIERED DISCUSSION PROMPTS

Use these prompts to help students understand Zaroff's strength as an adversary as shown in lines 586–612:

**Connect** How do you feel about Zaroff at this point in the story? *Accept all reasonable answers.*

**Analyze** Zaroff knows that Rainsford is nearby. Why does Zaroff choose to end the day's hunt, rather than try to finish off Rainsford as soon as possible? *Possible answer: He knows that it is smarter to conserve his own strength and wear Rainsford down. Also, he may enjoy Rainsford's torment.*

**Synthesize** How does Zaroff's personality add tension to the scene? *Possible answer: Zaroff is both calm and cruel. He is a focused predator who understands that his prey can be worn down psychologically as well as physically. The reader is left in suspense about what he will do when he comes back.*

## FOR STRUGGLING READERS

⑤ **Targeted Passage** [Lines 586–612]

This passage, which describes how one of Rainsford's traps goes off but fails to kill Zaroff, vividly captures the story's tensions and the deadly seriousness of the hunt.

• What has Rainsford set up? (lines 608–610)

• What happens to Zaroff when he encounters the trap? (lines 592–599)

• What does Zaroff promise Rainsford? (line 612)

UNIT 1: NARRATIVE STRUCTURE

READING STRATEGY: *Review*

**P PREDICT**

***Possible answer:*** *No. The trap apparently is at the edge of the quicksand, and Zaroff has already spoken of the importance of staying away from that area. Furthermore, Zaroff has proven himself to be aware of traps (and now, having been slightly wounded, he is likely to be even more alert). In addition, given Zaroff's years of hunting around the world, it is likely that he is familiar with all manner of exotic traps.*

**IF STUDENTS NEED HELP . . .** Encourage them to make a chart in which they record story details related to the question. Then they can examine those details and add their own prior knowledge to them to make predictions. Remind students that their predictions should be based on story details.

---

**TEXT ANALYSIS**

COMMON CORE
**RL 5**

**Q *Model the Skill:* CONFLICT**

Model for students how to identify the suspense created from conflict. Explain that up to this point, Zaroff has escaped two traps Rainsford created. Tell students that this increases the tension because readers see how frantic Rainsford becomes after each trap fails. Now that Zaroff is bringing a pack of hounds, Rainsford's options and chances for survival have become even more limited.

***Possible answer:*** *The only escape route at this point seems to be the sea, where the dogs cannot follow.*

---

earth had given him an idea. He stepped back from the quicksand a dozen feet or so, and like some huge prehistoric beaver, he began to dig.

Rainsford had dug himself in in France when a second's delay meant death. That had been a placid pastime compared to his digging now. The pit grew deeper; when it was above his shoulders, he climbed out and from some hard saplings cut stakes and sharpened them to a fine point. These stakes he planted in the bottom of the pit with the points sticking up. With flying fingers he
630 wove a rough carpet of weeds and branches, and with it he covered the mouth of the pit. Then, wet with sweat and aching with tiredness, he crouched behind the stump of a lightning-charred tree. **P**

He knew his pursuer was coming; he heard the padding sound of feet on the soft earth, and the night breeze brought him the perfume of the general's cigarette. It seemed to Rainsford that the general was coming with unusual swiftness; he was not feeling his way along, foot by foot. Rainsford, crouching there, could not see the general, nor could he see the pit. He lived a year in a minute. Then he felt an impulse to cry aloud with joy, for he heard the sharp crackle of the breaking branches as the cover of the pit gave way; he heard the
640 sharp scream of pain as the pointed stakes found their mark. He leaped up from his place of concealment. Then he cowered back. Three feet from the pit a man was standing, with an electric torch in his hand.

"You've done well, Rainsford," the voice of the general called. "Your Burmese tiger pit[20] has claimed one of my best dogs. Again you score. I think, Mr. Rainsford, I'll see what you can do against my whole pack. I'm going home for a rest now. Thank you for a most amusing evening."

At daybreak Rainsford, lying near the swamp, was awakened by a sound that made him know that he had new things to learn about fear. It was a distant sound, faint and wavering, but he knew it. It was the baying of a
650 pack of hounds. **Q**

Rainsford knew he could do one of two things. He could stay where he was and wait. That was suicide. He could flee. That was postponing the inevitable. For a moment he stood there, thinking. An idea that held a wild chance came to him, and, tightening his belt, he headed away from the swamp.

The baying of the hounds grew nearer, then still nearer, nearer, ever nearer. On a ridge Rainsford climbed a tree. Down a watercourse, not a quarter of a mile away, he could see the bush moving. Straining his eyes, he saw the lean figure of General Zaroff; just ahead of him, Rainsford made out another figure whose wide shoulders surged through the tall jungle weeds; it was the giant
660 Ivan, and he seemed pulled forward by some unseen force; Rainsford knew that Ivan must be holding the pack in leash.

They would be on him any minute now. His mind worked frantically. He thought of a native trick he had learned in Uganda.[21] He slid down the tree.

---

20. **Burmese** (bər-mēz') **tiger pit:** a trap used for catching tigers in Myanmar, a country in Southeast Asia formerly called Burma.

21. **Uganda** (yōō-găn'də): a country in central Africa.

**78**    UNIT 1: NARRATIVE STRUCTURE

**P PREDICT**
Will the trap ensnare the general? Give reasons for your prediction.

**Q CONFLICT**
The introduction of the pack of hounds poses a new complication. What recourse does Rainsford have?

---

## DIFFERENTIATED INSTRUCTION

### FOR STRUGGLING READERS

**Concept Building: World War I** Explain that Rainsford's having "dug himself in in France" (line 625) is a reference to military service in Europe during World War I (1914–1918). The Germans' early attempt to sweep westward across France was met by the resistance of Allied forces, and both sides "dug in," creating a system of opposing trenches from which most of the war was fought, with high casualties and little movement. More than any other war, before or after, World War I was known for its trench warfare, and the dismal conditions in the trenches (including rats and lice, disease, and constant concern about enemy shellfire and snipers) probably toughened Rainsford's survival skills.

He caught hold of a springy young sapling, and to it he fastened his hunting knife, with the blade pointing down the trail; with a bit of wild grapevine he tied back the sapling. Then he ran for his life. The hounds raised their voices as they hit the fresh scent. Rainsford knew now how an animal at bay feels.

He had to stop to get his breath. The baying of the hounds stopped abruptly, and Rainsford's heart stopped, too. They must have reached the knife.

670   He shinned excitedly up a tree and looked back. His pursuers had stopped. But the hope that was in Rainsford's brain when he climbed died, for he saw in the shallow valley that General Zaroff was still on his feet. But Ivan was not. The knife, driven by the recoil of the springing tree, had not wholly failed.

THE MOST DANGEROUS GAME   **79**

**Analyze Visuals**

**Activity** This photograph of crashing waves (called *Wakes on Sea*) presents the sea as a forbidding place. Have students suggest why an image of the sea appears at this point in the story. *Possible answer: This image may be a reminder that the sea is how Rainsford got to this island and put him into a life-threatening position; it also may be a foreshadowing of an escape route.*

**REVISIT THE BIG QUESTION**

## What does it take to be a **SURVIVOR?**

**Discuss** In line 662–669, how has Rainsford changed since the beginning of the story, when he talked with Whitney about hunting? *Possible answer: Rainsford seemed arrogant and insensitive when he spoke with Whitney about hunting; now he understands what it is to be vulnerable and how a hunted animal must feel.* Discuss how circumstances have tested Rainsford's survival skills in ways he could not have predicted or trained for.

**FOR RELUCTANT READERS**

**Connect to the Text** Have students each choose a short passage in the story that interests them. Tell them to translate their passages to a story board, comic strip, photo montage, or other visual medium. Encourage students to use their imaginations when interpreting the descriptive language in their passages. Ask for volunteers to share their completed work with the class.

 **VISUALIZE**

*Possible answer: The contrast between the desperate Rainsford and the nonchalant Zaroff makes a dramatic impact: It reminds readers that although these characters seemed at first to be kindred spirits, they differ in one important value—and, at this point, readers do not yet know whose value will triumph.*

**IF STUDENTS NEED HELP...** Have them work in small groups to add details to their Visualizing charts that help them form mental images of the story's characters, settings, and events.

## SELECTION WRAP–UP

**READ WITH A PURPOSE** Now that students have read the selection, ask them to describe what the most dangerous game is and why General Zaroff considers this game to be so dangerous. Then have students discuss what statement the author might be making about hunting. *Possible answers: The most dangerous game is humankind. General Zaroff considers humans the most dangerous because humans can reason and are resourceful. The author might be making the statement that hunting is cruel for the hunted.*

★ **CRITIQUE** Have students tell what they think are the most believable and unbelievable parts of this story.

## INDEPENDENT READING

Students may also enjoy reading Joseph Conrad's *Heart of Darkness*, a story featuring an exotic, treacherous setting.

---

Rainsford had hardly tumbled to the ground when the pack took up the cry again.

"Nerve, nerve, nerve!" he panted, as he dashed along. A blue gap showed between the trees dead ahead. Ever nearer drew the hounds. Rainsford forced himself on toward that gap. He reached it. It was the shore of the sea. Across a cove he could see the gloomy gray stone of the château. Twenty feet below him
680  the sea rumbled and hissed. Rainsford hesitated. He heard the hounds. Then he leaped far out into the sea. . . .

When the general and his pack reached the place by the sea, the Cossack stopped. For some minutes he stood regarding the blue-green expanse of water. He shrugged his shoulders. Then he sat down, took a drink of brandy from a silver flask, lit a perfumed cigarette, and hummed a bit from *Madama Butterfly.*[22] **R**

General Zaroff had an exceedingly good dinner in his great paneled dining hall that evening. With it he had a bottle of Pol Roger and half a bottle of Chambertin.[23] Two slight annoyances kept him from perfect enjoyment. One
690  was the thought that it would be difficult to replace Ivan; the other was that his quarry had escaped him; of course the American hadn't played the game— so thought the general as he tasted his after-dinner liqueur. In his library he read, to soothe himself, from the works of Marcus Aurelius.[24] At ten he went up to his bedroom. He was deliciously tired, he said to himself, as he locked himself in. There was a little moonlight, so before turning on his light he went to the window and looked down at the courtyard. He could see the great hounds, and he called "Better luck another time" to them. Then he switched on the light.

A man, who had been hiding in the curtains of the bed, was standing there.
700  "Rainsford!" screamed the general. "How in God's name did you get here?"

"Swam," said Rainsford. "I found it quicker than walking through the jungle."

The general sucked in his breath and smiled. "I congratulate you," he said. "You have won the game."

Rainsford did not smile. "I am still a beast at bay," he said, in a low, hoarse voice. "Get ready, General Zaroff."

The general made one of his deepest bows.

"I see," he said. "Splendid! One of us is to furnish a repast[25] for the hounds. The other will sleep in this very excellent bed. On guard, Rainsford. . . ."

710  He had never slept in a better bed, Rainsford decided. ◞

**R VISUALIZE**
Picture in your mind the contrasting images of Rainsford's dramatic escape and Zaroff's "civilized" actions at the edge of the water. What is the impact of this contrast?

**❻ Targeted Passage**

---

22. **Madama Butterfly:** a famous opera by the Italian composer Giacomo Puccini.
23. **Pol Roger** (pôl′ rō-zhā′) **...Chambertin** (shăm-bĕr-tăn′): Pol Roger is a French champagne. Chambertin is a red French wine.
24. **Marcus Aurelius** (mär′kəs ô-rē′lē-əs): an ancient Roman emperor and philosopher.
25. **furnish a repast:** serve as a meal.

**80**    UNIT 1: NARRATIVE STRUCTURE

---

## DIFFERENTIATED INSTRUCTION

**FOR STRUGGLING READERS**

**❻ Targeted Passage** [Lines 694–710]

This passage concludes the story with a plot twist: Rainsford wins the "most dangerous game" by confronting Zaroff in the general's own bedroom.

- How did Rainsford get to the château? (lines 700–702)

- How does Rainsford respond when Zaroff congratulates him? (lines 705–706)

**Comprehension Support** Explain that the phrase "a beast at bay" (line 705) means "an animal that is unable to retreat and forced to face danger," and that an animal "at bay" is extremely dangerous. Point out that Rainsford calls himself "a beast at bay"; then ask

- How has Rainsford changed? Has he become an animal?

- Was he always an animal?

Students can discuss their ideas in groups.

## Comprehension

1. **Recall** Before arriving at the island, what is Rainsford's position on hunting?

2. **Recall** Why has Zaroff begun hunting human "game"?

3. **Clarify** What happens at the end of the story?

## Text Analysis

4. **Draw Conclusions** In your opinion, why does Rainsford choose to confront Zaroff in the end, rather than simply ambush him? What does this reveal about his personality? Cite evidence.

5. **Compare and Contrast Characters** Use a Venn diagram to compare and contrast Rainsford and Zaroff. Start by listing each man's **character traits** in the appropriate circle. Then note their similarities where the circles overlap.

Rainsford    Zaroff

6. **Analyze Conflict** Reread lines 473–484. Connell does not reveal the main conflict until a good deal of the story has passed. Why? Support your answer.

7. **Examine Foreshadowing** Connell makes use of foreshadowing to help readers predict future events in the story. Find at least three examples of foreshadowing in the story. How does this technique add to the **suspense** of this story? Cite evidence.

8. **Visualize Description** Look back at the descriptive details you recorded as you read. Choose at least two details that evoked the most striking sensory images in your mind. Which particular words helped make each of these images so vivid?

9. **Make Judgments** At the end of the story, do you think Rainsford has changed his mind about hunting? Support your opinion.

## Text Criticism

10. **Critical Interpretations** One critic has remarked that "ironically, Zaroff's belief in his invincibility as a hunter weakens him and causes his defeat." Cite evidence from the story to support or challenge this statement.

### What does it take to be a SURVIVOR?

What characteristics help people survive dangerous situations?

---

COMMON CORE

**RL 4** Analyze the cumulative impact of specific word choices on meaning and tone. **RL 5** Analyze how an author's choices concerning how to structure a text, order events within it, and manipulate time create such effects as mystery, tension, or surprise.

# Practice and Apply

For preliminary support of post-reading questions, use these copy masters:

**R** RESOURCE MANAGER—Copy Masters
Reading Check p. 52
Conflict p. 45
Question Support p. 53

Additional selection questions are provided for teachers on page 39.

### ANSWERS

## Comprehension

1. *He calls it "the best sport in the world."*

2. *Zaroff has come to the conclusion that it is too easy to catch animals; he wants the challenge of a quarry that can reason.*

3. *Rainsford eludes Zaroff and returns to the château. He hides in the general's bedroom, where he surprises and kills Zaroff.*

## Text Analysis

COMMON CORE **RL 4, RL 5**

**Possible answers:**

4. *Rainsford plays by the rules. Earlier in the story he called Zaroff's game "murder" (line 335), so he will not kill Zaroff in cold blood; rather, he will fight Zaroff face to face. Rainsford's insistence on playing by the rules, telling the general to "get ready" (line 706), reveals that he is honorable.*

5. *Rainsford: American, plays by the rules*

   *Zaroff: Russian, lives on island, breaks rules*

   *Both: great hunters, high social status, wealthy, both become the hunted*

6. ● **COMMON CORE FOCUS** *Analyze Conflict Throughout the first part of the story, Connell is busy establishing character and setting and building suspense. He does this to intensify the surprise and underscore the horror of the main conflict when it is revealed.*

7. *Whitney's recounting of sailor's lore (lines 4–5, 30–51) foreshadows the accident; finding the spent cartridges (lines 116–120) foreshadows an unusual quarry; the appearance of Zaroff's château (lines 132–140) suggests a place where secretive events occur. This technique creates suspense by building uncertainty, suspicion, and fear for Rainsford.*

---

8. ■ **COMMON CORE FOCUS** *Visualize Description The dining room's paneling, high ceiling, refectory table, and numerous trophies are vividly described (lines 213–219). So is Rainsford's flight through the Death Swamp's rank vegetation, savage insects, and leech-like ooze (lines 615–620).*

9. *not changed: slept well after killing Zaroff; changed: has new understanding of how an "animal at bay" feels (line 667)*

## Text Criticism

**Possible answer:**

10. *Before retiring, Zaroff ate well, drank, and read without worry, underestimating Rainsford by assuming that his quarry had drowned (lines 687–698).*

### What does it take to be a SURVIVOR? *Possible answers:*
alertness, quick thinking, creativity, calmness

# ANSWERS

## Vocabulary in Context

▲ **VOCABULARY PRACTICE**

| | | |
|---|---|---|
| 1. *tangible* | 5. *amenity* | 9. *droll* |
| 2. *disarming* | 6. *solicitously* | 10. *condone* |
| 3. *imperative* | 7. *scruples* | 11. *zealous* |
| 4. *cultivated* | 8. *quarry* | 12. *uncanny* |

 **RESOURCE MANAGER—Copy Master**
Vocabulary Practice p. 50

### ACADEMIC VOCABULARY IN WRITING

*Possible answer: The story's* **structure** *involves a* **sequence** *of events and* **elements** *that build upon themselves, adding more and more tension by having the reader be unaware of what will happen at the end, until it finally climaxes with a surprise ending.*

### VOCABULARY STRATEGY: DENOTATION AND CONNOTATION

**COMMON CORE L 5b**

- For additional instruction on connotation and denotation, focus on the word *syrupy*. Explain that the denotation, or meaning, of *syrupy* is "sweet," but the word has the negative connotation of "overly sweet," as in *Nancy did not trust the girl's syrupy compliments.*

- Explain that *solicitous* also can signal a behavior that is a bit too concerned or overdone, as in *That morning, I tried to avoid running into my ever-smiling, solicitous neighbor.*

- Ask students to imagine the tone of voice in which each sentence is spoken. Have volunteers read the sentences aloud in these different tones and describe the different connotative values of *syrupy* and *solicitous*.

**Possible answers:**

| | |
|---|---|
| 1. *reckless* | 4. *bizarre* |
| 2. *reactionary* | 5. *impudent* |
| 3. *tightfisted* | |

 **RESOURCE MANAGER—Copy Master**
Vocabulary Strategy p. 51

**THINK central**
**Interactive Vocabulary**

Keywords direct students to a **WordSharp** tutorial on **thinkcentral.com** or to other types of vocabulary practice and review.

---

# Vocabulary in Context

▲ **VOCABULARY PRACTICE**

Choose the word from the list that best completes each sentence.

1. As Rainsford swam ashore, the air was so humid it was almost _____.
2. He spoke in a(n) _____ way in order to try not to anger Zaroff's guard.
3. For his own safety, Rainsford felt it _____ not to come across as an intruder.
4. Zaroff's love of fine food and wine made him seem a(n) _____ person.
5. His house offered every _____ that could make a guest comfortable.
6. In the morning, Zaroff inquired _____ whether Rainsford had slept well.
7. But Zaroff lacked the ____ that moral people have.
8. He saw nothing wrong with hunting a human _____.
9. In fact, with an odd, or a(n) _____, smile he stalked his prisoners.
10. Rainsford strongly disagreed with Zaroff and refused to ____ his hunting.
11. Zaroff was _____ in tracking down his victims.
12. Rainsford soon found that Zaroff had a(n) _____ ability to follow difficult trails.

**WORD LIST**

amenity
condone
cultivated
disarming
droll
imperative
quarry
scruple
solicitously
tangible
uncanny
zealous

### ACADEMIC VOCABULARY IN WRITING

- analyze  • element  • infer  • sequence  • structure

Write a short paragraph about the story's **structure**. Do you think the structure helped the author build tension throughout the story? Use at least three of the Academic Vocabulary words in your response.

### VOCABULARY STRATEGY: DENOTATION AND CONNOTATION

A word's **denotation** is its basic dictionary meaning; its **connotations** are the overtones of meaning that it may take on. For example, the vocabulary word *cultivated* means "cultured"; so does *highbrow*. However, *cultivated* has mostly positive overtones; *highbrow* has negative connotations of snobbishness.

**PRACTICE** Use the context of each sentence below to determine which of the two words conveys a negative connotation. Then, use that word to fill in the blank.

1. The quarterback's _____ move lost his team the game. (bold/reckless)
2. My brother was grounded for his _____ response to having his allowance taken away. (conservative/reactionary)
3. I would ask my mom for the money to buy that bike, but she is very _____. (tightfisted/thrifty)
4. The magician's _____ act was too much for us, so we left. (unique/bizarre)
5. Joanne tends to get into trouble for being too _____ with her teacher. (outspoken/impudent)

**COMMON CORE**

**L 5b** Analyze nuances in the meaning of words with similar denotations.

 **Interactive Vocabulary**
**THINK central**
Go to **thinkcentral.com**.
KEYWORD: HML9-82

---

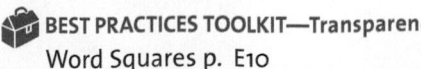

## DIFFERENTIATED INSTRUCTION

### FOR ENGLISH LANGUAGE LEARNERS

**Vocabulary: Multiple-Meaning Words** Before students complete Vocabulary practice, use Word Squares to help them understand the meanings of these multiple-meaning words:

- *quarry* (line 122)
- *disarming* (line 152)
- *cultivated* (line 165)
- *imperative* (line 533)

**BEST PRACTICES TOOLKIT—Transparency**
Word Squares p. E10

### FOR ADVANCED LEARNERS/PRE–AP

**Rank Connotations** Have students use a thesaurus to locate three synonyms for a vocabulary word of their choice. Ask students to rank the synonyms on a continuum in order from negative to positive connotations or to put them in a chart according to their connotations. *Example for* zealous: rabid *(negative);* enthusiastic *(neutral);* ardent *(positive).* Encourage students to share and explain their work.

# Language

◆ **GRAMMAR AND STYLE: Add Descriptive Details**

Review the **Grammar and Style** note on page 75. Writers often use **prepositional phrases** to add descriptive details that show what events are taking place and where, when, and how they are taking place. Here is an example from the story:

> *He executed a series of intricate loops; he doubled on his trail again and again, recalling all the lore of the fox hunt, and all the dodges of the fox. Night found him leg-weary, with hands and face lashed by the branches, on a thickly wooded ridge.* (lines 528–531)

Notice how the revisions in blue add descriptive details that show how, when, and where in this diary entry. Revise your response to the prompt below by using the same techniques.

**STUDENT MODEL**

~~in a cold sweat in the middle of the night,~~

Even though it's been several weeks, I still wake up, trembling

~~like a chill in my veins~~
with fear. The feeling of panic is ~~intense~~, and I can't move.

## READING-WRITING CONNECTION

YOUR TURN

Explore the themes of "The Most Dangerous Game" by responding to this prompt. Then use the **revising tip** to improve your writing.

| **WRITING PROMPT** | **REVISING TIP** |
|---|---|
| **Short Constructed Response: Diary Entry** In the dialogue at the beginning of the story, Whitney empathizes with hunted animals. What does Rainsford learn about the feelings of hunted animals from his experience of being hunted? Write **one or two paragraphs** of a diary entry that Rainsford might write on this subject after his experience. | Review your diary entry. Did you use prepositional phrases to help the reader get a sense of what happened, and where, when, and how everything occurred? |

**Interactive Revision**
Go to **thinkcentral.com**.
KEYWORD: HML9-83

---

## FOR STRUGGLING WRITERS

- Have students work in pairs to brainstorm a list of words that describe the feelings that Rainsford experienced when he became Zaroff's quarry (lines 519–681).

- Have students reread the paragraph where Rainsford comes to an understanding of how an animal at bay feels (lines 662–667).

---

 **COMMON CORE**

**L 1b** Use prepositional phrases to convey meanings and add variety and interest to writing.

# Language

COMMON CORE **L 1b**

◆ **GRAMMAR AND STYLE**

- Discuss the revisions to the student model, eliciting the kind of information that each added phrase provides. (For more on prepositional phrases, see **Grammar Handbook**, page R60.)

- Have students add prepositional phrases to this sentence:

  When Rainsford returns, he hides. ***Possible answer:*** *When Rainsford returns to the château, he hides in Zaroff's bedroom until the general's return.*

 **RESOURCE MANAGER**—Copy Master
Add Descriptive Details p. 54

**READING-WRITING CONNECTION**

- Suggest that students brainstorm or freewrite to recapture the feeling of being hunted.

 **BEST PRACTICES TOOLKIT**—Transparency
Main Idea and Details p. B6

| **Writing Online** THINK central |
|---|
| The following tools are available online at **thinkcentral.com** and on **WriteSmart** CD-ROM: • **Interactive Graphic Organizers** • **Interactive Student Models** • **Interactive Revision Lessons** For additional grammar instruction, see **GrammarNotes** on **thinkcentral.com**. |

## Assess and Reteach

### Assess

**DIAGNOSTIC AND SELECTION TESTS**
Selection Test A pp. 27–28
Selection Test B/C pp. 29–30

**Interactive Selection Test** on **thinkcentral.com**

### Reteach

**Level Up Online Tutorials** on **thinkcentral.com**

**Reteaching Worksheets** on **thinkcentral.com**
Literature Lesson 6: Conflict and Suspense
Literature Lesson 9: Setting and Its Roles
Vocabulary Lesson 17: Denotation and Connotation

## COMMON CORE FOCUS

**RL 1** Cite textual evidence to support analysis of what the text says explicitly as well as inferences drawn from the text. **RL 3** Analyze how complex characters interact with other characters and advance the plot. **RL 4** Determine the figurative meaning of phrases as they are used in a text. **L 3** Apply knowledge of language to make effective choices for meaning or style. **L 4c** Consult reference materials to determine or clarify a word's meaning. **W 3d** Use precise words and phrases to convey a vivid picture of the experiences, events, settings, and characters.

## SUMMARY

The narrator, an immigrant, is chosen to write a speech for school. The girl's father finds the speech disrespectful and tears it up. Her mother writes an alternate speech that pleases the father, but not the speech-giver herself.

## What is a
# GENERATION GAP?

Direct students to the question. Together, discuss differences between students' generation and the ones that preceded it. Ask students how a generation gap contributes to parent-child conflicts. Continue the exploration by having students complete and discuss the *ROLE-PLAY.*

# Daughter of Invention
Short Story by Julia Alvarez

# What is a
# GENERATION GAP?

## COMMON CORE

**RL 1** Cite textual evidence to support analysis of what the text says explicitly as well as inferences drawn from the text. **RL 3** Analyze how complex characters interact with other characters and advance the plot. **RL 4** Determine the figurative meaning of phrases as they are used in a text.

What causes parent-child conflicts? Is it inevitable that parents and teenagers disagree? In "Daughter of Invention," a father and his teenage daughter confront this issue head-on.

*ROLE-PLAY* With a small group of classmates, develop a list of subjects that may trigger disagreements between parents and teenagers. With a partner, role-play a dialogue between a parent and a teenager on one of these subjects. Then switch roles and have the conversation again. What insights do you gain?

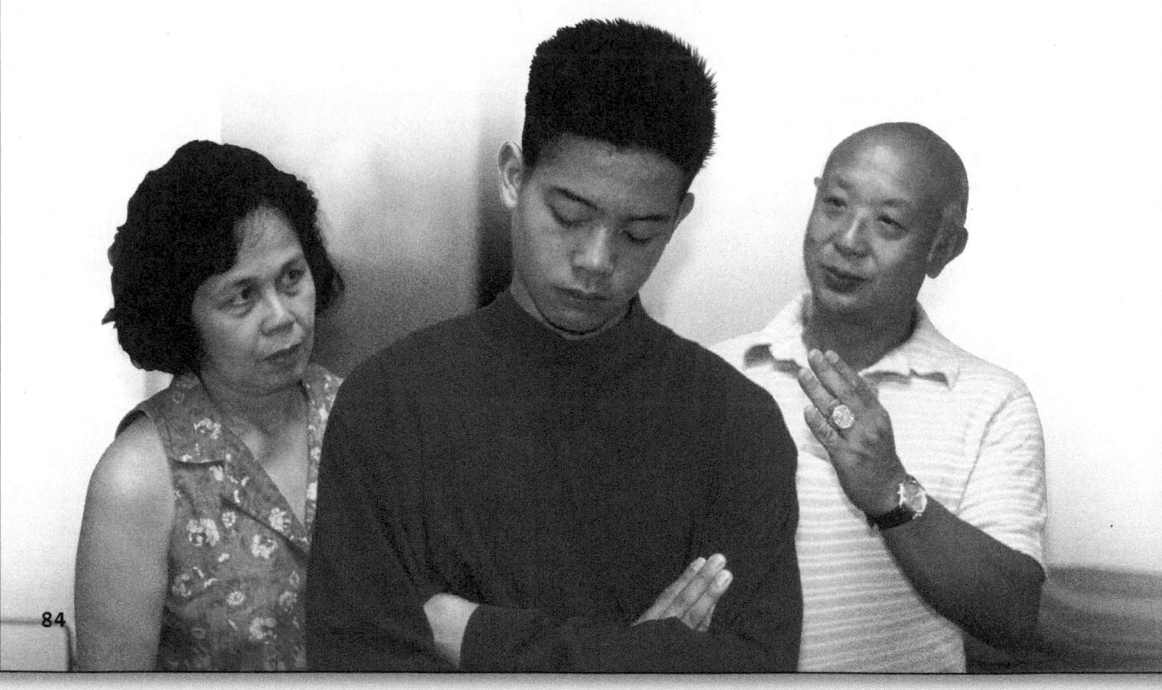

84

See resources on the **Teacher One Stop DVD-ROM** and on **thinkcentral.com**.

### RESOURCE MANAGER UNIT 1
Plan and Teach, pp. 57–64
Summary, pp. 65–66†‡*
Text Analysis and Reading
    Skill, pp. 67–70†*
Vocabulary, pp. 71–73
Grammar and Style, p. 76*

### DIAGNOSTIC AND SELECTION TESTS
Selection Tests, pp. 31–34

### BEST PRACTICES TOOLKIT
Two-Column Chart, p. A25
Sequence Chain, p. B21
Word Squares, p. E10

### TECHNOLOGY
⊘ **Teacher One Stop DVD-ROM**
⊘ **Student One Stop DVD-ROM**
⊘ **Audio Anthology CD**
⊘ **GrammarNotes DVD-ROM**
⊘ **ExamView Test Generator**
   on the **Teacher One Stop**

* Resources for Differentiation        † Also in Spanish        ‡ In Haitian Creole and Vietnamese

## TEXT ANALYSIS: PLOT AND CHARACTER

The plot of a story is shaped by the problems, or **conflicts**, that the main character faces. As the main character responds to the conflict—by making decisions, taking actions, and interacting with other characters—the plot moves forward and engages the reader.

*The poet's words shocked and thrilled me. . . . That night, at last, I started to write, recklessly, three, five pages, looking up only once. . . .*

As you read "Daughter of Invention," notice how the narrator's actions and interactions influence the plot.

## READING SKILL: MAKE INFERENCES

Often a writer will not tell you everything that is going on in a character's mind. Instead, you may need to **make inferences**, or logical guesses, about what the character thinks and feels. To do this, you need to combine story details with what you know from your own experiences.

As you read, look for clues to how the narrator and her parents feel about living in the United States. For each character, use a chart like the one shown to record your observations and inferences.

| Mother | | |
|---|---|---|
| Details from Text | My Own Experience | Inference |
| • She begins inventing in the U.S. | New surroundings could lead to a fresh perspective. | → |
| • | | |
| • | | |

**Review: Clarify**

## ▲ VOCABULARY IN CONTEXT

The following words all have negative connotations. Try writing definitions in your *Reader/Writer Notebook* for as many of these words as you can.

1. disclaimer
2. inhospitable
3. insubordinate
4. misnomer
5. noncommittal
6. plagiarized

 Complete the activities in your **Reader/Writer Notebook**.

---

## Meet the Author

### Julia Alvarez
**born 1950**

**Immigrant Experience**
Like the narrator in "Daughter of Invention," Julia Alvarez emigrated with her family from the Dominican Republic to the United States. As a ten-year-old in New York City, she felt out of place and was sometimes subjected to name-calling. It was at this time that Alvarez began to write, finding comfort in recording memories of her old life in the Dominican Republic. "I found myself turning more and more to writing as the one place where I felt I belonged," Alvarez has said.

**Literary Success**
Alvarez has won many awards for her writing, which includes novels and poetry as well as short stories. Her fiction often centers on the grim political history of the Dominican Republic, as well as the experiences of Hispanic immigrants in New York City. Her poetry and short stories have appeared in numerous magazines and anthologies.

**BACKGROUND TO THE STORY**
**The Dominican Republic Under Trujillo**
In 1960, Alvarez's family fled the Dominican Republic after the discovery of her father's involvement in a plot to overthrow Rafael Trujillo (rä-fä-ĕl' trōō-hē'ō). Trujillo, a brutal dictator, ruled the Dominican Republic from 1930 to 1961, staying in power by suppressing all political opposition. Those who criticized him simply "disappeared"—often after the black Volkswagens of the SIM, Trujillo's secret police, drove up to their homes.

**Authors Online**
Go to **thinkcentral.com**. KEYWORD: HML9-85

**THINK**central

85

---

## Teach

### ● *Model the Skill:* PLOT AND CHARACTER

To model how to determine ways a character's actions influence the plot, read aloud this example:

> Carl works all weekend, trying to prove to his doubting parents that he can follow through on something he starts.

Point out that Carl responds to his conflict with his parents by working hard to disprove their doubts. His response to the conflict moves the plot forward.

**GUIDED PRACTICE** Ask students to predict what actions Carl's parents might take in response to his efforts to prove himself.

### ● *Model the Skill:* MAKE INFERENCES

Use the text under Background to model how to make inferences.

- I know from my own experience that people in the United States can express political views without "disappearing."
- I can infer that the author's family fled the Dominican Republic because they were afraid the father might "disappear."

**GUIDED PRACTICE** Ask students to make inferences about "disappearing."

**R** RESOURCE MANAGER—Copy Master
Make Inferences p. 69

---

## ▲ VOCABULARY IN CONTEXT

**DIAGNOSE WORD KNOWLEDGE** Have all students complete Vocabulary in Context. Check their definitions against the following:

**disclaimer** (dĭs-klā'mər) *n.* a denial of responsibility or knowledge
**inhospitable** (ĭn-hŏs'pĭ-tə-bəl) *adj.* not welcoming; hostile
**insubordinate** (ĭn'sə-bôr'dn-ĭt) *adj.* disobedient to a superior

**misnomer** (mĭs-nō'mər) *n.* an inaccurate or incorrect name
**noncommittal** (nŏn'kə-mĭt'l) *adj.* not committing oneself; not revealing what one thinks
**plagiarized** (plā'jə-rīzd') *adj.* copied from someone else's writings; **plagiarize** *v.*

**PRETEACH VOCABULARY** Use the following copy master to help students analyze word meanings, using context clues.

**R** RESOURCE MANAGER—Copy Master
Vocabulary Study p. 71

1. Read the first item aloud, emphasizing *disclaimer*.
2. Point out the word *denied* in the first sentence and the phrase "is not responsible" in the second sentence. Discuss possible meanings for *disclaimer*, such as "denial."
3. Repeat the procedure for items b–f.

### READ WITH A PURPOSE

*Help students set a purpose for reading. Tell them to read "Daughter of Invention" to learn how the narrator's relationship with her parents changes.*

# Daughter of Invention

### JULIA ALVAREZ

**READING SKILL**

COMMON CORE
RL 1

### Ⓐ MAKE INFERENCES

**Possible answer:** *Story details suggest that the mother is at home attending to the house and children during the day, while the father goes to work, doing what "was for men to do." Therefore, when it is night-time, and she finally has time for herself, the mother wants to engage her mind and creative talents.*

**IF STUDENTS NEED HELP . . .** Have them reread the first and last sentences of paragraph 2. Ask them why the mother might wait to invent until after "settling her house down."

She wanted to invent something, my mother. There was a period after we arrived in this country, until five or so years later, when my mother was inventing. They were never pressing, global needs she was addressing with her pencil and pad. She would have said that was for men to do, rockets and engines that ran on gasoline and turned the wheels of the world. She was just fussing with little house things, don't mind her.

She always invented at night, after settling her house down. On his side of the bed my father would be conked out for an hour already, his Spanish newspaper draped over his chest, his glasses, propped up on his bedside table,

10 looking out eerily at the darkened room like a disembodied guard. But in her lighted corner, like some devoted scholar burning the midnight oil, my mother was inventing, sheets pulled to her lap, pillows propped up behind her, her reading glasses riding the bridge of her nose like a schoolmarm's. On her lap lay one of those innumerable pads of paper my father always brought home from his office, compliments of some pharmaceutical company, advertising tranquilizers or antibiotics or skin cream; in her other hand, my mother held a pencil that looked like a pen with a little cylinder of lead inside. She would work on a sketch of something familiar, but drawn at such close range so she could attach a special nozzle or handier handle, the thing looked peculiar.

20 Once, I mistook the spiral of a corkscrew for a nautilus shell, but it could just as well have been a galaxy forming. Ⓐ

### Analyze Visuals ▶

Examine the portrait. What details help you **draw conclusions** about the woman's personality?

**❶ Targeted Passage**

Ⓐ **MAKE INFERENCES**
Why might the mother spend her evenings sketching inventions?

*Reader with Green Hat* (1909), Henri Charles Manguin. Musée d'Art Moderne de la Ville de Paris, Paris. © Giraudon/Art Resource, New York/2007 Artists Rights Society (ARS), New York/ADAGP, Paris.

---

## DIFFERENTIATED INSTRUCTION

### FOR ENGLISH LANGUAGE LEARNERS

**Options for Reading** Have students read pages 86–94 together. Then have them write four questions related to the reading. Students can discuss the answers with a partner. Finally, have students read the rest of the story together.

### FOR STRUGGLING READERS

Use one or more Targeted Passages (pp. 86, 88, 91, 93, 96) to ensure that students focus on key story events, concepts, and skills. Targeted Passages are also good for English learners.

**❶ Targeted Passage [Lines 1–7]**

This passage provides significant information about the mother in the story and her drive to invent.

**Family Structure** In 1960, Dominican Republic society held strong expectations for women to stay at home and for men to work, typically in the fields or in construction. Starting in the 1960s in the United States, however, the role of women began to change and expand, a change that has profound effects on the family described in "Daughter of Invention."

**Cultural Connection** Historically, fixed division of labor between men and women was found in other agrarian societies, including Ireland, Mexico, and China. Have students discuss division of labor in contemporary society.

## Analyze Visuals

*Possible answer: The woman's facial expression and posture reflect her absorption in the book and suggest her intellectual curiosity.*

**About the Art** In this painting, French Fauve artist Henri Charles Manguin (1874–1949) uses color to present the subject as the focal point of the portrait. The dark shades of paint on the wall and table contrast with the lighter tints of the woman's shawl to create an intimate and cozy world where she sits calmly reading. Similarly, the mother in the story absorbs herself in solitary and creative activity.

- Who is the narrator in relation to the mother? (line 1)

- What do you learn about the mother? (lines 1–7)

- What connection can you make between this passage and the title of the story? (line 1)

**FOR ADVANCED LEARNERS/PRE–AP**

**Analyze** Have students discuss what they have learned so far about the story's characters, plot, and setting. Then have students analyze the author's word choice and sentence structure. Ask how use of these stylistic techniques affects students' perceptions of the characters, especially the narrator. Ask students to name adjectives they think describe the narrator and then make inferences about the narrator's age, thoughts and feelings, and relationship with her parents.

It was the only time all day we'd catch her sitting down, for she herself was living proof of the *perpetuum mobile*[1] machine so many inventors had sought over the ages. My sisters and I would seek her out now when she seemed to have a moment to talk to us: We were having trouble at school or we wanted her to persuade my father to give us permission to go into the city or to a shopping mall or a movie—in broad daylight! My mother would wave us out of her room. "The problem with you girls . . ." I can tell you right now what the problem always boiled down to: We wanted to become Americans and my
30 father—and my mother, at first—would have none of it.

"You girls are going to drive me crazy!" She always threatened if we kept nagging. "When I end up in Bellevue,[2] you'll be safely sorry!"

She spoke in English when she argued with us, even though, in a matter of months, her daughters were the fluent ones. Her English was much better than my father's, but it was still a mishmash of mixed-up idioms and sayings that showed she was "green behind the ears," as she called it.

If my sisters and I tried to get her to talk in Spanish, she'd snap, "When in Rome, do unto the Romans . . ."

I had become the spokesman for my sisters, and I would stand my ground
40 in that bedroom. "We're not going to that school anymore, Mami!"

"You have to." Her eyes would widen with worry. "In this country, it is against the law not to go to school. You want us to get thrown out?"

"You want us to get killed? Those kids were throwing stones today!"

"Sticks and stones don't break bones . . ." she chanted. I could tell, though, by the look on her face, it was as if one of those stones the kids had aimed at us had hit her. But she always pretended we were at fault. "What did you do to provoke them? It takes two to tangle, you know."

"Thanks, thanks a lot, Mom!" I'd storm out of that room and into mine. I never called her *Mom* except when I wanted her to feel how much she had
50 failed us in this country. She was a good enough Mami, fussing and scolding and giving advice, but a terrible girlfriend parent, a real failure of a Mom.

Back she'd go to her pencil and pad, scribbling and tsking and tearing off paper, finally giving up, and taking up her *New York Times*. Some nights, though, she'd get a good idea, and she'd rush into my room, a flushed look on her face, her tablet of paper in her hand, a cursory knock on the door she'd just thrown open: "Do I have something to show you, Cukita!"

This was my time to myself, after I'd finished my homework, while my sisters were still downstairs watching TV in the basement. Hunched over my small desk, the overhead light turned off, my lamp shining poignantly on
60 my paper, the rest of the room in warm, soft, uncreated darkness, I wrote my secret poems in my new language.

---

1. *perpetuum mobile* (pĕr-pĕt′ōō-əm mō′bĭ-lĕ) *Latin:* perpetual motion (operating continuously without a sustained input of energy).

2. **Bellevue** (bĕl′vyōō′): a large hospital in New York City, with a well-known psychiatric ward.

**B PLOT AND CHARACTER**

*Possible answer: The narrator feels that her mother is not living up to her image of an American mom. The narrator feels that such a mother would be sympathetic to her daughters' concerns and try to solve them.*

**IF STUDENTS NEED HELP . . .** Read aloud lines 48–51, beginning with the words "Thanks, thanks a lot, Mom!" Help students use a Two-Column Chart to show the narrator's two perceptions of her mother—one as a Mami and one as a Mom.

 BEST PRACTICES TOOLKIT—Transparency
Two-Column Chart p. A25

**C GRAMMAR AND STYLE**    COMMON CORE L 3

**Analyze the Use of Modifiers** Good writers use modifiers, which include adjectives and adverbs, to make their writing more descriptive and therefore more interesting. To highlight the impact of the modifiers used by the author in lines 57–61, invite a volunteer to read aloud the passage, omitting the adjectives and adverb. Then discuss the difference in the passage with and without modifiers. Have students look for other modifiers in the selection and notice how they add to the descriptions of characters, settings, and events.

---

COMMON CORE RL 4

**Language Coach**

**Idioms** An **idiom** is an expression that cannot be understood literally. In line 36, the mother mixes the metaphor "green" with the idiom "wet behind the ears." Both expressions mean "young and inexperienced." What do the idioms "break a leg" and "in your face" mean?

**2 Targeted Passage**

**B PLOT AND CHARACTER**
Why was the narrator disappointed in her mother?

**C GRAMMAR AND STYLE**
Reread lines 57–61. Alvarez uses **modifiers** such as *poignantly, warm, soft,* and *secret* to convey the special atmosphere that surrounds the narrator as she writes.

---

## DIFFERENTIATED INSTRUCTION

### FOR STRUGGLING READERS

**2 Targeted Passage [Lines 39–51]**

This passage sets up the conflict between the daughters and their mother.

- What problem do the children face at school? (line 43)

- How do you think the mother's reaction to the problem makes the narrator feel? What clues in the passage help you know this? (lines 48–51)

### FOR ENGLISH LANGUAGE LEARNERS

**Language Coach**     COMMON CORE RL 4

**Meanings of Idioms** Have students reread lines 33–36 to understand the idiom the mother uses. The narrator's mother uses two other mixed-up idioms and sayings: "When in Rome, do unto the Romans" and "Sticks and stones don't break bones." What do students think these phrases mean?

"You're going to ruin your eyes!" My mother would storm into my room, turning on the overly bright overhead light, scaring off whatever shy passion I had just begun coaxing out of a labyrinth of feelings with the blue thread of my writing.

"Oh Mami!" I'd cry out, my eyes blinking up at her. "I'm writing."

"Ay, Cukita." That was her communal pet name for whoever was in her favor. "Cukita, when I make a million, I'll buy you your very own typewriter." (I'd been nagging my mother for one just like the one father had bought her
70 to do his order forms at home.) "Gravy on the turkey" was what she called it when someone was buttering her up. She'd butter and pour. "I'll hire you your very own typist."

Down she'd plop on my bed and hold out her pad to me. "Take a guess, Cukita?" I'd study her rough sketch a moment: soap sprayed from the nozzle head of a shower when you turned the knob a certain way? Coffee with creamer already mixed in? Time-released water capsules for your plants when you were away? A key chain with a timer that would go off when your parking meter was about to expire? (The ticking would help you find your keys easily if you mislaid them.) The famous one, famous only in hindsight, was the stick
80 person dragging a square by a rope—a suitcase with wheels? "Oh, of course," we'd humor her. "What every household needs: a shower like a car wash, keys ticking like a bomb, luggage on a leash!" By now, as you can see, it'd become something of a family joke, our Thomas Edison Mami, our Benjamin Franklin Mom.[3]

Her face would fall. "Come on now! Use your head." One more wrong guess, and she'd tell me, pressing with her pencil point the different highlights of this incredible new wonder. "Remember that time we took the car to Bear Mountain,[4] and we re-ah-lized that we had forgotten to pack an opener with our pick-a-nick?" (We kept correcting her, but she insisted this is how
90 it should be said.) "When we were ready to eat we didn't have any way to open the refreshments cans?" (This before fliptop lids, which she claimed had crossed her mind.) "You know what this is now?" A shake of my head. "Is a car bumper, but see this part is a removable can opener. So simple and yet so necessary, no?"

"Yeah, Mami. You should patent it." I'd shrug. She'd tear off the scratch paper and fold it, carefully, corner to corner, as if she were going to save it. But then, she'd toss it in the wastebasket on her way out of the room and give a little laugh like a **disclaimer.** "It's half of one or two dozen of another . . ."

I suppose none of her daughters was very encouraging. We resented her
100 spending time on those dumb inventions. Here, we were trying to fit in America among Americans; we needed help figuring out who we were, why these Irish kids whose grandparents were micks two generations ago, why they

**disclaimer**
(dĭs-klā'mər) *n.* a denial of responsibility or knowledge

---

3. **Thomas Edison Mami . . . Benjamin Franklin Mom:** Edison and Franklin were celebrated inventors.
4. **Bear Mountain:** a state park not far from New York City.

---

Use these prompts to help students understand the irony of the mother's inventive ideas in lines 73–94:

**Connect** Which of the mother's inventive ideas have you seen either in person or in an advertisement? *Students should cite evidence from their lives (lines 74–80, 87–94).*

**Analyze** What is the narrator's intent in comparing her mother to Thomas Edison and Benjamin Franklin? Cite evidence. *Possible answer: Her mother is so passionate about her ideas for inventions that the family jokingly compares her to two historically significant inventors (lines 82–84).*

**Synthesize** What is ironic about the way the narrator perceives her mother's ideas for inventions and the destinies of those same concepts? Possible answer: Many of the invention ideas the mother conceived and later disregarded were eventually patented and produced by other people. Many of these products are sold today.

**REVISIT THE BIG QUESTION**

What is a

# GENERATION GAP?

**Discuss** In lines 99–107, how does limited understanding of a situation or of another's perspective contribute to the parent-child conflicts in this story? *The daughters have no understanding of their mother's need to invent (lines 99–100); the mother doesn't have enough understanding of American culture to know how to help her daughters fit in (lines 104–107).*

---

**FOR ENGLISH LANGUAGE LEARNERS**

**Reading: Background** Explain that in the United States, inventors can register their ideas with the Patent Office to prevent someone from stealing them.

**FOR STRUGGLING READERS**

**Comprehension Support** Direct students to lines 99–103. Point out how this passage gives insight into the conflicts between the daughters and their mother. The daughters are upset that the mother devotes so much attention and time to her inventions. They feel she should be helping them figure out how to fit in.

**VOCABULARY**                    COMMON CORE
L 4

**OWN THE WORD**

**disclaimer:** Remind students that *dis-* means "opposite of." Have them use the meaning of *dis-* to explain the meaning of *disclaimer.* Then, have students create a list of other words that begin with *dis-.*

*Possible answers: disabled, disadvantage, disagree, discomfort, disrespectful*

## D MAKE INFERENCES

**Possible answer:** *Although Papi is successful in America, he continues to struggle with memories of his terrifying past. He dreams about it (line 118) and secretly fears the Dominican authorities will come after him and his family (line 120).*

**IF STUDENTS NEED HELP . . .** Have students list the story details in lines 112–116 that tell about life in the Dominican Republic.

## ADDITIONAL TEACHING OPPORTUNITY

**Flashback** Recall that a flashback is usually an account of a conversation, an episode, or an event that happened before the beginning of the story, one that often shows how past events led up to the present situation. In lines 110–120, how does this flashback about Papi's experiences in the Dominican Republic help you understand his behavior in this scene?

## TIERED DISCUSSION PROMPTS

Direct students to lines 108–143. Use these prompts to help students understand the narrator's mother:

**Connect** How do you feel about the mother? Explain. *Accept all reasonable responses.*

**Analyze** What are the mother's personality traits? Cite evidence. *Possible answers: The way she calls out at night while her husband is sleeping shows that she is lively and emotional (line 110). She is creative and invents things (lines 125–127). She is a hard worker (lines 140–143).*

**Evaluate** How does the author bring the mother's personality to life? *Possible answer: The author effectively shows that the mother is excitable through her lively language with all of its mixed-up American sayings (lines 125–132, 136–137).*

---

were calling us spics.[5] Why had we come to the country in the first place? Important, crucial, final things, you see, and here was our own mother, who didn't have a second to help us puzzle any of this out, inventing gadgets to make life easier for American moms. Why, it seemed as if she were arming our own enemy against us!

One time, she did have a moment of triumph. Every night, she liked to read *The New York Times* in bed before turning off her light, to see what the
110 Americans were up to. One night, she let out a yelp to wake up my father beside her, bolt upright, reaching for his glasses which, in his haste, he knocked across the room. "*Que pasa? Que pasa?*" What is wrong? There was terror in his voice, fear she'd seen in his eyes in the Dominican Republic before we left. We were being watched there; he was being followed; he and mother had often exchanged those looks. They could not talk, of course, though they must have whispered to each other in fear at night in the dark bed. Now in America, he was safe, a success even; his Centro Medico[6] in Brooklyn was thronged with the sick and the homesick. But in dreams, he went back to those awful days and long nights, and my mother's screams confirmed his secret fear: we had
120 not gotten away after all; they had come for us at last. **D**

"Ay, Papi, I'm sorry. Go back to sleep, Cukito. It's nothing, nothing really." My mother held up the *Times* for him to squint at the small print, back page headline, one hand tapping all over the top of the bedside table for his glasses, the other rubbing his eyes to wakefulness.

"Remember, remember how I showed you that suitcase with little wheels so we would not have to carry those heavy bags when we traveled? Someone stole my idea and made a million!" She shook the paper in his face. She shook the paper in all our faces that night. "See! See! This man was no *bobo*! He didn't put all his pokers on a back burner. I kept telling you, one of these days
130 my ship would pass me by in the night!" She wagged her finger at my sisters and my father and me, laughing all the while, one of those eerie laughs crazy people in movies laugh. We had congregated in her room to hear the good news she'd been yelling down the stairs, and now we eyed her and each other. I suppose we were all thinking the same thing: Wouldn't it be weird and sad if Mami did end up in Bellevue as she'd always threatened she might?

"*Ya, ya!* Enough!" She waved us out of her room at last. "There is no use trying to drink spilt milk, that's for sure."

It was the suitcase rollers that stopped my mother's hand; she had weather vaned a minor brainstorm. She would have to start taking herself seriously.
140 That blocked the free play of her ingenuity. Besides, she had also begun working at my father's office, and at night, she was too tired and busy filling in columns with how much money they had made that day to be fooling with gadgets!

---

5. **micks . . . spics:** derogatory terms for people of Irish descent and people of Hispanic descent, respectively.
6. **Centro Medico** (sĕn′trō mĕ′dē-kō): medical center.

**D** MAKE INFERENCES
What **internal conflict** does the narrator's father struggle with? Include thorough evidence from the text to support your answer.

**Language Coach**

**Idioms** In line 129, the mother mixes the idioms "don't put all your pokers in one fire" (which means not to risk everything) and "put on a back burner" (meaning to set aside). What thought is she trying to express to her family?

---

## DIFFERENTIATED INSTRUCTION

### FOR ENGLISH LANGUAGE LEARNERS

**Language Coach**

COMMON CORE RL 4

**Idioms** Students may struggle with the meanings of the numerous mixed-up idioms in the story. Point out the idiom in line 130. Ask students what they think it means. Have students restate, or paraphrase, what the mother says in lines 128–130.

### FOR ADVANCED LEARNERS/PRE–AP

**Research Activity** Have students research the adjustment process of recent immigrants to the United States, especially those from repressive dictatorships. Ask students to compare the experiences of these families with the experience of the family described in "Daughter of Invention," especially with regard to recent immigration policies, educational opportunities, and how families grapple with redefining traditional roles of authority.

**❸**

She did take up her pencil and pad one last time to help me out. In ninth grade, I was chosen by my English teacher, Sister Mary Joseph, to deliver the teacher's day address at the school assembly. 150 Back in the Dominican Republic, I was a terrible student. No one could ever get me to sit down to a book. But in New York, I needed to settle somewhere, and the natives were unfriendly, the country **inhospitable,** so I took root in the language. By high school, the nuns were reading my stories and compositions out loud 160 to my classmates as examples of imagination at work.

This time my imagination jammed. At first I didn't want and then I couldn't seem to write that speech. I suppose I should have thought of it as a "great honor," as my father called it. But I was mortified. I still had a pronounced lilt to my accent, and I did not like 170 to speak in public, subjecting myself to my classmates' ridicule. Recently, they had begun to warm toward my sisters and me, and it took no great figuring to see that to deliver a eulogy for a convent full of crazy, old overweight nuns was no way to endear myself to the members of my class.

But I didn't know how to get out of it. Week after week, I'd sit down, hoping to polish off some quick, **noncommittal** little speech. I couldn't get 180 anything down.

The weekend before our Monday morning assembly I went into a panic. My mother would just have to call in and say I was in the hospital, in a coma. I was in the Dominican Republic. Yeah, that was it! Recently, my father had been talking about going back home to live.

*La Mère de l'artiste* (1889), Paul Gauguin. Oil on canvas. Staatsgalerie, Stuttgart. Photo © akg-images, London.

**inhospitable**
(ĭn-hŏs′pĭ-tə-bəl) *adj.* not welcoming; hostile

**noncommittal**
(nŏn′kə-mĭt′l) *adj.* not committing oneself; not revealing what one thinks

DAUGHTER OF INVENTION  **91**

## Analyze Visuals

**Activity** Point out the concerned expression on the face of the young woman in the painting. Discuss a time when, up to this point in the story, the narrator might have worn a similar expression. ***Possible answer:*** *The narrator might have looked this way when she thought about giving her speech to her class (lines 163–171).*

**About the Art** Post-impressionist painter Paul Gauguin (1848–1903) was a pioneer in the use of color and the expression of feeling in art. This painting is titled *The Artist's Mother*, but its subject has a young, unlined face with pink cheeks and a youthful ribbon in her hair. Her eyes, which seem to look directly at the viewer, are filled with feeling. Her looks may strike many students as Latina; in fact, Gauguin's mother was of Peruvian descent.

### OWN THE WORD

- **inhospitable:** Have students find a context clue in the sentence to help determine the meaning of *inhospitable*. Then have students cite synonyms for *inhospitable*. ***Possible answers:*** *unfriendly, ungracious*

- **noncommittal:** Have students look within the following sentence to find clues about the meaning of *noncommittal: I knew my friends did not share my opinion about the rule changes at school, so I was careful to make only a few noncommittal remarks about them.*

---

**FOR STRUGGLING READERS**

**❸ Targeted Passage [Lines 144–171]**

This passage provides the reader with background information that is important to the upcoming climax of the story. It also hints at future events between the daughter and her mother.

- What kind of student was the narrator in the Dominican Republic? What kind of student is she now? (lines 150–161)

- How does the narrator feel about being chosen to give the speech? (lines 165–168)

- Reread lines 144–145. How do you predict the mother will help out the narrator? (lines 144–145)

**E** **CLARIFY**

Help students understand the meaning of the quotation "Necessity is the mother of invention." Discuss why the author may have chosen to have the mother misquote this saying when she states, "Necessity is the daughter of invention." ***Possible answer:*** *Throughout the story, the mother mixes up familiar phrases, a behavior the daughters might find endearingly humorous. Because the mother has many ideas for inventing gadgets that are "necessities," it makes sense that the narrator is thought of as a daughter of invention.*

---

**TEXT ANALYSIS**

COMMON CORE

RL 3

**F** **PLOT AND CHARACTER**

***Possible answer:*** *The quotation from Whitman shows that the poet "sings" about himself. In other words, he writes about himself in his own words. He learns to "destroy the teacher"; that is, he does not look to others to find out what he should say. Whitman seems more real to the narrator than other poets she has read.*

---

My mother tried to calm me down. "Just remember how Mister Lincoln couldn't think of anything to say at the Gettysburg, but then, Bang! 'Four score and once upon a time ago,'"[7] she began reciting. Her version of history was half invention and half truths and whatever else she needed to prove a point. "Something is going to come if you just relax. You'll see, like the Americans
190 say, 'Necessity is the daughter of invention.' I'll help you." **E**

All weekend, she kept coming into my room with help. "Please, Mami, just leave me alone, please," I pleaded with her. But I'd get rid of the goose only to have to contend with the gander. My father kept poking his head in the door just to see if I had "fulfilled my obligations," a phrase he'd used when we were a little younger, and he'd check to see whether we had gone to the bathroom before a car trip. Several times that weekend around the supper table, he'd recite his valedictorian speech from when he graduated from high school. He'd give me pointers on delivery, on the great orators and their tricks. (Humbleness and praise and falling silent with great emotion were his favorites.)
200 My mother sat across the table, the only one who seemed to be listening to him. My sisters and I were forgetting a lot of our Spanish, and my father's formal, florid diction was even harder to understand. But my mother smiled softly to herself, and turned the Lazy Susan at the center of the table around and around as if it were the prime mover, the first gear of attention.

That Sunday evening, I was reading some poetry to get myself inspired: Whitman in an old book with an engraved cover my father had picked up in a thrift shop next to his office a few weeks back. "I celebrate myself and sing myself . . ." "He most honors my style who learns under it to destroy the teacher."[8] The poet's words shocked and thrilled me. I had gotten used to the
210 nuns, a literature of appropriate sentiments, poems with a message, expurgated texts. But here was a flesh and blood man, belching and laughing and sweating in poems. "Who touches this book touches a man."

That night, at last, I started to write, recklessly, three, five pages, looking up once only to see my father passing by the hall on tiptoe. When I was done, I read over my words, and my eyes filled. I finally sounded like myself in English! **F**

As soon as I had finished that first draft, I called my mother to my room. She listened attentively, as she had to my father's speech, and in the end, her eyes were glistening too. Her face was soft and warm and proud. "That is a beautiful, beautiful speech, Cukita. I want for your father to hear it before he
220 goes to sleep. Then I will type it for you, all right?"

Down the hall we went, the two of us, faces flushed with accomplishment. Into the master bedroom where my father was propped up on his pillows, still awake, reading the Dominican papers, already days old. He had become interested in his country's fate again. The dictatorship had been toppled. The

---

7. **"Four score and once upon a time ago":** Mami is misquoting President Abraham Lincoln's Gettysburg Address, which begins "Four score and seven years ago, . . ."

8. **"I celebrate . . . destroy the teacher":** lines from the long poem "Song of Myself," by the American poet Walt Whitman (1819–1892).

**E** **CLARIFY**
Reread lines 185–190. The correct proverb is "Necessity is the mother of invention." Note that the title of the story is taken from the mother's misquotation.

**F** **PLOT AND CHARACTER**
Why do you think the experience of reading Whitman finally freed the narrator to write her speech?

---

## DIFFERENTIATED INSTRUCTION

**FOR ENGLISH LANGUAGE LEARNERS**

**Vocabulary: Idioms and Sayings** Explain that throughout this story, Mami misuses or misstates common English sayings. For each example, introduce the correct form or saying, and explain its meaning.

**Examples:**

- *It takes two to tangle* (line 47), original saying: "It takes two to tango." Meaning: it takes two to create an argument.

- *It's half of one or two dozen of another* (line 98), original saying: "Six of one, half a dozen of the other." Meaning: it doesn't matter which choice you make, both are equal.

- *Necessity is the daughter of invention* (line 190), original saying: "Necessity is the mother of invention." Meaning: our needs cause us to invent devices.

interim government was going to hold the first free elections in thirty years. There was still some question in his mind whether or not we might want to move back. History was in the making, freedom and hope were in the air again! But my mother had gotten used to the life here. She did not want to go back to the old country where she was only a wife and a mother (and a
230 failed one at that, since she had never had the required son). She did not come straight out and disagree with my father's plans. Instead, she fussed with him about reading the papers in bed, soiling those sheets with those poorly printed, foreign tabloids. "*The Times* is not that bad!" she'd claim if my father tried to humor her by saying they shared the same dirty habit. **G**

**G** MAKE INFERENCES
How has the mother changed since coming to the United States? Cite evidence.

The minute my father saw my mother and me, filing in, he put his paper down, and his face brightened as if at long last his wife had delivered a son, and that was the news we were bringing him. His teeth were already grinning from the glass of water next to his bedside lamp, so he lisped when he
240 said, "Eh-speech, eh-speech!"

"It is so beautiful, Papi," my mother previewed him, turning the sound off on his TV. She sat down at the foot of the bed. I stood before both of them, blocking their view of the soldiers in helicopters landing amid silenced gun reports and explosions. A few weeks ago it had been the shores of the Dominican Republic. Now it was the jungles of Southeast Asia they were saving. My mother gave me the nod to begin reading.

250 I didn't need much encouragement. I put my nose to the fire, as my mother would have said, and read from start to finish without looking up. When I was done, I was a little embarrassed at my pride in my own words. I pretended to quibble with a phrase or two I was sure I'd be talked out of changing. I looked questioningly to my mother. Her face was radiant. She turned to share her pride with my father.

But the expression on his face shocked us both.
260 His toothless mouth had collapsed into a dark zero. His eyes glared at me, then shifted to my mother, accusingly. In barely audible Spanish, as if secret microphones or informers were all about, he whispered, "You will permit her to read *that?*"

④ **Targeted Passage**

*Pedro Mañach* (1901), Pablo Picasso. Oil on linen, 41½″ × 27″; framed: 53″ × 38⅛″ × 4″. National Gallery of Art, Washington, D.C., Chester Dale Collection. © 2004 Board of Trustees of the National Gallery of Art/2007 Estate of Pablo Picasso/Artists Rights Society (ARS), New York (1963.10.53).

DAUGHTER OF INVENTION    **93**

**READING SKILL**   **COMMON CORE**
RL 1

**G MAKE INFERENCES**

*Possible answer:* *The mother has expanded herself beyond her roles as wife and mother. She has asserted her creative side as an inventor (line 1), has begun working at the father's office (lines 140–141), and does not measure herself by the standards of the old country (lines 229–230). She also asserts her desires, though indirectly, by distracting her husband with talk about the messy paper, instead of agreeing with him (lines 230–234).*

## Analyze Visuals

**Activity**  Ask students in what way the father and the man in the painting seem alike at this point in the story. *Possible answer: Both seem authoritarian and unyielding.*

**About the Art**  Spanish painter Pablo Picasso (1881–1973), who employed many styles in his long career, is known for using geometric shapes in many of his paintings. Here, Picasso takes the curved lines of the human body and turns them into squares, rectangles, and angles. With his pointed eyebrow and the right angle of his arm and body, the man looks quite the opposite of warm and approachable.

**FOR STRUGGLING READERS**

④ **Targeted Passage** [Lines 250–264]

This passage depicts the contrast between the mother and father in terms of how far they've come in adapting to the mores of their new culture.

• How does the mother feel about her daughter's speech? (lines 257–258)

• How does the father feel about the speech? (lines 259–264)

• How do you think the father's reaction makes the daughter feel? (lines 259, 264)

**Concept Support: Cultural Differences**
[small-group option]  Have students use a Two-Column Chart to show differences between the Dominican culture that the parents know and the American culture the children are being raised in.

🧰 **BEST PRACTICES TOOLKIT—Transparency** Two-Column Chart p. A25

## What is a
# GENERATION GAP?

**Discuss** In lines 265–268, what aspect of the parents' history widens the generation gap in the story and contributes to the family's conflicts? *Possible answer: The narrator's parents lived most of their lives in a country where questioning authority was frowned upon and where interactions between parent and child were more formal than in the United States.*

---

###  MAKE INFERENCES

*Possible answer: One emotion is fear, stemming from the father's anxiety about the Dominican Republic authorities' cruelty. He also wants to teach his daughter the value of being respectful in her new country. He may even be worried that his own authority is being threatened by a house full of independent women.*

**IF STUDENTS NEED HELP...** Have students reread lines 286–288 and use their Making Inferences charts to help them answer the question.

| | Father | |
|---|---|---|
| Details | My Own Experience | Inference |
| mother joining forces with daughters | father feeling outnumbered | conflict building between females in family and father |

---

### OWN THE WORD

- **plagiarized:** Have students read the definition of the adjective *plagiarized*. Remind them that the verb is *plagiarize*, and the noun is *plagiarism*.

- **insubordinate:** Have students use the context clues in line 275 to find adjectives for *insubordinate*. *Possible answers: improper, disrespecting*

---

My mother's eyebrows shot up, her mouth fell open. In the old country, any whisper of a challenge to authority could bring the secret police in their black V.W.'s. But this was America. People could say what they thought. "What is wrong with her speech?" my mother questioned him.

"What ees wrrrong with her eh-speech?" My father wagged his head at
270 her. His anger was always more frightening in his broken English. As if he had mutilated the language in his fury—and now there was nothing to stand between us and his raw, dumb anger. "What is wrong? I will tell you what is wrong. It shows no gratitude. It is boastful. 'I celebrate myself?' 'The best student learns to destroy the teacher'?" He mocked my **plagiarized** words. "That is **insubordinate**. It is improper. It is disrespecting of her teachers—" In his anger he had forgotten his fear of lurking spies: Each wrong he voiced was a decibel higher than the last outrage. Finally, he was yelling at me, "As your father, I forbid you to say that eh-speech!"

My mother leapt to her feet, a sign always that she was about to make a
280 speech or deliver an ultimatum. She was a small woman, and she spoke all her pronouncements standing up, either for more protection or as a carry-over from her girlhood in convent schools where one asked for, and literally took, the floor in order to speak. She stood by my side, shoulder to shoulder; we looked down at my father. "That is no tone of voice, Eduardo—" she began.

By now, my father was truly furious. I suppose it was bad enough I was rebelling, but here was my mother joining forces with me. Soon he would be surrounded by a house full of independent American women. He too leapt from his bed, throwing off his covers. The Spanish newspapers flew across the
290 room. He snatched my speech out of my hands, held it before my panicked eyes, a vengeful, mad look in his own, and then once, twice, three, four, countless times, he tore my prize into shreds.

"Are you crazy?" My mother lunged at him. "Have you gone mad? That is her speech for tomorrow you have torn up!"

"Have *you* gone mad?" He shook her away. "You were going to let her read that . . . that insult to her teachers?"

"Insult to her teachers!" My mother's face had crumpled up like a piece of paper. On it was written a love note to my father. Ever since they had come to this country, their life together was a constant war. "This is America, Papi,
300 America!" she reminded him now. "You are not in a savage country any more!"

I was on my knees, weeping wildly, collecting all the little pieces of my speech, hoping that I could put it back together before the assembly tomorrow morning. But not even a sibyl[9] could have made sense of all those scattered pieces of paper. All hope was lost. "He broke it, he broke it," I moaned as I picked up a handful of pieces.

---

9. **sibyl** (sĭb′əl): a female prophet. (According to the Roman poet Virgil, the sibyl of Cumae recorded the words of her prophecies on tree leaves, which she arranged on the floor of her cave. If the wind scattered the leaves, the prophecies became unintelligible.)

**94**   UNIT 1: NARRATIVE STRUCTURE

---

**plagiarized**
(plā′jə-rīzd′) *adj.* copied from someone else's writings **plagiarize** *v.*

**insubordinate**
(ĭn′sə-bôr′dn-ĭt)
*adj.* disobedient to a superior

---

 MAKE INFERENCES
Reread lines 269–292. What emotions besides anger might be behind the father's action?

---

## DIFFERENTIATED INSTRUCTION

### FOR ADVANCED LEARNERS/PRE–AP
**External or Internal Conflict** Have students list the various conflicts in the story, identify them as external or internal, and explain the reasoning behind their choices. For example:

- *Mother versus daughters:* The mother says the girls will drive her crazy. (external)

- *Father versus daughter:* He disapproves of the first draft of the narrator's speech. (external)

- *Mother versus father:* The mother disagrees with Papi's reaction to the narrator's speech. (external)

- *Father's past versus father's present:* Papi is still haunted by his experiences in the Dominican Republic. (internal)

- *Daughter versus father:* She weeps as she gathers up the shreds of her speech. (external)

- *Daughter versus writing speech:* At first she is mortified to write her speech. (internal)

---

Probably, if I had thought a moment about it, I would not have done what I did next. I would have realized my father had lost brothers and comrades to the dictator Trujillo. For the rest of his life, he would be haunted by blood in the streets and late night disappearances. Even after he had been in the
310 states for years, he jumped if a black Volkswagen passed him on the street. He feared anyone in uniform: the meter maid giving out parking tickets, a museum guard approaching to tell him not to touch his favorite Goya[10] at the Metropolitan.

I took a handful of the scraps I had gathered, stood up, and hurled them in his face. "Chapita!" I said in a low, ugly whisper. "You're just another Chapita!"

It took my father only a moment
320 to register the hated nickname of our dictator, and he was after me. Down the halls we raced, but I was quicker than he and made it to my room just in time to lock the door as my father threw his weight against it. He called down curses on my head, ordered me on his authority as my father to open that door this very instant! He throttled
330 that doorknob, but all to no avail. My mother's love of gadgets saved my hide that night. She had hired a locksmith to install good locks on all the bedroom doors after our house had been broken into while we were away the previous summer. In case burglars broke in again, and we were in the house, they'd have a second round of locks to contend with before they got to us. ❶

"Eduardo," she tried to calm him down. "Don't you ruin my new locks."

He finally did calm down, his anger spent. I heard their footsteps retreating
340 down the hall. I heard their door close, the clicking of their lock. Then, muffled voices, my mother's peaking in anger, in persuasion, my father's deep murmurs of explanation and of self-defense. At last, the house fell silent, before I heard, far off, the gun blasts and explosions, the serious, self-important voices of newscasters reporting their TV war.

A little while later, there was a quiet knock at my door, followed by a tentative attempt at the doorknob. "Cukita?" my mother whispered. "Open up, Cukita."

"Go away," I wailed, but we both knew I was glad she was there, and I needed only a moment's protest to save face before opening that door.

---

10. **Goya** (goi′ə): a painting by the Spanish artist Francisco de Goya y Lucientes (1746–1828).

▼ **Analyze Visuals**

This painting depicts the execution of a group of Spaniards by Napoleon's occupying army. Why do you think a painting like this might appeal to someone like Papi? Explain.

*The Third of May, 1808* (1814), Francisco de Goya y Lucientes. Oil on canvas, 266 cm × 345 cm. Museo del Prado, Madrid. Photo © Erich Lessing/Art Resource, New York.

❶ **PLOT AND CHARACTER**
Why does the narrator's father become enraged at her?

DAUGHTER OF INVENTION    95

---

## Analyze Visuals

*Possible answer:* *Papi would probably relate to the painting's strong depiction of violence and tyranny. Having lived through political terror in the Dominican Republic, Papi may have witnessed such scenes (lines 308–309). His fear of anyone in uniform is so great it carries over to his early years in the United States (lines 311–313).*

**About the Art** Spanish painter Francisco de Goya y Lucientes (1746–1828) depicts the horror of political tyranny in this painting called *The Third of May, 1808.*

**TEXT ANALYSIS**  COMMON CORE  RL 3

❶ *Model the Skill:* **PLOT AND CHARACTER**

To model how to determine why the narrator's father becomes enraged at her, review with students the events that followed the narrator's reading of her speech to her parents and how she and her parents interacted.

1. Direct students to lines 272–275 and lines 290–292, and then ask them how the narrator's father responded to the speech.

2. Have students reread lines 306–318, and ask students how the narrator responded to her father.

Point out that the conflict between father and daughter escalates with each action and response until the father is enraged and chasing his daughter down the hall.

*Possible answer:* *The speech itself threatens the father's view of authority. He doesn't want his daughter to be disrespectful to her teachers, and he feels that her speech does just that (lines 272–275). The fact that his daughter calls him "Chapita" reminds him of his life in the Dominican Republic. There, he fought against a dictator (nicknamed "Chapita") who was cruel and brutal to citizens. Hearing his daughter compare him to the dictator is very hurtful and insulting (lines 316–321).*

---

## FOR ENGLISH LANGUAGE LEARNERS

**Comprehension: Transitions** Reread lines 339–347. Point out the signal words that help readers keep track of the sequence of events: *finally, then, at last, later, followed by.* Have students use a Sequence Chain to list these events in the order they occurred, using the signal words.

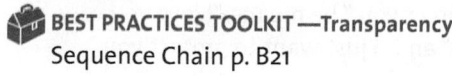 **BEST PRACTICES TOOLKIT —Transparency**
Sequence Chain p. B21

## FOR STRUGGLING READERS

**Develop Reading Fluency** In lines 326–329 the author tells readers what the narrator's father says to her instead of writing the words as direct discourse. Have students rewrite the lines as dialogue and read their lines aloud, using appropriate intonation and expression. Then have student pairs read the dialogue between mother and daughter aloud, contrasting the tone of this exchange with the way the father spoke.

 *Model the Skill:* **MAKE INFERENCES**

To model how to make inferences about what the narrator's mother thinks and feels, direct students to lines 354–355. Ask students what the lines say about how the narrator was feeling. Then have students recall the mother's response when the narrator's father tore up the original speech. Tell students that these story details and students' experiences can help them make inferences about why the mother helped write the speech.

***Possible answer:*** *The narrator is "too upset" to do it herself (line 354). The mother liked her daughter's original speech and didn't agree with her husband's reaction to it. She wants to support her daughter in their new country (lines 299–300) yet respect her husband.*

**VOCABULARY**

**OWN THE WORD**

**misnomer:** Tell students that the prefix *mis-* means "badly" or "wrongly." Have students list three other words that begin with *mis-*.

***Possible answers:*** *misinform, misspell, misprint*

**SELECTION WRAP–UP**

**READ WITH A PURPOSE** Have students describe the parent-child conflicts and how they are resolved. How does the child-parent relationship change? ***Possible answer:*** *The narrator initially humors her mother and challenges her father's authority. By the end, they have a new understanding of one another and recognize the love they share.*

⭐ **CRITIQUE** Have students evaluate the story by rating it from 1 (an inaccurate portrayal of parent-child conflicts in the United States) to 5 (accurate portrayal).

---

350    What we ended up doing that night was putting together a speech at the last moment. Two brief pages of stale compliments and the polite commonplaces on teachers, wrought by necessity without much invention by mother for daughter late into the night in the basement on the pad of paper and with the same pencil she had once used for her own inventions, for I was too upset to compose the speech myself. After it was drafted, she typed it up while I stood by, correcting her **misnomers** and mis-sayings. ◗

She was so very proud of herself when I came home the next day with the success story of the assembly. The nuns had been flattered, the audience had stood up and given "our devoted teachers a standing ovation," what my
360   mother had suggested they do at the end of my speech.

She clapped her hands together as I recreated the moment for her. "I stole that from your father's speech, remember? Remember how he put that in at the end?" She quoted him in Spanish, then translated for me into English.

That night, I watched him from the upstairs hall window where I'd retreated the minute I heard his car pull up in front of our house. Slowly, my father came up the driveway, a grim expression on his face as he grappled with a large, heavy cardboard box. At the front door, he set the package down carefully and patted all his pockets for his house keys—precisely why my mother had invented her ticking key chain. I heard the snapping open of the
370   locks downstairs. Heard as he struggled to maneuver the box through the narrow doorway. Then, he called my name several times. But I would not answer him.

"My daughter, your father, he love you very much," he explained from the bottom of the stairs. "He just want to protect you." Finally, my mother came up and pleaded with me to go down and reconcile with him. "Your father did not mean to harm. You must pardon him. Always it is better to let bygones be forgotten, no?"

I guess she was right. Downstairs, I found him setting up a brand new electric typewriter on the kitchen table. It was even better than the one I'd
380   been begging to get like my mother's. My father had outdone himself with all the extra features: a plastic carrying case with my initials, in decals, below the handle, a brace to lift the paper upright while I typed, an erase cartridge, an automatic margin tab, a plastic hood like a toaster cover to keep the dust away. Not even my mother, I think, could have invented such a machine!

But her inventing days were over just as mine were starting up with my schoolwide success. That's why I've always thought of that speech my mother wrote for me as her last invention rather than the suitcase rollers everyone else in the family remembers. It was as if she had passed on to me her pencil and pad and said, "Okay, Cukita, here's the buck. You give it a shot."

**misnomer** (mĭs-nō′mər) *n.* an inaccurate or incorrect name

◗ **MAKE INFERENCES** Why does the narrator's mother write the speech for her?

**⑤ Targeted Passage**

---

**DIFFERENTIATED INSTRUCTION**

**FOR STRUGGLING READERS**

**⑤ Targeted Passage** [Lines 350–384]
This passage depicts the resolution in conflict between the narrator and her parents.

- How does the mother show that she is proud of her daughter? How does the father show his pride? (lines 350–356; lines 373–374, 378–383)

- How do you think the narrator's view of her parents changes at the end of the story?

How do you think this new view will affect the relationship between them? (lines 357–360, 373–377, 384)

**FOR ENGLISH LANGUAGE LEARNERS**

**Culture: Clarify** Call students' attention to the pronouns used by the father in lines 373 and 374. Point out that when he says, "he love you very much" and "He just want to protect you," he means, "I love you very much" and "I just want to protect you."

## Comprehension

1. **Recall** How do the daughters respond to their mother's inventions?

2. **Recall** What difficulties do the daughters face in their new country?

3. **Clarify** How does the narrator's father react to his daughter's speech?

4. **Represent** Create a timeline showing key events in the order they occur. Circle the event that represents the **climax** of the story.

**COMMON CORE**

**RL 1** Cite strong and thorough textual evidence to support analysis of what the text says explicitly as well as inferences drawn from the text. **RL 3** Analyze how complex characters interact with other characters and advance the plot.

## Text Analysis

5. **Make Inferences** Review the inference chart you created for each character. How do the cultural differences between the Dominican Republic and the United States contribute to the parent-child conflicts between the narrator and her father? Include sufficient evidence to support your answer.

6. **Plot and Character** What do you learn about the narrator from the way she resolves the conflict with her father? If she had acted differently, how might the conflict have been resolved?

7. **Make Judgments** Does the mother do the right thing by composing a flattering speech for her daughter to give? Explore this question in a chart like the one shown.

| Pros | Cons |
|------|------|
| No one's feelings are hurt. | |

8. **Compare and Contrast Characters** Compare the narrator's qualities with her mother's. Are mother and daughter more alike or more different? Support your interpretation with strong evidence from the story.

9. **Draw Conclusions** Reread lines 385–389. In what ways might the narrator's future be different from her past?

10. **Synthesize** Reread lines 378–384. A **symbol** is a person, place, object, or activity that stands for something beyond itself. What does the typewriter represent in this story?

## Text Criticism

11. **Critical Interpretations** One critic has said that at the end of this story, the reader is left with the impression that the narrator "is living in a new world where even the old obstacles of culture can be overcome." Do you agree with this interpretation? Support your answer.

### What is a GENERATION GAP?

Why might children and parents find it difficult to understand one another?

---

8. *They are more alike. Although the mother invents and the daughter writes, both like a quiet time alone at night (lines 7, 57–58). Both are generally strong and determined, but they accept Papi's will about the speech.*

9. *In the future, the narrator will be writing more. She may be better accepted at school.*

10. *It symbolizes Papi's love for his daughter and his desire to see her succeed. It also symbolizes the narrator's potential as a writer.*

### Text Criticism
**Possible answers:**
11. *Agree: The end of the story points to the narrator's social acceptance and success in writing in the English language.* **Disagree:** *The narrator will always be influenced by her own memories and by her parents.*

### What is a GENERATION GAP?
*Students might compare and contrast factors, including where and when they grew up, with the same factors in their parents' lives to better understand the generation gap.*

---

# Practice and Apply

For preliminary support of post-reading questions, use these copy masters:

**R** RESOURCE MANAGER—Copy Masters
Reading Check p. 74
Plot and Character p. 67
Question Support p. 75

Additional selection questions are provided for teachers on page 61.

### ANSWERS

## Comprehension

1. *The girls gently mock or criticize her when discussing the inventions (lines 80–84).*

2. *Other students call the girls names (lines 100–103). Some throw stones (line 43).*

3. *The father is greatly upset and he forbids her to read it (lines 259–264, 275–278). He tears it up into tiny pieces (lines 290–292).*

4. *Possible answer: First, narrator is asked to write speech (lines 146–149); next, she finds inspiration (lines 205–214); next, she reads speech to father (lines 250–252); next, father rips up speech (climax) (lines 290–292); next, narrator and mother write a new speech (lines 350–356); next, narrator delivers speech (lines 357–360); last, father apologizes and buys her a typewriter (lines 373–374, 378–379).*

## Text Analysis

**COMMON CORE RL 1, RL 3**

**Possible answers:**

5. ■ **COMMON CORE FOCUS** *Make Inferences The mother and father experienced great terror in the Dominican Republic that affects their lives in the United States. In the Dominican Republic, people who questioned authority "disappeared." Papi still "feared anyone in uniform: the meter maid giving out parking tickets" (lines 308–311). He did not want his daughter showing disrespect to her teachers in her speech.*

6. ● **COMMON CORE FOCUS** *Plot and Character By calling her father "Chapita," the nickname of the hated dictator, the narrator reveals that she is angry and hurt. Had she tried to reason with her father, he might have understood her better.*

7. *Pros: The speech gets done on time and is a success. Cons: The narrator does not do her own work or express her own thoughts; the women do not stand up for what is meaningful to them.*

## ANSWERS
## Vocabulary in Context
▲ VOCABULARY PRACTICE

1. *c*     4. *b*
2. *b*     5. *b*
3. *a*     6. *c*

 **RESOURCE MANAGER—Copy Master**
Vocabulary Practice p. 72

### ACADEMIC VOCABULARY IN WRITING

Suggest to students that they put themselves in the narrator's place as they write their paragraphs. Remind them to consider the narrator's family history and the generation gap that often causes conflict between the daughter and her mother.

### VOCABULARY STRATEGY: THE LATIN PREFIX *in-*

COMMON CORE L 4c

- Model for students how the prefix *in-* changes form depending on the word it precedes.

- Ask students to predict what form the prefix *in-* takes when added to these words: *possible* (im), *mature* (im), *respective* (ir), *legible* (il).

**Possible answers:**

1. *informal*—"not formal, casual"
   *inedible*—"not fit to be eaten"

2. *illegible*—"not readable"
   *illegal*—"not legal"

3. *immobile*—"not moveable"
   *improbable*—"not likely to occur"

4. *irregular*—"not following a usual procedure"
   *irresistible*—"impossible to resist"

5. *incapable*—"not able"
   *insufferable*—"not to be endured or tolerated"

6. *imbalance*—"without balance"
   *immature*—"lacking maturity or growth"

 **RESOURCE MANAGER—Copy Master**
Vocabulary Strategy p. 73

**Interactive Vocabulary**     THINK central

Keywords direct students to a **WordSharp** tutorial on **thinkcentral.com** or to other types of vocabulary practice and review.

---

## Vocabulary in Context

▲ VOCABULARY PRACTICE

Write the word with a meaning closest to that of each boldfaced vocabulary word.

1. **inhospitable:** (a) inoperable, (b) unnecessary, (c) unwelcoming
2. **misnomer:** (a) mission, (b) misidentification, (c) misspent
3. **plagiarized:** (a) copied, (b) returned, (c) postmarked
4. **disclaimer:** (a) importance, (b) denial, (c) theory
5. **noncommittal:** (a) loyal, (b) cautious, (c) nonsensical
6. **insubordinate:** (a) inaccurate, (b) buried, (c) defiant

**WORD LIST**
disclaimer
inhospitable
insubordinate
misnomer
noncommittal
plagiarized

### ACADEMIC VOCABULARY IN WRITING

• analyze  • element  • infer  • sequence  • structure

To better understand the literary **element** of character, **analyze** the narrator's relationship with her mother. Early in the story, the narrator describes her mother as "a real failure of a Mom." Would the narrator evaluate her differently at the end of the story? Write one or two paragraphs expressing your opinion. Use one or more of the Academic Vocabulary words in your response.

### VOCABULARY STRATEGY: THE LATIN PREFIX *in-*

*In-* at the beginning of a word may be a prefix meaning "not," as in the vocabulary words *inhospitable* and *insubordinate*. If you can identify a root or a base word in words like these, you can easily figure out their meanings. (When the prefix *in-* precedes certain letters, it is spelled *il-*, *im-*, or *ir-*.)

**PRACTICE** Use a dictionary to help you find two words in each group that contain a prefix meaning "not." Write a short denotative definition (based on the definition in the dictionary) of each word. Then list any connotations—or feelings and associations connected with the word—that come to mind.

1. informal, internal, inedible
2. illegible, illegal, illness
3. imperial, immobile, improbable
4. irritate, irregular, irresistible
5. intellect, incapable, insufferable
6. imbalance, imagine, immature

○ **COMMON CORE**

**L 4c** Consult reference materials to determine or clarify a word's meaning.

Interactive Vocabulary | THINK central

Go to **thinkcentral.com**.
KEYWORD: HML9-98

---

## *DIFFERENTIATED INSTRUCTION*

### FOR ENGLISH LANGUAGE LEARNERS

**Task Support: Reteach** Use Word Squares to reteach the vocabulary words before students begin the Vocabulary in Context activities.

 **BEST PRACTICES TOOLKIT—Transparency** Word Squares p. E10

### FOR ADVANCED LEARNERS/PRE–AP

**Vocabulary in Writing** Have students write a closing paragraph of a speech that the narrator of this story might give in her school assembly, using as many vocabulary words as possible. *Example: Although my words may have seemed insubordinate to my father, I indeed have a sincere respect for him and my teachers.*

# Language

◆ **GRAMMAR AND STYLE:** Modifiers

Review the **Grammar and Style** note on page 88. Alvarez has carefully chosen **modifiers** that describe not only the physical details but also the atmosphere of the room.

Modifiers, which include **adjectives** and **adverbs,** are words and phrases that give information about other words. When describing a scene, incorporate modifiers that will paint a vivid picture for your audience. Here is another example of Alvarez's effective use of modifiers to enhance a scene:

> . . . *My father would be conked out for an hour already, his Spanish newspaper draped over his chest, his glasses, propped up on his bedside table, looking out eerily at the darkened room like a disembodied guard. But in her lighted corner, like some devoted scholar burning the midnight oil, my mother was inventing . . .* (lines 8–12)

Now study this model. Notice how the revisions in blue help to make the images more vivid. Use similar techniques to revise your own writing.

---

**STUDENT MODEL**

As I sat down at the table, I slid my fingers over the typewriter keys. What was I going to write? Would my father insist on reading every word again? I loaded a piece of paper into the typewriter and stared at its emptiness.

*trembling   black*
*well-meaning*
*smooth, cream-colored   longingly*

---

## READING-WRITING CONNECTION

Increase your understanding of "Daughter of Invention" by responding to this prompt. Then use the **revising tip** to improve your writing.

| WRITING PROMPT | REVISING TIP |
|---|---|
| **Extended Constructed Response: Scene** It's a year later, and the narrator has been asked to write another speech for school. Will the parent-child conflicts resume? Write **three to five paragraphs** describing the scene. | Review your scene. How have you used modifiers to describe the physical details and atmosphere of the setting? |

**Interactive Revision** THINK central
Go to **thinkcentral.com.**
KEYWORD: HML9-99

---

COMMON CORE

**L 3** Apply knowledge of language to make effective choices for meaning or style. **W 3d** Use precise words and phrases to convey a vivid picture of the experiences, events, settings, and characters.

---

## FOR STRUGGLING WRITERS

- Introductory paragraph describes the scene.
- Second paragraph gives examples of parent-child relationship.
- Third paragraph (a) compares old parent-child relationship with new and (b) reaffirms opinion.

---

# Language

COMMON CORE **L 3, W 3d**

◆ **GRAMMAR AND STYLE**

- After students examine the student model, list the modifiers in blue on the board. Point out that the modifier *longingly* is an adverb because it tells about the verb *stared*. Then point out that the modifier *trembling* is an adjective because it describes the noun *fingers*.

- Have students say whether each word listed on the board is used to modify a noun or a verb.

- Have students replace the modifiers in blue in the student model with a new set of modifiers. Discuss whether or not the new modifiers changed the feel of the student model.

**R** **RESOURCE MANAGER**—Copy Master
Set the Scene p. 76

**READING-WRITING CONNECTION**

- Distribute a Sequence Chain for use in planning or mapping the scene.

**BEST PRACTICES TOOLKIT**—Transparency
Sequence Chain p. B21

---

**Writing Online** THINK central

The following tools are available online at **thinkcentral.com** and on **Write*Smart*** CD-ROM:
- **Interactive Graphic Organizers**
- **Interactive Student Models**
- **Interactive Revision Lessons**
For additional grammar instruction, see **GrammarNotes** on **thinkcentral.com.**

---

# Assess and Reteach

## Assess

**DIAGNOSTIC AND SELECTION TESTS**
Selection Test A pp. 31–32
Selection Test B/C pp. 33–34

**Interactive Selection Test** on **thinkcentral.com**

## Reteach

**Level Up Online Tutorials** on **thinkcentral.com**

**Reteaching Worksheets** on **thinkcentral.com**
Literature Lesson 6: Conflict and Suspense
Reading Lesson 8: Making Inferences
Vocabulary Lesson 2: Prefixes

# Focus and Motivate

## SUMMARY

"The Gift of the Magi" recounts the sacrifices a young couple make for each other. Each sells a prized possession to buy the other a Christmas gift—but ironically, each sells the very thing that makes the other's gift special.

## What are you willing to SACRIFICE?

Explore the question by asking students to describe sacrifices they have made for others, as well as sacrifices others have made for them. Extend the discussion by having students complete the *DISCUSS* activity.

---

**Essential Course of Study**

# The Gift of the Magi
Short Story by O. Henry

 Video link at thinkcentral.com

VIDEO TRAILER **THINK** central KEYWORD: HML9-100

# What are you willing to SACRIFICE?

Have you ever made a sacrifice in order to help others or make someone happy? In "The Gift of the Magi," a young couple have to decide what each is willing to do to show love for the other.

*DISCUSS* With a small group, list examples of sacrifices that people make for those they love. Consider examples in real life as well as those in books, movies, and television shows. Do all the sacrifices involve material items? Which are the hardest ones to make? Which sacrifice shows the greatest love?

Sacrifices for Someone You Love
1. Spending a week's allowance to buy a gift
2.
3.
4.
5.

100

---

## Selection Resources

## TEXT ANALYSIS: IRONY

**Irony** is a contrast between what is expected to happen and what actually occurs. There are three types of irony commonly used in literary works:

- **Situational irony:** when a character or the reader expects one thing to happen but something else happens instead
- **Verbal irony:** when what is said is the opposite of what is meant
- **Dramatic irony:** when what a character knows contrasts with what the audience knows

O. Henry is well-known for writing stories in which situational irony results in **surprising plot twists.** As you read "The Gift of the Magi," be ready for the unexpected.

## READING STRATEGY: PREDICT

If a story is well written, it will keep you wondering what happens next. You may ask yourself questions and find yourself **predicting** possible answers. In this story, for example, what can you predict from the title?

As you read "The Gift of the Magi," jot down two or three predictions. Then see whether you were right—or whether O. Henry managed to surprise you.

## ▲ VOCABULARY IN CONTEXT

The following words are key to understanding this story of love and sacrifice. To see how many words you already know, substitute a different word or phrase for each boldfaced term. Then, in your *Reader/Writer Notebook*, write a brief definition of each word you're familiar with.

1. **instigate** a rebellion
2. a package in the **vestibule**
3. as **agile** as a gymnast
4. **falter** in his determination
5. **ransack** the entire house
6. show **prudence** in her decisions
7. a face marked by the **ravage** of time
8. an **assertion** that can't be proved
9. win the **coveted** prize
10. a **chronicle** of the year's events

 Complete the activities in your **Reader/Writer Notebook.**

## *Meet the Author*

# O. Henry
### 1862–1910

**A Life Like His Fiction**
Using the pen name O. Henry, William Sydney Porter wrote hundreds of short stories. In some ways, his own life reflected the twists and turns of his stories. Born in Greensboro, North Carolina, and raised by his grandmother and aunt after his mother's death, Porter left school at age 15 to work in a drugstore. At age 20, he moved to Texas and worked on a ranch. After he married and had a child, he went to work as a bank clerk. Then, after leaving this position, he was accused of having embezzled bank funds. Porter fled to Central America to avoid trial. When he returned to visit his dying wife, he was arrested, convicted, and imprisoned for three years. He always maintained his innocence.

**From Prison to Fame**
Porter refined his short story style while serving time in prison. By the time of his release, he was already selling stories to magazines. Today the most renowned annual collection of new American short stories bears his pen name—the O. Henry Awards.

**BACKGROUND TO THE STORY**
**Bearers of Gifts**
In this story, O. Henry makes an **allusion,** or reference, to the Magi. According to Christian tradition, the Magi were three wise men or kings who traveled to Bethlehem, guided by a miraculous star, to present gifts of gold, frankincense, and myrrh to the infant Jesus. These gifts were prized possessions, having monetary, medicinal, and ceremonial value.

**Author Online**
**THINK**central
Go to **thinkcentral.com.**
KEYWORD: HML9-101

101

---

# *Teach*

## ● *Model the Skill:* IRONY

To model how to identify irony, read this example:

> Ana didn't see Emilio anywhere in the station. She was sure that he had left, as he had said he would if she was late. Sadly, Ana started home. When Emilio ran in seconds later, his fear about being late turned to anger. "I meant what I said," he thought, and he boarded the train.

Point out that the irony in this situation is that Ana did not wait for Emilio because she thought she was too late, when, in fact, it was Emilio who was late.

**GUIDED PRACTICE** Have students cite ironies they have read about or experienced.

## ■ *Model the Skill:* PREDICT

To model making predictions, discuss the story title with students.

- The title offers clues about the story.
- The words *magi* and *gift* help me predict that the story focuses on a Christmas gift.

**GUIDED PRACTICE** After students read Background, ask what prediction they can make about the nature of a gift or gifts in the story.

**R RESOURCE MANAGER**—Copy Master Predict p. 89 (for student use while reading the selection)

---

## VOCABULARY SKILL

## ▲ VOCABULARY IN CONTEXT

**DIAGNOSE WORD KNOWLEDGE** Have all students complete Vocabulary in Context. Check their definitions against the following:

**agile** (ăj′əl) *adj.* able to move quickly and easily
**assertion** (ə-sûr′shən) *n.* a statement
**chronicle** (krŏn′ĭ-kəl) *n.* a record of events
**coveted** (kŭv′ĭ-tĭd) *adj.* greedily desired or wished for **covet** *v.*
**falter** (fôl′tər) *v.* to hesitate from lack of courage or confidence

**instigate** (ĭn′stĭ-gāt′) *v.* to stir up; provoke
**prudence** (prōōd′ns) *n.* the use of good judgment and common sense
**ransack** (răn′săk′) *v.* to search or examine vigorously
**ravage** (răv′ĭj) *n.* serious damage
**vestibule** (vĕs′tə-byōōl′) *n.* a small entryway within a building

**PRETEACH VOCABULARY** Use the copy master to help students predict meanings.

**R RESOURCE MANAGER**—Copy Master Vocabulary Study p. 91

**READ WITH A PURPOSE**

*Help students set a purpose for reading. Tell them to read "The Gift of the Magi" to find out how a couple's affection influences the giving and receiving of gifts.*

**VOCABULARY**   COMMON CORE L 4

**OWN THE WORD**

**instigate:** Remind students that *instigate* is a verb that means "to stir up or provoke." Have students list antonyms for *instigate*. **Possible answers:** repress, squelch, suppress, stop

# The Gift of the Magi

### O. Henry

One dollar and eighty-seven cents. That was all. And 60 cents of it was in pennies. Pennies saved one and two at a time by bulldozing the grocer and the vegetable man and the butcher until one's cheeks burned with the silent imputation of parsimony[1] that such close dealing implied. Three times Della counted it. One dollar and eighty-seven cents. And the next day would be Christmas.

There was clearly nothing to do but flop down on the shabby little couch and howl. So Della did it. Which **instigates** the moral reflection that life is made up of sobs, sniffles, and smiles, with sniffles predominating.

10     While the mistress of the home is gradually subsiding from the first stage to the second, take a look at the home. A furnished flat at $8 per week. It did not exactly beggar description, but it certainly had that word on the lookout for the mendicancy squad.[2]

**Analyze Visuals ▸**

From this painting, what can you **infer** about the characters in this story?

**① Targeted Passage**

**instigate** (ĭn'stĭ-gāt')
*v.* to stir up; provoke

---

1. **imputation** (ĭm'pyŏŏ-tā'shən) **of parsimony** (pär'sə-mō'nē): suggestion of stinginess.
2. **mendicancy** (mĕn'dĭ-kən-sē) **squad:** a police unit assigned to arrest beggars.

*The Kiss* (1891), Édouard Vuillard. Philadelphia Museum of Art, The Louis E. Stern Collection, 1963. © 2007 Artists Rights Society (ARS), New York/ADAGP, Paris (1963-181-76).

## DIFFERENTIATED INSTRUCTION

**FOR ENGLISH LANGUAGE LEARNERS**

**Options for Reading** Use Read Aloud/Think Aloud to introduce the story. Then have learners listen to the *Audio Anthology CD* as they read along.

 **BEST PRACTICES TOOLKIT—Transparency** Read Aloud/Think Aloud p. A34

**FOR STRUGGLING READERS**

In combination with the *Audio Anthology CD*, use one or more Targeted Passages (pp. 102, 105, 106, 108) to ensure that students focus on key story events, concepts, and skills. Targeted Passages are also good for English language learners.

**① Targeted Passage [Lines 1–8]**

This passage introduces conflict in the plot: Della has no money at Christmas time.

• How has Della managed to save $1.87? (lines 1–4)

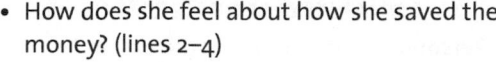

**Reading Support**

This selection on **thinkcentral.com** includes embedded **ThinkAloud** models—students "thinking aloud" about the story to model the kinds of questions a good reader would ask about a selection.

## BACKGROUND

**Christmas Gifts**  The custom of gift giving on Christmas goes back to the pre-Christian, Roman festivals of Saturnalia and Kalends.  At first, gifts were simple items such as twigs from a sacred grove that were believed to bring good luck.  Soon, food, jewelry, and candles were considered appropriate gifts.  Early Christians frowned upon Christmas gift giving, which they saw as a pagan holdover.  The Church found justification in the gift giving by the magi, the three wise men.  By the Middle Ages, Christians accepted gift giving at Christmas.

**Cultural Connection**  Holiday gift giving traditions differ around the world.  On January 6 (Epiphany or Three Kings Day), Brazilian and Spanish children put their shoes on the window sill or outdoors and find them filled with treats the next day.  Many Russian families decorate trees and exchange gifts at New Year's.  Invite students to share their gift giving traditions or their knowledge of gift giving traditions in other cultures.

## Analyze Visuals

*Possible answer:  The characters in the story are deeply in love and treat each other with affection.*

**About the Art**  Édouard Vuillard (1868–1940) was a French painter and lithographer known for his scenes of Montmartre in Paris and of intimate home life.  Vuillard was a member of the Nabis, a group of artists influenced by Paul Gauguin.  Their style features boldly outlined surface patterns and use of bright color.

- How does she feel about how she saved the money? (lines 2–4)
- Why does Della burst into tears? (lines 7–8)

**FOR ADVANCED LEARNERS/PRE–AP**

**Compare and Contrast**  Have students compare and contrast the author's description of daily life in New York City at the turn of the 20th century with their knowledge of life in today's cities.  Ask them to consider such factors as income, expenses, male and female role models, and relationships.  Ask students to take notes and to summarize their conclusions in  a paragraph.

## Analyze Visuals

**Activity** Ask students to discuss how Degas's image visually echoes the description of Della in lines 50–52. *Possible answer: The woman's flowing hair corresponds to O. Henry's description of Della's hair.*

**About the Art** French painter and sculptor Edgar Degas (1834–1917) is celebrated for combining traditional painting styles with a more relaxed style known as impressionism.

**TEXT ANALYSIS**  COMMON CORE  RL 5

### 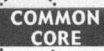 Model the Skill: IRONY

To model how to identify the irony of such an elegant name applying to Jim's current financial status, read aloud lines 18–24. Point out the change in material circumstances that the Youngs have undergone.

Lead students to notice the playful link between the impressive-sounding middle name and the "former period of prosperity" (lines 18–19).

*Possible answer: No, he is not. Although Mr. James Dillingham Young is a distinguished-sounding name, Jim and Della live in a simple apartment that has a broken letterbox and doorbell (lines 14–16). Jim's salary has also just been reduced from $30 per week to $20.*

**VOCABULARY**  COMMON CORE  L 4

### OWN THE WORD

**vestibule:** Tell students that *vestibule* is not used as frequently as it once was. Today, "lobby" or "entrance hall" are more commonly used. Have students name buildings where *vestibules* are commonly found and their purposes. *Possible answers: apartment buildings, office buildings*

*Woman Combing Her Hair*, Edgar Degas. Charcoal and pastel. © The Fine Art Society, London/Bridgeman Art Library.

In the **vestibule** below belonged to this flat a letterbox into which no letter would go and an electric button from which no mortal finger could coax a ring. Also appertaining thereunto was a card bearing the name "Mr. James Dillingham Young."

The "Dillingham" had been flung to the breeze during a former period of prosperity when its possessor was being paid $30 per week. Now, when
20 the income was shrunk to $20, the letters of "Dillingham" looked blurred, as though they were thinking seriously of contracting to a modest and unassuming D. But whenever Mr. James Dillingham Young came home and reached his flat above, he was called "Jim" and greatly hugged by Mrs. James Dillingham Young, already introduced to you as Della. Which is all very good.

Della finished her cry and attended to her cheeks with the powder rag. She stood by the window and looked out dully at a gray cat walking a gray fence in a gray backyard. Tomorrow would be Christmas Day, and she had only $1.87

**vestibule** (věs′tə-byōōl′) *n.* a small entryway within a building

**A IRONY**
You might expect someone named Mr. James Dillingham Young to be rich. Is he?

---

## DIFFERENTIATED INSTRUCTION

### FOR ENGLISH LANGUAGE LEARNERS

**Vocabulary Support** Use Definition Mapping to teach these words: *period* (line 18), *income* (line 20), *obtain* (line 36), *accurate* (line 37), *conception* (line 37), *task* (line 83).

 BEST PRACTICES TOOLKIT—Transparency Definition Mapping p. E6

### FOR ADVANCED LEARNERS/PRE–AP

**Personification** To convey the extent to which the Youngs' financial status has recently dwindled, in lines 19–22, O. Henry humorously paints a picture with words—literally—in the description of the letters in *Dillingham* on the mailbox. Have students sketch the mailbox, showing the Dillingham name as it might have appeared after Jim's cut in salary.

with which to buy Jim a present. She had been saving every penny she could
for months, with this result. Twenty dollars a week doesn't go far. Expenses
30 had been greater than she had calculated. They always are. Only $1.87 to buy
a present for Jim. Her Jim. Many a happy hour she had spent planning for
something nice for him. Something fine and rare and sterling—something just
a little bit near to being worthy of the honor of being owned by Jim.

There was a pier glass[3] between the windows of the room. Perhaps you
have seen a pier glass in an $8 flat. A very thin and very **agile** person may, by
observing his reflection in a rapid sequence of longitudinal strips, obtain a
fairly accurate conception of his looks. Della, being slender, had mastered
the art.

Suddenly she whirled from the window and stood before the glass. Her eyes
40 were shining brilliantly, but her face had lost its color within twenty seconds.
Rapidly she pulled down her hair and let it fall to its full length.

Now, there were two possessions of the James Dillingham Youngs in which
they both took a mighty pride. One was Jim's gold watch that had been his
father's and his grandfather's. The other was Della's hair. Had the Queen of
Sheba[4] lived in the flat across the air shaft, Della would have let her hair hang
out the window some day to dry and mocked at Her Majesty's jewels and gifts.
Had King Solomon[5] been the janitor, with all his treasures piled up in the
basement, Jim would have pulled out his watch every time he passed, just to
see him pluck at his beard from envy. **B**

50 So now Della's beautiful hair fell about her, rippling and shining like a
cascade of brown waters. It reached below her knee and made itself almost a
garment for her. And then she did it up again nervously and quickly. Once she
**faltered** for a minute and stood still while a tear or two splashed on the worn
red carpet.

On went her old brown jacket; on went her old brown hat. With a whirl of
skirts and with the brilliant sparkle still in her eyes, she fluttered out the door
and down the stairs to the street.

Where she stopped, the sign read "Mme. Sofronie. Hair Goods of All
Kinds." One flight up Della ran and collected herself, panting, before
60 Madame, large, too white, chilly, and hardly looking the "Sofronie."

"Will you buy my hair?" asked Della.

"I buy hair," said Madame. "Take yer hat off and let's have a sight at the
looks of it."

Down rippled the brown cascade.

"Twenty dollars," said Madame, lifting the mass with a practiced hand.

"Give it to me quick," said Della.

Oh, and the next two hours tripped by on rosy wings. Forget the hashed
metaphor. She was **ransacking** the stores for Jim's present.

---

3. **pier glass:** a large mirror set in a wall section between windows.
4. **Queen of Sheba:** in the Bible, a rich Arabian queen.
5. **King Solomon:** a Biblical king of Israel, known for his wisdom and wealth.

THE GIFT OF THE MAGI **105**

**agile** (ăj′əl) *adj.* able to move quickly and easily

**②** Targeted Passage

**B** PREDICT
What events might occur involving these prized possessions?

**falter** (fôl′tər) *v.* to hesitate from lack of courage or confidence

**ransack** (răn′săk′) *v.* to search or examine vigorously

**B** PREDICT

*Possible answer: Because Della wants to buy Jim a gift, it is possible that she will sell her hair to raise money.*

**IF STUDENTS NEED HELP . . .** Have students use a Predicting chart, or a chart like this one, to help them make predictions about story events:

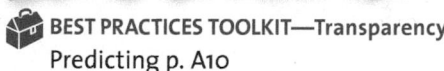

| Predicting Chart | | |
|---|---|---|
| Clues | Inference(s) | Predictions |
| Della did up her hair again nervously. | She is anxious because she might trade it for money. | She will probably explore such a trade. |

**BEST PRACTICES TOOLKIT—Transparency**
Predicting p. A10

**REVISIT THE BIG QUESTION**

## What are you willing to SACRIFICE?

**Discuss** Why do you think that in line 67 O. Henry portrays Della as happy after she makes the sacrifice of selling her hair? *Possible answer: Della's sacrifice has made it possible to buy a special gift for Jim.*

VOCABULARY    COMMON CORE    L 4

**OWN THE WORD**

- **agile:** Reinforce students' understanding of *agile* by asking them to describe the following: an *agile* football player; an *agile* animal; an *agile* mind. *Possible answers: a football player who moves nimbly about the field; a monkey; a mind that quickly analyzes facts and draws conclusions*

- **falter:** Review the definition of *falter* with students. Then have them cite instances when people might *falter* before taking action.

- **ransack:** Remind students that the connotation of *ransack* is vigorous action, pillaging.

**FOR STRUGGLING READERS**

**②** Targeted Passage [Lines 42–57]

This passage marks a significant event in the plot: Della cuts her hair to buy a present for Jim.

- What has Della decided to do? (lines 50–54)

- Why do you think Della made that decision? (lines 42–49)

- Why do you think Della faltered for a minute, stood still, and cried? (lines 42–46)

**FOR ENGLISH LANGUAGE LEARNERS**

**Language: Pronoun Referents** Explain the referent for the pronoun *it* in line 63: "Take yer hat off and let's have a sight at the looks of it." (*It* refers to Della's hair.) Then have learners work in mixed-language groups to identify referents for the pronouns in lines 69–79.

## What are you willing to **SACRIFICE?**

**Discuss** How do the details in lines 98–100 hint that Jim, as well as Della, is capable of sacrifice? ***Possible answer:*** *Rather than spend money on himself, Jim sacrifices by going without a much-needed new overcoat and gloves.*

---

**READING STRAGEGY**

**COMMON CORE RL 1**

### **C** PREDICT

***Possible answer:*** *He will express his confusion, but he will not criticize Della, because of his deep love for her.*

**IF STUDENTS NEED HELP . . .** Read aloud lines 103–105, beginning "It was not anger . . .". Help students see that Jim will not express anger, because he respects Della's decisions.

---

**VOCABULARY**

**COMMON CORE L 4**

### OWN THE WORD

- **prudence:** Have students describe ways that they exercise *prudence*. ***Possible answers:*** *wearing a seatbelt, saving money*

- **ravage:** Have students review lines 81–82 and identify the context clue that helps determine the meaning of *ravage*. ***Possible answer:*** *repair; something that was damaged would need to be repaired.*

---

---

She found it at last. It surely had been made for Jim and no one else.
70 There was none other like it in any of the stores, and she had turned all of them inside out. It was a platinum fob chain[6] simple and chaste in design, properly proclaiming its value by substance alone and not by meretricious ornamentation[7]—as all good things should do. It was even worthy of The Watch. As soon as she saw it, she knew that it must be Jim's. It was like him. Quietness and value—the description applied to both. Twenty-one dollars they took from her for it, and she hurried home with the 87 cents. With that chain on his watch Jim might be properly anxious about the time in any company. Grand as the watch was, he sometimes looked at it on the sly on account of the old leather strap that he used in place of a chain.

80    When Della reached home, her intoxication gave way a little to **prudence** and reason. She got out her curling irons and lighted the gas and went to work repairing the **ravages** made by generosity added to love. Which is always a tremendous task, dear friends—a mammoth task.

Within forty minutes her head was covered with tiny, close-lying curls that made her look wonderfully like a truant schoolboy. She looked at her reflection in the mirror long, carefully, and critically.

"If Jim doesn't kill me," she said to herself, "before he takes a second look at me, he'll say I look like a Coney Island[8] chorus girl. But what could I do—oh, what could I do with a dollar and eighty-seven cents!"

90    At 7 o'clock the coffee was made, and the frying pan was on the back of the stove hot and ready to cook the chops.

Jim was never late. Della doubled the fob chain in her hand and sat on the corner of the table near the door that he always entered. Then she heard his step on the stair away down on the first flight, and she turned white for just a moment. She had a habit of saying little silent prayers about the simplest everyday things, and now she whispered: "Please, God, make him think I am still pretty."

The door opened, and Jim stepped in and closed it. He looked thin and very serious. Poor fellow, he was only twenty-two—and to be burdened with a 100 family! He needed a new overcoat, and he was without gloves.

Jim stopped inside the door, as immovable as a setter at the scent of a quail. His eyes were fixed upon Della, and there was an expression in them that she could not read, and it terrified her. It was not anger, nor surprise, nor disapproval, nor horror, nor any of the sentiments that she had been prepared for. He simply stared at her fixedly with that peculiar expression on his face. **C**

Della wriggled off the table and went for him.

"Jim, darling," she cried, "don't look at me that way. I had my hair cut off and sold it because I couldn't have lived through Christmas without giving you a present. It'll grow again—you won't mind, will you? I just had to do it. My

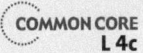 **3 Targeted Passage**

**C** PREDICT
What will Jim say about Della's hair?

---

6. **fob chain:** a short chain for a pocket watch.
7. **meretricious** (mĕr′ĭ-trĭsh′əs) **ornamentation:** cheap, gaudy decoration.
8. **Coney Island:** a resort district of Brooklyn, New York, famous for its amusement park.

---

### Language Coach

**Homophones** The adjective *chaste*, from line 71, and the past-tense verb *chased* are **homophones**—words that sound alike but have very different meanings. Using a dictionary to help you, jot down the meanings of these two words.

**prudence** (prōōd′ns) *n.* the use of good judgment and common sense

**ravage** (răv′ĭj) *n.* serious damage

---

## DIFFERENTIATED INSTRUCTION

**FOR STRUGGLING READERS**

**3 Targeted Passage [Lines 92–105]**
This passage sets up new tension in the plot, through an event that Della does not predict: Jim says nothing about her hair.

- Why does Della whisper a prayer? (lines 96–97)
- Why is Della terrified? (lines 102–103)

**FOR ENGLISH LANGUAGE LEARNERS**

### Language Coach

**COMMON CORE L 4c**

**Homophones**
Ask students to work in pairs to develop a list of homophones—words that sound alike but have very different meanings. Have volunteers read their lists aloud; write the words on the board. Then, have students use dictionaries to look up the meaning of each word on the list.

110 hair grows awfully fast. Say 'Merry Christmas!' Jim, and let's be happy. You don't know what a nice—what a beautiful, nice gift I've got for you."

"You've cut off your hair?" asked Jim, laboriously, as if he had not arrived at that patent fact yet even after the hardest mental labor.

"Cut it off and sold it," said
120 Della. "Don't you like me just as well, anyhow? I'm me without my hair, ain't I?"

Jim looked about the room curiously.

"You say your hair is gone?" he said, with an air almost of idiocy.

"You needn't look for it," said Della. "It's sold, I tell you—sold and gone too. It's Christmas Eve,
130 boy. Be good to me, for it went for you. Maybe the hairs of my head were numbered," she went on with a sudden serious sweetness, "but nobody could ever count my love for you. Shall I put the chops on, Jim?"

Out of his trance Jim seemed to quickly wake. He enfolded his Della. For ten seconds let us
140 regard with discreet scrutiny[9] some inconsequential object in the other direction. Eight dollars a week or a million a year—what is the difference? A mathematician or a wit would give you the wrong answer. The magi brought valuable gifts, but that was not among them. This dark **assertion** will be illuminated later on.

Jim drew a package from his overcoat pocket and threw it upon the table.

"Don't make any mistake, Dell," he said, "about me. I don't think there's
150 anything in the way of a haircut or a shave or a shampoo that could make me like my girl any less. But if you'll unwrap that package, you may see why you had me going awhile at first."

---

9. **discreet scrutiny:** cautious observation.

**assertion** (ə-sûr′shən)
*n.* a statement

**D PREDICT**
What do you predict Jim's gift will be? Explain.

---

## FOR STRUGGLING READERS

**Develop Reading Fluency** Use the exchange between Della and Jim, beginning with "Say 'Merry Christmas!'" (line 110) to give students practice in reading dialogue. Remind students that dialogue represents a conversation. Tell them that fluent readers read dialogue with expression, using punctuation marks to show them when to pause or make changes in their intonation to indicate statements or questions. First, model for students an effective reading of the dialogue. Have a proficient reader read aloud one character while you read the other. Then have students work in mixed-ability groups to practice reading the dialogue. Conclude by having students discuss how taking note of the punctuation helped them in their reading.

---

## Analyze Visuals

**Activity** Ask students, "How does this image relate to this point in the story?" *Possible answer: Della has sold her hair to buy a chain for Jim's watch. The size and blurred appearance of the watch make it seem important and mysterious. The watch is likely to figure in an important, but as yet unclear, way in the rest of the story.*

## TIERED DISCUSSION PROMPTS

In lines 115–136, use these prompts to help students understand how the author builds tension in this passage:

**Analyze** What is Della feeling? *Possible answer: She is eager for Jim's reaction and to enjoy Christmas Eve with him.*

**Evaluate** How does suspense contribute to this story? *Possible answer: It heightens reader interest in the actions of Jim and Della.*

---

**READING STRATEGY**  COMMON CORE  RL 1

**D** *Model the Skill:* **PREDICT**

Model for students how to predict this story event. State that we already know that Della's hair is a prized possession. Explain that while reading lines 115–126 students can further understand how dumbfounded Jim is to find that Della has sold her hair. Have students consider the cause-and-effect relationship between Della's haircut and Jim's confusion.

*Possible answer: Jim's gift will have something to do with Della's hair.*

**R** RESOURCE MANAGER—Copy Master
Reading Fluency p. 97

---

**VOCABULARY**  COMMON CORE  L 4

## OWN THE WORD

**assertion:** Remind students that the connotation of *assertion* is a forceful statement. For example, a baseball fan might make an *assertion* that a particular team will win the World Series. Have students create two related sentences that show how an *assertion* is stronger than a statement.

## SELECTION WRAP–UP

**READ WITH A PURPOSE** Now that students have read the selection, have them analyze how Della's and Jim's love influenced their decisions about giving gifts. Then have students discuss what statement the author might be making about gifts and relationships. *Possible answer: Della's and Jim's love influenced them to sacrifice their most treasured possessions to buy gifts for each other. The author might be making the statement that in loving relationships material gifts are less meaningful than emotional or spiritual gifts, such as love and kindness.*

★ **CRITIQUE** Ask students what lasting impressions they will take away from this story. Ask them to share favorite images or passages.

---

White fingers and nimble tore at the string and paper. And then an ecstatic scream of joy, and then, alas! a quick feminine change to hysterical tears and wails, necessitating the immediate employment of all the comforting powers of the lord of the flat.

For there lay The Combs—the set of combs, side and back, that Della had worshiped for long in a Broadway window. Beautiful combs, pure tortoise shell, with jeweled rims—just the shade to wear in the beautiful vanished hair. 160 They were expensive combs, she knew, and her heart had simply craved and yearned over them without the least hope of possession. And now, they were hers, but the tresses that should have adorned the **coveted** adornments were gone. **E**

But she hugged them to her bosom, and at length she was able to look up with dim eyes and a smile and say, "My hair grows so fast, Jim!"

And then Della leaped up like a little singed cat and cried, "Oh, oh!"

Jim had not yet seen his beautiful present. She held it out to him eagerly upon her open palm. The dull, precious metal seemed to flash with a reflection of her bright and ardent spirit.

170 "Isn't it a dandy, Jim? I hunted all over town to find it. You'll have to look at the time a hundred times a day now. Give me your watch. I want to see how it looks on it."

Instead of obeying, Jim tumbled down on the couch and put his hands under the back of his head and smiled.

"Dell," said he, "let's put our Christmas presents away and keep 'em a while. They're too nice to use just at present. I sold the watch to get the money to buy your combs. And now suppose you put the chops on." **F**

The magi, as you know, were wise men—wonderfully wise men—who brought gifts to the Babe in the manger. They invented the art of giving 180 Christmas gifts. Being wise, their gifts were no doubt wise ones, possibly bearing the privilege of exchange in case of duplication. And here I have lamely related to you the uneventful **chronicle** of two foolish children in a flat who most unwisely sacrificed for each other the greatest treasures of their house. But in a last word to the wise of these days let it be said that of all who give gifts these two were of the wisest. Of all who give and receive gifts, such as they are the wisest. Everywhere they are the wisest. They are the magi.

**coveted** (kŭv′ĭ-tĭd) *adj.* greedily desired or wished for **covet** *v.*

**chronicle** (krŏn′ĭ-kəl) *n.* a record of events

---

## DIFFERENTIATED INSTRUCTION

### FOR STRUGGLING READERS

**4 Targeted Passage** [Lines 167–186]

This passage concludes the story with a plot twist and reveals the irony: the two characters have sacrificed their most prized possessions to buy now useless gifts for each other.

- What is ironic about the gifts Jim and Della have bought? (lines 175–177)
- What is O. Henry's opinion of the actions of Jim and Della? (lines 184–186)

### FOR ADVANCED LEARNERS/PRE–AP

**Evaluate** Have students evaluate the tone of the story by rating it on a scale of 1 (not sentimental) to 5 (overly sentimental). Ask students to cite evidence from the story to support their opinions.

## Comprehension

**1. Recall** Why is Della unhappy when the story begins?

**2. Recall** What two possessions do Della and Jim treasure?

**3. Summarize** What sacrifices do the Youngs make to buy each other gifts?

## Text Analysis

■ **4. Predict** Reexamine the predictions you made as you read the story. Were you able to predict the outcome of the story, or were you surprised? Go back through the story to find passages that hint at the surprise ending.

● **5. Analyze Irony** This story contains **situational irony,** in which characters, or the reader, expect one thing to happen but something entirely different occurs. To explore the situational irony in this story, make a chart like the one shown.

| What Della Plans: | What Actually Happens: |
|---|---|
| What Jim Plans: | What Actually Happens: |

For each character, identify what is expected to happen and what actually does happen. There is a double irony here. How are the two ironies related?

**6. Draw Conclusions About the Narrator** Reread lines 22–24. In this and many other passages, the narrator speaks directly to the reader. How would you describe the narrator's personality? Cite evidence.

**7. Make Judgments** Reread lines 178–186. Here the narrator uses an **allusion,** or indirect reference to a person, place, event, or literary work. Why does the narrator compare Della and Jim to the Magi? What does this imply about the characters and the events in this story?

**8. Synthesize** What does this story seem to be saying about material possessions? Cite evidence to support your answer.

## Text Criticism

**9. Critical Interpretations** For several years in the early 1900s, O. Henry was one of the most widely read short story writers in the United States. Even today, some of his stories are considered classics. What elements in "The Gift of the Magi" might account for his continued popularity?

### What are you willing to SACRIFICE?

What material possessions could you do without?

**COMMON CORE**

**RL 1** Cite textual evidence to support inferences drawn from the text. **RL 5** Analyze how an author's choices concerning how to structure a text and order events within it create surprise. **RL 10** Read and comprehend stories.

# Practice and Apply

For preliminary support of post-reading questions, use these copy masters:

**R** RESOURCE MANAGER—Copy Masters
Reading Check p. 94
Irony p. 87
Question Support p. 95

Additional selection questions are provided for teachers on page 81.

### ANSWERS

## Comprehension

**1.** *She has only $1.87 to buy Jim a present.*

**2.** *Della treasures her hair, Jim his watch.*

**3.** *Della sells her hair and Jim sells his watch.*

## Text Analysis

COMMON CORE RL 1, RL 5, RL 10

*Possible answers:*

**4.** ■ **COMMON CORE FOCUS** *Predict*
*Students' responses about their predictions will vary. The following passages may provide hints about the surprise ending:*
- *"But what could I do—oh, what could I do with a dollar and eighty-seven cents!" (lines 88–89)*
- *"It was not anger, nor surprise, nor disapproval, nor horror, nor any of the sentiments that she had been prepared for." (lines 103–105)*
- *"The magi brought valuable gifts, but that was not among them. This dark assertion will be illuminated later on." (lines 146–147)*

**5.** ● **COMMON CORE FOCUS** *Analyze Irony*
*What Della Plans: to sell her hair in order to buy a chain for Jim's watch;*
*What Actually Happens: Jim has sold his watch, which makes the chain a useless gift.*
*What Jim Plans: to sell his watch to buy combs for Della's hair;*
*What Actually Happens: Della has sold her hair, which makes the combs a useless gift. The double irony is that the couple is still poor but no longer has their prized possessions.*

**6.** *The narrator's personality is affectionate (lines 22–24), amused (lines 44–49), and a bit moralizing (lines 82–83). Students should cite supporting evidence.*

**7.** *He compares them to the magi because their sacrifices demonstrated wisdom and love. The comparison implies Jim and Della were wise rather than foolish.*

**8.** *The story implies that material possessions are less important than love and sacrifice. The author reinforces this in the closing paragraph, calling the Youngs "the wisest" and "the magi" (line 186).*

## Text Criticism

*Possible answer:*
**9.** *O. Henry's appeal might be based on the appealing characters, surprise ending, and use of irony.*

### What are you willing to SACRIFICE? *Possible answers:*
*television, cell phone*

## ANSWERS

## Vocabulary in Context

▲ **VOCABULARY PRACTICE**

1. *d*          6. *c*
2. *a*          7. *b*
3. *d*          8. *c*
4. *a*          9. *d*
5. *b*          10. *a*

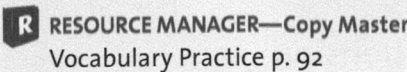 **RESOURCE MANAGER—Copy Master**
Vocabulary Practice p. 92

**ACADEMIC VOCABULARY IN SPEAKING**

Point out to students that the words are associated with the author's craft in writing the story: for example, the author heightens suspense during the *sequence* in which Jim is confused by Della's unexpected haircut (lines 101–136).

**VOCABULARY STRATEGY:**
**THE GREEK WORD ROOT** *chron*

- To help students understand word roots, focus on the vocabulary words *chronometer* and *synchronize*.
- Model for students how the word *chronometer* contains two roots (*chron* and *meter*) and that *synchronize* contains a prefix and a root (*syn* and *chron*).

**Possible answers:**

1. *chronic*

2. *chronological*

3. *chronicle*

4. *Synchronize*

5. *chronometer*

 **RESOURCE MANAGER—Copy Master**
Vocabulary Strategy p. 93

**Interactive Vocabulary**

Keywords direct students to a **WordSharp** tutorial on **thinkcentral.com** or to other types of vocabulary practice and review.

---

## Vocabulary in Context

**VOCABULARY PRACTICE**

Write the letter of the word that is most different in meaning from the others.

1. (a) destruction, (b) ravage, (c) ruin, (d) creation
2. (a) stop, (b) stir, (c) urge, (d) instigate
3. (a) desired, (b) coveted, (c) craved, (d) unwanted
4. (a) cellar, (b) vestibule, (c) foyer, (d) entryway
5. (a) waver, (b) proceed, (c) falter, (d) hesitate
6. (a) assertion, (b) declaration, (c) denial, (d) statement
7. (a) limber, (b) clumsy, (c) flexible, (d) agile
8. (a) loot, (b) plunder, (c) organize, (d) ransack
9. (a) history, (b) record, (c) chronicle, (d) prediction
10. (a) carelessness, (b) caution, (c) prudence, (d) wisdom

**WORD LIST**

agile
assertion
chronicle
coveted
falter
instigate
prudence
ransack
ravage
vestibule

**ACADEMIC VOCABULARY IN SPEAKING**

- analyze  - element  - infer  - sequence  - structure

What **elements** of "The Gift of the Magi" create suspense? With a partner, discuss how O. Henry's writing affected you as you read. Use at least three of the Academic Vocabulary words in your discussion.

**COMMON CORE**

**L 4c** Consult reference materials to determine or clarify a word's etymology.

**VOCABULARY STRATEGY: THE GREEK WORD ROOT** *chron*

The vocabulary word *chronicle* contains the Greek root *chron*, which means "time." This root is found in many English words used by historians and scientists.

**PRACTICE** Write the word from the word web that best completes each sentence. Use context clues to help you or, if necessary, consult a dictionary.

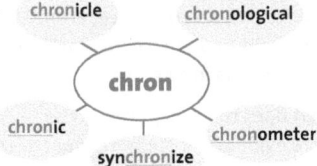

1. Scientists have discovered cures for many _____ illnesses.
2. Most history books present events in _____ order.
3. The professor read the _____ of an ancient king's life.
4. _____ your watches so the experiment's results are accurate.
5. A _____ in a ship is an aid in determining longitude.

**Interactive Vocabulary**

Go to **thinkcentral.com**.
KEYWORD: HML9-110

---

## DIFFERENTIATED INSTRUCTION

**FOR ENGLISH LANGUAGE LEARNERS**
**Vocabulary: Cognates** Remind Spanish speakers that in Spanish, the equivalent of *chron* (as in *chronicle*) is *cron*, and that the *h* is silent in the English root.

**FOR ADVANCED LEARNERS/PRE-AP**
**Vocabulary as Character Clues** Have students take the characters' personalities into account in their retellings. *Example: Della, who is impulsive and emotional, might use words with strong connotations, such as* ransack, coveted, *and* ravages. Ask students to take notes about strong words used by Della or Jim and summarize their findings in a paragraph.

# Language

◆ **GRAMMAR AND STYLE: Make Effective Word Choices**

**COMMON CORE**

L 3 Make effective choices for meaning or style. **W 3b** Use description to develop characters.

Review the **Grammar and Style** note on page 108. Throughout the story, O. Henry uses **precise verbs** to descriptively convey the thoughts, feelings, and actions of his characters. By incorporating precise verbs into your own writing, you can give readers a greater and more accurate sense of your characters and their behavior.

In the following excerpts, notice how O. Henry uses verbs that help create vivid images for the reader:

> *With a whirl of skirts and with the brilliant sparkle still in her eyes, she fluttered out the door and down the stairs to the street.* (lines 55–57)
>
> *Instead of obeying, Jim tumbled down on the couch....* (line 173)

Now study this model. Notice how the revisions in blue help you to better visualize Jim's trip to the shop. Use similar methods to revise your response to the prompt below.

---

**STUDENT MODEL**

         *scurried*
Jim ~~walked~~ to the shop; the store would close in just an hour. He reached

                  *yanked*                      *clasped*
into his right pocket, ~~took~~ out the watch, and ~~held~~ it in his hands.

---

## READING-WRITING CONNECTION

**YOUR TURN** Demonstrate your understanding of "The Gift of the Magi" by responding to this prompt. Then use the **revising tip** to improve your writing.

| **WRITING PROMPT** | **REVISING TIP** |
|---|---|
| **Extended Constructed Response: Description** What do you imagine Jim's shopping trip was like? Write **three to five paragraphs** describing Jim's actions and thoughts as he sells his watch and buys the combs for Della. | Review your response. Are the verbs you used precise? If not, replace them with more descriptive choices. |

**Interactive Revision** **THINK central**
Try it at **thinkcentral.com.**
KEYWORD: HML9-111

---

## FOR STRUGGLING WRITERS

Have students work in pairs to brainstorm Jim's thoughts, emotions, and actions to build drama and suspense in the following paragraphs.

- The introductory paragraph presents Jim's decision to purchase a gift for Della.

- The body describes Jim's sale of the watch and purchase of the combs.

- The last paragraph gives Jim's thoughts as he travels home with the gift.

---

# Language

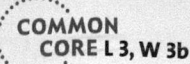
**COMMON CORE L 3, W 3b**

● **GRAMMAR AND STYLE**

- List these words on the board: *scurried, ambled, scuttled, fluttered, tumbled, sprang, hustled, burst into, pounded.*

- Write this passage on the board. Have students suggest more precise verbs to replace the underlined verbs. (For more information on using language effectively, see pages R34–35 of the **Grammar Handbook.**)

> *Jim <u>walked</u> out of the pawnshop and headed to the store. As he <u>entered,</u> his heart <u>beat quickly.</u>*

> **Possible answers:** *ambled, burst in, fluttered*

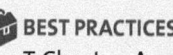
**RESOURCE MANAGER—Copy Master**
Make Effective Word Choices p. 96

**READING-WRITING CONNECTION**

**WRITING PROMPT**

Have students list strong, precise action verbs and sensory details. Have them orally present their paragraphs.

🧳 **BEST PRACTICES TOOLKIT—Transparency**
T Chart p. A25

---

**Writing Online** **THINK central**

The following tools are available online at **thinkcentral.com** and on **WriteSmart** CD-ROM:
- **Interactive Graphic Organizers**
- **Interactive Student Models**
- **Interactive Revision Lessons**

For additional grammar instruction, see **GrammarNotes** on **thinkcentral.com**.

---

# Assess and Reteach

## Assess

**DIAGNOSTIC AND SELECTION TESTS**
    Selection Test A pp. 35–36
    Selection Test B/C pp. 37–38

**Interactive Selection Test** on **thinkcentral.com**

## Reteach

**Level Up Online Tutorials** on **thinkcentral.com**

**Reteaching Worksheets** on **thinkcentral.com**
    Literature Lessons 37, 38, Reading Lesson 1

## Focus and Motivate

*from* **The Lord of the Rings**
Film Clip on **Media** **Smart** DVD-ROM

### COMMON CORE FOCUS

**RL 7** Analyze the representation of a key scene in two different artistic mediums, including what is emphasized or absent in each treatment.
**W 9a (RL 7)** Draw evidence from literary texts; analyze a key scene in two different artistic mediums. **SL 2** Integrate multiple sources presented in diverse media or formats. **SL 5** Make strategic use of digital media in presentations.

### SUMMARY

In this film clip from *The Lord of the Rings*, two hobbits, Frodo and Sam, begin their mission to take a mysterious and powerful ring to a safer location. As they travel through a forest, they encounter two other hobbits, Merry and Pippin. Suddenly, an ominous wind blows, and Frodo senses an approaching threat. A Black Rider—a shadowy, deadly being who is pursuing the ring—stops to search the area. The hobbits run and hide, eventually escaping the Black Rider by raft.

### What keeps you in SUSPENSE?

Ask students to discuss any suspense-filled movies they've seen recently. What filmmaking techniques helped make the movies suspenseful? Did they include music, fast-paced action, or the slow, agonizing way in which directors prolong tense situations?

### BACKGROUND

*The Lord of the Rings*, by J. R. R. Tolkien, is an epic fantasy that was first published in 1954. Although it is one long story, it was originally published in three volumes: *The Fellowship of the Ring, The Two Towers*, and *The Return of the King*. Together, the books tell the story of a hobbit, Frodo Baggins. As part of a fellowship that includes an elf, a dwarf, several humans, and other hobbits, Frodo goes on a quest to destroy the One Ring, which the powers of evil want to ensure their victory. The book became wildly popular in the 1960s, inspiring a whole genre of fantasy books that dealt with imaginary lands and mythical races of creatures. It also inspired several movies, of which director Peter Jackson's are the most famous.

 **COMMON CORE**

**RL 7** Analyze the representation of a key scene in two different artistic mediums, including what is emphasized or absent in each treatment.

# What keeps you in SUSPENSE?

Have you ever been thrust into a situation that made your heart pound and your palms sweat? In this scene, Frodo Baggins, a young hobbit, has hardly started on a mission when he senses something ominous. Notice how the director builds suspense as danger reveals itself.w

## Background

**Imagining Tolkien's World** In 1999 the director Peter Jackson began to transform J. R. R. Tolkien's fantasy epic *The Lord of the Rings* into one of the most critically acclaimed movies of all time. As one reviewer stated, "This astounding movie accomplishes what no other fantasy film has been able to do: transport viewers to an entirely different reality, immerse them in it, and maroon them there...."

In the first installment, *The Fellowship of the Ring,* Frodo Baggins inherits a ring that has the power to destroy civilization. Frodo accepts the challenge of taking the ring to Rivendell, a place where a council will decide the ring's fate. He is joined on this mission by his loyal friend Sam and two other hobbits.

112

## Media Study Resources

> **R** **RESOURCE MANAGER UNIT 1**
> Plan and Teach pp. 99–108
> Summary pp. 103†*, 104‡*
> Viewing Guide p. 105
> Close Viewing p. 106
> Media Activity p. 107
> Produce Your Own Media p. 108
>
> **TECHNOLOGY**
> 🔘 **Teacher One Stop DVD-ROM**
> 🔘 **Student One Stop DVD-ROM**
> 🔘 **Media***Smart* **DVD-ROM**
> MediaScope on **thinkcentral.com**
>
> *See resources on the* **Teacher One Stop DVD-ROM** *and on* **thinkcentral.com**.

\* Resources for Differentiation    † Also in Spanish    ‡ In Haitian Creole and Vietnamese

## Media Literacy: Suspense in Movies

**Suspense** is a feeling of growing tension and excitement. Writers build suspense by making readers feel uncertain about what will happen next. Like writers, directors have the ability to make viewers feel excited or nervous as events unfold from one scene to the next. A skillful director can use basic filmmaking techniques, such as **camera shots, editing,** and **sound,** to create suspense and draw viewers into the action.

| FILM TECHNIQUES | STRATEGIES FOR VIEWING | |
|---|---|---|
| A **camera shot** is a single, continuous view filmed by a camera. A director sets up shots that will advance a story's plot and tell the story in a compelling way. | • Pay attention to **point-of-view shots;** they show what characters see. In suspenseful scenes, they can make viewers sympathize with the characters and feel as if they are in danger themselves.<br>• Notice how **high-angle shots,** in which the camera looks down on objects or persons, can make characters seem helpless. **Low-angle shots,** with the camera looking up, can make characters seem powerful or threatening. |  |
| **Editing** is the process of selecting and arranging shots in a sequence. Editors and directors build tension by increasing the pace from one shot to the next. | Be aware of **pace,** which is influenced by the length of time each shot stays on the screen. As suspense increases, the length of shots gets shorter. **Quick cuts,** which may last no longer than a second, perhaps even less, are used to create excitement and build viewers' anticipation. |  |
| **Sound** consists of the **music, sound effects,** and **dialogue** used in a scene. Sounds can be manipulated to increase viewers' emotional response to the scene. | • Listen for the use of **music.** Shrill tones or quick, steady beats often signal danger. Even **background music** can contribute to the atmosphere of a scene or create a certain feeling in the viewer.<br>• In particular, notice how any prolonged **absence of sound** affects you. Silence can heighten a tense moment. |  |

# Teach

## Media Literacy

COMMON CORE **RL 7**

Review with students the definition of *suspense* and ask them to recall particularly suspenseful moments from movies they have seen. Ask what made those episodes so gripping. On the board, list any answers students might generate, such as *eerie music, sound effects,* and *lighting.* Make sure *camera shots, editing,* and *sound* are included on the list. Then discuss the chart on this page.

- **Camera Shots** To reinforce the importance of camera shots and angles, present a common situation, such as an encounter with an angry dog. Ask students, How would the scene be presented from the point of view of an outsider? of the person encountering the dog? of the dog? Would the dog look more or less menacing if seen head on or from above?

- **Editing** Mention to students that in an action scene, shots and camera angles can change several times in just a few moments. Challenge them to actually count the changes the next time they watch this kind of scene.

- **Sound** Have students think about the range of sound effects they've been exposed to through video games, TV, and movies. Speculate with them about the kinds of sounds or music they might expect to hear in a fantasy that involves intense action and a variety of strange creatures. List the sound effects for students to revisit once they've viewed the clip.

---

## MEDIA STUDY: TEACHING OPTIONS

**Teaching Option 1: The Basics (1–2 Days)**
1. Begin the Media Study using the material provided on pages 112–113.
2. Show the Introduction on Media*Smart.* Then show the First Viewing. As they watch, have students use the Viewing Guide on page 114, along with the corresponding copy master on page 105 of the Resource Manager. Discuss their responses.
3. Return to the pupil book for the extension activities on page 115.

**Teaching Option 2: In-Depth Study (2–3 Days)**
1. Begin the Media Study using pages 112–113.
2. Show the Introduction and First Viewing from Media*Smart.* Then continue on Media*Smart* with the Media Lessons, using the teacher notes available in the Resources section.
3. Show the Guided Analysis presentation. Have students record their observations on the Student Viewing Guide available in the Resources section from Media*Smart.*
4. Return to the pupil book, page 115.

# Practice and Apply

## VIEWING GUIDE

1. As students prepare to view the clip, tell them that they will be asked to identify techniques used to build suspense and help the viewer identify with the hobbits. Encourage them to watch and listen for these elements:

   - the types of shots that make it clear that Frodo is the main character, at the center of the action

   - editing that shows how the hobbits are reacting to the unexpected danger

   - sound effects and music that reflect the mysterious nature of what the hobbits confront and that guide the audience's expectations

2. Some students may have difficulty ignoring the narrative to focus on the technical aspects of this scene. To help students analyze the visuals, have them watch the clip without sound. To help them pay attention to the music and sound effects, suggest they listen to the scene without viewing the action.

**R** RESOURCE MANAGER—Copy Masters
Viewing Guide p. 105
Close Viewing p. 106
Media Activity p. 107

Use this resource with the Viewing Guide:

💿 Media*Smart* DVD-ROM

Media*Scope* on **thinkcentral.com**

## ANSWERS

### FIRST VIEWING: Comprehension

1. *The hobbits hide and then run, finally making their way to Buckleberry Ferry and escaping on a raft.*

2. *At the start of the scene, it is daytime, and the setting looks peaceful. By the end of the scene, it is presumably nighttime, and the setting appears threatening.*

### CLOSE VIEWING: Media Literacy

**Possible answers:**

3. *Sound: howling wind; loud, eerie choral music; screeching horse; low, rumbling horns*

   *Editing and shots: quick cuts, high-angle shots, close-up shots*

4. *At key moments, the director uses the absence of sound to build suspense. Music and sound effects are used to signal the presence*

**Media⬤Smart** DVD-ROM
- **Film Clip:** *The Lord of the Rings*
- **Director:** Peter Jackson
- **Rating:** PG-13
- **Genre:** Fantasy
- **Running Time:** 4 minutes

114

## Viewing Guide for
# The Lord of the Rings

In this scene Frodo and the other hobbits take a peaceful break from their journey only to discover that a Black Rider is pursuing them.

As you watch this clip, pay attention to particular moments that draw you into the action and create suspense. Plan on watching the scene several times. To help you analyze suspense, refer to the questions that follow.

### NOW VIEW

#### FIRST VIEWING: Comprehension

1. **Recall** How do the hobbits escape the Black Rider?

2. **Summarize** How does the setting change as the scene progresses?

#### CLOSE VIEWING: Media Literacy

3. **Make Inferences** What techniques does the director use to lead you to believe that the Black Rider is evil?

4. **Analyze Sound** How does the director use sound to increase tension in the scene? Think about sound effects, music, changes in volume, and absence of sound.

5. **Analyze Camera Shots** How does the director use **point-of-view shots** and **high-angle** and **low-angle shots** to influence viewers' perception of the events? Think about the following shots:

   - Frodo's view of the road
   - Frodo's view of the horse's mouth and bit and hoof
   - the shot of the Black Rider standing directly above the hobbits' hiding place

6. **Evaluate Editing** Toward the end of the scene, the Black Rider is closing in on Frodo and the other hobbits. What effect do the **pace** and the use of **quick cuts** have on viewers?

of danger; the volume of the music increases as the situation worsens.

5. *Point-of-view shots show what the characters see. Frodo's view of the road indicates that something is coming. Low-angle shots convey that the Black Rider is powerful or menacing. High-angle shots convey helplessness and danger.*

6. *The pace and quick cuts increase the suspense. Viewers probably become anxious about Frodo's fate as the hobbit nearly comes within reach of the Black Rider.*

# Write or Discuss

**Analyze Suspense in Different Media** Why might a film's visual presentation of a suspenseful scene differ from the written version? Compare the beginning of the scene you just viewed with the way that Tolkien describes the Black Rider's approach in the book:

*The sound of hoofs stopped. As Frodo watched he saw something dark pass across the lighter space between two trees, and then halt. It looked like the black shade of a horse led by a smaller black shadow. The black shadow stood close to the point where they had left the path, and it swayed from side to side. Frodo thought he heard the sound of snuffling. The shadow bent to the group, and then began to crawl towards him.*

# Produce Your Own Media

**Create a Storyboard** A **storyboard** is a device used to plan the shooting of a film and to help the director envision what the finished product will look like. Create a storyboard revisiting the beginning of the *Fellowship of the Ring* scene. Your storyboard should emphasize the Black Rider's point of view and should include between eight and ten shots.

*HERE'S HOW* Think of your storyboard as a set of rough sketches that includes descriptions of each shot. Here are some tips to get you started:

- Break down the incident shot by shot, in chronological order.
- Consider using a variety of shots and angles, including close-ups, high-angle and low-angle shots, and point-of-view shots.
- Once you establish the scene, use point-of-view shots to show what the Black Rider sees.
- Think about the sounds you want to accompany each shot.

**STUDENT MODEL**

**Shot type:** LS (long shot)
**Action:** Black Rider races dangerously fast.
**Audio:** Horse screeches. Silence.

**Shot type:** MS (medium shot)
**Action:** Camera zooms in to show image of Black Rider. **Audio:** Music plays to indicate danger.

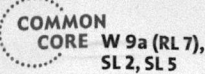
**COMMON CORE**

**W 9a (RL 7)** Draw evidence from literary texts; analyze a key scene in two different artistic mediums. **SL 2** Integrate multiple sources presented in diverse media or formats. **SL 5** Make strategic use of digital media in presentations.

**Media Tools** THINK central

Go to **thinkcentral.com**.
KEYWORD: HML9-115

**Production Tip**

Use abbreviations of shot types in your storyboard.

**POV** = point-of-view shot
**LS** = long shot
**MS** = medium shot
**CU** = close-up shot
**ELS** = extreme long shot

---

# Produce Your Own Media

**Rubric: Create a Storyboard** A strong storyboard should have

- an establishing shot, such as a long shot or an extreme long shot
- a variety of shots that show events in chronological order
- point-of-view shots to reflect what the Black Rider sees
- an accurate description of the action
- appropriate sounds to match each shot when necessary
- properly labeled shot types

**R** RESOURCE MANAGER—Copy Master
Produce Your Own Media p. 108

---

# Write or Discuss

COMMON CORE **W 9a (RL 7), SL 2, SL 5**

**Analyze Suspense in Different Media** Guide students to note that while the film version of this key scene can integrate images and sound effects simultaneously, the written format has a more measured approach to introducing each visual and auditory element into the scene. Discuss students' views about which medium creates a more suspenseful scene.

## MEDIA STUDY WRAP-UP

Have students summarize what they have learned about visual, sound, and editing techniques that filmmakers use to create suspense. Encourage students to use terms such as *high-angle shots* and *quick cuts* in their explanations.

## RETEACH

For students who are unable to apply the Media Study skills, select from these reteaching options:

- **Camera Shots** Provide students with a familiar movie image, such as King Kong. Ask, How would King Kong look to a viewer from a low-angle shot? *(mighty and ferocious)* from a high-angle shot? *(smaller and not so ferocious)*
- **Editing** Have students consider reality TV shows they've seen. Ask, In what ways do producers distort the "reality" of the show? *(They use flashbacks, tell stories out of order, or slow down time to prolong a suspenseful or dramatic moment.)*
- **Sound** Make a two-column chart on the board. In one column, write types of movies and TV shows such as: horror movie and sitcom. In the other column, write "Sounds." Have students list the types of sounds and sound effects they would be likely to hear in each type of show.

**Media Tools** THINK central

Media study keywords point to **MediaScope**, a Web site that helps students strengthen media analysis and production skills.

# Focus and Motivate

## ○ COMMON CORE FOCUS

**RI 1** Cite textual evidence to support analysis of what the text says explicitly as well as inferences drawn from the text. **RI 3** Analyze how the author unfolds a series of events, including how they are introduced and developed and the connections that are drawn between them. **RI 4** Determine the figurative meaning of phrases as they are used in a text. **W 5** Strengthen writing by revising, focusing on what is most significant for a specific purpose and audience. **L 3** Apply knowledge of language to make effective choices for meaning or style. **L 4c** Consult specialized reference materials to clarify a word's meaning.

## SUMMARY

In this excerpt from his autobiography, *Black Boy,* Richard Wright recalls a turning point in his childhood. Sent to buy groceries, Wright fends off a gang and returns home with a new sense of self-respect.

## What is worth FIGHTING FOR?

Discuss the question with students by examining the meaning of *convictions* ("strong beliefs"). After students complete the *DISCUSS* activity, have them compare their lists. Were there any recurring issues?

## Selection Resources

---

## The Rights to the Streets of Memphis
Autobiography by Richard Wright

# What is worth FIGHTING FOR?

## ○ COMMON CORE

**RI 1** Cite textual evidence to support analysis of what the text says explicitly as well as inferences drawn from the text. **RI 3** Analyze how the author unfolds a series of events, including how they are introduced and developed and the connections that are drawn between them. **RI 4** Determine the figurative meaning of phrases as they are used in a text.

An important part of becoming an adult is learning to stand up for yourself and maintain your convictions. In "The Rights to the Streets of Memphis," Richard Wright recalls an episode from his early childhood when he was threatened by a neighborhood gang.

*DISCUSS* What would draw you to a rally or make you speak out in a crowd? With a small group, generate a list of issues or values that you would defend at any cost. Why is each one so important to you? Choose a spokesperson to present the one your group cares about the most.

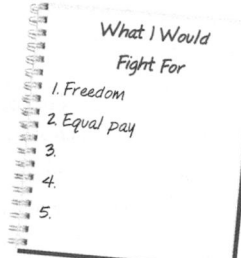

What I Would Fight For
1. Freedom
2. Equal pay
3.
4.
5.

116

---

See resources on the **Teacher One Stop DVD-ROM** and on **thinkcentral.com**.

**R RESOURCE MANAGER UNIT 1**
Plan and Teach, pp. 109–116
Summary, pp. 117–118†‡*
Text Analysis and Reading
   Skill, pp. 119–122†*
Vocabulary, pp. 123–125*
Grammar and Style, p. 128

**DIAGNOSTIC AND SELECTION TESTS**
Selection Tests, pp. 39–42

**📁 BEST PRACTICES TOOLKIT**
Word Questioning, p. E9
Cause and Effect Graphics,
   p. B16
New Word Analysis, p. E8

**TECHNOLOGY**
⊘ **Teacher One Stop DVD-ROM**
⊘ **Student One Stop DVD-ROM**
⊘ **Audio Anthology CD**
⊘ **GrammarNotes DVD-ROM**
⊘ **ExamView Test Generator**
   on the Teacher One Stop

---

\* Resources for Differentiation      † Also in Spanish      ‡ In Haitian Creole and Vietnamese

## TEXT ANALYSIS: AUTOBIOGRAPHY

An **autobiography** is the story of a person's life, written by that person. Writers of autobiographies generally use the same narrative techniques that are found in fiction. This makes the events they relate come to life for the reader. As you read "The Rights to the Streets of Memphis," notice how Richard Wright employs these and other narrative techniques:

- describes the **conflict** he faced
- builds **suspense** as events reach a **climax**
- uses realistic **dialogue** to reveal events and personalities

## READING SKILL: IDENTIFY CAUSE AND EFFECT

Writers of autobiographies often explain the **causes** and **effects** of important events in their lives in order to help readers understand the full significance of their experiences. For example, to describe the magnitude of his hunger, Wright explains:

*The hunger I had known before this ... had made me beg constantly for bread. ... But this new hunger ... scared me ...*

Recognizing cause-and-effect organizational patterns helps you connect events and make inferences and draw conclusions about important ideas in the narrative.

As you read Wright's autobiography, jot down the cause-and-effect relationships he points out.

| Cause | Effect |
|-------|--------|
| Father leaves. | Family is without food. |

## ▲ VOCABULARY IN CONTEXT

Use an appropriate vocabulary word to complete each phrase. Then, in your *Reader/Writer Notebook,* write a brief definition of each word you're familiar with.

| WORD LIST | clamor | flay | stark |
|-----------|--------|------|-------|
| | dispirited | retaliate | |

1. _____, absolute fear
2. a loud _____
3. _____ with a whip
4. _____, or get even
5. depressed and _____

 Complete the activities in your **Reader/Writer Notebook.**

## Meet the Author

# Richard Wright
### 1908–1960

**A Hard Beginning**

Richard Wright's life began in poverty. His father, a Mississippi sharecropper, abandoned his family when Wright was five. His mother, a teacher, had to support herself and her children. Because his family moved often and his mother became ill, Wright attended school irregularly. He dropped out of high school after only a few weeks and then traveled the country, working at odd jobs. Brilliant but troubled, he read widely. He also wrote powerful stories that earned him respect and recognition.

**French Citizenship**

After establishing himself as a writer with the success of his novel *Native Son,* Wright moved to France in 1947 to get away from the racism he had experienced in the United States. He settled in Paris and became a French citizen, continuing to write until his death.

**BACKGROUND TO THE SELECTION**

**Memphis in the Early 1900s**

This excerpt from Wright's autobiography *Black Boy* deals with a time when Wright was living in a tenement in Memphis, Tennessee. In the early 1900s, African Americans experienced harsh economic conditions in Memphis and other cities throughout the South. Federal welfare efforts, such as subsidized housing, food stamps, and aid to dependent children, did not exist. Most of the jobs available to black men and women paid very low wages. Like Wright's mother, many black women worked as poorly paid domestic servants.

**Author Online**

**THINK** central

Go to **thinkcentral.com**.
KEYWORD: HML9-117

**117**

**TEXT ANALYSIS**

COMMON CORE

RI 3

● *Model the Skill:* **AUTOBIOGRAPHY**

To model how to analyze autobiographical narrative techniques, read this passage aloud:

> "If you believe in something," Dad told me, "you have to speak out." When I said I feared making people angry, he replied, "Maybe so, Maria. But what is important is being true to yourself."

Point out that the father's dialogue explains some of his beliefs (speaking out and being true to oneself) and his hope of instilling those in his daughter.

**GUIDED PRACTICE** Ask students what the passage reveals about the author.

**READING SKILL**

COMMON CORE

RI 1, RI 3

■ *Model the Skill:* **IDENTIFY CAUSE AND EFFECT**

Use **A Hard Beginning** to model cause and effect relationships.

- **Cause:** Wright's family moved often, and his mother became ill.
- **Effect:** Wright attended school irregularly.
- The word *because* in the passage signals a cause-effect relationship.

**GUIDED PRACTICE** After students read **French Citizenship**, ask what caused Wright to move to France.

---

**VOCABULARY SKILL**

COMMON CORE

L 4

## ▲ VOCABULARY IN CONTEXT

**DIAGNOSE WORD KNOWLEDGE** Have all students complete Vocabulary in Context. Check their definitions against the following:

**clamor** (klăm′ər) *n.* a noisy outburst; outcry
**dispirited** (dĭ-spĭr′ĭ-tĭd) *adj.* dejected
**flay** (flā) *v.* to whip or lash
**retaliate** (ri-′tə-lē-āt) *v.* to pay back an injury in kind

**stark** (stärk) *adj.* complete or utter; extreme
*Answers:* **1.** stark, **2.** clamor, **3.** flay, **4.** retaliate, **5.** dispirited

**PRETEACH VOCABULARY** Use the copy master to help students predict meanings.

1. Read aloud item 1, emphasizing *clamor.*
2. Point out "loud enough for everyone to hear" and elicit meanings for *clamor.*

**R** RESOURCE MANAGER—Copy Master
Vocabulary Study p. 123

**READING SKILL**

COMMON CORE RI 1

**Ⓐ CAUSE AND EFFECT**

*Possible answer:* Wright began to recognize that the new, more frightening kind of hunger was causing him to feel different. Students may cite evidence in the text such as he "became less active" in play and "had to pause and think what was happening."

**IF STUDENTS NEED HELP ...** Have students reread lines 6–10. Ask them to describe the "new" hunger that Wright is experiencing. Then have students reread lines 11–13 and describe the effect that the "new" hunger has on Wright.

**Extend the Discussion** What does Wright mean when he writes that the hunger he had known before had not been a stranger? What does this tell you about his life?

**VOCABULARY**

COMMON CORE L 4

**OWN THE WORD**

**clamor:** Have students complete the following sentence to show an understanding of the noun. There was a *clamor* when ...

*Possible answers: I dropped a glass. the baby began to cry.*

# THE Rights TO THE Streets OF Memphis

## RICHARD WRIGHT

Hunger stole upon me so slowly that at first I was not aware of what hunger really meant. Hunger had always been more or less at my elbow when I played, but now I began to wake up at night to find hunger standing at my bedside, staring at me gauntly. The hunger I had known before this had been no grim, hostile stranger; it had been a normal hunger that had made me beg constantly for bread, and when I ate a crust or two I was satisfied. But this new hunger baffled me, scared me, made me angry and insistent. Whenever I begged for food now my mother would pour me a cup of tea which would still the **clamor** in my stomach for a moment or two; but a little later I would feel
10 hunger nudging my ribs, twisting my empty guts until they ached. I would grow dizzy and my vision would dim. I became less active in my play, and for the first time in my life I had to pause and think of what was happening to me. Ⓐ

"Mama, I'm hungry," I complained one afternoon.

"Jump up and catch a kungry," she said, trying to make me laugh and forget.

"What's a *kungry*?"

"It's what little boys eat when they get hungry," she said.

"What does it taste like?"
20 "I don't know."

"Then why do you tell me to catch one?"

"Because you said that you were hungry," she said, smiling.

I sensed that she was teasing me, and it made me angry.

"But I'm hungry. I want to eat."

**Analyze Visuals ▶**

What impressions of tenement life does the painting on page 119 convey?

**❶ Targeted Passage**

**clamor** (klăm′ər) *n.* a noisy outburst; outcry

COMMON CORE RI 1

**Ⓐ CAUSE AND EFFECT**
After only the first paragraph, you can already begin drawing conclusions about Wright's early life and the ideas he expresses in this autobiography. At this point, what cause-and-effect relationship did Wright start to recognize? Cite evidence in your response.

*Alley* (1942), Jacob Lawrence. Courtesy of Clark Atlanta University Art Galleries. © 2007 Gwendolyn Knight Lawrence/ Artists Rights Society (ARS), New York.

**118** UNIT 1: NARRATIVE STRUCTURE

---

## DIFFERENTIATED INSTRUCTION

**FOR ENGLISH LANGUAGE LEARNERS**

**Vocabulary Support** Use Word Questioning to teach these words: *aware* (line 1), *constantly* (line 5), *vision* (line 11), *restrictions* (line 45), *image* (line 57).

🧰 **BEST PRACTICES TOOLKIT—Transparency** Word Questioning p. E9

**FOR STRUGGLING READERS**

In combination with the *Audio Anthology CD*, use one or more Targeted Passages (pp. 118, 120, 121, 122) to ensure that students focus on key story events, concepts, and skills. Targeted Passages are also good for English learners.

**❶ Targeted Passage [Lines 1–13]**

This passage establishes one of the difficult circumstances of Wright's young life.

- What hardship is the author describing? What might this suggest about the kind of childhood Wright experienced? (lines 1–6)
- In what way is this hardship greater now than ever before? (lines 6–13)

## FOR ADVANCED LEARNERS/PRE–AP

**Evaluate** This passage from Wright's autobiography provides details about the social and economic aspects of life in the tenements of Memphis during the early 20th century. What can students infer about the health and social issues affecting the author during this period? As they read, have students make note of health, developmental, and social aspects detailed in the passage. Then have students discuss how such influences may have affected the author's wellbeing and character.

## BACKGROUND

**Tenement Housing** In the late 19th and early 20th centuries, many of the thousands of immigrants who came to America lived in tenements such as the one shown in the painting on this page. Tenement landlords were more concerned with making a profit than with providing comfortable living conditions. As a result, urban tenements were typically run-down, dirty, crowded buildings, with no electricity, heat, or indoor plumbing. Living conditions gradually improved with the passage of tenement housing laws in the early 1900s.

## Analyze Visuals

*Possible answer: The angle, shadows, and dominant grayness of the scene convey a sense of hardship. Most of the people in the painting are shown with downcast heads. This posture suggests boredom, weariness, and discontent.*

**About the Art** Jacob Lawrence (1917–2000) was an American painter best known for his series of paintings that deal with African-American people and subjects. Lawrence's art was influenced by the abstract elements of cubism and by his experiences living in New York City's Harlem, where he witnessed scenes of tenement life such as the one shown in *Alley.*

## REVISIT THE BIG QUESTION

What is worth

# FIGHTING FOR?

Why does the mother cry when her son repeatedly asks for food? Why does she bring up the topic of the absent father? ***Possible answer:*** *It hurts her for the children to go hungry. With her husband gone, she must find a job before she can purchase food for the children.*

## Analyze Visuals

**Activity** After students read the selection, ask them to compare and contrast the woman in the portrait with the author's mother. *Possible answer: The woman in the portrait appears to have endured hardship, as did Wright's mother. Although the woman seems weary and sad, like Wright's mother, she projects strength.*

**About the Art** Charles White (1918–1979) was an American painter known for his paintings of African Americans, such as *Woman Worker*, shown here.

## TIERED DISCUSSION PROMPTS

In lines 39–59, use these discussion prompts to help students understand the author's character development:

**Analyze** What do you think the author was like before his father's departure? *Possible answer: He seems to have been high-spirited but repressed by his father's "restrictions" (line 45).*

**Synthesize** How does the author's attitude about his father's departure change from line 40 to line 59? *Possible answer: Initially, he enjoyed the freedom to make noise. But that turned to a "deep, biological bitterness" (lines 58–59) when he realized that his father wasn't coming home to provide food.*

---

"You'll have to wait."

"But I want to eat now."

"But there's nothing to eat," she told me.

"Why?"

"Just because there's none," she explained.

30 "But I want to eat," I said, beginning to cry.

"You'll just have to wait," she said again.

"But why?"

"For God to send some food."

"When is He going to send it?"

"I don't know."

"But I'm hungry!"

She was ironing, and she paused and looked at me with tears in her eyes.

"Where's your father?" she asked me.

40 I stared in bewilderment. Yes, it was true that my father had not come home to sleep for many days now and I could make as much noise as I wanted. Though I had not known why he was absent, I had been glad that he was not there to shout his restrictions at me. But it had never occurred to me that his absence would mean that there would be no food.

"I don't know," I said.

"Who brings food into the house?" my mother

50 asked me.

"Papa," I said. "He always brought food."

"Well, your father isn't here now," she said.

"Where is he?"

"I don't know," she said.

"But I'm hungry," I whimpered, stomping my feet.

"You'll have to wait until I get a job and buy food," she said.

As the days slid past the image of my father became associated with my pangs of hunger, and whenever I felt hunger I thought of him with a deep biological bitterness.[1]

60 My mother finally went to work as a cook and left me and my brother alone in the flat each day with a loaf of bread and a pot of tea. When she returned at evening she would be tired and **dispirited** and would cry a lot. Sometimes, when she was in despair, she would call us to her and talk to us for hours, telling us that we now had no father, that our lives would be different from those of other children, that we must learn as soon as possible to take care of ourselves, to dress ourselves, to prepare our own food; that we must take upon ourselves the responsibility of the flat while she worked. Half frightened, we

*Woman Worker* (1951), Charles White. © 1951 The Charles White Archive.

 **AUTOBIOGRAPHY**
Reread lines 39–56. What life-changing event does Wright reveal through **dialogue?**

**dispirited** (dĭ-spĭr′ĭ-tĭd) *adj.* dejected

 **Targeted Passage**

---

1. **deep, biological bitterness:** bitterness caused by the pangs of hunger.

---

## DIFFERENTIATED INSTRUCTION

### FOR STRUGGLING READERS

 **Targeted Passage** [Lines 60–67]

This passage continues to paint a picture in the reader's mind of the hardships faced by the author as a result of being abandoned by his father.

- Why are the author and his brother left alone in the flat each day? How do you think the mother feels about this? (lines 60–62)

- How are the boys' lives now "different from those of other children"? (lines 62–67)

### FOR STRUGGLING READERS

**Develop Reading Fluency** Use parts of the exchange between Wright and his mother to give students practice in reading dialogue. Fluent readers read dialogue with expression, using punctuation marks to show them when to pause or make changes in their intonation. Have a proficient reader read aloud one character while you read the other. Have students practice reading the dialogue.

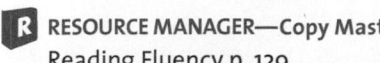

would promise solemnly. We did not understand what had happened between
our father and our mother and the most that these long talks did to us was to
make us feel a vague dread. Whenever we asked why father had left, she would
tell us that we were too young to know.

One evening my mother told me that thereafter I would have to do the
shopping for food. She took me to the corner store to show me the way. I
was proud; I felt like a grownup. The next afternoon I looped the basket over
my arm and went down the pavement toward the store. When I reached the
corner, a gang of boys grabbed me, knocked me down, snatched the basket,
took the money, and sent me running home in panic. That evening I told my
mother what had happened, but she made no comment; she sat down at once,
wrote another note, gave me more money, and sent me out to the grocery
again. I crept down the steps and saw the same gang of boys playing down the
street. I ran back into the house.

"What's the matter?" my mother asked.

"It's those same boys," I said. "They'll beat me."

"You've got to get over that," she said. "Now, go on."

"I'm scared," I said.

"Go on and don't pay any attention to them," she said.

I went out of the door and walked briskly down the sidewalk, praying that
the gang would not molest me. But when I came abreast of them someone
shouted.

"There he is!"

They came toward me and I broke into a wild run toward home. They
overtook me and flung me to the pavement. I yelled, pleaded, kicked, but they
wrenched the money out of my hand. They yanked me to my feet, gave me a
few slaps, and sent me home sobbing. My mother met me at the door.

"They b-beat m-me," I gasped. "They t-t-took the m-money."

I started up the steps, seeking the shelter of the house.

"Don't you come in here," my mother warned me.

I froze in my tracks and stared at her.

"But they're coming after me," I said.

"You just stay right where you are," she said in a deadly tone. "I'm going to
teach you this night to stand up and fight for yourself."

She went into the house and I waited, terrified, wondering what she was
about. Presently she returned with more money and another note; she also had
a long heavy stick.

"Take this money, this note, and this stick," she said. "Go to the store and
buy those groceries. If those boys bother you, then fight."

I was baffled. My mother was telling me to fight, a thing that she had never
done before.

"But I'm scared," I said.

"Don't you come into this house until you've gotten those groceries,"
she said.

**© AUTOBIOGRAPHY**
Why do you suppose
Wright includes such
specific details about
this experience?

**Ⓓ GRAMMAR AND STYLE**
Reread lines 91–94.
Wright uses **strong verbs
in a series**—like *yelled*,
*pleaded*, and *kicked*—to
help readers visualize
the attack.

**❸ Targeted Passage**

**COMMON CORE RI 4**

**Language Coach**

**Idioms** An **idiom** is an
expression that cannot
be understood literally.
In lines 102–103, the
expression "what
she was about" is an
idiomatic expression.
Based on the clues in
the story, what do you
think this idiom means?

---

**FOR STRUGGLING READERS**

**❸ Targeted Passage** [Lines 91–106]

This passage shows how Wright's mother
makes him stand up for himself against the
boys who are chasing him.

- What is Wright hoping will happen when he
  climbs the steps to his home? (line 96)

- Why is the reaction of Wright's mother
  surprising? (lines 97–103)

- What does Mrs. Wright hope to accomplish
  by giving Wright the stick? (lines 105–106)

**FOR ENGLISH LANGUAGE LEARNERS**

**Language Coach**     **COMMON CORE RI 4**

**Idioms** *Answer: The idiom means that
he wonders what his mother was thinking
or planning.* Have students reread lines
100–101, putting themselves in the situation.

**BEST PRACTICES TOOLKIT**—Transparency
New Word Analysis p. E8

---

**© Model the Skill:
AUTOBIOGRAPHY**

To model for students why Wright may
have used such specific detail, read aloud
lines 75–81, beginning with "When I
reached…." Point out that Wright brings
the narrative to life by using a string of action verbs, vividly painting a picture of the
encounter and building the tension of the
violent scene.

**Possible answer:** *Wright most likely
includes the details so readers can vividly
"see" the events he describes. The details
also build suspense and set the scene for
Wright's next encounter with the gang.*

**Extend the Discussion** Why do you think
the author is able to recall these events
in such detail many years later?

**Ⓓ GRAMMAR
AND STYLE**     **COMMON CORE L 3**

**Strong Verbs in a Series** Guide students to
identify other effective word choices the
author makes to help readers understand
and visualize the attack and its aftermath.
(Possible answers *yanked, sobbed, gasped*)

**REVISIT THE BIG QUESTION**
What is worth

# FIGHTING FOR?

**Discuss** What do lines 100–101 suggest about
the convictions of Wright's mother? *Possible
answer: She believes that people should stand
up for themselves and even use physical force if
necessary.*

**E** *Model the Skill:* **CAUSE AND EFFECT**

To model for students the effect that the fighting had on Wright, read aloud lines 137–145. Point out the change from Wright's earlier response to the bullies. Have students add details to their chart on page 117 about the difference in Wright's attitude and behavior following the fight.

*Possible answer: The fighting gave Wright confidence and self-respect; it showed that he could stand up and defend himself.*

## SELECTION WRAP-UP

**READ WITH A PURPOSE** Have students analyze how the circumstances in Wright's life caused him to stand up for himself. *Possible answer: Wright knew his mother would whip him if he came home without the groceries and that he would have to use the stick to fight off the gang.*

### OWN THE WORD

- **retaliate:** *Retaliate* is made up of the prefix *re-*, meaning "again," and the Latin word *talio,* "punishment in kind."

- **flay:** Have students provide synonyms for *flay.* **Possible answers:** *smack, strike, whack*

- **stark:** Ask students to use *stark* in different contexts.

---

"They'll beat me; they'll beat me," I said.

"Then stay in the streets; don't come back here!"

I ran up the steps and tried to force my way past her into the house. A stinging slap came on my jaw. I stood on the sidewalk, crying.

"Please, let me wait until tomorrow," I begged.

"No," she said. "Go now! If you come back into this house without those groceries, I'll whip you!"

120 She slammed the door and I heard the key turn in the lock. I shook with fright. I was alone upon the dark, hostile streets and gangs were after me. I had the choice of being beaten at home or away from home. I clutched the stick, crying, trying to reason. If I were beaten at home, there was absolutely nothing that I could do about it; but if I were beaten in the streets, I had a chance to fight and defend myself. I walked slowly down the sidewalk, coming closer to the gang of boys, holding the stick tightly. I was so full of fear that I could scarcely breathe. I was almost upon them now.

"There he is again!" the cry went up.

They surrounded me quickly and began to grab for my hand.

"I'll kill you!" I threatened.

130 They closed in. In blind fear I let the stick fly, feeling it crack against a boy's skull. I swung again, lamming another skull, then another. Realizing that they would **retaliate** if I let up for but a second, I fought to lay them low, to knock them cold, to kill them so that they could not strike back at me. I **flayed** with tears in my eyes, teeth clenched, **stark** fear making me throw every ounce of my strength behind each blow. I hit again and again, dropping the money and the grocery list. The boys scattered, yelling, nursing their heads, staring at me in utter disbelief. They had never seen such frenzy. I stood panting, egging them on, taunting them to come on and fight. When they refused, I ran after them and they tore out for their homes, screaming. The parents of the

140 boys rushed into the streets and threatened me, and for the first time in my life I shouted at grownups, telling them that I would give them the same if they bothered me. I finally found my grocery list and the money and went to the store. On my way back I kept my stick poised for instant use, but there was not a single boy in sight. That night I won the right to the streets of Memphis.  **E**

**④ Targeted Passage**

**retaliate** (rĭ-tăl′ē-āt′) *v.* to pay back an injury in kind

**flay** (flā) *v.* to whip or lash

**stark** (stärk) *adj.* complete or utter; extreme

**E CAUSE AND EFFECT**
What effect did the fighting have on Wright's personality?

---

## DIFFERENTIATED INSTRUCTION

### FOR STRUGGLING READERS

**④ Targeted Passage [Lines 127–145]**

This passage concludes the excerpt with the author's momentous experience: he defends himself.

- What happens when the gang starts to attack Wright again? (lines 130–139)

- What do Wright's actions suggest about how he's changed? (lines 138–142)

- How do you think Wright feels after the encounter? (lines 143–145)

### FOR ADVANCED LEARNERS/PRE-AP

**Synthesize** Have students reread *Meet the Author* (p. 117). Then ask them to speculate about how the incident described in this autobiography and Wright's later success as a writer might be connected. Have students write a paragraph citing their conclusion.

## Comprehension

1. **Recall** Why does Richard's mother have no food for him?

2. **Recall** What choice does Richard have to make?

3. **Clarify** What does the **title** refer to?

## Text Analysis

4. **Identify Cause and Effect** Review the cause-and-effect relationships you listed as you read. What are the main causes of Richard's predicament? Cite evidence from the text to support your answer.

5. **Examine Language** Reread lines 1–10 and note the words and phrases that Wright uses to make hunger seem human. What effect does this **personification** have on the reader?

6. **Analyze Dialogue** Wright not only narrates events but also uses dialogue to bring a sense of reality to his narrative. Review the conversations between Wright and his mother. What does it suggest about their relationship and the way it changes?

7. **Predict** Reread the last paragraph of the selection. Will Richard be different after fighting the street gang? Cite evidence to support your prediction.

8. **Interpret Autobiography** In an autobiography, the writer must choose which life experiences to include and which to leave out. In your opinion, why did Wright choose to share this particular episode in his life? Support your opinion.

9. **Evaluate Narrative Techniques** Find examples of each narrative technique listed in the graphic shown. Which narrative techniques does Wright make the best use of in this autobiography? Explain your evaluation.

| Techniques | Examples |
|---|---|
| • Describes conflict | |
| • Uses believable dialogue | |
| • Builds suspense | |
| • Develops personalities | |

## Text Criticism

10. **Critical Interpretations** When this autobiography was published in 1945, a critic wrote, "It is not easy for those who have had happier childhoods, with little restraint or fear in them, to face up to the truth of this childhood of Richard Wright." Do you agree with this statement? Explain why or why not.

### What is worth FIGHTING FOR?

What are the issues or values that you would fight to defend?

THE RIGHTS TO THE STREETS OF MEMPHIS  123

---

**COMMON CORE**

**RI 1** Cite textual evidence to support analysis of what the text says explicitly as well as inferences drawn from the text. **RI 3** Analyze how the author unfolds a series of events, including how they are introduced and developed and the connections that are drawn between them.

---

# Practice and Apply

For preliminary support of post-reading questions, use these copy masters:

 **RESOURCE MANAGER—Copy Masters**
Reading Check p. 126
Autobiography p. 119
Question Support p. 127

Additional selection questions are provided for teachers on page 113.

## ANSWERS

### Comprehension

1. *Richard's father had provided the food, but he abandoned the family.*

2. *Richard must choose between standing up for himself against bullies or getting punished by his mother.*

3. *The title refers to Richard's having earned the right to walk safely on the streets of his neighborhood.*

### Text Analysis

**COMMON CORE RI 1, RI 3**

*Possible answers:*

4. ■ **COMMON CORE FOCUS** *Identify Cause and Effect Students should note that the main causes cited in the text are his father's abandonment of the family, the gang's assaults on him, and his mother's conviction that Richard has to learn to fight for himself.*

5. *Personifying hunger by describing it as if it were a living creature makes the hunger and its effects seem more vivid to the reader.*

6. *The dialogue portrays a comfortable relationship. The later dialogue reveals that the mother exerts strong control when an important issue is at stake, which forces the son to change.*

7. *It is likely that Richard will be more self-confident. He is now aware of his own power (lines 136–142) and the victory it has brought him (lines 144–145).*

8. ● **COMMON CORE FOCUS** *Interpret: Autobiography This episode marks the point at which Wright overcomes his fear and stands up for himself. Vivid detail and the dramatic way the episode is portrayed show how important the episode was to Wright.*

9. *Describes conflict: lines 72–81, 91–94, 130–142. Uses believable dialogue: lines 14–56, 82–118. Builds suspense: lines 100–108, 119–130. Develops personalities:*

---

*lines 1–13, 60–71, 100–118. Students may choose any of these techniques, but should provide reasons for their choices.*

## Text Criticism

*Possible answer:*

10. *Agree: A person fortunate enough to have a happy childhood may find it difficult to relate to the hardship that Wright suffered. Disagree: Students who have not suffered hardships may still feel sympathy, because most people have faced some type of difficulty in their lives.*

### What is worth FIGHTING FOR? *Possible answers: freedom, equality*

# ANSWERS

## Vocabulary in Context

### ▲ VOCABULARY PRACTICE

1. *dispirited*
2. *stark*
3. *clamor*
4. *retaliate*
5. *flay*

 **RESOURCE MANAGER—Copy Master**
Vocabulary Practice p. 124

### ACADEMIC VOCABULARY IN SPEAKING

Students' answers will vary, but should take into account the level of reasoning displayed by Wright in the passage, as well as his behavior. Student answers should include academic vocabulary words and supporting evidence from the text.

### VOCABULARY STRATEGY: SYNONYMS AND ANTONYMS

◌ COMMON CORE L 4c ◌

- Point out that words such as *and* in the example phrase "tired and dispirited" offer clues as to whether an unknown word could be a synonym or antonym of another word in the sentence.
- After students complete the practice, discuss the clue words in each sentence.

#### Possible answers:

1. *containing plenty*
2. *puzzled*
3. *rich*
4. *lying*
5. *unwillingness to compromise*

 **RESOURCE MANAGER—Copy Master**
Vocabulary Strategy p. 125

---

**Interactive Vocabulary**  **THINK** central

Keywords direct students to a **WordSharp** tutorial on **thinkcentral.com** or to other types of vocabulary practice and review.

---

## Vocabulary in Context

### ▲ VOCABULARY PRACTICE

Write the word from the list that best completes each sentence.

1. Alone and hungry, Richard felt _____ as he walked the streets.
2. He knew it would be hard to rise above his family's _____ poverty.
3. He tried to concentrate amid the _____ as several older boys shouted at him.
4. If they tried to harm him, he intended to _____ immediately.
5. He would _____ them with his stick if necessary.

**WORD LIST**
clamor
dispirited
flay
retaliate
stark

### ACADEMIC VOCABULARY IN SPEAKING

- analyze  • element  • infer  • sequence  • structure

**Analyze** the selection to **infer**, or make an educated guess, about how old Wright was when this incident happened. Discuss your guess with a partner, providing evidence from the text for support. Use at least one of the Academic Vocabulary words in your response.

### VOCABULARY STRATEGY: SYNONYMS AND ANTONYMS

**Synonyms** are words with the same, or almost the same, meaning. **Antonyms** are words with opposite meanings. Recognizing synonyms and antonyms can help you figure out the meanings of unknown words. For example, Wright says his mother felt "tired and dispirited." Though *tired* is not an exact synonym of *dispirited*, it is close enough in meaning to help you figure out what *dispirited* means.

*PRACTICE* In each sentence, the boldfaced word is either a synonym or an antonym of the underlined word. Use the boldfaced word to help you figure out the meaning of the underlined word. Then write a definition of the underlined word. You may consult a thesaurus for help determing whether the words in each pair are synonyms or antonyms.

1. The table was **overflowing** with <u>bountiful</u> platters of food.
2. Though Alice was <u>nonplused</u> by his remarks, I was **unsurprised**.
3. The <u>affluent</u> Henleys were sometimes shunned by their **poorer** neighbors.
4. She wasn't **deceiving** anyone with her <u>prevaricating</u>.
5. <u>Intransigence</u> and **stubbornness** won't help us overcome this problem.

⚬ **COMMON CORE**

**L 4c** Consult specialized reference materials to clarify a word's meaning.

**Interactive Vocabulary**  **THINK** central

Go to **thinkcentral.com**.
KEYWORD: HML9-124

---

## DIFFERENTIATED INSTRUCTION

### FOR ENGLISH LANGUAGE LEARNERS

**Vocabulary: Cognates** For speakers of Romance languages, point out that the word *incident* in the **Academic Vocabulary in Speaking** directions is a cognate.

### FOR ADVANCED LEARNERS/PRE–AP

**Vocabulary in Writing** Have students use at least three vocabulary words in a paragraph written from the point of view of one of the boys in the gang.

# Language

◆ **GRAMMAR AND STYLE:** Emphasize Action

Review the **Grammar and Style** note on page 121. There, Wright uses **strong verbs in a series** to emphasize the actions taking place. By incorporating similar techniques into your own writing, you can help readers to easily visualize events, as Wright does.

Here is another example from the story:

> *When I reached the corner, a gang of boys grabbed me, knocked me down, snatched the basket, took the money, and sent me running home in panic.*
> (lines 75–77)

Now study this model. Notice how the revisions in blue make the sentence much stronger, yet still concise. Revise your response to the prompt below by using the same techniques.

STUDENT MODEL

To help her son survive, Mrs. Wright ~~used several tactics to make~~ *urged, commanded, and finally compelled* him ^to^ face his deepest fears.

**READING-WRITING CONNECTION**

 Demonstrate your understanding of the characters in "The Rights to the Streets of Memphis" by responding to this prompt. Then use the **revising tip** to improve your writing.

| WRITING PROMPT | REVISING TIP |
|---|---|
| **Extended Constructed Response: Interpretation** Mrs. Wright left her two young sons alone during the day. She ordered Richard to bring home groceries even if he has to fight a gang to do so. Why did she act as she did? Write a **three-to-five-paragraph response,** describing her actions and explaining her motives. | Review your response. Have you used strong verbs to describe Mrs. Wright's actions? Have you explained the reasons for her actions? If not, revise your response. |

**Interactive Revision**  THINK central

Go to **thinkcentral.com**. KEYWORD: HML9N-125

---

**FOR STRUGGLING WRITERS**

- Help students visualize the sequence of events.

- Help students express each step in a separate sentence. For example: *Richard swung the stick and hit one boy. Then another boy grabbed the stick.*

- Encourage students to continue the sequence of action through the point when Richard ultimately returns home.

---

# Language

◆ **GRAMMAR AND STYLE**

After students examine the revisions in the student model, discuss the effect of the word choices, *urged, commanded,* and *compelled.* Ask students what these strong verbs help them to visualize, and why the words are more effective choices for meaning than *used.*

**R RESOURCE MANAGER—Copy Master**
Use Subjunctive Mood p. 128

**READING-WRITING CONNECTION**

**WRITING PROMPT**

- Encourage students to review what they know about the Wright family's situation, and to consider the alternatives available to Mrs. Wright. Then have them think about her actions and motives.

**BEST PRACTICES TOOLKIT—Transparency**
Cause and Effect Graphics p. B16

**COMMON CORE**

**L 3** Apply knowledge of language to make effective choices for meaning or style.
**W 5** Strengthen writing by revising, focusing on what is most significant for a specific purpose and audience.

**Writing Online**  THINK central

The following tools are available online at **thinkcentral.com** and on **Write*Smart* CD-ROM:**
- **Interactive Graphic Organizers**
- **Interactive Student Models**
- **Interactive Revision Lessons**
For additional grammar instruction, see **GrammarNotes** on **thinkcentral.com**.

## Assess and Reteach

### Assess

**DIAGNOSTIC AND SELECTION TESTS**
Selection Test A pp. 39–40
Selection Test B/C pp. 41–42

**Interactive Selection Test** on **thinkcentral.com**

### Reteach

**Level Up Online Tutorials** on **thinkcentral.com**

**Reteaching Worksheets** on **thinkcentral.com**
Literature Lessons 5, 43
Vocabulary Lesson 18

# Focus and Motivate

## COMMON CORE FOCUS

**RI 3** Analyze how the author unfolds a series of events, including the order in which points are made and how they are introduced and developed. **RI 6** Determine an author's purpose in a text. **L 4c** Consult reference materials to determine or clarify a word's meaning or etymology.

## SUMMARY

In this excerpt from *Seabiscuit: An American Legend*, the biography of a racehorse, Laura Hillenbrand recounts the 1937 Santa Anita Handicap. Rivals Seabiscuit and Rosemont compete in a hard-fought race, but Seabiscuit falters at the end and loses. Hillenbrand suggests that the loss may have been due to jockey Red Pollard's partial blindness, which he had kept secret.

## What makes a WINNER?

Have students identify qualities that characterize a winner. Extend the discussion by asking how a person might be a "winner" even without participating in a competition. Then have students complete the *PRESENT* activity.

---

# from Seabiscuit: An American Legend

Biography by Laura Hillenbrand

# What makes a WINNER?

## COMMON CORE

**RI 3** Analyze how the author unfolds a series of events, including the order in which points are made and how they are introduced and developed. **RI 6** Determine an author's purpose in a text.

In the heat of competition, what separates a winner from a loser? That's the question explored in *Seabiscuit*, the story of the legendary racehorse that won the hearts of millions of Americans.

**PRESENT** With a partner, choose someone you consider to be a winner. Create a "portrait" of the person in words and images, labeling the qualities that you feel led to his or her success. Share your portrait with the rest of the class.

126

---

# Selection Resources

See resources on the **Teacher One Stop DVD-ROM** and on **thinkcentral.com**.

 **RESOURCE MANAGER UNIT 1**
   Plan and Teach, pp. 131–138
   Summary, pp. 139–140†‡*
   Text Analysis and Reading
      Skill, pp. 141–144†*
   Vocabulary, pp. 145–147*

**DIAGNOSTIC AND SELECTION TESTS**
   Selection Tests, pp. 43–46

 **BEST PRACTICES TOOLKIT**
   Word Sorts, p. E5
   New Word Analysis, p. E8
   Predicting, p. A10

**TECHNOLOGY**
- **Teacher One Stop DVD-ROM**
- **Student One Stop DVD-ROM**
- **Audio Anthology CD**
- **GrammarNotes DVD-ROM**
- **ExamView Test Generator** on the Teacher One Stop

 **THINK** central

**Find it Online!**

Features on **thinkcentral.com** that support the selection include
- **PowerNotes** presentation
- **ThinkAloud** models to enhance comprehension
- **WordSharp** vocabulary tutorials
- interactive writing and grammar instruction

---

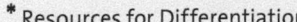 * Resources for Differentiation      † Also in Spanish      ‡ In Haitian Creole and Vietnamese

## ● TEXT ANALYSIS: SUSPENSE IN BIOGRAPHY

A **biography** is a true account of someone's life. The following biography is unusual in that the author has chosen to make the life of a famous horse the focus of her work.

Though biographers must research and report facts accurately, a good biographer is also a storyteller who engages readers. Through the use of **foreshadowing**, for example, the biographer can build **suspense** in the same way that a fiction writer does. Notice how the first sentence sets up a feeling of tension and concern about future events:

*Quiet trepidation settled over the Howard barn in the week before the Santa Anita Handicap.*

As you read this selection from *Seabiscuit*, pay attention to the way Laura Hillenbrand unfolds a series of events.

## ● READING SKILL: IDENTIFY AUTHOR'S PURPOSE

An **author's purpose** is the reasons the author has for writing a particular work. An author typically has one or more of these basic purposes in mind:

- to inform or explain
- to express thoughts or feelings
- to persuade
- to entertain

Understanding an author's purpose for writing can provide insight into the central idea, or most important idea, conveyed by a nonfiction text. It can also help you decide *how* to read. For example, if you realize that an author is trying to inform or explain by including detailed information, you might decide to take notes as you read in order to revisit the most important details later on.

As you read this selection, try to decide Hillenbrand's purpose, and look for details that support it. Record your findings in your *Reader/Writer Notebook.*

***Review: Predict***

## ▲ VOCABULARY IN CONTEXT

Try to figure out the meaning of each boldfaced word.

1. felt **trepidation** waiting
2. mumbled **inaudibly**
3. looking for the **optimal** solution
4. tiny **increment** of speed
5. a slow, steady **cadence**
6. clumsy and **inept**
7. **inexplicably** slowed down
8. finally reached an **unequivocal** decision

 Complete the activities in your **Reader/Writer Notebook.**

## Meet the Author

# Laura Hillenbrand
**born 1967**

**The Will to Overcome**
At the age of 19, Laura Hillenbrand's life changed forever. Up until then, she had been physically active, swimming competitively, riding horses, and playing tennis. Suddenly, she was stricken with chronic fatigue syndrome, an illness that sometimes made her too weak even to feed herself. To find purpose in her life and "a way to endure the suffering," Hillenbrand started writing. As she wrote *Seabiscuit*, she found a link between herself and her subject—a horse who had the will to overcome obstacles.

**A Thorough Researcher**
Although her illness sometimes left her bedridden, Hillenbrand meticulously researched the life of Seabiscuit. She placed ads in horseracing magazines, interviewed aging jockeys by phone, and sought information from the Library of Congress. Her research paid off in a best-selling biography filled with suspenseful events and memorable details.

**BACKGROUND TO THE BIOGRAPHY**
**Horseracing**
Known as the sport of kings, horseracing is one of the oldest of all spectator sports. A popular type of horserace is the handicap, a race in which the horses carry different amounts of weight based on factors such as age and past performances. Faster horses carry more weight; slower horses carry less. The goal is to give all the horses an equal chance of winning. To ride a racehorse, a jockey needs balance, coordination, strength, and quick reflexes. According to Hillenbrand, "The extraordinary athleticism of the jockey is unparalleled."

Author Online
Go to **thinkcentral.com.**
KEYWORD: HML9-127

127

---

**TEXT ANALYSIS** — COMMON CORE — RI 3

## ● *Model the Skill:* SUSPENSE IN BIOGRAPHY

To model how to identify suspense in a biography, read aloud this example:

> Maria has trained hard for months, yet everyone insists she has no chance. She is older than all the other runners and has not competed since her injury.

Explain to students that although the odds are stacked against Maria, she has been training hard to win. The suspense lies in the question of whether she can beat the odds and prove the naysayers wrong.

**GUIDED PRACTICE** Ask students to describe suspenseful moments in stories.

**READING SKILL** — COMMON CORE — RI 6

## ■ *Model the Skill:* IDENTIFY AUTHOR'S PURPOSE

To model how to identify an author's purpose for writing, explain that the author suffers from chronic fatigue syndrome. To find purpose in her life, Hillenbrand decided to write about Seabiscuit. So, her purpose for writing the biography was to find purpose in her life.

**GUIDED PRACTICE** Ask students to pick one of their favorite books and identify possible purposes for it being written.

 **RESOURCE MANAGER—Copy Master**
Identify Author's Purpose p. 143

---

**VOCABULARY SKILL** — COMMON CORE — L 4

## ▲ VOCABULARY IN CONTEXT

**DIAGNOSE WORD KNOWLEDGE** Have all students complete Vocabulary in Context. Check their definitions against the following:

**cadence** (kād′ns) *n.* a balanced, rhythmic flow
**inaudibly** (ĭn-ô′də-blē) *adv.* in a way that is impossible to hear
**increment** (ĭn′krə-mənt) *n.* a small, slight growth or increase
**inept** (ĭn-ĕpt′) *adj.* generally incompetent

**inexplicably** (ĭn-ĕk′splĭ-kə-blē) *adv.* in a way that is difficult or impossible to explain
**optimal** (ŏp′tə-məl) *adj.* most favorable; best
**trepidation** (trĕp′ĭ-dā′shən) *n.* nervous fear
**unequivocal** (ŭn′ĭ-kwĭv′ə-kəl) *adj.* allowing no doubt or misunderstanding

**PRETEACH VOCABULARY** Use the copy master to help students predict meanings.

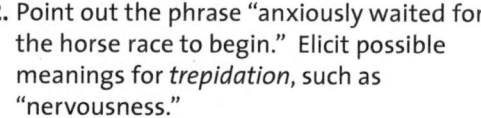 **RESOURCE MANAGER—Copy Master**
Vocabulary Study p. 145

1. Read the first item aloud, emphasizing *trepidation*.

2. Point out the phrase "anxiously waited for the horse race to begin." Elicit possible meanings for *trepidation*, such as "nervousness."

3. Repeat the procedure for the other items.

### READ WITH A PURPOSE

*Help students set a purpose for reading. Tell them to read* Seabiscuit: An American Legend *to find out whether the author focuses on the horse or the jockey and what effect it has.*

**READING SKILL**   COMMON CORE   RI 6

### A AUTHOR'S PURPOSE

*Possible answer: The detailed account in the opening of the biography shows that the author's main purpose is to inform readers about the rivalry between Seabiscuit and Rosemont. Her style of writing and choice of engaging details suggests that she also intends to entertain her readers with a fascinating, true story.*

**IF STUDENTS NEED HELP . . .**

• Have students identify factual information that the author presents in the first three paragraphs. Also note the author's explanation of how the racetrack is prepared (lines 3–4). Remind students about the extensive research that was required to unearth so many details.

**Extend the Discussion** *Seabiscuit* was the basis for a popular movie. How can you tell that Hillenbrand's account might make an exciting film?

**VOCABULARY**   COMMON CORE   L 4

### OWN THE WORD

**trepidation:** Point out that the root word for trepidation is *trepidus*, which is Latin for "anxious." Have students make a list of things that might cause them *trepidation.*

# Seabiscuit:
## AN AMERICAN LEGEND

### Laura Hillenbrand

Quiet **trepidation** settled over the Howard barn in the week before the Santa Anita Handicap.[1] Late in the week, a long, soaking shower doused the racing oval. When the rain stopped, asphalt-baking machines droned over the course, licking flames over the surface to dry the soil. Rosemont emerged from the barn three days before the race and scorched the track in his final workout. Reporters waited for Smith[2] to give his horse a similar workout, but they never saw Seabiscuit doing anything more than stretching his legs. Rumors swirled around the track that Seabiscuit was lame. Rosemont's stock rose; Seabiscuit's dropped.

10　Smith had fooled them. At three o'clock one morning shortly before the race, he led Seabiscuit out to the track and gave him one last workout in peace and isolation. The horse ran beautifully.

On February 27, 1937, Charles and Marcela Howard[3] arrived at Santa Anita to watch their pride and joy go for the hundred-grander. They were giddy with anticipation. "If Seabiscuit loses," mused a friend, "Mrs. Howard is going to be so heartbroken that I'll have to carry her out. If he wins, Charley'll be so excited that I'll have to carry him." Howard couldn't keep still. He trotted up to the press box and made the wildly popular announcement that if his horse won, he'd send up a barrel of champagne for the reporters. He went down 20　to the betting area, and seeing that the line was too long to wait, he grabbed a bettor and jammed five $1,000 bills into his hand. "Put it all on Seabiscuit's nose,[4] please," he told the bewildered wagerer before trotting off again. **A**

**trepidation**
(trĕp′ĭ-dā′shən)
*n.* nervous fear

**Analyze Visuals ▶**
Examine the photograph of Seabiscuit. What details convey his strength and will to win?

**① Targeted Passage**

**A AUTHOR'S PURPOSE**
From what you have read so far, what do you think is the author's main purpose for writing?

---

1.  **Santa Anita Handicap:** a race at the Santa Anita track in California, with a prize of $100,000.
2.  **Smith:** Tom Smith, Seabiscuit's trainer.
3.  **Charles and Marcela Howard:** Seabiscuit's owners.
4.  **"put it . . . nose":** bet all the money on Seabiscuit's coming in first.

---

## DIFFERENTIATED INSTRUCTION

### FOR ENGLISH LANGUAGE LEARNERS

**Vocabulary Support**  Use New Word Analysis to teach these words: *similar* (line 6), *virtually* (line 48), *minimizing* (line 81), *focus* (line 95), *professional* (line 167).

📦 BEST PRACTICES TOOLKIT—Transparency
New Word Analysis p. E8

### FOR STRUGGLING READERS

In combination with the *Audio Anthology CD*, use one or more Targeted Passages (pp. 128, 131, 133, 135) to ensure that students focus on key story events, concepts, and skills. Targeted Passages are also good for English learners.

**① Targeted Passage [Lines 1–14]**

This passage establishes the conflict and the setting and introduces several key characters, including the two rival horses.

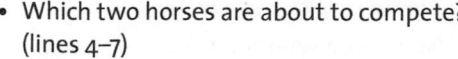

## Reading Support

This selection on **thinkcentral.com** includes embedded **ThinkAloud** models–students "thinking aloud" about the story to model the kinds of questions a good reader would ask about a selection.

## BACKGROUND

**Racehorses** Thoroughbreds, prized for their strength and endurance, are the breed most commonly used for horseracing. Thorough-bred racehorses like Seabiscuit are specially bred to race; they are visually lightweight, intelligent, and very fast. The ancestry of each horse is carefully recorded by horse breeders, who have created the breed by crossing Arabian and Turkish stallions with English mares. In most cases, when a successful horse retires from racing, he is used to breed more horses in hopes of raising another champion.

## Analyze Visuals

*Possible answer: Seabiscuit's muscular body and powerful legs, as he surges forward, convey his strength and will to win. He appears totally focused, ears alert and forward. In addition, the angle of the photograph suggests that Seabiscuit is leading the race.*

- Which two horses are about to compete? (lines 4–7)
- What did Tom Smith do to fool the reporters? Why? (lines 10–12)
- How do the Howards feel about Seabiscuit? (lines 13–14)

**FOR ADVANCED LEARNERS/PRE–AP**

**Hypothesize** After students have read the first page, tell them they are going to work in pairs and discuss why they think Seabiscuit is considered an American legend. You might wish to point out the economic and social conditions in the United States at the time (*Great Depression, war brewing in Europe*). Ask pairs to share their discussions with the class. Have students keep their discussions in mind and compare them to what they find out from reading the selection.

**Activity** Ask students what physical attributes of a successful jockey the photograph highlights. What other traits might a trainer look for in a jockey? *Possible answer: A successful jockey needs to be small-framed and lightweight. Other traits that a trainer might look for are physical strength and endurance, determination, and the ability to communicate with horses.*

---

TEXT ANALYSIS

**COMMON CORE**

**RI 3**

### B SUSPENSE IN BIOGRAPHY

*Possible answer: The writer builds tension by spotlighting the two main competitors, describing the particular challenges that each horse and each rider must face, and emphasizing their rivalry.*

---

**READING STRATEGY: *Review***

### C PREDICT

*Possible answer: Seabiscuit seems likely to win, based on his good start in the race, Pollard's confidence, and the horse's present lead on Rosemont. Also, the passage implies that the "speed horses" won't be able to maintain their pace.*

**IF STUDENTS NEED HELP . . .** Review lines 52–63 with students, and help them use Predicting to predict the winner.

**BEST PRACTICES TOOLKIT—Transparency** Predicting p. A10

---

**VOCABULARY**

**COMMON CORE**

**L 4**

### OWN THE WORD

**optimal:** Remind students that *optimal* means "most favorable"; an antonym is *unfavorable*. Have students use both words in sentences.

---

At a little past 4:00 P.M. Pollard[5] and Seabiscuit parted from Smith at the paddock gate and walked out onto the track for the Santa Anita Handicap. A record crowd of sixty thousand fans had come to see eighteen horses try for the richest
30 purse in the world. Millions more listened on radio.

As Pollard felt Seabiscuit's hooves sink into the russet soil, he had reason to worry. The baking machines had not completely dried the surface. Rain and dirt had blended into a heavy goo along the rail; breaking from the three post,[6] Seabiscuit would be right
40 down in it. Far behind him in the post parade, jockey Harry Richards was contemplating a different set of obstacles for Rosemont. He had drawn the seventeenth post position. He was going to have the luxury of a hard, fast track, but his problem would be traffic. As a late runner, Rosemont would have to pick his way through the cluttered field.

The two jockeys virtually bookended the field as they moved to the post. Pollard feared nothing but Richards and Rosemont. Richards feared nothing
50 but Pollard and Seabiscuit. The two horses stood motionless while the field was loaded around them.

At the sound of the bell, Seabiscuit bounded forward. To his outside, a crowd of horses rushed inward to gain **optimal** position. The field doubled over on itself, and the hinge was Seabiscuit, who was pinched back to ninth. In a cloud of horses, Pollard spotted daylight five feet or so off the rail. He banked Seabiscuit out into it, holding him out of the deep part of the track. He slipped up to fourth position, just off of front-running Special Agent. On the first turn Seabiscuit was crowded back down to the rail. As the field straightened into the backstretch, Pollard found another avenue and eased him
60 outward again, to firmer ground. Ahead, Special Agent was setting a suicidal pace, but Pollard sensed how fast it was and was not going to be lured into it. He sat back and waited. Behind him, Rosemont was tugging along toward the back of the field, waiting for the speed horses to crumble.

Seabiscuit owner C. S. Howard, jockey Red Pollard, and trainer Tom Smith.

### B SUSPENSE IN BIOGRAPHY

Reread lines 32–51. What technique does the writer use to build suspense?

**optimal** (ŏp′tə-məl) *adj.* most favorable; best

### C PREDICT

Which horse do you predict will win the race? Why do you think so?

---

5. **Pollard:** Red Pollard, Seabiscuit's jockey.

6. **the three post:** in the starting gate, the third position out from the railing.

---

## DIFFERENTIATED INSTRUCTION

### FOR ENGLISH LANGUAGE LEARNERS

**Vocabulary: Multiple-Meaning Words**
Remind students that a word can have two different meanings with the same spelling. Use New Word Analysis to teach these multiple-meaning words from the selection: *purse* (line 30), *post* (line 48), *field* (line 53), *banked* (line 56), *track* (line 56), *avenue* (line 59), *move* (line 65), *fold* (line 72), *rump* (line 74), *wire* (line 79), *rest* (line 87), *toy* (line 97), *rail* (line 101).

**BEST PRACTICES TOOLKIT—Transparency** New Word Analysis p. E8

**Media and Concepts** Use a recorded book version of *Seabiscuit* or another suspenseful story to build and reinforce the concept of suspense. Have students listen to a section; then, ask them to work in small groups to discuss the following questions: What part of the story kept you on the edge of your seat? How does the author create this suspense?

With a half mile to go, Pollard positioned Seabiscuit in the clear and readied for his move. Behind him, Richards sensed that the moment had come to shoot for Seabiscuit. He began threading Rosemont through the field, cutting in and out, picking off horses one by one, talking in his horse's ear as clumps of dirt cracked into his face. His luck was holding; every hole toward which he guided his horse held open just long enough for him to gallop through. On
70 the far turn he reached Seabiscuit's heels and began looking for a way around him. Ahead of him, Pollard crouched and watched Special Agent's churning hindquarters, waiting for him to fold.

At the top of the stretch Special Agent faltered. Pollard pulled Seabiscuit's nose to the outside and slapped him on the rump. Seabiscuit pounced. Richards saw him go and gunned Rosemont through the hole after him, but Seabiscuit had stolen a three-length advantage. Special Agent gave way grudgingly along the inside as Indian Broom rallied up the outside, not quite quick enough to keep up.

Lengthening stride for the long run to the wire, Seabiscuit was alone on the
80 lead in the dry, hard center of the track. Pollard had delivered a masterpiece of reinsmanship, avoiding the traps and saving ground while minimizing his run along the boggy rail. He had won the tactical battle with Richards. He was coming into the homestretch of the richest race in the world with a strong horse beneath him. Behind them were seventeen of the best horses in the nation. To the left and right, sixty thousand voices roared. Ahead was nothing but a long strip of red soil.

The rest of the field peeled away, scattered across thirty-two lengths of track behind them. It was down to Rosemont and Seabiscuit.

Seabiscuit was moving fastest. He charged down the stretch in front with
90 Pollard up over his neck, moving with him, driving him on. Rosemont was obscured behind him. He was gaining only by **increments**. Seabiscuit sailed through midstretch a full length ahead of Rosemont. Up in the stands, the Howards and Smith were thinking the same thing: Rosemont is too far behind. Seabiscuit is going to win.

Without warning, horse and rider lost focus. Abruptly, **inexplicably**, Pollard wavered. He lay his whip down on Seabiscuit's shoulder and left it there.

Seabiscuit paused. Perhaps he slowed in hopes of finding an opponent to toy with. Or maybe he sensed Pollard's hesitation. His composure, which Smith had patiently schooled into him over six months, began to unravel. Seabiscuit
100 suddenly took a sharp left turn, veering ten feet across the track and back down into the deep going, straightening himself out just before hitting the rail. He had given away several feet of his lead. The **cadence** of his stride dropped. What had been a seamless union was now only a man and a horse, jangling against each other.

### Language Coach

**Oral Fluency** The suffix *-tion* is pronounced "shuhn." Work with a partner to pronounce *positioned* (line 64). Then practice saying these other words from the selection: *nation, hesitation, celebration, anticipation, exhaustion.*

**increment** (ĭn′krə-mənt) *n.* a small, slight growth or increase

**inexplicably** (ĭn-ĕk′splĭ-kə-blē) *adv.* in a way that is difficult or impossible to explain

**cadence** (kād′ns) *n.* a balanced, rhythmic flow

---

**REVISIT THE BIG QUESTION**

## What makes a WINNER?

**Discuss** In lines 73–85, what qualities do you see in Pollard and Seabiscuit that suggest they may win this race? *Possible answer: Pollard has "delivered a masterpiece of reinsmanship" (lines 80–81), and Seabiscuit is a fast, responsive horse (lines 73–74).*

## TIERED DISCUSSION PROMPTS

Use these prompts to help students explore the sudden shift in the narrative that occurs in lines 89–104:

**Connect** Have you ever seen a competition in which a person or team that had been poised to win suddenly no longer looked like a sure thing? What was your reaction? *Accept all reasonable responses.*

**Evaluate** In lines 97–98, the author offers two possible reasons why Seabiscuit lost his composure. Which reason seems more likely? Why? *Possible answer: It seems more likely that Seabiscuit "sensed Pollard's hesitation." Up until this point, the jockey had been firmly in control, but then he abruptly wavered (lines 95–96). Since the horse takes his cues from the rider, Seabiscuit probably faltered in response.*

**VOCABULARY** · COMMON CORE · L 4

### OWN THE WORD

- **increment:** Tell students that the word *increment* is related to the word *increase*. Both words share a root that means "to grow." Ask students to identify words and phrases in the surrounding sentences that help them understand the meaning of *increment*. *Possible answer: gaining only; sailed through midstretch a full length ahead; too far behind*

- **inexplicably:** Have students complete this sentence: Nadia was always afraid of horses, so it was strange when she inexplicably... *Possible answer: ... volunteered at a horse farm.*

- **cadence:** Point out that the word *cadence* comes from the Latin *cadere*, meaning "to fall," and can refer to rhythmic flow or movement.

---

**FOR STRUGGLING READERS**

② **Targeted Passage [Lines 64–72]**

This passage highlights the point in the race when both Pollard and Richards begin to make their final moves to win.

- What is Pollard waiting for? (lines 71–72)
- What does Richards decide to do at this moment? (lines 66–69)
- How does Pollard's decision work out? (lines 68–71)
- Which three horses are in the lead by the end of this passage? (lines 69–72)

**FOR ENGLISH LANGUAGE LEARNERS**

### Language Coach

**Oral Fluency** Place students in pairs and tell them that they are going to practice using the words *nation, hesitation, celebration, anticipation,* and *exhaustion* in sentences. Tell students to use each word in a sentence about the selection, and to alternate between partners until they have used each word.

What makes a
# WINNER?

**Discuss** Based on the sequence in lines 105–112, does the Richards-Rosemont combination have the characteristics of a **winner**? Explain. *Possible answer: The Richards-Rosemont combination does, indeed. Richards is a skilled jockey ready to take advantage of any weakness in the competition, and Rosemont is a fast horse that responds well to the jockey.*

---

## READING SKILL

**COMMON CORE** RI 6

### D AUTHOR'S PURPOSE

*Possible answer: The author layers an astonishing amount of detail to describe a few seconds of the race. Specific numbers help readers to visualize the action ("fifteen strides," "ten feet," "six feet"), as does mention of "half-moon blinker cups" that limit Seabiscuit's vision. Hillenbrand also describes "the roar from the grandstand" (lines 119–120) and the shrieking crowd (line 123). This detailed, sensory account is both informative and entertaining.*

**IF STUDENTS NEED HELP...** Work with students to brainstorm details that appeal to sight and to sound. Record their ideas, using concept webs.

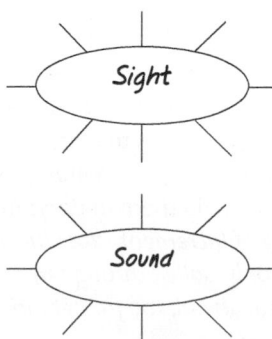

**Extend the Discussion** How do the short, clipped sentences in lines 121–123 help to build the excitement?

---

From between Rosemont's ears, Richards saw Seabiscuit's form disintegrate. He looked toward the wire. It seemed close enough to touch, but Rosemont still wasn't past Seabiscuit's saddlecloth. He had been riding on instinct, reflex, but now his heart caught in his throat: *I am too late.* Desperate, he flung himself over Rosemont's neck, booting and whipping and screaming,
110 "Faster, baby, faster!" Striding high in the center of the track, Rosemont was suddenly animated by Richards's raging desire. He dropped his head and dug in. Seabiscuit's lead, stride by stride, slipped away.

For a few seconds at the most critical moment of their careers, Pollard and Seabiscuit faltered. For fifteen strides, more than the length of a football field, Pollard remained virtually motionless. Rosemont was some ten feet to his outside, leaving plenty of room for Pollard to swing Seabiscuit out of the rail-path's slow going, but Pollard didn't take the opportunity. From behind his half-moon blinker cups,[7] Seabiscuit could see nothing but an empty track ahead of him, nor is it likely that he could hear Rosemont over the roar from
120 the grandstand. Or perhaps he was waiting for him. His left ear swung around lazily, as if he were paying attention to something in the infield. His stride slowed. His mind seemed scattered. The lead was vanishing. A length. Six feet. A neck. The wire was rushing at them. The crowd was shrieking. **D**

**D AUTHOR'S PURPOSE**
Reread lines 113–123. What details make this passage not only informative but entertaining?

---

7. **blinker cups:** flaps put over a horse's eyes to keep it from seeing sideways.

---

## DIFFERENTIATED INSTRUCTION

### FOR STRUGGLING READERS

**Language Support** Elicit or provide the meaning of the idiomatic phrase *his heart caught in his throat* (line 108), "felt intense, momentary worry or despair." Ask volunteers to share examples of experiences that caused their hearts to catch in their throats.

### FOR ADVANCED LEARNERS/PRE–AP

**Analyze Style** Hillenbrand uses literary techniques to convey information while simultaneously creating an exciting account of the neck-and-neck race. Have students work in small groups to identify and discuss examples of characterization, point of view, and dialogue. How do these techniques help the author to accomplish both purposes?

Rosemont edges out Seabiscuit to win the Santa Anita Handicap by a nose.

◄ **Analyze Visuals**

What elements of the dramatic finish are captured by this photograph? What does the photo add to your understanding of the story? Be specific.

With just a few yards to go, Pollard broke out of his limbo. He burst into frenzied motion. Seabiscuit's ears snapped back and he dived forward. But Rosemont had momentum. The lead shrank to nothing. Rosemont caught Seabiscuit, then took a lead of inches. Seabiscuit was accelerating, his rhythm building, his mind narrowed down to his task at the urgent call of his rider. But Richards was driving harder, scratching and yelling and pleading for 130 Rosemont to run. Seabiscuit cut the advantage away. They drew even again.

Rosemont and Seabiscuit flew under the wire together. **E**

Up in their box, the Howards leapt up. Charles ran to the Turf Club bar, calling for champagne for everyone. Voices sang out and corks popped and a wild celebration began.

Gradually, the revelers went silent. The crowd had stopped cheering. The stewards posted no winner. They were waiting for the photo. The exhausted horses returned to be unsaddled, and the fans sat in agonized anticipation. Two minutes passed. In the hush, a sibilant sound attended the finish photo as it slid down to the stewards. There was a terrible pause. The numbers blinked up 140 on the board.

Rosemont had won.

**E SUSPENSE IN BIOGRAPHY**
Reread lines 124–131. What words does the writer use to build excitement in this passage?

**3 Targeted Passage**

---

**FOR STRUGGLING READERS**

**3 Targeted Passage** [Lines 131–141]

This passage presents the climax of the race: a photo finish victory for Rosemont.

- Which two horses cross the finish line at the same time? (line 131)
- Why were the fans sitting "in agonized anticipation" (line 137)? (lines 135–136)
- What does the photo finish show? (line 141)

**FOR ENGLISH LANGUAGE LEARNERS**

**Media and Language** To reinforce language attainment, show a video about Seabiscuit or another famous racehorse. Have students note down words that relate to the sport of horseracing. Ask students to look up the meaning of each word. Challenge them to use these terms in a discussion about Laura Hillenbrand's biography.

---

**Analyze Visuals**

*Possible answer:* *The photograph shows just how close Rosemont and Seabiscuit are and how far ahead of the pack these two lead horses are. The photo highlights the intensity, speed, and demands of the race in the horses' strained efforts and the jockeys' athletic contortions. It contributes to the viewer's understanding of the astonishing skill required to win such a race.*

**TEXT ANALYSIS**
**COMMON CORE**
**RI 3**

**E SUSPENSE IN BIOGRAPHY**

*Possible answer:* *The writer uses action words and phrases to build excitement, such as* broke out, burst into frenzied motion, snapped back, dived forward, accelerating, urgent call, driving harder, scratching and yelling and pleading, *and* flew under the wire.

**Extend the Discussion** What effect does line 131 have on the reader?

**BACKGROUND**

**Photo Finish** A photograph taken at the moment that the horses cross the finish line must be examined before officials announce the winner of a close race. As in the 1937 Santa Anita Handicap, a horse may win by such a small margin that the winner can be determined only by studying the photograph taken at the wire, literally making the race a "photo finish." The term is also used informally to describe any very close contest.

## What makes a
# WINNER?

**Discuss** It has been said that true winners must also know how to lose. How might this saying apply to the behavior of Charles, Marcela, and Pollard in lines 148–160? *Possible answers: True winners are gracious in defeat. Charles and Marcela smile bravely and continue passing out champagne. Pollard goes directly to Richards and congratulates him on his victory.*

## Analyze Visuals

*Possible answer: Pollard's smile shows his fondness for Seabiscuit. That he appears to be putting a blanket on the horse suggests that he takes good care of the animal. Seabiscuit seems calm and content. The photograph reflects their strong, close bond and the communication generated by this connection.*

---

**VOCABULARY**  COMMON CORE L 4

### OWN THE WORD

**unequivocal:** Ask students to provide synonyms for *unequivocal*. **Possible answers:** *clear-cut, definite, specific, unambiguous*

---

A howl went up from the grandstand. Thousands of spectators were certain that the stewards had it wrong, that Seabiscuit had been robbed. But the photo was **unequivocal:** Rosemont's long bay muzzle hung there in the picture, just a wink ahead of Seabiscuit's. "Dame Fortune," wrote announcer Joe Hernandez, "made a mistake and kissed the wrong horse—Rosemont—in the glorious end of the Santa Anita Handicap."

Charles and Marcela collected themselves. The length of Rosemont's nose had cost them $70,700. They continued passing out the champagne, brave
150 smiles on their faces.

Pollard didn't need to look at the tote board. He knew he had lost from the instant the noses hit the line. Wrung to exhaustion and deathly pale, he slid from Seabiscuit's back. He walked over to Richards, who was being smothered in kisses by his tearful wife. Pollard's face was blank, his voice barely above a whisper. All around him, people regarded him with expressions of cool accusation.

**unequivocal**
(ŭn′ĭ-kwĭv′ə-kəl)
*adj.* allowing no doubt or misunderstanding

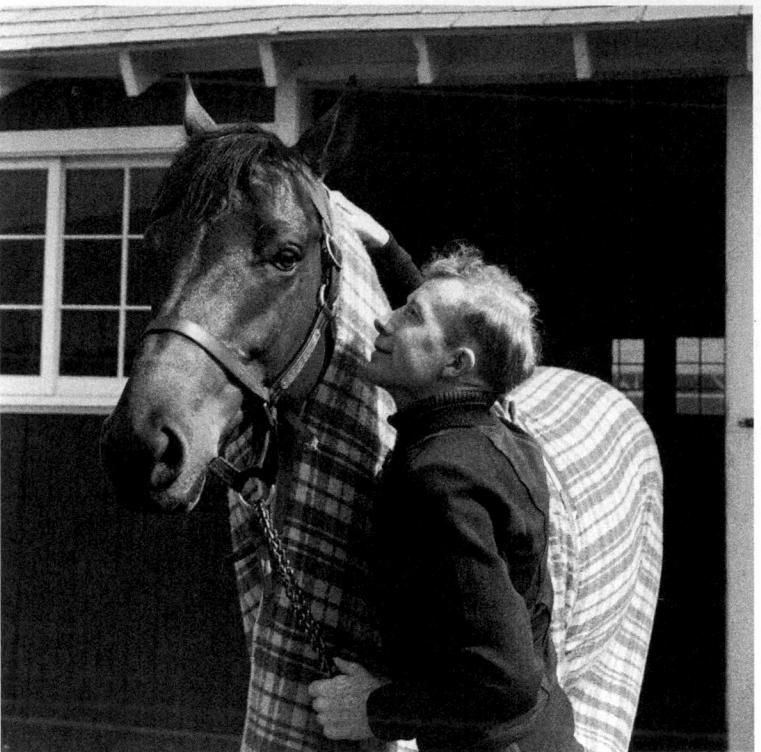

◄**Analyze Visuals**
What does this photo of Seabiscuit and Red Pollard show you about their relationship? Be specific.

---

## DIFFERENTIATED INSTRUCTION

### FOR STRUGGLING READERS

**Language Support** Elicit or provide the meaning of the phrase *Dame Fortune ... kissed the wrong horse* (lines 145–146)—"the less talented horse (that is, Rosemont) had better luck." Explain that this kind of figure of speech is called *personification*, attributing human characteristics to animals, objects, places, or forces of nature. Ask students to suggest other examples.

### FOR ENGLISH LANGUAGE LEARNERS

**Vocabulary: Cognates** Remind students that the prefix *un–* means "not." Then call attention to the vocabulary word *unequivocal* (line 144). Point out that the Spanish cognate *equivocar* means "to mistake," so *unequivocal* means "no mistaking" (or "unmistakable"). Have students who speak Latin-based languages identify other words similar to those in their language and share their findings.

"Congratulations, Harry, you rode a swell race," Pollard said.

"Thanks," said Richards, his face covered in lipstick and his voice breaking; he had shouted it away urging Rosemont on. "But it was very close."

160 "Close, yes," said Pollard almost **inaudibly**, "but you won."

Pollard saw Howard hovering nearby, waiting for him. The jockey went to him.

"What happened?" Howard asked gently. Ashen and spent, Pollard said that the rail had been slow, and that he had been unable to get outside without fouling Rosemont. If he and Rosemont had switched positions, he was sure Seabiscuit would have won.

It was a thin excuse. Pollard must have known that to save his professional standing, he would have to offer more that than, say something that would explain how he had allowed Rosemont to come to him without fighting back

170 until the last moment. Already, harsh words were being hung on him: *arrogant*, **inept**, *overconfident*. He could not have mistaken the reproach on the faces of those around him. His reputation was tumbling. But Pollard gave the public nothing to make them reconsider.

Perhaps he couldn't. He had a secret to keep, a gamble he had made years earlier and remade with each race. But he could no longer think that its risks affected only himself.

Perhaps Pollard didn't see Rosemont coming because of the blindness of his right eye.

It is unlikely that he could have heard Rosemont over the din from the

180 crowd. Rosemont's surge, unexpected and sudden, may have eluded Pollard until very late in the race. Pollard did not begin urging Seabiscuit in earnest until Rosemont was alongside him, just forward enough for Pollard to see him with his left eye, upon turning his head. One good eye offers little depth perception, so he may not have been able to judge whether Rosemont was far enough to his right to allow Seabiscuit to move outward.

If this explanation is correct, then Pollard was trapped. He was publicly accused of inexcusable failure in the most important race of his career, but he could not defend himself. Had he let on that he was blind in one eye, his career would have been over. Like most jockeys in the 1930s, he had nowhere

190 else to go, nothing else to live on, nothing else he loved. For Red Pollard, there was no road back to Edmonton. If his blindness was the cause of the loss, his frustration and guilt must have been consuming.

Howard accepted Pollard's explanation without criticism. Neither he nor Smith blamed him.

Almost everyone else did. ❧

---

inaudibly (ĭn-ô′də-blē) *adv.* in a way that is impossible to hear

inept (ĭn-ĕpt′) *adj.* generally incompetent

**F** SUSPENSE IN BIOGRAPHY
Notice that the writer withholds this important piece of information from the reader until after the race is over. If the writer had revealed this information before describing the race, would the suspense have been greater or less? Explain.

④ **Targeted Passage**

---

VOCABULARY — COMMON CORE — L 4

**OWN THE WORD**

- **inaudibly:** Point out that the word *inaudibly* is made up of the prefix *in–*, which means "not," and the Latin word *audire*, which means "hear."

- **inept:** The connotation for *inept* is that a person does something wrong or unsuitable for a task. What made people call Pollard *inept*? ***Possible answer:*** *Seabiscuit lost the race due to Pollard's mistake.*

TEXT ANALYSIS — COMMON CORE — RI 3

**F SUSPENSE IN BIOGRAPHY**

***Possible answer:*** **less:** *Readers might have expected something would go wrong as a result of Pollard's partial blindness.* **greater:** *The possibility of the partially blind jockey missing important visual information would have created tension. Readers would have wondered if Pollard could overcome his limitation.*

**SELECTION WRAP-UP**

**READ WITH A PURPOSE** Now that students have read the selection, ask them to explain if they think the story would be more or less interesting if the author had not discussed Pollard. Why? ***Possible answers: more:*** *story would have focused on the race and the horses;* ***less:*** *horse and rider are both important to understanding the race*

⭐ **CRITIQUE** Ask students: What did you admire most about Seabiscuit? about Pollard? Ask them to give reasons that support their answers.

**INDEPENDENT READING**

Students may also enjoy reading *It's Not About the Bike: My Journey Back to Life* by Lance Armstrong with contributor Sally Jenkins. This memoir describes Armstrong's battle with cancer and includes information on bicycle racing.

---

**FOR STRUGGLING READERS**

④ **Targeted Passage [Lines 170–195]**

This passage reveals Pollard's secret: his partial blindness, which may have cost him the race.

- Who does the public blame for Seabiscuit's loss? (lines 170–173)

- Why doesn't Pollard say more in his own defense? (lines 186–190)

- What secret has Pollard been hiding? (lines 177–178)

- Why has he been hiding it? (lines 188–189)

- What consequence may this secret have had? (line 191)

**FOR ADVANCED LEARNERS/PRE-AP**

**Make Judgments** Have students work in small groups to debate whether or not Pollard was justified in concealing his partial blindness. Encourage students to consider what they might have done in his situation.

# Practice and Apply

For preliminary support of post-reading questions, use these copy masters:

**R** RESOURCE MANAGER—Copy Masters
Reading Check p. 148
Suspense in Biography p. 141
Question Support p. 149

Additional selection questions are provided for teachers on page 135.

## ANSWERS

## Comprehension

1. *Rosemont was Seabiscuit's main challenger in the race.*

2. *The stewards studied a photograph of the horses crossing the finish line.*

3. *If Pollard's secret got out, his career would be over, because no one would hire a jockey who was blind in one eye.*

## Text Analysis

COMMON CORE RI 3, RI 6

*Possible answers:*

4. ■ **COMMON CORE FOCUS** *Identify Author's Purpose Hillenbrand's main purpose was to inform—that is, to tell Seabiscuit's story. To do this, she provided researched facts and explanations. However, the author also hoped to entertain, as evidenced by her lively narrative style, use of suspense, and other literary techniques.*

5. ● **COMMON CORE FOCUS** *Analyze Suspense in Biography Raising questions in reader's mind: "Rumors swirled . . . that Seabiscuit was lame" (lines 7–8). Foreshadowing: "Rain and dirt had blended into a heavy goo along the rail . . . Seabiscuit would be right down in it. . . . [Rosemont's] problem would be traffic" (lines 36–46). Withholding certain information: "Perhaps Pollard didn't see Rosemont coming because of the blindness of his right eye" (lines 180–181).*

6. *In desperation, Richards intensified his efforts as they approached the finish line, and Rosemont was "animated" by Richardson's "raging desire" (line 111) to win. In contrast, Pollard "inexplicably . . . wavered" and "lay his whip down" (lines 95–96); Seabiscuit then lost his composure.*

---

## Comprehension

COMMON CORE

RI 3 Analyze how the author unfolds a series of events, including the order in which points are made and how they are introduced and developed. RI 6 Determine an author's purpose in a text.

1. **Recall** Which horse was Seabiscuit's main challenger in the race?

2. **Recall** How did the stewards determine which horse had won the race?

3. **Clarify** Why did Pollard keep the blindness in his right eye a secret?

## Text Analysis

4. **Identify Author's Purpose** Review your notes. What do you think Hillenbrand's main **purpose** was in writing this biography? What other purposes might she have had? Include important details from the text to support your answer.

5. **Analyze Suspense in Biography** How does the author unfold events and create suspense in this biography? In a chart like the one shown, give examples of each of her narrative techniques.

| Narrative Technique | Example |
|---|---|
| Raising questions in reader's mind | • Rosemont's stock rose |
| Foreshadowing | |
| Withholding certain information | |

6. **Compare and Contrast** Compare Seabiscuit and Pollard with Rosemont and Richards. What qualities made the difference between the winner and the loser of the Santa Anita Handicap?

7. **Make Judgments** Reread lines 186–195. Was it fair to blame Pollard for losing the race? Support your answer with reasons and evidence.

8. **Evaluate** How does the revelation about Pollard's blindness in his right eye affect your evaluation of Seabiscuit as a racing horse?

## Text Criticism

9. **Historical Context** Commenting on *Seabiscuit,* Hillenbrand said, "The subjects that I've written about—the men and the horse—were radically different individuals, but the one thread that pulls through all of their lives . . . is this struggle between overwhelming hardship and the will to overcome it." When Seabiscuit raced, the United States was reeling from the Great Depression, a catastrophic economic collapse that began in 1929 and continued through the 1930s. What might Seabiscuit have represented to the country at that time?

### What makes a WINNER?

How does Seabiscuit live up to your idea of a winner?

---

7. *It probably was fair to blame him because the partially blind jockey "did not begin urging Seabiscuit in earnest until Rosemont was alongside him, just forward enough for Pollard to see him with his left eye . . ." (lines 181–183).*

8. *Revealing Pollard's blindness makes the reader wonder if Seabiscuit could have performed better with a different jockey.*

## Text Criticism

*Possible answer:*

9. *Seabiscuit may have represented hope for the country—that hard work, perseverance, and luck would ultimately enable people to overcome hardships.*

### What makes a WINNER?

*Possible answers: He is a winner because he raced well and only lost because Pollard saw Rosemont too late.*

# Vocabulary in Context

## ▲ VOCABULARY PRACTICE

1. A person who speaks **inaudibly** can easily be heard.
2. The **optimal** time to spot Mars is on a cloudy night.
3. To honor your ancestors, you might build an **increment.**
4. An **inept** person is not a good choice to manage a project.
5. If you have **trepidation** about heights, you may not like skydiving.
6. Troops might march to the **cadence** of a band.
7. If an event occurs **inexplicably,** it is hard to understand why it happens.
8. An **unequivocal** "no" answer indicates that you have not made up your mind.

**WORD LIST**

cadence
inaudibly
increment
inept
inexplicably
optimal
trepidation
unequivocal

## ACADEMIC VOCABULARY IN SPEAKING

• analyze   • element   • infer   • sequence   • structure

Working with a partner, **analyze** the **sequence** of events in the race (lines 52–141) and then create a timeline to represent these events graphically. Note where the horses are in each segment of your timeline (for example, all the horses are in the same place at the race's start). Discuss with your partner the details in the text that help you create your timeline. Use at least two Academic Vocabulary words in your discussion.

## VOCABULARY STRATEGY: THE *aud* WORD FAMILY

The word *inaudibly* can be traced back to the Latin root *aud,* which means "to hear." Many other words belong to the same word family as *inaudibly.* If you can recognize the root in these words, you can understand how they are related in meaning.

**COMMON CORE**

**L 4c** Consult reference materials to determine or clarify a word's meaning or etymology.

**PRACTICE** Use each word below in a sentence that shows its connection in meaning to *inaudibly.* If necessary, consult a dictionary.

1. audit
2. audiology
3. audience
4. audio-visual
5. auditorium
6. audition

Interactive Vocabulary

**THINK** central

Go to **thinkcentral.com.**
KEYWORD: HML9-137

---

# Vocabulary in Context

## ▲ VOCABULARY PRACTICE

| | |
|---|---|
| 1. *false* | 5. *true* |
| 2. *false* | 6. *true* |
| 3. *false* | 7. *true* |
| 4. *true* | 8. *false* |

**R** RESOURCE MANAGER—Copy Master
Vocabulary Practice p. 146

## ACADEMIC VOCABULARY IN SPEAKING

Suggest that students first make a numbered list of the events in the race and then use that list to create their timelines.

## VOCABULARY STRATEGY: THE *aud* WORD FAMILY

COMMON CORE **L 4c**

• To help students with the **PRACTICE** activity, work with them on the first item: *audit.* Begin by eliciting or explaining its meaning ("a careful examination of financial records").

• Ask how *audit* might relate to the meaning of *aud.* Model the thinking process with this example: A tax examiner conducting an *audit* of a business would want to *hear* an explanation of the records.

**R** RESOURCE MANAGER—Copy Master
Vocabulary Strategy p. 147

**Interactive Vocabulary**

**THINK** central

Keywords direct students to a **WordSharp** tutorial on **thinkcentral.com** or to other types of vocabulary practice and review.

# Assess and Reteach

## Assess

**DIAGNOSTIC AND SELECTION TESTS**
Selection Test A pp. 43–44
Selection Test B/C pp.45–46

**Interactive Selection Test on thinkcentral.com**

## Reteach

**Level Up Online Tutorials** on **thinkcentral.com**

**Reteaching Worksheets** on **thinkcentral.com**
Literature Lesson 6, Reading Lesson 43, Vocabulary Lesson 7

---

## DIFFERENTIATED INSTRUCTION

### FOR ENGLISH LANGUAGE LEARNERS

**Vocabulary: Prefixes** Have students use Word Sorts to sort vocabulary words in these two categories: those that *do* have a prefix that means "not," and those that *don't* have a prefix that means "not." Explain to students that the *in* in *increment* is not a prefix.

BEST PRACTICES TOOLKIT—Transparency
Word Sorts p. E5

### FOR ADVANCED LEARNERS/PRE–AP

**Vocabulary in Writing** Challenge students to use as many vocabulary words as they can in a brief news story recounting the Santa Anita Handicap. Remind them that news writing attempts to address the Reporter's Questions: *who, what, where, when, why, and how.*

# Focus and Motivate

## COMMON CORE FOCUS

**RI 1** Cite textual evidence to support analysis of what the text says explicitly. **RI 2** Determine a central idea of a text; provide an objective summary of the text. **RI 4** Analyze the cumulative impact of specific word choices on meaning and tone. **RI 7** Analyze various accounts of a subject told in different mediums. **W 9b (RI 7)** Draw evidence from informational texts to support analysis; analyze various accounts of a subject told in different mediums.

### SUMMARY

"Horse of the Century" consists of three brief pieces about Seabiscuit: a magazine article excerpt describing the horse's amazing popularity; a timeline tracing Seabiscuit's racing career; and a radio transcript of the exciting 1937 Santa Anita Handicap, which was the focus of the previous excerpt from *Seabiscuit: An American Legend*.

## What's the Connection?

Use a KWL chart to prepare students for the three brief selections. For the first column, have students recall what they already know about Seabiscuit. In the second column, have them write questions about what they want to know. After reading, have students write what they have learned.

**BEST PRACTICES TOOLKIT—Transparency**
KWL p. A21

# Teach

## Standards Focus: Synthesize

- Explain that synthesizing information from different sources is a little like assembling a puzzle. Each source presents different pieces, and the pieces taken together form a total picture.

- Encourage students to think about the genre of each piece before they read it. Have them consider what kind of information they can expect to find. For example, a magazine article is likely to provide interesting details, while a timeline will give dates of significant events.

**R RESOURCE MANAGER—Copy Master**
Synthesize pp. 157-160

---

## Reading for Information

## Horse of the Century · Essential Course of Study ECOS

- Magazine Article, page 139
- Timeline, page 140
- Radio Transcript, page 141

Use with *Seabiscuit: An American Legend*, page 128.

**COMMON CORE**

**RI 1** Cite textual evidence to support analysis of what the text says explicitly. **RI 2** Determine a central idea of a text; provide an objective summary of the text. **RI 4** Analyze the cumulative impact of specific word choices on meaning and tone. **RI 7** Analyze various accounts of a subject told in different mediums.

## What's the Connection?

In the selection from *Seabiscuit: An American Legend*, you read about one of the most famous horseraces of the 20th century. The following selections will help you get a sense of what it was like to actually be at that race and why many Americans practically held their breath as they listened to it on the radio.

## Standards Focus: Synthesize

When you read different texts on the same topic, you **synthesize** information—that is, you put together the facts, ideas, and details you get from each of them. As a result, you gain a fuller understanding of the topic than you would from reading only one text. Here's how you can synthesize the ideas and information in the pieces about Seabiscuit:

- **Summarize** the central ideas and details in each piece. An effective summary reports what the original writer intended, without opinions or embellishment.

- Jot down any questions that come to you as you read.

- When information in one source conflicts with information in another, jot down these conflicts as questions, too.

- Look for **textual evidence**—facts and details from the selections—to help you make logical connections and to support your conclusions.

For more help synthesizing, complete a chart like the one started here as you read the following selections.

| Source | Central Ideas | New Information & Questions |
|---|---|---|
| From *Seabiscuit: An American Legend* | Jockey, owner, and fans were surprised by his defeat in the Santa Anita Handicap. | Why was this horse so popular? |
| From "Four Good Legs Between Us" | Even though Seabiscuit lost this race, he was fast becoming a celebrity. | Howard made him popular by racing him all over the country. What was going on in Europe? |

---

## Selection Resources

See resources on the **Teacher One Stop DVD-ROM** *and on* <u>thinkcentral.com</u>.

 **RESOURCE MANAGER UNIT 1**
Lesson Support,* pp. 151–162

**INTERACTIVE READER**

**ADAPTED INTERACTIVE READER**

**ELL ADAPTED INTERACTIVE READER**

**TECHNOLOGY**

- **Teacher One Stop DVD-ROM**
- **Student One Stop DVD-ROM**
- **PowerNotes DVD-ROM**
- **Audio Anthology CD**
- **ExamView Test Generator** on the **Teacher One Stop**

* Resources for Differentiation

## from
# Four Good Legs Between Us
### Laura Hillenbrand

Though Seabiscuit had lost [the Santa Anita Handicap], he was rapidly becoming a phenomenal celebrity. Two factors converged to create and nourish this. The first was Charles Howard. A born adman, Howard courted the nation on behalf of his horse much as he had hawked his first Buicks, undertaking exhaustive promotion that presaged the modern marketing of athletes. Crafting daring, unprecedented coast-to-coast racing campaigns, he shipped Seabiscuit over fifty thousand railroad miles to showcase his talent at eighteen tracks in seven states and Mexico. The second factor was timing. The nation was sliding from economic ruin into the whirling eddy of Europe's cataclysm. Seabiscuit, Howard, Pollard, and Smith, whose fortunes
10 swung in epic parabolas, would have resonated in any age, but in cruel years the peculiar union among the four transcended the racetrack. **Ⓐ**

The result was stupendous popularity. In one year Seabiscuit garnered more newspaper column inches than Roosevelt, Hitler, or Mussolini. *Life* even ran a pictorial on his facial expressions. Cities had to route special trains to accommodate the invariably record-shattering crowds that came to see him run. Smith, fearing Seabiscuit wouldn't get any rest, hoodwinked the press by trotting out a look-alike. Such fame fueled the immediate, immense success of Howard's Santa Anita and California's new racing industry, today a four-billion-dollar business.

**Ⓐ SYNTHESIZE**
**Summarize** the two causes of Seabiscuit's popularity.

---

**INFORMATIONAL ANALYSIS**  COMMON CORE

RI 1, RI 2, RI 7

**Ⓐ SYNTHESIZE**

***Possible answer:*** *Charles Howard was an outstanding promoter who built Seabiscuit's popularity by showcasing the horse "at eighteen tracks in seven states and Mexico" (line 7). In addition, during difficult economic and political times, people found inspiration in the team of Seabiscuit, Howard, Pollard, and Smith.*

---

**Find it Online!**

Features on **thinkcentral.com** that support the selection include
• **PowerNotes** presentation
• **ThinkAloud** models to enhance comprehension
• **WordSharp** vocabulary tutorials
• interactive writing and grammar instruction

---

## DIFFERENTIATED INSTRUCTION

### FOR ENGLISH LANGUAGE LEARNERS

**Options for Reading** Read the first two sentences of the first paragraph, making sure students understand their meaning. Explain that these sentences state the paragraph's central idea. Call on volunteers to read the supporting sentences. Repeat this procedure with the second paragraph, pointing out that the first sentence states the paragraph's central idea.

Use these prompts to help students reflect on information displayed in the timeline:

**Connect** Which event shown on the timeline did you read about in *Seabiscuit: An American Legend* (pp. 128–135)? *Possible answer: The timeline shows Seabiscuit's loss to Rosemont in the Santa Anita Handicap of 1937.*

**Apply** Which horse other than Rosemont does the timeline imply was a major rival of Seabiscuit? *Possible answer: War Admiral was also a major rival.*

**Evaluate** Who was Seabiscuit's jockey in 1940? Does this surprise you in light of the events you read about in *Seabiscuit: An American Legend?* Give reasons for your answer. *Possible answer: Red Pollard was the jockey. Students should support their answers with thoughtful reasoning.*

---

**INFORMATIONAL ANALYSIS**

COMMON CORE
RI 1, RI 2, RI 7

**B** *Model the Skill:* **SYNTHESIZE**

Explain to students that a timeline can help you synthesize information from several sources by providing clues or new information that complements what you already know from other sources. Tell students that they already know that in his first try at the Santa Anita Handicap, Seabiscuit lost to Rosemont. Explain that knowing this will help students identify new pieces of information about Seabiscuit. *Answers may vary, but students may point to new information related to the selection they read from* Seabiscuit: An American Legend; *Seabiscuit beat Rosemont in the Brooklyn Handicap on June 26, 1937, four months after losing to him in the Santa Anita Handicap; Seabiscuit won his third try at the Santa Anita Handicap, on March 2, 1940.*

---

## Timeline: Seabiscuit

**1937** ○ *February 27:* In his first try at the Santa Anita Handicap, Seabiscuit loses to Rosemont by a nose, in a photo finish.

○ *March 6:* Seabiscuit draws a crowd of 45,000 excited fans and wins the San Juan Capistrano Handicap by seven lengths, smashing the track record.

○ *May 6:* The German airship *Hindenburg* bursts into flames as it is about to land in Lakehurst, New Jersey.

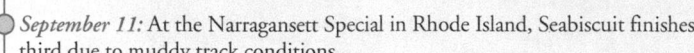

○ *June 5:* War Admiral captures the Triple Crown after a win at the Belmont Stakes.

○ *June 26:* Seabiscuit runs in the Brooklyn Handicap, beating rival Rosemont and local horse Aneroid.

○ *July:* Seabiscuit wins the Butler Handicap and the Yonkers Handicap easily, despite carrying far more weight than his competitors in both races.

○ *September 11:* At the Narragansett Special in Rhode Island, Seabiscuit finishes third due to muddy track conditions.

○ *October 12:* Seabiscuit wins the Continental Handicap in New York, gaining the top spot in the 1937 winnings race with $152,780 earned, $8,000 ahead of War Admiral.

○ *October 30:* Seabiscuit and War Admiral are slated to meet on the track, but Seabiscuit is scratched from the Washington Handicap due to muddy track conditions, allowing an easy victory for his rival.

○ *December 7:* War Admiral is named horse of the year by *Turf and Sport Digest.*

**1938** ○ *October 30:* Orson Welles's radio broadcast of *The War of the Worlds,* the tale of a Martian invasion on Earth, creates panic among listeners who mistake it for news.

○ *November 1:* With 40 million listeners tuned in across the country, Seabiscuit beats War Admiral by four lengths in just over a minute fifty-six for the mile and three-sixteenths, a new Pimlico record.

**1939** ○ *February 14:* Seabiscuit injures his suspensory ligament in a prep race for Santa Anita.

○ *September 3:* Britain and France declare war on Germany.

**1940** ○ *March 2:* Seabiscuit wins in his third try at the $100,000 Santa Anita Handicap. He clocks the fastest mile and a quarter in Santa Anita's history, the second fastest ever run in the United States. The most people ever to attend an American horse race—75,000—watch as Pollard leads Seabiscuit from behind to victory.

○ *April 10:* Seabiscuit retires to Charles Howard's Ridgewood Ranch. **B**

**B** **SYNTHESIZE**
Identify one or two new ideas or pieces of information that this timeline provides about Seabiscuit.

**140** UNIT 1: NARRATIVE STRUCTURE

---

## DIFFERENTIATED INSTRUCTION

### FOR ENGLISH LANGUAGE LEARNERS

**Vocabulary: Idioms** Use New Word Analysis to teach the meanings of the idioms in the timeline: *slated to* (October 30, 1937), "scheduled to"; *is scratched* (October 30, 1937), "dropped from or taken out"; *tuned in* (November 1, 1938), "listened to the broadcast."

**BEST PRACTICES TOOLKIT—Transparency**
New Word Analysis p. E8

### FOR ADVANCED LEARNERS/PRE–AP

**Expand Timeline** Challenge students to identify other notable national or international events that occurred between February 27, 1937, and April 10, 1940, and add them to the timeline. Discuss which events were the most significant and why.

# Races on the Radio
## Santa Anita Handicap (1937)
## with Clem McCarthy and Buddy Twist

**CLEM McCARTHY:**

Eddy Thomas won't take the start until he's on his toes and the jockey is ready. Then he'll push that button, the bell will ring, and they'll be on their way. We don't have any starting barriers now, as you know. Here they go. And they're on their way down the stretch. The break was good; every horse got a chance just as they left there. **C**

As they come down here to the eighth pole, it is Time Supply and Special Agent. Special Agent is trying to force his way to the front and he's going to do a good job of it as they pass the stands. Here on the outside comes Rosemont in a good position. And as they go by me it is 10 Special Agent on the lead by one length. Special Agent has the lead and then comes Time Supply in second place right along beside him. Going to the first turn is Special Agent by a length. Time Supply is second and on the outside of him is Accolade. And Boxthorn is close up. Far back in the crowd, on the inside, in about twelfth place is Red Rain. Up there close is Rosemont in about sixth place.

They're going into the stretch; they've gone half a mile. And the time for the first quarter over this track was 22 and two fifths seconds, the half in 45 and four. They're turning into the backstretch with Special Agent on the lead. Special Agent has a lead now of one length 20 and a half. Right behind him comes Time Supply. And in there, slipping through on the inside is . . . Indian Broom is going up on the inside now in a good position. Around that far turn, there's still no change in the positions. Rosemont is having a hard time working his way through, he's now in sixth position going around on the inside, he's saving ground, he's got plenty left. If he's enough horse, he may get home.

**C** SYNTHESIZE
Read all or part of this transcript aloud, using the tone and style of a sports announcer. Where do you speed up the pace?

---

INFORMATIONAL ANALYSIS · COMMON CORE

**C** SYNTHESIZE   RI 1, RI 2, RI 7

*Possible answer: Readers will speed up the pace when something exciting or unexpected occurs, as in lines 21–22, lines 28–29, and lines 30–38. In a close race such as this one, an announcer would naturally tend to pick up the pace as the horses approach the finish line.*

**Extend the Discussion**  In what ways is listening to a radio broadcast of a horse race different from reading about the event in a newspaper?

---

**FOR STRUGGLING READERS**

**Vocabulary Support**  Have students point out racing-related terms: *stretch* (line 4), *pole* (line 6), *length* (line 10), and *backstretch* (line 18). Ask them to define these terms using context, and check their responses in a dictionary.

**Develop Reading Fluency**  Remind students that this is a transcript of a play-by-play of the race, and as a result, it should be read differently from dialogue between characters. To give students an example, model an effective reading of lines 6–9 by using expression, pacing, and intonation. Then, ask students to echo your reading of each sentence in lines 10–15. Finally, have students work in mixed-ability pairs, and tell one partner to read lines 30–37 while the other should read lines 38–45. Have students practice their lines until they can read them fluently. Observe students as they work, and offer constructive feedback as necessary.

Use these prompts to help students understand how the announcers bring the horse race to life in lines 26–38:

**Connect** Have you ever listened to a radio broadcast of a sporting event? Describe it. *Students' answers will vary.*

**Analyze** How does McCarthy build the excitement? *Possible answer: He describes the rapidly changing positions of the horses as they maneuver for position. He also uses exciting phrases, such as "challenging head-and-head" (line 30), "challenging boldly" (line 35), and "the battle is on" (lines 35–36).*

**Synthesize** Did reading this transcript help you to understand the information you read about in the excerpt from *Seabiscuit* in a new way? Explain. *Students may respond that the transcript provided a sense of what it was like to actually witness the race and experience the confusion many must have felt in trying to determine who won.*

---

**INFORMATIONAL ANALYSIS** · **COMMON CORE** RI 1, RI 2, RI 7

**D SYNTHESIZE**

*Possible answer: The transcript reveals the time of the race (2:02 and four-fifths) and the fact that the track was about the same as two years earlier. The transcript also describes news photographers waiting to learn the winner and people cheering.*

Have students add to the synthesizing information chart they already started. Remind them to summarize the central idea and note any new questions or information they have.

---

**COMMON CORE** RI 4

**Language Coach**

**Informal Language**
Because this selection is a radio transcript, it uses informal language. Informal language often includes contractions, sentence fragments, and slang. Reread lines 30–39 and identify three examples of informal speech.

---

And on the outside, here comes the other one, Indian Broom. And Goldeneye is moving up from the rear. Here comes Accolade in second position. And Seabiscuit is now moving up and is challenging as they turn for home.

30    It's Special Agent and Seabiscuit challenging head-and-head as they swing into the stretch. And they've only got a quarter of a mile to come. They've stepped the first mile in 1:36 and four-fifths—and that shows you what this pace is. He can't live at it. Seabiscuit has got the lead half way down the stretch. But here comes one of the Baroni entries challenging on the outside, challenging boldly. And the battle is on. Indian Broom is coming fast and here comes Rosemont between horses. And Rosemont may take it all. It's gonna be a photograph finish. And it's anybody's race right to the end.

    I think Rosemont got the money. I think Rosemont was first. It
40  was an eyebrow finish. And Seabiscuit was the second horse. Seabiscuit was second and one of the Taylor entries; I think Indian Broom, was third. It was very close. That was an eyelash finish. Rosemont was closing strong, but Seabiscuit hung on. The time of the race was 2:02 and four-fifths, which makes the track almost identically like the track of two years ago . . .

**BUDDY TWIST:**

Oh boy, one of the most thrilling finishes I think that I've ever seen in a horse race in my life, Clem. The crowd down here has gone completely mad. The photographers are outside the charm circle, which is a white circle here, where the winner will come up in just a moment. Newsreel
50  photographers are setting up on every hand. The horses are just coming back now. And everybody, depending on who was their favorite, was shouting "Rosemont," "Seabiscuit"—one would call Rosemont, one Seabiscuit. There were half-a-dozen here who were just as sure Rosemont won as Seabiscuit, they don't know what to think of it. One of the most beautiful driving finishes I think I've ever seen.

**CLEM McCARTHY:**

Here's the photograph finish. Hold it now. Get ready for it. Just a few seconds and we'll know the winner of this race. I think Rosemont won it, but that's only my guess from where I stand. The photograph will tell us the actual winner. The naked eye is not as good as the photograph,
60  we'll have it in a second. They're looking at it down there. I know it was an eyelash finish. Either horse won by a whisker and that's all. Just about a quarter of an inch, I can't see any more between them. I really shouldn't express an opinion on a finish that close. And they're still waiting. That shows you what a difficult . . . There it is, Rosemont is the winner. Rosemont by a nose. Seabiscuit is second. Just a minute Buddy until I get it. Rosemont is the winner—I want you to get that jockey if you got him—Seabiscuit is second. And the Taylor entry finished third and fourth. They haven't put up the distinguishing numbers and they finished very close together. **D**

**D SYNTHESIZE**
What does this transcript reveal about the end of the race that was not included in the other texts?

---

## DIFFERENTIATED INSTRUCTION

### FOR ENGLISH LANGUAGE LEARNERS

**Language Coach** · **COMMON CORE** RI 4

**Informal Language** Have students work in pairs to rewrite the informal language they spotted to formal language. Tell students to write new sentences using the rewritten language. Ask each pair to share two rewritten informal language examples and two new sentences using those examples.

### FOR ADVANCED LEARNERS/PRE–AP

**Compare and Contrast** Use a Venn Diagram with students to help them compare Hillenbrand's account of the Santa Anita Handicap in *Seabiscuit: An American Legend* with the radio transcript. Then have students write a brief essay summarizing similarities and differences and share their essays with the class.

 **BEST PRACTICES TOOLKIT—Transparency** Venn Diagram p. A26

## Comprehension

1. **Recall** Which horse won the Santa Anita Handicap in 1937? What kind of a finish was it?

2. **Recall** How many times did Seabiscuit enter the Santa Anita Handicap before winning?

3. **Summarize** What major world events took place during Seabiscuit's rise to fame?

## Text Analysis

4. **Analyze Mood and Tone** What elements of the radio transcript contribute to the sense of excitement? Be specific.

5. **Synthesize** Review the ideas and information you noted in your chart. How did the world events of the day contribute to Seabiscuit's popularity? Use evidence from the texts to support your answer.

**COMMON CORE**

**RI 1** Cite textual evidence to support analysis of what the text says explicitly. **RI 2** Determine a central idea of a text; provide an objective summary of the text. **W 9b (RI 7)** Draw evidence from informational texts to support analysis; analyze various accounts of a subject told in different mediums.

## Read for Information: Draw Conclusions

**WRITING PROMPT**
In a paragraph, state and support your conclusions about one of the following topics:

- horseracing as a spectator sport
- Seabiscuit's popularity
- jockeys

To answer this prompt, you will need to pick your topic and follow these steps:

1. Gather information about your topic from the three selections, as well as from Hillenbrand's biography of Seabiscuit.

2. Consider the central ideas and information you have collected. Ask yourself what conclusion(s) you can draw from them.

3. State your conclusion(s) in a topic sentence. Then, support those conclusions with ideas and information from the texts.

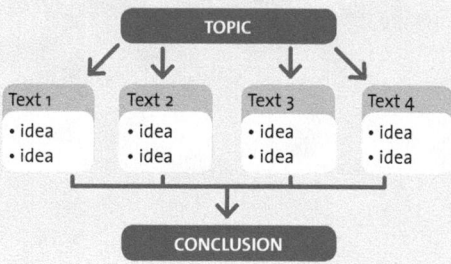

---

## Practice and Apply

For preliminary support of post-reading questions, use these copy masters:

**R** RESOURCE MANAGER—Copy Masters
Reading Check p. 161
Question Support p. 162
Additional selection questions are provided for teachers on page 153.

### ANSWERS

## Comprehension

1. *Rosemont won the race in a photo finish.*

2. *Seabiscuit won on his third try.*

3. *The Great Depression occurred, the Hindenburg burst into flames, and Britain and France declared war on Germany.*

## Text Analysis

**COMMON CORE RI 1, RI 2**

**Possible answers:**

4. *McCarthy details how the horses compete for position as they race. He uses strong verbs, such as challenge, and Twist includes comments such as "one of the most thrilling finishes ... I've ever seen ... in my life."*

5. **COMMON CORE FOCUS** *Synthesize People found inspiration and escape in Seabiscuit's races during the "cruel years," when the "nation was sliding from economic ruin" (page 139, lines 8–11).*

## Read for Information: Draw Conclusions

**COMMON CORE W 9b (RI 7)**

**Writing Prompt** *Responses will vary, but students should state their conclusions in a topic sentence and support them.*

## Assess and Reteach

### Assess

**DIAGNOSTIC AND SELECTION TESTS**
Selection Tests A pp. 47-48
Selection Tests B/C pp. 49-50

**Interactive Selection Test** on **thinkcentral.com**

### Reteach

**Level Up Online Tutorials** on **thinkcentral.com**

---

**FOR STRUGGLING WRITERS**

**Read for Information**

- Direct students to narrow their topic. For example, if they choose "jockeys," they should think in terms of a complete statement, such as "The life of a jockey is exciting but difficult."

- Encourage students to begin by writing their conclusions in a topic sentence. Explain that they can revise their sentences later, but starting with a conclusion will help them stay focused.

**FOR ADVANCED LEARNERS/PRE–AP**

**Author's Purpose** Challenge students to write two separate paragraphs accomplishing different main purposes: to inform or explain, to express their thoughts or feelings, to persuade, or to entertain. Have them share their paragraphs with a partner.

# Focus and Motivate

## COMMON CORE FOCUS

**RL 4** Determine the connotative meaning of words as they are used in a text; analyze the cumulative impact of specific word choices on meaning and tone. **RL 5** Analyze how an author's choices concerning how to structure a text create mystery and surprise. **RL 10** Read and comprehend poetry.

## SUMMARY

**"The Raven"** The speaker in Edgar Allan Poe's classic poem is a man grieving over the death of his beloved Lenore. A raven mysteriously flies into his study late one dreary night and responds with the word "Nevermore" to each of the man's questions, adding to his torment. In the end, the man demands that the raven leave, but the bird remains.

**"Incident in a Rose Garden"** In Donald Justice's ironic poem, a man discovers that Death has come not for his gardener, but for him.

## Why are we fascinated by the UNKNOWN?

Discuss the question. Elicit examples of different kinds of the unknown, such as speculation about life on other planets and questions about the existence of ghosts. Extend the exploration by having students complete the *DISCUSS* activity. Then ask volunteers to share their favorite stories with the class.

## Selection Resources

---

 **Essential Course of Study ECOS**

### The Raven
Poem by Edgar Allan Poe

**HISTORY** Video link at thinkcentral.com

### Incident in a Rose Garden
Poem by Donald Justice

**VIDEO TRAILER THINK central** KEYWORD: HML9-144

# Why are we fascinated by the UNKNOWN?

## COMMON CORE

**RL 4** Determine the connotative meaning of words as they are used in a text; analyze the cumulative impact of specific word choices on meaning and tone. **RL 5** Analyze how an author's choices concerning how to structure a text create mystery and surprise. **RL 10** Read and comprehend poetry.

Have you ever skimmed the strange headlines of a tabloid newspaper when standing in line at the supermarket? Do you channel-surf for television shows about strange phenomena? Our fascination with weird or unexplained events makes us part of a long tradition of writers and readers who enjoy speculating on the unknown or the unexplainable. The writers of the two poems you are about to read relied on that universal fascination when they introduced us to two strange, and perhaps imaginary, visitors.

*DISCUSS* With a partner, share the story of a movie, television show, or urban legend that you find fascinating or unbelievable.

144

---

*See resources on the* **Teacher One Stop DVD-ROM** *and on* **thinkcentral.com**.

**HISTORY** Video link at thinkcentral.com

 **RESOURCE MANAGER UNIT 1**
Plan and Teach, pp. 163–170
Text Analysis and Reading
Skill, pp. 171–174†*

**DIAGNOSTIC AND SELECTION TESTS**
Selection Tests, pp. 51–54

 **BEST PRACTICES TOOLKIT**
Comparison Matrix, p. A24

**INTERACTIVE READER**

**ADAPTED INTERACTIVE READER**

**ELL ADAPTED INTERACTIVE READER**

**TECHNOLOGY**

- **Teacher One Stop DVD-ROM**
- **Student One Stop DVD-ROM**
- **PowerNotes DVD-ROM**
- **Audio Anthology CD**
- **GrammarNotes DVD-ROM**
- **Audio Tutor CD**
- **ExamView Test Generator** on the Teacher One Stop

 **THINK central**

## Video Trailer

Go to **thinkcentral.com** to preview the **Video Trailer** introducing this selection. Other features that support the selection include
- **PowerNotes** presentation
- **ThinkAloud** models to enhance comprehension
- **WordSharp** vocabulary tutorials
- interactive writing and grammar instruction

---

\* Resources for Differentiation       † Also in Spanish       ‡ In Haitian Creole and Vietnamese

## TEXT ANALYSIS: NARRATIVE POETRY

Like fiction, a **narrative poem** contains the elements of plot, conflict, character, and setting that combine to create a story. Because of the nature of poetry, these elements are often condensed into images and compact descriptions. For example, notice that this line contains information about setting, plot, and character:

*Once upon a midnight dreary, while I pondered, weak and weary*

In each of the following narrative poems, the **speaker**, or voice that talks to the reader, is also the main character in the story. As you read, note what events each speaker describes and how these create a compelling story in verse form.

## READING SKILL: READING POETRY

When you read a narrative poem, certain reading strategies will help you understand the poem's story and meaning.

- First, read the poem silently to grasp the basic story line.
- Look for instances of **irony** with which the poet may use to add extra levels of depth and creativity to the poem.
- Then read the poem aloud several times, and listen to how it sounds. Pay attention to sound devices, such as **rhyme**, **rhythm**, and **repetition**. Does the poem include **alliteration**, the repetition of consonant sounds at the beginning of words? How do these sound devices add to the effect of the poem? (To review the definitions of these sound-device terms, see the **Glossary of Literary and Nonfiction Terms**, page R102.)
- Look for clues that reveal something about the **speaker**. What does the speaker feel about the poem's characters and events?

As you read each poem, record the most striking examples of sound devices in a chart similar to the following:

| Sound Device | "The Raven" | "Incident in a Rose Garden" |
|---|---|---|
| alliteration | "nodded, nearly napping" | |

 Complete the activities in your **Reader/Writer Notebook**.

## Meet the Authors

### Edgar Allan Poe
**1809–1849**

**A Life of Tragedy**
One of America's literary giants, Edgar Allan Poe has fascinated generations of readers with his haunting poetry and tales of horror. (See "The Cask of Amontillado" on page 370.) Poe suffered many tragic losses in his short life. He was orphaned at the age of 2 and taken in by foster parents, but never formally adopted. Poe later quarreled bitterly with his foster father. At the age of 27, Poe married a 13-year-old cousin, Virginia Clemm. She died about ten years later, after an agonizing battle with tuberculosis.

**Death-Haunted Poetry**
Poe's poetry often deals with the subject of death. According to Poe, the "death then of a beautiful woman is, unquestionably, the most poetical topic in the world."

### Donald Justice
**1925–2004**

**From Music to Poetry**
Donald Justice originally intended to become a composer and studied for a degree in music before deciding to become a writer. He then earned a doctorate in creative writing, participating in the Iowa Writers' Workshop. A Pulitzer Prize–winning poet, Justice taught English at a number of universities.

**Authors Online**
Go to thinkcentral.com. KEYWORD: HML9-145

**THINK central**

145

---

---

# Teach

**READ WITH A PURPOSE**

*Help students set a purpose for reading. Tell them to read "The Raven" to find out what the raven repeatedly says to the speaker and then read "Incident in a Rose Garden" to learn the identity of the stranger.*

**TEXT ANALYSIS**                    COMMON CORE
RL 5

**Ⓐ NARRATIVE POETRY**

*Possible answer:* The speaker's internal conflict is that he is trying, without success, to get over the grief he feels for his "lost Lenore" (line 10), who has died.

**TIERED DISCUSSION PROMPTS**

Use these prompts to help students explore the speaker's changing state of mind in lines 1–18:

**Connect** Have you ever had an experience in which familiar surroundings suddenly seemed unfamiliar or even frightening? Explain. *Students may mention returning to their old house, neighborhood, or school, and feeling that the once-familiar place looked different.*

**Analyze** Why do the speaker's surroundings suddenly seem strange to him? *Possible answer: It is a cold night. The fire is dying, but the room seems strangely alive with "sad, uncertain rustling" curtains (line 13) and a strange tapping noise.*

**Synthesize** How does the speaker's state of mind change during the first three stanzas of the poem? Cite details to support your answer. *Possible answer: At the beginning of the poem, the speaker is sorrowful, weak, and weary (lines 1 and 10), but he is not nervous or scared. By the third stanza, however, his state of mind has changed, and he is now frightened and agitated because of the tapping on his door. He is filled with "fantastic terrors never felt before" (line 14), and his heart is beating heavily (line 15). The familiar setting of his chamber has become a source of terror; even the rustling of the curtains scares him (lines 13–14).*

# The RAVEN

### Edgar Allan Poe

**Analyze Visuals ▶**
What **mood** is conveyed by the style of the drawing?

Once upon a midnight dreary, while I pondered, weak and weary,
Over many a quaint and curious volume of forgotten lore—
While I nodded, nearly napping, suddenly there came a tapping,
As of someone gently rapping, rapping at my chamber door.
5 "'Tis some visitor," I muttered, "tapping at my chamber door—
    Only this and nothing more."

Ah, distinctly I remember it was in the bleak December;
And each separate dying ember wrought its ghost upon the floor.
Eagerly I wished the morrow;—vainly I had sought to borrow
10 From my books surcease of sorrow[1]—sorrow for the lost Lenore—
For the rare and radiant maiden whom the angels name Lenore—
    Nameless *here* forevermore. Ⓐ

And the silken, sad, uncertain rustling of each purple curtain
Thrilled me—filled me with fantastic terrors never felt before;
15 So that now, to still the beating of my heart, I stood repeating
"'Tis some visitor entreating entrance at my chamber door;—
Some late visitor entreating entrance at my chamber door;—
    That it is and nothing more."

Presently my soul grew stronger; hesitating then no longer,
20 "Sir," said I, "or Madam, truly your forgiveness I implore;
But the fact is I was napping, and so gently you came rapping,
And so faintly you came tapping, tapping at my chamber door,
That I scarce was sure I heard you"—here I opened wide the door;—
    Darkness there and nothing more.

**Ⓐ NARRATIVE POETRY**
With what **internal conflict** does the speaker struggle?

---

1. **from my books surcease of sorrow:** from reading, an end to sorrow.

*Raven* (1994), Jim Dine. Charcoal on wall, 128″ × 98½″.
Kunstverein Ludwigsburg, Germany, destroyed.
© 2007 Jim Dine/Artists Rights Society (ARS), New York.

## DIFFERENTIATED INSTRUCTION

**FOR ENGLISH LANGUAGE LEARNERS**
**Vocabulary: Word Associations** Students may have difficulty understanding the 19th-century vocabulary in the poem. Tell students that an unknown word may contain a familiar word part or be similar to a word they already know. For example, in line 9 the word *morrow* is similar to *tomorrow*. Then tell students that context clues can also help them understand unfamiliar words. For example, students can reason that the word *chamber* means "bedroom," because the speaker tells us he was napping when he heard tapping on his door.

**Media and Language** To help build and reinforce understanding of the sound devices in "The Raven," have students listen to a tape recording or CD of the poem from the school's media center. Play the recording of the first two stanzas once; then, ask students to identify two to four rhyming words they heard (such as *lore, door, floor, Lenore*). Then, play the recording again and ask students to identify two to four examples of alliteration (such as *napping, tapping, borrow, sorrow*). Students can also listen to the recording for the poem's rhythm.

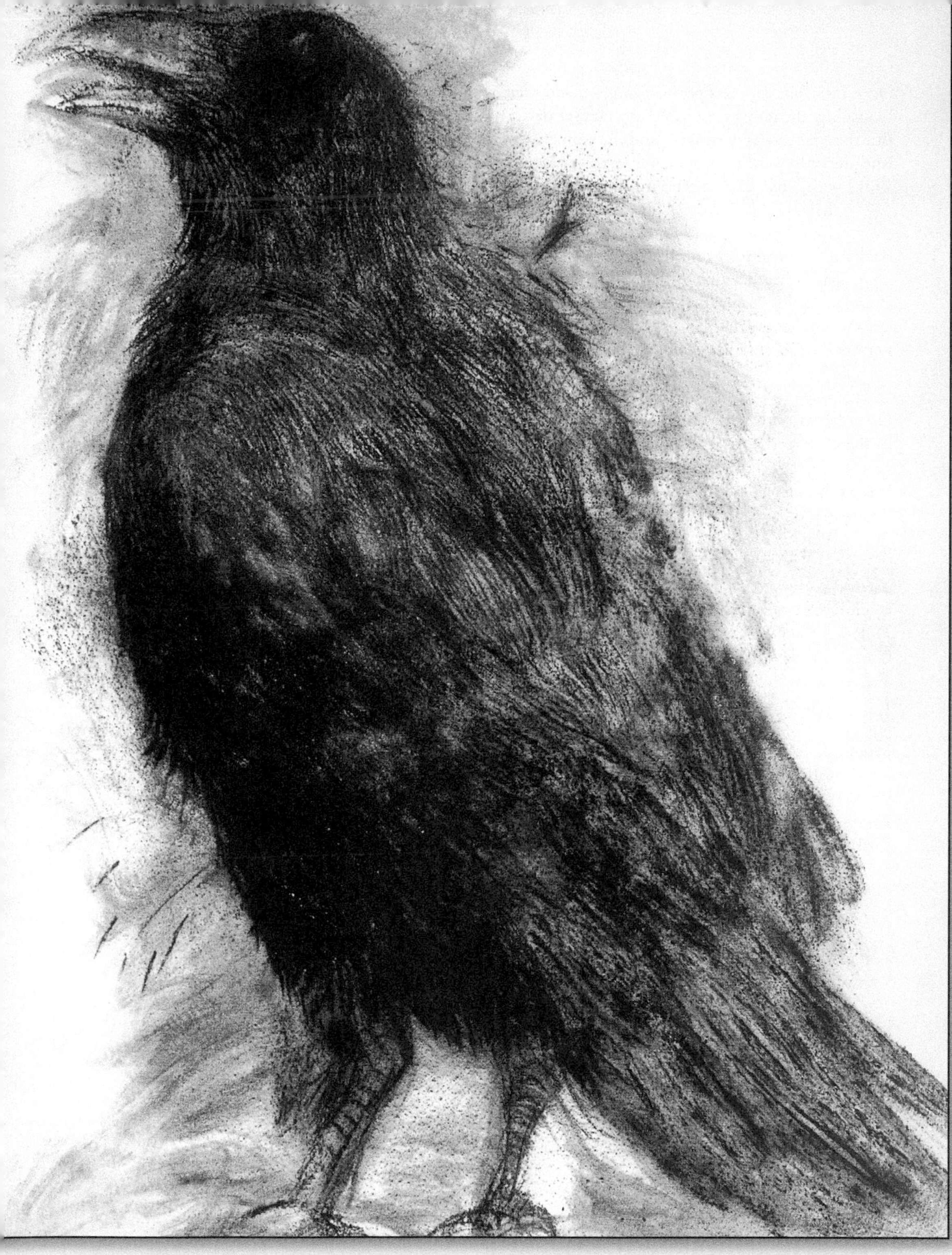

**Reading Support** THINK central

This selection on thinkcentral.com includes embedded **ThinkAloud** models–students "thinking aloud" about the story to model the kinds of questions a good reader would ask about a selection.

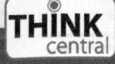

## BACKGROUND

**The Raven** In Western culture, the raven has a symbolic association with evil omens, mystery, and death. Poe initially considered using a parrot or an owl in the poem, but he chose the raven instead because of the bird's cultural associations. In addition, the raven seemed a more suitable choice for the dark and melancholy mood of the poem.

## Analyze Visuals

***Possible answer:*** *The smudges and indistinct features of the drawing almost seem to vibrate, creating a mood of agitation and even menace.*

**About the Art** Contemporary painter Jim Dine (b. 1935) uses charcoal to create a deep, dense blackness with smudges and seemingly random marks.

**REVISIT THE BIG QUESTION**

## Why are we fascinated by the UNKNOWN?

**Discuss** In lines 13–24, how does Poe build suspense about the unknown source of the tapping on the door? ***Possible answer:*** *He builds suspense by creating tension between the speaker's increasingly uneasy mental state and the origin of strange sounds he hears outside his door. The speaker is filled with "fantastic terrors" (line 14) and is aware of "the beating of [his] heart" (line 15) as he tries to reassure himself that the tapping is nothing more than "some visitor" (line 16). When at last he opens the door, he finds "Darkness there and nothing more" (line 24). The speaker—and the reader—is left in suspense about who or what is tapping on the door.*

**FOR STRUGGLING READERS**

**Options for Reading** Read "The Raven" aloud as the class follows along. Emphasize the dramatic narrative elements, building the mood as you read. Because "The Raven" is a long poem, students may benefit from your pausing every few stanzas to make a comment or ask a question. However, their primary purpose for this first reading should be listening to the sound and rhythm of the poem and its haunting, melancholy quality.

## B Model the Skill: READING POETRY

- Read lines 25–48 aloud to the class to model how to read poetry that has alliteration. Have students listen for the repetition of consonant sounds at the beginning of words as you read.

- Have students in groups of four practice the skill by taking turns reading a stanza aloud while the others listen. Then have student groups record what they decide are the most striking examples of alliteration in their sound device charts.

**Possible answer:** *Alliteration occurs in line 25—"Deep into that darkness"—but line 26 provides a better example: "Doubting, dreaming dreams . . . dared to dream . . . ." Poe uses alliteration throughout the poem (for example: "weak and weary" [line 1], "lost Lenore" [line 10], "flirt and flutter" [line 37], "shorn and shaven" [line 45]) to create a rhythmic, almost hypnotic, effect; an atmosphere of melancholy; and a feeling of inevitability.*

## C NARRATIVE POETRY

**Possible answer:** *The speaker reacts to the raven's entrance with a smile, finding the raven "beguiling" (line 43), and asks the bird his name (line 47). He seems to welcome this visitor as a source of relief from his "sad fancy" (line 43). We can conclude from this reaction that the speaker feels lonely and is grateful for a distraction from his low spirits.*

---

25  Deep into that darkness peering, long I stood there wondering, fearing,
    Doubting, dreaming dreams no mortal ever dared to dream before;
    But the silence was unbroken, and the stillness gave no token,
    And the only word there spoken was the whispered word, "Lenore!"
    This I whispered, and an echo murmured back the word "Lenore!"
30          Merely this and nothing more.

    Back into the chamber turning, all my soul within me burning,
    Soon again I heard a tapping somewhat louder than before.
    "Surely," said I, "surely that is something at my window lattice;
    Let me see, then, what thereat is, and this mystery explore—
35  Let my heart be still a moment and this mystery explore;—
            'Tis the wind and nothing more!"

    Open here I flung the shutter, when, with many a flirt and flutter,
    In there stepped a stately Raven of the saintly days of yore.[2]
    Not the least obeisance made he;[3] not a minute stopped or stayed he;
40  But, with mien of lord or lady,[4] perched above my chamber door—
    Perched upon a bust of Pallas[5] just above my chamber door—
            Perched, and sat, and nothing more.

    Then this ebony bird beguiling[6] my sad fancy into smiling,
    By the grave and stern decorum of the countenance[7] it wore,
45  "Though thy crest be shorn and shaven, thou," I said, "art sure no craven,[8]
    Ghastly grim and ancient Raven wandering from the Nightly shore—
    Tell me what thy lordly name is on the Night's Plutonian[9] shore!"
            Quoth the Raven, "Nevermore."

    Much I marveled this ungainly fowl to hear discourse so plainly,
50  Though its answer little meaning—little relevancy bore;
    For we cannot help agreeing that no living human being
    Ever yet was blessed with seeing bird above his chamber door—
    Bird or beast upon the sculptured bust above his chamber door,
            With such name as "Nevermore."

---

2. **saintly days of yore:** sacred days of the past.

3. **not the least obeisance** (ō-bā'səns) **made he:** he did not bow or make any other gesture of respect.

4. **with mien of lord or lady:** with the appearance of a noble person.

5. **bust of Pallas:** statue of the head and shoulders of Athena, Greek goddess of war and wisdom.

6. **this ebony bird beguiling** (bĭ-gī'lĭng): this black bird that is charming or delighting.

7. **grave and stern decorum . . . countenance** (koun'tə-nəns): serious and dignified expression on the face.

8. **art sure no craven:** are surely not cowardly.

9. **Plutonian:** having to do with Pluto, Roman god of the dead and ruler of the underworld.

### B READING POETRY
Reread lines 25–30. Identify examples of **alliteration**, the repetition of consonant sounds at the beginning of words. Notice how often this **sound device** occurs in this narrative poem. What is the effect?

### C NARRATIVE POETRY
What can you conclude about the **speaker** from the way he reacts to the raven's entrance?

---

## DIFFERENTIATED INSTRUCTION

### FOR STRUGGLING READERS

**Vocabulary Support**

**Line 34:** *thereat*—poetic expression for "at that place"

**Lines 49, 71:** *ungainly*—"awkward-looking"

**Concept Support** To build understanding of alliteration, give students an opportunity to create their own alliterative phrases. Have them begin by pairing up adjectives or making adjective-noun combinations, as in "beautiful blue butterfly" or "delicious dinner."

### FOR ENGLISH LANGUAGE LEARNERS

**Language: Modifiers** Explain that poets often do not follow customary language patterns. For example, adjectives usually precede the word they modify, as in "bleak December" (line 7) and "purple curtain" (line 13), but Poe reverses the order in "midnight dreary" (line 1) and "land enchanted" (line 87). Explore how Poe departs from the usual word order in such lines as 37–38, 49, and 57. Have small groups find other examples of unusual word order in the poem and share them with the class.

55 But the Raven, sitting lonely on the placid bust, spoke only
That one word, as if his soul in that one word he did outpour.
Nothing farther then he uttered—not a feather then he fluttered—
Till I scarcely more than muttered, "Other friends have flown before—
On the morrow *he* will leave me, as my hopes have flown before."
60       Then the bird said, "Nevermore."

Startled at the stillness broken by reply so aptly spoken,
"Doubtless," said I, "what it utters is its only stock and store
Caught from some unhappy master whom unmerciful Disaster **D**
Followed fast and followed faster till his songs one burden bore—
65 Till the dirges of his Hope[10] that melancholy burden bore
      Of 'Never—nevermore.'"

But the Raven still beguiling all my fancy into smiling,
Straight I wheeled a cushioned seat in front of bird and bust and door;
Then, upon the velvet sinking, I betook myself to linking
70 Fancy unto fancy, thinking what this ominous bird of yore—
What this grim, ungainly, ghastly, gaunt, and ominous bird of yore
      Meant in croaking, "Nevermore."

This I sat engaged in guessing, but no syllable expressing
To the fowl whose fiery eyes now burned into my bosom's core;
75 This and more I sat divining,[11] with my head at ease reclining
On the cushion's velvet lining that the lamp-light gloated o'er,
But whose velvet violet lining with the lamp-light gloating o'er,
      *She* shall press, ah, nevermore!

Then, methought, the air grew denser, perfumed from an unseen censer
80 Swung by Seraphim[12] whose foot-falls tinkled on the tufted floor.
"Wretch," I cried, "thy God hath lent thee—by these angels he hath sent thee
Respite—respite and nepenthe[13] from thy memories of Lenore;
Quaff, oh quaff this kind nepenthe[14] and forget this lost Lenore!"
      Quoth the Raven, "Nevermore."

---

10. **dirges** (dûr′jĭz) **of his Hope:** funeral hymns mourning the loss of hope.

11. **divining** (dĭ-vī′nĭng): guessing or speculating.

12. **censer swung by Seraphim** (sĕr′ə-fĭm): container of burning incense swung by angels of the highest rank.

13. **he hath sent thee respite** (rĕs′pĭt) **... nepenthe** (nĭ-pĕn′thē): God has sent you relief and forgetfulness of sorrow.

14. **quaff, oh quaff this kind nepenthe:** drink this beverage that eases pain.

**D** **READING POETRY**
Reread line 63. Notice the **internal rhyme**—similar or identical sounds within a line—of the words *master* and *disaster*. Find examples of internal rhyme in other stanzas, and notice how they help emphasize certain words.

**COMMON CORE RL 4**

**Language Coach**

**Denotation/Connotation** Many words have positive or negative emotional associations, or **connotations.** Reread line 74. Does the word *fiery* have a positive or negative connotation?

**D** **READING POETRY**
      RL 4, RL 10

***Possible answer:*** *Poe uses internal rhyme to enhance the melodic and rhythmic quality of the poem and draw attention to certain words. Examples of internal rhyme include* peering, fearing *(line 25);* unbroken, token *(line 27);* turning, burning *(line 31);* shutter, flutter *(line 37);* beguiling, smiling *(line 43);* shaven, craven *(line 45);* ungainly, plainly *(line 49);* uttered, fluttered *(line 57);* broken, spoken *(line 61).*

**REVISIT THE BIG QUESTION**

# Why are we fascinated by the **UNKNOWN?**

**Discuss** In lines 37–78, how does Poe use the raven to make the unknown seem increasingly frightening? ***Possible answer:*** *He uses the raven to emphasize the speaker's deteriorating mental state. When the mysterious raven first appears, the bird seems harmless to the speaker. He welcomes the raven with a smile and talks with the bird as though he were a friend. However, the raven's repeated single-word response of "Nevermore" frustrates the speaker and turns his initial calm into torment. Poe emphasizes the speaker's fear and agitation by using alarming adjectives to describe the raven, as in line 71: "grim, ungainly, ghastly, gaunt, and ominous."*

---

**FOR ENGLISH LANGUAGE LEARNERS**

**Language Coach**    COMMON CORE RL 4

**Denotation/Connotation**

*negative connotation;* Tell students that a word's denotation is its meaning; its connotation is the word's emotional association. Have students identify three words in lines 58–81 that are used in dialogue to mean "said." Have students decide whether each word carries a positive or negative connotation. ***Possible answers:*** *muttered (line 58), croaking (line 72), cried (line 81); negative*

**FOR ADVANCED LEARNERS/PRE–AP**

**Compare and Contrast** Have students work in small groups to analyze the speaker's changing reactions to the raven, from the time the bird first appears until the end of the poem. Ask students to use a Comparison Matrix to compare how the speaker feels at the end of each stanza and explain both how and why his feelings change as the poem progresses.

**BEST PRACTICES TOOLKIT—Transparency**
Comparison Matrix p. A24

## Analyze Visuals

**Activity** After students finish reading the poem, ask them to explain which of the two art pieces seems to better match the mood of the selection—the charcoal drawing of the raven on page 147 or this cardboard relief which pictures both a raven and a heart. *Students' responses should reflect an understanding of the poem's mysterious and melancholy mood.*

**About the Art** Jim Dine (b. 1935) is known for his emotional style and recurrent subjects— hearts, birds, robes, flowers, and portraits. After receiving a B.F.A. at the University of Ohio, Athens, Dine moved to New York City where he began his career as a Pop artist. During his prolific career, Dine has worked as a painter, sculptor, print-maker, and photographer.

| READING SKILL | COMMON CORE |
| --- | --- |
| | RL 4, RL 10 |

###  READING POETRY

***Possible answer:*** *Through repetition of "is there," "tell me," and "I implore," the poet shows the speaker's increasing urgency and desperation in seeking answers and consolation from the raven.*

| TEXT ANALYSIS | COMMON CORE |
| --- | --- |
| | RL 5 |

### **F** *Model the Skill:* **NARRATIVE POETRY**

Model for students how to determine whether the speaker's conflict is resolved and how to make inferences about the speaker's future. Point out that in line 100, the speaker tells readers that he is still lonely ("Leave my loneliness unbroken!"). Then explore the meaning of the final two lines (107–108). Ask what the speaker implies when he says that his soul shall be lifted "from out that shadow … nevermore!"

***Possible answer:*** *The speaker's conflict is left unresolved. He still feels grief for his loss of Lenore, and the raven has given him no real comfort, reassurance, or relief. On the contrary, the raven's maddening repetition of the same one-word response has agitated the speaker even more. The future appears bleak for the speaker; his sorrow is likely to continue unabated.*

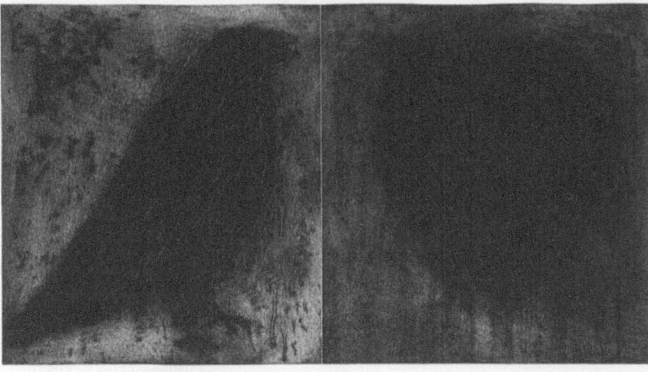

*Red Passion* (1996), Jim Dine. Cardboard relief intaglio. Image size 33 ¹/₈″ × 59″. Paper size 39 ½″ × 63 ⁷/₈″. Published by Pace Editions, Inc. Edition of 12. © 2007 Jime Dine/Artists Rights Society (ARS), New York.

85 "Prophet!" said I, "thing of evil!—prophet still, if bird or devil!—
  Whether Tempter sent, or whether tempest tossed[15] thee here ashore,
  Desolate yet all undaunted,[16] on this desert land enchanted—
  On this home by Horror haunted—tell me truly, I implore—
  Is there—*is* there balm in Gilead?[17]—tell me—tell me, I implore!" **E**
90     Quoth the Raven, "Nevermore."

  "Prophet!" said I, "thing of evil!—prophet still, if bird or devil!
  By that Heaven that bends above us—by that God we both adore—
  Tell this soul with sorrow laden if, within the distant Aidenn,[18]
  It shall clasp a sainted maiden whom the angels name Lenore—
95 Clasp a rare and radiant maiden whom the angels name Lenore."
      Quoth the Raven, "Nevermore."

  "Be that word our sign of parting, bird or fiend!" I shrieked, upstarting—
  "Get thee back into the tempest and the Night's Plutonian shore!
  Leave no black plume as a token of that lie thy soul hath spoken!
100 Leave my loneliness unbroken!—quit the bust above my door!
  Take thy beak from out my heart, and take thy form from off my door!"
      Quoth the Raven, "Nevermore."

  And the Raven, never flitting, still is sitting, *still* is sitting
  On the pallid bust of Pallas just above my chamber door;
105 And his eyes have all the seeming of a demon's that is dreaming,
  And the lamp-light o'er him streaming throws his shadow on the floor;
  And my soul from out that shadow that lies floating on the floor
      Shall be lifted—nevermore! **F**

---

15. **whether Tempter sent … tempest tossed:** whether the devil sent or a violent storm carried.
16. **desolate yet all undaunted:** alone and yet unafraid.
17. **balm in Gilead** (gĭl′ē-əd): relief from suffering.
18. **Aidenn** (ād′n): heaven.

**E** **READING POETRY**
What does the **repetition** in lines 88–89 help the poet achieve?

**F** **NARRATIVE POETRY**
Think about whether the speaker's **conflict** is resolved at the end of the poem. What can you **infer** about his future?

## DIFFERENTIATED INSTRUCTION

### FOR STRUGGLING READERS

**Comprehension Support** To make sure students understand lines 97–108, ask what the speaker demands that the raven do in lines 97–101 and whether the raven does as the speaker asks. Have students cite specific lines and phrases to support their responses. To extend the discussion, ask students to paraphrase one or both stanzas.

### FOR ADVANCED LEARNERS/PRE–AP

**Analyze** Explain that "The Raven" is open to various interpretations. For example, some readers think that the poem is not meant to be taken too literally—that its meaning is mainly symbolic. Others believe that the poem is a study in madness—that the raven exists only in the grief-stricken speaker's mind. Have students write a brief essay giving their own interpretations, with supporting details from the poem. Have volunteers share their essays with the class.

# Incident *in a* Rose Garden

## DONALD JUSTICE

*The Back of a Man with a Rose,* René Magritte. Private Collection Bloch, Santa Monica, CA. © 2007 C. Herscovici, Brussels/Artists Rights Society (ARS), New York. Photo © Superstock, Inc.

The gardener came running,
An old man, out of breath.
Fear had given him legs.
　*Sir, I encountered Death*
5　*Just now among the roses.*
　*Thin as a scythe he stood there.*
　*I knew him by his pictures.*
　*He had his black coat on,*
　*Black gloves, a broad black hat.*
10　*I think he would have spoken,*
　*Seeing his mouth stood open.*
　*Big it was, with white teeth.*
　*As soon as he beckoned, I ran.*
　*I ran until I found you.*
15　*Sir, I am quitting my job.*
　*I want to see my sons*
　*Once more before I die.*
　*I want to see California.* Ⓖ
　We shook hands; he was off.

> Ⓖ **NARRATIVE POETRY**
> In lines 4–18, the gardener (whose words are italicized) describes Death as a **character.** What do these lines suggest the **conflict** of this poem will be?

---

## Analyze Visuals

**Activity** After students read the poem, have them compare Justice's representation of Death with the "man with a rose" in this painting. How are the two alike? How do they differ? *Possible answer: Both wear a black coat and hat, although the hat in the poem is described as "broad," unlike the one shown in the painting. Both figures hold a rose.*

**About the Art** The paintings of surrealist artist René Magritte (1898–1967) are misleading in their apparent simplicity. Like so much of Magritte's work, *The Back of a Man with a Rose* raises many questions in the viewer's mind but provides few answers. Magritte once remarked that his paintings "evoke mystery and, indeed, when one sees one of my pictures, one asks oneself this simple question 'What does that mean?' It does not mean anything, because mystery means nothing either, it is unknowable."

---

**TEXT ANALYSIS** 　COMMON CORE RL 5

### Ⓖ NARRATIVE POETRY

*Possible answer: By describing Death as a character, these lines suggest that the conflict will be between the character of Death and another character who does not want to die.*

**Extend the Discussion** What specific details in these lines personify Death as a character?

---

**REVISIT THE BIG QUESTION**

## Why are we fascinated by the **UNKNOWN?**

**Discuss** In lines 1–18, how does the gardener react to his encounter with the unknown, represented by the figure of Death? *Possible answer: Frightened, the gardener runs away and quits his job, hoping to "see [his] sons once more before [he dies]."*

---

### FOR STRUGGLING READERS

**Develop Reading Fluency** Read "Incident in a Rose Garden" aloud. Use your tone of voice to emphasize the differences among the three characters in the poem—the gardener, the speaker, and Death—and to help demonstrate the ominous atmosphere of the poem. Then have students listen to the poem on the *Audio Anthology CD* as they read along.

Distribute the copy master and have students work in pairs or groups to practice fluency.

**R** RESOURCE MANAGER—Copy Master
Reading Fluency p. 176

**Comprehension Support** To make sure that students understand the poet's technique, ask what the italic type represents (someone speaking). As students read the second and third stanzas, elicit or explain that the italic type continues to serve the same purpose, but the speaker changes. Have students identify the three speakers.

## **H** READING POETRY

**Possible answer:** *The rhythm adds emphasis to the slow and deliberate actions of Death as he pinches off one bloom after another, apparently enjoying—like a "connoisseur" (line 28).*

**Extend the Discussion** Why do you think the poet tells us that Death holds the blooms to his nose before discarding them?

## **I** READING POETRY

**Possible answer:** *Several details in the poem contribute to creating an ironic effect. In line 13, the gardener flees before giving Death a chance to speak, perhaps suggesting that Death's purpose may prove to be other than expected. In addition, when the gardener runs off, Death does not pursue him, but instead waits patiently (lines 20–25), perhaps suggesting that he has other business to attend to. Finally, referring to Death's hand as a "cage of bone" (line 42) suggests that the hand may capture the person who shakes it.*

## SELECTION WRAP–UP

**READ WITH A PURPOSE** Now that students have read both poems, ask them how the raven's repeated phrase affects the speaker in "The Raven." Then ask students to list adjectives and similies that the poet uses to describe Death in "Incident in a Rose Garden."
**Possible answers:** "Nevermore" agitates and frustrates the speaker; drives him mad. "thin as a scythe," "white teeth," "dressed like a Spanish waiter," "a connoisseur of roses," "stranger"

⭐ **CRITIQUE** Ask students to explain which poem's ending they found more satisfying, and why.

## INDEPENDENT READING

Students who want to further explore the works of Poe may enjoy "The Murders in the Rue Morgue," a "locked room" mystery with a surprising conclusion.

20 And there stood Death in the garden,
   Dressed like a Spanish waiter.
   He had the air of someone
   Who because he likes arriving
   At all appointments early
25 Learns to think himself patient.
   I watched him pinch one bloom off
   And hold it to his nose—
   A connoisseur of roses—
   One bloom and then another. **H**
30 They strewed the earth around him.
      *Sir, you must be that stranger*
      *Who threatened my gardener.*
      *This is my property, sir.*
      *I welcome only friends here.*

35 Death grinned, and his eyes lit up
   With the pale glow of those lanterns
   That workmen carry sometimes
   To light their way through the dusk.
   Now with great care he slid
40 The glove from his right hand
   And held that out in greeting,
   A little cage of bone.
      *Sir, I knew your father,*
      *And we were friends at the end.*
45    *As for your gardener,*
      *I did not threaten him.*
      *Old men mistake my gestures.*
      *I only meant to ask him*
      *To show me to his master.*
50    *I take it you are he?* **I**

*for Mark Strand*

## **H** READING POETRY
Read aloud lines 26–29, and note the **rhythm** created by the words. What effect does this add to the image presented?

COMMON CORE RL 5

## **I** READING POETRY
For most readers, lines 48–50 reveal a **surprise** ending. The poet uses **irony,** a difference between what the reader expects and what actually occurs. In this case, the reader's understanding that Death has come for the gardener is overturned when it is revealed that it is the narrator himself who is Death's victim. What details in the poem contribute to creating this ironic effect?

## DIFFERENTIATED INSTRUCTION

### FOR STRUGGLING READERS
**Comprehension Support** Elicit or explain that Justice uses personification in his poem—representing death as a character. Direct students' attention to lines 6–13, 20–30, and 35–50, and have them identify details that the poet uses to portray death in human form.

### FOR ADVANCED LEARNERS/PRE–AP
**Imagery** [small-group option] Have students discuss how the descriptive images in lines 6–9, 22–30, and 35–42 give a sinister air to Death. Ask which image seems most menacing, and why. Extend the discussion by asking whether Death's politeness in the third stanza makes him seem more or less sinister.

## Comprehension

1. **Recall** What is the **setting** of each poem?

2. **Recall** In "The Raven," what loss is the speaker trying to recover from?

3. **Recall** In "Incident in a Rose Garden," for whom has Death really come?

4. **Clarify** What happens at the end of each poem?

## Text Analysis

5. **Analyze** Reread lines 7–12 of "The Raven." The **speaker** has tried to forget his sadness and loss. What is his mental state at the end of the poem? Do you think the raven is real or just a figment of his imagination? Support your views with details from the poem.

6. **Identify Irony** Explain the **ironies,** or unexpected twists, in "Incident in a Rose Garden."

7. **Interpret Narrative Poetry** Use a chart to identify the narrative elements found in these poems. In each poem, which element plays the largest role? Support your answer.

| Narrative Element | "The Raven" | "Incident in a Rose Garden" |
|---|---|---|
| Characters | | |
| Setting | | |
| Conflict | | |
| Resolution (How does it end?) | | |

8. **Reading Poetry** Review the chart you filled in as you read the poems. Which poet depends more heavily on **sound devices** to help convey mood and meaning? Cite evidence.

## Text Criticism

9. **Critical Interpretations** With the publication of "The Raven" in 1845, Poe became famous overnight. More than 160 years later, the poem is still considered a classic. What accounts for its continued appeal? Be specific in your answer.

### Why are we fascinated by the UNKNOWN?

What is it about unexplained events or occurrences that people find intriguing?

**COMMON CORE**

**RL 4** Analyze the cumulative impact of specific word choices on meaning and tone. **RL 5** Analyze how an author's choices concerning how to structure a text create mystery and surprise. **RL 10** Read and comprehend poetry.

# Practice and Apply

For preliminary support of post-reading questions, use these copy masters:

 **RESOURCE MANAGER—Copy Masters**
Narrative Poetry p. 171
Question Support p. 175

Additional selection questions are provided for the teacher on page 167.

## ANSWERS

### Comprehension

1. *"The Raven": the speaker's "chamber," on "a midnight dreary" in "bleak December"; "Incident in a Rose Garden": a rose garden*

2. *the death of his beloved Lenore*

3. *the speaker*

4. *"The Raven": The raven remains in the speaker's chamber, casting his shadow forever over the speaker's soul. "Incident in a Rose Garden": Death reveals that he has come not for the gardener but for "his master."*

### Text Analysis

COMMON CORE **RL 4, RL 5, RL 10**

*Possible answers:*

5. *The speaker is in a state of utter despair at the end. Whether students respond that the raven is real or imaginary, they should support their opinions with evidence.*

6. *The central irony is that Death has come not for the gardener, who fears him, but for the speaker, who bravely orders Death to leave. It is also ironic to call Death a "connoisseur of roses," because Death's enjoyment of roses involves killing them.*

7. ● **COMMON CORE FOCUS** *Interpret Narrative Poetry After students have used the chart to identify the different*

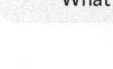 *narrative elements in the poems, they may choose these elements as the most important:* **"The Raven":** *the characters, because their interaction creates the poem's conflict and sustains its eerie mood;* **"Incident in a Rose Garden":** *the resolution, because the surprise ending provides the poem's central irony and meaning*

8. ● **COMMON CORE FOCUS** *Reading Poetry Poe uses sound devices—rhyme, rhythm, repetition, alliteration—much more than Justice to convey mood and meaning.*

## Text Criticism

*Possible answer:*

9. *Poe's poem deals with timeless themes, such as love and loss; its sound devices and eeriness make it entertaining; its ambiguity (is the raven real or imaginary?) teases the reader and encourages discussion.*

### Why are we fascinated by the UNKNOWN?

Have students consider what excites them or makes them fearful—or both—about the unknown.

# Assess and Reteach

### Assess

**DIAGNOSTIC AND SELECTION TESTS**
Selection Test A pp. 51–52
Selection Test B/C pp. 53–54

**Interactive Selection Test** on **thinkcentral.com**

### Reteach

**Level Up Online Tutorials** on **thinkcentral.com**

**Reteaching Worksheets** on **thinkcentral.com**
Literature Lesson 20: Speaker
Literature Lesson 21: Rhyme

# Focus and Motivate

## COMMON CORE FOCUS

**RL 5** Analyze how an author's choices concerning how to structure a text and order events within it create such effects as mystery, tension, or surprise. **RL 10** Read and comprehend dramas. **L 3** Apply knowledge of language to make effective choices for meaning or style.

## SUMMARY

"Sorry, Right Number" is the suspenseful tale of Katie Weiderman, who receives an alarming phone call from an unidentified, though somehow familiar, caller. Five years after her husband's fatal heart attack, Katie learns that the message was a warning from the future, and that she herself was the caller.

## What sends a **CHILL** down your spine?

Discuss the question with students. Ask students to think about books and movies that they find scary. Discuss how suspense, the supernatural, and sudden surprises affect the "chill factor." Have students complete the *QUICKWRITE.* Follow up by asking why an unknown or unseen force can be more frightening or suspenseful than a known one.

# Selection Resources

---

# Sorry, Right Number

Teleplay by Stephen King

# What sends a CHILL down your spine?

**COMMON CORE**

**RL 5** Analyze how an author's choices concerning how to structure a text and order events within it create such effects as mystery, tension, or surprise. **RL 10** Read and comprehend dramas.

Not all horror stories give readers a fright by portraying gory scenes. Some present ordinary people doing ordinary things—until something creepy, or even supernatural, happens. In *Sorry, Right Number*, a family is puzzled by a mysterious phone caller pleading for help.

*QUICKWRITE* Supernatural events play a part in many stories of fantasy, mystery, and horror. Work with a group to generate a list of supernatural occurrences in stories, movies, and TV programs. Arrange them in a "chill factor" chart according to how powerfully they affect you.

Chill Factor
10. (Terrifying)
9.
8.
7. (Nail biter)
6.
5.
4.
3. (Tame)
2.
1.

154

---

See resources on the **Teacher One Stop DVD-ROM** and on <u>thinkcentral.com</u>.

 **RESOURCE MANAGER UNIT 1**
Plan and Teach, pp. 177–184
Summary, pp. 185–186†‡*
Text Analysis and Reading Skill, pp. 187–190†*
Grammar and Style, p. 193

**DIAGNOSTIC AND SELECTION TESTS**
Selection Tests, pp. 55–58

**BEST PRACTICES TOOLKIT**
Readers' Theater, A1
Knowledge Rating, p. E3
New Word Analysis, p. E8
Storyboard, p. C11
Two-Column Chart, p. A25

**TECHNOLOGY**
⊘ **Teacher One Stop DVD-ROM**
⊘ **Student One Stop DVD-ROM**
⊘ **Audio Anthology CD**
⊘ **ExamView Test Generator on the Teacher One Stop**

\* Resources for Differentiation      † Also in Spanish      ‡ In Haitian Creole and Vietnamese

## TEXT ANALYSIS: PLOT IN DRAMA

As you probably know, a **drama** is basically a story told in dialogue form. Like a work of fiction, drama establishes a setting, presents a series of **plot** events, and centers around one or more **conflicts** that the characters must cope with. Because a drama does not use a narrator to describe what happens, the plot unfolds through the characters' words and actions. As you read this drama, note what the dialogue and camera directions reveal about the setting, the conflict, and the unusual events that surround the cast of characters. Also, be ready for Stephen King's special brand of suspense.

## READING SKILL: READING A TELEPLAY

Reading a teleplay is different from reading a script for a stage play. Your mind's eye will be challenged to **visualize** what the camera is focusing on. For example, in *Sorry, Right Number*, when a camera direction calls for an extreme close-up and then takes you inside a telephone receiver, you have to imagine not only how this looks but also what effect it creates. In addition, in a teleplay, you don't have to wait for formal scene changes to have changes in setting, as you do with a regular stage play. You can be instantly thrown from one setting to the next, even from one time period to another, by a camera direction that reads "slam cut to."

Standard **dramatic conventions** in teleplays can also help you visualize the action. Like plays, teleplays begin with a list of characters, and each character's name is identified before his or her lines of dialogue. Additionally, stage directions—passages of italicized text—describe the location and action of the scene, as well as some sounds. By combining the two in your mind, you can "see" what is happening in the scene.

Before you read *Sorry, Right Number*, study Stephen King's note at the beginning of the teleplay to familiarize yourself with common teleplay terms. As you read, use your experience watching TV and movies to help you visualize what the camera wants you to see.

 Complete the activities in your **Reader/Writer Notebook**.

## Meet the Author

## Stephen King
**born 1947**

**From the Trash Can to the Bestseller List**
Stephen King nearly threw away his writing career before it began. He dumped the manuscript of his first horror novel, *Carrie*, into the trash, but his wife retrieved it and urged him to continue working on it. Later, after *Carrie* became a hit movie, King went on to have six titles on the *New York Times* bestseller list at the same time. Credited with reviving the market for both horror fiction and horror films, King has been called a "one-man entertainment industry."

**From Brain to Screen**
King has written that the idea for *Sorry, Right Number* came to him "one night on my way home from buying a pair of shoes." He wrote the script in two sittings and about a week later submitted it to a friend who produced a TV series called *Tales from the Darkside*. The friend bought the teleplay the day he read it and had it in production a week or two later; and it was broadcast a month after that—"one of the fastest turns from in-the-head to on-the-screen that I've ever heard of," King commented.

**BACKGROUND TO THE DRAMA**
**Writing for Television**
Mixed in with the camera directions in *Sorry, Right Number* are passages in King's own voice. King acts as both author and "narrator" of the play, frequently addressing the reader. He explains abbreviations, points out things he wants the reader to know, and comments on situations.

**Author Online**
Go to **thinkcentral.com**.
KEYWORD: HML9-155

155

## Teach

**TEXT ANALYSIS** — COMMON CORE — RL 5

### ● *Model the Skill:* PLOT IN DRAMA

To model how narrative prose and dialogue convey similar information in different ways, give these examples to students:

> The creature moved toward the two girls. They wanted to run, but the door was locked.

> "The creature's moving toward us, Amy!"

> "Run!"

> "It's no use. The door is locked."

Explain that the dialogue has more impact upon the reader because it conveys the emotions of the characters and intensifies the suspense as a result.

**GUIDED PRACTICE** Ask which approach—narrative prose or dialogue—reveals plot mainly through characters' words.

**READING SKILL** — COMMON CORE — RL 10

### ■ *Model the Skill:* READING A TELEPLAY

Tell students to imagine having to "watch" a scary movie or TV show with their eyes closed. Ask them how the experience would affect their enjoyment and their understanding of the plot. Tell students that because a teleplay is written to be performed on television, it is important for readers to think visually when reading one. Readers must "keep their eyes open" to see the events that are unfolding on the page.

**GUIDED PRACTICE** Ask students which they think would be scarier, and why: watching a scary movie without the sound or listening to it without the picture.

**R** RESOURCE MANAGER—Copy Master Reading a Teleplay p. 189 (for student use while reading the selection)

---

## DIFFERENTIATED INSTRUCTION

### FOR ENGLISH LANGUAGE LEARNERS
**Language: Skill Words** Make sure students understand the meanings of these words related to plot in drama:
- *drama:* a literary form in which dialogue—the words the characters say—tells the story
- *characters:* the people who take part in the story
- *plot:* the sequence of events in the story
- *conflicts:* the struggles that the characters face

**Media and Concepts** To build and reinforce the concept of plot sequence, show a video, such as *Back to the Future* or one you have in your classroom. Stop the video periodically to confirm that students understand the chronological shifts in the plot sequence. Ask students to respond orally to the following questions: What is the time period at the beginning of the video? When does the time period shift? What happens when this shift occurs? What is the time period at the end of the video?

### READ WITH A PURPOSE

*Help students set a purpose for reading. Tell them to read "Sorry, Right Number" to find out how the author creates suspense in a teleplay.*

### TIERED DISCUSSION PROMPTS

Use these prompts to help students understand the characters who have been introduced in lines 1–20, and the format of the teleplay:

**Connect** Think of your favorite television programs. How are the stories typically set up at the beginning? *Possible answer: They usually begin by establishing where the action is going to take place and who one or more of the main characters are, and hint at what the conflict will be that will drive the action. Students may give examples.*

**Analyze** What can you tell about Bill from Katie's conversation? *Possible answer: It seems as if Bill is a writer. He is prone to chronic worry and complains about his health.*

**Evaluate** How do setting and character work in this scene to point toward future conflicts? *Possible answer: The setting suggests that the Weidermans are well off; they have a comfortable home with modern conveniences. The dialogue suggests that potential problems may lie ahead for the Weidermans, possibly with regard to Bill's health.*

# SORRY, RIGHT NUMBER

## Stephen King

### CAST OF CHARACTERS

| | |
|---|---|
| Katie Weiderman | Polly Weiderman |
| Jeff Weiderman | Operator |
| Connie Weiderman | Dawn |
| Dennis Weiderman | Minister |
| Bill Weiderman | Groundskeeper |
| | Hank |

**Author's note:** Screenplay abbreviations are simple and exist, in this author's opinion, mostly to make those who write screenplays feel like lodge brothers.[1] In any case, you should be aware that *CU* means *close-up; ECU* means *extreme close-up; INT.* means *interior; EXT.* means *exterior; B.G.* means *background; POV* means *point of view.* Probably most of you knew all that stuff to begin with, right?

**Act I**                                    **Targeted Passage** ❶

(*Fade in on* Katie Weiderman's *mouth, ECU*)

(*She's speaking into the telephone. Pretty mouth; in a few seconds we'll see that the rest of her is just as pretty.*)

**Katie.** Bill? Oh, he says he doesn't feel very well, but he's always like that between books . . . can't

sleep, thinks every headache is the first symptom of a brain tumor . . . once he gets going on something new, he'll be fine.

10 (*Sound, B.G.: the television*)

(*The camera draws back.* Katie *is sitting in the kitchen phone nook, having a good gab with her sister while she idles through some catalogues. We should notice one not-quite-ordinary thing about the phone she's on: it's the sort with two lines. There are lighted buttons to show which ones are engaged. Right now only one—*Katie's*—is. As* Katie *continues her conversation, the camera swings away from her, tracks across the kitchen, and through the arched*

20 *doorway that leads into the family room.*)

**Katie** (*voice, fading*). Oh, I saw Janie Charlton today . . . yes! Big as a *house!* . . .

---

1. **lodge brothers:** members of the same men's social organization. Lodges sometimes have special rituals or vocabularies.

## DIFFERENTIATED INSTRUCTION

### FOR ENGLISH LANGUAGE LEARNERS

**Reading: Background** Tell students that they will be reading a teleplay, a play written for television. Have students share any experiences they have had watching a stage play.

**Options for Reading** Use the Readers Theater strategy to introduce the play. Assign the roles to groups of students.

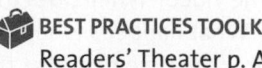 **BEST PRACTICES TOOLKIT**
Readers' Theater p. A1

### FOR STRUGGLING READERS

In combination with the *Audio Anthology CD*, use one or more Targeted Passages (pp. 156, 159, 167, 169, 170) to ensure that students focus on key story events, concepts, and skills. Targeted Passages are also good for English learners.

❶ **Targeted Passage [Lines 1–22]**
This passage sets the scene of the teleplay. It introduces one of the main characters

## BACKGROUND

**Television in the 1980s** "Sorry, Right Number" was written in 1987, a time when network television achieved new levels of realism in its prime-time progams. Even comedies like *Cheers* and *Wings* (mentioned on p. 158) focused on relationships between family and friends and gave a more accurate portrayal of American life than did the more idealized comedies of the 1950s and early 1960s. "Sorry, Right Number" portrays a family held together by strong relationships, but those bonds are about to be tested in some dramatic, even extraordinary ways.

## Analyze Visuals

**Activity** Ask students how the photograph relates to both the title and the opening scene of the teleplay. *Possible answer: The photograph shows a woman on the telephone; the teleplay opens with Katie Weiderman on the phone. The title is a play on the familiar phrase "sorry, wrong number," which a caller might say after dialing incorrectly.*

and gives readers an important piece of information.

- What "not-quite-ordinary" thing does the author want readers to take note of? (line 15)

- What significance do you think this detail might have for the rest of the story? (line 15)

**FOR ADVANCED LEARNERS/PRE–AP**

**Compare Genres** Remind students that this teleplay is a drama filled with suspense. Tell them that after reading the teleplay, they will work in small groups to pick a scene and rewrite it for another genre. Students might consider genres such as comedy, action, romance, or documentary. Have groups share their reworked scenes with the class and lead a class discussion on how the change in genre affects the impact and telling of the story.

Use these prompts to help students understand the interrelationships of the Weiderman family members as shown in lines 28–80:

**Connect** Based on your experience, do the relationships among the Weiderman children seem realistic? *Students will probably answer yes.*

**Analyze** Based on the dialogue among the children, what do you learn about the Weidermans as a family? *Possible answer: They are creatures of habit—they watch the same TV programs every week—but they are also thoughtful and close-knit.*

**Evaluate** What kind of mother is Katie? *Possible answer: She is caring and concerned, attentive even to the tone of her family's voices.*

---

**READING SKILL**

COMMON CORE
RL 10

**■ *Model the Skill*: READING A TELEPLAY**

Model for students how to read a teleplay. Point out that the author calls for two close-up (CU) shots on this page. Tell students that the first close-up is of the Dracula poster on the door to Bill's study (lines 81–87), while the second is of photographs of Katie and the Weiderman children (lines 88–92). Explain that since the two close-ups come so quickly after the other, the author has linked them in the mind of the reader. This creates suspense because readers wonder if the eerie caption on the poster hints at events in the plot that are yet to come.

---

(*She fades. The TV gets louder. There are three kids: Jeff,* eight, *Connie,* ten, *and Dennis,* thirteen. *Wheel of Fortune is on, but they're not watching. Instead they're engaged in that great pastime, Fighting About What Comes On Later.*)

**Jeff.** Come *onnn!* It was his first *book!*

**Connie.** His first *gross* book.

30 **Dennis.** We're gonna watch *Cheers* and *Wings,*[2] just like we do every week, Jeff.

(*Dennis speaks with the utter finality only a big brother can manage. "Wanna talk about it some more and see how much pain I can inflict on your scrawny body, Jeff?" his face says.*)

**Jeff.** Could we at least tape it?

**Connie.** We're taping CNN[3] for Mom. She said she might be on the phone with Aunt Lois for quite a while.

40 **Jeff.** How can you tape CNN, for God's sake? It *never stops!*

**Dennis.** That's what she likes about it.

**Connie.** And don't say God's sake, Jeffie—you're not old enough to talk about God except in church.

**Jeff.** Then don't call me Jeffie.

**Connie.** Jeffie, Jeffie, Jeffie.

(*Jeff gets up, walks to the window, and looks out into the dark. He's really upset. Dennis and Connie, in*
50 *the grand tradition of older brothers and sisters, are delighted to see it.*)

**Dennis.** Poor Jeffie.

**Connie.** I think he's gonna commit suicide.

**Jeff** (*turns to them*). It was his *first* book! Don't you guys even *care?*

**Connie.** Rent it down at the Video Stop tomorrow, if you want to see it so bad.

**Jeff.** They don't rent R-rated pictures to little kids and you know it!

60 **Connie** (*dreamily*). Shut up, it's Vanna! I *love* Vanna!

**Jeff.** Dennis—

**Dennis.** Go ask Dad to tape it on the VCR in his office and quit being such a totally annoying little booger.

(*Jeff crosses the room, poking his tongue out at Vanna White as he goes. The camera follows as he goes into the kitchen.*)

**Katie.** . . . so when he asked me if *Polly* had tested strep positive,[4] I had to remind him she's away at
70 prep school[5] . . . Lois, I miss her . . .

(*Jeff is just passing through, on his way to the stairs.*)

**Katie.** Will you kids *please* be quiet?

**Jeff** (*glum*). They'll be quiet. *Now.*

(*He goes up the stairs, a little dejected. Katie looks after him for a moment, loving and worried.*)

**Katie.** They're squabbling again. Polly used to keep them in line, but now that she's away at school . . . I don't know . . . maybe sending her to Bolton wasn't such a hot idea. Sometimes when
80 she calls home she sounds so *unhappy* . . .

(*INT. Bela Lugosi*[6] *as Dracula, CU*)

(*Drac's standing at the door of his Transylvanian castle. Someone has pasted a comic-balloon coming out of his mouth which reads: "Listen! My children of the night! What music they make!" The poster is on a door but we only see this as Jeff opens it and goes into his father's study.*)

(*INT. a photograph of Katie, CU*)

(*The camera holds, then pans slowly right. We pass
90 another photo, this one of Polly, the daughter away at school. She's a lovely girl of sixteen or so. Past Polly is Dennis . . . then Connie . . . then Jeff.*)

---

2. ***Cheers* and *Wings*:** popular television sitcoms of the 1980s and 1990s.

3. **CNN:** the Cable News Network.

4. **had tested strep positive:** had strep throat, an infection caused by bacteria called streptococci.

5. **prep school:** a private high school that prepares students for college.

6. **Bela Lugosi:** a Hungarian-born actor (1882–1956) best known for his roles in U.S. horror films of the 1930s and 1940s.

---

**DIFFERENTIATED INSTRUCTION**

**FOR ENGLISH LANGUAGE LEARNERS**

**Vocabulary Support** Use Knowledge Rating to teach these words: *tape* (line 36), *tradition* (line 50), *positive* (line 69), *residence* (line 133), *network* (line 116), *area* (line 314).

🧰 BEST PRACTICES TOOLKIT— Transparency Knowledge Rating p. E3

**Culture: Connect** Explain to students that *residence* means "home." Then point out that Katie's phone greeting, "Hello, Weiderman residence," is a common way to answer the phone in the United States. Have volunteers share phone greetings used in their own culture. Then have them repeat the phone greeting used by Katie Weiderman, replacing *Weiderman* with their own surnames.

(*The camera continues to pan and also widens out so we can see Bill Weiderman, a man of about forty-four. He looks tired. He's peering into the word-processor on his desk, but his mental crystal ball must be taking the night off, because the screen is blank. On the walls we see framed book-covers. All of them are spooky. One of the titles is* Ghost Kiss.)

100 (*Jeff comes up quietly behind his dad. The carpet muffles his feet. Bill sighs and shuts off the word-cruncher. A moment later Jeff claps his hands on his father's shoulders.*)

**Jeff.** BOOGA-BOOGA!

**Bill.** Hi, Jeffie.

(*He turns in his chair to look at his son, who is disappointed.*)

**Jeff.** How come you didn't get scared?

**Bill.** Scaring is my business. I'm case-hardened.
110 Something wrong?

**Jeff.** Daddy, can I watch the first hour of *Ghost Kiss* and you tape the rest? Dennis and Connie are hogging *everything*.

(*Bill swivels to look at the book-jacket, bemused.*)

**Bill.** You sure you want to watch *that*, champ? It's pretty—

**Jeff.** *Yes!*

**Targeted Passage** ②

(*INT.* Katie, *in the phone nook*)

(*In this shot, we clearly see the stairs leading to her*
120 *husband's study behind her.*)

**Katie.** I *really* think Jeff needs the orthodontic work but you know Bill—

(*The other line rings. The other light stutters.*)

**Katie.** That's just the other line, Bill will—

(*But now we see* Bill *and* Jeff *coming downstairs behind her.*)

**Bill.** Honey, where're the blank videotapes? I can't find any in the study and—

**Katie** (*to* Bill). *Wait!*
130 (*to* Lois). Gonna put you on hold a sec, Lo.

(*She does. Now both lines are blinking. She pushes the top one, where the new call has just come in.*)

**Katie.** Hello, Weiderman residence.

(*Sound: desperate sobbing*)

**Sobbing voice** (*filter*). Take . . . please take . . . t-t-

**Katie.** Polly? Is that you? What's wrong?

(*Sound: sobbing. It's awful, heartbreaking.*)

**Sobbing voice** (*filter*). Please—quick—

(*Sound: sobbing . . . Then, click! A broken*
140 *connection.*)

**Katie.** Polly, calm down! Whatever it is can't be that b—

(*hum of an open line*)

(*Jeff has wandered toward the TV room, hoping to find a blank tape.*)

**Analyze Visuals**

**Activity** Ask students how the doorway in the photograph functions as a transitional tool. *Possible answer: The door helps guide the reader from one scene to another.*

**REVISIT THE BIG QUESTION**
What sends a **CHILL** down your spine?
**Discuss** Up until the time Katie answers the other phone line in lines 133–143, the events described have been ordinary. What is it about the phone call that changes the mood of the story? *Possible answer: The voice on the phone is accompanied by "desperate sobbing," described as "awful, heartbreaking," and the connection is suddenly lost. The mood is now disturbing and unsettling.*

**FOR STRUGGLING READERS**

② **Targeted Passage** [Lines 118–143]

This passage brings readers back to the two-line telephone that was introduced on page 156. It marks a turning point in the plot as Katie puts a caller on hold to take another call.

- Why does Katie put her call on hold? (lines 123–130)

- Whose voice does Katie think she hears on the other line? (line 136)

- Why does the call end abruptly? (lines 138–140)

- What effect does this call have on the teleplay's level of suspense? (line 123)

## Analyze Visuals

**Activity** Ask students how the photograph relates to plot events. *Possible answer: The photograph shows a telephone keypad, underscoring the fact that a phone call has driven the plot so far.*

TEXT ANALYSIS  COMMON CORE

RL 5

● *Model the Skill:* **PLOT IN DRAMA**

Model for students how to identify conflict in dialogue in a teleplay. Explain that a key event in the plot is the mysterious phone call Katie receives. The author uses dialogue to make the reader feel how upset Katie is as she tries to figure out who was calling and why. Readers then learn from what Katie says that her first choice as to the identity of the caller is Polly (lines 136–157). Throughout this scene, Katie's tone is emotional while Bill remains calm. His attempts to calm Katie down only seem to make things worse, which intensifies the sense of conflict (lines 168–201).

**Extend the Discussion** How does Jeff add tension to the scene?

---

**Bill.** Who was that?

(*Without looking at her husband or answering him,* Katie *slams the lower button in again.*)

**Katie.** Lois? Listen, I'll call you back. That was
150 Polly, and she sounded very upset. No . . . she hung up. Yes. I will. Thanks.

(*She hangs up.*)

**Bill** (*concerned*). It was Polly?

**Katie.** Crying her head off. It sounded like she was trying to say "Please take me home" . . . I knew that school was bumming her out . . . Why I ever let you talk me into it . . .

(*She's rummaging frantically on her little phone desk. Catalogues go slithering to the floor around*
160 *her stool.*)

**Katie.** Connie did you take my address book?

**Connie** (*voice*). No, Mom.

(Bill *pulls a battered book out of his back pocket and pages through it.*)

**Bill.** I got it. Except—

**Katie.** I know, dorm phone is always busy. Give it to me.

**Bill.** Honey, calm down.

**Katie.** I'll calm down after I talk to her. She is
170 sixteen, Bill. Sixteen-year-old girls are prone to depressive interludes. Sometimes they even k . . . just give me the number!

**Bill.** 617-555-8641.

(*As she punches the numbers, the camera slides in to CU.*)

**Katie.** Come on, come on . . . don't be busy . . . just this once . . .

(*Sound: clicks. A pause. Then . . . the phone starts ringing.*)

180 **Katie** (*eyes closed*). Thank You, God.

**Voice** (*filter*). Hartshorn Hall, this is Frieda.

**Katie.** Could you call Polly to the phone? Polly Weiderman? This is Kate Weiderman. Her mother.

**Voice** (*filter*). hang on, please, Mrs. Weiderman.

(*Sound: the phone clunks down.*)

**Voice** (*filter, and very faint*). Polly? Pol? . . . Phone call! . . . It's your mother!

(*INT. a wider angle on the phone nook, with* Bill)

190 **Bill.** Well?

**Katie.** Somebody's getting her. I hope.

(Jeff *comes back in with a tape.*)

**Jeff.** I found one, Dad. Dennis hid em. As usual.

**Bill.** In a minute, Jeff. Go watch the tube.

**Jeff.** But—

**Bill.** I won't forget. Now go *on.*

(Jeff *goes.*)

**Katie.** Come on, come on, come on . . .

**Bill.** Calm down, Katie.

200 **Katie** (*snaps*). If you'd heard her, you wouldn't tell me to calm down! She sounded—

**Polly** (*filter, cheery voice*). Hi, mom!

**Katie.** Pol? Honey? Are you all right?

---

## DIFFERENTIATED INSTRUCTION

**FOR ENGLISH LANGUAGE LEARNERS**

**Vocabulary: Idioms** Use New Word Analysis to teach these idioms: *crying her head off* (line 154), "crying loudly"; *let it go* (line 199), "forget about it"; *getting her feet under her* (lines 193–194), "getting to know" or "getting used to".

 **BEST PRACTICES TOOLKIT—** Transparency New Word Analysis p. E8

**Polly** (*happy, bubbling voice*). Am I *all right?* I aced my bio exam, got a B on my French Conversational Essay, and Ronnie Hansen asked me to the Harvest Ball. I'm so all right that if one more good thing happens to me today, I'll probably blow up like the *Hindenburg.*[7]

210 **Katie.** You didn't just call me up, crying your head off?

(*We see by* Katie's *face that she already knows the answer to this question.*)

**Polly** (*filter*). Heck no!

**Katie.** I'm glad about your test and your date, honey. I guess it was someone else. I'll call you back, okay?

**Polly** (*filter*). 'Kay. Say hi to Dad!

**Katie.** I will.

220 (*INT. the phone nook, wider*)

**Bill.** She okay?

**Katie.** Fine. I could have *sworn* it was Polly, but . . . *she's* walking on air.

**Bill.** So it was a prank. Or someone who was crying so hard she dialed a wrong number . . . "through a shimmering film of tears," as we veteran hacks like to say.

**Katie.** It was not a prank and it was not a wrong number! It was someone in *my family!*

230 **Bill.** Honey, you can't know that.

**Katie.** No? If Jeffie called up, just crying, would you know it was him?

**Bill** (*struck by this*). Yeah, maybe. I guess I might.

(*She's not listening. She's punching numbers, fast.*)

**Bill.** Who you calling?

(*She doesn't answer him. Sound: phone rings twice. Then:*)

**Older Female Voice** (*filter*). Hello?

**Katie.** Mom? Are you . . . (*She pauses.*) Did you 240 call just a few seconds ago?

**Voice** (*filter*). No, dear . . . why?

**Katie.** Oh . . . you know these phones. I was talking to Lois and I lost the other call.

**Voice** (*filter*). Well, it wasn't me. Kate, I saw the *prettiest* dress in La Boutique today, and—

**Katie.** We'll talk about it later, Mom, okay?

**Voice** (*filter*). Kate, are you all right?

**Katie.** I have . . . Mom, I think maybe I've got diarrhea. I have to go. 'Bye.

250 (*She hangs up.* Bill *hangs on until she does; then he bursts into wild donkey-brays of laughter.*)

**Bill.** Oh boy . . . diarrhea . . . I gotta remember that the next time my agent calls . . . oh Katie, that was so cool—

**Katie** (*almost screaming*). *This is not funny!*

(Bill *stops laughing.*)

(*INT. the TV room*)

(Jeff *and* Dennis *have been tussling. They stop. All three kids look toward the kitchen.*)

260 (*INT. the phone nook, with* Bill *and* Katie)

**Katie.** *I tell you it was someone in my family and she sounded*—oh, you don't understand. I *knew* that voice.

**Bill.** But if Polly's okay and your mom's okay . . .

**Katie** (*positive*). It's Dawn.

**Bill.** Come on, hon, a minute ago you were sure it was Polly.

**Katie.** It *had* to be Dawn. I was on the phone with Lois and Mom's okay, so Dawn's the only other 270 one it *could* have been. She's the youngest . . . I could have mistaken her for Polly . . . and she's out there in that farmhouse alone with the baby!

**Bill** (*startled*). What do you mean, alone?

**Katie.** Jerry's in Burlington! It's Dawn! *Something's happened to Dawn!*

(Connie *comes into the kitchen, worried.*)

**Connie.** Mom? Is Aunt Dawn okay?

**Bill.** So far as we know, she's fine. Take it easy, doll. Bad to buy trouble before you know it's on sale.

---

7. *Hindenburg:* an airship that exploded, crashed, and burned spectacularly in 1937.

## TIERED DISCUSSION PROMPTS

Use these prompts to help students understand the author's technique for building suspense as shown in lines 224–265:

**Connect** After Katie speaks with Polly, Bill concludes that the sobbing phone call was either "a prank" or "someone who . . . dialed a wrong number." Katie, however, strongly disagrees. Do you agree with Bill or with Katie? Why? *Responses should reflect an understanding of the situation.*

**Analyze** How does the author maintain the tension level after Katie talks to Polly? *Possible answer: Katie insists that the call "was not a prank and it was not a wrong number! It was someone in my family!" Then she concludes that something must have happened to Dawn, her younger sister.*

**Evaluate** How does the difference in the way that Katie and Bill react to the phone call add to the suspense? *Possible answer: The contrast between Bill's relative calmness and Katie's apprehension heightens the suspense. The reader isn't sure who more accurately grasps what's going on, Bill or Katie.*

## FOR ADVANCED LEARNERS/PRE–AP

**Draw Conclusions About Characterization**
[paired-activity option] Bill tells Katie, "Bad to buy trouble before you know it's on sale." Discuss with students whether they think this is an appropriate comment. Use a Storyboard to help pairs of students write and perform an extended dialogue between Bill and Katie on this topic.

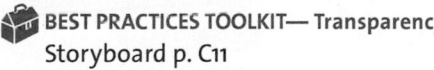 **BEST PRACTICES TOOLKIT**— Transparency Storyboard p. C11

## TIERED DISCUSSION PROMPTS

Use these prompts to help students understand how the author builds suspense in lines 287–326 through a progression of events and attitudes:

**Connect** Do you feel that the operator acted appropriately in this scene? Explain. *Responses should reflect an understanding of the situation and how the operator's actions did or did not reflect the situation.*

**Analyze** How is Bill's attitude changing? What is the effect of this change on the level of tension? **Possible answer:** *Previously, Bill seemed relatively unconcerned. He no longer seems quite as confident that nothing is wrong, which makes readers wonder whether Katie's fears may be well-founded.*

**Evaluate** Why do you think King includes the operator's personal comments about Bill's books? **Possible answer:** *The operator's chatty conversation—broken off when Bill abruptly hangs up—contrasts sharply with the stress that Katie and Bill are feeling, which helps heighten the suspense.*

### REVIST THE BIG QUESTION

## What sends a **CHILL** down your spine?

**Discuss** A supernatural event is an event that could not happen naturally in our world under any circumstances. What natural and supernatural reasons might account for the phone at the farmhouse being off the hook as shown in lines 323–329? **Possible answers:** *Natural— someone took the phone off the hook because he or she didn't want to be disturbed; the phone was knocked off the hook during a struggle; an intruder cut the phone wires so no one could call for help. Supernatural— some type of energy from space or another dimension is interfering with the phone lines.*

---

280 (Katie *punches numbers and listens. Sound: the dah-dah-dah of a busy signal.* Katie *hangs up.* Bill *looks a question at her with raised eyebrows.*)

**Katie.** Busy.

**Bill.** Katie, are you sure—

**Katie.** She's the only one left—it had to be her. Bill, I'm scared. Will you drive me out there?

(Bill *takes the phone from her.*)

**Bill.** What's her number?

**Katie.** 555-6169.

290 (Bill *dials. Gets a busy. Hangs up and punches 0.*)

**Operator** (*filter*). Operator.

**Bill.** I'm trying to reach my sister-in-law, operator. The line is busy. I suspect there may be a problem. Can you break into the call, please?

(*INT. the door to the TV room*)

(*All three kids are standing there, silent and worried.*)

(*INT. the phone nook, with* Bill *and* Katie)

**Operator** (*filter*). What is your name, sir?

**Bill.** William Weiderman. My number is—

300 **Operator** (*filter*). Not the William Weiderman that wrote *Spider Doom?!*

**Bill.** Yes, that was mine. If—

**Operator** (*filter*). Oh, I just *loved* that book! I love *all* your books! I—

**Bill.** I'm delighted you do. But right now my wife is very worried about her sister. If it's possible for you to—

**Operator** (*filter*). Yes, I can do that. Please give me your number, Mr. Weiderman, for the records.

310 (*She giggles.*) I *promise* not to give it out.

**Bill.** It's 555-4408.

**Operator** (*filter*). And the call number?

**Bill** (*looks at* Katie). Uh . . .

**Katie.** 555-6169.

**Bill.** 555-6169.

**Operator** (*filter*). Just a moment, Mr. Weiderman . . . *Night of the Beast* was also great, by the way. Hold on.

(*Sound: telephonic clicks and clacks*)

---

320 **Katie.** Is she—

**Bill.** Yes. Just . . .

(*There's one final click.*)

**Operator** (*filter*). I'm sorry, Mr. Weiderman, but that line is not busy. It's off the hook. I wonder if I sent you my copy of *Spider Doom*—

(Bill *hangs up the phone.*)

**Katie.** Why did you hang up?

**Bill.** She can't break in. Phone's not busy. It's off the hook.

330 (*They stare at each other bleakly.*)

(*EXT. A low-slung sports car passes the camera. Night.*)

(*INT. the car, with* Katie *and* Bill)

(Katie*'s scared.* Bill, *at the wheel, doesn't look exactly calm.*)

**Katie.** Hey, Bill—tell me she's all right.

**Bill.** She's all right.

**Katie.** Now tell me what you really think.

**Bill.** Jeff snuck up behind me tonight and put the

340 old booga-booga on me. He was disappointed as hell when I didn't jump. I told him I was case-hardened. (*pause*) I lied.

**Katie.** Why did Jerry have to move out there when he's gone half the time? Just her and that little tiny baby? *Why?*

**Bill.** Shh, Kate. We're almost there.

**Katie.** Go faster.

(*EXT. the car*)

(*He does. That car is smokin.*)

350 (*INT. the Weiderman TV room*)

(*The tube's still on and the kids are still there, but the horsing around has stopped.*)

**Connie.** Dennis, do you think Aunt Dawn's okay?

**Dennis** (*thinks she's dead, decapitated by a maniac*). Yeah. Sure she is.

(*INT. the phone, POV from the TV room*)

(*just sitting there on the wall in the phone nook, lights dark, looking like a snake ready to strike*)

(*Fade out.*)

---

## DIFFERENTIATED INSTRUCTION

### FOR ENGLISH LANGUAGE LEARNERS

**Culture: Clarify** Explain that the words *booga-booga* are common children's language for magic spells and scary things in general. Point out other uniquely American references and explain their meanings. For example:

- *R-rated pictures* (line 58): films meant for adult audiences. *R* stands for "restricted."

- *Harvest Ball* (line 207): a school dance that takes place in the fall

- *Huey Lewis and the News* (line 62): a musical group popular in the 1980s

- *It's network* (line 116): The program is on a channel that is available to all.

- *boogeyman* (line 135): an imaginary monster

**Analyze Visuals**

Activity Ask students how the photograph relates to the atmosphere of the story.
*Possible answer: The photograph shows how isolated and vulnerable the house is, visually suggesting that the occupants may be in danger.*

**READING SKILL**    COMMON CORE   RL 10

**■ READING A TELEPLAY**

How do the first two camera directions at the beginning of Act II build suspense?
*Possible answer: The first two camera directions at the beginning of Act II connect an exterior shot of Dawn's isolated farmhouse with an interior shot in which Katie says how scared she is (line 1–7). Given what the reader now knows about the location of the farmhouse, Katie's fear may be justified.*

**Act II**

(*EXT. an isolated farmhouse*)

(*A long driveway leads up to it. There's one light on in the living room. Car lights sweep up the driveway. The Weiderman car pulls up close to the garage and stops.*)

(*INT. the car, with* Bill *and* Katie)

**Katie.** I'm scared.

(Bill *bends down, reaches under his seat, and brings out a pistol.*)

10 **Bill** (*solemnly*). Booga-booga.

**Katie** (*total surprise*). How long have you had that?

**Bill.** Since last year. I didn't want to scare you or the kids. I've got a license to carry. Come on.

(*EXT.* Bill *and* Katie)

(*They get out.* Katie *stands by the front of the car while* Bill *goes to the garage and peers in.*)

**Bill.** Her car's here.

(*The camera tracks with them to the front door. Now we can hear the TV, playing loud.* Bill *pushes the*

**FOR ENGLISH LANGUAGE LEARNERS**

**Vocabulary: Word Associations and Phrasal Verbs** As students read, help them identify and understand words that typically occur together in the English language, such as these:

• *right now* (line 17): "at the present time"

• *hot idea* (line 79): "great suggestion"

• *calm down* (lines 141, 168): "relax"

• *take it easy* (line 278): "relax"

• *come on* (line 13): "follow me"

• *heart attack* (lines 264–265): a sudden blockage of blood flow to the heart

• *learning process* (p. 171): the method or steps involved in learning something

**FOR ADVANCED LEARNERS/PRE–AP**

**Apply Similar Similes** [paired-activity option]
At the end of Act I, King compares the phone to "a snake ready to strike." Discuss what King is trying to communicate with this simile. Have students write two original similes or metaphors that would convey a similar feeling.

Use these prompts to help students understand plot structure and development as shown in Act II, lines 1–65.

**Connect** Have you or someone you know ever encountered something unusually suspicious or out of the ordinary? Did your encounter turn out to be easily explained or did it remain a mystery? *Accept all reasonable responses.*

**Analyze** What chain of events has intensified the suspense at this point in the plot? *Possible answers: King increases the suspense through a sequence of events: Bill takes out a gun; there is no answer to the doorbell; the lock has been tampered with; as Bill enters the house, he tells the "terrified" Katie to "be ready to run."*

**Evaluate** How have the roles of Bill and Katie changed as a result of plot development at this point? *Possible answer: Earlier, it was mainly Katie who set plot events into motion. Now it is Bill who is controlling the action.*

20 doorbell. *We hear it inside. They wait.* Katie *pushes it. Still no answer. She pushes it again and doesn't take her finger off.* Bill *looks down at:)*

(*EXT. the lock,* Bill's *POV*)

(*big scratches on it*)

(*EXT.* Bill *and* Katie)

**Bill** (*low*). The lock's been tampered with.

(Katie *looks, and whimpers.* Bill *tries the door. It opens. The TV is louder.*)

**Bill.** Stay behind me. Be ready to run if something 30 happens. I wish I'd left you home, Kate.

(*He starts in.* Katie *comes after him, terrified, near tears.*)

(*INT.* Dawn *and Jerry's living room*)

(*From this angle we see only a small section of the room. The TV is much louder.* Bill *enters the room, gun up. He looks to the right . . . and suddenly all the tension goes out of him. He lowers the gun.*)

**Katie** (*draws up beside him*). Bill . . . what . . . (*He points.*)

40 (*INT. the living room, wide,* Bill *and* Katie's *POV*)

(*The place looks like a cyclone hit it . . . but it wasn't robbery and murder that caused this mess; only a healthy eighteen-month-old baby. After a strenuous day of trashing the living room, Baby got tired and Mommy got tired and they fell asleep on the couch together. The baby is in* Dawn's *lap. There is a pair of Walkman earphones on her head. There are toys—tough plastic Sesame Street and PlaySkool stuff, for the most part—scattered hell to breakfast. The baby 50 has also pulled most of the books out of the bookcase. Had a good munch on one of them, too, by the look.* Bill *goes over and picks it up. It is* Ghost Kiss.)

**Bill.** I've had people say they just eat my books up, but this is ridiculous.

(*He's amused.* Katie *isn't. She walks over to her sister, ready to be mad . . . but she sees how really exhausted* Dawn *looks and softens.*)

(*INT.* Dawn *and the baby,* Katie's *POV*)

(*Fast asleep and breathing easily, like a Raphael 60 painting of Madonna and Child.[8] The camera pans down to: the Walkman. We can hear the faint strains of Huey Lewis and the News. The camera pans a bit further to a Princess telephone[9] on the table by the chair. It's off the cradle. Not much; just enough to break the connection and scare people to death.*)

(*INT.* Katie)

(*She sighs, bends down, and replaces the phone. Then she pushes the stop button on the Walkman.*)

(*INT.* Dawn, Bill, *and* Katie)

70 (Dawn *wakes up when the music stops. Looks at* Bill *and* Katie, *puzzled.*)

**Dawn** (*fuzzed out*). Well . . . hi.

(*She realizes she's got the Walkman phones on and removes them.*)

**Bill.** Hi, Dawn.

**Dawn** (*still half asleep*). Shoulda called, guys. Place is a mess.

(*She smiles. She's radiant when she smiles.*)

**Katie.** We *tried.* The operator told Bill the phone 80 was off the hook. I thought something was wrong. How can you sleep with that music blasting?

**Dawn.** It's restful. (*Sees the gnawed book* Bill's *holding*) Oh Bill, I'm sorry! Justin's teething and—

**Bill.** There are critics who'd say he picked just the right thing to teethe on. I don't want to scare you, beautiful, but somebody's been at your front door lock with a screwdriver or something. Whoever it was forced it.

**Dawn.** Gosh, no! That was Jerry, last week. I 90 locked us out by mistake and he didn't have his key and the spare wasn't over the door like it's supposed to be. He was mad because he had to take a whiz real bad and so he took the screwdriver to it. It didn't work, either—that's one tough lock. (*pause*) By the time I found my key he'd already gone in the bushes.

---

8. **Raphael . . . Madonna and Child:** Raphael (1483–1520) was a well-known painter of mostly religious subjects in the period known as the Renaissance.

9. **Princess telephone:** an early type of compact telephone, popular in the 1960s.

## DIFFERENTIATED INSTRUCTION

### FOR ENGLISH LANGUAGE LEARNERS

**Media and Language** Show an excerpt of the television production of *Sorry, Right Number* or another suspenseful teleplay, and ask students to note unfamiliar words. After students look up the meaning of each word, have them write a paragraph about the teleplay that includes at least three of the words.

### FOR ADVANCED LEARNERS/PRE–AP

**First-Person Narrative** Ask students to write a first-person narrative from Dawn's point of view describing Bill and Katie's entrance. Use details from the narrator's commentary as well as what you have learned about the characters to develop the scene. Then have students read their narratives aloud.

**Bill.** If it wasn't forced, how come I could just open the door and walk in?

**Dawn** (*guiltily*). Well . . . sometimes I forget to
100 lock it.

**Katie.** You didn't call me tonight, Dawn?

**Dawn.** Gee, no! I didn't call *anyone!* I was too busy chasing Justin around! He kept wanting to eat the fabric softener! Then he got sleepy and I sat down here and thought I'd listen to some tunes while I waited for your movie to come on, Bill, and I fell asleep—

(*At the mention of the movie* Bill *starts visibly and looks at the book. Then he glances at his watch.*)

110 **Bill.** I promised to tape it for Jeff. Come on, Katie, we've got time to get back.

**Katie.** Just a second.

(*She picks up the phone and dials.*)

**Dawn.** Gee, Bill, do you think Jeffie's old enough to watch something like that?

**Bill.** It's network. They take out the blood-bags.

**Dawn** (*confused but amiable*). Oh. That's good.

(*INT.* Katie, *CU*)

**Dennis** (*filter*). Hello?

120 **Katie.** Just thought you'd like to know your Aunt Dawn's fine.

**Dennis** (*filter*). Oh! Cool. Thanks, Mom.

(*INT. the phone nook, with* Dennis *and the others*)

(*He looks* very *relieved.*)

**Dennis.** Aunt Dawn's okay.

(*INT. the car, with* Bill *and* Katie)

(*They drive in silence for awhile.*)

**Katie.** You think I'm a hysterical idiot, don't you?

**Bill** (*genuinely surprised*). No! I was scared, too.

130 **Katie.** You sure you're not mad?

**Bill.** I'm too relieved. (*laughs*) She's sort of a scatterbrain, old Dawn, but I love her.

**Katie** (*leans over and kisses him*). I love *you*. You're a sweet man.

---

**Bill.** I'm the *boogeyman!*

**Katie.** I am not fooled, sweetheart.

(*EXT. the car*)

(*Passes the camera and we dissolve to:*)

(*INT.* Jeff, *in bed*)

140 (*His room is dark. The covers are pulled up to his chin.*)

**Jeff.** You *promise* to tape the rest?

(*Camera widens out so we can see* Bill, *sitting on the bed.*)

**Bill.** I promise.

**Jeff.** I especially liked the part where the dead guy ripped off the punk rocker's head.

**Bill.** Well . . . they *used* to take out all the blood-bags.

150 **Jeff.** What, Dad?

**Bill.** Nothing. I love you, Jeffie.

**Jeff.** I love you, too. So does Rambo.

(Jeff *holds up a stuffed dragon of decidedly unmilitant aspect.*[10] Bill *kisses the dragon, then* Jeff.)

**Bill.** 'Night.

**Jeff.** 'Night. (*as* Bill *reaches his door*) Glad Aunt Dawn was okay.

**Bill.** Me too.

(*He goes out.*)

160 (*INT. TV, CU*)

(*A guy who looks like he died in a car crash about two weeks prior to filming [and has since been subjected to a lot of hot weather] is staggering out of a crypt. The camera widens to show* Bill, *releasing the VCR pause button.*)

**Katie** (*voice*). Booga-booga.

(Bill *looks around companionably. The camera widens out more to show* Katie, *wearing a nightgown.*)

170 **Bill.** Same to you. I missed the first forty seconds or so after the break. I had to kiss Rambo.

**Katie.** You sure you're not mad at me, Bill?

---

10. **unmilitant aspect:** unaggressive appearance.

## ● PLOT IN DRAMA

King has ruled out characters who could have been responsible for the mysterious call—Polly, Katie's mother, and Dawn. How does he use dialogue to maintain suspense? ***Possible answer:*** *The reader's attention has been drawn more and more to the character of Bill. The reader learns that Bill has had health problems (line 5) and that he secretly obtained a permit to carry a gun (Act II, lines 8–13). Now, on page 166, Bill is going to be alone in his study.*

**Extend the Discussion** How do repeated references to the horror movie based on Bill's book add suspense?

---

**FOR ADVANCED LEARNERS/PRE–AP**

**Analyze Plot Devices** King structures the plot to sustain the mood and keep readers involved.

1. Have students discuss how King uses patterns of rising and falling action that result in alternating periods of tension and relaxation.

2. Have pairs of students make a Two-Column Chart listing excerpts that demonstrate tension or relaxation.

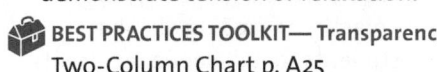 **BEST PRACTICES TOOLKIT—** Transparency Two-Column Chart p. A25

## What sends a **CHILL** down your spine?

**Discuss** What, if any, supernatural events have taken place so far? *Possible answers: Some students may think that all the events so far have been ordinary. Others may think that the phone call came from a supernatural source that has yet to be explored.*

---

(*He goes to her and kisses her.*)

**Bill.** Not even a smidge.

**Katie.** It's just that I could have sworn it was one of mine. You know what I mean? One of mine?

**Bill.** Yes.

**Katie.** I can still hear those sobs. So lost . . . so heartbroken.

180 **Bill.** Kate, have you ever thought you recognized someone on the street, and called her, and when she finally turned around it was a total stranger?

**Katie.** Yes, once. In Seattle. I was in a mall and I thought I saw my old roommate. I . . . oh. I see what you're saying.

**Bill.** Sure. There are sound-alikes as well as look-alikes.

**Katie.** But . . . *you know your own.* At least I thought so until tonight.

190 (*She puts her cheek on his shoulder, looking troubled.*)

**Katie.** I was so *positive* it was Polly . . .

**Bill.** Because you've been worried about her getting her feet under her at the new school . . . but judging from the stuff she told you tonight, I'd say she's doing just fine in that department. Wouldn't you?

**Katie.** Yes . . . I guess I would.

**Bill.** Let it go, hon.

200 **Katie** (*looks at him closely*). I hate to see you looking so tired. Hurry up and have an idea, you.

**Bill.** Well, I'm trying.

**Katie.** You coming to bed?

**Bill.** Soon as I finish taping this for Jeff.

**Katie** (*amused*). Bill, that machine was made by Japanese technicians who think of near everything. It'll run on its own.

**Bill.** Yeah, but it's been a long time since I've seen this one, and . . .

210 **Katie.** Okay. Enjoy. I think I'll be awake for a little while.

(*She starts out, then turns in the doorway as something else strikes her.*)

**Katie.** If they show the part where the punk's head gets—

**Bill** (*guiltily*). I'll edit it.

**Katie.** 'Night. And thanks again. For everything.

(*She leaves. Bill sits in his chair.*)

(*INT. TV, CU*)

220 (*A couple is necking in a car. Suddenly the passenger door is ripped open by the dead guy and we dissolve to:*)

(*INT. Katie, in bed*)

(*It's dark. She's asleep. She wakes up . . . sort of.*)

**Katie** (*sleepy*). Hey, big guy—

(*She feels for him, but his side of the bed is empty, the coverlet still pulled up. She sits up. Looks at:*)

(*INT. a clock on the night-table, Katie's POV*)

(*It says 2:03 A.M. Then it flashes to 2:04.*)

(*INT. Katie*)

230 (*Fully awake now. And concerned. She gets up, puts on her robe, and leaves the bedroom.*)

(*INT. the TV screen, CU*)

(*snow*)

**Katie** (*voice, approaching*). Bill? Honey? You okay? Bill? Bi—

(*INT. Katie, in Bill's study*)

(*She's frozen, wide-eyed with horror.*)

(*INT. Bill, in his chair*)

(*He's slumped to one side, eyes closed, hand inside his*
240 *shirt. Dawn was sleeping. Bill is not.*)

(*EXT. a coffin, being lowered into a grave*)

**Minister** (*voice*). And so we commit the earthly remains of William Weiderman to the ground, confident of his spirit and soul. "Be ye not cast down, brethren . . ."

(*EXT. graveside*)

---

## DIFFERENTIATED INSTRUCTION

### FOR STRUGGLING READERS

**Develop Reading Fluency** Use the exchange between Katie and Bill (page 166) to give students practice in reading dialogue. Remind students that dialogue represents a conversation between people. Tell them that fluent readers read dialogue with expression, using punctuation marks and character directions to show them when to pause or when to make changes in their intonation to indicate statements or questions.

First model for students an effective reading of the dialogue. (You might ask a proficient reader to read aloud one character while you read the other.) Then have students work in mixed-ability groups to practice reading the dialogue on p. 166. Conclude the activity by asking students to discuss how taking note of the punctuation and character directions helped them in their reading.

**R** RESOURCE MANAGER—Copy Masters
Reading Fluency p. 194

(*All the Weidermans are ranged here.* Katie *and* Polly *wear identical black dresses and veils.* Connie *wears a black skirt and white blouse.* Dennis *and*
250 Jeff *wear black suits.* Jeff *is crying. He has Rambo the Dragon under his arm for a little extra comfort.*)

(*Camera moves in on Katie. Tears course slowly down her cheeks. She bends and gets a handful of earth. Tosses it into the grave.*)

**Katie.** Love you, big guy.

(*EXT.* Jeff)

(*weeping*)                                    **Targeted Passage**

(*EXT. looking down into the grave*)

(*scattered earth on top of the coffin*)

260 (*Dissolve to:*)

(*EXT. the grave*)

(*A* Groundskeeper *pats the last sod into place.*)

**Groundskeeper.** My wife says she wishes you'd written a couple more before you had your heart attack, mister. (*pause*) I like Westerns, m'self.

(*The* Groundskeeper *walks away, whistling.*)

(*Dissolve to:*)

(*EXT. A church. Day.*)

(*Title card: Five Years Later*)

270 (*The Wedding March is playing.* Polly, *older and radiant with joy, emerges into a pelting shower of rice. She's in a wedding gown, her new husband by her side.*)

(*Celebrants throwing rice line either side of the path. From behind the bride and groom come others. Among them are* Katie, Dennis, Connie, *and* Jeff . . . *all five years older. With* Katie *is another man. This is* Hank. *In the interim,* Katie *has also taken a husband.*)

⓷

## Analyze Visuals

How does the photograph relate to the action described on page 167? *Possible answer: The rows of tombstones in the photograph suggest death and the passage of time, which is fitting for a passage that deals with both Bill's funeral and Polly's wedding five years later.*

**READING SKILL**

COMMON CORE

RL 10

### ● READING A TELEPLAY

Like other narratives, teleplays need to condense the passage of time but not leave out important events. What devices does King use on page 167 to disclose important events that happen to the Weidermans over a period of time? *Possible answer: King links a series of exterior shots with a brief monologue and narrator's commentary to move from Bill's death to Polly's wedding. The first three shots disclose Bill's death by building from the shot of Katie using the nickname "big guy," an affectionate term she had for her husband, to a shot of Jeff crying, to a shot of a coffin in a grave. The fourth exterior shot, accompanied by a short monologue by a groundskeeper, discloses that Bill died from a heart attack. The fifth exterior shot of the church shows Polly emerging in a wedding gown and the title card tells us that it is five years later.*

---

**FOR ADVANCED LEARNERS/PRE–AP**

**Research Activity: The Undead** Throughout the teleplay, King has included references to horror stories and movies, such as *Ghost Kiss*, written by the character Bill, and *Dracula*. Have students research classic horror stories and legends about the undead and present their findings to the class.

**FOR STRUGGLING READERS**

⓷ **Targeted Passage** [Lines 263–279]

This brief section explains the passage of time and describes very important events that have occurred in the interim.

• To whom is the groundskeeper speaking? (lines 263–266)

• How much time passes between the funeral and Polly's wedding? How do you think this passage of time has changed the Weiderman family? (line 269)

## TIERED DISCUSSION PROMPTS

Use these prompts to help students understand the relationship between Polly and Hank as shown in lines 270–289:

**Connect**  Do you feel that the Weidermans are depicted as behaving in a realistic manner following Bill's death? *Accept thoughtful answers.*

**Analyze**  What might have caused problems between Polly and Hank in the past? *Possible answer: Judging from Hank's comment to Polly, it is likely that Polly missed her natural father and resented Hank because he took the father's place in the household.*

**Evaluate**  How does the reference to the tension between Hank and Polly contribute to the plot? *Possible answer: The tension indicates that Bill is very much missed and his death is still unresolved for the family.*

---

280  (Polly *turns and her mother is there.*)

**Polly.** Thank you, Mom.

**Katie** (*crying*). Oh doll, you're so welcome.

(*They embrace. After a moment* Polly *draws away and looks at* Hank. *There is a brief moment of tension, and then* Polly *embraces* Hank, *too.*)

**Polly.** Thank you too, Hank. I'm sorry I was such a creep for so long . . .

**Hank** (*easily*). You were never a creep, Pol. A girl only has one father.

290  **Connie.** Throw it! Throw it!

(*After a moment,* Polly *throws her bouquet.*)

(*EXT. the bouquet, CU, slow motion*)

(*turning and turning through the air*)

(*dissolves to:*)

(*INT. The study, with* Katie. *Night.*)

(*The word-processor has been replaced by a wide lamp looming over a stack of blueprints. The book jackets have been replaced by photos of buildings.*)

## DIFFERENTIATED INSTRUCTION

### FOR ADVANCED LEARNERS/PRE–AP

**Create a Monologue**  Write a monologue in Polly's voice that might be used as a voice-over for the shot of her tossing the bouquet. The monologue should include questions she might have about past events as well as concerns she might have about the future. Have students perform their monologues for the class.

Ones that have first been built in Hank's mind, presumably.)

(Katie *is looking at the desk, thoughtful and a little sad.*)

**Hank** (*voice*). Coming to bed, Kate?

(*She turns and the camera widens out to give us Hank.* *He's wearing a robe over pajamas. She comes to him and gives him a little hug, smiling. Maybe we notice a few streaks of gray in her hair; her pretty pony has done its fair share of running since Bill died.*)

**Katie.** In a little while. A woman doesn't see her first one get married every day, you know.

**Hank.** I know.

(*The camera follows as they walk from the work area of the study to the more informal area. This is much the same as it was in the old days, with a coffee table, stereo, TV, couch, and Bill's old easy-chair. She looks at this.*)

**Hank.** You still miss him, don't you?

**Katie.** Some days more than others. You didn't know, and Polly didn't remember.

**Hank** (*gently*). Remember what, doll?

**Katie.** Polly got married on the five-year anniversary of Bill's death.

**Hank** (*hugs her*). Come on to bed, why don't you?

**Katie.** In a little while.

**Hank.** Okay. Maybe I'll still be awake.

(*He kisses her, then leaves, closing the door behind him. Katie sits in Bill's old chair. Close by, on the coffee table, is a remote control for the TV and an extension phone. Katie looks at the blank TV, and the camera moves in on her face. One tear rims one eye, sparkling like a sapphire.*)

**Katie.** I *do* still miss you, big guy. Lots and lots. Every day. And you know what? It hurts.

(*The tear falls. She picks up the TV remote and pushes the on button.*)

(*INT. TV, Katie's POV*)

(*An ad for Ginsu Knives comes to an end and is replaced by a star logo.*)

④

**Targeted Passage**

---

**Announcer** (*voice*). Now back to Channel 63's Thursday night Star Time Movie . . . *Ghost Kiss.*

(*The logo dissolves into a guy who looks like he died in a car crash about two weeks ago and has since been subjected to a lot of hot weather. He comes staggering out of the same old crypt.*)

(*INT. Katie*)

(*Terribly startled—almost horrified. She hits the off button on the remote control. The TV blinks off.*)

(*Katie's face begins to work. She struggles against the impending emotional storm, but the coincidence of the movie is just one thing too many on what must have already been one of the most emotionally trying days of her life. The dam breaks and she begins to sob . . . terrible, heartbroken sobs. She reaches out for the little table by the chair, meaning to put the remote control on it, and knocks the phone onto the floor.*)

(*Sound: the hum of an open line*)

(*Her tear-stained face grows suddenly still as she looks at the telephone. Something begins to fill it . . . an idea? an intuition? Hard to tell. And maybe it doesn't matter.*)

(*INT. the telephone, Katie's POV*)

(*The camera moves in to ECU . . . moves in until the dots in the off-the-hook receiver look like chasms.*)

(*sound of open-line buzz up to loud*)

(*We go into the black . . . and hear:*)

**Bill** (*voice*). Who are you calling? Who do you *want* to call? Who *would* you call, if it wasn't too late?

(*INT. Katie*)

(*There is now a strange hypnotized look on her face. She reaches down, scoops the telephone up, and punches in numbers, seemingly at random.*)

(*Sound: ringing phone*)

(*Katie continues to look hypnotized. The look holds until the phone is answered . . . and she hears herself on the other end of the line.*)

**Katie** (*voice; filter*). Hello, Weiderman residence.

(*Katie—our present-day Katie with the streaks of gray in her hair—goes on sobbing, yet an expression of*

---

300

310

320

330

340

350

360

370

380

## Analyze Visuals

**Activity** Ask students how the photograph relates to both the story's atmosphere and plot.

*Possible answer:* *The mood of the photograph suggests the eerie events that occur on page 169, which is where the television comes into play.*

## TIERED DISCUSSION PROMPTS

Use these prompts to help students understand the events that take place in lines 340–369:

**Connect** Have you ever experienced any extraordinary coincidences in your life? Explain. *Answers will vary.*

**Analyze** How does the TV announcer's reference to the movie *Ghost Kiss* add a creepy, supernatural element to the plot?
*Possible answer: Ghost Kiss is a horror movie made from Bill's first book. It is also the same movie that was playing on TV—and that Bill was recording for his son Jeff—when Bill died from a heart attack exactly five years earlier.*

**Synthesize** At what point does King move out of the realm of "ordinary events"? How does he signal this shift in the teleplay?
*Possible answer: The camera moves into the telephone receiver. Then we hear Bill's voice, prompting Katie to make a phone call, which turns out to be to herself.*

---

**FOR STRUGGLING READERS**

④ **Targeted Passage** [Lines 322–377]

This passage builds suspense and also leads to the resolution of the plot.

- Why does Katie begin sobbing? (lines 349–354)
- How do the camera directions add to the drama before Katie picks up the telephone? (lines 362–364)
- What suggests that something supernatural is occurring? (lines 358–377)

**Using Content-area Vocabulary** To provide students with practice in writing using content-area vocabulary, ask them to write a response to this prompt: Write a paragraph in which you trace how King builds suspense in this teleplay. Be sure to discuss the conflict and its resolution, using evidence from the teleplay to support your ideas.

## What sends a CHILL down your spine?

What does Katie realize that is pivotal to the plot? *Possible answer: The mysterious phone call turns out to be Katie from the future trying to warn herself in the past about Bill's imminent heart attack.*

## SELECTION WRAP–UP

**READ WITH A PURPOSE** Now that students have read the selection, ask them to detail one or two techniques that the author uses to build suspense. Then have students discuss how the story might differ if it was written in another format, like a short story. *Possible answers: The author uses ominous references to horror movies as well as the mystery of who called Katie to build suspense gradually over the course of the story. The story might differ as a short story in that there would be no camera shots, there might be more detailed descriptions of the characters and settings, and readers might get to read the internal thoughts of the characters.*

★ **CRITIQUE** Ask students to evaluate King's story for believability. Have them identify specific places where the author either gains or loses credibility. Encourage students to share and compare their reactions regarding the "surprise" ending.

### INDEPENDENT READING

Students may also enjoy reading Stephen King's "Thinner," a suspenseful story about the unusual effects an accident has on one man.

---

*desperate hope is trying to be born on her face. On some level she understands that the depth of her grief has allowed a kind of telephonic time-travel. She's trying to talk, to force the words out.)*

**Katie** *(sobbing).* Take . . . please take . . . t-t-

*(INT. Katie, in the phone nook, reprise)*

*(It's five years ago, Bill is standing beside her, looking concerned. Jeff is wandering off to look for a blank tape in the other room.)*

390 **Katie.** Polly? What's wrong?

*(INT. Katie, in the study)*

**Katie** *(sobbing).* Please—quick—

*(Sound: click of a broken connection)*

**Katie** *(screaming).* Take him to the hospital! If you want him to live, take him to the hospital! He's going to have a heart attack! He—

*(Sound: hum of an open line)*

*(Slowly, very slowly, Katie hangs up the telephone. Then, after a moment, she picks it up again. She*
400 *speaks aloud with no self-consciousness whatever. Probably doesn't even know she's doing it.)*

**Katie.** I dialed the old number. I dialed—

*(Slam cut to:)*

*(INT. Bill, in the phone nook with Katie beside him)*

*(He's just taken the phone from Katie and is speaking to the operator.)*

**Operator** *(filter, giggles).* I *promise* not to give it out.

410 **Bill.** It's 555-

*(Slam cut to:)*

*(INT. Katie, in Bill's old chair, CU)*

**Katie** *(finishes).* -4408.

*(INT. the phone, CU)*

*(Katie's trembling finger carefully picks out the number, and we hear the corresponding tones: 555-4408.)*

*(INT. Katie, in Bill's old chair, CU)*

*(She closes her eyes as the phone begins to ring. Her*
420 *face is filled with an agonizing mixture of hope and fear. If only she can have one more chance to pass the vital message on, it says . . . just one more chance.)*

**Katie** *(low).* Please . . . please . . .

**Recorded voice** *(filter).* You have reached a non-working number. Please hang up and dial again. If you need assistance—

*(Katie hangs up again. Tears stream down her cheeks. The camera pans away and down to the telephone.)*

430 *(INT. the phone nook, with Katie and Bill, reprise)*

**Bill.** So it was a prank. Or someone who was crying so hard she dialed a wrong number . . . "through a shimmering film of tears," as we veteran hacks like to say.

**Katie.** It was not a prank and it was not a wrong number! It was someone in *my family!*

*(INT. Katie [present day] in Bill's study)*

**Katie.** Yes. Someone in *my family.* Someone very close. *(pause)* Me.

440 *(She suddenly throws the phone across the room. Then she begins to sob again and puts her hands over her face. The camera holds on her for a moment, then dollies across to:)*

*(INT. the phone)*

*(It lies on the carpet, looking both bland and somehow ominous. Camera moves in to ECU—the holes in the receiver once more look like huge dark chasms. We hold, then:)*

*(Fade to black.)*

**⑤ Targeted Passage**

---

## DIFFERENTIATED INSTRUCTION

### FOR STRUGGLING READERS

**⑤ Targeted Passage** [Lines 385–439]

This passage marks a crucial turning point in the plot and concludes the story: Katie realizes it was her own voice in the initial call.

- Who was the mysterious caller? (lines 435–439)

- What was the purpose of the call? (lines 394–396)

- When Katie tries to call the second time, why is her face "filled with . . . hope and fear"? (lines 415–422)

**MEMOIR** Stephen King wrote a memoir of his life as a writer. Here are a few words of advice from the book.

*from*
# On Writing

## Stephen King

If you want to be a writer, you must do two things above all others: read a lot and write a lot. There's no way around these two things that I'm aware of, no shortcut.

I'm a slow reader, but I usually get through seventy or eighty books a year, mostly fiction. I don't read in order to study the craft; I read because I like to read. It's what I do at night, kicked back in my blue chair. Similarly, I don't read fiction to study the art of fiction, but simply because I like stories. Yet there is a learning process going on. Every book you pick up has its own lesson or lessons, and quite often the bad books have more to teach than the good ones.

Good writing, on the other hand, teaches the learning writer about style, graceful narration, plot development, the creation of believable characters, and truth-telling. A novel like *The Grapes of Wrath* may fill a new writer with feelings of despair and good old-fashioned jealousy— "I'll never be able to write anything that good, not if I live to be a thousand"—but such feelings can also serve as a spur, goading the writer to work harder and aim higher. Being swept away by a combination of great story and great writing—of being flattened, in fact—is part of every writer's necessary formation. You cannot hope to sweep someone else away by the force of your writing until it has been done to you.

## TIERED DISCUSSION PROMPTS

Use these prompts to help students understand how the author's views on writing had an impact on "Sorry, Right Number":

**Connect** How has reading some of King's thoughts on writing helped you appreciate the author's creation of "Sorry, Right Number"? *Possible answer: King is clearly enthusiastic about reading and writing fiction, and he views each book that he reads as part of a never-ending learning process. His enjoyment of writing and his broad background in fiction are reflected in his teleplay.*

**Analyze** King refers to the importance of "plot development" and "believable characters." How are these two aspects of good writing linked in "Sorry, Right Number"? *Possible answer: For the teleplay to succeed, the story must unfold in a logical and suspenseful manner. At the same time, the characters who move the plot must be credible in action and speech in order for readers to get caught up in the events.*

**Evaluate** Do you think that King was equally successful in plot development and character creation in the teleplay? Give reasons for your answer. *Answers will vary, but students should provide thoughtful reasons as support.*

# Practice and Apply

For preliminary support of post-reading questions, use these copy masters:

**R** RESOURCE MANAGER—Copy Masters
Reading Check p. 191
Plot in Drama p. 187
Question Support p. 192

Additional selection questions are provided for teachers on page 181.

## ANSWERS

## Comprehension

1. *She thinks the caller is her daughter Polly.*

2. *He has a fatal heart attack.*

3. *Polly gets married; an emotionally overwrought Katie subsequently experiences "a kind of telephonic time travel" during which she telephones herself in the past in a futile effort to warn of Bill's coming heart attack.*

4. *The sobbing caller is Katie herself.*

## Text Analysis

COMMON CORE RL 5, RL 10

*Possible answers:*

5. ■ **COMMON CORE FOCUS** *Reading a Teleplay* Page 169: "The camera moves in to ECU . . . until the dots in the off-the-hook receiver look like chasms." Page 170: The phone looks "somehow ominous. Camera moves in to ECU—the holes in the receiver once more look like huge dark chasms."*

6. ● **COMMON CORE FOCUS** *Analyze Plot in Drama*
*Exposition: Family members interact; Rising Action: Katie gets upsetting phone call; Katie and Bill try to identify caller without success; Bill has fatal heart attack; Katie has emotional breakdown after Polly's wedding; Climax: Katie makes emotional phone call; Falling Action: Katie tries in vain to call again; Resolution: Katie realizes that she herself had been the sobbing caller.*

7. *Foreshadowing: Page 156: Katie says that Bill "doesn't feel very well." Outcome: On pages 159 and 166, Bill is described as looking "tired"; he subsequently has a heart attack. Foreshadowing: Page 162: King compares the phone to "a snake ready to strike." Outcome: The phone does in a sense "strike" during the climax.*

8. *The realization that she is connecting with the past is dawning on her, along with the idea of warning about the heart attack.*

## Comprehension

1. **Recall** At first, whom does Katie believe the sobbing caller to be?

2. **Recall** Why doesn't Bill return to bed after watching the movie?

3. **Summarize** What happens on the fifth anniversary of Bill's death?

4. **Clarify** Who is the sobbing caller?

## Text Analysis

● 5. **Reading a Teleplay** Look back through the play. What clues do the camera and stage directions give you for interpreting the play's supernatural occurrences?

● 6. **Analyze Plot in Drama** Create a plot diagram like the one shown. Then place the events of *Sorry, Right Number* in their correct positions on the diagram.

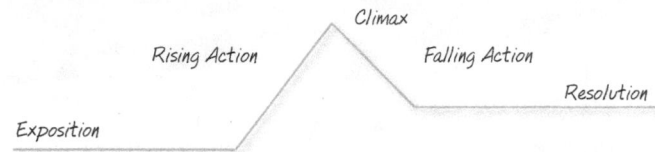

7. **Analyze Foreshadowing** In drama as in other fiction, foreshadowing can deepen a mood of suspense by hinting at future events. Go back through the teleplay and find examples of foreshadowing. For each example, provide a description of what eventually happens.

8. **Interpret** How would you explain the vague understanding—the "desperate hope . . . trying to be born"—that comes to Katie after she hears her own voice on the phone? Support your answer.

9. **Make Judgments** Could Katie be in any way responsible for Bill's death?

10. **Evaluate** Revisit the "chill factor" chart you created. Where would you place *Sorry, Right Number* on a scale of 1 to 10? Support your answer.

## Text Criticism

11. **Author's Style** In the excerpt from *On Writing* (page 171), Stephen King lists what he considers the qualities of good writing: "style, graceful narration, plot development, the creation of believable characters, and truth-telling." Which of these qualities does this teleplay best exemplify? Cite details, including lines of dialogue and examples of camera directions, to support your opinion.

### What sends a CHILL down your spine?

Describe a time when something ordinary seemed or became frightening.

**COMMON CORE**

**RL 5** Analyze how an author's choices concerning how to structure a text and order events within it create such effects as mystery, tension, or surprise. **RL 10** Read and comprehend dramas.

9. *Responsible: Her near-hysteria about the phone call certainly raised Bill's stress level. Not Responsible: Bill "doesn't feel very well" (p. 156) from the start; also, Bill was fated to have the heart attack—otherwise there would have been no call from the future!*

10. *Students should support their opinions with clear reasons.*

## Text Criticism

*Possible answer:*

11. *The teleplay best exemplifies "plot development" and "creation of believable characters." Students should support their opinions.*

**What sends a CHILL down your spine?** Ask students if they have been scared by something ordinary after seeing a horror movie.

# Language

◆ **GRAMMAR AND STYLE: Create Realistic Characters**

At various points, King uses **slang** to suggest the youth of a character. In writing dialogue, it is important to choose language that accurately reflects the characteristics of the people who are speaking; otherwise, your audience will find it difficult to believe what they are reading. Here is an example of King's use of slang in *Sorry, Right Number*:

> **Katie.** *Just thought you'd like to know your Aunt Dawn's fine.*
>
> **Dennis** (filter). *Oh! Cool. Thanks, Mom.* (Act II, lines 120–122)

Notice how the revisions in blue make the following dialogue more accurately reflect the ages of the speakers. Revise your response to the prompt below by making the same kinds of revisions.

> **STUDENT MODEL**
>
> **Katie.** Now, I know you're going to think this couldn't have happened. But five years ago, on the day Bill died, I got a call from myself.
>
> **Polly.** ~~That sounds really odd.~~ *Whatever, Mom.*
>
> **Dennis.** Mom, ~~that's a strange thing to say~~. *you're freaking out!*
>
> **Hank.** You're wrong, Katie. Let's talk about this.

## READING-WRITING CONNECTION

Increase your understanding of *Sorry, Right Number* by responding to this prompt. Then use the **revising tip** to improve your writing.

| **WRITING PROMPT** | **REVISING TIP** |
|---|---|
| **Short Constructed Response: Dialogue** Imagine that Katie tries to explain to her family what occurred with the phone call. What does she say? How does her family react? Write **one-half page** of the dialogue that you imagine would occur. | Review your dialogue. Do you use language and slang to reflect the age of the characters? If not, revise to make your dialogue match the speakers. |

**Interactive Revision**

Go to **thinkcentral.com**. KEYWORD: HML9-173

---

## COMMON CORE

**L3** Apply knowledge of language to make effective choices for meaning or style.

---

# Language

COMMON CORE **L3**

◆ **GRAMMAR AND STYLE**

- After students examine the student model, remind them that the children are now five years older, and their language, thinking, and manner of interacting should all reflect the passage of time. Jeff is now 13, Connie, 15, Dennis, 18, and Polly, 21.

- Point out that adults, such as Katie and Hank, might also use slang, but it's likely to differ from the slang used by younger people.

**R** RESOURCE MANAGER—Copy Master
Create Realistic Characters p. 193

**READING-WRITING CONNECTION**

- Encourage students to imagine themselves as each individual character in order to create realistic dialogue. Point out that the children are five years older than they were at the beginning of the teleplay, so their dialogue should sound more mature. Have students use their dialogue to write a scene for the teleplay. Remind them to include stage directions. Invite students to perform their scenes for the class.

**Writing Online**

The following tools are available online at **thinkcentral.com** and on **Write*Smart* CD-ROM:**
- **Interactive Graphic Organizers**
- **Interactive Student Models**
- **Interactive Revision Lessons**
For additional grammar instruction, see **GrammarNotes** on **thinkcentral.com**.

---

# Assess and Reteach

## Assess

**DIAGNOSTIC AND SELECTION TESTS**
Selection Test A pp. 55–56
Selection Test B/C pp. 57–58

**Interactive Selection Test** on **thinkcentral.com**

## Reteach

**Level Up Online Tutorials** on **thinkcentral.com**

---

## DIFFERENTIATED INSTRUCTION

### FOR STRUGGLING WRITERS

1. First speaker, Katie, summarizes what has happened.

2. Body of dialogue expresses disbelief.

3. Next speaker also expresses disbelief of Katie's claims.

# Focus and Motivate

**W 3a–e** Write narratives to develop real or imagined experiences or events using effective technique, well-chosen details, and well-structured event sequences. **W 4** Produce clear and coherent writing in which the development, organization and style are appropriate to task, purpose, and audience. **W 5** Develop and strengthen writing as needed by planning, revising, editing, rewriting, or trying a new approach. **W 10** Write routinely over shorter time frames for a range of tasks, purposes, and audiences. **L 2** Demonstrate command of the conventions of standard English capitalization, punctuation, and spelling. **L 3** Apply knowledge of language to make effective choices for meaning or style.

## WRITE WITH A PURPOSE

Tell students to choose experiences that changed their values, beliefs, or ideas in some way. Remind them that their purposes are to describe the experiences and to reflect on the significance of the experiences.

## COMMON CORE TRAITS

Review the *COMMON CORE TRAITS* with students, focusing primarily on development of ideas and organization of ideas. Compare the list of traits with the rubric on page 182.

## ADDITIONAL TASKS

**Write About a Community Event** Write a personal narrative about your experiences at a community event. Make sure to reflect on the significance of the event.
**Possible subjects:** government election, museum exhibit, charity event

**Write to a Review Committee** Write a personal narrative as part of an application to a school. Choose an experience that illustrates the character traits the review committee values. Then explain why this experience shows that you are a good candidate for the school.
**Possible subjects:** yearbook or newspaper staff, AP class, childcare assistant

### Writing Online

The following tools are available online at **thinkcentral.com** and on **Write*Smart* CD-ROM:**
• Interactive Graphic Organizers
• Interactive Student Models
• Interactive Revision Lessons

---

## Writing Workshop
### NARRATIVE

# Personal Narrative
### Essential Course of Study

Your life is a series of stories, all uniquely yours. Each story reveals something about you and the events that shape your life. When you write about yourself, you gain a deeper understanding of why certain experiences are important to you. In this workshop, you will write a personal narrative—a story that describes a memorable event from your past.

 Complete the workshop activities in your **Reader/Writer Notebook.**

### WRITE WITH A PURPOSE

**WRITING TASK**

Write a **personal narrative** in which you describe for a specific audience a meaningful experience in your life. Make sure to narrate the events of the experience and to reflect on its significance.

**Idea Starters**
• a memorable incident from your childhood
• a challenging experience that taught you a lesson
• an accomplishment you are proud of

**THE ESSENTIALS**

Here are some common purposes, audiences, and formats for narrative writing.

| PURPOSES | AUDIENCES | FORMATS |
|---|---|---|
| • to describe a meaningful experience<br>• to better understand yourself | • classmates and teacher<br>• family members<br>• Web users | • essay for class<br>• journal<br>• blog<br>• documentary<br>• podcast |

### COMMON CORE TRAITS

**1. DEVELOPMENT OF IDEAS**
• focuses on a **meaningful experience**
• provides **well-chosen details**
• uses narrative techniques such as **dialogue** and **description**
• establishes and reflects on the **significance of the experience**
• provides a **conclusion** that follows from the experience

**2. ORGANIZATION OF IDEAS**
• presents a **logical sequence** of events
• uses effective **pacing**

**3. LANGUAGE FACILITY AND CONVENTIONS**
• establishes and maintains a **first-person point of view**
• uses **precise words** and **sensory language**
• varies sentence structure with **compound sentences**
• employs correct **grammar, mechanics,** and **spelling**

### Writing Online
Go to **thinkcentral.com**.
KEYWORD: HML9N-174

---

## Writing Workshop Resources

**R RESOURCE MANAGER UNIT 1**
Plan and Teach pp. 195–198
Prewriting–Editing pp. 199–203
Scoring Rubric p. 204
Speaking and Listening p. 205
Writing Support p. 206*

**BEST PRACTICES TOOLKIT**
Writing Template: Personal Narrative pp. C16, C18

**TECHNOLOGY**
⊘ **Teacher One Stop DVD-ROM**
⊘ **Student One Stop DVD-ROM**
⊘ **Write*Smart* CD-ROM**
⊘ **GrammarNotes DVD-ROM**

**Writing Center on thinkcentral.com**

*See resources on the **Teacher One Stop** DVD-ROM and on **thinkcentral.com**.*

\* Resources for Differentiation

# Planning/Prewriting

 **COMMON CORE** W 3a-e Write narratives to develop real or imagined experiences or events using effective technique, well-chosen details, and well-structured event sequences. W 5 Develop and strengthen writing as needed by planning.

## Getting Started

### CHOOSE A STORY TO TELL

Think back over your life, recalling memorable or challenging experiences. Create a timeline of peaks and valleys in your life. Include the rewarding experiences and the ones that involved real challenges. Choose the **single experience** that you want to write about.

▶ **ASK YOURSELF:**

- What are the most memorable experiences of my life?
- What have been the greatest challenges of my life?
- What do I want to share in this personal narrative?

### THINK ABOUT AUDIENCE AND PURPOSE

As you begin to reflect on your topic more deeply, keep in mind your **purpose,** which is to describe a meaningful experience to your **audience.** Consider your audience so you know what type of language is appropriate. For example, a description of an experience aimed at parents will contain different language than a description of the same experience aimed at your classmates.

▶ **ASK YOURSELF:**

- Who is my target audience? Am I writing for more than one particular audience? What do I want people to understand about this experience?
- What kind of language will my audience best understand and be able to relate to?

### LIST THE EVENTS OF YOUR EXPERIENCE

Since this is a **personal narrative,** you will use first-person point of view to tell your story. Begin your planning by focusing on a **single experience.** Outline the **events** to create a smooth progression from first to last. The last event will be the resolution. Jot down details that you can use later to describe the **setting** (where the events took place), the **people** involved, and include a few lines of **dialogue.**

▶ **WHAT DOES IT LOOK LIKE?**

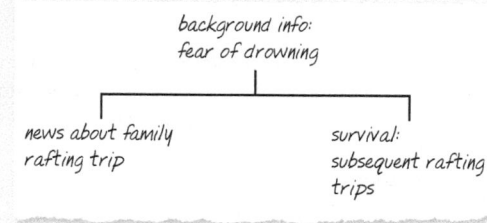

```
          background info:
          fear of drowning
         ┌──────────┴──────────┐
news about family        survival:
rafting trip             subsequent rafting
                         trips
```

### TELL WHY THE EVENT IS SIGNIFICANT

Reflect on why the event is **significant** or important to you. Think about what you learned. Identify how the experience changed you.

▶ **WHAT DOES IT LOOK LIKE?**

- faced a fear successfully
- discovered the pitfalls of worrying
- recognized inner strength
- learned that fear is normal

---

## DIFFERENTIATED INSTRUCTION

### FOR ENGLISH LANGUAGE LEARNERS

**Language: Reinforce Narrative Terms** Write these terms on the board and review them with students:

- *narrative:* writing that takes the form of a story
- *reflect:* to realize or understand after thought
- *significance:* importance

- *chronological:* in the order of time; order in which things happen: first, next, last
- *background:* events that come before another event
- *dialogue:* conversation between characters
- *sensory details:* details that describe what something feels, tastes, looks, sounds, or smells like

---

# Teach

## Planning/Prewriting

 **COMMON CORE** W 3a-e, W 5

▶ **CHOOSE A STORY TO TELL** Encourage students to illustrate their timelines with sketches or photographs. These visual prompts will aid students with sensory description when they begin drafting. Students may also choose to incorporate these visual elements into their narratives.

▶ **THINK ABOUT AUDIENCE AND PURPOSE** Illustrate the relationship between language and audience by having students think of recent experiences. Then, ask students to write one or two sentences describing the experiences to their peers. Tell students to rewrite the sentences for their parents. Invite volunteers to read the two descriptions aloud. Lead the class to discuss how audience affects language choice in each example.

▶ **LIST THE EVENTS OF YOUR EXPERIENCE** Make sure that students understand the need for a well-structured sequence of events in a narrative. Descriptions of people (including their words) and places infuse the narrative with depth and meaning.

▶ **TELL WHY THE EVENT IS SIGNIFICANT** Suggest that students respond to the following questions to explore the significance of their experiences:

- As a result of this experience, what did you learn about yourself? about others?
- How were you different after the experience than before the experience?
- Based on this experience, what advice would you give others?

**R** **RESOURCE MANAGER—Copy Masters**
Planning/Prewriting p. 199
Drafting p. 200
Revising and Editing pp. 201–202
Ask a Peer Reader p. 203
Rubric p. 204
Writing Support p. 206

## Planning/Prewriting *continued*

▶ **DESCRIBE YOUR EXPERIENCE** Make sure that students understand that sensory language helps the audience experience the events along with a narrator by engaging all five senses. When describing a person, for example, remind students to describe how the person looks, sounds, and smells. They can also describe the texture of an item of clothing or a hand. They might incorporate taste details by describing the reactions of others. For example, *When Mr. Smith walked into the room, Charles's mouth suddenly tasted of quarters.*

 **YOUR TURN** Suggest that students bring in pictures—either from magazines or family photograph albums—that relate to their narratives. Tell students to use these images to facilitate their use of sensory language. Have them describe what is happening in the pictures using all five senses: sight, sound, taste, touch, and smell. Suggest that students incorporate these descriptions into their narratives.

## Planning/Prewriting *continued*

**DESCRIBE YOUR EXPERIENCE** ▶

Your narrative should engage your audience by using **telling details** and **sensory language.** Create a web to record details and sensory language that you can use in your draft to describe people, places, and events.

**WHAT DOES IT LOOK LIKE?**

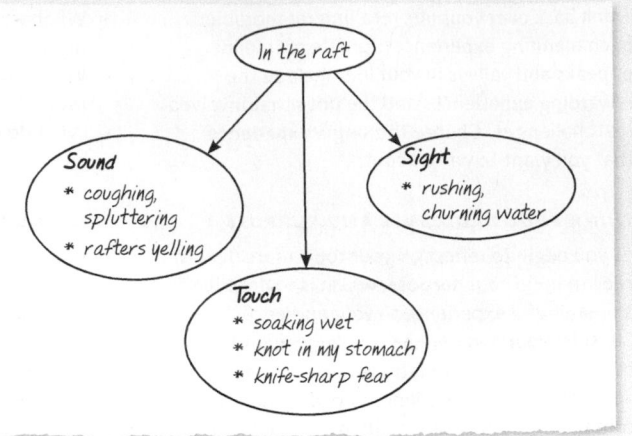

**PEER REVIEW** Describe to a peer the purpose and audience of your personal narrative. Then, ask for tips regarding language appropriate for such an audience.

 **YOUR TURN** In your *Reader/Writer Notebook,* develop your writing plan. Record a brief description of the experience you want to write about. Then, use an organizer such as the one on this page to jot down sensory language you will include in your narrative. Consider the following tips as you list sensory details to include:

- Think of the visual images that appear in your mind as you recall the experience.
- Consider the sounds during the experience. Remember that silence can also be described through sensory images.
- Remember whether there was a distinctive smell or feeling during the experience. For example, it may have been hot, cold, dry, or humid.
- Focus on sensory language that will emphasize your overall impression of the event, making the event vivid for the audience and making its significance clear.

## DIFFERENTIATED INSTRUCTION

### FOR STRUGGLING WRITERS

**Sensory Language** Choose an object in the room that can be easily described using sensory language. Have students take turns describing one aspect of the object. After each description, ask other students to identify the sense to which the description appeals. If students tend to focus on sight details, prompt them to expand their descriptions by asking questions such as *How does the object smell? How does the object feel? How might this object taste? How does the object sound?*

### FOR ADVANCED LEARNERS/PRE–AP

**Incorporate Foreshadowing and Flashback** As students draft their narratives, have them look for places to incorporate foreshadowing and flashback. For example, students might use foreshadowing to hint at the conflicts or resolutions. Students might use flashbacks to add background information. Reiterate that sensory details can be used to create foreshadowing and enhance flashbacks. Remind students to use transitions or other clues to help readers understand their sequences.

# Drafting

 **COMMON CORE** **W 4** Produce clear and coherent writing in which the development, organization, and style are appropriate to task, purpose, and audience. **L 2** Demonstrate command of the conventions of standard English punctuation.

The following chart shows a structure for organizing a clear and coherent personal narrative.

## Organizing Your Personal Narrative

### INTRODUCTION

- Orient your **audience** by introducing them to the **people**, **places**, and **events** you're writing about. Begin with an engaging action, exchange of **dialogue**, or reaction.
- Provide background information to help the audience understand the experience.

▼

### BODY

- **Sequence** your events so that they build on one another and create a **coherent** whole.
- Use **pacing** that keeps the action moving and creates a smooth progression of events.
- Include **precise words and phrases**, **telling details**, and **sensory language** to vividly describe the **people**, **places**, and **events** involved.
- Describe **thoughts** and **feelings**, and use **realistic dialogue** to develop events and characters.

▼

### CONCLUDING SECTION

- Narrate the **resolution** of the experience by telling how the events ended.
- Explain why the experience is **significant** by reflecting on what you learned or how the experience changed you.

## GRAMMAR IN CONTEXT: PUNCTUATING DIALOGUE

Speech between people in a narrative is called *dialogue*. Dialogue requires special punctuation that signals to the audience that these words are spoken aloud.

| Rule | Example |
|---|---|
| **Quotation Marks:** Place quotation marks (" ") around the exact words that someone says. | *"If you fall in, relax and go with the flow."* |
| **Comma:** Use a comma inside the second quotation mark to separate the quotation from its tag line. However, if the dialogue ends with a question mark or exclamation point, do not use a comma. | *"If you fall in, relax and go with the flow," one of the lean, sunburned tour guides said.* <br> *"This is gonna be awesome!" they hollered.* |

 **YOUR TURN** Develop a first draft of your personal narrative, following the structure outlined in the chart above. As you write, include some dialogue that you had with another person. Make sure to use proper punctuation.

## FOR ENGLISH LANGUAGE LEARNERS

**Identify the Speaker** Ask two students to read aloud to the class a dialogue exchange. Ask students to explain how they know that a character is talking and how they know which character is talking. *(They use their senses of sight and sound.)* Next, provide students with a written example of the same dialogue. Ask students to explain how they know that a character is talking and how they know which character is talking. *(They note quotation marks and tag lines.)*

## FOR STRUGGLING WRITERS

**Punctuating Dialogue** Place lines of dialogue (without quotation marks or commas but with question marks and exclamation marks as needed) written on sentence strips in one box. Place tag lines written on sentence strips in another box. Have students take turns selecting one sentence strip from each box. Tell students to post their strips on the board to form sentences. Ask volunteers to use quotation marks and commas as necessary to punctuate the sentences.

---

# Practice and Apply

## Drafting

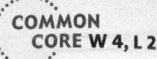 **COMMON CORE W 4, L 2**

▶ **INTRODUCTION** Tell students to read the dialogue introduction to the Student Draft on p. 179. Then ask students to work in pairs or small groups to rewrite the introduction two times, once beginning with action (My stomach knotted when . . . .) and once beginning with reaction (Are you crazy! I thought when my dad announced . . . .). Invite volunteers to read examples aloud to the class. Lead the class to discuss the pros and cons of each type of introduction for this particular story.

▶ **BODY** Suggest that students narrate the sequence of events first. Then, have students return to their drafts to identify places where they can use precise words and phrases or sensory language to describe people, places, and events.

▶ **CONCLUDING SECTION** Remind students that not all problems or conflicts are necessarily solved. The people may simply come to accept circumstances as they are.

Make sure that students understand the importance of reflecting on the significance of events. These explanations provide audience members with themes or messages that they may apply to their own lives.

## GRAMMAR IN CONTEXT: PUNCTUATING DIALOGUE

For additional practice, have students punctuate the following lines of dialogue.

- A rafting trip through the Grand Canyon? For a week? Really? I said, a grin pasted on my face.

- That's a great idea, Dad. I felt a knot forming in my stomach.

 **YOUR TURN** Ask students to complete the Your Turn activity independently. Remind students to punctuate dialogue correctly. Suggest that students write their drafts double-spaced so that they can make revisions easily later.

For interactive revision tools, see

 **Write*Smart* CD-ROM**

**Writing Center at <u>thinkcentral.com</u>**

# Revising

***Model the Skill*** Using a draft narrative on a transparency or electronic whiteboard, model how to use the questions, tips, and strategies suggested in the chart to evaluate and revise. You might use the narrative of a student from another class or from a previous year. Make sure to remove the student's name from the narrative so that the writer remains anonymous.

**YOUR TURN** Before students engage in partner reviews, suggest that they make lists of questions they wanted answered during their review sessions. For example, *How can I add taste details to my narrative? Can you think of a better title?* Tell students to leave spaces between questions for their partners to write responses. Instruct students to make certain that they respond to all of their partners' questions, preferably in colored ink, so that it is easy to distinguish questions from answers as they revise or rewrite their narratives.

For interactive revision tools, see

**Write*Smart* CD-ROM**

**Writing Center** on <u>thinkcentral.com</u>

---

# Revising

As you revise your narrative, consider both the sequence and the sensory details that make the people and places come to life. The goal is to determine whether you've achieved your purpose and effectively communicated your ideas to the intended audience. The following chart will help you determine which parts of your draft need revising, rewriting, or a new approach.

## PERSONAL NARRATIVE

| Ask Yourself | Tips | Revision Strategies |
|---|---|---|
| 1. Does the narrative focus on a single event that is explained through well-chosen details? | **Underline** each detail that is essential for the reader's understanding of the experience. | **Add** events as necessary to make the experience clear for your audience. **Delete** extra events and irrelevant details that are not underlined. |
| 2. Does the narrative follow a well-structured sequence of events? | **Number** the events in the order in which they occur. | **Rearrange** events so that they build on one another in a smooth progression. |
| 3. Does the pacing keep the action moving? | **Place an X** next to details or events that slow down the narrative. **Draw a star** where the action moves too quickly. | **Revise or remove** details that slow down the pace. **Add** details where the action jumps too quickly ahead. |
| 4. Is sensory language used to describe characters and setting? | **Draw an arrow** next to each sensory detail. | **Add** sensory language. **Include** details that appeal to a variety of senses. |
| 5. Do the people speak through dialogue? | **Bracket** examples of dialogue. | **Add** dialogue where possible to engage readers, reveal character traits, or show the conflict. |
| 6. Is the significance of the experience revealed through thoughts and feelings? | **Highlight** statements that describe thoughts or feelings. | **Add** specific thoughts and feelings that make clear to your audience why this experience is important to you. |

**YOUR TURN** **PEER REVIEW** Exchange your personal narrative with a classmate, or read it aloud to your partner. As you read and comment on your classmate's essay, focus on events and sensory language. Discuss whether you understand the events, the people, and the significance of the experience. If your narrative is not flowing smoothly, use the revision strategies in the chart to tighten your writing or try a new approach.

---

## DIFFERENTIATED INSTRUCTION

### FOR ENGLISH LANGUAGE LEARNERS

**Narrative Details** Review simple narrative elements: setting, plot, conflict, and characters. Write the following list on the board:

• clear the table
• put the dishes in the sink
• wash the dishes
• dry the dishes
• put the dishes away

Ask students to work with a partner to create a short narrative from the list by adding details that specify setting, characters, and conflict. Ask each pair to narrate their original story for the class.

## ANALYZE A STUDENT DRAFT

Read this draft; notice the comments on its strengths as well as suggestions for improvement.

**COMMON CORE**

**W 5** Develop and strengthen writing by revising, editing, rewriting, or trying a new approach, addressing what is most significant for a specific purpose and audience. **L 3** Use language to make effective choices for meaning or style.

### Facing My Fears: Riding the River
by Rick Rosario, Franklin High School

**❶** "A rafting trip through the Grand Canyon? For a week? Really?" I said, a grin pasted on my face. "That's a great idea, Dad." I felt a knot forming in my stomach.

**❷** My two brothers high-fived each other. "This experience is going to be very rewarding!" they hollered. My mother grinned her approval.

**❸** I'm not the best athlete at Franklin High, but I work hard, and I enjoy competition. However, I used to avoid rafting, sailing, kayaking, and similar sports. Here's why: When I was ten, I climbed a railing, slipped, and fell into the Dungeness River. My uncle jumped in immediately and fished me out. I came up coughing and spluttering, with a brand new fear of drowning. Rushing, churning water filled my nightmares.

**❹** The night my father told us about the vacation, I looked through the expedition catalog from Western Adventures, and my worst fears were confirmed. On the cover was a photograph of a huge orange raft vanishing into a giant rapid. The vacationers clung to the sides, tiny and powerless. Now, I'm an OK swimmer. But as I looked at the catalog, I wondered why anyone, even a champion swimmer, would want to go whitewater rafting. Does anyone really think that the guides can control everything that happens during the journey? I asked myself.

> Rick opens with **dialogue** that he contrasts with **sensory language.** This technique will have the audience wondering why Rick isn't really excited about the trip.

> Rick includes **dialogue** and gestures to describe the people involved. However, some of the dialogue needs to be revised to appear more **realistic.**

> Rick develops his narrative voice through **background information, thoughts,** and **feelings.**

**LEARN HOW** Create Realistic Dialogue  In his second paragraph, Rick includes dialogue from his brothers to draw the audience into the narrative. However, the dialogue doesn't really sound like something two boys would say. It is unrealistic. To create realistic dialogue, record as exactly as you can the person's words and manner of speaking. Does the person use slang or speak using formal language? When people talk in a personal narrative, they should sound the way they do in real life.

**RICK'S REVISION TO PARAGRAPH ❷**

*"This is gonna be awesome!"*

My two brothers high-fived each other. "~~This experience is going to be very rewarding!~~" they hollered. My mother grinned her approval.

---

## FOR ENGLISH LANGUAGE LEARNERS

**Dialogue Strategies**  Provide students with strategies for creating realistic dialogue in English.

- Have students interview some of the people included in their narratives, recording the words exactly as they hear them.

- Have students consult with native speakers to review and revise dialogue for realism.

- Review common aspects of dialogue with students, including contractions, slang, and idioms.

## FOR STRUGGLING WRITERS

**Create Realistic Dialogue**  Have students work in pairs to write a few lines of realistic dialogue, based on the following scenario:

- Hugo and Wes are walking home from school. Summer break has just begun. They are excitedly discussing their plans to build a skateboard ramp.

Tell each pair to read the dialogue aloud to determine how realistic it is. Have students in each pair share ideas for improvement.

## ANALYZE A STUDENT DRAFT

Explain that the Student Draft on this page is the first half of a personal narrative. Model reading the draft and the annotations in blue, explaining that the yellow highlighting illustrates the student's language choices. Explain that the following *Learn How* mini-lessons provide helpful information about ways to improve this student draft as well as students' own drafts.

**LEARN HOW**  Create Realistic Dialogue

- Make sure that students understand that audience members must care about the people in a narrative if they are to continue reading and enjoying a piece.

- One way writers ensure that the audience cares about the fates of the characters is to create realistic characters or characters who seem like real people.

- Using realistic dialogue is one way to achieve this goal. If the characters sound like people with whom the audience is familiar, the characters seem real.

- Have students read aloud to partners all instances of dialogue in their narratives. Ask partners to comment on whether or not the dialogue sounds "real." If not, have partners make suggestions for revision.

Explain that the Student Draft is continued and completed on this page. Read the draft and annotations aloud and discuss. Ask students to comment on the student writer's discussion of the significance of the experience.

**LEARN HOW** Use Correct Punctuation for Dialogue

- Make sure that students understand that quotation marks tell readers which words come directly from characters.

- Quotation marks help readers differentiate between dialogue and narration.

- Have students review their drafts to ensure that all dialogue is punctuated correctly.

**YOUR TURN** Ask students to complete the **Your Turn** activity independently. Remind students to examine every instance of dialogue carefully to ensure that it is realistic and punctuated correctly.

For interactive revision tools, see

**WriteSmart CD-ROM**

**Writing Center on thinkcentral.com**

---

**5** By the time we found ourselves rafting down the river, I had my answer: No. The guides cannot control everything that happens during a rafting trip. I could feel every bump and sway. I could hear the whoosh of the river all around me. The front of our raft was submerged in icy water. There was no doubt in my mind: I was going to drown.

**6** Seconds later, the front of the raft shot out of the water like a cannonball. And then, suddenly, it was all over. We had made it.

**7** The rafters erupted in wild shouts, all of us laughing about how we were soaking wet and what a thrill the ride had been. My brothers yelled, Let's do it again! The knot in my stomach eased a bit. We encountered many more rapids in the next five days, but my fear was never again as knife-sharp.

**8** During that vacation, I faced my worst fear not just once, but dozens of times. I learned that worrying about an experience can be worse than the experience itself. I realized that I am tougher than I thought. I found out that it's all right to express fear—even to scream if I need to. By the end of the week, I had a real smile on my face, not a pasted-on grin. And the knot in my stomach was long gone.

> Rick includes words and phrases throughout the narrative that signal a **well-structured sequence** of events.

> Notice how Rick includes **dialogue** in this paragraph. While dialogue can help engage the reader, Rick should be careful to use correct punctuation for dialogue.

> Rick's concluding paragraph states the **significance** of the experience. By using some of the same details as in the introduction, Rick connects the events of his narrative.

**LEARN HOW** Use Correct Punctuation for Dialogue In the seventh paragraph, Rick provides his brothers' dialogue after an exciting experience. However, he fails to punctuate the dialogue correctly because he leaves out quotation marks.

**RICK'S REVISION TO PARAGRAPH 7**

My brothers yelled, "Let's do it again!"

**YOUR TURN** Use the feedback from your peers and teacher as well as the two "Learn How" lessons to revise your essay. Evaluate how well you have described the experience and addressed the audience and purpose by examining your events, details, and techniques. Consider your use of dialogue, pacing, and sensory language. Ask yourself if you've painted a vivid picture and explained the significance of the events.

## Editing and Publishing

 **COMMON CORE** **W 5** Strengthen writing by revising, editing, rewriting, or trying a new approach. **L 2** Demonstrate command of the conventions of standard English capitalization, punctuation, and spelling. **L 2c** Spell correctly.

In the editing stage, you check your narrative to make sure that it is free of grammar, usage, and punctuation errors. Also, read carefully to catch any spelling errors, even after doing a word-processing spell-check. These kinds of mistakes distract your audience from focusing on the meaningful experience you describe.

### GRAMMAR IN CONTEXT: COMPOUND SENTENCES

To vary rhythm and emphasis, writers avoid using the same sentence structure over and over again. In most pieces of writing, you will find both simple and compound sentences. Writers use coordinating conjunctions such as *and, but,* or *or* to join independent clauses of equal importance. The result is a compound sentence. Examine the following compound sentences from Rick's draft:

> *The night my father told us about the vacation, I looked through the expedition catalog from Western Adventures, and my worst fears were confirmed.*

[This sentence uses the **coordinating conjunction** *and* to join two independent clauses into one **compound sentence**.]

As Rick edits his narrative, he notices two sentences that could be combined to form a compound sentence, making the thought flow better.

> *I could feel every bump and sway*, *and I could hear the whoosh of the river all around me.*

### PUBLISH YOUR WRITING

It's time to share your personal narrative with your audience. Try one of these ideas:

- Send your narrative to a magazine or Web site that accepts narratives from unpublished writers.
- Publish your narrative in a blog, or turn it into a digital story to post online.
- Present your narrative as a speech for your classmates.

 **YOUR TURN** Proofread your narrative and correct any errors. Make sure that compound sentences use a comma and a coordinating conjunction to join independent clauses. Then, publish your narrative for your audience.

## Editing and Publishing

 **COMMON CORE W 5, L 2, L 2c**

### GRAMMAR IN CONTEXT: COMPOUND SENTENCES

Provide students with further explanation regarding the use of coordinating conjunctions to form compound sentences.

- *and:* use to compare
- *but, yet:* use to contrast
- *for:* use to show cause
- *nor:* use to provide negative options
- *or:* use to provide options
- *so:* use to show effect

Have students work in pairs or small groups to practice writing compound sentences using different coordinating conjunctions to show different relationships between independent clauses. Invite volunteers to present sentences to the class.

### PUBLISH YOUR WRITING

Brainstorm with students additional ways to publish their narratives.

 **YOUR TURN** Allow students time to proofread their drafts. Remind them to create realistic dialogue and punctuate it correctly. In addition, suggest that students incorporate compound sentences into their drafts.

---

## DIFFERENTIATED INSTRUCTION

### FOR ENGLISH LANGUAGE LEARNERS

**Independent Clauses** Before introducing compound sentences, review with students the qualities of an independent clause:

- contains a subject
- contains a verb
- states a complete thought

Help students identify these qualities in the following examples:

- I looked through the expedition catalog from Western Adventures.

- My worst fears were confirmed.
- I could feel every bump and sway.
- I could hear the whoosh of the river all around us.

### FOR STRUGGLING WRITERS

**Complex-Compound Sentences** Help students understand that the clause "The night my father told us about the vacation" functions as a dependent clause because it does not express a complete thought. The following example is a complex sentence: *The night my father told*

*us about the vacation, I looked through the expedition catalog from Western Adventures.* The entire example is a complex-compound sentence. If students find this example confusing, have them cover the dependent clause with sticky notes and save explanations of complex and complex-compound sentences for another time.

## Scoring Rubric

Tell students that the best way to understand a scoring rubric is to use it to score actual writing. Provide the class with copies of a student's narrative with the student's name removed. Work as a class to evaluate the narrative by using the scoring rubric. Have students score the narrative and write brief paragraphs using the language of the scoring rubric to explain the reasons behind their scores. Take a class survey to determine whether there is a consensus regarding the score. If not, guide students toward a consensus using the sample narrative and the scoring rubric.

For Rubric Bank, see

 **WriteSmart CD-ROM**

**Writing Center on thinkcentral.com**

## Assess and Reteach

### Assess

 **RESOURCE MANAGER—Copy Master**
Rubric for Evaluation p. 204

**Online Essay Scoring at thinkcentral.com**

### Reteach

**Level Up Online Tutorial at thinkcentral.com**
**Reteaching Workshops on thinkcentral.com**

---

## Scoring Rubric

Use the rubric below to evaluate your personal narrative from the Writing Workshop or your response to the on-demand task on the next page.

### PERSONAL NARRATIVE

| SCORE | COMMON CORE TRAITS |
|---|---|
| **6** | • **Development** Skillfully conveys a real experience using well-chosen details; effectively uses dialogue and description; concludes by reflecting on the significance of the experience<br>• **Organization** Has a coherent sequence that builds to a strong conclusion; uses effective pacing<br>• **Language** Consistently maintains first-person point of view; effectively uses compound sentences for variety; weaves in sensory language; shows a strong command of conventions |
| **5** | • **Development** Effectively conveys a real experience; mainly uses well-chosen details; ably uses dialogue and description; reflects on the significance of the experience<br>• **Organization** Has a coherent sequence that builds to a conclusion; uses mostly effective pacing<br>• **Language** Maintains first-person point of view; varies sentence structure; includes sensory language; has a few errors in conventions |
| **4** | • **Development** Conveys a real experience; uses some well-chosen details; could use more dialogue or description<br>• **Organization** Includes some extraneous events, resulting in ineffective pacing<br>• **Language** Mostly maintains first-person point of view; generally varies sentence structure; needs more sensory language; has a few distracting errors in conventions |
| **3** | • **Development** Conveys a real experience, but it needs more development; could use more details; needs more dialogue or description<br>• **Organization** Has a confusing sequence caused by extraneous events; has a lagging pace at times<br>• **Language** Has a few lapses in first-person point of view; lacks variety in sentence structure; lacks sensory language; has some significant errors in conventions |
| **2** | • **Development** Conveys a real experience but does not develop it with details; lacks sufficient dialogue and description<br>• **Organization** Includes too many events that distract from the experience; has choppy pacing<br>• **Language** Uses inconsistent point of view; lacks variety in sentence structure; mostly lacks sensory language; has many distracting errors in conventions |
| **1** | • **Development** Has no identifiable experience; provides few details; lacks dialogue or description<br>• **Organization** Has no apparent organization<br>• **Language** Never establishes a clear point of view; uses only simple sentences; lacks sensory language; has major problems with conventions |

# Preparing for Timed Writing

**COMMON CORE** W 10 Write routinely over shorter time frames for a range of tasks, purposes, and audiences.

## 1. ANALYZE THE TASK 5 MIN

Read the task carefully. Then, read it again, making note of the words that tell the type of writing, the topic, the audience, and the purpose.

**WRITING TASK**

Much has been written and said about the meaning of courage. Write a <u>personal</u> *Type of* <u>narrative</u> about a time you were nervous or excited about an upcoming event and *writing* demonstrated <u>courage</u> that you may not have known you possessed. Use your narrative *Topic* to <u>describe a meaningful experience</u> to <u>classmates</u>. *Purpose* *Audience*

## 2. PLAN YOUR RESPONSE 10 MIN

Identify a personal experience during which you were nervous or excited. Then, list the people involved, the places, background information, and events. Finally, note what made the event meaningful for you and reflect on your newfound courage.

| Narrative Elements | Notes |
|---|---|
| People involved | |
| Places | |
| Background Information | |
| Events | |
| Outcome | |
| Significance of the event | |

## 3. RESPOND TO THE TASK 20 MIN

Begin drafting your narrative. Start with an engaging action, piece of dialogue, or reaction that introduces the experience. As you write, remember the following:

- In the introduction, present the people involved, places, and events and provide background information that a classmate might need.
- In the body, narrate the sequence of events in a well-structured, logical order. Remember to keep the action moving.
- In the concluding section, reflect on the significance of the experience.

## 4. IMPROVE YOUR RESPONSE 5–10 MIN

**Revising** Compare your draft with the task. Does your draft tell a personal story about courage that allows your classmates to better know you? Does your draft explain why this experience is significant to you?

**Proofreading** Find and correct any errors in grammar, mechanics, and spelling. Make sure that your narrative is correctly punctuated, and all edits are neatly written and legible.

**Checking Your Final Copy** Before you submit your personal narrative, examine it once more to make sure that you are presenting your best work.

---

## Preparing for Timed Writing

**COMMON CORE W 10**

1. **Analyze the Task** Before students begin writing, encourage them to answer the following questions:
   - What is my time limit?
   - What are the key skills assessed in the scoring rubric?
   - Who is my audience?
   - What is my purpose?

2. **Plan Your Response** Point out to students that the scoring rubric emphasizes focusing on a real experience. Remind students to use a well-structured sequence to introduce the people, places, and events in a smooth and logical progression, providing background information as necessary.

3. **Respond to the Task** Remind students to incorporate sensory details to describe people and places and to keep the action moving. In addition, they should include their own thoughts and feelings to convey the significance of the event thoroughly.

4. **Improve Your Response** Point out that the scoring rubric emphasizes the use of first-person point of view and dialogue. Remind students to punctuate dialogue correctly.

## Assess

Use the Scoring Rubric on p. 182 to assess students' personal narratives.

---

## DIFFERENTIATED INSTRUCTION

### FOR ENGLISH LANGUAGE LEARNERS

**Significance of Experiences** Explain to students that all experiences are set within the context of other experiences. To determine the significance of the experiences, students will need to think about these contexts. Give the following example:

- **Focal Experience:** Theo defends a new student who is being harassed.
- **Contextual Experience:** These bullies have previously harassed other students.

- **Significance:** Theo learns that the harassment will continue if no one stops it.

### FOR STRUGGLING WRITERS

**Relevant Details** Emphasize that when students choose specific experiences on which to focus, they should present readers with several relevant details that explain how and why students acted courageously. Have students make lists of relevant details. If students can only think of a few details, tell them that they may want to choose other experiences.

# Focus and Motivate

:::: COMMON CORE FOCUS

**SL 4** Present information clearly, concisely, and logically such that listeners can follow the line of reasoning. **SL 6** Adapt speech to a variety of contexts, demonstrating command of formal English.

## SPEAK WITH A PURPOSE

Help students identify purposes for their informal narrative speeches through a brainstorming session. Write *Audience: Classmates → Purposes: _____* on the board. Then list students' ideas regarding the purposes for informal narrative speaking. Students may suggest entertainment, establishment of personal connections, or communication of a lesson, theme, or advice.

## COMMON CORE TRAITS

As students prepare to deliver their speeches, remind them to keep in mind the **COMMON CORE TRAITS** of a strong informal speech.

# Practice and Apply

## Adapt Your Personal Narrative

### Model the Skill: AUDIENCE

Model for students how to add descriptive details to a passage one plans to read aloud. Write the following sentence on the board:

- It was hot, and we were by the edge of the pool.

Write the following revision on the board:

- The blazing sun poured down as we stood by the shimmering pool.

Additionally, suggest that students locate events in specific places. For instance, they should say "in the cafeteria line" or "by my locker" rather than "at school." This strategy will also help the audience visualize events.

**GUIDED PRACTICE** Write the following sentences on the board and work with students to add descriptive details.

- It was cold, so we sat close to the campfire. I laughed as my brother's marshmallow fell into the flames.

**R** RESOURCE MANAGER—Copy Master
Speaking and Listening p. 205

---

**Speaking & Listening Workshop**

# Presenting an Informal Speech

*Essential Course of Study*  **ECOS**

Imagine sitting at a lunch table with a friend who has just returned from an exciting vacation. Your friend relates the details of this personal narrative as an **informal speech**—a type of speech we give every day as we tell each other stories about our lives.

Complete the workshop activities in your **Reader/Writer Notebook**.

| SPEAK WITH A PURPOSE | COMMON CORE TRAITS |
|---|---|
| **TASK** Adapt your personal narrative to create a three- to five-minute **informal speech.** Practice your speech, and then present it to your class. | **A STRONG INFORMAL SPEECH . . .**<br>• includes story elements such as people, places, and narrative events<br>• uses sensory language to describe people and places<br>• presents ideas clearly so listeners can easily follow the sequence of events<br>• is delivered using effective verbal and nonverbal techniques |

:::: COMMON CORE

**SL 4** Present information clearly, concisely, and logically such that listeners can follow. **SL 6** Adapt speech to a variety of contexts, demonstrating command of formal English.

## Adapt Your Personal Narrative

Your audience will be listening to your narrative instead of reading it, so you will need to adapt the narrative to make it easy for listeners to follow. Keep in mind your audience—your classmates—and use these suggestions to translate your writing into an effective speech:

- **Language** Use short, concise sentences, connecting ideas with transitions.
- **Organization** Make sure the sequence of events is clear and that events build on one another logically. Eliminate minor characters and unnecessary dialogue.
- **Audience** Focus on details that describe people and places. This will help your audience "experience" the event and understand its importance.
- **Effective Communication** If you are using notes, mark your text to show where you will use a different voice, a certain facial expression, a gesture, or sound effects. Notice how Rick Rosario adapted parts of his personal narrative.

**THINK** central

**Speaking & Listening Online**

Go to thinkcentral.com. KEYWORD: HML9N-184

| Written Narrative | Informal Speech |
|---|---|
| "A rafting trip through the Grand Canyon? For a week? Really?" I said, a grin pasted on my face. "That's a great idea, Dad." I felt a knot forming in my stomach. | [grin] You should have seen the grin on my face when my dad told me about our next family vacation! [pause] It was a fake grin. We were going on a rafting trip through the Grand Canyon. [frown] Ugh! |

- **Practice** Pace your delivery so that you finish on time. You might have a friend time you as you practice.

---

## DIFFERENTIATED INSTRUCTION

### FOR ENGLISH LANGUAGE LEARNERS

**Language: Reinforce Narrative Terms** Explain to students that giving an informal narrative speech has the same goals as writing a personal narrative—to entertain and to convey a message or theme. Review key terms used in the Workshops:

- *informal:* casual; without prescribed rules or customs
- *sequence of events:* order in which actions take place

- *verbal:* by means of words
- *nonverbal:* by means other than words
- *pace:* speed or rate
- *gestures:* movements of the body
- *facial expressions:* movements of the face
- *posture:* position of the body

## Deliver Your Speech

### USE VERBAL TECHNIQUES

How you use your voice can give the audience as much information as what you say.

- **Use a Conversational Tone** Use some of the same inflections and gestures you use when you share an important event with a friend. Volume should be normal, as in a conversation.
- **Pace Your Presentation** You can engage your audience by speaking at a faster pace to describe exciting events and at a slower pace to create suspense or drama.

### USE NONVERBAL TECHNIQUES

Facial expressions and gestures add meaning to your informal speech.

- Use gestures or body language to emphasize high points of conflict or humor.
- Make frequent eye contact with your audience, using your eyes to convey feelings.
- Employ facial expressions such as smiling, frowning, or raising an eyebrow to add drama to your presentation.
- Pay attention to how your posture conveys your attitude toward events. For example, slumped shoulders may indicate a feeling of defeat.

**YOUR TURN**

**As a Speaker** Before you present, create note cards that contain short words or phrases that remind you of the sequence of events and the details you want to include. By using words and phrases rather than sentences, you will avoid sounding as if you are reading rather than speaking to your audience. Number the cards in the order in which you will present your ideas. As you give your presentation, use your notes to stay on track.

**As a Listener** Connect with the speaker's narrative by making mental comparisons between the speaker's experiences and your own. These connections engage you, the listener, in the speaker's story, creating interest and involvement.

---

---

## Deliver Your Speech

*Model the Skill:* **USE VERBAL TECHNIQUES**

Model for students how to slow their pacing when they come to turning points in their narratives so that the audience will understand that something important is taking place. Also, show students how variations in pacing can show changes in time and mood.

**GUIDED PRACTICE** Ask a volunteer to read a passage from his or her narrative that contains an important detail or turning point. Ask students whether they recognize when the turning point occurs. Then have students underline sentences in their narratives that contain turning points or important details. Students should plan to slow their pacing when reading the underlined sentences aloud.

**YOUR TURN**

Have students prepare their note cards. Instruct students to focus on nouns, verbs, adjectives, and adverbs. These types of words are content words that will provoke speakers' memories as they deliver their presentations.

## Assess and Reteach

### Assess

Use the **COMMON CORE TRAITS** to assess students' speeches.

A strong informal speech
- includes story elements
- uses sensory language
- presents the sequence of events clearly
- is delivered using effective verbal and nonverbal techniques

### Reteach

Some students may have trouble relaying the sequence of events. Post a transitions word bank that students may consult. Remind students to keep verb tenses consistent when relaying the sequence of events. In this case, students are likely to use past tense verbs. Have them work with partners to edit their narratives for consistent verb tense.

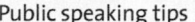

**Speaking and Listening Online** **THINK** central
- Public speaking tips
- Strategies for effective listening

## COMMON CORE FOCUS

**RL 1** Cite textual evidence to support analysis of what the text says explicitly as well as inferences drawn from the text. **RL 5** Analyze how an author's choices concerning how to structure a text create tension. **RI 1** Cite textual evidence to support analysis of what the text says explicitly as well as inferences drawn from the text. **RI 5** Analyze how an author's ideas are refined by particular sentences. **W 5** Strengthen writing by revising and editing to ensure that it demonstrates the conventions of standard English grammar and punctuation. **L 6** Acquire and use accurately general academic words; demonstrate independence in gathering vocabulary knowledge.

## CHECK READINESS

Read aloud the paragraph under **ASSESS** and stress to students that this is not the full Unit Test, but a way for them to check their readiness for it. Then have students examine the standards listed under **REVIEW** and look back in the unit or in the **Student Resource Bank** for any skills they need to review.

## READ THE TEXTS

Remind students to keep unit goals in mind as they read each passage, paying particular attention to these literary elements and reading skills:

- conflict
- plot stages and foreshadowing
- identifying main ideas

To help students focus on conflict while reading, encourage them to ask questions such as

- What external and internal conflicts exist between or within a character?

## ANSWER THE QUESTIONS

Direct students to pages R93–R101 of the **Handbook** to review test-taking strategies.

- When responding to multiple-choice items, suggest that students think of their answers before reading the answer choices.
- If students are unable to answer a question, suggest that they use a process of elimination for choosing the best answer.

---

## Assessment Practice

### ASSESS
Taking this practice test will help you assess your knowledge of these skills and determine your readiness for the Unit Test.

### REVIEW
After you take the practice test, your teacher can help you identify any standards you need to review.

#### COMMON CORE

**RL 1** Cite textual evidence to support analysis of what the text says explicitly as well as inferences drawn from the text. **RL 5** Analyze how an author's choices concerning how to structure a text create tension. **RI 1** Cite textual evidence to support analysis of what the text says explicitly as well as inferences drawn from the text. **RI 5** Analyze how an author's ideas are refined by particular sentences. **W 5** Strengthen writing by revising and editing to ensure that it demonstrates the conventions of standard English grammar and punctuation. **L 6** Acquire and use accurately general academic words; demonstrate independence in gathering vocabulary knowledge.

**Practice Test** THINK central

Take it at thinkcentral.com.
KEYWORD: HML9N-186

---

## Assessment Practice

**DIRECTIONS** Read the two texts and the public service advertisement. Then, answer the questions that follow.

# La Puerta *by José Antonio Burciaga*

1   It had rained in thundering sheets every afternoon that summer. A dog-tired Sinesio returned home from his job in a mattress sweat shop. With a weary step from the *autobús*, Sinesio gathered the last of his strength and darted across the busy *avenida* into the ramshackle *colonia* where children played in the meandering pathways that would soon turn into a noisy *arroyo* of rushing water. The rain drops striking the *barrio*'s tin, wooden and cardboard roofs would soon become a sheet of water from heaven.

2   Every afternoon Sinesio's muffled knock on their two-room shack was answered by Faustina, his wife. She would unlatch the door and return to iron more shirts and dresses of people who could afford the luxury. When thunder clapped, a frightened Faustina would quickly pull the electric cord, believing it would attract lightning. Then she would occupy herself with preparing dinner. Their three children would not arrive home for another hour.

3   On this day Sinesio laid down his tattered lunch bag, a lottery ticket and his week's wages on the oily tablecloth. Faustina threw a glance at the lottery ticket.

4   Sinesio's silent arrival always angered Faustina so she glared back at the lottery ticket, "Throwing money away! Buying paper dreams! We can't afford dreams, and you buy them!"

5   Sinesio ignored her anger. From the table, he picked up a letter, smelled it, studied the U.S. stamp, and with the emphatic opening of the envelope sat down at the table and slowly read aloud the letter from his brother Aurelio as the rain beat against the half tin, half wooden rooftop.

6   *Dear Sinesio,*

7   *I write to you from this country of abundance, the first letter I write from los Estados Unidos. After two weeks of nerves and frustration I finally have a job at a canning factory. It took me that long only because I did not have the necessary social security number. It's amazing how much money one can make, but just as amazing how fast it goes. I had to pay for the social security number, two weeks of rent, food, and a pair of shoes. The good pair you gave me wore out on our journey across the border. From the border we crossed two mountains, and the desert in between.*

8   *I will get ahead because I'm a better worker than the rest of my countrymen. I can see that already and so does the "boss." Coming here will be hard for you, leaving Faustina and the children. It was hard enough for me and I'm single without a worry in life. But at least you will have me here if you come and I'm*

---

## DIFFERENTIATED INSTRUCTION

### FOR ENGLISH LANGUAGE LEARNERS

**Assessment Practice: Work Backward**
Prepare students by having them read the questions *before* reading the passages. Have pairs find unfamiliar words in test directions and questions and follow these steps:

1. Write each word on an index card.
2. Look up the meaning in a dictionary and write it on the back of the card.
3. Use the cards to practice the words with your partner and to teach them to others.

**Assessment Practice: Pacing** Make sure that students understand that a test of reading is based on students' abilities to identify, understand, and analyze main ideas and important details. Therefore, although the test is timed, students must resist the urge to read quickly. Model for students how to read slowly by reading aloud from a transparency the first paragraph of "La Puerta", underlining important phrases and details and writing brief summaries (or key words and phrases) for each paragraph in the margin. Such notes

*sure I can get you a job. All you've heard about the crossing is true. Even the lies are true. "Saludos" from your "compadres" Silvio and Ramiro. They are doing fine. They're already bothering me for the bet you made against the Dodgers.*

9    *Next time we get together I will relate my adventures and those of my "compañeros" . . . things to laugh and cry about.*

10   Aurelio signed the letter *Saludos y abrazo*. Sinesio looked off into space and imagined himself there already. But this dreaming was interrupted by the pelting rain and Faustina's knife dicing *nopal*, cactus, on the wooden board.

11   *¿Qué crees?*—"What do you think?" Faustina asked Sinesio.

12   *¡No sé!*—"I don't know," Sinesio responded with annoyance.

13   "But you do know, Sinesio. How could you not know? There's no choice. We have turned this over and around a thousand times. That miserable mattress factory will never pay you enough to eat with. We can't even afford the mattresses you make!"

14   Sinesio's heart sank as if he was being pushed out or had already left his home. She would join her *comadres* as another undocumented widow. Already he missed his three children, Celso, Jenaro, and Natasia his eldest, a joy every time he saw her. "An absence in the heart is an empty pain," he thought.

15   Faustina reminded Sinesio of the inevitable trip with subtle statements and proverbs that went straight to the heart of the matter. "Necessity knows no frontiers," she would say. The dicing of the *nopal* and onions took on the fast clip of the rain. Faustina looked up to momentarily study a trickle of water that had begun to run on the inside of a heavily patched glass on the door. It bothered her, but unable to fix it at the moment she went back to her cooking.

16   Sinesio accepted the answer to a question he wished he had never asked. The decision was made. There was no turning back. "I will leave for *el norte* in two weeks," he said gruffly and with authority.

17   Faustina's heart sank as she continued to make dinner. After the rain, Sinesio went out to help his *compadre* widen a ditch to keep the water from flooding in front of his door. The children came home, and it became Faustina's job to inform them that *Papá* would have to leave for a while. None of them said anything. Jenaro refused to eat. They had expected and accepted the news. From their friends, they knew exactly what it meant. Many of their friends' fathers had already left and many more would follow.

18   Throughout the following days, Sinesio continued the same drudgery at work but as his departure date approached he began to miss even that. He secured his family and home, made all the essential home repairs he had put off and asked his creditors for patience and trust. He asked his sisters, cousins and neighbors to check on his family. Another *compadre* lent him money for

**GO ON** ➡️

## ITEM ANALYSIS

| COMPREHENSION AND WRITTEN RESPONSE | ITEMS | UNIT PAGES |
|---|---|---|
| Conflict | 2, 3 | 28–35, 59 |
| Narrative Techniques | 4, 14 | 28–35, 37 |
| Inferences | 6, 11, 12, 16, 17, 19, 20, 21, 22, 23 | 85 |
| Plot Development | 9, 10, 18 | 28–35 |
| Context Clues | 1, 5, 8, 13 | 82 |
| Word Roots | 7, 15 | 53 |

| WRITING AND GRAMMAR | ITEMS | UNIT PAGES |
|---|---|---|
| Revision | 1, 2, 6 | 178–183 |
| Punctuation | 3, 4 | 180 |
| Sentence Structure | 5, 7 | 54 |

**Practice Test**

On **thinkcentral.com** students can complete an interactive version of this practice test *and* receive remediation for the skills they have not yet mastered.

---

will help students return to particular paragraphs for rereading as they begin to respond to the questions. Then, have students work with partners to annotate the remainder of the story in this same way.

**FOR STRUGGLING READERS**

**Assessment Practice: Self-Questioning** Point out that literary texts often contain sentences or passages that are complex and difficult to understand. However, such passages are frequently important to the meaning of a story. Tell students that when they read such a sentence or passage, they should read and re-read it slowly. Then, students should ask themselves questions such as "What does this sentence or passage mean?" or "Why is

it important in the story?" Model this practice for students with Sinesio's thought: "An absence in the heart is an empty pain." Then, have students work with partners to ascertain the meaning and significance of the following line from Faustina: "Necessity knows no frontiers."

the trip and the coyote[1]. Sinesio did not know when he would return but told everyone, "One year, no more. Save enough money, buy things to sell here and open up a *negocio*, a small business the family can help with."

19     The last trip home from work was no different except for the going-away gift, a bottle of *mezcal*, and the promise of his job when he returned. As usual, the *autobús* was packed. And as usual, the only ones to talk were two loud young men, *sinvergüenzas*—without shame.

20     The two young men talked about the *Lotería Nacional* and a lottery prize that had gone unclaimed for a week. "*¡Cien millones de pesos!*—One hundred million pesos! *¡Caray!*" one of them kept repeating as he slapped the folded newspaper on his knees again and again. "Maybe the fool that bought it doesn't even know!"

21     "Or can't read!" answered the other. And they laughed with open mouths.

22     This caught Sinesio's attention. Two weeks earlier he had bought a lottery ticket. "Could . . . ? No!" he thought. But he felt a slight flush of blood rush to his face. Maybe this was his lucky day. The one day out of the thousands that he had lived in poverty.

23     The two jumped off the bus, and Sinesio reached for the newspaper they had left behind. There on the front page was the winning number. At the end of the article was the deadline to claim the prize: 8 that night.

24     Sinesio did not have the faintest idea if his ticket matched the winning number. So he swung from the highest of hopes and dreams to resigned despair as he wondered if he had won one hundred million pesos.

25     Jumping off the bus, he ran home, at times slowing to a walk to catch his breath. The times he jogged, his heart pounded, the newspaper clutched in his hand, the heavy grey clouds ready to pour down.

26     Faustina heard his desperate knock and swung the door open.

27     "*¿Dónde está?*" Sinesio pleaded. "Where is the lottery ticket I bought?" He said it slowly and clearly so he wouldn't have to repeat himself.

28     Faustina was confused, "What lottery ticket?"

29     Sinesio searched the table, under the green, oily cloth, on top of the dresser and through his papers, all the while with the jabbing question, "What did you do with the *boleto de lotería?*"

30     Thunder clapped. Faustina quit searching and unplugged the iron. Sinesio sounded off about no one respecting his papers and how no one could find anything in that house. "*¿Dónde está el boleto de lotería?*—Where is the lottery ticket?

31     They both stopped to think. The rain splashed into a downpour against the door. Faustina looked at the door to see if she had fixed the hole in the glass.

32     *¡La puerta!*—"The door!" blurted Faustina, "I put it on the door to keep the rain from coming in!"

---

1. **coyote:** slang for a smuggler.

## DIFFERENTIATED INSTRUCTION

**FOR ENGLISH LANGUAGE LEARNERS**
**Assessment Practice: Context Clues** Students who are not Spanish speakers may have difficulty with the use of Spanish in this story. Tell students that they can use context clues to determine the meanings of these words and phrases in the same way that they use context clues to determine the meanings of unfamiliar English vocabulary words. Model this practice for students.

• "open up a *negocio*, a small business the family can help with"

The author restates the meaning of *negocio* with the word *business*.

• "a bottle of *mezcal*"

*Mezcal* comes in a bottle and is given as a gift. Readers may infer that *mezcal* is an alcoholic beverage because people often give alcoholic beverages as gifts, and these beverages often come in bottles.

Have students work with partners to use context clues to understand the meanings of other Spanish terminology on this page.

33    Sinesio turned to see the ticket glued on the broken window pane. It was light blue with red numbers and the letters "*Lotería Nacional.*" Sinesio brought the newspaper up to the glued lottery ticket and with his wife compared the numbers off one by one—*Seis-tres-cuatro-uno-ocho-nueve-uno-¡SIETÉ—DOS!*—Sinesio yelled.

34    "¡No!" trembled a disbelieving and frightened Sinesio, "One hundred million pesos!" His heart pounded, afraid this was all a mistake, a bad joke. They checked it again and again only to confirm the matching numbers.

35    Sinesio then tried to peel the ticket off. His fingernail slid off the cold, glued lottery ticket. Faustina looked at Sinesio's stubby fingernails and moved in. But Faustina's thinner fingernails also slid off the lottery ticket. Sinesio walked around the kitchen table looking, thinking, trying to remain calm.

36    Then he grew frustrated and angry. "What time is it?"

37    "A quarter to seven," Faustina said looking at the alarm clock above the dresser. They tried hot water and a razor blade with no success. Sinesio then lashed out at Faustina in anger, "You! I never answered your mockery! Your lack of faith in me! I played the lottery because I knew this day would come! "*¡Por Dios Santo!*" and he swore and kissed his crossed thumb and forefinger. "And now? Look what you have done to me, to us, to your children!"

38    "We can get something at the *farmacia!* The doctor would surely have something to unglue the ticket."

39    "*¡Sí! ¡O sí!*" mocked Sinesio. "Sure! We have time to go there."

40    Time runs faster when there is a deadline. The last bus downtown was due in a few minutes. They tried to take the broken glass pane off the door but he was afraid the ticket would tear more. Sinesio's fear and anger mounted with each glance at the clock.

41    In frustration, he pushed the door out into the downpour and swung it back into the house, cracking the molding and the inside hinges. One more swing, pulling, twisting, splintering, and Sinesio broke the door completely off.

42    Faustina stood back with hands over her mouth as she recited a litany to all the *santos* and virgins in heaven as the rain blew into their home and splashed her face wet.

43    Sinesio's face was also drenched. But Faustina could not tell if it was from the rain or tears of anger, as he put the door over his head and ran down the streaming pathway to catch the *autobús.*

**GO ON** ➡

189

---

**FOR STRUGGLING READERS**

**Assessment Practice: Story Structure** Remind students that all stories follow the same basic structure: rising action, climax, falling action. Suggest that students draw triangles in the margin. At the top of the triangle tell students to write "fight between Sinesio and Faustina." Then, tell students to list significant events leading up to the fight on the left side of the triangle and significant events following the fight on the right side of the triangle. This quick story diagram will help students respond to questions regarding plot stages and conflict. Have students compare and contrast their event listings with partners. Tell students that they may add to or revise their diagrams as necessary after working with their partners.

# "Live Your Dreams"

**89th Connecticut College Commencement Address**
**Delivered May 20, 2007**
**by Robert D. Ballard**

1   We are here today to celebrate an important event in your life. A day you have worked so hard to have, a day that marks the end of one adventure in your life and the beginning of another.

2   For life truly is and should be a series of great adventures; a series of journeys within journeys.

3   Now, I am sure most of you have mixed emotions about today. You are glad your four-year journey in education is over but you are also nervous about what lies ahead. Are you sure about your next adventure in life? Have you made the right decision?

4   It is important to remember that all journeys in life begin with a dream, a dream to become someone; a dream to do something important in life that you and your friends and parents will be proud of. . . .

5   But all of us have different kinds of dreams, different goals in life to pursue. It is hard to know at times which dream to pursue since so many can run through your head while growing up. It is easy to question your decision to pursue one dream instead of another. To be paralyzed at times by indecision, fearful that you have made the wrong choice and that you may be going down the wrong road.

6   If you have such fears, put them aside, for life is the act of becoming; you never arrive. It's the journey that counts. Isn't it amazing how much time and energy mountain climbers spend planning and executing their ascent of Mount Everest and the meager amount of time they spend once they reach the summit taking in the view? It was the act of climbing that took them to the top, not a desire to get there and stay.

7   The question is which mountain in life should you pick to climb, which dream to pursue. I would like to share with you some important insights I have made which help me pick the mountains in life to climb.

8   The most important thing I have discovered is not whether the mountain is in Asia, or Europe, or under the sea.

9   The most important thing is that the mountain you choose to climb is high. I have discovered that if you climb a mountain that is say 1,000 feet tall and fall off its summit and break your neck you are just as dead as you would be had you fallen off a mountain that is 30,000 feet tall. You're dead all the same, so why did you pick a small mountain to fall off?

190

---

10  I have also discovered that it is just as hard to climb a 1,000-foot mountain, as it is to climb one 30,000 feet tall. People that climb tall mountains get up at the same time in the morning and go to bed at the same time in evening as those who climb little ones. They have to put up with the same amount of trials and tribulations each day. So what I learned was, it is just as easy or just as hard to climb a tall mountain as it is to climb a small mountain, so why not go for it!

11  When you walk up on the stage today to receive your diploma, having finally reached the summit of your present dream, a dream that has taken four or more years to reach, you will only spend a few seconds here. But when you look out at your parents and friends and see how proud they are, you will realize that this four-year journey was well worth the effort.

12  What is also important about climbing a tall mountain instead of a small one is that it takes a longer time to climb. This gives you a lot of time to think about what you are doing along the way and it gives you more time to enjoy the journey.

13  If you can reach the top of a mountain in just an hour or a day, it wasn't worth your time to climb.

14  I have found that if I pick a distant summit in the clouds to pursue, time is on my side and I can have a lot of fascinating side trips along the way. Side trips that enrich my life, but since I have that distant summit on the horizon to guide me, I find that I don't get lost along the way. I always know how to get back on the trail once my side trip has ended.

15  I also discovered that tall mountains frighten people off. As a result, there aren't many people climbing them. The path up to the summit is less crowded, less congested, and in fact easier to climb.

16  So I advise you to think big, have big dreams. Climb tall mountains.

GO ON

191

**FOR STRUGGLING READERS**

**Assessment Practice: Identify Genre, Purpose, and Audience** Remind students that taking a little time to describe a passage before reading it will help them with comprehension. Model for students how to identify the genre *(speech)*, purpose *(give advice to college graduates)*, and audience *(college graduates)* of this passage. Then, given this information, lead students to brainstorm what kind of content and language they expect to find in this passage. Record students' ideas on the board. Then, ask students to read the passage. Have students compare the passage with their initial expectations. Ask students to discuss how this process aids comprehension.

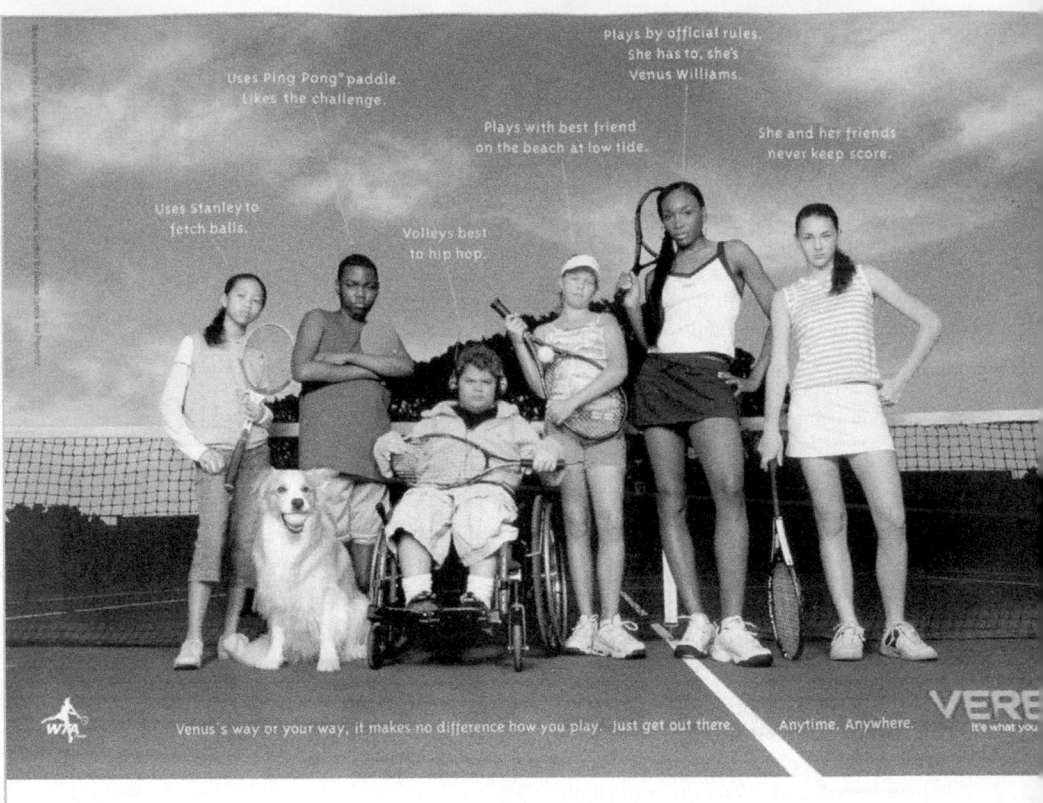

Uses Ping Pong® paddle.
Likes the challenge.

Plays by official rules.
She has to, she's
Venus Williams.

Plays with best friend
on the beach at low tide.

She and her friends
never keep score.

Uses Stanley to
fetch balls.

Volleys best
to hip hop.

Venus's way or your way, it makes no difference how you play. Just get out there. Anytime. Anywhere.

VERB
It's what you

---

## DIFFERENTIATED INSTRUCTION

### FOR ENGLISH LANGUAGE LEARNERS

**Assessment Support: Vocabulary** Using the VERB advertisement, introduce students to the following advertising terminology:

- *advertisement:* paid public announcement of goods, services, or ideas

- *copy:* words used in an advertisement

- *graphics:* illustrations, graphs, maps, or other visual elements

- *logo:* image or symbol that represents a company or organization

- *slogan:* memorable phrase used to advertise a product

- *target audience:* group of customers an advertisement is intended to appeal to

# Reading Comprehension

Use "La Puerta" (pp. 186–189) to answer
questions 1–10.

1. In paragraph 1, the word *meandering*
   means —
   - A. crowded
   - B. expensive
   - C. straight
   - D. twisting

2. In the beginning of the story, the conflict
   between Sinesio and Faustina is that —
   - A. Faustina thinks that she works harder
     than Sinesio
   - B. Faustina wants Sinesio to think more
     about the family's finances
   - C. Faustina is tired of ironing other people's
     clothing
   - D. Sinesio dislikes giving Faustina his
     paycheck every week

3. In paragraph 8, when Aurelio writes "It was
   hard enough for me and I'm single without
   a worry in life" it emphasizes —
   - A. Sinesio's internal conflict about leaving
     his family
   - B. the external conflict between Sinesio
     and Faustina
   - C. Faustina's internal conflict about her
     family's poverty
   - D. how hard it is to succeed in the face
     of obstacles

4. In paragraph 15, the author foreshadows
   that —
   - A. Sinesio will not travel across new frontiers
   - B. the window will be fixed with the lottery
     ticket
   - C. the family will become wealthier
   - D. the door will be replaced

5. In paragraph 18, the word *drudgery* means —
   - A. chores
   - B. entertainment
   - C. skills
   - D. failure

6. The reader can infer from the young men's
   reaction to the unclaimed lottery ticket in
   paragraphs 20–21 that —
   - A. they wish they had bought the winning
     ticket
   - B. they think uneducated people play
     the lottery
   - C. they know no one will claim the prize
   - D. they wish the prize money was larger

7. The word *desperate* comes from the Latin root
   *desperatus*, meaning "to despair." In paragraph
   26, *desperate* means —
   - A. calm
   - B. difficult
   - C. hopeful
   - D. urgent

GO ON →

## ANSWERS

## Reading Comprehension

Model a thinking process for answering
multiple-choice questions.

1. **D is correct.** Twisting *is a synonym for*
   meandering, *meaning "winding, as of a
   stream."* A *is incorrect because the* avenida *is
   busy or crowded, not the pathways.* B *and* C
   *are incorrect because the pathways are not
   well planned; they twist, wind, or meander.*

2. **B is correct.** *Faustina resents living in
   poverty while Sinesio spends their money
   on lottery tickets.* A *is not correct because
   Sinesio and Faustina both work hard.* C
   *is not correct because although Faustina
   is probably tired of ironing for others, she
   is willing to work to support her family.* D
   *is not correct because Sinesio cares about
   his family and accepts the responsibility of
   supporting them.*

3. **A is correct.** *Sinesio is reluctant to leave his
   family.* B *is not correct because Faustina
   supports Sinesio's decision to leave.* C *is not
   correct because Faustina is not conflicted
   over Sinesio's departure.* D *is not correct
   because Aurelio succeeds in the face of
   obstacles and offers Sinesio the opportunity
   to do the same.*

4. **B is correct.** *Faustina notices the leak on the
   glass of the patched door.* A *is not correct
   because Faustina and Sinesio believe the
   trip is inevitable.* C *is not correct because
   the paragraph focuses on the family's
   impoverished living conditions.* D *is not
   correct because the family has no money to
   replace the door.*

5. **A is correct.** *Chores is a synonym for* drudgery, *meaning "work that is hard or tiresome."
   Chores are tiresome, repetitious tasks, and
   the narrator describes the drudgery as being
   the same over time.* B *is not correct because
   Sinesio does not find his work entertaining.*
   C *is not correct because Sinesio uses skills to
   perform his tiresome work.* D *is not correct
   because Sinesio does not fail while working
   at the mattress factory.*

6. **B is correct.** *The use of the word* fool
   *suggests that the man thinks the lottery
   winner may be uneducated.* A *is not correct
   because the man uses the unclaimed lottery
   ticket as an opportunity to feel superior to
   the winner rather than as an opportunity
   to lament his own lack of action.* C *is not
   correct because the man does not comment
   on whether he thinks the prize will remain
   unclaimed.* D *is not correct because the
   man thinks the prize money is abundant.*

7. **D is correct.** *Sinesio needs to get in the
   house quickly to find the lottery ticket
   because time is short to claim the prize.* A
   *and* C *are not correct because Sinesio is not
   calm or hopeful regarding the lost lottery
   ticket.* B *is not correct because it is not
   difficult for Sinesio to knock on the door.*

**8. A is correct.** *Because Sinesio does manual labor and Faustina takes over the job of scraping the ticket from the window, it is likely that Sinesio's fingernails are short, not long. B and D are not correct because pretty or thin fingernails would not render Sinesio unsuccessful. C is not correct because short is a synonym for* stubby.

**9. C is correct.** *As the deadline nears, readers do not know whether Sinesio and Faustina will successfully redeem their winning lottery ticket, resulting in suspense. A is not correct because Sinesio and Faustina find the lottery ticket after a short search. B is not correct because readers already know about the leaky door and roof. D is not correct because readers do not yet know what has happened to the lottery ticket when Sinesio returns home.*

**10. D is correct.** *Readers do not learn the outcome of the story. A, B, and C are not correct because these details do not tell readers whether or not Sinesio is able to redeem his lottery ticket.*

**11. B is correct.** *The author says "all journeys in life begin with a dream." A is not correct because he is not talking about a vacation. C and D are not correct because the author advocates side trips while pursuing a dream.*

**12. A is correct.** *The author says that it's hard to choose among one's dreams. B is not correct because the author does not discuss this idea. C is not correct because the author focuses on what comes after this. D is not correct because the author emphasizes the importance of the journey and moving on to new challenges.*

**13. C is correct.** *The author contrasts the large amount of time spent planning and climbing with the little amount of time spent enjoying the summit. A is not correct because the climbers do not desire to stay on the mountaintop. B is not correct because* plenty *is an antonym of* meager. *D is not correct because the time at the top is short, not uncertain.*

**14. B is correct.** *Rhetorical questions involve the audience in the subject of the speech. A is not correct because the mountain is a metaphor. C is not correct because the speaker is not testing the audience's*

8. An antonym for the word *stubby* as it is used in paragraph 35 is —
   A. long
   B. pretty
   C. short
   D. thin

9. The author creates suspense at the climax of the story when —
   A. Sinesio and Faustina find the lottery ticket
   B. it starts to rain and the door and roof begin leaking
   C. the deadline for redeeming the lottery ticket nears
   D. Sinesio is returning from work

10. What is the resolution of the story?
    A. Sinesio breaks the door off the shack.
    B. Faustina prays to the saints.
    C. Sinesio runs down the street with the door.
    D. It is left to the reader's imagination.

> **Use "Live Your Dreams" (pp. 190–191) to answer questions 11–16.**

11. The author believes that the key element of any journey is —
    A. a destination
    B. a dream
    C. an itinerary
    D. good planning

12. In paragraph 5, the author describes the struggle to —
    A. choose the right dream
    B. grow up too quickly
    C. get a college education
    D. stay on the mountaintop

13. In paragraph 6, the word *meager* means —
    A. adequate
    B. plenty
    C. very little
    D. uncertain

14. The author includes a question at the end of paragraph 9 to —
    A. make the audience aware of the dangers of mountain climbing
    B. get the audience emotionally involved
    C. make sure the audience is still listening
    D. provoke an answer from the audience

15. The word *tribulations* comes from the Latin root *tribulare*, meaning "to oppress." In paragraph 10 *tribulations* means —
    A. burdens
    B. court battles
    C. judgments
    D. morals

16. The reader can conclude that the author —
    A. has climbed a mountain
    B. has traveled around the world
    C. has fulfilled some of his dreams
    D. has given this speech before

194

*listening skills. D is not correct because the speaker does not expect the audience to answer.*

**15. A is correct.** *Tribulations* are the burdens brought on by trials. *B is not correct because all people are not involved in court battles. C and D are not correct because judgments and morals are not the result of trials.*

**16. C is correct.** *The author speaks from his experiences of pursuing his dreams. A is not correct because the mountain is a metaphor. B is incorrect because the author says that the location of the mountain is not important. D is incorrect because the author does not refer to this.*

Use "La Puerta" and "Live Your Dreams" to answer questions 17–18.

**17.** Sinesio and Ballard would agree that —
  **A.** dreams can change over time
  **B.** difficult dreams are worth pursuing
  **C.** dreams are only important for young people
  **D.** there is only one dream that a person should follow

**18.** The tone at the end of both selections is one of —
  **A.** fear
  **B.** humor
  **C.** optimism
  **D.** suspense

Use the public service advertisement on page 192 to answer questions 19–20.

**19.** The purpose of this advertisement is to —
  **A.** encourage teens to be more physically active
  **B.** teach teens how to play tennis
  **C.** persuade Venus Williams to teach tennis
  **D.** keep the local community together

**20.** According to the advertisement, teens should play —
  **A.** on organized teams
  **B.** anytime, anywhere
  **C.** if they're physically able
  **D.** games they will win

**SHORT CONSTRUCTED RESPONSE**
Write a short response to each question, using text evidence to support your response.

**21.** In "La Puerta," what does the door symbolize? Support your response with evidence from the text.

**22.** Why does the speaker of "Live Your Dreams" use the metaphor of climbing a mountain? Support your response with evidence from the text.

Write a short response to this question, using evidence from **both** texts to support your response.

**23.** What is one similarity between Sinesio in "La Puerta" and Robert Ballard, the author of "Live Your Dreams"? Support your response with evidence from **both** texts.

GO ON

195

**23.** *Both men realize that dreams take time to be realized. Sinesio buys lottery tickets, hoping that one day he will win. He wants to be able to provide for his family and keep them together. Ballard believes dreams should take time to achieve because then there is more time to enjoy the journey.*

**17. B *is correct.*** *Sinesio pursues a better life despite the hardships, and Ballard encourages the audience to climb tall mountains. A is incorrect because Sinesio's dreams do not change. C is incorrect because Sinesio and Ballard are not young. D is not correct because Ballard advocates side trips during the pursuit of a dream.*

**18. C *is correct.*** *Despite the uncertainty at the end of both selections, both the characters in "La Puerta" and Robert Ballard show hope for a positive future. A is not correct because there is nothing to fear in either selection. B is not correct because neither selection is humorous. D is not correct because there is no suspense in Ballard's speech.*

**19. A *is correct.*** *The advertisement pictures teens dressed for tennis. B is incorrect because there is no information about how to play tennis. C is incorrect because Venus Williams is part of the ad as a role model rather than the intended audience. D is not correct because the advertisement is part of a national campaign to promote youth tennis.*

**20. B *is correct.*** *Anytime, anywhere is part of the slogan. A is incorrect because the advertisement does not mention organized sports. C is incorrect because some of the players have physical disabilities. D is not correct because one of the teens claims never to keep score.*

**SHORT CONSTRUCTED RESPONSE**

*Possible responses:*

**21.** *The door symbolizes the struggle with poverty. It has to be latched from the inside so that it stays closed. The glass is patched many times and water is still getting in. Faustina uses the lottery ticket to keep the rain from coming in. Further, toward the end of the story, it is a struggle to break the door off the hinge. The door is their hope, but it is also an obstacle to realizing their hope.*

**22.** *The speaker of "Live Your Dreams" uses the metaphor of the mountain to give the audience a visual image of his message. The metaphor helps the audience understand the idea that life is a journey that takes goals, plans, and work.*

# Revising and Editing

1. **B is correct.** *The length of the bus ride is not relevant to the memory of the paper war. A is not correct because it is the topic sentence. C and D are not correct because they are relevant to the experience of the paper war.*

2. **C is correct.** *This sentence includes sight and touch details relevant to the experience of the paper war. A, B, and D are not correct because these details are not relevant to the paper war.*

3. **B is correct.** *Deleting the comma and the phrase* it was *corrects the comma splice. A is not correct because there is no reason to place a comma after* bus. *C is not correct because the hyphen forms the compound adjective* shy-looking. *D is incorrect because the sentence contains an error.*

4. **A is correct.** *Adding a comma after* rolling *sets off the introductory phrase. B is not correct because* myself *is correct. C is not correct because there is no reason to add a comma after* raging. *D is not correct because the sentence contains an error.*

5. **D is correct.** *This sentence is an effective way to combine the sentences by making the second sentence a phrase. A is incorrect because this sentence suggests that the two events occur simultaneously rather than sequentially. B is not correct because it contains a comma splice. C is not correct because the coordinating conjunction* but *suggests an inaccurate contrast.*

---

# Revising and Editing

**DIRECTIONS** Read this passage, and answer the questions that follow.

> (1) Of all the events of my childhood the one I remember best is my first ride on the school bus. (2) It took our bus forty-five minutes to get from my house to the school. (3) As I stepped on and looked for an empty seat, I saw countless strange faces glaring back at me. (4) I sat near the back of the bus next to a shy-looking kid wearing a backpack, it was almost as big as he was. (5) As the bus got rolling I soon found myself in the middle of a raging paper war. (6) "Will this ever stop?" I wondered as a thick, wet paper wad struck my ear. (7) "Get under here!" the boy next to me shouted. (8) He signaled me to duck under the backpack with him. (9) As we crouched, we laughed together at the chaos around us. (10) I promised to meet him after school so we could ride home together.

1. Which sentence should be deleted to make the paragraph more coherent?
   A. Sentence 1
   B. Sentence 2
   C. Sentence 6
   D. Sentence 8

2. Which sentence should the writer add to include relevant sensory details?
   A. The bus had room for sixty-four students.
   B. I disliked waiting for the bus almost as much as riding it.
   C. I waded through crumpled litter and masses of students to get to my seat.
   D. My friend's mom worked at the school, so he didn't ride the bus.

3. What change, if any, should be made to sentence 4?
   A. Add a comma after *bus*
   B. Delete the comma and *it was*
   C. Change *shy-looking* to **shy looking**
   D. Make no change

4. What change, if any, should be made in sentence 5?
   A. Add a comma after *rolling*
   B. Change *myself* to **me**
   C. Add a comma after *raging*
   D. Make no change

5. What is the best way to combine sentences 7 and 8?
   A. "Get under here!" the boy next to me shouted when he signaled me to duck under the backpack with him.
   B. "Get under here!" the boy next to me shouted, he signaled me to duck under the backpack with him.
   C. "Get under here!" the boy next to me shouted, but he signaled me to duck under the backpack with him.
   D. "Get under here!" the boy next to me shouted, signaling me to duck under the backpack with him.

---

## DIFFERENTIATED INSTRUCTION

**FOR ENGLISH LANGUAGE LEARNERS**

**Assessment Support: Negative Words** When answering multiple-choice questions, caution students to pay attention to negative words in the question or stem. Negative words such as *not* ask test takers to reverse their thinking; they must identify a response that is untrue or undesirable. Point out the word *deleted* in question 1. The question asks students to identify which sentence does *not* belong in the passage. Tell students to review the first sentence of the passage to identify the main idea. Then, have students read all the answer choices, selecting the one that does not give further information or explanation regarding the main idea.

**6.** Which sentence should the writer add to explain the significance of the event?

**A.** That school bus ride was really awkward.

**B.** In the midst of flying trash, I had somehow found a friend.

**C.** The bus system was in need of stricter discipline.

**D.** The school bus was an efficient mode of transportation.

**7.** Which transitional word or phrase should be added to the beginning of sentence 10?

**A.** When we arrived,

**B.** As a matter of fact,

**C.** Before this all began,

**D.** However,

197

**6. B *is correct.*** *This sentence explains why the paper war is a memorable event in the writer's life.* A, C, and D *are not correct because these details do not support the story.*

**7. A *is correct.*** *This transition indicates that after the incident on the bus, the author wants to meet him for the ride home.* B, C, and D *are not correct because they indicate an inaccurate relationship between the events.*

**FOR STRUGGLING READERS**

**Assessment Support: Test Patterns** Instruct students to use their reasoning skills and knowledge to respond to each question on a standardized test. Caution students against looking for test patterns. A student who observes that the last three answers have been "B" should not change his or her answer based on this observation. In general, students should rely on their first responses unless they have good reasons for changing their answers.

## INTRODUCE *GREAT READS*

In Unit 1, students have discussed a number of big questions. Invite students to tell which question they found most intriguing and why, and then focus attention on the three that appear on this page. Discuss the recommended books and their summaries, pointing out how each connects to the related question. Encourage students to choose one or more of these "great reads" to read independently.

## Ideas for Independent Reading

Which of the questions in Unit 1 intrigued you the most? Continue exploring them through independent reading.

### What does it take to be a survivor?

**The Autobiography of Miss Jane Pittman**
*by Ernest J. Gaines*

This unusual novel is written as an autobiography. A 110-year-old woman tells the story of her life, from her childhood as a slave in Louisiana to the civil rights era of the 1960s.

**And Then There Were None**
*by Agatha Christie*

At certain points, this mystery novel might bring to mind the sizzling plot elements of "The Most Dangerous Game." Ten strangers are lured to an island from which there is no escape.

**In These Girls, Hope Is a Muscle**
*by Madeleine Blais*

This true account goes behind the scenes as a basketball team tries to survive the state playoffs.

### What is worth fighting for?

**Shoeless Joe**
*by W. P. Kinsella*

Against everyone's advice, Ray Kinsella builds a baseball diamond in a cornfield to give Shoeless Joe Jackson, a legendary outfielder done in by scandal and now dead, a chance to play.

**All Quiet on the Western Front**
*by Erich Maria Remarque*

This fictional antiwar classic follows Paul Baumer into the German army during World War I. While fighting the human enemy, Paul also fights a more deadly enemy—the hate that leads men into war.

**The Pact: Three Young Men Make a Promise and Fulfill a Dream**
*by Dr. Sampson Davis, et al.*

Three young men from the wrong side of the tracks in Newark, New Jersey, made a pact: they would all become doctors and they would do it together. Over-coming numerous obstacles, they all achieved their goal.

### What makes a winner?

**Bad Boy: A Memoir**
*by Walter Dean Myers*

The author of many novels about black characters remembers his own childhood in Harlem. Surrounded by poverty and drugs, he seeks escape and adventure in books and succeeds in becoming a writer.

**The Natural**
*by Bernard Malamud*

Roy Hobbs, a talented athlete whose promising career is cut short by his own misdeeds, makes a comeback in middle age. He struggles to be a great player and to fulfill his dream.

**The Miracle Worker**
*by William Gibson*

This play tells the true story of the dedicated Annie Sullivan's struggle to free Helen Keller from the prison of her dark and silent world. Convinced that she can give Helen the gift of language, Annie applies herself with fanatical dedication.

**Get Novel Wise** THINK central

Go to **thinkcentral.com**.
KEYWORD: HML9-198

198

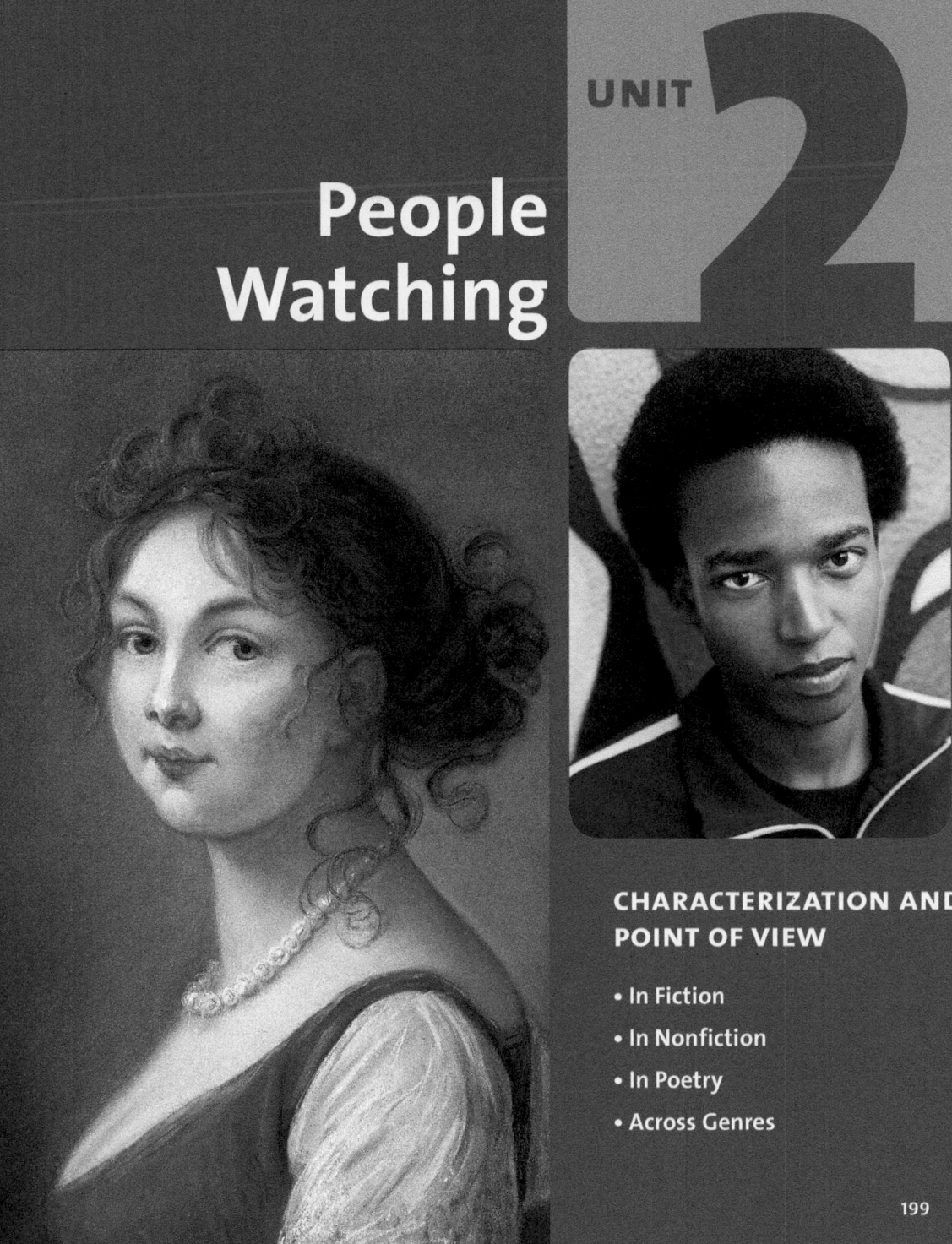

# People Watching

## CHARACTERIZATION AND POINT OF VIEW

- In Fiction
- In Nonfiction
- In Poetry
- Across Genres

199

## INTRODUCE THE UNIT

In a park, at the beach, or at the mall, observing the clothing, facial expressions, and body language of passersby is a great way to learn about people of all cultures, ages, and genders. Ask volunteers to tell about some of the interesting people they have observed. Question them about what they learned from their observations.

Invite students to use their people-watching skills to discuss the pictures on this page. To elicit ideas, ask:

- When might each person have lived?
- How would you describe each person's manner of dress? What can you learn from it?
- How might you describe each person's attitude?
- What might each person be thinking and feeling?
- If you wrote a story about each of them, what might be the title?

Discuss with students which of their ideas are facts and which are speculation. Point out that we can learn only so much from observing people in a portrait or book illustration or even in real life. In this unit, students will explore how **characterization, point of view,** and the other techniques an author uses to develop a character allow readers to get below the surface and truly know the character.

For help in planning this unit, see

**R** RESOURCE MANAGER UNIT 2
pp. 1–10

**About the Art** Marie Louise Élisabeth Vigée LeBrun (1755–1842) painted Louise Augusta, Queen of Prussia in 1801. For more information, see page 225 of the teacher's edition.

| | **Text Analysis Workshop: Character and Point of View** pp. 202–207 | **Pancakes** Short Story pp. 208–221 | *Comparing Texts* **The Necklace/ Spending Spree/ Is Debt Dragging You Down?** Short Story/Magazine Article/ Advertisement pp. 222–239 | **Hamadi** Short Story pp. 240–253 | from **I Know Why the Caged Bird Sings / Caged Bird** Autobiography pp. 254–267 |
|---|---|---|---|---|---|
| **COMMON CORE** **STRAND** | | *Lexile: 930* *Fry: 11* *Dale-Chall: 6.2* | *Lexile: 920* *Fry: 11* *Dale-Chall: 6.5* | *Lexile: 830* *Fry: 7* *Dale-Chall: 6.3* | *Lexile: 910* *Fry: 7* *Dale-Chall: 6.0* |
| **Reading Literature** | Point of View pp. 202–203 Character Traits and Motivation pp. 204–206 RL 3 Analyze the Text p. 207 | First-Person Point of View pp. 209, 213, 217, 219 RL 3 Sarcasm p. 216 RL 4 Draw Conclusions pp. 209, 210, 214, 215, 219 RL 1 Language Coach pp. 216, 218 RL 4 | Character Motivation pp. 223, 228, 231, 233, 234 RL 3 Make Inferences pp. 223, 224, 226, 234 RL 1 Language Coach p. 227 RL 4 | Third-Person Point of View pp. 241, 244, 245, 247, 251 RL 3 Figurative Language p. 250 RL 4 Monitor pp. 241, 242, 245, 248, 249, 251 | |
| **Reading Informational Text** | | | Magazine Article p. 237 Flier, p. 238 RI 7 | | Characterization in Autobiography pp. 255, 256, 260, 261, 263, 265 RI 5, RI 10 Analyze Perspectives pp. 255, 258, 263, 265 RI 6 |
| **Writing** | | Writing Prompt p. 221 W 4 | Quickwrite p. 222 Writing Prompt p. 236 | Writing Prompt p. 253 W 9a (RL 3) | Writing Prompt p. 267 W 2b, W 10 |
| **Speaking and Listening** | | Discuss p. 208 SL 1 | What's the Connection p. 222 SL 1 | Present p. 240 SL 1 | Discuss p. 254 SL 1 |
| **Language** | | Precise Adjectives pp. 212, 221 L 3 Latin Word Root *ben* p. 220 L 4c | Vary Sentence Beginnings pp. 230, 236 L 1b The Latin Word Root *spec* p. 235 L 4a | Language Coach pp. 246, 248 L 4, L 4c Using Repetition to Add Emphasis pp. 250, 253 L 3 Words from Greek Culture p. 252 L 6 | Language Coach p. 260 L 4c Descriptive Details pp. 261, 267 L 1b Multiple-Meaning Words p. 266 L 4 |

| Linked Selections | | *A Voice/My Father's Song* Poems pp. 286–291 | *from Rosa Parks/Rosa* Biography/Poem pp. 292–301 | *Writing Workshop:* Argument: Literary Criticism pp. 302–311 *Speaking and Listening Workshop:* Participating in a Discussion pp. 312–313 |
| *Blind to Failure* Magazine Article pp. 268–281 | *A Different Level of Competition* Newspaper Article pp. 282–285 | | | |
| *Lexile: 1200* *Fry: College* *Dale-Chall: 7.4* | *Lexile: 1040* *Fry: 12* *Dale-Chall: 7.6* | | *Lexile: 1320* *Fry: College* *Dale-Chall: 7.2* | |
| | | Speaker pp. 287–291 RL 1 Reading Poetry pp. 287, 288, 291 RL 10 | Characterization Across Genres pp. 293, 296, 297, 298, 299 RL 7 Purpose for Reading p. 293 RL 7 | |
| Character Study pp. 269, 270, 272, 274, 276, 280 RI 3 Language Coach p. 279 RI 4 | Main Ideas pp. 282–285 RI 1, RI 2, RI 5, RI 6 | | Characterization Across Genres pp. 293, 296, 297, 298, 299 RI 7 Purpose for Reading p. 293 RI 7 | |
| Quickwrite p. 268 | Writing Prompt p. 285 W 9b (RI 1) | Quickwrite p. 286 | Write for Assessment p. 301 W 4, W 9 (RL 7, RI 7), W 10 | Writing a Literary Criticism pp. 302–311 W 1a–e, W 2c, W 4, W 5, W 9a (RL 1, 3), W 10 |
| Interpret Graphic Aids pp. 269, 273, 278, 280 SL 2 | | | Discuss p. 292 SL 1 | Participating in a Discussion pp. 312–313 SL 1a–d, SL 3, SL 4 |
| Specialized Vocabulary, p. 281 L 6 | | | Language Coach p. 296 L 4a Paradox p. 298 L 5a Etymologies p. 300 L 4c | Editing and Publishing p. 309 L 1b, L 2 |

ECOS

To see the complete Essential Course of Study, see pp. T23–T28.

For additional lesson planning help, see **Teacher One Stop DVD.**

## Instructional Support

**Resource Manager Unit 2**

**UNIT SUPPORT**
Academic Vocabulary, p. 3
Additional Academic Vocabulary, p. 4
Grammar Focus pp. 5–6
Text Analysis Workshop pp. 9–10
Writing Workshop: Argument:
   Literary Criticism p. 165

**SELECTION SUPPORT\***

**Plan and Teach**
Lesson planning pages
Additional leveled selection questions
Extension activities

**Student Copy Masters**
Selection summaries in four languages
Skills copy masters in English and Spanish
Vocabulary preteaching and support
Reading Check and Question Support
Reading Fluency

\*Available for all selections

† Available on **thinkcentral.com**.

**Language Handbook**

**Vocabulary Practice**

**Best Practices Toolkit**†

**PowerNotes** DVD-ROM†

**Connections: Nonfiction for
Common Core** CD-ROM†

**Teacher One Stop** DVD-ROM

**Student One Stop** DVD-ROM

**Write*Smart*** CD-ROM†

**GrammarNotes** DVD-ROM†

**WordSharp** CD-ROM†

## Differentiated Instruction

### STRUGGLING READERS AND WRITERS

Resource Manager Unit 2
Additional Selection Questions
Question Support
Reading Fluency
**Interactive Reader**
**Adapted Interactive Reader**
**Level Up Online Tutorials**
**Audio Anthology**
(with Audio summaries)
**Diagnostic and Selection Tests**
Selection Tests A/B

### ENGLISH LANGUAGE LEARNERS

Resource Manager Unit 2
Selection Summaries in English,
Spanish, Vietnamese and Haitian Creole
Skills Copymasters in Spanish
**English Language Learner Adapted
Interactive Reader Teacher's Guide**
**ELL Adapted Interactive Reader**
**Audio Tutor**
**Guide to English for Newcomers**
**Audio Anthology**
**Audio Summaries in Multiple
Languages**
(on **thinkcentral.com**)

### ADVANCED LEARNERS

Resource Manager Unit 2
Additional Selection Questions
Ideas for Extension
**Diagnostic and Selection Tests**
Selection Tests B/C

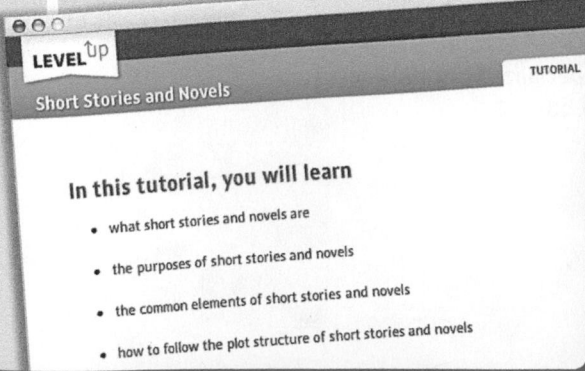

## Assessment and Reteaching

**Diagnostic and Selection Tests**

**Unit and Benchmark Tests**

**ThinkCentral Online Assessment:**

- All program assessments
- Level Up Online Tutorials

**ExamView Test Generator** on the Teacher One Stop DVD-ROM

**Online Essay Scoring** on **thinkcentral.com**

**ThinkCentral Online Reteaching:**

- Level Up Online Tutorials
- Reteaching Worksheets

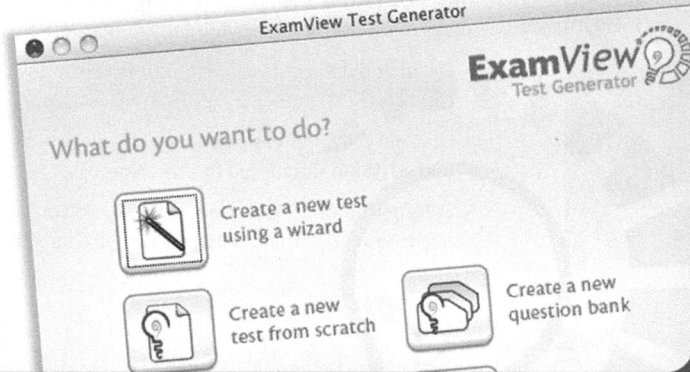

## Professional Development

**Video Center** Based on interviews with program consultants and other educational experts, these videos feature classroom-ready teaching strategies.

**Teacher Toolkit** Includes a Teacher Handbook as well as a range of articles and handouts by program consultants and other educators.

Janet Allen

Kylene Beers

Jim Burke

Carol Jago

## THINK central at a Glance

### One Location, Endless Resources

**Find Resources** Browse all *Holt McDougal Literature* components for the ones that meet your students' needs and match your teaching style.

**Assess Progress and Reteach** Assign electronic versions of program assessments to measure your students' mastery of the Common Core State Standards. On thinkcentral.com, some tests deliver online remediation tutorials to students who have not mastered skills.

 **Interactive Whiteboard Lessons**

Prepare your students for college and careers by teaching relevant, real-world skills through dynamic, interactive instruction. Go to **thinkcentral.com** to browse through all whiteboard lessons or to access the lessons, including the following:

- Character Development and Motivation
- Point of View
- Making Inferences

 Together Holt McDougal and HISTORY® are revolutionizing the study of English/language arts with video that helps students relive and re-imagine the people, places, and events they are discovering through reading. Look for selections with the HISTORY® icon.

## What makes a
# CHARACTER
## memorable?

To introduce the page, invite students to describe memorable characters from books or from TV shows, plays, or movies they have seen. Call on volunteers to describe or demonstrate how the character walked, spoke, gestured, or used facial expressions. As you proceed, discuss how these details help communicate the character's personality.

*ACTIVITY* Encourage students to be specific when responding to the questions. Guide students to conclude that a writer needs to have a strong sense of the character's physical appearance, manner of speaking and acting, personality, and even a sense of the character's past.

**CHECK UNDERSTANDING** Have students sum up what they have learned about characters.

**Find It Online!**

**THINK** central

Go to thinkcentral.com for the interactive version of this unit.

## What makes a
# CHARACTER
## memorable?

Any skilled actor knows that it takes more than costumes and makeup to create a memorable character. Everything from the voice to the walk to the simplest of gestures and facial expressions must be considered and carefully chosen.

*ACTIVITY* With a group of classmates, think of several complex and interesting characters that you remember from TV shows, books, or movies. Describe each one, including details about both looks and personality. Then consider the following questions:

• On what details did you base your first impression of each character?

• How did your impression change as you got to know the character better? What details led to this change?

• Considering your discussion, what would you imagine a writer needs to keep in mind when creating a character?

200

---

## Unit Resources

See resources on the **Teacher One Stop DVD-ROM** and on thinkcentral.com.

**R** RESOURCE MANAGER UNIT 2

UNIT AND BENCHMARK TESTS

**📁** BEST PRACTICES TOOLKIT

INTERACTIVE READER

ADAPTED INTERACTIVE READER

ELL ADAPTED INTERACTIVE READER

LANGUAGE HANDBOOK

VOCABULARY PRACTICE

**TECHNOLOGY**

💿 **Teacher One Stop DVD-ROM**

💿 **Student One Stop DVD-ROM**

💿 **PowerNotes DVD-ROM**

💿 **Write*Smart* CD-ROM**

💿 **Media*Smart* DVD-ROM**

💿 **GrammarNotes DVD-ROM**

💿 **Audio Anthology CD**

💿 **Audio Tutor CD**

**THINK** central

**Find It Online!**

The interactive version of this unit on **thinkcentral.com** includes

• video and **PowerNotes** introductions to key selections

• audio support—listen or download

• **ThinkAloud** models

• **WordSharp** vocabulary tutorials

• interactive review and remediation

## Preview Unit Goals

| | |
|---|---|
| **TEXT ANALYSIS** | • Identify and analyze point of view<br>• Analyze character traits and motivation<br>• Analyze the methods writers use to develop complex characters<br>• Analyze and compare characterization in a variety of texts |
| **READING** | • Make inferences and draw conclusions<br>• Recognize central ideas and supporting details<br>• Analyze the representation of a subject in different mediums |
| **WRITING AND LANGUAGE** | • Write an argument (literary criticism), using valid reasoning and evidence<br>• Use supporting and descriptive details; use precise adjectives<br>• Use various types of phrases and clauses<br>• Place commas correctly and use appropriate and varied transitions |
| **SPEAKING AND LISTENING** | • Present an argument (literary criticism) |
| **VOCABULARY** | • Use knowledge of word origins to determine or clarify word meanings<br>• Determine the correct meaning of multiple-meaning words and domain-specific vocabulary<br>• Determine figurative and connotative meanings of words |
| **ACADEMIC VOCABULARY** | • complex    • device    • evaluate<br>• interact    • perspective |

201

---

**UNIT GOALS**
Included in this unit: RL 1, RL 3-4, RL 6-7, RL 10, RI 1-7, RI 10, W 1a-e, W 2b-c, W 4-5, W 9a-b, W 10, SL 1a-d, SL 2-4, L 1b, L 2-4, L 4a, c, L 5a, L 6
Complete text of the Common Core State Standards is found in the correlation on p. T10. Standards covered in this unit are found in the standards overview (pp. 199A–199B) and on the lesson pages where they are taught.

## Preview Unit Goals

This page provides the big picture of the skills and strategies covered in this unit. Point out that each skill strand is a different color and that throughout the unit, the skills taught within a strand match the color of that strand. Encourage students to think about their ability to use each skill or strategy as they read the page.

Suggest that students copy the Academic Vocabulary terms in their **Reader/Writer Notebooks** and define them in their own words as they work through the unit. Encourage students to use these words in their discussion of the selections and in their writing.

---

## DIFFERENTIATED INSTRUCTION

### FOR ENGLISH LANGUAGE LEARNERS

**Academic Vocabulary** Provide students with definitions of each Academic Vocabulary word

**complex** (käm pleks') *adj.* made up of two or more parts; hard to understand or analyze

**device** (di vīs') *n.* a thing created; a mechanical invention or creation

**evaluate** (ĭ-văl´yōō-āt) *v.* to find out the value or worth of something; to judge or examine

**interact** (in´tər akt') *v.* to act or work with someone or something; to act with one another

**perspective** (pər spek'tiv) *adj.* point of view or mental view

Use the copy master to help students learn academic words they will use in this unit and on the Assessment Practice.

**R** RESOURCE MANAGER—Copy Masters
Academic Vocabulary p. 3

# Focus and Motivate

## COMMON CORE FOCUS

**RL 3** Analyze how complex characters develop over the course of a text, interact with other characters, and advance the plot or develop the theme.

# Teach

## Part 1: Point of View

**Point of View** Explain that point of view influences how a story is told. Have students imagine that a bank robbery has taken place in their town. Then discuss how each of these participants or onlookers might retell the event:

- the robber
- the driver of the getaway car
- a bank employee who faced the robber
- a customer who witnessed the robbery
- a police officer who pursued the robber
- a local newspaper reporter

Point out that details of the story would vary according to the point of view of the narrator. Ask students which persons might be expected to know the most and the least about the robbery. Then, discuss whose point of view might be more emotional or biased and whose might be more objective.

**BEST PRACTICES TOOLKIT—Transparency**
Analysis Frame: Character pp. D21, D26

---

# Character and Point of View  *Essential Course of Study* ECOS

When you read a book or watch a movie, you become involved on an emotional level with the characters. Like real people, complex characters can win your sympathy, make your blood boil with anger, get on your nerves, or give you insights into human nature. By asking some pointed questions, you can better understand why you are reacting the way you are. For example, through whose eyes are you experiencing events? Which details are shaping your impression of each character?

## COMMON CORE

Included in this workshop:
**RL 3** Analyze how complex characters develop over the course of a text, interact with other characters, and advance the plot or develop the theme.

## Part 1: Point of View

The perspective from which a story is told is called **point of view.** Think of point of view as the lens that a writer chooses for his or her readers to look through. Point of view determines what you learn about the characters and may shape how you feel about them. It also affects the choice of the **narrator**—the voice that tells the story. Knowing a work of fiction's point of view can help you evaluate the details you receive about characters and plot events.

| FIRST-PERSON POINT OF VIEW | THIRD-PERSON POINT OF VIEW |
|---|---|
| **The Narrator**<br>• is a main or minor character in the story<br>• refers to himself or herself as *I* or *me*<br>• presents his or her own thoughts and feelings<br>• does not have direct access to the thoughts and feelings of other characters | **The Narrator**<br>• is not a character in the story<br>• may not be an identifiable person but merely a voice that tells the story<br>• is called **omniscient** if he or she knows the thoughts and feelings of all the characters<br>• is called **limited** if he or she focuses on the thoughts and feelings of one character |
| ▼ | ▼ |
| **Impact on the Reader**<br>• Your understanding of characters and events is limited to what this narrator reveals about them.<br>• You can't necessarily trust the narrator's interpretation of events.<br>• The story seems real, almost as if the narrator were talking to you. | **Impact on the Reader**<br>• You are likely to learn more about characters and events than if the story were told by a first-person narrator.<br>• You might not feel as connected to the characters because the story is told in a less personal way. |

---

## DIFFERENTIATED INSTRUCTION

### FOR STRUGGLING READERS

**Note Taking** Read aloud the text below "Part 1: Point of View." Draw a T-chart on the board and label the left side *first-person point of view* and the right side *third-person point of view*. Have students do the same on a piece of paper. As you read the characteristics of a first-person narrator on p. 202, have students take notes under the *first-person point of view* heading. Ask volunteers to share their notes and record information in note form on the

T-chart on the board. Repeat the process for the right side and *third-person point of view*. Ask students to re-read p. 202 and add any missing information to their notes. Encourage students to refer back to their notes as they read the selections in this unit.

## MODEL 1: FIRST-PERSON POINT OF VIEW

A first-person narrator allows you to experience events from his or her perspective. Even though you are getting only one view of the action, you often feel as though you are right at the scene. As you read this excerpt, consider how the boy's thoughts affect the way you picture the room.

*from*
# GREAT EXPECTATIONS
### Novel by **Charles Dickens**

. . . I was half afraid. However, the only thing to be done being to knock at the door, I knocked, and was told from within to enter. I entered, therefore, and found myself in a pretty large room, well lighted with wax candles. No glimpse of daylight was to be seen in it. It was a dressing-room, as I supposed
5 from the furniture, though much of it was of forms and uses then quite unknown to me. But prominent in it was a draped table with a gilded looking-glass, and that I made out at first to be a fine lady's dressing-table.

Whether I should have made out this object so soon, if there had been no fine lady sitting at it, I cannot say. In an arm-chair, with an elbow resting on
10 the table and her head leaning on that hand, sat the strangest lady I have ever seen, or shall ever see.

**Close Read**

1. How does the first-person point of view influence the way you visualize this scene?

2. How do you think this scene would be different if the lady were the narrator?

## MODEL 2: THIRD-PERSON POINT OF VIEW

In a story told from the third-person point of view, an outside narrator tells you about the story's characters and events. As you read this excerpt, think about whether the character would describe himself in the same way the third-person narrator does.

*from*
# The Chocolate War
### Novel by **Robert Cormier**

The Goober was beautiful when he ran. His long arms and legs moved flowingly and flawlessly, his body floating as if his feet weren't touching the ground. When he ran, he forgot about his acne and his awkwardness and the shyness that paralyzed him when a girl looked his way. Even his thoughts
5 became sharper, and things were simple and uncomplicated—he could solve math problems when he ran or memorize football play patterns. Often he rose early in the morning, before anyone else, and poured himself liquid through the sunrise streets, and everything seemed beautiful, everything in its proper orbit, nothing impossible, the entire world attainable.

**Close Read**

1. Find an example of a direct comment about the Goober. Then find an example in which the narrator allows you to "see" his thoughts. An example of each has been boxed.

2. Identify a sentence that the Goober probably would not have used to describe himself and his running.

## MODEL 1: FIRST-PERSON POINT OF VIEW
### Close Read

1. **Possible answer:** *You are seeing everything through the boy's eyes and experiencing the eerie scene as he is experiencing it. His fear (line 1) probably influences his perception and description of the scene.*

2. **Possible answer:** *If you were seeing the scene through the woman's eyes, you might learn her thoughts and feelings about being interrupted by a strange boy at the door. Also, since the woman is in familiar surroundings, she would probably not describe its details as strange or eerie.*

## MODEL 2: THIRD-PERSON POINT OF VIEW
### Close Read

1. **Possible answer:** *Direct comment: "His long arms and legs moved flowingly and flawlessly" (lines 1–2). Narrator allows you to see Goober's thoughts: "He could solve math problems when he ran" (lines 5–6).*

   **If students need help . . .** Have students compare the two boxed examples. Note that the first boxed example is a comment, and the second uses the verb *forgot* to signal inner thoughts and feelings.

2. **Possible answer:** *The Goober probably wouldn't have written the first sentence to describe himself: "The Goober was beautiful when he ran."*

### FOR STRUGGLING READERS

**Comprehension: Story Elements** Write these story elements on the board and have students identify them by analyzing the first three sentences of the excerpt from *Great Expectations*:

Narrator: *a boy*
Main Character: *the narrator*
Setting: *large, candle-lit room*
Other Characters: *a woman in the room*

### FOR ADVANCED LEARNERS/PRE–AP

**Analyze Point of View** Have students read the workshop independently. Assign previously read selections to individuals. Direct students to identify and describe the points of view of the narrators in their assigned selections and to tell how these points of view affect what the reader learns.

**Online Remediation**

Are your students struggling with text analysis skills? Consider assigning them one or more **Level Up Online Tutorials** as remediation before beginning this unit. Log in to **thinkcentral.com** to view a list of the skills addressed by **Level Up**.

# Teach

## Part 2: Character Traits and Motivation

**Character Traits** Before reading the page, write the word *traits* on the board and record students' ideas about possible meanings. Then, ask students to recall memorable or complex characters from selections they have read and to describe the characters' traits—what the characters were like.

Explain that an author may directly identify a character's traits but that most characterization is indirect. The author reveals characters through methods such as appearance, words, thoughts, actions, and other characters' thoughts and actions.

**Methods of Characterization** After discussing the chart with students, read each example and have students identify the method.

- She arrived in a crisp white T-shirt and pressed jeans. *physical appearance*
- Alberto spoke in a booming voice accompanied by dramatic gestures. *speech, thoughts, and actions*
- Jenny had a multitude of friends in her orbit, all of them vying for her time. *other characters*

Invite volunteers to generate their own sample sentences or phrases, and have the class identify the method.

## CHECK UNDERSTANDING

Have students name three or more character traits.

---

## Part 2: Character Traits and Motivation

Authors develop complex and believable characters through a range of devices that reveal the characters' traits and sometimes conflicting motivations. By analyzing these traits and motivations, you can determine how the characters advance the story's plot or develop the theme.

### CHARACTER TRAITS

You have probably encountered characters who are athletic, shy, arrogant, or wise—words you might also use to describe people in your life. These words are descriptions of **character traits,** or qualities shown by characters. Sometimes a narrator directly identifies a character's traits, but more often, traits are revealed through indirect methods of characterization. This means that a writer *shows* you a character without telling you what kind of person he or she is. Using the clues in the text, you must form your own impression.

| METHODS OF CHARACTERIZATION | EXAMPLES |
|---|---|
|  **1. PHYSICAL APPEARANCE** Descriptions of the character's <br>• clothing <br>• physical characteristics <br>• body language and facial expressions <br>• gestures or mannerisms | • A character who usually wears unmatched socks and stained shirts might be described as **slovenly.** <br>• If a character is always smiling and making eye contact with others, you might infer that she is **warm** or **friendly.** |
|  **2. SPEECH, THOUGHTS, AND ACTIONS** Presentation of the character's <br>• speech patterns <br>• habits and tastes <br>• talents and abilities <br>• interaction with others | • A character who speaks so quietly that others can't hear might be described as **timid.** <br>• You might infer that a character who repeatedly misses softball practice without telling the coach is **irresponsible** or **unreliable.** |
| **3. OTHER CHARACTERS** Presentation of other characters' <br>• reactions to the character <br>• relationships with the character <br>• impression of the character's reputation <br>• traits that contrast with the character's traits | • If a character's girlfriend describes him as a "no-good lying jerk," you might infer that he is **insensitive** and **dishonest.** <br>• If people often confide their troubles to a character, you might conclude that she is **trustworthy.** |

---

## DIFFERENTIATED INSTRUCTION

### FOR STRUGGLING READERS

**Note Taking** For those students who need help, hand out the note-taking copy master for this page. Read this page. Assist students in completing the copy master as needed.

 RESOURCE MANAGER—Copy Master
Note Taking p. 10

### FOR ENGLISH LANGUAGE LEARNERS

**Classification Chart** Use a Classification Chart to show the difference between direct and indirect characterization. Label the first column *Direct* and the second column *Indirect*. In the first column, write "tells traits." In the second column, list "appearances"; "speech, thoughts, and actions"; and "other characters." Have students summarize the diagram.

 BEST PRACTICES TOOLKIT—TRANSPARENCY
Classification Chart p. B17

## MODEL 1: PHYSICAL APPEARANCE

Whether it is accurate or not, your first impression of a character may be based solely on his or her appearance. As you read this excerpt, consider how the narrator's description of her unique wardrobe affects your impression of her. How would you describe the narrator to others?

*from* Life Without **Go-Go** Boots

Personal essay by **Barbara Kingsolver**

. . . In fifth grade, when girls were wearing straight shifts with buttons down the front, I wore pastel shirtwaists with cap sleeves and a multitude of built-in petticoats. My black lace-up oxfords, which my parents perceived to have orthopedic value, carried their own weight in the spectacle. I suspected people
5 noticed, and I knew it for sure on the day Billy Stamps announced to the lunch line: "Make way for the Bride of Frankenstein."

**Close Read**

1. What do you learn about the narrator's traits from her own description of how she dresses? Find two details that reveal these traits.

2. Identify one trait that is revealed through Billy Stamps's reaction to the narrator.

## MODEL 2: SPEECH, THOUGHTS, AND ACTIONS

In this excerpt from the novel *To Kill a Mockingbird*, the writer creates a distinct portrait of Miss Maudie by showing her in action. As you read, think about how the writer reveals Miss Maudie's personality.

*from* To Kill a Mockingbird

Novel by **Harper Lee**

Miss Maudie hated her house: time spent indoors was time wasted. She was a widow, a chameleon lady who worked in her flower beds in an old straw hat and men's coveralls, but after her five o'clock bath she would appear on the porch and reign over the street in magisterial beauty.
5 She loved everything that grew in God's earth, even the weeds. With one exception. If she found a blade of nut grass in her yard it was like the Second Battle of the Marne: she swooped down upon it with a tin tub and subjected it to blasts from beneath with a poisonous substance she said was so powerful it'd kill us all if we didn't stand out of the way.

**Close Read**

1. What do you learn about Miss Maudie in this excerpt? Describe her as completely as you can.

2. Miss Maudie is both elegant and energetic. Which details in the text reveal these traits? One has been boxed.

**FOR STRUGGLING READERS**

**Draw the Contrast** To help students comprehend the passage in Model 1, have them work in pairs to illustrate what girls wore and what the narrator wore. You may need to explain terms such as *shifts, shirtwaists, cap sleeves,* and *petticoats.* Have them point out the differences between the two styles.

## MODEL 1: PHYSICAL APPEARANCE

### BACKGROUND

Go-go boots were popular in the 1960s, the time period described in Kingsolver's essay. These white, tight-fitting, calf-high boots were worn by dancers on afternoon discotheque shows on television and were quickly adopted by teenagers. These boots are in stark contrast to the black lace-up oxfords worn by the narrator.

#### Close Read

1. *Possible answer: The narrator was probably unpopular and embarrassed by her wardrobe, which was very different from that of the other girls. Details that reveal these traits: "when girls were wearing . . . I wore . . . ." Her self-conciousness and embarrassment are conveyed when she says that her oxfords "carried their own weight in the spectacle."*

2. *Possible answer: Billy Stamps's reaction to the narrator confirms that the narrator was considered strange by the other students and subject to their ridicule.*

## MODEL 2: SPEECH, THOUGHTS, AND ACTIONS

#### Close Read

1. *Possible answer: Miss Maudie hates the indoors. She has two sides: the rumpled gardener (lines 2–3) and the regal lady of the neighborhood (line 4). She loves all growing things except nut grass, which she exterminates mercilessly (lines 5–8).*

2. *Possible answer: Details that reveal her elegance: "magisterial beauty" (line 4); details that reveal her energy: "time spent indoors was time wasted" (line 1); "she swooped down upon it" (line 7).*

## CHARACTER MOTIVATION

**Character Motivation** Use a three-column chart such as the one below to explore character motivation in a selection that students have previously read.

| Action | Motivation | Clues |
|---|---|---|
| Scout fights at school. | A boy insults her father. | She is devoted to her father. |

### Close Read

1. *Possible answer:* The narrator's birth filled the parents with ambition and a desire to get ahead in the world.

2. *Possible answer:* The mother was motivated by stories of historical figures who rose from poverty to greatness. She thinks that her child will have more opportunities as the son of a businessman rather than as the son of a farmer (lines 9–10).

## CHECK UNDERSTANDING

Have students think of a character in a book or film they have read or seen recently and describe the character's motivation.

## CHARACTER MOTIVATION

Why does a character move across the country, steal money from a friend, go to war, or live alone on a mountaintop? Figuring out a character's **motivation**—the reasons behind his or her actions—is a key part of understanding the character. Love, hate, vengeance, ambition, and desperation are some of the emotions that drive characters' behavior. Sometimes a writer will directly tell you about a character's motivation, but more often you must look for details in the story that reveal the motivation. As you read any story, consider the following clues:

- the narrator's direct comments about a character's motivation
- the character's actions, thoughts, feelings, values, and interactions with other characters
- hints about internal conflicts that may motivate the character
- your own insights into human behavior

In the following excerpt, why does the mother persuade her husband to make some changes? As you read, use the clues in the text to uncover the mother's motivation.

---

*from* # THE EGG

Short story by **Sherwood Anderson**

It was in the spring of his thirty-fifth year that father married my mother, then a country school-teacher, and in the following spring I came wriggling and crying into the world. Something happened to the two people. They became ambitious. The American passion for getting up in the world took possession of 5 them.

It may have been that mother was responsible. Being a school-teacher she had no doubt read books and magazines. She had, I presume, read of how Garfield, Lincoln, and other Americans rose from poverty to fame and greatness, and as I lay beside her . . . she may have dreamed that I would some day rule men and 10 cities. At any rate she induced father to give up his place as a farmhand, sell his horse, and embark on an independent enterprise of his own. . . . For herself she wanted nothing. For father and myself she was incurably ambitious.

### Close Read

1. How does the narrator's birth change his parents?

2. Reread the boxed text. What does it tell you about the mother's motivation for convincing her husband to give up farming?

---

## DIFFERENTIATED INSTRUCTION

### FOR STRUGGLING READERS

**Vocabulary Support** Introduce these terms from "The Egg." Have students read the context for each word and suggest a synonym to replace it:

- *presume* (line 7), "assume," "guess"
- *induced* (line 10), "caused"
- *embark on* (line 11), "begin," "start"
- *enterprise* (line 11), "business," "undertaking"
- *incurably* (line 12), "hopelessly"

**Concept Support** To help students gain familiarity with the terms *motivate* and *motivation*, list the following the board:

- greed
- love of family
- being fired from a job
- peer pressure

Have students suggest an action or word for each emotion or situation that could cause someone to become motivated.

# Part 3: Analyze the Text

Use what you've just learned about point of view, character traits, and motivation to analyze this excerpt from a novel about Hana, a Japanese woman who comes to the United States in the early 20th century. In the excerpt, some neighbors visit the new home of Hana and her husband, Taro. As you read, notice how the writer reveals Hana's and Taro's personalities. How does the choice of the narrator shape your understanding of the scene?

*from*

# Picture *Bride*

### Novel by **Yoshiko Uchida**

The men glanced around the living room which Hana had taken great pains to decorate properly. A new flowered rug lay on the floor, and fresh white curtains that Kiku had helped Hana sew hung at the windows. The first tight buds of the flowering peach in their yard had begun to swell, and knowing
5  there would be callers, Hana had arranged a spray on the mantel.
   "We'll come right to the point," a tall red-headed man said without bothering to sit down. "There've been some complaints from the neighborhood about having Japanese on this block."
   Taro caught his breath. "I see. Can you tell me who it was that
10  complained?"
   "Just some of the neighbors."
   "What is it we have done to offend them?"
   "Well, nothing specific."
   Taro looked at each of the men in turn and tried to keep his voice steady.
15  "Gentlemen," he began. "My wife and I looked many, many months to find a home where we might raise our daughter. When the owner said there would be no objection to our moving in here, we trusted him. It was a dream come true for us. We have already spent much time and money to make this house our home. And now, you would ask us to leave?"
20  Taro dared not stop before he finished all he wanted to say. "I should like to meet those neighbors who object to us," he said. "Is it any of you gentlemen?"
   The men looked uncomfortable. "We're just here to represent them."
   "Then please invite them to come talk to me. If they can tell me why we aren't desirable or why we do not deserve their respect, I shall consider their
25  request. I am the proprietor of Takeda Dry Goods and Grocers on Seventh Street and I would be happy to have them visit my shop as well."
   The men glanced uneasily at one another and had nothing more to say.

## Close Read

1. From which point of view is this story told? Explain how you know.

2. What do you learn about Hana's traits from the description of the room in lines 1–5?

3. What kind of people are the men in Taro's and Hana's home? Find two details that reveal their traits. An example has been boxed.

4. Reread lines 14–19 and 23–26. What is Taro's motivation for bravely speaking his mind? Explain what his words tell you about his character.

5. How would the story be different if Taro were the narrator?

# Part 3: Analyze the Text

**Close Read**

1. ***Possible answer:*** *The story is told from the third-person omniscient point of view: the narrator is not a character in the story; the reader knows the thoughts of Taro, Hana, and, arguably, the men.*

2. ***Possible answer:*** *Hana is meticulous, enjoys decorating her home, takes pride in it, and is eager to impress visitors.*

3. ***Possible answer:*** *The men are rude, disrespectful, abrupt, prejudiced, possibly unable to be direct about their own issues, and unprepared for a confrontation. Supporting details: lines 6–8, 22, and 27.*

4. ***Possible answer:*** *Taro is motivated by the wish to stay in his home and by pride. Also, he was assured that he would have no problems moving into this neighborhood. He is proud, straightforward, hardworking, and frustrated by the situation.*

5. ***Possible answer:*** *If Taro were the narrator, readers might learn more about his inner reactions to the men entering his house and gain insight into his thoughts and feelings about the men's request.*

## Assess and Reteach

### Assess

Have students identify what motivates the main characters in *Picture Bride*. Also have them identify the narrator and reflect on what he or she knows about the characters, their thoughts, and their motivations.

### Reteach

For students who are unable to apply the workshop skills to the excerpt from *Picture Bride*, select from these reteaching options.

- Review the note-taking copy masters for this lesson. Have students choose one skill and explain it to a partner.

- Name a story the class has read recently. Have students identify the narrator, the point of view, and details that show the main character's traits and motivation.

## FOR STRUGGLING READERS

**Analysis Support: Character Traits**

1. Draw a three-column chart with the heads *Taro, Hana,* and *The Men.* Write these sideheads: *Words, Actions.*

2. Have students work in pairs to list the characters' words and actions and the traits they reveal.

3. Discuss what students know about the main characters in this excerpt. Ask from whose point of view the story is told.

## FOR ENGLISH LANGUAGE LEARNERS

**Vocabulary: Idioms** Help students use context clues to determine the meanings of these idioms in the story:

- *great pains* (line 1), "a lot of effort"
- *come right to the point* (line 6), "speak directly"
- *caught his breath* (line 9), "stopped breathing for a second"

# Focus and Motivate

## COMMON CORE FOCUS

**RL 1** Cite strong and thorough textual evidence to support analysis of what the text says explicitly as well as inferences drawn from the text. **RL 3** Analyze how complex characters develop over the course of a text and interact with other characters. **RL 4** Determine the figurative meaning of phrases as they are used in a text; analyze the cumulative impact of specific word choices on meaning. **W 4** Produce explanatory writing in which the style is appropriate to the task. **L 3** Apply knowledge of language to make effective choices for meaning or style. **L 4c** Consult reference material to determine or clarify a word's meaning or etymology.

## SUMMARY

"Pancakes" is Joan Bauer's comic account of a teenager's obsession with perfection. At a critical moment while working, Jill's ex-boyfriend and his parents arrive. Their offer of help teaches Jill a lesson about her priorities.

### Are you a
## PERFECTIONIST?

After students read the paragraph and take the quiz, have them give examples of being a perfectionist. Encourage them to use those examples in the *DISCUSS* activity.

---

# Selection Resources

---

## Pancakes
Short Story by Joan Bauer

# Are you a
# PERFECTIONIST?

**COMMON CORE**

**RL 1** Cite strong and thorough textual evidence to support analysis of what the text says explicitly as well as inferences drawn from the text. **RL 3** Analyze how complex characters develop over the course of a text and interact with other characters. **RL 4** Determine the figurative meaning of phrases as they are used in a text; analyze the cumulative impact of specific word choices on meaning.

The main character in "Pancakes" is a perfectionist—she needs everything to be perfect in order to be happy. Would you describe yourself this way? Take this true-false quiz to find out. If you answer "true" to three or more statements, you are flirting with perfectionism.

*DISCUSS* After you take the quiz, form a small group with two to four of your classmates to discuss the pros and cons of perfectionism. Is striving for perfection ever helpful or necessary? When might it be difficult to cope with this trait?

## quiz ⦵⦵ HOW PERFECT IS TOO PERFECT?
Answer the following questions to discover if a perfectionist lurks within you.

1. I won't even attempt to do something unless I know that I will be able to do it without a mistake.
   ☐ TRUE  ○ FALSE

2. I am so competitive that my best friends won't play sports with me.
   ☐ TRUE  ○ FALSE

3. I know what I will be wearing every day for the next week.
   ☐ TRUE  ○ FALSE

4. I won't eat food unless it's prepared exactly the way I like it.
   ☐ TRUE  ○ FALSE

5. I can't sleep if my bookshelf is not correctly categorized and in alphabetical order.
   ☐ TRUE  ○ FALSE

---

See resources on the **Teacher One Stop DVD-ROM** *and on* **thinkcentral.com**.

**R** **RESOURCE MANAGER UNIT 2**
Plan and Teach, pp. 11–18
Summary, pp. 19–20†‡*
Text Analysis and Reading
   Skill, pp. 21–24†*
Vocabulary, pp. 25–27*
Grammar and Style, p. 30

**DIAGNOSTIC AND SELECTION**
   **TESTS**
Selection Tests, pp. 59–62

**BEST PRACTICES TOOLKIT**
Definition Mapping, p. E6
Two-Column Chart, p. A25
Analysis Frame: Character,
   pp. D21, D26
New Word Analysis, p. E8
Open Mind, p. D9

**TECHNOLOGY**
 **Teacher One Stop DVD-ROM**
**Student One Stop DVD-ROM**
**Audio Anthology CD**
**GrammarNotes DVD-ROM**
**ExamView Test Generator**
on the **Teacher One Stop**

---

\* Resources for Differentiation          † Also in Spanish          ‡ In Haitian Creole and Vietnamese

## TEXT ANALYSIS: FIRST-PERSON POINT OF VIEW

"Pancakes" is told from a **first-person point of view.** Jill, the narrator, is a character in the story, and she describes events as she herself experiences them. You will see the other characters and the actions in the story through Jill's eyes and learn exactly what she thinks and how she feels. As you read "Pancakes," look for comments that reveal Jill's feelings about her life and help explain the causes of her perfectionism.

*Review:* **Character Traits**

## READING SKILL: DRAW CONCLUSIONS

After reading a story, you often add up the details you've read about and develop your own ideas about what they mean. This process is called **drawing conclusions.** A conclusion is a logical judgment that a reader makes. In order to be logical, your conclusions must be based on

- strong evidence from the text
- your own experience and knowledge

As you read "Pancakes," use a chart like the one shown to record important details about Jill's thoughts, actions, and relationships. Tell what these details reveal about Jill.

| Details About Jill | My Thoughts |
|---|---|
| She refers to her mother as "Ms. Subtlety" after her mother tapes an article on perfectionism to Jill's mirror. | Jill is being sarcastic. She might feel her mother is picking on her. |

After reading, you can use the information you've gathered to draw conclusions about Jill's perfectionism.

*Review:* **Predict**

## ▲ VOCABULARY IN CONTEXT

Joan Bauer makes use of the following boldfaced words to tell this amusing story. Try to figure out the meaning of each word from the context of the phrase given.

1. mustard and other **condiments**
2. a **degenerate** with no morals
3. the **benign** climate of Hawaii
4. ill-behaved and **crass**
5. **steel** yourself against insults
6. **rabid** with anger

 Complete the activities in your **Reader/Writer Notebook.**

---

## Meet the Author

### Joan Bauer
born 1951

**Comic Relief**
From a very young age, Joan Bauer knew she wanted to have a career making people laugh. She remembers having an early fascination with things that were funny—especially the stories told to her by her grandmother, whom she calls her greatest creative influence. Bauer often crafts characters who share the same anxieties she felt as a teenager—apprehension about her parents' divorce, worry about her appearance—and chronicles the relief and inspiration that humor can bring to adverse situations. Describing her motivation to write, Bauer says, "I want to create stories that link life's struggles with laughter."

**Accidents and Accolades**
Bauer's first novel, *Squashed,* began as a screenplay. When she suffered severe injuries in a car accident, however, she found herself unable to meet the tight schedule the film industry demanded. During her long recovery, she turned her screenplay into a prize-winning novel. "The humor in that story kept me going," Bauer explains.

**BACKGROUND TO THE STORY**
**Writing from Experience**
Like Jill in "Pancakes," Bauer, as a teenager, waited tables in a pancake restaurant. She vividly remembers the Sunday morning when she was the only waitress on duty, frantically trying to attend to all her customers. The memory still haunts her: "I remember the sheer terror of dozens of hungry people looking to me and me alone for breakfast. To this day, whenever I walk into a pancake house, I hyperventilate."

**Author Online**
Go to **thinkcentral.com.**
KEYWORD: HML9-209

209

---

## VOCABULARY SKILL

COMMON CORE
L 4

### ▲ VOCABULARY IN CONTEXT

**DIAGNOSE WORD KNOWLEDGE** Have all students complete Vocabulary in Context. Check their words and phrases against the following:

**benign** (bǐ-nīn′) *adj.* good; kindly
**condiment** (kŏn′də-mənt) *n.* a sauce, relish, or spice used to season food
**crass** (krăs) *adj.* crude; unrefined
**degenerate** (dǐ-jěn′ər-ǐt) *n.* a corrupt or vicious person

**rabid** (răb′ǐd) *adj.* uncontrollable; fanatical
**steel** (stēl) *v.* to make hard or strong

**PRETEACH VOCABULARY** Use the following copy master to help students create a word map for each boldfaced word.

**R** RESOURCE MANAGER—Copy Master
Vocabulary Study p. 25

1. Read the first phrase in Part A aloud.
2. Guide students in creating word maps.

---

# Teach

TEXT ANALYSIS
COMMON CORE
RL 3

## ● *Model the Skill:* FIRST-PERSON POINT OF VIEW

Read aloud this passage:

> I sat at my desk, surrounded by my new classmates, and smiled. I knew that everyone would like me.

Point out that this passage reveals the narrator's feelings. It shows that she is confident that she will make new friends.

**GUIDED PRACTICE** Ask students to name stories that they have read with a first-person point of view and to tell what they recall about the narrator.

READING SKILL
COMMON CORE
RL 1

## ■ *Model the Skill:* DRAW CONCLUSIONS

Read the text under **Comic Relief,** then model drawing conclusions. Tell the students:

1. The author wants to make people laugh.
2. From experience, I know that humor often helps people cope with problems.
3. I conclude that the humor in "Pancakes" helps students see problems in perspective.

**GUIDED PRACTICE** After students read **Accidents and Accolades,** ask what conclusion they can draw about Bauer's need to use humor in her stories.

**R** RESOURCE MANAGER—Copy Master
Draw Conclusions p. 23 (for student use while reading the selection)

## READ WITH A PURPOSE

*Help students set a purpose for reading. Ask them to observe how the narrator deals with the things that bother her. Ask them to consider whether they would react in the same ways.*

**READING SKILL**   **COMMON CORE**   **RL 1**

### Ⓐ DRAW CONCLUSIONS

***Possible answer:*** *Jill is self-confident and has a strong self-image. She boasts that she looks spectacular in the shirt because its color complements her hair and eyes (lines 23–25).*

**IF STUDENTS NEED HELP . . .** Have students add their thoughts about these prior details to their Reading Skills charts:

- comments about Allen (lines 6–8)
- interaction with the mirror (lines 8–11)

Discuss how their responses establish a strong self-image for Jill from the start.

**Extend the Discussion** Find some examples on this page of Jill's tendency to exaggerate. How do the exaggerations add to your impression of her self-image?

**VOCABULARY**   **COMMON CORE**   **L 4**

### OWN THE WORD

- **rabid:** Remind students of the other meaning of *rabid*: affected with rabies, an infectious, often fatal disease that attacks the central nervous system of mammals. Then have students write a pair of sentences showing an understanding of the two meanings of *rabid*.

- **benign:** Have students create a semantic map for *benign*. Write the word in a center circle and add the definition given: "good, kindly." Draw spider legs from the center circle and have students add synonyms to complete the map. ***Possible answers:*** *harmless, inoffensive, innocuous, pleasant, nice*

---

# Pancakes

## JOAN BAUER

The last thing I wanted to see taped to my bathroom mirror at five-thirty in the morning was a newspaper article entitled "Are You a Perfectionist?" But there it was, courtesy of my mother, Ms. Subtlety herself. I was instantly irritated because Allen Feinman had accused me of perfectionism when he broke up with me last month. The term he used was "**rabid** perfectionism," which I felt was a bit much—but then Allen Feinman had no grip on reality whatsoever. He was rabidly unaware, if the truth be known, like a **benign** space creature visiting Earth with no interest in going native. I tore the article off the mirror; this left tape smudges. Dirty mirrors drove me crazy. I grabbed
10 the bottle of Windex from the closet and cleaned off the gook until the mirror shined, freed of yellow journalism.[1]

I glowered at the six telltale perfectionist signs in the now crumpled article.

1. Do you have a driving need to control your environment?
2. Do you have a driving need to control the environment of others?
3. Are you miserable when things are out of place?
4. Are your expectations of yourself and others rarely met?
5. Do you believe if something is to be done right, only you are the one to do it?
6. Do you often worry about your performance when it is less
20 than perfect?

Number six had particular sting, for it was that very thing that Allen Feinman had accused me of the day he asked for his green and black lumberjack shirt back, a truly spectacular shirt that looked a lot more spectacular on me than it did on him because it brought out the intensity of my short black hair and my mysterious brown eyes. He had accused me Ⓐ of numbers one through five as well, but on this last fateful day he said, "The problem with you, Jill, is that if the least little thing goes wrong, you

---

1. **yellow journalism:** journalism that exploits or exaggerates the news to create sensations and attract readers.

**210**   UNIT 2: CHARACTERIZATION AND POINT OF VIEW

### ⓵ Targeted Passage

### *Analyze Visuals* ▶

What qualities of this photograph convey the fast-paced atmosphere of a busy restaurant? Explain how these qualities work together to convey a specific **mood**, or feeling.

**rabid** (răb′ĭd) *adj.* uncontrollable; fanatical

**benign** (bĭ-nīn′) *adj.* good; kindly

### Ⓐ DRAW CONCLUSIONS

Reread lines 21–25 to draw a conclusion about the narrator's sense of self. Do you think Jill has a strong or a weak self-image? Record your answer in your chart.

---

## DIFFERENTIATED INSTRUCTION

### FOR ENGLISH LANGUAGE LEARNERS

Show students how they can use Definition Mapping as a learning strategy for learning words like *consumed* (line 66), *challenge* (line 143), and *ultimate* (line 303).

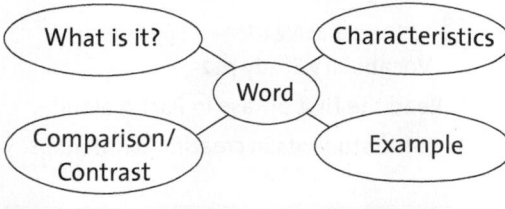

### FOR STRUGGLING READERS

In combination with the *Audio Anthology CD*, use one or more Targeted Passages (pp. 210, 212, 217, 218) to ensure that students focus on key story events, concepts, and skills. Targeted Passages are also good for English learners.

### ⓵ Targeted Passage [Lines 1–11]

This passage introduces Jill, the first-person narrator of the story, and reveals her strongest personality trait: her perfectionism.

**Teens at Work** According to U.S. Department of Labor Statistics, youth employment in America is booming. An estimated 5.9 million young people between the ages of 16 and 19 have jobs. Today, two-thirds of American high school students have jobs. Older male and female youths are equally likely to work in the restaurant trade, with boys employed primarily as cooks and busboys and girls as waitresses and cashiers. In "Pancakes," Jill opens the restaurant on weekends—an unusual responsibility for someone so young.

**Cultural Connection** Various forms of pancakes, a batter cake fried with oil or butter, are found in cultures around the world. Examples include French *crêpes*, Ethiopian *injire*, Egyptian *katief*, and the Russian *blintz*. Invite students to share examples of pancakes they are familiar with.

## Analyze Visuals

*Possible answer: The blurry background of a restaurant and the fuzzy image of a waitress carrying a loaded food tray convey a feeling of urgency, characterized by quick movements and a hectic pace.*

**About the Art** The photographer titled this composition *Speedy Service at Diner.* Focusing on the waitress in the foreground while using a slow shutter speed makes the background blurry and gives the photograph a feeling of rapid movement. The mood of the photograph matches the narrator's upcoming description of a busy pancake restaurant (starting at line 105).

- What does Jill find taped to her mirror? Why is she displeased about it? (lines 1–5)
- What does she call her mother? (line 3)
- Who is Allen? Why is Jill irritated with him? (lines 4–8)
- What does she do to the mirror? Why? (lines 9–11)

**FOR ADVANCED LEARNERS/PRE–AP**

**Analyze Adjectives** Remind students that precise adjectives enhance writing.

- Ask students to keep a running list of the adjectives that the narrator, Jill, uses to describe the following: herself, Allen Feinman, and her work situation.
- Ask student pairs to discuss what these adjectives reveal about Jill.
- Have them brainstorm additional adjectives they would use to describe Jill, Allen, and Jill's morning at work.

## B CHARACTER TRAITS

*Possible answer:* Her irritation with anything out of place, having and using a spot remover kit, and her expectation that Allen would have appreciated her planning and organization illustrate her perfectionism.

**IF STUDENTS NEED HELP . . .** Have students use a chart to match Jill's actions in lines 38–45 with the "telltale perfectionist signs" in lines 13–20.

| Jill's Actions | Perfectionist Signs |
|---|---|
| uses spot remover kit | miserable with disorder |
| fluffs pillows; removes spot, plucks dead leaf | needs to control environment |
| offered to organize Allen's CD collection | needs to control others |

 **BEST PRACTICES TOOLKIT—Transparency**
Two-Column Chart p. A25

## C GRAMMAR AND STYLE

COMMON CORE L 3

**Analyze Supporting Details** Discuss how *short clipped* hair (line 56) and *just-manicured* nail (line 57) suggest Jill's obsession for meticulous detail. Then ask students to read Mr. Halloran's statement in lines 55–56 and comment on what the precise adjectives *organized* and *competent* suggest about his view of Jill's personality. Encourage students to find other examples of precise adjectives in the story and discuss their effectiveness.

## VOCABULARY

COMMON CORE L 4

### OWN THE WORD

**condiment:** Remind students that the prefix *con-* comes from the Latin for "together" or "jointly." Have students explain the relationship between the meaning of *con-* and *condiment*. **Possible answer:** *Condiments go together with, and add flavor to, various foods.*

---

can't handle it. Everything has to follow this impossible path to perfection. Someday, and I hope it's soon for your sake, you're going to have to settle for
30 sub-par performance and realize that you're imperfect like the rest of us." He stormed off like an angry prophet who had just delivered a curse, muttering that if I was like this at seventeen, imagine what I would be like at thirty.

"Good riddance," I shouted. "I hope you find a messy, inconsiderate girlfriend who can never find her purse or her car keys, who has no sense of time, no aptitude for *planning,* and that you spend the rest of your adolescent years on your hands and knees looking for your contacts!"

I padded down the hall to my bedroom. It was Sunday morning. I was due at my waitress job at the Ye Olde Pancake House in forty-five minutes. I sat on my white down quilt, saw the chocolate smudge, quick got up and brushed the
40 smudge with my spot remover kit that I kept in my top dresser drawer, being careful to brush the nap against the grain. I put the kit back in the drawer, refluffed my two white pillows, plucked a dead leaf off my philodendron plant, and remembered my second to last fight with Allen when he went completely ballistic at my selfless offer to alphabetize his CD collection with a color-coded cross-reference guide by subject, title, and artist. B

Males.

I put on my Ye Olde Pancake House waitress uniform that I had ironed and starched the night before: blue, long-sleeved ankle-length dress, white apron, white-and-blue flowered bonnet. I could have done without the bonnet, but
50 when you're going for the ye olde look, you have to sacrifice style. I was lucky to have this job. I got it one week after my parents and I moved to town, got hired *because* I am a person of order who knows there is a right way and a wrong way to do things. I replaced a waitress who was a complete disorganized slob. As Howard Halloran, the owner of the Ye Olde Pancake House, said to me, "Jill, if you're half as organized and competent as you look, I will die happy." I smoothed back my short clipped hair, flicked a sesame seed off my just-manicured nail, and told him that I was. C

"I have a system for everything," I assured him. "Menu first, bring water when you come back to take the order, call it in, bring coffee immediately to
60 follow. Don't ever let customers wait." Then I mentioned my keen knack for alphabetizing **condiments,** which was always a bonus, particularly when things got busy, and how a restaurant storage closet should be properly organized to take full advantage of the space.

"You're hired," Howard Halloran said reverently, and put me in charge of opening and setting up the restaurant on Saturday and Sunday mornings, which is when nine-tenths of all pancakes in the universe are consumed and you don't want some systemless person at the helm. You want a waitress of grit with a strategic battle plan that never wavers. Sunday morning in a pancake house is war.

I tied my white apron in a perfect bow across my back, tiptoed past my
70 parents' bedroom, taking care not to wake them, even though my mother had taken an insensitive potshot at me without provocation.

It's not like my life had been all that perfect.

### B CHARACTER TRAITS
Both the narrator's mother and her former boyfriend have accused her of perfectionism. In what ways do Jill's own actions and emotions illustrate this character trait?

### 2 Targeted Passage

### C GRAMMAR AND STYLE
Reread lines 47–57. Bauer's use of the **precise adjectives** *short, clipped,* and *just-manicured* provide insight into Jill's personality.

**condiment** (kŏn′də-mənt) *n.* a sauce, relish, or spice used to season food

---

## DIFFERENTIATED INSTRUCTION

### FOR STRUGGLING READERS

### 2 Targeted Passage [Lines 50–68]
This passage not only shows how Jill got the job of which she is so proud but also underscores her perfectionism.

- What does Jill say about the person who used to have her job? (lines 53–54)
- What does Jill tell Mr. Halloran about her abilities and skills? (lines 57–63)
- What special task does he give her? How does she feel about this responsibility?

(lines 64–68)

### FOR ADVANCED LEARNERS/PRE–AP

**In-Depth Textual Analysis** [small-group option] Have students use the Analyzing Character part of the Analysis Frame to explore the way in which Jill responds to and is changed by her challenge in "Pancakes." Urge students to note relevant story details and to use those details as they discuss the story.

 **BEST PRACTICES TOOLKIT—Transparency**
Analysis Frame: Character pp. D21, D26

Did I ask to move three times in eighteen months because my father kept getting transferred? Did I ask to attend three high schools since sophomore year? Did I complain about being unfairly uprooted?

Well . . . I did complain a little. . . .

Didn't I figure out a way to handle the pressure? When my very roots were being yanked from familiar soil, I became orderly and organized. I did things in the new towns so that people would like me and want to hire me, would
80 want to be my friends. I baked world-class cookies for high school bake sales, even if it meant staying up till three A.M.; I joined clubs and volunteered for the grunge jobs that no one wanted; I always turned in a spectacular performance and people counted on me to do it. I made everything look easy. People looked up to me, or down, depending—I'm five four. And I sure didn't feel like defending all that success before dawn! **D**

I tiptoed out the back door to my white car (ancient, yet spotless) and headed for work.

Syrup, I tried explaining to Hugo, the busboy, must be poured slowly from the huge cans into the plastic pourers on the tables because if you pour it fast, you
90 can't control the flow and you get syrup everywhere, which never really cleans up. It leaves a sticky residue that always comes back to haunt you. Syrup, I told him, is our enemy, but like Allen Feinman, Hugo was a male without vision. He couldn't anticipate disaster, couldn't cope with forethought and prevention; he let life rule him rather than the other way around, which was why *I* personally filled the syrup containers on Sunday mornings—maple, strawberry, boysenberry, and pecan. **E**

I had just filled the last containers and was putting them on the tables in horizontal rows. I had lined up the juice glasses and coffee mugs for optimal efficiency, which some people who shall remain nameless would call
100 perfectionism, but when the place gets busy, trust me, you want everything at your fingertips or you'll lose control. I never lose control. Hugo had set the back tables and I followed him, straightening the silverware. You'd think he'd been born in a barn. Andy Pappas, the cook, was making the special hash browns with onion and green pepper that people loved.

I **steeled** myself for the hungry Sunday morning mob that would descend in two hours. I always mentally prepared for situations that I knew were going to be stressful—it helped me handle them right. I could see me, Shirl, and Lucy, the other waitresses, serving the crowd, handling the cash register. Usually Howard Halloran took the money, but he was taking a long-needed
110 weekend off since his wife said if he didn't she would sell the place out from under him. I could see myself watching my station like a hawk, keeping the coffee brewing, getting the pancakes delivered hot to the tables. Do it fast, do it right—that was my specialty.

It was seven o'clock. Shirl and Lucy were late, but I knew that Lucy's baby was sick and Shirl was picking her up, so I didn't worry. They'd been late before. I myself was never late. I unlocked the front door, and a few customers

**D POINT OF VIEW**
Reread lines 72–85. How, if at all, do the thoughts and feelings of the **narrator** change your perception of her? Explain your answer.

**E POINT OF VIEW**
Reread lines 88–96. Think about the way Jill's point of view affects your impression of Hugo. How might this passage be different if Hugo were the narrator?

**steel** (stēl) *v.* to make hard or strong

PANCAKES **213**

---

**FOR ENGLISH LANGUAGE LEARNERS**

**Vocabulary: Idioms** Use New Word Analysis to teach these idioms from the story: *went completely ballistic* (lines 43–44), "became extremely angry"; *world-class* (line 80), "excellent"; *dug in* (line 133), "began to eat"; *as good as dead* (lines 158–159), "certain to fail"; *on her way* (line 192), "coming"; *fall guy* (line 265), "person receiving the blame."

💼 **BEST PRACTICES TOOLKIT—Transparency**
New Word Analysis p. E8

**FOR ADVANCED LEARNERS/PRE–AP**

**Hypothesize About Plot** Jill is so proud of her efficiency that readers can guess that she is about to have it challenged in some way. Have students write a paragraph, supported by details on pages 212–213, in which they discuss specific hypotheses about (1) what that challenge will be and (2) how Jill will respond to it. Ask students to share their paragraphs with a partner.

---

**TEXT ANALYSIS** | COMMON CORE RL 3

**D POINT OF VIEW**

***Possible answer:*** *Jill's comments about trying to handle pressure and have people like her make her a more sympathetic character.*

**Extend the Discussion** Do you think that other people understand Jill's motivation? What leads you to that opinion?

---

**TEXT ANALYSIS** | COMMON CORE RL 3

**E *Model the Skill:* POINT OF VIEW**

Read aloud the two sentences beginning with "Syrup, I told . . ." on line 91. Point out that Jill's description of Hugo is fairly judgmental and that she compares him to Allen, of whom we already know she disapproves. Point out that we can understand what Jill dislikes about Hugo's actions, but we only learn Jill's thoughts about why Hugo does what he does. The story never reveals Hugo's feelings or even his words.

***Possible answer:*** *Since Jill sees Hugo as incompetent, readers may also. If Hugo were the narrator, he might explain how well he tries to do his job and what he thinks of Jill's attempts to improve him.*

---

**VOCABULARY** | COMMON CORE L 4

**OWN THE WORD**

**steel:** Ask students if they have ever *steeled* themselves for an event. Ask them to explain when and why. How did the situation turn out? Was it necessary for them to have *steeled* themselves beforehand? How did it help them manage?

## F Model the Skill: DRAW CONCLUSIONS

Model how to tell the difference between the facts in the paragraph (what Andy cooks and how he does it) and the one opinion that it contains (Jill's comment about Andy's "total focus").

**Possible answer:** *Jill admires Andy for his organizational and planning skills, as she comments that "the man had total focus" (line 123).*

**Extend the Discussion** How did Jill compliment Andy when she first spoke about him (lines 103–104)? Do you think that she sees Andy as a kindred soul—or just as a person who is somewhat less incompetent than most of the people around her?

## Analyze Visuals

**Possible answer:** *The huge numerals on the clock face and the sweeping second hand reinforce a feeling of time pressure and of time speeding by.*

### REVISIT THE BIG QUESTION

### Are you a

# PERFECTIONIST?

**Discuss** Why does such a perfectionist as Jill feel threatened by the arrival of a tour bus in lines 153–159? **Possible answers:** *She realizes that this group will push her system of organization to the limit; she knows that even with her system, she can't serve all these people by herself, and the other waitresses have not come in yet.*

---

came straggling in with their Sunday newspapers, settling into the booths. Nothing I couldn't handle. Things didn't start getting crazy until around eight-thirty. I had my system.

120    I took orders, walked quickly to the kitchen window. "Four over easy on eight with sausage," I said crisply. "Side of cakes." That was restaurant-speak for four plates of two eggs over easy with sausage and pancakes on the side. Andy tossed his spatula in the air, went to work. The man had total focus. He could have two dozen eggs cooking in front of him and he knew when to flip each one. F

A young family came in with three small children; gave them the big table by the window. Got them kid seats, took their order.

"Number three."

That was my waitress number. Andy called the number over the loudspeaker when my order was ready and I went and picked it up. A nice time-efficient
130    system. I walked quickly to the counter (running made the customers nervous), grabbed the eggs, sausage, and pancakes, carried them four up on my left arm to table six, smiled professionally. Everything all right here, folks? Everyone nodded happily and dug in. Everything was always merry and pleasant at the Ye Olde Pancake House. That's why people came. Merry people left big tips.

I checked the ye old wall clock. Seven forty-seven. Still no Shirl or Lucy. They'd never been this late. Allen Feinman had been more than an hour late plenty of times. Allen Feinman didn't care about time—his or anyone else's. I didn't understand the grave problems he had at first; I was so caught up in him—this cute, brainy, funny guy who really seemed to want a shot
140    of discipline. I put in my usual extra effort into the relationship—baked his favorite cookies (cappuccino chip), packed romantic picnics (French bread, brie,[2] and strawberries), thought about unusual things to do in Coldwater, Michigan, which was quite a challenge, but I went to the library and came up with a list of ten possible side trips around town that we could do for free.

"You're just so *organized*," he would say, which I thought was a true compliment. Later on, I realized, coming from him, it was the darkest insult.

Andy was flipping pancakes on the grill. I scanned my customers to make sure everyone was cared for, turned to dash into
150    the bathroom quickly when a screech of tires sounded in the parking lot. I looked out the window. A lump caught in my throat.

A large tour bus pulled to a grinding halt.

I watched in horror as an army of round, middle-aged women stepped from the bus and headed toward the restaurant like hungry lionesses stalking prey.

It was natural selection—I was as good as dead.

160    "Number three."

---

2. **brie** (brē): a soft French cheese.

**214**    UNIT 2: CHARACTERIZATION AND POINT OF VIEW

---

F DRAW CONCLUSIONS
Think about Jill's description of Andy. Does he seem like someone Jill would admire? Cite thorough evidence to support your conclusion.

**Analyze Visuals ▼**

As you examine the photograph below, think about why the photographer chose to take such an extreme close-up of the clock. What effect does this create?

---

## DIFFERENTIATED INSTRUCTION

### FOR ENGLISH LANGUAGE LEARNERS

**Vocabulary: Idioms and Sayings** Point out these sayings and explain their meanings: *people who shall remain nameless* (line 99), "people whose names I will not reveal"; *he'd been born in a barn* (line 103), "he never had learned proper manners"; *watching . . . like a hawk* (line 111), "watching very carefully"; *A lump caught in my throat* (line 152), "I was frightened and upset."

### FOR ADVANCED LEARNERS/PRE–AP

**Evaluate Author's Choices** In lines 136–146, in the middle of describing a busy Sunday morning, Jill interrupts herself to recall how she had tried to give Allen some discipline. Have pairs of students debate whether this interruption weakens the story, each student taking either the *pro* or the *con* side. Students also should discuss why they think Bauer included this interruption.

I looked at Andy, who raised his face to heaven.

"Call them," I shrieked. "Call Shirl and Lucy! Tell them to get here!"

Andy reached for the phone.

I turned to the front door as the tour bus women poured in. They were all wearing sweatshirts that read MICHIGAN WOMEN FOR A CLEANER ENVIRONMENT. "A table for sixty-six," said a woman, laughing.

My lungs collapsed. Sixty-six hungry environmentalists. I pointed to a stack of menus, remembering my personal Waitress Rule Number One: Never let a customer know you're out of control.

170 "Sit anywhere," I cooed. "I'll be right with you." **G**

"If you wrote the menu on a blackboard you wouldn't waste paper," one said.

"Number three." I raced back to the kitchen. Pancakes for table eight. I layered the plates on my left arm, plopped butter balls from the ye olde butter urn on the pancakes. Andy said he'd tried Shirl and Lucy and no one answered. At least they were on their way. I raced to table eight. The little girl took one look at her chocolate chip pancakes and burst into tears.

"They're not the little ones," she sobbed.

"Oh, now, precious," said her father, "I'm sure this nice young lady doesn't 
180 want you to be disappointed."

I looked at the environmentalists who needed coffee. Life is tough, kid.

"Tell the waitress what you want, precious."

Precious looked at me, loving the control. She scrunched up her dimples, dabbed her tears, and said, "I want the teeny weeny ones, pwease."

"Teeny weeny ones coming up," I chirped, and raced to Andy. "Chocolate silver dollars for the brat on eight," I snarled. "Make them perfect, or someone dies."

"You're very attractive when you get busy," Andy said laughing.

"Shut up."

190 The phone rang. I lunged for it. It was Lucy calling from the hospital. Her baby had a bronchial infection,[3] needed medicine. She couldn't come in, but Shirl was on her way, she should be pulling onto the interstate now.

"Are you all right there, Jill?"

"Of course," I lied. "Take care of that baby. That's the most important thing."

"You're terrific," she said, and hung up.

I'm terrific, I told myself. I can handle this because, as a terrific person, I have an organized system that always works. I grabbed two coffee pots and raced to the tour group, smiling. Always smile. Poured coffee. They'd only get 
200 water if they asked. We're so glad you came to see us this morning. Yes, we have many tours pass through, usually we have more waitresses, though. It's a safe bet that any restaurant on this earth has more waitresses than the Ye Olde Pancake House does at this moment. **H**

---

3. **bronchial infection:** an infection of the bronchial tubes—the tubes that connect the windpipe to the lungs.

**G DRAW CONCLUSIONS**
Consider the difference between what Jill is thinking and what she actually says. What does this indicate about her character? Explain how you came to this conclusion.

**H PREDICT**
Will Jill be able to handle the crisis at the pancake house? Make a prediction about what will happen as Jill struggles to cope with the teeming crowd of hungry customers.

READING SKILL    COMMON CORE

**G DRAW CONCLUSIONS**    RL 1

*Possible answer:* Jill wants people to like her and depend upon her, so she doesn't always tell the truth or say what she really thinks. You can make this conclusion based on the fact that Jill tries to do things perfectly so that people will like her (lines 78–84). We also know that she believes that a waitress must always appear to her customers to be in control (lines 168–169), and so she would never say anything that would suggest that she is feeling panicky.

**IF STUDENTS NEED HELP . . .** Call their attention to lines 133–134, where Jill describes Ye Old Pancake House as always being "merry and pleasant." Point out that this statement reveals that Jill considers it her responsibility to maintain that cheerful atmosphere, even if it means not always telling the truth.

READING STRATEGY: *Review*

**H PREDICT**

*Possible answers:* She will fail because she is overwhelmed and needs help but tries to manage on her own; she will succeed because someone (perhaps Shirl) will come to help her.

**FOR STRUGGLING READERS**

**Develop Reading Fluency** Remind students that dialogue is often labeled specifically so that the reader knows how the words are being spoken; *said* is less specific than *screamed, whispered,* or *sighed.* Have students find the lines of dialogue on this page that are described with words other than *said.* (*shrieked, cooed, sobbed, chirped, snarled, lied*) Point out that characters' ways of speaking vary depending on their mood. In addition, the tone or mood Jill uses depends on whether she feels she can reveal her real feelings (speaking to Andy) or wishes to appear calm and confident (speaking to customers, Lucy). Have student pairs decide how each line of dialogue should be spoken, and perform the lines for one another. Ask volunteers to perform the lines for the class.

I took their orders like a shotgunner shooting clay pigeons.
*Pull!*
Pigs in a blanket.
Steak and fried eggs.
Buttermilk pancakes.
Betsy Ross (buttermilks with strawberry and blueberry compote).
210 Colonial Corn Cakes (Allen Feinman's favorite).
A round-faced woman looked at me, grinning. "Everything looks so good."
She sighed. "What do you recommend?"

I recommend that you eat someplace else, ma'am, because I do not have
time for this. I looked toward the front of the restaurant; six large men were
waiting to be seated. Hugo was pouring syrup quickly into pourers to
torture me, sloshing it everywhere. I said, "Everything's great here, ma'am.
I'll give you a few seconds to decide." I turned to the woman in the next
booth. The round-faced woman grabbed my arm. I don't like being touched
by customers.

220 "Just a minute. Well . . . it all looks so good."
"Number three." I glared in Andy's direction. "And number three again."
A cook can make or break you.
The round-faced woman decided on buttermilk pancakes, a daring choice. ❶
I ran to the kitchen window. "Hit me," Andy said.

"I'd love to. You're only getting this once. Buttermilks on twelve. Pigs on
four, Betsy's on three. Colonials on seven." I threw the rest of the orders
at him.

"You have very small handwriting," he said. "That's often the sign of low
self-esteem."
230 I put my hand down in one of Hugo's syrup spills, pushed back my bangs
with it; felt syrup soak my scalp.

Andy said, "You're only one person, Jill."

I scanned the restaurant—juice glasses askew, hungry people waiting at
dirty tables. I could do anything if I worked hard enough. Shirl would be here
any minute.

"Waitress, we're out of syrup!" A man held his empty syrup container
up. I looked under the counter for the extra maple syrup containers I had
cleverly filled, started toward the man, tripped over an environmentalist's foot,
which sent the syrup container flying, caught midair, but upside down by a
240 trucker who watched dumbly as syrup oozed onto the floor in a great, sticky
glop. I lunged for the syrup container, slid on the spill, felt sugared muck coat
my exposed flesh.

"Hugo!" I screamed, pointing at the disaster. "Hot water!"

"Number three."

I moved in a daze as more and more people came. Got the tour bus groups
fed and out. Had they mentioned separate checks, one woman asked?
*Nooooooooo . . .*

---

**Language Coach**

**Multiple Meanings** *Pull*
normally means "the
opposite of *push*." In
clay-pigeon shooting, its
meaning is different. At
the command "Pull!" a
clay disk launches into
the air. Reread lines
204–205. What does this
use of *pull* say about how
the narrator takes orders?

---

COMMON CORE RL 4

❶ **SARCASM**

**Sarcasm** is a cutting,
often ironic remark. Jill
uses sarcasm when she
refers to the woman's
order as "a daring choice."
She actually means the
opposite—that it is
*not* daring to order the
buttermilk pancakes.
Ordinarily, a sarcastic
remark is intended to
wound the recipient.
Rather than speaking
it aloud, Jill keeps the
potentially offensive
remark to herself. Given
the context of the story
so far, why do you think
she does this?

---

## TEXT ANALYSIS

COMMON CORE RL 4

❶ **SARCASM**

Ask students to recall times when they
have heard others use sarcasm. How did it
make them feel? Did it make a difference
whether the sarcasm was aimed at them
or at someone else?

*Possible answer: Despite the frustration
and anger Jill is feeling, she is still a perfectionist who wants to do a good job. If she
offends a customer she will not be doing a
good job.*

**Extend the Discussion** Jill does not share
her sarcasm with the customer but does
share it with the reader. Does she use sarcasm with anyone else in the story? Why
do you think this is?

## TIERED DISCUSSION PROMPTS

Direct students to lines 220–244. Then use
these prompts to help students understand
Jill's increasing frustration:

**Connect** Have you ever felt overwhelmed
by a job or task? How does that help you
to understand Jill's situation? *Accept all
reasonable responses.*

**Analyze** How do the details show that Jill is
beginning to lose control? *Possible answer:
Jill throws orders at Andy (lines 226–227), trips
over a customer's foot (line 238), and screams
at Hugo (line 243).*

---

## DIFFERENTIATED INSTRUCTION

### FOR ENGLISH LANGUAGE LEARNERS

**Language Coach**  COMMON CORE RL 4

**Multiple-Meaning Words** *Answer:
Here the word* pull *suggests that the
narrator takes orders rapidly, precisely, and
with no nonsense.* Have groups determine
the correct meaning for each of these
words: *counter* (line 130), *felt* (line 241), *coat*
(line 241), *dead* (line 268), *grounds* (line
301), *missed* (line 333).

### FOR STRUGGLING READERS

**Support Ideas** Help students locate evidence
from this page that helps them realize that
Jill is trying to maintain a positive attitude
over the chaos in the restaurant. *Possible
answer: She announces that "everything's
great here" (line 216), despite the problems
swirling around her.*

Made coffee. More coffee. Told everyone I was the only waitress here,
250 if they were in a hurry, they might want to go someplace else. But no one left. They just kept coming, storming through the restaurant like Cossacks.[4] People were grabbing my arm as I ran by.

"What's your name, babe?" asked a lecherous man.

*"Miss,"* I snarled.

"Number three."

260 "I had a life when I woke up this morning! Everything was in place!"

Buckwheats on table three.

The man looked at them. . . . He said, "You call these buckwheats? Buckwheats are supposed to be enormous and hearty." I'm the fall guy for everything that happens in the restaurant. It's my tip that's floating down the river waving bye-bye. I embraced my personal Waitress Rule Number Two: The customer is always right, even if they're dead wrong. I said, "That's the way we do them here, sir," and he said he can't eat them, he can't look at them, he'll have
270 the buttermilks, not knowing the trouble he's caused me. Andy gets sensitive if someone sends the food back—he's an artist, can't handle criticism. You have to lie to him or he slows down. I raced back to the kitchen.

"The man's a **degenerate**," I said to Andy. "He wouldn't know a world-class buckwheat if it jumped in his lap. He doesn't deserve to be in the presence of your cooking."

The phone rang. I lunged for it. It's Shirl calling from someone's car phone on the interstate with impossible news. A trailer truck had jackknifed, spilling soda cans everywhere. There was a five-mile backup. She'd be hours getting to work.

"Are you all right?" Shirl asked.

280 I looked at the line of cars pulling into the parking lot, the tables bulging with hungry customers, the coffee cups raised in anticipation of being filled, the line at the cash register. I heard a woman say how the restaurant had gone downhill, and the people were looking at me like I was their breakfast savior, like I had all the power and knowing, like I could single-handedly make sure they were happy and fed. And I was ashamed that I couldn't do it, but no one could. ●

*Not even me!*

I tore off my ye olde bonnet. "I'm trapped in a pancake house!" I shrieked into the phone, and, like in all sci-fi stories, the connection went dead.

"Number three."

290 I limped toward him, a shadow of my former self.

"We're out of sausage," Andy said solemnly.

---

4. **Cossacks:** a people of southern Russia, known as fierce cavalrymen.

**degenerate** (dǐ-jěn'ər-ĭt) *n.* a corrupt or vicious person

● **POINT OF VIEW**
Reread lines 280–285. Consider how learning Jill's thoughts contributes to your understanding of her character. How would your reaction to Jill be different if you didn't know what Jill was thinking and feeling?

❸ **Targeted Passage**

## OWN THE WORD

**crass:** Review the definition of *crass* with students. Then have them list antonyms for *crass*. **Possible answers:** *refined, elegant, graceful, sympathetic, kind*

**READING STRATEGY:** *Review*

### K PREDICT

**Possible answers:** *Allen might laugh at Jill, too, for he still may be upset about her criticism of him; he might surprise Jill by helping her with the customers, even though earlier she had been critical of him.*

## SELECTION WRAP–UP

**READ WITH A PURPOSE** Now that students have read the selection, ask them to describe how Jill dealt with things that bothered her during the course of the story, and how and why those reactions changed. Then ask students whether they think the change in behavior Jill showed at the end of the story is temporary or permanent. **Possible answer:** *Jill's perfectionist habits are probably too strong to have disappeared completely due to one bad day at work. However, she may at least be able to recall these events when problems arise again and not be so self-critical.*

⭐ **CRITIQUE** Have students evaluate the author's use of humor in the story by rating it from 1 (did not care for it at all) to 5 (liked it a lot). Then ask them to indicate their favorite passage and explain why they liked it.

### INDEPENDENT READING

For students wanting to read more from Joan Bauer, suggest *Rules of the Road,* which chronicles the challenges of a high school student at home and work.

---

"Good. It's one less thing to carry." I stood on the counter, put my head back, and screamed, "We're out of sausage and it's not my fault!"

A man at a back table hollered that he needed ketchup for his eggs. I reached down in the K section under the counter. Nothing under K. I got on my knees, hands shaking, rifling through jams, jellies, lingonberries. *Hugo!* I shrieked.

He ran up to me.

"Ketchup, Hugo! Wake up! The sky is falling!"

He pointed to the C section. "Catsup," he said meekly.

300    I was falling down a dark, disorderly tunnel. There was no end in sight. Coffee grounds were in my eyebrows, my hands smelled like used tea bags. I was exhausted, syrup encrusted, I'd had to go to the bathroom for three hours. People were going to get their own coffee—the ultimate defeat for any waitress. I looked at my haggard reflection in the coffee urn. The only consolation was that I wouldn't live till noon.

"Waitress!"

I raced down the aisle to table twelve, seeing the hunted look in my customer's eyes. I wanted to be perfect for every one of you. I wanted you all to like me. I'm sorry I'm not better, not faster. Please don't hate me, I'm only one 310 person, not even a particularly tall person.

"I'm sorry," I said to a table of eight, "but I simply can't do everything!"

I felt a ripple of **crass** laughter in the air. I turned. Allen Feinman had walked in with his parents. **K**

No. . . . Anything but this.

Our eyes met. I could hear the taunts at school, the never-ending retelling of this, my ultimate nightmare.

"Can I help, Jill?" He rolled up his shirtsleeves. Allen Feinman was offering to help.

I grabbed his arm. "Can you work the register?"

320    "Of course." Allen organized the people into a line, made change, smiled. He had such a nice smile. Thanked everyone for their patience, got names on lists.

Mrs. Feinman took off her jacket and asked, "Can I make coffee, dear?"

"Mrs. Feinman, you don't have to—"

"We've always been so fond of you, Jill."

I slapped a bag of decaf in her sainted hands. Mr. Feinman poured himself a cup of coffee and went back to wait in the car.

We whipped that place into shape. All I needed was a little backup. My pockets were bulging with tips, and when Shirl raced in at eleven forty-five, I pushed a little girl aside who'd been waiting patiently by the bathroom door 330 and I lunged toward the toilet stall. Life is tough, kid.

By one-thirty the crowds had cleared. Lucy called—her baby was home and doing better. Allen Feinman and I were sitting at a back table eating pancakes. He said he'd missed me. I said I'd missed him, too. Hugo was speed-pouring boysenberry syrup, spilling everywhere—but somehow it didn't matter anymore. It was good enough.

And that, I realized happily, was fine by me. ❧

**crass** (krăs) *adj.* crude; unrefined

### K PREDICT

Predict what might happen with the arrival of Allen. Give reasons for your prediction.

④ **Targeted Passage**

**COMMON CORE** RL 4

**Language Coach**

**Idioms** An **idiom** is an expression that cannot be understood literally. Given the context of the story leading up to line 327, what do you think "we whipped that place into shape" means?

---

## DIFFERENTIATED INSTRUCTION

### FOR ENGLISH LANGUAGE LEARNERS

**Language Coach**

**COMMON CORE** RL 4

**Idioms** *Answer:* "*we whipped that place into shape" means that they quickly improved the conditions of the restaurant.* Have students share other related idioms they know. **Possible answers:** *making things shipshape, spic-and-span, sparkling; making events run like a top; getting one's ducks in a row*

### FOR STRUGGLING READERS

④ **Targeted Passage** [Lines 317–336]

In this concluding passage, Allen and his mother come to the rescue—and Jill decides that "good enough" is just fine.

- Who offers to help Jill, and how? Why does she accept their offers? (lines 317–325)
- How does Jill react to Hugo's mess? What is the significance of her response? (lines 333–335)

## Comprehension

1. **Recall** List two reasons why Jill is upset at the beginning of the story.

2. **Summarize** What crisis does Jill face in this story, and how is her crisis resolved?

3. **Clarify** What does Jill fear will happen when Allen Feinman shows up at the restaurant? Why does Allen's behavior surprise her?

## Text Analysis

● 4. **Draw Conclusions** Review the chart you made as you read. What drives Jill to constantly strive for perfection? Cite evidence to support your conclusion.

5. **Analyze Character** A **static character** is a character who changes very little, if at all, during the course of a story. A **dynamic character** is a character who changes significantly as a result of his or her experiences. In a chart like the one shown, list the character traits Jill exhibits at

| Jill's Traits at Beginning of Story | Jill's Traits at End of Story |
|---|---|
| 1. Critical of others 2. Meticulous | |

the beginning of the story and those she shows signs of as the story ends. Would you describe Jill as a static character or a dynamic character? Cite strong and thorough evidence from the text to support your answer.

● 6. **Analyze Point of View** With a **first-person narrator,** you see the story unfold through one character's eyes. Would a **third-person omniscient narrator**— a narrator who sees into the minds of all the characters in a story—have presented a more accurate picture of the events? Support your opinion.

7. **Evaluate Character Traits** "Pancakes" clearly points out the downside of perfectionism, but it suggests that this trait can be a positive force as well. Citing evidence from the story, decide whether perfectionism is an asset or a fault. Then compare your answer with the ideas you had about perfectionism before you read the story.

## Text Criticism

8. **Author's Style** In an essay titled "Humor, Seriously," Joan Bauer explains that her technique for creating humorous characters involves "layering nutty traits over serious personalities and situations." How effective is Bauer at developing a quirky character who confronts real-life problems in a humorous way? Cite specific dialogue and descriptions from "Pancakes" to explain your opinion.

### Are you a PERFECTIONIST?

In what activities are you most likely to seek perfection?

**COMMON CORE**

**RL 1** Cite strong and thorough textual evidence to support analysis of what the text says explicitly as well as inferences drawn from the text. **RL 3** Analyze how complex characters develop over the course of a text and interact with other characters.

# Practice and Apply

For preliminary support of post-reading questions, use these copy masters:

**R** RESOURCE MANAGER—Copy Masters
 Reading Check p. 28
 First-Person Point of View p. 21
 Question Support p. 29

 Additional selection questions are provided for teachers on page 15.

### ANSWERS

## Comprehension

1. *She resents her mother's implication that she is a perfectionist. She is irritated at being called a "rabid perfectionist" by Allen.*

2. *She is left to wait on an unusually large crowd at the restaurant by herself. The crisis is resolved when Allen and his parents arrive and Allen and his mother offer to help Jill.*

3. *She believes that Allen will humiliate her at school by telling people about her loss of control. Instead, he offers to help.*

## Text Analysis

**COMMON CORE RL 1, RL 3**

*Possible answers:*

4. ● **COMMON CORE FOCUS Draw Conclusions** *Jill wants people to like her and look up to her. Evidence may vary.*

5. *Jill is a dynamic character. At first, she demands perfection from herself and others. She is meticulous, controlling, and critical. However, when Jill gives up some control by accepting help and realizes that people like her for herself, being perfect no longer seems as important.*

6. ● **COMMON CORE FOCUS Analyze Point of View** *A third-person omniscient narrator would have explained how other characters saw events and each other. Because the story is meant to focus on Jill, such an in-depth picture may be unnecessary.*

7. *Answers will vary, but students should note that Jill's perfectionism helped her get a job and handle special responsibility.*

## Text Criticism

*Possible answer:*

8. *Students probably find Bauer quite effective in her character development. Support may include the following: "A large tour bus pulled to a grinding halt. I watched in horror as an army of round, middle-aged women stepped from the bus and headed toward the restaurant like hungry lionesses stalking prey" (lines 153–157); "'What do you recommend?' I recommend that you eat someplace else, ma'am . . ." (lines 212–213);*

*"'Hit me,' Andy said. 'I'd love to. You're only getting this once'" (lines 224–225).*

### Are you a PERFECTIONIST?

Remind students to refer to the questions in the newspaper article Jill received from her mother at the beginning of the story.

# ANSWERS
## Vocabulary in Context
▲ **VOCABULARY PRACTICE**

1. *degenerate*     4. *crass*
2. *rabid*          5. *condiment*
3. *steel*          6. *benign*

**RESOURCE MANAGER**—Copy Master
Vocabulary Practice p. 26

### ACADEMIC VOCABULARY IN WRITING

Jill is a complex character. At first she seems to have only one side. However, as Jill accepts the help of Allen and his mother, her **perspective** changes. She wants to do things right, has a sense of humor, is sensitive to others, and knows that she can't be perfect all of the time.

### VOCABULARY STRATEGY:
### THE LATIN WORD ROOT *ben*

- Point out that the words in the word web all begin with *ben* but are different parts of speech. *Benign* and *benevolent* are adjectives; *benediction, beneficiary,* and *benefactor* are nouns; *benefit* can be a noun or a verb.

- Using a dictionary, model for students how some of the words use *ben* to help make meaning.

  *benediction* = a "good" speaking; a blessing

  *benefactor* = one who does "well"; a helper or protector

  *benevolent* = wishing "good" for others; having a kindly character

**Possible answers:**

1. *benefit*        4. *beneficiary*
2. *benediction*    5. *benefactor*
3. *benign*         6. *benevolent*

**RESOURCE MANAGER**—Copy Master
Vocabulary Strategy p. 27

**Interactive Vocabulary**   THINK central

Keywords direct students to a **WordSharp** tutorial on **thinkcentral.com** or to other types of vocabulary practice and review.

---

# Vocabulary in Context

▲ **VOCABULARY PRACTICE**

Write the word from the list that best completes each sentence.

1. Allen Feinman may have been critical of Jill's attitude, but that did not make him a _____.
2. He did not have a _____ temper, nor was he outrageous in other ways.
3. Jill had to _____ herself against panic when she saw Allen walking into the restaurant.
4. Perhaps it was a bit _____ when he snickered at her plight.
5. Seeing each _____ lined up precisely would have made him laugh.
6. Still, the way he and his mother helped Jill out of a jam was quite _____.

**WORD LIST**
benign
condiment
crass
degenerate
rabid
steel

### ACADEMIC VOCABULARY IN WRITING

- complex   - device   - evaluate   - interact   - perspective

Do you think Jill is a **complex** character? Write a paragraph explaining why Jill is or is not a complex character. Be sure to cite examples of Jill's thoughts, words, or actions to support your explanation. Use at least one Academic Vocabulary word in your response.

### VOCABULARY STRATEGY: THE LATIN WORD ROOT *ben*

The vocabulary word *benign* contains the Latin root *ben*, which means "well." This root and the related form *bene* are found in a number of English words. To understand the meaning of words with *ben*, use context clues as well as your knowledge of the root.

**COMMON CORE**

L 4c Consult reference material to determine or clarify a word's meaning or etymology.

ben**ign**     bene**fit**

bene**volent**     **ben, bene**     bene**factor**

bene**diction**     bene**ficiary**

**PRACTICE** Write the word from the word web that best completes each sentence. Use context clues to help you or, if necessary, consult a dictionary.

1. One _____ of a good night's sleep is feeling rested in the morning.
2. The minister offered a _____ at the end of the prayer service.
3. He assured us that his intentions were entirely _____.
4. There was only one _____ listed in Grandma's will.
5. Jennifer's _____ offered to pay her way through college.
6. Most charities involve themselves in _____ works.

Interactive Vocabulary   THINK central
Go to **thinkcentral.com**.
KEYWORD: HML9-220

---

## DIFFERENTIATED INSTRUCTION

### FOR ENGLISH LANGUAGE LEARNERS

**Vocabulary: Cognates** Before completing the Vocabulary Strategy section, ask Spanish speakers what common words in their language have this same Latin root. **Possible answers:** benévolo (*benevolent*), bien (*good, well*), bienvenido (*welcome*), bueno/buena (*good*).

### FOR ADVANCED LEARNERS/PRE–AP

**Vocabulary in Writing** Have students create an advertisement for Ye Olde Pancake House that uses as many vocabulary words as reasonably possible. For example, students might promote the restaurant as "a place that caters to *rabid* breakfast appetites" or promise that "no one will call you *crass* if you ask for refills on our out-of-this-world coffee."

# Language

◆ **GRAMMAR AND STYLE: Add Supporting Details**

Review the **Grammar and Style** note on page 212. Joan Bauer uses **precise adjectives** to convey important physical details that support her characterization of Jill's personality. Here are some helpful adjective hints:

1. **Replace vague adjectives with more precise ones.** Some adjectives, such as *nice*, are too general. Instead, use adjectives that say exactly what you mean.

2. **Avoid using too many adjectives.** Too many adjectives can result in overwriting. Choose adjectives carefully, and you will need only a few.

Here are some additional examples of Bauer's use of precise adjectives:

> . . . *He went completely ballistic at my selfless offer to alphabetize his CD collection with a color-coded cross-reference guide. . . .* (lines 43–45)

> *I was exhausted, syrup-encrusted. . . .* (line 302)

Notice how the revisions in blue improve the precision of this first draft. You can revise your response to the prompt below by using similar techniques.

---

**STUDENT MODEL**

Jill and Andy both have ~~good~~ *excellent* attitudes toward their jobs. They are both ~~hard,~~ *diligent* ~~fast~~ workers. Jill makes *careful* preparations for Sunday's crowd by arranging all of the condiments neatly *alphabetical* in order. Andy fries his hash browns ahead of time, so that when customers walk in, they are greeted with ~~a nice~~ *an enticing* aroma.

---

## READING-WRITING CONNECTION

 **YOUR TURN**

Demonstrate your understanding of the characters in "Pancakes" by responding to this prompt. Then use the **revising tip** to improve your writing.

**WRITING PROMPT**

**Extended Constructed Response: Comparison**
Referring to details in the story, write **three to five paragraphs** comparing Jill's and Andy's attitudes toward their work at the restaurant. Make sure to include examples of Jill's **perfectionism.**

**REVISING TIP**

▶ Review your response. Did you use precise adjectives to convey the physical details of Jill and Andy's characters?

**Interactive Revision**

THINK central

Go to **thinkcentral.com**.
KEYWORD: HML9-221

---

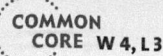 **COMMON CORE**

**L 3** Apply knowledge of language to make effective choices for meaning or style. **W 4** Produce explanatory writing in which the style is appropriate to the task and purpose.

# Language

**COMMON CORE  W 4, L 3**

◆ **GRAMMAR AND STYLE**

- Identify *many*, *great*, and *weird* as other examples of vague adjectives. Have students use each one in a sentence and then replace it with a more precise adjective.

- As you discuss the Student Model, invite suggestions about other precise adjectives that might have been used.

 **RESOURCE MANAGER—Copy Master**
Add Supporting Details p. 30

**READING-WRITING CONNECTION**

- Have students use Open Mind to explore Jill's and Andy's attitudes before comparing them. Students may find it easier to focus first on Jill's and then on Andy's attitude. Remind students to support their ideas with details from the story.

 **BEST PRACTICES TOOLKIT—Transparency**
Open Mind p. D9

---

**Writing Online**  THINK central

The following tools are available online at **thinkcentral.com** and on **Write***Smart* CD-ROM:
- **Interactive Graphic Organizers**
- **Interactive Student Models**
- **Interactive Revision Lessons**
For additional grammar instruction, see **GrammarNotes** on **thinkcentral.com**.

---

# Assess and Reteach

## Assess

**DIAGNOSTIC AND SELECTION TESTS**
Selection Test A pp. 59–60
Selection Test B/C pp. 61–62

**Interactive Selection Test** on **thinkcentral.com**

## Reteach

**Level Up Online Tutorials** on **thinkcentral.com**

**Reteaching Worksheets** on **thinkcentral.com**
Literature Lesson 10, Reading Lesson 9, Vocabulary Lesson 8

---

## FOR STRUGGLING WRITERS

- Limit the assignment to only two paragraphs.

- Help students recall three details about Jill and three details about Andy before organizing the information into paragraphs.

- If students need help getting their writing started, provide these prompts: *Andy and Jill both feel _____ about their work; Unlike Jill, Andy _____; Unlike Andy, Jill _____.*

# Focus and Motivate

## Comparing Texts

## The Necklace
Short Story by Guy de Maupassant

## Spending Spree
Magazine Article

## Is Debt Dragging You Down?
Flier

*Essential Course of Study* ECOS

VIDEO TRAILER **THINK** central KEYWORD: HML9-222

# How important is STATUS?

### COMMON CORE FOCUS

**RL 1** Cite textual evidence to support analysis of what the text says explicitly as well as inferences drawn from the text. **RL 3** Analyze how complex characters develop over the course of a text and interact with other characters. **RL 4** Determine the connotative meaning of words and phrases as they are used in a text. **RL 6** Analyze a particular point of view reflected in a work of world literature. **RI 7** Analyze various accounts of a subject told in different mediums. **L 1b** Use various types of phrases and clauses to convey specific meanings and add variety and interest to writing. **L 4a** Use context as a clue to the meaning of a word.

### SUMMARIES

**"The Necklace"** A wife borrows and then loses a necklace. The couple struggle to replace it.

**"Spending Spree"** This article describes how and why many teens fall into credit card debt.

**Advertisement** The print advertisement illustrates the suffering that debt causes.

### How important is STATUS?

Be sure students understand the meaning of *status*. Then, ask students who has status in our society.

### What's the Connection?

Discuss the connection between status and money. Are there other marks of status?

**COMMON CORE**

**RL 1** Cite textual evidence to support analysis of what the text says explicitly as well as inferences drawn from the text. **RL 3** Analyze how complex characters develop over the course of a text and interact with other characters. **RL 4** Determine the connotative meaning of words and phrases as they are used in a text. **RL 6** Analyze a particular point of view reflected in a work of world literature.

What happens to people who place too much importance on status, or the standing they have in a group? In "The Necklace," you'll meet Madame Loisel, an unforgettable character whose pursuit of status costs her more than she could ever have imagined.

### What's the Connection?

Like Madame Loisel, some people think material possessions are the key to status. However, buying all of the latest sought-after status symbols is a quick way to exceed one's budget. After "The Necklace," you'll read a magazine article and view an advertisement that explore the topics of overspending and debt.

222

---

## Selection Resources

*See resources on the* **Teacher One Stop DVD-ROM** *and on* **thinkcentral.com**.

 **RESOURCE MANAGER UNIT 2**
Plan and Teach, pp. 31–38
Summary, pp. 39–40†‡*
Text Analysis and Reading
   Skill, pp. 41–44†*
Vocabulary, pp. 45–47*
Grammar and Style, p. 50

**DIAGNOSTIC AND SELECTION TESTS**
Selection Tests, pp. 63–66

 **BEST PRACTICES TOOLKIT**
Word Squares, p. E10
Making Inferences, p. A13
New Word Analysis, p. E8
Two-Column Chart, p. A25

**INTERACTIVE READER**

**ADAPTED INTERACTIVE READER**

**ELL ADAPTED INTERACTIVE READER**

**TECHNOLOGY**
- **Teacher One Stop DVD-ROM**
- **Student One Stop DVD-ROM**
- **PowerNotes DVD-ROM**
- **Audio Anthology CD**
- **GrammarNotes DVD-ROM**
- **Audio Tutor CD**
- **ExamView Test Generator**
  on the **Teacher One Stop**

**THINK** central

### Video Trailer

Go to **thinkcentral.com** to preview the **Video Trailer** introducing this selection. Other features that support the selection include
- **PowerNotes** presentation
- **ThinkAloud** models to enhance comprehension
- **WordSharp** vocabulary tutorials
- interactive writing and grammar instruction

\* Resources for Differentiation     † Also in Spanish     ‡ In Haitian Creole and Vietnamese

## TEXT ANALYSIS: CHARACTER MOTIVATION

**Motivation** is the reason behind a character's behavior; it's what drives a complex character to think and act in a certain way. For example, a character might want the lead in a school play and perhaps to fit in with popular students. What the character says and does would reflect that desire. As you read "The Necklace," consider how Madame Loisel's words and actions reflect her motivation.

***Review:* Point of View**

## READING SKILL: MAKE INFERENCES

Instead of directly telling readers what a character is like, a writer often includes details that are clues to the character's personality. Readers can use these details, along with their own knowledge, to **make inferences,** or logical guesses, about the character's traits, values, and feelings.

In a chart like the one shown, record your inferences as you read, along with the details and experiences that helped you make them.

| Details About Characters | Personal Experience | My Inference |
|---|---|---|
| Madame Loisel married her husband because she had no other prospects. | People are usually frustrated when they do something simply because they feel they have no choice. | She didn't really choose to marry her husband and probably feels frustrated. |

***Review:* Predict**

## ▲ VOCABULARY IN CONTEXT

Restate each phrase, using a different word or words for the **boldfaced term.** Then, in your *Reader/Writer Notebook*, write a brief definition of each word you're familiar with.

1. few **prospects** for success
2. talked **incessantly** all day
3. **vexation** about their argument
4. a desperate **pauper**
5. **adulation** from her fans
6. **disconsolate** after losing his dog
7. **aghast** at her rude remarks
8. run the **gamut** of possibilities
9. a prisoner's **privation**
10. messy, with his tie all **askew**

Complete the activities in your **Reader/Writer Notebook.**

---

## Meet the Author

# Guy de Maupassant
### 1850–1893

**Master Storyteller**
Guy de Maupassant (gē' də mō-pä-säɴ') is considered by many to be the greatest French short story writer. He created his characters with remarkable precision, focusing on the exact gesture, feeling, or word that defined each character. As a result, his stories seem to be, in his words, "pieces of human existence torn from reality."

**Reversal of Fortune**
Although Maupassant was born into an upper-middle-class family in France, the family fortune ran out early. He was forced to work for a time as a government clerk, the position that the main character's husband holds in "The Necklace." Eventually, though, Maupassant turned to writing and managed to achieve some wealth and fame through his hundreds of stories. Sadly, his success was short-lived. After suffering from mental illness, Maupassant died in a Paris asylum at age 42.

### BACKGROUND TO THE STORY
**Status for Sale**
This story takes place in Paris in the second half of the 19th century. At the time Maupassant wrote "The Necklace," European societies were divided into upper, middle, and lower classes. Birth usually determined a person's class. Sometimes a man could buy his way into a higher class by acquiring wealth. A woman could improve her status by marrying into a higher class. One obstacle for women was the tradition of the dowry—money or property that a bride's family was expected to give her new husband, but that poorer families could not provide.

**Author Online**
THINK central
Go to **thinkcentral.com.**
KEYWORD: HML9-223

223

---

# Teach

**TEXT ANALYSIS**    COMMON CORE   RL 3

## ● *Model the Skill:* CHARACTER MOTIVATION

For instructional support, read aloud this example:

> Invited to a party given by the most popular girl at school, Lily used all her savings to buy designer jeans.

Point out that Lily is making a big sacrifice to get something impressive to wear to the party because she wanted to fit in with more popular girls.

**GUIDED PRACTICE** Name some actions of familiar characters. Ask students to suggest the characters' motivations.

**READING SKILL**    COMMON CORE   RL 1

## ■ *Model the Skill:* MAKE INFERENCES

Point out that the traits Maupassant gave his characters were very realistic. Explain that you can infer some things about the author from his ability to craft such precisely described characters, such as he was very observant and attentive to detail.

**GUIDED PRACTICE** Have students use **Reversal of Fortune** to infer themes found in Maupassant's writing.

**R**   RESOURCE MANAGER—Copy Master Make Inferences p. 43 (for student use while reading the selection)

---

## VOCABULARY SKILL

### ▲ VOCABULARY IN CONTEXT

**DIAGNOSE WORD KNOWLEDGE** Have all students complete Vocabulary in Context. Check their definitions against the following:

**adulation** (ăj'ə-lā'shən) *n.* excessive praise or flattery

**aghast** (ə-găst') *adj.* filled with shock or horror

**askew** (ə-skyoo') *adj.* crooked; to one side

**disconsolate** (dĭs-kŏn'sə-lĭt) *adj.* extremely depressed or dejected

**gamut** (găm'ət) *n.* an entire range or series

**incessantly** (ĭn-sĕs'ənt-lē) *adv.* without interruption; continuously

**pauper** (pô'pər) *n.* a poor person, especially one who depends on public charity

**privation** (prī-vā'shən) *n.* the lack of a basic necessity or a comfort of life

**prospects** (prŏs'pĕkts') *n.* chances or possibilities, especially for financial success

**vexation** (vĕk-sā'shən) *n.* irritation; annoyance

**PRETEACH VOCABULARY** Use the copy master to help students predict meanings for each boldfaced word.

COMMON CORE   L 4

**R**   RESOURCE MANAGER—Copy Master Vocabulary Study p. 45

## READ WITH A PURPOSE

*Help students set a purpose for reading. Remind students that they should read carefully to determine the major conflict in the story and how it affects the characters.*

### READING SKILL

COMMON CORE
RL 1

### A MAKE INFERENCES

***Possible answer:*** *Madame Loisel grieves over her shabby apartment and furnishings (lines 11–14), feels enraged by her middle-class existence (lines 14–17), and dreams of a life of wealth and luxury (lines 17–20). These feelings stem from her belief that she was born for such a life.*

**IF STUDENTS NEED HELP . . .** Call their attention to the sentence in lines 11–12. Help students understand that Madame Loisel expected more out of life. She believed that she deserved more than she had, and felt cheated.

**Extend the Discussion** How have you felt when you haven't gotten something you expected or thought you deserved?

### VOCABULARY

COMMON CORE
L 4

### OWN THE WORD

- **prospects:** Read the sentence with *prospects* aloud to students. Then have them identify words and phrases in the sentence that help them understand the meaning of the word. ***Possible answer:*** *chances; things to look forward to*

- **incessantly:** Help students break down the word into its parts. The prefix *in-* means "not," *cess* comes from cease, or stop, so *incessantly* means "nonstop."

# The Necklace

## Guy de Maupassant

She was one of those pretty and charming girls, born, as if by an accident of fate, into a family of clerks. With no dowry, no **prospects,** no way of any kind of being met, understood, loved, and married by a man both prosperous and famous, she was finally married to a minor clerk in the Ministry of Education.

She dressed plainly because she could not afford fine clothes, but was as unhappy as a woman who has come down in the world; for women have no family rank or social class. With them, beauty, grace, and charm take the place of birth and breeding. Their natural poise, their instinctive good taste, and their mental cleverness are the sole guiding principles which make daughters
10 of the common people the equals of ladies in high society.

She grieved **incessantly,** feeling that she had been born for all the little niceties and luxuries of living. She grieved over the shabbiness of her apartment, the dinginess of the walls, the worn-out appearance of the chairs, the ugliness of the draperies. All these things, which another woman of her class would not even have noticed, gnawed at her and made her furious. The sight of the little Breton[1] girl who did her humble housework roused in her disconsolate regrets and wild daydreams. She would dream of silent chambers, draped with Oriental tapestries and lighted by tall bronze floor lamps, and of two handsome butlers in knee breeches, who, drowsy from the heavy warmth
20 cast by the central stove, dozed in large overstuffed armchairs. **A**

---

1. **Breton** (brĕt′n): from Brittany, a region in northwestern France.

**224** UNIT 2: CHARACTERIZATION AND POINT OF VIEW

*Louise Augusta, Queen of Prussia (1801),*
*Marie Louise Élisabeth Vigée LeBrun. Pastel, 51 cm × 41 cm.*
*Stiftung Preussische Schlösser und Gärten*
*Berlin-Brandenburg. Photo by J. P. Anders.*

### Analyze Visuals ▶

Examine the portrait on page 225. What social class do you think the woman belongs to? Identify the details that helped you draw this **inference.**

**prospects** (prŏs′pĕkts′) *n.* chances or possibilities, especially for financial success

**incessantly** (ĭn-sĕs′ənt-lē) *adv.* without interruption; continuously

**A MAKE INFERENCES** Consider what you learn about Madame Loisel's situation in lines 11–20. Why do you think she feels the way she does?

**1 Targeted Passage**

## DIFFERENTIATED INSTRUCTION

### FOR ENGLISH LANGUAGE LEARNERS

**Vocabulary Support** Use Word Squares to teach these words: *prospects* (line 2), *minor* (line 4), *ministry* (line 4), *principles* (line 9), *convinced* (line 90), *consulted* (line 173).

**BEST PRACTICES TOOLKIT—Transparency** Word Squares p. E10

### FOR STRUGGLING READERS

In combination with the *Audio Anthology CD*, use one or more Targeted Passages (pp. 224, 226, 228, 233) to ensure that students focus on key story events, concepts, and skills. Targeted Passages are also good for English learners.

**1 Targeted Passage [Lines 11–20]**

This passage introduces Madame Loisel's frustration with her life, a frustration that will drive the rest of the story.

- What is Madame Loisel's home like? (lines 12–14)

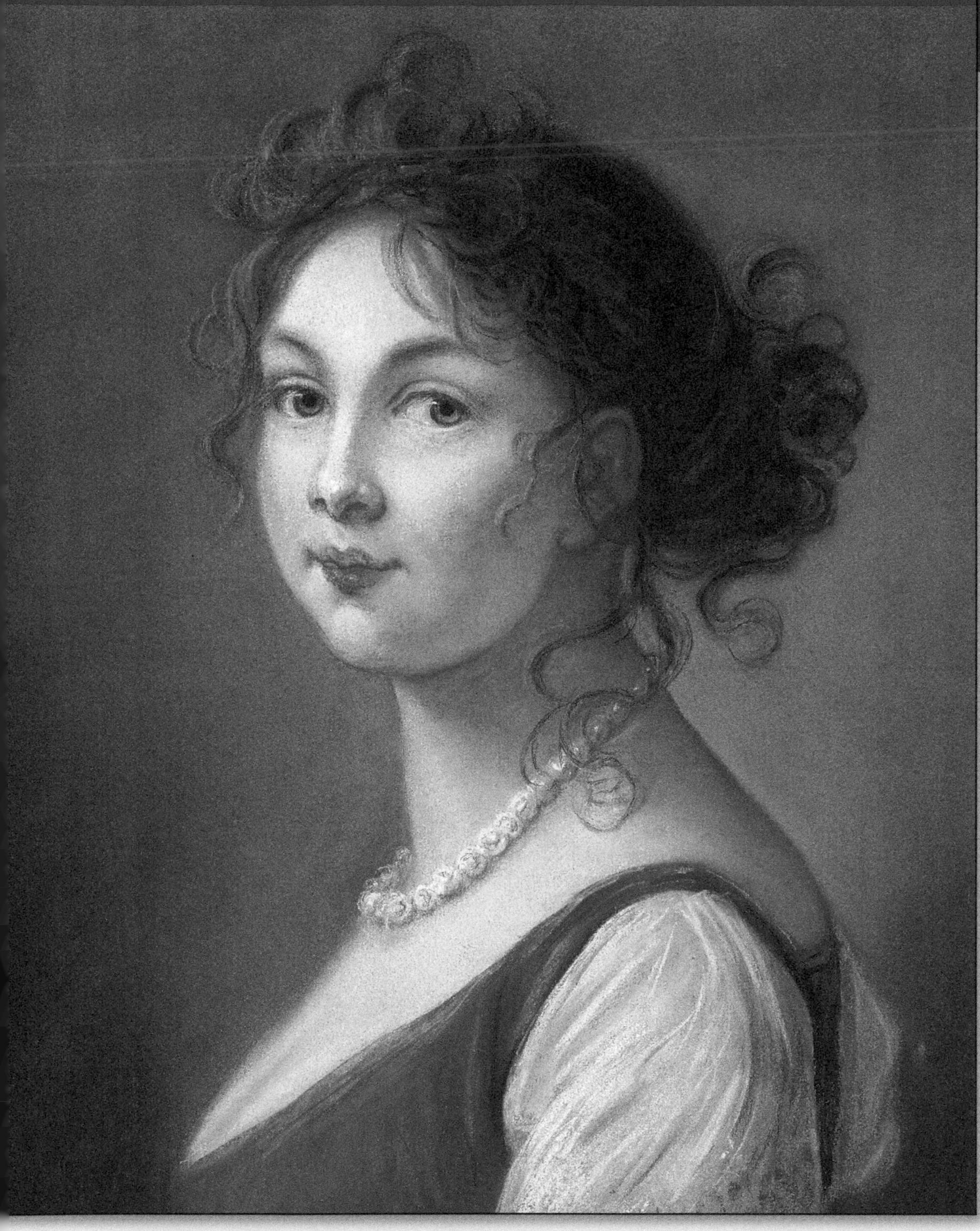

**Reading Support**

This selection on **thinkcentral.com** includes embedded **ThinkAloud** models–students "thinking aloud" about the story to model the kinds of questions a good reader would ask about a selection.

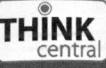

## BACKGROUND

**Arranged Marriages** Point out the phrase was *finally married to* in line 4. The use of the passive voice suggests that Madame Loisel did not have a strong role in choosing her husband. In the 1800s in France, marriages often were arranged, with parents matching couples who shared comparable education, values, and economic status.

**Cultural Connection** Today, marriages continue to be arranged in some traditional families and cultures. In contemporary Japan, for example, an estimated 10–12 percent of marriages are arranged. Invite students to share what they may know about arranged marriages in other cultures.

## Analyze Visuals

***Possible answer:*** *The woman's attractive hairstyle, elegant pearls, stylish dress, and smooth skin suggest that she is a member of the middle class or perhaps even the upper class.*

**About the Art** *Louise Augusta, Queen of Prussia* was one of many portraits of prominent Europeans and Russians that French neoclassical artist Marie Louise Élisabeth Vigée LeBrun (1755–1842) painted between 1770 and 1835. One of the most in-demand portrait artists of her time, she completed more than 900 paintings, including 700 portraits, during her career.

- What does she wish it were like? (lines 17–20)
- What might this tell you about Madame Loisel? (lines 12–20)

**FOR ADVANCED LEARNERS/PRE–AP**

Encourage students to explore alternate endings to the story. Assign individuals or groups to alter key events in the plot. Ask students to take on roles of key characters and act out the groups' plot changes for the class. For details, see

RESOURCE MANAGER
Ideas for Extension pp. 36–37

She would dream of great reception halls hung with old silks, of fine furniture filled with priceless curios, and of small, stylish, scented sitting rooms just right for the four o'clock chat with intimate friends, with distinguished and sought-after men whose attention every woman envies and longs to attract.

hen dining at the round table, covered for the third day with the same cloth, opposite her husband, who would raise the cover of the soup tureen, declaring delightedly, "Ah! A good stew! There's nothing I like better . . ." she would dream of fashionable dinner parties, of gleaming silverware, of tapestries making the walls 30 alive with characters out of history and strange birds in a fairyland forest; she would dream of delicious dishes served on wonderful china, of gallant compliments whispered and listened to with a sphinxlike[2] smile as one eats the rosy flesh of a trout or nibbles at the wings of a grouse.

She had no evening clothes, no jewels, nothing. But those were the things she wanted; she felt that was the kind of life for her. She so much longed to please, be envied, be fascinating and sought after. **B**

She had a well-to-do friend, a classmate of convent-school days whom she would no longer go to see, simply because she would feel so distressed on 40 returning home. And she would weep for days on end from **vexation,** regret, despair, and anguish.

Then one evening, her husband came home proudly holding out a large envelope.

"Look," he said, "I've got something for you."

She excitedly tore open the envelope and pulled out a printed card bearing these words:

"The Minister of Education and Mme. Georges Ramponneau[3] beg M. and Mme. Loisel[4] to do them the honor of attending an evening reception at the Ministerial Mansion on Friday, January 18."

50 Instead of being delighted, as her husband had hoped, she scornfully tossed the invitation on the table, murmuring, "What good is that to me?"

"But, my dear, I thought you'd be thrilled to death. You never get a chance to go out, and this is a real affair, a wonderful one! I had an awful time getting a card. Everybody wants one; it's much sought after, and not many clerks have a chance at one. You'll see all the most important people there."

**B MAKE INFERENCES**
Think about Madame Loisel's dreams and desires up to this point. What can you infer about her values?

**vexation** (vĕk-sā′shən) *n.* irritation; annoyance

**2 Targeted Passage**

---

2. **sphinxlike:** mysterious (from the Greek myth of the sphinx, a winged creature that killed those who could not answer its riddle).

3. **Mme. Georges Ramponneau** (zhôrzh′ răN-pô-nō′): *Mme.* is an abbreviation for *Madame* (mə-däm′), a title of courtesy for a French married woman.

4. **M. and Mme. Loisel** (lwä-zĕl′): *M.* is an abbreviation for *Monsieur* (mə-syœ′), a title of courtesy for a Frenchman.

226    UNIT 2: CHARACTERIZATION AND POINT OF VIEW

---

A Paris Street, Rain (1877), Gustave Caillebotte. Oil on canvas. The Art Institute of Chicago.
© Erich Lessing/Art Resource, New York.

She gave him an irritated glance and burst out impatiently, "What do you think I have to go in?"

He hadn't given that a thought. He stammered, "Why, the dress you wear when we go to the theater. That looks quite nice, I think."

60 He stopped talking, dazed and distracted to see his wife burst out weeping. Two large tears slowly rolled from the corners of her eyes to the corners of her mouth; he gasped, "Why, what's the matter? What's the trouble?"

By sheer will power she overcame her outburst and answered in a calm voice while wiping the tears from her wet cheeks:

"Oh, nothing. Only I don't have an evening dress and therefore I can't go to that affair. Give the card to some friend at the office whose wife can dress better than I can."

He was stunned. He resumed. "Let's see, Mathilde.[5] How much would a suitable outfit cost—one you could wear for other affairs too—something 70 very simple?"

She thought it over for several seconds, going over her allowance and thinking also of the amount she could ask for without bringing an immediate refusal and an exclamation of dismay from the thrifty clerk.

Finally, she answered hesitatingly, "I'm not sure exactly, but I think with four hundred francs[6] I could manage it."

---

5. **Mathilde** (mä-tēld').

6. **francs** (frăngks): The franc was the basic monetary unit of France.

THE NECKLACE 227

---

**COMMON CORE RL 4**

**Language Coach**

**Denotation/Connotation** Many words and fixed expressions have positive or negative emotional associations (**connotations**). These connotations are different from the word's dictionary definition (**denotation**). Reread lines 56–57. What is the denotation of *burst out* in this sentence? What are its connotations?

---

## Analyze Visuals

**Activity** Point out that the couple in the foreground is middle class, like the Loisels. Ask students if this information surprises them or affects their opinion of Madame Loisel.

**About the Art** This famous painting by French Impressionist Gustave Caillebotte (1848–1894) provides a glimpse of Paris during the time frame of "The Necklace." Like other Impressionistic works, this street scene captures a single moment in everyday life.

## TIERED DISCUSSION PROMPTS

Use these prompts to help students understand the relationship between the Loisels as described in lines 42–67.

**Connect** For whom do you feel more sympathy, Madame Loisel or her husband? Why? *Students may choose either character as long as their reasons accurately reflect story details about that character and his or her situation.*

**Analyze** How do these two characters react differently to the invitation? *Possible answer: He is proud and happy (lines 42–44, 52–55), but she is negative (lines 50–51, 56–57, 60–67).*

**Evaluate** Do both characters have valid reactions or feelings? Explain. *Students may cite evidence from their lives or from the text to support their evaluations.*

---

### FOR ENGLISH LANGUAGE LEARNERS

**Language Coach** **COMMON CORE RL 4**

**Denotation/Connotation**
*Answer:* Burst out *denotes "said" or "cried"; it connotes a sudden release of emotion.* Point out that *gasped*, another synonym for *said*, is used in line 62. Help students understand its particular connotation using the context of the story.

### FOR ADVANCED LEARNERS/PRE-AP

**Examine Perspectives** [small-group option] Guy de Maupassant has been called a misogynist (a hater of women) by some contemporary scholars. Have students look for evidence in the story that supports or contradicts that view and then present their findings in a class discussion.

##  CHARACTER MOTIVATION

**Possible answers:** *He wants to please his wife; he fears that she will be bitter and hard to live with if he doesn't give her the money.*

**Extend the Discussion** Maupassant does not include Madame Loisel's reaction to her husband's offer. Do you think that she was grateful? overjoyed? indifferent? Explain.

**REVISIT THE BIG QUESTION**

How important is

# STATUS?

**Discuss** In lines 88–91, Madame Loisel rejects the idea of wearing flowers rather than jewels. How does this response relate to her desire for status? *Possible answers: Madame Loisel thinks that flowers are too simple or affordable; she prefers to wear something that is a symbol of wealth.*

##  *Model the Skill:* CHARACTER MOTIVATION

Discuss with students Madame Loisel's dreams, desires, and values. Point out that Madame Loisel valued the status that she believed would be hers if she wore the diamond necklace.

**Possible answer:** *Madame Loisel's motivation for choosing an expensive and glittering diamond necklace comes from her desire to appear wealthy and to be noticed and admired by others.*

### OWN THE WORD

**pauper:** Have students complete this sentence to show that they understand the meaning of *pauper*. Mark said he felt like a *pauper* at the banquet held at the country club because . . .

**Possible answer:** *he wasn't wearing the fancy clothes everyone else wore.*

---

He turned a bit pale, for he had set aside just that amount to buy a rifle so that, the following summer, he could join some friends who were getting up a group to shoot larks on the plain near Nanterre.[7]

However, he said, "All right. I'll give you four hundred francs. But try to get 80 a nice dress." **C**

As the day of the party approached, Mme. Loisel seemed sad, moody, and ill at ease. Her outfit was ready, however. Her husband said to her one evening, "What's the matter? You've been all out of sorts for three days."

And she answered, "It's embarrassing not to have a jewel or a gem—nothing to wear on my dress. I'll look like a **pauper**: I'd almost rather not go to that party."

He answered, "Why not wear some flowers? They're very fashionable this season. For ten francs you can get two or three gorgeous roses."

90 She wasn't at all convinced. "No. . . . There's nothing more humiliating than to look poor among a lot of rich women."

But her husband exclaimed, "My, but you're silly! Go see your friend Mme. Forestier[8] and ask her to lend you some jewelry. You and she know each other well enough for you to do that."

She gave a cry of joy, "Why, that's so! I hadn't thought of it."

The next day she paid her friend a visit and told her of her predicament.

Mme. Forestier went toward a large closet with mirrored doors, took out a large jewel box, brought it over, opened it, and said to Mme. Loisel, "Pick something out, my dear."

100 At first her eyes noted some bracelets, then a pearl necklace, then a Venetian cross, gold and gems, of marvelous workmanship. She tried on these adornments in front of the mirror, but hesitated, unable to decide which to part with and put back. She kept on asking, "Haven't you something else?"

"Oh, yes, keep on looking. I don't know just what you'd like."

All at once she found, in a black satin box, a superb diamond necklace; and her pulse beat faster with longing. Her hands trembled as she took it up. Clasping it around her throat, outside her high-necked dress, she stood in ecstasy looking at her reflection.

Then she asked, hesitatingly, pleading, "Could I borrow that, just that and 110 nothing else?"

"Why, of course."

She threw her arms around her friend, kissed her warmly, and fled with her treasure. **D**

The day of the party arrived. Mme. Loisel was a sensation. She was the prettiest one there, fashionable, gracious, smiling, and wild with joy. All the

---

7. **Nanterre** (näɴ-tĕr'): a city of north central France.

8. **Forestier** (fô-rĕs-tyā').

**C** CHARACTER MOTIVATION
What do you think is Monsieur Loisel's motivation for giving the money to his wife? Include details from the story as you explain your answer.

**pauper** (pô'pər) *n.* a poor person, especially one who depends on public charity

**3** Targeted Passage

**D** CHARACTER MOTIVATION
Why does Madame Loisel choose the diamond necklace? Use details from the story to explain her motivation.

---

## DIFFERENTIATED INSTRUCTION

**FOR STRUGGLING READERS**

 **Targeted Passage [Lines 92–113]**
This passage introduces the object that gives the story its title.

- Why does Madame Loisel visit Madame Forestier? (lines 92–96)

- What does Madame Forestier say when Madame Loisel explains her situation? (lines 98–99)

- Name two things that Madame Loisel looks at but then discards. (lines 100–101)

- What does she finally borrow? (lines 105–111)

men turned to look at her, asked who she was, begged to be introduced. All the Cabinet officials wanted to waltz with her. The minister took notice of her.

120 She danced madly, wildly, drunk with pleasure, giving no thought to anything in the triumph of her beauty, the pride of her success, in a kind of happy cloud composed of all the **adulation,** of all the admiring glances, of all the awakened longings, of a sense of complete victory that is so sweet to a woman's heart.

She left around four o'clock in the morning. Her husband, since midnight, had been dozing in a small empty sitting room with three other gentlemen whose wives were having too good a time.

He threw over her shoulders the wraps he had brought for going home, modest garments of everyday life whose shabbiness clashed with the stylishness of her evening clothes. She felt this and longed to escape, unseen by the other women who were draped in expensive furs.

**adulation** (ăj′ə-lā′shən) *n.* excessive praise or flattery

**Analyze Visuals**

In your opinion, how well does this painting reflect the **setting** of the party? Describe the details that influenced your opinion.

*The Ball,* Victor Gabriel Gilbert. © Christie's Images/Corbis.

THE NECKLACE **229**

## Analyze Visuals

*Possible answer: The party that Madame Loisel attends probably is much like the one pictured, with women in beautiful evening gowns and men in tuxedoes dancing in an elegant, formal salon.*

**About the Art** French painter Victor Gabriel Gilbert (1847–1935) painted *The Ball* during the time period in which "The Necklace" was written. Like many other paintings by Gilbert, *The Ball* portrays the world of the rich in sumptuous detail.

---

**VOCABULARY**     COMMON CORE   L 4

### OWN THE WORD

**adulation:** Have students identify context clues in the sentence that help them determine the meaning of *adulation*.

*Possible answer: triumph, happy cloud, admiring glances, complete victory*

---

**FOR ENGLISH LANGUAGE LEARNERS**

**Vocabulary: Idioms and Sayings** Use New Word Analysis to teach the meanings of these idioms and sayings as you come across them in the reading:

- *thrilled to death* (line 52), "very excited and happy"
- *ill at ease* (line 82), "nervous"
- *all out of sorts* (line 84), "irritable"
- *paid a visit* (line 96), "went to see"

- *pick out* (lines 98–99), "choose"
- *in all her glory* (line 143), "looking her best"
- *her mind a blank* (line 160), "unable to think"
- *drove him* (line 163), "urged him," "suggested that he would be successful"

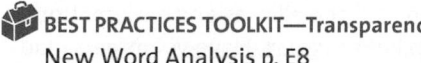 BEST PRACTICES TOOLKIT—Transparency New Word Analysis p. E8

## ⓔ POINT OF VIEW

*Possible answer: Telling the two characters' thoughts allows readers to learn about their different reactions and personalities and to emphasize how superficial Madame Loisel is.*

**IF STUDENTS NEED HELP . . .** Ask them what Madame Loisel's life will be like the next day. Ask whether going to the party changed her life in any lasting way. Help students understand that after the elegant party, Madame Loisel might be more disappointed than ever with her dreary life.

## ⓕ GRAMMAR AND STYLE

COMMON CORE **L 1b**

**Analyze Sentence Beginnings** Many good writers, such as Maupassant, vary their sentence beginnings to make their writing more interesting and lively. After students read the sentences beginning with *Before the mirror* (line 142) and *Suddenly* (line 143), discuss how the author's choices add rhythm and drama to the sentences. Encourage students to find other sentences in the selection that begin in interesting and dramatic ways and to tell how those sentences affect them as readers.

## VOCABULARY

COMMON CORE

**L 4**

## OWN THE WORD

- **disconsolate:** Remind students that *dis-* means "opposite of," and comes from the Latin for "apart." Have them explain the meaning of *disconsolate* using the meaning of *dis-*. Then have students list antonyms for *disconsolate*. **Possible answers:** *happy, comforted, joyous, cheerful*

- **aghast:** Ask students to think of situations that would make them feel *aghast*. Ask them to explain their reasoning. **Possible answers:** *being late to work; missing an airplane flight; learning that a relative or friend had been hurt in an accident*

---

130  Loisel held her back.

"Hold on! You'll catch cold outside. I'll call a cab."

But she wouldn't listen to him and went rapidly down the stairs. When they were on the street, they didn't find a carriage; and they set out to hunt for one, hailing drivers whom they saw going by at a distance.

They walked toward the Seine,[9] **disconsolate** and shivering. Finally on the docks they found one of those carriages that one sees in Paris only after nightfall, as if they were ashamed to show their drabness during daylight hours.

It dropped them at their door in the Rue des Martyrs,[10] and they climbed

140  wearily up to their apartment. For her, it was all over. For him, there was the thought that he would have to be at the Ministry at ten o'clock. ⓔ

Before the mirror, she let the wraps fall from her shoulders to see herself once again in all her glory. Suddenly she gave a cry. The necklace was gone. ⓕ

Her husband, already half-undressed, said, "What's the trouble?"

She turned toward him despairingly, "I . . . I . . . I don't have Mme. Forestier's necklace."

"What! You can't mean it! It's impossible!"

They hunted everywhere, through the folds of the dress, through the folds of the coat, in the pockets. They found nothing.

150  He asked, "Are you sure you had it when leaving the dance?"

"Yes, I felt it when I was in the hall of the Ministry."

"But if you had lost it on the street, we'd have heard it drop. It must be in the cab."

"Yes. Quite likely. Did you get its number?"

"No. Didn't you notice it either?"

"No."

They looked at each other **aghast.** Finally Loisel got dressed again.

"I'll retrace our steps on foot," he said, "to see if I can find it."

And he went out. She remained in her evening clothes, without the strength

160  to go to bed, slumped in a chair in the unheated room, her mind a blank.

Her husband came in about seven o'clock. He had had no luck.

He went to the police station, to the newspapers to post a reward, to the cab companies, everywhere the slightest hope drove him.

That evening Loisel returned, pale, his face lined; still he had learned nothing.

"We'll have to write your friend," he said, "to tell her you have broken the catch and are having it repaired. That will give us a little time to turn around."

She wrote to his dictation.

---

**disconsolate**
(dĭs-kŏn′sə-lĭt) *adj.* extremely depressed or dejected

## ⓔ POINT OF VIEW
What is the impact of having the narrator explain what Madame Loisel and her husband each think?

## ⓕ GRAMMAR AND STYLE
Reread lines 142–143. Notice how Maupassant varies his sentence beginnings by using words and phrases such as *before the mirror* and *suddenly*.

**aghast** (ə-găst′) *adj.* filled with shock or horror

---

9. **Seine** (sĕn): the principal river of Paris.

10. **Rue des Martyrs** (rü′ dā mär-tēr′): a street in Paris.

**230**   UNIT 2: CHARACTERIZATION AND POINT OF VIEW

---

## DIFFERENTIATED INSTRUCTION

**FOR ENGLISH LANGUAGE LEARNERS**

**Language: Punctuation and Print Clues** Remind students that authors often use punctuation in ways that help their readers understand how the characters are speaking. Point out the ellipses and exclamation points in lines 145–147. Have volunteers read the words aloud in the way they think the characters said them.

**FOR ADVANCED LEARNERS/PRE–AP**

**Contrast Characters** Have students write a paragraph in response to this question: *What details in the story thus far support the view that Madame Loisel is a romantic and Monsieur Loisel is a realist?* Invite students to compare their responses.

A t the end of a week, they had given up all hope.

And Loisel, looking five years older, declared, "We must take steps to replace that piece of jewelry."

The next day they took the case to the jeweler whose name they found inside. He consulted his records. "I didn't sell that necklace, madame," he said. "I only supplied the case."

Then they went from one jeweler to another hunting for a similar necklace, going over their recollections, both sick with despair and anxiety.

They found, in a shop in Palais Royal, a string of diamonds which seemed exactly like the one they were seeking. It was priced at forty thousand francs. They could get it for thirty-six.

180 They asked the jeweler to hold it for them for three days. And they reached an agreement that he would take it back for thirty-four thousand if the lost one was found before the end of February.

Loisel had eighteen thousand francs he had inherited from his father. He would borrow the rest.

He went about raising the money, asking a thousand francs from one, four hundred from another, a hundred here, sixty there. He signed notes, made ruinous deals, did business with loan sharks, ran the whole **gamut** of moneylenders. He compromised the rest of his life, risked his signature without knowing if he'd be able to honor it, and then, terrified by the outlook

190 for the future, by the blackness of despair about to close around him, by the prospect of all the **privations** of the body and tortures of the spirit, he went to claim the new necklace with the thirty-six thousand francs which he placed on the counter of the shopkeeper. **G**

When Mme. Loisel took the necklace back, Mme. Forestier said to her frostily, "You should have brought it back sooner; I might have needed it."

She didn't open the case, an action her friend was afraid of. If she had noticed the substitution, what would she have thought? What would she have said? Would she have thought her a thief?

Mme. Loisel experienced the horrible life the needy live. She played her
200 part, however, with sudden heroism. That frightful debt had to be paid. She would pay it. She dismissed her maid; they rented a garret under the eaves.

She learned to do the heavy housework, to perform the hateful duties of cooking. She washed dishes, wearing down her shell-pink nails scouring the grease from pots and pans; she scrubbed dirty linen, shirts, and cleaning rags which she hung on a line to dry; she took the garbage down to the street each morning and brought up water, stopping on each landing to get her breath. And, clad like a peasant woman, basket on arm, guarding sou[11] by sou her scanty allowance, she bargained with the fruit dealers, the grocer, the butcher, and was insulted by them.

---

11. **sou** (sōō): a French coin of small value.

**gamut** (găm'ət) *n.* an entire range or series

**privation** (prī-vā'shən) *n.* the lack of a basic necessity or a comfort of life

**G CHARACTER MOTIVATION**
Consider why the Loisels don't tell Mathilde's friend the truth. What motivates them to go into such debt?

---

**G CHARACTER MOTIVATION**

*Possible answer:* *The Loisels are ashamed of their carelessness, and they fear Madame Forestier's reaction. By replacing the necklace secretly, they hope to maintain their honor and dignity.*

**IF STUDENTS NEED HELP . . .** Ask students how they would feel if they lost something of great value that belonged to someone else. Have them name some of the thoughts that might go through their heads while they pondered what to do.

**Extend the Discussion** Discuss whether the Loisels made the right decision.

**TIERED DISCUSSION PROMPTS**

Use these prompts to help students understand what happens to Madame Loisel in lines 199–209:

**Connect** What is your opinion of Madame Loisel at this point? *Students should cite evidence to support their opinions.*

**Evaluate** Do you think that Madame Loisel is now a more admirable character than she was at the beginning of the story? Explain. *Students should defend their responses.*

**VOCABULARY** COMMON CORE L 4

**OWN THE WORD**

- **gamut:** Write the word *gamut* and the definition "an entire range or series" in a circle. Have students add synonyms to complete a semantic map. *Possible answers: progression, string, extent, scope*

- **privation:** Read lines 185–193 aloud to students. Have them cite the context clues that can help them determine the meaning of *privations*. *Possible answers: compromised life, risked signature, terrified by outlook for the future, tortures of the spirit.*

---

**FOR STRUGGLING READERS**

**Monitor Understanding** Ask students to check their understanding by having small groups prepare two lists, using details from this page:

- a list of ways in which Monsieur Loisel raises the money to buy the diamond necklace (lines 180–193)

- a list of ways in which Madame Loisel changes her life in order to set aside money to repay that amount (lines 201–209)

**FOR ADVANCED LEARNERS/PRE–AP**

**Analyze Plot Elements** [paired-activity option] A *contrivance* is an illogical or unlikely action or event in a plot. Upon reading it, the reader might exclaim, "That's ridiculous!" or "That never would happen in real life." Have students prepare a statement that considers (1) whether or not Madame Forestier's failure to open the jewelry case is a contrivance and (2) if there are other contrivances in this story.

## Analyze Visuals

*Possible answer:* The elegant hairdo, pearls, apparent leisure, and beautiful gown in the portrait on page 225 show a woman living a privileged life—the kind of life that Madame Loisel had dreamed of having. The messy hair, lack of jewelry, menial task, rough clothing, and weary appearance in the portrait on this page convey a life of drudgery—the kind of life that Madame Loisel lives now. Similarly, the contrast between the smooth brushstrokes of the earlier portrait and the rough style of this artwork suggests how Madame Loisel has changed from a relatively well-off, middle-class homemaker to a common worker.

**About the Art** Edgar Degas (1834–1917) is well known for artwork that shows people in daily activities such as bathing, combing their hair, and working in laundries. A French Impressionist, Degas often showed his subjects in natural, spontaneous poses.

◀ **Analyze Visuals**

**Compare** this artwork with the one shown on page 225. How do the details and styles of each reflect the changes that Madame Loisel endures?

*The Laundress* (1869), Edgar Degas. Pastel, white crayon, and charcoal. Musée d'Orsay, Paris. Photo © Jean Schormans/Réunion des Musées Nationaux/Art Resource, New York.

210    Each month notes had to be paid, and others renewed to give more time.
   Her husband labored evenings to balance a tradesman's accounts, and at night, often, he copied documents at five sous a page.
   And this went on for ten years.
   Finally, all was paid back, everything including the exorbitant rates of the loan sharks and accumulated compound interest.

---

## DIFFERENTIATED INSTRUCTION

### FOR ENGLISH LANGUAGE LEARNERS

**Vocabulary: Multiple-Meaning Words** Point out that some English words have more than one meaning. Have students use context clues and prior knowledge to determine how each of these words is used in the story:

- *raising* (line 185)
- *sharks* (line 187)
- *notes* (line 210)
- *compound* (line 215)
- *common* (line 233)
- *mean* (line 239)

### FOR STRUGGLING READERS

**Developing Oral Fluency** Ask students to look at lines 222–224. Point out that the first three sentences are questions, while the last two are exclamations. Ask students to listen closely as you read the paragraph aloud, emphasizing the differences between the sounds of questions and exclamations. Then pair struggling readers with fluent students who can listen as they read the sentences.

**R**  RESOURCE MANAGER—Copy Master
Reading Fluency p. 51

Mme. Loisel appeared an old woman, now. She became heavy, rough, harsh, like one of the poor. Her hair untended, her skirts **askew,** her hands red, her voice shrill, she even slopped water on her floors and scrubbed them herself. But, sometimes, while her husband was at work, she would sit near the
220 window and think of that long-ago evening when, at the dance, she had been so beautiful and admired.

What would have happened if she had not lost that necklace? Who knows? Who can say? How strange and unpredictable life is! How little there is between happiness and misery!

Then one Sunday when she had gone for a walk on the Champs Élysées[12] to relax a bit from the week's labors, she suddenly noticed a woman strolling with a child. It was Mme. Forestier, still young-looking; still beautiful, still charming. **H**

Mme. Loisel felt a rush of emotion. Should she speak to her? Of course. And
230 now that everything was paid off, she would tell her the whole story. Why not?

She went toward her. "Hello, Jeanne."

The other, not recognizing her, showed astonishment at being spoken to so familiarly by this common person. She stammered. "But . . . madame . . . I don't recognize . . . You must be mistaken."

"No, I'm Mathilde Loisel."

Her friend gave a cry, "Oh, my poor Mathilde, how you've changed!"

"Yes, I've had a hard time since last seeing you. And plenty of misfortunes—and all on account of you!" **I**

"Of me . . . How do you mean?"

240 "Do you remember that diamond necklace you loaned me to wear to the dance at the Ministry?"

"Yes, but what about it?"

"Well, I lost it."

"You lost it! But you returned it."

"I brought you another just like it. And we've been paying for it for ten years now. You can imagine that wasn't easy for us who had nothing. Well, it's over now, and I am glad of it."

Mme. Forestier stopped short, "You mean to say you bought a diamond necklace to replace mine?"

250 "Yes. You never noticed, then? They were quite alike."

And she smiled with proud and simple joy.

Mme. Forestier, quite overcome, clasped her by the hands. "Oh, my poor Mathilde. But mine was only paste.[13] Why, at most it was worth only five hundred francs!" ❦

**askew** (ə-skyōō′) *adj.* crooked; to one side

**H PREDICT**
Do you think Madame Loisel will tell her friend the truth? Why or why not?

**I CHARACTER MOTIVATION**
Think about what motivates Madame Loisel to approach her friend. Is this action believable, given Madame Loisel's earlier thoughts and actions? Explain your response.

④ **Targeted Passage**

---

12. **Champs Élysées** (shän zā-lē-zā′): a famous wide street in Paris.
13. **paste:** a hard, glassy material used in making imitation gems.

THE NECKLACE   **233**

**READING STRATEGY:** *Review*

**H PREDICT**

**Possible answer:** *She has kept the secret for ten years, to avoid shame; she is likely to keep it now.*

**IF STUDENTS NEED HELP . . .** Review lines 196–198 and discuss Madame Loisel's fear of losing status in Madame Forestier's eyes.

**TEXT ANALYSIS**   COMMON CORE   RL 3

**I CHARACTER MOTIVATION**

**Possible answers:** *Yes, it is surprising that Madame Loisel has decided to reveal her fall in status. No, it is not surprising that she would want to confront Madame Forestier, whom she blames (at least in part) for the reversal that she has suffered.*

**VOCABULARY**   COMMON CORE   L 4

**OWN THE WORD**

**askew:** Have students explain the image of "skirts *askew*." What would this look like? Then ask students to name other clothing items that could go *askew* if worn carelessly. **Possible answers:** *hats, caps, stockings, ties*

**SELECTION WRAP–UP**

**READ WITH A PURPOSE** Now that students know how the central conflict affected the main characters, ask them whether they think the effect on Mme. Loisel was good or bad. **Possible response:** *It was good, because even though it was physically difficult it made her less frivolous and petty.*

★ **CRITIQUE** Have students evaluate the story, telling which parts they liked or disliked and why. Have students revisit their evaluations after discussing the story to see if their original opinions change.

**INDEPENDENT READING**

If students are interested in reading other stories about social classes, they might enjoy *Jane Eyre* by Charlotte Brontë.

**FOR STRUGGLING READERS**

④ **Targeted Passage [Lines 240–254]**

As the story ends, this passage reveals a surprise: the true value of the necklace.

- What confession does Madame Loisel make? How does she feel as she does so? (lines 243–247)

- How does Madame Forestier react? (lines 248–252)

- How much was the lost necklace worth? Why was it worth so little? (lines 253–254)

**FOR ADVANCED LEARNERS/PRE–AP**

**Analyze Theme** Madame Loisel borrowed the necklace to look like the upper-class people she envied. Had she not lost the necklace, or felt the need to borrow it in the first place, the Loisels' life would have been much better. What lesson might the author be trying to convey about an excessive concern for status? What other lessons might readers learn from this story?

# Practice and Apply

For preliminary support of post-reading questions, use these copy masters:

**R** **RESOURCE MANAGER—Copy Masters**
Reading Check p. 48
Character Motivation p. 41
Question Support p. 49

Additional selection questions, are provided for teachers on page 35.

## ANSWERS

## Comprehension

1. *She dreams of a life of wealth and elegance, rather than her ordinary, middle-class life.*

2. *Madame Loisel loses the necklace.*

3. *Madame Loisel learns that the necklace was fake and was worth very little.*

## Text Analysis

COMMON CORE RL 1, RL 3, RL 6

**Possible answers:**

4. ■ **COMMON CORE FOCUS** *Make Inferences* *Madame Loisel has changed a great deal. At the start, she feels she was born for riches and hates her middle-class life (lines 11–20). She is also too proud to attend the ball in the dress she owns (lines 65–67). By the end of the story, she is able to admit to having "nothing" (line 246) and to have labored for ten years.*

5. *Madame Loisel, who had wanted a life of having much more, finds that it was unnecessary for her to have spent ten years getting by with so much less.*

6. *He does not seem as desperate. He thinks that the dress that his wife wears to the theater "looks quite nice" (line 59); he is not worried about attire or jewelry for the reception (lines 58–62, 88–89).*

7. ● **COMMON CORE FOCUS** *Interpret Motivation*
   *Motivation #1: She feels that she has no suitable dress and so cannot attend the ball.*
   *Motivation #2: She wants to appear wealthy.*
   *Motivation #3: He is ashamed of the loss; he needs to stall for time to figure out how to repay the debt.*

8. *Knowing that Monsieur Loisel also becomes "sick with despair and anxiety" over the lost necklace (line 176) makes Madame Loisel's foolish need seem all the worse.*

9. *Heroic: She does the housework herself, bargains with tradespeople, and sacrifices her refinement.* **Not heroic:** *The Loisels' problem is mostly her fault, so she should carry part of the burden.*

---

## Comprehension

1. **Recall** Why is Madame Loisel discontented at the beginning of the story?

2. **Recall** What causes the change in the Loisels' financial situation?

3. **Summarize** What twist occurs at the end of the story?

## Text Analysis

● 4. **Make Inferences** Review the inferences and evidence from the story you wrote down during reading. How much do you think Madame Loisel has changed by the time the story ends?

5. **Analyze Irony** Situational irony occurs when a character—or the reader—expects one thing to happen but something entirely different occurs. What is ironic about the ending of "The Necklace"?

6. **Compare and Contrast Characters** Does Monsieur Loisel long for status as desperately as his wife does? Cite evidence to support your opinions.

● 7. **Interpret Motivation** Consider what you know about the characters' feelings and goals. For each action described in the chart shown, decide on the character's motivation.

| Action | Motivation |
|---|---|
| Mme. Loisel weeps when she receives the invitation. (line 60) | |
| Mme. Loisel borrows jewelry rather than wear flowers. (line 109) | |
| Monsieur Loisel advises his wife not to tell her friend about the lost necklace. (line 166–167) | |

8. **Analyze Point of View** For most of "The Necklace," the narrator focuses on Madame Loisel's thoughts and feelings. However, since this story is told from the **third-person omniscient point of view,** the narrator also relays the thoughts of Monsieur Loisel. Did knowing Monsieur Loisel's inner thoughts affect your opinion of Madame Loisel? Explain your answer.

9. **Evaluate** Reread lines 199–201. Do you agree that Madame Loisel shows heroism in paying off her debt? Find examples to support your opinion.

## Text Criticism

10. **Critical Interpretations** The literary critic Edward D. Sullivan declared that "The Necklace" is not just a story pointing to a moral, such as "Honesty is the best policy," but a story showing that in people's lives "blind chance rules." Do you agree or disagree with Sullivan's argument? Cite strong and thorough evidence to support your opinion.

> **How important is STATUS?**
>
> What would you give up in order to pursue popularity?

**COMMON CORE**

RL 1 Cite textual evidence to support analysis of what the text says explicitly as well as inferences drawn from the text. RL 3 Analyze how complex characters develop over the course of a text and interact with other characters. RL 6 Analyze a particular point of view reflected in a work of world literature.

---

## Text Criticism

**Possible answers:**

10. *Agree: Chance is to blame, as seen in Madame Loisel's position at birth and the accidental loss of the necklace. Disagree: Dishonesty is to blame, as seen in Madame Loisel's pretense of wealth and the Loisels' cover-up of the item's loss.*

> **How important is STATUS?**
> Encourage students to explain what they would expect to gain as the result of the sacrifices they make.

# Vocabulary in Context

## ▲ VOCABULARY PRACTICE

For each item, choose the word from the list that relates in meaning.

1. dejected, miserable, low
2. irritation, displeasure, anger
3. opportunities, possibilities, chances
4. range, extent, scope
5. praise, worship, adoration
6. horrified, dismayed, appalled
7. loss, damage, hardship
8. slanting, sideways, crooked
9. beggar, debtor, have-not
10. steadily, ceaselessly, perpetually

**WORD LIST**

adulation
aghast
askew
disconsolate
gamut
incessantly
pauper
privation
prospects
vexation

## ACADEMIC VOCABULARY IN SPEAKING

- complex   - device   - evaluate   - interact   - perspective

Madame Loisel and Mme. Forestier **interact** only three times in this story. With a partner, discuss the ways in which the two women interact. If either of them had acted or responded differently, how would the story have changed? Use at least one Academic Vocabulary word in your discussion.

**COMMON CORE**

**L 4a** Use context as a clue to the meaning of a word.

## VOCABULARY STRATEGY: THE LATIN WORD ROOT *spec*

The word *prospect* contains the Latin root *spec* or *spect*, which means "look" or "see." How is the root reflected in the meanings of the other words in the word family shown on the right?

**PRACTICE** This chart lists two additional roots and example words from "The Necklace." Use the roots and context clues to figure out the meanings of the underlined words.

prospect   retrospect

perspective — **spec, spect** — spectator

inspect   speculate

| Root | Meaning | Example |
|------|---------|---------|
| *dict* = speak | **dictation** (line 168) |
| *grat* = thanks | **gracious** (line 115) |

1. The courtroom was silent as the judge announced the <u>verdict</u>.
2. The actress expressed <u>gratitude</u> in her acceptance speech.
3. The confused defendant <u>contradicted</u> his earlier testimony.
4. What an <u>ingrate</u>! Sam didn't acknowledge our gift.
5. The subjects were afraid to defy the king's <u>edict</u>.

**Interactive Vocabulary** **THINK** central

Go to **thinkcentral.com**.
KEYWORD: HML9-235

THE NECKLACE   **235**

---

## DIFFERENTIATED INSTRUCTION

### FOR ADVANCED LEARNERS/PRE–AP

**Vocabulary in Writing** [small-group option] Have students create headlines that reflect the plot of "The Necklace," using as many vocabulary words as possible. ***Example:*** *Loisels <u>Disconsolate</u> over Ruinous Debts*

### FOR ENGLISH LANGUAGE LEARNERS

**Media and Language** Have students work with a proficient English speaker to make recordings as they read aloud the sentences in the Practice activity. Then, have them listen to their recordings and identify any words they do not know or that they found difficult to pronounce. By listening to their recordings and discussing unknown or difficult words, students will build and reinforce their understanding of Latin root words such as *spec, dict,* and *grat.*

---

# Language

## ◆ GRAMMAR AND STYLE

- Point out the words *when, where,* and *how.* Have students brainstorm for words, phrases, and clauses that might answer these questions in a sentence.

- After discussing the student model, write this paragraph (in black) on the board and have students suggest revisions (in blue) to vary the sentence beginnings.

*On returning home from the ball,* ~~T~~*the Loisels discover that the borrowed necklace is missing. They search frantically but to no avail. After a few days,* ~~T~~*they are forced to give up. Without telling Madame Forestier what has happened,* ~~T~~*they purchase a new necklace.* ~~without telling Madame Forestier what has happened.~~

 **RESOURCE MANAGER—Copy Master**
Sentence Beginnings p. 50

### READING-WRITING CONNECTION

- Have students use a Two-Column Chart to organize the examples of characteristics of the relationship and the details that support their conclusions.

 **BEST PRACTICES TOOLKIT—Transparency**
Two-Column Chart p. A25

---

### Writing Online  THINK central

The following tools are available online at **thinkcentral.com** and on **WriteSmart CD-ROM:**
- **Interactive Graphic Organizers**
- **Interactive Student Models**
- **Interactive Revision Lessons**
For additional grammar instruction, see **GrammarNotes** on **thinkcentral.com**.

---

# Assess and Reteach

## Assess
**DIAGNOSTIC AND SELECTION TESTS**
Selection Test A pp. 63–64
Selection Test B/C pp. 65–66

**Interactive Selection Test** on **thinkcentral.com**

## Reteach
**Level Up Online Tutorials** on **thinkcentral.com**

---

# Language

COMMON CORE

L 1b Use various types of phrases and clauses to convey specific meanings and add variety and interest to writing.

## ◆ GRAMMAR AND STYLE: Vary Sentence Beginnings

Review the **Grammar and Style** note on page 230. Like Maupassant, you can vary your sentence beginnings to add interest to your writing. Keep the following techniques in mind when you respond to the writing prompt below.

1. **Avoid using too many pronouns and articles.** Don't fall into the trap of beginning all your sentences with the words *he, she, it,* and *the.*

2. **Use words, phrases, and clauses that let readers know when, where, or how.** By using a variety of words, phrases, and clauses, Maupassant added descriptive details and avoided repetitive beginnings. Here are two examples:

   *Finally, she answered hesitatingly . . .* (line 74)

   *As the day of the party approached, Mme. Loisel seemed sad. . . .* (line 81)

Notice how the revisions in blue improve the rhythm and flow of this first draft.

> **STUDENT MODEL**
>
> *Before the necklace is lost,*
> ∧The Loisels do not have a good marriage. Madame Loisel treats her husband
>     *Without a care for his feelings,  At the party,*
> poorly. ∧She frequently snaps at him. ∧She ignores him ~~at the party.~~
> *However,*        *Sensitive to her needs,*
> ∧He seems to always dote on her. ∧He does everything she wants.

### READING-WRITING CONNECTION

 **YOUR TURN**  Increase your understanding of "The Necklace" by responding to this prompt. Then use the **revising tip** to improve your writing.

| WRITING PROMPT | REVISING TIP |
|---|---|
| **Short Constructed Response: Analysis** How would you characterize the relationship between Monsieur and Madame Loisel at the beginning of the story? Using examples from the text, write **one or two paragraphs** to describe their marriage. Include details that show how they treat each other. | Review your response. Did you vary the beginnings and structure of your sentences to create a smooth and interesting writing style? If not, revise your response to add variation to your sentences. |

 **Interactive Revision  THINK central**
Go to **thinkcentral.com**.
KEYWORD: HML9-236

---

## DIFFERENTIATED INSTRUCTION

### FOR STRUGGLING WRITERS

*Possible Organization for the short response:*

1. The topic sentence describes the Loisels' marriage.

2. The body cites specific characteristics of that relationship and at least one detail that illustrates each characteristic.

3. The final sentence reviews and/or remarks on that relationship.

## Magazine Article

In "The Necklace," the Loisels borrow and buy their way into years of debt. Unfortunately, in their desire to achieve status, some teens today are falling into a similar cycle.

# $pending $pree

Been shopping lately? No matter which income bracket teens fall into, their general attitude stays the same: spend, don't save. On average, teens spend $100 a week on entertainment, clothing, and food. Perhaps this is why they're becoming the new target group of credit card marketers.

### Pay or Play

While many teens might find the lure of a credit card to be irresistible, spending comes with a price. More and more often, young people are joining the ranks of those in debt.

What's the cause for this? Teens are often pressured to wear the same clothes, buy the same music, and own the same products. The credit card industry feeds off of this need to consume by offering credit cards to those who are barely out of high school.

Since most 18-year-olds are still unfamiliar with handling their personal finances, many don't pay their credit card bills on time, if at all. The result is a rapid build-up of debt.

### Incentives for $aving

To help curb this financial downward spiral, one city has even established a "financial literacy" program. The Private Industry Council of Milwaukee County launched the pilot program, aimed at central-city teens. The training that teens receive through the program encourages them to save and instructs them in how to open a bank account.

### Payoff

Learning to handle money responsibly early on can reap great rewards down the line. Not only does it contribute to a person's peace of mind to know that he or she is financially secure, but it also helps to establish a good credit record. So count your pennies, and avoid becoming one of the many Americans who are currently in debt.

**Convenient or Costly?** The chart shows how credit card charges can accumulate, assuming you miss three monthly payments.

| | |
|---|---|
| VIDEO GAME | $40.00 |
| CLOTHES | $100.00 |
| LUNCH | $28.00 |
| Original total due: | $168.00 |
| Credit card late fees and finance charges: | **+** $83.00 |
| Credit card total due: | **=** $251.00 |

---

## DIFFERENTIATED INSTRUCTION

**FOR ENGLISH LANGUAGE LEARNERS**

**Language: Word Roots** Point out that the word *credit* includes the Latin root *cred*, which means "trust" or "believe." Explain that credit allows you to buy something now in the trust or belief that you will pay for it in the future.

**Culture: Clarify** Explain that credit card companies, banks, and stores make money by penalizing people who make late payments. People pay fees, called "interest" or "finance charges," which can be very costly. With a "revolving charge," for example, you make payments that are only part of what you owe. Thus, you end up paying interest on the interest. In addition, many companies charge a yearly fee for their credit cards.

---

## Magazine Article

Have students work in small groups to compare the similarities and differences about debt that this magazine article describes with the kind of debt portrayed in "The Necklace." Remind students to note the effects debt has on other areas of life aside from the financial aspect.

### READING FOR INFORMATION

Point out that "Spending Spree" is a magazine article. Have students preview the article, noting the title, photo, subheadings, and chart. Then ask:

- What information do the text features and graphic aids provide? ***Possible answer:*** *The title and photo suggest the topic. The blue subheadings introduce the key ideas, while the chart and the caption make clear how interest can accumulate and lead to increased debt.*

- What effect might the playful tone and style of the subheadings have on readers? ***Possible answer:*** *They add interest, make the text less intimidating, and focus attention on key ideas.*

- What is the main idea of this article? ***Possible answer:*** *Teens are becoming the new target of credit card marketers (lines 5–6).*

### DISCUSSION PROMPTS

Use the questions below to help students understand the issue of spiraling teen credit card debt:

**Evaluate** Based on this article, do you think that financial literacy programs are the answer to solving the problem of spiraling teen credit card debt? Explain your answer. ***Possible answer:*** *While financial literacy is one way to make teens aware of the dangers in taking on debt, teens also need to be taught ways to avoid taking on huge amounts of debt.*

**Synthesize** How might Madame Loisel's life have been different had she lived today and had easy credit available? ***Possible answers:*** *She would have been better off because she could have paid off her debt over time; her life would be no better because she still would have to pay back a huge debt plus the compounding interest.*

# Practice and Apply

○ COMMON CORE FOCUS

**RI 7** Analyze various accounts of a subject told in different mediums.

## Flier

Have students study the flier. Discuss with the class how the Consumer Debt Hotline might be able to help someone who is struggling with debt. Then, ask students if they feel that the hotline could have helped the Loisels manage their debt differently.

**ANALYZE VISUALS** — COMMON CORE RI 7

### 1. INFER

*Possible answer:* Debt is compared to imprisonment by representing it as a heavy, impeding object, similar to a ball and chain, attached to a person.

**ANALYZE VISUALS** — COMMON CORE RI 7

### 2. ANALYZE

*Possible answer:* The images show expensive, luxurious items such as those that might cause a person to get into debt.

**ANALYZE VISUALS** — COMMON CORE RI 7

### 3. CONNECT

Answers will vary. Students may say that the flier makes them think they should not make extravagant purchases on credit if they won't be able to responsibly pay back the debts.

## Flier

The magazine article you just read explores teenagers' spending habits, but teens aren't alone in taking on too much debt. Many adults also struggle to pay for financed purchases. Credit-counseling agencies, such as the one advertised on this flier, claim to help consumers make wiser spending decisions and ultimately get out of debt.

○ COMMON CORE

**RI 7** Analyze various accounts of a subject told in different mediums.

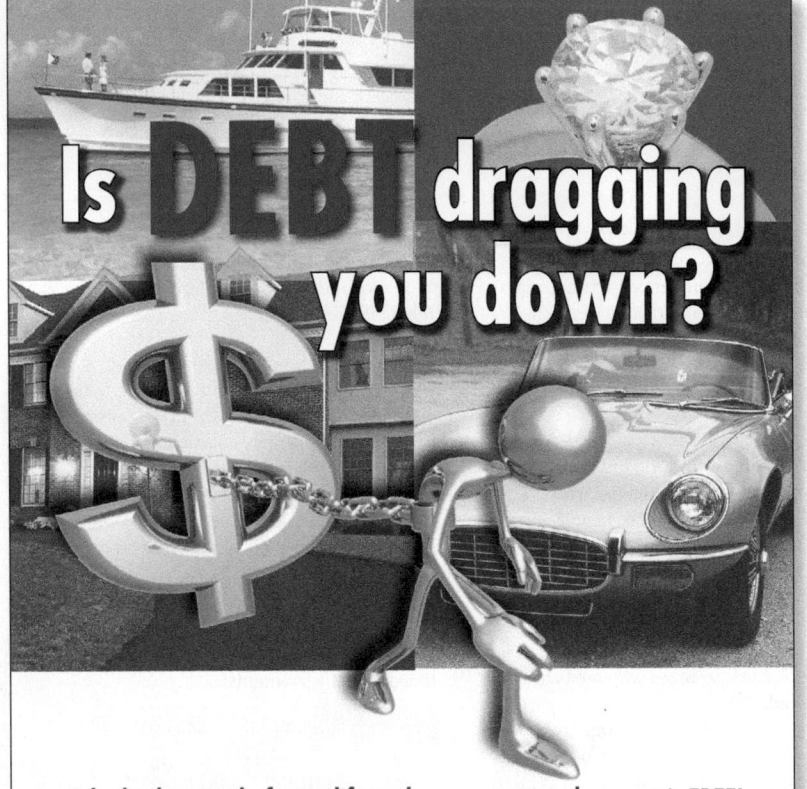

## Is DEBT dragging you down?

Take back control of your life and your money today . . . it's FREE!
### Call the Consumer Debt Hotline at
# 555-8753

1. **INFER**
In this flier, what image is used to represent debt? To what is debt being compared?

2. **ANALYZE**
What do the background images represent?

3. **CONNECT**
How does this flier affect your thoughts about extravagant purchases?

## Assessment Practice: Short Constructed Response

### LITERARY TEXT: "THE NECKLACE"

Certain assessment questions ask you about the changes that characters undergo in a literary text. To strengthen your understanding of character and plot development, apply the strategies below as you respond to the **short constructed response** question.

> How did Madame Loisel's perspective and attitude about life change over the ten years she spent repaying her debt? Support your answer with evidence from the story.

◀ **STRATEGIES IN ACTION**

1. *Clearly state the nature of Madame Loisel's change.*

2. *Supply strong evidence of Madame Loisel's perspective or attitude both before and after the change.*

3. *Remember that evidence from the text can take the form of a* **direct quotation**, *a* **paraphrase**, *or a specific* **synopsis**.

### NONFICTION TEXT: "SPENDING SPREE"

Drawing inferences from texts as you read is an important skill that you will be tested on in assessments. Practice this skill by answering the **short constructed response** question below.

> What benefits can a debt-free life offer you as you get older? Support your answer with evidence from the magazine article.

◀ **STRATEGIES IN ACTION**

1. *An* **inference** *is a conclusion you draw from the text that goes beyond what the text is saying.*

2. *Reread the article and consider what advantages might come from not having debts to pay back.*

3. *Use evidence from the text to support your ideas.*

### COMPARING LITERARY AND NONFICTION TEXTS

Assessments may ask you to identify thematic connections between literary and nonfiction texts. Practice this valuable skill by applying the following question to "The Necklace" and "Spending Spree."

> What causes both Madame Loisel and the teens mentioned in "Spending Spree" to borrow more than they can afford to repay? Support your answer with evidence from both texts.

◀ **STRATEGIES IN ACTION**

1. *First, consider examples from real life as you formulate an answer. Why do people you know borrow money?*

2. *Try to make a* **generalization** *that relates to both Madame Loisel and the teens.*

3. *Make sure that you include strong evidence from both texts to support your ideas.*

---

## Assessment Practice: Short Constructed Response

*LITERARY TEXT: "THE NECKLACE"*
**Possible answer:** *Before she goes into debt, Madame Loisel is distressed by her lack of a rich lifestyle. She is ashamed to visit her richer friend. Once she goes into debt, Mme. Loisel focuses intently and with determination on repaying the money: she "played her part . . . with sudden heroism. That frightful debt had to be paid. She would pay it." Once the debt is paid, she is proud of what she has accomplished. It is believable that she had to change as the result of the debt and the changes it brought to her life.*

*NONFICTION TEXT: "SPENDING SPREE"*
**Possible answer:** *Credit card companies charge late fees and finance charges, which increase an existing debt further. The money that is saved by not having to pay late fees and finance charges can instead go into savings and investments, which earn interest for the consumer, not the credit card company.*

*COMPARING LITERARY AND NONFICTION TEXTS* *Answers will vary, but should include the desire for a wealthier lifestyle, material goods, and popularity. Both characters are also young and careless.*

---

## DIFFERENTIATED INSTRUCTION

### FOR STRUGGLING WRITERS

**Analyze the Short Constructed Response Question** Explain to students that in order to address the short constructed response question, they must make a connection between the two selections. You may wish to discuss first how the two selections diverge; for example, the story takes place in 19th century France while the article is about contemporary American teens. Also, it is not Mme. Loisel's careless spending that gets her into trouble, but the loss of the necklace. Once you have identified the differences, discuss the similarities:

- *How is Mme. Loisel similar to an American teen of today?*
- *How is the system of borrowing the Loisels had to deal with similar to the credit system described in the article?*

Remind students that it is appropriate to acknowledge the differences even as they write about the similarities.

## Focus and Motivate

### COMMON CORE FOCUS

**RL 3** Analyze how complex characters develop over the course of a text. **RL 4** Determine the figurative meaning of words and phrases as they are used in the text. **W 9a (RL 3)** Draw evidence from literary texts; analyze how complex characters develop over the course of a text. **L 3** Apply knowledge of language to make effective choices for meaning or style. **L 4** Determine or clarify the meaning of unknown or multiple-meaning words and phrases. **L 4c** Consult reference materials to clarify a word's precise meaning or etymology. **L 6** Acquire and use accurately general academic and domain-specific words and phrases; demonstrate independence in gathering vocabulary knowledge.

### SUMMARY

In Naomi Shihab Nye's "Hamadi," high school freshman Susan is fond of her family's courtly, elderly friend Saleh Hamadi who comforts her like a grandparent during a difficult time.

### What makes someone REMARKABLE?

Ask the question. Explain that *remarkable* conveys the idea of being worth admiration. After students have completed the *PRESENT* activity, point out that this oral activity demonstrates the essence of *remarkable*.

---

## Selection Resources

---

## Hamadi

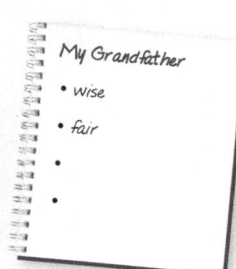

Video link at thinkcentral.com

Short Story by Naomi Shihab Nye

# What makes someone REMARKABLE?

**COMMON CORE**

**RL 3** Analyze how complex characters develop over the course of a text. **RL 4** Determine the figurative meaning of words and phrases as they are used in a text. **L 4** Determine or clarify the meaning of unknown or multiple-meaning words and phrases.

Whether it's an outrageous sense of humor or an aura of quiet confidence, some people have qualities that are hard not to notice. Susan, the main character in the short story "Hamadi," has a friend with a unique way of looking at the world. Susan finds Hamadi remarkable; she notices him because of his extraordinary personality.

*PRESENT* What makes individuals stand out to you? What traits give them striking personalities? Pick one remarkable person and list his or her traits. Then "introduce" this person to a classmate in a way that makes it clear why the individual is so extraordinary.

My Grandfather
• wise
• fair
•
•

240

---

See resources on the **Teacher One Stop DVD-ROM** *and on* **thinkcentral.com**.

 Video link at thinkcentral.com

 **RESOURCE MANAGER UNIT 2**
Plan and Teach, pp. 53–60
Summary, pp. 61–62†‡*
Text Analysis and Reading
  Skill, pp. 63–66†*
Vocabulary, pp. 67–69*
Grammar and Style, p. 72

**DIAGNOSTIC AND SELECTION TESTS**
Selection Tests, pp. 67–70

 **BEST PRACTICES TOOLKIT**
Readers Theater, p. A1
Word Questioning, p. E9
Analysis Frame: Character,
  pp. D21, D26
Venn Diagram, p. A26
Character Traits and Textual
  Evidence, p. D6

**TECHNOLOGY**
- **Teacher One Stop DVD-ROM**
- **Student One Stop DVD-ROM**
- **Audio Anthology CD**
- **GrammarNotes DVD-ROM**
- **ExamView Test Generator**
  on the **Teacher One Stop**

* Resources for Differentiation          † Also in Spanish          ‡ In Haitian Creole and Vietnamese

## TEXT ANALYSIS: THIRD-PERSON LIMITED POINT OF VIEW

"Hamadi" is told from a **third-person limited point of view.** The narrator is an outside voice that tells what only one character thinks, feels, and observes. The narrator of "Hamadi" zeroes in on the thoughts and feelings of a high school freshman named Susan. As you read "Hamadi," notice how the author develops the character of Susan—pay attention to what the narrator reveals about her, and consider how this affects your perception of her.

## READING STRATEGY: MONITOR

When you read, pause every few minutes to check, or **monitor,** how well you are understanding the story.

- **Visualize:** Picture characters, events, and settings.
- **Clarify:** Stop now and then to review what you understand.
- **Question:** Ask questions about the events and characters.
- **Predict:** Look for hints of what might happen next.
- **Connect:** Compare events with your own experiences.

As you read "Hamadi," use the "Monitor" annotations to help you gain insight into the characters.

*Review:* **Make Inferences**

## ▲ VOCABULARY IN CONTEXT

Which of the following words might be used to describe

1. an ornate piece of furniture?
2. an ancient language?
3. an empty room?
4. a subtle joke?
5. a meal after a long journey?

In your *Reader/Writer Notebook,* write a brief definition of each word in the Word List that you are not familiar with.

| WORD LIST | | | |
|---|---|---|---|
| anthem | lavish | sustenance |
| archaic | spartan | wry |
| expansive | surrogate | |

 Complete the activities in your **Reader/Writer Notebook.**

## Meet the Author

# Naomi Shihab Nye
**born 1952**

### More Than One Way to See
Naomi Shihab Nye was born in St. Louis, Missouri. Like Susan, the main character in "Hamadi," Nye grew up in an Arab-American family. In 1966 her family moved to the Middle East, and Nye spent her freshman year at a high school in East Jerusalem, then a part of Jordan. Nye says her year in the Middle East changed her irreversibly. "This is one of the best things about growing up in a mixed family or community," she says. "You never think only one way of doing or seeing anything is right."

### A Writer of Vision
Best known as a poet, Nye is also a short story writer, essayist, children's book author, novelist, and songwriter. In all of her work, Nye honors diverse viewpoints and celebrates the mixing of cultures. Literature, she believes, gives us "insight into all the secret territories of the human spirit."

### BACKGROUND TO THE STORY
**Seeking Refuge**
In this story, both the main character's father and her friend Hamadi come from a region torn by conflict. Hamadi is from Lebanon, a country devastated by a 16-year civil war. Susan's father is Palestinian. In 1947, the United Nations proposed a plan to partition what was then Palestine to create the state of Israel, a homeland for the Jewish people. More than 50 years later, the conflict between Israelis and Palestinians is still unresolved and often marked by violence. These situations have created millions of refugees—people who have fled their native lands in search of shelter and protection.

**Author Online**
THINK central
Go to thinkcentral.com.
KEYWORD: HML9-241

241

---

# Teach

**TEXT ANALYSIS**　　　　**COMMON CORE**
RL 3

● *Model the Skill:*
## THIRD-PERSON LIMITED POINT OF VIEW

To model how to identify point of view, read aloud this passage:

> Ten years went by, and Harris no longer remembered. He felt agitated when he saw Mrs. Coombs, but could not say why he felt this way. As to what Mrs. Coombs felt, one could not possibly know.

This passage shows third-person limited point of view. The narrator is not a character in the story and tells what only one character is thinking and feeling.

**GUIDED PRACTICE** Which character in the passage does the narrator zero in on?

---

**READING STRATEGY**

■ *Model the Skill:* **MONITOR**

Discuss monitoring strategies and model them using the suggestions to monitor your understanding of *Meet the Author.* Clarify that Nye lived in the Middle East, and predict that Susan will be similar in some ways to Nye.

**GUIDED PRACTICE** Have students use the *Background* text to model the skill.

**R** RESOURCE MANAGER—Copy Master Monitor p. 65

---

**VOCABULARY SKILL**　　　　**COMMON CORE**
L 4

## ▲ VOCABULARY IN CONTEXT

**DIAGNOSE WORD KNOWLEDGE** Have all students complete Vocabulary in Context. Check their answers against the following:

**anthem** (ăn′thəm) *n.* an uplifting song or hymn
**archaic** (är-kā′ĭk) *adj.* very old or unfashionable
**expansive** (ĭk-spăn′sĭv) *adj.* outgoing; showing feelings openly and freely
**lavish** (lăv′ĭsh) *adj.* extravagant; more than is needed
**spartan** (spär′tn) *adj.* simple, plain, and frugal

**surrogate** (sûr′ə-gĭt) *adj.* serving as a substitute
**sustenance** (sŭs′tə-nəns) *n.* food or provisions that sustain life
**wry** (rī) *adj.* dryly humorous, often with a bit of irony

**PRETEACH VOCABULARY** Use the following copy master to introduce students to the bold-faced words.

**R** RESOURCE MANAGER—Copy Master Vocabulary Study p. 67

1. Read the first sentence on the worksheet, emphasizing *anthem*.
2. Have students mark on the worksheet whether they have heard the word before.
3. Have students write their own sentence and a possible meaning.
4. Repeat the procedure for items 2–8.

### READ WITH A PURPOSE

*Help students set a purpose for reading. Tell them to pay attention to how the characters view Hamadi when they first meet him. Have students note whether these views change over the course of the story and why.*

**A** *Model the Skill:* **MONITOR**

Model for students how to monitor comprehension by displaying a photograph of the Sphinx. Use adjectives to describe it such as quiet, calm, wise, secretive, or mysterious. Then, read aloud lines 11–20. Note additional adjectives you might use to describe the grandmother such as steadfast or hardworking.

***Possible answer:*** *Susan's grandmother is calm, wise, slightly mysterious, steadfast, hardworking, and unhurried. She also may be religious.*

### OWN THE WORD

**wry:** Ask students if they have ever described someone or something as *wry*, perhaps a friend who had a wry sense of humor. Who was the person or what was the thing, and what qualities suggested the description as *wry*? Who do they know who could be described as *wry*?

# HAMADI
## Naomi Shihab Nye

*"It takes two of us to discover truth:
one to utter it and one to understand it."*

**KAHLIL GIBRAN,** *Sand and Foam*

Susan didn't really feel interested in Saleh Hamadi[1] until she was a freshman in high school carrying a thousand questions around. Why this way? Why not another way? Who said so and why can't I say something else? Those brittle women at school in the counselor's office treated the world as if it were a yardstick and they had a tight hold of both ends.

Sometimes Susan felt polite with them, sorting attendance cards during her free period, listening to them gab about fingernail polish and television. And other times she felt she could run out of the building yelling. That's when she daydreamed about Saleh Hamadi, who had nothing to do with any of it. Maybe she thought of him as escape, the way she used to think about the
10 Sphinx at Giza[2] when she was younger. She would picture the golden Sphinx sitting quietly in the desert with sand blowing around its face, never changing its expression. She would think of its **wry,** slightly crooked mouth and how her grandmother looked a little like that as she waited for her bread to bake in the old village north of Jerusalem.[3] Susan's family had lived in Jerusalem for three years before she was ten and drove out to see her grandmother every weekend. They would find her patting fresh dough between her hands, or pressing cakes of dough onto the black rocks in the *taboon,* the rounded old oven outdoors. Sometimes she moved her lips as she worked. Was she praying? Singing a secret
20 song? Susan had never seen her grandmother rushing. **A**

Now that she was fourteen, she took long walks in America with her father down by the drainage ditch at the end of their street. Pecan trees shaded the

---

1. **Saleh Hamadi** (sä′lĕкн hä-mä′dē).
2. **Sphinx at Giza** (gē′zə): a huge ancient statue with a man's head and a lion's body, near the city of Giza in northern Egypt.
3. **Jerusalem:** the capital of Israel and a holy city for Jews, Christians, and Muslims.

**242**   UNIT 2: CHARACTERIZATION AND POINT OF VIEW

**Analyze Visuals ▶**

Susan daydreams about Saleh Hamadi to escape from the everyday. What aspects of this painting have a dreamlike quality?

**① Targeted Passage**

**wry** (rī) *adj.* dryly humorous, often with a bit of irony

**A MONITOR**
Reread lines 8–20. As you read, **visualize** the scene Susan remembers. Describe Susan's grandmother's **traits.**

*Inspiration* (1994), Daniel Nevins. Oil, acrylic, and collage on wood, 6.6″ × 9.0″. Private collection. © Daniel Nevins/SuperStock.

---

### FOR ENGLISH LANGUAGE LEARNERS

**Options for Reading** Use Readers Theater to help students read this story. Assign a narrator to read non-highlighted text and individual students to read each character's part.

 **BEST PRACTICES TOOLKIT**
Readers Theater p. A1

### FOR STRUGGLING READERS

In combination with the *Audio Anthology* CD, use one or more Targeted Passages (pp. 242, 244, 247, 250) to ensure that students focus on key story events, concepts, and skills. Targeted Passages are also good for English learners.

**① Targeted Passage [Lines 1–10]**

This passage introduces Susan and Hamadi, the story's two main characters.

## B Model the Skill: POINT OF VIEW

Refer students to line 23 and note that Susan asks questions about her father's childhood. Explain that in this detail, you can infer that Susan is interested in her heritage.

*Possible answer:* Susan cares about her heritage; she is helpful, selfless, thoughtful, and generous.

## TIERED DISCUSSION PROMPTS

Direct students to lines 32–57. Use these prompts to help students see how details reveal Hamadi's appearance and personality:

**Connect** Think of someone you know who is unusual but admirable. How would you make those traits clear to someone who had never met that person? *Possible answer: by using precise and vivid language to describe the traits that seem the most distinctive or remarkable*

**Synthesize** How does this description of Hamadi's outlook on life make him seem remarkable? *Possible answer: Hamadi has endured loneliness and poverty while maintaining a life of dignity and thoughtfulness.*

### OWN THE WORD

- **spartan:** Tell students that the adjective *spartan* comes from the ancient Greek city-state of Sparta, which was known for rigor, discipline, and severe lifestyles. Have students explain why the room where Hamadi lives is described as *spartan*. *Possible answer: simple furnishing, basic necessities*

- **expansive:** Tell students that *expansive* comes from the Latin *expandere,* "to spread out." Have them name other things that could be described as *expansive*. *Possible answers: land holdings, a large house*

---

path. She tried to get him to tell stories about his childhood in Palestine.[4] She didn't want him to forget anything. She helped her American mother complete tedious kitchen tasks without complaining—rolling grape leaves around their lemony rice stuffing, scrubbing carrots for the roaring juicer. Some evenings when the soft Texas twilight pulled them all outside, she thought of her faraway grandmother and said, "Let's go see Saleh Hamadi. Wouldn't he like some of that cheese pie Mom made?" And they would wrap a slice of pie and
30 drive downtown. Somehow he felt like a good substitute for a grandmother, even though he was a man. **B**

Usually Hamadi was wearing a white shirt, shiny black tie, and a jacket that reminded Susan of the earth's surface just above the treeline on a mountain—thin, somehow purified. He would raise his hands high before giving advice. "It is good to drink a tall glass of water every morning upon arising!" If anyone doubted this, he would shake his head. "Oh Susan, Susan, Susan," he would say.

He did not like to sit down, but he wanted everyone else to sit down. He made Susan sit on the wobbly chair beside the desk and he made her father or
40 mother sit in the saggy center of the bed. He told them people should eat six small meals a day.

They visited him on the sixth floor of the Traveler's Hotel, where he had lived so long nobody could remember him ever traveling. Susan's father used to remind him of the apartments available over the Victory Cleaners, next to the park with the fizzy pink fountain, but Hamadi would shake his head, pinching kisses at his **spartan** room. "A white handkerchief spread across a tabletop, my two extra shoes lined by the wall, this spells 'home' to me, this says 'mi casa.' What more do I need?"

Hamadi liked to use Spanish words. They made him feel **expansive,** worldly.
50 He'd learned them when he worked at the fruits and vegetables warehouse on Zarzamora[5] Street, marking off crates of apples and avocados on a long white pad. Occasionally he would speak Arabic, his own first language, with Susan's father and uncles, but he said it made him feel too sad, as if his mother might step into the room at any minute, her arms laden with fresh mint leaves.

He had come to the United States on a boat when he was eighteen years old and he had never been married. "I married books," he said. "I married the wide horizon."

"What is he to us?" Susan used to ask her father. "He's not a relative, right? How did we meet him to begin with?"
60 Susan's father couldn't remember. "I think we just drifted together. Maybe we met at your uncle Hani's house. Maybe that old Maronite priest[6] who used to cry after every service introduced us. The priest once shared an apartment

**B POINT OF VIEW**
Reread lines 21–31. What important **character traits** of Susan's does the narrator reveal in this paragraph?

**② Targeted Passage**

**spartan** (spär'tn) *adj.* simple, plain, and frugal

**expansive** (ĭk-spăn'sĭv) *adj.* outgoing; showing feelings openly and freely

---

4. **Palestine:** a historical region at the east end of the Mediterranean Sea.

5. **Zarzamora** (zär'zə-môr'ə).

6. **Maronite priest:** The Maronites are a Christian group allied with the Roman Catholic Church. They live primarily in Lebanon, the country to the north of Israel.

---

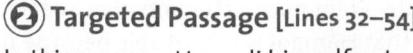

## DIFFERENTIATED INSTRUCTION

### FOR STRUGGLING READERS

**② Targeted Passage [Lines 32–54]**

In this passage, Hamadi himself enters the story, and many details about his life and personality are revealed.

- What clothing does Hamadi usually wear? (line 32)

- How do his words and actions show that he cares about people? (lines 35–41)

- How does Hamadi furnish his room? (lines 46–48)

- Why does Hamadi feel sad when he speaks Arabic? (line 53–54)

### FOR ENGLISH LANGUAGE LEARNERS

**Vocabulary Support** Use Word Questioning to teach these words: *substitute* (line 30), *distinctions* (line 79), *responded* (line 152), *significant* (line 237), *preliminary* (line 237), *immigrants* (line 244).

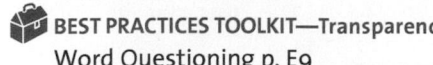 **BEST PRACTICES TOOLKIT—Transparency** Word Questioning p. E9

with Kahlil Gibran[7] in New York—so he said. And Saleh always says he stayed with Gibran when he first got off the boat. I'll bet that popular guy Gibran has had a lot of roommates he doesn't even know about."

Susan said, "Dad, he's dead."

"I know, I know," her father said.

Later Susan said, "Mr. Hamadi, did you really meet Kahlil Gibran? He's one of my favorite writers." Hamadi walked slowly to the window of his room and
70 stared out. There wasn't much to look at down on the street—a bedraggled flower shop, a boarded-up tavern with a hand-lettered sign tacked to the front, GONE TO FIND JESUS. Susan's father said the owners had really gone to Alabama.

Hamadi spoke patiently. "Yes, I met brother Gibran. And I meet him in my heart every day. When I was a young man—shocked by all the visions of the new world—the tall buildings—the wild traffic—the young people without shame—the proud mailboxes in their blue uniforms—I met him. And he has stayed with me every day of my life."

"But did you really meet him, like in person, or just in a book?"

He turned dramatically. "Make no such distinctions, my friend. Or your life
80 will be a pod with only dried-up beans inside. Believe anything can happen."

Susan's father looked irritated, but Susan smiled. "I do," she said. "I believe that. I want fat beans. If I imagine something, it's true, too. Just a different kind of true." **C**

Susan's father was twiddling with the knobs on the old-fashioned sink. "Don't they even give you hot water here? You don't mean to tell me you've been living without hot water?"

On Hamadi's rickety desk lay a row of different "Love" stamps issued by the post office.

"You must write a lot of letters," Susan said.

90 "No, no, I'm just focusing on that word," Hamadi said. "I particularly like the globe in the shape of a heart," he added.

"Why don't you take a trip back to your village in Lebanon?" Susan's father asked. "Maybe you still have relatives living there."

Hamadi looked pained. "'Remembrance is a form of meeting,' my brother Gibran says, and I do believe I meet with my cousins every day."

"But aren't you curious? You've been gone so long! Wouldn't you like to find out what has happened to everybody and everything you knew as a boy?" Susan's father traveled back to Jerusalem once each year to see his family.

"I would not. In fact, I already know. It is there and it is not there. Would
100 you like to share an orange with me?" **D**

His long fingers, tenderly peeling. Once when Susan was younger, he'd given her a **lavish** ribbon off a holiday fruit basket and expected her to wear it on her head. In the car, Susan's father said, "Riddles. He talks in riddles. I don't know why I have patience with him." Susan stared at the people talking and laughing in the next car. She did not even exist in their world.

---

7. **Kahlil Gibran** (kə-lēl′ jə-brän′): a Lebanese-American philosopher and mystic poet whose best known work is *The Prophet*.

HAMADI **245**

**C MONITOR**
Reread lines 68–83. As you read, **question** whether Hamadi actually met Gibran in person. What does Hamadi's own answer to this question reveal about his character?

**D POINT OF VIEW**
Reread lines 87–100. Although the **narrator** does not directly convey Hamadi's thoughts, the narrator does give the reader clues about how Hamadi thinks and feels. What are these clues, and what do they tell you about Hamadi?

**lavish** (lăv′ĭsh) *adj.* extravagant; more than is needed

## Analyze Visuals

*Possible answer:* *The mood in* Healing *is more peaceful than the mood in the painting on page 243. The female figure here appears relaxed, as indicated by her gentle smile, calm eyes, curving limbs, gentle gestures, wavy lines, and heart cradled within her chest. The male figure in* Inspiration *seems tense by comparison, with his unsmiling mouth, sad or wistful eyes, angular arms, and heart above his head.* Healing *has a soothing blue background with a smooth texture;* Inspiration *has a dreary greenish-blue background and a rough texture.*

*Healing* (1996), Daniel Nevins. Oil on wood, 7.4″ × 9.0″. © Daniel Nevins/SuperStock.

### ◀ Analyze Visuals

**Compare** the mood of this painting with the mood of the painting on page 243. Consider the colors, lines, and textures in each painting, as well as each figure's facial expression and gestures.

───

S usan carried *The Prophet* around on top of her English textbook and her Texas history. She and her friend Tracy read it out loud to one another at lunch. Tracy was a junior—they'd met at the literary magazine meeting where Susan, the only freshman on the staff, got assigned to do
110 proofreading. They never ate in the cafeteria; they sat outside at picnic tables with sack lunches, whole wheat crackers and fresh peaches. Both of them had given up meat.

### COMMON CORE L 4

### Language Coach

**Multiple Meanings** The phrase *given up* has more than one meaning. In line 112, it means "stopped (eating something, for example)." What does it mean in this sentence? *By the fourth quarter, the football team was so far behind they'd already given up.*

───

## DIFFERENTIATED INSTRUCTION

### FOR ENGLISH LANGUAGE LEARNERS

**Language Coach**  COMMON CORE L 4

**Multiple Meanings** *Answer:* *admit failure and stop trying*

Ask students to define the meaning of the phrase *given up* in the following sentences: *After fighting unsuccessfully for many days, the army had given up.* (surrendered) *Feeling sadness over the lost puppy, the child had given up.* (lost hope or faith)

### FOR ADVANCED LEARNERS/PRE–AP

**In-depth Textual Analysis** Have students use the Character Analysis Frame to explore this story and, in particular, the characters of Hamadi and Susan. Students may refer to the Analysis Frame as they discuss "Hamadi" in class or write about it after reading.

 **BEST PRACTICES TOOLKIT—Transparency**
Analysis Frame: Character pp. D21, D26

Tracy's eyes looked steamy. "You know that place where Gibran says, 'Hate is a dead thing. Who of you would be a tomb?'"

Susan nodded. Tracy continued. "Well, I hate someone. I'm trying not to, but I can't help it. I hate Debbie for liking Eddie and it's driving me nuts."

"Why shouldn't Debbie like Eddie?" Susan said. "*You* do."

Tracy put her head down on her arms. A gang of cheerleaders walked by giggling. One of them flicked her finger in greeting.

120 "In fact, we *all* like Eddie," Susan said. "Remember, here in this book—wait and I'll find it—where Gibran says that loving teaches us the secrets of our hearts and that's the way we connect to all of Life's heart? You're not talking about liking or loving, you're talking about owning."

Tracy looked glum. "Sometimes you remind me of a minister." **E**

Susan said, "Well, just talk to me someday when *I'm* depressed."

Susan didn't want a boyfriend. Everyone who had boyfriends or girlfriends seemed to have troubles. Susan told people she had a boyfriend far away, on a farm in Missouri, but the truth was, boys still seemed like cousins to her. Or brothers. Or even girls.

130 A squirrel sat in the crook of a tree, eyeing their sandwiches. When the end-of-lunch bell blared, Susan and Tracy jumped—it always seemed too soon. Squirrels were lucky; they didn't have to go to school.

Susan's father said her idea was ridiculous: to invite Saleh Hamadi to go Christmas caroling with the English Club. "His English is **archaic**, for one thing, and he won't know *any* of the songs."

"How could you live in America for years and not know 'Joy to the World' or 'Away in a Manger'?"

"Listen, I grew up right down the road from 'Oh Little Town of Bethlehem' and I still don't know a single verse."

140 "I want him. We need him. It's boring being with the same bunch of people all the time." **F**

So they called Saleh and he said he would come—"thrilled" was the word he used. He wanted to ride the bus to their house, he didn't want anyone to pick him up. Her father muttered, "He'll probably forget to get off." Saleh thought "caroling" meant they were going out with a woman named Carol. He said, "Holiday spirit—I was just reading about it in the newspaper."

Susan said, "Dress warm."

Saleh replied, "Friend, my heart is warmed simply to hear your voice."

All that evening Susan felt light and bouncy. She decorated the coffee can

150 they would use to collect donations to be sent to the children's hospital in Bethlehem. She had started doing this last year in middle school, when a singing group collected $100 and the hospital responded on exotic onion-skin stationery[8] that they were "eternally grateful."

---

8. **onion-skin stationery:** a thin, strong typing paper.

**E MAKE INFERENCES**
Consider what you know about Susan so far. Why does Tracy compare her to a minister? Explain your answer.

**3 Targeted Passage**

**archaic** (är-kā′ĭk) *adj.*
very old or unfashionable

**F POINT OF VIEW**
Why does Susan find Hamadi so interesting? Decide whether you would be able to answer this question if Susan were not the point-of-view character.

**E MAKE INFERENCES**

*Possible answer:* *Like a minister, Susan offers spiritual counsel. Tracy also may feel that Susan is telling her something that she knows is true but does not want to hear. People often say that they have been "preached at" in such situations.*

**TEXT ANALYSIS**
**F POINT OF VIEW**

*Possible answer:* *Hamadi is different from the people Susan knows. Readers could not answer the question if another character were the point of view character because readers would not know Susan's thoughts and feelings.*

**IF STUDENTS NEED HELP . . .** Use a Venn diagram to help them compare Hamadi to Susan's friends.

🧰 BEST PRACTICES TOOLKIT—Transparency Venn Diagram p. A26

**VOCABULARY**

**OWN THE WORD**

**archaic:** Have students name *archaic* consumer goods and their modern counterparts. For example, ice boxes have been replaced by refrigerators; record and cassette players have been replaced with iPods and MP3 players; and slide rules have been replaced by computer programs that perform the same function.

---

**FOR ENGLISH LANGUAGE LEARNERS**

**Culture: Clarify** Explain the tradition of Christmas caroling (line 134). Have groups of students list ten Christmas carols and then see which of the carols named in the story appear on their list: "Joy to the World" (lines 136–137); "Away in a Manger" (line 137); "Oh Little Town of Bethlehem" (line 138); "We Wish You a Merry Christmas" (lines 191–192); "What Child Is This?" (lines 225–226); "The Friendly Beasts" (line 226).

**FOR STRUGGLING READERS**

**3 Targeted Passage [Lines 116–143]**

This passage introduces a conflict: Tracy's competition with Debbie for Eddie's attention. It also develops the contrast between Hamadi and Susan's family and friends.

- What does Tracy say about Debbie? Why? (line 116)
- What idea does Susan's father ridicule? (lines 133–134)
- How do Susan and Hamadi both feel about going Christmas caroling? (line 142)

**G MONITOR**

*Possible answer: Hamadi offers Susan intellectual and emotional support, as a grandmother would. Like Susan's grandmother, Hamadi is an enigmatic, interesting person, who makes Susan pause, think, and ask questions.*

## TIERED DISCUSSION PROMPTS

Refer students to lines 173–179. Use these prompts to help students understand the relationship between Susan's ideas about holidays and her character:

**Connect** Do you ever have the feeling about holidays described in lines 175–176? Explain. *Various attitudes are acceptable. Responses may address the idea of not feeling "ready" for holidays, for example.*

**Synthesize** What generalization can you make about Susan's character, based on her attitude toward holidays? *Possible answer: She looks at life in a unique, even remarkable, way.*

## OWN THE WORD

- **surrogate:** Ask students if they have ever had friends who served as *surrogate* grandparents, aunts, or uncles. Then have students explain what these people did in the role of *surrogate* relatives.

- **sustenance:** Have students reread the sentence preceding the sentence with *sustenance* and have them identify the context clue that can help them determine the meaning of *sustenance*. **Possible answer: *sack of dates***

---

Her father shook his head. "You get something into your mind and it really takes over," he said. "Why do you like Hamadi so much all of a sudden? You could show half as much interest in your own uncles."

Susan laughed. Her uncles were dull. Her uncles shopped at the mall and watched TV. "Anyone who watches TV more than twelve minutes a week is uninteresting," she said.

160    Her father lifted an eyebrow.

"He's my **surrogate** grandmother," she said. "He says interesting things. **G** He makes me think. Remember when I was little and he called me The Thinker? We have a connection." She added, "Listen, do you want to go too? It's not a big deal. And Mom has a *great* voice. Why don't you both come?"

A minute later her mother was digging in the closet for neck scarves, and her father was digging in the drawer for flashlight batteries.

Saleh Hamadi arrived precisely on time, with flushed red cheeks and a sack of dates stuffed in his pocket. "We may need **sustenance** on our journey." Susan thought the older people seemed quite giddy as they drove down to the

170    high school to meet the rest of the carolers. Strands of winking lights wrapped around their neighbors' drainpipes and trees. A giant Santa tipped his hat on Dr. Garcia's roof.

Her friends stood gathered in front of the school. Some were smoothing out song sheets that had been crammed in a drawer or cabinet for a whole year. Susan thought holidays were strange; they came, and you were supposed to feel ready for them. What if you could make up your own holidays as you went along? She had read about a woman who used to have parties to celebrate the arrival of fresh asparagus in the local market. Susan's friends might make holidays called Eddie Looked at Me Today and Smiled.

180    Two people were alleluia-ing in harmony. Saleh Hamadi went around the group formally introducing himself to each person and shaking hands. A few people laughed silently when his back was turned. He had stepped out of a painting, or a newscast, with his outdated long overcoat, his clunky old man's shoes and elegant manners.

Susan spoke more loudly than usual. "I'm honored to introduce you to one of my best friends, Mr. Hamadi."

"Good evening to you," he pronounced musically, bowing a bit from the waist.

What could you say back but "Good evening, sir." His old-fashioned

190    manners were contagious.

They sang at three houses that never opened their doors. They sang "We Wish You a Merry Christmas" each time they moved on. Lisa had a fine, clear soprano. Tracy could find the alto harmony to any line. Cameron and Elliot had more enthusiasm than accuracy. Lily, Rita, and Jeannette laughed every time they said a wrong word and fumbled to find their places again. Susan

**surrogate** (sûr'ə-gĭt) *adj.* serving as a substitute

**G MONITOR**
After you read line 161, stop to **clarify**. Why does Susan call Hamadi her "surrogate grandmother"?

**sustenance** (sŭs'tə-nəns) *n.* food or provisions that sustain life

**Language Coach**

**Etymology** Reread line 180. The **etymology**, or history, of *alleluia* shows that it is a Middle English word expressing joy, praise, or thanks. It's from an even older Hebrew word still used today. In a dictionary, find the Hebrew word for *alleluia*.

## DIFFERENTIATED INSTRUCTION

**FOR ENGLISH LANGUAGE LEARNERS**

**Language Coach**          COMMON CORE
                                 L 4c

**Etymology**

*Answer: hallelujah* Have students consult dictionaries to learn the origin of *soprano* (line 193). (*Italian* < sopra, < *above Latin* supra) Then, ask students how this origin relates to the meaning of the word. *Soprano singers have high voices. They sing in the range of middle C to two or more octaves above.*

**FOR ADVANCED LEARNERS/PRE–AP**

**Synthesize** [small-group option] Challenge students to prepare a statement about how the Christmastime setting serves to reinforce ideas in this story. Then ask students to imagine that "Hamadi" was set during another religious or patriotic holiday. Have students discuss the new setting and prepare a statement about how the story might change.

loved to see how her mother knew every word of every verse without looking at the paper, and how her father kept his hands in his pockets and seemed more interested in examining people's mailboxes or yard displays than in trying to sing. And Saleh Hamadi—what language was he singing in? He didn't even
200 seem to be pronouncing words, but humming deeply from his throat. Was he saying, "Om"?[9] Speaking Arabic? Once he caught her looking and whispered, "That was an Aramaic[10] word that just drifted into my mouth—the true language of the Bible, you know, the language Jesus Christ himself spoke."

By the fourth block their voices felt tuned up and friendly people came outside to listen. Trays of cookies were passed around and dollar bills stuffed into the little can. Thank you, thank you. Out of the dark from down the block, Susan noticed Eddie sprinting toward them with his coat flapping, unbuttoned. She shot a glance at Tracy, who pretended not to notice. "Hey guys!" shouted Eddie. "The first time in my life I'm late and everyone else is
210 on time! You could at least have left a note about which way you were going." Someone slapped him on the back. Saleh Hamadi, whom he had never seen before, was the only one who managed a reply. "Welcome, welcome to our cheery group!"

Eddie looked mystified. "Who is this guy?"

Susan whispered, "My friend." **H**

Eddie approached Tracy, who read her song sheet intently just then, and stuck his face over her shoulder to whisper, "Hi." Tracy stared straight ahead into the air and whispered "Hi" vaguely, glumly. Susan shook her head. Couldn't Tracy act more cheerful at least?

220 They were walking again. They passed a string of blinking reindeer and a wooden snowman holding a painted candle.

Eddie fell into step beside Tracy, murmuring so Susan couldn't hear him anymore. Saleh Hamadi was flinging his arms up high as he strode. Was he power walking?[11] Did he even know what power walking was? Between houses, Susan's mother hummed obscure songs people hardly remembered: "What Child Is This?" and "The Friendly Beasts."

Lisa moved over to Eddie's other side. "I'm *so excited* about you and Debbie!" she said loudly. "Why didn't she come tonight?"

Eddie said, "She has a sore throat."

230 Tracy shrank up inside her coat. **I**

Lisa chattered on. "James said we should make our reservations *now* for dinner at the Tower after the Sweetheart Dance, can you believe it? In December, making a reservation for February? But otherwise it might get booked up!"

**H** MAKE INFERENCES
**Compare** how Susan answers Eddie's question in line 215 with how she introduces Hamadi in lines 185–186. Why does her attitude change?

**I** MONITOR
Think about how Tracy is feeling and why she acts the way she does. Can you **connect** her behavior to anything you've experienced?

---

9. **om:** a sacred syllable in certain Eastern religions, repeated to aid one's concentration while meditating.
10. **Aramaic** (ăr′ə-mā′ĭk).
11. **power walking:** fast walking with rhythmic swinging of the arms, done as a form of exercise.

HAMADI    **249**

## J FIGURATIVE LANGUAGE

**Possible answer:** *Personification can be used to add meaning to an abstract idea, making this abstraction (animal or object) appear more vivid to the reader. In this sense, any meaning the writer wants to convey in an imaginative or powerful way can be expressed using personification.*

Read this sentence for students: The sky is dark and looks sad. Explain that the sky is being described using personification. (*it looks sad*) Have students work in pairs to list two examples of personification from other books, movies, or other mediums.

## K GRAMMAR AND STYLE

COMMON CORE L 3

**Add Emphasis** After students have read this passage, point out that they already have seen several examples of repetition in this story. To illustrate, ask them to reread lines 115–123. Discuss how the repetition of "I hate" (lines 115–116) and "you're [not] talking about" (lines 122–123) adds emphasis to the characters' comments.

## VOCABULARY

COMMON CORE L 4

### OWN THE WORD

**anthem:** Tell students that *anthems* are often songs of loyalty. Have them identify the name and verses of the national *anthem* of the United States, and ask if they can identify names and verses of other national *anthems*. **Possible answer:** *United States: "Star-Spangled Banner"; Britain: "God Save the King/Queen"; Mexico: "al grito de guerra"; France: "La Marseillaise"*

## SELECTION WRAP–UP

**READ WITH A PURPOSE** The story ends with a few carolers seeing Hamadi in a new way. Ask students how Susan connects with Hamadi. **Possible answer:** *They have a common heritage and shared life philosophy.*

---

Saleh Hamadi tuned into this conversation with interest; the Tower was downtown, in his neighborhood. He said, "This sounds like significant preliminary planning! Maybe you can be an international advisor someday." Susan's mother bellowed, "Joy to the World!" and voices followed her, stretching for notes. Susan's father was gazing off into the sky. Maybe he 240 thought about all the refugees in camps in Palestine far from doorbells and shutters. Maybe he thought about the horizon beyond Jerusalem when he was a boy, how it seemed to be inviting him, "Come over, come over." **J** Well, he'd come all the way to the other side of the world, and now he was doomed to live in two places at once. To Susan, immigrants seemed bigger than other people, and always slightly melancholy. They also seemed doubly interesting. Maybe someday Susan would meet one her own age. **K**

Two thin streams of tears rolled down Tracy's face. Eddie had drifted to the other side of the group and was clowning with Cameron, doing a tap dance shuffle. "While fields and floods, rocks, hills and plains, repeat the sounding 250 joy, repeat the sounding joy . . ." Susan and Saleh Hamadi noticed her. Hamadi peered into Tracy's face, inquiring, "Why? Is it pain? Is it gratitude? We are such mysterious creatures, human beings!"

Tracy turned to him, pressing her face against the old wool of his coat, and wailed. The song ended. All eyes were on Tracy and this tall, courteous stranger who would never in a thousand years have felt comfortable stroking her hair. But he let her stand there, crying, as Susan stepped up firmly on the other side of Tracy, putting her arms around her friend. And Hamadi said something Susan would remember years later, whenever she was sad herself, even after college, a creaky **anthem** sneaking back into her ear, "We go on. On and on. 260 We don't stop where it hurts. We turn a corner. It is the reason why we are living. To turn a corner. Come, let's move."

Above them, in the heavens, stars lived out their lonely lives. People whispered, "What happened? What's wrong?" Half of them were already walking down the street. ❧

## J FIGURATIVE LANGUAGE

In line 242, the horizon beyond Jerusalem seems to invite Susan's father to "come over." By attributing a personal quality to the horizon, the author is employing **personification,** a type of **figurative language.** By using this instance of personification, Nye is expressing the particular historical and cultural situation of Susan's father, an immigrant from Palestine who grieves for his homeland. What else can be expressed using personification?

## K GRAMMAR AND STYLE

Reread lines 235–246. Nye repeats the phrase "Maybe he thought about" to add emphasis to her writing.

**anthem** (ăn'thəm) *n.* an uplifting song or hymn

④ **Targeted Passage**

Detail of *Inspiration* (1994), Daniel Nevins.     Detail of *Healing* (1996), Daniel Nevins.

---

## DIFFERENTIATED INSTRUCTION

**FOR STRUGGLING READERS**

④ **Targeted Passage** [Lines 247–264]

This concluding passage shows Hamadi and Susan at their most noble moment: joining forces to comfort Susan's friend Tracy.

- Why does Tracy start crying? (lines 247–248)
- To whom does Tracy turn for comfort? (line 253)
- What does Susan then do? (line 256)
- What does Hamadi say? (lines 259–261)

**FOR STRUGGLING READERS**

**Develop Reading Fluency** Read the paragraph beginning with line 235 aloud for students. Use intonation to add emphasis and emotion when the narrator employs the repeated phrasing "Maybe he thought about". Then, read the paragraph aloud a second time, having students echo your reading of each sentence. Lead students to discuss the power of the voice to convey emotion.

## Comprehension

1. **Recall** Why does Susan begin to feel interested in Hamadi?

2. **Recall** What does Susan invite Hamadi to do?

3. **Clarify** What happens to Tracy at the end of the story?

## Text Analysis

**COMMON CORE**

RL 3 Analyze how complex characters develop over the course of a text.

● 4. **Evaluate Monitoring Strategies** Review the monitoring strategies listed on page 241. Which strategy did you find most helpful as you read the story? Cite examples.

● 5. **Analyze Point of View** Think about how "Hamadi" might be different if it were told from a **first-person point of view,** with Hamadi himself as the narrator. How might your perception of Hamadi change?

6. **Draw Conclusions** Reread lines 257–261. Why do you think Hamadi's words have such a profound effect on Susan? Citing evidence from the text, explain why you think she finds Hamadi's words so meaningful.

7. **Analyze Characters** A **round character** is one who is complex and highly developed, displaying a variety of different traits in his or her personality. A **flat character** is not highly developed. He or she usually has one outstanding trait or role and exists mainly to advance the plot of a story. Identify one round character and one flat character in the story. Then explain how each fits the criteria above.

8. **Compare Literary Works** Compare Susan with Jill, the narrator of "Pancakes" on pages 210–218. Use a Venn diagram like the one shown to record Susan's and Jill's **traits.** Which character has the more remarkable personality?

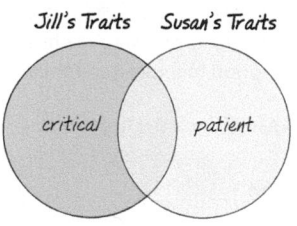

*Jill's Traits    Susan's Traits*

critical    patient

## Text Criticism

9. **Critical Interpretations** In reviewing *Habibi*, Nye's first novel, the critic Karen Leggett observed, "Adolescence magnifies the joys and anxieties of growing up even as it radically simplifies the complexities of the adult world.... Nye is meticulously sensitive to this rainbow of emotion...." Paraphrase this quotation. Then explain whether you think Leggett's comment applies to "Hamadi."

### What makes someone REMARKABLE?

What qualities must a person have in order to be considered remarkable?

---

8. *Susan: interested in life and people, compassionate, unusual point of view, self-confident;* **Jill:** *judgmental, sarcastic, self-absorbed, perfectionist, insecure;* **Both:** *responsible, straightforward. Opinions will vary as to who is more remarkable, but students may have more positive feelings toward Susan.*

## Text Criticism

**Possible answer:**

9. *Teenagers experience love and worry very intensely. They extend this black-and-white view to the adult world, oversimplifying the challenges they will face. The comment applies to Tracy.*

**What makes someone REMARKABLE?** Students might consider qualities that differentiate someone from others or that cause some to defy stereotypes or expectations.

---

# Practice and Apply

For preliminary support of post-reading questions, use these copy masters:

**R** **RESOURCE MANAGER—Copy Masters**
Reading Check p. 70
Third-Person Limited Point of View p. 63
Question Support p. 71

Additional selection questions are provided for teachers on page 57.

### ANSWERS

## Comprehension

1. *Hamadi is so different from the other people she knows that she sees him as an escape from her everyday life.*

2. *She invites him to go Christmas caroling with her friends from the English Club.*

3. *Tracy cries because Eddie does not return her affections. She turns to Hamadi for comfort, and he and Susan comfort her.*

## Text Analysis

**COMMON CORE RL 3**

**Possible answers:**

4. **Evaluate Monitoring Strategies** *Choices and examples will vary, but these strategies might be included.*
   **Visualize** *Imagining Hamadi's appearance or the Christmas caroling scene makes the story easier for students to understand.*

   **Question** *Students might respond to Susan's own questions in the story.*

   **Connect** *Students might grasp the story's situation better by remembering an unusual family friend or relative.*

5. ● **COMMON CORE FOCUS** **Analyze Point of View** *It might change quite a bit. Hamadi probably would not realize that other people think of him as odd. He also might not seem as remarkable because his actions and appearance would not be filtered through Susan's perception of him.*

6. *Hamadi's endurance, love, and optimism help answer Susan's questions about life (lines 1–20, 78–83).*

7. *Susan is a round character because she comes to a realization about life. Tracy is a flat character because she serves only to show the travails of unrequited teenage love.*

## ANSWERS

## Vocabulary in Context

▲ VOCABULARY PRACTICE

1. *true*
2. *false*
3. *false*
4. *true*
5. *true*
6. *true*
7. *true*
8. *false*

 **RESOURCE MANAGER—Copy Master**
Vocabulary Practice p. 68

### ACADEMIC VOCABULARY IN WRITING

*Possible answer:* I was very surprised, but pleased, when my young friend Susan called. She invited me to go caroling with her and her friends. I had never been caroling before, but I thought it would be interesting to **interact** with Susan and her friends.

### VOCABULARY STRATEGY: WORDS FROM GREEK CULTURE

 COMMON CORE L 6

To help students understand how these words are used, construct and discuss a chart like this:

| Word | Part of Speech | Meaning |
|------|----------------|---------|
| Hercules Herculean | noun adjective | Greek hero very difficult |
| Colossus of Rhodes colossal | noun adjective | statue enormous |
| Narcissus narcissistic | noun adjective | Greek figure self-absorbed |
| Titans titanic | noun adjective | Greek gods huge |

**Possible answers:**

1. *the Empire State Building; a cruise ship*
2. *himself or herself*
3. *earning a medical degree; building a house by oneself*
4. *that the ship was huge*

 **RESOURCE MANAGER—Copy Master**
Vocabulary Strategy p. 69

### Interactive Vocabulary

 THINK central

Keywords direct students to a **WordSharp** tutorial on **thinkcentral.com** or to other types of vocabulary practice and review.

---

## Vocabulary in Context

▲ VOCABULARY PRACTICE

Indicate whether each statement is true or false.

1. It can be hard to tell when someone with a **wry** sense of humor is kidding.
2. **Spartan** hotel rooms are very elaborately furnished.
3. Someone with an **expansive** personality is usually rather shy.
4. Six courses and two desserts would constitute a **lavish** meal.
5. A poem filled with **archaic** words might be hard to understand.
6. Your **surrogate** grandmother would not necessarily be related to you.
7. Seeds and berries provide **sustenance** for many birds.
8. An **anthem** is a song written for an old person's funeral.

**WORD LIST**

anthem
archaic
expansive
lavish
spartan
surrogate
sustenance
wry

### ACADEMIC VOCABULARY IN WRITING

• complex   • device   • evaluate   • interact   • perspective

What might Hamadi have thought about the events on the night he, Susan, and the English Club went caroling? Write a brief description of those events from his **perspective**. Include his thoughts about being invited and the actions of the other people. Use at least one Academic Vocabulary word in your response.

### VOCABULARY STRATEGY: WORDS FROM GREEK CULTURE

You may remember the original meaning of the vocabulary word *spartan* from a history class: someone from the Greek city-state of Sparta. *Spartans* were known for their rejection of luxury and comfort. Knowing the histories of other words related to ancient Greece can help you to understand their meanings.

**COMMON CORE**

L 6 Acquire and use accurately general academic and domain-specific words and phrases; demonstrate independence in gathering vocabulary knowledge.

*PRACTICE* Read the chart and then answer the questions.

| Character/Item | Description |
|----------------|-------------|
| Hercules | a mythological hero whose strength helped him perform almost impossible tasks |
| Colossus of Rhodes | an enormous statue of the Greek sun god |
| Narcissus | a mythological youth who fell in love with his own reflection |
| Titans | a race of mighty gods who preceded Zeus and his family |

1. What is a modern-day example of something **colossal**?
2. What would a **narcissistic** person most likely talk about?
3. What might be an example of a **herculean** task?
4. By calling their ship *Titanic*, what were the ship owners suggesting?

 Interactive Vocabulary

Go to **thinkcentral.com**.
KEYWORD: HML9-252

---

## DIFFERENTIATED INSTRUCTION

### FOR ENGLISH LANGUAGE LEARNERS

**Writing: Task Support** Encourage students to use the Character Traits and Textual Evidence chart to plan their sentences for the Vocabulary in Writing activity.

📦 BEST PRACTICES TOOLKIT—Transparency Character Traits and Textual Evidence p. D6

### FOR ADVANCED LEARNERS/PRE–AP

**Analyze Antonyms** Have students identify antonyms (opposites) for as many of the vocabulary words as possible. Allow them to check their responses in a dictionary or thesaurus. Then have students write three sentences, showing in each one a word and its opposite in a way that makes the difference clear. Offer this example: *Uncle David has an <u>expansive</u> personality, but Aunt Maria is rather <u>unsociable</u>.*

# Language

◆ **GRAMMAR AND STYLE: Add Emphasis**

Review the **Grammar and Style** note on page 250. Throughout the story, Nye uses **repetition** to impress upon the reader the thoughts and actions of her characters. Use repetition in your own writing when you want to add emphasis.

Here are some examples from the story. Note that Nye repeats the same pronouns, nouns, and verbs:

> *Her uncles were dull. Her uncles shopped at the mall and watched TV.* (lines 157–158)

> *A minute later her mother was digging in the closet for neck scarves, and her father was digging in the drawer for flashlight batteries.* (lines 165–166)

Notice how the revision in blue adds emphasis to this first draft. Use similar techniques to revise your response to the prompt below.

> **STUDENT MODEL**
> —*remarkable because*
> Susan is a remarkable person. She is observant and kind and curious about life.

## READING-WRITING CONNECTION

 Increase your understanding of "Hamadi" by responding to this prompt. Then use the **revising tip** to improve your writing.

| **WRITING PROMPT** | **REVISING TIP** |
|---|---|
| **Extended Constructed Response: Character Analysis**<br>Analyze how Nye develops the character of Susan. In **three to five paragraphs**, identify the traits Susan exhibits, as well as the methods of characterization Nye uses to show the reader these traits. | Review your response. Did you effectively emphasize Susan's character traits? If not, consider using repetition to help add emphasis to your analysis. |

**Interactive Revision** THINK central
Go to thinkcentral.com.
KEYWORD: HML9-253

---

**COMMON CORE**

**L 3** Apply knowledge of language to make effective choices for meaning or style.
**W 9a (RL 3)** Draw evidence from literary texts; analyze how complex characters develop over the course of a text.

---

# Language

COMMON CORE **W 9a** (RL 3), L 3

◆ **GRAMMAR AND STYLE**

- Have students locate the repetition in the examples (*her uncles* and *was digging*). Elicit that in both examples, Nye repeats a key phrase to stress the characters' identity and actions and help readers visualize the scenes.

- Invite students to use repetition to add emphasis to this passage.

> *Susan's heart ached with Tracy's pain. ~~Susan knew~~ It ached with the disappointment and embarrassment that Tracy felt.*

**R** RESOURCE MANAGER—Copy Master
Add Emphasis p. 72

**READING-WRITING CONNECTION**

- Have students list the character traits that first come to mind when they think about Susan.

**Writing Online**  THINK central

The following tools are available online at **thinkcentral.com** and on Write*Smart* CD-ROM:
- **Interactive Graphic Organizers**
- **Interactive Student Models**
- **Interactive Revision Lessons**
For additional grammar instruction, see **GrammarNotes** on **thinkcentral.com**.

## Assess and Reteach

### Assess

**DIAGNOSTIC AND SELECTION TESTS**
Selection Test A pp. 67–68
Selection Test B/C pp. 69–70

**Interactive Selection Test** on **thinkcentral.com**

### Reteach

**Level Up Online Tutorials** on **thinkcentral.com**

**Reteaching Worksheets** on **thinkcentral.com**
Literature Lesson 11, Reading Lesson 2, Vocabulary Lesson 6

---

**FOR STRUGGLING WRITERS**

**Introductory Paragraph:** Make a statement about the impact of Susan's character.
**Intermediate Paragraph(s):** Cite examples of Susan's curiosity, wisdom, generosity, and kindness. Refer to Susan's thoughts and actions and other characters' reactions to her.
**Concluding Paragraph:** Connect Susan's chief traits to the word *remarkable*.

# Focus and Motivate

## COMMON CORE FOCUS

**RI 5** Analyze how an author's ideas are developed.
**RI 6** Determine an author's point of view in a text. **RI 10** Read and comprehend literary nonfiction. **W 2b** Develop the topic with concrete details. **W 10** Write over shorter time frames.
**L 1b** Use various types of clauses to add variety and interest to writing. **L 4** Determine or clarify the meaning of multiple-meaning words. **L 4c** Consult reference materials to determine or clarify a word's meaning.

## SUMMARY

In this excerpt, Angelou recalls the day that the sophisticated Mrs. Flowers gave her lemonade, cookies, and "a little talking to." Mrs. Flowers gave the young, withdrawn Angelou reading assignments, lessons in living, and a sense of being liked that lasted a lifetime.

## What is a TEACHER?

Have students freewrite about a mentor they have known. They can use the results to complete the *DISCUSS* activity.

---

# Selection Resources

---

## Before Reading

**Essential Course of Study ECOS**

## from I Know Why the Caged Bird Sings
Autobiography by Maya Angelou

**VIDEO TRAILER THINK**central **KEYWORD: HML9-254**

# What is a TEACHER?

### COMMON CORE

**RI 5** Analyze how an author's ideas are developed.
**RI 6** Determine an author's point of view in a text. **RI 10** Read and comprehend literary nonfiction.
**L 4c** Consult reference materials to determine or clarify a word's meaning.

Your teachers at school are dedicated to helping you acquire knowledge, but are there individuals outside the classroom who teach you important things as well? In this selection, you'll meet Mrs. Flowers, a woman who acted as a mentor—a wise and trusted counselor or teacher—to a young Maya Angelou.

**DISCUSS** Think of people who have shared wisdom with you, helped you to see things in new ways, or pushed you when you needed encouragement. With a small group of classmates, discuss the impact a mentor can have, and then generate a word web detailing the most important traits of a mentor.

patience
Qualities of a Mentor
generosity

254

---

*See resources on the* **Teacher One Stop DVD-ROM** *and on* **thinkcentral.com**.

**R RESOURCE MANAGER UNIT 2**
Plan and Teach, pp. 73–80
Summary, pp. 81–82†‡*
Text Analysis and Reading Skill, pp. 83–86†*
Vocabulary, pp. 87–89*
Grammar and Style, p. 92

**DIAGNOSTIC AND SELECTION TESTS**
Selection Tests, pp. 71–74

**BEST PRACTICES TOOLKIT**
Predicting, p. A10
Knowledge Rating, p. E3

**INTERACTIVE READER**

**ADAPTED INTERACTIVE READER**

**ELL ADAPTED INTERACTIVE READER**

**TECHNOLOGY**
- Teacher One Stop DVD-ROM
- Student One Stop DVD-ROM
- PowerNotes DVD-ROM
- Audio Anthology CD
- GrammarNotes DVD-ROM
- Audio Tutor CD
- ExamView Test Generator on the Teacher One Stop

**THINK**central
**Video Trailer**

Go to **thinkcentral.com** to preview the **Video Trailer** introducing this selection. Other features that support the selection include
- **PowerNotes** presentation
- **ThinkAloud** models to enhance comprehension
- **WordSharp** vocabulary tutorials
- interactive writing and grammar instruction

\* Resources for Differentiation     † Also in Spanish     ‡ In Haitian Creole and Vietnamese

## ● TEXT ANALYSIS: CHARACTERIZATION IN AUTOBIOGRAPHY

When describing important individuals they have known, writers of **autobiography** often develop their ideas by using the same methods of **characterization** that fiction writers do. These include

- description of a person's physical appearance
- examples of the person's speech, thoughts, or feelings
- the speech, thoughts, or feelings of other people
- the narrator's ideas and comments about the person

As you read, look for details that reveal Mrs. Flowers's personality traits and ways she influenced the young Angelou.

## ● READING SKILL: ANALYZE PERSPECTIVES

Autobiographies often reflect two different **perspectives**, or viewpoints:

- that of the writer as he or she experiences events
- that of the writer looking back on these events years later

As you read this selection, use a chart like the one shown to record Angelou's thoughts and observations about Mrs. Flowers from both her childhood and adult perspectives.

| Child's Viewpoint | Adult's Viewpoint |
|---|---|
| "Why on earth did she insist on calling her Sister Flowers? Shame made me want to hide my face." (lines 25–26) | "She was one of the few gentlewomen I have ever known, and has remained throughout my life the measure of what a human being can be." (lines 18–19) |

**Review: Make Inferences**

## ▲ VOCABULARY IN CONTEXT

In your *Reader/Writer Notebook*, make a chart like the one shown, placing each word in the column where it fits.

| WORD LIST | | | |
|---|---|---|---|
| | cascade | illiteracy | sacrilegious |
| | clarity | infuse | taut |
| | homely | leer | |

| Know Word Well | Think I Know Word | Don't Know Word |
|---|---|---|
| | | |

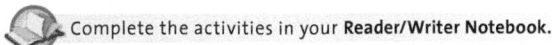

Complete the activities in your **Reader/Writer Notebook.**

---

## Meet the Author

## Maya Angelou
born 1928

**Marguerite Moves South**
Maya Angelou was born Marguerite Johnson in St. Louis, Missouri. The name Maya was originally given to her by her older brother, Bailey, who called her "mya sister" as a child. When their parents divorced, Marguerite and Bailey were sent to live with their grandmother in the small, rigidly segregated town of Stamps, Arkansas. Their grandmother, whom they called Momma, ran the only African American–owned store in her community, in a part of town referred to as Black Stamps.

**Childhood Trauma**
After being abused by a family friend when she was eight, Angelou withdrew into herself and spoke to no one but Bailey for five years. It is at this point in her life that this selection takes place.

**Never Defeated**
Angelou has come a long way since her early struggles. In 1993, when she read her poem "On the Pulse of Morning" to commemorate Bill Clinton's swearing in as president, she became only the second poet to speak at an inauguration. She served as a coordinator of Martin Luther King Jr.'s Southern Christian Leadership Conference and has taught in Africa and the United States. Her writings have achieved tremendous popularity, inspiring millions of people around the world. When asked what advice she'd like to pass on to her readers, Angelou replied, "You may encounter many defeats, but you must not be defeated."

**Author Online** THINK central
Go to **thinkcentral.com.**
KEYWORD: HML9-255

255

---

## *Teach*

## ● *Model the Skill:* CHARACTERIZATION IN AUTOBIOGRAPHY

To model how to identify methods of characterization, read this sentence:

She was young and had a childlike face; when she spoke, she seemed wise.

Point out that the first part of the sentence describes physical appearance. Ask what method the second part uses.

**GUIDED PRACTICE** Ask what method of characterization students would use in their own autobiography and why.

## ■ *Model the Skill:* ANALYZE PERSPECTIVES

Ask students to compare the two perspectives in the chart. Elicit that the child's view is self-centered and the adult's view shows a sense of "looking back."

**GUIDED PRACTICE** Discuss how Angelou's comment in **Never Defeated** is from an adult's viewpoint.

| Child's Viewpoint | Adult's Viewpoint |
|---|---|
| I didn't care if my lollipop was lying on the floor. I wanted it! | My dad never gave in to my tantrums. |

**R** RESOURCE MANAGER—Copy Master
Analyze Perspectives p. 85 (for student use while reading the selection)

---

## VOCABULARY SKILL

## ▲ VOCABULARY IN CONTEXT

**DIAGNOSE WORD KNOWLEDGE** Have all students complete **Vocabulary in Context.** Check their words and phrases against the following:

**cascade** (kă-skăd′) *v.* to fall or flow like a waterfall
**clarity** (klăr′ĭ-tē) *n.* clearness
**homely** (hōm′lē) *adj.* characteristic of home life; simple; everyday
**illiteracy** (ĭ-lĭt′ər-ə-sē) *n.* a lack of ability to read and write
**infuse** (ĭn-fyōōz′) *v.* to fill, as if by pouring

**leer** (lîr) *v.* to give a sly, evil glance
**sacrilegious** (săk′rə-lĭj′əs) *adj.* disrespectful toward a sacred person, place, or thing
**taut** (tôt) *adj.* pulled or drawn tight

**PRETEACH VOCABULARY** Use the Vocabulary Study copy master to help students predict meanings for each boldfaced word in the copy master.

**R** RESOURCE MANAGER—Copy Master
Vocabulary Study p. 87

1. Read item 1 aloud, emphasizing *cascade.*
2. Point out the words *flowing* and *down.* Discuss possible meanings for *cascade,* such as "to flow or fall like water."
3. Repeat the procedure for items 2–8.

### READ WITH A PURPOSE

*Help students set a purpose for reading. Tell them to look at ways that Marguerite's mentor teaches her as they read the selection.*

---

**TEXT ANALYSIS**  COMMON CORE  RI 5, RI 10

### Ⓐ CHARACTERIZATION

***Possible answer:*** *Mrs. Flowers seems more knowing and powerful than other people. She is unaffected by weather conditions, and her clothing matches her alone. She stays apart from others and, unlike them, wears gloves.*

**IF STUDENTS NEED HELP . . .** Have them identify the information in these lines:

- lines 4–6: her resistance to weather conditions
- lines 7–8: her "perfect" clothing
- lines 11–12: her distance from others
- lines 12–13: her lack of familiarity and her gloves

---

**VOCABULARY**  COMMON CORE  L 4

### OWN THE WORD

**taut:** Have students create a semantic map for *taut*. Write the word in a center circle and add the definition given, "pulled or drawn tight." Draw spider legs from the center circle and have students add synonyms to complete the map.
***Possible answers:*** *strained, tense, tight, inflexible*

---

# I KNOW WHY THE *Caged Bird* SINGS

## Maya Angelou

**Analyze Visuals ▶**

Examine this portrait. How does it compare with Angelou's description of Mrs. Flowers? Cite details from the painting and the text to support your answer.

For nearly a year, I sopped around the house, the Store, the school and the church, like an old biscuit, dirty and inedible. Then I met, or rather got to know, the lady who threw me my first life line.

Mrs. Bertha Flowers was the aristocrat of Black Stamps. She had the grace of control to appear warm in the coldest weather, and on the Arkansas summer days it seemed she had a private breeze which swirled around, cooling her. She was thin without the **taut** look of wiry people, and her printed voile dresses and flowered hats were as right for her as denim overalls for a farmer. She was our side's answer to the richest white woman in town.

10 Her skin was a rich black that would have peeled like a plum if snagged, but then no one would have thought of getting close enough to Mrs. Flowers to ruffle her dress, let alone snag her skin. She didn't encourage familiarity. She wore gloves too. Ⓐ

I don't think I ever saw Mrs. Flowers laugh, but she smiled often. A slow widening of her thin black lips to show even, small white teeth, then the slow, effortless closing. When she chose to smile on me, I always wanted to thank her. The action was so graceful and inclusively benign.

She was one of the few gentlewomen I have ever known, and has remained throughout my life the measure of what a human being can be.

20 Momma had a strange relationship with her. Most often when she passed on the road in front of the Store, she spoke to Momma in that soft yet carrying voice, "Good day, Mrs. Henderson." Momma responded with "How you, Sister Flowers?"

**taut** (tôt) *adj.* pulled or drawn tight

Ⓐ **CHARACTERIZATION**
Reread lines 4–13. What is distinctive about Mrs. Flowers's appearance and demeanor? What idea is the writer developing about Mrs. Flowers?

 **Targeted Passage**

*Woman with Umbrella,* Bill Farnsworth. © Images.com/Corbis.

---

## DIFFERENTIATED INSTRUCTION

**FOR ENGLISH LANGUAGE LEARNERS**
**Options for Reading** Have students listen to the entire selection on the *Audio Anthology CD*. Then divide the selection among student pairs. Have students look up unfamiliar words not explained in the text and then paraphrase and share their sections with the class.

**FOR STRUGGLING READERS**
In combination with the *Audio Anthology CD*, use one or more Targeted Passages (pp. 256, 261, 263) to ensure that students focus on key story events, concepts, and skills. Targeted Passages are also good for English learners.

**①** **Targeted Passage** [Lines 12–23]
This passage clarifies the fact that although Mrs. Flowers seems aristocratic, she is gracious and kind.

- What does Mrs. Flowers not encourage? (line 12)

**Reading Support**

This selection on **thinkcentral.com** includes embedded **ThinkAloud** models—students "thinking aloud" about the story to model the kinds of questions a good reader would ask about a selection.

## BACKGROUND

**Southern Stratification** This excerpt from Angelou's autobiography highlights the class distinctions within the African-American community in the South during the 1930s. Within that community, even the most genteel and educated African Americans were looked down upon by the white lower class. Explain that "powhitefolks" (line 56) is a phonetic spelling of "poor white folks." Marguerite is troubled by the idea that poor whites would address Mrs. Flowers disrespectfully as "Bertha"—just as she is embarrassed that her grandmother addresses her too familiarly as "Sister Flowers."

## Analyze Visuals

*Possible answer:* *Like Mrs. Flowers, the woman in the painting is "thin without the taut look of wiry people" (line 7) and has skin that is "a rich black" (line 10). She also wears a hat (line 8) and seems to have an aristocratic air (line 4). Unlike Mrs. Flowers, she carries an umbrella, and does not wear gloves.*

**About the Art** In *Woman with Umbrella*, Connecticut-born Bill Farnsworth (born 1958) creates an image of a woman set apart by her elegance and by the umbrella that forms the shadow in which she walks. Farnsworth explains, "Using light, color, and texture, I try to bring the viewer into the painting, so they too can feel the moment in time. . . . My goal is to tell the story 'without words.'"

## REVISIT THE BIG QUESTION

### What is a
# TEACHER?

**Discuss** Think about what it means to be a mentor. Based on what Angelou says in lines 18– 19, what did she learn from Mrs. Flowers? *Possible answer: She learned the meaning of being a gentlewoman and the standard of what it means to be a human being.*

- How does she smile? How does Angelou remember feeling when Mrs. Flowers smiled at her? (lines 14–17)
- What kind of "measure" is Mrs. Flowers? (lines 18–19)
- How does she greet Momma? (lines 20–23)

**FOR ADVANCED LEARNERS/PRE–AP**

**Creative Projects** Extend the lesson by having students choose one of the following creative projects:

- Create a model of a caged bird
- Write a diary entry from Marguerite's point of view
- Compose a song about Marguerite's experience

Mrs. Flowers didn't belong to our church, nor was she Momma's familiar.[1] Why on earth did she insist on calling her Sister Flowers? Shame made me want to hide my face. Mrs. Flowers deserved better than to be called Sister. Then, Momma left out the verb. Why not ask, "How *are* you, *Mrs.* Flowers?" With the unbalanced passion of the young, I hated her for showing her ignorance to Mrs. Flowers. It didn't occur to me for many years that they 30 were as alike as sisters, separated only by formal education.

Although I was upset, neither of the women was in the least shaken by what I thought an unceremonious greeting. Mrs. Flowers would continue her easy gait up the hill to her little bungalow, and Momma kept on shelling peas or doing whatever had brought her to the front porch.

Occasionally, though, Mrs. Flowers would drift off the road and down to the Store and Momma would say to me, "Sister, you go on and play." As I left I would hear the beginning of an intimate conversation, Momma persistently using the wrong verb, or none at all.

"Brother and Sister Wilcox is sho'ly the meanest—" "Is," Momma? "Is"? 40 Oh, please, not "is," Momma, for two or more. But they talked, and from the side of the building where I waited for the ground to open up and swallow me, I heard the soft-voiced Mrs. Flowers and the textured voice of my grandmother merging and melting. They were interrupted from time to time by giggles that must have come from Mrs. Flowers (Momma never giggled in her life). Then she was gone. **B**

She appealed to me because she was like people I had never met personally. Like women in English novels who walked the moors[2] (whatever they were) with their loyal dogs racing at a respectful distance. Like the women who sat in front of roaring fireplaces, drinking tea incessantly from silver trays full 50 of scones and crumpets.[3] Women who walked over the "heath"[4] and read morocco-bound[5] books and had two last names divided by a hyphen. It would be safe to say that she made me proud to be Negro, just by being herself.

She acted just as refined as whitefolks in the movies and books and she was more beautiful, for none of them could have come near that warm color without looking gray by comparison.

It was fortunate that I never saw her in the company of powhitefolks. For since they tend to think of their whiteness as an evenizer, I'm certain that I would have had to hear her spoken to commonly as Bertha, and my image of her would have been shattered like the unmendable Humpty-Dumpty. **C**

60 One summer afternoon, sweet-milk fresh in my memory, she stopped at the Store to buy provisions. Another Negro woman of her health and age would have been expected to carry the paper sacks home in one hand, but Momma said, "Sister Flowers, I'll send Bailey up to your house with these things."

---

1. **familiar:** a close friend or associate.
2. **moors:** broad open areas of countryside with marshes and patches of low shrubs.
3. **scones** (skōnz) **and crumpets** (krŭm'pĭts): Scones are small, biscuitlike pastries; crumpets are rolls similar to English muffins.
4. **heath** (hēth): another word for a moor.
5. **morocco-bound:** Morocco is a soft leather sometimes used for expensive book covers.

**258** UNIT 2: CHARACTERIZATION AND POINT OF VIEW

---

**READING SKILL**  COMMON CORE  RI 6

**B** *Model the Skill:* **ANALYZE PERSPECTIVES**

Model for students how to analyze perspectives by copying the graphic organizer from "Before You Read" onto the board. Have students reread line 39 aloud. Write "Brother and Sister Wilcox is sho'ly the meanest—(Momma) (line 39)" under adult perspective. Have students read the remainder of lines 39–45 slowly and complete the chart with one more example of each perspective.

**Possible answer:** *The embarrassment over Momma's grammatical errors (lines 39–41) reflects a child's viewpoint. The comment that "Momma never giggled in her life" (line 44) reflects an adult's viewpoint.*

**READING SKILL:** *Review*

**C** **MAKE INFERENCES**

**Possible answer:** *The reader can infer that race relations were strained and that segregation and discrimination were common. The lines suggest that "powhitefolks" would not have used a title of respect such as "Mrs. Flowers"; rather, they would have thought themselves to be superior to her merely because their skin was white. They would have "spoken to [her] commonly as Bertha." The reader would probably not be able to make such inferences if Angelou had not provided her adult perspective on what she felt as a child. Marguerite probably realized that poor whites would have felt superior to Mrs. Flowers because of their skin color, but she would not have been able to articulate the idea so clearly.*

**IF STUDENTS NEED HELP . . .** Have students consider what might happen if they called the school principal by his or her first name. What kind of attitude would that action convey?

**B ANALYZE PERSPECTIVES** Reread lines 39–45. Which parts of this passage are written from a child's perspective? Which are written from the viewpoint of an adult reflecting on the experience? Record your answers in your chart.

**C MAKE INFERENCES** In lines 56–59, what can you infer about race relations in Stamps, Arkansas, in the 1930s? Consider whether you would be able to make these inferences if Angelou did not comment on her childhood experiences from her adult viewpoint.

---

## DIFFERENTIATED INSTRUCTION

**FOR STRUGGLING READERS**

**Predict Plot** This narrative's action does not really begin until line 60. As students near that point, use Predicting to list key details from the exposition and predict why Mrs. Flowers might be important as the selection continues.

📦 **BEST PRACTICES TOOLKIT—Transparency** Predicting p. A10

**FOR ENGLISH LANGUAGE LEARNERS**

**Vocabulary Support** Use Knowledge Rating to teach these words: *occur* (line 29), *persistently* (line 37), *refined* (line 53), *equivalent* (line 73), *generations* (line 165), *conclusions* (line 194).

📦 **BEST PRACTICES TOOLKIT—Transparency** Knowledge Rating p. E3

She smiled that slow dragging smile, "Thank you, Mrs. Henderson. I'd prefer Marguerite, though." My name was beautiful when she said it. "I've been meaning to talk to her, anyway." They gave each other age-group looks.

Momma said, "Well, that's all right then. Sister, go and change your dress. You going to Sister Flowers's."

▼ **Analyze Visuals**

Does the girl in this painting look similar to how you envision Marguerite? Describe the **details** that influenced your answer.

*Ancilla with an Orange* (1956), Dod Procter. Oil on canvas. Royal West of England Academy, Bristol, UK. © The Bridgeman Art Library.

## Analyze Visuals

*Possible answer:* *The girls are somewhat similar. Marguerite is about to change into a nice dress, perhaps like the one in the picture. Also, in Mrs. Flowers's presence, Marguerite might look as pensive as the painting's subject.*

**About the Art** Inspired by impressionist and post-impressionist painters, British artist Dod Procter (1892–1972) created a light-filled canvas showing a young girl with an orange. As in many paintings by the impressionist master Renoir, her subject is a girl placed against a colorful background.

## TIERED DISCUSSION PROMPTS

Direct students to lines 39–68. Use these prompts to help students understand the role of Momma in this account:

**Recall** How does Momma treat Mrs. Flowers in the store? *Possible answer: Momma pays special attention to Mrs. Flowers, sending someone to deliver her groceries.*

**Analyze** How does Momma's attitude toward Mrs. Flowers seem to have influenced Marguerite? *Possible answer: Marguerite appears to be in awe of Mrs. Flowers, just as Momma is.*

**Synthesize** What does Momma probably think when Mrs. Flowers asks to have Marguerite carry her groceries home? Explain. *Possible answer: Momma may be proud that such a fine woman is paying attention to Marguerite. Also, since they now exchange "age-group looks" (line 66), Momma may be glad to see that something that she and Mrs. Flowers have planned is about to occur.*

## FOR ENGLISH LANGUAGE LEARNERS

**Vocabulary: Idioms and Sayings** Use New Word Analysis to teach the meanings of these idioms and sayings as you come across them in the reading:

- *sweet-milk fresh* (line 60), "vivid and pleasant"
- *what on earth* (line 69), "what (among all possible choices)"
- *handed out* (line 82), "given"
- *it would be fitting* (line 105), "it would be right for the situation"
- *bear in mind* (lines 118–119), "remember"
- *tried her hand at* (lines 150–151), "attempted"
- *pay me a visit* (line 182), "visit me"

 **BEST PRACTICES TOOLKIT—Transparency** New Word Analysis p. E8

##  Model the Skill:
## CHARACTERIZATION

Model for students how to locate details in the text that reveal Marguerite's character and then note how these details suggest specific character traits. Read lines 85–86 aloud. Point out that Marguerite turns around when Momma tells her to. That shows that she was obedient. Have students find other text details and identify the character traits they illustrate.

*Possible answer: Marguerite is extremely shy and modest, and she is obedient (lines 88, 100–103). She is perceptive of other people's feelings and attitudes, as well as sensitive about how others view her (lines 100–103). She also hides inside a rich interior life of unspoken thoughts and imagination (lines 104–106).*

🧰 BEST PRACTICES TOOLKIT—Transparency Two-Column Chart p. A25

**Extend the Discussion** What does Marguerite think, say, or do in this scene that reveals who she really is despite how she acts?

### OWN THE WORD

**sacrilegious:** Point out to students the spelling of *sacrilegious*, that it is not the same as *religious*. Then have them write a pair of sentences contrasting *religious* and *sacrilegious*. **Possible answer:** *Paul's family is quite religious, and they attend church at least twice a week; making fun of their beliefs would be sacrilegious.*

---

The chifforobe[6] was a maze. What on earth did one put on to go to
70 Mrs. Flowers's house? I knew I shouldn't put on a Sunday dress. It might be
**sacrilegious.** Certainly not a house dress, since I was already wearing a fresh
one. I chose a school dress, naturally. It was formal without suggesting that
going to Mrs. Flowers's house was equivalent to attending church.

I trusted myself back into the Store.

"Now, don't you look nice." I had chosen the right thing, for once.

"Mrs. Henderson, you make most of the children's clothes, don't you?"

"Yes, ma'am. Sure do. Store-bought clothes ain't hardly worth the thread
it take to stitch them."

"I'll say you do a lovely job, though, so neat. That dress looks professional."

80 Momma was enjoying the seldom-received compliments. Since everyone we
knew (except Mrs. Flowers, of course) could sew competently, praise was rarely
handed out for the commonly practiced craft.

"I try, with the help of the Lord, Sister Flowers, to finish the inside just like
I does the outside. Come here, Sister."

I had buttoned up the collar and tied the belt, apronlike, in back. Momma
told me to turn around. With one hand she pulled the strings and the belt fell
free at both sides of my waist. Then her large hands were at my neck, opening
the button loops. I was terrified. What was happening?

"Take it off, Sister." She had her hands on the hem of the dress.

90 "I don't need to see the inside, Mrs. Henderson, I can tell . . ." But the
dress was over my head and my arms were stuck in the sleeves. Momma said,
"That'll do. See here, Sister Flowers, I French-seams[7] around the armholes."
Through the cloth film, I saw the shadow approach. "That makes it last longer.
Children these days would bust out of sheet-metal clothes. They so rough."

"That is a very good job, Mrs. Henderson. You should be proud. You can
put your dress back on, Marguerite."

"No ma'am. Pride is a sin. And 'cording to the Good Book, it goeth
before a fall."

"That's right. So the Bible says. It's a good thing to keep in mind."

100 I wouldn't look at either of them. Momma hadn't thought that taking off
my dress in front of Mrs. Flowers would kill me stone dead. If I had refused,
she would have thought I was trying to be "womanish" and might have
remembered St. Louis. Mrs. Flowers had known that I would be embarrassed
and that was even worse. I picked up the groceries and went out to wait in the
hot sunshine. It would be fitting if I got a sunstroke and died before they came
outside. Just dropped dead on the slanting porch.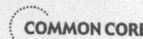

There was a little path beside the rocky road, and Mrs. Flowers walked in
front swinging her arms and picking her way over the stones.

---

6. **chifforobe** (shĭf'ə-rōb'): a chest of drawers combined with a small closet
for hanging clothes.

7. **French-seams:** sew seams that are turned in and stitched on the wrong side so
that the unfinished edges of the cloth are not visible.

**sacrilegious** (săk'rə-lĭj'əs)
*adj.* disrespectful toward
a sacred person, place,
or thing

**Language Coach**

**Homophones** Words that sound alike but have different meanings and sometimes spellings are called **homophones.** Reread line 80. *Compliments* are admiring remarks. What does the homophone *complements* mean? Use a dictionary to verify your answer.

🅓 **CHARACTERIZATION** In addition to describing her mentor in a compelling way, Angelou also presents a vivid portrait of herself as a child. List three traits Marguerite exhibits.

---

## DIFFERENTIATED INSTRUCTION

### FOR ENGLISH LANGUAGE LEARNERS

**Language Coach**

**Homophones** *Possible answer: two parts that complete each other or make a whole;* Ask students to come up with two examples of compliments (for example: "You look pretty") and two examples of complements (for example: salt and pepper).

### FOR ADVANCED LEARNERS/PRE–AP

**Compare and Contrast Allusions** [small-group option] This scene contains several allusions to beliefs in the Bible; indeed, it provides a reference for much of what Momma says. Later, Mrs. Flowers and Angelou allude to secular literature. After students have read the selection, ask them to compare and contrast these allusions and draw conclusions about what the allusions indicate about the account's main characters.

She said, without turning her head, to me, "I hear you're doing very good school work, Marguerite, but that it's all written. The teachers report that they have trouble getting you to talk in class." We passed the triangular farm on our left and the path widened to allow us to walk together. I hung back in the separate unasked and unanswerable questions.

"Come and walk along with me, Marguerite." I couldn't have refused even if I wanted to. She pronounced my name so nicely. Or more correctly, she spoke each word with such **clarity** that I was certain a foreigner who didn't understand English could have understood her.

"Now no one is going to make you talk—possibly no one can. But bear in mind, language is man's way of communicating with his fellow man and it is language alone which separates him from the lower animals." That was a totally new idea to me, and I would need time to think about it.

"Your grandmother says you read a lot. Every chance you get. That's good, but not good enough. Words mean more than what is set down on paper. It takes the human voice to **infuse** them with the shades of deeper meaning."

I memorized the part about the human voice infusing words. It seemed so valid and poetic.

She said she was going to give me some books and that I not only must read them, I must read them aloud. She suggested that I try to make a sentence sound in as many different ways as possible.

"I'll accept no excuse if you return a book to me that has been badly handled." My imagination boggled at the punishment I would deserve if in fact I did abuse a book of Mrs. Flowers'. Death would be too kind and brief.

The odors in the house surprised me. Somehow I had never connected Mrs. Flowers with food or eating or any other common experience of common people. There must have been an outhouse, too, but my mind never recorded it.

The sweet scent of vanilla had met us as she opened the door.

"I made tea cookies this morning. You see, I had planned to invite you for cookies and lemonade so we could have this little chat. The lemonade is in the icebox."

It followed that Mrs. Flowers would have ice on an ordinary day, when most families in our town bought ice late on Saturdays only a few times during the summer to be used in the wooden ice-cream freezers.

She took the bags from me and disappeared through the kitchen door. I looked around the room that I had never in my wildest fantasies imagined I would see. Browned photographs **leered** or threatened from the walls and the white, freshly done curtains pushed against themselves and against the wind. I wanted to gobble up the room entire and take it to Bailey, who would help me analyze and enjoy it.

"Have a seat, Marguerite. Over there by the table." She carried a platter covered with a tea towel. Although she warned that she hadn't tried her hand at baking sweets for some time, I was certain that like everything else about her the cookies would be perfect.

110

120

130

140

150

**clarity** (klăr′ĭ-tē) *n.* clearness

② **Targeted Passage**

**infuse** (ĭn-fyōōz′) *v.* to fill, as if by pouring

**E** **CHARACTERIZATION**
Reread lines 109–124. What does this passage reveal about the **conflict** developing in this selection? Summarize what you already know about Marguerite's conflict.

**leer** (lîr) *v.* to give a sly, evil glance

**F** **GRAMMAR AND STYLE**
Reread lines 143–148. Angelou uses the **adjective clause** "that I had never in my wildest fantasies imagined I would see" to convey with precision Marguerite's excitement.

I KNOW WHY THE CAGED BIRD SINGS **261**

---

TEXT ANALYSIS
**COMMON CORE**
RI 5, RI 10

**E** **CHARACTERIZATION**

*Possible answer:* The passage reveals that Marguerite has a great deal to say but has a hard time saying it. Marguerite says earlier that she "sopped around the house . . . like an old biscuit," suggesting that she has been unhappy and troubled. Her unhappiness may have something to do with her reticence.

**F** **GRAMMAR AND STYLE**
COMMON CORE L 1b

**Add Descriptive Details** Explain that adjective clauses modify nouns or pronouns, telling *what kind* or *which one*. In this sentence, the adjective clause modifies the noun *room*. Have students find other sentences in the selection that contain adjective clauses. To help students locate clauses, explain that adjective clauses often begin with *that, which, who,* or *whom* and immediately follow the noun or pronoun that they modify.

VOCABULARY
**COMMON CORE**
L 4

**OWN THE WORD**

- **clarity:** Tell students that the noun *clarity* is directly related to the adjective *clear*. Have students list other words or phrases that have *clear-* or *clair-* in their stems. *Possible answers: clearly, clearance, clear-cut, clearing, clairvoyant*

- **infuse:** Tell students that the prefix *in-* can mean "into," and that *fuse* means "to mix together." Have them write sentences that show an understanding of *infuse.*

- **leer:** Tell students that *leer* in Spanish and *lire* in French mean "to read." The English verb, however, means to look at someone in an evil way. Have students describe how it would feel to be leered at.

---

**FOR STRUGGLING READERS**

② **Targeted Passage** [Lines 109–129]

This passage reveals Mrs. Flowers's reason for inviting Marguerite to her home.

- According to Mrs. Flowers, what is Marguerite doing right at school? What problem is she having? (lines 109–111)

- What "totally new idea" does she present to Marguerite? (lines 119–121)

- What does she want Marguerite to do with the books that she borrows? (lines 127–128)

**FOR ENGLISH LANGUAGE LEARNERS**

**Vocabulary: Phrasal Verbs** Point out that some English verbs often "go together" with other words (words that otherwise may be prepositions or adverbs) to form phrasal verbs with unique meanings. Guide students to define some of the phrasal verbs on these pages: *put on* (line 70); *turn around* (line 86); *take off* (line 89); *picked up* (line 104); *hung back* (line 113); *set down* (line 123); *gobble up* (line 147).

## Analyze Visuals

**About the Art** Contemporary painter Michele Hausman (born 1952) represents nature in landscapes, florals, and still lifes. She believes that "seeing is the greatest joy of existence" and uses her paintings to express that joy.

**Activity** Marguerite regards her snack with Mrs. Flowers as a perfect interlude on a hot summer day. How does the painting suggest that perfection? *Possible answer: Its mood and colors are cool and refreshing.*

## TIERED DISCUSSION PROMPTS

Direct students to lines 153–159. Use these prompts to discuss how Angelou characterizes herself as a girl:

**Connect** Have you or someone you know ever been a guest in a fancy setting? What details stood out? Explain. *Encourage students to be as specific as possible in their descriptions.*

**Analyze** Why are the details about the cookies important? What do they show about Marguerite? *Possible answer: The details reveal her feelings at that moment—in particular, her delight in the special treatment that Mrs. Flowers gives her.*

**Evaluate** What is the value of such small details in an autobiography? *Possible answers: They show Marguerite's inner thoughts; they show how a child's mind might work; they give the reader a chance to visualize; they may help readers identify with Marguerite.*

*Lemonade* (2002), Michele Hausman. © Michele Hausman.

They were flat round wafers, slightly browned on the edges and butter-yellow in the center. With the cold lemonade they were sufficient for childhood's lifelong diet. Remembering my manners, I took nice little lady like bites off the edges. She said she had made them expressly for me and that she had a few in the kitchen that I could take home to my brother. So I jammed one whole cake in my mouth and the rough crumbs scratched the insides of my jaws, and if I hadn't had to swallow, it would have been a dream come true.

160 As I ate she began the first of what we later called "my lessons in living." She said that I must always be intolerant of ignorance but understanding of **illiteracy.** That some people, unable to go to school, were more educated and even more intelligent than college professors. She encouraged me to listen carefully to what country people called mother wit. That in those **homely** sayings was couched the collective wisdom of generations.

When I finished the cookies she brushed off the table and brought a thick, small book from the bookcase. I had read *A Tale of Two Cities*[8] and found it up to my standards as a romantic novel. She opened the first page and I heard poetry for the first time in my life.

**illiteracy** (ĭ-lĭt′ər-ə-sē) *n.* a lack of ability to read and write

**homely** (hōm′lē) *adj.* characteristic of home life; simple; everyday

---

8. ***A Tale of Two Cities:*** a novel by Charles Dickens, set in Paris and London during the French Revolution (1789–1799).

**262**   UNIT 2: CHARACTERIZATION AND POINT OF VIEW

## DIFFERENTIATED INSTRUCTION

**FOR ADVANCED LEARNERS/PRE–AP**

**Make Judgments** Have students reread the "lessons in living" discussed in lines 160–165. Is this the counsel that Marguerite most needs to hear? Is it practical? Ask students to respond to these questions by writing a paragraph that expresses a judgment about the quality of Mrs. Flowers's "lessons."

**FOR ENGLISH LANGUAGE LEARNERS**

**Media and Concepts** To build and reinforce the concept of characterization, show a scene from *Star Wars* or another film that you have in your classroom. As students watch, ask them to derive meaning from the characters' appearance, dialogue, facial expressions, and actions. Ask students to respond orally to the following questions: What did you learn about each character's personality? What clues in the film helped you understand what each character was like?

170 "It was the best of times and the worst of times . . ."[9] Her voice slid in and curved down through and over the words. She was nearly singing. I wanted to look at the pages. Were they the same that I had read? Or were there notes, music, lined on the pages, as in a hymn book? Her sounds began **cascading** gently. I knew from listening to a thousand preachers that she was nearing the end of her reading, and I hadn't really heard, heard to understand, a single word.

"How do you like that?"

It occurred to me that she expected a response. The sweet vanilla flavor was still on my tongue and her reading was a wonder in my ears. I had to speak.

180 I said, "Yes, ma'am." It was the least I could do, but it was the most also. **G**

"There's one more thing. Take this book of poems and memorize one for me. Next time you pay me a visit, I want you to recite."

> I have tried often to search behind the sophistication of years for the enchantment I so easily found in those gifts. The essence escapes but its aura remains.[10] To be allowed, no, invited, into the private lives of strangers, and to share their joys and fears, was a chance to exchange the Southern bitter wormwood for a cup of mead with Beowulf or a hot cup of tea and milk with Oliver Twist.[11] When I said aloud, "It is a far, far better thing that I do, than I have ever done . . ."[12] tears of love filled my eyes at my selflessness.
>
> 190 On that first day, I ran down the hill and into the road (few cars ever came along it) and had the good sense to stop running before I reached the Store.
>
> I was liked, and what a difference it made. I was respected not as Mrs. Henderson's grandchild or Bailey's sister but for just being Marguerite Johnson.
>
> Childhood's logic never asks to be proved (all conclusions are absolute). I didn't question why Mrs. Flowers had singled me out for attention, nor did it occur to me that Momma might have asked her to give me a little talking to. All I cared about was that she had made tea cookies for *me* and read to *me* from her favorite book. It was enough to prove that she liked me. **H**

---

**cascade** (kă-skād') v. to fall or flow like a waterfall

**G CHARACTERIZATION**
What does Angelou mean when she says that speaking was both the least and the most she could do?

**③ Targeted Passage**

**H ANALYZE PERSPECTIVES**
Reread lines 183–198. In which lines is Angelou directly narrating her actions and experiences as a child? In which lines is she sharing insights she learned later, as she grew up? Explain your answers.

---

9. **"It was . . . the worst of times . . .":** the famous opening sentence of *A Tale of Two Cities*.

10. **The essence . . . remains:** The basic quality of a thing or event escapes, but the feelings or atmosphere that it creates remains.

11. **a chance to exchange . . . with Oliver Twist:** Angelou compares her existence as a black child in the bigoted South to wormwood, a bitter herb. Mead (a liquor made from honey) and tea with milk were common drinks in the respective eras of Beowulf and Oliver Twist, two characters from English literature. Angelou suggests that reading about such characters provided an escape from her racist Southern surroundings.

12. **"It is a far . . . than I have ever done . . .":** the final line of *A Tale of Two Cities*, spoken by a man who sacrifices his own life to save that of another.

---

**FOR STRUGGLING READERS**

**③ Targeted Passage [Lines 183–198]**

In this concluding passage, Angelou reflects upon what Mrs. Flowers did for her.

- In line 184, what does Angelou call the things that Mrs. Flowers did for her?

- According to line 192, what now makes a difference to her?

- According to lines 197–198, what did she care about on that day? Why?

**FOR STRUGGLING READERS**

**Develop Reading Fluency** Read the first paragraph on this page aloud to model for students how to read aloud effectively. Then have students split into pairs and take turns reading alternate paragraphs to one another.

**R RESOURCE MANAGER—Copy Master**
Reading Fluency p. 93

---

**TEXT ANALYSIS**  COMMON CORE
RI 5, RI 10

**G CHARACTERIZATION**

***Possible answer:*** *Because Marguerite is so quiet, just saying "Yes, ma'am" is hard for her—perhaps the most she can do. The statement also refers to the respect that she owes: Mrs. Flowers has done so much for her, and she has been so moved by hearing Mrs. Flowers read, that answering is the least she can do in return.*

**Extend the Discussion** What is Marguerite feeling when she says, "Yes, ma'am"?

---

**READING SKILL**  COMMON CORE
RI 6

**H ANALYZE PERSPECTIVES**

***Possible answer:*** *Angelou narrates actions and experiences as a child in lines 190–193 and 197–198; Angelou shares adult insights in lines 183–189 and 194–197.*

---

**VOCABULARY** COMMON CORE
L 4

**OWN THE WORD**

**cascade:** Give students these examples: This part of the river is known as the *cascades* because there are a lot of small waterfalls. The lace in her wedding gown fell in *cascades* from her waist to the floor. That joyous summer seemed to be filled with a *cascade* of events, one after the other.

---

**SELECTION WRAP–UP**

**READ WITH A PURPOSE** Now that students have finished reading the selection, have them discuss the ways that people can teach other people. What did Mrs. Flowers teach Marguerite? ***Possible answer:*** *She taught her "lessons in living."*

**INDEPENDENT READING**

Students interested in reading more about race and class distinction might enjoy *To Kill a Mockingbird* by Harper Lee, a story set in a small Alabama town during the Depression.

## TIERED DISCUSSION PROMPTS

Use these prompts to help students explore the symbol of the "caged bird" and connect Angelou's poem to the autobiography:

**Connect** What connotations do you associate with the image of a caged bird? Explain. *Some students will say that the image has negative connotations because a cage suggests confinement and lack of freedom.*

**Analyze** What is the purpose of including the "free bird" in the poem (lines 1, 23)? How does it help to understand the function of the caged bird? Explain. **Possible answer:** *The free bird sets up a contrast with the caged bird. The free bird can experience nature such as the wind (line 2) and makes the sky its own (lines 7, 26). The caged bird sings out of frustration and longing.*

**Evaluate** Ask students to tell which selection they prefer and then to explain how effectively it portrays what it is like to be caged. *Students who prefer the excerpt from the autobiography may say that it vividly portrays a child who is trapped within herself and is unable to escape her torment without help. Students who prefer the poem may argue that it uses dramatic images and figures of speech to describe the rage, frustration, and pain of feeling trapped but, in doing so, shows us the power of the caged bird who expresses feelings in song.*

# Caged Bird  Maya Angelou

A free bird leaps
on the back of the wind
and floats downstream
till the current ends
5 and dips his wing
in the orange sun rays
and dares to claim the sky.

But a bird that stalks
down his narrow cage
10 can seldom see through
his bars of rage
his wings are clipped and
his feet are tied
so he opens his throat to sing.

15 The caged bird sings
with a fearful trill
of things unknown
but longed for still
and his tune is heard
20 on the distant hill
for the caged bird
sings of freedom.

The free bird thinks of another breeze
and the trade winds soft through the sighing trees
25 and the fat worms waiting on a dawn-bright lawn
and he names the sky his own

But a caged bird stands on the grave of dreams
his shadow shouts on a nightmare scream
his wings are clipped and his feet are tied
30 so he opens his throat to sing.

The caged bird sings
with a fearful trill
of things unknown
but longed for still
35 and his tune is heard
on the distant hill
for the caged bird
sings of freedom.

## Comprehension

1. **Recall** What is Mrs. Flowers's feeling about language?

2. **Summarize** What kinds of assignments does Mrs. Flowers give Marguerite?

3. **Clarify** What does Mrs. Flowers mean when she tells Marguerite that some people, though lacking formal schooling, are "more educated and even more intelligent than college professors"?

## Text Analysis

4. **Understand Motives** What motivates Mrs. Flowers to help Marguerite?

5. **Analyze Perspectives** Review the chart that you filled in while reading. How does Angelou's adult perspective help you to understand the long-range effect that Mrs. Flowers had on her life? Cite evidence.

6. **Evaluate Characterization in Autobiography** Skim the selection and find examples of the various methods of characterization used by Angelou in her autobiography. Which would you say is the most powerful method used to characterize Mrs. Flowers? Use the list shown to help you with your response.

> **Methods of Characterization**
>
> • description of a person's physical appearance
>
> • examples of the person's speech, thoughts, or feelings
>
> • the speech, thoughts, or feelings of other people
>
> • the narrator's ideas and comments about the person

7. **Compare Literary Works** Reread the poem "Caged Bird" on page 264. Does Mrs. Flowers teach the young Marguerite to "sing"? If so, in what way?

## Text Criticism

8. **Biographical Context** The title *I Know Why the Caged Bird Sings* is an allusion to the poem "Sympathy" by Paul Laurence Dunbar. The last stanza reads:

> I know why the caged bird sings, ah me,
>     When his wing is bruised and his bosom sore,—
> When he beats his bars and he would be free;
> It is not a carol of joy or glee,
>     But a prayer that he sends from his heart's deep core,
> But a plea, that upward to Heaven he flings—
> I know why the caged bird sings!

Why do you think Angelou refers to this poem in the title of her autobiography?

### What is a TEACHER?

What does it take for a person to be considered a teacher?

COMMON CORE

**RI 5** Analyze how an author's ideas are developed.
**RI 6** Determine an author's point of view in a text. **RI 10** Read and comprehend literary nonfiction.

---

# Practice and Apply

For preliminary support of post-reading questions, use these copy masters:

**R RESOURCE MANAGER**—Copy Masters
Reading Check p. 90
Characterization in Autobiography p. 83
Question Support p. 91

Additional selection questions are provided for teachers on page 77.

## ANSWERS

## Comprehension

1. *Mrs. Flowers says that language separates people from animals (line 120) and that the human voice gives meaning to words (line 124).*

2. *Marguerite is to read books aloud and to make each sentence sound in as many different ways as possible (lines 127–129). Marguerite also must memorize a poem to recite (lines 181–182).*

3. *She probably means that wisdom does not depend upon formal education.*

## Text Analysis

COMMON CORE **RI 5, RI 6, RI 10**

*Possible answers:*

4. *Momma probably asked Mrs. Flowers to help Marguerite (lines 196–197). Teachers' concerns are mentioned (lines 110–111), as well.*

5. ● **COMMON CORE FOCUS** *Analyze Perspectives Angelou recalls that Mrs. Flowers enabled her to hear "poetry for the first time in my life" (lines 168–169). She also remarks on the "enchantment I . . . found in those gifts" (line 184) and how it remains with her. She summarizes Mrs. Flowers's effect in lines 18–19.*

6. ● **COMMON CORE FOCUS** *Evaluate Characterization in Autobiography Angelou describes Mrs. Flowers's physical appearance, gives examples of her speech, and offers her own comments. The most powerful method may be Angelou's own poetic comments.*

7. *Yes; By requiring Marguerite to participate in the power of the spoken word, Marguerite is drawn out of her silence and will foster her ability to free herself through writing.*

## Text Criticism

*Possible answer:*

8. *Angelou, as a victim of abuse, was also "bruised." Just like the caged bird she did not sing, but was trapped in an isolating silence. She learns to sing to be free.*

### What is a TEACHER?
Students might mention not only teachers who teach them in school but also mentors who teach them values and life lessons.

# ANSWERS

## Vocabulary in Context

▲ VOCABULARY PRACTICE

| | |
|---|---|
| 1. *cascade* | 5. *sacrilegious* |
| 2. *leer* | 6. *clarity* |
| 3. *illiteracy* | 7. *taut* |
| 4. *homely* | 8. *infuse* |

 **RESOURCE MANAGER—Copy Master**
Vocabulary Practice p. 88

### ACADEMIC VOCABULARY IN WRITING

Maya Angelou uses the image of a singing bird in a cage as a device to symbolize someone who lacks freedom. Through the **perspective** of the bird who sings of "things unknown but longed for still," the reader understands the point of view of Angelou.

### VOCABULARY STRATEGY: MULTIPLE-MEANING WORDS

 **COMMON CORE L 4**

Explain that context clues are the best tool for distinguishing multiple meanings. Give this illustration.

> I sing in the choir.
> The poet sings of freedom.
> If she thinks she can avoid going to jail, the woman who helped with the crime might sing.

Have students use context clues to determine the meaning of *sing* in each sentence.

**Possible answers:**

| | |
|---|---|
| 1. *b* | 3. *c* |
| 2. *a* | 4. *c* |

 **RESOURCE MANAGER—Copy Master**
Vocabulary Strategy p. 89

**Interactive Vocabulary** THINK central

Keywords direct students to a **WordSharp** tutorial on **thinkcentral.com** or to other types of vocabulary practice and review.

---

# Vocabulary in Context

▲ VOCABULARY PRACTICE

Determine the relationship between the first pair of words in each analogy. Then write the word that best completes the second pair.

1. *Drift* is to *snow* as _____ is to *water*.
2. *Smile* is to *sweetness* as _____ is to *wickedness*.
3. *Disease* is to *medicine* as _____ is to *education*.
4. *Fancy* is to *special* as _____ is to *everyday*.
5. *Toxic* is to *environment* as _____ is to *religion*.
6. *Bewilderment* is to *confusion* as *understanding* is to _____.
7. *Untied* is to *tied* as *loose* is to _____.
8. *Help* is to *assist* as _____ is to *inject*.

**WORD LIST**
cascade
clarity
homely
illiteracy
infuse
leer
sacrilegious
taut

### ACADEMIC VOCABULARY IN WRITING

• complex • device • evaluate • interact • perspective

Maya Angelou uses the image of a singing bird in a cage as a symbol. Write a paragraph explaining how Angelou uses this **device** to share her experiences as a young black woman. Identify what the bird symbolizes and include examples of its use. Use at least one Academic Vocabulary word in your paragraph.

### VOCABULARY STRATEGY: MULTIPLE-MEANING WORDS

**COMMON CORE**

**L 4** Determine or clarify the meaning of multiple-meaning words.

Sometimes words, such as the vocabulary word *homely* in this selection, do not have the meanings you expect. Many English words have a number of meanings, and to understand what you are reading, you must decide which of these meanings the writer intends.

*PRACTICE* Write the letter of the best definition for each boldfaced word. If you need to, consult a dictionary or glossary.

1. She **distinguished** herself from her friends by wearing all black.
   (a) successful or commanding great respect, (b) set oneself apart, (c) recognized differences among several choices

2. **Channel** your energies into some worthwhile project.
   (a) direct into a particular course of action, (b) body of water connecting two larger bodies of water, (c) band of radio or television frequencies

3. The store sold **notions** as well as yarn and knitting needles.
   (a) beliefs about something, (b) vague understandings of something, (c) needles, buttons, and other sewing materials

4. Amassing **capital** was his primary goal.
   (a) city where government is located, (b) punishable by death, (c) money

**Interactive Vocabulary** THINK central

Go to **thinkcentral.com**.
KEYWORD: HML9-266

**266** UNIT 2: CHARACTERIZATION AND POINT OF VIEW

---

## DIFFERENTIATED INSTRUCTION

### FOR ENGLISH LANGUAGE LEARNERS

**Task Support: Reteach** Use Word Squares to reteach the vocabulary words before students begin the Vocabulary in Context activities.

 **BEST PRACTICES TOOLKIT—Transparency**
Word Squares p. E10

### FOR ADVANCED LEARNERS/PRE–AP

**Vocabulary Strategy** Have students determine the meaning of each of these words as it is used in the selection from *I Know Why the Caged Bird Sings* and then use a dictionary to find at least one additional meaning for each word: *measure* (line 19), *refined* (line 53), *provisions* (line 61), *finish* (line 83), *pronounced* (line 115), and *novel* (line 168).

# Language

◆ **GRAMMAR AND STYLE: Add Descriptive Details**

Review the **Grammar and Style** note on page 261. In her writing, Angelou uses **adjective clauses** to add interesting, vivid details about her characters and their emotions. Adjective clauses are subordinate clauses that, like adjectives, modify nouns and pronouns. They are introduced by **relative pronouns** such as *who, whom, whose, that,* and *which* and **relative adverbs** such as *when, where,* and *why.* Here are some examples from the selection:

> . . . *It seemed she had a private breeze which swirled around. . . .* (line 6)
>
> . . . *From the side of the building where I waited for the ground to open up and swallow me, I heard the soft-voiced Mrs. Flowers. . . .* (lines 40–42)

Notice how the revisions in blue make this first draft more descriptive. Use similar methods to revise your response to the prompt below.

**STUDENT MODEL**

*who goes out of her way to make Marguerite feel at ease*

Mrs. Flowers is a generous person. She invites Marguerite over to

*, where she serves cookies and lemonade*

her house and reads out loud from a book *that captivates the girl.*

## READING-WRITING CONNECTION

**YOUR TURN**

Broaden your understanding of the selection by responding to this prompt. Then use the **revising tip** to improve your writing.

| WRITING PROMPT | REVISING TIP |
|---|---|
| **Extended Constructed Response: Character Analysis**<br>Think about the most important character traits Mrs. Flowers exhibits. Then review the word web you created detailing the qualities a **mentor** should possess. Write **three to five paragraphs** describing Mrs. Flowers's traits and analyzing how these traits compare with the qualities you listed. | Review your response. Did you use adjective clauses to add interesting and vivid details to your description of Mrs. Flowers's traits? |

> **Interactive Revision** THINK central
> Go to **thinkcentral.com**.
> KEYWORD: HML9-267

---

**FOR STRUGGLING WRITERS**

*Possible Organizations:*

**Introductory Paragraph:** Make a statement about the impact of Mrs. Flowers's character.

**Intermediate Paragraphs:** Cite examples of Mrs. Flowers's generosity and kindness to Marguerite.

**Concluding Paragraph:** Connect Mrs. Flowers's chief traits to the word *mentor.*

---

COMMON CORE

**L 1b** Use various types of clauses to add variety and interest to writing. **W 2b** Develop the topic with concrete details. **W 10** Write over shorter time frames.

---

# Language

COMMON CORE W 2b, W 10, L 1b

◆ **GRAMMAR AND STYLE**

1. Discuss the revisions to the student model. Note how the added adjective clauses elaborate on the original sentences.

2. List nouns and have students add adjective clauses to expand them. Here are some examples.

   • the Store **Possible answer:** *that Momma runs*

   • the lemonade **Possible answer:** *which is deliciously cool on a hot summer day*

   • Marguerite **Possible answer:** *who doesn't speak*

**R** RESOURCE MANAGER—Copy Master
Add Descriptive Details p. 92

**READING-WRITING CONNECTION**

• Suggest students begin by listing the character traits that first come to mind when they think about Mrs. Flowers.

📁 BEST PRACTICES TOOLKIT—Transparency
Venn Diagram p. A26

> **Writing Online** THINK central
>
> The following tools are available online at **thinkcentral.com** and on **WriteSmart CD-ROM:**
> • **Interactive Graphic Organizers**
> • **Interactive Student Models**
> • **Interactive Revision Lessons**
> For additional grammar instruction, see **GrammarNotes** on **thinkcentral.com**.

# Assess and Reteach

## Assess

**DIAGNOSTIC AND SELECTION TESTS**
  Selection Test A, pp. 71-72
  Selection Test B/C, pp. 73-74

**Interactive Selection Test** on **thinkcentral.com**

## Reteach

**Level Up Online Tutorials** on **thinkcentral.com**

# Focus and Motivate

## COMMON CORE FOCUS

**RI 3** Analyze how the author unfolds an analysis, including how points are introduced and developed and the connections that are drawn between them. **RI 4** Determine the technical meaning of words as they are used in a text. **SL 2** Integrate multiple sources of information presented in diverse media or formats. **L 6** Acquire and use accurately general and domain-specific words; demonstrate independence in gathering vocabulary knowledge.

## SUMMARY

"Blind to Failure" is Karl Taro Greenfeld's report on blind mountaineer Erik Weihenmayer's remarkable climb to the summit of Mount Everest. Weihenmayer's determination helped him overcome doubts and triumph over the physical challenges and extreme dangers of the world's highest peak.

## When is **STRENGTH** more than muscle?

Introduce the question and have students read the text. Then together discuss what kinds of strength are required for bravery. Continue the exploration by having students complete the *QUICKWRITE* and compare their charts.

---

## Blind to Failure

Magazine Article by Karl Taro Greenfeld

# When is **STRENGTH** more than muscle?

### COMMON CORE

**RI 3** Analyze how the author unfolds an analysis, including how points are introduced and developed and the connections that are drawn between them. **RI 4** Determine the technical meaning of words as they are used in a text. **SL 2** Integrate multiple sources of information presented in diverse media or formats.

It's easy to think of people who are strong in body. Many famous athletes have tremendous physical strength. But some people are extremely strong in mind and spirit as well. In "Blind to Failure," you'll meet one such individual, Erik Weihenmayer, who was the first blind mountaineer to reach the top of Mount Everest. In scaling the world's highest peak, Weihenmayer became an inspiring portrait of bravery and determination.

*QUICKWRITE* Think of different types of strength—physical, emotional, spiritual, and so forth. Think of people who exemplify each type of strength and put them in categories in a chart like the one shown. Do any of the people belong in more than one category?

| Physical Strength | Emotional Strength | Spiritual Strength |
|---|---|---|
| • | • | • |
| • | • | • |
| • | • | • |

268

---

## Selection Resources

See resources on the **Teacher One Stop DVD-ROM** and on **thinkcentral.com**.

 **RESOURCE MANAGER UNIT 2**
Plan and Teach, pp. 95-102
Summary, pp. 103-104†‡*
Text Analysis and Reading
   Skill, pp. 105-106, 107-108†*
Vocabulary, pp. 109-111*

**DIAGNOSTIC AND SELECTION TESTS**
Selection Tests, pp. 75-78

 **BEST PRACTICES TOOLKIT**
Character Analysis Chart, p. D5
Word Squares, p. E10
New Word Analysis, p. E8

**TECHNOLOGY**
🔘 **Teacher One Stop DVD-ROM**
🔘 **Student One Stop DVD-ROM**
🔘 **Audio Anthology CD**
🔘 **GrammarNotes DVD-ROM**
🔘 **ExamView Test Generator**
   on the **Teacher One Stop**

---

\* Resources for Differentiation     † Also in Spanish     ‡ Also in Haitian Creole and Vietnamese

## Teach

## ● TEXT ANALYSIS: CHARACTER STUDY

Some nonfiction writers provide insight into the personalities of individuals by writing **character studies.** A character study usually includes factual information about its subject's appearance, speech, and actions, but the details the writer chooses to include can also suggest his or her personal ideas about the subject. As you read "Blind to Failure," note how the author unfolds his analysis about Erik Weihenmayer:

- actions that have made him newsworthy or famous and his own comments about those actions
- descriptions of his physical traits and facial expressions
- examples of others' reactions to his accomplishments

## ● READING SKILL: INTERPRET GRAPHIC AIDS

Magazine articles like "Blind to Failure" often include **graphic aids**—charts, graphs, and maps—that present important information in visual form. This article features a **diagram,** a drawing in which lines, symbols, and words are used to help the reader picture a process, an event, or the way something works. As you read "Blind to Failure," turn back and forth between the text and the diagram to better understand the difficulties of the climb and to follow the climbers' progress. Use a chart to record the information you learn from the diagram.

| Camp or Location | Elevation | Related Events/ Details of Climb | Other Information |
|---|---|---|---|
| Base Camp | 17,600 feet | Below Khumbu Icefall | |

*Review:* **Connect, Draw Conclusions**

## ▲ VOCABULARY IN CONTEXT

Which of these words do you already know? In your *Reader/Writer Notebook,* write a sentence for each of the words. Then check your understanding after you've read the selection.

| WORD LIST | | |
|---|---|---|
| acclimatization | crevasse | insurmountable |
| aplomb | demeanor | paramount |
| arduous | inevitability | transcend |
| banal | | |

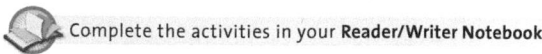 Complete the activities in your **Reader/Writer Notebook.**

## Meet the Author

# Karl Taro Greenfeld
**born 1965**

### Striking Stories
Karl Taro Greenfeld was born in Kobe, Japan, and grew up in Los Angeles, California. As a journalist, he has made his home in Hong Kong, China, investigating everything from entertainment fads to economic disasters. In June of 2001, Greenfeld set out for Nepal to interview members of the Everest expedition that included Erik Weihenmayer, the climber you will read about.

### BACKGROUND TO THE ARTICLE
**Reaching for the Peak**
At 29,035 feet, Mount Everest is the highest peak on earth. To reach the summit, mountaineers establish a series of camps at intervals up the mountain and then make numerous trips between them, carrying supplies from the base camp to the highest camp. When the highest camp is well stocked and the weather is favorable, the climbers make a push for the summit.

**The Perils of Everest**
Climbing Mount Everest is incredibly dangerous, even for the most experienced climbers. Extreme cold makes frostbite common. Sunshine reflected off the snow can cause temporary blindness and fatal falls. Climbers often suffer dizziness and confusion due to lack of oxygen. The region above 26,000 feet is called the Death Zone. At that altitude, blood thickens, the heart speeds up, and the brain can swell, with serious injury or death a possible result. Ninety percent of climbers attempting to scale Mount Everest fail to reach the summit.

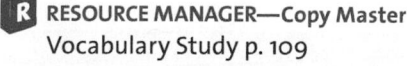
Author Online
THINK central
Go to **thinkcentral.com.**
KEYWORD: HML9-269

269

**TEXT ANALYSIS** COMMON CORE RI 3

## ● *Model the Skill:* CHARACTER STUDY

For instructional support, read aloud this passage:

Thompson raised the trophy triumphantly, his muscles bulging. "I am the best!" he roared, pumping his fist in the air. Spectators frowned at the new champion's boast.

Identify details that help provide a character study of Thompson such as his bulging muscles, and his bragging statement and gestures, and the spectators' unfavorable reaction.

**GUIDED PRACTICE** Have students identify similarly revealing details in previous selections from this text.

**READING SKILL** COMMON CORE SL 2

## ■ *Model the Skill:* INTERPRET GRAPHIC AIDS

After reading the page, identify types of graphic aids, such as *maps, illustrated user manuals,* or *scientific diagrams.*

**GUIDED PRACTICE** Brainstorm ideas about graphic aids that students might find in an article about a mountain climber.

 **RESOURCE MANAGER**—Copy Master Interpret Graphic Aids p. 107 (for student use while reading the selection)

---

## VOCABULARY SKILL

## ▲ VOCABULARY IN CONTEXT

**DIAGNOSE WORD KNOWLEDGE** Have all students complete **Vocabulary in Context.** Check their definitions against the following:

**acclimatization** (ə-klī'mə-tĭ-zā'shən) *n.* the act of getting accustomed to a new climate or environment

**aplomb** (ə-plŏm') *n.* poise; self-assurance

**arduous** (är'jōō-əs) *adj.* requiring much effort; difficult

**banal** (bə-năl') *adj.* commonplace; trite

**crevasse** (krĭ-văs') *n.* a deep crack or split in a glacier

**demeanor** (dĭ-mē'nər) *n.* a way of behaving; manner

**inevitability** (ĭn-ĕv'ĭ-tə-bĭl'ĭ-tē) *n.* something that is certain to happen

**insurmountable** (ĭn'sər-moun'tə-bəl) *adj.* impossible to overcome

**paramount** (păr'ə-mount') *adj.* of highest importance

**transcend** (trăn-sĕnd') *v.* to pass beyond the limits of

**PRETEACH VOCABULARY** Use the following copy master to help students predict the meaning of each boldfaced word, using context clues.

**COMMON CORE** L 4

**R** **RESOURCE MANAGER**—Copy Master Vocabulary Study p. 109

1. Read item 1, emphasizing *acclimatization.*
2. Elicit possible meanings for *acclimatization,* such as "adjustment."
3. Repeat the procedure for items 2–10.

### READ WITH A PURPOSE

*Help students set a purpose for reading. As students read, have them consider whether Weihenmayer achieves celebrity status and why or why not.*

---

**TEXT ANALYSIS** — COMMON CORE RI 3

### Ⓐ CHARACTER STUDY

**Possible answer:** *Such a person may be in good physical condition. He also is either very brave or very foolhardy.*

**IF STUDENTS NEED HELP . . .** Have students use a Character Analysis Chart or expand upon a chart like this to help them make inferences about Weihenmayer.

| Information from Article | My Knowledge and Experience | My Inferences |
|---|---|---|
| Erik planned to climb Mount Everest. | Few people have reached this goal. | Erik is daring and brave. |
| Erik had difficulty reaching Camp 1. | More difficult parts of the climb are to come. | Perhaps Erik is taking on too great a challenge. |

 **BEST PRACTICES TOOLKIT—** Transparency Character Analysis Chart p. D5

---

**VOCABULARY** — COMMON CORE L 4

### OWN THE WORD

**crevasse:** Have students complete this sentence: Falling into a *crevasse* when mountain climbing is extremely dangerous because . . . **Possible answers:** *the crevasse might be too deep for a partner to reach you*

---

# Blind to Failure

## KARL TARO GREENFELD

When he saw Erik Weihenmayer arrive that afternoon, Pasquale Scaturro[1] began to have misgivings about the expedition he was leading. Here they were on the first floor of Mount Everest, and Erik—the reason for the whole trip— was stumbling into Camp 1 bloody, sick, and dehydrated. "He was literally green," says fellow climber and teammate Michael O'Donnell. "He looked like George Foreman[2] had beaten him for two hours." The beating had actually been administered by Erik's climbing partner, Luis Benitez.[3] Erik had slipped into a **crevasse,** and as Benitez reached down to catch him, his climbing pole raked Erik across the nose and chin. Wounds heal slowly at that altitude
10 because of the thin air.

As Erik passed out in his tent, the rest of the team gathered in a worried huddle. "I was thinking maybe this is not a good idea," says Scaturro. "Two years of planning, a documentary movie, and this blind guy barely makes it to Camp 1?"

This blind guy. Erik Weihenmayer, thirty-three, wasn't just another yuppie trekker who'd lost a few rounds to the mountain. Blind since he was thirteen, the victim of a rare hereditary disease of the retina, he began attacking mountains in his early twenties. Ⓐ

But he had been having the same doubts as the rest of the team. On that
20 arduous climb to camp through the Khumbu Icefall,[4] Erik wondered for the first time if his attempt to become the first sightless person to summit Mount Everest was a colossal mistake, an act of Daedalian hubris[5] for which he would be punished. There are so many ways to die on that mountain, spanning

---

1. **Erik Weihenmayer** (wī'ən-mā'ər) . . . **Pasquale Scaturro** (päs-kwä'lā skä-tōō'rō).
2. **George Foreman:** a former heavyweight boxing champion.
3. **Luis Benitez** (lōō-ēs' bĕ-nē'tĕs).
4. **Khumbu** (kōōm'bōō) **Icefall:** a stretch of glacier beginning at about 18,000 feet and extending to the area of Camp 1 at 20,000 feet.
5. **Daedalian hubris** (dĭ-dā'lē-ən hyōō'brĭs): excessive pride like that of Daedalus, a master craftsman in Greek mythology. When Daedalus fashioned wings for himself and his son from feathers and wax, his son flew too near the sun, the wax in his wings melted, and he fell into the sea and drowned.

**270** UNIT 2: CHARACTERIZATION AND POINT OF VIEW

---

**Analyze Visuals** ▸

Examine the photograph of Weihenmayer. Identify three character **traits** you would attribute to him solely on the basis of this picture.

**crevasse** (krĭ-văs') *n.* a deep crack or split in a glacier

❶ **Targeted Passage**

Ⓐ **CHARACTER STUDY**
Think about the endeavor Weihenmayer undertook and his fellow climbers' descriptions of the expedition to this point. What **inferences** can you make about someone who would attempt such a feat?

---

## DIFFERENTIATED INSTRUCTION

### FOR ENGLISH LANGUAGE LEARNERS

**Vocabulary Support** Use Word Squares to teach these words: *teammate* (line 5), *partner* (line 7), *rely* (line 40), *achievement* (line 114), *capable* (line 157), *primarily* (line 244).

 **BEST PRACTICES TOOLKIT—Transparency** Word Squares p. E10

### FOR STRUGGLING READERS

In combination with the *Audio Anthology CD*, use one or more Targeted Passages (pp. 270, 272, 277, 279) to ensure that students focus on key events, concepts, and skills. Targeted Passages are also good for English learners.

❶ **Targeted Passage [Lines 1–14]**

This passage introduces Erik and reveals the almost insurmountable physical challenge that he faces.

## BACKGROUND

**Climbing Mount Everest** Until the early 20th century, people living near Mount Everest considered the Himalayas sacred, and no climbers ascended the mountains. Starting in the 1920s, however, foreign expeditions ventured into the Himalayas, assisted by people of the hardy Sherpa ethnic group. In 1953, Edmund Hillary of New Zealand and Sherpa Tenzing Norgay of Nepal were the first to reach the top of Mount Everest. The first woman to climb to the summit was Junko Tabei of Japan, in 1975.

## Analyze Visuals

Based upon his stance and appearance, Weihenmayer seems to exhibit determination, preparedness, and confidence.

**REVISIT THE BIG QUESTION**
## When is STRENGTH
### more than muscle?

**Discuss** Based on lines 19–23, do Erik's doubts show a lapse of bravery? Explain. *Student responses may vary but many may answer that bravery is often necessary for honestly facing the facts of a difficult situation.*

- In what condition is Erik Weihenmayer when he first arrives at Camp 1? Why? (lines 4–10)
- How do the other climbers react when they first see Erik? (lines 11–12)
- How does the group's leader feel about Erik being on the expedition? (lines 12–14)

**FOR ADVANCED LEARNERS/PRE–AP**
**Expert Groups** Allow students to become experts or members of expert groups by researching and choosing a way to share additional information about one of these topics:

- geographical facts about the Himalayas
- attempts to conquer Mount Everest
- facilities and activities for the blind in your community

banal (bə-năl') *adj.* commonplace; trite

30 Erik, as he stumbled through the icefall, was so far out of his comfort zone that he began to speculate on which of those fates might await him. For a moment he flashed on all those clichés about what blind people are supposed to do—become piano tuners or pencil salesmen—and thought maybe they were stereotypes for good reason. Blind people certainly shouldn't be out here, wandering through an ever changing ice field, measuring the distance over a 1,000-foot-deep crevasse with climbing poles and then leaping, literally, over and into the unknown.

The blind thrive on patterns: stairs are all the same height, city blocks roughly the same length, curbs approximately the same depth. They learn to identify the patterns in their environment much more than the sighted 40 population do, and to rely on them to plot their way through the world.

But in the Khumbu Icefall, the trail through the Himalayan glacier is patternless, a diabolically cruel obstacle course for a blind person. It changes every year as the river of ice shifts, but it's always made up of treacherously crumbly stretches of ice, ladders roped together over wide crevasses, slightly narrower crevasses that must be jumped, huge seracs,[7] avalanches, and—most frustrating for a blind person, who naturally seeks to identify patterns in his terrain—a totally random icescape.

In the icefall there is no system, no repetition, no rhyme or reason to the lay of the frozen land. On the other hand, "it is so specific in terms of where 50 you can step," Erik recalls. "Sometimes you're walking along and then boom, a crevasse is right there, and three more steps and another one, and then a snow bridge. And vertical up, then a ladder and then a jumbly section." It took Erik thirteen hours to make it from Base Camp through the icefall to Camp 1, at 20,000 feet. Scaturro had allotted seven.

A typical assault on Everest requires each climber to do as many as ten traverses through the icefall, both for **acclimatization** purposes and to help carry the immense amount of equipment required for an ascent. After Erik's accident, the rest of the National Federation of the Blind (NFB) team discussed letting him stay up in Camp 1, equipped with videotapes and food, while the rest of the team and 60 the Sherpas[8] did his carries for him. No way, said Erik. No way was he going to do this climb without being a fully integrated and useful member of the team. "I wasn't going to be carried to the top and spiked like a football," he says. The next day he forced himself to head back down through the icefall. He would eventually make ten passes through the Khumbu, cutting his time to five hours. **B**

② **Targeted Passage**

acclimatization (ə-klī'mə-tǐ-zā'shən) *n.* the act of getting accustomed to a new climate or environment

**B** CHARACTER STUDY
Reread lines 55–64. What do you learn about Weihenmayer from his reaction to his teammates' idea?

---

6. **cerebral edema** (sĕr'ə-brəl ǐ-dē'mə).
7. **seracs** (sə-răks'): large, pointed masses of ice isolated by intersecting crevasses.
8. **Sherpas**: a Himalayan people who live around the Nepal-Tibet border and often assist climbers of Everest.

272    UNIT 2: CHARACTERIZATION AND POINT OF VIEW

---

## TIERED DISCUSSION PROMPTS

Direct students to lines 29–54. Use these prompts to help students understand the challenges that a blind climber faces:

**Connect** Have you ever felt that you were out of your "comfort zone"? How does that memory help you understand Erik in these paragraphs? *Responses should reflect an understanding of Erik's uncertainty.*

**Analyze** What evidence does Greenfeld give to explain why the icefall terrain is so much more dangerous for Weihenmayer than for a sighted person? *Possible answer: "The blind thrive on patterns . . ." (lines 37–40), but "the trail through the Himalayan glacier is patternless . . ." (lines 41–49).*

**Evaluate** What is your opinion of Erik Weihenmayer up to this point? Defend your answer. *Opinions will vary but should be supported with solid reasons and information from the article.*

**B** **CHARACTER STUDY**

*Possible answer: Weihenmayer is tough and determined. He insists upon carrying his own weight rather than letting the rest of the team shoulder his load. He also cuts his time down to five hours (line 64) from the initial thirteen (line 53).*

**Extend the Discussion** Why is the comparison of being "carried to the top and spiked like a football" (line 62) an effective way to show Weihenmayer's reaction?

**OWN THE WORD**

- **banal:** Tell students that *banal* activities are normal, everyday ones like brushing your teeth, combing your hair, tying your shoes. Then have students name other *banal* activities and explain why they are *banal*.

- **acclimatization:** Review the definition with students, and then have them name instances when they had to *acclimate*. *Possible answers: when they attended a new school, moved to a new city, or travelled to a different region with different customs*

---

## DIFFERENTIATED INSTRUCTION

**FOR STRUGGLING READERS**

② **Targeted Passage [Lines 41–64]**
This largely descriptive passage reveals some dangerous climbing conditions—and Erik's refusal of special treatment.

- What makes the Khumbu Icefall dangerous? (line 41)

- Why are icefalls especially difficult for a blind person? (lines 42–47)

- What offer do his teammates make? Why does Erik turn them down? (lines 58–61)

**FOR ENGLISH LANGUAGE LEARNERS**

**Vocabulary: Word Associations** Explain these word associations, or "word chunks," as you come across them in the reading:

- *get waylaid* (line 24), "be stopped"

- *diabolically cruel* (line 42), "extremely difficult"

- *circus-freak variety* (line 111), "very strange type"

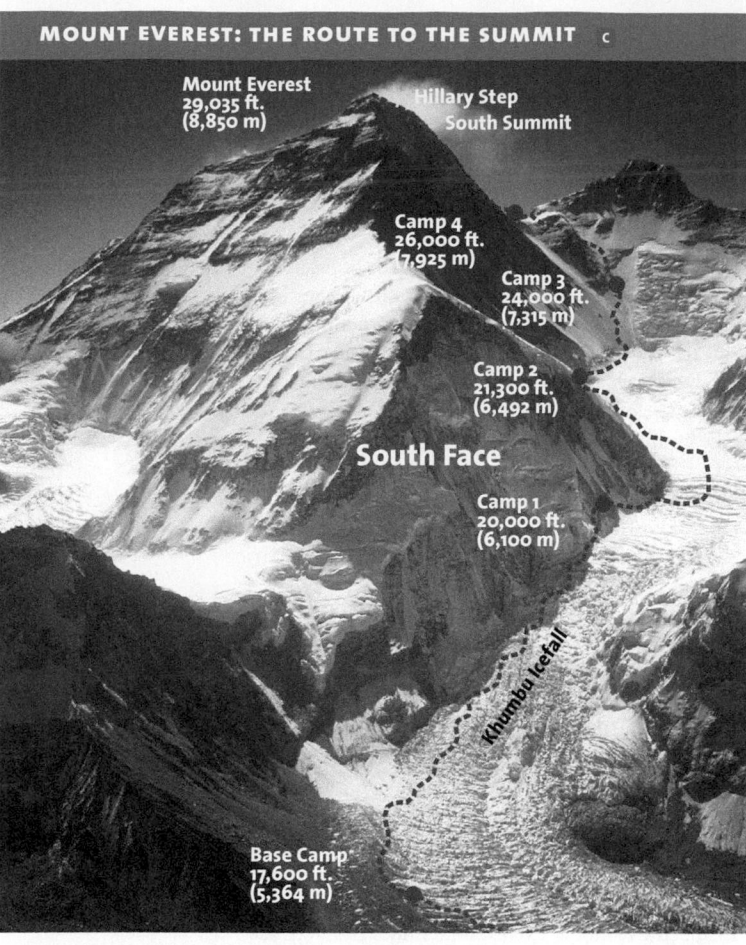

**MOUNT EVEREST: THE ROUTE TO THE SUMMIT**  C

- Mount Everest 29,035 ft. (8,850 m)
- Hillary Step
- South Summit
- Camp 4 26,000 ft. (7,925 m)
- Camp 3 24,000 ft. (7,315 m)
- Camp 2 21,300 ft. (6,492 m)
- **South Face**
- Camp 1 20,000 ft. (6,100 m)
- Khumbu Icefall
- Base Camp 17,600 ft. (5,364 m)

**C INTERPRET GRAPHIC AIDS**
What information about Camp 1 do you learn from this **diagram**? Record the information in your chart.

**C** *Model the Skill:* **INTERPRET GRAPHIC AIDS**

Model for students how to record this information on the chart that they began on page 269.

***Camp or Location:*** Camp 1

***Elevation:*** 20,000 feet

***Related Events/Details of Climb:*** Ascent from Camp 1 to Camp 2 is indirect.

***Other Information:*** On the South Face, above Khumbu Icefall; 2,400 feet above Base Camp; 1,300 feet below Camp 2

***Possible answer:*** *Camp 1 is located on the South Face of Mount Everest, above the Khumbu Icefall. The elevation of Camp 1 is 20,000 feet, placing it more than 2,000 feet above Base Camp. The ascent to Camp 2 (1,300 feet higher) is indirect.*

Sometimes, when Erik is giving a motivational speech for one of his corporate clients . . . a fat, balding, middle-aged middle manager will approach him and say, "Even I wouldn't do that stuff." Erik calls it the Even I Syndrome. And he has to resist an impulse to say, "You're fat, out of shape, and you smoke. Why would you even think of doing any of this stuff? Just because you
70 can see?" Erik is not impatient or smug, but he tires of people assuming that sight will trump all other attributes and senses combined.

By all accounts, Erik is gifted with strong lungs, a refined sense of balance, a disproportionately powerful upper body, rubbery legs, and flexible ankles. His conditioning is exemplary and his heart rate low. He is stockier than most mountaineers, who tend toward lanky, long muscles. But he possesses an

**REVISIT THE BIG QUESTION**
When is **STRENGTH** more than muscle?

**Discuss** In lines 65–71, how does Erik's encounter with someone who has the "Even I Syndrome" help show what **bravery** is—and is not? ***Possible answer:*** *It is a reminder that bravery is not just a matter of physical vision; although there is a physical factor, attitude plays a major role.*

**FOR STRUGGLING READERS**
**Develop Reading Fluency** When reading aloud, emphasize transitions to help listeners understand sequence of events. Model this by reading aloud lines 65–71, emphasizing the phrase *Sometimes, when . . . .* Point out that the article has focused on past events but that the phrase signals Erik's life in the present. Distribute the copy master and have students work in groups to practice fluency.

**R** **RESOURCE MANAGER—Copy Master**
Reading Fluency p. 114

**FOR ADVANCED LEARNERS/PRE–AP**
**Evaluate Assumptions** [small-group option] Greenfeld writes that Weihenmayer "tires of people assuming that sight will trump all other attributes and senses combined" (lines 70–71).

Ask students what other assumptions they think able-bodied people make about people with physical disabilities. Have them prepare a response and then present and defend it in class.

abundance of the one indispensable characteristic of a great mountaineer: mental toughness, the ability to withstand tremendous amounts of cold, discomfort, physical pain, boredom, bad food, insomnia, and tedious conversation when you're snowed into a pup tent for a week on a three-foot-
80 wide ice shelf at 20,000 feet. (That happened to Erik on Alaska's Denali.[9]) On Everest, toughness is perhaps the most important trait a climber can have. "Erik is mentally one of the strongest guys you will ever meet," says fellow climber Chris Morris.

Everybody gets sick on Everest. It's called the Khumbu Krud, brought on by a combination of high altitude, dirty food, fetid water, intestinal parasites, and an utterly alien ecosystem. On Erik's team, at any given moment, half the climbers were running fevers, the others were nauseated, and they all suffered from one form or another of dysentery, an awkward ailment when there's a driving snowstorm and it's thirty below outside the tent. . . .

90 Scaling Everest requires the enthusiasm and boosterism of a physical-education teacher combined with the survival instinct of a Green Beret.[10] You have to want that summit. And if you whine . . . your teammates might discard you before you get there. Erik, beneath his beard and quiet **demeanor,** was both booster and killer. "He was the heart and soul of our team," says Eric Alexander. "The guy's spirit won't let you quit."

**E**rik walks through these Kathmandu[11] streets with remarkable ease, his red-tipped cane searching out ahead of him, measuring distance, pitch, and angle. You give him little hints as he goes—"There's a doorway. Okay, now a right—no, left, sorry"—and he follows, his stride confident but easily arrested
100 when he bumps into an old lady selling shawls, and then into the wheel of a scooter. The physical confidence that he projects has to do with having an athlete's awareness of how his body moves through space. Plenty of sighted people walk through life with less poise and grace than Erik, unsure of their steps, second-guessing every move. And certainly most of the blind don't maneuver with Erik's **aplomb.** As he takes a seat in a crowded restaurant, ordering pizza, spaghetti, ice cream . . . —you work up an appetite climbing Everest—he smiles and nods as other diners ask, "Hey, aren't you the blind guy . . . ?"

With his Germanic, sculpted features and light brown hair, Erik looks a bit like a shaggy, youthful Kirk Douglas. He is a celebrity now: strangers ask for
110 his autograph, reporters call constantly, restaurants give him free meals. But is his celebrity the circus-freak variety—of a type with the Dogboy and the two-headed snake?

At its worst, Erik fears, it is. Casual observers don't understand what an achievement his Everest climb was, or they assume that if a blind guy can do it, anyone can. And indeed, improved gear has made Everest, at least in some

---

9. **Denali** (də-nä'lē): the highest peak in North America, also known as Mount McKinley.
10. **Green Beret:** a member of the U.S. Army Special Forces.
11. **Kathmandu** (kăt'măn-dōō'): the capital of Nepal.

**274** UNIT 2: CHARACTERIZATION AND POINT OF VIEW

---

**demeanor** (dĭ-mē'nər) *n.* a way of behaving; manner

 **CHARACTER STUDY**
Think about how your perception of Weihenmayer would be different if his teammates' descriptions of him were omitted. Why did the writer include these personal opinions in the article?

**aplomb** (ə-plŏm') *n.* poise; self-assurance

---

**D** *Model the Skill:* **CHARACTER STUDY**

Point out the description of the characteristics needed for climbers to do well when climbing in lines 76–81. Explain that this leads to Morris and Alexander's descriptions of Weihenmayer by letting readers know of the extreme conditions climbers face, and how most people fare when they climb the mountain. If this information was not present, it would be hard to put what Weihenmayer's teammates say about him in perspective.

*Possible answer: Without the descriptions, our judgment of Weihenmayer's character would be based only on what Greenfeld, an outside observer, says about him. The teammates' comments support what Greenfeld says about Weihenmayer being mentally and emotionally strong. They also strengthen the positive impression that Greenfeld has been crafting.*

---

**OWN THE WORD**

- **demeanor:** Have students reread the paragraph and list words or phrases that relate to an individual's *demeanor*. *Possible answers: enthusiasm, boosterism, survival instinct, whine, quiet*

- **aplomb:** Ask students to list ways that Erik acts with *aplomb*. *Possible answers: mountain climbs with confidence, did not give up when injured, walks with remarkable ease, has physical confidence, orders and eats many kinds of foods with ease*

---

**DIFFERENTIATED INSTRUCTION**

**FOR ENGLISH LANGUAGE LEARNERS**
**Vocabulary: Idioms** Use New Word Analysis to teach these idioms from this story: *work up an appetite* (line 106), "become hungry"; *work his way close to* (line 141), "move gradually toward"; *pass themselves off* (line 159), "present themselves to others (in a false way)"; *pick up* and *go for* (line 171), "meet" and "are attracted to"; *work against* and *took to it* (line 184), "hinder" and "became good at it"; *socking away* (line 254), "storing."

 **BEST PRACTICES TOOLKIT—Transparency**
New Word Analysis p. E8

---

people's minds, a bit smaller. In the climbing season there's a conga line[12] to the top, or so it seems, and the trail is a junkyard of discarded oxygen tanks and other debris. But Everest eats the unready and the unlucky. Almost 90 percent of Everest climbers fail to reach the summit. Many—at least 165 since 120 1953—never come home at all, their bodies lying uncollected where they fell. Four died in May. "People think because I'm blind, I don't have as much to be afraid of, like if I can't see a 2,000-foot drop-off I won't be scared," Erik says. "That's insane. Look, death is death, if I can see or not."

Everest expeditions break down into two types: those like Erik's, which are sponsored and united by a common goal, and those like the one described by Jon Krakauer in *Into Thin Air*,[13] in which gangs of climbers pay $65,000 each for the opportunity to stand on top of the world. But as conditions become more **arduous,** these commercial teams start squabbling, blaming weaker members for slowing them down and sometimes even refusing to help 130 teammates in distress.

Many pros wouldn't go near Erik's team, fearing they might have to haul the blind guy down. "Everyone was saying Erik was gonna have an epic," says Charley Mace, a member of the film crew. ("Epic" is Everest slang for disaster.) Another climber planned to stay close, boasting that he would "get the first picture of the dead blind guy."

For Erik, who knew almost as soon as he could speak that he would lose his vision in his early teens, excelling as an athlete was the result of accepting his disability rather than denying it. Growing up with two brothers in Hong Kong and then Weston, Connecticut, he was always an athletic kid, a tough gamer 140 who developed a bump-and-grind one-on-one basketball game that allowed him to work his way close to the hoop. He was, his father Ed says, "a pretty normal kid. While bike riding, he might have run into a few more parked cars than other kids, but we didn't dwell on his going blind."

His blindness was a medical **inevitability,** like a court date with a hanging judge.[14] "I saw blindness like this disease," he explains. "Like AIDS or something that was going to consume me." Think about that—being a kid, ten, eleven years old, and knowing that at some point in the near future your world is going to go dark. Certainly it builds character—that mental toughness his fellow climbers marvel at—but in a child, the natural psychological defense 150 would be denial. **E**

When he lost his vision, Erik at first refused to use a cane or learn Braille, insisting he could somehow muddle on as normal. "I was so afraid I would seem like a freak," he recalls. But after a few embarrassing stumbles—he couldn't even find the school rest rooms anymore—he admitted he needed help. For Erik, the key was acceptance—not to fight his disability but to learn to work within it; not to **transcend** it but to understand fully what he was

---

**arduous** (är'jōō-əs) *adj.* requiring much effort; difficult

**inevitability** (ĭn-ĕv'ĭ-tə-bĭl'ĭ-tē) *n.* something that is certain to happen

**E** **CONNECT**
Reread lines 136–150. Do you agree that denial would be the natural response to a situation like Weihenmayer's? Explain.

**transcend** (trăn-sĕnd') *v.* to pass beyond the limits of

---

12. **conga line:** The conga is a Latin American dance in which the dancers form a long, winding line.

13. ***Into Thin Air:*** a best-selling book about the 1996 climbing season at Mount Everest, during which eight climbers died.

14. **hanging judge:** a judge who always hands out very harsh sentences.

---

**TIERED DISCUSSION PROMPTS**
Direct students to lines 113–123. Use these prompts to help students appreciate the problem of underestimating Everest:

**Connect** Conquering Everest would make you a celebrity. Would that motivate you to climb? *Answers will vary but should recognize the difficulties involved in the attempt.*

**Apply** How might the statement that "Everest eats the unready and the unlucky" (line 118) affect a potential climber? *Possible answer: It might give him or her second thoughts.*

**READING STRATEGY:** *Review*

**E** **CONNECT**

*Possible answer:* **Agree:** *Because he lived for several years as a sighted person, young Erik probably felt some denial regarding his eventual loss of vision.* **Disagree:** *Some people may live in fear or prepare for the worst, knowing they will eventually lose their sight.*

**Extend the Discussion** Weihenmayer calls blindness "something that was going to consume [him]" (line 146). Do you think that he truly believed this as a child, or do these words express an adult's perspective?

**VOCABULARY**                     COMMON CORE
                                   L 4
**OWN THE WORD**

- **arduous:** Tell students that one synonym for *arduous* is *hard.* Then have students list other synonyms. *Possible answers: synonyms: difficult, laborious, tough, exhausting*

- **inevitability:** Remind students that the prefix *in-* means "not." Something that is *inevitable* cannot be avoided. Have students explain how a court date is *inevitable.* *Possible answer: If you are summoned, you must show up in court.*

- **transcend:** Tell students that the Latin word *trans* means "over" or "across." Have them explain the definition of *transcend* using the Latin *trans.*

---

**FOR ADVANCED LEARNERS/PRE–AP**
**Compare and Contrast** Lines 124–130 describe two types of Everest expeditions: those that are "united by a common goal" and those that are "commercial teams." Ask students to write an essay in which they contrast the two types of teams, making note of how words and details in the article (1) support the image of Erik's group as a unified team and (2) imply Greenfeld's disapproval of commercial teams.

**FOR ENGLISH LANGUAGE LEARNERS**
**Media and Concepts** To build and reinforce the concept of a character study, show students a documentary, such as one from the A&E *Biography* series. Have students derive meaning about the subject by noting his or her noteworthy actions, the reactions of others, and comments he or she has made about himself or herself. Then ask students to give their own impression of the subject and to explain what details from the biography contributed to their impression.

## When is **STRENGTH** more than muscle?

**Discuss** Based on lines 151–167, how did Weihenmayer show **bravery** in adjusting to his loss of vision? Cite evidence to support your answer. *Possible answer: He found the inner strength to accept his situation and to explore alternate avenues of achievement (lines 155–158). For example, he found that wrestling was a sport "where feel and touch mattered more than sight" (lines 163–164), and he was able to excel in it.*

---

**TEXT ANALYSIS**

COMMON CORE

RI 3

### **F** CHARACTER STUDY

*Possible answer: Weihenmayer's words show that he's basically "just like most guys" (line 175). Some students may suggest that Weihenmayer's comments about using his blindness to meet women (line 171) and devising a secret handshake to alert him to attractive women (lines 173–174) lower their opinion of him.*

---

**VOCABULARY**

COMMON CORE

L 4

### **OWN THE WORD**

**paramount:** Have students explain why senses of hearing and touch become *paramount* for someone who has lost the sense of sight. *Possible answer: Individuals must rely more heavily on the remaining senses when one sense is lost.*

---

capable of achieving within it; not to pretend he had sight but to build systems that allowed him to excel without it. "It's tragic—I know blind people who like to pass themselves off as being able to see," Erik says. 160 "What's the point of that?"

He would never play basketball or catch a football again. But then he discovered wrestling. "I realized I could take sighted people and slam them into the mat," he says. Grappling was a sport where feel and touch mattered more than sight: if he could sense where his opponent had his weight or how to shift his own body to gain better leverage, he could excel using his natural upper-body strength. As a high school senior he went all the way to the National Junior Freestyle Wrestling Championship in Iowa.

Wrestling gave him the confidence to reenter the teenage social fray. He began dating when he was seventeen; his first girlfriend was a sighted 170 woman three years older than he. Erik jokes that he is not shy about using his blindness to pick up women. "They really go for the guide dog," he explains. "You go into a bar, put the guide dog out there, and the girls just come up to you." He and his friends devised a secret handshake to let Erik know if the girl he was talking to was attractive. "Just because you're blind doesn't make you any more selfless or deep or anything. You're just like most guys, but you look for different things," Erik says. . . . And the voice becomes **paramount**. "My wife has the most beautiful voice in the world," Erik says. Married in 1997, he and his wife Ellie have a one-year-old daughter, Emma. **F**

Erik first went hiking with his father when he was thirteen, trying to tap his 180 way into the wild with a white cane and quickly becoming frustrated stubbing his toes on rocks and roots and bumping into branches and trunks. But when he tried rock climbing, at sixteen while at a camp for the disabled in New Hampshire, he was hooked. Like wrestling, it was a sport in which being blind didn't have to work against him. He took to it quickly, and through climbing gradually found his way to formal mountaineering.

Watching Erik scramble up a rock face is a little like watching a spider make its way up a wall. His hands are like antennae, gathering information as they flick outward, surveying the rock for cracks, grooves, bowls, nubbins, knobs, edges, and ledges, converting all of it into a road map etched into his 190 mind. "It's like instead of wrestling with a person, I am moving and working with a rock," he explains. "It's a beautiful process of solving a puzzle." He is an accomplished rock climber, rated 5.10 (5.14 being the highest), and has led teams up sections of Yosemite's notorious El Capitan.[15] On ice, where one wrong strike with an ice ax can bring down an avalanche, Erik has learned to listen to the ice as he pings it gently with his ax. If it clinks, he avoids it. If it makes a thunk like a spoon hitting butter, he knows it's solid ice.

**paramount**
(păr′ə-mount′) *adj.* of highest importance

**F** CHARACTER STUDY
Reread lines 168–178, and think about Weihenmayer's **traits**. How do his own words affect your opinion of him?

---

15. **Yosemite's** (yō-sĕm′ĭ-tēz) **notorious El Capitan:** a 3,604-foot granite peak with a sheer cliff face, in Yosemite National Park, California.

**276** UNIT 2: CHARACTERIZATION AND POINT OF VIEW

---

## DIFFERENTIATED INSTRUCTION

**FOR ADVANCED LEARNERS/PRE–AP**
**Evaluate Figurative Language** Have students reread the last paragraph on this page, then identify as many similes and metaphors in the paragraph as they can, and express an opinion about which are the most effective and least effective. Invite students to compare their responses.

Despite being an accomplished mountaineer—summiting Denali, Kilimanjaro in Africa, and Aconcagua[16] in Argentina, among other peaks, and, in the words of his friends, "running up 14ers" (14,000-foot peaks)—Erik viewed Everest as
200 **insurmountable** until he ran into Scaturro at a sportswear trade show in Salt Lake City, Utah. Scaturro, who had already summited Everest, had heard of the blind climber, and when they met the two struck an easy rapport. A geophysicist who often put together energy-company expeditions to remote areas in search of petroleum, Scaturro began wondering if he could put together a team that could help Erik get to the summit of Everest.

"Dude," Scaturro asked, "have you ever climbed Everest?"

"No."

"Dude, you wanna?"

210 Climbing with Erik isn't that different from climbing with a sighted mountaineer. You wear a bell on your pack, and he follows the sound, scuttling along using his custom-made climbing poles to feel his way along the trail. His climbing partners shout out helpful descriptions: "Death fall two feet to your right!" "Emergency helicopter-evacuation pad to your left!" He is fast, often running up the back of less experienced climbers. His partners all have scars from being jabbed by Erik's climbing poles when they slowed down.

For the Everest climb, Scaturro and Erik assembled a team that combined veteran Everest climbers and trusted friends of Erik's. Scaturro wrote up a Braille proposal for the Everest attempt and submitted it to Marc Maurer, president of
220 the National Federation of the Blind. Maurer immediately pledged $250,000 to sponsor the climb. . . . For Erik, who already had numerous gear and clothing sponsors, this was the greatest challenge of his life. If he failed, he would be letting down not just himself but all the blind, confirming that certain activities remained the preserve of the sighted.

He argued to anyone who would listen that he was an experienced mountaineer and that if he failed, it would be because of his heart or lungs or brain rather than his eyes. He wasn't afraid of physical danger—he had made dozens
230 of skydives and scaled some of the most dangerous cliff faces in the world—but he was frightened of how the world would perceive him. "But I knew that if I went and failed, that would feel better than if I didn't go at all," Erik says. "It could be like [the wrestling] Junior Nationals all over again. I went out to Iowa, and I got killed. But I needed to go to understand what my limits were."

---

16. **Kilimanjaro** (kĭl′ə-mən-jär′ō) ... **Aconcagua** (äk′ən-kä′gwə): the highest peaks in Africa and South America, respectively.

**insurmountable**
(ĭn′sər-moun′tə-bəl) *adj.* impossible to overcome

▼ **Analyze Visuals**

How does this photograph, which shows Weihenmayer and his teammates clambering over one of Everest's many crevasses, contribute to your understanding of Weihenmayer?

③ **Targeted Passage**

---

## Analyze Visuals

*Possible answer: The photograph helps readers visualize and appreciate the extraordinary effort required for a blind climber to ascend the mountain's icy, uneven terrain.*

### TIERED DISCUSSION PROMPTS

Direct students to lines 216–236. Use these prompts to help students understand why it was so important to Weihenmayer to succeed:

**Connect** What were the risks of attempting the Everest climb? Do you think you would try it? *Responses should reflect an understanding of the risks in the attempt.*

**Analyze** Why did Erik consider the Everest climb his greatest challenge (line 223)? *Possible answer: In climbing Mount Everest, Erik felt he was representing all blind people. He feared that his failure would confirm the belief that blind people should be restricted from certain activities.*

**Evaluate** Do you think that Weihenmayer put unrealistic pressure on himself? Explain your answer. *Possible answer: Perhaps he did; lines 223–225 and 231–232 indicate that he felt responsible for the way the world thought of all blind people.*

**VOCABULARY**          COMMON CORE
                              L 4

### OWN THE WORD

**insurmountable:** Remind students that the prefix *in-* means "not." Then have them list challenges that they have faced that they thought would be *insurmountable.* Were they, or did students find ways to meet the challenges? If so, how they did they overcome, or *surmount*, obstacles that stood in the way of success?

---

### FOR STRUGGLING READERS

③ **Targeted Passage [Lines 209–225]**

This passage emphasizes some practical and emotional factors involved in Erik's climb.

- How do bells and shouts help guide Erik during a climb? (lines 210–215)

- How and why did the National Federation of the Blind get involved in this climb? (lines 218–221)

- How did Erik feel about failing? What did he think failure would prove? (lines 223–225)

### FOR ENGLISH LANGUAGE LEARNERS

**Culture: Clarify** Some students may not be familiar with the role that sponsors (lines 218–221) play in various activities. Explain that members of this expedition did not have to pay all of the costs of the climb because they were "sponsored" or supported financially by the National Federation of the Blind.

 **INTERPRET GRAPHIC AIDS**

**Possible answer:** *Camp 4; perhaps Camp 3 as well*

**IF STUDENTS NEED HELP . . .** Have them reread lines 239–241 and then review the diagram to determine which camps are above or close to 25,000 feet.

READING SKILL      COMMON CORE   SL 2

 **INTERPRET GRAPHIC AIDS**

**Possible answer:** *We know that the unlabeled features must be above Camp 4 (line 251) but below the summit. We also know that they are reached via the South Face (line 264) and that the Southeast Ridge begins at 27,500 feet (line 264), whereas the diagram shows the summit to be at 29,035 feet. We know, too, that the Southeast Ridge leads up to the South Summit (lines 271–273).*

**REVISIT THE BIG QUESTION**

## When is **STRENGTH** more than muscle?

**Discuss** In lines 242–245, what does the statement "At that altitude, Erik could rely on no one but himself" say about Erik's **bravery**? Explain. *Possible answer: It says that he must be very brave. He has undertaken the ascent even though he knows that his teammates will not always be able to help him.*

---

Oxygen deprivation does strange things to the human body. Heart rates go haywire, brain function decreases, blood thickens, intestines shut down. Bad ideas inexplicably pop into your head, especially above 25,000 feet, where, 240 as Krakauer famously wrote in *Into Thin Air*, climbers have the "mind of a reptile." **G**

At that altitude, Erik could rely on no one but himself. His teammates would have to guide him, to keep ringing the bell and making sure Erik stayed on the trail, but they would be primarily concerned about their own survival in some of the worst conditions on earth. Ironically, Erik had some advantages as they closed in on the peak. For one thing, at that altitude all the climbers wore goggles and oxygen masks, restricting their vision so severely that they could not see their own feet—a condition Erik was used to. Also, the final push for the summit began in the early evening, so most of the climb was in pitch 250 darkness; the only illumination was from miner's lamps.

When Erik and the team began the final ascent from Camp 4—the camp **H** he describes as Dante's Inferno with ice and wind[17]—they had been on the mountain for two months, climbing up and down and then up from Base Camp to Camps 1, 2, and 3, getting used to the altitude and socking away enough equipment—especially oxygen canisters—to make a summit push. They had tried for the summit once but had turned back because of weather. At 29,000 feet, the Everest peak is in the jet stream, which means that winds can exceed one hundred miles per hour and that what looks from sea level like a cottony wisp of cloud is actually a killer storm at the summit. Bad weather 260 played a fatal role in the 1996 climbing season documented in *Into Thin Air*.

On May 24, with only seven days left in the climbing season, most of the NFB expedition members knew this was their last shot at the peak. That's why when Erik and Chris Morris reached the Balcony,[18] the beginning of the Southeast Ridge, at 27,500 feet, after a hard slog up the South Face,[19] they were terribly disappointed when the sky lit up with lightning, driving snow, and fierce winds. "We thought we were done," Erik says. "We would have been spanked if we made a push in those conditions." A few teammates gambled and went for it, and Jeff Evans and Brad Bull heroically pulled out fixed guidelines that had been frozen in the ice. By the time Base Camp radioed that 270 the storm was passing, Erik and the entire team were coated in two inches of snow. Inspired by the possibility of a break in the weather, the team pushed on up the exposed Southeast Ridge, an additional 1,200 vertical feet to the South Summit.[20] At that point the climbers looked like astronauts walking on some kind of Arctic moon. They moved slowly because of fatigue from their huge, puffy down suits, backpacks with oxygen canisters and regulators, and goggles.

---

17. **Camp 4 . . . ice and wind:** Camp 4, at 26,000 feet, is compared to the hell described in the *Inferno*, the first part of Dante Alighieri's long poem *The Divine Comedy*.
18. **Balcony:** a natural platform where climbers often stop to rest.
19. **South Face:** the whole side of Everest on which Erik's group climbed to get to the summit.
20. **South Summit:** a peak several hundred feet below the true summit of Everest.

**G** INTERPRET GRAPHIC AIDS
Turn back to the **diagram** on page 273. In which camp or camps would the climbers have been subject to oxygen deprivation if they had run out of supplemental oxygen?

**H** INTERPRET GRAPHIC AIDS
As you read about the group's push for the summit, use the **diagram** on page 273 to follow the climbers' progress after they left Camp 4. How can you **infer** the locations of unlabeled features, such as the Balcony and the Southeast Ridge?

With a 10,000-foot vertical fall into Tibet on one side and a 7,000-foot fall into Nepal on the other, the South Summit, at 28,750 feet, is where many climbers finally turn back. The 656-foot-long knife-edge ridge leading to the Hillary Step[21] consists of ice, snow, and fragmented shale, and the only way to
280 cross it is to take baby steps and anchor your way with an ice ax. "You can feel the rock chip off," says Erik. "And you can hear it falling down into the void."

The weather was finally clearing as they reached the Hillary Step, the 39-foot rock face that is the last major obstacle before the true summit. Erik clambered up the cliff, belly-flopping over the top. "I celebrated with the dry heaves," he jokes. And then it was forty-five minutes of walking up a sharply angled snow slope to the summit.

"Look around, dude," Evans told the blind man when they were standing on top of the world. "Just take a second and look around."

I t could be called the most successful Everest expedition ever, and not just
290 because of Erik's participation. A record nineteen climbers from the NFB team summited, including the oldest man ever to climb Everest—sixty-four-year-old Sherman Bull—and the second father-and-son team ever to do so—Bull and his son Brad.

What Erik achieved is hard for a sighted person to comprehend. What do we compare it with? How do we relate to it? Do we put on a blindfold and go hiking? That's silly, Erik maintains, because when a sighted person loses his vision, he is terrified and disoriented. And Erik is clearly neither of those things. Perhaps the point is really that there is no way to put what Erik has done in perspective because no one has ever done anything like it. It is a unique achievement, one
300 that in the truest sense pushed the limits of what man is capable of. Maurer of the NFB compares Erik to Helen Keller. "Erik can be a contemporary symbol for blindness," he explains. "Helen Keller lived one hundred years ago. She should not be our most potent symbol for blindness today." 🄸

Erik, sitting in the Kathmandu international airport, waiting for the flight out of Nepal that will eventually return him to Golden, Colorado, is surrounded by his teammates and the expedition's seventy-five pieces of luggage. Success has made the group jubilant. This airport lounge has become the mountaineering equivalent of a winning Super Bowl locker room. . . .

In between posing for photos and signing other passengers' boarding passes,
310 Erik talks about how eager he is to get back home. He says summiting Everest was great, probably the greatest experience of his life. But then he thinks about a moment a few months ago, before Everest, when he was walking down the street in Colorado with daughter Emma in a front pack. They were on their way to buy some banana bread for his wife, and Emma was pulling on his hand, her little fingers curled around his index finger. That was a summit, too, he says. There are summits everywhere. You just have to know where to look. ❧

---

21. **Hillary Step:** a spur named for Sir Edmund Hillary, who, with the Sherpa Tenzing Norgay, was the first successful climber of Everest.

COMMON CORE RI 4

**Language Coach**

**Antonyms** An **antonym** is a word that means the opposite of another word. Reread lines 276–278. Which word in this sentence is an antonym for *horizontal*, which means "parallel to the horizon"?

🄸 **DRAW CONCLUSIONS**
What value might Maurer's idea have?

④ **Targeted Passage**

---

**READING SKILL:** *Review*

🄸 **DRAW CONCLUSIONS**

*Possible answer: Erik, like Helen Keller, would show the world that blind people can take part in activities that sighted people enjoy. However, he would make the point for today's world, not just the world of a century ago.*

**SELECTION WRAP–UP**

**READ WITH A PURPOSE** Point out that Green-feld notes that Weihenmayer "is a celebrity now" (line 109). Ask students whether they think that Weihenmayer has earned celebrity status. Do they think that he wants to be treated as a celebrity? *Possible answer: Students may say that Weihenmayer has earned celebrity status due to his efforts. However, he doesn't want to be treated as a celebrity if people view him as a circus-freak.*

⭐ **CRITIQUE** On a scale of 1 to 5, how did you enjoy reading this story? What advantages, if any, does a nonfiction article like this have over fiction?

**INDEPENDENT READING**
Students may want to read the autobiography *There's Always a Way* by Kevin Saunders. He served on the President's Council on Physical Fitness.

---

## DIFFERENTIATED INSTRUCTION

### FOR STRUGGLING READERS

④ **Targeted Passage** [Lines 297–316]
This concluding passage celebrates Erik's achievement and puts it in the context of his everyday life.

- To whom does Marc Maurer compare Erik Weihenmayer, and why? (line 301)
- Why does Greenfeld compare the climbers to Super Bowl winners? (line 308)
- What happened to Erik at home, before Everest? Why is that scene important? (lines 312–315)

### FOR ENGLISH LANGUAGE LEARNERS

**Language Coach**   COMMON CORE RI 4

**Antonyms** *Answer: vertical*

Ask students to brainstorm examples of items that are horizontal (*horizon, desert, bed*) and items that are vertical (*elevator, skyscraper, rocket*).

# Practice and Apply

For preliminary support of post-reading questions, use these copy masters:

**R** **RESOURCE MANAGER—Copy Masters**
Reading Check p. 112
Character Study p. 105
Question Support p. 113

Additional selection questions are provided for teachers on page 99.

## ANSWERS

## Comprehension

1. *He wanted to be the first blind person to climb Mount Everest and show that such a feat is not restricted to sighted people.*

2. *He did accomplish his goal, for he reached the summit of Mount Everest despite the difficulties of the climb.*

3. ***Advantages:*** *not hampered by lack of visibility, highly sensitive to sound;* ***Disadvantages:*** *unable to see terrain or gauge distance*

## Text Analysis

COMMON CORE RI 3, SL 2

*Possible answers:*

4. ● **COMMON CORE FOCUS** *Analysis Character Study*
***Courage:*** *lines 229–231, 242–245;*
***Determination:*** *lines 60–64, 276–286;*
***Inner strength:*** *lines 75–80, 90–95*

5. *Textual evidence can support either view.* ***Internal struggle:*** *lines 29–36, 223–225, 229–233;* ***External struggle:*** *lines 19–28, 41–47, 199–200*

6. *His presence may have inspired the others. In the words of one teammate, he was "the heart and soul" of the team (line 94).*

7. ■ **COMMON CORE FOCUS** *Evaluate Graphic Aids In conjunction with the chart, the diagram helps readers visualize the challenge and the danger in the ascent. It might have been even more helpful if it had included callouts indicating how long the climbers took to advance from point to point.*

## Text Criticism

*Possible answer:*

8. *She probably would have praised him for having the courage to attempt what no other blind person had done before.*

---

## Comprehension

1. **Recall** What was Erik Weihenmayer's goal, and why did he take on that challenge?

2. **Recall** Did Weihenmayer reach his goal? Explain your response.

3. **Summarize** What were Weihenmayer's advantages and disadvantages in comparison with the sighted members of his expedition?

## Text Analysis

● 4. **Analyze a Character Study** In this character study, the writer describes events—and develops and shares his own ideas—that reveal Weihenmayer's outstanding traits. List three of those traits in a chart. For each, cite examples from the text.

| Outstanding Traits | Examples from Text |
|---|---|
| 1. | |
| 2. | |
| 3. | |

5. **Draw Conclusions** Think about the **conflicts** that Weihenmayer faced in "Blind to Failure." Which do you view as the main conflict—his internal struggle with his disability or his external struggle with the mountain? Support your conclusion with thorough evidence from the text.

6. **Analyze Cause and Effect** How might Weihenmayer's presence have contributed to the great success of the expedition, with 19 climbers reaching the summit? Cite strong evidence from the selection.

● 7. **Evaluate Graphic Aids** Review the chart you made as you read. How did the **diagram** help you understand this article? What other kinds of information, if any, would it have been useful to include in the graphic aid?

## Text Criticism

8. **Different Perspectives** Helen Keller once proclaimed, "No pessimist ever discovered the secret of the stars, or sailed to an uncharted land, or opened a new doorway for the human spirit." What might Keller say about Weihenmayer if she were alive today? Explain your answer.

### When is **STRENGTH** more than muscle?

How did Weihenmayer's feat reveal both internal and external strength?

**COMMON CORE**

**RI 3** Analyze how the author unfolds an analysis, including how points are introduced and developed and the connections that are drawn between them. **SL 2** Integrate multiple sources of information presented in diverse media or formats.

---

When is **STRENGTH** more than muscle? Weihenmayer's feat showed physical strength in climbing the mountain; the feat showed internal strength through perseverance and determination.

# Vocabulary in Context

## ▲ VOCABULARY PRACTICE

Identify the words in each pair as synonyms or antonyms.

1. acclimatization/adaptation
2. demeanor/appearance
3. inevitability/certainty
4. banal/unusual
5. paramount/insignificant
6. arduous/simple
7. transcend/exceed
8. insurmountable/impossible
9. aplomb/awkwardness
10. crevasse/summit

**WORD LIST**

acclimatization
aplomb
arduous
banal
crevasse
demeanor
inevitability
insurmountable
paramount
transcend

## ACADEMIC VOCABULARY IN WRITING

- complex • device • evaluate • interact • perspective

Climbing Mount Everest is difficult and **complex.** Write a paragraph explaining how being blind made the climb even more complex for Erik Weihenmayer. Identify at least three conditions that make the climb more complex, and use at least one Academic Vocabulary word in your response.

## VOCABULARY STRATEGY: SPECIALIZED VOCABULARY

Sports like mountaineering, as well as many occupations, have their own **specialized vocabularies.** A specialized vocabulary often includes words (like *crevasse*) that are used primarily within the particular field, as well as familiar words (like *face*) that are used with special meanings in the field. When familiar words have special meanings, it is often possible to figure out those meanings from the context. Otherwise, check a dictionary, looking for labels, such as *Mountaineering,* that may precede definitions giving special meanings of words.

**PRACTICE** Write the mountaineering term that matches each definition. If you need to, check a dictionary.

ascenders    chimney    crampons    face    saddle

1. devices attached to a rope to help one climb it
2. spiked iron plates on shoes to prevent slipping on ice
3. the sloping side of a mountain
4. a wide vertical crack into which the body of a climber can fit
5. a flat ridge connecting two higher elevations

**COMMON CORE**

**L 6** Acquire and use accurately general and domain-specific words; demonstrate independence in gathering vocabulary knowledge.

**Interactive Vocabulary** THINK central

Go to **thinkcentral.com.**
KEYWORD: HML9-281

BLIND TO FAILURE    **281**

---

## ANSWERS

# Vocabulary in Context

## ▲ VOCABULARY PRACTICE

| | |
|---|---|
| 1. *synonyms* | 6. *antonyms* |
| 2. *synonyms* | 7. *synonyms* |
| 3. *synonyms* | 8. *synonyms* |
| 4. *antonyms* | 9. *antonyms* |
| 5. *antonyms* | 10. *antonyms* |

**R** **RESOURCE MANAGER—Copy Master**
Vocabulary Practice p. 110

## ACADEMIC VOCABULARY IN WRITING

Any climb of Mount Everest is **complex,** but is more so for a person who is blind. Weihenmayer couldn't see the terrain ahead or his climbing team members. To **evaluate** Erik Weihenmayer's contributions to climbing, one must consider the complexity of his climb.

## VOCABULARY STRATEGY: SPECIALIZED VOCABULARY

**COMMON CORE L 6**

- Invite students explain specialized terms in areas such as sports or computers.
- Have students use context clues and logic to determine the meaning of the words.

**Answers:**

| | |
|---|---|
| 1. *ascenders* | 4. *chimney* |
| 2. *crampons* | 5. *saddle* |
| 3. *face* | |

**R** **RESOURCE MANAGER—Copy Master**
Vocabulary Strategy p. 111

**Interactive Vocabulary** THINK central

Keywords direct students to a **WordSharp** tutorial on **thinkcentral.com** or to other types of vocabulary practice and review.

# *Assess and Reteach*

## *Assess*

**DIAGNOSTIC AND SELECTION TESTS**
Selection Test A pp. 75–76
Selection Test B/C pp. 77-78

**Interactive Selection Test** on **thinkcentral.com**

## *Reteach*

**Level Up Online Tutorials** on **thinkcentral.com**

---

## DIFFERENTIATED INSTRUCTION

### FOR ENGLISH LANGUAGE LEARNERS

**Culture: Connect** To extend the Vocabulary Strategy discussion, invite students to share specialized vocabulary from their home language. For example, students might name terms relating to clothing, cuisine, arts and crafts, and sports. Interested students might create a bulletin board display on the basis of this discussion.

### FOR ADVANCED LEARNERS/PRE–AP

**Academic Vocabulary in Writing** Have students write their paragraphs as though Erik Weihenmayer were responding. Challenge students to use more than one vocabulary word in their paragraphs.

# Focus and Motivate

**RI 1** Cite strong and thorough textual evidence to support analysis of what the text says explicitly as well as inferences drawn from the text.
**RI 2** Determine a central idea of a text and analyze its development. **RI 5** Analyze in detail how an author's ideas are developed and refined by portions of a text. **RI 6** Determine an author's purpose in a text. **W 9b (RI 1)** Draw evidence from informational texts; cite strong and thorough textual evidence to support analysis of what the text says explicitly as well as inferences drawn from the text.

## SUMMARY

This article focuses on athletes with disabilities. It makes the point that these athletes are not any different from athletes without disabilities.

## What's the Connection?

Use an Anticipation Guide to prepare students for the selection. Write these statements on the transparency. Have students respond to each one before and after reading.

- Athletes with disabilities are less intense than athletes without disabilities.
- Athletes with disabilities can participate in most sports.

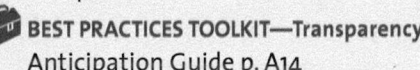 **BEST PRACTICES TOOLKIT—Transparency**
Anticipation Guide p. A14

# Teach

## Standards Focus: Identify Main Ideas
Guide students through the process of looking for key ideas. Explain that one clue to the key idea of a section, and ultimately to the main idea of the text, is information that is repeated or illustrated by examples. Use questions to guide students.

- What words identify the topic and tell what this section is about?
- What idea about athletes with disabilities is most important? What examples support it?
- What point are these athletes making? How has playing sports influenced their lives?
- Is there one sentence that sums up the information in this section?
- What is the author's purpose for writing?

 **RESOURCE MANAGER—Copy Master**
Identify Main Ideas p. 123

---

## Reading for Information

# A Different Level of Competition
Newspaper Article

Use with "Blind to Failure," page 270.

**COMMON CORE**

**RI 1** Cite strong and thorough textual evidence to support analysis of what the text says explicitly as well as inferences drawn from the text.
**RI 2** Determine a central idea of a text and analyze its development. **RI 5** Analyze in detail how an author's ideas are developed and refined by portions of a text. **RI 6** Determine an author's purpose in a text.

## What's the Connection?

In "Blind to Failure" you read about Erik Weihenmayer, a mountaineer who successfully climbed Mount Everest despite having lost his vision as a teenager. Now, in "A Different Level of Competition," you will read about other intensely driven athletes who are taking the sports world by storm—despite their disabilities.

## Standards Focus: Identify Main Ideas

The **main idea**, or central idea, of a nonfiction text is the most important idea the text expresses about its topic. It may be stated explicitly in a sentence in the text, or it may be implied. The main idea is often suggested by smaller key ideas, each developed in a paragraph or a longer section of the work. These ideas, too, may be stated or implied. Distinguishing important details from less important ones will help you identify key ideas even when they are not directly stated. Furthermore, important details support, and can often help you determine, the author's **purpose**—the reason or reasons that an author writes a text.

In the following article, various key ideas are developed one at a time over the course of several paragraphs. Use a chart like the one shown to note these key ideas.

| Section | Key Idea |
|---|---|
| Title | "A Different Level of Competition" |
| Lead-in | Sports help people with disabilities. |
| Section 1 (paragraphs 1–5) | |
| Section 2 (paragraphs 6–9) | |
| Section 3 (paragraphs 10–16) | |
| Section 4 (paragraphs 17–20) | |
| Section 5 (paragraphs 21–24) | |

*Review:* **Predict**

---

## Selection Resources

*See resources on the* **Teacher One Stop DVD-ROM** *and on* <u>thinkcentral.com</u>.

 **RESOURCE MANAGER UNIT 2**
Lesson Support,* pp. 115–128

**DIAGNOSTIC AND SELECTION TESTS**
Selection Tests, pp. 79–82

**BEST PRACTICES TOOLKIT**
pp. A14, E8

**TECHNOLOGY**
- Teacher One Stop DVD-ROM
- Student One Stop DVD-ROM
- Audio Anthology CD
- ExamView Test Generator on the Teacher One Stop

\* Resources for Differentiation

# A Different Level of Competition

by Anne Stein

**Sports for people with disabilities offer chances to build body and spirit** Ⓐ

Here's a secret about young guys with disabilities who play team sports: They talk trash. And depending on the sport, they throw punches and crash into each other so hard that games can look like gladiator competitions.

In other words, a competitive athlete with a disability isn't any less intense than a competitive athlete without a

10 disability. Ⓑ

Take sled hockey, for example. A player balances on two ice-skating blades mounted beneath a molded plastic sled/seat. Sitting just inches above the ice, the athlete holds two small hockey sticks with metal teeth on one end to whip his body and sled around the rink; the other end is used for puck-handling. The stick is rotated to hit the puck.

20 "There are games that are rougher than others, but our team tries to focus more on the puck than the body," said Sylvester Flis, 27, a member of the 2002 U.S. Paralympic sled hockey team. Flis, who was born with spina bifida, lives in Chicago and practices with the RIC Blackhawks, sponsored by the Chicago Blackhawks and the Rehabilitation Institute of Chicago.

30 "We don't have big fights often, but there's lots of pushing and shoving. You've got to be very strong and athletic. You have to be in top shape to perform at the national level," Flis said.

Champion skier Sandy Dukat's lower leg was amputated when she was four.

But fighting and body checking aren't what draw people with disabilities to sports and competition. Besides the social aspects, there is an attitude of encouragement often lacking in able-

40 bodied athletics.

Matt Coppens, 30, of Richton Park lost both legs when a teenage driver ran into his car as Coppens set up roadside traffic cones.

Coppens wasn't much of an athlete before the accident. Now he trains full time and will join Flis on the sled hockey team. He also represented the United States at the 2000 Sydney Paralympics

50 in volleyball.

"There's so much camaraderie here," he said. "No matter what team you're on, you can't help but feel a closeness." Ⓒ

Whether it's competitive or recreational, sports serve an important role for people with disabilities, just as it does for the able-bodied.

"The benefits of participating in team sports have been studied a lot over the

60 years, especially in terms of what it does for youth and people without disabilities. [Team sports] does all the same things, and more, for people with disabilities,"

---

Ⓐ **PREDICT**
From the title and the lead-in, what do you think will be the main idea of this article?

Ⓑ **MAIN IDEA**
What key idea does Stein convey in her introduction?

Ⓒ **MAIN IDEA**
Identify the key idea introduced in this paragraph. How is the anecdote about Matt Coppens related to this idea?

---

# Practice and Apply

**READING STRATEGY:** *Review*

Ⓐ **PREDICT**

*Possible answer:* The main idea of this article probably will be that people with disabilities participate in competitive sports.

**INFORMATIONAL ANALYSIS**     COMMON CORE

Ⓑ **MAIN IDEA**

*Possible answer:* Athletes with disabilities compete as intensely as non-disabled athletes.

RI 1,
RI 2,
RI 5,
RI 6

**INFORMATIONAL ANALYSIS**     COMMON CORE

Ⓒ *Model the Skill:* **MAIN IDEA**

RI 1,
RI 2,
RI 5,
RI 6

Clarify that an anecdote is a brief story and *camaraderie* means "friendly fellowship." Then identify the anecdote and tell how Coppens felt about sports before and after his accident. The anecdote in lines 41–53 shows Coppens's dis-interest before the accident and his full involvement afterward due to the camaraderie.

*Possible answer:* Camaraderie is important among athletes with disabilities. Athletes with disabilities grow very close to their teammates, as Coppens learned while training for sled hockey.

**Extend the Discussion** Discuss why being a member of an elite sports team might be so important to a handicapped athlete.

---

## DIFFERENTIATED INSTRUCTION

### FOR ENGLISH LANGUAGE LEARNERS

**Options for Reading** [paired activity] To complete the chart on page 282, have students read each set of paragraphs independently and share their understanding with a partner. Then have them work together to identify the key idea and state it in a one-sentence summary.

**Media and Concepts** To build and reinforce the concept of main ideas, have students listen to a podcast from the Texana Review or another source. Direct students to derive meaning about the topic by noting the most important ideas. Remind students that the main idea might be stated directly or it might be implied by the smaller ideas, and that they can pause and review the podcast at any point to clarify meaning. Then ask students to share with the class the main ideas expressed in the podcast.

## BACKGROUND

**Sports Events for People with Disabilities** Like the more well-known Special Olympics, Paralympics are local, state, national, and international athletic competitions. While the Special Olympics are for athletes with a cognitive disability who have varying athletic abilities, Paralympic events are for athletes with any type of permanent physical disability. The Paralympic Games, which are held shortly after the Olympic Games, are international events in which only the highest level, or elite, athletes are chosen to compete.

## INFORMATIONAL ANALYSIS

COMMON CORE RI 2, RI 5, RI 6

**D MAIN IDEA**

**Possible answer:** *The key idea is that participating in team sports offers the same benefits—and more—for people with disabilities as it does for participants without disabilities. The writer may have written this article to change the way people perceive disabled athletes and their skills.*

**Extend the Discussion** Have students identify the main idea of "Blind to Failure." Ask them how the main ideas of the two selections are similar and different.

## INFORMATIONAL ANALYSIS

COMMON CORE RI 1, RI 2, RI 5, RI 6

**E MAIN IDEA**

**Possible answer:** *People should not be surprised that disabled people can be athletes. Rather, it should be accepted as common knowledge.*

---

said Jeff Jones, director of the Galvin Center for Health and Fitness at the Rehabilitation Institute of Chicago.

"Team sports teaches cooperation, sportsmanship, socialization and how to win and lose," Jones said. "It also
70 teaches people with disabilities to challenge themselves. There's a phrase that's kicked around a lot among people with disabilities: 'If I can do this, I can do anything.'"

Jones said sled hockey players are some of the most conditioned, fit people he knows. They just happen to have a disability.

"They get what everyone gets out of
80 team sports: a sense of accomplishment, enjoyment, satisfaction, conditioning and better health. And that makes everyday activities easier, just like it does for someone without a disability. They just don't happen to have as many opportunities as people without disabilities have to participate in sports," Jones said. "Our athletes are much more appreciative of the opportunities than
90 those without disabilities. They can't just quit one team and go to another. The opportunities are few and far between."

Jerri Voda, who was born with cerebral palsy, races sailboats each summer through the Chicago-based Judd Goldman Adaptive Sailing Program.

"It's absolutely boosted my self-esteem," she said. "It's truly exhilarating for anyone with physical disabilities to
100 participate in an activity that an able-bodied person can participate in. And the feeling of being out on the water driving a boat has totally heightened my independence and made me feel capable of achieving more in the future." **D**

Nearly every sport, recreational or competitive, can be adapted to the physical capabilities of participants.

Among the hundreds of sports available
110 are wheelchair basketball, football and tennis; quadriplegic rugby; water and snow-skiing for the blind and visually impaired; and chair-based aerobics.

There are track and field and swimming events for every category of amputee, as well as blind softball and competitions for people with cerebral palsy and head injury. There is even a fledgling soccer league worldwide played
120 by amputees on crutches.

Chicagoan Sandy Dukat, 29, is a member of the U.S. disabled ski team. Born without a femur, her leg was amputated at the knee at age 4, but the disability never stopped her from being a jock. Dukat competed against able-bodied kids in baseball, basketball and high jump, where she used one leg to clear a very competitive 4 feet, 11 inches.
130 Now Dukat's sport is alpine skiing, where she reaches speeds up to 50 m.p.h. perched on one ski and two poles with tiny ski-like attachments called outriggers. She didn't ski growing up in Ohio, but her fearlessness and speed caught the eye of coaches who encouraged her to train.

Though Dukat loves the thrill of sport, she would like to be seen as an elite athlete, not an athlete with a disability.
140 She also would like people to stop clapping when she runs or skates along the lakefront path.

"People with disabilities are very capable," Dukat said. "We can work, have a family, a job, we can balance things."

She said someday people won't be shocked by the sight of her jogging with a prosthetic leg.

"It should be the norm. I don't look
150 at someone with two legs and say, 'That's so cool.' It shouldn't be a surprise to see someone with disabilities doing this." **E**

---

COMMON CORE RI 2, RI 5, RI 6

**D MAIN IDEA**
Notice the **important details** in this section: Disabled athletes are exceptionally fit, they get many benefits from participating in team sports, and they appreciate their opportunities to compete. What key idea is developed by these details? What does that key idea suggest about the author's **purpose** for writing this article?

**E MAIN IDEA**
What last point does the author make?

---

## DIFFERENTIATED INSTRUCTION

### FOR STRUGGLING READERS

**Vocabulary Support** Explain that an *elite* athlete (line 138) would be one of the best or most-skilled players in his or her sport. Ask students to name some athletes they would consider to be among the elite players of their favorite sport.

### FOR ENGLISH LANGUAGE LEARNERS

**Vocabulary: Idioms** Use New Word Analysis to teach these idioms from the story: *kicked around* (line 72), "discussed"; *jock* (line 126), "athlete"; *caught the eye* (line 135), "attracted the attention"; *balance things* (line 145), "keep a harmonious mix of elements in one's life"; *That's so cool* (lines 150–151), "That is very impressive."

**BEST PRACTICES TOOLKIT—Transparency** New Word Analysis p. E8

## Comprehension

1. **Recall** Name three sports that have been adapted for disabled athletes.

2. **Summarize** How are athletes with disabilities similar to other athletes?

## Text Analysis

3. **Identify Main Idea** Review the key ideas you recorded in your chart. On the basis of these ideas, what would you say is the entire article's main, or central, idea? Explain your answer.

4. **Compare and Contrast** What do the athletes described in this article have in common with Erik Weihenmayer? Are they different from him in any way? Give examples to support your comparison.

### COMMON CORE

**RI 2** Determine a central idea of a text and analyze its development. **RI 5** Analyze in detail how an author's ideas are developed and refined by portions of a text. **RI 6** Determine an author's purpose in a text. **W 9b (RI 1)** Draw evidence from informational texts; cite strong and thorough textual evidence to support analysis of what the text says explicitly as well as inferences drawn from the text.

## Read for Information: Make Generalizations

**WRITING PROMPT**

What do people with disabilities gain from participating in rigorous sports and undertaking other physical challenges? Use information from "Blind to Failure" and "A Different Level of Competition" to support your response.

To respond to this prompt, you will have to synthesize ideas from both texts and then make a generalization. A **generalization** is a broad statement about a category, based on a study of some members of that category. To make a generalization, follow these steps:

1. Gather strong and thorough evidence—anecdotes and direct statements—about what people with disabilities gain from playing sports.

2. Look for key ideas suggested by this evidence.

3. Make a general statement based on these key ideas.

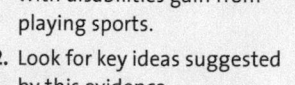

Review your evidence to make sure your generalization is true and fair; revise your generalization if necessary.

---

**FOR STRUGGLING WRITERS**

**Read for Information**

- Remind students to record evidence on index cards, one anecdote or direct statement per card, and then organize their cards according to the key idea each card supports.

- If students write an answer to the prompt, advise them to begin with their generalization, state the key ideas that led to the generalization, and support each idea with evidence from the article.

**FOR ADVANCED LEARNERS/PRE–AP**

**Read for Information** Encourage students to incorporate evidence from at least one additional source in their written response to the writing prompt.

---

# Practice and Apply

For preliminary support of post-reading questions, use these copy masters:

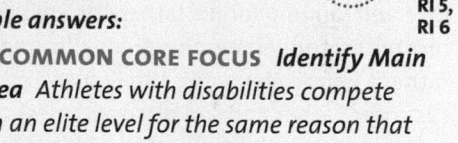 **RESOURCE MANAGER**—Copy Masters
Reading Check p. 127
Question Support p. 128
Additional selection questions are provided for teachers on page 118.

## ANSWERS

### Comprehension

1. *Possible answers:* basketball, football, tennis, sled hockey, sailboat racing

2. *They are competitive, fit, and interested in challenge. They receive the same benefits from sports.*

### Text Analysis

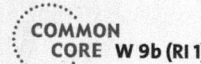 COMMON CORE **RI 2, RI 5, RI 6**

*Possible answers:*

3. ● **COMMON CORE FOCUS** *Identify Main Idea* Athletes with disabilities compete on an elite level for the same reason that people without disabilities do, but they appreciate the opportunities even more.

4. *Compare and Contrast* The athletes do not share Erik's disability or sport. However, like Erik, they are resolute and seek challenges.

## Read for Information: Make Generalizations

COMMON CORE **W 9b (RI 1)**

**Writing Prompt** *Possible answer:* Athletes with disabilities reap the same benefits as do other athletes, but they especially value the way physical challenge develops self-confidence.

# Assess and Reteach

## Assess

DIAGNOSTIC AND SELECTION TESTS
Selection Tests A pp. 79-80
Selection Tests B/C pp. 81-82

**Interactive Selection Test** on **thinkcentral.com**

## Reteach

**Level Up Online Tutorials** on **thinkcentral.com**

# Focus and Motivate

## SUMMARIES

**"A Voice"** In this poem, the speaker describes her admiration for her Mexican-born mother, who overcame challenges to become a fluent speaker and writer of English. The speaker recalls her mother's story of having gone onstage at the state capitol but being unable to speak when she saw the audience of strangers.

**"My Father's Song"** In this poem about a son's love and longing for his father, the speaker recounts a tender memory that epitomizes his father's gentle character. While planting corn together, father and son discover a nest of baby mice that they move to a safe place.

## What makes a MEMORY?

Direct students' attention to the question. Ask, "Think about your favorite or most vivid memory. What makes it stand out in your mind?" Extend the discussion by having students complete the *QUICKWRITE*.

# Selection Resources

---

## A Voice
Poem by Pat Mora

## My Father's Song
Poem by Simon J. Ortiz

# What makes a MEMORY?

Whether they're once-in-a-lifetime occurrences or everyday experiences, some things remain imprinted on your mind long after they happen. In "A Voice" and "My Father's Song," two poets write about old memories that remain vivid many years later.

*QUICKWRITE* Think of a memory that remains very clear to you. Write a paragraph describing the memory in as much detail as you can. In a small group, try to generalize about the kinds of memories that retain their sharpness. Do memories of extraordinary events remain more vibrant than those of ordinary events? Do positive memories stand out more than negative ones?

286

---

*See resources on the **Teacher One Stop DVD-ROM** and on **thinkcentral.com**.*

 **RESOURCE MANAGER UNIT 2**
Plan and Teach, pp. 129-136
Text Analysis and Reading
   Skill, pp. 137-138, 139-140†*

**DIAGNOSTIC AND SELECTION TESTS**
Selection Tests, pp. 83-86

 **BEST PRACTICES TOOLKIT**
Read Aloud/Think Aloud,
   p. A34

**TECHNOLOGY**
⊘ **Teacher One Stop DVD-ROM**
⊘ **Student One Stop DVD-ROM**
⊘ **Audio Anthology CD**
⊘ **GrammarNotes DVD-ROM**
⊘ **ExamView Test Generator**
   on the **Teacher One Stop**

---

\* Resources for Differentiation          † Also in Spanish          ‡ Also in Haitian Creole and Vietnamese

## TEXT ANALYSIS: SPEAKER

One of the elements of poetry is the **speaker**—the voice that "talks" to the reader. Like the narrator in a work of fiction, the speaker relates the ideas or the story of the poem from a specific **point of view.** The speaker can be detached from or intensely involved with the experience or ideas expressed in the poem. It is important to keep in mind that the speaker is not necessarily the poet, even when he or she uses the pronouns *I* and *me.* As you read "A Voice" and "My Father's Song," ask yourself these questions about each speaker:

- Whom is the speaker addressing?
- What is the speaker's relationship to the subject of the poem?
- How would I characterize the speaker's attitude toward the person being described?

By thinking about these questions as you read, you can make inferences about what the speaker is like and why he or she chose to share the experience described in the poem.

## READING STRATEGY: READING POETRY

There are two ways to read lines of poetry:

- Read the lines continuously—paying attention to entire sentences, regardless of line breaks or stanzas.
- Read each line in isolation—noting the ideas and images in it, regardless of sentence structure.

Try both approaches with the following passage from "A Voice":

*The family story says your voice is the voice
of an aunt in Mexico, spunky as a peacock.*

When the lines are read together, they read like a regular sentence. When they are read with a pause at the end of each line, what gets emphasized?

Read "A Voice" and "My Father's Song" aloud using the first method, then silently using the second. Note how the line breaks help bring emphasis to certain words and ideas.

 Complete the activities in your **Reader/Writer Notebook.**

## Meet the Authors

### Pat Mora
**born 1942**

**The Power of Words**
Pat Mora began writing poems while in elementary school in El Paso, Texas, where she was born and raised. Her mother, who dreamed of becoming a writer, won several speech contests while in school but was unable to continue her education when the Great Depression hit. She passed on her ambition and her love of language to her daughter—gifts that have played an integral part in Mora's career. Discussing her motives for writing, the poet, essayist, and short story writer explains, "I am fascinated by the pleasure and power of words."

### Simon J. Ortiz
**born 1941**

**A Voice of Inspiration**
Simon J. Ortiz, an Acoma Pueblo Indian, was born in Albuquerque, New Mexico, and raised in the Acoma Pueblo homeland about 65 miles outside the city. He attributes his love of words to his father, who sang and talked to his son while working. Another source of inspiration for Ortiz is his Native American heritage. His poems, short stories, and essays often center on themes of Native American history and culture. But they also explore more universal, personal subjects like identity and loneliness. Of his poetry, Ortiz says, "I tell you about me and my world so you may be able to see yourself."

**Authors Online**
Go to **thinkcentral.com.** KEYWORD: HML9-287

 THINK central

287

**TEXT ANALYSIS**  COMMON CORE RL 1

### ● Model the Skill: SPEAKER

After students read the page, read aloud these lines for instructional support:

> Grandmother's hugs were
> two parts furniture polish
> four parts curry powder
> One part damp garden dirt.

Tell students that the speaker is a grandson or granddaughter who is describing his or her grandmother.

**GUIDED PRACTICE** Does the speaker sound detached or involved with the subject of the poem?

**READING SKILL**  COMMON CORE RL 10

### ■ Model the Skill: READING POETRY

Tell students that long, obvious pauses at the ends of lines can make a poem sound choppy and can interrupt the flow of ideas. Explain that pausing slightly, particularly if a line ends with a punctuation mark, gives the poem a more natural rhythm. Model these two approaches for students by reading aloud a poem.

**GUIDED PRACTICE** Have partners take turns reading aloud stanzas from their favorite poems, trying to hear how different ways of pausing at the ends of lines can change the emphasis of certain words or images.

**R** RESOURCE MANAGER—Copy Master Reading Poetry p. 139 (for student use while reading the selection)

*Help students set a purpose for reading. Tell them to think about how the speakers' relationships with their parents affect their development as individuals.*

---

**TEXT ANALYSIS** · COMMON CORE · RL 1

 **SPEAKER**

*Possible answer:* *Readers can infer that the speaker knows the person she describes very well. The speaker gives readers intimate details about the person.*

---

**READING SKILL** · COMMON CORE · RL 10

 *Model the Skill:* **READING POETRY**

Read aloud lines 10–11. Pause at the end of line 10 before reading line 11. Tell students that the phrasing affects the meaning of the words. Explain that leaving *slow* at the end of the line emphasizes how slowly he walked and helps emphasize the image of the "hot river" at the beginning of the next line.

*Possible answer:* *The line break emphasizes the importance of speaking "about patriotism and democracy" for the person the speaker is addressing.*

---

**ADDITIONAL TEACHING OPPORTUNITY**

**Appreciate Oral Poetry:** Point out that the impact of poetry changes when it is heard rather than read silently. Choose students to read the poems in this lesson aloud. Tell students to listen for enjoyment during a first reading, and then listen for and note examples of rhyme, vivid imagery, and characterization. Invite students to comment on how their perceptions changed when the poems were read aloud. (To learn more about appreciating oral poetry, see **Reading Handbook,** page R2.)

---

# A Voice

### PAT MORA

Even the lights on the stage unrelenting
as the desert sun couldn't hide the other
students, their eyes also unrelenting,
students who spoke English every night

5 as they ate their meat, potatoes, gravy.
Not you. In your house that smelled like
rose powder, you spoke Spanish formal
as your father, the judge without a courtroom

in the country he floated to in the dark
10 on a flatbed truck. He walked slow
as a hot river down the narrow hall
of your house. You never dared to race past him,

to say, "Please move," in the language
you learned effortlessly, as you learned to run,
15 the language forbidden at home, though your mother
said you learned it to fight with the neighbors.

You liked winning with words. You liked
writing speeches about patriotism and democracy.
You liked all the faces looking at you, all those eyes.
20 "How did I do it?" you ask me now. "How did I do it

when my parents didn't understand?"
The family story says your voice is the voice
of an aunt in Mexico, spunky as a peacock.
Family stories sing of what lives in the blood.

 **SPEAKER**
What can you **infer** about the speaker's relationship with the person she describes?

 **READING POETRY**
By breaking the line after "you liked," what idea does the poet emphasize?

---

## DIFFERENTIATED INSTRUCTION

**FOR ENGLISH LANGUAGE LEARNERS**

**Comprehension Support** Ask students to explain in their own words what happened at the state capitol. Help them understand the meaning of these phrases:

- *their eyes were pinpricks* (line 30), "their stares were painful"
- *never at a loss for words* (lines 31–32), "always has a comment; always has something to say"
- *to speak up* (line 35), "to say something; to make a comment"

**FOR STRUGGLING READERS**

**Develop Reading Fluency** Read aloud "A Voice" to students. Tell students to pay attention to the mood of the poem as well as to what effect your pauses have on the story told in the poem. Finally, have students listen to the selection on the *Audio Anthology CD.*

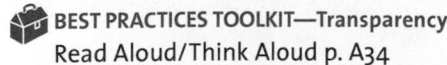 **BEST PRACTICES TOOLKIT—Transparency** Read Aloud/Think Aloud p. A34

**RESOURCE MANAGER—Copy Masters** Reading Fluency p. 142

25 You told me only once about the time you went
   to the state capitol, your family proud as if
   you'd been named governor. But when you looked
   around, the only Mexican in the auditorium,
   you wanted to hide from those strange faces.
30 Their eyes were pinpricks, and you faked
   hoarseness. You, who are never at a loss
   for words, felt your breath stick in your throat

   like an ice-cube. "I can't," you whispered.
   "I can't." Yet you did. Not that day but years later.
35 You taught the four of us to speak up.
   This is America, Mom. The undo-able is done 🅒

   in the next generation. Your breath moves
   through the family like the wind
   moves through the trees.

🅒 **SPEAKER**
What is revealed in lines 35–36 about the speaker's relationship to the person she is addressing?

▼**Analyze Visuals**

What do the sizes and positions of the two women in the painting suggest?

*Girls from Guadalupita, New Mexico,* Miguel Martinez. Oil pastel on paper, 30″ × 40″. Michael McCormick Gallery, Taos, New Mexico.

A VOICE  **289**

## BACKGROUND

Between 1900 and 1929, more than one million Mexicans migrated to the United States. Many found jobs as unskilled workers here. They also found discrimination. Mexicans were blamed for increases in crime and violence; they were the victims of physical and verbal attacks; and they were often regarded as inferior. It was the crushing weight of these stereotypes that the speaker's mother felt when she could not speak at the state capitol.

**TEXT ANALYSIS**   COMMON CORE
RL 1

🅒 *Model the Skill:* **SPEAKER**

Read lines 35–36 aloud. Point out that the speaker uses the English *Mom* instead of the Spanish *mama.* Explain that this reflects the speaker's life and experience in America and not the speaker's Mexican heritage.
***Possible answer:*** *The lines reveal that the* you *addressed by the speaker is her mother.*

## Analyze Visuals

*Possible answer: The larger size and fore-ground placement of the figure on the left suggest that she is stronger and more dominant than the figure on the right. Her attitude also seems protective. The figure on the left is the focus of the painting, as the mother in the poem is the focus of the family.*

**About the Art** For contemporary painter Miguel Martinez (born 1951), this work is typical: large, expressive faces of women fill the canvas.

**REVISIT THE BIG QUESTION**
## What makes a
# MEMORY?

**Discuss** Direct students to lines 25–34. Ask: Why is the memory of the trip to the state capitol an important one for the *you* of the poem? Why is it important for the speaker?
***Possible answer:*** *For the you of the poem, it is a painful memory of a rare moment of failure (lines 31–32), one that, years later, she overcame (line 34). For the speaker, that strength becomes a source of inspiration.*

**D SPEAKER**

*Possible answer:* *The speaker's attitude is one of love and longing for his father. He misses him, wishes he could speak to him (lines 1–2), and recalls endearing details about him (lines 3–5).*

**Extend the Discussion** Why do you think the poet refers to his father's speaking as a "song" (line 7)?

## Analyze Visuals

**Activity** After students finish reading the poem, ask them which details in this painting relate to the poem and which do not.

**About the Art** Contemporary Navajo artist Shonto Begay (born 1954) plays on the two meanings of *plant.* In the foreground, he paints a traditional Navajo man planting in the desert. In the background, a nuclear or other power plant is shown. The powerful relationship of the Navajo man to the earth is in sharp contrast to the ominous stacks creating power on the horizon.

## SELECTION WRAP–UP

**READ WITH A PURPOSE** Now that students have finished reading the selections, have them discuss the impact of parental influence on individual development. How do the parents affect each of the speakers? *Possible answer: Mora's speaker views herself as an extension of her mother. Ortiz's speaker learns from his father that masculinity can be both soft and expressive.*

## INDEPENDENT READING

Students may also enjoy Mora's *Adobe Odes,* a collection of poems about home and everyday life.

# My Father's Song

## SIMON J. ORTIZ

Wanting to say things,
I miss my father tonight.
His voice, the slight catch,
the depth from his thin chest,
5  the tremble of emotion
in something he has just said
to his son, his song: **D**

We planted corn one Spring at Acu[1]—
we planted several times
10  but this one particular time
I remember the soft damp sand
in my hand.

My father had stopped at one point
to show me an overturned furrow;[2]
15  the plowshare had unearthed
the burrow nest of a mouse
in the soft moist sand.

Very gently, he scooped tiny pink animals
into the palm of his hand
20  and told me to touch them.
We took them to the edge
of the field and put them in the shade
of a sand moist clod.

I remember the very softness
25  of cool and warm sand and tiny alive mice
and my father saying things.

---

1. **Acu** (ä′kōō): the Acoma people's name for the Acoma Pueblo.
2. **furrow** (fûr′ō): a long, shallow trench made in the ground by a plow.

**D SPEAKER**
From the description in this first stanza, what can you tell about the speaker's attitude toward the father?

*Navajo Power Plant* (1990). © Shonto Begay/Avery Collection of American Indian Painting.

## DIFFERENTIATED INSTRUCTION

**FOR STRUGGLING READERS**
**Options for Reading** Read aloud "My Father's Song" to students. Ask students to pay attention to the way the speaker describes his father and to the mood the memory of his father creates. Then have students listen to the *Audio Anthology CD* as they read along chorally.

**FOR ADVANCED LEARNERS/PRE–AP**
**Analyze Content and Meaning** [small-group option] Ask students what they think this particular memory of the son shows about his father's character. Have them present their ideas in one or two paragraphs.

## Comprehension

1. **Recall** Describe the incident related in "My Father's Song."

2. **Recall** What happens to the speaker's mother in "A Voice"?

3. **Clarify** In "A Voice," what is the speaker's mother referring to in line 20 when she asks, "How did I do it?"

## Text Analysis

● 4. **Compare Speakers** Review the questions listed on page 287. Then use a chart like this one to compare the two poems. What characteristics do they share?

|  | "A Voice" | "My Father's Song" |
|---|---|---|
| Person Being Addressed |  |  |
| Relationship to Subject |  |  |
| Attitude Displayed |  |  |
|  |  |  |

● 5. **Reading Poetry** Phrasing in poetry helps bring emphasis to certain words and ideas. It can also affect the interpretation of a poem. Why did Pat Mora choose to split certain sentences between lines or stanzas in "A Voice"? What does this call attention to? Cite strong and specific examples.

6. **Interpret Imagery** Poets often make use of **images** that appeal to the five senses: sight, sound, touch, smell, and taste. In "My Father's Song," which of these senses does the poet evoke? What is the effect of using such images? Support your answer.

7. **Evaluate** In your opinion, which poem does a better job of characterizing the person being remembered? Support your opinion with details.

## Text Criticism

8. **Biographical Context** Both Mora and Ortiz are known for their efforts to preserve the cultures from which they come. To what extent does each of these poems fulfill that mission? Support your opinion.

### What makes a MEMORY?
What is your earliest childhood memory?

**COMMON CORE**

RL 1 Cite strong and thorough textual evidence to support inferences drawn from the text.
RL 10 Read and comprehend poems.

---

# Practice and Apply

For preliminary support of post-reading questions, use these copy masters:

 **RESOURCE MANAGER—Copy Masters**
Speaker p. 137
Question Support p. 141

Additional selection questions are provided for teachers on page 133.

## ANSWERS

## Comprehension

1. *The speaker recalls a time when, while planting corn, his father unearthed a nest of mice and had the speaker touch them.*

2. *The mother goes to the state capitol and becomes too frightened to speak to the large, strange audience.*

3. *She is referring to learning to speak English when the language was forbidden in her home, and also standing out as she spoke it.*

## Text Analysis

COMMON CORE RL 1, RL 10

**Possible answers:**

4. ● **COMMON CORE FOCUS** *Compare Speakers* **"A Voice":** *addresses the speaker's mother; secondhand relationship to subject; attitude of respect, honor, pride;* **"My Father's Song":** *addresses the reader; firsthand experience; attitude of admiration*

5. ● **COMMON CORE FOCUS** *Reading Poetry The breaks in the sentences slow down the reader and tend to put emphasis on the word at the end of the line, such as "faked" at the end of line 30 and "done" in line 36.*

6. *Touch is foremost: the speaker recalls the soft damp sand, the shade of a moist sand clod, and the tiny, living mice he touched.*

---

7. *Students' opinions will vary.* **"A Voice"** *gives more details about the mother.* **"My Father's Song"** *evokes the gentle essence of the father's character.*

## Text Criticism

**Possible answer:**

8. *Mora expresses admiration and gratitude toward immigrants. Ortiz shows the gentle spirit of his father, who was connected to nature through his cultural heritage.*

### What makes a MEMORY?
*Students might recall seeing the ocean, starting school, or performing for others. Make sure that students support their descriptions with sensory details.*

---

# Assess and Reteach

## Assess

**DIAGNOSTIC AND SELECTION TESTS**
Selection Test A pp. 83–84
Selection Test B/C pp. 85–86

**Interactive Selection Test** on **thinkcentral.com**

## Reteach

**Level Up Online Tutorials** on **thinkcentral.com**

# Focus and Motivate

## COMMON CORE FOCUS

**RL 7** Analyze the representation of a subject in two different artistic mediums, including what is emphasized or absent in each treatment. **RI 7** Analyze various accounts of a subject told in different mediums, determining which details are emphasized in each account. **L 4a** Use context as a clue to the meaning of a word. **L 4c** Consult reference materials to determine a word's meaning or etymology. **L 5a** Interpret figures of speech in context and analyze their role in the text. **W 4** Produce informative writing in which the development and organization are appropriate to the task. **W 9 (RL 7, RI 7)** Draw evidence from literary or informational texts; analyze the representation of a subject in different mediums. **W 10** Write over shorter time frames.

## SUMMARY

**"Rosa Parks"** This selection from Douglas Brinkley's biography *Rosa Parks* chronicles the day on which Rosa Parks, an African-American seamstress, refused to give up her seat to a white passenger on a segregated bus in Montgomery, Alabama. Parks's quiet dignity served as an inspiration in the civil rights movement.

**"Rosa"** In this brief poem, Rita Dove presents impressions of Rosa Parks on the same historic day. She emphasizes Parks's dignity, everyday sensibilities, and symbolic importance.

## What is **DIGNITY?**

Have students read the paragraph. After students generate the list for the *DISCUSS* activity, ask them to identify the qualities that individuals with dignity have in common.

## Selection Resources

---

**Comparing Across Genres**

*from* **Rosa Parks**
Biography by Douglas Brinkley

Video link at
thinkcentral.com

**Essential Course of Study**
ECOS

**Rosa**
Poem by Rita Dove

# What is **DIGNITY?**

**COMMON CORE**

**RL 7** Analyze the representation of a subject in two different artistic mediums, including what is emphasized or absent in each treatment. **RI 7** Analyze various accounts of a subject told in different mediums, determining which details are emphasized in each account. **L 4a** Use context as a clue to the meaning of a word. **L 5a** Interpret figures of speech in context and analyze their role in the text.

Some people have it—quiet strength and an air of personal dignity. One such person was Rosa Parks. You are about to read two selections about Rosa Parks in different mediums—a biography and a poem. Both pieces portray her dignity and courage and the important role she played in the civil rights movement.

**DISCUSS** With a small group, generate a list of real people, living or dead, as well as characters in books, movies, or TV shows, whom you consider to have dignity. Then discuss whether dignity comes mainly from within or from the approval of others.

People or Characters with Dignity
1. Dr. Martin Luther King, Jr.
2. Mother Teresa
3.
4.
5.

---

Video link at
thinkcentral.com

**R RESOURCE MANAGER UNIT 2**
Plan and Teach, pp. 143–150
Summary, pp. 151–152†‡*
Text Analysis,
pp. 153–157†*
Vocabulary, pp. 158–160*

**DIAGNOSTIC AND SELECTION TESTS**
Selection Tests, pp. 87–90

**BEST PRACTICES TOOLKIT**
Outline, p. B19
**INTERACTIVE READER**
**ADAPTED INTERACTIVE READER**
**ELL ADAPTED INTERACTIVE READER**

**TECHNOLOGY**
- **Teacher One Stop DVD-ROM**
- **Student One Stop DVD-ROM**
- **PowerNotes DVD-ROM**
- **Audio Anthology CD**
- **GrammarNotes DVD-ROM**
- **Audio Tutor CD**
- **ExamView Test Generator**
  on the **Teacher One Stop**

**THINK central**

**Video Trailer**

Go to **thinkcentral.com** to preview the **Video Trailer** introducing this selection. Other features that support the selection include
- **PowerNotes** presentation
- **ThinkAloud** models to enhance comprehension
- **WordSharp** vocabulary tutorials
- interactive writing and grammar instruction

---

## TEXT ANALYSIS: CHARACTERIZATION ACROSS GENRES

As you know, fiction writers use methods of **characterization** to develop the made-up characters that populate their work. However, when writers of nonfiction and poetry portray real people, they cannot make up facts and details. Instead, writers in these **genres** shape readers' impressions of particular people by combining factual information with techniques unique to the genres in which they are working. The biography and the poem that follow both tell about Rosa Parks. The chart below shows the genre techniques each writer uses to characterize her.

| Techniques Used in the Biography | Techniques Used in the Poem |
|---|---|
| • facts and details about Rosa Parks's actions, thoughts, and appearance | • word choice to describe Rosa Parks's actions and appearance |
| • quotations from Rosa Parks | • images to depict Rosa Parks's traits |
| • quotations from others who knew Rosa Parks | |

As you read, notice the techniques each writer uses to portray this historic figure and try to synthesize the ideas expressed.

## READING STRATEGY: SET A PURPOSE FOR READING

When you **set a purpose** for reading, you choose specific reasons for reading a work. In this lesson, you will read a biography and a poem in order to compare and contrast the ways they portray Rosa Parks. As you read, think about your impressions of Rosa Parks. After you read, you will use the **Points of Analysis** chart on page 299 to make connections that will help you analyze the two accounts.

## ▲ VOCABULARY IN CONTEXT

Restate each phrase, using a different word or words for each boldfaced term. Then, in your *Reader/Writer Notebook*, write a brief definition of each word you're familiar with.

1. cheering **frenetically** during the suspenseful game
2. the master chef's **protégé**
3. letting the mind wander in a pleasant **reverie**
4. an **exhortation** to try harder to win
5. as **serene** as a calm summer day
6. **retrieve** a lost scarf

 Complete the activities in your **Reader/Writer Notebook**.

## Meet the Authors

### Douglas Brinkley
born 1961

**Historian and Educator**
Douglas Brinkley has written award-winning books about Henry Ford, Franklin Delano Roosevelt, and Jimmy Carter, among others. In 1993 Brinkley published *The Majic Bus: An American Odyssey*. In this first-person account, he described a class he taught aboard a cross-country bus. Visiting 30 states, his students attended lectures, read widely, listened to American music, toured historical sites, and met celebrated authors.

### Rita Dove
born 1952

**Honored Poet**
According to Rita Dove, "Poetry is language at its most distilled and most powerful." In 1993 she became the poet laureate of the United States—the youngest person and the first African American so honored.

### BACKGROUND TO THE SELECTIONS
**Civil Rights**
Southern states once had laws that enforced racial segregation. Among other injustices, African Americans were forced to sit in separate sections of buses. In 1955, Rosa Parks's refusal to give up her seat on a bus triggered a 382-day bus boycott by African Americans in Montgomery, Alabama. The boycott brought Rosa Parks, Dr. Martin Luther King, Jr., and their cause to national prominence. In 1956, the Supreme Court ruled that segregation on buses and other transportation was unconstitutional.

**Authors Online**
Go to **thinkcentral.com**. KEYWORD: HML9-293

## Teach

TEXT ANALYSIS    COMMON CORE   RL 7, RI 7

● **Model the Skill:**
## CHARACTERIZATION ACROSS GENRES

Read aloud this example from a poem:

"The players' dignity moved us all;
Despite defeat, they all stood tall."

Explain that the poet creates an image to show the players' acceptance of defeat. Then, read aloud this prose example:

"They're an impressive group," the coach said. "The players stayed positive, even after a 20-point loss."

Point out that the prose writer uses a quotation from the players' coach to show the players' attitude.

**GUIDED PRACTICE** Ask students which example they preferred, and why.

**R** RESOURCE MANAGER—Copy Master Characterization Across Genres p. 153 (for student use while reading the selections)

READING STRATEGY    COMMON CORE   RL 7, RI 7

■ **Model the Skill:**
## SET A PURPOSE FOR READING

Elicit that setting a purpose is a good reading strategy because it helps readers focus on what is important to them.

**GUIDED PRACTICE** Discuss purposes for reading a biography.

---

VOCABULARY SKILL    COMMON CORE   L 4

## ▲ VOCABULARY IN CONTEXT

**DIAGNOSE WORD KNOWLEDGE** Have all students complete **Vocabulary in Context**. Check their definitions against the following:

**exhortation** (ĕg′zôr-tā′shən) *n.* a communication strongly urging that something be done
**frenetically** (frə-nĕt′ĭk-lē) *adv.* in a frenzied or frantic way
**protégé** (prō′tə-zhā′) *n.* a person who is guided or supported by an older or more influential person

**retrieve** (rĭ-trēv′) *v.* to find and return safely
**reverie** (rĕv′ə-rē) *n.* a state of daydreaming
**serene** (sə-rēn′) *adj.* calm; peaceful

**PRETEACH VOCABULARY** Use the following copy master to help students predict the meaning of each boldfaced word.

**R** RESOURCE MANAGER—Copy Master Vocabulary Study p. 158

1. Read item 1 aloud, emphasizing *frenetically*.

2. Point out the phrases *busy season* and *to keep up with*. Elicit possible meanings for *frenetically*, such as "in an extremely excited manner."

3. Repeat the procedure for items 2–6.

### READ WITH A PURPOSE

*Help students set a purpose for reading. Tell them to look for ways the selection from the biography helps them understand the poem that follows.*

### TIERED DISCUSSION PROMPTS

Direct students to lines 13–21. Use these prompts to help students gain insight into Rosa Parks's attitudes and values:

**Connect** Have you ever felt conflicted about being in one place but wanting to be in another? How did you cope? *Answers will vary.*

**Analyze** How does Parks put her coffee-break time to good use? *Possible answer: She calls the university president to reserve a classroom for the workshop that she is organizing.*

**Synthesize** What does the fact that Parks can focus on NAACP activities despite the bustle at work tell you about her? *Possible answer: The work of the NAACP is very important to her, and she takes it seriously.*

---

**VOCABULARY**     COMMON CORE   L 4

### OWN THE WORD

**frenetically:** Have students review the passage and identify context clues that help them determine the meaning of *frenetically*.

*Possible answer: beehive of activity*

---

*from*

# Rosa Parks

### DOUGLAS BRINKLEY

Rosa Parks headed to work on December 1, 1955, on the Cleveland Avenue bus to Court Square. It was a typical prewinter morning in the Alabama capital, chilly and raw, topcoat weather. Outside the Montgomery Fair Department Store a Salvation Army Santa rang his bell for coins in front of window displays of toy trains and mannequins modeling reindeer sweaters. Every afternoon when school let out, hordes of children would invade the store to gawk at the giant Christmas tree draped with blinking lights, a mid-1950s electrical marvel. But Rosa Parks saw little of the holiday glitter down in the small tailor shop in the basement next to the huge steam presses, where the
10 only hint of Yuletide cheer came from a sagging, water-stained banner reading "Merry Christmas and a Happy New Year."

Not that many of Montgomery Fair's lower-level employees had the time to let the faded decoration make them sad. The department store rang up nearly half of its sales between Thanksgiving and New Year's Day, which turned the tailor shop into a beehive of activity every December. But even on days spent **frenetically** hemming, ironing, and steam-pressing, Parks's mind was more with the NAACP[1] than her workday duties. She was in the midst of organizing a workshop to be held at Alabama State University on December 3–4 and spent the morning during her coffee break telephoning H. Council Trenholm,
20 president of the university, applying enough quiet persuasion to be granted the use of a classroom over the weekend. "I was also getting the notices in the mail

**Analyze Visuals ▶**

What qualities of Rosa Parks does the photograph convey?

**① Targeted Passage**

**frenetically**
(frə-nĕt'ĭk-lē) *adv.* in a frenzied or frantic way

---

1. **NAACP:** a civil rights organization. The initials stand for National Association for the Advancement of Colored People.

**294**   UNIT 2: CHARACTERIZATION AND POINT OF VIEW

---

## DIFFERENTIATED INSTRUCTION

### FOR ENGLISH LANGUAGE LEARNERS

**Options for Reading** Ask a question about a set of paragraphs or range of numbered lines; then have pairs of students scan the designated text to find the answer.

### FOR STRUGGLING READERS

In combination with the *Audio Anthology* CD, use one or more Targeted Passages (pp. 294, 296, 297) to ensure that students focus on key events, concepts, and skills. Targeted Passages are also good for English learners.

**① Targeted Passage [Lines 13–21]**

This passage sets up the contrast between Rosa Parks's busy job and her participation in civil rights activities.

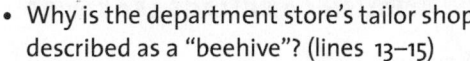

**Reading Support**

This selection on **thinkcentral.com** includes embedded **ThinkAloud** models—students "thinking aloud" about the story to model the kinds of questions a good reader would ask about a selection.

## BACKGROUND

**Transportation Discrimination** African Americans suffered many humiliations in Montgomery, Alabama. Under Montgomery's segregation laws, bus drivers could make black passengers pay the fare and then step off and board through the rear door, so as not to walk past white riders. Some other rules are mentioned in this selection. Black riders who violated these rules could be arrested and fined.

**Cultural Connection** When Rosa Parks made her momentous decision not to surrender her seat on the bus in Montgomery, Alabama, she joined a tradition of nonviolent resistance that spans many cultures. In the 1940s, Mohandas Karamchand Gandhi (1869–1948) used non-violent fasts and protests to lead the people of India to independence from British rule. In the 1980s, Lech Walesa (born 1943) led a strike that forced Poland's Communist government to legally recognize the Polish workers' union, Solidarity.

## Analyze Visuals

*Possible answer: The photograph conveys her seriousness, reserve, and perhaps determination.*

**About the Photo** No camera recorded Rosa Parks's historic bus ride. This picture was taken a little more than a year later, when the Montgomery bus boycott finally brought about the integration of the city's public transportation system (symbolized by the fact that a white man is seated behind Parks).

- Why is the department store's tailor shop described as a "beehive"? (lines 13–15)
- To what organization does Rosa Parks belong? What is its purpose? (lines 16–17)
- Who is Parks trying to impress? Why? (lines 19–21)

**FOR ADVANCED LEARNERS/PRE–AP**

**Research and Present** Assign students to small groups. Provide independent opportunities for groups to research the history of segregation in the United States. Have each group make a brief presentation about their findings.

for the election of officers of the senior branch of the NAACP, which would be [the] next week," Parks recalled. That afternoon, she lunched with Fred Gray, the lawyer who defended Claudette Colvin and was serving as Clifford Durr's[2] **protégé** at his law office above the Sears Auto Tire Store.

"When 1:00 P.M. came and the lunch hour ended, Mrs. Parks went back to her work as a seamstress," Gray would write in his civil rights memoir, *Bus Ride to Justice.* "I continued my work and left the office in the early afternoon for an out-of-town engagement."

30    Shortly after 5:00 P.M., Rosa Parks clocked out of work and walked the block to Court Square to wait for her bus home. It had been a hard day, and her body ached, from her feet swollen from the constant standing to her shoulders throbbing from the strain and her chronic bursitis. But the bus stand was packed, so Parks, disinclined to jockey for a rush-hour seat, crossed Dexter Avenue to do a little shopping at Lee's Cut-Rate Drug. She had decided to treat herself to a heating pad but found them too pricey. Instead, she bought some Christmas gifts, along with aspirin, toothpaste, and a few other sundries, and headed back to the bus stop wondering how her husband's day had been at the Maxwell Air Force Base Barber Shop and thinking about what her mother would cook for dinner. **B**

40    It was in this late-day **reverie** that Rosa Parks dropped her dime in the box and boarded the yellow-olive city bus. She took an aisle seat in the racially neutral middle section,[3] behind the movable sign which read "colored." She was not expecting any problems, as there were several empty spaces at the whites-only front of the bus. A black man was sitting next to her on her right and staring out the window; across the aisle sat two black women deep in conversation. At the next two stops enough white passengers got on to nearly fill up the front section. At the third stop, in front of the Empire Theater, a famous shrine to country-music fans as the stage where the legendary Hank Williams got his start, the last front seats were taken, with one man left standing.

50    The bus driver twisted around and locked his eyes on Rosa Parks. Her heart almost stopped when she saw it was James F. Blake, the bully who had put her off his bus twelve years earlier. She didn't know his name, but since that incident in 1943, she had never boarded a bus that Blake was driving. This day, however, she had absentmindedly stepped in. "Move y'all, I want those two seats," the driver barked on behalf of Jim Crow,[4] which dictated that all four blacks in that row of the middle section would have to surrender their seats to accommodate a single white man, as no "colored" could be allowed to sit parallel with him. A stony silence fell over the bus as nobody moved. "Y'all

---

2. **Claudette Colvin . . . Clifford Durr's:** Claudette Colvin was an African-American teenager who had refused to give up her seat on a Montgomery city bus earlier in 1955. Clifford Durr was a white lawyer who worked for civil rights.

3. **racially neutral middle section:** a section of the bus where African Americans could sit, as long as no whites needed or wanted seats there.

4. **Jim Crow:** a term referring to the segregation of African Americans.

**296**    UNIT 2: CHARACTERIZATION AND POINT OF VIEW

---

**protégé** (prō′tə-zhā′) *n.* a person who is guided or supported by an older or more influential person

**A** CHARACTERIZATION
How did Parks's work for the NAACP differ from her job at the store? Why do you think Brinkley chose to highlight these differences?

**B** CHARACTERIZATION
Reread lines 30–39. What do Rosa Parks's thoughts and actions reveal about her?

**reverie** (rĕv′ə-rē) *n.* a state of daydreaming

 **Targeted Passage**

---

COMMON CORE L 4a

**Language Coach**

**Word Roots**  The Latin root word *commodare* ("to make fit") has lent itself to the formation of many English words, such as *commodious* ("roomy"). Reread lines 54–58. Which word in this sentence comes from *commodare*? Based on context clues, what does the word mean?

---

## TEXT ANALYSIS

COMMON CORE
RL 7,
RI 7

**A CHARACTERIZATION**

*Possible answer:* At the store, Parks worked as a seamstress (lines 15–16), but her NAACP tasks called upon her organizational and communication skills (lines 17–25). Brinkley probably wanted to show that Parks had a strong commitment to both types of work.

## TEXT ANALYSIS

COMMON CORE
RL 7,
RI 7

**B CHARACTERIZATION**

*Possible answer:* She is practical and makes productive use of her time. She is also thoughtful and generous.

## VOCABULARY

COMMON CORE
L 4

**OWN THE WORD**

- **protégé:** Tell students that *protégé* is a French term derived from the verb "to protect." Have students explain the relationship between *to protect* and *protégé,* "a person who is guided or supported by an older person."

- **reverie:** Tell students that, like *protégé,* *reverie* has roots in French. *Rever* means "to dream."

---

## DIFFERENTIATED INSTRUCTION

### FOR STRUGGLING READERS

**Targeted Passage** [Lines 40–58]

This pivotal passage introduces this account's conflict: an irritated bus driver whose demand is about to change history.

- Where does Rosa Parks sit? Why? (lines 42–44)

- What happens at the front of the bus? (lines 46–49)

- What does Blake, the driver, want Parks and three other passengers to do? (lines 54–58)

### FOR ENGLISH LANGUAGE LEARNERS

**Language Coach**    COMMON CORE
L 4a

**Word Roots** *Answer:*

*Accommodate* here means to "give special consideration to." Have students reread lines 54–58. Ask students what word comes from the Old English root *surrenderen,* which means "to deliver." What does the word mean in this context?

better make it light on yourselves and let me have those seats," Blake sputtered,
60 more impatiently than before. Quietly and in unison, the two black women
sitting across from Parks rose and moved to the back. Her seatmate quickly
followed suit, and she swung her legs to the side to let him out. Then Parks slid
over to the window and gazed out at the Empire Theater marquee promoting
*A Man Alone,* a new Western starring Ray Milland. **C**

    The next ten seconds seemed like an eternity to Rosa Parks. As Blake
made his way toward her, all she could think about were her forebears, who,
Maya Angelou would put it, took the lash, the branding iron, and untold
humiliations while only praying that their children would someday "flesh out"
the dream of equality. But unlike the poet, it was not Africa in the days of the
70 slave trade that Parks was thinking about; it was racist Alabama in the here and
now. She shuddered with the memory of her grandfather back in Pine Level
keeping watch for the KKK[5] every night with a loaded shotgun in his lap,
echoing abolitionist John Brown's[6] **exhortation:** "Talk! Talk! Talk! That didn't
free the slaves. . . . What is needed is action! Action!" So when Parks looked up
at Blake, his hard, thoughtless scowl filled her with pity. She felt fearless, bold,
and **serene.** "Are you going to stand up?" the driver demanded. Rosa Parks
looked straight at him and said: "No." Flustered and not quite sure what to do,
Blake retorted, "Well, I'm going to have you arrested." And Parks, still sitting
next to the window, replied softly, "You may do that."
80     Her majestic use of "may" rather than "can" put Parks on the high ground,
establishing her as a protester, not a victim. "When I made that decision,"
Parks stated later, "I knew I had the strength of my ancestors with me," and
obviously their dignity as well. And her formal dignified "No," uttered on a
suppertime bus in the cradle of the Confederacy as darkness fell, ignited the
collective "no" of black history in America, a defiance as liberating as John
Brown's on the gallows in Harpers Ferry. **D**

**C CHARACTERIZATION**
Reread lines 50–64. What
do you learn about Rosa
Parks from the way she
reacted to the bus driver's
commands?

**❸ Targeted Passage**

**exhortation**
(ĕg′zôr-tā′shən) *n.* a
communication strongly
urging that something
be done

**serene** (sə-rēn′) *adj.*
calm; peaceful

**D CHARACTERIZATION**
How does Brinkley convey
Rosa Parks's dignity and
strength?

---

5. **back in Pine Level . . . KKK:** Pine Level is a town about 100 miles southeast of Birmingham. The KKK was
the Ku Klux Klan, an extremist secret society that often violently terrorized blacks in the South.

6. **abolitionist John Brown's:** Brown, a white militant, performed radical acts to force the abolition of
slavery, including a failed attempt to steal guns from the U.S. arsenal at Harpers Ferry, Virginia.

---

**FOR STRUGGLING READERS**

**❸ Targeted Passage** [Lines 65–85]

Brinkley reveals the climax and resolution of
Parks's clash with the driver. He also offers
ideas about the implications of that moment.

- As Blake approaches, what does Parks think
  about? (lines 65–69)

- What two things does she tell him? (lines
  77–79)

- Why does Brinkley compare Parks to John
  Brown? (lines 83–86)

**FOR ADVANCED LEARNERS/PRE–AP**

**Analyze Irony** [paired-activity option]  Have
students prepare and share a statement
about the irony in the title of the movie playing at the Empire Theater (*A Man Alone, line
64*).  If time permits, expand the activity by
having students discuss any other details in
the account that they find ironic.

---

TEXT ANALYSIS     COMMON CORE

**C CHARACTERIZATION**    RL 7, RI 7

*Possible answer: Parks is resolute and firm
but not aggressive.  She makes her feelings
known through silent disobedience—that is,
passive resistance.*

**REVISIT THE BIG QUESTION**
## What is DIGNITY?

**Discuss**  Based on lines 75–80, how does
Parks's manner toward Blake demonstrate her
dignity?  *Possible answer: Rather than be loudly
defiant, she simply meets his gaze and speaks
just a few soft words that are to the point.*

---

TEXT ANALYSIS     COMMON CORE

**D CHARACTERIZATION**    RL 7, RI 7

*Possible answer: He describes Parks's feel-
ings of courage and calmness, quotes her
later comments about the source of her
strength, and connects her action to the
larger story of "black history in America."*

**IF STUDENTS NEED HELP . . .** Copy the Text
Analysis chart onto the board.  Have students fill in the first column as they answer
the following questions.

- What words does Brinkley use in lines
  75–76 to describe Parks?  *Possible answer:
  He calls her "fearless, bold, and serene."*

- In line 82, what does Parks say about her
  strength?  *Possible answer: It was "the
  strength of [her] ancestors."*

---

VOCABULARY     COMMON CORE

**OWN THE WORD**    L 4

- **exhortation:** Remind students that *exhortation* has a connotation of a strong
  request.  Have students list synonyms of
  the root verb *exhort* with similar connotations.  *Possible answers: plead, advocate, press*

- **serene:** Review the meaning of *serene*
  with students.  Then have them list
  antonyms.  *Possible answers: disturbed,
  troubled, agitated*

## SELECTION WRAP–UP

**READ WITH A PURPOSE** Now that students have finished reading the selection, have them compare and contrast the characterization of Parks in the biography and in the poem. How does the excerpt from the biography help you understand the poem? ***Possible answer:*** *The excerpt describes Parks's refusal to give up her seat on the bus. Knowing that history makes it easier to understand what the poem refers to.*

⭐ **CRITIQUE** Have students evaluate and compare their reactions to these two works. In particular, have them explain which work made them think more, and why.

## INDEPENDENT READING

Students might also enjoy reading about a childhood spent with Mahatma Gandhi in *Gandhi Through a Child's Eyes: An Intimate Memoir* by Narayan Desai.

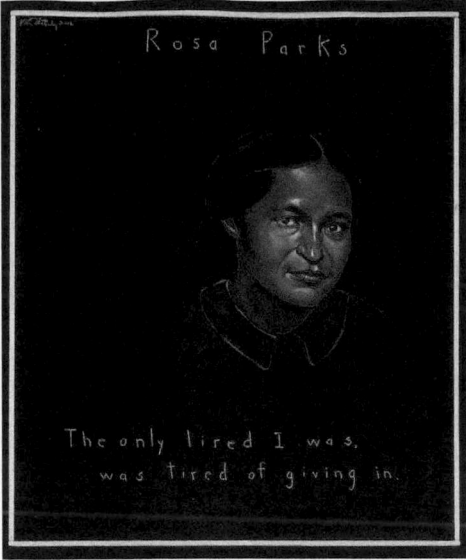

From *Americans Who Tell the Truth*, Robert Shetterly. Used by permission of Dutton Children's Books, a division of Penguin Young Readers Group, a member of Penguin Group, Inc. © Robert Shetterly.

# Rosa
## RITA DOVE

How she sat there,
the time right inside a place
so wrong it was ready.

That trim name with
5 its dream of a bench
to rest on. Her sensible coat.

Doing nothing was the doing: **E**
the clean flame of her gaze
carved by a camera flash.

10 How she stood up
when they bent down to **retrieve**
her purse. That courtesy. **F**

## DIFFERENTIATED INSTRUCTION

### FOR STRUGGLING READERS

**Develop Reading Fluency** Have students listen to the entire poem on the *Audio Anthology CD* (also good for English learners) as they read along. Then have student pairs take turns reading stanzas aloud to one another. Have each pair perform the poem for small groups or the entire class.

**R** RESOURCE MANAGER—Copy Master
Reading Fluency p. 163

### FOR ADVANCED LEARNERS/PRE–AP

**Analyze Imagery** Ask students to contrast the "clean flame" of Parks's gaze in line 8 with the camera flash in line 9. While both images relate to light, how do differences between them suggest a contrast between Parks and the society she is trying to reform? ***Possible answer:*** *The flame suggests Parks's constancy, strength, and purposefulness. The camera flash suggests the transitory nature of society, as well as its artificiality, invasiveness, and perhaps even destructiveness.*

## Comprehension

1. **Recall** Where did Rosa Parks sit after boarding the bus in the evening?

2. **Recall** Why did the bus driver order her to move?

3. **Summarize** What decision did Rosa Parks make?

## Text Analysis

4. **Draw Conclusions** Rosa Parks, an ordinary person, helped launch the civil rights movement. Why was she able to wield such enormous influence?

● 5. **Analyze Characterization** In both the biography and the poem, what words and actions convey Rosa Parks's dignity?

6. **Make Inferences** Reread lines 10–12 of the poem. Whom is the speaker calling courteous? Do you think the speaker's statement is sincere or ironic? Explain.

## Comparing Across Genres

Now that you have read both selections, think about the similarities and differences in the details used to portray Rosa Parks. Create a **Points of Analysis** chart like the one shown, and answer the questions. If a point of analysis is not covered in one of the selections, leave the relevant box blank.

| Points of Analysis | In the Biography | In the Poem |
|---|---|---|
| What did you learn about Rosa Parks's appearance? | | |
| What did you learn about her daily life? | | |
| What did you learn about her personality, thoughts, and feelings? | | |
| What did you learn about her values and the things she thought were important? | | |
| What genre techniques did the writer use to portray Rosa Parks? | | |

### What is **DIGNITY?**

Is dignity something you have or would like to have?

**COMMON CORE**

**RL 7** Analyze the representation of a subject in two different artistic mediums, including what is emphasized or absent in each treatment. **RI 7** Analyze various accounts of a subject told in different mediums, determining which details are emphasized in each account.

# Practice and Apply

For preliminary support of post-reading questions, use these copy masters:

 **RESOURCE MANAGER**—Copy Masters
Reading Check p. 161
Question Support p. 162

Additional selection questions are provided for teachers on page 147.

## ANSWERS

### Comprehension

1. *She sat in "the racially neutral middle section," where blacks were allowed unless seats were needed for whites.*

2. *The front of the bus filled up, leaving one white man standing. All four black riders in Parks's row were supposed to move so that the white man could sit there.*

3. *She decided not to move, even if her refusal led to her arrest.*

### Text Analysis

COMMON CORE **RL 7, RI 7**

*Possible answers:*

4. *The time had finally come for collective action, and Parks's refusal to move served as the igniting spark.*

5. ● **COMMON CORE FOCUS** *Analyze Characterization* "Rosa Parks looked straight at him and said: 'No'" (lines 76–77) and "You may do that" (line 79). "How she sat there" (line 1); "Her sensible coat" (line 6) and "the clean flame of her gaze" (line 8).

6. *The speaker is calling the people who "bent down to retrieve her purse" courteous. It seems ironic since they are doing so while forcing her to move from her seat.*

### What is **DIGNITY?** *Students might consider what qualities Rosa Parks possessed that showed her dignity and how they would like to have that in their own lives.*

## Comparing Across Genres

*Possible answer:*

(appearance)

*Biography:* (implied), appears tired

*Poem:* sensible coat

(daily life)

*Biography:* works as seamstress; commutes by bus

*Poem:* [not covered]

(personality, thoughts, feelings)

*Biography:* determined, brave, sincere, serious

*Poem:* modest, unextravagant (implied)

(values/what was important)

*Biography:* taking a stand against segregation

*Poem:* not moving from her seat ("doing nothing")

(genre techniques)

*Biography:* facts, details, quotations

*Poem:* word choice, imagery, metaphor

## ANSWERS

## Vocabulary in Context

▲ **VOCABULARY PRACTICE**

1. *reverie*
2. *frenetically*
3. *protégé*
4. *exhortation*
5. *serene*
6. *retrieve*

 **RESOURCE MANAGER—Copy Master**
Vocabulary Practice p. 159

**ACADEMIC VOCABULARY IN SPEAKING**

*Since this narrative includes little dialogue, suspense, or description of conflict, students' evaluations should identify character development as the most effective technique.*

**VOCABULARY STRATEGY: ETYMOLOGIES**

 COMMON CORE **L 4c**

*(also an EL language objective)*

Explain that etymologies vary somewhat from dictionary to dictionary. Most etymologies, however, show word history in reverse chronological order, tracing the word back, step by step, to its origins.

**Possible answers:**

1. Middle English, Anglo-French, Latin, Greek
2. "to dream"
3. *exhortari*, from *ex-*, meaning "out," + *hortari*, meaning "to urge or incite"
4. French

 **RESOURCE MANAGER—Copy Master**
Vocabulary Strategy p. 160

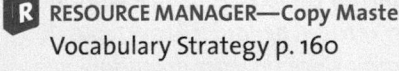

**Interactive Vocabulary** | THINK central

Keywords direct students to a **WordSharp** tutorial on **thinkcentral.com** or to other types of vocabulary practice and review.

---

## Vocabulary in Context

▲ **VOCABULARY PRACTICE**

Write the word that best completes each sentence.

1. Boarding the bus, Rosa Parks was lost in a private _____ of memories and wishes.
2. She had been working _____ all day because it was the busy Christmas season.
3. She lunched with a lawyer who was a _____ of a famous civil rights lawyer.
4. She recalled her grandfather's _____ to act.
5. Her belief in the rightness of her refusal made her calm and _____.
6. She knew that if she lost her self-respect now, she might never _____ it.

**WORD LIST**

exhortation
frenetically
protégé
retrieve
reverie
serene

**ACADEMIC VOCABULARY IN SPEAKING**

• complex • device • evaluate • interact • perspective

With a partner, **evaluate** the narrative techniques used in the biography. Which technique is used most effectively—dialogue, suspense, description of conflict, or development of character? Support your evaluation with at least three examples. Use at least one Academic Vocabulary word in your response.

**VOCABULARY STRATEGY: ETYMOLOGIES**

Researching a word's **etymology**—that is, its history and origin—can give you insight into the word's meaning. One easy way to learn a word's etymology is to look the word up in a dictionary. Information about the word's origin will appear near the beginning or end of the dictionary entry.

**COMMON CORE**

**L 4c** Consult reference materials to determine a word's meaning or etymology.

> **se•rene** (sə-rēn′) *adj.* **1.** Unaffected by disturbance; calm and unruffled. See synonyms at **calm. 2.** Unclouded; fair: *serene skies and a bright blue sea.* **3.** often **Serene** Used as a title and form of address for certain members of royalty: *Her Serene Highness; His Serene Highness.* [Middle English, from Latin *serenus*, serene, clear.] —**se•rene′ly** *adv.* —**se•rene′ness** *n.*

*PRACTICE* Use a dictionary to answer these questions.

1. Through what languages can the history of *frenetic* be traced?
2. Does the Old French verb that gave rise to *reverie* mean "to be happy" or "to dream"?
3. From what Latin word does *exhort* derive, and what does it mean?
4. What language is the source of *protégé*?

**Interactive Vocabulary** | THINK central

Go to **thinkcentral.com**.
KEYWORD: HML9-300

---

## DIFFERENTIATED INSTRUCTION

**FOR ENGLISH LANGUAGE LEARNERS**

**Vocabulary Strategy: Etymologies** To provide more instruction with etymologies, help students use a dictionary to find the etymologies of the word *signature*. Discuss how knowing the etymology can help students understand the meaning of the word. (Signature *comes from Latin* signum, *which means "sign" and is related to* signare, *"to mark." To put one's signature on something is to mark it with one's name, or to leave a sign of oneself.*)

**FOR ADVANCED LEARNERS/PRE–AP**

**Vocabulary in Writing** Have students use at least two vocabulary words in a paragraph written in the first person from the point of view of a white passenger on the bus.

# Writing for Assessment

**COMMON CORE**
W 4, W 9 (RL 7, RI 7), W 10

## 1. READ THE PROMPT

In writing assessments, you may be asked to compare and contrast how two writers treat the same subject. You are now going to practice writing an essay that requires this type of focus.

> Like many people, Douglas Brinkley and Rita Dove seem fascinated by Rosa Parks and the courage she displayed when she defied racist laws and refused to give up her bus seat. In a four- or five-paragraph essay, compare and contrast the portrayals of Rosa Parks. Do they emphasize the same details and create the same impression of her? In what ways do they differ? Give evidence to support your response.

◀ **STRATEGIES IN ACTION**

1. I need to write an essay that analyzes *similarities and differences* between the two works on Rosa Parks.
2. I have to consider how each writer *reveals Parks's traits* and personality.
3. I need to *include examples or quotations* from the two works.

## 2. PLAN YOUR WRITING

- Review the **Points of Analysis** chart you created on page 299.
- Using your chart, find examples to use as evidence for the points you will develop in your essay. If necessary, review the selections to identify more examples.
- Create an outline to organize your main points. You might base this outline on the categories used in the chart.

## 3. DRAFT YOUR RESPONSE

**Introduction** Introduce the topic, Rosa Parks, and then explain that you will be comparing portrayals of her in a biography and a poem. Be sure to include the title and author of each work.

**Body** Use the topics in your chart as a guide to the key points of your analysis. In one paragraph, for example, you might compare and contrast how each writer describes her appearance. Within each paragraph you write, give specific details to back up your points.

**Conclusion** Wrap up your essay with a restatement of your main idea and a brief summary of your main points.

**Revision** Check your use of transitional words and phrases to connect your ideas. Words and phrases such as *likewise, both,* and *in the same way* signal similarities. *On the other hand, instead, nevertheless,* and *however* signal differences.

---

## DIFFERENTIATED INSTRUCTION

### FOR STRUGGLING WRITERS

**Reinforce Outlining** Demonstrate different approaches to outlining, urging students to use the method that works best for them. For example, present an Outline and ask students to consider whether it meets their needs. Be sure to explain that each main point with its supporting information becomes a paragraph.

📋 **BEST PRACTICES TOOLKIT—** Transparency
Outline p. B19

---

# Writing for Assessment

**COMMON CORE** W 4, W 9 (RL 7, RI 7), W 10

## 1. READ THE PROMPT

- Remind students that comparing and contrasting means discussing both similarities and differences.
- Encourage students to read the prompt carefully, making sure they know exactly what they are being asked to discuss.

## 2. PLAN YOUR WRITING

- Explain that an outline helps writers gather and organize ideas and supporting details.
- Emphasize that ideas about this topic must be supported by examples (such as quotations or vivid details) from each work.

## 3. DRAFT YOUR RESPONSE

- Explain that students should choose the method that they feel best showcases the points they wish to make. For example, they might focus on the biography in one paragraph and the poem in the next paragraph. Alternatively, they might focus on similarities between the two works in one paragraph and differences in another.
- Point out that the use of transitional words and phrases is only one thing that students should check as they revise. They also should review the clarity of their main points, the accuracy of supporting details, and so on.

---

# Assess and Reteach

## Assess

**DIAGNOSTIC AND SELECTION TESTS**
Selection Test A pp. 87-88
Selection Test B/C pp. 89-90

**Interactive Selection Test** on **thinkcentral.com**

## Reteach

**Level Up Online Tutorials** on **thinkcentral.com**

# Focus and Motivate

## COMMON CORE FOCUS

**W 1a–e** Write arguments to support claims using valid reasoning and relevant evidence; establish and maintain a formal style and objective tone; provide a concluding section. **W 2c** Use appropriate and varied transitions to link the major sections of the text, create cohesion, and clarify relationships. **W 4** Produce clear and coherent writing appropriate to the task, purpose, and audience. **W 5** Develop and strengthen writing by planning, revising, editing, rewriting, or trying a new approach. **W 9a (RL 1, 3)** Cite textual evidence; analyze how complex characters develop over the course of a text. **W 10** Write routinely over shorter time frames for a range of tasks, purposes, and audiences. **L 1b** Use adjectival and adverbial phrases to convey specific meanings. **L 2** Demonstrate command of the conventions of punctuation and spelling.

## WRITE WITH A PURPOSE

Tell students that they should choose a character that has made a strong impression on them. When they evaluate the character's believability, they should be able to offer relevant evidence to support their claim.

## COMMON CORE TRAITS

Review the *COMMON CORE TRAITS* with students, focusing on the use of valid reasons and relevant evidence. Compare the list of traits with the rubric on page 310.

## ADDITIONAL TASKS

**Write About Social Studies** Think of a historical figure who has been portrayed in films. Write a literary criticism in which you compare how the person is characterized in books and films.

**Possible topics:** George Washington, Cleopatra, Amelia Earhart

**Write About Community** Write an essay in which you evaluate how the claims in a newspaper editorial are expressed and supported.

### Writing Online

The following tools are available online at **thinkcentral.com** and on **Write*Smart* CD-ROM**:
- **Interactive Graphic Organizers**
- **Interactive Student Models**
- **Interactive Revision Lessons**

---

## Writing Workshop
### ARGUMENT

# Literary Criticism

*Essential Course of Study*

"This character's actions and motivations are completely unrealistic." "That's *exactly* how I would react in a similar situation." Have you ever had similar thoughts or observations while reading a short story or a novel? Analyzing and evaluating characters is part of what makes reading literature so rewarding. In this workshop, you will learn how to write a work of literary criticism. You will evaluate a specific character's believability and support your **claim,** or position, with evidence.

Complete the workshop activities in your **Reader/Writer Notebook.**

---

### WRITE WITH A PURPOSE

#### WRITING TASK
Write a work of **literary criticism** in which you evaluate the believability of a specific character from literature. Use relevant evidence from the text to justify your claim.

#### Idea Starters
- Madame or Monsieur Loisel in "The Necklace"
- Jill in "Pancakes"
- Atticus or Scout Finch in *To Kill a Mockingbird*
- Okonkwo in *Things Fall Apart*

#### THE ESSENTIALS
Here are some common purposes, audiences, and formats for writing a work of literary criticism.

| PURPOSES | AUDIENCES | FORMATS |
|---|---|---|
| • to convince others to agree with your claim<br>• to better understand your reactions to characters in literature | • classmates and teacher<br>• friends<br>• book club members<br>• newspaper readers<br>• Web users | • essay for class<br>• book review in school or local newspaper<br>• online book review<br>• podcast<br>• blog posting |

### *COMMON CORE TRAITS*

#### 1. DEVELOPMENT OF IDEAS
- includes an **introduction** that states a **precise claim**
- provides **valid reasons** and **relevant evidence** to support the claim
- acknowledges **opposing claims** and includes **counterclaims**
- offers a **concluding section** that supports the argument presented

#### 2. ORGANIZATION OF IDEAS
- **organizes** reasons and evidence in a **logical way**
- uses **transitions** to create cohesion and clarify the relationships among ideas

#### 3. LANGUAGE FACILITY AND CONVENTIONS
- maintains a **formal style** and **objective tone**
- uses **adjectival** and **adverbial phrases** to add precise detail
- employs correct **grammar, mechanics,** and **spelling**

**Writing Online**

**THINK** central

Go to **thinkcentral.com.**
KEYWORD: HML9N-302

---

## Writing Workshop Resources

### RESOURCE MANAGER UNIT 2
Plan and Teach pp. 165–168
Prewriting–Editing pp. 169–173
Writing Rubric p. 174
Speaking and Listening p. 175
Writing Support p. 176*

### BEST PRACTICES TOOLKIT
Writing Template: Literary Analysis
p. C30

### TECHNOLOGY
- **Teacher One Stop DVD-ROM**
- **Student One Stop DVD-ROM**
- **Write*Smart* CD-ROM**
- **GrammarNotes DVD-ROM**

**Writing Center on thinkcentral.com**

*See resources on the **Teacher One Stop** DVD-ROM and on **thinkcentral.com**.*

\* Resources for Differentiation

# Planning/Prewriting

 **COMMON CORE** **W 1a-e** Write arguments to support claims using valid reasoning and relevant evidence. **W 5** Develop and strengthen writing as needed by planning. **W 9a (RL 1, 3)** Cite textual evidence; analyze how complex characters develop over the course of a text.

## Getting Started

### CHOOSE A CHARACTER

List characters that have made an impression on you. Consult the Idea Starters on page 302 for some sample characters. Review your list, and then choose a character that is complex enough to be the subject of a **substantive,** or meaningful, argument. Next, assess the character's believability using specific questions or criteria. Remember— you may not personally know anyone like the character you chose, but that does not mean he or she is unrealistic.

### ▶ ASK YOURSELF:

- In what ways does this character seem lifelike and three-dimensional?
- Does the character have emotions and flaws that are easy to relate to?
- Do this character's thoughts and actions make sense, given what I know about his or her personality traits?
- If the character does not seem believable, why not?

### THINK ABOUT AUDIENCE AND PURPOSE

To write an effective work of literary criticism, you must first identify your **purpose**—to convince your **audience** to accept your claim as a valid statement. To be successful, you need to consider your audience members' understanding of the character and their potential viewpoints. Then you can choose the reasons and evidence that will be most convincing to them.

### ▶ ASK YOURSELF:

- Who is my audience? What do I want my audience to think about this character?
- Do I expect my audience to agree or disagree with my claim? How will that impact the supporting details I include?
- What background information about the plot or the character will my audience need in order to understand my argument?

### STATE YOUR CLAIM AND REASONS

State your position in a **precise claim.** Your claim will guide every detail you include in your literary criticism. You should be able to prove your claim with **valid reasons**—ones that are logical and make sense. If you discover that your claim can't be supported well, then you should revise it or try a new approach.

### ▶ WHAT DOES IT LOOK LIKE?

**Claim:** *Madame Loisel is a realistic character, driven by emotions that many people share.*

| Reason 1 | Reason 2 | Reason 3 |
|---|---|---|
| Envy causes Madame Loisel to react in extreme ways. | Madame Loisel behaves impulsively like a real person might under great stress. | Madame Loisel's pride and insecurity affect her decision-making. |

---

# Teach

## Planning/ Prewriting

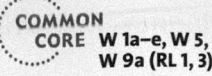 **COMMON CORE** W 1a–e, W 5, W 9a (RL 1, 3)

▶ **CHOOSE A CHARACTER** If students have difficulty choosing a character, have them skim through some stories they have read in class. Remind them that they each should choose a character that has made a strong impression, and that they should know enough about the character to be able to provide sufficient evidence to support a claim.

▶ **THINK ABOUT AUDIENCE AND PURPOSE** Explain to students that their audience may not agree with their claim. As they acknowledge any opposing claims in their literary criticism, they should be able to offer supporting statements. Encourage students to bolster their claim by providing their audience with meaningful background information.

▶ **STATE YOUR CLAIM AND REASONS** Encourage students to evaluate the validity of each of their reasons. Have them ask themselves: *Is this reason logical? Does it make sense?* If they answer *no* to any of these questions, have them replace the reason with a valid one.

**R** **RESOURCE MANAGER—Copy Masters**
Planning/Prewriting p. 169
Drafting p. 170
Revising and Editing pp. 171–172
Rubric p. 174
Writing Support p. 176

---

## DIFFERENTIATED INSTRUCTION

### FOR ENGLISH LANGUAGE LEARNERS

**Language: Reinforce Literary Terms** Write these terms on the board and review them with students:

- *claim:* a sentence that states the writer's position on an issue

- *reasons:* explanation of why the writer believes this position

- *evidence:* valid and relevant information that supports a reason. Evidence includes quotations, anecdotes, and examples.

- *opposing claim:* a viewpoint on the issue that is different from the writer's

- *counterclaim:* the writer's response to an opposing claim

## Planning/Prewriting *continued*

▶ *GATHER EVIDENCE* Tell students that they can use their own experiences as reasons that support their claim. To do so, they must first make sure their anecdotes or examples tie in with what is happening in the text. Encourage students to think of a time when they experienced something similar to what the character experiences. Were their actions similar to those of the character?

▶ *ANTICIPATE OPPOSING CLAIMS* Have students work in pairs, taking turns stating their claim and explaining their reasons. Each partner should then express an opposing claim. If students are unable to offer a convincing counterclaim, encourage them to rethink their stance on the character.

**YOUR TURN** Have students complete the **Your Turn** activity independently. Then ask them to exchange charts. Have partners identify the reasons and evidence for the claims. Allow time for students to add additional anecdotes, examples, and quotations.

For interactive graphic organizers, see

💿 **Write*Smart* CD-ROM**

**Writing Center** on **thinkcentral.com**

---

## Planning/Prewriting *continued*

### Getting Started

#### GATHER EVIDENCE

In order to craft a convincing argument, you should supply several strong **reasons** that clearly and directly support your claim. For literary criticism, it's important to closely examine the text for **evidence** that you can include to back up your reasons. Each of your reasons must be supported by at least one of the following kinds of **relevant,** or related, evidence.

- **anecdote**—a brief, personal story that illustrates the point you are making
- **example**—a specific instance that supports your point, such as an example of a character's thoughts or actions
- **quotation**—a phrase, sentence, or passage excerpted from the text

#### ▶ WHAT DOES IT LOOK LIKE?

> **Anecdote**
> Just as Madame Loisel is afraid to tell the truth, my little brother lost his baseball mitt last summer and was terrified to tell my parents about it.

> **Example**
> Many people feel just like Madame Loisel. For example, I sometimes envy other people's clothing or possessions.

> **Quotation**
> Madame Loisel is not content with her station in life, believing "that she had been born for all the little niceties and luxuries of living."

#### ANTICIPATE OPPOSING CLAIMS

Some readers may disagree with your assessment of the character. For your criticism to be persuasive, you need to address any **alternate** or **opposing claims** and explain their limitations. Brainstorm a list of possible opposing claims readers might have. For each opposing claim, list a **counterclaim** that refutes the opposition and explains why your viewpoint is more valid.

#### ▶ WHAT DOES IT LOOK LIKE?

> **Opposing Claim:** Wouldn't a real person tell his or her friend about the lost necklace instead of going into debt?
>
> **Counterclaim:** Madame Loisel is too proud and insecure to confess the truth to her friend.

**PEER REVIEW** Describe to a peer your audience, purpose, and claim. Then ask: What reasons and evidence will best support my claim?

**YOUR TURN** In your *Reader/Writer Notebook,* choose a character for evaluation. Decide whether that character is realistic, and write your position in a precise claim. Use a chart or graphic organizer to identify valid reasons and evidence. Make sure to state possible opposing claims and formulate counterclaims in response.

**304** UNIT 2: CHARACTERIZATION AND POINT OF VIEW

---

## DIFFERENTIATED INSTRUCTION

### FOR ENGLISH LANGUAGE LEARNERS

**Writing: Gather Support** Have students use these sentence starters to help them develop their claims and relevant evidence:

- My claim is _____.
- One reason for my claim is _____.
- This reason is supported by the following (example, anecdote, quotation): _____.

### FOR STRUGGLING WRITERS

**Providing Counterclaims** Explain that counterclaims address an opposing claim, explaining why the original claim is still valid. Have students write a list of possible opposing claims to their arguments. Then ask: How would you convince someone that this opposing claim is inaccurate? Students should provide evidence in the form of anecdotes, quotations, or examples.

## Drafting

◌ COMMON CORE

**W 2c** Use appropriate and varied transitions to link the major sections of the text, create cohesion, and clarify relationships. **W 4** Produce clear and coherent writing appropriate to the task, purpose, and audience.

The following chart shows how to organize your draft to create an effective work of literary criticism.

### Organizing Your Literary Criticism

**INTRODUCTION**

- Open with a **challenging question, compelling quotation,** or **relevant anecdote.**
- Introduce the **character,** the **author,** and the **literary work.** Provide any **background** that your audience might need to understand your criticism.
- State your position in a **precise claim.**

▼

**BODY**

- Present your reasons in **logical order,** such as by order of importance.
- Support each reason with **relevant** and **sufficient evidence,** including quotations from the text.
- Acknowledge **opposing claims** fairly. Provide **counterclaims** to emphasize the strength of your claim and the limitations of other viewpoints.
- Maintain a **formal style** by using a confident voice and avoiding slang. Use an **objective,** or controlled, **tone** that isn't defensive or dismissive of opposing claims.

▼

**CONCLUDING SECTION**

- **Restate your claim** so that it follows from and supports your argument.
- Leave the reader with something to think about, such as a **thought-provoking question.**

### GRAMMAR IN CONTEXT: USING TRANSITIONS

When your claim, reasons, and evidence are tied together well, your essay is **coherent,** or smooth and easy to follow. Use appropriate **transitions**—words, phrases, and clauses that show the relationship among your ideas—to link the major sections of your essay. Be sure to vary your transitions to strengthen the flow of your essay.

| Transitions that Create Cohesion | | Example |
|---|---|---|
| however | consequently | *Madame Loisel makes for a believable character.* **One reason** *I believe this is because she exhibits many of the same traits and emotions that we all experience, such as pride and envy.* **For example, although** *she lives well for a woman of her station, she is not content because she is consumed with envy of the wealthy class.* |
| if … then | for example | |
| furthermore | although | |
| one reason | so | |

**YOUR TURN** Develop a draft of your essay, using the plan outlined in the chart. Make sure you include appropriate and varied transitions to link your ideas.

### FOR ENGLISH LANGUAGE LEARNERS

**Language: Transitions** Students may struggle with using appropriate transitions. Write the sentence frames on the board and, using the list on page 305, help students complete them.

- _____, I also experience feelings of envy. *(however, for example, consequently, furthermore)*

- _____ I believe this is because Madame Loisel handles hardship in a realistic manner. *(one reason)*

- _____ she knew about the necklace's real value, _____ none of this would ever happen. *(if, so; then)*

Show students that punctuation and sentence structure often determine which transitions are appropriate.

---

## Practice and Apply

### Drafting

◌ COMMON CORE **W 2c, W 4**

▶ **INTRODUCTION** Tell students that their introductions should both interest and inform readers. As they state their claims and give essential background information about the literary works, encourage students to find ways to keep readers interested, such as by adding challenging questions.

▶ **BODY** Remind students that the details in the body of a literary criticism should all work to support the claim. In their own work, students will need to list reasons, acknowledge opposing claims, and provide counterclaims. Have students review their drafts and eliminate any extraneous details that do not support their claims.

▶ **CONCLUDING SECTION** Remind students that a concluding section should not only restate the claim, but also leave readers with something to think about. Have students work with partners to brainstorm ways to strengthen their concluding sections.

### GRAMMAR IN CONTEXT: USING TRANSITIONS

For practice, have each student think of a movie character and then write a short paragraph about why that character is important in the film. Students should state a claim, include three reasons that support it, and use transitions to create cohesion in their paragraphs. Have volunteers share their paragraphs with the class.

**YOUR TURN** Ask students to complete the **Your Turn** activity independently. Have them circle transitional words and phrases and insert more if there are not enough. Suggest that students write their drafts double-spaced so that they can make revisions more easily.

 **BEST PRACTICES TOOLKIT**—Transparency Writing Template: Literary Analysis, p. C30 For interactive revision tools, see

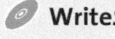 **Write*Smart* CD-ROM**

**Writing Center** on **thinkcentral.com**

**Model the Skill** Using a draft of a work of literary criticism on a transparency or electronic whiteboard, model how to use the questions, tips, and strategies suggested in the chart to evaluate and revise. Consider using literary criticism written by a student from a different class or from a previous year. Be sure to remove the writer's name so that the student remains anonymous.

Remind pairs to think of all possible opposing claims as they review each other's literary criticism. Have them identify any argument or evidence that needs strengthening by asking themselves: "Does this convince me that this claim is correct?"

For interactive revision tools, see

**WriteSmart CD-ROM**

**Writing Center** on <u>thinkcentral.com</u>

# Revising

When you revise, you evaluate the development, organization, and style of your draft. Use the chart shown to help you revise and rewrite where necessary. Check that you achieve your purpose and provide enough evidence to persuade your audience.

**LITERARY CRITICISM**

| Ask Yourself | Tips | Revision Strategies |
|---|---|---|
| 1. Do I capture the audience's attention in my opening lines? | ▶ **Bracket** thought-provoking statements, questions, quotations, or anecdotes. | ▶ **Add** an attention-getting statement, question, quotation, or anecdote. |
| 2. Does my introduction identify the character, author, and literary work? Do I state a precise claim? | ▶ **Draw boxes** around the names of the character, author, and title of the work. **Underline** the claim. | ▶ **Add** a sentence that names the character, author, and literary work. **Revise** the claim to more precisely describe your opinion of the character's believability. |
| 3. Are there at least two valid reasons that support my claim? Is there relevant evidence to support each reason? | ▶ **Highlight** the reasons that support the claim. **Circle** the evidence that supports each reason. **Draw an arrow** from the evidence to the reason. | ▶ If necessary, **add** valid reasons to support the claim. **Add** examples, anecdotes, or quotations to bolster unsupported reasons. **Elaborate** on pieces of evidence by adding more details or explanation. |
| 4. Do I use transitions to clarify the relationships among my claim, counterclaim, reasons, and evidence? | ▶ **Draw a star** next to each transitional word or phrase. | ▶ **Check** your starred transitions and **add** variety if necessary. **Reread** the parts that lack stars. **Add** appropriate transitions to link related ideas. |
| 5. Do I acknowledge opposing claims and present counterclaims? | ▶ **Draw a wavy line** under the opposing claims and your responses to them. | ▶ If necessary, **add** a counterclaim that acknowledges the merits of your opinion and the limitations of opposing claims. |
| 6. Does the concluding section restate my claim and give the reader something to think about? | ▶ **Put a check mark** next to the restatement. **Underline** the sentence that offers an important insight. | ▶ **Add** a restatement of the claim if it is missing. **Add** a thought-provoking question or statement about human nature. |

**YOUR TURN** **PEER REVIEW** Working with a peer, review your drafts together. Answer each question in the chart to decide how to improve your drafts and where to try a new approach.

---

## DIFFERENTIATED INSTRUCTION

**FOR ENGLISH LANGUAGE LEARNERS**

**Writing: Introduction** Provide students with the following sentence frames:

• My claim is _____.

• I strongly believe this because _____.

• My evidence to support this is _____.

Work with students to reorder the information in these sentences to create revised introductions that are compelling and attention-grabbing.

**FOR ADVANCED LEARNERS/PRE–AP**

**Analyze Concluding Sections** Provide students with several samples of literary criticism. Challenge them to write a brief description of the strategies each writer used to strengthen their concluding section. Work with students to prepare a format for sharing the strategies with the class.

## ANALYZE A STUDENT DRAFT

Read this student's draft and the comments about it as a model for revising your own work of literary criticism.

COMMON CORE

**W 1d** Establish and maintain a formal style and objective tone. **W 5** Strengthen writing by revising, editing, rewriting, or trying a new approach, focusing on addressing what is most significant for a specific purpose and audience.

### Madame Loisel: Driven by Emotion

by Mia Thompson, Holmes High School

**❶** Have you ever decided to hide a mistake rather than tell the truth and face the consequences? In Guy de Maupassant's "The Necklace," the character of Madame Loisel longs for an upper-class life. When she is unexpectedly invited to a party, she borrows an extravagant diamond necklace from a wealthy friend. Trouble begins when Madame Loisel discovers that she has lost the necklace. Rather than tell her friend the truth, she reacts rashly and decides to replace the necklace by going into debt. Envy, impulsiveness, and pride are universal emotions that drive Madame Loisel's decisions and motivations. In developing a complex character guided by these emotions, Maupassant has created a believable character.

**❷** From the beginning of the story, readers learn that Madame Loisel is consumed with envy. She feels that she was born into the wrong class and that her situation in life is unfair. For example, she will no longer visit her wealthy friend anymore. Because of her jealousy, "she would weep for days on end from vexation, regret, despair, and anguish." She is clearly out of her mind, because even though she has nice digs and a servant, she is still down in the dumps! Yet envy causes many people to act over the top. After all, just think of all the movies and TV shows that focus on characters whose jealousy leads to turmoil and conflict. Further, think of all the times that jealousy has negatively affected your life. Envy is a universal emotion.

Mia grabs the attention of her audience by beginning with an **interesting question.**

In her introduction, Mia clearly states a **precise claim.**

Mia provides **evidence** from the story to support her claim, but she needs to maintain the **formal style and objective tone** she establishes in her introduction.

**LEARN HOW** Use a Formal Style and Objective Tone Mia establishes a formal style and objective tone in her introduction. However, in her second paragraph, she lapses into informal language, which weakens the credibility of her ideas. Also, by including an exclamation point, Mia comes across as overly charged and emotional. Notice how Mia's revisions make her tone and style consistent.

**MIA'S REVISION TO PARAGRAPH ❷**

~~She is clearly out of her mind, because e~~ven though she has ~~nice digs~~ *nice house* a~~,~~ and a servant, she ~~is still down in the dumps!~~ *remains unhappy.* Yet envy causes many people to ~~act over the top~~ *have extreme reactions to even the most insignificant problems.*

## ANALYZE A STUDENT DRAFT

Explain that the Student Draft on this page is the first half of a literary criticism. Model reading the draft and the annotations in blue that explain the student's language choices. Explain that the *Learn How* mini-lesson has helpful information about a way to improve this student's draft as well as their own.

**LEARN HOW** Use a Formal Style and Objective Tone

- Remind students that a formal style and objective tone can strengthen the credibility of their literary criticism.

- Write the following sentences on the board: *Marie is the best ice skater in the world! She has so many medals and wins absolutely everything.* Ask students how they could revise and add details to these sentences to make them more credible. *(Possible answers: Toning down the use of informal language; giving details about Marie's awards and rank.)*

- Have students read through their drafts, looking for places where they can revise informal or dismissive language. Remind students to check for slang and the overuse of exclamation points.

## FOR STRUGGLING WRITERS

**Formal Style and Objective Tone** Explain to students that informal language, such as slang, is what most people use in casual conversation. In their literary criticisms, however, they should work to control their tone in order to make their arguments more convincing. Provide pairs of students with sample informal sentences. Have them take turns revising them to reflect a formal style and objective tone.

Explain that the Student Draft is continued and completed on this page. Read the draft and annotations aloud and discuss. Ask students how well the writer's response to an opposing claim addresses possible reader concerns.

 **LEARN HOW** Strengthen Your Concluding Section

- Remind students that a strong concluding section is one that is memorable to the reader. Read aloud the original draft of Mia's paragraph. Then read the revised version. Ask students how adding an observation and an insightful question improved the concluding section.

- Have volunteers suggest other observations or questions Mia could have added to her concluding section to make it stand out.

- Suggest students return to their own literary criticisms to see how they might strengthen their concluding sections.

**YOUR TURN** Before students complete the **Your Turn** activity, have them work in pairs to discuss each other's concluding sections. Ask partners to evaluate whether the concluding section is memorable and why. Partners should then brainstorm possible ways to strengthen or improve their concluding sections.

For interactive revision tools, see

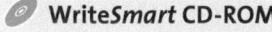 **WriteSmart CD-ROM**

**Writing Center** on **thinkcentral.com**

---

**3**   Jealousy isn't Madame Loisel's only realistic trait. Impulsiveness also leads to her downfall. After she and her husband discover the loss of the necklace, they are "aghast," desperate, and not thinking clearly. In times like these, people often don't make the most rational decisions. Rather, their impulsiveness leads them to act rashly. Had the Loisels taken the time to calmly assess the situation, they may have handled their predicament differently.

> Mia uses **appropriate transitions** to shift from discussion of one reason to the next.

**4**   Some readers might view Madame Loisel's decision to go into debt over the lost necklace as unrealistic, especially since it means she will have to live the rest of her life as a pauper—a life that would cause her agony and despair. Madame Loisel's decision, however, makes sense when readers consider how proud she is and how much she cares about what people think of her. Someone who is that insecure and proud would surely choose to keep her dignity, rather than be shamed or looked down upon by her friend.

> Mia addresses an **opposing claim** and offers a **valid counterclaim** in response.

**5**   A flawed woman who never realizes her dreams and lets her emotions get the best of her, Madame Loisel is as complex and three-dimensional as a real person.

> Mia could strengthen her concluding section by adding an insightful question or observation.

**LEARN HOW** Strengthen Your Concluding Section  Mia can improve her concluding section by providing more than a mere restatement of her claim. Ending with an insightful observation or question about human nature can make a work of literary criticism more memorable. In her revision, Mia prompts readers to put themselves in the character's shoes. This ending is more likely to resonate with her audience.

---

**MIA'S REVISION TO PARAGRAPH 5**

A flawed woman who never realizes her dreams and lets her emotions get the best of her, Madame Loisel is as complex and three-dimensional as a real person. *Her story serves as a warning to readers of what could happen if they let envy and pride rule their decisions. But are you sure, in a similar situation, that you wouldn't fall prey to the same emotions?*

---

 **YOUR TURN**  Use feedback from your peers and your teacher as well as the two "Learn How" lessons to revise your work of literary criticism. Evaluate how well you convince your audience to adopt your claim through compelling reasons, strong evidence, an acknowledgment of opposing viewpoints, and valid counterclaims.

---

## DIFFERENTIATED INSTRUCTION

### FOR ENGLISH LANGUAGE LEARNERS

**Writing: Strengthen Your Concluding Section**  Students may need help adding interesting observations or insightful questions to their concluding sections. Suggest that students free write or talk about the characters they have chosen and their claims about them. Listing any impressions or lingering questions they have. Work with students to identify any observations or questions they can include and expand on in their concluding sections.

# Editing and Publishing

In the editing stage, you proofread your essay to make sure it is free of grammar, spelling, and punctuation errors. You don't want mistakes to detract from your criticism and prevent your audience from accepting the validity of your claim.

**COMMON CORE**

**W 1e** Provide a concluding section that supports the argument. **W 5** Strengthen writing by editing. **L 1b** Use adjectival and adverbial phrases to convey specific meanings. **L 2** Demonstrate command of the conventions of punctuation and spelling.

## GRAMMAR IN CONTEXT: ADJECTIVAL AND ADVERBIAL PHRASES

Prepositional phrases can help you convey specific meanings and add detail to your writing. **Adjectival phrases** are prepositional phrases that modify nouns or pronouns. **Adverbial phrases** modify verbs, adjectives, or adverbs.

| Type of Phrase | Example |
|---|---|
| Adjectival |  *The star character in Maupassant's short story is the status-seeking Madame Loisel.* |
| Adverbial | ▶ *She didn't realize she had lost the necklace until that evening.* |

When Mia proofread her essay, she noticed that she could make her ideas more precise by adding adjectival and adverbial phrases.

> after the party
> Trouble begins when Madame Loisel discovers that she has lost the necklace of her dreams.

### PUBLISH YOUR WRITING

Share your literary criticism with an audience.
- Make copies of your writing and distribute them to your classmates.
- Submit your work for publication in your school newspaper or in a literary magazine.
- Participate in an informal discussion in which you and a small group debate the believability of the character.
- Post your criticism on a blog and invite other classmates to post their viewpoints. Elicit others' opinions on the character and your claim.

**YOUR TURN** Correct any errors in your literary criticism by carefully proofreading it. Make sure you add adjectival and adverbial phrases to make your ideas clear to readers. Then publish your writing where your audience is most likely to notice it.

---

## FOR ENGLISH LANGUAGE LEARNERS

**Language: Prepositional Phrases** Students may need practice in identifying and using prepositional phrases. List the words *jump, throw, girl,* and *hat* on the board. Work with students to create sentences for each of these words and identify what kind of prepositional phrase you are using.
[**Possible answers:** *Jump over the line (adverbial); The girl with the bangs was happy. (adjectival); Throw the letter through the slot (adverbial); The hat in the shop window was pretty (adjectival)*]

## FOR STRUGGLING WRITERS

**Prepositional Phrases** Review with students that adjectival and adverbial phrases help make their writing more precise. For practice, have students identify the phrases underlined in the following sentences.

- The <u>friend with the diamond necklace</u> arrived <u>late at night.</u> *(adjectival; adverbial)*

- She was <u>humbled by her kindness.</u> *(adverbial)*

---

# Editing and Publishing

**COMMON CORE** W 1e, W 5, L 1b, L 2

## GRAMMAR IN CONTEXT: ADJECTIVAL AND ADVERBIAL PHRASES

Explain to students that adjectival and adverbial phrases can help them support the claim they are making in their literary criticism. Using these types of phrases provides additional detail that will strengthen their writing and help their readers understand specific ideas.

- Have students read their final drafts and identify ideas that are not clear.

- Encourage them to add adjectival and adverbial phrases to these ideas.

## PUBLISH YOUR WRITING

Brainstorm with students about additional ways to publish their literary criticisms.

**YOUR TURN** Allow time for students to proofread their drafts. Remind them to add prepositional phrases to make their ideas more precise.

## Scoring Rubric

Tell students that the best way to understand a scoring rubric is to use it to score actual writing. Provide the class with copies of a literary criticism—either a student's from a previous year with the student's name removed or a sample from a state assessment. Have students work with partners to evaluate the essay by using the scoring rubric. Have students score the essay, and create bulleted lists of reasons and examples that support their scores. Take a class survey to determine whether there is a consensus regarding the score. If not, guide students toward a consensus using the sample essay and the scoring rubric. Make sure that students understand that consensus is important to ensure that all essays are scored fairly and equally. The purpose of a rubric is to eliminate subjectivity from the scoring process.

For Rubric Bank, see

 **Write*Smart* CD-ROM**

**Writing Center** on **thinkcentral.com**

## Assess and Reteach

### Assess

 **RESOURCE MANAGER—Copy Master**
Rubric for Evaluation p. 174

**Online Essay Scoring** at **thinkcentral.com**

### Reteach

**Level Up Online Tutorial** at **thinkcentral.com**

---

# Scoring Rubric

Use this rubric to evaluate your literary criticism from the Writing Workshop or your response to the on-demand writing task on the next page.

## LITERARY CRITICISM

| SCORE | COMMON CORE TRAITS |
|---|---|
|  6 | • **Development** Asserts a precise claim; supports the claim with valid reasons and relevant, sufficient evidence; ably counters opposing claims with counterclaims; ends powerfully<br>• **Organization** Is logically organized; uses appropriate and varied transitions to create cohesion and show the relationships among the claim, reasons, and evidence<br>• **Language** Consistently maintains a formal style and objective tone; shows a strong command of conventions |
|  5 | • **Development** States a precise claim; offers valid reasons and relevant evidence; counters opposing claims with counterclaims; ends with a strong concluding section<br>• **Organization** Is logically organized; uses appropriate transitions to show the relationships among the claim, reasons, and evidence<br>• **Language** Uses a formal style and objective tone; has a few errors in conventions |
|  4 | • **Development** States a clear claim; offers mostly valid reasons and evidence; needs to more fairly address opposing claims; has an adequate concluding section<br>• **Organization** Reflects a logical organization, with one or two exceptions; could use a few more transitions<br>• **Language** Mostly uses a formal style, but sounds defensive at times; includes a few distracting errors in conventions |
|  3 | • **Development** States a claim that could be more precise; provides some relevant support but not enough to be sufficient; unfairly dismisses other viewpoints; has a somewhat weak concluding section<br>• **Organization** Has some flaws in organization; needs more transitions to show how ideas are linked<br>• **Language** Often lapses into an informal style or defensive tone; has several errors in conventions |
|  2 | • **Development** Has a weak claim; offers some irrelevant reasons and insufficient evidence; fails to acknowledge other viewpoints; has a weak concluding section<br>• **Organization** Has major organizational flaws; lacks transitions throughout<br>• **Language** Uses an informal style and defensive tone; has many errors in conventions |
|  1 | • **Development** Lacks a claim; has no support; ignores opposing claims; ends abruptly<br>• **Organization** Has no organization and transitions<br>• **Language** Uses an inappropriate style and tone; has major problems with grammar, mechanics, and spelling |

# Preparing for Timed Writing

**COMMON CORE** **W 10** Write routinely over shorter time frames for a range of tasks, purposes, and audiences.

## 1. ANALYZE THE TASK 5 MIN

Read the writing task carefully. Then read it again, underlining words that tell the topic, the audience, and the purpose. Circle the type of writing you are being asked to do.

> **WRITING TASK**
>
> Your <u>school newspaper</u> wants you to write about <u>a book you've read recently</u>. Write (a work of literary criticism) in which you <u>evaluate the believability of the plot</u>.
>
> *Audience* · *Topic* · *Type of Writing* · *Purpose*

## 2. PLAN YOUR RESPONSE 10 MIN

First, jot down the **criteria,** or elements, of a realistic plot, such as a believable ending. Ask yourself: How does the plot of this book measure up to my criteria? Your answer will help you develop your claim, reasons, and evidence. Use a chart to list reasons and evidence. Also, note an opposing claim your readers might have. What counterclaim could you develop to address their concerns?

| Reasons | Evidence |
|---------|----------|
|         |          |
|         |          |
|         |          |

*Possible Opposing Claim:*

*My Counterclaim:*

## 3. RESPOND TO THE TASK 20 MIN

Use your notes to draft your work of literary criticism. As you write, keep these guidelines in mind:

- In the introduction, grab your audience's attention, provide background information about the book, and state your claim.
- In each body paragraph, provide a reason and relevant evidence.
- Acknowledge an opposing claim and refute it with a valid counterclaim.
- Conclude by restating your claim and sharing a relevant observation or insight.

## 4. IMPROVE YOUR RESPONSE 5–10 MIN

**Revising** Check your draft against the writing task. Do you state your claim precisely? Do you include valid reasons, relevant evidence, and counterclaims to address opposing claims?

**Proofreading** Neatly correct any errors in grammar, spelling, and mechanics.

**Checking Your Final Copy** Before you turn in your literary criticism, check for any errors you may have missed and apply finishing touches.

---

## Preparing for Timed Writing

 **COMMON CORE W 10**

1. **Analyze the Task** Before students begin writing, encourage them to answer the following questions:
   - What is my time limit?
   - What are the key skills assessed in the scoring rubric?
   - Who is my audience?
   - What are my topic and purpose?

2. **Plan Your Response** Remind students that the literary criticism rubric emphasizes supporting a claim with reasons and evidence. Tell students that they should state their claim in their introduction and that every detail in their literary criticism should support their claim.

3. **Respond to the Task** Tell students that the rubric stresses the importance of addressing opposing claims. Tell them that within the body of their literary criticism, they should acknowledge a possible opposing claim and refute it with a counterclaim that addresses the concern.

4. **Improve Your Response** Point out that the scoring rubric emphasizes the use of transitions to create cohesion and link ideas. Encourage students to check that they have included transitional words and phrases that show the organization of their literary criticism and link their ideas logically.

## Assess

Use the scoring rubric on p. 310 to assess students' literary criticisms.

---

## DIFFERENTIATED INSTRUCTION

### FOR ENGLISH LANGUAGE LEARNERS

**Writing: Plan a Response** Have students write their claims in the center of a word web. Help them identify three reasons that support their claims and record them in the web. Then ask students to work in pairs to identify evidence for each of their reasons before writing their literary criticism.

### FOR STRUGGLING WRITERS

**Organize Ideas** Have students use the following outline to record details they will include in their literary criticisms.

**Introduction**
- Attention-grabbing question, fact, anecdote, or example: _____
- Claim: _____

**Body**
- Reason 1: _____
- Evidence: _____
- Reason 2: _____
- Evidence: _____

**Concluding Section**
- Restatement of claim: _____
- Interesting observation or intriguing question: _____

# Focus and Motivate

## COMMON CORE FOCUS

**SL 1a–d** Participate effectively in group discussions. **SL 3** Evaluate a speaker's point of view, reasoning, and use evidence. **SL 4** Present information and supporting evidence clearly, concisely, and logically.

### SPEAK WITH A PURPOSE

Tell students that they will be using the character evaluations from their literary criticism to participate in a discussion. Students should be prepared to defend their claims to their peers and offer counterclaims.

### COMMON CORE TRAITS

As students plan their discussions, remind them to keep in mind the *COMMON CORE TRAITS* of an effective discussion.

# Practice and Apply

## Planning the Discussion

### Model the Skill: SET GOALS FOR THE DISCUSSION

Students may struggle to determine how to adapt and present their written essays during the discussion. Explain that in a discussion, they may modify, or change, their views if they feel a speaker has made a valid and convincing claim. Unlike the written essay, the point of the discussion is not to prove that their own view is right. Instead, they should engage in a conversation with an open mind to build upon their own understanding while also evaluating others' points of view.

**R** RESOURCE MANAGER—Copy Master
Speaking and Listening p. 175

---

## Speaking & Listening Workshop

# Participating in a Discussion

Have you talked to any of your classmates about your literary criticism? Perhaps you even quoted evidence from the text to support your ideas. That's an example of an informal **discussion**, in which two or more well-informed people thoroughly analyze a topic orally. In fact, any time you talk with friends on a topic of interest, you are participating in an informal discussion.

Complete the workshop activities in your **Reader/Writer Notebook**.

| SPEAK WITH A PURPOSE | COMMON CORE TRAITS |
|---|---|
| **TASK** <br><br> Participate in a **discussion** about the character you evaluated in your literary criticism. State whether you feel the character is believable or unrealistic, and defend your claim with reasons and evidence. | **PARTICIPANTS IN AN EFFECTIVE DISCUSSION . . .** <br><br> • come to the conversation prepared and work with peers to set rules, goals, and deadlines <br><br> • respond thoughtfully to diverse perspectives and actively incorporate others into the discussion <br><br> • evaluate each speaker's point of view, reasons, and evidence, noting any flawed reasoning or irrelevant evidence <br><br> • present relevant information supported by evidence |

**COMMON CORE**

**SL 1a–d** Participate effectively in group discussions. **SL 3** Evaluate a speaker's point of view, reasoning, and use of evidence. **SL 4** Present information and supporting evidence clearly, concisely, and logically.

## Planning the Discussion

In your informal discussion, remember to adapt your written criticism to reflect the purpose, audience, and context of the discussion. Use the following guidelines to help you plan your discussion.

- **Identify Group Members** Form groups based on the character you evaluated or the story you chose.

- **Prepare Discussion Notes** Outline your claim, reasons, and supporting evidence. Refer to these notes during your discussion.

- **Set Goals for the Discussion** Determine what your group hopes to accomplish as a result of this discussion. Will you reach a consensus on whether or not the character is believable? Or will you summarize points of agreement and disagreement? Decide as a group how you will achieve these goals, such as by taking a vote or allowing each participant a chance to present an alternate view. Remember to set a deadline for each part of your discussion and to agree on any needed roles, such as note-taker.

- **Create Rules for the Discussion** Participants should develop a list of rules such as the following: speak clearly and concisely; listen without interrupting; respect alternate views; and avoid arguing or going off on tangents.

**Speaking & Listening Online**

Go to **thinkcentral.com**.
KEYWORD: HML9N-312

---

## DIFFERENTIATED INSTRUCTION

### FOR ENGLISH LANGUAGE LEARNERS

**Language: Reinforce Literary Terms** Explain to students that participating in a discussion about their literary criticism has the same basic goals as writing the essay, namely to make a claim and support it with relevant reasons and evidence. The difference, of course, is that the discussion allows people to discuss opposing claims immediately. To assist students in their discussion, review these terms:

- *unrealistic:* not believable

- *peers:* a group of people who have equal ability, such as classmates

- *irrelevant:* not to the point or relating to the subject

- *consensus:* a shared agreement

- *tangents:* information that is not relevant or to the point

## Holding the Discussion

Use the tips and strategies on this page to present your viewpoint effectively and evaluate other speakers' ideas.

### PRESENTING AND EVALUATING IDEAS

During a productive discussion, all participants have a chance to state, clarify, verify, and challenge each other's viewpoints. Keep the following in mind:

| Topic | Strategies That Work |
|---|---|
| **Point of View** <br><br> Does the speaker clearly state his or her viewpoint in a precise claim? | **For Speakers** Use a confident voice and decisive, direct language to state your claim. For example, avoid statements like, "Madame Loisel might be a believable character." Words such as *might* or *maybe* make you appear less credible and assured. <br><br> **For Listeners** Listen for a wavering tone or indecisive language. Such clues may indicate that the speaker is not confident in all aspects of his or her claim. |
| **Support** <br><br> Does the speaker use logical support rather than **fallacious**—flawed—reasoning? Is each reason supported with evidence? | **For Speakers** State your findings clearly, concisely, and logically, so that listeners can follow your line of reasoning. Support every statement you assert with evidence. <br><br> **For Listeners** Think about whether other speakers' reasons make sense. For instance, consider this example of flawed reasoning: "Since I don't know anyone like Madame Loisel, she is not a believable character." Politely challenge any speaker whose reasons lack logic. Also, notice when the evidence provided is not relevant to the reason or sufficient enough to prove the point. |
| **Other Perspectives** <br><br> What are the major points of agreement or disagreement? How do the viewpoints discussed modify speakers' ideas? | **For Speakers** Publicly acknowledge when you agree with another speaker's viewpoint. For instance, you might say something like, "While I agree that Madame Loisel's jealousy is realistic, I think her choices are far-fetched. What person would go into debt for years because of what one person might think of her?" <br><br> **For Listeners** Listen closely while other speakers respond to your claim. Ask yourself: In what way, if any, do other perspectives change or modify my viewpoint? What new connections can I make in light of others' reasons and evidence? |

 **As a Speaker** After sharing your viewpoint, encourage others to respond by asking questions or making comments. Answer any questions posed concisely but completely.

**As a Listener** Keep an open mind, and consider other perspectives. Don't hesitate to modify your viewpoint when another speaker makes a convincing case.

SPEAKING AND LISTENING WORKSHOP **313**

### FOR STRUGGLING STUDENTS

**Politely Challenging Others** Explain that when a listener challenges a speaker's reasons or logic, it keeps a discussion lively and thought-provoking. Both the speaker and listener may learn something new from this exchange. Have pairs work together to politely challenge each other's claims and reasons. Suggest that they use the following format: *While I agree that _____, I think _____.*

### Holding the Discussion

*Model the Skill:* **PRESENTING AND EVALUATING IDEAS**

Model presenting and evaluating ideas by asking three students to briefly discuss a claim in front of the class. Ask one student to make a claim about a character in a commonly known children's tale, for example, Goldilocks. Remind the student to speak confidently. Then have the other two students evaluate the first students' claim using the ideas from the chart in the student book.

**GUIDED PRACTICE** Have students take notes during the practice discussion and use them to respond to questions and opposing claims.

 After the discussion, have students evaluate their roles as speakers and listeners. Students should ask themselves: *As a speaker, did I answer questions and address comments? As a listener, did I consider other perspectives?* Have students suggest ways they can improve future discussions.

## Assess and Reteach

### Assess

Use the **COMMON CORE TRAITS** to assess students' discussions.

A strong participant in a discussion
- speaks clearly and directly to state a claim
- listens to and evaluates other points of view
- uses logical support and reasoning
- agrees and disagrees respectfully with diverse viewpoints

### Reteach

Remind students that they should look at their own opposing claims and counterclaims to see if they relate to the discussion. Students should also listen closely to each speaker and determine whether the speaker's claim, reasons, and evidence are logical and make sense.

**Speaking and Listening Online**
- Public speaking tips
- Strategies for effective listening

SPEAKING AND LISTENING WORKSHOP **313**

# Assessment Practice

## COMMON CORE FOCUS

**RL 1** Cite strong and thorough textual evidence to support analysis of what the text says explicitly as well as inferences drawn from the text. **RL 3** Analyze how complex characters develop over the course of a text, interact with other characters, and advance the plot or develop the theme. **RI 1** Cite strong and thorough textual evidence to support analysis of what the text says explicitly as well as inferences drawn from the text. **RI 3** Determine a central idea of a text. **W 5** Strengthen writing by revising and editing to ensure that it demonstrates conventions of standard English grammar and usage. **L 6** Acquire and use accurately general academic words; demonstrate independence in gathering vocabulary knowledge.

## CHECK READINESS

Read aloud the paragraph under **ASSESS** and stress to students that this is not the full Unit Test, but a way for them to check their readiness for it. Then have students examine the standards listed under **REVIEW** and look back in the unit or in the **Student Resource Bank** for any skills they need to review.

## READ THE TEXTS

Remind students to keep unit goals in mind as they read each passage, paying particular attention to these literary and reading skills:

- main ideas and supporting details
- characterization
- make inferences and draw conclusions
- point of view

To help students focus on the character's tone while reading, encourage them to ask

- What are Samir and Hoda like in "Airport"? What do I learn about them from their actions and words?
- What is Annie Johnson like? What does she want to do?

## ANSWER THE QUESTIONS

Direct students to pages R93–R101 of the **Handbook** to review test-taking strategies.

- As students prepare to answer multiple-choice questions, remind them not to choose the first answer that seems to fit. Instead, they should read all choices, eliminate any that are clearly wrong, and choose the one that is the most accurate and complete.

**314** UNIT 2

---

**COMMON CORE**

# Assessment Practice

**ASSESS**
Taking this practice test will help you assess your knowledge of these skills and determine your readiness for the Unit Test.

**REVIEW**
After you take the practice test, your teacher can help you identify any standards you need to review.

**COMMON CORE**

**RL 1** Cite strong and thorough textual evidence to support analysis of what the text says explicitly as well as inferences drawn from the text. **RL 3** Analyze how complex characters develop over the course of a text, interact with other characters, and advance the plot or develop the theme. **RI 1** Cite strong and thorough textual evidence to support analysis of what the text says explicitly as well as inferences drawn from the text. **RI 3** Determine a central idea of a text. **W 5** Strengthen writing by revising and editing to ensure that it demonstrates conventions of standard English grammar and usage. **L 6** Acquire and use accurately general academic words; demonstrate independence in gathering vocabulary knowledge.

**Practice Test**

**THINK**central

Take it at **thinkcentral.com**.
KEYWORD: HML9N-314

---

**DIRECTIONS** Read the two texts and the poster. Then, answer the questions that follow.

# Airport  *by Pauline Kaldas*

1   He paced the airport waiting room, his steps marking a path in the carpet between the rows of seats. At first those sitting down looked up at this man who could not hold his feet still like the rest of them and curb his agitation. After a while, some returned to their own thoughts or families. A few kept their gaze on his coming and going, perhaps to ease their own turmoil. Even after he left, a few repeated his path with their eyes as if permanently held by the ghost of his movement.

2   Samir was about five feet seven, with black hair cut short because otherwise it would frizz and wave. His nose was rather large, but his eyes compensated, their brown glimmer and long lashes giving his face an unexpected beauty. He was slender, his physique almost that of a young boy. But around the middle a slight roundness was beginning, probably because for the past year he had been going to a Chinese restaurant and ordering pupu platters for dinner. Once, his coworkers had talked him into going out after work. He was frightened at the prospect of having to understand the menu and perhaps not having enough money. When they ordered something to be shared, he was relieved. The assortment of fried foods soothed him. Although some of the tastes were unfamiliar, he had grown up with the smell of food frying. His mother fried fish, potatoes, cauliflower, so now he could eat with a certain security. He asked a couple of times what this was called, his tongue moving silently in his mouth to repeat the words *pupu platter*. After that, occasionally, he would go to the restaurant alone and order the same thing. He didn't catch the odd twist of the waiter's face, and he ate confidently.

3   It was eleven o'clock Sunday morning. He had woken early, a little before six, despite having stayed up late cleaning his small apartment thoroughly. Glancing at his watch, he noted there was still another hour before the plane was due. He stretched his pacing out of the waiting area to look at one of the arrival terminals. Flight 822 from Egypt via Switzerland. Yes, the arrival time was still twelve o'clock P.M. He turned his gaze around the airport until his eyes fell on some tables and chairs that he hoped were part of a coffee shop. He headed over, lengthening his stride a little. Ordering the coffee, he was tempted to get something to eat but was afraid his stomach would turn, so he settled at a small table with the Styrofoam cup awkwardly balanced in his hand. It was too hot to drink so he could only sit, the sounds of the airport mingling together till they became a steady hum in his head.

**314**   UNIT 2: CHARACTERIZATION AND POINT OF VIEW

---

## DIFFERENTIATED INSTRUCTION

### FOR ENGLISH LANGUAGE LEARNERS

**Assessment Practice: Work Backward**
Prepare students by having them read the questions *before* reading the passages. Have pairs find unfamiliar words in test directions and questions and follow these steps:

1. Write each word on an index card.

2. Look up the meaning in a dictionary and write it on the back of the card.

3. Use the cards to practice words with your partner and to teach them to others.

4  She stared at the empty suitcase on her bed. How do you pack for moving to another country? she thought. She circled the room, stopping to sift through open dresser drawers, to flip through clothes hung in the closet, to slightly rearrange items on top of dressers, only to find herself back in front of an empty suitcase.

5  Her mother appeared at the door. "Hoda, you haven't done anything! The suitcase is empty."

6  Hoda shifted her eyes to the suitcase as if seeing its open cavity for the first time. "I will. I'm just organizing," Hoda replied to appease her mother.

7  "You leave early in the morning," her mother said as if ringing a bell.

8  As her mother stepped out of the room, Hoda sat on the bed, giving her back to the suitcase. She was an attractive woman, but not in the traditional Egyptian sense. Her body was slim without the usual roundness around the hips and legs, probably because she insisted on walking everywhere. Taxis are too expensive and buses are too crowded, she argued. Her black hair was cut straight just above her shoulders. She never put anything in it, didn't use henna,[1] and wore it simply as it was. Her mother had tried to coax her a little, to style it in some way, but after all these years, she knew it was a useless effort. Her face held the energy of youth, and people often found themselves looking at her. It was her mouth that was her most prominent feature. Although it was considered slightly large, there was still something captivating about it, the way her smile pulled you in and made you listen to whatever she was saying.

9  It was eleven o'clock Saturday morning. She had woken early, a little before six, despite having stayed up late saying good-bye to friends and relatives. The first thing she did was call the airport to check the departure time. Flight 822 to Boston via Switzerland. Yes, it was leaving at two o'clock A.M. in the morning and due to arrive at twelve o'clock P.M. American Eastern time. After she hung up, she made herself a cup of coffee although she rarely drank it. The traffic outside began its erratic rhythm of fitful stops and starts accentuated by the loud honks of impatient drivers. She sat in the kitchen almost in a trance until her ears tuned the noise outside to a steady hum in her head.

10  Would she be on the plane? It was his brother who had written with the flight information. He had received one letter from her parents, accepting his proposal and giving their blessing. Everything else, signing the church marriage papers, processing the immigration documents, had been done through his brother. And it had taken longer than expected, almost two years of filling out

---

1. **henna** (hĕn'ə) n.: reddish brown dye made from the leaves of the henna plant.

 **GO ON**

## ITEM ANALYSIS

| COMPREHENSION AND WRITTEN RESPONSE | ITEMS | UNIT PAGES |
|---|---|---|
| Character Traits and Motivations | 1, 3, 12, 17, 21 | 202–207 |
| Make Inferences and Draw Conclusions | 4, 5, 6, 8, 16, 19, 22, 23 | 209 |
| Generalizations | 10, 18 | 285 |
| Main Ideas and Details | 2, 3, 12, 13, 14, 17, 20 | 282 |
| Multiple-Meaning Words and Specialized Vocabulary | 7, 9, 11, 15 | 266 |

| WRITING AND GRAMMAR | ITEMS | UNIT PAGES |
|---|---|---|
| Supporting and Descriptive Details | 1, 6 | 267 |
| Vary Sentence Beginnings | 2, 3, 4, 5 | 236 |

### Practice Test

On **thinkcentral.com** students can complete an interactive version of this practice test *and* receive remediation for the skills they have not yet mastered.

---

## FOR STRUGGLING READERS

**Assessment Support**  Consider these options for completing the Assessment Practice:

- Have students "work backward" to review the test questions before reading the passages.

- Select random questions in the Assessment and have students demonstrate *how* and *where* to look for answers.

- Ask students to locate unfamiliar vocabulary words in the Assessment. Elicit the words' meanings from the class.

- Have students record useful testing words and definitions in their journal for later reference.

- Read the selections or parts of them aloud to aid in student comprehension.

forms, presenting proof of this and that, till he felt his life had transformed into a sheaf of papers. He sometimes forgot the purpose behind all this, that it would eventually lead to marrying someone whom he didn't know. At times, fear chimed through Samir's body. Perhaps he should've listened when his brother had urged him to return to Egypt, to choose for himself. But Samir was reluctant to leave his new job.

11    In the meantime, all he could do was wait and work. He had arrived in this country with little money and little education. The only school that would accept him in Egypt was the agricultural college. For two years, he sat and listened to professors lecturing about crops, soil, irrigation till his mind blurred and he knew if he didn't leave, he would end up another man with a college degree selling cigarettes in a kiosk.[2] He was not a lucky person, but he entered the green card[3] lottery anyway. It was free and they only asked for your name and address. The rumor said fifty thousand each year would be chosen to come to America. And he had heard of people who won and actually went. What a strange country, he thought, to make its immigration decisions through a lottery. He curbed his joy when he received notification that he had been selected. It was clear that the process would be long. Now came the applications to be filled, the requests for documents, the interview which, in halting English, he felt sure would eliminate him, but the end was indeed permission to immigrate, to chance his life in another country.

12    Would he be there? What was she doing going to another country to marry a man she didn't even know? Her parents had helped convince her that this would be best for her. "He's from a good family and after all he's in America and not many people can get there." "Besides," her father added, "this America is more suited to your independent nature." "Yes," her mother added, in a resigned tone, "and they like educated people there." It was true that in Egypt Hoda often felt like a piece of rough wood that needed to be sanded down. No one understood her desire to continue for a master's degree in chemistry. "You have a college degree," her parents argued, "and you're twenty-one now. Look for a husband. It's time to settle down." When a young man approached her parents to propose marriage, she accepted, thinking this would keep people quiet. But she had been naive. The young man was insistent that she quit school and devote her time to setting up their new home. Finally their heated arguments led to a breakup of the engagement, and not surprisingly this only worsened her reputation. She knew her parents feared that now she would never marry.

---

2. **kiosk** (kē'ŏsk') *n.:* small structure, used as a newsstand or booth, which is open at one or more sides.

3. **green card** *n.:* document granting a foreigner permission to live and work in the United States.

316

13    When the proposal from America came, she hesitated. She had one more year until she completed her degree. But everyone assured her the paperwork would allow her enough time to finish. And they were right. Things dragged out for so long that at times she forgot she was engaged or that she was going to America. So when Samir's brother appeared at their door two weeks ago with the plane tickets and the approved visa,[4] her head spun like a top.

14    He had arrived with some hope and trepidation. The process had been difficult, but each time he pictured himself standing inside the kiosk, his body trapped and his arms reaching for cigarettes, he was able to push himself and do what was requested. Surely in America there would be more possibilities. But that first year, America kept him dog-paddling and gasping for air. The language confounded him, quick mutterings with hardly any gestures or even a direct look. He took an English class, but the rules of grammar and the purposely slow pronunciation of the teacher did little to improve his understanding. He found a job washing dishes in a restaurant where contact was limited to *Good morning, How are you* and *See you later*. When the radio in the kitchen broke one day, followed by the mumbled swearing of the cook, he offered to fix it. The cook gave him a perplexed look and tossed the radio to him with a *Go ahead*. The dishes piled up a bit as he fiddled with the switches, found a knife to use as a screwdriver, and then managed to make the music reemerge. After that, other radios and sometimes clocks, telephones, or calculators were handed to him. Most of the time he could fix them, and the added conversations made him more confident.

15    Fixing things was the one thing he could do. It was like a sixth sense to him. When he was a child, if something broke at home, they couldn't afford to buy another one. Since it was already not working, his family figured there was no harm in letting him fiddle with it, and so he learned how everything was put together, how to take it apart, and how to reconnect the parts so it worked. He was most comfortable staring at the inside of a machine with its intricate weaving of wires and knobs. But he had never perceived his ability as a skill; it was simply an instinct.

16    When the restaurant manager caught wind of his reputation, he approached him with a request to fix his stereo, adding, *I took it to the shop but they couldn't do anything*.

17    He spent a day at the manager's house, surrounded by components with wires stretching like a web of animal tails. Every time the manager walked by, Samir saw him shaking his head with a look of doubt clouding his face. By the end of the day, the tails had been untangled, and when Samir pressed the

---

4.  **visa** (vē′zə) *n.*: certificate granting official approval to enter a country.

GO ON ➡

317

power button, the music spread through the house. *Thank you, thank you,* the manager repeated, and Samir stood puzzled by how a boss could lower himself to thank an employee. The manager sent Samir to the same shop that couldn't fix his stereo. He was hired on a trial basis, but he proved himself quickly. He had found his niche[5] in this country that could make many things, but didn't know how to fix what it broke.

18    It wasn't that she didn't want to get married. She had always hoped her life would be with a partner, and at some point she expected to have children. But she knew she didn't want the life she saw around her. Women dragging their chores like chains, cleaning house, washing clothes, cooking food, all for others. She had watched friends marry at eighteen and nineteen, sometimes even men of their own choosing whom they loved. Within the first year, their spirits dissipated like sugar crystals in water. It frightened her to envision her life in this way, her days filled with the care of home and family, her body growing heavy with the idleness of her brain.

19    That is why, against everyone's understanding, she enrolled in the master's program in chemistry. She was one of two women, but the other was there only to pass the time until she found a husband. Her family had determined that it would be more respectable for her to continue her studies than to remain at home waiting. But for Hoda, it was a different matter. Chemistry had caught her fancy and it was the only thing she wanted to do. As a child her mother had to pull her out of the kitchen, where she would find her sitting cross-legged on the floor with a bowl in front of her, mixing starch and water, baking soda and vinegar, or some new combination. "Just to see what would happen," she answered her mother's shouting inquiries. Finally, her mother banished her from the kitchen. The result, aside from Hoda never learning how to cook, was that she began borrowing chemistry books from her friend's older brother who was studying at the university and moved the experiments to more secluded parts of the house. She struggled through the master's program, where the male students laughed directly at her and the professors didn't take her seriously. Still she persisted and gained high marks. It was an act of faith since she knew the only job Egypt would give her would be in a lab analyzing blood and urine samples.

20    Perhaps that's why she accepted the roll of dice that would lead her to America. There might be a chance there of having a real job, of doing research, of working with someone who would take her seriously, not turn everything back around to her femininity. Her English was strong since all the sciences were taught in English, and she had occasionally had American or British professors with whom she had no trouble communicating. What concerned

---

5. **niche** (nĭch) *n.*: position or situation that is especially appropriate for a person.

318

her was this man who had extended his proposal across the ocean. What kind of man would marry a woman without even seeing her, would choose as if picking a number out of a hat?

21    After two years in America and turning thirty, Samir knew he had to get married. And he also knew he needed a certain kind of woman, not one who would lean on him, who would expect to be at home while he worked. He needed someone who could stand in this world next to him, perhaps even lead him a little. He sent his request to his brother: a woman who was educated, who knew English well, who wanted to work; a woman who could swim in deep water, he added. His brother argued with him that he was asking for trouble, that such a woman should remain unmarried. But Samir was insistent and said he would accept nothing else.

22    Hoda was twenty-five years old. If she didn't marry soon, she would be looked on with either pity or suspicion. And if she remained in Egypt and married the next man who proposed, her life would inevitably fall into the repeated pattern of other women. She couldn't articulate what she wanted, only that it was not here. Hoda caught her breath like the reins of a horse and began to fill the suitcases. She counted the number of dresses, skirts, and pants she had, then divided by half: that's how many she would take. Then she proceeded to do the same with all other items. Within a few hours the two permitted suitcases were filled.

# New Directions    *by Maya Angelou*

1    In 1903 the late Mrs. Annie Johnson of Arkansas found herself with two toddling sons, very little money, a slight ability to read and add simple numbers. To this picture add a disastrous marriage and the burdensome fact that Mrs. Johnson was a Negro.

2    When she told her husband, Mr. William Johnson, of her dissatisfaction with their marriage, he conceded that he too found it to be less than he expected, and had been secretly hoping to leave and study religion. He added that he thought God was calling him not only to preach but to do so in Enid, Oklahoma. He did not tell her that he knew a minister in Enid with whom he could study and who had a friendly, unmarried daughter. They parted amicably, Annie keeping the one-room house and William taking most of the cash to carry himself to Oklahoma.

**GO ON** ➡

319

---

**Comprehension: Time Sequence** Explain that actions in the story go both backward and forward in time. Give examples of past events that explain Samir and Hoda's background (*he wins the immigration lottery; she studies at the university*) as well as example of events that seem to take place in the present time (*he paces the floor at the airport; she packs her suitcase*).

**Vocabulary: Roots** Point out that the root of *insistent* (paragraph 21) is the Latin word *insister,* which means "to stand." Help students understand the connection between "demanding or continuing to make demands" and a root meaning "to stand."

3    Annie, over six feet tall, big-boned, decided that she would not go to work as a domestic[1] and leave her "precious babes" to anyone else's care. There was no possibility of being hired at the town's cotton gin[2] or lumber mill, but maybe there was a way to make the two factories work for her. In her words, "I looked up the road I was going and back the way I come, and since I wasn't satisfied, I decided to step off the road and cut me a new path." She told herself that she wasn't a fancy cook but that she could "mix groceries well enough to scare hungry away and keep from starving a man."

4    She made her plans meticulously and in secret. One early evening to see if she was ready, she placed stones in two five-gallon pails and carried them three miles to the cotton gin. She rested a little, and then, discarding some rocks, she walked in the darkness to the saw mill five miles farther along the dirt road. On her way back to her little house and her babies, she dumped the remaining rocks along the path.

5    That same night she worked into the early hours boiling chicken and frying ham. She made dough and filled the rolled-out pastry with meat. At last she went to sleep.

6    The next morning she left her house carrying the meat pies, lard, an iron brazier,[3] and coals for a fire. Just before lunch she appeared in an empty lot behind the cotton gin. As the dinner noon bell rang, she dropped the savors into boiling fat and the aroma rose and floated over to the workers who spilled out of the gin, covered with white lint, looking like specters.[4]

7    Most workers had brought their lunches of pinto beans and biscuits or crackers, onions and cans of sardines, but they were tempted by the hot meat pies which Annie ladled out of the fat. She wrapped them in newspapers, which soaked up the grease, and offered them for sale at a nickel each. Although business was slow, those first days Annie was determined. She balanced her appearances between the two hours of activity.

8    So, on Monday if she offered hot fresh pies at the cotton gin and sold the remaining cooled-down pies at the lumber mill for three cents, then on Tuesday she went first to the lumber mill presenting fresh, just-cooked pies as the lumbermen covered in sawdust emerged from the mill.

9    For the next few years, on balmy spring days, blistering summer noons, and cold, wet, and wintry middays, Annie never disappointed her customers, who could count on seeing the tall, brown-skin woman bent over her brazier, carefully turning the meat pies. When she felt certain that the workers had

---

1. **domestic** (də měs'tĭk) *adj.:* household servant, such as a maid or cook.

2. **cotton gin** *n.:* factory in which machines are used to separate the seeds from the fibers of cotton.

3. **brazier** (brā'zhər) *n.:* cooking device used to grill food over burning coals.

4. **specters** (spěk'tərz) *n.:* ghosts.

320

---

## DIFFERENTIATED INSTRUCTION

**FOR STRUGGLING READERS**

**Comprehension Support** Direct students to the first two paragraphs of the story on page 319. Point out that Annie must make a change in her life because her husband leaves her with two children to support. Explain that her husband's departure is the *cause* of Annie's decision. Choosing to cook for working people is the *effect* of her decision.

**Concept Support** After students read paragraph 3, discuss what is involved in "cutting a new path." Ask students for examples of what it means to "step off the road" to make a change. Ask students for examples of these kinds of changes from their own experience, and help them connect with Annie's decision to make a change.

become dependent on her, she built a stall between the two hives of industry and let the men run to her for their lunchtime provisions.

10    She had indeed stepped from the road which seemed to have been chosen for her and cut herself a brand-new path. In years that stall became a store where customers could buy cheese, meal, syrup, cookies, candy, writing tablets, pickles, canned goods, fresh fruit, soft drinks, coal, oil, and leather soles for worn-out shoes.

11    Each of us has the right and the responsibility to assess the roads which lie ahead, and those over which we have traveled, and if the future road looms ominous or unpromising, and the roads back uninviting, then we need to gather our resolve and, carrying only the necessary baggage, step off that road into another direction. If the new choice is also unpalatable,[5] without embarrassment, we must be ready to change that as well.

5. **unpalatable** (ŭn păl'ə tə bəl) *adj.:* unpleasant; unacceptable.

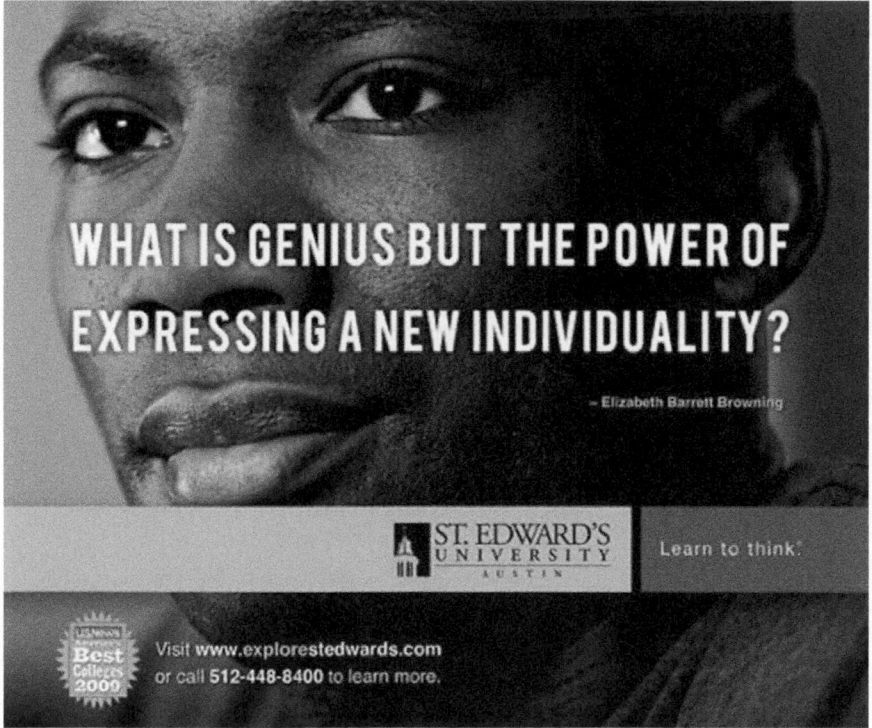

321

# Reading Comprehension

Model a thinking process for answering multiple-choice questions.

1. **A is correct.** *Both Samir and Hoda are unsatisfied with their lives, and they see marriage as one opportunity for improvement.* B *is incorrect because Samir is not studying for a graduate degree.* C *is incorrect because neither character needs to get away from family.* D *is incorrect because the characters do not send money home.*

2. **D is correct.** *Samir's brother selects Hoda to be Samir's wife.* A *is incorrect because Samir chooses when to enter the lottery.* B *is a weak choice because Samir agrees to go to the shop to fix things.* C *is incorrect because Samir chooses to enter the agricultural college.*

3. **B is correct.** *Samir is waiting in the airport for his future wife to arrive.* A *is incorrect because Samir is staying in the United States.* C *is incorrect because Samir's attitude about flying is not mentioned in the story.* D *is incorrect because Samir does not consider returning to Egypt.*

4. **C is correct.** *Samir originally eats the* pupu platter *with friends and doesn't realize it is meant to be shared.* A *is incorrect because Samir's pronunciation is not ironic.* B *is incorrect because he is used to eating fried foods.* D *is incorrect because the food does not make Samir sick.*

5. **B is correct.** *The airport is a place of arrivals and departures, and it symbolizes change.* A *is a weaker choice because Samir and Hoda will continue to face problems.* C *is incorrect because Samir and Hoda's choices do not guarantee security.* D *is incorrect because the airport is not a cause of delays in Hoda's arrival.*

6. **A is correct.** *Samir is afraid that his nervousness will upset his stomach.* B *is incorrect because Samir continues to want to marry Hoda.* C *is incorrect because Samir's trip to the airport is not discussed in the story.* D *is incorrect because Samir does not drink the hot coffee.*

7. **A is correct.** *Hoda tells her mother she will pack her suitcase to keep her mother from worrying.* B *is incorrect because it does not make sense in the context of the sentence.*

---

# Reading Comprehension

> **Use "Airport" (pp. 314–319) to answer questions 1–11.**

1. Samir and Hoda enter into an arranged marriage because they both —
   A. want to improve their lives
   B. are pursuing graduate degrees
   C. need to get away from their families
   D. must send money home

2. What choice about Samir's life was made for him?
   A. When to enter the green card lottery
   B. Where to work at fixing things
   C. Where to go to school in Egypt
   D. Which woman to marry

3. In the beginning of the story, Samir seems agitated because —
   A. he is waiting to fly somewhere
   B. he is waiting to meet his future wife
   C. he is frightened about flying
   D. he is anxious about returning home to Egypt

4. In paragraph 2, Samir's food order at the Chinese restaurant is ironic because —
   A. he has trouble pronouncing *pupu platter*
   B. the food does not taste as he expects
   C. the *pupu platter* is meant to be shared, not eaten alone
   D. the food makes him sick although it reminds him of home

5. The airport symbolizes —
   A. running away from problems
   B. a chance for new beginnings
   C. security in life's decisions
   D. procrastination and delays

6. In paragraph 3, the author uses the phrase "afraid his stomach would turn" to show that Samir —
   A. felt sick with nervousness
   B. changed his mind about the marriage
   C. drove too fast to the airport
   D. drank coffee that was too strong

7. In paragraph 6, the word *appease* means —
   A. to calm
   B. to express
   C. to frustrate
   D. to provoke

8. The phrases "felt like a piece of rough wood . . . ," "her head spun like a top," "spirits dissipated like sugar crystals," "wires stretching like a web of animal tails," and "caught her breath like the reins of a horse" are all examples of —
   A. analogies
   B. metaphors
   C. similes
   D. symbols

9. In paragraph 14, the word *trepidation* means —
   A. composure
   B. expectation
   C. lukewarm
   D. nervousness

10. What does paragraph 20 suggest about the choices people make?
    A. Preparation is important.
    B. The results are unknown.
    C. There are few risks involved.
    D. Let fate decide what to do.

---

C *and* D *are incorrect because they mean the opposite of what Hoda is attempting to accomplish, which is to soothe her mother.*

8. **C is correct.** *All the phrases are similes because they compare unlike items using* like *or* as. A *is a weaker answer because the phrases are similes, which are a specific type of analogy.* B *is incorrect because metaphors do not include* like *or* as. D *is incorrect because the phrases make comparisons, rather than standing as symbols.*

9. **D is correct.** *Samir faces many difficulties, which contribute to his nervousness.* A *is incorrect because* composure *means the opposite of* trepidation. B *is incorrect because it does not indicate the slightly negative connotation implied by* trepidation. C *is incorrect because it does not make sense in the context of the sentence.*

10. **B is correct.** *The phrase "roll of the dice" indicates that many choices are the result of chance.* A *is a weaker answer because the paragraph indicates Hoda's preparation cannot determine her future.* C *is incorrect because Hoda's arranged marriage involves risk.* D *is incorrect because Hoda's preparation is the opposite of letting "fate" decide.*

**11.** Which phrase in paragraph 21 helps the reader understand the meaning of *insistent*?

   **A.** *who would lean on him*

   **B.** *even lead him a little*

   **C.** *he was asking for trouble*

   **D.** *he would accept nothing else*

> **Use "New Directions" (pp. 319–321) to answer questions 12–15.**

**12.** Annie Johnson is motivated to start her own business because she —

   **A.** doesn't like working for others

   **B.** wants to put her many skills to use

   **C.** needs to be able to supervise others

   **D.** must support her family

**13.** Annie knows she is ready to start her business by —

   **A.** selling all her meat pies on the first day

   **B.** being sure she can carry her supplies to the factories

   **C.** how much her children enjoy her food

   **D.** building a stall between the factories

**14.** Which of the following statements best expresses a main idea about the passage?

   **A.** Life is hard, and people need to make sacrifices to be successful.

   **B.** If the road you are on in life is not the one you want, make a new path for yourself.

   **C.** Only a few people can overcome great obstacles to create a successful life.

   **D.** With hard work and perseverance, it is possible to overcome discrimination.

**15.** When Annie Johnson made her plans *meticulously*, she —

   **A.** started learning how to cook

   **B.** cooked the meat pies at night

   **C.** practiced her daily routine

   **D.** arrived at the factory at lunchtime

> **Use "Airport" and "New Directions" to answer questions 16–18.**

**16.** One message in "Airport" and "New Directions" is that people —

   **A.** should not take great risks in life

   **B.** can achieve success easily

   **C.** can only count on themselves

   **D.** have to overcome fears to move forward in life

**17.** In both texts, the women —

   **A.** rely on others for their success

   **B.** are married

   **C.** are independent

   **D.** have immigrated from another country

**18.** Which of the following themes do the texts share?

   **A.** Hopes for a new life may help you achieve what you did not know you could.

   **B.** Taking chances is too dangerous for people with high expectations for themselves.

   **C.** Love adds meaning to relationships, whether we seek it or not.

   **D.** One should hold onto one's ideals and values to be successful.

 **GO ON**

323

**11. D is correct.** The phrase "accept nothing else" indicates Samir's refusal to compromise or abandon his request. A is incorrect because it implies giving assistance, not insistence. B is incorrect because it indicates Samir will receive assistance, not make a demand. C is incorrect because insistence does not imply trouble, only steadiness of purpose.

**12. D is correct.** Annie begins her own business when her husband leaves and she must provide for her children. A is a weaker choice because it does not address Annie's main reason for working, which is to earn money for her family. B is incorrect because Annie wants to employ her skills in the service of making a living. C is incorrect because Annie does not supervise others at her job.

**13. B is correct.** Annie practices carrying weighted buckets before she begins her business. A is incorrect because Annie does not sell all her meat pies the first day. C is incorrect because the story does not depict Annie's children eating her food. D is incorrect because Annie does not build a stall until later.

**14. B is correct.** The passage emphasizes people's ability to change in order to overcome difficulties. A is a weaker choice because change, not sacrifice, is the main idea of the passage. C is incorrect because the passage emphasizes Annie's ordinariness and lack of resources as she overcomes obstacles. D is incorrect because discrimination is not the main idea of the passage.

**15. C is correct.** Meticulously *implies great care and practice. A is incorrect because Annie already knows how to cook. B and D are incorrect because they describe the time that Annie completed her actions, not the care and planning she took in her work.*

**16. D is correct.** In both stories, characters must make changes to improve their conditions in life. A is incorrect because characters in both selections take risks. B is incorrect because the characters are not assured of easy success. C is incorrect because Samir and Hoda count on their families.

**17. C is correct.** *Hoda shows her independence by attending the university and breaking off her engagement, while Annie shows her independence by beginning a new business to support her children. A is incorrect because relying on others is the opposite of independence. B is incorrect because Hoda is not yet married and Annie is separated from her husband. D is incorrect because only Hoda immigrates to another country.*

**18. A is correct.** *Both Hoda and Annie believe that they can create new lives for themselves. B is incorrect because both texts emphasize the need for taking chances. C is incorrect because none of the stories' main characters are in love. D is incorrect because the characters in the stories do not have their values challenged in the texts.*

**19. A is correct.** Words such as "genius" and "Learn to think" emphasize a search for knowledge. B is incorrect because the poster is serious and emphasizes learning. C is incorrect because the emphasis on individuality is the opposite of fitting in. D is incorrect because the focus of the poster is on self-development, not selflessness.

**20. B is correct.** The poster indicates that self-exploration can lead to self-knowledge and development. A is incorrect because the poster does not mention the need for studying. C and D are incorrect because the poster does not mention the possibility of outward success.

## SHORT CONSTRUCTED RESPONSE

*Possible responses:*

**21.** The text indicates that Hoda's wish for independence and education conflicts with her culture's expectations of women. The conflict leads her father to point out that the United States is better suited for her "independent nature" (paragraph 12). She also faces the possibility of conflict with a husband that she has not met, as she wonders "what kind of a man" would marry her without knowing her (paragraph 20).

**22.** The author admires Annie's ability to "step off the road" in order to take care of her children (paragraph 3). She appreciates Annie's ability to work hard in "blistering summer noons, and cold, wet, and wintry middays" to make her business succeed (paragraph 9).

**23.** In both texts, the main characters believe that they can change their lives for the better. They have hopes and dreams in which they imagine a future better than the life they are living. Samir, for example, dreams that he can have a future other than "selling cigarettes in a kiosk" (paragraph 11). Hoda hopes that by studying chemistry, she can find work she enjoys while avoiding a family life that makes her body "heavy with the idleness of her brain" (paragraph 18). Annie dreams that she can find a kind of work that will allow her to support her family without leaving her "'precious babes' to anyone else's care" (paragraph 3).

---

Use the poster on p. 321 to answer questions 19–20.

**19.** This poster appeals to the viewer's —
- **A.** quest for self-knowledge
- **B.** need for entertainment
- **C.** desire to fit in with others
- **D.** impulse to help others

**20.** What is the main message of the poster?
- **A.** Study hard to do your best.
- **B.** Believe in who you are and who you can become.
- **C.** Attend our school and find great employment.
- **D.** Be smarter and you will go far in life.

### SHORT CONSTRUCTED RESPONSE
Write a short response to each question, using strong and thorough text evidence to support your response.

**21.** What is one conflict Hoda faces in "Airport"? Support your response with evidence from the text.

**22.** What does the writer of "New Directions" think of Annie Johnson? Support your response with evidence from the text.

Write a short response to this question, using strong and thorough evidence from both texts to support your response.

**23.** How does the idea of hopes and dreams apply to "Airport" and "New Directions"? Support your response with evidence from **both** texts.

324

---

## DIFFERENTIATED INSTRUCTION

### FOR ENGLISH LANGUAGE LEARNERS

**Test-Taking Strategies: Understanding Instructions** Read aloud the test instructions on pages 322–324.

- Explain words such as *visual representation* ("image or picture") and *text evidence* ("examples, or sample words and phrases").
- For short-answer questions, help students identify the types of passages from the text that would support their answers.

# Revising and Editing

**DIRECTIONS** Read this passage, and answer the questions that follow.

> (1) Mary Kingsley was an Englishwoman born in 1862. (2) She spent years traveling in Africa. (3) Her family expected her to stay home to care for her mother. (4) Her mother was sick at the time. (5) After their deaths, she went to West africa. (6) Her parents died in 1892. (7) Kingsley hacked through jungles in the heat. (8) Even then, she dressed like a proper English matron. (9) She always wore a dress made out of thick fabric. (10) She also wore boots and a hat. (11) She fell onto the spikes of an animal trap. (12) It is at these moments you realize the blessings of a good thick skirt," she wrote later.

1. What is the best way to combine sentences 1 and 2?
   A. Mary Kingsley, an Englishwoman born in 1862, spent years traveling in Africa.
   B. Born in 1862, Mary Kingsley, who was an Englishwoman, spent years traveling in Africa.
   C. Mary Kingsley was an Englishwoman, born in 1862, she spent years in Africa.
   D. Mary Kingsley, English and born in 1862, spent years traveling in Africa.

2. What is the most effective way to improve the organization of this paragraph?
   A. Delete sentence 3
   B. Move sentence 6 before sentence 5
   C. Delete sentence 7
   D. Move sentence 11 before sentence 10

3. What is the best way to combine sentences 3 and 4?
   A. Expecting her to stay at home, her mother was sick.
   B. She stayed at home, as her family expected, to care for her mother.
   C. Her family expected her to stay home to care for her sick mother.
   D. Mary's mother was sick, so she was expected to stay home.

4. What change, if any, should be made to sentence 5?
   A. Change *africa* to **Africa**
   B. Delete the comma after **deaths**
   C. Change *West* to **west**
   D. Make no change

5. What transitional word should be added to the beginning of sentence 11?
   A. Instead,          C. Once,
   B. Next,             D. Subsequently,

6. What change, if any, should be made to sentence 12?
   A. Insert open quotation marks before *It*
   B. Change *blessings* to **blessing's**
   C. Delete the closed quotation marks after *skirt*,
   D. Make no change

STOP

325

## ANSWERS
## Revising and Editing

1. **A is correct.** *The sentence uses precise adjectives and combines the sentences effectively, using few commas. B is a weaker answer because the inclusion of phrases requires awkward additional commas. C is incorrect because it includes a comma splice. D is a weaker answer because it creates the awkward phrase "English and born in 1862."*

2. **B is correct.** *Sentence 6 should come before sentence 5 because "her parents" (sentence 6) is the referent for "their deaths" (sentence 5). A is incorrect; the information provided adds important detail to Mary Kingsley's story. C is incorrect because the information about Mary Kingsley's dress is important to the end of the paragraph. D is incorrect because sentence 10 should stay in its current position to complete the description of Kingsley's costume.*

3. **C is correct.** *The revision combines the sentences to show cause and effect. A is incorrect because the revision creates a dangling participle. B is incorrect because it changes the meaning of the original sentences. D is a weaker answer because the phrase "she was expected" is in passive voice.*

4. **A is correct.** *The proper noun Africa should be capitalized. B is incorrect because the comma is required following an introductory element. C is incorrect because the region of West Africa is a proper noun. D is incorrect because the revision is required for proper capitalization.*

5. **C is correct.** *Once should be added to indicate that an example follows. A is incorrect because it implies contrast. B and D are incorrect because they imply a sequence of events.*

6. **A is correct.** *The phrase "she wrote later" indicates that sentence should be set off with quotation marks. B is incorrect because blessings is used as a plural, not as a possessive. C and D are incorrect because the sentence should be set off as a quotation.*

## COMMON CORE FOCUS

**RL 10** Read and comprehend literature. **RI 10** Read and comprehend literary nonfiction.

## INTRODUCE *GREAT READS*

In Unit 2, students have discussed a number of big questions. Invite students to tell which question they found most intriguing and why, and then focus attention on the three that appear on this page. Discuss the recommended books and their summaries, pointing out how each connects to the related question. Encourage students to choose one or more of these "great reads" to read independently.

## UNIT 2
# *Great Reads*

**COMMON CORE**

**RL 10** Read and comprehend literature. **RI 10** Read and comprehend literary nonfiction.

## Ideas for Independent Reading

What makes a character grow and change? How many ways can you define strength? Find out by reading these additional works.

## *Are you a perfectionist?*

### Into the Wild
*by Jon Krakauer*

This true account of an idealistic young man tells of his wish to give up the trappings of wealth and privilege. He leaves a comfortable life to live a simple one in the wilderness. And he almost makes it.

### The Chosen
*by Chaim Potok*

Two neighbor boys live with different sets of parental expectations. Reuven, the narrator, slowly comes to understand the weight of responsibility that rests on his best friend Danny's shoulders.

### Pride and Prejudice
*by Jane Austen*

The mother of five daughters, Mrs. Bennet wants to find the perfect husband for each of them. As you read this Jane Austen novel, see if Mrs. Bennet and her daughters need to compromise their rather unrealistic standards.

## *How important is status?*

### The Outsiders
*by S. E. Hinton*

In this classic young-adult novel, the "greasers" are the poor kids' gang and the "socs" are a gang of rich kids. Tragedy forces Ponyboy, a greaser, to change the way he lives.

### A Connecticut Yankee in King Arthur's Court
*by Mark Twain*

Hank Morgan lives in 19th-century Connecticut. After a head injury he wakes up in the England of King Arthur, where he is definitely not one of the privileged. Twain's social satire is still relevant to today's world.

### Kaffir Boy
*by Mark Mathabane*

This is the true story of a black youth's coming of age under the apartheid policy in South Africa.

## *When is strength more than muscle?*

### Finding Fish
*by Antwone Fisher*

Fisher's autobiography tells of his life in a foster home, where he was humiliated and abused. Fisher escaped, first into the navy and then into a life of writing, where his talent flourished. His award-winning screenplay *Antwone Fisher* became a feature film.

### Coming of Age in Mississippi
*by Anne Moody*

Moody's autobiographical classic describes her childhood in the Mississippi of the 1950s. She was unwilling to accept the racist world of that time and challenged it through her work in the civil rights movement.

### O Pioneers!
*by Willa Cather*

After her father dies, Alexandra inherits the family farm—over the protests of her brothers. She struggles to overcome tragedy and hardship while keeping her family together and forging a living on the hard Nebraska prairie.

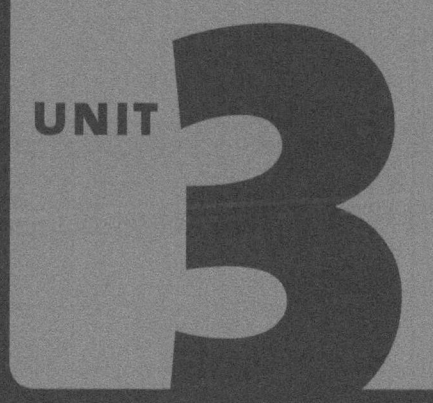

# A Sense of Place

## SETTING, MOOD, AND IMAGERY

- In Fiction
- In Media
- In Nonfiction
- In Poetry

327

**About the Art** This photograph depicts the Catacomb of Saint Callisto, Rome, Italy. See also page 377.

# UNIT 3

## COMMON CORE

**STRAND**

| | ECOS<br>**Text Analysis Workshop: Setting, Mood, and Imagery**<br>pp. 330–335 | ECOS<br>**A Christmas Memory**<br>Short Story<br>pp. 336–353<br><br>*Lexile: 830*<br>*Fry: 7*<br>*Dale-Chall: 6.6* | ECOS<br>**Through the Tunnel**<br>Short Story<br>pp. 354–369<br><br>*Lexile: 860*<br>*Fry: 4*<br>*Dale-Chall: 5.5* | ECOS<br>**The Cask of Amontillado**<br>Short Story<br>pp. 370–383<br><br>*Lexile: 830*<br>*Fry: 11*<br>*Dale-Chall: 7.5* |
|---|---|---|---|---|
| **Reading Literature** | Setting pp. 330–331 **RL 3, RL 4**<br>Imagery and Mood pp. 332–333 **RL 4**<br>Analyze the Text pp. 334–335 | Details of Setting pp. 337, 338, 342, 347, 349, 351 **RL 4**<br>Flashback p. 350 **RL 5**<br>Analyze Imagery pp. 337, 341, 342, 345, 351 **RL 4** | Setting as Symbol pp. 355, 358, 363, 367 **RL 3**<br>Analyze Details pp. 355, 356, 358, 360, 363, 367 **RL 4** | Mood pp. 371, 374, 376, 379, 381, 383 **RL 4**<br>Irony p. 375 **RL 5**<br>Paraphrase pp. 371, 372, 379<br>Formal Language pp. 376, 383 **RL 4** |
| **Reading Informational Text** | | | | Read for Information p. 380 |
| **Writing** | | Quickwrite p. 336<br>Writing Prompt p. 353 | Writing Prompt p. 369 | Writing Prompt p. 383 **W 4** |
| **Speaking and Listening** | | | Discuss p. 354 **SL 1** | Present p. 370 **SL 1** |
| **Language** | | Effective Verb Tense pp. 344, 353 **L 3**<br>Language Coach p. 348<br>Connotation and Denotation p. 352 **L 5b** | Write Concisely p. 359, 369 **L 1, L 3**<br>Language Coach p. 366 **L 4b**<br>Latin Roots (*quest, quer, quisit*) p. 368 **L 4d** | Language Coach p. 374 **L 4**<br>Formal Language pp. 376, 383 **L 2, L 3**<br>Foreign Words and Phrases p. 379 **L 4c**<br>The *clud* Word Family p. 382 **L 4c** |

| Media Study: from **The Cask of Amontillado** Film Clip pp. 384–387 | Linked Selections | | The Sharks/The Peace of Wild Things Poems pp. 406–411 | Writing Workshop: Short Story pp. 412–421 Technology Workshop: Producing a Story Trailer pp. 422–423 |
|---|---|---|---|---|
| | *from* **A Walk in the Woods** Travel Narrative pp. 388–399 | **Wilderness Letter** Letter pp. 400–405 | | |
| Lexile: 1140 Fry: College Dale-Chall: 6.6 | Lexile: 1140 Fry: College Dale-Chall: 6.6 | | | |
| Setting and Mood pp. 385–386 **RL 7** | | | Imagery and Mood pp. 407, 408, 411 **RL 4** Connect pp. 407, 410, 411 **RL 4, RL 10** | |
| | Setting and Mood pp. 389, 390, 392, 396, 398 **RI 4** Author's Perspective pp. 389, 390, 394, 398 **RI 4, RI 6** | Primary Sources pp. 400–405 **R 1, RI 6** Central Idea p. 401 **R 1, RI 2, RI 6** | | |
| Write or Discuss p. 387 **W 9a** | Quickwrite p. 388 | Writing Prompt p. 405 **W 2b** | | Writing a Short Story pp. 412–421 **W 3a–e, W 4, W 5, W 10** Producing a Story Trailer pp. 422–423 **W 6** |
| Write or Discuss p. 387 **SL 2, SL 5** | | | Discuss p. 406 **SL 1** | Producing a Story Trailer pp. 422–423 **SL 2, SL 5** |
| | Language Coach pp. 393, 396 **L 4b, L 4c** Context Clues p. 399 **L 4a** | Language Coach p. 402 **L 4** | | Drafting p. 415 **L 1b** Editing and Publishing p. 419 **L 2, L 2c** |

**ECOS**

To see the complete Essential Course of Study, see pp. T23–T28.

 For additional lesson planning help, see **Teacher One Stop DVD.**

# Instructional Support

**Resource Manager Unit 3**

**UNIT SUPPORT**
Academic Vocabulary, p. 3
Additional Academic Vocabulary, p. 4
Grammar Focus p. 5
Text Analysis Workshop pp. 9–10
Writing Workshop: Short Story p. 133

**SELECTION SUPPORT***

**Plan and Teach**
Lesson planning pages
Additional leveled selection questions
Extension activities

**Student Copy Masters**
Selection summaries in four languages
Skills copy masters in English and Spanish
Vocabulary preteaching and support
Reading Check and Question support
Reading Fluency

*Available for all selections

† Available on **thinkcentral.com**

**Language Handbook**
**Vocabulary Practice**
**Best Practices Toolkit**†
**PowerNotes** DVD-ROM†
**Connections: Nonfiction for Common Core** CD-ROM†

**Teacher One Stop** DVD-ROM
**Student One Stop** DVD-ROM
**MediaSmart** DVD-ROM
*from* The Cask of Amontillado
**WriteSmart** CD-ROM†
**GrammarNotes** DVD-ROM†
**WordSharp** CD-ROM†

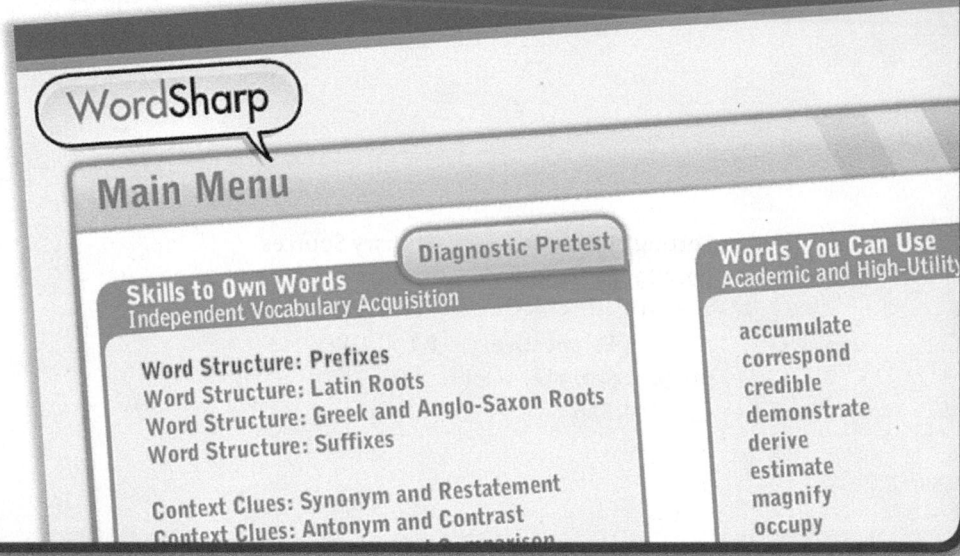

# Differentiated Instruction

| *STRUGGLING READERS AND WRITERS* | *ENGLISH LANGUAGE LEARNERS* | *ADVANCED LEARNERS* |
|---|---|---|
| **Resource Manager Unit 3**<br>Additional Selection Questions<br>Question Support<br>Reading Fluency<br>**Interactive Reader**<br>**Adapted Interactive Reader**<br>**Level Up Online Tutorials**<br>**Audio Anthology**<br>(with Audio summaries)<br>**Diagnostic and Selection Tests**<br>Selection Tests A/B | **Resource Manager Unit 3**<br>Selection Summaries in English, Spanish, Vietnamese and Haitian Creole<br>Skills Copymasters in Spanish<br>**English Language Learner Adapted Interactive Reader Teacher's Guide**<br>**ELL Adapted Interactive Reader**<br>**Audio Tutor**<br>**Guide to English for Newcomers**<br>**Audio Anthology**<br>**Audio Summaries in Multiple Languages**<br>(on **thinkcentral.com**) | **Resource Manager Unit 3**<br>Additional Selection Questions<br>Ideas for Extension<br>**Diagnostic and Selection Tests**<br>Selection Tests B/C |

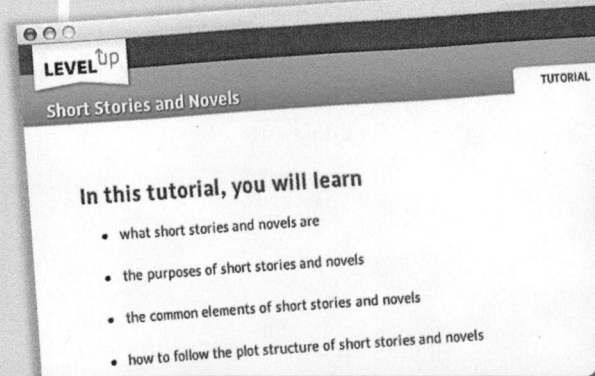

**Diagnostic and Selection Tests**

**Unit and Benchmark Tests**

**ThinkCentral Online Assessment:**

- All program assessments
- Level Up Online Tutorials

**ExamView Test Generator** on the Teacher One Stop DVD-ROM

**Online Essay Scoring** on **thinkcentral.com**

**ThinkCentral Online Reteaching:**

- Level Up Online Tutorials
- Reteaching Worksheets

**Holt McDougal** Online Essay Scoring

Welcome to Holt McDougal Online Essay Scoring!

This site is designed to help you improve your writing skills and prepare for standardized writing tests. When you write and submit a response to one of the writing prompts on this site, the computerized scoring system will immediately score and deliver feedback on your essay. Other resources on this site will help you prepare, develop, and revise your essay.

STUDENTS

Get started by entering the

Writing Zone →

**Find Resources** Browse all *Holt McDougal Literature* components for the ones that meet your students' needs and match your teaching style.

**Assess Progress and Reteach** Assign electronic versions of program assessments to measure your students' mastery of the Common Core State Standards. On thinkcentral.com, some tests deliver online remediation tutorials to students who have not mastered skills.

 *Interactive Whiteboard Lessons*

Prepare your students for college and careers by teaching relevant, real-world skills through dynamic, interactive instruction. Go to **thinkcentral.com** to browse through all white-board lessons, including the following:

- Role of Setting
- Figurative Language and Imagery
- Word Choice and Tone

## Professional Development

**Video Center** Based on interviews with program consultants and other educational experts, these videos feature classroom-ready teaching strategies.

**Teacher Toolkit** Includes a Teacher Handbook as well as a range of articles and handouts by program consultants and other educators.

**Janet Allen**

**Kylene Beers**

**Jim Burke**

**Carol Jago**

 **HISTORY**

Together Holt McDougal and HISTORY® are revolutionizing the study of English/language arts with video that helps students relive and re-imagine the people, places, and events they are discovering through reading. Look for selections with the HISTORY® icon.

## How can you **TRAVEL** without leaving home?

To introduce the page, ask the question and have students read the paragraph. Then have them think of two settings: a familiar one in which they probably would feel very comfortable (for example, their best friend's home) and an unfamiliar one in which they might feel very uncomfortable (for example, a concert hall for a performance of music that they dislike). Ask students to make some notes about sights, sounds, and other sensory details that they associate with each setting.

*ACTIVITY* Call on volunteers to share their responses. Discuss which details and images provided them with an especially strong sense of place. Help students draw the conclusion that in a well-presented setting, vivid images and accurate details work together to create a believable world—even if the setting is imaginary—and a specific mood.

**CHECK UNDERSTANDING** Have students define the term *setting* and explain how setting is related to imagery and mood.

---

## How can you **TRAVEL** without leaving home?

We can experience the sights and sounds of a war-torn country long ago or a bustling city in the modern day. We can visit any place in the world—past, present, or future—because talented writers transport us to settings we have never seen and can only imagine.

*ACTIVITY* Recall a story you have read or a film you have viewed that you felt transported you to another place or time period. Concentrate on the setting of the story and think about all the ways in which the writer or director brought the setting to life. Then answer the following questions:

- How was the time period suggested?
- What details were used to portray the location?
- What information made the setting vivid and engaging?
- If the setting was completely imaginary, how was it made believable?

**Find It Online!** THINK central
Go to thinkcentral.com for the interactive version of this unit.

---

## Unit Resources

See resources on the **Teacher One Stop DVD-ROM** *and on* **thinkcentral.com**.

**R** **RESOURCE MANAGER UNIT 3**

**UNIT AND BENCHMARK TESTS**

**BEST PRACTICES TOOLKIT**

**INTERACTIVE READER**

**ADAPTED INTERACTIVE READER**

**ELL ADAPTED INTERACTIVE READER**

**LANGUAGE HANDBOOK**

**VOCABULARY PRACTICE**

**TECHNOLOGY**

- **Teacher One Stop DVD-ROM**
- **Student One Stop DVD-ROM**
- **PowerNotes DVD-ROM**
- **Write*Smart* CD-ROM**
- **Media*Smart* DVD-ROM**
- **GrammarNotes DVD-ROM**
- **Audio Anthology CD**
- **Audio Tutor CD**

**Find It Online!** THINK central

The interactive version of this unit on **thinkcentral.com** includes
- video and **PowerNotes** introductions to key selections
- audio support—listen or download
- **ThinkAloud** models
- **WordSharp** vocabulary tutorials
- interactive review and remediation

## Preview Unit Goals

| | |
|---|---|
| **TEXT ANALYSIS** | • Identify and analyze setting and its impact on conflict and character<br>• Identify and analyze imagery<br>• Identify mood and tone and analyze how writers convey mood and tone through word choice |
| **READING** | • Make inferences and cite evidence<br>• Identify author's perspective and purpose<br>• Distinguish between primary and secondary sources |
| **WRITING AND LANGUAGE** | • Write a short story<br>• Write concisely by using compound predicates<br>• Bring immediacy to writing by using an effective verb tense<br>• Use participial phrases to add interest and detail |
| **VOCABULARY** | • Use context clues to unlock meaning<br>• Understand and use connotative meanings of words |
| **ACADEMIC VOCABULARY** | • aspect    • circumstance    • contribute<br>• distinct    • perceive |
| **MEDIA AND VIEWING** | • Compare the film and written versions of a key scene<br>• Analyze how visual and sound techniques convey meaning<br>• Plan and produce a story trailer |

## Media Smart DVD-ROM

### Great Stories on Film

Compare authors' use of sensory language with filmmakers' methods of creating setting and mood. View a clip from a film version of "The Cask of Amontillado." Page 384

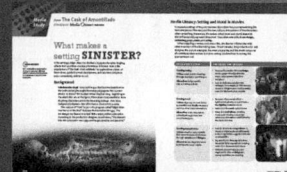

329

---

COMMON **UNIT GOALS**
CORE    Included in this unit: RL 1, RL 3-5, RL 7, RL 10, RI 1-2, RI 4, RI 6, W 2b, W 3a-e, W 4-6, W 9a, W 10, SL 1-2, SL 5, L 1, L 1b, L 2, L 2c, L 3-4, L 4a-d, L 5b, L 6

Complete text of the Common Core State Standards is found in the correlation on p. T10. Standards covered in this unit are found in the standards overview (pp. 327A–327B) and on the lesson pages where they are taught.

## Preview Unit Goals

This page introduces the major skills and strategies that this unit will cover. Have students preview the categories and skills, making note of the color-coding that identifies each strand throughout the unit.

Remind students to copy the Academic Vocabulary into their **Reader/Writer Notebooks**. Throughout the unit, model using the vocabulary. Have students use it in discussions and in writing, as well. By the end of the unit, students should have developed a clear, accurate, and useful definition of each term.

---

## DIFFERENTIATED INSTRUCTION

### FOR ENGLISH LANGUAGE LEARNERS

**Academic Vocabulary** Provide students with definitions of each Academic Vocabulary word.

**aspect** (as'pekt') *n.* a quality, part, or element

**circumstance** (sur kem' stans') *n.* a happening, event, or fact occurring near or in company with another

**contribute** (kən trib'yōōt) *v.* to provide or give ideas, knowledge, material goods, etc.

**distinct** (di stinkt') *adj.* separate or different; defined clearly

**perceive** (pər sēv') *v.* to observe or become aware of

Use the copy master to help students learn academic words they will use in this unit and on the Assessment Practice.

**R** RESOURCE MANAGER—Copy Masters
Academic Vocabulary p. 3
Additional Academic Vocabulary p. 4

# Setting, Mood, and Imagery

**Essential Course of Study** ✓ ECOS

A good story is much more than the events that happen or the conflicts between characters. When and where a story takes place also affects your reading experience. Consider, for example, a story about two lost hikers who are fighting for survival. It's the setting details—the towering trees, the stark winter sky, and the approaching snowstorm—that make you care about the conflict. By creating an unforgettable setting, a writer seizes your imagination and whisks you into the world of a story.

## COMMON CORE FOCUS

**RL 3** Analyze how complex characters develop over the course of a text, interact with other characters, and advance the plot. **RL 4** Analyze the cumulative impact of specific word choices on meaning and tone.

# Teach

## Part 1: Setting

**Setting** To introduce the topic of setting, ask students to identify the time and place of a book or movie. Remind students that setting includes *when* and *where* a story takes place. For example, a story set in the Great Plains in the late 19th century will be different from a story set in the Great Plains today. Next, focus on ideas associated with seasons, certain times of day, historical periods, and places by having students complete a chart such as the one shown here.

| Time, Place | Association |
|---|---|
| fall | harvest, increasing darkness |
| dawn | fresh starts, the beginning |
| 1849 Gold Rush | adventure, hope, trust |
| Los Angeles | creativity, urban sprawl |

**Role of Setting** Review how setting can

- influence character: Ask students how being in a war might affect one's character.
- create conflicts: Ask students what conflicts occur in their lives that would not have occurred in the early 1900s.
- serve as a symbol: Have students tell what these settings might represent—a jungle, a tower, a futuristic laboratory.

🧰 **BEST PRACTICES TOOLKIT—Transparency** Analysis Frame: Setting pp. D21, D30

## COMMON CORE

Included in this workshop:
**RL 3** Analyze how complex characters develop over the course of a text, interact with other characters, and advance the plot. **RL 4** Analyze the cumulative impact of specific word choices on meaning and tone.

## Part 1: Setting

You know that the **setting** of a story is the time and place in which the action occurs. The time could be a particular year, a specific season, a time of day, or a historical period. The place could be anywhere—from a bustling ancient city to a deserted tropical island.

In addition to describing the time and location of a story, setting is another literary element authors use to develop complex, believable characters. Setting details often reveal information about the characters' lives, their occupations, their values, and their relationships. Setting may also play a more active role by creating conflicts for the characters or by influencing the decisions they make.

| ROLE OF SETTING | EXAMPLE SETTING |
|---|---|
| **Setting can influence characters by**  <br> • determining the living conditions and jobs available to them <br> • shaping their personalities, their dreams, and their values | ***A poor, drought-stricken Midwestern farm town in the 1930s*** <br> Despite months of grueling work, Joe's crops are failing again. Realizing that his life may never improve, he becomes bitter and angry. |
| **Setting can create conflicts by**  <br> • exposing the characters to dangerous weather, such as a storm or a drought <br> • making characters endure a difficult time period, such as the Great Depression | The drought has lasted seven years, and most of the farms are failing. People have begun to sell their most prized possessions because they need money. Recently, Mrs. Wilkes sold her wedding band to buy shoes for her daughter. |
| **Setting can serve as a symbol by**  <br> • representing an important idea <br> • representing a character's hopes, future, or predicament | Some people have planted a small flower garden in the town square. The garden is a symbol of their hope that their community can still thrive. |

## DIFFERENTIATED INSTRUCTION

### FOR STRUGGLING READERS

**Note Taking** Students can better understand the role setting plays in a literary work by taking notes about the specific characteristics that define that setting in the form of a list. Ask students to look for descriptive words and phrases that identify the time and location of the story and record them in a list as they read. When their list is complete, ask students to write a brief summary defining the setting based on their list.

## MODEL 1: SETTING AND CHARACTERS

*Nervous Conditions* takes place in a British colony in Africa during the 1960s. Nhamo has left his village to attend school at a mission. How has this opportunity affected him?

### from Nervous **Conditions**

#### Novel by **Tsitsi Dangarembga**

. . . Nhamo was forced once a year to return to his squalid homestead, where he washed in cold water in an enamel basin or a flowing river, not in a bathtub with taps gushing hot water and cold; where he ate *sadza* regularly with his fingers and meat hardly at all, never with a knife or fork; where there was no
5 light beyond the flickering yellow of candles and homemade paraffin lamps to enable him to escape into his books when the rest of us had gone to bed.

All this poverty began to offend him, or at the very least to embarrass him after he went to the mission, in a way that it had not done before.

**Close Read**

1. Identify two details that help you understand Nhamo's life in both settings—the mission and the homestead. An example has been boxed.

2. How has Nhamo's experience at the mission influenced his perception of life on the homestead?

## MODEL 2: SETTING AND CONFLICT

In George Orwell's novel *1984,* the country is run by a government that monitors citizens' every move and demands loyalty to its leader—Big Brother. As you read this excerpt, pay attention to the description of this society. How might the setting create conflicts for the characters?

### from **1984**

#### Novel by **George Orwell**

Outside, even through the shut window pane, the world looked cold. Down in the street little eddies of wind were whirling dust and torn paper into spirals, and though the sun was shining and the sky a harsh blue, there seemed to be no color in anything except the posters that were plastered everywhere.
5 The black-mustachio'd face gazed down from every commanding corner. There was one on the house front immediately opposite. BIG BROTHER IS WATCHING YOU, the caption said, while the dark eyes looked deep into Winston's own. Down at street level another poster, torn at one corner, flapped fitfully in the wind. . . . In the far distance a helicopter skimmed down between
10 the roofs, hovered for an instant like a blue-bottle, and darted away again with a curving flight. It was the Police Patrol, snooping into people's windows. The patrols did not matter, however. Only the Thought Police mattered.

**Close Read**

1. In what kind of world does this story take place? Identify four details that help you visualize the setting. One has been boxed.

2. What conflicts might this society create for Winston and other citizens? Explain your answer.

TEXT ANALYSIS WORKSHOP **331**

## MODEL 1: SETTING AND CHARACTERS

**Close Read**

1. *Possible answer:* Two details that help readers understand Nhamo's life in both settings are: "where he ate *sadza* regularly with his fingers [home], never with a knife and fork" [as he does at school] and "where there was no light beyond the flickering yellow of candles and homemade paraffin lamps [home] to enable him to escape into his books" [as he does at school, with ample light].

2. *Possible answer:* Readers learn that Nhamo is now offended and embarrassed by the "squalid" conditions of his family's homestead. Students may say that living in better conditions at the mission probably opened Nhamo's eyes to "all this poverty" at home.

## MODEL 2: SETTING AND CONFLICT

**Close Read**

1. *Possible answer:* The story takes place in an eerie and unsettling world. Four of the details that help readers visualize the setting are "eddies of wind were whirling dust and torn paper into spirals" (lines 2–3); "though the sun was shining and the sky a harsh blue, there seemed to be no color in anything" (lines 3–4); "the dark eyes looked deep into Winston's own" (lines 7–8); "snooping into people's windows" (line 11).

2. *Possible answer:* People are probably unable to live freely and do what they want. They have to operate as if their every move is being watched and monitored. This could create major conflicts. People must choose between following the rules and doing what they want at the risk of getting caught.

---

### FOR STRUGGLING READERS

**Illustrate Setting** Have students quickly sketch the scene or part of the scene from the *1984* excerpt. Then ask them to imagine themselves in the scene and to discuss how the setting might affect them. Guide them to focus on conflicts that they might feel.

### FOR ENGLISH LANGUAGE LEARNERS

**Language: Skill Words** On the board, list the literary terms shown in italics. Then give the examples in random order for students to classify.

- *setting:* mountaintop; beach; classroom
- *conflict:* fight between friends; desire to leave home and to please parents
- *symbol:* flag; sword; heart

**Online Remediation**

Are your students struggling with text analysis skills? Consider assigning them one or more **Level Up Online Tutorials** as remediation before beginning this unit. Log in to **thinkcentral.com** to view a list of the skills addressed by **Level Up.**

## Part 2: Imagery and Mood

### IMAGERY

**Sensory Language** Tell students that sensory language helps a reader create images, or pictures, in his or her mind. The more precise a writer's details, the better a reader is able to form mental images of story characters, settings, and events. As students read the models on page 333, have them look for specific words and phrases that appeal to the senses and record them in a chart like this.

| Sense | Words and Phrases |
|---|---|
| Sight | |
| Hearing | |
| Smell | |
| Taste | |
| Touch | |

### MOOD

**Mood** Point out that imagery and setting combine to create the mood in the picture. For additional practice, display another image—such as a forest in spring, an abandoned city street, or a lavish, busy dining room—and elicit examples of sensory language that combine to create a single mood, such as hope, despair, or festivity.

### CHECK UNDERSTANDING

Have partners write a short description of a scene at school using sensory language to create a mood.

---

## Part 2: Imagery and Mood

To create a setting that stays with you long after a story ends, a writer paints pictures with words. With the right choice of details and the **tone** of the language, a writer can transport you to any scene and affect how you feel about a story.

### IMAGERY

**Imagery** consists of vivid descriptions that recreate sensory experiences for readers. Rather than detailing every aspect of a setting, a writer may use **sensory language**—specific words and phrases that appeal to the senses of sight, hearing, smell, taste, and touch—to help you visualize a scene. For example, in the *1984* excerpt on the previous page, Orwell uses phrases like these to appeal to the senses of sight and hearing:

- *"eddies of wind were whirling dust"*
- *"another poster . . . flapped fitfully in the wind"*

Armed with these details, your imagination fills in the rest of the scene. While Orwell does not mention anxious people and wailing sirens, you can picture these details as part of the setting.

### MOOD

A writer also uses imagery and setting details to create the **mood,** or atmosphere, of a story. Whether it is lighthearted, hopeful, or mysterious, a story's mood can affect your emotional reaction to the characters and events. For example, the bleak, eerie mood established in *1984* might prompt you to sympathize with the characters as you are drawn into their unsettling world.

How do the sensory details in the graphic convey a mood of terror and fear?

SIGHT: "Flashes of lightning illuminated the **ink-black sky.**"

TOUCH: "Another cobweb stuck to her **cold, clammy skin.**"

TASTE: "She could not get the **metallic taste of fear** out of her mouth."

SOUND: "Her **heart thumped wildly** when she heard an **ominous scratching** on the door."

SMELL: "The foul smell of **dead mice** hung in the air."

332

---

**FOR STRUGGLING READERS**

**Note Taking** For those students who need help, hand out the note-taking copy master for this page. Read and discuss the page. Assist students in completing the note-taking copy master as needed.

**R** RESOURCE MANAGER—Copy Master
Note Taking p. 10

**FOR ENGLISH LANGUAGE LEARNERS**

**Language: Skill Words** On the board, list the literary terms shown in italics. Then give examples in random order for students to classify.

- *sensory detail:* flash of lightning, buzzing of bees, smell of bread baking
- *mood:* happy, solemn or serious, suspenseful

## MODEL 1: IMAGERY

This excerpt is from a chilling story by H. P. Lovecraft, a master of horror and suspense. As you read, pay attention to the sensory details he uses to describe an unusual street.

*from*

# The Music of Erich Zann

### Short story by **H. P. Lovecraft**

The Rue d'Auseil lay across a dark river bordered by precipitous brick blear-windowed warehouses and spanned by a ponderous bridge of dark stone. It was always shadowy along that river, as if the smoke of neighboring factories shut out the sun perpetually. The river was also odorous with evil stenches
5 which I have never smelled elsewhere. . . . Beyond that bridge were narrow cobbled streets with rails; and then came the ascent, at first gradual, but incredibly steep as the Rue d'Auseil was reached.

I have never seen another street as narrow and steep as the Rue d'Auseil. It was almost a cliff, closed to vehicles, consisting in several places of flights
10 of steps, and ending at the top in a lofty ivied wall. Its paving was irregular, sometimes stone slabs, sometimes cobblestones, and sometimes bare earth with struggling greenish-grey vegetation. The houses were tall, peaked-roofed, incredibly old, and crazily leaning backward, forward, and sidewise.

### Close Read

1. The boxed detail appeals to the sense of smell. Find three more details and identify the sense each one appeals to.

2. What mood does this setting create? Point out specific examples of imagery that contributes directly to the mood.

## MODEL 2: MOOD

The imagery in this excerpt evokes a very different atmosphere. Notice the specific sensory details that contribute to the mood.

*from*

# Their Eyes Were Watching God

### Novel by **Zora Neale Hurston**

It was a spring afternoon in West Florida. Janie had spent most of the day under a blossoming pear tree in the back-yard. She had been spending every minute that she could steal from her chores under that tree for the last three days. That was to say, ever since the first tiny bloom had opened. It had called her to
5 come and gaze on a mystery. From barren brown stems to glistening leaf-buds; from the leaf-buds to snowy virginity of bloom. It stirred her tremendously.

### Close Read

1. How would you describe the mood of this excerpt?

2. Find four details that help to convey the mood. One has been boxed.

TEXT ANALYSIS WORKSHOP **333**

---

## MODEL 1: IMAGERY
### Close Read

1. ***Possible answer:*** *Sight: "a dark river bordered by precipitous brick blear-windowed warehouses" (lines 1–2); sight and smell: "shadowy along that river, as if the smoke of neighboring factories shut out the sun perpetually" (lines 3–4); sight: "the houses were tall, peaked-roofed . . . crazily leaning backward, forward, and sidewise" (lines 12–13).*

2. ***Possible answer:*** *The mood created by the setting is eerie and ominous. Examples of imagery that contribute to this mood are "odorous with evil stenches" (line 4); "sometimes bare earth with struggling greenish-grey vegetation" (lines 11–12); and "the houses were tall, peaked-roofed . . . crazily leaning backward, forward, and sidewise" (lines 12–13).*

**IF STUDENTS NEED HELP . . .** To reinforce that every detail has meaning, examine choices made by the writer:

- "precipitous . . . warehouses" instead of small, cozy houses on gently rolling hills
- a "lofty ivied wall" instead of a fragrant garden path
- "struggling greenish-grey vegetation" instead of delicate pink flowers

## MODEL 2: MOOD
### Close Read

1. ***Possible answer:*** *The mood might be described as wondrous, uplifting, or hopeful.*

2. ***Possible answer:*** *Four details that convey mood are "spring afternoon" (line 1); "first tiny bloom" (line 4); "from barren brown stems to glistening leaf-buds" (line 5); and "it stirred her tremendously" (line 6).*

---

## DIFFERENTIATED INSTRUCTION

### FOR ENGLISH LANGUAGE LEARNERS

**Comprehension: Analysis** To help students comprehend Model 1, explain that the prepositions *across*, *along*, and *beyond* tell *where* and enable readers to visualize the setting. Draw a wavy line, label it "dark river," and draw the Rue d'Auseil *across* it. Then have students point out the location of shadows or smoke *along* the river (line 3) and the narrow cobbled streets *beyond* it (lines 5–6).

# Practice and Apply

## Part 3: Analyze the Text

### Close Read

1. **Possible answer:** *The introduction says that the setting is in the mountains of New Mexico. Details reveal that the setting is near ranches and a cowboy camp, during the late afternoon in summer when the temperature is fairly hot. The narrator is a cowboy or ranch hand who spends his evenings with other cowboys after a hard day of work.*

2. **Possible answer:** *Images include "the forests were fresh, green, and gay" (line 8); "the cattle moved slowly, fat and sleek in the August sun and shadow" (lines 8–9); "the sun was setting behind me in a riot of streaks and colors" (lines 13–14); and "deep, harmonious silence" (line 14). These details create a mood of laziness and calm.*

3. **Possible answer:** *The mood changes from calm to intense excitement and even mystery. Words or phrases conveying this change include "a deafening quiet" (line 16), "comes to a standstill" (line 16), and "sun flares hotly" (line 17).*

   **IF STUDENTS NEED HELP ...** Reread lines 8–14. Have students find details that point to the relaxed or sleepy mood, including words like *drowsy, lethargy,* and *dozing.* Then ask how "a deafening quiet" is different from a sleepy feeling.

4. **Possible answer:** *Exclamation points let the reader know that the narrator is excited to see the horse and that spotting the Wonder Horse is a rare occurrence. Details such as "pride, prestige, and art incarnate in animal flesh" and "an ideal" show that the narrator is enthralled by the beauty and intrigue of the horse. The words* statue *and* engraving *emphasize the narrator's perception of the horse as a work of art.*

UNIT 3: SETTING, MOOD, AND IMAGERY

---

## Part 3: Analyze the Text

Using what you've learned in this workshop, analyze setting, mood, and imagery in these two short story excerpts.

The first excerpt is from a story that takes place in the mountains of New Mexico, where people tell tales about a legendary white horse that roams the wild. As you read, notice the details that the writer uses to describe the setting and create a distinct mood.

*from*

# My Wonder Horse

Short story by **Sabine R. Ulibarrí**

I was fifteen years old. Although I had never seen the Wonder Horse, he filled my imagination and fired my ambition. I used to listen open-mouthed as my father and the ranch hands talked about the phantom horse who turned into mist and air and nothingness when he was trapped. I joined in the
5   universal obsession—like the hope of winning the lottery—of putting my lasso on him some day, of capturing him and showing him off on Sunday afternoons when the girls of the town strolled through the streets.

It was high summer. The forests were fresh, green, and gay. The cattle moved slowly, fat and sleek in the August sun and shadow. Listless and drowsy in the
10   lethargy of late afternoon, I was dozing on my horse. It was time to round up the herd and go back to the good bread of the cowboy camp. Already my comrades would be sitting around the campfire, playing the guitar, telling stories of past or present, or surrendering to the languor of the late afternoon. The sun was setting behind me in a riot of streaks and colors. Deep, harmonious silence.

15   I sit drowsily still, forgetting the cattle in the glade. Suddenly the forest falls silent, a deafening quiet. The afternoon comes to a standstill. The breeze stops blowing, but it vibrates. The sun flares hotly. The planet, life, and time itself have stopped in an inexplicable way. For a moment, I don't understand what is happening.

20   Then my eyes focus. There he is! The Wonder Horse! At the end of the glade, on high ground surrounded by summer green. He is a statue. He is an engraving. Line and form and white stain on a green background. Pride, prestige, and art incarnate in animal flesh. A picture of burning beauty and virile freedom. An ideal, pure and invincible, rising from the eternal dreams of humanity. Even
25   today my being thrills when I remember him.

### Close Read

1. Describe the setting in this excerpt. Find details that reveal the season, the weather, and the narrator's lifestyle.

2. Find four examples of imagery in lines 8–14. One has been boxed. What mood do these details create?

3. How does the mood change in lines 15–19? Find three words or phrases that convey this change.

4. Notice the tone, or attitude toward a subject, revealed in lines 20–25. Which details help you understand how the narrator feels about the horse?

**334**   UNIT 3: SETTING, MOOD, AND IMAGERY

---

## DIFFERENTIATED INSTRUCTION

### FOR STRUGGLING READERS
**Analysis Support: Setting and Mood**

1. Have students reread lines 8–10, one sentence at a time. As they read the sentences, write on the board the words that provide clues to the time of the setting: *summer, August,* and *late afternoon.*

2. Have partners complete a Two-Column Chart with words and phrases that demonstrate the change in mood. Have them label the headings of their chart *Before*

and *After.* Refer them to lines 8–14 for the beginning mood and lines 20–25 for the ending mood.

  **BEST PRACTICES TOOLKIT—Transparency**
  Two-Column Chart p. A25

Now read this excerpt, taken from a story that is based on an experience from the writer's life. In 1897, Crane was a passenger on a ship that sank off the coast of Florida. He and three other men rowed back to shore in a flimsy lifeboat. How does Crane's use of imagery help convey a different setting and mood?

*from*

# The OPEN BOAT

Short story by **Stephen Crane**

None of them knew the color of the sky. Their eyes glanced level, and were fastened upon the waves that swept toward them. These waves were of the hue of slate, save for the tops, which were of foaming white, and all of the men knew the colors of the sea. The horizon narrowed and
5  widened, and dipped and rose, and at all times its edge was jagged with waves that seemed thrust up in points like rocks.

Many a man ought to have a bathtub larger than the boat which here rode upon the sea. These waves were most wrongfully and barbarously abrupt and tall, and each froth-top was a problem in small-boat navigation. The cook
10  squatted in the bottom, and looked with both eyes at the six inches of gunwale which separated him from the ocean. His sleeves were rolled over his fat forearms, and the two flaps of his unbuttoned vest dangled as he bent to bail out the boat. Often he said, "That was a narrow clip." As he remarked it he invariably gazed eastward over the broken sea.
15  The oiler, steering with one of the two oars in the boat, sometimes raised himself suddenly to keep clear of water that swirled in over the stern. It was a thin little oar, and it seemed often ready to snap. The correspondent, pulling at the other oar, watched the waves and wondered why he was there.

The injured captain, lying in the bow, was at this time buried in that
20  profound dejection and indifference which comes, temporarily at least, to even the bravest and most enduring when, willy-nilly, the firm fails, the army loses, the ship goes down.

## Close Read

1. Using details from the text, describe the setting as completely as you can.

2. Identify five sensory details. One has been boxed. What senses do they appeal to?

3. How would you describe the mood of this excerpt? Explain how the sensory details you found help to create this mood.

4. In which excerpt does setting play a more important role? Support your opinion with specific details.

## Close Read

1. *Possible answer: The setting is a small boat in the ocean during rough weather. The smallness of the boat is shown by the sentence "Many a man ought to have a bathtub larger than the boat" (line 7). The rough water is shown by the phrases "jagged with waves" (line 5) and "barbarously abrupt and tall" (lines 8–9).*

2. *Possible answer: Sight: waves "barbarously abrupt and tall" (lines 8–9) and "sleeves were rolled over his fat forearms" (lines 11–12); sight and touch: "foaming white" (line 3) and "jagged with waves" (line 5); sight and sound: "water that swirled in over the stern" (line 16).*

3. *Possible answer: The mood is one of danger and excitement. Details listed for question 2 emphasize the rough waters and the dangerous situation. Details about the passengers, such as "raised himself suddenly" (lines 15–16), convey a readiness for action.*

4. *Possible answer: The setting plays a more important role in "The Open Boat," because the rough weather causes a life-or-death conflict for the passengers.*

## Assess and Reteach

### Assess

Have students describe the setting and mood of "My Wonder Horse" and "The Open Boat."

### Reteach

For students who are unable to apply the workshop skills to the stories, select from these reteaching options:

- Have students review the information on the note-taking copy masters and choose one skill to describe using a cluster.

- Have students identify the setting and mood of a scene from a recently read story.

## DIFFERENTIATED INSTRUCTION

### FOR STRUGGLING READERS
**Vocabulary Support** Introduce these terms from "The Open Boat." Have students use context or structural clues to suggest synonyms.

- *hue* (line 3), "color"
- *thrust* (line 6), "pushed"
- *invariably* (line 14), "always"
- *dejection* (line 20), "hopelessness"

### FOR ENGLISH LANGUAGE LEARNERS
**Vocabulary: Idioms and Sayings** Help students use context clues to determine the meanings of these phrases:

- *save for* (line 3), "except"
- *many a man* (line 7), "many men"
- *a narrow clip* (line 13), "an accident that almost happens"
- *keep clear of* (line 16), "stay away from"

# Focus and Motivate

## COMMON CORE FOCUS

**RL 4** Analyze the cumulative impact of specific word choices on meaning and tone. **RL 5** Analyze an author's choices concerning how to manipulate time. **L 3** Apply knowledge of language to make effective choices for meaning or style. **L 5b** Analyze nuances in the meaning of words with similar denotations.

## SUMMARY

The adult narrator recalls the days leading up to Christmas when he was seven years old and his best friend was an elderly but childlike cousin. On Christmas Day, they fly the kites they have made for each other. It would be their last Christmas together: Buddy is sent to military school, and his friend dies a few years later.

## What do you look for in a FRIEND?

After students have read the cartoon, ask the question and record responses. Then discuss how difficult situations can lead to or strengthen friendships. Finally, have students complete the *QUICKWRITE* and discuss their insights.

**Essential Course of Study ECOS**

## A Christmas Memory
Short Story by Truman Capote

# What do you look for in a FRIEND?

**COMMON CORE**

**RL 4** Analyze the cumulative impact of specific word choices on meaning and tone. **RL 5** Analyze an author's choices concerning how to manipulate time.

Think about your current friends as well as friends from the past. What draws you to someone and creates that special bond of friendship? Does a friend have to be your age? Do you always share the same interests and values? "A Christmas Memory" shows how important friendship can be to two very different individuals.

*QUICKWRITE* With a partner, write a "top ten" list of the key qualities you look for in a friend. Then compare your list with those of your classmates. Does everyone list similar qualities? Are physical traits and intellectual or emotional factors equally important?

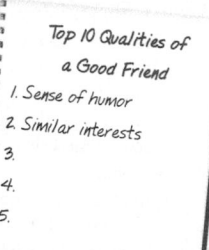

Top 10 Qualities of a Good Friend
1. Sense of humor
2. Similar interests
3.
4.
5.

**PEANUTS.**

WE'VE BEEN PALS FOR A LONG TIME, HAVEN'T WE, SNOOPY?

I THINK IT'S BECAUSE WE NOT ONLY LIKE EACH OTHER, BUT WE RESPECT EACH OTHER..

DON'T FORGET THE SUPPER DISH..

Peanuts: © United Feature Syndicate, Inc.

336

# Selection Resources

See resources on the **Teacher One Stop DVD-ROM** and on **thinkcentral.com**.

 **RESOURCE MANAGER UNIT 3**
Plan and Teach, pp. 11–18
Summary, pp. 19–20†‡*
Text Analysis and Reading
Skill, pp. 21–22, 23–24†*
Vocabulary, pp. 25–27*
Grammar and Style, p. 30

**DIAGNOSTIC AND SELECTION TESTS**
Selection Tests, pp. 91–94

 **BEST PRACTICES TOOLKIT**
Definition Mapping, p. E6
New Word Analysis, p. E8
Observation Chart, p. C7

**INTERACTIVE READER**

**ADAPTED INTERACTIVE READER**

**ELL ADAPTED INTERACTIVE READER**

**TECHNOLOGY**
- Teacher One Stop DVD-ROM
- Student One Stop DVD-ROM
- PowerNotes DVD-ROM
- Audio Anthology CD
- GrammarNotes DVD-ROM
- Audio Tutor CD
- ExamView Test Generator on the **Teacher One Stop**

\* Resources for Differentiation        † Also in Spanish        ‡ In Haitian Creole and Vietnamese

## TEXT ANALYSIS: DETAILS OF SETTING

In "A Christmas Memory," the adult narrator focuses on describing a particular period in his childhood. In fact, the narrator seems more interested in recreating the **setting** of this period than in telling about events. Through the use of **details,** the narrator describes not only the time and place of his childhood but also the historical era—the buildings, people, customs, and rituals that existed. The richness of the details makes the setting seem real and helps readers understand its importance to the narrator. Notice the vivid words used to describe walking through the woods:

*Always, the path unwinds through lemony sun pools and pitch-black vine tunnels.*

As you read, look for details that reveal the setting.

## READING SKILL: ANALYZE IMAGERY

Good descriptive writing is usually filled with **imagery**—words and phrases that appeal to the senses. Capote gives readers a lasting impression of a holiday memory by using language that appeals to one or more senses. For example, note how this phrase appeals to your sense of hearing:

*Lovely dimes, the liveliest coin, the one that really jingles.*

As you read, use a chart like the one below to jot down specific words and phrases that you find especially striking. Check off the senses that are appealed to in each case.

| Description | Sight | Smell | Hearing | Taste | Touch |
|---|---|---|---|---|---|
| Cracking open the pecans | ✓ | | ✓ | ✓ | |
| | | | | | |

*Review:* Make Inferences

## ▲ VOCABULARY IN CONTEXT

To see how many words you know, restate each phrase, using a different word or words for the boldfaced word.

1. to **inaugurate** a project
2. a day that **exhilarates**
3. party **paraphernalia**
4. **squander** your money
5. ordinary, **prosaic** ideas
6. **suffuse** with perfume
7. a **potent** medicine
8. **goad** her to action
9. **cavort** in the park
10. **sever** all contact

 Complete the activities in your **Reader/Writer Notebook.**

---

## Meet the Author

## Truman Capote
### 1924–1984

**Early Ambitions**
Raised by elderly relatives in a small Alabama town, Capote started writing to fill the loneliness. He began publishing his short stories in his teens. As he later explained, "I always knew that I wanted to be a writer and that I wanted to be rich and famous." By the time his first novel, *Other Voices, Other Rooms,* was published in 1948, he was on his way to achieving these goals.

**The Nonfiction Novel**
Capote enjoyed the celebrity that followed other successful publications, including the novel *Breakfast at Tiffany's* (1958). Then his career took a dramatic turn when he began what he called a nonfiction novel, a factual story written in the form of a novel. The result, *In Cold Blood* (1965), was an instant bestseller and made him a multimillionaire. Still, the six years he spent on this book took a toll on him.

**Personal Decline**
Capote's life ultimately descended into a haze of addiction, illness, and writer's block. Although some critics contend he threw away his talent in the pursuit of celebrity, most acknowledge his talent as a storyteller.

**BACKGROUND TO THE STORY**

**The Facts Behind the Fiction**
This story is based on Capote's childhood during the Great Depression of the 1930s. His friend was a much older cousin named Sook Faulk. Writing in the voice of an adult, Capote condenses years of experiences with his cousin into one memorable Christmas.

**Author Online** THINKcentral
Go to thinkcentral.com.
KEYWORD: HML9-337

337

---

# Teach

**TEXT ANALYSIS**  COMMON CORE  RL 4

## ● *Model the Skill:* DETAILS OF SETTING

Read this sentence aloud:

That ancient six-by-six tree house, with its creaking, moldy boards and leaking roof, was our secret hideaway.

To model the skill, point out the words in the sentence that help you picture the tree house: *ancient, creaking, moldy, leaking.* Explain that these details help you imagine how the tree house looks, feels, sounds, and even smells.

**GUIDED PRACTICE** Have students list and discuss stories and novels that have vivid settings.

**READING SKILL**  COMMON CORE  RL 4

## ■ *Model the Skill:* ANALYZE IMAGERY

Point out that not all images are mental pictures. Ripples of thunder or fluttering wings are images, too. Discuss the types of images in this passage:

*Plunk!* The second after Jenna dropped her keys, the jets of water whooshed them away in a jangling whirl of silver.

**GUIDED PRACTICE** Ask students what senses they associate with a holiday.

**R** RESOURCE MANAGER—Copy Master Analyze Imagery p. 28 (for student use while reading the selection)

---

**VOCABULARY SKILL**  COMMON CORE  L 4

## ▲ VOCABULARY IN CONTEXT

**DIAGNOSE WORD KNOWLEDGE** Have students complete Vocabulary in Context. Check their definitions against the following:

**cavort** (kə-vôrt') *v.* to leap or romp about
**exhilarate** (ĭg-zĭl'ə-rāt') *v.* to make merry or lively
**goad** (gōd) *v.* to drive or urge
**inaugurate** (ĭn-ô'gyə-rāt') *v.* to make a formal beginning of

**paraphernalia** (păr'ə-fər-nāl'yə) *n.* the articles needed for a particular event or activity
**potent** (pōt'nt) *adj.* powerful
**prosaic** (prō-zā'ĭk) *adj.* dull; commonplace
**sever** (sĕv'ər) *v.* to cut off
**squander** (skwŏn'dər) *v.* to spend or use wastefully
**suffuse** (sə-fyooz') *v.* to gradually spread through or over

**R** RESOURCE MANAGER—Copy Master Vocabulary Study p. 25

## READ WITH A PURPOSE

*Help students set a purpose for reading. Point out that the events in the story took place more than twenty years before the author wrote them down. Ask students to determine why the events remained so memorable to the author.*

---

**TEXT ANALYSIS**     COMMON CORE   **RL 4**

### Ⓐ DETAILS OF SETTING

**Possible answer:** *The setting is late November (line 1) in a large old house in the country (lines 2–3). The weather has just begun to get cold enough to use the fireplace (lines 4–5).*

**Extend the Discussion** In what way does the dialogue—such as "It's fruitcake weather! Fetch our buggy" (lines 27–28)—help you understand the setting?

---

**VOCABULARY**     COMMON CORE   **L 4**

### OWN THE WORD

- **inaugurate:** Ask students what the woman in the story is inaugurating with the declaration "It's fruitcake weather!"
  **Possible answer:** *the Christmas season*
  Then ask students to complete this sentence: I'm *inaugurating . . .* by *. . . .*
  **Possible answer:** *I'm* inaugurating *summer by swimming in the lake.*

- **exhilarate:** Tell students that the prefix *ex-* is from the Greek for "out of" or "from." Then point out that the Greek *hilaros* means "cheerful." Have students explain the relationship between the meaning of *exhilarate* and its Greek roots.

---

# A Christmas Memory

## Truman Capote

Imagine a morning in late November. A coming of winter morning more than twenty years ago. Consider the kitchen of a spreading old house in a country town. A great black stove is its main feature; but there is also a big round table and a fireplace with two rocking chairs placed in front of it. Just today the fireplace commenced its seasonal roar.

A woman with shorn white hair is standing at the kitchen window. She is wearing tennis shoes and a shapeless gray sweater over a summery calico dress. She is small and sprightly, like a bantam hen; but, due to a long youthful illness, her shoulders are pitifully hunched. Her face is remarkable—not
10   unlike Lincoln's, craggy like that, and tinted by sun and wind; but it is delicate too, finely boned, and her eyes are sherry-colored and timid. "Oh my," she exclaims, her breath smoking the windowpane, "it's fruitcake weather!"

> The person to whom she is speaking is myself. I am seven; she is sixty-something. We are cousins, very distant ones, and we have lived together—well, as long as I can remember. Other people inhabit the house, relatives; and though they have power over us, and frequently make us cry, we are not, on the whole, too much aware of them. We are each other's best friend. She calls me Buddy, in memory of a boy who was formerly her best friend. The other Buddy died in the 1880's, when she was still a child. She is still a child.

20   "I knew it before I got out of bed," she says, turning away from the window with a purposeful excitement in her eyes. "The courthouse bell sounded so cold and clear. And there were no birds singing; they've gone to warmer country, yes indeed. Oh, Buddy, stop stuffing biscuit and fetch our buggy. Help me find my hat. We've thirty cakes to bake."

It's always the same: a morning arrives in November, and my friend, as though officially **inaugurating** the Christmas time of year that **exhilarates** her imagination and fuels the blaze of her heart, announces: "It's fruitcake weather! Fetch our buggy. Help me find my hat." Ⓐ

### Analyze Visuals ▶

How does the woman in this painting compare with your image of Buddy's friend? Cite details from the story, such as the sensory language in lines 6–11, to support your answer.

**①**   **Targeted Passage**

**inaugurate** (ĭn-ô′gyə-rāt′) *v.* to make a formal beginning of

**exhilarate** (ĭg-zĭl′ə-rāt′) *v.* to make merry or lively

Ⓐ **DETAILS OF SETTING** Use the details on this page to figure out as much as you can about the setting.

*Anna Kuerner* (1971), Andrew Wyeth. Tempera on panel. Private collection. Photo © 1995 Andrew Wyeth.

---

## DIFFERENTIATED INSTRUCTION

### FOR ENGLISH LANGUAGE LEARNERS

**Vocabulary Support** Use Definition Mapping to teach these words: *commenced* (line 5), *contracted* (line 107), *lectured* (line 167), *locate* (line 288), *succession* (line 355).

🧰 **BEST PRACTICES TOOLKIT—Transparency** Definition Mapping p. E6

### FOR STRUGGLING READERS

In combination with the *Audio Anthology CD,* use one or more Targeted Passages (pp. 338, 342, 346–347, 350) to ensure that students focus on key story events, concepts, and skills. Targeted Passages are also good for English learners.

**①** **Targeted Passage [Lines 13–19]**

This passage introduces the theme of friendship, as seen in Buddy's description

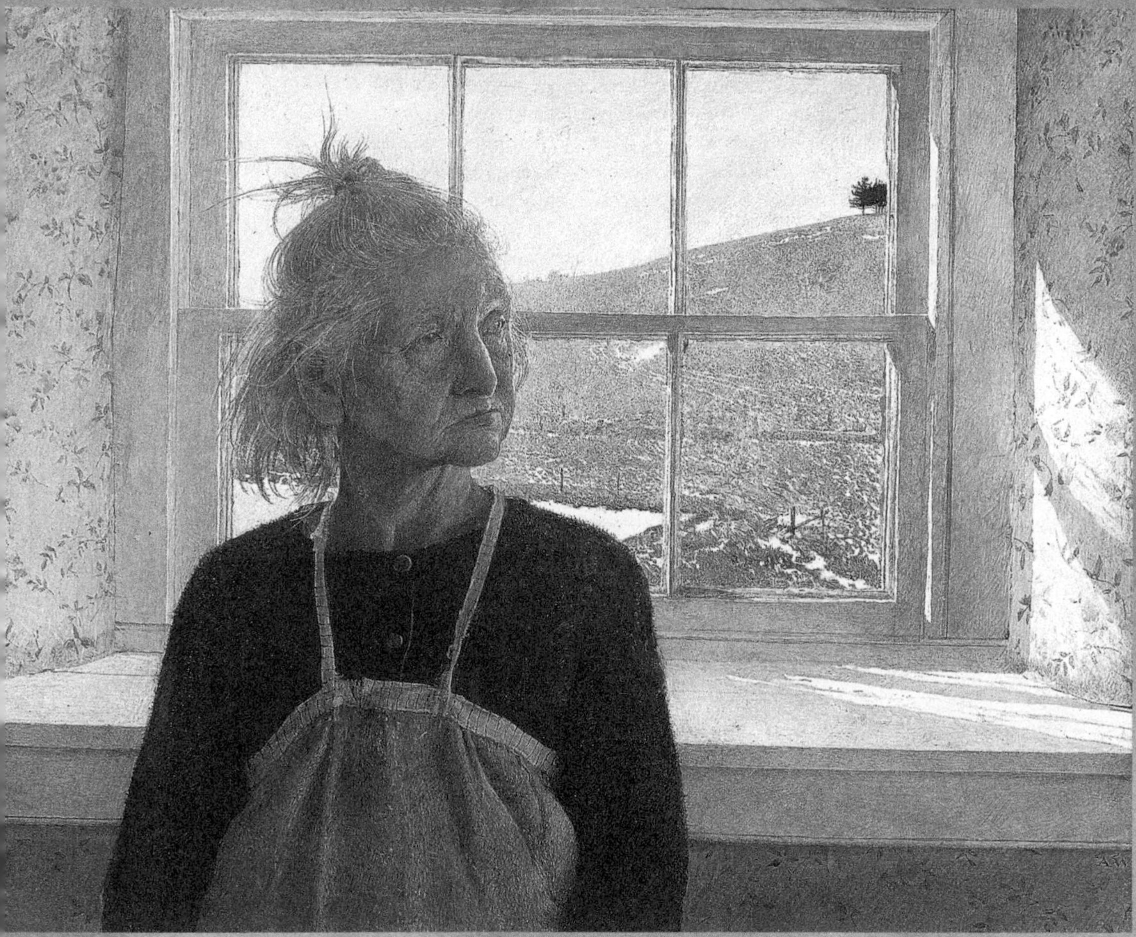

## Reading Support

This selection on **thinkcentral.com** includes embedded **ThinkAloud** models–students "thinking aloud" about the story to model the kinds of questions a good reader would ask about a selection.

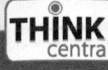

## BACKGROUND

**Rural America and the Depression** Although many segments of the U.S. population had prospered in the years just before the Great Depression, farmers had not. Their economic difficulties increased beginning in late 1929. New Deal programs were established to provide relief by regulating farm production and raising prices for agricultural products.

**Cultural Connection** Fruitcake is one of the culinary traditions of Christmas. Other traditional Christmas desserts include plum puddings in Australia; the *bûche de Noël*, or yule log cake, in France; and the *panettone* cake of Italy. Call on volunteers to tell about treats that are a part of their holiday traditions.

## Analyze Visuals

***Possible answer:*** *Like the woman in the story, the woman in the painting is small, has white hair, and is standing at a window (lines 6–8). The woman in the painting is also wearing mainly shapeless clothing. Students may express different opinions about whether the woman in the painting fits the story.*

**About the Art** American painter Andrew Wyeth (1917-2009) is known for his realistic, earth-toned paintings. Here he takes a realistic look at a person whose farm was the subject of his first painting. Wyeth shows how life has left its mark both on the human subject and on the old house.

of his older cousin and friend.

- What is the age difference between Buddy and his friend? Does the difference seem to matter to them? (lines 13–17)
- Who else lives in the house? How do Buddy and his friend feel about them? (lines 15–17)
- How strong is the friendship between Buddy and his cousin? How can you tell? (lines 17–19)

**FOR ADVANCED LEARNERS/PRE–AP**

**Analyze Character and Setting** The narrator explains that he and his friend do not have much contact with the other members of the household. Ask students to note any mentions of these absent characters throughout the story and to use these details to make inferences about Buddy's living situation and place in the household.

**B MAKE INFERENCES**

*Possible answers: Buddy and his friend do many things with the buggy together and are year-round friends. They share in both work and play. In addition, their life does not seem to be easy. For example, they must haul firewood, and the buggy, the only tool that they have for that purpose, is old and poorly suited to the task.*

## REVISIT THE BIG QUESTION

# What do you look for in a FRIEND?

**Discuss** In lines 31–40, Buddy speaks of the older woman as if they were equals. What obstacle or obstacles might they have had to overcome to establish their friendship? Explain. *Possible answer: Their age difference might have been the main obstacle. However, since the older woman had a childlike personality, age was not the issue that it might have been for other people.*

## Analyze Visuals

**Activity** Ask students how well they think this painting resembles the setting where Buddy and his friend gather pecans for the fruitcakes. *Answers will vary, but students may note Capote's reference to "concealing leaves" (line 44).*

**About the Art** Contemporary artist Bob Timberlake (born 1933) paints realistic rural landscapes, including wooded lots and rolling hills, of his native North Carolina. In *Wild Dog Mushroom* he conveys not only the look but the texture of the leaf-covered ground in autumn.

### OWN THE WORD

**paraphernalia:** Ask students to name *paraphernalia* that would be needed for a picnic in the woods. *Possible answer: blanket or towels, folding chairs, cups, plates, napkins*

---

The hat is found, a straw cartwheel corsaged with velvet roses out-of-doors
30 has faded: it once belonged to a more fashionable relative. Together, we guide our buggy, a dilapidated baby carriage, out to the garden and into a grove of pecan trees. The buggy is mine; that is, it was bought for me when I was born. It is made of wicker, rather unraveled, and the wheels wobble like a drunkard's legs. But it is a faithful object; springtimes, we take it to the woods and fill it with flowers, herbs, wild fern for our porch pots; in the summer, we pile it with picnic **paraphernalia** and sugar-cane fishing poles and roll it down to the edge of a creek; it has its winter uses, too: as a truck for hauling firewood from the yard to the kitchen, as a warm bed for Queenie, our tough little orange and white rat terrier who has survived distemper and two rattlesnake bites. Queenie
40 is trotting beside it now. **B**

Three hours later we are back in the kitchen hulling a heaping buggyload of windfall pecans. Our backs hurt from gathering them: how hard they were to find (the main crop having been shaken off the trees and sold by the orchard's owners, who are not us) among the concealing leaves, the frosted, deceiving grass. Caarackle! A cheery crunch, scraps of miniature thunder sound as the shells collapse and the golden mound of sweet oily ivory meat mounts in the milk-glass bowl. Queenie begs to taste, and now and again my friend sneaks her a mite, though insisting we deprive ourselves. "We mustn't, Buddy. If we start, we won't stop. And there's scarcely enough as there is. For thirty
50 cakes." The kitchen is growing dark. Dusk turns the window into a mirror: our reflections mingle with the rising moon as we work by the fireside in the firelight. At last, when the moon is quite high, we toss the final hull into the

**paraphernalia**
(păr′ə-fər-nāl′yə) *n.* the articles needed for a particular event or activity

**B MAKE INFERENCES**
Reread lines 30–40. What do you learn about Buddy and his friend from their activities with the buggy?

Detail of *Wild Dog Mushroom* (1974), Bob Timberlake. © Bob Timberlake.

---

## DIFFERENTIATED INSTRUCTION

**FOR ENGLISH LANGUAGE LEARNERS**
**Vocabulary: Multiple-Meaning Words**
Explain that some words in English have more than one meaning and even can be used as more than one part of speech. Discuss how each of these words is used in the selection: *object* (line 34), *hard* (line 42), *leaves* (line 44), *bowl* (line 47), *jam* (line 55), *kind* (line 56), *prize* (line 66), *slide* (line 73).

**FOR ADVANCED LEARNERS/PRE–AP**
**Research Activity** Have students research famous friendships in literature, such as that of Huck and Jim in *The Adventures of Huckleberry Finn*. After they have finished reading "A Christmas Memory," ask them to compare the friendship between Buddy and his friend with the friendship they researched.

fire and, with joined sighs, watch it catch flame. The buggy is empty, the bowl is brimful.

We eat our supper (cold biscuits, bacon, blackberry jam) and discuss tomorrow. Tomorrow the kind of work I like best begins: buying. Cherries and citron, ginger and vanilla and canned Hawaiian pineapple, rinds and raisins and walnuts and whiskey and oh, so much flour, butter, so many eggs, spices, flavorings: why, we'll need a pony to pull the buggy home.

60 But before these purchases can be made, there is the question of money. Neither of us has any. Except for skinflint sums persons in the house occasionally provide (a dime is considered very big money); or what we earn ourselves from various activities: holding rummage sales, selling buckets of hand-picked blackberries, jars of homemade jam and apple jelly and peach preserves, rounding up flowers for funerals and weddings. Once we won seventy-ninth prize, five dollars, in a national football contest. Not that we know a fool thing about football. It's just that we enter any contest we hear about: at the moment our hopes are centered on the fifty-thousand-dollar Grand Prize being offered to name a new brand of coffee (we suggested "A.M.";
70 and, after some hesitation, for my friend thought it perhaps sacrilegious, the slogan "A.M.! Amen!"). To tell the truth, our only *really* profitable enterprise was the Fun and Freak Museum we conducted in a back-yard woodshed two summers ago. The Fun was a stereopticon[1] with slide views of Washington and New York lent us by a relative who had been to those places (she was furious when she discovered why we'd borrowed it); the Freak was a three-legged biddy chicken hatched by one of our own hens. Everybody hereabouts wanted to see that biddy: we charged grownups a nickel, kids two cents. And took in a good twenty dollars before the museum shut down due to the decease of the main attraction.

80 But one way and another we do each year accumulate Christmas savings, a Fruitcake Fund. These moneys we keep hidden in an ancient bead purse under a loose board under the floor under a chamber pot under my friend's bed. The purse is seldom removed from this safe location except to make a deposit or, as happens every Saturday, a withdrawal; for on Saturdays I am allowed ten cents to go to the picture show. My friend has never been to a picture show, nor does she intend to: "I'd rather hear you tell the story, Buddy. That way I can imagine it more. Besides, a person my age shouldn't **squander** their eyes. When the Lord comes, let me see him clear." In addition to never having seen a movie, she has never: eaten in a restaurant, traveled more than five miles
90 from home, received or sent a telegram, read anything except funny papers and the Bible, worn cosmetics, cursed, wished someone harm, told a lie on purpose, let a hungry dog go hungry. Here are a few things she has done, does do: killed with a hoe the biggest rattlesnake ever seen in this county (sixteen rattles), dip snuff[2] (secretly), tame hummingbirds (just try it) till they balance

---

1. **stereopticon** (stĕr'ē-ŏp'tĭ-kŏn'): an early slide projector that could merge two images of the same scene on a screen, resulting in a 3-D effect.

2. **dip snuff:** to place a small amount of finely ground tobacco (snuff) in one's mouth.

**C** ANALYZE IMAGERY
What words and phrases in this passage appeal to the senses and help you imagine the characters shelling pecans?

**squander** (skwŏn'dər) *v.* to spend or use wastefully

READING SKILL | COMMON CORE
RL 4

**C** ANALYZE IMAGERY

*Possible answer:* The "Caarackle!" and "cheery crunch" (line 45), as well as the "joined sighs" (line 53), appeal to the sense of hearing. The changing light and the play of firelight and reflection (lines 50–53), as well as the empty buggy and full bowl (lines 53–54), appeal to the sense of sight.

**IF STUDENTS NEED HELP . . .** Have pairs of students use details from lines 41–54 to expand upon the chart shown on page 337.

**BEST PRACTICES TOOLKIT—Transparency** Observation Chart p. C7

VOCABULARY | COMMON CORE
L 4

**OWN THE WORD**

**squander:** Have students complete one or both of the following sentences with a real or imagined event: *I squandered my money when I . . . . I squandered my time when I . . . Possible answers:* bought a cheap watch that quickly broke; waited for over an hour for a bus that never came.

**FOR STRUGGLING READERS**
**Locate Supporting Details** On this page, Capote characterizes Buddy's friend as both a child and an adult. Help students find some of the details that suggest her childishness (for example, running the Fun and Freak Museum and reading the funny pages) and some that remind readers that she is an adult (such as her thoughts about dying and her courage in killing a large rattlesnake).

**FOR ENGLISH LANGUAGE LEARNERS**
**Vocabulary: Idioms and Sayings** Explain these sayings, using New Word Analysis:

- *on the whole* (lines 16–17), "mostly"
- *a fool thing* (line 67), "anything at all"
- *set about* (line 243), "began"
- *gets my goat* (line 286), "annoys me"
- *makes me boil* (line 324), "angers me"

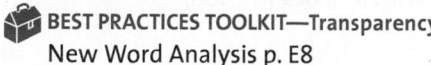 **BEST PRACTICES TOOLKIT—Transparency** New Word Analysis p. E8

on her finger, tell ghost stories (we both believe in ghosts) so tingling they chill you in July, talk to herself, take walks in the rain, grow the prettiest japonicas in town, know the recipe for every sort of old-time Indian cure, including a magical wart remover. D

Now, with supper finished, we retire to the room in a faraway part of the house where my friend sleeps in a scrap-quilt-covered iron bed painted rose pink, her favorite color. Silently, wallowing in the pleasures of conspiracy, we take the bead purse from its secret place and spill its contents on the scrap quilt. Dollar bills, tightly rolled and green as May buds. Somber fifty-cent pieces, heavy enough to weight a dead man's eyes.[3] Lovely dimes, the liveliest coin, the one that really jingles. Nickels and quarters, worn smooth as creek pebbles. But mostly a hateful heap of bitter-odored pennies. Last summer others in the house contracted to pay us a penny for every twenty-five flies we killed. Oh, the carnage of August: the flies that flew to heaven! Yet it was not work in which we took pride. And, as we sit counting pennies, it is as though we were back tabulating dead flies. Neither of us has a head for figures; we E count slowly, lose track, start again. According to her calculations, we have $12.73. According to mine, exactly $13. "I do hope you're wrong, Buddy. We can't mess around with thirteen. The cakes will fall. Or put somebody in the cemetery. Why, I wouldn't dream of getting out of bed on the thirteenth." This is true: she always spends thirteenths in bed. So, to be on the safe side, we subtract a penny and toss it out the window.

Of the ingredients that go into our fruitcakes, whiskey is the most expensive, as well as the hardest to obtain: State laws forbid its sale. But everybody knows you can buy a bottle from Mr. Haha Jones. And the next day, having completed our more **prosaic** shopping, we set out for Mr. Haha's business address, a "sinful" (to quote public opinion) fish-fry and dancing café down by the river. We've been there before, and on the same errand; but in previous years our dealings have been with Haha's wife, an iodine-dark Indian woman with brassy peroxided hair and a dead-tired disposition. Actually, we've never laid eyes on her husband, though we've heard that he's an Indian too. A giant with razor scars across his cheeks. They call him Haha because he's so gloomy, a man who never laughs. As we approach his café (a large log cabin festooned inside and out with chains of garish-gay naked light bulbs and standing by the river's muddy edge under the shade of river trees where moss drifts through the branches like gray mist) our steps slow down. Even Queenie stops prancing and sticks close by. People have been murdered in Haha's café. Cut to pieces. Hit on the head. There's a case coming up in court next month.

Naturally these goings-on happen at night when the colored lights cast crazy patterns and the Victrola[4] wails. In the daytime Haha's is shabby and deserted. I knock at the door, Queenie barks, my friend calls: "Mrs. Haha, ma'am? Anyone to home?" F

**D MAKE INFERENCES**
Reread lines 80–98. What do these details reveal about Buddy's friend?

**② Targeted Passage**

**E ANALYZE IMAGERY**
Notice how imagery adds depth to ordinary objects such as coins and dollar bills.

**prosaic** (prō-zā'ĭk) *adj.* dull; commonplace

**F DETAILS OF SETTING**
Reread the description of Mr. Haha's café in lines 119–136. Which specific words and details indicate that the café is a dangerous and "sinful" place?

3. **heavy enough to weight a dead man's eyes:** from the custom of putting coins on the closed eyes of corpses to keep the eyelids from opening.
4. **Victrola:** a trademark for a brand of old record player.



READING SKILL: *Review*

## D MAKE INFERENCES

***Possible answer:*** *She has religious faith and has led a sheltered life (lines 88–91); she is gentle and kind (lines 91–92); she is tough (lines 92–98); she is willing to work to achieve her goals (lines 80–83).*

**IF STUDENTS NEED HELP . . .** Ask
- How far has Buddy's friend traveled?
- What unusual things has she done?
- What are her beliefs?
- How does she treat other people?

READING SKILL — COMMON CORE RL 4

## E *Model the Skill:* ANALYZE IMAGERY

Model an analysis of one of the author's descriptive details. Point out the words "hateful heap of bitter-odored pennies." Explain that pennies are made with copper, unlike other coins, and do smell metallic. The narrator probably finds them "hateful" both because they are worth the least and because of the memory of how they were earned: by killing flies, "not work in which we took pride."

TEXT ANALYSIS — COMMON CORE RL 4

## F DETAILS OF SETTING

***Possible answer:*** *dancing (line 121); grisly murders (lines 131–132); the wailing Victrola (line 134); the garish, naked light bulbs (line 128); and the shabby, deserted appearance of Haha's in the daytime (line 134)*

VOCABULARY — COMMON CORE L 4

## OWN THE WORD

**prosaic:** Write the word and the definition "dull; commonplace" in a circle. Have students add synonyms around the circle to create a semantic map. ***Possible answers:*** *humdrum, boring, routine, uninteresting*

342 UNIT 3: SETTING, MOOD, AND IMAGERY

## DIFFERENTIATED INSTRUCTION

### FOR STRUGGLING READERS

**② Targeted Passage [Lines 99–116]**

By focusing on a shared activity, this descriptive passage underscores the bond between Buddy and his friend.

- Where do the friends go after dinner? (lines 99–100)
- What have they hidden? What do they plan to do with it? (lines 103–106)
- What job did they share to earn money? (lines 106–108)

### FOR ENGLISH LANGUAGE LEARNERS

**Culture: Connect** In most Latin American and European countries, the number 13 implies bad luck. Ask students if they know of other numbers or actions that are considered bad luck in their home cultures.

Footsteps. The door opens. Our hearts overturn. It's Mr. Haha Jones himself! And he *is* a giant; he *does* have scars; he *doesn't* smile. No, he glowers at us through Satan-tilted eyes and demands to know: "What you want
140 with Haha?"

For a moment we are too paralyzed to tell. Presently my friend half-finds her voice, a whispery voice at best: "If you please, Mr. Haha, we'd like a quart of your finest whiskey."

His eyes tilt more. Would you believe it? Haha is smiling! Laughing, too. "Which one of you is a drinkin' man?"

"It's for making fruitcakes, Mr. Haha. Cooking."

This sobers him. He frowns. "That's no way to waste good whiskey." Nevertheless, he retreats into the shadowed café and seconds later appears carrying a bottle of daisy-yellow unlabeled liquor. He demonstrates its sparkle
150 in the sunlight and says: "Two dollars."

We pay him with nickels and dimes and pennies. Suddenly, as he jangles the coins in his hand like a fistful of dice, his face softens. "Tell you what," he proposes, pouring the money back into our bead purse, "just send me one of them fruitcakes instead."

"Well," my friend remarks on our way home, "there's a lovely man. We'll put an extra cup of raisins in *his* cake."

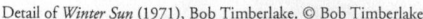
Detail of *Winter Sun* (1971), Bob Timberlake. © Bob Timberlake.

Use these prompts to help students understand the scene at Haha's, described in lines 127–156.

**Connect** Have you ever misjudged anyone because of his or her physical appearance? Explain. *Answers will vary.*

**Analyze** Why doesn't Mr. Haha take the money for the whiskey? *Possible answers: He is amused by these visitors; he is touched to think that his whiskey will be used in fruitcakes that will bring people Christmas cheer.*

**Synthesize** What does this scene show about Buddy's friend? *Possible answer: She is capable of charming someone as fearsome as Haha. But she also has poor judgment. She takes a seven-year-old to visit a bootlegger, and she thinks that a man who may be a criminal is "lovely" because he gives her the bottle of whiskey for free.*

## Analyze Visuals

**Activity** Ask students whether what they learn about Buddy is, like this painting, illuminated in some ways but dark and closed off in others. Have students explain their answers.

**About the Art** In addition to painting the rural landscapes of North Carolina, Bob Timberlake (see page 340) also paints its rural structures, such as log cabins and porches. This experiment in the use of light presents the side of the house in clear detail, but its entrance is obscured in shadow.

**FOR STRUGGLING READERS**

**Monitor Comprehension** If students seem to be having trouble tracking the plot, urge them to think of it as a series of key scenes. For each scene (perhaps corresponding with the Targeted Passages), have them fill in an Open Mind chart. They should record the key details of the scene and any comments that they wish to make about the scene.

**BEST PRACTICES TOOLKIT—Transparency**
Open Mind p. D9

**FOR ENGLISH LANGUAGE LEARNERS**

**Language: Conversational English Patterns** Explain that *We hear* is left out but understood in the sentence in line 137: *Footsteps.* Discuss these unusual language patterns in the rest of the story:

• *send me one of them fruitcakes* (lines 153–154)

• *giveya two-bits cash for that ol tree* (line 254)

• *out it goes* (line 312)

## Analyze Visuals

*Possible answer:* *The black stove (line 157) is the most obvious detail. The many pots on the stove suggest a flurry of cooking activity, as described in the paragraph. The stack of wood suggests that this stove, like the stove in the story, was stoked with firewood.*

**About the Art** In *Mrs. Dorsett's Kitchen*, North Carolina artist Bob Timberlake (see pages 340 and 343) focuses on a country kitchen, where a large cast-iron stove takes the viewer back to a former way of life. The setting is complete with cooking pots that also recall an earlier era. The scene suggests an old farmhouse, with its pine floors and old-time shelves in lieu of cabinets and counters.

*Mrs. Dorsett's Kitchen* (1973), Bob Timberlake. © Bob Timberlake.

◀ **Analyze Visuals**
What **details** in this painting evoke the scene described in lines 157–162?

The black stove, stoked with coal and firewood, glows like a lighted pumpkin. Eggbeaters whirl, spoons spin round in bowls of butter and sugar, vanilla sweetens the air, ginger spices it; melting, nose-tingling odors saturate
160 the kitchen, **suffuse** the house, drift out to the world on puffs of chimney smoke. In four days our work is done. Thirty-one cakes, dampened with whiskey, bask on windowsills and shelves.

Who are they for?

Friends. Not necessarily neighbor friends: indeed, the larger share is intended for persons we've met maybe once, perhaps not at all. People who've struck our fancy. Like President Roosevelt. Like the Reverend and Mrs. J. C. Lucey, Baptist missionaries to Borneo[5] who lectured here last winter. Or the little knife grinder who comes through town twice a year. Or Abner Packer, the driver of the six o'clock bus from Mobile, who exchanges waves with
170 us every day as he passes in a dust-cloud whoosh. Or the young Wistons, a

**suffuse** (sə-fyōōz′) *v.* to gradually spread through or over

 **GRAMMAR AND STYLE**
Notice how Capote makes use of the **present tense** even though the memory is part of the narrator's past. This creates a sense of immediacy for the reader.

5. **Borneo** (bôr′nē-o′): a large island in the South China Sea, southwest of the Philippines.

**344** UNIT 3: SETTING, MOOD, AND IMAGERY

 **GRAMMAR AND STYLE** COMMON CORE L3

**Choose Effective Verb Tense** Point out that present-tense verbs dominate "A Christmas Memory" but that present tense is not the traditional tense used to narrate past events. The traditional tense is past tense. To illustrate, have one or more students read aloud lines 157–162, changing the present-tense verbs to past-tense verbs. Discuss how the paragraph now resembles a traditional story—interesting, but not quite as immediate as it sounded with present-tense verbs. For an extra challenge, have students change the present-tense verbs to future-tense verbs; then discuss how the paragraph now conveys a sense of anticipation.

**VOCABULARY** COMMON CORE L4

**OWN THE WORD**

**suffuse:** Ask students to list kitchen fragrances that can *suffuse* the air in the house. *Possible answers: onions cooking, turkey roasting, coffee brewing, toast burning*

## DIFFERENTIATED INSTRUCTION

**FOR ADVANCED LEARNERS/PRE–AP**

**Analyze Style** [small-group option] Have students analyze Capote's **style** in "A Christmas Memory"—his particular way of writing and communicating ideas. Suggest that they begin by examining this page and the next and then draw from other passages in the story to develop and support their analysis. Have students consider these stylistic elements and record their ideas in a journal or two-column chart:

• diction (word choice)

• active vs. passive verbs

• sentence length and structure

• imagery and figurative language

• sound devices (such as alliteration)

• tone

• use of dialogue

To conclude the activity, ask students to deliver a brief class presentation that summarizes their analysis of Capote's style.

California couple whose car one afternoon broke down outside the house and who spent a pleasant hour chatting with us on the porch (young Mr. Wiston snapped our picture, the only one we've ever had taken). Is it because my friend is shy with everyone *except* strangers that these strangers, and merest acquaintances, seem to us our truest friends? I think yes. Also, the scrapbooks we keep of thank-you's on White House stationery, time-to-time communications from California and Borneo, the knife grinder's penny post cards, make us feel connected to eventful worlds beyond the kitchen with its view of a sky that stops.

180     Now a nude December fig branch grates against the window. The kitchen is empty, the cakes are gone; yesterday we carted the last of them to the post office, where the cost of stamps turned our purse inside out. We're broke. That rather depresses me, but my friend insists on celebrating—with two inches of whiskey left in Haha's bottle. Queenie has a spoonful in a bowl of coffee (she likes her coffee chicory-flavored and strong). The rest we divide between a pair of jelly glasses. We're both quite awed at the prospect of drinking straight whiskey; the taste of it brings screwed-up expressions and sour shudders. But by and by we begin to sing, the two of us singing different songs simultaneously. I don't know the words to mine, just: *Come on along,*
190 *come on along, to the dark-town strutters' ball.* But I can dance: that's what I mean to be, a tap dancer in the movies. My dancing shadow rollicks on the walls; our voices rock the chinaware; we giggle: as if unseen hands were tickling us. Queenie rolls on her back, her paws plow the air, something like a grin stretches her black lips. Inside myself, I feel warm and sparky as those crumbling logs, carefree as the wind in the chimney. My friend waltzes round the stove, the hem of her poor calico skirt pinched between her fingers as though it were a party dress: *Show me the way to go home,* she sings, her tennis shoes squeaking on the floor. *Show me the way to go home.*

    Enter: two relatives. Very angry. **Potent** with eyes that scold, tongues that
200 scald. Listen to what they have to say, the words tumbling together into a wrathful tune: "A child of seven! whiskey on his breath! are you out of your mind? feeding a child of seven! must be loony! road to ruination! remember Cousin Kate? Uncle Charlie? Uncle Charlie's brother-in-law? shame! scandal! humiliation! kneel, pray, beg the Lord!"

    Queenie sneaks under the stove. My friend gazes at her shoes, her chin quivers, she lifts her skirt and blows her nose and runs to her room.

    Long after the town has gone to sleep and the house is silent except for the chimings of clocks and the sputter of fading fires, she is weeping into a pillow already as wet as a widow's handkerchief.
210     "Don't cry," I say, sitting at the bottom of her bed and shivering despite my flannel nightgown that smells of last winter's cough syrup, "don't cry," I beg, teasing her toes, tickling her feet, "you're too old for that."

    "It's because," she hiccups, "I *am* too old. Old and funny."

A CHRISTMAS MEMORY    **345**

---

**H** MAKE INFERENCES
Why do you think Buddy and his friend send their fruitcakes to strangers?

**I** ANALYZE IMAGERY
In lines 187–198, Capote appeals to four out of the five senses. Identify as many of these sensory details as you can, and note which sense each appeals to.

**potent** (pōt'nt) *adj.* powerful

**J** MAKE INFERENCES
Reread lines 199–206. What impression do you get of the relatives?

---

READING SKILL: *Review*

**H** MAKE INFERENCES

*Possible answer: They probably have few friends of their own. They live an isolated life and mainly have only each other.*

**IF STUDENTS NEED HELP . . .** Ask them to list other characters they have met so far (the other people in the house; Mr. Haha). Have them make a statement gauging how emotionally close each one is to Buddy and his friend.

**Extend the Discussion** Does it seem more pathetic or more charming that Buddy and his friend send their fruitcakes to strangers? How does the narrator feel about it as a child? as an adult looking back?

READING SKILL     COMMON CORE   RL 4

**I** ANALYZE IMAGERY

*Possible answer: Sight: rollicking shadow, paws "plowing" the air; Hearing: singing, rocking voices and giggling, the wind in the chimney, squeaking shoes; Taste: whiskey; Touch: tickling and "sparky" warmth, "pinched" calico skirt*

READING SKILL: *Review*

**J** MAKE INFERENCES

*Possible answer: They are angry and judgmental; they appear to notice only problems and mistakes.*

**Extend the Discussion** Do you think this description of the relatives is formed more from accurate recall or from the one-sided impressions of a seven-year-old? Explain.

---

**FOR STRUGGLING READERS**
**Make Inferences** For help with making inferences, such as those presented in the lettered questions on this page, help students use an inference chart or other graphic organizer that requires them to analyze details in a step-by-step fashion.

📋 **BEST PRACTICES TOOLKIT—Transparency**
Making Inferences p. A13

**FOR ENGLISH LANGUAGE LEARNERS**
**Culture: Clarify** Explain Buddy's reference to tap dancing in lines 190–191. Point out that tap dancing, singing, and chorus lines were popular features in movies of the 1930s because they helped distract people's minds from the worries of the Great Depression. Indeed, many people, like Buddy, came to equate tap dancing with fame and fortune.

## Analyze Visuals

**Activity** When students have finished reading, ask them if this painting accurately reflects their ideas about the setting. Urge them to support their answers with story details.

**About the Art** This painting by Bob Timberlake (see pages 340, 343, and 344) underscores rural isolation. It presents the viewer with a foreground that is empty and a wooded background that seems a natural barrier to human contact. Note how dull or muted the light is and how little variation there is in color.

**REVISIT THE BIG QUESTION**

## What do you look for in a **FRIEND?**

**Discuss** One reason that Buddy can turn his cousin's sadness and self-pity into eager anticipation is that both of them understand friendship. Review your *QUICKWRITE* list, "Top 10 Qualities of a Good Friend" (page 336). What qualities on that list are reflected in this turnaround? *Answers will vary from list to list but may include qualities such as these: no fear of displaying personal thoughts and feelings; understanding me better than just about anyone else; wanting me to be happy or optimistic.*

Detail of *Another World* (1974), Bob Timberlake. © Bob Timberlake.

"Not funny. Fun. More fun than anybody. Listen. If you don't stop crying you'll be so tired tomorrow we can't go cut a tree."

She straightens up. Queenie jumps on the bed (where Queenie is not allowed) to lick her cheeks. "I know where we'll find real pretty trees, Buddy. And holly, too. With berries big as your eyes. It's way off in the woods. Farther than we've ever been. Papa used to bring us Christmas trees from there:
220 carry them on his shoulder. That's fifty years ago. Well, now: I can't wait for morning."

Morning. Frozen rime⁶ lusters the grass; the sun, round as an orange and orange as hot-weather moons, balances on the horizon, burnishes the silvered winter woods. A wild turkey calls. A renegade hog grunts in the undergrowth. Soon, by the edge of knee-deep, rapid-running water, we have to abandon the buggy. Queenie wades the stream first, paddles across barking complaints at the swiftness of the current, the pneumonia-making coldness of it. We follow, holding our shoes and equipment (a hatchet, a burlap sack) above our heads. A mile more: of chastising thorns, burrs and briers that catch at

**③ Targeted Passage**

---

6. **rime:** a white frost.

**346** UNIT 3: SETTING, MOOD, AND IMAGERY

our clothes; of rusty pine needles brilliant with gaudy fungus and molted
feathers. Here, there, a flash, a flutter, an ecstasy of shrillings remind us that
not all the birds have flown south. Always, the path unwinds through lemony
sun pools and pitch-black vine tunnels. Another creek to cross: a disturbed
armada of speckled trout froths the water round us, and frogs the size of plates
practice belly flops; beaver workmen are building a dam. On the farther shore,
Queenie shakes herself and trembles. My friend shivers, too: not with cold but
enthusiasm. One of her hat's ragged roses sheds a petal as she lifts her head and
inhales the pine-heavy air. "We're almost there; can you smell it, Buddy?" she
says, as though we were approaching an ocean. **K**

240      And, indeed, it is a kind of ocean. Scented acres of holiday trees, prickly-
leafed holly. Red berries shiny as Chinese bells: black crows swoop upon
them screaming. Having stuffed our burlap sacks with enough greenery and
crimson to garland a dozen windows, we set about choosing a tree. "It should
be," muses my friend, "twice as tall as a boy. So a boy can't steal the star." The
one we pick is twice as tall as me. A brave handsome brute that survives thirty
hatchet strokes before it keels with a creaking rending cry. Lugging it like a
kill, we commence the long trek out. Every few yards we abandon the struggle,
sit down and pant. But we have the strength of triumphant huntsmen; that
and the tree's virile, icy perfume revive us, **goad** us on. Many compliments

250 accompany our sunset return along the red clay road to town; but my friend
is sly and noncommittal when passers-by praise the treasure perched in our
buggy: what a fine tree, and where did it come from? "Yonderways," she
murmurs vaguely. Once a car stops, and the rich mill owner's lazy wife leans
out and whines: "Giveya two-bits⁷ cash for that ol tree." Ordinarily my friend
is afraid of saying no; but on this occasion she promptly shakes her head: "We
wouldn't take a dollar." The mill owner's wife persists. "A dollar, my foot! Fifty
cents. That's my last offer. Goodness, woman, you can get another one." In
answer, my friend gently reflects: "I doubt it. There's never two of anything." **L**
     Home: Queenie slumps by the fire and sleeps till tomorrow, snoring loud

260 as a human.
     A trunk in the attic contains: a shoebox of ermine tails (off the opera cape
of a curious lady who once rented a room in the house), coils of frazzled tinsel
gone gold with age, one silver star, a brief rope of dilapidated, undoubtedly
dangerous candylike light bulbs. Excellent decorations, as far as they go, which
isn't far enough: my friend wants our tree to blaze "like a Baptist window,"
droop with weighty snows of ornament. But we can't afford the made-in-Japan
splendors at the five-and-dime. So we do what we've always done: sit for days
at the kitchen table with scissors and crayons and stacks of colored paper. I
make sketches and my friend cuts them out: lots of cats, fish too (because

270 they're easy to draw), some apples, some watermelons, a few winged angels
devised from saved-up sheets of Hershey-bar tin foil. We use safety pins to
attach these creations to the tree; as a final touch, we sprinkle the branches

---

7. **two-bits:** 25 cents.

A CHRISTMAS MEMORY    **347**

**❸ Targeted Passage**
*continued*

**K** DETAILS OF SETTING
Reread lines 222–239.
What is the effect of
including such vivid
details of this natural
setting?

**goad** (gōd) *v.* to drive
or urge

**L** MAKE INFERENCES
Reread lines 253–258.
What do you learn about
Buddy's friend from her
response to the mill
owner's wife?

---

TEXT ANALYSIS     COMMON CORE
RL 4

**K DETAILS OF SETTING**

***Possible answer:** The details combine to
make getting the tree sound like a wonderful adventure in a beautiful, isolated, and
almost magical place.*

**IF STUDENTS NEED HELP...** Have them
add the following details to their imagery
charts and then discuss which senses each
detail addresses:

- "lemony sun pools" (lines 232–233)
  ***Possible answer:** sight, smell, taste*
- "froths the water" (line 234) ***Possible
  answer:** sight, hearing*
- "pine-heavy air" (line 238) ***Possible
  answer:** smell, touch*

---

READING SKILL: *Review*

**L MAKE INFERENCES**

***Possible answer:** She is proud; she thinks
little of people whom she sees as lazy; she
appreciates the value of hard work.*

**IF STUDENTS NEED HELP...** Recall the
description in lines 210–221 of how the
promise of cutting down a tree with Buddy
cheered up his friend. What can you
infer from that scene as well as from this
one about how much the tree means to
Buddy's friend?

---

VOCABULARY     COMMON CORE
L 4

**OWN THE WORD**

**goad:** Ask students to list forces or moti-
vators that *goad* scholars and athletes to
excel. ***Possible answers:** the desire to receive public recognition, gain acceptance
into an outstanding college, be recruited
by a college or professional sports team*

---

**FOR STRUGGLING READERS**

**❸ Targeted Passage [Lines 222–249]**

By recounting the search for a Christmas tree,
this passage prepares readers for the friends'
last Christmas Day together.

- Where do the friends go to find a tree?
  What kind of day is it? (lines 222–243)
- Why does Buddy's friend shiver? (lines
  236–237)
- What kind of tree do they finally choose?
  (lines 243–245)

- Why do they go on, even though the hard
  work has tired them? (lines 247–249)

**FOR ENGLISH LANGUAGE LEARNERS**

**Culture: Clarify** Explain that what Buddy refers to as "Hershey-bar tin foil" (line 271) is the
shiny foil paper in which candy makers used
to wrap chocolate candy. Point out that Her-
shey is a chocolate-manufacturing company
located in Pennsylvania. Its mass-production
techniques made chocolate candy affordable
for almost all Americans, even during the
Great Depression.

Use these prompts to explore how the scene described in lines 284–293 illuminates the character of Buddy's friend:

**Connect** What do you think is important in choosing a gift for someone? *Answers will vary.*

**Analyze** What does the comment made by Buddy's friend about what "gets [her] goat" (line 286) show about her? *Possible answer: She has a generous, selfless nature. She is frustrated that she cannot do as much as she would like to do for Buddy.*

**Evaluate** How well does Capote present a child's perspective by describing the presents that Buddy and his friend give to each other? Defend your answer. *Possible answer: He presents it rather well. By showing someone who seems almost too good to be true, Capote captures a child's limited understanding and tendency to idolize or simplify.*

### REVIST THE BIG QUESTION

## What do you look for in a **FRIEND?**

**Discuss** How is the bond between these two stronger than mere friendship? Defend your answer. *Possible answer: They are quite comfortable with one another. They love each other, and Buddy's friend seems as if she would do anything for Buddy. In some ways, they are more like a mother and son, or a grandmother and grandchild, than friends.*

---

with shredded cotton (picked in August for this purpose). My friend, surveying the effect, clasps her hands together. "Now honest, Buddy. Doesn't it look good enough to eat?" Queenie tries to eat an angel.

After weaving and ribboning holly wreaths for all the front windows, our next project is the fashioning of family gifts. Tie-dye scarves for the ladies, for the men a home-brewed lemon and licorice and aspirin syrup to be taken "at the first Symptoms of a Cold and after Hunting." But when it comes time for
280 making each other's gift, my friend and I separate to work secretly. I would like to buy her a pearl-handled knife, a radio, a whole pound of chocolate-covered cherries (we tasted some once, and she always swears: "I could live on them, Buddy, Lord yes I could—and that's not taking his name in vain"). Instead, I am building her a kite. She would like to give me a bicycle (she's said so on several million occasions: "If only I could, Buddy. It's bad enough in life to do without something *you* want; but confound it, what gets my goat is not being able to give somebody something you want *them* to have. Only one of these days I will, Buddy. Locate you a bike. Don't ask how. Steal it, maybe"). Instead, I'm fairly certain that she is building me a kite—the same as last year
290 and the year before: the year before that we exchanged slingshots. All of which is fine by me. For we are champion kite fliers who study the wind like sailors; my friend, more accomplished than I, can get a kite aloft when there isn't enough breeze to carry clouds.

Christmas Eve afternoon we scrape together a nickel and go to the butcher's to buy Queenie's traditional gift, a good gnawable beef bone. The bone, wrapped in funny paper, is placed high in the tree near the silver star. Queenie knows it's there. She squats at the foot of the tree staring up in a trance of greed: when bedtime arrives she refuses to budge. Her excitement is equaled by my own. I kick the covers and turn my pillow as though it were a
300 scorching summer's night. Somewhere a rooster crows: falsely, for the sun is still on the other side of the world.

"Buddy, are you awake?" It is my friend, calling from her room, which is next to mine; and an instant later she is sitting on my bed holding a candle. "Well, I can't sleep a hoot," she declares. "My mind's jumping like a jack rabbit. Buddy, do you think Mrs. Roosevelt will serve our cake at dinner?" We huddle in the bed, and she squeezes my hand I-love-you. "Seems like your hand used to be so much smaller. I guess I hate to see you grow up. When you're grown up, will we still be friends?" I say always. "But I feel so bad, Buddy. I wanted so bad to give you a bike. I tried to sell my cameo Papa gave
310 me. Buddy"—she hesitates, as though embarrassed—"I made you another kite." Then I confess that I made her one, too; and we laugh. The candle burns too short to hold. Out it goes, exposing the starlight, the stars spinning at the window like a visible caroling that slowly, slowly daybreak silences. Possibly we doze; but the beginnings of dawn splash us like cold water: we're up, wide-eyed and wandering while we wait for others to waken. Quite deliberately my friend drops a kettle on the kitchen floor. I tap dance in front of closed doors. One

**Language Coach**

**Oral Fluency** Many words in English begin with the letter combinations *kn-* or *gn-*, in which the first letter is silent. Correctly pronounce these words: *knickers, gnash, gnarl, knuckle*. Now say the word in lines 294–295 that follows this pattern.

---

## DIFFERENTIATED INSTRUCTION

### FOR ENGLISH LANGUAGE LEARNERS

**Language Coach**

**Oral Fluency** *Answer: gnawable* Tell students that *gnaw* means "to chew on persistently," as a dog chews a bone.

### FOR STRUGGLING READERS

**Develop Reading Fluency** Remind students that italics have two different uses in a text: they indicate special words such as titles or quotes, and they show emphasis. Model reading aloud the sentences containing italicized words on page 349. Point out that the magazine title does not get special emphasis while the words *says* and *is* do. Have students read the sentences aloud after you.

**R** RESOURCE MANAGER—Copy Master
Reading Fluency p. 31

*Christmas Orange* (1975), Bob Timberlake. © Bob Timberlake.

by one the household emerges, looking as though they'd like to kill us both; but it's Christmas, so they can't. First, a gorgeous breakfast: just everything you can imagine—from flapjacks and fried squirrel to hominy grits and honey-in-the-comb. Which puts everyone in a good humor except my friend and me. Frankly, we're so impatient to get at the presents we can't eat a mouthful.

Well, I'm disappointed. Who wouldn't be? With socks, a Sunday school shirt, some handkerchiefs, a hand-me-down sweater, and a year's subscription to a religious magazine for children, *The Little Shepherd*. It makes me boil. It really does.

My friend has a better haul. A sack of satsumas,[8] that's her best present. She is proudest, however, of a white wool shawl knitted by her married sister. But she *says* her favorite gift is the kite I built her. And it *is* very beautiful; though not as beautiful as the one she made me, which is blue and scattered with gold and green Good Conduct stars;[9] moreover, my name is painted on it, "Buddy."

"Buddy, the wind is blowing."

The wind is blowing, and nothing will do till we've run to a pasture below the house where Queenie has scooted to bury her bone (and where, a winter hence, Queenie will be buried, too). There, plunging through the healthy waist-high grass, we unreel our kites, feel them twitching at the string like sky

**M DETAILS OF SETTING**
What do the gifts received by Buddy and his friend tell you about the economic circumstances of the household?

---

8. **satsumas** (săt-sōō′mez): fruit similar to tangerines.

9. **Good Conduct stars:** small, shiny, glued paper stars often awarded to children for good behavior or perfect attendance in school.

---

## Analyze Visuals

**Activity** Have students locate story details that relate to the key elements of this painting. *Possible answer: Lines 240–243 describe bags filled with holly; line 326 reveals that Buddy's friend receives a sack of satsumas as a Christmas gift.* Students also might comment on whether or not they consider the painting's overall effect to be merry and on how well its mood relates to the mood of the Christmas in Capote's story.

**About the Art** Here contemporary American painter Bob Timberlake (see pages 340, 343, 344, and 346) presents the viewer with some traditional images of Christmas. Oranges were common gifts or stocking stuffers when times were harder and citrus less commonly available. Holly with red berries is a typical example of Christmas greenery.

**TEXT ANALYSIS**                    COMMON CORE
                                      RL 4

### M *Model the Skill:* DETAILS OF SETTING

Model analyzing the evidence revealed by the gifts. Point out that Buddy's presents are all practical except for the homemade kite. His friend's gifts include fruit as her "best" gift (in Buddy's opinion) and a handmade wool shawl.

*Possible answer:* The gifts indicate that the family is struggling. The most obvious example of this may be the hand-me-down sweater presented as a gift (line 323).

---

**FOR ENGLISH LANGUAGE LEARNERS**

**Culture: Connect** Point out the elements of what Buddy calls "a gorgeous breakfast" (line 318) in that past era and rural locale. Have students compare and contrast the meal with the supper described in line 55. Then encourage students to describe foods they enjoy for breakfast, supper, or special occasions in their home cultures.

**FOR RELUCTANT READERS**

Ask students to imagine the anticipation, followed by disappointment, that Buddy experiences on Christmas morning. Ask them to guess what Buddy wants to say to his relatives about his gifts, and then to think about what he probably should say. Have each student write or say one sentence for each response.

fish as they swim into the wind. Satisfied, sun-warmed, we sprawl in the grass and peel satsumas and watch our kites **cavort**. Soon I forget the socks and hand-me-down sweater. I'm as happy as if we'd already won the fifty-thousand-dollar Grand Prize in that coffee-naming contest.

340 "My, how foolish I am!" my friend cries, suddenly alert, like a woman remembering too late she has biscuits in the oven. "You know what I've always thought?" she asks in a tone of discovery and not smiling at me but a point beyond. "I've always thought a body would have to be sick and dying before they saw the Lord. And I imagined that when he came it would be like looking at the Baptist window: pretty as colored glass with the sun pouring through, such a shine you don't know it's getting dark. And it's been a comfort: to think of that shine taking away all the spooky feeling. But I'll wager it never happens. I'll wager at the very end a body realizes the Lord has already shown himself. That things as they are"—her hand circles in a gesture that gathers

350 clouds and kites and grass and Queenie pawing earth over her bone—"just what they've always seen, was seeing him. As for me, I could leave the world with today in my eyes."

This is our last Christmas together.

Life separates us. Those who Know Best decide that I belong in a military school. And so follows a miserable succession of bugle-blowing prisons, grim reveille-ridden[10] summer camps. I have a new home too. But it doesn't count. Home is where my friend is, and there I never go.

And there she remains, puttering around the kitchen. Alone with Queenie. Then alone. ("Buddy dear," she writes in her wild hard-to-read script,

360 "yesterday Jim Macy's horse kicked Queenie bad. Be thankful she didn't feel much. I wrapped her in a Fine Linen sheet and rode her in the buggy down to Simpson's pasture where she can be with all her Bones . . ."). For a few Novembers she continues to bake her fruitcakes single-handed; not as many, but some: and, of course, she always sends me "the best of the batch." Also, in every letter she encloses a dime wadded in toilet paper: "See a picture show and write me the story." But gradually in her letters she tends to confuse me with her other friend, the Buddy who died in the 1880's; more and more, thirteenths are not the only days she stays in bed: a morning arrives in November, a leafless birdless coming of winter morning, when she cannot

370 rouse herself to exclaim: "Oh my, it's fruitcake weather!"

And when that happens, I know it. A message saying so merely confirms a piece of news some secret vein had already received, **severing** from me an irreplaceable part of myself, letting it loose like a kite on a broken string. That is why, walking across a school campus on this particular December morning, I keep searching the sky. As if I expected to see, rather like hearts, a lost pair of kites hurrying toward heaven. ❧

---

10. **reveille-ridden** (rĕv'ə-lē-rĭd'n): dominated by an early-morning signal, as on a bugle, to wake soldiers or campers.

**cavort** (kə-vôrt') v. to leap or romp about

 **FLASHBACK**
As a recollection of the narrator's childhood, most of this story functions as a **flashback**—in this case, an episode that occurred before the narrator's present time. How does the narrator's quick summary of life-changing events leading back to the present ("this particular December morning" in line 374) contribute to the nostalgic tone of the story?

④ **Targeted Passage**

**sever** (sĕv'ər) v. to cut off

---

 **FLASHBACK**

Have students focus on one event and think about how it adds to the nostalgic tone of the story. Then discuss with students how each of these events together creates a strong nostalgic tone.

*Possible answer: The events leading back to the present sharply contrast with the narrator's idealized recollection of his childhood. Even though the events are summarized quickly, they tell of sad changes in the lives of the two friends, so it is easy to see why the narrator is nostalgic about their last Christmas together.*

---

**VOCABULARY**    COMMON CORE    L 4

**OWN THE WORD**

- **cavort:** Tell students that common synonyms for *cavort* are "romp" and "play." Have students name three places where children might be found cavorting. *Possible answer: schoolyard, park, beach*

- **sever:** Tell students that a common synonym for *sever* is "cut off." Antonyms include "unite" and "join." Have students use both *sever* and one of its antonyms in a sentence. *Possible answer: His finger was severed in an accident but was later surgically joined back to his hand.*

---

**SELECTION WRAP–UP**

**READ WITH A PURPOSE** Ask students whether they think the author's memory provided all of the details for this story. They should support their answers with reasoning. *Possible answers: No; The author is unlikely to remember an event that happened so long ago so clearly, so he creatively filled in many details.*

⭐ **CRITIQUE** Ask students to respond to the story as a whole. Have them point out what they liked best and least, providing examples to support and clarify their responses.

**INDEPENDENT READING**

Students might also enjoy Willa Cather's *My Antonia*, a story about a man remembering his childhood in Nebraska.

---

**DIFFERENTIATED INSTRUCTION**

**FOR STRUGGLING READERS**

④ **Targeted Passage** [Lines 353–376]
This bittersweet passage reveals what has happened to Buddy and his friend since the time of the narrative.

- Where did Buddy go for the next several years after this Christmas? (lines 354–356)

- What happened to Queenie? (lines 360–362)

- Why did the friend's letters change? (lines 366–368)

- How does Buddy learn about his friend's death? How does he react? (lines 371–376)

## Comprehension

1. **Clarify** How is Buddy's friend different from most people her age?

2. **Recall** What makes Christmas with his friend so memorable for Buddy?

3. **Summarize** What happens to the two friends after this particular Christmas?

## Text Analysis

4. **Examine Character** Think about your impression of Buddy's friend. What **details** helped create this character portrait?

5. **Draw Conclusions About Characters** Buddy is 7; his friend is over 60. Why are they such good friends? Give examples from the story to support your answer.

6. **Interpret Symbols** A symbol is a person, place, or object that represents something beyond itself. What might the kites at the end of the story represent, or symbolize? Give reasons for your interpretation.

● 7. **Evaluate Imagery** Look over the examples of imagery that you noted in your chart. Which example seemed the most vivid? What sense or senses did it appeal to? Explain your choice.

● 8. **Examine Details of Setting** Locate two passages in which the description of setting helps you understand something about the **historical era,** or time period, in which the story takes place. Then explain what the details tell you about the historical era.

● 9. **Analyze Influence of Setting** Think about the impact of setting on the events and characters in this story. What might change if the story were set in a city instead of the country or in contemporary times instead of the past? Choose one detail of time or place from the story and explain how the story would be different if this detail were altered.

10. **Make Judgments** In your opinion, is this story merely a vivid portrayal of a memory, or does it also convey a **theme,** or message?

## Text Criticism

11. **Biographical Context** Since its publication, "A Christmas Memory" has stirred debate among readers and critics. If it is based to a large degree on actual people and events, why is it called fiction? Explain why Capote might have chosen to call this work fiction as opposed to autobiography.

### What do you look for in a FRIEND?

How have particular friendships defined these qualities for you?

A CHRISTMAS MEMORY **351**

COMMON CORE

RL 4 Analyze the cumulative impact of specific word choices on meaning and tone.

---

# Practice and Apply

For preliminary support of post-reading questions, use these copy masters:

**R** **RESOURCE MANAGER—Copy Masters**
Reading Fluency pp. 31–32
Details of Setting p. 21
Question Support p. 29

Additional selection questions are provided for teachers on page 15.

## ANSWERS

## Comprehension

1. *Although she is in her sixties, the woman is childlike in her attitudes and some of her actions.*

2. *It is a time—the last time—that he shares pleasant, familiar tasks and the spirit of Christmas with the only person to whom he seems deeply connected.*

3. *They are separated soon afterward, and they never see each other again.*

## Text Analysis

COMMON CORE RL 4

*Possible answers:*

4. *She is childlike and enjoys children's pastimes, like flying kites; she is generous (she gives Buddy a dime every Saturday for the movies); she thinks the best of people (calling bootlegger Mr. Haha "a lovely man").*

5. *They are friends because they enjoy each other's company and like the same activities. They also appear to be isolated from the rest of the family and thus have no one else.*

6. *Buddy compares the kites to hearts. They may represent the hearts or souls of Buddy and his friend, rising toward heaven, where they would be reunited forever. Buddy's wish is to be once more with his friend.*

7. ● **COMMON CORE FOCUS** *Evaluate Imagery The image of counting out the money seemed most vivid. One can "see" the rolled bills, feel the weight of the half-dollars, and smell the bitter odor of the pennies.*

8. ● **COMMON CORE FOCUS** *Examine Details of Setting Lines 84–85 show that a movie ticket cost a dime. The thank-you notes (line 176) point to the Franklin Roosevelt administration.*

9. ● **COMMON CORE FOCUS** *Analyze Influence of Setting In a city, Buddy and his friend would not chop down a Christmas tree for free.*

---

10. *The story portrays how deeply a caring person and simple activities can affect a child. It also expresses themes about acceptance, imagination, and the power of friendship.*

## Text Criticism

*Possible answer:*

11. *Calling the work fiction enabled Capote to embellish it for literary or dramatic effect.*

### What do you look for in a FRIEND?

Students should describe specific events in detail.

A CHRISTMAS MEMORY **351**

## ANSWERS

## Vocabulary in Context

▲ VOCABULARY PRACTICE

| | |
|---|---|
| 1. *d* | 6. *c* |
| 2. *c* | 7. *a* |
| 3. *b* | 8. *c* |
| 4. *b* | 9. *d* |
| 5. *a* | 10. *c* |

 **RESOURCE MANAGER—Copy Master**
Vocabulary Practice p. 26

### ACADEMIC VOCABULARY IN WRITING

***Possible answer:*** Buddy's friend **contributes** many things to their friendship. She shares her money and time. She gives Buddy attention, teaching him how to make and give fruitcakes. Most of all, she shares her enthusiasm for life, such as when making and flying kites.

Given his **circumstances**, Buddy doesn't have as much to contribute to the friendship. He gives a gift at Christmas, and he shares some chores. However, he does give two things that are extremely important: his time and his love.

### VOCABULARY STRATEGY: CONNOTATION AND DENOTATION

COMMON CORE L 5b

Ask students to explain the connotations of the underlined words in this sentence:

> The odor in the old house was so <u>potent</u> that my eyes began to water.

As you review the Practice items, have students explain each choice in terms of its connotation as well as its denotation.

**Possible answers:**

1. *spent*
2. *foolhardy*
3. *unassuming*
4. *fraud*
5. *thin*

 **RESOURCE MANAGER—Copy Master**
Vocabulary Strategy p. 27

**Interactive Vocabulary**

THINK central

Keywords direct students to a **WordSharp** tutorial on **thinkcentral.com** or to other types of vocabulary practice and review.

---

## Vocabulary in Context

▲ VOCABULARY PRACTICE

Identify the word that is not related in meaning to the other words in the set.

1. (a) gear, (b) paraphernalia, (c) materials, (d) notice
2. (a) vigorous, (b) robust, (c) prosaic, (d) forceful
3. (a) start, (b) finish, (c) begin, (d) inaugurate
4. (a) destroy, (b) suffuse, (c) demolish, (d) consume
5. (a) depress, (b) invigorate, (c) energize, (d) exhilarate
6. (a) squander, (b) waste, (c) conserve, (d) misuse
7. (a) retreat, (b) urge, (c) spur, (d) goad
8. (a) potent, (b) mighty, (c) possible, (d) strong
9. (a) cavort, (b) prance, (c) frolic, (d) fight
10. (a) cut, (b) separate, (c) join, (d) sever

**WORD LIST**

cavort
exhilarate
goad
inaugurate
paraphernalia
potent
prosaic
sever
squander
suffuse

### ACADEMIC VOCABULARY IN WRITING

• aspect   • circumstance   • contribute   • distinct   • perceive

Buddy and his friend have a wonderful relationship because they each **contribute** to their friendship. Write two short paragraphs. In one paragraph, tell what Buddy contributes to their friendship. In the other paragraph, tell what his friend contributes. Use at least one Academic Vocabulary word in your paragraphs.

### VOCABULARY STRATEGY: CONNOTATION AND DENOTATION

A word's **denotation** is its basic dictionary meaning; its **connotations** are the overtones of meaning that it may take on. For example, the vocabulary word *goad* means "to urge," but it has connotations of physically forcing or bullying that *urge* does not have. When you choose words in writing, be sure to consider whether their connotations fit the context.

**COMMON CORE**

**L 5b** Analyze nuances in the meaning of words with similar denotations.

***PRACTICE*** Choose the word that works best in the context of each sentence.

1. Though the Smiths (spent, squandered) a lot of money, they thought putting their son through college was worth it.
2. It was (brave, foolhardy) of Karen not to study before final exams.
3. Al has a modest, (unassuming, groveling) manner that puts people at ease.
4. Anyone treating patients without a medical degree is a (fraud, pretender).
5. The haircut framed her (thin, emaciated) face quite nicely.

**Interactive Vocabulary** THINK central

Go to **thinkcentral.com.**
KEYWORD: HML9-352

---

## DIFFERENTIATED INSTRUCTION

### FOR STRUGGLING LEARNERS

**Task Support: Reinforce** Use Word Sorts to reinforce understanding of the Word List before students begin the **Vocabulary Practice** activity.

BEST PRACTICES TOOLKIT—Transparency
Word Sorts p. E5

### FOR ADVANCED LEARNERS/PRE–AP

**Multiple Connotations** Elicit from students that some words can have more than one connotation, depending on the context of the sentence. For example, the word *paraphernalia* is often used to describe paperwork, or it can describe a random collection of things. Ask students what kinds of connotations those two meanings bring to mind. Then, lead a similar discussion using the rest of the words.

## Language

◆ **GRAMMAR AND STYLE: Choose Effective Verb Tense**

Review the **Grammar and Style** note on page 344. By choosing to tell his the **present tense,** Capote invites the reader to relive the memory along with the narrator. Here is an example from the story:

*Long after the town has gone to sleep and the house is silent except for the chimings of clocks and the sputter of fading fires, she is weeping into a pillow . . .* (lines 207–208)

Notice how the revisions in blue, changing past to present tense, bring an immediacy to the writing, as though the events were occurring now. Try using a similar technique as you revise your response to the prompt below.

> **STUDENT MODEL**
>
> My friend jam~~med~~ her hat down on her head and recklessly navigate~~d~~ the
>
> $\overset{s}{\phantom{}}$ $\overset{s}{\phantom{}}$
>
> baby buggy across the frosty grass. The pecans we ~~sought were~~ hiding under
>
> $\overset{seek\ are}{\phantom{}}$
>
> rotting leaves and twigs.

### READING-WRITING CONNECTION

 Increase your understanding of "A Christmas Memory" by responding to this prompt. Then use the **revising tip** to improve your writing.

| **WRITING PROMPT** | **REVISING TIP** |
|---|---|
| **Short Constructed Response: Description** Imitation is a good way to learn from a master stylist like Truman Capote. Pick your favorite scene from the story and create a **one- or two-paragraph description** of it, using your own sensory language to create imagery. | Review your description. Does it clearly evoke the time and place and include vivid imagery? Does it convey a sense of immediacy? If not, revise your response. Add more sensory language, and remember to experiment with present-tense narration. |

**Interactive Revision**
Go to **thinkcentral.com.**
KEYWORD: HML9-353

---

### FOR STRUGGLING WRITERS

- Urge students to generate their own details rather than reusing Capote's.

- Remind students that even though their writing is descriptive, it still needs a topic sentence for each paragraph and a main idea that unifies the details.

---

## Language

◆ **GRAMMAR AND STYLE**

Discuss the revisions to the student model. In particular, point out the spelling changes. (For information on present-tense verbs, see **Grammar Handbook**, page R55.)

- *Jammed* drops the doubling of a letter to become *jams*.

- *Navigated* changes its last letter but not its stem to become *navigates*.

- *Sought* and *were* change form completely to become *seek* and *are*.

**R** **RESOURCE MANAGER—Copy Master**
Choose Effective Verb Tense p. 30

**READING-WRITING CONNECTION**
Have students visualize the scene, using Sensory Notes to record details and images. Urge students to capture details that appeal to various senses.

**BEST PRACTICES TOOLKIT—Transparency**
Sensory Notes p. B9

>
> **Writing Online**
>
> The following tools are available online at **thinkcentral.com** and on **Write*Smart* CD-ROM:**
> - **Interactive Graphic Organizers**
> - **Interactive Student Models**
> - **Interactive Revision Lessons**
>
> For additional grammar instruction, see **GrammarNotes** on **thinkcentral.com.**

## Assess and Reteach

### Assess

**DIAGNOSTIC AND SELECTION TESTS**
Selection Test A, pp. 91–92
Selection Test B/C, pp. 93–94

**Interactive Selection Test** on **thinkcentral.com**

### Reteach

**Level Up Online Tutorials** on **thinkcentral.com**

**Reteaching Worksheets** on **thinkcentral.com**
Literature Lesson 9, Language and Literary Devices Lesson 28, Vocabulary Lesson 17

### COMMON CORE FOCUS

**RL 1** Cite textual evidence to support analysis of what the text says explicitly as well as inferences drawn from the text. **RL 3** Analyze how complex characters develop over the course of a text. **RL 4** Analyze the cumulative impact of specific word choices on meaning. **L 1** Demonstrate command of the conventions of standard English grammar and usage. **L 3** Apply knowledge of language to make effective choices for meaning or style. **L 4b, d** Identify patterns of word changes; verify the preliminary determination of the meaning of a word.

### SUMMARY

While vacationing with his mother at a beach resort, 11-year-old Jerry decides that he must swim through an underwater tunnel. When he makes the dangerous swim, he keeps his accomplishment a secret from his mother.

### When is a **RISK** worth taking?

After you ask the question, invite students to define *risk*. Have them read the paragraph and suggest examples of risks. Wrap up by having students complete the *DISCUSS* activity.

---

Essential Course of Study **ECOS** **Through the Tunnel** Short Story by Doris Lessing  Video link at thinkcentral.com

VIDEO TRAILER THINK central KEYWORD: HML9-354

# When is a **RISK** worth taking?

#### COMMON CORE

**RL 1** Cite textual evidence to support analysis of what the text says explicitly as well as inferences drawn from the text. **RL 3** Analyze how complex characters develop over the course of a text. **RL 4** Analyze the cumulative impact of specific word choices on meaning. **L 4b** Identify patterns of word changes.

In "Through the Tunnel," Jerry risks his personal safety. Sometimes people take such risks to prove something to themselves or others. The risks can be physical, emotional, or social. But when is an action too risky to attempt? More importantly, how do you calculate risk?

**DISCUSS** Think about a time when you or someone you know took a risk to prove something. Create a balance scale like the one shown to weigh that risk. In the base of the scale, write down the dangerous or risky activity. Jot down the risks in one box and the possible benefits in the other. Share your balance scale with your classmates, and discuss with them whether the possible benefits outweighed the risks of the behavior.

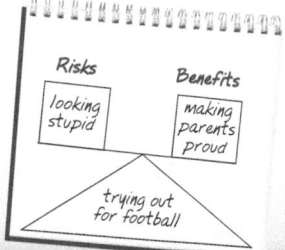

*Risks* — looking stupid
*Benefits* — making parents proud
*trying out for football*

354

---

*See resources on the **Teacher One Stop DVD-ROM** and on **thinkcentral.com**.*

 Video link at **thinkcentral.com**

 **THINK** central

 **RESOURCE MANAGER UNIT 3**
Plan and Teach, pp. 33–40
Summary, pp. 41–42†‡*
Text Analysis and Reading
   Skill, pp. 43–44, 45–46†*
Vocabulary, pp. 47–49*
Grammar and Style, p. 52

**DIAGNOSTIC AND SELECTION TESTS**
Selection Tests, pp. 95–98

 **BEST PRACTICES TOOLKIT**
Word Questioning, p. E9
New Word Analysis, p. E8

**INTERACTIVE READER**

**ADAPTED INTERACTIVE READER**

**ELL ADAPTED INTERACTIVE READER**

**TECHNOLOGY**
- **Teacher One Stop DVD-ROM**
- **Student One Stop DVD-ROM**
- **PowerNotes DVD-ROM**
- **Audio Anthology CD**
- **GrammarNotes DVD-ROM**
- **Audio Tutor CD**
- **ExamView Test Generator**
  on the **Teacher One Stop**

### Video Trailer

Go to **thinkcentral.com** to preview the **Video Trailer** introducing this selection. Other features that support the selection include
- **PowerNotes** presentation
- **ThinkAloud** models to enhance comprehension
- **WordSharp** vocabulary tutorials
- interactive writing and grammar instruction

---

* Resources for Differentiation      † Also in Spanish      ‡ In Haitian Creole and Vietnamese

## ● TEXT ANALYSIS: SETTING AS SYMBOL

A **symbol** is a person, place, object, or activity that stands for something beyond itself. For example, a star often symbolizes hope or excellence. A handshake communicates goodwill.

In "Through the Tunnel," various **settings** symbolize important ideas. As symbols, these settings help characterize Jerry by subtly revealing his thoughts about himself. As you read, think about what the beach, the bay, the tunnel, and the events that take place in each location might symbolize to Jerry and what these symbols tell you about his character.

## ● READING SKILL: ANALYZE DETAILS

In order to understand the symbolic significance of each setting in "Through the Tunnel," you must analyze the **descriptive details** and pay attention to the larger meanings they imply. For example, the big beach is a familiar place where Jerry's mother goes. What might this represent to Jerry? As you read, keep track of words and phrases from the text that describe each setting by using a chart similar to the one shown.

| Beach | Bay | Tunnel |
|---|---|---|
| crowded | wild and rocky | |
| familiar | | |

**Review:** Draw Conclusions

## ▲ VOCABULARY IN CONTEXT

Lessing uses the numbered words in her story about coming of age. Try to match each word with a synonym. Then, in your *Reader/Writer Notebook*, write an example that shows the meaning of each vocabulary word you know.

| | | |
|---|---|---|
| **1.** contrition | | **a.** cliff |
| **2.** incredulous | | **b.** perseverance |
| **3.** inquisitive | | **c.** regret |
| **4.** persistence | | **d.** request |
| **5.** promontory | | **e.** questioning |
| **6.** supplication | | **f.** unbelieving |

 Complete the activities in your **Reader/Writer Notebook.**

## Meet the Author

### Doris Lessing
**born 1919**

**Distinguished Writer**
Doris Lessing has been celebrated as one of the 20th century's "most powerful and compelling novelists." In sheer size and variety, her body of work is impressive: over 45 books ranging from novels and short story collections to essays, a thus far two-volume autobiography, and a book about cats.

**Crossing Boundaries**
Born in Persia (now Iran), Lessing grew up on a farm in Southern Rhodesia (now Zimbabwe) with her British parents. As part of the small community of white settlers in Africa, she saw firsthand the injustices of white minority rule and racial segregation. In 1949, Lessing left Rhodesia for London to start a new life as a writer. Her first novel, *The Grass Is Singing* (1950), and many of her other early works are set in Rhodesia and deal critically with the colonial society she had known. Her best-known novel is *The Golden Notebook* (1962), a story about a woman writer in London struggling to come to terms with her life and times.

**Child of Africa**
Lessing insists, "Whatever I am, I have been made so by central Africa." Her self-confidence, strength, and independence can be traced to her youth in the rough, unforgiving country of the African bush. There she could roam freely but, like other African children, had to deal at an early age with dangerous thunderstorms, droughts, snakes, scorpions, and insects. Survival—emotional, intellectual, and physical—is at the heart of her life and work.

**Author Online**  **THINK** central

Go to **thinkcentral.com**.
KEYWORD: HML9-355

355

# *Teach*

### TEXT ANALYSIS
**COMMON CORE**
**RL 3**

## ● *Model the Skill:* SETTING AS SYMBOL

Model recognizing and understanding symbols. Ask students to picture a soldier waving a white flag on a battlefield. Explain that the white flag symbolizes surrender.

**GUIDED PRACTICE** Have students imagine a courtroom statue of a blindfolded woman holding a scale. Ask them to explain what this statue symbolizes. ***Possible answer:*** *equal treatment under the law*

### READING SKILL
**COMMON CORE**
**RL 4**

## ■ *Model the Skill:* ANALYZE DETAILS

Point out that there can be more than one larger meaning to a given detail or group of details. Model analyzing details by asking students to picture a lush garden filled with blooming flowers. Explain that this image could suggest several different ideas, such as peace, beauty, romance, or extravagance.

**GUIDED PRACTICE** Ask students what a dark forest or a sunny beach suggests to them.

 RESOURCE MANAGER—Copy Master Analyze Details p. 45 (for student use while reading the selection)

### VOCABULARY SKILL
**COMMON CORE**

## ▲ VOCABULARY IN CONTEXT

**DIAGNOSE WORD KNOWLEDGE** Have all students complete the Vocabulary in Context. Check their definitions against the following.

**contrition** (kən-trĭsh'ən) *n.* a feeling of regret for doing wrong
**incredulous** (ĭn-krĕj'ə-ləs) *adj.* doubtful; disbelieving
**inquisitive** (ĭn-kwĭz'ĭ-tĭv) *adj.* curious; inquiring
**persistence** (pər-sĭs'təns) *n.* the act of refusing to stop or be changed

**promontory** (prŏm'ən-tôr'ē) *n.* a high ridge of land or rock jutting out into a body of water
**supplication** (sŭp'lĭ-kā'shən) *n.* a humble request or prayer

**PRETEACH VOCABULARY** Use the copy master to help students predict the meaning of each boldfaced word.

R RESOURCE MANAGER—Copy Master Vocabulary Study p. 47

**L 4**

**1.** Read aloud the first sentence in Part A.

**2.** Point out the phrase "did not mean to hurt her feelings." Elicit possible meanings for *contrition*.

**3.** Repeat the procedure for the other words.

### READING SKILL

COMMON CORE

RL 4

**Ⓐ *Model the Skill:* ANALYZE DETAILS**

Model how to analyze descriptive details. Point out that the beach is described as *crowded* and also *safe*. Explain that the larger meaning this implies is that the beach is a safe place for the boy. Tell students to put other descriptive details about the beach and bay in their Analyze Details charts.

**Possible answer:** *The beach is safe and crowded; the bay is wild and dangerous.*

### VOCABULARY

COMMON CORE

L 4

#### OWN THE WORD

**contrition:** Ask students to explain why Jerry is filled with *contrition* and then runs after his mother. Then, have students name times when their actions have made them feel *contrite*.

# THROUGH THE
# Tunnel

## DORIS LESSING

Going to the shore on the first morning of the vacation, the young English boy stopped at a turning of the path and looked down at a wild and rocky bay, and then over to the crowded beach he knew so well from other years. His mother walked on in front of him, carrying a bright striped bag in one hand. Her other arm, swinging loose, was very white in the sun. The boy watched that white, naked arm, and turned his eyes, which had a frown behind them, toward the bay and back again to his mother. When she felt he was not with her, she swung around. "Oh, there you are, Jerry!" she said. She looked impatient, then smiled. "Why, darling, would you rather not come with
10  me? Would you rather—" She frowned, conscientiously worrying over what amusements he might secretly be longing for, which she had been too busy or too careless to imagine. He was very familiar with that anxious, apologetic smile. **Contrition** sent him running after her. And yet, as he ran, he looked back over his shoulder at the wild bay; and all morning, as he played on the safe beach, he was thinking of it. Ⓐ

Next morning, when it was time for the routine of swimming and sunbathing, his mother said, "Are you tired of the usual beach, Jerry? Would you like to go somewhere else?"

**Analyze Visuals ▶**
What elements of this painting are emphasized by its **composition**—the sizes, shapes, and arrangement of its parts?

**❶ Targeted Passage**

**contrition** (kən-trĭsh′ən) *n.* a feeling of regret for doing wrong

**Ⓐ ANALYZE DETAILS**
From what you've learned so far, what contrast exists between the beach and the bay?

356  UNIT 3: SETTING, MOOD, AND IMAGERY

## DIFFERENTIATED INSTRUCTION

### FOR ENGLISH LANGUAGE LEARNERS
**Options for Reading** Ask a question about a set of paragraphs or range of numbered lines. Have pairs of students scan the designated text to find the answer.

### FOR STRUGGLING READERS
In combination with the *Audio Anthology CD*, use one or more Targeted Passages (pp. 356, 359, 362, 363, 366) to ensure that students focus on key story events, concepts, and skills. Targeted Passages are also good for English learners.

**❶ Targeted Passage [Lines 1–15]**
This passage introduces the setting of the rocky bay and the attraction that it has for Jerry, the main character.

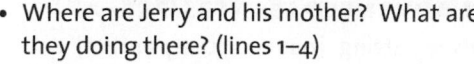

## Reading Support

This selection on **thinkcentral.com** includes embedded **ThinkAloud** models—students "thinking aloud" about the story to model the kinds of questions a good reader would ask about a selection.

## BACKGROUND

**Cultural Connection** "Through the Tunnel" describes how Jerry becomes more mature by reaching a difficult goal. Many cultures have formal celebrations of maturity. In Judaism, children become adult members of the congregation upon their thirteenth birthday. Similarly, traditional Apaches often celebrate *Na'ii'ees*—"the Sunrise Dance"—for girls of about the same age. Its eight phases symbolize the passage from childhood to adulthood. Invite students to share what they may know about other coming-of-age ceremonies.

## Analyze Visuals

*Possible answer:  The beach is bright, crowded, and lively. The bay is dark and rocky; possibly dangerous.*

**About the Art**  Ken Howard (1932–   ) is an English artist known for his paintings of Cornish beaches.

---

- Where are Jerry and his mother?  What are they doing there? (lines 1–4)

- What does Jerry keep looking at? (lines 2–7)

- Why does his mother frown? (lines 10–12)

- What does Jerry think about all morning? (lines 14–15)

**FOR ADVANCED LEARNERS/PRE–AP**

**Analyze Character**  Ask students to observe the character of the mother throughout the story. Based on what is revealed about her, how do they think she would react if Jerry told her what he has achieved?  Would her reaction be different if she learned about it through some other source?  After finishing the story, students should write a short scene showing the mother learning about Jerry's feat and reacting to it.

## **B** *Model the Skill:* SETTING AS SYMBOL

Model how to identify events in a setting as a symbol. Tell students that in lines 24–27 the boy almost follows his mother back to the beach. Explain that this event indicates that their separation might symbolize the boy's first step towards maturation.

***Possible answer:*** *The beach might symbolize the safety of childhood; the bay, the excitement and dangers of adulthood.*

**IF STUDENTS NEED HELP...** Guide them through specific lines in the passage.

- At line 21, note that Jerry wants to see the rocks, which can stand for danger.

- At line 22, point out that the bay's wildness is in the mother's thinking, not Jerry's.

- After reading lines 23–30, discuss why the mother urges Jerry to go to the bay. Help them connect her thinking to the symbolism of the bay and the beach.

## **C** ANALYZE DETAILS

***Possible answer:*** *The cold, deep water that "shocked his limbs" (lines 45–46) suggests this is "the real sea," not the sheltered cove. Furthermore, Jerry crossed "a middle region," with monsterlike rocks, to reach it (lines 43–45).*

## OWN THE WORD

**promontory:** Reread the definition of *promontory* to students. Then, have students write sentences explaining the differences among a *promontory*, a hill, and a mountain. ***Possible answer:*** *A hill has gentler slopes and is less high than a mountain; a promontory always juts into water.*

---

20 "Oh, no!" he said quickly, smiling at her out of that unfailing impulse of contrition—a sort of chivalry. Yet, walking down the path with her, he blurted out, "I'd like to go and have a look at those rocks down there."

She gave the idea her attention. It was a wild-looking place, and there was no one there; but she said, "Of course, Jerry. When you've had enough, come to the big beach. Or just go straight back to the villa, if you like." She walked away, that bare arm, now slightly reddened from yesterday's sun, swinging. And he almost ran after her again, feeling it unbearable that she should go by herself, but he did not.

She was thinking, Of course he's old enough to be safe without me. Have I been keeping him too close? He mustn't feel he ought to be with me. I must be 30 careful. **B**

He was an only child, eleven years old. She was a widow. She was determined to be neither possessive nor lacking in devotion. She went worrying off to her beach.

As for Jerry, once he saw that his mother had gained her beach, he began the steep descent to the bay. From where he was, high up among red-brown rocks, it was a scoop of moving bluish green fringed with white. As he went lower, he saw that it spread among small **promontories** and inlets of rough, sharp rock, and the crisping, lapping surface showed stains of purple and darker blue. Finally, as he ran sliding and scraping down the last few yards, 40 he saw an edge of white surf and the shallow, luminous movement of water over white sand, and, beyond that, a solid, heavy blue.

He ran straight into the water and began swimming. He was a good swimmer. He went out fast over the gleaming sand, over a middle region where rocks lay like discolored monsters under the surface, and then he was in the real sea—a warm sea where irregular cold currents from the deep water shocked his limbs. **C**

When he was so far out that he could look back not only on the little bay but past the promontory that was between it and the big beach, he floated on the buoyant surface and looked for his mother. There she was, a speck of 50 yellow under an umbrella that looked like a slice of orange peel. He swam back to shore, relieved at being sure she was there, but all at once very lonely.

On the edge of a small cape that marked the side of the bay away from the promontory was a loose scatter of rocks. Above them, some boys were stripping off their clothes. They came running, naked, down to the rocks. The English boy swam toward them, but kept his distance at a stone's throw. They were of that coast; all of them were burned smooth dark brown and speaking a language he did not understand. To be with them, of them, was a craving that filled his whole body. He swam a little closer; they turned and watched him with narrowed, alert dark eyes. Then one smiled and waved. It was enough. In 60 a minute, he had swum in and was on the rocks beside them, smiling with a

**B** SETTING AS SYMBOL
Reread lines 21–30. What might the beach symbolize? The bay?

**promontory**
(prŏm′ən-tôr′ē) *n.*
a high ridge of land or rock jutting out into a body of water

**C** ANALYZE DETAILS
Reread lines 42–46. Why might Jerry consider this area "the real sea"?

---

## DIFFERENTIATED INSTRUCTION

**FOR ENGLISH LANGUAGE LEARNERS**

**Vocabulary Support** Use Word Questioning to provide instruction and practice for these Key Academic Vocabulary words: *region* (line 43), *proceeded* (line 63), *visible* (line 82), *inspection* (line 93), *impact* (line 133), *brief* (line 262)

 **BEST PRACTICES TOOLKIT—Transparency**
Word Questioning p. E9

**FOR ADVANCED LEANERS/PRE–AP**

**Analyze Setting** [paired activity option] Ask students to sketch the setting described in lines 34–51 from the perspective of either Jerry or his mother. Include only those details each would see from his or her perspective. Then ask each student to explain his or her choices of representation.

desperate, nervous **supplication**. They shouted cheerful greetings at him; and then, as he preserved his nervous, uncomprehending smile, they understood that he was a foreigner strayed from his own beach, and they proceeded to forget him. But he was happy. He was with them.

They began diving again and again from a high point into a well of blue sea between rough, pointed rocks. After they had dived and come up, they swam around, hauled themselves up, and waited their turn to dive again. They were big boys—men, to Jerry. He dived, and they watched him; and when he swam around to take his place, they made way for him. He felt he was accepted and
70 he dived again, carefully, proud of himself.

Soon the biggest of the boys poised himself, shot down into the water, and did not come up. The others stood about, watching. Jerry, after waiting for the sleek brown head to appear, let out a yell of warning; they looked at him idly and turned their eyes back toward the water. After a long time, the boy came up on the other side of a big dark rock, letting the air out of his lungs in a sputtering gasp and a shout of triumph. Immediately the rest of them dived in. One moment, the morning seemed full of chattering boys; the next, the air and the surface of the water were empty. But through the heavy blue, dark shapes could be seen moving and groping.
80 Jerry dived, shot past the school of underwater swimmers, saw a black wall of rock looming at him, touched it, and bobbed up at once to the surface, where the wall was a low barrier he could see across. There was no one visible; under him, in the water, the dim shapes of the swimmers had disappeared. Then one, and then another of the boys came up on the far side of the barrier of rock, and he understood that they had swum through some gap or hole in it. He plunged down again. He could see nothing through the stinging salt water but the blank rock. When he came up the boys were all on the diving rock, preparing to attempt the feat again. And now, in a panic of failure, he yelled up, in English, "Look at me! Look!" and he began splashing and kicking
90 in the water like a foolish dog.

They looked down gravely, frowning. He knew the frown. At moments of failure, when he clowned to claim his mother's attention, it was with just this grave, embarrassed inspection that she rewarded him. Through his hot shame, feeling the pleading grin on his face like a scar that he could never remove, he looked up at the group of big brown boys on the rock and shouted, *"Bonjour! Merci! Au revoir! Monsieur, monsieur!"*[1] while he hooked his fingers round his ears and waggled them.

Water surged into his mouth; he choked, sank, came up. The rock, lately weighted with boys, seemed to rear up out of the water as their weight was
100 removed. They were flying down past him, now, into the water; the air was full of falling bodies. Then the rock was empty in the hot sunlight. He counted one, two, three. . . .

---

1. *Bonjour! Merci! Au revoir! Monsieur, monsieur!* (bôn-zhŏŏr′ mĕr-sē′ ō′rə-vwär′ mə-syœ′ mə-syœ′) French: Good day! Thank you! Goodbye! Sir, sir!

THROUGH THE TUNNEL **359**

---

**supplication**
(sŭp′lĭ-kā′shən) *n.* a humble request or prayer

② **Targeted Passage**

◆ **GRAMMAR AND STYLE**
Reread lines 80–81. Notice how Lessing uses a **compound predicate** to concisely describe several actions taking place.

---

---

At fifty, he was terrified. They must all be drowning beneath him, in the watery caves of the rock! At a hundred, he stared around him at the empty hillside, wondering if he should yell for help. He counted faster, faster, to hurry them up, to bring them to the surface quickly, to drown them quickly— anything rather than the terror of counting on and on into the blue emptiness of the morning. And then, at a hundred and sixty, the water beyond the rock was full of boys blowing like brown whales. They swam back to the shore
110 without a look at him.

He climbed back to the diving rock and sat down, feeling the hot roughness of it under his thighs. The boys were gathering up their bits of clothing and running off along the shore to another promontory. They were leaving to get away from him. He cried openly, fists in his eyes. There was no one to see him, and he cried himself out. **E**

It seemed to him that a long time had passed, and he swam out to where he could see his mother. Yes, she was still there, a yellow spot under an orange umbrella. He swam back to the big rock, climbed up, and dived into the blue pool among the fanged and angry boulders. Down he went, until he
120 touched the wall of rock again. But the salt was so painful in his eyes that he could not see. **F**

He came to the surface, swam to shore, and went back to the villa to wait for his mother. Soon she walked slowly up the path, swinging her striped bag, the flushed, naked arm dangling beside her. "I want some swimming goggles," he panted, defiant and beseeching.

She gave him a patient, **inquisitive** look as she said casually, "Well, of course, darling."

But now, now, now! He must have them this minute, and no other time. He nagged and pestered until she went with him to a shop. As soon as she had
130 bought the goggles, he grabbed them from her hand as if she were going to claim them for herself, and was off, running down the steep path to the bay.

Jerry swam out to the big barrier rock, adjusted the goggles, and dived. The impact of the water broke the rubber-enclosed vacuum, and the goggles came loose. He understood that he must swim down to the base of the rock from the surface of the water. He fixed the goggles tight and firm, filled his lungs, and floated, face down, on the water. Now, he could see. It was as if he had eyes of a different kind—fish eyes that showed everything clear and delicate and wavering in the bright water.

Under him, six or seven feet down, was a floor of perfectly clean, shining
140 white sand, rippled firm and hard by the tides. Two grayish shapes steered there, like long, rounded pieces of wood or slate. They were fish. He saw them nose toward each other, poise motionless, make a dart forward, swerve off, and come around again. It was like a water dance. A few inches above them the water sparkled as if sequins were dropping through it. Fish again—myriads of

Analyze
Visuals ▶

How would you describe the **mood** of this painting? What elements of color, content, and composition contribute to this mood?

**E** DRAW CONCLUSIONS
Why is Jerry upset? Cite details that support your answer.

**F** ANALYZE DETAILS
What do the specific words used to describe the boulders in line 119 suggest about the tunnel?

**inquisitive** (ĭn-kwĭz′ĭ-tĭv) *adj.* curious; inquiring

*Reflections* (1970), Ken Danby. Original egg tempera, 38″ × 52″. © Ken Danby/Gallery Moos, Toronto, Canada.

---

READING SKILL: *Review*

COMMON CORE
RL 1

**E** DRAW CONCLUSIONS

**Possible answer:** *Jerry is upset because he feels that the boys are deliberately abandoning him (lines 113–114).*

READING SKILL

COMMON CORE
RL 4

**F** ANALYZE DETAILS

**Possible answer:** *The reference to "fanged and angry boulders" suggests that the tunnel is treacherous, like a wild, predatory animal.*

**Extend the Discussion** The expression "fanged and angry boulders" implies that the boulders are alive. Is this type of language an effective way to describe something that is not alive? Defend your answer.

## Analyze Visuals

**Possible answer:** *The monotone brown palette, the boy's contemplative stance, and the craggy, overhanging rocks create a quiet, thoughtful mood. (The fact that the name of the painting is* Reflections *reinforces this interpretation.)*

**About the Art** *Reflections* is typical of the work of contemporary Canadian painter Ken Danby because of its realistic style and naturalistic setting.

VOCABULARY

COMMON CORE
L 4

**OWN THE WORD**

**inquisitive:** Tell students that the prefix *in-* comes from the Latin for "into" Have students explain the actions of an *inquisitive* individual, someone who is inquiring or asking questions about or into a particular matter.

---

## *DIFFERENTIATED INSTRUCTION*

**FOR ENGLISH LANGUAGE LEARNERS**

**Vocabulary: Suffixes** Have students explain the meaning of *grayish* in line 140. Point out that the suffix *-ish* often means "like." Then ask Jigsaw Reading groups to list five other adjectives with the *-ish* suffix that they think fit the story (for example, *childish, foolish, doggish, feverish,* and *nightmarish*). Instruct groups to look up and discuss their words. Then ask group representatives to tell the class what the words mean and how they

relate to "Through the Tunnel." Repeat this activity for the word *motionless* (line 142) and the suffix *-less,* meaning "without."

🧰 **BEST PRACTICES TOOLKIT**—Transparency Jigsaw Reading p. A1

## When is a RISK worth taking?

**Discuss** Direct students to lines 118–121. The boulders are "fanged and angry." The salt stings Jerry's eyes so badly that he cannot see. However, Jerry keeps diving, trying to find the tunnel. Why does Jerry take this painful, dangerous risk? ***Possible answer:*** *He feels compelled to prove his maturity because he senses that the older boys have rejected him.*

### FOR ADVANCED LEARNERS/PRE–AP

**Research Activity** Have students research rituals that use water as a symbol of rebirth, such as the Christian rite of baptism or the Hindu practice of bathing in the sacred waters of the Ganges River. Note how, for many of these rituals, a symbolic death is a key element of the rite of transformation.

minute fish, the length of his fingernail, were drifting through the water, and in a moment he could feel the innumerable tiny touches of them against his limbs. It was like swimming in flaked silver. The great rock the big boys had swum through rose sheer out of the white sand—black, tufted lightly with greenish weed. He could see no gap in it. He swam down to its base.

150　　Again and again he rose, took a big chestful of air, and went down. Again and again he groped over the surface of the rock, feeling it, almost hugging it in the desperate need to find the entrance. And then, once, while he was clinging to the black wall, his knees came up and he shot his feet out forward and they met no obstacle. He had found the hole.

He gained the surface, clambered about the stones that littered the barrier rock until he found a big one, and, with this in his arms, let himself down over the side of the rock. He dropped, with the weight, straight to the sandy floor. Clinging tight to the anchor of stone, he lay on his side and looked in under the dark shelf at the place where his feet had gone. He could see the hole.

160　It was an irregular, dark gap; but he could not see deep into it. He let go of his anchor, clung with his hands to the edges of the hole, and tried to push himself in.

He got his head in, found his shoulders jammed, moved them in sidewise, and was inside as far as his waist. He could see nothing ahead. Something soft and clammy touched his mouth; he saw a dark frond moving against the grayish rock, and panic filled him. He thought of octopuses, of clinging weed. He pushed himself out backward and caught a glimpse, as he retreated, of a harmless tentacle of seaweed drifting in the mouth of the tunnel. But it was enough. He reached the sunlight, swam to shore, and lay on the diving rock.

170　He looked down into the blue well of water. He knew he must find his way through that cave, or hole, or tunnel, and out the other side.

First, he thought, he must learn to control his breathing. He let himself down into the water with another big stone in his arms, so that he could lie effortlessly on the bottom of the sea. He counted. One, two, three. He counted steadily. He could hear the movement of blood in his chest. Fifty-one, fifty-two. . . . His chest was hurting. He let go of the rock and went up into the air. He saw that the sun was low. He rushed to the villa and found his mother at her supper. She said only "Did you enjoy yourself?" and he said "Yes."

All night the boy dreamed of the water-filled cave in the rock, and as soon 180　as breakfast was over he went to the bay.

That night, his nose bled badly. For hours he had been underwater, learning to hold his breath, and now he felt weak and dizzy. His mother said, "I shouldn't overdo things, darling, if I were you."

That day and the next, Jerry exercised his lungs as if everything, the whole of his life, all that he would become, depended upon it. Again his nose bled at night, and his mother insisted on his coming with her the next day. It was

---

**DRAW CONCLUSIONS**
Reread lines 155–171. How does Jerry's perception of the tunnel change? What does this tell you about him?

**3 Targeted Passage**

---

## DIFFERENTIATED INSTRUCTION

### FOR STRUGGLING READERS

**3 Targeted Passage [Lines 169–185]**

This passage reveals the challenges involved in preparing for a swim through the tunnel.

- As he looks into the water, what goal does Jerry set for himself? (lines 170–171)

- How does he learn to control his breathing? (lines 172–176)

- Why does he start getting nosebleeds? (lines 181–182)

- What advice does his mother give him?

(lines 182–183)

### FOR ENGLISH LANGUAGE LEARNERS

**Vocabulary: Multiple-Meaning Words** Have students work in groups to identify the correct meaning and part of speech for each of these words as used in the story: *rose* (line 148), *down* (line 150), *lie* (line 173), *safe* (line 189), *count* (line 192), *strain* (line 203), *open* (line 222), *clear* (line 234), *crack* (line 253), *sink* (line 269).

---

### G DRAW CONCLUSIONS

***Possible answer:*** *Initially, Jerry feels panic over imagined danger. When he sees the tunnel for what it is, he becomes more determined than ever to find a way through. This change in perception suggests Jerry's growing maturity.*

**IF STUDENTS NEED HELP . . .** Use the Comparison Matrix to help them draw conclusions about the change in Jerry.

**BEST PRACTICES TOOLKIT**—Transparency Comparison Matrix p. A24

## TIERED DISCUSSION PROMPTS

Use these prompts to explore Jerry's first attempt to swim the tunnel, as described in lines 163–171:

**Connect** Do you know of any scary passageways, like a cave or a tunnel? What details stand out in your mind? ***Possible answer:*** *Students may draw from personal experience or from television or movies.*

**Analyze** How might the tunnel be symbolic of the passage from childhood to adulthood? ***Possible answer:*** *It is mysterious and scary.*

**Synthesize** How does this symbolism reflect the idea that Jerry is changing? ***Possible answer:*** *Jerry decides to be more grown up. If he can pass through the tunnel, perhaps he will be grown up, like the older boys he saw earlier.*

a torment to him to waste a day of his careful self-training, but he stayed with her on that other beach, which now seemed a place for small children, a place where his mother might lie safe in the sun. It was not his beach.

190  He did not ask for permission, on the following day, to go to his beach. He went, before his mother could consider the complicated rights and wrongs of the matter. A day's rest, he discovered, had improved his count by ten. The big boys had made the passage while he counted a hundred and sixty. He had been counting fast, in his fright. Probably now, if he tried, he could get through that long tunnel, but he was not going to try yet. A curious, most unchildlike **persistence,** a controlled impatience, made him wait. In the meantime, he lay underwater on the white sand, littered now by stones he had brought down from the upper air, and studied the entrance to the tunnel. He knew every jut and corner of it, as far as it was possible to see. It was as if he

200  already felt its sharpness about his shoulders.

He sat by the clock in the villa, when his mother was not near, and checked his time. He was **incredulous** and then proud to find he could hold his breath without strain for two minutes. The words "two minutes," authorized by the clock, brought close the adventure that was so necessary to him.

In another four days, his mother said casually one morning, they must go home. On the day before they left, he would do it. He would do it if it killed him, he said defiantly to himself. But two days before they were to leave—a day of triumph when he increased his count by fifteen—his nose

210  bled so badly that he turned dizzy and had to lie limply over the big rock like a bit of seaweed, watching the thick red blood flow on to the rock and trickle slowly down to the sea. He was frightened. Supposing he turned dizzy in the tunnel? Supposing he died there, trapped? Supposing—his head went around, in the hot sun, and he almost gave up. He thought he would return to the house and lie down, and next summer, perhaps, when he had another year's growth in him—*then* he would go through the hole.

But even after he had made the decision, or thought he had, he found himself sitting up on the rock and looking down into the water; and he knew that now, this moment, when his nose had only just stopped bleeding, when his head was still sore and throbbing—this was the moment when he would

220  try. If he did not do it now, he never would. He was trembling with fear that he would not go; and he was trembling with horror at that long, long tunnel under the rock, under the sea. Even in the open sunlight, the barrier rock seemed very wide and very heavy; tons of rock pressed down on where he would go. If he died there, he would lie until one day—perhaps not before next year—those big boys would swim into it and find it blocked.

He put on his goggles, fitted them tight, tested the vacuum. His hands were shaking. Then he chose the biggest stone he could carry and slipped over the

---

**H SETTING AS SYMBOL**
What does the big beach symbolize to Jerry now? Cite details in this paragraph that support your interpretation.

**persistence** (pər-sĭs'təns) *n.* the act of refusing to stop or be changed

**incredulous** (ĭn-krĕj'ə-ləs) *adj.* doubtful; disbelieving

④ **Targeted Passage**

**I ANALYZE DETAILS**
Reread lines 205–225. How dangerous is the tunnel? Point out details that reveal this.

THROUGH THE TUNNEL  363

---

---

**FOR STRUGGLING READERS**

④ **Targeted Passage** [Lines 211–222]

This passage describes the internal conflict that Jerry must overcome to swim through the tunnel.

• What "supposing" questions go through Jerry's mind? (lines 211–212)

• What does he think about doing instead of swimming through the tunnel? (lines 213–215)

• At what moment does he decide to make the swim? Why is he trembling at that moment? (lines 216–222)

## Analyze Visuals

**Activity** As a class, discuss what specific details in this painting reinforce the sense of danger and risk that Jerry experiences at this point in the story. *Possible answer: The turbulence of the water, the absence of people in the scene, the rocky ledges and outcroppings, and the overhead vantage point reflect the sense of danger and risk.*

**About the Art** Artist Susan Shatter (born 1943) paints in both oils and watercolors. Educated at New York's Pratt Institute and at Boston University, Shatter uses art to express emotional responses to nature. *Ice Blue* is typical of her work because it shows her ability to capture what she calls the flow of water.

### REVISIT THE BIG QUESTION
## When is a RISK
### worth taking?

**Discuss** What hints does the author include in lines 234–243 to suggest the danger in the risk that Jerry has taken? *Possible answer: "a sharp pain dizzied him" (lines 237–238); "water seemed to press upon him with the weight of rock" (line 239); "his head was pulsing" (line 241)*

*Ice Blue* (1981), Susan Shatter. Oil on canvas, 40″ × 90″. Private collection. Courtesy of the Fischback Gallery, New York.

edge of the rock until half of him was in the cool, enclosing water and half in the hot sun. He looked up once at the empty sky, filled his lungs once, twice, 230 and then sank fast to the bottom with the stone. He let it go and began to count. He took the edges of the hole in his hands and drew himself into it, wriggling his shoulders in sidewise as he remembered he must, kicking himself along with his feet.

Soon he was clear inside. He was in a small rock-bound hole filled with yellowish-gray water. The water was pushing him up against the roof. The roof was sharp and pained his back. He pulled himself along with his hands—fast, fast—and used his legs as levers. His head knocked against something; a sharp pain dizzied him. Fifty, fifty-one, fifty-two. . . . He was without light, and the water seemed to press upon him with the weight of rock. Seventy-one, seventy-240 two. . . . There was no strain on his lungs. He felt like an inflated balloon, his lungs were so light and easy, but his head was pulsing.

He was being continually pressed against the sharp roof, which felt slimy as well as sharp. Again he thought of octopuses, and wondered if the tunnel might be filled with weed that could tangle him. He gave himself a panicky,

---

convulsive kick forward, ducked his head, and swam. His feet and hands moved freely, as if in open water. The hole must have widened out. He thought he must be swimming fast, and he was frightened of banging his head if the tunnel narrowed.

    A hundred, a hundred and one. . . . The water paled. Victory filled him.
250 His lungs were beginning to hurt. A few more strokes and he would be out. He was counting wildly; he said a hundred and fifteen, and then, a long time later, a hundred and fifteen again. The water was a clear jewel-green all around him. Then he saw, above his head, a crack running up through the rock. Sunlight was falling through it, showing the clean, dark rock of the tunnel, a single mussel shell, and darkness ahead.

    He was at the end of what he could do. He looked up at the crack as if it were filled with air and not water, as if he could put his mouth to it to draw in air. A hundred and fifteen, he heard himself say inside his head—but he had said that long ago. He must go on into the blackness ahead, or he would
260 drown. His head was swelling, his lungs cracking. A hundred and fifteen, a hundred and fifteen pounded through his head, and he feebly clutched at rocks

## TIERED DISCUSSION PROMPTS
Use these prompts to focus on the suspense in the story's climax at lines 249–267:

**Connect**  Can you think of a time when you or someone you know was pushed to the limit and yet had to keep going? *Answers will vary, but students should recognize the struggle between determination and panic that a person would probably feel in such a situation.*

**Apply**  How does your answer to the previous question help you understand that this passage is the climax of "Through the Tunnel"? *Possible answer: Jerry feels the same kind of struggle. This passage represents the climax of the story because it is the moment of greatest emotional intensity and suspense about the outcome of Jerry's struggle: he will either swim through the tunnel or die inside it.*

**Evaluate**  Does Lessing's language here effectively emphasize the tension in the plot? Explain. *Possible answer: Her language is effective. She creates tension with vivid modifiers ("water paled," "counting wildly," "lungs cracking") and repetition ("he said a hundred and fifteen, and then, a long time later, a hundred and fifteen again. . . . A hundred and fifteen, he heard himself say inside his head . . . a hundred and fifteen pounded through his head").*

### FOR ADVANCED LEARNERS/PRE–AP
**Analyze Details**  Ask students to recall the research that they gathered for the activity on page 361. Then ask them in what ways Jerry symbolically dies and is reborn in the story. Make sure students notice details such as images of darkness and light.

### FOR RELUCTANT READERS
**Accomplishing Goals**  Point out that Jerry's goal of swimming through the tunnel is one he set for himself. Ask students to think of a time they set a goal for themselves. What was the goal? What did they have to do to accomplish it? Did they do so? Did it help that they set the goal themselves? Students can share their stories in small groups or write paragraphs describing their goals.

## ADDITIONAL TEACHING OPPORTUNITY

**Evaluate Theme:** Ask students to identify the story's **theme**—its underlying message about life or human nature. Then have students evaluate that theme—decide whether they think it is valid. Tell students to use these questions as their evaluation criteria:

- Does the theme express a broad insight into life or human nature, or simply an idea that applies only to a few people?

- Does the theme offer a meaningful insight, or is it too obvious or clichéd?

- Is the theme a realistic observation, or is it too optimistic, cynical, or narrow-minded?

Point out to students that a theme may be valid even if they do not personally agree with it. (To learn more about evaluating theme, see **Reading Handbook**, page R2.)

## SELECTION WRAP-UP

**READ WITH A PURPOSE** Now that students have finished the story, ask them to explain why the risk was one Jerry felt he had to take. *Possible response: He felt he had to take the risk in order to grow up or prove himself to be grown up.*

★ **CRITIQUE** Ask students to consider how Jerry changes during the story, and whether they think the change is realistic. Have students defend their evaluations.

## INDEPENDENT READING

For another story about great risk, recommend Sook Nayul Choi's *Year of Impossible Goodbyes*.

---

in the dark, pulling himself forward, leaving the brief space of sunlit water behind. He felt he was dying. He was no longer quite conscious. He struggled on in the darkness between lapses into unconsciousness. An immense, swelling pain filled his head, and then the darkness cracked with an explosion of green light. His hands, groping forward, met nothing; and his feet, kicking back, propelled him out into the open sea.

He drifted to the surface, his face turned up to the air. He was gasping like a fish. He felt he would sink now and drown; he could not swim the few feet
270 back to the rock. Then he was clutching it and pulling himself up onto it. He lay face down, gasping. He could see nothing but a red-veined, clotted dark. His eyes must have burst, he thought; they were full of blood. He tore off his goggles and a gout of blood went into the sea. His nose was bleeding, and the blood had filled the goggles.

He scooped up handfuls of water from the cool, salty sea, to splash on his face, and did not know whether it was blood or salt water he tasted. After a time, his heart quieted, his eyes cleared, and he sat up. He could see the local boys diving and playing half a mile away. He did not want them. He wanted nothing but to get back home and lie down.

280 In a short while, Jerry swam to shore and climbed slowly up the path to the villa. He flung himself on his bed and slept, waking at the sound of feet on the path outside. His mother was coming back. He rushed to the bathroom, thinking she must not see his face with bloodstains, or tearstains, on it. He came out of the bathroom and met her as she walked into the villa, smiling, her eyes lighting up.

"Have a nice morning?" she asked, laying her hand on his warm brown shoulder a moment.

"Oh, yes, thank you," he said.

"You look a bit pale." And then, sharp and anxious, "How did you bang
290 your head?"

"Oh, just banged it," he told her.

She looked at him closely. He was strained; his eyes were glazed-looking. She was worried. And then she said to herself, Oh, don't fuss! Nothing can happen. He can swim like a fish.

They sat down to lunch together.

"Mummy," he said, "I can stay under water for two minutes—three minutes, at least." It came bursting out of him.

"Can you, darling?" she said. "Well, I shouldn't overdo it. I don't think you ought to swim any more today."

300 She was ready for a battle of wills, but he gave in at once. It was no longer of the least importance to go to the bay. ✎

---

---

**COMMON CORE** L 4b

**Language Coach**

**Derivations** Many words are derived, or generated, from the addition of prefixes or suffixes to a common root. The Latin root *-sci-* ("knowledge") gives rise to many related words, such as *science* and *scientific*. Reread lines 263–264. Which words in these lines are related through *-sci-*?

⑤ **Targeted Passage**

---

## DIFFERENTIATED INSTRUCTION

### FOR ENGLISH LANGUAGE LEARNERS

**Language Coach**    COMMON CORE L 4b

**Derivations**

*Answer: conscious, unconsciousness*
Have students choose and use two words with the *–sci–* root in two sentences. Ask for volunteers to share their words and sentences with the class.

### FOR STRUGGLING READERS

⑤ **Targeted Passage** [Lines 280–301]

This passage presents the falling action of the story and hints that Jerry's accomplishment has changed him profoundly.

- What does Jerry do when he hears his mother coming? Why? (lines 282–284)

- What kinds of answers does he give to her questions? (lines 288–291)

- When she advises him not to swim again that day, why does he give in? (lines 300–301)

## Comprehension

1. **Recall** Describe Jerry's age and family situation.

2. **Summarize** What happens between Jerry and the older boys?

3. **Clarify** Why is it so important for Jerry to swim through the tunnel? Explain what he is trying to prove.

## Text Analysis

4. **Identify Conflicts** Identify the external and internal conflicts Jerry faces in the story. How are these conflicts resolved?

5. **Analyze Suspense** Reread lines 234–267. How does Lessing build suspense in this passage? What other techniques does she use to build suspense in this story? Give examples to support your answers.

6. **Analyze Relationships** Explain Jerry's relationship with his mother. How has their relationship changed by the end of the story?

● 7. **Analyze Details** Look over the chart you made as you read. What are the major differences between the big beach and the bay? What does each place **symbolize** to Jerry?

● 8. **Interpret Setting as Symbol** What does Jerry's swim through the tunnel symbolize? Cite descriptions of the tunnel, its connection to the older boys, and Jerry's feelings about the tunnel to support your interpretation.

9. **Draw Conclusions About Motive** Does Jerry accomplish what he wants by swimming through the tunnel? To decide, create a chart, briefly describing Jerry before and after his swim.

| Before, Jerry is... | After, Jerry is... |
|---|---|
| anxious to please his mother lonely | |

10. **Evaluate** Do the benefits of Jerry's accomplishment outweigh the risks? Base your decision on evidence from the story, such as Jerry's preparation, as well as on your own knowledge and experience.

## Text Criticism

11. **Critical Interpretations** The critic Martha Duffy once praised Lessing for the "unsparing clarity and frankness" of her writing. What evidence do you find in "Through the Tunnel" to support this assessment of Lessing's work?

> ### When is a **RISK** worth taking?
> How would you decide if the potential rewards of a risk are worth taking the risk?

**COMMON CORE**

**RL 1** Cite textual evidence to support analysis of what the text says explicitly as well as inferences drawn from the text. **RL 3** Analyze how complex characters develop over the course of a text. **RL 4** Analyze the cumulative impact of specific word choices on meaning.

---

# Practice and Apply

For preliminary support of post-reading questions, use these copy masters:

**R RESOURCE MANAGER—Copy Masters**
Reading Check p. 50
Setting as Symbol p. 43
Question Support p. 51

Additional selection questions are provided for teachers on page 37.

## ANSWERS

## Comprehension

1. *Jerry is an 11-year-old English boy being raised by his widowed mother.*

2. *The boys are friendly at first, but ignore Jerry after he clowns around.*

3. *Jerry wants to prove that he belongs with the older boys and is worthy of their friendship and admiration.*

## Text Analysis

*Possible answers:*

COMMON CORE **RL 1, RL 3, RL 4**

4. *Jerry's internal conflict against his physical and psychological limitations is resolved when he swims through the tunnel. His external conflicts with the older boys, his mother, and the tunnel also are resolved at that point (lines 278–279 and 300–301).*

5. *Lessing traces Jerry's injuries, pain (lines 237–242, 261–266), and fear (lines 244–248). Vivid modifiers (as in lines 242–245) make the scene more suspenseful and terrifying.*

6. *At first, Jerry and his mother are emotionally attached. By the end of the story, Jerry asserts his independence, and his mother begins to accept his assertion.*

7. ■ **COMMON CORE FOCUS** *Analyze Details The big beach is crowded and safe; the bay is desolate and dangerous. The beach symbolizes childhood and dependency; the bay, adulthood and independence.*

8. ● **COMMON CORE FOCUS** *Interpret Setting as Symbol It symbolizes rebirth, a journey, and a passage to adulthood that the older boys have experienced. The descriptions in lines 234–235, 245–246, and 254 suggest the birth process. Jerry's mix of fear and determination suggests that he must undergo this journey to mature.*

9. *Draw Conclusions About Motive Jerry accomplishes what he wants. He still agrees to his mother's request, but now he*

---

*does so for his own reason (lines 300–301). Similarly, he still may be alone, but he no longer feels the need for the companionship of the older boys.*

10. *Students who felt the risk was worth it may argue that Jerry has matured because of the experience. Students who disagree may argue that he might have died.*

## Text Criticism

*Possible answer:*
11. *The description of Jerry's trip through the tunnel (lines 226–267) is just one example that supports the assessment.*

> ### When is a **RISK** worth taking?
> *Students may calculate that the ratio of upside (reward) versus downside (danger) must be high.*

## ANSWERS

## Vocabulary in Context

▲ VOCABULARY PRACTICE

1. *false*
2. *true*
3. *false*
4. *true*
5. *true*
6. *true*

 **RESOURCE MANAGER—Copy Master**
Vocabulary Practice p. 48

### ACADEMIC VOCABULARY IN WRITING

***Possible response:*** *Jerry's mother perceives that he needs to feel more independent. What she doesn't recognize is how much he wants to have some friends and to be respected by them. She also doesn't understand the risks he is willing to take to prove that he is worthy of that approval. She knows Jerry is a good swimmer so she can't imagine a* **circumstance** *in which he would be risking his life.*

### VOCABULARY STRATEGY: THE LATIN ROOTS *quest,* *quer,* AND *quisit*

COMMON CORE L 4d

- Help students pronounce each word, especially *conquistador* and *query.*
- As you discuss each word to be defined, guide students to use what they know of these Latin roots and other roots to determine word meaning. For example, *conquistador* is a Spanish word that contains the root for *conquer.*

***Possible answers:***
*acquire,* "to gain"; *requisite,* "necessary"; *inquisition,* "official investigation"; *query,* "question"; *conquistador,* "one of the 16th-century Spanish conquerors of the Americas"; *inquest,* "legal or judicial inquiry"; *Sentences will vary but should present the words accurately.*

 **RESOURCE MANAGER—Copy Master**
Vocabulary Strategy p. 49

**Interactive Vocabulary** THINK central

Keywords direct students to a **WordSharp** tutorial on **thinkcentral.com** or to other types of vocabulary practice and review.

---

## Vocabulary in Context

▲ VOCABULARY PRACTICE

Drawing on your understanding of the words, write *true* or *false* for each item.

1. If you feel **contrition** for something you did, you feel proud of your actions.
2. You should not live on a **promontory** if you are afraid of heights.
3. An **inquisitive** child will rarely ask why.
4. You might hear a **supplication** at a prayer service.
5. A person shows **persistence** by repeating a job until she gets it right.
6. If you are **incredulous** about a friend's advice, you likely will ignore it.

**WORD LIST**
contrition
incredulous
inquisitive
persistence
promontory
supplication

### ACADEMIC VOCABULARY IN WRITING

- aspect
- circumstance
- contribute
- distinct
- perceive

Which changes in Jerry does his mother **perceive** during their beach vacation? Which changes does she *not* perceive? Answer these questions in a paragraph, using at least one Academic Vocabulary word from the list.

### VOCABULARY STRATEGY: THE LATIN ROOTS *quest,* *quer,* AND *quisit*

**COMMON CORE**

**L 4d** Verify the preliminary determination of the meaning of a word.

The word *inquisitive* contains the root of the Latin word *quaerere,* meaning "to seek." Common forms of this root include *quest, quer,* and *quisit.* When the Latin prefix *in-* ("into") and the suffix *-ive* ("tending toward a specific action") are added to *quisit,* they make the word *inquisitive,* which literally means "inclining to seek into." Remembering the meaning of *quest, quer,* and *quisit* will help you understand words in this family, which you are likely to encounter in many contexts. In history classes, for example, you may read about the Spanish conquistadors.

***PRACTICE*** Try your hand at writing a definition for each of these words in the *quest, quer,* and *quisit* family. Use a dictionary to confirm your definitions. Then, for each word, write a sentence that shows its meaning.

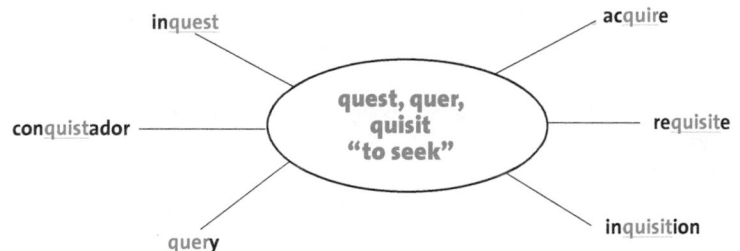

**Interactive Vocabulary** THINK central
Go to **thinkcentral.com.**
KEYWORD: HML9-368

---

## DIFFERENTIATED INSTRUCTION

### FOR ENGLISH LANGUAGE LEARNERS

**Vocabulary: Prefixes** Before completing the Vocabulary Strategy section, explain that the prefix *in-* in the word *inquisitive* means "into" but that *in-* sometimes means "not." Provide these additional examples:
***in-* = "into":** *inspect, inform, intelligent*
***in-* = "not":** *incredulous, inept, inadequate*

### FOR ADVANCED LEARNERS/PRE–AP

**Vocabulary in Writing** Ask students to use at least three vocabulary words in a journal entry. Have them write as a diver who is concerned about the dangers for the boys who have been seen swimming through the tunnel.

# Language

◆ **GRAMMAR AND STYLE: Write Concisely**

Review the **Grammar and Style** note on page 359. Like Lessing, you can use **compound predicates** to make your writing more concise and Improve the flow of your sentences.

A predicate indicates what a subject is or does or what happens to the subject. By combining predicates, you can avoid writing a series of short, choppy sentences that begin with the same noun or pronoun.

Here is an example of how Lessing uses this technique:

*He looked up once at the empty sky, filled his lungs once, twice, and then sank fast to the bottom with the stone. He let it go and began to count.* (lines 229–231)

Notice how the revisions in blue improve sentence flow.

> **STUDENT MODEL**
>
> I think Jerry's mom is a responsible parent. She pays attention to Jerry. ~~She~~
>                                                                              *and*
> tries to figure out what he wants. ~~He wants her to~~ give him more freedom.
>                                                                   *s*   *when he asks for it*
>                                *and*
> She knows he is a good swimmer. ~~She~~ decides to let him go to the bay.

## READING-WRITING CONNECTION

**YOUR TURN** Further explore the characters in "Through the Tunnel" by responding to the writing prompt below. Then use the **revising tip** to improve your writing.

| WRITING PROMPT | REVISING TIP |
|---|---|
| **Short Constructed Response: Analysis** Do you think Jerry's mother is right to trust him by himself? Consider the **risks** Jerry takes, as well as his **success**, and then write a **one- or two-paragraph response** that explains your answer. | Review your response. Have you used compound predicates to connect related ideas? If not, revise your writing. |

**Interactive Revision**

**THINK** central

Go to **thinkcentral.com**.
KEYWORD: HML9-369

---

**COMMON CORE**

**L 1** Demonstrate command of the conventions of standard English grammar and usage. **L 3** Apply knowledge of language to make effective choices for meaning or style.

# Language

**COMMON CORE L1, L3**

◆ **GRAMMAR AND STYLE**

- Model the finding of predicates in "Through the Tunnel." Then, as you discuss the student model, call on volunteers to isolate each part of the compound predicate.

- Write these sentences on the board. Have students suggest ways to use compound predicates to revise the short sentences.

  *Jerry swam a little closer to the older boys,* ~~.~~ *~~Then he~~ turned quickly,* ~~. Next, he~~ *waved to them eagerly, and* ~~. In addition, he~~ *watched them closely.*

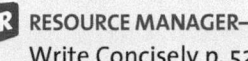 **RESOURCE MANAGER—Copy Master** Write Concisely p. 52

**READING-WRITING CONNECTION**

Encourage students to reread lines 296–301 to assess Jerry's level of maturity. Suggest that students spend five minutes or so freewriting about Jerry and his swim.

> **Writing Online**  **THINK** central
>
> The following tools are available online at **thinkcentral.com** and on **Write*Smart* CD-ROM:**
> - **Interactive Graphic Organizers**
> - **Interactive Student Models**
> - **Interactive Revision Lessons**
>
> For additional grammar instruction, see **GrammarNotes** on **thinkcentral.com**.

## Assess and Reteach

### Assess

**DIAGNOSTIC AND SELECTION TESTS**
Selection Test A, pp. 95–96
Selection Test B/C, pp. 97–98

**Interactive Selection Test** on **thinkcentral.com**

### Reteach

**Level Up Online Tutorials** on **thinkcentral.com**

**Reteaching Worksheets** on **thinkcentral.com**
Language and Literary Devices Lesson 31: Symbol and Symbolism
Vocabulary Lesson 10: Word Families and Derivatives

---

**FOR STRUGGLING WRITERS**

Help students make a jotted outline.

I. Topic Sentence: Jerry's mother is wise to trust her son.
II. Reason #1: The risks are minor.
  A. Lines 84–88: The other boys succeed easily.
  B. Lines 269–279: Jerry recovers quickly from his swim.
III. Reason #2: Jerry's achievement is great.
  A. Lines 278–279: Jerry no longer needs to impress the local boys.
  B. Lines 300–301: Jerry has matured, so he no longer needs to fight with his mother.

# Focus and Motivate

## COMMON CORE FOCUS

**RL 1** Cite textual evidence to support analysis of what the text says explicitly as well as inferences drawn from the text. **RL 4** Analyze the cumulative impact of specific word choices on meaning and tone. **RL 5** Analyze how an author's choices concerning how to structure a text create tension or surprise. **L 2** Demonstrate command of the conventions of standard English punctuation. **L 3** Apply knowledge of language to make effective choices for meaning or style. **L 4** Determine the meaning of unknown and multiple-meaning words and phrases. **L 4c** Consult reference materials to determine a word's etymology. **W 4** Produce narrative writing in which the style is appropriate to the task and purpose.

## SUMMARY

Montresor tricks Fortunato into accompanying him deep within the catacombs beneath his palace. Once there, Montresor walls Fortunato up inside a crypt, leaving him there to die.

## Is **REVENGE** ever justified?

Discuss different opinions students may have on the subject of revenge. Have students complete the *PRESENT* activity.

---

## Selection Resources

*See resources on the **Teacher One Stop DVD-ROM** and on **thinkcentral.com**.*

 **RESOURCE MANAGER UNIT 3**
Plan and Teach, pp. 55–62
Summary, pp. 63–64†‡*
Text Analysis and Reading
   Skill, pp. 65–66, 67–68†*
Vocabulary, pp. 69–71*
Grammar and Style, p. 74

**DIAGNOSTIC AND SELECTION TESTS**
Selection Tests, pp. 99–102

 **BEST PRACTICES TOOLKIT**
Word Questioning, p. E9
Jigsaw Reading, p. A1

**INTERACTIVE READER**

**ADAPTED INTERACTIVE READER**

**ELL ADAPTED INTERACTIVE READER**

Video link at
**thinkcentral.com**

**TECHNOLOGY**
- Teacher One Stop DVD-ROM
- Student One Stop DVD-ROM
- PowerNotes DVD-ROM
- Audio Anthology CD
- GrammarNotes DVD-ROM
- Audio Tutor CD
- ExamView Test Generator on the **Teacher One Stop**

### Video Trailer

 **THINK** central

Go to **thinkcentral.com** to preview the **Video Trailer** introducing this selection. Other features that support the selection include
- **PowerNotes** presentation
- **ThinkAloud** models to enhance comprehension
- **WordSharp** vocabulary tutorials
- interactive writing and grammar instruction

\* Resources for Differentiation     † Also in Spanish     ‡ In Haitian Creole and Vietnamese

---

*Essential Course of Study* **ECOS**    **The Cask of Amontillado**     Video link at thinkcentral.com
Short Story by Edgar Allan Poe

**VIDEO TRAILER**  **THINK** central | KEYWORD: HML9-370

# Is **REVENGE** ever justified?

### COMMON CORE

**RL 1** Cite textual evidence to support analysis of what the text says explicitly as well as inferences drawn from the text. **RL 4** Analyze the cumulative impact of specific word choices on meaning and tone. **RL 5** Analyze how an author's choices concerning how to structure a text create tension or surprise. **L 4** Determine the meaning of unknown and multiple-meaning words and phrases.

Montresor, the narrator of "The Cask of Amontillado," feels that revenge is necessary to right a wrong. Some would argue that two wrongs never make a right and that revenge leads only to more wrongdoing. Do acts of revenge ever resolve conflicts?

**PRESENT** An act of revenge often causes a chain reaction, and the repercussions can go on for months or years. With a group, think of one act of revenge and chart out the possible chain of effects. Share your chain of events with the rest of the class.

> **Event**
> Girl makes fun of boy.
> ↓
> **Act of Revenge**
> Boy spills ink on her uniform.
> ↓
> **Effects**
> • Uniform is ruined.
> • Girl's parents have to buy a new one.

370

## TEXT ANALYSIS: MOOD

In "The Cask of Amontillado," Edgar Allan Poe creates an unforgettable **mood** of suspense and horror. From the beginning, the narrator's talk of injuries borne, unforgivable insults, and threatened revenge conveys a sinister feeling. Poe develops this mood by means of

- the sensory details and imagery used to convey the setting
- the repetition of words and the rhythm and **tone** of the language
- words describing thoughts, feelings, and actions

As you read, notice how Poe's descriptions of the setting and his use of language combine to create a memorably dark tale.

## READING SKILL: PARAPHRASE

Poe often uses long, formal, complex sentences that are especially challenging to modern readers. To make sure that you understand the events in this story, try paraphrasing. To **paraphrase** is to restate information in one's own words. A paraphrase is about the same length as the original text. It includes all the details of the original but is written in simpler language. As you read this story, take time to paraphrase difficult passages. Here is an example.

| Text | Paraphrase |
|------|-----------|
| "It must be understood, that neither by word nor deed had I given Fortunato cause to doubt my good-will." (lines 9–10) | You must understand that I said and did nothing to make Fortunato mistrust me. |

**Review: Make Inferences**

## ▲ VOCABULARY IN CONTEXT

The boldfaced words help create a mood of horror. Use context clues to figure out the meaning of each word. Then use each word in a sentence. Write your sentences in your *Reader/Writer Notebook*. After reading the selection, check to see whether you used the words correctly.

1. to **preclude** pain
2. to lie with **impunity**
3. **immolation** of an enemy
4. **abscond** with money
5. everlasting **repose**
6. **termination** of a job
7. to help anger to **subside**
8. to close off an **aperture**

 Complete the activities in your **Reader/Writer Notebook**.

---

## Meet the Author

### Edgar Allan Poe
1809–1849

**The Genius of Poe**
Edgar Allan Poe started out as a poet but turned to writing short fiction to earn a living. His career in fiction officially began in 1833, with a $50 prize for his story "MS. Found in a Bottle." At the time he was living in poverty with his beloved aunt Maria Clemm and her daughter, Virginia. With the prize money came recognition and a job offer from a literary magazine. By 1838, Poe had married Virginia and moved the family to Philadelphia, where he worked for several leading literary magazines.

**Master of the Macabre**
Poe may have started writing horror fiction because that's what the reading public wanted. Gothic tales were popular at the time, and newspapers regularly printed sensational reports of bizarre murders. Poe adapted elements of Gothic fiction, took a few story ideas from news headlines, added his psychological insights into the mix, and soon became the undisputed master of the genre.

**BACKGROUND TO THE STORY**
**A Different Burial Ground**
Although this story begins during a time of carnival festivities, the setting soon shifts to the dark, cool burial vaults under the narrator's palace, where he also stores his wine. In such underground cemeteries, called catacombs, bodies were placed in carved recesses along the walls of burial chambers. The largest and most famous are those of Rome, in which early Christians were entombed.

**Author Online** THINK central
Go to thinkcentral.com.
KEYWORD: HML9-371

371

---

## Teach

**TEXT ANALYSIS** — **COMMON CORE RL 4**

### ● Model the Skill: MOOD

To model analyzing mood, read aloud this example:

> A cold wind sliced across the silent and empty graveyard. Stanton shivered and glanced up at the moon, a pale sliver behind dark clouds. He heard footsteps, then more footsteps, and his stomach knotted. *Shouldn't have come*, he thought.

Point out that the paragraph conveys fear and mystery through sensory details and imagery ("pale sliver," "stomach knotted"), repetition ("footsteps"), and thoughts ("Shouldn't have come").

**GUIDED PRACTICE** Elicit from students other words or phrases that could be used to create a mood of fear.

---

**READING STRATEGY**

### ■ Model the Skill: PARAPHRASE

Explain that paraphrasing is a way to reword information so that it is easier to understand yet retains the original meaning.

**GUIDED PRACTICE** Provide several examples of formal language for students to paraphrase.

**R** RESOURCE MANAGER—Copy Master Paraphrase p. 67 (for student use while reading the selection)

---

## VOCABULARY SKILL

### ▲ VOCABULARY IN CONTEXT

**DIAGNOSE WORD KNOWLEDGE** Have all students complete Vocabulary in Context. Check their definitions against the following:

**abscond** (ăb-skŏnd') *v.* to go away suddenly and secretly

**aperture** (ăp'ər-chər) *n.* an opening, such as a hole or a gap

**immolation** (ĭm'ə-lā'shən) *n.* death or destruction

**impunity** (ĭm-pyōō'nĭ-tē) *n.* freedom from penalty or harm

**preclude** (prĭ-klōōd') *v.* to make impossible, especially by taking action in advance

**repose** (rĭ-pōz') *v.* to lie dead or at rest

**subside** (səb-sīd') *v.* to decrease in amount or intensity; settle down

**termination** (tûr'mə-nā'shən) *n.* an end, limit, or edge

**PRETEACH VOCABULARY** Use the copy master to help students predict meanings of each

boldfaced word.

**R** RESOURCE MANAGER—Copy Master Vocabulary Study p. 69

1. Read item 1 aloud, emphasizing *abscond*.
2. Point out the phrase "he told them not to leave." Elicit possible meanings for *abscond*.
3. Have students record their predictions.
4. Repeat the procedure for items 2–8.

**COMMON CORE L 4**

## READ WITH A PURPOSE

*Encourage students to set a purpose for reading. Explain that this is a story of one man taking revenge on another. Ask students to determine why the man wants revenge, what form it takes, and why he chooses that particular form.*

### READING STRATEGY

**A** *Model the Skill:* **PARAPHRASE**

Explain that to paraphrase you will restate the information more simply. Read the first sentence of the story aloud. Then tell students that the paraphrase version would read "I had put up with Fortunato's abuse as well as I could, but when he insulted me, I was determined to get even."

*Possible answer:* However, I did not threaten him or give him any reason to worry. I would get my revenge, all right, but in due time and without risk to myself. Getting even is not worth it if the person getting even is punished for what he has done. It is also not worth it unless the target of the revenge understands that the person he has wronged is paying him back for what he did.

The narrator vows revenge because Fortunato has insulted him. He considers revenge to be successful if the "avenger" escapes punishment and if the victim knows that he has been paid back for his wrong.

### VOCABULARY

**COMMON CORE**
L 4

### OWN THE WORD

- **preclude:** Write the word and definition "to make impossible." Have students add synonyms to create a semantic map. *Possible answers: prohibit, hinder, thwart*

- **impunity:** Ask students to think of a situation where they would like *impunity* for their actions. *Possible answer: when questioning an authority figure*

- **immolation:** Explain that the verb *immolate* means "to kill" or "destroy" with a connotation of burning. Tell students that when they burn leaves, they are *immolating* them.

---

# The Cask of Amontillado
### Edgar Allan Poe

The thousand injuries of Fortunato I had borne as I best could; but when he ventured upon insult, I vowed revenge. You, who so well know the nature of my soul, will not suppose, however, that I gave utterance to a threat. *At length* I would be avenged; this was a point definitively settled—but the very definitiveness with which it was resolved, **precluded** the idea of risk. I must not only punish, but punish with **impunity**. A wrong is unredressed when retribution overtakes its redresser. It is equally unredressed when the avenger fails to make himself felt as such to him who has done the wrong. **A**

10 It must be understood, that neither by word nor deed had I given Fortunato cause to doubt my good-will. I continued, as was my wont, to smile in his face, and he did not perceive that my smile *now* was at the thought of his **immolation.**

He had a weak point—this Fortunato—although in other regards he was a man to be respected and even feared. He prided himself on his connoisseurship[1] in wine. Few Italians have the true virtuoso spirit. For the most part their enthusiasm is adopted to suit the time and opportunity—to practice imposture upon the British and Austrian *millionaires.* In painting and gemmary[2] Fortunato, like his countrymen, was a quack—but in the matter of old wines he was sincere. In this respect I did not differ from him materially; I 20 was skillful in the Italian vintages myself, and bought largely whenever I could.

It was about dusk, one evening during the supreme madness of the carnival[3] season, that I encountered my friend. He accosted me with excessive warmth, for he had been drinking much. The man wore motley.[4] He had on a tight-fitting parti-striped dress, and his head was surmounted by the conical cap and bells. I was so pleased to see him, that I thought I should never have done wringing his hand.

---

1. **connoisseurship** (kŏn′ə-sûr′shĭp): expertise or authority, especially in the fine arts or in matters of taste.
2. **gemmary** (jĕm′ə-rē): knowledge of precious gems.
3. **carnival:** a festival before the fasting period of Lent, characterized by fanciful costumes, masquerades, and feasts.
4. **motley:** the costume of a court jester.

**372** UNIT 3: SETTING, MOOD, AND IMAGERY

**①** **Targeted Passage**
*Analyze Visuals* ▶
Would you describe the mood of this photograph as festive or sinister? Explain.

**preclude** (prĭ-klōōd′) *v.* to make impossible, especially by taking action in advance

**impunity** (ĭm-pyōō′nĭ-tē) *n.* freedom from penalty or harm

**A** **PARAPHRASE**
Paraphrase the opening paragraph. Why does the narrator vow revenge? What does he consider a successful revenge?

**immolation** (ĭm′ə-lā′shən) *n.* death or destruction

---

## DIFFERENTIATED INSTRUCTION

### FOR ENGLISH LANGUAGE LEARNERS

**Vocabulary Support** Use Word Questioning to teach these words: *resolved* (line 5), *impose* (line 47), *explicit* (line 61), *sufficient* (line 62), *indication* (line 175).

📖 BEST PRACTICES TOOLKIT—Transparency Word Questioning p. E9

### FOR STRUGGLING READERS

In combination with the *Audio Anthology CD*, use one or more Targeted Passages (pp. 372, 375, 378, 379) to ensure that students focus on key story events, concepts, and skills. Targeted Passages are also good for English learners.

**①** **Targeted Passage** [Lines 1–12]
This passage establishes the narrator's feelings and intentions toward Fortunato.

- Why does the narrator, Montresor, want revenge against Fortunato? (lines 1–2)

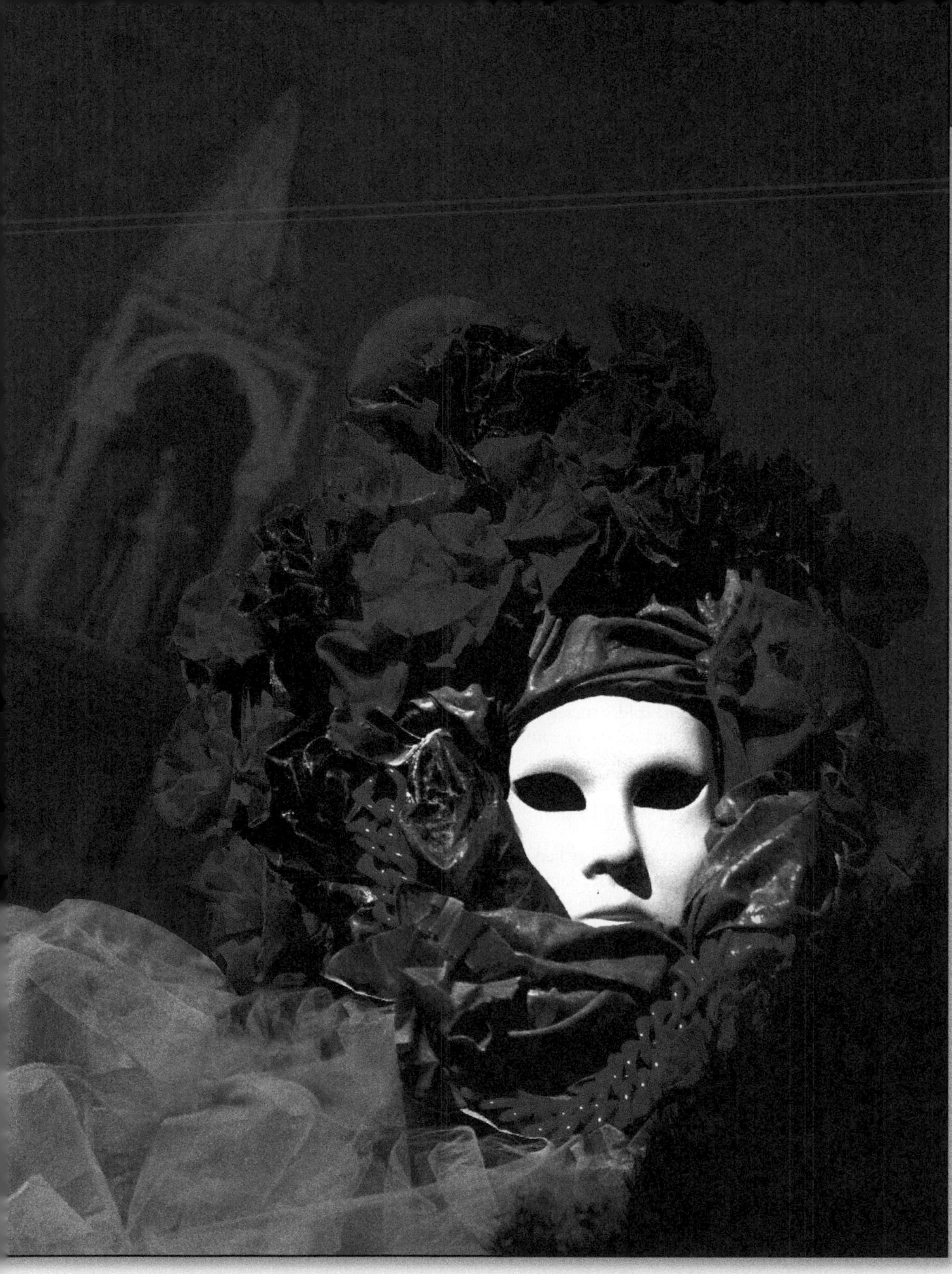

## Reading Support

THINK central

This selection on **thinkcentral.com** includes embedded **ThinkAloud** models–students "thinking aloud" about the story to model the kinds of questions a good reader would ask about a selection.

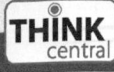

## BACKGROUND

***Carnival Season*** The "supreme madness of the carnival season" (lines 21–22) is a time of merrymaking, feasting, costumes, and parades celebrated just before Lent. Festive carnival traditions remain popular today in many parts of the world, from New Orleans, Louisiana (where it is known as Mardi Gras), to Rio de Janeiro, Brazil. In "The Cask of Amontillado," the narrator's choice of this time of year to exact his revenge was probably deliberate, not only because people would be distracted, but also because Fortunato would likely have been drinking and celebrating and therefore unlikely to suspect any foul play.

## Analyze Visuals

***Possible answer:*** *Though the mask and colorful costume may suggest a festive event, the photo's overall mood is sinister. The mask is unsmiling, with a disquieting contrast between the bright white face and black eye sockets. The dark background adds to the sinister mood, as does the angle of the tower behind the subject.*

- What does the narrator mean when he says that he "must not only punish, but punish with impunity"? (lines 5–6)
- How does the narrator feel about Fortunato? How does he act toward him? What does this contrast suggest? (lines 9–12)

**FOR ADVANCED LEARNERS/PRE–AP**

**Write the Prequel** Students will notice that the insult Montresor has suffered is never described. As students read the story, ask them to observe the personalities of Montresor and Fortunato and their relationship. Then ask them to write a "prequel" to the story, using Poe's heightened style, in which the insult is given.

## OWN THE WORD

**abscond:** Have students reread the paragraph containing *abscond.* Then have them identify context clues that help determine the meaning of the word.

*Possible answer: no attendants at home, immediate disappearance*

---

TEXT ANALYSIS  COMMON CORE RL 4

### Ⓑ *Model the Skill:* MOOD

Model how to identify details that contribute to mood. Point out that in line 27 the narrator addresses Fortunato warmly. This is in stark contrast to the opening paragraph, and leads to a dark mood that the narrator has evil plans for Fortunato.

*Possible answer: Readers know that the narrator intends revenge by getting Fortunato to his mansion, but Fortunato does not. Suspense is built in this conversation by the narrator's manipulation of Fortunato with his false concern about Fortunato's health and his need to be elsewhere, the repetition of the word* friend, *and the narrator's appeal to Fortunato's vanity by his mention of Luchesi several times. In the end, the reader still does not know what the narrator plans to do at his palazzo.*

**REVISIT THE BIG QUESTION**

## Is REVENGE
### ever justified?

**Discuss** In lines 56–63, the narrator puts on a mask and wraps himself in a cloak. He also explains that he was able "to insure" there would be "no attendants at home." What do these actions suggest about his plan for revenge? *Possible answer: The narrator has carefully laid the groundwork for whatever he is planning. These actions will most likely prevent anyone from identifying him or witnessing his crime. They will allow him to go unpunished, an important factor for him, as he gets his revenge.*

---

I said to him: "My dear Fortunato, you are luckily met. How remarkably well you are looking to-day! But I have received a pipe of what passes for Amontillado,[5] and I have my doubts."

30 "How?" said he. "Amontillado? A pipe? Impossible! And in the middle of the carnival!"

"I have my doubts," I replied; "and I was silly enough to pay the full Amontillado price without consulting you in the matter. You were not to be found, and I was fearful of losing a bargain."

"Amontillado!"

"I have my doubts."

"Amontillado!"

"And I must satisfy them."

"Amontillado!"

40 "As you are engaged, I am on my way to Luchesi.[6] If anyone has a critical turn, it is he. He will tell me—"

"Luchesi cannot tell Amontillado from Sherry."

"And yet some fools will have it that his taste is a match for your own."

"Come, let us go."

"Whither?"

"To your vaults."

"My friend, no; I will not impose upon your good nature. I perceive you have an engagement. Luchesi—"

"I have no engagement;—come."

50 "My friend, no. It is not the engagement, but the severe cold with which I perceive you are afflicted. The vaults are insufferably damp. They are encrusted with niter."[7]

"Let us go, nevertheless. The cold is merely nothing. Amontillado! You have been imposed upon. And as for Luchesi, he cannot distinguish Sherry from Amontillado." Ⓑ

Thus speaking, Fortunato possessed himself of my arm. Putting on a mask of black silk, and drawing a *roquelaure*[8] closely about my person, I suffered him to hurry me to my palazzo.[9]

There were no attendants at home; they had **absconded** to make merry in
60 honor of the time. I had told them that I should not return until the morning, and had given them explicit orders not to stir from the house. These orders were sufficient, I well knew, to insure their immediate disappearance, one and all, as soon as my back was turned.

---

5. **a pipe ... Amontillado** (ə-mŏn'tl-ä'dō): a barrel of a wine that is supposed to be a type of pale, dry sherry, named for a town in southern Spain.

6. **Luchesi** (lōō-kā'sē).

7. **niter:** a white, gray, or colorless mineral, consisting of potassium nitrate.

8. **roquelaure** (rôk-lōr') *French:* a man's knee-length cloak, popular during the 18th century.

9. **palazzo** (pə-lät'sō): a palace or mansion.

---

COMMON CORE L 4

**Language Coach**

**Fixed Expressions** Many verbs take on a special meaning when followed by a particular preposition. *Impose* means "to establish by authority" (*impose a tax*). Followed by *upon,* though, it has a different meaning. Reread line 47. What does the expression *impose upon* mean here?

Ⓑ **MOOD**
Reread lines 27–55. How does Poe build a mood of suspense in this conversation between the narrator and Fortunato?

**abscond** (ăb-skŏnd') *v.* to go away suddenly and secretly

---

## DIFFERENTIATED INSTRUCTION

### FOR ENGLISH LANGUAGE LEARNERS

**Language Coach** 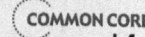 COMMON CORE L 4

**Fixed Expresssions** *Answer: take advantage of*

Have students work in pairs to list an example of when someone would *impose* something and when something would be *imposed upon.*

### FOR ADVANCED LEARNERS/PRE–AP

**Analyze Dialogue** After reading the story, have students reread lines 27–55. Have them explain exactly how Montresor uses psychology to manipulate Fortunato into doing what he wants him to do.

I took from their sconces two flambeaux,[10] and giving one to Fortunato, bowed him through several suites of rooms to the archway that led into the vaults. I passed down a long and winding staircase, requesting him to be cautious as he followed. We came at length to the foot of the descent and stood together on the damp ground of the catacombs of the Montresors.

**② Targeted Passage**

The gait of my friend was unsteady, and the bells upon his cap jingled as he strode.

"The pipe?" said he.

"It is farther on," said I; "but observe the white web-work which gleams from these cavern walls."

He turned toward me, and looked into my eyes with two filmy orbs that distilled the rheum of intoxication.[11]

"Niter?" he asked, at length.

"Niter," I replied. "How long have you had that cough?"

"Ugh! ugh! ugh!—ugh! ugh! ugh!—ugh! ugh! ugh!—ugh! ugh! ugh!—ugh! ugh! ugh!"

80 My poor friend found it impossible to reply for many minutes.

"It is nothing," he said, at last.

"Come," I said, with decision, "we will go back; your health is precious. You are rich, respected, admired, beloved; you are happy, as once I was. You are a man to be missed. For me it is no matter. We will go back; you will be ill, and I cannot be responsible. Besides, there is Luchesi—"

"Enough," he said; "the cough is a mere nothing; it will not kill me. I shall not die of a cough."

"True—true," I replied; "and, indeed, I had no intention of alarming you unnecessarily; but you should use all proper caution. A draft of this Medoc[12]

90 will defend us from the damps."

Here I knocked off the neck of a bottle that I drew from a long row of its fellows that lay upon the mold. **C**

"Drink," I said, presenting him the wine.

He raised it to his lips with a leer. He paused and nodded to me familiarly, while his bells jingled.

"I drink," he said, "to the buried that **repose** around us."

"And I to your long life."

He again took my arm, and we proceeded.

"These vaults," he said, "are extensive."

100 "The Montresors," I replied, "were a great and numerous family."

"I forget your arms."

"A huge human foot d'or,[13] in a field azure; the foot crushes a serpent rampant whose fangs are imbedded in the heel."

10. **from their sconces two flambeaux** (flăm'bōz'): from their wall brackets two lighted torches.

11. **filmy...intoxication:** eyes clouded and glazed over from drunkenness.

12. **Medoc** (mā-dôk'): a red wine from the Bordeaux region of France.

13. **d'or** (dôr) *French:* colored gold. (Montresor is describing his coat of arms, the distinctive emblem of his family.)

THE CASK OF AMONTILLADO **375**

---

**COMMON CORE RL 5**

**C IRONY**

**Verbal irony** occurs when a character *says* one thing but *means* another. Another kind of irony, **situational irony**, is when a character or reader expects something to happen but the opposite takes place. Look back over lines 74–92. What is ironic about the conversation between Fortunato and Montresor?

**repose** (rĭ-pōz') *v.* to lie dead or at rest

---

**C IRONY**

Have students work in pairs to write down what the characters expect to happen during their conversation. Explain that this will help them note the opposite, and thus the irony of these parts of the conversation.

*Possible answer: The conversation is ironic in three ways. First, the narrator expresses great concern for the welfare of his "poor friend" (line 80), when in reality he means him only harm. Second, Fortunato says that he "shall not die of a cough" (lines 86–87), and the narrator agrees. However, the two men have very different reasons for that belief. Third, the narrator urges Fortunato to be careful, as he carefully lures him into the catacombs.*

**TIERED DISCUSSION PROMPTS**

Use these prompts to help students understand how setting and character help to create the dark mood in lines 64–99.

**Connect** Based on the narrator's words, would you trust him? *Possible answer: Students should recognize that the narrator has done little to arouse Fortunato's suspicions.*

**Analyze** How does the change in setting contribute to the mood of the story? *Possible answer: The catacombs are dark, damp, and isolated. This is in sharp contrast to the crowded, merry carnival setting.*

---

**VOCABULARY**      COMMON CORE   L 4

**OWN THE WORD**

**repose:** Have students identify the context clue that can help them determine the meaning of *repose*. Tell them that the word can be used in other contexts as well. Then, have students write sentences that show an understanding of the word. *Possible answer: We can* repose *for a while under this tree before continuing our hike.*

---

**FOR STRUGGLING READERS**

**② Targeted Passage [Lines 64–70]**

This passage introduces a change of setting and sets up the events that follow.

• Where does the narrator lead Fortunato? (lines 65–68)

• Why does the narrator feel the need to take with them "two flambeaux"? (lines 64–68)

• Why is Fortunato's "gait . . . unsteady"? (line 69)

**Vocabulary: Multiple-Meaning Words** Help students use their prior knowledge in combination with context clues to determine the meaning of these words as they are used in the story: *accosted* (line 22), "greeted"; *warmth* (line 22) , "friendliness"; *engaged* (line 40), "busy"; *imposed upon* (line 54), "take advantage of"; *possessed* (line 56), "took"; *suffered* (line 57), "allowed"; *arms* (line 101), "family symbol"; *extremity* (line 155), "farthest point"; *arrested* (line 155), "stopped"; *depended* (line 158), "hung."

**ⓓ MOOD**

*Possible answer:* *Poe's use of sensory details—"walls of piled bones," "inmost recesses of the catacombs," "hangs like moss," "drops of moisture trickle among the bones"—helps the reader visualize the setting and creates a dark and sinister mood.*

**Extend the Discussion** What irony may there be in the narrator's suggestion to Fortunato that they "go back ere it is too late" (line 114)?

**ⓔ GRAMMAR AND STYLE** · COMMON CORE RL 4, L 2, L 3

**Formal Language** Poe's use of formal language gives an air of seriousness to the story—for example, "Then you are not of the brotherhood" (line 122). This formal style is appropriate for the manner in which Montresor and Fortunato interact. Have students write a one-paragraph response to this question: If Montresor and Fortunato were truly close friends, would formal language be as effective in the telling of the story? Why or why not?

*Possible answer:* *Responses may vary but should include a basis for students' opinions.*

---

"And the motto?"

*"Nemo me impune lacessit."* [14]

"Good!" he said.

The wine sparkled in his eyes and the bells jingled. My own fancy grew warm with the Medoc. We had passed through walls of piled bones, with casks and puncheons[15] intermingling, into the inmost recesses of the catacombs. I

110 paused again, and this time I made bold to seize Fortunato by an arm above the elbow.

"The niter!" I said; "see, it increases. It hangs like moss upon the vaults. We are below the river's bed. The drops of moisture trickle among the bones. Come, we will go back ere it is too late. Your cough—" ⓓ

"It is nothing," he said; "let us go on. But first, another draft of the Medoc."

I broke and reached him a flagon of De Grâve.[16] He emptied it at a breath. His eyes flashed with a fierce light. He laughed and threw the bottle upward with a gesticulation I did not understand.

I looked at him in surprise. He repeated the movement—a grotesque one.

120 "You do not comprehend?" he said.

"Not I," I replied.

"Then you are not of the brotherhood."

"How?"

"You are not of the masons."[17]

"Yes, yes," I said; "yes, yes."

"You? Impossible! A mason?"

"A mason," I replied.

"A sign," he said.

"It is this," I answered, producing a trowel[18] from beneath the folds of my

130 *roquelaure.*

"You jest," he exclaimed, recoiling a few paces. "But let us proceed to the Amontillado."

"Be it so," I said, replacing the tool beneath the cloak, and again offering him my arm. He leaned upon it heavily. We continued our route in search of the Amontillado. We passed through a range of low arches, descended, passed on, and descending again, arrived at a deep crypt, in which the foulness of the air caused our flambeaux rather to glow than flame.

At the most remote end of the crypt there appeared another less spacious. Its walls had been lined with human remains, piled to the vault overhead,

140 in the fashion of the great catacombs of Paris. Three sides of this interior ⓔ

**ⓓ MOOD** In lines 108–114, note the sensory details and imagery that help you visualize the setting. What mood do they create?

**ⓔ GRAMMAR AND STYLE** Notice Poe's use of **formal language**, including complex sentence structures.

---

14. ***Nemo me impune lacessit*** (nā′mō mā ĭm-pōō′nĕ lä-kĕs′ĭt) *Latin:* No one injures me with impunity.

15. **casks and puncheons:** large storage containers for wine.

16. **De Grâve** (də gräv′): a red wine from the Bordeaux region of France.

17. **of the masons:** a Freemason, a member of a social organization with secret rituals and signs.

18. **producing a trowel:** Montresor is playing on another meaning of *mason*—"one who builds with stone or brick."

---

## DIFFERENTIATED INSTRUCTION

### FOR STRUGGLING READERS

**Vocabulary Support** Encourage students to use context clues to unlock the meaning of these words: *flagon* (line 116), "a container for liquids"; *grotesque* (line 119), "strange"; *trowel* (line 129), "a tool used for spreading mortar"; *crypt* (line 136), "an underground room or vault."

**Develop Reading Fluency** Explain to students how conversation and dialogue can be identified by the use of opening and closing quotation marks and, often, the identification of the speaker.

Have students work in pairs to identify who is speaking in lines 120–133. They can color-code or initial each piece of dialogue. With a fluent volunteer, perform a reading of the dialogue only from these lines. Then have student pairs practice similar readings.

**ℝ RESOURCE MANAGER—Copy Master** Reading Fluency p. 75

◄ **Analyze Visuals**
What qualities of the catacomb are emphasized by the two arches? Explain.

## Analyze Visuals

*Possible answer:* *The arches emphasize that the catacomb is deep underground and that within it there are chambers within chambers. These qualities are described in the text in lines 135–148.*

**REVISIT THE BIG QUESTION**

## Is REVENGE
### ever justified?

**Discuss** After reading lines 149–154, what revenge do you predict Montresor has in mind?

*Possible answer: He plans to trap Fortunato in the recess.*

crypt were still ornamented in this manner. From the fourth the bones had been thrown down, and lay promiscuously upon the earth, forming at one point a mound of some size. Within the wall thus exposed by the displacing of the bones, we perceived a still interior recess, in depth about four feet, in width three, in height six or seven. It seemed to have been constructed for no especial use within itself, but formed merely the interval between two of the colossal supports of the roof of the catacombs, and was backed by one of their circumscribing walls of solid granite.

It was in vain that Fortunato, uplifting his dull torch, endeavored to pry
150 into the depth of the recess. Its **termination** the feeble light did not enable us to see.

"Proceed," I said; "herein is the Amontillado. As for Luchesi—"

"He is an ignoramus," interrupted my friend, as he stepped unsteadily forward, while I followed immediately at his heels. In an instant he had

**termination**
(tûr′mə-nā′shən) *n.* an end, limit, or edge

THE CASK OF AMONTILLADO    **377**

**VOCABULARY**    COMMON CORE    L 4

### OWN THE WORD

**termination:** Give students extra practice using the term. Have them complete the following sentences: *At the termination of class, the teacher . . . **Possible answer:** quickly reminded us of tomorrow's test.* My mother was not unhappy when she received a termination notice from her office, because she. . . ***Possible answer:** had already found another job.*

**FOR ENGLISH LANGUAGE LEARNERS**

**Vocabulary: Idioms and Sayings** Explain that in this story Poe uses many idioms, expressions that have a different meaning from the individual words. Have students use context clues to determine the meaning of these idioms or sayings.

- *at his heels* (line 154), "behind him"
- *in a great measure* (line 174), "mostly"
- *worn off* (line 174), "gone away"

Have students work in pairs to create sentences with each idiom.

**FOR ADVANCED LEARNERS/PRE–AP**

**Analyze** Ask students to reread lines 117–131. Have them work in pairs to discuss why Poe included this exchange between Montresor and Fortunato about the brotherhood of Freemasons. What do these lines add to our understanding of the characters? How does the exchange add to the suspense of the story?

**Activity** Ask students how the image supports the events described. *Possible answer: The massiveness of the chain and handcuffs underscore the seriousness of Fortunato's situation, suggesting that escape will be impossible.*

## ADDITIONAL TEACHING OPPORTUNITY

**Evaluate Theme:** Ask students to identify the story's **theme**—its underlying message about life or human nature. Then have students evaluate that theme—decide whether they think it is valid. Tell students to use these questions as their evaluation criteria.

- Does the theme express a broad insight into life or human nature, or simply an idea that applies only to a few people?

- Does the theme offer a meaningful insight, or is it too obvious or clichéd?

- Is the theme a realistic observation, or is it too optimistic, cynical, or narrow-minded?

Point out to students that a theme may be valid even if they do not personally agree with it. (To learn more about evaluating theme, see **Reading Handbook**, page R2.)

---

### VOCABULARY

COMMON CORE

L 4

#### OWN THE WORD

**subside:** Tell students that subside comes from the Latin *sub-*, which means "down" and *sidere*, "*to settle.*" Have students explain the definition of *subside* using the Latin roots.

---

reached the extremity of the niche, and finding his progress arrested by the rock, stood stupidly bewildered. A moment more and I had fettered him to the granite. In its surface were two iron staples, distant from each other about two feet, horizontally. From one of these depended a short chain, from the other a padlock. Throwing the links about his waist, it was but the work of a few 160 seconds to secure it. He was too much astounded to resist. Withdrawing the key I stepped back from the recess.

"Pass your hand," I said, "over the wall; you cannot help feeling the niter. Indeed it is *very* damp. Once more let me *implore* you to return. No? Then I must positively leave you. But I must first render you all the little attentions in my power."

"The Amontillado!" ejaculated my friend, not yet recovered from his astonishment.

"True," I replied; "the Amontillado."

As I said these words I busied myself among the pile of bones of which I 170 have before spoken. Throwing them aside, I soon uncovered a quantity of building stone and mortar. With these materials and with the aid of my trowel, I began vigorously to wall up the entrance of the niche.

I had scarcely laid the first tier of the masonry when I discovered that the intoxication of Fortunato had in a great measure worn off. The earliest indication I had of this was a low moaning cry from the depth of the recess. It was not the cry of a drunken man. There was then a long and obstinate silence. I laid the second tier, and the third, and the fourth; and then I heard the furious vibrations of the chain. The noise lasted for several minutes, during which, that I might hearken to it with the more satisfaction, I ceased 180 my labors and sat down upon the bones. When at last the clanking **subsided,**

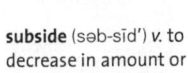 **Targeted Passage**

**subside** (səb-sīd′) *v.* to decrease in amount or intensity; settle down

378  UNIT 3: SETTING, MOOD, AND IMAGERY

## DIFFERENTIATED INSTRUCTION

### FOR STRUGGLING READERS

**Targeted Passage [Lines 156–172]**

This passage reveals Montresor's planned revenge and underscores his cruel nature.

- What does Montresor do to Fortunato when they reach the end of the niche? (lines 156–160)

- What revenge does Montresor appear to be taking against Fortunato? (lines 170–172)

### FOR ENGLISH LANGUAGE LEARNERS

**Comprehension: Transitions** Discuss the use of *but* to signal contrasting ideas in these sentences: "I must not only punish, but ..." (lines 5–6); "I had no intention of alarming you unnecessarily; but ..." (lines 88–89); "Then I must positively leave you. But ..." (lines 163–164). Have Jigsaw Reading groups paraphrase the sentences.

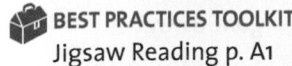 **BEST PRACTICES TOOLKIT**
Jigsaw Reading p. A1

I resumed the trowel, and finished without interruption the fifth, the sixth, and the seventh tier. The wall was now nearly upon a level with my breast. I again paused, and holding the flambeaux over the mason-work, threw a few feeble rays upon the figure within. **F**

A succession of loud and shrill screams, bursting suddenly from the throat of the chained form, seemed to thrust me violently back. For a brief moment I hesitated—I trembled. Unsheathing my rapier,[19] I began to grope with it about the recess; but the thought of an instant reassured me. I placed my hand upon the solid fabric of the catacombs, and felt satisfied. I reapproached the wall. I
190 replied to the yells of him who clamored. I re-echoed—I aided—I surpassed them in volume and in strength. I did this, and the clamorer grew still. **G**

It was now midnight, and my task was drawing to a close. I had completed the eighth, the ninth, and the tenth tier. I had finished a portion of the last and the eleventh; there remained but a single stone to be fitted and plastered in. I struggled with its weight; I placed it partially in its destined position. But now there came from out the niche a low laugh that erected the hairs upon my head. It was succeeded by a sad voice, which I had difficulty in recognizing as that of the noble Fortunato. The voice said—

"Ha! ha! ha!—he! he!—a very good joke indeed—an excellent jest. We will
200 have many a rich laugh about it at the palazzo—he! he! he! —over our wine—he! he! he!"

"The Amontillado!" I said.

"He! he! he!—he! he! he!—yes, the Amontillado. But is it not getting late? Will not they be awaiting us at the palazzo, the Lady Fortunato and the rest? Let us be gone."

"Yes," I said, "let us be gone."

*"For the love of God, Montresor!"*

"Yes," I said, "for the love of God!" **H**

But to these words I hearkened in vain for a reply. I grew impatient. I called
210 aloud,

"Fortunato!"

No answer. I called again,

"Fortunato!"

No answer still. I thrust a torch through the remaining **aperture** and let it fall within. There came forth in return only a jingling of the bells. My heart grew sick—on account of the dampness of the catacombs. I hastened to make an end of my labor. I forced the last stone into its position; I plastered it up. Against the new masonry I re-erected the old rampart of bones. For the half of a century no mortal has disturbed them. *In pace requiescat!*[20]  **④**

**Targeted Passage**

---

19. **rapier** (rā′pē-ər): a long, slender sword.

20. *In pace requiescat* (ĭn pä′kĕ rĕ-kwē-ĕs′kät) *Latin:* May he rest in peace.

THE CASK OF AMONTILLADO  **379**

---

**F MOOD**
Reread this paragraph. What **details** make this description especially horrifying?

**G PARAPHRASE**
Restate what happens in lines 185–191. What emotions does Montresor experience at this point in the story?

**H MOOD**
Reread lines 192–208. Point out **images** and other **details** that convey the mood of the scene.

**aperture** (ăp′ər-chər) *n.* an opening, such as a hole or a gap

**COMMON CORE L 4c**

**⚠ FOREIGN WORDS AND PHRASES**
Poe uses several words and phrases from other languages in this story. For example, "In pace requiescat" (line 219) is a Latin phrase meaning "Rest in peace." Identify the foreign word in line 204 and look up its origin and meaning in a dictionary.

---

**TEXT ANALYSIS**  COMMON CORE  RL 4

**F MOOD**
*Possible answer:* "low moaning cry" (line 175), "furious vibrations of the chain" (line 178), "that I might hearken to it with the more satisfaction, I ceased my labors and sat down upon the bones" (lines 179–180), "threw a few feeble rays upon the figure within" (lines 183–184)

**READING STRATEGY**

**G PARAPHRASE**
*Possible answer:* Fortunato begins to scream, which briefly unnerves Montresor, and he reaches for his rapier. But then Montresor realizes that Fortunato is trapped and yells back at him until he is silent. A feeling of triumph has replaced Montresor's moment of doubt.

**TEXT ANALYSIS**  COMMON CORE  RL 4

**H MOOD**
*Possible answer:* "It was now midnight" (line 192), "there remained but a single stone to be fitted and plastered in" (lines 194–195), "there came from out the niche a low laugh that erected the hairs upon my head" (lines 196–197), "'For the love of God, Montresor!'" (line 207).

**VOCABULARY SKILL**  COMMON CORE  L 4c

**⚠ FOREIGN WORDS AND PHRASES**
*Possible Answer:* palazzo; origin: Italy; meaning: "palace"

---

**FOR STRUGGLING READERS**

**④ Targeted Passage [Lines 214–219]**
This passage concludes the story, hinting at Montresor's momentary remorse.

- What revenge does Montresor carry out against Fortunato? (line 217)
- Why does Montresor claim that his "heart grew sick" (lines 215–216)? Do you accept his explanation? Why or why not? (lines 215–216)
- Does Montresor get away with his crime?

How do you know? (lines 218–219)

**FOR ENGLISH LANGUAGE LEARNERS**
**Language: Pronoun Referents** Ask students whom the phrases "him who clamored" (line 190) and "the clamorer" (line 191) refer to. (*Both refer to Fortunato.*) Then have students read lines 203–205. Have pairs discuss and share their ideas about whom or what each of these pronouns refers to: in line 203, *it* (*the time*); in line 204, *they* ("the *Lady Fortunato and the rest*"); in line 205, *us* (*Fortunato and Montresor*).

**SELECTION WRAP-UP**

**READ WITH A PURPOSE** Ask the students what they now know about Montresor's motive for revenge and how it contributes to their experience of the story. *Possible answers: Fortunato's supposed insult is never really explained. This makes the story more frightening because the reader sympathizes with Fortunato.*

## TIERED DISCUSSION PROMPTS

Use these prompts to help students understand the connection between "The Cask of Amontillado" and the murder that may have inspired Poe to create his short story:

**Connect** How has "The Story Behind 'The Cask of Amontillado'" affected your appreciation of Poe's story? *Possible answer: Poe was inspired by real-life events, just as many writers are today. This does not diminish his talent as a writer or storyteller. Rather, it highlights his ability to explore the darker side of human behavior.*

**Analyze** What details does Edward Rowe Snow use to make his narrative read like a horror story? Be specific. *Possible answer: Snow uses details like "moonless night," "ancient dungeons," "subterranean casemate," and "heavy iron handcuffs and footcuffs" to evoke a scary setting and atmosphere.*

**Evaluate** In what ways does "The Story Behind 'The Cask of Amontillado'" stand out as distinct from "The Cask of Amontillado"? *Possible answer: "The Story Behind 'The Cask of Amontillado'" has more details. While the reader never learns what Fortunato's mysterious "insult" actually was, Snow reveals specifically why the officers sought revenge on Captain Green—he killed Lieutenant Massie, a beloved fellow officer. Captain Green was also a livelier character than Fortunato. Student answers may vary about which narrative they like best.*

# THE STORY BEHIND
# *The* CASK
# *of Amontillado*
### EDWARD ROWE SNOW

While at Fort Independence, Poe [who was a private there in 1827] became fascinated with the inscriptions on a gravestone on a small monument outside the walls of the fort. . . .

*Beneath this stone are deposited the remains of Lieut. ROBERT F. MASSIE, of the U. S. Regt. of Light Artillery. . . .*

During the summer of 1817, Poe learned, twenty-year-old Lieutenant Robert F. Massie of Virginia had arrived at Fort Independence as a newly appointed officer. Most of the men at the post came to enjoy Massie's friendship, but one officer, Captain Green, took a violent dislike to him. Green was known at the fort as a bully and a dangerous swordsman.

When Christmas vacations were allotted, few of the officers were allowed to leave the fort, and Christmas Eve found them up in the old barracks hall, playing cards. Just before midnight, at the height of the card game, Captain Green sprang to his feet, reached across the table and slapped Lieutenant Massie squarely in the face. "You're a cheat," he roared, "and I demand immediate satisfaction!" . . .

The duel began. Captain Green, an expert swordsman, soon had Massie at a disadvantage and ran him through. Fatally wounded, the young Virginian was carried back to the fort, where he died that afternoon. His many friends mourned the passing of a gallant officer. . . .

Feeling against Captain Green ran high for many weeks, and then suddenly he completely vanished. Years went by without a sign of him, and Green was written off the army records as a deserter.

According to the story which Poe finally gathered together, Captain Green had been so detested by his fellow officers at the fort that they decided to take a terrible revenge on him for Massie's death. . . .

Visiting Captain Green one moonless night, they pretended to be friendly and plied him with wine until he was helplessly intoxicated. Then, carrying the captain down to one of the ancient dungeons, the officers forced his body through a tiny opening which led into the subterranean casemate.[1] . . .

His captors began to shackle him to the floor, using the heavy iron handcuffs and footcuffs fastened into the stone. Then they all left the dungeon and proceeded to seal the captain up alive inside the windowless casemate, using bricks and mortar. . . .

Captain Green shrieked in terror and begged for mercy, but his cries fell on deaf ears. The last brick was finally inserted, mortar applied, and the room sealed up, the officers believed, forever. . . .

[In 1905, workmen repairing the fort found a skeleton inside, shackled to the floor with a few fragments of an old army uniform clinging to the bones.]

---

1. **subterranean casemate** (sŭb′tə-rā′nē-ən kăs′māt′): a fortified underground or partly underground room.

## Comprehension

1. **Recall** Why does Montresor, the narrator, want revenge?

2. **Recall** How does Montresor trick Fortunato into joining him?

3. **Summarize** What does Montresor do to ensure the success of his plan?

4. **Summarize** What happens to Fortunato?

## Text Analysis

5. **Make Inferences About Character** What kind of man is Montresor? Think of four or five character traits that you can infer from his words and actions. Record your answers in a chart like this one.

| Montresor's Character Traits | Words/Actions |
|---|---|
| 1. shrewdness | He knows how to take advantage of Fortunato's pride. |
| 2. | |

● 6. **Analyze Mood** What is the overall mood, or atmosphere, of this story? In your opinion, what contributes most to the mood—the setting, the rhythm and tone of the language, or the descriptions of Montresor's thoughts, feelings, and actions? Provide details from the story to support your opinion.

7. **Make Judgments** Review your **paraphrase** of lines 1–8. Does Montresor achieve the kind of revenge he wants? Cite details to support your answer.

8. **Evaluate Narrator** Consider whether Montresor is a **reliable** or an **unreliable narrator.** Is the reader to believe, as Montresor does, that his revenge is justified? Give evidence from the story.

9. **Evaluate Dramatic Irony** **Dramatic irony** occurs when the reader knows something that a character does not. Identify three examples of dramatic irony in this story. What is the effect of the irony on your experience as a reader?

10. **Compare and Contrast** Poe often drew inspiration for his tales from the real world. Compare the details of "The Story Behind 'The Cask of Amontillado'" on page 380 with Poe's story. How similar are these accounts?

## Text Criticism

11. **Critical Interpretations** In defining the short story as a literary form, Poe emphasized that every word should contribute to a "unity of effect or impression." How well does Poe achieve a "unity of effect" in this story? Give examples from the text to support your answer.

> ## Is **REVENGE** ever justified?
> What do you think is the right way to address a wrong?

**COMMON CORE**

**RL 1** Cite textual evidence to support analysis of what the text says explicitly as well as inferences drawn from the text. **RL 4** Analyze the cumulative impact of specific word choices on meaning and tone.

THE CASK OF AMONTILLADO    **381**

---

(line 87). When Fortunato approves of the Montresor family motto (lines 105–106), the reader understands its true, murderous meaning. These dramatic ironies heighten the reader's anticipation of the murder.

10. In both accounts a man is given wine, chained, walled in, and left to die while he pleads for mercy. The stories differ in setting, and in Poe's story the revenge is carried out by one person, not a group.

## Text Criticism

11. Students should support their responses with relevant examples.

> ## Is **REVENGE** ever justified?
> Suggest that students support their opinions with specific, reasoned examples as though arguing in a debate or before a jury.

---

# Practice and Apply

For preliminary support of post-reading questions, use these copy masters:

**R** RESOURCE MANAGER—Copy Masters
Reading Check p. 72
Mood p. 65
Question Support p. 73

Additional selection questions are provided for teachers on page 59.

## ANSWERS

## Comprehension

1. *Montresor wants revenge because he feels that Fortunato has insulted him.*

2. *Montresor plays on Fortunato's pride and vanity, pretending to need his expertise to judge some Amontillado he has purchased.*

3. *Montresor pretends to be Fortunato's friend. He carries out his plan when there are "no attendants at home." He gives Fortunato wine to drink.*

4. *Montresor lures Fortunato deep into the catacombs in his mansion, then chains him up, walls him in, and leaves him there to die.*

## Text Analysis

COMMON CORE **RL 1, RL 4**

*Possible answers:*

5. *Make Inferences About Character Trait (T): vengeful, Words/Actions (W/A): lines 1–8; T: calculating, W/A: carefully plans revenge; T: devious, W/A: manipulates Fortunato through flattery; T: heartless, W/A: lines 178–180*

6. ● COMMON CORE FOCUS *Analyze Mood The overall mood is sinister, created mainly by Montresor's diabolical thoughts, feelings, and actions. For example, he carries out his revenge while pretending to be Fortunato's friend; he taunts Fortunato (lines 162–165) and enjoys his suffering (lines 177–191).*

7. *Yes. He kills Fortunato without getting caught. His victim dies knowing who killed him, but perhaps not why.*

8. *Unreliable; Montresor never explains the "thousand injuries" or "insult," so we can't judge whether his revenge is justified—if murder is ever justified.*

9. *When Montresor urges his "friend" to turn back because his "health is precious" (lines 80–82), the reader suspects he is really luring his enemy to the vaults to kill him, and that Fortunato will "not die of a cough"*

THE CASK OF AMONTILLADO    **381**

## ANSWERS

## Vocabulary in Context

▲ VOCABULARY PRACTICE

| | |
|---|---|
| 1. *a* | 5. *a* |
| 2. *b* | 6. *b* |
| 3. *a* | 7. *a* |
| 4. *b* | 8. *a* |

 RESOURCE MANAGER—Copy Master
Vocabulary Practice p. 70

### ACADEMIC VOCABULARY IN SPEAKING

***Possible response:*** Student responses will vary, but discussion should be supported by events in the story.

### VOCABULARY STRATEGY:
### THE *clud* WORD FAMILY

COMMON CORE **L 4c**

• To help students with the **PRACTICE** activity, work with them on the first item: *include.* Begin by eliciting or providing its meaning ("to take in or contain as part of a whole or group").

• Ask how *include* might relate to the meaning of *clud.* Model the thinking process with this example: A book that *includes* names and dates would contain useful information.

• Additional words in the *clud* family: *exclude, disclose, enclosure.*

 RESOURCE MANAGER—Copy Master
Vocabulary Strategy p. 71

**Interactive Vocabulary** THINK central

Keywords direct students to a **WordSharp** tutorial on **thinkcentral.com** or to other types of vocabulary practice and review.

---

## Vocabulary in Context

▲ VOCABULARY PRACTICE

Choose the situation that most closely relates to each vocabulary word.

1. **aperture:** (a) a crack in a building's foundation, (b) a large stack of lumber
2. **subside:** (a) two cars racing through traffic, (b) a heavy wind lessening in force
3. **impunity:** (a) getting away with a personal foul in football, (b) a tiny hole in a shirt
4. **termination:** (a) someone starting a new job, (b) someone being fired
5. **repose:** (a) lying on a deserted beach, (b) carrying a heavy load of books
6. **abscond:** (a) making a public announcement, (b) sneaking out of a meeting
7. **immolation:** (a) fatalities in a train accident, (b) cartons of spoiled produce
8. **preclude:** (a) getting vaccinated against polio, (b) planting bulbs in fall

WORD LIST
abscond
aperture
immolation
impunity
preclude
repose
subside
termination

### ACADEMIC VOCABULARY IN SPEAKING

• aspect  • circumstance  • contribute  • distinct  • perceive

What **aspects** of Fortunato's character allow him to be fooled by Montresor's intentions? With a partner, identify two or three aspects and discuss how they affect the outcome. Use at least one Academic Vocabulary word in your discussion.

### VOCABULARY STRATEGY: THE *clud* WORD FAMILY

The root of the word *preclude* can be traced back to a Latin word meaning "to close." This root—the spellings of which include *clud, clos, clus,* and *claus*—has given rise to a large word family. *Preclude,* in which the root is combined with the prefix *pre-,* literally means "to close before." If you can recognize the root in the family of words, you can understand how they are related in meaning.

***PRACTICE*** Use each word in a sentence that shows the connection between its meaning and that of *preclude.* Then, using a dictionary, identify three additional words in the *clud* family.

| | |
|---|---|
| 1. include | 5. closet |
| 2. recluse | 6. clause |
| 3. foreclosure | 7. seclusion |
| 4. exclusive | 8. conclude |

COMMON CORE

L 4c Consult reference materials to determine a word's etymology.

 Interactive Vocabulary THINK central

Go to **thinkcentral.com.**
KEYWORD: HML9-382

---

## DIFFERENTIATED INSTRUCTION

### FOR ENGLISH LANGUAGE LEARNERS

**Vocabulary: Prefixes** Encourage students to use their knowledge of the prefixes *im-* (meaning "not") and *sub-* (meaning "under" or "below") to help them remember the definitions of *impunity* and *subside.*

### FOR ADVANCED LEARNERS/PRE–AP

**Practice Vocabulary** Challenge students to write a coherent paragraph using as many of the vocabulary words as they can. Have volunteers share their paragraphs with the class.

# Language

◆ **GRAMMAR AND STYLE: Use Appropriate Language**

Review the **Grammar and Style** note on page 376. Poe uses **formal language** to tell his suspenseful tale. This style of language contains challenging vocabulary, includes complex sentence structures and standard punctuation, and avoids contractions. Use formal language when you want your writing to have a serious quality. Here is an example from the story:

> *I continued, as was my wont, to smile in his face, and he did not perceive that my smile now was at the thought of his immolation.* (lines 10–12)

Notice how the revisions in blue make use of formal language that better reflects Poe's style. Use similar methods to revise your response to the prompt.

> **STUDENT MODEL**
>
> *I soon realized, to my horror,*
> It hadn't occurred to me that Montresor ~~would~~ actually wall up the entrance
>                                            was                              ~ing
> to the niche. *Surely this was merely a jest. After all, how could*
> ~~Where'd he think he was going? I couldn't believe~~ he ~~would~~
> *wretched, cavernous enclosure?*
> leave me in this ~~damp place!~~

**COMMON CORE**

**RL 4** Analyze the cumulative impact of specific word choices on meaning and tone. **L 2** Demonstrate command of the conventions of standard English punctuation. **L 3** Apply knowledge of language to make effective choices for meaning or style. **W 4** Produce narrative writing in which the style is appropriate to the task and purpose.

## READING-WRITING CONNECTION

**YOUR TURN** Expand your understanding of "The Cask of Amontillado" by responding to this prompt. Then use the **revising tip** to improve your writing.

| **WRITING PROMPT** | **REVISING TIP** |
|---|---|
| **Extended Constructed Response: Monologue** What do you think goes through Fortunato's mind after he realizes what has happened to him? Why doesn't he try to reason with Montresor? Use what you know about Fortunato to write a **three-to-five-paragraph monologue**, retelling the last part of the story from his point of view. | Look back over your monologue. Did you use formal language to convey Fortunato's perspective? If not, revise your response to better reflect Poe's style. |

**Interactive Revision** — **THINK**central

Go to **thinkcentral.com**.
KEYWORD: HML9-383

---

**FOR STRUGGLING WRITERS**

- Limit the length of the monologue to no more than three paragraphs.

- Encourage students to imagine themselves in Fortunato's situation. Have pairs or small groups of students share their thoughts and feelings orally before committing them to paper.

---

# Language

**COMMON CORE** RL 4, L 2, L 3, W 4

◆ **GRAMMAR AND STYLE**

After students examine the student model, write these sentences on the board, and have students suggest revisions. (For information on formal language, see **Grammar Handbook.**)

> What had I done to make Montresor so mad? I couldn't remember a thing. Besides, nothing I might have said or done would have deserved this!

***Possible answer:*** *What wrong had I committed to provoke such anger in Montresor? No injustice or insult of any sort occurred to me. Moreover, no word or deed merited such punishment.*

**R** **RESOURCE MANAGER—Copy Master**
Use Appropriate Language p. 74

**READING-WRITING CONNECTION**

Have students reread lines 173–215 and reflect on Fortunato's reactions to what has happened to him. Suggest that students consider at what point Fortunato finally realizes Montresor's intent to kill him.

**Writing Online** — **THINK**central

The following tools are available online at **thinkcentral.com** and on **Write*Smart* CD-ROM:**
- **Interactive Graphic Organizers**
- **Interactive Student Models**
- **Interactive Revision Lessons**

For additional grammar instruction, see **GrammarNotes** on **thinkcentral.com**.

---

# Assess and Reteach

## Assess

**DIAGNOSTIC AND SELECTION TESTS**
Selection Test A, pp. 99–100
Selection Test B/C, pp. 101–102

**Interactive Selection Test** on **thinkcentral.com**

## Reteach

**Level Up Online Tutorials** on **thinkcentral.com**

**Reteaching Worksheets** on **thinkcentral.com**
Language and Literary Devices Lesson 44, Language and Literary Devices Lesson 38, Research and Study Skills Lesson 12

# Focus and Motivate

○ COMMON CORE FOCUS

**RL 7** Analyze the representation of a key scene in two different artistic mediums, including what is emphasized or absent in each treatment.
**W 9a (RL 7)** Draw evidence from literary texts; analyze a key scene in two different artistic mediums. **SL 2** Integrate multiple sources presented in diverse media formats. **SL 5** Make strategic use of digital media in presentations.

## SUMMARY

In this film clip from *The Cask of Amontillado*, Montresor and the "friend," Fortunato, on whom he has vowed revenge, descend into the catacombs beneath Montresor's palazzo. There Montresor shackles the dumbfounded Fortunato to the wall and takes his revenge by walling him into the niche.

## What makes a setting SINISTER?

To help students explore the question, ask them what the word *sinister* means. Invite them to share moments from film or TV that felt sinister. Have them describe elements of the lighting, music, and setting that created the sinister mood. For example, perhaps the lighting was shadowy, the music was ominous, or the setting included sinister places, such as dark attics. Ask how these elements contributed to the sinister mood.

## BACKGROUND

This version of "The Cask of Amontillado" is one of many TV and film adaptations of Poe's works. Horror filmmaker Roger Corman produced versions of Poe's stories "The Fall of the House of Usher," "The Pit and the Pendulum," and "The Masque of the Red Death." Poe's works have also been used in satires, as in the popular TV series The *Simpsons*. One Halloween episode was based on Poe's poem "The Raven," and an episode titled "The Tell-Tale Head" was loosely based on Poe's "The Tell-Tale Heart."

---

**Media Study**

*from* **The Cask of Amontillado**
Film Clip on **Media ◉ Smart** DVD-ROM

*Essential Course of Study* **ECOS**

# What makes a setting SINISTER?

○ **COMMON CORE**

**RL 7** Analyze the representation of a key scene in two different artistic mediums, including what is emphasized or absent in each treatment.

In his writings, Edgar Allan Poe drafted a blueprint for spine-tingling effects that countless creative artists have followed. View a film adaptation of "The Cask of Amontillado" to explore how a team of filmmakers, guided by Poe's descriptions, evoked a time and place and a consistently sinister mood.

## Background

**Tale from the Crypt** One could argue that had Poe been born in the 20th century, he might have enjoyed page-to-film success similar to that of the modern writer Stephen King. Beginning in the silent-film era of the 1920s, filmmakers saw potential in Poe's shadowy characters and in his haunting settings. Over time, Hollywood adapted a few of his horror classics into movies.

This version of "Cask" is part of a program called "Edgar Allan Poe: Terror of the Soul" that was first broadcast in 1995. The set design was based on actual 18th-century Italian catacombs. According to the production designer, David Wasco, "The descent into the catacombs was supposed to get spookier and spookier."

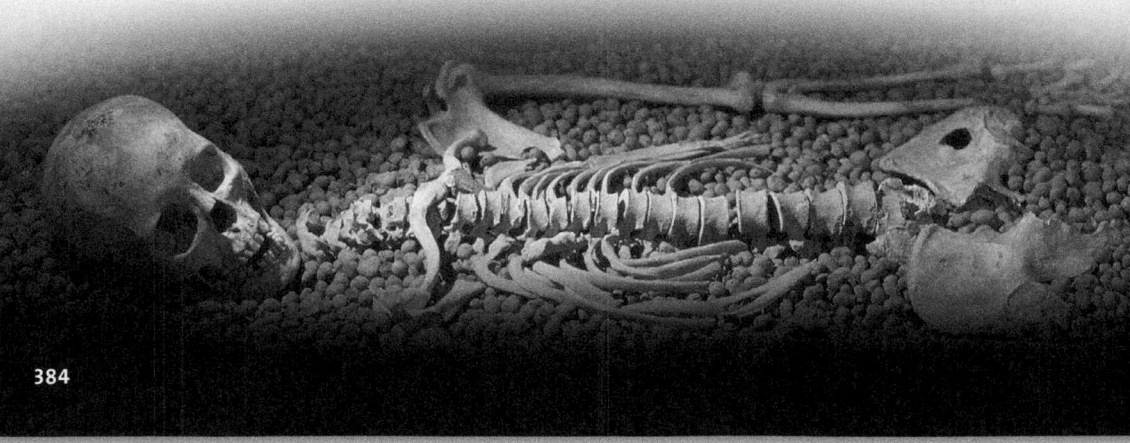

384

---

## Media Study Resources

See resources on the **Teacher One Stop DVD-ROM** *and on* <u>thinkcentral.com</u>.

**R** **RESOURCE MANAGER UNIT 3**
Plan and Teach, pp. 77–80
Summary, pp. 81-82†‡*
Viewing Guide, p. 83
Close Viewing, p. 84
Media Activity, p. 85
Produce Your Own Media, p. 86

**TECHNOLOGY**
⊘ **Teacher One Stop DVD-ROM**
⊘ **Student One Stop DVD-ROM**
⊘ **MediaSmart DVD-ROM**
**MediaScope** on <u>thinkcentral.com</u>

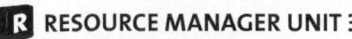

\* Resources for Differentiation     † Also in Spanish     ‡ In Haitian Creole and Vietnamese

# Media Literacy: Setting and Mood in Movies

To recreate settings of the past onscreen, filmmakers focus on representing the time and place of the story and the class, culture, and customs of the characters. After researching these areas, filmmakers select visual and sound elements that will accurately represent the period. These elements include **set design, costuming, props, music,** and **acting.**

When adapting a written work into a film, the director collaborates with other members of the filmmaking team. The art director, the production (or set) designer, the costume designer, the cinematographer, and the music composer all contribute ideas on how to make a setting vivid and how to convey the appropriate mood.

| FROM PAGE TO FILM | STRATEGIES FOR VIEWING | |
|---|---|---|
| **Creating Setting**<br>**Writers** reveal details of settings through description and dialogue.<br><br>**Filmmakers** design specific sets and enhance them. | • Focus on the details of the **set design.** Are the **props**—the objects in the scene—appropriate to the time and place?<br>• Look for distinctive details in the **costumes.** For example, an 18th-century character of high status would probably wear rich fabrics of velvet and silk. |  |
| **Creating Mood**<br>**Writers** often rely on word choice to describe vivid **details**—factual or sensory—that create atmosphere.<br><br>**Filmmakers** create atmosphere primarily through visual and sound techniques. | • Be aware of the overall effect—lighthearted, gloomy, or mysterious—that **lighting** creates in scenes.<br>• Notice how the **music** varies in tone.<br>• Listen for **sound effects.** Creaking floorboards or hollow echoes can enhance an atmosphere established by the visual elements. |  |
| **Creating Dramatic Irony**<br>**Writers** reveal to readers details that some characters don't know through **narration** and **dialogue.**<br><br>**Filmmakers** use visual and sound techniques to reveal details. | • Look for clues in the **compositions.** A character might be placed deliberately in the foreground to suggest weakness or vulnerability.<br>• Pay attention to **close-ups** that show characters' facial expressions revealing what other characters don't know.<br>• Notice the tone of voice an actor might use in a line of **dialogue** to convey more than one meaning. |  |

MEDIA STUDY **385**

---

## MEDIA STUDY: TEACHING OPTIONS

**Teaching Option 1: The Basics (1–2 Days)**
1. Begin the Media Study using the material provided on pages 384–385.
2. Show the Introduction on Media*Smart*. Then, show the First Viewing. As they watch, have students use the Viewing Guide on page 386, along with the corresponding copy master on page 83 of the Resource Manager. Discuss students' responses.
3. Return to the pupil book for the extension activities on page 387.

**Teaching Option 2: In-Depth Study (2–3 Days)**
1. Begin the Media Study using pages 384–385.
2. Show the Introduction and First Viewing from Media*Smart*. Then continue on Media*Smart* with the Media Lessons, using the teacher notes available in the Resources section.
3. Show the Guided Analysis presentation. Have students record their observations on the Student Viewing Guide available in the Resources section from Media*Smart*.
4. Return to the pupil book, page 387.

---

# *Teach*

## Media Literacy

COMMON CORE RL 7

Review with students the elements that filmmakers use to create story setting and mood. Ask the class to recall scenes from a familiar movie set in either the distant past or the future. On the board, list "Set Design and Props," "Costumes," "Lighting," "Music and Sound Effects," and "Acting." List students' descriptions of each aspect of the film. Link the listed features to the overall mood in the film. Then discuss the chart on page 385.

- **Creating Setting** To emphasize the impact of set design, have students imagine a male and female actor in front of a blank blue screen. The actors are fleeing from something. Then ask students to add (1) these different backgrounds: first an army of giant ants in a desert, then a battalion of Roman warriors; (2) these costumes: first sleek silver futuristic flight suits, then loose togas; and (3) these props: first X-ray weapons, then swords. Ask how each change of background, costumes, and props changes the viewer's experience.

- **Creating Mood** Ask students to recall kinds of music and sound effects that make a movie viewer uneasy or frightened. List these ideas on the board. Revisit the list after students view the clip, and allow time to add new ideas.

- **Creating Dramatic Irony** Point out that film shots may position characters near objects, such as an ax hanging on the wall, that predict something to the audience but not to the character. Ask students for additional examples of this technique. Have students explore the impact of tone of voice. Ask volunteers to say these words, first as if having an ordinary conversation and then as if hinting at something unspoken: "This will be an interesting day."

# Practice and Apply

## VIEWING GUIDE

1. Before students view the clip, tell them that they will be asked to identify techniques used to convey a sinister setting and mood. Encourage them to watch and listen for these elements:

   - **set design** and **props** and the way they combine to create a sense of impending doom for Fortunato

   - **costumes** and how they provide information about the time period in which Fortunato and Montresor live

   - **lighting** in the catacombs and how it creates a somber mood

   - **music** and **sound effects** that add to the gloomy atmosphere in the catacombs

   - **composition, close-ups,** and **dialogue** that show Montresor's sinister intentions and Fortunato's ultimate terror

2. Some students may have difficulty isolating the elements that go into creating the clip's sinister mood. Before they view the clip, you might encourage them to make a chart with these headings: "Set Design and Props," "Costumes," "Lighting," "Music and Sound Effects," "Composition," "Close-Ups," and "Dialogue." Urge students to take notes during the viewing.

**R** RESOURCE MANAGER—Copy Masters
Viewing Guide p. 83
Close Viewing p. 84
Media Activity p. 85

Use this resource with the Viewing Guide:

⊘ **MediaSmart DVD-ROM**

**MediaScope** on **thinkcentral.com**

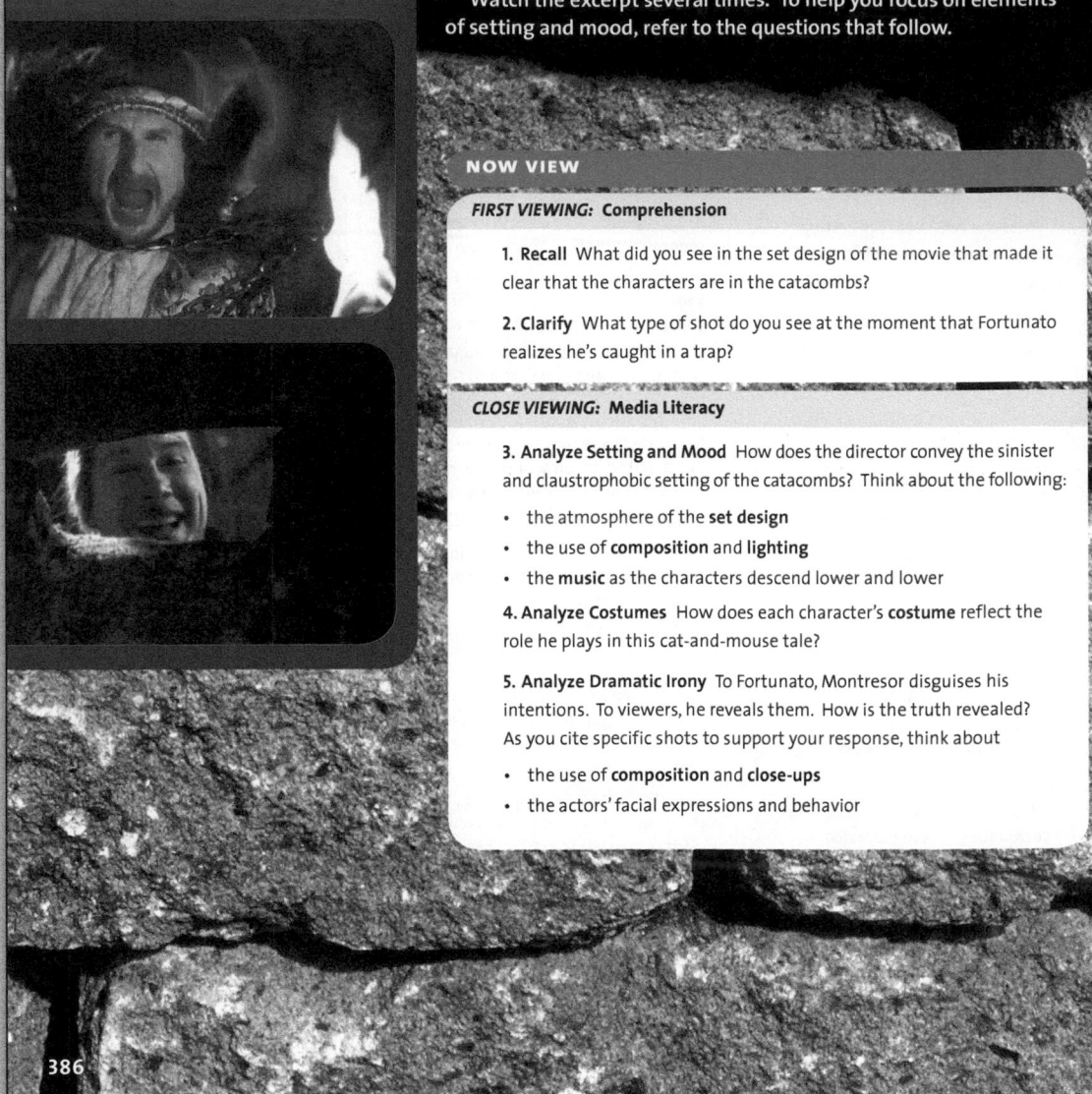

**Media ◉ Smart** DVD-ROM
- **Film Clip:** *The Cask of Amontillado*
- **Director:** Joyce Chopra
- **Production Designer:** David Wasco
- **Genre:** Horror
- **Running Time:** 10.5 minutes

386

## Viewing Guide for
# The Cask of Amontillado

This film excerpt from "The Cask of Amontillado" begins with the search for the Amontillado. You already know how this tale of revenge ends. So, as you watch the adaptation, focus on how film techniques create a sinister atmosphere and evoke a particular mood.
    Watch the excerpt several times. To help you focus on elements of setting and mood, refer to the questions that follow.

### NOW VIEW

**FIRST VIEWING: Comprehension**

1. **Recall** What did you see in the set design of the movie that made it clear that the characters are in the catacombs?

2. **Clarify** What type of shot do you see at the moment that Fortunato realizes he's caught in a trap?

**CLOSE VIEWING: Media Literacy**

3. **Analyze Setting and Mood** How does the director convey the sinister and claustrophobic setting of the catacombs? Think about the following:

   - the atmosphere of the **set design**
   - the use of **composition** and **lighting**
   - the **music** as the characters descend lower and lower

4. **Analyze Costumes** How does each character's **costume** reflect the role he plays in this cat-and-mouse tale?

5. **Analyze Dramatic Irony** To Fortunato, Montresor disguises his intentions. To viewers, he reveals them. How is the truth revealed? As you cite specific shots to support your response, think about

   - the use of **composition** and **close-ups**
   - the actors' facial expressions and behavior

## ANSWERS

### FIRST VIEWING: Comprehension

1. *stone and brick walls, dim lighting, exposed skeletons in crypts, narrow passages, descending stairways, the niter seeping through cracks*

2. *close-up shot of Fortunato's face lit by the dim, flickering flame of a torch*

### CLOSE VIEWING: Media Literacy
**Possible answers:**

3. **set design:** *conveys the cramped space of the catacombs, with the low ceiling often visible;* **composition:** *shows close proximity of characters;* **lighting:** *dim throughout the story;* **music:** *more foreboding as the characters descend*

4. *Fortunato wears a silk jester's costume, suggesting both wealth and buffoonery. Montresor's black cloak suggests foreboding; it is the dress of a criminal and an executioner.*

5. *As Montresor follows Fortunato deeper into the catacombs, close-up shots reveal Montresor's anger and distaste toward Fortunato. As the men near the end of the catacombs, Montresor appears increasingly anxious.*

## Write or Discuss

**COMMON CORE**

**W 9a (RL 7)** Draw evidence from literary texts; analyze a key scene in two different artistic mediums. **SL 2** Integrate multiple sources presented in diverse media formats. **SL 5** Make strategic use of digital media in presentations.

**Compare Film and Written Versions** Edgar Allan Poe was a master at using words to create eerie and frightening story settings. In your opinion, does the film adaptation of "The Cask of Amontillado" effectively portray the story's sinister setting? To compare the film and written versions, note the following:

- Poe's description of the catacombs versus the visual presentation
- the sequence of events in the catacombs
- the film techniques used to enhance the scenes, including sound, lighting, and camera shots

## Produce Your Own Media

**Create a Production Design Board** Imagine that you're part of a production team assigned to design sets for an adaptation of "The Cask of Amontillado." You'll use a production design board to present ideas for creating a sinister setting. A production design board visually represents different elements of a set, such as scenery, costumes, and props. The board displays small parts or drawings of these elements.

*HERE'S HOW* Work with a partner to review the short story and decide what scene (or scenes) to depict and how to present it. Consider these suggestions:

- Keep the presentation simple. Use labels to identify key elements.
- Using foam board as the background, apply photos or sketches of design elements and fabric samples (or magazine clippings of patterns).
- Attach quotations from the tale that inspired your selections.

**Media Tools** THINK central

Go to **thinkcentral.com**.
KEYWORD: HML9-387

**STUDENT MODEL**

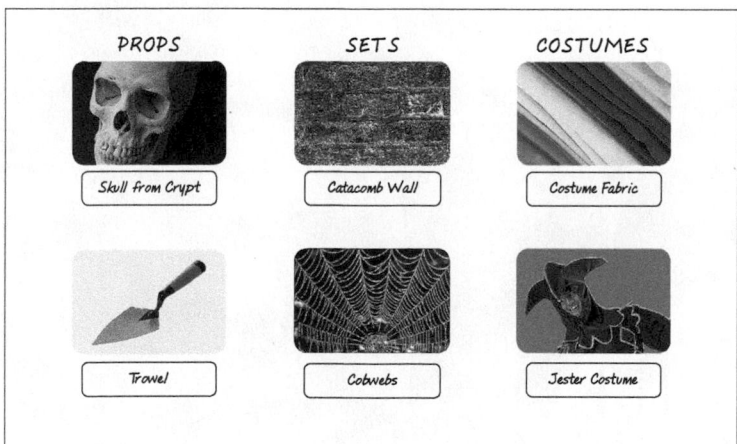

PROPS — Skull from Crypt — Trowel

SETS — Catacomb Wall — Cobwebs

COSTUMES — Costume Fabric — Jester Costume

**Tech Tip**

Use a clip-art program as a source of images of props and other elements of a set's design.

MEDIA STUDY **387**

## Produce Your Own Media

**Rubric: Create a Production Design Board**
A strong production design board should have

- a variety of set elements, such as props and costumes, with a label for each
- design elements such as sketches, fabric samples, magazine clippings, and clip art
- quotations from the story that relate to the design elements
- a clear identification of the scene or scenes
- a strong focus on the scene or scenes

- a simple and easy-to-understand format

**R** RESOURCE MANAGER—Copy Master
Produce Your Own Media p. 86

## Write or Discuss

**COMMON CORE** **W 9a (RL 7), SL 2, SL 5**

**Compare Film and Written Versions** In their evaluations, students should address techniques used by set, costume, sound, and lighting designers as well as film techniques such as camera shots. Make sure students recognize the impact that elements of setting and film technique have on mood. In addition, encourage students to include their own personal reactions to the written story versus the filmed version.

### MEDIA STUDY WRAP-UP

Have students summarize what they have learned about set, costume, sound, and lighting design for film and how these elements contribute to mood. Encourage students to use such terms as *set design, props, costuming, lighting, music, sound effects, composition, close-up,* and *dialogue* in their explanations.

### RETEACH

If students are having difficulty applying the Media Study skills, use one of these reteaching options:

- **Setting and Mood** Ask students to imagine they are going to film a version of this story locally. Ask where they would film in order to capture both the mood and logic of the original setting. *(Possible answer: an abandoned warehouse or underground tunnel like a sewer, so that, as in the catacombs, nobody can hear Fortunato's cries)*
- **Costumes** Ask students what sorts of modern dress, if any, would capture the same mood as the costumes used in the film. *(Possible answer: a silly costume for Fortunato and a black suit or trenchcoat for Montresor)*
- **Dramatic Irony** Remind students that dramatic irony gives the words or images in a story or film a second level of meaning. Review the class's answers to Question 5 on page 386. Then, ask the students to work in pairs to choose one of the ironic moments from the film and decide what the film might have shown if that moment was *not* meant to be ironic.

# Focus and Motivate

○ COMMON CORE FOCUS

**RI 4** Analyze the cumulative impact of specific word choices on meaning and tone. **RI 6** Determine an author's point of view in a text and analyze how an author uses rhetoric to advance that point of view. **L 4a-c** Use context as a clue to the meaning of a word; Identify patterns of word changes; consult a dictionary to find the pronunciation of a word.

## SUMMARY

In this excerpt from *A Walk in the Woods*, travel writer Bill Bryson presents a harrowing account of his encounter with a furious snowstorm while hiking the Appalachian Trail.

## Where do you find
## ADVENTURE?

Pose the question, and then have students share and compare their concepts of adventure. Ask whether they think adventure must entail an element of risk. Continue the exploration by having students complete the *QUICKWRITE*. Have volunteers describe their adventures.

---

## Selection Resources

---

**Essential Course of Study** ECOS

## *from* **A Walk in the Woods**
Travel Narrative by Bill Bryson

# Where do you find
# ADVENTURE?

○ COMMON CORE

**RI 4** Analyze the cumulative impact of specific word choices on meaning and tone. **RI 6** Determine an author's point of view in a text and analyze how an author uses rhetoric to advance that point of view. **L 4b, c** Identify patterns of word changes; consult a dictionary to clarify a word's pronunciation.

Do you find adventure in physically risky activities, such as rock climbing and skateboarding, or in everyday pursuits? In this selection, you'll read about the adventures of Bill Bryson, a well-known travel writer whose hike along the Appalachian Trail took some unexpected turns.

*QUICKWRITE* With a small group, generate a list of adventures you've had or would like to have. Then select one adventure and write a short paragraph explaining how you would prepare for it.

388

---

See resources on the **Teacher One Stop DVD-ROM** *and on* <u>thinkcentral.com</u>.

 **RESOURCE MANAGER UNIT 3**
   Plan and Teach, pp. 87–94
   Summary, pp. 95–96†‡*
   Text Analysis and Reading
      Skill, pp. 97–98, 99–100†*
   Vocabulary, pp. 101–103*

**DIAGNOSTIC AND SELECTION TESTS**
   Selection Tests, pp. 103–106

 **BEST PRACTICES TOOLKIT**
   Definition Mapping, p. E6
   Two-Column Chart, p. A25
   New Word Analysis, p. E8
   Jigsaw Reading, p. A1

**INTERACTIVE READER**

**ADAPTED INTERACTIVE READER**

**ELL ADAPTED INTERACTIVE READER**

**TECHNOLOGY**
   ⊘ **Teacher One Stop DVD-ROM**
   ⊘ **Student One Stop DVD-ROM**
   ⊘ **PowerNotes DVD-ROM**
   ⊘ **Audio Anthology CD**
   ⊘ **GrammarNotes DVD-ROM**
   ⊘ **Audio Tutor CD**
   ⊘ **ExamView Test Generator**
      on the **Teacher One Stop**

---

\* Resources for Differentiation          † Also in Spanish          ‡ In Haitian Creole and Vietnamese

## TEXT ANALYSIS: SETTING AND MOOD

**Setting** can play an important role in creating a **mood.** In this selection, Bill Bryson describes the Appalachian Trail by using sensory language and precise verbs. These, in turn, convey a mood to the reader and help bring Bryson's experience to life. As you read, think about how the mood influences your impressions of the Appalachian Trail and those who travel it.

## READING SKILL: IDENTIFY AUTHOR'S PERSPECTIVE

People often look at a subject from different perspectives. For example, a person living in Florida may react negatively to a 40-degree day, while a person raised in Minnesota might view such weather as a blessing. The combination of beliefs, values, and feelings that influence how a writer looks at situations and events is called the **author's perspective.** In order to figure out an author's perspective, it's important to pay attention to

- statements of opinion—personal ideas that cannot be proved true
- details and examples the writer chooses to include
- the writer's **tone,** or attitude (such as humorous or serious)

As you read Bill Bryson's account of hiking the Appalachian Trail, try to figure out his perspective by completing a chart like the one shown.

| Statement, Detail, or Tone | What It Reveals About Bryson |
|---|---|
| "Life takes on a neat simplicity. . . ." (line 6) | He values a lack of complication. |

**Review:** Cause and Effect, Make Inferences

## ▲ VOCABULARY IN CONTEXT

Put each vocabulary word in the appropriate column, and then write a brief definition of each word you're familiar with.

| WORD LIST | abysmal | reconnoiter | unnerving |
|---|---|---|---|
| | buffeted | singularity | veneer |
| | daunted | superannuated | |

| Know Well | Think I Know | Don't Know At All |
|---|---|---|
| | | |

 Complete the activities in your **Reader/Writer Notebook.**

## Meet the Author

# Bill Bryson
born 1951

**Native Son**
Bill Bryson (brī′sən) is a popular travel writer whose hiking stories combine humor and human interest with a sense of adventure. Bryson spent more than 20 years of his adult life in England, touring the countryside and writing best-selling books. In 1995 Bryson returned to the United States and settled in New Hampshire near a branch of the famous Appalachian Trail. Soon after, he became inspired to hike the length of the trail, hoping to improve his fitness and become better acquainted with his homeland. *A Walk in the Woods* records Bryson's adventures with his friend Stephen Katz as they traveled the trail.

**A Challenging Trip**
When he and Katz began their trip, Bryson was used to casual walks through the English countryside. He knew little about the rugged conditions to be found in the U.S. wilderness. As a result, Bryson and Katz were ill prepared for the many challenges they faced, including carrying 40-pound packs, making their own meals, and sleeping outdoors. Much of the humor and suspense in *A Walk in the Woods* stems from their lack of preparation.

**BACKGROUND TO THE SELECTION**
**A Path for the People**
The Appalachian Trail is a footpath that spans more than 2,100 miles from Mount Katahdin in Maine to Springer Mountain in Georgia. It passes through 14 states. The idea for the trail began in 1921 with a proposal by conservationist Benton MacKaye. On August 14, 1937, the trail was completed.

**Author Online**
**THINK** central
Go to **thinkcentral.com.**
KEYWORD: HML9-389

389

# Teach

**TEXT ANALYSIS**  COMMON CORE  RI 4

● *Model the Skill:* **SETTING AND MOOD**

To model recognizing the connection between setting and mood, read aloud this example:

> The crumbling tombstones cast long shadows in the pale dawn light. An icy wind slashed across the graveyard as a piercing scream shattered the silence.

Point out the following sensory details and precise verbs that convey setting and mood: "crumbling tombstones," "long shadows in the pale dawn light," "icy wind," "piercing scream shattered."

**GUIDED PRACTICE** Have students help you identify the mood evoked by these details. *Possible answers:* spooky, scary

**READING SKILL**  COMMON CORE  RI 4, RI 6

■ *Model the Skill:* **IDENTIFY AUTHOR'S PERSPECTIVE**

Tell students why you do or do not enjoy outdoor activities. Then explain how your statements, supporting details, and tone reveal your perspective.

**GUIDED PRACTICE** Ask volunteers to share their opinions about outdoor activities.

**R** RESOURCE MANAGER—Copy Master Identify Author's Perspective p. 99 (for student use while reading the selection)

## VOCABULARY SKILL

### ▲ VOCABULARY IN CONTEXT

**DIAGNOSE WORD KNOWLEDGE** Have all students complete the Vocabulary in Context. Check their definitions against the following:

**abysmal** (ə-bĭz′məl) *adj.* very bad
**buffeted** (bŭf′ĭ-tĭd) *adj.* knocked about or struck **buffet** *v.*
**daunted** (dôn′tĭd) *adj.* discouraged **daunt** *v.*
**reconnoiter** (rē′kə-noi′tər) *v.* to make a preliminary inspection

**singularity** (sĭng′gyə-lăr′ĭ-tē) *n.* something peculiar or unique
**superannuated** (soo′pər-ăn′yoo-ā′tĭd) *adj.* obsolete with age
**unnerving** (ŭn-nûr′vĭng) *adj.* causing loss of courage **unnerve** *v.*
**veneer** (və-nîr′) *v.* to cover with a thin layer of material

**PRETEACH VOCABULARY** Use the copy master to help students predict meanings for each boldfaced word.

COMMON CORE  L 4

**R** RESOURCE MANAGER—Copy Master Vocabulary Study p. 101

1. Read aloud the first two sentences in Part A, emphasizing *unnerving.*

2. Point out "courage" and "sense of adventure" in contrast to *unnerving.* Elicit possible meanings for *unnerving.*

3. Repeat the process for remaining words.

# Practice and Apply

## READ WITH A PURPOSE

*Ask students to set a purpose for reading. Point out the Big Question and the selection's title. Have students read to find out how "A Walk in the Woods" can be an adventure.*

**TEXT ANALYSIS**  COMMON CORE
RI 4

### A SETTING AND MOOD

*Possible answer:* Bryson's description of the woods creates a mood of pleasant monotony—the feeling that you're experiencing the same things over and over again, and it's OK.

**READING SKILL** COMMON CORE
RI 4,
RI 6

### B *Model the Skill:* AUTHOR'S PERSPECTIVE

To model how to identify author's purpose, point out line 8, "It's quite wonderful, really." Explain that this is a statement of opinion that shows the author enjoys the different cycle of time while hiking.

*Possible answer:* At this point, Bryson has a very positive attitude about hiking, finding it a most relaxing activity (lines 6–13, 23–25).

**Extend the Discussion** What does Bryson mean in lines 26–28?

**VOCABULARY**  COMMON CORE
L 4

### OWN THE WORD

**singularity:** Remind students that the base of *singularity* is *single*. Have them explain the meaning of *singularity* based on the meaning of *single,* "solitary, only one, or individual."

---

# A Walk in the Woods

## BILL BRYSON

Distance changes utterly when you take the world on foot. A mile becomes a long way, two miles literally considerable, ten miles whopping, fifty miles at the very limits of conception. The world, you realize, is enormous in a way that only you and a small community of fellow hikers know. Planetary scale is your little secret.

Life takes on a neat simplicity, too. Time ceases to have any meaning. When it is dark, you go to bed, and when it is light again you get up, and everything in between is just in between. It's quite wonderful, really.

You have no engagements, commitments, obligations, or duties; no special
10 ambitions and only the smallest, least complicated of wants; you exist in a tranquil tedium,[1] serenely beyond the reach of exasperation, "far removed from the seats of strife," as the early explorer and botanist William Bartram[2] put it. All that is required of you is a willingness to trudge.

There is no point in hurrying because you are not actually going anywhere. However far or long you plod, you are always in the same place: in the woods. It's where you were yesterday, where you will be tomorrow. The woods is one boundless **singularity.** Every bend in the path presents a prospect indistinguishable from every other, every glimpse into the trees the same tangled mass. For all you know, your route could describe a very large,
20 pointless circle. In a way, it would hardly matter. **A**

At times, you become almost certain that you slabbed this hillside three days ago, crossed this stream yesterday, clambered over this fallen tree at least twice today already. But most of the time you don't think. No point. Instead, you exist in a kind of mobile Zen mode,[3] your brain like a balloon tethered with string, accompanying but not actually part of the body below. Walking for hours and miles becomes as automatic, as unremarkable, as breathing. At the end of the day you don't think, "Hey, I did sixteen miles today," any more than you think, "Hey, I took eight-thousand breaths today." It's just what you do. **B**

---

1. **tranquil tedium:** calm and peaceful boredom.
2. **William Bartram** (bär'trəm): one of the first explorers of the Appalachian Mountains, who wrote about his experiences in a book published in 1791.
3. **mobile Zen mode:** walking, perfectly in tune with one's environment to the point of feeling at one with the surroundings.

**390** UNIT 3: SETTING, MOOD, AND IMAGERY

### Analyze Visuals ▶
How does the angle of this photograph affect the **mood** conveyed?

**① Targeted Passage**

**singularity**
(sĭng'gyə-lăr'ĭ-tē) *n.* something peculiar or unique

**A SETTING AND MOOD**
Reread lines 14–20. What mood is created by Bryson's description of the woods?

**B AUTHOR'S PERSPECTIVE**
What was Bryson's attitude about hiking at this point? Cite details that helped you draw your **conclusion.**

---

## DIFFERENTIATED INSTRUCTION

### FOR ENGLISH LANGUAGE LEARNERS

**Vocabulary Support** Use Definition Mapping to teach these words: *route* (line 19), *accompanying* (line 25), *accumulating* (line 59), *vary* (line 76), *intensely* (line 215).

**📦 BEST PRACTICES TOOLKIT—Transparency**
Definition Mapping p. E6

### FOR STRUGGLING READERS

In combination with the *Audio Anthology CD,* use one or more Targeted Passages (pp. 390, 393, 394, 397) to ensure that students focus on key selection events, concepts, and skills. Targeted Passages are also good for English learners.

**① Targeted Passage [Lines 1–20]**

This passage describes the setting and establishes the author's attitude about his adventure.

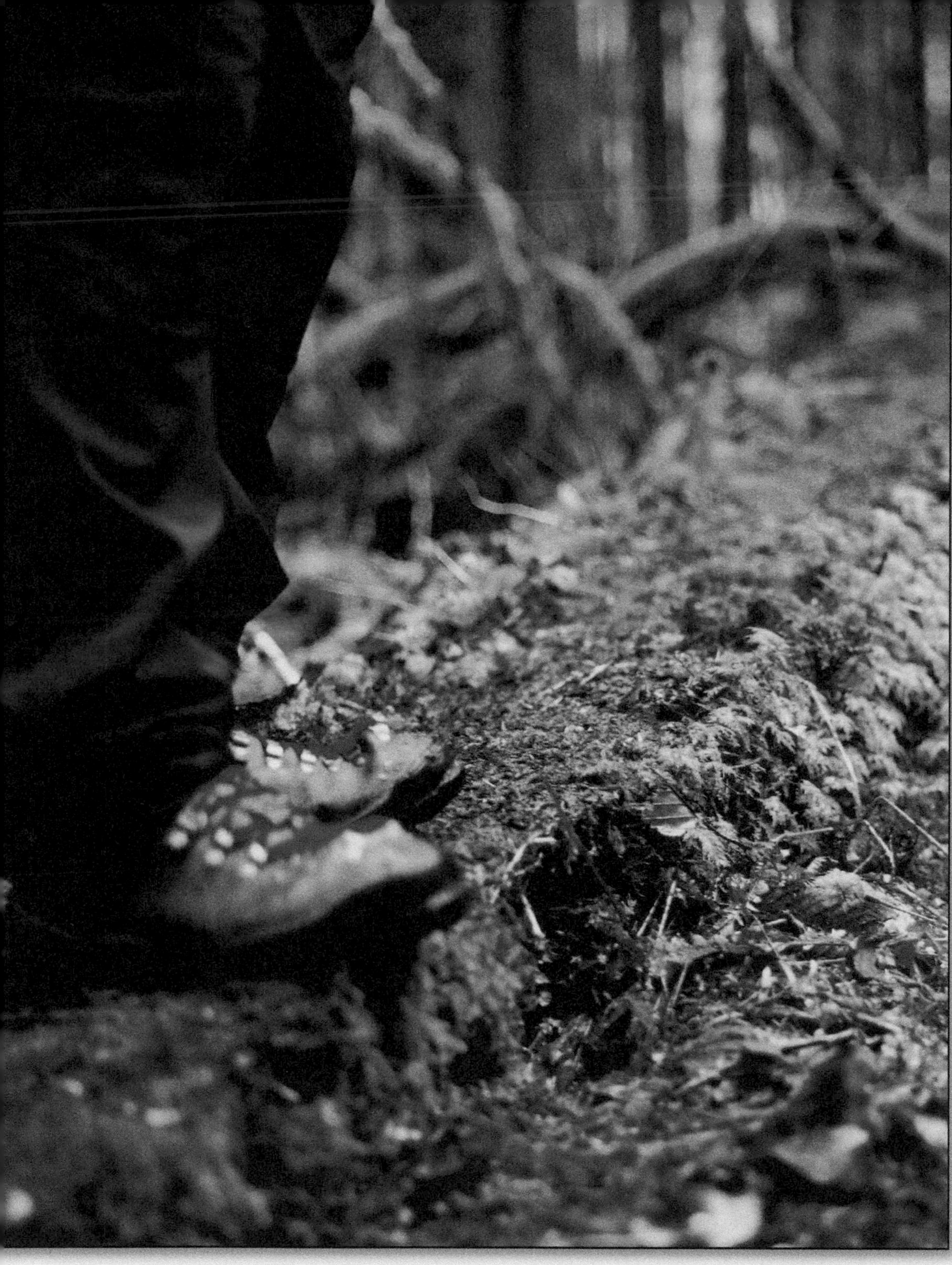

Reading Support

THINK central

This selection on **thinkcentral.com** includes embedded **ThinkAloud** models–students "thinking aloud" about the story to model the kinds of questions a good reader would ask about a selection.

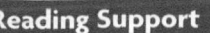

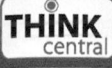

## BACKGROUND

**The Appalachian National Scenic Trail** This trail is part of America's national park system. However, unlike most national parks, the AT, as hikers call it, is not located in one state. Instead, it is in 14 different states, passing through some 60 different parks and forests. Hiking the entire length of the AT usually takes five to seven months. While the national parks are patrolled and maintained by paid government workers, numerous volunteers devote their time to preserving the AT through "trail maintenance clubs" throughout the Appalachian Mountains.

## Analyze Visuals

***Possible answer:*** *The angle of the photograph conveys a feeling of ruggedness by focusing on the hiker's boots, standing on a rough path in the woods. By focusing on only the hiker's legs and boots as well as the path, the photograph also conveys the immediacy of the natural world.*

- What is the setting of this narrative? (lines 15–16)
- How is the author traveling? What does this suggest about the author? (line 1)
- What clues help you identify the author's attitude about hiking in the woods? (lines 8–20)

**FOR ADVANCED LEARNERS/PRE–AP**

**Author's Perspective** [small-group option] As they read the selection, ask students to observe the tone in which Bryson describes his adventures. Ask students if they think the tone of his narrative accurately reflects his feelings at the time. Have them write their thoughts, supported with evidence from the text.

##  CAUSE AND EFFECT

***Possible answer:*** *The increasing snow, furious wind, and falling temperature made it much more difficult for Bryson and Katz to hike. Just as the weather got worse, the terrain became more treacherous.*

**Extend the Discussion** What details does Bryson include to describe the terrain? Have students put their notes into the chart they started on page 389.

---

**TEXT ANALYSIS**

*COMMON CORE*
*RI 4*

##  Model the Skill: SETTING AND MOOD

To model how to identify the effect setting can have on mood, read the sentence that begins, "The skies grew..." in lines 31–32. Explain that the phrase "skies grew sullen and the air chillier" makes the weather seem ominous and gives a sense that it will soon become a dangerous force for the hikers. This makes for a serious mood, because the hikers will encounter great obstacles as they continue to climb.

***Possible answer:*** *Bryson's description of the setting (lines 39–43; 49–51) and of Katz's experience (lines 53–56) makes the mood tense and alarming.*

---

**VOCABULARY**

*COMMON CORE*
*L 4*

### OWN THE WORD

- **veneer:** Have students find context clues to help them determine the meaning of the word *veneer*. ***Possible answer:*** *thin layer*

- **unnerving:** Write the word *unnerving* and the definition "causing loss of courage" in a circle. Have students add synonyms around it to complete a semantic map. ***Possible answers:*** *upsetting, unsettling, daunting, frightening*

---

And so we walked, hour upon hour, over rollercoaster hills, along knife-edge
30 ridges and over grassy balds, through depthless ranks of oak, ash, chinkapin,
and pine. The skies grew sullen and the air chillier, but it wasn't until the third
day that the snow came. It began in the morning as thinly scattered flecks,
hardly noticeable. But then the wind rose, then rose again, until it was blowing
with an end-of-the-world fury that seemed to have even the trees in a panic,
and with it came snow, great flying masses of it. By midday we found ourselves
plodding into a stinging, cold, hard-blowing storm. Soon after, we came to a
narrow ledge of path along a wall of rock. **C**

    Even in ideal circumstances this path would have required delicacy and care.
It was like a window ledge on a skyscraper, no more than fourteen or sixteen
40 inches wide, and crumbling in places, with a sharp drop on one side of perhaps
eighty feet, and long, looming stretches of vertical granite on the other. Once
or twice I nudged foot-sized rocks over the side and watched with faint horror
as they crashed and tumbled to improbably remote resting places. The trail
was cobbled with rocks and threaded with wandering tree roots against which
we constantly stubbed and stumbled, and **veneered** everywhere with polished
ice under a thin layer of powdery snow. At exasperatingly frequent intervals,
the path was broken by steep, thickly bouldered streams, frozen solid and
ribbed with blue ice, which could only be negotiated in a crablike crouch. And
all the time, as we crept along on this absurdly narrow, dangerous perch, we
50 were half-blinded by flying snow and jostled by gusts of wind, which roared
through the dancing trees and shook us by our packs. This wasn't a blizzard; it
was a tempest. We proceeded with painstaking deliberativeness, placing each
foot solidly before lifting the one behind. Even so, twice Katz made horrified,
heartfelt, comic-book noises ("AIEEEEE!" and "EEEARGH!") as his footing
went, and I turned to find him hugging a tree, feet skating, his expression bug-
eyed and fearful. **D**

    It was deeply **unnerving**. It took us over two hours to cover six-tenths of
a mile of trail. By the time we reached solid ground at a place called Bearpen
Gap, the snow was four or five inches deep and accumulating fast. The whole
60 world was white, filled with dime-sized snowflakes that fell at a slant before

**C CAUSE AND EFFECT**
Reread lines 29–37 and note the changes in **setting**. How did these changes affect Bryson and his friend Katz?

**veneer** (və-nîr′) *v.* to cover with a thin layer of material

**D SETTING AND MOOD**
Reread lines 38–56. How does Bryson's use of sensory language in his description of the setting and of Katz influence the mood in this paragraph? Cite details to support your answer.

**unnerving** (ŭn-nûr′vĭng) *adj.* causing loss of courage **unnerve** *v.*

---

## DIFFERENTIATED INSTRUCTION

**FOR ADVANCED LEARNERS/PRE–AP**
**Author's Perspective** In lines 53–56, the author uses humorous language in his description of Katz: "comic-book noises ('AIEEEEE!' and 'EEEARGH!')"; "bug-eyed." Have students discuss how this touch of humor affects the suspense of the narrative, even though the situation is filled with danger.

**FOR STRUGGLING READERS**
**Develop Reading Fluency** Demonstrate how the author conveys tension through his use of language. Read aloud lines 38–56, using expression and phrasing to dramatize the text. (You may also wish to give a flat, monotonous reading for contrast.) Then assign each sentence in the paragraph to a student. Have students read the paragraph aloud using appropriate phrasing and emphasis.

**R** RESOURCE MANAGER—Copy Master
Reading Fluency p. 106

being caught by the wind and hurled in a variety of directions. We couldn't see more than fifteen or twenty feet ahead, often not even that.

The trail crossed a logging road, then led straight up Albert Mountain,[4] a bouldered summit 5,250 feet above sea level, where the winds were so wild and angry that they hit the mountain with an actual wallop sound and forced us to shout to hear each other. We started up and hastily retreated. Hiking packs leave you with no recognizable center of gravity at the best of times; here we were literally being blown over. Confounded, we stood at the bottom of the summit and looked at each other. This was really quite grave. We were caught
70 between a mountain we couldn't climb and a ledge we had no intention of trying to renegotiate. Our only apparent option was to pitch our tents—if we could in this wind—crawl in, and hope for the best. I don't wish to reach for melodrama, but people have died in less trying circumstances.

I dumped my pack and searched through it for my trail map. Appalachian Trail maps are so monumentally useless that I had long since given up using them. They vary somewhat, but most are on an **abysmal** scale of 1:100,000, which ludicrously compresses every kilometer of real world into a mere centimeter of map. Imagine a square kilometer of physical landscape and all that it might contain—logging roads, streams, a mountaintop or two, perhaps
80 a fire tower, a knob or grassy bald, the wandering AT,[5] and maybe a pair of important side trails—and imagine trying to convey all that information on an area the size of the nail on your little finger. That's an AT map.

Actually, it's far, far worse than that because AT maps—for reasons that bewilder me beyond speculation—provide less detail than even their meager scale allows. For any ten miles of trail, the maps will name and identify perhaps only three of the dozen or more peaks you cross. Valleys, lakes, gaps, creeks, and other important, possibly vital, topographical features are routinely left unnamed. Forest Service roads are often not included, and, if included, they're inconsistently identified. Even side trails are frequently left

4. **Albert Mountain:** a peak in western North Carolina.
5. **AT:** Appalachian Trail.

---

COMMON CORE L 4b

**Language Coach**

**Suffixes** Recall that a **suffix** is a word part attached to the end of a base word. In line 66, Bryson uses the adverb *hastily*—which is made up of the noun *haste* (meaning "speed") and the suffix *-ly* (meaning "in a certain manner")—to indicate that their retreat was fast. The adverb suffix *-ly* can be traced back to Old English. Bryson uses many other adverbs formed with this suffix to describe his actions and circumstances as he tries to survive the rugged geography and harsh climate of the region. What other *-ly* adverbs can you find on this page? What do they mean?

**abysmal** (ə-bĭz′məl) *adj.* very bad

**Targeted Passage**

---

**Analyze Visuals**

**Activity** Ask students how the setting and mood of the photograph differ from the setting and mood of the narrative. *Possible answer: The setting and mood of the photo are bright and calm, while those of the narrative are stormy and ominous.*

**About the Photograph** The photograph on these two pages shows a portion of the Great Smoky Mountains in Tennessee. The Appalachian Trail passes through these mountains, which are part of the Appalachian mountain chain.

**REVISIT THE BIG QUESTION**

## Where do you find
# ADVENTURE?

**Discuss** An adventure usually involves some danger or risk. Does Bryson's experience here, in lines 63–73, qualify as an adventure? Explain. *Possible answer: Bryson is in a very dangerous and risky situation; he is truly experiencing an adventure. As he comments in line 73, "people have died in less trying circumstances."*

---

**VOCABULARY** COMMON CORE L 4

**OWN THE WORD**

**abysmal:** Have students name things that could be described as *abysmal* and explain why the adjective *abysmal* fits. *Possible answers: abysmal weather: cold, gray, rainy, or snowy; abysmal job: boring, dreary, poorly paid; abysmal picture: out of focus, unflattering; abysmal lighting: too poor to see; abysmal car: won't start, doesn't run well*

---

**FOR STRUGGLING READERS**

**2 Targeted Passage [Lines 63–73]**

This passage sets up the key conflict in the narrative: The hikers' struggle with decisions about how to survive the dangerous storm.

- Why does Bryson choose not to return to safer conditions at a lower altitude? (lines 69–71)

- Why does Bryson tell the reader, "people have died in less trying circumstances"? (lines 71–73)

---

**FOR ENGLISH LANGUAGE LEARNERS**

**Language Coach** COMMON CORE L 4b

**Suffixes**

*Possible Answers:* literally, actually; really, truly; monumentally, highly; ludicrously, laughably; possibly, conceivably; inconsistently, incongruously

## READING SKILL

### E AUTHOR'S PERSPECTIVE

**Possible answer:** Bryson finds AT maps "monumentally useless" (line 75) and "seriously inadequate" (lines 91–92).

**Extend the Discussion** Summarize the reasons for Bryson's opinion of AT maps. Do you think his feelings are justified? Why, or why not?

## TIERED DISCUSSION PROMPTS

Use these prompts to help students understand the perilous situation Bryson and Katz find themselves in in lines 93–127:

**Summarize** What options are available to Bryson and Katz at this moment in their journey? What is your opinion of those options? **Possible answer:** *They can either follow the Forest Service road, which might lead to a shelter, or they can go back downhill and try to camp. Either journey would be difficult in a blizzard.*

**Analyze** How does Bryson reach a decision about what to do? **Possible answer:** *He evaluates the alternatives and then asks Katz for his opinion (lines 108–114). Katz, apparently agreeing with Bryson's logic, continues walking along the logging road, and Bryson follows (lines 115–116).*

**Evaluate** How well do you think Bryson and Katz work as a team? Explain. **Possible answer:** *Bryson and Katz don't seem to work well as a team. Katz doesn't appear to be of much help. He seems to rely on Bryson (line 107) and doesn't offer any suggestions of his own (line 115). Meanwhile, Bryson himself is uncertain of what to do (line 108).*

## VOCABULARY

### OWN THE WORD

**buffeted:** Ask students if they have ever been *buffeted* by winds just as Katz and the narrator were during their hike. How did students respond to the wind?

---

90  off. There are no coordinates, no way of directing rescuers to a particular place, no pointers to towns just off the map's edge. These are, in short, seriously inadequate maps. **E**

In normal circumstances, this is merely irksome. Now, in a blizzard, it seemed closer to negligence. I dragged the map from the pack and fought the wind to look at it. It showed the trail as a red line. Nearby was a heavy, wandering black line, which I presumed to be the Forest Service road we stood beside, though there was no actual telling. According to the map, the road (if a road is what it was) started in the middle of nowhere and finished half a dozen miles later equally in the middle of nowhere, which clearly made no sense—

100  indeed, wasn't even possible. (You can't start a road in the middle of forest; earth-moving equipment can't spontaneously appear among the trees. Anyway, even if you could build a road that didn't go anywhere, why would you?) There was, obviously, something deeply and infuriatingly wrong with this map.

"Cost me eleven bucks," I said to Katz a little wildly, shaking the map at him and then crumpling it into an approximately flat shape and jabbing it into my pocket.

"So what're we going to do?" he said.

I sighed, unsure, then yanked the map out and examined it again. I looked from it to the logging road and back. "Well, it looks as if this logging road

110  curves around the mountain and comes back near the trail on the other side. If it does and we can find it, then there's a shelter we can get to. If we can't get through, I don't know, I guess we take the road back downhill to lower ground and see if we can find a place out of the wind to camp." I shrugged a little helplessly. "I don't know. What do you think?"

He issued a single bitter guffaw and returned to the hysterical snow. I hoisted my pack and followed.

We plodded up the road, bent steeply, **buffeted** by winds. Where it settled, the snow was wet and heavy and getting deep enough that soon it would be impassable and we would have to take shelter whether we wanted to or not.

120  There was no place to pitch a tent here, I noted uneasily—only steep, wooded slope going up on one side and down on the other. For quite a distance—far longer than it seemed it ought to—the road stayed straight. Even if, farther on, it did curve back near the trail, there was no certainty (or even perhaps much likelihood) that we would spot it. In these trees and this snow you could be ten feet from the trail and not see it. It would be madness to leave the logging road and try to find it. Then again, it was probably madness to be following a logging road to higher ground in a blizzard.

Gradually, and then more decidedly, the trail began to hook around behind the mountain. After about an hour of dragging sluggishly through ever-

130  deepening snow, we came to a high, windy, level spot where the trail—or at least *a* trail—emerged down the back of Albert Mountain and continued on into level woods. I regarded my map with bewildered exasperation. It didn't give any indication of this whatever, but Katz spotted a white blaze twenty yards into the woods, and we whooped with joy. We had refound the AT.

**E** AUTHOR'S PERSPECTIVE
What is Bryson's opinion of AT maps?

**buffeted** (bŭf'ĭ-tĭd) *adj.* knocked about or struck **buffet** *v.*

**3** Targeted Passage

---

## DIFFERENTIATED INSTRUCTION

### FOR STRUGGLING READERS

**3** Targeted Passage [Lines 108–134]

In this passage, Bryson decides how to progress: They will take the logging road to get around the mountain.

- What causes Bryson to feel uneasy as they follow the logging road? (lines 120–122)
- At what point does Bryson know he has made the right decision? (lines 132–134)
- What insight into hiking does Bryson and Katz's predicament give you? (lines 122–126)

### FOR ENGLISH LANGUAGE LEARNERS

**Vocabulary: Multiple-Meaning Words** Have students use context clues and prior knowledge to figure out the meanings of these multiple-meaning words from the selection:

- *trying* (line 73), "difficult"
- *scale* (line 85), "size"
- *bitter* (line 115), "unhappy"
- *affair* (line 140), "object"

A shelter was only a few hundred yards farther on. It looked as if we would live to hike another day.

The snow was nearly knee deep now, and we were tired, but we all but pranced through it, and Katz whooped again when we reached an arrowed sign on a low limb that pointed down a side trail and said "BIG SPRING SHELTER."

140 The shelter, a simple wooden affair, open on one side, stood in a snowy glade—a little winter wonderland—150 yards or so off the main trail. Even from a distance we could see that the open side faced into the wind and that the drifting snow was nearly up to the lip of the sleeping platform. Still, if nothing else, it offered at least a sense of refuge.

We crossed the clearing, heaved our packs onto the platform, and in the same instant discovered that there were two people there already—a man and a boy of about fourteen. They were Jim and Heath, father and son, from Chattanooga,[6] and they were cheerful, friendly, and not remotely **daunted** by the weather. They had come hiking for the weekend, they told us (I hadn't

150 even realized it was a weekend), and knew the weather was likely to be bad, though not perhaps quite this bad, and so were well prepared. Jim had brought a big clear plastic sheet, of the sort decorators use to cover floors, and was trying to rig it across the open front of the shelter. Katz, uncharacteristically, leapt to his assistance. The plastic sheet didn't quite reach, but we found that with one of our groundcloths lashed alongside it we could cover the entire front. The wind walloped ferociously against the plastic and from time to time tore part of it loose, where it fluttered and snapped, with a retort like gunshot, until one of us leaped up and fought it back into place. The whole shelter was, in any case, incredibly leaky of air—the plank walls and floors were full

160 of cracks through which icy wind and occasional blasts of snow shot—but we were infinitely snugger than we would have been outside.

So we made a little home of it for ourselves, spread out our sleeping pads and bags, put on all the extra clothes we could find, and fixed dinner from a reclining position. Darkness fell quickly and heavily, which made the wildness outside seem even more severe. Jim and Heath had some chocolate cake, which they shared with us (a treat beyond heaven), and then the four of us settled down to a long, cold night on hard wood, listening to a banshee[7] wind and the tossing of angry branches.

When I awoke, all was stillness—the sort of stillness that makes you sit up

170 and take your bearings. The plastic sheet before me was peeled back a foot or so and weak light filled the space beyond. Snow was over the top of the platform and lying an inch deep over the foot of my sleeping bag. I shooed it off with a toss of my legs. Jim and Heath were already stirring to life. Katz slumbered heavily on, an arm flung over his forehead, his mouth a great open hole. It was not quite six.

daunted (dôn'tǐd) *adj.* discouraged daunt *v.*

---

6. **Chattanooga** (chăt'ə-nōō'gə): a city in southeastern Tennessee.

7. **banshee** (băn'shē): in Gaelic folklore, a female spirit who wails as a sign that death is coming.

Use these prompts to help students compare Bryson and Katz with Jim and his son in lines 145–161:

**Connect** Can you think of an experience when you or someone you know was surprised by unexpected support during a tense situation? How does that help you understand Bryson and Katz's reaction to Jim and Heath? *Accept all reasonable responses.*

**Compare** How does Jim and Heath's state of mind differ from Bryson's? *Possible answer: Jim and Heath are "cheerful . . . and not remotely daunted by the weather" (lines 148–149), while Bryson is no doubt physically and emotionally drained by the situation.*

**Evaluate** Why have Jim and his son apparently fared better than Bryson and Katz? *Possible answer: Jim and Heath are better prepared and perhaps more experienced hikers. For example, they anticipated the weather (line 150) and had packed a plastic sheet (lines 151–152).*

**REVISIT THE BIG QUESTION**

## Where do you find
# ADVENTURE?

**Discuss** What lesson might Bryson have learned from his adventure thus far? *Possible answer: Bryson has probably learned that he needs to be better prepared when hiking the AT and that he has to expect the unexpected.*

**VOCABULARY**   COMMON CORE   **L 4**

### OWN THE WORD

**daunted:** Tell students that common synonyms for *daunted* are "intimidated" or "discouraged." Have students name antonyms for *daunted. Possible answers: encouraged, emboldened, undaunted, unintimidated*

---

**FOR ENGLISH LANGUAGE LEARNERS**

**Vocabulary: Word Associations** Have students work in groups to figure out the meanings of these common word groups, using context clues: *all but* (line 137), "nearly"; *make a move* (line 199), "begin moving"; *as well as* (line 220), "in addition to"; *set off* (line 236), "went."

**FOR ADVANCED LEARNERS/PRE–AP**

**Characterization** On this page (lines 153–154, 173–175), as in a number of other places in the narrative, Bryson depicts his friend Stephen Katz in an unflattering way. Ask students to consider why the author may have made this choice. Does it add humor or does it detract from the narrative? Ask students to explain their responses in a short paragraph.

##  SETTING AND MOOD

*Possible answer: The mood is mixed. On the one hand, it's more relaxed now that the immediate danger has passed. There is a feeling of appreciation for the beautiful surroundings (lines 182–185). On the other hand, the mood reflects Bryson's uneasiness about moving on (lines 181–182, 189–190).*

**IF STUDENTS NEED HELP . . .** Have students use the information in lines 176–190 to complete a Two-Column Chart.

| Setting Details | Effect on Mood |
|---|---|
| • snow is more than waist deep (lines 177–178) | • surprising and worrisome |
| • | • |

 **BEST PRACTICES TOOLKIT—Transparency**
Two-Column Chart p. A25

---

**REVISIT THE BIG QUESTION**

## Where do you find
# ADVENTURE?

**Discuss** How do lines 215–221 highlight both positive and negative aspects of Bryson's hiking adventure? *Possible answer: While the hikers experience the beauty of the woods (lines 216–217), they must also cope with difficulties caused by the snow (lines 217–221).*

## OWN THE WORD

**reconnoiter:** Have students complete this sentence, showing that they understand the meaning of *reconnoiter.* We were afraid that the Boy Scout troop was lost, but we were sure that the troop leader would reconnoiter and . . . *Possible answer: find shelter or guide the troop safely home.*

---

I decided to go out to **reconnoiter** and see how stranded we might be. I hesitated at the platform's edge, then jumped out into the drift—it came up over my waist and made my eyes fly open where it slipped under my clothes and found bare skin—and pushed through it into the clearing, 180 where it was slightly (but only slightly) shallower. Even in sheltered areas, under an umbrella of conifers, the snow was nearly knee deep and tedious to churn through. But everywhere it was stunning. Every tree wore a thick cloak of white, every stump and boulder a jaunty snowy cap, and there was that perfect, immense stillness that you get nowhere else but in a big woods after a heavy snowfall. Here and there clumps of snow fell from the branches, but otherwise there was no sound or movement. I followed the side trail up and under heavily bowed limbs to where it rejoined the AT. The AT was a plumped blanket of snow, round and bluish, in a long, dim tunnel of overbent rhododendrons. It looked deep and hard going. I walked a few yards as a test. 190 It was deep and hard going.

When I returned to the shelter, Katz was up, moving slowly and going through his morning groans, and Jim was studying his maps, which were vastly better than mine. I crouched beside him and he made room to let me look with him. It was 6.1 miles to Wallace Gap and a paved road, old U.S. 64. A mile down the road from there was Rainbow Springs Campground, a private campsite with showers and a store. I didn't know how hard it would be to walk seven miles through deep snow and had no confidence that the campground would be open this early in the year. Still, it was obvious this snow wasn't going 200 to melt for days and we would have to make a move sometime; it might as well be now, when at least it was pretty and calm. Who knew when another storm might blow in and really strand us?

Jim had decided that he and Heath would accompany us for the first couple of hours, then turn off on a side trail called Long Branch, which descended steeply through a ravine for 2.3 miles and emerged near a parking lot where they had left their car. He had hiked the Long Branch trail many times and knew what to expect. Even so, I didn't like the sound of it and asked him hesitantly if he thought it was a good idea to go off on a little-used side trail, into goodness knows what conditions, where no one would come across him and his son if they got in trouble. Katz, to my relief, agreed with me. "At least 210 there's always other people on the AT," he said. "You don't know what might happen to you on a side trail." Jim considered the matter and said they would turn back if it looked bad.

Katz and I treated ourselves to two cups of coffee, for warmth, and Jim and Heath shared with us some of their oatmeal, which made Katz intensely happy. Then we all set off together. It was cold and hard going. The tunnels of boughed rhododendrons, which often ran on for great distances, were exceedingly pretty, but when our packs brushed against them they dumped volumes of snow onto our heads and down the backs of our necks. The three adults took it in turns to walk in front because the lead person always received 220 the heaviest dumping, as well as having all the hard work of dibbing holes in the snow.

**reconnoiter** (rē′kə-noi′tər) *v.* to make a preliminary inspection

**F SETTING AND MOOD**
Reread lines 176–190. Describe the mood in this paragraph. What sensory details of the setting contribute to the mood?

**COMMON CORE L 4c**

**Language Coach**

**Oral Fluency** The letter combination *ough* has several different pronunciations. It is pronounced /AW/ in *bought* but /UF/ in *rough,* /OH/ in *dough* but /OW/ in *doughty* ("brave"). Reread lines 215–218. Which pronunciation above applies to *boughed?* Use a dictionary to confirm your answer.

---

## DIFFERENTIATED INSTRUCTION

### FOR STRUGGLING READERS

**Figurative Language** Remind students that a metaphor is a figure of speech that makes a comparison between two unlike things without using *like* or *as.* Have students identify the metaphors in lines 182–183 and 187–188. Model the process of determining the comparison in lines 182–183 by asking: If the trees are described as wearing a cloak and a cap, what are they being compared to?

### FOR ENGLISH LANGUAGE LEARNERS

**Language Coach**   COMMON CORE   L 4c

**Oral Fluency *Answer:*** "/OW/(BOWD)" Have students work in pairs to brainstorm one more word for each pronunciation of *ough.* Then have students use the words in sentences they read to their partners.

The Long Branch trail, when we reached it, descended steeply through bowed pines—too steeply, it seemed to me, to come back up if the trail proved impassable, and it looked as if it might. Katz and I urged Jim and Heath to reconsider, but Jim said it was all downhill and well-marked, and he was sure it would be all right. "Hey, you know what day it is?" said Jim suddenly and, seeing our blank faces, supplied the answer. "March twenty-first."

Our faces stayed blank.

"First day of spring," he said.

230 We smiled at the pathetic irony of it, shook hands all around, wished each other luck, and parted. **G**

Katz and I walked for three hours more, silently and slowly through the cold, white forest, taking it in turns to break snow. At about one o'clock we came at last to old 64, a lonesome, **superannuated** two-lane road through the mountains. It hadn't been cleared, and there were no tire tracks through it. It was starting to snow again, steadily, prettily. We set off down the road for the campground and had walked about a quarter of a mile when from behind there was the crunching sound of a motorized vehicle proceeding cautiously through snow. We turned to see a big jeep-type car rolling up beside us. The

240 driver's window hummed down. It was Jim and Heath. They had come to let us know they had made it, and to make sure we had likewise. "Thought you might like a lift to the campground," Jim said. ❧

**G** MAKE INFERENCES
What does Bryson mean by "the pathetic irony" of its being the first day of spring?

**superannuated**
(soo′pər-ăn′yoo-ā′tĭd) *adj.* obsolete with age

④ Targeted Passage

---

## FOR STRUGGLING READERS

④ **Targeted Passage** [Lines 232–242]

This passage concludes the excerpt. Everyone appears to have made it through the adventure safely.

- How do you think Bryson and Katz felt when they made it to the road and found that it hadn't been cleared? (line 235)
- Do you think they took the ride to the campground? Explain your answer. (lines 240–242)

## FOR ENGLISH LANGUAGE LEARNERS

**Vocabulary: Idioms** Use New Word Analysis to teach students the following idioms:

- *here and there (line 185)*, "in a few places"
- *hard going (line 190)*, "difficult"
- *ran on (line 216)*, "extended"
- *made it (line 241)*, "succeeded"
- *a lift (line 242)*, "a ride"

📦 **BEST PRACTICES TOOLKIT—Transparency**
New Word Analysis p. E8

## Analyze Visuals

**Activity** Ask students how the scene in the photo might compare to the setting of the selection. ***Possible answer:*** *The snowy trail in the photo is beautiful, but it probably does not reflect the much snowier terrain on the AT. Here, the sun is out and the path is clear. In the text, we read that the road was not plowed and that it started snowing again.*

**READING SKILL:** *Review*

**G MAKE INFERENCES**

***Possible answer:*** *Spring usually brings with it warmer temperatures, but the hikers find themselves in a wintry, snow-covered world.*

**VOCABULARY**                    COMMON CORE
                                        L 4

### OWN THE WORD

**superannuated:** Tell students that *superannuated* is formed of two Latin words, *super*, meaning "over or above" and *annus*, meaning "one year." Have students explain the relationship of "over one year old" with the definition of *superannuated*, "obsolete with age."

## SELECTION WRAP–UP

**READ WITH A PURPOSE** What sort of adventure was described in this narrative? How does Bryson's experience compare to your own idea of what makes an adventure? *Students' answers should indicate how their ideas of adventure compare to Bryson's experience.*

⭐ **CRITIQUE** In his narrative, Bryson uses several writing techniques normally associated with fiction, such as dialogue and figurative language. Have students evaluate the author's writing style and explain why it does or does not make the narrative more effective.

### INDEPENDENT READING

Students might enjoy reading about a young man's struggle to survive in Alaska in Jon Krakauer's *Into the Wild*.

# Practice and Apply

For preliminary support of post-reading
questions, use these copy masters:

**R** **RESOURCE MANAGER**—Copy Masters
Reading Check p. 104
Setting and Mood p. 97
Question Support p. 105

Additional selection questions are
provided for teachers on page 91.

## ANSWERS
## Comprehension

1. *They have set out to hike the length of the
Appalachian Trail.*

2. *They encounter a fierce snowstorm.*

3. *They follow a logging road around the
mountain, which leads them to a shelter.*

## Text Analysis

COMMON CORE RI 4, RI 6

*Possible answers:*

4. ● **COMMON CORE FOCUS** *Analyze
Setting and Mood The details about the
woods (lines 14–20), the terrain (lines
29–31, 38–56), and the snow and wind
(lines 32–37, 58–62, 117–127) contribute to
the mood in the selection.*

5. ■ **COMMON CORE FOCUS** *Identify
Author's Perspective Bryson found it
peaceful, relaxing, and beautiful (lines 6–13,
23–25, 182–185). However, through this
experience, Bryson also realized that hiking
can be dangerous (lines 72–73) and that it's
important to be prepared (lines 149–152,
192–193).*

6. *Unlike Jim's maps—"vastly better than
mine" (lines 192–193)—Bryson's maps were
"monumentally useless" (line 75) and "seriously inadequate" (lines 91–92). As a result,
readers aren't sure if he can find his way to
the shelter.*

7. *Bryson seems uncertain and unprepared
for the circumstances he encounters. Katz
is not much help. He relies on Bryson and
seems to offer no suggestions of his own
(lines 68–69, 107–108, 115). Together, they
do not build confidence in the reader that
they are a winning combination.*

## Comprehension

1. **Recall** What have Bill Bryson and Stephen Katz set out to do?

2. **Recall** What stands in their way?

3. **Summarize** How do they survive the ordeal?

## Text Analysis

● 4. **Analyze Setting and Mood** What elements of setting most strongly
contribute to the mood in this selection? Consider the time of day, the season,
the weather, and the natural landscape. Cite details from the text to support
your answer.

■ 5. **Identify Author's Perspective** Review the chart you completed as you
read. In a sentence or two, summarize Bryson's perspective on walking the
Appalachian Trail. Explain whether you think his perspective changes in any
way as the episode unfolds. Support your ideas with evidence from the text.

6. **Interpret Suspense** How do Bryson's poor preparations for his adventure
contribute to the suspense of this selection? Explain.

7. **Evaluate Personality Traits** In what way do Bryson and Katz make unlikely
heroes in this adventure story? Cite examples from the text.

8. **Make Judgments** In *A Walk in the Woods*, as in many outdoor adventure
stories, nature is the **antagonist**—that is, the force that the central figure, or
**protagonist**, struggles against. To what degree is nature really responsible for
the troubles Bryson and Katz face? Use a graphic like this one in your evaluation.

| Problem or Conflict | Caused by Nature | Caused by Hikers |
|---|---|---|
| Bryson and Katz are caught in a snowstorm. | ✓ | |

## Text Criticism

9. **Critical Interpretations** Bill Bryson has been described by one critic as a writer
"who could wring humor from a clammy sleeping bag." Judging by this
selection, do you agree or disagree with that statement? Cite details from the
selection to support your opinion.

### Where do you find ADVENTURE?

What types of activities or pursuits do you find adventurous?

COMMON CORE

**RI 4** Analyze the cumulative
impact of specific word choices on
meaning and tone. **RI 6** Determine
an author's point of view in a text
and analyze how an author uses
rhetoric to advance that point
of view.

8. *Students should recognize that while
the snowstorm and the rugged terrain
are natural obstacles, the troubles that
Bryson and Katz face are aggravated by
their lack of experience and preparation.
For example, they brought poor maps,
apparently did not check the weather
forecast, and did not bring emergency
items, such as the plastic sheet that Jim had
with him.*

## Text Criticism

*Possible answer:*

9. *Bryson writes with a dry sense of humor,
even when describing a dangerous situation
(lines 51–56, 72–73, 104–106, 166, 177–179).*

### Where do you find
**ADVENTURE?** *Answers will vary
but should match criteria of adventure as
agreed upon by the class.*

# Vocabulary in Context

## ▲ VOCABULARY PRACTICE

Decide whether the words in each pair are synonyms or antonyms. You may consult a thesaurus to check your answers.

1. buffeted/battered
2. veneer/uncover
3. reconnoiter/inspect
4. superannuated/rejuvenated
5. daunted/inspired
6. unnerving/encouraging
7. abysmal/wonderful
8. singularity/commonality

**WORD LIST**

abysmal
buffeted
daunted
reconnoiter
singularity
superannuated
unnerving
veneer

## ACADEMIC VOCABULARY IN WRITING

- aspect • circumstance • contribute • distinct • perceive

The hikers in *A Walk in the Woods* encounter a variety of events. Write a paragraph in which you identify and explain at least one **distinct circumstance** that creates danger for the hikers and one that provides safety. Use at least one Academic Vocabulary word in your paragraph.

**COMMON CORE**

L 4a  Use context as a clue to the meaning of a word.

## VOCABULARY STRATEGY: CONTEXT CLUES

Often you can figure out the meaning of an unfamiliar word by examining the words and sentences that surround it. Three types of context clues that can help you determine the meanings of unfamiliar words in *A Walk in the Woods* are

- **general context clues,** which allow you to infer the meaning of an unfamiliar word by reading information in the sentences that surround it
- **comparison clues,** in which the unknown word is likened to something known
- **example clues,** in which one or more examples are included in the text to suggest the meaning of the unfamiliar word

Not only can these types of context clues help you determine a word's **denotation**, or basic dictionary meaning, but they are also helpful in determining a word's **connotations**, or the overtones of meaning a word may take on.

*PRACTICE* Use context clues to figure out the meaning of each word that follows. First identify the type of context clue that helps you determine the meaning of the word. Then write a definition of the word.

slabbed (line 21)
renegotiate (line 71)
topographical (line 87)
retort (line 157)

**Interactive Vocabulary**  **THINK** central

Go to **thinkcentral.com**.
KEYWORD: HML9-399

---

## DIFFERENTIATED INSTRUCTION

### FOR ENGLISH LANGUAGE LEARNERS

**Task Support: Simplify** Use Jigsaw Reading to divide among student pairs or groups the words listed in **VOCABULARY STRATEGY: CONTEXT CLUES.** Have each pair or group identify the context clues that help them figure out the meaning of each word. Then have students share their word meanings with the class.

**BEST PRACTICES TOOLKIT**
Jigsaw Reading p. A1

### FOR ADVANCED LEARNERS/PRE–AP

**Vocabulary in Writing** Have students use at least two vocabulary words in a paragraph written in the first person from Jim's viewpoint to describe his first meeting with Bryson and Katz (page 395).

---

# ANSWERS

## Vocabulary in Context

### ▲ VOCABULARY PRACTICE

1. *synonyms*
2. *antonyms*
3. *synonyms*
4. *antonyms*
5. *antonyms*
6. *antonyms*
7. *antonyms*
8. *antonyms*

**R** RESOURCE MANAGER—Copy Master
Vocabulary Practice p. 102

### ACADEMIC VOCABULARY IN WRITING

Suggest that students list dangerous circumstances from the story, and then those that provide safety. Students can then decide which they can describe most clearly.

### VOCABULARY STRATEGY: CONTEXT CLUES

**COMMON CORE** L 4a

To model using context clues, use the vocabulary word *reconnoiter* (line 176). Point out how information in lines 169–170 and 177–190 can help them infer the meanings.

***Possible answers:***
*slabbed*—"crossed"
*renegotiate*—"cross again"
*topographical*—"having to do with physical features of land"
*retort*—"a reply"

**R** RESOURCE MANAGER—Copy Master
Vocabulary Strategy p. 103

**Interactive Vocabulary**  **THINK** central

Keywords direct students to a **WordSharp** tutorial on **thinkcentral.com** or to other types of vocabulary practice and review.

# Assess and Reteach

## Assess

**DIAGNOSTIC AND SELECTION TESTS**
Selection Test A, pp. 103–104
Selection Test B/C, pp. 105–106

**Interactive Selection Test** on **thinkcentral.com**

## Reteach

**Level Up Online Tutorials** on **thinkcentral.com**

A WALK IN THE WOODS  **399**

# Focus and Motivate

## COMMON CORE FOCUS

**RI 1** Cite textual evidence to support analysis of what the text says explicitly as well as inferences drawn from the text. **RI 2** Determine a central idea of a text and analyze its development; provide a summary of the text. **RI 6** Determine an author's purpose in a text. **W 2b** Develop the topic with well-chosen, relevant, and sufficient facts, quotations, or other information and examples. **L 4** Determine or clarify the meaning of multiple-meaning words.

### SUMMARY

This selection is a letter in which the writer argues for preserving wilderness for historic significance and people's spiritual health.

## What's the Connection?

Use a KWL chart to prepare students. For the first column, help students brainstorm a list of things they already know about wilderness. In the second column, write questions about what they want to know about wilderness.

**BEST PRACTICES TOOLKIT—Transparency**
KWL p. A21

# Teach

## Standards Focus: Read Primary Sources

Guide students in their analysis of Wallace Stegner's letter. To help them complete the chart as they read, encourage students to pay attention to details. Use these questions to get students started:

- To whom did Stegner write the letter?
- What is Stegner's purpose for writing?

**R RESOURCE MANAGER—Copy Master**
Read Primary Sources p. 113

Use with *A Walk in the Woods*, page 390.

## COMMON CORE

**RI 1** Cite textual evidence to support analysis of what the text says explicitly as well as inferences drawn from the text. **RI 2** Determine a central idea of a text and analyze its development; provide a summary of the text. **RI 6** Determine an author's purpose in a text. **L 4** Determine or clarify the meaning of multiple-meaning words.

---

**Reading for Information**

# Wilderness Letter

*Essential Course of Study* **ECOS**

## What's the Connection?

In *A Walk in the Woods*, you read about some of the pleasures and perils of hiking the Appalachian Trail in a government-protected wilderness area. Now, in a letter from Wallace Stegner, you will read one of many arguments that have been made in favor of preserving such wilderness areas.

## Standards Focus: Read Primary Sources

**Primary sources** are materials written by people who witnessed the events portrayed. These sources can give us unique insights into a subject. Letters, speeches, interviews, public documents, and other texts—whether published, archived, or only saved in someone's attic—are all types of primary sources. To get the most out of a primary source, consider

- the form and purpose of the text
- where and when it was written
- the intended audience
- the author's position in his or her family, society, or profession

To further analyze a primary source, summarize its main points. Then complete a chart such as the one here to help you analyze how the source fits in with what you have read or learned elsewhere. Try doing this as you read Wallace Stegner's letter.

| | |
|---|---|
| What is the form and purpose of this document? | |
| What, if anything, do I already know about the author and his times? | |
| What seems to be the relationship between the author and his audience? | |
| What does the document tell me about life at the time it was written? | |

---

# Selection Resources

*See resources on the **Teacher One Stop DVD-ROM** and on **thinkcentral.com**.*

**R RESOURCE MANAGER UNIT 3**
Lesson Support*, pp. 107–110

**DIAGNOSTIC AND SELECTION TESTS**
Selection Tests, pp. 107–110

**INTERACTIVE READER**

**ADAPTED INTERACTIVE READER**

**ELL ADAPTED INTERACTIVE READER**

**TECHNOLOGY**
- Teacher One Stop DVD-ROM
- Student One Stop DVD-ROM
- PowerNotes DVD-ROM
- Audio Anthology CD
- Audio Tutor CD
- ExamView Test Generator
  on the **Teacher One Stop**

* Resources for Differentiation

# Practice and Apply

# Wilderness Letter

### Wallace Stegner

Los Altos, Calif.
Dec. 3, 1960

David E. Pesonen
Wildland Research Center
Agricultural Experiment Station
243 Mulford Hall
University of California
Berkeley 4, Calif.

Dear Mr. Pesonen:

I believe that you are working on the wilderness portion of the Outdoor Recreation Resources Review Commission's report. If I may, I should like to urge some arguments for wilderness preservation that involve recreation, as it is ordinarily conceived, hardly at all. Hunting, fishing, hiking, mountain-climbing, camping, photography, and the enjoyment of natural scenery will all, surely, figure in your report. So will the wilderness as a genetic reserve, a scientific yardstick by which we may measure the world in its natural balance against the world in its man-
10 made imbalance. What I want to speak for is not so much the wilderness uses, valuable as those are, but the wilderness idea, which is a resource in itself. Being an intangible and spiritual resource, it will seem mystical to the practical-minded—but then anything that cannot be moved by a bulldozer is likely to seem mystical to them.

I want to speak for the wilderness idea as something that has helped form our character and that has certainly shaped our history as a people. . . . **A**

**COMMON CORE** RI 1, RI 2, RI 6

**A CENTRAL IDEA**
The **central idea** is the most important idea that a text or part of a text conveys. This idea may be stated outright, or it may be merely implied by the details the author has chosen to include. To analyze the development of a central idea—and to determine an author's purpose, or reason, for writing—consider what the specific details "add up" to suggest. What central idea and purpose for writing are suggested by Stegner's first two paragraphs?

## AUTHOR BIOGRAPHY

Although not all of his stories are set in the West, Wallace Stegner (1909–1993) is called the dean of Western writers. A passionate environmentalist, Stegner not only wrote about the importance of preserving the West, he fought for it. In 1960, Stegner wrote *Wilderness Letter*. In his letter, he stated that wild places were in need of federal protection. Four years later, *Wilderness Letter* was influential in the passage of the Wilderness Act.

## TIERED DISCUSSION PROMPTS

Use these prompts to help students understand Stegner's viewpoint in lines 1–15:

**Connect** What is your experience of the wilderness? Cite memorable examples from movies, television, or your own life. *Responses will vary.*

**Compare and Contrast** What does Stegner mean when he refers to measuring "the world in its natural balance against the world in its man-made imbalance" (lines 9–10)? *Possible answer: The untouched wilderness represents a natural balance of living things; the rest of the world is imbalanced because people have altered the natural state.*

**Evaluate** How does Stegner's tone suggest the direction his letter is taking? Cite evidence to support your answer. *Possible answer: Stegner's tone suggests that he disapproves of some people's view of the environment. For example, he remarks, "anything that cannot be moved by a bulldozer is likely to seem mystical" to people who are "practical-minded."*

**INFORMATIONAL ANALYSIS**

**COMMON CORE** RI 1, RI 2, RI 6

**A CENTRAL IDEA**

*Possible answer: Stegner is writing to argue in favor of wilderness preservation. However, he is basing his arguments on "not so much the wilderness uses . . . but the wilderness idea, which is a resource in itself" (lines 10–12).*

## DIFFERENTIATED INSTRUCTION

### FOR STRUGGLING READERS
**Build Comprehension** Explain that Stegner's style includes challenging sentence structures. Encourage students to reread sentences that seem confusing.

- Discuss how the words "hardly at all" at the end of the second sentence alter the sentence's meaning. Help students rewrite the sentence in their own words.

- Discuss what the pronoun "it" in line 13 refers to.

### FOR ENGLISH LANGUAGE LEARNERS
**Reading: Background** Explain that U.S. citizens often tell government leaders about changes they want to see. Point out that this is a letter from a citizen who wanted the government to preserve the wilderness.

**Options for Reading** Read aloud selected sections to students. After discussing the sections, have students listen to the rest of the selection in the *Audio Anthology CD*.

## B Model the Skill: PRIMARY SOURCES

Model how to analyze the letter. Read the following phrase: "Without any remaining wilderness we are committed . . . to a headlong drive into our technological termite-life . . ." Explain that this phrase indicates that the author's purpose for saying this is that it is important to conserve our natural resources. It also hints that life in the United States was focused on technology.

***Possible answer:*** *Stegner's description suggests that litter, pollution, and highway construction are destroying the wilderness, while people are rushing toward a world dominated by technology.*

---

**COMMON CORE L 4**

### Language Coach

**Homographs** Words that have the same spelling but different meanings or pronunciations are **homographs**. Consider *permit*. Pronounced "PER mit," it means "a license." Pronounced "per MIT," it means "allow." Reread lines 19–22. Which meaning and pronunciation of *permit* is used in this passage?

---

**B PRIMARY SOURCES**
What does Stegner's description suggest about life in the United States at the time he wrote this?

---

Something will have gone out of us as a people if we ever let
20  the remaining wilderness be destroyed; if we permit the last
virgin forests to be turned into comic books and plastic cigarette
cases; if we drive the few remaining members of the wild species
into zoos or to extinction; if we pollute the last clear air and
dirty the last clean streams and push our paved roads through
the last of the silence, so that never again will Americans be free
in their own country from the noise, the exhausts, the stinks of
human and automotive waste. And so that never again can we
have the chance to see ourselves single, separate, vertical and
individual in the world, part of the environment of trees and
30  rocks and soil, brother to the other animals, part of the natural
world and competent to belong in it. Without any remaining
wilderness we are committed wholly, without chance for even
momentary reflection and rest, to a headlong drive into our
technological termite-life, the Brave New World[1] of a completely
man-controlled environment. We need wilderness preserved—as
much of it as is still left, and as many kinds—because it was the
challenge against which our character as a people was formed.
The reminder and the reassurance that it is still there is good for
our spiritual health even if we never once in ten years set foot
40  in it. It is good for us when we are young, because of the
incomparable sanity it can bring briefly, as vacation and rest, into
our insane lives. It is important to us when we are old simply
because it is there—important, that is, simply as idea. **B**

We are a wild species. . . . Nobody ever tamed or domesticated
or scientifically bred us. But for at least three millennia we have
been engaged in a cumulative and ambitious race to modify and
gain control of our environment, and in the process we have
come close to domesticating ourselves. Not many people are
likely, any more, to look upon what we call "progress" as an
50  unmixed blessing. Just as surely as it has brought us increased
comfort and more material goods, it has brought us spiritual
losses, and it threatens now to become the Frankenstein that will
destroy us. One means of sanity is to retain a hold on the
natural world, to remain, insofar as we can, good animals.
Americans still have that chance, more than many peoples; for
while we were demonstrating ourselves the most efficient and
ruthless environment-busters in history, and slashing and
burning and cutting our way through a wilderness continent, the
wilderness was working on us. It remains in us as surely as
60  Indian names remain on the land. If the abstract dream of
human liberty and human dignity became, in America, something

---

1. **Brave New World:** a reference to Aldous Huxley's 1932 science fiction novel, *Brave New World*, depicting a society in which happiness and the most basic natural life functions are controlled by technology.

---

## DIFFERENTIATED INSTRUCTION

### FOR ENGLISH LANGUAGE LEARNERS

### Language Coach     COMMON CORE L 4

**Homographs Answer:** *per-MIT; "allow"*
Have students work in pairs to identify one other homograph. Have volunteers share both meanings of their homographs.

### FOR ADVANCED LEARNERS/PRE–AP

**Evaluate** [paired-activity option] Stegner suggests that progress may "become the Frankenstein that will destroy us" (lines 52–53). What do you think he means by this dramatic statement?

more than an abstract dream, mark it down at least partially to the fact that we were in subtle ways subdued by what we conquered. . . . **C**

The American experience has been the confrontation by old peoples and cultures of a world as new as if it had just risen from the sea. That gave us our hope and our excitement, and the hope and excitement can be passed on to newer Americans, Americans who never saw any phase of the frontier. But only so 70 long as we keep the remainder of our wild as a reserve and a promise—a sort of wilderness bank. . . .

We need to demonstrate our acceptance of the natural world, including ourselves; we need the spiritual refreshment that being natural can produce. And one of the best places for us to get that is in the wilderness where the fun houses, the bulldozers, and the pavements of our civilization are shut out.

Sherwood Anderson, in a letter to Waldo Frank in the 1920's, said it better than I can. "Is it not likely that when the country was new and men were often alone in the fields and the forest 80 they got a sense of bigness outside themselves that has now in some way been lost . . . Mystery whispered in the grass, played in the branches of trees overhead, was caught up and blown across the American line in clouds of dust at evening on the prairies . . . I am old enough to remember tales that strengthen my belief in a deep semi-religious influence that was formerly at work among our people. The flavor of it hangs over the best work of Mark Twain . . . I can remember old fellows in my home town speaking feelingly of an evening spent on the big empty plains. It had taken the shrillness out of them. They had learned the trick 90 of quiet . . ."

We could learn it too, even yet; even our children and grand-children could learn it. But only if we save, for just such absolutely non-recreational, impractical, and mystical uses as this, all the wild that still remains to us. . . .

For myself, I grew up on the empty plains of Saskatchewan and Montana and in the mountains of Utah, and I put a very high valuation on what those places gave me. And if I had not been able periodically to renew myself in the mountains and deserts of western America I would be very near bughouse. Even 100 when I can't get to the back country, the thought of the colored deserts of southern Utah, or the reassurance that there are still stretches of prairie where the world can be instantaneously perceived as disk and bowl, and where the little but intensely important human being is exposed to the five directions and the thirty-six winds, is a positive consolation. The idea alone can

**C** PRIMARY SOURCES
What does Stegner say is one potential cost of "progress"?

---

INFORMATIONAL ANALYSIS    COMMON CORE
RI 1, RI 6

## **C** PRIMARY SOURCES

***Possible answer:** Stegner writes that progress has caused us "spiritual losses" (lines 51–52), taking us farther and farther away from the natural world.*

### IF STUDENTS NEED HELP . . .

- Have students read lines 48–60.
- Ask: What are the positive aspects of progress? *(lines 50–51)* What are the negative aspects? *(lines 51–53)*
- Ask: What represents "sanity" for Stegner? *(lines 53–54)*

## TIERED DISCUSSION PROMPTS

Use these prompts to help students understand Stegner's view of the value of nature:

**Connect** What effect does the experience of a peaceful natural environment—such as a forest or a seashore—have on your emotions? *Accept all thoughtful responses.*

**Analyze** Why does Stegner believe that preservation of the existing wilderness is so important? ***Possible answer:** The existing wilderness is all that remains of the wild that was. We need to preserve what's left of the natural world so that we can pass it on to future generations.*

**Synthesize** Do you think Stegner approves of national parks? Why or why not? ***Possible answers: Yes—** They protect the environment while allowing people to enjoy nature in a relatively unspoiled state. **No—** By allowing cars, concession stands, and the like, we are reducing nature to a poor imitation of the wild.*

---

## FOR ENGLISH LANGUAGE LEARNERS

**Language: Conversational English Patterns**
Help students understand some of the unusual word groups used by the author. Explain that the phrase *speaking feelingly* means "speaking with feeling" (line 88) and the phrase *as good a place as any* means "this place is as good as any other place" (line 134).

sustain me. But as the wilderness areas are progressively exploited or "improved," as the jeeps and bulldozers of uranium prospectors scar up the deserts and the roads are cut into the alpine timberlands, and as the remnants of the unspoiled and
110 natural world are progressively eroded, every such loss is a little death in me. In us. . . . **D**

Let me say something on the subject of the kinds of wilderness worth preserving. Most of those areas contemplated are in the national forests and in high mountain country. For all the usual recreational purposes, the alpine and forest wildernesses are obviously the most important, both as genetic banks and as beauty spots. But for the spiritual renewal, the recognition of identity, the birth of awe, other kinds will serve every bit as well. Perhaps, because they are less friendly to life, more abstractly
120 nonhuman, they will serve even better. On our Saskatchewan prairie, the nearest neighbor was four miles away, and at night we saw only two lights on all the dark rounding earth. The earth was full of animals—field mice, ground squirrels, weasels, ferrets, badgers, coyotes, burrowing owls, snakes. I knew them as my little brothers, as fellow creatures, and I have never been able to look upon animals in any other way since. The sky in that country came clear down to the ground on every side, and it was full of great weathers, and clouds, and winds, and hawks. I hope I learned something from knowing intimately the creatures of the
130 earth; I hope I learned something from looking a long way, from looking up, from being much alone. A prairie like that, one big enough to carry the eye clear to the sinking, rounding horizon, can be as lonely and grand and simple in its forms as the sea. It is as good a place as any for the wilderness experience to happen; the vanishing prairie is as worth preserving for the wilderness idea as the alpine forests.

So are great reaches of our western deserts, scarred somewhat by prospectors but otherwise open, beautiful, waiting. . . .

These are some of the things wilderness can do for us. That is
140 the reason we need to put into effect, for its preservation, some other principle than the principles of exploitation or "usefulness" or even recreation. We simply need that wild country available to us, even if we never do more than drive to its edge and look in. For it can be a means of reassuring ourselves of our sanity as creatures, a part of the geography of hope. **E**

Very sincerely yours,

Wallace Stegner

**D** PRIMARY SOURCES
Reread this paragraph. **Paraphrase** what Stegner is saying about the benefits of wilderness to his own life.

**E** PRIMARY SOURCES
Reread Stegner's closing paragraph. In a sentence, **summarize** his conclusion.

**DIFFERENTIATED INSTRUCTION**

**FOR STRUGGLING READERS**

**Vocabulary Support** Point out the words *exploited* (line 107) and *exploitation* (line 141). Explain that the base word *exploit* means "to make productive use of." Next, point out the words *improved* and *usefulness,* which follow *exploited* and *exploitation.* Explain that the author places quotation marks around these words to show that while others may believe that the tearing down of our wilderness has improved the usefulness of space, he doesn't.

## Comprehension

1. **Summarize** In Stegner's view, what is the danger for humans in losing touch with nature?

## Text Analysis

2. **Identify Author's Purpose** What does Stegner want Pesonen to understand?

● 3. **Analyze Primary Sources** Review the chart you developed as you read Stegner's letter. What was being done to wilderness areas at that time? Explain.

4. **Evaluate Author's Message** Stegner makes a point of distinguishing between the recreational value of the wilderness and its value as a source of spiritual renewal. Do you agree that this is an important difference? Include specific references to the text in your answer.

**COMMON CORE**

**RI 1** Cite textual evidence to support analysis of what the text says explicitly as well as inferences drawn from the text. **RI 2** Provide a summary of the text. **RI 6** Determine an author's purpose in a text. **W 2b** Develop the topic with well-chosen, relevant, and sufficient facts, quotations, and other information and examples.

## Read for Information: Cite Evidence

**WRITING PROMPT**
Bill Bryson and Wallace Stegner, each in his own way, have written in favor of wilderness areas. How are the pieces similar in this regard? How are they different? Support your response with specific quotations, ideas, and facts from Stegner's letter and Bryson's account.

The following steps will help you respond to the prompt:

1. Reread Bryson's narrative and Stegner's letter, looking for direct statements, facts, and anecdotes about wilderness areas.

2. Record direct quotations and summarize longer passages that seem relevant to your comparison. Note the author, source, and page numbers.

3. Review your notes and evaluate each item's usefulness in writing your comparison.

4. As you write your comparison, support your statements with direct quotations and citations of facts or anecdotes from these two sources. Always credit your sources and be sure to use quotation marks around direct quotations.

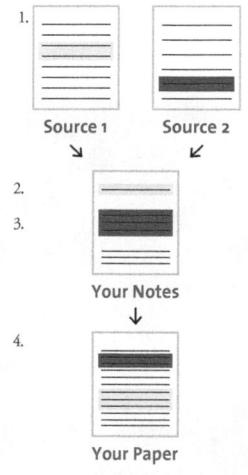

Source 1    Source 2

Your Notes

Your Paper

**FOR STRUGGLING WRITERS**
**Read for Information**

• Suggest that students first summarize similarities between the two pieces. Then have students explain the differences.

• Remind students to use quotation marks for direct quotations—that is, when they quote a person's exact words.

---

# Practice and Apply

For preliminary support of post-reading questions, use these copy masters:

 **RESOURCE MANAGER**—Copy Masters
Reading Check p. 117
Question Support p. 118
Cite Evidence p. 114

Additional selection questions are provided for teachers on page 109.

## ANSWERS

## Comprehension

1. *Possible answer: Stegner fears that people will not be able to connect with their history.*

## Text Analysis

*Possible answers:*

COMMON CORE RI 1, RI 2, RI 6

2. *Identify Author's Purpose The wilderness is a precious spiritual resource and has intrinsic value beyond practical uses.*

3. ● **COMMON CORE FOCUS** *Analyze Primary Sources Technological "progress" was causing the destruction of wilderness areas. For example, trees were being cut so paved roads could be built through wooded areas.*

4. *Evaluate Author's Message Students may agree or disagree but should develop their answers using specific textual references.*

## Read for Information: Cite Evidence

COMMON CORE W 2b

**Writing Prompt** *Students should support their comparisons with evidence from both texts.*

# Assess and Reteach

## Assess

**DIAGNOSTIC AND SELECTION TESTS**
Selection Test A, pp. 107–108
Selection Tests B/C, pp. 109–110

**Interactive Selection Test** on **thinkcentral.com**

## Reteach

**Level Up Online Tutorials** on **thinkcentral.com**

**Reteaching Worksheets** on **thinkcentral.com**
Vocabulary Lesson 20: Homonyms and Homographs

# Focus and Motivate

## COMMON CORE FOCUS

**RL 4** Analyze the cumulative impact of specific word choices on meaning and tone. **RL 10** Read and comprehend poems.

## SUMMARY

**"The Sharks"** The speaker of this poem by Denise Levertov dares to swim into deep water on her last day at the ocean. At sundown, the ocean fills with sharks, evoking fear and worry.

**"The Peace of Wild Things"** In this lyric poem by Wendell Berry, the speaker awakens, troubled by the state of the world. Lying down by a lake, he finds peace in proximity to nature's "wild things" that do not despair about the future.

## What are the different faces of NATURE?

Introduce the question and ask students to respond to it. Invite them to identify and describe different natural settings that display the different faces of nature before going on to complete the *DISCUSS* activity. Students can arrange their list of elements on a continuum from extremely soothing to terrifying.

---

## The Sharks
Poem by Denise Levertov

## The Peace of Wild Things
Poem by Wendell Berry

# What are the different faces of NATURE?

**COMMON CORE**

**RL 4** Analyze the cumulative impact of specific word choices on meaning and tone. **RL 10** Read and comprehend poems.

What do you think of when you hear the word *nature?* Storms? Flowers? Insects? Nature can have a variety of associations, such as peace, beauty, danger, and destruction. In the poems "The Sharks" and "The Peace of Wild Things," two poets describe sharply different faces of nature.

*DISCUSS* List eight elements of nature, four that you view as unsettling or frightening and four that you view as peaceful or soothing. After you have completed your list, get together with one or two classmates and compare notes.

406

---

# Selection Resources

See resources on the **Teacher One Stop DVD-ROM** *and on* <u>thinkcentral.com</u>.

 **RESOURCE MANAGER UNIT 3**
Plan and Teach, pp. 119–126
Text Analysis and Reading
Skill, pp. 127–130†‡

**DIAGNOSTIC AND SELECTION TESTS**
Selection Tests, pp. 111–114

**BEST PRACTICES TOOLKIT**
Draw It, p. A2

**TECHNOLOGY**
- Teacher One Stop DVD-ROM
- Student One Stop DVD-ROM
- Audio Anthology CD
- GrammarNotes DVD-ROM
- ExamView Test Generator on the **Teacher One Stop**

---

\* Resources for Differentiation       † Also in Spanish       ‡ In Haitian Creole and Vietnamese

## TEXT ANALYSIS: IMAGERY AND MOOD

To create **mood** in poetry, writers rely on **imagery**—words and phrases that appeal to the reader's senses.

*Dark fins appear, innocent*
*as if in fair warning.*

In the above example from "The Sharks," note how the visual image of "dark fins" helps establish a mood of sinister foreboding.

As you read each poem in this lesson, use a chart to keep track of words and phrases that evoke a particular mood.

| Imagery | Mood Created |
|---------|--------------|
| "Dark fins appear, innocent as if in fair warning." | foreboding, threatening |

## READING STRATEGY: CONNECT

Reading poetry can be a meaningful experience when you **connect** your own experiences and knowledge with the thoughts and feelings expressed in a poem. For example, consider the speaker's **tone** in "The Peace of Wild Things," the attitude the speaker takes toward nature. Your experiences in nature may have led you to form similar feelings—or left you with a different impression altogether.

By allowing yourself to connect with the experience revealed in a poem, you enhance your understanding of the speaker and the ideas conveyed. As you read, make use of the "connect" strategy whenever appropriate.

 Complete the activities in your **Reader/Writer Notebook**.

## Meet the Authors

### Denise Levertov
**1923–1997**

**Destined for Poetry**
Born in England, Denise Levertov (lĕv′ər-tôv′) grew up in a home full of books, reading, and lively conversation. She began writing when she was five, and once said that she knew "from an early age—perhaps by 7 . . . that I was an artist-person and had a destiny." She wrote all of her life, publishing more than 30 volumes of poetry and prose. In commenting on her work, she emphasized the need for "precision in poetry." Levertov immigrated to the United States in 1948 and, in addition to her writing, was passionately committed to causes of peace and social justice.

### Wendell Berry
**born 1934**

**A Love for the Land**
A novelist, essayist, and poet, Wendell Berry grew up on a farm in Kentucky. After starting a promising career as a writer and college professor in California and then New York City, Berry chose to return to Kentucky. There he has combined farming and writing in a life committed to conserving the land and preserving the values of small farms and communities. Berry's novels, essays, and poems reflect his love of nature, the richness of farm and family life, and his concerns about the world and its problems. He writes in a direct style that evokes the rural world he knows so well.

**Authors Online**
Go to thinkcentral.com. KEYWORD: HML9-407

**THINK** central

**407**

**TEXT ANALYSIS**          COMMON CORE
                                  RL 4

### Model the Skill: IMAGERY AND MOOD

For instructional support, read aloud this example:

A feathery fog settled upon the valley like a lazy lapdog. At high noon, it slipped away, searching for shade.

Help students identify words or images that appeal to the senses, such as "feathery fog settled," "like a lazy lapdog." Explain that they elicit a light-hearted mood.

**GUIDED PRACTICE** Ask students to suggest how to change the image to create a malevolent mood; they might start with "black choking smoke" instead of "feathery fog."

**R** RESOURCE MANAGER—Copy Master
Imagery and Mood p. 127 (for student use while reading the selection)

**READING SKILL**          COMMON CORE
                                 RL 4,
                                 RL 10

### Model the Skill: CONNECT

Encourage students to look at and respond to the photograph of the lightning storm on page 406 as you describe your own response to the photo. *(Example: The photo makes me feel awe at the beauty of nature, and a little scared also. It reminds me of the times I have seen lightning strike and makes me think of the sound that makes.)*

**GUIDED PRACTICE** Have students describe their reaction to the photograph, then cover up the lightning. What reaction do they have to the picture now? Are their feelings different with the lightning covered up? Why or why not?

## DIFFERENTIATED INSTRUCTION

### FOR STRUGGLING READERS

**Imagery and Mood** Have students close their eyes and imagine walking in a meadow on a sunny summer afternoon. What images do they see, hear, and smell? How does this scene make them feel? Ask them to be as specific as possible. Continue this activity by having students picture the changes that a sudden storm would create. Use Draw It to have students create on paper the images they imagined.

 **BEST PRACTICES TOOLKIT**
Draw It, p. A2

## READ WITH A PURPOSE

*Ask students to set a purpose for reading. Remind them that poets use language to express tone and mood as well as ideas. Encourage students to read closely to identify the tone or mood expressed in each poem.*

**TEXT ANALYSIS**

COMMON CORE
RL 4

###  *Model the Skill:* IMAGERY AND MOOD

To model the skill, remind students that mood is the feeling the author creates through images and specific words. Discuss the meaning of *warning* in line 3 ("an alert") and *sinister* in line 4 ("evil or threatening") before asking students how these words and the image of dark fins in line 2 make them feel.

***Possible answer:*** *The image of dark fins (line 2) and the words* warning *and* sinister *help to establish the ominous mood.*

# THE
# SHARKS
### Denise Levertov

Well then, the last day the sharks appeared.
Dark fins appear, innocent
as if in fair warning. The sea becomes
sinister, are they everywhere? **Ⓐ**
5 I tell you, they break six feet of water.[1]
Isn't it the same sea, and won't we
play in it any more?
I liked it clear and not
too calm, enough waves
10 to fly in on. For the first time
I dared to swim out of my depth.
It was sundown when they came, the time
when a sheen of copper stills the sea,
not dark enough for moonlight, clear enough
15 to see them easily. Dark
the sharp lift of the fins.

**Ⓐ** IMAGERY AND MOOD
Reread lines 1–4. What is the mood at the beginning of this poem? Which words and images help establish this mood?

**Analyze Visuals ▶**
How does the photograph reflect the mood of the poem?

1. **they break ... water:** Sharks often show their dorsal fin if water is shallow enough.

## DIFFERENTIATED INSTRUCTION

### FOR ENGLISH LANGUAGE LEARNERS
**Language: Idiom** Remind students that *depth* is how deep something is. *Out of my depth* can literally mean "deeper than I can comfortably swim in." The expression can also be used idiomatically to refer to a feeling of discomfort or of being overwhelmed. Tell students that in this context both the literal and figurative meanings make sense.

### FOR STRUGGLING READERS
**Develop Reading Fluency** Read aloud each poem, emphasizing the dark, sinister mood of "Sharks" and the transcendent, mystical feeling of "The Peace of Wild Things." Point out that neither poem rhymes and that the end of a line does not necessarily indicate the end of a thought. Assign each poem to three or four students and ask them to divide it among themselves using logical breaks. They should then practice and present a reading.

**R** RESOURCE MANAGER—Copy Master
Reading Fluency p. 132

Use these prompts to focus on how the speaker's actions reveal the poem's theme in lines 8–16:

**Connect** Have you ever seen the ocean? If not, what do you imagine that it looks like? Describe. *Students may describe personal experiences as well as what they know from movies or television.*

**Analyze** What kind of person likes "enough waves / to fly in on" ( lines 9–10)? *Possible answer: These lines describe a somewhat timid person who seems to long for adventure (for a sea that is "not / too calm") but takes only moderate risk, maintaining safe parameters.*

**Evaluate** How do the speaker's actions and attitude help us infer the poem's theme? *Possible answer: The speaker is like many people who take measured risks: when she ventures too far, she confronts real or imagined danger. The poem's theme, taking risks (and venturing beyond one's comfort zone), means confronting dangerous situations and our fears of them.*

**REVISIT THE BIG QUESTION**

## What are the different faces of **NATURE?**

**Discuss** What faces of nature does Levertov portray in "The Sharks"? *Possible answer: She portrays nature as unpredictable and frightening.*

## Analyze Visuals

*Possible answer: The large, menacing black fin slicing through the clear blue water and the shadows around it capture the poem's frightening mood.*

**FOR STRUGGLING READERS**

**Characterization** To help students understand the speaker's apprehension, ask: Would a fearless person swim close to shore? What kind of water would a fearless person want to swim in? Why did the speaker wait until the last day to dare to swim out of her depth (lines 10–11)?

**FOR ADVANCED LEARNERS/PRE–AP**

**Symbolism** Discuss how the sharks symbolize the speaker's fears about becoming an adult and accepting the responsibilities, as well as the independence, of adulthood. Which time words in the poem reinforce the idea that the speaker is on the verge of a change or major transition in her life? Invite students to speculate about why the speaker asks, "won't we / play in it [the sea] any more?" (lines 6–7)

READING SKILL

COMMON CORE

**B** *Model the Skill:* **CONNECT**  RL 4, RL 10

To model connecting to the poem, describe for students a specific time when you enjoyed nature. Include a description of how exposure to the natural world affected your mood. Then connect it to the poem. *Example: When I go to the beach, I find the rhythm and sound of the waves soothing. The ocean also reminds me of how large the earth is and shows that it is all connected. The poet expresses this same feeling of oneness with the natural world.*

*Possible answer: Students are likely to share the speaker's feeling that nature is a comfort and refuge from everyday life.*

**Extend the Discussion** How do the images in lines 8–10 convey the poem's peaceful and comforting mood?

**REVISIT THE BIG QUESTION**

## What are the different faces of **NATURE?**

**Discuss** What aspects of nature give the speaker the greatest comfort? ***Possible answer:*** *The speaker finds comfort lying near a marsh or lake with the stars shining overhead.*

## Analyze Visuals

**Activity** How does this photo reflect the poem's mood? ***Possible answer:*** *It shows a duck afloat in still water. The mood is peaceful and soothing.*

## SELECTION WRAP–UP

**READ WITH A PURPOSE** Now that students have read both poems ask: what do the poems have in common? ***Possible answer:*** *They both have a reverence for nature.*

⭐ **CRITIQUE** Nature is the setting for both poems. How effectively does each poem use this setting to develop its theme?

## INDEPENDENT READING

For more poems on nature, recommend Adrienne Adams' *Poetry of Earth and Sky.*

# The Peace of Wild Things
## Wendell Berry

When despair for the world grows in me
and I wake in the night at the least sound
in fear of what my life and my children's lives may be,
I go and lie down where the wood drake[1]
5 rests in his beauty on the water, and the great heron feeds.
I come into the peace of wild things
who do not tax their lives with forethought
of grief. I come into the presence of still water.
And I feel above me the day-blind stars
10 waiting with their light. For a time
I rest in the grace of the world, and am free. **B**

---

1. **wood drake:** a type of male duck.

**B** CONNECT
Think about how you feel when you walk in the woods, alongside a lake, or through a scenic park. In what ways does your experience connect with the speaker's ideas?

## DIFFERENTIATED INSTRUCTION

**FOR ADVANCED LEARNERS/PRE–AP**

**Analyze Language** Ask students to consider the last sentence of the poem. Ask them to write a short paragraph in which they explain their understanding of what the author means by "the grace of the world" and why and how it provides rest and freedom for him.

## Comprehension

1. **Recall** What situation is presented in "The Sharks"?

2. **Summarize** What problem does the speaker in "The Peace of Wild Things" experience, and what does he do about it?

## Text Analysis

● 3. **Connect** As you read the poems, what connections were you able to make? Which of these had the strongest impact? Explain why, citing specific words and details in each poem.

4. **Identify Speaker** In "The Sharks," whom do you imagine the speaker to be? Consider the evidence in the poem about the speaker's age and situation. Remember that the speaker and the poet are not necessarily the same person.

5. **Analyze Speaker** Reread line 1 of "The Peace of Wild Things." Considering the speaker's "despair for the world," how would you describe the speaker?

6. **Compare and Contrast** Describe the faces of nature presented in each poem. What differences do you see in the comfort level each speaker has with his or her natural surroundings? Are there any similarities in their attitudes toward nature? Support your conclusions.

● 7. **Evaluate Mood** Review the charts you filled in as you read the poems. What overall mood is created by each poem? How effective are the **images** in creating each mood? Explain your opinion.

8. **Compare Literary Works** Reread Wallace Stegner's "Wilderness Letter" on pages 401–404. Which of Stegner's ideas does "The Peace of Wild Things" support?

## Text Criticism

9. **Historical Perspective** Reread "The Peace of Wild Things." Is Berry's perspective strictly a modern one? Might a person living 200 years ago, for example, have felt this same "despair for the world"? Give reasons for your opinions.

> ### What are the different faces of NATURE?
> How does your definition of nature influence the way you interact with it?

**COMMON CORE**

RL 4 Analyze the cumulative impact of specific word choices on meaning and tone. RL 10 Read and comprehend poems.

---

# Practice and Apply

For preliminary support of post-reading questions, use these copy masters:

**R** **RESOURCE MANAGER—Copy Masters**
Imagery and Mood p. 127
Question Support p. 131

Additional selection questions are provided for teachers on page 123.

## ANSWERS

## Comprehension

1. *The speaker has ventured too far into the ocean and is surrounded by sharks.*

2. *Unable to sleep because of his despair over the state of the contemporary world, the speaker eases his distress by going into nature.*

## Text Analysis

COMMON CORE RL 4, RL 10

*Possible answers:*

3. ● **COMMON CORE FOCUS** *Connect Answers and details will vary, but students may connect with fear in the first poem, peace in the second.*

4. *The speaker in "The Sharks" is likely a timid person on the verge of maturity, at the end of a vacation (lines 1, 6–7, 11).*

5. *The speaker is a parent who worries about the world that he and his generation are bequeathing to their heirs (lines 1–3).*

6. *"The Sharks" presents nature's terrifying face; "The Peace of Wild Things," nature's soothing face. The first speaker's fears keep her from venturing far from shore. The second speaker's ease in nature enables him to find solace near a marsh. Both speakers acknowledge nature's power and influence on their feelings (lines 3–5 of the first poem and lines 8–11 of the second).*

---

7. ● **COMMON CORE FOCUS** *Evaluate Mood The frightening mood of the first poem is created by alarming images of "Dark fins." The calm, comforting mood of the second poem is created by the peaceful images of a wood drake resting on water and a great heron feeding, and by the consoling image of "the day-blind stars / waiting with their light."*

8. *According to both selections, nature is important for spiritual well-being.*

## Text Criticism
*Possible answer:*

9. *People 200 years ago may have felt a similar despair because the Industrial Revolution was disrupting lives.*

> ### What are the different faces of NATURE?
> *Students may recognize that our feelings about nature depend on whether we see ourselves as part of nature or separate from it in a given situation.*

---

# Assess and Reteach

## Assess

**DIAGNOSTIC AND SELECTION TESTS**
Selection Test A, pp. 111–112
Selection Test B/C, pp. 113–114

**Interactive Selection Test** on **thinkcentral.com**

## Reteach

**Level Up Online Tutorials** on **thinkcentral.com**

# Focus and Motivate

## COMMON CORE FOCUS

**W 3a–e** Write narratives to develop real or imagined experiences or events using effective techniques, well-chosen details, and well-structured event sequences. **W 4** Produce clear and coherent writing in which the development, organization, and style are appropriate to task, purpose, and audience. **W 5** Develop and strengthen writing as needed by planning, revising, editing, rewriting, or trying a new approach. **W 10** Write routinely over shorter time frames for a range of tasks, purposes, and audiences. **L 1b** Use participial phrases to convey specific meanings and add variety and interest to writing. **L 2** Demonstrate command of the conventions of standard English capitalization, punctuation, and spelling.

## WRITE WITH A PURPOSE

Recommend that students choose real-world events or characters to inspire their stories. Such choices will enhance students' abilities to develop their plots and fulfill the purpose of expressing a theme or observation about life.

## COMMON CORE TRAITS

Review the **COMMON CORE TRAITS** with students, focusing primarily on development of ideas and organization of ideas. Compare the list of traits with the rubric on page 420.

## ADDITIONAL TASKS

**Write About Art** Identify a work of art that suggests a story to you. Create a story revolving around one of the characters, the setting, or the situation depicted.

**Possible subjects:** *The Mysteries of Harris Burdick* by Chris Van Allsburg, people in transit, people in conversation

**Write as an Advertiser** Write an advertisement in which a product speaks and tells a story that illustrates one of its features.

**Possible subjects:** telephone that can call 9-1-1 or a backpack with a tracking device

### Writing Online

The following tools are available online at **thinkcentral.com** and on **Write*Smart* CD-ROM:**
- Interactive Graphic Organizers
- Interactive Student Models
- Interactive Revision Lessons

---

## Writing Workshop
**NARRATIVE**

# Short Story
**Essential Course of Study**  **ECOS**

The power of storytelling is evident in the literature you have read in this unit and in the stories you encounter in everyday life. Now, you have an opportunity to invent a story of your own. In this workshop, you will write a **short story**—a narrative that includes characters, a setting, a plot, a conflict, a resolution, and a theme. You will use techniques such as dialogue, description, and pacing to develop your story and engage readers.

Complete the workshop activities in your **Reader/Writer Notebook.**

### WRITE WITH A PURPOSE

#### WRITING TASK

Write a **short story** in which you develop characters, a setting, plot events, a conflict, a resolution, and a theme. You can use real-world or imagined events, issues, or people to inspire your story.

**Idea Starters**
- newspaper articles on events, scientific discoveries, or weather disasters
- magazine features that profile interesting people
- situations that you have observed or experienced, such as a conflict among siblings

#### THE ESSENTIALS

Here are some common purposes, audiences, and formats for short story writing.

| PURPOSES | AUDIENCES | FORMATS |
|---|---|---|
| • to entertain<br>• to express a theme or observation about life | • classmates and teacher<br>• contest judges<br>• younger students | • literary magazine<br>• school newspaper<br>• student writing contest<br>• blog readers |

### COMMON CORE TRAITS

**1. DEVELOPMENT OF IDEAS**
- introduces, develops, and resolves a **central conflict**
- introduces and develops a **narrator** and **characters**
- uses **dialogue** and **description** to develop the plot
- provides a **conclusion** that follows from story events
- reflects a **theme,** or message, about life

**2. ORGANIZATION OF IDEAS**
- presents a smooth **sequence of events** to create a coherent story
- uses effective **pacing**

**3. LANGUAGE FACILITY AND CONVENTIONS**
- maintains a **point of view**
- uses the **active voice** consistently
- includes **precise words and phrases, telling details,** and **sensory language**
- uses **quotation marks** and **participles** correctly
- employs correct **grammar, mechanics,** and **spelling**

**Writing Online** THINK central

Go to **thinkcentral.com.**
KEYWORD: HML9N-412

---

## Writing Workshop Resources

**R RESOURCE MANAGER UNIT 3**
Plan and Teach pp. 133–136
Prewriting–Editing pp. 137–141
Writing Rubric p. 142
Technology p. 143
Writing Support p. 144*

 **BEST PRACTICES TOOLKIT**
Writing Template: Short Story pp. C16, C39

**TECHNOLOGY**
- 🔘 **Teacher One Stop DVD-ROM**
- 🔘 **Student One Stop DVD-ROM**
- 🔘 **Write*Smart* CD-ROM**
- 🔘 **GrammarNotes DVD-ROM**

**Writing Center on thinkcentral.com**

*See resources on the* **Teacher One Stop DVD-ROM** *and on* **thinkcentral.com.**

* Resources for Differentiation

## Planning/Prewriting

 COMMON CORE

**W 3a-e** Write narratives to develop real or imagined experiences or events using effective techniques, well-chosen details, and well-structured event sequences. **W 5** Develop and strengthen writing as needed by planning.

### Getting Started

**CHOOSE A STORY TO TELL**

Brainstorm ideas for possible **plots, characters, settings,** or **themes.** Use a web diagram to record these ideas. Then, highlight the ideas that seem most promising. You can also choose a photograph, a print advertisement, or another visual as a prompt for story writing.

▶ **WHAT DOES IT LOOK LIKE?**

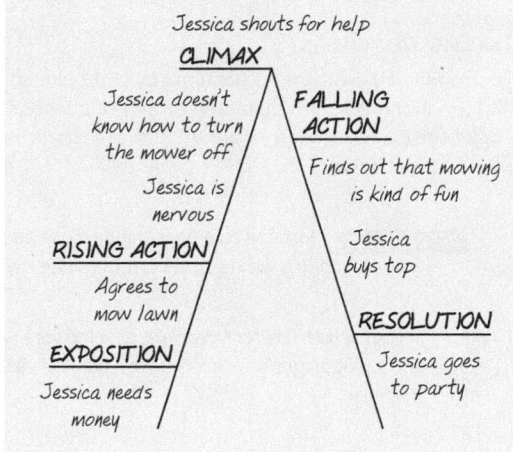

```
songwriter gets          girl finds out she's
rich, can't write        tougher than she
songs anymore                thought
              Story Ideas
boy gets revenge         pet dog saves
on brother who           child from
   ignores him             drowning
```

**FLESH OUT YOUR CHARACTERS**

You want your **characters** to seem like real people. To accomplish this goal, you will want to include well-chosen details that show how each character looks, speaks, and relates to other characters. You will also want to determine what conflicts each character faces. Creating a character chart can help you plan and develop distinct and interesting characters.

▶ **WHAT DOES IT LOOK LIKE?**

| Characters | Details |
|---|---|
| Jessica | has manicure; likes to look good; favorite color is pink; goes to lots of parties; doesn't like to be viewed as weak |
| John | older; teases his sister but thinks she's OK; willing to help her |

**MAP YOUR STORY**

Create a diagram to plan the **plot** of your story. Begin with the **exposition** by introducing the **characters** and **setting** and by setting out a **conflict**—a problem or situation to be solved. Identify the complications you will introduce in the **rising action.** Then, determine the **climax,** or the most important or exciting event in the plot. Finally, chart the **falling action** and **resolution**—how the conflict is resolved or solved.

As you begin to plan your story, keep **pacing** in mind. In a well-paced story, the action keeps moving from one event to the next and the writer doesn't linger too long on unimportant details.

**TIP** If you plan to write a longer short story, experiment with **multiple plot lines,** or subplots that relate to the main plot or central conflict.

▶ **WHAT DOES IT LOOK LIKE?**

```
                Jessica shouts for help
                      CLIMAX
Jessica doesn't              FALLING
know how to turn             ACTION
the mower off
                          Finds out that mowing
Jessica is                  is kind of fun
nervous
                          Jessica
RISING ACTION             buys top

Agrees to                      RESOLUTION
mow lawn
EXPOSITION                Jessica goes
                          to party
Jessica needs
money
```

WRITING WORKSHOP **413**

---

## DIFFERENTIATED INSTRUCTION

### FOR ENGLISH LANGUAGE LEARNERS

**Using Content-area Vocabulary** To provide students with practice in writing using content-area vocabulary, ask them to write a response to this prompt: Write a paragraph that tells about the most memorable story you have read. Be sure to include the following information: the story's title and author, the main characters, the setting, the conflict and its resolution, and the story's theme.

Before students write their paragraphs, give a brief review of the following terms: conflict, resolution, character, setting, and theme. Tell students that the story they select can be one in their native language or a story they have read in English. Have students share their completed paragraphs in a small group.

---

## Teach

### Planning/Prewriting

 COMMON CORE **W 3a-e, W 5**

▶ **CHOOSE A STORY TO TELL** Tell students that another way to brainstorm ideas for a story is to recall familiar plots from fables or books. Then, students can change important elements, such as characters or settings. For example, the fable of the tortoise and the hare might be retold through human characters who race toward a distant star. Have pairs of students work together to brainstorm familiar stories and various ways they might be changed.

▶ **FLESH OUT YOUR CHARACTERS** List several famous people who are familiar to the entire class such as musicians, actors, or athletes. Have students take turns describing unspecified people from the list. Ask the class to identify each person being described. Make sure that students understand the significance of revealing well-chosen character details.

▶ **MAP YOUR STORY** Urge students to experiment with a variety of graphic organizers, including Story Frames and Sequence Chains. Point out that story graphic organizers do not have to be completed sequentially. Students may start at any point and then work backward or forward as needed. Explain that the completed graphic organizers will provide a focus on key events, which will help the pacing of their stories.

**BEST PRACTICES TOOLKIT—Transparencies**

Story Map p. D59
Sequence Chain p. B45

**R RESOURCE MANAGER—Copy Masters**

Planning/Prewriting p. 137
Drafting p. 138
Revising and Editing pp. 139–140
Ask a Peer Reader p. 141
Rubric p. 142
Writing Support p. 144

## Planning/Prewriting *continued*

▶ **CHOOSE A POINT OF VIEW** Make sure that students understand that point of view is linked to purpose. With which characters do writers want readers to sympathize and why? If writers want readers to sympathize with one character more than any other, they should choose a first-person or limited third-person point of view. If writers want readers to understand how a particular event impacts several characters, they may want to choose an omniscient third-person narrator. Point out that another effective storytelling strategy is to tell the story from multiple points of view by having more than one narrator.

▶ **CREATE SUSPENSE** Make sure that students understand that suspense propels readers through a story. In other words, suspense keeps readers reading because they must continue reading the story to find out what will happen next. Ask students whether they've ever read a book or seen a movie that they couldn't leave without finding out how the story ended. Lead students to discuss how the writer or producer created suspense in each example. List students' ideas on the board.

**YOUR TURN** As students work to develop a writing plan, suggest that they mentally fill each character role with a familiar actor. They may also obtain photographs of these actors from magazines or the Internet. These visual images will help students assign ages, educational backgrounds, mannerisms, and so on to each character.

For interactive revision tools, see

💿 **Write*Smart* CD-ROM**

**Writing Center** on **thinkcentral.com**

---

## Planning/Prewriting *continued*

### Getting Started

**CHOOSE A POINT OF VIEW**
Decide who will tell your story. Consider the following information as you choose your narrator.

**First-Person Narrator**
**Who:** a character in the story
**Pronouns:** *I, we, my*
**Knows:** only what character knows
**Effect:** creates sympathy for one character

**Third-Person Limited Narrator**
**Who:** not a character in the story
**Pronouns:** *he, she, they*
**Knows:** only what one character knows
**Effect:** creates sympathy for one character and distance from other characters

**Third-Person Omniscient Narrator**
**Who:** not a character in the story
**Pronouns:** *he, she, they*
**Knows:** what all characters know
**Effect:** broad view of characters and events

> **TIP** If you are writing a longer short story, you might create sections told by different first-person narrators. Weaving in **multiple points of view** can give readers more than one perspective on the characters, setting, and plot.

▶ **WHAT DOES IT LOOK LIKE?**

**First-Person Narrator**

> *We went to the garage, and John pulled out the mower for me.*

▶ **Third-Person Limited Narrator**

> *Jessica, relieved to get some help from her brother, went to the garage to retrieve the mower.*

▶ **Third-Person Omniscient Narrator**

> *John was amused that his sister couldn't operate a lawn mower. Jessica was not amused.*

**CREATE SUSPENSE**
Use point of view to create **suspense** by withholding information from both characters and the audience, or let the audience know information that a character does not yet know.

▶ **WHAT DOES IT LOOK LIKE?**

> *"John!" she shouted, but there was no way he could hear her. Watching from an upstairs window, John moved to help Jessica but then stopped.*

**PEER REVIEW** Describe to a peer the purpose and audience of your short story. Then, ask: Which point of view would best communicate my purpose?

**YOUR TURN** In your *Reader/Writer Notebook*, develop your writing plan. Create a character chart and a plot diagram. Then, choose a point of view and think about how you might build suspense.

---

## DIFFERENTIATED INSTRUCTION

### FOR STRUGGLING WRITERS
**Use Dialogue** To help students create lively dialogue, suggest that they follow these tips:

- Write each character's words first. When you are satisfied with the words, go back to insert punctuation and speaker tags.

- Use precise words to create speaker tags: *begged, insisted, snapped, hollered, squeaked,* and so on. Develop a reference bank of words that can be used in place of the word *said.*

- Vary the placement of speaker tags. These tags can come at the beginning or end of dialogue. They can also be inserted within a line of dialogue: "Stop running!" Beth shouted. "You're going to trip."

### FOR ADVANCED LEARNERS/PRE–AP
**In-Depth Analysis** Have students use the Analysis Frame to analyze a favorite author's style. Challenge students to employ some of these same style elements in their short stories.

 **BEST PRACTICES TOOLKIT—Transparency** Analysis Frame: Author's Craft pp. D24, D25

# Drafting

 **COMMON CORE** W 4 Produce clear and coherent writing in which the development, organization, and style are appropriate to task, purpose, and audience. L 1b Use participial phrases to convey specific meanings and add variety and interest to writing.

The following chart shows a structure for organizing an effective short story.

## Organizing Your Short Story

### EXPOSITION

- Engage and orient your readers with **action** or **dialogue** that sets up a **central conflict,** problem, or situation.
- Establish a **point of view** by introducing a **narrator,** or the voice that tells the story.
- Introduce the audience to the **characters** and **setting.**

### RISING ACTION AND CLIMAX

- Include the **plot** events that build suspense and lead up to a **climax.** Do not include events that do not move the plot forward.
- Use **pacing** that keeps the action moving and smoothly progresses from one event to the next.
- Employ techniques such as **dialogue** to develop events, characters, and suspense.
- Use **precise words and phrases, telling details,** and **sensory language** to convey a vivid picture of the setting, events, and characters.

### FALLING ACTION AND RESOLUTION

- Explain how the **conflict** is resolved or solved.
- Tie up loose **plot points,** and add a **surprise** for the audience.
- Leave the audience with something to reflect on, perhaps by clarifying your story's **theme,** or central message.

## GRAMMAR IN CONTEXT: PARTICIPLES

A *participle* is a verb form that can be used as an adjective. Verbals, such as participles, add color and telling details to writing. A present participle ends with *-ing*. Past participles use the same form as the past tense of the verb; these usually end with *-ed*.

| | |
|---|---|
| Present Participle | She pulled tentatively, and the mower let out a brief, *unnerving* growl. |
| Past Participle | "In this heat?" she asked, fanning herself with *manicured* nails. |
| Irregular Past Participle | Jessica, *known* for her girlish ways, was not interested in mowing the lawn. |

 **YOUR TURN** Develop a first draft of your short story following the structure outlined in the chart above. As you write, use participles to add colorful details to your story.

## FOR ENGLISH LANGUAGE LEARNERS

**Verb Bank** Display a list of English verbs: *ask, burn, cry, deal, eat, save, see, shake,* and *smile.* Have students work with partners to create and record present and past participles for each verb. Help students with irregular past participles as needed. Then, have students create sentences using the participles. Invite partners to present some of their sentences to the class. Leave the list on display so that students may reference it during the writing process.

## FOR STRUGGLING WRITERS

**Word Search** Provide students with copies of a page from a fiction text. Have partners use colored pens to circle any participle examples they find on the page. Then, tell students to discuss the impact of these examples on the author's writing and the reader's reaction to the text. To facilitate this discussion, tell students to read the sentences aloud first without the participles and then again with them. Have each pair present a few textual examples and a summary of their discussion to the class.

---

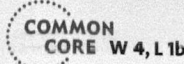

# Practice and Apply

## Drafting

**COMMON CORE** W 4, L 1b

▶ *EXPOSITION* Model for students how to begin the same story using action, dialogue, and sensory description. Lead students to discuss the benefits and disadvantages of each lead for this particular story. Then suggest that students also write more than one exposition for their stories. Have students meet with partners to discuss the benefits and disadvantages of each lead before selecting one. Suggest that students save any rejected expositions for possible later use.

▶ *RISING ACTION AND CLIMAX* Remind students that all the events in a plot should be linked tightly to the climax. Each preceding event should lead logically to the next as these events build toward the climax. The subsequent events should lead logically toward the resolution. Any extraneous events should be eliminated. Suggest that students think about these events as links in a chain. Each link is essential to maintaining the chain; extraneous links are unnecessary.

▶ *FALLING ACTION AND RESOLUTION* Explain that although a resolution may prove surprising for readers, it should not introduce ideas or characters that are entirely new. Such resolutions undermine the credibility of the preceding stories. For example, no reader wants to spend time reading a mystery only to find that the culprit is a character who has never appeared in the story.

### GRAMMAR IN CONTEXT: PARTICIPLES

For additional practice, have students add different participles to the following sentences.

- She pulled tentatively, and the mower let out a brief, _____ growl.
- "In this heat?" she asked, fanning herself with _____ nails.

 **YOUR TURN** Ask students to complete the **Your Turn** activity independently. Remind students to use participles to add color and telling details to their writing. Suggest that students write their drafts double-spaced so that they can make revisions easily later.

For interactive revision tools, see

 **Write*Smart* CD-ROM**

**Writing Center** on <u>thinkcentral.com</u>

## Revising

**Model the Skill** Using a draft short story on a transparency or electronic whiteboard, model how to use the questions, tips, and strategies suggested in the chart to evaluate and revise. You might use the story of a student from another class or from a previous year. Make sure to remove the student's name from the story so that the writer remains anonymous.

**YOUR TURN** During peer review, remind students to look directly into the eyes of their partners during the discussion. Students should nod their heads from time to time as their partners speak. These nonverbal techniques send the message that one is listening and interested in participating.

For interactive revision tools, see

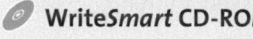

**WriteSmart CD-ROM**

**Writing Center** on thinkcentral.com

---

## Revising

As you revise, consider the characters, setting, pacing, and plot elements of your short story. The goal is to determine whether you've achieved your purpose and effectively communicated your ideas to the intended audience. The following chart will help you determine which parts of your draft need rewriting or a new approach.

### SHORT STORY

| Ask Yourself | Tips | Revision Strategies |
|---|---|---|
| 1. Does the exposition grab the attention of the audience? | ▶ **Draw a box** around the dialogue, action, or description that engages readers. | ▶ **Add** dialogue, action, or description. Provide just enough details to force the audience to ask a question that will be answered only if they continue to read. |
| 2. Are the characters believable? | ▶ **Place a star** next to each instance of dialogue and realistic character description. | ▶ **Add** believable dialogue that includes contractions, slang, pauses, jargon, or exclamations that match each character's age and personality. |
| 3. Is the setting vivid? | ▶ **Draw** an arrow next to each sensory detail. | ▶ **Add** sensory details to describe the time and place of action. **Include** details that appeal to a variety of senses. |
| 4. Is the conflict clear? Do the plot events build toward a climax? | ▶ **Underline** each detail that tells something about the conflict. **Bracket** the climax. **Draw a line** from each event in the rising action to the climax. | ▶ **Add** details to develop the conflict. **Add** transitions or details to create a smooth progression of events, so that each event clearly leads to the climax. |
| 5. Does the pacing keep the action moving? | ▶ **Draw a wavy line** under any details that are unrelated to the central conflict. | ▶ **Delete** any unnecessary details to tighten the pace and propel the action forward. |
| 6. Does the resolution contain a message or lesson for the audience as well as the characters? | ▶ **Write** the theme of the story on a sticky note. **Ask** your partner to write the theme of the story on another sticky note. **Compare** the two statements of theme for similarities. | ▶ **Add** concluding dialogue or action that makes the story's theme clear. |

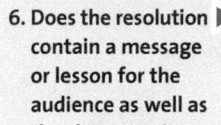

**YOUR TURN**  **PEER REVIEW** Exchange your short story with a classmate, or read your story aloud to your partner. As you read and discuss the two stories, make sure to focus on character and plot. Discuss how each writer develops these elements through dialogue, suspense, and sensory detail. If your story is not flowing smoothly, use the revision strategies in the chart to rework and tighten your writing.

---

## DIFFERENTIATED INSTRUCTION

### FOR ENGLISH LANGUAGE LEARNERS

**Transitions** Make sure that students recognize signal words and phrases that indicate sequence. Explain that many stories are told in the order in which events happen. Writers use signal words and phrases to make this order of events clear. Provide the following examples, and point out that they appear in chronological order: *At first, Jessica was afraid of the mower. Later, she lost her fear. She imagined mowing flowers some day.* Finally, display an illustration of a sequence, such as a seed sprouting or a child growing older. Ask students to tell what is happening and to use signal words and phrases to make the order clear.

## ANALYZE A STUDENT DRAFT

Read this draft; notice the comments on its strengths as well as suggestions for improvement.

**COMMON CORE**

**W 5** Develop and strengthen writing as needed by revising, editing, rewriting, or trying a new approach, focusing on addressing what is most significant for a specific purpose and audience.

### Tough Enough

by Sarah Yovovich, Evanston Township High School

"Just lend me ten bucks, John," Jessica begged. "Come on!"

"I'm sure the shirt is very cute and pink and perfect, Sis, but I don't have the ten. Now move—I gotta mow the lawn."

"In this heat?" she asked, fanning herself with manicured nails.

"You know, Mom and Dad pay me ten bucks to mow," John said.

"Oh! So you can lend it to me after you finish?"

He snorted. "Yeah, right. I'll let you mow the lawn, though."

"No way! That mower's heavy!" Jessica said, her eyes wide.

"What's that I hear? Oh, it's the sound of a thousand cute tops crying!"

"Shut up and show me how this thing works," she snapped. They went to the garage, and John pulled out the mower for her.

"So, I just pull this cord?" She pulled tentatively, and the mower let out a brief, unnerving growl. Jessica jumped back and let out an "Eep!"

"It's fine, Jess. Pull as hard as you can," John said. Jessica braced herself and pulled. The mower roared to life. Her confident look amused John.

"Good job!" he hollered. "Go to it!"

"Wait!" she squeaked, but he was gone. She took a deep breath and nudged the mower forward a few inches. It made a hideous *crrrunch* as twigs were chewed and spat out. She shrieked, thinking of how "cute" she would look with missing toes. The mower kept roaring, and she realized that she didn't know how to turn it off.

> **Dialogue** and **descriptive details** reveal the characters' personalities.

> The narrative maintains a consistent third-person **point of view.**

> Sarah uses lively **sensory language** to show readers how it felt to mow the lawn. However, the story would be more engaging if Sarah used the **active voice** throughout the narrative.

**LEARN HOW** Use Active Voice When the subject performs the action, the verb is in the active voice: *Jessica mowed the lawn.* In the passive voice, the subject is acted upon: *The lawn was mowed by Jessica.* In the paragraph above, Sarah lapses into the passive voice; her story will be livelier if she uses the active voice.

#### SARAH'S REVISION

"Wait!" she squeaked, but he was gone. She took a deep breath and nudged the mower forward a few inches. It made a hideous *crrrunch* as ~~twigs were chewed and spat out.~~ *it chewed up some twigs and spat out their remains.*

WRITING WORKSHOP **417**

---

## ANALYZE A STUDENT DRAFT

Explain that the Student Draft on this page is the first half of a short story. Model reading the draft and the annotations in blue, explaining that the yellow highlighting illustrates the student's language choices. Explain that the following *Learn How* mini-lessons provide helpful information about ways to improve this student draft as well as students' own drafts.

**LEARN HOW** Use Active Voice

Explain that passive verbs include a form of the verb *be*. Have students identify passive verbs in these examples and restate the ideas in the active voice.

- The grass was thrown everywhere by the mower.
- John was moved by Jessica's plea.
- The silk top was finally bought by Jessica.

---

**FOR ENGLISH LANGUAGE LEARNERS**

**Active Voice** Present the following examples to students:

- The mower was pulled out of the garage by John.
- John pulled the mower out of the garage.

Regarding the first example, ask students to identify who pulls the mower out of the garage. Discuss the effect on meaning when the actor appears at the end of the sentence.

(*It makes the action more important than the actor.*) Lead students to compare and contrast the first example with the second. How does the emphasis of the sentence change? (*The actor becomes more important than the action.*)

**FOR STRUGGLING WRITERS**

**Passive Voice** Explain to students that there are two ways to identify passive voice: 1) the presence of a *be* verb such as *am, are, been, is, was,* or *were*; and 2) the use of a *by*

(*the*) . . . phrase following the verb. Present the following example:

- The mower <u>was</u> pulled out of the garage <u>by</u> John.

To shift the sentence into the active voice, the writer simply needs to make the *by* agent the subject of the sentence:

- John pulled the mower out of the garage.

Explain that the Student Draft is continued and completed on this page. Read the draft and annotations aloud and discuss. Ask students to comment on the student writer's resolution and theme.

"John!" she shouted, but there was no way he could hear her. She nudged the evil machine forward and watched grass spew out the side. It was kind of cool. Terrifying, but cool.

She kept pushing all the way to the other side of the lawn. The mower was heavy, but she was strong enough. Turning around was another issue. Still, she was tough, even if she liked pink. She pushed down on the handle, and the mower tilted up surprisingly easily. The sound was much louder. Slowly, she turned, and then she pushed forward to mow the next strip of grass. The grass fell as she mowed. By the time she got to the end of the lawn, she had perfected the turning technique so that it was one fluid motion.

No longer afraid of the mower, she moved her sweaty face closer to examine the controls. She found the switch and cut the engine.

John emerged from inside and surveyed the lawn. "Nice job, Jess."

"Thank you. Excuse me, but I have money to collect, a shower to take, and a top to buy," she said as she walked past him.

That night, she looked amazing in her new pink top. Her friend Alice said, "You look beautiful! Like a flower or something!"

"Thank you!" Jessica replied, thinking about how much fun it would be to mow right through a field of flowers, petals flying everywhere.

> Sarah develops a **plot** and **central conflict** that make the text a story rather than a description. However, the story would be more effective if Sarah included more sensory details.

> Sarah uses the **sequence of events** to **resolve the conflict** in a believable way.

> The lighthearted **conclusion** shows how the character of Jessica has changed. This character change reinforces the story's **theme** or message.

---

**LEARN HOW** Add Sensory Details

- Review with students that sensory details appeal to the five senses.
- Invite students to name the senses (*sight, smell, touch, taste, and hearing*) and to identify examples in the Student Draft.
- Discuss how these details affect readers.

 **YOUR TURN** Ask students to complete the **Your Turn** activity independently. Remind students to add sensory details to involve the audience in the experiences of their stories.

For interactive revision tools, see

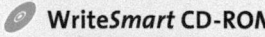 Write*Smart* CD-ROM

Writing Center on thinkcentral.com

**LEARN HOW** Add Sensory Details Sensory details help to paint a vivid picture of the setting and the conflict. Sarah adds sensory details to transport readers to the scene and to involve them in Jessica's experience.

**SARAH'S REVISION**

*Her tense muscles relaxed, and she let out a loud sigh.*
She pushed down on the handle, and the mower tilted up. ~~surprisingly easily.~~
*No longer muffled by the grass, the mower's chainsaw roar increased to jackhammer level.*
~~The sound was much louder.~~ . . . The grass fell as she mowed.
              *shaggy*

 **YOUR TURN** Use the feedback from your peers and teacher as well as the two "Learn How" lessons to revise and rework your short story, paying special attention to plot elements, characterization, pacing, and sensory details.

---

## DIFFERENTIATED INSTRUCTION

**FOR ENGLISH LANGUAGE LEARNERS**

**Sensory Details** Help students develop a vocabulary of precise sensory language to use during the revision process. Record the five senses. Then, list words that describe sights, sounds, tastes, feelings, and smells.

- sights: orange, crooked, curved
- sounds: shrill, muffled, thumping
- tastes: acid, tart, salty
- feelings: bumpy, sticky, slippery
- smells: burnt, smoky, perfumed

To help students generate more words for the list, display pictures for students to describe. Encourage them to use this list to add sensory details to their drafts.

**FOR STRUGGLING WRITERS**

**Sensory Experience** Provide each student with an apple or orange. Have students prepare five-column charts, labeling each column with a sense. Tell students to list words in each column to describe their fruits. Encourage students to move beyond obvious descriptors such as *smooth* or *tart*. Students may also record comparative phrases, such as *green as a new leaf in spring*. Invite students to present several entries to the class.

# Editing and Publishing

During the editing process, proofread your short story to make sure that it is free of any grammar, usage, and punctuation errors. Also, read carefully to catch any spelling errors, even after doing a word-processing spell-check. These kinds of mistakes will distract your audience from focusing on the conflict you describe.

**COMMON CORE** W 5 Strengthen writing by revising, editing, rewriting, or trying a new approach. L 2 Demonstrate command of the conventions of standard English capitalization, punctuation, and spelling. L 2c Spell correctly.

## GRAMMAR IN CONTEXT: QUOTATION MARKS

**Sarcasm** and **irony** occur when a speaker says one thing but means another. However, there is a distinction between communicating sarcasm and irony in speaking versus writing. Readers can't hear the sarcasm in your voice as listeners do. To make sure they don't misinterpret your writing and take a sarcastic or ironic comment literally, you can draw attention to the comment by using **quotation marks.**

> *It made a hideous crrrunch as twigs were chewed and spat out. She shrieked, thinking of how "cute" she would look with missing toes.*

Here, Sarah uses quotation marks to indicate sarcasm or irony. She says that she will look cute with missing toes, but she means that she will *not* look cute with missing toes. The quotation marks help Sarah convey this meaning to her audience.

As Sarah edits her story, she identifies another opportunity to use quotation marks to indicate the use of sarcasm or irony.

> *Her "confident" look amused John.*

## PUBLISH YOUR WRITING

It's time to share your short story with your audience. Try one of these ideas:

- Submit your short story to the school literary magazine, yearbook, or newspaper.
- Enter your short story in a creative writing contest for secondary students.
- Use your short story as part of an application for a creative writing class, writing workshop, or writers' group.
- Produce a **trailer,** or a short video, that communicates the plot of your story and convinces your audience to read it.

 **YOUR TURN** Correct any errors in your short story. Make sure to use participles to add details to your writing. Also, use quotation marks to indicate sarcasm or irony where appropriate. Then, publish your short story for your audience.

---

# Editing and Publishing

**COMMON CORE** W 5, L 2, L 2c

## GRAMMAR IN CONTEXT: QUOTATION MARKS

Explain to students that sarcasm is a "taunting, sneering, or cutting remark." Irony occurs when someone says one thing but means the opposite. Have students explain the irony in the following examples:

- as soft as ice
- as humorous as a tax audit
- as enjoyable as getting a vaccination shot

Model for students how to indicate irony using your voice. Make sure that students understand that they can use quotation marks to translate these vocal cues to paper.

## PUBLISH YOUR WRITING

Brainstorm with students additional ways to publish their stories.

 **YOUR TURN** Allow students time to proofread their drafts. Remind them to use quotation marks to indicate sarcasm or irony. This technique will help make the intended meaning clear for readers.

---

## FOR ENGLISH LANGUAGE LEARNERS

**Understand Sarcasm** Explain to students that an ironic comment can be delivered sarcastically as an insult. For example, a teacher may say to a lazy student, "Don't study too hard." The comment is ironic because the teacher means the opposite of what she says. She means that the lazy student should study. The comment may be delivered insultingly, making it sarcastic. Ask students to identify which word in the dialogue might take quotation marks to make the intended meaning clear (*"study"*). Have pairs of students work together to invent other examples. Have students present their examples aloud to the class.

## FOR STRUGGLING WRITERS

**Identify Irony in Popular Culture** Play for students the song "Ironic" by Alanis Morissette. Tell students that the song has been widely criticized because the examples are not necessarily ironic. Lead students to discuss and evaluate whether or not each example in the song is ironic. Finally, lead students to discuss the message or theme of the song. Does the speaker intend to offer examples of irony, or is it ironic—given the song's title—that the examples are not necessarily ironic? Have students discuss the effect of placing quotation marks around the song's title.

## Scoring Rubric

Tell students that the best way to understand a scoring rubric is to use it to score actual writing. Ask students to evaluate their own stories using the rubric. Have students write paragraphs explaining and defending their scores using the language of the rubric. Review students' stories and scoring paragraphs, noting whether or not you agree with students' assessments and why.

For Rubric Bank, see

**WriteSmart CD-ROM**

**Writing Center** on **thinkcentral.com**

## Assess and Reteach

### Assess

**R** RESOURCE MANAGER—Copy Masters
Rubric for Evaluation p. 142

**Online Essay Scoring** at **thinkcentral.com**

### Reteach

**Level Up Online Tutorials** at **thinkcentral.com**

**Reteaching Workshops** on **thinkcentral.com**

Writing Lesson 22: Elaborate with Sensory Details

Writing Lesson 32: Writing Dialogue

---

## Scoring Rubric

Use the rubric below to evaluate your short story from the Writing Workshop or your response to the on-demand task on the next page.

**SHORT STORY**

| SCORE | COMMON CORE TRAITS |
|---|---|
|  | • **Development** Skillfully introduces, develops, and resolves a conflict; develops compelling, believable characters; effectively uses dialogue and description<br>• **Organization** Has a smooth, coherent event sequence that builds to a strong conclusion; uses effective pacing<br>• **Language** Consistently maintains a point of view; effectively uses active voice; weaves in sensory language; shows a strong command of conventions |
|  | • **Development** Effectively introduces, develops, and resolves a conflict; develops interesting, believable characters; ably uses dialogue and description<br>• **Organization** Has a coherent event sequence that builds to a conclusion; uses mostly effective pacing<br>• **Language** Maintains a point of view; uses active voice; includes sensory language; has a few errors in conventions |
|  | • **Development** Introduces, develops, and resolves a conflict; has interesting characters with some believable traits; could use some more dialogue or description<br>• **Organization** Includes some extraneous events, resulting in ineffective pacing<br>• **Language** Mostly maintains a point of view; generally uses active voice; needs more sensory language; has a few distracting errors in conventions |
|  | • **Development** Introduces and resolves a conflict, but it needs more development; has some underdeveloped characters; needs more dialogue or description<br>• **Organization** Has a confusing sequence caused by some extraneous events; has a lagging pace at times<br>• **Language** Has a few lapses in point of view; includes too much passive voice; lacks enough sensory language; has some significant errors in conventions |
|  | • **Development** Introduces a conflict but does not develop or resolve it; inadequately develops characters; lacks sufficient dialogue and description<br>• **Organization** Includes too many events that distract from the plot; has choppy pacing<br>• **Language** Uses inconsistent point of view; relies on passive voice; mostly lacks sensory language; has many distracting errors in conventions |
|  | • **Development** Has no identifiable conflict; includes underdeveloped characters; lacks any dialogue or description<br>• **Organization** Has no apparent organization<br>• **Language** Never establishes a clear point of view; uses only passive voice; lacks sensory language; has major problems with conventions |

# Preparing for Timed Writing

**COMMON CORE** W 10 Write routinely over shorter time frames for a range of tasks, purposes, and audiences.

## 1. ANALYZE THE TASK — 5 MIN

Read the task carefully. Then, read it again, noting the words in the task that tell the type of writing, the topic, the audience, and the purpose.

> **WRITING TASK**
>
> The best stories are often the ones that spring from life's big questions. Write a <u>short story</u> that illustrates your response to one of the following questions. *← Type of writing*
> • <u>When is a risk worth taking?</u> • <u>Where do you find adventure?</u> *← Topic*
> Your story will <u>appear on a blog</u> titled "Short Stories, Big Ideas." *← Purpose/Audience*

## 2. PLAN YOUR RESPONSE — 10 MIN

First, answer one of the questions in a sentence or two. This answer will be the theme of your story. Then, identify a personal or fictional event that illustrates your answer. Finally, use this chart to develop the characters, setting, conflict, events, and resolution.

| Story Elements | Notes |
|---|---|
| Answer to Question/Theme | * One can find adventure by _____. |
| Characters | |
| Setting | |
| Conflict | |
| Events | |
| Resolution | |

## 3. RESPOND TO THE TASK — 20 MIN

Begin drafting your story. Start with engaging action or dialogue that introduces the conflict, problem, or situation. As you write, keep these points in mind:

- In the exposition, present the characters, setting, and conflict.
- In the rising action and climax, narrate the sequence of events in chronological, or other logical order. Remember to keep the action moving.
- In the falling action and resolution, resolve the conflict.

## 4. IMPROVE YOUR RESPONSE — 5–10 MIN

**Revising** Compare your draft with the task. Does your draft tell a well-paced story that includes characters, setting, plot, conflict, and theme?
**Proofreading** Correct any errors, and make sure your writing is legible.
**Checking Your Final Copy** Before you submit your short story, examine it once more to make sure that you are presenting your best work.

---

# Preparing for Timed Writing

 COMMON CORE W 10

1. **Analyze the Task** Before students begin writing, encourage them to answer the following questions:
   - What is my time limit?
   - What are the key skills assessed in the scoring rubric?
   - Who is my audience?
   - What is my purpose?

2. **Plan Your Response** Point out to students that the scoring rubric emphasizes a smooth, coherent event sequence in which all events are clearly linked. Suggest that students identify their climaxes and then work backward to define essential characters, settings, and events.

3. **Respond to the Task** Remind students to resolve their central conflicts in ways that point toward clear themes. Tell students that if a character learns a lesson as a result of the plot events, the audience will learn this lesson, too, resulting in theme.

4. **Improve Your Response** Point out that the scoring rubric emphasizes a consistent narrative point of view and effective dialogue. Remind students that a third-person narrator can use shifting perspectives to reveal several characters' thoughts, feelings, and attitudes toward other characters or events. A first-person narrator must maintain a single perspective throughout the story. Tell students to review their dialogue for realism by reading it aloud.

## Assess

Use the Scoring Rubric on p. 420 to assess students' narratives.

---

# DIFFERENTIATED INSTRUCTION

### FOR ENGLISH LANGUAGE LEARNERS

**Engaging Plot Sequence** Have students use sentence starters to help them create story maps:

- My characters are _____.
- My story takes place _____.
- The main conflict is _____.
- The most exciting part of my story will be when _____.
- The major events will be _____.
- The story ends with _____.
- The message of my story is _____.

### FOR STRUGGLING WRITERS

**Natural Dialogue** Write this example on the board:

- "I am only asking for a loan of ten dollars, John," Jessica begged. "Please reconsider my request."

Ask a student to read the dialogue aloud. Discuss why the dialogue does not sound natural, listing students' ideas on the board. Have pairs of students work together to revise the dialogue for naturalism. Ask each pair to present its revision to the class.

# Focus and Motivate

## COMMON CORE FOCUS

**W 6** Use technology to display information flexibly and dynamically. **SL 2** Integrate multiple sources of information presented in diverse media. **SL 5** Make strategic use of digital media to add interest.

### PRODUCE WITH A PURPOSE

Ask volunteers to describe memorable trailers that they've seen in theaters, on the Web, or on television. Help students brainstorm a list of qualities found in good trailers. Encourage them to incorporate these features in their own work.

### COMMON CORE TRAITS

As students plan their productions, remind them to keep in mind the **COMMON CORE TRAITS** of a successful trailer.

# Practice and Apply

## Planning a Trailer

Distribute Sequence Chain graphic organizers for students to use when creating their storyboards. Ask students to sketch each scene or to insert printed images into the frames. Explain that a storyboard doesn't require detailed artwork; it only has to convey basic information about how each shot will look. Demonstrate this by drawing on the board two panels containing a medium and a wide view of two stick figures. Have students add the script that accompanies each scene below its corresponding image.

**R** RESOURCE MANAGER—Copy Master
Technology p. 143

**BEST PRACTICES TOOLKIT**
Sequence Chain pp. B21, B45

---

**Technology Workshop**

# Producing a Story Trailer

*Essential Course of Study*

Have you ever watched **trailers,** the scenes of coming attractions that advertise new films? The goal of any trailer is to make viewers want to see a film, without giving away critical details, such as the surprise ending. Of course, trailers aren't limited to movies. In this workshop, you will produce a trailer designed to make others want to read your short story.

Complete the workshop activities in your **Reader/Writer Notebook.**

| PRODUCE WITH A PURPOSE | COMMON CORE TRAITS |
|---|---|
| **TASK**<br>Create a **story trailer** that introduces potential readers to your short story and entices them to read it. | **A SUCCESSFUL STORY TRAILER . . .**<br>• introduces the characters and outlines the basic plot in an engaging way<br>• incorporates digital media, such as text, graphics, audio, and visual elements<br>• is appropriate for the audience |

COMMON CORE

**W 6** Use technology to display information flexibly and dynamically. **SL 2** Integrate multiple sources of information presented in diverse media. **SL 5** Make strategic use of digital media to add interest.

## Planning a Trailer

Your trailer should run for about one minute. Make sure that it introduces the important characters and basic plot elements of your story. Remember that your goal is to make viewers want to read your story. Follow the guidelines below to plan your story trailer.

- **Write a Script** Identify scenes in your story that quickly communicate plot and conflict. In a story about sports, for example, scenes in which characters discuss a game and its importance quickly establish the plot for viewers. Determine the best way to present your information. Will you record a voice-over narrator highlighting plot points or asking intriguing questions? Will you show live action, still images, or both? Remember—don't give too much information. You only need enough material for about a minute of viewing.

- **Choose a Cast** After creating the script for your story trailer, choose friends and classmates to play the roles of your characters and voice-over narrator. Help them rehearse their lines.

- **Create a Mood** Music can help establish the mood of your trailer. Think about the music you've heard during suspenseful moments in a movie. Music adds to the viewer's understanding of what is happening on screen. Review your script and select clips of music that reflect the mood you want to establish.

**Media Tools** **THINK** central
Go to thinkcentral.com.
KEYWORD: HML9N-422

---

## DIFFERENTIATED INSTRUCTION

### FOR ENGLISH LANGUAGE LEARNERS

**Language: Reinforce Transitions** As students prepare their storyboards, review transitional words and phrases that can help clarify the order and sequence of scenes. List the following words on the board: *first, second, next, then, after, before,* and *last.* Model the use of transitions in describing storyboard frames:

*First we see a boy and a girl walking on the side of a road. Then a medium shot shows another boy hiding behind a tree, watching them. Next, a close-up shows that this boy is very angry. . . .*

Encourage students to use transitions as they describe and ask questions about each other's storyboards.

## Producing the Trailer

Your first step in producing a trailer is to create the storyboard. A **storyboard** visually shows each scene in the trailer through a series of panels, like a comic strip. Creating a storyboard lets you determine how to shoot each scene. Below are a few types of shots you can use.

| Close-Up | Medium Shot | Wide Shot |
|---|---|---|
| When you want to present a detail, such as a facial expression, use a tight, close-up shot. This focuses the viewer's attention. | Use a medium shot when you want to emphasize interaction, such as characters talking to each other. | A wide shot establishes the setting for viewers. A view from a distant perspective can communicate the scope of the story and the characters it contains. |

**AS YOU FILM YOUR TRAILER, KEEP THE FOLLOWING TIPS IN MIND:**

- Follow the storyboard.
- Remind your cast members to memorize and practice their lines.
- Re-shoot scenes as needed until you are happy with them.

**AS YOU EDIT YOUR TRAILER, USE THESE GUIDELINES TO HELP YOU:**

- Add music or voice-over narration to create a mood and move the plot along.
- Edit the pace to reflect the mood: Short, quick cuts can emphasize action or conflict. Longer clips help create a reflective mood.
- Delete any parts of scenes that interrupt the pace.

 **YOUR TURN** Play a "rough cut" of your edited trailer for a few classmates. Ask for feedback. Does the trailer make them want to read your story? If not, ask them to identify parts of your trailer that need improvement, such as its pacing or music. Try to incorporate these changes into the final edit of your story trailer.

# Assessment Practice

## COMMON CORE FOCUS

**RL 1** Cite textual evidence to support analysis of what the text says explicitly. **RL 4** Determine the connotative meaning of words as they are used in a text; analyze the cumulative impact of specific word choices on meaning and tone. **W 5** Strengthen writing by revising and editing to ensure that it demonstrates the conventions of standard English grammar, usage, and capitalization. **L 4a** Use context as a clue to the meaning of a word.

### CHECK READINESS

Read aloud the paragraph under **ASSESS** and stress to students that this is not the full Unit Test, but a way for them to check their readiness for it. Then have students examine the standards listed under **REVIEW** and look back in the unit or in the **Student Resource Bank** for any skills they need to review.

### READ THE TEXTS

Remind students to keep the unit goals in mind as they read the passage, paying particular attention to these literary elements and reading skills:

- setting and mood
- sensory language and imagery
- paraphrasing

To help students focus on sensory language and imagery, tell them to ask questions like

- What image do these details create?
- How do the sensory details affect the mood?

### ANSWER THE QUESTIONS

Direct students to pages R93–R101 of the **Handbook** to review test-taking strategies.

- When responding to multiple-choice items, tell students to look for descriptive details in the answer choices.
- Point out that when two answer choices share common traits, it is probable that one is right.

---

### ASSESS

Taking this practice test will help you assess your knowledge of these skills and determine your readiness for the Unit Test.

### REVIEW

After you take the practice test, your teacher can help you identify any standards you need to review.

**COMMON CORE**

**RL 1** Cite textual evidence to support analysis of what the text says explicitly. **RL 4** Determine the connotative meaning of words as they are used in a text; analyze the cumulative impact of specific word choices on meaning and tone. **W 5** Strengthen writing by revising and editing to ensure that it demonstrates the conventions of standard English grammar, usage, and capitalization. **L 4a** Use context as a clue to the meaning of a word.

**Practice Test** **THINK central**

Take it at thinkcentral.com.
KEYWORD: HML9N-424

---

# Assessment Practice

**DIRECTIONS** Read the following text, and then answer the questions.

## *from* The Hobbit
## Chapter VIII: Flies and Spiders
*by J. R. R. Tolkien*

1    They walked in single file. The entrance to the path was like a sort of arch leading into a gloomy tunnel made by two great trees that leaned together, too old and strangled with ivy and hung with lichen to bear more than a few blackened leaves. The path itself was narrow and wound in and out among the trunks. Soon the light at the gate was like a little bright hole far behind, and the quiet was so deep that their feet seemed to thump along while all the trees leaned over them and listened.

2    As their eyes became used to the dimness they could see a little way to either side in a sort of darkened green glimmer. Occasionally a slender beam of sun that had the luck to slip in through some opening in the leaves far above, and still more luck in not being caught in the tangled boughs and matted twigs beneath, stabbed down thin and bright before them. But this was seldom, and it soon ceased altogether.

3    There were black squirrels in the wood. As Bilbo's sharp inquisitive eyes got used to seeing things he could catch glimpses of them whisking off the path and scuttling behind tree-trunks. There were queer noises too, grunts, scufflings, and hurryings in the undergrowth, and among the leaves that lay piled endlessly thick in places on the forest-floor; but what made the noises he could not see. The nastiest things they saw were the cobwebs: dark dense cobwebs with threads extraordinarily thick, often stretched from tree to tree, or tangled in the lower branches on either side of them. There were none stretched across the path, but whether because some magic kept it clear, or for what other reason they could not guess.

4    It was not long before they grew to hate the forest as heartily as they had hated the tunnels of the goblins, and it seemed to offer even less hope of any ending. But they had to go on and on, long after they were sick for a sight of the sun and of the sky, and longed for the feel of wind on their faces. There was no movement of air down under the forest-roof, and it was everlastingly still and dark and stuffy. Even the dwarves felt it, who were used to tunneling, and lived at times for long whiles without the light of the sun; but the hobbit, who liked holes to make a house in but not to spend summer days in, felt that he was being slowly suffocated.

---

## DIFFERENTIATED INSTRUCTION

### FOR ENGLISH LANGUAGE LEARNERS

**Assessment Practice: Work Backward**
Prepare students by having them read the questions *before* reading the passages. Have pairs find unfamiliar words in test directions and questions and follow these steps:

1. Write each word on an index card.
2. Look up the meaning in a dictionary and write it on the back of the card.
3. Use the cards to practice the words with your partner and to teach them to others.

**Assessment Support: Vocabulary** Provide students with a summary of *The Hobbit* and clarify story-related vocabulary.

Bilbo Baggins, a little person, leads a band of dwarves on a dangerous adventure toward their ancient home in the Lonely Mountains to rescue a stolen fortune. Along the way, Bilbo obtains a magical ring that will become the central focus of subsequent books.

- *Bilbo:* a hobbit and the main character of the story

5    The nights were the worst. It then became pitch-dark—not what you call pitch-dark, but really pitch: so black that you really could see nothing. Bilbo tried flapping his hand in front of his nose, but he could not see it at all. Well, perhaps it is not true to say that they could see nothing: they could see eyes. They slept all closely huddled together, and took it in turns to watch; and when it was Bilbo's turn he would see gleams in the darkness round them, and sometimes pairs of yellow or red or green eyes would stare at him from a little distance, and then slowly fade and disappear and slowly shine out again in another place. And sometimes they would gleam down from the branches just above him; and that was most terrifying. But the eyes that he liked the least were horrible pale bulbous sort of eyes. "Insect eyes," he thought, "not animal eyes, only they are much too big."

6    Although it was not yet very cold, they tried lighting watch-fires at night, but they soon gave that up. It seemed to bring hundreds and hundreds of eyes all round them, though the creatures, whatever they were, were careful never to let their bodies show in the little flicker of the flames. Worse still it brought thousands of dark-grey and black moths, some nearly as big as your hand, flapping and whirring round their ears. They could not stand that, nor the huge bats, black as a top-hat, either; so they gave up fires and sat at night and dozed in the enormous uncanny darkness.

7    All this went on for what seemed to the hobbit ages upon ages; and he was always hungry, for they were extremely careful with their provisions. Even so, as days followed days, and still the forests seemed just the same, they began to get anxious. The food would not last for ever: it was in fact already beginning to get low. They tried shooting at the squirrels, and they wasted many arrows before they managed to bring one down on the path. But when they roasted it, it proved horrible to taste, and they shot no more squirrels.

8    They were thirsty too, for they had none too much water, and in all the time they had seen neither spring nor stream. This was their state when one day they found their path blocked by a running water. It flowed fast and strong but not very wide right across the way, and it was black, or looked it in the gloom. It was well that Beorn had warned them against it, or they would have drunk from it, whatever its color, and filled some of their emptied skins at its bank.

GO ON →

## ITEM ANALYSIS

| COMPREHENSION AND WRITTEN RESPONSE | ITEMS | UNIT PAGES |
| --- | --- | --- |
| Setting | 1, 4, 12, 14, 15 | 330–335 |
| Mood | 2, 9 | 330–335 |
| Paraphrase | 6, 8 | 371 |
| Imagery | 2, 3, 5, 7, 9, 10, 11, 13 | 337 |

| VOCABULARY | ITEMS | UNIT PAGES |
| --- | --- | --- |
| Connotative and Denotative Meanings | 1, 2, 3, 4, 5, 6, 7, 8 | 352 |

| WRITING AND GRAMMAR | ITEMS | UNIT PAGES |
| --- | --- | --- |
| Sentence Structure | 1, 3 | 412–420 |
| Compound Predicate | 2, 5 | 369 |
| Participles | 4, 6 | 412–420 |

### Practice Test

On **thinkcentral.com** students can complete an interactive version of this practice test *and* receive remediation for the skills they have not yet mastered.

---

- *goblins:* evil or mischievous spirits, often humanlike, ugly, and misshapen
- *dwarves:* human beings who are much smaller than the typical person
- *hobbit:* a little person or a dwarf
- *Beorn:* a man able to assume the form of a bear who helps Bilbo and the others during their quest

**FOR STRUGGLING READERS**

**Assessment Practice: Sensory Language**
Model for students how to classify descriptive details in a five-column chart in the margin of the text. For example, use the first paragraph of the excerpt.

**sight:** "arch leading into a gloomy tunnel"

**sound:** "quiet was so deep"

**touch:** "strangled with ivy"

Lead students to discuss how they visualize this setting. Ask them how they would draw this setting. What colors and shapes would they use? Invite students to take turns contributing to a class drawing on a transparency or the board. Then, lead students to discuss how these images make them feel. Explain that these feelings describe the mood of the passage.

# Reading Comprehension

Model a thinking process for answering multiple-choice questions.

1. **B is correct.** *Paragraph 3 identifies the setting as a forest floor. A is not correct because the narrator compares the entrance to the forest to a tunnel. C and D are incorrect because no details refer to a park or a desert.*

2. **A is correct.** *The narrator creates a feeling of unease with words like "strangled," "blackened," and "darkened green glimmer." B is not correct because the characters feel fear. C is not correct because the characters are surrounded by many unfamiliar noises. D is not correct because the impression is one of eeriness rather than crowding.*

3. **D is correct.** *The sunlight soon disappears, leaving the travelers to battle the elements of the forest. A is incorrect because the sunlight disappears. B is not correct because the travelers do not appear lucky. C is not correct because the travelers appreciate the sunlight.*

4. **D is correct.** *The travelers have negative reactions to the forest and felt they were being "slowly suffocated." The characters do not have positive feelings like the excitement in A, confidence in B, or comfort in C.*

5. **A is correct.** *Grunts are sounds; scufflings, and hurryings are acts that the travelers can hear rather than see, smell, or touch. Therefore, B, C, and D are not correct.*

6. **C is correct.** *Bilbo hears grunts, scufflings, and hurryings in the undergrowth and among the leaves, but he cannot see what makes these noises. A is not correct because Bilbo becomes accustomed to these constant noises. B and D are incorrect because they leave out Bilbo and his perceptions.*

---

# Reading Comprehension

> **Use the excerpt from *The Hobbit* (pp. 424–425) to answer questions 1–12.**

1. Which of these best describes the setting of "Flies and Spiders"?
   A. Gloomy tunnel
   B. Large, dense forest
   C. Squirrel-filled park
   D. Waterless desert

2. The description in paragraphs 1 and 2 creates a mood of —
   A. unease because the stillness and darkness seem abnormal
   B. happiness because the travelers are going for a walk
   C. quiet because the leaves muffle footsteps
   D. crowdedness because the path is so narrow

3. How does the description of the sunlight in paragraph 2 reflect the travelers' conflict?
   A. The sun shows sneakiness by slipping through the leaves.
   B. The sun is lucky to reach the ground, just as the travelers are lucky.
   C. The sun seems threatening to the travelers when it stabs down through the leaves.
   D. The sun is soon defeated by the darkness, which hints at what will happen to the travelers.

4. The way the characters react to the setting reveals —
   A. that they are excited by the prospect of an adventure
   B. that they are confident that they will get through the forest
   C. that they are comfortable with the closeness of their surroundings
   D. that they are disturbed by the dark stuffiness of the forest

5. The phrase "grunts, scufflings, and hurryings" in paragraph 3 appeals to the sense of —
   A. hearing
   B. sight
   C. smell
   D. touch

6. In paragraph 3, which is the best way to paraphrase Bilbo's experience with the noises?
   A. Bilbo was startled by the scuffling noises the squirrels made.
   B. The leaves were piled so thick that they muffled all sounds.
   C. Bilbo heard strange noises but couldn't get a good look at what made them.
   D. Strange animals rushed through the undergrowth, grunting and scuffling.

---

## DIFFERENTIATED INSTRUCTION

### FOR ENGLISH LANGUAGE LEARNERS

**Assessment Support: Practice** Model for students how to evaluate the answer choices for multiple-choices questions by labeling each as *true* or *false*. Use question 1 as an example. *The setting is a gloomy tunnel* is false. You can eliminate answer choice A. The setting is a forest; true. Answer choice B is a good possibility, but check answers C and D to verify. The setting is a park; false. The setting is a desert; false. B is the best choice. Have students work with partners to apply this method to item 2. Provide students with this sentence starter: The mood is one of _____ *(unease, happiness, quiet, crowdedness).*

7. The image of cobwebs in paragraph 3 suggests —
   A. ropes hanging from trees
   B. a trap about to spring
   C. woven fabric
   D. a work of art

8. Which is the best way to paraphrase the sentence that describes Bilbo's experience at night in paragraph 5?
   A. They slept crowded together, and when it was Bilbo's turn to watch, he could see pairs of yellow or red or green eyes staring at him.
   B. They slept crowded together, and yellow or red or green eyes stared at Bilbo, then faded and shone out again elsewhere.
   C. When it was Bilbo's turn, pairs of yellow or red or green eyes stared at him.
   D. When they slept crowded together, pairs of yellow or red or green eyes stared at Bilbo.

9. The image of the eyes in paragraph 5 creates a mood of —
   A. eager expectation
   B. admiration for their beauty
   C. curiosity and interest
   D. fear and anxiety

10. The details about strange noises, extraordinarily thick cobwebs, and watching eyes suggest that —
    A. the travelers are looking for trouble
    B. other travelers are lost in the forest
    C. strange creatures are watching the travelers
    D. the forest is a very noisy place

11. Which is an example of imagery in paragraph 6 used to describe the moths?
    A. *Worse still*
    B. *Flapping and whirring*
    C. *Black as a top-hat*
    D. *Uncanny*

12. The stream crossing the path when the travelers are most thirsty is ironic because —
    A. the travelers are relieved to finally find water
    B. the water does not look good to drink but tastes fine
    C. the water is moving too fast for the travelers to catch in their skins
    D. the travelers have been warned not to drink the water and must remain thirsty

**SHORT CONSTRUCTED RESPONSE**
**Write three or four sentences to answer each question.**

13. Identify four sensory details in paragraph 6 and explain to which sense each appeals.

14. Why was night the most difficult time for the travelers? Support your response with details from the story.

**Write two to three paragraphs to answer this question.**

15. Describe some problems the characters face in this passage. Explain how the setting causes each problem.

**GO ON ➡**

427

---

7. **B** *is correct.* *Spiders use their webs to trap prey.* A *is not correct because the cobwebs are not hanging.* C *and* D *are not correct because there is no suggestion of weaving or artistry.*

8. **A** *is correct.* *It includes important details including sleeping arrangements, the watch schedule, and the setting.* B *is incorrect because the action seems to occur while Bilbo is sleeping in the group.* C *is not correct because it omits that the characters slept crowded together.* D *is not correct because it suggests the pairs of yellow or green eyes belong to those who were sleeping.*

9. **D** *is correct.* *The eyes are creepy and make the characters uneasy, creating an atmosphere of fear. This cancels out the possibility of positive moods described in* A, B, *and* C.

10. **C** *is correct.* *The eyes suggest witnesses; the noises suggest another presence; the cobwebs suggest activity by others.* A *is incorrect because the travelers do not challenge the creatures.* B *is incorrect because the details and clues do not suggest other travelers.* D *is not correct because the noises described are not loud but more like noises made when sneaking about.*

11. **B** *is correct.* *"Worse still it brought thousands of dark-grey and black moths, some nearly as big as your hand, flapping and whirring round their ears."* A *is not correct because it is not a description.* C *is not correct because it describes the bats.* D *is not correct because it describes the darkness.*

12. **D** *is correct.* *One would expect thirsty travelers to drink from a stream. Yet, they cannot.* A *is incorrect because they know they have to remain thirsty.* B *is not correct because the travelers do not drink the water.* C *is not correct because the travelers do not attempt to catch the water.*

## SHORT CONSTRUCTED RESPONSE

*Possible responses:*

13. *Watch-fires appeal to the senses of sight and touch (due to the heat they generate). The description of "hundreds of eyes" appeals to the sense of sight; of "flapping and whirring" moths, to the senses of sight and sound; and of squirrels "horrible to taste," to the sense of taste.*

14. *The night is so dark that the characters cannot see anything but frightening eyes that "slowly fade and disappear and slowly shine out again in another place." They also cannot make a fire because it will attract creatures such as moths and bats, "flapping and whirring round their ears."*

15. *The characters run short of food and water because the forest is vast and it takes them a long time to get through it. They are hungry, but they cannot eat the horrible-tasting squirrels. They are thirsty, but they have been warned not to drink from the stream. They feel threatened at all times by creatures they cannot see but whose eyes shine from the darkness.*

# Vocabulary

1. **D is correct.** *The connotation is one of sneakiness because the creatures are barely glimpsed. Scuttling and sneaking both have negative connotations. A and C are not correct because these words have positive connotations. B can be eliminated because the travelers, not the creatures, are threatened.*

2. **B is correct.** *The thicknesses of the cobwebs surprise the travelers. A is not correct because the cobwebs inspire fear rather than hope. C is not correct because the cobwebs are unusual, not typical. D is not correct because the travelers have no use for the cobwebs.*

3. **B is correct.** *The travelers huddle because they are scared. A is not correct because the travelers feel fear. C is incorrect because the travelers are not alone. D is not correct because the primary purpose for huddling is to offset fear rather than to create warmth.*

4. **D is correct.** *The darkness takes on a life of its own that the travelers find overwhelming. A is not correct because the travelers do not feel as if they are welcome guests. B is not correct because the darkness creates fear rather than irritation. C is not correct because the darkness is not ordinary.*

5. **A is correct.** *Bilbo tries to determine the source of the noises. B is not correct because Bilbo is doing more than seeing. C is not correct because although Bilbo may feel fear, he is trying to determine the source of the noises. D is incorrect because there are no context clues to support it.*

6. **D is correct.** *Bulbous is an adjective that means "enlarged." A is not correct because it tells about Bilbo rather than the eyes. B is not correct because it doesn't describe size and is not supported by the text. C is not correct because the eyes are too big to be traditional insect eyes.*

7. **A is correct.** *Paragraph 7 relates hunger to provisions and restates the term as "food." B is not correct because these words describe time. C is not correct because these words describe the state of the travelers and the setting. D is not correct because these words describe the travelers.*

8. **A is correct.** *If the travelers had not been warned against the stream, they would have filled their skins, or containers, with water. B, C, and D are not correct because these items cannot be filled with water.*

## Vocabulary

> **Use your knowledge of connotation and denotation to answer the following questions.**

1. The denotation of *scuttling* in paragraph 3 is "running hastily." Which word below best describes its connotation?
   A. Celebrating
   B. Escaping
   C. Jumping with joy
   D. Sneaking

2. What connotation does *extraordinarily* have in paragraph 3?
   A. Hopefully
   B. Surprisingly
   C. Typically
   D. Usefully

3. The author uses the word *huddled* in paragraph 5 with a connotation of —
   A. coziness
   B. fear
   C. privacy
   D. warmth

4. What connotation does *enormous* have in paragraph 6?
   A. Generous
   B. Irritating
   C. Ordinary
   D. Overwhelming

> **Use your knowledge of context clues to answer the following questions.**

5. Based on the context clues in paragraph 3, *inquisitive* means —
   A. curious
   B. far-seeing
   C. fearful
   D. pale

6. Which words give the strongest clue to the meaning of *bulbous* in paragraph 5?
   A. *He liked the least*
   B. *Horrible pale*
   C. *Insect eyes*
   D. *Much too big*

7. Which words give the strongest clue to the meaning of *provisions* in paragraph 7?
   A. *hungry, food*
   B. *ages, days*
   C. *always, same*
   D. *careful, anxious*

8. Based on the context clues in paragraph 8, *skins* means —
   A. containers
   B. fur coats
   C. hands
   D. money

# Revising and Editing

**DIRECTIONS** Read this passage, and answer the questions that follow.

> (1) It was crowded at Briscoe park. (2) Parkgoers enjoyed a variety of activites.
> (3) People were racing models. (4) People were playing chess. (5) People were jogging.
> (6) A group was playing bocce, a game brought over from Italy many years ago.
> (7) Grace brings her collie, Jake, to the park. (8) She throws sticks for him to fetch.
> (9) The dog ran circles around Grace. (10) Jake ran over to the bocce game. (11) He
> grabbed the ball in his mouth. (12) He takes off as Grace and the bocce players run
> after him.

1. What change, if any, should be made in sentence 1?
   A. Change *crowded* to **a crowd**
   B. Change *park* to **Park**
   C. Change *was* to **were**
   D. Make no change

2. What is the best way to rewrite sentences 3–5, using a compound predicate?
   A. People were racing models. They were playing chess. People jogged.
   B. People were racing models. People were playing chess. Some were jogging.
   C. People were racing models, playing chess, and jogging.
   D. People were racing models; people were playing chess; people were jogging.

3. What change, if any, should be made to sentence 6?
   A. A group playing bocce, a game brought over from Italy many years ago.
   B. A group was playing, a game brought over from Italy many years ago, bocce.
   C. A group was playing bocce, many years ago a game brought over from Italy.
   D. Make no change

4. What is the best way to change sentences 7 and 8 to the past tense?
   A. Change *brings* to **brought** and change *throws* to **threw**.
   B. Change *brings* to **was bringing** and *throws* to **was throwing**.
   C. Change *brings* to **had brought** and *throws* to **had thrown**.
   D. Sentence 7 is already in the past tense.

5. What is the best way to rewrite sentences 10 and 11, using a compound predicate?
   A. Jake ran over to the bocce game. Jake grabbed the ball in his mouth.
   B. Jake ran over to the bocce game and grabbed the ball in his mouth.
   C. Jake ran over to the bocce game, and grabbing the ball in his mouth.
   D. Jake ran over to the bocce game. He grabbed the ball in his mouth.

6. What is the best way to write sentence 12 in the past tense?
   A. Change *takes* to **had taken** and change *run* to **had run**.
   B. Change *takes* to **taking** and *run* to **running**.
   C. Change *takes* to **took** and *run* to **ran**.
   D. Sentence 12 is already in the past tense.

STOP

429

## DIFFERENTIATED INSTRUCTION

### FOR STRUGGLING READERS

**Assessment Support: Test Strategy** Point out to students that the revising and editing questions require them to examine one, two, or three sentences at a time. During this task, the other sentences may prove distracting. Suggest that students use scratch paper to cover all but the sentences in question. Then, tell students to concentrate on mentally (or physically) making each change suggested by the answer choices, eliminating wrong answers as they work. Also, tell students to trust their instincts when answering such questions. It is acceptable to choose the response "Make no change" if students feel reasonably certain the other answer choices are incorrect.

### INTRODUCE *GREAT READS*

In Unit 3, students have discussed a number of big questions. Invite students to tell which question they found most intriguing and why, and then focus attention on the three that appear on this page. Discuss the recommended books and their summaries, pointing out how each connects to the related question. Encourage students to choose one or more of these "great reads" to read independently.

# UNIT 3
## Great Reads

## Ideas for Independent Reading

Are there different kinds of adventure? Does seeking revenge lead to justice? Consider these questions when you read these works.

### What do you look for in a friend?

**The Moves Make the Man**
*by Bruce Brooks*

"Jayfox," the only black student in his school, loves basketball. Bix, a white student, worships baseball. The two meet in a home ec class where each is learning to cook because his mother is ill.

**The Friends**
*by Rosa Guy*

When Phyllisia arrives in New York City from the West Indies, her classmates ridicule her. Only Edith tries to befriend her, but Phyllisia is not interested. Eventually, tragedies in her family change Phyllisia's mind about the meaning of friendship.

**Sula**
*by Toni Morrison*

Sula and Nel, both black and poor, meet as young girls in an Ohio town. For years they share everything, until life separates them. They meet years later to renew their friendship and heal old wounds.

### Is revenge ever justified?

**In the Middle of the Night**
*by Robert Cormier*

Denny's father was the usher when a theater tragedy killed many children. His family endures hate mail and threats. When Denny answers the phone one night, a survivor initiates a plot for revenge, using Denny himself.

**Hamlet**
*by William Shakespeare*

Shakespeare's dramatic classic describes the agony of Hamlet, the prince of Denmark, as he determines how best to revenge his father's murder at the hands of his uncle.

**One Flew over the Cuckoo's Nest**
*by Ken Kesey*

McMurphy never intends to end up in a mental health ward. Once there, he organizes the inmates to resist the cruel Nurse Ratched. His plan for revenge against her humiliations has tragic consequences.

### Where do you find adventure?

**The Call of the Wild**
*by Jack London*

London's classic novel tells the story of Buck, a domesticated dog stolen from his home and made to work as a sled dog during the Alaskan gold rush.

**The Last Unicorn**
*by Peter Beagle*

Beagle's classic fantasy tells of a lonely unicorn who searches for more of her own kind. She's aided in her thrilling and dangerous adventure by the totally incompetent magician Schmendrick, along with Molly Grue, a human girl.

**The Birthday Boys**
*by Beryl Bainbridge*

This historical novel is based on the diaries of five explorers, led by Robert Falcon Scott, who tried to be the first to reach the South Pole. They were beaten to the pole, and bad weather and poor planning led to their deaths on their way back to base camp.

**Get Novel Wise**

**THINK** central

Go to **thinkcentral.com**.
KEYWORD: HML9-430

430

### NovelWise
**THINK** central

The keyword on this page points to **NovelWise**, a Web site that helps students choose a novel or other book-length work to read. **NovelWise** also provides

• study guides
• reading strategies and literary elements instruction
• presentations to introduce classic novels
• project ideas

# Getting the Message

## THEME AND SYMBOL

- In Fiction
- In Nonfiction
- In Poetry
- Across Genres

431

### INTRODUCE THE UNIT

If you want to share a message, you might make a speech, whisper a few words, or send a note by e-mail. Ask students to name some messages that might be conveyed in these ways. Point out that artists share messages, too, through the visual images that they create.

Invite students to consider how the painting and the photograph on this page convey a similar message. To elicit ideas, ask:

- How are the figures in the painting and the photograph similar?
- How are the mother figures different?
- What message do you get when you look at each image separately?
- How does the message change when you look at the images together?

Point out that looking for a message in an image is similar to looking for a message in a story, poem, or other piece of writing. A reader notices an overall effect and then reads carefully for details. Tell students that the over-riding message of a piece of writing is called a **theme.** In this unit, students will consider the theme of each selection by looking for details and synthesizing the overall idea of each selection. The better they understand a theme, the more they will appreciate the writing that expresses it.

For help in planning this unit, see

**R** RESOURCE MANAGER UNIT 4
 pp. 1–10

**About the Art** April Harrison's *Mama's Cradle* focuses on the warmth and comfort of family love. For more information on Harrison and her work, see page 495.

Dorothea Lange's 1936 photograph, known as "Migrant Mother," shows a destitute mother of seven children in California.

# COMMON CORE

**STRAND**

| | ✓ ECOS<br>Text Analysis Workshop: Theme and Symbol<br>pp. 434–439 | Comparing Texts<br>*Marigolds*<br>Short Story<br>pp. 440–453, 459 | *Sowing Change/*<br>*In Our Hands*<br>Newspaper Article<br>Book Cover<br>pp. 454–459 | ✓ ECOS<br>*The Scarlet Ibis/Woman*<br>*With Flower*<br>Short Story<br>pp. 460–479 | *Math and After Math*<br>Essay<br>pp. 480–491 |
|---|---|---|---|---|---|
| | | Lexile: 1140<br>Fry: 9<br>Dale-Chall: 6.8 | Lexile: 1230<br>Fry: College<br>Dale-Chall: 8.1 | Lexile: 1060<br>Fry: 8<br>Dale-Chall: 6.0 | Lexile: 970<br>Fry: 10<br>Dale-Chall: 6.4 |
| **Reading Literature** | Themes in Literature pp. 434–435 **RL 2**<br>Determine Theme p. 436 **RL 2, RL 3**<br>Analyze the Text pp. 437–439 | Theme and Setting pp. 441, 442, 446, 447, 449, 450, 452 **RL 2, RL 4**<br>Draw Conclusions pp. 441, 444, 445, 448, 449, 451, 452 **RL 1, RL 4** | Book Cover p. 458 **RL 7** | Symbol pp. 461, 464, 473, 474, 477 **RL 2**<br>Make Inferences pp. 461, 462, 464, 466–468, 471, 475, 477 **RL 1, RL 3** | |
| **Reading Informational Text** | | | Outline pp. 455–457 **RI 2, RI 3, RI 5** | | Implied Main Idea pp. 481, 485, 486, 488, 489, 490 **RI 1, RI 2**<br>Sequence of Events pp. 481, 484, 486, 490 **RI 3**<br>Language Coach p. 485 **RI 4** |
| **Writing** | | | Writing Prompt p. 457 **W 2f** | Writing Prompt p. 479 **W 9a (RL 3)** | |
| **Speaking and Listening** | | What's the Connection? p. 440 **SL 1** | What's the Connection? p. 454 **SL 1** | Discuss p. 460 **SL 1** | Discuss p. 480 **SL 1** |
| **Language** | | Language Coach pp. 445, 448 **L 4b, L 4c**<br>The Suffix –or p. 453 **L 4b, L 4d** | Language Coach p. 455 **L 4a** | Language Coach p. 465 **L 4a**<br>Vary Sentence Structure pp. 468, 479 **L 1b**<br>Language Coach p. 470 **L 4b**<br>Denotation and Connotation p. 478 **L 5b** | Analogies p. 489 **L 5**<br>Using Context Clues p. 491 **L 4a** |

| *The Future in My Arms* Essay pp. 492–499 | *Poem On Returning to Dwell in the Country/My Heart Leaps Up/The Sun* Poems pp. 500–505 | *Two Kinds/Rice and Rose Bowl Blues* Short Story/Poem pp. 506–523 | *Writing Workshop:* Informative Text: Analysis of Literary Nonfiction pp. 524–533 *Speaking and Listening Workshop:* Participating in a Panel Discussion pp. 534–535 |
|---|---|---|---|
| Lexile: 1420 Fry: 11 Dale-Chall: 6.6 | | Lexile: 880 Fry: 7 Dale-Chall: 6.1 | |
| | Universal Theme pp. 501, 503–505  RL 2, RL 6 Reading Poetry pp. 501, 502, 504, 505  RL 4 | Theme Across Genres pp. 507, 508, 510–512, 514, 515, 517, 520, 521  RL 2, RL 3 Purpose for Reading p. 507 Language Coach p. 516  RL 4 Draw Conclusions  p. 519  RL 4 | |
| Author's Perspective pp. 493, 494, 496, 498  RI 6 Monitor pp. 493, 494, 496, 498  RI 2 | | | |
| Quickwrite p. 492 Writing Prompt p. 499 W 4 | Quickwrite p. 500 | Writing for Assessment p. 523  W 2a–c, f, W 4, W 5, W 9a (RL 1, 2) | Writing an Analysis of Literary Nonfiction pp. 524–533 W 2a–e, W 4, W 5, W 9b (RI 1), W 10 |
| | | Discuss p. 506  SL 1 | Participating in a Panel Discussion pp. 534–535  SL 1a–d, SL 4 |
| Rhetorical Questions pp. 496, 499  L 3 Language Coach p. 497  L 4a | | Language Coach p. 513  L 4c Word Origins p. 522  L 4c | Drafting p. 527  L 1b Editing and Publishing p. 531  L 2, L 2c |

ECOS

To see the complete Essential Course of Study, see pp. T23–T28.

For additional lesson planning help, see **Teacher One Stop DVD.**

## Instructional Support

**Resource Manager Unit 4**

**UNIT SUPPORT**

Academic Vocabulary, p. 3

Additional Academic Vocabulary, p. 4

Grammar Focus p. 5

Text Analysis Workshop pp. 9–10

Writing Workshop: Informative Text: Analysis of Literary Nonfiction p. 145

**SELECTION SUPPORT***

**Plan and Teach**

Lesson planning pages

Additional leveled selection questions

Extension activities

**Student Copy Masters**

Selection summaries in four languages

Skills copy masters in English and Spanish

Vocabulary preteaching and support

Reading Check and Question support

Reading Fluency

*Available for all selections

† Available on **thinkcentral.com**.

**Language Handbook**

**Vocabulary Practice**

**Best Practices Toolkit**†

**PowerNotes** DVD-ROM†

**Connections: Nonfiction for Common Core** CD-ROM†

**Teacher One Stop** DVD-ROM

**Student One Stop** DVD-ROM

**Write*Smart*** CD-ROM†

**GrammarNotes** DVD-ROM†

**WordSharp** CD-ROM†

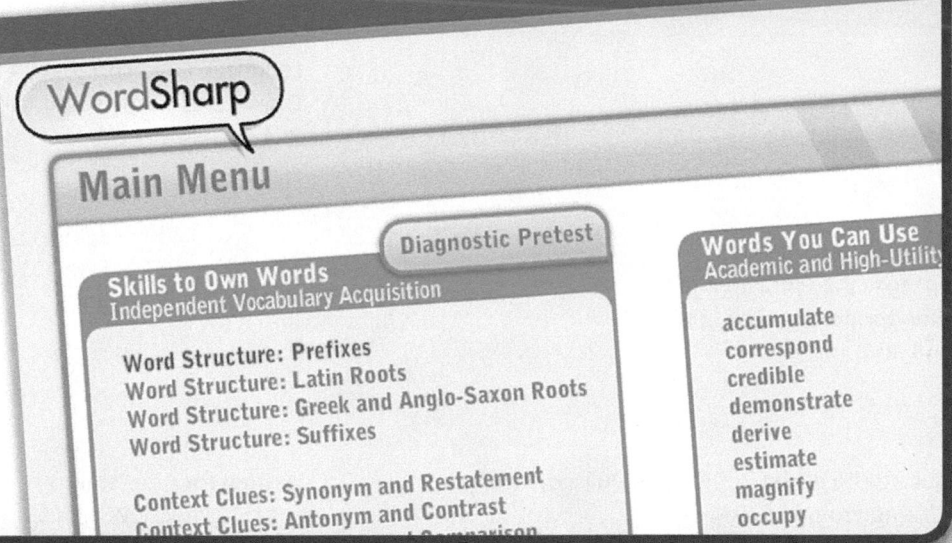

## Differentiated Instruction

### STRUGGLING READERS AND WRITERS

**Resource Manager Unit 4**

Additional Selection Questions

Question Support

Reading Fluency

**Interactive Reader**

**Adapted Interactive Reader**

**Level Up Online Tutorials**

**Audio Anthology**
(with Audio summaries)

**Diagnostic and Selection Tests**

Selection Tests A/B

### ENGLISH LANGUAGE LEARNERS

**Resource Manager Unit 4**

Selection Summaries in English, Spanish, Vietnamese and Haitian Creole

Skills Copymasters in Spanish

**English Language Learner Adapted Interactive Reader Teacher's Guide**

**ELL Adapted Interactive Reader**

**Audio Tutor**

**Guide to English for Newcomers**

**Audio Anthology**

**Audio Summaries in Multiple Languages**
(on **thinkcentral.com**)

### ADVANCED LEARNERS

**Resource Manager Unit 4**

Additional Selection Questions

Ideas for Extension

**Diagnostic and Selection Tests**

Selection Tests B/C

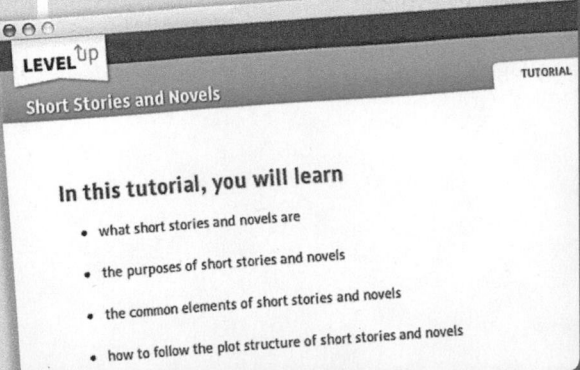

## Assessment and Reteaching

**Diagnostic and Selection Tests**

**Unit and Benchmark Tests**

**ThinkCentral Online Assessment:**
- All program assessments
- Level Up Online Tutorials

**ExamView Test Generator** on the Teacher One Stop DVD-ROM

**Online Essay Scoring** on **thinkcentral.com**

**ThinkCentral Online Reteaching:**
- Level Up Online Tutorials
- Reteaching Worksheets

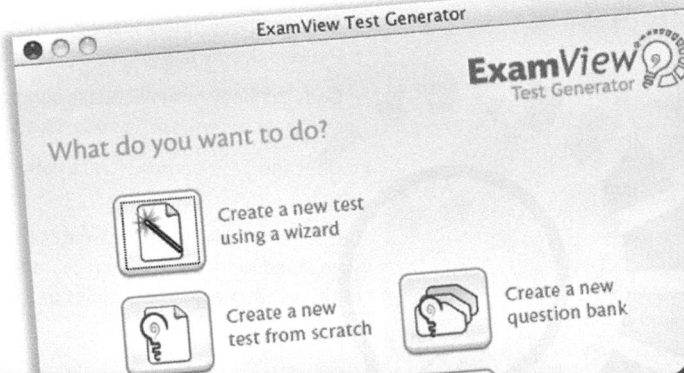

## Professional Development

**Video Center** Based on interviews with program consultants and other educational experts, these videos feature classroom-ready teaching strategies.

**Teacher Toolkit** Includes a Teacher Handbook as well as a range of articles and handouts by program consultants and other educators.

Janet Allen

Kylene Beers

Jim Burke

Carol Jago

## THINKcentral at a Glance

### One Location, Endless Resources

**Find Resources** Browse all *Holt McDougal Literature* components for the ones that meet your students' needs and match your teaching style.

**Assess Progress and Reteach** Assign electronic versions of program assessments to measure your students' mastery of the Common Core State Standards. On thinkcentral.com, some tests deliver online remediation tutorials to students who have not mastered skills.

 **Interactive Whiteboard Lessons**

Prepare your students for college and careers by teaching relevant, real-world skills through dynamic, interactive instruction. Go to **thinkcentral.com** to browse through all whiteboard lessons, including the following:

- Theme/Central Idea
- Citing Textual Evidence
- Word Choice and Tone

 Together Holt McDougal and HISTORY® are revolutionizing the study of English/language arts with video that helps students relive and re-imagine the people, places, and events they are discovering through reading. Look for selections with the HISTORY® icon.

431D

## What **MESSAGES**
### are timeless?

Introduce the page by reading the first paragraph. Explain that a theme is expressed most accurately as a sentence rather than as a single word such as *loyalty* or *patriotism*. To extend discussion of timeless messages, have students look carefully at the image of the eagle and the flag. Offer this example of the message, or theme of this image:

> Being like the eagle—proud, alert, and fiercely determined—will help a person handle any situation.

Discuss students' responses to this theme and suggestions for alternate themes.

*ACTIVITY* Suggest that students name books and movies that will be familiar to other students. As students compare their lists, ask them to name a theme or message that they noticed in their selections. Explain that time-less themes may occur in very different stories.

**CHECK UNDERSTANDING** After compiling the group list, ask volunteers to identify themes that they feel are timeless.

**Find It Online!**

**THINK** central

Go to **thinkcentral.com** for the interactive version of this unit.

## What **MESSAGES**
### are timeless?

"Beauty is in the eye of the beholder." "Love conquers all." These statements may have been communicated to you by family, friends, teachers, or others who wanted to send you messages about life and human nature. Those messages, called themes when they appear in works of fiction or movies, are often expressed in similar ways by writers across different cultures or time periods.

*ACTIVITY* Think about three or four of your favorite books or movies. For each, write down the theme that you think the author or director was trying to express. Consider the following questions:

- Does the book or movie have something to say about the way people behave under particular circumstances?
- Does the book or movie teach something about an abstract concept, such as war, love, or friendship?
- Does the book or movie try to convince you to act in a specific way?

Get together with your classmates to see how many of your listed items have similar themes. Make a group list of titles that are good examples of a particular theme.

432

## Unit Resources

*See resources on the* **Teacher One Stop DVD-ROM** *and on* **thinkcentral.com**.

**R** **RESOURCE MANAGER UNIT 4**

**UNIT AND BENCHMARK TESTS**

**BEST PRACTICES TOOLKIT**

**INTERACTIVE READER**

**ADAPTED INTERACTIVE READER**

**ELL ADAPTED INTERACTIVE READER**

**LANGUAGE HANDBOOK**

**VOCABULARY PRACTICE**

**READER/WRITER NOTEBOOK**

**TECHNOLOGY**

- **Teacher One Stop DVD-ROM**
- **Student One Stop DVD-ROM**
- **PowerNotes DVD-ROM**
- **Write*Smart* CD-ROM**
- **Media*Smart* DVD-ROM**
- **GrammarNotes DVD-ROM**
- **Audio Anthology CD**
- **Audio Tutor CD**

**Find It Online!**

The interactive version of this unit on **thinkcentral.com** includes

- video and **PowerNotes** introductions to key selections
- audio support—listen or download
- **ThinkAloud** models
- **WordSharp** vocabulary tutorials
- interactive review and remediation

## Preview Unit Goals

| | |
|---|---|
| **TEXT ANALYSIS** | • Determine a theme or central idea and analyze its development<br>• Compare and contrast universal themes<br>• Identify and interpret symbolism<br>• Analyze an author's perspective |
| **READING** | • Make inferences and draw conclusions; cite evidence<br>• Analyze sequence of events<br>• Outline a text and analyze key ideas |
| **WRITING AND LANGUAGE** | • Write an analysis of literary nonfiction<br>• Effectively select, organize, and analyze content<br>• Use rhetorical questions for effect<br>• Use and punctuate various types of clauses correctly |
| **SPEAKING AND LISTENING** | • Participate in a panel discussion |
| **VOCABULARY** | • Use suffixes to determine the meaning of words<br>• Determine the connotative meaning of words<br>• Use context as a clue to meaning<br>• Use a dictionary to find the pronunciation of words or determine their etymology |
| **ACADEMIC VOCABULARY** | • context     • interpret     • reveal<br>• significant   • tradition |
| **MEDIA AND VIEWING** | • Analyze representations in different mediums |

433

---

**COMMON UNIT GOALS**
Included in this unit: **RL 1-4, RL 6-7, RL 10, RI 1-6, RI 10, W 2a-f, W 4-5, W 9a-b, W 10, SL 1a-d, SL 4, L 1b, L 2c, L 3, L 4a-d, L 5, L 5b, L 6**

Complete text of the Common Core State Standards is found in the correlation on p. T10. Standards covered in this unit are found in the standards overview (pp. 431A–431B) and on the lesson pages where they are taught.

## Preview Unit Goals

The goals on this page highlight the main concepts that will be covered in the unit. Encourage students to skim the list as they prepare for the unit. Remind students that the color-coded skill strand will be repeated throughout the unit.

Have students record the Academic Vocabulary terms in their journals, with a preliminary definition for each term. Urge students to confirm and perhaps refine the definitions as they read and discuss or write about the selections in the unit.

---

## DIFFERENTIATED INSTRUCTION

### FOR ENGLISH LANGUAGE LEARNERS

**Academic Vocabulary** Provide students with definitions of each Academic Vocabulary word.

**context** (kŏn′tĕkst′) *n.* the words that surround a particular word or passage and make the meaning of that word or passage clear; the circumstances in which an event occurs

**interpret** (ĭn tûr′prĭt) *v.* to explain the meaning of or translate

**reveal** (rĭ vēl′) *v.* to show, make known, or expose

**significant** (sĭg nĭf′ə kənt) *adj.* having meaning; important

**tradition** (trə-dĭsh′ən) *n.* a practice passed down from generation to generation

Use the copy master to help students learn academic words they will use in this unit and on the Assessment Practice.

 **RESOURCE MANAGER—Copy Masters**
Academic Vocabulary p. 3

Additional Academic Vocabulary p. 4

# Focus and Motivate

**RL 2** Determine a theme or central idea of a text and analyze in detail its development over the course of the text, including how it emerges and is shaped and refined by specific details; provide an objective summary of the text. **RL 3** Analyze how complex characters develop the theme.

# Teach

## Part 1: Themes in Literature

**Universal Themes** Explain to students that universal themes are based on experiences and feelings that everyone goes through. Ask them to name some feelings, such as love, hate, happiness, sadness, and loss, that everyone understands. Use the following activity to reinforce the concept of universal themes:

1. Have small groups choose one of the universal themes in the box on page 434 or identify a new one.

2. Ask each group to list at least two literary works or movies that share the theme.

3. Have each group write its theme in the center circle of a web and examples in adjoining circles.

4. Guide a discussion of the groups' webs.

**Symbols** Explain that objects, places, and events in works of literature are often used as symbols to stand for something else. However, students should be careful not to over-interpret such details. For example, a rainstorm may symbolize sadness, or it may simply be a rainstorm. Have small groups revisit the universal themes they placed in their word webs. Ask each group to identify a color, an object, and an event that might be used as symbols to develop their themes.

🧰 **BEST PRACTICES TOOLKIT—Transparency**
Analysis Frame: Theme pp. D21, D32

---

# Theme and Symbol

A dramatic plot, heart-pounding action, intriguing characters—one or all of these elements may play a part in capturing, and holding, your interest in a story. Often, though, stories resonate most when they provide insights into life or human nature. The meaning behind a work of literature is the **theme,** the underlying message or **central idea** that the writer wants you to remember. Understanding this message and the writer's view of the world is the payoff you'll earn for reading carefully.

COMMON CORE

Included in this workshop:
**RL 2** Determine a theme or central idea of a text and analyze in detail its development over the course of the text, including how it emerges and is shaped and refined by specific details; provide an objective summary of the text. **RL 3** Analyze how complex characters develop the theme.

## Part 1: Themes in Literature

Some very old stories have such enduring appeal that they influence works written many centuries later. One reason these stories remain relevant is that they feature themes about emotions and experiences that are common across virtually all time periods and cultures. These **universal themes** show up again and again in literature—from ancient myths and folktales to today's bestsellers.

**EXAMPLES OF UNIVERSAL THEMES**

- People can learn from the mistakes and triumphs of past generations.

- When it comes to war, there are no winners.

- Difficult choices are part of growing up.

- Love binds people together.

A writer can use virtually every element of a story—characters, plot, and setting—to develop a theme. To convey a theme about the challenges of growing up, for example, a writer might craft a story about an insecure teenager who is plagued by difficult choices. As the character struggles to resolve the conflicts, he or she may learn a lesson about life.

A writer may also develop a theme through the use of symbols. A **symbol** is a person, place, object, or activity that stands for something beyond itself. In the same story about the doubt-ridden teenager, a writer may use the following symbols to communicate the theme without having to directly state it:

- a fork in the road (an important decision)

- the color red (a character's anger at the world)

- a torrential rainstorm (an emotional upheaval)

---

## DIFFERENTIATED INSTRUCTION

### FOR STRUGGLING READERS

**Note Taking** For students who need help with note taking, hand out the note-taking copy master before reading the first paragraphs. Then read them aloud. As you discuss theme, have students record a definition for *theme* on the copy master. Continue with the rest of the page, giving students time to record definitions and examples.

📕 **RESOURCE MANAGER—Copy Master**
Note Taking p. 9

## MODEL: THEME AND SYMBOL

Some symbols, like the ivy leaf in this story, are hard *not* to notice. The story is about Johnsy and Sue, two artists who become friends while living in New York City. When Johnsy becomes sick with pneumonia, she sinks into a deep depression. How does the symbol help you to understand Johnsy's emotions?

### *from* The Last Leaf

Short story by **O. Henry**

"Couldn't you draw in the other room?" asked Johnsy, coldly.

"I'd rather be here by you," said Sue. "Besides, I don't want you to keep looking at those silly ivy leaves."

5 "Tell me as soon as you have finished," said Johnsy, closing her eyes, and lying white and still as a fallen statue, "because I want to see the last one fall. I'm tired of waiting. I'm tired of thinking. I want to turn loose my hold on everything, and go sailing down, down, just like one of those poor, tired leaves." . . .

When Sue awoke from an hour's sleep the next morning she found Johnsy
10 with dull, wide-open eyes staring at the drawn green shade.

"Pull it up; I want to see," she ordered, in a whisper.

Wearily Sue obeyed.

But, lo! after the beating rain and fierce gusts of wind that had endured through the livelong night, there yet stood out against the brick wall one ivy
15 leaf. It was the last on the vine. Still dark green near its stem, but with its serrated edges tinted with the yellow of dissolution and decay, it hung bravely from a branch some twenty feet above the ground.

"It is the last one," said Johnsy. "I thought it would surely fall during the night. I heard the wind. It will fall to-day, and I shall die at the same time." . . .

20 The day wore away, and even through the twilight they could see the lone ivy leaf clinging to its stem against the wall. And then, with the coming of the night the north wind was again loosed, while the rain still beat against the windows and pattered down from the low Dutch eaves.

When it was light enough Johnsy, the merciless, commanded that the shade
25 be raised.

The ivy leaf was still there.

Johnsy lay for a long time looking at it. And then she called to Sue, who was stirring her chicken broth over the gas stove.

"I've been a bad girl, Sudie," said Johnsy. "Something has made that last leaf
30 stay there to show me how wicked I was. It is a sin to want to die."

### Close Read

1. Reread lines 4–8. How do the ivy leaves symbolize Johnsy and her feelings about life?

2. Examine the boxed description of the last leaf. Which words or phrases might also be used to describe Johnsy? Explain.

3. The theme emerges in lines 29–30. Summarize and explain what the writer is saying about how people should view life. How does the symbol help to convey the theme?

## MODEL: THEME AND SYMBOL

**Close Read**

1. *Possible answer: Johnsy is waiting to die, and she sees herself as a "tired" leaf ready to fall down.*

2. *Possible answer: "Yellow of dissolution and decay" (line 16) might apply to Johnsy because she is sick. Also, the last leaf is "still dark green near its stem" (line 15), which is evidence of some life. Johnsy also has some life left in her, despite her wanting to die. And, "it hung bravely" (line 16) might also apply to Johnsy, who seems as if she is hanging on to life by a thread.*

3. *Possible answer: The theme of the story is that people should never give up on life. According to Johnsy, it is a sin to want to die. The last leaf, symbolizing life (no matter how fragile), helps to show Johnsy the error of her ways and helps to communicate the theme as well.*

---

**FOR STRUGGLING READERS**

**Language Support: Vocabulary** Use Word Squares to provide instruction and practice for these words: "serrated" (line 16), "dissolution" (line 16), "twilight" (line 20), and "merciless" (line 24).

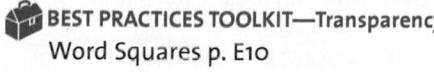 **BEST PRACTICES TOOLKIT—Transparency** Word Squares p. E10

**FOR ADVANCED LEARNERS/PRE–AP\***

**Analyze Symbols** Have students reread lines 13–17. Ask them what the "beating rain" and "fierce gusts of wind" might stand for *(life's hardships)*. Ask students to suggest other symbols for the hardships of life.

\* Pre-AP is a registered trademark of the College Entrance Examination Board. Use of the trademark does not constitute production, participation, sponsorship, or endorsement by the College Board.

**Online Remediation**

Are your students struggling with text analysis skills? Consider assigning them one or more **Level Up Online Tutorials** as remediation before beginning this unit. Log in to **thinkcentral.com** to view a list of the skills addressed by **Level Up**.

## Part 2: Determine Theme

**Theme** Point out that the theme of a work is like a lesson that the author is trying to teach. Remind students to begin determining a theme by summarizing or retelling the story. Then, show students how to use a work's topic to determine and evaluate its theme. To find the topic, students should answer in a word or phrase, "What is the work about?" (You might provide an example of a topic such as "growing up.") After determining the topic of the work, students should ask, "What is the writer trying to teach about the topic?" The answer to this question is often the work's theme. ("Learning to take responsibility for one's actions is part of growing up.") To evaluate the theme, students can ask, "How was the author successful in addressing the theme?"

**Clues to Theme** Students can use story elements as clues to figure out theme. They can also use story elements to evaluate their preliminary ideas about theme. They might assess whether an idea about theme is on target by answering these questions:

- How does the title relate to this theme?
- How do the story conflicts support it?
- How do the characters' actions or statements hint at the theme?
- How does the setting support it?
- Which symbols support the theme?

## CHECK UNDERSTANDING

Have students explain theme in their own words.

---

## Part 2: Determine Theme

Writers rarely state a work's theme directly. More often, the theme is implied. You have to analyze layers of clues to see what they reveal about the theme. As you try to uncover the theme of a work, keep these guidelines in mind:

- It is helpful to summarize the text before you determine its theme. Briefly retell the story's events, identifying important details, without including your own opinions.

- The theme is not the subject of a work; it is what the work means. Love is a subject or topic. A theme is the writer's insight or idea about love, best expressed in a sentence or two, such as "Love conquers all."

- Some works of literature have more than one theme, but in short stories, usually one theme stands out.

- The genre of a work affects the way its theme emerges. For example, a poem may share a common theme with a story, but the poet uses different techniques to express that theme.

### CLUES TO A STORY'S THEME

**TITLE**
The title may reflect a story's subject or a significant idea. Ask
- What in the story does the title refer to?
- Does the title have more than one meaning?
- What ideas does the title highlight?

**CHARACTERS**
Characters can reflect theme by what they do or say. Ask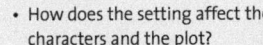
- What do the main character's thoughts and actions reveal about him or her?
- How does the main character change?
- What lessons does the character learn?

**PLOT AND CONFLICT**
A story revolves around conflicts that are central to the theme. Ask
- What conflicts do the characters face?
- How are the conflicts resolved?
- Is the resolution portrayed positively or negatively?

**SETTING**
Setting can convey theme because of what it means to the characters and readers. Ask
- How does the setting affect the characters and the plot?
- What might the setting represent?

**IMPORTANT STATEMENTS**
The narrator or the characters may make statements that hint at the theme. Ask
- What key statements are made by the characters or the narrator?
- What ideas do these statements emphasize?

**SYMBOLS**
Characters, conflicts, and settings can serve as symbols that support the theme. Ask
- What might the characters, conflicts, and setting represent?
- What ideas do these symbols communicate?

---

## DIFFERENTIATED INSTRUCTION

### FOR ENGLISH LANGUAGE LEARNERS
**Language: Skill Words** On the board, list the literary terms shown in italics. Then give the examples in random order for students to classify.

- *conflict:* The two students glared at each other with hate in their eyes.
- *setting:* The beach stretched for miles under a cloudless sky.
- *characters:* Alison nervously whistled her favorite song as she walked to her first job interview.

### FOR STRUGGLING READERS
**Note Taking** Provide the note-taking copy master to students who experience difficulty with note taking. Read and discuss the top of the page. Then review the "Clues to Theme" section. Ask students to fill in the copy masters after you review each feature.

**R** RESOURCE MANAGER—Copy Master
Note Taking p. 10

## Part 3: Analyze the Text

This story takes place in Dublin, Ireland, during a civil war that erupted in 1922. Hidden by darkness, a sniper waits for his next target. As you read, track the clues to the theme. What message about war is the writer communicating?

# The Sniper
Short story
by **Liam O'Flaherty**

The long June twilight faded into night. Dublin lay enveloped in darkness, but for the dim light of the moon, that shone through fleecy clouds, casting a pale light as of approaching dawn over the streets and the dark waters of the Liffey. Around the beleaguered Four Courts the heavy guns roared. Here and
5 there through the city machine guns and rifles broke the silence of the night, spasmodically, like dogs barking on lone farms. Republicans and Free Staters[1] were waging civil war.

On a roof-top near O'Connel Bridge, a Republican sniper lay watching. Beside him lay his rifle and over his shoulders were slung a pair of field-glasses.
10 His face was the face of a student—thin and ascetic, but his eyes had the cold gleam of the fanatic. They were deep and thoughtful, the eyes of a man who is used to looking at death.

He was eating a sandwich hungrily. He had eaten nothing since morning. He had been too excited to eat. He finished the sandwich, and taking a flask
15 of whiskey from his pocket, he took a short draught. Then he returned the flask to his pocket. He paused for a moment, considering whether he should risk a smoke. It was dangerous. The flash might be seen in the darkness and there were enemies watching. He decided to take the risk. Placing a cigarette between his lips, he struck a match, inhaled the smoke hurriedly and put out
20 the light. Almost immediately, a bullet flattened itself against the parapet[2] of the roof. The sniper took another whiff and put out the cigarette. Then he swore softly and crawled away to the left.

Cautiously he raised himself and peered over the parapet. There was a flash and a bullet whizzed over his head. He dropped immediately. He had
25 seen the flash. It came from the opposite side of the street.

He rolled over the roof to a chimney stack in the rear, and slowly drew himself up behind it, until his eyes were level with the top of the parapet. There was nothing to be seen—just the dim outline of the opposite housetop against the blue sky. His enemy was under cover.
30 Just then an armored car came across the bridge and advanced slowly up the street. It stopped on the opposite side of the street fifty yards ahead. The sniper could hear the dull panting of the motor. His heart beat faster. It was an enemy car. He wanted to fire, but he knew it was useless. His bullets would never pierce the steel that covered the grey monster.

---

1. **Republicans and Free Staters:** The Irish Republican Army (Republicans) wanted complete independence from England. The Irish Free Staters wanted Ireland to govern itself but still remain part of the British Empire.

2. **parapet:** a low wall along the edge of a roof or balcony.

### Close Read

1. Which setting details in the first paragraph help convey a grim, dangerous picture of war? One detail has been boxed.

2. Reread the description of the sniper in lines 8–18. Through the character of the sniper, what might the writer be saying about soldiers who fight in wars?

---

## Part 3: Analyze the Text
### Close Read

1. *Possible answer:* Details include "lay enveloped in darkness" (line 1), "dark waters of the Liffey" (lines 3–4), "beleaguered Four Courts" (line 4), "rifles broke the silence of the night" (line 5), and "like dogs barking on lone farms" (line 6). All these details show how war is disrupting a once-peaceful city.

2. *Possible answer:* O'Flaherty characterizes the sniper as being indifferent to death. As a risk-taker, he gets an adrenaline rush from the dangerous situations he often finds himself in. The writer describes the sniper as a "fanatic," hardly a favorable impression of soldiers who fight in wars. The writer is probably trying to emphasize the cold-blooded, indifferent nature of soldiers who have been programmed to kill.

### ADDITIONAL TEACHING OPPORTUNITY

**Evaluate Theme:** Ask students to identify the story's theme—its underlying message about life or human nature. Then have students evaluate that theme and decide whether they think it is valid. Tell students to use these questions as their evaluation criteria:

- Does the theme express a broad insight into life or human nature, or simply an idea that applies only to a few people?

- Does the theme offer a meaningful insight, or is it too obvious or clichéd?

- Is the theme a realistic observation, or is it too optimistic, cynical, or narrow-minded?

Point out to students that a theme may be valid even if they do not personally agree with it. (To learn more about evaluating theme, see **Reading Handbook,** page R2.)

---

**FOR ADVANCED LEARNERS/PRE-AP**

**Analyze Title** Have students discuss what ideas the title highlights. Why doesn't the author use the sniper's name in the story?

**3. Possible answer:** *The sniper thinks the woman is an informer—someone who told the man in the car about the sniper's location. The sniper thought that the man was preparing to shoot him, so the sniper acted first.*

**4. Possible answer:** *The enemy shoots the sniper in the arm, and the sniper feels immense pain. He has to bandage his wound and continue to be discreet so that his cover is not blown.*

**5. Possible answer:** *By thinking about the other sniper as only "the enemy," the sniper dehumanizes his target. As a soldier, it's probably best not to think of your target as a human being.*

---

35    Then round the corner of a side street came an old woman, her head covered by a tattered shawl. She began to talk to the man in the turret of the car. She was pointing to the roof where the sniper lay. An informer.

    The turret opened. A man's head and shoulders appeared, looking towards the sniper. The sniper raised his rifle and fired. The head fell heavily on the
40  turret wall. The woman darted towards the side street. The sniper fired again. The woman whirled round and fell with a shriek into the gutter.

    Suddenly from the opposite roof a shot rang out and the sniper dropped his rifle with a curse. The rifle clattered to the roof. The sniper thought the noise would wake the dead. He stopped to pick the rifle up. He couldn't lift it. His
45  forearm was dead. . . . He muttered, "I'm hit."

    Dropping flat on to the roof, he crawled back to the parapet. With his left hand he felt the injured right forearm. The blood was oozing through the sleeve of his coat. There was no pain—just a deadened sensation, as if the arm had been cut off.

50    Quickly he drew his knife from his pocket, opened it on the breastwork of the parapet and ripped open the sleeve. There was a small hole where the bullet had entered. On the other side there was no hole. The bullet had lodged in the bone. It must have fractured it. He bent the arm below the wound. The arm bent back easily. He ground his teeth to overcome the pain.

55    Then, taking out his field dressing, he ripped open the packet with his knife. He broke the neck of the iodine bottle and let the bitter fluid drip into the wound. A paroxysm of pain swept through him. He placed the cotton wadding over the wound and wrapped the dressing over it. He tied the end with his teeth.

60    Then he lay still against the parapet, and closing his eyes, he made an effort of will to overcome the pain.

    In the street beneath all was still. The armored car had retired speedily over the bridge, with the machine gunner's head hanging lifeless over the turret. The woman's corpse lay still in the gutter.
65    The sniper lay for a long time nursing his wounded arm and planning escape. Morning must not find him wounded on the roof. The enemy on the opposite roof covered his escape. He must kill that enemy and he could not use his rifle. He had only a revolver to do it. Then he thought of a plan.

    Taking off his cap, he placed it over the muzzle of his rifle. Then he pushed
70  the rifle slowly upwards over the parapet, until the cap was visible from the opposite side of the street. Almost immediately there was a report, and a bullet pierced the center of the cap. The sniper slanted the rifle forward. The cap slipped down into the street. Then, catching the rifle in the middle, the sniper dropped his left hand over the roof and let it hang, lifelessly. After a few
75  moments he let the rifle drop to the street. Then he sank to the roof, dragging his hand with him.

    Crawling quickly to the left, he peered up at the corner of the roof. His ruse had succeeded. The other sniper seeing the cap and rifle fall, thought that

**3.** Why does the sniper shoot the man in the armored car and the woman? Explain how you think the writer wants you to feel about the sniper's actions.

**4.** What conflicts are created by the presence of the enemy sniper?

**5.** Notice how the sniper refers to the other sniper only as "the enemy" in lines 65–68. In what ways might this help the sniper be effective in war?

---

## DIFFERENTIATED INSTRUCTION

### FOR STRUGGLING READERS

**Concept Support** To help students understand how the sniper depersonalized his enemy, ask them to suppose the sniper knew his enemy's name. Guide a discussion of their responses to the following questions:

- Would he be more likely or less likely to hate the other sniper?

- Would he be more likely or less likely to want to hurt the other sniper?

- Would he be more likely or less likely to want to kill the other sniper?

### FOR ADVANCED LEARNERS/PRE–AP

**Analyzing Symbols** Ask students what the woman symbolizes. *Possible answer: She symbolizes all the faceless victims of war, innocent people who die simply because they are in the wrong place at the wrong time.*

he had killed his man. He was now standing before a row of chimney pots,
80 looking across, with his head clearly silhouetted against the western sky.

The Republican sniper smiled and lifted his revolver above the edge of the parapet. The distance was about fifty yards—a hard shot in the dim light, and his right arm was paining him. . . . He took a steady aim. His hand trembled with eagerness. Pressing his lips together, he took a deep breath through his
85 nostrils and fired. He was almost deafened with the report and his arm shook with the recoil.

Then, when the smoke cleared, he peered across and uttered a cry of joy. His enemy had been hit. He was reeling over the parapet in his death agony. He struggled to keep his feet, but he was slowly falling forward,
90 as if in a dream. The rifle fell from his grasp, hit the parapet, fell over, bounded off the pole of a barber's shop beneath and then clattered on to the pavement.

Then the dying man on the roof crumpled up and fell forward. The body turned over and over in space and hit the ground with a dull thud. Then it lay still.

95 The sniper looked at his enemy falling and he shuddered. The lust of battle died in him. He became bitten by remorse. The sweat stood out in beads on his forehead. Weakened by his wound and the long summer day of fasting and watching on the roof, he revolted from the sight of the shattered mass of his dead enemy. His teeth chattered. He began to gibber to himself, cursing the
100 war, cursing himself, cursing everybody.

He looked at the smoking revolver in his hand and with an oath he hurled it to the roof at his feet. The revolver went off with the concussion, and the bullet whizzed past the sniper's head. He was frightened back to his senses by the shock. His nerves steadied. The cloud of fear scattered from his mind and
105 he laughed.

Taking the whiskey flask from his pocket, he emptied it at a draught. He felt reckless under the influence of the spirits. He decided to leave the roof and look for his company commander to report. Everywhere around was quiet. There was not much danger in going through the streets. He picked up his
110 revolver and put it in his pocket. Then he crawled down through the sky-light to the house underneath.

When the sniper reached the laneway on the street level, he felt a sudden curiosity as to the identity of the enemy sniper whom he had killed. He decided that he was a good shot whoever he was. He wondered if he knew
115 him. Perhaps he had been in his own company before the split in the army. He decided to risk going over to have a look at him. He peered around the corner into O'Connell Street. In the upper part of the street there was heavy firing, but around here all was quiet.

The sniper darted across the street. A machine gun tore up the
120 ground around him with a hail of bullets, but he escaped. He threw himself face downwards beside the corpse. The machine gun stopped.

Then the sniper turned over the dead body and looked into his brother's face.

### Close Read

6. How does the Republican sniper resolve his conflict with the second sniper?

7. Reread the boxed text. How does the sniper change after seeing his enemy fall?

8. Which details in lines 112–116 tell you that the sniper starts to realize his fallen enemy is a human being? Explain.

9. Consider the last line of the story and the clues you noticed while reading. What is the writer saying about war? State the theme and summarize details that helped you understand it.

TEXT ANALYSIS WORKSHOP **439**

### Close Read

6. *Possible answer: The sniper tricks his enemy by sticking his cap on the top of his rifle. Seeing the cap and thinking it is the sniper himself, the enemy shoots his target. The sniper lets the cap fall and dangles his arm so that it looks like he's been shot. Thinking the sniper is now dead, the enemy comes out of hiding. The sniper takes aim and successfully kills his enemy.*

7. *Possible answer: After the sniper kills his enemy, he starts to develop a conscience. He is no longer interested in the rush he gets from battles and killing. Partly due to his wound and his hunger, he briefly questions the point of the war. Also, he is disgusted by the sight of the dead enemy.*

8. *Possible answer: Details revealing that the sniper sees his enemy as a human being include "sudden curiosity as to the identity," "he was a good shot," and "wondered if he knew him." These details contrast with the sniper's earlier thoughts about the "enemy." For the first time, the sniper starts thinking of his enemy as "he" and "him"—another human being.*

9. *Possible answer: War is pointless and brutal; it literally pits brother against brother. Details that help to convey this theme: the change in the sniper's character, the powerful last line, the details about the dangerous setting.*

## Assess and Reteach

### Assess

Have students explain how the theme of "The Sniper" is revealed through the conflicts, characters, and setting.

### Reteach

Select from these reteaching options to help students who experienced difficulty applying the workshop skills to "The Sniper":

1. Review the note-taking copy masters. Have students define terms and explain how each story feature gives clues to the theme.

2. Ask students to name a familiar story and to suggest ideas for its theme. Have them discuss how the story's conflicts, characters, setting, and symbols support the theme they suggested.

**FOR STRUGGLING READERS**

**Language Support: Vocabulary** Have partners find and define two unfamiliar verbs from "The Sniper." Make sure they find descriptive, vivid verbs. Ask students to quickly draw a sketch showing the action of each verb. Then have them share their sketches and definitions with another pair.

# Focus and Motivate

## COMMON CORE FOCUS

**RL 1** Cite textual evidence to support analysis of what the text says explicitly as well as inferences drawn from the text. **RL 2** Determine a theme of a text and analyze its development. **RL 4** Determine the figurative meaning of words and phrases as they are used in a text. **L 4b–d** Identify patterns of word changes that indicate different meanings; consult reference materials to determine or clarify a word's etymology; verify the preliminary determination of the meaning of a word or phrase.

## SUMMARIES

**"Marigolds"** Lizabeth lives during the Depression. Her family's difficulties frustrate and frighten her, and she vents her stress by destroying a cherished marigold garden. Years later, she still regrets the act, but from it she has learned about compassion.

**"Sowing Change"** Donna Freedman's article explains how neighbors worked together to turn a barren lot into a garden.

**Book Cover** The cover of *In Our Hand*s, a book about social change, shows a pair of hands holding a green seedling.

## What if life had a RESET button?

Explore the question by asking students what actions people often regret.

## What's the Connection

Lead students in a discussion of how people take and show pride in their environment.

## Selection Resources

---

**Marigolds**
Short Story by Eugenia Collier

**Sowing Change**
Newspaper Article by Donna Freedman

**In Our Hands**
Book Cover

# What if life had a RESET button?

### COMMON CORE

**RL 1** Cite textual evidence to support analysis of what the text says explicitly as well as inferences drawn from the text. **RL 2** Determine a theme of a text and analyze its development. **RL 4** Determine the figurative meaning of words and phrases as they are used in a text. **L 4b, c** Identify patterns of word changes that indicate different meanings; consult reference materials to determine or clarify a word's etymology.

It's a terrible thing to drop your grandmother's prized china vase on the kitchen floor. And did you really have to be so mean to your little brother yesterday? At one time or another, we've all done or said something that makes us cringe with regret. We wish we could turn back the clock by a minute or a day and just do the whole thing over.

## What's the Connection?

The literary text that follows will explore not only regret but other concepts that shape the way we see and experience the world—poverty, pride, and beauty, to name a few. After you read "Marigolds," you'll read a nonfiction text and a visual that explore similar topics.

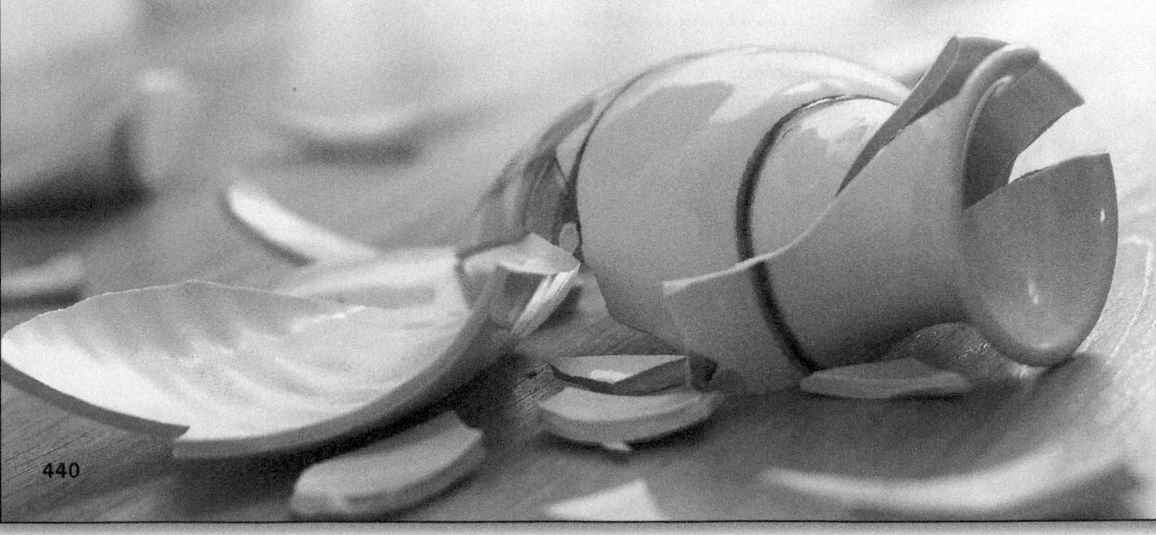

440

---

*See resources on the* **Teacher One Stop DVD-ROM** *and on* <u>thinkcentral.com</u>.

 **RESOURCE MANAGER UNIT 4**
Plan and Teach, pp. 11–18
Summary, pp. 19–20 † ‡*
Text Analysis and Reading
  Skill, pp. 21–24† *
Vocabulary, pp. 25–27*

**DIAGNOSTIC AND SELECTION TESTS**
Selection Tests, pp. 115–118

 **BEST PRACTICES TOOLKIT**
Word Squares, p. E10
Open Mind, p. D9
Cause-and-Effect Graphics
  Chain, p. B39

**TECHNOLOGY**
🔘 **Teacher One Stop DVD-ROM**
🔘 **Student One Stop DVD-ROM**
🔘 **Audio Anthology CD**
🔘 **ExamView Test Generator**
  on the **Teacher One Stop**

---

*\* Resources for Differentiation*      † In Spanish      ‡ In Haitian Creole and Vietnamese

## TEXT ANALYSIS: THEME AND SETTING

"Marigolds" takes place in a rural African-American community during the 1930s—a time of racial segregation, poverty, and limited opportunity. This **setting** offers important clues about the development of the story's **theme,** or underlying message. For example, the figurative, or nonliteral, description of "futile waiting" as "the sorrowful background music of our impoverished little community" powerfully describes the setting and hints at the hopelessness of the narrator's situation. As you read the story, think about how the setting influences the narrator's experiences and the conflicts she faces. What message do those experiences teach us about life?

## READING SKILL: DRAW CONCLUSIONS

A **conclusion** is a logical judgment based on information in the text and on your own experience and prior knowledge. As you read "Marigolds," create a graphic organizer like the one shown. Include information from the text and your thoughts about the information. Then record your conclusions.

| Text Information | + Prior Knowledge | = Conclusion |
|---|---|---|
| All the narrator remembers about her hometown is the dust. | + Most people recall pleasant memories of their past. | = She must not have many pleasant memories, or she would have remembered them. |

**Review:** Paraphrase

## ▲ VOCABULARY IN CONTEXT

In your *Reader/Writer Notebook,* create a chart like the one below and place the following words from the story in the chart according to your knowledge of them. Then write a brief definition of each word you know.

| WORD LIST | | |
|---|---|---|
| bravado | impotent | poignantly |
| degradation | nostalgia | retribution |
| exuberance | ostensibly | squalor |
| futile | perverse | stoicism |

| Know Well | Think I Know | Don't Know |
|---|---|---|
| | | |

 Complete the activities in your **Reader/Writer Notebook.**

## Meet the Author

# Eugenia Collier
### born 1928

**Respect for Education**
Eugenia Collier grew up in the segregated part of Baltimore, Maryland, the city where she still lives today. From her parents, a doctor and a teacher, Collier learned the value of education at a young age. This led her to graduate with high honors from Howard University. She then received a master of arts from Columbia University.

**Award-Winning Teacher and Writer**
After working for five years as a caseworker for the Baltimore Department of Public Welfare, Collier became a college professor and started her writing career. She credits her African-American heritage as her inspiration. "The fact of my blackness is the core and center of my creativity." "Marigolds," one of her first stories, won the Gwendolyn Brooks Award for fiction in 1969. Since then, her stories, poems, and essays have appeared in many anthologies and magazines. She was selected as an outstanding educator from 1972–75 and won a Distinguished Writers Award in 1984.

**BACKGROUND TO THE STORY**
**Hard Times**
During the Great Depression of the 1930s, millions of Americans suffered from unemployment. Government programs, such as the unemployment insurance available today, did not yet exist to help people get through the tough times. Although many Americans suffered, African Americans were particularly hard hit. In an age of racial segregation and prejudice, black people generally had fewer job opportunities and experienced higher unemployment rates.

Author Online
**THINK** central
Go to **thinkcentral.com.**
KEYWORD: HML9-441

441

# Teach

TEXT ANALYSIS
COMMON CORE
RL 2, RL 4

## ● *Model the Skill:* THEME AND SETTING

Read aloud this example:

> Lakeside was a town of mansions and luxury cars. Its residents spoke of wealth but never of wisdom or regret.

Discuss how the setting might be connected to a theme. Point out that the setting suggests rich residents; the theme might be their materialism or arrogance.

**GUIDED PRACTICE** Have students name settings and themes from other stories.

READING SKILL
COMMON CORE
RL 1

## ■ *Model the Skill:* DRAW CONCLUSIONS

Use the information about the author to model drawing conclusions.

- The Depression affected African Americans quite severely.
- Collier's parents were a doctor and a teacher, and therefore less likely to be unemployed than other workers.
- Collier probably did not suffer as much as other African-American children did.

**GUIDED PRACTICE** Discuss how the **Meet the Author** subheads express conclusions about the text.

**R** RESOURCE MANAGER—Copy Master Draw Conclusions p. 23 (for student use while reading the selection)

VOCABULARY SKILL
COMMON CORE
L 4

## ▲ VOCABULARY IN CONTEXT

**DIAGNOSE WORD KNOWLEDGE** Have all students complete Vocabulary in Context. Check their definitions against the following:

**bravado** (brə-vä'dō) *n.* a false show of courage or defiance

**degradation** (dĕg'rə-dā'shən) *n.* condition of being brought to a lower level; humiliation

**exuberance** (ĭg-zōō'bər-əns) *n.* condition of unrestrained joy

**futile** (fyōot'l) *adj.* having no useful result

**impotent** (ĭm'pə-tənt) *adj.* powerless; lacking strength or vigor

**nostalgia** (nŏ-stăl'jə) *n.* bittersweet longing for things from the past

**ostensibly** (ŏ-stĕn'sə-blē) *adv.* seemingly; to all outward appearances

**perverse** (pər-vûrs') *adj.* stubbornly contrary; wrong; harmful

**poignantly** (poin'yənt-lē) *adv.* in a profoundly moving manner

**retribution** (rĕt'rə-byōō'shən) *n.* something given in repayment, usually as a punishment

**squalor** (skwŏl'ər) *n.* a filthy, shabby, and wretched condition, as from poverty

**stoicism** (stō'ĭ-sĭz'əm) *n.* indifference to pleasure or pain; a lack of visible emotion

**PRETEACH VOCABULARY** Use the copy master to help students predict the meaning of each boldfaced word in the copy master, using context clues.

**R** RESOURCE MANAGER—Copy Master Vocabulary Study p. 25

### READ WITH A PURPOSE

*Help students set a purpose for reading.
Ask them to compare the narrator with the
14-year-old version of herself that she describes
in the story.*

---

**TEXT ANALYSIS**  |  **COMMON CORE**

**Ⓐ THEME AND SETTING**  RL 2, RL 4

*Possible answer: The author helps readers
visualize the setting by describing in detail
the late-summer dust (lines 1–4) and summing up the setting as "the dry September
of the dirt roads and grassless yards of the
shanty-town" (lines 8–9). She contrasts
this setting with her town's lush lawns and
shade trees (lines 5–6), which she knows
must have existed but which she does not
remember. She also contrasts the "arid,
sterile dust" (line 2) that she does remember with the marigolds' "brilliant splash of
sunny yellow" (lines 10–11).*

---

**VOCABULARY**  |  **COMMON CORE**  L 4

**OWN THE WORD**

- **nostalgia:** Ask students the following
  questions: *Have you ever had an experience that made you feel* nostalgic? *What
  memory did the experience trigger? How
  did the* nostalgia *make you feel? Did it
  make you long for the past?*

- **futile:** Have students complete this sentence: *Although we worked hard on our
  invention, our work was* futile *because ...*
  **Possible answer:** *our invention never
  worked, and other students had far more
  creative ideas.*

---

# Marigolds
### Eugenia Collier

When I think of the home town of my youth, all that I seem to remember is
dust—the brown, crumbly dust of late summer—arid, sterile dust that gets
into the eyes and makes them water, gets into the throat and between the
toes of bare brown feet. I don't know why I should remember only the dust.
Surely there must have been lush green lawns and paved streets under leafy
shade trees somewhere in town; but memory is an abstract painting—it does
not present things as they are, but rather as they *feel*. And so, when I think of
that time and that place, I remember only the dry September of the dirt roads
and grassless yards of the shanty-town where I lived. And one other thing I
10 remember, another incongruency of memory—a brilliant splash of sunny
yellow against the dust—Miss Lottie's marigolds. Ⓐ

Whenever the memory of those marigolds flashes across my mind, a strange
**nostalgia** comes with it and remains long after the picture has faded. I feel
again the chaotic emotions of adolescence, illusive as smoke, yet as real as the
potted geranium before me now. Joy and rage and wild animal gladness and
shame become tangled together in the multicolored skein of 14-going-on-15
as I recall that devastating moment when I was suddenly more woman than
child, years ago in Miss Lottie's yard. I think of those marigolds at the strangest
times; I remember them vividly now as I desperately pass away the time
20 waiting for you, who will not come.

I suppose that **futile** waiting was the sorrowful background music of our
impoverished little community when I was young. The Depression that
gripped the nation was no new thing to us, for the black workers of rural
Maryland had always been depressed. I don't know what it was that we were
waiting for; certainly not for the prosperity that was "just around the corner,"
for those were white folks' words, which we never believed. Nor did we wait
for hard work and thrift to pay off in shining success as the American Dream[1]
promised, for we knew better than that, too. Perhaps we waited for a miracle,

---

1. **American Dream:** the belief that through hard work one will achieve a comfortable and prosperous life.

**442**   UNIT 4: THEME AND SYMBOL

Detail of *Full Spittoon* (1974),
Bob Timberlake. Watercolor.
Private Collection.
© Bob Timberlake.

---

**Analyze Visuals ▶**

How would you describe
the **mood** created by this
painting?

**❶ Targeted Passage**

**Ⓐ THEME AND SETTING**
Identify details that help
you visualize the setting.
What contrasts are
presented?

**nostalgia** (nŏ-stăl′jə) *n.*
bittersweet longing for
things from the past

**futile** (fyōōt′l) *adj.* having
no useful result

---

## DIFFERENTIATED INSTRUCTION

**FOR ENGLISH LANGUAGE LEARNERS**

**Vocabulary Support**  Use Word Squares to
teach these words: *community* (line 22),
*Depression* (line 22), *strategy* (line 92), *reinforce*
(line 92), *exploits* (line 123), *ignorant* (line 307).

🧰 **BEST PRACTICES TOOLKIT—Transparency**
Word Squares p. E10

**FOR STRUGGLING READERS**

In combination with the *Audio Anthology CD*,
use one or more Targeted Passages
(pp. 442, 448, 449, 451) to ensure that students
focus on key story events, concepts, and skills.
Targeted Passages are also good for English
learners.

**❶ Targeted Passage** [Lines 8–24]

This passage establishes "Marigolds" as a
recollection of events from the narrator's

**REVISIT THE BIG QUESTION**

What if life had a

## RESET button?

**Discuss** Which words and phrases in lines 12–20 suggest that the narrator feels some regret about the past? *Possible answer: The narrator's reference to her nostalgia as "strange" (lines 12–13) may hint at regret. The negative terms "chaotic emotions" (line 14) and "rage" (line 15) are stronger, and they lead to the most telling word: "shame" (line 16). The connection between shame and the "devastating moment" that she recalls (line 17) suggests a strong sense of regret about the past—specifically, about some past action.*

## Analyze Visuals

*Possible answer: The bright colors of the flowers create a cheerful mood. The fact that a spittoon is used as a flowerpot for the blooms also adds to the upbeat feeling.*

**About the Art** If students have read "A Christmas Memory" in Unit 3, they already have met North Carolina artist Bob Timberlake (born 1933). Known for his realistic style, Timberlake has painted many scenes of the rural South. The bright marigolds in this painting help students envision this story's title and the description of Miss Lottie's marigolds as "a brilliant splash of sunny yellow" (lines 10–11).

troubled adolescence.

- What time in her life is the narrator recalling? How can you tell? (lines 14–17)
- Why was her life difficult at that time? (lines 22–24)
- What details suggest that Miss Lottie and her marigolds will be important in the story that the narrator is about to tell? (lines 9–13)

**FOR ADVANCED LEARNERS/PRE–AP**

**Explore Cultural Context** Have students research different aspects of the Depression and present their findings to the class. Possible topics include:

- Governmental action and inaction that may have exacerbated the crisis at first
- Programs created under the New Deal that are still in place today
- Maryland's or their own state's specific economic problems and solutions

wander about in the September dust, offering one's sweat in return for some
meager share of bread. But God was chary[2] with miracles in those days, and so
we waited—and waited.

We children, of course, were only vaguely aware of the extent of our poverty.
Having no radios, few newspapers, and no magazines, we were somewhat
unaware of the world outside our community. Nowadays we would be called
"culturally deprived" and people would write books and hold conferences
about us. In those days everybody we knew was just as hungry and ill-clad as
we were. Poverty was the cage in which we all were trapped, and our hatred
40 of it was still the vague, undirected restlessness of the zoo-bred flamingo who
knows that nature created him to fly free.

As I think of those days I feel most **poignantly** the tag-end of summer, the
bright dry times when we began to have a sense of shortening days and the
imminence of the cold.

By the time I was 14 my brother Joey and I were the only children left at our
house, the older ones having left home for early marriage or the lure of the city,
and the two babies having been sent to relatives who might care for them better
than we. Joey was three years younger than I, and a boy, and therefore vastly
inferior. Each morning our mother and father trudged wearily down the dirt
50 road and around the bend, she to her domestic job, he to his daily unsuccessful
quest for work. After our few chores around the tumbledown shanty, Joey and I
were free to run wild in the sun with other children similarly situated.

For the most part, those days are ill-defined in my memory, running
together and combining like a fresh water-color painting left out in the rain.
I remember squatting in the road drawing a picture in the dust, a picture that
Joey gleefully erased with one sweep of his dirty foot. I remember fishing for
minnows in a muddy creek and watching sadly as they eluded my cupped
hands, while Joey laughed uproariously. And I remember, that year, a strange
restlessness of body and of spirit, a feeling that something old and familiar was
60 ending, and something unknown and therefore terrifying was beginning. C

One day returns to me with special clarity for some reason, perhaps because
it was the beginning of the experience that in some inexplicable way marked
the end of innocence. I was loafing under the great oak tree in our yard, deep
in some reverie which I have now forgotten except that it involved some secret,
secret thoughts of one of the Harris boys across the yard. Joey and a bunch of
kids were bored now with the old tire suspended from an oak limb which had
kept them entertained for a while.

"Hey, Lizabeth," Joey yelled. He never talked when he could yell. "Hey,
Lizabeth, let's us go somewhere."

---

2. **chary** (châr'ē): sparing or stingy.

---

**B DRAW CONCLUSIONS**
Based on what you've
read so far, what
conclusions can you draw
about the narrator's life?
Cite details to support
your answer.

**poignantly**
(poin'yənt-lē) *adv.*
in a profoundly
moving manner

**C DRAW CONCLUSIONS**
Reread lines 58–60.
Lizabeth, the narrator,
is almost 15 at this point
in the story. What
changes are taking place
in her life?

---

### B DRAW CONCLUSIONS

*Possible answer:* The narrator is poor, as
suggested in references to the shanty-town
(line 9) and to being hungry and ill-clad
(line 38). Her family has suffered financially
for some time, for "The Depression . . . was
no new thing to us . . ." (lines 22–23).
The comment that "God was chary with
miracles" (line 32) and the comparison of
poverty to a cage (line 39) indicate that the
narrator does not expect her life to improve.

**Extend the Discussion** Why do you think
the narrator compares her life to that of a
"zoo-bred flamingo" (line 40)?

---

### C *Model the Skill:* DRAW CONCLUSIONS

Have students reread lines 13–18 and
58–60. Model adding this information to
their Reading Skill charts:

*Text Information:* Lizabeth, who is almost
15, is restless. She feels that part of her life
is ending and another part is beginning.

*Prior Knowledge:* At 14 and 15, people are
no longer children, but they are not yet
adults. It can be an unsettling time.

*Conclusion:* Lizabeth senses that she is
moving toward adulthood.

*Possible answer:* The changes are that Lizabeth feels restless and worried that familiar
things in her life are being replaced with
things that are unknown and frightening.
In short, Lizabeth is moving toward young
adulthood.

---

### OWN THE WORD

**poignantly:** Ask students if they have
*poignant* memories of a summer or of a
special holiday celebrated with friends or
family. What about the event make the
memories *poignant*?

---

## DIFFERENTIATED INSTRUCTION

**FOR ENGLISH LANGUAGE LEARNERS**
**Language: Pronoun Referents** Explain the
usage of *one* in lines 28–32. There, *one* is the
formal equivalent of the informal *you* or the
impersonal *someone*. Reinforce the concept
by discussing the use of *one* and *one's* in
lines 307–308.

**FOR ADVANCED LEARNERS/PRE–AP**
**Analyze Figurative Language** [paired-activity
option] Eugenia Collier uses two linked
metaphors in this statement: "Poverty was
the cage in which we all were trapped, and
our hatred of it was still the vague, undirected restlessness of the zoo-bred flamingo
who knows that nature created him to fly
free" (lines 39–41). Have students analyze the
metaphors and explain why the metaphors
are effective.

---

70    I came reluctantly from my private world. "Where you want to go? What you want to do?"

The truth was that we were becoming tired of the formlessness of our summer days. The idleness whose prospect had seemed so beautiful during the busy days of spring now had degenerated to an almost desperate effort to fill up the empty midday hours.

"Let's go see can we find some locusts on the hill," someone suggested.

Joey was scornful. "Ain't no more locusts there. Y'all got 'em all while they was still green."

The argument that followed was brief and not really worth the effort.

80    Hunting locust trees wasn't fun any more by now.

"Tell you what," said Joey finally, his eyes sparkling. "Let's go over to Miss Lottie's."

The idea caught on at once, for annoying Miss Lottie was always fun. I was still child enough to scamper along with the group over rickety fences and through bushes that tore our already raggedy clothes, back to where Miss Lottie lived. I think now that we must have made a tragicomic spectacle, five or six kids of different ages, each of us clad in only one garment—the girls in faded dresses that were too long or too short, the boys in patchy pants, their sweaty brown chests gleaming in the hot sun. A little cloud of dust followed

90    our thin legs and bare feet as we tramped over the barren land.

When Miss Lottie's house came into view we stopped, **ostensibly** to plan our strategy, but actually to reinforce our courage. Miss Lottie's house was the most ramshackle of all our ramshackle homes. The sun and rain had long since faded its rickety frame siding from white to a sullen gray. The boards themselves seemed to remain upright not from being nailed together but rather from leaning together like a house that a child might have constructed from cards. A brisk wind might have blown it down, and the fact that it was still standing implied a kind of enchantment that was stronger than the elements. There it stood, and as far as I know is standing yet—a gray rotting thing with

100    no porch, no shutters, no steps, set on a cramped lot with no grass, not even any weeds—a monument to decay. **D**

In front of the house in a squeaky rocking chair sat Miss Lottie's son, John Burke, completing the impression of decay. John Burke was what was known as "queer-headed." Black and ageless, he sat, rocking day in and day out in a mindless stupor, lulled by the monotonous squeak-squawk of the chair. A battered hat atop his shaggy head shaded him from the sun. Usually John Burke was totally unaware of everything outside his quiet dream world. But if you disturbed him, if you intruded upon his fantasies, he would become enraged, strike out at you, and curse at you in some strange enchanted

110    language which only he could understand. We children made a game of thinking of ways to disturb John Burke and then to elude his violent **retribution**.

---

**COMMON CORE** L 4b

**Language Coach**

**Derivations** Words that are formed from another word or base are **derivations**. The word *generate*, meaning "bring into existence," has many derivations, including *generation* and *regenerate*. Reread lines 73–75 to find another derivation of *generate*. Guess the word's meaning.

---

**ostensibly** (ŏ-stĕn'sə-blē) *adv.* seemingly; to all outward appearances

---

**D DRAW CONCLUSIONS**
Reread lines 91–101. What does this description of Miss Lottie's home add to your understanding of her and her social and financial standing?

---

**retribution**
(rĕt'rə-byōō'shən) *n.* something given in repayment, usually as a punishment

---

**TIERED DISCUSSION PROMPTS**
Use these prompts to help students explore the children's attitudes in lines 72–90:

**Connect** Have you ever had too much free time on your hands? Describe how you felt. *Answers should show an understanding of the children's boredom.*

**Synthesize** The narrator notes that "we must have made a tragicomic spectacle" (line 86). What does she mean? Do you think that she felt this way when she was 14? *Possible answer: The group is tragicomic in that the children's ragtag appearance is funny to behold, but sad in that it reflects their poverty. At 14, Lizabeth might not have had the maturity to make this observation.*

---

**READING SKILL**    **COMMON CORE**
                     **RL 1**

**D DRAW CONCLUSIONS**

*Possible answer:* The narrator says that Miss Lottie's decaying house was "the most ramshackle of all our ramshackle homes" (line 93). As the owner of the worst-looking house in an impoverished community, Miss Lottie probably has a very low social and financial standing.

---

**VOCABULARY**    **COMMON CORE**
                  **L 4**

**OWN THE WORD**

- **ostensibly:** Write *ostensibly* and the definition "seemingly; to all outward appearances" in a circle. Have students add synonyms to complete a semantic map. *Possible answers: apparently, presumably, outwardly, evidently*

- **retribution:** Remind students that the prefix *re-* means "again" or "back," and that in ancient times, *tribute* was often paid to leaders in goods or money. Have students determine the meaning of *retribution* from its root words.

---

**FOR STRUGGLING READERS**

**Comprehension Support** Make sure that students understand the moment in lines 70–83 that sets the rising action of the plot into motion. Ask students to explain why the children decide to annoy Miss Lottie, even though they probably know that it is not nice to do.

**FOR ENGLISH LANGUAGE LEARNERS**

**Language Coach**    **COMMON CORE**
                      **L 4b**
**Derivations** *Possible answers: degenerated, "sunk to a lower state";* Have students use a dictionary to confirm or refine their definitions.

**REVISIT THE BIG QUESTION**

## What if life had a
# RESET button?

**Discuss** Lizabeth does not gather pebbles in lines 148–155. Might she sense that she will regret participating? If so, why does she change her mind? *Possible answer: The more adult part of Lizabeth realizes the silliness of the activity (line 152) and may sense that she will regret participating. She changes her mind because she doesn't want the younger children to think that she is scared (lines 153–154).*

### E THEME AND SETTING

*Possible answer: To Miss Lottie, the marigolds represent beauty in her difficult life. They may also represent one of the few things in her life that she can control. To the children, the marigolds represent the beauty that is absent from their lives. As a result, the children hate the flowers, without understanding why (lines 136–143).*

**IF STUDENTS NEED HELP . . .** Ask them to work in small groups to discuss the characters' actual or probable thoughts about the marigolds. Have groups use the results to complete and then compare two Open Mind diagrams—one to represent Miss Lottie, the other to represent the children.

 **BEST PRACTICES TOOLKIT—Transparency** Open Mind p. D9

### OWN THE WORD

- **stoicism:** Tell students that *stoicism* comes from the Greek *Stoic*, the name for a school of philosophy that advocated the calm acceptance of all occurrences.

- **perverse:** Tell students that a common antonym of *perverse is cooperative*. Have students name other antonyms and synonyms for *perverse*.

- **bravado:** Have students give other examples of someone showing "false *bravado*" like Lizabeth.

---

But our real fun and our real fear lay in Miss Lottie herself. Miss Lottie seemed to be at least a hundred years old. Her big frame still held traces of the tall, powerful woman she must have been in youth, although it was now bent and drawn. Her smooth skin was a dark reddish-brown, and her face had Indian-like features and the stern <u>stoicism</u> that one associates with Indian faces. Miss Lottie didn't like intruders either, especially children. She never left her yard, and nobody ever visited her. We never knew how she managed those

120 necessities that depend on human interaction—how she ate, for example, or even whether she ate. When we were tiny children, we thought Miss Lottie was a witch and we made up tales, that we half believed ourselves, about her exploits. We were far too sophisticated now, of course, to believe the witch-nonsense. But old fears have a way of clinging like cobwebs, and so when we sighted the tumble-down shack, we had to stop to reinforce our nerves.

"Look, there she is," I whispered, forgetting that Miss Lottie could not possibly have heard me from that distance. "She's fooling with them crazy flowers."

"Yeh, look at 'er."

Miss Lottie's marigolds were perhaps the strangest part of the picture.

130 Certainly they did not fit in with the crumbling decay of the rest of her yard. Beyond the dusty brown yard, in front of the sorry gray house, rose suddenly and shockingly a dazzling strip of bright blossoms, clumped together in enormous mounds, warm and passionate and sun-golden. The old black witch-woman worked on them all summer, every summer, down on her creaky knees, weeding and cultivating and arranging, while the house crumbled and John Burke rocked. For some <u>perverse</u> reason, we children hated those marigolds. They interfered with the perfect ugliness of the place; they were too beautiful; they said too much that we could not understand; they did not make sense. There was something in the vigor with which the old woman destroyed

140 the weeds that intimidated us. It should have been a comical sight—the old woman with the man's hat on her cropped white head, leaning over the bright mounds, her big backside in the air—but it wasn't comical, it was something we could not name. We had to annoy her by whizzing a pebble into her flowers or by yelling a dirty word, then dancing away from her rage, reveling in our youth and mocking her age. Actually, I think it was the flowers we wanted to destroy, but nobody had the nerve to try it, not even Joey, who was usually fool enough to try anything. **E**

"Y'all git some stones," commanded Joey now, and was met with instant giggling obedience as everyone except me began to gather pebbles from the

150 dusty ground. "Come on, Lizabeth."

I just stood there peering through the bushes, torn between wanting to join the fun and feeling that it was all a bit silly.

"You scared, Lizabeth?"

I cursed and spat on the ground—my favorite gesture of phony **bravado**. "Y'all children get the stones; I'll show you how to use 'em."

**stoicism** (stō′ĭ-sĭz′əm) *n.* indifference to pleasure or pain; a lack of visible emotion

**perverse** (pər-vûrs′) *adj.* stubbornly contrary; wrong; harmful

### E THEME AND SETTING
What do the marigolds represent to Miss Lottie? to the children?

**bravado** (brə-vä′dō) *n.* a false show of courage or defiance

---

## DIFFERENTIATED INSTRUCTION

**FOR ENGLISH LANGUAGE LEARNERS**
**Language: Conversational English Patterns** Explain that some contractions in the story, such as "'er" (line 128), "y'all" (line 148), "'em" (line 155), and "gonna" (line 215), are regional and/or nonstandard contractions. They are found most often in writing that imitates casual conversation. Encourage students to identify other examples of nonstandard contractions in the story.

**FOR ADVANCED LEARNERS/PRE–AP**
**Analyze Syntax** Have students reread the sentence in lines 131–133. Challenge them to explain why the author uses such an unusual sentence structure—placing the subject (*strip*) in the middle of the sentence, after two prepositional phrases and the verb (*rose*). Then ask students to identify the adjectives and adverbs in the sentence and to explain their significance.

*Field of Hope*, Charly Palmer. Mixed media collage on canvas, 24″ × 18″. © Charly Palmer.

I said before that we children were not consciously aware of how thick were the bars of our cage. I wonder now, though, whether we were not more aware of it than I thought. Perhaps we had some dim notion of what we were, and how little chance we had of being anything else. Otherwise, why would we
160 have been so preoccupied with destruction? Anyway, the pebbles were collected quickly, and everybody looked at me to begin the fun. **F**

"Come on, y'all."

We crept to the edge of the bushes that bordered the narrow road in front of Miss Lottie's place. She was working placidly, kneeling over the flowers, her

◀ **Analyze Visuals**
How does this image compare with the narrator's description of the setting and Miss Lottie?

**F THEME AND SETTING**
What connection is made between poverty—described metaphorically as a cage—and destruction in lines 156–161?

MARIGOLDS   **447**

## Analyze Visuals

*Possible answer:* **Miss Lottie:** *Like Miss Lottie in her youth, the woman in the painting is a "tall, powerful woman" (line 115). Unlike Miss Lottie today, who wears a "man's hat on her cropped white head" (line 141) as she gardens, the woman in the painting is young, slender, and dressed for Sunday church services.* **Setting:** *The setting in the story is a dusty "dry September"(line 8) in a "shanty-town" with "dirt roads and grassless yards" (lines 8–9); whereas the setting in the image is a bright, summer day in a churchyard. The flowers provide the most striking similarity of the two settings. In both, a "dazzling strip of bright blossoms" are showcased as "warm and passionate and sun-golden" (line 133).*

**About the Art** Charly "Carlos" Palmer (b. 1960) describes his artworks as social and political in nature. Over his 25-year career, he has often focused on African-American historical subjects, including the Middle Passage, slavery, the Jim Crow era, and the civil rights movement.

---

**TEXT ANALYSIS**   COMMON CORE

**F THEME AND SETTING**   RL 2, RL 4

*Possible answer:* *The narrator suggests that people trapped in poverty (in this case, the children) may feel so frustrated that they lash out with destructive behavior (in this case, vandalizing Miss Lottie's garden).*

---

### FOR ENGLISH LANGUAGE LEARNERS

**Culture: Connect** Review why the marigold garden was important to Miss Lottie. Then point out that many cultures value various styles of gardening for artistic reasons (as in Japanese or English formal gardens), for practical reasons (as in the floating gardens of Mexico or the *dacha* of Russia), or for both. Invite students to describe the role that gardening plays in the cultures that they know best.

### FOR STRUGGLING READERS

**Develop Reading Fluency** Point out the unusual syntax (word order) used by the author in lines 156–161. Demonstrate a fluent reading of the paragraph and help students determine the subject, verb, and object(s) in each sentence. Then have student pairs read the paragraph to each other.

 **RESOURCE MANAGER**—Copy Master Reading Fluency p. 30

## What if life had a
# RESET button?

**Discuss** What role does regret play in Lizabeth's bad mood in lines 188–191? *Possible answer: Lizabeth is in a bad mood because she regrets her part in the attack on Miss Lottie (lines 189–190) and feels ashamed of herself (line 188).*

---

**READING SKILL**  COMMON CORE  RL 1

**G DRAW CONCLUSIONS**

*Possible answer: The childish part of Lizabeth sees fun in such wild behavior. Lizabeth is torn, however, because the more adult part of her realizes that she has maliciously attacked an elderly woman without provocation.*

**IF STUDENTS NEED HELP . . .** Direct them to the conjunction *but* in line 189. Point out that *but* signals a contrast and that conflicting feelings are a type of contrast. After students reread the sentence in lines 188–190, elicit that it provides the best information for answering the question.

**Extend the Discussion** Why do you think Lizabeth's conflicting feelings led her to argue with Joey (lines 194–195)?

---

**VOCABULARY**  COMMON CORE  L 4

**OWN THE WORD**

- **impotent:** Remind students that the prefix *im-* means "not," so someone or something that is *impotent* is not powerful. Have students use *impotent* and *potent* in a pair of sentences that show an understanding of the meaning of both words.

- **exuberance:** Ask students if they have ever felt *exuberant*. Have them explain the reason or the event that triggered their *exuberance*.

---

dark hand plunged into the golden mound. Suddenly "zing"—an expertly-aimed stone cut the head off one of the blossoms.

"Who out there?" Miss Lottie's backside came down and her head came up as her sharp eyes searched the bushes. "You better git!"

170 We had crouched down out of sight in the bushes, where we stifled the giggles that insisted on coming. Miss Lottie gazed warily across the road for a moment, then cautiously returned to her weeding. "Zing"—Joey sent a pebble into the blooms, and another marigold was beheaded.

Miss Lottie was enraged now. She began struggling to her feet, leaning on a rickety cane and shouting, "Y'all git! Go on home!" Then the rest of the kids let loose with their pebbles, storming the flowers and laughing wildly and senselessly at Miss Lottie's **impotent** rage. She shook her stick at us and started shakily toward the road crying, "Git 'long! John Burke! John Burke, come help!"

180 Then I lost my head entirely, mad with the power of inciting such rage, and ran out of the bushes in the storm of pebbles, straight toward Miss Lottie chanting madly, "Old witch, fell in a ditch, picked up a penny and thought she was rich!" The children screamed with delight, dropped their pebbles and joined the crazy dance, swarming around Miss Lottie like bees and chanting, "Old lady witch!" while she screamed curses at us. The madness lasted only a moment, for John Burke, startled at last, lurched out of his chair, and we dashed for the bushes just as Miss Lottie's cane went whizzing at my head.

I did not join the merriment when the kids gathered again under the oak in our bare yard. Suddenly I was ashamed, and I did not like being ashamed. The child in me sulked and said it was all in fun, but the woman in me flinched 190 at the thought of the malicious attack that I had led. The mood lasted all afternoon. When we ate the beans and rice that was supper that night, I did not notice my father's silence, for he was always silent these days, nor did I notice my mother's absence, for she always worked until well into evening. Joey and I had a particularly bitter argument after supper; his **exuberance** got on my nerves. Finally I stretched out upon the palette in the room we shared and fell into a fitful doze. **G**

When I awoke, somewhere in the middle of the night, my mother had returned, and I vaguely listened to the conversation that was audible through the thin walls that separated our rooms. At first I heard no words, only voices. 200 My mother's voice was like a cool, dark room in summer—peaceful, soothing, quiet. I loved to listen to it; it made things seem all right somehow. But my father's voice cut through hers, shattering the peace.

"Twenty-two years, Maybelle, twenty-two years," he was saying, "and I got nothing for you, nothing, nothing."

"It's all right, honey, you'll get something. Everybody's out of work now, you know that."

"It ain't right. Ain't no man ought to eat his woman's food year in and year out, and see his children running wild. Ain't nothing right about that."

---

**impotent** (ĭm′pə-tənt) *adj.* powerless; lacking strength or vigor

**Targeted Passage**

COMMON CORE  L 4c

**Language Coach**

**Etymology** The Latin word *malus* means "bad." Words that come from *malus* include the verbs *malfunction* ("fail to work properly") and *malign* ("speak badly of"). What adjective in line 190 shares this **etymology**, or origin? What other words can you think of that might come from *malus*? Check a dictionary to see how many you have identified correctly.

**exuberance** (ĭg-zoo′bər-əns) *n.* condition of unrestrained joy

**G DRAW CONCLUSIONS** Reread lines 187–196. Why is the narrator torn between conflicting feelings?

---

## DIFFERENTIATED INSTRUCTION

**FOR STRUGGLING READERS**

**2 Targeted Passage [Lines 179–190]**
This passage targets the adolescent child-adult conflict with which Lizabeth struggles.

- How does Lizabeth feel while she and the other children are taunting Miss Lottie? (line 179)

- How are her feelings different afterward? (lines 187–188)

- In line 189, what two people does she say are "in me"? What does she mean? (lines 189–190)

**FOR ENGLISH LANGUAGE LEARNERS**

**Language Coach**  COMMON CORE  L 4c
**Etymology** *Possible answers: malicious; malcontent, maladjusted, malformed* Have students use the root and context to define *malicious*. *Possible answer: with bad intent*

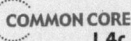

"Honey, you took good care of us when you had it. Ain't nobody got
210 nothing nowadays."

"I ain't talking about nobody else, I'm talking about me. God knows I try."
My mother said something I could not hear, and my father cried out louder,
"What must a man do, tell me that?"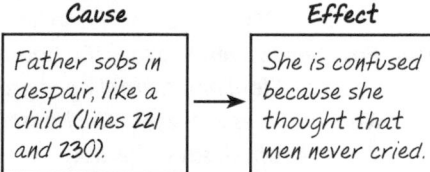

"Look, we ain't starving. I git paid every week, and Mrs. Ellis is real nice
about giving me things. She gonna let me have Mr. Ellis' old coat for you
this winter—"

"Damn Mr. Ellis' coat! And damn his money! You think I want white folks'
leavings? Damn, Maybelle"—and suddenly he sobbed, loudly and painfully,
and cried helplessly and hopelessly in the dark night. I had never heard a man
220 cry before. I did not know men ever cried. I covered my ears with my hands
but could not cut off the sound of my father's harsh, painful, despairing sobs.
My father was a strong man who would whisk a child upon his shoulders and
go singing through the house. My father whittled toys for us and laughed so
loud that the great oak seemed to laugh with him, and taught us how to fish
and hunt rabbits. How could it be that my father was crying? But the sobs
went on, unstifled, finally quieting until I could hear my mother's voice, deep
and rich, humming softly as she used to hum to a frightened child.

The world had lost its boundary lines. My mother, who was small and soft,
was now the strength of the family; my father, who was the rock on which
230 the family had been built, was sobbing like the tiniest child. Everything
was suddenly out of tune, like a broken accordion. Where did I fit into this
crazy picture? I do not now remember my thoughts, only a feeling of great
bewilderment and fear. ●

Long after the sobbing and the humming had stopped, I lay on the palette,
still as stone with my hands over my ears, wishing that I too could cry and
be comforted. The night was silent now except for the sound of the crickets
and of Joey's soft breathing. But the room was too crowded with fear to allow
me to sleep, and finally, feeling the terrible aloneness of 4 A.M., I decided to
awaken Joey.

240 "Ouch! What's the matter with you? What you want?" he demanded
disagreeably when I had pinched and slapped him awake.

"Come on, wake up."

"What for? Go 'way."

I was lost for a reasonable reply. I could not say, "I'm scared, and I don't want
to be alone," so I merely said, "I'm going out. If you want to come, come on."

The promise of adventure awoke him. "Going out now? Where to,
Lizabeth? What you going to do?"

I was pulling my dress over my head. Until now I had not thought of going
out. "Just come on," I replied tersely.

250 I was out the window and halfway down the road before Joey caught
up with me.

MARIGOLDS **449**

**Ⓗ DRAW CONCLUSIONS**
From the dialogue in lines
203–213, what can you
conclude is bothering
Lizabeth's father?

**❸ Targeted Passage**

**Ⓘ THEME AND SETTING**
How does the
conversation between
Lizabeth's parents affect
her? Cite details to
support your answer.

---

READING SKILL  COMMON CORE  RL 1

**Ⓗ DRAW CONCLUSIONS**

**Possible answer:** The father's grieving
outcries show that he wants to take care of
his family but is frustrated that he cannot
find a job.

**Extend the Discussion** Why does the
mother's attempt at comforting her
husband (lines 209–210) fail?

---

TEXT ANALYSIS  COMMON CORE  RL 2, RL 4

**Ⓘ *Model the Skill:* THEME AND SETTING**

Use Cause-and-Effect Graphics to explore
details from lines 217–234 and their effect
on Lizabeth.

| Cause | Effect |
|-------|--------|
| Father sobs in despair, like a child (lines 221 and 230). | She is confused because she thought that men never cried. |

| Cause | Effect |
|-------|--------|
| Mother hums to him as she would to a child (lines 226–227). | She feels that everything in her world is "out of tune" (line 231). |

**Possible answer:** The conversation confuses
and frightens Lizabeth, for it suggests that
her parents have switched their traditional
roles. Her mother, the breadwinner, now
seems stronger than her unemployed father,
whom the mother now comforts like a little
child (lines 228–230).

**BEST PRACTICES TOOLKIT**—Transparency
Cause-and-Effect Graphics p. B39

---

**FOR STRUGGLING READERS**

**❸ Targeted Passage** [Lines 218–245]
This passage establishes Lizabeth's
emotional state, which will lead her to
take an important action.

• In what ways has Lizabeth's world "lost its
boundary lines"? (line 228)

• What does she wish for? (lines 235–236)

• Why does Lizabeth awaken Joey? (lines
237–245)

**FOR ENGLISH LANGUAGE LEARNERS**
**Vocabulary: Multiple-Meaning Words** Point
out that certain words have more than one
meaning and that students must determine
the appropriate definition in a given use.
Help students use context clues to figure out
the meaning of "madly" (line 181); "thin" (line
199); "cried" (line 212); "whisk" (line 222); "rich"
(line 227); and "soft" (lines 228 and 237, with
different meanings).

## Analyze Visuals

**Activity** Invite students to study the girl in the foreground of *New Dreams* and to describe her mood. Then, ask them to scan the story "Marigolds" up to this point. Which passage(s) could best be illustrated by the picture? *Possible answer: The girl appears to be deep in thought, creating a serious, quiet, and reflective mood. The picture could illustrate the narrator reflecting guiltily on the "malicious attack" that she had led.*

**About the Art** Once described as a "visual storyteller," Ernest Crichlow (1914–2005) first attained national distinction in the 1930s. He was born in Brooklyn to immigrants from Barbados, and the immigrant experience was often a subject in his art.

### REVISIT THE BIG QUESTION
## What if life had a
## **RESET** button?

**Discuss** How does regret influence the way that Lizabeth sees Miss Lottie's house in lines 256–259? *Possible answer: She sees the house as she sees her life: "foul and crumbling, a grotesque caricature" (lines 257–258). The house looked haunted, Lizabeth says, "because I was haunted too" (lines 258–259).*

---

| TEXT ANALYSIS | COMMON CORE |
|---|---|
| | **RL 2, RL 4** |

### ● THEME AND SETTING

*Possible answer: Lizabeth's circumstances utterly frustrate and confuse her (lines 261–262). Her emotions overwhelm her, too (lines 261–265). Needing a way to vent these feelings, Lizabeth feels compelled to destroy the beautiful flowers that stand in contrast to the ugliness of her life.*

---

| VOCABULARY | COMMON CORE |
|---|---|
| | **L 4** |

### OWN THE WORD

**degradation:** Ask students to reread lines 261–265. Then have them list words that contribute to their understanding of the connotation of *degradation*. **Possible answers:** *great need, hopelessness, poverty, bewilderment, fear*

---

*New Dreams* (2002), Ernest Crichlow. Lithograph (Edition 150), 24¾" × 16¾". Photo by Maureen Turci, Mojo Portfolio. Courtesy of the Ernest Crichlow Estate.

"Wait, Lizabeth, where you going?"

I was running as if the Furies[3] were after me, as perhaps they were—running silently and furiously until I came to where I had half-known I was headed: to Miss Lottie's yard.

The half-dawn light was more eerie than complete darkness, and in it the old house was like the ruin that my world had become—foul and crumbling, a grotesque caricature.[4] It looked haunted, but I was not afraid because I was haunted too.

260     "Lizabeth, you lost your mind?" panted Joey.

I had indeed lost my mind, for all the smoldering emotions of that summer swelled in me and burst—the great need for my mother who was never there, the hopelessness of our poverty and **degradation,** the bewilderment of being neither child nor woman and yet both at once, the fear unleashed by my father's tears. And these feelings combined in one great impulse toward destruction. ●

**degradation**
(dĕg′rə-dā′shən) *n.* condition of being brought to a lower level; humiliation

**● THEME AND SETTING**
Reread lines 261–265. Why do the narrator's emotions produce an urge to destroy?

---

3. **Furies:** In Greek and Roman mythology, the Furies were three goddesses of vengeance, or revenge.

4. **a grotesque caricature** (grō-tĕsk′ kăr′ĭ-kə-chŏŏr′): a bizarre and absurdly exaggerated representation of something.

**450**    UNIT 4: THEME AND SYMBOL

---

## DIFFERENTIATED INSTRUCTION

### FOR ADVANCED LEARNERS/PRE–AP

**Analyze Allusions** Use the reference to the Furies in line 253 as the springboard for a mini-lesson about allusions. Have a small group of students work together to prepare a presentation in which they define the term, analyze the power of the allusion in terms of the theme of the selection, and discuss a few examples of allusions from other works that they have read.

"Lizabeth!"

I leaped furiously into the mounds of marigolds and pulled madly, trampling and pulling and destroying the perfect yellow blooms. The fresh smell of early morning and of dew-soaked marigolds spurred me on as I went
270 tearing and mangling and sobbing while Joey tugged my dress or my waist crying, "Lizabeth stop, please stop!"

And then I was sitting in the ruined little garden among the uprooted and ruined flowers, crying and crying, and it was too late to undo what I had done. Joey was sitting beside me, silent and frightened, not knowing what to say. Then, "Lizabeth, look."

I opened my swollen eyes and saw in front of me a pair of large calloused feet; my gaze lifted to the swollen legs, the age-distorted body clad in a tight cotton night dress, and then the shadowed Indian face surrounded by stubby white hair. And there was no rage in the face now, now that the garden was
280 destroyed and there was nothing any longer to be protected.

④ **Targeted Passage**

"M-miss Lottie!" I scrambled to my feet and just stood there and stared at her, and that was the moment when childhood faded and womanhood began. That violent, crazy act was the last act of childhood. For as I gazed at the immobile face with the sad, weary eyes, I gazed upon a kind of reality that is hidden to childhood. The witch was no longer a witch but only a broken old woman who had dared to create beauty in the midst of ugliness and sterility. She had been born in **squalor** and lived in it all her life. Now at the end of that life she had nothing except a falling-down hut, a wrecked body, and John Burke, the mindless son of her passion. Whatever verve there was left in her,
290 whatever was of love and beauty and joy that had not been squeezed out by life, had been there in the marigolds she had so tenderly cared for. ⓚ

Of course I could not express the things that I knew about Miss Lottie as I stood there awkward and ashamed. The years have put words to the things I knew in that moment, and as I look back upon it, I know that that moment marked the end of innocence. People think of the loss of innocence as meaning the loss of virginity, but this is far from true. Innocence involves an unseeing acceptance of things at face value, an ignorance of the area below the surface. In that humiliating moment I looked beyond myself and into the depths of another person. This was the beginning of compassion, and one cannot have
300 both compassion and innocence. ⓛ

The years have taken me worlds away from that time and that place, from the dust and squalor of our lives and from the bright thing that I destroyed in a blind childish striking out at God-knows-what. Miss Lottie died long ago and many years have passed since I last saw her hut, completely barren at last, for despite my wild contrition she never planted marigolds again. Yet, there are times when the image of those passionate yellow mounds returns with a painful poignancy. For one does not have to be ignorant and poor to find that one's life is barren as the dusty yards of one's town. And I too have planted marigolds. ∾

**squalor** (skwŏl'ər) *n.* a filthy, shabby, and wretched condition, as from poverty

**COMMON CORE** RL 4

ⓚ **DRAW CONCLUSIONS**
The narrator uses fairy-tale metaphors to describe Miss Lottie throughout the story, repeatedly calling her a witch and referring to "enchantment" surrounding her home. Reread lines 285–291, in which a change takes place in Lizabeth. Why is she suddenly able to see Miss Lottie as she really is?

ⓛ **PARAPHRASE**
Paraphrase the narrator's thoughts about innocence and compassion in lines 295–300.

---

**FOR STRUGGLING READERS**

④ **Targeted Passage** [Lines 276–300]

This passage presents the moment at which Lizabeth's perspective changes and she begins thinking like an adult.

- As she looks at Miss Lottie, what does Lizabeth see instead of a witch? (lines 285–286)

- What does Lizabeth realize about the marigolds' importance to Miss Lottie? (lines 289–291)

- Why does Lizabeth see this moment as the end of her innocence? (lines 295–300)

**FOR ENGLISH LANGUAGE LEARNERS**

**Comprehension: Contrast** Discuss how Collier uses "no longer . . . but only" to set up a contrast in lines 285–286. Also discuss the extended contrast in lines 228–230, which does not use words that traditionally signal contrast. Invite students to identify other contrasts of details or ideas in the story.

---

**READING SKILL** COMMON CORE

ⓚ **DRAW CONCLUSIONS** RL 4

**Possible answer:** *The realization of what she has done, the purging of her pent-up emotions, and the shock of her encounter with Miss Lottie have enabled Lizabeth to see "a kind of reality that is hidden to childhood" (lines 284–285).*

Have students go back through the story and note the other instances of fairy-tale metaphors that are used to describe Miss Lottie. Ask students how these metaphors compare to fairy tales they know.

**READING STRATEGY:** *Review*

ⓛ **PARAPHRASE**

**Possible answer:** *In its truest form, innocence means accepting things as they appear to be on the surface, without thought or question. Compassion, however, involves looking beneath the surface.*

**VOCABULARY** COMMON CORE

**OWN THE WORD** L 4

**squalor:** Have students explain the relationship between the context clues "ugliness," "sterility," and "falling-down hut" to help them determine the meaning of *squalor*.

**SELECTION WRAP–UP**

**READ WITH A PURPOSE** Now that students have read the story, ask them how the narrator must have changed between the time described in the story and the time at which she narrates it. *Possible answer: She has risen out of poverty and ignorance.* How has she not changed? *Possible answer: She still remembers and regrets her actions.*

★ **CRITIQUE** Ask students what parts of the story they liked most. Why? What parts did they like least? Why?

# Practice and Apply

For preliminary support of post-reading questions, use these copy masters:

**R** RESOURCE MANAGER—Copy Masters
Reading Check p. 28
Theme and Setting p. 21
Question Support p. 29

Additional selection questions are provided for teachers on page 15.

## ANSWERS

## Comprehension

1. *The narrator is 14, almost 15 (line 16).*

2. *They do not fit in with their environment—Miss Lottie's ugly, decaying property.*

3. *She destroys Miss Lottie's marigolds.*

## Text Analysis

COMMON CORE RL 1, RL 2, RL 4

**Possible answers:**

4. ***Understand the Influence of Setting*** *The story takes place in an impoverished rural black community when the Depression "gripped the nation." The dreary setting shapes the narrator's hopeless outlook.*

5. ● **COMMON CORE FOCUS** *Draw Conclusions Lizabeth's act results from frustration at feeling trapped in poverty (lines 39–41 and 136–139). It also comes from the emotional pressure of seeing her parents struggling with financial problems (lines 228–233).*

6. *The climax occurs when Lizabeth destroys the marigolds, only to come face to face with Miss Lottie (lines 267–291). For Lizabeth, this is "the moment when childhood faded and womanhood began" (line 282). For Miss Lottie, it is the end of the last spark of beauty in her life (lines 289–291 and 305).*

7. *Charts will vary. Associating details like the "brilliant splash of sunny yellow" (lines 10–11) with the sun's energy suggests that the marigolds symbolize beauty that has life-affirming power.*

8. ● **COMMON CORE FOCUS** *Analyze Theme and Setting The story suggests that poverty limits people's lives and deprives them of much of life's beauty. It also suggests that a barren life can take different forms but that people can find ways to create beauty and counteract such barrenness.*

9. *Students may agree or disagree but should support their responses with thoughtful, well-supported reasons.*

## Text Criticism

**Possible answer:**

10. *Students should recognize that the strongest indication of segregation lies in the parents' job situations. Opinions will vary but should be clearly stated and reasonably defended.*

---

## Comprehension

1. **Recall** How old is the narrator in the story?

2. **Recall** What is unusual about Miss Lottie's marigolds?

3. **Summarize** What does the narrator do that she later regrets?

## Text Analysis

4. **Understand the Influence of Setting** Note the most prominent features of the story's setting and the figurative language the narrator often uses to describe them. How do they affect the narrator's outlook on life?

5. **Draw Conclusions** Review the chart you made as you read. What leads the young Lizabeth to destroy Miss Lottie's marigolds? Support your conclusions with evidence from the story.

6. **Analyze Climax** Identify the climax of the story. What change does this turning point initiate in the narrator? in Miss Lottie? Cite evidence to support your answers.

7. **Analyze Symbolism** Miss Lottie's marigolds are central to the story. What do they symbolize? To help you interpret their meaning, create a chart like the one shown to record descriptions of the marigolds and the ideas you associate with them.

| Description of Marigolds | Associations |
|---|---|
| "a brilliant splash of sunny yellow" (lines 10–11) | "sunny yellow," like the sun, gives energy and life |

8. **Analyze Theme and Setting** The narrator and Miss Lottie respond to their impoverished surroundings in very different ways. What message does the story convey about the impact of poverty on people's lives? What other themes does the story impart?

9. **Evaluate Ideas** Reread the next-to-last paragraph (lines 292–300). Do you agree with what the narrator says about innocence and compassion? Use evidence from the story as well as your own experiences to explore your answer.

## Text Criticism

10. **Social Context** Can "Marigolds" be considered social commentary on racial segregation? Cite evidence to support your opinion.

### What if life had a RESET button?

If you had another chance, what in your past would you do differently?

**COMMON CORE**

**RL 1** Cite textual evidence to support analysis of what the text says explicitly as well as inferences drawn from the text. **RL 2** Determine a theme of a text and analyze its development. **RL 4** Determine the figurative meaning of words and phrases as they are used in a text.

---

**What if life had a RESET button?**
To encourage students' thoughtful responses, let them know that they do not need to share their answers with the class.

## Vocabulary in Context

▲ **VOCABULARY PRACTICE**

Decide whether the words in each pair are similar or different in meaning.

1. perverse/agreeable
2. squalor/splendor
3. exuberance/enthusiasm
4. retribution/retaliation
5. nostalgia/homesickness
6. futile/effective
7. poignantly/indifferently
8. bravado/timidity
9. degradation/humiliation
10. ostensibly/apparently
11. impotent/powerless
12. stoicism/emotionalism

**WORD LIST**

bravado
degradation
exuberance
futile
impotent
nostalgia
ostensibly
perverse
poignantly
retribution
squalor
stoicism

### ACADEMIC VOCABULARY IN WRITING

- context  - interpret  - reveal  - significant  - tradition

Marigolds play a **significant** role in the lives of both Miss Lottie and the narrator. Think of one thing—it could be an object or a place—that has been significant in your life. Write a paragraph expressing what you feel about it and why you feel that way. Use at least one Academic Vocabulary word in your paragraph.

### VOCABULARY STRATEGY: THE SUFFIX *-or*

Many words have endings called **suffixes** that can help you determine a word's meaning. For example, the word *squalor* ends with *-or,* a noun suffix derived from Latin meaning "state or condition of." You may recognize *squalor* as similar to the word *squalid,* meaning "very dirty or filthy." These two insights can help you conclude that *squalor* means "a filthy condition." Recognizing this suffix in other unfamiliar words can provide clues to the meanings of those words.

**PRACTICE** Use each numbered word in a sentence. Then use your knowledge of the suffix *-or* to figure out the meaning of each word. Use a dictionary to check your work.

1. terror
2. furor
3. candor
4. stupor
5. fervor
6. pallor

**COMMON CORE**

**L 4b, d** Identify and correctly use patterns of word changes that indicate different meanings or parts of speech; verify the preliminary determination of the meaning of a word.

**Interactive Vocabulary** THINK central

Go to **thinkcentral.com**.
KEYWORD: HML9-453

---

### DIFFERENTIATED INSTRUCTION

**FOR ENGLISH LANGUAGE LEARNERS**

**Vocabulary: Prefixes and Suffixes** Have students work in small groups to review the Word List. Group members should teach each other the prefixes and suffixes whose meanings they know, using a dictionary for confirmation. They should then use the dictionary to explore the meanings of word parts that are unfamiliar to them.

**FOR ADVANCED LEARNERS/PRE–AP**

**Vocabulary Practice** Ask students to use five pairs of words in sentences that compare or contrast people, places, or events. Have students compare the uses that they found for these words.

---

**ANSWERS**

## Vocabulary in Context

▲ **VOCABULARY PRACTICE**

1. *different*
2. *different*
3. *similar*
4. *similar*
5. *similar*
6. *different*
7. *different*
8. *different*
9. *similar*
10. *similar*
11. *similar*
12. *different*

**R** **RESOURCE MANAGER—Copy Master**
Vocabulary Practice p. 26

### ACADEMIC VOCABULARY IN WRITING

Allow students to use concept webs to help them brainstorm different items and examples of their significance.

### VOCABULARY STRATEGY: THE SUFFIX *-or*

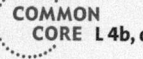

**COMMON CORE L 4b, d**

Encourage students to use context in combination with suffix clues to figure out the meaning of unfamiliar words.

***Possible definitions:***

1. *condition of great fear*
2. *furious state or condition*
3. *candid condition or expression*
4. *condition of dulled sense*
5. *state of intense feeling*
6. *pale condition*

**R** **RESOURCE MANAGER—Copy Master**
Vocabulary Strategy p. 27

**Interactive Vocabulary** THINK central

Keywords direct students to a **WordSharp** tutorial on **thinkcentral.com** or to other types of vocabulary practice and review.

## Assess and Reteach

### Assess

**DIAGNOSTIC AND SELECTION TESTS**
Selection Test A, B/C pp. 115–116, 117–118

**Interactive Selection Test** on **thinkcentral.com**

### Reteach

**Level Up Online Tutorials** on **thinkcentral.com**

# Focus and Motivate

## COMMON CORE FOCUS

**RI 2** Determine a central idea of a text and analyze its development; provide an objective summary of the text. **RI 3** Analyze how the author unfolds an analysis, including the order in which the points are made. **RI 5** Analyze how an author's ideas are developed and refined. **L 4a** Use context as a clue to the meaning of a word.

### SUMMARY

Donna Freedman's article explains how members of a Chicago neighborhood worked together to turn a barren lot into a garden that beautifies the community and celebrates African-American heritage.

## What's the Connection?

Use a Comparison Matrix to prepare students for the selection. Have students note these aspects of Miss Lottie's garden: who created it, who maintained it, what it looked like, what plants it contained, and what it meant to people. Then, have them fill in details about the African Heritage Garden as they read. Discuss comparisons and contrasts.

| Items to Compare | Who Created the Garden |
|---|---|
| Miss Lottie's garden | Miss Lottie |
| African Heritage Garden | North Lawndale neighborhood |

 **BEST PRACTICES TOOLKIT—Transparency**
Comparison Matrix p. A24

# Teach

## Standards Focus: Outline

Guide students through the process of outlining "Sowing Change." Explain that a main idea and its supporting details may span more than one paragraph. Point out that some main ideas are stated directly, while others are implied.

**R RESOURCE MANAGER—Copy Master**
Outline p. 41

---

## Sowing Change
Newspaper Article

**COMMON CORE**

**RI 2** Determine a central idea of a text and analyze its development; provide an objective summary of the text. **RI 3** Analyze how the author unfolds an analysis, including the order in which the points are made. **RI 5** Analyze how an author's ideas are developed and refined. **L 4a** Use context as a clue to the meaning of a word.

## What's the Connection?

In "Marigolds," Miss Lottie's garden is the only bright spot in her difficult life. In the North Lawndale neighborhood of Chicago, Illinois, a garden has also become a bright spot for residents. To find out more about this garden and its impact, read "Sowing Change."

## Standards Focus: Outline

When you need to understand and summarize a great many ideas and facts, outlining can help. An **outline** is a way of organizing a text's **main ideas** and **supporting details** according to their levels of importance. Since the main ideas and supporting details are written in the form of brief phrases, an outline can be considered a text's skeleton. You can take notes in outline form by following these steps:

- Skim the text to figure out its main topic, subtopics, and pattern of organization.
- Draft a basic outline by restating the main topics (numbered with Roman numerals) and the subtopics (lettered with capital letters) in the order presented by the writer, excluding your own opinions.
- Then, as you read the text closely, determine which supporting details are most important and which are less important in supporting the **author's purpose** and **central idea**. Add these details at the appropriate levels of importance. Use Arabic numerals and lower-case letters to show further levels of detail.

Follow the steps above to take notes on "Sowing Change" in outline form. You can use the outline begun here as your starting point or create a new one. (For more information on outlining, see the **Reading Handbook,** page R4.)

> The African Heritage Garden in North Lawndale
>   I. What the Garden Looks Like
>     A. Covers a large corner lot
>     B. Contains many plants and special features
>       1.
>         a.
>         b.
>       2.
>   II. What It Took to Create the Garden

## Selection Resources

See resources on the **Teacher One Stop DVD-ROM** *and on* **thinkcentral.com**.

**R RESOURCE MANAGER UNIT 4**
Lesson Support, pp. 33–47

**DIAGNOSTIC AND SELECTION TESTS**
Selection Tests, pp. 119–122

**BEST PRACTICES TOOLKIT**
pp. A24, E8

**TECHNOLOGY**
- 💿 **Teacher One Stop DVD-ROM**
- 💿 **Student One Stop DVD-ROM**
- 💿 **Audio Anthology CD**
- 💿 **GrammarNotes DVD-ROM**
- 💿 **ExamView Generator** on the **Teacher One Stop**

\* Resources for Differentiation      † Also in Spanish      ‡ In Haitian Creole and Vietnamese

# Sowing Change

### DONNA FREEDMAN

Many hands join to transform a barren city lot into a thriving green space for plants—and people in North Lawndale **A**

The 20-by-32-foot bed of marigolds is not just a sea of orange blooms, but a Rorschach blot. Back up a few feet, look again and the shape of the African continent emerges on a North Lawndale street corner.

A pair of doorway-like arbors invite passersby off the sidewalk and into a garden where raised beds are a glory of
10 lilies, daisies, hibiscus, nicotiana, shrub roses and other plants. In some places, flowers fight for space among broccoli, sweet potatoes and purple kale that are almost treelike in their vigor.

Three low, bark-covered mounds, plus a limestone-terraced hill at the rear of the site, give a sense of terrain. Shrubs, ornamental grasses and young hackberry, black locust, crab apple and magnolia trees
20 also provide vertical uplift on this city lot.

"This is what we need: open space, a place to sit and talk, to think a while," says North Lawndale resident Gerald Earles, sitting in the garden at 12th Place and Central Park Avenue. The 130-by-100-foot garden seemed to spring up in a single day in late April. **B**

In reality, it took more than two years, about 400 volunteers and $200,000 in
30 donated materials and expertise to create the African Heritage Garden.

"I've always known that the community [was] capable of a project of this magnitude. We just needed a focus," says Valerie Leonard, executive director of the non-profit North Lawndale Small Grants Human Development Corp.

The corporation's attempts to garden on the site withered and died due to lack
40 of water. But things finally came together this year after the Chicago Botanic Garden NeighborSpace, a non-profit land trust, and The Enterprise Companies, a residential real estate development firm, provided financial and design support.

About 200 people, including about 25 people from the community, attended a design session in March to determine

**A** OUTLINE
Before you begin taking notes, skim the entire article to see what its main topics and subtopics are.

**B** OUTLINE
What important information in this paragraph is not covered in the draft outline on page 454? Add it to your own outline.

⸨COMMON CORE⸩ L 4a
**Language Coach**

**Word Origins** Many botanical terms, such as the names of certain plants, are derived from Latin. Some terms, however, have their linguistic roots in other languages. *Withered* (line 39) comes from the Middle English root *widren*, which is related to another Middle English word meaning "weathered." Based on this information and the context clues in lines 38–40, what does *withered* mean?

SOWING CHANGE **455**

---

---

**C** *Model the Skill:* **OUTLINE**

Read the paragraph aloud. Focus on Gladys Woodson's comment in lines 63–65. Discuss her background and how her words might also apply to the African Heritage Garden.

**Possible answer:** *The comparison to Unity Park suggests that one purpose of the African Heritage Garden is to improve the quality of the neighborhood by discouraging the presence of criminals.*

**D** **OUTLINE**

**Possible answer:** *The community continues to care for the garden.*

---

**C** OUTLINE
What do lines 63–67 add to your understanding of the purpose of this garden?

**D** OUTLINE
What new topic is introduced in lines 95–98?

---

what the garden would become. All
50 agreed that the site should have a bed shaped like the African continent and incorporate a number of plants that grow in Africa. Both ideas were part of Leonard's original plan, which was inspired by Unity Park, another Lawndale project.

That park was created five years ago by residents fed up with crime near 19th Street and Kostner Avenue. Gladys Woodson, who spearheaded that project,
60 says that once the site became a well-used and neatly maintained park, the criminal element left.

"If you get enough good people to come out, the bad people are going to leave," Woodson says. She and other Unity Park organizers are helping at the African Heritage Garden as well. **C**

In fact, the heritage garden is thriving under the care and nurturing of a variety
70 of groups, including the North Lawndale Greening Committee, the Combined Block Club, and Slumbusters. Neighbor-Space, which purchased the land from the city and leases it to North Lawndale, also paid to install a water hookup.

The plants and landscape materials, design, and onsite supervision were paid for by a grant from the Chicago Botanic Garden's Neighborhood Gardens
80 program. Each year, the Chicago Botanic Garden awards money to community groups interested in greening their neighborhoods.

It all came together on April 26 when about five dozen volunteers of varying ages, mostly neighborhood residents, planted hundreds of flowers and vegetable seedlings under the supervision of the Chicago Botanic Garden's Community
90 Gardens division. The Safer Foundation, which helps men make the transition from prison to the outside world, sent clients to build arbors and a half-dozen large raised beds.

With regular watering, the garden has thrived—as have the weeds. Scheduled work parties and neighborhood residents keep the weeds at bay. **D**

In late June, the Chicago Botanic
100 Garden brought more trees and flowers, which were planted by about 30 volunteers, including 9-year-old Nikky Pierce. Nikky, who lives down the street from the garden, is pleased with the results.

"Before, it was just dirty and trashy," she says. "It looks pretty when there are flowers in it."

Elder plantswoman and neighborhood resident Annie Lott lends a hand as well as
110 her expertise. At 92, she is an avid gardener who grows numerous flowers and 16 kinds of vegetables. It was her suggestion to put "some food, something that's healthy" in the flower beds.

"I love this garden because it brings back memories of how I was raised," says Lott, who is from Mississippi. "I was raised on a farm and our father taught us to do things for others and share."
120 The African Heritage Garden is a work in progress. Areas among the beds and mounds still need to be covered with stones. A shelter symbolizing a tribal hut, made with thatch and other materials from Africa, is in the works. Park benches also are likely.

But the progress has been huge, says Leonard, even though some of the volunteers had no gardening experience.
130 "They were involved, and now they're asking, 'When can we do it again?'

"That's music to my ears," Leonard says. "When you see how it was being used before and how it's being used now, that's an awesome feeling. It belongs to the community now."

---

## DIFFERENTIATED INSTRUCTION

### FOR STRUGGLING READERS

**Vocabulary Support** Explain that *expertise* (lines 30 and 110) means "special skill or knowledge." Discuss what kinds of expertise would be needed to create a community garden. Then invite students to identify areas in which they think that they have expertise (for example, in a sport or hobby).

### FOR ENGLISH LANGUAGE LEARNERS

**Vocabulary: Idioms** Use New Word Analysis to teach these idioms from the article:

- *withered and died* (line 39), "failed"
- *spearheaded* (line 59), "led"
- *at bay* (line 98), "under control"
- *music to my ears* (line 132), "something that I am happy to hear"

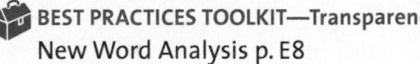 BEST PRACTICES TOOLKIT—Transparency New Word Analysis p. E8

## Comprehension

1. **Summarize** After initial setbacks, how did the African Heritage Garden come to be?

## Text Analysis

● 2. **Analyze Your Outline** Using the outline you created, summarize the article's main ideas and supporting details.

3. **Make Inferences** What are some of the values held by the North Lawndale community? How does the garden represent these values? Cite details from the article to support your answer.

4. **Make Judgments** Consider what you know about crime as well as what the article tells you about this particular community garden. Why would something as simple as a garden reduce crime in an area?

> **COMMON CORE**
>
> **RI 2** Determine a central idea of a text and analyze its development; provide an objective summary of the text. **RI 3** Analyze how the author unfolds an analysis, including the order in which the points are made. **RI 5** Analyze how an author's ideas are developed and refined. **W 2f** Provide a concluding statement or section that follows from the information presented.

## Read for Information: Analyze Ideas

> **WRITING PROMPT**
>
> Both "Marigolds" and "Sowing Change" feature gardeners and their work. Write a brief analysis of the benefits of gardens. Use details from the short story and the article to support your ideas.

Writing an **analysis** involves identifying and explaining the parts of a subject and, finally, arriving at a conclusion. For help, follow these steps:

1. To analyze the benefits of gardens, review the benefits and consider how you might break them down. For example, the benefits might split naturally into "benefits to gardeners" and "benefits to the community."

2. Reread the selections to take notes on the particular benefits you want to address.

3. Review your notes. Identify any conclusions you can draw about gardening and its benefits.

As you write your analysis, be systematic. Introduce each main idea, identify its parts, and then elaborate on those parts before arriving at your conclusion.

**Introduce Subject** → **Examine Part of Subject** → **Draw a Conclusion**

---

4. **Make Judgments** *Criminals tend to plan and act in secrecy. A beautiful public space that residents frequent would probably become a place where secretive activity would be difficult to conduct.*

## Read for Information: Analyze Ideas

 COMMON CORE **W 2f**

**Writing Prompt** *Possible answer: Gardens provide beauty and tranquility. Gardens also provide the people who tend them with a satisfying activity. In "Marigolds," Miss Lottie's garden was an island of beauty in her bleak life. In "Sowing Changes," a garden transformed a barren lot and refreshed the community's spirit.*

---

# Practice and Apply

For preliminary support of post-reading questions, use these copy masters:

**R** RESOURCE MANAGER—Copy Masters
Reading Check p. 45
Question Support p. 46

Additional selection questions are provided for teachers on page 36.

## ANSWERS

## Comprehension

1. *Possible answer: The garden has provided residents with an attractive, peaceful space in place of a barren lot.*

## Text Analysis

> COMMON CORE **RI 2, RI 3, RI 5**

*Possible answers:*

2. ● **COMMON CORE FOCUS** *Analyze Your Outline Summaries should include the following main ideas and details:* **Main Ideas:** *What the Garden Looks Like, What It Took to Create the Garden, How the Garden Continues to Be Cared For, What the Garden Means to the Community Today;* **Important supporting details:** *Covers a large corner lot, Contains many plants and special features; Numerous volunteers from the community, Support from non-profit groups . . .*

3. *Make Inferences The North Lawndale community values safety and beauty. The garden represents these values by providing an attractive place for residents (lines 21–22 and 105–107) that may also discourage the presence of criminals (lines 63–65).*

# Assess and Reteach

## Assess

**DIAGNOSTIC AND SELECTION TESTS**
Selection Tests A, B/C pp. 119–120, 121–122

**Interactive Selection Test** on **thinkcentral.com**

## Reteach

**Level Up Online Tutorials** on **thinkcentral.com**

**Reteaching Worksheets** on **thinkcentral.com**
Study Skills Lesson 15: Outlining Your Reading

# Practice and Apply

## COMMON CORE FOCUS

**RL 7** Analyze the representation of a subject in two different mediums.

## Book Cover

Have students look at the Comparison Matrix they completed for "Marigolds" and "Sowing Change." Ask them to look at this book cover and discuss the symbolic value of the seedling. What does this have in common with the short story and the article? ***Possible answer: The seedling serves as a symbol of social change, as it does in "Marigolds" and "Sowing Change."***

**ANALYZE VISUALS**
COMMON CORE · RL 7

### 1. INTERPRET

***Possible answer:*** *The book's authors may want readers to take personal responsibility for doing good things in their community. "In Our Hands" suggests that it's up to us—citizens and residents—to take care of our communities.*

**ANALYZE VISUALS**
COMMON CORE · RL 7

### 2. ANALYZE DETAILS

***Possible answer:*** *One hand appears to be female and the other appears to be male. The man's hand is darker skinned than the woman's. These differences convey the idea that people can work together despite superficial differences.*

**ANALYZE VISUALS**
COMMON CORE · RL 7

### 3. SYNTHESIZE

***Possible answer:*** *Grassroots probably means what it does because small community organizations need to nurture involvement, much like gardeners need to nurture plants, as in this picture on the book cover. Also, these small community organizations can be the root of movements that have far-reaching effects.*

---

## Book Cover

As you've seen in the preceding literary and nonfiction texts, plants can possess beauty and vitality that make them potent symbols. Consider the image on the book cover below. The questions on the right will help you analyze what this image suggests about communities and cooperation.

COMMON CORE

**RL 7** Analyze the representation of a subject in two different mediums.

1. **INTERPRET**
   Think about the title *In Our Hands*. What might the book's authors want to persuade readers to think or do?

2. **ANALYZE DETAILS**
   What differences do you notice between the two hands pictured on the book cover? What idea might these differences convey?

3. **SYNTHESIZE**
   The term *grassroots* refers to organizations and movements that operate at the local level. With this book cover in mind, explain why *grassroots* likely means what it does.

## Assessment Practice: Short Constructed Response

### LITERARY TEXT: "MARIGOLDS"

On assessments, you will need to answer questions that focus on particular passages from a story. To strengthen your close-reading skills, read the **short constructed response** question below and pay attention to the strategies suggested at right.

> The narrator recalls exactly when "childhood faded and womanhood began" (lines 281–282). Explain why she considers this incident to be her coming-of-age experience. Support your answer with evidence from the story.

◀ **STRATEGIES IN ACTION**

1. Read the passage closely before deciding on your interpretation.

2. Remember that evidence from the text can take the form of a **direct quotation**, a **paraphrase**, or a specific **synopsis**.

3. Make sure that any assertion you make is directly supported by evidence.

### NONFICTION TEXT: "SOWING CHANGE"

You will also need to draw conclusions about nonfiction texts as you read. Practice this skill by answering the **short constructed response** question below.

> In what ways have community gardens changed the North Lawndale neighborhood for the better? Support your answer with evidence from the article.

◀ **STRATEGIES IN ACTION**

1. Reread the article and note the positive changes taking place in the community.

2. Draw insightful **conclusions** by connecting these changes to the creation of parks.

3. Include evidence for *each* connection you make. Relevant quotations make solid evidence in support of your conclusions.

### COMPARING LITERARY AND NONFICTION TEXTS

To compare and contrast a literary and a nonfiction text, apply the following **short constructed response** question to "Marigolds" and "Sowing Change."

> How is the children's behavior in "Marigolds" different from that of the community members in "Sowing Change"? What factors might account for these differences? Support your answer with evidence from both texts.

◀ **STRATEGIES IN ACTION**

1. After stating generally how the behaviors differ, give a specific example of each.

2. Notice that the second part of the question is asking you to make an **inference**—an educated guess based on your own knowledge and the information in the text. As evidence, you must cite the information from the text that led you to your inference.

---

## Assessment Practice: Short Constructed Response

*LITERARY TEXT: "MARIGOLDS"*
***Possible answer:*** *The narrator considers the incident to be her coming-of-age experience because it caused her to see "a kind of reality that is hidden to childhood." She is able to look past herself, past the selfishness of childhood, and understand another person's motivations. She realizes that Miss Lottie is a poor old woman simply trying to bring beauty to her environment.*

*NONFICTION TEXT: "SOWING CHANGE"*
***Possible answer:*** *The park improved the neighborhood by causing residents to take more pride in their community and by bringing people together. In the article, a nine-year-old resident notes that the area used to be "dirty and trashy" but now "looks pretty." The article includes many other positive comments by residents, one of whom calls it "what we need: open space, a place to sit and talk . . . "*

*COMPARING LITERARY AND NONFICTION TEXTS* ***Possible answer:*** *The children's behavior is different from the residents' behavior in that the children destroy something beautiful while the residents create beauty. The fact that the children are young and most of the residents are adults could account for their different behavior. Also, the community members are encouraged in their project by each other and by various aid organizations; the children in "Marigolds" have nobody to guide or help them toward a creative rather than destructive course of action.*

---

## DIFFERENTIATED INSTRUCTION

### FOR STRUGGLING WRITERS

**Analyze the Short Constructed Response Question** Explain to students that in order to answer the short constructed response question thoughtfully, they should consider both how the two groups differ and how they are alike. Have students identify what the groups have in common. ***Possible answers:*** *They are primarily African American; they do not have a lot of financial resources; they do not know much about gardening at first.*

Now ask students, given those similarities, why the outcomes of the two stories are so different. Have students use their ideas to answer the question.

**459**

# Focus and Motivate

## SUMMARY

The narrator of "The Scarlet Ibis" recounts major events in the short life of Doodle, his disabled younger brother.

## Why do we **HURT** the ones we **LOVE?**

Write the term *mixed emotions* on the board, and elicit students' ideas about its meaning. Discuss reasons for mixed emotions in real-life situations. Then ask and discuss the Big Question. Conclude by having students complete the *DISCUSS* activity, perhaps with a focus on sibling relationships.

---

Essential Course of Study **ECOS**

# The Scarlet Ibis

Short Story by James Hurst

VIDEO TRAILER **THINK** central KEYWORD: HML9-460

# Why do we **HURT** the ones we **LOVE?**

Cruelty can intrude on the most loving relationship, often in moments of anger or disappointment. How do you deal with mixed emotions like these? Adults usually control such urges, but children are more likely to act on their immediate feelings. What harm can come from a thoughtless word or action?

**DISCUSS** Sometimes we are harder on loved ones than on anyone else. Why do you think this is? Discuss this question with a small group of your classmates.

FoxTrot BILL AMEND

FOXTROT © 1997 Bill Amend. Reprinted with permission of UNIVERSAL PRESS SYNDICATE. All rights reserved.

460

---

# Selection Resources

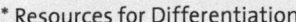 

## TEXT ANALYSIS: SYMBOL

A **symbol** is a literary device in which a person, animal, place, object, or activity stands for something beyond itself. Writers use symbols to emphasize important ideas and character traits in a story, which can act as clues to the story's **theme.** In "The Scarlet Ibis," for example, a swamp comes to symbolize the love between two brothers. To identify other symbols in this story, use these strategies as you read:

- Look for ideas that the writer emphasizes.
- Note striking images and character descriptions.
- Ask yourself what associations each one brings to mind.

*Review:* Mood, Theme

## READING SKILL: MAKE INFERENCES ABOUT CHARACTERS

When you make an **inference,** you make a logical guess based on observations or evidence and on your own knowledge and experience. Sometimes called "reading between the lines," making inferences is an essential step in understanding theme, characters, and the story itself. Use a chart like the one shown to record evidence from the text and your inferences about the relationship between the narrator and his brother.

| Quotations and Evidence | Inferences About Relationship |
|---|---|
| "Doodle ... was a nice crazy, like someone you meet in your dreams". | Narrator basically liked his brother, but thought he was odd. |

## ▲ VOCABULARY IN CONTEXT

The following boldfaced words are important to understanding "The Scarlet Ibis." To see which words you already know, restate each phrase, using a different word for the boldfaced word.

1. **exotic** flowers from the tropics
2. **reiterate** your idea for emphasis
3. **evanesce,** like smoke into thin air
4. in **imminent** danger of falling
5. claimed **infallibility** in his deeply-held beliefs
6. worked hard and with **doggedness**
7. balanced **precariously** on the edge
8. dangerous beliefs that bordered on **heresy**

 Complete the activities in your **Reader/Writer Notebook.**

## Meet the Author

## James Hurst
**born 1922**

### A Man of Many Talents
James Hurst lives near the North Carolina coast, not far from the farm where he was born. After attending college and serving in the U.S. Army during World War II, he studied singing at New York's famous Juilliard School. Hoping for an operatic career, he also studied in Rome, Italy, but soon gave up on this goal. Then, in 1951, he settled into a long career at a large New York bank.

### A Tribute to the Human Spirit
During his early years at the bank, Hurst published short stories and a play. "The Scarlet Ibis" received national attention after appearing in the *Atlantic Monthly* in July 1960 and winning the Atlantic First award that same year. When asked about the meaning of the story, Hurst once replied, "I hesitate to respond, since authors often do not understand what they write. That is why we have critics. I venture to say, however, that it comments on the tenacity and the splendor of the human spirit."

### BACKGROUND TO THE STORY
**Drawn from Nature**
"The Scarlet Ibis" takes its title from a tropical bird rarely found in coastal North Carolina, where the story takes place. The lush natural environment of this setting is prominent in the story. In addition to the ibis, Hurst uses the local names of plants for the power of their symbolic associations. For example, the exotic ibis lands in a "bleeding tree," a type of pine that oozes a white sap when cut. "Graveyard flowers" are fragrant white gardenias often planted in cemeteries because they bloom year after year.

**Author Online THINK**central
Go to **thinkcentral.com.**
KEYWORD: HML9-461

461

### TEXT ANALYSIS
COMMON CORE
RL 2

## ● *Model the Skill:* SYMBOL

To help students understand symbols, write this sentence on the board:

> James Hurst fought for his flag during World War II.

Explain that in this sentence the word *flag* stands as a symbol for his country, the United States.

**GUIDED PRACTICE** Have students name symbols that could represent love.

### READING SKILL
COMMON CORE
RL 1, RL 3

## ■ *Model the Skill:* MAKE INFERENCES ABOUT CHARACTERS

Remind students that not all actions or emotions are clearly explained in stories. They may need to make inferences. Have students imagine a parent who is raging with anger at one moment and then hugging his or her child the next. Explain that you will use what you know about parent-child relationships to infer that the parent loves the child, but the child has misbehaved.

**GUIDED PRACTICE** Invite students to make inferences about the characters in the *FoxTrot* comic strip on page 460.

**R** RESOURCE MANAGER—Copy Master Make Inferences About Characters p. 61 (for student use while reading the selection)

---

### VOCABULARY SKILL
COMMON CORE
L 4

## ▲ VOCABULARY IN CONTEXT

**DIAGNOSE WORD KNOWLEDGE** Have all students complete Vocabulary in Context. Check their answers against the following:

**doggedness** (dô′gĭd-nĭs) *n.* persistence; stubbornness
**evanesce** (ĕv′ə-nĕs′) *v.* to disappear; vanish
**exotic** (ĭg-zŏt′ĭk) *adj.* excitingly strange
**heresy** (hĕr′ĭ-sē) *n.* an action or opinion contrary to what is generally thought of as right
**imminent** (ĭm′ə-nənt) *adj.* about to occur

**infallibility** (ĭn-făl′ə-bĭl′ĭ-tē) *n.* an inability to make errors
**reiterate** (rē-ĭt′ə-rāt′) *v.* to repeat
**precariously** (prĭ-kâr′ē-əs-lē) *adv.* insecurely; in a dangerous or unstable way

**PRETEACH VOCABULARY** Use the copy master to help students predict the meaning of each boldfaced word using context clues.

**R** RESOURCE MANAGER—Copy Master Vocabulary Study p. 63

1. Read item 1 aloud,
2. Point out the phrase "did not give up." Elicit possible meanings for *doggedness*.
3. Repeat the procedure for items 2–8.

**READ WITH A PURPOSE**

*Encourage students to set a purpose for reading. Have them read to find out what a scarlet ibis is and how it is important to this story of two brothers.*

---

**TEXT ANALYSIS:** *Review*    COMMON CORE   RL 2

### Ⓐ MOOD

**Possible answer:** *the description that "summer was dead but autumn had not yet been born"; words like "stained," "rotting," and "rank" (lines 2–3); details of the "empty cradle" (line 5) of the nest and the graveyard flowers whose scent was "speaking softly the names of our dead" (line 7)*

**IF STUDENTS NEED HELP . . .** Model for students how to find some of the details that relate to things that are dying, disappearing, or missing.

---

**READING SKILL**    COMMON CORE   RL 1, RL 3

### Ⓑ MAKE INFERENCES

**Possible answer:** *We can infer that Doodle was born with some illness or disability. We can make this inference based on these text details: he "seemed all head, with a tiny body which was red and shriveled" (lines 20–21); everybody thought he would die (line 21).*

---

# The Scarlet Ibis

### James Hurst

It was in the clove of seasons,[1] summer was dead but autumn had not yet been born, that the ibis lit in the bleeding tree. The flower garden was stained with rotting brown magnolia petals and ironweeds grew rank amid the purple phlox. The five o'clocks by the chimney still marked time, but the oriole nest in the elm was untenanted and rocked back and forth like an empty cradle. The last graveyard flowers were blooming, and their smell drifted across the cotton field and through every room of our house, speaking softly the names of our dead. Ⓐ

It's strange that all this is still so clear to me, now that that summer has long since fled and time has had its way. A grindstone stands where the bleeding
10 tree stood, just outside the kitchen door, and now if an oriole sings in the elm, its song seems to die up in the leaves, a silvery dust. The flower garden is prim, the house a gleaming white, and the pale fence across the yard stands straight and spruce. But sometimes (like right now), as I sit in the cool, green-draped parlor, the grindstone begins to turn, and time with all its changes is ground away—and I remember Doodle.

Doodle was just about the craziest brother a boy ever had. Of course, he wasn't a crazy crazy like old Miss Leedie, who was in love with President Wilson and wrote him a letter every day, but was a nice crazy, like someone you meet in your dreams. He was born when I was six and was, from the
20 outset, a disappointment. He seemed all head, with a tiny body which was red and shriveled like an old man's. Everybody thought he was going to die—everybody except Aunt Nicey, who had delivered him. She said he would live because he was born in a caul,[2] and cauls were made from Jesus' nightgown. Daddy had Mr. Heath, the carpenter, build a little mahogany coffin for him. But he didn't die, and when he was three months old, Mama and Daddy decided they might as well name him. They named him William Armstrong, which was like tying a big tail on a small kite. Such a name sounds good only on a tombstone. Ⓑ

---

1. **the clove of seasons:** a time between two seasons, in this case, summer and autumn.
2. **born in a caul:** born with a thin membrane covering the head.

Ⓐ MOOD
What words or images contribute to the mood of sadness and longing in lines 1–7?

① **Targeted Passage**

**Analyze Visuals** ▶
What qualities does the boy in the painting seem to have? Point to details of color, line, shape, and texture to support your answer.

Ⓑ MAKE INFERENCES
What inferences can you make about Doodle from the **details** offered in this paragraph? Explain your thought process.

*Richard at Age Five* (1944), Alice Neel. Oil on canvas, 26" × 14". © Estate of Alice Neel. Courtesy Robert Miller Gallery, New York.

---

## DIFFERENTIATED INSTRUCTION

**FOR ENGLISH LANGUAGE LEARNERS**

**Options for Reading** Read the first Targeted Passage aloud and explain that "The Scarlet Ibis" is a personal and emotional journey back into childhood. Then have learners listen to the *Audio Anthology CD* as they read along.

**FOR STRUGGLING READERS**

In combination with the *Audio Anthology CD*, use one or more Targeted Passages (pp. 462, 467, 469, 473, 475) to ensure that students focus on key story events, concepts, and skills. Targeted Passages are also good for English learners.

① **Targeted Passage [Lines 8–16]**

This passage helps to establish the setting and narrator of the story.

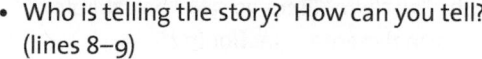

**Reading Support**

This selection on **thinkcentral.com** includes embedded **ThinkAloud** models—students "thinking aloud" about the story to model the kinds of questions a good reader would ask about a selection.

## BACKGROUND

**The Summer of 1918** The climax of "The Scarlet Ibis" is set in July and August of 1918, a time crucial to American involvement in World War I. During those months, American forces played a key role in the Second Battle of the Marne, a series of battles involving German, British, French, and American forces. Hundreds of thousands of soldiers were killed or wounded. The battle defeated the last major German offensive of the war, resulting in the German surrender the following November.

### REVISIT THE BIG QUESTION

# Why do we **HURT**
## the ones we **LOVE?**

**Discuss** How do lines 16–20 show that the narrator had mixed emotions about Doodle from the boy's birth? ***Possible answer:*** *He says that Doodle was both "a nice crazy" (line 18) and "from the outset, a disappointment" (lines 19–20).*

## Analyze Visuals

*Possible answer: With his seated position, large eyes and ears, delicate features, and closed mouth, the boy appears more of an observer and thinker than a doer. The roughness of the lines and the lack of detail in the solid-colored clothing give the impression that the boy is not quite realized.*

**About the Art** American portrait artist Alice Neel (1900–1984) created this oil painting.

---

- Who is telling the story? How can you tell? (lines 8–9)

- What do you learn about the narrator from these sentences? In particular, who is Doodle? (lines 13–16)

- When did the events that the narrator is about to retell take place? (lines 8–11)

**FOR ADVANCED LEARNERS/PRE–AP**

Ask students to find examples of exotic wildlife that can be found in coastal North Carolina and then explain how each example could be used symbolically in the story. See

**R** **RESOURCE MANAGER**
Ideas for Extension pp. 54–55

I thought myself pretty smart at many things, like holding my breath, 30 running, jumping, or climbing the vines in Old Woman Swamp, and I wanted more than anything else someone to race to Horsehead Landing, someone to box with, and someone to perch with in the top fork of the great pine behind the barn, where across the fields and swamps you could see the sea. I wanted a brother. But Mama, crying, told me that even if William Armstrong lived, he would never do these things with me. He might not, she sobbed, even be "all there." He might, as long as he lived, lie on the rubber sheet in the center of the bed in the front bedroom where the white marquisette curtains billowed out in the afternoon sea breeze, rustling like palmetto fronds.[3]

It was bad enough having an invalid brother, but having one who possibly 40 was not all there was unbearable, so I began to make plans to kill him by smothering him with a pillow. However, one afternoon as I watched him, my head poked between the iron posts of the foot of the bed, he looked straight at me and grinned. I skipped through the rooms, down the echoing halls, shouting, "Mama, he smiled. He's all there! He's all there!" and he was. **C**

When he was two, if you laid him on his stomach, he began to move himself, straining terribly. The doctor said that with his weak heart this strain would probably kill him, but it didn't. Trembling, he'd push himself up, turning first red, then a soft purple, and finally collapse back onto the bed like an old worn-out doll. I can still see Mama watching him, her hand 50 pressed tight across her mouth, her eyes wide and unblinking. But he learned to crawl (it was his third winter), and we brought him out of the front bedroom, putting him on the rug before the fireplace. For the first time he became one of us.

As long as he lay all the time in bed, we called him William Armstrong, even though it was formal and sounded as if we were referring to one of our ancestors, but with his creeping around on the deerskin rug and beginning to talk, something had to be done about his name. It was I who renamed him. When he crawled, he crawled backward, as if he were in reverse and couldn't change gears. If you called him, he'd turn around as if he were going in the 60 other direction, then he'd back right up to you to be picked up. Crawling backward made him look like a doodlebug, so I began to call him Doodle, and in time even Mama and Daddy thought it was a better name than William Armstrong. Only Aunt Nicey disagreed. She said caul babies should be treated with special respect since they might turn out to be saints. Renaming my brother was perhaps the kindest thing I ever did for him, because nobody expects much from someone called Doodle. **D**

Although Doodle learned to crawl, he showed no signs of walking, but he wasn't idle. He talked so much that we all quit listening to what he said. It was about this time that Daddy built him a go-cart and I had to pull him around.

**C** MAKE INFERENCES
Compare the narrator's initial reaction to Doodle with his response to Doodle's grin. What can you infer about the change in the narrator's attitude?

**D** SYMBOL
Reread lines 60–66. A nickname can sometimes be a kind of symbol. What does Doodle's nickname tell you about the feelings and expectations others have for him?

---

3. **palmetto fronds:** the fanlike leaves of a kind of palm tree.

---

## DIFFERENTIATED INSTRUCTION

**FOR ENGLISH LANGUAGE LEARNERS**

**Vocabulary Support** Use Word Squares to teach these words: *reverse* (line 58), *reveal* (line 164), *surveying* (line 235), *schedule* (line 247), *contrarily* (line 275), *parallel* (line 378).

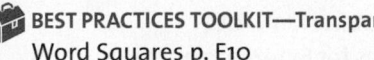 **BEST PRACTICES TOOLKIT—Transparency** Word Squares p. E10

**Language: Conversational Patterns** Adapt the New Word Analysis strategy to teach these conversational phrases:

- *be "all there"* (lines 35–36), "be capable of normal mental functioning"

- *if I so much as* (line 72), "if I even"

- *when the going got rough* (line 81), "when challenges arose"

- *he was a sight* (line 82), "he looked ridiculous"

- *barring rain* (line 161), "if it didn't rain"

 **BEST PRACTICES TOOLKIT—Transparency** New Word Analysis p. E8

*Cypress Swamp, Texas* (1940), Florence McClung. Oil on masonite, 24″ × 30″. Gift of the Roger H. Ogden Collection. The Ogden Museum of Southern Art.

70 At first I just paraded him up and down the piazza, but then he started crying to be taken out into the yard, and it ended up by my having to lug him wherever I went. If I so much as picked up my cap, he'd start crying to go with me, and Mama would call from wherever she was, "Take Doodle with you."

He was a burden in many ways. The doctor had said that he mustn't get too excited, too hot, too cold, or too tired and that he must always be treated gently. A long list of don'ts went with him, all of which I ignored once we got out of the house. To discourage his coming with me, I'd run with him across the ends of the cotton rows and careen him around corners on two wheels. Sometimes I accidentally turned him over, but he never told Mama. His skin
80 was very sensitive, and he had to wear a big straw hat whenever he went out. When the going got rough and he had to cling to the sides of the go-cart, the hat slipped all the way down over his ears. He was a sight. Finally, I could see I was licked. Doodle was my brother and he was going to cling to me forever, no matter what I did, so I dragged him across the burning cotton field to share with him the only beauty I knew, Old Woman Swamp. I pulled the go-cart through the sawtooth fern, down into the green dimness where the palmetto

> ◠ COMMON CORE L 4a
>
> **Language Coach**
>
> **Word Definitions**
> Writers sometimes give clues to a word's meaning by placing a definition or example nearby. Reread lines 77–78. What words give you clues to the meaning of *careen*?

THE SCARLET IBIS **465**

---

**FOR ADVANCED LEARNERS/PRE–AP**
**Analyze Style** [paired-activity option] Have students mine pages 464–465 for characteristics of Hurst's style, including the way he varies sentence lengths, places lists within sentences, uses poetic language, and creates a unique voice through the use of rhetorical devices and through the tone of the narrator. Have students share their findings and look for additional examples as they continue reading.

**FOR ENGLISH LANGUAGE LEARNERS**

> **Language Coach**　　◠ COMMON CORE L 4a
> **Word Definitions** *Answer:*
> *"around corners on two wheels"* Have students look up the definition of *careen* to confirm their choice. Then, have them use context to determine the meaning of *licked* in line 83.

---

**TIERED DISCUSSION PROMPTS**
Use these prompts to help students understand the narrator's attitude toward Doodle in lines 74–85:

**Connect** How would you feel about having a younger sibling who wanted to go everywhere you went? *Students might mention the responsibilities and stresses that such a situation would create.*

**Analyze** How does the narrator respond to his role as a caretaker? *Possible answer: He sees his brother as a burden (line 74) and mistreats him sometimes (lines 76–79), but eventually he shares what he loves with Doodle (lines 82–85).*

**Synthesize** How does the point of view help to tone down the mistreatment and resentment expressed in these lines? *Possible answer: The first-person point of view reveals a narrator whose resentments seem understandable for a child of his age. Nevertheless, there is a cruelty in turning over the helpless Doodle and in making him "cling" to the sides of the go-cart.*

**Analyze Visuals**

**Activity** Ask students how this scene helps them visualize Old Woman Swamp. *Possible answer: The painting shows huge trees and standing water; it shows exotic-looking vegetation. Yet, there is a house in sight, so while the swamp seems unspoiled, like Old Woman Swamp, it is not entirely separated from human life.*

**About the Art** American painter Florence McClung (1894–1992) is known for her regional paintings. Like many of her other works, *Cypress Swamp, Texas* documents an environment for which she felt affection. The huge cypress trees, standing in water and hung with mosses, suggest a world that is strange yet wonderful—much like the world of Old Woman Swamp in this story.

## E MAKE INFERENCES

*Possible answer: The brothers find ways to enjoy their shared time. One reason may be that they have only each other; they must adapt. Another reason may be that Doodle lets his brother lead.*

TEXT ANALYSIS: *Review* · COMMON CORE · RL 2

## F THEME

*Possible answer: Inside me (and inside others, too), some cruelty mixes with love, just as life always contains the possibility of death, and sometimes I was cruel to Doodle.*

**IF STUDENTS NEED HELP . . .** Have students ignore the parenthetical material at first. Note that *borne* means "carried."

**REVISIT THE BIG QUESTION**

## Why do we HURT the ones we LOVE?

**Discuss** What mixed emotions do you see in the brothers' relationship when the narrator shows Doodle the coffin in lines 100–118?
*Possible answer: The narrator is cruel when he shows Doodle his own coffin and when he threatens to leave his brother alone with it in the barn, but he is also caring when he carries Doodle outside. Doodle is defiant in resisting his brother's demand to touch the coffin, but dependent in his pleading not to be left alone.*

---

fronds whispered by the stream. I lifted him out and set him down in the soft rubber grass beside a tall pine. His eyes were round with wonder as he gazed about him, and his little hands began to stroke the rubber grass. Then he
90 began to cry.

"For heaven's sake, what's the matter?" I asked, annoyed.

"It's so pretty," he said. "So pretty, pretty, pretty."

After that day Doodle and I often went down into Old Woman Swamp. I would gather wildflowers, wild violets, honeysuckle, yellow jasmine, snakeflowers, and water lilies, and with wire grass we'd weave them into necklaces and crowns. We'd bedeck ourselves with our handiwork and loll about thus beautified, beyond the touch of the everyday world. Then when the slanted rays of the sun burned orange in the tops of the pines, we'd drop our jewels into the stream and watch them float away toward the sea. **E**
100 There is within me (and with sadness I have watched it in others) a knot of cruelty borne by the stream of love, much as our blood sometimes bears the seed of our destruction, and at times I was mean to Doodle. One day I took **F** him up to the barn loft and showed him his casket, telling him how we all had believed he would die. It was covered with a film of Paris green[4] sprinkled to kill the rats, and screech owls had built a nest inside it.

Doodle studied the mahogany box for a long time, then said, "It's not mine."

"It is," I said. "And before I'll help you down from the loft, you're going to have to touch it."

"I won't touch it," he said sullenly.
110 "Then I'll leave you here by yourself," I threatened, and made as if I were going down.

Doodle was frightened of being left. "Don't go leave me, Brother," he cried, and he leaned toward the coffin. His hand, trembling, reached out, and when he touched the casket he screamed. A screech owl flapped out of the box into our faces, scaring us and covering us with Paris green. Doodle was paralyzed, so I put him on my shoulder and carried him down the ladder, and even when we were outside in the bright sunshine, he clung to me, crying, "Don't leave me. Don't leave me."

When Doodle was five years old, I was embarrassed at having a brother of
120 that age who couldn't walk, so I set out to teach him. We were down in Old Woman Swamp and it was spring and the sick-sweet smell of bay flowers hung everywhere like a mournful song. "I'm going to teach you to walk, Doodle," I said.

He was sitting comfortably on the soft grass, leaning back against the pine. "Why?" he asked.

I hadn't expected such an answer. "So I won't have to haul you around all the time."

"I can't walk, Brother," he said.

---

**E MAKE INFERENCES**
Describe the relationship that develops between the brothers. What do you think is the reason that Doodle wins the narrator over?

**F THEME**
In lines 100–102, the narrator makes a direct statement that offers clues to the theme. Paraphrase the message he expresses.

---

4. **Paris green:** a poisonous green powder used to kill pests.

---

## DIFFERENTIATED INSTRUCTION

**FOR STRUGGLING READERS**

**Concept Support** As you review lines 119–128, discuss the idea that teaching Doodle to walk seems noble—until we understand the narrator's reason for doing so (a reason that he both thinks to himself and says to Doodle). Point out this mix of the narrator's positive action and negative motivation as students read on.

**FOR ENGLISH LANGUAGE LEARNERS**

**Vocabulary: Phrasal Verbs** Explain that *set out* (line 120) can mean "begin" (as with a literal or figurative journey) but it also can mean "to put" or "to place," as in "to set out the dinner plates." Have students find one or more definitions for the phrasal verbs "give up" (line 141), "took up" (line 188), "work out" (line 208), and "broke into" (line 225) and determine which meaning is used in context.

"Who says so?" I demanded.

130 "Mama, the doctor—everybody."

"Oh, you can walk," I said, and I took him by the arms and stood him up. He collapsed onto the grass like a half-empty flour sack. It was as if he had no bones in his little legs.

"Don't hurt me, Brother," he warned.

"Shut up. I'm not going to hurt you. I'm going to teach you to walk." I heaved him up again, and again he collapsed.

This time he did not lift his face up out of the rubber grass. "I just can't do it. Let's make honeysuckle wreaths."

"Oh yes you can, Doodle," I said. "All you got to do is try. Now come on,"
140 and I hauled him up once more.

It seemed so hopeless from the beginning that it's a miracle I didn't give up. But all of us must have something or someone to be proud of, and Doodle had become mine. I did not know then that pride is a wonderful, terrible thing, a seed that bears two vines, life and death. Every day that summer we went to the pine beside the stream of Old Woman Swamp, and I put him on his feet at least a hundred times each afternoon. Occasionally I too became discouraged because it didn't seem as if he was trying, and I would say, "Doodle, don't you *want* to learn to walk?" **G**

He'd nod his head, and I'd say, "Well, if you don't keep trying, you'll never
150 learn." Then I'd paint for him a picture of us as old men, white-haired, him with a long white beard and me still pulling him around in the go-cart. This never failed to make him try again.

Finally one day, after many weeks of practicing, he stood alone for a few seconds. When he fell, I grabbed him in my arms and hugged him, our laughter pealing through the swamp like a ringing bell. Now we knew it could be done. Hope no longer hid in the dark palmetto thicket but perched like a cardinal in the lacy toothbrush tree, brilliantly visible.

"Yes, yes," I cried, and he cried it too, and the grass beneath us was soft and the smell of the swamp was sweet.

160 With success so **imminent**, we decided not to tell anyone until he could actually walk. Each day, barring rain, we sneaked into Old Woman Swamp, and by cotton-picking time Doodle was ready to show what he could do. He still wasn't able to walk far, but we could wait no longer. Keeping a nice secret is very hard to do, like holding your breath. We chose to reveal all on October eighth, Doodle's sixth birthday, and for weeks ahead we mooned around the house, promising everybody a most spectacular surprise. Aunt Nicey said that, after so much talk, if we produced anything less tremendous than the Resurrection,[5] she was going to be disappointed.

At breakfast on our chosen day, when Mama, Daddy, and Aunt Nicey were
170 in the dining room, I brought Doodle to the door in the go-cart just as usual and had them turn their backs, making them cross their hearts and hope to

---

5. **the Resurrection:** the rising of Jesus Christ from the dead after his burial.

**G** MAKE INFERENCES
Why does the narrator try so hard to teach Doodle to walk? Point out statements in lines 141–148 that support your answer.

**imminent** (ĭm′ə-nənt) *adj.* about to occur

**②** **Targeted Passage**

die if they peeked. I helped Doodle up, and when he was standing alone I let them look. There wasn't a sound as Doodle walked slowly across the room and sat down at his place at the table. Then Mama began to cry and ran over to him, hugging him and kissing him. Daddy hugged him too, so I went to Aunt Nicey, who was thanks praying in the doorway, and began to waltz her around. We danced together quite well until she came down on my big toe with her brogans,[6] hurting me so badly I thought I was crippled for life.

180  Doodle told them it was I who had taught him to walk, so everyone wanted to hug me, and I began to cry.

"What are you crying for?" asked Daddy, but I couldn't answer. They did not know that I did it for myself; that pride, whose slave I was, spoke to me louder than all their voices, and that Doodle walked only because I was ashamed of having a crippled brother.

Within a few months Doodle had learned to walk well and his go-cart was put up in the barn loft (it's still there) beside his little mahogany coffin. Now, when we roamed off together, resting often, we never turned back until our destination had been reached, and to help pass the time, we took up lying. From the beginning Doodle was a terrible liar and he got me in the habit. Had 190 anyone stopped to listen to us, we would have been sent off to Dix Hill.[7]

My lies were scary, involved, and usually pointless, but Doodle's were twice as crazy. People in his stories all had wings and flew wherever they wanted to go. His favorite lie was about a boy named Peter who had a pet peacock with a ten-foot tail. Peter wore a golden robe that glittered so brightly that when he walked through the sunflowers they turned away from the sun to face him. When Peter was ready to go to sleep, the peacock spread his magnificent tail, enfolding the boy gently like a closing go-to-sleep flower, burying him in the gloriously iridescent, rustling vortex.[8] Yes, I must admit it. Doodle could beat me lying. ◆

200  Doodle and I spent lots of time thinking about our future. We decided that when we were grown we'd live in Old Woman Swamp and pick dog-tongue for a living. Beside the stream, he planned, we'd build us a house of whispering leaves and the swamp birds would be our chickens. All day long (when we weren't gathering dog-tongue) we'd swing through the cypresses on the rope vines, and if it rained we'd huddle beneath an umbrella tree and play stickfrog. Mama and Daddy could come and live with us if they wanted to. He even came up with the idea that he could marry Mama and I could marry Daddy. Of course, I was old enough to know this wouldn't work out, but the picture he painted was so beautiful and serene that all I could do was whisper Yes, yes.

---

6. **brogans** (brō′gənz): heavy, ankle-high work shoes.
7. **Dix Hill:** common name for a mental hospital in Raleigh, North Carolina.
8. **iridescent rustling vortex:** the shimmering, rainbow-colored peacock feathers are in a funnel shape, like a whirlpool or whirlwind (vortex).

**468**  UNIT 4: THEME AND SYMBOL

---

**H MAKE INFERENCES**
Reread lines 181–184. Why is the narrator ashamed of himself?

**I GRAMMAR AND STYLE**
Reread lines 194–199. Hurst uses a variety of sentence structures, containing **independent** and **subordinate clauses,** to add rhythm and interest to his writing.

---

---

**DIFFERENTIATED INSTRUCTION**

**FOR ENGLISH LANGUAGE LEARNERS**
**Vocabulary: Multiple-Meaning Words** Have pairs of students use a dictionary and a Cluster Diagram to find and present multiple meanings of these story words: "licked" (line 83), "living" (line 202), "drive" (line 249), "rail" (line 347), and "rustling" (line 359). Discuss how context determines the story meaning in each instance of use.

💼 **BEST PRACTICES TOOLKIT—Transparency**
Cluster Diagram p. B18

**FOR ADVANCED LEARNERS/PRE–AP**
**Hypothesize About Setting** [small-group option] Would the relationships and conflicts that we see in this story have developed if there had been no swamp (which, as is pointed out in lines 200–209, shapes the brothers' dreams about the future as well as their present lives) or if the events had taken place in a city of that time or in today's world? Have students gather story evidence to argue their case.

**Analyze Visuals**

**Activity** Ask students to explain how this painting compares to and contrasts with story events. *Possible answer: Contrast: There are five rather than two children; the setting appears to be a quarry, not a swamp; all of the children appear equally capable. Comparison: One boy seems to be the leader; the situation could be one in which timid children are encouraged or pressured to act beyond their comfort zone.* Ask students why the painting is appropriate, even if its details do not match the story exactly. *Possible answer: It is a scene that the narrator and Doodle may imagine being a part of if Doodle's progress continues.*

**About the Art** In this painting, Canadian artist Vincent McIndoe shows five children at a swimming hole, one of whom is the focus of activity at the moment. Though the scene is one of natural beauty, the setting is not entirely inviting, with its steep rocks and unsupervised, somewhat risky diving activity.

210      Once I had succeeded in teaching Doodle to walk, I began to believe in my own **infallibility,** and I prepared a terrific development program for him, unknown to Mama and Daddy, of course. I would teach him to run, to swim, to climb trees, and to fight. He, too, now believed in my infallibility, so we set the deadline for these accomplishments less than a year away, when, it had been decided, Doodle could start to school.

     That winter we didn't make much progress, for I was in school and Doodle suffered from one bad cold after another. But when spring came, rich and warm, we raised our sights again. Success lay at the end of summer like a pot of gold, and our campaign got off to a good start. On hot days, Doodle

220 and I went down to Horsehead Landing, and I gave him swimming lessons or showed him how to row a boat. Sometimes we descended into the cool greenness of Old Woman Swamp and climbed the rope vines or boxed

**infallibility**
(ĭn-făl′ə-bĭl′ĭ-tē) *n.* an inability to make errors

❸ **Targeted Passage**

THE SCARLET IBIS    **469**

**REVISIT THE BIG QUESTION**

# Why do we **HURT** the ones we **LOVE?**

**Discuss** What mixed emotions does the narrator seem to feel as he prepares his development program for Doodle in lines 210–219? Explain. *Possible answer: He is pleased enough with the program to call it "terrific" (line 211) but concerned enough to leave it "unknown to Mama and Daddy" (line 212). In addition, he may be glad that it might do Doodle some good—but he already has admitted that pride is his motivation, and here he proudly speaks of his "infallibility" (line 211).*

**VOCABULARY**     COMMON CORE   L 4

**OWN THE WORD**

**infallibility:** Tell students that the prefix *in-* means "not" or "without." *Fallibility* means "ability to make a mistake," so *infallibility* means "not having the ability to make a mistake."

**FOR STRUGGLING READERS**

❸ **Targeted Passage** [Lines 210–219]

This passage sets up increased tension, as the narrator pushes Doodle toward a specific goal.

- What four things does the narrator plan to teach Doodle to do? (lines 212–213)

- From whom does he keep this plan a secret? Why? (line 212)

- At the end of this passage, about how close are they to their deadline? (lines 216–219)

**FOR ENGLISH LANGUAGE LEARNERS**

**Comprehension: Comparisons** Have small groups find what is being compared in these similes and record their comparisons in a Two-Column Chart: "like a closing go-to-sleep flower" (line 197); "like a pot of gold" (lines 218–219); "like a hawk at the entrails of a chicken" (line 231); "like a broken vase of red flowers" (line 305).

 **BEST PRACTICES TOOLKIT—Transparency** Two-Column Chart p. A25

**Possible answer:** *The dull browns and greens combine with the images of dying plants and falling leaves to create a mood of loss or sorrow. The brushstrokes that depict decaying plant matter are quick and fleeting, like the decomposing life itself.*

**About the Art** The influential American landscape artist Charles Burchfield (1893–1967) blended the feelings and atmosphere of a landscape with the spiritual qualities of the objects within them.

## TIERED DISCUSSION PROMPTS

Use these prompts to help students understand how details of the scene in lines 226–241 foreshadow disaster:

**Connect** Have you ever experienced nature in a particularly destructive way? Describe. *Students may mention hurricanes, tornadoes, thunderstorms, floods, or even earthquakes.*

**Analyze** How would you describe the roles of the brothers in this scene? ***Possible answer:*** *The brothers are figures of innocence and perhaps unfounded optimism, giggling and having fun, "knowing that everything would be all right" (lines 240–241), despite the signs of blight and sorrow around them.*

**Synthesize** What function does this passage serve for the story? Explain your answer. ***Possible answer:*** *It shifts the mood. The previous pages have been full of the joy of Doodle's learning to walk and the narrator's confidence in his own infallibility. In this passage, death and destruction enter in, uninvited and invincible. Their presence foretells of their power in scenes to come.*

*Autumn Embers (Frosted Scarlet Sage)* (1944), Charles Burchfield. Watercolor on paper, 22 1/2" x 28".
Courtesy DC Moore Gallery, New York.

◀ **Analyze Visuals**
How do the color, brush strokes, and subject matter of this painting create a **mood** of sorrow and despair?

scientifically beneath the pine where he had learned to walk. Promise hung about us like the leaves, and wherever we looked, ferns unfurled and birds broke into song.

    That summer, the summer of 1918, was blighted. In May and June there was no rain and the crops withered, curled up, then died under the thirsty sun. One morning in July a hurricane came out of the east, tipping over the oaks in the yard and splitting the limbs of the elm trees. That afternoon it roared
230 back out of the west, blew the fallen oaks around, snapping their roots and tearing them out of the earth like a hawk at the entrails of a chicken. Cotton bolls were wrenched from the stalks and lay like green walnuts in the valleys between the rows, while the cornfield leaned over uniformly so that the tassels touched the ground. Doodle and I followed Daddy out into the cotton field, where he stood, shoulders sagging, surveying the ruin. When his chin sank down onto his chest, we were frightened, and Doodle slipped his hand into mine. Suddenly Daddy straightened his shoulders, raised a giant knuckly fist, and with a voice that seemed to rumble out of the earth itself began cursing heaven, hell, the weather, and the Republican Party.[9] Doodle and I, prodding
240 each other and giggling, went back to the house, knowing that everything would be all right.

---

9. **Republican Party:** In 1918, most Southerners were Democrats.

**470**    UNIT 4: THEME AND SYMBOL

COMMON CORE L 4b

**Language Coach**

**Prefixes** Word parts that come before base words are **prefixes**. The base word *furled* in line 224 means "rolled up." The prefix *un-*, which comes from Old English, means "the opposite of," or "not." What is the definition of *unfurled*? What other words include the prefix *un-*?

## DIFFERENTIATED INSTRUCTION

### FOR ADVANCED LEARNERS/PRE–AP

**Analyze Metaphor** Have students write a paragraph or two explaining *blight* as a metaphor in "The Scarlet Ibis." Encourage them to analyze the wider context of the story, including the war in Europe, as well as the more narrow world of the characters. Also ask students to reflect on how the concept of blight does or does not fit in with some of the other seasonal and natural imagery in the story.

### FOR ENGLISH LANGUAGE LEARNERS

**Language Coach**    COMMON CORE L 4b

**Prefixes** *Answer:* *unfurled*
Ask students what objects other than leaves might be furled or unfurled.
***Possible answers:*** *flags, curtains* Have students pantomime or demonstrate how they would *furl* and *unfurl* a flag.

And during that summer, strange names were heard through the house: Château-Thierry, Amiens, Soissons, and in her blessing at the supper table, Mama once said, "And bless the Pearsons, whose boy Joe was lost at Belleau Wood."[10]

So we came to that clove of seasons. School was only a few weeks away, and Doodle was far behind schedule. He could barely clear the ground when climbing up the rope vines, and his swimming was certainly not passable. We decided to double our efforts, to make that last drive and reach our pot of
250 gold. I made him swim until he turned blue and row until he couldn't lift an oar. Wherever we went, I purposely walked fast, and although he kept up, his face turned red and his eyes became glazed. Once, he could go no further, so he collapsed on the ground and began to cry.

"Aw, come on, Doodle," I urged. "You can do it. Do you want to be different from everybody else when you start school?"

"Does it make any difference?"

"It certainly does," I said. "Now, come on," and I helped him up.

As we slipped through dog days,[11] Doodle began to look feverish, and Mama felt his forehead, asking him if he felt ill. At night he didn't sleep well,
260 and sometimes he had nightmares, crying out until I touched him and said, "Wake up, Doodle. Wake up."

It was Saturday noon, just a few days before school was to start. I should have already admitted defeat, but my pride wouldn't let me. The excitement of our program had now been gone for weeks, but still we kept on with a tired **doggedness.** It was too late to turn back, for we had both wandered too far into a net of expectations and had left no crumbs behind.

Daddy, Mama, Doodle, and I were seated at the dining-room table having lunch. It was a hot day, with all the windows and doors open in case a breeze should come. In the kitchen Aunt Nicey was humming softly. After a long
270 silence, Daddy spoke. "It's so calm, I wouldn't be surprised if we had a storm this afternoon."

"I haven't heard a rain frog," said Mama, who believed in signs, as she served the bread around the table.

"I did," declared Doodle. "Down in the swamp."

"He didn't," I said contrarily.

"You did, eh?" said Daddy, ignoring my denial.

"I certainly did," Doodle **reiterated,** scowling at me over the top of his iced-tea glass, and we were quiet again.

Suddenly, from out in the yard, came a strange croaking noise. Doodle
280 stopped eating, with a piece of bread poised ready for his mouth, his eyes popped round like two blue buttons. "What's that?" he whispered.

---

**J MAKE INFERENCES**
What is happening to Doodle?

**doggedness**
(dô′gĭd-nĭs)
*n.* persistence; stubbornness

**reiterate** (rē-ĭt′ə-rāt′)
*v.* to repeat

---

10. **Château-Thierry** (shä-tō-tyĕ-rē′), **Amiens** (ä-myăn′), **Soissons** (swä-sōn′), ... **Belleau** (bel′ō) **Wood:** places in France where famous battles were fought near the end of World War I (1914–1918).

11. **dog days:** the hot, uncomfortable days between early July and early September (named after the Dog Star, Sirius, which rises and sets with the sun at this time).

THE SCARLET IBIS **471**

---

**FOR ENGLISH LANGUAGE LEARNERS**
**Comprehension: Contrast** Have students locate the contrasts signaled by "different from" (line 255) and by "but" (lines 263 and 264) and explain what is being contrasted. *Possible answer:* line 255: Doodle and everyone else; line 263: defeat and pride; line 264: doggedness and lack of excitement

**FOR STRUGGLING READERS**
**Develop Reading Fluency** Point out the series of compound and complex sentences in the long paragraph on page 470. Explain that the commas within each sentence are a guide both to its sense and to how it should be read aloud. Read the paragraph aloud as a demonstration. Point out that you took short breaks at the commas and longer ones at the periods. Next, ask students to read the entire paragraph aloud, one sentence per student.

**R RESOURCE MANAGER—Copy Master**
Reading Fluency p. 69

---

*Possible answer: Doodle may be getting ill. He appears to be showing signs of exhaustion from the demanding schedule that his brother has set. There even is a small chance that Doodle, who has been associated with death since his birth, and whose coffin (though now too small) seems to await him in the barn, is dying.*

**REVISIT THE BIG QUESTION**
# Why do we **HURT** the ones we **LOVE?**

**Discuss** Why do you think the narrator presses Doodle so hard with his program of physical exercise in lines 246–266? *Possible answer: After his success at teaching Doodle to walk, the narrator truly believes that he can teach his brother to run, swim, and do other physical activities so that he will not be "different from everybody else" when he starts school. But the narrator has mixed emotions: he is motivated by selfishness as well as love. He is ashamed of Doodle's disability and wants him to be like everybody else so that his brother won't embarrass him—not because fitting in is that important for Doodle's own happiness or development.*

**VOCABULARY** COMMON CORE L 4

**OWN THE WORD**

- **doggedness:** Tell student that common synonyms for *doggedness* are "stubbornness" and "tenaciousness." Have students name common antonyms. *Possible answers: docility, flexibility*

- **reiterate:** Point out that *reiterate* means "to repeat." Ask students to explain why writers or speakers might *reiterate* specific information.

## Analyze Visuals

**Activity** Invite comments about this dramatic image; in particular, ask students what makes the bird seem both wonderful and terrible. Have them consider the three main colors (red, green, and black), as well as the foreground and background. *Possible answer: The bird is both beautiful and dramatic because of its bright red color, its curved neck, and its long beak. The background against which it is set, however, is far more somber: The bird is framed by a black, perhaps menacing, tree trunk and a blurred sea of muted green. This background is just as large as, if not larger than the foreground image.*

## DIFFERENTIATED INSTRUCTION

**FOR STRUGGLING READERS**

**Identify Key Facts** The arrival of the scarlet ibis is an important moment in this story. Help students check their comprehension of the scene by answering a set of Reporter's Questions about it.

- *Who* are the people in this scene? **Possible answer:** *the narrator, Doodle, Daddy, and Mama*

- *When* does the scene take place? **Possible answer:** *lunchtime*

- *What* unexpected event happens? **Possible answer:** *A scarlet ibis comes to their yard.*

- *Where* does the scarlet ibis land? **Possible answer:** *at the top of the bleeding tree*

- *Why* does it fall to the ground? **Possible answer:** *It is dying.*

- *How* does Doodle react to what has happened? **Possible answer:** *He wants to bury it, and Mama reluctantly agrees.*

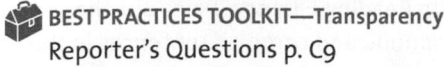 **BEST PRACTICES TOOLKIT—Transparency** Reporter's Questions p. C9

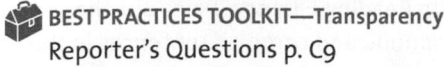

I jumped up, knocking over my chair, and had reached the door when Mama called, "Pick up the chair, sit down again, and say excuse me."

By the time I had done this, Doodle had excused himself and had slipped out into the yard. He was looking up into the bleeding tree. "It's a great big red bird!" he called. **K**

The bird croaked loudly again, and Mama and Daddy came out into the yard. We shaded our eyes with our hands against the hazy glare of the sun and peered up through the still leaves. On the topmost branch a bird the size
290 of a chicken, with scarlet feathers and long legs, was perched **precariously.** Its wings hung down loosely, and as we watched, a feather dropped away and floated slowly down through the green leaves.

"It's not even frightened of us," Mama said.

"It looks tired," Daddy added. "Or maybe sick."

Doodle's hands were clasped at his throat, and I had never seen him stand still so long. "What is it?" he asked.

Daddy shook his head. "I don't know, maybe it's—"

At that moment the bird began to flutter, but the wings were uncoordinated, and amid much flapping and a spray of flying feathers, it
300 tumbled down, bumping through the limbs of the bleeding tree and landing at our feet with a thud. Its long, graceful neck jerked twice into an S, then straightened out, and the bird was still. A white veil came over the eyes and the long white beak unhinged. Its legs were crossed and its clawlike feet were delicately curved at rest. Even death did not mar its grace, for it lay on the earth like a broken vase of red flowers, and we stood around it, awed by its **exotic** beauty. **L**

"It's dead," Mama said.

"What is it?" Doodle repeated.

"Go bring me the bird book," said Daddy.
310 I ran into the house and brought back the bird book. As we watched, Daddy thumbed through its pages. "It's a scarlet ibis," he said, pointing to a picture. "It lives in the tropics—South America to Florida. A storm must have brought it here."

> Sadly, we all looked back at the bird. A scarlet ibis! How many miles it had traveled to die like this, in *our* yard, beneath the bleeding tree.
> "Let's finish lunch," Mama said, nudging us back toward the dining room.
> "I'm not hungry," said Doodle, and he knelt down beside the ibis.
> "We've got peach cobbler for dessert," Mama tempted from the doorway.
> Doodle remained kneeling. "I'm going to bury him."

④ **Targeted Passage**

320 "Don't you dare touch him," Mama warned. "There's no telling what disease he might have had."

"All right," said Doodle. "I won't."

Daddy, Mama, and I went back to the dining-room table, but we watched Doodle through the open door. He took out a piece of string from his pocket

THE SCARLET IBIS **473**

---

**K** **SYMBOL**
What clues suggest that the appearance of the bird might be important?

**precariously**
(prĭ-kâr′ē-əs-lē) *adv.* insecurely; in a dangerous or unstable way

**exotic** (ĭg-zŏt′ĭk) *adj.* excitingly strange

**L** **SYMBOL**
What characteristics of the scarlet ibis are emphasized in lines 298–306?

---

**FOR STRUGGLING READERS**

④ **Targeted Passage** [Lines 314–319]

This passage sets up a connection between Doodle and the ibis that has just died.

- When Mama says, "Let's finish lunch," what does Doodle say and do? (line 317)

- How does Mama try to get Doodle's mind off the ibis? (line 318)

- What does Doodle announce that he is going to do? (line 319)

**FOR ENGLISH LANGUAGE LEARNERS**

**Comprehension: Transitions** Explain that some words and phrases signal time; they tell *when* or in *what order*. Have students find these and other sequence words in the selection: "at first … but then" (line 70); "as" (line 258); "by the time" (line 284); "at that moment" (line 298); "after" (line 350). Discuss how each word or phrase signals time or time order.

---

**K** *Model the Skill:* **SYMBOL**

Reread lines 279–286 and have students list the actions described there. Discuss how these actions compare with ordinary responses that they might have to seeing a bird land in a tree.

*Possible answer:* *The appearance of the bird is important because it is unexpected and startling. It causes the narrator to jump up, knock over his chair, and run for the door. Doodle, too, is amazed by the bird; he acts on his own to see it and speaks up about it, both of which are uncharacteristic of him. In addition, the story's title is "The Scarlet Ibis," so the first appearance of the title character is probably important.*

---

**L** **SYMBOL**

*Possible answer:* *The lines mention the bird's lack of coordination (line 299), its collapse to the ground (lines 299–301), the jerking of its graceful neck (line 301), the filming over of its eyes (line 302), its delicate feet (lines 303–304), and its exotic, flower-like quality (lines 304–306). Taken together, the details emphasize the bird's graceful beauty—and the fact that it has died.*

---

**OWN THE WORD**

- **precariously:** Ask students to describe situations in which a person is perched *precariously*. *Possible answers: standing or sitting on a rickety chair, wobbly ladder, or broken bench*

- **exotic:** Tell students that the connotation of *exotic* is "foreign" or from a different part of the world. Have students explain why the ibis is described as *exotic*. *Answers will vary depending on students' experiences.*

and, without touching the ibis, looped one end around its neck. Slowly, while singing softly "Shall We Gather at the River," he carried the bird around to the front yard and dug a hole in the flower garden, next to the petunia bed. Now we were watching him through the front window, but he didn't know it. His awkwardness at digging the hole with a shovel whose handle was twice as long
330  as he was made us laugh, and we covered our mouths with our hands so he wouldn't hear.

When Doodle came into the dining room, he found us seriously eating our cobbler. He was pale and lingered just inside the screen door. "Did you get the scarlet ibis buried?" asked Daddy.

Doodle didn't speak but nodded his head.

"Go wash your hands, and then you can have some peach cobbler," said Mama.

"I'm not hungry," he said.

"Dead birds is bad luck," said Aunt Nicey, poking her head from the
340  kitchen door. "Specially *red* dead birds!"

As soon as I had finished eating, Doodle and I hurried off to Horsehead Landing. Time was short, and Doodle still had a long way to go if he was going to keep up with the other boys when he started school. The sun, gilded with the yellow cast of autumn, still burned fiercely, but the dark green woods through which we passed were shady and cool. When we reached the landing, Doodle said he was too tired to swim, so we got into a skiff and floated down the creek with the tide. Far off in the marsh a rail was scolding, and over on the beach locusts were singing in the myrtle trees. Doodle did not speak and kept his head turned away, letting one hand trail limply in the water.

350  After we had drifted a long way, I put the oars in place and made Doodle row back against the tide. Black clouds began to gather in the southwest, and he kept watching them, trying to pull the oars a little faster. When we reached Horsehead Landing, lightning was playing across half the sky and thunder roared out, hiding even the sound of the sea. The sun disappeared and darkness descended, almost like night. Flocks of marsh crows flew by, heading inland to their roosting trees; and two egrets, squawking, arose from the oyster-rock shallows and careened away.

Doodle was both tired and frightened, and when he stepped from the skiff he collapsed onto the mud, sending an armada of fiddler crabs rustling off into
360  the marsh grass. I helped him up, and as he wiped the mud off his trousers, he smiled at me ashamedly. He had failed and we both knew it, so we started back home, racing the storm. We never spoke (What are the words that can solder[12] cracked pride?), but I knew he was watching me, watching for a sign of mercy. The lightning was near now, and from fear he walked so close behind me he kept stepping on my heels. The faster I walked, the faster he walked, so

---

12. **solder** (sŏd′ər): to join or bond together.

---

---

*Possible answer:* Both are exotic creatures that have landed in a time or place that is not entirely hospitable to them. Both are delicate, frail, unusual beauties with short lives and tragic deaths.

## TIERED DISCUSSION PROMPTS

Use these prompts to help students understand details in lines 358–370 that will lead to the climax and resolution of the story:

**Connect** Think about a time when you let someone down. How does that experience help you understand what Doodle feels at this moment? *Answers may address emotions such as guilt, dependence, and despair.*

**Analyze** What makes this scene so challenging for Doodle? *Possible answer: The thunder and lightning would frighten anyone near or in water. Doodle is also extremely exhausted; feels shame at having let his brother down; and still has a terrible need for his brother, as evidenced by his cries of "Don't leave me!" (line 370)*

**Evaluate** Why is Hurst's reference to a "sign of mercy" (lines 363–364) effective? *Possible answer: It reminds readers how cruel the narrator has been—pushing Doodle mercilessly for weeks and now working him into such a state of exhaustion that he has collapsed onto the mud.*

---

## DIFFERENTIATED INSTRUCTION

### FOR ENGLISH LANGUAGE LEARNERS

**Comprehension: Prepositions** Explain that some prepositions signal place. Invite students to use simple drawings to explain the concepts of place signaled by "across the burning cotton field" (line 84); "down into the green dimness where the palmetto fronds whispered by the stream" (lines 86–87); "far off . . . and over on the beach" (lines 347–348); "was playing across half the sky" (line 353).

### FOR ADVANCED LEARNERS/PRE–AP

**Make Judgments** It is unlikely that a storm could have brought a scarlet ibis to North Carolina. In fact, the comment that the bird ranges as far north as Florida (line 312) is inaccurate. Does this create a serious flaw in this story? To make their judgments, students should build a case for what the story might have lost or gained had there been no scarlet ibis or had it been replaced by some other creature.

I began to run. The rain was coming, roaring through the pines, and then, like a bursting Roman candle, a gum tree ahead of us was shattered by a bolt of lightning. When the deafening peal of thunder had died, and in the moment before the rain arrived, I heard Doodle, who had fallen behind, cry out,

370 "Brother, Brother, don't leave me! Don't leave me!"

The knowledge that Doodle's and my plans had come to naught[13] was bitter, and that streak of cruelty within me awakened. I ran as fast as I could, leaving him far behind with a wall of rain dividing us. The drops stung my face like nettles, and the wind flared the wet glistening leaves of the bordering trees. Soon I could hear his voice no more. **N**

I hadn't run too far before I became tired, and the flood of childish spite **evanesced** as well. I stopped and waited for Doodle. The sound of rain was everywhere, but the wind had died and it fell straight down in parallel paths like ropes hanging from the sky. As I waited, I peered through the downpour, but no

380 one came. Finally I went back and found him huddled beneath a red nightshade bush beside the road. He was sitting on the ground, his face buried in his arms, which were resting on his drawn-up knees. "Let's go, Doodle," I said.

He didn't answer, so I placed my hand on his forehead and lifted his head. Limply, he fell backward onto the earth. He had been bleeding from the mouth, and his neck and the front of his shirt were stained a brilliant red.

"Doodle! Doodle!" I cried, shaking him, but there was no answer but the ropy rain. He lay very awkwardly, with his head thrown far back, making his vermilion[14] neck appear unusually long and slim. His little legs, bent sharply at the knees, had never before seemed so fragile, so thin.

390 I began to weep, and the tear-blurred vision in red before me looked very familiar. "Doodle!" I screamed above the pounding storm and threw my body to the earth above his. For a long long time, it seemed forever, I lay there crying, sheltering my fallen scarlet ibis from the **heresy** of rain. ◡

**N** MAKE INFERENCES
Why does the narrator continue to run when he knows Doodle has fallen behind him?

**evanesce** (ĕv′ə-nĕs′) v. to disappear; vanish

⑤ **Targeted Passage**

**heresy** (hĕr′ĭ-sē) n. an action or opinion contrary to what is generally thought of as right

---

13. **had come to naught:** had resulted in nothing.
14. **vermilion** (vər-mĭl′yən): bright red to reddish orange.

THE SCARLET IBIS  **475**

THE SCARLET IBIS  **475**

---

**FOR STRUGGLING READERS**

⑤ **Targeted Passage** [Lines 380–393]

This passage presents the story's resolution and clarifies its title.

- Where does the narrator find Doodle? (lines 380–381)

- What happens when he tries to get Doodle up? Why does Doodle not respond? (lines 384–385)

- How are Doodle's neck and legs described? Why is the description familiar? (lines 388–389)

**FOR RELUCTANT READERS**

**Connect to the Text** Ask students to connect to the narrator's experience: Have they ever had to take care of a younger (or perhaps an elderly) relative or family friend? What sacrifices did they have to make, if any? Did they learn anything from the experience, either about themselves or the other person? Have students discuss their experiences in small groups.

---

**READING SKILL**  COMMON CORE  RL 1, RL 3

**N** **MAKE INFERENCES**

**Possible answer:** *The narrator is frustrated or irritated with Doodle, and running away seems to be his way of punishing him. Also, the reference to "cracked pride" (line 363) suggests that the narrator has given up on helping Doodle out of a sense of pride.*

**VOCABULARY**  COMMON CORE  L 4

**OWN THE WORD**

- **evanesce:** Read the definition of *evanesce* aloud to students: "to disappear, vanish." Then, tell students that antonyms include *appear, materialize, emerge, become visible, arise.*

- **heresy:** Tell students that the connotation of *heresy* often includes an opinion that is at variance with religious doctrine. Explain that a *heretic* is a person who holds unorthodox opinions.

**SELECTION WRAP-UP**

**READ WITH A PURPOSE** Now that students have read the story, ask them what they think the scarlet ibis represented to each of the boys, and whether the two boys had different perspectives. **Possible answer:** *Both boys recognized the ibis as representing Doodle's death, but Doodle seemed to see the connection before his brother did.*

★ **CRITIQUE** "The Scarlet Ibis" is stuffed with symbols and loaded with imagery. Ask students whether they find the dense details and multiple symbols effective and interesting or over the top. Encourage them to cite details that support their answers.

**INDEPENDENT READING**

Students who enjoy reading short stories will find other selections of interest in the anthology *Great American Stories* by C. G. Draper.

THE SCARLET IBIS  **475**

## Analyze Visuals

**Activity** Ask students how well this image matches the instructions for plant care given in the poem. *Possible answer: The flower does seem to have been left alone or even abandoned, for it sits by an icy window in relative darkness. Still, the bloom is not seeking "the sunlight for itself"; instead, it has been turned to face the viewer.*

## TIERED DISCUSSION PROMPTS

Use these prompts to help students make thematic and symbolic connections between "The Scarlet Ibis" and "Woman with Flower":

**Connect** How do you react to the concluding statement, "The things we love we have to learn to leave alone"? *Students may discuss the virtues of, or problems with, noninterference. They may argue that people are not plants.*

**Apply** Do the terms "careful prodding" (line 7) and "eager tenderness" (line 8) apply to events and characters in "The Scarlet Ibis"? Explain. *Possible answers: Yes, there was careful prodding as the narrator helped Doodle walk and then eagerly goaded him on to the possibility of greater accomplishments; No, the prodding was not careful or tender but arose from the narrator's pride and self-interest and was often cruel.*

**Synthesize** How do you think Doodle, the narrator, and their parents would react to the idea that the "leaf's inclined to find its own direction; / Give it a chance to seek the sunlight for itself"? Why? *Possible answer: All but the narrator might have agreed with this statement. They were content to let Doodle be who and what he would be; they did not have ambitions for him. Only the narrator saw things differently.*

# WOMAN
## *with* Flower

Naomi Long Madgett

I wouldn't coax the plant if I were you.
Such watchful nurturing may do it harm.
Let the soil rest from so much digging
And wait until it's dry before you water it.
5 The leaf's inclined to find its own direction;
Give it a chance to seek the sunlight for itself.

Much growth is stunted by too careful prodding,
Too eager tenderness.
The things we love we have to learn to leave alone.

**476** UNIT 4: THEME AND SYMBOL

## Comprehension

1. **Clarify** How is Doodle different from other children?

2. **Recall** What are the narrator's motives for teaching Doodle?

3. **Summarize** What happens to Doodle, and why?

## Text Analysis

● 4. **Make Inferences** Look back at the chart you made as you read. Review the inferences you made about the relationship between Doodle and the narrator. How would you describe their relationship over the course of the story?

5. **Analyze Character** The narrator has mixed emotions about Doodle. How might he answer the big question on page 460?

● 6. **Interpret Symbol** The narrator sees Doodle as the scarlet ibis at the end, but Doodle identifies with the exotic bird immediately. To explore this symbolic connection, identify as many similarities between the ibis and Doodle as you can. Record your comparison in a chart like the one shown.

> Scarlet Ibis and Doodle
>
> Both are unusual and don't fit in their surroundings.

● 7. **Analyze Theme and Symbol** Which of the following themes does the **symbolism** of the ibis support? Find details to support your answer.

   a. Selfish pride generally causes more harm than good.

   b. Delicate creatures need to be protected and cared for.

   c. Spiteful cruelty toward a loved one often stems from wounded pride.

8. **Examine Foreshadowing and Mood** Reread lines 298–306. The dramatic death of the ibis foreshadows Doodle's death. Find at least three other examples of such foreshadowing. What mood do they create?

9. **Compare Literary Works** What advice does the speaker in "Woman with Flower" seem to offer the narrator of "The Scarlet Ibis"? In what ways are the themes of these works similar? In what ways are they different?

## Text Criticism

10. **Author's Style** "The Scarlet Ibis" is an example of Southern literature, which is characterized in part by its emphasis on details of time and place, the importance of family and community, an exploration of the past, and a sense of moral dilemma. How are these characteristics evident in this story?

> ### Why do we HURT the ones we LOVE?
>
> What consequences can arise from being cruel to loved ones?

**COMMON CORE**

RL 1 Cite textual evidence to support inferences drawn from a text. RL 2 Determine a theme of a text and analyze its development over the course of the text. RL 3 Analyze how complex characters interact with other characters and develop the theme.

## Practice and Apply

For preliminary support of post-reading questions, use these copy masters:

**R RESOURCE MANAGER**—Copy Masters
Reading Check p. 66
Symbol p. 59
Question Support p. 67

Additional selection questions are provided for teachers on page 53.

### ANSWERS

## Comprehension

1. *He is physically weaker than other children.*

2. *The narrator is motivated by embarrassment about his brother and by pride and self-interest.*

3. *Doodle dies in a storm. He tried to keep up with his brother, who ran from him, but the effort was too much for his frail body.*

## Text Analysis

COMMON CORE RL 1, RL 2, RL 3

*Possible answers:*

4. ● **COMMON CORE FOCUS** *Make Inferences They love each other, but Doodle is more innocent and needy, while the narrator is full of pride and self-interest. In many ways, their relationship is somewhat normal for children.*

5. *The narrator might say that we hurt the ones we love because we have the power to do so or because we may not be thinking about anyone but ourselves.*

6. ● **COMMON CORE FOCUS** *Interpret Symbol Both are exotic. Both are out of place. Both are victims of storms; both die. Both are associated with red (Doodle is red with blood when he dies).*

7. ● **COMMON CORE FOCUS** *Analyze Theme and Symbol All three fit the story, but the symbolism of the ibis specifically supports theme b because both the ibis and Doodle are delicate creatures. For evidence, see lines 45–53, 250–253, and 287–306.*

8. *Doodle's touching the coffin and his cry of "Don't leave me" immediately afterward are foreshadowing, as is the narrator's early comment that Doodle's real name, William Armstrong, "sounds good only on a tombstone." These details, all related to death and loss, create a mood of impending tragedy.*

9. *The speaker's advice is not to coax but to "learn to leave alone" the things we love. The narrator coaxed too eagerly, which, given the outcome of the story, suggests that too much interference is a bad thing. Nevertheless, the story presents mixed results of noninterference, whereas the poem suggests only its virtues.*

## Text Criticism

*Possible answer:*

10. *Time and place: lines 1–3, 85–99; family and community: lines 16–22, 169–180; the past: lines 5–15; moral dilemma: lines 74–85, 100–118*

> ### Why do we HURT the ones we LOVE? *Possible response:* The loved one can end up feeling far more hurt than we intended, due to the fact that they care so much about what we think.

## ANSWERS

## Vocabulary in Context

▲ VOCABULARY PRACTICE

1. *b*          5. *b*
2. *d*          6. *b*
3. *b*          7. *b*
4. *c*          8. *d*

 **RESOURCE MANAGER—Copy Master**
Vocabulary Practice p. 64

### ACADEMIC VOCABULARY IN WRITING

*Possible answer: I decided to **reveal** my secret place to him, the most beautiful place in the city. I dragged him and his wagon down the elevator of our building and across ten blocks of heavy traffic. Finally, we made it to the park. The green canopy parted and I pulled the wagon to a grassy bank along a small pond.*

### VOCABULARY STRATEGY: DENOTATION AND CONNOTATION

⟨ **COMMON CORE L 5b** ⟩

Students may have an easier time placing the words if they first associate each word with a tone of voice, facial expression, or other indicator of attitude. For example, for the first item, they might think about the tone of voice and volume that might be used to talk, vent, or articulate and relate that to positive or negative feelings.

**Possible answers:**
1. *highly negative: vent; neutral: talk, articulate*
2. *neutral: new; positive: fresh, original*
3. *negative: finicky; negative to neutral: choosy; positive: particular*
4. *negative: smirk; positive: grin, smile*
5. *neutral: responsibility, obligation; neutral to positive: duty*

 **RESOURCE MANAGER—Copy Master**
Vocabulary Strategy p. 65

---

**Interactive Vocabulary**    **THINK** central

Keywords direct students to a **WordSharp** tutorial on **thinkcentral.com** or to other types of vocabulary practice and review.

---

## Vocabulary in Context

▲ **VOCABULARY PRACTICE**

Identify the word that is not related in meaning to the other words in the set.

1. (a) exotic, (b) ordinary, (c) unusual, (d) foreign
2. (a) impending, (b) imminent, (c) approaching, (d) remote
3. (a) fidelity, (b) heresy, (c) conformity, (d) compliance
4. (a) echo, (b) repeat, (c) originate, (d) reiterate
5. (a) errancy, (b) infallibility, (c) inaccuracy, (d) imperfection
6. (a) insecurely, (b) cleverly, (c) precariously, (d) dangerously
7. (a) disappear, (b) float, (c) vanish, (d) evanesce
8. (a) doggedness, (b) perseverance, (c) tenacity, (d) casualness

**WORD LIST**
doggedness
evanesce
exotic
heresy
imminent
infallibility
precariously
reiterate

### ACADEMIC VOCABULARY IN WRITING

• context  • interpret  • reveal  • significant  • tradition

This story takes place in the **context** of the rural South in the early 1900s. What would have been different if the context were of a city in 2010? Take one incident from the story and rewrite it, making the changes that would be necessary. Use at least one Academic Vocabulary word in your response.

### VOCABULARY STRATEGY: DENOTATION AND CONNOTATION

While a word's **denotation** refers to a word's definition, a word's **connotation** refers to the attitudes or feelings associated with a word. For example, *doggedness* and *stubbornness* could both be defined as "the quality of not giving in readily," but, in the context of the story, the use of the word *doggedness* to describe Doodle's efforts conveys positive connotations not associated with *stubbornness*. Writers use connotation to communicate certain feelings and to evoke a mood. Being aware of these connotations can enrich your understanding of what you read.

**· · · COMMON CORE**
**L 5b** Analyze nuances in the meaning of words with similar denotations.

**PRACTICE** Place the words in each group on a continuum like the one shown to show the positive or negative associations each word connotes. Then compare your answers with those of a classmate.

*highly negative* ⟵⟶ *highly positive*

1. talk, vent, articulate
2. new, fresh, original
3. choosy, finicky, particular
4. smile, smirk, grin
5. responsibility, obligation, duty

**Interactive Vocabulary**    **THINK** central
Go to **thinkcentral.com**.
KEYWORD: HML9-478

---

## DIFFERENTIATED INSTRUCTION

### FOR ENGLISH LANGUAGE LEARNERS

**Vocabulary: Modifiers** To review words that describe verbs, ask students to identify which words in the Vocabulary Practice describe verbs. **Possible answer:** *all the words in item 6* Ask students how they know this; if needed, review *-ly* endings for many words that describe verbs.

### FOR ADVANCED LEARNERS/PRE–AP

**Vocabulary in Writing** Have students use some or most of the vocabulary words in two ways: one in a sentence that James Hurst might have written and the other in a sentence that another writer whose work they have read (such as Ray Bradbury in "A Sound of Thunder" [Unit 1]) might have written.

# Language

◆ **GRAMMAR AND STYLE:** Vary Sentence Structure

Review the **Grammar and Style** note on page 468. Hurst uses a variety of sentence structures in his writing. Using only one type of sentence can make your writing sound dull.

All complete sentences contain at least one **independent clause,** which can stand on its own. (*Doodle went to sleep.*) Some combine the independent clause or clauses with one or more **subordinate clauses,** which cannot stand alone. (*Doodle went to sleep while the family ate dinner.*) This kind of variety, as found in this passage from Hurst's story, makes for better-sounding prose:

> *I lifted him out and set him down in the soft rubber grass beside a tall pine. His eyes were round with wonder as he gazed about him, and his little hands began to stroke the rubber grass.* (lines 87–89)

Below, notice how the revisions in blue improve the rhythm of this first draft. Revise your response to the prompt below by incorporating a variety of sentence structures.

**STUDENT MODEL**

The narrator sometimes shows he cares for Doodle. ^but He also seems to enjoy making his brother feel trapped and alone. ^as if He treats Doodle ^were like an animal. In reality, Doodle is just a child. ^who He does his best to overcome a serious illness.

## READING-WRITING CONNECTION

Add to your understanding of "The Scarlet Ibis" by responding to this prompt. Then use the **revising tip** to improve your writing.

| **WRITING PROMPT** | **REVISING TIP** |
|---|---|
| **Extended Constructed Response: Character Analysis** Do you blame the narrator for what happens to Doodle? Consider his age, his mixed emotions, and what he says about himself. Write a **three- to five-paragraph response** analyzing his role in Doodle's death. | ▶ Review your response. How have you used independent and subordinate clauses to make your prose sound better? |

**Interactive Revision**

Go to **thinkcentral.com.**
KEYWORD: HML9-479

---

**FOR STRUGGLING WRITERS**

1. Have pairs discuss the issue and take notes.

2. Ask them to list quotations from the text that support their discussion points.

3. Have them refer to their notes as they write.

---

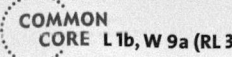 **COMMON CORE**

**L 1b** Use various types of clauses to add variety and interest to writing. **W 9a (RL 3)** Draw evidence from literary texts; analyze how complex characters interact with other characters.

# Language

 **COMMON CORE** L 1b, W 9a (RL 3)

◆ **GRAMMAR AND STYLE**

1. Point out that the first sentence in the sample passage is a simple sentence, even though it has a compound predicate. The second sentence is compound-complex because it contains two independent clauses and a subordinate clause. (To learn more about clauses, see **Grammar Handbook,** page R62.)

2. Discuss how dull the student model is as a series of short sentences. Note that the first new sentence is compound-complex and that the second is complex.

3. Invite students to suggest other ways of revising the student model.

**R** RESOURCE MANAGER—Copy Master
Vary Sentence Structure p. 68

**READING-WRITING CONNECTION**

Urge students to state their opinions and give three reasons for their opinions before they begin to write out their response.

**Writing Online** THINK central

The following tools are available online at **thinkcentral.com** and on **Write*Smart* CD-ROM:**
- **Interactive Graphic Organizers**
- **Interactive Student Models**
- **Interactive Revision Lessons**

For additional grammar instruction, see **GrammarNotes** on **thinkcentral.com.**

## Assess and Reteach

*Assess*

**DIAGNOSTIC AND SELECTION TESTS**
Selection Test A pp. 123–124
Selection Test B/C pp. 125–126

**Interactive Selection Test** on **thinkcentral.com**

*Reteach*

**Level Up Online Tutorials** on **thinkcentral.com**

## Math and After Math

Essay by Lensey Namioka

### COMMON CORE FOCUS

**RI 1** Cite textual evidence to support analysis of what the text says explicitly as well as inferences drawn from the text. **RI 2** Determine a central idea of a text and analyze how it emerges and is shaped and refined by specific details. **RI 3** Analyze how the author unfolds a series of ideas or events. **RI 4** Determine the meaning of words as they are used in a text. **L 4a** Use context as a clue to the meaning of a word or phrase. **L 5** Demonstrate understanding of word relationships.

### SUMMARY

In "Math and After Math," Lensey Namioka describes how she finally discovered her true talent. After a shaky start learning the abacus in China, Namioka immigrated to the United States and excelled in math, despite American gender prejudices. Over time, however, she came to realize that writing, rather than math, inspired her.

### What are you really **GOOD** at?

To lead into the Big Question, ask students why they enjoy certain activities more than others. Have students link their enjoyment or success to a talent. Continue the dialogue by having partners complete the *DISCUSS* activity.

# What are you really **GOOD** at?

**COMMON CORE**

**RI 1** Cite textual evidence to support analysis of what the text says explicitly as well as inferences drawn from the text. **RI 2** Determine a central idea of a text and analyze how it emerges and is shaped and refined by specific details. **RI 3** Analyze how the author unfolds a series of ideas or events. **RI 4** Determine the meaning of words as they are used in a text. **L 5** Demonstrate understanding of word relationships.

Knowing what you're good at can take you a long way toward finding work and activities that you enjoy. In "Math and After Math," Lensey Namioka describes how she first embarked on one career path and then later discovered her true talent.

*DISCUSS* Make a list of activities you particularly enjoy. For each one, list the skills that help you succeed at the activity. With a partner, brainstorm career possibilities that could make use of those skills.

Cooking
• ability to follow recipes
• knack for combining ingredients

480

*See resources on the* **Teacher One Stop DVD-ROM** *and on* **thinkcentral.com**.

**R** **RESOURCE MANAGER UNIT 4**
Plan and Teach, pp. 71–78
Summary, pp. 79–80 † ‡*
Text Analysis and Reading
Skill, pp. 81–82, 83–84† *
Vocabulary, pp. 85–87*

**DIAGNOSTIC AND SELECTION TESTS**
Selection Tests, pp. 127–130

**BEST PRACTICES TOOLKIT**
Jigsaw Reading, p. A1
New Word Analysis, p. E8

**TECHNOLOGY**
⊘ **Teacher One Stop DVD-ROM**
⊘ **Student One Stop DVD-ROM**
⊘ **Audio Anthology CD**
⊘ **ExamView Test Generator**
on the **Teacher One Stop**

---

\* Resources for Differentiation     † In Spanish     ‡ In Haitian Creole and Vietnamese

## ● TEXT ANALYSIS: IMPLIED MAIN IDEA

In nonfiction, the writer's **central idea,** or overall message, is often referred to as the main idea. This **main idea** may be stated directly, or it may be implied by the factual details and personal examples and ideas that the writer chooses to include.

In "Math and After Math," Lensey Namioka shares a series of anecdotes—episodes from her life through which she develops a main idea. To identify the implied main idea as you read, ask yourself, What important idea is conveyed by the anecdotes? How does this idea relate to the author's conclusion?

## ■ READING SKILL: ANALYZE SEQUENCE OF EVENTS

The events in a memoir are not always described in the same sequence in which they occurred. When describing or explaining events, a writer may move back and forth in time to make a point. This skipping around in time can be confusing, however, so it's important for the reader to keep track of how the **sequence of events** actually unfolded. Signal words, such as *when, by the time,* or *for years,* help to clarify this sequence.

As you read "Math and After Math," use a chart to jot down the important events in each stage of Namioka's life. Then number them in the order they occurred in time.

| Stage in Life | Order | Event |
|---|---|---|
| Second grade | | Namioka suffers "abacus anxiety." |
| Years later | | Family emigrates to America. Math is best subject. |

## ▲ VOCABULARY IN CONTEXT

Lensey Namioka uses the following boldfaced words to tell her tale of personal discovery. Use context clues to determine the meaning of each one.

1. The speaker's **dialect** revealed that he was not a native of the area.
2. The movie's **scenario** included no plot twists or surprises.
3. Her ability to act is **intuitive;** she has never had a lesson.
4. The detective's **analytic** approach to solving problems led him to the killer.
5. Your **hypothesis** will not stand up to further testing.

Complete the activities in your **Reader/Writer Notebook.**

## Meet the Author

# Lensey Namioka
### born 1929

**Always an Outsider**
Lensey Namioka was born in China and moved to the United States when she was nine years old. She has lived in many places and, consequently, has felt herself to be something of an outsider wherever she has lived. It's not surprising, then, that the protagonists in her stories for young adults are usually outsiders too.

**Multicultural Author**
Namioka's writing draws on both her Chinese heritage and her husband's Japanese heritage. She has written humorous novels about young Chinese immigrants in America, as well as a series of adventure-mystery books about two 16th-century Japanese samurai.

**BACKGROUND TO THE ESSAY**
**Girls and Math**
In "Math and After Math," Namioka describes how she stood out in her American classrooms as a girl who was good at math. Researchers have long sought to determine whether the differences in math performance between girls and boys stem from biology or culture. In elementary school, girls tend to outperform boys in many subjects, including math. In high school, however, the situation changes. Statistics show that, as a group, boys score slightly higher than girls on math aptitude tests. Also, boys tend to choose math-related college majors and careers more often than girls do, although this is changing. Researchers continue to debate various hypotheses that explain these gender differences.

**Author Online**
**THINK** central
Go to **thinkcentral.com.**
KEYWORD: HML9-481

**481**

TEXT ANALYSIS — COMMON CORE — RI 1, RI 2

## ● *Model the Skill:* IMPLIED MAIN IDEA

To support instruction, read aloud this anecdote, and ask what it implies about the character's musical interest and talent:

> Every afternoon, Dave listened to the jazz station on the radio. After he got a keyboard for his birthday, he spent every free minute learning his favorite pieces. Soon he was jamming with a band.

Point out that Dave's involvement in music increases and his interest remains high. This implies that Dave's interest and talent in jazz are serious and may lead to continued involvement.

**GUIDED PRACTICE** Ask what the *Background* implies about the current status of the biology–culture debate.

READING SKILL — COMMON CORE — RI 3

## ■ *Model the Skill:* ANALYZE SEQUENCE OF EVENTS

Model appropriate statements using the time signal phrases *the other day, last week,* and *a long time ago.*

**GUIDED PRACTICE** Ask students what each of these terms might signal: *now, a few years ago, on a recent outing.*

**R RESOURCE MANAGER—Copy Master**
Analyze Sequence of Events p. 103

---

VOCABULARY SKILL — COMMON CORE — L 4

## ▲ VOCABULARY IN CONTEXT

**DIAGNOSE WORD KNOWLEDGE** Have all students complete Vocabulary in Context. Check their words and phrases against the following:

**analytic** (ăn′ə-lĭt′ĭk) *adj.* using logical reasoning or analysis
**dialect** (dī′ə-lĕkt′) *n.* a variety of a standard language unique to a certain region or social group

**hypothesis** (hī-pŏth′ĭ-sĭs) *n.* an assumption made in order to test its possible consequences
**intuitive** (ĭn-tōō′ĭ-tĭv) *adj.* based on what seems to be true without conscious reasoning; instinctive
**scenario** (sĭ-nâr′ē-ō′) *n.* a description of a possible course of action or events

**PRETEACH VOCABULARY** Help students explore meaning, using a word map, for each boldfaced word in the copy master.

**R RESOURCE MANAGER—Copy Master**
Vocabulary Study p. 85

1. Read the phrases with boldfaced vocabulary words.
2. Help students fill out a word map for *hypothesis.*
3. Have them create word maps for the other vocabulary words.

*Have students set a purpose for reading. Ask them to read to discover what the author means by the phrase "after math."*

**REVISIT THE BIG QUESTION**

## What are you really **GOOD** at?

**Discuss** How might the circumstances Namioka describes in lines 6–11 affect her mathematical talent? *Possible answer: Moving to a strange part of the country under traumatic circumstances, as well as trying to adjust to an unfamiliar dialect, have created "abacus anxiety," a kind of nervous reaction that undercuts her ability to perform well in class.*

---

**VOCABULARY**

COMMON CORE L 4

### OWN THE WORD

**dialect:** Tell students that the connotation of *dialect* is a regional variation of the language. Have them identify *dialects* of English that they are familiar with. *Possible answer: Australians and British people have different dialects; there are some regional dialects in the United States.*

---

# Math *and* After Math

## LENSEY NAMIOKA

"Seven!" shouted the teacher.

Or did he shout "Four"?

I shrank down in my seat. Math class was an absolute nightmare. The teacher scared me so much that my hands got sweaty, and my fingers slipped on the abacus[1] beads.

I was in the second grade when I discovered that I suffered from abacus anxiety. The trouble was that I was going to a school where the teacher spoke a different **dialect**. I grew up with Mandarin, the dialect spoken by the majority of the Chinese. When the eastern part of China was occupied by the Japanese,
10 our family moved inland, to a region where I could barely understand the local dialect.

Writing was pretty much the same in any dialect, so in language and history classes I didn't have trouble with what was on the blackboard. My problems started in the math class, where we had to learn the abacus. Before the days of the calculator, the abacus was the main tool for adding and multiplying. It still is, in many parts of China (as well as in countries like Japan and Russia).

The abacus teacher would shout out the numbers he wanted us to add or multiply. My ears didn't always understand what he said, so *seven*, for instance, sounded a lot like *four*.

---

1. **abacus** (ăb'ə-kəs): a manual computing device consisting of rods hung within a frame and strung with movable counters.

**Analyze Visuals ▶**

What elements of the photograph reflect the writer's attitude toward math?

**① Targeted Passage**

**dialect** (dī'ə-lĕkt') *n.*
a variety of a standard language unique to a certain region or social group

---

## DIFFERENTIATED INSTRUCTION

**FOR ENGLISH LANGUAGE LEARNERS**

**Options for Reading** Have students use a Jigsaw Reading strategy to read sections of the essay and then come together to share what they have learned.

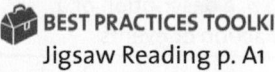 **BEST PRACTICES TOOLKIT**
Jigsaw Reading p. A1

**FOR STRUGGLING READERS**

In combination with the *Audio Anthology CD*, use one or more Targeted Passages (pp. 482, 485, 488, 489) to ensure that students focus on key events, concepts, and skills. Targeted Passages are also good for English learners.

**① Targeted Passage [Lines 1–7]**

This passage establishes the topic of Namioka's essay—the causes of girls' success or failure in math.

## BACKGROUND

**The Abacus** This calculating device may have originated in ancient Babylon more than 2,000 years ago. Originally it was probably a board or slab with sand spread on top for tracing letters. The abacus developed into a board marked with lines and equipped with counters. The positions of the counters indicated numerical values, such as ones, tens, and hundreds. Today, the counters of an abacus are usually strung on wires. Experts possess the skill to compete on the abacus with modern mechanical calculators.

## Analyze Visuals

*Possible answer:* *The girl in the photograph is poised to complete the problem on the black-board, but her fingers have yet to write the answer. Perhaps, like the writer, she is stalled by anxiety. An abacus, like the one the writer describes in line 5, is in the upper right corner.*

- Where does the opening anecdote take place? (line 3)
- What grade was Namioka in at the time? (line 6)
- Why did she suffer from anxiety in math class? (lines 6–9)

**FOR ADVANCED LEARNERS/PRE-AP**

**Gain Expertise** Have students work individually or in pairs to research and then choose a way to share information about one of these topics:

- the Japanese occupation of China
- U.S. immigration patterns since World War II
- the Cultural Revolution

20    Until that class, math was one of my better subjects, especially when it came to multiplication. Years later, when we emigrated to America, I was astounded to hear one of my American friends recite the multiplication table:

"Two times one is two. Two times two is four. Two times three is six . . ." It seemed to take forever.

The multiplication table is much shorter in Chinese. One reason is that the Chinese names for numbers are all one-syllable. We don't have numbers like *seven*.

Also, we omit words like *times* and *equals* while reciting. Instead of "Seven times two equals fourteen," we say, *Er qi shi si,* or literally, *two seven fourteen.* So we do it in four syllables instead of eight.

30    The best trick is that we memorize only half as many entries, because we know that seven times two is the same as two times seven. (I learned later this was called the Commutative Law.)

This meant I could rattle off the multiplication table about three times faster than my American classmates. But I learned the table even faster than my *Chinese* classmates. The reason was that I sang it.

"You can remember a tune better than a string of numbers," my father told me. "So I want you to sing the multiplication table."

The standard way to teach musical notation in Chinese schools was to give numbers to the diatonic scale:[2] *do* was one (not a female deer), *re* was two (not 40 a ray of sunshine), *mi* was three, and so on. When I had to remember that two times seven was fourteen, my father told me to hum the little tune *re ti do fa.* This was not a pretty tune, but it certainly stuck in my mind.

---

2. **diatonic** (dī′ə-tŏn′ĭk) **scale:** the standard musical scale of seven tones, often referred to as *do, re, mi, fa, sol, la,* and *ti.*

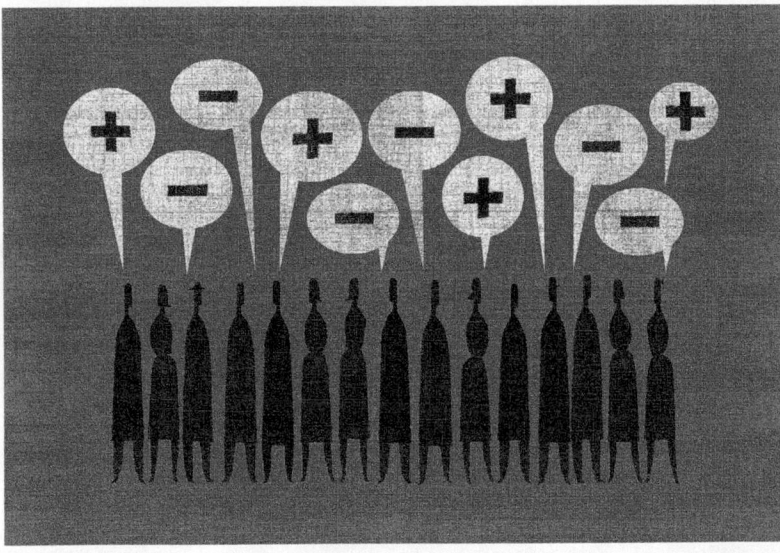

© Images.com/Corbis

**A SEQUENCE OF EVENTS**

*Possible answer:* "Until," "Years later," "when," "forever"

**Extend the Discussion** Have students put the information revealed in lines 20–24 into their Reading Skill charts. Then ask them which of these time words does not actually describe the sequence of events in the story. *(forever)*

**A SEQUENCE OF EVENTS**
Reread lines 20–24. Which words indicate the passage of time?

---

## DIFFERENTIATED INSTRUCTION

### FOR ENGLISH LANGUAGE LEARNERS

**Multiple-Meaning Words** Explain that *string* (line 36) refers here to a "series" or "sequence." As a noun, *string* can also mean "a thin piece of twisted fiber." Have mixed-language-ability Jigsaw Reading groups investigate these other multiple-meaning words and report their findings: "top" (line 72), "slip" (line 100), "addressed" (line 104), "argument" (line 108), "manage" (line 133), "crept" (line 136), and "squeeze" (line 202).

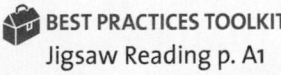 **BEST PRACTICES TOOLKIT**
Jigsaw Reading p. A1

### FOR STRUGGLING READERS

**Develop Reading Fluency** Use the conversation between the narrator's mother and the realtor to demonstrate the difference in tone used by the two speakers. Help students identify the words that tell how each speaker feels. (**realtor:** *rushed, frantic;* **mother:** *turned him down, stubborn*) Remind students that how we feel is shown in how we speak. Read lines 78–82 aloud to demonstrate this. Then ask volunteers to give their own readings of the conversation.

Following Father's suggestion, I learned the multiplication table very quickly, and even now I still hum. The other day, when I was in the store buying candy bars, I noticed another customer staring at me. I was trying to figure out if my fistful of change was enough for four candy bars, and I must have been humming as I multiplied.

When I entered American schools, my best subject was math. I didn't need to know much English to manage the Arabic numbers,[3] and my Chinese
50 school had been a year ahead of American schools in math (because of shorter multiplication tables, maybe). **B**

After a while I realized that my classmates found me weird. During our early years in America, my family lived in towns where there weren't too many Asians, and I looked different from everybody else in class. It turned out that my weirdness wasn't just because I looked different, or because I hummed funny tunes.

"How come you're so good at math?" asked one of my classmates.

"Why shouldn't I be?" I asked.

"You're a girl!"

60 In America, apparently, it was unusual for a girl to be good at math. It was different in China, where women were good at figures. They regularly kept the household accounts and managed the family budget.

A few years ago, I saw a movie about Chinese-Americans called *Dim Sum*.[4] A Chinese man who ran a restaurant in Chinatown brought his receipts to a woman friend, who figured out his accounts for him.

My American friends found the situation strange. "It's not unusual at all," I told them. "In my family, for instance, my mother made the major financial decisions."

In fact, my mother made a financial killing when we were living in Berkeley,
70 California. A neighbor took her to a land auction. A piece of land near our house was offered for sale, and Mother thought it would be fun to bid on it. Someone was bound to top her bid, she thought.

She was stunned when nobody else made a bid, and Mother found herself the owner of a large plot of land.

As she and her friend prepared to leave the auction room, a man rushed up to them. He was a realtor who had planned to bid for the land, but had arrived at the auction too late.

"I'll give you whatever you paid, plus something extra!" he told Mother.

"No, thank you," said Mother. "I'm quite happy with the purchase."
80 The realtor raised his offer, but Mother still turned him down. He became frantic. "Look, I'll go as high as two thousand dollars above your bid!"

This just made Mother more stubborn. "No, I want to keep the land."

The realtor obtained our address and phone number, and immediately called our house.

---

3. **Arabic numbers:** the numerical symbols 1, 2, 3, 4, 5, 6, 7, 8, 9, and 0.

4. ***Dim Sum:*** the movie title refers to a Chinese cuisine in which small portions of a variety of foods, including an assortment of dumplings, are served.

---

**B IMPLIED MAIN IDEA**
Consider Namioka's childhood success with math. What is she implying about Chinese math education?

**2 Targeted Passage**

---

COMMON CORE RI 4
**Language Coach**
**Word Definitions** You often have to read several definitions in a dictionary to find one that fits. Reread line 69. Which definition fits the use of *killing* in this line? (1) the act of one who kills, (2) a sudden gain, (3) very funny

---

TEXT ANALYSIS — COMMON CORE RI 1, RI 2

**B** *Model the Skill:* **IMPLIED MAIN IDEA**

Point out that in line 48 Namioka says that her best subject was math. Explain that the implication is that her education in this area was very strong and built her confidence and skills in math.

***Possible answer:*** *Namioka implies that Chinese math education is more efficient, interesting, and fun.*

**REVISIT THE BIG IDEA**
What are you really
**GOOD** at?

**Discuss** What does this anecdote by Namioka in lines 69–82 suggest about her mother's talent? ***Possible answer:*** *The anecdote suggests that Namioka's mother had a talent for spotting a profitable real estate investment.*

---

**FOR STRUGGLING READERS**

**2 Targeted Passage** [Lines 52–59]

This passage introduces the conflicts generated by cultural differences and gender stereotypes.

- In what ways did Namioka's classmates find her "weird"? (lines 52–59)
- What was distinctive about the towns Namioka lived in at that time? (lines 52–54)
- What did Namioka's classmates say about her talent for math? (lines 57–59)

**FOR ENGLISH LANGUAGE LEARNERS**

**Language Coach** — COMMON CORE RI 4
**Word Definitions** *Answer:*
"(2) a sudden gain" Ask students to discuss how the word *kill* is usually used and to speculate about how this use of *kill* came about. Point out the realtor's distress as a possible clue.

When Father answered the phone, the realtor shouted, "Do you know what your wife just did? She threw away a chance to make two thousand dollars!"

"I'm sure she had her reasons," Father answered calmly. Nothing that the realtor said could disturb him.

The land turned out to be an excellent investment, and helped to provide a
90   tidy nest egg for my parents in their old age.

In many other Asian countries, too, the housewife is the one who manages money. It's normal for the husband to hand over his paycheck to his wife, and out of it she gives him an allowance. Perhaps it's the result of Confucius's teaching[5] that a gentleman is above money, so it's the woman's duty to be concerned with such petty matters.

Things were very different in America. An American husband would hit the roof if his wife did what my mother had done. Women here were supposed to be hopeless when it came to money matters and figures.

Many girls got good math grades in elementary school, but their grades
100  began to slip when they entered middle school. By then they were getting interested in boys, and they didn't want the boys to think they were weird.

I was weird in elementary and middle school because I was a real whiz at multiplication. In high school, I continued to be a whiz in my geometry and algebra classes. I was lucky to have a geometry teacher who addressed us by last name and didn't care whether you were a boy or a girl, as long as you agreed with Euclid.[6]

My high school geometry class was also the first place where the word *argument* meant something good. My parents complained that I was always arguing. In geometry class, making an argument meant presenting something
110  in an orderly, logical manner.

I also liked the story or word problems in my algebra class. Years later, when I was teaching math, I couldn't understand why many students complained bitterly about them. To me, story problems meant fiction, romance. The most exciting one involved an army column marching forward at a certain speed. A messenger at the head of the column was sent back to the rear. If the column was so many miles long, would he be able to deliver his message in time? I pictured the following **scenario:**

"We expect to engage the enemy in half an hour," the commander told the messenger. "You have to get word to the men in the rear of the column!"
120  The mud-splashed rider desperately lashed his horse, while arrows fell on him from ambushers. How fast did he have to ride so that he would reach the rear guard in time to deliver his message?

Attacking these story problems with relish, I was usually one of the first in the class to finish, and I was often sent to the board to write out the solution.

---

5. **Confucius's** (kən-fyōo′shəs-ĭz) **teaching:** the Chinese philosopher Confucius (551–479 B.C.) taught ideas about practical moral values that are still widely followed in China today.

6. **Euclid** (yōo′klĭd): a third-century-B.C. Greek mathematician upon whose ideas much of the study of geometry in schools is based.

**486**   UNIT 4: THEME AND SYMBOL

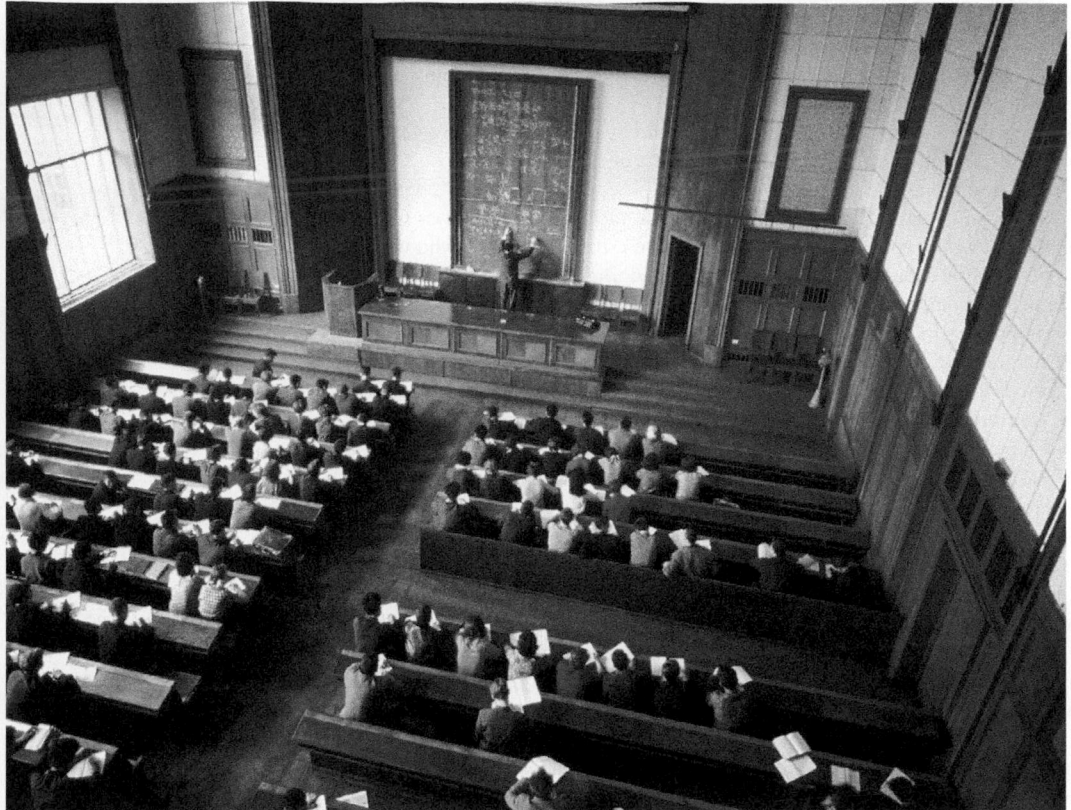

A math lecture in a university lecture hall

By the time I started college, I began to realize that it was unusual, unnatural—maybe even unhealthy—for girls to be good at math. I entered Radcliffe College, which was connected with Harvard. Some of my laboratory courses were taken together with the Harvard students, but classes such as English and math were taught separately on the small Radcliffe campus.

130     The English classes usually had around twenty students, but my beginning calculus class had only five of us. According to rumor, new instructors at Harvard were assigned to teach Radcliffe math classes as a test.

"If they manage to get through the year without breaking down, they're allowed to go on to higher things," we heard.

On the first day of our math class, the instructor (who later became a famous mathematician) crept into the room without looking at us, and spent the whole period mumbling into the blackboard. In fact, he spent the whole year mumbling into the blackboard.

"He's awfully shy, isn't he?" I remarked to a friend.

"Maybe he's just scared of girls who study math," she said.

Things got better when I entered the University of California, which was co-ed. The math classes were larger, and five girls in a class of forty boys weren't enough to scare the instructors.

By this time I knew that in America a girl who was good at math was not only unusual, unnatural, unhealthy, but—worst of all—unattractive.

"Boys don't date you if you're a math whiz," I was told. **E**

The situation was different for me. First of all, racial cross-dating was still rare when I was in college, so I dated only Chinese-American boys, who were hardened to the sight of their mothers or sisters doing math.

I got very good grades in math throughout my school years and majored in mathematics in college. I had a head start in the multiplication table, and I loved arguing and proving things. By the time I learned that I wasn't supposed to do well in math, it was too late.

A hot topic when I was in graduate school was the right-brain, left-brain debate. Scientists decided that men tended to use their left brain, which was the reasoning part, while women used their right brain, the **intuitive** part.

"That's why we're good at hard sciences and math," the boys in my classes assured us. "You girls should stick with poetry, history, art, and things like that. It's a matter of genes or hormones."

Then, later studies showed that the Japanese listened to insect sounds with their left (**analytic**) brain, while Westerners listened to insects with their right brain. Still other studies showed that professional musicians (both male and female) listened to music with the analytic side of their brain, while the general public listened with their intuitive side.

It began to seem that training and social pressure, not genes and hormones, influenced which side of the brain was used. I eagerly followed the debate and could hardly wait for the day when it was okay for women to study science and math in America. **F**

Today, attitudes are finally beginning to change. My daughters tell me that girls in high school math classes are less afraid to do well, and many women go into science and math in college. (One of my daughters is a computer scientist, and the other is an engineer.)

For years, I seemed to be doing well in math because of my Chinese background, because I wasn't afraid to get good math grades in school. I did all the assigned problems without much trouble. But it wasn't enough to do all the problems assigned by the teacher. To be a creative mathematician, you also have to make up problems. I finally learned that I would never do really original work in mathematics.

I found that, for math at least, I lacked what the Chinese call *huo qi*,[7] literally "fiery breath," in other words, ambition and drive. In English the

**E IMPLIED MAIN IDEA**
What do Namioka's anecdotes about college suggest is the main reason that American girls do poorly in math?

**intuitive** (ĭn-to͞o′ĭ-tĭv) *adj.* based on what seems to be true without conscious reasoning; instinctive

**analytic** (ăn′ə-lĭt′ĭk) *adj.* using logical reasoning or analysis

**F IMPLIED MAIN IDEA**
Reread lines 160–168. How does this factual information about brain research support Namioka's main idea?

**3 Targeted Passage**

7. ***huo qi*** (hwō chē).



**TEXT ANALYSIS** COMMON CORE RI 1, RI 2

### E IMPLIED MAIN IDEA

***Possible answer:*** *The anecdotes suggest that American girls do poorly in math because of prejudice, narrow-mindedness, and gender stereotypes that equate success in math to unattractiveness.*

**TEXT ANALYSIS** COMMON CORE RI 1, RI 2

### F IMPLIED MAIN IDEA

***Possible answer:*** *The studies referred to in these lines support Namioka's main idea that talent and success are not "built-in" or "hard-wired" features in an individual. Instead, to a large degree, they are products of training and social expectations.*

**REVISIT THE BIG QUESTION**

## What are you really GOOD at?

**Discuss** Why does Namioka believe, according to lines 169–172, that attitudes today are changing, and that girls and women are less afraid to show their talent in math and science? ***Possible answer:*** *Namioka believes what her daughters tell her: Girls do well in high school math classes and then pursue careers in science and math. Her daughters' own careers are proof. One daughter is a computer scientist, and the other is an engineer.*

**VOCABULARY** COMMON CORE L 4

### OWN THE WORD

- **intuitive:** Tell students that the Latin root of *intuitive* is *intuit-*, which means "contemplate." Have students explain the relationship between *intuitive* and *contemplate*. ***Possible answer:*** *If you contemplate a problem, you will get an intuitive sense of the correct answer.*
- **analytic:** Tell students that the root of *analytic* is the verb *analyze*. Have them name synonyms for *analyze*. ***Possible answers:*** *examine, investigate, question, evaluate*

## DIFFERENTIATED INSTRUCTION

### FOR STRUGGLING READERS

**3 Targeted Passage** [Lines 173–180]

This passage introduces the last section of the essay, where Namioka's focus shifts from prejudice and social pressure to her honest evaluation of her true talents.

- Why was Namioka not afraid to do well in math in school? (lines 173–174)
- What do you need in order to become a creative mathematician? (lines 176–177)
- What did Namioka find she lacked in the field of mathematics? (lines 179–180)

### FOR ENGLISH LANGUAGE LEARNERS

**Vocabulary: Phrasal Verbs** Explain that *threw away* (line 86) means "wasted." Assign students these phrasal verbs to look up in a dictionary and have them share definitions: "make up" (line 177), "dried up" (line 189), "thrown in" (line 206), "worked out" (line 207).

expression "fire in the belly" comes close. I didn't think I was creative enough in mathematics to do good research, nor did I have the drive. **G**

My immediate excuse for getting out of math was the difficulty of arranging for childcare. To be completely honest, I have to admit that I left mathematics because I wasn't all that good, despite my early impressive grades.

I made the transition from mathematics to freelance writing through translation work. For a brief period, I translated mathematical papers from Chinese into English.

My work dried up, however, when the Cultural Revolution[8] swept over
190 China. Mathematicians, like other scholars, were ordered to stop research and write papers confessing their political shortcomings. (These were the lucky ones. The unlucky ones spent their time cleaning latrines.) With no mathematical papers to translate, I eventually took up freelance writing.

My parents reproached me. "How can you give up a beautiful subject like mathematics?"

"We can admire beautiful pictures or music," I told them. "But we don't all have the gift to paint or compose."

"You spent so many years studying math," some people say. "Does it help you at all in your writing?"

200 Math has taught me the useful lesson of thrift. I've met hundreds of mathematicians, and not one of them was a spendthrift. In math you're taught to squeeze the strongest possible result out of the weakest possible **hypothesis**—in other words, you try to get the most value for your money.

This thrifty habit stayed with me after I became a writer. When I put people or events into a book, I squeeze the most out of them. Very few things are thrown in and then forgotten later. As a result my plots seem to be carefully worked out in advance, instead of being made up as I go along. **A**

Years ago, I enjoyed story problems because the stories fired my imagination. In fact, writing fiction was where I finally found my "fiery breath." Instead
210 of story problems, I can write problem stories. And that's what I'm still doing today. ❧

---

8. **Cultural Revolution:** a political upheaval in China in the 1960s that resulted in many attacks on intellectuals.

MATH AND AFTER MATH **489**

---

**G IMPLIED MAIN IDEA**
What does Namioka suggest is needed in order for a person to express a true talent?

**Targeted Passage**
**hypothesis** (hī-pŏth'ĭ-sĭs) *n.* an assumption made in order to test its possible consequences

**COMMON CORE L 5**

**A ANALOGIES**
An **analogy** is a comparison of two things that are alike in certain ways. In lines 200–207, Namioka uses analogies to describe the effect of studying math on her writing. She first explains that math teaches behaviors similar to thrifty spending habits. Then she explains how her writing style is also "thrifty"—nothing is wasted or cast aside. Create your own analogy by comparing either math or writing to something else.

---

**TEXT ANALYSIS** COMMON CORE RI 1, RI 2

**G IMPLIED MAIN IDEA**
***Possible response:*** *Namioka suggests that a person needs ambition and drive, or "fire in the belly," to express a true talent.*

**VOCABULARY** COMMON CORE L 5

**A ANALOGIES**
***Possible answer:*** *Sometimes math looks like a foreign language to me, but I know it's really the universal language of the world.*

Suggest that students think about how they use math or writing when they create their analogies. For example, tell them that the step-by-step nature of solving math problems is like following instructions to install computer software.

**SELECTION WRAP-UP**

**READ WITH A PURPOSE** Now that students have read the nonfiction text, ask them to explain its title. ***Possible answers:*** *Much of the narrator's early life was devoted to math because she was good at it, but eventually she realized her true gift and her passion was for storytelling and her life moved into a new, after-math phase.*

★ **CRITIQUE** Have students evaluate Namioka's ideas about talent and ability. Ask them to explain whether they agree with her and to give reasons.

**INDEPENDENT READING**
Students who want to explore their own goals and talents may enjoy *What Do You Really Want? How to Set a Goal and Go for It! A Guide for Teens* by Beverly K. Bachel.

---

**FOR STRUGGLING READERS**

**4 Targeted Passage** [Lines 200–211]

This passage concludes the essay by drawing a parallel between Namioka's enjoyment of math and her discovery of her true talent: writing stories.

- What does Namioka mean by "thrift"? (lines 200–202)

- How does Namioka's "thrifty habit" help her with developing characters and plots? (lines 204–207)

- When did Namioka finally find her "fiery breath"? (line 209)

**FOR ADVANCED LEARNERS/PRE-AP**

**Apply** [small-group option] Have students consider how Namioka's essay might apply to other fields or careers besides math. Ask them how stereotypes contribute to lower expectations and prevent people from developing their true talents. Ask them to write a small paragraph expressing their responses.

# Practice and Apply

For preliminary support of post-reading questions, use these copy masters:

**R** **RESOURCE MANAGER—Copy Masters**
Reading Check p. 88
Implied Main Idea p. 81
Question Support p. 89

Additional selection questions are provided for teachers on page 75.

## ANSWERS

## Comprehension

1. *She learned math under the easier Chinese system, where expectations were high for girls' performance in math.*

2. *They regarded her talent as unusual, even weird, because, in America, girls were not expected to do well in math.*

3. *The Chinese typically assume that girls and women have an aptitude for math, and so they exhibit a relaxed and evenhanded attitude toward them.*

4. *She realized that she lacked the creativity needed for research and the ambition and drive necessary for high achievement.*

## Text Analysis

COMMON CORE RI 1, RI 2, RI 3

*Possible answers:*

5. *The main cultural difference is in the different expectations of girls learning math. In China, girls are expected to perform well in math. Namioka's experiences at school and college in America, as well as her story about her mother's financial dealing, illustrate this difference.*

6. *The internal conflict concerns Namioka's self-image as a member of an ethnic minority and as a talented student of math—an unusual strength for girls in America. The external conflict revolves around the expectations of Namioka's peers and of her parents.*

7. ● **COMMON CORE FOCUS** *Identify Implied Main Idea The main idea is that gender stereotypes lead to poor performance, which in turn contributes to low expectations for success. This damaging cycle has little to do with true talent or ability. Most of the anecdotes in the essay support this idea.*

## Comprehension

1. **Recall** Why did Namioka do so well in math as a young child?

2. **Recall** In the United States, how did Namioka's classmates regard her talent for math? Why?

3. **Summarize** According to Namioka, what is the typical Chinese attitude about girls' and women's abilities in the area of math?

4. **Clarify** Why did Namioka finally give up her work in mathematics?

## Text Analysis

5. **Compare and Contrast Cultures** What is the main cultural difference discussed in this selection? Support your answer with details from the text.

6. **Analyze Conflict** In this essay, Namioka traces her struggle to determine her true talent. What part of this conflict is **internal?** What part is **external?** Give reasons for your responses.

● 7. **Identify Implied Main Idea** In your own words, state the main idea, the central idea or message, of this essay. Cite evidence from the text to support your answer.

■ 8. **Evaluate Sequence** On your sequence chart, review the parts of the essay where Namioka describes events out of chronological order. In each case, evaluate the effect of this change of sequence. Do you think this is a good technique? Cite evidence to explain your opinion.

9. **Make Judgments** How do contemporary views on women's talent in math compare with those discussed in this essay? Cite evidence to support your claim.

### What are you really GOOD at?

Will you follow a career that utilizes your talents?

COMMON CORE

RI 1 Cite textual evidence to support analysis of what the text says explicitly as well as inferences drawn from the text. RI 2 Determine a central idea of a text and analyze how it emerges and is shaped and refined by specific details. RI 3 Analyze how the author unfolds a series of ideas or events.

8. ■ **COMMON CORE FOCUS** *Evaluate Sequence Students may cite anecdotes such as Namioka's surprise about the recital of the multiplication table when she first emigrated to America (lines 21–24), or the reference to the Chinese movie (lines 63–65). In each case, the departure from chronological sequence helps Namioka elaborate or flesh out the main idea.*

9. *Contemporary views about girls and women in math are more tolerant and relaxed than they used to be. As evidence, Namioka cites her daughters' experiences and the fact that one is a computer scientist, and the other is an engineer (lines 169–172).*

### What are you really GOOD at?

*Possible response: Students' responses should identify the talents they know themselves to have and explain the reasoning behind either a "yes" or "no" answer.*

## Vocabulary in Context

▲ **VOCABULARY PRACTICE**

Decide whether these statements are true or false.

1. If you have an **intuitive** understanding of a procedure, you will probably check each step as you go.
2. Spanish is a **dialect** of English.
3. A student asking for more homework is an unlikely **scenario.**
4. A **hypothesis** is often the first step in an investigation.
5. A person with an **analytic** mind could probably be a successful mathematician.

*WORD LIST*

analytic

dialect

hypothesis

intuitive

scenario

### ACADEMIC VOCABULARY IN WRITING

- context
- interpret
- reveal
- significant
- tradition

Namioka talks about the Chinese **tradition** related to the handling of household finances. With a partner, discuss other traditions she identifies and what they **reveal** about the culture of China or the culture of the United States. Use at least one Academic Vocabulary word in your discussion.

### VOCABULARY STRATEGY: USING CONTEXT CLUES

*Dialect* refers to a variety of speech that differs from the standard speech patterns of a given culture. Vocabulary is one element of dialect. For example, a person might refer to a sweet, carbonated beverage as a *soda*, a *pop*, or a *soft drink*, depending on where he or she lives in the United States. You can often infer the meaning of a word in dialect by noting **context clues** in the sentences and paragraphs that surround the word.

**COMMON CORE**

**L 4a** Use context as a clue to the meaning of a word or phrase.

*PRACTICE* Identify the meaning of the underlined term in each sentence. Use context clues and your own knowledge to determine its meaning. Work with other students to try to identify where or by whom the term is mostly used.

1. Put a <u>schmear</u> of cream cheese on that bagel.
2. The <u>gum bands</u> holding the papers together were old and frayed.
3. You can pack your lunch in that little <u>poke</u>.
4. My grandparents lived on the top floor of the <u>two-flat</u> where I grew up.
5. That <u>plug</u> ought to be put out to pasture.
6. After drinking the chocolate <u>frappé</u>, he wasn't hungry for dinner.
7. Leon is getting together with his <u>homeboys</u>.
8. You can get some water from the <u>bubbler</u> in the hallway.

**Interactive Vocabulary**

**THINK** central

**Go to thinkcentral.com.**
KEYWORD: HML9-491

---

## DIFFERENTIATED INSTRUCTION

### FOR ENGLISH LANGUAGE LEARNERS

**Vocabulary: Cognates**  Point out that all the items in the Word List have cognates in Latin-based languages, such as Spanish, French, and Italian. Have students provide the equivalents in their home languages on the board under each English word. Then have them discuss similarities among the words in the different languages.

### FOR ADVANCED LEARNERS/PRE–AP

**Vocabulary in Writing**  Have students use at least three vocabulary words in a paragraph about a possible career choice.

---

## ANSWERS

### Vocabulary in Context

▲ **VOCABULARY PRACTICE**

| | | |
|---|---|---|
| **1.** *false* | **3.** *true* | **5.** *true* |
| **2.** *false* | **4.** *true* | |

**R** **RESOURCE MANAGER—Copy Master**
Vocabulary Practice p. 86

### ACADEMIC VOCABULARY IN WRITING

**Possible response:** *The phone call to the father from the realtor reveals the American tradition that men handle the family finances.*

**VOCABULARY STRATEGY:**
**USING CONTEXT CLUES**

**COMMON CORE L 4a**

Have students work with a partner during this activity, taking turns substituting a meaning for each underlined word.

**Possible answers:**

1. small portion (Yiddish)
2. rubber bands (Pennsylvania)
3. sack; carrying bag (Southern)
4. two-story (Chicago)
5. old horse (Western)
6. partly iced drink; milk shake (Eastern)
7. close friends; buddies (urban)
8. water cooler (Wisconsin, Australia)

**R** **RESOURCE MANAGER—Copy Master**
Vocabulary Strategy p. 87

**Interactive Vocabulary**

**THINK** central

Keywords direct students to a **WordSharp** tutorial on **thinkcentral.com** or to other types of vocabulary practice and review.

---

## Assess and Reteach

### Assess

**DIAGNOSTIC AND SELECTION TESTS**
Selection Test A pp. 127–128
Selection Test B/C pp. 129–130

**Interactive Selection Test** on **thinkcentral.com**

### Reteach

**Level Up Online Tutorials** on **thinkcentral.com**

# Focus and Motivate

## COMMON CORE FOCUS

**RI 2** Determine a central idea of a text; provide a summary of the text. **RI 6** Determine an author's point of view in a text and analyze how an author uses rhetoric to advance that point of view. **W 4** Produce argumentative writing in which the style is appropriate to the task, purpose, and audience. **L 3** Apply knowledge of language to make effective choices for meaning or style. **L 4a** Use context as a clue to the meaning of a word.

## SUMMARY

In her essay "The Future in My Arms," Haitian-born writer Edwidge Danticat recalls becoming an aunt at the age of thirty. Holding her new-born niece, Danticat feels both protective and humbled as she reflects on the responsibility of adults to provide a *repozwa*—a sacred place of refuge—for their community's children.

## What does a community OWE its CHILDREN?

Read and discuss the question with students. Ask students to paraphrase the African proverb and suggest the kinds of responsibility involved in raising a child. Then use the proverb to introduce the *QUICKWRITE*, in which students think about the "village" that has raised them. Suggest that students jot down some notes about the person they choose before they start writing.

## Selection Resources

---

# The Future in My Arms
Essay by Edwidge Danticat

# What does a community OWE its CHILDREN?

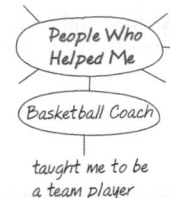

**COMMON CORE**

**RI 2** Determine a central idea of a text; provide a summary of the text. **RI 6** Determine an author's point of view in a text and analyze how an author uses rhetoric to advance that point of view. **L 4a** Use context as a clue to the meaning of a word.

Parents, of course, have a huge commitment to their children. But what is the responsibility of a community to its young? A familiar African proverb states, "It takes a village to raise a child." Do you agree?

*QUICKWRITE* In a small group, discuss how people in your community have influenced your life. Did someone teach you to play soccer or baseball? What about the person who always made a point of asking how you were doing? Create a concept web, as shown, with people who have helped you. Then choose one person and write a paragraph describing how he or she has made a difference in your life.

People Who Helped Me

Basketball Coach

taught me to be a team player

492

---

*See resources on the **Teacher One Stop DVD-ROM** and on **thinkcentral.com**.*

**R RESOURCE MANAGER UNIT 4**
Plan and Teach, pp. 91–98
Summary, pp. 99–100 † ‡ *
Text Analysis and Reading
   Skill, pp. 101–102, 103–105 †*
Grammar and Style, p. 107

**DIAGNOSTIC AND SELECTION TESTS**
Selection Tests, pp. 131–134

**BEST PRACTICES TOOLKIT**
Two-Column Chart, p. A25
Word Squares, p. E10

**TECHNOLOGY**
⦿ **Teacher One Stop DVD-ROM**
⦿ **Student One Stop DVD-ROM**
⦿ **Audio Anthology CD**
⦿ **GrammarNotes DVD-ROM**
⦿ **ExamView Test Generator**
   on the **Teacher One Stop**

---

* Resources for Differentiation     † In Spanish     ‡ In Haitian Creole and Vietnamese

## TEXT ANALYSIS: AUTHOR'S PERSPECTIVE

An **author's perspective** is the lens through which a writer views a subject. This lens is made up of the writer's ideas, values, feelings, and beliefs—products of the writer's life experiences and cultural upbringing. For example, in "Math and After Math" (page 480), Lensey Namioka writes from the perspective of a Chinese-American female who has a talent for math and was raised to believe that it is "not unusual at all" for a woman to excel at mathematics. Readers learn her perspective from direct statements as well as anecdotes that illustrate her views.

As you read "The Future in My Arms," determine Edwidge Danticat's point of view by examining the following:

- statements of opinion
- tone, or attitude
- diction, or word choice
- repeated words or ideas
- the descriptions of cultural customs
- the portrayal of her niece

## READING STRATEGY: MONITOR

**Monitoring** is the strategy of checking your comprehension as you read and intentionally using other strategies to improve it. For example, if as you read you realize that you are not understanding the text very well, you might decide you need to slow down your reading pace, reread, or skim the next section before reading it. With "The Future in My Arms," the following strategies may be especially helpful:

- **Predict** what will happen later in the selection.
- **Question** the events described and their significance.
- **Reread** passages that you find confusing.
- **Summarize** what you have read by briefly restating the central ideas in your own words.

As you read, keep track of your thoughts, ideas, and questions by jotting them down.

 Complete the activities in your **Reader/Writer Notebook**.

 **Author Online**
**THINK** central
Go to **thinkcentral.com**.
KEYWORD: HML9-493

493

## Teach

● *Model the Skill:* **AUTHOR'S PERSPECTIVE**

Discuss what the quotation in **One Voice in a Million** suggests about Danticat's perspective. Help students recognize that Danticat is proud of her Haitian heritage and is eager to share her experiences as an immigrant. Discuss what students might expect the essay to be like, based on that perspective. *Possible answer: The essay might present Haitian culture in a way that is appealing and that shows Danticat's pride in her people and their traditions.*

**GUIDED PRACTICE** Have students choose two passages from this essay and discuss the author's perspective in each one.

■ *Model the Skill:* **MONITOR**

Show how to use the strategies to monitor understanding of the background information. For example, predict that the essay will give a sense of what the Haitian community is like, question the events that led Haitians to leave their homeland, and reread the final sentence to clarify the meaning of *Haitian Diaspora*.

**GUIDED PRACTICE** Have students repeat the process you modeled, using **An Early Start**.

**R** RESOURCE MANAGER—Copy Master Monitor p. 103 (for student use while reading the selection)

## DIFFERENTIATED INSTRUCTION

### FOR ENGLISH LANGUAGE LEARNERS
**Culture: Connect** The references on this page to Edwidge Danticat's immigrant experience will resonate with many students who are learning English. Invite students who were born (or whose parents were born) outside the United States to add their special insights to class discussions of "The Future in My Arms."

### FOR ADVANCED LEARNERS/PRE–AP
**Evaluate a Quotation** When students have finished reading "The Future in My Arms," have them return to this page and reread the Danticat quotation in **One Voice in a Million.** Ask them if they think that this essay has fulfilled what Danticat calls her "greatest hope" by sharing her experiences in an artistic but clear manner. Urge students to cite textual details that support their views.

# THE FUTURE IN *My Arms*

### Edwidge Danticat

I had never held any living thing so tiny in my hands. Six pounds and one ounce, lighter than my smallest dumbbell was my newborn niece, her face bright pink, her eyes tightly shut, her body coiled around itself in a fetal position, still defiantly resisting the world into which she'd just been thrust. I had been awaiting her birth with feverish anticipation; I was going away for the summer, and I didn't want to leave before she was born, only to come back eight weeks later and find that she had grown accustomed to most things in the world except her only auntie on her father's side, the sole woman child in a family of men, who all her life had dreamed of having a sister. **B**

10   She arrived the day before I was to leave. I was at the Brooklyn Public Library researching an article when I called to check my messages. In a breathless voice, my brother Andre announced, "You are now the proud aunt of Nadira Amahs Danticat.[1] Her name means, 'She whom God has chosen.'"

  I ran out of the library and headed toward a flower shop on Flatbush Avenue. As I approached, I heard someone call out my name. It was my brother Karl and Mia, who were expecting their own child in a few months. They, too, were heading to the hospital to see Nadira.

  On the way there, I remembered a message that a girlfriend of mine, a new mother, had sent me for my thirtieth birthday a few months before. "May 20 your arms always be a repozwa, a place where a child can rest her head," it said. I had told her that two of my brothers were becoming fathers, and she wanted me to share those words with them. But I'd decided to wait until both my niece and nephew were born to share this with their parents—that we had each become a *repozwa*,[2] the Haitian Creole[3] term for "sacred place," in whose shelter children would now seek rest.

---

1. **Nadira Amahs Danticat** (nä-dĭr′ä ä-mäs′ dän-tĭ-kä′).
2. *repozwa* (rä-pōz-wä′).
3. **Haitian Creole:** the French-based language spoken in Haiti.

**Repozwa** In Haitian popular religion, a *repozwa* was originally a kind of sanctuary, often in a natural setting, where one went to seek spiritual communion, guidance, and healing. A spiritual gathering place, the *repozwa* was a cultural gathering place as well, as it was descended from African, European, and Native American influences.

**Cultural Connection** In many cultures, child rearing is considered a communal responsibility. In some cultures it is fulfilled by an extended kin not tied to the child by blood; in other cultures child rearing is done by extended family who impress upon the child the values and traditions of the culture.

## Analyze Visuals

*Possible answer:* *The* repozwa *concepts of "sacred place," "shelter," and "a place where a child can rest her head," are suggested by the peaceful embrace of the woman and the quiet sleep of the child on her shoulder.*

**About the Art** April Harrison's art features an intricate mix of layered artistic materials. Harrison often focuses her work on the warmth, strength, and comfort of bonded relationships, especially of motherly love.

**REVISIT THE BIG QUESTION**

## What does a community
## OWE its CHILDREN?

**Discuss** How does Danticat's unwillingness to go away until her niece has been born, described in lines 5–9, reflect a sense of responsibility? *Possible answer: Her unwillingness arises from her desire to be physically present to greet the newborn and to join in celebrating this important event.*

- Why did Danticat decide to wait to share the message with her brothers? (lines 22–24)
- What does *repozwa* mean? (lines 24–25)
- What does using the term suggest about Danticat's values? (lines 18–25)

**FOR ADVANCED LEARNERS/PRE–AP**

**Extend** Many cultures and religions have traditional practices for welcoming newborns. Students can research the practices of one culture or religion and present their findings to the class. Students should explain where in the world the practice is used, its traditional or religious significance, and how old the baby is when it is performed.

By the time we got to the hospital, my sister-in-law, Carol, had already had a few visitors. She appeared exhausted but in good spirits as she and Andre took us down the corridor to the maternity-ward window. Which one was Nadira? Andrew wanted us to guess, to pick her out of the rows of infants

30 like a long-lost relative in a crowd of strangers. We were aided in our task by the small pink name tag glued to her bassinet. Carol asked if we wanted to have a closer look. We went back to the room and waited for the nurse to bring her in.

We all stood up when she was carried in. I knew I was getting ahead of myself, but this made me think of a wedding where everyone immediately—and almost instinctively—rises to greet the bride. She was passed from loving hand to loving hand, but I kept her longer. I would soon have to leave, so I wanted to hold her, to cradle her in my arms, let her tiny head rest in the crook of my elbow. I wanted to watch her ever so slightly open her eyes and

40 tighten her mouth as she battled to make sense of all the new sounds around her, all the laughter, the wild comparisons with relatives living and gone, all so very present in her face. I wanted to read her lines from Sonia Sanchez's "Poem at Thirty": "i am here waiting / remembering that / once as a child / i walked two / miles in my sleep. / did i know / then where i / was going? / traveling. i'm always traveling. / i want to tell / you about me . . . / here is my hand."

Nadira's presence had already transformed the room. Her opening her eyes was like a Hollywood press conference, with all the video and picture cameras going off, trying to capture something that perhaps none of us knew how to express, that we had suddenly been allowed a closer view of one of life's great

50 wonders, and by being there, were an extension of a miracle that happened every second of every day in every part of the world, but had generously now granted us a turn.

That day, when we lined up for a glance, a touch, a picture, and tried to imagine a life for Nadira in a new country, we each made our own silent promises not to let her face that new world alone. We were telling her and her parents that we were her village with our offers of baby-sitting favors, our giant teddy bears, our handfuls of flowers, and the crooks of our arms and necks and laps, which we hoped that she would run to if she ever needed a refuge.

Looking back on my own thirty years, having crossed many borders, loved

60 and lost many family and friends, young and old, to time, migrations, illnesses, I couldn't help but worry for Nadira, and for my nephew yet to be born. Are there ahead for them wars, a depression, a holocaust, a new civil-rights struggle as there were for those children born at the dawn of the last century? Will they have to face the colonization of new planets, genetic cloning, new forms of slavery, and other nightmares we have yet to imagine? Will we, their tiny village, give them enough love and assurance to help them survive, thrive, and even want to challenge those things?

Before handing Nadira back to her parents, I felt torn between wanting her to grow up quickly so that her body might match the wits she'd need to face

70 her future and at the same time wanting her to stay small so that she might be

**C MONITOR**
**Reread** lines 42–45. What significance might these lines of poetry have for Danticat?

**2 Targeted Passage**

**D AUTHOR'S PERSPECTIVE**
What do Danticat's promises suggest about her beliefs concerning the responsibility adults have toward children?

**E GRAMMAR AND STYLE**
**Reread** lines 62–67. Notice how Danticat poses a series of **rhetorical questions** about the future to prompt readers to share her concern.

---

**READING STRATEGY**

**C *Model the Skill*: MONITOR**

Note the title of the poem and remind students that Danticat herself is thirty years old (line 19). Call on a volunteer to read the lines of poetry aloud. Ask students to describe the speaker and guess who "you" might be in the lines "i want to tell / you about me . . . / here is my hand."

***Possible answer:*** *The lines might signify that older family or community members share a common destiny—traveling through life's journey—with children.*

---

**TEXT ANALYSIS**

**D AUTHOR'S PERSPECTIVE**

***Possible answer:*** *Danticat's promises indicate a belief that adults have a responsibility to love, protect, and shelter the children in their community.*

**Extend the Discussion** Does this idea conflict with the belief that adults should help children learn to become responsible adults? Why or why not?

---

**E GRAMMAR AND STYLE**

**Rhetorical Questions** Explain that readers are expected to think about rather than answer rhetorical questions. Also note that a series of rhetorical questions can increase a writer's emotional impact. Have students identify the list of items in each question and discuss their importance.

---

## DIFFERENTIATED INSTRUCTION

**FOR STRUGGLING READERS**

 **Targeted Passage [Lines 46–52]**

This passage focuses on Danticat's love for her infant niece.

• Why does Danticat compare the scene at the hospital to a Hollywood press conference? (lines 47–49)

• What effect does Nadira have on the hospital room? (lines 46–47)

• What "miracle" is happening all the time, everywhere? Why, then, is it so special to

Danticat? (lines 50–52)

**Develop Reading Fluency** Explain that lines 43–45 show a quoted poem; when contained within other text, poems are often written like this. The slashes show where the line breaks should appear. Remind students that line breaks have significance but do not necessarily indicate where a thought or sentence ends. Then read the poem aloud for the students. Ask volunteers to give their own readings for the class or a small group.

*Circle of Joy,* Keith Mallett. © Keith Mallett Studio, Inc./www.keithmallett.com.

easier to shield and carry along the length of our elbows to the reach of our palms. I wanted to tell her parents that though I had never held any living thing so tiny in my hands, I had never held anything so grand either, a bundle so elaborately complex and yet fragile, encompassing both our past and our future.

Though Nadira and my soon-to-arrive nephew were not created specifically with me in mind, I felt as though they were the most magical gifts that could ever have blessed my thirtieth year of life. Humbled by my responsibility to them, I silently promised their parents that for the next thirty years and the thirty after that, my heart and soul would be their children's repozwa, a sacred place where they would always find rest. ❧

80

③ **Targeted Passage**

---

## Analyze Visuals

**Activity** Ask students how the image high-lights Danticat's overall theme of adult responsibility toward children. *Possible answer: The three women (who may be the child's mother, grandmother, and great-grandmother) tenderly cradle the infant in their arms. The image conveys a sense that multigenerational family members are creating a strong safety net for the child. The image relates well to Danticat's concluding promise to be Nadira's repozwa at all times (lines 78–81).*

**About the Art** The subject matter of American artist Keith Mallet (b. 1948) ranges from figurative to still life and abstracts.

## SELECTION WRAP-UP

**READ WITH A PURPOSE** Now that students have read the selection, ask them what Danticat anticipates for her niece's future. *Possible answers: Her own presence, but also uncertainty and potential worries.* **What does this reveal about the author?** *Possible answer: She is very aware of problems and potential problems in the world, partly as the result of her own experiences.*

⭐ **CRITIQUE** Ask students to state whether they felt that Danticat made a compelling argument. Do students feel that it is realistic to ask adults to help care for other people's children? What are some benefits and advantages that adults derive from mentoring youngsters?

## INDEPENDENT READING

Students can read more about community life in *An Hour Before Daylight: Memories of a Rural Boyhood* by Jimmy Carter.

---

## FOR STRUGGLING READERS

③ **Targeted Passage** [Lines 76–81]

As the essay concludes, this passage sets a tone of loving determination.

- What kind of "gifts" does Danticat call her niece and nephew? (lines 77–78)

- Why does she say that she is blessed? Why does she say that she is humbled? (lines 77–79)

- What promise does she make? If she keeps that promise, what can her niece and nephew expect of her in the future? (lines 79–81)

## FOR ENGLISH LANGUAGE LEARNERS

# Practice and Apply

For preliminary support of post-reading questions, use these copy masters:

**R** RESOURCE MANAGER—Copy Masters
Reading Check p. 105
Author's Perspective p. 101
Question Support p. 106

Additional selection questions are provided for teachers on page 95.

## ANSWERS

### Comprehension

1. *Danticat is the baby's aunt.*

2. *Danticat regards the baby as "one of life's great wonders" (lines 49–50) and as one of "the most magical gifts" that she could receive (line 77).*

3. *Besides the author, the baby is the only female child in a family of men.*

4. *She hopes to be a repozwa, a place where the girl always can find safety and rest.*

### Text Analysis

COMMON CORE RI 2, RI 6

**Possible answers:**

5. ● COMMON CORE FOCUS *Determine Central Idea Adults in a community have a responsibility to protect and care for the community's children, even if these children are not their own.*

6. ● COMMON CORE FOCUS *Make Inferences About Author's Perspective Danticat believes that adults must give children "love and assurance to help them . . . thrive" (line 66). Adults also must convey a sense of identity and cohesiveness to the community's children by accepting the responsibility of care and concern (lines 55–58).*

7. *Origin: Haitian Creole*
*Literal Meaning: "sacred place"*
*Connotations: shelter, refuge, love, concern, protection, spirituality*
*Significance in Essay: sums up writer's thesis or main idea*

8. *Nadira encompasses the past because she is the descendant of relatives, both living and dead (line 41). She encompasses the future because she will confront challenges that present-day adults may not even imagine (lines 62–65).*

---

## Comprehension

1. **Recall** What is Danticat's relationship to the baby she holds?

2. **Recall** How does Danticat regard the baby and her birth?

3. **Clarify** Why is the baby so special to her?

4. **Summarize** What role does she hope to play in the baby's life?

## Text Analysis

■ 5. **Determine Central Idea** Review the questions, thoughts, and ideas you noted as you monitored your reading. Then, using this information as a guide, state the central idea, or thesis, of "The Future in My Arms."

● 6. **Make Inferences About Author's Perspective** What can you infer about Danticat's values, feelings, and beliefs concerning the role of adults in children's lives? Support your inferences with details from the text.

7. **Analyze Concept** Complete a concept chart like the one shown for the word *repozwa*. What is the significance of the word in this essay? Give evidence to support your answer.

| Repozwa |
|---|
| Origin: |
| Literal Meaning: |
| Connotations: |
| Significance in Essay: |

8. **Interpret Text** Reread lines 72–75. What does Danticat mean when she states that the baby Nadira encompasses "both our past and our future"? Support your answer with details from the essay.

## Text Criticism

9. **Social Context** How do your community's views on the responsibility of adults toward children compare with those in this selection? Consider the role of institutions such as parks, schools, daycare facilities, and neighborhood-watch programs in your area. What role do neighbors and extended families have in the care of children? Cite evidence to support your evaluation.

### What does a community OWE its CHILDREN?

How should this commitment to children extend *beyond* the community?

COMMON CORE

RI 2 Determine a central idea of a text; provide a summary of the text. RI 6 Determine an author's point of view in a text and analyze how an author uses rhetoric to advance that point of view.

---

## Text Criticism

9. *Accept any response that is adequately supported by specific details and that makes a reasonable comparison.*

What does a community **OWE** its **CHILDREN?** *Answers will vary, but students may argue that all children deserve the chance to meet their full potential, whatever their community.*

# Language

◆ **GRAMMAR AND STYLE:** Add Rhetorical Questions

Review the **Grammar and Style** note on page 496. Here, the author uses **interrogative sentences** to ask **rhetorical questions** that not only express her own concerns but also prompt similar concerns in her readers. Unlike other questions, **rhetorical questions** do not require answers; they are used for effect. For example, notice how the following rhetorical questions make this paragraph more powerful than it would be with only declarative statements:

> *A community is only as strong as its members. Our community needs to reach out to all children who live in our town. What are their needs? What will help them grow strong? How can we help them become responsible citizens who will, in turn, make this a better community?*

Now study the following model. Notice how the revisions in blue make this first draft more powerful and effective.

**STUDENT MODEL**

*What is my responsibility to this child? What is our responsibility to all children in the community?*

Recently, I became an aunt to a beautiful baby girl. This joyous occasion caused me to reflect upon my role in her life, ~~I started to consider my~~ ~~responsibilities to her and the other children in our community.~~

**COMMON CORE**

**L 3** Apply knowledge of language to make effective choices for meaning or style. **W 4** Produce argumentative writing in which the style is appropriate to the task, purpose, and audience.

## READING-WRITING CONNECTION

Increase your understanding of "The Future in My Arms" by responding to this prompt. Then use the **revising tip** to improve your writing.

| WRITING PROMPT | REVISING TIP |
|---|---|
| **Extended Constructed Response: Letter** How might Danticat encourage a community to become a *repozwa* for its children? Drawing on ideas in her essay, write a **three- to five-paragraph letter** that Danticat might send to a local newspaper encouraging that community to examine its **responsibilities** to its children. | Review your letter. Does it make a strong case? Consider adding rhetorical questions to make your writing more powerful. |

**Interactive Revision** THINK central

Go to thinkcentral.com.
KEYWORD: HML9-499

---

## DIFFERENTIATED INSTRUCTION

### FOR STRUGGLING WRITERS

- Suggest that students limit their response to two or three paragraphs.

- Help students generate persuasive arguments relating to two civic or community organizations or programs.

- Have students brainstorm in small groups to develop arguments that relate to the specific needs of their community.

---

# Language

**COMMON CORE L 3, W 4**

◆ **GRAMMAR AND STYLE**

After students examine the paragraph and the student model, have them rewrite the rhetorical questions in the paragraph as declarative sentences. When students compare the two versions, they probably will agree that the rhetorical questions strengthen the persuasive appeal of the paragraph.

**R** RESOURCE MANAGER—Copy Master
Add Rhetorical Questions p. 107

**READING-WRITING CONNECTION**

- Suggest that students look for ideas about community responsibility in their answer to question 9 on page 498. Students can use lines 62–67 as a model for their rhetorical questions.

**BEST PRACTICES TOOLKIT—Transparency**
Two-Column Chart p. A25

**Writing Online** THINK central

The following tools are available online at **thinkcentral.com** and on **WriteSmart CD-ROM:**
- **Interactive Graphic Organizers**
- **Interactive Student Models**
- **Interactive Revision Lessons**
For additional grammar instruction, see **GrammarNotes** on **thinkcentral.com**.

## Assess and Reteach

### Assess

**DIAGNOSTIC AND SELECTION TESTS**
Selection Test A pp. 131–132
Selection Test B/C pp. 133–134

**Interactive Selection Test** on **thinkcentral.com**

### Reteach

**Level Up Online Tutorials** on **thinkcentral.com**

**Reteaching Worksheets** on **thinkcentral.com**
Language and Literacy Devices Lesson 47: Author's Perspective

# Focus and Motivate

## COMMON CORE FOCUS

**RL 2** Determine a theme of a text and analyze its development over the course of the text, including how it emerges and is shaped and refined by details. **RL 4** Analyze the cumulative impact of specific word choices on meaning and tone. **RL 6** Analyze a particular point of view or cultural experience reflected in a work of world literature.

## SUMMARIES

**"Poem on Returning to Dwell in the Country"** The speaker explains that he was once ambitious and materialistic, but has now given up such entrapments. He will return to the mountains and hills that he loved as a child and will live simply in a cottage.

**"My Heart Leaps Up"** The speaker shares that he would prefer death to losing his ability to feel joy in nature.

**"The Sun"** The speaker describes the pleasure the sun gives to those who are open to its beauty.

## Where do you go to GET AWAY from it all?

Read the question and discuss the paragraph. Ask students to name aspects of nature that many people enjoy (such as mountains, beaches, and sunsets). After students complete the *QUICKWRITE,* invite volunteers to share their paragraphs.

## Selection Resources

## Before Reading

### Poem on Returning to Dwell in the Country
Poem by T'ao Ch'ien

**Essential Course of Study EGOS**

### My Heart Leaps Up
Poem by William Wordsworth

### The Sun
Poem by Mary Oliver

**VIDEO TRAILER THINK central** KEYWORD: HML9-500

# Where do you go to GET AWAY from it all?

### COMMON CORE

**RL 2** Determine a theme of a text and analyze its development over the course of the text, including how it emerges and is shaped and refined by details. **RL 4** Analyze the cumulative impact of specific word choices on meaning and tone. **RL 6** Analyze a particular point of view or cultural experience reflected in a work of world literature.

What does nature do for you? Whether it's staring at a fishbowl, escaping to the mountains, or simply taking a walk in the park, many people look to nature for beauty, serenity, or rejuvenation. The poems that follow reflect on the experience of basking in the natural world.

**QUICKWRITE** Make a concept web like the one shown, identifying a part of nature you enjoy and how it makes you feel. Then write a paragraph explaining your thoughts.

*Requires patience; slows me down*

*Going Fishing*

*Makes me feel self-sufficient*  *Quiet is soothing*

500

---

*See resources on the* **Teacher One Stop DVD-ROM** *and on* **thinkcentral.com**.

**R RESOURCE MANAGER UNIT 4**
   Plan and Teach, pp. 109–116
   Text Analysis and Reading
      Skill, pp. 117–118, 119–120 †*
**DIAGNOSTIC AND SELECTION TESTS**
   Selection Tests, pp. 135–138

**INTERACTIVE READER**

**ADAPTED INTERACTIVE READER**

**ELL ADAPTED INTERACTIVE READER**

**TECHNOLOGY**
   🖉 **Teacher One Stop DVD-ROM**
   🖉 **Student One Stop DVD-ROM**
   🖉 **PowerNotes DVD-ROM**
   🖉 **Audio Anthology CD**
   🖉 **GrammarNotes DVD-ROM**
   🖉 **Audio Tutor CD**
   🖉 **ExamView Test Generator**
      on the **Teacher One Stop**

---

*** Resources for Differentiation     † In Spanish     ‡ In Haitian Creole and Vietnamese**

## TEXT ANALYSIS: UNIVERSAL THEME

Some poems have a **universal theme;** they express ideas that people from many cultures and times have found to be true. The poems you are about to read all describe a love of nature. Although written by poets who lived centuries apart and in very different cultures, all three poems touch upon the same theme. As you read each poem, use these strategies to identify their shared message:

- Think about the idea each poem is expressing about nature. What theme does each poem convey?
- Examine each poet's approach to the subject and look for similarities and differences.

Modern-day poets often write with an awareness of mythic, classical, or traditional poems and are influenced by the language and themes of poems from earlier historical periods. For example, someone writing about nature in the 20th or 21st century would likely have been influenced by England's Romantic poets, who had a deep reverence for nature. When reading the following three poems, consider the influences each earlier poem may have had on the later ones.

## READING STRATEGY: READING POETRY FOR THEME

The words in a poem are carefully chosen and arranged to convey the poet's message. As a result, to understand **theme** in poetry, you need to look at details differently than you would when reading prose. The strategies that follow can help you discover the theme in each poem in this lesson:

- Identify the **speaker,** or voice, that "talks" to the reader. What attitude does the speaker have toward the subject of the poem?
- Notice key **images** and think about their meanings.
- Identify words and phrases that are emphasized or repeated or that strike you as important. Consider what ideas and feelings the words and phrases convey.

As you read, keep a list of significant words, images, and phrases from each poem.

> "Poem on Returning to Dwell in the Country"
>
> "For my nature always/loved the hills and mountains." (lines 3–4)

 Complete the activities in your **Reader/Writer Notebook.**

## T'ao Ch'ien
### 365–427

**Grandfather of Chinese Wilderness Poetry**
T'ao Ch'ien worked for the government before he returned to his family farm to live as a farmer—a radical decision at the time. His poetry reflects Taoist philosophy, which emphasizes living simply and close to nature. Both his life and his natural, conversational style of poetry inspired many later Chinese writers.

## William Wordsworth
### 1770–1850

**England's Poet of Nature**
William Wordsworth grew up in the Lake District of northern England. As a boy, he loved being outdoors and appreciated the natural beauty of the region; this love of nature never left him. His poetry introduced a new view of the relationship between people and nature. Wordsworth became one of the leaders of the Romantic movement in English literature.

## Mary Oliver
### born 1935

**American Celebrant of Nature**
Mary Oliver became a distinguished poet and professor without ever having finished college. Her poetry, which links the worlds of people, animals, and plants, has won the Pulitzer Prize and the National Book Award.

**Authors Online**
THINK central
Go to thinkcentral.com. KEYWORD: HML9-501

501

---

**TEXT ANALYSIS**                    COMMON CORE
                                     RL 2,
                                     RL 6

### ● *Model the Skill:* UNIVERSAL THEME

To help students recognize a universal theme, write these lines on the board:

> Filled with excitement and yet with fear,
> I drop my toys and approach the door.
> Stepping through, I face a year
> Of change, of growth, of wonders in store!

Elicit that this stanza suggests **universal themes** related to growing up and/or facing the future.

**GUIDED PRACTICE** Ask students to name other themes that they would consider universal.

---

**READING STRATEGY**                COMMON CORE
                                     RL 4

### ● *Model the Skill:* READING POETRY FOR THEME

Apply the strategies in the text to the stanza in the **Text Analysis** teaching activity. Ask students what feelings are suggested by *fear* and *change* and by *excitement, growth,* and *wonders.* Then discuss why certain words stand out and why the image of stepping through an open doorway is effective.

**GUIDED PRACTICE** Have students work with partners to present a **theme** from the same stanza in their own words, following the strategies in the text.

**R** RESOURCE MANAGER—Copy Master Reading Poetry for Theme p. 119 (for student use while reading the selections)

---

## DIFFERENTIATED INSTRUCTION

### FOR STRUGGLING READERS

**Clarify Concepts** As the text notes, part of determining a poem's theme involves examining the poet's approach to his or her subject. Make sure that students understand what is meant by an "approach."

- Define *approach* as "the methods that an author uses to accomplish his or her purpose." If writing is meant to persuade, for example, then *approach* refers to the ways in which the author tries to get readers to agree with him or her.

- Explain that many poems are meant to describe. In this case, *approach* refers to the ways in which the poet tries to help readers experience sensory impressions.

- Explain that poets use various methods to achieve their purposes. Vivid images, precise word choices, repetition, and unusual comparisons are just a few methods in a poet's approach.

## READ WITH A PURPOSE

*Help students set a purpose for reading. Remind them that all three poems share the universal theme of a love for nature. Ask students to read closely to determine the specific images each poet uses to indicate "nature."*

**READING STRATEGY**

**COMMON CORE**

**RL 4**

 **A** *Model the Skill:* **READING POETRY**

Point out the key words *tame* and *house-pond*. Point out that both words suggest captivity. Then ask:

- Why would a tame bird long for his old forest (lines 9–10)? *Possible answer: He yearns for the freedom of nature.*

- Why does the fish in the house-pond think of his ancient pool (lines 11–12)? *Possible answer: He wants to return to his home in nature.*

*Possible answer: Both the tame bird and the fish are in an artificial, restrictive setting, and both miss their natural environment. Similarly, the speaker is trapped in the artificial, restrictive "Dusty Net" (lines 5–6). He misses his natural environment of hills and mountains (lines 3–4).*

*Viewing Plum Blossoms by Moonlight,*
Ma Yuan. Ink and color on silk,
9-7/8" x 10-1/2". Gift of John M.
Crawford, Jr. (1986.493.2). Photo
by Malcolm Varon © Metropolitan
Museum of Art, New York/Art
Resource, New York.

# Poem on Returning to Dwell in the Country

### T'ao Ch'ien

In youth I had nothing
    that matched the vulgar tone,[1]
For my nature always
    loved the hills and mountains.
5 Inadvertently I fell
    into the Dusty Net,[2]
Once having gone
    it was more than thirteen years.
The tame bird
10    longs for his old forest—
The fish in the house-pond
    thinks of his ancient pool. **A**
I too will break the soil
    at the edge of the southern moor,
15 I will guard simplicity
    and return to my fields and garden.
My land and house—
    a little more than ten acres,
In the thatched cottage—
20    only eight or nine rooms.
Elms and willows
    shade the back verandah,
Peach and plum trees
    in rows before the hall.

**A** **READING POETRY**
Consider the **images** in
lines 9–12. Why does
the speaker mention the
tame bird and the fish in
the house-pond?

---

1. **matched the vulgar tone:** The speaker is saying that
he was never coarse or raucous in his youth.

2. **Dusty Net:** a term that refers to being caught up in
professional ambition and materialism.

## DIFFERENTIATED INSTRUCTION

### FOR ENGLISH LANGUAGE LEARNERS

**Comprehension: Transitions** Understanding these terms that signal spatial relationships in T'ao Ch'ien's poem will help students appreciate the scope and vividness of its description of nature: "at the edge of" (line 14), "in" (lines 19, 24, 26, 27, and 35), "before" (line 24), "amidst" (line 30), "atop" (line 32), "within" (lines 34 and 38).

### FOR STRUGGLING READERS

**Develop Reading Fluency** Before helping students analyze each of the poems in this lesson, read each poem aloud. Encourage students to enjoy the images, sounds, and ideas that each poet expresses. Students can also work in pairs or small groups to analyze each poem in order to comprehend its organization—the lengths of lines and stanzas, rhyme scheme (if any), and places where complete thoughts begin and end. After students have examined the poems, allow individuals to

25 Hazy and dimly seen
    a village in the distance,
Close in the foreground
    the smoke of neighbors' houses.
A dog barks
30     amidst the deep lanes,
A cock is crowing
    atop a mulberry tree.
No dust and confusion
    within my doors and courtyard;
35 In the empty rooms
    more than sufficient leisure.
Too long I was held
    within the barred cage.
Now I am able
40     to return again to Nature. **B**
      *Translated by William Acker*

**B UNIVERSAL THEME**
Reread the last four lines. What is the "barred cage"?

# My Heart Leaps Up

W I L L I A M   W O R D S W O R T H

My heart leaps up when I behold
    A rainbow in the sky:
So was it when my life began;
So is it now I am a man;
5 So be it when I shall grow old,
    Or let me die! **C**
The Child is father of the Man;
And I could wish my days to be
Bound each to each by natural piety.[1]

**C UNIVERSAL THEME**
Paraphrase what the speaker reveals in lines 1–6 about his feelings toward nature.

---

1. **piety** (pī′ĭ-tē): the quality of showing devotion or being reverent.

---

## Analyze Visuals

**Activity** Ask students to describe how the painting captures the key idea of nature. *Possible answer: The painting presents a beautiful natural landscape, but it also emphasizes the appreciation of nature by showing a person admiring that landscape.*

**About the Art** *Viewing Plum Blossoms by Moonlight* by Ma Yuan (C.A.D. 1190–C.A.D. 1225) shows a scholar contemplating the moon beyond a plum tree.

**REVISIT THE BIG QUESTION**

## Where do you go to **GET AWAY** from it all?

**Discuss** Review the details about the speaker's new setting in lines 21–32. What generalization can you make about why he will enjoy returning to nature? *Possible answer: The natural setting will be beautiful and serene.*

**TEXT ANALYSIS**     COMMON CORE   RL 2, RL 6

**B UNIVERSAL THEME**

*Possible answer: The "barred cage" is the way of life that the speaker is giving up—his life of being trapped in the "Dusty Net" (line 6) of ambition and materialism.*

**Prereading for "My Heart Leaps Up" is found on page 500.**

**TEXT ANALYSIS**    COMMON CORE   RL 2, RL 6

**C UNIVERSAL THEME**

*Possible answer: I feel joy when I see a rainbow. It is a feeling I have had since childhood, and it continues today. I will feel the same pleasure in rainbows when I am old; if I cannot, I don't want to live!*

give a dramatic reading of one of the poems or have small groups plan and present a choral reading.

**R RESOURCE MANAGER—Copy Master** Reading Fluency p. 122

**FOR ADVANCED LEARNERS/PRE–AP**

**Synthesize** Wordsworth ends "My Heart Leaps Up" with a statement that includes the expression "natural piety" (line 9). After students have read all three poems in this lesson, come back to this statement. Ask students to write an extended definition of *natural piety* based on details in the three poems. Have students compare their definitions in small groups.

## Analyze Visuals

**Activity** This photograph by Bill Binzen is titled *The Heart of Trees*. Ask students how the image whimsically captures Wordsworth's attitude toward nature. *Possible answer: The heart in the photograph provides a literal window into nature, while the speaker's heart leaps up in response to nature.*

Prereading for this poem is found on page 500.

**D READING POETRY**

*Possible answer: Images such as the sun's relaxed floating toward the horizon (lines 5–8), the "rumpled sea" (line 10), and the sun's rising "like a red flower" (lines 12–16) suggest that the speaker looks at nature with a mix of wonder and joy.*

**E *Model the Skill:* UNIVERSAL THEME**

Help students identify similarities among the themes of the poems:

- joy in and reverence for nature
- sadness or disgust at the idea of rejecting nature in favor of material things

Remind students that Oliver may have read both earlier poems.

*Possible answer: Oliver would likely have found similarities in their work to the way she feels about nature. All want to preserve it and all feel a profound connection with it. This may have inspired her to write a poem about the love of nature, but in her own, modern style.*

## SELECTION WRAP–UP

**READ WITH A PURPOSE** Now that students have read the poems, ask them what images each poet uses to evoke nature. *Possible answers: T'ao: hills and mountains, trees; Wordsworth: a rainbow; Oliver: the sunset/sunrise* Ask: How do these images help the poets achieve their shared purpose? *Possible answer: They are universal images that any reader can imagine and relate to.*

⭐ **CRITIQUE** Have students choose one element of each poet's technique and evaluate its effectiveness.

---

# The SUN
### Mary Oliver

Have you ever seen
anything
in your life
more wonderful

5 than the way the sun,
every evening,
relaxed and easy,
floats toward the horizon

and into the clouds or the hills,
10 or the rumpled sea,
and is gone—
and how it slides again

out of the blackness,
every morning,
15 on the other side of the world,
like a red flower

streaming upward on its heavenly oils,
say, on a morning in early summer,
at its perfect imperial distance—
20 and have you ever felt for anything **D**

such wild love—
do you think there is anywhere, in any language,
a word billowing enough
for the pleasure

25 that fills you,
as the sun
reaches out,
as it warms you

as you stand there,
30 empty-handed—
or have you too
turned from this world—

or have you too
gone crazy
35 for power,
for things? **E**

**D READING POETRY**
Note the **imagery** in lines 5–20. What can you **infer** about the speaker's attitude toward nature from this description of the sun?

**E UNIVERSAL THEME**
List the similarities among the three poems. How might Oliver have been influenced by the other two poems?

---

## DIFFERENTIATED INSTRUCTION

**FOR STRUGGLING READERS**
**Clarify Structure** Mary Oliver presents "The Sun" as a single long sentence. Help students break the poem into the five questions that form its true structure. Have them locate the occurrences of "have you"—the words that introduce questions in lines 1, 20, 31, and 33. Then point out "do you," which signals the question in line 22. Note, too, that the first four questions end with a dash instead of a question mark.

**FOR ADVANCED LEARNERS/PRE–AP**
**Analyze Style** [small-group option] Point out that "The Sun" is an example of free verse. Since the poem lacks rhyme, meter, and a fixed form such as that of a sonnet, the poet must unify ideas using various other methods. Challenge students to analyze how Oliver uses repetition, the sounds of words, and other literary elements to unify ideas in this poem.

## Comprehension

1. **Recall** In "Poem on Returning to Dwell in the Country," what change does the speaker make in his life?

2. **Recall** In "My Heart Leaps Up," what does the speaker wish for?

3. **Summarize** In "The Sun," what does the speaker regard as the most wonderful thing in life?

## Text Analysis

4. **Compare and Contrast** In "Poem on Returning to Dwell in the Country," contrast the speaker's feelings about his former life in the city and his new life in the country. Why does the speaker prefer the country life? Provide evidence from the poem to support your answer.

5. **Interpret Meaning** "My Heart Leaps Up" includes the famous line "The Child is father of the Man." Think about how childhood experiences influence the person one becomes as an adult. What do you think the speaker means?

6. **Make Inferences** What possible influences from the other poems do you see in "The Sun"? Record your answers in a chart like the one shown.

| | Influences in "The Sun" |
|---|---|
| from "Poem on Returning to Dwell in the Country" | |
| from "My Heart Leaps Up" | |

● 7. **Analyze Universal Theme** Record on a piece of paper the theme reflected in each poem. Then come up with a single theme that all three poems share.

8. **Evaluate** In your opinion, which poem makes the strongest statement about the power of nature? Cite evidence to support your choice.

## Text Criticism

9. **Historical Context** England's Romantic poets had a deep reverence for nature. Their work shows an emphasis on imagination, the expression of emotions, and wonder at the world around them. How does Wordsworth's poem reflect this tradition? To what extent do these traits appear in T'ao Ch'ien's and Mary Oliver's poems? Cite evidence to support your answer.

### Where do you go to GET AWAY from it all?

Do you have a special place that is all your own?

COMMON CORE

RL 2 Determine a theme of a text and analyze its development over the course of the text, including how it emerges and is shaped and refined by details. RL 4 Analyze the cumulative impact of specific word choices on meaning and tone. RL 6 Analyze a particular point of view or cultural experience reflected in a work of world literature.

# Practice and Apply

For preliminary support of post-reading questions, use these copy masters:

**R** RESOURCE MANAGER—Copy Masters
Universal Theme p. 117
Question Support p. 121

Additional selection questions are provided for the teacher on page 113.

## ANSWERS

### Comprehension

1. *The speaker leaves his materialistic lifestyle and moves to the country.*

2. *The speaker wishes that he will always rejoice in rainbows and that his days will be linked by devotion to nature.*

3. *The speaker regards the sun, especially sunrises and sunsets, as the most wonderful thing in life.*

### Text Analysis

COMMON CORE RL 2, RL 4, RL 6

*Possible answers:*

4. *The speaker prefers country life for its simplicity (line 15), beauty (lines 21–32), lack of dust and confusion (lines 33–34), leisure (lines 35–36), and freedom (lines 37–40).*

5. *Our childhood experiences and attitudes shape (or should shape) our adulthood.*

6. *From ". . . Country": seeing love of nature in contrast to love for power and material things; From "My Heart . . .": a physical, joyful response to a natural wonder*

7. ● COMMON CORE FOCUS *Analyze Universal Theme Connecting to the natural world provides a simple but powerful joy.*

8. *Students may choose "My Heart Leaps Up" because the speaker would rather die than live untouched by nature.*

## Text Criticism

*Possible answer:*

9. *Wordsworth's poem typifies romanticism by expressing the speaker's love of nature and wonder in its power to move him (lines 1–6). Similarly, T'ao Ch'ien's poem shows the speaker's love of nature, especially in lines 21–32. Oliver's poem also expresses the speaker's deep emotional connection to nature, notably in lines 20–30.*

**Where do you go to GET AWAY from it all?** Students should describe their special places using sensory details.

# Assess and Reteach

## Assess

DIAGNOSTIC AND SELECTION TESTS
Selection Test A pp. 135–136
Selection Test B/C pp. 137–138

**Interactive Selection Test** on <u>thinkcentral.com</u>

## Reteach

**Level Up Online Tutorials** on <u>thinkcentral.com</u>

### COMMON CORE FOCUS

**RL 2** Determine a theme of a text and analyze its development, including how it emerges and is shaped and refined by specific details. **RL 3** Analyze how complex characters develop the theme. **RL 4** Determine the figurative meaning of words and phrases as they are used in a text; analyze the cumulative impact of word choices on meaning. **L 4c** Consult reference materials to find the pronunciation of a word or determine its etymology. **W 2a-c** Introduce a topic; organize complex ideas, concepts, and information; develop the topic with details, quotations, and examples; use appropriate transitions. **W 2f** Provide a concluding statement that follows from the explanation presented. **W 4** Produce clear and coherent explanatory writing in which the organization is appropriate to the purpose and audience. **W 5** Develop and strengthen writing by planning and revising. **W 9a (L 1, 2)** Cite textual evidence; determine a theme of a text.

### SUMMARIES

**"Two Kinds"** Pushed to become a musical prodigy, the narrator rebels. Years later, the narrator accepts the family piano as a sign of her mother's love and forgiveness.

**"Rice and Rose Bowl Blues"** The speaker in this poem is a girl who wants to play football but whose mother wants her to learn to cook.

### How do EXPECTATIONS affect performance?

Explore the question by having small groups complete the *DISCUSS* activity.

---

**Comparing Across Genres**

**Two Kinds**
Short Story by Amy Tan

**Rice and Rose Bowl Blues**
Poem by Diane Mei Lin Mark

HISTORY Video link at thinkcentral.com

*Essential Course of Study* ECOS

VIDEO TRAILER **THINK**central KEYWORD: HML9-506

# How do EXPECTATIONS affect performance?

### COMMON CORE

**RL 2** Determine a theme of a text and analyze its development, including how it emerges and is shaped and refined by specific details. **RL 3** Analyze how complex characters develop the theme. **RL 4** Determine the figurative meaning of words and phrases as they are used in a text; analyze the cumulative impact of specific word choices on meaning. **L 4c** Consult reference materials to find the pronunciation of a word.

Think of a time when someone in authority set a very high goal for you. Perhaps a coach expected you to be the team's top scorer, or a parent expected you to get straight A's. How did you respond to these expectations? Were you motivated to work harder? Did you inwardly rebel?

**DISCUSS** With a small group of classmates, discuss why parents in particular might have high expectations of their children. Record three or more reasons from your discussion and then share them with other groups.

506

---

*See resources on the* **Teacher One Stop DVD-ROM** *and on* **thinkcentral.com**.

HISTORY Video link at thinkcentral.com

**R** **RESOURCE MANAGER UNIT 4**
Plan and Teach, pp. 123–130
Summary, pp. 131–132†‡*
Text Analysis, pp. 133–137†*
Vocabulary, pp. 138–140*

**DIAGNOSTIC AND SELECTION TESTS**
Selection Tests, pp. 139–142

**BEST PRACTICES TOOLKIT**
Word Squares, p. E10
Comparison Matrix, p. A24

**INTERACTIVE READER**

**ADAPTED INTERACTIVE READER**

**ELL ADAPTED INTERACTIVE READER**

**TECHNOLOGY**
- Teacher One Stop DVD-ROM
- Student One Stop DVD-ROM
- PowerNotes DVD-ROM
- Audio Anthology CD
- GrammarNotes DVD-ROM
- Audio Tutor CD
- ExamView Test Generator on the **Teacher One Stop**

**THINK** central

### Video Trailer

Go to **thinkcentral.com** to preview the **Video Trailer** introducing this selection. Other features that support the selection include
- **PowerNotes** presentation
- **ThinkAloud** models to enhance comprehension
- **WordSharp** vocabulary tutorials
- interactive writing and grammar instruction

---

\* Resources for Differentiation     † Also in Spanish     ‡ In Haitian Creole and Vietnamese

## ● TEXT ANALYSIS: THEME ACROSS GENRES

The short story and the poem you are about to read are literary works about young people struggling to be themselves in the face of parental expectations. Each has a specific **theme,** or message, about that topic. The fiction writer and the poet use different techniques to express the theme of the work. The chart shows the techniques each writer uses.

As you read, try to infer the theme of each work by paying attention to the following.

| In the Short Story | In the Poem |
|---|---|
| • details about the main character's traits, motivations, and values | • words and phrases describing the speaker's thoughts and feelings |
| • details about how the characters change and the lessons they learn | • key images |
| • the major internal and external conflicts | • stanzas and lines that present an idea or compare images |
| • information about the setting | • sound devices, such as alliteration and repetition, that may emphasize an idea |
| • the story's title | • the poem's title |

## ● READING STRATEGY: SET A PURPOSE FOR READING

When you **set a purpose for reading,** you establish specific reasons to read a work. For example, your purpose for reading "Two Kinds" and "Rice and Rose Bowl Blues" is to identify the theme of each so that you can compare and contrast them. As you read, think about the important struggles each main character faces. After you read, you will use the **Points of Comparison** chart on page 521 to help you analyze and compare the two selections.

*Review:* Draw Conclusions

## ▲ VOCABULARY IN CONTEXT

Decide whether each word in the list has a positive or a negative connotation, and record your thoughts in your *Reader/Writer Notebook*.

| WORD LIST | debut | fiasco | prodigy |
|---|---|---|---|
| | discordant | lament | reproach |
| | encore | mesmerizing | |

 Complete the activities in your **Reader/Writer Notebook.**

---

## Meet the Authors

### Amy Tan
born 1952

**Late Bloomer**
Like the narrator in "Two Kinds," Amy Tan is the daughter of Chinese immigrants. Raised in the San Francisco Bay area, she spent most of her high school years traveling through Europe with her family after the death of her father and brother. Although she had studied literature and worked as a business writer, Tan did not turn to fiction writing until age 33 when her analyst fell asleep during a session for the third time. At that point, she abandoned therapy in favor of fiction.

**Overnight Success**
After publishing a handful of short stories, Tan came out with *The Joy Luck Club,* a collection of related short stories about four Chinese women friends and their daughters. Critically acclaimed, the book became a bestseller and was made into a movie. Her work has been translated into more than 20 languages, including Chinese.

### Diane Mei Lin Mark

**Maker of Images**
A fifth-generation Chinese American, Diane Mark is a successful writer and filmmaker. She co-produced the film *Picture Bride,* a lyrical depiction of Hawaii's plantation culture in the early 20th century. The film won the Audience Award for Best Dramatic Film at the 1995 Sundance Film Festival.

**Authors Online**
Go to **thinkcentral.com.** KEYWORD: HML9-507

THINK central

---

## Teach

TEXT ANALYSIS
COMMON CORE
RL 2, RL 3

### ● *Model the Skill:* THEME ACROSS GENRES

Remind students to pay attention to meaningful statements made by the main characters. Model by reading aloud this example:

> "You always stick by me," Lisa told Nan. "I don't know what would happen if you treated me like my other so-called friends."

Explain that Lisa's statement might hint at the story's theme or message. It emphasizes the importance of Nan's friendship. This suggests that the story's theme or message is "Friends can make a difference in the worst of times."

**R** RESOURCE MANAGER—Copy Master
Theme Across Genres p. 133

---

READING STRATEGY

### ■ *Model the Skill:* SET A PURPOSE FOR READING

Point out that two selections have been paired. This suggests two key purposes for reading these selections: first, to identify the theme of each, and second, to compare and contrast these themes.

**GUIDED PRACTICE** Ask students to suggest another purpose for reading "Two Kinds."

---

VOCABULARY SKILL
COMMON CORE
L 4

## ▲ VOCABULARY IN CONTEXT

**DIAGNOSE WORD KNOWLEDGE** Have all students complete Vocabulary in Context.

Check their identification of the words' connotations against the following:

**debut** (dā-byōō′) *n.* first public performance or showing

**discordant** (dĭ-skôr′dnt) *adj.* having a disagreeable or clashing sound

**encore** (ŏn′kôr′) *n.* a repeated or additional performance

**fiasco** (fē-ăs′kō) *n.* a complete failure

**lament** (lə-mĕnt′) *v.* to express grief or deep regret

**mesmerizing** (mĕz′mə-rīz′ĭng) *adj.* holding one's attention in an almost hypnotic manner **mesmerize** *v.*

**prodigy** (prŏd′ə-jē) *n.* a person who is exceptionally talented or intelligent

**reproach** (rĭ-prōch′) *n.* blame; criticism

**PRETEACH VOCABULARY** Use the copy master to help students predict meanings for each boldfaced word.

**R** RESOURCE MANAGER—Copy Master
Vocabulary Study p. 138

1. Read item 1 aloud, emphasizing *prodigy*.
2. Invite a volunteer to find the context clue ("her exceptional talent").
3. Ask students to record their ideas.
4. Repeat the procedure for items 2–10.

## READ WITH A PURPOSE

*Help students set a purpose for reading. Explain that this story is about a girl's relationship with her mother. Ask them to monitor how that relationship changes during the course of the story.*

### TEXT ANALYSIS

COMMON CORE — RL 2, RL 3

### Ⓐ THEME

**Possible answer:** *The narrator's mother wants wealth and success for her daughter (lines 3–4). Her aspirations suggest that she is optimistic as well as ambitious.*

**IF STUDENTS NEED HELP . . .** Ask them to find evidence in the story's first paragraph that reveals the mother's longings.

### VOCABULARY

COMMON CORE — L 4

### OWN THE WORD

**prodigy:** Tell students that *prodigy* comes from the Latin word *prodigium*, which described something so wonderful that it was thought to be an omen. When you call someone a *prodigy*, you are indicating that he or she has an unusual gift of some type. Have students list well known or historical figures who are *prodigies*.

---

# *Two* Kinds

## Amy Tan

My mother believed you could be anything you wanted to be in America. You could open a restaurant. You could work for the government and get good retirement. You could buy a house with almost no money down. You could become rich. You could become instantly famous.

"Of course you can be **prodigy**, too," my mother told me when I was nine. "You can be best anything. What does Auntie Lindo know? Her daughter, she is only best tricky."

America was where all my mother's hopes lay. She had come here in 1949 after losing everything in China: her mother and father, her family home, her
10 first husband, and two daughters, twin baby girls. But she never looked back with regret. There were so many ways for things to get better. Ⓐ

We didn't immediately pick the right kind of prodigy. At first my mother thought I could be a Chinese Shirley Temple.[1] We'd watch Shirley's old movies on TV as though they were training films. My mother would poke my arm and say, *"Ni kan"*—You watch. And I would see Shirley tapping her feet, or singing a sailor song, or pursing her lips into a very round O while saying, "Oh my goodness."

*"Ni kan,"* said my mother as Shirley's eyes flooded with tears. "You already know how. Don't need talent for crying!"
20 Soon after my mother got this idea about Shirley Temple, she took me to a beauty training school in the Mission district[2] and put me in the hands of a student who could barely hold the scissors without shaking. Instead of getting big fat curls, I emerged with an uneven mass of crinkly black fuzz. My mother dragged me off to the bathroom and tried to wet down my hair.

"You look like Negro Chinese," she lamented, as if I had done this on purpose.

The instructor of the beauty training school had to lop off these soggy clumps to make my hair even again. "Peter Pan is very popular these days,"

**prodigy** (prŏd'ə-jē) *n.* a person who is exceptionally talented or intelligent

### ❶ Targeted Passage

Ⓐ **THEME**
Reread lines 1–11. What does the narrator's mother want for her daughter? Consider what this suggests about the mother's **character**.

### Analyze Visuals ▶

What do the posture, facial expressions, dress, and printed background suggest about the mother and daughter in this picture? Explain.

---

1. **Shirley Temple:** a popular child movie star of the 1930s.
2. **Mission district:** a residential neighborhood in San Francisco.

**508** UNIT 4: THEME AND SYMBOL

---

## DIFFERENTIATED INSTRUCTION

### FOR ENGLISH LANGUAGE LEARNERS

**Vocabulary Support** Use Word Squares to teach these words: *instructor* (line 27), *quoted* (line 55), *predicting* (line 65), *conduct* (line 165), *layered* (line 239), *assumed* (line 289).

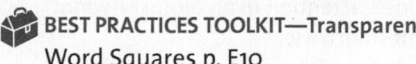 BEST PRACTICES TOOLKIT—Transparency Word Squares p. E10

### FOR STRUGGLING READERS

In combination with the *Audio Anthology CD*, use one or more Targeted Passages (pp. 508, 513, 517, 519) to ensure that students focus on key story events, concepts, and skills. Targeted Passages are also good for English learners.

### ❶ Targeted Passage [Lines 5–14]

This passage establishes the major story elements: the main characters, setting, conflicts, and theme.

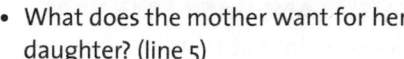

**Reading Support**

This selection on **thinkcentral.com** includes embedded **ThinkAloud** models—students "thinking aloud" about the story to model the kinds of questions a good reader would ask about a selection.

## BACKGROUND

**Confucius's Influence** The primacy of the parent-child relationship has been deeply embedded in Chinese thinking for 2,500 years. In Confucian philosophy, children are duty-bound to care for their parents and, more important, to love and revere them. According to Confucius, filial piety is the most primary of all virtues. Confucianism spread throughout China after Confucius's death in 479 B.C., and has remained linked with the Chinese way of life ever since. In "Two Kinds," Amy Tan explores the relationship between a mother and daughter in the context of Chinese-American culture.

## Analyze Visuals

*Possible answer: The pose and clothing are both traditional, with the daughter standing dutifully by her mother. Both have calm, mysterious expressions. However, there is a hint of mischief and longing in the girl's demeanor, which is neither as stiff nor as formal as her mother's.*

- What does the mother want for her daughter? (line 5)
- When did the mother come to America? (line 8)
- What do you learn about the mother's past? (lines 9–10)
- What do mother and daughter watch on TV together? Why is that important? (lines 12–14)

**FOR ADVANCED LEARNERS/PRE–AP**

**Learn More** Point out that the narrator's mother came to the United States from China shortly after World War II. Interested students can research China's experiences during and after that war and present their findings to the class. Ask them to speculate on the possible connection between the mother's experiences and the war.

## B Model the Skill: THEME

To model recognizing the narrator's conflict, reread lines 39–45. Point out that she is excited about the idea of being a prodigy. Point to the word *But* at the beginning of line 42. Remind students that this word indicates a contradiction of the previous statement. Have students help identify the narrator's other feeling besides excitement (*impatience*).

**Possible answer:** *Although the narrator yearns for her mother's approval and is excited by what her future might hold, she is impatient and insecure about the likelihood of success.*

## C THEME

**Possible answer:** *The narrator fails one impossible test after another (lines 57–58, 63–69). Given her mother's unrealistic expectations, the narrator seems doomed for failure.*

**IF STUDENTS NEED HELP . . .** Analyze the tests that the mother has set up for the narrator by working together to complete a Two-Column Chart. Continue it throughout the story.

| Test | Why It Is Unrealistic |
|---|---|
| national capitals | hasn't studied them |
| finding queen | need to know trick |

 **BEST PRACTICES TOOLKIT**—Transparency Two-Column Chart p. A25

## OWN THE WORD

**reproach:** Tell students that *reproach* is both a noun and a verb. Write in a circle the word and the definition for the noun, "blame, criticism." Have students add synonyms to create a semantic map with nouns and verbs. **Possible answers:** *noun: scolding, rebuke; verb: chide, admonish, reprimand*

---

the instructor assured my mother. I now had hair the length of a boy's, with
30 straight-across bangs that hung at a slant two inches above my eyebrows. I liked the haircut, and it made me actually look forward to my future fame.

In fact, in the beginning, I was just as excited as my mother, maybe even more so. I pictured this prodigy part of me as many different images, trying each one on for size. I was a dainty ballerina girl standing by the curtains, waiting to hear the right music that would send me floating on my tiptoes. I was like the Christ child lifted out of the straw manger, crying with holy indignity. I was Cinderella stepping from her pumpkin carriage with sparkly cartoon music filling the air.

In all of my imaginings, I was filled with a sense that I would soon become
40 *perfect.* My mother and father would adore me. I would be beyond **reproach.** I would never feel the need to sulk for anything.

But sometimes the prodigy in me became impatient. "If you don't hurry up and get me out of here, I'm disappearing for good," it warned. "And then you'll always be nothing." **B**

Every night after dinner, my mother and I would sit at the Formica[3] kitchen table. She would present new tests, taking her examples from stories of amazing children she had read in *Ripley's Believe It or Not,* or *Good Housekeeping, Reader's Digest,* and a dozen other magazines she kept in a pile in our bathroom. My mother got these magazines from people whose houses
50 she cleaned. And since she cleaned many houses each week, we had a great assortment. She would look through them all, searching for stories about remarkable children.

The first night she brought out a story about a three-year-old boy who knew the capitals of all the states and even most of the European countries. A teacher was quoted as saying the little boy could also pronounce the names of the foreign cities correctly.

"What's the capital of Finland?" my mother asked me, looking at the magazine story.

All I knew was the capital of California, because Sacramento was the name
60 of the street we lived on in Chinatown. "Nairobi!"[4] I guessed, saying the most foreign word I could think of. She checked to see if that was possibly one way to pronounce "Helsinki" before showing me the answer.

The tests got harder—multiplying numbers in my head, finding the queen of hearts in a deck of cards, trying to stand on my head without using my hands, predicting the daily temperatures in Los Angeles, New York, and London.

One night I had to look at a page from the Bible for three minutes and then report everything I could remember. "Now Jehoshaphat[5] had riches and honor in abundance and . . . that's all I remember, Ma," I said. **C**

---

3. **Formica** (fôr-mī′kə): a heat-resistant material used on kitchen counters, table tops, and similar surfaces.
4. **Nairobi** (nī-rō′bē): the capital of the African nation of Kenya.
5. **Jehoshaphat** (jə-hŏsh′ə-făt′): a king of the ancient Biblical land of Judah in the ninth century B.C.

**reproach** (rĭ-prōch′) *n.* blame; criticism

**B** THEME
Reread lines 32–44. What are the narrator's conflicting feelings about being a prodigy?

**C** THEME
Reread lines 45–69. How successfully does the narrator perform the tests given by her mother?

---

## DIFFERENTIATED INSTRUCTION

### FOR STRUGGLING READERS

**Comprehension Support** Make a list of the words that the narrator uses to describe herself at different times. Depending on her mood, she felt "sad," "ugly," and "crazed" (lines 74–75), or "angry," "powerful," and "willful" (lines 79–80).

### FOR ENGLISH LANGUAGE LEARNERS

**Culture: Clarify** Point out that the magazines mentioned in lines 47–48 were all popular at the time of the story and some still are today. Also, explain that the "Chinese Shirley Temple" was a real child who performed regularly on *The Ed Sullivan Show* in the 1950s.

70 And after seeing my mother's disappointed face once again, something inside of me began to die. I hated the tests, the raised hopes and failed expectations. Before going to bed that night, I looked in the mirror above the bathroom sink and when I saw only my face staring back—and that it would always be this ordinary face—I began to cry. Such a sad, ugly girl! I made high-pitched noises like a crazed animal, trying to scratch out the face in the mirror.

And then I saw what seemed to be the prodigy side of me—because I had never seen that face before. I looked at my reflection, blinking so I could see more clearly. The girl staring back at me was angry, powerful. This girl and I

80 were the same. I had new thoughts, willful thoughts, or rather thoughts filled with lots of won'ts. I won't let her change me, I promised myself. I won't be what I'm not. **D**

So now on nights when my mother presented her tests, I performed listlessly, my head propped on one arm. I pretended to be bored. And I was. I got so bored I started counting the bellows of the foghorns out on the bay while my mother drilled me in other areas. The sound was comforting and reminded me of the cow jumping over the moon. And the next day, I played a game with myself, seeing if my mother would give up on me before eight bellows. After a while I usually counted only one, maybe two bellows at most.

90 At last she was beginning to give up hope.

Two or three months had gone by without any mention of my being a prodigy again. And then one day my mother was watching The *Ed Sullivan Show*[6] on TV. The TV was old and the sound kept shorting out. Every time my mother got halfway up from the sofa to adjust the set, the sound would go back on and Ed would be talking. As soon as she sat down, Ed would go silent again. She got up, the TV broke into loud piano music. She sat down. Silence. Up and down, back and forth, quiet and loud. It was like a stiff, embraceless dance between her and the TV set. Finally she stood by the set with her hand on the sound dial.

100 She seemed entranced by the music, a little frenzied piano piece with this **mesmerizing** quality, sort of quick passages and then teasing lilting ones before it returned to the quick playful parts.

"*Ni kan,*" my mother said, calling me over with hurried hand gestures, "Look here."

I could see why my mother was fascinated by the music. It was being pounded out by a little Chinese girl, about nine years old, with a Peter Pan haircut. The girl had the sauciness of a Shirley Temple. She was proudly modest like a proper Chinese child. And she also did this fancy sweep of a curtsy, so that the fluffy skirt of her white dress cascaded slowly to the floor

110 like the petals of a large carnation.

---

6. The *Ed Sullivan Show*: a popular television variety show in the 1950s and 1960s.

TWO KINDS **511**

**D THEME**
Reread lines 70–82. What causes the narrator to rebel against her mother? Point out statements that reveal her new insights and provide clues to the theme.

**mesmerizing**
(měz′mə-rīz′ĭng) *adj.* holding one's attention in an almost hypnotic manner **mesmerize** *v.*

---

**TEXT ANALYSIS**  COMMON CORE

**D THEME**  RL 2, RL 3

**Possible answer:** *After being set up for failure, the narrator moves from self-hatred ("Such a sad, ugly girl!," line 74) to rebellion ("The girl staring back at me was angry, powerful. This girl and I were the same. I had new thoughts, willful thoughts, or rather thoughts filled with lots of won'ts," lines 79–81).*

**REVISIT THE BIG QUESTION**
How do
## EXPECTATIONS
affect performance?

Why might the child on the *Ed Sullivan Show* described in lines 100–110 appeal to the mother's expectations for her daughter? **Possible answer:** *Unlike Shirley Temple, this child star is Chinese, and so the mother's expectations for her daughter seem more realistic.*

**VOCABULARY**  COMMON CORE

**OWN THE WORD**  L 4

**mesmerizing:** Read aloud to students the sentence with *mesmerizing*. Point out that the word captures the mother's interest in the piano piece. Have students rewrite the sentence using a synonym for *mesmerizing*. **Possible answer:** *... a little frenzied piano piece with this enchanting quality ...*

---

**FOR ADVANCED LEARNERS/PRE-AP**
**Analyze Figurative Language** [small-group option] Use the Comparison Matrix with students to analyze the similes on this page. Encourage students to discuss how each simile contributes to characterization and to the story's emotional texture.

- "like a crazed animal" (line 75)
- "like a stiff, embraceless dance between her and the TV set" (lines 97–98)
- "like the petals of a large carnation" (line 110)

After discussing the similes, direct students to the metaphor in lines 70–82, and ask what the two faces in the mirror stand for. How do the two faces connect to the title and the theme?

**BEST PRACTICES TOOLKIT—Transparency**
Comparison Matrix p. A24

## Analyze Visuals

**Activity** Ask students how the photograph helps to establish the story's setting. *Possible answer: The TV set helps to date the setting in the 1950s, when most sets showed only black-and-white images and needed attached antennae for reception. The image on the screen is Ed Sullivan himself, striking a typical pose.*

TEXT ANALYSIS

COMMON CORE

RL 2,
RL 3

 **THEME**

*Possible answer: These lines reveal a conflict between the narrator and her mother over the relationship between talent and effort. The mother believes that her daughter is not "the best" (line 129) and not even the best that she could be (lines 148–149) simply because she is not trying hard enough (line 129). Her daughter, on the other hand, believes that she is not and never will be a genius no matter how hard she tries, and that her mother should accept her for who she is (line 145). The mother continues to push her daughter because she equates talent with effort and also because she wants her daughter to achieve her full potential.*

**IF STUDENTS NEED HELP . . .** Ask them to explain why the narrator comes to the defense of the little girl on TV (lines 122–125). Does the narrator believe that she herself deserves credit for trying hard?

VOCABULARY

COMMON CORE

L 4

**OWN THE WORD**

**encore:** Ask students if they have ever been to a concert where the performing group performed an *encore*. What triggered the extra performance? How did the audience react? How did the performers react?

In spite of these warning signs, I wasn't worried. Our family had no piano and we couldn't afford to buy one, let alone reams of sheet music and piano lessons. So I could be generous in my comments when my mother bad-mouthed the little girl on TV.

120 "Play note right, but doesn't sound good! No singing sound," complained my mother.

"What are you picking on her for?" I said carelessly. "She's pretty good. Maybe she's not the best, but she's trying hard." I knew almost immediately I would be sorry I said that.

"Just like you," she said. "Not the best. Because you not trying."

130 She gave a little huff as she let go of the sound dial and sat down on the sofa.

The little Chinese girl sat down also to play an **encore** of "Anitra's Dance" by Grieg.[7] I remember the song, because later on I had to learn how to play it.

Three days after watching *The Ed Sullivan Show*, my mother told me what my schedule would be for piano lessons and piano practice. She had talked to Mr. Chong, who lived on the first floor of our apartment building. Mr. Chong
140 was a retired piano teacher and my mother had traded housecleaning services for weekly lessons and a piano for me to practice on every day, two hours a day, from four until six.

When my mother told me this, I felt as though I had been sent to hell. I whined and then kicked my foot a little when I couldn't stand it anymore.

"Why don't you like me the way I am? I'm *not* a genius! I can't play the piano. And even if I could, I wouldn't go on TV if you paid me a million dollars!" I cried.

My mother slapped me. "Who ask you be genius?" she shouted. "Only ask
150 you be your best. For you sake. You think I want you be genius? Hnnh! What for! Who ask you!"

"So ungrateful," I heard her mutter in Chinese. "If she had as much talent as she has temper, she would be famous now."

**encore** (ŏn'kôr') *n.* a repeated or additional performance

 **THEME**
Examine the **conflict** between the characters as revealed in lines 128–132 and lines 145–152. Why does the mother continue to push her daughter?

---

7. **Grieg** (grēg): Norwegian composer Edvard Grieg (1843–1907).

## DIFFERENTIATED INSTRUCTION

**FOR ENGLISH LANGUAGE LEARNERS**
**Vocabulary: Idioms** Use New Word Analysis to teach these idioms from the story: *bad-mouthed* (line 117), "say something bad about"; *picking on* (line 122), "criticizing"; *couldn't stand it* (line 144), "could not bear or tolerate it"; *get away with* (line 186), "not get punished or blamed for something one did."

 **BEST PRACTICES TOOLKIT—Transparency** New Word Analysis p. E8

**FOR ADVANCED LEARNERS/PRE–AP**
**Evaluate Allusions** [small-group options] Discuss the composers mentioned on pages 512–514: Grieg (line 135), Beethoven (lines 164–165), and Schumann (line 218). Encourage volunteers to research one of these composers and share what they discover about the composer and his music. After they finish the story, have students discuss how Amy Tan uses music history to enrich the story and develop her characters.

Mr. Chong, whom I secretly nicknamed Old Chong, was very strange, always tapping his fingers to the silent music of an invisible orchestra. He looked ancient in my eyes. He had lost most of the hair on top of his head and he wore thick glasses and had eyes that always looked tired and sleepy. But he must have been younger than I thought, since he lived with his mother and was not yet married.

160 I met Old Lady Chong once and that was enough. She had this peculiar smell like a baby that had done something in its pants. And her fingers felt like a dead person's, like an old peach I once found in the back of the refrigerator; the skin just slid off the meat when I picked it up.

I soon found out why Old Chong had retired from teaching piano. He was deaf. "Like Beethoven!" he shouted to me. "We're both listening only in our head!"[8] And he would start to conduct his frantic silent sonatas.

Our lessons went like this. He would open the book and point to different things, explaining their purpose: "Key! Treble! Bass! No sharps or flats! So this is C major! Listen now and play after me!"

And then he would play the C scale a few times, a simple chord, and then, 170 as if inspired by an old, unreachable itch, he gradually added more notes and running trills and a pounding bass until the music was really something quite grand.

I would play after him, the simple scale, the simple chord, and then I just played some nonsense that sounded like a cat running up and down on top of garbage cans. Old Chong smiled and applauded and then said, "Very good! But now you must learn to keep time!"

So that's how I discovered that Old Chong's eyes were too slow to keep up with the wrong notes I was playing. He went through the motions in half-time. To help me keep rhythm, he stood behind me, pushing down on my 180 right shoulder for every beat. He balanced pennies on top of my wrists so I would keep them still as I slowly played scales and arpeggios.[9] He had me curve my hand around an apple and keep that shape when playing chords. He marched stiffly to show me how to make each finger dance up and down, staccato[10] like an obedient little soldier.

He taught me all these things, and that was how I also learned I could be lazy and get away with mistakes, lots of mistakes. If I hit the wrong notes because I hadn't practiced enough, I never corrected myself. I just kept playing in rhythm. And Old Chong kept conducting his own private reverie.

So maybe I never really gave myself a fair chance. I did pick up the basics 190 pretty quickly, and I might have become a good pianist at that young age.

---

8. **Beethoven . . . in our head!** (bā′tō′vən): Ludwig van Beethoven (1770–1827) continued to compose great music even after becoming totally deaf during the last years of his life.

9. **arpeggios** (är-pĕj′ē-ōz′): chords in which the notes are played separately in quick sequence rather than at the same time.

10. **staccato** (stə-kä′tō): producing distinct, abrupt breaks between successive tones.

TWO KINDS    **513**

---

**COMMON CORE** L 4c

**Language Coach**

**Oral Fluency** Certain English letter combinations are pronounced differently in different words. Usually *ch* is pronounced /CH/, as in *cheese*. Sometimes, though, it is pronounced /K/, as in *character*. Reread lines 169–172. Find examples where *ch* is pronounced as /K/ and as /CH/. Use a dictionary to check the pronunciations of the words you find.

② **Targeted Passage**

---

**TIERED DISCUSSION PROMPTS**

Use these prompts to help students understand the narrator's dilemma in lines 163–184:

**Connect** How would you feel if your parents forced you to take unwanted lessons and to practice two hours each day in your free time? What would you do? *Responses should reflect an understanding of the conflicts that such a situation would likely engender.*

**Analyze** The narrator nicknames her piano teacher "Old Chong." What does this nickname suggest about the narrator's attitude? *Possible answer: The nickname suggests that she is not respectful toward her teacher or serious about her lessons.*

**Evaluate** What is your opinion of the narrator's actions? Does she have any alternatives? *Possible answer: The narrator's mother leaves little room for compromise, making rebellion or capitulation her only alternatives.*

---

**FOR STRUGGLING READERS**

② **Targeted Passage** [Lines 185–190]

This passage reflects the narrator's inner conflict: her mixed feelings about fooling Old Chong.

- What does the narrator do when she hits the wrong notes? (lines 186–187)

- What is Old Chong's reaction to the narrator's mistakes? (line 188)

- What does the narrator say she might have become ? (line 190)

---

**FOR ENGLISH LANGUAGE LEARNERS**

**Language Coach**     **COMMON CORE** L 4c

**Oral Fluency** *Answer:* /CH/: *unreachable;* /K/: *chord* Students may find it helpful to keep a running 2-column list of words they encounter with each pronunciation.

##  THEME

*Possible answer: Because her mother's expectations are so high and her demands so unreasonable, the narrator feels helpless and angry, and she rebels by performing poorly at her piano lessons. The narrator's disrespectful treatment of her teacher is a way of getting back at her mother.*

**Extend the Discussion** Why does the narrator say that she practiced "dutifully in my own way" (line 193)?

---

### READING STRATEGY: *Review*

## ⑥ DRAW CONCLUSIONS

*Possible answer: Foolish pride may be one motivation: her mother wants the narrator to outshine Waverly. However, her ambition, optimism, and love also drive her.*

---

### VOCABULARY

COMMON CORE

L 4

## OWN THE WORD

- **discordant:** Point out that when there is *discord* (noun form) between people they often quarrel or clash. In music, *discordant* (adjective form) notes clash and may sound like a musical argument. Have students offer examples of music that is intentionally clashing and *discordant*.

- **lament:** Have students complete this sentence: My aunt *lamented* that her only daughter . . . *Possible answers: failed to make the honor roll at school; did not want to learn to play the piano*

---

But I was so determined not to try, not to be anybody different, that I learned to play only the most ear-splitting preludes,[11] the most **discordant** hymns. ⒡

Over the next year, I practiced like this, dutifully in my own way. And then one day I heard my mother and her friend Lindo Jong both talking in a loud, bragging tone of voice so others could hear. It was after church, and I was leaning against the brick wall wearing a dress with stiff white petticoats. Auntie Lindo's daughter, Waverly, who was about my age, was standing farther down the wall about five feet away. We had grown up together and shared all the closeness of two sisters squabbling over crayons and dolls. In other words,
200 for the most part, we hated each other. I thought she was snotty. Waverly Jong had gained a certain amount of fame as "Chinatown's Littlest Chinese Chess Champion."

"She bring home too many trophy," **lamented** Auntie Lindo that Sunday. "All day she play chess. All day I have no time do nothing but dust off her winnings." She threw a scolding look at Waverly, who pretended not to see her.

"You lucky you don't have this problem," said Auntie Lindo with a sigh to my mother.

And my mother squared her shoulders and bragged: "Our problem worser
210 than yours. If we ask Jing-mei[12] wash dish, she hear nothing but music. It's like you can't stop this natural talent."

And right then, I was determined to put a stop to her foolish pride. ⒢

A few weeks later, Old Chong and my mother conspired to have me play in a talent show which would be held in the church hall. By then, my parents had saved up enough to buy me a secondhand piano, a black Wurlitzer spinet[13] with a scarred bench. It was the showpiece of our living room.

For the talent show, I was to play a piece called "Pleading Child" from Schumann's[14] *Scenes from Childhood*. It was a simple, moody piece that sounded more difficult than it was. I was supposed to memorize the whole
220 thing, playing the repeat parts twice to make the piece sound longer. But I dawdled over it, playing a few bars and then cheating, looking up to see what notes followed. I never really listened to what I was playing. I daydreamed about being somewhere else, about being someone else.

The part I liked to practice best was the fancy curtsy: right foot out, touch the rose on the carpet with a pointed foot, sweep to the side, left leg bends, look up and smile.

---

11. **preludes** (prĕl′yōōdz′): short piano compositions, each usually based on a single musical theme.
12. **Jing-mei** (jĭng′mā′).
13. **Wurlitzer spinet:** Wurlitzer was a well-known manufacturer of organs and pianos, including the small upright piano known as a spinet.
14. **Schumann's** (shōō′mänz′): composed by Robert Schumann (1810–1856), a German composer famous for his piano works.

---

### ⒡ THEME
Why does the narrator intentionally do poorly in her piano lessons?

**discordant** (dĭ-skôr′dnt) *adj.* having a disagreeable or clashing sound

**lament** (lə-mĕnt′) *v.* to express grief or deep regret

### ⒢ DRAW CONCLUSIONS
After overhearing her mother's conversation with Auntie Lindo in lines 203–211, the narrator concludes that "foolish pride" motivates her mother. Based on what you know about the mother so far, do you agree? Explain your answer.

---

## DIFFERENTIATED INSTRUCTION

### FOR STRUGGLING READERS

**Concept Support** Help students to understand how the narrator is feeling when she decides to put a stop to her mother's "foolish pride."

Have students reread the dialogue leading up to her decision (lines 203–212) before asking these questions:

- How does the narrator feel about her piano lessons?

- What does her mother say that is probably untrue?

- How does this untruth make the narrator feel?

- What might the narrator be planning?

---

**Analyze Visuals**

**Activity** This photograph shows San Francisco's Chinatown, the setting of the story. Ask students what aspects of that setting the photograph highlights. **Possible answer:** *The photograph shows that the story takes place in a lively, urban setting with lots of restaurants.*

My parents invited all the couples from the Joy Luck Club[15] to witness my **debut.** Auntie Lindo and Uncle Tin were there. Waverly and her two older brothers had also come. The first two rows were filled with children both
230 younger and older than I was. The littlest ones got to go first. They recited simple nursery rhymes, squawked out tunes on miniature violins, twirled Hula-Hoops,[16] pranced in pink ballet tutus, and when they bowed or curtsied, the audience would sigh in unison, "Awww," and then clap enthusiastically.

When my turn came, I was very confident. I remember my childish excitement. It was as if I knew, without a doubt, that the prodigy side of me really did exist. I had no fear whatsoever, no nervousness. I remember thinking to myself, This is it! This is it! I looked out over the audience, at my mother's blank face, my father's yawn, Auntie Lindo's stiff-lipped smile, Waverly's sulky expression. I had on a white dress layered with sheets of lace, and a pink bow
240 in my Peter Pan haircut. As I sat down I envisioned people jumping to their feet and Ed Sullivan rushing up to introduce me to everyone on TV. **⊕**

And I started to play. It was so beautiful. I was so caught up in how lovely I looked that at first I didn't worry how I would sound. So it was a surprise to me when I hit the first wrong note and I realized something didn't sound quite right. And then I hit another and another followed that. A chill started at the top of my head and began to trickle down. Yet I couldn't stop playing, as though my hands were bewitched. I kept thinking my fingers would adjust themselves back, like a train switching to the right track. I played this strange jumble through two repeats, the sour notes staying with me all the way
250 to the end.

---

15. **Joy Luck Club:** the social group to which the family in this story belongs.
16. **Hula-Hoops:** plastic hoops that are whirled around the body by means of hip movements.

**debut** (dā-byōō') *n.* first public performance or showing

**⊕ THEME**
Reread lines 234–241. What **internal conflict** is revealed by the narrator's expectations of her own performance?

TWO KINDS    **515**

**TEXT ANALYSIS**    COMMON CORE

**⊕ THEME**    RL 2, RL 3

**Possible answer:** *These lines reveal the narrator's internal conflict about being a prodigy: Though she resents her mother's pushing, she longs for the adulation and approval that extraordinary talent would bring her.*

**VOCABULARY**    COMMON CORE

**OWN THE WORD**    L 4

**debut:** Remind students that a *debut* is the first public appearance, and that it usually refers to performers, actors, artists, or musicians. Have students name times they have had *debuts* to showcase their own skills to an audience.

**FOR ENGLISH LANGUAGE LEARNERS**

**Language: Multiple-Meaning Words** Remind students that two words can have the same spelling but different meanings. Use New Word Analysis to teach these multiple-meaning words from the story: *bars* (line 221), *sweep* (line 225), *hit* (line 244), *sour* (line 249).

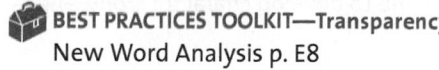 **BEST PRACTICES TOOLKIT—Transparency** New Word Analysis p. E8

**FOR ADVANCED LEARNERS/PRE–AP**

**Analyze Irony** The narrator was determined to put an end to her mother's foolish pride. How is this determination ironic in light of the narrator's surprise during her terrible performance (lines 234–250)? Ask students to write a paragraph explaining their responses.

Use these prompts to help students understand the shame that the narrator caused
herself and her parents in lines 251–288:

**Connect** Think about a time when you were
embarrassed or when you observed someone else's embarrassment. How does that
experience help you understand the narrator's feelings after her terrible performance?
*Answers should demonstrate an understand-
ing of her shame, guilt, and disappointment.*

**Analyze** Why did the narrator suddenly realize how many people were in the audience?
*Possible answer: The jolt of shame shook her
out of her daydream, so she noticed the other
people around her (lines 260–262).*

**Evaluate** The narrator reports that her
mother gave her "a quiet, blank look that
said she had lost everything. I felt the same
way" (lines 279–280). What does she mean?
*Possible answer: She was identifying with her
mother's sense of loss and shame.*

---

**VOCABULARY**   COMMON CORE L 4

### OWN THE WORD

**fiasco:** Ask students to list other words
or phrases that are synonyms for *fiasco*.
Encourage students to think of words
that are colorful or dramatic. *Possible
answers: disaster, complete washout,
catastrophe*

---

When I stood up, I discovered my legs were shaking. Maybe I had just been
nervous and the audience, like Old Chong, had seen me go through the right
motions and had not heard anything wrong at all. I swept my right foot out,
went down on my knee, looked up and smiled. The room was quiet, except for
Old Chong, who was beaming and shouting, "Bravo! Bravo! Well done!" But
then I saw my mother's face, her stricken face. The audience clapped weakly,
and as I walked back to my chair, with my whole face quivering as I tried not
to cry, I heard a little boy whisper loudly to his mother, "That was awful," and
the mother whispered back, "Well, she certainly tried."

260   And now I realized how many people were in the audience, the whole world
it seemed. I was aware of eyes burning into my back. I felt the shame of my
mother and father as they sat stiffly throughout the rest of the show.

We could have escaped during intermission. Pride and some strange sense
of honor must have anchored my parents to their chairs. And so we watched it
all: the eighteen-year-old boy with a fake mustache who did a magic show and
juggled flaming hoops while riding a unicycle. The breasted girl with white
makeup who sang from *Madama Butterfly*[17] and got honorable mention. And
the eleven-year-old boy who won first prize playing a tricky violin song that
sounded like a busy bee.

270   After the show, the Hsus,[18] the Jongs, and the St. Clairs from the Joy Luck
Club came up to my mother and father.

"Lots of talented kids," Auntie Lindo said vaguely, smiling broadly.

"That was somethin' else," said my father, and I wondered if he was
referring to me in a humorous way, or whether he even remembered what I
had done.

Waverly looked at me and shrugged her shoulders. "You aren't a genius like
me," she said matter-of-factly. And if I hadn't felt so bad, I would have pulled
her braids and punched her stomach.

But my mother's expression was what devastated me: a quiet, blank look
280   that said she had lost everything. I felt the same way, and it seemed as if
everybody were now coming up, like gawkers at the scene of an accident, to
see what parts were actually missing. When we got on the bus to go home,
my father was humming the busy-bee tune and my mother was silent. I kept
thinking she wanted to wait until we got home before shouting at me. But
when my father unlocked the door to our apartment, my mother walked in
and then went to the back, into the bedroom. No accusations. No blame. And
in a way, I felt disappointed. I had been waiting for her to start shouting, so I
could shout back and cry and blame her for all my misery.

I assumed my talent-show **fiasco** meant I never had to play the piano again.
290   But two days later, after school, my mother came out of the kitchen and saw
me watching TV.

---

17. *Madama Butterfly:* a famous opera by the Italian composer Giacomo Puccini.
18. **Hsus** (shüz).

---

○ COMMON CORE RL 4

**Language Coach**

**Fixed Expressions** A
preposition at the end
of a verb can change its
meaning. Reread line
261. The phrase "eyes
burning" usually refers
to itchy or irritated
eyes, but "eyes burning
into my back" means
something else. How
does the narrator feel
here?

**fiasco** (fē-ăs′kō) *n.*
a complete failure

---

## DIFFERENTIATED INSTRUCTION

### FOR ENGLISH LANGUAGE LEARNERS

**Language Coach**   COMMON CORE RL 4

**Fixed Expressions** *Possible answer: as
if unfriendly eyes are watching her* Make
sure students understand that she does
not literally feel a burning sensation, but
feels intensely self-conscious.

### FOR ADVANCED LEARNERS/PRE–AP

**Evaluate Dialogue** Many characters make
comments about the narrator's piano performance, but only a little boy (line 258) speaks
with complete honesty, and only her mother,
who is usually talkative, says nothing. Have
students discuss how Amy Tan uses dialogue
in this scene to develop character, irony, and
humor.

"Four clock," she reminded me as if it were any other day. I was stunned, as though she were asking me to go through the talent-show torture again. I wedged myself more tightly in front of the TV.

"Turn off TV," she called from the kitchen five minutes later.

I didn't budge. And then I decided. I didn't have to do what my mother said anymore. I wasn't her slave. This wasn't China. I had listened to her before and look what happened. She was the stupid one.

300 She came out from the kitchen and stood in the arched entryway of the living room. "Four clock," she said once again, louder.

"I'm not going to play anymore," I said nonchalantly. "Why should I? I'm not a genius."

She walked over and stood in front of the TV. I saw her chest was heaving up and down in an angry way.

"No!" I said, and I now felt stronger, as if my true self had finally emerged. So this was what had been inside me all along.

"No! I won't!" I screamed.

She yanked me by the arm, pulled me off the floor, snapped off the TV. She was frighteningly strong, half pulling, half carrying me toward the piano 310 as I kicked the throw rugs under my feet. She lifted me up and onto the hard bench. I was sobbing by now, looking at her bitterly. Her chest was heaving even more and her mouth was open, smiling crazily as if she were pleased I was crying.

"You want me to be someone that I'm not!" I sobbed. "I'll never be the kind of daughter you want me to be!"

"Only two kinds of daughters," she shouted in Chinese. "Those who are obedient and those who follow their own mind! Only one kind of daughter can live in this house. Obedient daughter!" ❶

"Then I wish I wasn't your daughter. I wish you weren't my mother," I 320 shouted. As I said these things I got scared. It felt like worms and toads and slimy things crawling out of my chest, but it also felt good, as if this awful side of me had surfaced, at last.

"Too late change this," said my mother shrilly.

> And I could sense her anger rising to its breaking point. I wanted to see it spill over. And that's when I remembered the babies she had lost in China, the ones we never talked about. "Then I wish I'd never been born!" I shouted. "I wish I were dead! Like them."
>
> It was as if I had said the magic words. Alakazam!—and her face went blank, her mouth closed, her arms went slack, and she backed out of the 330 room, stunned, as if she were blowing away like a small brown leaf, thin, brittle, lifeless.

❶ **THEME**
The **title** of a story is often a clue to its theme. The title of this story comes from the exchange between mother and daughter in lines 314–318. How do the narrator's values differ from her mother's? Cite examples in your answer.

**❸ Targeted Passage**

---

TEXT ANALYSIS ⏣ COMMON CORE · RL 2, RL 3

**❶ THEME**

*Possible answer: The title suggests their conflict in values: The narrator is the kind of daughter who follows her own mind, while her mother expects the other kind, an obedient daughter. This conflict derives in part from cultural differences, as the mother embodies traditional Chinese values that demand reverence for parents, while the daughter has been inculcated with American pride in the individual. At every turn, the narrator's strong will clashes with her mother's demands for obedience.*

**Extend the Discussion** The daughter was born and raised in America, while the mother grew up in China. To what extent are cultural differences responsible for their conflicts?

**REVISIT THE BIG QUESTION**

How do
# EXPECTATIONS
affect performance?

**Discuss** The narrator's mother tells her in lines 316–318 that there are only two kinds of daughters. What does this statement reveal about the mother's expectations? *Possible answer: The statement reveals the fact that the mother is rigid in her expectations; she expects them to be shared and fulfilled without question.*

---

**FOR STRUGGLING READERS**

**❸ Targeted Passage [Lines 324–331]**

This passage reflects the climax of the narrator's conflict with her mother.

- Why does the narrator mention the babies her mother had lost? What does the narrator wish for herself? (lines 325–327)

- How does the mother react to her daughter's words? (lines 328–331)

**FOR ENGLISH LANGUAGE LEARNERS**

**Culture: Connect** Read aloud the word *Alakazam* (line 328), and explain that it is a nonsense word, like *abracadabra*, sometimes used by magicians in fairy tales. Ask volunteers to name similar words in their home languages.

**Activity** The photograph shows an immigrant with portraits of her parents. Ask students what it suggests about how people integrate their past history with their current lives. *Possible answer: The photograph suggests that for many immigrants their hearts and memories are with their home country and its culture. Despite her American clothing, the woman remains connected with the culture of China, where ancestors are honored.*

## TIERED DISCUSSION PROMPTS

Use these prompts to help students understand the narrator's relationship with her mother in lines 332–337:

**Connect** How do you feel about the narrator's mother by this point in the story? Does she still exert a strong influence over her daughter? Should she? Explain. *Accept all reasonable responses.*

**Analyze** What does the narrator mean when she says in lines 336–337, "I did not believe I could be anything I wanted to be. I could only be me"? *Possible answer: The narrator means that she no longer believes she can achieve whatever her mother expects from her simply by trying hard, regardless of her own natural abilities or interests.*

**Synthesize** Why do you think that the narrator falls short of her mother's expectations for her in high school and college? *Possible answer: The narrator rebels against her mother's unrealistic expectations for her as a way of "asserting [her] own will" (line 333). She may also have been trying to punish her mother by deliberately achieving less than she was capable of or by pursuing interests that did not meet her mother's ideas of success.*

It was not the only disappointment my mother felt in me. In the years that followed, I failed her so many times, each time asserting my own will, my right to fall short of expectations. I didn't get straight A's. I didn't become class president. I didn't get into Stanford. I dropped out of college.

For unlike my mother, I did not believe I could be anything I wanted to be. I could only be me.

And for all those years, we never talked about the disaster at the recital or my terrible accusations afterward at the piano bench. All that remained 340 unchecked, like a betrayal that was now unspeakable. So I never found a way to ask her why she had hoped for something so large that failure was inevitable.

And even worse, I never asked her what frightened me the most: Why had she given up hope?

## DIFFERENTIATED INSTRUCTION

### FOR ENGLISH LANGUAGE LEARNERS

**Comprehension: Sequence** Use a Timeline to review key events in the story. Make sure students understand that the narrator's conflicts with her mother (lines 332–341) continue for years after her piano fiasco.

BEST PRACTICES TOOLKIT—Transparency
   Timeline p. B23

### FOR ADVANCED LEARNERS/PRE–AP

**Compare Characters** Throughout the story, the narrator stresses the differences between herself and her mother. Have students work in small groups to discuss how they are alike.

For after our struggle at the piano, she never mentioned my playing again. The lessons stopped. The lid to the piano was closed, shutting out the dust, my misery, and her dreams.

So she surprised me. A few years ago, she offered to give me the piano, for my thirtieth birthday. I had not played in all those years. I saw the offer as a sign of forgiveness, a tremendous burden removed.

350 "Are you sure?" I asked shyly. "I mean, won't you and Dad miss it?"

"No, this your piano," she said firmly. "Always your piano. You only one can play."

"Well, I probably can't play anymore," I said. "It's been years."

"You pick up fast," said my mother, as if she knew this was certain. "You have natural talent. You could been genius if you want to."

"No I couldn't."

"You just not trying," said my mother. And she was neither angry nor sad. She said it as if to announce a fact that could never be disproved. "Take it," she said. **J**

360 But I didn't at first. It was enough that she had offered it to me. And after that, every time I saw it in my parents' living room, standing in front of the bay windows, it made me feel proud, as if it were a shiny trophy I had won back.

Last week I sent a tuner over to my parents' apartment and had the piano reconditioned, for purely sentimental reasons. My mother had died a few months before and I had been getting things in order for my father, a little bit at a time. I put the jewelry in special silk pouches. The sweaters she had knitted in yellow, pink, bright orange—all the colors I hated—I put those in mothproof boxes. I found some old Chinese silk dresses, the kind with little slits up the sides. I rubbed the old silk against my skin, then wrapped them

370 in tissue and decided to take them home with me.

After I had the piano tuned, I opened the lid and touched the keys. It sounded even richer than I remembered. Really, it was a very good piano. Inside the bench were the same exercise notes with handwritten scales, the same secondhand music books with their covers held together with yellow tape.

I opened up the Schumann book to the dark little piece I had played at the recital. It was on the left-hand side of the page, "Pleading Child." It looked more difficult than I remembered. I played a few bars, surprised at how easily

380 the notes came back to me.

And for the first time, or so it seemed, I noticed the piece on the right-hand side. It was called "Perfectly Contented." I tried to play this one as well. It had a lighter melody but the same flowing rhythm and turned out to be quite easy. "Pleading Child" was shorter but slower; "Perfectly Contented" was longer, but faster. And after I played them both a few times, I realized they were two halves of the same song. ✎ **K**

**J DRAW CONCLUSIONS**
In fiction, some characters remain **static,** or don't change, while others are **dynamic,** or change through the course of the story. Reread lines 354–359. Has the mother changed? Explain your answer.

**④ Targeted Passage**

COMMON CORE RL 4

**K DRAW CONCLUSIONS**
A **paradox** is a statement that appears to be a contradiction but reveals some truth. What paradox is expressed in the story's final paragraph? What truth do you find in it?

TWO KINDS  **519**

---

**READING STRATEGY:** *Review*

**J DRAW CONCLUSIONS**

***Possible answer:*** *The mother's attitude toward her daughter hasn't changed, as she still insists that her daughter could have been a genius, if only she had tried (lines 355–357). In offering her daughter the piano, however, she seems to have come to some level of acceptance. This gesture also reflects her enduring love and affection for her child.*

**READING STRATEGY:** *Review*  COMMON CORE RL 4

**K DRAW CONCLUSIONS**

Remind students that a paradox can be true while appearing contradictory. ***Possible answer:*** *The paradox is that the two songs don't seem to go together. Pleading and being contented are different emotional states, and the two songs have different sounds. One might expect "Pleading Child" to be the faster song and "Perfectly Contented" to be slower, but the opposite is the case. This reveals there are two parts to life and we change as we grow, hopefully finding contentment along the way.*

**REVISIT THE BIG QUESTION**

## How do EXPECTATIONS affect performance?

How do the two song titles in lines 377–386 show how the narrator has changed in her response to her mother's expectations? ***Possible answer:*** *At the beginning of the story, the narrator is pleading for her mother's love and acceptance by attempting to meet her expectations. Later in the story, the narrator rebels against those expectations yet is still pleading for her mother to love her for who she is. At the end of the story, the narrator is perfectly contented because her mother's gift of the piano is a peace offering that signals that she does love her for who she is, even though she still believes that her daughter could have met her high expectations if she had tried harder.*

---

**FOR STRUGGLING READERS**

**④ Targeted Passage [Lines 377–386]**

This passage concludes the story with a discovery of two important piano pieces.

- What is the first piece the narrator plays? What does she remember about it? (lines 377–380)
- What is the second piece? What does she notice about it? (lines 381–383)
- What does the narrator conclude after she plays both piano pieces a few times? (lines 385–386)

**FOR ADVANCED LEARNERS/PRE–AP**

**Evaluate Symbols** Have students discuss the symbolic meaning of the Schumann piano pieces.

- How are the two piano pieces like the two kinds of daughters?
- How do the two pieces symbolize the narrator and her conflict with her mother?
- What symbolic resolution do the two pieces provide?

Prereading for this poem is found on page 506.

## Analyze Visuals

**Activity** This photograph shows a rice bowl and chopsticks. Ask students what image they might select to illustrate a poem about their own cultural or family traditions. *Students may mention images of specific types of food, clothing, or ceremonial objects.*

**REVISIT THE BIG QUESTION**

How do
# EXPECTATIONS
affect performance?

**Discuss** What is the significance of Mama's expectation in lines 6–8 that her daughter learn to wash rice? ***Possible answer:*** *Learning to wash rice, a woman's job, signals a coming of age that will usher in new roles and new duties.*

| TEXT ANALYSIS | COMMON CORE |
| --- | --- |
| | RL 2, RL 3 |

 **THEME**

***Possible answer:*** *The text in parentheses reveals that the speaker's heart is still with the players on the football field. The parentheses underscore her need for secretiveness about her true feelings.*

| TEXT ANALYSIS | COMMON CORE |
| --- | --- |
| | RL 2, RL 3 |

 **THEME**

***Possible answer:*** *The speaker's reaction to Roland shows that she feels rebellious and angry about the changes in her life.*

## SELECTION WRAP–UP

**READ WITH A PURPOSE** Ask students to compare and contrast the mother-daughter relationships in the story and the poem. ***Possible answer:*** *In both, the mothers require their daughters to do things that do not interest them. Both the mother and the daughter in "Two Kinds" express their feelings more harshly than the mother and daughter in the poem.*

# RICE
*and*
# ROSE BOWL BLUES

**DIANE MEI LIN MARK**

I remember the day
Mama called me in from
the football game with brothers
and neighbor boys
5 in our front yard

said it was time
I learned to
wash rice for dinner

glancing out the window
10 I watched a pass interception
setting the other team up
on our 20
 *Pour some water*
 *into the pot,*
15  she said pleasantly,
 turning on the tap
 *Rub the rice*
 *between your hands,*
 *pour out the clouds,*
20  *fill it again*
 (I secretly traced
 an end run through
 the grains in
 between pourings)
25 with the rice
settled into a simmer
I started out the door
but was called back

the next day
30 Roland from across the street
sneeringly said he heard
I couldn't play football
anymore

I laughed loudly,
35 asking him
where
he'd heard
such a thing

**THEME**
Reread lines 21–24. What does the text in parentheses tell you about the speaker's feelings and interests? Why do you think the poet used parentheses here?

**THEME**
What can you tell about the speaker's feelings from her reaction to Roland?

## DIFFERENTIATED INSTRUCTION

**FOR STRUGGLING READERS**

**Comprehension Support** Because there are no periods and only minimal capitalization in the poem, students may need help understanding its structure. Read the poem aloud, emphasizing the flow of ideas. Then work with students to divide the poem into sentences by deciding where complete thoughts end and where they continue into the next line or stanza. If necessary, have students "edit" the poem by suggesting where to add periods and capitalization.

**FOR ENGLISH LANGUAGE LEARNERS**

**Culture: Clarify** Point out that the Rose Bowl is a famous college football championship played in California on New Year's Day. Also explain the football terminology *pass interception* (line 10), "a throw that is caught by the other team"; *on our 20* (line 12), "20 yards from our goal."

## Comprehension

1. **Recall** In "Two Kinds," what does the narrator's mother want her to become?

2. **Recall** What does the narrator's mother offer her on her 30th birthday?

3. **Summarize** What can you tell about the character of the speaker in "Rice and Rose Bowl Blues"?

## Text Analysis

4. **Make Inferences** In lines 18–19, Jing-mei's mother says, "You already know how. Don't need talent for crying!" What does her comment reveal about Jing-mei?

5. **Analyze Conflict** In "Two Kinds," why does the narrator's conflict with her mother last so long and become so bitter? Is it ever resolved? Cite evidence from the story to support your answer.

6. **Evaluate Characters** Just like people in real life, characters in fiction can behave in ways that surprise you. However, authors still attempt to create credible, or believable, characters. Do you find the characters of Jing-mei and her mother to be credible? Why or why not? Support your answers with details from the text.

7. **Analyze Gender Roles** In "Rice and Rose Bowl Blues," how does gender play a role in the tension between the speaker and her mother? Use evidence from the poem to support your answer.

## Comparing Across Genres

Now that you have read both selections about parental expectations, you are ready to identify each writer's **theme**, or message. The **Points of Comparison** chart will help you get started.

| Points of Comparison | In the Short Story | In the Poem |
|---|---|---|
| How would you describe the main conflict? | | |
| What lesson does the narrator or the speaker learn? | | |
| What idea does the title emphasize? | | |
| Write a sentence stating the theme as you interpret it. | | |
| Which techniques are important in conveying the theme? | | |

### How do EXPECTATIONS affect performance?

What best motivates you to succeed?

---

### COMMON CORE

**RL 2** Determine a theme of a text and analyze its development, including how it emerges and is shaped and refined by specific details. **RL 3** Analyze how complex characters develop the theme.

---

# Practice and Apply

For preliminary support of post-reading questions, use these copy masters:

**R** RESOURCE MANAGER—Copy Masters
Reading Check p. 141
Theme Across Genres p. 133
Question Support p. 142

Additional selection questions are provided for teachers on page 127.

## ANSWERS

## Comprehension

1. *The narrator's mother wants her to be "the best"—in other words, a prodigy or a genius.*

2. *The narrator's mother offers her the family piano on her 30th birthday.*

3. *The speaker is a self-assured tomboy and a reluctantly obedient daughter.*

## Text Analysis

COMMON CORE RL 2, RL 3

*Possible answers:*

4. *Jing-mei cries frequently.*

5. *The mother's unrealistically high expectations make failure likely, and her unwillingness to compromise gives the daughter reason to feel bitter. Even after the piano fiasco, the conflict continues as mother and daughter fight this same battle through high school and college (lines 332–335). A resolution comes with the gift of the piano, which represents the mother's love, the only kind of acceptance she can offer.*

6. *Yes; I have friends who have similar relationships with their mothers. In the story, Jing-mei's mother pushes her to excel, and some of my friends' mothers push my friends in much the same way.*

7. *The speaker's mother has gender-specific expectations that clash with the speaker's interests and create tension between the two of them. When forced to stop playing football for a cooking lesson, the speaker's heart is still with her football team.*

## Comparing Across Genres

*Possible answers:*

**Main Conflict: Short Story** *The mother's expectations conflict with the daughter's desire to be herself.* **Poem** *The mother's expectations conflict with the daughter's wish for freedom.*

**Lesson: Short Story** *The narrator learns that*

---

her mother loves her despite disappointments. **Poem** *The speaker learns that she can find ways to claim her freedom.*

**Title: Short Story** *It emphasizes the conflicts between the obedient daughter and the willful daughter.* **Poem** *It emphasizes the conflict between traditional female roles and the freedom of childhood.*

**Theme: Short Story** *Unrealistic expectations create bitterness.* **Poem** *Expectations don't always stifle treasured freedoms.*

**Techniques: Short Story** *figurative language, humor, contrasts* **Poem** *alliteration, metaphor*

### How do EXPECTATIONS affect performance?

Suggest that students think about their proudest accomplishments, then consider what forces motivated them to achieve those accomplishments.

## ANSWERS

## Vocabulary in Context

▲ VOCABULARY PRACTICE

1. *no; an early bloomer*
2. *your dog's death*
3. *knocking over a bookcase*
4. *feel bad*
5. *a rerun*
6. *blaring car horns*
7. *a shiny toy*
8. *excited*

### ACADEMIC VOCABULARY IN WRITING

**Possible answer:** *The narrator's mother does have some personal pride connected to her daughter's success, but that's not her most **significant** motivation. She is not asking her daughter to be perfect, but to be the best she can be.*

### VOCABULARY STRATEGY: WORD ORIGINS

1. *Adolphe Sax (1814–1894) invented the saxophone.*
2. *Charles C. Boycott (1832–1897) was an English land agent who refused to lower his rents.*
3. *Joel R. Poinsett (1799–1851) discovered this tropical American flower.*
4. *Frankfurt, Germany, is a city known for smoked sausage.*
5. *Bedlam Hospital of St. Mary of Bethlehem, London, was an infamous insane asylum.*
6. *General Henry Shrapnel (1761–1842) invented artillery shells that contained metal balls.*
7. *Tangier, Morocco, in North Africa produces this orange citrus fruit.*
8. *George W. G. Ferris (1859–1896) invented this amusement park ride.*

**R** RESOURCE MANAGER—Copy Master
Vocabulary Strategy p. 140

**Interactive Vocabulary**

Keywords direct students to a **WordSharp** tutorial on **thinkcentral.com** or to other types of vocabulary practice and review.

---

## Vocabulary in Context

▲ VOCABULARY PRACTICE

Answer the questions to show your understanding of the vocabulary words.

1. Is a **prodigy** considered a late bloomer?
2. Which would you be more likely to **lament**—your dog's death or an A on a test?
3. Which might be a **fiasco**—enjoying a vacation or knocking over a bookcase?
4. Would a **reproach** cause someone to rejoice or feel bad?
5. If a television show is an **encore** presentation, is it a new program or a rerun?
6. Which are **discordant** sounds—blaring car horns or softly rippling waves?
7. Which might be **mesmerizing** to a child—a newspaper or a shiny toy?
8. If someone is making a **debut**, is he or she likely to be excited or bored?

**WORD LIST**
debut
discordant
encore
fiasco
lament
mesmerizing
prodigy
reproach

### ACADEMIC VOCABULARY IN WRITING

• context • interpret • reveal • significant • tradition

The narrator **interprets** her mother's expectations in a negative way, thinking her mother expects too much. Write a paragraph in which you discuss whether you think the narrator's interpretation is correct or incorrect. Use at least one Academic Vocabulary word in your response.

### VOCABULARY STRATEGY: WORD ORIGINS

Words that derive from the names of people or places are called **eponyms.** For example, the vocabulary word *mesmerizing* (the present participle of *mesmerize*) comes from the name Franz Mesmer, an Austrian doctor who popularized hypnotism. The etymology in the dictionary entry of an eponym will help you understand the term's origin.

**COMMON CORE**

**L 4c** Consult reference materials to determine a word's etymology.

> **mes•mer•ize** (mĕz′mə-rīz′) *tr.v.* **-ized, -iz•ing, -iz•es 1.** To spellbind; enthrall.
> **2.** To hypnotize. [After Franz Mesmer, Austrian physician, 1734–1815.]

**PRACTICE** Use an unabridged dictionary to identify the person or place from which each word derives. Then write a brief explanation of the connection.

1. saxophone
2. boycott
3. poinsettia
4. frankfurter

5. bedlam
6. shrapnel
7. tangerine
8. Ferris wheel

**Interactive Vocabulary**

Go to **thinkcentral.com**.
KEYWORD: HML9-522

---

## DIFFERENTIATED INSTRUCTION

### FOR ENGLISH LANGUAGE LEARNERS

**Vocabulary: Word Origins** Invite students to share eponyms from their languages and to explain the origins of each word.

### FOR ADVANCED LEARNERS/PRE–AP

**Vocabulary Research** Have students further investigate one of the eponyms. Ask them to report their findings to the class.

## Writing for Assessment

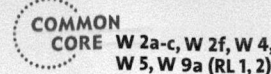

COMMON CORE
W 2a–c, W 2f, W 4, W 5, W 9a (RL 1, 2)

### 1. READ THE PROMPT

In writing assessments, you will often be asked to **compare and contrast** the themes in works of different genres. You are now going to practice writing an essay that requires this type of focus.

> The conflict between parents and children is an age-old problem, explored here by Amy Tan and Diane Mei Lin Mark. In Tan's story "Two Kinds," what is the theme expressed by the mother-daughter struggle? What is the theme of Mark's poem "Rice and Rose Bowl Blues"? In a three- or four-paragraph essay, explore how their messages are similar or different. Do you think the similarities have anything to do with culture? Support your analysis with evidence.

◀ **STRATEGIES IN ACTION**

1. I have to state the **theme** of each work.
2. I need to **compare and contrast** the themes.
3. I need to consider the **genre** of each work as I look for evidence of the themes I've identified.
4. I need to include **details and quotations** from each work.

### 2. PLAN YOUR WRITING

- Review the **Points of Comparison** chart you created on page 521.
- Decide whether the themes are basically similar or markedly different.
- Using your chart, find examples to use as evidence for the points you develop in your essay. If necessary, review the texts again to identify more examples.
- Create an outline to organize your ideas. You may want to discuss each text separately and then compare them, or you may choose to discuss each point of comparison in its own paragraph.

> I. Conflict
>   A. Tan piece
>   B. Mark piece
>
> II. Lesson learned
>   A. Tan piece
>   B. Mark piece

### 3. DRAFT YOUR RESPONSE

**Introduction** Introduce the topic—parental expectations—and then explain that you will discuss what the two works say about it. Include the titles and authors of the texts.

**Body** State and explain Amy Tan's theme in the second paragraph and Diane Mei Lin Mark's in the third. In a fourth paragraph, compare the two themes.

**Conclusion** Wrap up your essay with a final thought about parental expectations.

**Revision** Check your use of transitional words and phrases to connect ideas within and between paragraphs. Words and phrases such as *likewise, both,* and *in the same way* signal similarities. *On the other hand, however, in contrast,* and *nevertheless* signal differences.

TWO KINDS / RICE AND ROSE BOWL BLUES    **523**

### FOR STRUGGLING WRITERS

- Help students find two quotations that give clues to the theme from each text.
- Suggest that students highlight the introduction, body, and conclusion in their outlines.
- Review students' statements of theme from their **Points of Comparison** charts.
- Limit the length of the assignment to no more than four paragraphs.

## Writing for Assessment

COMMON CORE  W 2a-c, W 2f, W 4, W 5, W 9a (RL 1, 2)

### 1. READ THE PROMPT

Review with students how different features of a story or poem give clues to its theme. Remind them that characters, conflict, and symbols support the theme.

### 2. PLAN YOUR WRITING

- After students have reviewed the Points of Comparison chart on page 521, ask them to write a statement or two that compares and contrasts the themes in the two texts.
- Have students look at the outline on this page. Remind them that one way to organize an essay is to use a point-by-point organization that compares and contrasts the two texts. They can also organize their essay by comparing and contrasting the texts in separate paragraphs, using a subject-by-subject organization.
- Have students determine which organization suits their purpose and have them create an outline for their essay.

### 3. DRAFT YOUR RESPONSE

Ask students to check their outlines to make sure they allow for an introduction, body, and conclusion. Point out that they can identify in their outlines where they will plug in quotes from each work.

## Assess and Reteach

### Assess

**DIAGNOSTIC AND SELECTION TESTS**
  Selection Test A, B/C, pp. 139–140, 141–142

**Interactive Selection Test** on **thinkcentral.com**

### Reteach

**Level Up Online Tutorials** on **thinkcentral.com**

**Reteaching Worksheets** on **thinkcentral.com**
  Literature Lesson 12: Theme

# Focus and Motivate

## COMMON CORE FOCUS

**W 2a–e** Write informative/explanatory texts to examine complex ideas clearly and accurately through the effective selection, organization, and analysis of content. **W 4** Produce clear and coherent writing. **W 5** Develop and strengthen writing as needed by planning, revising, editing, rewriting, or trying a new approach. **W 9b (RI 1)** Draw evidence from literary nonfiction to support analysis. **W 10** Write routinely over shorter time frames for a range of tasks, purposes, and audiences. **L 1b** Use various types of clauses to convey specific meanings and add variety and interest. **L 2** Demonstrate command of the conventions of standard English capitalization, punctuation, and spelling.

## WRITE WITH A PURPOSE

Recommend that students select essays that they enjoy reading. Suggest that students cut apart copies of essay paragraphs. Students may cut the paragraphs into individual sentences. Then, they may cut the sentences into phrases and clauses and even single words. Tell students to begin lists of descriptors regarding the author's word choice, sentence structure, and so on. This will help students focus on style elements rather than content.

## COMMON CORE TRAITS

Review the *COMMON CORE TRAITS* with students, focusing primarily on the development of ideas and the organization of ideas. Compare the list of traits with the rubric on page 532.

## ADDITIONAL TASKS

**Write to the Author** Write a letter to the author of a literary nonfiction text commenting on the effect of the author's style choices. **Possible subjects:** "The Future in My Arms," "Math and After Math," or another essay

**Write to a Fan** Write an e-mail to a fan of a particular author of literary nonfiction, commenting on the effect of the author's style choices. **Possible subjects:** "The Future in My Arms," "Math and After Math," or another essay

### Writing Online

The following tools are available online at **thinkcentral.com** and on **WriteSmart CD-ROM:**
- Interactive Graphic Organizers
- Interactive Student Models
- Interactive Revision Lessons

---

## Writing Workshop
**INFORMATIVE TEXT**

*Essential Course of Study* **ECOS**

# Analysis of Literary Nonfiction

Every author—whether writing truth or fiction—makes choices about the way he or she conveys information. These style choices affect the meaning of the text and the understanding of readers. In this workshop, you will write an **analysis of literary nonfiction** as a way of understanding the effects of an author's choices.

Complete the workshop activities in your **Reader/Writer Notebook.**

### WRITE WITH A PURPOSE

**WRITING TASK**

Choose an essay, and write a **literary analysis.** Your analysis should help the audience understand one element of the author's style and its effects on readers.

**Idea Starters**
- Edwidge Danticat's sentence structure in "The Future in My Arms"
- Lensey Namioka's word choice in "Math and After Math"
- an author's tone in an essay you find inspiring, funny, or sad

**THE ESSENTIALS**

Here are some common purposes, audiences, and formats for literary analysis.

| PURPOSES | AUDIENCES | FORMATS |
|---|---|---|
| • to better understand a work of literary nonfiction and explain it to others<br>• to examine how a writer uses language to affect readers | • classmates and teacher<br>• author<br>• Internet users | • essay for class<br>• e-mail to an author<br>• blog for people interested in the author or the subject matter of essay<br>• message-board posting |

### COMMON CORE TRAITS

**1. DEVELOPMENT OF IDEAS**
- presents an **engaging introduction**
- develops a **controlling idea** that offers an **analysis** of the author's style
- supports main points of analysis with **relevant details** and **quotations from the text**
- concludes with a **summary of main points** and **insights**

**2. ORGANIZATION OF IDEAS**
- **organizes** ideas in a logical way
- uses varied **transitions** to create **cohesion** and **connect ideas**

**3. LANGUAGE FACILITY AND CONVENTIONS**
- establishes and maintains a **formal style** and **objective tone**
- includes **precise language**
- uses **commas** correctly
- employs correct **grammar, mechanics,** and **spelling**

**Writing Online**

Go to **thinkcentral.com**.
KEYWORD: HML9N-524

---

## Writing Workshop Resources

**RESOURCE MANAGER UNIT 4**

Plan and Teach pp. 145–148
Prewriting–Editing pp. 149–153
Writing Rubric p. 154
Speaking and Listening p. 155
Writing Support p. 156*

**BEST PRACTICES TOOLKIT**

Writing Template: Informative Essay pp. C16, C29

**TECHNOLOGY**

 **Teacher One Stop DVD-ROM**
**Student One Stop DVD-ROM**
**WriteSmart CD-ROM**
**GrammarNotes DVD-ROM**

**Writing Center on thinkcentral.com**

*See resources on the **Teacher One Stop** DVD-ROM and on **thinkcentral.com**.*

\* Resources for Differentiation

## Planning/Prewriting

 **COMMON CORE** **W 2a-e** Write informative/explanatory texts to examine complex ideas clearly and accurately through the effective selection, organization, and analysis of content. **W 5** Develop and strengthen writing as needed by planning.

### Getting Started

#### CHOOSE AN ESSAY FOR ANALYSIS

Choose an essay for analysis. Once you define the purpose of the essay, you can better examine how a writer achieves a particular effect through **style**—his or her unique way of expressing ideas. To begin, use a graphic organizer to identify your overall impression of the essay, as well as its effect on you as a reader. This step enables you to understand *what* the writer has done before discussing *how* he or she does it.

#### ▶ WHAT DOES IT LOOK LIKE?

*Essay:* "The Future in My Arms"

*Purpose:* to describe the impact of her niece Nadira's birth on Danticat's life and family

| My Overall Impression | Effect on Reader |
|---|---|
| • Danticat wants to protect her niece. <br>• Danticat feels responsible for her niece. | For Danticat, past, present, and future are combined in caring for and protecting one's family. |

#### THINK ABOUT AUDIENCE AND PURPOSE

As you begin to analyze the essay, keep in mind your own **purpose** for writing. In this case, it is to help your **audience** understand the effects of the author's style. Identify a specific audience for your writing, such as the writer, fans of the writer, or people interested in the subject matter of the essay. Understanding your audience will in turn help you form appropriate ideas for your essay.

#### ▶ ASK YOURSELF:

- Who is my audience? What do I want people to understand about the essay?
- What stylistic elements might have the strongest impact on my audience?
- What **domain-specific,** or specialized, vocabulary will my audience need to know in order to understand my analysis?

#### IDENTIFY STYLISTIC ELEMENTS

Now, consider how the writer uses stylistic elements, such as repetition or allusion, to achieve particular effects on readers. Use another graphic organizer to list examples of stylistic elements that you noticed as you read the essay. Then, choose the element that affected you most. Ask yourself: How does the author's use of this element affect the meaning or message of the essay? Jot down your thoughts in your graphic organizer.

#### ▶ WHAT DOES IT LOOK LIKE?

| Element | Examples |
|---|---|
| (Listing) | • "new sounds around her, all the laughter, the wild comparisons with relatives"<br>• "to hold her, to cradle her … to watch her … to read her lines"<br>• "wars, a depression, a holocaust, a new civil rights struggle" |
| Allusions | repozwa, Sonia Sanchez, African proverb |

*Effect of Listing:* Combines past (family history), present (birth) and future (wars, depression, and so on)—stopping time to protect niece.

---

## Teach

### Planning/Prewriting **COMMON CORE W 2a-e, W 5**

▶ **CHOOSE AN ESSAY FOR ANALYSIS**
Remind students that authors write for a variety of purposes: to persuade, inform, entertain, describe, or explain. Make sure that students understand that an author's purpose will directly affect the style choices he or she makes. For example, if Danticat's purpose is to describe, readers may expect to find sensory details or figurative language in the essay.

▶ **THINK ABOUT AUDIENCE AND PURPOSE**
Make sure that students understand that their purpose for writing is to explain. They will explain the effects of an author's style choices. Remind them that they are explaining cause-and-effect relationships. An author's style choice causes a particular effect on readers.

▶ **IDENTIFY STYLISTIC ELEMENTS** Once students have identified a stylistic element to analyze, it may help them to use cause-and-effect graphic organizers to explore the effects of these devices. For example: *Cause: Danticat's lists > Effect: link past, present, and future in single moment*

🧰 **BEST PRACTICES TOOLKIT—Transparencies**
Cause-and-Effect Chain p. B39

Ⓡ **RESOURCE MANAGER—Copy Masters**
Planning/Prewriting p. 149
Drafting p. 150
Revising and Editing pp. 151–152
Ask a Peer Reader p. 153
Rubric p. 154
Writing Support p. 156

---

### DIFFERENTIATED INSTRUCTION

#### FOR ENGLISH LANGUAGE LEARNERS
**Language: Reinforce Terms** Write these terms on the board and review them with students:

- *analysis:* the expression of a writer's understanding of a textual work
- *literary nonfiction:* a written work that contains an explanation

- *stylistic effect:* the resulting beauty based on the way an author uses language to express his or her ideas
- *elements of style:* the language elements an author uses to express his or her ideas

## Planning/Prewriting *continued*

▶ **DEVELOP A CONTROLLING IDEA**
Provide students with frames to help them develop their controlling idea:

- In [title of essay], [author of essay]'s [stylistic element] has (have) the effect of _____.

Make sure that students understand that they can make changes to the frame as necessary to suit their needs.

▶ **ORGANIZE YOUR IDEAS** After students have written their controlling ideas, tell them to write two or three reasons that their controlling ideas are true. Each of these reasons can be developed into a body paragraph. Once students' reasons are listed, tell them to select an order for presenting these reasons. If they follow the order of the original text, they are using sequential order.

▶ **PROVIDE EVIDENCE FROM THE TEXT** Have students select at least one quotation from the original essays for each idea or reason they will present. Under each quotation, tell students to write why the quotation explains the reason or idea it will support. For example: *The baby—born in the present—brings back to life the relatives who have passed with her expressions or facial features.*

 **YOUR TURN** As students work to analyze an author's style choices, remind them to pose questions. For example, *Why does Danticat include a series of lists in her essay? How do people usually use lists? Does Danticat use lists in this way, or does she create a new purpose for her lists?* The strategy of asking and answering self-generated questions will help students better understand the work of literary nonfiction and their reaction to it.

---

## Planning/Prewriting *continued*

### Getting Started

**DEVELOP A CONTROLLING IDEA**
Your **controlling idea,** or thesis statement, should identify the effect of the author's stylistic element. Continue modifying or reworking this statement as you draft.

▶ **WHAT DOES IT LOOK LIKE?**

*In "The Future in My Arms," Danticat's lists have the effect of suspending time.*

**ORGANIZE YOUR IDEAS**
Think about how you can present your ideas to achieve your purpose and make your analysis clear to the audience. You will want to organize your ideas in a **logical** and **cohesive** way. For example, you can discuss examples of a single stylistic element in the **sequence** in which they appear in the essay.

▶ **WHAT DOES IT LOOK LIKE?**

*Sequential Order*
1. *Past becomes the present*
   *family's past and birth of niece happen at same time*
2. *Future becomes the present*
   *Nadira's birth and future happen at the same time*

**PROVIDE EVIDENCE FROM THE TEXT**
Every point you make about the author's style must be supported with well-chosen evidence, including **concrete details** and **quotations** from the text. Your evidence should be **relevant,** or related, to your controlling idea and **sufficient** enough to help your audience understand your analysis.

▶ **WHAT DOES IT LOOK LIKE?**

1. *Past becomes the present*
   *"relatives living and gone, all so very present in her face"*
2. *Future becomes the present*
   *"wars, a depression, a holocaust, a new civil rights struggle"*

**PEER REVIEW** Describe to a peer the purpose and audience for your analysis. Then, ask: What is my main point? Which statements should be supported with more evidence from the text? If your statements cannot be sufficiently supported, revisit and rework them.

**YOUR TURN** In your *Reader/Writer Notebook*, develop your writing plan. Create charts and outlines such as those on pages 525–526 to choose and then analyze an element of style. Consider the following questions as you analyze the effect of this stylistic element:

- Why does the author choose to use this particular element?
- How does this element affect readers?
- How does this element relate to the purpose and structure of the work?

---

## DIFFERENTIATED INSTRUCTION

### FOR ENGLISH LANGUAGE LEARNERS
**Outline Frame** To help students plan their responses, provide them with annotated outline frames:

**I. Introduction**

**A.** What idea will get readers interested in your thesis statement? _____

**B.** Controlling idea: _____

**II. Body**

**A.** Reason or idea #1: _____

**B.** Supporting quotation: _____

**C.** Explanation of relationship between reason/idea and quotation: _____

(Repeat structure for idea #2 and beyond)

**III. Concluding Section**

**A.** Restatement of controlling and main ideas: _____

**B.** Final thought: _____

### FOR STRUGGLING WRITERS
**Use Quotations** Review how to incorporate quotations into students' writing using quotation marks, colons, ellipses, and commas.

# Drafting

The following chart shows a structure for organizing a clear and coherent literary analysis.

 **COMMON CORE** W 9b (RI 1) Draw evidence from literary nonfiction to support analysis. W 4 Produce clear and coherent writing. L 1b Use various types of clauses to convey specific meanings and add variety and interest.

## Organizing Your Literary Analysis

**INTRODUCTION**
- Begin with an engaging **question** or a **comment** to help the audience connect to the topic.
- Identify the **author** and **title** of the essay.
- Provide a **controlling idea** that describes the effects of a stylistic element.

▼

**BODY**
- Introduce relevant **textual evidence**, such as **quotations** and **concrete details**, to illustrate the controlling idea.
- Use **precise language** to explain the **effect** of each example from the text. If necessary, define any **domain-specific vocabulary**, such as literary terms.
- Organize your essay in a logical **sequence**, and use **varied transitions** to connect related ideas.
- Maintain a **formal style** and **objective tone** by avoiding contractions and biased language.

▼

**CONCLUDING SECTION**
- Summarize the **main ideas** of your analysis.
- Offer an overall **insight** about the author's style and its effects on readers.

### GRAMMAR IN CONTEXT: RESTRICTIVE AND NONRESTRICTIVE RELATIVE CLAUSES

To provide readers with additional information, you can insert a relative clause. Relative clauses begin with relative pronouns: *that, when, where, which, who, whom, whose,* and *why.*

Use a **restrictive relative clause** to state information that is essential to sentence meaning. Use a **nonrestrictive relative clause** to state information that is not essential to sentence meaning.

| Type of Relative Clause | Example |
|---|---|
| Restrictive Relative Clause ▶ | *It begins to seem as if all of these actions are possible in this one moment for this little girl* **who brings the past into the present with her face:** *"relatives living and gone, all so very present in her face."* |
| Nonrestrictive Relative Clause ▶ | *This listing creates momentum,* **which stops the flow of time.** |

 **YOUR TURN**  Develop a draft of your analysis by following the structure above. Use restrictive and nonrestrictive relative clauses to add information to your sentences.

## FOR ENGLISH LANGUAGE LEARNERS

**Restrictive and Nonrestrictive Clauses** Write the following phrases and clauses on separate sentence strips: *It begins to seem as if all of these actions are possible in this one moment for this little girl; who brings the past into the present with her face; "relatives living and gone, all so very present in her face"; This listing creates momentum; which stops the flow of time.* Have volunteers hold the strips to form sentences without the restrictive and nonrestrictive clauses. Make sure that students understand that these sentences are complete.

Then, have additional volunteers place the restrictive and nonrestrictive clauses into the sentences. Discuss how each of these clauses adds information to the sentences.

## FOR STRUGGLING WRITERS

**Relative Clauses** Place a variety of complete sentences in one box and a variety of relative clauses in another box. Have students take turns drawing one entry from each box and forming sentences. Have the class identify whether each relative clause is restrictive or nonrestrictive and why.

---

# Practice and Apply

## Drafting

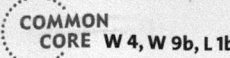 **COMMON CORE** W 4, W 9b, L 1b

▶ **INTRODUCTION** Make sure that students understand that the introduction to a literary analysis serves the same purpose as the introduction to any other type of writing: get readers interested in reading. Tell students to identify the real subject of their controlling ideas, which is *lists* in the case of the Student Draft. Then, have students experiment with ways to introduce these topics to readers.

▶ **BODY** Post a bank of cause-and-effect transition words for students to consult as they draft:

- *as, because, consequently, due to, for, since, so, therefore*

▶ **CONCLUDING SECTION** Make sure that students understand that the concluding section should do more than simply summarize main points. It should offer readers something about which to think as they finish reading. Writers should ask themselves this question: What do I want my readers thinking about at the end of my essay?

### GRAMMAR IN CONTEXT: RESTRICTIVE AND NONRESTRICTIVE RELATIVE CLAUSES

For additional practice, have students add restrictive and nonrestrictive clauses to the following sentences.
- The baby girl holds the hopes of her family.
- The relatives feel responsible for the baby's future.

 **YOUR TURN**  Ask students to complete the Your Turn activity independently. Remind students to use restrictive and nonrestrictive clauses to add details to their writing. Suggest that students write their drafts double-spaced so that they can make revisions easily later.

For interactive revision tools, see

🖉 **Write*Smart* CD-ROM**

**Writing Center on <u>thinkcentral.com</u>**

## Revising

**Model the Skill** Using a draft literary analysis on a transparency or electronic whiteboard, model how to use the questions, tips, and strategies suggested in the chart to evaluate and revise. You might use the response of a student from another class or from a previous year. Make sure to remove the student's name from the story so that the writer remains anonymous.

**YOUR TURN** During peer review, remind students that it is not the job of a partner to solve a writer's problems. It is the job of a partner to point out where a writer's ideas have gone astray. Nevertheless, a good partner is certainly willing to brainstorm possible solutions with a writer. Ultimately, however, the responsibility for revising or rewriting lies with the writer.

For interactive revision tools, see

⊘ **WriteSmart CD-ROM**

**Writing Center** on **thinkcentral.com**

---

## Revising

As you revise, determine whether you've achieved your purpose and effectively communicated your ideas to the intended audience. The questions, tips, and strategies in the following chart will help you revise, rewrite, and improve your draft.

### LITERARY ANALYSIS

| Ask Yourself | Tips | Revision Strategies |
|---|---|---|
| 1. Does the introduction grab readers' interest? | ▶ **Underline** the opening question or comment. | ▶ **Add** a question or comment about the subject of the essay to engage the audience. |
| 2. Does the controlling idea identify the effect of one specific stylistic element? | ▶ **Put check marks** above the element and its overall effect. | ▶ **Elaborate** on your controlling idea by describing a stylistic element and interpreting its effect. |
| 3. Are examples presented in sequential order with clear and varied transitions between related ideas? | ▶ **Number** the examples in the order in which they appear in the essay. **Circle** the transitional words that clarify relationships among ideas. | ▶ **Rearrange** examples as necessary to achieve sequential order. **Add** varied transitions to connect ideas as needed. |
| 4. Is each idea supported by relevant and sufficient textual evidence? | ▶ **Draw a line** from each quotation or detail to the idea it supports. | ▶ **Add** quotations or details as necessary so that you have at least one piece of supporting evidence per idea. |
| 5. Do I maintain a formal style throughout the analysis? | ▶ **Bracket** contractions, casual slang, or informal language. | ▶ **Reword** text to avoid contractions. **Replace** instances of informal language with precise, formal words. |
| 6. Does the concluding section summarize key ideas and provide an insight into the effect of the author's style? | ▶ **Place stars** above each key idea listed in the concluding section. **Circle** the insight. | ▶ **Add** a summary of main ideas or a statement that articulates the connection between the author's style and its effect. |

**YOUR TURN**

**PEER REVIEW** Exchange your analysis with a partner, or read it aloud to your partner. As you read and comment on the essays, make sure to focus on textual evidence and quotations. Discuss whether the writer effectively supports his or her controlling idea. If necessary, provide concrete suggestions for improvement or reworking, using the revision strategies in the chart.

---

## DIFFERENTIATED INSTRUCTION

### FOR STRUGGLING WRITERS

**Organization** Help students make copies of their drafts, and provide them with chart paper. Tell students to cut apart their drafts, pasting their controlling ideas at the tops of their charts. Then, have students paste under their controlling ideas any ideas or sentences from their drafts that explain their controlling ideas. Tell students that any remaining sentences or ideas should be deleted from their responses or revised to make connections to the controlling ideas clear.

### FOR ADVANCED LEARNERS/PRE–AP

**Revision** Have students sketch out new organizational plans for their drafts. Ask students to consider whether these new plans improve the original plans and why. Ask students to respond to the following questions in the form of journal writing: Is there a logic to how your supporting evidence is organized? Do you want to begin or end with your strongest point and why? Tell students to revise their drafts as necessary based on these self-studies.

## ANALYZE A STUDENT DRAFT

Read this draft; notice the comments on its strengths as well as suggestions for improvement.

**COMMON CORE**

**W 5** Strengthen writing as needed by revising, editing, rewriting, or trying a new approach, focusing on addressing what is most significant for a specific purpose and audience.

### Listing in Edwidge Danticat's "The Future in My Arms"
by Malik Smith, Kingwood High School

**❶**     Do you ever make lists? Of course you do! What is the purpose of these lists? Often, people make lists because they want to remember things. In "The Future in My Arms," writer Edwidge Danticat makes lists as she describes meeting her newborn niece for the first time. Danticat's lists may help her remember that moment, but they also have the effect of suspending time. It is as if all aspects of Nadira's past, present, and future are captured in the moment of her birth.

**❷**     When she holds her niece for the first time, Danticat is overwhelmed by the emotion of a bridegroom who waits to hold his bride. She wants to perform many actions during this one moment in time as she meets her niece for the first time: "to hold her, to cradle her . . . let her tiny head rest . . . to watch her . . . to read her lines . . . a glance, a touch, a picture. . . ." This listing creates momentum, which stops the flow of time. It begins to seem as if all of these actions are possible in this one moment for this little girl who brings the past into the present with her face: "relatives living and gone, all so very present in her face."

> The **introduction** includes an unexpected question and identifies the author and the work. The **controlling idea** identifies the effect of a style element.

> Malik supports a main idea about the effect of author's style with relevant **quotations** from the text. However, his essay will be more compelling if he eliminates wordiness.

**LEARN HOW**   **Eliminate Wordiness**   The goal of analytical writing is to make ideas clear for readers. However, writers can sometimes over-explain a point, resulting in wordiness. As Malik edits his essay, he finds a place where he can revise his style to make his ideas clearer.

#### MALIK'S REVISION TO PARAGRAPH ❷

When she holds her niece for the first time, Danticat is overwhelmed by the emotion of a bridegroom who waits to hold his bride. ~~She wants to perform many actions during this one moment in time as she meets her niece for the first time:~~ *She wants many things at once:* "to hold her, to cradle her . . . let her tiny head rest . . . to watch her . . . to read her lines . . . a glance, a touch, a picture. . . ."

---

## ANALYZE A STUDENT DRAFT

Explain that the Student Draft on this page is the first half of a literary analysis. Model reading the draft and the annotations in blue, explaining that the yellow highlighting illustrates the student's language choices. Explain that the following *Learn How* mini-lessons provide helpful information about ways to improve this student draft as well as students' own drafts.

**LEARN HOW**   **Eliminate Wordiness**

Provide students with the following tips for eliminating wordiness:

- delete empty words such as *really*, *a lot*, and *very*
- replace adverbs with stronger verbs and adjectives
- use synonyms to avoid repetition
- revise sentences that are difficult to read aloud
- review sections that were difficult to write for unnecessary words

---

### FOR ENGLISH LANGUAGE LEARNERS

**Language Partners** Wordiness may also result from writing in a non-native language as students work to express complex ideas with unfamiliar language constructions. Have students work with native English speakers to revise their drafts for wordiness.

### FOR STRUGGLING WRITERS

**Revise for Wordiness** Have students work with partners to revise the following sentences to eliminate wordiness:

- Completing the essay by Monday is an impossibility without some kind of reduction in other assignments.
- Mrs. Smith, who teaches accounting, suggested during a staff meeting the requirement of accounting classes for all students who plan to graduate from high school.
- The study method that is most successful and useful requires students to spend one hour each evening in review of previously taught concepts.

## ANALYZE A STUDENT DRAFT *continued*

Explain that the Student Draft is continued and completed on this page. Read the draft and annotations aloud and discuss. Ask students to comment on the student writer's observation regarding the ultimate effect of the author's use of a list.

**❸** Danticat who serves as a representative of the family adds things to her list that the family will give Nadira: "baby-sitting favors . . . giant teddy bears . . . handfuls of flowers . . . the crooks of our arms and necks and laps . . . a refuge." With these gifts, Danticat "imagine[s] a life for Nadira," creating the future in the present. These items represent not a mere list of things, but the keys to that future.

**❹** Danticat finishes her list: "wars, a depression, a holocaust, a new civil-rights struggle . . . colonization of new planets, genetic cloning, new forms of slavery." Again, Danticat uses the list to make the future part of the present. This list, however, reflects the negative possibilities that might one day dim the brightness of this moment.

**❺** As Danticat hands Nadira back to her parents, the list ends, and the normal flow of time resumes. Nadira is left with years rather than moments to grow through the items on Danticat's list. Danticat's essay "The Future in My Arms" now takes on the function of a traditional list—something that will remind both Danticat and Nadira of Danticat's promises.

> Malik offers an **analysis of the author's style.**

> Malik uses **restrictive clauses** to add information to his sentences. He can also add **prepositional phrases** to provide the audience with details.

> Malik concludes with an **insightful observation** regarding the effect of the author's style.

**LEARN HOW** Add Prepositional Phrases Prepositions are combined with other words to form prepositional phrases. These phrases show relationships between words in a sentence. Use prepositional phrases to add important details that will help your audience better understand your analysis.

| Preposition Word Bank |
| --- |
| about, across, after, along, among, around, at, before, between, beyond, but, by, despite, during, except, for, from, in, into, like, near, of, on, out, outside, over, past, since, throughout, to, toward, until, upon, with, within |

**MALIK'S REVISION TO PARAGRAPH ❹**

with her worries for Nadira's future

Danticat finishes her list: "wars, a depression, a holocaust, a new civil-rights struggle . . . colonization of new planets, genetic cloning, new forms of slavery."

 **YOUR TURN** Use the feedback from your peers and teacher as well as the two "Learn How" lessons to revise your essay. Evaluate how well you have analyzed the effect of the author's style and addressed the audience by examining your controlling idea, evidence, and quotations.

### LEARN HOW   Add Prepositional Phrases

- Tell students that they can use prepositional phrases to indicate time, place, or direction.
- They can also use prepositional phrases to introduce objects.
- Additionally, they can utilize prepositional phrases to show spatial relationships.
- Explain that when students use prepositional phrases to begin sentences, the phrases should be followed by commas.

 **YOUR TURN** Ask students to complete the Your Turn activity independently. Remind students to add prepositional phrases to illuminate relationships between words.

For interactive revision tools, see

⊘ **Write***Smart* CD-ROM

**Writing Center on thinkcentral.com**

## DIFFERENTIATED INSTRUCTION

**FOR ENGLISH LANGUAGE LEARNERS**

**Understand Prepositions** Provide pairs of students with boxes and toy or paper animals. Tell students to construct sentences using prepositional phrases to describe possible relationships between the box and the animal. For example, *the mouse ran across the box.* Invite students to present some of their sentences to the class.

**FOR STRUGGLING WRITERS**

**Make a Chart** Have pairs of students create five-column charts. Tell students to label the columns as follows: time, place, direction, object, and spatial relationship. Instruct students to write three sentences for each column using prepositional phrases to indicate the assigned relationships. Before students begin working, provide them with a sample sentence for each category. Have students present their charts to the class.

# Editing and Publishing

COMMON CORE

W 5 Strengthen writing by editing.
L 2 Demonstrate command of the conventions of standard English capitalization, punctuation, and spelling.
L 2c Spell correctly.

In the editing stage, you proofread your essay to rid it of grammar, usage, and punctuation errors. You also should read your essay slowly and carefully to correct any lingering misspelled words that your word-processing spell-check did not catch. With these final steps, you prepare your essay for public appearance.

## GRAMMAR IN CONTEXT: COMMAS WITH NONRESTRICTIVE PHRASES AND CLAUSES

When you use a nonrestrictive phrase or clause to add nonessential information to a sentence, use commas to set off the phrase or clause from the rest of the sentence. The commas provide a cue for the reader that what comes after the comma is additional information.

If you are not sure whether the phrase or clause is nonrestrictive, read the sentence aloud without it. If the shortened version of the sentence doesn't make sense, then the information is essential and should not be set off from the rest of the sentence by commas. If the shorter version maintains its basic meaning, though, the information is not essential and should be set off from the rest of the sentence by commas.

> This listing creates momentum, *which stops the flow of time.*

As Malik edits his essay, he realizes he has incorrectly punctuated a nonrestrictive clause.

> *Danticat, who serves as a representative of the family, adds things to her list that the family will give Nadira: "baby-sitting favors . . . giant teddy bears . . . handfuls of flowers . . . the crooks of our arms and necks and laps . . . a refuge."*

## PUBLISH YOUR WRITING

Share your analysis with others in one of the following ways:
- Organize a panel discussion in which you and a group of classmates talk about your interpretations of the essay.
- Submit your essay as part of an application to an academic program.
- Post a blog for people interested in the subject matter of the essay.
- Send your essay to a school newspaper or Web site.

**YOUR TURN** Correct any errors in your essay. Check your use of restrictive and nonrestrictive relative clauses, and make sure that all nonrestrictive phrases and clauses are set off with commas. Then, publish your final essay for your audience.

---

## FOR ENGLISH LANGUAGE LEARNERS
**Understand Commas** Discuss with students the following examples:
- Danticat has two nieces who are babies.
- Danticat has two nieces, who are babies.

In the first example, Danticat has more than two nieces—two of whom are babies while the others are not. In the second example, Danticat has only two nieces who happen to be babies.

## FOR STRUGGLING WRITERS
**Nonrestrictive Phrases and Clauses** Explain to students that they can create nonrestrictive

clauses and phrases in reference to possession, subjects, or objects. Present the following examples:
- **Possession:** Edwidge Danticat, **whose** works are well-regarded, is the author of the essay.
- **Subject:** Nadira, **who** is born into a rich cultural tradition, claims the hearts of her family members.
- **Object:** The hospital, **which** is near the end of the avenue, is Nadira's birthplace.

---

# Editing and Publishing

COMMON CORE W 5, L 2, L 2c

## GRAMMAR IN CONTEXT: COMMAS WITH NONRESTRICTIVE PHRASES AND CLAUSES

Tell students that the relative pronoun *that* may not be used to introduce a nonrestrictive phrase or clause. The other relative pronouns may be used as follows:
- people: *who, whom, whose*
- things/ideas: *which*
- places: *where*
- times: *when*
- reasons: *why*

Point out that Malik uses nonrestrictive clauses in reference to an idea and a person.

## PUBLISH YOUR WRITING

Brainstorm with students additional ways to publish their essays.

**YOUR TURN** Allow students time to proofread their drafts. Remind them to use commas to indicate nonrestrictive phrases and clauses. This strategy tells readers that the information is not essential to the meaning of the sentence.

## Scoring Rubric

Tell students that the best way to understand a scoring rubric is to use it to score actual writing. Ask students to work with partners to evaluate each other's literary analyses. For each point on the scoring rubric, tell students to write examples from the essays to support their scores. Point out that students can use these notes to revise their essays before submitting them for official scoring. The purpose of a rubric is to eliminate subjectivity from the scoring process.

For Rubric Bank, see

 **Write*Smart* CD-ROM**

**Writing Center on thinkcentral.com**

## Assess and Reteach

### Assess

 RESOURCE MANAGER—Copy Masters
Rubric for Evaluation p. 154

**Online Essay Scoring at thinkcentral.com**

### Reteach

**Level Up Online Tutorials at thinkcentral.com**

**Reteaching Worksheets on thinkcentral.com**

Writing Lesson 3: Thinking About Purpose, Audience, and Form

Writing Lesson 21: Integrating Quotations

## Scoring Rubric

Use the rubric below to evaluate your literary analysis from the Writing Workshop or your response to the on-demand task on the next page.

### LITERARY ANALYSIS

| SCORE | COMMON CORE TRAITS |
|---|---|
| 6 | • **Development** Has an engaging introduction; includes a controlling idea with an insightful analysis of the author's style; supports main points with relevant evidence; ends powerfully<br>• **Organization** Arranges ideas in an effective, logical order; uses varied transitions to create cohesion and link ideas<br>• **Language** Consistently maintains a formal style; uses precise language; shows a strong command of conventions |
| 5 | • **Development** Has an effective introduction; provides a controlling idea that offers an original analysis of the author's style; supports main points with evidence; has a strong concluding section<br>• **Organization** Arranges ideas logically; uses transitions to link ideas<br>• **Language** Maintains a formal style; uses precise language; has minimal errors |
| 4 | • **Development** Has an introduction that could be more engaging; includes a controlling idea that states an analysis of the author's style; could use some more evidence; has an adequate concluding section<br>• **Organization** Arranges ideas logically; could vary transitions more<br>• **Language** Mostly maintains a formal style; needs more precise language at times; has a few distracting errors in conventions |
| 3 | • **Development** Has an adequate, though not memorable, introduction; has a controlling idea that makes an obvious statement about the author's style; lacks sufficient support; has a routine concluding section<br>• **Organization** Reflects flaws in organization; needs transitions to link related ideas<br>• **Language** Frequently lapses into an informal style; uses some vague word choices; has some significant errors in conventions |
| 2 | • **Development** Has a weak introduction and a controlling idea that does not relate to the writing task; lacks specific evidence; has a weak concluding section<br>• **Organization** Has organizational flaws; lacks transitions throughout<br>• **Language** Uses an informal style and vague language; has many errors in conventions |
| 1 | • **Development** Has no introduction or controlling idea; offers unrelated evidence; ends abruptly<br>• **Organization** Includes a string of disconnected ideas with no overall organization<br>• **Language** Uses an inappropriate style and vague, tired language; has major problems with grammar, mechanics, and spelling |

# Preparing for Timed Writing

COMMON CORE

**W 10** Write routinely over shorter time frames for a range of tasks, purposes, and audiences.

## 1. ANALYZE THE TASK — 5 MIN

Read the task carefully. Then, read it again, noting the words in the task that tell the type of writing, the topic, the audience, and the purpose.

> **WRITING TASK**
>
> *Type of writing/Topic* → "It takes a village to raise a child." –African Proverb *Purpose*
>
> Write an <u>analysis of this quotation</u> by <u>explaining the meaning of the quotation and offering specific examples</u> from works you have read or experiences from your life that illustrate the idea presented in the quotation. You will give your essay as a gift to a <u>parent, guardian, or another important adult in your life.</u> ← *Audience*

## 2. PLAN YOUR RESPONSE — 10 MIN

First, paraphrase the quotation by stating it in your own words. A paraphrase is generally longer than the original text. Then, list examples from your reading or experiences that support or explain the paraphrase.

| | |
|---|---|
| Paraphrase of Quotation | |
| Supporting Example #1 | |
| Supporting Example #2 | |
| Supporting Example #3 | |

## 3. RESPOND TO THE TASK — 20 MIN

Begin drafting your analysis of the quotation. Start with an engaging question or comment to grab your audience's attention. As you write, keep these points in mind:

- In the introduction, include a controlling idea, or thesis statement, that explains your overarching analysis of the quotation.
- In the body, present concrete details from your reading or your own experiences that support the controlling idea.
- In the concluding section, provide an insightful comment regarding the responsibility of a community in raising its children.

## 4. IMPROVE YOUR RESPONSE — 5–10 MIN

**Revising** Check your draft against the writing task. Do you offer an analysis of the quotation? Do you support that analysis with concrete details? Do you end with an insightful comment about the subject matter?

**Proofreading** Find and correct any errors in grammar, usage, and mechanics. Make sure that your analysis and any edits are neatly written and legible.

**Checking Your Final Copy** Before you submit your analysis, examine it once more to make sure that you are presenting your best work.

---

## Preparing for Timed Writing

COMMON CORE W 10

1. **Analyze the Task** Before students begin writing, encourage them to answer the following questions:
   - What is my time limit?
   - What are the key skills assessed in the scoring rubric?
   - Who is my audience?
   - What is my purpose?

2. **Plan Your Response** Point out to students that the scoring rubric emphasizes supporting main points of analysis with relevant evidence. Make sure that students understand that once they paraphrase the proverb, they need to list examples from texts or their own experiences that prove that the proverb is true.

3. **Respond to the Task** Remind students that an analysis is focused on a strong controlling idea. Tell students that they can use their paraphrases of the proverb to develop their controlling idea. For example, the ancient Africans believed that everyone in a community must contribute to the development and well-being of a child. This belief is as true today as it was in ancient Africa.

4. **Improve Your Response** Point out that the scoring rubric emphasizes a powerful conclusion. To engage readers, a concluding section must do more than summarize main points or restate the controlling idea. It must offer readers a final comment that they may apply to their own lives. Suggest that students use this question to develop and revise their conclusions: What is the reader's responsibility in raising the children of the community?

## Assess

Use the Scoring Rubric on p. 532 to assess students' literary analyses.

---

# DIFFERENTIATED INSTRUCTION

## FOR ENGLISH LANGUAGE LEARNERS

**Paraphrasing** Help students paraphrase the proverb by asking questions and having students brainstorm responses.

- What are other words for *village*?
- Who makes up a village?
- What does it mean to raise a child?
- What responsibilities are involved in raising a child?
- Who generally fulfills these responsibilities?

Model for students how to use their responses to write a paraphrase of the proverb. Then, have students write their own paraphrases.

## FOR STRUGGLING WRITERS

**Prepare to Write** Before students begin the timed writing, have them freewrite for five minutes about the people who have helped raise them. Tell students to consider whether or not anyone beyond their family members have aided in this process. Suggest that students may use these ideas as they develop their responses to the timed-writing prompt.

# Focus and Motivate

**SL 1a-d** Participate effectively in collaborative group discussions. **SL 4** Present information, findings, and supporting evidence clearly, concisely, and logically such that listeners can follow the line of reasoning.

## SPEAK WITH A PURPOSE

Help students identify purposes for their panel discussions. Write this question on the board: Why do people gather to discuss important topics of interest? Ask students to respond to this question. Record students' ideas on the board. Make sure that students understand that such discussions help people analyze information to improve understanding and decide on courses of action.

## COMMON CORE TRAITS

As students prepare to hold their discussions, remind them to keep in mind the *COMMON CORE TRAITS* of a strong panel discussion.

# Practice and Apply

## Planning the Discussion

### Model the Skill: PREPARE DISCUSSION NOTES

Use a transparency to model for students how to prepare notes as they think about and re-search topics for their discussions by suggest-ing the following categories of information:

- **Facts:** *who, what, when, where,* and *why*
- **Causes and Effects:** Who or what caused the event? What are the effects?
- **Questions:** What questions do I have about the causes or effects?

**GUIDED PRACTICE** As students prepare their notes, suggest that they consult newspapers.

**R** RESOURCE MANAGER—Copy Master
Speaking and Listening p. 155

---

**Speaking & Listening Workshop**

*Essential Course of Study* **ECOS**

# Participating in a Panel Discussion

If you wrote about the same essay as some of your classmates, you might have chatted about your analysis and even quoted evidence from the text to bolster your ideas. That's an example of an informal **panel discussion,** in which well-informed participants thoroughly analyze a topic. In fact, you join a panel discussion each time you talk with friends about a book, movie, or sporting event. When you have a group conversation on a topic of interest, you are participating in a panel discussion.

Complete the workshop activities in your **Reader/Writer Notebook.**

| SPEAK WITH A PURPOSE | COMMON CORE TRAITS |
|---|---|
| **TASK** | **PARTICIPANTS IN A STRONG PANEL DISCUSSION . . .** |
| Participate in a **panel discussion** based on an analysis of a recent school or community event. (This may require some research.) | • follow rules that result from peer discussion<br>• present relevant information supported by evidence or logical inferences<br>• respond thoughtfully to diverse perspectives and justify their own views<br>• speak clearly with appropriate speed, volume, and pronunciation<br>• listen, take notes, ask questions, and evaluate ideas |

**SL 1a-d** Participate effectively in collaborative group discussions. **SL 4** Present information, findings, and supporting evidence clearly, concisely, and logically such that listeners can follow the line of reasoning.

## Planning the Discussion

Informal discussions are governed by rules of politeness. While these same rules may guide a formal discussion, participants in a formal setting also need formal rules to keep the discussion on track. Keeping in mind the purpose, audience, and context for this panel discussion, follow these suggestions to plan the discussion.

- **Identify Panel Members** Form groups of about five members based on the events you want to analyze. As a group, select a date and time for your panel discussion and decide on the specific information that participants must gather or research for the discussion.

- **Appoint a Moderator** Panel members should ask for a volunteer or appoint one student from another panel to moderate each discussion. The moderator will propel the conversation by posing, redirecting, and clarifying questions; making connections among stated ideas; summarizing important points; and enforcing the rules.

- **Set Goals for the Discussion** Discuss with the moderator the goals for your discussion. Does your panel wish to reach some consensus as a result of its discussion, such as a decision or a statement of the panel's position? Or does your panel want to summarize points of agreement and disagreement? Decide as a group how the panel will achieve these goals, such as by taking a vote or by giving each member the chance to voice a final opinion.

**Speaking & Listening Online**
**THINK** central
Go to **thinkcentral.com.**
KEYWORD: HML9-534

---

## DIFFERENTIATED INSTRUCTION

### FOR ENGLISH LANGUAGE LEARNERS
**Language: Reinforce Discussion Terms**
Explain to students that participating in a panel discussion has the same goal as writing a literary analysis—to analyze or interpret a topic. Review key terms used in this Work-shop:

- *panel:* a multiple-meaning word that in this case means "a group of persons selected for a specific purpose, such as discussing a topic"

- *moderator:* person who presides over a formal discussion

- *consensus:* opinion held by all or most of a group of people

- *forum:* place for discussion

- **Create Rules for the Discussion** Participants should come to a consensus on rules such as the following: speak clearly and concisely; listen respectfully without interrupting; ask thoughtful questions; and avoid arguing or going off on tangents.
- **Prepare Discussion Notes** After you complete your research, jot down your main ideas and supporting evidence regarding your analysis of the current event. Use these notes during the discussion.

## Holding the Discussion

### LET'S GET TALKING

A well-run discussion is an excellent forum for participants to build on each other's ideas. This process helps all participants clarify and elaborate their understandings of the topic.

- **Get Started** The moderator should identify the topic, introduce the panelists, and state the goals for the discussion. For example, he or she might say, "Our goal today is to identify and analyze the effects of the new school rules."
- **State Your Ideas** Respond to the questions posed by the moderator with appropriate speaking volume, speed, and enunciation. Present your claim first, followed by your most compelling and logical reasons and evidence. You want to make sure listeners can follow your points.
- **Give Others the Opportunity to Respond** Listen while another speaker summarizes your ideas and adds his or her own viewpoint. Evaluate the reasons and evidence presented, and then decide whether this new information changes or modifies your opinion.
- **Be Respectful** Take notes that summarize, synthesize, or highlight other participants' ideas, and wait for your turn to share the comments you've jotted down. Respond thoughtfully to other perspectives.
- **Wrap It Up** Summarize your points of agreement and disagreement for the panelists and the audience.

**As a Panel Speaker** Make sure to speak clearly and pointedly. Use questions posed by the moderator and other panelists to make adjustments to your argument.

**As a Listener** As a member of the panel, pay attention to each speaker's analysis. Listen carefully to make sure you can follow the ideas and evidence, and ask questions for clarification and elaboration.

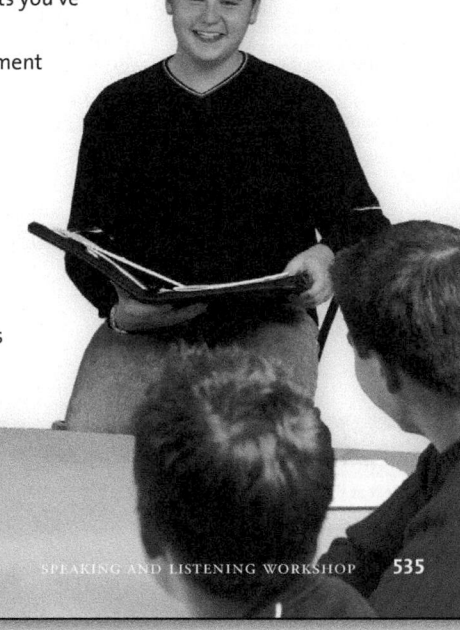

SPEAKING AND LISTENING WORKSHOP **535**

### FOR STRUGGLING STUDENTS

**Use Details** Work with students to help them select topics for their discussions that are familiar, such as a football game or a homecoming dance. By selecting such topics, students will avoid the need for significant research. Ask students to brainstorm a list of reasons why they enjoy the particular activity they have chosen. Have students choose three reasons from the list and explain each to a partner. Encourage the listening partner to ask questions to elicit more detail. Then, have students explain their reasons a second time, adding details and increasing specificity in their explanation.

## Holding the Discussion

### Model the Skill: BE RESPECTFUL

Use a transparency to model for students how to use a colored pen to add notations to discussion notes during a panel discussion. Point out that during the course of a discussion, you may add alternative points of view and additional questions. These notes will help panelists think through and plan their responses, which will aid them in maintaining respectful behavior.

**GUIDED PRACTICE** Have students work with partners to practice listening to a speaker, waiting for the final word to be uttered, and then using hand gestures to signal that they would like to respond. Students may practice these skills by stating ideas from their notes.

**YOUR TURN** Using students' discussion notes, have students work with partners to rehearse stating their ideas with appropriate speed, volume, and enunciation. Remind students to use respectful tones when responding to another panelist's ideas. Ask partners to provide speakers with feedback.

## Assess and Reteach

### Assess

Use the **COMMON CORE TRAITS** to assess students' panel discussions.

A participant in a strong panel discussion
- follows rules for discussion
- presents relevant information, evidence, and logical inferences
- responds thoughtfully to diverse perspectives and justifies his or her own views
- speaks clearly and pointedly
- listens, takes notes, asks questions, and evaluates ideas

### Reteach

Some students may have trouble summarizing the ideas of others and adding their own thoughts. Provide students with sentence starters:

*You're saying that _____ I agree that _____. However, I think that _____ because _____.*

# Assessment Practice

## COMMON CORE FOCUS

**RL 2** Determine a theme of a text and analyze its development over the course of the text.
**RI 2** Determine a central idea of a text and analyze its development over the course of the text.
**W 5** Strengthen writing by revising and editing to ensure that it demonstrates the conventions of standard English grammar and spelling. **L 1b** Use various types of clauses. **L 4a** Use context as clue to the meaning of a word or phrase. **L 4c** Consult reference materials to determine a word's precise meaning. **L 6** Demonstrate independence in gathering vocabulary knowledge.

## CHECK READINESS

Read aloud the paragraph under **ASSESS** and stress to students that this is not the full Unit Test, but a way for them to check their readiness for it. Then have students examine the standards listed under **REVIEW** and look back in the unit or in the **Student Resource Bank** for any skills they need to review.

## READ THE TEXTS

Remind students to keep unit goals in mind as they read each passage, paying particular attention to these literary and reading skills:

- analyze theme
- identify and interpret a symbol
- identify author's perspective
- make inferences and draw conclusions

To help students focus on characters while reading, encourage them to ask questions such as

- What conclusions can you draw about the characters' behavior?
- What do you think motivates the characters to behave in the ways that they do?

## ANSWER THE QUESTIONS

Direct students to page R93–R101 of the **Handbook** to review test-taking strategies.

- As students prepare to answer multiple-choice questions, remind them not to choose the first alternative that seems to fit. Instead, they should read through all the choices, eliminate any that are clearly wrong, and then choose the most accurate answer.

---

**COMMON CORE**

**ASSESS**
Taking this practice test will help you assess your knowledge of these skills and determine your readiness for the Unit Test.

**REVIEW**
After you take the practice test, your teacher can help you identify any standards you need to review.

 **COMMON CORE**

**RL 2** Determine a theme of a text and analyze its development over the course of the text. **RI 2** Determine a central idea of a text and analyze its development over the course of the text. **W 5** Strengthen writing by revising and editing to ensure that it demonstrates the conventions of standard English grammar and spelling. **L 1b** Use various types of clauses. **L 4a** Use context as clue to the meaning of a word or phrase. **L 4c** Consult reference materials to determine a word's precise meaning. **L 6** Demonstrate independence in gathering vocabulary knowledge.

**Practice Test**
**THINK**central
Take it at thinkcentral.com.
KEYWORD: HML9N-536

---

## Assessment Practice

**DIRECTIONS** Read the two texts and the poster. Then, answer the questions that follow.

# The Golden Kite, the Silver Wind *by Ray Bradbury*

1   "In the shape of a *pig*?" cried the Mandarin.[1]

2   "In the shape of a pig," said the messenger, and departed.

3   "Oh, what an evil day in an evil year," cried the Mandarin. "The town of Kwan-Si, beyond the hill, was very small in my childhood. Now it has grown so large that at last they are building a wall."

4   "But why should a wall two miles away make my good father sad and angry all within the hour?" asked his daughter quietly.

5   "They build their wall," said the Mandarin, "in the shape of a pig! Do you see? Our own city wall is built in the shape of an orange. That pig will devour us, greedily!"

6   "Ah."

7   They both sat thinking.

8   Life was full of symbols and omens.[2] Demons lurked everywhere, Death swam in the wetness of an eye, the turn of a gull's wing meant rain, a fan held *so,* the tilt of a roof, and, yes, even a city wall was of immense importance. Travelers and tourists, caravans, musicians, artists, coming upon these two towns, equally judging the portents,[3] would say, "The city shaped like an orange? No! I will enter the city shaped like a pig and prosper, eating all, growing fat with good luck and prosperity!"

9   The Mandarin wept. "All is lost! These symbols and signs terrify. Our city will come on evil days."

10   "Then," said the daughter, "call in your stonemasons[4] and temple builders. I will whisper from behind the silken screen and you will know the words."

11   The old man clapped his hands despairingly. "Ho, stonemasons! Ho, builders of towns and places!"

---

1. **Mandarin** (măn′də rĭn) *n.:* high-ranking government official in the Chinese empire.
2. **omens** (ō′mənz) *n.:* things or events believed to be signs of future occurrences.
3. **portents** (pôr′tĕnts) *n.:* things that warn of events about to occur.
4. **stonemasons** (stōn′mā′sənz) *n.:* people who build with stones.

---

## DIFFERENTIATED INSTRUCTION

**FOR ENGLISH LANGUAGE LEARNERS**
**Assessment Practice: Work Backward**
Prepare students by having them read the questions *before* reading the passages. Have pairs find unfamiliar words in test directions and questions and follow these steps:

1. Write each word on an index card.

2. Look up the meaning in a dictionary and write it on the back of the card.

3. Use the cards to practice words with your partner and to teach them to others.

12  The men who knew marble and granite and onyx and quartz[5] came quickly. The Mandarin faced them most uneasily, himself waiting for a whisper from the silken screen behind his throne. At last the whisper came.

13  "I have called you here," said the whisper.

14  "I have called you here," said the Mandarin aloud, "because our city is shaped like an orange, and the vile city of Kwan-Si has this day shaped theirs like a ravenous pig—"

15  Here the stonemasons groaned and wept. Death rattled his cane in the outer courtyard. Poverty made a sound like a wet cough in the shadows of the room.

16  "And so," said the whisper, said the Mandarin, "you raisers of walls must go bearing trowels[6] and rocks and change the shape of *our* city!"

17  The architects and masons gasped. The Mandarin himself gasped at what he had said. The whisper whispered. The Mandarin went on: "And you will change our walls into a club which may beat the pig and drive it off!"

18  The stonemasons rose up, shouting. Even the Mandarin, delighted at the words from his mouth, applauded, stood down from his throne. "Quick!" he cried. "To work!"

19  When his men had gone, smiling and bustling, the Mandarin turned with great love to the silken screen. "Daughter," he whispered, "I will embrace you." There was no reply. He stepped around the screen, and she was gone.

20  Such modesty, he thought. She has slipped away and left me with a triumph, as if it were mine.

21  The news spread through the city; the Mandarin was acclaimed. Everyone carried stone to the walls. Fireworks were set off and the demons of death and poverty did not linger, as all worked together. At the end of the month the wall had been changed. It was now a mighty bludgeon[7] with which to drive pigs, boars, even lions, far away. The Mandarin slept like a happy fox every night.

22  "I would like to see the Mandarin of Kwan-Si when the news is learned. Such pandemonium[8] and hysteria; he will likely throw himself from a mountain! A little more of that wine, oh Daughter-who-thinks-like-a-son."

23  But the pleasure was like a winter flower; it died swiftly. That very afternoon the messenger rushed into the courtroom. "Oh Mandarin, disease, early sorrow, avalanches, grasshopper plagues, and poisoned well water!"CC

---

5. **marble and granite and onyx** (ŏn´ĭks) **and quartz** *n.:* high-quality stones.

6. **trowels** (trou´əlz) *n.:* tools for laying plaster or mortar.

7. **bludgeon** (blŭj´ən) *n.:* short club.

8. **pandemonium** (păn´də mō´nē əm) *n.:* great confusion; chaos.

GO ON ▶

## ITEM ANALYSIS

| COMPREHENSION AND WRITTEN RESPONSE | ITEMS | UNIT PAGES |
| --- | --- | --- |
| Identify and Analyze Theme | 19, 20, 25 | 434–439 |
| Compare and Contrast Universal Themes | 25 | 434–439 |
| Identify and Interpret Symbols | 1, 7 | 434–439 |
| Identify Author's Perspective | 17, 22, 24 | 493 |
| Make Inferences and Draw Conclusions | 3, 8, 12, 18, 22, 23 | 461 |
| Identify an Implied Main Idea | 5, 10, 15, 20, 21 | 481 |

| VOCABULARY | ITEMS | UNIT PAGES |
| --- | --- | --- |
| Analyze Context Clues | 2, 4, 6, 11, 13, 14, 16 | 491 |
| Use a Dictionary | 9 | 522 |

| WRITING AND GRAMMAR | ITEMS | UNIT PAGES |
| --- | --- | --- |
| Develop Ideas Logically | 1, 2, 3, 4, 5, 6 | 524–532 |
| Use Independent and Subordinate Clauses | 1, 3, 6 | 524–532 |

### Practice Test

On **thinkcentral.com** students can complete an interactive version of this practice test *and* receive remediation for the skills they have not yet mastered. Tests in the **Texas Assessment Practice Workbooks** are also available as online interactive tests with remediation.

## FOR STRUGGLING READERS

**Assessment Support** Consider these options for completing the Assessment Practice:

- Have students "work backward" to review the test questions before reading the passages.

- Select random questions in the Assessment and have students demonstrate how and where to look for answers.

- Ask students to locate unfamiliar vocabulary words in the Assessment. Elicit the words' meanings from the class.

- Have students record useful testing words and definitions in their journal for later reference.

- Read the selections or parts of them aloud to aid in student comprehension.

24  The Mandarin trembled.

25  "The town of Kwan-Si," said the messenger, "which was built like a pig and which animal we drove away by changing our walls to a mighty stick, has now turned triumph to winter ashes. They have built their city's walls like a great bonfire to burn our stick!"

26  The Mandarin's heart sickened within him, like an autumn fruit upon the ancient tree. "Oh, gods! Travelers will spurn[9] us. Tradesmen, reading the symbols, will turn from the stick, so easily destroyed, to the fire, which conquers all!"

27  "No," said a whisper like a snowflake from behind the silken screen.

28  "No," said the startled Mandarin.

29  "Tell my stonemasons," said the whisper that was a falling drop of rain, "to build our walls in the shape of a shining lake."

30  The Mandarin said this aloud, his heart warmed.

31  "And with this lake of water," said the whisper and the old man, "we will quench the fire and put it out forever!"

32  The city turned out in joy to learn that once again they had been saved by the magnificent Emperor of ideas. They ran to the walls and built them nearer to this new vision, singing, not as loudly as before, of course, for they were tired, and not as quickly, for since it had taken a month to rebuild the wall the first time, they had had to neglect business and crops and therefore were somewhat weaker and poorer.

33  There then followed a succession of horrible and wonderful days, one in another like a nest of frightening boxes.

34  "Oh, Emperor," cried the messenger, "Kwan-Si has rebuilt their walls to resemble a mouth with which to drink all our lake!"

35  "Then," said the Emperor, standing very close to his silken screen, "build our walls like a needle to sew up that mouth!"

36  "Emperor!" screamed the messenger. "They make their walls like a sword to break your needle!"

37  The Emperor held, trembling, to the silken screen. "Then shift the stones to form a scabbard to sheathe that sword!"[10]

38  "Mercy," wept the messenger the following morn, "they have worked all night and shaped their walls like lightning which will explode and destroy that sheath!"

39  Sickness spread in the city like a pack of evil dogs. Shops closed. The population, working now steadily for endless months upon the changing of

---

9.  **spurn** (spûrn) v.: reject someone or something for being unworthy; scorn.

10. **scabbard . . . sword** n.: a scabbard is a case for a sword's blade. To sheathe a sword means to put it in a case.

538

## DIFFERENTIATED INSTRUCTION

**FOR STRUGGLING READERS**

**Build Comprehension** Review with students the cultural context of the story, explaining the competition between the Mandarin's city and the city of Kwan-Si. Have students create a comparison and contrast chart to organize information about the shape of the cities' walls and the importance of their symbolism. Discuss these questions:

• Why are the cities in such competition?

• Why are symbols so important to the city officials?

• What strategies can help people overcome their disagreements?

**FOR ENGLISH LANGUAGE LEARNERS**

**Culture: Clarify** Explain the importance of symbols and omens in Chinese culture, reviewing how colors, shapes, and animals have special significance. Point out the examples listed in paragraph 8, and have students give other examples of symbols from other cultures, such as good luck when a person finds a penny, or bad luck when someone walks under a ladder.

the walls, resembled Death himself, clattering his white bones like musical instruments in the wind. Funerals began to appear in the streets, though it was the middle of summer, a time when all should be tending and harvesting. The Mandarin fell so ill that he had his bed drawn up by the silken screen and there he lay, miserably giving his architectural orders. The voice behind the screen was weak now, too, and faint, like the wind in the eaves.

40    "Kwan-Si is an eagle. Then our walls must be a net for that eagle. They are a sun to burn our net. Then we build a moon to eclipse their sun!"

41    Like a rusted machine, the city ground to a halt.

42    At last the whisper behind the screen cried out:

43    "In the name of the gods, send for Kwan-Si!"

44    Upon the last day of summer the Mandarin Kwan-Si, very ill and withered away, was carried into our Mandarin's courtroom by four starving footmen. The two mandarins were propped up, facing each other. Their breaths fluttered like winter winds in their mouths. A voice said:

45    "Let us put an end to this."

46    The old men nodded.

47    "This cannot go on," said the faint voice. "Our people do nothing but rebuild our cities to a different shape every day, every hour. They have no time to hunt, to fish, to love, to be good to their ancestors and their ancestors' children."

48    "This I admit," said the mandarins of the towns of the Cage, the Moon, the Spear, the Fire, the Sword, and this, that, and other things.

49    "Carry us into the sunlight," said the voice.

50    The old men were borne out under the sun and up a little hill. In the late summer breeze a few very thin children were flying dragon kites in all the colors of the sun, and frogs and grass, the color of the sea, and the color of coins and wheat.

51    The first Mandarin's daughter stood by his bed.

52    "See," she said.

53    "Those are nothing but kites," said the two old men.

54    "But what is a kite on the ground?" she said. "It is nothing. What does it need to sustain it and make it beautiful and truly spiritual?"

55    "The wind, of course!" said the others.

56    "And what do the sky and the wind need to make *them* beautiful?"

57    "A kite, of course—many kites, to break the monotony, the sameness of the sky. Colored kites, flying!"

GO ON

## FOR ENGLISH LANGUAGE LEARNERS

**Transitions: Continuation** Copy the sequence charts to help students follow the many changes to the walls of the story's two cities.

**Mandarin's Walls:**
Orange→Club→Lake→Needle→
Scabbard →Net→Moon

**Kwan-Si's Walls:**
Pig→Bonfire→Mouth→Sword→
Lightning→Eagle→Sun

Review the vocabulary to make sure students understand the definitions of the different shapes.

## FOR ADVANCED LEARNERS/PRE–AP

The Mandarin's daughter says the kite and wind give one another "purpose and meaning. One without the other is nothing. Together, all will be beauty and cooperation" (paragraph 58). Have students discuss this quotation and explore its meaning in the story. Ask students to think of other examples of things or people that together create "purpose and meaning."

58 "So," said the Mandarin's daughter. "You, Kwan-Si, will make a last rebuilding of your town to resemble nothing more nor less than the wind. And we shall build like a golden kite. The wind will beautify the kite and carry it to wondrous heights. And the kite will break the sameness of the wind's existence and give it purpose and meaning. One without the other is nothing. Together, all will be beauty and cooperation and a long and enduring life."

59 Whereupon the two mandarins were so overjoyed that they took their first nourishment in days, momentarily were given strength, embraced, and lavished praise upon each other, called the Mandarin's daughter a boy, a man, a stone pillar, a warrior, and a true and unforgettable son. Almost immediately they parted and hurried to their towns, calling out and singing, weakly but happily.

60 And so, in time, the towns became the Town of the Golden Kite and the Town of the Silver Wind. And harvestings were harvested and business tended again, and the flesh returned, and disease ran off like a frightened jackal. And on every night of the year the inhabitants of the Town of the Kite could hear the good clear wind sustaining them. And those in the Town of the Wind could hear the kite singing, whispering, rising, and beautifying them.

61 "So be it," said the Mandarin in front of his silken screen.

540

# The Arms Race

*by Albert Einstein*
***from* Einstein on Peace**

*Although the United States and the former Soviet Union were allies during World War II, they later became involved in a power struggle known as the Cold War. The two superpowers engaged in an arms race—a competition to develop more and more powerful nuclear weapons. In 1952, the United States successfully tested the first hydrogen bomb, a weapon much more powerful than the atomic bomb. In 1953, the Soviet Union exploded its own hydrogen bomb.*

1 The belief that it is possible to achieve security through armaments on a national scale is, in the present state of military technology, a disastrous illusion. In the United States, this illusion has been strengthened by the fact that this country was the first to succeed in producing an atomic bomb. This is why people tended to believe that this country would be able to achieve permanent and decisive military superiority which, it was hoped, would deter any potential enemy and thus bring about the security, so intensely sought by us as well as by the rest of the world. The maxim we have followed these last five years has been, in short, security through superior force, whatever the cost.

2 This technological as well as psychological orientation in military policy has had its inevitable consequences. Every action related to foreign policy is governed by one single consideration: How should we act in order to achieve the utmost superiority over the enemy in the event of war? The answer has been: Outside the United States, we must establish military bases at every possible, strategically important point of the globe as well as arm and strengthen economically our potential allies. And inside the United States, tremendous financial power is being concentrated in the hands of the military; youth is being militarized; and the loyalty of citizens, particularly civil servants, is carefully supervised by a police force growing more powerful every day. People of independent political thought are harassed. The public is subtly indoctrinated by the radio, the press, the schools. Under the pressure of military secrecy, the range of public information is increasingly restricted.

3 The arms race between the United States and the Soviet Union, initiated originally as a preventive measure, assumes hysterical proportions. On both sides, means of mass destruction are being perfected with feverish haste and behind walls of secrecy. And now the public has been advised that the production of the hydrogen bomb is the new goal which will probably be accomplished. An accelerated development toward this end has been solemnly proclaimed by the President. If these efforts should prove successful, radioactive poisoning of the atmosphere and, hence, annihilation[1] of all life on earth will have been brought within the range of what is technically

---

1. **annihilation** (ə nī′ə lā′shən) *n.:* absolute destruction.

**GO ON**

---

possible. The weird aspect of this development lies in its apparently inexorable[2] character. Each step appears as the inevitable consequence of the one that went before. And at the end, looming ever clearer, lies general annihilation.

4    Is there any way out of this impasse[3] created by man himself? All of us, and particularly those who are responsible for the policies of the United States and the Soviet Union, must realize that, although we have vanquished an external enemy,[4] we have proved unable to free ourselves from the war mentality. We shall never achieve real peace as long as every step is taken with a possible future conflict in view, especially since it becomes ever clearer that such a war would spell universal annihilation. The guiding thought in all political action should therefore be: What can we do in the prevailing situation to bring about peaceful coexistence among all nations? The first goal must be to do away with mutual fear and distrust. Solemn renunciation of the policy of violence, not only with respect to weapons of mass destruction, is without doubt necessary. Such renunciation, however, will be effective only if a supranational judicial and executive agency is established at the same time, with power to settle questions of immediate concern to the security of nations. Even a declaration by a number of nations that they would collaborate loyally in the realization of such a "restricted world government" would considerably reduce the imminent danger of war.

5    In the last analysis the peaceful coexistence of peoples is primarily dependent upon mutual trust and, only secondarily, upon institutions such as courts of justice and the police. This holds true for nations as well as for individuals. And the basis of trust is a loyal relationship of give-and-take.

---

2. **inexorable** (ĭn ĕk′sər ə bəl) *adj.*: unable to be stopped.

3. **impasse** (ĭm′păs) *n.*: difficult situation or problem with no obvious solution.

4. **vanquished** (văng′kwĭsht) **an external enemy** *v.*: defeated hostile relations. Einstein is referring to Germany, Japan, and their allies in World War II, which were defeated by the United States, Great Britain, and their allies.

542

---

landscaping ◆ office work ◆ cleaning ◆ painting

*CHOOSE A JOB THAT'S GOOD FOR YOU –*
*MAKE A DIFFERENCE THAT'S GOOD FOR ALL*

I don't know what your destiny will be, but one thing I do know: the only ones among you who will be really happy are those who have sought and found how to serve.

- *Dr. Albert Schweitzer (1875-1965)*

**SAVE THE DATE:**
*Saturday, April 22   8:00-4:00*
Call **512-555-1212** for more details

**Fulfills Community Service requirements:**
check with your counselor

543

---

**FOR ENGLISH LANGUAGE LEARNERS**

**Reading: Preview** Help English learners preview the image in the poster to determine its general meaning. Elicit from volunteers information that they can gather from the image alone: a group of students are working together; they seem to be cleaning up or making improvements; the recycling symbol on the boy's shirt indicates that he cares about the environment. Then point out words from the poster that support concepts students have already identified from the images: *work, cleaning, job, serve*.

**Vocabulary: Word Associations** Help English learners identify the word play in the poster's headline by reviewing the associations among *U, Unity,* and *Community*. Explain that *Unity*, which means "being in harmony," is contained in *Community*, which means "a group of people living together." Point out that *U* stands for the sound made by *you*, and explain why the author chose this alternative spelling. Ask students to explain how the bold typeface of the headline helps them see the connections between the three words.

# Reading Comprehension

Model a thinking process for answering multiple-choice questions.

1. **C is correct.** *According to paragraph 8, pigs symbolize greed, "eating all and growing fat." A, B and D are incorrect because the pig does not symbolize courage, danger, or wisdom.*

2. **A is correct.** *Travelers and tourists imply movement, just as caravan has associations of travel. B is incorrect because money and luck are not associated with travel. C is incorrect because importance is not associated with travel. D is incorrect because warnings do not help the reader understand a moving caravan.*

3. **D is correct.** *The Mandarin thinks that the other city's pig-shaped wall is more important-looking than his wall. A is incorrect because there is no indication that the city walls are unsound. B is incorrect because the Mandarin rebuilds the wall in the shape of a club, not another animal. C is incorrect because there are no community complaints.*

4. **B is correct.** *A "ravenous pig" is one that will eat much food to satisfy its hunger. A, C, and D are incorrect because they all describe appearance, rather than the condition of having a great hunger.*

5. **A is correct.** *The daughter whispers from behind a curtain so that no one will know that the ideas are hers, not her father's. B is incorrect because he takes her advice, rather than ignoring it. C is incorrect because the Mandarin thinks the advice is both good and right. D is incorrect because the Mandarin does accept her advice, even though she is a woman.*

6. **A is correct.** *The Mandarin thought he had outwitted the other city. B and C are incorrect because the Mandarin is competitive, not evil or greedy. D is incorrect because the Mandarin has shown himself to be less intelligent than his daughter.*

7. **B is correct.** *Cold weather makes fall and winter times of dormancy and death. A is incorrect because the season of spring is associated with new beginnings. C and D are incorrect because they are the opposite of what happens in fall and winter,*

when things get weaker and die.

8. **A is correct.** *The Mandarin is celebrated for his wisdom even though all his ideas come from his daughter. B is incorrect because the people focus on making their city wall the best at that time, not on the possibility of the other kingdom changing its wall. C is incorrect because the Mandarin's daughter, not the Mandarin, chose the next shape of the wall. D is incorrect because the wall's symbolism is very important to the Mandarin.*

9. **D is correct.** *The Mandarin wants to build a wall that will seem more important than the neighboring kingdom's wall. A, B and C are incorrect because they refer to the actions of an actual sun and moon; in the selection, eclipse refers to walls in the shape of a sun and moon, rather than heavenly bodies.*

---

# Reading Comprehension

> Use "The Golden Kite, the Silver Wind" (pp. 536–540) to answer questions 1–13.

1. In paragraph 5, the author uses the pig-shaped wall to represent —
   - **A.** courage
   - **B.** danger
   - **C.** greed
   - **D.** wisdom

2. Which words from paragraph 8 help the reader understand the meaning of the word *caravan*?
   - **A.** travelers and tourists
   - **B.** good luck and prosperity
   - **C.** immense importance
   - **D.** the portents

3. What prompts the Mandarin to have the city wall rebuilt?
   - **A.** His city wall is crumbling and is in need of repair.
   - **B.** He likes the idea of rebuilding it in the shape of a different animal.
   - **C.** People in the community are complaining about the wall's appearance.
   - **D.** He views the other city's wall as more impressive than his city's wall.

4. The word *ravenous* in paragraph 14 means —
   - **A.** extremely heavy
   - **B.** really hungry
   - **C.** very thin
   - **D.** somewhat birdlike

5. How does the Mandarin use his daughter's advice?
   - **A.** He takes the advice but pretends it was his idea.
   - **B.** He thanks her but dismisses her advice.
   - **C.** He thinks it is good advice but isn't the right advice.
   - **D.** He can't accept her advice because she is not a man.

6. In paragraph 21, the author uses the word *fox* to show that the Mandarin is —
   - **A.** clever
   - **B.** evil
   - **C.** greedy
   - **D.** intelligent

7. What do the seasons fall and winter symbolize in the story?
   - **A.** new beginnings and life
   - **B.** sickness and death
   - **C.** power
   - **D.** immortality and good fortune

8. In what way is this story ironic?
   - **A.** The people know the shapes of the wall are not the Mandarin's idea.
   - **B.** The people think the other kingdom won't change the shape of its wall.
   - **C.** The Mandarin knows what the next shape of the wall will be.
   - **D.** The Mandarin doesn't think the shape of the wall is important.

9. Read the following dictionary entry.

   **eclipse** \ē klĭps'\ *n* **1.** the blockage of the light of the moon by the sun or the blocking of the light of the sun by the moon **2.** any blockage of light *v* **3.** to cause an eclipse **4.** to overshadow, hide from view

   Which definition best fits the word *eclipse* as it is used in paragraph 40?
   - **A.** Definition 1
   - **B.** Definition 2
   - **C.** Definition 3
   - **D.** Definition 4

**10.** The author implies that the competition between the two kingdoms —

    **A.** will make the kingdoms stronger and more wealthy

    **B.** will never end and probably destroy each kingdom

    **C.** will unite the kingdoms into one large kingdom

    **D.** will have no effect

**11.** Which word from paragraph 57 helps the reader understand the meaning of the word *monotony*?

    **A.** break

    **B.** colored

    **C.** flying

    **D.** sameness

**12.** The praises the mandarins give the daughter in paragraph 59 suggest that in ancient China —

    **A.** women and men were treated equally

    **B.** men were more valued and respected than women

    **C.** there weren't any differences in gender roles

    **D.** women were more valued and respected than men

**13.** In paragraph 60, the author uses the word *flesh* to refer to —

    **A.** the townspeople

    **B.** the skin of an animal

    **C.** the fruit of the harvest

    **D.** renewed life

---

> **Use "The Arms Race"** from *Einstein on Peace* (pp. 541–542) to answer questions 14–18.

**14.** The word *inevitable* in paragraph 2 means —

    **A.** totally defeated

    **B.** uncontrolled

    **C.** quick

    **D.** unavoidable

**15.** Paragraph 3 is mainly about —

    **A.** the destructive path both nations are pursuing

    **B.** different uses for the hydrogen bomb

    **C.** the President's desire to slow down the production of the hydrogen bomb

    **D.** the increased need for secrecy while developing the hydrogen bomb

**16.** Which word or phrase from paragraph 4 helps the reader understand the meaning of the word *renunciation*?

    **A.** universal annihilation

    **B.** peaceful coexistence

    **C.** achieve real peace

    **D.** do away with

**17.** What sort of tone does Einstein create?

    **A.** Fearful

    **B.** Humorous

    **C.** Mysterious

    **D.** Sentimental

**18.** The reader can conclude that Einstein was a —

    **A.** political leader

    **B.** peacemaker

    **C.** revolutionary

    **D.** soldier

**GO ON** ➡

545

---

**10. B *is correct.*** The leaders show no signs of negotiating to stop building walls, and the people of the kingdoms become weak and poor. A and D are incorrect because the kingdoms become poorer and weaker. C is incorrect because the constant changing of the wall weakened their people.

**11. D *is correct.*** Monotony arises from sameness, or a lack of change or variety. A and C are incorrect because break and flying describe actions, not an unchanging condition. B is incorrect because colored implies brightness, not sameness.

**12. B *is correct.*** The masculine names of "boy," "man," and "unforgettable son" are delivered as if they are the Mandarin's highest praise. A and C are incorrect because the praise of an "unforgettable son" shows unequal treatment of men and women, and differences in gender roles. D is incorrect because the Mandarin's praises shows women to be less valued and respected than men.

**13. A *is correct.*** The author says that the "flesh returned," meaning that the townspeople gained weight and their health was restored. B and C are incorrect because flesh refers to people, not to foods to be eaten. D is incorrect because flesh refers specifically to the people of the town, not to renewed life in general.

**14. D *is correct.*** The passage refers to consequences that cannot be controlled or avoided. A and C are incorrect because an inevitable thing is not necessarily defeated or quick. B is incorrect because inevitable implies something that cannot be changed, rather than something that cannot be controlled.

**15. A *is correct.*** The description indicates that the hydrogen bomb has a negative social and psychological impact. B is incorrect because the bomb's only use is to destroy. C is incorrect because the selection does not indicate the President wishes to slow down bomb production. D is incorrect because until then, the bomb had been developed in secret.

**16. D *is correct.*** The author wants to renounce, or do away with, a policy of violence. A is incorrect because annihilation refers to widespread death and tragedy, not "doing away with" a policy. B and C are incorrect because the author wants to achieve peace, not renounce it.

**17. A *is correct.*** Einstein warns that the development of weapons can lead to widespread destruction. B is incorrect because Einstein's topic and message are serious. C and D are incorrect because Einstein's message is based on fact, not fiction or emotion.

**18. B *is correct.*** Einstein argues for renouncing war, weaponry, and violence. A and C are incorrect because Einstein does not discuss his views of politics or government. D is incorrect because Einstein asks for peace, not war.

## ANSWERS

19. **D is correct.** *Both texts emphasize the benefits of working together, rather than working against another city or country. A is incorrect because the texts show that pride can harm people and nations. B is incorrect because only "The Arms Race" emphasizes caution. C is incorrect because neither text promotes the idea that peace can be achieved through defense.*

20. **A is correct.** *When cities and nations trust one another, there is no need for violence or negative competition. B and C are incorrect because only "The Arms Race" mentions treaties and alliances, which are based on trust. D is incorrect because suspicion is the opposite of trust.*

21. **A is correct.** *The poster emphasizes the benefit of working to improve one's community. B is incorrect because it does not include the purpose for working. C is incorrect because the poster does not attempt to minimize the seriousness of work. D is incorrect because the poster does not address the idea of peace.*

22. **C is correct.** *The "U" is an appropriate symbol because the poster features young people, who would be familiar with text messaging symbols. A is incorrect because "U" does not repeat the recycling symbol shape. B is incorrect because "U" does not address work and service. D is incorrect because the designer's job is to create a poster, not to monitor ink usage.*

## SHORT CONSTRUCTED RESPONSE

*Possible responses:*

23. *The Mandarins work together to find a compromise that is in both their interests. When they change their walls to the shapes of a kite and the wind, they give one another "purpose and meaning" (paragraph 58).*

24. *I agree with Einstein that countries must work to establish trust in order to build treaties and achieve peace throughout the world in order to avert "mass destruction" and "radioactive poisoning of the atmosphere" (paragraph 3).*

25. *In "The Golden Kite," the kingdoms work together to build walls that complement and enhance one another, so that "[t]ogether, all will be beauty and cooperation" (paragraph 58). In "The Arms Race," Einstein hopes that countries can cooperate to build a trust that will transcend treaties or laws, since "the basis of trust is a loyal relationship of give-and-take" (paragraph 5).*

---

> **Use "The Golden Kite, the Silver Wind" and "The Arms Race" to answer questions 19–20.**

19. Which of the following themes or central ideas do the texts share?
    - **A.** Pride inspires confidence.
    - **B.** Caution leads to failure.
    - **C.** Defense creates peace.
    - **D.** Cooperation promotes security.

20. Both texts suggest that peaceful coexistence is based on —
    - **A.** mutual trust
    - **B.** treaties
    - **C.** alliances
    - **D.** mutual suspicion

> **Use the poster to answer questions 21–22.**

21. The main or central message of the poster is that —
    - **A.** together, you can help your community
    - **B.** work can be fun
    - **C.** you shouldn't take work too seriously
    - **D.** cooperation leads to peace

22. The designer probably chose to spell "you" as "U" in the slogan to —
    - **A.** repeat the shape of the recycling symbol
    - **B.** emphasize the concept of service
    - **C.** appeal to a teen audience using text messaging symbols
    - **D.** save space and ink on the poster

---

### SHORT CONSTRUCTED RESPNOSE
**Write a short response to each question, using text evidence to support your response.**

23. "The Golden Kite, the Silver Wind" focuses on the conflict between two Mandarins (rulers) from neighboring kingdoms. How do the Mandarins resolve their conflict? Support your response with evidence from the text.

24. Do you agree with Einstein's views? Support your response with evidence from the text.

**Write a short response to this question, using evidence from both texts to support your response.**

25. How does the idea of cooperation apply to "The Golden Kite, the Silver Wind" and "The Arms Race"? Support your response with evidence from **both** texts.

---

## DIFFERENTIATED INSTRUCTION

### FOR ENGLISH LANGUAGE LEARNERS
**Assessment Vocabulary** To help students understand the Comprehension questions, teach or review these key vocabulary words:

- Item 3: *prompts*—"encourages, moves, or motivates"
- Item 10: *implies*—"suggests, states indirectly"
- Item 23: *resolve*—"settle, bring to an end"

**546** UNIT 4: THEME AND SYMBOL

# Revising and Editing

**DIRECTIONS** Read this passage, and answer the questions that follow.

> (1) Nadia walked down the street. (2) She heard a noise behind her. (3) She considers her options. (4) But it was dark now. (5) She was in an unfamiliar part of town. (6) She decided to run. (7) Suddenly, she felt hot breathe on the back of her leg. (8) She poised herself to kick. (9) She realized it was just a dog. (10) She wondered if she had really been so afraid of a friendly little beagle. (11) Had something else been behind her too?

**1.** What is the most effective way to combine sentences 1 and 2 into a complex sentence?
- **A.** Nadia walked down the street, she heard a noise behind her.
- **B.** Nadia walked down the street and heard a noise behind her.
- **C.** As Nadia walked down the street, she heard a noise behind her.
- **D.** Nadia walked down the street; also, she heard a noise behind her.

**2.** What change, if any, should be made in sentence 3?
- **A.** Change *considers* to **considered**
- **B.** Insert *one* after **her**
- **C.** Change *options* to **opts**
- **D.** Make no change

**3.** Where is the best place to insert the subordinate clause *because she had been visiting her cousin's new house*?
- **A.** At the beginning of the paragraph
- **B.** At the end of sentence 3
- **C.** At the end of sentence 5
- **D.** At the end of sentence 7

**4.** What change, if any, should be made in sentence 7?
- **A.** Change *back* to **backs**
- **B.** Insert comma after *breathe*
- **C.** Change *breathe* to **breath**
- **D.** Make no change

**5.** Which transitional word or phrase should be added to the beginning of sentence 9?
- **A.** At first,     **C.** In fact,
- **B.** Finally,       **D.** Then,

**6.** What is the most effective way to combine sentences 10 and 11 into a complex sentence?
- **A.** She had been afraid of a friendly little beagle; however, something else had been behind her too.
- **B.** Although she wondered if she had really been afraid of a friendly little beagle, perhaps something else had been behind her too.
- **C.** She wondered if she had really been afraid of a friendly little beagle, and if something else had been behind her too.
- **D.** Wondering if she had been afraid of a friendly little beagle, something else had been behind her too.

STOP

547

## ANSWERS

# Revising and Editing

1. **C is correct.** *The sentence is the only example of a complex sentence, combining an independent clause ("she heard") with a dependent clause ("As Nadia walked down the street").* A is incorrect because it contains two independent clauses separated by a comma splice. B is incorrect because it is a simple sentence with a compound verb. D is incorrect because it contains two independent clauses.

2. **A is correct.** *The verb should be changed to the past tense to remain consistent with the other verbs in the passage.* B is incorrect because *one* would not agree in number with the plural *options*. C is incorrect because it replaces a noun with a verb, which does not make logical sense in the sentence. D is incorrect because the verb tense of *considers* is incorrect and should be changed.

3. **C is correct.** *Nadia could be alarmed in part because her "cousin's new house" was "in an unfamiliar part of town."* A, B, and D are incorrect because the information does not fit logically in these places.

4. **C is correct.** *The noun* breath *should replace the verb* breathe. A is incorrect because the plural *backs* would not agree in number with the singular *leg*. B is incorrect because a comma is not required before a prepositional phrase. D is incorrect because the verb *breathe* is incorrect in the sentence and should be changed.

5. **D is correct.** Then *helps convey the sequence of events in the passage.* A is incorrect because it would be out of sequence, since this action occurs near the end of the passage. B is incorrect because sentence 9 is not the final action in the passage. C is incorrect because Nadia has not yet verified what created the alarming noise.

6. **B is correct.** *The sentence is the only example of a complex sentence, containing the independent clause "something else had been" and the dependent clause "Although she wondered."* A is incorrect because it is a compound sentence made of two independent clauses. C is incorrect because it incorrectly adds a comma before a dependent clauses. D is incorrect because it creates a dangling participle.

---

**FOR STRUGGLING READERS**

**Assessment Support: Use Independent and Subordinate Clauses** Provide students with practice identifying independent and subordinate clauses and using them in sentences. Write the following independent and subordinate clauses on the board:

*I went to class*
*Because I went to class*
*After I went to class*
*While I went to class*

Have students identify the independent clause *(I went to class)* and modify it by adding a descriptive subordinate clause. Then have students add independent clauses to the remaining subordinate clauses. Have students compare sentences, identifying the dependent and independent clauses in their work. **Possible answer:** *Because I went to class (dependent clause), I missed seeing the accident in the parking lot (independent clause).*

**RL 10** Read and comprehend literature. **RI 10** Read and comprehend literary nonfiction.

## INTRODUCE *GREAT READS*

In Unit 4, students have discussed a number of big questions. Invite students to tell which question they found most intriguing and why, and then focus attention on the three that appear on this page. Discuss the recommended books and their summaries, pointing out how each connects to the related question. Encourage students to choose one or more of these "great reads" to read independently.

## Ideas for Independent Reading

Which of the themes in this unit has the most importance in your life? Discover how these themes affect others in the following books.

○ COMMON CORE

**RL 10** Read and comprehend literature. **RI 10** Read and comprehend literary nonfiction.

### How do expectations affect performance?

**Music of the Heart**
*by Roberta Gaspari*

No one expected Gaspari's students to succeed at the violin. But she and her kids—more than one thousand over the years—proved that expectations and talent can lead to good music.

**Gifted Hands**
*by Ben Carson, M.D. with Cecil Murphy*

Carson's mother expected him to do something worthwhile with his life. He did not disappoint her. In 1987, the surgeon helped complete the first successful separation of Siamese twins joined at the head.

**Lanterns: A Memoir of Mentors**
*by Marian Wright Edelman*

The lawyer, civil rights activist, and founder of the Children's Defense Fund honors the famous and not-so-famous people in her life who kept her expectations high while she struggled to make a difference.

### Why do we hurt the ones we love?

**The Kite Runner**
*by Khaled Hosseini*

Amir and Hassan grow up together in Afghanistan. Amir fails his friend Hassan before leaving for America. He returns years later to try to make up for his betrayal.

**The Once and Future King**
*by T. H. White*

In this retelling of the legend of King Arthur, Queen Guinevere loves both her husband Arthur and the knight Lancelot, Arthur's best friend. Though each one loves the other two, all three suffer terribly.

**This Boy's Life**
*by Tobias Wolff*

Divorce may be necessary for adults, but the children in the family often get hurt. The award-winning author remembers his struggle to grow up and find himself while frequently separated from his father.

### What are you really good at?

**One Writer's Beginnings**
*by Eudora Welty*

In this memoir, Welty brings to life her family, her younger self, and the American South in the early 1900s. She also conveys her love for stories—those she found in books as well as those she heard on long, hot summer afternoons.

**I'd Rather Teach Peace**
*by Colman McCarthy*

As a *Washington Post* columnist, McCarthy has written for many years on nonviolence as a way of life. Here he talks about teaching peace to students, prisoners, and others.

**The Other Side of the Mountain**
*by Evans G. Valens*

Valens tells the inspiring true story of skier Jill Kinmont, who found a way to reshape her life after a crippling accident.

**Get Novel Wise** [THINK central]

Go to **thinkcentral.com**.
KEYWORD: HML9-548

548

[THINK central]

**NovelWise**

The keyword on this page points to **NovelWise**, a Web site that helps students choose a novel or other book-length work to read. **NovelWise** also provides

- study guides
- reading strategies and literary elements instruction
- presentations to introduce classic novels
- project ideas

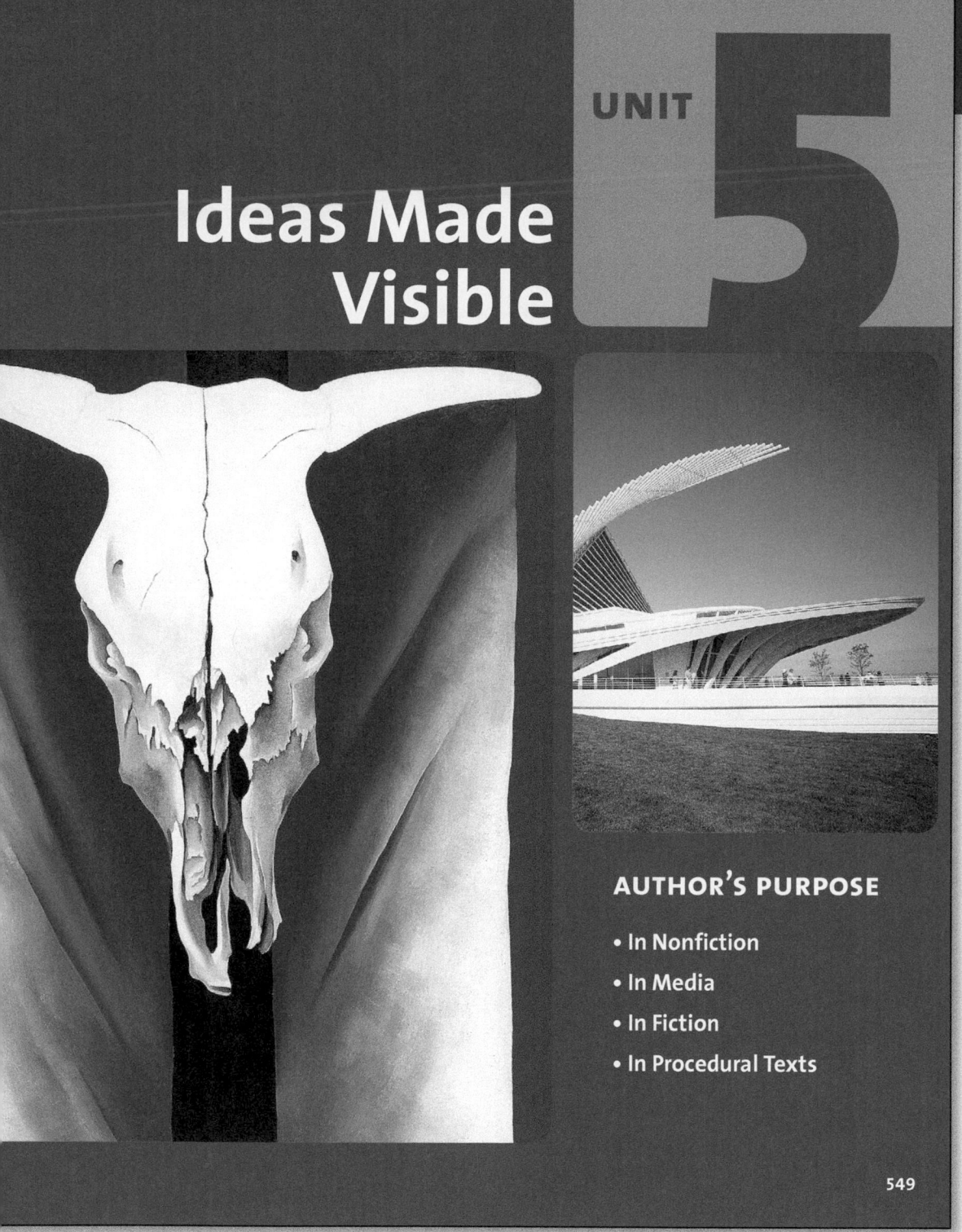

# 5

# Ideas Made Visible

## AUTHOR'S PURPOSE

- In Nonfiction
- In Media
- In Fiction
- In Procedural Texts

549

**About the Art** Georgia O'Keeffe (1887–1986) painted *Cow's Skull: Red, White, and Blue* in 1931. For more information, see page 573.

## INTRODUCE THE UNIT

An idea is an abstract concept; it is personal and internal. Yet some people share their ideas with the world—and they often do so in ways that are clear and memorable. For example, painters, photographers, and architects make their ideas come alive through paint, film, and construction materials. Writers bring their ideas to life through words.

Invite students to describe how they express their ideas. Ask them to identify purposes that prompt them to bring their ideas to life. Then have students consider how the pictures on this page share ideas. Discuss these questions:

- What colors are in the painting? What might those colors mean?
- What is memorable about the architecture in the photograph?
- Does either image strike you as strongly positive or negative? Explain.
- Why do you think each artist whose work is represented on this page decided to share a visual idea in the way shown?

Tell students that as they read this unit, they will explore not only *how* writers make their ideas visible for readers but also *why* they do so. In each selection, therefore, students will consider the author's purpose for writing.

For help in planning this unit, see

**R** RESOURCE MANAGER UNIT 5
pp. 1–10

# UNIT 5

## COMMON CORE

| STRAND | Text Analysis Workshop: Author's Purpose pp. 552–557 (ECOS) | Island Morning Descriptive Essay pp. 558–567 | Georgia O'Keeffe Biographical Essay pp. 568–577 | Who Killed the Iceman?/Skeletal Sculptures Magazine Article/ Process Description pp. 578–589 (ECOS) | The Lost Boys Magazine Article pp. 590–599 (ECOS) |
|---|---|---|---|---|---|
| | | Lexile: 1230 Fry: 10 Dale-Chalh: 6.2 | Lexile: 1160 Fry: 10 Dale-Chall: 6.9 | Lexile: 1070/1070 Fry: College/College Dale-Chall: 8.4/7.6 | Lexile: 1060 Fry: College Dale-Chall: 7.0 |
| **Reading Literature** | | | | | |
| **Reading Informational Text** | Author's Purpose and Perspective pp. 552–554 **RI 4, RI 6** Organization and Format pp. 554–555 **RI 3, RI 5** Compare Texts pp. 556–557 | Diction pp. 559, 560, 562, 563, 566 **RI 4** Analyze Patterns of Organization pp. 559, 563, 564, 566 **RI 3, RI 5** Language Coach p. 562 **RI 4** Tone p. 564 **RI 4** | Tone pp. 569, 574, 575 **RI 4** Irony p. 572 **RI 5** Implied Main Ideas pp. 569, 570, 575 **RI 2, RI 5** | Text Features pp. 579–581, 587, 588 **RI 2, RI 5** Take Notes pp. 579, 580, 581, 585, 588 **RI 2, RI 5** | Author's Purpose pp. 591, 592, 596, 598 **RI 6** Tone p. 595 **RI 4** |
| **Writing** | | Quickwrite p. 558 Writing Prompt p. 567 **W 4** | Quickwrite p. 568 Writing Prompt p. 577 | Writing Prompt p. 588 | Writing Prompt p. 598 |
| **Speaking and Listening** | | | | Discuss p. 578 **SL 1** Graphic Sources pp. 582, 588 **SL 2** | Discuss p. 590 **SL 1** Interpret Graphic Aids pp. 591, 592, 594, 597, 598 **SL 2** |
| **Language** | | Improve Sentence Flow pp. 562, 567 **L 1b** | Language Coach p. 572 **L 4b** Use Descriptive Language pp. 573, 577 **L 1b** Word Root gen p. 576 **L 4c** | Language Coach pp. 581, 584 **L 4, L 4a, c** Suffix –ologies p. 589 **L 6** | Language Coach p. 596 **L 4b** Latin Root fract p. 599 **L 4b, c** |

549A

| Media Study: News Reports | The Open Window | from The House on Mango Street | Consumer Documents: From the Manufacturer to You | Adding Graphics to Your Web Site | Writing Workshop: |
|---|---|---|---|---|---|
| TV Newscast/ Web News Report pp. 600–603 | Short Story pp. 604–611 | Fiction pp. 612–619 | Product Information, Safety Information, Warranty pp. 620–625 | Technical Directions pp. 626–631 | Informative Text: Business Letter pp. 632–641 Speaking and Listening Workshop: Creating an Online Professional Profile pp. 642–643 |
| | Lexile: 1070 Fry: 10 Dale-Chall: 7.0 | Lexile: 890 Fry: 6 Dale-Chall: 5.1 | Lexile: 1100 Fry: 10 Dale-Chall: 9–10 | Lexile: 910 Fry: 7 Dale-Chall: 7–8 | |
| | Tone and Author's Purpose pp. 605, 606, 609, 610 **RL 4, RL 6** Background p. 607 **RL 6** Predict pp. 605, 608, 610 Language Coach p. 608 **RL 4** Text Analysis p. 610 **RL 10** | Author's Perspective pp. 613, 617, 618, 619 **RL 4** Make Inferences About Character pp. 613, 614, 616, 619 **RL 1, RL 3** | | | |
| Media Literacy pp. 601–602 **RI 7** | | | Consumer Documents pp. 621, 623–625 **RI 5, RI 6** Adjust Reading Rate pp. 621, 623–625 Language Coach p. 622 **RI 4** | Technical Directions pp. 627, 629–631 **RI 3, RI 4** Skim and Scan pp. 627, 628, 630, 631 Analogy p. 628 **RI 4** Language Coach p. 629 **RI 4** | |
| Write or Discuss p. 603 **W 9b** (RI 7) | Writing Prompt p. 611 | | Quickwrite p. 620 | Writing Prompt p. 631 **W 2c, W 10** | Writing a Business Letter pp. 632–641 **W 2a–f, W 4, W 5, W 7, W 10** Creating an Online Professional Profile pp. 642–643 **W 2a, W 6** |
| Write or Discuss p. 603 **SL 2, SL 5** | Discuss p. 604 **SL 1** | Present p. 612 **SL 1** | | Discuss p. 626 **SL 1** | |
| | Add Descriptive Details pp. 609, 611 **L 1b** | Language Coach p. 616 **L 5a** Paradox p. 618 **L 5a** | | | Drafting p. 635 **L 2** Editing and Publishing p. 639 **L 1b, L 2c** |

To see the complete Essential Course of Study, see pp. T23–T28.

 For additional lesson planning help, see **Teacher One Stop DVD.**

# Instructional Support

**Resource Manager Unit 5**

**UNIT SUPPORT**

Academic Vocabulary, p. 3

Additional Academic Vocabulary, p. 4

Grammar Focus p. 5

Text Analysis Workshop pp. 9–10

Writing Workshop: Informative Text:
  Business Letter p. 163

**SELECTION SUPPORT***

**Plan and Teach**

  Lesson planning pages

  Additional leveled selection questions

  Extension activities

**Student Copy Masters**

  Selection summaries in four languages

  Skills copy masters in English and Spanish

  Vocabulary preteaching and support

  Reading Check and Question Support

  Reading Fluency

  *Available for all selections

  † Available on **thinkcentral.com**.

**Language Handbook**

**Vocabulary Practice**

**Best Practices Toolkit**†

**PowerNotes** DVD-ROM†

**Connections: Nonfiction for
Common Core** CD-ROM†

**Teacher One Stop** DVD-ROM

**Student One Stop** DVD-ROM

**Media*Smart*** DVD-ROM

News Reports

**Write*Smart*** CD-ROM†

**GrammarNotes** DVD-ROM†

**WordSharp** CD-ROM†

CREDITS   HELP   QUIT

Create, customize, or print a variety of graphic organizers and writing templates to help your students brainstorm ideas and organize their writing.

Ideas for Writing
Interactive Student Models
Interactive Graphic Organizers
Interactive Revision Lessons
Writing Model Bank
Rubric Generator

TOOL BOX
SHAPE
LINK
Rock
Types of Music

# Differentiated Instruction

## STRUGGLING READERS AND WRITERS

**Resource Manager Unit 5**

Additional Selection Questions

Question Support

Reading Fluency

**Interactive Reader**

**Adapted Interactive Reader**

**Level Up Online Tutorials**

**Audio Anthology**
(with Audio summaries)

**Diagnostic and Selection Tests**

Selection Tests A/B

## ENGLISH LANGUAGE LEARNERS

**Resource Manager Unit 5**

Selection Summaries in English,
Spanish, Vietnamese and Haitian Creole

Skills Copymasters in Spanish

**English Language Learner Adapted
Interactive Reader Teacher's Guide**

**ELL Adapted Interactive Reader**

**Audio Tutor**

**Guide to English for Newcomers**

**Audio Anthology**

**Audio Summaries in Multiple
Languages**
(on **thinkcentral.com**)

## ADVANCED LEARNERS

**Resource Manager Unit 5**

Additional Selection Questions

Ideas for Extension

**Diagnostic and Selection Tests**

Selection Tests B/C

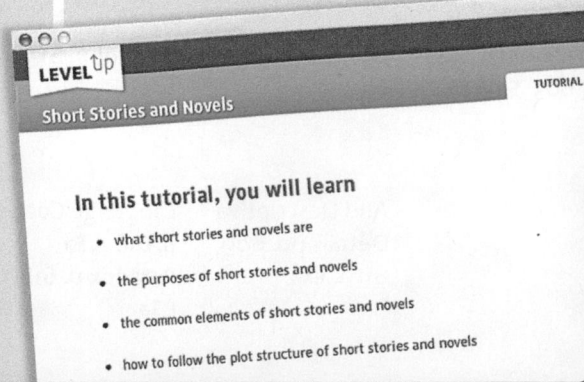

LEVEL up   TUTORIAL
Short Stories and Novels

In this tutorial, you will learn

• what short stories and novels are

• the purposes of short stories and novels

• the common elements of short stories and novels

• how to follow the plot structure of short stories and novels

## Assessment and Reteaching

**Diagnostic and Selection Tests**

**Unit and Benchmark Tests**

**ThinkCentral Online Assessment:**
- All program assessments
- Level Up Online Tutorials

**ExamView Test Generator** on the Teacher One Stop DVD-ROM

**Online Essay Scoring** on **thinkcentral.com**

**ThinkCentral Online Reteaching:**
- Level Up Online Tutorials
- Reteaching Worksheets

**Holt McDougal** Online Essay Scoring

Welcome to Holt McDougal Online Essay Scoring!

This site is designed to help you improve your writing skills and prepare for standardized writing tests. When you write and submit a response to one of the writing prompts on this site, the computerized scoring system will immediately score and deliver feedback on your essay. Other resources on this site will help you prepare, develop, and revise your essay.

**STUDENTS**

Get started by entering the **Writing Zone**

## Professional Development

**Video Center** Based on interviews with program consultants and other educational experts, these videos feature classroom-ready teaching strategies.

**Teacher Toolkit** Includes a Teacher Handbook as well as a range of articles and handouts by program consultants and other educators.

**Janet Allen**

**Jim Burke**

**Kylene Beers**

**Carol Jago**

---

 **at a Glance**

**One Location, Endless Resources**

**Find Resources** Browse all *Holt McDougal Literature* components for the ones that meet your students' needs and match your teaching style.

**Assess Progress and Reteach** Assign electronic versions of program assessments to measure your students' mastery of the Common Core State Standards. On thinkcentral.com, some tests deliver online remediation tutorials to students who have not mastered skills.

 *Interactive Whiteboard Lessons*

Prepare your students for college and careers by teaching relevant, real-world skills through dynamic, interactive instruction. Go to **thinkcentral.com** to browse through all whiteboard lessons, including the following:

- Author's Purpose and Perspective
- Text Structure and Meaning
- Analyzing Informational Text
- Summarizing Text

 Together Holt McDougal and HISTORY® are revolutionizing the study of English/language arts with video that helps students relive and re-imagine the people, places, and events they are discovering through reading. Look for selections with the HISTORY® icon.

## Why do writers WRITE?

Read and discuss the question and the first paragraph. Point out that a writer's purpose sometimes is fairly obvious, as in these examples:

- an ad for a new car (to persuade)
- a story about a funny event at school (to entertain)
- a bicycle repair manual (to inform)

*ACTIVITY* Have some students read their Activity answers aloud. Encourage classmates to ask questions about main points and details of their classmates' answers. Encourage students to talk about topics and contexts that are both familiar and unfamiliar to them.

**CHECK UNDERSTANDING** Have students name the purposes for writing that have been introduced on this page. Ask them to give an additional example of a form of writing meant to fulfill each purpose.

# Why do writers WRITE?

A letter to the editor. A research paper. An e-mail to a friend. Any of these writing products might come from your pen or computer and be shared with others or kept to yourself. The reasons that any individual writes are as varied as the personality and goals of the writer. But the writer always has a purpose for crafting words in a particular form and in a particular way.

*ACTIVITY* List five things you have read and five things you have written in the last month. Answer the following:

- Which did you read to get information? Which did you write to provide information?
- Which tried to persuade you? Which did you write to persuade someone else?
- Which did you write to express how you felt?

Think about your answers. For which purpose did you most often read? For which purpose did you most often write? Are you surprised?

**Find It Online!**
**THINK**central

Go to thinkcentral.com for the interactive version of this unit.

550

## Unit Resources

See resources on the **Teacher One Stop DVD-ROM** *and on* **thinkcentral.com**.

**R** RESOURCE MANAGER UNIT 5

UNIT AND BENCHMARK TESTS

BEST PRACTICES TOOLKIT

INTERACTIVE READER

ADAPTED INTERACTIVE READER

ELL ADAPTED INTERACTIVE READER

LANGUAGE HANDBOOK

VOCABULARY PRACTICE

**TECHNOLOGY**

- Teacher One Stop DVD-ROM
- Student One Stop DVD-ROM
- PowerNotes DVD-ROM
- Write*Smart* CD-ROM
- Media*Smart* DVD-ROM
- GrammarNotes DVD-ROM
- Audio Anthology CD
- Audio Tutor CD

**THINK**central

**Find It Online!**

The interactive version of this unit on **thinkcentral.com** includes

- video and **PowerNotes** introductions to key selections
- audio support—listen or download
- **ThinkAloud** models
- **WordSharp** vocabulary tutorials
- interactive review and remediation

## Preview Unit Goals

| | |
|---|---|
| **TEXT ANALYSIS** | • Identify and analyze tone and diction<br>• Recognize and analyze an author's perspective or purpose<br>• Analyze functional texts, such as consumer documents and technical directions |
| **READING** | • Analyze patterns of organization<br>• Interpret graphic aids<br>• Analyze how an author's ideas are developed and refined |
| **WRITING AND LANGUAGE** | • Write an informational text—business letter<br>• Use nouns, adverbs, and conjunctions correctly |
| **VOCABULARY** | • Use word roots to determine or clarify the meaning of words<br>• Use Greek suffixes to understand domain-specific vocabulary<br>• Determine the technical meanings of words and phrases |
| **ACADEMIC VOCABULARY** | • conclude • construct • implicit<br>• primary • specific |
| **MEDIA AND VIEWING** | • Analyze how events and information are presented in different mediums<br>• Create an online professional profile<br>• Create a news segment |

## Media Smart DVD-ROM

### News with a Purpose

Experience a daring rescue as you explore the features that make TV and Web news informative. Page 600

**UNIT GOALS**

Included in this unit: **RL 1, RL 3–4, RL 6, RL 10, RI 2–7, RI 10, W 2a–f, W 4–7, W 9b, W 10, SL 1–2, SL 5, L 1b, L 2, L 2c, L 4, L 4a–c, L 5a, L 6**

Complete text of the Common Core State Standards is found in the correlation on p. T10. Standards covered in this unit are found in the standards overview (pp. 549A–549B) and on the lesson pages where they are taught.

## Preview Unit Goals

These goals outline the main skills addressed in this unit. Have students familiarize themselves with the list in preparation for the selections. Remind students of the use of color coding to distinguish the skill strands.

Draw students' attention to the Academic Vocabulary terms. Ask volunteers to define any familiar words. Have students record the terms in their **Reader/Writer Notebooks**, along with a preliminary definition for each. Throughout the unit, have students review each term and confirm the definitions by using the terms in writing and speaking.

## DIFFERENTIATED INSTRUCTION

### FOR ENGLISH LANGUAGE LEARNERS

**Academic Vocabulary** Provide students with definitions of each Academic Vocabulary word.

**conclude** (kən klōōd′) *v.* to decide or infer by reasoning

**construct** (kən strukt′) *v.* to systematically create or build

**implicit** (im plis′it) *adj.* not plainly obvious or exhibited; suggested or implied

**primary** (prī′mĕr-ē) *adj.* highest in rank, or first in importance

**specific** (spĭ-sĭf′k) *adj.* definite; of a special sort

Use the copy master to help students learn academic words they will use in this unit and on the Assessment Practice.

**R** **RESOURCE MANAGER—Copy Masters**
Academic Vocabulary p. 3
Additional Academic Vocabulary p. 4

# Focus and Motivate

## COMMON CORE FOCUS

**RI 3** Analyze how an author unfolds an analysis or series of ideas or events, including the order in which the points are made, how they are introduced and developed, and the connections that are drawn between them. **RI 4** Analyze the cumulative impact of specific word choices on meaning and tone. **RI 5** Analyze in detail how an author's ideas or claims are developed and refined by sentences, paragraphs, or larger portions of a text. **RI 6** Determine an author's point of view or purpose in a text and analyze how an author uses rhetoric to advance that point of view or purpose.

# Teach

## Part 1: Author's Purpose and Perspective

**Author's Purpose** Explain that students can identify an author's purpose by thinking about the author's main reason for writing.

To identify and analyze author's purpose, readers may want to consider

- subject
- author's tone
- intended audience
- details and words
- effect on readers

Using this chart as a model, help students analyze various works, such as a newspaper article, an editorial, a short story, and an essay.

| Title | Purpose |
|---|---|
| Subject | |
| Author's tone | |
| Intended audience | |
| Details, words | |
| Effect | |

**BEST PRACTICES TOOLKIT—Transparency**
Analysis Frame: Author's Craft
pp. D21, D24

---

# Author's Purpose
*Essential Course of Study* **ECOS**

Before architects draft their blueprints, they need to understand the purpose of the proposed building. Are they designing a stadium to seat screaming spectators or a library for quiet study? This purpose drives every decision that architects make, from the layout of their buildings to the design. Like architects, writers carefully construct their stories and essays with a specific purpose in mind.

## COMMON CORE

Included in this workshop:
**RI 3** Analyze how an author unfolds an analysis or series of ideas or events, including the order in which the points are made, how they are introduced and developed, and the connections that are drawn between them.
**RI 4** Analyze the cumulative impact of specific word choices on meaning and tone. **RI 5** Analyze in detail how an author's ideas or claims are developed and refined by sentences, paragraphs, or larger portions of a text. **RI 6** Determine an author's point of view or purpose in a text and analyze how an author uses rhetoric to advance that point of view or purpose.

## Part 1: Author's Purpose and Perspective

An **author's purpose** is what the writer hopes to achieve by crafting a particular work. Although a writer may have more than one purpose, usually one purpose stands out. A writer's purpose could be any of the following:

- to inform or explain
- to express thoughts or feelings
- to persuade
- to entertain

You can uncover an author's purpose by looking at the choices the writer made. Every choice—from the subject and the tone to the particular words and other **important details**—is a clue that can reveal the purpose. Another clue is your reaction to what you read. For instance, if you are convinced by an argument to fight for a cause, then the author's **central idea,** or main point, is probably that people should support that cause. Thus, the author's primary purpose is to persuade.

| AUTHOR'S PURPOSE | CLUES IN THE WRITING |
|---|---|
| **TO INFORM OR EXPLAIN**<br>Examples: encyclopedia or magazine articles, documentaries, instruction manuals, warranties, Web sites | • facts and statistics<br>• steps in a process<br>• diagrams or illustrated explanations |
| **TO PERSUADE**<br>Examples: editorials, TV ads, political speeches | • a statement of opinion<br>• supporting evidence<br>• appeals to emotion<br>• a call to action |
| **TO ENTERTAIN**<br>Examples: short stories, novels, plays, humorous essays, movies | • suspenseful or exciting situations<br>• humorous or fascinating details<br>• intriguing characters |
| **TO EXPRESS THOUGHTS OR FEELINGS**<br>Examples: personal essays, poems, diaries, journals | • thoughtful descriptions<br>• insightful observations<br>• the writer's personal feelings |

**552** UNIT 5: AUTHOR'S PURPOSE

---

## DIFFERENTIATED INSTRUCTION

### FOR STRUGGLING READERS

**Note Taking** For students who need help with note taking, hand out the note-taking copy master for Part 1 before reading the text. Have students read each paragraph silently. Then, as you discuss the main points of the text, have students record them on the copy master.

**Visualize** Have students use free-form mapping to associate the author's purposes on this page with examples and writing clues for these purposes.

**RESOURCE MANAGER—Copy Master**
Note Taking p. 9

## MODEL 1: TO INFORM OR EXPLAIN

Writing that informs or explains typically leaves you feeling more knowledgeable. As you read this article, look for clues that suggest its purpose.

### from WEB MASTERS

Nonfiction article by **Joe Bower**

Spiderwebs are flexible yet strong, ultrasensitive, adaptable to different settings, and able to span great distances (compared with the size of their makers). They perform a variety of impressive functions, the most obvious of which is capturing prey.

5   Not all of the world's estimated 37,000 known spider species make webs. In fact, arachnologists categorize spiders based on this ability. Tarantulas and jumping spiders belong to the large group that doesn't make webs. Instead, these arachnids, which are sometimes referred to as wandering spiders, stalk or ambush their prey.

**Close Read**

1. Which words and phrases suggest that this is an informative article? One word has been boxed.

2. Identify one other important detail that suggests the author's purpose is to inform or explain. How does this detail advance the author's purpose?

## MODEL 2: TO EXPRESS THOUGHTS OR FEELINGS

This essay also focuses on spiders, but the writer includes minimal facts. How do the details, the language, and the writer's tone help you understand her feelings about spiders?

### from *Weaving* THE WORLD

Personal essay by **Janisse Ray**

Every night the spiders weave the world back together. This morning I see webs whole again, shining freshly gossamer in the new sun, webs we tore down last night accidentally, setting up the tent on the platform. All day paddling, we have been watching for them—zippers and bananas and crabs, colorful and intriguing.

5 They are everywhere, stitching leaves to trees, and trees to shrubs, and shrubs to ground. . . .

  The spiders have adapted to their fragility, their vulnerability; when we humans bungle into their webs, they scurry off, up a single thread into a sweet bay. They have no new technologies, no new economies. Across the

10 prairies they spin and spin, as they have done for thousands of years, holding this outrageously glorious world together.

**Close Read**

1. Examine the boxed details that the writer uses to describe spiders and their webs. How do these details differ from those in "Web Masters"?

2. Is the writer's attitude toward spiders admiring or matter-of-fact? Support your answer.

TEXT ANALYSIS WORKSHOP   **553**

## MODEL 1: TO INFORM OR EXPLAIN

**Close Read**

1. *Possible answer: Words and phrases that suggest that this is an informative article include "estimated 37,000 known spider species" (line 5), "in fact," "arachnologists" (line 6), and "which are sometimes referred to as wandering spiders" (line 8).*

2. *Possible answer: Other important details that suggest the author's purpose are his inclusion of a statistic, the "nonfiction article" byline, the matter-of-fact tone, and facts presented in a straightforward manner. These details advance the author's purpose by presenting facts in a format consistent with the genre of expository nonfiction.*

## MODEL 2: TO EXPRESS THOUGHTS OR FEELINGS

**Close Read**

1. *Possible answer: The boxed details are the writer's personal observations rather than verifiable facts and statistics. Words and phrases all have very positive—not neutral—connotations. Readers can tell that the writer is marveling at spiders and their place in the world.*

2. *Possible answer: The writer's tone is admiring, not matter-of-fact, as evidenced by words and phrases such as "spiders weave the world back together" (line 1), "colorful and intriguing" (line 4), and "holding this outrageously glorious world together" (line 11). The writer makes spiders seem both graceful in their movements and an important part of this world.*

---

### FOR STRUGGLING READERS

**Analysis Support: Author's Purpose** Have students list as many facts and statistics as they can find in "Web Masters."
***Possible answer:*** *Spiderwebs are flexible, strong, ultrasensitive, adaptable, and "able to span great distances"; webs capture prey; there are 37,000 spider species; tarantulas and jumping spiders "stalk or ambush their prey" rather than make webs.*

Next, challenge students to identify facts and statistics in "Weaving the World." Elicit that Model 2 has few, if any, facts and no statistics. Ask what this difference suggests about the author's purpose. ***Possible answer:*** *The purpose is not to inform or explain.*

**Online Remediation** THINK central

Are your students struggling with text analysis skills? Consider assigning them one or more **Level Up Online Tutorials** as remediation before beginning this unit. Log in to **thinkcentral.com** to view a list of the skills addressed by **Level Up**.

# *Teach*

## RECOGNIZING AUTHOR'S PERSPECTIVE

**Different Perspectives** To highlight the idea that perspectives may differ sharply even when purposes are the same, write this sentence on the board, or use another one that focuses on an issue over which students are divided:

> It is dangerous to talk on a cell phone while driving.

- Have the class form groups based on whether they agree or disagree with the statement.

- Have groups complete this chart by suggesting perspective-specific examples suitable for a persuasive essay on the subject. Then have them compare their charts.

| Perspective Clues | Examples |
|---|---|
| Focus | |
| Word choice | |
| Tone | |

 **BEST PRACTICES TOOLKIT—Transparency** Two-Column Chart p. A25

## Part 2: Organization and Format

**Patterns of Organization** After students read the chart, discuss with them that these patterns of organization can vary. For example, although chronological order usually proceeds forward in time, an author of a nonfiction article may begin by describing an event and then explaining what led up to it, while an author of fiction may use flashback. Similarly, an author using comparison-contrast may first present similarities and then describe differences. Or, the author may focus on differences first and then discuss similarities. Point out that authors choose the approach that best serves their purpose.

## CHECK UNDERSTANDING

Have students describe two reasons for using a particular pattern of organization.

---

## RECOGNIZING AUTHOR'S PERSPECTIVE

Even if they have similar purposes, no two writers will approach a topic in the same way. Their perspectives influence what they write and how they write it. An **author's perspective** is the lens through which a writer looks at a topic. This lens is colored by the writer's experiences, values, and feelings.

Consider the two excerpts on the previous page. Factual articles, such as "Web Masters," usually don't reveal a writer's viewpoint. However, literary essays, such as "Weaving the World," include clues that convey an author's perspective. Even though the author of "Weaving the World" includes *some* factual information, personal examples and opinions play a greater role in her description. Notice how the following clues reveal a writer who appreciates nature.

- **Word Choice** Words and phrases such as "colorful and intriguing" and "vulnerability" reveal the writer's fascination with the wonders of nature.

- **Tone** A writer's **tone** is his or her attitude toward a subject. The writer does not focus on spiders' creepy qualities. Her tone is admiring, not fearful.

## Part 2: Organization and Format

To achieve their purpose, writers of both literary and expository nonfiction choose particular patterns of organization, such as **cause-effect** and **classification.** Recognizing these patterns can help you determine an author's purpose, locate information, and understand the connections between ideas. Here are two common patterns.

| CHRONOLOGICAL | COMPARISON-CONTRAST |
|---|---|
| **What It Does** <br> • Describes events in time order | **What It Does** <br> • Highlights similarities and differences between two or more subjects |
| **Why Writers Use It** <br> • To explain a sequence of events in an easy-to-follow way <br> • To tell a suspenseful or exciting story | **Why Writers Use It** <br> • To show the benefits of one subject over another <br> • To compare an unfamiliar subject with a familiar one |
| **How to Recognize It** <br> • Look for signal words such as *before, finally, first, next,* and *then.* | **How to Recognize It** <br> • Look for signal words such as *also, and, but, in contrast, unlike,* and *while.* |

In addition to these patterns, nonfiction writers use **text features** to help you understand a topic. Imagine a scientific article without **subheadings, captions,** and **boldfaced type** to guide you. Who wouldn't be confused?

---

## DIFFERENTIATED INSTRUCTION

### FOR STRUGGLING READERS

**Note Taking** For those students who need help, hand out the note-taking copy master for Part 2. Read and discuss the text. Assist students in completing their note-taking copy master as needed.

**R** RESOURCE MANAGER—Copy Master Note Taking p. 10

### FOR ADVANCED LEARNERS/PRE–AP

**Identify Pattern Combinations** Have students identify works they have read in which the author combines two or more patterns of organization. Challenge students to explain how the pattern combinations help the authors accomplish their purpose.

**MODEL: CLASSIFICATION ORGANIZATION**

In this scientific article, the writer uses classification organization to group information by common characteristics. As you read, think about how this organization, with the help of the text features, helps you digest the information.

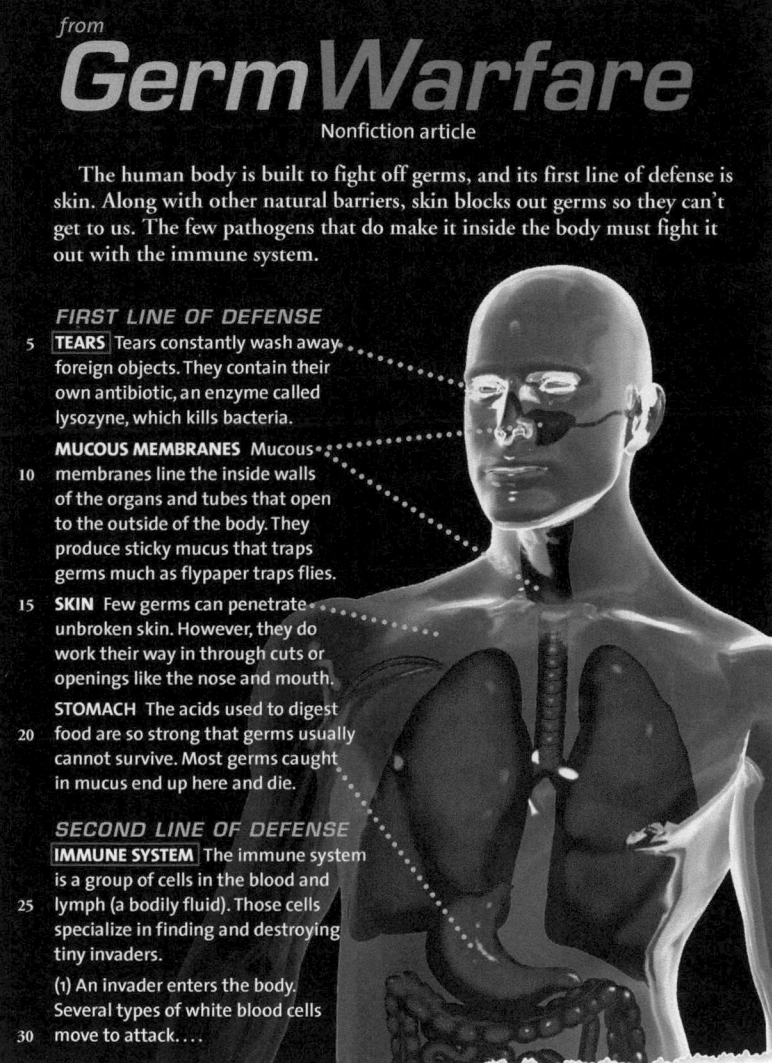

*from*

# GermWarfare

Nonfiction article

The human body is built to fight off germs, and its first line of defense is skin. Along with other natural barriers, skin blocks out germs so they can't get to us. The few pathogens that do make it inside the body must fight it out with the immune system.

*FIRST LINE OF DEFENSE*

5 **TEARS** Tears constantly wash away foreign objects. They contain their own antibiotic, an enzyme called lysozyne, which kills bacteria.

**MUCOUS MEMBRANES** Mucous
10 membranes line the inside walls of the organs and tubes that open to the outside of the body. They produce sticky mucus that traps germs much as flypaper traps flies.

15 **SKIN** Few germs can penetrate unbroken skin. However, they do work their way in through cuts or openings like the nose and mouth.

**STOMACH** The acids used to digest
20 food are so strong that germs usually cannot survive. Most germs caught in mucus end up here and die.

*SECOND LINE OF DEFENSE*

**IMMUNE SYSTEM** The immune system
25 is a group of cells in the blood and lymph (a bodily fluid). Those cells specialize in finding and destroying tiny invaders.

(1) An invader enters the body. Several types of white blood cells
30 move to attack. . . .

**Close Read**

1. Into what two main categories is the information grouped? Explain how you can tell.

2. Notice the boldfaced words used throughout the article. Two have been boxed. What purpose do they serve?

3. What does the information in the annotated diagram add to your understanding of mucous membranes?

**MODEL: CLASSIFICATION ORGANIZATION**

Close Read

1. ***Possible answer:*** *Information is presented in two categories: the body's two lines of defense against intrusive germs. The heads "First Line of Defense" and "Second Line of Defense" are clues to the organization.*

2. ***Possible answer:*** *Boldfaced words identify each element of the body's first and second lines of defense. Readers can see at a glance which parts of the body help fight germs.*

3. ***Possible answer:*** *The annotated diagram shows readers exactly where mucous membranes are located—information many readers might not know. The annotation (lines 9–14) explains how the mucous membranes function to trap germs.*

---

## DIFFERENTIATED INSTRUCTION

**FOR STRUGGLING READERS**

**Comprehension: Classification** Write these items on the board and have students explain what the items have in common that enables the writer to group them together: *tears, mucous membranes, skin, stomach.*

**Concept Support** On the board, list the italicized terms. Then give the examples in random order for students to classify.

- *cause-effect:* The rainstorm flooded roads.
- *classification:* There are two kinds of medicine for the illness.
- *chronological order:* Jake arrived at the party after Emily.
- *comparison-contrast:* It is generally warmer in Florida than in Vermont.

## Part 3: Compare Texts

### Close Read

1. **Possible answer:** Alvarez is sharing her personal thoughts and feelings. Through these details, she is probably trying to recreate for readers a common fear: having something go awry on an airplane. The details that Alvarez includes are probably intended to make readers smile or at least see the humor in the situation. Alvarez is describing an experience—facing an emergency on a plane and not having paid attention to the emergency procedures and drills—that many people can relate to.

2. **Possible answer:** Alvarez's tone might be described as honest and lightly humorous. Three details that convey the tone include "Oh Lord, I thought, this is it!" (line 3), "something that really worries me: when confident-looking businessmen look worried" (lines 13–14), and "I would have already died of terror" (line 21).

3. **Possible answer:** Alvarez's purpose is to express her thoughts and feelings. The details mentioned above are all observations about a personal experience.

4. **Possible answer:** Alvarez is writing from the perspective of someone who has been through this suspenseful, fearful situation and can still find something to smile about. She has a good-natured perspective on this experience.

**IF STUDENTS NEED HELP . . .** Have students reread lines 19–21. Discuss how these lines reveal that the author has flown before ("I never paid attention") and how her lighthearted tone suggests that she can laugh about such experiences.

## Part 3: Compare Texts

What happens when lightning strikes an airplane? Both of the following excerpts answer this question, but their similarities end there. As you read, use what you have just learned about clues—details, tone, and choice of words—to determine each author's purpose and perspective.

from
# Aha Moment

### Essay by Julia Alvarez

I was in the tiny bathroom in the back of the plane when I felt the slamming jolt, then the horrible swerve that threw me against the door. Oh Lord, I thought, this is it! Somehow I managed to unbolt the door and scramble out. The flight attendants, already strapped in, waved wildly for me
5 to sit down. As I lunged ahead toward my seat, passengers looked up at me with the stricken expression of creatures who know they are about to die.

"I think we got hit by lightning," the girl in the seat next to mine said. She was from a small town in east Texas, and this was only her second time on an airplane. She had won a trip to England by competing in a high school
10 geography bee and was supposed to make a connecting flight when we landed in Newark.

In the next seat, at the window, sat a young businessman who had been confidently working. Now he looked worried—something that really worries me: when confident-looking businessmen look worried. The laptop was put
15 away. "Something's not right," he said.

The pilot's voice came over the speaker. I heard vaguely through my fear, "Engine number two . . . hit . . . emergency landing . . . New Orleans." When he was done, the voice of a flight attendant came on, reminding us of the emergency procedures she had reviewed before takeoff. Of course I never paid
20 attention to this drill, always figuring that if we ever got to the point where we needed to use life jackets, I would have already died of terror.

Now we began a roller-coaster ride through the thunderclouds. I was ready to faint, but when I saw the face of the girl next to me I pulled myself together. I reached for her hand and reassured her that we were going to make it. "What a
25 story you're going to tell when you get home!" I said. "After this, London's going to seem like small potatoes."

### Close Read

1. Reread the boxed details. Is Alvarez reporting "just the facts" or is she sharing personal impressions as well? Explain the intended effect of these details.

2. Although Alvarez describes a frightening experience, her tone is not fearful. Identify the tone and three details that convey it.

3. Do you think Alvarez's primary purpose is to persuade, to entertain, to inform, or to express thoughts and feelings? What important details from the essay advance this purpose?

4. Consider the descriptions in lines 1–3 and 19–21, as well as Alvarez's tone. What can you infer about her perspective?

## DIFFERENTIATED INSTRUCTION

### FOR STRUGGLING READERS

**Vocabulary Support** Introduce these words from "Aha Moment." Have students read the context for each word and suggest a synonym to replace it:

- *jolt* (line 2), "bump"
- *swerve* (line 2), "sharp turn"
- *lunged* (line 5), "dove"
- *stricken* (line 6), "worried" or "scared"

### FOR ENGLISH LANGUAGE LEARNERS

**Vocabulary: Idioms** Help students use context clues to determine the meanings of these idioms in the essay: *pulled myself together* (line 23), "calmed myself down"; *make it* (line 24), "survive"; *like small potatoes* (line 26), "not very difficult."

Now read this article, and compare it to Alvarez's dramatic account.
Use the clues in the text to identify the author's purpose and perspective.

# Aircraft Built to Shrug Off Lightning Strike

Newspaper article by **Tom McNamee**

Lightning strikes airplanes now and again, but seldom with tragic results.

In a typical year, lightning
5 causes only a handful of aircraft accidents in the United States, and occasionally none at all. From 1983 through 1995, 29 accidents resulted in 37 deaths. But a 30th
10 accident proved the exception. On Aug. 2, 1985, lightning struck a Lockheed L-1011 as it came in for a landing at Dallas-Fort Worth International Airport, slamming
15 the jet to the ground and killing 137 passengers.

One witness on the ground, an aviation weather expert, recalled seeing "lightning from cloud to
20 cloud." Another witness said the plane exploded even before crashing into "just a big ball of fire."

**A Plane's Built-in Protection**

As a rule, however, the laws of nature favor aircraft in a collision
25 with lightning. Lightning's electrical charge usually spreads across the entire outer skin of the craft, robbing it of its concentrated power, before it is shed like rainwater.
30 The metallic skin of some aircraft is ideal for conducting and diluting an electrical charge. And planes with skins made of lighter-weight composite materials, such as

The most common areas for lightning to strike a plane include the wing tips and the fuselage nose.

35 graphite, are commonly fitted with an underlying metal mesh to collect and route the charge. . . .

**Aircraft Size and Condition**

As a rule, larger planes are least threatened by lightning, said Donald
40 Kemp, retired chief of accident investigations for the Federal Aviation Administration. Larger aircraft have more surface area to absorb lightning's electrical charge,
45 and they are fitted with pencil-like "shedders" on the back of the wings to collect and "bleed off" electricity.

"If a plane is in proper condition, you shouldn't have a problem,"
50 Kemp said.

**Close Read**

1. How do the boxed details in this article differ from those in "Aha Moment"?

2. Identify two text features that the writer uses. What information do these features convey?

3. What is the author's purpose? Describe two clues that helped you determine that purpose.

4. Consider the writer's tone and the details in this article. Do they tell you anything about the writer's perspective? Explain your answer.

---

**Close Read**

1. *Possible answer:* The boxed details are facts and statistics rather than personal observations.

2. *Possible answer:* The title of the article conveys the main idea—generally what the article is about. The subheads tell the main idea of each section. Students might also identify the caption and the photo as text features.

3. *Possible answer:* The author's purpose is to inform and explain. Two clues are the statistics about aircraft accidents; the "newspaper article" byline; straight-forward, objective language; and quotes from experts and witnesses.

4. *Possible answer:* Readers do not get a sense of the writer behind the words. The tone is objective, the details factual; the writer is simply reporting the facts in a neutral way without revealing anything about himself.

## Assess and Reteach

### Assess

Ask students to identify the purpose and perspective of previously read works of nonfiction and fiction. Have them identify organization patterns and text features in these works.

### Reteach

For students who are unable to apply the workshop skills to previously read works, select from these reteaching options.

1. Review with students the note-taking copy masters for this lesson. Have students restate the information in the copy masters in their own words and provide examples.

2. Refer students to one or more recently read selections. Help students identify the author's purpose and perspective by asking questions such as these:
   - Why did the author write this selection?
   - For what audience is the selection written?
   - What is the subject of the selection?
   - What is the author's tone?

Next, ask questions to guide students' identification of organization patterns and text features.

---

**FOR STRUGGLING READERS**

**Analysis Support: Author's Purpose and Perspective** Have students create a chart to compare and contrast the models on pages 556 and 557 in terms of facts, details, focus, tone, and language. Then, using the information in the chart, help students draw conclusions about differences in the authors' purposes and perspectives.

**FOR ENGLISH LANGUAGE LEARNERS**

**Comprehension: Generalization** Write these words and phrases on the board: *seldom* (line 2), *typical* (line 4), *As a rule* (lines 23 and 38), *usually* (line 26), and *most common* (photo caption). Have students find these words and phrases in the text and then use Think-Pair-Share to clarify what generalization the writer is making in each context.

💼 **BEST PRACTICES TOOLKIT—Transparency** Think-Pair-Share p. A18

# Focus and Motivate

## COMMON CORE FOCUS

**RI 3** Analyze how an author unfolds a series of ideas or events. **RI 4** Determine the figurative meaning of phrases as they are used in a text; analyze the cumulative impact of specific word choices on meaning and tone. **RI 5** Analyze in detail how an author's ideas are developed and refined. **W 4** Produce informative writing in which the organization and style are appropriate to task and purpose. **L 1b** Use various types of clauses to convey specific meanings and add variety and interest to writing.

## SUMMARY

Jamaica Kincaid recalls how she spent mornings in Antigua. She goes on to describe mornings on the island where she lives now: Manhattan.

## What place do you call HOME?

Pose the question. Elicit details that students associate with home. Extend the discussion by asking what elements—for example, family members and possessions—combine to create the feeling that a place is "home." Conclude by having students complete the *QUICKWRITE* and share their responses.

---

## Island Morning

Descriptive Essay by Jamaica Kincaid

# What place do you call HOME?

### COMMON CORE

**RI 3** Analyze how an author unfolds a series of ideas or events. **RI 4** Determine the figurative meaning of phrases as they are used in a text; analyze the cumulative impact of specific word choices on meaning and tone. **RI 5** Analyze in detail how an author's ideas are developed and refined.

The word *home* can mean many different things. When you think about your home, you might envision the building you live in or your own familiar neighborhood. You may picture the streets of your hometown or the landscape of your home country. *Home* can include the people you care about and your memories of growing up. It can even be a place where you no longer live that still feels more like home than where you live today.

*QUICKWRITE* What does the word *home* bring to mind? In a short paragraph, describe the first image—be it person, place, or thing—you picture when you think of *home*. If you'd like, attach a sketch to accompany your description.

558

---

## Selection Resources

*See resources on the* **Teacher One Stop DVD-ROM** *and on* underline{thinkcentral.com}.

**RESOURCE MANAGER UNIT 5**
Plan and Teach, pp. 11–18
Summary pp. 19–20†‡*
Text Analysis and Reading
   Skill, pp. 21–25†*
Grammar and Style, p. 27

**DIAGNOSTIC AND SELECTION TESTS**
Selection Tests, pp. 143–146

**BEST PRACTICES TOOLKIT**
Word Squares p. E10
Three-Column Journal, p. B10
Comparison Matrix, p. A24
Classification Chart, p. B17

**TECHNOLOGY**
- Teacher One Stop DVD-ROM
- Student One Stop DVD-ROM
- Audio Anthology CD
- GrammarNotes DVD-ROM
- ExamView Test Generator
  on the **Teacher One Stop**

\* Resources for Differentiation     † Also in Spanish     ‡ In Haitian Creole and Vietnamese

## TEXT ANALYSIS: DICTION

**Diction** includes both a writer's choice of words as well as syntax, or the way those words are arranged into sentences. Jamaica Kincaid arranges words in unique ways, often using repetition to create rhythmic sounds. Describing her neighbors' morning routine, she writes,

*All of these different people doing all these different things did this one thing: they were all up and about by half past five in the morning.*

As you read, look for other passages in which Kincaid creates unusual sentences or chooses words to establish rhythm as well as imagery.

**Review: Tone**

## READING SKILL: ANALYZE PATTERNS OF ORGANIZATION

To show connections between ideas, writers arrange their information in an order that emphasizes those connections. In this essay, Kincaid uses both **comparison and contrast** and **chronological order.**

- When organizing according to comparison and contrast, Kincaid presents all of the details about one subject or place and then all of the details about another.
- When Kincaid uses chronological order, she presents events in the order in which they typically occur.

As you read, record **signal words** that help you identify both patterns of organization that Kincaid uses in this essay.

| Signal Words | Pattern of Organization |
|---|---|
| "by six o'clock" (line 29) | chronological order |
| "I now live in ..." (line 93) | comparison and contrast |
| | |

 Complete the activities in your **Reader/Writer Notebook.**

## Meet the Author

# Jamaica Kincaid
**born 1949**

### Leaving the Island
Jamaica Kincaid is the name Elaine Potter Richardson chose for herself when she began writing. Born on Antigua, a small Caribbean island that was then a British colony, Kincaid was educated in British schools. Although she was often at the top of her class, her mother removed her from school at age 17 against her wishes and sent her to America to support the family.

### Musical Musings
When she arrived in America, Kincaid explains, "I didn't know there was such a world as the literary world. I didn't know anything, except maybe how to put one foot in front of the other." She broke ties with her family and took a number of different jobs— and was fired from each one. In 1976, Kincaid landed a job at the *New Yorker,* a literary magazine, where her unique and resilient writing voice emerged. Much of Kincaid's writing expresses her anger at colonialism and the British disregard for her identity as an African-Caribbean woman. Her prose is celebrated for its lyrical beauty. "My work," she says, "is a chord that develops in many different ways."

### BACKGROUND TO THE ESSAY
**History of Antigua**
Kincaid's birthplace, a small island in the eastern Caribbean, was a British colony for over 300 years. In 1981, Antigua united with a small neighboring island to become Antigua and Barbuda, an independent state. Most Antiguans have African heritage, as they are descendants of slaves brought to the island centuries ago to work in the tobacco and sugarcane fields.

Author Online  THINK central
Go to **thinkcentral.com.**
KEYWORD: HML9-559

559

---

# Teach

TEXT ANALYSIS
COMMON CORE
RI 4

## ● *Model the Skill:* DICTION

To help students understand how a writer's diction helps set a tone, read aloud this example:

> Home should be a place of safety, a shelter from life's storms. Home should be a refuge, a sanctuary, a fortress.

Point out the rhythm Kincaid creates by using commas in this selection, as well as her repetition of the word "home." Tell students that Kincaid uses the words *shelter, refuge, sanctuary,* and *fortress* as synonyms for "home." Explain that word choice, rhythm and repetition establish a comforting tone.

**GUIDED PRACTICE** Have pairs of students use this example or the example on page 559 as the model for an original sentence. Discuss the results.

READING SKILL
COMMON CORE
RI 3,
RI 5

## ■ ANALYZE PATTERNS OF ORGANIZATION

Review the explanation, making sure that students understand the difference in purpose between the two patterns. After discussing the examples of signal words, share other words and phrases that signal patterns of organization, such as these:

**Comparison and contrast:** *similarly, like, both, however, on the other hand*

**Chronological order:** *first, next, later, then, in the morning, after supper*

**GUIDED PRACTICE** Discuss the type and effectiveness of the pattern of organization in the text about the author.

**R** RESOURCE MANAGER—Copy Master Analyze Patterns of Organization p. 23 (for student use while reading the selection)

---

## DIFFERENTIATED INSTRUCTION

### FOR STRUGGLING READERS
**Reinforce the Concept** Explain that comparison emphasizes *similarities* between people, places, or things, whereas contrast emphasizes *differences.* Point out that comparisons and contrasts sometimes are directly stated but at other times must be inferred from details.

### FOR ADVANCED LEARNERS/PRE–AP
**Extend the Concept** Point out that both patterns of organization can have variations. For example, a writer who uses comparison and contrast may make point-by-point comparisons instead of exhausting one topic before describing the other. A writer using chronological order may include flashbacks. Have students name topics whose development might use these variations.

**READ WITH A PURPOSE**

*Help students set a purpose for reading. Tell them to look for differences between Kincaid's two island homes.*

**TEXT ANALYSIS**      **COMMON CORE**   **RI 4**

**Ⓐ DICTION**

**Possible answer:** *By listing each fruit and vegetable separately, Kincaid emphasizes the abundance and diversity of items grown on the island. Listing the items in this way, repeating the word* and *instead of using commas to separate the items, strengthens the stylistic rhythm of her language.*

# Island
## MORNING
### Jamaica Kincaid

I grew up on an island in the West Indies which has an area of a hundred and eight square miles. On the island were many sugarcane fields and a sugar-making factory and a factory where both white and dark rum were made. There were cotton fields, but there were not as many cotton fields as there were sugarcane fields. There were arrowroot[1] fields and tobacco fields, too, but there were not as many arrowroot fields and tobacco fields as there were cotton fields. Some of the fifty-four thousand people who lived on the island grew bananas and mangoes and eddoes and dasheen and christophine[2] and sweet potatoes and white potatoes and plums and guavas and papaws and
10 limes and lemons and oranges and grapefruits, and every Saturday they would bring them to the market, which was on Market Street, and they would sell the things they had grown. This was the only way many of them could make Ⓐ a living, and, though it sounds like farming, they weren't farmers in the way a Midwestern wheatgrower is a farmer, and they don't think of the plots of land on which they grew these things as The Farm. Instead, the plots of land were called The Ground. They might say, "Today, me a go up ground." The Ground was often many miles away from where they lived, and they got there not by taking a truck or some other kind of automotive transportation but by riding a donkey or by walking. A small number—a very small number—of the fifty-
20 four thousand people worked in banks or in offices. The rest of them—the ones who didn't grow things that were sold in the market on Saturday or work in the factories or in the fields, the banks or the offices—were carpenters or

1. **arrowroot:** a West Indian plant from which a starch is derived, for use in cooking and medicine.
2. **eddoes and dasheen and christophine:** eddoes and dasheen are plants with edible corms, or small bulblike growths. Christophine is a fruit-growing plant.

**Analyze Visuals ▶**

Examine the painting on page 561. What **mood** do the bright colors, busy people, and whimsical animals create? Explain your answer.

**❶ Targeted Passage**

**Ⓐ DICTION**
Reread lines 7–12 aloud. What is the effect of listing each fruit and vegetable separately instead of simply referring to the crops as a group?

Detail of *Harvest Scene with Twelve People,* R. Mervilus. Oil on canvas. Private collection. © SuperStock.

## DIFFERENTIATED INSTRUCTION

**FOR ENGLISH LANGUAGE LEARNERS**

**Vocabulary Support** Use Word Squares to teach these words: *transportation* (line 18), *automatic* (line 28), *devotion* (line 72), *definition* (line 94), *vehicles* (line 102), *identically* (line 106).

📐 **BEST PRACTICES TOOLKIT—Transparency** Word Squares p. E10

**FOR STRUGGLING READERS**

In combination with the *Audio Anthology CD,* use one or more Targeted Passages (pp. 560, 564, 565) to ensure that students focus on key events, concepts, and skills. Targeted Passages are also good for English learners.

**❶ Targeted Passage [Lines 1–12]**

This passage introduces Kincaid's childhood home.

• Where did Jamaica Kincaid grow up? (lines 1–2)

## B Model the Skill: DICTION

Show students how to analyze repetition by putting the details in these lines into chart form, as shown:

| Got up . . . | On . . . | To go to . . . |
|---|---|---|
| early | weekdays | work or school |
| early | Saturdays | market |
| early | Sundays | church |

**Possible answer:** *By repeating the phrase, the author emphasizes the routine, active lives of the people. The repetition also maintains the kind of rhythm that is characteristic of Kincaid's style.*

 **BEST PRACTICES TOOLKIT—Transparency**
Three-Column Journal p. B10

**Extend the Discussion** How does Kincaid keep the idea of getting up early every day from sounding unpleasant?

## C GRAMMAR AND STYLE

**Coordinating Conjunctions** Writers use coordinating conjunctions to connect elements of equal or nearly equal status and to combine ideas. For example, in lines 33–35, Kincaid uses *but* to combine the idea of the sun's rising with the idea that the air remains cool. Combining these ideas into one sentence creates a more flowing style than a series of short, simple sentences would do. Ask students to locate the appearances of *and* and *but* in these lines. Urge them to watch for other places in the text in which Kincaid uses co-ordinating conjunctions to combine ideas and make sentences flow.

---

masons or servants in the new hotels for tourists which were appearing suddenly all over the island, or servants in private homes, or seamstresses, or tailors, or shopkeepers, or fishermen, or dockworkers, or schoolchildren. All of these different people doing all these different things did this one thing: they were all up and about by half past five in the morning, and they did this without the help of an alarm clock or an automatic clock radio. Every morning—workday, Saturday, or Sunday—the whole island was alive by six o'clock. People got up
30 early on weekdays to go to work or to school; they got up early on Saturday to go to market; and they got up early on Sunday to go to church. **B**

    It is true that the early morning is the most beautiful time of day on the island. The sun has just come up and is immediately big and bright, the way the sun always is on the island, but the air is still cool from the night; the sky is deep, cool blue (like the sea, it gets lighter as the day wears on, and then it gets darker, until by midnight it looks black); the red in the hibiscus and the flamboyant[3] flowers seems redder; the green of the trees and grass seems greener. If it is December, there is dew everywhere: dew on the painted red galvanized rooftops;[4] dew on my mother's upside-down washtubs; dew on the stones that
40 make up her stone heap (a round mound of big and little stones in the middle of our yard; my mother spreads out soapy white laundry on these stones, so that the hot sun will bleach them even whiter); dew on the vegetables in my mother's treasured (to her, horrible to me) vegetable garden. But it wasn't to admire any of these things that people got up so early. I had never, in all the time I lived there, heard anyone say, "What a beautiful morning." Once, just the way I had read it in a book, I stretched and said to my mother, "Oh, isn't it a really lovely morning?" She didn't reply to that at all, but she pulled my eyelids this way and that and then said that my sluggish liver was getting even more sluggish. I don't know why people got up so early, but I do know that they took great pride in
50 this. It wasn't unusual at all to hear one woman say to another, "Me up since **C** way 'fore day mornin'," and for the other woman to say back to her, with a laugh, "Yes, my dear, you know de early bird ketch de early worm."

    In our house, we got up every day at half past five. This is what got us up: every morning, Mr. Jarvis—a dockworker who lived with his wife (she sold sweets she made herself to schoolchildren at the bus depot just before they boarded buses that would take them back to their homes in the country) and their eight children in a house at the very end of our street—would take his herd of goats to pasture. At exactly half past five, he and his goats reached our house. We heard the cries of the goats and the sound the stake at the end of the chain tied around their
60 necks made as it dragged along the street. Above the sound of what my mother called "the early morning racket," we could hear Mr. Jarvis whistling. Mostly, he whistled the refrain of an old but popular calypso[5] tune. The words in the refrain were "Come le' we go, Soukie, Come le' we go." If we heard only the crying of

---

3. **flamboyant:** another name for the royal poinciana (poin'sē-ăn'ə) tree, known for its huge red flowers.
4. **galvanized rooftops:** metal roofs coated with a layer of zinc to prevent rust.
5. **calypso** (kə-lĭp'sō): a type of West Indian music based on African rhythms, often with lyrics about local events or personalities.

**B DICTION**
Reread lines 28–31. What effect is created by the **repetition** of the phrase "got up early"?

**C GRAMMAR AND STYLE**
Reread lines 32–50. Kincaid creates long, fluid sentences by using the **coordinating conjunctions** *and* and *but*.

**Language Coach**

**Idioms** Groups of words that have a special meaning different from the meaning of each separate word are **idioms.** Lines 53 and 58 contain the same idiom for a time expression. Identify the idiom and tell what it means.

---

## DIFFERENTIATED INSTRUCTION

### FOR ENGLISH LANGUAGE LEARNERS

**Language Coach**  COMMON CORE RI 4

**Idioms** *Possible answer: half past five = 5:30* Have students reread lines 29–31. Ask students what the phrase "got up early" means. *Possible answer: It means woke up and started the day early.*

### FOR STRUGGLING READERS

**Develop Reading Fluency** Point out the colloquial speech found in lines 50–63. Model for students an effective way to read the lines. Have students practice reading the following sentences in small groups, with particular attention to the cadences of the colloquial language. Then have student volunteers read the colloquial phrases to the entire class.

**R RESOURCE MANAGER—Copy Master**
Reading Fluency p. 28

*Farm in Haiti,* Roosevelt. Oil on canvas. Private collection. © SuperStock.

the goats and the sound of their chain, we knew it was Mr. Jarvis's son Nigel, a rude wharf-rat boy, who was taking the goats to pasture. **D**

We weren't the only ones who got up to the sound of Mr. Jarvis and his goats. Mr. Gordon, a man who grew lettuce and sold most of it to the new hotels and who lived right next to us, would get up soon after Mr. Jarvis passed. He would throw open all the windows and all the doors in his house, and he would turn on 70 his radio and tune it to a station in St. Croix,[6] a station which at that hour played American country-and-Western music. It may have been from this that my mother developed her devotion to the music of Hank Williams.[7] Mr. Gordon was very nice to my family, but that didn't prevent me from deciding that he resembled a monkey, and so I nicknamed him Monkey Lettuce. I called him this only behind his and my parents' back, of course. We never tuned our radio to the station in St. Croix. Instead, at exactly seven o'clock, my parents turned on our radio and tuned it to the station on our island. A man's voice would say, "It is seven o'clock." Then another voice, a completely different voice, would say, "This is BBC London."[8] Then we would listen to the news being broadcast. At 80 around that time, we sat down to eat breakfast. **E**

---

6. **St. Croix** (kroi): an island in the Caribbean Sea, one of the U.S. Virgin Islands.
7. **Hank Williams:** American songwriter, known for many country-and-Western hits, who died at the age of 29.
8. **BBC London:** the British Broadcasting Corporation, based in London, broadcasts in many areas that are part of the Commonwealth of Nations.

**D DICTION**
Reread lines 61–65. Compare the dialect in the song Kincaid quotes with Kincaid's own words, such as "a rude wharf-rat boy." Describe how they differ.

**E PATTERNS OF ORGANIZATION**
Identify the pattern of organization used in lines 75–80, and cite the specific words that signal this pattern. How does the organization help you to follow the events Kincaid describes?

ISLAND MORNING    **563**

Between the time I got up and eight o'clock, I would have helped my mother fill her washtubs with water, swept up the yard, fed the chickens, taken a bath in cold water, polished my shoes, pressed my school uniform (gray pleated-linen tunic, pink poplin blouse), gone to the grocer (Mr. Richards) to buy fresh bread (two fourpence loaves, one each for my mother and father; a twopence loaf for me; and three penny loaves, one each for my little brothers) and also to buy butter and cheese (made in New Zealand), gone to Miss Roma to have my hair freshly braided, and eaten a breakfast of porridge, eggs, bread and butter, cheese, and hot Ovaltine.[9] By that time, it was no longer early morning on our island, 90 and half an hour later, together with two hundred and ninety-nine other girls and three hundred boys, I would be in my school auditorium singing, "All things bright and beautiful, All creatures great and small."

 **Targeted Passage**

I now live in Manhattan. The only thing it has in common with the island where I grew up is a geographical definition. Certainly no one I know gets up at half past five, at six o'clock, at seven o'clock, at half past seven, at eight o'clock. I know one person who sleeps all day and stays up all night. I know another person who has to take a nap if he gets up before noon. And how easy it is, I have noticed, to put a great distance between you and a close friend if you should call that friend before ten in the morning. **F**

100 I wake up, still, without an alarm, at half past five. In the neighborhood in which I live, it is very quiet at that hour. It is not romantic at all to hear nothing in the city. At around six o'clock, I begin to hear the sound of moving vehicles. Trucks. I know they are trucks because the sound I hear is a rumbling sound that only trucks make. The sound sometimes comes from streets far away. If I get up and look out, I might not see anyone. If I see anyone, it is always two or three men together, dressed identically, in tight black leather pants, a black leather jacket, a black leather cap, and black leather boots. They will walk very quickly down my street as if they are in a great hurry. When I look out, I never notice the early light playing on the street or on the brownstone houses across 110 the street from me. In Manhattan, I notice only whether it is sunny or bright or cloudy and gray or raining or snowing. I never notice things like gradations of light,[10] but my friends tell me that they are there.

Between six and seven, I sit and read women's magazines. I read articles about Elizabeth Taylor's new, simple life, articles about Mary Tyler Moore, articles about Jane Pauley, articles about members of the Carter family, articles about Candice Bergen, articles about Doris Day, articles about Phyllis Diller, and excerpts from Lana Turner's autobiography.[11] I know many things about these people—things that they may have forgotten themselves and things that, should we ever meet, they might wish I would forget also. At seven o'clock, I **G**

---

9. **Ovaltine:** a nutritious chocolate drink.

10. **gradations of light:** shades of light; light that changes by very small degrees from lighter to darker.

11. **Elizabeth Taylor's . . . Turner's autobiography:** The people named are actors, journalists, musicians, and other celebrities of the time, whose exploits would have made it into the pages of popular magazines.

**F PATTERNS OF ORGANIZATION** Reread lines 93–99. Which pattern of organization does the author use to highlight the differences between Antigua and Manhattan? Identify the word or phrase that signals a shift in subject.

**G TONE** How would you describe Kincaid's tone, or attitude, in lines 113–119? Explain your answer.

---

---

*Brownstones*, Patti Mollica. © Patti Mollica/SuperStock.

### Targeted Passage ③

120 watch the morning news for one whole hour. I watch the morning news for two reasons: it makes me feel as if I am living in Chicago, and on the morning news I see and hear the best reports on anything having to do with pigs. I don't know why the morning news makes me feel as if I am living in Chicago and not, say, Cleveland, but there it is. I love Chicago and would like to live there, but only for an hour. Some days, after watching the morning news, my head is filled with useless (to me) but interesting information about pigs. Some of the information, though, is good only for a day. Then, for half an hour, I watch Captain Kangaroo. I love Captain Kangaroo and have forgiven him for saying to Chastity Bono, when they were both guests on her parents' television

130 show,[12] "Now, let me lay this on you, Chastity."[13] Surely a grown man, even if he is a children's hero (perhaps because he is a children's hero), shouldn't talk like that.

   Then it is half past eight and no longer early morning in Manhattan, either. ◆

*October 17, 1977*

---

12. **Captain Kangaroo . . . television show:** Captain Kangaroo, a.k.a. Bob Keeshan, was the host of a long-running television program for children. Chastity Bono is the daughter of Sonny Bono and Cher, pop singers who hosted a variety TV show in the 1970s.

13. **"Now, let me . . . Chastity":** Captain Kangaroo was using a slang expression of the time. Used mostly by young people, it meant, "Now, let me tell you something."

### ▲ Analyze Visuals

**Compare** this painting with the one on page 563. How well does each capture the **setting** Kincaid describes? Consider the colors and lines in both paintings, as well as each artist's depiction of light.

## Analyze Visuals

*Possible answer:* The painting on this page captures some of the feeling of the setting but only a few of Kincaid's details. For example, Kincaid talks about the early-morning quiet, broken by the sound of trucks, and about the few pedestrians she might see. The buildings in the painting (brownstones, as in Kincaid's description) seem to be bathed in early-morning light, but no streets, vehicles, or pedestrians are shown. Similarly, through its use of light and color, the painting on page 563 captures the farming life and the feeling of the island setting that Kincaid describes.

**About the Art** New York artist Patti Mollica is known for her urban landscapes. *Brownstones*, which dramatically highlights the buildings' shapes, angles, patterns, and colors, is typical of her work. Perhaps the buildings in this painting are similar to those that Kincaid mentions in lines 109–110.

## SELECTION WRAP–UP

**READ WITH A PURPOSE** Now that students have finished reading the selection, ask them which island home Kincaid likes better. How do they know? *Possible answer: Kincaid likes her Antigua home better. When she compares it with Manhattan, Antigua is more beautiful and life, especially morning life, seems to have more meaning.*

⭐ **CRITIQUE** Have students decide whether Kincaid's descriptions provide a balanced account of both places.

### INDEPENDENT READING

   Students may enjoy reading more from Jamaica Kincaid in *Annie John: A Novel,* a coming of age story of a young girl in Antigua.

---

### FOR STRUGGLING READERS

③ **Targeted Passage [Lines 120–128]**

This passage describes how Kincaid spends part of her early mornings in Manhattan. It contrasts with the description in the Targeted Passage on page 564.

• Why does Kincaid watch the morning news? (lines 120–122)

• How does she describe the information she watches about pigs? Why do you think she says this? (lines 126–127)

### FOR ENGLISH LANGUAGE LEARNERS

**Language: Punctuation** Point out Kincaid's use of parentheses in lines 54–56, 83–87, 126, and 131. Explain that these parentheses add interesting but not essential explanations and observations to her descriptions. Then work with students to write two or three original sentences that include information in parentheses.

# Practice and Apply

For preliminary support of post-reading questions, use these copy masters:

**R** RESOURCE MANAGER—Copy Masters
Reading Check p. 25
Diction p. 21
Question Support p. 26

Additional selection questions are provided for teachers on page 15.

## ANSWERS

## Comprehension

1. *Kincaid compares and contrasts her childhood home, the island of Antigua, with her current home, Manhattan.*

2. *Most people were up by 5:30 A.M. and busy by 6:00 A.M. (lines 26–29).*

3. *Life in Manhattan is nothing like life on Antigua. The times of getting up are different, as are the early-morning sights and sounds and people's priorities.*

## Text Analysis

COMMON CORE RI 3, RI 4, RI 5

*Possible answers:*

4. ■ **COMMON CORE FOCUS** *Analyze Patterns of Organization* Answers will vary but will probably focus on the early-morning activities in the two places. Opinions should be supported with specific evidence.*

5. *Kincaid grew up in an agricultural environment on a Caribbean island (lines 1–12). Manhattan life, with its big buildings and rumbling trucks (lines 100–112), must seem somewhat confining and grim. If she had grown up in a big city, she would be more accustomed to her surroundings.*

6. *Unlike her friends, Kincaid grew up in a place where the weather usually was bright and sunny (lines 33–34). Manhattan weather conditions are far more variable, so Kincaid focuses simply on whether the day is bright or gray (lines 110–111). The fact that she doesn't notice things like gradations of light suggests that she feels somewhat detached from her Manhattan home.*

---

## Comprehension

1. **Recall** What does Kincaid compare and contrast in this essay?

2. **Recall** What time did most people in Kincaid's home country start their day?

3. **Clarify** Explain why the author feels that the only thing Manhattan and Antigua share is "a geographical definition" of being an island.

## Text Analysis

■ 4. **Analyze Patterns of Organization** To **compare and contrast** Antigua and Manhattan, Kincaid includes many of the same kinds of details in her description of each place. Use the chart you created as you read to find examples of these points of comparison. Then explain which one you think best highlights the similarities and differences between the two islands.

5. **Analyze Author's Perspective** An author's perspective is the way he or she looks at a topic. How might Kincaid's childhood experiences in Antigua have influenced her perspective on living in a big city like New York? Use evidence from the text to support your answer.

6. **Draw Conclusions** Reread lines 100–112. Why do the author's friends in Manhattan notice the gradations of light, while she herself does not? What might this tell you about her feelings toward Manhattan as her home?

● 7. **Evaluate Diction** Kincaid frequently uses lists and repetition to achieve her unique style. Record three examples of such usage in a chart. Then complete your chart by briefly explaining the effect each example creates.

| Example of Kincaid's Diction | Effect Created |
|---|---|
| "Certainly no one I know gets up at half past five, at six o'clock, at seven o'clock, at half past seven, at eight o'clock" (lines 94–96) | Kincaid's use of repetition here helps emphasize how solitary her mornings in New York are. It gives the paragraph a reflective, lonely tone. |

## Text Criticism

8. **Critical Interpretations** The literary critic Suzanne Freeman has said that Kincaid's "singsong style" produces "images that are as sweet and mysterious as the secrets that children whisper in your ear." In your opinion, does this comment apply to Kincaid's depiction of her island birthplace? Explain.

> ### What place do you call HOME?
> What makes a place a "home"?

---

COMMON CORE

RI 3 Analyze how an author unfolds a series of ideas or events. RI 4 Analyze the cumulative impact of specific word choices on meaning and tone. RI 5 Analyze in detail how an author's ideas are developed and refined.

---

7. ● **COMMON CORE FOCUS** *Evaluate Diction* Examples of such usage include lines 7–10, which spotlight Antigua's agricultural variety and create a sense of satisfaction and delight; lines 20–25, which emphasize diversity through a range of occupations; and lines 113–117, which present the subjects of magazine articles to suggest why Kincaid finds them trivial.

## Text Criticism

*Possible answer:*

8. *Answers will vary, but students should support their opinions by suggestions of a "singsong style" (such as the lists in lines 5–10 and 22–25).*

> ## What place do you call HOME?
> Have students think about what about their home they value.

# Language

◆ **GRAMMAR AND STYLE: Improve Sentence Flow**

Review the **Grammar and Style** note on page 562. Jamaica Kincaid uses **coordinating conjunctions** to join independent clauses and connect ideas. She creates long sentences and achieves a conversational style.

Like Kincaid, use the coordinating conjunctions *and, but, for, nor, or, so,* and *yet* when you want to combine shorter sentences or connect ideas. In the following excerpt, notice how the author uses *and* to join two independent clauses and *but* to connect ideas:

> *The Ground was often many miles away from where they lived, and they got there not by taking a truck or some other kind of automotive transportation but by riding a donkey or by walking.* (lines 16–19)

Notice how the revisions in blue help to improve the flow of this first draft. Revise your response to the prompt below by using similar techniques.

> **STUDENT MODEL**
>
> My house is home to a family of seven. ^but^ There is only one bathroom. ^so^ All five of us kids race crazily down the hall every weekday morning. My older sister almost always gets there first. ^so^ The rest of us stand blinking and yawning in the hallway. ^or^ We drift slowly downstairs to the kitchen.

## READING-WRITING CONNECTION

 **YOUR TURN** Expand your knowledge of "Island Morning" by responding to this prompt. Then use the **revising tip** to improve your writing.

| WRITING PROMPT | REVISING TIP |
|---|---|
| **Extended Constructed Response: Comparison-Contrast** Choose one of the two mornings Kincaid describes and compare it with your own daily routine. Use the rich details presented in the selection to write a **three-to-five-paragraph comparison.** | Review your response. How have you used coordinating conjunctions to connect your ideas and achieve a conversational style? |

**Interactive Revision** THINK central
Go to **thinkcentral.com.**
KEYWORD: HML9-567

 **COMMON CORE**

**L 1b** Use various types of clauses to convey specific meanings and add variety and interest to writing. **W 4** Produce informative writing in which the organization and style are appropriate to task and purpose.

---

## DIFFERENTIATED INSTRUCTION

### FOR STRUGGLING WRITERS

- Suggest that students limit their responses to three paragraphs.

- Present some details to which students might relate. For example, point out the early-morning activities on Antigua or the television viewing in Manhattan.

- Encourage peer reviews in which students can consider ways to make their comparisons clearer.

---

# Language

 **COMMON CORE L 1b, W 4**

◆ **GRAMMAR AND STYLE**

- Elicit, or be prepared to share, sentences that illustrate the use of the coordinating conjunctions.

- After discussing the student model, write this paragraph on the board. Have students use coordinating conjunctions to improve the flow. (For more on coordinating conjunctions, see **Grammar Handbook,** page R46.)

  > My alarm goes off at 6:30, but I don't leap out of bed. There's no point. My sister is already in the bathroom, so I'll have to wait anyway.

**R RESOURCE MANAGER—Copy Master**
Improve Sentence Flow p. 27

**READING-WRITING CONNECTION**
Have students adapt the Comparison Matrix or the Classification Chart for use as they identify and group details. Remind students to choose a main idea for the comparison as a whole as well as a topic sentence for each paragraph.

**BEST PRACTICES TOOLKIT—Transparencies**
Comparison Matrix p. A24
Classification Chart p. B17

> **Writing Online** THINK central
>
> The following tools are available online at **thinkcentral.com** and on **Write*Smart*** CD-ROM:
> - **Interactive Graphic Organizers**
> - **Interactive Student Models**
> - **Interactive Revision Lessons**
> For additional grammar instruction, see **GrammarNotes** on **thinkcentral.com.**

---

# Assess and Reteach

## Assess

**DIAGNOSTIC AND SELECTION TESTS**
Selection Test A pp. 143–144
Selection Test B/C pp. 145–146

**Interactive Selection Test** on **thinkcentral.com**

## Reteach

**Level Up Online Tutorials** on **thinkcentral.com**

# Focus and Motivate

## COMMON CORE FOCUS

**RI 2** Determine a central idea of a text and analyze its development. **RI 4** Analyze the cumulative impact of specific word choices on meaning and tone. **RI 5** Analyze how an author's ideas are developed and refined. **L 1b** Use various types of clauses to convey specific meanings and add variety and interest to writing. **L 4b** Identify patterns of word changes that indicate different parts of speech. **L 4c** Consult reference materials to determine or clarify a word's meaning or etymology.

## SUMMARY

Spending much of her life in the relative isolation of the southwest United States, Georgia O'Keeffe used bold colors to paint subjects that many critics of the time considered unworthy. Today, however, her work is viewed as imaginative and inspiring.

## What is the source of INSPIRATION?

Ask the question. Elicit that an inspiration is anyone or anything (an object, an event, a thought) that sparks a creative idea. Introduce the *QUICKWRITE* and the varied applications of the term *artist*. Then have students complete the activity and share the results.

---

*Selection Resources*

---

## Georgia O'Keeffe
Biographical Essay by Joan Didion

# What is the source of INSPIRATION?

### COMMON CORE

**RI 2** Determine a central idea of a text and analyze its development. **RI 4** Analyze the cumulative impact of specific word choices on meaning and tone. **RI 5** Analyze how an author's ideas are developed and refined. **L 4b** Identify patterns of word changes that indicate different parts of speech.

What drives painters to create vibrant pictures? What compels movie directors to invent alien worlds or makes songwriters dream up meaningful lyrics? Artists find inspiration in their daily lives, in nature, or even in the work of other artists.

*QUICKWRITE* Think of the most powerful work by your favorite artist, be it a painter, a dancer, an actor, an author, or a musician. What do you think inspired the artist to create this work? Whether it's a song about the person who broke his heart or a huge mural of her neighborhood, try to imagine the inspiration behind the art. Describe your artist's source of inspiration in a short paragraph.

568

---

*See resources on the **Teacher One Stop DVD-ROM** and on **thinkcentral.com**.*

**R RESOURCE MANAGER UNIT 5**
Plan and Teach, pp. 29–36
Summary p. 37†* p. 38‡*
Text Analysis and Reading
   Skill, pp. 39–42†*
Vocabulary, pp. 43–45*
Grammar and Style, p. 48

**DIAGNOSTIC AND SELECTION TESTS**
Selection Tests, pp. 147–150

**BEST PRACTICES TOOLKIT**
Definition Mapping, p. E6

**TECHNOLOGY**
🖊 **Teacher One Stop DVD-ROM**
🖊 **Student One Stop DVD-ROM**
🖊 **Audio Anthology CD**
🖊 **GrammarNotes DVD-ROM**
🖊 **ExamView Test Generator**
on the **Teacher One Stop**

---

\* Resources for Differentiation     † Also in Spanish     ‡ In Haitian Creole and Vietnamese

## TEXT ANALYSIS: TONE

**Tone** is a writer's attitude toward his or her subject. Just as people often speak in a particular tone of voice, such as sarcastic or amused, writers create a tone with their choice of words. As you read "Georgia O'Keeffe," record details that help you identify Joan Didion's tone. Look for the following:

- unusual words Didion uses to describe O'Keeffe
- emphasized or repeated words and phrases
- details about O'Keeffe's life Didion chooses to include

| Details from the Text | Tone Established |
|---|---|
| Didion describes O'Keeffe as "this angelic rattlesnake." (lines 63–64) | |

## READING SKILL: IDENTIFY IMPLIED MAIN IDEAS

The **main, or central, idea** is the most important idea in a paragraph or essay. Often, the main idea is not directly stated but **implied** by supporting details. As you read, use these strategies to identify and understand Didion's main ideas:

- Identify the specific topic of each paragraph or section.
- Examine all the details the author includes in that section.
- Ask what idea or message the details convey about the topic.
- State the idea or message in a sentence.

## ▲ VOCABULARY IN CONTEXT

Didion's vibrant portrait of Georgia O'Keeffe is enhanced by her use of the words shown in bold. To see how many words you already know, restate each phrase, using a different word or words for each boldfaced term. Then, in your *Reader/Writer Notebook*, write a brief definition of each word you're familiar with.

1. a **condescending** attitude toward teenagers
2. witness the **genesis** of an idea
3. scorned with a **derisive** laugh
4. bitter **rancor** between enemies
5. painted with bright, **immutable** colors

 Complete the activities in your **Reader/Writer Notebook**.

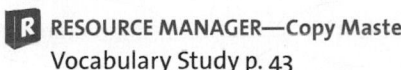
## Teach

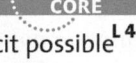

## READ WITH A PURPOSE

*Help students set a purpose for reading. Tell them look for ways to describe Georgia O'Keeffe as they read the story.*

READING SKILL

**COMMON CORE**
RI 2,
RI 5

**A** *Model the Skill:* **IMPLIED MAIN IDEAS**

Help students find the implied main idea by pointing out that often the main idea of a paragraph is stated or suggested in the first sentence or two. Explain that in the second paragraph, the focus is on Didion's daughter. Tell students to focus on key comments like "the painting was the painter as the poem is the poet."

***Possible answer:*** *Didion's daughter realized that style is character and that the boldness of O'Keeffe's painting reflected O'Keeffe's bold character.*

## REVISIT THE BIG QUESTION

What is the source of
# INSPIRATION?

**Discuss** Based on lines 7–13, in what sense was the "Sky Above Clouds" canvas an inspiration to Didion's daughter? ***Possible answer:*** *It filled her with awe and made her feel that talking to O'Keeffe was very important—presumably, because she wanted to know the artist better, perhaps because the painting stirred her own creative impulses.*

VOCABULARY

**COMMON CORE**
L 4

## OWN THE WORD

**condescending:** Ask students if they have ever acted *condescendingly* toward another individual? If so, what was the circumstance? How did the person react to the *condescending* attitude?

---

# Georgia O'Keeffe

## JOAN DIDION

"Where I was born and where and how I have lived is unimportant," Georgia O'Keeffe told us in the book of paintings and words published in her ninetieth year on earth. She seemed to be advising us to forget the beautiful face in the Stieglitz photographs.[1] She appeared to be dismissing the rather **condescending** romance that had attached to her by then, the romance of extreme good looks and advanced age and deliberate isolation. "It is what I have done with where I have been that should be of interest." I recall an August afternoon in Chicago in 1973 when I took my daughter, then seven, to see what Georgia O'Keeffe had done with where she had been. One of the vast O'Keeffe "Sky Above Clouds"

10 canvases floated over the back stairs in the Chicago Art Institute that day, dominating what seemed to be several stories of empty light, and my daughter looked at it once, ran to the landing, and kept on looking. "Who drew it," she whispered after a while. I told her. "I need to talk to her," she said finally.

My daughter was making, that day in Chicago, an entirely unconscious, but quite basic assumption about people and the work they do. She was assuming that the glory she saw in the work reflected a glory in its maker, that the painting was the painter as the poem is the poet, that every choice one made alone—every word chosen or rejected, every brush stroke laid or not laid down—betrayed one's character. *Style is character.* It seemed to me that afternoon that I had rarely

20 seen so instinctive an application of this familiar principle, and I recall being pleased not only that my daughter responded to style as character but that it was Georgia O'Keeffe's particular style to which she responded: this was a hard woman who had imposed her 192 square feet of clouds on Chicago. **A**

---

1. **Stieglitz** (stĕg'lĭts) **photographs:** American photographer Alfred Stieglitz, O'Keeffe's husband, took and exhibited many photographs of O'Keeffe.

**condescending**
(kŏn'dĭ-sĕn'dĭng) *adj.*
assuming an air of
superiority

**①** **Targeted Passage**

***Analyze Visuals ▶***

Examine this 1932 Stieglitz photograph of O'Keeffe. List three **traits** you would attribute to O'Keeffe based solely on this photograph.

**A** IMPLIED MAIN IDEAS
Reread lines 14–23 and think about the details Didion includes about her daughter's reaction to O'Keeffe's work. What is the main idea of the paragraph?

---

## DIFFERENTIATED INSTRUCTION

### FOR ENGLISH LANGUAGE LEARNERS

Show students how they can use Definition Mapping as a learning strategy for words like *isolation* (line 6), *dominating* (line 11), and *appreciation* (line 37).

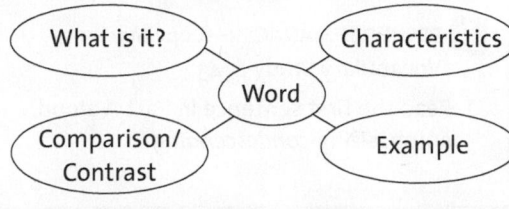

### FOR STRUGGLING READERS

In combination with the *Audio Anthology CD*, use one or more Targeted Passages (pp. 570, 572, 574) to ensure that students focus on key events, concepts, and skills. Targeted Passages are also good for English learners.

**①** Targeted Passage [Lines 1–7]

This passage introduces the subject of Didion's essay, focusing on that subject's individualistic view of life.

"Hardness" has not been in our century a quality much admired in women, nor in the past twenty years has it even been in official favor for men. When hardness surfaces in the very old we tend to transform it into "crustiness" or eccentricity, some tonic pepperiness to be indulged at a distance. On the evidence of her work and what she has said about it, Georgia O'Keeffe is neither "crusty" nor
30 eccentric. She is simply hard, a straight shooter, a woman clean of received wisdom and open to what she sees. This is a woman who could early on dismiss most of her contemporaries as "dreamy," and would later single out one she liked as "a very poor painter." (And then add, apparently by way of softening the judgment: "I guess he wasn't a painter at all. He had no courage and I believe that to create one's own world in any of the arts takes courage.") This is a woman who in 1939 could advise her admirers that they were missing her point, that their appreciation of her famous flowers was merely sentimental. "When I paint a red hill," she observed coolly in the catalogue for an exhibition that year, "you say it is too bad that I don't always paint flowers.
40 A flower touches almost everyone's heart. A red hill doesn't touch everyone's heart." This is a woman who could describe the **genesis** of one of her most well-known paintings—the "Cow's Skull: Red, White and Blue" owned by the Metropolitan—as an act of quite deliberate and **derisive** orneriness. "I thought of the city men I had been seeing in the East," she wrote. "They talked so often of writing the Great American Novel—the Great American Play—the Great American Poetry. . . . So as I was painting my cow's head on blue I thought to myself, 'I'll make it an American painting. They will not think it great with the red stripes down the sides—Red, White and Blue—but they will notice it.'"

50 The city men. The men. They. The words crop up again and again as this astonishingly aggressive woman tells us what was on her mind when she was making her astonishingly aggressive paintings. It was those city men who stood accused of sentimentalizing her flowers: "I made you take time to look at what I saw and when you took time to really notice my flower you hung all your associations with flowers on my flower and you write about my flower as if I think and see what you think and see—and I don't." *And I don't.* Imagine those words spoken, and the sound you hear is *don't tread on me.* "The men" believed it impossible to paint New York, so Georgia O'Keeffe painted New York. "The men" didn't think much
60 of her bright color, so she made it brighter. The men yearned toward Europe so she went to Texas, and then New Mexico. The men talked about Cézanne,[2] "long involved remarks about the 'plastic quality' of his form and color," and took one another's long involved remarks, in the view of this angelic rattlesnake in their midst, altogether too seriously. "I can paint one of those **B**

---

2. **Cézanne** (sā-zăn′): Paul Cézanne, late-19th-century French painter whose style and study of shapes influenced new art movements in the early 20th century.

---

② **Targeted Passage**

**genesis** (jĕn′ĭ-sĭs) *n.* the origin or coming into being (of something)

**derisive** (dĭ-rī′sĭv) *adj.* expressing contempt or ridicule

**COMMON CORE L 4b**

**Language Coach**

**Derivations** Many adverbs are **derived**, or formed, by adding -*ly* to an adjective. Reread lines 50–52. What -*ly* adverb can you identify? What adjective is it derived from? Use a dictionary to find the meaning of both words.

**COMMON CORE RI 5**

**B IRONY**
Reread lines 59–65 and look for **irony**, or the difference between the actual result and the expected one. In this instance, O'Keeffe is doing the opposite of what one might expect in response to the expectations of the art world. Why do you think the author focused on O'Keeffe's ironic behavior in this section of the essay? Explain your answer.

---

**TEXT ANALYSIS** **COMMON CORE RI 5**

**B IRONY**

*Possible answer: Using the ironic language and focusing on the ironic aspect of O'Keeffe's life highlights how far O'Keeffe strayed from what was expected of her as both an artist and a woman. The language gives a clear, incident-by-incident idea of O'Keeffe taking the opposite direction from what was expected.*

Have students work in pairs to give examples of irony from songs, television shows, movies, books, or other mediums. Ask for volunteers to share.

---

**VOCABULARY** **COMMON CORE L 4**

**OWN THE WORD**

- **genesis:** Tell students that *genesis* comes from a Greek suffix that means "origin."
- **derisive:** Tell students that synonyms for *derisive* include *disparaging*, *belittling*, and *mocking*. Have students name antonyms for *derisive*. **Possible answers:** *praising, complimentary, appreciative*

---

**DIFFERENTIATED INSTRUCTION**

**FOR STRUGGLING READERS**

② **Targeted Passage [Lines 24–38]**
In this passage, Didion identifies and begins to support her interpretation of O'Keeffe's essential trait: her hardness.

- What are two other words for *hardness*? How well does Didion think these other words describe O'Keeffe? Explain. (lines 24–31)
- How did O'Keeffe show hardness to most of her contemporaries? to her admirers? (lines 31–38)

**FOR ENGLISH LANGUAGE LEARNERS**

**Language Coach** **COMMON CORE L 4b**

**Derivations** *Answer:*
*astonishingly = shockingly; astonishing = shocking* Have students reread lines 97–103. Ask students to find two more adjectives in the text that can be turned into -*ly* adverbs and to use a dictionary to find their definitions.

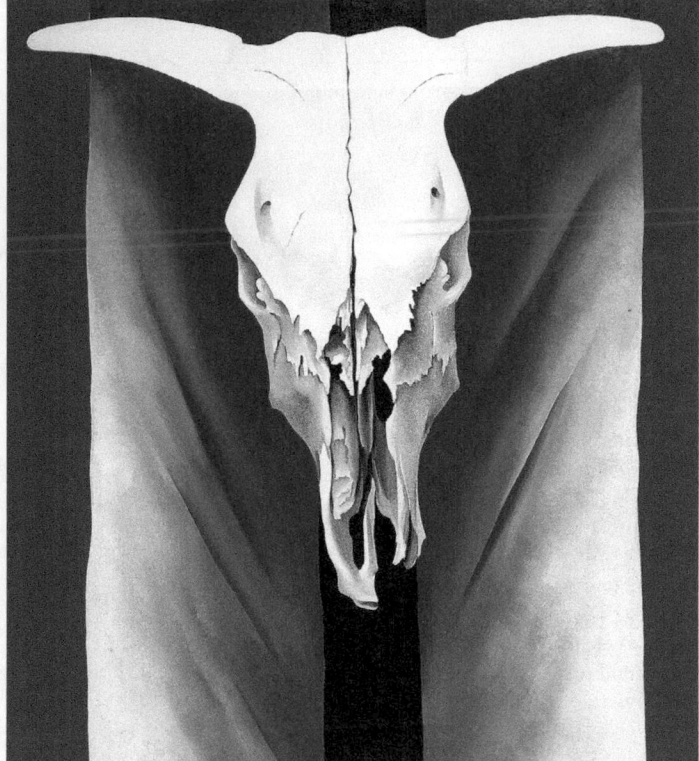

*Cow's Skull: Red, White, and Blue* (1931), Georgia O'Keeffe. Oil on canvas, 39⅞" × 35⅞". The Metropolitan Museum of Art, Alfred Stieglitz Collection, 1952. © 2007 Georgia O'Keeffe Museum/Artists Rights Society (ARS), New York. Photo © Georgia O'Keeffe/Metropolitan Museum of Art (52.203).

◀ **Analyze Visuals**

Reread lines 41–49. What message do you think O'Keeffe was sending to the "city men" when she painted this piece? Explain your answer, citing details from the text as well as the painting.

dismal-colored paintings like the men," the woman who regarded herself always as an outsider remembers thinking one day in 1922, and she did: a painting of a shed "all low-toned and dreary with the tree beside the door." She called the act of **rancor** "The Shanty" and hung it in her next show. "The men seemed to approve of it," she reported fifty-four years later, her contempt undimmed. "They seemed to think that maybe I was beginning to paint. That was my only low-toned dismal-colored painting."

Some women fight and others do not. Like so many successful guerrillas[3] in the war between the sexes, Georgia O'Keeffe seems to have been equipped early with an **immutable** sense of who she was and a fairly clear understanding that she would be required to prove it. On the surface her upbringing was conventional. She was a child on the Wisconsin prairie who played with china dolls and painted watercolors with cloudy skies because sunlight was too hard to paint and, with her brother and sisters, listened every night to her mother read stories of the Wild West, of Texas, of Kit Carson and Billy the Kid.[4] She

70

**rancor** (răng'kər) *n.* bitter and deep ill will

**immutable** (ĭ-myōō'tə-bəl) *adj.* unchanging

 **GRAMMAR AND STYLE**
Reread lines 76–77. Didion is using a **restrictive clause** ("She was a child . . . *who played with china dolls and painted watercolors . . .*") to impart necessary information to the reader as well as to enhance her description of O'Keeffe.

---

3. **guerrillas** (gə-rĭl'əz): members of irregular military units who work to undermine the enemy using tactics such as surprise raids.

4. **Kit Carson and Billy the Kid:** Carson was a scout in the American West; Billy the Kid was an outlaw.

---

**Analyze Visuals**

*Possible answer:* *The painting was her way of saying that what makes a painting American is the independent spirit of its painter. Didion says that, for O'Keeffe, the painting was "an act of quite deliberate and derisive orneriness" (line 43).*

**About the Art** O'Keeffe painted this work—one of her most famous—in 1931. It depicts one of several bones that she shipped to New York State as subjects for her paintings.

## TIERED DISCUSSION PROMPTS

Direct students to lines 72–89. Help students explore the childhood experiences that shaped O'Keeffe's career:

**Connect** What examples of art and literature are you familiar with? *Students should identify relevant personal experiences.*

**Analyze** Would you call O'Keeffe's childhood exposure to art and literature narrow, or broad? Explain. *Possible answer: Narrow; she saw little art and heard folktales.*

**Evaluate** Do you think that her exposure to art and literature limited or freed O'Keeffe? *Possible answer: It freed her to express art in her own way.*

---

**◉ GRAMMAR AND STYLE**  COMMON CORE L 1b

**Restrictive Clause** Have students work in pairs to write two sentences using restrictive clauses. Remind students that restrictive clauses are important to the basic meaning of the sentence and are not set off by commas or dashes.

---

**VOCABULARY**  COMMON CORE L 4

### OWN THE WORD

- **rancor:** Ask students to list situations that would give rise to feelings of *rancor*. *Possible answers: malicious gossip, being bullied*

- **immutable:** Remind students that the prefix *im-* means "not." *Mutable* means "subject to change." Tell students that both the verb *mutate* and the noun *mutation* refer to change.

---

### FOR STRUGGLING READERS

**Develop Reading Fluency** Model for students an effective way to read lines 50–58. Point out that the sentences are choppy, and certain words and phrases are italicized and repeated for emphasis. Have students take turns reading the sentences, with emphasis on the italicized phrases.

### FOR ADVANCED LEARNERS/PRE–AP

**Compare and Contrast** Have students reread **Meet the Author** on page 569 and then meet in small groups to discuss the similarities and differences between Georgia O'Keeffe and Joan Didion. Offer these topics for discussion:

- their opinions about art
- their opinions about themselves
- their position as women artists in American society and culture

## Analyze Visuals

*Possible answer: O'Keeffe places the flower in the center and makes it so large that it dominates the painting. Her colors focus attention on the dramatically bright flower.*

**About the Art** The jimson weed is a common desert plant in the American Southwest. Its flowers are large and beautiful, but all parts of the plant are toxic and can be fatal if eaten.

## SELECTION WRAP–UP

**READ WITH A PURPOSE** Now that students have finished reading the selection, have them describe Georgia O'Keeffe. *Possible answer: O'Keeffe is strong-willed and even aggressive, with an unchanging view of who she is.*

⭐ **CRITIQUE** Ask students if they found reading this biography inspirational. Ask them to explain their responses.

### INDEPENDENT READING

Students interested in reading other works by Didion might enjoy *We Tell Ourselves Stories in Order to Live: Collected Nonfiction*, which includes various essays about cultural events of the last two centuries.

---

80 told adults that she wanted to be an artist and was embarrassed when they asked what kind of artist she wanted to be: she had no idea "what kind." She had no idea what artists did. She had never seen a picture that interested her, other than a pen-and-ink Maid of Athens[5] in one of her mother's books, some Mother Goose illustrations printed on cloth, a tablet cover that showed a little girl with pink roses, and the painting of Arabs on horseback that hung in her grandmother's parlor.
90 At thirteen, in a Dominican convent, she was mortified when the sister corrected her drawing. At Chatham Episcopal Institute in Virginia she painted lilacs and sneaked time alone to walk out to where she could see the line of the Blue Ridge Mountains on the horizon. At the Art Institute in Chicago she was shocked by the presence of live models and wanted to abandon anatomy lessons. At the Art Students League in New York one of her fellow students advised her that, since he
100 would be a great painter and she would end up teaching painting in a girls' school, any work of hers was less important than modeling for him. Another painted over her work to show her how the Impressionists[6] did trees. She had not before heard how the Impressionists did trees and she did not much care.

*Jimson Weed* (1932), Georgia O'Keeffe. The Georgia O'Keeffe Museum, Santa Fe, New Mexico. © 2007 Georgia O'Keeffe Museum/Artists Rights Society (ARS), New York. Photo © Art Resource, New York.

At twenty-four she left all those opinions behind and went for the first time to live in Texas, where there were no trees to paint and no one to tell her how not to paint them. In Texas there was only the horizon she craved. In Texas
110 she had her sister Claudia with her for a while, and in the late afternoons they would walk away from town and toward the horizon and watch the evening star come out. "That evening star fascinated me," she wrote. "It was in some way very exciting to me. My sister had a gun, and as we walked she would throw bottles in the air and shoot as many as she could before they hit the ground. I had nothing but to walk into nowhere and the wide sunset space with the star. Ten watercolors were made from that star." In a way one's interest is compelled as much by the sister Claudia with the gun as by the painter Georgia with the star, but only the painter left us this shining record. Ten watercolors were made from that star. ∾ ⓓ

**Targeted Passage** ③

▲ **Analyze Visuals**

O'Keeffe is celebrated for her ability to make even flowers look strong and imposing. Explain how she creates this air of strength, considering elements such as the flower's size, position, and color.

ⓓ **TONE**
Reread lines 107–119. What is the "shining record" Didion refers to? Describe the tone conveyed by the writer's **word choice**.

5. **Maid of Athens:** the subject of a love poem by 19th-century English writer George Gordon, Lord Byron.

6. **Impressionists:** members of an influential 19th-century French school of painting who focused on depicting quick visual impressions and conveying how light influenced the scenes they painted.

---

## DIFFERENTIATED INSTRUCTION

### FOR STRUGGLING READERS

③ **Targeted Passage [Lines 107–119]**

This concluding passage ties O'Keeffe's independent spirit and love of beauty to the American Southwest.

- When O'Keeffe went to Texas, what did she leave behind? What things and attitudes did she want to find there? (lines 107–109)

- What did she do in the late afternoons? (lines 110–112)

- How can you tell that the evening star was important to her? (line 116)

### FOR ENGLISH LANGUAGE LEARNERS

**Culture: Clarify** Tell students that *evening star* (lines 111–119) is another name for the planet Venus, which can be seen in the western sky in most parts of the United States. Ask them to name some well-known astronomical features in the sky over their home countries. For example, in South America, the brightest stars in the group that we call the Big Dipper are known as Las Tres Marías.

## Comprehension

COMMON CORE

RI 2 Determine a central idea of a text and analyze its development. RI 4 Analyze the cumulative impact of specific word choices on meaning and tone. RI 5 Analyze how an author's ideas are developed and refined.

1. **Recall** What anecdote, or short personal story, does Didion tell at the beginning of this essay?

2. **Clarify** What did O'Keeffe's critics tend to think of her work?

## Text Analysis

3. **Paraphrase** O'Keeffe asserts, "Where I was born and where and how I have lived is unimportant. It is what I have done with where I have been that should be of interest." Paraphrase this quotation. Then explain what O'Keeffe meant.

4. **Understand Motives** What inspired O'Keeffe to act the way she did? For each action described in the chart, identify O'Keeffe's motive, or inspiration. Use a graphic organizer like the one shown to record your answers.

| Motive    ⟶ | Action |
|---|---|
| | O'Keeffe paints "Cow's Skull: Red, White, and Blue" (line 42). |
| | O'Keeffe uses even brighter colors in her paintings (line 60). |
| | O'Keeffe moves to the Southwest (line 108). |

5. **Identify Implied Main Idea** Reread lines 72–106. Examine the details in this paragraph. What is the implied main idea conveyed by these details? Use evidence from the text to support your answer.

6. **Analyze Characterization** Didion reveals her subject's traits using the same methods of characterization used by fiction writers. Identify at least two methods of characterization Didion uses in this selection. Then explain which of O'Keeffe's traits are revealed in each case, citing evidence from the text.

7. **Analyze Tone** Review the chart you filled in as you read. How does Didion's tone help convey the ideas she wants to express about O'Keeffe?

## Text Criticism

8. **Author's Style** Joan Didion has remarked that "writing is hostile in that you're trying to make somebody see something the way you see it, trying to impose your idea, your picture." In what ways might this essay be considered "hostile"? Did Didion achieve her goal of making you see Georgia O'Keeffe the same way she does? Explain your answer.

### What is the source of INSPIRATION?

In what other areas besides the arts is inspiration important?

---

7. ● **COMMON CORE FOCUS** *Analyze Tone* Didion's serious, informative tone shows the respect and admiration that she feels and wants readers to feel for O'Keeffe.

## Text Criticism
*Possible answer:*

8. The essay is "hostile" in that Didion tried to overcome O'Keeffe's early critics. Didion achieved her goal by showing the reader the reasons for O'Keeffe's orneriness and the great art that resulted from her defiance of convention.

### What is the source of INSPIRATION?
*Students may name strong emotions, beautiful things and landscapes, and a desire to make a difference in the world.*

---

# Practice and Apply

For preliminary support of post-reading questions, use these copy masters:

**R** **RESOURCE MANAGER—Copy Masters**
Reading Check p. 46
Identify Implied Main Ideas p. 41
Question Support p. 47

Additional selection questions are provided for teachers on page 33.

## ANSWERS

## Comprehension

1. *She tells how her daughter was impressed by an O'Keeffe painting while visiting an art museum.*

2. *They thought that her colors were too bright and that she sentimentalized her flowers.*

## Text Analysis

COMMON CORE RI 2, RI 4, RI 5

*Possible answers:*

3. *"Don't look at where I have come from. Look at what I have accomplished." O'Keeffe meant that her achievements show her character and strength better than her background does.*

4. *Row 1: She wanted to paint an American painting, to make it noticeable, and to be ornery.*

   *Row 2: She wanted to defy the men who did not like her use of bright colors.*

   *Row 3: She wanted to be in a place where no one would tell her what or how to paint.*

5. ■ **COMMON CORE FOCUS** *Identify Implied Main Idea In spite of obstacles, O'Keeffe was determined to be an artist. Those obstacles included her narrow exposure to art and literature and the discouraging comments that came from teachers and other art students.*

6. *Just as fiction writers use dialogue to reveal character traits, Didion uses O'Keeffe's words to show her independence and defiance of convention (lines 34–35, 54–57) and her love for nature (lines 112–116). Just as fiction writers give background information that illuminates character traits, Didion gives details about O'Keeffe's childhood and education that shaped her independent artistic spirit (lines 72–106).*

## ANSWERS

# Vocabulary in Context

▲ **VOCABULARY PRACTICE**

1. *condescending*    4. *rancor*
2. *derisive*    5. *genesis*
3. *immutable*

 **RESOURCE MANAGER—Copy Master**
Vocabulary Practice p. 44

**ACADEMIC VOCABULARY IN WRITING**

*Answers will vary, but students' dialogues should be supported by details in Didion's essay.*

**VOCABULARY STRATEGY:**    **COMMON CORE L 4c**
**THE WORD ROOT** *gen*

• Point out that the root *gen* is pronounced differently in different words. Ask volunteers to demonstrate by pronouncing each word in the web.

• For each item in the activity, help students use their knowledge of the root in combination with context clues (such as *family tree* in item 1 and *brand names* in item 2) to determine word meaning.

**Possible answers:**

1. *genealogist*    4. *Genocide*
2. *Generic*    5. *generate*
3. *gene*

 **RESOURCE MANAGER—Copy Master**
Vocabulary Strategy p. 45

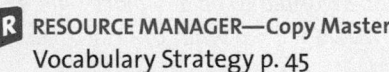

**Interactive Vocabulary**

Keywords direct students to a **WordSharp** tutorial on **thinkcentral.com** or to other types of vocabulary practice and review.

---

# Vocabulary in Context

▲ **VOCABULARY PRACTICE**

Determine the relationship between the first pair of words in each analogy. Then write the vocabulary word that best completes the second pair.

1. *Tolerant* is to *easygoing* as *smug* is to _____.
2. *Contemptuous* is to *speech* as _____ is to *remark*.
3. *Filth* is to *squalor* as _____ is to *permanent*.
4. *Embrace* is to *affection* as *insult* is to _____.
5. *Birth* is to *death* as _____ is to *termination*.

**WORD LIST**
condescending
derisive
genesis
immutable
rancor

**ACADEMIC VOCABULARY IN WRITING**

• conclude   • construct   • implicit   • primary   • specific

**Construct** an imaginary dialogue between Didion and O'Keeffe. Include **specific** details from Didion's essay to show how the two women react to each other. Use at least one Academic Vocabulary word in your response.

**VOCABULARY STRATEGY: THE WORD ROOT** *gen*

The vocabulary word *genesis* contains the Greek root *gen*, which means "birth, race, or origin." *Gen* is also a Latin root with a similar meaning. You will encounter the root *gen* not only in your English class but in readings for other classes as well, such as science and social studies. To understand the meaning of words with *gen*, use context clues as well as your knowledge of the root.

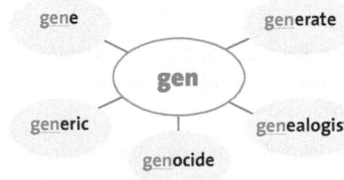

**COMMON CORE**

**L 4c** Consult reference materials to determine or clarify a word's meaning or etymology.

**PRACTICE** Choose the word from the word web that best completes each sentence. Use context clues to help you or, if necessary, consult a dictionary.

1. They hired a _____ to trace their family tree.
2. _____ products are usually less expensive than those with brand names.
3. The defective _____ that he inherited led to a serious blood disease.
4. _____ is the attempt to destroy a race of people.
5. They could not _____ enough interest in their project to get financial backing for it.

**Interactive Vocabulary**

Go to **thinkcentral.com**.
KEYWORD: HML9-576

---

## DIFFERENTIATED INSTRUCTION

**FOR ENGLISH LANGUAGE LEARNERS**

**Vocabulary: Roots** Have students work with dictionaries in home language groups to create word webs like the one in the Vocabulary Strategy section, showing these additional English words with the root *gen*: *gender, generation, genetics, genome, pathogen, primogeniture, progeny,* and *regenerate*.

**FOR ADVANCED LEARNERS/PRE–AP**

**Vocabulary Practice** Challenge students to use the vocabulary words listed in the **FOR ENGLISH LANGUAGE LEARNERS** note on page T570 to write their own analogies. Have students trade their analogies with a partner to complete.

# Language

◆ **GRAMMAR AND STYLE:** Use Descriptive Language

Review the **Grammar and Style** note on page 573. A **restrictive clause** is necessary to the basic meaning of a sentence; it is not set off by commas or dashes. A **nonrestrictive clause** gives only additional information and is not necessary to the meaning of a sentence; it is set off by commas or dashes (like commas, dashes are often used to emphasize parenthetical information).

Didion makes effective use of the restrictive clause in her short, concise description about Georgia O'Keeffe. Didion also uses restrictive clauses stylistically to make the essay more descriptive.

**Restrictive Clause:** *She was a child on the Wisconsin prairie* **who played with**
**china dolls and painted watercolors**.... (lines 76–77)

The revisions in blue incorporate restrictive clauses to lend clarity and enhance the description. Use similar techniques to revise your response to the prompt below.

> **STUDENT MODEL**
>
> Joan Didion effectively illustrates the character traits of an aggressive artist *who possessed a particular "hardness" of character and who desired* ~~and her desire~~ to paint, and live, in unexpected ways.

## READING-WRITING CONNECTION

 Improve your understanding of "Georgia O'Keeffe" by responding to this prompt. Then use the **revising tip** to improve your writing.

| WRITING PROMPT | REVISING TIP |
|---|---|
| **Short Constructed Response: Evaluation**<br>What character trait does Didion highlight in her essay on Georgia O'Keeffe? How effective are the details the author includes to illustrate this trait? Write a **one- or two-paragraph response**, citing evidence from the text. | Review your response. How have you used restrictive clauses in your evaluation of Didion's characterization of Georgia O'Keeffe? |

**Interactive Revision**
Go to **thinkcentral.com**.
KEYWORD: HML9-577

---

## FOR STRUGGLING WRITERS

- List several character traits that might be chosen as the topic for the essay.

- Have students choose one trait and look for three details that show this trait. Remind students to give the line numbers of supporting details that they cite.

---

**COMMON CORE**

**L 1b** Use various types of clauses to convey specific meanings and add variety and interest to writing.

# Language  COMMON CORE **L 1b**

◆ **GRAMMAR AND STYLE**

After students examine the student model, have them explain how the details improve the description.

Write the following sentences on the board and ask students to improve them, using restrictive clauses to give meaning and style to the sentences.

*Cara Marie is the only senior. (Cara Marie is the only senior who was offered a scholarship to an Ivy League college.)*

*Mercury is the planet. (Mercury is the planet that is closest to the sun.)*

*The squirrel was nibbling on an acorn. (The squirrel with its bushy tail twitching was nibbling on an acorn.)*

**R** **RESOURCE MANAGER—Copy Master**
Use Descriptive Language p. 48

**READING-WRITING CONNECTION**
Have students review the O'Keeffe quotations in lines 1–7 and 54–57, which point to her independence and defiance of convention.

**Writing Online** **THINK central**

The following tools are available online at **thinkcentral.com** and on **WriteSmart CD-ROM:**
- **Interactive Graphic Organizers**
- **Interactive Student Models**
- **Interactive Revision Lessons**
For additional grammar instruction, see **GrammarNotes** on **thinkcentral.com**.

# Assess and Reteach

## Assess

**DIAGNOSTIC AND SELECTION TESTS**
Selection Test A pp. 147–148
Selection Test B/C pp. 149–150

**Interactive Selection Test** on **thinkcentral.com**

## Reteach

**Level Up Online Tutorials** on **thinkcentral.com**

**Reteaching Worksheets** on **thinkcentral.com**
Literature Lesson 45: Tone

# Focus and Motivate

Before Reading

## COMMON CORE FOCUS

**RI 2** Analyze a central idea's development over the course of a text, including how it emerges and is shaped and refined by details; provide an objective summary of the text. **RI 5** Analyze how an author's ideas or claims are developed and refined. **SL 2** Integrate multiple sources of information presented in diverse formats. **L 4** Determine or clarify the meaning of unknown and multiple-meaning words. **L 6** Acquire and use accurately general academic and domain-specific words; demonstrate independence in gathering vocabulary knowledge.

## SUMMARIES

**"Who Killed the Iceman?"** This *National Geographic* article presents the mystery of a 5,000-year-old mummy found frozen in an Italian glacier.

**"Skeletal Sculptures"** Donna M. Jackson's article explains how forensic anthropologists reconstruct facial features on a skull cast to help detectives identify human remains.

## How do scientists UNLOCK the past?

Have students read the paragraph and complete the *DISCUSS* activity, then have them write a definition of investigate.

# Selection Resources

---

## Who Killed the Iceman?
Magazine Article

 Video link at thinkcentral.com

**Essential Course of Study ECOS**

## Skeletal Sculptures
Process Description by Donna M. Jackson

**VIDEO TRAILER** THINKcentral KEYWORD: HML9-578

# How do scientists UNLOCK the past?

### COMMON CORE

**RI 2** Analyze a central idea's development over the course of a text, including how it emerges and is shaped and refined by details; provide an objective summary of the text. **RI 5** Analyze how an author's ideas or claims are developed and refined. **SL 2** Integrate multiple sources of information presented in diverse formats. **L 4** Determine or clarify the meaning of unknown and multiple-meaning words.

Everyone knows bones and corpses can't talk. Or can they? As you may know from true-crime shows or sci-fi thrillers, human remains often have their own stories to tell. As police detectives unravel intricate cases and scientists investigate unexplained phenomena, these remains often tell stories that help piece the past together.

**DISCUSS** What types of criminal or scientific investigation do you know about? With a partner, choose a type to discuss. List the methods investigators use to track down the truth. Then briefly explain the purpose of each method.

| Criminal Investigation | |
|---|---|
| Method | Purpose |
| 1. Finger-printing | Identify suspect |
| 2. | |
| 3. | |

578

---

See resources on the **Teacher One Stop DVD-ROM** *and on* thinkcentral.com.

 **RESOURCE MANAGER UNIT 5**
Plan and Teach, pp. 49–56
Summary pp. 57–58†‡*
Text Analysis and Reading
   Skill, pp. 59–62†*
Vocabulary, pp. 63–65*

**DIAGNOSTIC AND SELECTION TESTS**
Selection Tests, pp. 151–154

 **BEST PRACTICES TOOLKIT**
Word Squares, p. E10
Classification Chart, p. B17
Venn Diagram, p. A26
Two-Column Chart, p. A25

**INTERACTIVE READER**

**ADAPTED INTERACTIVE READER**

**ELL ADAPTED INTERACTIVE READER**

 Video link at thinkcentral.com

**TECHNOLOGY**
⊘ **Teacher One Stop DVD-ROM**
⊘ **Student One Stop DVD-ROM**
⊘ **PowerNotes DVD-ROM**
⊘ **Audio Anthology CD**
⊘ **GrammarNotes DVD-ROM**
⊘ **Audio Tutor CD**
⊘ **ExamView Test Generator**
   on the **Teacher One Stop**

 **Video Trailer**

Go to thinkcentral.com to preview the **Video Trailer** introducing this selection. Other features that support the selection include
• **PowerNotes** presentation
• **ThinkAloud** models to enhance comprehension
• **WordSharp** vocabulary tutorials
• interactive writing and grammar instruction

---

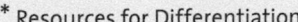 * Resources for Differentiation      † Also in Spanish      ‡ In Haitian Creole and Vietnamese

## TEXT ANALYSIS: TEXT FEATURES

**Text features** are design elements that highlight the organization and key information of a text. They can help you preview what you'll read and recognize central ideas.

- **Subheadings** signal the beginning of a new topic or section. They often identify the focus of the text that follows them.
- **Graphic aids,** such as maps and photographs, present information visually. They are frequently accompanied by **captions,** which describe or clarify the information.
- **Numbered lists** often consist of steps in a process that should be followed in order.

As you read, use text features to help you analyze how claims and ideas are developed in each article.

## READING STRATEGY: TAKE NOTES

When you **take notes,** your goal should be to summarize a text's claims, central ideas, and details in a way that is easy to understand and remember. Since text features highlight central ideas and key information, including them in your notes can help.

As you read each section of "Who Killed the Iceman?" jot down its subheading. Then record the important details included in the section.

As you read "Skeletal Sculptures," note the key information in each step.

**Review:** Monitor

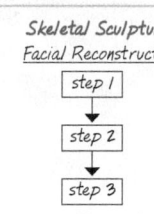

*Who Killed the Iceman?*
Background
- He was froz-en for 5,000 years.
- Hikers found him in 1991 on the border between Austria and Italy.

*Skeletal Sculptures*
Facial Reconstruction
step 1
↓
step 2
↓
step 3

## ▲ VOCABULARY IN CONTEXT

Find a word that could be used in each newspaper headline.

| WORD LIST | anthropology | compile | refute |
|---|---|---|---|
| | artifact | presumed | |

1. Woman **Thought** Guilty of Murder
2. New Study to **Pull Together** Years of Research
3. Unusual **Object** Found in Archaeological Dig
4. **Science** Spotlight: Ancient Tribes
5. Scholar to **Deny Accuracy of** Theory

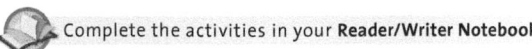 Complete the activities in your **Reader/Writer Notebook.**

### Stumbling onto a Mummy

"Who Killed the Iceman?" chronicles some of the theories surrounding the death of a man who met his demise around 3000 B.C. The "Iceman," the oldest frozen mummy ever found, was discovered by German hikers vacationing in the Alps. When they spied a body embedded in the ice, the hikers assumed they had found the remains of a mountain climber who'd met a dismal fate. They had no idea they'd stumbled onto a 5,000-year-old relic. The Iceman now resides at the South Tyrol Museum of Archaeology in Bolzano, Italy.

**Rescue workers and forensic experts examine the Iceman.**

### Crime-Fighting Scientists

"Skeletal Sculptures" describes how forensic anthropologists help police track down the truth. Anthropology is the scientific study of humans—our origins, behavior, environment, and physical features. Forensics is the use of science to solve crimes. Forensic anthropologists use their knowledge of human characteristics to assist in cracking tough cases involving human remains. The scientists identify the victim's age, sex, race, and physical characteristics. They also determine the likely cause of death, which makes them an integral part of many murder investigations.

### TEXT ANALYSIS   COMMON CORE   RI 2, RI 5

## ● *Model the Skill:* TEXT FEATURES

Scan the first page of "Who Killed the Iceman" and point out the "Background" subheading and the photograph and its caption. Then have students scan the rest of the two selections to see that all of the features mentioned in the text are used. Have students brainstorm for other types of writing that might include the text features listed, including history and science texts, encyclopedias, magazine articles, and product information manuals.

**GUIDED PRACTICE** Have students suppose that such text features were missing from the genres that they listed. Discuss why the absence might make the writing more difficult to understand.

### READING STRATEGY   COMMON CORE   RI 2, RI 5

## ■ *Model the Skill:* TAKE NOTES

Tell students that by taking notes, they are making use of text features. A note should express an idea clearly and reference a page number.

**GUIDED PRACTICE** Ask students how they might use their notes in the future.

**R** RESOURCE MANAGER—Copy Master Take Notes p. 61

---

### VOCABULARY SKILL   COMMON CORE   L 4

## ▲ VOCABULARY IN CONTEXT

**DIAGNOSE WORD KNOWLEDGE** Have all students complete Vocabulary in Context. Check their words against the following:

**anthropology** (ăn′thrə-pŏl′ə-jē) *n.* the science or study of human beings, including their physical characteristics and cultures

**artifact** (är′tə-făkt′) *n.* something created by humans, usually for a practical purpose

**compile** (kəm-pīl′) *v.* to put together by gathering from many sources

**presumed** (prĭ-zoomd′) *adj.* thought to be true
    **presume** *v.*

**refute** (rĭ-fyoot′) *v.* to prove false by argument or evidence

**PRETEACH VOCABULARY** Use the following copy master to help students predict meanings for each boldfaced word.

**R** RESOURCE MANAGER—Copy Master Vocabulary Study p. 63

1. Read aloud the first pair of sentences.
2. Point out "human cultures and their characteristics." Elicit meanings for *anthropology,* such as "the study of human cultures and characteristics."
3. Repeat the procedure for the other items.

## READ WITH A PURPOSE

*Help students set a purpose for reading. Tell them to look for the different methods that scientists use to discover what happened to people in the past.*

### TEXT ANALYSIS
COMMON CORE
RI 2, RI 5

**Ⓐ** *Model the Skill:* TEXT FEATURES

Explain that the photograph and its caption clarify the title of the article. Ask students to identify the Iceman and to explain their reasoning.

*Possible answer:* The mummy looks more lifelike than would be expected from a 5,000-year-old body. It is surprising that the body is a mummy, with skin, rather than just a skeleton.

### READING STRATEGY
COMMON CORE
RI 2, RI 5

**Ⓑ** *Model the Skill:* TAKE NOTES

Explain that one way to take notes is to paraphrase sentences. Then tell students that paraphrasing the first and last sentences of a paragraph often gives them its central idea. Have students do this for the first paragraph and then add this information to their Take Notes graphic organizers.

*Possible answer:* The most important information is that the Iceman is 5,000 years old, that he was found in 1991 in a mountain glacier on the border of Austria and Italy, and that scientists have determined that he died in battle or was murdered or sacrificed.

**IF STUDENTS NEED HELP . . .** Help them paraphrase the first sentence and the last sentence of the paragraph. Model turning the paraphrases into notes, deciding which details to include and which to omit.

---

*FROM NATIONAL GEOGRAPHIC MAGAZINE*

# WHO KILLED THE ICEMAN?

**Ⓐ** **TEXT FEATURES**
Examine this **photograph** and its accompanying **caption.** Does the 5,000-year-old mummy look as you expected him to, or does his appearance surprise you? Explain your answer.

Among the first to reach the scene, these mountaineers used makeshift tools to help free the mummy.

### Background

He spent some 5,000 years frozen in a mountain glacier on the Austro-Italian border before passing hikers discovered him, sprawled in the melting snow, in 1991. He now resides in a refrigerated room at a museum in Italy. Over the 11 years since his discovery the Iceman mummy has been examined from every possible angle. But not until this past summer did those studying his still frozen body notice a crucial piece of evidence that dramatically rewrites his story: "Ötzi," nicknamed for the Ötztal Alps where he was found, didn't freeze to death in a sudden snow storm while tending sheep as some had suggested. Instead he was killed, a victim of warfare, murder, or human sacrifice. **Ⓑ**

**Ⓑ** **TAKE NOTES**
What is the most important information provided in the section labeled "Background"? Be sure to record each section's essential details in your notes.

**Targeted Passage** **①**

---

## DIFFERENTIATED INSTRUCTION

### FOR ENGLISH LANGUAGE LEARNERS
**Vocabulary Support** Use Word Squares to teach these words: *evidence* (line 6), *interpretation* (line 31), *experts* (line 59), *controversial* (line 69), *perspective* (line 70), *contexts* (line 72).

📦 **BEST PRACTICES TOOLKIT—Transparency** Word Squares p. E10

### FOR STRUGGLING READERS
In combination with the *Audio Anthology CD*, use one or more Targeted Passages (pp. 580, 583, 584, 587) to ensure that students focus on key events, concepts, and skills. Targeted Passages are also good for English learners.

**①** **Targeted Passage** [Lines 5–9]
This passage sets up the mystery in this true story: the fact that the understanding of the Iceman's death has changed.

### Clues Discovered

10 X-rays reveal an arrowhead buried deep in the Iceman's left shoulder—an injury that could not possibly have been self-inflicted. This discovery consequently led archaeologists to believe that the Iceman had been killed. The wound, visible as a small dark smudge beneath the mummy's leathery skin, had been overlooked in all previous examinations. Though no arrow shaft protrudes from the wound and no blood marks the arrow's entrance, it's now clear that the Iceman was shot in the back. But who did it? And why?

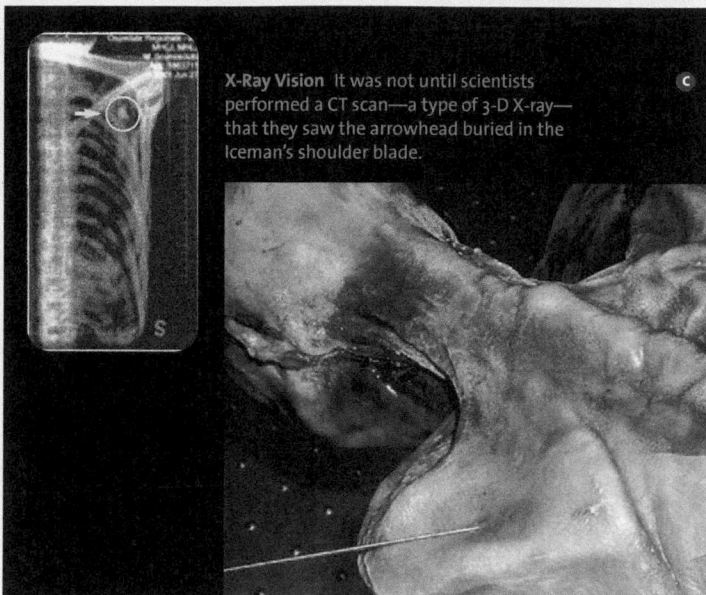

**X-Ray Vision** It was not until scientists performed a CT scan—a type of 3-D X-ray—that they saw the arrowhead buried in the Iceman's shoulder blade.  **C**

### Differing Theories  **D**

"There's no way anyone can ever really know," says archaeologist Johan Reinhard, a National Geographic Society explorer-in-residence. "It might have been murder. Or it might have been ritual sacrifice."[1]

20 Reinhard knows mummies. Among the many he has discovered is the Inca "ice maiden," a victim of sacrifice, on the frozen slopes of Peru's Nevado Ampato[2] in 1995. His experience studying mountain cultures in the Andes, the Himalayas, and elsewhere has convinced him that the Iceman's death was not a random killing.

---

1. **ritual sacrifice:** a sacrifice that is part of a religious ceremony.
2. **Nevado Ampato** (nə-vä'dō äm-pä'tô): a volcano in the Central Andes.

COMMON CORE L 4a, c

### Language Coach

**Roots and Affixes** A prefix is an affix (word part) added before a root or base word. One meaning of the prefix *pro-* is "forward." What do you think *protrudes* in line 15 means? (Hint: the root *-trud-* means "thrust.") Check your answer in a dictionary.

**C  TEXT FEATURES** How do these photographs support the **central idea** of the "Clues Discovered" section? Explain, citing details from the text and the photos.

**D  TAKE NOTES** As you begin reading the section about the controversy surrounding Ötzi's death, take careful notes to keep track of the differing theories.

---

 **THINK** central

### Reading Support

This selection on **thinkcentral.com** includes embedded **ThinkAloud** models—students "thinking aloud" about the story to model the kinds of questions a good reader would ask about a selection.

### BACKGROUND

**When Did the Iceman Die?** Scientists extracted a tiny amount of food from the mummy's intestines, revealing the contents of his last meal. A botanist examined the food and found the remnants of bread, plants, and meat. He also found many varieties of pollen. Most of the pollen came from the hop hornbeam tree. That fact reveals that the Iceman died in springtime, for the hop hornbeam tree releases pollen only from March to June.

**TEXT ANALYSIS**    COMMON CORE RI 2, RI 5

**C  TEXT FEATURES**

*Possible answer:* *The right image shows the arrowhead that probably killed the Iceman. The text describes a telltale smudge beneath his skin (line 13). The left image supports the description by pointing out the smudge and showing the same location on the X-ray.*

**READING STRATEGY**    COMMON CORE RI 2, RI 5

**D  TAKE NOTES**

*Notes may vary but should include details that support each of the two main theories.*

**IF STUDENTS NEED HELP...** Assist them in using a Classification Chart to distinguish details that support the "murder" theory from details that support the "ritual sacrifice" theory.

💼 **BEST PRACTICES TOOLKIT**—Transparency Classification Chart p. B17

---

- What did scientists originally think caused the Iceman's death? For how long was that the accepted view? (lines 5–9)
- What is the new explanation of his death? Be specific. (line 9)

### FOR ENGLISH LANGUAGE LEARNERS

**Language Coach**   COMMON CORE L 4a, c

**Roots and Affixes**
*Possible answer: thrusts forward;* Ask students to find other words with prefixes and suffixes on this page and look up their meanings.

### FOR ADVANCED LEARNERS/PRE-AP

**Developing Expertise** Support students in becoming experts or members of expert groups by guiding them in researching one of these topics further:

- human civilization in Europe 5,000 years ago
- various methods of mummification
- other recent mummy investigations
- mummies in folklore and film

Have students share their information with the class.

COMMON CORE SL 2

## ⓔ GRAPHIC SOURCES

*Possible answer: The map indicates where the mummy was found. The caption gives the altitude of that location. The photograph shows what the Iceman's dagger looked like.*

Walk students through reading the map. Ask, "What is the title of the map? What does that tell you about what the map is about?" Ask students to read the caption. Point out that the red star indicates where Ötzi was found. Point out that students can get a sense of where the mummy was found in relation to modern-day countries.

## TIERED DISCUSSION PROMPTS

Direct students to lines 31–41. Use these prompts to help students grasp the importance of artifacts in learning more about the Iceman:

**Connect** How might artifacts that you carry provide information about your life? Give examples. *Possible answer: Textbooks might show students' grade level and approximate age. Certain jewelry might indicate their religion. Certain clothing might show that they live in a cold place or a warm place.*

**Synthesize** What artifacts might help prove one theory about the Iceman's death over another? Explain. *Possible answer: If the Iceman had been found with more religious tokens, the "ritual sacrifice" theory would be more plausible. If he had carried arrows that were different from the broken ones, the "murder" theory would be more plausible.*

COMMON CORE L 4

## OWN THE WORD

**artifact:** Tell students to reread the paragraph with the word *artifact.* Then have them cite context clues that helped them determine the meaning of *artifact.* *Possible answers: found with the mummy, broken arrows, copper ax*

---

"Look at where he died," Reinhard says. "It's a prominent pass, between two of the highest peaks in the Ötztal Alps. This is the kind of place where people from mountain cultures have traditionally made offerings to their mountain gods. We know that mountain worship was important in prehistoric Europe during the Bronze Age," he says. "And there is good
30 evidence that it may also have played a role earlier, in the Copper Age."[3]

Reinhard's interpretation seems to answer questions about **artifacts** found with the mummy that have long puzzled experts. For example, breaking objects was a ceremonial practice in Neolithic[4] Europe. This might explain the broken arrows lying near the mummy. The Iceman's copper ax—the oldest prehistoric ax in Europe with its bindings and handle intact—is also significant. Its copper had to have been mined, and mountains, as the source of valuable metals used to make tools, "were worshiped by miners throughout the world," says Reinhard. "This helps explain why the ax was left with the body after the killing." Murderers would likely have taken something so
40 useful with them. But people performing a ritual might have left it for the Iceman's use in the afterlife or as a tribute to the gods.

**artifact** (är′tə-făkt′) *n.* something created by humans, usually for a practical purpose

COMMON CORE SL 2

## ⓔ GRAPHIC SOURCES

Examine the map that accompanies this article. **Graphic sources** such as maps clarify information in the text and present additional factual data. What information does this map convey? List two details you can learn from this graphic source.

ⓔ **Where Ötzi Died**

SWITZERLAND · Innsbruck · AUSTRIA · Ötztal Alps · Venice · ITALY

Ötzi was found at approximately 10,500 feet in the Ötztal Alps on the border between Austria and Italy. After closely examining Ötzi's clothing and possessions—including a sheath and dagger (shown at right)—archaeologists realized they had uncovered a 5,300-year-old find.

3. **Bronze Age . . . Copper Age:** The Bronze Age in Europe, when bronze tools began to be used, lasted roughly from 3500 B.C. to 1000 B.C. The Copper Age overlaps with the earliest part of the Bronze Age.

4. **Neolithic** (nē′ə-lĭth′ĭk): having to do with the prehistoric period when food growing began, but before metal tools were used—about 4000 B.C. in Europe.

---

## DIFFERENTIATED INSTRUCTION

### FOR ENGLISH LANGUAGE LEARNERS

**Language: Verb Tenses** Point out these verbs used in lines 36–41:

- *had to have been mined* (line 36)
- *were worshiped* (line 37)
- *would . . . have taken* (line 39)
- *might have left* (line 40)

Explain that some of these verb forms are common in language used to express theories and hypotheses.

### FOR ADVANCED LEARNERS/PRE–AP

**Hypothesize** Ask students to reread this page, paying particular attention to details about where the Iceman was discovered. Have students use these details to propose an alternative hypothesis that explains the location of the find, the artifacts that accompanied the body, and the Iceman's wound. Students' hypotheses should draw upon textual evidence for support. Discuss hypotheses that volunteers offer to share.

Another clue: The Iceman's body was found in a naturally formed trench along the pass. Prior explanations had him taking shelter there from sudden bad weather. "But the trench is not deep and is at a high point of the pass. It 50 would have been a poor place to sit out a storm," explains Reinhard. Perhaps, instead, the Iceman was buried there by whoever killed him, which would account for the body's being so well preserved. **F**

Reinhard's ideas have not been met with enthusiasm by European experts. In contrast 60 with his beliefs, the mummy's caretaker, pathologist Eduard Egarter Vigl of South Tyrol Museum of Archaeology, believes that Ötzi may have been fleeing from an attacker, saying, "The Iceman was hit by an arrow from behind." Others maintain that arrows aren't efficient means of ritual killing and that no clear evidence of any other Copper Age sacrifice exists.

A scientist examines the skeletal remains of the Iceman.

**So Who Killed the Iceman?**

"They view the idea of human sacrifice as too sensational," says Reinhard. "But they can't **refute** what I've pointed out, and I believe my theory better explains the known facts.

"I know it's controversial," he admits. "But it's time to **compile** all the 70 evidence and reexamine it from a different perspective. Let's look at these artifacts not only relative to each other but also within social, sacred, and geographical contexts."

**F MONITOR**
One important part of monitoring your reading is **evaluating** the information that's provided. Do you find Reinhard's theory convincing? Why or why not?

**2 Targeted Passage**

**refute** (rĭ-fyo͞ot′) *v.* to prove false by argument or evidence

**compile** (kəm-pīl′) *v.* to put together by gathering from many sources

---

**FOR STRUGGLING READERS**

**2 Targeted Passage [Lines 59–65]**

This passage presents arguments against Reinhard's theory of ritual sacrifice as the cause of the Iceman's death.

- What are the professional qualifications of Eduard Egarter Vigl? (lines 61–62)

- What does Vigl believe the Iceman was doing when he was killed? (lines 62–63)

- How do others argue against ritual killing as the cause of his death? (lines 64–65)

**Develop Reading Fluency** Model for students an effective way to read text containing quotes in lines 57–73. Demonstrate how fluent readers set apart the quotes from the rest of the test by using pauses. Next have students break into pairs to practice reading this section aloud to each other.

---

How do scientists

**UNLOCK** the past?

**Discuss** Based on lines 42–56, how have researchers' investigations helped refute the idea that the Iceman died while taking shelter from bad weather? *Possible answer: In studying the location where the mummy was found, researchers have learned that the pass was an exposed place, not one where the Iceman might have taken shelter from a storm.*

**READING STRATEGY: Review**

**F MONITOR**

*Possible answer: Reinhard's theory is convincing. He points out that the Iceman died in the kind of place where prehistoric people made human sacrifices. He argues that the Iceman's valuable copper ax, found near his body, would probably have been taken by murderers, while it might have been left by people performing a ritual killing. Finally, Reinhard argues that the trench where the Iceman's body was found suggests that he was buried there after his death and was not taking shelter from a storm.*

**IF STUDENTS NEED HELP . . .**

1. Guide students as they record the clues in lines 25–56.

2. Have students note Reinhard's professional qualifications.

3. Discuss the reputation of *National Geographic*, the publisher of the article.

**VOCABULARY**   COMMON CORE  L 4

**OWN THE WORD**

- **refute:** Ask students if they have ever tried to *refute* another person's statement. How was the student able to *refute* the other person's remark?

- **compile:** Remind students that the Latin prefix *com-* means "together; jointly," so *compile* means literally "to pile together."

## G MONITOR

**Possible answer:** *Facial reconstruction is a "last resort" because it is a guess at the victim's appearance, meant to trigger the memory of someone who can identify the victim when no other clues point to the victim's identity.*

**IF STUDENTS NEED HELP . . .** Work through a diagram such as this to clarify the reasons for and results of facial reconstruction.

```
          A skeleton is
          unidentified.

   The police need          Police want to
   a new lead in a          publish a likeness
   crime case.              in the media.

            SKELETAL
            SCULPTURE

   The sculpture            Details can
   hints at the             provide clues to
   identity of the          investigators.
   victim.

       Someone recognizes
       the likeness and has
       information about
       the victim.
```

### OWN THE WORD

**anthropology:** Tell students that *anthropos* is a Greek word meaning "human being"; the suffix *-logy* comes from Greek and means "science or study." Have students name other fields of study that end with the suffix *-logy*. **Possible answers:** *sociology, psychology, archaeology, theology, musicology*

---

**anthropology**
(ăn′thrə-pŏl′ə-jē) *n.* the science or study of human beings, including their physical characteristics and cultures

---

COMMON CORE   L 4

### Language Coach

**Multiple Meanings**
Many words have more than one meaning. Reread lines 11–15. *Likeness* can mean "portrait," "similarity," or "appearance." Which meaning best fits the word's use in these lines?

---

## G MONITOR

As you read, stop to **clarify:** why does Dr. Charney call facial reconstruction "a last resort at identification"?

---

# Skeletal SCULPTURES

Dr. Michael Charney is an expert in forensic[1] **anthropology.** His expertise has enabled him to take a few pieces of a skeleton found in Missouri and compile a portrait of a five-foot, 120-pound Asian woman in her mid-twenties. Still, that isn't enough to identify her.

10   The dead woman's "face" needs to be brought back to life.

Reconstructing the likeness of a person in clay, using the skull as a guide, is a last resort at identification, Dr. Charney says. It gives police a new lead to follow, a visual clue that can be photographed and displayed in the media.

Facial reconstruction is not 20 an identifying tool, he warns. The goal is to trigger someone to recognize the model and to identify the person through scientific means.

"All that's needed is a general recognition that it looks like so-and-so," he says. **G**

Before re-creating a face, Dr. Charney and forensic sculptor 30 Nita Bitner search the skull for signs of disease, injury, and structural defects.

"We look for things that shouldn't be there," Bitner says. "Sometimes we find broken noses, cuts, or dentures." These

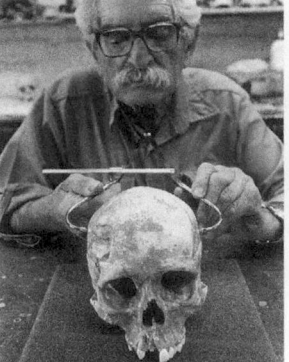

Dr. Michael Charney measures a skull with spreading calipers.

affect the face's appearance and aid in the identification process. If the nose bone is curved to one 40 side, for example, it's important to show it in the face because it's a distinguishing feature.

"We have to be careful, however, not to include anything that happened at the time of death," Bitner notes, "because it wouldn't be recognizable to others."

Age also influences how a face is built. Wrinkled skin, which 50 might help illustrate an older person, is often incorporated into a sculpture for accuracy.

After studying the Missouri woman's skull, Bitner makes a latex mold and pours a plaster cast. Now she's ready to sculpt the face.

**① Targeted Passage**

---

1. **forensic:** having to do with applying scientific methods to crime investigation.

---

## DIFFERENTIATED INSTRUCTION

### FOR STRUGGLING READERS

**① Targeted Passage** [Lines 43–56]

This passage identifies challenges in the work of Nita Bitner, the forensic sculptor.

- How does Bitner prepare to sculpt a face? Why do you think that she doesn't use the victim's actual skull? (lines 43–56)

- Why is it important for her to include wrinkles on some sculptures? (lines 48–52)

- What kinds of details would she want to avoid? Why? (lines 43–47)

### FOR ENGLISH LANGUAGE LEARNERS

**Language Coach**    COMMON CORE L 4

**Multiple Meanings** **Possible answer:** *appearance* Ask students to find other words with more than one meaning on this page. Have students look up the meanings of the words in the dictionary. (examples: lead, line 15; means, line 24; cast, line 55)

1. Forensic sculptor Nita Bitner begins a facial restoration by cutting round rubber pegs into different lengths. The pegs, called landmarks, represent the thickness of the soft tissue (muscle, fat, and skin) at different points on the face. These tissue depths, which vary for men and women of varying ages, were first calculated from corpses by nineteenth-century scientists and later updated. ⓗ

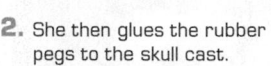

2. She then glues the rubber pegs to the skull cast.

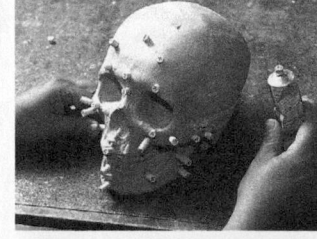

3. Bitner "connects the dots" with strips of modeling clay. When attaching the strips of clay, she begins at the forehead and works her way down to the cheekbones, nasal area, chin, and mouth.

4. Once the dots are connected, Bitner fills in the spaces with clay and fleshes out the face. Now the prominent cheekbones of the Missouri woman become strikingly clear. Suddenly her broad face and delicate nose emerge.

**ⓗ TAKE NOTES**
As you read the numbered items in this section, record the steps of the process in your notes. For each step, include only the **details** that are most important.

SKELETAL SCULPTURES **585**

---

**READING STRATEGY** COMMON CORE

RI 2, RI 5

**ⓗ TAKE NOTES**

***Possible answer: Step 1*—*Bitner cuts rubber pegs as landmarks. Step 2*—*She glues the pegs to the skull cast. Step 3*—*She uses clay strips to connect the pegs. Step 4*—*She fills in the gaps. Step 5*—*She smooths the clay. Step 6*—*She sets the eyes. Step 7*—*She sculpts eyelids. Step 8*—*She sculpts the sides of the nose. Step 9*—*She measures the width of the nose. Step 10*—*She molds the upper lip. Step 11*—*She adds a wig and scarf. Step 12*—*The finished sculpture is photographed.***

**IF STUDENTS NEED HELP . . .** Assist them in using the Take Notes chart to list the steps in sculpting a face.

**REVISIT THE BIG QUESTION**

How do scientists

**UNLOCK** the past?

**Discuss** Based on steps 1–4, how does Bitner use forensic investigation to help her reconstruct a victim's face? *Possible answer: Bitner combines what she knows about the subject's race, gender, and approximate age with calculations of tissue depth, which differ for men and women of varying ages. Based upon this information, she uses rubber pegs and modeling clay to flesh out a likeness of the deceased person.*

---

**FOR ENGLISH LANGUAGE LEARNERS**

**Comprehension: Transitions** Point out that the word *step* indicates a sequence of details. Then help students pick out these other words in the steps that help clarify the sequence: *begins* (Step 1); *then* (Step 2); *When* (Step 3); *Once, Now* (Step 4); *As* (Step 5); *Next* (Step 7); *then* (Step 8); *Now* (Step 10); *will, will then* (Step 11); *now* (Step 12).

**FOR RELUCTANT READERS**

Group students into pairs. Then tell them that they are going to create their own version of the Iceman's face. Remind pairs to look over the details about the Iceman in the article and encourage them to visualize what they feel the Iceman looked like. Tell pairs to create the Iceman's face in a sketch, painting, collage, clay, or other medium. Have each pair present their Iceman face to the class.

Direct students to steps 1–12. Use these prompts to help students grasp the difficulty of facial reconstruction:

**Connect** Think about the distinguishing features of your face. How would an acquaintance describe you? *Students should identify characteristics of their appearance that are unique.*

**Analyze** What are some possible problems with facial reconstruction? *Possible answer: The sculptor might not know about such distinguishing features as scars, tattoos, or hairstyles. Furthermore, if the sculptor does not have enough information about the victim, the reconstruction might present the victim as looking too old or too young.*

**Evaluate** What qualities must sculptor Nita Bitner have in order to be good at her work? How can you tell? *Possible answer: Bitner must be meticulous about details, for she has to notice very small irregularities on each skull. She must be logical, for she is required to use clues to interpret facts. She must be artistic, for she needs to visualize tissues and shapes that are not present.*

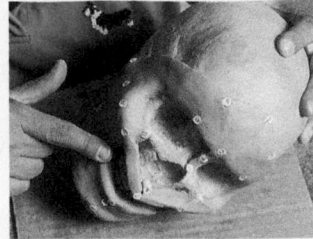

**5.** As Bitner smooths the clay with her thumb and fingers, the face develops like a photograph.

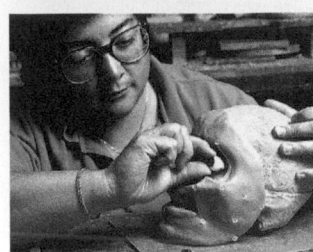

**6.** Bitner sets the plastic brown eyes in their sockets.

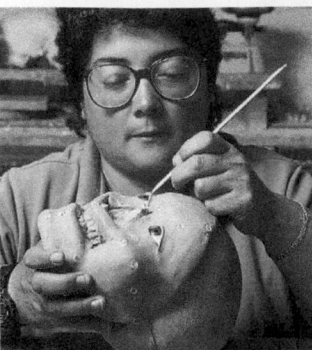

**7.** Next come the eyelids.

**8.** Bitner then sculpts the sides of the nose.

**9.** She measures the nose with a ruler to ensure it is the correct width.

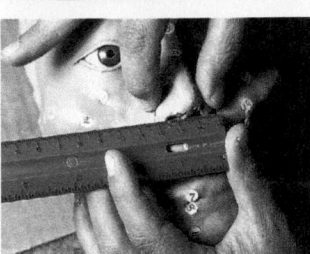

## DIFFERENTIATED INSTRUCTION

### FOR STRUGGLING READERS

**Use Visuals** Discuss how the photographs clarify details or give additional details about the process of facial reconstruction. For example, the photographs show how the face is sculpted by hand rather than by machine, how the sculptor uses specialized tools to create details, and how precise measurements are important to completing the sculpture.

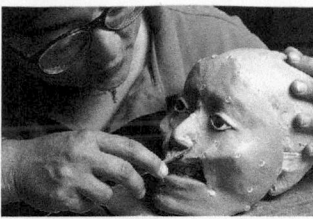

**10.** Now it's time to mold the upper lip.

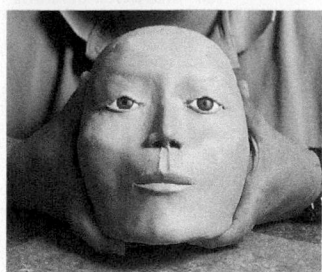

**11.** The face is nearly complete. Because the Missouri woman is **presumed** to be Asian, Bitner will add a black wig. She will then add a scarf for a finishing touch.

**presumed** (prĭ-zoomd′) *adj.* thought to be true
**presume** *v.*

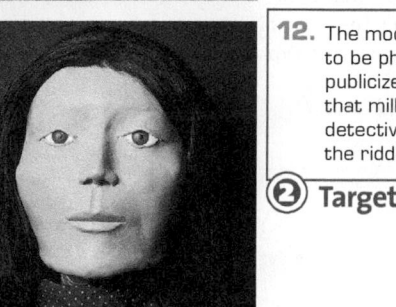

**12.** The model is now ready to be photographed and publicized in the media so that millions of amateur detectives can help solve the riddle of her identity. ●

② **Targeted Passage**

● **TEXT FEATURES**
Review the **photographs** illustrating the process. Which step do you think is the most critical for transforming a skull into a recognizable human face? Explain your answer.

---

**FOR STRUGGLING READERS**

② **Targeted Passage** [Step 12]

This passage explains how the sculpture will be used after it is completed.

- What will happen to the sculpture now?
- How will the media use the photograph of the sculpture?
- Who will be interested in viewing the sculpture? Which viewers are most likely to interest police, and why?

**FOR ADVANCED LEARNERS/PRE–AP**

**Compare and Contrast** [small-group option] Ask students whether a forensic sculptor is primarily an artist or a scientist and how the skills are different. Have students list the aspects of the job that require one or both sets of skills. Invite students to share their responses; then come to a class consensus.

---

**OWN THE WORD**

**presumed:** have students create a semantic map for *presumed*. Write the word in a center circle and add the definition given, "thought to be true." Draw spider legs from the center circle and have students add synonyms to complete the map. *Possible answers: believed, hypothesized, surmised, deduced*

● **TEXT FEATURES**

*Possible answer: Step 4 is important because it is fundamental—the basic fleshing out of the face. Step 7, the creation of eyelids, would be especially important for an Asian face. The nose (Step 8) and the lips (Step 10) are also important because the unique characteristics of these features would be crucial to identifying a face.*

**Extend the Discussion** Even with a very skilled sculptor, the finished face might look different from the face of the victim. Do you think that facial reconstruction could hinder the investigation of a crime? Explain.

**SELECTION WRAP–UP**

**READ WITH A PURPOSE** Now that students have finished reading the selection, have them describe how forensic anthropologists attempt to identify individuals. *Possible answer: Forensic anthropologists create models of people's faces.*

★ **CRITIQUE** Have students explain whether they found each article interesting. Then ask them to rate the effectiveness of the two articles together.

**INDEPENDENT READING**

For students wanting to read more about the Iceman, suggest *Iceman: Uncovering the Life and Times of a Prehistoric Man Found in an Alpine Glacier* by Brenda Fowler.

# Practice and Apply

For preliminary support of post-reading questions, use these copy masters:

**R** RESOURCE MANAGER—Copy Masters
Reading Check p. 66
Text Features p. 60
Question Support p. 67

Additional selection questions are provided for teachers on page 53.

## ANSWERS

## Comprehension

1. *The Iceman was found in the Ötztal Alps. "Ötzi" is short for "Ötztal."*

2. *Reinhard theorizes that the Iceman was killed as part of a ritual sacrifice.*

3. *Facial reconstruction is the re-creation of a face from a skull cast. Detectives use it to help identify skeletal remains.*

## Text Analysis

COMMON CORE RI 2, RI 5, SL 2

*Possible answers:*

4. ● **COMMON CORE FOCUS** *Summarize Notes Paragraphs should include key points from the 12 steps.*

5. *Disagreement is helpful because it encourages deeper inquiry. Without disagreement, for instance, Reinhard might have accepted the original theory about the Iceman's death and might never have discovered the arrowhead in the mummy's back.*

6. ● **COMMON CORE FOCUS** *Analyze Text Features The reader would have gotten an accurate idea about how and where the mummy was found and about the discovery of the arrowhead. The reader would have missed details about Reinhard's theory.*

7. *X-rays of Ötzi's shoulder: shows the arrowhead lodged in the Iceman's back; Analysis of where the body was found: suggests that the Iceman was not seeking shelter from a storm; Evaluation of artifacts found with Iceman's body: helps date the Iceman and suggests that his death had a religious significance. Students should provide reasonable support for their choices of most effective method.*

## Comprehension

1. **Recall** Why is the Iceman nicknamed Ötzi?

2. **Summarize** What is Johan Reinhard's theory about how the Iceman died?

3. **Clarify** What is facial reconstruction, and for what is it used?

## Text Analysis

4. **Summarize Notes** Review the notes you took as you read "Skeletal Sculptures." Using these, summarize the process of facial reconstruction.

5. **Draw Conclusions** In your opinion, is disagreement between scientists helpful or harmful to further investigation? Use evidence from "Who Killed the Iceman?" to support your conclusion.

6. **Analyze Text Features** If you had simply scanned the text features—the title, subheads, and graphic aids—of "Who Killed the Iceman?" would you have had an accurate idea of what the article was about? Explain your answer.

7. **Evaluate** Complete the chart below, noting the information that each method of investigation provided to the scientists studying the Iceman. Which method do you think yielded the most crucial information? Explain.

| Method of Investigation | Information Provided |
|---|---|
| X-rays of Ötzi's shoulder | |
| Analysis of where the body was found | |
| Evaluation of artifacts found with the Iceman's body | |

### READING-WRITING CONNECTION

| WRITING PROMPT | REVISING TIP |
|---|---|
| **Short Constructed Response: Comparison and Contrast** How do Reinhard's theories about the mummy's death and the evidence he offers differ from those of the other scientists mentioned in "Who Killed the Iceman?" Using your notes and examples from the text, write **one or two paragraphs** comparing and contrasting Reinhard's theories with the other scientists' beliefs. | Review your response. Did you clearly explain each of the differing theories? Did you include the evidence each theory relies upon? |

### How do scientists UNLOCK the past?

How does learning about the past give us insight into our own time?

COMMON CORE

RI 2 Analyze a central idea's development over the course of a text, including how it emerges and is shaped and refined by details; provide an objective summary of the text. RI 5 Analyze how an author's ideas or claims are developed and refined. SL 2 Integrate multiple sources of information presented in diverse formats.

**READING-WRITING CONNECTION**

- Provide students with a Venn Diagram. Encourage them to reread the article, noting Reinhard's theories in one circle and other scientific theories in the other circle. Where the circles overlap, students should note any similarities between the two camps.

- Suggest that students organize their essays by explaining all the similarities first and the differences next.

 **BEST PRACTICES TOOLKIT—Transparency** Venn Diagram p. A26

**How do scientists UNLOCK the past?** Have students think about why scientists study past cultures and what their discoveries might teach us.

## Vocabulary in Context

▲ **VOCABULARY PRACTICE**

Decide whether these statements are true or false.

1. A wildflower originally identified centuries ago is an ancient **artifact.**
2. If I **refute** an argument, I make a convincing case against it.
3. To write a good report, you should **compile** information from several sources.
4. A person interested in animal behavior might want to study **anthropology.**
5. Someone **presumed** to be at fault has already been proved wrong.

**WORD LIST**

anthropology

artifact

compile

presumed

refute

### ACADEMIC VOCABULARY IN SPEAKING

- conclude
- construct
- implicit
- primary
- specific

When you listen to oral instructions, you can't rely on illustrated steps like those in "Skeletal Sculptures," but you can include clarifying questions in your notes to ask the speaker directly. Use at least two Academic Vocabulary words each as you practice giving and following oral instructions: Think of a task or process you've performed or a **specific** problem you've solved by following steps. Prepare the steps as instructions and present them orally to a partner. Then switch roles. Can you **conclude** that you understood each other's instructions? Explain.

### VOCABULARY STRATEGY: SPECIALIZED FIELDS, OR "OLOGIES"

The words for many fields of study, such as *anthropology,* end with the Greek suffix *-ology,* meaning "study of." The word for the person doing the studying often ends in *-ologist,* as in *anthropologist.* Many of these words, such as *toxicology* (the study of poisons), are recognizable because they have a familiar root. Others, like *penology* (the study of prisons), have a Greek or Latin root you may have to learn.

**PRACTICE** Choose the word in parentheses that fits each sentence. Use context clues, your knowledge of roots, or, if necessary, a dictionary.

1. Because his grandfather had Alzheimer's disease, Jeremy decided to specialize in (gerontology, geology).
2. A (cosmetologist, criminologist) was brought in to examine the murder scene.
3. If you study (ornithology, psychology), you will become an expert on birds.
4. Please have your hearing checked by an (audiologist, ecologist).
5. Ed, an amateur (cytologist, herpetologist), viewed lizards, snakes, and turtles near the beach.
6. Learning a little about (meteorology, oncology) helped me anticipate thunderstorms.

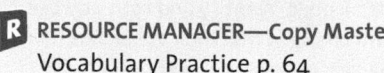

**COMMON CORE**

**L 6** Acquire and use accurately general academic and domain-specific words; demonstrate independence in gathering vocabulary knowledge.

**Interactive Vocabulary**

Go to **thinkcentral.com.**
KEYWORD: HML9-589

---

## DIFFERENTIATED INSTRUCTION

### FOR ENGLISH LANGUAGE LEARNERS

**Vocabulary: Cognates** Create a Two-Column Chart on the board. Help students list more fields of study in the first column and titles of people who study them in English in the second column. In both columns, allow students to list the home-language equivalents of each field.

 **BEST PRACTICES TOOLKIT—Transparency**
Two-Column Chart p. A25

### FOR ADVANCED LEARNERS/PRE–AP

**Analyze Terminology** Challenge students to locate similar-seeming words that end with *-ology,* along with a definition for each word, as in *ethnology* (the study of race)/*ethology* (the study of animal behavior) and *nephology* (the study of clouds)/*nephrology* (the study of kidneys). Have students exchange lists and try to match each word with its definition.

---

## ANSWERS

## Vocabulary in Context

▲ **VOCABULARY PRACTICE**

1. *false*
2. *true*
3. *true*
4. *false*
5. *false*

 **RESOURCE MANAGER—Copy Master**
Vocabulary Practice p. 64

### ACADEMIC VOCABULARY IN SPEAKING

**Possible answer:** *Historians and scientists have drawn different conclusions about the Iceman's history. With evidence on both sides, the debate could go on for a long time.*

### VOCABULARY STRATEGY: SPECIALIZED FIELDS, OR "OLOGIES"

**COMMON CORE L 6**

After students have read the paragraph, help them use their knowledge of word parts and context clues to complete the **PRACTICE** activity. Urge students to use a dictionary to identify any unfamiliar fields of study.

**Possible answers:**

1. *gerontology*
2. *criminologist*
3. *ornithology*
4. *audiologist*
5. *herpetologist*
6. *meteorology*

**R RESOURCE MANAGER—Copy Master**
Vocabulary Strategy p. 65

**Interactive Vocabulary**

**THINK** central

Keywords direct students to a **WordSharp** tutorial on **thinkcentral.com** or to other types of vocabulary practice and review.

---

## Assess and Reteach

### Assess

**DIAGNOSTIC AND SELECTION TESTS**
Selection Test A, B/C, pp. 151–152, 153–154

**Interactive Selection Test** on **thinkcentral.com**

### Reteach

**Level Up Online Tutorials** on **thinkcentral.com**

## Focus and Motivate

### SUMMARY

"The Lost Boys" describes the plight of orphaned African boys who fled Sudan during a hostile civil war. Sara Corbett's article presents the challenges faced by the roughly 10,000 survivors. It then focuses on the three Dut brothers, refugees who have been resettled in Fargo, North Dakota.

### How far would you go to find FREEDOM?

Have students read the paragraph. Make sure that students understand the term *refugee* before they begin the *DISCUSS* activity.

## Selection Resources

---

**Essential Course of Study ECOS**

## The Lost Boys
Magazine Article by Sara Corbett

VIDEO TRAILER **THINK** central | KEYWORD: HML9-590

# How far would you go to find FREEDOM?

It's impossible for most of us to imagine what it would be like to be a refugee—someone who faces terrible danger in his or her home country and flees in search of freedom and protection. What would you do if you were imprisoned for your religious or political beliefs or harassed about the color of your skin? What would it take to make you leave your home and seek refuge in a strange, new place?

**DISCUSS** With a partner, discuss what it might be like to be forced to leave your home, your friends, your family, and everything familiar to you. Describe the one thing you would take with you if you had to leave quickly, and explain what you think you would miss most.

590

---

## TEXT ANALYSIS: AUTHOR'S PURPOSE

An **author's purpose** is what he or she hopes to achieve by writing a particular work. An author might write for any of several purposes:

- to persuade
- to inform or explain
- to entertain
- to express thoughts and feelings

In fact, an author may have more than one purpose for writing a given piece. For example, an author could be attempting to persuade you to register to vote while also expressing feelings about democracy. Understanding both the purpose of a text and how the author uses rhetoric to support that purpose is essential to getting the most out of what you read. As you read "The Lost Boys," use a chart to identify the purpose of key passages in the text.

| Passage | Purpose |
|---------|---------|
| "According to U.S. State Department estimates, some 17,000 boys were separated from their families..." (lines 27–29) | inform |

## READING SKILL: INTERPRET GRAPHIC AIDS

Magazine articles like "The Lost Boys" often include **graphic aids**—such as charts, maps, and photographs—that present key information and events.

- As you read, examine the **photographs** in this article. Consider the subjects' body language and facial expressions. What do they tell you about the subjects' feelings or experiences?
- As you study the **map** in this article, note details about Sudan. Where is this country? What features appear on the map? What else does the map communicate?

*Review:* Connect

## ▲ VOCABULARY IN CONTEXT

The words listed here are crucial to understanding the Lost Boys' journey to freedom. Place each word in the column where it belongs. Define each word you know.

| WORD LIST | boon | fractious | posse |
|-----------|------|-----------|-------|
|  | exodus | marauding | subsist |

| Know Well | Think I Know | Don't Know |
|-----------|--------------|------------|
|  |  |  |

Complete the activities in your **Reader/Writer Notebook.**

---

## Background

**A Devastating Division**

The young refugees profiled in this article are from Sudan, the largest country in Africa. Sudan has been torn apart by Africa's longest-running civil war. Their country has been devastated by war and ravaged by religious conflicts. Over 4 million Sudanese people have been driven from their homes, 2 million have died, and thousands more have been forced into slavery. Since 1955, Sudan's Islamic fundamentalist government has fought against groups of rebels from southern Sudan. The government is intent on imposing Islamic law on the people of Sudan, while the southern Sudanese groups demand religious freedom and economic power. Peace talks aimed at ending the war have produced glimmers of hope, and on May 26, 2004, a power-sharing agreement was signed by both sides. However, further crisis broke out in western Sudan shortly thereafter, plunging the country back into chaos and creating more orphans and refugees.

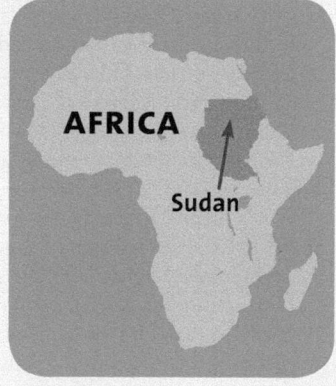

AFRICA

Sudan

---

## Teach

### ● *Model the Skill:* AUTHOR'S PURPOSE

Explain that an author's purpose might vary for different kinds of writing. Write examples on the board. A newspaper editorial might be written to persuade or inform. A story's purpose might be to entertain. An article's purpose might be to inform. And a letter might be written to express thoughts, inform, or persuade.

**GUIDED PRACTICE** Ask students to identify the author's purpose or purposes in other selections that they have read as a class.

**R** RESOURCE MANAGER—Copy Master
Author's Purpose p. 79

### ■ *Model the Skill:* INTERPRET GRAPHIC AIDS

Have students preview "The Lost Boys" by answering the questions about the graphic aids. Explain that a chart might be used to present information in a simple, easy-to-understand fashion. Call on volunteers to explain why they might choose a map or photograph to illustrate a piece of writing.

**GUIDED PRACTICE** Have students identify examples of graphic aids in one of their other textbooks and explain how each one facilitates understanding.

---

### ▲ VOCABULARY IN CONTEXT

**DIAGNOSE WORD KNOWLEDGE** Have all students complete **Vocabulary in Context.** Check their definitions against the following:

**boon** (bo͞on) *n.* a benefit; blessing
**exodus** (ĕk′sə-dəs) *n.* a mass departure
**fractious** (frăk′shəs) *adj.* hard to manage or hold together; unruly
**marauding** (mə-rô′dĭng) *adj.* roaming about in search of plunder **maraud** *v.*

**posse** (pŏs′ē) *n.* a band
**subsist** (səb-sĭst′) *v.* to support oneself at a minimal level

**PRETEACH VOCABULARY** Use the following copy master to help students predict meanings for each boldfaced word.

**R** RESOURCE MANAGER—Copy Master
Vocabulary Study p. 83

1. Read the first item aloud, emphasizing *boon.*

2. Point out the words *drink* and *thirsty.* Elicit possible meanings for *boon,* such as "an advantage that meets a need."

3. Repeat the procedure for the other items.

### READ WITH A PURPOSE

*Help students set a purpose for reading. Ask them to look for what the Lost Boys left behind, and what life was like when they arrived in the United States.*

---

**READING SKILL**  COMMON CORE SL 2

### A GRAPHIC AIDS

*Possible answer: Their facial expressions and body language suggest that the brothers feel uneasy in their new surroundings.*

---

**TEXT ANALYSIS**  COMMON CORE RI 6

### B AUTHOR'S PURPOSE

*Possible answer: Beginning with an anecdote helps readers better perceive the subject matter in human terms—that is, to see Sudan's victims as real people.*

**IF STUDENTS NEED HELP . . .** Relate the question to a topic from students' social studies curriculum. For example, discuss how reading a timeline of events that led to the American Revolution is different from reading stories about the men and women who were part of the move to independence. Which kind of reading would students prefer, and why? *Answers will vary, but students should recognize that real-life stories encourage a personal connection.*

**Extend the Discussion** Does beginning the article with an anecdote help Sara Corbett, the writer, achieve her purpose? Explain.

---

# THE LOST BOYS

### SARA CORBETT

**THESE YOUNG AFRICAN REFUGEES SURVIVED LIONS, CROCODILES, AND STARVATION. NOW THEY'RE STARTING LIFE OVER IN AMERICA.**

One evening in late January, Peter Dut, 21, leads his two teenage brothers through the brightly lit corridors of the Minneapolis airport, trying to mask his confusion. Two days earlier, the brothers, refugees from Africa, had encountered their first light switch and their first set of stairs. An aid worker in Nairobi[1] had demonstrated the flush toilet to them—also the seat belt, the shoelace, the fork. And now they find themselves alone in Minneapolis, three bone-thin African boys confronted by a swirling river of white faces and rolling suitcases.

Finally, a traveling businessman recognizes their uncertainty. "Where are you flying to?" he asks kindly, and the eldest brother tells him in halting,
10  bookish English. A few days earlier, they left a small mud hut in a blistering-hot Kenyan refugee camp, where they had lived as orphans for nine years after walking for hundreds of miles across Sudan.[2] They are now headed to a new home in the U.S.A. "Where?" the man asks in disbelief when Peter Dut says the city's name. "Fargo? North Dakota? You gotta be kidding me. It's too cold there. You'll never survive it!"

Finally and then he laughs. Peter Dut has no idea why. **B**

In the meantime, the temperature in Fargo has dropped to 15 below. The boys tell me that, until now, all they have ever known about cold is what they felt grasping a bottle of frozen water. An aid worker handed it to them one day
20  during a "cultural orientation" session at the Kakuma[3] Refugee Camp, a place where the temperature hovers around 100 degrees.

Peter Dut and his two brothers belong to an unusual group of refugees referred to by aid organizations as the Lost Boys of Sudan, a group of roughly 10,000 boys who arrived in Kenya in 1992 seeking refuge from their country's

---

1. **Nairobi** (nī-rō′bē): the capital city of Kenya, a country in Africa.
2. **Sudan:** a country in eastern Africa northwest of Kenya.
3. **Kakuma** (kə-kōō′mä).

**592**  UNIT 5: AUTHOR'S PURPOSE

**A GRAPHIC AIDS**
This **photograph** was taken shortly after the Dut brothers arrived in North Dakota. What do their facial expressions and body language suggest about their comfort level in their new surroundings?

**1 Targeted Passage**

**B AUTHOR'S PURPOSE**
The writer begins this article with an **anecdote** instead of immediately presenting statistics about Sudan. How does this choice affect your perception of the subject matter?

---

## DIFFERENTIATED INSTRUCTION

### FOR ENGLISH LANGUAGE LEARNERS

**Vocabulary Support**  Use Word Questioning to teach these words: *survive* (line 15), *cultural* (line 20), *displaced* (line 68), *transition* (line 102), *coordinates* (line 102), *identity* (line 110).

🧰 **BEST PRACTICES TOOLKIT—Transparency**  Word Questioning p. E9

### FOR STRUGGLING READERS

In combination with the *Audio Anthology CD*, use one or more Targeted Passages (pp. 592, 594, 597) to ensure that students focus on key events, concepts, and skills. Targeted Passages are also good for English learners.

**1 Targeted Passage [Lines 1–16]**

This passage introduces the Dut brothers. It addresses the challenges that they have faced in the past and are facing now.

## BACKGROUND

**Sudan's People** The great majority of the Sudanese people are Muslims. Most of northern Sudan is made up of Muslims and dominated by Islamic culture, while most of southern Sudan consists of Christians and followers of indigenous religions.

**The Dinka** Many of the Lost Boys were from the Dinka tribe. These native people of Sudan make up approximately 12 percent of the total population. The Dinka derive their living mainly from raising cattle, sheep, and goats. They are generally tall, have a thin build, and are known for their courage.

## Analyze Visuals

**Activity** After students have read the article, ask them to suggest other photographs that might have appeared here. *Possible answers: a photograph of the brothers in Africa, boarding the airplane, or walking through the airport in Minneapolis*

**REVISIT THE BIG QUESTION**

### How far would you go to find FREEDOM?

**Discuss** In lines 8–16, how well does the businessman understand what it means to be a refugee? How can you tell? *Possible answer: He probably has little true understanding of the boys' life as refugees. Anything that he may have grasped about their circumstances from what Peter tells him seems to be lost in his amusement at their destination. It also is unlikely that the businessman has ever had to flee danger in his home country.*

---

- From where have the Dut brothers come? Where are they going? (lines 1–4)
- What changes in climate will the brothers experience? (lines 10–15)
- What else about life in the United States do you know will be new to them? (lines 3–7)

**FOR ADVANCED LEARNERS/PRE-AP**

**Anchor Activity** Allow students to do research in the library and on the Internet on the Lost Boys and how their lives have changed since arriving in the United States. When they have completed their research, ask them to share their results in a five-minute presentation to the class. Require each student to provide a graphic aid as part of their presentation.

**C GRAPHIC AIDS**

*Possible answer: The map shows that Ethiopia is east of Sudan. It shows that Sudan also borders the Central African Republic, the Democratic Republic of Congo, Uganda, and Kenya. The most important information may be the locations of Sudan, Ethiopia, and Kenya because this information enables readers to better visualize the Lost Boys' trek.*

## TIERED DISCUSSION PROMPTS

Direct students to lines 27–41. Use these prompts to help students grasp the gravity of the refugees' circumstances:

**Analyze** What challenges did the boys face on their journey, and what conclusion can you draw about the impact of such an experience on the survivors? *Possible answer: Challenges, such as lack of food and water, bandits, wild animals, risk of drowning, and witnessing so much death would make the experience traumatic.*

**Evaluate** These refugees were named "the Lost Boys" after the orphans in *Peter Pan*. Is this a fitting name? Why or why not? *Possible answers: Yes—because the refugees were orphans with nowhere to go. No—because their situation was too horrendous to be compared to a children's tale.*

## OWN THE WORD

- **fractious:** Tell students that a synonym for *fractious* is "rebellious" and that antonyms include "agreeable" and "good-humored."

- **posse:** Tell students that *posse* generally refers to a group of people summoned by the sheriff to help in law enforcement.

- **exodus:** Tell students that *exodus* comes from the Greek word *exodos*, and that the prefix *exo-* means "outside of."

- **marauding:** Remind students that *maraud* and *marauder*, the individual doing the action, have a connotation of unlawful activities.

---

**fractious** civil war. The fighting pits a northern Islamic government against rebels in the south who practice Christianity and tribal religions.

The Lost Boys were named after Peter Pan's **posse** of orphans. According to U.S. State Department estimates, some 17,000 boys were separated from their families and fled southern Sudan in an **exodus** of biblical proportions after 30 fighting intensified in 1987. They arrived in throngs, homeless and parentless, having trekked about 1,000 miles from Sudan to Ethiopia, back to Sudan, and finally to Kenya. The majority of the boys belonged to the Dinka or Nuer tribes, and most were between the ages of 8 and 18. (Most of the boys don't know for sure how old they are; aid workers assigned them approximate ages after they arrived in 1992.)

Along the way, the boys endured attacks from the northern army and **marauding** bandits, as well as lions who preyed on the slowest and weakest among them. Many died from starvation or thirst. Others drowned or were eaten by crocodiles as they tried to cross a swollen Ethiopian river. By the time 40 the Lost Boys reached the Kakuma Refugee Camp, their numbers had been cut nearly in half.

**fractious** (frăk'shəs) *adj.* hard to manage or hold together; unruly

**posse** (pŏs'ē) *n.* a band

**exodus** (ĕk'sə-dəs) *n.* a mass departure

**②Targeted Passage**

**marauding** (mə-rô'dĭng) *adj.* roaming about in search of plunder **maraud** *v.*

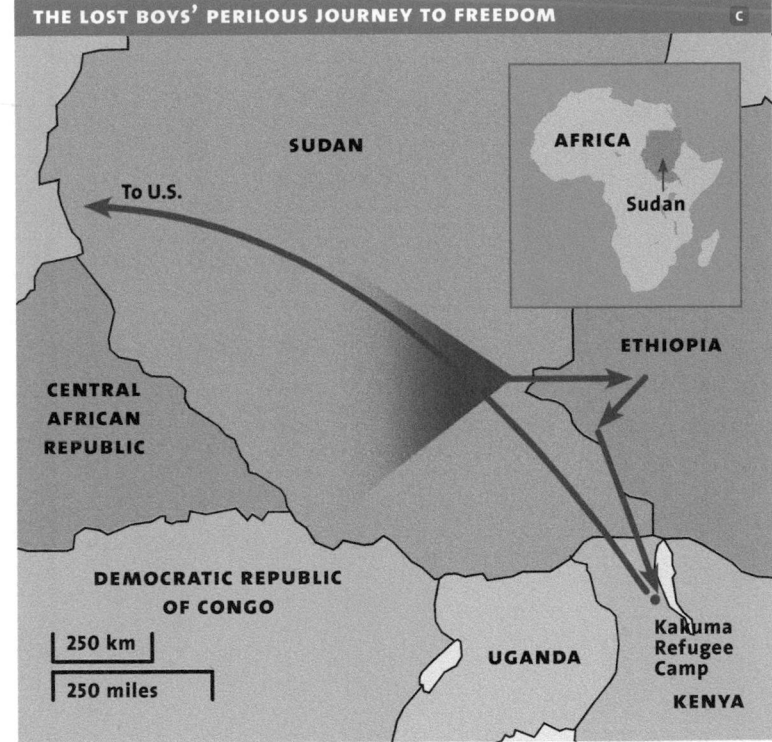

THE LOST BOYS' PERILOUS JOURNEY TO FREEDOM

SUDAN

To U.S.

AFRICA

Sudan

ETHIOPIA

CENTRAL AFRICAN REPUBLIC

DEMOCRATIC REPUBLIC OF CONGO

250 km

250 miles

UGANDA

Kakuma Refugee Camp

KENYA

**C GRAPHIC AIDS**
List two details included on the **map** that are not provided in the article. What do you think is the most important piece of information communicated by this map?

---

## DIFFERENTIATED INSTRUCTION

### FOR STRUGGLING READERS

**②Targeted Passage [Lines 27–35]**
This passage introduces the Lost Boys and the extremity of their situation.

- Why have the Lost Boys left Sudan? (lines 29–30)

- What does the writer mean when she calls their journey "an exodus of biblical proportions"? (line 29)

- What was the boys' condition when they arrived in Kenya? (lines 30–35)

### FOR RELUCTANT READERS

**Connect** Ask students if they or someone they know have ever journeyed to a new place without a family member. Have them imagine traveling to a place where everyone looks different from them, the food and weather are unfamiliar, and where they didn't know the language. Ask: What feelings and challenges might be involved? Have students discuss these questions in small groups.

In 1992, roughly 10,000 boys from Sudan poured into a refugee camp in Kenya.

Now, after nine years of **subsisting** on rationed corn mush and lentils and living largely ungoverned by adults, the Lost Boys of Sudan are coming to America. In 1999, the United Nations High Commissioner for Refugees, which handles refugee cases around the world, and the U.S. government agreed to send 3,600 of the boys to the U.S.—since going back to Sudan was out of the question. About 500 of the Lost Boys still under the age of 18 will be living in apartments or foster homes across the U.S. by the end of this year. The boys will start school at a grade level normal for their age, thanks to a
50 tough English-language program at their refugee camp. The remaining 3,100 Lost Boys will be resettled as adults. After five years, each boy will be eligible for citizenship, provided he has turned 21. **D**

**NIGHTTIME IN AMERICA?**
On the night that I stand waiting for Peter Dut and his brothers to land in Fargo, tendrils of snow are snaking across the tarmac. The three boys file through the gate without money or coats or luggage beyond their small backpacks. The younger brothers, Maduk, 17, and Riak, 15, appear petrified. As a social worker passes out coats, Peter Dut studies the black night through the airport window. "Excuse me," he says worriedly. "Can you tell me, please, is it now night or day?"
60　This is a stove burner. This is a can opener. This is a brush for your teeth. The new things come in a tumble. The brothers' home is a sparsely furnished, two-bedroom apartment in a complex on Fargo's south side. Rent is $445 a month. It has been stocked with donations from area churches and businesses: toothpaste, bread, beans, bananas.

**subsist** (səb-sĭst′) *v.* to support oneself at a minimal level

COMMON CORE RI 4

**D TONE**
**Tone** is the attitude a writer or speaker takes toward a subject. In a written work, tone is conveyed by the writer's choice of words and details. The tone of magazine articles can vary widely based on the author's purpose as well as his or her **audience**— the people intended to read the article. Most articles, however, can be described as either formal or informal in tone. Compared to other magazine articles you've read, is this one formal or informal? Explain.

THE LOST BOYS  **595**

How far would you go to find **FREEDOM?**
**Discuss** In lines 42–52, how might the Lost Boys' experience of being refugees in the United States differ from their experiences in the Kakuma Refugee Camp? *Possible answer: The settlement process may separate friends and even families. After "living largely ungoverned by adults" (line 43), those under the age of 18 will experience supervision in foster homes (line 48) and schools (line 49). Hopefully, their diet will be more plentiful than the rationed corn mush and lentils (line 42) they lived on before.*

**Analyze Visuals**

**Activity** How does the photograph help you understand the experience of the Lost Boys as they arrived in the Kakuma Refugee Camp? *Possible answer: The photograph shows that many of the Lost Boys are quite young and their arms are thin, suggesting that they have gone without proper nourishment. Their faces and bodies suggest both fear and hope. Their arms are raised, as if in surrender, but they are moving forward, as if in anticipation of safety and the hope of a new life.*

**TEXT ANALYSIS**　　COMMON CORE　RI 4

**D TONE**
*Possible answer: This article starts out formal, with objective facts, but changes to informal when the point of view shifts.*

Have students discuss what impact the tone has on the article.

**VOCABULARY**　　COMMON CORE　L 4

**OWN THE WORD**

**subsist:** Give students these examples: The boys *subsisted* on meager food supplies. The homeless family *subsisted* in a city shelter during the winter months. After the hurricane, we lacked the basic essentials needed to *subsist* in our home.

**FOR ENGLISH LANGUAGE LEARNERS**
**Developing Reading Fluency** Point out the different lengths of sentences in lines 54–65. Remind students that fluent readers pause between sentences to create a rhythm in the piece. Model for students an effective reading of this section. Then have students work in mixed-ability groups to practice reading the section. Conclude by asking students why they think the author included several short sentences in this selection.

**FOR ADVANCED LEARNERS/PRE-AP**
**Evaluate Point of View** In line 53, Corbett shifts to a first-person point of view. Have students discuss why Corbett does so. Ask whether using a first-person point of view is necessary or desirable in this article, and why or why not.

A caseworker empties a garbage bag full of donated clothing, which looks to have come straight from the closet of an elderly man. I know how lucky the boys are: The State Department estimates that war, famine, and disease in southern Sudan have killed more than 2 million people and displaced another 4 million. Still I cringe to think of the boys showing up for school in these clothes.

70  The next day, when I return to the apartment at noon, the boys have been up since 5 and are terribly hungry. "What about your food?" I ask, gesturing to the bread and bananas and the box of cereal sitting on the counter.

Peter grins sheepishly. I suddenly realize that the boys, in a lifetime of cooking maize and beans over a fire pit, have never opened a box. I am placed in the role of teacher. And so begins an opening spree. We open potato chips. We open a can of beans. We untwist the tie on the bagged loaf of bread. Soon, the boys are seated and eating a hot meal.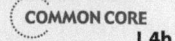

**LIVING ON LEAVES AND BERRIES**

The three brothers have come a long way since they fled their village in Sudan with their parents and three sisters—all of whom were later killed by Sudanese
80  army soldiers. The Lost Boys first survived a 6- to 10-week walk to Ethiopia, often subsisting on leaves and berries and the occasional **boon** of a warthog carcass. Some boys staved off dehydration by drinking their own urine. Many fell behind; some were devoured by lions or trampled by buffalo.

The Lost Boys lived for three years in Ethiopia, in UN-supported camps, before they were forced back into Sudan by a new Ethiopian government no longer sympathetic to their plight. Somehow, more than 10,000 of the boys miraculously trailed into Kenya's UN camps in the summer of 1992—as Sudanese government planes bombed the rear of their procession.

For the Lost Boys, then, a new life in America might easily seem to be the
90  answer to every dream. But the real world has been more complicated than that. Within weeks of arriving, Riak is placed in a local junior high; Maduk starts high school classes; and Peter begins adult-education classes.

**REFUGEE BLUES**

Five weeks later, Riak listens quietly through a lesson on Elizabethan history at school, all but ignored by white students around him.

Nearby at Fargo South High School, Maduk is frequently alone as well, copying passages from his geography textbook, trying not to look at the short skirts worn by many of the girls.

Peter Dut worries about money. The three brothers say they receive just $107 in food stamps each month and spend most of their $510 monthly cash
100  assistance on rent and utilities.

Resettlement workers say the brothers are just undergoing the normal transition. Scott Burtsfield, who coordinates resettlement efforts in Fargo through Lutheran Social Services, says: "The first three months are always the toughest. It really does get better."

---

**AUTHOR'S PURPOSE**
What is Corbett's purpose in lines 70–77? Explain, citing specific details from the passage.

**boon** (bo͞on) *n.* a benefit; blessing

**COMMON CORE**   L 4b
**Language Coach**
**Roots and Affixes**
A suffix is an affix at the end of a root or base. Reread lines 93–94. In *Elizabethan*, the suffix *-an*, which comes from French and can be traced back to Latin, means "belonging to." The base word, *Elizabeth*, refers to England's queen from 1558–1603. What is *Elizabethan history*?

---

 *Model the Skill:* **AUTHOR'S PURPOSE**

Draw the Author's Purpose chart on the board. Have students read lines 67–69. Write "2 million killed, 4 million displaced" in the first column. Explain that the author's purpose in these lines is to inform the reader about the disaster in Sudan. Write "to inform" in the second column. Continue with the next paragraph, eliciting student responses and filling in the chart as you read.

*Possible answer:* Corbett's main purpose is to inform or explain—specifically, to make clear to the reader just how drastically different the boys' new environment is from the life they have known. For example, the boys are used to "a lifetime of cooking . . . over a fire pit" and "have never opened a box" (lines 73–74).

**Extend the Discussion**  How does Sara Corbett hold her readers' attention while presenting this information?

**OWN THE WORD**

**boon:** Tell students that a *boon* is a benefit, and the opposite is a loss. Have students use both words in a sentence.
*Possible answer:* The unexpected gift from my uncle was a boon, but it became a loss when my wallet was stolen.

---

**DIFFERENTIATED INSTRUCTION**

**FOR ENGLISH LANGUAGE LEARNERS**

 **Language Coach**   COMMON CORE
L 4b
**Roots and Affixes**
*Possible answer:* the history of England from 1558–1603 Have students reread lines 101–102. Ask students what the root word is in "resettlement." What does the word mean? *Possible answer:* the process of "settling" in a place again

**FOR ADVANCED LEARNERS/PRE–AP**

**Compare and Contrast Presentations**  Peter Dut is also one of the subjects of *Lost Boys of Sudan* (2003), an award-winning documentary by Megan Mylan and Jon Shenk. If a copy of the film is available from a local library, have a group of students watch it critically. Ask group members to show a clip in class and to compare and contrast Corbett's print article with the film.

Riak Dut, shown here in his school lunch line, eats alone most days.

The Lost Boys can only hope so; they have few other options. A return to southern Sudan could be fatal. "There is nothing left for the Lost Boys to go home to—it's a war zone," says Mary Anne Fitzgerald, a Nairobi-based relief consultant.

Some Sudanese elders have criticized sending boys to the U.S. They worry
110 their children will lose their African identity. One afternoon, an 18-year-old Lost Boy translated a part of a tape an elder had sent along with many boys: "He is saying: 'Don't drink. Don't smoke. Don't kill. Go to school every day, and remember, America is not your home.'" **G**

But if adjustment is hard, the boys also experience consoling moments.

One of these comes on a quiet Friday night last winter. As the boys make a dinner of rice and lentils, Peter changes into an African outfit, a finely woven green tunic, with a skullcap to match, bought with precious food rations at Kakuma.

Just then, the doorbell rings unexpectedly. And out of the cold tumble four
120 Sudanese boys—all of whom have resettled as refugees over the last several years. I watch one, an 18-year-old named Sunday, wrap his arms encouragingly around Peter Dut. "It's a hard life here," Sunday whispers to the older boy, "but it's a free life, too." ✹

**F GRAPHIC AIDS**
What can you **infer** about Riak's experiences at his junior high in North Dakota based on this photograph? Explain your answer.

**G CONNECT**
Think about what it's like to receive instructions from a parent or other adult. Do you think these taped messages will influence the boys? Explain.

**❸ Targeted Passage**

THE LOST BOYS **597**

---

## FOR STRUGGLING READERS

**❸ Targeted Passage [Lines 114–123]**

This concluding passage sets a positive tone as Peter Dut considers both his past and his future.

- On the Friday night described, how do Peter's clothing and dinner show that he values his African heritage? (lines 115–118)

- What does Peter have in common with the visitors who arrive? (lines 119–121)

- How might Sunday's words help Peter adjust to life in the United States? (lines 122–123)

## FOR ENGLISH LANGUAGE LEARNERS

**Comprehension: Transitions** Discuss the examples of contrast using the conjunction *but* in lines 90, 114, and 122–123. Then point out the idiomatic phrase *all but* in line 94. Explain that *all but* does not show contrast; instead, it is another way of saying *mostly* or *almost.*

**F *Model the Skill:* GRAPHIC AIDS**

Illustrate how to use a photograph to better understand reading selections. Point out that Riak is standing apart from the other students. The other students have their backs to him.

***Possible answer:*** *It can be inferred that Riak is having trouble being accepted socially by the other students. As a result, he is isolated.*

**READING SKILL:** *Review*

**G CONNECT**

***Possible answer:*** *The taped messages may have some influence, especially if the boys' culture encourages the respect of elders. However, the elders are far away. Peer pressure—and the desire for acceptance in a new environment—may be more influential.*

## SELECTION WRAP–UP

**READ WITH A PURPOSE** Now that students have finished reading the selection, have them compare and contrast the life that the Lost Boys left behind with the life they found in the United States. ***Possible answer:*** *The selection describes the trauma and risk of death the boys left behind. Even though life was difficult in the United States, they were free.*

⭐ **CRITIQUE** Have students evaluate the writer's presentation. Did Corbett provide enough information that readers truly could understand the Lost Boys' plight? What questions did she leave unanswered, and why?

## INDEPENDENT READING

Suggest students read *God Grew Tired of Us: A Memoir* by John Bul Dau. The book tells about the author's years in refugee camps and his new life in the United States.

THE LOST BOYS **597**

# Practice and Apply

For preliminary support of post-reading questions, use these copy masters:

 **RESOURCE MANAGER—Copy Masters**
Reading Check p. 86
Interpret Graphic Aids p. 81
Question Support p. 87

Additional selection questions are provided for teachers on page 73.

## ANSWERS

## Comprehension

1. *The Lost Boys were seeking safety from a devastating civil war in their homeland.*

2. *The boys faced death from the northern army, bandits, and wild animals; from drowning; and from starvation or thirst.*

3. *He told Peter that life in America was difficult but "free." He meant that Peter now could make a life for himself without facing the daily dangers of civil war.*

## Text Analysis
### COMMON CORE RI 6, SL 2
*Possible answers:*

4. *Regardless of their view, students should support their responses with thoughtful reasons and details from the text.*

5. *Students should base their impressions on textual details and the photographs. Students may describe the brothers as uncertain in their new circumstances but determined to try their best.*

6. ■ **COMMON CORE FOCUS** *Interpret Graphic Aids Students should recognize the usefulness of each graphic aid. For example, the map helps them visualize the boys' journey; the photographs emphasize the differences between the boys' lives as wandering refugees and their lives as students in the United States.*

7. ● **COMMON CORE FOCUS** *Evaluate Author's Purpose Corbett's primary purpose is to inform and explain. She achieves this purpose by presenting facts and details that teach readers about the plight of the Lost Boys.*

---

## Comprehension

1. **Recall** Why did the Lost Boys leave Sudan?

2. **Summarize** What hardships did the boys endure as they fled from their homes in Sudan to the refugee camp in Kenya?

3. **Clarify** How did Peter Dut's friend comfort him at the end of the article?

## Text Analysis

4. **Connect** Think back to the discussion you had about what it might be like to be forced from your home. Did reading about these young refugees change your feelings at all? Explain why or why not, citing details from the selection.

5. **Analyze Characterization** How would you describe the Dut brothers? What details caused you to form this impression? Use a spider map like the one shown to record the details before responding in a few sentences.

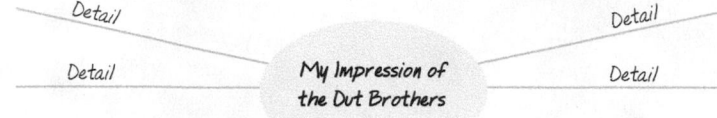

Detail     Detail

Detail     My Impression of the Dut Brothers     Detail

6. ● **Interpret Graphic Aids** Examine the **map** on page 594 and the **photographs** on pages 593, 595, and 597. Which was most effective at helping you understand the Lost Boys' experiences? Was the article more effective with the graphics than it would have been without? Explain your answer.

7. ● **Evaluate Author's Purpose** Review the chart you filled in as you read. What do you think is Corbett's primary purpose? Which purpose does she achieve most effectively? Explain your answers, citing evidence from the text.

### READING-WRITING CONNECTION

| WRITING PROMPT | REVISING TIP |
|---|---|
| **Short Constructed Response: Analysis** Of all the struggles these refugees faced in America, which do you think must have been the most difficult? Consider the alienation caused by culture shock, financial hardship, loneliness, and the new climate. Write **one or two paragraphs** explaining your view, citing evidence. | Review your response. Did you incorporate relevant and convincing examples from the text to support your opinion? Add more support if necessary. |

### How far would you go to find FREEDOM?

When is freedom worth other sacrifices?

<constCOMMON CORE

RI 6 Determine an author's purpose in a text and analyze how the author uses rhetoric to advance that purpose. SL 2 Integrate multiple sources of information presented in diverse formats.

---

**READING-WRITING CONNECTION**

- Review lines 1–7, 53–77, and 93–123, which emphasize the boys' alienation.

- Urge students to project themselves into the refugees' situation. Which challenges in their new life would students find most difficult? Why?

- Remind students to use textual evidence to support their views.

**How far would you go to find FREEDOM?** Students should consider the trauma the Lost Boys faced in Sudan and the difficulties they faced in the United States when answering this question.

## Vocabulary in Context

### ▲ VOCABULARY PRACTICE

Choose the word that is not related in meaning to the other words.

1. migration, exodus, consolation, flight
2. boon, building, structure, edifice
3. conspiring, ravaging, plundering, marauding
4. amusement, posse, recreation, entertainment
5. subsist, survive, manage, reconsider
6. irritable, divisive, fractious, connected

**WORD LIST**

boon

exodus

fractious

marauding

posse

subsist

### ACADEMIC VOCABULARY IN SPEAKING

- conclude • construct • implicit • primary • specific

The author's admiration for the lost boys is **implicit** in this article. With a partner, discuss and identify **specific** characteristics and achievements she admires. Use at least one Academic Vocabulary word in your discussion.

### VOCABULARY STRATEGY: THE LATIN ROOT *fract*

The vocabulary word *fractious* contains the Latin root *fract*, which means "to break." This root may also appear as *frag* and *fring*. To understand the meaning of words with these root forms, use context clues and your knowledge of the root.

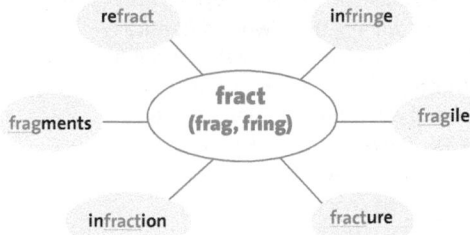

refract   infringe   fragments   **fract (frag, fring)**   fragile   infraction   fracture

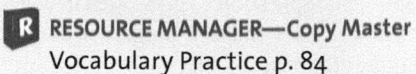
**COMMON CORE**

**L 4b, c** Identify and correctly use patterns of word changes that indicate different meanings; consult reference materials to determine or clarify a word's meaning or etymology.

**PRACTICE** Choose the word from the word web that best completes each sentence. Use context clues to help you or, if necessary, check a dictionary.

1. Don't put _____ objects where children can reach them.
2. _____ of the shattered glass still lay on the floor.
3. The protesters feared that the police would _____ on their rights.
4. Because water will _____ light, a pencil in a glass of water will look broken.
5. Any serious _____ of the rules will be punished by a two-day suspension.
6. He suffered a hairline _____ of his collarbone.

**Interactive Vocabulary**   **THiNK** central

Go to **thinkcentral.com**.
KEYWORD: HML9-599

THE LOST BOYS   **599**

---

## ANSWERS

## Vocabulary in Context

### ▲ VOCABULARY PRACTICE

1. *consolation*     4. *posse*
2. *boon*            5. *reconsider*
3. *conspiring*      6. *connected*

 **RESOURCE MANAGER—Copy Master**
Vocabulary Practice p. 84

### ACADEMIC VOCABULARY IN SPEAKING

*Answers will vary but should be supported by facts from the article.*

### VOCABULARY STRATEGY: THE LATIN ROOT *fract*

**COMMON CORE** **L 4b, c**

- As you discuss the examples, point out that the root may appear anywhere in a word and that it can have prefixes and suffixes attached to it.
- As you review the **PRACTICE** items, call on volunteers to explain how they chose the correct word for each sentence.

*Possible answers:*

1. *fragile*       4. *refract*
2. *Fragments*     5. *infraction*
3. *infringe*      6. *fracture*

 **RESOURCE MANAGER—Copy Master**
Vocabulary Strategy p. 85

**Interactive Vocabulary**   **THiNK** central

Keywords direct students to a **WordSharp** tutorial on **thinkcentral.com** or to other types of vocabulary practice and review.

---

## Assess and Reteach

### Assess

**DIAGNOSTIC AND SELECTION TESTS**
Selection Tests A, B/C pp. 155–156, 157–158

**Interactive Selection Test** on **thinkcentral.com**

### Reteach

**Level Up Online Tutorials** on **thinkcentral.com**

---

## DIFFERENTIATED INSTRUCTION

### FOR ENGLISH LANGUAGE LEARNERS

**Vocabulary: Cognates** Have students find all words in the Vocabulary Practice that have a similar form in their home language. You may want to point out that some words starting with *s* in English add an *e* at the beginning of the Spanish word (as in *structure/estructura*). As an alternative, have students think of words in their home languages with the root *fract* (*frag/fring*) and make word webs for each language.

### FOR ADVANCED LEARNERS/PRE–AP

**Vocabulary in Writing** Ask students to use at least four vocabulary words in a paragraph to accompany one of their headlines. Have students compare their paragraphs to see how they used the words.

**News Reports**

TV Newscast Clip / Web News Report on **Media Smart** DVD-ROM

### ⌁ COMMON CORE FOCUS

**RI 7** Analyze various accounts of a subject told in different mediums, determining which details are emphasized in each account. **W 9b (RI 7)** Draw evidence from informational texts; analyze accounts of a subject told in different mediums. **SL 2** Integrate multiple sources presented in diverse media or formats. **SL 5** Make strategic use of digital media in presentations.

### SUMMARY

These news reports recount the rescue of nine Pennsylvania coal miners to tell the following basic story. On Day 1 the men are trapped and nearly drown. On Day 2 rescuers drill an airshaft, providing oxygen and warmth to the miners. On Day 3, the rescuers start to drill a rescue tunnel, but their drill bit breaks. The trapped men begin writing farewell notes. That night the broken bit is replaced, and on Day 4 the drill breaks through. The men are soon brought one by one up to safety.

## How do you get the NEWS?

Ask students what news sources they use to get information about the world around them. For each news source mentioned, ask what techniques the source uses. Discuss how news on different media uses features such as photographs, diagrams, video, interviews, press conferences, and other elements.

### BACKGROUND

How did teens learn about the trapped Pennsylvania miners? A 2003 study of more than 65,000 teens aged 13–18 showed the following: 48% ranked TV as their main news source; 9% cited the Internet; and 18% cited newspapers. Teens said newspapers were most accurate, fair, and informative, but TV news was most entertaining and easiest to use.

# How do you get the NEWS?

### ⌁ COMMON CORE

**RI 7** Analyze various accounts of a subject told in different mediums, determining which details are emphasized in each account.

When you need to know the latest news, where do you turn? To the nearest TV or radio? To the Internet? To the nearest friend? Some people get their news through brief summaries, while others seek forms that are chock-full of details. The two news formats you'll explore, a segment of a TV newscast and an article from a news Web site, will shed light on the different ways the news media can cover the same event and the advantages and disadvantages of news formats.

## Background

**Digging for News** The news event you'll investigate took place in Somerset, Pennsylvania, in 2002. Nine coal miners were trapped nearly 240 feet underground in a mineshaft that was filling up rapidly with icy water. Mining crews worked frantically to drill a rescue shaft and construct a basket of steel-wire mesh to transport each miner. During four very tense days, new developments about the rescue effort flowed from a variety of news sources, including TV- and radio-network newscasts, newspaper reports, and Internet news services.

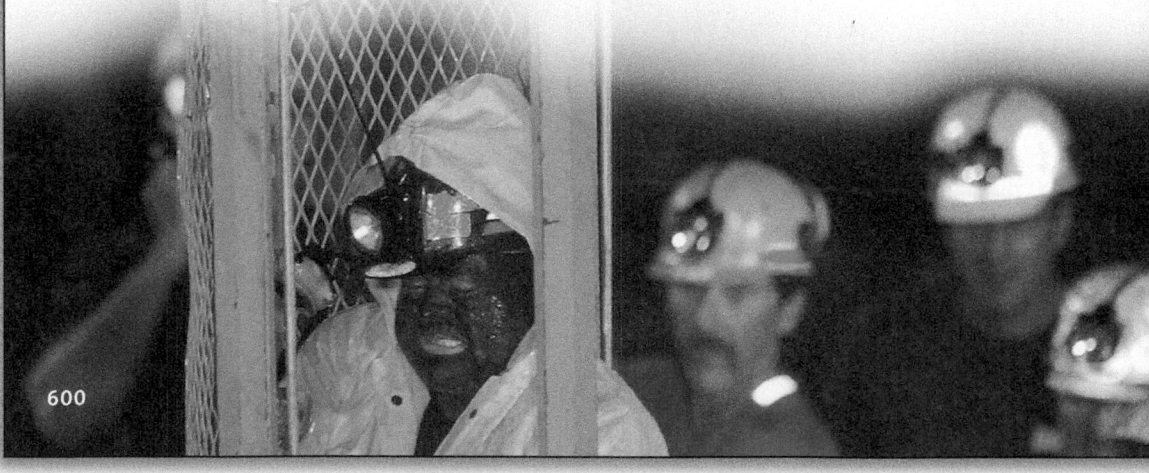

600

## Media Study Resources

**R RESOURCE MANAGER UNIT 5**

Plan and Teach pp. 89–92
Summary pp. 93†*, 94‡*
Viewing Guide p. 95
Close Viewing p. 96
Media Activity p. 97
Produce Your Own Media p. 98

**TECHNOLOGY**

 **Teacher One Stop DVD-ROM**
**Student One Stop DVD-ROM**
**Media*Smart* DVD-ROM**
**MediaScope** on **thinkcentral.com**

*See resources on the **Teacher One Stop DVD-ROM** and on **thinkcentral.com**.*

* Resources for Differentiation    † Also in Spanish    ‡ In Haitian Creole and Vietnamese

# Media Literacy: News Formats

News formats are packaged in a variety of ways, not only to deliver information but to get and keep an audience's attention. Shown below are features of two electronic news sources.

## FEATURES OF A TV NEWSCAST

**1** The **anchor** introduces the news story with a **lead-in.**

**2** Then the scene cuts to **video footage,** which is shot and edited to illustrate the events of the news story. As the footage plays, the anchor or a **field reporter** describes the details.

**3** The **voice-over** is the unseen reporter's voice that plays over the images. A voice-over makes a news story easy to follow.

**4** **Sound bites,** brief statements from interviews with experts or witnesses, can provide details and stir emotions.

**Advantages**
- TV news stories can be aired as soon as the event is known.
- A typical news segment lasts 30 seconds to 2 minutes. This allows more news stories to be reported in a short period of time.
- Video and audio give a story immediacy and drama.

**Disadvantages**
- Because a news segment is short, it may not cover an event thoroughly enough.
- Sometimes stations "go live," or air a story, before all the facts are gathered.

## FEATURES OF A WEB NEWS REPORT

**1** **Menus** on the page help users to navigate the site.

**2** The **lead,** the first sentence (or first few sentences), starts the report.

**3** **Captions** explain the photographs or other visuals.

**4** **Hyperlinks**—typically, highlighted words, phrases, or images—allow users to jump directly to updates or more information.

**Quotations** from those involved add human interest.

**Advantages**
- Breaking stories can be posted and updated at any time.
- Space is usually not a limitation. A Web news report can run for an indefinite length.
- **Streaming video** or **animations** bring the scene to life.

**Disadvantages**
- Web articles may not be accessible to everyone.
- Sometimes stories are posted so quickly that the facts may be inaccurate.

## STRATEGIES FOR VIEWING
- In any news format, consider what key details are included. Look for answers to the *5 W's* and the *H* questions: Who? What? Where? When? Why? and How?
- Be sure you can spot the **lead.** Try restating the lead in your own words to be sure it covers all the essential details.

---

## MEDIA STUDY: TEACHING OPTIONS

**Teaching Option 1: The Basics (1–2 Days)**
1. Begin the Media Study using the material provided on pages 600–601.
2. Show the Introduction on MediaSmart. Then show the First Viewing. As they watch, have students use the Viewing Guide on page 602, along with the corresponding copy master on page 95 of the Resource Manager. Discuss their responses.
3. Return to the pupil book for the extension activities on page 603.

**Teaching Option 2: In-Depth Study (2–3 Days)**
1. Begin the Media Study using pages 600–601.
2. Show the Introduction and First Viewing from MediaSmart. Continue on MediaSmart with the Media Lessons, using the teacher notes in the Resources.
3. Show the Guided Analysis presentation. Have students record their observations on the Student Viewing Guide available in the Resources section from MediaSmart.
4. Return to the pupil book, page 603.

---

## Media Literacy

COMMON CORE RI 7

Discuss both TV newscasts and Web news reports. Ask students how TV newscasts generally progress. Who presents the news? Who and what do viewers see besides the newscasters? List terms on the board as students mention them, adding *anchor, video, reporter, voice-over,* and *sound bites* if necessary. Then ask students what elements they expect to find on a Web news report. How do they locate stories of interest? How can they find more details? Add terms to the board list, such as *menus* and *hyperlinks.* Then discuss the chart on page 601.

- **TV Newscast** To reinforce how different features of a TV newscast come together, ask students to improvise presenting a story about a football game. Have one student act as the anchor and provide a lead-in. Ask students what video footage they might see and what kind of commentary a field reporter might provide. Ask how voice-over might be used and what kinds of sound bites a reporter might try to get.

- **Web News Report** Ask students to imagine that they are getting information about the same football game, this time using an Internet news site. Ask how they would locate sports news and then specifically football news. Have students describe the screen on which the football story appears.

- **Advantages and Disadvantages** Have students describe the advantages and disadvantages of learning about the football story in each of these two formats.

# Practice and Apply

## VIEWING GUIDE

1. Before students view the TV news report and examine the Web news report, tell them that they will be asked to compare the way the two media deliver information and try to capture the audience's attention. Encourage them to watch and listen for these elements:

   - **leads** and how these draw audiences into the miners' dramatic story
   - **video footage** on TV that gives visual information about the rescue progress
   - **voice-overs** that help TV viewers follow the story and **captions** that explain Web images of the miners and the rescue
   - **sound bites** on TV and **quotations** on the Web that help viewers get to know the miners, their families, and their rescuers
   - **menus** and **hyperlinks** that help Web news readers locate information

2. Some students may not be able to link the labels for various TV news techniques with what they see in the news report. Help these students identify video footage, voice-over, and sound bite elements. Help them differentiate between an anchor and a field reporter.

**R** **RESOURCE MANAGER—Copy Masters**
Viewing Guide p. 95
Close Viewing p. 96
Viewing Activity p. 97

Use this resource with the Viewing Guide:

🔘 **Media*Smart* DVD-ROM**
**MediaScope** on **thinkcentral.com**

## ANSWERS

### FIRST VIEWING: Comprehension

1. *A 240-foot shaft was drilled down to where the miners were trapped. They were raised through the shaft in a 21"-wide basket, one miner at a time.*

2. *Click on the link—the blue underlined words— "Randy Fogle."*

### CLOSE VIEWING: Media Literacy

**Possible answers:**

3. *This story's unique and dramatic life-and-death qualities appealed to a national audience. The audience grew as the story played out over four days.*

---

**Media🔘Smart** DVD-ROM
- **News Format 1:** "Nine Coal Miners Brought Up Safely"
- **Genre:** TV newscast
- **Running Time:** 4.5 minutes

- **News Format 2:** "All Nine Pulled Alive from Mine"
- **Genre:** Web news report

SOMERSET, Pennsylvania (CNN) -- One by one, nine soggy and exhausted miners, their faces blackened with coal dust, were pulled early Sunday from a flooded Pennsylvania coal mine after being trapped underground for more than three days.

The last one pulled from the 240-foot deep shaft was 41-year-old Mark Popernack, who emerged at 2:45 a.m. and gave his rescuers a thumbs-up.

All nine men were taken to hospitals where they will remain under observation for at least 24 hours, officials said. They will be reunited with their families at the medical facilities.

The first miner, Randy Fogle, who had complained of chest pains, was taken by helicopter to Conemaugh Hospital.

Dr. Richard Saluzzo said Fogle was hypothermic, meaning his temperature was

John Philippi was the fifth miner to be pulled from the Pennsylvania mine on Sunday.

602

---

## Viewing Guide for
# News Reports

Both the NBC video clip and the CNN.com news report were originally presented the day after the rescue. The video clip, as an in-depth news feature, lasts longer than a typical news segment.

View the clip several times and take as much time as you need to look over the Web report. As you explore these two news formats, consider how each delivers the facts and take note of the specific techniques each uses to capture attention.

**NOW VIEW**

### FIRST VIEWING: Comprehension

1. **Summarize** In a brief statement, describe how the coal miners were rescued. Base the statement on the TV newscast.

2. **Clarify** In using the Web news site, what would you need to do to find additional information about Randy Fogle?

### CLOSE VIEWING: Media Literacy

3. **Draw Conclusions** By TV news standards, the newscast you've viewed is much longer than a typical news story. Basic news stories range in length from 30 seconds to 2 minutes. Why do you think so much time is devoted to this story?

4. **Analyze Techniques** The TV newscast includes **sound bites** from two rescued miners and from certain officials. The Web news report includes **quotations** from similar sources. Why do you think both news formats included such information?

5. **Compare Formats** You've examined how two news formats covered the same event. Use a Venn diagram to compare how the TV news segment and the Web news report are alike and different.

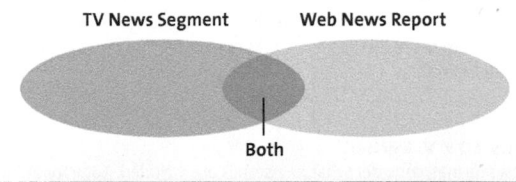

TV News Segment        Web News Report

Both

---

4. *Quoting participants provides human interest and eyewitness details. Quoting others, such as experts, spokespeople, or the governor, gives different perspectives and details from other points of view.*

5. ***TV news segment:** extensive visuals and narrative convey the on-the-scene experience, provide a strong sense of the atmosphere, introduce people involved; perhaps more engaging because easier to watch; **Web news report:** dedicates more space to more thorough coverage of the event; allows for interactive links for more in-depth detail*

*about the people and technology involved in the story; **Both:** use credible sources; relay essential facts and details; provide visual images of the event*

# Write or Discuss

**Compare the News Formats** Which news format—the TV news segment or the Web news report—is more effective at covering the rescue? Explain your opinion. Keep the following criteria in mind:

- the effectiveness of the lead in each format in delivering and emphasizing the important facts about the rescue
- the techniques used to capture and keep your interest
- the time or space limitations of each format

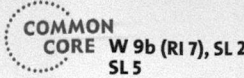
**COMMON CORE**

**W 9b (RI 7)** Draw evidence from informational texts; analyze accounts of a subject told in different mediums. **SL 2** Integrate multiple sources presented in diverse media or formats. **SL 5** Make strategic use of digital media in presentations.

# Produce Your Own Media

**Create a News Segment** Select an article from your school newspaper or from a community newspaper. Determine how you would create an update to the article in the form of a TV news segment. Then divide into teams to draft a script, conduct interviews, and plan to shoot the video footage of the segment.

*HERE'S HOW* Work in the assigned planning groups to address these questions:

- Who would be the anchor and the on-camera reporter?
- Whom would you interview for sound bites?
- What lead-in would your anchor provide?
- What voice-over would you need to include to structure the story?
- What video footage would you shoot?

**Media Tools** THINK central

Go to **thinkcentral.com**.
KEYWORD: HML9-603

### STUDENT MODEL

| WHAT VIEWERS SEE | WHAT VIEWERS HEAR | SHOT KEY | |
|---|---|---|---|
| ON-CAMERA REPORTER BIANCA EXT—DAY 1. LS of reporter standing with a group of student protesters in a parking lot. | BIANCA: Since the start of the school year, a growing group of students at Optima High believe the school parking lot to be in need of a makeover. . . . | **LS** Long Shot **MS** Medium Shot **VWS** Very Wide Shot **EXT** Exterior | |
| CUT TO: MS of BIANCA 2. Quickly zoom out to a VWS that reveals the potholes—some rather deep—dotting the lot. | BIANCA: . . . an extreme makeover. | | |

**Tech Tip**
You might use a design program to create a graphic for the report.

A LOT OF TROUBLE

603

## Produce Your Own Media

**Rubric: Create a News Segment** A strong plan for a TV news segment should have a script that clearly tells

- what viewers see and hear
- what the anchor's lead-in will be
- what the field reporter will say and do
- when sound bites will be used
- how and when voice-over will be used
- what video footage will be used

- the kinds of shots used when showing the anchor, the on-camera reporter, and the content of any video footage

**R** RESOURCE MANAGER—Copy Master
Produce Your Own Media p. 98

---

# Assess and Reteach

## Write or Discuss

COMMON CORE **W 9b (RI 7), SL 2, SL 5**

**Compare the News Formats** In their evaluations, students should address how well each medium conveyed the basic facts and identify techniques each medium used to capture audience interest. Students should also show an awareness of the general advantages and disadvantages of the two media. For example, students might point out how well the animations in the TV newscast conveyed information about drilling down to the miners but how time constraints limited the information given about the individual miners. They might note that the Web report enabled them to easily find additional information about Randy Fogle but that its minimal visuals reduced its impact. In addition, encourage students to include their own personal reactions to the TV newscast and the Web news report.

### MEDIA STUDY WRAP—UP

Have students summarize what they have learned about TV newscasts and Web news reports. Encourage students to use terms such as *anchor, field reporter, lead-in, video footage, voice-over, sound bites, menu, lead, caption, hyperlink,* and *quotations* in the summary.

### RETEACH

Select from these reteaching options:

- **Web News:** Have students choose a current news story and investigate how two different Internet news Web sites report that story. Have students identify the following pieces of the stories: leads, captions, hyperlinks, and quotations.
- **Television News:** Have students watch the first news story on a national news program. Ask, How long is the story? What does the newscast include? Have students identify the anchor, field reporter, lead-in, video footage, and voice-over.

**Media Tools** THINK central

Media study keywords point to **MediaScope**, a Web site that helps students strengthen media analysis and production skills.

# Focus and Motivate

## SUMMARY

Framton Nuttel visits an acquaintance of his sister whom he has never met. He is greeted by the woman's niece, Vera, who invents a story about her aunt in which the woman daily awaits the return of her long lost husband and brothers. When the husband and brothers arrive after a day of hunting, Nuttel believes he is seeing ghosts and flees.

## How should you treat a **GUEST?**

Ask students to describe a time when they were a guest in someone's home and were treated well. What did the host do? Extend the discussion by having students complete the *DISCUSS* activity.

---

*Before Reading*

## The Open Window
Short Story by Saki

# How should you treat a GUEST?

You're sitting at home when the doorbell rings. Instead of the pizza-delivery guy you were expecting, it's an uninvited guest. If that guest happens to be your best friend, you now have someone fun to share your pizza with. If, however, that guest is someone you would rather not hang out with, what should you do?

*DISCUSS* In your opinion, do you have an obligation to treat a guest, invited or not, with hospitality? Discuss your opinion with a small group of classmates. Talk about the obligations you have as a host—especially to a guest you would rather not spend time with. Are there minimum standards you have to meet in order not to be rude? After you've discussed these questions, think about whether or not your opinion has changed and, if so, why.

---

## TEXT ANALYSIS: TONE AND AUTHOR'S PURPOSE

A writer's **tone**, or attitude toward a subject, can often reveal his or her **perspective** and **purpose**. Just as you might use one tone of voice to make a joke and another to criticize someone, writers choose their words to convey different tones and accomplish different purposes. A writer's tone may be playful or solemn, sarcastic or admiring. Figuring out the writer's tone can help you decide what his or her purpose might be. As you read Saki's famous short story "The Open Window," ask yourself

- Does the narrator's description of other characters reveal whether Saki is portraying them in a favorable or an unfavorable light?
- Does Saki use formal or informal language? What effect does this create?

*Review:* Point of View

## READING STRATEGY: PREDICT

To make **predictions** about characters, try the following strategies:

- Think about each character's personality. How might someone with these traits respond to conflict or to new situations?
- Consider different characters' actions. What might happen as a result of these actions?
- Use your own experience. If you were ever in a situation similar to the one in the story, how did it turn out?

As you read "The Open Window," stop occasionally to predict what might happen next. Record text clues that help you make reasonable guesses, and check your predictions against what actually happens.

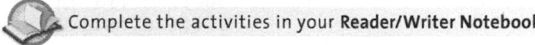

| Text Clues | My Prediction | Actual Outcome |
|---|---|---|
| Mrs. Sappleton has had a "great tragedy." (line 26) | She will still be very sad, even though it happened years ago. | |

 Complete the activities in your **Reader/Writer Notebook.**

---

## Meet the Author

### Saki
1870–1916

**Also Known As ...**
"Saki" is the pen name of Hector Hugo Munro, a British author best known for his satirical short stories. Munro was born in Burma, a country in Asia then controlled by the British. When he was very young, his mother was killed in an accident. His father sent Munro and his siblings to England to be raised by their aunts, two old women who believed in old-fashioned discipline.

**Saki's Saga**
When he was 23, Munro returned to Burma to join the military police. Stricken with malaria a year later, he gave up his badge and his pet tiger cub and returned to England to try his hand at writing. As he embarked on his literary career, he picked up the name Saki from the *Rubáiyát*, a long poem by 12th-century Persian writer Omar Khayyám. Although he wrote nonfiction, political cartoons, novels, and plays, Saki is most famous for his short stories, which are praised for their whimsical humor and shrewd social criticism. When World War I began, the writer rushed to enlist. During a night march through France in 1916, he was shot and killed by a German sniper.

**BACKGROUND TO THE STORY**
**Ridiculing the Rich**
"The Open Window" depicts the world of the British upper class in the early 1900s. Saki, himself a member of the upper class, often ridiculed the customs of high society. For instance, he made fun of the fact that people were expected to present formal letters of introduction when visiting strangers and poked fun at the "nerve cure," a trip to the countryside to treat anxiety.

**Author Online**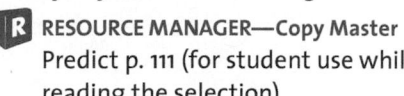
Go to **thinkcentral.com.**
KEYWORD: HML9-605

605

---

# Teach

**TEXT ANALYSIS**   COMMON CORE   RL 4, RL 6

## ● *Model the Skill:* TONE AND AUTHOR'S PURPOSE

Write some common author's purposes on the board, such as to inform, to persuade, and to entertain. Point out that if an author is trying to persuade a reader, the tone might be personal and positive. If an author is trying to inform readers, the tone might be deliberate and serious. Elicit that if an author is trying to entertain readers, the tone might be informal and humorous.

**GUIDED PRACTICE** Have students compare the tone and author's purpose they might find in a textbook, a newspaper editorial, and a children's book.

---

**READING STRATEGY**

## ▣ PREDICT

To support instruction, read this passage aloud to students.

> Erica's two brothers had been arguing constantly lately. Her ten-year-old brother Ethan had threatened to do anything to get a room of his own. Now Erica wondered where he might be. Suddenly, a loud pounding came from the attic. Erica raced upstairs, flung open the door, and stared. There stood her brother, hammer in hand.

Tell students that you can predict that Ethan is building his own room in the attic.

**GUIDED PRACTICE** Have students define *prediction*, using a dictionary if necessary. Clarify any misunderstanding.

**R** RESOURCE MANAGER—Copy Master Predict p. 111 (for student use while reading the selection)

---

## DIFFERENTIATED INSTRUCTION

### FOR STRUGGLING READERS

**Concept Support** After students read the discussion on tone and author's purpose, point out that they use and respond to tone every day. Read this statement aloud twice, using tone of voice first to express the imperative, and then excitement: "Class is beginning now." Ask students to identify the tone and the purpose it may imply. Have students provide other examples of how tone of speaking expresses a purpose or meaning.

### FOR ENGLISH LANGUAGE LEARNERS

**Frayer Model** To help students construct meaning and clarify understanding of the literary analysis and reading strategy concepts on this page, construct a Frayer Model on the board. Work with students to complete the organizer for each of the terms.

🧰 BEST PRACTICES TOOLKIT—Transparency Frayer Model p. A30

### READ WITH A PURPOSE

*Help students set a purpose for reading. Tell them to keep a list of Vera's character traits.*

---

TEXT ANALYSIS   

**COMMON CORE**

RL 4, RL 6

**A Model the Skill: TONE AND AUTHOR'S PURPOSE**

Help students identify tone and author's purpose by first reading aloud lines 3–7. Ask whether Nuttel is portrayed in a positive or a negative manner. Point out the formal language in the passage as well. This language helps convey the impression that Nuttel has a nervous condition.

***Possible answer:*** *Framton Nuttel tries to think of something appropriate to say. In fact, he starts to wonder whether visiting total strangers will help him get over his nervous condition. Saki's tone shows that the character is thoughtful and kind. He shows this by including Nuttel's thoughts and his concern for the feelings of the niece.*

---

# The Open Window

### SAKI

"My aunt will be down presently, Mr. Nuttel," said a very self-possessed young lady of fifteen; "in the mean-time you must try and put up with me."

Framton Nuttel endeavored to say the correct something that should duly flatter the niece of the moment without unduly discounting the aunt that was to come. Privately he doubted more than ever whether these formal visits on a succession of total strangers would do much toward helping the nerve cure[1] which he was supposed to be undergoing. **A**

"I know how it will be," his sister had said when he was preparing to migrate to this rural retreat; "you will bury yourself down there and not speak
10 to a living soul, and your nerves will be worse than ever from moping. I shall just give you letters of introduction to all the people I know there. Some of them, as far as I can remember, were quite nice."

Framton wondered whether Mrs. Sappleton, the lady to whom he was presenting one of the letters of introduction, came into the nice division.

"Do you know many of the people round here?" asked the niece, when she judged that they had had sufficient silent communion.

"Hardly a soul," said Framton. "My sister was staying here, at the rectory,[2] you know, some four years ago, and she gave me letters of introduction to some of the people here."

20 He made the last statement in a tone of distinct regret.

"Then you know practically nothing about my aunt?" pursued the self-possessed young lady.

"Only her name and address," admitted the caller. He was wondering whether Mrs. Sappleton was in the married or widowed state. An undefinable something about the room seemed to suggest masculine habitation.[3]

---

1. **nerve cure:** a treatment for nervousness or anxiety.
2. **the rectory** (rĕk′tə-rē): the parish priest's house.
3. **masculine habitation:** that men lived there.

---

**A TONE AND AUTHOR'S PURPOSE**

**Paraphrase** lines 3–7. So far, how would you describe Saki's tone, or his attitude toward this character? Explain your answer, citing evidence.

**1 Targeted Passage**

**Analyze Visuals ▶**

The narrator describes the niece as "self-possessed," or confident and in control. In your opinion, does the young woman in this painting look self-possessed? Explain, citing the **details** that influenced your opinion.

*Veil of Elegance,* Peter Miller. Private Collection. © Bridgeman Art Library.

---

## DIFFERENTIATED INSTRUCTION

**FOR ENGLISH LANGUAGE LEARNERS**

**Journal** As they read, ask students to keep a journal noting questions, observations, and reflections about characters and situations. Ask students to refer to their notes when completing other activities that accompany the selection.

**FOR STRUGGLING READERS**

In combination with the *Audio Anthology CD,* use one or more Targeted Passages (pp. 606, 608, 609) to ensure that students focus on key story events, concepts, and skills. Targeted Passages are also good for English learners.

**1 Targeted Passage [Lines 15–22]**

This passage shows what Nuttel knows about his host. It also introduces the character of the niece, giving her the information she needs to create a convincing tale.

## BACKGROUND

**Letters of Recommendation** During Victorian times, letter writing was an art as well as a necessity. Letters were written for both social and business purposes, and people always took care to write properly and to show good breeding. Each type of letter had its own rules and style. Letters of introduction were often written to introduce a friend to another friend or relative. Of course, the letter writers had to be careful for whom they wrote letters. It would not do to introduce someone of a different social standing or improper character to someone of a higher standing. Letters were supposed to be short and concise because they were usually hand-delivered, and it would have been awkward for a guest to sit quietly while someone read a lengthy letter.

## Analyze Visuals

*Possible answer: Yes, the subject looks self-possessed because she has a thoughtful expression on her face and sits in a relaxed, easy posture. She does not appear worried or tense.*

**About the Art** The contemporary English artist Peter Miller uses light and color to create a thoughtful, serene mood in his work. In the painting, light streams from both the window and the lamp. The light is created with flickering colors that create a softness on the flowers, the outdoor scene, and the girl's clothing. In contrast, the sharp lines and underlying structure of the furniture add strength to the overall softness of the painting.

---

- What two questions does the niece ask Nuttel? (lines 15, 21)
- How does Nuttel know Mrs. Sappleton? (lines 17–19)
- How does Nuttel feel about meeting people his sister has recommended? (line 20)

### FOR STRUGGLING READERS

**Develop Reading Fluency** Model for students and effective way to read conversation by reading lines 15–25 aloud. You might ask for a

volunteer to read the dialogue of one character while you read the other. Have students take the parts of the narrator and characters and read parts of the story aloud. Allow the students opportunities to practice in pairs or small groups before they read in front of the class.

**R** RESOURCE MANAGER—Copy Master
Reading Fluency p. 116

### FOR ADVANCED LEARNERS/PRE–AP

**Journal** Have students take notes on their favorite character in this story. Then have them write a one-page journal entry about this event from that character's perspective using their notes on character to help them.

**B POINT OF VIEW**

*Possible answer:* *The story is told from the third-person point of view. The characters are referred to as "he," "she," "him," and "her." If the story were in the first person, the pronouns* I, my, we, *and* mine *would be used.*

**REVISIT THE BIG QUESTION**

## How should you
## treat a GUEST?

**Discuss** Based on lines 15–50, how does Vera treat Nuttel when he is a guest in her home?
*Possible answer: Vera is polite and friendly, showing genuine interest in him. However, her attitude seems excessive as she shares intimate details about her family with a man she has never met before.*

**READING STRATEGY**

**C** *Model the Skill:* **PREDICT**

Point out what Vera says in lines 35–50. Explain that her words might affect Nuttel's decision to ask Mrs. Sappleton about her tragedy. Then have students write each clue from the text in their Predict charts and tell them to mark their predictions about what Nuttel will do in column two. Instruct them to write the actual outcomes in their charts as they read further.

*Possible answer: Nuttel will not say anything to Mrs. Sappleton about her tragedy. He is a sensitive and nervous character who would be careful not to upset Mrs. Sappleton.*

---

"Her great tragedy happened just three years ago," said the child; "that would be since your sister's time."

"Her tragedy?" asked Framton; somehow in this restful country spot tragedies seemed out of place.

30 "You may wonder why we keep that window wide open on an October afternoon," said the niece, indicating a large French window[4] that opened on to a lawn.

"It is quite warm for the time of the year," said Framton; "but has that window got anything to do with the tragedy?" **B**

"Out through that window, three years ago to a day, her husband and her two young brothers went off for their day's shooting. They never came back. In crossing the moor to their favorite snipe-shooting ground they were all three engulfed by a treacherous piece of bog. It had been that dreadful wet summer, you know, and places that were safe in other years gave way suddenly without 40 warning. Their bodies were never recovered. That was the dreadful part of it." Here the child's voice lost its self-possessed note and became falteringly human. "Poor aunt always thinks that they will come back some day, they and the little brown spaniel that was lost with them, and walk in that window just as they used to do. That is why the window is kept open every evening till it is quite dusk. Poor dear aunt, she has often told me how they went out, her husband with his white waterproof coat over his arm, and Ronnie, her youngest brother, singing 'Bertie, why do you bound?' as he always did to tease her, because she said it got on her nerves. Do you know, sometimes on still, quiet evenings like this, I almost get a creepy feeling that they will all walk 50 in through that window—"

She broke off with a little shudder. It was a relief to Framton when the aunt bustled into the room with a whirl of apologies for being late in making her appearance.

"I hope Vera has been amusing you?" she said.

"She has been very interesting," said Framton. **C**

"I hope you don't mind the open window," said Mrs. Sappleton briskly; "my husband and brothers will be home directly from shooting, and they always come in this way. They've been out for snipe in the marshes today, so they'll make a fine mess over my poor carpets. So like you menfolk, 60 isn't it?"

She rattled on cheerfully about the shooting and the scarcity of birds, and the prospects for duck in the winter. To Framton it was all purely horrible. He made a desperate but only partially successful effort to turn the talk on to a less ghastly topic; he was conscious that his hostess was giving him only a fragment of her attention, and her eyes were constantly straying past him to the open window and the lawn beyond. It was certainly an unfortunate coincidence that he should have paid his visit on this tragic anniversary.

---

4. **French window:** a pair of windows that extend to the floor and open like doors.

608   UNIT 5: AUTHOR'S PURPOSE

**B POINT OF VIEW**
Is this story told from the **first-person** or the **third-person** point of view? Explain how you determined this, citing evidence.

**COMMON CORE** RL 4

**Language Coach**

**Idioms** Groups of words that have a special meaning different from the combined literal meaning of each separate word are **idioms**. Reread lines 45–48. What idiom in line 48 explains the cause of Bertie's teasing? What does it mean?

**C PREDICT**
Will Nuttel say anything to Mrs. Sappleton about her "great tragedy"? Give reasons for your prediction.

**2 Targeted Passage**

---

## DIFFERENTIATED INSTRUCTION

**FOR STRUGGLING READERS**

**2 Targeted Passage** [Lines 56–60]
This passage reveals how Mrs. Sappleton explains the "great tragedy" to her guest.

- Why is the window open? (lines 57–58)
- Where does Mrs. Sappleton believe her husband and brothers are? (line 58)
- What has Nuttel been told about Mrs. Sappleton's husband and brothers? (line 36)

**FOR ENGLISH LANGUAGE LEARNERS**

**Language Coach**   **COMMON CORE** RL 4

**Idioms** *Possible answer: it got on her nerves = it irritated her* Have students read lines 61–67. Ask students to find an idiom and define it. *Possible answer: rattled on = talked constantly about nothing.*

"The doctors agree in ordering me complete rest, an absence of mental excitement, and avoidance of anything in the nature of violent physical
70 exercise," announced Framton, who labored under the tolerably widespread delusion that total strangers and chance acquaintances are hungry for the least detail of one's ailments and infirmities, their cause and cure. "On the matter of diet they are not so much in agreement," he continued. **D**

"No?" said Mrs. Sappleton, in a voice which only replaced a yawn at the last moment. Then she suddenly brightened into alert attention—but not to what Framton was saying.

"Here they are at last!" she cried. "Just in time for tea, and don't they look as if they were muddy up to the eyes!"

Framton shivered slightly, and turned toward the niece with a look intended
80 to convey sympathetic comprehension. The child was staring out through the open window with dazed horror in her eyes. In a chill shock of nameless fear Framton swung round in his seat and looked in the same direction.

In the deepening twilight three figures were walking across the lawn toward the window; they all carried guns under their arms, and one of them was additionally burdened with a white coat hung over his shoulders. A tired brown spaniel kept close at their heels. Noiselessly they neared the house, and then a hoarse young voice chanted out of the dusk:

"I said, Bertie, why do you bound?"

Framton grabbed wildly at his stick and hat; the hall door, the gravel drive, and
90 the front gate were dimly noted stages in his headlong retreat. A cyclist coming along the road had to run into the hedge to avoid imminent collision.

"Here we are, my dear," said the bearer of the white mackintosh, coming in through the window; "fairly muddy, but most of it's dry. Who was that who bolted out as we came up?"

"A most extraordinary man, a Mr. Nuttel," said Mrs. Sappleton; "could only talk about his illnesses, and dashed off without a word of goodbye or apology when you arrived. One would think he had seen a ghost."

"I expect it was the spaniel," said the niece calmly; "he told me he had a horror of dogs. He was once hunted into a cemetery somewhere on the banks
100 of the Ganges[5] by a pack of pariah dogs[6], and had to spend the night in a newly dug grave with the creatures snarling and grinning and foaming just above him. Enough to make anyone lose his nerve." **E**

Romance[7] at short notice was her specialty.

---

5. **Ganges** (gănˈjēzˈ): a large river in northern India.

6. **pariah** (pə-rīˈə) **dogs:** dogs that have escaped from their owners and become wild.

7. **romance:** highly imaginative fiction.

THE OPEN WINDOW **609**

**D TONE AND AUTHOR'S PURPOSE**
Is the language Saki uses to describe Nuttel's endless discussion of his health formal or informal? Explain the tone this language helps convey.

**3 Targeted Passage**

**E GRAMMAR AND STYLE**
Reread lines 99–102. Saki uses the **participles** *snarling, grinning,* and *foaming* to emphasize Vera's talent for choosing imaginative details.

---

## FOR STRUGGLING READERS
**3 Targeted Passage [77–88]**
This passage reveals the plot twist.

- Who does Mrs. Sappleton see coming toward the window? (lines 77–88)
- How does Vera react? (lines 80–81)
- How does this affect Framton? (lines 81–82)

## FOR ADVANCED LEARNERS/PRE–AP
**Hypothesize** [paired-activity option] After students finish reading the story, have them imagine a scene between Nuttel and his sister after his visit. During the visit, Nuttel shares the shocking details about Mrs. Sappleton's "great tragedy." Have students write the scene as a dialogue or skit. Ask students to share their work with the class by reading their stories or performing their dialogues or skits.

---

TEXT ANALYSIS     COMMON CORE   RL 4, RL 6

## D TONE AND AUTHOR'S PURPOSE

*Possible answer:* The language is formal. The formality conveys a feeling of respect and distance among the characters.

## TIERED DISCUSSION PROMPTS
Direct students to lines 89–103. Use these prompts to help students understand the surprise ending:

**Connect** How would you feel if a guest suddenly bolted from your home without a word of goodbye or apology? *Students might say that they would feel confused or angry.*

**Analyze** Why does Mr. Nuttel bolt from the house? *Possible answer: He thinks the people nearing the house are ghosts.*

**Synthesize** Why do you think Vera lies to Nuttel? *Possible answer: Vera is bored, enjoys inventing stories, and perhaps also enjoys making Mr. Nuttel look ridiculous.*

## E GRAMMAR AND STYLE   COMMON CORE L 1b

**Adverbs** An adverb is a word that modifies a verb, an adjective, or another adverb. Some adjectives, such as *wild* and *dim,* change to adverbs by adding the suffix *-ly.* Have students read lines 89–103 and find six adverbs other than *wildly* and *dimly.*

## SELECTION WRAP–UP

**READ WITH A PURPOSE** Now that students have finished reading the selection, have them describe the character of Vera. *Possible answer: Vera likes to toy with people, is very smart and cunning, and dishonest.*

⭐ **CRITIQUE** Have students evaluate the ending of the story and explain why it is or is not effective. Ask students to explain Saki's message about manners and social interactions.

# Practice and Apply

For preliminary support of post-reading questions, use these copy masters:

**R** RESOURCE MANAGER—Copy Masters
Reading Check p. 113
Tone and Author's Purpose p. 109
Question Support p. 114

Additional selection questions are provided for teachers on page 103.

## ANSWERS

## Comprehension

1. *She keeps the window open because she believes her husband and brothers will return from their hunting trip, one that took place three years before and during which they drowned.*

2. *Nuttel leaves abruptly because he believes he is seeing the ghosts of the husband and brothers. Vera explains his departure by inventing a story about his fear of dogs.*

3. *Vera is good at making up stories on the spur of the moment.*

## Text Analysis

COMMON CORE RL 4, RL 6, RL 10

*Possible answers:*

4. **First question:** *Vera wanted to know if he could have heard that she was good at inventing stories.* **Second question:** *She wanted to find out what information she would not be able to contradict in her invented story to make it plausible.*

5. **Evaluate Predictions** *Students should evaluate their predictions for accuracy and explain why any of their predictions were wrong.*

6. *We would not learn what happened after Nuttel left the room, nor would we learn of Vera's specialty for inventing stories at short notice.*

7. ● **COMMON CORE FOCUS** *Analyze Tone and Author's Purpose* *Saki's purpose was to make fun of silly people like Nuttel. He might be trying to tell his readers that people like Mr. Nuttel are gullible, inexperienced, and dull witted. In the passage in lines 89–91, Mr. Nuttel believes he is seeing the ghosts of the hunters. He is not clever enough to see through Vera's joke.*

## Text Criticism

*Possible answer:*

8. *Corb is correct because if the reader thinks that Vera is not telling the truth, the ending is not surprising. Saki skillfully repeats the details of Vera's story—the clothing, the dog, and the hunting expedition three times: in Vera's story, when Mrs. Sappleton appears, and when the hunters appear. The repetition helps convince the reader that Vera's story is true.*

---

## Comprehension

COMMON CORE

RL 4 Analyze the cumulative impact of specific word choices on meaning and tone. RL 6 Analyze a particular point of view or cultural experience reflected in a work of world literature. RL 10 Read and comprehend stories.

1. **Recall** Describe the "great tragedy" that Vera relates to Mr. Nuttel. According to Vera, why does her aunt keep the window open?

2. **Recall** Why does Nuttel leave so abruptly, and how does Vera explain his frantic departure?

3. **Paraphrase** Reread the story's final line. Then restate it in your own words.

## Text Analysis

4. **Draw Conclusions** A **surprise ending** is an unexpected twist at the end of a story. Reread lines 15–25 and think about Vera's behavior. Now that you know how "The Open Window" ends, what would you say was Vera's **motive** for asking Nuttel each question listed in the chart shown?

| Vera's Question | Motive |
|---|---|
| "Do you know many of the people round here?" (line 15) | |
| "Then you know practically nothing about my aunt?" (line 21) | |

5. **Evaluate Predictions** How accurate were your predictions? Using the chart you created as you read, describe the clues that allowed you to make on-target guesses or explain how Saki caught you by surprise.

6. **Analyze Point of View** Saki uses a **third-person omniscient narrator** in "The Open Window." The narrator is an outside voice that gives you access to the thoughts and feelings of all the characters and relates events that may be happening simultaneously. How would the end of this story be different if it were told exclusively from Nuttel's point of view? Explain your answer.

7. **Analyze Tone and Author's Purpose** Think about Saki's use of formal language to describe silly situations, as well as his depiction of Mr. Nuttel. From Saki's tone, what can you infer about his purpose? Explain.

## Text Criticism

8. **Critical Interpretations** According to critic Rena Corb, the "successful ending" of this story depends on "the reader's belief, along with Nuttel's, that Vera is telling the truth." Do you agree or disagree with Corb's assertion? Support your opinion with evidence from the selection.

### How should you treat a GUEST?

What rules of hospitality do you follow?

---

### How should you treat a GUEST?

Ask students if their families have taught them any rules about how to treat guests.

# Language

◆ **GRAMMAR AND STYLE: Add Descriptive Details**

Review the **Grammar and Style** note on page 609. Through his use of descriptive **participles,** Saki gives the reader a greater sense of Vera's ability to create fanciful stories.

**Participles** and **participial phrases** can help your writing become more vivid. A participle is a verb form that can be used as an adjective. Present participles end in *-ing*, and past participles end in *-ed* or *-en*. A participial phrase is made up of a participle and its modifiers and complements.

Here are examples of Saki's use of a participle and a participial phrase in "Open Window":

> The child was *staring* out through the open window with dazed horror in her eyes. (lines 80–81)

> A cyclist *coming along the road* had to run into the hedge to avoid imminent collision. (lines 90–91)

Notice how the revisions in blue make this first draft more descriptive. Revise your response to the prompt below by using similar techniques.

> **STUDENT MODEL**
>
> *Embarrassed by his abrupt departure from the Sappleton's home,*
> ^Nuttel will most likely leave the village or, at the very least, remain hidden
> *mocking*
> from a ~~harsh~~ public.
> ^

## READING-WRITING CONNECTION

**YOUR TURN**

Extend your interaction with "The Open Window" by responding to this prompt. Then use the **revising tip** to improve your writing.

| WRITING PROMPT | REVISING TIP |
|---|---|
| **Short Constructed Response: Prediction** Imagine that Framton Nuttel learned the truth about the Sappleton "tragedy." How might he respond to the news? Write **one or two paragraphs** describing how Nuttel might feel and act upon learning that he had been tricked. Base your response on the traits Nuttel exhibits in the story. | Review your response. Did you add descriptive details to your response by using participles and participial phrases? If not, revise your response to make your writing more vivid. |

**Interactive Revision** THINK central

Go to **thinkcentral.com.**
KEYWORD: HML9-611

---

## DIFFERENTIATED INSTRUCTION

### FOR STRUGGLING WRITERS

- Offer the following sentence frame as a paragraph starter: *When Nuttel learns that Vera has tricked him, he reacts by _____. The reason he reacts this way is _____.*

- Suggest that the first paragraph focus on Nuttel's reaction. The second paragraph should focus on quotations from the text that led to the prediction.

---

**COMMON CORE**

**L 1b** Use various types of phrases to convey specific meanings and add variety and interest to writing.

# Language

**COMMON CORE L 1b**

◆ **GRAMMAR AND STYLE**

After students examine the model, ask them how the participles affect the writing. Then write these sentences on the board and have students revise them using participles.

*Many immigrants faced long months of waiting at Ellis Island. (Many immigrants, weakened by their journeys, faced. . .)*

*We ran inside to get out of the rain. (We ran inside to get out of the pouring rain.)*

*That cucumber was delicious. (That peeled, sliced cucumber was delicious.)*

(For more information on using participles, see **Grammar Handbook,** page R55.)

**READING-WRITING CONNECTION**

- Encourage students to list words that describe Nuttel's character. As students write, they should use these character traits as a guide. Nuttel's reaction to being tricked should be consistent with the overriding character traits.

> **Interactive Vocabulary** THINK central
>
> Keywords direct students to a **WordSharp** tutorial on **thinkcentral.com** or to other types of vocabulary practice and review.

# Assess and Reteach

## Assess

**DIAGNOSTIC AND SELECTION TESTS**
> Selection Test A pp. 159–160
> Selection Test B/C pp. 161–162

**Interactive Selection Test** on **thinkcentral.com**

## Reteach

**Level Up Online Tutorials** on **thinkcentral.com**

**Reteaching Worksheets** on **thinkcentral.com**
> Literature Lesson 45: Tone
>
> Reading Lesson 3: Determining Author's Purpose
>
> Reading Lesson 1: Predicting

### COMMON CORE FOCUS

**RL 1** Cite textual evidence to support analysis of what the text says explicitly as well as inferences drawn from the text. **RL 3** Analyze how complex characters develop over the course of a text. **RL 4** Analyze the cumulative impact of specific word choices on meaning and tone. **L 5A** Interpret figures of speech in context and analyze their role in the text.

### SUMMARY

In the first of three excerpts from *The House on Mango Street,* the narrator recalls how the house her family finally moved into did not live up to her expectations. In the second vignette, she reflects on the life of her great-grandmother, for whom she was named. In the final vignette, the narrator describes how and why she likes to make up stories.

## What STORIES will you tell your children?

Point out that every family has its own particular legacy. Then introduce the question, and have students complete the *PRESENT* activity. Extend the discussion by asking why it is important for families to have and pass on legacies.

---

## *from* The House on Mango Street
### Fiction by Sandra Cisneros

# What STORIES will you tell your children?

### COMMON CORE

**RL 1** Cite textual evidence to support analysis of what the text says explicitly as well as inferences drawn from the text. **RL 3** Analyze how complex characters develop over the course of a text. **RL 4** Analyze the cumulative impact of specific word choices on meaning and tone. **L 5a** Interpret figures of speech in context and analyze their role in the text.

Whether it's a tale about the sweet taste of victory or a description of a devastating loss, you have important stories to tell. These stories, if you choose to tell them, will someday be the next generation's legacy—stories, beliefs, and traditions passed on from one generation to the next.

*PRESENT* With a classmate, share a few stories you might want to tell your kids someday. Then pick your favorite—maybe it's the funniest, or the most outrageous, or the one that says the most about you. With a small group, take turns telling your chosen tales. Explain why these are the stories you would pass on to the next generation.

612

---

See resources on the **Teacher One Stop DVD-ROM** *and on* **thinkcentral.com**.

 **RESOURCE MANAGER UNIT 5**
    Plan and Teach, pp. 117–124
    Summary pp. 125–126†‡*
    Text Analysis and Reading
      Skill, pp. 127–131†*

**DIAGNOSTIC AND SELECTION**
    **TESTS**
    Selection Tests, pp. 163–166

**BEST PRACTICES TOOLKIT**
    Context Clues (Comparison),
      p. E16

**TECHNOLOGY**

- **Teacher One Stop DVD-ROM**
- **Student One Stop DVD-ROM**
- **Audio Anthology CD**
- **GrammarNotes DVD-ROM**
- **ExamView Test Generator**
  on the **Teacher One Stop**

---

**\* Resources for Differentiation**      **† Also in Spanish**      **‡ In Haitian Creole and Vietnamese**

## TEXT ANALYSIS: AUTHOR'S PERSPECTIVE

Just as your own experiences influence the way you think about different issues, a writer's personal experiences affect the way he or she approaches a topic. When you analyze an **author's perspective,** or point of view, you work to figure out how the writer looks at his or her subject. As you read this excerpt from *The House on Mango Street,* think about Sandra Cisneros's perspective on the narrator's circumstances.

- Pay attention to the writer's choice of details. In these vignettes, Cisneros describes a rundown house in vivid detail. What do her descriptions of its small windows, crumbling bricks, and tiny yard help emphasize?
- Consider direct statements of the narrator's thoughts or feelings. What kind of person is she?

As you read, consider what these details and statements reveal about Cisneros's ideas, as well as her feelings about what it's like to grow up in a place like the house on Mango Street.

*Review:* Tone

## READING SKILL: MAKE INFERENCES ABOUT CHARACTER

Writers don't usually spell out every single thing their characters are thinking and feeling. They often leave it up to the reader to **make inferences** about what isn't directly stated. As you read the following vignettes, keep track of significant details that tell you something about the narrator's background, personality, and feelings. Then record the inferences you can draw from these details.

| Details from the Text | My Inferences |
|---|---|
| Esperanza's family has moved around a lot, and she doesn't sound very happy about that. (lines 1–3) | Esperanza probably wishes her family could just stay in one place and not move around so much. |
| When the family moves to Mango Street, they finally get their own house. But Esperanza says that "it's not the house we'd thought we'd get." (line 9) | |

 Complete the activities in your **Reader/Writer Notebook.**

## Meet the Author

### Sandra Cisneros
**born 1954**

**Defining Her Destiny**
Sandra Cisneros grew up in a male-dominated household where her father and six brothers were the authority figures. She quietly rebelled against the traditional role she was expected to play as a Mexican-American female, writing in secret until she went away to college. The author now uses her work to give voice to the experiences of Mexican-American women. "I'm trying to write the stories that haven't been written," Cisneros explains. "I'm determined to fill a literary void."

**Latina Power**
Much of Cisneros's writing deals with the shame of poverty and the guilt that comes with rejecting certain aspects of one's culture. Her poetry and prose have received critical acclaim. "I am a woman and I am a Latina," the author says proudly. "Those are the things that make my writing distinctive. Those are the things that give my writing power."

**BACKGROUND TO THE SELECTION**
**No Place Like Home**
When Cisneros was young, her family moved frequently from Chicago to Mexico City and back again. She never remained in one place long enough to make close friends, and she longed for a "perfect" house like the ones she read about and saw on TV. When she was 11, Cisneros and her family finally moved into a shabby house in a poor Chicago neighborhood. The rundown house was not the dream home she had longed for. Esperanza Cordero, the narrator of *The House on Mango Street,* faces similar issues.

Author Online
THINK central
Go to **thinkcentral.com.**
KEYWORD: HML9-613

613

## DIFFERENTIATED INSTRUCTION

### FOR STRUGGLING READERS

**Vocabulary Support** Elicit or provide the meanings of these words: *vignette*—"short descriptive literary sketch"; *inference*—"conclusion drawn from information in combination with personal knowledge and experience." Explain that *inference* comes from the verb *infer.*

# Teach

## ● *Model the Skill:* AUTHOR'S PERSPECTIVE

To help students understand author's perspective, read this excerpt from the vignette:

> "I knew then I had to have a house. A real house. One I could point to. But this isn't it." (lines 44–45)

Explain that the author expresses the narrator's disappointment and shame about living in this house. She has aspirations to have a house of her own about which she can be proud.

**GUIDED PRACTICE** Ask students how the author's perspective might be different had she grown up in a family with more economic resources.

## ■ *Model the Skill:* MAKE INFERENCES ABOUT CHARACTER

Tell students that making inferences involves making guesses about something that is not explicitly stated. Reread the passage above aloud. Explain that one inference you can make based on these lines about Esperanza is that she cares very much about appearances. Encourage students to confirm or revise their inferences about Esperanza as they read further and gather more information about her.

**GUIDED PRACTICE** Have students use the details from the second row of the chart to make an inference from Esperanza's statements about how she feels about the house.

**R** RESOURCE MANAGER—Copy Master Make Inferences About Character p. 129 (for student use while reading the selection)

### READ WITH A PURPOSE

*Help students set a purpose for reading. Ask them to pay attention to how poverty affected Esperanza.*

**A** *Model the Skill:* **MAKE INFER-ENCES ABOUT CHARACTER**

Demonstrate how to make inferences by copying the Make Inferences About Character chart on the board. Copy details from the story into the first column: "The water pipes broke... house was too old" (lines 10–11). Explain that one inference is that the family did not have enough money to live in a newer place without broken plumbing. Write the inference in column two of the chart. Repeat the process, eliciting details and inferences from the students.

*Possible answer:* *The reader can infer that the family has limited financial resources, which compels them to live in a building that has broken pipes, and as a result, they had to use the washroom next door and carry water in empty milk jugs to use.*

---

# The House on Mango Street

## Sandra Cisneros

### The House on Mango Street

We didn't always live on Mango Street. Before that we lived on Loomis on the third floor, and before that we lived on Keeler. Before Keeler it was Paulina, and before that I can't remember. But what I remember most is moving a lot. Each time it seemed there'd be one more of us. By the time we got to Mango Street we were six—Mama, Papa, Carlos, Kiki, my sister Nenny and me.

The house on Mango Street is ours, and we don't have to pay rent to anybody, or share the yard with the people downstairs, or be careful not to make too much noise, and there isn't a landlord banging on the ceiling with a broom. But even so, it's not the house we'd thought we'd get.

10     We had to leave the flat[1] on Loomis quick. The water pipes broke and the landlord wouldn't fix them because the house was too old. We had to leave fast. We were using the washroom next door and carrying water over in empty milk gallons. That's why Mama and Papa looked for a house, and that's why we moved into the house on Mango Street, far away, on the other side of town. **A**

They always told us that one day we would move into a house, a real house that would be ours for always so we wouldn't have to move each year. And our house would have running water and pipes that worked. And inside it would have real stairs, not hallway stairs, but stairs inside like the houses on TV. And

---

1. **flat:** an apartment on one floor of a building.

*Analyze Visuals* ▶
What effect is created by the heightened colors and blurred lines in this image? Explain your answer.

 **Targeted Passage**

**A** MAKE INFERENCES ABOUT CHARACTER
Reread lines 6–14. What can you infer about the family's economic circumstances? Explain your answer.

---

## DIFFERENTIATED INSTRUCTION

### FOR ENGLISH LANGUAGE LEARNERS

**Develop Reading Fluency** Read aloud lines 6–9. As you read, emphasize the connecting words *and, or,* and *but.* Point out that these conjunctions and the commas will help the student read fluently and understand meaning. Ask students to read these lines to a partner once, exaggerating the connecting words. Then, have students read the lines aloud fluently a second time without exaggeration.

### FOR STRUGGLING READERS

In combination with the *Audio Anthology CD,* use one or more Targeted Passages (pp. 614, 616, 617, 618) to ensure that students focus on key story events, concepts, and skills. Targeted Passages are also good for English learners.

 **Targeted Passage [Lines 6–14]**

This passage explains how the family came to live in the house on Mango Street and describes the flat they used to live in.

## ⓑ MAKE INFERENCES ABOUT CHARACTER

*Possible answer:* When the nun says "there," the narrator looks up and notices the paint peeling and wooden bars on the windows. Her reaction reveals that she feels ashamed and embarrassed to live there.

### IF STUDENTS NEED HELP...

- Have students reread lines 34–36 and 40–41. Discuss the descriptive details, and ask what kind of mental image they create.

- Have students reread line 42. Ask them to paraphrase the narrator's reaction: "The way she said it made me feel like nothing."

**Extend the Discussion** Why do you think the author put the word *there* in italics (lines 39, 40, 42, and 43)?

## ⓒ TONE

*Possible answer:* Striking words and phrases include "like the number nine" and "A muddy color" (line 48) and "songs like sobbing" (line 50). Cisneros's word choice conveys a sad, disconsolate tone, the feeling of longing for something that may never come.

**Extend the Discussion** The author makes several comparisons in lines 47–50. How do these comparisons express the narrator's feelings about her name?

---

we'd have a basement and at least three washrooms so when we took a bath we
20 wouldn't have to tell everybody. Our house would be white with trees around it, a great big yard and grass growing without a fence. This was the house Papa talked about when he held a lottery ticket and this was the house Mama dreamed up in the stories she told us before we went to bed.

But the house on Mango Street is not the way they told it at all. It's small and red with tight steps in front and windows so small you'd think they were holding their breath. Bricks are crumbling in places, and the front door is so swollen you have to push hard to get in. There is no front yard, only four little elms the city planted by the curb. Out back is a small garage for the car we don't own yet and a small yard that looks smaller between the two buildings
30 on either side. There are stairs in our house, but they're ordinary hallway stairs, and the house has only one washroom. Everybody has to share a bedroom— Mama and Papa, Carlos and Kiki, me and Nenny.

Once when we were living on Loomis, a nun from my school passed by and saw me playing out front. The laundromat downstairs had been boarded up because it had been robbed two days before and the owner had painted on the wood YES WE'RE OPEN so as not to lose business.

Where do you live? she asked.

There, I said pointing up to the third floor.

You live *there?*

40 *There.* I had to look to where she pointed—the third floor, the paint peeling, wooden bars Papa had nailed on the windows so we wouldn't fall out. You live *there?* The way she said it made me feel like nothing. *There.* I lived *there.* I nodded. ⓑ

I knew then I had to have a house. A real house. One I could point to. But this isn't it. The house on Mango Street isn't it. For the time being, Mama says. Temporary, says Papa. But I know how those things go.

## *My Name*

In English my name means hope. In Spanish it means too many letters. It means sadness, it means waiting. It is like the number nine. A muddy color. It is the Mexican records my father plays on Sunday mornings when he is
50 shaving, songs like sobbing. ⓒ

It was my great-grandmother's name and now it is mine. She was a horse woman too, born like me in the Chinese year of the horse[2]—which is supposed to be bad luck if you're born female—but I think this is a Chinese lie because the Chinese, like the Mexicans, don't like their women strong.

My great-grandmother. I would've liked to have known her, a wild horse of a woman, so wild she wouldn't marry. Until my great-grandfather threw a sack over her head and carried her off. Just like that, as if she were a fancy chandelier. That's the way he did it.

---

2. **Chinese year of the horse:** In the traditional Chinese calendar, each succeeding year is named after 1 of 12 animals. People born in the year of the horse are thought to be energetic and quick-witted.

### Language Coach

**Fixed Expressions** A **fixed expression** offers a ready-made way of saying something. Reread lines 24–26. How does the fixed expression *holding their breath* help you "see" what the windows look like?

**Targeted Passage** *continued*

### ⓑ MAKE INFERENCES ABOUT CHARACTER

Reread lines 33–43. Consider the narrator's reaction to the nun's remark. What do these lines reveal about the narrator's feelings?

### ⓒ TONE

Reread lines 47–50. Identify striking words or phrases in this paragraph. What tone does Cisneros's **word choice** convey? Explain your answer.

---

## DIFFERENTIATED INSTRUCTION

### ② Targeted Passage [Lines 24–32]

This passage contrasts the house on Mango Street with the narrator's expectations.

- What does the house look like? (lines 24–31)

- How is the house different from what the narrator had expected? (line 24)

- How does the narrator feel about living in the house on Mango Street? (lines 24–32)

### Language Coach

**Fixed Expressions** *Possible answer: They look puckered and squinty, not letting in much light.* Have students reread lines 21–23. Ask students what "when he held a lottery ticket" means. *"when we get rich."*

*The Cashier* (2003), Lisa Reinke. Oil on canvas, 5″ × 7″. © Lisa Reinke.

And the story goes she never forgave him. She looked out the window her
60 whole life, the way so many women sit their sadness on an elbow. I wonder if
she made the best with what she got or was she sorry because she couldn't be
all the things she wanted to be. Esperanza. I have inherited her name, but I
don't want to inherit her place by the window. ⓓ

ⓓ **AUTHOR'S
PERSPECTIVE**
Reread lines 51–63.
What cultural
expectations and values
does Cisneros reveal in
these paragraphs?

❸ **Targeted Passage**

---

**FOR STRUGGLING READERS**

❸ **Targeted Passage [Lines 59–63]**

This passage tells the story of what happened
to Esperanza's great-grandmother and shows
Esperanza's feelings about it.

- What does the narrator wonder about her
  great-grandmother? (lines 60–62)

- What does the narrator inherit from her
  great-grandmother? What does she not
  want to inherit? (lines 62–63)

**FOR ADVANCED LEARNERS/PRE–AP**

**Hypothesize** Have students discuss to what
extent the thoughts and observations on
lines 59–63 are the fictional Esperanza's or
Cisneros's own feelings. Ask students if they
believe that the vignette of Esperanza's great-
grandmother is a made-up tale or an account
of events that actually happened in Cisneros's
family.

---

# What **STORIES** will you tell your children?

**Discuss** Refer students to lines 55–63. In what
ways is the story of her great-grandmother
a legacy to the narrator? *Possible answer:
The narrator acknowledges her great-grandmother's defiance when she says that the older
woman never forgave her husband for carrying
her off to marry him. But, the narrator also
expresses her determination not to "inherit her
[great-grandmother's] place by the window"
(line 63), meaning her sadness about how her
life turned out.*

## Analyze Visuals

**Activity** Ask students whether they think
the mood of the painting reflects Cisneros's
tone. Why or why not? *Answers will vary, but
students should support their responses with
thoughtful reasons.*

**About the Art** Artist Lisa Reinke's *The Cashier*
is typical of her brightly colored portraits. This
bold, bright painting and the wavy lines emphasize the profile of a girl, whose serious and
seemingly sad appearance may suggest the
narrator of *The House on Mango Street.*

---

**TEXT ANALYSIS**

**COMMON CORE**
RL 4

ⓓ *Model the Skill:* **AUTHOR'S PERSPECTIVE**

Begin by reading line 54 aloud. Point out
that this detail shows that the narrator
values strong women.

*Possible answer: Cisneros's narrative
implies the dominant position of men when
Cisneros describes how the "great-grandfather . . . carried her off . . . as if she were
a fancy chandelier" (lines 56–58). The narrator then remarks that "so many women
sit their sadness on an elbow" (line 60) and
wonders if the great-grandmother was
"sorry because she couldn't be all the things
she wanted to be" (lines 61–62).*

At school they say my name funny as if the syllables were made out of tin and hurt the roof of your mouth. But in Spanish my name is made out of a softer something, like silver, not quite as thick as sister's name—Magdalena—which is uglier than mine. Magdalena who at least can come home and become Nenny. But I am always Esperanza.

70 I would like to baptize myself under a new name, a name more like the real me, the one nobody sees. Esperanza as Lisandra or Maritza or Zeze the X. Yes. Something like Zeze the X will do.

## Mango Says Goodbye Sometimes

I like to tell stories. I tell them inside my head. I tell them after the mailman says, Here's your mail. Here's your mail he said.

I make a story for my life, for each step my brown shoe takes. I say, "And so she trudged up the wooden stairs, her sad brown shoes taking her to the house she never liked."

I like to tell stories. I am going to tell you a story about a girl who didn't want to belong.

80 We didn't always live on Mango Street. Before that we lived on Loomis on the third floor, and before that we lived on Keeler. Before Keeler it was Paulina, but what I remember most is Mango Street, sad red house, the house I belong but do not belong to.

I put it down on paper and then the ghost does not ache so much. I write it down and Mango says goodbye sometimes. She does not hold me with both arms. She sets me free. **E**

One day I will pack my bags of books and paper. One day I will say goodbye to Mango. I am too strong for her to keep me here forever. One day I will go away.

90 Friends and neighbors will say, What happened to that Esperanza? Where did she go with all those books and paper? Why did she march so far away?

They will not know I have gone away to come back. For the ones I left behind. For the ones who cannot out. 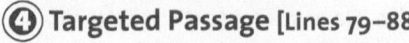 **F**

---

**E AUTHOR'S PERSPECTIVE**
Reread lines 83–85. What might the author be saying about the power of writing? Explain your answer.

④ **Targeted Passage**

**COMMON CORE** L 5a

**F PARADOX**
A **paradox** is a statement that contradicts itself. Paradoxes are often like riddles, with meanings that are difficult to interpret. In line 91, when the narrator says that she has "gone away to come back," she seems to be contradicting herself. What do you think this statement means? Explain your answer.

---

**TEXT ANALYSIS**

**COMMON CORE** RL 4

**E AUTHOR'S PERSPECTIVE**

*Possible answer:* *The author may be saying that writing for her is a way of expressing and releasing her feelings and a means to feel free of the difficult circumstances that constrain her.*

**Extend the Discussion** Do you think that addressing the subject matter of *The House on Mango Street* in a *nonfiction* selection would have the same liberating power for the author? Why or why not?

---

**TEXT ANALYSIS**

**COMMON CORE** L 5a

**F PARADOX**

*Possible answer:* *Student answers will vary.*

Have students work in small groups to list two paradoxes from movies, television shows, books, or other mediums. Ask each group to share their paradoxes with the class.

---

**SELECTION WRAP-UP**

**READ WITH A PURPOSE** Now that students have finished reading the selection, ask them about Esperanza's family circumstances. What are her dreams for the future? *Possible answers:* *Esperanza's family is poor. She dreams of leaving the house on Mango Street and becoming a writer. Leaving the house would represent leaving poverty behind.*

★ **CRITIQUE** The three vignettes are excerpts from a book-length work. Have students consider ways in which the vignettes are—and are not—related. Ask students to evaluate how well the three vignettes work together as a selection.

**INDEPENDENT READING**

For students interested in reading about the Mexican-American experience, suggest *Parrot in the Oven: Mi vida* by Victor Martinez.

---

## DIFFERENTIATED INSTRUCTION

**FOR STRUGGLING READERS**

④ **Targeted Passage** [Lines 79–88]

This passage reveals Esperanza's feelings about the house on Mango Street, her reason for writing, and her intention to move away.

- Why does the narrator say that she does "not belong to" the house? (lines 79–82)

- What does she mean when she says, "I write it down and Mango says goodbye sometimes" (lines 83–84)?

**FOR ENGLISH LANGUAGE LEARNERS**

**Comprehension: Comparisons** Tell students that they will find many comparisons in the story. Point out "a wild horse of a woman" (lines 55–56), "as if ... mouth" (lines 64–65), and "like silver" (line 66). Divide students into Context Clues groups, assign each group a section of text, and have them identify other comparisons.

**BEST PRACTICES TOOLKIT**
Context Clues (Comparison), p. E16

## Comprehension

1. **Recall** Describe Esperanza's house on Mango Street.

2. **Recall** What does Esperanza's name mean in English?

3. **Clarify** What does Esperanza mean when she refers to her home as "the house I belong but do not belong to"?

## Text Analysis

4. **Make Inferences About Character** Review the inferences you made about Esperanza as you read. Based on your inferences, what **conclusions** can you draw about this character? List the adjectives you would use to describe Esperanza, and then explain why you chose each. Cite evidence to support your conclusions.

5. **Understand Tone** How would you describe Cisneros's tone in these vignettes? Jot down words and phrases that stood out to you, and think about the tone they help create. Describe Cisneros's tone in a sentence or two.

6. **Interpret Text** Reread lines 51–63 and consider Esperanza's feelings about her legacy. She says she doesn't want to inherit her great-grandmother's "place by the window." What does she mean? What else doesn't she want to inherit? Explain your answer.

7. **Draw Conclusions** Consider Cisneros's statement on page 613 that she strives to "write the stories that haven't been written." On the basis of what you know about her, why do you think Cisneros chose to tell Esperanza's story? Explain your answer, citing evidence.

8. **Analyze Author's Perspective** Think about the details Cisneros includes in these vignettes, as well as Esperanza's feelings about her life. Then consider what you learned about Cisneros in the biography and background on page 613. What do you think is Cisneros's perspective on growing up poor? Use evidence from the text as well as details from the biography to support your answer.

## Text Criticism

9. **Author's Style** Cisneros says that in writing *The House on Mango Street* she "was trying to write something that was a cross between fiction and poetry." In your opinion, are these vignettes more like verse or more like fiction? Consider the author's choice of words and details as well as what she communicates with each vignette. Defend your answer with evidence from the text.

### What **STORIES** will you tell your children?

Is it important to share one's life experiences with the next generation? Why?

COMMON CORE

**RL 1** Cite textual evidence to support analysis of what the text says explicitly as well as inferences drawn from the text. **RL 3** Analyze how complex characters develop over the course of a text. **RL 4** Analyze the cumulative impact of specific word choices on meaning and tone.

---

# Practice and Apply

For preliminary support of post-reading questions, use these copy masters:

 **RESOURCE MANAGER—Copy Masters**
Reading Check p. 131
Author's Perspective p. 127
Question Support p. 132

Additional selection questions are provided for teachers on page 121.

## ANSWERS

## Comprehension

1. *It was a small, red house with tight steps, little windows, and crumbling bricks.*

2. *Esperanza means "hope" in English.*

3. *It is the house in which she lives with her family, but she does not feel a part of it.*

## Text Analysis

COMMON CORE **RL 1, RL 3, RL 4**

*Possible answers:*

4. ■ **COMMON CORE FOCUS** *Make Inferences About Character Esperanza's sensitivity, sense of legacy, and determination are shown by her feelings about the "sad red house," her connection to her great-grandmother, and her commitment to writing.*

5. *Cisneros's tone is sad and wistful. For example, the narrator describes the house on Mango Street as "not the way they told it at all" (line 24). She says the house is "sad" and she does "not belong to it." She writes so the "ghost does not ache so much" (lines 81–83).*

6. *She doesn't want to be restricted in her activities by a dominating husband, or to inherit a lifetime of regret, unable to pursue the things that she wants.*

7. *Esperanza's story is an example of giving "voice to the experiences of Mexican-American women" (page 613). Cisneros suggests that Mexican-American females need not feel restricted to traditional roles; they need not "sit their sadness on an elbow" (line 60).*

8. ● **COMMON CORE FOCUS** *Analyze Author's Perspective Cisneros's childhood experience of moving into "a shabby house" in a poor Chicago neighborhood shaped her perspective on the pain of poverty and allowed her to depict Esperanza's situation and feelings.*

## Text Criticism

9. *Students may choose either answer, but they should support their opinions with evidence from the text.*

### What **STORIES** will you tell your children?
Ask students what memories from their childhoods they feel will be important to share with their children. Why?

---

# Assess and Reteach

## Assess

**DIAGNOSTIC AND SELECTION TESTS**
Selection Test A pp. 163–164
Selection Test B/C pp. 165–166

**Interactive Selection Test** on **thinkcentral.com**

## Reteach

**Level Up Online Tutorials** on **thinkcentral.com**

**Reteaching Workshops** on **thinkcentral.com**
Literature Lesson 47: Author's Perspective
Reading Lesson 8: Making Inferences

# Focus and Motivate

## COMMON CORE FOCUS

**RI 4** Determine the technical meaning of words as they are used in a text. **RI 5** Analyze how an author's ideas are developed and refined. **RI 6** Determine an author's purpose in a text.

### SUMMARY

The purpose of most consumer documents is to help you learn to use the product effectively, safely, and happily. This selection presents an assortment of consumer documents—product information, instructions, safety information, warranties—and describes how to read and use them.

## Why are **FUNCTIONAL** texts necessary?

After students haves completed the *QUICKWRITE,* ask them to describe personal experiences with consumer documents. If they had some advice to give to the writers of these texts, what would it be?

---

**Essential Course of Study ECOS**

## Consumer Documents: From the Manufacturer to You

Product Information, Safety Information, Warranty

# Why are **FUNCTIONAL** texts necessary?

**COMMON CORE**

**RI 4** Determine the technical meaning of words as they are used in a text. **RI 5** Analyze how an author's ideas are developed and refined. **RI 6** Determine an author's purpose in a text.

Have you tried to read a product warranty or an instruction manual and found yourself utterly confused? Sometimes functional texts—documents that provide instructions or other detailed, step-by-step information—can be difficult to understand. Good readers know not to panic. They slow down the pace of their reading, look up critical vocabulary, and pay attention to graphic representations of data such as charts and diagrams. In short, they make sure to find the information they *need*.

*QUICKWRITE* What was the last product you bought that came with information you needed to read before using the product? Did you find the information helpful? Why or why not? Record your thoughts in a brief paragraph.

620

---

# Selection Resources

See resources on the **Teacher One Stop DVD-ROM** and on **thinkcentral.com**.

**R RESOURCE MANAGER UNIT 5**
Plan and Teach, pp. 135–140
Summary, pp. 141–142†‡*
Text Analysis and Reading
Skill, pp. 143–146†*

**DIAGNOSTIC AND SELECTION TESTS**
Selection Tests, pp. 167–170

**INTERACTIVE READER**

**ADAPTED INTERACTIVE READER**

**ELL ADAPTED INTERACTIVE READER**

**TECHNOLOGY**
- Teacher One Stop DVD-ROM
- Student One Stop DVD-ROM
- PowerNotes DVD-ROM
- GrammarNotes DVD-ROM
- Audio Tutor CD
- ExamView Test Generator
  on the **Teacher One Stop**

\* Resources for Differentiation     † Also in Spanish     ‡ In Haitian Creole and Vietnamese

## TEXT ANALYSIS: CONSUMER DOCUMENTS

A **consumer** is someone who uses a product or service. You, your parents, and your classmates are all consumers. Many of the things you buy—even a product as simple as a backpack—come with **consumer documents**. The more complicated the product is, the more complex the documents that come with it.

The **purpose** of most consumer documents is to give you information so that you can use the product effectively, safely, and—the company hopes—happily. Designers of consumer documents try to organize information well and explain the product clearly so that their documents meet this objective. As you read the consumer documents that follow, consider their purpose and how well they achieve it.

## READING STRATEGY: ADJUST READING RATE

When reading consumer documents, you must learn how to **adjust your reading rate.** You may read quickly through information you think you already know, but you should slow down when you come across technical or quantitative data that are more difficult to understand. Often, you'll find this kind of data in graphics, such as charts, tables, and computer screen shots, to which you should pay close, careful attention.

As you read these documents, take notes about your reading rate in a chart like the one below. An example has been filled in for you.

| Product Information | Safety Information | Warranty |
|---|---|---|
| I quickly scanned the row headings in the table, but then I slowed down to compare the numbers to what I expected from the product. | | |

 Complete the activities in your **Reader/Writer Notebook.**

---

### Reading for Life

So many of the things that you'll want to do in life—such as make purchases, find a job, and be involved in your community—require you to read and understand **functional texts,** procedural and work-related documents that serve a practical purpose. Consumer documents are not the only sort of functional texts that you'll encounter in your daily life. Among the other types with which you should familiarize yourself are public documents and workplace documents.

### Public Documents

Simply stated, a **public document** is a document that is made public—for all to read. Government agencies, schools, libraries, fire and police departments, transit departments, and even movie theaters all produce public documents. Public documents come in many forms. Here are some you may be familiar with:

- Fliers or posters
- Travel advisories
- Legal records
- Congressional proceedings

### Workplace Documents

Documents that are created for and by employees are called **workplace documents.** When you look for a job, for example, you may write a business letter in which you state your qualifications and ask for an interview. You might include a **résumé,** a formal listing of your educational and work experience, or fill in an **application** supplied by the employer. If you are hired, you may have to sign an employment **contract.** On the job, you may communicate with your coworkers by using **e-mails, memos,** and **reports.**

For more information on functional texts, see the **Reading Handbook,** pages R16–R19.

---

### ● Model the Skill: CONSUMER DOCUMENTS

Point out that consumer documents need to be clearly organized because users of the product often return to them to answer questions they may have as they learn to use the product. Describe an experience you have had with a consumer product document. Then ask what other special challenges the writer of consumer documents might face. ***Possible answer: People may not read them carefully, so the writer must think of ways to make them easily understood.***

### READING STRATEGY

### ■ Model the Skill: ADJUST READING RATE

To model the skill of adjusting your reading rate, read aloud the safety instructions on page 623 and slow down when reading critical information. Have students point out to you where you slowed down and why. Then fill in the space on the chart on this page to describe how you adjusted your reading rate to read the safety instructions. ***Possible answer: I slowed down when I read about how I should never block or cover the vents because it's important to allow the unit to cool.***

**GUIDED PRACTICE** Have students read the warranty information on page 624 and fill in the chart.

**R** RESOURCE MANAGER—Copy Master Adjust Reading Rate p. 145 (for student use while reading the selection)

---

## DIFFERENTIATED INSTRUCTION

### FOR ENGLISH LANGUAGE LEARNERS

Ask students to discuss with a partner the "joke" in the comic strip on page 620. Provide these sentence frames to encourage discussion:

The funny thing is ___.

The cell phone is ___ and the manual is ___.

I understand this joke because ___.

I like/don't like this comic strip because ___.

## READ WITH A PURPOSE

*Help students set a purpose for reading. Tell them to look for information they can use to make a list of tips on becoming a better reader and user of consumer documents.*

### REVISIT THE BIG QUESTION

## Why are FUNCTIONAL texts necessary?

Have students read the bulleted list that describes three types of functional texts that accompany most products. Then have them speculate on what other kinds of texts they might like to have when purchasing and learning to use a new product.

---

# CONSUMER DOCUMENTS:

## From the Manufacturer to You

Picture before you an unopened box. In it is the latest and greatest computer game console. In your hurry to get it out of the box, you let a sheaf of papers slide to the floor. There they lie in danger of being thrown out with all the packing materials. Be sure you retrieve and read them carefully. These

5 **consumer documents** can make a big difference in how much you enjoy your new game.

### Elements and Features of Consumer Documents

Here are some types of consumer documents and the elements, or types of information, that each document provides:

- **product information**—descriptions of what the product will do
10 - **instruction manual**—information on how to use the product, often including safety information and any directions required for installation
- **warranty**—details of company and owner responsibilities if the product does not work

COMMON CORE  RI 4

**Language Coach**

**Multiple Meanings**
The noun *manual* in line 10 has a **technical** meaning—that is, a meaning specific to a specialized field, such as electronics. Its technical meaning here is "a guide or reference book." (As an adjective, *manual* has a more general, everyday meaning: "done or used with the hands.") What is the technical meaning of the word *console* as it is used in line 2? Use a dictionary for help if necessary.

---

## DIFFERENTIATED INSTRUCTION

### FOR ENGLISH LANGUAGE LEARNERS

**Language Coach**   COMMON CORE RI 4

**Multiple Meanings  *Possible answer:*** Students should note that in a technical context, the noun *console* refers to a piece of equipment on which switches or other controls are located. Prompt students to recognize that as a verb *console* means to comfort someone who is upset or sad. If students are unfamiliar with either meaning, encourage them to check a dictionary.

### FOR STRUGGLING READERS

**Build Vocabulary**  Help students to use each vocabulary term in a sentence:

*itemize:* to specify the items of something (line 14); *safeguard:* a precaution or protection (page 623); *ventilation:* allowing air to get to something (page 623); *warrant:* to guarantee the quality (line 5, p. 624); *defect:* a flaw, imperfection, or weakness (line 6, p. 624 )

Consumer documents itemize, or detail, the unique **features** of each
15    product. Here are some samples.

## Product Information Ⓐ

| WYSIWYGAME ARTS | | |
|---|---|---|
| | CPU | 800MHz |
| | Video card | 250 MHz GPU |
| | Resolution | 1920 × 1080 maximum |
| | Memory | 128 MB |
| | Storage | Memory Card—Hard Drive |
| | Sound card | 64 Channels |
| | DVD | Yes |
| | Media | 12 × DVD-ROM 6.2 GB Capacity |
| | Hard drive | 8 GB |
| | Modem | Yes |
| | Ethernet port | Yes |
| | Controllers | 4 |

## Safety Information

Please follow these safeguards regarding the installation and use of your game console:

1. When installing your game console, be certain that the unit receives proper ventilation. Vents in the console covering are provided for this purpose. Never block or cover these vents with any objects, such as fabric, books, or magazines.
2. Do not install your game console in a bookcase or entertainment rack where it cannot receive proper ventilation.
3. Do not place the game console in direct sunlight or near a heat source, such as a radiator or hot-air duct.
4. Do not set the game console on a soft surface, such as a bed, sofa, or rug, since doing so may result in damage to the appliance.
5. Unplug this appliance from the wall outlet and contact a qualified service person under the following conditions:
   a. The power-supply cord or plug is damaged.
   b. Liquid has been spilled on, or objects have fallen into, the game console.
   c. The game console has been exposed to rain or water.
   d. The game console does not operate normally after you follow the operating instructions.
   e. The game console has been dropped, or the cabinet has been damaged.
   f. The game console exhibits a distinct change in performance.

*Do not attempt to service this product yourself. Opening or removing the outside covers may expose you to dangerous voltage or other hazards. All service must be done by qualified service personnel.* Ⓑ

**Ⓐ ADJUST READING RATE**
If you are seriously considering buying a video computer game, you should slow down and pay careful attention to the data listed in this table. If you want a game console with 128 MB of memory and 10 GB of hard-drive space, does this product have what you need? Explain.

**Ⓑ CONSUMER DOCUMENTS**
This page from an instruction manual lists safety information. How is the safety information organized for ease of use by readers?

---

**READING STRATEGY**

**Ⓐ Model the Skill: ADJUST READING RATE**

Model the skill of slowing your reading rate to check the specifications of the console by asking yourself a question and then thinking out loud as you read the table to find the answer. For example, say, "I need a console with four controllers. Does this one have what I need? Yes, according to the last row in the spec table."

*Answer:* No, the product does not have what I need. The WYSIWYGame Arts console has only an 8 GB hard drive, and I want 10 GB of hard drive space.

**TEXT ANALYSIS**    COMMON CORE   RI 5, RI 6

**Ⓑ Model the Skill: CONSUMER DOCUMENTS**

Ask students to explain why reading the safety information that comes with a product is especially important. Lead them to understand that many products use electricity, which can be dangerous or fatal if used improperly.

*Possible answer:* The safety information is organized in a numbered and lettered list. It's easier to understand each safeguard when they are separated into individual warnings instead of being lumped together in one long paragraph.

**FOR STRUGGLING READERS**
**Develop Reading Fluency** Point out to students that reading a difficult instruction aloud and emphasizing key points is a way to increase understanding. Model reading some of the numbered points in the safety information the way you would if you were trying to emphasize certain points. For example, you might read, "DO NOT INSTALL your game console in a BOOKCASE or ENTERTAINMENT RACK where it CANNOT RECEIVE PROPER VENTILATION."

**FOR ADVANCED LEARNERS/PRE–AP**
**Analyze** Have students read the safety information under number 5 and the italicized note following point 5. Then have them suggest possible reasons why the manufacturer recommends contacting a qualified service person under so many different circumstances. *Possible answer: Most of the circumstances need a professional repair and the company is afraid users will cause harm to themselves or to the unit if they try to fix it themselves.*

## C CONSUMER DOCUMENTS

**Possible answer:** *Key disclaimers: The warranty extends only to the original purchaser or recipient of the product as a gift by the original purchaser. The warranty against defects in materials and workmanship is good only for 90 days. For replacement during this time, you must return the product to the place of purchase.*

READING STRATEGY

## D ADJUST READING RATE

**Possible answers:** *You install or operate the product incorrectly; you don't send in the warranty card or it doesn't reach the company within the time specified.*

## SELECTION WRAP–UP

**READ WITH A PURPOSE** Now that students have finished reading the selection, have them share their tips on how to become a more effective user of consumer documents.

⭐ **CRITIQUE** Have students discuss why it is important to read and understand consumer documents.

---

## WARRANTY

### Limited Warranty

WYSIWYGame Arts makes the following limited warranties. These limited warranties extend to the original consumer purchaser or any person receiving this product as a gift from the original consumer purchaser and to no other purchaser or transferee.

### Limited Ninety [90] Day Warranty

5   WYSIWYGame Arts warrants this product and its parts against defect in materials and workmanship for a period of ninety [90] days after the dated or original retail purchase. During this period, WYSIWYGame Arts will replace any defective product or part without charge to you. For replacement you must deliver the entire
10   product to the place of purchase. C

### Limited One [1] Year Warranty of Parts

WYSIWYGame Arts further warrants the parts of this product against defects in materials or workmanship for a period of one [1] year after the date of original retail purchase. During this period, WYSIWYGame Arts will replace a defective part without charge to
15   you, except that if a defective part is replaced after ninety [90] days from the date of original purchase, you pay labor charges involved in the replacement. You must also deliver the entire product to an authorized WYSIWYGame Arts service station. You pay all transportation and insurance charges for the product to and from the
20   service station.

### Owner's Manual and Warranty Registration

Read the owner's manual thoroughly before operating this product. WYSIWYGame Arts does not warrant any defect caused by improper installation or operation. Complete and mail the attached registration card within fourteen [14] days; the warranty is effective only if your
25   name, address, and date of purchase are on file as the new owner of a WYSIWYGame Arts product. D

**C CONSUMER DOCUMENTS**
Important features of warranties include **disclaimers—** exceptions and special conditions placed upon how the warranty is upheld. What disclaimers do you find in these first two paragraphs (lines 1–10)?

**D ADJUST READING RATE**
Given the many disclaimers and important details in the warranty, you may want to go back and read it again. After rereading the warranty *slowly,* think of a circumstance under which your warranty might end up being invalid.

---

## *DIFFERENTIATED INSTRUCTION*

### FOR ENGLISH LANGUAGE LEARNERS

Have students use these sentence frames to write a warranty claim letter to the manufacturer of the game console.

I bought ___ on ___.

The problem with the product is ___.

I would like you to ___ and ___.

You can contact me at ___.

### FOR STRUGGLING WRITERS

Have students make a list of questions they would like to ask about this warranty. To get the list started, suggest this question: *What percentage of consoles need service during the 90-day warranty period?* After students have listed several more questions, have them discuss how the answers to these questions might affect their decision to purchase the product or not.

## Comprehension

1. **Recall** What types of information does a warranty provide?

2. **Clarify** What should you do if your WYSIWYGame Arts console malfunctions?

3. **Summarize** What time limits does the WYSIWYGame Arts console's warranty impose?

## Text Analysis

● 4. **Analyze Reading Rate** While reading these consumer documents, when did you find yourself speeding up? When did you find yourself slowing down? Explain why you adjusted your reading rate when you did.

5. **Draw Conclusions** Consider the safety information you read about the WYSIWYGame Arts console. For what age group might this game be appropriate? Use evidence from the document to support your conclusion.

● 6. **Evaluate Consumer Documents** Is the information in these consumer documents well-organized and easy to understand? What features of the documents are intended to help them accomplish their purpose? Support your answer with examples from the documents.

7. **Synthesize Information** Suppose that you were comparing the WYSIWYGame Arts console with a competing product. Some of that product's features are listed in the left column in the graphic below. Complete the graphic by filling in the corresponding features of the WYSIWYGame Arts console.

| CompuBlaze Designz Console | WYSIWYGame Arts Console |
|---|---|
| CPU: 820MHz | |
| Hard drive: 4 GB | |
| Memory: 256 MB | |
| Media: 8 X DVD-ROM 62 GB capacity | |
| Length of warranty: Limited six-month warranty on parts and service | |

### Why are FUNCTIONAL texts necessary?

How are they different from other things you read?

**7.**

| CompuBlaze Designz Console | WYSIWYGame Arts Console |
|---|---|
| CPU: 820MHz | CPU: 800MHz |
| Hard drive: 4 GB | Hard drive: 8 GB |
| Memory: 256 MB | Memory: 128 MB |
| Media: 8 X DVD-ROM 6.2 GB capacity | Media: 12 X DVD-ROM 6.2 GB capacity |
| Length of warranty: Limited six-month warranty on parts and service | Length of warranty: Limited ninety-day warranty on parts and service; limited one-year warranty on parts |

### Why are FUNCTIONAL texts necessary? *Possible answer:*

*They explain how to perform certain tasks; they give us information needed to use products.*

For preliminary support of post-reading questions, use these copy masters:

**R** RESOURCE MANAGER—Copy Master
Consumer Documents p. 143
Question Support p. 147
Additional selection questions are provided for teachers on page 138.

### ANSWERS

## Comprehension

1. *Details of the company's responsibilities if the product malfunctions.*

2. *Unplug it and call a professional service technician.*

3. *The limited warranty on parts and workmanship is good for ninety days. The limited warranty on parts, with a charge for labor beyond ninety days, is good for one year. You must mail in your warranty registration card within fourteen days.*

## Text Analysis

COMMON CORE  RI 5, RI 6

**COMMON CORE**
RI 5 Analyze how an author's ideas are developed and refined.
RI 6 Determine an author's purpose in a text.

*Possible answers:*

4. **Analyze Reading Rate** *Answers may vary. Students might say that they slowed down when they needed to read something carefully to understand it or when they were looking for specific information.*

5. *I think this game console is appropriate only for people age 10 and older. Its safety precautions are very detailed, and younger children might have a hard time following safe practices while using the console.*

6. ● **COMMON CORE FOCUS** *Evaluate Consumer Documents* Answers will vary. *Possible answer: I think the documents are very well organized. The numbered lists and boldface headings make the documents easy to navigate when you're looking for particular information. The fact that the technical specifications are in a chart also helps the documents convey information clearly.*

# Assess and Reteach

### Assess

**DIAGNOSTIC AND SELECTION TESTS**
Selection Tests A, B/C pp. 167–170

**Interactive Selection Test** on **thinkcentral.com**

### Reteach

**Level Up Online Tutorials** on **thinkcentral.com**

### Adding Graphics to Your Web Site
Technical Directions

### SUMMARY

This selection provides step-by-step instructions for adding graphics to a Web site.

## What features make instructions **USEFUL?**

After students haves completed the *DISCUSS* activity, have students describe personal experiences with technical instructions. What kinds of problems have they encountered? What advice would they give to people reading technical instructions?

# What features make instructions **USEFUL?**

You often follow directions when you cook, participate in sports, play music, or dance. When you're dealing with technology, however, following directions carefully is essential. You can sometimes improvise in the kitchen or on the dance floor, but missed steps during a technical task can cause a device to malfunction and may even damage it.

*DISCUSS* Suppose that you were building a home on a desert island. What technical directions or instruction manuals would you find useful? What features would you expect them to have? Share your thoughts with a small group of classmates.

626

*See resources on the* **Teacher One Stop DVD-ROM** *and on* **thinkcentral.com**.

 **RESOURCE MANAGER UNIT 5**
  Plan and Teach, pp. 149–154
  Summary, pp. 155–156†‡*
  Text Analysis and Reading
    Skill, pp. 157–160†*

**DIAGNOSTIC AND SELECTION TESTS**

  Selection Tests, pp. 171–174

**TECHNOLOGY**
  🔘 **Teacher One Stop DVD-ROM**
  🔘 **Student One Stop DVD-ROM**
  🔘 **GrammarNotes DVD-ROM**
  🔘 **ExamView Test Generator**
    on the **Teacher One Stop**

* Resources for Differentiation     † Also in Spanish     ‡ In Haitian Creole and Vietnamese

## TEXT ANALYSIS: TECHNICAL DIRECTIONS

Instructions for using computers as well as other scientific, mechanical, and electronic products and activities are called **technical directions.** You follow technical directions when you read instructions on how to do an experiment in a chemistry lab, fix a flat tire on your bicycle, program the remote control for your television, operate your new microwave oven, or install software on your computer. Technical directions may seem complicated at first, but if you pay attention and follow each step carefully, you can accomplish the task. You will also need to make sure you understand any technical terms used in the directions, so use context clues or a dictionary to help you. Keep these tips in mind as you read "Adding Graphics to Your Web Site."

## READING STRATEGY: SKIM AND SCAN

These skills can help you when you first encounter any kind of informational document.

- **Skimming** helps you get an overview of the document. You glance at titles, heads, subheads, and graphics and read the first line or two of each paragraph to get a general idea of what information is provided, what order it is in, and how it might be connected.

- **Scanning** helps you locate information in the document. You search for boldface or italic terms, technical and quantitative data in graphics, particular terms in headings, and other important details for specific pieces of information.

As you read the directions that follow, skim to get the general idea and scan to find specific information. In your *Reader/Writer Notebook*, you can record the general idea and the specific details you find in a chart like the one below.

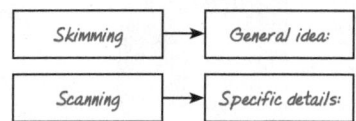

 Complete the activities in your **Reader/Writer Notebook.**

## Background

### Digital Photography

Can you imagine a world without pictures? People have been creating images since the days of cave paintings, but today, photographs shape the way we document history, relive personal memories, and learn about places we've never visited. The technology that made photographic images possible evolved in simpler forms for hundreds of years, but it wasn't until the late eighteenth century that photography truly came into being. Now, new technology is again revolutionizing how we create—and what we can do with—images.

Digital cameras record images not as light signatures on film but as files on rewritable media. The images can be viewed instantly, without the need for developing, and the image files can be easily transferred to a computer. Thus, professionals and novices alike can use software to edit pictures in ways ranging from simple touch-ups and adjustments to beautiful artistic re-renderings.

### Web Presence

Nowadays, it may seem as if everyone has a Web page, blog (Web log), or profile on a social-networking site. In reality, Internet access is far from universal. As more and more young people gain access to the Internet, however, they continually find new ways to let their personalities shine in cyberspace. Adding photographs to Web sites is an easy way to personalize your little corner of the Internet.

ADDING GRAPHICS TO YOUR WEB SITE **627**

## Teach

TEXT ANALYSIS — COMMON CORE RI 3, RI 4

### ● Model the Skill: TECHNICAL DIRECTIONS

Describe for students a problem you have had with understanding a set of technical directions. Explain the techniques or problem-solving steps you used to eventually apply them (for example, "dividing and conquering," rereading, taking notes).

**GUIDED PRACTICE** Have volunteers share their own problem-solving tips on understanding technical directions.

### READING STRATEGY

### ■ Model the Skill: SKIM AND SCAN

- To model the skill of *skimming* text, skim the text on pages 628–629, calling out the title, heads, subheads, and content of the graphics. Read the first line or two of several paragraphs so students can see the technique described in action.

- To model the skill of *scanning* text, and to differentiate it from skimming, announce that you are scanning the text on pages 628–629 to find out quickly at what percentage of the original you should scan your image. Model looking for a percentage symbol as a way of quickly locating this information.

**GUIDED PRACTICE** Have students scan the information on page 629 to find out what resolution the text recommends.

**R** RESOURCE MANAGER—Copy Master Skim and Scan p. 159 (for student use while reading the selection)

## DIFFERENTIATED INSTRUCTION

### FOR ENGLISH LANGUAGE LEARNERS

Provide these sentence frames to help students practice skimming and scanning text:

After skimming the text, I learned the general idea is ___.

A specific detail I found by scanning is ___.

I found these details by scanning the ___.

### READ WITH A PURPOSE

*Help students set a purpose for reading. Tell them to look for information they could use to describe the format, or general organizational structure, of technical directions.*

### Ⓐ SKIM

**Possible answer:** *A quick read reveals that the document gives instructions for editing an image so that you can add it to a Web site.*

**Extend the Discussion** Have students fill in the top right column of their Reading Strategy graphic organizers with the general idea of what the selection is about, based on skimming the entire selection. Have students share their general idea statements with the class. *Possible answer: Skimming the selection reveals that it tells how to add graphics to a Web site.*

### Ⓑ ANALOGY

**Possible answer:** *A scanner is like a copy machine, but instead of printing what it "copies," it saves the image to your computer.*

Tell students that analogies often contain the words *is, like,* or *a.* Have them state other analogies about the scanner or another technical device they are familiar with. If necessary, write this sentence frame on the board: A ___ is like a ___.

---

Ⓐ **SKIM**
What does a quick read of the title, first paragraph, and first graphic tell you about the topic of this document?

Ⓑ **ANALOGY**
An **analogy** is a comparison between two things to show how they are alike, as in this example: *The new robot is like a spider, using its eight titanium legs to crawl over obstacles.* An analogy is a useful way of describing something when the comparison is to something else well-known and more easily understood. What is a scanner? Create your own analogy to describe a scanner and what it does. Continue reading these instructions first if necessary.

---

# Adding Graphics to Your Web Site

The following technical directions show how to scan, edit, and save an image for your Web site using a made-up photo-editing program called FotoEdit. The directions assume you have a scanner and it is set up properly to work with your computer. Reading through these instructions will make you
5  familiar with the process of following **technical directions** so that when you choose your own picture-editing program, you'll have no trouble getting the results you want. Ⓐ

### Setting Up

1. Make sure the scanner is turned on.
2. Place your image in the scanner. The image should lie face down on the
10    glass, aligned according to the page-size indicators on the scanner. Ⓐ
3. Open up the FotoEdit program.

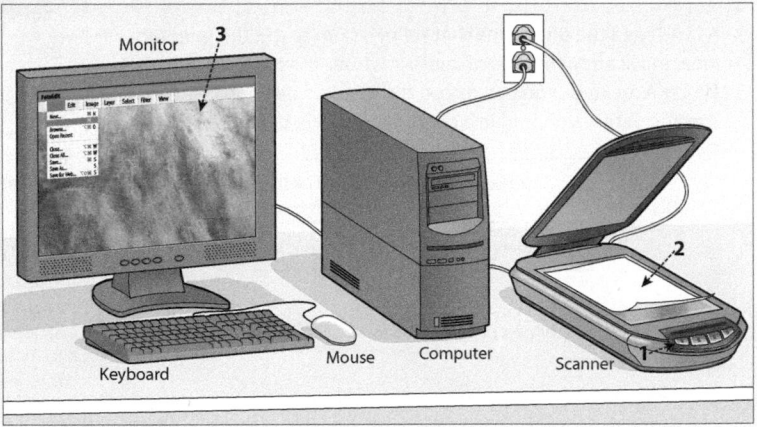

Monitor · 3 · Keyboard · Mouse · Computer · Scanner

---

## DIFFERENTIATED INSTRUCTION

### FOR STRUGGLING READERS

Pair a more-proficient and a less-proficient student. Have pairs each bring to class some technical directions from products they own. Have them create a list of three questions they expect to have answered by the directions. Then have them work together to read the directions and find answers to the questions.

**Develop Reading Fluency** Remind students that reading a difficult instruction aloud, to emphasize key points, is a way to increase understanding. Model reading steps 4 and 5 the way you would if you were trying to emphasize certain points. For example, give extra emphasis to the terms printed in boldface and the capitalized terms. Then ask volunteers to read the same steps as if they were reading them aloud to a person carrying out the steps.

## Scanning

4. In FotoEdit, under the File menu, choose Import; then select your scanner's name under the list of options. This will open up a scanning dialogue box within FotoEdit. A preview of your picture will also appear. **Do not remove original image from the scanner.**

5. With the cursor, select the area of the image you want scanned.

6. Set the size and resolution of the image. In general, scan your image at a larger size than the original (such as 200%) to provide more options for editing later on. For Web use, it is best to set the resolution to 72 dpi (dots per inch).

7. Click on SCAN. Your image will now open as an untitled document in FotoEdit, ready to be edited.

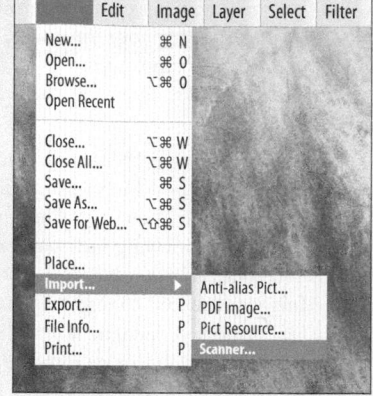

 **TECHNICAL DIRECTIONS**

Why is the statement in lines 18–19 boldface?

---

**COMMON CORE RI 4**

**Language Coach**

**Acronyms** In technical writing, you'll often encounter **acronyms**, initials used to stand for words. Sometimes they'll be defined—as "dpi" is in line 27. Often, if they are not defined, you may need to look them up in a current dictionary to determine their meanings. For example, look up the definition of the technical acronym CPU.

---

---

##  Model the Skill: SCAN

Tell students that if you wanted to find tips on image size when scanning, you would scan the section with the boldface head "Scanning."

**Possible answer:** *The image width and height in the first graphic (800 pixels x 600 pixels) would probably catch my eye. I would stop and read step 9 carefully because it provides in-depth information about the editing process.*

## TECHNICAL DIRECTIONS

**Possible answer:** *The graphic illustrates the menus that are verbally described in the saving instructions. The graphic would help you find the File menu and Save As option if you didn't already know where they were.*

## SELECTION WRAP–UP

**READ WITH A PURPOSE** Now that students have finished reading the selection, have them describe the general format of technical directions. **Possible answer:** *These, like many other sets of technical directions, reflect the order in which the steps are done.*

⭐ **CRITIQUE** Have students discuss with a partner the qualities that make technical instructions easy to understand. Then discuss with the class ways students can incorporate these qualities into their own writing.

---

## SCAN

If you were scanning through the directions to find out how to resize an image, what data in a graphic on this page would catch your attention? What steps would you be sure to read carefully?

## TECHNICAL DIRECTIONS

How does the graphic above help you understand the directions for saving that follow?

---

### Editing

30  8. You may now perform any number of edits to ready your image for Web use. You can crop, adjust the color, retouch, and sharpen the image in FotoEdit.

35  9. In order to resize the image, you must decide how big you want it to appear on the Web page. First, make sure you are viewing the image at 100% (actual size). Next, go to the

40  Image menu and choose the Image Size option. A dialogue box will open. If you want your image to be large, you may set the pixel size to 800 width × 600 height. If you would like your image to be a thumbnail size, set the width to a size of around 180 pixels. If the "Constrain proportions" option

45  is enabled in this box, the image height will be set automatically.

10. Once you have entered the desired values, hit OK. You will now see the resized image.

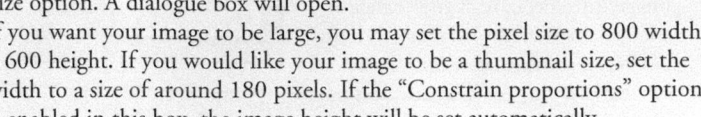

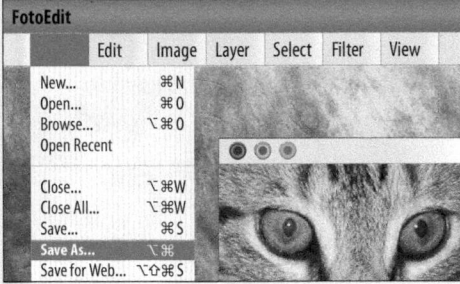

### Saving

11. When you are satisfied with the way your image looks, go to the File menu and select Save As.

50  12. When you name your file, be sure not to exceed 31 characters, including the file extension.

13. Choose JPEG under file format (a JPEG is a compressed version of the file, suitable for Web use). When saving an image as a JPEG, you will have the option of setting the image quality and file size. For the Internet, it is best

55  to choose a "medium" setting for these options.

14. Click OK. Your image is now ready to be uploaded onto your Web site.

---

## DIFFERENTIATED INSTRUCTION

### FOR ENGLISH LANGUAGE LEARNERS

Have students work in a group to discuss changes they would have to make to these technical directions if they were teaching an older relative how to edit photos on a computer. What background might they need to provide? Which terms would be unfamiliar? Which skills would have to be taught or reviewed?

### FOR ADVANCED LEARNERS/PRE-AP

Have students create a set of technical directions, complete with graphics, for a common procedure such as making popcorn, shooting a free throw in basketball, or using a personal music player. Have students share their directions with the class, explaining the reasons for the choices they made in creating the document.

## Comprehension

1. **Recall** To what resolution should you set an image for Web use?

2. **Clarify** What units are used in the measurement of resolution?

## Text Analysis

● 3. **Follow Technical Directions** After you have placed your image in the scanner and opened up FotoEdit, what are the first two things you should do in order to scan the image? What will appear on your screen after you do so?

◗ 4. **Skim and Scan** Go back and scan the directions for graphics that show functions available from the File menu. Does either graphic include content that the other does not? Explain.

5. **Make Inferences** When might you want to check the "Constrain proportions" option in the Image Size dialogue box? What does the word *proportions* refer to? Support your inferences with details from the document.

6. **Draw Conclusions** What organizational pattern did the writer of these directions follow? Explain.

### READING-WRITING CONNECTION

| WRITING PROMPT | REVISING TIP |
|---|---|
| **Extended Constructed Response: Technical Directions** Write directions that explain how to perform a task that involves a machine or a tool. You may, for example, choose to write instructions for sending a text message on a cell phone, using a compass, or tuning up your bicycle. | Review your response. Is the purpose of your document clear? Are the steps easy to follow? Add transitional words such as *next*, *then*, and *finally* to clarify the order of your steps. Also, consider adding helpful sketches to your instructions if they are particularly complex. |

Instructions for How to . . .
1.
2.
3.
4.

## What features make instructions USEFUL?

How can you clarify confusing instructions?

ADDING GRAPHICS TO YOUR WEB SITE    631

# Practice and Apply

For preliminary support of post-reading questions, use these copy masters:

 **RESOURCE MANAGER—Copy Master**
Technical Directions p. 157
Question Support p. 161
Additional selection questions are provided for teachers on page 152.

## ANSWERS

### Comprehension

1. *The document recommends a resolution of 72 dpi for images intended for Web use.*

2. *Resolution is measured in dpi, or dots per inch.*

### Text Analysis

COMMON CORE RI 3, RI 4

*Possible answers:*

3. ● **COMMON CORE FOCUS** *Follow Technical Directions You should choose Import from the File menu and then select your scanner's name. A scanning dialogue box and a preview of your picture will appear on your screen after you do so.*

4. *Skim and Scan Yes; the first graphic includes more of the File menu, including the Import option and its menu. The second graphic includes a window with an image of a cat.*

5. *You would want to check the "Constrain proportions" box when you don't want to adjust the height after inputting the width. Proportions refers to the ratio of height to width. The document says that "the image height will be set automatically." This probably keeps the height-width proportion the same as the original.*

6. *The writer of these directions organized the steps by the order in which they should be performed. The steps are listed numerically throughout, so clearly they should be performed in the order the numbers suggest.*

# Assess and Reteach

## Assess

**DIAGNOSTIC AND SELECTION TESTS**
Selection Tests A, B/C pp. 167–170

**Interactive Selection Tests** on <u>thinkcentral.com</u>

## Reteach

**Level Up Online Tutorials** on <u>thinkcentral.com</u>

**READING-WRITING CONNECTION**    COMMON CORE W 2c, W 10

*Possible response:* To retrieve phone messages, press the "play messages" button on your answering machine. Then listen for instructions on how to save and delete messages.

What features make instructions **USEFUL?** *Possible answer: You can use graphics, numbers, arrange data in step-by-step lists, define unfamiliar terms, and make important information stand out in the text.*

# Focus and Motivate

**W 2a–f** Write informative/explanatory texts to convey ideas and information clearly through accurate selection and organization. **W 4** Produce clear and coherent writing. **W 5** Develop and strengthen writing as needed by planning, revising, editing, rewriting, or trying a new approach. **W 7** Conduct research to answer a question or solve a problem. **W 10** Write routinely over shorter time frames for a range of tasks, purposes and audiences. **L 1b** Use various types of phrases and clauses to convey specific meanings and add variety and interest to writing. **L 2** Demonstrate command of the conventions of standard English capitalization, punctuation, and spelling.

## WRITE WITH A PURPOSE

To help students identify with a business audience, ask them to list on the board what they know about the business world and the people who work in it. Help students differentiate between useful information and misleading stereotypes. Then, ask students to brainstorm the characteristics of language that would be appropriate for communicating with individuals in the business world.

## COMMON CORE TRAITS

Review the *COMMON CORE TRAITS* with students, focusing primarily on development of ideas and organization of ideas. Compare the list of traits with the rubric on page 640.

## ADDITIONAL TASKS

**Write to a Local Representative or City Council Member** Write a letter to a local government official about an issue that concerns you.
**Possible subjects:** need for a traffic light, improved public transportation, or a city-wide recycling program

**Write to a Businessperson** Write a letter to the manager of a local business to inquire about a part-time job and the qualifications for this job.
**Possible subjects:** local restaurants, music stores, or grocery stores

### Writing Online  THINK central

The following tools are available online at **thinkcentral.com** and on **WriteSmart** CD-ROM:
• **Interactive Graphic Organizers**
• **Interactive Student Models**
• **Interactive Revision Lessons**

---

## Writing Workshop
**INFORMATIVE TEXT**

# Business Letter

*Essential Course of Study* **ECOS**

You communicate every day with different people in different settings. Each act of communication is crafted for a specific audience with a specific purpose in mind. When you communicate in a workplace setting, the purpose is often to provide or inquire about information. In this workshop, you will write a business letter to request information from an organization.

 Complete the workshop activities in your **Reader/Writer Notebook**.

### WRITE WITH A PURPOSE

**WRITING TASK**
Write a **business letter** to an organization in which you explain your interest in the organization and request information for further action.

**Idea Starters**
• college or university regarding admission, financial aid, or scholarship requirements
• local business regarding an internship position
• organization that sponsors foreign exchange students or athletes

**THE ESSENTIALS**
Here are some common purposes, audiences, and formats for business letters.

| PURPOSES | AUDIENCES | FORMATS |
|---|---|---|
| • to provide information<br>• to request information | • employees of private, public, or government organizations<br>• clients of a particular business organization | • letters<br>• e-mails<br>• memoranda |

### COMMON CORE TRAITS

**1. DEVELOPMENT OF IDEAS**
• has a clearly stated **purpose**
• develops the letter with well-chosen and relevant **facts** and **examples,** limiting details to essential information
• has a **concluding section** that supports the information and expresses appreciation

**2. ORGANIZATION OF IDEAS**
• **logically organizes** information
• uses appropriate and varied **transitions** to link ideas
• has correct **formatting**
• includes the **contact information** for the sender and the recipient

**3. LANGUAGE FACILITY AND CONVENTIONS**
• maintains a **formal style** and **objective, respectful tone**
• uses **precise language** and **domain-specific vocabulary**
• includes **complex sentences**
• employs correct **grammar, mechanics,** and **spelling**

**Writing Online** **THINK central**
Go to **thinkcentral.com**.
KEYWORD: HML9N-632

---

## Writing Workshop Resources

**R** **RESOURCE MANAGER UNIT 5**
Plan and Teach pp. 163–166
Prewriting–Editing pp. 167–171
Writing Rubric p. 172
Speaking and Listening p. 173
Writing Support p. 174*

**BEST PRACTICES TOOLKIT**
Writing Template: Business Writing: Letter p. C41

**TECHNOLOGY**
⊘ **Teacher One Stop DVD-ROM**
⊘ **Student One Stop DVD-ROM**
⊘ **WriteSmart CD-ROM**
⊘ **GrammarNotes DVD-ROM**

**Writing Center on thinkcentral.com**

*See resources on the* **Teacher One Stop DVD-ROM** *and on* **thinkcentral.com**.

* Resources for Differentiation

# Planning/Prewriting

**COMMON CORE** **W 2a-f** Write informative/explanatory texts to convey ideas and information clearly through accurate selection and organization. **W 5** Develop and strengthen writing by planning. **W 7** Conduct research to answer a question or solve a problem.

## Getting Started

### CHOOSE AN ORGANIZATION

Consider your educational, career, and recreational interests and goals. Choose an organization that has something to offer you in expanding these interests or meeting these goals.

▶ **ASK YOURSELF:**

- Where would I like to work or complete an internship?
- Where might I obtain a grant or scholarship to pursue my studies or interests?
- What organization might I like to join as a member?
- What organization might sponsor me as a foreign exchange student, athlete, or something else?

### RESEARCH RELEVANT FACTS

Once you've determined an area of interest and a related organization, you need to locate the information that is already available regarding your topic.

As you research, be alert to **precise language** and **domain-specific terms** that are common to the field. For example, an organization involved with developing software would use technological terms and abbreviations that are specific to that field. You can use such language and terms to make a good impression and demonstrate your familiarity with the topic or field.

▶ **ASK YOURSELF:**

- What information is readily available on this topic via the organization's Web site?
- What do I already know about the organization's involvement with this topic?
- Do I know anyone who is involved with this organization that I might consult for additional information or cite as a reference?
- What work-related words, terms, and abbreviations are repeated as I research this organization?

### THINK ABOUT AUDIENCE AND PURPOSE

Once you've chosen an organization, you need to identify the person, the department, and the office location that deals with your area of interest. Consider your **purpose** as you research your **audience.**

▶ **WHAT DOES IT LOOK LIKE?**

| What department in this organization handles my area of interest? | YWW/Applications |
|---|---|
| Where is the office for this department located, including the mailing address? | Young Writers' Workshop 10902 Payne Ave. Raleigh, NC 27601 |
| Who is the manager of this department? | Evan Thomas |
| What is the e-mail address of this department or this manager? | EThomas@yww.org |

WRITING WORKSHOP **633**

## DIFFERENTIATED INSTRUCTION

### FOR ENGLISH LANGUAGE LEARNERS

**Language: Reinforce Business Terms** Write these terms on the board or label a transparency of a business letter. Review the terms with students, drawing attention to words with multiple-meanings.

- *heading:* text used to form the top of a letter
- *salutation:* words used in greeting
- *body:* main or central part of a letter
- *closing:* words used to say goodbye
- *signature:* handwritten name
- *tone:* writer's attitude toward the subject or audience expressed through word choice

---

# Teach

## Planning/ Prewriting

**COMMON CORE** **W 2a-f, W 5, W 7**

▶ *CHOOSE AN ORGANIZATION* Point out to students that as young adults in secondary school, there are many prospects now available to them, including employment and study abroad. Encourage students to use this assignment to investigate opportunities in which they have genuine interests.

▶ *RESEARCH RELEVANT FACTS* Remind students that business letters may both provide and request information. Suggest that students prepare two-column charts with the following headings: *Facts I Know* and *Questions I Have.* Tell students that they may use some of what they already know to provide background information in their introductions. They can use their questions to formulate specific requests.

Explain to students that showing an understanding of language that is common to the organization or business tells the recipient of the letter that the writer is either knowledgeable about the field, or has taken the time to do some preliminary research. Point out that familiarity with the language of the organization makes it more likely that the letter will be taken seriously. Caution students to be sure they are using precise language and domain-specific vocabulary correctly.

▶ *THINK ABOUT AUDIENCE AND PURPOSE* Tell students that the audience of a business letter is specific—usually a particular person or group. Often, writers do not personally know the letter's recipient. Ask students to think about how they generally introduce themselves to someone new. Will any of these traditional behaviors prove useful for letter writing?

**R** **RESOURCE MANAGER—Copy Masters**
Planning/Prewriting p. 167
Drafting p. 168
Revising and Editing p. 169–170
Ask a Peer Reader p. 171
Rubric p. 172
Writing Support p. 174

WRITING WORKSHOP **633**

## Planning/Prewriting *continued*

▶ **IDENTIFY WHAT YOU NEED TO KNOW**
Remind students that one purpose of their letters is to persuade the recipients to act by providing information or accepting them into a program, for example. Students should state their requests clearly and deliberately and then provide the reasons that the recipients should fulfill these requests.

▶ **EXPLAIN YOUR INTEREST** Make sure that students understand that background information provides the reader with a context for a writer's interest in an organization. It is also an opportunity to impress the reader with one's qualifications. Background information should be focused, succinct, and persuasive.

 **YOUR TURN** As students work on their planning charts, suggest that they add the rows for specific requests and explanation of interest. Students may also find it helpful to list domain-specific vocabulary, such as technical terms, in one section of their charts.

---

## Planning/Prewriting *continued*

### Getting Started

**IDENTIFY WHAT YOU NEED TO KNOW**
Once you've become familiar with the existing information, it's time to determine what you still want or need to know. Form a specific request, which will function the way a controlling idea, or thesis statement, does in an essay.

▶ **WHAT DOES IT LOOK LIKE?**

> *Specific Request:* Please accept me into the Young Writers' Workshop.

**EXPLAIN YOUR INTEREST**
Explain your interest in the field or subject of the organization to whom you are writing. Provide background information or relevant experience or coursework.

▶ **WHAT DOES IT LOOK LIKE?**

> *Explanation of Interest:* I enjoy reading and writing poetry both individually and collaboratively. My stepmother attended this writers' workshop. I would like to improve my writing skills through feedback

**PEER REVIEW** Describe to a peer the purpose and audience of your business letter. Then ask: What background information should I provide to explain my interest and capture the attention of my recipient?

**YOUR TURN** In your *Reader/Writer Notebook,* develop your writing plan. Record a brief description of the letter you want to write. Then, use a chart such as the one on page 633 to record contact information and the ideas that will make up the body of your letter. Consider the following tips as you outline your letter:

- Research as much information as possible about your audience, including facts about the organization, so that you can focus the body of the document and make the request as specific as possible. Additionally, you don't want to waste the audience's time by asking for information that may be readily available.
- Business letters are usually one page in length, which means that you must limit the details to essential or well-chosen facts and relevant information.
- List precise words and terms that are commonly used in the information you've researched about the organization. Refer to your list as you write and try to incorporate some of this domain-specific vocabulary.
- Because you are not likely to know the recipient of a business letter personally, use formal language, an objective, respectful tone, and standard formatting to make a good impression.

---

## DIFFERENTIATED INSTRUCTION

### FOR STRUGGLING WRITERS
**Letter Outlines** Provide students with business letter outlines that contain labels and write-on-lines for the following elements: heading, inside address, salutation, body, closing, and signature. Make sure that students understand the importance of proper formatting when writing business letters. The standardized format ensures that reader expectations are met. It also demonstrates the writer's professionalism.

### FOR ADVANCED LEARNERS/PRE-AP
**Extend Business Experience** Extend students' experiences with business communications by providing the following prompt:

Find a meeting you can attend. Consider groups in your community as well as local councils and school boards. Contact organizers to find out where and when the meeting will occur. Prepare a chart for notetaking that includes places for the following information: name of the organization, date of the meet-

ing, people in attendance, call to order, and business conducted. You may add or modify categories as needed.

# Drafting

**COMMON CORE**

W 4 Produce clear and coherent writing in which the development, organization, and style are appropriate to the task, purpose, and audience. L 2 Demonstrate command of the conventions of standard English capitalization.

The following chart shows a structure for organizing a clear and coherent business letter.

## Organizing Your Business Letter

**INTRODUCTION**
- Introduce yourself, and then provide relevant **background information** as necessary.
- State the **purpose** for writing the letter.

**BODY**
- Establish and maintain a **formal style** and **objective, respectful tone.** Avoid slang and casual language.
- Include **specific questions** or **requests** for information.
- Use a **business letter format.** (Refer to the model on pages 637–638.)
- Organize ideas in a **clear and logical** way.
- Include **precise language** and **domain-specific vocabulary** that shows your understanding of the organization or its work.
- Use appropriate and varied **transitions** to link ideas.

**CONCLUDING SECTION**
- Express **appreciation** to the recipient for reading your letter and honoring your request.

### GRAMMAR IN CONTEXT: CAPITALIZATION

Proper names, including names of organizations, competitions, awards, and programs, are capitalized. When proper names are abbreviated or referred to by acronyms, all the capital letters remain capitalized. *Abbreviations* are shortened forms of words that usually begin with a capital letter and end with a period. *Acronyms* are words created from the first or first few letters of several words in a name and are written with capital letters and no periods. For example, you may need to use abbreviations or acronyms as you refer to the names of states or organizations.

| Word Form | Examples |
|---|---|
| abbreviation | • Avenue > Ave.  • Corporation > Corp.  • Mister > Mr. |
| acronym | • Mothers Against Drunk Driving > MADD<br>• National Aeronautics and Space Administration > NASA<br>• Young Writers' Workshop > YWW |

**YOUR TURN**

Develop a first draft of your business letter, following the structure outlined in the chart above. As you write, make sure to keep the information purposeful, clear, and brief. Use abbreviations and acronyms as necessary, making sure to use capitalization correctly.

## FOR ENGLISH LANGUAGE LEARNERS

**Proper Nouns** Point out that proper nouns name specific items and are therefore capitalized. Present and explain the following examples:

- The avenue was cleaned.
- Jayme Avenue (or Ave.) was cleaned.
- The man gave me a quarter.
- Mister (or Mr.) Smith gave me a quarter.

## FOR STRUGGLING WRITERS

**Abbreviations and Acronyms** Tell students that one purpose of abbreviations and acronyms is to save typesetting space within a document. They also shorten sentences, allowing readers to focus on meaning. However, while abbreviations may be used without first writing out the terms, acronyms should be spelled out when first used. Frequently, writers include the acronym in parenthesis after the first use and then use the acronym only in subsequent citations: Mothers Against Drunk Driving (MADD).

# Practice and Apply

## Drafting

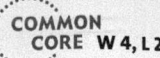

**COMMON CORE W 4, L 2**

▶ *INTRODUCTION* Help students differentiate between relevant and irrelevant background information by modeling how to characterize details. For instance, does a particular detail provide the reader with an example or an explanation that relates to the request? If so, it is relevant. If not, it may not be relevant and should be deleted.

▶ *BODY* Make sure that students understand that writers convey a tone or attitude through the words they choose and the details they include. If a writer uses words with negative connotations or includes unpleasant details, the writing will take on a negative tone. In this case, a negative tone reflects unfavorably on the writer. Explain that maintaining a formal style and an objective tone shows that the writer respects the recipient and the organization.

▶ *CONCLUDING SECTION* Remind students that the recipient has many job-related tasks on which to spend his or her time. The recipient is not necessarily required to read or respond to letters of inquiry. Therefore, it is appropriate for the writer to express appreciation and gratitude.

### GRAMMAR IN CONTEXT: CAPITALIZATION

For additional practice, have students rewrite the following sentences, using abbreviations, acronyms, and correct capitalization.

- Miss Lawton lives on Elm Street.
- Mister Petrocelli is in charge of Dynamo Corporation.
- Doctor Chen invites published poets to speak at Young Writer's Workshop.

**YOUR TURN**

Ask students to complete the *Your Turn* activity independently. Remind students to use abbreviations and acronyms accurately by employing correct capitalization. Suggest that students write their drafts double-spaced so that they can make revisions easily later.

For interactive revision tools, see

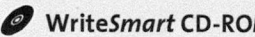

**WriteSmart CD-ROM**

**Writing Center on thinkcentral.com**

## Revising

**Model the Skill** Using a draft business letter on a transparency or electronic whiteboard, model how to use the questions, tips, and strategies suggested in the chart to evaluate and revise. You might use the letter of a student from another class or from a previous year. Make sure to remove the student's name from the letter so that the writer remains anonymous.

**YOUR TURN** Point out to students the value in working with different peer review partners during each writing workshop. Different people will offer different points of view with regard to improving one's writing. These varying points of view may prove invaluable. Tell students that if they choose to work with someone whom they do not know well, they should begin by learning their partners' names along with a few personal details. Students should also smile and treat their partners as friends. These strategies will facilitate a valuable working relationship.

For interactive revision tools, see

**WriteSmart CD-ROM**

**Writing Center on thinkcentral.com**

---

## Revising

As you revise, consider the content, tone, and formatting of your business letter. The goal is to determine if you've achieved your purpose and effectively communicated your ideas to the intended audience. The following chart will help you determine which parts of your draft need revising, rewriting, or a new approach.

### BUSINESS LETTER

| Ask Yourself | Tips | Revision Strategies |
|---|---|---|
| 1. Does the introduction provide relevant information about the writer's interest in the organization and purpose for writing? | ▶ **Bracket** information regarding the writer's interest in the organization. | ▶ **Add, delete,** or **revise** this information to keep the introduction purposeful, clear, and brief. |
| 2. Is the request for information clearly stated in the body? | ▶ **Place a box** around the request for information. | ▶ **Add** a request for information if necessary. |
| 3. Is precise language and domain-specific vocabulary used? | ▶ **Underline** precise language and domain-specific vocabulary. | ▶ **Add** precise language and domain-specific vocabulary as needed to show a knowledge of the field or organization. |
| 4. Does the concluding section express appreciation for the recipient's assistance in this matter? | ▶ **Circle** any statement of appreciation in the closing. | ▶ **Add** a sentence that thanks the recipient for taking the time to read and respond to the request. |
| 5. Is the tone objective and the language formal? | ▶ **Place an X** next to casual phrasing or slang. | ▶ **Use** formal language to reword any casual phrasing or slang. |
| 6. Is the letter formatted correctly? | ▶ **Put a check mark** next to each formatting element: sender's address, recipient's address, date, salutation, body, closing, and signature. | ▶ **Add** any elements that are missing. |

**YOUR TURN**  **PEER REVIEW** Exchange your business letter with a classmate, or read your letter aloud to a partner. As you read and comment on the letters, focus on content and formatting. Make sure to discuss whether the tone is objective and the language of the letter is clear and appropriate. If your business letter is not clear, use the revision strategies in the chart to clarify your writing or try a new approach.

---

## DIFFERENTIATED INSTRUCTION

### FOR STRUGGLING WRITERS

**Peer Review** Suggest that students work silently in pairs to review each other's drafts. Tell readers to record positive comments and constructive criticisms on sticky notes and to place them in appropriate locations on the letters. Tell students to commit themselves to four notes—two positive comments and two constructive criticisms. Remind students to use the language of the revision chart in composing their comments.

### FOR ADVANCED LEARNERS/PRE-AP

**Response and Revision** Tell students to read their partners' drafts as if they are addressed to the readers. Then, have students write letters of response to the writers, noting whether the purposes are clear and whether or not the letters are persuasive. Is the reader compelled to fulfill the writer's request? Why or why not? Encourage students to use the feedback in these letters of response to aid them in the revision process.

## ANALYZE A STUDENT DRAFT

Read this draft; notice the comments on its strengths as well as suggestions for improvement.

 **COMMON CORE** — **W 2e** Establish and maintain a formal style. **W 5** Develop and strengthen writing as needed by revising, editing, rewriting or trying a new approach.

James Kolditz
35 Oakdale Rd.
Morrisville, NC 27560

May 5, 2012

Evan Thomas
Young Writers' Workshop
10902 Payne Ave.
Raleigh, NC 27601

Dear Mr. Thomas:

**❶**    I love reading and writing poetry. I love to throw down rhymes with my stepmom. She's a Young Writers' Workshop alum. She told me some crazy stories. I would love to join the group.

> Using the **block-style format,** James includes the proper information in the header of his letter.

> In the introduction, James explains his **interest in the organization** and **establishes a personal connection** to the organization through his stepmother. However, some of the language is repetitive and informal. James should revise his letter to include formal language.

> In the introduction, James states his **purpose** for writing—to take part in the Young Writers' Workshop.

**LEARN HOW** Use Formal Language  To improve the effectiveness of his letter, James needs to revise the language to be more specific and more formal. This revision will also improve the style and tone of the letter. After all, James wants to make a good impression in order to reach his goal of being accepted into the workshop.

### JAMES'S REVISION TO PARAGRAPH ❶

~~I love reading and writing poetry. I love to throw down rhymes with my stepmom. She's a Young Writers' Workshop alum. She told me some crazy stories. I would love to join the group.~~

*Although I love reading and writing poetry as an individual, I also enjoy writing collaboratively with my stepmother, Tameka Williams. When my stepmother was a young woman. She attended the Young Writers' Workshop. Her stories have encouraged me, and I would very much like to take part in your poetry workshop.*

## ANALYZE A STUDENT DRAFT

Explain that the Student Draft on this page is the first half of a business letter. Model reading the draft and the annotations in blue, explaining that the yellow highlighting illustrates the student's language choices. Explain that the following *Learn How* mini-lessons provide helpful information about ways to improve this student draft as well as students' own drafts.

**LEARN HOW** Use Formal Language

- Explain to students that using formal language positively affects the tones of their letters.

- Lead students to discuss the differences in formality in the original draft and in James's revision.

- Point out that in revising, James replaces informal language that does not contribute to the formal tone he wants to establish.

### FOR ENGLISH LANGUAGE LEARNERS

**Understand Idioms and Slang**  Help students comprehend the language in the original student draft and understand why such informal language is inappropriate for business communications. Explain that idioms are expressions that hold meanings that are separate from the meanings of the Individual words and that slang is informal speech. Both types of language are inappropriate for business writing.

- *throw down rhymes:* compose or write poetry

- *alum:* abbreviated form of the word *alumnus* or *alumna,* which means "person who is a graduate of a particular school or program"

- *crazy:* used informally as an adjective to mean "wild or fantastic"

### FOR STRUGGLING WRITERS

**Revise Informal Word Choice**  Work as a class to generate a list of vague, informal words that regularly appear in students' writing. The list may include words and phrases such as *lots, a lot of, stuff, very, truly, great, awesome, things,* and *a while back.* Challenge students to think of more formal and precise language to use. Then, have students meet with partners. Together, they can review each other's drafts to find examples of the words and phrases on the list and either delete them or replace them with more formal and precise language.

## ANALYZE A STUDENT DRAFT *continued*

Explain that the Student Draft is continued and completed on this page. Read the draft and annotations aloud and discuss. Ask students to comment on the student writer's explanation of why he is a good candidate for the workshop.

---

**2**    At school, I like the poetry unit the most. I want to improve my poetry writing skills. The Young Writers' Workshop could help me develop my creativity and writing skills. At YWW, other students' opinions on the effectiveness of my work could be given to me. I cannot get this kind of feedback anywhere else.

**3**    Please send me the workshop application materials, including the deadline and the criteria for eligibility. I appreciate your help, and I am looking forward to the opportunity to join the group at YWW.

Sincerely,

*James Kolditz*

James Kolditz

In the body, James explains why he is a good candidate for the workshop. However, James can improve the effectiveness of his letter by using **active and passive tenses** appropriately.

James states his **request for information** that will help him achieve his goal.

Throughout the letter, James conveys an **objective** and **respectful tone**, ends on a cordial and appreciative note, and includes a **closing** and his **signature**.

---

 **LEARN HOW** Use Active and Passive Tenses

- Tell students that in order to change the passive voice to the active voice, they should ask the following question of each sentence: The action is performed by whom?

- Then, students should make this actor the subject of the sentence and alter the verb as necessary.

- If the actor is not clear, students may need to use context clues to determine the acting agent.

 **LEARN HOW** Use Active and Passive Tenses   When the subject of the sentence performs the action, the verb is in the **active** voice. When the subject is acted upon, the verb is in the **passive** voice. In most writing situations, the active voice is preferable because it is straightforward. However, a writer may choose the passive voice to focus on the action or the object receiving the action rather than the subject.

| Tense | Active Voice | Passive Voice |
|---|---|---|
| present | I want to improve my poetry writing skills. | My poetry writing skills will be improved. |
| past | I did not get this kind of feedback anywhere else. | This kind of feedback had not been given to me before. |
| future | I will get other students' opinions on the effectiveness of my work. | The effectiveness of my work will be evaluated by other students. |

**JAMES'S REVISION TO PARAGRAPH 2**

*I could get other students' opinions on the effectiveness of my work*

At YWW, ~~other students' opinions on the effectiveness of my work could be given to me.~~

**YOUR TURN** Ask students to complete the Your Turn activity independently. Remind students to focus on using active tenses.

**YOUR TURN** Use the feedback from your peers and teacher as well as the two "Learn How" lessons to revise your letter. Evaluate how clearly you have communicated your ideas to your audience.

**638**   UNIT 5: AUTHOR'S PURPOSE

---

## DIFFERENTIATED INSTRUCTION

### FOR ENGLISH LANGUAGE LEARNERS

**Illustrate Active and Passive Voice** Help students understand active and passive voices through the use of graphic representations. Use the following examples:
**Active Voice:** the subject performs the action
The boy wrote the story.
**Passive Voice:** the subject receives the action
The story was written by the boy.
Then, have student pairs create other examples. Have each pair present one example to the class.

### FOR STRUGGLING WRITERS

**Voice Shifts in Compound Sentences** Tell students to examine compound sentences for unneeded shifts in voice. Present the following example:

- The students provided valuable feedback, but it was difficult to apply.

- The students provided valuable feedback, but I found it difficult to apply.

Ask students to revise this example:

- I will get other students' opinions on the effectiveness of my work, and my work will improve. *(I will get other students' opinions on the effectiveness of my work, and I will improve my work.)*

## Editing and Publishing

In the editing stage, you check your business letter to make sure that it is free of grammar, usage, and punctuation errors. Also, read carefully to check for any spelling errors, even after doing a word-processing spell-check. These kinds of mistakes distract your audience from the content of your letter.

 **W 5** Strengthen writing by revising, editing, rewriting, or trying a new approach. **L 1b** Use various types of phrases and clauses to convey specific meanings and add variety and interest to writing. **L 2c** Spell correctly.

### GRAMMAR IN CONTEXT: COMPLEX SENTENCES

Before you edit and proofread for the final time, consider improving sentence structure to strengthen your letter. In James's draft, he uses a sentence fragment—a group of words that does not have a subject or a verb or that does not express a complete thought.

> *When my stepmother was a young woman.*
>
> [This sentence is a fragment because it does not express a complete thought. The word *when* is a **subordinating conjunction,** making this sentence a **dependent clause.**]

As James edits his letter, he recognizes the sentence fragment. He corrects the problem by creating a complex sentence.

> *When my stepmother was a young woman, she attended the Young Writers' Workshop.*

A dependent clause must be attached to an independent clause to form a complete sentence. This type of sentence is called a **complex sentence.** Notice that a comma follows a dependent clause that appears at the beginning of a complex sentence.

### PUBLISH YOUR WRITING

Consider these options for publishing your letter:

- Mail your letter to its intended recipient.
- E-mail your letter to its intended recipient.
- Sharpen your other business communication skills by writing an online professional profile.
- Publish a classroom book for secondary students that includes instructions for and models of work-related writing.

 **YOUR TURN** Proofread your business letter and correct any errors. Add variety to your sentence structures by including complex sentences. Make sure that each sentence has a subject and a verb and expresses a complete thought. Then, publish your letter for your audience.

### FOR ENGLISH LANGUAGE LEARNERS

**Sentence Fragments** Place a variety of clauses in one box and a variety of sentence fragments in another box. Have student pairs take turns drawing one item from each box. Then, ask students to create complex sentences by attaching the fragments to the clauses. Model this process for students ahead of time. Make sure that students understand that while the clauses may stand alone as sentences, the fragments may not.

### FOR STRUGGLING WRITERS

**Complex Sentences** Place a variety of silly clauses in two boxes. Have students take turns drawing a clause from each box. Then, have students use the subordinating conjunction word bank to form complex sentences. Tell students to write their complex sentences on the board. Lead the class to identify the relationship being expressed in each example.

---

## Practice and Apply

### Editing and Publishing

COMMON CORE W 5, L 1b, L 2c

#### GRAMMAR IN CONTEXT: COMPLEX SENTENCES

Provide students with a bank of subordinating conjunctions that they can use to form dependent clauses and complex sentences: *after, although, as, because, before, since, so, where, whether, while, unless.*

Point out that subordinating conjunctions and dependent clauses can be used to show the following relationships within a sentence: cause, choice, concession, condition, effect, location, and time. Using the words in the bank, provide students with a sample sentence for each condition.

- **Cause:** Danticat is happy *because* her niece was born.
- **Choice:** Danticat must decide *whether* she wants to protect *or* guide her niece.
- **Concession:** *Although* Danticat wants to protect her niece, she must allow the little girl to live her own life.
- **Condition:** Danticat will not be able to protect her niece *unless* she allows others to help.
- **Effect:** Danticat holds the baby *so* the mother can rest.
- **Location:** Danticat loves the library *where* she finds wisdom.
- **Time:** *After* Danticat visits the hospital, she goes to the library.

#### PUBLISH YOUR WRITING

Brainstorm with students additional ways to publish their business letters.

 **YOUR TURN** Allow students time to proofread their drafts. Remind them to create sentence variety by constructing complex sentences. A variety of sentence structures makes writing interesting for readers.

## Scoring Rubric

Tell students that the best way to understand a scoring rubric is to use it to score actual writing. Provide small student groups with models of business letters found online at state assessment Web sites. Have students use the rubric to score the models. Then, ask each group to present its model to the class, using the language of the rubric to explain its scoring. When all groups have presented, lead students to discuss how the state models compare and contrast with their drafts. The purpose of a rubric is to eliminate subjectivity from the scoring process.

For Rubric Bank, see

 **Write*Smart* CD-ROM**

**Writing Center on thinkcentral.com**

## Assess and Reteach

### Assess

**R** RESOURCE MANAGER—Copy Master
Rubric for Evaluation p. 172

**Online Essay Scoring at thinkcentral.com**

### Reteach

**Level Up Online Tutorials at thinkcentral.com**

**Reteaching Worksheets on thinkcentral.com**

Writing Lesson 10: Using Active and Passive Voice

Writing Lesson 31: Tone and Voice

## Scoring Rubric

Use the rubric below to evaluate your business letter from the Writing Workshop or your response to the on-demand task on the next page.

| BUSINESS LETTER | |
|---|---|
| **SCORE** | **COMMON CORE TRAITS** |
| **6** | • **Development** Has a compelling, clearly stated purpose; limits details to essential information; provides a strong concluding section that expresses appreciation<br>• **Organization** Has a logical organization; includes appropriate formatting; uses varied transitions; includes contact information<br>• **Language** Maintains a formal style and objective, respectful tone; uses precise language and domain-specific vocabulary; shows a strong command of conventions |
| **5** | • **Development** Competently states a purpose; includes mostly essential information; expresses appreciation in conclusion<br>• **Organization** Has a logical organization; includes appropriate formatting; uses transitions; includes contact information<br>• **Language** Uses precise words; generally maintains a formal style and objective, respectful tone; has a few errors in conventions |
| **4** | • **Development** Sufficiently states a purpose; includes some nonessential information; expresses appreciation<br>• **Organization** Has a mostly logical organization; some formatting is incorrect; needs a few more transitions; includes contact information<br>• **Language** Uses vague words in some places; mostly maintains a formal style and objective, respectful tone; includes a few distracting errors in conventions |
| **3** | • **Development** States the purpose for writing, but could be clearer; includes nonessential information; implies but does not state appreciation<br>• **Organization** Has some flaws in organization; some formatting is missing or incorrect; more transitions are needed; contact information is missing details<br>• **Language** Needs more precise words; has frequent lapses in style and tone; has some critical errors in conventions |
| **2** | • **Development** Weakly states the purpose for writing; much of the information is not essential; lacks expression of appreciation<br>• **Organization** Has organizational flaws; lacks formatting; important transitions missing; contact information incomplete<br>• **Language** Lacks precise words or uses them incorrectly; uses informal style and a personal tone; has many distracting errors in conventions |
| **1** | • **Development** Lacks a clear purpose for writing; question or request missing or unclear<br>• **Organization** Has no apparent organization; omits formatting and contact information<br>• **Language** Has an inappropriate style and tone; has major problems in conventions |

# Preparing for Timed Writing

**COMMON CORE** W 10 Write routinely over shorter time frames for a range of tasks, purposes, and audiences.

### 1. ANALYZE THE TASK    5 MIN

Read the task carefully, noting the type of writing, the topic, and the purpose.

> **WRITING TASK**
> *← Topic*
> You purchased an item that turned out to be defective. Your task is to write a
> *← Type of writing    ← Audience    ← Purpose*
> business letter to the (manufacturer) that explains the problem and requests that the item
> be replaced.

### 2. PLAN YOUR RESPONSE    10 MIN

The task requires that you explain the problem with the merchandise and that you request a specific outcome (that the defective merchandise be replaced). Use a graphic organizer to describe the problem. In addition, you will need to include the elements of a business letter: sender's address, date, recipient's address, salutation, body, closing, and signature. Use your imagination to create the company name, the product name, and the recipient's address.

| | |
|---|---|
| *Defective Element* | |
| *Steps Taken to Work Around Problem* | |
| *Effect of Not Having Problem Resolved* | |

### 3. RESPOND TO THE TASK    20 MIN

Begin drafting your letter. As you write, keep the following points in mind:

- Clearly state the problem with the device and provide supporting details. Make your request for a new device clear and reasonable.
- Maintain an objective, respectful tone through formal language.
- Follow the prescribed format for a business letter.

### 4. IMPROVE YOUR RESPONSE    5–10 MIN

**Revising**  Review your draft by comparing it with the task. Does your draft state the problem through explanation and supporting details? Does your draft make a clear request for a replacement? Is the tone of the letter objective and respectful? Does your draft follow correct formatting for a business letter?

**Proofreading**  Find and correct any errors in grammar, usage, mechanics, or spelling. Make sure that your letter is neatly written and legible.

**Checking Your Final Copy**  Before submitting your letter, examine it once more to make sure that you have done your best work.

---

## DIFFERENTIATED INSTRUCTION

### FOR ENGLISH LANGUAGE LEARNERS

**Transitions**  Have students work in small groups to generate lists of transitional words and phrases that they can use to show cause and effect in their letters, including *as a result, because, consequently, due to, since, so,* and *therefore*. Point out that many of these transitions can be used to create complex sentences, which will help students establish the smooth and logical flow cited in the rubric.

### FOR STRUGGLING WRITERS

**Structure First**  Suggest that students begin by developing the format or structure of the letter first, placing the required formatting elements and leaving space to add the body. This technique enables students to create their own templates for writing, which makes the task of writing in a timed situation less daunting.

---

## Preparing for Timed Writing

**COMMON CORE** W 10

1. **Analyze the Task**  Before students begin writing, encourage them to answer the following questions:
   - What is my time limit?
   - What are the key skills assessed in the scoring rubric?
   - Who is my audience?
   - What is my purpose?

2. **Plan Your Response**  Point out to students that the scoring rubric emphasizes the need for a clearly stated purpose for writing. Explain that in this case the purpose for writing is specified in the writing task: to make a request for a replacement item. Emphasize that by explaining the steps taken to work around the problem, students will support that request.

3. **Respond to the Task**  Remind students of the importance of expressing appreciation to the recipient of the letter. Point out that this type of polite and respectful gesture makes it more likely that their requests will be honored.

4. **Improve Your Response**  Point out that the scoring rubric emphasizes formatting and tone. Suggest that students use the formatting elements listed in step 2 as a checklist for reviewing their drafts. They can place small checkmarks next to each existing element and add any missing elements. Tell students to review their word choice to assess tone. To remain objective and respectful, students should revise any words with negative connotations.

## Assess

Use the Scoring Rubric on p. 640 to assess students' business letters.

## Focus and Motivate

**W 2a** Include formatting, graphics, and multimedia to aid comprehension. **W 6** Use technology to update individual writing products and display information flexibly and dynamically.

### PRODUCE WITH A PURPOSE

Ask students to think about the type of information that would interest business professionals and potential employers. Reinforce the purpose of creating a profile that will help students find employment, establish professional contacts, and network with colleagues.

### COMMON CORE TRAITS

As students plan their online professional profiles, remind them to keep in mind the *COMMON CORE TRAITS* of a strong profile.

## Practice and Apply

### Creating Your Profile

Students with limited work experience might struggle with identifying appropriate information to include in their profiles. Suggest that they focus their approach on attracting potential employers. Help students brainstorm to create a list of abilities that an employer might value, such as interpersonal or technical skills. Remind students to consider any experience gained through volunteer activities, community organizations, school projects, events, and coursework.

---

**Technology Workshop**

**Essential Course of Study ECOS**

# Creating an Online Professional Profile

Some Web sites blend business communications with social networking, allowing users to connect with people they know and with people their connections know. On sites like these, you can upload a résumé, network with others, join interest groups, and post recommendations from and for others. Joining a professional community can help you find a summer job or connect with future employers. In this workshop, you will learn how to create and update your own online professional profile.

 Complete the workshop activities in your **Reader/Writer Notebook**.

| PRODUCE WITH A PURPOSE | COMMON CORE TRAITS |
|---|---|
| **TASK**<br>Create an **online professional profile** for the purpose of networking, finding a job, and helping potential employers find you. | **A SUCESSFUL ONLINE PROFILE . . .**<br>• contains all relevant information for networking or job-seeking<br>• maintains a formal, professional tone<br>• includes formatting features, such as bullets and headings<br>• reflects current information through frequent updates |

COMMON CORE

**W 2a** Include formatting, graphics, and multimedia to aid comprehension. **W 6** Use technology to update individual writing products and display information flexibly and dynamically.

## Creating Your Profile

Most professional networking sites allow you to create a profile for free. After choosing a networking site, follow these guidelines to create a dynamic profile:

- **Open an Account** Follow the site's instructions to set up a username and password for your profile. Be sure to get your parents' and teacher's approval before choosing a site and opening an account.

- **Enter Your Information** Decide which details to provide, such as education, experience, and abilities. Be concise and clear, including only information that reflects your professional goals. If you want to work for a veterinarian, for example, highlight classes and volunteer experience that involve animals. Be sure to maintain a formal and professional tone.

- **Format Your Profile** Use headings and bullets to organize your information so that it is easy to read and scan. Common headings include *Education, Experience,* and *Skills.* If you include a photo of yourself, choose an appropriate one.

- **Publish Your Profile** Follow the site's instructions to publish your profile. Then invite other members to connect with you. You can also join groups that share your professional interests and ask people to write recommendations for you.

 Media Tools **THINK**central
Go to **thinkcentral.com**.
KEYWORD: HML9N-642

---

### FOR ENGLISH LANGUAGE LEARNERS

**Language: Reinforce Business Terms** Explain that like all business communications, an online profile should maintain a professional tone. This means that students should avoid slang and colloquial expressions and only use formal language. Write the following business terms on the board and review them with students:

- *colleagues:* coworkers
- *network:* to communicate with people for professional reasons, such as finding work
- *online profile:* a personal web page found on a professional networking site
- *qualifications:* the training and experience necessary to do a specific job

- *recommendation:* a written statement explaining why a person is qualified for a certain job
- *résumé:* a document that outlines a job applicant's education, experience, and professional skills

## Updating Your Profile

To make sure that your professional profile is as effective as possible, you must regularly update it to reflect any new skills, certificates, recommendations, or job titles you attain. Frequent updates will increase your chances of receiving a job inquiry or connection from a potential employer. Update your profile by logging in to the site and selecting the "Edit Profile" function. You might update the following sections of your profile:

| Profile Section | What to Update |
|---|---|
| **Contact Information** <br> Have you moved to another city or changed your email address? | If your contact information is not current, use the *Edit* function to update it. This allows potential connections or employers to contact you easily. |
| **Education** <br> Have you completed new courses, graduated from a school, or earned a certificate? | Completing courses and training programs can prepare you for a job which you wouldn't otherwise be qualified for. By adding these details to your profile, you increase your chances of finding a better job. |
| **Experience** <br> Have you learned a new skill, taken on more responsibility at school or at your job, or developed a new interest? | Every job requires a particular set of skills. Your computer proficiency or leadership abilities will appeal to employers looking for candidates with those skills. |
| **Connections** <br> Do you have any pending requests of people hoping to connect to your profile? | Co-workers and acquaintances may send requests, asking to be added to your professional network. You can accept or deny any requests you receive. |

 **YOUR TURN** Be sure to visit your online professional profile often. Write brief recommendations for connections whose talents and work you value. Recommendations should maintain a professional tone and highlight specific skills. Ask these connections to then write a recommendation for you.

### FOR STRUGGLING STUDENTS

**Organizing Profiles** Some students may have trouble organizing the information in their professional profiles. Distribute three index cards to each student. Have students write a label on each of their cards: *Education, Experience,* and *Skills.* Explain that they will use these headings to organize the information on their profiles. Then have students list relevant information on each card. For example, students could include their school name, relevant courses, GPA, and extracurricular activities on the *Education* card. Students can then refine the information from the index cards as they create their profile.

---

### Updating Your Profile

Model the process of updating an online profile with the following scenario: Explain that after setting up your profile, you earned a certificate in cooking and gained experience using a popular software program. Demonstrate how to update the information in the Education and Skills sections of your profile. Remind students that regularly updating their profiles can help them qualify for more jobs.

 **YOUR TURN** Have students work in pairs to write brief recommendations for each other. Remind them to focus only on the professional skills and talents that would interest a potential employer. For example, they might mention time-management or organizational skills, such as: *When Marisa was employed at Coffee Hut, she always completed her orders promptly and efficiently.*

## Assess and Reteach

### Assess

Use the *COMMON CORE TRAITS* to assess students' profiles.

A strong online professional profile
- includes effective formatting, graphics, and multimedia
- uses technology to update and display information

### Reteach

Some students may have trouble following the online instructions for setting up a professional profile. Model the first few actions and then have students try again.

**Media Tools**  THINK central

Keywords for using technology direct students to **MediaScope,** a Web site that helps them strengthen media analysis and production skills.

# Assessment Practice

COMMON CORE

## COMMON CORE FOCUS

**RI 2** Analyze development of a central idea over the course of a text. **RI 3** Analyze how the author unfolds an analysis or series of ideas or events. **RI 4** Determine the technical meaning of words as they are used in a text; analyze the cumulative impact of specific word choices on meaning and tone. **RI 5** Analyze how an author's ideas are developed and refined. **RI 6** Determine an author's point of view or purpose. **W 5** Strengthen writing by editing to ensure that it demonstrates the conventions of standard English grammar, usage, and capitalization. **L 4a** Use context as a clue to the meaning of a word. **L 6** Demonstrate independence in gathering vocabulary knowledge.

## CHECK READINESS

Read aloud the paragraph under **ASSESS** and stress to students that this is not the full Unit Test, but a way for them to check their readiness for it. Then have students examine the standards listed under **REVIEW** and look back in the unit or in the **Student Resource Bank** for any skills they need to review.

## READ THE TEXTS

Remind students to keep the unit goals in mind as they read each passage, paying particular attention to these literary elements and reading skills:

- author's purpose and tone
- textual organization

To help students focus on tone while reading, encourage them to ask questions such as

- How does the author's tone affect my understanding of the main ideas?

## ANSWER THE QUESTIONS

Direct students to pages R93–R101 of the **Handbook** to review test-taking strategies.

- When responding to multiple-choice items, tell students to maintain consistent pacing.
- Suggest that students place marks next to challenging items and return to these items for review if they have time.

**ASSESS**
Taking this practice test will help you assess your knowledge of these skills and determine your readiness for the Unit Test.

**REVIEW**
After you take the practice test, your teacher can help you identify any standards you need to review.

COMMON CORE

**RI 2** Analyze development of a central idea over the course of a text. **RI 3** Analyze how the author unfolds an analysis or series of ideas or events. **RI 4** Determine the technical meaning of words as they are used in a text; analyze the cumulative impact of specific word choices on meaning and tone. **RI 5** Analyze how an author's ideas are developed and refined. **RI 6** Determine an author's point of view or purpose. **W 5** Strengthen writing by editing to ensure that it demonstrates the conventions of standard English grammar, usage, and capitalization. **L 4a** Use context as a clue to the meaning of a word. **L 6** Demonstrate independence in gathering vocabulary knowledge.

Practice Test — THINK central
Take it at thinkcentral.com.
KEYWORD: HML9N-644

# Assessment Practice

**DIRECTIONS** Read the following texts, and then answer the questions.

## His Name Was Pete  *by William Faulkner*

1   His name was Pete. He was just a dog, a fifteen-months-old pointer, still almost a puppy even though he had spent one hunting season learning to be the dog he would have been in another two or three if he had lived that long.

2   But he was just a dog. He expected little of the world into which he came without past and nothing of immortality either:—food (he didn't care what nor how little just so it was given with affection—a touch of a hand, a voice he knew even if he could not understand and answer the words it spoke); the earth to run on; air to breathe, sun and rain in their seasons and the covied quail which were his heritage long before he knew the earth and felt the sun, whose scent he knew already from his staunch and faithful ancestry before he himself ever winded it. That was all he wanted. But that would have been enough to fill the eight or ten or twelve years of his natural life because twelve years are not very many and it doesn't take much to fill them.

3   Yet short as twelve years are, he should normally have outlived four of the kind of motorcars which killed him—cars capable of climbing hills too fast to avoid a grown pointer dog. But Pete didn't outlive the first of his four. He wasn't chasing it; he had learned not to do that before he was allowed on highways. He was standing on the road waiting for his little mistress on the horse to catch up, to squire her safely home. He shouldn't have been in the road. He paid no road tax, held no driver's license, didn't vote. Perhaps his trouble was that the motorcar which lived in the same yard he lived in had a horn and brakes on it and he thought they all did. To say he didn't see the car because the car was between him and the late afternoon sun is a bad excuse because that brings the question of vision into it and certainly no one unable with the sun at his back to see a grown pointer dog on a curveless two-lane highway would think of permitting himself to drive a car at all, let alone one without either horn or brakes because next time Pete might be a human child and killing human children with motorcars is against the law.

4   No, the driver was in a hurry: that was the reason. Perhaps he had several miles to go yet and was already late for supper. That was why he didn't have time to slow or stop or drive around Pete. And since he didn't have time to do that, naturally he didn't have time to stop afterward; besides Pete was only a dog flung broken and crying into a roadside ditch and anyway the car had passed him by then and the sun was at Pete's back now, so how could the driver be expected to hear his crying?

---

## DIFFERENTIATED INSTRUCTION

### FOR ENGLISH LANGUAGE LEARNERS

**Assessment Practice: Tone** Draw a two-column chart on the board. At the top of each column, write the following questions:

- How does the narrator feel about Pete the dog? How do you know?
- How does the narrator feel about the driver who kills Pete? How do you know?

Help students identify words and phrases from the story to support each of their re-sponses. Make sure that students understand that word choice reveals tone. For example, the narrator discusses Pete with positive phrases such as "earth to run on" and "air to breathe." The narrator describes the driver's behavior with negative phrases such as "in a hurry" and "didn't have time."

5    But Pete has forgiven him. In his year and a quarter of life he never had anything but kindness from human beings; he would gladly give the other six or eight or ten of it rather than make one late for supper.

# Dog Proves as Smart as Average Toddler    *by Margaret Munro*

1    A nine-year-old border collie with a 200-word "vocabulary" has provided scientific proof that dogs understand what their masters are saying, according to new research.

### Knows Word Meanings

2    Rico knows the meaning of about 200 words and can infer and remember the meaning of new ones with the same ability as very young children, according to a report published in the journal *Science* yesterday. Rico, who lives in Germany, can retrieve randomly chosen items from a collection of balls and toys. He understands requests to put toys in boxes and bring them to certain people.

3    He can also fetch, by name, objects that he has never seen before. A month after seeing them just once, he still remembered and fetched the new objects on demand, reported Julia Fischer and her colleagues with the Max Planck Institute for Evolutionary Anthropology.

### Makes Inferences

4    The scientists say Rico's abilities provide evidence that dogs are capable of a type of learning and inference that has long been considered the domain of humans.

5    "There are some things that some people believe are uniquely human, such as language acquisition," said Ms. Fischer. "Maybe it's not so special after all." She said dogs appear to have innate and superior word-learning skills, which could help explain why they are such popular pets.

6    One of Canada's leading dog experts is impressed.

7    "It doesn't surprise me, but it's wonderful someone actually set out and spent all the time to plug that stuff into [Rico's] mind," said Dr. Stanley Coren, a psychologist at the University of British Columbia who has written extensively about the intelligence of dogs.

**GO ON** ➡

## ITEM ANALYSIS

| COMPREHENSION AND WRITTEN RESPONSE | ITEMS | UNIT PAGES |
| --- | --- | --- |
| Tone | 1, 3, 10 | 569 |
| Author's Purpose | 4, 5 | 552–553, 591 |
| Textual Organization | 6 | 554–555 |
| Main Idea | 2, 7, 11 | 569 |

| VOCABULARY | ITEMS | UNIT PAGES |
| --- | --- | --- |
| Word Roots | 1, 2, 3, 4 | 576 |
| Context Clues | 5, 6, 7, 8 | 576 |

| WRITING AND GRAMMAR | ITEMS | UNIT PAGES |
| --- | --- | --- |
| Sentences | 1, 2, 4, 5 | 567 |
| Clauses and Descriptive Language | 3, 6 | 577 |

### Practice Test

On **thinkcentral.com** students can complete an interactive version of this practice test *and* receive remediation for the skills they have not yet mastered.

---

**FOR STRUGGLING READERS**

**Assessment Practice: Identify Main Ideas**
Remind students that nonfiction is generally organized according to main ideas and supporting details. Main ideas are often stated near the beginnings of paragraphs. Subheadings, too, frequently provide clues regarding main ideas. Model for students how to draw a main ideas and details graphic organizer in the margin of the story. Tell students they can use this strategy for identifying main

ideas and details during testing situations. Provide students with the following main ideas based on the subheadings:

• Rico knows word meanings.

• Rico makes inferences.

Have students work with partners to supply supporting details for each main idea. Ask volunteers to present their details to the class.

## ANSWERS

### Reading Comprehension

Model a thinking process for answering multiple-choice questions.

1. **C *is correct.*** *The narrator's straightforward style understates his sorrow, adding to the essay's impact.* A *is not correct because the narrator expresses only sorrow, not longing for the past.* B *is not correct because the narrator focuses on Pete rather than his anger at the driver.* D *is not correct because the narrator does not suggest that he is superior to the reader or to Pete.*

2. **D *is correct.*** *The narrator cites details that suggest that Pete behaves responsibly and the driver does not.* A *is not correct because the fact that Pete does not chase cars is a supporting detail.* B *is not correct because Pete was looking after his "little mistress."* C *is not correct because it provides a detail that supports the idea that the driver behaved dangerously.*

3. **B *is correct.*** *The narrator is angry with the driver over his behavior before, during, and after the accident.* A *is not correct because the narrator sympathizes with Pete, not the driver.* C *is not correct because the narrator blames the driver, not the car, for Pete's death.* D *is not correct because the narrator admires Pete.*

4. **B *is correct.*** *The narrator both informs readers about the events surrounding Pete's death and expresses his feelings over the loss of the dog.* A *is not correct because the piece is not entertaining.* C *and* D *are not correct because the piece does not overtly attempt to persuade readers to act or change their thinking.*

Chris Lassiter/News Leader

## Reading Comprehension

> **Use "His Name Was Pete" (pp. 644–645) to answer questions 1–4.**

1. The author's tone throughout this essay is —
   - **A.** nostalgic
   - **B.** sarcastic
   - **C.** straightforward
   - **D.** superior

2. The main idea of paragraph 3 is that —
   - **A.** Pete didn't chase cars
   - **B.** Pete shouldn't have been on the road
   - **C.** running over children is illegal
   - **D.** there is no excuse for running over a dog

3. In the last line of paragraph 4, the phrase "how could the driver" reveals the author's —
   - **A.** sympathy with the driver
   - **B.** anger at the driver
   - **C.** feelings about cars
   - **D.** impatience with Pete

4. The author's two purposes in writing this essay were to —
   - **A.** inform and entertain
   - **B.** inform and express feelings
   - **C.** persuade and express feelings
   - **D.** persuade and entertain

646

Use "Dog Proves as Smart as Average Toddler" (p. 645) to answer questions 5–6.

5. The subheadings "Knows Word Meanings" and "Makes Inferences" are clues that the author's primary purpose is to —
   A. inform or explain
   B. persuade
   C. entertain
   D. express feelings

6. One way the author organizes the article is by comparing and contrasting —
   A. words and toys
   B. dogs and children
   C. scientists and research projects
   D. pets and language acquisition

Use "His Name Was Pete" and "Dog Proves as Smart as Average Toddler" to answer question 7.

7. Which one of the following statements would most likely be supported by both authors?
   A. Most dogs are not as smart as Rico.
   B. A dog should always be on a leash or inside a fence.
   C. Dogs and people can form strong connections.
   D. Dogs are patient animals.

Use the Web page on page 646 to answer questions 8–9.

8. From the information on the Web page, you can identify that the hero of the story is —
   A. an elderly woman who fell down
   B. someone who needed medical attention
   C. a large black dog called a labradoodle
   D. Valerie Locklear, a dog owner who lives in Staunton

9. Which of the following could you find by selecting a hyperlink from the menu on this Web site?
   A. The lead to this story
   B. A video clip of Oakley's rescue
   C. More local news
   D. More pictures of Oakley

**SHORT CONSTRUCTED RESPONSE**
Write a short response to the following question, using text evidence to support your response.

10. What was Faulkner's attitude toward the dog's death in "His Name Was Pete"? Support your response with evidence from the essay.

Write a short response to the following question, using evidence from both texts to support your response.

11. Compare and contrast the main ideas of "His Name Was Pete" and "Dog Proves as Smart as Average Toddler." Name one way in which the texts are alike and one way in which they are different. Support your response with two details from each of the texts.

GO ON

---

## ANSWERS

5. **A is correct.** The purpose of the piece is to inform readers about a research study. B is not correct because the piece does not ask readers to act or change their thinking. C is not correct because the piece is not narrative. D is not correct because the writer does not express her feelings regarding the study.

6. **B is correct.** The writer compares dogs and children with regard to their abilities to make inferences and remember the meanings of words. A is not correct because words and toys are part of a research study. C is not correct because the article focuses on one research study. D is not correct because the article focuses on one dog.

7. **C is correct.** One narrator feels a strong bond with Pete, and the other narrator understands why dogs are popular pets. A is not correct because Pete, too, is smart. B is not correct because Rico's living situation is not discussed. D is not correct because Rico's patience is not discussed.

8. **C is correct.** The photograph and the caption tell that a heroic, large, black dog called a labradoodle alerted his owner that an elderly neighbor needed medical attention. A is not correct because the woman is the object of the hero's actions. B is not correct because the dog facilitates getting medical attention for a woman. D is not correct because the dog alerts Locklear to the situation regarding the neighbor.

9. **C is correct.** The left margin contains hyperlinks to more local news. A is not correct because the lead to this story appears on this page. B is not correct because the story was written after the rescue so no video exists. D is not correct because there is no reference to additional pictures of Oakley.

## SHORT CONSTRUCTED RESPONSE

*Possible responses:*

10. *The narrator is sad and angry that the car hit Pete. He is sad because the dog is doing a good thing when he is hit. He is standing in the road waiting for the little girl on her horse to catch up with him so he can escort her home safely (lines 18-19). The driver is too*

---

busy to slow down for Pete or to stop when he hits him. Recalling Pete's kindness, the narrator implies that the dog gladly sacrifices his life so that the driver won't be late for supper. Readers can feel the narrator's anger when he says, sarcastically, that Pete has no right to be in the road because he doesn't pay taxes, hold a driver's license, or vote (line 20). His anger is apparent when he points out that the driver shouldn't be driving a car "without either horn or brakes" (line 27).

11. *Students' responses should clearly state similarities and differences between the selections. Similarities might include that the main ideas of both selections focus on praiseworthy and intelligent dogs. Supporting details might include Pete's learning not to chase cars and Rico's understanding of 200 words. Differences might include that one tells about a personal experience and the other tells about a scientific study.*

# Vocabulary

1. **A is correct.** The prefix im- means "not." The word immortality means "not death" or "eternal life." B, C, and D are not correct because they do not have anything to do with death.

2. **C is correct.** A dog's word learning skills appear to be "present from birth." A, B, and D are not correct because they do not have anything to do with birth.

3. **D is correct.** Scientific proof is based on facts. A is not correct because the root -scient- does not relate to animals. B is not correct because scientific proof is based on facts, not the imagination. C is not correct because a theory must be proven through facts.

4. **A is correct.** People believe that language and reasoning belong exclusively to one species: humans. B is not correct because lonely doesn't make sense in this context. C is not correct because people believe these traits to be exclusively, not partially, human. D is not correct because these traits are not superficial.

5. **D is correct.** Anthropologists conduct studies, which require analysis, not instruction, dissection, or monitoring. A, B, and C are not correct.

6. **C is correct.** The journal is a magazine or newspaper where a report is published. A and B are not correct because the sentence describes a place where a report is published rather than records. D is not correct because the word is used as a noun rather than a verb.

## Vocabulary

| Use your knowledge of context clues and the word-root definitions to answer the following questions. |
| --- |

1. The Latin root -mort- means "death." The word *immortality* in the sentence below means —

   *He expected little of the world into which he came without past and nothing of immortality either.*

   **A.** eternal life
   **B.** great fame
   **C.** good behavior
   **D.** a promising future

2. The Latin root -nat- means "born." The word *innate* in paragraph 5 of "Dog Proves as Smart as Average Toddler" means —

   **A.** taught by humans
   **B.** learned over time
   **C.** present from birth
   **D.** taken from memory

3. The Latin root -scient- means "knowing." The word *scientific* in paragraph 1 of "Dog Proves as Smart as Average Toddler" means —

   **A.** from animals
   **B.** from imagination
   **C.** based on theory
   **D.** based on facts

4. The Latin prefix uni- means "one." The word *uniquely* in paragraph 5 of "Dog Proves as Smart as Average Toddler" means —

   **A.** exclusively
   **B.** lonely
   **C.** partially
   **D.** superficially

| Use your knowledge of context clues to help you answer the following questions. |
| --- |

5. *Anthropology* is the study of the origins, behavior, and development of humans. If anthropologists studied dogs instead of people, they would most likely —

   **A.** attempt to teach dogs to perform tricks
   **B.** dissect dogs who have died from an illness
   **C.** monitor the level of protein in dogs' diets
   **D.** analyze the actions and reactions of dogs

   **journal** \jûr′nəl\ *noun* **1.** a record of current transactions **2.** a record of experiences, ideas, or reflections kept regularly for private use **3.** a newspaper or magazine *verb* **1.** to record experiences, ideas, or private reflections in notebook

6. In paragraph 2 of the article, the term *journal* means —

   **A.** Definition *noun* 1
   **B.** Definition *noun* 2
   **C.** Definition *noun* 3
   **D.** Definition *verb* 1

7. The word *Institute* in paragraph 3 refers to —

   **A.** a pattern of behavior
   **B.** an authoritative rule
   **C.** an organization
   **D.** a workshop

8. In paragraph 7 the word *psychologist* refers to a person who studies —

   **A.** obedience in dogs
   **B.** vocabulary words
   **C.** word-learning skills
   **D.** mental processes and behavior

7. **C is correct.** Julia Fischer and her colleagues work in an institution or organization. A is not correct because the scientists study patterns of behavior, not work in them. B is not correct because Fischer works with her colleagues; she does not rule over them. D is not correct because Fischer works with colleagues in a large organization, not a small workshop.

8. **D is correct.** Coren studies intelligence, not obedience. A is not correct. B and C are not correct because psychologist describes Coren, not the details of the study described in this article.

# Revising and Editing

**DIRECTIONS** Read this passage, and answer the questions that follow.

> (1) For years, many people claimed that animals were not emotional. (2) Recently, scientists have documented what every pet owner already knows. (3) Animals can, indeed, feel emotions. (4) The author and former psychoanalyst Jeffrey Masson studies animal emotions in his book *When elephants weep*. (5) Masson describes an elephant that feels happy when drawing pictures. (6) He tells of a chimp that nursed its sick owner back to health. (7) The proof has been well documented. (8) Some scientists resist Masson's conclusions, but many believe that animals do feel emotions.

1. Which is the best coordinating conjunction to use to combine sentences 1 and 2?
   - **A.** And
   - **B.** But
   - **C.** Or
   - **D.** So

2. What change, if any, should be made in sentence 4?
   - **A.** Change *in his book* When elephants weep to *in his book* "When elephants weep"
   - **B.** Change *in his book* When elephants weep to *in his book:* When elephants weep
   - **C.** Change *in his book* When elephants weep to *in his book* When Elephants Weep
   - **D.** Make no change

3. What is the best way to rewrite sentence 5 using an adverb?
   - **A.** Masson describes an elephant that feels happy when playfully drawing pictures.
   - **B.** Masson describes an elephant that feels happy when drawing fanciful pictures.
   - **C.** Masson describes a talented elephant that feels happy when drawing pictures.
   - **D.** Masson describes an elephant that draws happy pictures.

4. Which is the best coordinating conjunction to use to combine sentences 5 and 6?
   - **A.** And
   - **B.** For
   - **C.** Or
   - **D.** Yet

5. What is the most effective way to improve the organization of the paragraph?
   - **A.** Move sentence 7 to follow sentence 1
   - **B.** Move sentence 7 to follow sentence 3
   - **C.** Move sentence 7 to follow sentence 4
   - **D.** Delete sentence 7

6. What is the best way to rewrite sentence 8 using an adverb?
   - **A.** Some stubborn scientists resist Masson's conclusions, but many believe that animals do feel emotions.
   - **B.** Some scientists resist Masson's conclusions, and many believe that animals do feel emotions.
   - **C.** Some scientists resist Masson's conclusions, but many believe that animals do feel something.
   - **D.** Some scientists resist Masson's conclusions, but many strongly believe that animals do feel emotions.

STOP

649

## Revising and Editing

1. **B** *is correct. The word* but *shows a contrast between previous thinking and current thinking.* A *is not correct because* and *shows equal importance.* C *is not correct because* or *shows a choice.* D *is not correct because* so *shows cause and effect.*

2. **C** *is correct. The words in a title are capitalized.* A *is not correct because the title is a book, not an article.* B *is not correct because the title is not an example.* D *is not correct because there is an error in capitalization.*

3. **A** *is correct.* Playfully *is an adverb that tells how the elephant draws.* B *is not correct because* fanciful *is an adjective that describes the pictures.* C *is not correct because* talented *is an adjective that describes the elephant.* D *is not correct because it changes the meaning of the original sentence and does not include an adverb.*

4. **A** *is correct. The word* and *joins two ideas of equal importance.* B *is not correct because* for *shows a cause.* C *is not correct because* or *suggests a choice.* D *is not correct because* yet *suggests contrast.*

5. **B** *is correct. Sentence 7 supports the idea that animals can feel emotions.* A *is not correct because Sentence 7 does not support the idea that animals are not emotional.* C *is not correct because Sentence 7 does not tell about Masson.* D *is not correct because Sentence 7 relates to the content of the paragraph.*

6. **D** *is correct.* Strongly *is an adverb that describes the scientists' beliefs.* A *is not correct because* stubborn *is an adjective that describes the scientists.* B *and* C *are not correct because they do not contain adverbs and feature inaccurate coordinating conjunctions.*

## DIFFERENTIATED INSTRUCTION

### FOR STRUGGLING READERS

**Assessment Support: Reading Items** Remind students to read test items carefully, underlining or circling key words, phrases, or details. Tell students that they cannot respond accurately if they are not certain how they are being asked to respond. For example, point out that the word *adverb* is critical in items 3 and 6. A given answer may offer a good revision of the sentence. However, if the answer does not contain an adverb, it is not correct. Point out that the phrase *coordinating conjunction* is critical in items 1 and 4. Students should first verify that all answer choices contain coordinating conjunctions. Any that do not may be immediately eliminated.

## COMMON CORE FOCUS

**RL 10** Read and comprehend literature. **RI 10** Read and comprehend literary nonfiction.

### INTRODUCE *GREAT READS*

In Unit 5, students have discussed a number of big questions. Invite students to tell which question they found most intriguing and why, and then focus attention on the three that appear on this page. Discuss the recommended books and their summaries, pointing out how each connects to the related question. Encourage students to choose one or more of these "great reads" to read independently.

**COMMON CORE**

**RL 10** Read and comprehend literature. **RI 10** Read and comprehend literary nonfiction.

## Ideas for Independent Reading

What ideas does each writer communicate in the following works?

## What place do you call home?

**Desert Solitaire**
*by Edward Abbey*

Abbey's love song to the deserts of the southwestern United States has become a touchstone for writing about a place. This volume shows readers why the desert was Abbey's spiritual home.

**Barrio Boy**
*by Ernesto Galarza*

In this autobiography, Galarza describes his early years in western Mexico and his childhood in a barrio in Sacramento, California.

**My Place**
*by Sally Morgan*

Morgan was not told of her aboriginal heritage until she was 15. She wrote this highly personal memoir to show readers what Australian aboriginal people have endured as outsiders in their own land.

## Why would people leave their homelands?

**Picture Bride**
*By Yoshiko Uchida*

In this novel, Hana Omiya journeys from Japan to the United States to escape a more restricted life in Japan. She finds that life in America has its own barriers to happiness and freedom.

**Of Beetles and Angels: A Boy's Remarkable Journey from a Refugee Camp to Harvard**
*by Mawi Asgedom*

Asgedom and his family fled civil war in Ethiopia in 1983. In 1999, he graduated from Harvard. His father's words, "Treat all people—even the most unsightly beetles—as though they were angels from heaven," have guided him.

**How the García Girls Lost Their Accents**
*by Julia Alvarez*

After the four García girls leave the Dominican Republic, they eagerly embrace American culture, often to the dismay of their old-world parents.

## What stories will you tell your children?

**The Kitchen God's Wife**
*by Amy Tan*

In this contemporary novel, a woman tries to communicate with her daughter by telling of her struggle for survival in the harsh world of China before and during World War II.

**A Yellow Raft in Blue Water**
*by Michael Dorris*

Three generations of Native American women share their lives and their secrets in three interwoven fictional narratives.

**Fahrenheit 451**
*by Ray Bradbury*

Four hundred fifty-one degrees Fahrenheit is the temperature at which books burn. Bradbury's classic novel considers an unnamed society in which ideas are so dangerous that people must be "protected" from the stories of the past.

**Get Novel Wise**

Go to **thinkcentral.com**.
KEYWORD: HML9-650

650

**NovelWise**

The keyword on this page points to **NovelWise,** a Web site that helps students choose a novel or other book-length work to read. **NovelWise** also provides

• study guides
• reading strategies and literary elements instruction
• presentations to introduce classic novels
• project ideas

# 6

# Taking Sides

### ARGUMENT AND PERSUASION

- In Nonfiction
- In Media
- In Fiction

651

**INTRODUCE THE UNIT**

Civil rights hero Martin Luther King, Jr., is considered one of the most powerful speakers of all time. His impassioned words persuaded hundreds of thousands of people to join in his peaceful demand for justice. Still, many people disagreed with King, and he had to argue his position often.

King's example suggests that people argue most strongly over issues that matter greatly to them. Invite students to apply that thought to the images on this page. Ask:

- What do you think is happening in each scene? If you were in that scene, what might you see and hear?
- Which scene shows "Taking Sides" in a calm, controlled way? in an angry way?
- Suppose that you were to create a scene of people arguing or being persuasive about something that matters greatly to them. Which of these images would it resemble more? Why?

Tell students that as they read this unit, they will learn some important techniques of **persuasive writing.** They will analyze how writers and speakers seek to influence. They also will practice being influential as they defend their own positions.

For help in planning this unit, see

**R** RESOURCE MANAGER UNIT 6
pp. 1–10

**About the Art** Detail from *A Tempestuous Evening at the Maison de la Culture* by Albert Laforet (1937).

# UNIT 6

## COMMON CORE

**STRAND**

| | *Text Analysis Workshop: Argument and Persuasion* pp. 654–659 | *I Have a Dream* Speech pp. 660–669 | *Testimony Before the Senate* Speech pp. 670–679 | *How Private Is Your Private Life?/The Privacy Debate: One Size Doesn't Fit All* Magazine Article/Newspaper Editorial pp. 680–693 |
|---|---|---|---|---|
| | | Lexile: 1120 Fry: 10 Dale-Chall: 7.3 | Lexile: 1100 Fry: College Dale-Chall: 7.5 | Lexile: 1390/1260 Fry: College/College Dale-Chall: 8.2/9.3 |
| **Reading Literature** | | | | |
| **Reading Informational Text** | Elements of an Argument pp. 654–655  RI 2, RI 5, RI 8 The Craft of Persuasion pp. 656–658  RI 6, RI 8 | Argument pp. 661, 662, 666, 668  RI 8 Seminal U.S. Documents pp. 666, 668  RI 9 Rhetorical Devices pp. 661, 664, 666, 668  RI 6 Language Coach p. 666  RI 4 | Persuasive Techniques pp. 671, 672, 674, 677  RI 5, RI 8 Summarize pp. 671, 673, 675, 677  RI 2 | Fact and Opinion pp. 681, 683, 684, 686, 688, 690, 691  RI 4, RI 8 Recognize Bias pp. 681, 683, 687, 691  RI 8 Language Coach p. 685  RI 4 Series of Events p. 684  RI 3 Sarcasm p. 689  RI 4 |
| **Writing** | | Quickwrite p. 660 Writing Prompt p. 668  W 9b (RI 9) | Writing Prompt p. 679  W 9a (RI 8) | Writing Prompt p. 693  W 4 |
| **Speaking and Listening** | Analyze the Text p. 659  SL 3 | | Discuss p. 670  SL 1 | Debate p. 680  SL 1 |
| **Language** | | Analogies p. 669  L 5a | Persuasive Techniques p. 674  L 1a Language Coach p. 675  L 4c Imperative Sentences pp. 676, 679  L 3 Foreign Words p. 678  L 4c | Language Coach p. 690 Use Rhetorical Devices pp. 690, 693  L 1a Internet Words p. 692  L 6 |

| Media Study: Billy Thomas/Life Is Calling<br>Public Service Announcements<br>pp. 694–697 | Comparing Texts<br><br>**Primal Screen/The Pedestrian/TV Master**<br>Essay/Short Story/Advertisement<br>pp. 698–710<br><br>Lexile: 990/1100<br>Fry: 9/12<br>Dale-Chall: 6.5/5.9 | Writing Workshop:<br>Argument: Persuasive Essay<br>pp. 712–721<br><br>**Speaking and Listening Workshop:**<br>Debating an Issue<br>pp. 722–723 |
|---|---|---|
| | Writer's Message pp. 699–702, 704–708 **RL 2**<br>Language Coach p. 707 **RL 4** | |
| Persuasion in PSAs pp. 695–697 **RI 7** | Writer's Message pp. 699–702, 704–708 **RI 2, RI 5**<br>Set a Purpose for Reading pp. 699, 708<br>Language Coach p. 700 **RI 4**<br>Advertisement p. 710 **RI 7** | |
| Write or Discuss p. 697 **W 9b (RI 7)** | Writing Prompt p. 709 **W 5**<br>Write for Assessment p. 711 | Writing a Persuasive Essay<br>pp. 712–721 **W 1a–e, W 4, W 5, W 10** |
| Media Literacy pp. 695–696<br>Write or Discuss p. 697 **SL 2, SL 3** | What's the Connection? p. 698 **SL 1** | Debating an Issue pp. 722–723<br>**SL 1a–d, SL 3, SL 6** |
| | Language Coach p. 704 **L 4**<br>Capitalize Dialogue pp. 707, 709 **L 2** | Drafting p. 715 **L 1a, L 3**<br>Revising pp. 716–718 **L 1**<br>Editing and Publishing p. 719 **L 2, L 2c** |

To see the complete Essential Course of Study, see pp. T23–T28.

For additional lesson planning help, see **Teacher One Stop DVD.**

## Instructional Support

**Resource Manager Unit 6**

**UNIT SUPPORT**

Academic Vocabulary, p. 3

Additional Academic Vocabulary, p. 4

Grammar Focus p. 5

Text Analysis Workshop pp. 9–10

Writing Workshop: Argument:
  Persuasive Essay p. 103

**SELECTION SUPPORT***

**Plan and Teach**

Lesson planning pages

Additional leveled selection questions

Extension activities

**Student Copy Masters**

Selection summaries in four languages

Skills copy masters in English and Spanish

Vocabulary preteaching and support

Reading Check and Question Support

Reading Fluency

*Available for all selections

† Available on **thinkcentral.com**.

Language Handbook

Vocabulary Practice

Best Practices Toolkit†

**PowerNotes** DVD-ROM†

**Connections: Nonfiction for
Common Core** CD-ROM†

**Teacher One Stop** DVD-ROM

**Student One Stop** DVD-ROM

**Media*Smart*** DVD-ROM
Billy Thomas / Life is Calling

**Write*Smart*** CD-ROM†

**GrammarNotes** DVD-ROM†

**WordSharp** CD-ROM†

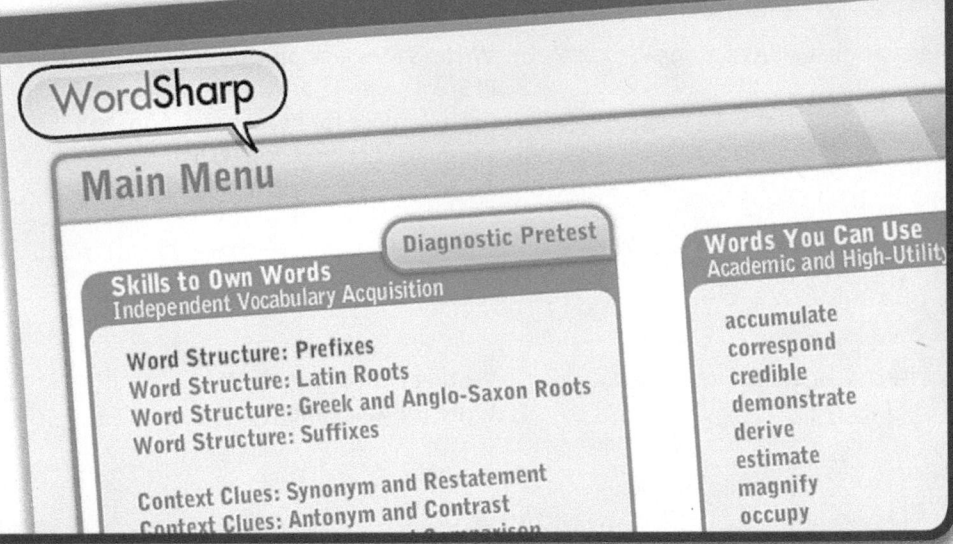

## Differentiated Instruction

| STRUGGLING READERS AND WRITERS | ENGLISH LANGUAGE LEARNERS | ADVANCED LEARNERS |
|---|---|---|
| **Resource Manager Unit 6** | **Resource Manager Unit 6** | **Resource Manager Unit 6** |
| Additional Selection Questions | Selection Summaries in English, Spanish, Vietnamese and Haitian Creole | Additional Selection Questions |
| Question Support | Skills Copymasters in Spanish | Ideas for Extension |
| Reading Fluency | **English Language Learner Adapted Interactive Reader Teacher's Guide** | **Diagnostic and Selection Tests** |
| **Interactive Reader** | **ELL Adapted Interactive Reader** | Selection Tests B/C |
| **Adapted Interactive Reader** | **Audio Tutor** | |
| **Level Up Online Tutorials** | **Guide to English for Newcomers** | |
| **Audio Anthology** | **Audio Anthology** | |
| (with Audio summaries) | **Audio Summaries in Multiple Languages** | |
| **Diagnostic and Selection Tests** | (on **thinkcentral.com**) | |
| Selection Tests A/B | | |

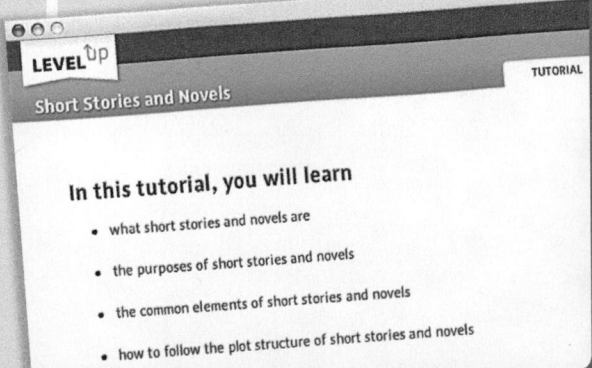

## Assessment and Reteaching

**Diagnostic and Selection Tests**

**Unit and Benchmark Tests**

**ThinkCentral Online Assessment:**

- All program assessments
- Level Up Online Tutorials

**ExamView Test Generator** on the Teacher One Stop DVD-ROM

**Online Essay Scoring** on **thinkcentral.com**

**ThinkCentral Online Reteaching:**

- Level Up Online Tutorials
- Reteaching Worksheets

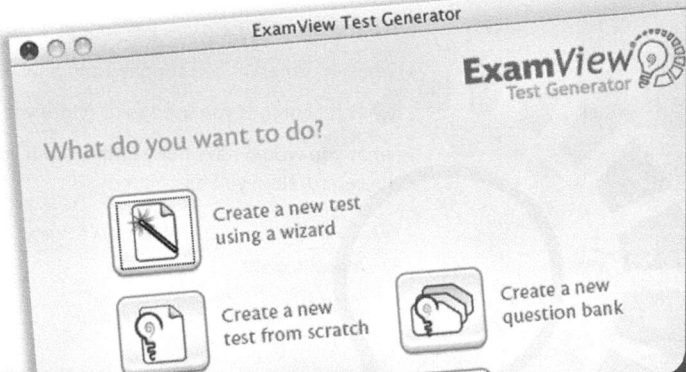

## Professional Development

**Video Center** Based on interviews with program consultants and other educational experts, these videos feature classroom-ready teaching strategies.

**Teacher Toolkit** Includes a Teacher Handbook as well as a range of articles and handouts by program consultants and other educators.

Janet Allen

Jim Burke

Kylene Beers

Carol Jago

 **THINK** central **at a Glance**

**One Location, Endless Resources**

**Find Resources** Browse all *Holt McDougal Literature* components for the ones that meet your students' needs and match your teaching style.

**Assess Progress and Reteach** Assign electronic versions of program assessments to measure your students' mastery of the Common Core State Standards. On thinkcentral.com, some tests deliver online remediation tutorials to students who have not mastered skills.

 *Interactive Whiteboard Lessons*

Prepare your students for college and careers by teaching relevant, real-world skills through dynamic, interactive instruction. Go to **thinkcentral.com** to browse through all white-board lessons, including the following:

- Evaluating Arguments
- Writing Effective Arguments
- Using Parallel Structure

 **HISTORY** Together Holt McDougal and HISTORY® are revolutionizing the study of English/language arts with video that helps students relive and re-imagine the people, places, and events they are discovering through reading. Look for selections with the HISTORY® icon.

## How can we
# INFLUENCE others?

Read and discuss the question and the paragraph. Help students connect to the explanation by asking them to think of times that they have seen advertising techniques like these used to influence an audience:

- citing a doctor's opinion of a product
- urging the audience to "join the crowd" by using a product
- citing facts and statistics
- appealing to the audience's fears

Ask students to explain how the poster and pins on this page attempt to influence an audience. *Possible answer: The poster and pins are meant to persuade people to vote. They influence their audience by suggesting that people can make their ideas heard and can solve problems by voting.*

*ACTIVITY* Urge students to make some notes or to freewrite about the occasion that they have in mind before they begin work on the chart. Afterward, use volunteers' responses to compile a list of persuasive "do's" and "don'ts."

**CHECK UNDERSTANDING** Elicit that the goal of persuasive writing is to influence the reader to take the writer's side.

## How can we
# INFLUENCE others?

**Find It Online!** THINK central
Go to **thinkcentral.com** for the interactive version of this unit.

You convince your friend to see your side in an argument. You get your teacher to give you an extension on an assignment. You influence your classmates to vote for you in a school election. Each time you succeed in getting someone to side with you on an idea, a plan, or an action, you have practiced the art of persuasion. Similarly, whenever you purchase a product you saw advertised or go see a movie after viewing its trailer, the art of persuasion has influenced you.

*ACTIVITY* Recall a time when you were determined to get your way. Then fill in a chart like the one shown. Think about

- what worked to help you get your point across
- what information you supplied and how you organized it
- what techniques you used to convince your audience
- what you would have done differently if you were less successful than you had hoped

| What Worked | What Didn't Work |
|---|---|
| • a logical argument | • whining |

652

---

## Unit Resources

*See resources on the* **Teacher One Stop DVD-ROM** *and on* **thinkcentral.com**.

 **RESOURCE MANAGER UNIT 6**

**UNIT AND BENCHMARK TESTS**

**BEST PRACTICES TOOLKIT**

**INTERACTIVE READER**

**ADAPTED INTERACTIVE READER**

**ELL ADAPTED INTERACTIVE READER**

**LANGUAGE HANDBOOK**

**VOCABULARY PRACTICE**

**TECHNOLOGY**

- **Teacher One Stop DVD-ROM**
- **Student One Stop DVD-ROM**
- **PowerNotes DVD-ROM**
- **Write***Smart* **CD-ROM**
- **Media***Smart* **DVD-ROM**
- **GrammarNotes DVD-ROM**
- **Audio Anthology CD**
- **Audio Tutor CD**

 **Find It Online!** THINK central

The interactive version of this unit on **thinkcentral.com** includes
- video and **PowerNotes** introductions to key selections
- **audio support**—listen or download
- **ThinkAloud** models
- **WordSharp** vocabulary tutorials
- interactive review and remediation

652

## Preview Unit Goals

| | |
|---|---|
| **TEXT ANALYSIS** | • Analyze how an author's claims are developed and refined<br>• Analyze and evaluate the elements of an argument—proposition, support, reasons, evidence, and counterclaims<br>• Distinguish fact from opinion<br>• Analyze persuasive techniques, including emotional appeals |
| **READING** | • Provide an objective summary of a text<br>• Analyze rhetorical structures and devices—repetition, parallelism, and analogy<br>• Recognize bias |
| **WRITING AND LANGUAGE** | • Write an argument (persuasive essay)<br>• Use parallel structure; structure sentences correctly |
| **SPEAKING AND LISTENING** | • Participate effectively in a debate |
| **VOCABULARY** | • Understand and use specialized and technical vocabulary<br>• Determine the meaning of words and phrases in a text |
| **ACADEMIC VOCABULARY** | • coherent     • evident     • differentiate<br>• relevant     • technique |
| **MEDIA AND VIEWING** | • Analyze and create persuasive media<br>• Integrate multiple sources of information presented in diverse media or formats |

## Media Smart DVD-ROM

**Persuasion in Advertising**
Analyze the techniques in public service announcements that are designed to move you to action. Page 694

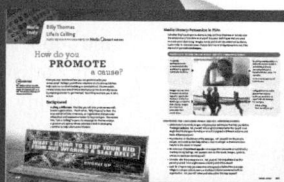

653

Complete text of the Common Core State Standards is found in the correlation on p. T10. Standards covered in this unit are found in the standards overview (pp. 651A–651B) and on the lesson pages where they are taught.

## Preview Unit Goals

The goals on this page identify the main skills and strategies that students will meet in this unit's reading selections. Have students scan the list and consider what they already know about each goal. As you note the color-coding of each strand, urge students to watch for the colors to be repeated throughout the unit.

Point out the Academic Vocabulary at the bottom of the page. Call on volunteers to define familiar terms and to look up unfamiliar terms in a dictionary. Have students use their **Reader/Writer Notebooks** to record the terms and a definition for each. Throughout the unit, remind students to reinforce their understanding by using these terms in speaking and writing about the selections.

## DIFFERENTIATED INSTRUCTION

### FOR ENGLISH LANGUAGE LEARNERS

**Academic Vocabulary** Provide students with definitions of each Academic Vocabulary word.

**coherent** (kō hir'ənt) *adj.* logical, consistent, or connected

**differentiate** (dif´ər en'shē āt´) *v.* to perceive or create a difference between

**evident** (ev'ə dənt) *adj.* obvious, easy to see or understand

**relevant** (rel'ə vənt) *adj.* related or pertinent to the matter at hand

**technique** (tek nēk´) *n.* a method of procedure or a manner of doing something

Use the copy master to help students learn academic words they will use in this unit and on the Assessment Practice.

**R** RESOURCE MANAGER—Copy Masters
Academic Vocabulary p. 3
Additional Academic Vocabulary p. 4

# Focus and Motivate

## COMMON CORE FOCUS

**RI 2** Determine a central idea of a text and analyze its development over the course of the text, including how it emerges and is shaped and refined by specific details. **RI 5** Analyze in detail how an author's ideas or claims are developed and refined. **RI 6** Analyze how an author uses rhetoric to advance that point of view or purpose. **RI 8** Delineate and evaluate the argument and specific claims in a text, assessing the reasoning and evidence; identify false statements and fallacious reasoning. **SL 3** Evaluate a speaker's use of evidence and rhetoric.

# Teach

## Part 1: The Elements of an Argument

**Claim and Support** Explain that arguments are meant to influence readers or listeners—in other words, to cause them to think or act in a certain way. For example, campaigners offer arguments to support a candidate. An editorial may call for a change in an existing law. Stress that unless a claim is supported by valid reasons and relevant evidence, it remains nothing more than an opinion.

Ask students to cite examples of arguments meant to influence thought or action, such as advertisements, speeches, and letters to the editor. Have students use a chart to analyze the intent of two of these arguments.

| Argument | Intent |
|---|---|
| This soap cleans better than any other soap. | To convince consumers to buy the soap |
| | |

**Reading an Argument** To reinforce the notion that claims must be supported, draw a parallel with the legal system. Elicit that attorneys represent opposing positions or points of view, for which they provide relevant, credible evidence. This evidence is meant to influence a judge or jury.

📖 **BEST PRACTICES TOOLKIT —Transparency** Analysis Frame: Persuasion pp. D21, D44

# Argument and Persuasion  *Essential Course of Study*

You encounter arguments and opinions everywhere. Friends share their views on controversial issues. Politicians explain why they deserve your vote. Ads claim that products can fix your problems. Which arguments have merit, and which are just cleverly persuasive? So many decisions you make depend on your ability to analyze arguments and recognize the techniques that are being used to persuade you.

## Part 1: The Elements of an Argument

You've heard the word *argument* all your life. It suggests heated discussions characterized by strong feelings and loud voices. In formal speaking and writing, however, an argument is not emotional. An **argument** expresses a point of view or position on an issue and supports the position with reasons and evidence. Sound arguments appeal strictly to reason, not emotions. They include these elements:

- the **claim**—the writer's or speaker's position on an issue
- the **support**—valid reasons and relevant and sufficient evidence

In addition to supporting the claim, strong arguments anticipate objections that opponents might raise and counter those objections with evidence.

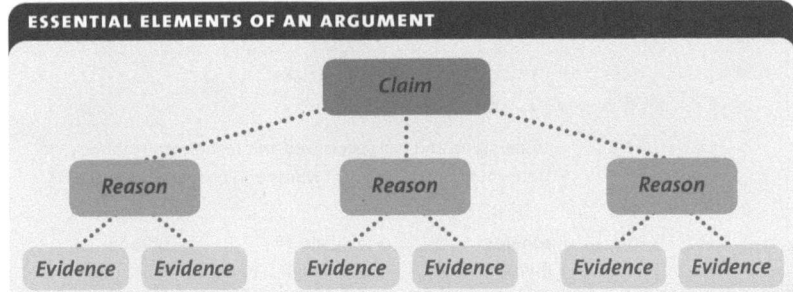

**ESSENTIAL ELEMENTS OF AN ARGUMENT**

### STRATEGIES FOR READING AN ARGUMENT

- **Look for the claim.** Often, the claim is stated in the introduction or the conclusion of an argument. Make sure you look for clues in the title, too. When the claim is not stated directly, ask yourself: What does the evidence tell me about the writer's or speaker's position or point of view?

- **Track the evidence.** Convincing arguments include a great deal of support. As a result, most arguments are not short. To keep track of how a writer or speaker develops his or her claims and ideas, jot down his or her reasons and supporting evidence—in the same order in which they appear. Look for facts, statistics, examples, anecdotes, and quotations from experts. Analyze the quality, credibility (believability), and relevance of the evidence—both in support of the position and in opposition to possible counterarguments.

COMMON CORE

Included in this workshop:
**RI 2** Determine a central idea of a text and analyze its development over the course of the text, including how it emerges and is shaped and refined by specific details.
**RI 5** Analyze in detail how an author's ideas or claims are developed and refined.
**RI 6** Analyze how an author uses rhetoric to advance that point of view or purpose.
**RI 8** Delineate and evaluate the argument and specific claims in a text, assessing the reasoning and evidence; identify false statements and fallacious reasoning. **SL 3** Evaluate a speaker's use of evidence and rhetoric.

## DIFFERENTIATED INSTRUCTION

### FOR STRUGGLING READERS

**Note Taking** Have students read p. 654 silently, taking notes on the definitions of *claim* and *support*. Then, have students copy the graphic organizer on p. 654 on a piece of paper. Go over the chart and its parts with the class. Then, ask students to close their books while you read aloud the excerpt from "Motorcycle Helmet Bill" on p. 655. As students listen to the text, pause and allow them time to fill in *Claim, Reasons,* and *Evidence* in the appropriate box in their charts. When you complete the reading, ask for volunteers to share the contents of their own charts with the class. Make any necessary corrections to students' note taking.

## MODEL: THE ELEMENTS OF AN ARGUMENT

In this testimony given before the Maryland Senate, the speaker makes a strong claim about the state's motorcycle helmet law. As you read, look for the elements that she uses to effectively prove her position.

# from MOTORCYCLE HELMET BILL

### Testimony before the Maryland Senate by **Janice Golec**

I respectfully urge you to oppose any legislation that weakens Maryland's current "all riders" motorcycle helmet law. Motorcycle helmets help save lives and reduce critical head injuries, and laws requiring helmet use have a dramatic life-saving effect. This has been
5 proven in Maryland and every other state where all riders are required to wear helmets. In such states, death rates from head injuries are half what they are among cyclists in states with no helmet laws or laws which only apply to minors. Where helmet [laws] have been enacted, then repealed, death rates for motorcyclists rise in the absence of a helmet law.

10 This is hardly a fluke; the General Accounting Office, a non-partisan research agency of the U.S. Government, reviewed 46 studies of motorcycle helmets and helmet laws, and reported that every study comparing helmeted with non-helmeted crash victims found that helmeted riders had lower fatality rates, ranging from 28 percent to 73 percent lower. . . .

15 Helmet laws save taxpayers money, too. Studies in six states show that public funds pay up to 82 percent of the costs to treat orthopedic injuries sustained by motorcyclists. A Maryland study showed that acute care costs to non-helmeted riders averaged three times those of helmeted riders. . . .

A partial law is almost as bad as no law at all. Statistically speaking, there is
20 negligible difference in death and injury rates between states with no helmet law and states with partial laws. Because partial helmet laws are difficult for police to enforce, helmet-use rates for all riders remain low in states with restricted helmet laws.

Helmet law opponents love to talk about motorcyclists' right to decide whether
25 or not they will wear helmets, but some rights are not worth having. . . . To weaken Maryland's helmet law is to condemn 28—or more—Maryland motorcyclists to death. That's a right nobody should have.

### Close Read

1. Who is the speaker's audience?

2. What is the speaker's claim, or position?

3. One reason that the speaker uses to prove her claim is boxed. Cite two pieces of evidence that support this reason.

4. Find another reason that the speaker uses to support her claim. What evidence supports this reason?

5. The speaker anticipates opponents' arguments in lines 19–27. How does she counter these viewpoints?

---

## MODEL: THE ELEMENTS OF AN ARGUMENT

### Close Read

1. **Possible answer:** *The speaker's audience is the Maryland Senate.*

2. **Possible answer:** *Legislators should oppose laws that weaken Maryland's "all riders" motorcycle helmet law.*

3. **Possible answer: Evidence 1:** *In other states with all-rider laws, death rates from head injuries are half what they are in states with no helmet laws.* **Evidence 2:** *Helmeted riders have a lower fatality rate than non-helmeted crash victims, as reported in 46 studies of motorcycle helmets and helmet laws.*

4. **Possible answer:** *Another reason to oppose legislation that weakens the "all riders" law is that such laws save taxpayers money. Golec cites studies in six states that found that taxpayers pay for costs related to motorcyclists' orthopedic injuries.*

**IF STUDENTS NEED HELP . . .** Remind students that paragraphs often have topic sentences that state the main idea. Encourage them to find the topic sentence in the paragraph that begins on line 15. Point out that the other sentences in the paragraph develop the topic sentence with supporting details.

5. **Possible answer:** *Golec maintains that a partial law is almost as bad as no motorcycle helmet law. She says that partial laws are difficult for police to enforce, and therefore, many motorcyclists do not wear helmets. Golec also mentions the minimal difference between death and injury rates for motorcyclists in states with partial helmet laws and those with no laws. Finally, Golec anticipates that opponents will mention motorcyclists' right to decide whether to wear their helmets. She says that some rights are not worth having, especially when they put people's lives at risk.*

**Online Remediation**

If your students are struggling with text analysis skills, consider assigning them one or more **Level Up Online Tutorials** as remediation before beginning this unit. Log in to **thinkcentral.com** to view a list of the skills addressed by **Level Up**.

---

### FOR STRUGGLING READERS

**Comprehension: Opposing Viewpoints** Explain that in lines 19–27, the speaker is anticipating two arguments that opponents might make. Help students use paragraph context to identify the opposing viewpoints. *(A partial helmet law would be adequate; motorcyclists have the right to decide whether they will wear helmets.)*

### Concept Support

1. Draw a diagram similar to the one on page 654, but write each heading above the lozenge.

2. Help students list on the board key phrases from "Motorcycle Helmet Bill" that correspond to *claim, reason,* and *evidence.*

3. Have students write the phrases in the correct places in the diagram.

## Part 2: The Craft of Persuasion

### PERSUASIVE TECHNIQUES

**Persuasion** As students read the chart, have them reflect on each of the techniques and examples described. Elicit the purpose of each appeal—for example, to get someone's vote, to sell a product, to solicit money for charity, to encourage volunteers—and have students discuss whether the example is effective. To add to the discussion, some students may enjoy acting out each example in a way that exaggerates its appeal.

As you guide a discussion about the effectiveness of each example, ask students to describe an audience to which each might appeal. Extend the discussion by asking students to consider whether certain appeals work best with particular age groups. Ask, for example, which techniques might work best with teenagers, and why.

During your discussion, elicit from students additional examples for each of the techniques in the chart. Encourage students to draw from various sources, such as television and radio commercials, print advertisements, political speeches, essays, and editorials.

### CHECK UNDERSTANDING

Have students brainstorm examples of persuasive techniques used in everyday interactions, as when peers urge one another to participate in an activity because "everyone's doing it."

---

## Part 2: The Craft of Persuasion

Never underestimate the power of **persuasion**—that is, the art of swaying people's feelings, opinions, and actions. With compelling language, writers and speakers can enhance strong arguments or disguise the flaws in weak ones. To evaluate the real strength of an argument, you first need to recognize the persuasive techniques and rhetorical structures and devices that are being used to sway you. Then you can objectively examine the evidence and determine your position.

### PERSUASIVE TECHNIQUES

Consider where you have encountered the following persuasive techniques. What are their intended effects on readers, listeners, and viewers?

| TECHNIQUES | EXAMPLES |
|---|---|
| **Appeals by Association** | |
| **Bandwagon Appeal** <br> Taps into people's desire to belong | You have to come to the concert. Everyone's going to be there. |
| **"Plain Folks" Appeal** <br> Implies that ordinary people are on "our side" or that a candidate is like an ordinary person | Senator Jacobs knows what it's like to struggle to make ends meet. |
| **Testimonial** <br> Relies on endorsements from well-known people or satisfied customers | As an Olympic athlete, I need all the energy I can get. That's why I start my day with Grain Puffs. |
| **Transfer** <br> Connects a product, a candidate, or a cause with a positive image or idea | Freedom is in your hands the minute you hit the road in a Mountainback XRV. |
| **Emotional Appeals** | |
| **Appeals to Pity, Fear, or Vanity** <br> Uses words that evoke strong feelings, rather than facts and evidence, to persuade | Appeal to Pity <br> For just one dollar a day, you can give a stray pet a second chance. |
| **Appeal to Values** | |
| **Ethical Appeal** <br> Taps into people's values or moral standards | Volunteer today—because it's the right thing to do. |
| **Word Choice** | |
| **Loaded Language** <br> Uses words with strongly positive or negative connotations to stir people's emotions | For the safety of our innocent children, we must protect our community from rampant crime. |

---

## DIFFERENTIATED INSTRUCTION

### FOR STRUGGLING READERS

**Note Taking** For students who need help, hand out the note-taking copy master for Part 2. Read and discuss the text. Assist students in completing their note-taking copy master as needed.

**R** RESOURCE MANAGER—Copy Master Note Taking p. 10

### FOR ENGLISH LANGUAGE LEARNERS

**Language: Skill Words** On the board, list the italicized terms. Then give the examples in random order for students to classify.

- *Bandwagon Appeal:* Try Slick Gloss—it's what all the cool kids are wearing.
- *Testimonial:* I'm a fashion model, and I eat Fruit Flakes for breakfast every day.
- *Appeal to Fear:* The new Super-12 Lock will keep the bad guys out of your home!

## MODEL 1: PERSUASION IN SPEECHES

In this speech, a government official pledges his commitment to promoting organ donation. What techniques does he use to try to convince you of his proposition?

*from* The Gift of Life

Speech by **Tommy Thompson**

This month in Fresno, California, members of the Hispanic community gathered . . . to remember 19-year-old Maribel Cordova. Maribel had received an identification card this year and told her mother she wanted to become a donor.

5  Two weeks later, a damaged blood vessel in her head tragically cut her life short.

Because of Maribel's selfless act, others lived. A 35-year-old man from Northern California received her lungs. A 66-year-old Southern California woman got her liver. . . .

10  These are the human experiences of hope out of loss, of life out of death, that touch and motivate us, that drive us to do everything within our power to promote organ and tissue donation. Through education, outreach, science and the vitally important work of people like you, we will reach that future when organ donation is, quite simply, a fact of life.

**Close Read**

1. Find two examples of loaded language. One has been boxed.
2. Identify one other persuasive technique used in this speech. Cite details that helped you find it.

## MODEL 2: PERSUASION IN THE MEDIA

Persuasive techniques are also at work in TV and magazine ads. How do the words and the visual in this print ad help convey a powerful message?

Make your home defensible against wildfires. Visit Firewise.org, where you can discover some simple things you can do to help protect your home and your loved ones. What have you got to lose, except everything.

**FIREWISE**
COMMUNITIES

**Close Read**

1. What persuasive technique is used in this ad? Cite specific details to support your answer.
2. Describe the intended effect of the ad on viewers.

---

## MODEL 1: PERSUASION IN SPEECHES

**Close Read**

1. ***Possible answer:*** *Other examples of loaded language include "Maribel's selfless act" and "hope out of loss, of life out of death."*
2. ***Possible answer:*** *One other persuasive technique is ethical appeal, as evidenced by "through education, outreach, science and the vitally important work of people like you, we will reach that future . . . ."*

## MODEL 2: PERSUASION IN THE MEDIA

**Close Read**

1. ***Possible answer:*** *Emotional appeals to fear include "What have you got to lose, except everything" and the image of an ordinary home in flames.*
2. ***Possible answer:*** *The intended effect is to scare viewers into taking precautions with their homes. Also, the ad might prompt viewers to visit the Firewise Web site so they can find out other simple ways to protect their home from fires.*

---

## DIFFERENTIATED INSTRUCTION

### FOR STRUGGLING READERS

**Analysis Support: Loaded Language** Discuss with students how the title "The Gift of Life" is a metaphor that is an example of loaded language. Elicit or explain that both *gift* and *life* are words with positive connotations and that the phrase "gift of life" suggests the most valuable gift a person could give. Point out, too, that the speaker repeats the word *life* in lines 5, 9, and 13.

### FOR ADVANCED LEARNERS/PRE–AP

**Analyze Extended Meanings** Explain that *donor, donate,* and *donation* all come from a Latin word meaning "gift." Ask students to identify words used in medical contexts (blood donor, for example).

## RHETORICAL STRUCTURE AND DEVICES

**Repetition** Elicit or provide other examples of the use of repetition for effect. For example, many students will be familiar with Martin Luther King, Jr.'s "I Have a Dream" speech. Discuss how repetition not only emphasizes certain phrases and ideas but also creates a rhythm that makes key words more memorable.

**Parallelism** Have students read the Lyndon Baines Johnson quotation aloud to get a feeling for the rhythm created. Point out that repetition and parallelism are techniques often used together.

**Analogy** Elicit or explain the meaning of the Billy Joel analogy. Ask students to state whether the analogy expresses Joel's approval or disapproval of "American popular music today" and to explain why. Then ask why such an analogy is effective. ***Possible answers:*** *It expresses disapproval. It implies the music is not fresh. It creates a strong image in the listener's mind.*

**Close Read**

1. ***Possible answer:*** *The repeated question helps emphasize Truth's message about just how wrong "that man over there" is. Essentially, she is disproving the man's claim that women need to be helped because she does not need help.*

   **IF STUDENTS NEED HELP . . .** Have students read Truth's words aloud, while listening for the repetition. Elicit that the phrase *And ain't I a woman?* underscores each point she makes.

2. ***Possible answer:*** *Parallelism occurs in the first two sentences: "helped into carriages"/ "helps me into carriages"; "lifted over ditches"/ "over mud-puddles"; "have the best place everywhere"/ "give me any best place." Also, many sentences begin with "I have" and "I could."*

---

### RHETORICAL STRUCTURES AND DEVICES

In addition to employing persuasive techniques, writers and speakers use **rhetorical devices,** which can shape the structure of sentences and paragraphs within a persuasive work in ways that make the work's message resonate. In these examples, notice how the wording makes the message memorable.

| RHETORICAL DEVICE | EXAMPLE |
|---|---|
| **REPETITION** Uses the same word or words more than once for emphasis | Let there be justice for all. Let there be peace for all. Let there be work, bread, water and salt for all. —from "Glory and Hope" by Nelson Mandela |
| **PARALLELISM** Uses similar grammatical constructions to express ideas that are related or equal in importance. Often creates a rhythm. | We cannot, we must not, refuse to protect the right of every American to vote in every election. . . . And we ought not, and we cannot, and we must not wait another eight months before we get a bill. —from "We Shall Overcome" by Lyndon Baines Johnson |
| **ANALOGY** Makes a comparison between two subjects that are alike in some ways | Have you heard the canned, frozen and processed product being dished up to the world as American popular music today? —from a commencement address by Billy Joel |

In the speech below, Sojourner Truth, a 19th-century leader in the antislavery and women's rights movements, responds to men who had spoken against women's rights. How does her use of rhetorical devices enhance her message?

## *from* And Ain't I a *Woman?*
### Speech by **Sojourner Truth**

That man over there say that women needs to be helped into carriages, and lifted over ditches, and to have the best place everywhere. Nobody ever helps me into carriages, or over mud-puddles, or give me any best place! And ain't I a woman? Look at me! Look at my arm! I have ploughed, and planted, and
5 gathered into barns, and no man could head me! And ain't I a woman? I could work as much and eat as much as a man—when I could get it—and bear the lash as well! And ain't I a woman? I have borne thirteen children, and seen 'em mos' all sold off to slavery, and when I cried out with my mother's grief, none but Jesus heard me! And ain't I a woman?

**Close Read**

1. Notice the boxed question that the speaker repeats. What is the effect of the repetition?

2. Find an example of parallelism. Identify the words, phrases, or sentences that exhibit parallel structure.

---

## DIFFERENTIATED INSTRUCTION

### FOR ADVANCED LEARNERS/PRE–AP

**Use Rhetorical Devices** Sojourner Truth used repetition and parallelism to make her speech more powerful. Challenge students to rewrite Truth's speech in more contemporary language while preserving her rhetorical devices. Have volunteers read their updated versions to the class. Discuss whether or not the students' versions are as powerful as the original.

## Part 3: Analyze the Text

In 1962, when President John F. Kennedy gave this stirring speech about space exploration, people were feeling threatened by the possibility of war with the Soviet Union. Using what you've just learned, analyze Kennedy's argument. What techniques does he use to persuade his audience?

# from The New Frontier

Speech by **John F. Kennedy**

No man can fully grasp how far and how fast we have come, but condense, if you will, the 50,000 years of man's recorded history in a time span of but a half century. Stated in these terms, we know very little about the first 40 years, except at the end of them advanced man had learned to use the skins
5  of animals to cover them. Then about 10 years ago, under this standard, man emerged from his caves to construct other kinds of shelter. Only five years ago man learned to write and use a cart with wheels. Christianity began less than two years ago. The printing press came this year, and then less than 2 months ago, during this whole 50-year span of human history, the steam engine
10  provided a new source of power.

Newton explored the meaning of gravity. Last month electric lights and telephones and automobiles and airplanes became available. Only last week did we develop penicillin and television and nuclear power, and now if America's new spacecraft succeeds in reaching Venus, we will have literally reached the
15  stars before midnight tonight.

This is a breathtaking pace, and such a pace cannot help but create new ills as it dispels old, new ignorance, new problems, new dangers. Surely the opening vistas of space promise high costs and hardships, as well as high reward. . . .

If this capsule history of our progress teaches us anything, it is that man, in
20  his quest for knowledge and progress, is determined and cannot be deterred. The exploration of space will go ahead, whether we join in it or not, and it is one of the great adventures of all time, and no nation which expects to be the leader of other nations can expect to stay behind in this race for space.

Those who came before us made certain that this country rode the first
25  waves of the industrial revolutions, the first waves of modern invention, and the first wave of nuclear power, and this generation does not intend to founder in the backwash of the coming age of space. We mean to be a part of it—we mean to lead it. For the eyes of the world now look into space, to the moon and to the planets beyond, and we have vowed that we shall not see it governed
30  by a hostile flag of conquest, but by a banner of freedom and peace. We have vowed that we shall not see space filled with weapons of mass destruction, but with instruments of knowledge and understanding.

**Close Read**

1. Summarize Kennedy's claim.

2. Does this speech mostly appeal to reason or to emotion? Explain your answer.

3. In lines 1–15, Kennedy uses a "capsule history" to describe a span of 50,000 years. Why might he begin by producing this analogy describing time?

4. Identify one persuasive technique that Kennedy uses. Cite evidence to support your answer.

5. One example of parallelism has been boxed. What is its effect? Identify another example.

TEXT ANALYSIS WORKSHOP  **659**

**FOR STRUGGLING READERS**
**Comprehension: Analogy** After students read lines 1–15, discuss the idea of condensing "50,000 years . . . in a time span of but a half century" (lines 1–3). Display a timeline to help students visualize the concept, and guide students in locating on the timeline the events Kennedy mentions in his speech.

**FOR ENGLISH LANGUAGE LEARNERS**
**Comprehension: Contrast** Call students' attention to the use of *but* in lines 30 and 31. Have students identify the items being contrasted (*hostile flag of conquest / banner of freedom and peace; weapons of mass destruction / instruments of knowledge and understanding*). Elicit or explain that the phrase *we shall not see* is used with *but* to form the parallel construction.

# Practice and Apply

## Part 3: Analyze the Text

**Close Read**

1. **Possible answer:** *Kennedy's claim is that the United States needs to emerge as a leader in the race for space.*

2. **Possible answer:** *Answers will vary, but students may say that Kennedy's speech appeals more to emotion than to reason. Instead of facts and statistics, he opens with an analogy about progress, speaks about "high reward," stresses that the country cannot afford to stay behind, and says that space must be governed by a "banner of freedom and peace," not "a hostile flag of conquest."*

3. **Possible answer:** *Kennedy may want to emphasize the "breathtaking pace" of past progress and to show how far the country has come in a short time.*

4. **Possible answers:** *He appeals to the emotion of fear by saying that space could be "governed by a hostile flag of conquest" (lines 29–30). He also uses bandwagon appeal by implying that those who came before made sure that the U. S. "rode the first waves" (lines 24–25) of progress and that this generation should do likewise.*

5. **Possible answers:** *The parallelism emphasizes that our predecessors were leaders in progress, which supports Kennedy's claim that the country should take a leadership role in exploring space. Other examples occur in lines 29–32.*

# Assess and Reteach

### Assess

Have students define and give examples of the persuasive techniques (page 656) and rhetorical devices (page 658) discussed.

### Reteach

For students who are unable to apply the workshop skills to "The New Frontier," select from these reteaching options:

• Have students review the note-taking copy masters and restate the information in their own words. Help them identify examples.

• Have small groups summarize the persuasive techniques and rhetorical devices and identify examples of each.

## COMMON CORE FOCUS

**RI 4** Analyze the impact of word choices on meaning and tone. **RI 6** Determine an author's purpose in a text; analyze how an author uses rhetoric to advance that purpose. **RI 8** Delineate and evaluate the argument and specific claims in a text. **RI 9** Analyze seminal U.S. documents of historical significance. **W 9b (RI 9)** Draw evidence from informational texts to support analysis of seminal U.S. documents of historical significance. **L 5a** Interpret figures of speech in context.

### SUMMARY

In his historic "I Have a Dream" speech, delivered at the Lincoln Memorial in 1963, Dr. Martin Luther King, Jr., presents a promise of freedom that has yet to be realized.

## Can a **DREAM** change the world?

Ask the question. Help students to understand that vision means seeing with the mind and heart what the world could become rather than seeing with the eyes what the world is now. After students have completed the *QUICKWRITE,* allow volunteers to share their responses.

---

*Essential Course of Study* **ECOS**

## I Have a Dream
 Video link at thinkcentral.com

Speech by Dr. Martin Luther King Jr.

**VIDEO TRAILER** THINK central   KEYWORD: HML9-660

# Can a **DREAM** change the world?

**COMMON CORE**

**RI 4** Analyze the impact of word choices on meaning and tone. **RI 6** Determine an author's purpose in a text; analyze how an author uses rhetoric to advance that purpose. **RI 8** Delineate and evaluate the argument and specific claims in a text. **RI 9** Analyze seminal U.S. documents of historical significance.

Time and again someone has a dream, or vision, of how to make the world a better place. That vision finds expression in powerful words—words that stir others to find ways to improve our lives. In the speech you are about to read, Dr. Martin Luther King Jr. eloquently sets forth the vision he had for the future.

*QUICKWRITE* What is your vision for a better world? Does it involve better schools? safer communities? cleaner air? Write a paragraph describing your vision of how to change one aspect of the world.

660

---

See resources on the **Teacher One Stop DVD-ROM** and on **thinkcentral.com**.

 Video link at thinkcentral.com

 **RESOURCE MANAGER UNIT 6**
Plan and Teach, pp. 11–18
Summary pp. 19–20†‡*
Text Analysis and Reading
    Skill, pp. 21–24†*
Vocabulary, pp. 25–27*

**DIAGNOSTIC AND SELECTION TESTS**
Selection Tests, pp. 175–178

 **BEST PRACTICES TOOLKIT**
Two-Column Chart, p. A25
Definition Mapping, p. E6
New Word Analysis, p. E8

**INTERACTIVE READER**

**ADAPTED INTERACTIVE READER**

**ELL ADAPTED INTERACTIVE READER**

**TECHNOLOGY**
 **Teacher One Stop DVD-ROM**
💿 **Student One Stop DVD-ROM**
💿 **PowerNotes DVD-ROM**
💿 **Audio Anthology CD**
💿 **GrammarNotes DVD-ROM**
💿 **Audio Tutor CD**
💿 **ExamView Test Generator**
on the **Teacher One Stop**

### Video Trailer
 THINK central

Go to **thinkcentral.com** to preview the **Video Trailer** introducing this selection. Other features that support the selection include
• **PowerNotes** presentation
• **ThinkAloud** models to enhance comprehension
• **WordSharp** vocabulary tutorials
• interactive writing and grammar instruction

---

\* Resources for Differentiation          † Also in Spanish          ‡ In Haitian Creole and Vietnamese

## TEXT ANALYSIS: ARGUMENT

In an **argument,** a writer or speaker takes a position on an issue and provides support for the position by appealing strictly to reason. The position is referred to as the **claim,** or proposition. The **support** for the claim may be reasons, evidence, or both—but this support should be credible, relevant to the claim, and of sufficient quality to be persuasive. In "I Have a Dream," King makes this claim about the status of African Americans:

*But one hundred years later* [after the Emancipation Proclamation], *the Negro still is not free. . . .*

As you read the speech, look for this claim and the reasons and evidence King provides to support it.

## READING SKILL: UNDERSTAND RHETORICAL DEVICES

Writers and speakers typically use more than just arguments to persuade. They also use **rhetorical devices** such as these three:

- **Repetition** is the repeated use of the same word or phrase. It is used primarily for emphasis.
- **Parallelism** is the repetition of similar grammatical structures, words, phrases, or sentences. It is used to show that ideas are related or equal in importance.
- An **analogy** is a point-by-point comparison of two subjects. It can help convey ideas that are hard to grasp, such as how a complex object looks or functions.

As you read, write down examples of these devices and describe their effects, using a chart like the one shown.

| Word, Phrase, or Sentence | Type of Device | Effect |
|---|---|---|
| "one hundred years later" | repetition | emphasizes how long African Americans have been denied their rights |

## ▲ VOCABULARY IN CONTEXT

King chose the words shown in boldface to inspire his audience. Use the context to figure out their meanings.

1. a **momentous** occasion
2. miss payments and **default** on a loan
3. turned from protest to **militancy**
4. two evils **inextricably** joined
5. a **legitimate** excuse

Complete the activities in your **Reader/Writer Notebook.**

---

## Meet the Author

### Dr. Martin Luther King Jr.
#### 1929–1968

**Crusader for Justice**
Preaching a philosophy of nonviolence, Dr. Martin Luther King Jr. became a catalyst for social change in the 1950s and 1960s. He galvanized people of all races to participate in boycotts, marches, and demonstrations against racial injustice. His moral leadership stirred the conscience of the nation and helped bring about the passage of the Civil Rights Act of 1964. In that same year he was awarded the Nobel Peace Prize. King continued his work for justice and equality until he was assassinated in 1968.

**Inspirational Speaker**
An eloquent Baptist minister from Atlanta, King often used religious references in his speeches. On the night before his death, he told an audience in Memphis, Tennessee: "I've seen the Promised Land. I may not get there with you, but I want you to know tonight, that we as a people will get to the Promised Land."

**BACKGROUND TO THE SPEECH**
**March on Washington**
In August 1963, thousands of Americans marched on Washington, D.C., to urge Congress to pass a civil rights bill. King delivered his "I Have a Dream" speech on the steps of the Lincoln Memorial before more than 200,000 people.

Author Online
Go to **thinkcentral.com.**
KEYWORD: HML9-661

661

---

## Teach

**TEXT ANALYSIS** — COMMON CORE — RI 8

### ● *Model the Skill:* ARGUMENT

Tell students that your vision for changing the world involves ending hunger. Tell them this statement is an accurate claim, or proposition, for your vision: *Even though we have the technology to feed everyone, many people still go hungry.* Have them state another proposition for your vision. ***Possible answer:*** *We have enough food; hungry people need to receive it.*

**GUIDED PRACTICE** Ask students to explain what role a claim has in an argument.

---

**READING SKILL** — COMMON CORE — RI 6

### ■ *Model the Skill:* UNDERSTAND RHETORICAL DEVICES

Discuss the terms *repetition, parallelism,* and *analogy.* Have students look ahead to see how *one hundred years later* is repeated in lines 8–13. Then, have students locate and explain the purpose of a repeated term in the quotation in **Inspirational Speaker.** ***Possible answer:*** *King repeats "Promised Land" to emphasize his vision.*

**GUIDED PRACTICE** Discuss why repetition, parallelism, and analogies can help make a speech effective.

**R** RESOURCE MANAGER—Copy Master Understand Rhetorical Devices p. 23

---

## VOCABULARY SKILL
COMMON CORE — L 4

### ▲ VOCABULARY IN CONTEXT

**DIAGNOSE WORD KNOWLEDGE** Have all students complete Vocabulary in Context. Check their words and phrases against the following:

**default** (dĭ-fôlt′) *v.* to fail to keep a promise, especially a promise to repay a loan
**inextricably** (ĭn-ĕk′strĭ-kə-blē) *adv.* in a way impossible to untangle
**legitimate** (lə-jĭt′ə-mĭt) *adj.* justifiable; reasonable

**militancy** (mĭl′ĭ-tənt-sē) *n.* the act of aggressively supporting a political or social cause
**momentous** (mō-mĕn′təs) *adj.* of great importance

**PRETEACH VOCABULARY** Use the following copy master to help students self-assess their knowledge of each boldfaced word.

**R** RESOURCE MANAGER—Copy Master Vocabulary Study p. 25

1. Read item 1 aloud, emphasizing *default.*
2. Point out the clues *promise to pay, promise,* and *does not give.* Elicit possible meanings for *default,* such as "fail to fulfill a commitment."
3. Repeat the procedure for the other items in Part A.

## READ WITH A PURPOSE

*Help students set a purpose for reading. Ask them to decide what King's goal was in delivering his speech to the crowd.*

### Ⓐ *Model the Skill:* ARGUMENT

Suggest that students use a Two-Column Chart to paraphrase King's claims. Model the first example below from lines 10–11. Then fill in the second quotation from line 13 and have students provide a paraphrase similar to the one provided.

| I Read | My Paraphrase |
|---|---|
| "lives on a lonely island of poverty" | is isolated by being poor |
| "finds himself in exile" | set apart and sent away |

 **BEST PRACTICES TOOLKIT—Transparency** Two-Column Chart p. A25

*Possible answer: King cites segregation (line 9), discrimination (line 10), and poverty (line 11) as evidence that African Americans do not enjoy complete freedom.*

### OWN THE WORD

- **momentous:** Ask students to name *momentous* occasions in their own lives, perhaps when a sibling was born, they were honored for accomplishments in a particular field, gave a speech in front of a large audience, or scored a goal in a crucial soccer game.

- **default:** Ask students to list reasons why a nation or an individual might *default* on a promissory note. *Possible answers: did not have money to pay back the lender, chose to ignore the loan, refused to acknowledge that money was due*

# I Have a Dream

**DR. MARTIN LUTHER KING JR.**

I am happy to join with you today in what will go down in history as the greatest demonstration for freedom in the history of our nation.

Five score[1] years ago, a great American, in whose symbolic shadow we stand today, signed the Emancipation Proclamation.[2] This **momentous** decree came as a great beacon light of hope to millions of Negro slaves who had been seared in the flames of withering injustice. It came as a joyous daybreak to end the long night of their captivity.

10 But one hundred years later, the Negro still is not free; one hundred years later, the life of the Negro is still sadly crippled by the manacles of segregation and the chains of discrimination; one hundred years later, the Negro lives on a lonely island of poverty in the midst of a vast ocean of material prosperity; one hundred years later, the Negro is still languishing in the corners of American society and finds himself in exile in his own land. Ⓐ

So we've come here today to dramatize a shameful condition. In a sense we've come to our nation's capital to cash a check. When the architects of our republic wrote the magnificent words of the Constitution and the Declaration of Independence, they were signing a promissory note[3] to which every American was to fall heir. This note was the promise that all men, yes, black men as well as white men, would be guaranteed the unalienable rights of life,
20 liberty, and the pursuit of happiness.

It is obvious today that America has **defaulted** on this promissory note insofar as her citizens of color are concerned. Instead of honoring this sacred obligation, America has given the Negro people a bad check, a check which has come back marked "insufficient funds." But we refuse to believe that the bank of justice is bankrupt. We refuse to believe that there are insufficient funds in

---

1. **five score:** 100; *score* means "twenty." (This phrasing recalls the beginning of Abraham Lincoln's Gettysburg Address: "Four score and seven years ago …")
2. **Emancipation Proclamation:** a document signed by President Lincoln in 1863, during the Civil War, declaring that all slaves in states still at war with the Union were free.
3. **promissory** (prŏm′ĭ-sôr′ē) **note:** a written promise to repay a loan.

### Analyze Visuals ▶

What impression do you get of Martin Luther King Jr. from this photograph?

**momentous** (mō-měn′təs) *adj.* of great importance

 **Targeted Passage**

### Ⓐ ARGUMENT

Reread lines 8–13. What evidence does King provide to **support** the **claim** that "the Negro still is not free"? Is the evidence relevant and credible? Explain.

**default** (dĭ-fôlt′) *v.* to fail to keep a promise, especially a promise to repay a loan

August 28, 1963: Dr. Martin Luther King Jr. delivers his speech at the Lincoln Memorial during the March on Washington, D.C.

---

## DIFFERENTIATED INSTRUCTION

### FOR ENGLISH LANGUAGE LEARNERS

**Vocabulary Support** Use Definition Mapping to practice these words: *demonstration* (line 2), *symbolic* (line 3), *discrimination* (line 10), *pursuit* (line 20), *insufficient* (line 24), *foundations* (line 43).

 **BEST PRACTICES TOOLKIT—Transparency** Definition Mapping p. E6

### FOR STRUGGLING READERS

In combination with the *Audio Anthology CD*, use one or more Targeted Passages (pp. 662, 665, 667) to ensure that students focus on key ideas, concepts, and skills. Targeted Passges are also good for English learners.

**①** Targeted Passage [Lines 1–7]

This introductory passage establishes the historical context of King's speech.

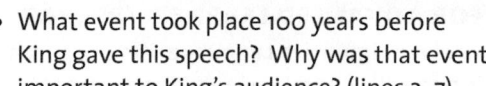

## Reading Support

This selection on **thinkcentral.com** includes embedded **ThinkAloud** models–students "thinking aloud" about the story to model the kinds of questions a good reader would ask about a selection.

## BACKGROUND

**"I Have a Dream"** Ironically, the phrase that has come to define King's famous speech was not in the prepared version that he intended to deliver to the approximately 200,000 listeners who had gathered in front of the Lincoln Memorial on August 28, 1963 to protest racial injustice. As he stepped toward the podium after a long program of speeches and musical performances, King was informed that time would allow for him to speak extemporaneously if he wished. He delivered his prepared remarks and then, he reported later, a phrase came to him: "I have a dream." He had used it in speeches in Birmingham and Detroit in April and June of that year. But now, King repeated the phrase over and over, each time using it to introduce a vision of a more just nation, each time stirring the emotional response of his listeners. When he finished to thunderous applause, King had transformed his audience with the inspiration of his words and the power of his dream.

## Analyze Visuals

*Possible answer: King is calm, confident, and in control.*

- What event took place 100 years before King gave this speech? Why was that event important to King's audience? (lines 3–7)

- What does King say about the historic importance of the event at which he is speaking? Do you think that he was right? Why or why not? (lines 8–20)

**Options for Reading** Read aloud the first two paragraphs of "I Have a Dream." Review the author and purpose of the speech. Then have learners listen to the *Audio Anthology CD* as they read along.

### FOR ADVANCED LEARNERS/PRE–AP

**Multimedia Display** Challenge students to create a "Dream on Display" museum exhibit. Include copies of historic photos, re-creations of signs the marchers carried, and the buttons they wore. Use the Internet to find background information on the march, the civil rights movement, and Dr. King and other leaders.

Use these prompts to help students focus on King's tone in lines 39–44:

**Connect** If you had been in the audience, how might you have reacted to these words? Why? *Answers will vary, but students should consider responses to the resolute, even defiant, attitude in King's statements.*

**Analyze** In terms of content and emotion, what is the purpose of this paragraph? *Possible answer: The purpose is to bring King's introductory focus to a point of tension, some of which will be released in the next paragraph.*

**Synthesize** How does King use tone to appeal to his audience? *Possible answer: King's tone is both revolutionary and unifying. When he says that the struggle for equality will continue (lines 41–42) and will shake the country (line 43), his determined tone appeals to the need for radical change. He then appeals to a sense of unity, however, by looking optimistically to a "bright day of justice" (line 44) for all.*

---

**VOCABULARY**

COMMON CORE
L 4

**OWN THE WORD**

**legitimate:** Tell students that the Latin word *lex* means "law," and that this is the key to understanding the meaning of *legitimate*, whose connotation is something that is legal or right.

---

**READING SKILL**

COMMON CORE
RI 6

**B RHETORICAL DEVICES**

*Possible answer: King uses repetition. By repeating "now is the time" (lines 31, 32, 33, and 35), he stresses the urgency of the situation.*

**IF STUDENTS NEED HELP . . .** Read the lines aloud so that students can hear the repetition.

**Extend the Discussion** What else does King do in this paragraph to hold his listeners' attention and emphasize his message?

More than 200,000 marchers gather on the mall between the Washington Monument and the Lincoln Memorial. To the right, civil rights leaders march with King.

the great vaults of opportunity of this nation. And so we've come to cash this check, a check that will give us upon demand the riches of freedom and the security of justice.

We have also come to this hallowed spot to remind America of the fierce
30 urgency of now. This is no time to engage in the luxury of cooling off or to take the tranquilizing drug of gradualism.[4] Now is the time to make real the promises of democracy; now is the time to rise from the dark and desolate valley of segregation to the sunlit path of racial justice; now is the time to lift our nation from the quicksands of racial injustice to the solid rock of brotherhood; now is the time to make justice a reality for all of God's children. It would be fatal for the nation to overlook the urgency of the moment. This sweltering summer of the Negro's **legitimate** discontent will not pass until there is an invigorating autumn of freedom and equality. **B**

Nineteen sixty-three is not an end, but a beginning. And those who hope
40 that the Negro needed to blow off steam and will now be content will have a rude awakening if the nation returns to business as usual. There will be neither rest nor tranquility in America until the Negro is granted his citizenship rights. The whirlwinds of revolt will continue to shake the foundations of our nation until the bright day of justice emerges.

**legitimate** (lə-jĭt'ə-mĭt)
*adj.* justifiable; reasonable

**B RHETORICAL DEVICES**
Reread lines 29–38. What rhetorical device does King use, and what is the effect of using it?

---

4. **gradualism:** a policy of seeking to reach a goal slowly, in gradual stages.

**664** UNIT 6: ARGUMENT AND PERSUASION

---

## DIFFERENTIATED INSTRUCTION

**FOR ENGLISH LANGUAGE LEARNERS**
**Vocabulary: Idioms** Use New Word Analysis to teach these idioms: *cooling off* (line 30), "calming down"; *blow off steam* (line 40), "release anger"; *rude awakening* (line 41), "shocking realization"; *business as usual* (line 41), "the normal routine"; *tied up with* (line 55), "connected to."

BEST PRACTICES TOOLKIT—Transparency
New Word Analysis p. E8

**FOR ADVANCED LEARNERS/PRE–AP**
**Analyze Figurative Language** King's speech is rich with figurative language, such as "the tranquilizing drug of gradualism," which he refers to in line 31. Ask students to choose one example of figurative language from King's speech and write a paragraph about how their choices helped them to understand King's message.

A young woman participates in the demonstration.

But there is something that I must say to my people, who stand on the worn threshold which leads into the palace of justice. In the process of gaining our rightful place we must not be guilty of wrongful deeds. Let us not seek to satisfy our thirst for freedom by drinking from the cup of bitterness and hatred. We must forever conduct our struggle on the high plain of dignity
50 and discipline. We must not allow our creative protests to degenerate into physical violence. Again and again we must rise to the majestic heights of meeting physical force with soul force. The marvelous new **militancy**, which has engulfed the Negro community, must not lead us to a distrust of all white people. For many of our white brothers, as evidenced by their presence here today, have come to realize that their destiny is tied up with our destiny. And they have come to realize that their freedom is **inextricably** bound to our freedom. We cannot walk alone. And as we walk, we must make the pledge that we shall always march ahead. We cannot turn back.

There are those who are asking the devotees of civil rights, "When will you
60 be satisfied?" We can never be satisfied as long as the Negro is the victim of the unspeakable horrors of police brutality; we can never be satisfied as long as our bodies, heavy with the fatigue of travel, cannot gain lodging in the motels of the highways and the hotels of the cities; we cannot be satisfied as long as the Negro's basic mobility is from a smaller ghetto to a larger one; we can never be satisfied as long as our children are stripped of their selfhood and robbed of

## ▲ Analyze Visuals

What do these photographs suggest about King's effectiveness as an orator and a leader? Explain.

## ❷ Targeted Passage

**militancy** (mĭl′ĭ-tənt-sē) *n.* the act of aggressively supporting a political or social cause

**inextricably** (ĭn-ĕk′strĭ-kə-blē) *adv.* in a way impossible to untangle

---

## FOR STRUGGLING READERS

### ❷ Targeted Passage [Lines 45–58]

Several statements in this passage illustrate the dignity and highmindedness of the civil rights movement under King's leadership.

- What actions does King oppose? (line 51)
- According to King, what thoughts should the Negro community have—and not have—toward white people? (lines 53–58)
- What does he mean when he uses the term *soul force*? (line 52)

## FOR ADVANCED LEARNERS/PRE–AP

**Analyze Style** [paired-activity option]
Have students reread these two pages, considering how King's sentences vary in length, structure, and placement of key elements. As students comment, encourage them to note variations in sentence structures (simple, compound, complex, compound-complex) and sentence beginnings, in particular.

---

## Analyze Visuals

*Possible answers:* The photograph of the huge crowd suggests that King was a powerful draw and a good speaker. The photograph of the marchers suggests that he understood how to work with others. The photograph of the young woman suggests that people looked to him as a leader and found hope in his words.

**Activity** Have students discuss why King and his fellow marchers wore suits. *Possible answer:* King presented civil rights as a struggle for human dignity. Wearing suits was a way of symbolizing the dignity of that cause.

## TIERED DISCUSSION PROMPTS

Use these prompts, which focus on lines 45–58, to help students understand the audience for this speech:

**Connect** How do you react to King's words about violence? *Students might mention how violence could harm the cause of civil rights.*

**Analyze** What does King do in these lines to show that whites and blacks in his audience must work together? *Possible answer: King says that the freedom and destiny of whites are linked to that of blacks (lines 55–57).*

**Synthesize** How do these lines both send a message to King's followers and gain the support of a wider audience? *Possible answer: These lines show that hatred and bitterness are not the answer to the problem of racial inequality. They show the need for trust and cooperation.*

---

**VOCABULARY**

COMMON CORE

L 4

### OWN THE WORD

- **militancy:** Tell students that *militancy* is based on the Latin root *milit-*, which means "soldier." Ask students to name other words with this root. *Possible answers: military, militia*

- **inextricably:** Remind students that the prefix *in-* means "not." Therefore, *inextricable* often refers to a situation from which you cannot *extricate* or untangle yourself.

TEXT ANALYSIS

COMMON CORE

RI 8

**© ARGUMENT**

*Possible answer:* police brutality, segregation, ghettos, "For Whites Only" signs, voting restrictions, and lack of concern for African-Americans' voting issues

READING SKILL

COMMON CORE

RI 6

**Ⓓ *Model the Skill:* RHETORICAL DEVICES**

Remind students that parallelism is the idea that similar ideas should be expressed using similar grammatical forms. Point out the example in lines 73–74. Tell students that "battered by" and "staggered by" are the same grammatical format; the parallelism makes King's ideas more vivid.

*Possible answer:* "sweltering with the heat of injustice, sweltering with the heat of oppression" (lines 88–89); and "by the color of their skin . . . by the content of their character" (lines 91–92)

**REVISIT THE BIG QUESTION**

## Can a **DREAM**

### change the world?

**Discuss** In lines 81–106, King introduces his dream. Why is it appropriate to speak of his dream as a vision—that is, as something more than a dream? *Possible answer:* King's dream is not just a fantasy; it is a vision because King has a plan to make America a better place.

TEXT ANALYSIS

COMMON CORE

RI 9

**Ⓔ SEMINAL U.S. DOCUMENTS**

*Possible answer:* Dr. King's speech is significant because he uses the words of America's foundational document, the Declaration of Independence, to make his point. His speech prompted major changes in American laws and customs.

---

their dignity by signs stating For Whites Only; we cannot be satisfied as long as the Negro in Mississippi cannot vote and a Negro in New York believes he has nothing for which to vote. No! No, we are not satisfied, and we will not be satisfied until "justice rolls down like waters and righteousness like a
70 mighty stream." **ⓒ**

I am not unmindful that some of you have come here out of great trials and tribulations. Some of you have come fresh from narrow jail cells. Some of you have come from areas where your quest for freedom left you battered by the storms of persecution and staggered by the winds of police brutality. You have been the veterans of creative suffering. Continue to work with the faith that unearned suffering is redemptive.[5] Go back to Mississippi. Go back to Alabama. Go back to South Carolina. Go back to Georgia. Go back to Louisiana. Go back to the slums and ghettos of our Northern cities, knowing that somehow this situation can and will be changed. Let us not wallow in the
80 valley of despair.

I say to you today, my friends, even though we face the difficulties of today and tomorrow, I still have a dream. It is a dream deeply rooted in the American dream. I have a dream that one day this nation will rise up and live out the true meaning of its creed, "We hold these truths to be self-evident; that all men are created equal." I have a dream that one day on the red hills of Georgia, sons of former slaves and the sons of former slave owners will be able to sit down together at the table of brotherhood. I have a dream that one day even the state of Mississippi, a state sweltering with the heat of injustice, sweltering with the heat of oppression, will be transformed into an oasis of freedom and
90 justice. I have a dream that my four little children will one day live in a nation where they will not be judged by the color of their skin, but by the content of their character. **Ⓓ**

I have a dream today!

I have a dream that one day down in Alabama—with its vicious racists, with its Governor having his lips dripping with the words of interposition and nullification[6]—one day right there in Alabama, little black boys and black girls will be able to join hands with little white boys and white girls as sisters and brothers.

I have a dream today!

I have a dream that one day every valley shall be exalted, and every hill and
100 mountain shall be made low. The rough places will be plain and the crooked places will be made straight, "and the glory of the Lord shall be revealed, and all flesh shall see it together." **Ⓔ**

This is our hope. This is the faith that I go back to the South with. With this faith we will be able to hew out of the mountain of despair a stone of hope. With this faith we will be able to transform the jangling discords of our nation into a beautiful symphony of brotherhood. With this faith we will

---

5.  **unearned suffering is redemptive:** undeserved suffering is a way of earning freedom or salvation.

6.  **Governor . . . nullification:** Rejecting a federal order to desegregate the University of Alabama, Governor George Wallace claimed that the principle of nullification (a state's alleged right to refuse a federal law) allowed him to resist federal "interposition," or interference, in state affairs.

**ⓒ ARGUMENT**

Identify the examples of racial injustice that King provides as strong, relevant, and credible **evidence** to convince his audience to share his views.

COMMON CORE   RI 4

**Language Coach**

**Formal Language** The formal language of public speeches differs from everyday language in several ways. For one, it contains fewer contractions (such as *I'm* or *you'll*). How might you rephrase the sentence in lines 79–80 informally?

**Ⓓ RHETORICAL DEVICES**

Reread lines 71–92. What examples of **parallel** grammatical structures help make the expression of ideas memorable?

COMMON CORE   RI 9

**Ⓔ SEMINAL U.S. DOCUMENTS**

Lines 81–102 of Dr. King's speech include his most familiar and stirring words in support of civil rights, emphasizing repeatedly that the dream of justice and equality can be realized for all Americans. Why do you think these lines establish Dr. King's speech as a significant text in American history?

---

## DIFFERENTIATED INSTRUCTION

### FOR STRUGGLING READERS

**Comprehension Support** [lines 81–92] To make sure that students understand this key paragraph, have them write the word *dream* six times on a sheet of paper, once for each appearance of *dream* as King describes it in the paragraph. In each case, ask students to note one thing that King says about his dream. Compare and discuss students' notes.

### FOR ENGLISH LANGUAGE LEARNERS

**Language Coach**   COMMON CORE   RI 4

**Formal Language** *Possible answer: Let's not feel sorry for ourselves.* Have students work in pairs to find other examples of formal speech in the text. Then have them decide how the sentences might be pronounced informally using contractions and everyday words. Remind students that the formal language King uses is appropriate for a public speech that conveys serious ideas. Informal language is appropriate in everyday situations, such as conversations with friends and family.

be able to work together, to pray together, to struggle together, to go to jail together, to stand up for
110 freedom together, knowing that we will be free one day. And this will be the day. This will be the day when all of God's children will be able to sing with new meaning, "My country 'tis of thee, sweet land of liberty, of thee I sing. Land where my fathers died, land of the pilgrims' pride, from every mountainside, let freedom ring."
120 And if America is to be a great nation, this must become true.

So let freedom ring from the prodigious hilltops of New Hampshire; let freedom ring from the mighty mountains of New York; let freedom ring from the heightening Alleghenies of Pennsylvania; let freedom ring from the snowcapped Rockies of
130 Colorado; let freedom ring from the curvaceous slopes of California. But not only that. Let freedom ring from Stone Mountain of Georgia; let freedom ring from Lookout Mountain of Tennessee; let freedom ring from every hill and molehill of Mississippi. "From every mountainside, let freedom ring."

And when this happens, and
140 when we allow freedom to ring, when we let it ring from every village and every hamlet, from every state and every city, we will be able to speed up that day when all of God's children— black men and white men, Jews and Gentiles, Protestants and Catholics—will be able to join hands and sing in the words of the old Negro spiritual, "Free at last. Free at last. Thank God Almighty, we are free at last." ❧

❸ Targeted Passage

January 20, 2003: Marchers in St. Louis celebrate King's birthday, a national holiday.

## Analyze Visuals

**Activity** Ask students why they think *I Have a Dream* appears on the sign that the woman is carrying. *Possible answer: The sign honors King's life, as noted by the dates at the bottom. "I Have a Dream" may be the most important speech that King ever gave; furthermore, it captures all that he worked for in the civil rights movement.*

### REVISIT THE BIG QUESTION
## Can a DREAM
### change the world?

**Discuss** Point out lines 139–145. What is King's ultimate, or greatest, vision? *Possible answer: King's ultimate vision is an America in which all people can come together in freedom, no longer concerned that their differences are counted against them.*

## SELECTION WRAP–UP

**READ WITH A PURPOSE** Now that students have finished reading the selection, have them decide how successful King was in meeting his goal in giving his speech. What role did use of language play in his success? *Possible answer: By referring to the Bible and other sources his readers would be familiar with, he elevated their spirits and energized them.*

★ **CRITIQUE** Have students identify what they feel is the most powerful, persuasive, or inspiring part of this speech.

### INDEPENDENT READING
Students may want to read more about the quest for civil rights as explained in *Why We Can't Wait,* by Martin Luther King, Jr.

---

**FOR STRUGGLING READERS**

❸ **Targeted Passage** [Lines 122–138]

As this powerful passage helps bring the speech to its emotional close, it reminds the listener of a bell, tolling its message.

• In what order does King name U.S. states? Why? (lines 122–138)

**FOR ENGLISH LANGUAGE LEARNERS**

**Develop Reading Fluency** Point out lines 122–138 to students and remind them that this passage brings the speech to its emotional close. Demonstrate an impassioned reading using inflection and tone. Use choral reading for the passage and then ask students how their use of inflection and tone helps bring the speech to its emotional close in this passage.

**R** RESOURCE MANAGER—Copy Master Reading Fluency p. 30

# Practice and Apply

For preliminary support of post-reading questions, use these copy masters:

**R** **RESOURCE MANAGER—Copy Masters**
Reading Check p. 28
Argument p. 21
Question Support p. 29

Additional selection questions are provided for teachers on page 15.

## ANSWERS

## Comprehension

1. *King describes poverty (lines 8–13), police brutality (line 61), segregation (lines 61–66), ghettos (lines 63–64), and voting inequalities (lines 66–68).*

2. *King predicts that the struggle for civil rights will continue, disturbing the very foundations of the country (lines 39–44).*

3. *King's dream is of an America where all people live in brotherhood, justice, and freedom (lines 81–92 and 143–145).*

## Text Analysis

COMMON CORE RI 6, RI 8, RI 9

*Possible answers:*

4. ● **COMMON CORE FOCUS** *Analyze the Argument Example: "For Whites Only" signs (lines 65–66); Example: voting inequities (lines 66–68); Example: slums and ghettos (line 78)*

5. ■ **COMMON CORE FOCUS** *Understand Rhetorical Devices Repetition: "No! No, we are not satisfied, and we will not be satisfied . . ." (lines 68–69). The repeated no and not satisfied emphasize King's frustration. Parallelism: "This is no time . . . . Now is the time . . ." (lines 30–35). The parallel structure sets up a contrast that stresses the urgency of the situation.*

6. *King means that America promised "unalienable rights" to all but has not honored that promise for African Americans. Instead, America has segregated African Americans and treated them unfairly.*

7. *This allusion is effective because the Declaration of Independence is familiar to all Americans. Furthermore, King alludes to the document in lines 14–20, when he discusses how America has failed to keep its promise to African Americans; by quoting it again now, he is saying that the failure can be rectified.*

---

## Comprehension

1. **Recall** What examples of racial injustice does King describe?

2. **Clarify** What does King predict will happen if justice is denied African Americans?

3. **Summarize** What is King's dream?

## Text Analysis

● 4. **Analyze the Argument** On a graphic organizer like the one shown, list at least three examples of racial injustice that King uses as effective **support** for his **claim** that African Americans are not free.

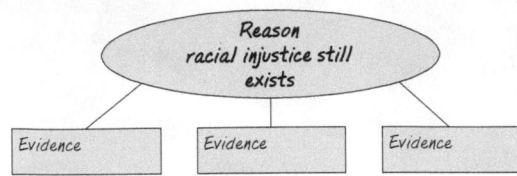

Reason racial injustice still exists → Evidence | Evidence | Evidence

■ 5. **Understand Rhetorical Devices** Review the chart you created as you read. Then identify an example of **repetition** or **parallelism** and explain its effect.

6. **Understand an Analogy** Reread lines 14–28. In these paragraphs, King uses an analogy to compare a familiar object—a promissory note—to something abstract—the promise of equal rights. What does King mean when he says that America has given African Americans a "bad check"? Explain your answer.

7. **Evaluate an Allusion** Reread lines 81–85. An allusion is an indirect reference, within a work, to something that the audience or reader is expected to know. As King begins to explain his vision, he alludes to the Declaration of Independence, quoting its famous lines. How effective is this allusion? Support your evaluation.

### READING-WRITING CONNECTION

| WRITING PROMPT | REVISING TIP |
|---|---|
| **Extended Constructed Response: Analysis** How would you account for the extraordinary acclaim King's speech has received, not only when it was first delivered but many years later? Write a **three-to-five-paragraph analysis** of the effectiveness of King's address. Consider both the strength of its logic and its emotional power. | Review your analysis. Did you state the qualities that make the speech memorable? Did you provide relevant examples from the speech? |

## Can a DREAM change the world?

How can you turn a dream for change into a reality?

COMMON CORE

**RI 6** Determine an author's purpose in a text; analyze how an author uses rhetoric to advance that purpose. **RI 8** Delineate and evaluate the argument and specific claims in a text. **RI 9** Analyze seminal U.S. documents of historical significance. **W 9b (RI 9)** Draw evidence from informational texts to support analysis of seminal U.S. documents of historical significance.

---

**READING-WRITING CONNECTION**

COMMON CORE W 9b(RI 9)

Have students use an Argumentation frame to explore the logic of King's speech. Pairs or small groups of students might work together to find and discuss examples of its emotional power. Students also may use Mapping Main Ideas and Details to plan their essays.

💼 BEST PRACTICES TOOLKIT—Transparencies
Argumentation p. B11
Mapping Main Ideas and Details p. C6

Can a **DREAM** change the world? *Possible answer: Many students may say that if enough people believe in the dream it can, in fact, bring about big changes. Students should cite specific examples from history or current events.*

# Vocabulary in Context

## ▲ VOCABULARY PRACTICE

Answer the questions to show your understanding of the vocabulary words.

1. Which would be more **momentous**—the birth of a baby or the first snow of the season in upstate New York?

2. If you **default** on a loan, do you sign up to borrow money or fail to make a payment?

3. If your teacher judges your doctor's note to be **legitimate,** would you be sent to the principal's office or allowed to miss gym?

4. Who would be more likely to support a course of **militancy**—a person starting a new job or a person unfairly denied an opportunity to work?

5. Which items are more likely to be **inextricably** linked—the products on a shelf at a grocery store, or the necklaces kept in a dresser drawer?

## ACADEMIC VOCABULARY IN WRITING

- coherent   • differentiate   • evident   • relevant   • technique

The **technique,** or rhetorical device, of repetition is **evident** in Dr. King's speech. Using the technique of repetition, write a paragraph or two on a topic you care about, such as the environment or education. Use at least one Academic Vocabulary word in your writing.

## VOCABULARY STRATEGY: ANALOGIES

Recall that an **analogy** is a comparison between two things that are alike in some way. Writers often use analogies to explain a complicated idea or describe the appearance or function of an object. Here is another analogy from King's speech:

> *Five score years ago, a great American . . . signed the Emancipation Proclamation. This momentous decree came as a great beacon light of hope to millions of Negro slaves. . . .* (lines 3–5)

In this instance, King is saying that the Emancipation Proclamation was like a beacon—the proclamation spread hope much as a beacon spreads light.

**PRACTICE** Identify the analogy in each of the following sentences by noting what two things are being compared. Then produce your own analogy by comparing the first thing to something else.

1. Reading a poem is like opening an oyster; you may find a pearl within.

2. The Internet works like a system of roads, transporting information at different speeds depending on the traffic and each road's "speed limit."

3. In the NASA photograph, the distant moon looks like a half-peeled potato.

**COMMON CORE**

**L 5a** Interpret figures of speech in context.

**Interactive Vocabulary**  **THINK**central

Go to **thinkcentral.com.**
KEYWORD: HML9-669

---

## ANSWERS

# Vocabulary in Context

## ▲ VOCABULARY PRACTICE

1. *the birth of a baby*
2. *fail to make a payment*
3. *allowed to miss gym*
4. *person denied work opportunity*
5. *necklaces kept in a dresser drawer*

**R** RESOURCE MANAGER—Copy Master
Vocabulary Practice p. 26

## ACADEMIC VOCABULARY IN WRITING

**Possible answer:** *By educating citizens, we strengthen our country. By educating citizens, we* differentiate *our country from others.*

## VOCABULARY STRATEGY: ANALOGIES

**COMMON CORE L 5a**

**Possible answers:**

1. *A poem is like a riddle because both require work to understand.*
2. *The Internet is like a living creature because it changes and evolves.*
3. *The moon is like a sponge because both have craters and are round.*

**R** RESOURCE MANAGER—Copy Master
Vocabulary Strategy p. 27

**Interactive Vocabulary**  **THINK**central

Keywords direct students to a **WordSharp** tutorial on **thinkcentral.com** or to other types of vocabulary practice and review.

---

## DIFFERENTIATED INSTRUCTION

### FOR ENGLISH LANGUAGE LEARNERS

**Vocabulary: Related Words** Have students work with partners and use a dictionary to find words that are related to some of these vocabulary words. For example, for *militancy,* students might note the related words *military, militant,* and *militia.* Interested pairs of students might work together to create a poster or other visual aid that catalogs their findings.

### FOR ADVANCED LEARNERS/PRE–AP

**Vocabulary in Writing** Challenge students to write a coherent paragraph, with a clear main idea, that uses all the words. Allow students to share their paragraphs in small groups and discuss the ways in which they used the words.

---

# Assess and Reteach

## Assess

**DIAGNOSTIC AND SELECTION TESTS**
Selection Test A, pp. 175–176
Selection Test B/C, pp. 177–178

**Interactive Selection Test** on **thinkcentral.com**

## Reteach

**Level Up Online Tutorials** on **thinkcentral.com**

**Reteaching Workshops** on **thinkcentral.com**
Literature Lesson 36

# Focus and Motivate

COMMON CORE FOCUS

**RI 2** Analyze the development of a central idea in a text and provide an objective summary of the text. **RI 5** Analyze in detail how an author's ideas or claims are developed. **RI 8** Delineate and evaluate the argument and specific claims in a text. **W 9a (RI 8)** Draw evidence from informational texts to support an evaluation of the specific claims in a text. **L 1a** Use parallel structure. **L 3** Apply knowledge of language to make effective choices for meaning or style. **L 4c** Consult reference materials to determine a word's meaning and etymology.

## SUMMARY

Actor Michael J. Fox urges an increase in federal funding for Parkinson's disease research. Fox describes his expectation that a cure could be found soon—if the research were better funded.

### How do you
### SELL AN IDEA?

Introduce the question. Have students read the question and comment on memorable commercials. After students complete the *DISCUSS* activity, compile a master list of persuasive techniques used to pitch products.

## Selection Resources

---

# How do you
# SELL AN IDEA?

COMMON CORE

**RI 2** Analyze the development of a central idea in a text and provide an objective summary of the text. **RI 5** Analyze in detail how an author's ideas or claims are developed. **RI 8** Delineate and evaluate the argument and specific claims in a text. **L 1a** Use parallel structure. **L 4c** Consult reference materials to determine a word's meaning and etymology.

Teenagers are a hot market—companies are always trying to convince them to buy something. You're familiar with commercials and ads that try to sell you a product. But are you aware that a great deal of energy and money is spent trying to sell you on people and ideas? People in almost every business work hard at crafting their pitch.

**DISCUSS** With a partner, brainstorm a list of times when you realized someone was trying to sell you an idea, an image, or a person's expertise. What techniques were used? Which ones worked?

| Idea | Pitch Used |
|------|------------|
| Say "no" to drugs. | Commercial about saving a friend who's drowning; features the slogan "Friends, the anti-drug." |

670

---

See resources on the **Teacher One Stop DVD-ROM** *and on* **thinkcentral.com**.

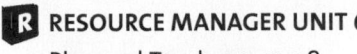 **RESOURCE MANAGER UNIT 6**
   Plan and Teach, pp. 31–38
   Summary pp. 39–40†‡*
   Text Analysis and Reading
      Skill, pp. 41–44†*
   Vocabulary, pp. 45–47*
   Grammar and Style, p. 50

**DIAGNOSTIC AND SELECTION TESTS**
   Selection Tests, pp. 179–182

 **BEST PRACTICES TOOLKIT**
   Word Questioning, p. E9

**INTERACTIVE READER**

**ADAPTED INTERACTIVE READER**

**ELL ADAPTED INTERACTIVE READER**

**TECHNOLOGY**
- **Teacher One Stop DVD-ROM**
- **Student One Stop DVD-ROM**
- **PowerNotes DVD-ROM**
- **Audio Anthology CD**
- **GrammarNotes DVD-ROM**
- **Audio Tutor CD**
- **ExamView Test Generator**
   on the **Teacher One Stop**

**Video Trailer**

Go to **thinkcentral.com** to preview the **Video Trailer** introducing this selection. Other features that support the selection include
- **PowerNotes** presentation
- **ThinkAloud** models to enhance comprehension
- **WordSharp** vocabulary tutorials
- interactive writing and grammar instruction

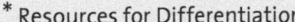 * Resources for Differentiation     † Also in Spanish     ‡ In Haitian Creole and Vietnamese

## TEXT ANALYSIS: PERSUASIVE TECHNIQUES

Writers and speakers typically use more than just arguments to persuade. To develop their ideas or claims, they use rhetorical devices and **persuasive techniques**—that is, messages and descriptions that appeal to people's emotions, values, and desires to belong to a particular group or be like a particular person.

In "Testimony Before the Senate," Michael J. Fox often uses the persuasive techniques that are classified as emotional appeals. **Emotional appeals** are descriptions designed to win support by appealing to people's feelings of compassion or, sometimes, fear. Here Fox appeals to our sense of pity:

*There are doctors, teachers, policemen, nurses, and parents who are no longer able to work, to provide for their families, and live out their dreams.*

As you read, look for other examples of emotional appeals.

## READING STRATEGY: SUMMARIZE

A **summary** is a brief retelling of the main ideas of a written or spoken text. When you summarize, use your own words to restate the main ideas without including your own opinions. As you read Fox's speech, prepare to summarize it by jotting down main ideas and important details on a chart like the one shown. Your summary will help you evaluate the text's arguments.

> *Paragraph/Section 1*
> | Main Idea: |
> | Important Details: |
>
> ↓
>
> *Paragraph/Section 2*
> | Main Idea: |
> | Important Details: |
>
> ↓

## ▲ VOCABULARY IN CONTEXT

The following boldfaced words are key to understanding Michael J. Fox's persuasive plea. Restate each phrase, using a different word or words for the boldfaced term.

1. rejecting the **status quo**
2. a **meager** salary, which doesn't allow for luxuries
3. a **neurological** disorder causing tremors
4. **eradicate** poverty and other social problems

 Complete the activities in your **Reader/Writer Notebook**.

---

## Meet the Author

# Michael J. Fox
born 1961

**Actor and Crusader**
A successful actor in both film and television—he received four Emmy Awards—Michael J. Fox was diagnosed with Parkinson's disease at the age of 30. In order to spend more time with his family and to promote Parkinson's research, he retired from acting in 2000. He went on to establish the Michael J. Fox Foundation for Parkinson's Research.

**BACKGROUND TO THE SPEECH**
**Parkinson's Disease**
Parkinson's disease results from a loss of brain cells that produce dopamine, a chemical that transmits brain signals. The disease's many symptoms include tremors, slowness of movement, and problems with balance. Over time, walking and other ordinary activities become more and more difficult. The cause of Parkinson's is still unknown, and as yet no cure has been found. Unfortunately, the medications used to treat the disease often have serious side effects.

**Authors Online**
Go to **thinkcentral.com**. KEYWORD: HML9-671

THINK central

---

# Teach

TEXT ANALYSIS — COMMON CORE — RI 5, RI 8

## ● Model the Skill: PERSUASIVE TECHNIQUES

To model the use of an emotional appeal, read aloud this example:

> If you care about fire safety, vote to save Engine 12.

Point out that this emotional appeal is persuasive because it appeals to people's concerns for their safety in the event of a fire.

**GUIDED PRACTICE** Ask students to give an example of an emotional appeal about another topic.

READING SKILL — COMMON CORE — RI 2

## ■ Model the Skill: SUMMARIZE

Model this skill by summarizing **Author Online**:

> After he was diagnosed with Parkinson's disease, Michael J. Fox eventually gave up his successful acting career. He has become a powerful advocate for finding a cure for the disease.

Discuss which details from the text were included and which were omitted.

**GUIDED PRACTICE** Have students summarize the **Background** text.

**R** RESOURCE MANAGER—Copy Master Summarize p. 43 (for student use while reading the selection)

---

VOCABULARY SKILL — COMMON CORE — L 4

## ▲ VOCABULARY IN CONTEXT

**DIAGNOSE WORD KNOWLEDGE** Have all students complete Vocabulary in Context. Check their words and phrases against the following:

**eradicate** (ĭ-răd'ĭ-kāt') *v.* to do away with completely
**meager** (mē'gər) *adj.* lacking in quantity or quality
**neurological** (noŏr'ə-lŏj'ĭ-kəl) *adj.* having to do with the nervous system

**status quo** (stăt'əs kwō) *n.* the existing state of affairs

**PRETEACH VOCABULARY** Use the following copy master to help students predict the meaning of each boldfaced word.

**R** RESOURCE MANAGER—Copy Master Vocabulary Study p. 45

1. Read the first sentence in Part A aloud, emphasizing *status quo*.
2. Point out the phrase *resigned to accept*. Elicit possible meanings for *status quo*.
3. Repeat the procedure for the other items in Part A.

# Practice and Apply

## READ WITH A PURPOSE

*Help students set a purpose for reading. Tell them to look for reasons Fox decided to become a spokesperson for Parkinson's.*

**REVISIT THE BIG QUESTION**

How do you
# SELL AN IDEA?

Point out lines 1–12. **Discuss** How does Senator Specter indicate that the Subcommittee is open to listening to the pitch that Fox is about to make? *Possible answer: Specter mentions the acclaim that Fox has received (lines 1–5) and the fact that Fox has Parkinson's disease (lines 5–6), suggesting that Fox comes before the Subcommittee with some authority to address the issue. Specter also admits the need to cure the disease (lines 10–11). Finally, he thanks Fox for coming and says that the Subcommittee is looking forward to hearing Fox's testimony (lines 11–12).*

---

**TEXT ANALYSIS**  COMMON CORE  RI 5, RI 8

### Ⓐ *Model the Skill:* PERSUASIVE TECHNIQUES

Model an appeal to vanity by praising your students' ability to read critically. Ask them how they felt being praised.

*Possible answer: The persuasive technique is an appeal to vanity. Fox is trying to win over the senators, in part, by praising their leadership.*

**Extend the Discussion** It is not uncommon for people who come before Congress to begin their testimony with words like these. Why is Fox's technique an effective opening for a speech to such an audience?

---

## PARKINSON'S DISEASE RESEARCH AND TREATMENT

# HEARING

BEFORE A
### SUBCOMMITTEE OF THE
### COMMITTEE ON APPROPRIATIONS
### UNITED STATES SENATE
ONE HUNDRED SIXTH CONGRESS

FIRST SESSION

### SPECIAL HEARING

Printed for the use of the Committee on Appropriations

**Senator SPECTER.** We have with us today Mr. Michael J. Fox, a successful actor for many years. First, as Alex P. Keaton, on the television series "Family Ties." You always work with a middle initial, do you not, Mr. Fox? Later in many movies, including "Back to the Future," and, most recently, on television again in the highly acclaimed "Spin City." Michael was diagnosed with Parkinson's in 1991, at the age of 30.

He has become very, very active in Parkinson's advocacy. One of the facts of life is that when someone like Michael J. Fox steps forward, it very heavily personalizes the problem, focuses a lot of public attention on it,
10 and has the public understanding of the need for doing whatever we can as a country to conquer this disease and many, many others. So we thank you for being here, Michael J. Fox, and look forward to your testimony.

Again, we will put the lights on, for 5 minutes, on testimony.

**Ⓐ PERSUASIVE TECHNIQUES**
What persuasive technique mentioned on page 656 in the Text Analysis Workshop is Fox using in lines 14–18?

**Targeted Passage ①**

**Mr. FOX.** Mr. Chairman, Senator Harkin, and members of the Subcommittee—thank you for inviting me to testify today about the need for a greater federal investment in Parkinson's research. I would like to thank you, in particular, for your tremendous leadership in the fight to double funding for the National Institutes of Health.[1] Ⓐ

---

1. **National Institutes of Health:** a government organization that conducts and supports research designed to improve the health of the nation.

---

## DIFFERENTIATED INSTRUCTION

**FOR ENGLISH LANGUAGE LEARNERS**

**Vocabulary Support** Use Word Questioning to practice these words: *advocacy* (line 7), *federal* (line 16), *funding* (line 18), *techniques* (line 27), *adequately* (line 49), *medical* (line 65).

🧰 **BEST PRACTICES TOOLKIT—Transparency**
Word Questioning p. E9

**FOR STRUGGLING READERS**

In combination with the *Audio Anthology CD*, use one or more Targeted Passages (pp. 672, 675, 676) to ensure that students focus on key ideas, concepts, and skills. Targeted Passages are also good for English learners.

**① Targeted Passage [Lines 14–18]**

This passage presents Fox's first words and the goal for his speech.

- Who is Fox's audience? (lines 14–15)

Michael J. Fox testifies before the U.S. Senate.

**Reading Support**

This selection on **thinkcentral.com** includes embedded **ThinkAloud** models—students "thinking aloud" about the story to model the kinds of questions a good reader would ask about a selection.

◄ **Analyze Visuals**

Think about your reaction to seeing a famous actor linked with a cause or product. Are you more willing to read this speech and consider its message because the author is a celebrity? Explain your answer.

## Analyze Visuals

*Possible answer:* *Yes; people generally would be more willing to consider a message coming from a celebrity whom they know and like than from a stranger.*

## BACKGROUND

**Fox's Foundation** The Michael J. Fox Foundation for Parkinson's Research looks for a cure through drug development, cell replacement therapy, and genetic discoveries. Since its founding, less than a year after Fox's 1999 testimony before the Senate, the organization has funded or directed more than $50 million in research.

Some, or perhaps most of you are familiar with me from 20 years of
20 work in film and television. What I wish to speak to you about today has little or nothing to do with celebrity—save for this brief reference.

When I first spoke publicly about my 8 years of experience as a person with Parkinson's, many were surprised, in part because of my age (although 30 percent of all Parkinson's patients are under 50, and 20 percent are under 40, and that number is growing). I had hidden my symptoms and struggles very well, through increasing amounts of medication, through surgery, and by employing the hundreds of little tricks and techniques a person with Parkinson's learns to mask his or her condition for as long as possible.

30 While the changes in my life were profound and progressive, I kept them to myself for a number of reasons: fear, denial for sure, but I also felt that it was important for me to just quietly "soldier on." **B**

When I did share my story, the response was overwhelming, humbling, and deeply inspiring. I heard from thousands of Americans affected by Parkinson's, writing and calling to offer encouragement and to tell me of their experience. They spoke of pain, frustration, fear and hope. Always hope.

**B** **SUMMARIZE**
Reread lines 22–32, and record the passage's important details in your chart. Then restate the main idea of the passage in your own words.

*Possible answer:* *Important details may include the facts that many people were surprised when Fox spoke about his illness; that Fox was young when diagnosed; that he hid his symptoms well, like others who are able to hide their illness; and that he used a variety of methods to keep the secret for as long as possible. The main idea is that Fox, like many other Parkinson's victims, kept his illness a secret so successfully that many were surprised when they learned the truth.*

**IF STUDENTS NEED HELP . . .** Explain that the main idea must be inferred by combining several details. Guide students as they record the details in their Main Idea/Details chart.

TESTIMONY BEFORE THE SENATE **673**

- What does Fox give as the reason for his testimony? What does that reason tell you about his purpose for speaking? (lines 15–16)
- To whom is he grateful? Why do you think that he opens his speech by expressing gratitude? (line 17)

## FOR ADVANCED LEARNERS/PRE–AP

**Make Judgments** Begin a class discussion about the role of celebrities as endorsers of products or opinions. Why are people willing to accept celebrities' opinions on subjects about which they have little or no expertise? In advertising, should celebrities be required to disclose how much they are being paid to endorse a product? What kinds of celebrities might have credibility in what areas?

## C PERSUASIVE TECHNIQUES

**Possible answer:** *Fox is making a "plain folks" appeal, pointing out that Parkinson's disease affects a wide range of everyday Americans. Fox's list reminds senators that not all victims are celebrities.*

## Analyze Visuals

**Activity** In scenes such as this one, how does Fox come across to television viewers? *Possible answer: Fox appears responsible, pleasant, socially conventional, and healthy.*

---

TEXT ANALYSIS

COMMON CORE

L 1a

## D PERSUASIVE TECHNIQUES

**Possible answer:** *I think he repeats Parkinson's over and over to emphasize the importance of the issue. He wants to leave a strong impression on the Senate about the need for increased funding for Parkinson's.*

Have students work in pairs to find one other example of repetition or parallelism in Fox's speech. Ask pairs to share their examples and explain what impact they have on the speech.

---

VOCABULARY

COMMON CORE

L 4

## OWN THE WORD

**status quo:** Tell students that *status quo* is a Latin term meaning "state in which." Have students explain the relationship between the Latin and English meanings of the term.

*Possible answer: In English, the term refers to the way things are right now, or the state they are in.*

---

## C PERSUASIVE TECHNIQUES

In additon to appealing to the senators' pity, what does Fox appeal to by referring to the specific categories of "doctors, teachers, policemen, nurses, and parents"?

COMMON CORE L 1a

## D PERSUASIVE TECHNIQUES

Persuasive speakers strengthen the impact of their emotional appeals through the use of rhetorical devices and structures. In lines 51–55, Fox uses repetition and **parallelism** to emphasize the challenges that people with Parkinson's face. He repeats the word *too* in three straight sentences, the first two of which are parallel in grammatical structure. Elsewhere, Fox repeats the word *Parkinson's* over and over instead of using *it* or *the disease*. Why do you think he does this?

**status quo** (stăt′əs kwō) *n.* the existing state of affairs

---

What I understood very clearly is that the time for quietly "soldiering on" is through. The war against Parkinson's is a winnable war, and I am
40 resolved to play a role in that victory.

What celebrity has given me is the opportunity to raise the visibility of Parkinson's disease and focus more attention on the desperate need for more research dollars. While I am able, for the time being, to continue to do what I love best, others are not so fortunate. There are doctors, teachers, policemen, nurses, and parents who are no longer able to work, to provide for their families, and live out their dreams. **C**

Fox starred in the sitcom *Spin City* from 1996 to 2000, when he retired from acting.

The one million Americans living with Parkinson's want to beat this disease. So do millions more Americans who have family members suffering from Parkinson's. But it won't happen until Congress adequately funds
50 Parkinson's research.

For many people with Parkinson's, managing their disease is a full-time job. It is a constant balancing act. Too little medicine causes tremors and stiffness. Too much medicine produces uncontrollable movement and slurring. And far too often, Parkinson's patients wait and wait for the medicines to "kick-in." New investigational therapies have helped some people like me control my symptoms, but in the end, we all face the same reality: the medicines stop working. **D**

For people living with Parkinson's, the **status quo** isn't good enough.

As I began to understand what research might promise for the future,
60 I became hopeful I would not face the terrible suffering so many with Parkinson's endure. But I was shocked and frustrated to learn that the

---

## DIFFERENTIATED INSTRUCTION

### FOR ENGLISH LANGUAGE LEARNERS

**Language: Pronoun Referents** Ask students to identify the referents, either explicit or implicit, for the following pronouns: *you* (line 20); *many* (line 23); *his, her* (line 28); *They* (line 36); *others* (line 44); *their* (line 46); *it* (lines 49, 52, 99); *we* (lines 65, 66); *one* (line 86); *some* (line 89); *your* (line 94). If students cannot identify referents accurately, review the topic, using as models the sentences in which these pronouns appear.

### FOR STRUGGLING READERS

**Develop Reading Fluency** Point out to students that when people speak, they can emphasize the key points they are making. Model this skill by reading a paragraph from this page, a sentence at a time, and having students repeat after you. Emphasize important words and phrases by slowing down, increasing your volume, and enunciating more clearly.

**R** RESOURCE MANAGER—Copy Master
Reading Fluency p. 51

amount of funding for Parkinson's research is so **meager**. Compared with the amount of federal funding going to other diseases, research funding for Parkinson's lags far behind.

In a country with a $15 billion investment in medical research we can and we must do better.

At present, Parkinson's is inadequately funded, no matter how one cares to spin it. Meager funding means a continued lack of effective treatments, slow progress in understanding the cause of the disease, and little chance
70 that a cure will come in time. I applaud the steps we are taking to fulfill the promise of the Udall Parkinson's Research Act, but we must be clear—we aren't there yet.

If, however, an adequate investment is made, there is much to be hopeful for. We have a tremendous opportunity to close the gap for Parkinson's. We are learning more and more about this disease. The scientific community
80 believes that with a significant investment in Parkinson's research, new discoveries and improved treatments strategies are close-at-hand. Many have called Parkinson's the most curable **neurological** disorder and the one expected to produce a breakthrough first. Scientists tell me that a cure is possible, some say even by the end
90 of the next decade—if the research dollars match the research opportunity. **E**

Fox is greeted by Senators Paul Wellstone and Arlen Specter.

Mr. Chairman, you and the members of the Subcommittee have done so much to increase the investment in medical research in this country. I thank you for your vision. Most people don't know just how important this research is until they or someone in their family faces a serious illness. I know I didn't.

The Parkinson's community strongly supports your efforts to double medical research funding. At the same time, I implore you to do more for people with Parkinson's. Take up Parkinson's as if your life depended on it.
100 Increase funding for Parkinson's research by $75 million over current levels for the coming fiscal year.[2] Make this a down payment for a fully funded

---

2. **fiscal year:** a 12-month period—which may or may not coincide with the calendar year—during which a company or organization keeps accounting records.

meager (mē'gər) adj. lacking in quantity or quality

**2 Targeted Passage**
neurological
(nŏŏr'ə-lŏj'ĭ-kəl) adj. having to do with the nervous system

**E SUMMARIZE**
According to Fox, why should we be hopeful about Parkinson's? Cite specific details.

COMMON CORE L 4c

**Language Coach**

**Cognates** Words from different languages with similar meaning and spellings are called **cognates.** The Latin root *-plor-* ("cry out") appears in many Spanish-English cognates, such as *deplore/deplorar.* What cognate of the Spanish *imploro* appears in line 98? What other cognates contain this root? Use a dictionary to check your answers.

---

**TIERED DISCUSSION PROMPTS**
Use these prompts to help students understand Fox's balanced tone in lines 58–72:

**Connect** Think of a time when something on which you had set your hopes fell apart. How does that experience help you grasp what Fox says in lines 58–64? *Students should consider the disappointment and frustration implied in Fox's statement.*

**Evaluate** Did Fox take an appropriate tone in this passage? Explain. *Possible answer: Fox's tone was appropriate. If he were not critical, his plea would seem unimportant. At the same time, he needed to be respectful because of his audience's status and its power to grant his request.*

READING SKILL

COMMON CORE
RI 2

**E SUMMARIZE**

*Possible answer:* Fox says we should be hopeful about Parkinson's because we are learning a lot about the disease and doctors believe it is the most curable neurological disorder—if Parkinson's research gets adequate funding.

**Analyze Visuals**

**Activity** How do the senators appear to respond to Fox in the photograph? *Possible answer: They appear interested in him and appreciative of his attention.*

VOCABULARY

COMMON CORE
L 4

**OWN THE WORD**

- **meager:** Have students reread the paragraph with *meager.* Then have them identify context clues in the surrounding sentences that can help them determine the meaning of the word. *Possible answers: shocked, frustrated, lags far behind*

- **neurological:** Tell students that *neurology* is the medical science that deals with the nervous system and disorders that affect it.

---

**FOR STRUGGLING READERS**

**2 Targeted Passage** [Lines 73–91]
In this passage, Fox discusses the effect that increased funding could have on Parkinson's research.

- Why are scientists hopeful about finding a cure for Parkinson's disease? (lines 85–87)

- How soon might they find a cure? (lines 89–90)

- What do scientists need to make progress in finding a cure? (lines 90–91)

**FOR ENGLISH LANGUAGE LEARNERS**

**Language Coach** COMMON CORE L 4c
**Cognates** *Possible answer: implore; explore/explorar* What other cognates for Spanish words can you find on this page?

*Possible answers: medical (line 65), progress (line 69), promise (line 71), opportunity (line 76)*

## Analyze Visuals

**Activity** What can you infer about Parkinson's disease research from the photograph? *Possible answer: The research requires advanced technology.*

### GRAMMAR AND STYLE

COMMON CORE L3

**Imperative Sentences** Point out that Fox could have used declarative sentences (for example, *I would like you to increase funding . . .*). The imperative sentences, however, express respectful commands, making the plea direct and urgent. To check understanding, elicit that the second sentence in this group is imperative and that it seems more forceful than the other two:

> This research needs more funding.
> Increase funding for this research.
> Could you increase research funding?

---

### VOCABULARY

COMMON CORE L4

**OWN THE WORD**

**eradicate:** Tell students that the connotation of *eradicate* is to thoroughly wipe out or destroy. Then, have students create a semantic map for *eradicate*.

*Possible answers: eliminate, purge, wipe out, exterminate*

---

### SELECTION WRAP–UP

**READ WITH A PURPOSE** Have students decide if Fox gave an effective presentation in favor of increased funding for Parkinson's research. Have them support their answers. *Possible answer: Most students will say yes, and cite Fox's celebrity, personal experiences with the disease, and knowledge.*

⭐ **CRITIQUE** Have students evaluate the ending of the speech. Ask students how else Fox might have concluded his testimony.

---

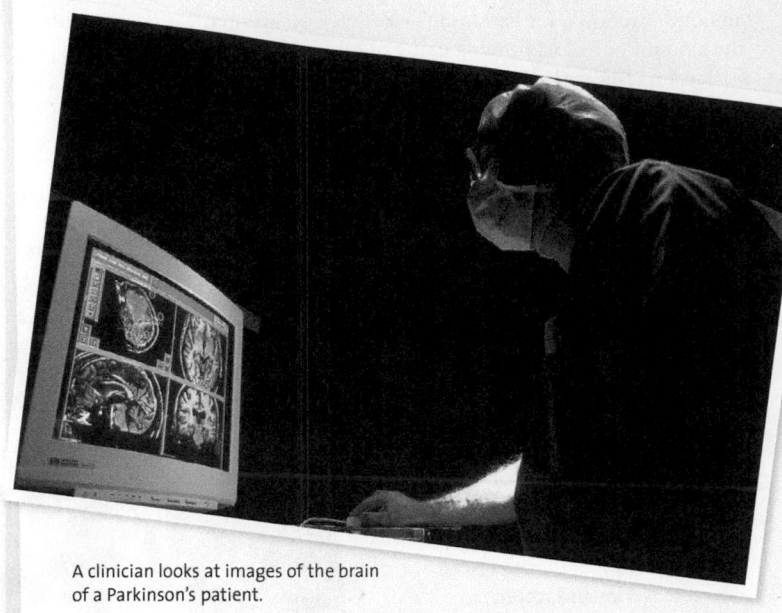

A clinician looks at images of the brain of a Parkinson's patient.

### GRAMMAR AND STYLE
Reread lines 97–103. Fox uses **imperative sentences** to urge Congress to increase research funding.

### Targeted Passage ❸

**eradicate** (ĭ-răd'ĭ-kāt')
*v.* to do away with completely

Parkinson's research agenda that will make Parkinson's nothing more than a footnote in medical textbooks.

I would like to close on a personal note. Today you will hear from, or have already heard from, more than a few experts, in the fields of science, book-keeping and other areas. I am an expert in only one—what it is like to be a young man, husband, and father with Parkinson's disease. With the help of daily medication and selective exertion, I can still perform my job, in my case in a very public arena. I can still help out with the daily
110 tasks and rituals involved in home life. But I don't kid myself . . . that will change. Physical and mental exhaustion will become more and more of a factor, as will increased rigidity, tremor and dyskinesia.[3] I can expect in my 40s to face challenges most wouldn't expect until their 70s and 80s—if ever. But with your help, if we all do everything we can to **eradicate** this disease, in my 50s I'll be dancing at my children's weddings. And mine will be just one of millions of happy stories.

Thank you again for your time and attention.

**Senator SPECTER.** Thank you very much, Mr. Fox, for those very profound and moving words.

---

3. **dyskinesia** (dĭs'kə-nē'zhə): inability to control bodily movements.

---

## DIFFERENTIATED INSTRUCTION

### FOR STRUGGLING READERS

❸ **Targeted Passage [Lines 110–116]**

This passage wraps up the speech and looks toward the future.

- At the end of the speech, what does Fox ask the senators to do? (lines 114–116)

- What will Fox be able to do if the disease is eradicated? (lines 115–116)

- Do you think the senators care if Fox dances at his children's weddings? Why is this ending effective? (lines 110–116)

### FOR RELUCTANT READERS

Tell students to imagine that they are one of the senators Fox is trying to sell his idea on. Have students discuss with a partner whether or not they feel that Fox's speech convinced them to support his cause and why. Have volunteers share their responses and then ask students who were not persuaded by his speech what Fox could have done to better persuade them.

## Comprehension

1. **Recall** How did other people with Parkinson's disease respond to Fox when he made his condition known?

2. **Recall** What did Fox resolve to do after he shared his situation with the public?

3. **Clarify** Why is managing the disease a full-time job for people with Parkinson's?

**COMMON CORE**

**RI 2** Analyze the development of a central idea in a text; provide an objective summary of the text. **RI 5** Analyze in detail how an author's ideas or claims are developed. **RI 8** Delineate and evaluate the argument and specific claims in a text.

## Text Analysis

4. **Summarize** Review the notes you took as you read. Then summarize what you learned about Parkinson's disease from reading Fox's testimony.

5. **Draw Conclusions** How does Fox's personal experience with Parkinson's help him make his pitch to his audience? Explain your answer.

6. **Analyze the Argument** Fox's **claim** is that Congress should increase federal spending for Parkinson's research. What reasons and evidence does he provide as **support** for his claim? Write them on a graphic organizer like the one shown.

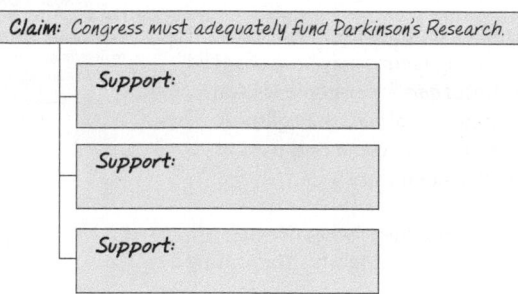

**Claim:** Congress must adequately fund Parkinson's Research.

> Support:
>
> Support:
>
> Support:

7. **Analyze the Counterargument** What potential objection is Fox countering in lines 90–101?

8. **Evaluate Persuasive Techniques** Reread lines 102–114. Fox concludes his testimony by describing two contrasting visions of his future. What emotion does each vision create? What is the effect of concluding his speech with this **emotional appeal?**

9. **Synthesize** Does it strengthen or weaken a cause to have a celebrity associated with it? Would a plea from an ordinary person carry as much weight as one from a celebrity? Consider Michael J. Fox's association with Parkinson's research and think of other celebrities who support particular causes.

### How do you SELL AN IDEA?

What makes some ideas easier—or harder—to sell than others?

---

emotional appeal is to make the senators feel the urgency of doing more to help find a cure.

9. *Celebrity association strengthens a cause. A plea from an ordinary person would not carry as much weight as a plea from a celebrity because people immediately recognize the celebrity and may be influenced by his or her opinions.*

### How do you SELL AN IDEA?

**Possible answer:** *Students might cite existing public resistance or support of an idea, which spokespersons are supporting the idea, or competing claims on public support.*

---

# Practice and Apply

For preliminary support of post-reading questions, use these copy masters:

**R** **RESOURCE MANAGER**—Copy Masters
Reading Check p. 48
Persuasive Techniques p. 41
Question Support p. 49

Additional selection questions are provided for teachers on page 35.

## ANSWERS

## Comprehension

1. *Other people with Parkinson's contacted Fox to encourage him and tell him of their experiences with the disease.*

2. *Fox resolved to dedicate himself to finding a cure for the disease.*

3. *Managing the disease is a full-time job because people with Parkinson's must monitor their condition all the time. They must constantly adjust their medications to control their symptoms.*

## Text Analysis

**COMMON CORE** RI 2, RI 5, RI 8

*Possible answers:*

4. ● **COMMON CORE FOCUS** *Summarize Parkinson's disease causes dyskinesia, or loss of bodily control. People with Parkinson's must manage their medications carefully and constantly. Eventually, medications become ineffective and sufferers can expect to display the severest symptoms of the disease.*

5. *Fox's personal experience makes him an expert on the difficulties of living with the disease. His pitch is more convincing because of his personal experience.*

6. *Support: Parkinson's research is inadequately funded. Support: Scientists believe that a rapid cure is possible if research is sufficiently funded. Support: The disease has devastated about a million American victims and their families.*

7. *Fox is countering the potential objection that the Subcommittee has already provided enough funding.*

8. ● **COMMON CORE FOCUS** *Evaluate Persuasive Techniques The first vision, with Fox becoming more disabled, is sad and frightening. The second, with Fox dancing at his children's weddings, is happy and hopeful. The effect of this concluding*

## ANSWERS

## Vocabulary in Context

### ▲ VOCABULARY PRACTICE

1. *neurological*     3. *meager*

2. *eradicate*     4. *status quo*

 **RESOURCE MANAGER—Copy Master**
Vocabulary Practice p. 46

### ACADEMIC VOCABULARY IN WRITING

Responses should reference Fox's celebrity status and his knowledge of the disease.

### VOCABULARY STRATEGY: FOREIGN WORDS

Model how to locate etymology in a dictionary, using *status quo* as an example.

***Possible answers:***

1. ***Original Language:*** *French;* ***Original Meaning:*** *by the bill of fare;* ***Meaning in English:*** *with a separate price for each menu item*

2. ***Original Language:*** *Italian;* ***Original Meaning:*** *to the tooth;* ***Meaning in English:*** *cooked but still chewy*

3. ***Original Language:*** *Latin;* ***Original Meaning:*** *something for something;* ***Meaning in English:*** *one thing in return for another*

4. ***Original Language:*** *Spanish;* ***Original Meaning:*** *a pot;* ***Meaning in English:*** *a papier-mâché container filled with treats*

5. ***Original Language:*** *French;* ***Original Meaning:*** *false step;* ***Meaning in English:*** *a social blunder*

6. ***Original Language:*** *Latin;* ***Original Meaning:*** *to this;* ***Meaning in English:*** *for this specific purpose*

7. ***Original Language:*** *Latin;* ***Original Meaning:*** *let the buyer beware;* ***Meaning in English:*** *one buys at one's own risk*

8. ***Original Language:*** *Italian;* ***Original Meaning:*** *in the cool;* ***Meaning in English:*** *outdoors*

 **RESOURCE MANAGER—Copy Master**
Vocabulary Strategy p. 47

**Interactive Vocabulary**

Keywords direct students to a **WordSharp** tutorial on **thinkcentral.com** or to other types of vocabulary practice and review.

---

## Vocabulary in Context

### ▲ VOCABULARY PRACTICE

Write the word from the Word List that best completes each sentence.

1. _____ diseases can damage the brain.
2. The goal of medical research is to _____ these diseases.
3. A _____ increase in funding might slow progress toward finding a cure.
4. Clearly, it is important to progress instead of maintaining the _____.

**WORD LIST**
eradicate
meager
neurological
status quo

### ACADEMIC VOCABULARY IN WRITING

• coherent   • differentiate   • evident   • relevant   • technique

With a partner, discuss how Michael J. Fox **differentiates** his experience with Parkinson's from that of non-celebrities. How does he differentiate his knowledge from that of scientists and financial experts? Use at least one Academic Vocabulary word in your discussion.

### VOCABULARY STRATEGY: FOREIGN WORDS

A dictionary is an important tool for understanding terms that come directly from another language. The meaning of some foreign terms may have changed slightly since they were brought into English. *Status quo,* for example, is Latin for "the state in which" but means "the existing state of affairs" in English. A dictionary will have the definitions of many foreign terms commonly used in English, and some will include the term's etymology, or history.

**PRACTICE** Create a four-column chart with these headings: "Foreign Term," "Original Language," "Original Meaning," and "Meaning in English." Then, using a dictionary, fill in the chart for each term.

1. à la carte     5. faux pas
2. al dente     6. ad hoc
3. quid pro quo     7. caveat emptor
4. piñata     8. alfresco

**COMMON CORE**

**L 4c** Consult reference materials to determine a word's precise meaning and etymology.

**Interactive Vocabulary**

Go to **thinkcentral.com**.
KEYWORD: HML9-678

---

## DIFFERENTIATED INSTRUCTION

### FOR ENGLISH LANGUAGE LEARNERS

**Culture: Connect** Invite students to think of words or expressions from their home languages or another language they know that they have heard used in English. Have them add these words to their Vocabulary Strategy Practice chart.

### FOR ADVANCED LEARNERS/PRE–AP

**Vocabulary in Writing** Have students use each of the words from the Word List in a brief scripted dialogue. Ask students to exchange their dialogues with a partner for review and, if necessary, revision.

# Language

◆ **GRAMMAR AND STYLE: Set The Tone**

Review the **Grammar and Style** note on page 676. Fox uses **imperative sentences**—sentences that express a command or request—in his testimony. By using imperative sentences, rather than other sentence types, Fox creates a sense of directness and urgency. (The subject of imperative sentences is usually *you*, often understood rather than stated.)

Here is an example of one student's use of imperative sentences:

> *Take up the cause with me. Give full support to the Parkinson's community by increasing research funding.*

Now study the model. Notice how the revisions in blue make the tone stronger and more urgent. Revise your response to the prompt below by employing similar techniques.

---

**STUDENT MODEL**

<del>You can</del> make a difference in the war against Parkinson's disease. Your donation <del>will go to research for a cure.</del> *Send in*

---

**READING-WRITING CONNECTION**

**YOUR TURN** Broaden your understanding of "Testimony Before the Senate" by responding to this prompt. Then use the **revising tip** to improve your writing.

| **WRITING PROMPT** | **REVISING TIP** |
|---|---|
| **Extended Constructed Response: Write a Memo** Imagine you are a senator who has just heard Fox's testimony. How would you respond? Write a **three-to-five-paragraph memo** to a fellow senator, describing your reaction and identifying the most convincing parts of Fox's testimony. | Review your memo. Did you use imperative sentences to give your writing a sense of directness and urgency? |

**Interactive Revision** **THINK** central
Go to **thinkcentral.com**.
KEYWORD: HML9-679

---

**COMMON CORE**

**L 3** Apply knowledge of language to make effective choices for meaning or style.
**W 9a (RI 8)** Draw evidence from informational texts to support an evaluation of the specific claims in a text.

---

# Language

**COMMON CORE** L 3, W 9a (RI 8)

◆ **GRAMMAR AND STYLE**

- Discuss how the tone of Fox's testimony would have seemed angrier and been more unpleasant if most of his sentences had been imperative. (For more on tone, see **Reading Handbook**, page R21.)

- Have students rewrite some declarative sentences from Fox's testimony as imperative sentences. Discuss the results. (For more on imperative sentences, see **Grammar Handbook**, page R59.)

**R** RESOURCE MANAGER—Copy Master
Set the Tone p. 50

**READING-WRITING CONNECTION**
Urge students to use Fox's speech as a model, but remind them that the memo must be concise. Students should use effective verbal strategies—vivid and descriptive language, imperative sentences, clear persuasive techniques—in preparing the message.

**Writing Online** **THINK** central

The following tools are available online at **thinkcentral.com** and on **Write*Smart* CD-ROM:**
- **Interactive Graphic Organizers**
- **Interactive Student Models**
- **Interactive Revision Lessons**
For additional grammar instruction, see **GrammarNotes** on **thinkcentral.com**.

---

# Assess and Reteach

## Assess

**DIAGNOSTIC AND SELECTION TESTS**
Selection Test A, B/C pp. 179–180, 181–182

**Interactive Selection Test** on **thinkcentral.com**

## Reteach

**Level Up Online Tutorials** on **thinkcentral.com**

**Reteaching Workshops** on **thinkcentral.com**
Research and Study Skill Lesson 13, Informational Texts Lesson 15, Writing Lesson 31, Vocabulary Lesson 24

---

**FOR STRUGGLING WRITERS**

- Suggest that students follow this structure: (1) define the disease; (2) explain how donations can help; (3) appeal for donations; and (4) explain how donations will be collected.

- Review Fox's call to action (lines 90–101), but remind students to make their message personal, not a mere parroting of Fox's message.

# Focus and Motivate

**Before Reading**

## COMMON CORE FOCUS

**RI 3** Analyze how the author unfolds a series of events, including the order in which the points are made. **RI 4** Determine the meaning of words as they are used in a text; analyze the impact of word choices on meaning and tone. **RI 8** Delineate and evaluate the argument and specific claims in a text; identify false statements and fallacious reasoning. **W 4** Produce clear and coherent writing in which the style is appropriate to the task, purpose, and audience. **L 1a** Use parallel structure. **L 6** Acquire and use accurately general academic and domain-specific words.

### SUMMARIES

In "How Private Is Your Private Life?," Andrea Rock shows that it is practically impossible to keep personal information private.

In "The Privacy Debate: One Size Doesn't Fit All," Arthur M. Ahalt, a retired judge, explains the benefits of access to public records.

## Is PRIVACY
### an illusion?

Read the question. Urge students to use their responses as a basis for their work on the *DEBATE* activity.

# Selection Resources

---

## How Private Is Your Private Life?
Magazine Article by Andrea Rock

**Essential Course of Study ECOS**

## The Privacy Debate:
## One Size Doesn't Fit All
Newspaper Editorial by Arthur M. Ahalt

**VIDEO TRAILER THINKcentral** KEYWORD: HML9-680

### COMMON CORE

**RI 3** Analyze how the author unfolds a series of events, including the order in which the points are made. **RI 4** Determine the meaning of words as they are used in a text; analyze the impact of word choices on meaning and tone. **RI 8** Delineate and evaluate the argument and specific claims in a text; identify false statements and fallacious reasoning.

## Is PRIVACY
### an illusion?

Your phone number appears in a hundred databases. Your favorite Web site keeps track of your every click. Do these advances in technology pose a threat to your privacy? Big Brother (along with 30 of his closest friends) may be watching you.

**DEBATE** With a small group, break into two teams and stage a debate over the question of personal privacy in today's society. Is your privacy at risk, or isn't it? Be prepared to back up your opinions with examples and other evidence.

**PRIVATE PROPERTY KEEP OUT**

**TRESPASSERS WILL BE PROSECUTED**

680

---

See resources on the **Teacher One Stop DVD-ROM** and on **thinkcentral.com**.

**R RESOURCE MANAGER UNIT 6**
- Plan and Teach, pp. 53–60
- Summary pp. 61–62†‡*
- Text Analysis and Reading Skill, pp. 63–66†*
- Vocabulary, pp. 67–69*
- Grammar and Style, p. 72

**DIAGNOSTIC AND SELECTION TESTS**
- Selection Tests, pp. 183–186

**BEST PRACTICES TOOLKIT**
- Definition Mapping, p. E6
- Think-Pair-Share, p. A18

**INTERACTIVE READER**

**ADAPTED INTERACTIVE READER**

**ELL ADAPTED READER**

**TECHNOLOGY**
- Teacher One Stop DVD-ROM
- Student One Stop DVD-ROM
- PowerNotes DVD-ROM
- Audio Anthology CD
- GrammarNotes DVD-ROM
- Audio Tutor CD
- ExamView Test Generator on the **Teacher One Stop**

### THINKcentral
### Video Trailer

Go to **thinkcentral.com** to preview the **Video Trailer** introducing this selection. Other features that support the selection include
- **PowerNotes** presentation
- **ThinkAloud** models to enhance comprehension
- **WordSharp** vocabulary tutorials
- interactive writing and grammar instruction

## ● TEXT ANALYSIS: FACT AND OPINION

Most persuasive writers use facts and opinions to support their claims. A **fact** is a statement that can be proved, or verified. An **opinion** is a statement that cannot be proved because it expresses a person's beliefs, feelings, or thoughts. It's important to distinguish facts from opinions because facts tend to be less disputable than opinions—unless the opinions come from experts and are well **substantiated,** or established by evidence. Can you distinguish the fact from opinion here?

*The constant invasion of our privacy is an outrage.*

*According to a 1999* Wall Street Journal *poll, loss of privacy is the number-one concern of Americans.*

The first statement is an opinion. The second is a fact; it can be proved by consulting the 1999 *Wall Street Journal* poll. As you read each of the following texts, identify the significant facts and opinions in a chart like the one shown.

| Location | Example | Fact/Opinion |
|---|---|---|
| lines 2–3 | A 1999 poll found that loss of privacy is the number-one concern of Americans. | Fact |

## ■ READING SKILL: RECOGNIZE BIAS

**Bias** is an unfair preference for or against a particular topic or issue. To detect bias, be on the lookout for the following:

- an argument in which the evidence is unbalanced, giving one side stronger or more adequate support than the other
- the presence of **loaded language**—words with intensely positive or negative connotations
- opinions stated as if they were facts
- the use of overgeneralizations, such as **stereotyping,** and other faulty reasoning (See **Reading Handboook,** page R24.)

## ▲ VOCABULARY IN CONTEXT

Which of the following words can be used to discuss

- the promotion of a cause?
- an unbiased discussion?
- something unsettling?
- a skilled talker?

| WORD LIST | | | |
|---|---|---|---|
| | affiliate | awry | nonpartisan |
| | anonymity | browser | pervasive |
| advocacy | articulate | disconcerting | surveillance |

 Complete the activities in your **Reader/Writer Notebook.**

### Technology and Privacy

Many Americans are becoming increasingly concerned that the miracles of technology have come at a high cost—namely, the loss of personal privacy. Internet companies, for example, can monitor Web sites to gather information about their visitors— information that can be sold to other companies for marketing purposes. In many large corporations, computer software can screen workers' e-mail messages. Some Americans want Congress to pass stronger privacy laws like those that have been established in other countries. In the United States, however, corporate opponents have lobbied successfully against such legislation.

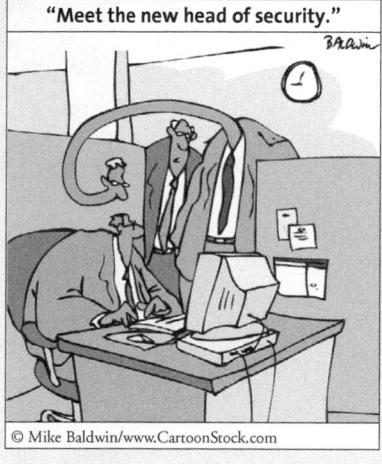

"Meet the new head of security."

© Mike Baldwin/www.CartoonStock.com

## ● *Model the Skill:* FACT AND OPINION

After students read the **Background,** read the first statement below and classify it as fact. Then ask students to classify the second statement.

> Internet companies can gather information about their visitors by monitoring Web sites. *(Fact)*
>
> Technology is not worth the price we pay in privacy. *(Opinion)*

**GUIDED PRACTICE**  Elicit that this statement is a fact: *Computer software can screen workers' e-mail.* Have students suggest an opinion related to that fact.

**R** RESOURCE MANAGER—Copy Master Fact and Opinion p. 63 (for student use while reading the selections)

## ■ *Model the Skill:* RECOGNIZE BIAS

For instructional support, write this chapter title on the board: *Government Snooping and You.* Elicit that *snooping* is loaded language. Discuss how the title might suggest a book whose author is biased.

**GUIDED PRACTICE**  Ask students to suggest another chapter title that might appear in the same book.

## ▲ VOCABULARY IN CONTEXT

**DIAGNOSE WORD KNOWLEDGE**  Have all students complete Vocabulary in Context. Check their words and phrases against the following:

**advocacy** (ăd′və-kə-sē) *adj.* involving public support for an idea or policy

**affiliate** (ə-fĭl′ē-ĭt) *n.* a person or an organization officially connected to a larger body

**anonymity** (ăn′ə-nĭm′ĭ-tē) *n.* the condition of being unknown

**articulate** (är-tĭk′yə-lĭt) *adj.* able to speak clearly and coherently; well-spoken

**awry** (ə-rī′) *adj.* off course; wrong

**browser** (brou′zər) *n.* a program used to navigate the Internet

**disconcerting** (dĭs′kən-sûr′tĭng) *adj.* causing one to feel confused or embarrassed **disconcert** *v.*

**nonpartisan** (nŏn-pär′tĭ-zən) *adj.* not supporting or controlled by any political group

**pervasive** (pər-vā′sĭv) *adj.* spreading widely through an area or group of people

**surveillance** (sər-vā′ləns) *adj.* having to do with close observation

**R** RESOURCE MANAGER—Copy Master Vocabulary Study p. 67

L 4

# Practice and Apply

## READ WITH A PURPOSE

*Help students set a purpose for reading. Ask them to evaluate the information they read in this selection to decide how great the threat to their privacy is today.*

## BACKGROUND

**A "Right" to Privacy?** Students may be surprised to learn that the U.S. Constitution nowhere specifies privacy as a right. However, many Supreme Court cases have addressed a range of privacy issues. Court decisions and public discussion about the issues addressed have tended to give privacy Constitutional status. In particular, the Fourth Amendment (which protects Americans from "unreasonable searches and seizures") and the Fifth Amendment (which guards against self-incrimination and the taking of private property for public use) have been linked to privacy issues. Still, their application has not been interpreted consistently. As both Rock and Ahalt suggest, privacy remains difficult both to define and to protect.

## Analyze Visuals

**Activity** Have students explain what the boy in the picture is doing and what personal information he might be giving away. *Possible answer: The boy is using a telephone and a computer. He is holding a card—perhaps a library card, a membership card, or even a credit card. He may be giving away personal data, such as his address or date of birth. If the card is a credit card, he might be giving away private financial information. The boy also might be revealing such things as personal interests or preferences as a consumer.*

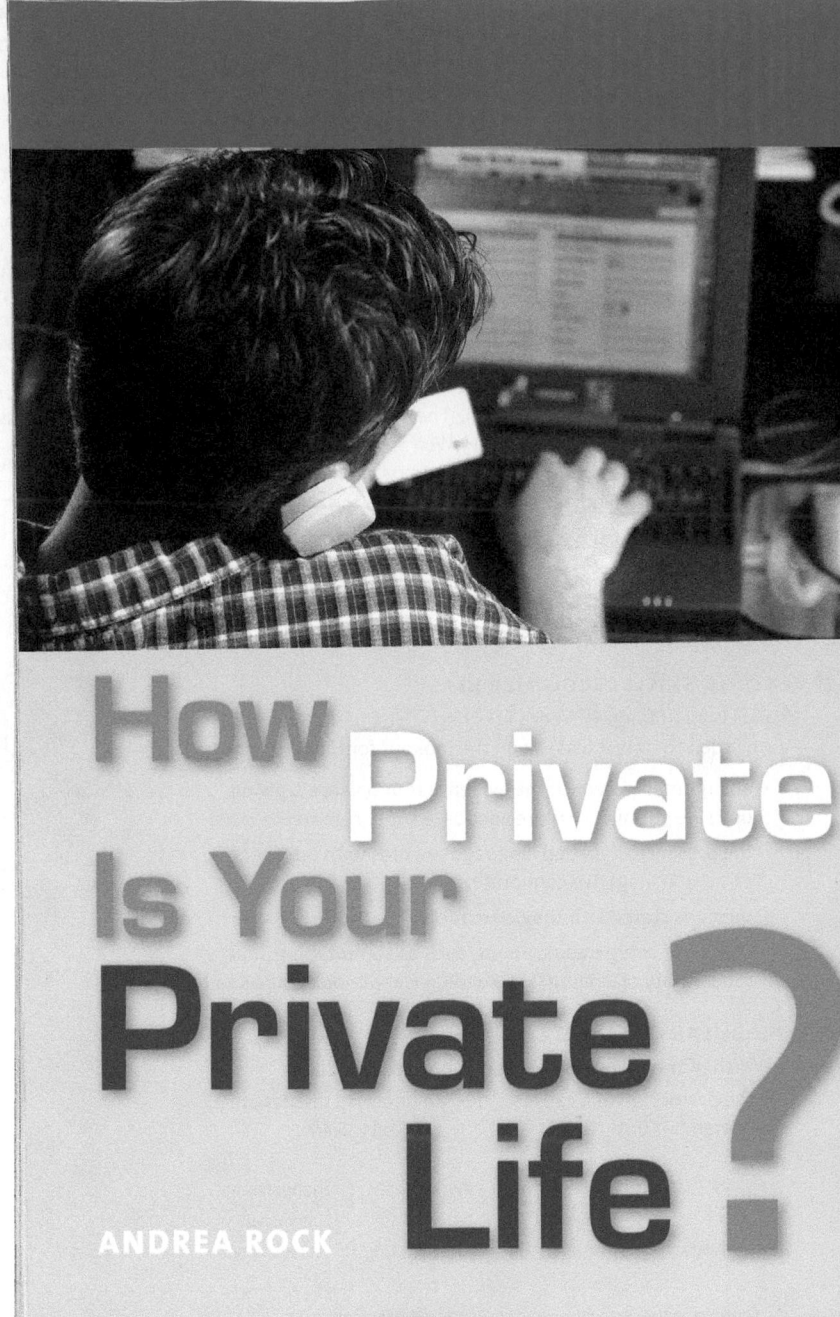

# How Private Is Your Private Life?

**ANDREA ROCK**

## DIFFERENTIATED INSTRUCTION

### FOR ENGLISH LANGUAGE LEARNERS

**Vocabulary Support** Use Definition Mapping to teach these words: *technology* (line 1), *legal* (line 12), *policy* (line 20), *computer* (line 74), *security* (line 82).

🧰 BEST PRACTICES TOOLKIT—Transparency Definition Mapping p. E6

### FOR STRUGGLING READERS

In combination with the *Audio Anthology CD*, use one or more Targeted Passages (pp. 683, 684, 687, 688, 690) to ensure that students focus on key ideas, concepts, and skills. Targeted Passages are also good for English learners.

*When you go online, file an insurance claim or even eat out, you reveal personal information to strangers. Here's what you need to know about who's watching you—and how to protect yourself.*

Rapid advances in technology have fostered an ever-growing assault on our private lives. A 1999 *Wall Street Journal* poll found that loss of privacy **A** ranked as Americans' number-one concern for the new century—ahead of depression, war and terrorism.

Regulators and lawmakers alike have proposed measures to safeguard privacy, but they face strong opposition from businesses whose aim is to collect as much information as possible about consumers' financial and medical histories, their shopping habits and other personal details. Companies profit by selling this information to advertisers and other businesses, or simply by using it to tailor their own advertising.

To find out how **pervasive** the system really is, the editors of LHJ[1] asked me to see how often in a single day my activities resulted in a legal invasion of privacy. I was surprised by what I learned:

**9:00 A.M.**

After sending my two sons off to school, I go to the grocery store. At the register, I hand the cashier my supermarket discount card. Later, I discover that this card allows retailers to track exactly what I've purchased, how much I spend and how often I shop. These details can then be shared with product manufacturers so that coupons and other offers can be targeted to me. "People should be aware that when they use these cards, they are literally selling their privacy," says Ari Schwartz, senior policy analyst at the Center for Democracy and Technology, an **advocacy** organization in Washington, D.C. Schwartz adds that his group has already seen cases where these records have been used in lawsuits. **B**

**9:25 A.M.**

After returning a video, I stop at the post office to mail an insurance claim form. Amazingly, the privacy of my video-rental records is protected by federal law, but not the data in my medical records. By signing the claim form, I authorize doctors to release sensitive information about myself to insurers and other third parties,[2] such as the Medical Information Bureau, which keeps records of health problems reported on some insurance applications and informs insurers (on request) about pre-existing conditions.

1. **editors of LHJ:** The author was given this assignment by the editors of *Ladies' Home Journal*.
2. **release sensitive information . . . other third parties:** Congress attempted to address this problem by passing the Health Insurance Portability and Accountability Act, which makes the unauthorized release of medical information a crime.

**A RECOGNIZE BIAS**
Notice the phrase "ever-growing assault on our private lives." Does this **loaded language** portray technology as positive or negative? Explain.

**① Targeted Passage**

**pervasive** (pər-vā'sĭv) *adj.* spreading widely through an area or group of people

**advocacy** (ăd'və-kə-sē) *adj.* involving public support for an idea or policy

**B FACT AND OPINION**
Reread lines 14–23. What facts are included here? Cite examples from the text.



## ① Targeted Passage [Lines 1–13]

This introductory passage establishes the purpose of the article.

- What kinds of information about consumers do businesses want to collect? Why? (lines 7–8)
- How do many Americans feel about that practice? Why? (lines 2–3)
- What has Andrea Rock, the writer, been asked to find out? Who has asked her? (lines 11–13)

## FOR ADVANCED LEARNERS/PRE–AP

**Creative Writing** Have students write a short story on the theme of "threats to privacy." Point out that the story could be satirical, realistic, or fantastic, and that it could portray an event that might really happen or one that is exaggerated to make a point. Have volunteers share their stories with the class and discuss issues that their stories bring up.

### Reading Support

THINK central

This selection on thinkcentral.com includes embedded **ThinkAloud** models–students "thinking aloud" about the story to model the kinds of questions a good reader would ask about a selection.

### READING SKILL

COMMON CORE RI 8

## A RECOGNIZE BIAS

***Possible answer:*** *The phrase portrays technology as negative. The word* assault *suggests harm, and Rock says that the assault is an ever-growing, or increasing, danger.*

**Extend the Discussion** How might you rewrite this phrase if you wanted to portray technology as positive?

### TEXT ANALYSIS

COMMON CORE RI 4, RI 8

## B FACT AND OPINION

***Possible answer:*** *Rock notes that retailers track how much has been purchased, when, and how often; that these details can be shared and can make the consumer a target for advertising; and that Ari Schwartz, a senior policy analyst at the Center for Democracy and Technology, says that people who use supermarket discount cards are selling their privacy.*

### VOCABULARY

COMMON CORE L 4

## OWN THE WORD

- **pervasive:** Tell students that the Latin prefix *per-* means "through." Have students name things or situations that are *pervasive.*
- **advocacy:** Review the definition of *advocacy* with students. Then have them name *advocacy* groups that exist in their community. ***Possible answers:*** *veterans affairs, civil rights*

# Is **PRIVACY**
### an illusion?

**Discuss** Based on lines 26–34, what good can come from sharing medical records? In your opinion, does that make the loss of privacy a good thing? Explain. *Possible answer: It is good that records are shared with insurers so that medical bills can be paid. It also is good that they are shared with other doctors and specialists so that the best care can be given. Opinions about the loss of privacy will vary but should be reasonably supported.*

---

**TEXT ANALYSIS** | COMMON CORE RI 3

### **C SERIES OF EVENTS**

*Possible answer:* The chronological presentation emphasizes the idea that even typical daily activities can compromise privacy.

Ask students to suggest ideas about how the writer might have protected her privacy during each event.

---

**TEXT ANALYSIS** | COMMON CORE RI 4, RI 8

### **D FACT AND OPINION**

*Possible answer:* The statement could be verified by reading the text of the law, either in a book or online.

---

## Analyze Visuals

**Activity** Have students match the photograph to the text in lines 44–48. Then ask them to make an inference, based on the photograph. *Possible answer: The E-Z Pass makes it possible to create travel records for both individuals (the cars) and businesses (the trucks).*

---

COMMON CORE RI 3

**C SERIES OF EVENTS**
By line 34, you have followed the author through two time periods in her day. How does this chronological presentation of her interactions with technology develop her argument about the loss of privacy?

**Targeted Passage 2**

**D FACT AND OPINION**
How could the statement in lines 41–43 be verified?

Although my medical records can be shared with people I don't know, in about half the states in the U.S., I don't have the legal right to see them myself. **C**

**10:00 A.M.**
I call the car dealer about the 1997 Subaru I just purchased. When I register a car or apply for a driver's license in New York, my name, address, date of birth and the model of my car may be sold to marketers, private investigators and others who access the state's database. Policies may vary by state, with some selling Social Security numbers, too.

40     The federal Driver's Privacy Protection Act of 1994 requires application forms to inform consumers that personal information may be disclosed to third parties and that they must be given an opportunity to prohibit such disclosures. **D**

---

## DIFFERENTIATED INSTRUCTION

**FOR STRUGGLING READERS**

**2 Targeted Passage [Lines 35–43]**
This passage typifies the article's structure.

- What does the heading *10:00 A.M.* mean?
- What does the writer do at 10:00 A.M.? (line 35)
- How does she relate that action to the release of personal information? (lines 36–39)
- What kind of factual information does Rock present next? Why? (lines 40–43)

**FOR ENGLISH LANGUAGE LEARNERS**

**Language: Print Cues** Point out the conventions related to writing out numbers in *third parties* (line 42), *45th Street and Fifth Avenue* (line 49), and *twenty-second intervals* (line 50). Explain that numbers ten and below usually are written as words but that numbers above ten usually are written as numerals. Elicit that this practice has been followed in the first two examples but not in the third.

**10:20 A.M.**

On my way into New York City to meet a friend for lunch, I save time by paying the toll with my E-Z Pass, a radio tag that deducts the toll from my account. But using the pass means that a record of my travels is being kept. While it can help track criminals, the data could also be used to legally obtain personal information about law-abiding citizens.

**11:30 A.M.**

As I'm waiting to cross the corner of 45th Street and Fifth Avenue, I'm
50 being filmed by a hidden video camera. At twenty-second intervals, the device transmits the images onto an Internet site. The camera is operated by a private company simply for the use of promotional purposes and entertainment on its Web site, but **surveillance** cameras are increasingly being used by police and merchants to fight crime, as well.

**surveillance** (sər-vā'ləns) *adj.* having to do with close observation

"By the end of the decade, I imagine most public places will have surveillance cameras connected to a computer that spontaneously compares faces shown on a monitor with mug shots of people wanted by the police," says John Pike, a security analyst at the Federation of American Scientists, a private policy group in Washington D.C.

**NOON**

60 My friend Diane joins me at Daniel, a lovely French restaurant. In my research, I found out that tiny cameras strategically positioned in the

COMMON CORE RI 4

**Language Coach**

**Word Definitions** You often have to read several definitions in a dictionary to find the one that fits. Reread lines 55–57. Which definition fits the use of *spontaneously* in this quotation? (1) impulsively, (2) automatically, (3) instinctively

---

**FOR ENGLISH LANGUAGE LEARNERS**

**Language Coach**   COMMON CORE RI 4

**Word Definitions**

***Possible answer:*** *automatically* Ask students to look up the definitions for "strategically" in the dictionary and decide which one best fits the word's use in line 61.

**FOR ADVANCED LEARNERS/PRE–AP**

**Make Judgments** [small-group option]  Have students record the number of invasions of privacy that Rock experiences in the hours that her article covers. Then have students discuss whether her presentation is realistic. Students might compare and contrast her claims with their own experiences or the likely experiences of people they know.

---

**TIERED DISCUSSION PROMPTS**

Use these prompts to help students link surveillance with technology, focusing on the text in lines 49–59:

**Connect**  Where have you seen surveillance devices? *Students may mention places such as convenience stores and banks.*

**Analyze**  How does the author contrast the use of the hidden camera on the corner of 45th Street and Fifth Avenue with surveillance cameras used by the police? ***Possible answer:*** *The camera that films the author transmits images to a private company for promotional and entertainment purposes; surveillance cameras fight crime.*

**Evaluate**  How does the quotation from John Pike influence your views on the use of surveillance cameras?  Explain. *Student answers may vary.*

### Analyze Visuals

**Activity**  Have students note the relative size, placement, and clarity of the cars and cameras in this scene.  Then have students use this information to analyze the photographer's purpose. ***Possible answer:*** *The cameras are in the foreground; they also are in focus and appear very large in relation to the cars.  The photographer's purpose is to emphasize the watchfulness of the cameras.*

**VOCABULARY**   COMMON CORE   L 4

**OWN THE WORD**

**surveillance:** Tell students that *surveillance* means close observation, carefully watching.  Have them write a pair of sentences that show an understanding of the word. ***Possible answer:*** *After the corner apartment was broken into, the neighbors decided to form a* surveillance *group.  The building owner also said he would hire a watchman to continue the* surveillance *of the building at night.*

**E** *Model the Skill:* **FACT AND OPINION**

Point out lines 69–70 and explain that the author's use of Diane's cell phone is a fact that can be proven by looking at call records. Then have students fill in another row on their Elements of Nonfiction charts.

*Possible answer:* **fact:** *Cameras allow chefs to watch diners (lines 61–62);* **opinion:** *"it's disconcerting to know that every bite I take is being filmed" (lines 63–64); Answers will vary. Possible answer: The opinion can't be fully substantiated because it refers to the writer's personal feelings. It does seem to be a reasonable reaction though.*

**REVISIT THE BIG QUESTION**

Is **PRIVACY** an illusion?

**Discuss** Reread lines 69–73. Do you worry about your privacy when you use a cell phone? Why, or why not? *Possible answers: Yes; I didn't know that a radio receiver could pick up the signal. No; almost no one is really interested in my phone conversations.*

**VOCABULARY** COMMON CORE

L 4

**OWN THE WORD**

**disconcerting:** Ask students to explain why it would be *disconcerting* to be continuously filmed while eating.
*Possible answer: It would provide a full picture of every bite you take and could be embarrassing.*

**disconcerting**
(dĭs'kən-sûr'tĭng) *adj.*
causing one to feel confused or embarrassed
**disconcert** *v.*

**E** **FACT AND OPINION**
Identify at least one fact and one opinion in lines 60–64. Is the opinion you identified **substantiated** (supported by evidence)? Explain.

ceiling allow the chefs to watch diners eating so that they can time their delivery of the courses. The food is delicious, but it's **disconcerting** to know that every bite I take is being filmed. **E**

Diane tells me that a friend of hers just received a ticket by mail for running a red light six months earlier in Los Angeles. A police surveillance camera caught the license plate of the rental car, which the authorities used to track down his name and address.

**1:30** P.M.

70 I use Diane's cell phone to leave a message for a friend, aware that my conversation could be intercepted by someone with a radio receiver. Says Pike: "If you are discussing something highly sensitive that you wouldn't want your prying neighbor or worst enemy to know, don't have that conversation on a cell or portable phone."

**4:00** P.M.

After I check my e-mail on my home-office computer, my older son, Adam, visits a site that provides all the research he needs for his fifth-grade science project. I feel much more comfortable about his use of the Internet

---

## DIFFERENTIATED INSTRUCTION

**FOR ENGLISH LANGUAGE LEARNERS**

**Vocabulary: Multiple-Meaning Words** Using a dictionary for support, discuss the meaning in context for some or all of these multiple-meaning words: *records* (line 32), *right* (line 33), *parties* (line 42), *pass* (line 46), *track* (line 47), *twenty-second* (line 50), *simply* (line 52), *wanted* (line 57), *time* (line 62), *courses* (line 63), *caught* (line 67), *prying* (line 72), *cell* (line 73), *check* (line 74), and *check out* (line 94).

**FOR ADVANCED LEARNERS/PRE–AP**

**Analyze an Allusion** Review this statement from the first paragraph on page 680: "Big Brother . . . may be watching you." Explain that the term *Big Brother,* from George Orwell's novel *1984,* refers to a government that allows its citizens no privacy. Have students write and share a paragraph in which they discuss how the allusion applies to Rock's article.

now that a new federal law prohibits commercial Web sites from collecting personal information from children under thirteen without parental consent.

**6:11 P.M.**

80 I use online banking services to see if a recent deposit has been credited to my account. When I first signed up for this service, I was instructed to use my Social Security number as my customer access code. I avoid giving out that number when possible, but in this case, I had no choice. The bank protects my account information from hackers and other unauthorized third parties, but it does share that data with inside **affiliates,** such as brokerage partners.[3]

Consumer advocates say financial privacy has been further endangered by a federal law that made it easier for banks to merge with other financial firms, such as brokerages and insurance companies. Though the law 90 includes provisions to protect consumer privacy, critics say there are loopholes that could lead, for example, to a bank denying a loan to a customer because its health-insurance affiliate's data reveals that he or she is being treated for a life-threatening illness.

**9:35 P.M.**

When I visit *Amazon.com* to check out a book, a message on my computer screen says that the Web site is trying to place a "cookie," a tag that identifies me to an Internet company whenever I visit its site, on my hard drive. Normally, consumers don't receive this alert, but I've learned how to activate a feature on my computer's **browser** that will warn me every time a cookie is about to be placed, giving me the option of accepting it or not. 100 Adam and I have visited eleven Web sites today, accumulating forty-nine cookies in all.

Cookies can give you more than you bargained for. A Web site may share its data with an ad network, such as DoubleClick, which places banner ads on more than 1,800 Web sites. An online profile of you is created, which associates your computer with any sites you visit on that ad network, noting what you look at or buy. Your profile continues to expand and can be sold to anyone without your knowledge or consent. Visiting a gardening Web site just to learn about varieties of roses might trigger a deluge of seed catalogs in your mailbox later. **F**

**10:45 P.M.**

110 To wrap up, I return to my Excite home page to read my horoscope. "Your home is your castle," it says, "and you are the supreme ruler within its walls." After today, I'm not so sure.

---

3. **brokerage partners:** individuals or companies that buy and sell stocks or other assets for others.

---

**affiliate** (ə-fĭl′ē-ĭt) *n.* a person or an organization officially connected to a larger body

**browser** (brou′zər) *n.* a program used to navigate the Internet

**3 Targeted Passage**

**F** RECOGNIZE BIAS
Reread lines 102–109. Loaded language can sometimes take the form of **hyperbole,** or exaggeration. Find an example of hyperbole in this paragraph. How might this influence a reader?

---

**FOR STRUGGLING READERS**

**3 Targeted Passage [Lines 94–109]**

This passage explains how privacy is compromised on the Internet.

- What is a cookie? How does Rock gather cookies? (lines 95–96)
- Why does Rock have a browser alert about cookies? (lines 98–99)
- How can cookies be used to invade personal privacy? (lines 102–107)

**FOR ENGLISH LANGUAGE LEARNERS**

**Comprehension: Transitions** Talk about how Rock incorporates examples into her article. Discuss her use of signal words or transitional words and phrases like *for example* (line 91) and *such as* (line 103), as well as her presentation of examples without such words (as in lines 107–109).

---

**TIERED DISCUSSION PROMPTS**

Use these prompts to help students understand the privacy issues related to sharing one's Social Security number, as discussed in lines 80–86:

**Connect** When have you been asked for your Social Security number? *Answers will vary.*

**Apply** Why do you think that Rock usually avoids giving out that number (lines 82–83)? *Possible answer: The number is an important part of her identity. It also may be the best means of access to official and private data.*

**Evaluate** Based on the information that Rock presents, are her worries about giving out her Social Security number justified? Why or why not? *Possible answers: Yes; the information can be shared. No; she does not present enough facts about the abuse of the information.*

---

**READING SKILL**

**COMMON CORE**

**RI 8**

**F Model the Skill: RECOGNIZE BIAS**

Point out lines 69–73. Explain that the phrases "highly sensitive," "prying neighbor," and "worst enemy" are examples of loaded language. These phrases help indicate to the reader the bias that Pike has for privacy.

*Possible answer:* Visiting a gardening Web site "might trigger a deluge of seed catalogs" (lines 107–109). Deluge (meaning "flood") is an example of hyperbole.

---

**VOCABULARY**

**COMMON CORE**

**L 4**

**OWN THE WORD**

- **affiliate:** Read the definition of *affiliate* to students. Then have them name television station *affiliates* that they are familiar with. Point out that most local television stations are *affiliated* with and are owned by a parent network.
- **browser:** Have students identify their favorite Web browser and explain why they prefer it. *Accept reasonable responses.*

Prereading for this newspaper article is found on pages 680–681.

## TIERED DISCUSSION PROMPTS

Use these prompts to help students understand Ahalt's purpose, as discussed in lines 1–10:

**Connect** What comes to your mind when you hear the phrase "privacy debate"? *Answers will vary.*

**Analyze** How does the Emerson quotation help clarify the title? How does Ahalt use the idea in that quotation? *Possible answer: The quotation suggests that people look at issues in different ways. Ahalt uses it to conclude that debates can be complex.*

**Synthesize** How does Ahalt probably view the idea of public use of private data? *Possible answer: Ahalt probably sees some reason to have access to private data.*

---

### TEXT ANALYSIS
COMMON CORE
RI 4, RI 8

###  FACT AND OPINION

*Possible answer: fact:* "There are now 280 million Americans" (lines 32–33); *opinion:* "we're long past doing business at the corner store" (lines 33–35); "where everybody knew your name" (lines 35–36); Answers will vary. Possible answer: The opinion is substantiated by the fact that America's population is now very large and the economy is changing.

---

### VOCABULARY
COMMON CORE
L 4

### OWN THE WORD

- **anonymity:** Tell students that the adjective form is *anonymous*. Have students use the word in a short paragraph describing a situation in which they would prefer to remain *anonymous*.

- **articulate:** Tell students that the verb *articulate* is pronounced differently than the adjective and that the verb means "to pronounce distinctly." Have students write a sentence using both the verb and the adjective form of *articulate*.

---

---

# The Privacy Debate

Arthur M. Ahalt

## One Size Doesn't Fit All

"One man's justice is another man's injustice," said Ralph Waldo Emerson, neatly summarizing the complexity of most debates.

Unfortunately, the current debate over privacy issues rarely illuminates both sides of this complex issue. Instead, we are told there should be no debate over the 10 need for privacy.

This article will explore the other side of the privacy debate and demonstrate the benefit of access and openness, particularly in the area of public records.

As a retired state circuit court judge with 17 years on the bench, I've observed firsthand the benefits to our judicial, government and 20 economic systems of open access to public records. Unfortunately, too many Americans seem willing to reduce such access in the name of privacy.

Why is the siren call[1] of privacy so strong?

Maybe it stems from the impersonal nature of modern society, lack of community and 30 the rise of the global economy, all of which makes us wish for more **anonymity.** There now are 280 million Americans, and we're long past doing business at the corner store where everybody knew your name.

Maybe technology is to blame, with credit cards and consumer information automated to move 40 consumers from the practical obscurity of paper records to huge computer databases.

Maybe it's some politicians, the media and any number of self-styled advocates and experts who traffic in scare headlines, breathless press releases and emotional soapbox speeches. It's no mystery—privacy concerns affect **articulate** middle 50 class citizens who buy papers and vote—creating a "squeaky" wheel that gets the grease.

---

**anonymity**
(ă-nə-nĭm′ĭ-tē) *n.* the condition of being unknown

###  FACT AND OPINION
Identify a fact and an opinion in lines 27–36. Is the opinion you identified well substantiated? Explain.

**articulate** (är-tĭk′yə-lĭt) *adj.* able to speak clearly and coherently; well-spoken

**Targeted Passage**

---

1. **siren call:** alluring but possibly dangerous appeal (after the Sirens, mythological creatures whose irresistible songs lured sailors into danger).

---

## DIFFERENTIATED INSTRUCTION

### FOR STRUGGLING READERS

 **Targeted Passage [Lines 25–52]**
This passage helps explain the public's worries about privacy. At the same time, it undermines the argument in favor of privacy.

- What three reasons does Arthur M. Ahalt, the writer, give to explain why people are so concerned about privacy? (lines 28, 37, 43)

- Does Ahalt believe that these are valid reasons? Do you agree? (lines 28, 37, 43)

### FOR ENGLISH LANGUAGE LEARNERS

**Culture: Connect** Discuss the meaning of these expressions from page 688:

- *siren call* (line 25)
- *corner store* (lines 34–35)
- *soapbox speeches* (lines 47–48)
- *a "squeaky" wheel that gets the grease* (lines 51–52)

Invite students to tell how they would describe a situation that each term suggests in their home languages or cultures.

Privacy is also a **nonpartisan** concern which neither political party owns, and represents an issue where conservatives and liberals often meet in unison. Media stories about privacy issues often are human-interest heart-tuggers that sell and
60 gather an audience. Think tanks, clearinghouses[2] and "experts"  flock to issue press releases, hold seminars, appear on television and generally stoke the fires of paranoia[3] and emotionalism.

In this atmosphere, confusion, fear and concern replace a balanced view of the privacy issue.

Politicians and the media quote
70 polls—"93 percent of people are concerned about privacy." Well, no doubt. (I would like to know about the 7 percent who are not concerned about privacy, but that is another matter.) Those polls, however, don't appear to probe the trade-offs, such as "would you prefer a bank loan in three days or three months?" Most Americans
80 not only prefer to obtain immediate credit and debt, they demand it.

But instant credit and debt is more than a convenience; it's also the very basis of the underlying strength and power of our economic system, which moves at the speed of light as a direct result of the transparency of information available to economic decision
90 makers. Car, home and bank loans and the issuance of credit and debit cards can be made quickly because information about most of us is available. It's the source of our

---

2. **think tanks, clearinghouses:** A think tank is a research institute organized to investigate social problems; a clearinghouse is an organization that collects and distributes information.

3. **stoke the fires of paranoia:** increase fear and suspicion.

**nonpartisan**
(nŏn-pär'tĭ-zən) *adj.* not supporting or controlled by any political group

COMMON CORE RI 4

**SARCASM**
Reread the sentence that starts on line 60. The author uses quotation marks to indicate **sarcasm**—a form of wit characterized by cutting, ironic language—to show the reader that these "experts" actually lack genuine expertise. Why do you think the author is using sarcasm here?

---

**Analyze Visuals**

**Activity** Have students tell what the image shows and explain how it relates to the text on this page. *Possible answer: The image shows a credit card being scanned. It illustrates the idea of instant credit, which Ahalt calls "the very basis of the underlying strength and power of our economic system" (lines 84–86).*

**SARCASM**                                  COMMON CORE RI 4
*Possible answer:  The author is using sarcasm to back up the point that media stories about privacy issues are human-interest pieces and not written by experts; rather, they are written by people who want to "stoke the fires of paranoia and emotionalism."*

Lead a discussion with students about whether the use of sarcasm is more effective or harmful in a debate.

**REVIST THE BIG QUESTION**
Is **PRIVACY** an illusion?
**Discuss** Refer students to lines 69–81. Ask: How is privacy at odds with our high-tech, commercial world? *Possible answer: Privacy may need to be traded for some benefits. For example, the ability to get credit fast depends on knowing quickly whether someone is a good credit risk.*

**VOCABULARY**                              COMMON CORE L 4

**OWN THE WORD**
**nonpartisan:** Read the sentence containing *nonpartisan* aloud to students and have them identify context clues that can help them determine the meaning of the word. *Possible answers: neither political party; conservatives and liberals meet in unison*

---

**FOR STRUGGLING READERS**

**Develop Reading Fluency** Model for students an effective way to read the sentence containing the sarcastic use of the term "experts" in line 61. Point out to students how you inflect your voice to get across the idea that the term is being used sarcastically. Then have volunteers read the sentence and make up sentences of their own using a similar term.

**FOR ADVANCED LEARNERS/PRE–AP**

**Compare and Contrast Tone** [paired-activity option] Have students compare and contrast the tone of Ahalt's article with that of Rock's piece. Which writer seems more personal? more scornful? more sure of himself or herself? Have students identify several differences, as well as similarities. Remind students to support their points with textual evidence.

## Analyze Visuals

**Activity** Ask what the man is studying and how the photograph relates to the article. *Possible answer: The man is examining a fingerprint. Fingerprints are a means of identification that can be used to track a person's activities.*

**VOCABULARY** COMMON CORE **L 4**

### OWN THE WORD

**awry:** Tell students that *awry* means "wrong or amiss," and that antonyms are "right; perfect." Have students use both *awry* and one of its antonyms in a sentence that shows an understanding of the meaning of the words.

### ❶ GRAMMAR AND STYLE

Have students locate the infinitive phrases in these lines, beginning with *"to find . . ."* (line 109). Discuss how the parallelism creates a rhythm that helps readers distinguish—and remember—Ahalt's points.

**TEXT ANALYSIS** COMMON CORE **RI 4, RI 8**

### ❶ FACT AND OPINION

*Possible answer:* These lines state an opinion because they tell what Ahalt believes. His statement cannot be proved.

## SELECTION WRAP–UP

**READ WITH A PURPOSE** Have students discuss how great they feel the threat to privacy is. *Possible answer: While the threat is real, it can be controlled and information used responsibly.*

⭐ **CRITIQUE** Have students compare their reactions to the two articles. For example, which did they find more informative? more interesting? more personally useful?

---

**awry** (ə-rī′) *adj.*
off course; wrong

**Language Coach**

**Oral Fluency** Part of fluent reading is correct pronunciation. Words from French ending in *-que*, like *technique* and *antique*, end with a hard /k/ sound. Reread lines 138–145, and say the word that follows this rule.

❶ **GRAMMAR AND STYLE**
Reread lines 106–119. By using a series of infinitive phrases, the author establishes a **parallel structure** that emphasizes the benefits of open access to information.

❶ **FACT AND OPINION**
Is the author stating a fact or expressing an opinion in lines 133–137? How do you know?

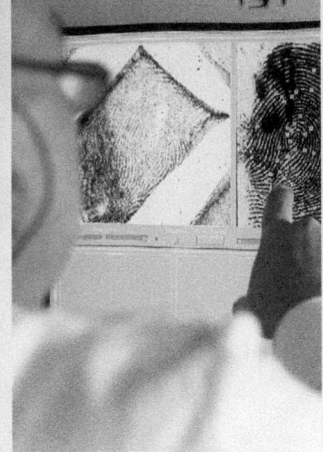

retail sector's⁷ strength. It's the reason we can buy and sell property in weeks; not months or years. Federal Trade Commission Chairman Tim Muris calls this system, which we 100 all take for granted, "the miracle of instant credit."

Economist Walter Kitchenman says that our consumer credit system is the "secret ingredient of the U.S. economy's resilience."

Aside from economic benefits, transparency also provides other specific benefits. It makes it possible to find absent spouses and 110 enforce child support payments; to screen day care workers and school bus drivers to keep our kids safe from substance abusers and child molesters; to check the background of bank tellers to avoid embezzlement; to connect heirs with fortunes; and to help prevent identity theft, and make it easier to fix if it occurs. ❶

120 There are real problems that affect real people in the privacy arena, but it's the classic case of bad news always selling, and good news remaining invisible.

Each day, billions of financial transactions occur in our economy. Do some go **awry?** Of course, but it is a small percentage. Unfortunately, no one wants 130 to read a headline "Today 299,999,033 Americans Did Not Suffer Privacy-Related Problems."

There is also a need to segment privacy from one huge ball of confusion into separate, more manageable and different issues, which require different approaches. ❶

Tracking Internet surfing and purchases is different from identity 140 theft, which is different from telemarketing calls, which is different from access to public records, which is also different from the use of Social Security numbers as a unique identifier.

Privacy supporters would have us believe that "one size fits all" when it comes to addressing matters of privacy.

150 I hold no portfolio on some of these issues, but as one who now is working directly in the area of public records accessibility, I am vitally concerned about access to these records and their contents.

Remember the old adage when you hear self-styled privacy experts expound on the need to keep information hidden: "for every 160 problem, there is a simple solution, which is usually wrong."

**Targeted Passage** ❺

7. **retail sector's:** of the branch of the nation's economy that deals with products people buy and use.

---

## DIFFERENTIATED INSTRUCTION

### FOR STRUGGLING READERS

❺ **Targeted Passage [Lines 146–161]**

This concluding passage restates Ahalt's main idea.

- Where else in this article have you seen the expression *one size fits all*? Why does Ahalt repeat it here? (lines 146–149)

- What does Ahalt say about himself as an authority on the subject of privacy? (lines 150–151)

- What adage does Ahalt quote? Why? (lines 159–161)

### FOR ENGLISH LANGUAGE LEARNERS

**Language Coach**

**Oral Fluency** *Possible answer: unique (yoo-NEEK)* Point out to students that another family of words that come from French includes words that end in *-tion*, pronounced /shun/. Have students locate words on this page with this spelling and pronunciation. *commission, line 98; transactions, line 126; information, line 159; solution, line 160.*

## Comprehension

1. **Recall** According to the author of "How Private Is Your Private Life?" what happens when a driver uses an E-Z Pass to pay a toll?

2. **Clarify** In the context of the Internet, what is a **cookie?**

3. **Summarize** According to the author of "The Privacy Debate: One Size Doesn't Fit All," how do we benefit from sacrificing some part of our privacy?

## Text Analysis

● 4. **Distinguish Fact from Opinion** Review the chart you filled in as you read. Does Andrea Rock rely more on fact or opinion in making her case? What about Arthur M. Ahalt? Do the opinions you identified tend to be substantiated? Cite evidence from the texts to support your answers.

5. **Analyze Argument** What question does Andrea Rock set out to explore? What conclusions does the bulk of her evidence support? How does she let readers know what she thinks by the end of her research day?

● 6. **Analyze Bias** Any piece of persuasive writing is likely to reflect the bias of its author. Which of the two articles do you think reflects a stronger bias? Support your answer with evidence from the texts.

7. **Identify Modes of Reasoning** The process of piecing together facts and other evidence to arrive at a logical conclusion or generalization is called **inductive reasoning.** Which of the two arguments you just read reaches its conclusion using inductive reasoning? Explain. (To learn more about inductive reasoning, see **Reading Handbook,** pages R22–R23.)

8. **Compare Texts** Which article do you find more convincing, and why?

9. **Make Judgments** How have these articles helped shape your thinking on the privacy issue? What does your reading experience suggest about the role that magazine articles and newspaper editorials can serve in civic life? Explain your answer.

> ### Is **PRIVACY** an illusion?
>
> What steps do you regularly take to ensure your privacy?

United States go awry (lines 125–128), but he does not give specifics. On the other hand, Rock doesn't only say that Web sites share data; she presents facts about DoubleClick (lines 102–107).

7. Rock's argument uses inductive reasoning. She gathers evidence throughout her day and then uses it to draw a conclusion.

8. Ahalt is more convincing because he, as a judge, is an authority. Rock is more convincing because she gathers so many verifiable facts.

9. Rock's article shows how our privacy can be invaded. Ahalt's article gives us good reasons to allow the invasion of privacy in some cases. Both articles serve a civic role in that they help readers think through the issue of privacy, which relates to citizenship.

> ### Is **PRIVACY** an illusion?
> **Possible answer:** Students should show an understanding of reasonable steps that help ensure privacy.

# Practice and Apply

For preliminary support of post-reading questions, use these copy masters:

**R RESOURCE MANAGER—Copy Masters**
Reading Check p. 70
Fact and Opinion p. 63
Question Support p. 71

Additional selection questions are provided for teachers on page 57.

## ANSWERS

## Comprehension

1. *The E-Z Pass establishes a travel record.*

2. *A cookie is a kind of ID tag that identifies users to those who create and maintain Web sites.*

3. *We benefit by being able to get credit quickly, a practice that keeps the economy strong. Other benefits are the ability to screen individuals for certain jobs (lines 111–116) and to help prevent identity theft (lines 117–118).*

## Text Analysis

*Possible answers:*

4. ● **COMMON CORE FOCUS** *Distinguish Fact from Opinion Rock relies heavily upon facts; Ahalt uses facts and opinions but emphasizes opinions. His opinions are mostly substantiated, however.* **How Private . . .?:** *fact: In about half of the states, citizens have no legal right to view their medical records (lines 33–34). opinion: "The [restaurant] food is delicious" (line 63).* **The Privacy Debate:** *fact: Access to records makes enforcing child support payments easier (lines 108–110). opinion: "[C]onfusion, fear and concern replace a balanced view of the privacy issue" (lines 66–68). Ahalt substantiates his opinion that the privacy issue isn't always balanced by giving privacy-related questions that polls don't ask.*

5. *Rock wants to find out how often her privacy is legally invaded during a typical day. Her evidence supports the conclusion that the invasion is constant. She lets readers know of her concerns by stating that she is no longer sure that her home is her castle.*

6. ■ **COMMON CORE FOCUS** *Analyze Bias Ahalt reflects a stronger bias. His writing is loaded with opinions but has few facts. For example, Ahalt says that only a few of the billions of daily financial transactions in the*

## ANSWERS

## Vocabulary in Context

▲ **VOCABULARY PRACTICE**

1. *assemble*
2. *fretfulness*
3. *inspiring*
4. *browser*
5. *arrogant*
6. *enemy*
7. *broadcasting*
8. *uneasy*
9. *illogical*
10. *advocacy*

 **RESOURCE MANAGER—Copy Master**
Vocabulary Practice p. 68

### ACADEMIC VOCABULARY IN WRITING

***Possible answer:*** *Although I've heard of people whose identities have been stolen, their problems don't seem* relevant *to my life. I think the advantages of modern communication definitely outweigh the potential risks.*

### VOCABULARY STRATEGY: INTERNET WORDS

**COMMON CORE L 6**

Explain that the Internet itself can provide definitions of Internet words. Suggest that students try *Internet glossary* as a search term. Note that definitions may vary from source to source.

***Possible answers:***
1. *a computer that stores information for client computers*
2. *a site that is a port of entry to the Web*
3. *a URL embedded in a document, meant to provide direct access to that URL*
4. *transmission of sounds and images via the Internet*
5. *a guide to accessing a site's content*
6. *wireless data communication; wireless networking (also called Wi-Fi)*

*Other terms may include* applet, blog, bookmark, domain name, FTP, netiquette, phishing, podcast, spyware, *and* worm.

 **RESOURCE MANAGER—Copy Master**
Vocabulary Strategy p. 69

---

**Interactive Vocabulary** **THINK** central

Keywords direct students to a **WordSharp** tutorial on **thinkcentral.com** or to other types of vocabulary practice and review.

---

---

## Vocabulary in Context

▲ **VOCABULARY PRACTICE**

Choose the word that is not related in meaning to the other words.

1. awry, amiss, assemble, astray
2. namelessness, disguise, anonymity, fretfulness
3. distressing, embarrassing, disconcerting, inspiring
4. electrician, browser, plumber, carpenter
5. pervasive, widespread, arrogant, extensive
6. enemy, associate, affiliate, partner
7. broadcasting, spying, observing, surveillance
8. impartial, uneasy, nonpartisan, unbiased
9. articulate, illogical, eloquent, expressive
10. rejection, advocacy, rebuff, disdain

### ACADEMIC VOCABULARY IN WRITING

- coherent
- differentiate
- evident
- relevant
- technique

Decide whether the arguments these two writers make about privacy are **relevant** to your life. In a paragraph or two, state your opinion and support it with evidence and a **coherent** argument. Use at least one Academic Vocabulary word in your response.

### VOCABULARY STRATEGY: INTERNET WORDS

You often hear Internet terms, whether in computer class or in your daily interactions, but do you know what they actually mean? Some terms, like the vocabulary word *browser* (a word that can be traced back to an Indo-European base), are common words used in specialized ways. Other terms are unique to discussion of the Internet. To be Web literate, you need a working knowledge of basic Internet terms.

***PRACTICE*** With a partner, write definitions for each term, and check them in a current dictionary or Web site glossary. Then list three other Internet terms you think your classmates should know, and define them.

1. server
2. portal
3. hyperlink
4. Webcast
5. site map
6. wireless fidelity

**WORD LIST**

advocacy
affiliate
anonymity
articulate
awry
browser
disconcerting
nonpartisan
pervasive
surveillance

**COMMON CORE**

**L 6** Acquire and use accurately general academic and domain-specific words.

**Interactive Vocabulary** **THINK** central

Go to **thinkcentral.com**.
KEYWORD: HML9-692

---

## DIFFERENTIATED INSTRUCTION

### FOR ENGLISH LANGUAGE LEARNERS

**Vocabulary** Have students write the part of speech of each word on the Word List. Also ask students to identify any words in the list that have cognates in their home languages (such as the English *affiliate* and the Spanish *afiliado*).

### FOR ADVANCED LEARNERS/PRE–AP

**Vocabulary in Writing** Have students consider the connotations of the words on the Word List. Then ask them to rank each word along a continuum for positive, neutral, or negative connotation. Invite students to compare and discuss their ideas.

# Language

◆ **GRAMMAR AND STYLE:** Use Rhetorical Devices

Review the **Grammar and Style** note on page 690. **Parallelism**—the use of similar grammatical constructions to express ideas that are related or equal in importance—can add rhythm or emphasis to speech or writing. In the following example from "The Privacy Debate: One Size Doesn't Fit All," notice how the author uses a series of adjective clauses, all beginning with "which is," to emphasize how privacy needs differ:

> *Tracking Internet surfing and purchases is different from identity theft, which is different from telemarketing calls, which is different from access to public records, which is also different from the use of Social Security numbers as a unique identifier.* (lines 138–145)

Now study the model. Notice how the revisions in blue add emphasis to the writer's ideas. Revise your response to the prompt below by using parallel structures.

> **STUDENT MODEL**
>
> You speak to the benefits of sharing public records. However, ~~I feel~~
> *why do you fail to mention*
> ∧                                                    ∧ ?
> ~~you do not sufficiently explore~~ the problems, such as identity theft. ~~You~~
> *Why do you fail to*                                *identify theft*        ?
> ∧ ~~allude to identity theft, but do not~~ mention how many lives ~~it~~ has ruined. ∧

## READING-WRITING CONNECTION

**YOUR TURN**

Explore the arguments presented in "How Private is Your Private Life?" and "The Privacy Debate: One Size Doesn't Fit All" by responding to this prompt. Then use the **revising tip** to improve your writing.

| WRITING PROMPT | REVISING TIP |
|---|---|
| **Extended Constructed Response: Critique** Write a letter to one of the authors in which you explain how his or her piece could be made more convincing. In your critique, write **three to five paragraphs** describing your reaction to the article and your suggestions for improvement. Make sure your critique goes beyond a mere summary and includes your feelings and observations about the piece. | Review your critique. Did you use parallelism to add rhythm and/or emphasis to your letter? If not, revise your response. |

**Interactive Revision** THINK central
Go to thinkcentral.com.
KEYWORD: HML9-693

---

**COMMON CORE**

**L 1a** Use parallel structure.
**W 4** Produce clear and coherent writing in which the style is appropriate to the task, purpose, and audience.

---

# Language

COMMON CORE W 4, L 1a

◆ **GRAMMAR AND STYLE**

After students analyze the two models, ask them to revise their passage for parallelism. Note that there may be more than one way to create parallelism in a given passage.

 **RESOURCE MANAGER**—Copy Master
Use Rhetorical Devices p. 72

**READING-WRITING CONNECTION**
Have students who are writing to the same person approach the prewriting stage of the assignment as a Think-Pair-Share activity.

 **BEST PRACTICES TOOLKIT**—Transparency
Think-Pair-Share p. A18

> **Writing Online**    THINK central
>
> The following tools are available online at **thinkcentral.com** and on **WriteSmart CD-ROM**:
> • **Interactive Graphic Organizers**
> • **Interactive Student Models**
> • **Interactive Revision Lessons**
> For additional grammar instruction, see **GrammarNotes** on **thinkcentral.com**.

# Assess and Reteach

## Assess

**DIAGNOSTIC AND SELECTION TESTS**
  Selection Test A pp. 183–184
  Selection Test B/C pp. 185–186

**Interactive Selection Test** on **thinkcentral.com**

## Reteach

**Level Up Online Tutorials** on **thinkcentral.com**

**Reteaching Workshops** on **thinkcentral.com**
  Reading Lesson 5: Distinguishing Fact
   from Opinion

---

**FOR STRUGGLING WRITERS**
Model this structure for the body of the letter:

> I enjoyed the article, but I feel that a few changes would make it even more convincing. For example, I think that _____ because _____. I also think that _____ because _____. Finally, I think that _____ because _____.

### Billy Thomas
### Life Is Calling

Public Service Announcements on **Media Smart** DVD-ROM

---

 **COMMON CORE FOCUS**

**RI 7** Analyze various accounts of a subject, determining which details are emphasized in each. **W 9b (RI 7)** Draw evidence from informational texts to support analysis of various accounts of a subject told in different mediums. **SL 2** Integrate multiple sources of information presented in diverse media or formats. **SL 3** Evaluate a speaker's use of evidence and rhetoric.

## SUMMARIES

The first PSA, "Billy Thomas," seeks support of Boys and Girls Clubs of America. Images of children having fun contrast with warning images such as police cars, and are interspersed with images of celebrity spokesman Denzel Washington expressing gratitude to his childhood Club and its leader, Billy Thomas. The second PSA, "Life Is Calling," asks people to join the Peace Corps. A voiceover asks questions about how far the viewer would go to help someone and for how long. Images take the viewer to very distant places with exotic peoples and landscapes.

## How do you
## PROMOTE a cause?

Have students share PSAs and their causes. Ask students what images, words, and music were used and what emotions were appealed to. You might focus on PSAs aimed at teens, such as about staying in school, drug use, underage drinking, or smoking.

## BACKGROUND

PSAs began in the 1940s when the War Advertising Council was established to persuade Americans to support World War II. Messages such as "Keep 'em Rolling" and "Loose Lips Sink Ships" were designed to promote patriotism, security, and confidence. Today, non-profit organizations and government agencies use PSAs to promote awareness of issues such as literacy and human rights.

---

# How do you
# PROMOTE
## a cause?

 **COMMON CORE**

**RI 7** Analyze various accounts of a subject, determining which details are emphasized in each. **SL 3** Evaluate a speaker's use of evidence and rhetoric.

Have you ever wondered how you can get involved in your community? Perhaps you'd like to volunteer at a local soup kitchen, help restore a rundown building, or donate blood. The two public service announcements (PSAs) in this lesson promote worthy causes by inspiring viewers to get involved. See if they motivate you to take action.

## Background

**Making a Difference** The PSAs you will view promote two well-known organizations. The first PSA, "Billy Thomas," is from the Boys and Girls Clubs of America, an organization that provides afterschool and weekend activities for boys and girls. The second PSA, "Life Is Calling," is part of a campaign for the Peace Corps, a government agency whose volunteers work in developing countries to help advance world peace.

694

---

## Media Study Resources

**R RESOURCE MANAGER UNIT 6**
Plan and Teach pp. 73–76
Summary pp. 77–78†‡*
Viewing Guide p. 79
Close Viewing p. 80
Media Activity p. 81
Produce Your Own Media p. 82

**TECHNOLOGY**
⊙ **Teacher One Stop DVD-ROM**
⊙ **Student One Stop DVD-ROM**
⊙ **MediaSmart DVD-ROM**
**MediaScope** on **thinkcentral.com**

*See resources on the* **Teacher One Stop DVD-ROM** *and on* **thinkcentral.com**.

\* **Resources for Differentiation**    † **Also in Spanish**    ‡ **In Haitian Creole and Vietnamese**

## Media Literacy: Persuasion in PSAs

Whether they're asking an audience to help end homelessness or to help save the environment, PSAs draw on many of the same techniques that are used in commercial advertising. Images, words, and music can attract an audience, but in order to raise awareness of important issues and get people to act, PSAs depend on **persuasive techniques.**

### PERSUASIVE TECHNIQUES IN PUBLIC SERVICE ANNOUNCEMENTS

A **celebrity spokesperson** who possesses admirable qualities may appeal to a particular audience.

By giving a **testimonial,** or a personal recommendation, an individual directly associates himself or herself with the cause. For example,

Voice-over: Does it work? It did for me.

**Images** may represent ideas and values that appeal to a particular audience. Notice how this image conveys the idea of unity. Images are often more persuasive than words alone.

A **slogan** is a memorable phrase that helps an audience remember an organization's message. For example,

Life is calling. How far will you go?

### STRATEGIES FOR ANALYZING PUBLIC SERVICE ANNOUNCEMENTS

- Make note of any words, images, and persuasive techniques that help you define the **target audience.** Ask yourself: Who might be interested in this cause? How might the PSA change in formality or tone if it targeted a different audience and had a different purpose?
- Pay attention to the delivery of the **message.** Ask yourself: Do the people, images, and words spoken help deliver a clear message? Is the information helpful to the viewer or listener?
- Be conscious of **emotional appeals**—messages that persuade an audience by creating strong feelings. Ask yourself: How do the words, images, symbols, and music create emotional appeal?
- Consider who the spokesperson is. Ask yourself: What qualities does this person possess? How might viewers identify with this person?
- Look for a logo to help you determine what group is behind the message. A **logo** is a unique symbol, name, or trademark that is associated with an organization. Ask yourself: When and where does the logo appear?

MEDIA STUDY    **695**

---

## Media Literacy

Review with students the meaning of *persuasion* and ask them to recall especially persuasive PSAs. Ask what made these ads so persuasive. What kind of images and music were used? Was there a spokesperson and, if so, who was it? Was there a memorable slogan or symbol? Then, discuss the techniques and strategies on this page.

- **Celebrity Spokesperson and Testimonial** To reinforce the effect of celebrity spokespeople and testimonials, ask students to imagine an ad campaign to end world hunger. Ask them to contrast the impact of a celebrity such as Bono as spokesperson with that of an anonymous speaker.
- **Images** Recall the old adage "a picture is worth a thousand words." Help students recognize that PSAs, like all ads, need to be short. Strong images help PSAs convey ideas and values quickly and memorably.
- **Slogan** Review some highly successful slogans, such as "Only you can prevent forest fires" and "Friends don't let friends drive drunk." Stress that the slogans work because they are short, catchy, memorable, and make a clear point.
- **Target Audience** Discuss the difference between ads addressed to teens and ads addressed to their parents, both about a single issue such as drug use. Help students see that PSAs target particular audiences with different persuasive techniques.
- **Emotional Appeals** Point out that PSAs use emotional appeals to stress that support for the cause will bring personal satisfaction. Ask students to name values and desires that they think PSAs try to appeal to, such as self-respect and desires to be healthy, live in safety, and feel useful and helpful.
- **Logo** To be sure students recognize logos, have them identify the publisher's logo on this book. What does it mean?

---

### MEDIA STUDY: TEACHING OPTIONS

**Teaching Option 1: The Basics (1–2 Days)**
1. Begin the Media Study using the material provided on pages 694–695.
2. Show the Introduction on MediaSmart. Then show the First Viewing. As they watch, have students use the Viewing Guide on page 696, along with the corresponding copy master on page 79 of the Resource Manager. Discuss their responses.
3. Return to the pupil book for the extension activities on page 697.

**Teaching Option 2: In-Depth Study (2–3 Days)**
1. Begin the Media Study using pages 694–695.
2. Show the Introduction and First Viewing from MediaSmart. Then continue on MediaSmart with the Media Lessons, using the teacher notes available in the Resources section.
3. Show the Guided Analysis presentation. Have students record their observations on the Student Viewing Guide available in the Resources section from MediaSmart.
4. Return to the pupil book, page 697.

MEDIA STUDY    **695**

# Practice and Apply

## VIEWING GUIDE

1. Before students view the two PSAs, tell them they will be asked to compare and contrast how the ads persuade people to support their causes. Encourage students to watch and listen for these elements and techniques:

   - a **celebrity spokesperson** and a **testimonial** that reflect a well-known actor's endorsement of the Boys and Girls Clubs

   - **images** that appeal to childhood memories or imagination of travel

   - **slogans** that deliver a message and encourage participation in life

   - how the interests and desires of the **target audiences** are addressed

   - how each **message** is delivered through words, images, and music, such as the continual line on maps and chalkboards that connects efforts of the Peace Corps

   - how **emotional appeals** that show young, impressionable children encourage viewers to act

   - **logos** that try to create unique symbols to associate with a cause

2. After students have viewed the PSAs, help them focus on different elements by showing the PSAs first with no sound, and then with only sound and no images.

   **R** RESOURCE MANAGER—Copy Masters
   Viewing Guide p. 79
   Close Viewing p. 80
   Media Activity p. 81

Use this resource with the Viewing Guide:

 MediaSmart DVD-ROM

MediaScope on **thinkcentral.com**

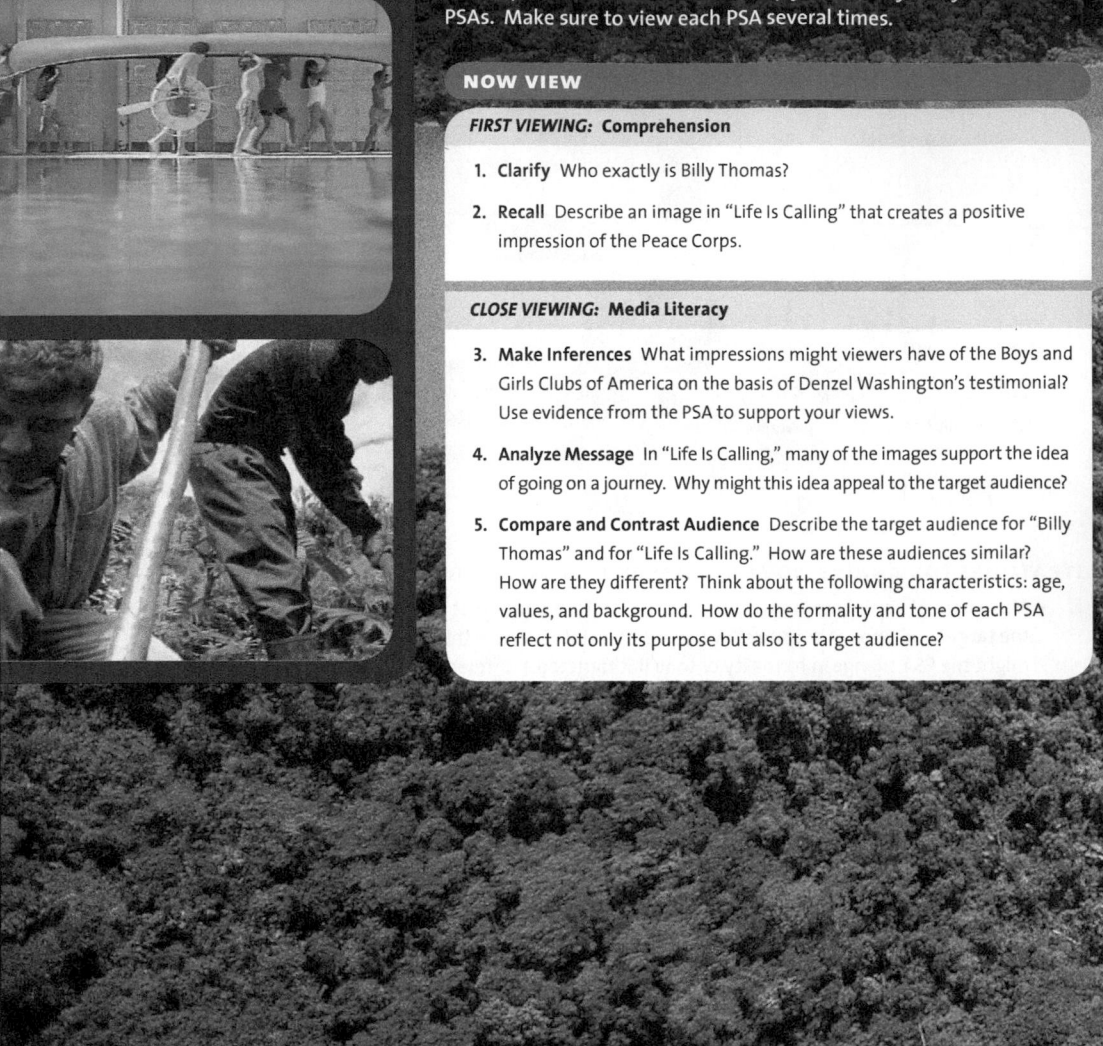

**Media Smart DVD-ROM**
- **PSA 1:** "Billy Thomas" from the Boys and Girls Clubs of America
- **PSA 2:** "Life Is Calling" from Peace Corps
- **Genre:** Public Service Announcements

### Viewing Guide for
# Public Service Announcements

In "Billy Thomas," Denzel Washington, a highly regarded actor who has won two Academy Awards, recalls a childhood experience. The second PSA, "Life Is Calling," poses a number of rhetorical questions designed to persuade viewers to volunteer and help those in need.
   The questions that follow will help you critically analyze these PSAs. Make sure to view each PSA several times.

#### NOW VIEW

**FIRST VIEWING: Comprehension**

1. **Clarify** Who exactly is Billy Thomas?

2. **Recall** Describe an image in "Life Is Calling" that creates a positive impression of the Peace Corps.

**CLOSE VIEWING: Media Literacy**

3. **Make Inferences** What impressions might viewers have of the Boys and Girls Clubs of America on the basis of Denzel Washington's testimonial? Use evidence from the PSA to support your views.

4. **Analyze Message** In "Life Is Calling," many of the images support the idea of going on a journey. Why might this idea appeal to the target audience?

5. **Compare and Contrast Audience** Describe the target audience for "Billy Thomas" and for "Life Is Calling." How are these audiences similar? How are they different? Think about the following characteristics: age, values, and background. How do the formality and tone of each PSA reflect not only its purpose but also its target audience?

696

## ANSWERS

### FIRST VIEWING: Comprehension
**Possible answers:**

1. *He ran the Club that Denzel Washington belonged to as a child.*

2. *A Peace Corps volunteer works in a field with local people.*

### CLOSE VIEWING: Media Literacy
**Possible answers:**

3. *The Clubs are caring organizations—**Images:** children and Club volunteers together; they are possible refugees from danger—**Images:** Club children in safe surroundings but police car lights; Club children can learn and have fun—**Images:** children dancing and swimming*

4. *The Peace Corps' traditional audience is young people who might want to travel.*

5. ***"Billy Thomas":** primarily parents or adults who can contribute time or money*

   ***"Life Is Calling":** primarily young adults*

   ***Similarities:** Both appeal to people with a desire to help others in need.* ***Differences:** "Billy Thomas" uses a famous person's personal experience and calls for help close to home. "Life Is Calling" has a more global view and calls for help around the world.*

   *Answers will vary, but should reflect the tone and formality of each PSA as it relates to the target audience.*

## Write or Discuss

**Evaluate Emotional Appeal** The PSAs in this lesson use emotional appeal to persuade viewers. Choose one of the PSAs and make a list of the techniques that are used to create emotional appeal. In your opinion, which of these elements is most effective? As part of your evaluation, consider the following:

• the use of celebrity endorsement or voice-over to deliver the message
• the target audience and techniques used to appeal to this audience
• how visuals communicate information differently than a non-visual text might
• your reaction to the PSA and how you think the intended audience might react

## Produce Your Own Media

**Create a PSA** The PSA shown in the professional model is from the National Crime Prevention Council. It is part of a campaign that encourages teens to get involved by taking an activity they enjoy and using it to help others in their community. Your job is to create a PSA like the one shown that presents your own distinct point of view on an issue.

*HERE'S HOW* Think of a well-known organization or charity that supports an issue you care about. For example, if you're interested in helping cancer patients, you might want to create a PSA for the American Cancer Society.

• Consider the layout of your PSA, including the size and placement of visuals, text, and a slogan.
• Use catchy words and images that grab your specific audience's attention.

**PROFESSIONAL MODEL**

**1** "Before" and "after" images give visual support to the message.
**2** A catchy slogan describes the message.
**3** A sign identifies the volunteer activity.
**4** The logo identifies the organization.

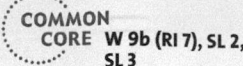

**COMMON CORE**

**W 9b (RI 7)** Draw evidence from informational texts to support analysis of various accounts of a subject told in different mediums. **SL 2** Integrate multiple sources of information presented in diverse media or formats. **SL 3** Evaluate a speaker's use of evidence and rhetoric.

**Media Tools** **THINK** central

Go to **thinkcentral.com**.
KEYWORD: HML9-697

**Tech Tip**

Use your own photographs and photo-editing software to give your PSA a professional quality.

---

want to hire them and for consumers to buy the products they endorse? Then ask students to name ineffective or unsuccessful spokespersons. Why are they unsuccessful? *Student responses may focus on credibility, likableness, or other personal qualities.*

• **Emotional Appeals** Have students discuss this question: Is it appropriate to use emotional appeals to convince people to support a cause? Why, or why not?

## Produce Your Own Media

**Rubric: Create a PSA** A strong PSA should have

• a clear message identifying the cause and encouraging action
• a catchy slogan that grabs viewers' attention
• eye-catching images that give information and/or call up an emotional response
• a clearly identifiable teen target audience
• a logo that clearly relates to the cause

**R** RESOURCE MANAGER—Copy Master
Produce Your Own Media p. 82

---

# Assess and Reteach

## Write or Discuss

COMMON CORE **W 9b (RI 7), SL 2, SL 3**

Produce a multimedia presentation with graphics and images that conveys a distinctive point of view and appeals to a specific audience.

**Evaluate Emotional Appeal** In their evaluations, students should address the persuasive techniques used to create emotional appeal, such as the relationship of a celebrity to the cause; images, music, and words that target the particular audience; and the specific emotions to which the ad appeals. They should compare how effective these techniques are in reaching viewers' emotions. For example, students might find Denzel Washington's personal relationship with the Boys Club and his memories highly effective. In "Life Is Calling," students may note that images of exotic faraway places successfully appeal to young people's urge for travel and adventure. Encourage students to include their own emotional reactions to the ad they choose.

## MEDIA STUDY WRAP-UP

Have students summarize what they have learned about the use of images, words, and music as persuasive techniques in PSAs. Encourage them to use terms such as *persuasion/persuasive, celebrity spokesperson, testimonial, image, slogan, target audience, message, emotional appeal,* and *logo* in their explanations.

## RETEACH

For students who are unable to apply the Media Study skills, select from these reteaching options:

• **Celebrity Spokespersons** Ask students to consider celebrity spokespersons they have seen on commercials and in advertisements. Have them give examples of people they consider effective spokespersons for a product or service. What makes these people effective? What qualities, experiences, or other attributes do they possess for companies to

**Media Tools**

Media study keywords point to **MediaScope**, a Web site that helps students strengthen media analysis and production skills.

# Focus and Motivate

## COMMON CORE FOCUS

**RL 2** Determine a central idea and analyze its development, including how it emerges and is shaped by details. **RI 2** Determine a central idea and analyze its development, including how it emerges and is shaped by details. **RI 4** Determine the connotative meanings of words and phrases as they are used in a text. **RI 5** Analyze in detail how an author's ideas or claims are developed and refined. **W 5** Develop and strengthen writing by editing to demonstrate conventions of standard English capitalization. **L 2** Demonstrate command of the conventions of standard English capitalization. **L 4** Determine the meaning of multiple-meaning words.

## SUMMARIES

The author of "Primal Screen" argues that family life is declining because Americans spend too much watching television.

In "The Pedestrian," Leonard Mead is arrested and taken to a psychiatric center when he is found talking a walk instead of watching television.

**Advertisement** The ad for "TV Master" shows a television remote control.

## Could we live without TELEVISION?

Read the question. Then, ask students to describe how big a part TV watching plays in their life.

## What's the Connection?

Lead students in a discussion about the future of television viewing. Do they think people in the future will watch more or less TV than we do today? Why, or why not?

## Selection Resources

---

*Comparing Texts*

**Primal Screen**
Essay by Ellen Goodman

**The Pedestrian**
Short Story by Ray Bradbury

**TV Master**
Advertisement

Video link at thinkcentral.com

# Could we live without TELEVISION?

### COMMON CORE

**RL 2** Determine a central idea and analyze its development, including how it emerges and is shaped by details. **RI 2** Determine a central idea and analyze its development, including how it emerges and is shaped by details. **RI 4** Determine the connotative meanings of words and phrases as they are used in a text. **RI 5** Analyze in detail how an author's ideas or claims are developed and refined. **L 4** Determine the meaning of multiple meaning words.

Some of us spend a lot of our time watching television. According to research, the average American family is glued to the screen for more than seven hours a day. Is this television habit helping us or hurting us?

## What's the Connection?

The essay that follows, "Primal Screen," focuses on problems associated with watching too much television. After reading the essay, you will read a literary text and view an advertisement that explore the topic of television watching in other ways.

698

---

See resources on the **Teacher One Stop DVD-ROM** and on **thinkcentral.com**.

**RESOURCE MANAGER UNIT 6**
Plan and Teach, pp. 83–90
Summary pp. 91–92†‡*
Text Analysis, pp. 93–97†*

**DIAGNOSTIC AND SELECTION TESTS**
Selection Tests, pp. 187–190

**BEST PRACTICES TOOLKIT**
Main Idea and Details, p. B6
Observation Chart, p. C7

**TECHNOLOGY**
Video link at thinkcentral.com
- Teacher One Stop DVD-ROM
- Student One Stop DVD-ROM
- Audio Anthology CD
- GrammarNotes DVD-ROM
- ExamView Test Generator on the **Teacher One Stop**

---

\* Resources for Differentiation     † Also in Spanish     ‡ In Haitian Creole and Vietnamese

## TEXT ANALYSIS: WRITER'S MESSAGE

The essay and short story you are about to read are works of **social criticism,** or literature that addresses real-life issues—political, religious, economic, or social. However, while both texts comment on the same topic, the impact of television viewing, each has a different message, or central idea, and conveys it through different methods. As you read, try to determine each **writer's message** by paying attention to the following:

| In the Essay | In the Short Story |
|---|---|
| • direct statements | • setting and imagery |
| • facts, statistics, and other evidence, such as descriptions of people's behavior and interactions | • mood, sensory details, and word choice |
| • explanations of causes and effects | • characters |
| • word choice | • dialogue |
| • tone | • plot—especially the nature of the conflict and its resolution |
| • the writer's call to action at the end | • the lesson you take from the story |

## READING STRATEGY: SET A PURPOSE FOR READING

When you **set a purpose for reading,** you identify specific goals to accomplish as you read. For example, after reading these next two selections, you'll be asked to compare and contrast them. You'll also be asked to repond to short constructed response questions, including one that requires cross-textual synthesis. Thus, you'll want to read with the following goals in mind:

• to determine each writer's message or central idea
• to identify the similarities and differences in the two messages, including how each message emerges and is shaped by details
• to identify evidence for your conclusions

Take a moment now to consider how you will accomplish these goals. Will you try to keep track of similarities and differences in the writers' messages as you read? Or do you need to determine each writer's message first and then review the selections to discover ways in which the messages differ and to find evidence?

 Complete the activities in your **Reader/Writer Notebook.**

## Meet the Authors

### Ellen Goodman
born 1941

**Newswoman**
After beginning her career as a research trainee at *Newsweek* in the early 1960s, Ellen Goodman broke into reporting and eventually became a columnist for the *Boston Globe.* Today her columns cover a wide range of topics—from politics to parenting—and appear in more than 450 newspapers across the country. Goodman rewards her readers with both good laughs and something to think about.

### Ray Bradbury
born 1920

**Social Prognosticator**
Ray Bradbury is one of the best-known and most highly regarded writers of science fiction. His stories have been termed "warning fictions" because they often explore the dire consequences of society's dependence on technology. Though his stories are serious, Bradbury relishes writing them. "I write for fun," he has said. "I have fun with ideas."

**Authors Online**
Go to thinkcentral.com. KEYWORD: HML9-699

699

## Teach

## READ WITH A PURPOSE

*Help students set a purpose for reading. Tell them to read to determine the author's general attitude about TV.*

### Ⓐ Model the Skill: WRITER'S MESSAGE

Point out that the TV family is communicating and solving its problems. Then note that the real family is not solving problems or communicating at all, except perhaps during commercials. Explain that in this contrast, readers see how different the families are and the issue the author is trying to highlight.

*Possible answer: By making this contrast, Goodman introduces the issue that real families, unlike the sitcom ones they are watching on TV, have trouble communicating and problem solving precisely because they are spending too much time watching TV.*

## TIERED DISCUSSION PROMPTS

Direct students to lines 23–26. Use these prompts to help students grasp the main point of Goodman's argument:

**Connect** Does Goodman's description remind you of families you know? Explain. *Answers will vary.*

**Analyze** According to Goodman, which is worse: what families watch on TV, or how long they watch TV? Why? *Possible answer: How long they watch is worse, according to Goodman. She believes that the more time family members watch TV, the less time they spend interacting with each other.*

**Evaluate** Do you think that Goodman's view is valid? Why or why not? *Possible answers: Yes, because the longer the TV is on, the less time there is for homework, conversation, hobbies, reading, or sleep. No, because people sometimes do other things even though a TV is on.*

---

# Primal Screen
## Ellen Goodman

Someday, I would like to see a television series about a family that sits around the set watching a series about a family that sits around the set.

It might not make the Nielsen top ten,[1] but it isn't such a strange idea. Especially when you think about what's going on right now.

Night after night, inside the tube, warm and wiggly families spend their prime time "communicating" like crazy and "solving problems" together like mad. Meanwhile, outside the tube, real families sit and wait for a commercial break just to talk to each other. Ⓐ

About the only subject that never comes up before our glazed eyes
10 is what the medium does to our family life. But, I suppose we already know that.

According to a recent Gallup Poll, television comes out as a major heavy in our family lives. On the scale of problems, TV didn't rate as bad as inflation, but it ran neck-and-neck with unemployment.

According to a recent Roper Poll, it even causes fights. When people were asked what husbands and wives argued about, money was the champion. But television was a strong contender. Considering how much more time we spend in front of the tube, that may not be such a shock.

To a certain extent, we blame the programs. In the Gallup Poll, for
20 example, people worried most about the overemphasis on sex and violence. But surely half of those fights between husbands and wives must be about the more fundamental issue of turning it off.

Deep down below our poll-taking consciousness, we know that the worst aspect of our addiction isn't what's on TV, but how long the TV is on. We can't help but be aware of what happens when we spend more time facing the screen than facing each other.

In that same Gallup Poll, a large number of us said that the way to improve family life is by sharing—sharing family needs, recreational activities and chores. But when you are watching, you aren't doing.
30 The only experience you are sharing is a vicarious one.

I am absolutely convinced that the average wife feels tuned out by the twelfth consecutive weekend sports event because she *is* being tuned out.

---

1. **Nielsen top ten:** the ten most-watched television shows, as determined by the Nielsen rating service.

### Ⓐ WRITER'S MESSAGE

Reread lines 5–8. What issue does the author introduce by contrasting sitcom families and real-life ones?

### Language Coach

**Slang** Informal, sometimes made-up words that substitute for formal words are called **slang.** Reread lines 5–7 and 17–18. What does the word *tube* refer to in these sentences? Look up *tube* in a dictionary and try to determine where its slang meaning comes from. Then, decide whether *tube* has a positive or negative connotation (the feeling associated with a word) in the context of this essay.

---

## DIFFERENTIATED INSTRUCTION

### FOR ENGLISH LANGUAGE LEARNERS

#### Language Coach

**Slang** *Possible answer:* Tube *refers to television. Students' answers should reflect the etymology of* tube. Have students work in pairs to use *tube* in sentences that have positive and negative connotations of the word.

### FOR STRUGGLING READERS

In combination with the *Audio Anthology CD,* use one or more Targeted Passages (pp. 701, 702, 705, 707) to ensure that students focus on key ideas, concepts, and skills. Targeted Passages are also good for English learners.

❶ **Targeted Passage [Lines 49–58]**

This passage presents Goodman's call to action.

The average kid develops that distant, slack-jawed, hypnotic, hooked stare because he or she *is* hooked.

In the same way, the people who spend night after night in front of the tube should worry about it. They've become an audience and not a family. Television simply presents us with one model of family life. Watching it makes us fit another model.

But the striking thing in all of this research about how we feel and
40 behave is the role of choice. On the one hand, we have real anxiety about what TV's doing to us. On the other hand, we allow it to happen. **B**

We choose to turn it on and each other off. We choose peace and quiet when we let the kids watch TV instead of running around the living room. We choose to "relax" in the semi-comatose slump.

The average viewing time of the American child between six and sixteen years of age is twenty to twenty-four hours a week. A large percentage of parents place no restrictions on either the number of hours watched or the type of program viewed.

At the very least, we behave as if we were powerless to wrench each
50 other away.

I grant you that there are a lot of things that touch on our families that are totally out of our individual control. We can't regulate foreign affairs. We can't set the price for oil.

But a television set has a dial and a plug. And we have hands. It is absurd to let our feelings of impotence in the world start creeping into our private lives. **C**

Just once, we ought to create a private show about a real-life family that kicked the habit.

**B WRITER'S MESSAGE**
What is Goodman's message about excessive TV viewing?

**◄ Analyze Visuals**
What are your impressions of the family in this photograph?

**COMMON CORE** RI 2

**C WRITER'S MESSAGE**
This writer reveals her message through strong statements of **opinion**— how she personally feels about people's TV habits. Opinions are either **substantiated** (backed up by facts) or **unsubstantiated** (inadequately supported). Are the opinions expressed in this essay generally substantiated or unsubstantiated? Support your answer with specific details from the text.

**① Targeted Passage**

- What are some things in our lives that we cannot control, according to Goodman? In contrast, what can we control? (lines 52–53)
- What facts does she present to prove that we have control over the TV? (line 54)
- What does she mean when she suggests creating a private show? (line 57)

**FOR ADVANCED LEARNERS/PRE–AP**
**Determine Attitudes** Have students create and administer a short survey to family members and neighbors on their attitudes toward television. You may want to pre-screen students' survey questions. After students have tabulated and analyzed their results, have them share their findings and conclusions with the class.

---

**TEXT ANALYSIS** | **COMMON CORE** RL 2, RI 2, RI 5

**B WRITER'S MESSAGE**
*Possible answer: Goodman's message is that despite our anxiety about watching too much TV, we feel powerless to change.*

## BACKGROUND
**More Viewing Stats** In 1999, the Kaiser Family Foundation studied the presence and effects of television. It found that 53 percent of all children had a television in their bedroom. It further found that students in grades seven through twelve spent just 22 minutes per day on leisure reading and 25 minutes reading for homework. In addition, the study showed that people who watched more TV were less contented than people who watched less.

## Analyze Visuals
*Possible answer: This family is obsessed with TV. It has spent a lot of money to have nine TV sets. Each person is watching his or her own show in a dark, uninviting room.*

**TEXT ANALYSIS** | **COMMON CORE** RI 2

**C WRITER'S MESSAGE**
*Possible answer: The opinions are mostly substantiated. For example, she backs up her opinion in lines 54–56.*

Tell students to work in pairs to find one other opinion that is either substantiated or unsubstantiated. Discuss with students what effect each type of opinion generally has on the author's argument.

**READ WITH A PURPOSE**

*Help students set a purpose for reading. Tell them to read "The Pedestrian" to find out how society deals with a person who is different.*

# The Pedestrian

Ray Bradbury

COMMON CORE

RL 2,
RI 2,
RI 5

**TEXT ANALYSIS**

**D WRITER'S MESSAGE**

*Possible answer:* The imagery and figurative language compare the houses in which people are watching TV to death (the graveyard; the tomblike building) and to the supernatural (the flickering light; the gray phantoms). They suggest that Bradbury equates TV viewing with lifelessness.

To enter out into that silence that was the city at eight o'clock of a misty evening in November, to put your feet upon that buckling concrete walk, to step over grassy seams and make your way, hands in pockets, through the silences, that was what Mr. Leonard Mead most dearly loved to do. He would stand upon the corner of an intersection and peer down long moonlit avenues of sidewalk in four directions, deciding which way to go, but it really made no difference; he was alone in this world of A.D. 2053, or as good as alone, and with a final decision made, a path selected, he would stride off, sending patterns of frosty air before him like the smoke of a cigar.

10  Sometimes he would walk for hours and miles and return only at midnight to his house. And on his way he would see the cottages and homes with their dark windows, and it was not unlike walking through a graveyard where only the faintest glimmers of firefly light appeared in flickers behind the windows. Sudden gray phantoms seemed to manifest upon inner room walls where a curtain was still undrawn against the night, or there were whisperings and murmurs where a window in a tomblike building was still open. **D**

Mr. Leonard Mead would pause, cock his head, listen, look, and march on, his feet making no noise on the lumpy walk. For long ago he had wisely changed to sneakers when strolling at night, because the dogs in intermittent
20  squads would parallel his journey with barkings if he wore hard heels, and lights might click on and faces appear and an entire street be startled by the passing of a lone figure, himself, in the early November evening.

**Analyze Visuals ▶**

What details in the painting help create a somber mood?

**D WRITER'S MESSAGE**

Reread lines 10–16. What do the **imagery** and the **figurative language** in this passage suggest about Bradbury's position on TV viewing?

**2 Targeted Passage**

Detail of *Tourists Beware: New Buffalo Speed Trap* (1985), Roger Brown. Oil on canvas, 48″ × 48″. © The School of the Art Institute of Chicago and the Brown family.

---

## DIFFERENTIATED INSTRUCTION

**FOR STRUGGLING READERS**

**2 Targeted Passage [Lines 17–22]**

This passage emphasizes the difference between Leonard Mead, the main character, and the future world in which he lives.

- Why does Mr. Mead wear sneakers? For how long has he been doing so? (lines 18–20)

- Where are all the other people in this town? (line 21)

- How would people react if they saw him taking his walk? Why? (line 21)

**FOR ADVANCED LEARNERS/PRE–AP**

**Analyze Imagery** Point out that Bradbury uses many images of the natural world in this story. As students read, have them list examples in which the natural world is described or used in a comparison. Then ask students to write an analysis of these nature images that explains how Bradbury uses those references to make a point about the world of A.D. 2053.

## BACKGROUND

**Must-Have TV** The technology that made today's TV possible was developed in the late 1920s. It was not until World War II ended, however, that the production of TV sets and the establishment of TV stations and programming began in earnest. By the end of 1950, the year in which Ray Bradbury wrote "The Pedestrian," there were 10.5 million TV sets in American homes—one set for every fourteen or fifteen Americans. It seemed that everyone wanted to be the first in the neighborhood to own a TV and to watch whatever limited programming was available. By 1950, too, the A. C. Nielsen Company was already surveying TV viewers' preferences—and some people were already warning about the influence of what by 1960 was called the "idiot box."

## Analyze Visuals

*Possible answer: The dark, threatening sky; the lonely figure; and the plain, featureless homes create a somber mood.*

**About the Art** Roger Brown (1941–1997), a prolific modern artist, lived and worked mainly in Chicago. His work includes painting, architecture, landscape design, theater sets, murals, and printmaking. Brown also created sculptures out of found, assembled, and painted objects.

**REVISIT THE BIG QUESTION**

Could we live without

# TELEVISION?

**Discuss** Refer students to lines 10–16. "The Pedestrian" gives one writer's idea about how people would behave if a **television habit** took control of society. Is this scene of empty streets really possible, in your opinion? Explain. ***Possible answer:** Some students may argue that the scene does not seem possible. There always will be people who go out for entertainment or other reasons in the evenings.*

---

**FOR RELUCTANT READERS**
**A World Without TV** Ask students to describe a typical day for a young person in a world in which TV was never invented. Have them address how young people might fill their free time. Encourage them to use their creativity to propose alternate scenarios.

**FOR ENGLISH LANGUAGE LEARNERS**
**Comprehension: Transitions** Explain that writers often tell about something by giving an example of what it is like. Point out a few of the many comparisons with forms of *like* in this story: "like" (line 9), "not unlike" (line 12), and the adjective "tomblike" (line 16). Ask small groups to search the rest of the story for comparisons and to share their findings.

**Activity** Point out that the painting on this page was created by the same artist, Roger Brown, who created the one on page 703. Ask students to tell how the paintings are similar and to name some adjectives that describe the artist's style. *Possible answer: Each painting features multiple houses that are identical to one another, and the multiple houses are the same in both paintings except for their color. In both paintings, the artist has used similar colors and tones, and the sky in each includes swirls and bright light shining behind dark shapes. The artist's style might be described using the adjectives cartoon-like, stylized, fun, or funky.*

---

**TEXwT ANALYSIS**    **COMMON CORE**   RL 2, RI 2, RI 5

### ⓔ WRITER'S MESSAGE

***Possible answer:*** *Mead never encounters anyone because everyone else spends evenings indoors, watching TV. This detail indicates Bradbury's view that television is powerful enough to control people's behavior and alienate them from the real world.*

**IF STUDENTS NEED HELP . . .** Review lines 31–34 and elicit that the people are watching TV. Then suggest possible interpretations of Bradbury's message—for example, "TV is entertaining," "TV is better than nature/real life," "TV provides everything that people need," and "Walking is useless." Allow students to reject each interpretation and to give reasons for their rejection before arriving at a more reasonable interpretation.

**Extend the Discussion** How would the people inside the houses probably react to Bradbury's message? Explain.

*Clouds Over Alabama or Midnight in Alabama* (1994), Roger Brown. Oil on canvas, 48″ × 72″. © The School of the Art Institute of Chicago and the Brown family.

On this particular evening he began his journey in a westerly direction, toward the hidden sea. There was a good crystal frost in the air; it cut the nose and made the lungs blaze like a Christmas tree inside; you could feel the cold light going on and off, all the branches filled with invisible snow. He listened to the faint push of his soft shoes through autumn leaves with satisfaction, and whistled a cold quiet whistle between his teeth, occasionally picking up a leaf as he passed, examining its skeletal pattern in the infrequent lamplights as he 30 went on, smelling its rusty smell.

"Hello, in there," he whispered to every house on every side as he moved. "What's up tonight on Channel 4, Channel 7, Channel 9? Where are the cowboys rushing, and do I see the United States Cavalry over the next hill to the rescue?"

The street was silent and long and empty, with only his shadow moving like the shadow of a hawk in midcountry. If he closed his eyes and stood very still, frozen, he could imagine himself upon the center of a plain, a wintry, windless Arizona desert with no house in a thousand miles, and only dry river beds, the streets, for company.

40 "What is it now?" he asked the houses, noticing his wrist watch. "Eight-thirty P.M.? Time for a dozen assorted murders? A quiz? A revue? A comedian falling off the stage?"

Was that a murmur of laughter from within a moon-white house? He hesitated, but went on when nothing more happened. He stumbled over a particularly uneven section of sidewalk. The cement was vanishing under flowers and grass. In ten years of walking by night or day, for thousands of miles, he had never met another person walking, not one in all that time. ⓔ

**704**    UNIT 6: ARGUMENT AND PERSUASION

---

## DIFFERENTIATED INSTRUCTION

### FOR STRUGGLING READERS

**Identify Sensory Details** Have students use an Observation Chart to record details in lines 23–30 that involve human senses, such as sight (line 29), hearing (lines 26–28), touch (lines 24–26), and smell (line 30). Elicit that these details help establish the setting as a cold, pleasant autumn evening.

📁 **BEST PRACTICES TOOLKIT—Transparency** Observation Chart p. C7

### FOR ENGLISH LANGUAGE LEARNERS

**Language Coach**    ⌐ **COMMON CORE** L 4

**Multiple Meanings** *Answer:* "*Large, flat land*" Review the fact that some English words have several meanings and that a reader must determine the correct meaning for a given context. Present these examples: *moved* (line 31), *plain* (line 37), *streams* (line 53), *block* (line 55), *force* (line 67), and *ill* (line 81). Ask students to define each word as used in context, using a dictionary to check.

He came to a cloverleaf intersection which stood silent where two main highways crossed the town. During the day it was a thunderous surge of cars,
50 the gas stations open, a great insect rustling and a ceaseless jockeying for position as the scarab-beetles,[1] a faint incense puttering from their exhausts, skimmed homeward to the far directions. But now these highways, too, were like streams in a dry season, all stone and bed and moon radiance.

He turned back on a side street, circling around toward his home. He was within a block of his destination when the lone car turned a corner quite suddenly and flashed a fierce white cone of light upon him. He stood entranced, not unlike a night moth, stunned by the illumination, and then drawn toward it.

A metallic voice called to him:
60 "Stand still. Stay where you are! Don't move!"
He halted.
"Put up your hands!"
"But—" he said.
"Your hands up! Or we'll shoot!"

The police, of course, but what a rare, incredible thing; in a city of three million, there was only one police car left, wasn't that correct? Ever since a year ago, 2052, the election year, the force had been cut down from three cars to one. Crime was ebbing; there was no need now for the police, save for this one lone car wandering and wandering the empty streets.

70 "Your name?" said the police car in a metallic whisper. He couldn't see the men in it for the bright light in his eyes.
"Leonard Mead," he said.
"Speak up!"
"Leonard Mead!"
"Business or profession?"
"I guess you'd call me a writer."
"No profession," said the police car, as if talking to itself. The light held him **F** fixed, like a museum specimen, needle thrust through chest.
"You might say that," said Mr. Mead. He hadn't written in years. Magazines
80 and books didn't sell any more. Everything went on in the tomblike houses at night now, he thought, continuing his fancy. The tombs, ill-lit by television light, where the people sat like the dead, the grey or multicolored lights touching their faces, but never really touching *them*.
"No profession," said the phonograph voice, hissing. "What are you doing out?"
"Walking," said Leonard Mead.
"Walking!"
"Just walking," he said simply, but his face felt cold.
"Walking, just walking, walking?"
90 "Yes, sir."

---
1. **scarab-beetles:** large beetles considered to be sacred in ancient Egypt.

**③ Targeted Passage**

**F** **WRITER'S MESSAGE**
Why does the voice reply "No profession" when Mead says he is a writer?

---

## TIERED DISCUSSION PROMPTS

Use these prompts, which refer to lines 70–90, to help students grasp Mead's encounter with the police:

**Connect** Would you react as calmly as Mead seems to be reacting to the police car's challenge? *Students may feel that they would be more defensive.*

**Analyze** Why does the police car treat Mead with suspicion? *Possible answer: The car considers walking a suspicious activity because it is abnormal in this society.*

**Synthesize** Why might taking a walk be considered a threat to this society? *Possible answer: A society that values conformity would be threatened by any behavior outside the norm because that behavior would encourage independent thinking.*

### TEXT ANALYSIS COMMON CORE

**F WRITER'S MESSAGE**    RL 2, RI 2, RI 5

*Possible answer: Since people in this world rarely buy magazines and books (lines 79–80), there seems to be no reason for anyone to be a writer.*

**IF STUDENTS NEED HELP . . .** Have them search for a clue in the next paragraph. Discuss the thoughts that might have led the police car to its conclusion.

**Extend the Discussion** Which other professions would be obsolete in Mead's world? Which would be most important?

---

## FOR STRUGGLING READERS

**③ Targeted Passage [Lines 54–69]**

This passage introduces the conflict that takes the story to its climax.

- What confronts Mead just before he gets home? Why is this challenger unusual? (lines 54–56, 66)

- What does this challenger want Mead to do? Why? (lines 59–62)

- What is this challenger's job? What might happen to Mead? (line 68)

## FOR ADVANCED LEARNERS/PRE–AP

**Analyze Characterization** [paired-activity option] Ask students to reread Bradbury's description in lines 81–83 of the people inside the houses. Have them explain what Bradbury means by comparing the people to the dead and by saying that the television lights do not touch them. Then ask students to support an opinion about why Bradbury might have chosen to characterize people in this way.

**Activity** When students have finished reading "The Pedestrian," have them come back to this painting, also by Roger Brown (see **About the Art**, page 703). Ask them to explain how its details correspond with details in the text. *Possible answer: Only one person is on the street. In addition, the car seems to be in operation but apparently is unoccupied (unlike the houses).*

Detail of *Tourists Beware: New Buffalo Speed Trap* (1985), Roger Brown. Oil on canvas, 48″ × 48″. © The School of the Art Institute of Chicago and the Brown family.

---

**G WRITER'S MESSAGE**

*Possible answer: The fact that the voice is suspicious and then accusingly quiet suggests that to the people of the future, TV viewing is so important that it is a requirement for acceptable behavior.*

**IF STUDENTS NEED HELP . . .** Encourage students to cite at least one detail from the text that clarifies the importance of TV in this society.

---

**REVISIT THE BIG QUESTION**

## Could we live without
# TELEVISION?

**Discuss** Look at the word choice in the car's question in line 97. What does it suggest about this society's perception of the world? *Possible answer: Calling TV "a viewing screen . . . to see with" suggests that this society's perceptions are strictly controlled by television. The only "real" way of looking at the world is the way that TV presents it.*

---

"Walking where? For what?"

"Walking for air. Walking to see."

"Your address!"

"Eleven South Saint James Street."

"And there is air in your house, you have an air *conditioner*, Mr. Mead?"

"Yes."

"And you have a viewing screen in your house to see with?"

"No."

"No?" There was a crackling quiet that in itself was an accusation. **G**

100   "Are you married, Mr. Mead?"

"No."

"Not married," said the police voice behind the fiery beam. The moon was high and clear among the stars and the houses were gray and silent.

"Nobody wanted me," said Leonard Mead with a smile.

"Don't speak unless you're spoken to!"

Leonard Mead waited in the cold night.

**G WRITER'S MESSAGE**
Notice the voice's reaction when Mead admits to not having a viewing screen. How important is TV viewing to the people of the future?

---

## DIFFERENTIATED INSTRUCTION

**FOR STRUGGLING READERS**

**Develop Reading Fluency** To give students practice reading dialogue, use the conversation between Mead and the man in the car that begins on line 59. Remind students that prose often mixes dialogue with narration. If students see quotation marks, then they know that a character is speaking. They should use the action occurring at that point in the story to determine the appropriate expression and timing to use while reading the dialogue.

First, read the passage aloud to students, modeling the power relationship between the two men with your voice. Then, have students work with a partner to take turns reading the passage aloud. Conclude the activity by having several students read the passage aloud to the class.

**R RESOURCE MANAGER—Copy Masters**
Reading Fluency p. 100

"Just *walking,* Mr. Mead?"

"Yes."

"But you haven't explained for what purpose."

110   "I explained; for air, and to see, and just to walk."

"Have you done this often?"

"Every night for years."

The police car sat in the center of the street with its radio throat faintly humming.

"Well, Mr. Mead," it said.

"Is that all?" he asked politely.

"Yes," said the voice. "Here." There was a sigh, a pop. The back door of the police car sprang wide. "Get in."

"Wait a minute, I haven't done anything!"

120   "Get in."

"I protest!"

"Mr. Mead."

He walked like a man suddenly drunk. As he passed the front window of the car he looked in. As he had expected, there was no one in the front seat, no one in the car at all.

"Get in."

He put his hand to the door and peered into the back seat, which was a little cell, a little black jail with bars. It smelled of riveted steel. It smelled of harsh antiseptic; it smelled too clean and hard and metallic. There was nothing

130  soft there.

"Now if you had a wife to give you an alibi," said the iron voice. "But—"

"Where are you taking me?"

The car hesitated, or rather gave a faint whirring click, as if information, somewhere, was dripping card by punch-slotted card[2] under electric eyes. "To the Psychiatric Center for Research on Regressive Tendencies."[3] ●

He got in. The door shut with a soft thud. The police car rolled through the night avenues, flashing its dim lights ahead.

> They passed one house on one street a moment later, one house in an entire city of houses that were dark, but this one particular house had all of its
> 140  electric lights brightly lit, every window a loud yellow illumination, square and warm in the cool darkness.
>
> "That's *my* house," said Leonard Mead.
>
> No one answered him.
>
> The car moved down the empty river-bed streets and off away, leaving the empty streets with the empty sidewalks, and no sound and no motion all the rest of the chill November night. ❧

**Targeted Passage** ④

---

2.  **punch-slotted card:** At the time this story was written, cards punched with coded holes were used to feed data into computers.

3.  **Regressive Tendencies:** habits of acting in ways that belong to an earlier stage of human development, such as childhood.

**● GRAMMAR AND STYLE**
Reread lines 117–122. Notice how Bradbury capitalizes the first word of every line of dialogue, even if it is a sentence fragment. The first word of any quotation should always be capitalized.

**● WRITER'S MESSAGE**
What "crime" has Leonard Mead committed?

**COMMON CORE RL 4**

**Language Coach**

**Repetition** Writers often use **repetition,** the act of repeating a word, phrase, or sentence, to emphasize an idea. Notice how the word *empty* is repeated in lines 144–145. What idea is the writer trying to highlight by repeating this word?

THE PEDESTRIAN   **707**

---

**FOR ENGLISH LANGUAGE LEARNERS**

**Language Coach**   **COMMON CORE RI 4**

**Repetition** *Possible answer: everyone else is inside watching TV and thereby leading empty lives* Ask students what other word is repeated three times in lines 143–146. What might the author be communicating by the repetition of this word? *Possible answer: no; he may be emphasizing the negative quality of life in the future*

**FOR STRUGGLING READERS**

**④ Targeted Passage [138–146]**

This passage wraps up the story and reminds readers once again of the contrast between Mead and the rest of his society.

- What is different about Mead's house? (lines 140–141)
- What are the streets like after Mead is taken away? (lines 144–146)
- Who in Mead's world is aware of what has happened to him? (lines 142–143)

**● GRAMMAR AND STYLE**   **COMMON CORE L 2**

**Capitalization** Have students write four short lines of dialogue between two characters. Remind them to capitalize the first word of every line of dialogue.

**TEXT ANALYSIS**   **COMMON CORE RL 2, RI 2, RI 5**

**● WRITER'S MESSAGE**

*Possible answer: Mead's "crime" is that he does not want to watch a viewing screen.*

**Extend the Discussion** Why is Mead being taken to a facility that researches regressive tendencies (line 135)?

**SELECTION WRAP-UP**

**READ WITH A PURPOSE** Now that students have read the selections, ask them to describe how the society portrayed in this story deals with people who are different. Then, have students decide how this society is similar to ours and different. *Possible answer: The society Bradbury shows is similar to ours in that it can sometimes enforce its will on rebels; it is different in that there seems to be no way for people like Mead to survive outside of society.*

**★ CRITIQUE** Ask students how these selections made them feel about television, about the future, or about both.

**INDEPENDENT READING**

If students enjoy reading science fiction, recommend *Ender's Game,* Orson Scott Card's futuristic novel about genetically modified children exploited for intergalactic wars.

# Practice and Apply

For preliminary support of post-reading questions, use these copy masters:

**R** RESOURCE MANAGER—Copy Masters
Reading Check p. 98
Writer's Message Across Genres p. 93
Question Support p. 99

Additional selection questions are provided for teachers on page 87.

## ANSWERS

## Comprehension

1. *The city is busy by day. At night, however, everyone stays home watching TV, leaving the streets empty.*

2. *Mead seems suspicious because he is out walking at night, does not have a viewing screen, and is unmarried. These factors deviate from society's norm.*

3. *Goodman urges Americans to turn off the TV. By implication, she wants them to interact with their families more.*

## Text Analysis

COMMON
CORE  **RL 2, RI 2, RI 5**

*Possible answers:*

4. *To support her claim, Goodman says that half of married couples' fights about TV must be about whether to have the TV on at all rather than what to watch (lines 15–22). She also cites the statistic that American children watch 20–24 hours of TV each week and notes that parents allow that excessive viewing to happen (lines 42–48).*

5. *The title suggests that Goodman is using her essay to vent her deep (primal) frustration with the overuse of television (the screen).*

6. *The response that gets Mead into the most trouble is his revelation that he does not have a viewing screen. This fact makes Mead different from everyone else.*

7. ● **COMMON CORE FOCUS** *Draw Conclusions About Writer's Message* Bradbury *uses imagery and figurative language to suggest that people of the future have given up thinking for themselves and accept whatever the TV shows them. The implication is that people today may wind up like that if they fail to control their TV habit.*

---

## Comprehension

1. **Recall** Describe the city where Leonard Mead walks in "The Pedestrian."

2. **Clarify** Why does Mead seem especially suspicious to the police car?

3. **Clarify** In "Primal Screen," what does Goodman urge Americans to do?

## Text Analysis

4. **Analyze Support** In "Primal Screen," Goodman claims that the habit of television watching is a more serious problem than the content of the programs. What evidence does she use to support this claim?

5. **Make Inferences** The title of Goodman's essay, "Primal Screen," is a **pun**, or a play on words. It refers to primal scream therapy, a type of treatment in which patients scream to vent frustrations. Why did Goodman choose this title?

6. **Make Judgments** Of Leonard Mead's several responses to the police car, which do you think gets him into the most trouble? Why?

● 7. **Draw Conclusions About Writer's Message** Reread lines 79–83 in "The Pedestrian." Bradbury uses **imagery** and **figurative language** to describe the people of the future. In describing the future, what does he imply about the people of today?

■ 8. **Reflect on Your Purpose** Now that you have read each text, it is time to compare and contrast the writers' messages, or central ideas. Write your observations on a chart like the one shown.

| Points of Comparison | In the Essay | In the Short Story |
|---|---|---|
| What is the writer's focus? | what television watching is doing to family life | what television is doing to American society in general |
| What problems are identified or portrayed? | | |
| What solutions are recommended or suggested? | | |
| What methods are used to convey the message? | | |

### Could we live without TELEVISION?

Does watching television have a positive or negative effect on your life?

COMMON CORE

**RL 2** Determine a central idea and analyze its development, including how it emerges and is shaped by details. **RI 2** Determine a central idea and analyze its development, including how it emerges and is shaped by details. **RI 5** Analyze in detail how an author's ideas or claims are developed and refined.

---

8. ● **COMMON CORE FOCUS** *Reflect on Your Purpose In the Essay:* Problem(s): *the overuse of television and the perceived powerlessness to turn it off;* Solution(s): *turning off the set;* Methods: *persuasive language, statistics and other facts, and a strong call to action*

*In the Short Story:* Problem(s): *the taking over of society by mind-numbing television programming;* Solution(s): *experiencing nature and thinking independently;* Methods: *setting, characters, dialogue, imagery, word choice*

Could we live without **TELEVISION?** *Answers will vary, but students should be able to provide sound reasons for their response.*

# Language

◆ **GRAMMAR AND STYLE:** Capitalize Dialogue Correctly

Review the **Grammar and Style** note on page 707. Bradbury effectively communicates dialogue by following the first rule below. Pay attention to the second rule as well, which you'll need to use in your own writing.

1. The first word of a quoted sentence or quoted sentence fragment begins with a capital letter.

   *"I guess you'd call me a writer."* (Line 76)

   *"Your hands up! Or we'll shoot"* (Line 64)

2. If an interrupting expression divides a quoted sentence or fragment into two parts, the second part begins with a lowercase letter. If the second part of a quotation is a complete sentence, however, it begins with a capital letter.

   *"What part of the story," she asked, "was your favorite part?"*

   *"The ending," he responded. "Can you believe the police car took him away?"*

Now study the model. Notice how the revisions in blue correct this writer's dialogue. You can revise your response to the prompt below similarly to ensure correct capitalization.

> **STUDENT MODEL**
>
> I asked him, "do you feel television is a waste of people's time?"
>
> "I do," he replied, "Especially if they are watching TV instead of interacting with others." He then asked me how many hours of TV I watch each day, and I said, "four."

**READING-WRITING CONNECTION**

 Explore Bradbury's message in the "The Pedestrian" by responding to the prompt below. Then use the **revising tip** to improve your writing.

**WRITING PROMPT**

**Extended Constructed Response: Write Dialogue**
Imagine that you are having a conversation with Ray Bradbury about his views on television. Write **one to two pages** that reveal what he might think about how television affects people's lives.

**REVISING TIP**

Reread your response. Did you use correct capitalization to help you communicate your ideas clearly? If not, revise your response.

**Interactive Revision**

Go to **thinkcentral.com**. KEYWORD: HML9-709.

---

## DIFFERENTIATED INSTRUCTION

**FOR STRUGGLING WRITERS**

- Suggest that students look over their notes about the class discussion of "The Pedestrian" to remind themselves what Bradbury's opinions about television are.
- They may also want to reread parts of the story and look again at the illustrations. Help students identify relevant excerpts from the story to help them gauge the author's feelings about TV and its effects on people.

- Suggest that students include a short introduction to their response that sets the stage and identifies the speakers.

---

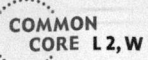

# Language

◆ **GRAMMAR AND STYLE**

- Students may benefit from writing on an index card the rules for capitalization of direct quotations. Have them look over their responses using the index card to make sure they have used proper capitalization.

- Write these sentences on the board and have students correctly capitalize them:

  "we can't regulate foreign affairs," stated Goodman. "we can't set the price for oil."

  *["We can't regulate foreign affairs," stated Goodman. "We can't set the price for oil."]*

  "no profession," said the phonograph voice, hissing. "what are you doing out?" "walking," said Leonard Mead.

  *["No profession," said the phonograph voice, hissing. "What are you doing out?" "Walking," said Leonard Mead.]*

**READING-WRITING CONNECTION**

Students will be writing a conversation between two people (Bradbury and themselves). Encourage them to make the two voices "sound" different, so that readers will know who is speaking just by the words and tone.

>
>
> **Writing Online**
>
> The following tools are available online at **thinkcentral.com** and on **WriteSmart** CD-ROM:
> - **Interactive Graphic Organizers**
> - **Interactive Student Models**
> - **Interactive Revision Lessons**
>
> For additional grammar instruction, see **GrammarNotes** on **thinkcentral.com**.

## Assess and Reteach

### Assess

**DIAGNOSTIC AND SELECTION TESTS**
   Selection Test A pp. 187–188
   Selection Test B/C pp. 189–190

**Interactive Selection Test** on **thinkcentral.com**

### Reteach

**Level Up Online Tutorials** on **thinkcentral.com**

---

**COMMON CORE**

**L 2** Demonstrate command of the conventions of standard English capitalization. **W 5** Develop and strengthen writing by editing to demonstrate conventions of standard English capitalization.

# Practice and Apply

## COMMON CORE FOCUS

**RI 7** Analyze various accounts of a subject told in different mediums.

## Advertisement

Have students look at the Comparison Matrix they filled out for "Primal Screen" and "The Pedestrian." Ask them to look at this advertisement and discuss the tone of the text and photographs. What does this have in common with the article and the short story? *Possible answer: All three are about television and its effects on people and society.*

---

**ANALYZE VISUALS**  COMMON CORE **RI 7**

### 1. INFER

*Possible answer: A remote control would be appealing to people who have TVs that require a button to press on the TV set to power on and off.*

---

**ANALYZE VISUALS**  COMMON CORE **RI 7**

### 2. ASSESS

*Possible answer: The exaggerated expressions on the faces exemplify the capitalized words* amaze *and* astound *and grab the attention of anyone looking at the ad.*

---

**ANALYZE VISUALS**  COMMON CORE **RI 7**

### 3. EVALUATE

*Possible answer: Yes; the reactions are what I would expect because the ability to power a TV on and off without having to get up and walk to the TV is an amazing technological advancement.*

---

## Reading for Information

### Advertisement

The essay and short story you just read explore the topic of television in different ways, but both texts communicate messages about excessive viewing. As you examine the advertisement below, consider what messages it conveys.

COMMON CORE

**RI 7** Analyze various accounts of a subject told in different mediums.

1. **INFER**
   Why might someone find a remote control that can only turn televisions on and off appealing?

2. **ASSESS**
   Why do you think this ad's designer chose faces with such exaggerated expressions?

3. **EVALUATE**
   Are the reactions pictured and described in the ad the result you would expect from using the TV Master? Explain.

## Assessment Practice: Short Constructed Response

### LITERARY TEXT: "PRIMAL SCREEN"

On assessments, you'll be expected to recognize an author's purpose for writing. Practice this skill by answering the **short constructed response** question below.

> What is the author's primary purpose in writing "Primal Screen"? Support your answer with evidence from the essay.

◀ **STRATEGIES IN ACTION**

1. Skim the essay looking at the author's choice of **words** and important **details**.

2. Decide if the words and details are meant to inform, persuade, entertain, or express feelings.

3. Include specific evidence to support your assertion about the author's purpose.

### NONFICTION TEXT: "THE PEDESTRIAN"

Analyzing important details in literary texts will make you a better critical reader. Practice this skill by answering the **short constructed response** question below.

> At the end of "The Pedestrian," why is it significant that Leonard Mead's house is the only house that is not completely dark? Support your answer with evidence from the story.

◀ **STRATEGIES IN ACTION**

1. Think about the story and consider why only one house might be lit. Then consider why this detail is significant.

2. The evidence from the text can be in the form of a **direct quotation**, a **paraphrase**, or a **specific synopsis**.

3. Include the evidence you find in your answer.

### COMPARING LITERARY AND NONFICTION TEXTS

Assessments will require you to identify and analyze the literary techniques that authors use. Practice analyzing imagery by applying the following **short constructed response** question to "Primal Screen" and "The Pedestrian."

> In "Primal Screen" and "The Pedestrian," how do the authors use imagery to help convey their messages about TV viewing? Support your answer with evidence from both texts.

◀ **STRATEGIES IN ACTION**

1. Reread the texts and think about the authors' views on watching TV.

2. Look for words and phrases in both texts that appeal to the senses and create images that support the authors' views. Use the specific examples as evidence in your answer.

PRIMAL SCREEN / THE PEDESTRIAN / TV MASTER **711**

---

## Assessment Practice: Short Constructed Response

*NONFICTION TEXT: "PRIMAL SCREEN"*
***Possible answer:*** *Students should respond that the author's primary purpose is to persuade readers to limit the amount of television viewing, citing evidence from the text that supports a persuasive purpose. An example of such evidence could include the final sentence, "Just once, we ought to create a private show about a real-life family that kicked the habit."*

*LITERARY TEXT: "THE PEDESTRIAN"*
***Possible answer:*** *Answers will vary, but students may respond that the fact that Leonard Mead's house is well lit emphasizes the difference between him, a person who does not own a "viewing screen," and his neighbors, people who do own and watch television all night. The illuminated windows in Mead's house are "warm in the cool darkness," whereas his neighbors' windows are for the most part dark, making the houses appear as "tomblike buildings."*

*COMPARING LITERARY AND NONFICTION TEXTS* ***Possible answer:*** *Students may discuss how both texts suggest that there should be limits to TV viewing because watching too much television can become an unhealthy habit. Images used as evidence that help convey this message are: "The average kid develops that distant, slack-jawed, hypnotic, hooked stare because he or she is hooked" and "The tombs, ill-lit by television light, where people sat like the dead, the grey or multicolored lights touching their faces, but never really touching them."*

---

### DIFFERENTIATED INSTRUCTION

#### FOR STRUGGLING WRITERS

**Cite Text Evidence** Many students will benefit from a review of how to identify and effectively cite text evidence, such as imagery, in their short constructed responses. To model the skill, have students locate the imagery in lines 5–6 (long moonlit avenues of sidewalk in four directions). Ask: What type of mood or feeling does this image create? Lead students to understand that the image Bradbury uses helps create a mood of loneliness and solitariness, as well as a feeling that Leonard Mead is different from all the other people in his society. Ask students to locate other instances of imagery in "The Pedestrian" that help reinforce Bradbury's theme.

# Focus and Motivate

## COMMON CORE FOCUS

**W 1a-e** Write arguments to support claims in an analysis of substantive topics, using valid reasoning and relevant and sufficient evidence. **W 4** Produce clear and coherent writing appropriate to task, purpose, and audience. **W 5** Develop and strengthen writing as needed by planning, revising, editing, rewriting, or trying a new approach, addressing what is most significant for a specific purpose and audience. **W 10** Write routinely over shorter time frames for a range of tasks, purposes, and audiences. **L 1** Demonstrate command of the conventions of standard English grammar and usage. **L 1a** Use parallel structure. **L 2** Demonstrate command of the conventions of standard English capitalization, punctuation, and spelling. **L 2c** Spell correctly. **L 3** Apply knowledge of language to make effective choices for meaning or style.

## WRITE WITH A PURPOSE

Tell students to choose issues that are important to them and about which they have strong opinions. Remind them that their purpose is to persuade their audiences to accept their views.

## COMMON CORE TRAITS

Review the *COMMON CORE TRAITS* with students, focusing primarily on development of ideas and organization of ideas. Compare the list of traits with the rubric on page 720.

## ADDITIONAL TASKS

**Write to a Business Leader** Write a persuasive essay directed to a business leader in response to an issue discussed in a newspaper or television editorial.
**Possible subjects:** global warming, the energy crisis, or online privacy

**Write About Fine Art** Choose a type of artwork or music you think is valuable and deserves recognition. Write an essay that persuades your audience to agree with you.
**Possible subjects:** graffiti art, a style of music (such as sampling), quilting

---

## Writing Workshop
### ARGUMENT

# Persuasive Essay

*Essential Course of Study* **ECOS**

As you have seen in this unit, persuasive words can be powerful. They can change people's minds, inspire others to take action, or even make a difference in the world. In this workshop, you will learn how to add power to your ideas and words by writing a persuasive essay.

Complete the workshop activities in your **Reader/Writer Notebook**.

### WRITE WITH A PURPOSE

**WRITING TASK**

Write a **persuasive essay** that asserts a claim, or position, on an issue. Support your claim with reasons and evidence that will convince your audience to act or think a certain way.

**Idea Starters**
• the link between fast food and obesity
• social problems, such as stereotyping
• cell phone use in schools
• mandatory recycling in a community

**THE ESSENTIALS**

Here are some common purposes, audiences, and formats for persuasive writing.

| PURPOSES | AUDIENCES | FORMATS |
|---|---|---|
| • to persuade people to agree with your claim<br><br>• to motivate others to take action | • classmates and teacher<br>• parents<br>• community members<br>• school board<br>• customer service department<br>• Web users | • essay for class<br>• editorial<br>• speech<br>• commercial/PSA<br>• message-board posting<br>• business proposal<br>• blog |

### COMMON CORE TRAITS

**1. DEVELOPMENT OF IDEAS**
• includes an **introduction** that identifies an issue and states a **precise claim**
• fairly develops the claim with **valid reasons** and **relevant evidence**
• anticipates **opposing claims** and counters them with well-supported **counterclaims**
• offers a **concluding section** that supports the claim

**2. ORGANIZATION OF IDEAS**
• establishes **clear, logical relationships** among claims, counterclaims, reasons, and evidence
• uses **transitions**—words, phrases, and clauses—to create **cohesion** and link ideas

**3. LANGUAGE FACILITY AND CONVENTIONS**
• maintains a **formal style** and **objective tone**
• uses effective **sentence types** and **structures**
• employs correct **grammar, mechanics,** and **spelling**

---

## Writing Workshop Resources

# Planning/Prewriting

**COMMON CORE** W 1a-e Write arguments to support claims in an analysis of substantive topics, using valid reasoning and relevant and sufficient evidence. W 5 Develop and strengthen writing as needed by planning.

## Getting Started

### CHOOSE A SUBSTANTIVE ISSUE

For your essay, consider **substantive issues,** or those that matter to a great deal of people. List a few issues. Make sure to choose an issue about which people have differing opinions. Persuasion always deals with opposing viewpoints, not with issues on which most people already agree.

▶ **ASK YOURSELF:**
- Which issue do I care about the most?
- What reasons can I think of to support my **claim,** or position?
- What are some opposing claims that other people might have?

### THINK ABOUT AUDIENCE AND PURPOSE

As you begin to probe your topic more deeply, keep in mind your **purpose**—to convince your **audience** to accept your claim. To be successful, you need to understand your audience's knowledge level of the topic and their potential concerns. Then you can choose the reasons and evidence that will be most convincing for them.

▶ **ASK YOURSELF:**
- Who is my audience? What do I want my audience to believe or do?
- What concerns might my audience have? How will my issue look from their point of view?
- What aspects of the issue might my audience want to know more about?

### STATE YOUR CLAIM

Adopt a viewpoint on the issue and confidently state your position in a **precise,** or clear, claim. You should be able to prove your claim with reasons and evidence. If you discover that your claim can't be supported easily, then you should rework it.

▶ **WHAT DOES IT LOOK LIKE?**

> *Claim:* School begins too early.
>
> ✔ **Issue:** when school begins
> ✔ **Writer's Position:** too early

### GATHER SUPPORT FOR YOUR CLAIM

To be convincing, you need to provide several strong **reasons,** or statements made to justify or support your claim. Be sure that each reason is **valid** (makes sense) and can be supported with evidence.

You also want to consider any **opposing,** or alternate, **claims** that your audience might raise. In your essay, you will need to distinguish your claim from opposing claims and explain the limitations of other viewpoints. You should address opposing claims in a **counterclaim**—a statement that refutes the opposition and explains why your claim is more valid.

▶ **WHAT DOES IT LOOK LIKE?**

> *Claim:* School begins too early.
>
> | Reason 1 | Reason 2 | Reason 3 |
> |---|---|---|
> | Teenagers need more sleep. | Walking to the bus stop in the dark is dangerous. | |
> | • Evidence: | • Evidence: | |
> | • Evidence: | • Evidence: | |
>
> *Opposing Claim:* What about the extra hour of school?
>
> *Counterclaim:* Keeping students in school for an hour later each day is a safer option.

---

## DIFFERENTIATED INSTRUCTION

### FOR ENGLISH LANGUAGE LEARNERS

**Language: Reinforce Persuasive Terms** Write these terms on the board and review them with students.

- *position:* an opinion regarding an issue
- *expert opinions:* opinions or facts given by people who know a lot about a subject
- *facts and statistics:* information that can be proven, and numerical information such as the time of day when most juvenile crime takes place

- *opposing claim:* the evidence given by others who have the opposite view from the writer
- *counterclaims:* arguments made to oppose another argument
- *call to action:* the writer's request to readers to do, think, or say something in response to an essay
- *ethical belief:* a view based on ideas about right and wrong

---

# Teach

## Planning/Prewriting

**COMMON CORE** W 1a-e, W 5

▶ **CHOOSE A SUBSTANTIVE ISSUE** Remind students that to be effective, their issue must have at least two sides. Advise students to narrow their topics to specific issues. For example,

- "backpack searches" instead of "school rules"
- "discrimination against student athletes" instead of "discrimination at school"

▶ **THINK ABOUT AUDIENCE AND PURPOSE**
Make sure that students understand that they need to craft their arguments to meet the needs of their audiences. Tell students they may need to include background information for people who are unfamiliar with their issues.

▶ **STATE YOUR CLAIM** Have students identify two or more reasons in support of their claims. Urge them to think of opposing claims as they list points of support. Make sure students have workable plans before they begin drafting their essays.

▶ **GATHER SUPPORT FOR YOUR CLAIM**
Explain that students should rebut counterclaims with facts, statistics, and expert opinions. Write this ineffective counterclaim on the board: *Her claim is wrong. Curfews don't prevent crime. We don't need curfews because they don't stop crime. They keep people glued to clocks.* Point out that the statement includes several reasoning errors. The second sentence is an overgeneralization that can't be proven. The third sentence proves nothing and repeats earlier text.

**R RESOURCE MANAGER—Copy Masters**
Planning/Prewriting p. 107
Drafting p. 108
Revising and Editing pp. 109–110
Ask a Peer Reader p. 111
Rubric p. 112
Writing Support p. 114

## Planning/Prewriting *continued*

▶ **COLLECT EVIDENCE** Tell students that they will need to do research before they write their essays. Even though their feelings about an issue may be valid, they need to present views that are supported by evidence.

Remind students that an effective persuasive essay will include a wide range of evidence, including evidence to counter claims of people who will disagree with the position. Stress also the need to accurately cite facts, statistics, and expert opinions.

**YOUR TURN** Give students time to choose issues, form precise claims, and begin charts. Have students research and find additional evidence independently.

For interactive revision tools, see

💿 **Write*Smart* CD-ROM**

**Writing Center** on **thinkcentral.com**

---

## Planning/Prewriting *continued*

### Getting Started

#### COLLECT EVIDENCE

Reasons get their strength from the evidence that supports them. Effective evidence is **relevant** (related) to your issue and **sufficient,** or clear and varied enough to back up your reasons. Here are some types of evidence:

**WHAT DOES IT LOOK LIKE?**

**Analogies:** comparisons that show similarities between otherwise unrelated ideas

▶ *We should be as concerned about disturbing students' natural sleep patterns as we are about skipping school.*

**Anecdotes:** personal examples or stories that illustrate a point

▶ *My grandfather says that when he was in school, students went to school later and were better rested.*

**Commonly accepted beliefs:** ideas that most people share

▶ *Most people recognize that walking to school in the dark poses dangers.*

**Examples:** specific instances or illustrations of a general idea

▶ *For example, motorists might not see pedestrians in the pre-dawn darkness.*

**Expert opinion:** statement made by an authority on the subject

▶ *Our principal said, "Students in first period classes tend to score lower on standardized math tests than their peers who take the same classes later in the day."*

**Facts:** statements that can be proven true, such as **statistics,** or numerical information

▶ *According to a recent study, eighty-five percent of teens in America aren't getting the sleep they need.*

**PEER REVIEW** Describe to a peer your audience and purpose. Then ask: Which kinds of evidence will best support my claim?

**YOUR TURN** In your *Reader/Writer Notebook,* develop your claim. Then, use a chart like the one on page 713 to track your reasons, evidence, opposing claims, and counterclaims. Consider the following tips as you gather evidence:

- Search encyclopedias, books, or magazine articles for relevant facts to back up your claim.
- Use reliable and trustworthy Web sites to locate articles that support or counter your claim on the issue.
- Write down any personal experiences that relate to your topic.

---

## DIFFERENTIATED INSTRUCTION

### FOR ENGLISH LANGUAGE LEARNERS

**Culture: Clarify** Students from some cultures may hesitate to express personal opinions. Clarify that opinions are acceptable within this classroom setting when they are expressed respectfully and are supported by facts, statistics, or expert opinions. Review types of opinions that can and cannot be supported.

- Blue is the best color. *(unsupportable)*
- Students should wear uniforms. *(supportable)*
- Lunches should be free. *(supportable)*

### FOR STRUGGLING WRITERS

**Collect Evidence** Have students brainstorm lists of key words they might use in Internet searches on their chosen issues and lists of categories for possible experts, such as teachers, scientists, and so on. Emphasize that an individual's expertise is usually limited to a specific field. Thus, a scientist is most likely an expert only in his or her specialty, not in other scientific areas.

## Drafting

**COMMON CORE** 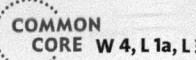 W 4 Produce clear and coherent writing appropriate to task, purpose, and audience. L 1a Use parallel structure. L 3 Apply knowledge of language to make effective choices for meaning or style.

This chart shows how to organize your draft to create a clear essay.

### Organizing Your Persuasive Essay

**INTRODUCTION**
- Grab the audience's attention with a startling **statistic, fact,** or **anecdote.**
- Identify the issue, and state a **precise claim**.

▼

**BODY**
- **Logically sequence ideas** to show how the claim, counterclaims, and evidence relate.
- Develop reasons with **relevant** and **sufficient evidence.**
- Fairly address opposing claims by acknowledging their strengths and limitations. Include a **well-supported counterclaim.**
- Use **transitions,** such as *furthermore* or *another reason,* to create **cohesion,** or flow.
- Maintain a **formal style** by using a confident voice and persuasive words. Use an **objective,** or controlled, **tone** that isn't defensive.

▼

**CONCLUDING SECTION**
- **Restate your claim,** and remind members of your audience why their support matters.
- End with a **call to action** — tell readers what they should do if they agree with your position.

### GRAMMAR IN CONTEXT: PARALLEL STRUCTURE

One technique you can use to emphasize your reasons is parallel structure. **Parallel structure** refers to words, phrases, and sentences with the same grammatical form.

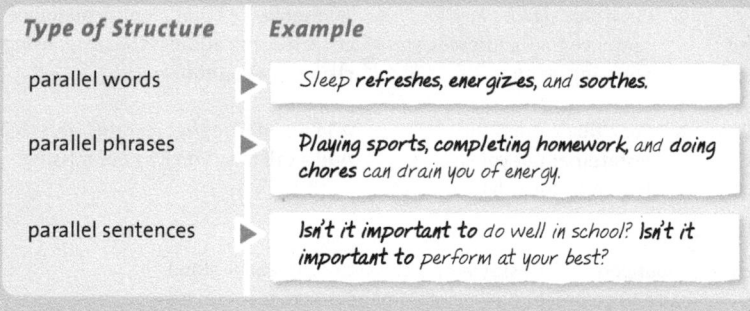

| Type of Structure | Example |
|---|---|
| parallel words | ► Sleep **refreshes, energizes,** and **soothes.** |
| parallel phrases | ► **Playing sports, completing homework,** and doing **chores** can drain you of energy. |
| parallel sentences | ► **Isn't it important to** do well in school? **Isn't it important to** perform at your best? |

**YOUR TURN**   Develop a first draft of your essay, following the structure outlined in the chart above. As you write, try to include at least one example of parallel structure.

---

### FOR ENGLISH LANGUAGE LEARNERS

**Parallel Structure** Provide students with several examples and non-examples of parallel structure. Discuss why each one is or is not parallel.

- **Parallel:** Seeing is believing. (verb form)
- **Not:** Seeing something will make you believe it.
- **Parallel:** Waste not, want not. (verb + not)
- **Not:** Do not waste, so you have what you want.
- **Parallel:** To live is to love. (to + verb)

- **Not:** All living people love.

### FOR ADVANCED LEARNERS/PRE–AP

**Synthesize Support Material** Have students use *Analysis Frame: Persuasion* to explore their topics in depth. Urge them to research creatively, such as by conducting interviews or citing published editorials, films, or exhibits. Have students cite sources with parenthetical notes and lists of works cited in the style of the MLA guidelines.

 **BEST PRACTICES TOOLKIT**
Analysis Frame: Persuasion pp. D44, D45

---

## Practice and Apply

### Drafting
**COMMON CORE** W 4, L 1a, L 3

▶ **INTRODUCTION** Tell students to look at the Student Draft on p. 717 for an example of an attention-grabbing introduction. Remind students that their introductions should engage readers' interests and establish the importance of their issues.

▶ **BODY** Explain that the best persuasive essays use a variety of appeals. Point out that emotional appeals are effective because they can instantly create sympathy or enthusiasm for an issue; however, the crux of a claim should be based on logical appeals.

▶ **CONCLUDING SECTION** Stress that after reading a writer's reasons and evidence, the audience should be convinced that the issue is important enough to merit action. Explain that the call to action directs readers toward concrete efforts, harnessing the energy the writer has created.

### GRAMMAR IN CONTEXT: PARALLEL STRUCTURE

For additional practice, have students rewrite the following sentences using parallel structure.
- People today are recycling plastics, reusing old clothes, and they drive their cars less often. *(People today are recycling plastics, reusing old clothes, and driving their cars less often.)*
- Lawmakers should be concerned with clean energy. Conserving resources should also concern lawmakers. *(Lawmakers should be concerned with clean energy. Lawmakers should also be concerned with energy conservation.)*

**YOUR TURN**   Ask students to complete the **Your Turn** activity independently. Remind students to include at least one example of parallel structure. Suggest that students write their drafts double-spaced so that they can make revisions easily later.

For interactive revision tools, see

💿 **Write*Smart* CD-ROM**

**Writing Center** on <u>thinkcentral.com</u>

## Revising

***Model the Skill*** Using a draft persuasive essay on a transparency or electronic whiteboard, model how to use the questions, tips, and strategies suggested in the chart to evaluate and revise. You might use the essay of a student from another class or from a previous year. Make sure to remove the student's name from the essay so that the writer remains anonymous.

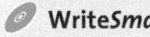 **YOUR TURN** Suggest that students, after reading their partners' drafts, take one minute to freewrite responses that explain why they are or are not persuaded by the texts. Then, allow students a few minutes to share their responses with one another. Students should begin by making positive comments about the drafts, followed by clear suggestions regarding how their partners can make their cases more persuasive.

For interactive revision tools, see

💿 **WriteSmart CD-ROM**
**Writing Center** on **thinkcentral.com**

---

## Revising

When you revise, you evaluate the development, organization, and style of your essay. Your goal is to determine if you've achieved your purpose and effectively communicated your ideas to the intended audience. The questions, tips, and strategies in the following chart can help you revise and rewrite where necessary.

**PERSUASIVE ESSAY**

| Ask Yourself | Tips | Revision Strategies |
|---|---|---|
| 1. Does the introduction grab the audience's attention and include a precise claim? | **Draw a wavy line** under the attention-grabbing text. **Bracket** the claim. | **Add** an attention-grabber. **Add** a claim or **rework** the existing one to make it more precise. |
| 2. Do at least two valid reasons support the claim? Is each reason supported by relevant and sufficient evidence? | **Underline** each reason. **Circle** each piece of evidence, and **draw an arrow** to the reason it supports. | **Add** reasons or revise existing ones to make them more valid. **Add** relevant evidence to ensure that your support is sufficient. |
| 3. Do transitions create cohesion and link related parts of my argument? | **Put a star** next to each transition. | **Add** words, phrases, or clauses to connect related ideas that lack transitions. |
| 4. Are the reasons in the order that is most persuasive? | **Number** the reasons in the margin, ranking them by their strength and effectiveness. | **Rearrange** the reasons into a more logical order, such as order of importance. |
| 5. Are opposing claims fairly acknowledged and refuted with counterclaims? | **Put a plus sign** by any sentence that addresses an opposing claim. | **Add** sentences that identify audience concerns, and address those opposing claims in a counterclaim. |
| 6. Does the concluding section restate the claim? Does it include a call to action? | **Put a box** around the restatement of your claim. **Highlight** the call to action. | **Add** a sentence that restates your claim. **Add** a call to action if one is missing. |

 **YOUR TURN** **PEER REVIEW** Exchange your persuasive essay with a classmate, or read it aloud to your partner. As you read and comment on your classmate's essay, focus on logic, organization, and evidence—not on whether you agree with the author's claim. Help each other identify parts of the drafts that need strengthening, reworking, or a new approach.

---

## DIFFERENTIATED INSTRUCTION

### FOR ENGLISH LANGUAGE LEARNERS

**Writing: Concluding Section** Provide students with sentence frames such as the following to help them develop their concluding sections.

- My topic is _____.
- To restate my position, I _____.
- The issue could be resolved by _____.
- I hope that my audience will _____.

### FOR STRUGGLING WRITERS

**Use Anecdotes** Have students meet with partners to talk informally about their essays. Tell students to ask each other questions such as "How does this issue affect you?" or "Why is this issue important to you?" Have students share personal anecdotes about the issues. Listening partners should jot down notes while the other students speak. Tell students to add these anecdotes to their essays.

## ANALYZE A STUDENT DRAFT

Read this draft; notice the comments on its strengths as well as suggestions for improvement.

**COMMON CORE**

**W 5** Strengthen writing by revising, editing, rewriting, or trying a new approach, addressing what is most significant for a specific purpose and audience. **L 1** Demonstrate command of the conventions of standard English grammar and usage.

### Should School Start Later?
by Jon Attridge, Quincy High School

**1**　Beep! You shut off the alarm. It's 6:00 a.m.—time to get ready for school, but you don't have the energy. You, like 85 percent of teens in America, aren't getting the sleep you need. Is this the morning you want to experience for the rest of your school career? No. School should start later.

**2**　Getting up too early, has serious consequences. Studies from the American Psychological Association show that the frontal lobe (the section of the brain in charge of learning ability and memory) is still developing in many adolescents. Disturbing REM (rapid eye movement) sleep can slow the development of this vital portion of the brain. This can result in much lower test scores. Starting school later would ensure that students would get plenty of uninterrupted sleep. Students could concentrate more on school and less on getting enough sleep.

**3**　Grades aren't the only thing that might improve. An additional hour of sleep can affect a student's mood and attitude. A later schedule doesn't just help students to be more positive and productive; teachers are in a better mood, providing more skilled teaching. With both students' and teachers' moods boosted, everyone gets along in stress-free situations.

> Jon grabs his audience's attention with his introduction. Both his topic and his **claim** are clear.

> Here, Jon uses **relevant facts** to support his reason that getting up too early has consequences.

> Although this is a good set of reasons, hopes for the future such as these could be expressed more clearly using the **subjunctive mood.**

**LEARN HOW** Use Subjunctive Mood　The third paragraph presents possibilities as though they were facts. To avoid confusing his readers, Jon should express these possibilities using the **subjunctive mood.**

#### JON'S REVISION TO PARAGRAPH 3

　Grades aren't the only thing that might improve. An additional hour of

*If school were to start an hour later,*

sleep can affect a student's mood and attitude. A~~ later schedule doesn't just~~

*would*　　　　　　　　　　　　*, and*　　*would be*

~~help~~ students ~~to~~ be more positive and productive~~;~~ teachers ~~are~~ in a better

*The boost in*

mood, providing more skilled teaching. ~~With~~ both students' and teachers'

*would ensure that*

moods ~~boosted,~~ everyone gets along in stress-free situations.

---

## ANALYZE A STUDENT DRAFT

Explain that the Student Draft on this page is the first half of a persuasive essay. Model reading the draft and the annotations in blue, explaining that the yellow highlighting illustrates the student's language choices. Explain that the following *Learn How* mini-lessons provide helpful information about ways to improve this student draft as well as students' own drafts.

**LEARN HOW**　Use Subjunctive Mood

Make sure that students understand that there are three moods in English.

- Indicative, which expresses truth or actuality—*I want to swim.*
- Imperative, which expresses a request or command—*Swim to me!*
- Subjunctive, which can express doubts, wishes, possibilities, or necessities—*If I were a dedicated athlete, I would swim every day.*

---

### FOR ENGLISH LANGUAGE LEARNERS

**Subjunctive** Make sure that students understand that they should employ the subjunctive mood when they speculate about the possible effects of their proposed solutions. These effects are imagined rather than actual. For example, *If school started later, grades might improve.*

Provide students with this graphic organizer:

| Solution | Possible Effects |
|---|---|
|  |  |

### FOR STRUGGLING WRITERS

**Verb Tense** Make sure that students understand that they must use past tense or past perfect tense verbs to express the subjunctive mood.

- If he came, . . .
- If he had come, . . .

Have students take turns completing these sentence starters. Then, ask students to develop their own examples.

## ANALYZE A STUDENT DRAFT *continued*

Explain that the Student Draft is continued and completed on this page. Read the draft and annotations aloud and discuss. Ask students to comment on the student writer's use of a transition to create cohesion.

**LEARN HOW** Add Cause-Effect Reasoning

- Explain that a common mistake students make when writing persuasive essays is not giving examples to illustrate each reason.

- Point out that the example the student writer adds clarifies why the extra hour of school is a good thing: it keeps children safe.

- Have students place asterisks next to places in their drafts that might be strengthened by adding cause-effect reasoning.

 **YOUR TURN** Ask students to complete the **Your Turn** activity independently. Remind students to find places in their essays where they can effectively use the subjunctive mood and cause-effect reasoning.

For interactive revision tools, see

**Write*Smart* CD-ROM**

**Writing Center** on **thinkcentral.com**

---

## ANALYZE A STUDENT DRAFT *continued*

**4** Furthermore, many students have to walk a lengthy distance to the bus stop or to school. It is often dark between 6:45 and 7:20 a.m. To be outside and walking in this minute amount of light can pose a danger to pedestrians. It's quite possible that drivers wouldn't be able to see a student walking along the side of the road. With school starting around 8:30 a.m., this risk would be much less likely to occur.

> Jon uses an effective **transition** to create cohesion and signal the introduction of another reason.

**5** "What about the extra hour of school?" you ask. It is, in fact, a good thing that students would be in school for another hour at the end of the day.

> Although Jon addresses an **opposing claim** in a **counterclaim**, the cause-effect relationship is unclear.

**6** Now imagine that morning again. It's 7:00 a.m. You say to yourself, "Wow, I feel great, and I've got plenty of time to get ready." Just one hour can make a huge difference in your mood and your day.

> Jon creates a strong **concluding section** that follows from and supports the argument presented.

**LEARN HOW** Add Cause-Effect Reasoning In the fifth paragraph, Jon anticipates an opposing claim by addressing the question, "What about the extra hour of school?" Jon added cause-effect reasoning to strengthen his counterclaim and clearly explain why it is a good idea to keep students in school for an hour longer each day. Cause-effect reasoning is particularly effective in crafting an argument because the writer can assert: If this **cause** occurs (kids are in school later), then this will be the **effect** (students will be safer).

> **JON'S REVISION TO PARAGRAPH 5**
>
> "What about the extra hour of school?" you ask. It is, in fact, a good thing that students will be in school for another hour at the end of the day.
>
> *Many parents have to work until 5:00 pm or later. For them, that one additional hour of school is one less hour that their child is home alone in the afternoon. Instead, their child is safe at school for one more hour.*

 **YOUR TURN** Use the feedback from your peers and teacher as well as the two "Learn How" lessons to revise your essay. Evaluate how well your essay convinces your audience to adopt your claim through compelling reasons, strong evidence, and a rousing call to action.

---

## DIFFERENTIATED INSTRUCTION

### FOR ENGLISH LANGUAGE LEARNERS

**Writing: Subordinating Conjunctions** Work with students to create a list of words and phrases they may use to describe cause-effect relationships. The list might include the following subordinating conjunctions: *therefore, if, when, once, because, then, so, as a result,* or *consequently.*

Give students sentence frames and have them fill in the blanks with appropriate words or phrases. For example,

- (If) you study hard, (then) you will get good grades.
- The school board was pleased (because) grades improved.

### FOR STRUGGLING WRITERS

**Add Cause-Effect Reasoning** Explain to students that they should avoid oversimplification when using cause-effect reasoning. Oversimplification often results from failing to consider more than one cause. Clues to oversimplification include words such as *only, never,* and *always.* Advise students to limit, or qualify, their cause-effect statements with phrases such as *an important factor, the three major effects,* or *one of the main reasons.*

# Editing and Publishing

**COMMON CORE** **W 5** Strengthen writing by revising, editing, rewriting, or trying a new approach. **L 2** Demonstrate command of the conventions of standard English capitalization, punctuation, and spelling. **L 2c** Spell correctly.

In the editing stage, you proofread your essay to make sure that it is free of grammar, spelling, and punctuation errors. You don't want mistakes to distract your audience from focusing on your claim and support. Misspellings may make readers doubt your credibility, so be sure to check a dictionary or other resource to confirm the spelling of any word you are uncertain about.

## GRAMMAR IN CONTEXT: GERUNDS

Good persuasive ideas can lose their impact if the audience gets bored by monotonous writing. One way to add variety and interest to your writing is to use **gerunds,** or verb forms used as nouns. For instance, examine the following sentence from Jon's draft:

> *Disturbing REM (rapid eye movement) sleep can slow the development of this vital portion of the brain.*
> [The **gerund phrase** is the subject of the verb *can slow*.]

Gerunds in the subject position are not followed by a comma as introductory phrases are.

> *Sleeping soundly, I was awakened by the alarm.*
> [The **introductory phrase** modifies the subject *I*.]

As Jon edited his essay, he realized he had incorrectly punctuated a gerund phrase. A comma is not necessary, because "getting up too early" is the subject.

> *Getting up too early͵has serious consequences.*

## PUBLISH YOUR WRITING

Finally, you will share your persuasive essay with your intended audience.
- Send your essay to an organization with an interest in your issue or with the power to make the change you want.
- Participate in a class debate on your issue.
- Publish your essay on a school or community Web site or on a Web site devoted to the issue you addressed.
- Adapt your essay into a persuasive speech that you deliver to your audience.

 **YOUR TURN** Correct any errors in your essay. Add variety to your sentence beginnings using gerunds. Edit carefully so that you do not separate a gerund from the rest of the sentence with commas. Then, publish your final essay where your audience is most likely to see it.

## FOR ENGLISH LANGUAGE LEARNERS

**Gerunds** Before introducing a verb form that can be used as a noun, review with students the basic function of nouns.

- A subject is the main part of a sentence or a clause and must have a predicate; it is the *doer* of the action:
  That **book** changed my life.

- A predicate nominative follows a linking verb and restates, identifies, or defines that subject:
  Treasure Island *is a great* **book**.

- A direct object completes the verb by answering the question *what* or *whom:*
  *I would like to write a* **book** *someday.*

- An object of a preposition is linked by a preposition to another part of a sentence:
  *Jared sat down with a good* **book**.

---

# Editing and Publishing

**COMMON CORE** W 5, L 2, L 2c

## GRAMMAR IN CONTEXT: GERUNDS

Remind students that a *gerund* is a verb form that ends in *–ing* and acts as a noun. Like other nouns, gerunds are used as subjects, predicate nominatives, direct objects, indirect objects, and objects of prepositions. A *gerund phrase* consists of a gerund plus its modifiers and complements. For practice, have students identify the gerunds and gerund phrases in the following sentences.

1. Lawmakers have proposed a law against <u>playing a car stereo</u> too loud.
2. <u>Singling out car stereos</u> is a form of discrimination because many other public noises are just as loud.
3. <u>Looking at all forms of noise pollution</u> would be a good idea.

## PUBLISH YOUR WRITING

Brainstorm with students additional ways to publish their persuasive essays.

 **YOUR TURN** Allow students time to proofread their drafts. Remind them to pay close attention to sentences that begin with gerunds. Also remind students to use parallel structure in their essays to strengthen their appeals.

## Scoring Rubric

Tell students that the best way to understand a scoring rubric is to use it to score actual writing. Provide the class with copies of a student's essay with the student's name removed. Work as a class to evaluate the essay by using the scoring rubric. Have students score the essay and write brief paragraphs using the language of the rubric to explain the reasons for their scores. The purpose of a rubric is to eliminate subjectivity from the scoring process.

For Rubric Bank, see

**WriteSmart CD-ROM**

**Writing Center** on **thinkcentral.com**

# Assess and Reteach

## Assess

R **RESOURCE MANAGER—Copy Masters**
Rubric for Evaluation p. 112

**Online Essay Scoring** at **thinkcentral.com**

## Reteach

**Level Up Online Tutorials** at **thinkcentral.com**

**Reteaching Worksheets** on **thinkcentral.com**

Writing Lesson 3: Thinking About Purpose, Audience, and Form

Writing Lesson 9: Revising for Parallelism

---

## Scoring Rubric

Use the rubric below to evaluate your persuasive essay from the Writing Workshop or your response to the on-demand writing task on the next page.

**PERSUASIVE ESSAY**

| SCORE | COMMON CORE TRAITS |
|-------|--------------------|
|  | • **Development** Asserts a precise claim on a substantive topic; supports the claim with valid reasons and relevant evidence; ably counters opposing claims with counterclaims; ends powerfully<br>• **Organization** Is logically organized to persuasive effect; uses transitions to create cohesion and show the relationships among the claim, reasons, and evidence<br>• **Language** Consistently maintains a formal style and objective tone; shows a strong command of conventions |
|  | • **Development** States a precise claim; offers valid reasons and evidence; counters opposing claims with counterclaims; ends with a strong concluding section<br>• **Organization** Is logically organized; uses transitions to show the relationships among the claim, reasons, and evidence<br>• **Language** Uses a formal style and objective tone; has a few errors in conventions |
|  | • **Development** States a clear claim; offers mostly valid support; needs to more fairly address opposing claims; has an adequate concluding section<br>• **Organization** Reflects a logical organization, with one or two exceptions; could use a few more transitions<br>• **Language** Mostly uses a formal style, but sounds defensive at times; includes a few distracting errors in conventions |
|  | • **Development** States a claim that could be more precise; provides some relevant support but not enough to be sufficient; unfairly dismisses other viewpoints; has a somewhat weak concluding section<br>• **Organization** Has some flaws in organization; needs more transitions to show how ideas relate<br>• **Language** Often lapses into an informal style or defensive tone; has several errors in conventions |
|  | • **Development** Has a weak claim; offers irrelevant reasons and insufficient evidence; fails to acknowledge other viewpoints; has a weak concluding section<br>• **Organization** Has major organizational flaws; lacks transitions throughout<br>• **Language** Uses an informal style and defensive tone; has many errors in conventions |
| 1 | • **Development** Lacks a claim; has no support; ignores opposing claims; ends abruptly<br>• **Organization** Has no organization and transitions<br>• **Language** Uses an inappropriate style and tone; has major problems with grammar, mechanics, and spelling |

# Preparing for Timed Writing

**COMMON CORE**

**W 10** Write routinely over shorter time frames for a range of tasks, purposes, and audiences.

## 1. ANALYZE THE TASK · 5 MIN

Read the task carefully. Then, read it again, noting on your own paper the words that tell the type of writing, the topic, the audience, and the purpose.

> **WRITING TASK**
>
> Imagine that your school board is planning to implement <u>coed physical education classes</u>—classes with boys and girls instead of single-gender classes. Write a <u>persuasive essay</u> convincing (parents) to support or oppose this plan.
>
>
>
> ↑ Topic
> ↑ Type of Writing   ↖ Purpose   ↖ Audience

## 2. PLAN YOUR RESPONSE · 10 MIN

Think about the reasons for each side of the issue. Make a list of pros and cons for coed physical education classes. Which side of the issue do you support? Which side can you defend more effectively with examples and reasoning? After you decide on your claim, make a chart to help you gather support. Note a possible opposing claim, and think about how you could you counter it.

| Reasons | Evidence |
|---------|----------|
|         |          |
|         |          |
|         |          |
| *Possible Opposing Claim:* | |

## 3. RESPOND TO THE TASK · 20 MIN

Begin drafting your essay. You may want to start by simply stating your claim. As you write, keep the following points in mind:

- In the introduction, grab your audience's attention and state your claim.
- In each body paragraph, give one reason for your claim, with relevant evidence and specific examples for that reason.
- Acknowledge and counter an opposing claim.
- Conclude by restating your claim and proposing some action that your audience should take.

## 4. IMPROVE YOUR RESPONSE · 5–10 MIN

**Revising** Review key aspects of the essay. Do you state your claim clearly? Do you include valid reasons, relevant evidence, and a call to action?

**Proofreading** Neatly correct any errors in grammar, usage, spelling, and mechanics.

**Checking Your Final Copy** Before you turn in your essay, examine it once more to catch any errors you may have missed.

## Preparing for Timed Writing

**COMMON CORE W 10**

1. **Analyze the Task** Before students begin writing, encourage them to answer the following questions:
   - What is my time limit?
   - What are the key skills assessed in the scoring rubric?
   - Who is my audience?
   - What are my topic and purpose?

2. **Plan Your Response** Point out to students that the scoring rubric emphasizes the importance of asserting a precise claim in their essays. Remind students to state their claims clearly in the first paragraphs of their essays.

3. **Respond to the Task** Remind students to consider opposing claims in their essays. They should include opposing claims and possible counterclaims to address those views.

4. **Improve Your Response** Point out that the scoring rubric emphasizes using a logical organization. Remind students to use transitions to ensure smooth and clear writing styles.

## Assess

Use the Scoring Rubric on p. 720 to assess students' persuasive essays.

---

## DIFFERENTIATED INSTRUCTION

### FOR ENGLISH LANGUAGE LEARNERS

**Writing: Call to Action** Explain to students that a call to action in a persuasive essay usually contains words that indicate judgment, such as *would, should,* and *ought.* For practice, have students brainstorm issues that interest them. Then, have them write opinion statements about three of their issues, using *would, should,* and *ought.*

### FOR STRUGGLING WRITERS

**Use Reasons and Evidence** Tell students that the number of reasons they can think of to support their opinions is not as important as how convincing these reasons are. Remind students not to choose the side of an issue with the most reasons overall, but to choose the side with the most convincing reasons.

# Focus and Motivate

## COMMON CORE FOCUS

**SL 1a–d** Participate effectively in collaborative group discussions. **SL 3** Evaluate a speaker's point of view, reasoning, and use of evidence and rhetoric. **SL 6** Adapt speech to a variety of contexts, demonstrating command of formal English.

## SPEAK WITH A PURPOSE

Help students understand that a debate may have multiple purposes. One purpose is to win the debate by presenting the most convincing evidence in support of a claim. Another purpose is to allow audience members to consider multiple perspectives regarding a particular issue.

## COMMON CORE TRAITS

As students prepare their debates, remind them to keep in mind the **COMMON CORE TRAITS** of an effective debate.

# Practice and Apply

## Planning the Debate

### Model the Skill: RESEARCH AND PREPARE NOTES

Model for students how to prepare notes. In your sample notes, be sure to create places for each reason followed by supporting evidence. Include labels for facts, statistics, anecdotes, and so on to ensure a variety of supporting evidence. Include columns or boxes where you may write summaries, questions, or notes regarding possible opposing claims.

**GUIDED PRACTICE** As students prepare their debate notes, provide research time and recommend source material, including reputable Internet sites, books, and media articles.

**R** RESOURCE MANAGER—Copy Master
Speaking and Listening p. 113

---

*Speaking & Listening Workshop*

# Debating an Issue
*Essential Course of Study*

If you have ever used persuasive speech to convince your parents to allow you to do something, or to appeal to a friend to lend his or her help, you have probably engaged in a **debate**—a discussion in which opposing sides of a question are argued.

Complete the workshop activities in your **Reader/Writer Notebook**.

| SPEAK WITH A PURPOSE | COMMON CORE TRAITS |
| --- | --- |
| **TASK**<br><br>Participate in a **debate** over a substantive issue involving your school or community, or a social issue. Note that such a debate will require some research. | **PARTICIPANTS IN AN EFFECTIVE DEBATE . . .**<br><br>• work productively with others in teams<br>• present precise claims, supported by reasons and evidence<br>• respond thoughtfully to diverse perspectives and justify their own views<br>• speak clearly and persuasively using standard formal English<br>• evaluate other speakers' viewpoints, reasoning, evidence, and **rhetoric**, or language |

**COMMON CORE**

**SL 1a–d** Participate effectively in collaborative group discussions. **SL 3** Evaluate a speaker's point of view, reasoning, and use of evidence and rhetoric. **SL 6** Adapt speech to a variety of contexts, demonstrating command of formal English.

**Speaking & Listening Online**

Go to **thinkcentral.com**.
KEYWORD: HML9-722

## Planning the Debate

The purpose of a debate is to allow participants and audience members to consider both sides of an issue. Follow these planning suggestions:

• **Identify Debate Teams** Form groups of six members based on the issues that you want to debate. Consider using topics from students' persuasive essays. Three members of the team will argue for the affirmative side of the issue. The other three members will argue for the negative side of the issue.

  *Affirmative:* Yes, school should begin later.

  *Negative:* No, school should not begin later.

• **Appoint a Moderator** The moderator will present the topic and goals of the debate, keep track of the time, and introduce and thank participants.

• **Research and Prepare Notes** Search print and online sources for valid reasons and evidence to support your team's claim. Be sure to anticipate possible opposing claims and compile evidence to counter those claims. You will use notes from your research during the debate.

• **Assign Debate Roles** One member will introduce the team's claim and supporting evidence. Another team member will respond to questions and opposing claims in an exchange with a member of the opposing team. The last member will present a strong closing argument.

---

## DIFFERENTIATED INSTRUCTION

### FOR ENGLISH LANGUAGE LEARNERS

**Language: Reinforce Debate Terms** Explain to students that participating in a debate shares one goal with writing a persuasive essay—to persuade others to agree with one's claim by offering supporting evidence. Review key terms used in this Workshop:

• *debate:* discussion during which opposing sides of a question are argued

• *substantive:* important, or of interest and concern to other people

• *research:* study or investigation in some field of knowledge for the purpose of discovering information

• *affirmative:* saying that something stated is true

• *negative:* saying that something stated is not true

• *moderator:* person who presides over a debate

## Holding the Debate

A well-run debate is an excellent forum for participants to express their viewpoints, build on others' ideas, and have a thoughtful, well-reasoned exchange of ideas.

### GETTING STARTED

The moderator will begin by stating the topic and introducing the participants. Participants should follow the instructions from the moderator concerning whose turn it is to speak and how much time each speaker has.

Use the following format to hold your debate:

| Speaker | Role | Time |
|---|---|---|
| Affirmative Speaker 1 | Present the claim and supporting evidence for the affirmative ("pro") side of the argument. | 5 minutes |
| Negative Speaker 1 | Ask probing questions that will prompt the other team to address flaws in the argument. | 3 minutes |
| Affirmative Speaker 2 | Respond to the questions posed by the opposing team and counter any concerns. | 3 minutes |
| Negative Speaker 2 | Present the claim and supporting evidence for the negative ("con") side of the argument. | 5 minutes |
| Affirmative Speaker 3 | Summarize the claim and evidence for the affirmative side and explain why your reasoning is more valid. | 3 minutes |
| Negative Speaker 3 | Summarize the claim and evidence for the negative side of the argument and explain why your reasoning is more valid. | 3 minutes |

**YOUR TURN**

**As a Speaker** Follow the moderator's instructions. Make sure to speak clearly and persuasively, using formal English appropriate for a structured debate. Maintain a respectful tone regardless of your perspective.

**As a Listener** When the other team is presenting its side, evaluate each speaker's point of view, claim, and evidence. Jot down notes, summarizing points of disagreement and identifying any **fallacious**— flawed—reasoning. Listen for persuasive rhetoric that is disguising exaggerated or distorted evidence. Be prepared to address these flaws when it's your team's turn to respond.

SPEAKING AND LISTENING WORKSHOP **723**

### FOR STRUGGLING STUDENTS

**Use Anecdotes** Remind students that anecdotes are effective during a debate because the audience identifies with the human aspects of the issues being discussed. These anecdotes can appeal to either reason or emotions. While anecdotes need to be realistic and related to the topic, they can come from personal experience or the imagination. Have students identify at least two places in their debate notes where they can add anecdotes to support a main idea.

## Holding the Debate

### Model the Skill: GETTING STARTED

Read aloud a paragraph from a persuasive essay on a transparency or the board. Tell students to imagine that Affirmative Speaker 1 has just delivered this information during a debate. Model for students how you would respond with a series of questions. Point out that many good debaters will insert critical commentary into the questioning process. The purpose here is to point out weaknesses in the affirmative argument.

**GUIDED PRACTICE** Provide pairs of students with another paragraph from the same persuasive essay. Have one student read the paragraph aloud. Ask the other student to respond with questions. Tell students to exchange roles and repeat the process.

**YOUR TURN** During the debate, provide the moderator with a stopwatch. Remind students to show respect by waiting for recognition from the moderator before beginning to speak. Make sure that students do not speak out of turn or interrupt one another.

## Assess and Reteach

### Assess

Use the **COMMON CORE TRAITS** to assess students' debates.

Participants in an effective debate
- work productively with others in teams
- present precise claims, supported by evidence
- respond thoughtfully and justify their views
- speak persuasively using standard English
- evaluate other speakers' viewpoints

### Reteach

Some students may have trouble identifying potential objections and counterclaims. Have students work with partners, taking different sides on the issue each has chosen to debate. Students should informally debate the issues. This insight will help students prepare their debate notes.

**Speaking and Listening Online**
- Public speaking tips
- Strategies for effective listening

# Assessment Practice

## COMMON CORE FOCUS

**RL 1** Cite evidence to support inferences drawn from the text. **RL 2** Determine a theme of a text. **RI 1** Cite evidence to support analysis of what the text says explicitly as well as inferences drawn from the text. **RI 2** Determine a central idea of a text. **RI 6** Analyze how an author uses rhetoric to advance a point of view or purpose. **RI 8** Evaluate the argument and specific claims in a text. **L 1a** Use parallel structure. **L 4a** Use context as a clue to the meaning of a word or phrase. **W 5** Develop and strengthen writing by editing to ensure that it demonstrates the conventions of standard English grammar and punctuation.

## CHECK READINESS

Read aloud the paragraph under **ASSESS** and stress to students that this is not the full Unit Test, but a way for them to check their readiness for it. Then have students examine the standards listed under **REVIEW** and look back in the unit or in the **Student Resource Bank** for any skills they need to review.

## READ THE TEXTS

Remind students to keep unit goals in mind as they read each passage, paying particular attention to these literary and reading skills:

- distinguish fact from opinion
- recognize and analyze bias
- analyze the elements of an argument
- analyze rhetorical structures and devices

To help students focus on elements of an argument, encourage them to ask themselves:

- What evidence does the author use to support his/her argument?
- What persuasive techniques or emotional appeals does the author use?

## ANSWER THE QUESTIONS

Direct students to pages R93–R101 of the **Handbook** to review test-taking strategies.

- As students prepare to answer multiple-choice questions, remind them to read through all choices, eliminate any that are clearly wrong, and then choose the most accurate answer.

---

**ASSESS**
Taking this practice test will help you assess your knowledge of these skills and determine your readiness for the Unit Test.

**REVIEW**
After you take the practice test, your teacher can help you identify any standards you need to review.

**COMMON CORE**

**RL 1** Cite evidence to support inferences drawn from the text. **RL 2** Determine a theme of a text. **RI 1** Cite evidence to support analysis of what the text says explicitly as well as inferences drawn from the text. **RI 2** Determine a central idea of a text. **RI 6** Analyze how an author uses rhetoric to advance a point of view or purpose. **RI 8** Evaluate the argument and specific claims in a text. **L 1a** Use parallel structure. **L 4a** Use context as a clue to the meaning of a word or phrase. **W 5** Develop and strengthen writing by editing to ensure that it demonstrates the conventions of standard English grammar and punctuation.

**Practice Test** **THINK** central
Take it at thinkcentral.com.
KEYWORD: HML9N-724

---

## Assessment Practice

**DIRECTIONS** Read the two texts and the book cover. Then, answer the questions that follow.

# The Happy Man's Shirt

*retold by Italo Calvino*
*translated by George Martin*

1  A king had an only son that he thought the world of. But this prince was always unhappy. He would spend days on end at his window staring into space.

2  "What on earth do you lack?" asked the king. "What's wrong with you?"

3  "I don't even know myself, Father."

4  "Are you in love? If there's a particular girl you fancy, tell me, and I'll arrange for you to marry her, no matter whether she's the daughter of the most powerful king on earth or the poorest peasant girl alive!"

5  "No, Father, I'm not in love."

6  The king tried in every way imaginable to cheer him up, but theaters, balls, concerts, and singing were all useless, and day by day the rosy hue drained from the prince's face.

7  The king issued a decree,[1] and from every corner of the earth came the most learned philosophers, doctors, and professors. The king showed them the prince and asked for their advice. The wise men withdrew to think, then returned to the king. "Majesty, we have given the matter close thought and we have studied the stars. Here's what you must do. Look for a happy man, a man who's happy through and through, and exchange your son's shirt for his."

8  That same day the king sent ambassadors to all parts of the world in search of the happy man.

---

1. **decree:** official order.

---

## DIFFERENTIATED INSTRUCTION

### FOR ENGLISH LANGUAGE LEARNERS

**Assessment Practice: Work Backward** Prepare students by having them read the questions *before* reading the passages. Have pairs find unfamiliar words in test directions and questions and follow these steps:

1. Write each word on an index card.

2. Look up the meaning in a dictionary and write it on the back of the card.

3. Use the cards to practice words with your partner and to teach them to others.

9    A priest was taken to the king. "Are you happy?" asked the king.

10   "Yes, indeed, Majesty."

11   "Fine. How would you like to be my bishop?"

12   "Oh, Majesty, if only it were so!"

13   "Away with you! Get out of my sight! I'm seeking a man who's happy just as he is, not one who's trying to better his lot."

14   Thus the search resumed, and before long the king was told about a neighboring king, who everybody said was a truly happy man. He had a wife as good as she was beautiful and a whole slew of children. He had conquered all his enemies, and his country was at peace. Again hopeful, the king immediately sent ambassadors to him to ask for his shirt.

15   The neighboring king received the ambassadors and said, "Yes, indeed, I have everything anybody could possibly want. But at the same time I worry because I'll have to die one day and leave it all. I can't sleep at night for worrying about that!" The ambassadors thought it wiser to go home without this man's shirt.

16   At his wit's end, the king went hunting. He fired at a hare but only wounded it, and the hare scampered away on three legs. The king pursued it, leaving the hunting party far behind him. Out in the open field he heard a man singing a refrain. The king stopped in his tracks. "Whoever sings like that is bound to be happy!" The song led him into a vineyard, where he found a young man singing and pruning the vines.

17   "Good day, Majesty," said the youth. "So early and already out in the country?"

18   "Bless you! Would you like me to take you to the capital? You will be my friend."

19   "Much obliged, Majesty, but I wouldn't even consider it. I wouldn't even change places with the Pope."

 GO ON

## ITEM ANALYSIS

| COMPREHENSION AND WRITTEN RESPONSE | ITEMS | UNIT PAGES |
| --- | --- | --- |
| Authors' Messages | 1, 14 | 699 |
| Summarize | 1, 4, 7, 8, 9, 10, 11, 16, 17, 21, 23, 24, 27 | 671 |
| Distinguish Fact from Opinion | 3, 15, 28 | 681 |
| Elements of an Argument | 7, 11, 14, 22, 23, 26 | 661 |
| Rhetorical Structures and Devices | 2, 3, 12, 13, 20, 25 | 661 |
| Persuasive Techniques | 15, 25, 26, 29 | 654–659 |
| Word Roots | 6, 18, 19 | 675 |

| WRITING AND GRAMMAR | ITEMS | UNIT PAGES |
| --- | --- | --- |
| Sentence Structure | 1, 2, 3, 4, 5 | 679 |
| Gerunds | 1, 5 | 719 |
| Subjunctive Mood | 7 | 717 |

### Practice Test

On **thinkcentral.com** students can complete an interactive version of this practice test *and* receive remediation for the skills they have not yet mastered.

## FOR STRUGGLING READERS

**Assessment Support** Consider these options for completing the Assessment Practice:

- Have students "work backward" to review the test questions before reading the passages.

- Select random questions in the Assessment and have students demonstrate *how* and *where* to look for answers.

- Ask students to locate unfamiliar vocabulary words in the Assessment. Elicit the words' meanings from the class.

- Have students record useful testing words and definitions in their journal for later reference.

- Read the selections or parts of them aloud to aid in student comprehension.

20    "Why not? Such a fine young man like you . . ."

21    "No, no, I tell you. I'm content with just what I have and want nothing more."

22    "A happy man at last!" thought the king. "Listen, young man. Do me a favor."

23    "With all my heart, Majesty, if I can."

24    "Wait just a minute," said the king, who, unable to contain his joy any longer, ran to get his retinue.[2] "Come with me! My son is saved! My son is saved!" And he took them to the young man. "My dear lad," he began, "I'll give you whatever you want! But give me . . . give me . . ."

25    "What, Majesty?"

26    "My son is dying! Only you can save him. Come here!"

27    The king grabbed him and started unbuttoning the youth's jacket. All of a sudden he stopped, and his arms fell to his sides.

28    The happy man wore no shirt.

---

2. **retinue:** assistants attending an important person.

## DIFFERENTIATED INSTRUCTION

### FOR STRUGGLING READERS

**Build Comprehension** Review with students the fable format of the story, in which characters often represent types, rather than complex, realistic people. Discuss these questions.

- How does the king's response to the prince differ from a real father's response to a son?

- How much do the learned advisors actually help the king?

- What does the poor youth in the story represent?

### FOR ENGLISH LANGUAGE LEARNERS

**Culture: Connect** Explain to language learners that this fable explores what things can and cannot make people happy. Point out that the king offers to provide his son with any material possession, yet the son remains sad. Help students connect the selection with displays of merchandise or elaborate advertisements they may have seen. Ask students why they think people are moved to buy expensive, unnecessary things, and how much enjoyment they think consumers derive from their unneeded purchases.

COMMENTARY

# A Story Full of the Stuff of Sorrow

*by Leonard Pitts Jr.*
**THE MIAMI HERALD**
Friday, December 5, 2008

1   I like stuff as much as the next guy.

2   My closet is stuffed with stuff, my shelves groan with stuff, boxes full of stuff jam my garage. I like stuff just fine.

3   But I would not kill for it.

4   Last week, a 34-year-old man was trampled to death by a mob rushing into a discount store to buy stuff. Jdimytai Damour was a seasonal worker manning the door of a store in Valley Stream, N.Y., as shoppers eager for so-called "Black Friday" bargains massed outside. The store was scheduled to open at 5 A.M., but that was not early enough for the 2,000 would-be shoppers. At five minutes before the hour, they were banging their fists and pressing their weight against the glass doors, which bowed and then broke in a shower of glass. The mob stormed in.

5   Four people, including a pregnant woman, were injured. And Damour was killed as people stomped over him, looking for good prices on DVDs, winter coats and game systems. Nor was the mob sobered by his death. As authorities sought to clear the store, some defiantly kept shopping; others complained that they had been on line since the night before.

6   And here, it seems appropriate to observe the obvious irony: Black Friday is the traditional beginning of the Christmas shopping season, Christmas being the holiday when, Christians believe, hope was born into the world in the form of a baby who became a man who preached a gospel of service to, and compassion for, our fellow human beings.

7   It is hard to see evidence of either in the mob's treatment of Jdimytai Damour and if your inclination is to heap scorn upon them, I don't blame you. But I would caution against regarding them as freaks or aberrations whose callous madness would never be seen in sane and normal people like ourselves. That would be false comfort.

727

---

**FOR ENGLISH LANGUAGE LEARNERS**
**Vocabulary: Multiple-Meaning Words** Point out examples of nouns that have verb forms in the selection. For example, a *man* is a male person, but *manning* means "working in a place." *Stuff* is a noun describing miscellaneous objects, but the verb *to stuff* means "to fill up something." Have students show their understanding by using both the noun and verb forms in sentences.

**FOR ADVANCED LEARNERS/PRE–AP**
Have students discuss the phenomenon of "Black Friday" and its role in Christmas shopping in the United States. Ask students to describe any experience they may have of "Black Friday" or any other crowded shopping event. Then have them suggest "Black Friday" alternatives and hypothesize how other pre-Christmas activities could become as popular as shopping for merchandise.

8    You may think I'm talking about mob psychology and to a degree, I am. From soccer riots to the Holocaust itself, human beings have always had a tendency to lose individual identity and accountability when gathered in groups. You will do things as part of a crowd that you never would as an individual. Theoretically, anyone who lacked a strong enough moral center and sense of self could have been part of that mob in Valley Stream.

9    But it's not just our common vulnerability to mob psychology that ties the rest of us to last week's tragedy. It is also our common love of stuff. Indeed, it is hard to imagine a starker illustration of our true priorities. Oh, we pay lip service to other things. We say children are a priority, but when did people ever press against the door for Parents' Night at school? We say education is a priority, but when did people ever bang against the windows of the library? We say faith is a priority, but when did people ever surge into a temple of worship as eagerly as they do a temple of commerce?

10   No, sale prices on MP3 players, that's our true priority. Jdimytai Damour died because too many of us have bought, heart and soul, into the great lie of American consumerism: acquiring stuff will make you whole. "You, Happier," is how a sign at my local electronics store puts it. As if owning a CD, a DVD, an HDTV, will elevate you to a level of joy otherwise impossible to attain.

11   Hey, you might be a total loser, might not have a friend, might not have an education, might not have a job, might not have a clue, but it will all be OK as soon as you get that new digital camera, especially if you get it for 50 percent off.

12   It would be nice to think—I will not hold my breath—that Damour's death would lead at least some of us to finally see that for the obscene lie it is, to realize that seeking wholeness in consumer goods is an act of emptiness, not joy.

13   You, Happier? No.

14   Just you, with more stuff.

728

---

# SIMPLE LIFE: FAMILY
## LIVE BETTER TOGETHER BY LIVING WITH LESS

by HOPE JOHNSTON

BOOK of the YEAR
Real Life Magazine

*Simple Life: Family will help you discover what you really need and what you don't, what you have in each other, and how to make the most of your time together.*

—Jeanne Michaels,
Weekly Review of Books

729

**FOR ENGLISH LANGUAGE LEARNERS**

**Vocabulary: Multiple-Meaning Words** Review with students the different definitions and connotations of *simple*. A *simple* piece of machinery might have few moving parts. A person with a *simple* mind might be naïve or unsophisticated. Point out that the book in the illustration is promoting the positive aspects of a *simple* life, meaning that people would live in a way that would be plain, natural, and without unneeded distractions or complications.

**Concept Support** Discuss with students the illustration on page 729, and identify it as the cover of a book titled *Simple Life: Family*. Point out that the illustration emphasizes relationships by showing people walking with their arms around one another. Have students point out what is missing from this illustration: buildings, automobiles, cell phones, and any merchandise with a brand name. Ask students to look at the illustration and explain what they think makes the people in the illustration happy.

## Reading Comprehension

Model a thinking process for answering multiple-choice questions.

1. **C is correct.** Despite the king's many resources, he cannot buy the poor young man's happiness. A is incorrect because the story does not fault the king for trying to help his son. B is incorrect because the story focuses on finding happiness, not how many tries it takes to find it. D is incorrect because the story includes no examples of friendship.

2. **B is correct.** The king assumes that his unhappy son will be cheered when he has the right gift. A, C, and D are incorrect because the prince is not shown to be ill nor full of pride or respect, just sad.

3. **A is correct.** The story is a fable because the characters are not realistic, and it illustrates a lesson, or moral. B is incorrect because interaction between the king, the prince, and the advisors is not true to life. C is incorrect because the characters are not based on a true story. D is incorrect because the story is fiction.

4. **B is correct.** The king's advisors announce that the prince will be happy if he exchanges shirts with a happy man. A is incorrect because the prince declares that he is not in love. C is incorrect because the king tries throwing parties before getting advice from his advisors. D is incorrect because the wise men advise action, not waiting.

5. **A is correct.** The prince's face loses its rosy color. B and D are incorrect because they refer to parts of the prince's body. C is incorrect because while makeup may have color, it is not a synonym for color.

6. **D is correct.** Philosopher is a combination of "loving" and "wise." A is incorrect because sophos does not mean "people." B is incorrect because sophos does not mean "flattery." C is incorrect because philos does not mean "elder."

7. **B is correct.** The king is searching for someone who is content with his station in life. Although the priest says he is happy, he thinks becoming a bishop would make him happier. A is incorrect because the king is searching for a person who wants noth-

ing at all. C is incorrect because the king is unhappy as long as his son is unhappy. D is incorrect because the king's statement does not make a connection between love and happiness.

8. **A is correct.** The prince and the neighboring king do not find satisfaction in their material wealth. B is incorrect because the prince states he is not in love. C is incorrect because the prince does not claim to be afraid of dying. D is incorrect because the neighboring king is not sad.

---

## Reading Comprehension

> **Use "The Happy Man's Shirt" (pp. 724–726) to answer questions 1–13.**

1. One theme of "The Happy Man's Shirt" is that —
   A. people should solve their problems themselves
   B. if at first you don't succeed, try, try again
   C. true happiness is not something you can buy
   D. true friendship is the most important thing there is

2. The unhappy prince is a symbol for —
   A. courage in illness
   B. greed
   C. pride
   D. respect

3. This story is an example of —
   A. a fable
   B. a realistic story
   C. historical fiction
   D. a nonfiction story

4. The wise men advise the king to —
   A. find the prince a bride
   B. have the prince wear a happy man's shirt
   C. throw a party for the prince
   D. let the prince grow out of his mood

5. In paragraph 6, the word *hue* means —
   A. color
   B. hair
   C. makeup
   D. voice

6. The word *philosophers* in paragraph 7 comes from the Greek words *philos*, which means "loving," and *sophos*, which means "wise." Therefore, a *philosopher* is a —
   A. lover of people
   B. lover of flattery
   C. wise elder
   D. lover of wisdom

7. In paragraph 13, when the king says to the priest "I'm seeking a man who's happy just as he is, not one who's trying to better his lot," he means that —
   A. people want what they cannot have
   B. things and titles cannot bring a person happiness
   C. he is happy with his own life
   D. the search for love

8. The prince and the neighboring king are alike because —
   A. both seem to have everything they could want, but they are not happy
   B. both are in love, which makes them unhappy
   C. both are worried about dying, which makes them unhappy
   D. both are sad and do not know why

9. In paragraph 16, the king goes hunting because he —
   A. was hungry and needed something to eat
   B. needed a new trophy in the castle
   C. wanted to visit the fields
   D. didn't know what else to do

10. When the king finds him, the happy young man is —
    A. singing to his sweetheart
    B. counting his money
    C. pruning grape vines
    D. plowing a field

11. The king decides that the young man is truly happy because the young man is —
    A. working outdoors
    B. healthy and young
    C. satisfied with his life
    D. a good farmer

12. The author uses dialogue —
    A. to establish the setting
    B. to describe the prince as unhappy
    C. to reveal the complicating incident
    D. to show how the king tried to cheer up his son

13. The story's ending is ironic because —
    A. the shirt is a symbol of material wealth
    B. the wise men are proven right
    C. the wise men learn a lesson
    D. the shirt is a symbol of happiness

---

**Use "A Story Full of the Stuff of Sorrow" (pp. 727–728) to answer questions 14–22.**

14. One message of "A Story Full of the Stuff of Sorrow" is that —
    A. people have too many possessions
    B. people should not buy anything but essentials
    C. happiness comes from having more than others do
    D. happiness does not come from things

15. This article is an example of —
    A. explanatory writing
    B. persuasive writing
    C. descriptive writing
    D. narrative writing

16. According to the article, Jdimytai Damour was —
    A. an employee
    B. a mobster
    C. a police officer
    D. a shopper

17. The author notes that when shoppers learned that a man had been crushed to death by the mob, some people —
    A. took up a collection for his family
    B. were upset that they had to quit shopping
    C. did not believe it was true
    D. fled the store in fear

GO ON

9. **D is correct.** The king is "at his wit's end" and goes hunting for a change of pace. A is incorrect because the story does not describe the king's hunger. B is incorrect because the story does not indicate the king's lack of trophies. C is incorrect because the king goes to the countryside specifically to hunt.

10. **C is correct.** The king discovers the young man in a vineyard, pruning the vines. A is incorrect because the young man is singing, but not to his sweetheart. B is incorrect because the young man is not shown to have money. D is incorrect because the young man is pruning, not plowing.

11. **C is correct.** The young man is content with his life and does not want anything in the way of money or power. A, B, and D are incorrect because while outdoor work and being healthy and young might make the young man a good farmer, they are not his source of happiness.

12. **D is correct.** Dialogue reveals the king's many efforts to help his son. Choices A, B, and C are incorrect because these plot elements are explained through narration.

13. **D is correct.** The ending reveals that the young man is happy despite him not having a shirt, which was the symbol of happiness. B and C are incorrect because the ending does not refer to the wise men. A is incorrect because the shirt was intended to be a symbol of happiness, not material wealth.

14. **D is correct.** The author argues that while things may be attractive or desirable, they do not independently create happiness. A is incorrect because the author does not explicitly argue about excessive possessions. B is incorrect because the author does not make suggestions on what consumers should buy. C is incorrect because it is the opposite of the author's argument.

15. **B is correct.** The author's primary goal is to persuade readers that buying things will not make them happy. A, C, and D are incorrect because the author's goal is to persuade readers of his point, not to explain a process or procedure, describe, or tell a story.

16. **A is correct.** Jdimytai Damour worked at a discount store. B is incorrect because the selection gives no indication that Damour was associated with crime. C is incorrect

because Damour was a seasonal worker, not a police officer. D is incorrect because Damour was trampled by shoppers at the store where he worked.

17. **B is correct.** People continued to shop because they had spent the night in line. A is incorrect because the article emphasizes shoppers' lack of concern. C is incorrect because the article indicates the shoppers' indifference, not their doubt. D is incorrect because the article emphasizes that people continued shopping.

**18. C is correct.** *"To suffer with" someone means to feel sympathy for them. A is incorrect because it does not mean "to touch" or "to express emotions." B is incorrect because it is the opposite of compassion. D is incorrect because "to compare" is an action that does not imply sympathy.*

**19. D is correct.** *The condition of having "hard skin" would impair one's ability to feel. A and B are incorrect because they are opposites of being "hard." C is incorrect because severity refers to a degree of something, not the ability to feel.*

**20. B is correct.** *The rhetorical questions illustrate that large groups of people swarm to stores, but not to schools and places of worship. A is incorrect because the questions point out where mobs are not likely to be found. C is incorrect because the questions draw attention to locations, not possessions. D is incorrect because the questions do not address personal responsibility.*

**21. D is correct.** *The author explains that people act differently when they are in a crowd because they do not feel responsible for their actions. A is incorrect because everyone is susceptible to mob psychology. B is incorrect because although everyone is vulnerable, people with strong moral centers may resist mob psychology. C is incorrect because a "mob" by definition must be a group, not individuals.*

**22. A is correct.** *The author points out the difference between the condition of possessing an object and being happy. B is incorrect because the author's observation is about advertising's message of happiness. C is incorrect because the message is not about the economy. D is incorrect because the author's message is not about the effects of buying stuff regardless of nationality.*

**23. D is correct.** *"The Happy Man's Shirt" focuses on one thing, while "A Story Full of the Stuff of Sorrow" looks at consumer goods in general. A is incorrect because the stories do not analyze friendship. B is incorrect because the stories look at what money can buy, not just the state of having money. C is incorrect because "The Happy Man's Shirt" does not address the tradition of pre-Christmas shopping.*

---

18. The word *compassion* in paragraph 6 combines the Latin prefix *com-*, which means "together" or "with," and the Latin root *-pati-*, meaning "to suffer." The word *compassion* means —
    A. to feel
    B. to be unfeeling
    C. to feel sympathy
    D. to compare

19. The word *callous* in paragraph 7 comes from the Latin word *callum*, which means "hard skin." *Callous* means —
    A. charitable
    B. gentle
    C. severe
    D. unfeeling

20. In paragraph 9, the author uses rhetorical questions to show —
    A. how vulnerable everyone is to mob psychology
    B. that people generally don't value children, education, and faith as much as they say
    C. how most people do not love their stuff
    D. that everyone is responsible for the tragedy, not only the people in the crowd

21. The author defines *mob psychology* as —
    A. things that you do, but that most people do not
    B. things everybody does
    C. things people do by themselves
    D. things people do because they are in a crowd

22. The author says that "the great lie of American consumerism" is that —
    A. bigger and better things will make you happy
    B. advertising convinces consumers to buy
    C. spending money is good for the economy
    D. Americans are "born consumers"

> **Use "The Happy Man's Shirt" and "A Story Full of the Stuff of Sorrow" to answer questions 23–24.**

23. Both "The Happy Man's Shirt" and "A Story Full of the Stuff of Sorrow" consider the value of —
    A. friends
    B. money
    C. tradition
    D. things

24. The king and the shoppers are similar because —
    A. both are wealthy
    B. both are trying to save their children
    C. both are trying to find happiness
    D. both are insensitive to other people

> **Use the book cover on page 729 to answer questions 25–26.**

25. The purpose of the photograph on the book cover is most likely to —
    A. show a family enjoying time together
    B. encourage an appreciation of nature
    C. illustrate the companionship of a dog
    D. encourage people to take up hiking

732

---

**24. C is correct.** *The king is trying to find what will make his son happy, while shoppers are trying to buy their own happiness. A is incorrect because not all the shoppers are wealthy. B is incorrect because the shoppers are not trying to save their children. D is incorrect because the king is not insensitive to others.*

**25. A is correct.** *The body language of the people in the photograph shows that they are relaxed and having a good time. B is incorrect because although the picture is taken outdoors, it does not focus on specific plants or animals. C is incorrect because there is no dog in the photograph. D is incorrect because the picture's focus is on the people's relationship, not on the activity of hiking.*

**26.** Which of these elements of the book jacket supports the author's credibility?

   **A.** The title, *Simple Life: Family*

   **B.** Live Better Together by Living with Less

   **C.** Jeanne Michaels, *Weekly Review of Books*

   **D.** Book of the Year, *Real Life Magazine*

### SHORT CONSTRUCTED RESPONSE
**Write a short response to each question, using text evidence to support your response.**

**27.** Do you think the king's advisers would be surprised that the happy man wore no shirt? Support your response with evidence from the text.

**28.** How effectively does the author of "A Story Full of the Stuff of Sorrow" support his central argument? Use evidence from the text to support your answer.

**Write a short response to the following question, using evidence from both texts to support your response.**

**29.** What impact does setting have on the mood of "The Happy Man's Shirt" and "A Story Full of the Stuff of Sorrow"? Support your response with evidence from **both** texts.

GO ON →

---

**26. D *is correct.*** The book award given by an outside source adds to the author's credibility. A and B are incorrect because the title and subtitle of the book may not reflect its true content. C is incorrect because a book's reviewer is not necessarily as objective as a group that gives a book award.

## SHORT CONSTRUCTED RESPONSE

***Possible responses:***

**27.** The king's advisers state that the king's son must exchange his shirt with a happy man (paragraph 7). So, yes they would be surprised to find that the happy man had no shirt.

**28.** The author effectively supports his central argument that people have come to value "stuff" more than children, education, or friendship through the use of facts (such as specific details from the incident), examples ("We say education is a priority, but when did people ever bang against the windows of the library?"), and emotional appeal ("Four people, including a pregnant woman, were injured.").

**29.** The kingdom setting of "The Happy Man's Shirt" gives it a folk or fairy tale mood. The modern, holiday shopping setting of "A Story Full of the Stuff of Sorrow" makes its mood realistic and urgent.

---

## DIFFERENTIATED INSTRUCTION

### FOR ENGLISH LANGUAGE LEARNERS
**Review Assessment Vocabulary** List the italicized assessment vocabulary on the board. Give examples in random order and have students match them with the terms. Elicit additional examples from the students.

- *credibility:* The book received an award from a magazine
- *fact:* A store worker was killed by a mob of shoppers.
- *opinion:* People shop too much.

- *summary:* "The Happy Man's Shirt" is about a king who wants to help his son find happiness.
- *rhetorical question:* Why do people shop so much?
- *persuasive writing:* This candidate is the best, and you should vote for her.
- *irony:* I thought the book would end in tragedy, but a twist in the end saved the character's life.
- *fable:* That story teaches a lesson or moral.
- *symbol:* That tree stands for stability and endurance.

# Revising and Editing

1. **D is correct.** *The sentence uses correct grammar, punctuation, and spelling. A is incorrect because "stepped" is an incorrect spelling. B is incorrect because "circles" should not be possessive. C is incorrect because the punctuation is correct for a question.*

2. **C is correct.** *The two examples of student groups should be together. A is incorrect because sentence 1 provides an opening statement and should be first. B and D are incorrect because moving other sentences would interrupt the passage's logical order.*

3. **D is correct.** *"Every day in class" provides a transition. A is incorrect because this revision deletes the transition phrase. B and C are incorrect because there is no transition phrase at the beginning of the sentence.*

4. **C is correct.** *A comma should follow the introductory phrase "Even though we might have different interests." A is incorrect because "I" would not agree with the "we" used later in the sentence. B is incorrect because the comma should occur after the entire introductory phrase, not the first word. D is incorrect because the sentence has an error.*

---

## Revising and Editing

**DIRECTIONS** Read this passage, and answer the questions that follow.

> (1) Why are people so afraid of stepping outside their social circles? (2) Every day in class, I notice how students congregate in separate groups. (3) Cheerleaders are in one corner. (4) Even though we might have different interests that doesn't mean we can't try to find some common ground. (5) Breaking out of your mold can be good for you. (6) I recommend that you try speaking to someone you don't usually speak to. (7) There are art students who are in another corner. (8) Just go up to someone start a conversation. (9) You might find that it's not so bad. (10) It's even possible that the two of you might like each other.

1. What change, if any, should be made to sentence 1?
   A. Change *of stepping* to **stepped**
   B. Change *circles* to **circle's**
   C. Change *?* to **.**
   D. Make no change

2. What is the most effective way to improve the organization of the paragraph?
   A. Move sentence 1 to follow sentence 5.
   B. Move sentence 2 to follow sentence 8.
   C. Move sentence 7 to follow sentence 3.
   D. Move sentence 8 to follow sentence 10.

3. What is the most effective way to revise sentence 2 to include a transition?
   A. I notice how students congregate in separate groups.
   B. Students congregate in separate groups every day in class.
   C. Students, every day in class, congregate in separate groups.
   D. Make no change because it already has a transition.

4. What change, if any, should be made in sentence 4?
   A. Change *we* to **I**
   B. Insert a comma after *Even*
   C. Insert a comma after *interests*
   D. Make no change

734

---

### FOR STRUGGLING READERS

**Assessment Support: Parallel Structure** Remind students that writers use parallel structure, or similar grammatical forms, to express related ideas. Have them identify the parallel elements of these sentences.

- Cara likes *to sing, to dance,* and *to paint.*
- *Every morning, Van walks to school,* and *every afternoon he walks to work.*

**Assessment Support: Gerunds** Review with students the *–ing* verb form and give them practice identifying which verbs are gerunds, or verbs acting as nouns.

- He is running in a marathon tomorrow. *Running* is his passion. (gerund)
- *Playing* with blocks can occupy the children for hours. (gerund) They are playing at the school's sand pile.
- *Learning* about history is fascinating to me. (gerund) I think that *learning* about another culture teaches us about ourselves. (gerund)

5. What is the most effective way to combine sentences 5 and 6 to form one complex sentence?

   **A.** Because breaking out of your mold can be good for you, I recommend that you try speaking to someone you don't usually speak to.

   **B.** Breaking out of your mold can be good for you, thus I recommend that you try speaking to someone you don't usually speak to.

   **C.** If breaking out of your mold can be good for you, I would recommend that you try speaking to someone you don't usually speak to.

   **D.** Breaking out of your mold can be good for you, but I recommend that you try speaking to someone you don't usually speak to.

6. What change, if any, should be made in sentence 8?

   **A.** Insert *and* after **someone**

   **B.** Change *start* to **starting**

   **C.** Insert a comma after **someone**

   **D.** Make no change

7. What is the most effective way to rewrite sentence 10 so that its structure is parallel to that of sentence 9?

   **A.** It would be impossible that the two of you wouldn't like each other.

   **B.** That the two of you might like each other is a possibility.

   **C.** How could you not like each other?

   **D.** You might even find that the two of you like each other.

**STOP**

735

5. **A *is correct.*** *This combination creates a complex sentence with an independent and a dependent clause. B and D are incorrect because they contain two independent clauses. C is incorrect because the relationship between ideas is less effective than answer A.*

6. **A *is correct.*** *The sentences needs the conjunction* and *to create a compound sentence. B is incorrect because* start *should keep the same form to be parallel with* go. *C is incorrect because inserting a comma would create a comma splice. D is incorrect because there is an error in the sentence.*

7. **D *is correct.*** *Sentence 9 begins with the words* You might find *followed by a noun clause. A, B, and C are incorrect because they do not follow the same pattern as sentence 9.*

---

**FOR STRUGGLING READERS**

**Assessment Support: Subjunctive Mood**
Review the subjunctive mood with students, which is used to express a condition contrary to fact, such as a wish or a phrase beginning with *if*. Give students practice selecting the proper verb forms to create the subjunctive mood.

- If he (*were*) more organized, he could finish quicker.

- She acted as if she (*were*) disappointed in the decision.

- He wishes that the program (*were*) scheduled earlier in the day.

**Assessment Support: Sentence Structure**   Provide students with additional practice creating complex sentences, which contain both a dependent and an independent clause. Ask students to combine the sentence pairs below into complex sentences.

- I have to wake up early. I'll set my alarm. (*Because I have to wake up early, I'll set my alarm.*)

- I'll pack my bag. Then I'll pack my briefcase. (*After I pack my bag, I'll pack my briefcase.*)

- I want to catch the 7 a.m. bus. It is always on time. (*I want to catch the 7 a.m. bus because it is always on time.*)

## COMMON CORE FOCUS

**RL 10** Read and comprehend literature.
**RI 10** Read and comprehend literary nonfiction.

### INTRODUCE *GREAT READS*

In Unit 6, students have discussed a number of big questions. Invite students to tell which question they found most intriguing and why, and then focus attention on the three that appear on this page. Discuss the recommended books and their summaries, pointing out how each connects to the related question. Encourage students to choose one or more of these "great reads" to read independently.

## Ideas for Independent Reading

How do you persuade others that your ideas have value? Read the following works to see how various individuals made their case.

COMMON CORE

**RL 10** Read and comprehend literature. **RI 10** Read and comprehend literary nonfiction.

### Can a dream change the world?

**Mountains Beyond Mountains**
*by Tracy Kidder*

Kidder writes about Dr. Paul Farmer, whose dream of medical care as a human right—untied to financial status—has taken root in places such as Haiti, Russian and Peruvian prisons, and inner-city Boston.

**Eco-Heroes: Twelve Tales of Environmental Victory**
*by Aubrey Wallace*

These 12 crusaders had dreams of saving forests, cleaning up toxic waste, and preventing the slaughter of dolphins. All 12 have motivated others to dream and to work for change.

**Eyes on the Prize: America's Civil Rights Years, 1954–1965**
*by Juan Williams*

The dream to end Jim Crow segregation has deep roots. This book chronicles *Brown v. Board of Education*, the Montgomery bus boycott, sit-ins and freedom rides, and the courage of those engaged in the struggle.

### How do you sell an idea?

**Silent Spring**
*by Rachel Carson*

In this groundbreaking book, Carson brought to the world's attention the fragility of our modern-day environment.

**Still Me**
*by Christopher Reeve*

Severely paralyzed in an accident, popular actor Reeve wrote and spoke eloquently about his condition. His activism led to increased research and breakthroughs in treating spinal cord injuries.

**How the Other Half Lives**
*by Jacob Riis*

Riis's writings and photographs of the poor in New York tenements of the late 19th century led to social reforms in the areas of housing and fire prevention.

### Is privacy an illusion?

**The Right to Privacy**
*by Ellen Alderman and Caroline Kennedy*

The authors present an overview of the ways in which our privacy has been invaded over the years, including the recent threats to privacy posed by cyberspace.

**The Firm**
*by John Grisham*

In this contemporary thriller, Mitch McDeere begins his legal career with a firm that seems to offer him everything—until he and his wife learn that their every move is under surveillance.

**1984**
*by George Orwell*

This novel portrays a chilling vision of a totalitarian society, a world in which the government can control individual thought and even reality itself.

**Get Novel Wise**

**THINK** central

Go to **thinkcentral.com**.
KEYWORD: HML9-736

736

### NovelWise

**THINK** central

The keyword on this page points to **NovelWise**, a Web site that helps students choose a novel or other book-length work to read. **NovelWise** also provides

- study guides
- reading strategies and literary elements instruction
- presentations to introduce classic novels
- project ideas

# UNIT 7

## Special Effects

**THE LANGUAGE OF POETRY**

737

**About the Art** Christopher Myers created this image for his book *Wings* in 2000. For more information, see page 777.

## INTRODUCE THE UNIT

When you hear the term *special effects*, you may think of *Star Wars*, *The Lord of the Rings*, or another blockbuster action movie. Moviemakers have their own bag of tricks to make ideas seem real or fantastic, but moviemaking is not the only genre to use special effects. Indeed, many people feel that poetry is the most effective of all genres for making unreal things seem real. Poets use imaginative language to evoke intense emotion, to help readers visualize improbable scenes, and to glorify even common objects. In poetry, language is the medium for creating special effects.

Invite students to consider how the term *special effects* applies to the images on this page. Ask:

- Which picture makes an impossible thing seem real?
- How is the boy in the artwork like the butterfly?
- What makes the photograph of the butterfly special?
- In what way is each image inspirational?

Explain to students that as they read the selections in this unit, they will see how the **language of poetry** creates special effects. They will learn to recognize and use these techniques—and, as a result, they will gain a greater appreciation for this special genre.

For help in planning this unit, see

**R** RESOURCE MANAGER UNIT 7
pp. 1–10

**737**

# UNIT 7

ECOS   ECOS

| COMMON CORE STRAND | Text Analysis Workshop: The Language of Poetry pp. 740–747 | My Papa's Waltz/I Ask My Mother to Sing/ Grape Sherbet Poems pp. 748–755 | Spring is like a perhaps hand/Elegy for the Giant Tortoises/Today/U.S. Poet Laureates: Getting the Word Out Poems pp. 756–763 | **Linked Selections** 400-Meter Free Style/ Bodybuilders' Contest Poems pp. 764–769 | The Night Poetry Rocked the House Magazine Article pp. 770–773 Lexile: 1130 Fry: 7 Dale-Chall: 7.6 |
|---|---|---|---|---|---|
| **Reading Literature** | Form pp. 740–741 RL 10 Poetic Elements pp. 742–743 RL 4 Imagery and Figurative Language pp. 744–745 | Lyric Poetry pp. 749, 750, 753, 754 RL 4 Imagery pp. 749, 752, 754 RL 4 Make Inferences pp. 749, 752, 753, 754 RL 1 | Elegy pp. 757, 760, 763 RL 4 Diction pp. 757, 758, 761, 763 RL 4 Paraphrase pp. 757, 760, 763 RL 10 | Concrete Poetry pp. 765, 767, 769 RL 10 Form pp. 765, 766, 768, 769 RL 10 Connect pp. 765, 766, 769 RL 10 | |
| **Reading Informational Text** | | | Magazine Article p. 762 | | Synthesize pp. 770–773 RI 2 Language Coach p. 771 RI 4 |
| **Writing** | | Quickwrite p. 748 Writing Prompt p. 755 W 4 | Writing Prompt p. 763 W 1b, W 9a (RL 10) | Writing Prompt p. 769 W 5, W 10 | Writing Prompt p. 773 W 1a-b |
| **Speaking and Listening** | | | Present p. 756 SL 1 | Discuss p. 764 SL 1 | |
| **Language** | Imagery and Figurative Language pp. 744–745 | Use Descriptive Language p. 755 L 1b | | Language Coach p. 767 L 4 | |

| For Poets/Ode to My Socks/egg horror poem Poems pp. 774–785 | O What Is That Sound Poem pp. 786–791 | The Seven Ages of Man/The Road Not Taken Poems pp. 792–797 | Writing Workshop: Informative Text: Analysis of a Poem pp. 798–807<br><br>Speaking and Listening Workshop: Presenting a Literary Analysis pp. 808–809 |
|---|---|---|---|
| Ode pp. 775, 781, 784 **RL 4** Figurative Language pp. 775, 776, 778, 779, 782, 784 **RL 4** Overstatement p. 780 **RL 4** Visualize pp. 775, 776, 780, 783, 784 **RL 10** Language Coach p. 779 **RL 4** | Ballad pp. 787, 790, 791 **RL 10** Sound Devices pp. 787, 788, 790, 791 **RL 4** Analyze Speakers pp. 787, 788, 791 **RL 3** | Dramatic Monologue pp. 793, 794, 797 **RL 3** Meter pp. 793, 794, 796, 797 **RL 10** Analyze Ideas pp. 793, 796, 797 **RL 2** | |
| Quickwrite p. 774 Writing Prompt p. 785 | Quickwrite p. 786 | | Writing an Analysis of a Poem pp. 798–807 **W 2a–f, W 4, W 5, W 9a (RL 1, 4), W 10** |
| | | Role-Play p. 792 **SL 1** | Presenting a Literary Analysis pp. 808–809 **SL 4, SL 6** |
| Write Concisely p. 785 **L 1b** | | Foreign Words p. 795 **L 4c** | Drafting p. 801 **L 1** Revising pp. 802–804 **L 2c** Editing and Publishing p. 805 **L 2, L 2c** |

To see the complete Essential Course of Study, see pp. T23–T28.

 For additional lesson planning help, see **Teacher One Stop DVD.**

# Instructional Support

## Resource Manager Unit 7

### UNIT SUPPORT
Academic Vocabulary, p. 3

Additional Academic Vocabulary, p. 4

Grammar Focus p. 5

Text Analysis Workshop pp. 9–10

Writing Workshop: Informative Text:
Analysis of a Poem p. 113

### SELECTION SUPPORT*

**Plan and Teach**

Lesson planning pages

Additional leveled selection questions

Extension activities

**Student Copy Masters**

Selection summaries in four languages

Skills copy masters in English and Spanish

Vocabulary preteaching and support

Reading Check and Question Support

Reading Fluency

*Available for all selections

† Available on **thinkcentral.com**.

---

**Language Handbook**

**Vocabulary Practice**

**Best Practices Toolkit†**

**PowerNotes** DVD-ROM†

**Connections: Nonfiction for Common Core** CD-ROM†

---

**Teacher One Stop** DVD-ROM

**Student One Stop** DVD-ROM

**WriteSmart** CD-ROM†

**GrammarNotes** DVD-ROM†

**WordSharp** CD-ROM†

Create, customize, or print a variety of graphic organizers and writing templates to help your students brainstorm ideas and organize their writing.

---

# Differentiated Instruction

| STRUGGLING READERS AND WRITERS | ENGLISH LANGUAGE LEARNERS | ADVANCED LEARNERS |
|---|---|---|
| **Resource Manager Unit 7**<br>Additional Selection Questions<br>Question Support<br>Reading Fluency<br>**Interactive Reader**<br>**Adapted Interactive Reader**<br>**Level Up Online Tutorials**<br>**Audio Anthology**<br>(with Audio summaries)<br>**Diagnostic and Selection Tests**<br>Selection Tests A/B | **Resource Manager Unit 7**<br>Selection Summaries in English, Spanish, Vietnamese and Haitian Creole<br>Skills Copymasters in Spanish<br>**English Language Learner Adapted Interactive Reader Teacher's Guide**<br>**ELL Adapted Interactive Reader**<br>**Audio Tutor**<br>**Guide to English for Newcomers**<br>**Audio Anthology**<br>**Audio Summaries in Multiple Languages**<br>(on **thinkcentral.com**) | **Resource Manager Unit 7**<br>Additional Selection Questions<br>Ideas for Extension<br>**Diagnostic and Selection Tests**<br>Selection Tests B/C |

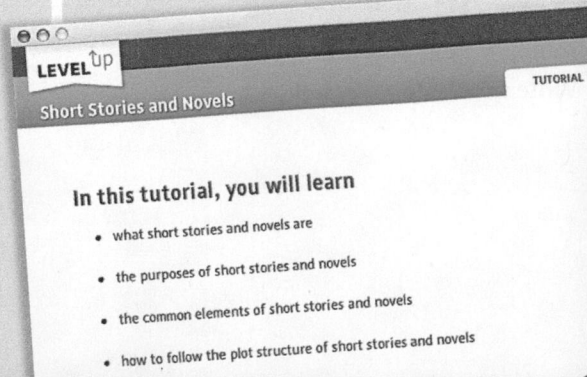

In this tutorial, you will learn

- what short stories and novels are
- the purposes of short stories and novels
- the common elements of short stories and novels
- how to follow the plot structure of short stories and novels

## Assessment and Reteaching

**Diagnostic and Selection Tests**

**Unit and Benchmark Tests**

**ThinkCentral Online Assessment:**

- All program assessments
- Level Up Online Tutorials

**ExamView Test Generator** on the Teacher One Stop DVD-ROM

**Online Essay Scoring** on **thinkcentral.com**

**ThinkCentral Online Reteaching:**

- Level Up Online Tutorials
- Reteaching Worksheets

**Holt McDougal** Online Essay Scoring

Welcome to Holt McDougal Online Essay Scoring!

This site is designed to help you improve your writing skills and prepare for standardized writing tests. When you write and submit a response to one of the writing prompts on this site, the computerized scoring system will immediately score and deliver feedback on your essay. Other resources on this site will help you prepare, develop, and revise your essay.

**STUDENTS**

Get started by entering the **Writing Zone**

## Professional Development

**Video Center** Based on interviews with program consultants and other educational experts, these videos feature classroom-ready teaching strategies.

**Teacher Toolkit** Includes a Teacher Handbook as well as a range of articles and handouts by program consultants and other educators.

**Janet Allen**

**Kylene Beers**

**Jim Burke**

**Carol Jago**

 **THiNK** central **at a Glance**

**One Location, Endless Resources**

**Find Resources** Browse all *Holt McDougal Literature* components for the ones that meet your students' needs and match your teaching style.

**Assess Progress and Reteach** Assign electronic versions of program assessments to measure your students' mastery of the Common Core State Standards. On thinkcentral.com, some tests deliver online remediation tutorials to students who have not mastered skills.

 *Interactive Whiteboard Lessons*

Prepare your students for college and careers by teaching relevant, real-world skills through dynamic, interactive instruction. Go to **thinkcentral.com** to browse through all white-board lessons, including the following:

- Poetry: Language and Form
- Figurative Language and Imagery
- Synthesizing Information

 Together Holt McDougal and HISTORY® are revolutionizing the study of English/language arts with video that helps students relive and re-imagine the people, places, and events they are discovering through reading. Look for selections with the HISTORY® icon.

**HISTORY**

## What POEMS
### do you remember?

To introduce the page and illustrate the question, recite the opening lyrics of a few familiar songs, such as "This Land Is Your Land" and "You Are My Sunshine." Call on volunteers to answer each question. After students have read the first paragraph on this page, ask them why these songs—these poems set to music—are easy to remember. ***Possible answers:*** *The lines have a catchy rhythm or interesting rhymes; they bring a happy occasion to mind; they have been heard so often that they are hard to forget.*

***ACTIVITY*** Point out that students need not choose a literary "classic"; rather, their choice should be a poem that is meaningful to them and that they can recite easily. As students share and discuss their examples, ask them to note the common qualities. Urge them to look for those qualities to reappear in the selections in this unit.

**CHECK UNDERSTANDING** Have students write a one- or two-sentence summary that explains why the poem they chose is a favorite.

**Find It Online!** THINK central

Go to **thinkcentral.com** for the interactive version of this unit.

## What POEMS
### do you remember?

Snippets of a nursery rhyme, verses from a favorite bedtime story, lines from an old favorite song or commercial jingle—chances are that the words from these poems linger in your memory because you have heard them over and over again.

*ACTIVITY* Write down the words to one of your favorite poems. Choose from poems you have read, heard, or memorized. Answer the following questions:

- What is your poem about?
- Has it been set to music?
- Are there any words that rhyme or repeat?
- Do you picture anything when you read or hear the poem?
- What is your favorite part of the poem?

Discuss with your classmates the qualities your favorites have in common.

738

---

## *Unit Resources*

See resources on the **Teacher One Stop DVD-ROM** *and on* **thinkcentral.com**.

 **RESOURCE MANAGER UNIT 7**

**UNIT AND BENCHMARK TESTS**

 **BEST PRACTICES TOOLKIT**

**INTERACTIVE READER**

**ADAPTED INTERACTIVE READER**

**ELL ADAPTED INTERACTIVE READER**

**LANGUAGE HANDBOOK**

**VOCABULARY PRACTICE**

**TECHNOLOGY**

- **Teacher One Stop DVD-ROM**
- **Student One Stop DVD-ROM**
- **PowerNotes DVD-ROM**
- **Write*Smart* CD-ROM**
- **Media*Smart* DVD-ROM**
- **GrammarNotes DVD-ROM**
- **Audio Anthology CD**
- **Audio Tutor CD**

 THINK central

**Find It Online!**

The interactive version of this unit on **thinkcentral.com** includes
- video and **PowerNotes** introductions to key selections
- audio support—listen or download
- **ThinkAloud** models
- **WordSharp** vocabulary tutorials
- interactive review and remediation

## Preview Unit Goals

**TEXT ANALYSIS**
- Recognize characteristics of a variety of forms of poetry, including lyric poetry, elegy, concrete poetry, ode, ballad, dramatic monologue, sonnet, and free verse
- Analyze imagery
- Analyze diction and the impact of word choices on meaning and tone
- Analyze structure and form, including line and stanza
- Analyze figurative language, including metaphor, simile, and personification
- Analyze sound devices, including repetition, alliteration, assonance, onomatopoeia, rhyme, rhythm, and meter

**READING**
- Use reading strategies, including visualizing and connecting
- Make inferences and cite evidence
- Determine a main idea or theme
- Synthesize ideas from multiple sources
- Analyze how characters, including a poem's speaker, develop and interact

**WRITING AND LANGUAGE**
- Write an analysis of a poem
- Write a concrete poem
- Support key ideas with details and quotations
- Use descriptive language effectively; write concisely
- Use participles and participial phrases to add interest to writing
- Use infinitives and infinitive phrases to add interest to writing

**SPEAKING AND LISTENING**
- Present a literary analysis

COMMON
CORE

**UNIT GOALS**

Included in this unit:
RL 1–4, RL 10, RI 2, RI 4, RI 10, W 1a–b, W 2a–f, W 4–5, W 9a, W 10, SL 1, SL 4, SL 6, L 1, L 1b, L 2, L 2c, L 4, L 4c, L 5
Complete text of the Common Core State Standards is found in the correlation on p. T10. Standards covered in this unit are found in the standards overview (pp. 737A–737B) and on the lesson pages where they are taught.

## Preview Unit Goals

The goals on this page present an overview of this unit's skills and strategies. Encourage students to preview the skills as they prepare for the upcoming selections. Remind students that the colors for each skill strand create a code that students can track throughout the unit.

## Focus and Motivate

### COMMON CORE FOCUS

**RL 4** Determine the meaning of words and phrases as they are used in a text, including figurative and connotative meanings; analyze the cumulative impact of specific word choices on meaning and tone. **RL 10** Read and comprehend poems. **L 5** Demonstrate understanding of figurative language, word relationships, and nuances in word meanings.

## Teach

### Part 1: Form

**Traditional Poetry** Read the Dickinson poem aloud, then explain that traditional poems are popular because of their regular, predictable rhythm and rhyme. Point out that other forms of traditional poetry also follow "rules," but these rules are more complex. Elicit or provide brief definitions and examples of these forms:

- *epic:* a long, narrative poem; examples: Homer's *Odyssey, The Song of Hiawatha*
- *ode:* a meditative or commemorative lyric poem; examples: poems of Keats and Shelley
- *ballad:* a narrative poem written to be sung or recited; example: Longfellow's *The Wreck of the Hesperus*
- *sonnet:* a 14-line poem having a set pattern of rhythm and rhyme; example: Shakespeare's sonnets
- *haiku:* a form of Japanese poetry having a set number of lines and syllables; example: poems of Matsuo Bashō
- *limerick:* a light or humorous poem with a particular rhyme scheme; example: Ogden Nash's *Requiem*

**Organic Poetry** Explain that organic poetry is unpredictable; it doesn't follow the rules of traditional poetry. Elicit or provide brief definitions and examples of these forms:

- *free verse:* poetry that does not have regular meter
- *concrete poetry:* poetry that conveys meaning visually through the arrangement of letters and words

As students explore traditional and organic poetry, they may want to use a Classification Chart to record differences between the two forms.

📦 **BEST PRACTICES TOOLKIT—Transparency**
Classification Chart p. B17

---

### Text Analysis Workshop

# The Language of Poetry

The poet Samuel Taylor Coleridge once described poetry as "the best words in their best order." Poets sear images into readers' minds, create unforgettable rhythms, and experiment with poetic forms. Whether they embrace the traditional rules of poetry, play with them, or break them altogether, poets use the techniques of their craft to inspire readers and communicate ideas. Experience these techniques in action by immersing yourself in the poetry of this unit.

### COMMON CORE

Included in this workshop:
**RL 4** Determine the meaning of words and phrases as they are used in a text, including figurative and connotative meanings; analyze the cumulative impact of specific word choices on meaning and tone. **RL 10** Read and comprehend poems. **L 5** Demonstrate understanding of figurative language, word relationships, and nuances in word meanings.

## Part 1: Form

Poetry is as much about form as it is about language and sound. **Form** refers to a poem's structure, or the way the words are arranged on the page. All poems are made up of series of **lines.** The length of the lines, where they break, and how they are punctuated all contribute to a poem's rhythm and meaning. In many poems, the lines are grouped into **stanzas,** which function like paragraphs in prose. Each stanza plays a part in conveying the overall message of a poem.

Poems come in a variety of forms, but they are usually talked about in terms of two categories—traditional and organic.

| **TRADITIONAL** | **ORGANIC** |
|---|---|
| *Characteristics*<br>• follows fixed rules, such as a specified number of lines<br>• has a regular pattern of rhythm and/or rhyme | *Characteristics*<br>• does not follow established rules for form<br>• does not have a regular pattern of rhythm and may not rhyme at all<br>• may use unconventional spelling, punctuation, and grammar |
| *Forms*<br>epic, ode, ballad, sonnet, haiku, limerick | *Forms*<br>free verse, concrete poetry |
| *Example*<br>Surgeons must be very careful<br>When they take the knife!<br>Underneath their fine incisions<br>Stirs the Culprit—*Life!*<br><br>—by Emily Dickinson | *Example*<br>we're everyanything more than believe<br>(with a spin<br>leap<br>alive we're alive)<br>we're wonderful one times one<br><br>—from "If Everything Happens That Can't Be Done" by E. E. Cummings |

---

## DIFFERENTIATED INSTRUCTION

### FOR STRUGGLING READERS

**Note Taking** To help students improve their reading comprehension, focus on note-taking skills. Tell students to use the boldface terms and the heads to organize their notes; to summarize the main ideas on this page; and to include only details that are important.

### FOR ADVANCED LEARNERS/PRE–AP

**Explore Forms** Have students work independently to identify examples of the forms listed in the chart. Ask them to share their examples in small groups or with the class by reading the poem aloud, classifying it as traditional or organic, and identifying its characteristics.

## MODEL 1: TRADITIONAL FORM

For centuries, poets have written sonnets that explore everything from unrequited love to the mysteries of nature. There are several types of sonnets, but all of them have 14 lines and are written in a strict pattern of rhythm and rhyme. Read this poem, which is a **Petrarchan sonnet,** to determine the characteristics of this particular form.

### Pretty Words
#### Poem by **Elinor Wylie**

Poets make pets of pretty, docile words:
I love smooth words, like gold-enamelled fish
Which circle slowly with a silken swish,
And tender ones, like downy-feathered birds:
5  Words shy and dappled, deep-eyed deer in herds,
Come to my hand, and playful if I wish,
Or purring softly at a silver dish,
Blue Persian kittens, fed on cream and curds.

I love bright words, words up and singing early;
10  Words that are luminous in the dark, and sing;
Warm lazy words, white cattle under trees;
I love words opalescent, cool, and pearly,
Like midsummer moths, and honied words like bees,
Gilded and sticky, with a little sting.

**Close Read**

1. How many lines make up the first stanza? How many are in the second stanza?

2. In the first stanza, each group of end-rhyming words is highlighted in the same color. Identify the end-rhyming words in the second stanza.

3. Compare the ideas expressed in the first stanza with those in the second one.

## MODEL 2: ORGANIC FORM

Poems written in **free verse,** like the one shown, do not adhere to a regular pattern of rhythm and rhyme.

### from **Beware: Do Not Read This Poem**
#### Poem by **Ishmael Reed**

the hunger of this poem is legendary
it has taken in many victims
back off from this poem
it has drawn in yr feet
5  back off from this poem
it has drawn in yr legs
back off from this poem

**Close Read**

1. Identify three characteristics that make this poem unconventional.

2. Even though the poet does not use punctuation, this poem has a natural rhythm. Read the poem aloud, using the rhythm you think is appropriate.

TEXT ANALYSIS WORKSHOP   **741**

## MODEL 1: TRADITIONAL FORM
**Close Read**

1. *There are eight lines in the first stanza, six in the second.*

2. *The end-rhyming words in the second stanza are "early" (line 9) and "pearly" (line 12); "trees" (line 11) and "bees" (line 13); "sing" (line 10) and "sting" (line 14).*

3. *Possible answer: In the first stanza, the poet expresses her love of "pretty, docile words"—words that are "smooth," "tender," "shy and dappled." In the second stanza, the poet expresses her love of "bright words"— words that "are luminous . . . opalescent . . . with a little sting." In both stanzas, she uses similes and metaphors to compare words to animals.*

## MODEL 2: ORGANIC FORM
**Close Read**

1. *Possible answer: The poem has no punctuation or capitalization; the word your is abbreviated as "yr" (lines 4 and 6); the poem does not rhyme; the lines do not have a consistent pattern of syllables.*

2. *Possible answer: Make sure students' readings emphasize the staccato, pronounced rhythm that results from the end-stopped nature of the lines and the repetition of "back off from this poem."*

**FOR STRUGGLING READERS**

**Language: Modifiers** Call attention to the poet's use of adjectives in "Pretty Words" to describe words that she loves. Have students identify places where she uses pairs of adjectives (lines 1, 5, 11, 12, 14) and hyphenated adjectives (lines 2, 4, 5). Help students link each modifier to the noun it describes. Then discuss how the poet's careful choice of descriptive words helps to create images that convey her meaning.

**FOR ADVANCED LEARNERS/PRE–AP**

**Synthesize: Free Verse** Challenge students to write a free-verse poem about a person they admire. Encourage them to give their poems a natural rhythm rather than one based on a set pattern. Have volunteers read their poems to the class.

**THINK** central

**Online Remediation**

Are your students struggling with text analysis skills? Consider assigning them one or more **Level Up Online Tutorials** as remediation before beginning this unit. Log in to **thinkcentral.com** to view a list of the skills addressed by **Level Up**.

# Teach

## Part 2: Poetic Elements

### SOUND DEVICES

After students read the Sound Device chart on this page, draw this chart on the board to help them reflect on the function of rhyme, rhythm, and sound devices in poems, prose, and popular music:

|          | Rhyme | Rhythm | Sound Devices |
|----------|-------|--------|---------------|
| Poetry   | ✓     | ✓      | ✓             |
| Prose    |       |        |               |
| Music    |       |        |               |

- Place a check mark in each box as you review sound devices and their use in each literary form. Emphasize the characteristics that make poetry unique as you discuss similarities and differences. For example, poems are generally written in lines rather than in sentences, and poets tend to convey their ideas and feelings through strong images and comparatively few words.

- Help students understand that poetry, prose, and songs all use rhyme, rhythm, and sound devices, but to different degrees and for different purposes. For example, a poet might use alliteration and assonance to convey a particular mood or to establish a distinct tone. A speechwriter might use repetition and rhythm to stress certain persuasive points. A songwriter might use alliteration to create a memorable phrase or lyric. Elicit or provide examples of the various techniques. (Edgar Allan Poe's "The Bells" is one excellent source. See page 743.)

### CHECK UNDERSTANDING

Have students create their own examples of repetition, alliteration, assonance, and consonance.

---

## Part 2: Poetic Elements

For a poet, deciding on a subject and form is just the beginning. Will the poem hum along at a steady beat or charge ahead with a bold rhythm? What images or sounds will convey a mood or establish a distinct tone? Using sound devices and language, poets can convey meaning, make music, and tap into the senses.

### SOUND DEVICES

Like music, language has rhythm. In poetry, the pattern of stressed and unstressed syllables in each line is what creates the **rhythm. Rhyme** also enhances the musical quality of a poem. It can occur at the ends of lines as **end rhyme** or within lines as **internal rhyme.**

A regular pattern of rhythm is called a **meter.** A regular pattern of rhyme is called a **rhyme scheme.** Meter is charted in a process called **scansion,** where stressed syllables are marked with a ´ and unstressed syllables with a ˘. A rhyme scheme is charted by assigning a letter of the alphabet to matching end rhymes. Notice how the meter and rhyme scheme are marked in these lines from "A Birthday" by Christina Rossetti:

| | |
|---|---|
| Mў héart / ĭs líke / ă síng / ĭng bírd | a |
| Whŏse nést / ĭs ín / ă wá / tĕred shóot: | b |
| Mў héart / ĭs líke / ăn áp / plĕ-trée | c |
| Whŏse bóughs / ăre bént / wĭth thíck / sĕt frúit; | b |

Here are some other techniques that poets use to create sound effects.

| SOUND DEVICE | EXAMPLE |
|--------------|---------|
| **REPETITION** a sound, word, phrase, or line that is repeated for emphasis and unity | back off from this poem it has drawn in yr feet back off from this poem  —from "Beware: Do Not Read This Poem" |
| **ALLITERATION** repetition of consonant sounds at the beginnings of words | Which circle slowly with a silken swish  —from "Pretty Words" |
| **ASSONANCE** repetition of vowel sounds in words that don't end with the same consonant | Words shy and dappled, deep-eyed deer in herds  —from "Pretty Words" |
| **CONSONANCE** repetition of consonant sounds within and at the ends of words | Whose nest is in a watered shoot  —from "A Birthday" |

---

## DIFFERENTIATED INSTRUCTION

### FOR STRUGGLING READERS

**Note Taking** For students who need help, hand out the note-taking copy master for Part 2. Read and discuss the text. Assist students in completing their note-taking copy master as needed.

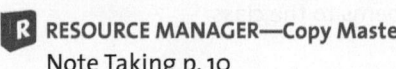 **RESOURCE MANAGER—Copy Master**
Note Taking p. 10

**Analysis Support: Sound Devices** To build understanding of sound devices, work with student pairs or small groups to create examples of repetition, alliteration, assonance, and consonance. If necessary, generate initial examples and have students identify them and add to them. For example, you might describe a "silent, slithery snake" and have students add alliteration, repetition, assonance, or consonance to the phrase. Ask volunteers to share the resulting examples.

## MODEL 1: METER

To identify a poem's meter, you have to break each line into smaller units, called feet. A **foot** consists of one stressed syllable and one or two unstressed ones. Look at the type and the number of feet in each line. Then combine the terms listed on the side—for example, **trochaic trimeter** or **iambic pentameter**—to describe what you find. Scan this poem to determine its meter.

---

# FIRE AND ICE
### Poem by **Robert Frost**

Some say the world will end in fire,
Some say in ice.
From what I've tasted of desire
I hold with those who favor fire.
5   But if it had to perish twice,
I think I know enough of hate
To say that for destruction ice
Is also great
And would suffice.

---

**METER**

**TYPES OF FEET**
iamb (rĕSÍST)
trochee (ÁBsĕnt)
spondee (GÓAL LÍNE)

**NUMBER OF FEET**
trimeter (3)
tetrameter (4)
pentameter (5)

**Close Read**

1. What is the metrical pattern of the lines in the box?

2. What is the poem's rhyme scheme?

## MODEL 2: OTHER SOUND DEVICES

Edgar Allan Poe wrote "The Bells" to experiment with the musical qualities of language. Read this excerpt aloud to get the full impact.

---

*from* # The Bells
### Poem by **Edgar Allan Poe**

Hear the sledges with the bells—
      Silver bells!
*What* a world of merriment their melody foretells!
      How they tinkle, tinkle, tinkle,
5         In the icy air of night!
      While the stars that oversprinkle
      All the Heavens, seem to twinkle
         With a crystalline delight;
      Keeping time, time, time,
10    In a sort of Runic rhyme, . . .

**Close Read**

1. Identify four examples of sound devices used in this poem.

2. What effects do these sound devices create? Explain how they add to Poe's description of the bells.

---

## MODEL 1: METER
**Close Read**
1. *iambic tetrameter*

**IF STUDENTS NEED HELP . . .** Have students read the boxed lines aloud, exaggerating the phrasing and stresses. Have them count the syllables, noting that there are eight syllables and that the first syllable in each foot is unstressed.

2. *abaabcbcb*

## MODEL 2: OTHER SOUND DEVICES
**Close Read**
1. *Possible answer: Repetition: "tinkle, tinkle, tinkle" (line 4); alliteration: "__W__hat a __w__orld of __m__erriment their __m__elody" (line 3); assonance: "the icy air of night" (line 5); consonance: "crysta__ll__ine delight" (line 8)*

2. *Possible answer: The devices suggest the sound of the bells, conveying their cheery, crisp, regular ringing. Use of the sound devices makes Poe's description come alive.*

---

## DIFFERENTIATED INSTRUCTION

### FOR ENGLISH LANGUAGE LEARNERS
**Language: Skill Words**  Point out the Greek combining forms *tri-*, in *trimeter*, meaning "three"; *tetra-*, in *tetrameter*, meaning "four"; and *penta-*, in *pentameter*, meaning "five." Also explain that *-meter* is a combining form too, meaning "measure." Have students define each complete word—*trimeter, tetrameter*, and *pentameter*—and put them in order from smallest to largest.

### FOR ADVANCED LEARNERS/PRE–AP
**Analyze Imagery**  Have students work in small groups to discuss Frost's imagery in "Fire and Ice," noting the senses to which the poet appeals. Then ask students to reflect on what feelings Frost associates with fire and what feelings he associates with ice. Also encourage students to discuss why it is often said that Frost's poems are deceptive in their apparent simplicity.

## IMAGERY AND FIGURATIVE LANGUAGE

**Word Pictures** Explain that imagery, diction, and figurative language bring poetry to life by creating vivid pictures in the reader's mind. Have students practice understanding figurative language, using familiar figures of speech from everyday conversation. Ask them to identify the figure of speech in each of these expressions, explain its meaning, and describe the mood it conveys:

- March comes in like a lion, goes out like a lamb. *(simile; March begins with bad weather, but ends with good weather; wild, then gentle)*

- He's got a heart of stone. *(metaphor; He's unfeeling; emotionally cold)*

- The stack of bills was a mile high. *(hyperbole; There were too many bills; despair)*

- The morning sun smiled upon our arrival. *(personification; Our arrival went well; cheerful)*

Challenge students to provide additional examples of similes, metaphors, personification, and hyperbole or to identify examples in selections they have read.

You might also point out that sometimes metaphors are "extended." For example, a poet may write an entire poem in which a person's life is compared to a ship at sea, tossed about on the waves, sailing for points unknown, and so on.

---

## IMAGERY AND FIGURATIVE LANGUAGE

Unlike prose, poetry is very concise: a limited number of words must carry a great deal of meaning. Therefore, **diction**, or word choice, is especially important. Poets must choose their words carefully in order to create certain effects. One of the ways poets expand their ability to make meaning and to achieve intended effects is by using imagery and figurative language.

You've already learned how **imagery** in fiction evokes sensory experiences for readers by appealing to the five senses. Poets also use sensory details to illustrate and elaborate on their ideas and feelings. For example, look again at "Fire and Ice" on the preceding page. Robert Frost uses two powerful sensory details—fire and ice—to help you picture the end of the world. Not only can you probably visualize the world engulfed in flames or numbed by ice, but you can also probably imagine what each type of destruction would feel like. These details are enough to spark unsettling images in your mind.

Like imagery, **figurative language** opens up the mind to more than the literal meanings of words. In this example, notice how the figurative expression not only is more descriptive but also conveys a stronger emotion:

**Literal:** He was angry.

**Figurative:** He burned with anger.

| FIGURATIVE LANGUAGE | EXAMPLE |
|---|---|
| **SIMILE** a comparison between two unlike things, containing the words *like*, *as*, or *as if* ▶ | My heart is like a singing bird —from "A Birthday" |
| **METAPHOR** a comparison between two unlike things without the word *like* or *as* ▶ | Poets make pets of pretty, docile words —from "Pretty Words" |
| **PERSONIFICATION** a description of an object, an animal, a place, or an idea in human terms ▶ | it [this poem] has taken in many victims —from "Beware: Do Not Read This Poem" |
| **HYPERBOLE** an exaggeration for emphasis or humorous effect ▶ | the hunger of this poem is legendary —from "Beware: Do Not Read This Poem" |

---

## DIFFERENTIATED INSTRUCTION

### FOR STRUGGLING READERS

**Concept Connect** On the board, list the boldfaced terms. Then give the examples in random order for students to classify.

- *simile:* My uncle is as stubborn as a child.

- *metaphor:* Nicole is a machine at work, never needing to rest.

- *personification:* The black storm clouds rumbled their anger.

- *hyperbole:* Jim's arm is so strong he can throw a ball a mile.

**Comprehension: Figurative Language** To reinforce the difference between the four types of figurative language, write this sentence on the board:

My heart is like a stone.

Ask students to identify the figurative language *(simile)*. Then help them change it into a metaphor. *(My heart is a stone.)* Work with students to change the base sentence to reflect personification and hyperbole.

## MODEL 3: IMAGERY AND FIGURATIVE LANGUAGE

In this poem, the writer uses sensory details and figurative language to acquaint you with a vivid character. As you read, notice the contrasting images of Miss Rosie—what she was and what she has become. Also, pay attention to the poem's **speaker,** the voice that describes the character, as well as the speaker's tone. How does the speaker's impression of Miss Rosie affect your perception of her?

# miss rosie

### Poem by **Lucille Clifton**

when i watch you
wrapped up like garbage
sitting, surrounded by the smell
of too old potato peels
5   or
when i watch you
in your old man's shoes
with the little toe cut out
sitting, waiting for your mind
10  like next week's grocery
i say
when i watch you
you wet brown bag of a woman
who used to be the best looking gal in georgia
15  used to be called the Georgia Rose
i stand up
through your destruction
i stand up

### Close Read

1. Point out three unusual comparisons and identify them as similes or metaphors. What image of Miss Rosie does this figurative language convey?

2. Find the hyperbole and explain its effect.

3. Reread the boxed lines. What is the speaker's attitude toward Miss Rosie? Explain how it affects your impression of Miss Rosie.

## MODEL 3: IMAGERY AND FIGURATIVE LANGUAGE

### Close Read

1. *Possible answer: Comparisons: "wrapped up like garbage" (line 2)—simile; "like next week's grocery" (line 10)—simile; "wet brown bag of a woman" (line 13)—metaphor. The language shows Miss Rosie as being alone, deteriorated, senile, pathetic.*

2. *"used to be the best looking gal in georgia" (line 14); effect: emphasizes just how far Miss Rosie has declined*

   **IF STUDENTS NEED HELP . . .** Ask students what the image of Miss Rosie as "the best looking gal in georgia" suggests. Have them contrast this image with the one presented in lines 1–13.

3. *Possible answer: The speaker feels both saddened and distressed to witness Miss Rosie's "destruction," and also stands to honor Miss Rosie and what she was. Because we see Miss Rosie through the speaker's eyes, we tend to share the speaker's feelings.*

## DIFFERENTIATED INSTRUCTION

### FOR STRUGGLING READERS

**Analysis Support: Speaker**  Read the poem aloud to the class. Then help students see how various sound devices contribute to the overall effect created by the speaker. For example, elicit or explain that the poem's stop-and-go rhythm and the speaker's repetition of the lines "when i watch you" and "i stand up" convey the speaker's feelings of distress.

## Part 3: Analyze the Text

**Close Read**

1. *The rhyme scheme is ababcdcdefefgg.*

2. ***Possible answer:*** *Two lines that reflect iambic pentameter are lines 2 and 11; lines that vary from the pattern include lines 1, 5, 9, and 14. Stressing words such as "Not" (lines 1, 5), "Love" (line 9), and "Look" (line 14) emphasizes the speaker's point that she's not like other girls who lock their loves away or harbor secrets behind a promise of fidelity.*

   **IF STUDENTS NEED HELP . . .** Have students read the poem aloud, listening for the metric pattern in each line. Remind students that iambic pentameter consists of five metric feet, each foot having one unstressed syllable followed by one stressed syllable.

3. ***Possible answer:*** *Lines 1–8 contain images of elaborate, bejeweled enclosures, locks, and secrecy; lines 9–12 contain images of openness, simplicity, kindness, and sharing.*

## Part 3: Analyze the Text

Now that you've learned about poetic forms and techniques, you're ready to see how everything works together in two distinctly different love poems.

The first poem is a Shakespearean sonnet, which has a rhyme scheme and organization different from those of the Petrarchan sonnet on page 741. This form of sonnet was introduced by 16th-century English poets and popularized by Shakespeare, but many modern poets still use the form today. A **Shakespearean sonnet** consists of three **quatrains**, or four-line units, and a final **couplet**, or pair of rhyming lines. Read the sonnet aloud first to understand what it is saying. Then read it again to analyze its poetic elements. What techniques are used to complement and extend the poem's meaning?

# NOT IN A SILVER CASKET...

Poem by **Edna St. Vincent Millay**

Not in a silver casket cool with pearls
Or rich with red corundum[1] or with blue,
Locked, and the key withheld, as other girls
Have given their loves, I give my love to you;
5  Not in a lovers'-knot, not in a ring
Worked in such fashion, and the legend plain—
*Semper fidelis,*[2] where a secret spring
Kennels a drop of mischief for the brain:
Love in the open hand, no thing but that,
10  Ungemmed, unhidden, wishing not to hurt,
As one should bring you cowslips[3] in a hat
Swung from the hand, or apples in her skirt,
I bring you, calling out as children do:
"Look what I have!—And these are all for you."

---

1. **corundum:** an extremely hard mineral, red and blue forms of which are rubies and sapphires.
2. *Semper fidelis Latin:* always faithful.
3. **cowslips:** plants that have fragrant yellow flowers.

**Close Read**

1. Identify the rhyme scheme of the poem.

2. This poem is written in iambic pentameter. Find and scan two lines that reflect this meter. Then find two lines that vary from the pattern. What is the effect of the change in rhythm?

3. How do the images in lines 1–8 contrast with those in lines 9–12?

## DIFFERENTIATED INSTRUCTION

**FOR STRUGGLING READERS**

**Analysis Support: Form** Draw a simple graphic organizer to help students visualize the Shakespearean sonnet's structure: three large boxes for each quatrain stacked above a smaller box for the couplet. Help students analyze the poem's meaning box by box. Write the meaning in the organizer.

- *first quatrain* (lines 1–4): other girls' love is elaborate love, but they keep it locked up.

- *second quatrain* (lines 5–8): the speaker gives her love plainly and forever, but with a hint of mystery

- *third quatrain* (lines 9–12): the speaker's love is open and simple like nature

- *couplet* (lines 13–14): the speaker feels that love should be expressed simply, freely, and openly

Now read this poem, which offers another perspective on love. As you read, notice how the sound devices, figurative language, and form help convey a heartfelt and sincere message.

# I AM OFFERING THIS POEM

Poem by **Jimmy Santiago Baca**

I am offering this poem to you,
since I have nothing else to give.
Keep it like a warm coat
when winter comes to cover you,
5  or like a pair of thick socks
the cold cannot bite through,

      I love you,

I have nothing else to give you,
so it is a pot full of yellow corn
10  to warm your belly in winter,
it is a scarf for your head, to wear
over your hair, to tie up around your face,

      I love you,

Keep it, treasure this as you would
15  if you were lost, needing direction,
in the wilderness life becomes when mature;
and in the corner of your drawer,
tucked away like a cabin or hogan[1]
in dense trees, come knocking,
20  and I will answer, give you directions,
and let you warm yourself by this fire,
rest by this fire, and make you feel safe,

      I love you,

It's all I have to give,
25  and all anyone needs to live,
and to go on living inside,
when the world outside
no longer cares if you live or die;
remember,
30        I love you.

---

1. **hogan:** a one-room Navajo building that is used as a dwelling or for ceremonial purposes.

### Close Read

1. Is this poem traditional or organic in form? Explain how you can tell.

2. Find four specific sound devices in the poem that give it unity and rhythm.

3. Identify the similes and metaphors in lines 1–12. A simile has been boxed. What qualities of the love poem do these comparisons help to emphasize?

4. Compare what these poems say about love. Cite similarities as well as differences.

### Close Read

1. *Possible answer: The poem is organic in form. It has no regular pattern of rhythm or rhyme.*

2. *Possible answer: Repetition: "I love you" (lines 7, 13, 23, 30); alliteration: "when winter comes to cover you" (line 4); consonance: "like a pair of thick socks" (line 5); rhyme: "wear"/ "hair" (lines 11–12), "give"/ "live" (lines 24–25)*

3. *Possible answer: Similes: "like a warm coat" (line 3), "like a pair of thick socks" (line 5); metaphors: "[this poem] is a pot full of yellow corn" (line 9), "a scarf" (lines 11–12). The comparisons help to emphasize such qualities as warmth, comfort, nurturing, and protection.*

4. *Possible answer: Both poems suggest that love is something to be given freely and openly. Both also disparage ostentation in the expression of love and prefer simple and sincere declarations and offerings. Baca's poem suggests that love nurtures, protects, and directs in a harsh world and is "all anyone needs to live" (line 25); Millay's sonnet contrasts her simple, demonstrative love with the more calculated expression of "other girls" (line 3).*

## Assess and Reteach

### Assess

List on the board the boldfaced terms from pages 740–746. Have students explain the meaning of each term and, as appropriate, give examples from the poems.

### Reteach

For students who are unable to apply the workshop skills to the poems, select from these reteaching options:

- Provide specific examples of troublesome terms. Have students read these and follow your guidance in recognizing and analyzing the poetic forms and elements. Ask students to read poems aloud to hear sound devices.

- Review with students the note-taking copy masters for this lesson. Have students restate the information in the copy masters in their own words. Help them identify examples.

---

**FOR STRUGGLING READERS**

**Analysis Support: Meaning** Help students explore the meaning of the last stanza. Explain what the poet means by the phrase "to go on living inside" (line 26). Note the contrast of "inside" with "outside" in line 27. Lead students to understand that the poet is speaking figuratively about feelings. Help students to paraphrase the stanza. *(Love is what I have to give. Love will help us feel okay even when the world ignores us.)*

**FOR ENGLISH LANGUAGE LEARNERS**

**Language: Pronoun Referents** Make sure that students understand that the phrase "this poem" is the referent for the word *it* in lines 3, 9, 11, 14, and 24. Elicit or explain that the poem is also symbolic of the speaker's love, especially in the final stanza, when the speaker says that it's "all anyone needs." Thus, *it* refers to both the poem and the speaker's love.

# Focus and Motivate

## SUMMARIES

**"My Papa's Waltz"** In this poem, the speaker shares a memory about his father.

**"I Ask My Mother to Sing"** The speaker of this poem describes how his mother and grandmother sing about a beautiful place in China.

**"Grape Sherbet"** The speaker reflects upon the importance of cherishing family memories and honoring the dead.

## Who lives in your MEMORY?

Ask the question as a lead-in to discussion. Then have students jot down some notes about a vivid memory to use as they complete the *QUICKWRITE.*

---

## My Papa's Waltz
Poem by Theodore Roethke

## I Ask My Mother to Sing
Poem by Li-Young Lee

## Grape Sherbet
Poem by Rita Dove

# Who lives in your MEMORY?

What are some of your most vivid family memories? They might include a raucous pillow fight with your sister or a rained-out picnic with your cousins. These memories can take a special shape in your mind; some might linger as stories to tell, but others might remain simply a series of images. The following poems contain such images, boiled down to their essential qualities.

*QUICKWRITE* Choose a memory involving someone close to you and write a brief sketch of your recollection. Include sensory details as well as events that present a clear picture of your subject.

748

---

## Selection Resources

## POETIC FORM: LYRIC POETRY

These three poems are all examples of **lyric poetry,** brief poems in which the speakers share personal thoughts and feelings on a subject. In ancient Greek, the word *lyric* referred to a type of poetry that expressed the feelings of a single singer, accompanied by a lyre, a small harplike instrument. Though no longer sung, lyric poems have a lot in common with songs, including

- a sense of rhythm and melody
- imaginative word choice, or **diction**
- the creation of a single, unified impression

Read the poems aloud to experience the sounds of the language.

## TEXT ANALYSIS: IMAGERY

One of the most important elements of any poem is its **imagery**—the words and phrases that appeal to one or more of the five senses. In addition to re-creating sensory experiences, however, imagery calls up particular ideas and emotions. In the following lines from "My Papa's Waltz," the imagery appeals to sight and hearing but also suggests certain feelings:

*We romped until the pans*
*Slid from the kitchen shelf*

These lines call up a sense of rowdy, out-of-control playtime.

## READING SKILL: MAKE INFERENCES

Lyric poems tend to be very condensed; in many cases, more is suggested than directly stated. It's important, then, to make inferences about their meanings. Think about the ideas and emotions suggested by the poet's word choices and the poem's images. As you read each poem, write down the images and your inferences on a chart like the one shown.

| *"Grape Sherbet"* | | |
|---|---|---|
| *Image* | *My Associations* | *Inference* |
| *"[Memorial Day] morning we galloped / through the grassed-over mounds / and named each stone / for a lost milk tooth."* | *• Memorial Day commemorates the dead.*<br>*• Grassy mounds and stones are found in cemeteries* | *They are running through a cemetery.* |

 Complete the activities in your **Reader/Writer Notebook.**

### Theodore Roethke
**1908–1963**

**Self-Taught Poet** Theodore Roethke learned to write verse by imitating other poets; he sought inspiration from his notebooks, where he had recorded his thoughts, feelings, and observations. He went on to earn a Pulitzer Prize and two National Book Awards. He once advised his readers to "listen" to his poems, "for they are written to be heard."

### Li-Young Lee
**born 1957**

**Son of Chinese Exiles** After his parents fled China to escape political persecution, Li-Young Lee's family lived in several Asian countries before arriving in the United States in 1964. After college, Lee began to write poetry—about love, family, and ordinary experiences.

### Rita Dove
**born 1952**

**Poet Laureate** Rita Dove's first attempts as a writer came early: in third or fourth grade, she composed a science-fiction novel based on her classroom spelling lists. Her poetry collections have won many awards, including a Pulitzer Prize in 1987. From 1993 to 1995, she served as U.S. poet laureate. Asked to name the most important quality for success, Dove replied, "I think that without imagination, we can go nowhere."

**Authors Online**
Go to thinkcentral.com. KEYWORD: HML9-749

THINK central

749

### Model the Skill: IMAGERY

For instructional support, read aloud this poem:

> Mama singing, children giggling,
> Daddy chortling, stew bubbling;
> Lightning flashing, rain dripping—
> Darkness coming.

Identify details that appeal to the senses: **Sight:** "Lightning flashing," "Darkness coming"; **Sound:** "Mama singing," "children giggling," "stew bubbling," "Daddy chortling," "rain dripping"; **Taste or smell:** "stew bubbling"; **Touch:** "rain dripping"

**GUIDED PRACTICE** Have students discuss the feelings that these images evoke.

### Model the Skill: MAKE INFERENCES

Use the text under **Rita Dove: Poet Laureate** to model making inferences.

1. Dove had an imaginative childhood.
2. She says that she values imagination.
3. Her poems may offer an imaginative way of looking at life.

**GUIDED PRACTICE** Ask students to make an inference about Li-Young Lee or Theodore Roethke, based on the text about the authors.

**R** RESOURCE MANAGER—Copy Master Make Inferences p. 23 (for student use while reading the selections)

---

## DIFFERENTIATED INSTRUCTION

### FOR STRUGGLING READERS

**Skill Words** Review these terms that are often used in a discussion of poetry: *speaker, stanza, rhyme scheme, line length, impression, rhythm,* and *meter.* Call on volunteers to define any terms they know. Have students use a dictionary to locate the meanings of unfamiliar terms. Urge them to watch for some of these terms as they read and to use these terms as they discuss and write about the poems.

### FOR ADVANCED LEARNERS/PRE–AP

**Extend Poetic Form** As you discuss what is meant by *lyric poetry,* challenge students to find examples of prose that could be described as lyrical because it reflects the qualities listed in the text. Descriptive short stories are a good starting place, but essays and "literary" nonfiction may yield rich examples too. Invite volunteers to read aloud a passage that they have found and to tell how it is marked by imagery, rhythm, and a unified impression.

## READ WITH A PURPOSE

*Help students set a purpose for reading. Tell them to consider the importance of family and family memories as they read the poems.*

**POETIC FORM**

COMMON CORE

RL 4

**Ⓐ** *Model the Skill:* **LYRIC POETRY**

Explain that the image in the first two lines is one of a father who has been drinking heavily, yet the boy hangs on to his father despite this. It conveys the feeling of the boy's innocence and the love he has for his father.

***Possible answer:*** *The speaker seems to cherish the memory. The poem has a jaunty rhythm and tender, loving images of the speaker having fun with his rough, rowdy father. However, some details give the memory a slightly troubling edge: the whiskey on his father's breath (line 1) and the steps he misses as they dance (line 11). The speaker's feelings about his mother's frowning disapproval (lines 7–8) are open to interpretation.*

## REVISIT THE BIG QUESTION

## Who lives in your
# MEMORY?

**Discuss** Why do you think the scene in "My Papa's Waltz" was so vivid among the poet's memories? ***Possible answer:*** *The scene was vivid and memorable because it was a happy time that the poet shared with his father. It was also emotionally charged, with a sometimes daring energy.*

# My Papa's Waltz

## THEODORE ROETHKE

The whiskey on your breath
Could make a small boy dizzy;
But I hung on like death:
Such waltzing was not easy.

5 We romped until the pans
Slid from the kitchen shelf;
My mother's countenance[1]
Could not unfrown itself.

The hand that held my wrist
10 Was battered on one knuckle;
At every step you missed
My right ear scraped a buckle.

You beat time on my head
With a palm caked hard by dirt,
15 Then waltzed me off to bed
Still clinging to your shirt. **Ⓐ**

**Analyze Visuals ▶**

What are your impressions of the characters depicted in the painting? Cite the details that create this impression.

**Ⓐ** **LYRIC POETRY**
How does the **speaker** feel about his bedtime waltz with his father? Use details from the poem to help explain why you think as you do.

_____

1. **countenance:** face or facial expression.

*Tender Moments* (2000), Francks Deceus. Mixed media, 101.6 cm x 101.6 cm. Haitian. Private Collection. Photo © The Bridgeman Art Library.

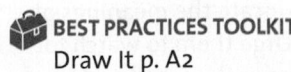

## DIFFERENTIATED INSTRUCTION

### FOR ENGLISH LANGUAGE LEARNERS

**Vocabulary Support** Point out to students the word *unfrown*. Explain that the prefix *un-* means "not or opposite of." The speaker means that the mother cannot stop frowning. Note, however, that *unfrown* is not a word typically used in English. The poet takes liberties with language to create a new perspective for readers on a familiar topic—the unhappy mother.

### FOR STRUGGLING READERS

**Options for Reading** Use the Draw It strategy to help students visualize the images in "My Papa's Waltz." Ask partners to read the poem aloud and share visual representations of what they read.

📋 **BEST PRACTICES TOOLKIT**
Draw It p. A2

## BACKGROUND

**Roethke's Father** Theodore Roethke was the son of Helen (Huebner) and Otto Roethke, a German immigrant who owned large commercial greenhouses in Saginaw, Michigan. Roethke's father was firm—sometimes fierce—with strangers, but affectionate and loyal to his family. Young Theodore viewed his father with a mixture of love and awe—characteristics that are reflected in "My Papa's Waltz."

## Analyze Visuals

*Possible answer: The larger character is protective of the smaller character, as suggested by the fact that his very large hands encircle the child's hands. The scene may capture a memory from the painter's youth, as suggested by the photograph.*

**About the Art** The poem scratched into the paint may be hard to read. It says

| | |
|---|---|
| Ride by | Step by Step |
| from now | Life |
| and forever | Love |
| Back to Back | the journey |

The words reflect the continuity of life that Haitian-American artist Francks Deceus (b. 1966) creates by juxtaposing the childhood photograph with the father and son—who seem to be dancing, like Roethke's speaker and his father.

## ADDITIONAL TEACHING OPPORTUNITY

**Appreciate Oral Poetry** Point out that the impact of poetry changes somewhat when it is heard instead of read silently. To illustrate, read the poems in this lesson aloud, or choose students to read them aloud. Urge students to listen for enjoyment during a first reading. On a second reading, have them listen for and note examples of rhyme, vivid language and imagery, and characterization. Invite students to comment about how their perceptions changed when the poems were read aloud. (To learn more about appreciating oral poetry, see **Reading Handbook,** page R2.)

### FOR ADVANCED LEARNERS/PRE–AP

**Set a Poem to Music** [small-group option] Remind students that lyric poetry was originally performed as song. Have interested students set to music a poem from this lesson or another poem of their choice. The music should mirror the emotions evoked by the poetry. Ask students to share their music by playing a recording or by performing it live for the class.

Prereading for this poem is found on page 748.

## Analyze Visuals

**Activity** Does this painting match the mood and imagery of the poem? Why, or why not?
*Possible answer: Yes, but in a suggestive rather than literal way. The painting reflects the poem's dreamy, nostalgic, and mournful mood. The painting's central image of a mother and child suggests the speaker's mother. The painting's fluid, translucent background suggests the poem's images of "spilling water" (line 11) and tears (line 13). The boat in the background evokes the poem's image of the speaker's father, who would "sway like a boat" if he were still alive to hear the singing (line 4).*

**About the Art** Hung Liu (b. 1948) emigrated from China to the United States in 1984. She mixes real and symbolic elements in paintings that explore personal subjects and her Chinese heritage.

---

**TEXT ANALYSIS** **COMMON CORE**
RL 4

###  IMAGERY

*Possible answer: The speaker can describe the images because they are described in the song. The feelings evoked are positive: awe at the sight of the structures and the lake and pleasure in the picnickers.*

---

**READING SKILL** **COMMON CORE**
RL 1

### **C** *Model the Skill:* MAKE INFERENCES

Explain to students that making inferences requires readers to combine text details with personal knowledge or experience. Tell students that you sometimes cry when you miss something or someone. Point out text details such as the references to another country and the fact that the speaker—the son and grandson of the singers—has never been there. You can infer that the women cry because they miss their homeland.

*Possible answer: The women cry because the song evokes strong memories and a sense of longing for their homeland.*

**752** UNIT 7: THE LANGUAGE OF POETRY

---

# I Ask My Mother to Sing

## LI-YOUNG LEE

*Mother and Child by Grand Canal* (2000), Hung Liu. Oil on canvas, 80″ × 80″. Courtesy Rena Bransten Gallery.

She begins, and my grandmother joins her.
Mother and daughter sing like young girls.
If my father were alive, he would play
his accordion and sway like a boat.

5  I've never been in Peking, or the Summer Palace,
nor stood on the great Stone Boat to watch
the rain begin on Kuen Ming Lake, the picnickers
running away in the grass. **B**

But I love to hear it sung;
10  how the waterlilies fill with rain until
they overturn, spilling water into water,
then rock back, and fill with more.

Both women have begun to cry.
But neither stops her song. **C**

**B** IMAGERY
Reread lines 5–9. How is the **speaker** able to describe images of a place he's never seen? Describe the feelings evoked by the images.

**C** MAKE INFERENCES
Why do the speaker's mother and grandmother start to cry during their song?

**752** UNIT 7: THE LANGUAGE OF POETRY

---

## DIFFERENTIATED INSTRUCTION

**FOR STRUGGLING READERS**
**Question the Poem** Model the Question Frames strategy to help students better understand this poem. Pose such questions as these: "Are the women sad?" "Do they wish to go home?" and "Why don't they stop singing?" Have students read each stanza and pose their own questions about the events and emotions that the words evoke.

**BEST PRACTICES TOOLKIT— Transparency** Question Frames p. A33

**FOR ENGLISH LANGUAGE LEARNERS**
**Culture: Clarify** Help students look in reference books and online sources to learn more about the references in lines 5–7: Peking, the Summer Palace, the great Stone Boat, and Kuen Ming Lake. In particular, help them locate images of some or all of these places. Discuss how knowing what the mother and grandmother are singing about affects their reading of the poem.

# Grape Sherbet

RITA DOVE

The day? Memorial.
After the grill
Dad appears with his masterpiece—
swirled snow, gelled light.
5 We cheer. The recipe's
a secret and he fights
a smile, his cap turned up
so the bib resembles a duck.

That morning we galloped
10 through the grassed-over mounds
and named each stone
for a lost milk tooth. Each dollop
of sherbet, later,
is a miracle,
15 like salt on a melon that makes it sweeter.

Everyone agrees—it's wonderful!
It's just how we imagined lavender
would taste. The diabetic grandmother
stares from the porch,
20 a torch
of pure refusal. **D**

We thought no one was lying
there under our feet,
we thought it
25 was a joke. I've been trying
to remember the taste,
but it doesn't exist.
Now I see why
you bothered,
30 father. **E**

*Ice Cream Dessert* (1959), Andy Warhol. Photo © Andy Warhol Foundation/Corbis. © 2007 Andy Warhol Foundation for the Visual Arts/ARS, New York.

**D** **MAKE INFERENCES**
Reread lines 18–21. What does the image of the grandmother suggest about her actions?

**E** **LYRIC POETRY**
What feeling is the **speaker** expressing in this poem?

Prereading for this poem is found on page 748.

## Analyze Visuals

**Activity** In his depiction of an ice-cream cone, what other objects does the artist suggest?
*Possible answer: The ice-cream cone looks like a fancy urn or building, and the scoop of ice cream looks like a jewel.*

**About the Art** Andy Warhol (1928–1987) was one of the pioneers of the pop art movement of the 1960s. *Ice Cream Dessert* is an early work that shows Warhol's fascination with the decorative qualities of popular objects.

---

**READING SKILL**   COMMON CORE   RL 1

**D** **MAKE INFERENCES**

*Possible answer: The image of the "torch of pure refusal" suggests that the grand-mother acts with burning determination and perhaps some resentment at being left out.*

---

**POETIC FORM**   COMMON CORE   RL 4

**E** **LYRIC POETRY**

*Possible answer: The speaker is expressing gratitude to her father for giving her happy memories and helping her see the importance of honoring the dead.*

---

## SELECTION WRAP–UP

**READ WITH A PURPOSE** Now that students have finished reading the selections, have them compare the poems. What do all three poems convey about the importance of family and family memories? *Possible answer: The poems suggest that family memories keep the speakers connected to their families and their cultural heritages.*

⭐ **CRITIQUE** Which poem affects you most strongly? Explain your response.

**INDEPENDENT READING**
Students may enjoy reading Lee's memoir of his family experiences, *The Winged Seed: A Remembrance.*

---

**FOR ENGLISH LANGUAGE LEARNERS**
**Vocabulary and Language** Identify and define confusing words, concepts, and cultural details in "Grape Sherbet." Make sure students know what sherbet is. Discuss the meaning of Memorial Day and ask for parallels from students' home cultures. Also discuss the meaning of "fights a smile" (lines 6–7), "bib" (line 8), "grassed-over mounds" (line 10), "lost milk tooth" (line 12), and "salt on a melon" (line 15).

**Develop Reading Fluency** Read aloud for students "Grape Sherbet," modeling how to pause for two beats at each dash and using intonation to indicate questions and exclamations. Read the poem aloud a second time, having students echo your reading of meaningful line groupings. In addition, distribute the copy master and have students work in pairs or groups to practice fluency.

**R** **RESOURCE MANAGER—Copy Master**
Reading Fluency p. 27

# Practice and Apply

For preliminary support of post-reading questions, use these copy masters:

**R** **RESOURCE MANAGER**—Copy Masters
Imagery p. 21
Question Support p. 25
Additional selection questions are provided for teachers on page 17.

## ANSWERS

## Comprehension

1. *The speaker's mother frowns because she disapproves of the rowdy dancing.*

2. *The mother's song is about scenes from her homeland of China, especially a scene of rain filling the waterlilies at Kuen Ming Lake.*

3. *The main setting of "Grape Sherbet" is a backyard in which a cookout is taking place on a Memorial Day afternoon. In stanza 2, the setting is a cemetery.*

## Text Analysis

COMMON CORE **RL 1,** **RL 4**

*Possible answers:*

4. ■ **COMMON CORE FOCUS** *Make Inferences* **"My Papa's Waltz":** *The father's battered knuckle (line 10) and dirty palm (line 14) imply that the father works with his hands.* **"I Ask My Mother to Sing":** *The words "I've never been in Peking" (line 5) imply that the mother and grandmother are singing about China and longing for their homeland.* **"Grape Sherbet":** *The words "he fights a smile" (lines 6–7) suggest that the father was proud of his dessert.*

5. *The experiences are alike in that both are happy memories of a lighthearted father. The experiences differ because in "Grape Sherbet," the speaker learns a life lesson from her father ("Now I see why / you bothered, / father"), but in "My Papa's Waltz," the speaker just has fun ("waltzed me off to bed / Still clinging to your shirt.").*

6. ● **COMMON CORE FOCUS** *Interpret Imagery* *The image of the waterlilies suggests that life is a cycle of happy and difficult events. The women's tears (line 13) reveal that their song of a happy memory also contains nostalgic sorrow.*

7. ● **COMMON CORE FOCUS** *Analyze Lyric Poetry* *The lyric qualities are that the poem is brief, personal, imaginative, and unified.*

---

## Comprehension

1. **Recall** In "My Papa's Waltz," why is the speaker's mother frowning?

2. **Clarify** In "I Ask My Mother to Sing," what is the mother's song about?

3. **Summarize** Describe the setting of "Grape Sherbet" as you visualize it.

## Text Analysis

● 4. **Make Inferences** Review the charts you made as you read. What key inferences helped you understand each poem? What clues did you use to make these inferences?

5. **Compare and Contrast** In "My Papa's Waltz" and "Grape Sherbet," the speakers recall childhood memories. How are their experiences with their fathers alike? How are they different? Cite evidence from each poem to support your answer.

● 6. **Interpret Imagery** Reread lines 9–12 in "I Ask My Mother to Sing." What idea is suggested by the image of the water lilies filling with water, spilling it into the lake, and filling up again? Consider the event described in the final stanza.

● 7. **Analyze Lyric Poetry** Review the definition of lyric poetry on page 749. Then identify the qualities of a lyric poem found in "I Ask My Mother to Sing."

8. **Make Judgments** In "My Papa's Waltz," how do you judge the father's behavior toward the **speaker**? Consider the word choices used in the descriptions as you cite evidence to support your answer.

## Text Criticism

9. **Critical Interpretations** In writing about "My Papa's Waltz," one critic remarked that Roethke reveals "something of his own joy, and bafflement, as the victim of his father's exuberant energy." Do you consider *victim* too harsh a word to describe the boy's part in the evening waltz? Why or why not?

### Who lives in your MEMORY?

What is your favorite way to share important family memories?

**COMMON CORE**

**RL 1** Cite textual evidence to support analysis of what the text says explicitly as well as inferences drawn from the text. **RL 4** Analyze the cumulative impact of specific word choices on meaning and tone.

---

8. *The father's behavior is loving and fun, even if he has whiskey on his breath and is a bit rough. The father "beats time" on the boy's head (line 13) in an affectionate way and puts his son to bed (line 15) in a tender way.*

## Text Criticism

*Possible answer:*

9. *The boy may be a "victim" in that he feels dizzy from the whiskey on his father's breath (lines 1–2) and has his ear scraped by his father's buckle (line 12). However, the scene seems to be a happy memory in which the boy participates willingly in the horseplay.*

### Who lives in your MEMORY?

Students might suggest storytelling during meals, creating scrapbooks or photo albums, or shooting video.

# Language

◆ **GRAMMAR AND STYLE: Use Descriptive Language**

One way to add interesting details to your writing is by using **participles** and **participial phrases.** A participle is a verb form that acts as an adjective. Present participles, as in "the *crying* baby," end in -*ing*, and past participles, as in "the freshly *washed* car," often end in -*ed*. A participial phrase consists of a participle and its modifiers and complements.

Here is an example of Rita Dove's use of participles in "Grape Sherbet":

> *Dad appears with his masterpiece—*
> *swirled snow, gelled light.* (lines 3–4)

Theodore Roethke uses a participial phrase in his poem "My Papa's Waltz":

> *You beat time on my head*
> *With a palm caked hard by dirt* (lines 13–14)

Notice how the revisions in blue use participles to make this first draft more descriptive. Revise your response to the prompt below by using a similar technique.

> **STUDENT MODEL**
>
>              *touching*
> Li-Young Lee describes a ~~sweet~~ scene between mother and son. The son
>                                    *, deceased but not forgotten*
> shows an appreciation for his mother's past and the memory of his father.

## READING-WRITING CONNECTION

Increase your understanding of the family poems by responding to this prompt. Then use the **revising tip** to improve your writing.

| **WRITING PROMPT** | **REVISING TIP** |
|---|---|
| **Extended Constructed Response: Analysis** What message does each poem convey about the relationship between parents and children? Write **three to five paragraphs** discussing the ways this relationship is depicted in the three poems. | Review your response. How effectively did you use participles and participial phrases to add interesting details to your writing? |

**Interactive Revision** THINK central

Go to **thinkcentral.com**.
KEYWORD: HML9-755

COMMON CORE

**W 4** Produce explanatory writing in which the style is appropriate to the purpose and audience. **L 1b** Use various types of phrases to add interest to writing.

## DIFFERENTIATED INSTRUCTION

### FOR STRUGGLING WRITERS

Suggest that students approach each poem in a single paragraph. Paragraphs should cite the main theme and then show how this theme is demonstrated by giving examples from the poem.

---

# Language

 COMMON CORE W 4, L 1b

◆ **GRAMMAR AND STYLE**

1. As students examine the student model, point out that participles add variety to descriptions. They can also enhance the rhythm in writing, especially in poetry.

2. For practice, write the verbs *chill* and *amaze* on the board. Have students give the present participle and past participle of each. Then have them create a phrase using one of the new forms. **Possible answer: chill:** *chilling, chilled; the sweet, chilled dessert;* **amaze:** *amazing, amazed; an amazing accomplishment*

**R** **RESOURCE MANAGER—Copy Master**
    Use Descriptive Language p. 26

**READING-WRITING CONNECTION**
Have students work in groups to state a theme for each poem. Have students freewrite individually about the parent/child relationship.

> **Writing Online**  THINK central
>
> The following tools are available online at **thinkcentral.com** and on **Write*Smart*** CD-ROM:
> • **Interactive Graphic Organizers**
> • **Interactive Student Models**
> • **Interactive Revision Lessons**
> For additional grammar instruction, see **GrammarNotes** on **thinkcentral.com**.

# Assess and Reteach

## Assess

**DIAGNOSTIC AND SELECTION TESTS**
    Selection Test A pp. 191–192
    Selection Test B/C pp. 193–194

**Interactive Selection Test** on **thinkcentral.com**

## Reteach

**Level Up Online Tutorials** on **thinkcentral.com**

**Reteaching Workshops** on **thinkcentral.com**
    Literature Lesson 18: Narrative vs. Lyric Poetry

    Literature Lesson 28: Imagery

    Reading Lesson 8: Making Inferences

    Writing Lesson 22: Elaborate with Sensory Details

## Focus and Motivate

### COMMON CORE FOCUS

**RL 4** Analyze the cumulative impact of specific word choices on meaning and tone. **RL 10** Read and comprehend poems. **W 1b** Develop claims fairly, citing evidence for each. **W 9a (RL 10)** Draw evidence from poems to support analysis and reflection.

### SUMMARIES

**"Spring is like a perhaps hand"** In this poem, the speaker likens the arrival of spring to a hand placing and rearranging things so that everything looks different.

**"Elegy for the Giant Tortoises"** In this elegy, the speaker laments the likely extinction of the giant tortoise. She has trouble visualizing them in the urban settings that surround her but is able to imagine them on the last day of their earthly existence.

**"Today"** In this poem, the speaker describes a spring day that is so perfect it fills him with a surging joy that makes him want to liberate everything around him.

Can you think
## OUT OF THE BOX?

Read the question aloud. Then ask students, "What situations inspire your sense of creativity? Why?" Extend the discussion by having students complete the *PRESENT* activity.

## Selection Resources

---

### Before Reading

Essential Course of Study **ECOS**

**Spring is like a perhaps hand**
Poem by E. E. Cummings

**Elegy for the Giant Tortoises**
Poem by Margaret Atwood

**Today**
Poem by Billy Collins

# Can you think
# OUT OF THE BOX?

**COMMON CORE**

**RL 4** Analyze the cumulative impact of specific word choices on meaning and tone. **RL 10** Read and comprehend poems.

Some of the best things in life are those unlike anything ever thought of before. Whether it's a brilliant invention (light bulb), a playful game (lizard boat), or an entertaining story (dog bites man), a new idea makes life more interesting and worthwhile. Creativity is a poet's bread and butter; a good poet always looks at things in a new way.

*PRESENT* With a small group, draw up a design for a new tool. Then share your invention with other groups and explain how it works.

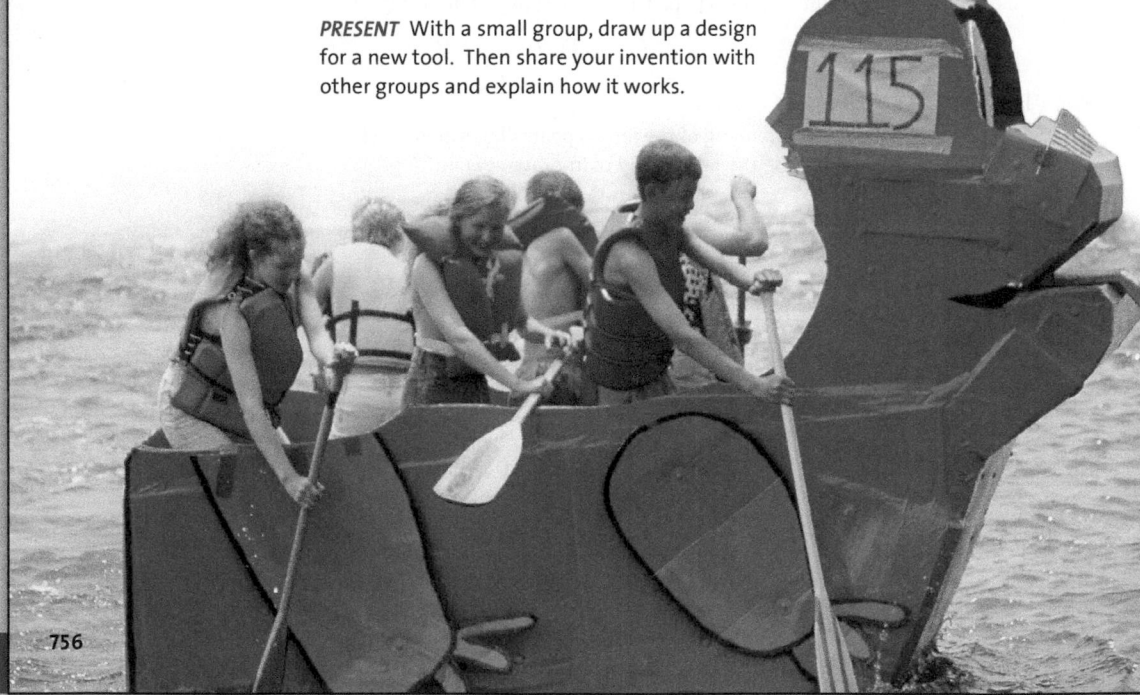

756

---

See resources on the **Teacher One Stop DVD-ROM** and on **thinkcentral.com**.

 **RESOURCE MANAGER UNIT 7**
Plan and Teach, pp. 29–36
Text Analysis and Reading
   Skill, pp. 37–40†

**DIAGNOSTIC AND SELECTION TESTS**
Selection Tests, pp. 195–198

**INTERACTIVE READER**

**ADAPTED INTERACTIVE READER**

**ELL ADAPTED INTERACTIVE READER**

**TECHNOLOGY**
- **Teacher One Stop DVD-ROM**
- **Student One Stop DVD-ROM**
- **PowerNotes DVD-ROM**
- **Audio Anthology CD**
- **GrammarNotes DVD-ROM**
- **Audio Tutor CD**
- **ExamView Test Generator**
  on the **Teacher One Stop**

### Video Trailer
 THINK central

Go to **thinkcentral.com** to preview the **Video Trailer** introducing this selection. Other features that support the selection include
- **PowerNotes** presentation
- **ThinkAloud** models to enhance comprehension
- **WordSharp** vocabulary tutorials
- interactive writing and grammar instruction

---

\* Resources for Differentiation      † Also in Spanish      ‡ Also in Haitian Creole and Vietnamese

## POETIC FORM: ELEGY

An **elegy** is a specific type of lyric poem. In an elegy, the speaker meditates about death, usually as a tribute to one who has recently died. Generally the **tone** is serious and the diction is formal. The second poem in this lesson is an elegy.

## TEXT ANALYSIS: DICTION

Poetry is known for its concise and exact use of language. When reading poetry, notice the **diction** (the choice of words) and the syntax (the order in which the words appear). For example, in "Today," Billy Collins describes his reaction to a spring day:

> . . . it made you want to throw
> open all the windows in the house

This particular use of words creates a sense of joy, freedom, and movement—more so than if he had simply said he felt like opening a window. Like any good poet, Collins has chosen his words carefully to create an intended effect. As you read these poems, notice the diction and the effects it creates.

## READING SKILL: PARAPHRASE

Sometimes poems can be difficult to understand because of an unusual sentence structure. When you **paraphrase** a line or stanza in a poem, you rephrase the poet's words with your own words. Unlike a summary, a paraphrase is not necessarily shorter than the original text; it is simply a recasting of the same ideas. To paraphrase, you should

- find the main ideas and important details
- think of simpler or more familiar ways of saying what the writer has written
- rewrite sentences in standard, subject-verb order

As you read each of the poems that follow, create a chart in which you paraphrase difficult passages.

### "Elegy for the Giant Tortoises"

| Original Wording | Paraphrase |
|---|---|
| "on the road where I stand they will materialize, / plodding past me in a straggling line / awkward without water" | They [the tortoises] will appear on the road where I stand, walking slowly by in a scattered line, looking clumsy because they are not in the water. |

 Complete the activities in your **Reader/Writer Notebook**.

## Meet the Authors

### E. E. Cummings
1894–1962

**Innovative and Popular**
Critics who praise Cummings rank him among the most innovative 20th-century poets. Believing in individuality and free expression, Cummings played with language, shaping it to fit his ideas. Though one of the most experimental of poets, he was enormously popular with the general public.

### Margaret Atwood
born 1939

**Canada's Treasure**
Margaret Atwood, a poet, novelist, essayist, and short story writer, has been called "a national heroine of the arts" in her native Canada. Her novels feature female characters searching for identity in a confusing and often threatening world. She is especially popular in Canada, where she has gained the status usually accorded only to movie stars and musicians.

### Billy Collins
born 1941

**"Most Popular Poet in America"**
Billy Collins's poetry appeals to a wide and ever-growing audience: high school students, fellow poets, literary critics, and general readers. According to one critic, "With his books selling briskly and his readings packing them in, Mr. Collins is the most popular poet in America."

**Authors Online**

**THINK** central

Go to thinkcentral.com. KEYWORD: HML9-757

757

## Teach

TEXT ANALYSIS
COMMON CORE
RL 4

### ● *Model the Skill:* DICTION

For instructional support, write these lines on the board, and read them aloud:

> In the museum of glass flowers
> nature's clock is stilled: forever
> flowers bud, arch, stretch, bloom
> this year, next year, a hundred years
> inside their cases: airless, dustless,
> colors unfading, leaves unwilted,
> upturned pollen faces
> forever unkissed by sun.

Identify the effect of the words *stilled, forever, airless, dustless, unfading, unwilted,* and *unkissed.* Point out that the words convey a sense of timelessness, permanence, and perhaps staleness.

**GUIDED PRACTICE** Ask students to identify the effect of the words *bud, arch, stretch,* and *bloom.*

READING SKILL
COMMON CORE
RL 10

### ■ *Model the Skill:* PARAPHRASE

Paraphrase the lines from the poem on the board. At the natural history museum, flowers made of glass look as though they are growing and changing, but, in fact, they don't change at all.

**GUIDED PRACTICE** Have students paraphrase another short poem.

**R** RESOURCE MANAGER—Copy Master Paraphrase p. 39 (for student use while reading the selection)

## DIFFERENTIATED INSTRUCTION

### FOR STRUGGLING READERS

**Literary Terms** Explain that the word *elegy* comes from the ancient Greek *elegos*, which means "song of mourning." Note that "mourning" is the process by which people come to terms with the death of someone they loved or admired. Explain that "Elegy for the Giant Tortoises" expresses sadness not about the death of a person but about the possible loss of a species of animals.

## READ WITH A PURPOSE

*Help students set a purpose for reading. Ask students to think about how each poem reflects "out of the box" thinking. Tell students to consider content, style, and form.*

### TEXT ANALYSIS

COMMON CORE

RL 4

**Ⓐ Model the Skill: DICTION**

Explain that the word *inch* is used not in a literal sense but rather to connote a measure or increment small enough to be barely noticeable.

***Possible answer:*** *The words* fraction *and* inch *suggest small things or amounts; their use suggests that spring makes everything look new and different while making only small changes.*

## REVISIT THE BIG QUESTION

### Can you think OUT OF THE BOX?

**Discuss** How does Cummings's creative use of capitalization and punctuation help convey meaning? ***Possible answer:*** *By capitalizing "spring" and "hand" in one place and not another, Cummings changes the emphasis. He also adds emphasis to the words "nowhere," "new," and "old." By using no punctuation until the end of the last line, Cummings creates a breathless, nonstop rhythm that echoes the changes that the poem is describing.*

# Spring  is like a perhaps hand

E. E. Cummings

Spring is like a perhaps hand
(which comes carefully
out of Nowhere) arranging
a window, into which people look (while
5 people stare
arranging and changing placing
carefully there a strange
thing and a known thing here) and

changing everything carefully

10 spring is like a perhaps
Hand in a window
(carefully to
and fro moving New and
Old things, while
15 people stare carefully
moving a perhaps
fraction of flower here placing
an inch of air there) and Ⓐ

without breaking anything.

**Analyze Visuals ▶**

What springlike elements do you find in this image? State your answer in terms of subject matter, color, shape, and texture.

**Ⓐ DICTION**
Reread lines 16–18. What do the words *fraction* and *inch* suggest about the concept of spring presented in the poem?

Untitled (2001), Laura Owens. Watercolor, color pencil, and photo on paper, 14″ × 10″. Courtesy Gavin Brown's enterprise, New York (LO 185d).

## DIFFERENTIATED INSTRUCTION

### FOR ENGLISH LANGUAGE LEARNERS

**Comprehension: Content** Create and supply small groups with visual outlines that contain a hand reaching in to arrange a picture window. Tell students to cut images from magazines that correspond with words in the poem and to paste these images in collage fashion into the visual outlines. Have each group present its collage to the class.

**Develop Reading Fluency: Options for Reading** Read the poem aloud, stressing pacing and intonation as you read the parenthetical lines. Then have pairs of students reread the poem, with one student reading the parts that are outside the parentheses and the other student reading the parts that are inside the parentheses. Have students discuss how the two parts work together.

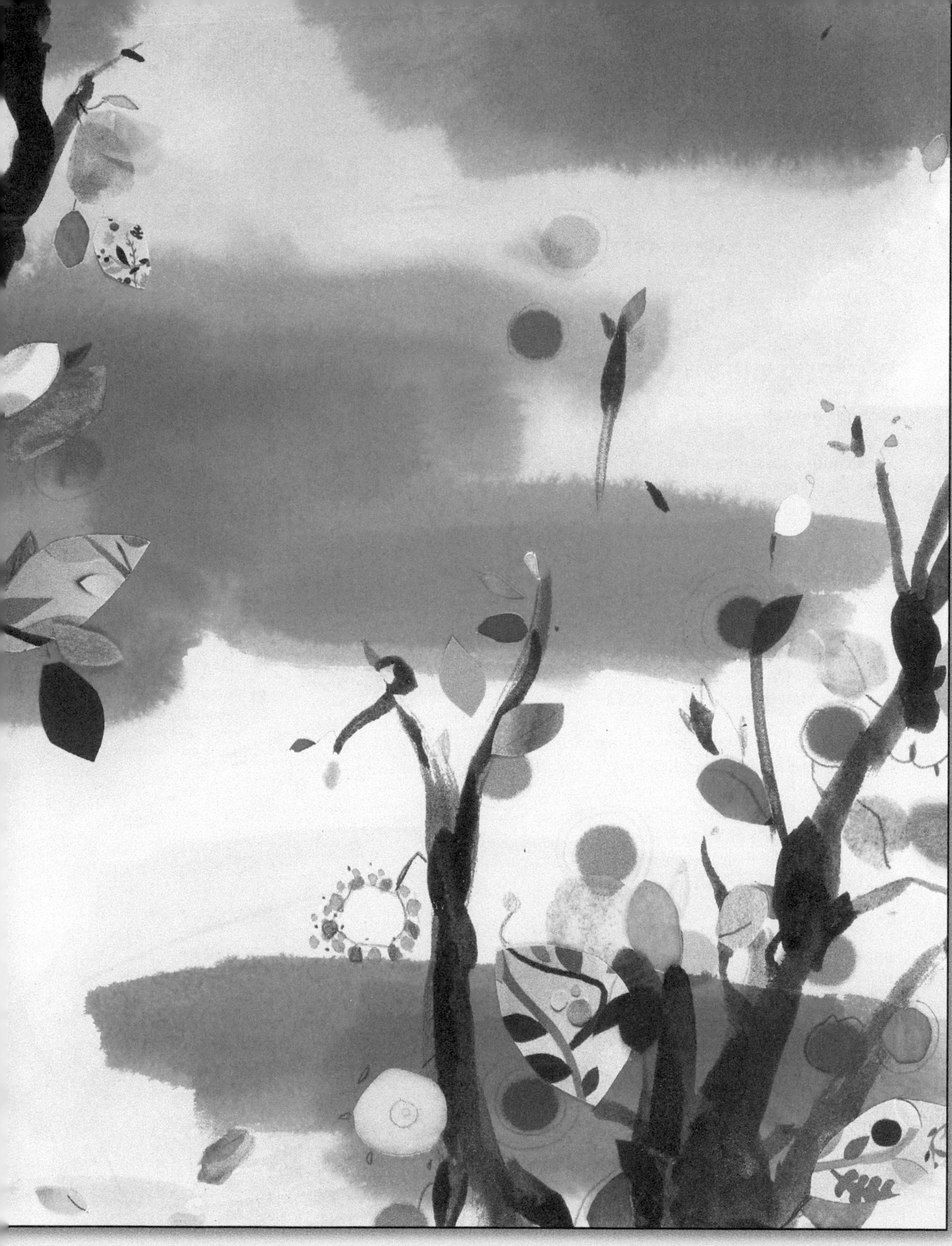

## Reading Support

This selection on **thinkcentral.com** includes embedded **ThinkAloud** models–students "thinking aloud" about the story to model the kinds of questions a good reader would ask about a selection.

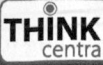

## Analyze Visuals

***Possible answers:*** *Springlike elements in the painting include trees and leaves rendered in vibrant shades of pink, yellow, blue, orange, and brown; leaf and branch shapes; and textures that suggest clouds, sky, and water.*

**About the Art** California artist Laura Owens (b. 1970) is inspired by many sources, including film, computer, and television imagery. Her creative rendering of color is evident in this mixed-media painting, whose delicate and vivid hues suggest the spirit of springtime.

## TIERED DISCUSSION PROMPTS

Draw students' attention to lines 1–9. Use these prompts to help students understand the comparisons the speaker makes:

**Connect** Describe how something that you regularly observe in nature, such as a garden or a tree, changes from the last days of winter to the first days of spring. ***Possible answer:*** *Students might describe the brightening of colors and the way flowers and the leaves on trees suddenly appear.*

**Analyze** According to the speaker, in what ways is spring is like a hand? ***Possible answer:*** *Like a hand, spring arranges, changes, and places things. Both can rearrange things so that they appear entirely different. Moreover, a hand can move things quietly, gently, gradually, and delicately, much as spring gradually and delicately changes the world of nature.*

**Synthesize** Explain how Cummings arranges and rearranges his words to reinforce the idea of his comparison. ***Possible answer:*** *By arranging his words in unusual ways, Cummings makes his words spring to life, just as nature does in spring. The poet is "like a perhaps hand" that rearranges the conventional placement of words.*

### FOR STRUGGLING READERS

**Comprehension Support**

- Explain that Cummings often uses parts of speech in unconventional ways. For example, the adverb *perhaps* is used as an adjective to modify the noun *hand*. Discuss possible reasons for using *perhaps* as an adjective. Ask students to think of conventional adjectives that a poet might have used instead (*light, hesitant, unsure*).
- Point out Cummings's repetition of the adverb *carefully* (lines 2, 7, 9, and 15). Explain that in line 15, *carefully* is modifying *moving* in line 16, not *stare* in line 15. Ask students why Cummings might have chosen to break line 15 after *carefully* instead of *stare*. ***Possible answer:*** *He is being playful. By breaking the line after carefully, he keeps the reader off-balance, because at first we assume that "people are staring carefully."*

Prereading for this poem is found on page 756.

## READING SKILL

**COMMON CORE** RL 10

### B Model the Skill: PARAPHRASE

Model for students how to substitute synonyms for *peripheries*, such as *margins, edges, borders, fringes*. Then, choose the synonym that makes sense within this context. Remind students to utilize the charts they began on page 757.

*Possible answer:* In subway stations and parks, I try to visualize the tortoises. However, it's as if they move to the edges of my eyes, keeping me from seeing them. Yet, on their "last day" of existence, that's where they'll be. I can already imagine the event.

## POETIC FORM

**COMMON CORE** RL 4

### C ELEGY

*Possible answer:* Religious language is appropriate in an elegy because, as a meditation about death, an elegy prompts religious thoughts (about the meaning of life and death) and often takes place in a religious setting.

## Analyze Visuals

**Activity** Ask students what the image of the turtle in the print adds to their appreciation of the poem. *Possible answer: The image emphasizes how big and ponderous the related giant tortoise is, and how helpless, sad, and defenseless it would be in the face of extinction. The unusual color of the background suggests that the turtle in the print, like the one in the poem, is from the artist's imagination.*

**About the Art** Andy Warhol (1928–1987) is well known for his art of everyday objects. The starkly contrasting and unreal colors in this print help grab the viewer's attention and convey the strangeness of this creature.

# Elegy for the GIANT TORTOISES

### MARGARET ATWOOD

*Sea Turtle* (about 1985), Andy Warhol. Synthetic polymer paint and silkscreen ink on canvas, 42" × 50". © Art Resource, New York/2007 Andy Warhol Foundation for the Visual Arts/Artists Rights Society (ARS), New York.

Let others pray for the passenger pigeon
the dodo, the whooping crane,[1] the eskimo:
everyone must specialize

I will confine myself to a meditation
5 upon the giant tortoises
withering finally on a remote island.

I concentrate in subway stations,
in parks, I can't quite see them,
they move to the peripheries of my eyes

10 but on the last day they will be there;
already the event
like a wave travelling shapes vision:

on the road where I stand they will materialize,
plodding past me in a straggling line
15 awkward without water

their small heads pondering
from side to side, their useless armour
sadder than tanks and history,

in their closed gaze ocean and sunlight paralysed,
20 lumbering up the steps, under the archways
toward the square glass altars

where the brittle gods are kept,
the relics of what we have destroyed,
our holy and obsolete symbols.

**B PARAPHRASE**
Paraphrase lines 7–12. What does "the last day" refer to?

**C ELEGY**
Reread lines 20–24. Notice the religious language—*altars, gods, relics,* and *holy.* Why is such language appropriate in an elegy?

---

1. **the passenger pigeon / the dodo, the whooping crane:** extinct or extremely endangered birds.

## DIFFERENTIATED INSTRUCTION

### FOR STRUGGLING READERS

**Comprehension Support** Remind students that there is no need to pause at the end of a line when reading poetry unless there is punctuation or a natural stopping point.

Read the poem aloud a few lines at a time, and have students repeat the lines with the same intonation and rhythm.

### FOR ADVANCED LEARNERS/PRE–AP

**Irony** Have students discuss what the speaker means when she says, "their useless armour / sadder than tanks and history" (lines 17–18). *Example: Armor is used for defense, but the tortoises are defenseless against their extinction, just as seemingly invincible armies (and their tanks) have been defeated.* Then have students identify the ultimate irony in the poem. *Example: After destroying the tortoises, we then honor and preserve them as relics in museum displays.*

# Today

**Billy Collins**

If ever there were a spring day so perfect,
so uplifted by a warm intermittent breeze

that it made you want to throw
open all the windows in the house

5   and unlatch the door to the canary's cage,
indeed, rip the little door from its jamb,

a day when the cool brick paths
and the garden bursting with peonies

seemed so etched in sunlight
10  that you felt like taking

a hammer to the glass paperweight
on the living room end table,

releasing the inhabitants
from their snow-covered cottage

15  so they could walk out,
holding hands and squinting

into this larger dome of blue and white,
well, today is just that kind of day.

*Flower* (1964), Andy Warhol. Screenprint printed on white paper, 23″ × 23″.
© 2007 Andy Warhol Foundation for the Visual Arts/Artists Rights Society
(ARS), New York. © Art Resource, New York.

**D DICTION**
Reread lines 13–17. What
words does the speaker
use to characterize the
inhabitants of the glass
paperweight? What
sense or feeling is evoked
by this language?

---

## Analyze Visuals

**Activity** Ask students how the print of the flowers conveys the imagery of the poem. *Possible answer: The sharp color contrast makes the flowers appear to be bursting from the grass, just as the peonies in the poem are bursting from the garden (line 8). The crisp outlines of the flowers also make them appear to be "etched in sunlight" (line 9).*

### REVISIT THE BIG QUESTION

## Can you think
# OUT OF THE BOX?

**Discuss** The speaker says that the day is so perfect that it makes you feel like "taking a hammer to the glass paperweight . . . releasing the inhabitants" (lines 10–13). How is this a creative way to describe a perfect day? *Possible answer: It is unusual to feel like smashing something in response to a perfect day. The speaker's violent image shows he can't bear the idea of any creature being confined and unable to enjoy the day.*

---

**TEXT ANALYSIS**   COMMON CORE   RL 4

**D DICTION**

*Possible answer:* The speaker uses the words "holding hands and squinting / into this larger dome of blue and white" to characterize the inhabitants of the paperweight. The language evokes a sense of innocence and discovery before a vast new world.

---

### FOR STRUGGLING READERS

**Comprehension Support** Ask students how many sentences there are in the poem (*one*). Have a capable reader read aloud the first two stanzas and the last line of the poem to simplify structure and meaning.

### FOR ENGLISH LANGUAGE LEARNERS

**Culture: Clarify** Focus on the image of the glass paperweight and its inhabitants (lines 10–14). Ask students if they have seen such a paperweight. If not, you may want to bring in one with "inhabitants" and ask students to imagine them walking out of their small dome into the larger world.

### SELECTION WRAP–UP

**READ WITH A PURPOSE** Now that students have finished reading the poems, have them compare them. How does each poem represent "out of the box" thinking? *Possible answer: Cummings's poem includes unconventional language and grammar usage; Atwood's poem utilizes the elegiac form in an unconventional way; Collins's poem describes people acting in unconventional ways.*

**MAGAZINE ARTICLE** Several poets in this unit have served as U.S. poet laureate. Read the following article to learn about this honorable and worthwhile position.

## TIERED DISCUSSION PROMPTS

Use these prompts to help students understand the connection between poetry and the role of the Poet Laureate:

**Connect** Have you ever felt "terrified" of poetry, as Rita Dove claims many people are? Why or why not? If so, do you feel this way now? Explain your answer. *Encourage students to refer to specific poems in their responses.*

**Analyze** Billy Collins encourages students to read poems aloud so they can "be simply enjoyed—not analyzed or interpreted." Do you think that it is possible to enjoy a poem fully without analyzing or interpreting it? Why or why not? *Some students might argue that a poem is best enjoyed as an immediate experience, without stopping to think about meanings. Other students might argue that poetry can be difficult to understand, and that it is hard to enjoy something you don't completely "get." Analyzing and interpreting a poem would therefore increase your enjoyment of it.*

**Evaluate** What can poets do to make poetry more popular? Are the kinds of things that Rita Dove and Billy Collins do effective? Give reasons for your answers. *Most students will say that visiting schools, giving readings, and hosting Web sites are all good ways to spread an appreciation and understanding of poetry. Students may also mention poetry slams and online magazines. Encourage students to be creative in thinking of other things poets might do to reach a wider audience.*

# U.S. POET LAUREATES

# Getting the Word Out

What should be the job of a national poet? Many readers suspect poets of being deliberately mysterious—of placing a hidden meaning behind a smokescreen of random line breaks and cryptic symbols. If that were true, then wouldn't a national poet keep these secrets under lock and key?

Not so. Every year since 1937, the U.S. Library of Congress has appointed a poet laureate to serve as the national poet. Apart from a few official duties, the poet is encouraged to continue to develop his or her own projects as well as promote the general appreciation of poetry. Some poet laureates have taken seriously their mission to dispel the poetry mystique.

**Rita Dove,** Poet Laureate from 1993–1995, visited schools and gave readings, presenting her complex poems in a down-to-earth manner.

"I really began to think about how poetry can reach every person. . . . If I can reduce the anxiety level of the audience out there and just read the poem as if it's an everyday thing . . . people would come up and say, 'I didn't realize poetry could be like that!' They [are] just terrified, that's all."

**Billy Collins,** Poet Laureate from 2001–2003, developed "Poetry 180," a website (www.loc.gov/poetry/180) featuring one poem for each day of the school year. He encourages students and teachers to read aloud a poem a day, with the strict rule that the poems are to be simply enjoyed—not analyzed or interpreted. Collins even helped establish a poetry channel for Delta Airlines.

"Well, there is always a temptation just to go to Washington and sit in this office and blow smoke rings for a year while I look out at the Capitol. But because of the excessive activism of my predecessors, it seems that an obligation falls my way to get out and light poetry bonfires and to spread the word of poetry."

## DIFFERENTIATED INSTRUCTION

### FOR RELUCTANT READERS

Tell students to imagine that Congress has appointed them U.S. Poet Laureates and charged them with the responsibility of promoting a general appreciation of poetry. Have small student groups work to together to draft proposals for poetry projects such as Poetry 180. Have each group present its proposal to the class. Then, choose one project to implement as a class.

## Comprehension

1. **Recall** When does the speaker of "Elegy for the Giant Tortoises" expect to actually see these reptiles?

2. **Clarify** In "Today," what does "this larger dome" refer to?

3. **Clarify** What is the hand in "Spring is like a perhaps hand" doing?

## Text Analysis

● 4. **Paraphrase** Review your paraphrasing charts. Then read aloud one of your paraphrases and the original passage. Which version has the stronger impact?

● 5. **Examine Diction** What words and phrases in each poem strike you as vivid or unusual? What effect do they have on your understanding of the poem?

● 6. **Analyze an Elegy** Review the definition of an elegy on page 757. What characteristics of an elegy are found in "Elegy for the Giant Tortoises"? Why might Atwood have chosen this form for a poem about an endangered species?

7. **Draw Conclusions** In "Spring is like a perhaps hand," what qualities of spring does the **speaker** emphasize?

8. **Compare and Contrast** Tone is an expression of the writer's attitude toward his or her subject. For each poem, choose an adjective that best describes the tone, such as *bitter, sad, lighthearted,* or *playful.* Then list the words and phrases in each poem that help convey the tone. Which two poems are most different in tone? Explain your answer.

*"Spring is like a perhaps hand"*

Tone: _____

Words and Phrases:
- 
- 
- 

### READING-WRITING CONNECTION

| WRITING PROMPT | REVISING TIP |
|---|---|
| **Extended Constructed Response: Opinion** Which of the poems displays the most **creativity** in its treatment of its subject? Write **three to five paragraphs**, citing evidence to support your view. | Review your response. Did you evaluate each poem in terms of its creativity? Did you present supporting evidence such as diction, imagery, and figurative language? If not, revise your response. |

### Can you THINK OUT OF THE BOX?

Why is innovative thinking so important?

---

# Practice and Apply

For preliminary support of post-reading questions, use these copy masters:

 **RESOURCE MANAGER—Copy Masters**
Diction p. 37
Question Support p. 41

Additional selection questions are provided for teachers on page 33.

## ANSWERS

## Comprehension

1. *She expects to see the tortoises on their last day of existence.*

2. *It refers to the sky above the real world.*

3. *The hand is arranging and placing the elements of spring.*

## Text Analysis

COMMON CORE **RL 4, RL 10**

*Possible answers:*

4. ■ **COMMON CORE FOCUS** *Paraphrase Answers will vary, but should show an understanding of the passage's meaning.*

5. ● **COMMON CORE FOCUS** *Examine Diction In "Spring . . ." vivid and unusual phrases include "inch of air." In "Elegy . . ." the phrase "sadder than tanks and history" is vivid. In "Today" the image of "taking a hammer to the glass paperweight" is forceful.*

6. ● **COMMON CORE FOCUS** *Analyze an Elegy An elegy is about death, and "Elegy . . ." is about the impending death of an entire species.*

7. *The speaker emphasizes the novelty,*

---

# Assess and Reteach

## Assess

**DIAGNOSTIC AND SELECTION TESTS**
Selection Test A pp. 195–196
Selection Test B/C pp. 197–198

**Interactive Selection Test** on **thinkcentral.com**

**Reteaching Worksheets** on **thinkcentral.com**
Literature Lesson 16: Ode and Elegy

---

*subtlety, and delicacy of spring.*

8. *"Spring": playful; "fraction of flower"; "Elegy": somber; "obsolete symbols"; "Today": joyful; "releasing the inhabitants." "Elegy . . ." and "Today" are the most different in tone.*

### READING-WRITING CONNECTION

COMMON CORE **W 1b, W 9**

To prepare for the assignment, have students list original or unusual uses of language from each poem. Have students use these examples to support their answers.

Can you think **OUT OF THE BOX?** *Possible answer: Innovative thinking breeds creativity and problem solving.*

## Focus and Motivate

### ⟨ COMMON CORE FOCUS

**RL 10** Read and comprehend poems.
**W 5** Strengthen writing by revising, focusing on what is most significant for a specific purpose.
**W 10** Write over shorter time frames for a range of tasks and purposes. **L 4** Determine or clarify the meaning of multiple-meaning words.

### SUMMARIES

**"400-Meter Free Style"** Maxine Kumin's concrete poem captures the simple, economical movements of a swimmer competing in a race, concentrating his efforts on achieving the fastest possible time.

**"Bodybuilders' Contest"** Wislawa Szymborska's humorous poem focuses on a muscular bodybuilder posing for, and winning, a competition.

### What makes a great
# COMPETITOR?

Introduce the question. Encourage students to explore the idea that a competitor's success usually involves some combination of talent, hard work, and luck. Have students complete the *DISCUSS* activity, giving reasons for the qualities they list. Then try to arrive at a class consensus regarding the most important qualities of a great competitor.

## Selection Resources

---

## 400-Meter Free Style
Poem by Maxine Kumin

## Bodybuilders' Contest
Poem by Wislawa Szymborska

# What makes a great
# COMPETITOR?

### ⟨ COMMON CORE

**RL 10** Read and comprehend poems. **L 4** Determine or clarify the meaning of multiple-meaning words.

Does a great competitor's success mainly rely on natural talent? hard work? luck? The next two poems describe the experiences of two athletes pursuing athletic achievement.

**DISCUSS** With a partner, discuss your favorite kinds of competition. Then generate a list of qualities you think great competitors have in common. Present your list to other pairs to compare your ideas.

Qualities of a Great Competitor

1.
2.
3.
4.
5.

764

---

*See resources on the **Teacher One Stop DVD-ROM** and on <u>thinkcentral.com</u>.*

**R** **RESOURCE MANAGER UNIT 7**
Plan and Teach, pp. 43–50
Text Analysis and Reading
Skill, pp. 51–54†

**DIAGNOSTIC AND SELECTION TESTS**
Selection Tests, pp. 199–202

**BEST PRACTICES TOOLKIT**
Jigsaw Reading, p. A1
Cluster Diagram, p. B18
Read-and-Say-Something, p. D3

**TECHNOLOGY**
⌾ **Teacher One Stop DVD-ROM**
⌾ **Student One Stop DVD-ROM**
⌾ **Audio Anthology CD**
⌾ **GrammarNotes DVD-ROM**
⌾ **ExamView Test Generator**
  on the **Teacher One Stop**

---

\* Resources for Differentiation     † Also in Spanish     ‡ Also in Haitian Creole and Vietnamese

● **POETIC FORM: CONCRETE POETRY**

Some poets go beyond the usual structural elements of line and stanza to write concrete poems. A **concrete poem** is one in which the poet uses visible shape to create a picture related to the poem's subject. For example, a concrete poem about stars might be written in the shape of a star. One of the poems you're about to read, "400-Meter Free Style," is a concrete poem.

● **TEXT ANALYSIS: FORM**

In poetry, **form** is the arrangement of words on a page. Poets use form deliberately to organize their thoughts, to help create rhythm, and to emphasize ideas and images. The two basic elements of form in poetry are **lines** and **stanzas.**

- **Lines:** The lines of a poem may be long or short. Poets manipulate line length to emphasize words and ideas and to establish rhythm.

- **Stanzas:** The lines of a poem may be grouped together in clusters known as stanzas. Poets use stanzas to organize important ideas and, in some cases, to develop rhyme schemes.

To understand how form can create a sense of rhythm in a poem, ask yourself the following questions:

- How long are the lines?

- Do the lines rhyme?

- Do the sentences always end at the end of a line?

- How many lines are in each stanza?

The two poems you are about to read have very different forms. "Bodybuilders' Contest" contains **couplets,** rhyming pairs of lines of equal length. "400-Meter Free Style," on the other hand, contains no rhyme but still has a strong rhythm. In each case, the form supports the poet's ideas.

As you read the poems, notice the elements of form and how they affect meaning and support the poet's ideas.

● **READING STRATEGY: CONNECT**

The poems you read will be more meaningful if you **connect** your own experiences to the ideas and feelings they express. For example, you might be on a swim team, or perhaps you have watched a swim meet like the one described in "400-Meter Free Style." Your own experience can help you understand the ideas expressed. As you read the following poems, make use of this strategy whenever appropriate.

 Complete the activities in your **Reader/Writer Notebook.**

## Meet the Authors

### Maxine Kumin
**born 1925**

**Late Bloomer**
Maxine Kumin didn't truly begin to write poetry until she was in her 30s. She did, however, have a few false starts before this. As a college freshman, she gave some of her poems to an instructor for comments. He returned the poems with a note that read, "Say it with flowers, but … don't try to write poems." Kumin didn't write poetry again for six years.

**Despite Bad Advice**
Kumin published her first poetry collection in 1961. Since then, she has published 14 volumes of poetry, as well as novels, essays, and children's books. She received a Pulitzer Prize in 1973 and was U.S. poet laureate from 1981 to 1982.

### Wislawa Szymborska
**born 1923**

**Poland's Quiet Poet**
Wislawa Szymborska was a renowned poet in her native Poland for many years before she became known in other countries. She was awarded the Nobel Prize in literature in 1996, which brought her international fame. Being thrust into the spotlight made the shy poet very uncomfortable. Today she lives quietly in Poland, where she continues to write and publish her poetry.

**THINK** central

**Authors Online**
Go to thinkcentral.com. KEYWORD: HML9-765

765

---

# Teach

**POETIC FORM** | **COMMON CORE** | **RL 10**

● ***Model the Skill:* CONCRETE POETRY**

For instructional support, write these lines of poetry on the board, and then read them aloud:

> **The Runner**
> A few more yards, she told herself,
>     her hunger for air was dire;
> I'm nearly there, she urged herself,
>     breathless
>         gasping
>             lungs on fire

Discuss how the lines of the poem help to create rhythm and emphasize the image of the runner. *The three short lines at the end seem to mimic the breathless pace of the runner, as if she doesn't have enough breath to speak one long line and is actually gasping the words. The way these short lines are stretched from left to right across the page also suggests the image of a runner in motion.*

**GUIDED PRACTICE** Ask students how the rhythm of this example would change if the poet had used one long line instead of three short ones.

**READING STRATEGY** | **COMMON CORE** | **RL 10**

■ ***Model the Skill:* CONNECT**

Reread the lines of poetry you wrote on the board for the **POETIC FORM** activity. Explain what experiences help you connect to the action and sensations that the poet describes.

**GUIDED PRACTICE** Elicit examples of poems or songs that students have connected to because of their own experiences.

**R** RESOURCE MANAGER—Copy Master Connect p. 53 (for student use while reading the selection)

---

## DIFFERENTIATED INSTRUCTION

### FOR STRUGGLING READERS

**Concept Support** Explore with students the idea that form helps to create rhythm. Read aloud a succession of short sentences. Then read aloud several long, flowing sentences. (If the text is available, have students follow along as you read.) Discuss how sentence length affects rhythm. Then ask why a writer might use one rhythm to describe a beautiful forest, for example, but a different rhythm to describe a battle scene.

**Concept Support** To help students connect with what they read, encourage them to use their imagination and their five senses to project themselves into a given situation. For example, if they are reading about a swimmer, they should imagine themselves in the swimmer's place and ask themselves, "What am I seeing? hearing? feeling?" Pose several situations to students, and help them project themselves into each one.

## READ WITH A PURPOSE

*Help students set a purpose for reading. Tell them to consider the conflict in each of the poems. Are the conflicts internal or external? How would students describe each conflict?*

---

**TEXT ANALYSIS**    COMMON CORE   RL 10

 **FORM**

*Possible answer: The poem's lines have endings in the same sense that each completed lap of the swimming pool has an "ending"—a brief pause that also marks the beginning of the next lap.*

---

**READING STRATEGY**    COMMON CORE   RL 10

 *Model the Skill:* **CONNECT**

Model for students how to connect to a poem by telling about a goal that captured your undivided attention.

*Students' responses should reflect the understanding that total concentration on a goal can maximize the likelihood of achieving that goal, while distractions can hamper performance.*

---

## REVISIT THE BIG QUESTION

## What makes a great COMPETITOR?

**Discuss** Draw students' attention to lines 13–29. How do these lines convey the amount of preparation this competitor has done for the race? *Possible answer: Through hard work, the competitor has "schooled out all extravagance" (line 17), meaning that there are no wasted movements. All of the swimmer's energy is applied toward the achievement of his goal.*

---

# 400-Meter Free Style

## Maxine Kumin

THE GUN full swing the swimmer catapults[1] and cracks

         s
         i
         x

5   feet away onto that perfect glass he catches at   **A**
  a
  n
  d

throws behind him scoop after scoop cunningly moving

10                t
               h
               e

water back to move him forward. Thrift is his wonderful
s
15 e
  c

ret; he has schooled out all extravagance. No muscle   **B**
           r
           i
20            p

ples without compensation wrist cock to heel snap to
h
i
s

25   mobile mouth that siphons[2] in the air that nurtures
              h
              i
              m

at half an inch above sea level so to speak.

---

1. **catapults** (kăt′ə-pŭlts′): springs.
2. **siphons** (sī′fənz): draws in, as if with a tube.

**A** **FORM**
Would you say that the **lines** in this poem have endings, or does the poem consist of one long line? Explain.

**B** **CONNECT**
The swimmer is completely focused on moving through the water as quickly and efficiently as possible. Think about a time when all your attention was focused on a single goal. Did it help you attain the goal?

---

## DIFFERENTIATED INSTRUCTION

**FOR ENGLISH LANGUAGE LEARNERS**

**Figurative Language** Point out to students that the word *glass* is used in the poem to mean swimming pool water, suggesting that the water is shiny like glass. Have students work in pairs to list other items that they might describe using the word *glass* such as fingernail polish, car paint, or cellophane wrap.

**Develop Reading Fluency: Options for Reading** Have students listen to "400-Meter Free Style" on the *Audio Anthology CD* as they read along silently. Ask students why they think the poem is displayed on the page the way it is. Next, read the poem aloud a sentence at a time. Have students repeat what you have read, using the same intonation and rhythm.

Additionally, distribute the copy master and have students work in pairs or groups to develop fluency.

**R**   **RESOURCE MANAGER—Copy Master**
Reading Fluency p. 56

30  T
    h
    e
    astonishing   whites   of   the   soles   of   his   feet   rise
                                                                   a
35                                                                 n
                                                                   d
    salute  us on the turns.  He  flips,  converts,  and  is  gone
    a
    l
40  l
    in one. We watch him for signs. His arms are steady at
                                                          t
                                                          h
                                                          e
45  catch, his cadent[3] feet tick in the stretch, they know
    t
    h
    e
    lesson well. Lungs know, too; he does not list for
50                                                    a
                                                      i
                                                      r
    he drives along on little sips carefully expended
    b
55  u
    t
    that plum red heart pumps hard cries hurt how soon
                                                       i
                                                       t
                                                       s
60  near one more and makes its final surge  Time: 4:25:9 **C**

---

3. **cadent** (kād'nt): moving in a rhythmic pattern, or cadence.

Prereading for this poem is found on page 764.

## Analyze Visuals

*Possible answer: The painting suggests strength, power, and robust health.*

**About the Art** Asian Pacific American artist Byron Spicer grew up in San Francisco in the 1960s and 1970s. The energy and diversity of the city influenced and inspired his imaginative artwork. Spicer paints numerous images at the same time and then assembles them in three-dimensional layers onto one panel. *Municipal Bonds* depicts a muscular physique suggestive of Szymborska's bodybuilder.

---

**TEXT ANALYSIS**

 *Model the Skill:* **FORM**

**COMMON CORE**
**RL 10**

Model how to use a Cluster Diagram to visualize the ideas presented in each of the three stanzas.

*Possible answer: The poet divides her poem into three stanzas. The first stanza focuses on the bodybuilder's rippling muscles—the "ocean of his torso" (line 2). The second stanza describes his choreographed onstage movements for the contest. The third stanza reveals that he wins the competition.*

 **BEST PRACTICES TOOLKIT—Transparency**
Cluster Diagram p. B18

---

## SELECTION WRAP–UP

**READ WITH A PURPOSE** Now that students have finished reading the selections, have them compare and contrast the poems. What is the conflict in each poem? *Possible answer: In the first poem, the swimmer battles internally against the weaknesses of his body and externally against the water and other swimmers. In the second poem, the bodybuilder battles externally against imagined wildlife and other bodybuilders.*

## INDEPENDENT READING

Students interested in reading poems about sports might enjoy *Extra Innings: Baseball Poems* edited by Lee Bennett Hopkins and illustrated by Scott Medlock.

---

# BODYBUILDERS' CONTEST

### Wislawa Szymborska

*Municipal Bonds* (2004), Byron Spicer. Mixed media, 45″ × 45″. © Byron Spicer.

From scalp to sole, all muscles in slow motion.
The ocean of his torso drips with lotion.
The king of all is he who preens[1] and wrestles
with sinews twisted into monstrous pretzels.

5  Onstage, he grapples with a grizzly bear
the deadlier for not really being there.
Three unseen panthers are in turn laid low,
each with one smoothly choreographed[2] blow.

He grunts while showing his poses and paces.
10  His back alone has twenty different faces.
The mammoth fist he raises as he wins
is tribute to the force of vitamins. ⓓ

*Translated by Stanislaw Baranczak and Clare Cavanagh*

---

1. **preens:** makes himself attractive and then shows off his appearance.
2. **choreographed** (kôr′ē-ə-grăft′): with the movements planned and arranged, as in a dance.

▲ **Analyze Visuals**

What qualities of a bodybuilder are reflected in the painting? Cite details.

ⓓ **FORM**
Notice the form of this poem. How has the poet used **stanzas** to organize her ideas?

**768** UNIT 7: THE LANGUAGE OF POETRY

---

## DIFFERENTIATED INSTRUCTION

### FOR STRUGGLING READERS

**Support Comprehension** Have students use the Read-and-Say-Something strategy to analyze the meaning and explain the humor in these lines: "From scalp to sole, all muscles in slow motion" (line 1); "sinews twisted into monstrous pretzels" (line 4); "a grizzly bear the deadlier for not really being there" (lines 5–6); "His back alone has twenty different faces" (line 10).

**BEST PRACTICES TOOLKIT**
Read-and-Say-Something p. D3

### FOR ADVANCED LEARNERS/PRE–AP

**Synthesize** "Bodybuilders' Contest" was translated into English from Polish. Ask students what challenges the translators must have faced and why translating poetry is so much more difficult than translating prose. You may want to remind students that the English version consists of rhyming couplets. You may also want to point out that humor in one language does not always translate easily into another.

## Comprehension

1. **Recall** In "Bodybuilders' Contest," what does the bodybuilder look like he is doing onstage?

2. **Recall** What is the very first thing that happens in "400-Meter Free Style"?

3. **Clarify** What "signs" has the speaker been watching for in "400-Meter Free Style"?

## Text Analysis

■ 4. **Connect** What connections were you able to make to these two poems? Which athlete did you think was the better competitor? Explain.

● 5. **Analyze a Concrete Poem** In what ways does the shape of "400-Meter Free Style" reflect the poem's subject? Would the poem have as much impact if it were written in **stanzas** with clear line breaks? Explain.

6. **Interpret Imagery** Reread lines 30–41 in "400-Meter Free Style." How is the "salute" of the swimmer's feet in keeping with his other movements?

7. **Examine Sound Devices** In Kumin's poem, there are a number of sound devices, including **alliteration,** the repetition of consonant sounds at the beginning of words. Identify at least five examples of alliteration. What effect do they have when the poem is read aloud?

8. **Analyze Rhyme** "Bodybuilders' Contest" uses rhyming **couplets** to call attention to certain images in each stanza and to create humor. What humorous images are emphasized in the poem?

● 9. **Examine Form** The form of "Bodybuilders' Contest" is very controlled. In what ways does this form fit the subject of the poem?

### READING-WRITING CONNECTION

| WRITING PROMPT | REVISING TIP |
|---|---|
| **Extended Constructed Response: Concrete Poem** Write your own **concrete poem** by first choosing a topic that suggests an object or an action, such as a bird or someone jumping. Then think of a simple **shape** that reflects that object or action. Draw an outline of the object, and write a poem to fit into the shape. | Review your poem. Did you focus on a single object or action and ▶ choose a shape that closely connects to the subject? If not, revise your poem accordingly. |

### What makes a great COMPETITOR?

What competitor do you relate to the most? Why?

---

COMMON CORE

RL 10 Read and comprehend poems. W 5 Strengthen writing by revising, focusing on what is most significant for a specific purpose. W 10 Write over shorter time frames for a range of tasks and purposes.

# Practice and Apply

For preliminary support of post-reading questions, use these copy masters:

**R** RESOURCE MANAGER—Copy Masters
Form p. 51
Question Support p. 55

Additional selection questions are provided for teachers on page 47.

### ANSWERS

## Comprehension

1. *The bodybuilder looks like he is grappling with animals.*

2. *A gun fires, starting the race.*

3. *The speaker has been watching for signs that the swimmer is tiring.*

## Text Analysis  COMMON CORE RL 10

*Possible answers:*

4. ■ **COMMON CORE FOCUS** *Connect Students should connect their own experiences to ideas in both poems and give reasons for their choices of the better competitor.*

5. ● **COMMON CORE FOCUS** *Analyze a Concrete Poem The shape of the poem suggests a swimmer swimming laps, providing a visual connection.*

6. *The "salute" is part of the swimmer's flip turn, described in lines 37–41.*

7. *Students should identify five examples of alliteration, including: "swing," "swimmer" (line 1). The poem's alliteration unifies the flow of words.*

8. *The rhymes emphasize humorous images, such as the torso dripping with "lotion" (line 2), and muscles twisting into "pretzels" (line 4).*

# Assess and Reteach

### Assess

**DIAGNOSTIC AND SELECTION TESTS**
Selection Test A pp. 199–200
Selection Test B/C pp. 201–202

**Interactive Selection Test** on **thinkcentral.com**

### Reteach

**Level Up Online Tutorials** on **thinkcentral.com**

**Reteaching Workshops** on **thinkcentral.com**
Literature Lesson 19: Structure of Poetry

---

9. ● **COMMON CORE FOCUS** *Examine Form The poem's controlled form matches the bodybuilder's controlled physique.*

**READING-WRITING CONNECTION** COMMON CORE W 5, W 10
Tell students that they can also use the words and lines of their poems to form a shape. For example, a poem about baseball might be arranged to form a baseball diamond.

What makes a great **COMPETITOR?** *Students are more likely to relate to the swimmer because they have probably participated in similar competitions.*

# Focus and Motivate

### COMMON CORE FOCUS

**RI 2** Determine a central idea of a text and analyze its development, including how it emerges and is shaped and refined by details. **RI 4** Determine the connotative meaning of words and phrases as they are used in a text. **W 1a-b** Introduce precise claims, supplying evidence for each.

## SUMMARY

In this article, a teenage girl recounts her experience as a participant in the finals of the National Youth Poetry Slam. She describes how, even though her team did not win, the competition provided an exciting and rewarding opportunity for self-expression.

## What's the Connection?

Use the SQ3R graphic organizer to help students preview and read the article. Direct students to

- Scan the article for title, headings, and pictures. Also note the use of italics.
- Skim the article, and make predictions about what they think they will learn.
- Write questions based on their skim of the text. Example: What is a "poetry slam"?
- Answer the questions as they read.
- Summarize central points of the article.

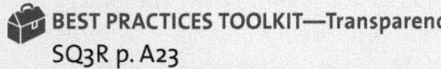 **BEST PRACTICES TOOLKIT—Transparency** SQ3R p. A23

# Teach

## Standards Focus: Synthesize

- Explain that a sidebar is meant to complement the main article—that is, extend the information in some way. Point out that "Not Your Father's Poetry" was written by someone other than the author of the main article, but that sometimes authors write one or more sidebars for their own articles.
- After students have read the article and the sidebar, discuss how the sidebar complements the main article.

**R** **RESOURCE MANAGER—Copy Master** Synthesize p. 65

---

# The Night Poetry Rocked the House
Magazine Article

Use with "400-Meter Free Style" and "Bodybuilders' Contest," pages 766 and 768.

### COMMON CORE

**RI 2** Determine a central idea of a text and analyze its development, including how it emerges and is shaped and refined by details. **RI 4** Determine the connotative meaning of words and phrases as they are used in a text.

## What's the Connection?

The last two poems brought to life two athletic competitions: a swim meet and a bodybuilders' contest. The article you are about to read will give you an idea of what it feels like to compete at a very different sort of event—a poetry slam.

## Standards Focus: Synthesize

Magazine articles often include **sidebars**—news items or short features inserted near the main text. When you read a magazine article that has a sidebar, you need to **synthesize** the information from both the article and its sidebar. By putting together the facts, ideas, and details from each, you'll get a fuller understanding of the topic.

How do you do that? What do you read first? Do you interrupt your reading of one piece to read the other? Here's how you can synthesize the ideas and details from "The Night Poetry Rocked the House" and the accompanying sidebar, "Not Your Father's Poetry."

- **Skim** both the main article and the sidebar to get a basic idea of what each is about and how each is organized.
- **Read** the main article from start to finish; then **summarize** its central ideas and details for yourself.
- **Note** any questions you have after reading the main article.
- **Read** the sidebar. As you read, ask yourself: What am I learning here that I did not learn from the main article?

After reading the sidebar, think about why the information in it was given separately from the main article. The answers you come up with may help you recognize the focus and strengths of the main article. For more help synthesizing the article and sidebar that follow, complete a chart like the one started here.

| Source | Central Ideas & Information | Questions & New Information |
|---|---|---|
| 1. "The Night Poetry Rocked the House" | Rachel Shapiro's last performance in the National Youth Poetry Slam in San Francisco is amazing. | What exactly is a poetry slam? |

---

# Selection Resources

See resources on the **Teacher One Stop DVD-ROM** and on **thinkcentral.com**.

**R** **RESOURCE MANAGER UNIT 7**
Lesson Support,* pp. 57–61

**DIAGNOSTIC AND SELECTION TESTS**
Selection Tests, pp. 203–206

 **BEST PRACTICES TOOLKIT**
SQ3R p. A23
New Word Analysis p. E8

**TECHNOLOGY**
- Teacher One Stop DVD-ROM
- Student One Stop DVD-ROM
- Audio Anthology CD
- ExamView Test Generator on the Teacher One Stop

* Resources for Differentiation

# The NIGHT POETRY ROCKED the HOUSE

**Rachel Shapiro**

We may not have won the national poetry slam—but that wasn't the point. **A**

We were brimming and overflowing with excitement. We had made it to the finals of the National Youth Poetry Slam in San Francisco, where more than 100 of the top teenage poets from across the country gathered to perform. It was 1 A.M., the last performance of the third and final round, and my team, representing
10 New York City, was about to go on, ending the entire weekend of inspiring words.

Onome, Casey, and I planned to perform a group piece that the three of us had written about women. *A girl thinks rich, thorough thoughts . . . Why doesn't she speak up in class?* We knew we would have points deducted because our piece was well over the
20 three-minute limit. But it didn't matter. We had something to say. We had a message to leave with San Francisco.

**ELOQUENT WORDS**
The three of us walked out on the stage gazing at the chandeliers and the 1,200 faces who cheered, who came to hear the voices of the young poets of the country. We performed on a stage blessed with the eloquent words of
30 skinny girls with proud, deep voices,

13-year-olds who roused the entire crowd, round women from Atlanta who sang amid their poetry; it was a stage ridden with confusion, rebirth, inspiration, talent, and pride.

Many words that night had shocked us with their brilliance. Now it was our turn. *Does she learn to dismiss her anger when/ he says he's sick of male-
40 bashing poems/ did she dump him when he bashed her?*

We had an open stage, a free forum to share the plight of the young girl who doesn't speak up in class—*who could never realize she was brilliant*—to speak of the silencing and submission of women—*Was she always this numb? Was she always this quiet?*—the abuse, the sellouts, and the lack of respect—
50 *Did her tears fall like raindrops/ outside a soundproof window?*

The words poured out with emotion and house-rocking force. We traded solos like a jazz trio; we jammed in counterpoint, in unison, in rhythm. *She was brilliant. Was she always this?* **B**

The second after we released the last word, the crowd was frozen, stunned. And then the room started to
60 shake with energy—in an instant my coach was onstage, people whom I had never met were hugging me, someone

**A SYNTHESIZE**
What do the title and the statement below it suggest the **central idea** of the article will be?

**Language Coach**
**Denotation/Connotation**
Many words have positive or negative associations (connotations). Reread lines 42–44. The word *plight* has a negative connotation. What similar word would have a less negative connotation? Use a dictionary to confirm your answer.

**B SYNTHESIZE**
Based on what you've read so far, how would you describe this poetry slam?

---

## READ WITH A PURPOSE
*Help students set a purpose for reading. Ask students to consider why so many young people have found their voices on the stages of America's poetry slams.*

**INFORMATIONAL ANALYSIS**  **COMMON CORE** RI 2

**A** *Model the Skill:* **SYNTHESIZE**
Explain the meaning of *rocked the house*: "caused great excitement in a theater or auditorium." Point out the word *won* in the statement, and explain that this word implies a competition or contest. Remind students to use the Synthesize charts they began on page 770 to help them.

*Possible answer:* The title and the statement below it suggest that the article is about some kind of poetry competition—a competition that the writer did not win but from which she did gain some benefit.

**INFORMATIONAL ANALYSIS**  **COMMON CORE** RI 2

**B** **SYNTHESIZE**
*Possible answer:* The poetry slam is an exciting competition ("1,200 faces who cheered" [line 26]; "words poured out with emotion and house-rocking force" [line 53] and "inspiring" [line 11]). It is also entertaining to watch and listen to ("We traded solos like a jazz trio; we jammed in counterpoint, in unison, in rhythm" [lines 54–55]).

---

## DIFFERENTIATED INSTRUCTION

**FOR ENGLISH LANGUAGE LEARNERS**
**Vocabulary: Idioms** Use New Word Analysis to teach these idioms from the article: *had made it to* (line 2), "had reached"; *ridden with* (line 34), "full of"; *male-bashing* (lines 39–40), "verbally attacking males"; *dump him* (line 40), "get rid of him"; *sellouts* (line 49), "acts of betrayal or giving in."

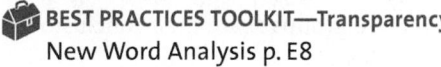 **BEST PRACTICES TOOLKIT—Transparency**
New Word Analysis p. E8

**Language Coach**
**Denotation/Connotation**
**Possible answer:**
situation; problem Ask students whether the word *eloquent* (line 29) has a positive or negative connotation. (*positive*) Ask students to think of a word with a negative connotation that might be used to describe someone's words. (*brash*)

## Not Your Father's Poetry
By Bruce Weber/*The New York Times*

C   Poetry slams have come of age. As poetry in general has surged in popularity in the United States, this offshoot has emerged as a way for passionate, mostly young people—representing a wide ethnic and racial range—to air their voices and for an evidently eager audience to hear and embrace them.

10    Slamming is a weird and lively amalgam of performance art, hip-hop concert, and—with its judges holding up numerical score cards—Olympic figure skating. It's a national grassroots movement, which began when a Chicago poet named Marc Smith held the first competitions in a bar in 1984.

The 11th annual National Poetry Slam was held in August, and the 3rd annual
20 National Youth Poetry Slam was held last spring.

Slam poetry has been boosted by, among other things, the popularity of rap music, the boom in stand-up comedy, and the proliferation of stage monologuists. At the same time, sales of poetry books have soared 30 percent in the last three years.

Watching others perform, says
30 Danny Solis, who has competed out of Albuquerque, New Mexico, "showed me that poetry could be something that lifts an audience to another place, like jazz, salsa or dance."

came up to us crying, saying, "Thank you. As a woman, I knew that had to be said, and you all said it so beautifully."

### ARENAS OF SUPPORT

I knew then that it was real, and that it was necessary to find creative ways to express yourself, so that people,
70 especially adults, will take you seriously and realize that you have some monumental things to say as well. Poetry slams give poets arenas full of excitement and support that

encourage us, urge us to tell them what we have to say. D

We didn't win, but it couldn't have mattered less to me. When I think of the young men and women with
80 whom I shared the stage, and especially of my team, I think of an Adrienne Rich poem:

> *No one has imagined us. We want to*
> *live like trees,*
> *Sycamores blazing through the*
> *sulfuric air,*
> *dappled with scars still exuberantly*
> *budding.*

---

## DIFFERENTIATED INSTRUCTION

### FOR STRUGGLING READERS
**Develop Reading Fluency** Read the last paragraph of the article aloud. Use intonation to emphasize the shift from narration to the lines of poetry. Read the paragraph aloud a second time and have students echo your reading of each sentence or meaningful line grouping.

### FOR ADVANCED LEARNERS/PRE–AP
**Evaluate Comparison** Have students reread lines 10–14. Then have them reflect on the accuracy of the writer's description of slamming. Direct students to work in small groups to do the research necessary to judge whether slamming can indeed be thought of as an "amalgam of performance art, hip-hop concert, and . . . Olympic figure skating" (lines 11–14). Have groups share their conclusions with the class.

## Comprehension

1. **Recall** Why have these young poets gathered as described in "The Night Poetry Rocked the House"?

2. **Summarize** How was the National Youth Poetry Slam a rewarding experience for the author?

## Text Analysis

3. **Synthesize** Review the chart you filled in as you read the main article and the sidebar. What does the sidebar add to your understanding of Shapiro's poetry slam experience? Explain.

4. **Analyze Tone** Describe the tone of the main article and the tone of the sidebar. Why do you suppose their tones differ?

> **COMMON CORE**
> **RI 2** Determine a central idea of a text and analyze its development, including how it emerges and is shaped and refined by details. **W 1a-b** Introduce precise claims, supplying evidence for each.

## Read for Information: Support an Opinion

> **WRITING PROMPT**
> You have just read three very different portrayals of three very different forms of competition—a swim meet, a bodybuilders' contest, and a poetry slam. Which portrayal do you find the most compelling? What elements of that piece make it more interesting to you than the others?

To answer this prompt, follow these steps:

1. Decide which piece you find yourself caring the most about. Write a brief statement explaining why. This statement will be your **claim.**

2. Write down the elements of this piece that make it the most compelling of the three. These will be the **reasons** for your choice.

3. Find details and quotations in the selection that illustrate each of your reasons. These will be your **evidence.**

4. State your opinion and support it with your reasons and evidence. You may want to mention any strengths of the other selections, but also point out the reasons why—despite these strengths—they don't match up to your favorite.

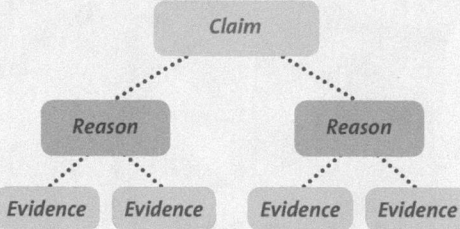

---

## DIFFERENTIATED INSTRUCTION

### FOR STRUGGLING READERS

**Read for Information** To help students determine which piece they found most compelling and why, suggest that they jot down thoughts about each of the three as a brainstorming prewriting activity. Have students use three separate sheets of paper and then compare the results. The piece that generated the most specific and detailed notes is probably the one that made the strongest impression.

### FOR ADVANCED LEARNERS/PRE–AP

**Make Judgments** Rachel Shapiro writes, "We didn't win, but it couldn't have mattered less to me" (lines 77–78). Have students discuss whether the swimmer in "400-Meter Free Style" or the bodybuilder in "Bodybuilders' Contest" would have felt the same way. Also have them explore whether Shapiro is being disingenuous in her statement.

---

# Practice and Apply

For preliminary support of post-reading questions, use these copy masters:

**R** RESOURCE MANAGER—Copy Masters
Reading Check p. 69
Question Support p. 70
Support an Opinion p. 66

Additional selection questions are provided for teachers on page 60.

## ANSWERS

## Comprehension

1. *They are competing in the finals of a national poetry slam.*

2. *The author was inspired by the words of other poets and rewarded by the audience's positive response to her own performance.*

## Text Analysis

> **COMMON CORE RI 2**

*Possible answers:*

3. ● **COMMON CORE FOCUS** *Synthesize The sidebar explains what poetry slams are, how they began, and why they've become so popular. These details flesh out Shapiro's account of her participation in a poetry slam.*

4. *The tone of the main article is enthusiastic and personal because it is a first-person account written by an actual participant. The tone of the sidebar is more subdued and objective because it is a newspaper article written by an observer.*

## Read for Information: Support an Opinion

> **COMMON CORE W 1a-b**

**Writing Prompt** *Students should support their opinions with evidence from the selections.*

# Assess and Reteach

## Assess

DIAGNOSTIC AND SELECTION TESTS
Selection Test A pp. 203–204
Selection Test B/C pp. 205–206

**Interactive Selection Test** on **thinkcentral.com**

## Reteach

**Level Up Online Tutorials** on **thinkcentral.com**

**Reteaching Workshops** on **thinkcentral.com**
Informational Texts Lesson 1, Reading Lesson 14

# Focus and Motivate

## COMMON CORE FOCUS

**RL 4** Determine the figurative meaning of words and phrases as they are used in text; analyze the cumulative impact of specific word choices on meaning and tone. **RL 10** Read and comprehend poems. **L 1b** Use various types of phrases to convey specific meanings and add variety and interest to writing.

## SUMMARIES

**"For Poets"** The speaker in this poem encourages poets to reach within themselves but also to "fly" with imagination.

**"Ode to My Socks"** In this ode, presented in English and Spanish, the speaker praises the virtues of a pair of hand-knit socks.

**"egg horror poem"** This poem describes the terror that refrigerated eggs feel as they wait to be made into meals for people.

### What makes your IMAGINATION soar?

Ask the question and relate it to the photograph. After students have completed the *QUICKWRITE*, call on volunteers to share responses, and ask how imagination influenced their descriptions.

---

## For Poets
Poem by Al Young

## Ode to My Socks
Poem by Pablo Neruda

## egg horror poem
Poem by Laurel Winter

# What makes your IMAGINATION soar?

### COMMON CORE

**RL 4** Determine the figurative meaning of words and phrases as they are used in a text; analyze the cumulative impact of specific word choices on meaning and tone. **RL 10** Read and comprehend poems.

It's easy to see why people might be inspired to creativity by something grand, like love or mountains, but imagination is not limited to the grand. A poet might see something as simple as a shoelace in a completely new way.

*QUICKWRITE* Write a short description of a familiar object as though you'd never seen it before. What does it make you think of? Use your imagination.

774

---

## Selection Resources

See resources on the **Teacher One Stop DVD-ROM** and on **thinkcentral.com**.

**R RESOURCE MANAGER UNIT 7**
Plan and Teach, pp. 71–78
Text Analysis and Reading
  Skill, pp. 79–82†
Grammar and Style, p. 84

**DIAGNOSTIC AND SELECTION TESTS**
Selection Tests, pp. 207–210

**BEST PRACTICES TOOLKIT**
Read Aloud/Think Aloud,
  p. A34
Venn Diagram, p. A26
Cluster Diagram, p. B18
Question Frames, p. A33

**TECHNOLOGY**
- **Teacher One Stop DVD-ROM**
- **Student One Stop DVD-ROM**
- **Audio Anthology CD**
- **GrammarNotes DVD-ROM**
- **ExamView Test Generator** on the **Teacher One Stop**

* Resources for Differentiation    † Also in Spanish    ‡ In Haitian Creole and Vietnamese

## POETIC FORM: ODE

A traditional **ode** is a poem that highly praises something—usually a person, an event, or an idea. Traditional odes are about serious subjects, and they have a formal **tone**. In this lesson, you'll read an ode by Pablo Neruda, who broke with tradition by writing odes about everyday objects—in this case a pair of cozy socks.

## TEXT ANALYSIS: FIGURATIVE LANGUAGE

**Figurative language** goes beyond the literal meaning of words, creating a comparison between two things not usually associated with one another. Such **figures of speech** allow the writer to characterize one of the two items in a particular, often unusual, way. Figurative language has three basic types, all found in Pablo Neruda's "Ode to My Socks."

- A **simile** compares two unlike things that have something in common, using the word *like* or *as*.

  *two socks soft / as rabbits*

- A **metaphor** directly compares two unlike things by saying that one thing actually *is* the other.

  *my feet became / two woolen / fish*

- **Personification** lends human qualities to an object, animal, or idea.

  *my feet seemed / unacceptable to me, / two tired old / fire fighters*

As you read, identify the figurative language used, and think of the qualities the comparison gives to the subject being described.

| Poem | Passage | Figure of Speech | Meaning of Comparison |
|------|---------|------------------|----------------------|
| "For Poets" | "Breathe in trees" | metaphor | |

## READING STRATEGY: VISUALIZE

The process of creating a sensory image in your mind is called **visualizing.** Good readers visualize the images and comparisons in a poem to help them understand the poet's ideas. As you read the next three poems, pause frequently to visualize the images and comparisons you find.

 Complete the activities in your **Reader/Writer Notebook.**

## Meet the Authors

### Al Young
**born 1939**

**A Man of Many Talents**
In his varied life, Al Young has written screenplays, essays, and novels, but poetry is his first love. "Poetry sweetens the tongue, deepens the heart, and expands the mind," he once said. "Even a writer of annual reports may draw richly from the conventions and techniques of poetry."

### Pablo Neruda
**1904–1973**

**Poetry and Politics**
Acclaimed both in his native Chile and internationally, Pablo Neruda's life was a mix of poetry and politics. After writing love poetry early in his career, Neruda turned to more political verse in the 1930s and 1940s. In the 1950s he began writing about everyday objects in a simple style that many people could understand and enjoy. Neruda was awarded the Nobel Prize in literature in 1971.

### Laurel Winter
**born 1959**

**Sci-Fi/ Fantasy Poet**
"I grew up as an odd kid in the mountains of Montana," writes Laurel Winter. "I was klutzy and bookwormish and didn't always fit in." Today Winter is an award-winning writer. On writing science fiction and fantasy, she said, "To me as a writer, in fantasy everything is available. If you can think of it, you can write it."

**Authors Online**

Go to **thinkcentral.com.** KEYWORD: HML9-775

775

## Teach

**TEXT ANALYSIS**

COMMON CORE
RL 4

### ● *Model the Skill:* FIGURATIVE LANGUAGE

For instructional support, identify the figurative language in this sentence:

The weeds are stubborn, like children who want their own way.

*Simile: weeds like children; Personification: stubborn weeds*

**GUIDED PRACTICE** Have students rephrase the simile as a metaphor. Then have them write an original example of each type of figurative language.

**R** RESOURCE MANAGER—Copy Master Figurative Language p. 79 (for student use while reading the selections)

**READING STRATEGY**

COMMON CORE
RL 10

### ● *Model the Skill:* VISUALIZE

For instructional support, give this example:

A delicate, pale green teacup balanced its tiny foot on a chipped porcelain saucer.

Point out the details that help you visualize the description: words like "delicate," "pale green," and "chipped"; the comparison of the teacup to a person balancing and its bottom to a foot

**GUIDED PRACTICE** Have students sketch what they visualize.

## DIFFERENTIATED INSTRUCTION

### FOR STRUGGLING READERS

**Distinguish Types of Language** Use the Think Aloud strategy with this example to differentiate figurative language from precise language that appeals to the senses:

My heavy brown loafers thudded to the floor and lay snoozing, like friendly, lazy dogs, near the door.

 BEST PRACTICES TOOLKIT—Transparency Read Aloud/Think Aloud p. A34

### FOR ADVANCED LEARNERS/PRE–AP

**Research Figures of Speech** Explain to students that there are several other kinds of figures of speech besides those listed on this page. These include apostrophe, hyperbole, litotes, metonymy, and synecdoche. Have students research and define these terms and then write an example of each one. Invite students to share their work in small groups.

**TEXT ANALYSIS**

COMMON CORE
RL 4

**A** *Model the Skill:* **FIGURATIVE LANGUAGE**

Discuss the figurative meaning of specific details. A "mole" (line 3) could mean a person who stays isolated in artistic work and hides from life experiences or other people. "Sunlight" (line 7) could stand for life with all its brightness and energy. Remind students to use the charts they began on page 775.

**Possible answer:** *The speaker is really suggesting that poets extend themselves. In particular, they should become aware of the natural world that surrounds them.*

**READING STRATEGY**

COMMON CORE
RL 10

**B** **VISUALIZE**

**Possible answer:** *These lines create mental pictures of creatures that move out of their comfort zone and extend themselves, as the speaker wants poets to do.*

# For Poets

## AL YOUNG

Stay beautiful
but dont stay down underground too long
Dont turn into a mole
or a worm
5 or a root
or a stone

Come on out into the sunlight
Breathe in trees
Knock out mountains
10 Commune[1] with snakes
& be the very hero of birds

Dont forget to poke your head up
& blink
think
15 Walk all around
Swim upstream

Dont forget to fly

### Analyze Visuals ▶

What elements of this image express the sentiments of this poem? Be specific.

**A** **FIGURATIVE LANGUAGE**
In lines 7–11, the speaker is not offering literal advice. What is he really suggesting?

**B** **VISUALIZE**
Reread lines 12–16. What mental pictures do these lines create?

From *Wings* (2000), Christopher Myers. © 2000 by Christopher Myers. Reprinted by permission of Scholastic, Inc.

1. **commune** (kə-myōōn'): communicate intimately.

## DIFFERENTIATED INSTRUCTION

**FOR ENGLISH LANGUAGE LEARNERS**

**Language: Punctuation and Print Clues** Note that in "For Poets," poet Al Young does not use any periods, apostrophes, or commas. He does use print cues, however, such as the ampersand (&) and capital letters. Suggest that Young may have kept the capital letters to mark his various thoughts but may have made the punctuation choices to emphasize a sense of urgency in sharing those thoughts with poets.

**Develop Reading Fluency: Options for Reading** Read "For Poets" aloud, emphasizing pacing to help students appreciate rhythm. Have students echo your reading of meaningful line groupings during a second reading. Follow the same plan for "Ode to My Socks" and "egg horror poem".

Prereading for this poem is found on page 774.

## TEXT ANALYSIS

COMMON CORE

RL 4

### C FIGURATIVE LANGUAGE

**Possible answer:** *The similes are "soft as rabbits" (lines 6–7) and "slipped my feet into them as if into jewel cases" (lines 8–12). The first simile describes the socks' softness, as if the wool were as soft as the fur of rabbits. The second simile suggests the fine craftsmanship of the socks that were knit by Maru Mori and the value that the speaker places upon them as gifts.*

**IF STUDENTS NEED HELP . . .** Have students search for the signal words *like* or *as*. Brainstorm for possible comparisons, then ask students to choose the comparisons that make the most sense to them.

**Extend the Discussion** Use a Venn Diagram to focus on one of the comparisons. For example, write *Socks* in one circle and *Jewel Cases* in the other. Have students fill in the diagram with details that show how the two objects are similar and different.

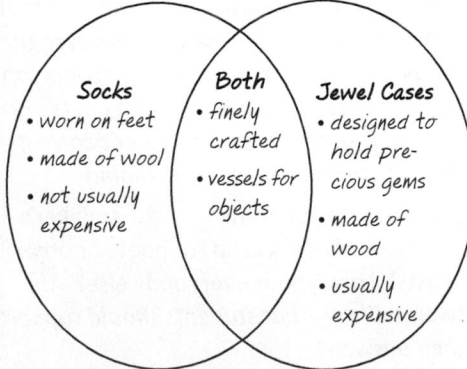

**Socks**
• worn on feet
• made of wool
• not usually expensive

**Both**
• finely crafted
• vessels for objects

**Jewel Cases**
• designed to hold precious gems
• made of wood
• usually expensive

📦 **BEST PRACTICES TOOLKIT—Transparency**
Venn Diagram p. A26

# ODE TO MY SOCKS

PABLO NERUDA

Maru Mori brought me
a pair
of socks
knitted with her own
5 shepherd's hands,
two socks soft
as rabbits.
I slipped
my feet into them
10 as if
into
jewel cases
woven
with threads of
15 dusk
and sheep's wool. **C**

Me trajo Maru Mori
un par
de calcentines
que tejió con sus manos
de pastora,
dos calcentines suaves
como liebres.
En ellos
metí los pies
como en
dos
estuches
tejidos
con hebras del
crepúsculo
y pellejo de ovejas.

**C FIGURATIVE LANGUAGE**
Identify the two **similes** in lines 1–16. What qualities of the socks are suggested by each simile?

## DIFFERENTIATED INSTRUCTION

**FOR STRUGGLING READERS**

**Track Details** As students read, have them complete a Cluster Diagram with comparisons and descriptive words that Neruda uses to describe the socks. Invite students to share their thoughts about the comparison or description that they consider the most imaginative, precise, unrealistic, and so on.

📦 **BEST PRACTICES TOOLKIT—Transparency**
Cluster Diagram p. B18

**FOR ENGLISH LANGUAGE LEARNERS**

**Culture: Connect** If any English learners speak Spanish as their first language, have them read aloud part or all of the Spanish version of this poem to the class. Have the rest of the class listen for the rhythm, alliteration, and assonance that is part of the original version of the poem.

Audacious[1] socks,
my feet became
two woolen
20 fish,
two long sharks
of lapis[2] blue
shot
with a golden thread,
25 two mammoth blackbirds,
two cannons,
thus honored
were
my feet
30 by
these
celestial[3]
socks. **D**
They were
35 so beautiful
that for the first time
my feet seemed
unacceptable to me,
two tired·old
40 fire fighters

Violentos calcentines,
mis pies fueron
dos pescados
de lana,
dos largos tiburones
de azul ultramarino
atravesados
por una trenza de oro,
dos gigantescos mirlos,
dos cañones:
mis pies
fueron honrados
de este modo
por
estos
celestiales
calcentines.
Eran
tan hermosos
que por primera vez
mis pies me parecieron
inaceptables
como dos decrépitos
bomberos, bomberos

---

1. **audacious** (ô-dā'shəs): bold or original.
2. **lapis:** the color of the stone lapis lazuli (lăp'ĭs lăz'ə-lē); bright blue.
3. **celestial** (sə-lĕs'chəl): heavenly.

---

### What makes your
# IMAGINATION soar?

**Discuss** Direct students' attention to lines 17–40. Ask: Why do you think Neruda described his socks and feet with such imagination? *Possible answer: Neruda may have wanted to show his appreciation to Maru Mori, who made the socks for him. He also may have wanted readers to understand that there is something wonderful about even the most ordinary objects.*

---

**COMMON CORE** RL 4

**Language Coach**

**Cognates** Words from different languages with similar meaning and spellings are **cognates.** Reread line 17. The Spanish word *violentos* has an obvious English cognate. Why do you think the translator chose *audacious* over *violent*?

---

**D** **FIGURATIVE LANGUAGE**
Reread lines 17–33. What unusual **metaphors** does the speaker use to emphasize the amazing nature of the socks?

---

**TEXT ANALYSIS**      COMMON CORE RL 4

**D** *Model the Skill:* **FIGURATIVE LANGUAGE**

Remind students that a metaphor is a comparison in which one thing is said to be the same as another thing. (That is, one thing *is* the other, not one thing is *like* the other.) Identify such comparisons. Remind students to continue filling out the charts they began on p. 775.

*Possible answer:* The speaker says that his socks have the power to transform his feet into "fish," "sharks," "blackbirds," and "cannons."

---

## FOR ENGLISH LANGUAGE LEARNERS

**Language Coach**     COMMON CORE RL 4

**Cognates** *Answer: Perhaps* violentos *is used more often to describe clothing (or its color) in Spanish than* violent *is in English.*

These are a few other words that you might explore in this poem:

- *cannons/cañones* (line 26)
- *honored/honrados* (lines 27 and 28)
- *unacceptable/inaceptables* (line 38)
- *temptation/tentación* (line 48)

## FOR ADVANCED LEARNERS/PRE–AP

**Compare and Contrast Poets** [small-group option] Tell students that Pablo Neruda's poetry is often compared to that of American poet Walt Whitman (1819–1892); in fact, Neruda said that Whitman was a source of great inspiration to him. Ask students to do some research on the connection, such as poetic style and choice of subject matter, and to share their findings with the class.

**Possible answers:** *Overstatement lends the poem irony and its tongue-in-cheek take on a traditional ode. Overstatement also helps the reader see the metaphors the poet is getting at when describing how he feels about the socks.*

Discuss with students how different the poem would be if overstatement was not used.

READING STRATEGY

COMMON CORE RL 10

**F** *Model the Skill:* **VISUALIZE**

Model how to focus on one image at a time (lines 50–52, 53–55, and 56–63). Point out that each image shows someone saving something special.

**Possible answer:** *All of the images describe delicate, exotic objects or creatures, protected or preserved in some way. The speaker is saying that even though his socks are special, he will resist the urge to enshrine them as sacred objects. Instead, he will wear them.*

---

not worthy
of the woven
fire
of those luminous
45  socks. **E**

Nonetheless,
I resisted
the strong temptation
to save them
50  the way schoolboys
bottle
fireflies,
the way scholars
hoard
55  sacred documents.
I resisted
the wild impulse
to place them
in a cage
60  of gold
and daily feed them
birdseed
and rosy melon flesh. **F**
Like explorers
65  who in the forest
surrender a rare
and tender deer
to the spit
and eat it
70  with remorse,
I stuck out
my feet
and pulled on
the
75  handsome
socks,
and
then my shoes.

indignos
de aquel fuego
bordado,
de aquellos luminosos
calcetines.

Sin embargo
resistí
la tentación aguda
de guardarlos
como los colegiales
preservan
las luciérnagas,
como los cruditos
coleccionan
documentos sagrados,
resistí
el impulso furioso
de ponerlos
en una jaula
de oro
y darles cada día
alpiste
y pulpa de melón rosado.
Como descubridores
que en la selva
entregan el rarísimo
venado verde
al asador
y se lo comen
con remordimiento,
estiré
los pies
y me enfundé
los
bellos
calcetines
y
luego los zapatos.

COMMON CORE RL 4

**E OVERSTATEMENT**
Most people would not describe their socks as *audacious, mammoth, celestial,* or *luminous.* Pablo Neruda's use of these words is an example of **overstatement,** or exaggeration for a particular effect. How do the overstatements affect the poem?

**F VISUALIZE**
Reread lines 46–63. As you visualize the images in these lines, think about what they have in common. What is the speaker saying about his socks?

---

## DIFFERENTIATED INSTRUCTION

**FOR STRUGGLING READERS**
**Clarify Comparisons** Students may need help understanding the images in lines 46–70. Read each image aloud, and ask students to explain the comparison it makes. For lines 56–63, make sure students understand the unstated part of the metaphor: the speaker is comparing his socks to birds. Also point out that the image of the explorers (lines 64–70) is different from the other three images because it describes how the speaker feels about wearing, rather than saving, his special socks.

So this is
80 the moral of my ode:
twice beautiful
is beauty
and what is good doubly
good
85 when it is a case of two
woolen socks
in wintertime. **G**

Y es ésta
la moral de mi oda:
dos veces es belleza
la belleza
y lo que es bueno es doblemente
bueno
cuando se trata de dos calcentines
de lana
en el invierno.

*Translated by Margaret Sayers Peden*

**G** ODE
Traditional odes have a
serious **tone**, or attitude
toward the subject. What
is the tone of this ode?

Prereading for this poem is found on page 774.

# egg horror poem

## LAUREL WINTER

small
white
afraid of heights
whispering
5 in the cold, dark carton
to the rest of the dozen.
They are ten now.
Any meal is dangerous,
but they fear breakfast most.
10 They jostle in their compartments
trying for tiny, dark-veined cracks—
not enough to hurt much,
just anything to make them unattractive
to the big hands that reach in
15 from time to random time.
They tell horror stories
that their mothers,
the chickens,
clucked to them—
20 meringues,
omelettes,
egg salad sandwiches,
that destroyer of dozens,
the homemade angel food cake.
25 The door opens.
Light filters into the carton,
"Let it be the milk,"
they pray.

**TEXT ANALYSIS** — COMMON CORE RL 4

**H FIGURATIVE LANGUAGE**

*Possible answer:* An egg is being personified. The words "afraid" and "whispering" convey human qualities.

**IF STUDENTS NEED HELP . . .** Ask them which words in lines 3–4 go beyond what we normally associate with eggs.

**H FIGURATIVE LANGUAGE**

In lines 1–6, what object is being **personified?** Identify the words that convey human qualities.

**TEXT ANALYSIS** — COMMON CORE RL 4

**I FIGURATIVE LANGUAGE**

*Possible answer:* All of these foods use eggs as a main ingredient. The eggs would be horrified because becoming part of such foods would mean that they would die.

**I FIGURATIVE LANGUAGE**

Reread lines 16–24. Why might meringues, omelettes, and the other foods mentioned in these lines seem horrifying to an egg?

## DIFFERENTIATED INSTRUCTION

**FOR STRUGGLING READERS**

**Clarify Meaning** Winter uses some unusual but vivid verbs and verb forms in this poem, including *jostle* (line 10), *clucked* (line 19), *whirring* (line 41), and *huddle* (line 42). To check and refine understanding, invite volunteers to act out these verbs and verb forms as they imagine the action occurring in the poem.

**FOR ENGLISH LANGUAGE LEARNERS**

**Culture: Clarify** Some students may be unfamiliar with meringues (line 20), omelettes (line 21), egg salad (line 22), or angel food cake (line 24). Describe each food, focusing on the importance of eggs as the main ingredient. You may wish to bring in a simple recipe for each food or provide samples of the food for students to taste. Students may also suggest how eggs are used in their home cultures.

But the carton opens,
30 a hand reaches in—
once,
twice.
Before they can even jiggle,
they are alone again,
35 in the cold,
in the dark,
new spaces hollow
where the two were.
Through the heavy door
40 they hear the sound of the mixer,
deadly blades whirring.

They huddle,
the eight,
in the cold,
45 in the dark,
and wait.

** VISUALIZE**
Reread lines 29–41. What events do you picture happening inside and outside the refrigerator?

# Practice and Apply

For preliminary support of post-reading questions, use these copy masters:

**R** RESOURCE MANAGER—Copy Masters
Visualize p. 81
Question Support p. 83

Additional selection questions are provided for teachers on page 75.

## ANSWERS

## Comprehension

1. *The danger is in turning into a mole, worm, root, or stone (lines 3–6).*

2. *The speaker compares his feet to "fish", "sharks", "mammoth blackbirds", and "cannons" (lines 20–26) and to "two tired old fire fighters" (lines 39–40).*

3. *The eggs' great fear is that they will be taken and cooked for people's food.*

## Text Analysis

COMMON CORE RL 4, RL 10

*Possible answers:*

4. ■ **COMMON CORE FOCUS** *Visualize Students should support their answers with examples.*

5. *The speaker means that poets should try to reach their highest potential. Flying may represent being imaginative and reaching artistic heights.*

6. *For the eggs, life is a scary waiting game (lines 3–5 and 46) in a cold, dark place (lines 35–36). They feel desperate and miserable, as shown in their prayer not to be taken (lines 27–28).*

7. *The onomatopoeic words are "whispering" (line 4), "jostle" (line 10), "cracks" (line 11), "clucked" (line 19), "jiggle" (line 33), and "whirring" (line 41).*

8. ● **COMMON CORE FOCUS** *Analyze an Ode "Ode to My Socks" is like a traditional ode because it offers praise. It is different from a traditional ode because its subject is an ordinary object, and its tone is light. Neruda's intent was for readers to become more appreciative of the world around them.*

9. ● **COMMON CORE FOCUS** *Evaluate Figurative Language The comparisons in lines 46–63 of "Ode to My Socks" are compelling, as they compare the speaker's desire to save the socks to a schoolboy's desire to bottle fireflies, a scholar's desire to hoard documents, and a bird-lover's desire to cage and pamper a bird.*

10. *Accept either opinion, but make sure that students have supported their choices with evidence from the poems, including specific figures of speech and images.*

## Comprehension

1. **Recall** According to the speaker in "For Poets," what is the danger of staying underground too long?

2. **Recall** What two comparisons in "Ode to My Socks" involve the speaker's feet rather than his socks?

3. **Clarify** What is the eggs' great fear in "egg horror poem"?

## Text Analysis

4. **Visualize** Which poem creates the most vivid pictures in your mind? What specific images and comparisons in the poem create these pictures?

5. **Interpret Metaphor** What does the speaker in "For Poets" mean by telling poets, "Dont forget to fly"? What activity does flying represent?

6. **Interpret Personification** What is life like for the eggs described in "egg horror poem"? Describe your impressions and support your ideas with details from the poem.

7. **Identify Onomatopoeia** When words have sounds that echo their own meaning, as in *buzz* and *gargle,* it is known as onomatopoeia. Reread "egg horror poem" and identify the onomatopoetic words.

8. **Analyze an Ode** Reread the description of an ode on page 775, and then think about some of the specific words and phrases used in "Ode to My Socks." In what ways is "Ode to My Socks" like a traditional ode? In what ways is it different? What do you think Neruda's intent was in writing an ode to a pair of socks?

9. **Evaluate Figurative Language** Review the examples of figurative language and their meanings that you recorded in your chart. Which figures of speech do you find the most effective or compelling? Explain your preferences.

10. **Evaluate Ideas** Skim "Ode to My Socks" and "egg horror poem." Which poet shows more imagination in making an everyday object seem new or unusual? Support your opinion with details from the poems.

## Text Criticism

11. **Critical Interpretations** The critic Dean Rader wrote that "'Ode to My Socks' is a poem about poetry." He believes that Neruda's ode is commenting on "what poetry is and what it should be." If this is true, what is Neruda saying about poetry? Explain your ideas.

### What makes your IMAGINATION soar?

How do *you* best express what is in your imagination?

COMMON CORE

**RL 4** Determine the figurative meaning of words and phrases as they are used in a text; analyze the cumulative impact of specific word choices on meaning and tone. **RL 10** Read and comprehend poems.

## Text Criticism

*Possible answer:*

11. *Neruda is saying that poetry has the power to bring attention to and beautify the smallest, most unimportant object.*

### What makes your IMAGINATION soar?

Students may suggest art forms such as painting, sketching, writing, playing music, and so on.

# Language

◆ **GRAMMAR AND STYLE: Write Concisely**

Because poetry typically consists of a compact, carefully chosen group of words, it benefits from the use of concise language. Other types of writing can also be improved when made concise. By incorporating **infinitives** and **infinitive phrases** into your writing, you can avoid unnecessary words and make your writing more interesting. An infinitive is a verb form that begins with *to* and functions as a noun, an adjective, or an adverb. An infinitive phrase consists of an infinitive plus its modifiers and complements. Note the following examples:

> *Dont forget to fly* ("For Poets," line 17)
>
> *I resisted / the wild impulse / to place them / in a cage / of gold*
> ("Ode to My Socks," lines 56–60)

In the revisions in blue, infinitives and infinitive phrases are used to combine sentences, making the writing more concise. Revise your response to the prompt below by making similar changes.

---

**STUDENT MODEL**

The kitchen at last settles down. ~~It wants~~ to nap.

The refrigerator hums softly in slumber.

It is happy. ~~It wishes~~ to do nothing for a while.

---

## READING-WRITING CONNECTION

**YOUR TURN** Add to your understanding of the poems by responding to this prompt. Then use the **revising tip** to improve your writing.

| WRITING PROMPT | REVISING TIP |
|---|---|
| **Short Constructed Response: Poem** Using "egg horror poem" as a model, write a **five- to ten-line poem** using an extended example of personification. | Reread your poem. How did you use infinitives and infinitive phrases to make your writing more concise? |

**Interactive Revision** THINK central
Go to **thinkcentral.com**.
KEYWORD: HML9-785

---

## DIFFERENTIATED INSTRUCTION

### FOR STRUGGLING WRITERS

- Urge students to choose a common object.

- Have students make two lists: surprising things that their subject might do, and feelings and thoughts that their subject might have.

---

# Language

◆ **GRAMMAR AND STYLE**

Have students analyze the examples and the student model. Then ask them to use infinitives or infinitive phrases to combine these pairs of sentences:

> When I read poems, I feel inspired. ~~I want~~ to write poetry of my own.

> I have a few minutes. ~~I can~~ to write some poetry right now.

**R** RESOURCE MANAGER—Copy Master
Write Concisely p. 84

### READING-WRITING CONNECTION

- Provide class time for students to perform their finished poems. Remind them to use verbal techniques (such as pitch, rate, pause, and volume) and nonverbal techniques (such as posture and gestures) to enhance their presentations. Invite listeners to offer constructive feedback.

---

**Writing Online** THINK central

The following tools are available online at **thinkcentral.com** and on **WriteSmart** CD-ROM:
- **Interactive Graphic Organizers**
- **Interactive Student Models**
- **Interactive Revision Lessons**
For additional grammar instruction, see **GrammarNotes** on **thinkcentral.com**.

---

# Assess and Reteach

## Assess

**DIAGNOSTIC AND SELECTION TESTS**
> Selection Test A pp. 207–208
> Selection Test B/C pp. 209–210

**Interactive Selection Test** on **thinkcentral.com**

## Reteach

**Level Up Online Tutorials** on **thinkcentral.com**

**Reteaching Worksheets** on **thinkcentral.com**
> Literature Lessons 16, 19, 30

---

COMMON CORE

L 1b Use various types of phrases to convey specific meanings and add variety and interest to writing.

### O What Is That Sound
Poem by W. H. Auden

# What triggers a sense of ALARM?

**COMMON CORE FOCUS**

**RL 3** Analyze how characters interact and advance the plot. **RL 4** Analyze the cumulative impact of specific word choices on meaning and tone. **RL 10** Read and comprehend poems.

### SUMMARY

W. H. Auden's ballad "O What Is That Sound" is a dialogue between two speakers who may be a husband and wife or a pair of lovers. Watching the advance of "scarlet soldiers," the more apprehensive first speaker asks a series of questions, which the second speaker calmly answers. However, when it becomes clear that the soldiers are headed for their house, the second speaker takes flight, abandoning the other.

### What triggers a sense of ALARM?

Ask the question. After students read the paragraph, ask what might cause a sense of alarm to gradually become more intense. Then have students complete the *QUICK-WRITE,* and ask volunteers to share their paragraphs with the class.

**COMMON CORE**

**RL 3** Analyze how characters interact and advance the plot. **RL 4** Analyze the cumulative impact of specific word choices on meaning and tone. **RL 10** Read and comprehend poems.

Strange noises, flashing lights, the smell of something burning—any of these things would catch your attention. But would they set your heart pounding? At what point does something unusual become threatening? The following poem describes someone reacting to an approaching threat with a growing sense of alarm.

*QUICKWRITE* Imagine a situation that might cause you to panic. It could be something as dangerous as getting lost in the woods or as mild as forgetting to study for a quiz. Write a short paragraph describing your physical and mental reaction.

786

*See resources on the* **Teacher One Stop DVD-ROM** *and on* **thinkcentral.com**.

**R** **RESOURCE MANAGER UNIT 7**
   Plan and Teach, pp. 85–92
   Text Analysis and Reading Skill,
   pp. 93–96†

**DIAGNOSTIC AND SELECTION TESTS**
   Selection Tests, pp. 211–214

**TECHNOLOGY**
- **Teacher One Stop DVD-ROM**
- **Student One Stop DVD-ROM**
- **Audio Anthology CD**
- **GrammarNotes DVD-ROM**
- **ExamView Test Generator**
  on the **Teacher One Stop**

* Resources for Differentiation     † Also in Spanish     ‡ Also in Haitian Creole and Vietnamese

## POETIC FORM: BALLAD

W. H. Auden was a modern poet, but he used a traditional ballad form for "O What Is That Sound." A **ballad** is a narrative poem that is meant to be sung or recited. Typically, a traditional ballad focuses on a single tragic event and usually implies more than it tells explicitly. A ballad typically includes

- a plot, characters, and setting
- dialogue and repetition
- a regular and simple rhyme scheme (such as *abb* or *aabb*)

## TEXT ANALYSIS: SOUND DEVICES

Poets choose their words carefully, as word choice, or diction, affects a poem's meaning, its tone, and the way it sounds. **Sound devices** such as repetition and rhyme can create rhythm and mood and emphasize the poet's ideas. In "O What Is That Sound," W. H. Auden uses these sound devices to create suspense, an anxious tone, and meaning:

- **Rhyme:** similar sounds at the ends of lines **(end rhyme)** or within lines **(internal rhyme)**
- **Repetition:** repeated words or phrases (*morning, morning*)
- **Assonance:** repetition of vowel sounds within words that don't rhyme (*only soldiers*)

As you read this poem, look for examples of sound devices, and notice how they help create a feeling of anxiety.

## READING SKILL: ANALYZE SPEAKERS

In this poem, everything you learn about the story and the characters' feelings comes from the dialogue between the two speakers. As you read, use the reactions of the speakers to imagine what is happening; also look for changes in either speaker's attitude. In a chart like the one shown, record what you infer about the speakers, including who they are and how they react to events—both early and then later on.

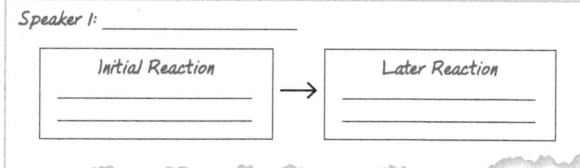

 Complete the activities in your **Reader/Writer Notebook**.

## Meet the Author

# W. H. Auden
### 1907–1973

**Admiration and Controversy**
W. H. Auden is one of the giants of 20th-century poetry. Born in northern England, he first intended to study science but soon realized his talent for poetry. His early poems, among them "O What Is That Sound," attracted both admiration and controversy. Perhaps Auden's most controversial act was moving to New York in 1939; he ultimately became a U.S. citizen. Some Englishmen never forgave him for leaving his country on the eve of World War II.

**An Enduring Legacy**
In his poetry, Auden confronted the tumultuous ideas and events that rocked his age—Freudian psychology, Marxism, fascism, civil war, and world war. In winning the National Medal for Literature in 1967 he was praised for illuminating "our lives and times with grace, wit and vitality." After the terrorist attacks of September 11, 2001, Web sites and New York subway walls displayed two of his finest poems, "Musée des Beaux Arts" and "September 1, 1939."

**BACKGROUND TO THE POEM**
**Long Ago and Far Away?**
The references to drums, horses, and the red uniforms of soldiers in "O What Is That Sound" suggest a faraway time, perhaps around the time of the American Revolution. However, the poem was written in the 1930s, a decade that Auden called "the age of anxiety." Frightened by worldwide economic depression and the rise of fascism in Italy and Germany, ordinary citizens felt vulnerable to events beyond their control.

**Author Online** **THINK** central
Go to **thinkcentral.com**.
KEYWORD: HML9-787

787

# Teach

TEXT ANALYSIS | COMMON CORE
RL 4

## ● Model the Skill: SOUND DEVICES

For instructional support, write this example on the board and read it aloud:

### The Storm

Rumble . . . rumble, a crack and a flash—
Take my hand, and for cover we'll dash.
Rumble . . . rumble, another bright flash—
Run for shelter from the cold wind's lash.

Discuss how sound devices create rhythm and mood and emphasize ideas in this poem. *The repetition of "Rumble . . . rumble" and the end rhymes create rhythm; the repetition of the words rumble and flash emphasizes the approaching storm; the use of short, rhyming words underscores a mood of haste.*

**GUIDED PRACTICE** Elicit examples from poems and songs that create rhythm and mood through sound devices.

READING SKILL | COMMON CORE
RL 3

## ■ Model the Skill: ANALYZE SPEAKERS

Explain that in prose, quotation marks generally show that a character is speaking. However, poets may choose not to use quotation marks. They may indicate who is speaking by other means—for example, by arrangement of lines or the use of italics. For example, in the lines of poetry used for the **TEXT ANALYSIS** activity, the spoken lines (lines 2 and 4) are indented. Explain what you can infer about the speaker's attitude in this example. *The speaker appears to be frightened by a storm.*

**GUIDED PRACTICE** Elicit examples of poems or songs that feature two or more speakers.

**R** RESOURCE MANAGER—Copy Master Analyze Speakers p. 95 (for student use while reading the selection)

---

## DIFFERENTIATED INSTRUCTION

### FOR STRUGGLING READERS

**Comprehension Support** Write on the board these boldfaced terms used on this page, and have students review their meaning: *rhyme, end rhyme, internal rhyme, repetition, assonance.* Elicit or provide examples of these sound devices from popular songs and familiar poems. Discuss how the devices help to create rhythm and mood and emphasize ideas in the songs and poems.

### FOR ADVANCED LEARNERS/PRE–AP

**Use Sound Devices** Challenge students to write a poem of at least four lines using as many of the sound devices described on this page as possible. Have volunteers write their poems on the board and then read them to the class. Have the class identify the sound devices used.

# Practice and Apply

## READ WITH A PURPOSE

*Help students set a purpose for reading. Ask students to pay attention to how Auden reveals the relationship between the speakers.*

---

# O What Is That Sound

### W. H. AUDEN

O what is that sound which so thrills the ear
    Down in the valley drumming, drumming?
Only the scarlet soldiers,[1] dear,
    The soldiers coming.

5 O what is that light I see flashing so clear
    Over the distance brightly, brightly?
Only the sun on their weapons, dear,
    As they step lightly.

O what are they doing with all that gear,
10     What are they doing this morning, this morning?
Only their usual maneuvers,[2] dear,
    Or perhaps a warning. Ⓐ

O why have they left the road down there,
    Why are they suddenly wheeling, wheeling?[3]
15 Perhaps a change in their orders, dear.
    Why are you kneeling? Ⓑ

**Analyze Visuals ▶**

What is the **mood** created by this painting? Identify the elements of subject matter, shape, and color that contribute to this mood.

Ⓐ **SOUND DEVICES**
Reread lines 9–12 aloud. Which of the lines in this stanza contains **assonance**? Identify the assonance, and explain its effect.

Ⓑ **ANALYZE SPEAKERS**
Do the two speakers seem to feel the same way about the approaching soldiers? Explain.

---

1. **scarlet soldiers:** a reference suggesting British soldiers, who wore bright red coats.
2. **maneuvers:** training exercises carried out by troops.
3. **wheeling:** turning around quickly so as to face in the opposite direction.

*Returning to the Trenches* (1914–15), C. R. W. Nevinson. © National Gallery of Canada, Ottawa/ The Nevinson Estate/Bridgeman Art Library.

**788** UNIT 7: THE LANGUAGE OF POETRY

---

## DIFFERENTIATED INSTRUCTION

### FOR ENGLISH LANGUAGE LEARNERS

**Color Synonyms** Explain to students that the word *scarlet* is a synonym for the word *red*. There are many synonyms for *red*, including *crimson, ruby, burgundy,* and *cherry*. Help students locate examples of each of these shades of red and label them with sticky notes. Then lead students to discuss the connotations associated with each synonym.

**Develop Reading Fluency: Options for Reading** Divide students into two groups in preparation for a choral reading of the poem. Have one group take the role of the first speaker, reading the first two lines of each stanza. Have the second group take the role of the second speaker, reading the last two lines of each stanza.

Remind students to use pacing, intonation, and expression. Model these practices as necessary. In addition, provide students with the copy master, and have students work in pairs or groups to practice fluency.

Ⓡ **RESOURCE MANAGER—Copy Master**
Reading Fluency p. 98

## What triggers a sense of **ALARM**?

**Discuss** Direct students' attention to lines 1–16. Ask: How do the questions asked by the first speaker convey a growing sense of alarm? *Possible answer: The questions suggest unexplained, possibly threatening behavior on the part of the soldiers. The questions in the fourth stanza, in particular, suggest alarm, because the soldiers have suddenly left the road, making the reader wonder where they are headed, and why.*

### Analyze Visuals

*Possible answer: The mood created by the painting is serious and purposeful. The slanted lines and angular shapes, suggesting rapid, unified motion toward a particular goal, contribute to this mood. The subject matter—armed soldiers quickly marching forward—also contributes to this mood, as does the artist's use of blue, red, and gray battlefield colors.*

**About the Art** British artist Christopher Richard Wynne Nevinson (1889–1946) created some of the most striking paintings of World War I. His experiences as a volunteer ambulance driver during that war affected him deeply. His paintings tend to portray soldiers not as heroic fighters but as mechanized masses of men caught up in warfare. *Returning to the Trenches* suggests the relentless forward movement of troops heading into battle.

**FOR STRUGGLING READERS**

**Concept Support** Reinforce students' understanding of the ballad form by helping them complete a chart identifying narrative elements of the plot, setting, and characters in "O What Is That Sound."

| Lines | Plot | Setting | Characters |
|-------|------|---------|------------|
| 1–4 | soldiers coming | | two speakers talking |
| 5–8 | they have weapons | daytime sun | |
| 9–12 | | morning | |

## C SOUND DEVICES

**Answer:** *Lines 17 and 19—"care" and "dear"—create slant rhyme.*

POETIC FORM  COMMON CORE RL 10

### D *Model the Skill:* BALLAD

Create a chart on the board with the following ballad characteristics listed in rows: repetition, rhythm, rhyme scheme, characters, dialogue, and implication. List examples from the poem for each characteristic.

**Possible answer:** *"O What Is That Sound" is a traditional ballad—that is, it tells a story. The repetition, regular rhythm, and simple rhyme scheme are such that the poem lends itself to singing or recitation. The poem contains characters and dialogue, and, like many traditional ballads, it implies more than it explicitly states.*

TEXT ANALYSIS  COMMON CORE RL 4

### E SOUND DEVICES

**Possible answer: Rhyme:** *"door" (line 33) and "floor" (line 35); "turning" (line 34) and "burning" (line 36).* **Repetition:** *"turning, turning" in line 34*

## SELECTION WRAP-UP

**READ WITH A PURPOSE** Now that students have finished the selection, have them consider the relationship between the speakers. How does Auden reveal the relationship between the speakers? **Possible answer:** *Speaker 2 addresses speaker 1 as dear, a term of endearment. In lines 29–31, the two speakers discuss vows of love. The speakers are likely husband and wife.*

★ **CRITIQUE** Ask students whether they think the simplicity of the poem's language and structure adds to, or detracts from, the story the poem tells. Have students support their answers with details from the poem.

Detail of *Returning to the Trenches.* © National Gallery of Canada, Ottawa.

> O haven't they stopped for the doctor's care,
>     Haven't they reined their horses, their horses?
> Why, they are none of them wounded, dear.
> 20     None of these forces. C
>
> O is it the parson they want, with white hair,
>     Is it the parson, is it, is it?
> No, they are passing his gateway, dear,
>     Without a visit.
>
> 25 O it must be the farmer who lives so near.
>     It must be the farmer so cunning, so cunning?
> They have passed the farmyard already, dear,
>     And now they are running. D
>
> O where are you going? Stay with me here!
> 30     Were the vows you swore deceiving, deceiving?
> No, I promised to love you, dear,
>     But I must be leaving.
>
> O it's broken the lock and splintered the door,
>     O it's the gate where they're turning, turning;
> 35 Their boots are heavy on the floor
>     And their eyes are burning. E

**C SOUND DEVICES**
**Slant rhyme** refers to end rhymes that are not exact, as in "chair" and "cheer." Which two lines in this stanza create slant rhyme?

**D BALLAD**
What characteristics of a ballad do you find in this poem?

**E SOUND DEVICES**
Reread lines 33–36 aloud. What words in this stanza are emphasized by **rhyme** and **repetition**?

## DIFFERENTIATED INSTRUCTION

### FOR ENGLISH LANGUAGE LEARNERS

**Vocabulary: Multiple-Meaning Words** Have students look up these words in their dictionaries: *"gear"* (line 9); *"orders"* (line 15); *"forces"* (line 20); *"cunning"* (line 26); *"swore"* (line 30); *"burning"* (line 36). Then, for each word, have pairs of students write the meaning that best fits the context. Have volunteers read their definitions aloud. Discuss with the class whether the meaning chosen is correct.

### FOR ADVANCED LEARNERS/PRE-AP

**Interpret** Throughout the poem, the second speaker has been an enigma, no less so in this last stanza. Ask students these questions: Is the second speaker a coward? Does the second speaker really love the first speaker as stated in line 31? If so, why does the second speaker place the first speaker in danger by not being more forthright about the troops? Ask students to write a short paragraph explaining their views on this mysterious figure.

## Comprehension

1. **Recall** Whom do the speakers observe in the distance?

2. **Clarify** Which speaker seems calmer?

3. **Clarify** Reread the last stanza. What happens to the second speaker?

## Text Analysis

4. **Understand Poetry** What is happening in this poem? Briefly describe the actions that take place. Give possible reasons for these actions.

5. **Analyze Speakers** Review the chart you completed as you read. Who are the two speakers in the poem? What is their relationship? Be sure to support your **answers** with details from the poem.

6. **Analyze Sound Devices** Reread the poem, looking for examples of **rhyme, repetition,** and **assonance.** Use a chart like the one shown to record two examples of each sound device. Which sound device is most effective in conveying a sense of anxiety and drama in the poem? Explain your thinking.

| Sound Devices | Examples |
|---|---|
| Rhyme (internal or end) | |
| Repetition | |
| Assonance | |

7. **Interpret Imagery** Reread lines 33–36 and note the description of the soldiers and their actions. Based on this imagery, what is your impression of the soldiers? Will they defend the speakers or attack them? Explain.

8. **Evaluate a Ballad** In this ballad, one speaker asks a series of questions, and a second speaker gives answers. How does this pattern of **repetitive dialogue** affect the level of tension throughout the poem? Explain your answer.

## Text Criticism

9. **Historical Context** Auden wrote this poem in the 1930s. During this decade, many European countries, including Germany and Italy, were being taken over by fascist dictators. These tyrannical leaders exercised complete control over every aspect of public and private life and used force to crush opposition. In what ways does the poem reflect these political realities of the 1930s?

### What triggers a sense of ALARM?

What is the best way to handle a threatening situation?

**COMMON CORE**

**RL 3** Analyze how characters interact and advance the plot. **RL 4** Analyze the cumulative impact of specific word choices on meaning and tone. **RL 10** Read and comprehend poems.

O WHAT IS THAT SOUND   **791**

---

## Practice and Apply

For preliminary support of post-reading questions, use these copy masters:

**R** **RESOURCE MANAGER**—Copy Masters
Sound Devices p. 93

Question Support p. 97

Additional selection questions are provided for teachers on page 89.

### ANSWERS

## Comprehension

1. *The speakers see "scarlet soldiers"—probably British redcoats.*

2. *The second speaker seems calmer.*

3. *The second speaker abandons the first.*

## Text Analysis

COMMON CORE  RL 3, RL 4, RL 10

*Possible answers:*

4. *Two people watch as soldiers approach. One person is apprehensive, while the other is calm. When it becomes clear that the soldiers pose a threat, the latter runs away. The soldiers then break down the door.*

5. **COMMON CORE FOCUS** *Analyze Speakers The two speakers are probably married or lovers, as shown by the second speaker's use of the word* dear. *While no clear threat is apparent, the second speaker remains calm. However, when the soldiers threaten their house (line 28), the second speaker abandons the first (lines 31–32), who expresses shock at this betrayal of "vows" (lines 29–30).*

6. **COMMON CORE FOCUS** *Analyze Sound Devices Rhyme: "ear"/"dear," "drumming"/"coming"; Repetition: "this morning, this morning," "wheeling,*

---

*wheeling"; Assonance: "stopped"/"doctor's," "must"/ "cunning." Most students will probably identify repetition as the most effective device for conveying anxiety and drama, because it emphasizes key words and phrases, as in lines 14, 22, 30, and 34.*

7. *The soldiers are on the attack, as evidenced by the fact that they broke the lock and splintered the door without ever calling out.*

8. **COMMON CORE FOCUS** *Evaluate a Ballad The pattern heightens the tension, making readers feel as though they are sharing the experience with the speakers as it unfolds.*

## Text Criticism

9. *Students should recognize that the brutal home invasion reflects the use of force in a totalitarian regime.*

### What triggers a sense of ALARM?

*Students might suggest fleeing, negotiating, or fighting.*

---

## Assess and Reteach

### Assess

**DIAGNOSTIC AND SELECTION TESTS**
Selection Test A pp. 211–212
Selection Test B/C pp. 213–214

**Interactive Selection Test** on **thinkcentral.com**

### Reteach

**Level Up Online Tutorials** on **thinkcentral.com**

**Reteaching Workshops** on **thinkcentral.com**
Literature Lessons 14: Ballad

# Focus and Motivate

## COMMON CORE FOCUS

**RL 2** Determine a theme or central idea of a text and analyze in detail its development over the course of the text. **RL 3** Analyze how complex characters develop over the course of a text. **RL 10** Read and comprehend poems. **L 4c** Consult reference materials to determine or clarify a word's etymology.

## SUMMARIES

**"The Seven Ages of Man"** In this dramatic monologue from Shakespeare's play *As You Like It*, a character named Jaques describes people as players on the world's stage who go through seven major periods, or "ages in their lives."

**"The Road Not Taken"** In this metaphorical poem, the speaker describes the choice he made when faced with two roads in a wood. By choosing to go down the less traveled road, he made a decision that affected the rest of his life.

## Do you set your own COURSE?

Present the question. Ask students for examples of choices they or someone they know made that had strong impacts on their life journeys. Then have students complete the *ROLE-PLAY*.

---

# Do you set your own COURSE?

## COMMON CORE

**RL 2** Determine a theme or central idea of a text and analyze in detail its development over the course of the text. **RL 3** Analyze how complex characters develop over the course of a text. **RL 10** Read and comprehend poems. **L 4c** Consult reference materials to determine or clarify a word's etymology.

If life is a journey, then who's driving? Some people feel that they make their own choices about where to turn and how far to drive, while others feel they are simply following a course set by someone else. The poems that follow suggest two very different views of this question.

*ROLE-PLAY* Imagine that you are applying for a job or preparing for a college interview. With a partner, take turns interviewing one another about your life goals. Where do you see yourself in 5 years? in 10 years? in 15 years? When answering these questions, explain what choices you may have to make in order to achieve these goals.

792

---

## Selection Resources

See resources on the **Teacher One Stop DVD-ROM** *and on* **thinkcentral.com**.

 **RESOURCE MANAGER UNIT 7**
Plan and Teach, pp. 99–106
Text Analysis and Reading
   Skill, pp. 107–110†

**DIAGNOSTIC AND SELECTION TESTS**
Selection Tests, pp. 215–218

**BEST PRACTICES TOOLKIT**
Cluster Diagram, p. B18

**TECHNOLOGY**
- **Teacher One Stop DVD-ROM**
- **Student One Stop DVD-ROM**
- **Audio Anthology CD**
- **GrammarNotes DVD-ROM**
- **ExamView Test Generator**
  on the **Teacher One Stop**

---

\* Resources for Differentiation        † Also in Spanish        ‡ Also in Haitian Creole and Vietnamese

## POETIC FORM: DRAMATIC MONOLOGUE

A **dramatic monologue** is a poem in which the speaker addresses a silent or absent listener, as if engaged in a private conversation. The speaker often reveals his or her own feelings, attitudes, motivations, and character traits in a moment of high intensity or deep emotion. "The Seven Ages of Man" is an example of a dramatic monologue; it is delivered by a character in Shakespeare's play *As You Like It*.

## TEXT ANALYSIS: METER

**Rhythm** is the pattern of stressed and unstressed syllables in a line of poetry. Rhythm that follows a regular pattern from line to line is called **meter**. Shakespeare used a very even meter:

They have their exits and their entrances;

And one man in his time plays many parts.

In the next example, from Frost, notice that the number of accents is the same in each line, but the rhythm varies slightly:

I shall be telling this with a sigh

Somewhere ages and ages hence

Poets use meter for the same reasons that a songwriter does: it sounds nice, it's easy to remember, and it allows for extra emphasis. Read the following poems aloud and tap your foot as you go. Then ask yourself these questions:

- Is the meter obvious or subtle? Is it close to normal speech?
- Where does the emphasis fall in each line?

***Review:*** Rhyme Scheme

## READING SKILL: ANALYZE IDEAS IN POETRY

You can better understand poems by looking for the **main idea** in each section. "The Seven Ages of Man" can be divided into seven sections—one for each "age." "The Road Not Taken" is already divided into four stanzas. As you read each poem, record the main idea of each "age" or stanza.

| "The Seven Ages of Man" | |
|---|---|
| Age | Main Idea |
| 1. infancy | |
| 2. school-boy days | |

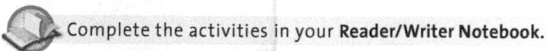 Complete the activities in your **Reader/Writer Notebook**.

---

## Meet the Authors

### William Shakespeare
#### 1564–1616

**Timeless Greatness**
Shakespeare is certainly the most famous writer in the world and arguably the greatest writer who ever lived. He wrote 37 plays, ranging from comedies to tragedies. He also published some of the most beautiful lyric poetry in the English language, including 154 sonnets, before he died at age 52. In his own time, theater audiences loved him and critics praised his incredible talent. But his contemporary Ben Jonson foresaw Shakespeare's indelible mark on the future: "He was not of an age, but for all time!"

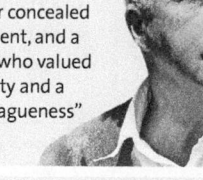

### Robert Frost
#### 1874–1963

**Beloved American Poet**
Declared America's poet laureate before the official creation of such a position, Robert Frost had become a beloved public figure by the time he died. The U.S. Senate passed a resolution honoring him, the state of Vermont named a mountain after him, and he was the first poet ever invited to recite his work at a presidential inauguration. Still, Frost is something of a puzzle. He was a modern poet who often used traditional rhyme and meter, a New England farmer whose folksy manner concealed an inner torment, and a man of ideas who valued both objectivity and a "tantalizing vagueness" in poetry.

**Authors Online**
Go to **thinkcentral.com**. KEYWORD: HML9-793

**THINK**central

793

---

# Teach

TEXT ANALYSIS · COMMON CORE RL 10

## ● *Model the Skill:* METER

For instructional support, write these lines on the board and read them aloud. Tap your feet to mark each stressed syllable.

> The church bell peals so rich and strong,
> The city's noise just melts away;
> And here amid a crushing throng,
> My thoughts have drifted far astray.

Explain that there are four stressed syllables.

**GUIDED PRACTICE** Provide students with examples of poems with regular meters, and have them identify where the emphasis falls in each line.

---

READING SKILL · COMMON CORE RL 2

## ■ *Model the Skill:* ANALYZE IDEAS IN POETRY

For instructional support, identify the main idea of the stanza written on the board. The sound of church bells in a busy city sends the speaker's thoughts far from the surrounding noise and crowds.

**GUIDED PRACTICE** Have students examine another stanza from a poem and state its main idea.

 **RESOURCE MANAGER**—Copy Master Analyze Ideas in Poetry p. 109 (for student use while reading the selection)

---

## DIFFERENTIATED INSTRUCTION

### FOR STRUGGLING READERS

**Dramatic Monologue** Ask students to think of examples of songs in which a "speaker" expresses views as if engaged in a private conversation. Help students recognize the parallel between songs in which a speaker reveals his or her feelings and poems in which the speaker delivers a dramatic monologue.

# Practice and Apply

## READ WITH A PURPOSE

*Help students set a purpose for reading. Ask students to consider how the speaker in each poem feels about people's choices in life.*

### A *Model the Skill:* DRAMATIC MONOLOGUE

Model how to use a Cluster Diagram to focus on how the speaker describes what happens during each stage.

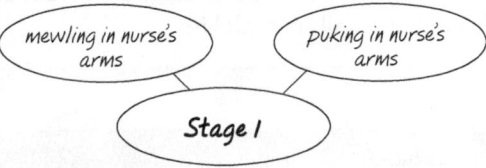

**Possible answer:** *Jaques's descriptions of the infant as "Mewling and puking" (lines 5–6) and the schoolboy as "whining" and "creeping like snail unwillingly to school" (lines 7 and 8–9) show his negative attitude toward childhood.*

**BEST PRACTICES TOOLKIT—Transparency**
Cluster Diagram p. B18

### B *Model the Skill:* METER

Model for students again how to tap your foot to count stressed syllables.

**Answer:** *five*

### TEXT ANALYSIS: *Review*

### C RHYME SCHEME

**Possible answer:** *No; lines 21 and 22 rhyme, but the other lines do not.*

---

# THE SEVEN AGES OF MAN

### WILLIAM SHAKESPEARE

JAQUES:
All the world's a stage,
And all the men and women merely players:
They have their exits and their entrances;
And one man in his time plays many parts,
5 His acts being seven ages. At first the infant,
Mewling[1] and puking in the nurse's arms.
And then the whining school-boy, with his satchel,
And shining morning face, creeping like snail
Unwillingly to school. And then the lover, **A**
10 Sighing like furnace, with a woeful ballad[2]
Made to his mistress' eyebrow. Then a soldier,
Full of strange oaths, and bearded like the pard,[3]
Jealous in honor, sudden and quick in quarrel,
Seeking the bubble reputation[4]
15 Even in the cannon's mouth. And then the justice, **B**
In fair round belly with good capon lin'd,[5]
With eyes severe, and beard of formal cut,
Full of wise saws and modern instances;[6]
And so he plays his part. The sixth age shifts
20 Into the lean and slipper'd pantaloon,[7]
With spectacles on nose and pouch on side,
His youthful hose well sav'd, a world too wide **C**

---

1. **mewling:** crying or whimpering.
2. **woeful ballad:** sad, sentimental song.
3. **pard:** leopard.
4. **bubble reputation:** reputation, which disintegrates as quickly as a bubble.
5. **with good capon** (kā'pŏn') **lin'd:** full of chicken.
6. **saws...instances:** old sayings and examples showing how they still apply.
7. **pantaloon** (păn'tə-loon'): a foolish old man.

**A DRAMATIC MONOLOGUE**
Reread lines 5–9. Notice how Jaques describes the infant and the schoolboy. What do these descriptions reveal about his attitude toward childhood?

**B METER**
Read aloud lines 10–15, tapping your foot at each stressed syllable. How many stressed syllables are in each line?

**C RHYME SCHEME**
Does Shakespeare employ a rhyme scheme for this poem? Support your answer.

---

## DIFFERENTIATED INSTRUCTION

### FOR ENGLISH LANGUAGE LEARNERS

**Understand Content** Draw a series of seven boxes on the board. Work with students to find photographs that illustrate each age of man in magazines. Then cut out and tape the photographs above each box. Ask students to take turns filling each box with words from the poem that describe each age.

### FOR STRUGGLING READERS

**Develop Reading Fluency** Read the poems aloud, using intonation, pacing, and expression to convey mood and drama. You might also have students echo-read the poems in sections—by "ages" for the Shakespeare poem and by stanzas for the Frost poem.

In addition, distribute the copy master, and have students work in pairs or groups to practice fluency.

**R RESOURCE MANAGER—Copy Master**
Reading Fluency p. 112

*The First and the Last Steps*, Emilio Longoni. Private Collection. © Alinari/Art Resource, New York.

◀ **Analyze Visuals**

After reading the poem, what connection can you see between the poem and this image?

For his shrunk shank;[8] and his big manly voice,
Turning again toward childish treble,[9] pipes
25 And whistles in his sound. Last scene of all,
That ends this strange eventful history,
Is second childishness and mere oblivion,[10]
Sans teeth, sans eyes, sans taste, sans everything. ⚠

---

8. **youthful hose . . . shank:** The stockings of his youth are too large for his shrunken calves.

9. **treble:** a high-pitched voice.

10. **oblivion** (ə-blĭv′ē-ən): complete forgetfulness.

---

**COMMON CORE** L 4c

⚠ **FOREIGN WORDS**
The word *sans* is a French word that means "without." In this instance, Shakespeare is saying the seventh age takes away everything you have, including your teeth, sight, taste, and memory. What other common English words can you think of that have foreign origins? Use a dictionary to confirm your answers.

---

## BACKGROUND

**Jaques** In Shakespeare's comedy *As You Like It*, the character Jaques has a melancholy view of life and judges others from the sidelines.

## Analyze Visuals

*Possible answer: The painting, like the poem, focuses on stages of life, connecting childhood and old age.*

**About the Art** Italian artist Emilio Longoni lived from 1859 to 1932.

---

**VOCABULARY**                    COMMON CORE L 4c

⚠ **FOREIGN WORDS**

***Possible answers:*** *bon voyage (French), bon appétit (French), mano a mano (Spanish), bona fide (Latin), en route (French), etcetera (Latin).*

Have students use their words in two or three sentences. Ask for volunteers to share their sentences.

---

## TIERED DISCUSSION PROMPTS

Direct students' attention to lines 1–5. Use these prompts to help students understand the metaphor that "All the world's a stage":

**Connect** In what situations are people like actors playing a part? *Students may mention jobs or family life.*

**Analyze** What "exits" and "entrances" do people make in life? *Possible answer: We exit at death and enter at birth; we also enter and exit various stages of life.*

**Synthesize** Jaques's view is that men and women are "merely players" (line 2). Is he a pessimist or a realist? Explain. *Some students may argue that Jaques is overly pessimistic because life involves more than just acting out a predetermined role. Others may argue that Jaques has a realistic view of our place in the world.*

---

## FOR STRUGGLING READERS

**Vocabulary Support** Point out that "second childishness" (line 27) is meant to connote helplessness and dependency. The connotations are different from those of the modern term *second childhood*, which suggests carefree playfulness.

## FOR ADVANCED LEARNERS/PRE–AP

**Analyzing** Ancient Greek philosophers wrestled with the question as to whether fate determines character or character determines fate. Have students discuss which of these viewpoints the speaker in "The Seven Ages of Man" expresses. Which viewpoint do students support, and why?

Prereading for this poem is found on page 792.

## Analyze Visuals

**Activity** Ask students how the scenes in the poem and painting are similar. *Possible answer: In both scenes, a "road" goes through a wood, and one side of the road seems less grassy than the other.*

**About the Art** British artist William Samuel Jay lived from 1843 to 1933.

---

### READING SKILL
**COMMON CORE**
**RL 2**

**E** *Model the Skill:* **ANALYZE IDEAS**

Remind students that the main idea is not always explicitly stated. In this case, tell students to focus on the concept of the two roads. Then, remind students to add the main idea to their Reading Skill charts.

***Possible answer:*** *The main idea is that people have to make choices (represented by the two roads).*

---

### TEXT ANALYSIS
**COMMON CORE**
**RL 10**

**F** **METER**

***Answer:*** *four pulses per line; words: "took," "other," "just," "fair" (line 6); "having," "perhaps," "better," "claim" (line 7); "because," "grassy," "wanted," "wear" (line 8); "as," "that," "passing," "there" (line 9); "worn," "really," "about," "same" (line 10)*

---

### TEXT ANALYSIS: *Review*

**G** **RHYME SCHEME**

***Answer:*** *The rhyme scheme is abaab.*

---

## SELECTION WRAP–UP

**READ WITH A PURPOSE** Have students compare and contrast the poems. How does each speaker feel about people's choices in life? *Possible answer: Shakespeare's speaker: choices have no effect on the inevitability of death; Frost's speaker: choices affect the qualities of their lives*

★ **CRITIQUE** Have students choose the poem they feel is most relevant to their own life.

---

# The Road Not Taken

### Robert Frost

*In the Beechwoods*, William Samuel Jay. Oil on canvas, 91.4 × 122 cm. Private collection. © Bourne Gallery, Reigate, Surrey/The Bridgeman Art Library.

Two roads diverged[1] in a yellow wood,
And sorry I could not travel both
And be one traveler, long I stood
And looked down one as far as I could
5 To where it bent in the undergrowth; **E**

Then took the other, as just as fair,
And having perhaps the better claim,
Because it was grassy and wanted wear;
Though as for that the passing there
10 Had worn them really about the same, **F**

And both that morning equally lay
In leaves no step had trodden[2] black.
Oh, I kept the first for another day!
Yet knowing how way leads on to way,
15 I doubted if I should ever come back.

I shall be telling this with a sigh
Somewhere ages and ages hence:
Two roads diverged in a wood, and I—
I took the one less traveled by,
20 And that has made all the difference. **G**

---

1. **diverged:** branched out; went in different directions.
2. **trodden:** walked on or trampled.

**E** **ANALYZE IDEAS**
Reread lines 1–5. What main idea is the poet expressing here?

**F** **METER**
Read aloud lines 1-10, tapping your foot with each stressed syllable. How many pulses are in each line? Which words in the second stanza are emphasized by the pulses?

**G** **RHYME SCHEME**
What rhyme scheme does Frost use in this poem?

---

## DIFFERENTIATED INSTRUCTION

### FOR STRUGGLING READERS

**Vocabulary Support** Assign pairs of students to find a definition for each of the underlined words or phrases from the poem: "a yellow <u>wood</u>" (line 1), "<u>long</u> I stood" (line 3), "just as <u>fair</u>" (line 6), "<u>wanted wear</u>" (line 8), and "<u>ages and ages hence</u>" (line 17). Have students write their definitions on the board. Then ask other students to challenge these definitions until students arrive at a consensus.

### FOR ENGLISH LANGUAGE LEARNERS

**Media and Concepts** To build and reinforce the concept of meter in poetry, have students listen to an audio recording of this poem. Have students listen to the complete poem once or twice; then, ask students to clap their hands to indicate the stressed syllables in the poem. You may also ask small groups of students to clap the stressed syllables for different stanzas.

## Comprehension

1. **Recall** In "The Seven Ages of Man," which two stages follow childhood?

2. **Paraphrase** According to Jaques, what happens to people in the last stage of life?

3. **Recall** In "The Road Not Taken," where do Frost's roads diverge?

4. **Clarify** Which road does the speaker choose?

## Text Analysis

5. **Analyze Ideas** Look at your chart of main ideas. On the basis of these ideas taken together, what do you think is the **theme** of each poem?

6. **Interpret Extended Metaphor** An extended metaphor compares two unlike things at length and in a number of ways, sometimes throughout an entire work. In "The Seven Ages of Man," the speaker compares the world to a stage. What does this comparison imply about the speaker's view of life?

7. **Analyze Dramatic Monologue** "The Seven Ages of Man" comes from Shakespeare's play *As You Like It.* Other characters in this play refer to Jaques as "the melancholy Jaques." Do you agree that Jaques has a gloomy outlook on life? Support your answer with details from his **dramatic monologue.** What else can you **infer** about Jaques from his speech?

8. **Interpret Symbol** In "The Road Not Taken," both roads lead into the woods, so the speaker cannot see where they go. What do the woods symbolize?

9. **Compare Themes** How would Frost's speaker respond to Jaques's statement "All the world's a stage, / And all the men and women merely players"? Cite evidence to support your answer.

10. **Evaluate Meter** "The Seven Ages of Man" is written in **iambic pentameter,** which has five stressed syllables alternating with five unstressed syllables per line. It is said to be the closest meter to human speech in English. "The Road Not Taken" is written loosely in **iambic tetrameter,** which has only four stresses instead of five. Which poem is easier to read aloud? Explain.

## Text Criticism

11. **Author's Style** In many of Shakespeare's plays, there is a character who comments philosophically on the world of the characters and on the world at large. It is sometimes thought that this character is speaking for Shakespeare himself. Could Jaques's monologue be an example of this? Explain.

> ### Do you set your own COURSE?
> Why is it important to make your own choices in life?

---

# Practice and Apply

For preliminary support of post-reading questions, use these copy masters:

**R** RESOURCE MANAGER—Copy Masters
Meter p. 107
Question Support p. 111

Additional selection questions are provided for teachers on page 103.

### ANSWERS

## Comprehension

1. *the lover and the soldier*

2. *People decline into a second childhood—forgetful and without teeth, sight, taste, or anything else.*

3. *in a forest*

4. *the road less traveled*

## Text Analysis

**COMMON CORE** RL 2, RL 3, RL 10

*Possible answers:*

5. ■ **COMMON CORE FOCUS** *Analyze Ideas* **"The Seven Ages of Man"**: *People's lives have seven predetermined stages.* **"The Road Not Taken"**: *People make choices in life without knowing what these choices will mean, but these choices often make all the difference in their lives.*

6. *The comparison implies that the speaker believes that people just play prescribed roles, with each role dictated by a given stage of life.*

7. ● **COMMON CORE FOCUS** *Analyze Dramatic Monologue His gloomy outlook is suggested by the ridicule he heaps upon man at each of his seven ages, from the puking*

---

*infant to the debilitated old man; readers can infer that Jaques respects few people, if any.*

8. *The woods symbolize the unexplored and unmapped future—choices in life.*

9. *Frost's speaker would respond that people are able to shape the course of their own lives—that they are not simply playing an assigned role, predetermined by their age.*

10. ● **COMMON CORE FOCUS** *Evaluate Meter Students should support their answers by citing specific examples of the different meters.*

## Text Criticism

11. *Some students may cite Jaques's conviction and eloquence as evidence that he is giving voice to Shakespeare's own views.*

> ### Do you set your own COURSE?
> *Students may say that one's choices affect the courses or qualities of their lives.*

---

# Assess and Reteach

### Assess

**DIAGNOSTIC AND SELECTION TESTS**
Selection Test A pp. 215–216
Selection Test B/C pp. 217–218

**Interactive Selection Test** on **thinkcentral.com**

### Reteach

**Level Up Online Tutorials** on **thinkcentral.com**

**Reteaching Workshops** on **thinkcentral.com**
Literature Lesson 22; Rhythm and Meter

# Focus and Motivate

## COMMON CORE FOCUS

**W 2a–f** Write informative/explanatory texts to examine complex ideas, concepts, and information through effective selection, organization, and analysis of content. **W 4** Produce clear and coherent writing. **W 5** Develop and strengthen writing as needed by planning, revising, editing, rewriting, or trying a new approach. **W 9a (RL 1, 4)** Cite textual evidence; analyze the impact of specific word choices on meaning and tone. **W 10** Write routinely over shorter time frames for a range of tasks, purposes, and audiences. **L 1** Demonstrate command of the conventions of standard English grammar and usage. **L 2** Demonstrate command of the conventions of standard English capitalization and punctuation. **L 2c** Spell correctly.

## WRITE WITH A PURPOSE

To achieve the purpose, make sure that students understand that an analysis identifies, examines, and explains the effects of an author's style choices.

## COMMON CORE TRAITS

Review the *COMMON CORE TRAITS* with students, focusing primarily on the development of ideas and the organization of ideas. Compare the list of traits with the rubric on page 806.

## ADDITIONAL TASKS

**Write About World Languages** Write an analysis in which you compare and contrast style elements in a poem written in a language other than English with its English translation. **Possible subjects:** Poem by Pablo Neruda or Gary Soto

**Write About Music** Write an analysis of a song—a poem set to music. In your analysis, consider not only the song's lyrics but also the music and how it affects the way the words are expressed. Make sure the song you choose is appropriate for class.

### Writing Online

The following tools are available online at **thinkcentral.com** and on **Write*Smart* CD-ROM**:
- Interactive Graphic Organizers
- Interactive Student Models
- Interactive Revision Lessons

*Writing Workshop*
*INFORMATIVE TEXT*

# Analysis of a Poem

*Essential Course of Study*

In this unit, you've focused on elements of poetry, such as word choice, imagery, and figurative language. In this workshop, you will write **an analysis of a poem** in which you examine one or two elements of the author's style and its effect upon readers.

 Complete the workshop activities in your **Reader/Writer Notebook.**

## WRITE WITH A PURPOSE

### WRITING TASK

Choose a poem and write an **analysis of the author's style.** Your analysis should help the audience understand one or two elements of the author's style and its effect on readers.

### Idea Starters
- interpret figurative language in "I Ask My Mother to Sing"
- interpret form in "Elegy for the Giant Tortoises" or "Ode to My Socks"
- interpret structure in "400-Meter Freestyle"

### THE ESSENTIALS

Here are some common purposes, audiences, and formats for literary analysis.

| PURPOSES | AUDIENCES | FORMATS |
|---|---|---|
| • to better understand a poem and to explain it to others | • classmates and teacher | • essay for class |
| | • poets | • letter or e-mail to a poet |
| • to understand the effects of a writer's choices | • poetry magazine readers | • review for a student literary magazine |
| | • Web users | • blog for fans of the poet |

## COMMON CORE TRAITS

### 1. DEVELOPMENT OF IDEAS
- presents an **engaging introduction**
- develops a **controlling idea** that offers an **analysis** of one or two elements of the author's style
- supports main points of analysis with **relevant details** and **quotations from the text**
- concludes with a **summary of main points** and **insights**

### 2. ORGANIZATION OF IDEAS
- **organizes** ideas in a logical way
- uses varied **transitions** to create **cohesion** and **connect ideas**

### 3. LANGUAGE FACILITY AND CONVENTIONS
- establishes and maintains a **formal style** and **objective tone**
- includes **precise language**
- uses **singular and plural possessives** correctly
- employs correct **grammar, mechanics,** and **spelling**

**Writing Online** THINK central

Go to **thinkcentral.com**.
KEYWORD: HML9N-798

## Writing Workshop Resources

 **RESOURCE MANAGER UNIT 7**
Plan and Teach pp. 113–116
Prewriting–Editing pp. 117–121
Writing Rubric p. 122
Speaking and Listening p. 123
Writing Support p. 124*

 **BEST PRACTICES TOOLKIT**
Writing Template: Poem p. C35
Analysis Frame: Poetic Language and
  Style p. D38

**TECHNOLOGY**
- **Teacher One Stop DVD-ROM**
- **Student One Stop DVD-ROM**
- **Write*Smart* CD-ROM**
- **GrammarNotes DVD-ROM**

**Writing Center on thinkcentral.com**

*See resources on the **Teacher One Stop DVD-ROM** and on **thinkcentral.com**.*

\* Resources for Differentiation

# Planning/Prewriting

 **COMMON CORE** W 2a-f Write informative/explanatory texts to examine complex ideas through the effective, selection, organization, and analysis of content. W 5 Develop and strengthen writing by planning.

## Getting Started

### CHOOSE A POEM FOR ANALYSIS

Choose a poem for analysis that contains sufficient elements to analyze. Then, use a graphic organizer to list elements of the work that catch your attention. Also, note questions and observations.

▶ **WHAT DOES IT LOOK LIKE?**

| Interesting Elements in "Spring is like a perhaps hand" | Questions and Observations |
|---|---|
| "perhaps hand" | What does Cummings mean by a "perhaps hand?" |
| parentheticals | Why use parentheses? Maybe the poem is an afterthought. |
| "window" "people stare" | What is the window, and why are people staring at it? |

### THINK ABOUT AUDIENCE AND PURPOSE

Your **audience** includes people who have read the poem or who are interested in the poet's work. Your **purpose** is to share your ideas about the effects of the stylistic elements.

▶ **ASK YOURSELF**

- What will people who haven't read the poem need to know?
- How can I support my ideas to appeal to readers who have different views about the poet's style?

### IDENTIFY KEY STYLISTIC ELEMENTS

Identify the elements of the author's style, such as figurative language, repetition, and unusual word choice, that make the poem so interesting. What is the cumulative effect of these elements on the poem? Do the word choices make the poem funny or sad? Does the figurative language create a vivid image? Use a graphic organizer to list **style elements** and **evidence** from the poem. Then choose the elements that most influenced you.

▶ **WHAT DOES IT LOOK LIKE?**

| Style Elements | Evidence |
|---|---|
| Figurative Language | Simile: "Spring is like a perhaps hand" |
| Unusual Word Choice | "perhaps hand" |
| Capitalization and Punctuation | Spring, Nowhere, Hand, Old, New three parentheticals, two commas, one period |

### DEVELOP A CONTROLLING IDEA

Your **controlling idea,** or thesis statement, should identify the main points of your analysis. Continue modifying or refining this statement as you draft.

▶ **WHAT DOES IT LOOK LIKE?**

In "Spring is like a perhaps hand," E. E. Cummings uses language and punctuation to suggest that the arrival of spring creates a shift in the way that people view the world that is both familiar and fresh.

WRITING WORKSHOP **799**

---

## DIFFERENTIATED INSTRUCTION

### FOR ENGLISH LANGUAGE LEARNERS

**Language: Reinforce Terms** Write these terms on the board and review them with students:

- *literary analysis:* the expression of a writer's understanding of a textual work
- *elements of style:* the language elements an author uses to express his or her ideas
- *tone:* the speaker's attitude toward the subject as expressed through word choice

- *figurative language:* words that have meaning beyond their literal translations
- *imagery:* language that appeals to the five senses
- *form:* type of poetry and its associated traits such as an ode or an elegy
- *structure:* the way lines and words are arranged on a page
- *diction:* a poet's choice of words
- *sound devices:* patterns of sound that occur when a poem is read aloud

---

# Teach

## Planning/ Prewriting

 **COMMON CORE** W 2a-f, W 5

▶ **CHOOSE A POEM FOR ANALYSIS** Tell students that poems that are between ten and twenty lines that are rich in meaning are well-suited for this assignment. Recommend that students re-read the poems in this unit; ask for recommendations from teachers, friends, family members or librarians; skim and scan poetry anthologies; or search the Internet to locate poems.

▶ **THINK ABOUT AUDIENCE AND PURPOSE** Point out to students that people who want to read a literary analysis are likely to be interested in poetry and in the work of the poet who is the subject of the analysis, but readers may have varying degrees of expertise. Remind them that to share their ideas effectively, they should provide examples and explanations that will aid understanding for those who are not well-versed in the subject matter.

▶ **IDENTIFY KEY STYLISTIC ELEMENTS** Remind students that they will have to read their poems several times before they find all the elements they might wish to include in their analyses. Also, tell students that their analyses of a poem may change as they read and re-read it.

▶ **DEVELOP A CONTROLLING IDEA** Remind students that a controlling idea should do two things—offer an analysis of the poem's style, and identify the key elements that support the analysis. Tell students to draw on the notes they make in their graphic organizers as they formulate their controlling idea. They should focus on the elements in their charts that are most important to their poems. Make sure that students understand that there is more than one way to interpret and analyze a poem. However, the lines and style elements chosen from the poem should support their ideas.

**R** **RESOURCE MANAGER—Copy Masters**
Planning/Prewriting p. 117
Drafting p. 118
Revising and Editing pp. 119–120
Ask a Peer Reader p. 121
Rubric p. 122
Writing Support p. 124

WRITING WORKSHOP **799**

## Planning/Prewriting continued

▶ *ORGANIZE YOUR IDEAS* Recommend that students number each style element they have identified in order of importance. Tell students to consider importance within the poems and importance in supporting their controlling ideas. Finally, have students use their rankings to decide how they will organize their ideas.

▶ *PROVIDE EVIDENCE FROM THE TEXT* Make sure that students understand that each body paragraph should include a quotation or example from their poems and an explanation of how the quotation or example supports their controlling ideas. Point out that the writer of the Student Draft will devote at least one paragraph to Cummings's use of parentheses (an example). She will explain that Cummings uses the parentheses to frame the window he describes. This idea helps support the point that Cummings uses punctuation to create a shift in perspective or people's views of the world.

 **YOUR TURN** As students work to analyze the author's style choices, remind them to pose questions. For example, *What do the parentheses have to do with the shift from winter to spring? What do the parentheses have to do with the window Cummings describes? How are parentheses traditionally used? How does Cummings use them?* The act of questioning will help students deconstruct their poems, allowing them to view each poem as a series of style choices.

For interactive revision tools, see

**WriteSmart CD-ROM**

**Writing Center** on **thinkcentral.com**

---

## Planning/Prewriting continued

### Getting Started

**ORGANIZE YOUR IDEAS**

Think about how you can present your ideas to make the purpose of your analysis clear to the audience. You will want to organize your ideas in a logical and cohesive way. An effective option for this type of writing is to arrange your ideas in **order of importance,** beginning with the least important element and building toward what you consider the most important one.

▶ **WHAT DOES IT LOOK LIKE?**

> Order of Importance
> 1. Figurative Language
>    • simile
>    • unusual word choice
> 2. Capitalization
>    • used sparingly
>    • five words only
> 3. Punctuation
>    • limited
>    • three parentheticals

**PROVIDE EVIDENCE FROM THE TEXT**

Every point you make about the author's style must be supported with well-chosen **evidence,** including **concrete details** and **quotations** from the text. Your evidence should be relevant to your controlling idea and sufficient enough to help your audience understand your analysis.

▶ **WHAT DOES IT LOOK LIKE?**

> Parentheticals
> **Evidence:** The bulk of the poem is enclosed in three sets of parentheses.
> **Effect:** The parentheses frame the window of spring at which the people stare.

**PEER REVIEW** Describe to a peer the purpose and audience of your analysis. Then, ask: What are the main points of my analysis? Which statements need to be supported with more evidence?

 **YOUR TURN** In your *Reader/Writer Notebook,* develop your writing plan. Create charts and outlines such as those on pages 799–800 to list and analyze stylistic elements. Consider the following questions as you analyze stylistic elements.

- How does the poet's choice of words create a cumulative effect in the poem? What is that effect?
- Does the poet use **figurative language,** such as metaphors or similes, to make comparisons?
- What **sound devices,** such as rhythm, rhyme, or repetition, does the poet use? What are their effects?

---

## DIFFERENTIATED INSTRUCTION

### FOR ENGLISH LANGUAGE LEARNERS

**Controlling Ideas** Students may have trouble formulating their controlling ideas. Give them the following starter formula: "In (title of poem), (poet's name) uses (style elements) to suggest that _____." Tell students to jump-start their drafts by using this formula and to base their body paragraphs on it. Later, they can revise their controlling ideas as necessary to enhance the flow of their writing.

### FOR STRUGGLING WRITERS

**Opinions versus Supportable Claims** Remind students that an analysis of a poem is not the same thing as an opinion. Tell them that analyses are more like claims than opinions. Opinions are often based on emotions and not always supported by facts. Claims should be based on evidence. In this case, students should base their claims on style elements that appear in the poems. Have students work with partners to identify claims that can be supported by their poems.

# Drafting

The following chart shows a structure for organizing a clear and coherent literary analysis.

 **COMMON CORE** W 4 Produce clear and coherent writing. W 9a (RL 1, 4) Cite textual evidence; analyze the impact of specific word choices on meaning and tone. L 1 Demonstrate command of the conventions of standard English grammar and usage when writing.

## *Organizing Your Literary Analysis*

**INTRODUCTION**
- Begin with an engaging **question** or a **comment** about the poem.
- Identify the **poet** and **literary work**.
- Provide a **controlling idea** that describes the effect of the stylistic element being examined.

▼

**BODY**
- Introduce **relevant evidence**, such as **quotations** and concrete **details** to support the controlling idea.
- Organize your main points in **order of importance** and use **varied transitions** to create cohesion and connect related ideas.
- Use **precise language** to explain the effect of each example cited. If necessary, define any **domain-specific vocabulary,** such as literary terms.
- Incorporate a **variety of sentence structures** into your response.
- Maintain a **formal style** and **objective tone** by avoiding slang and by supporting your analysis with evidence from the text.

▼

**CONCLUDING SECTION**
- Summarize the **main points** of your analysis.
- Offer an overall **insight** about the author's style and its effects.

## GRAMMAR IN CONTEXT: SINGULAR AND PLURAL POSSESSIVES

Part of analytical writing includes the ability to attribute a poem correctly to the writer. Treat the name of the poet as a singular noun.

| Rules | Examples |
|---|---|
| To form the possessive of a singular noun, add an apostrophe and an s—even when the singular noun ends in an s. ▶ | *Margaret Atwood's poem* *E. E. Cummings's poem* |
| To form the possessive case of a plural noun ending in s, add only the apostrophe. To form the possessive case of a plural noun that does not end in s, add an apostrophe and an s. ▶ | *the poets' interests in nature* *the people's intent stare* |

 **YOUR TURN** Develop a first draft of your analysis, following the structure outlined in the *Organizing Your Literary Analysis* chart above. As you write, pay attention to how you form possessives. To choose the correct possessive, decide whether the noun is singular or plural.

---

**FOR ENGLISH LANGUAGE LEARNERS**

**Possessives** Work with students to form possessive phrases based on the classroom setting. For example, Sue's book, Chris's backpack, the class's work, and so on. Record students' ideas on the board without the appropriate apostrophes to show possession. Then, have students take turns identifying whether a particular phrase is singular or plural and adding the appropriate apostrophe to show possession. Tell students that they may consult their peers for help as needed.

**FOR STRUGGLING WRITERS**

**Singular and Plural Subjects** Tell students that *Cummings* is a singular subject that ends with an *s*. To form a singular possessive, the writer must add an apostrophe and another *s*: Cummings's poem. However, if a plural subject ends with an *s*, the writer simply adds the apostrophe: poets' works. Emphasize that it is crucial to identify whether a possessive subject is singular or plural before placing an apostrophe. Have students work with partners to create further examples.

---

# Practice and Apply

## Drafting  **COMMON CORE** W 4, W 9a (RL 1, 4), L 1

▶ *INTRODUCTION* Suggest that students grab the attention of their readers by relating the content of their poems to experiences that people share. For example, everyone witnesses the shift from winter to spring each year. Lead students to discuss how a writer might introduce Cummings's poem in a way that will interest readers.

▶ *BODY* Tell students to quote only the necessary parts of a poetic line or series of lines. The bulk of each body paragraph should contain the writer's own words as he or she explains how a particular quotation supports the controlling idea.

▶ *CONCLUDING SECTION* To offer an overall insight, tell students to think about how their poems are connected to broader themes in the lives in their readers. For example, how does the subtle change in seasons affect the lives of the people in Cummings's poem? This effect probably extends to readers, as well.

### GRAMMAR IN CONTEXT: SINGULAR AND PLURAL POSSESSIVES

For additional practice, have students correct the singular and plural possessives in the sentences below.

- That poets book won most critics highest praises. (*That poet's book won most critics' highest praises.*)
- The reading of Ted Hughes poem moved listeners to tears. (*The reading of Ted Hughes's poem moved listeners to tears.*)
- The poets signed all their fans copies of their books. (*The poets signed all their fans' copies of their books.*)

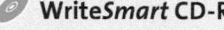 **YOUR TURN** Ask students to complete the **Your Turn** activity independently. Remind them to form possessives correctly. Suggest that students write their drafts double-spaced so that they can make revisions easily later.

For a literary analysis writing template, see

**Write*Smart* CD-ROM**

**Writing Center** on **thinkcentral.com**

# Revising

**Model the Skill** Using a draft analysis on a transparency or electronic whiteboard, model how to use the questions, tips, and strategies suggested in the chart to evaluate and revise. You might use the analysis of a student from another class or from a previous year. Make sure to remove the student's name from the analysis so that the writer remains anonymous.

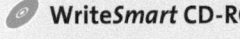

**YOUR TURN** During peer review, remind students to avoid telling their partners what to do. Instead, they should offer suggestions and ask questions without appearing bossy. Remind students that the goal is to help other students make their writing clear and effective. However, the ultimate decision regarding revisions is the writer's.

For interactive revision tools, see

**Write*Smart* CD-ROM**

**Writing Center** on **thinkcentral.com**

---

# Revising

As you revise, consider the controlling idea, points of analysis, and textual evidence. The following chart will help you revise, rewrite, and improve your draft.

## LITERARY ANALYSIS

| Ask Yourself | Tips | Revision Strategies |
|---|---|---|
| 1. Does the introduction contain a question or comment that will interest readers? | ▶ **Underline** the opening question or comment. | ▶ **Add** a question or comment about the subject of the poem to engage the audience. |
| 2. Does the controlling idea introduce readers to the stylistic element or elements to be discussed? | ▶ **Underline** the title and author. **Put a check mark** above the element and its overall effect. | ▶ **Elaborate** on your controlling idea by describing a stylistic element and explaining its effect. |
| 3. Are points presented in order of importance with clear and varied transitions between related ideas? | ▶ **Label** each paragraph with a **plus, check, or minus** to rate the importance of its point. **Circle** the transitions that link the points. | ▶ **Rearrange** body paragraphs as needed to present points in order of importance. **Add** varied transitions to connect ideas as needed. |
| 4. Is each point illustrated with relevant textual evidence? | ▶ **Place a star** next to each quotation or detail from the poem. | ▶ **Add** quotations or details as necessary. Make sure you have at least one piece of supporting evidence for each idea. |
| 5. Do I maintain a formal style throughout the analysis? | ▶ **Bracket** slang and informal language. | ▶ **Reword** text to avoid slang and replace informal language with precise, formal words. |
| 6. Does the concluding section summarize the writer's ideas and provide an insight into the effect of the author's style? | ▶ **Place a check mark** above the restatement of the controlling idea and **circle** the concluding insight. | ▶ **Add** a summary of main points or a statement that makes the connection between the author's stylistic elements and their effect. |

 **YOUR TURN**

**PEER REVIEW** Exchange your analysis with a partner, or read your analysis aloud to your partner. As you read and comment, make sure to focus on textual evidence and quotations. Discuss whether the writer effectively supports his or her controlling idea. Provide concrete suggestions for improvement or reworking, using the revision strategies in the chart. If necessary, suggest that the writer try a new approach.

---

## DIFFERENTIATED INSTRUCTION

### FOR ENGLISH LANGUAGE LEARNERS
**Revision** Have students go back to the graphic organizers they filled out during the prewriting stage and write the examples, quotations, or explanations they have not included in their drafts on sticky notes. As they revise their drafts, tell students to place the sticky notes next to paragraphs where the examples, quotations, or explanations will support the points they are making. Challenge students to make sure that they have found the best places to include the examples or quotations.

### FOR STRUGGLING WRITERS
**Supporting Evidence** Students may have trouble identifying appropriate textual evidence to add to their analyses of poetry. Have students work in pairs to read aloud each other's drafts. After each paragraph, students should stop and ask, "Which example or quotation from the poem will help prove this point?" Students should go together to the poems to identify examples or quotations that can be added to each paragraph.

## ANALYZE A STUDENT DRAFT

Read this draft; notice the comments on its strengths as well as suggestions for improvement.

COMMON CORE

**W 5** Strengthen writing as needed by revising, editing, rewriting, or trying a new approach, focusing on addressing what is most significant for a specific purpose and audience. **L 2c** Spell correctly.

### Winter Becomes Spring

Adrienne Ramirez, Parkland High School

**1**     E. E. Cummings's poem "Spring is like a perhaps hand" captures a moment in time that is subtle and delicate—the shift from winter to spring. Cummings uses unusual and unexpected language to suggest that the arrival of spring creates a shift in the way that people view the world that is both familiar and fresh.

**2**     Using a simile, Cummings compares the coming of spring to a hand arranging items in a window: "Spring is like a perhaps hand / . . . arranging / a window." The hand arranges, changes, and places items in the window at which "people stare." Some of the items are "strange," and some of the items are "known." The act of "arranging and changing placing" creates a shift in perspective—or point of view. For example, the people may recognize a "known" tree that has stood in the same spot for years. Yet, suddenly, as if from nowhere, "strange" green leaf buds appear that were not there yesterday, or were they? The speaker uses his flare for language to describe the subtlety of spring as well. Spring is not a hand but a "perhaps hand." The shift from winter to spring is so delicate that the hand moves a "fraction of a flower" or places "an inch of air."

> The **introduction** identifies the poet and the literary work. The **controlling idea** presents the stylistic elements to be analyzed.

> Adrienne supports a main point about the author's style with a **quotation.** She elaborates on this **textual evidence** to explain the effect of the text on a reader.

> The analysis includes **precise language** such as "speaker" rather than *poet* or *writer.* However, the writer makes a mistake involving commonly confused words.

---

**LEARN HOW** **Distinguish Between Commonly Confused Words** Some words have similar pronunciations but different spellings and meanings. Other words share common meanings, although they are pronounced and spelled differently. Use the following chart or a dictionary to choose between commonly confused words.

| | |
|---|---|
| accept (agree) | except (excluding) |
| affect (to influence) | effect (to cause) |
| imminent (looming) | eminent (superior) |
| flair (talent) | flare (emergency signal) |
| than (contrast) | then (next in time) |

**ADRIENNE'S REVISION TO PARAGRAPH 2**

The speaker uses his ~~flare~~ _flair_ for language to describe the subtlety of spring as well.

---

## ANALYZE A STUDENT DRAFT

Explain that the Student Draft on this page is the first half of a literary analysis. Model reading the draft and the annotations in blue, explaining that the yellow highlighting illustrates the student's language choices. Explain that the following *Learn How* mini-lessons provide helpful information about ways to improve this student draft as well as students' own drafts.

**LEARN HOW** Distinguish Between Commonly Confused Words

Tell students that there are no tricks for correcting commonly confused words. Recommend that students review prior writing to identify the particular words that they commonly confuse. Then, tell students to create personal banks of these words to use as reference guides during the writing process.

---

### FOR ENGLISH LANGUAGE LEARNERS

**Homophones** Explain to students that words that have similar sounds but different spellings and meanings are called homophones. To familiarize students with common English homophones, develop playing cards for a "Go Fish" game where students are expected to match homophone pairings. When the game is complete, have students work together to identify the meanings of the words in each pairing. Students may consult dictionaries as needed.

### FOR STRUGGLING WRITERS

**Word Games** Have students work with partners to develop silly jokes or riddles that illustrate the meanings of the commonly confused word pairings. For example, *How would you describe a talented emergency worker?* Someone with a flair for flares. Invite students to share their best jokes or riddles aloud with the class.

Explain that the Student Draft is continued and completed on this page. Read the draft and annotations aloud and discuss. Ask students to comment on the student writer's concluding connection between style and effect.

❸     To reinforce this delicate seasonal shift, Cummings uses capitalization sparingly and deliberately to draw attention to five words: "Spring," "Nowhere," "Hand," "Old," and "New." These five words convey the bulk of Cummings's message. For instance, in the midst of winter, as if from "Nowhere," people may begin to see the purple buds of spring's first flower. These buds are a familiar sign of spring. However, they appear suddenly in places where no one remembers seeing them: "moving New and / Old things." Here again, spring creates a subtle shift in perspective.

Adrienne supports her points with quotations from the text. However, her analysis will be more effective if she incorporates evidence from the text into her own sentence structures.

❹     Cummings also uses punctuation sparingly. In addition to two commas and one period, the poem contains three parenthetical expressions. Generally, a writer uses parentheses to add extra, nonessential information to a sentence. In the first case, Cummings uses parentheses in this traditional way: "(which comes carefully / out of Nowhere)." However, Cummings goes on to enclose most of the remainder of the poem in parentheses. Shifting the purpose of the parentheses, Cummings uses them to frame the window he describes: "(while / people stare / arranging and changing placing / carefully there a strange / thing and a known thing here)." The phrase "people stare" appears in both the second and third parenthetical expressions, emphasizing that the parentheses frame the picture window at which people stare.

The writer organizes her analysis by discussing elements in **order of importance**—from least important to most important.

❺     The change in seasons and perspective that Cummings describes is so slight that the world shifts from winter to spring as people stare, nearly unable to perceive the moment during which the shift occurs. Fortunately, Cummings has captured this moment for them.

In the concluding section, Adrienne restates her controlling idea and makes an **insightful connection** between style and effect.

**LEARN HOW**  Embed Quotations  Every quotation you use should advance your analysis. To make it clear how a quotation supports your ideas, embed it within your own sentence.

**ADRIENNE'S REVISION TO PARAGRAPH ❸**

. . . they appear suddenly in places where no one remembers seeing them: ~~"moving New and / Old things,"~~ *, creating something both "Old" and "New."*

 **YOUR TURN**  Use the feedback from your peers and teacher as well as the two "Learn How" lessons to revise your essay. Evaluate how well you have analyzed the effects of the author's style and addressed the audience.

**LEARN HOW**  Embed Quotations

- Tell students that adding quotations to their sentences helps show that they understand the poems.
- Tell students that they can simply add quotations to their own sentences, but they must ensure that any quoted material is enclosed in quotation marks.
- Remind students to use ellipses if they want to shorten the interior of a quotation.
- Explain that students can use brackets to insert affixes, transitional words, verbs, or subjects into a quotation if necessary for logic.

 **YOUR TURN**  Ask students to complete the **Your Turn** activity independently. Remind students to embed quotations within their own sentences to make their analyses interesting to read and to show that they understand their subjects.

For interactive revision tools, see

💿 **WriteSmart CD-ROM**

**Writing Center** on <u>thinkcentral.com</u>

## DIFFERENTIATED INSTRUCTION

**FOR ENGLISH LANGUAGE LEARNERS**

**Sentence Construction**  Ask a volunteer to offer an explanatory point involving a style element from his or her draft for the class to discuss. Then, ask the class to suggest quotations from the poem that support this point. Model how to create a sentence that states the point and embeds a supporting quotation. Then, have student pairs work together to create additional sentences using the other possible quotations discussed. Help students with punctuation as necessary.

**FOR STRUGGLING WRITERS**

**Embed Quotations**  Have students work with partners to highlight each quotation in their drafts and examine how each is introduced. Is the quotation embedded in a sentence or is it an independent clause? Does the quotation simply appear on its own without any attachment to an explanatory sentence? Have students discuss each non-embedded example, considering whether there is a way to effectively embed the quotation in the sentence that precedes or follows it.

# Editing and Publishing

In the editing stage, you check your analysis to make sure that it is free of grammar, usage, and punctuation errors. Also, read carefully to check for any spelling errors, even after doing a word-processing spell-check. These kinds of mistakes distract your audience from focusing on the content of your analysis.

**COMMON CORE** W 5 Strengthen writing by revising, editing, rewriting, or trying a new approach. L 2 Demonstrate a command of the conventions of standard English capitalization and punctuation when writing. L 2c Spell correctly.

### GRAMMAR IN CONTEXT: DASHES

Sometimes words, phrases, and sentences are used parenthetically; that is, they break into the main thought of a sentence. Most parenthetical elements are set off by commas or parentheses.

> *Yet, suddenly, as if from nowhere, "strange" green leaf buds appear.*

> *The act of "arranging and changing placing" creates a shift in perspective (or point of view).*

Sometimes, parenthetical elements are such an interruption that a stronger mark is needed. In such cases, a dash is used.

> *E. E. Cummings's poem "Spring is like a perhaps hand" captures a moment in time that is subtle and delicate—the shift from winter to spring.*

### PUBLISH YOUR WRITING

An analysis becomes complete when you share it with someone. Consider these publication ideas:

- Present your analysis of the poem in a formal speech to your class.
- Submit your analysis as part of an application to an academic program.
- Send your analysis to a magazine or newspaper that publishes literary reviews.
- Write a blog to share with fans of the poet.

 **YOUR TURN** Proofread your analysis and correct any errors you find. Experiment with using dashes in place of parentheses or commas. Consider the effect of these subtle changes in punctuation. Which choice best supports your intended meaning? Then, publish your analysis.

---

## Editing and Publishing

**COMMON CORE** W 5, L 2, L 2c

### GRAMMAR IN CONTEXT: DASHES

Point out to students that text set off by a dash appears more forceful and important to the main clause than information set off by commas or parentheses. Therefore, students should use dashes sparingly for emphasis. The overuse of dashes will undermine this sense of emphasis. Lead students to discuss whether Adrienne's use of the dash in the sample sentence is appropriate. Make sure that students support their responses with reasoning.

### PUBLISH YOUR WRITING

Brainstorm with students additional ways to publish their literary analyses.

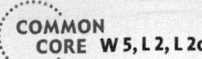 **YOUR TURN** Allow students time to proofread their drafts. Remind them to use dashes sparingly in place of commas or parentheses to create emphasis. This strategy tells readers that the information is essential to the meaning of the sentence.

---

## FOR ENGLISH LANGUAGE LEARNERS

**Understand Commas** Present to students the following sentences.

- Yet, suddenly, "strange" green leaf buds appear.
- The act of "arranging, and changing placing" creates a shift in perspective.
- E. E. Cummings's poem "Spring is like a perhaps hand" captures a moment in time that is subtle and delicate.

Explain that writers sometimes want to add extra information to their sentences (as if from nowhere; or point of view; the shift from winter to spring). There are three ways to add this information: commas, parentheses, and dashes. Each technique is correct, but each technique affects the meaning of the sentence slightly. Have pairs of students experiment with adding information to each of these sentences using all three techniques. Then, using sample sentences on the board, lead students to discuss the subtle meaning of each example.

## FOR STRUGGLING WRITERS

**Dashes** Lead students to discuss each example below for the appropriate use of the dash.

- Yet, suddenly, as if from nowhere, "strange" green leaf buds appear.
- Yet, suddenly—as if from nowhere—"strange" green leaf buds appear.
- The act of "arranging and changing placing" creates a shift in perspective (or point of view).
- The act of "arranging and changing placing" creates a shift in perspective—or point of view.

## Scoring Rubric

Tell students that the best way to understand a scoring rubric is to use it to score actual writing.

Distribute copies of a literary analysis with the student's name removed. Work as a class to evaluate the analysis based on the rubric. Then, ask students to individually assign final scores to the analysis accompanied by written explanations using the language of the rubric. Take a quick survey to learn whether there is a consensus regarding the score. If not, discuss these discrepancies with the goal of achieving a final consensus. The purpose of a rubric is to eliminate subjectivity from the scoring process.

For Rubric Bank, see

 **WriteSmart CD-ROM**

**Writing Center** on **thinkcentral.com**

---

## Assess and Reteach

### Assess

**R** **RESOURCE MANAGER—Copy Masters**
Rubric for Evaluation p. 122

**Online Essay Scoring** at **thinkcentral.com**

### Reteach

**Level Up Online Tutorials** at **thinkcentral.com**

**Reteaching Worksheets** on **thinkcentral.com**
Writing Lesson 29: Imagery and Figurative Language

---

## Scoring Rubric

Use the rubric below to evaluate your literary analysis from the Writing Workshop or your response to the on-demand task on the next page.

### LITERARY ANALYSIS

| SCORE | COMMON CORE TRAITS |
|---|---|
| **6** | • **Development** Has an engaging introduction; includes a controlling idea with an insightful analysis of the author's style; supports main points with relevant evidence; ends powerfully<br>• **Organization** Arranges ideas in an effective, logical order; uses varied transitions to create cohesion and link ideas<br>• **Language** Consistently maintains a formal style; uses precise language; shows a strong command of conventions |
| **5** | • **Development** Has an effective introduction; provides a controlling idea that offers an original analysis of the author's style; supports main points with evidence; has a strong concluding section<br>• **Organization** Arranges ideas logically; uses transitions to link ideas<br>• **Language** Maintains a formal style; uses precise language; has a few errors in conventions |
| **4** | • **Development** Has an introduction that could be more engaging; includes a controlling idea that states an analysis of the author's style; could use some more evidence; has an adequate concluding section<br>• **Organization** Arranges ideas logically; could vary transitions more<br>• **Language** Mostly maintains a formal style; needs more precise language at times; has a few distracting errors in conventions |
| **3** | • **Development** Has an adequate, though not memorable, introduction; has a controlling idea that makes an obvious statement about the author's style; lacks sufficient support; has a routine concluding section<br>• **Organization** Reflects some flaws in organization; needs more transitions to link ideas<br>• **Language** Frequently lapses into an informal style; uses some vague word choices; has some significant errors in conventions |
| **2** | • **Development** Has a weak introduction and a controlling idea that does not relate to the writing task; lacks specific evidence; has a weak concluding section<br>• **Organization** Has organizational flaws; lacks transitions throughout<br>• **Language** Uses an informal style and vague language; has many distracting errors in conventions |
| **1** | • **Development** Has no introduction or controlling idea; offers unrelated points as evidence; ends abruptly<br>• **Organization** Includes a string of disconnected ideas with no overall organization<br>• **Language** Uses an inappropriate style and vague, tired language; has major problems with grammar, mechanics, and spelling |

# Preparing for Timed Writing

**COMMON CORE** **W 10** Write routinely over shorter time frames for a range of tasks, purposes, and audiences.

## 1. ANALYZE THE TASK · 5 MIN

Read the task carefully. Then, read it again, noting the words in the task that tell the type of writing, the topic, the audience, and the purpose.

> **WRITING TASK**
>
> Harvest moon—
> walking around the pond
> all night long.
> —Bashō
>
> *Type of writing/Topic* → *Purpose* ↙
>
> Write <u>an analysis of this haiku poem</u> by <u>explaining the effects of stylistic elements.</u> Make sure to include textual evidence and quotations in your analysis. You will post your essay as a blog for <u>fans of haiku poetry.</u> ← *Audience*

## 2. PLAN YOUR RESPONSE · 10 MIN

First, note stylistic elements and examples from the poem. Then, list the effect of each. Finally, draft a controlling idea.

| Stylistic Element | Example | Effect |
|---|---|---|
|  |  |  |
|  |  |  |
|  |  |  |
| Controlling Idea: | | |

## 3. RESPOND TO THE TASK · 20 MIN

Begin drafting your analysis. Start with a question or comment about the subject of the poem. As you write, keep the following points in mind.

- In the introduction, include a controlling idea that explains your overarching analysis of the effect of stylistic elements in the poem.
- In the body, present textual evidence and quotations that support the controlling idea.
- In the concluding section, provide an insightful comment regarding the relationship between stylistic elements and their effect on the audience.

## 4. IMPROVE YOUR RESPONSE · 5–10 MIN

**Revising** Check your draft against the writing task. Do you provide an analysis of the poem? Do you support your analysis with concrete details? Do you end with an insightful comment?

**Proofreading** Find and correct any errors in grammar, usage, and mechanics. Make sure that your analysis and any edits are neatly written and legible.

**Checking Your Final Copy** Before you submit your analysis, examine it once more to make sure that you are presenting your best work.

---

## DIFFERENTIATED INSTRUCTION

### FOR ENGLISH LANGUAGE LEARNERS

**Haiku Poetry** Explain to students that the purpose of haiku poetry is to create word pictures rather than convey meaning. Suggest that students first draw pictures based on the details in the poem. Then tell students to ask themselves how the poet uses language to create these pictures or visual images. Help students identify visual details and personification. Have students work with partners to craft their controlling ideas. Provide sentence frames as necessary.

### FOR STRUGGLING WRITERS

**Punctuation in Poetry** Remind students that punctuation is important in poetry. Poets use punctuation to emphasize purpose and meaning. Point out that the poet uses a dash and a period and review their traditional functions. Then lead students to discuss how the poet uses punctuation to emphasize the vision he describes. Explain that the punctuation slows the time of the poem. Then model how to develop a controlling idea based on this analysis.

---

## Preparing for Timed Writing

**COMMON CORE W 10**

1. **Analyze the Task** Before students begin writing, encourage them to answer the following questions:
   - What is my time limit?
   - What are the key skills assessed in the scoring rubric?
   - Who is my audience?
   - What is my purpose?

2. **Plan Your Response** Point out to students that the scoring rubric emphasizes an insightful controlling idea. Remind students that their controlling idea should contain references to the poem and the poet as well as analysis of elements of the author's style such as word choice, sensory details, punctuation, and so on. For example, In Bashō's poem, he uses language and punctuation to create a unique visual image for readers.

3. **Respond to the Task** Remind students that the body of a literary analysis must contain explanation that is supported by textual evidence and quotations. For example, Bashō personifies the harvest moon who is "walking around the pond." The explanation must focus on why this statement is true.

4. **Improve Your Response** Point out that the scoring rubric emphasizes precise language. Tell students to make sure that they are using domain-specific literary terms in their analyses, including *speaker, stanza, line break, poet, personification, sensory detail,* and so on.

## Assess

Use the Scoring Rubric on p. 806 to assess students' literary analyses.

**SL 4** Presents information clearly, concisely, and logically such that listeners can follow the line of reasoning. **SL 6** Adapt speech to a variety of contexts and tasks.

### SPEAK WITH A PURPOSE

Help students identify purposes for their formal presentations through a brainstorming session. Write *Audience: Classmates* ⟶ *Purposes:* \_\_\_\_ on the board. Then list students' ideas regarding the purposes for formal presentations. Students may suggest informing listeners about the effects of a poet's style or describing how a poet uses style elements to create particular effects.

### COMMON CORE TRAITS

As students prepare to deliver their presentations, remind them to keep in mind the **COMMON CORE TRAITS** of a strong formal presentation.

# Practice and Apply

## Adapt Your Literary Analysis

### Model the Skill: ORGANIZATION

Explain that sentences may be more effective when they are short and direct. Sentences that use the noun-verb-object construction are easier for listeners to understand and remember than those that begin with phrases and clauses. Still, speakers should strive for a balance. Model the following.

- E. E. Cummings's poem "Spring is like a perhaps hand" captures the shift from winter to spring.
- Yet, suddenly, as if from nowhere, "strange" green leaf buds appear that were not there yesterday, or were they?

**GUIDED PRACTICE** Ask students to work at simplifying most of the sentences.

**R** RESOURCE MANAGER—Copy Master
Speaking and Listening p. 123

---

**Speaking & Listening Workshop**

*Essential Course of Study* **ECOS**

# Presenting a Literary Analysis

Not only can you write an analysis of a poem, you can also talk about it:

"What did you think of Michael's poem that he read in second period?"

"He had some cool sound effects. They made me feel like I was really there."

Discussing your analysis of a poem is similar to **presenting a literary analysis**.

 Complete the workshop activities in your **Reader/Writer Notebook**.

| SPEAK WITH A PURPOSE | COMMON CORE TRAITS |
|---|---|
| **TASK** Adapt your literary analysis into a **formal presentation**. Practice your presentation, and then present it to your classmates. | **A STRONG FORMAL PRESENTATION . . .** <br>• engages the audience from the start by relating the controlling idea to relevant aspects of the listeners' lives <br>• focuses clearly and concisely on the main points of the controlling idea <br>• relates stylistic elements to the effects of the work and offers evidence from the text and quotations to illustrate points <br>• delivers a concluding section that restates the controlling idea and offers an insight regarding style and effect <br>• employs effective eye contact, rate, volume, enunciation, and gestures |

**COMMON CORE**

**SL 4** Presents information clearly, concisely, and logically such that listeners can follow the line of reasoning. **SL 6** Adapt speech to a variety of contexts and tasks.

**THINK central**

Speaking & Listening Online

Go to thinkcentral.com.
KEYWORD: HML9-808

## Adapt Your Literary Analysis

Your audience will listen to your analysis of a poem rather than read it, so you'll need to adapt it by shortening sentences and focusing on your strongest ideas. Keep in mind that your classmates are your audience, and follow these tips:

- **Word Choice** Apart from literary terms, such as *simile* or *metaphor*, try to keep your vocabulary simple, but expressive. Use vivid verbs to describe actions.
- **Introduction** Adapt the introduction of your essay to capture your audience's attention quickly. Opening with a candid statement of personal response or a colorful detail from the poet's life will draw listeners in. Then, you can move on to your controlling idea.
- **Organization** Review the body of your analysis, and add transitional words and phrases where necessary to help your audience follow the line of reasoning and the progression of your thoughts.
- **Analysis** Try to relate the effects in the work you analyzed to your classmates' lives. For example, in response to "Spring is like a perhaps hand," you might relate Cummings's subject—spring—to the end of the school year.
- **Concluding Section** Close your presentation with a crisp restatement of your controlling idea. Quoting a line from the poem to reinforce your controlling idea is often effective.

---

## DIFFERENTIATED INSTRUCTION

### FOR ENGLISH LANGUAGE LEARNERS

**Language: Reinforce Analytical and Presentation Terms** Explain to students that presenting an analysis of a poem has the same goal as writing a literary analysis—to explain the effects of the author's style choices. Review key terms used in the Workshop:

- *formal:* according to prescribed rules or customs
- *simile:* comparison between two items using the word *like* or *as*

- *diction:* word choice
- *tone:* speaker's attitude toward the subject
- *enunciation:* pronunciation of words
- *emphasis:* special stress given to a syllable, word, or phrase when speaking

## Deliver Your Literary Analysis

Your attitude can have a great impact on your audience. How will you use your voice to convey tone? Will you sound academic? serious? breezy? How will you make your points clear and interesting? Consider these ideas:

### Verbal Techniques

| | |
|---|---|
| **Enunciation** | Enunciation refers to the clarity of your pronunciation. Speak clearly and carefully. |
| **Emphasis** | Stress key words by saying them in a different volume or tone than that of the overall presentation. |
| **Pauses** | Use pauses to give listeners time to digest your ideas or to add emphasis. |

You can make your presentation clear and interesting by using gestures and facial expressions in addition to spoken words. Review these tips:

### Nonverbal Techniques

| | |
|---|---|
| **Eye Contact** | Look into the eyes of audience members. Eye contact conveys confidence and sincerity. |
| **Facial Expression** | Be relaxed and natural, using expressions like a smile, a nod, or a raised eyebrow to convey meaning. |
| **Gestures** | Make natural gestures with your head and hands. Move around a bit. Try writing lines of poetry that are essential to your presentation on the board. |

**As a Speaker** When presenting your analysis to classmates, stay on topic. Make note cards with short reminder phrases, and arrange the cards logically, numbering them for easy reference.

**As a Listener** Evaluate the presentation. Listen carefully to identify the controlling idea. Then, think about whether the speaker effectively supports the controlling idea with clear textual evidence and quotations. Note whether the speaker's eye contact, rate, volume, enunciation, and gestures are appropriate and effective for the context and purpose of this presentation.

809

**FOR STRUGGLING STUDENTS**
**Verbal Techniques** Make sure students understand the meanings and distinctions among the terms *diction, pause,* and *emphasis.* Have volunteers read aloud drafts of their analyses, while experimenting with these three concepts. For example, for diction, they might insert a variety of synonyms for a particular word. For pause, they might pause at an inappropriate place where there is no punctuation. For emphasis, they might place stress on the wrong syllable of an ordinary word. Discuss how the three techniques can improve an oral presentation when used correctly.

## Teach

### Deliver Your Literary Analysis

*Model the Skill:* **VERBAL TECHNIQUES: EMPHASIS**
Remind students that when they present their analyses, they will have to clearly indicate when they are quoting from the original poems. Model for students how to modulate your voice or pause before delivering a quotation. You might also say "quote" and "unquote" as cues for listeners. Additionally, you might provide visuals of quotations to distinguish between your words and the poet's words.

**GUIDED PRACTICE** As students prepare for their presentations, tell them to practice with different ways of verbally or visually introducing quotations to find the methods with which they are most comfortable.

 Have students prepare their note cards. Instruct them to use underlining or highlighting to indicate key words within their short, reminder phrases.

## Assess and Reteach

### Assess

Use the **COMMON CORE TRAITS** to assess students' presentations.

A strong formal presentation
- focuses on the main points of the controlling idea
- offers evidence and quotations
- delivers a strong concluding section that restates the controlling idea and offers insight
- employs effective eye contact, rate, volume, enunciation, and gestures

### Reteach

If students struggle with the concept of tone, ask volunteers to read passages from the textbook using different tones of voice. Students might use tone to suggest that they are serious, bored, or sad. Ask students how they are able to "read" each tone of voice.

| Speaking and Listening Online |  |
|---|---|
| • Public speaking tips | |
| • Strategies for effective listening | |

# Assessment Practice

## COMMON CORE FOCUS

**RL 4** Determine the figurative meaning of words and phrases as they are used in a text; analyze the cumulative impact of specific word choices on meaning and tone. **RL 10** Read and comprehend poems. **W 5** Develop and strengthen writing by revising and editing to ensure that it demonstrates the conventions of standard English grammar, usage, and spelling. **L 1b** Use various types of phrases to convey specific meanings.

## CHECK READINESS

Read aloud the paragraph under **ASSESS** and stress to students that this is not the full Unit Test, but a way for them to check their readiness for it. Then have students examine the standards listed under **REVIEW** and look back in the unit or in the **Student Resource Bank** for any skills they need to review.

## READ THE TEXTS

Remind students to keep unit goals in mind as they read each passage, paying particular attention to these literary and reading skills:

- **poetic structure and form**
- **sound devices**
- **figurative language**
- **imagery**
- **make inferences**
- **visualize**

To help students focus on poetic elements, encourage them to ask questions like these:

- What tells you that these selections are poems? What poetic features do you notice even before you read the poems?
- How are these poems different from short stories or nonfiction articles? What is special about the way poets use language?

## ANSWER THE QUESTIONS

Direct students to pages R93–R101 of the **Handbook** to review test-taking strategies.

- Remind students not to choose the first answer that seems to fit. Instead, they should read all choices, eliminate any that are clearly wrong, and then choose the *best* answer.

---

### ASSESS

Taking this practice test will help you assess your knowledge of these skills and determine your readiness for the Unit Test.

### REVIEW

After you take the practice test, your teacher can help you identify any standards you need to review.

#### COMMON CORE

**RL 4** Determine the figurative meaning of words and phrases as they are used in a text; analyze the cumulative impact of specific word choices on meaning and tone. **RL 10** Read and comprehend poems. **W 5** Develop and strengthen writing by revising and editing to ensure that it demonstrates the conventions of standard English grammar, usage, and spelling. **L 1b** Use various types of phrases to convey specific meanings.

Practice Test
**THINK** central
Take it at thinkcentral.com.
KEYWORD: HML9N-810

---

## Assessment Practice

**DIRECTIONS** Read the following poems, and then answer the questions.

# The Sower    *by Victor Hugo*

Peaceful and cool, the twilight grey
Draws a dim curtain o'er the day,
While in my cottage-porch I lurk
And watch the last lone hour of work.

5   The fields around are bathed in dew,
And, with emotion filled, I view
An old man clothed in rags, who throws
The seed amid the channeled rows.

His shadowy form is looming now
10  High o'er the furrows of the plough;
Each motion of his arm betrays
A boundless faith in future days.

He stalks along the ample plain,
Comes, goes, and flings abroad the grain;
15  Unnoted, through the dreamy haze
With meditative soul I gaze.

At last, the vapours of the night
Dilate to heav'n the old man's height,
Till every gesture of his hand
20  Seems to my eyes sublimely grand!

*Translated by George Murray*

---

## DIFFERENTIATED INSTRUCTION

### FOR ENGLISH LANGUAGE LEARNERS

**Assessment Practice: Work Backward**
Prepare students by having them read the questions *before* reading the passages. Have pairs find unfamiliar words in test directions and questions and follow these steps:

1. Write each word on an index card and divide the cards among pairs of students. Tell students that they are going to define these words.

2. Instruct students to work individually to make an initial determination of each word's meaning. Then have students confer with their partners and check their work by using a dictionary.

3. Have students then share the words and definitions with the entire class, who can confirm the definitions or suggest others.

## To Be of Use   *by Marge Piercy*

The people I love the best
jump into work head first
without dallying in the shallows
and swim off with sure strokes almost out of sight.
5  They seem to become natives of that element,
the black sleek heads of seals
bouncing like half-submerged balls.

I love people who harness themselves, an ox to a heavy cart,
who pull like water buffalo, with massive patience,
10  who strain in the mud and the muck to move things forward,
who do what has to be done, again and again.

I want to be with people who submerge
in the task, who go into the fields to harvest
and work in a row and pass the bags along,
15  who are not parlor generals and field deserters
but move in a common rhythm
when the food must come in or the fire be put out.

The work of the world is common as mud.
Botched, it smears the hands, crumbles to dust.
20  But the thing worth doing well done
has a shape that satisfies, clean and evident.
Greek amphoras for wine or oil,
Hopi vases that held corn, are put in museums
but you know they were made to be used.
25  The pitcher cries for water to carry
and a person for work that is real.

**GO ON** ➡

## ITEM ANALYSIS

| COMPREHENSION AND WRITTEN RESPONSE | ITEMS | UNIT PAGES |
|---|---|---|
| Poetic Structure/Form | 1, 2, 11, 12, 18, 22, 24, 25 | 740–747 |
| Sound Devices | 19, 20 | 740–747 |
| Figurative Language | 6, 15 | 740–747 |
| Imagery | 21 | 740–747 |
| Make Inferences | 8, 13, 16 | 749 |
| Visualize | 4, 5, 9, 10, 17, 23 | 775 |

| WRITING AND GRAMMAR | ITEMS | UNIT PAGES |
|---|---|---|
| Descriptive Language | 4, 5, 10 | 755 |
| Participles and Participial Phrases | 2, 3, 8, 9 | 755 |
| Infinitives and Infinitive Phrases | 1, 6, 7 | 785 |

### Practice Test

On **thinkcentral.com** students can complete an interactive version of this practice test *and* receive remediation for the skills they have not yet mastered.

### FOR STRUGGLING READERS

**Assessment Support** Consider these options for completing the Assessment Practice:

- Have students "work backward" to review the test questions *before* reading the poems.

- Select random questions in the Assessment, and have students demonstrate how and where to look for the answers.

- Ask students to locate unfamiliar vocabulary words in the Assessment. Elicit the words' meanings from the class.

- Have students record useful testing words and definitions in their journals for later reference.

- Read the poems or parts of them aloud to aid in student comprehension.

## ANSWERS

# Reading Comprehension

Model a thinking process for answering multiple-choice questions.

1. **B is correct.** *It is the only metaphor among the answer choices. A and C are incorrect because they describe the setting. D is incorrect because it describes the sower's job.*

2. **C is correct.** *Each stanza is made up of one complete sentence. A is incorrect because each stanza is a complete sentence. B is incorrect because each stanza contains only one complete sentence. D is incorrect because each stanza is a complete sentence.*

3. **B is correct.** *A, C, and D are incorrect because the last two lines of each stanza end with the same sound (bb), not two different sounds (ab or cd).*

4. **C is correct.** *The consonant sound d is repeated at the beginning of* draws *and* dim. *A is incorrect because it is an example of consonance. B is incorrect because it is an example of rhyme. D is incorrect because it could be construed as words that create an image.*

5. **D is correct.** *The words "heav'n" and "sublimely" suggest nobility. A is a weaker answer because it might be inferred from the entire poem but not from the specified lines. B is incorrect because the shadows only enhance the man's stature. C is incorrect because the idea of dreaming cannot be inferred from the passage.*

6. **A is correct.** *The long o sound appears in both words of choice A. B and D are incorrect because they are examples of consonance. The words in C appear unrelated in sound.*

7. **A is correct.** *Every word in the answer choice describes an action that can be pictured. B, C and D are weaker answers because they contain at least one word that cannot be pictured:* along, soul, through.

8. **B is correct.** *The metaphor compares seals swimming in water to people "diving into" their work. A is incorrect because seals are not mentioned in line 3. C is incorrect because the poem does not mention the work habits of seals. D is incorrect because the poem does not say the seals are having fun.*

---

# Reading Comprehension

Use **"The Sower"** (p. 810) to answer questions 1–7.

1. In lines 1–4, the speaker uses a metaphor to compare the twilight to —
   - **A.** a peaceful workplace
   - **B.** a dim curtain
   - **C.** a cottage-porch
   - **D.** a lonely job

2. Each stanza in "The Sower" is made up of —
   - **A.** four lines that are incomplete sentences
   - **B.** four complete sentences that rhyme with each other
   - **C.** one complete sentence with rhyming parts
   - **D.** one part of a sentence that concludes in the last stanza

3. The rhyme scheme in every stanza of "The Sower" is —
   - **A.** *abab*       **C.** *abba*
   - **B.** *aabb*       **D.** *abcd*

4. Which pair of words is an example of alliteration in the poem?
   - **A.** *form, arm* (lines 9, 11)
   - **B.** *haze, gaze* (lines 15, 16)
   - **C.** *Draws, dim* (line 2)
   - **D.** *furrows, plough* (line 10)

5. From the image in lines 17–20, you can infer that the speaker —
   - **A.** thinks that the old man is a powerful person
   - **B.** is frightened by the shadows that are on the field
   - **C.** hopes that he is not just dreaming about the farm
   - **D.** believes that the work of planting grain is noble

6. Which pair of words is an example of assonance in the poem?
   - **A.** *old, clothed* (line 7)
   - **B.** *seed, amid* (line 8)
   - **C.** *stalks, ample* (line 13)
   - **D.** *Seems, eyes* (line 20)

7. Which group of words in lines 13–16 helps you visualize what the old man is doing in the field?
   - **A.** *stalks, comes, goes, flings*
   - **B.** *along, ample, abroad, unnoted*
   - **C.** *plain, grain, dreamy, soul*
   - **D.** *He, through, haze, meditative*

Use **"To Be of Use"** (p. 811) to answer questions 8–14.

8. The most likely meaning of the metaphor in lines 1–7 is that —
   - **A.** seals and people like to swim long distances instead of wading in shallow water
   - **B.** some people immerse themselves in work in the way that seals immerse themselves in water
   - **C.** seals and people dive right into their work and have the same good work habits
   - **D.** some people have as much fun at work as seals do when they play around in the water

9. Which of the following is an example of a simile in the poem?
   - **A.** *I love people who harness themselves*
   - **B.** *The work of the world is common as mud*
   - **C.** *I want to be with people who submerge / in the task*
   - **D.** *But the thing worth doing well done / has a shape that satisfies*

9. **B is correct.** *The passage compares the work of the world to mud. A, C, and D are incorrect because they do not express a comparison using* like *or* as.

10. **A is correct.** *The repetition of "who" shows the emphasis on the people that willingly choose to work. B is incorrect because the emphasis is on people, not animals. C is incorrect because the speaker is making an analogy and not describing an actual task. D is incorrect because the speaker emphasizes not strength but "massive patience,"*

"muck," and the repetition of tasks, as shown by "again."

11. **B is correct.** *The repeated m sound emphasizes endurance and accomplishment. A is incorrect because "strain" does not necessarily suggest clumsiness. C and D are incorrect because "who" refers to humans, not animals.*

12. **C is correct.** *The sound at the beginning of "worth" and "well" shows their connection. A, B, and D are incorrect because no reward, difference, or beginning is mentioned or suggested.*

UNIT 7: THE LANGUAGE OF POETRY

**10.** In lines 8–11, the speaker uses the repetition of "who" and "again" to emphasize an image of —

   **A.** people who diligently struggle to do their work

   **B.** sturdy animals that are trained to haul heavy loads

   **C.** the type of work that the speaker prefers to do

   **D.** people who are required to be physically strong to do their work

**11.** The alliteration in line 10 creates an image of —

   **A.** people who are clumsy when they perform physical labor

   **B.** people who struggle against obstacles to accomplish their work

   **C.** animals that are forced to perform dangerous tasks

   **D.** animals that work alongside people on farms

**12.** The repetition of forms of the verb *do* in "But the thing worth doing well done" (line 20) emphasizes —

   **A.** the importance of rewarding people who do a good job

   **B.** the different ways that people perform their jobs

   **C.** the connection between working and doing a good job

   **D.** the necessity of carrying out a job from the beginning to the end

**13.** The phrase "work that is real" in line 26 most likely refers to work that —

   **A.** has a meaningful purpose

   **B.** is physically challenging

   **C.** includes making objects

   **D.** takes place outdoors

**14.** Which one of the following objects is personified in lines 22–26?

   **A.** Amphoras    **C.** Pitcher

   **B.** Corn       **D.** Vase

> **Use "The Sower" and "To Be of Use" to answer questions 15–16.**

**15.** Which type of work can you visualize from images in both poems?

   **A.** Building

   **B.** Farming

   **C.** Fishing

   **D.** Logging

**16.** The speakers of both poems would most likely agree that —

   **A.** outdoor occupations are dangerous

   **B.** workers' relationships are important

   **C.** the best workers love their work

   **D.** work is something to be valued

**SHORT CONSTRUCTED RESPONSE**
**Write three or four sentences to answer this question.**

**17.** List five words or phrases that help you visualize the time of day at which "The Sower" takes place. Explain why visualizing that particular time of day is important to this poem.

**Write two or three paragraphs to answer this question.**

**18.** Compare the form of the poem "The Sower" with that of "To Be of Use." Explain how the line length, meter, and rhyme help convey the ideas and images of each poem.

---

**13. A is correct.** *All of the poem's images relate to concrete, useful tasks. No answer but A relates to the totality of tasks. B, C, and D are incorrect because they describe only details of individual types of work.*

**14. C is correct.** *The pitcher's crying is a human activity. A, B, and D are incorrect because the corn, amphoras, and vase do nothing human.*

**15. B is correct.** *"The Sower" describes planting; "To Be of Use" describes harvesting. A and C are incorrect because neither building nor fishing are mentioned in "The Sower." D is incorrect because logging is not mentioned in either poem.*

**16. D is correct.** *The comment that every gesture seems grand ("The Sower," lines 19-20) shows that the speaker values work. The remarks about loving hard workers shows the speaker of "To Be of Use" to value work. A and B are incorrect because the poems do not mention danger or relationships among workers. C is incorrect because Hugo's poem does not support that inference.*

## SHORT CONSTRUCTED RESPONSE

*Possible responses:*

**17.** *Words and phrases that help you visualize the time of day:* *"twilight grey," "dim curtain," "last lone hour of work," "shadowy farm," "dreamy haze," "vapours of the night"*

**18.** *Line lengths:* *"The Sower" has equal lines and stanzas (each stanza states one sentence), reinforcing the sower's steady progress. "To Be of Use" has variable line and stanza lengths, making up one or two sentences. The lengths underscore the variety of jobs.*

*Meter:* *"The Sower" has the same meter line to line. The steadiness conveys grandeur, like regal music. The image of the farmer waving an arm underscores steadiness. "To Be of Use" has an uneven meter. The meter reflects different kinds of work.*

*Rhyme:* *"The Sower" uses a common, predictable rhyme scheme. It soothes as the words suggest a reliable worker. "To Be of Use" relies on alliteration and assonance; these devices also comfort us as we read about what the speaker values.*

---

## ANSWERS
## Revising and Editing

1. **C is correct.** To pursue *is an infinitive. A is incorrect because it is a third-person present-tense verb, not an infinitive. B is incorrect because it is an example of a participle. D is incorrect because the original sentence contains no infinitive.*

2. **A is correct.** Lacking meter *or* end rhymes *is a participial phrase. B is incorrect because it contains a subordinate clause. C is incorrect because it contains an infinitive. D is incorrect because the original sentence contains no participial phrase.*

3. **C is correct.** *The word* arresting *is used as a participle. A, B, and the original sentence do not contain a participle, so all are incorrect. D is incorrect because the original sentence does not contain a participle.*

4. **C is correct.** *The transition word* However *provides a contrast, showing that the stanzas are strong even though they may be hard to memorize. A is incorrect because* Eventually *implies a chronology which is not present in the passage. B is incorrect because* For instance *would imply that the sentence contains examples. D is incorrect because* Similarly *implies that sentence 4 supports or is in agreement with sentence 3, rather than contrasting with it.*

## Revising and Editing
**DIRECTIONS** Read this passage, and answer the questions that follow.

(1) In her poem "For the Young Who Want To," Marge Piercy encourages young people who are in pursuit of their passion. (2) As is the case with many of Piercy's poems, the structure of this poem is organic. (3) Since it has no meter or end rhymes, it is difficult to memorize. (4) Its six stanzas are filled with strong statements that grab the reader's attention. (5) "Talent is what they say / you have after the novel / is published and favorably / reviewed," the poet states. (6) This assertion reflects Piercy's belief that artists receive praise from the public only after they have received the admiration of critics. (7) During the countless years that artists sacrifice so much time working on their art, their friends think it's just a hobby. (8) They keep asking artists when they are going to search for a real job. (9) Finally, Piercy concludes that what drives an artist is loving the work, with or without recognition. (10) As a result of this indirect form of criticism, artists sometimes seek to prove the legitimacy of their craft. (11) Piercy suggests that even though artists don't have licenses, they are still experts in their feild. (12) She then points out that the real writer is the one who practices the craft of writing.

1. What is the best way to revise sentence 1 to include an infinitive?
   A. Change *encourages* to **convinces**
   B. Change *who are in pursuit of* to **pursuing**
   C. Change *who are in pursuit of* to **to pursue**
   D. Make no change

2. What is the best way to rewrite sentence 3 using a participial phrase?
   A. Lacking meter or end rhymes, it is difficult to memorize.
   B. Since it lacks both meter and end rhymes, it is difficult to memorize.
   C. The lack of meter or end rhymes makes it difficult to memorize.
   D. No change is needed.

3. What is the best way to change sentence 4 to include a participle?
   A. Change *grab* to **demand**
   B. Change *strong* to **vivid**
   C. Change *strong* to **arresting**
   D. Make no change

4. Which transitional word or phrase could be added to the beginning of sentence 4?
   A. Eventually,
   B. For instance,
   C. However,
   D. Similarly,

## DIFFERENTIATED INSTRUCTION

### FOR STRUGGLING READERS
**Assessment Support: Participles** Most participles end in *–ing* or *–ed*. They may appear alone or as part of a phrase. Have students identify the participle, if any, acting as an adjective in these sentences.

- Chen is a underlined published poet (*participle*)
- The underlined standing student is Flo. (*participle*)
- Nora is reading a poetry book. (*none*)
- Otis sat, underlined waiting quietly. (*participle*)
- The students had prepared well. (*none*)

**Assessment Support: Infinitives** Infinitives may appear alone or in phrases. Most contain the word to. Help students to distinguish infinitives and infinitive phrases from prepositional phrases in the following sentences:

- Mr. Gomez is able to teach. (*infinitive*)
- Julia walked to the front of the room (*prepositional phrase*)
- To illustrate meter, Gil wrote two lines. (*infinitive phrase*)
- Pat likes to write sonnets. (*infinitive phrase*)

5. What is the most effective way to improve the organization of the paragraph?
   - **A.** Move sentence 10 to after sentence 11.
   - **B.** Move sentence 9 to after sentence 12.
   - **C.** Move sentence 1 to after sentence 2.
   - **D.** Make no change

6. What is the best way to change sentence 7 to include an infinitive?
   - **A.** Change *working* to **to work**
   - **B.** Change *sacrifice* to **are sacrificing**
   - **C.** Change *During the countless years* to **For the years**
   - **D.** Make no change

7. What is the best way to change sentence 8 to include an infinitive?
   - **A.** Change *They keep asking artists* to **They wonder**
   - **B.** Change *going to search* to **searching**
   - **C.** Change *going to search* to **looking**
   - **D.** Make no change

8. What is the best way to rewrite sentence 9 using an infinitive phrase?
   - **A.** Finally, Piercy draws the conclusion that what drives an artist is loving the work, with or without recognition.
   - **B.** Finally, Piercy concludes that what drives an artist is the ability to love the work, with or without recognition.
   - **C.** Finally, Piercy concludes that what drives an artist is loving the work, whether or not the art is recognized.
   - **D.** No change is needed.

9. What is the best way to rewrite sentence 10 using a participle?
   - **A.** As a result of this implied criticism, artists sometimes seek to prove the legitimacy of their craft.
   - **B.** As a result of this indirect form of criticism, artists sometimes seek to prove that their craft is legitimate.
   - **C.** As a result of this indirect form of criticism, artists sometimes are forced to prove the legitimacy of their craft.
   - **D.** No change is needed.

10. What change, if any, should be made to sentence 11?
    - **A.** Change *artists* to **artist's**
    - **B.** Change *doesn't* to **does not**
    - **C.** Change *feild* to **field**
    - **D.** Make no change

STOP

815

5. **B is correct.** *The word* Finally *indicates that sentence 9 should be the conclusion to the passage.* A *is incorrect because sentence 9 should precede sentence 10.* C *is incorrect because sentence 1 contains introductory information and should remain the first sentence of the passage.* D *is incorrect because sentence 9 should be the passage's concluding sentence.*

6. **A is correct.** To work *is an infinitive.* B *is incorrect because it changes the present form of the verb to present progressive, which includes a participle.* C *is incorrect because it replaces the prepositional phrase with another prepositional phrase.* D *is incorrect because the original sentence has no infinitive.*

7. **D is correct.** *The original sentence already contains an infinitive, to search.* A *is incorrect because it replaces one verb with another, without adding an infinitive.* B *and* C *are both incorrect because they remove an infinitive.*

8. **B is correct.** To love the work *is an infinitive phrase that acts as an adjective modifying* ability. A, C, *and the original do not contain an infinitive phrase, so they are incorrect.* D *is incorrect because the original sentence does not use an infinitive phrase.*

9. **A is correct.** *This revision changes the phrase "indirect form of criticism" to the more concise participle "implied criticism."* B *and* C *are incorrect because they do not add participles.* D *is incorrect because the revising with a participle improves the sentence.*

10. **C is correct.** *Field is misspelled* feild. A *is incorrect because* artists *should be plural, not possessive.* B *is incorrect because spelling out* don't *does not correct an error.* D *is incorrect because* feild *is misspelled.*

---

**FOR STRUGGLING READERS**

**Test-Taking Strategies: Understanding Instruction** Read aloud the instructions for item 1, and model the steps students must take to answer such questions. Help them recognize that the first task is to see whether sentence 1 contains an infinitive. Students who do not understand the term *infinitive* should review it. Then do a think-aloud to show how to substitute the A, B, and C options and to select the correct choice.

Give students support as they go through the same steps for item 6. Ask what they should look for and where. Then work together to identify the changes in each answer choice. Finally, ask a student to do a think-aloud as he or she tries to determine the correct answer.

## COMMON CORE FOCUS

**RL 10** Read and comprehend literature. **RI 10** Read and comprehend literary nonfiction.

### INTRODUCE *GREAT READS*

In Unit 7, students have discussed a number of big questions. Invite students to tell which question they found most intriguing and why, and then focus attention on the three that appear on this page. Discuss the recommended books and their summaries, pointing out how each connects to the related question. Encourage students to choose one or more of these "great reads" to read independently.

## Ideas for Independent Reading

Writers use poetic language in both the poetry and prose of the following selections.

**COMMON CORE**

**RL 10** Read and comprehend literature. **RI 10** Read and comprehend literary nonfiction.

### *What makes a strong competitor?*

**The Old Man and the Sea**
*by Ernest Hemingway*

Hemingway's concise style depicts Santiago, a Cuban fisherman, as he battles a giant marlin. The competition does not end when Santiago lands the huge creature.

**The Hot Zone**
*by Richard Preston*

This suspenseful true account of dealing with an outbreak of Ebola virus serves as a warning to humankind. The struggle between viruses and humans is likely to intensify in the future.

**The Big Year: A Tale of Man, Nature, and Fowl Obsession**
*by Mark Obmascik*

A birding marathon in 1998 lasted for 365 days, during which bird watchers tried to set a new record for number of species seen worldwide. The author describes the marathon and three of the passionate competitors.

### *Where can your imagination take you?*

**About This Life**
*by Barry Lopez*

The author's ability to see the natural world in fresh and startling ways makes him one of the nation's most valued naturalists and writers.

**19 Varieties of Gazelle**
*by Naomi Shihab Nye*

A Palestinian-American poet, Nye writes of animals, people, food, war and peace, and how life has changed in painful ways for Palestinians living in the occupied West Bank.

**Spoon River Anthology**
*by Edgar Lee Masters*

Under the sod of a Midwestern cemetery lie 244 souls. In this poetic classic, they speak to readers about their lives—full of disappointment and loss—and their inevitable deaths, some peaceful and some violent.

### *Do you set your own course?*

**We Die Alone: A WWII Epic of Escape and Endurance**
*by David Howarth*

Norwegian commandos race for the Swedish border to escape from Nazi pursuers. This true account demonstrates the strength and endurance of the human spirit.

**Great Expectations**
*by Charles Dickens*

Set in 19th-century England, this novel depicts the rags-to-riches story of the orphan Pip. Pip dreams of becoming a gentleman, and a secret patron arranges for this to happen. When Pip moves to London to fulfill his "great expectations," he learns the true meaning of nobility and love.

**In the Shadow of Man**
*by Jane Goodall*

From her memoir we learn that when Goodall began chimpanzee research in 1960, women didn't do primate studies. Her scientific discoveries paved the way for other women to do similar work.

**Get Novel Wise** **THiNK** central

Go to **thinkcentral.com**.
KEYWORD: HML9-816

**NovelWise** **THiNK** central

The keyword on this page points to **NovelWise**, a Web site that helps students choose a novel or other book-length work to read. **NovelWise** also provides
• study guides
• reading strategies and literary elements instruction
• presentations to introduce classic novels
• project ideas

# A Way with Words

## AUTHOR'S STYLE AND VOICE

- In Fiction
- In Media
- In Nonfiction
- In Poetry
- In Drama

817

**About the Art** Hyacinth Manning-Carner created *Tumbling Flowers* in 1954. For more information, see page 877.

## INTRODUCE THE UNIT

A person who speaks smoothly and easily is said to be "fluent." A person who chooses tactful, courteous words often is described as "well-spoken." A person who is said to have "a way with words" skillfully expresses ideas in clear, interesting ways. Ask students to think of someone they know or have read about who, in their opinion, has "a way with words." On the basis of those thoughts, invite students to share their ideas about what "a way with words" means.

Invite students to consider how the images on this page suggest various ways of using words. Use these discussion prompts:

- How are the people in the photograph using words?
- What details characterize the style of the artwork on the page?
- How does the artwork convey an idea?
- How does the style of communication in these images differ?

Tell students that as they read this unit, they will consider the various styles that writers use to express their ideas. They will look at different media and compare the **author's style and voice** in several literary selections.

For help in planning this unit, see

**R** RESOURCE MANAGER UNIT 8
pp. 1–10

**ECOS** ✓ **ECOS** ✓

| COMMON CORE STRAND | Text Analysis Workshop: Author's Style and Voice pp. 820–825 | Comparing Texts<br>Where Have You Gone, Charming Billy?/Tim O'Brien: The Naked Soldier/Be a Marine<br>Short Story/Interview/Poster pp. 826–840<br>Lexile: 930 | The Princess and the Tin Box<br>Fable pp. 842–847<br>Lexile: 1260 | Media Study: from The Birds<br>Film Clip pp. 848–851 | Going to Japan<br>Essay pp. 852–859<br>Lexile: 940<br>Fry: 10<br>Dale-Chall: 7.1 |
|---|---|---|---|---|---|
| **Reading Literature** | Author's Style and Voice pp. 820–825 **RL 4** | Realism pp. 827, 828, 830, 831, 837 **RL 4**<br>Sequence pp. 827, 831, 834, 835, 837 **RL 5**<br>Language Coach pp. 833, 835 **RL 4**<br>Recruitment Poster p. 840 **RL 7** | Parody pp. 843, 844, 846, 847 **RL 4, RL 5**<br>Predict pp. 843, 846, 847 **RL 5** | | |
| **Reading Informational Text** | Author's Style and Voice pp. 820–825 **RI 4** | Interview p. 836 | | | Humor pp. 853, 854, 856, 857, 858 **RI 4, RI 6**<br>Summarize pp. 853, 857, 858 **RI 2** |
| **Writing** | | Writing Prompt p. 839 | Writing Prompt p. 847 | Write or Discuss p. 851 **W 1b** | Quickwrite p. 852 |
| **Speaking and Listening** | | What's the Connection? p. 826 **SL 1** | Present p. 842 **SL 1** | Media Literacy p. 850 **SL 1a**<br>Write or Discuss p. 851 **SL 2, SL 4**<br>Produce Your Own Media p. 851 | |
| **Language** | Author's Style and Voice pp. 820–825 **L 3** | Supporting Details pp. 831, 839 **L 3**<br>Realism p. 834 **L 3**<br>Words That Start with *in-* p. 838 **L 4c** | Parody p. 846 **L 5a** | | Language Coach p. 856 **L 4b**<br>Foreign Words p. 857 **L 4c**<br>Appropriate Word Choice p. 859 **L 5b** |

| A Few Words<br>Essay<br>pp. 860–867 | A narrow Fellow in the Grass/"Hope" is the thing with feathers—<br>Poems<br>pp. 868–873 | Luxury/Kidnap Poem<br>Poems<br>pp. 874–879 | The Sneeze<br>Drama<br>pp. 880–889 | Writing Workshop:<br>Informative Text: Analysis of an Author's Style<br>pp. 890–899<br><br>Technology Workshop:<br>Creating a Podcast<br>pp. 900–901 |
|---|---|---|---|---|
| Lexile: 950<br>Fry: 6<br>Dale-Chall: 6.4 | | | | |
| | Dickinson's Style pp. 869, 870, 871, 873 RL 4<br>Reading Poetry pp. 869, 871, 873 RL 10 | Giovanni's Style pp. 875, 876, 878, 879 RL 4<br>Interpret Ideas in Poetry pp. 875, 876, 879 RL 2<br>Language Coach p. 878 RL 4 | Farce pp. 881, 886, 888, 889 RL 10<br>Visualize pp. 881, 882, 885, 889 RL 10 | |
| Tone pp. 861, 862, 865 RI 4<br>Paraphrase pp. 861, 864, 865 RI 10 | Journal Article p. 872 | | | |
| Writing Prompt p. 867 W 1a–b | | Quickwrite p. 874 | Quickwrite p. 880 | Writing an Analysis of an Author's Style pp. 890–899 W 2a–f, W 4, W 5, W 10<br>Creating a Podcast pp. 900–901 W 6 |
| Debate p. 860 SL 1 | Present p. 868 SL 1 | | | Creating a Podcast pp. 900–901 SL 5 |
| Language Coach p. 862 L 4a<br>Vary Sentence Types pp. 864, 867 L 3<br>Homonyms p. 866 L 4c | Dickinson's Style pp. 869–871, 873 L 5<br>Language Coach p. 870 L 4 | | | Drafting p. 893 L 1<br>Editing and Publishing p. 897 L 1b, L 2 |

ECOS

To see the complete Essential Course of Study, see pp. T23–T28.

 For additional lesson planning help, see Teacher One Stop DVD.

# Instructional Support

**Resource Manager Unit 8**

**UNIT SUPPORT**

Academic Vocabulary, p. 3

Additional Academic Vocabulary, p. 4

Grammar Focus p. 5

Text Analysis Workshop pp. 9–10

Writing Workshop: Informative Text: Analysis of an Author's Style p. 145

**SELECTION SUPPORT***

**Plan and Teach**

Lesson planning pages

Additional leveled selection questions

Extension activities

**Student Copy Masters**

Selection summaries in four languages

Skills copy masters in English and Spanish

Vocabulary preteaching and support

Reading Check and Question Support

Reading Fluency

*Available for all selections

† Available on **thinkcentral.com**.

Language Handbook

Vocabulary Practice

Best Practices Toolkit†

PowerNotes DVD-ROM†

Connections: Nonfiction for Common Core CD-ROM†

Teacher One Stop DVD-ROM

Student One Stop DVD-ROM

Media*Smart* DVD-ROM *from* The Birds

Write*Smart* CD-ROM†

GrammarNotes DVD-ROM†

WordSharp CD-ROM†

# Differentiated Instruction

## STRUGGLING READERS AND WRITERS

**Resource Manager Unit 8**

Additional Selection Questions

Question Support

Reading Fluency

**Interactive Reader**

**Adapted Interactive Reader**

**Level Up Online Tutorials**

**Audio Anthology** (with Audio summaries)

**Diagnostic and Selection Tests**

Selection Tests A/B

## ENGLISH LANGUAGE LEARNERS

**Resource Manager Unit 8**

Selection Summaries in English, Spanish, Vietnamese and Haitian Creole

Skills Copymasters in Spanish

**English Language Learner Adapted Interactive Reader Teacher's Guide**

**ELL Adapted Interactive Reader**

**Audio Tutor**

**Guide to English for Newcomers**

**Audio Anthology**

**Audio Summaries in Multiple Languages** (on **thinkcentral.com**)

## ADVANCED LEARNERS

**Resource Manager Unit 8**

Additional Selection Questions

Ideas for Extension

**Diagnostic and Selection Tests**

Selection Tests B/C

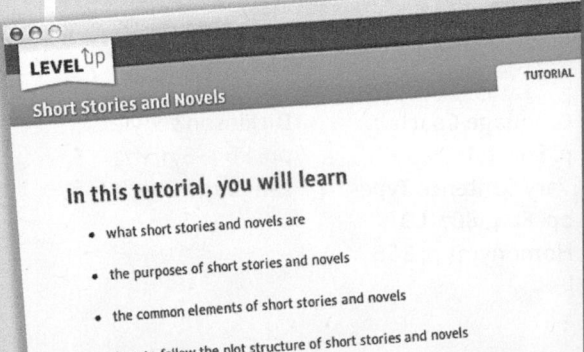

## Assessment and Reteaching

**Diagnostic and Selection Tests**

**Unit and Benchmark Tests**

**ThinkCentral Online Assessment:**
- All program assessments
- Level Up Online Tutorials

**ExamView Test Generator** on the Teacher One Stop DVD-ROM

**Online Essay Scoring** on **thinkcentral.com**

**ThinkCentral Online Reteaching:**
- Level Up Online Tutorials
- Reteaching Worksheets

**Holt McDougal Online Essay Scoring**

Welcome to Holt McDougal Online Essay Scoring!

This site is designed to help you improve your writing skills and prepare for standardized writing tests. When you write and submit a response to one of the writing prompts on this site, the computerized scoring system will immediately score and deliver feedback on your essay. Other resources on this site will help you prepare, develop, and revise your essay.

**STUDENTS**

Get started by entering the

**Writing Zone** →

## Professional Development

**Video Center** Based on interviews with program consultants and other educational experts, these videos feature classroom-ready teaching strategies.

**Teacher Toolkit** Includes a Teacher Handbook as well as a range of articles and handouts by program consultants and other educators.

**Janet Allen**

**Jim Burke**

**Kylene Beers**

**Carol Jago**

---

 **THINK** central **at a Glance**

**One Location, Endless Resources**

**Find Resources** Browse all *Holt McDougal Literature* components for the ones that meet your students' needs and match your teaching style.

**Assess Progress and Reteach** Assign electronic versions of program assessments to measure your students' mastery of the Common Core State Standards. On thinkcentral.com, some tests deliver online remediation tutorials to students who have not mastered skills.

 ***Interactive Whiteboard Lessons***

Prepare your students for college and careers by teaching relevant, real-world skills through dynamic, interactive instruction. Go to **thinkcentral.com** to browse through all whiteboard lessons, including the following:

- Figurative Language and Imagery
- Word Choice and Tone
- Poetry: Language and Form

 **HISTORY**

Together Holt McDougal and HISTORY® are revolutionizing the study of English/language arts with video that helps students relive and re-imagine the people, places, and events they are discovering through reading. Look for selections with the HISTORY® icon.

## What is
## STYLE?

Read and discuss the question and the paragraph. To illustrate differences in style, have students name a creative work that fits each of these stylistic descriptions:

- a movie that features extreme stunts and explosive action
- a song about personal thoughts, sung to subtle, possibly acoustic, accompaniment
- a clothing line known for its "retro" influences

Discuss how students chose their examples.

*ACTIVITY* Before students can answer these questions in groups, they need to choose an artist. Students should think of an artist whose work they are familiar with and about whom they can speak. Then, the student should present that artist's style to the group since some students may be unfamiliar with the artist's work. Remind students to define important terms or vocabulary that might be unfamiliar to other group members. Each group should then select an artist and answer all three questions. Have group representatives summarize the group's answers for a whole-class comparison.

**CHECK UNDERSTANDING** Have students define style in their own words and give an example of an artistic style.

## What is **STYLE?**

What draws you to a certain band's songs, a specific director's movies, or a particular writer's work? The answer to these questions can often be attributed to style. Style is what makes the work of writers and other creative people distinctive.

*ACTIVITY* With a small group, list artists—actors, songwriters, painters, authors, or directors—who have unique styles. Then pick one of these people and answer the following questions:

- What about the artist's work is distinctive? Are there characteristics that make his or her work immediately recognizable?
- What ties all of the artist's work together? For example, maybe your favorite songwriter uses the same imagery in all of his or her lyrics.
- What three words would you use to describe your artist's style?

**Find It Online!**  Go to thinkcentral.com for the interactive version of this unit.

818

---

## Unit Resources

See resources on the **Teacher One Stop DVD-ROM** *and on* **thinkcentral.com**.

 **RESOURCE MANAGER UNIT 8**

**UNIT AND BENCHMARK TESTS**

**BEST PRACTICES TOOLKIT**

**INTERACTIVE READER**

**ADAPTED INTERACTIVE READER**

**ELL ADAPTED INTERACTIVE READER**

**LANGUAGE HANDBOOK**

**VOCABULARY PRACTICE**

**TECHNOLOGY**

- **Teacher One Stop DVD-ROM**
- **Student One Stop DVD-ROM**
- **PowerNotes DVD-ROM**
- **WriteSmart CD-ROM**
- **MediaSmart DVD-ROM**
- **GrammarNotes DVD-ROM**
- **Audio Anthology CD**
- **Audio Tutor CD**

**Find It Online!** THINK central

The interactive version of this unit on **thinkcentral.com** includes
- video and **PowerNotes** introductions to key selections
- audio support—listen or download
- **ThinkAloud** models
- **WordSharp** vocabulary tutorials
- interactive review and remediation

## Preview Unit Goals

| | |
|---|---|
| **TEXT ANALYSIS** | • Analyze elements of style, including word choice, tone, sentence structure, sensory language, and figurative language<br>• Analyze the impact of style on meaning<br>• Analyze writers' styles<br>• Analyze humor, parody, and farce |
| **READING** | • Use reading strategies, including visualizing and predicting<br>• Analyze sequence, including flashbacks<br>• Objectively summarize and paraphrase<br>• Interpret ideas in poetry |
| **WRITING AND LANGUAGE** | • Write an analysis of an author's style<br>• Develop a topic with sufficient information and examples<br>• Use a variety of sentence types |
| **SPEAKING AND LISTENING** | • Deliver an effective presentation as a podcast |
| **VOCABULARY** | • Use prefixes to determine or clarify meaning<br>• Understand and use homonyms |
| **ACADEMIC VOCABULARY** | • appreciate     • attribute<br>• indicate      • unique<br>• vary |
| **MEDIA AND VIEWING** | • Analyze style and visual techniques in film<br>• Create a production still<br>• Create a podcast |

## Media Smart DVD-ROM

### Masterful Style in Film

Study a classic scene from *The Birds* to explore the style of Alfred Hitchcock, a master of movie suspense. Page 848

---

**UNIT GOALS**

Included in this unit: RL 1-2, RL 4-5, RL 7, RL 10, RI 1-2, RI 4, RI 6, RI 10, W 1a-b, W 2a-f, W 4-6, W 10, SL 1, SL 1a, SL 2, SL 4-5, L 1, L 1b, L 2, L 3, L 4, L 4a-c, L 5, L 5a-b, L 6

Complete text of the Common Core State Standards is found in the correlation on p. T10. Standards covered in this unit are found in the standards overview (pp. 817A–817B) and on the lesson pages where they are taught.

## Preview Unit Goals

This page expresses the main skills and strategies for Unit 8 as a set of goals. Have students preview the categories and goals, considering what experience they may already have with each goal. Be sure to point out the color-coding that identifies each strand throughout the unit.

Call on a volunteer to read the Academic Vocabulary terms aloud. Write definitions for the terms on the board, and have students record each term and its definition in their **Reader/Writer Notebooks**. As students read the selections in Unit 8, have them refer to their definitions as needed. Also encourage students to use these terms as they talk and write about the selections.

---

## DIFFERENTIATED INSTRUCTION

### FOR ENGLISH LANGUAGE LEARNERS

**Academic Vocabulary** Provide students with definitions of each Academic Vocabulary word.

**appreciate** (ə prē'shē āt') *v.* to think highly of; to recognize favorably the quality or value of

**attribute** (ə'-trĭb'yōōt') *n.* a quality thought of as a natural part of someone or something

**indicate** (in'di kāt') *v.* to point out or show

**unique** (yōō nēk') *adj.* the only one; having no equal

**vary** (vâr'ē) *v.* to modify or alter; to change the characteristics of something

Use the copy master to help students learn academic words they will use in this unit and on the Assessment Practice.

**R** RESOURCE MANAGER—Copy Masters
Academic Vocabulary p. 3
Additional Academic Vocabulary p. 4

# Focus and Motivate

## COMMON CORE FOCUS

**RL 4** Determine the figurative and connotative meanings of words and phrases as they are used in a text; analyze the cumulative impact of specific word choices on meaning and tone. **RI 4** Determine the connotative meaning of words and phrases as they are used in a text; analyze the cumulative impact of specific word choices on meaning and tone. **L 3** Apply knowledge of language to understand how language functions in different contexts, to make effective choices for meaning or style, and to comprehend more fully when reading or listening.

# Teach

## Part 1: What Is Style?

**Common Style** Tell students that the four types of style are not rigid distinctions, but that thinking about them sharpens readers' awareness of the choices authors make.

Discuss the styles most likely to be found in these four examples:

- a graduation speech *(Style: formal because of serious occasion; might include informal elements, such as humorous anecdotes)*

- a mystery about a 12-year-old detective, set in 2012 *(Style: informal to mirror the speech and behavior of young people today; would include literary elements)*

- an article on the health effects of traffic congestion *(Style: journalistic because author's main purpose is to convey information; level of formality would vary by publication)*

- a novel set during the Civil War *(Style: literary to create a rich portrayal of historical setting and the dramatic, complex experiences of characters)*

List books, articles, and documents with different styles in a chart. Have students check the style or styles that apply to each. Discuss why the style suits the author's purpose.

| Title | Formal | Informal |
|-------|--------|----------|
|       |        |          |
|       |        |          |

**BEST PRACTICES TOOLKIT—Transparency**
Analysis Frame: Author's Craft pp. D21, D24

---

# Author's Style and Voice

**Essential Course of Study**

What makes classical music different from rap? How can you tell the difference between a spine-tingling Edgar Allan Poe story and a Stephen King thriller? The answer is style, or the unique elements that make everything—from music to writing—distinctive. Style is what helps you tell *Newsweek* from the *National Enquirer* or a Shakespearean sonnet from a poem by E. E. Cummings. Often, the style of what you read can affect you just as much as the substance.

### COMMON CORE

Included in this workshop:
**RL 4** Determine the figurative and connotative meanings of words and phrases as they are used in a text; analyze the cumulative impact of specific word choices on meaning and tone. **RI 4** Determine the connotative meaning of words and phrases as they are used in a text; analyze the cumulative impact of specific word choices on meaning and tone. **L 3** Apply knowledge of language to understand how language functions in different contexts, to make effective choices for meaning or style, and to comprehend more fully when reading or listening.

## Part 1: What Is Style?

In literature, **style** is the way a particular work is written—not what is said, but *how* it's said. A writer's style, often reflecting the context in which the work is written, depends on many elements, including the writer's choice of words, tone, and sentence structures. Does the writer use long sentences packed with flowery details or ones that are short and to the point? Is the tone sincere or is it laced with sarcasm?

| COMMON STYLE | EXAMPLE |
|--------------|---------|
| **FORMAL**<br>• uses sophisticated, abstract language<br>• may use complex sentence structures<br>• carefully observes rules of grammar | And was Mr. Rochester now ugly in my eyes? No, reader: gratitude and many associations, all pleasurable and genial, made his face the object I best liked to see. . . .<br>—from *Jane Eyre* by Charlotte Brontë |
| *Informal*<br>• sounds like everyday conversation<br>• may use contractions and slang<br>• may use simple sentences and fragments | Remember that boy you thought you could not live without? What was his name? Randy. You don't remember?<br>—from *The Kitchen God's Wife* by Amy Tan |
| Journalistic<br>• uses neutral words to report facts<br>• often includes simple sentences<br>• reader notices what's said, not who's talking | A lightning flash can happen in half a second. In that instant, the lightning flash superheats the surrounding air to a temperature five times hotter than that on the surface of the sun.<br>—from *nationalgeographic.com* |
| *Literary*<br>• may use imagery to convey a mood<br>• often includes long, elaborate sentences<br>• reader often gets to know the narrator—the voice that tells the story | The lightning quivered about the pinnacles of the ancient Hôtel de Ville, and shed flickering gleams over the open space in front.<br>—from "The Adventure of the German Student" by Washington Irving |

---

## DIFFERENTIATED INSTRUCTION

### FOR STRUGGLING READERS

**Note Taking** Ask students to fold a piece of notebook paper in half and half again to make four distinct sections. Then, have students write the following four words as the heading of each section: *formal*, *informal*, *journalistic*, and *literary*. Direct students to close their books and listen and take notes as you read the information about each style of writing. Emphasize that students should include in their notes key words to identify each style. Ask for volunteers to share their notes with the class. Then, have students compare their responses with the information on p. 820.

## MODEL 1: STYLE

This excerpt comes from a famous novel about life on the Nebraska prairie. As you read, consider the common styles listed on the preceding page. Which style or styles do you think characterize the writing?

*from*

# My Ántonia

Novel by **Willa Cather**

While the train flashed through never-ending miles of ripe wheat, by country towns and bright-flowered pastures and oak groves wilting in the sun, we sat in the observation car, where the woodwork was hot to the touch and red dust lay deep over everything. The dust and heat, the burning wind, reminded us of many things. We were talking about what it is like to spend one's childhood in little towns like these, buried in wheat and corn, under stimulating extremes of climate: burning summers when the world lies green and billowy beneath a brilliant sky, when one is fairly stifled in vegetation, in the color and smell of strong weeds and heavy harvests; blustery winters with little snow, when the whole country is stripped bare and gray as sheet-iron.

**Close Read**

1. Notice the sentence length and the use of imagery in the boxed text. On the basis of these details, how would you describe the style of this excerpt?

2. Identify another detail that helped you determine the style.

## MODEL 2: STYLE

Here, another writer offers a different description of a prairie. As you read, consider how the writer's style compares with Willa Cather's in the excerpt from *My Ántonia*.

*from*

# PRAIRYERTH

Nonfiction by **William Least Heat-Moon**

The Flint Hills are the last remaining grand expanse of tallgrass prairie in America. On a geologic map, their shape something like a stone spear point, they cover most of the two-hundred-mile longitude of Kansas from Nebraska to Oklahoma, a stony upland twenty to eighty miles wide. At their western edge, the mixed-grass prairie begins and spreads a hundred or so miles to the shortgrass country of the high plains.

**Close Read**

1. Is this excerpt literary or journalistic? Support your answer.

2. Contrast Heat-Moon's style with Cather's. Identify at least two specific differences.

TEXT ANALYSIS WORKSHOP **821**

## MODEL 1: STYLE

**Close Read**

1. ***Possible answer:*** *The style of this excerpt is literary. The entire passage is one long, graceful sentence filled with images that convey the power and beauty of summer's lushness (lines 6–9) and contrast it with the harsh barrenness of winter (lines 9–10).*

2. ***Possible answer:*** *Another clue to the literary style is the sentence "The dust and heat, the burning wind, reminded us of many things" (lines 4–5). This portrays the narrator as a person—someone who grew up in this setting and whose memories bring feelings of peace and nostalgia.*

## MODEL 2: STYLE

**Close Read**

1. ***Possible answer:*** *This excerpt is journalistic, not literary. The writer focuses on specific facts, such as the shape, location, and width of the hills (lines 2–4) and how and where the vegetation changes (lines 4–6). Although he uses one simile, "like a stone spear point" (line 2), he mostly uses simple description, such as measurements— "twenty to eighty miles wide" (line 4)—and geographic terms, such as "tallgrass prairie" (line 1), "stony upland" (line 4), and "high plains" (line 6).*

2. ***Possible answer:*** *One specific difference between Heat-Moon's and Cather's styles is that Cather uses a great deal of imagery, whereas Heat-Moon uses very little. Another difference is in their sentence structures: Cather's sentences are much longer and more complex than Heat-Moon's. A third difference is that Cather's style gives the reader a sense of the narrator, whereas Heat-Moon's objective style draws little attention to the person behind the words.*

TEXT ANALYSIS WORKSHOP **821**

# *Teach*

## Part 2: Style and Voice

**Word Choice, Sentence Structure, and Tone**
Point out to students that people speak in different styles and voices to friends, parents, teachers, strangers, and so on, and that writers also adjust their voice to suit their purposes and audiences. Challenge students to compose these sentences using an effective and appropriate voice:

- a teenage narrator of a humorous story describing a scary experience to a friend *(Example: It was—I mean, you can't believe how big that spider was! I was, like, let me out of here!)*

- a high-school student thanking a committee for an award or scholarship *(Example: Your generous gift allows me to fulfill my lifelong dream of attending college, and I will dedicate the next four years to making use of this opportunity.)*

- the anonymous narrator of a literary-style novel describing the weather *(Example: Lightning splintered the sky, thunder rumbled like barrels rolling down an alley, and the rain spilled down in sheets and raced along the gutters.)*

- a journalist writing about the background of a celebrity *(Example: She took her first ballet lesson at the age of three and performed in The Nutcracker Suite with the London Royal Ballet at the age of six.)*

Then discuss with students their choices of words, sentence structure, and tone in crafting the voice of each sentence. If necessary, have them review the chart on page 820 for terms that refer to different styles and their characteristics.

### CHECK UNDERSTANDING

Have students describe their understanding of voice.

---

## Part 2: Style and Voice

Almost every choice a writer makes contributes to the style of his or her work. These choices also help to create a **voice,** the personality that comes across on the page. The voice may be the writer's, or it may belong to a fictional character in a story.

Here, two writers express feelings about their craft. A close look at three key elements—word choice, sentence structure, and tone—in these passages can help you better understand each writer's unique style.

### COMPARING STYLES

It is [the writer's] privilege to help man endure by lifting his heart, by reminding him of the courage and honor and hope and pride and compassion and pity and sacrifice which have been the glory of his past.
—William Faulkner, Nobel Prize acceptance speech, 1950

The very first thing I tell my new students on the first day of a workshop is that good writing is about telling the truth. We are a species that needs and wants to understand who we are. Sheep lice do not seem to share this longing, which is one reason they write so very little.
—Anne Lamott, *Bird by Bird*

### WORD CHOICE

If you've ever struggled to find the perfect words to describe something, then you know how important **word choice** can be. A short person can be *compact, shrimpy,* even *Lilliputian*—or just *short.* The **denotation** (literal meaning) is the same, but the **connotations** (emotional associations) are quite different.

In his speech, Faulkner uses formal, dramatic words and phrases—for example, "the glory of his past"—to emphasize the serious responsibility of writers. Lamott's writing, however, is more conversational. Her use of *I* and *we,* as well as phrases like "the very first thing," contributes to her personable style.

### SENTENCE STRUCTURE

Sentences can be short and to the point (like Lamott's) or long and complex (like Faulkner's). In fact, the Faulkner excerpt is one long sentence that strings together *hope, courage,* and other weighty words with a series of *and*'s. This structure adds to the dramatic impact of the writing and helps to create its formal style.

### TONE

**Tone** is a writer's attitude toward a subject, as expressed through choice of words and details. Faulkner's focus on the writer's "privilege" conveys a formal tone. Lamott, however, scampers playfully from truth to sheep lice. Such incongruous details help to create a humorous tone.

**822**   UNIT 8: AUTHOR'S STYLE AND VOICE

---

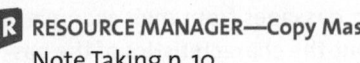

## DIFFERENTIATED INSTRUCTION

### FOR STRUGGLING READERS

**Note Taking** For students who need help, hand out the note-taking copy master for this page. As students read and discuss the main points, have them record them on the copy master.

**RESOURCE MANAGER—Copy Master**
Note Taking p. 10

**Concept Support** Tell students that an attitude is a feeling toward something. For example, anger, kindness, and respect can be attitudes. Suggest a familiar subject, such as a neighbor's dog. Help students list positive and negative attitudes that a writer's tone could reflect toward the subject *(admiring, disapproving, caring, irritated).* Have students describe the subject, choosing words to craft a tone that reflects one of the attitudes listed.

## MODEL 1: ELEMENTS OF STYLE

Sandra Cisneros has a unique and recognizable style of writing. As you read this excerpt, pay attention to her word choice and the structure of the sentences. To get the full effect of Cisneros's style, read the excerpt aloud. Does it sound like someone writing or like someone talking?

*from* **Geraldo**
# No Last Name

Vignette by **Sandra Cisneros**

She met him at a dance. Pretty too, and young. Said he worked in a restaurant, but she can't remember which one. Geraldo. That's all. Green pants and Saturday shirt. Geraldo. That's what he told her.

And how was she to know she'd be the last one to see him alive. An accident, don't you know. Hit-and-run. Marin, she goes to all those dances. Uptown. Logan. Embassy. Palmer. Aragon. Fontana. The Manor. She likes to dance. She knows how to do cumbias and salsas and rancheras even. And he was just someone she danced with. Somebody she met that night. That's right.

That's the story. That's what she said again and again. Once to the hospital people and twice to the police. No address. No name. Nothing in his pockets.

**Close Read**

1. Describe the structure of the sentences in the box. What effect do these sentences have on the style of the excerpt and the narrator's voice?

2. Find an example of word choice that would not belong in a story written in a formal style.

## MODEL 2: ELEMENTS OF STYLE

Jane Austen is known for her "novels of manners," in which she recorded the details of 19th-century middle-class British life with irony and humor. How does her style of writing differ from Cisneros's?

*from* *Pride* and *Prejudice*

Novel by **Jane Austen**

Elizabeth Bennet had been obliged by the scarcity of gentlemen to sit down for two dances; and during part of that time, Mr. Darcy had been standing near enough for her to overhear a conversation between him and Mr. Bingley, who came from the dance for a few minutes to press his friend to join it.

"Come, Darcy," said he, "I must have you dance. I hate to see you standing about by yourself in this stupid manner. You had much better dance."

"I certainly shall not. You know how I detest it, unless I am particularly acquainted with my partner. At such an assembly as this, it would be insupportable. Your sisters are engaged, and there is not another woman in the room whom it would not be a punishment to me to stand up with."

**Close Read**

1. What specific words and details in this excerpt help to convey a prim and proper tone?

2. Reread lines 1–4. What sentence structure does the writer use for the narrator's voice?

3. Rewrite the boxed text in a conversational style.

---

## MODEL 1: ELEMENTS OF STYLE
**Close Read**

1. **Possible answer:** *The "sentences" in the box are mostly short fragments. The phrase "don't you know" (line 5) is an informal expression, and the double subject "Marin, she . . ." (line 5) is improper grammar. All of these elements give the passage an informal style and emphasize the voice of the narrator, which has the breathless, stream-of-consciousness sound of someone telling upsetting news to a friend.*

2. **Possible answer:** *Examples of word choice that would not belong in a story written in a formal style are "Saturday shirt" (line 3) and "hospital people" (lines 9–10). In a formal style, the narrator would have described what the shirt looked like and used the exact title of the person she spoke with at the hospital or a more formal term, such as "hospital staff."*

## MODEL 2: ELEMENTS OF STYLE
**Close Read**

1. **Possible answer:** *Some of the words that convey a prim and proper tone are "obliged by the scarcity of gentlemen" (line 1), "particularly acquainted" (lines 7–8), "assembly" (line 8), and "insupportable" (line 9).*

2. **Possible answer:** *The passage begins with a long, complex sentence, which gives the narrator's voice a formal, literary quality.*

3. **Possible answer:** *Rewritten in a modern, informal, conversational style, the boxed text might read: "Absolutely not. I can't stand dancing with someone I don't know. Especially at this kind of party."*

---

## DIFFERENTIATED INSTRUCTION

### FOR STRUGGLING READERS

**Comprehension: Plot** If students have trouble following the fragmented style of the narrator in Model 1, have them work in pairs to list the events in order.

1. Marin went to a dance.

2. She danced with a boy named Geraldo.

3. Later that night, Geraldo was killed in a car accident.

4. Marin reported what she knew about him to the hospital staff and the police.

### FOR ENGLISH LANGUAGE LEARNERS

**Vocabulary: Multiple-Meaning Words**
Discuss the most common meanings of these words in Model 2: *obliged* (line 1), *press* (line 4), *engaged* (line 9).

1. Have students generate sentences using the different meanings of the words.

2. Ask students to identify the meaning intended in the model. (For *engaged*, accept either "occupied" or "pledged to marry" as a reasonable answer.)

# Practice and Apply

## Part 3: Analyze the Text

**Close Read**

1. *Possible answer: In addition to the boxed phrases, three other examples of Wells's many vivid images are "big, grayish rounded bulk, the size, perhaps, of a bear, was rising slowly and painfully" (lines 1–2), "the lipless brim of which quivered ... and dropped saliva" (lines 6–7), and "something fungoid in the oily brown skin" (lines 16–17).*

2. *Possible answer: The long string of repulsive images, linked in a single sentence, helps to emphasize the narrator's sense of fascination and horror.*

3. *Possible answer: Wells's style is literary. One literary element is his use of long, elaborate sentences, such as the one in lines 10–16. Another is his word choice. Wells describes the Martian in words chosen to convey the narrator's feelings, such as "strange horror" (lines 9–10), "Gorgon groups of tentacles" (line 12), "vital, intense, inhuman, crippled and monstrous" (line 16), and "unspeakably nasty" (line 18). Wells's style also contains formal elements. He uses sophisticated words such as "steadfastly" (line 4), "tentacular appendage" (line 8), "incessant" (line 12), and "tumultuous" (line 13), as well as proper grammar.*

---

## Part 3: Analyze the Text

Apply what you've just learned about style as you analyze these two excerpts. Though both writers take on the subject of outer space, they have distinctly different styles.

The first excerpt comes from a classic science fiction novel first published in 1898. As you read, pay attention to the elements—word choice, sentence structure, and tone—that reveal the writer's style.

### from THE WAR OF THE WORLDS

Novel by **H. G. Wells**

A big, grayish rounded bulk, the size, perhaps, of a bear, was rising slowly and painfully out of the cylinder. As it bulged up and caught the light, it glistened like wet leather.

Two large dark-colored eyes were regarding me steadfastly. The mass that
5 framed them, the head of the thing, was rounded, and had, one might say, a face. There was a mouth under the eyes, the lipless brim of which quivered and panted, and dropped saliva. The whole creature heaved and pulsated convulsively. A lank tentacular appendage gripped the edge of the cylinder, another swayed in the air.

Those who have never seen a living Martian can scarcely imagine the strange
10 horror of its appearance. The peculiar V-shaped mouth with its pointed upper lip, the absence of brow ridges, the absence of a chin beneath the wedgelike lower lip, the incessant quivering of this mouth, the Gorgon groups of tentacles, the tumultuous breathing of the lungs in a strange atmosphere, the evident heaviness and painfulness of movement due to the greater gravitational energy of the
15 earth—above all, the extraordinary intensity of the immense eyes—were at once vital, intense, inhuman, crippled and monstrous. There was something fungoid in the oily brown skin, something in the clumsy deliberation of the tedious movements unspeakably nasty.

### Close Read

1. One aspect of Wells's style is his use of vivid images to help you visualize the Martian. Three examples are boxed. Identify three additional examples.

2. Reread the sentence in lines 10–16. What do its structure and length help to emphasize?

3. Review the styles of writing on page 820. Which style or styles does Wells's writing display? Support your answer.

---

## DIFFERENTIATED INSTRUCTION

**FOR STRUGGLING READERS**

**Analysis Support: Sentence Structure and Word Choice** Have students work in small groups to rewrite the sentence in lines 10–16 as a paragraph made up of short sentences in simple, neutral language. Paragraphs might begin "It had a V-shaped mouth with a pointed upper lip. Its lower lip was wedge-shaped, and it had no chin ...." Ask a group to read its paragraph aloud, then help students compare its effect with Wells's version.

**Comprehension: Imagery** Explain that a Gorgon is a character in Greek mythology who has snakes for hair. Anyone who looks into her eyes turns to stone. Then ask students to create a picture of the Martian. Urge them to capture the emotional content as well as the details of Wells's imagery.

In the next excerpt, the astronaut Sally Ride describes her feelings and impressions as she looked down on her home planet from space. How does her style compare with the one Wells used in *The War of the Worlds*?

*from*

# Single Room, Earth View

### Essay by **Sally Ride**

Everyone I've met has a glittering, if vague, mental image of space travel. And naturally enough, people want to hear about it from an astronaut: "How did it feel . . . ?" "What did it look like . . . ?" "Were you scared?" Sometimes, the questions come from reporters, their pens poised and their tape recorders
5 silently reeling in the words; sometimes, it's wide-eyed, ten-year-old girls who want answers. I find a way to answer all of them, but it's not easy.

Imagine trying to describe an airplane ride to someone who has never flown. An articulate traveler could describe the sights but would find it much harder to explain the difference in perspective provided by the new view from
10 a greater distance, along with the feelings, impressions, and insights that go with that new perspective. And the difference is enormous: Space flight moves the traveler another giant step farther away. Eight and one-half thunderous minutes after launch, an astronaut is orbiting high above the Earth, suddenly able to watch typhoons form, volcanos smolder, and meteors streak through
15 the atmosphere below.

While flying over the Hawaiian Islands, several astronauts have marveled that the islands look just like they do on a map. When people first hear that, they wonder what should be so surprising about Hawaii looking the way it does in the atlas. Yet, to the astronauts it is an absolutely startling sensation:
20 The islands really *do* look as if that part of the world has been carpeted with a big page torn out of Rand-McNally, and all we can do is try to convey the surreal quality of that scene.

In orbit, racing along at five miles per second, the space shuttle circles the Earth once every 90 minutes. I found that at this speed, unless I kept my nose
25 pressed to the window, it was almost impossible to keep track of where we were at any given moment—the world below simply changes too fast. If I turned my concentration away for too long, even just to change film in a camera, I could miss an entire land mass. It's embarrassing to float up to a window, glance outside, and then have to ask a crewmate, "What continent is this?"

## Close Read

1. Reread the boxed sentence. What do you notice about its structure and Ride's choice of words? Explain whether these elements indicate a conversational style or a formal, academic one.

2. Consider the tone that Ride takes toward her subject. Is it enthusiastic or detached? Cite evidence to support your answer.

3. How would you characterize Ride's voice—the personality revealed through her writing? Explain.

4. Using examples from both excerpts, contrast Ride's and Wells's styles. Find three differences.

## Close Read

1. *Possible answer:* The boxed text contains a simple sentence followed by three very short questions. The words are also simple, and the sentence begins with "And." These elements create a conversational style.

2. *Possible answer:* Ride's tone is enthusiastic, as evidenced by words and phrases such as "marveled" (line 16), "absolutely startling sensation" (line 19), "surreal quality" (line 22), and "nose pressed to the window" (lines 24–25).

3. *Possible answer:* Ride's voice is candid, friendly, and enthusiastic. She is eager to answer questions (line 6), shows excitement in her descriptions (lines 12–15; 20–22), and has a sense of humor (lines 28–29).

4. *Possible answer:* Ride's style is informal and journalistic, while Wells's style is formal and literary. Specifically, Wells uses long, elaborate sentences, many sophisticated words, and a great deal of mood-evoking imagery. Ride uses simple sentences and familiar words, and she limits imagery in favor of more factual, neutral language.

## Assess and Reteach

### Assess

Name two contrasting literature selections that the class has recently read. Ask students to describe the style and voice of each.

### Reteach

For students who are unable to apply the workshop skills to recently read selections, use these reteaching options:

1. On the board, make a chart with columns headed *formal, informal, journalistic,* and *literary* and rows labeled *words, sentence structures, grammar, imagery,* and *sense of narrator.* Help students list the attributes of each style; for example, in the *words* row, write "sophisticated, abstract" under *formal* and "easy, familiar" under *informal.*

2. Ask students to review page 822 and its accompanying copy master. Have them meet in small groups to compose an answer to this question: What is voice, and what elements does a writer use to craft it? Have students share and refine their answers as a class.

## FOR ENGLISH LANGUAGE LEARNERS

**Comprehension: Transitions** Tell students that writers often make points by contrasting one thing or idea with another. Have students reread the sentence in line 6 of Ride's essay. Point out that in English the word *but* signals a contrast. In this sentence, Ride is contrasting her ability to answer questions with her struggle in doing it. Tell students that *yet* also signals a contrast.

Have students find other instances of *but* and *yet* in the selection and explain what is being contrasted. *Possible answers: contrast between ease of describing visual images and difficulty of describing thoughts and feelings associated with flight (line 8); contrast between what people would expect to experience and what astronauts actually experience (line 19)*

# Focus and Motivate

## SUMMARIES

**"Where Have You Gone, Charming Billy?"** A soldier in Vietnam reflects on a soldier who died of a heart attack because he was scared.

**"The Naked Soldier"** In an interview, author Tim O'Brien talks about bravery and courage.

**"Be a Marine"** A poster for the Marines from World War II appeals to recruits.

## Is **FEAR** our worst enemy?

Discuss the question with students. How do people behave while in the throes of fear?

## What's the Connection?

Discuss what it means to be a hero.

---

## Comparing Texts

### Where Have You Gone, Charming Billy?
Short Story by Tim O'Brien

### Tim O'Brien: The Naked Soldier
Interview from *Verbicide* Magazine

### Be a Marine
Recruitment Poster

*Essential Course of Study* **ECOS**

Video link at thinkcentral.com

VIDEO TRAILER **THINK**central | KEYWORD: HML9-826

## Is **FEAR** our worst enemy?

Your heart pounds. Your hands shake. Your stomach churns. Adrenaline floods your body. You are gripped by fear, and the way you react to it is as unique as your fingerprints. In "Where Have You Gone, Charming Billy?" a young soldier struggling through his first night in Vietnam tries desperately to combat his growing terror.

### What's the Connection?

Experiencing the tragedies of war can frighten and permanently scar even the bravest of soldiers, so why do people go to war? Is it heroic to fight despite fear? After reading the following short story, you'll read an interview and view a poster that each convey certain messages about honor, heroism, and war.

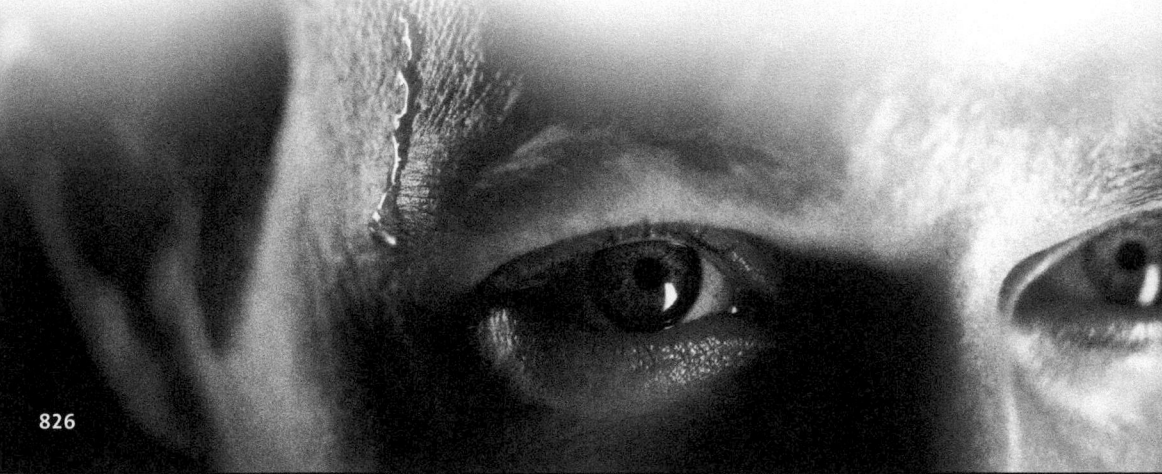

826

---

## Selection Resources

See resources on the **Teacher One Stop DVD-ROM** and on **thinkcentral.com**.

 Video link at thinkcentral.com

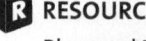 **RESOURCE MANAGER UNIT 8**
Plan and Teach, pp. 11–18
Summary pp. 19–20†‡*
Text Analysis and Reading Skill, pp. 21–24†*
Vocabulary, pp. 25–27*
Grammar and Style, p. 30

**DIAGNOSTIC AND SELECTION TESTS**
Selection Tests, pp. 219–222

 **BEST PRACTICES TOOLKIT**
Word Squares, p. E10
Sensory Notes, p. B9
New Word Analysis, p. E8

**INTERACTIVE READER**

**ADAPTED INTERACTIVE READER**

**ELL ADAPTED INTERACTIVE READER**

**TECHNOLOGY**

- **Teacher One Stop DVD-ROM**
- **Student One Stop DVD-ROM**
- **PowerNotes DVD-ROM**
- **Audio Anthology CD**
- **GrammarNotes DVD-ROM**
- **Audio Tutor CD**
- **ExamView Test Generator** on the **Teacher One Stop**

**Video Trailer** **THINK**central

Go to **thinkcentral.com** to preview the **Video Trailer** introducing this selection. Other features that support the selection include
- **PowerNotes** presentation
- **ThinkAloud** models to enhance comprehension
- **WordSharp** vocabulary tutorials
- interactive writing and grammar instruction

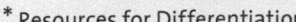 Resources for Differentiation     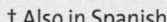 Also in Spanish     ‡ In Haitian Creole and Vietnamese

## TEXT ANALYSIS: REALISM

You know that just as you and your friends have a style all your own, so do writers. A writer's style is the unique way he or she communicates ideas. This style is reflected in the dialogue, word choice, and sentence structure of every piece of writing. In this story, Tim O'Brien uses the style of **realism** to depict the horrors of combat as seen through the eyes of a young soldier. To make the story seem real to the reader, he uses

- dialogue that sounds natural, like actual speech
- vivid, realistic descriptions of what the soldier sees
- a mix of long and short sentences to communicate the soldier's thoughts and feelings

As you read, think about the way the characters talk to each other, and consider O'Brien's word choice and sentence structure. Note passages that seem particularly realistic to you.

*Review:* **Point of View**

## READING SKILL: ANALYZE SEQUENCE

The sequence of a story is the order in which events occur. Sometimes a writer interrupts this linear order with a **flashback,** an account of an event that happened before the beginning of the story's action. A flashback provides more background information about the current situation and helps the reader understand the story's events. To identify a flashback, look for sudden changes in scene. As you read this story, note how its flashbacks help create a tense and frightening mood. Keep track of the story's order of events by filling in a sequence chain like the one shown.

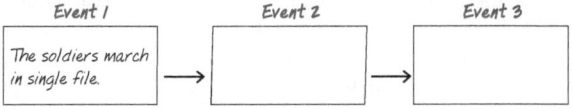

| Event 1 | Event 2 | Event 3 |
|---------|---------|---------|
| The soldiers march in single file. | | |

## ◆ VOCABULARY IN CONTEXT

In your *Reader/Writer Notebook,* try to restate each phrase, using a different word or words for the boldfaced term.

1. a secret mission depending on **stealth**
2. huge stalks of corn in the rich, **fecund** field
3. an argument too **diffuse** to understand
4. lying around in a state of **inertia**

 Complete the activities in your **Reader/Writer Notebook.**

---

## Meet the Author

### Tim O'Brien
born 1946

**From Dull to Dangerous**
"If you look in a dictionary under the word *boring,*" Tim O'Brien says sarcastically, "you will find a little pen-and-ink illustration of Worthington, Minnesota, where I grew up." As a kid, O'Brien escaped from the quiet predictability of his hometown by burying himself in books. Just after he graduated from a small Minnesota college, O'Brien's life got more exciting—but not in a way he ever would have chosen. He was drafted and sent to Vietnam.

**Combat Zone**
O'Brien was strongly opposed to the Vietnam War and considered fleeing to Canada to avoid serving in the army. He knew, however, that failing to enlist would make him an outcast in his hometown. "That's a tough thing to do when you're that old," O'Brien says, "to decide to walk away from your whole history." He was shipped to Vietnam in 1969, and though some of his experiences there were gruesome, they inspired him to write. In 1973, O'Brien published his first book, an account of his time in Vietnam. The war has been the main subject of his writing ever since.

**BACKGROUND TO THE STORY**
**Vietnam War**
This story takes place in the Southeast Asian country of Vietnam during a war in which over 58,000 Americans died. Rebels backed by Communist-ruled North Vietnam tried to take over South Vietnam in 1957. The U.S. entered the war as a South Vietnamese ally in 1964. Between 1965 and 1973, over 2 million Americans were sent to Vietnam. Few were prepared for the fear and anxiety that would overcome them.

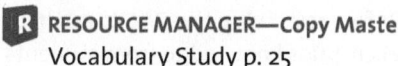
Author Online
Go to **thinkcentral.com.**
KEYWORD: HML9-827

827

---

**PRETEACH VOCABULARY** Use the following copy master to help students predict meanings for each boldfaced word.

**R RESOURCE MANAGER—Copy Master**
Vocabulary Study p. 25

1. Read item 1 aloud, emphasizing *stealth*.
2. Point out the context clues. Elicit possible meanings for *stealth*.
3. Have students fill in the chart.
4. Repeat the procedure for items 2–4.

---

## *Teach*

## ● *Model the Skill:* **REALISM**

For instructional support, read aloud this example:

> "I dunno. Folks aren't careful like they once was," said the man.
>
> "Nope," said the second man. "Nobody's got the time—not a free minute."

Explain that short interrupted sentences, slang, and inaccurate grammar make the conversation seem real.

**GUIDED PRACTICE** Have students suggest how the first man might answer the second man in the example.

## ■ *Model the Skill:* **ANALYZE SEQUENCE**

To support instruction, write these sentences on the board:

> Jake sat on a park bench, watching some kids playing baseball. A lanky boy raced to left field and made a diving catch. It reminded Jake of the last time he played ball with his brother.

Explain that the shift in scene comes when Jake thinks of the last time he played ball with his brother.

**GUIDED PRACTICE** Have students tell what the writer might describe next.

**R RESOURCE MANAGER—Copy Master**
Analyze Sequence p. 23

### READ WITH A PURPOSE

*Help students set a purpose for reading. Tell them to look for what it is that Paul Berlin is afraid of.*

**TEXT ANALYSIS**   COMMON CORE   RL 4

**Ⓐ Model the Skill: REALISM**

To model realistic thought processes, "think out loud" in a stream of consciousness for students as if you were ordering from a menu, walking down the street, or starting your car. Ask students why an author might choose to show a character's inner thoughts.

**Possible answer:** *The mix of sentences mimics the way a real person might think about things. It provides a realistic depiction of a soldier trying to cope with the horrors he's confronting. It also helps to emphasize how desperately Paul longs to think about anything but war.*

**VOCABULARY**   COMMON CORE   L 4

**OWN THE WORD**

**stealth:** Introduce the adverb *stealthily*, which is formed from the noun *stealth*. Remind students that adverbs tell how an action is done. Then, define *stealthily* as "in a secretive way." Ask students to describe other actions they or others might do *stealthily*. **Possible answers:** *look at or watch someone or something; take something; eat something*

# Where Have You Gone, Charming Billy?

## Tim O'Brien

The platoon of twenty-six soldiers moved slowly in the dark, single file, not talking.

One by one, like sheep in a dream, they passed through the hedgerow, crossed quietly over a meadow and came down to the rice paddy.[1] There they stopped. Their leader knelt down, motioning with his hand, and one by one the other soldiers squatted in the shadows, vanishing in the primitive **stealth** of warfare. For a long time they did not move. Except for the sounds of their breathing, . . . the twenty-six men were very quiet: some of them excited by the adventure, some of them afraid, some of them exhausted from the long night

10 march, some of them looking forward to reaching the sea where they would be safe. At the rear of the column, Private First Class Paul Berlin lay quietly with his forehead resting on the black plastic stock of his rifle, his eyes closed. He was pretending he was not in the war, pretending he had not watched Billy Boy Watkins die of a heart attack that afternoon. He was pretending he was a boy again, camping with his father in the midnight summer along the Des Moines River. In the dark, with his eyes pinched shut, he pretended. He pretended that when he opened his eyes, his father would be there by the campfire and they would talk softly about whatever came to mind and then roll into their sleeping bags, and that later they'd wake up and it would be morning and there would

20 not be a war, and that Billy Boy Watkins had not died of a heart attack that afternoon. He pretended he was not a soldier. Ⓐ

---

1. **hedgerow . . . rice paddy:** A hedgerow is a thick hedge separating fields or farms; a rice paddy is a flooded field in which rice is grown.

**828**   UNIT 8: AUTHOR'S STYLE AND VOICE

*Infantry* (1997), James E. Faulkner. Oil on canvas. Collection of Nature's Nest Gallery, Golden, Colorado. Photo courtesy of the artist.

**Analyze Visuals ▶**

Would you describe this painting as **realistic** or **abstract?** Cite details about the painting's subject, setting, and mood, as well as the artist's use of light and color.

**stealth** (stĕlth) *n.* cautious or secret action or movement

**❶ Targeted Passage**

**Ⓐ REALISM**
Reread lines 11–21, and consider O'Brien's use of both long and short sentences to convey Paul Berlin's thoughts. What effect does this stylistic choice create?

---

## DIFFERENTIATED INSTRUCTION

**FOR ENGLISH LANGUAGE LEARNERS**

**Reading: Background** Students may need to know some basic facts about the Vietnam War. Before reviewing the **BACKGROUND** note, elicit prior knowledge from students.

**Options for Reading** Ask a question and have students scan designated text for the answer.

**FOR STRUGGLING READERS**

In combination with the *Audio Anthology CD*, use one or more Targeted Passages (pp. 828, 834, 835) to ensure that students focus on key story events, concepts, and skills. Targeted Passages can also help for English learners.

## BACKGROUND

**Vietnam's Geography** Vietnam is generally mountainous with thick forests. South Vietnam, where this story takes place, is tropical with hot, wet summers. Winters tend to be dry and somewhat cooler. Flooding is common in some parts of the country. At the time of the Vietnam War, most Vietnamese were farmers, living in villages. The walls and roofs of their homes were made of palm leaves or straw. Rice has long been Vietnam's basic food; this crop grows in the kind of rice paddy that Paul Berlin wades through in the story.

## Analyze Visuals

*Possible answer: The painting is somewhat realistic. The soldier's posture is lifelike, and his clothing and ammunition look authentic. The setting is realistically depicted, though brushy and impressionistic in style. The dappled patches of greens, yellows, and browns suggest that the soldier is emerging from a dense forest into the sunlight—or perhaps into the glow of explosives. The mood of the painting is realistic in that it captures a soldier's exhaustion and despair. However, the painting is not realistic in the sense of portraying graphic violence or the gritty details of a soldier's life.*

**About the Art** Colorado artist James E. Faulkner (b. 1945) has received awards for his wildlife paintings. His rich depiction of jungle foliage in this painting reflects his skill with natural backgrounds. Soldiers like Paul Berlin marched through similar terrain while on duty in Vietnam.

**① Targeted Passage** [Lines 1–21]

This passage introduces the setting, the main character, and his internal conflict.

- Who is Paul Berlin? (line 11)
- Where is he, and what is he doing? (line 4)
- What is Paul Berlin pretending? (lines 13–20)
- Why is he pretending? (lines 13–21)

**FOR ADVANCED LEARNERS/PRE–AP**

**Interest Stations** Post these assignments for students to work on independently.

- **Create a Landscape: Realism** Illustrate a scene from the story.
- **Exploring Viewpoints: Speech** Write a speech Paul might give after serving for a year in the Vietnam War.

**R** RESOURCE MANAGER
Ideas for Extension pp. 16–17

## ⓑ REALISM

*Possible answer: Specific features that make the dialogue sound realistic include the use of short questions (line 30), short answers (line 31), interjections ("Hey!"), informal diction ("You got a lot to learn, buddy"), contractions, and shortened words ("sleepin'").*

## TIERED DISCUSSION PROMPTS

Use these prompts to help students understand Paul's thoughts in lines 36–44 about what he will and will not tell his mother:

**Analyze** Why would Paul plan to tell his mother about how things looked and smelled but not about how frightened he was? *Possible answer: He would want to share a part of his experience with her, but not upset her or make her think less of him.*

**Synthesize** Why is Paul so focused on what he will and will not tell his mother? *Possible answer: It's a way of coping by removing himself mentally to a safer place.*

## REVISIT THE BIG QUESTION

Is **FEAR** our worst enemy?

**Discuss** In lines 52–63, what does Paul Berlin now know about fear? *Possible answer: He sees that fear can be as intense as the "bundled and tight" fear (line 59) that he felt when he watched Billy Boy Watkins die. But he also realizes that there are less intense, less specific fears.*

## OWN THE WORD

- **fecund:** Tell students that common synonyms of *fecund* are "fruitful" and "productive." Antonyms include "barren" and "infertile."
- **diffuse:** Tell students that the prefix *dif-* and the root *-fus* come from Latin. *Dif-* means "in different directions" and *-fus* means "pour."

---

In the morning, when they reached the sea, it would be better. The hot afternoon would be over, he would bathe in the sea and he would forget how frightened he had been on his first day at the war. The second day would not be so bad. He would learn.

There was a sound beside him, a movement and then a breathed: "Hey!" He opened his eyes, shivering as if emerging from a deep nightmare. "Hey!" a shadow whispered. "We're *moving*. . . . Get up."

"Okay."

30 "You sleepin', or something?"

"No." He could not make out the soldier's face. With clumsy, concrete hands he clawed for his rifle, found it, found his helmet.

The soldier-shadow grunted. "You got a lot to learn, buddy. I'd shoot you if I thought you was sleepin'. Let's go." ⓑ

Private First Class Paul Berlin blinked.

Ahead of him, silhouetted against the sky, he saw the string of soldiers wading into the flat paddy, the black outline of their shoulders and packs and weapons. He was comfortable. He did not want to move. But he was afraid, for it was his first night at the war, so he hurried to catch up, stumbling once, 40 scraping his knee, groping as though blind; his boots sank into the thick paddy water and he smelled it all around him. He would tell his mother how it smelled: mud and algae and cattle manure and chlorophyll, decay, breeding mosquitoes and leeches as big as mice, the **fecund** warmth of the paddy waters rising up to his cut knee. But he would not tell how frightened he had been.

Once they reached the sea, things would be better. They would have their rear guarded by three thousand miles of ocean, and they would swim and dive into the breakers and hunt crayfish and smell the salt, and they would be safe.

He followed the shadow of the man in front of him. It was a clear night. Already the Southern Cross² was out. And other stars he could not yet name— 50 soon, he thought, he would learn their names. And puffy night clouds. There was not yet a moon. Wading through the paddy, his boots made sleepy, sloshing sounds, like a lullaby, and he tried not to think. Though he was afraid, he now knew that fear came in many degrees and types and peculiar categories, and he knew that his fear now was not so bad as it had been in the hot afternoon, when poor Billy Boy Watkins got killed by a heart attack. His fear now was **diffuse** and unformed: ghosts in the tree line, nighttime fears of a child, a boogieman in the closet that his father would open to show empty, saying "See? Nothing there, champ. Now you can sleep." In the afternoon it had been worse: the fear had been bundled and tight and he'd been on his hands and knees, crawling like an insect, 60 an ant escaping a giant's footsteps and thinking nothing, brain flopping like wet cement in a mixer, not thinking at all, watching while Billy Boy Watkins died.

Now as he stepped out of the paddy onto a narrow dirt path, now the fear was mostly the fear of being so terribly afraid again.

He tried not to think.

---

2. **Southern Cross:** a cross-shaped group of stars visible in the Southern Hemisphere.

### ⓑ REALISM
Reread lines 26–34. What specific features of the characters' speech make this **dialogue** sound realistic? Explain, citing evidence to support your answer.

**fecund** (fē′kənd) *adj.* producing much growth; fertile

**diffuse** (dĭ-fyo͞os′) *adj.* unfocused

---

## DIFFERENTIATED INSTRUCTION

### FOR STRUGGLING READERS
**Comprehension: Clarify Meaning** Focus students' attention on the use of the conditional "would" in lines 22–25 and lines 41–44. Help students recognize that this usage refers to things that someone might hope will happen but which may not necessarily occur.

### FOR ENGLISH LANGUAGE LEARNERS
**Vocabulary Support** Use Word Squares to teach these words: *categories* (line 53), *seek* (line 75), *adjust* (line 81), *enormous* (line 180), *stress* (line 180), *finally* (line 189).

 **BEST PRACTICES TOOLKIT**—Transparency Word Squares p. E10

There were tricks he'd learned to keep from thinking. Counting: He counted his steps, concentrating on the numbers, pretending that the steps were dollar bills and that each step through the night made him richer and richer, so that soon he would become a wealthy man, and he kept counting and considered the ways he might spend the money after the war and what he would do. He

70 would look his father in the eye and shrug and say, "It was pretty bad at first, but I learned a lot and I got used to it." Then he would tell his father the story of Billy Boy Watkins. But he would never let on how frightened he had been. "Not so bad," he would say instead, making his father feel proud. **C**

Songs, another trick to stop from thinking: *Where have you gone, Billy Boy, Billy Boy, Oh, where have you gone, charming Billy? I have gone to seek a wife, she's the joy of my life, but she's a young thing and cannot leave her mother,* and other songs that he sang in his thoughts as he walked toward the sea. And when he reached the sea he would dig a deep hole in the sand and he would sleep like the high clouds, and he would not be afraid any more.

80 The moon came out. Pale and shrunken to the size of a dime.

The helmet was heavy on his head. In the morning he would adjust the leather binding. He would clean his rifle, too. Even though he had been frightened to shoot it during the hot afternoon, he would carefully clean the breech and the muzzle and the ammunition so that next time he would be ready and not so afraid. In the morning, when they reached the sea, he would begin to make friends with some of the other soldiers. He would learn their names and laugh at their jokes. Then when the war was over he would have war buddies, and he would write to them once in a while and exchange memories. **D**

Walking, sleeping in his walking, he felt better. He watched the moon

90 come higher.

Once they skirted a sleeping village. The smells again—straw, cattle, mildew. The men were quiet. On the far side of the village, buried in the dark smells, a dog barked. The column stopped until the barking died away; then they marched fast away from the village, through a graveyard filled with conical-shaped burial mounds and tiny altars made of clay and stone. The graveyard had a perfumy smell. A nice place to spend the night, he thought. The mounds would make fine battlements, and the smell was nice and the place was quiet. But they went on, passing through a hedgerow and across another paddy and east toward the sea. **E**

He walked carefully. He remembered what he'd been taught: Stay off the

100 center of the path, for that was where the land mines and booby traps were planted, where stupid and lazy soldiers like to walk. Stay alert, he'd been taught. Better alert than inert. Ag-ile, mo-bile, hos-tile.[3] He wished he'd paid better attention to the training. He could not remember what they'd said about how to stop being afraid; they hadn't given any lessons in courage—not that he could remember—and they hadn't mentioned how Billy Boy Watkins would die of a heart attack, his face turning pale and the veins popping out.

---

3. **Better alert . . . hos-tile:** sayings and chants reminding soldiers to pay attention rather than be lifeless (inert), and to be light on their feet (agile), ready to move (mobile), and aggressive (hostile).

WHERE HAVE YOU GONE, CHARMING BILLY?  **831**

---

**C SEQUENCE**
Summarize the story's events up to this point. Which events take place in Vietnam? Which are scenes the narrator imagines will happen in the future or remembers from his past?

**D GRAMMAR AND STYLE**
Reread lines 81–88. Notice O'Brien's repetition of "he would," which reflects Paul's way of coping with his current situation.

**E REALISM**
Reread lines 91–98. Identify the **sensory details**—details that appeal to the five senses—O'Brien includes. How do these details contribute to the vivid, realistic style of this story?

---

**FOR ENGLISH LANGUAGE LEARNERS**
**Culture: Clarify** You may wish to have students listen to a recording of the folk song "Billy Boy." Provide a lyric sheet if necessary. Explain that it is actually a humorous song that has nothing to do with war.

**FOR ADVANCED LEARNERS/PRE–AP**
**Repetition and Suspense** Ask students to estimate and check how many times O'Brien has mentioned Billy Boy Watkins's death up to this point in the story. Discuss how this repetition builds suspense. What other effects does it have?

---

**C** *Model the Skill:* **SEQUENCE**

Remind students that this story has scenes set in the present, future, and the past. Explain that the scene between Paul and his father is in an imagined future. Tell students to use their Sequence charts to add events.

*Possible answer:* *Paul is marching at night with a platoon of soldiers in Vietnam. While the platoon stops by a rice paddy, Paul pretends he is still a boy, camping with his father. Another soldier chides Paul for daydreaming when he should be paying attention. As the platoon begins wading through the paddy, Paul recalls his terror over the death of a fellow soldier who died of a heart attack. He thinks of his father again and how he will tell him, when he's home again, that he wasn't afraid.*

---

**D GRAMMAR AND STYLE**     COMMON CORE L 3

**Analyze Repetition** Repetition involves the repeated use of any language element. A writer may repeat sounds, words, phrases, clauses, sentences, or rhythmic patterns. Ask students to count the number of times O'Brien repeats "he would." What point do they think he is making? Have students look for other examples of repetition.

---

**E REALISM**

*Possible answers:* **Smells:** *straw, cattle, mildew, dark smells, perfumy graveyard, nice smell.* **Sound:** *dog barking, quiet place.* **Sight:** *conical-shaped burial mounds, tiny clay and stone altars, hedgerow, paddy. These sensory details make Paul's experience in Vietnam come alive for the reader.*

**IF STUDENTS NEED HELP . . .** Have them use the Sensory Notes chart.

 BEST PRACTICES TOOLKIT—Transparency Sensory Notes p. B9

---

## TEXT ANALYSIS: *Review*

### ❺ POINT OF VIEW

*Possible answer: The story is told from the third-person limited point of view, with the narrator describing Paul's thoughts and feelings. Without this detailed description, the reader would not develop such a strong attachment to Paul or understand his struggle to cope with his intense fear.*

**REVISIT THE BIG QUESTION**

## Is FEAR our worst enemy?

**Discuss** In lines 118–122, whom is Berlin trying to convince that he is not afraid? *Possible answer: He imagines how he will convince his father in the future, while trying to convince himself in the present.*

## TIERED DISCUSSION PROMPTS

Use these prompts for lines 143–146 to help students understand why soldiers might avoid getting to know one another too well:

**Analyze** Why doesn't Paul care that he can't make out the man's face or know his name? *Possible answer: He does not want to get close to someone who may soon die.*

**Evaluate** Is Paul's strategy of not getting to know the other soldier a good one? Why or why not? *Possible answer: If the man dies, Paul is unlikely to feel shock, loss, and despair. On the other hand, Paul could benefit from connecting with another soldier.*

---

VOCABULARY                                          COMMON CORE  L 4

## OWN THE WORD

**inertia:** Have students create a semantic map for *inertia*. Write the word in a center circle and then add the definition given, "tendency to do what one has been doing." Draw spider legs from the center circle and have students add synonyms to complete the map. *Possible answers: listlessness, languor, sluggishness, passivity*

---

Private First Class Paul Berlin walked carefully.

Stretching ahead of him like dark beads on an invisible chain, the string of shadow-soldiers whose names he did not yet know moved with the silence and
110 slow grace of smoke. Now and again moonlight was reflected off a machine gun or a wrist watch. But mostly the soldiers were quiet and hidden and far-away-seeming in a peaceful night, strangers on a long street, and he felt quite separate from them, as if trailing behind like the caboose on a night train, pulled along by **inertia**, sleepwalking, an afterthought to the war.

So he walked carefully, counting his steps. When he had counted to three thousand, four hundred and eighty-five, the column stopped.

One by one the soldiers knelt or squatted down.

The grass along the path was wet. Private First Class Paul Berlin lay back and turned his head so that he could lick at the dew with his eyes closed,
120 another trick to forget the war. He might have slept. "I *wasn't* afraid," he was screaming or dreaming, facing his father's stern eyes. "I *wasn't* afraid," he was saying. When he opened his eyes, a soldier was sitting beside him, quietly chewing a stick of Doublemint gum. ❺

"You sleepin' again?" the soldier whispered.

"No," said Private First Class Paul Berlin. . . .

The soldier grunted, chewing his gum. Then he twisted the cap off his canteen, took a swallow and handed it through the dark.

"Take some," he whispered.

"Thanks."

130 "You're the new guy?"

"Yes." He did not want to admit it, being new to the war.

The soldier grunted and handed him a stick of gum. "Chew it quiet—okay? Don't blow no bubbles or nothing."

"Thanks. I won't." He could not make out the man's face in the shadows.

They sat still and Private First Class Paul Berlin chewed the gum until all the sugars were gone; then the soldier said, "Bad day today, buddy."

Private First Class Paul Berlin nodded wisely, but he did not speak.

"Don't think it's always so bad," the soldier whispered. "I don't wanna scare you. You'll get used to it soon enough. . . . They been fighting wars a long
140 time, and you get used to it."

"Yeah."

"You will."

They were quiet awhile. And the night was quiet, no crickets or birds, and it was hard to imagine it was truly a war. He searched for the soldier's face but could not find it. It did not matter much. Even if he saw the fellow's face, he would not know the name; and even if he knew the name, it would not matter much.

"Haven't got the time?" the soldier whispered.

"No."

"Rats. . . . Don't matter, really. Goes faster if you don't know the time,
150 anyhow."

"Sure."

---

*inertia* (ĭ-nûr′shə) *n.* tendency to continue to do what one has been doing

### ❺ POINT OF VIEW

Identify the point of view from which this story is told. How might your impression of Paul be different if you didn't receive such detailed descriptions of his thoughts and feelings?

---

## *DIFFERENTIATED INSTRUCTION*

**FOR ENGLISH LANGUAGE LEARNERS**

**Vocabulary: Idioms and Sayings** Use New Word Analysis to teach these idioms from the story: *let on* (line 72), "reveal"; *tough as nails* (line 171), "strong, hard, tough"; *scared stiff* (lines 195, 229–230), "deeply afraid." Also point out the slang term *rats* (line 149), meaning "too bad." Encourage students to watch for additional slang expressions.

🧰 **BEST PRACTICES TOOLKIT—Transparency** New Word Analysis p. E8

**FOR ADVANCED LEARNERS/PRE–AP**

**Figurative Language** Have students reread and discuss O'Brien's description of the soldiers walking ahead of him (lines 108–110). Challenge students to imitate the author's style by using figurative language to describe a scene they have witnessed. Have them share their descriptions with the class.

"What's your name, buddy?"

"Paul."

"Nice to meet ya," he said, and in the dark beside the path they shook hands. "Mine's Toby. Everybody calls me Buffalo, though." The soldier's hand was strangely warm and soft. But it was a very big hand. "Sometimes they just call me Buff," he said.

And again they were quiet. They lay in the grass and waited. The moon was very high now and very bright, and they were waiting for cloud cover.

160    The soldier suddenly snorted.

"What is it?"

"Nothin'," he said, but then he snorted again. "A bloody *heart attack!*" the soldier said. "Can't get over it—old Billy Boy croaking from a lousy heart attack. . . . A heart attack—can you believe it?"

The idea of it made Private First Class Paul Berlin smile. He couldn't help it. "Ever hear of such a thing?"

"Not till now," said Private First Class Paul Berlin, still smiling.

"Me neither," said the soldier in the dark.

". . . Dying of a heart attack. Didn't know him, did you."

170    "No."

"Tough as nails."

*Class of '67* (1987), Charlie Shobe. Oil on canvas. © Michael Tropea/National Vietnam Veterans Art Museum.

WHERE HAVE YOU GONE, CHARMING BILLY?    **833**

Use these prompts to help students understand Paul's giggling about Billy Boy's death in lines 174–182:

**Connect** Have you ever giggled nervously in a situation where laughter was inappropriate? Explain. *Answers will vary.*

**Analyze** Why does Paul suddenly start giggling uncontrollably? *Possible answer: It strikes him as absurd that Billy Boy died of a "natural cause" while in the midst of mortal danger. The telegram he imagines seems laughably ironic. Paul is also giggling from nervousness.*

**Synthesize** What can you tell about Paul's own mental state from his sudden fit of giggling? *Possible answer: Paul is deeply shaken by Billy Boy's death and surprised by the intensity of his own fear.*

---

## TEXT ANALYSIS

**COMMON CORE** L 3

### REALISM

*Possible answer: The writer of a government telegram might use the passive voice to emphasize* son *because Billy Boy is more important to the imaginary reader, Billy Boy's father, than what scared him. Also, government officials probably wouldn't want to be specific about the horrors of war in such a telegram by emphasizing exactly what scared Billy Boy.*

Have students work in pairs to rewrite the imaginary telegram using the active voice. When they have finished, ask students how the impact of the telegram is changed by the switch in voice.

---

## READING SKILL

**COMMON CORE** RL 5

### SEQUENCE

*Possible answer: The story's sequential order of events is interrupted with a flashback to the events of the afternoon when Billy Boy stepped on a mine. The word "remembering" is a clue that Paul is going back to the past in his mind.*

---

"Yeah."

"And what happens? A heart attack. Can you imagine it?"

"Yes," said Private First Class Paul Berlin. He wanted to laugh. "I can imagine it." And he imagined it clearly. He giggled—he couldn't help it. He imagined Billy's father opening the telegram: SORRY TO INFORM YOU THAT YOUR SON BILLY BOY WAS YESTERDAY SCARED TO DEATH IN ACTION IN THE REPUBLIC OF VIETNAM, VALIANTLY SUCCUMBING TO[4] A HEART ATTACK SUFFERED WHILE UNDER
180 ENORMOUS STRESS, AND IT IS WITH GREATEST SYMPATHY THAT . . . He giggled again. He rolled onto his belly and pressed his face into his arms. His body was shaking with giggles. **G**

The big soldier hissed at him to shut up, but he could not stop giggling and remembering the hot afternoon, and poor Billy Boy, and how they'd been drinking Coca-Cola from bright-red aluminum cans, and how they'd started on the day's march, and how a little while later poor Billy Boy stepped on the mine, and how it made a tiny little sound—*poof*—and how Billy Boy stood there with his mouth wide-open, looking down at where his foot had been blown off, and how finally Billy Boy sat down very casually, not saying a word,
190 with his foot lying behind him, most of it still in the boot.

He giggled louder—he could not stop. He bit his arm, trying to stifle it, but remembering: "War's over, Billy," the men had said in consolation, but Billy Boy got scared and started crying and said he was about to die. "Nonsense," the medic said, Doc Peret, but Billy Boy kept bawling, tightening up, his face going pale and transparent and his veins popping out. Scared stiff. Even when Doc Peret stuck him with morphine,[5] Billy Boy kept crying. **H**

"Shut up!" the big soldier hissed, but Private First Class Paul Berlin could not stop. Giggling and remembering, he covered his mouth. His eyes stung, remembering how it was when Billy Boy died of fright.
200 "Shut up!"

But he could not stop giggling, the same way Billy Boy could not stop bawling that afternoon.

Afterward Doc Peret had explained: "You see, Billy Boy really died of a heart attack. He was scared he was gonna die—so scared, he had himself a heart attack—and that's what really killed him. I seen it before."

So they wrapped Billy in a plastic poncho, his eyes still wide-open and scared stiff, and they carried him over the meadow to a rice paddy, and then when the Medevac helicopter[6] arrived they carried him through the paddy and put him aboard, and the mortar rounds[7] were falling everywhere, and the
210 helicopter pulled up and Billy Boy came tumbling out, falling slowly and then faster, and the paddy water sprayed up as if Billy Boy had just executed a long

---

4. **valiantly succumbing** (sə-kŭm′ĭng) **to:** bravely dying from.
5. **morphine** (môr′fēn′): a powerful drug used as a painkiller.
6. **Medevac** (mĕd′ĭ-văk′) **helicopter:** a helicopter used for transporting injured people to places where they can receive medical care. "Medevac" is a contraction of "medical evacuation."
7. **mortar rounds:** shells fired from small, portable cannons.

---

### REALISM

The imaginary telegram includes a past-tense verb in the **passive voice,** meaning that the subject *son* receives the action of the verb *was scared.* When a verb is in the **active voice,** the subject performs the action. Although the passive voice should be used sparingly in formal writing, it is realistic here because it emphasizes the person rather than what scared him to death. Why might the writer of a government telegram use the passive voice to emphasize *son?*

### SEQUENCE

Reread lines 183–196. What happens to the story's order of events in these lines? Identify the clues that helped you form your answer.

 **Targeted Passage**

---

## DIFFERENTIATED INSTRUCTION

### FOR STRUGGLING READERS

**Targeted Passage [Lines 183–205]**

This passage explains the mystery of Billy Boy's death.

- How did Billy Boy Watkins lose his foot? (lines 186–189)
- What was his reaction? (line 189)
- Why did the men say, "War's over, Billy"? (line 192)
- What really killed Billy Boy? (lines 203–205)

### Develop Reading Fluency

Remind students that how characters speak is as meaningful as what they say. Model for students an effective way to read a conversation between characters in this story (e.g., lines 124–142 or lines 160–175). You might ask for a volunteer to read the dialogue of one character while you read the other. Then have pairs of students practice reading the dialogue aloud together.

**R RESOURCE MANAGER**—Copy Master Reading Fluency p. 31

and dangerous dive, as if trying to escape Graves Registration, where he would be tagged and sent home under a flag, dead of a heart attack.

"Shut up, . . . !" the soldier hissed, but Paul Berlin could not stop giggling, remembering: scared to death.

220     Later they waded in after him, probing for Billy Boy with their rifle butts, elegantly and delicately probing for Billy Boy in the stinking paddy, singing—some of them—*Where have you gone, Billy Boy, Billy Boy, Oh, where have you gone, charming Billy?* Then they found him. Green and covered with algae, his eyes still wide-open and scared

230     stiff, dead of a heart attack suffered while— **ⓘ**

"Shut up, . . . !" the soldier said loudly, shaking him.

But Private First Class Paul Berlin could not stop. The giggles were caught in his throat, drowning him in his own laughter: scared to death like Billy Boy.

Giggling, lying on his back, he saw the moon move, or the clouds moving across the moon. Wounded in action, dead of fright. A fine war story. He would tell it to his father, how Billy Boy had been scared to death, never letting on . . . He could not stop.

The soldier smothered him. He tried to fight back, but he was weak from the giggles.

240     The moon was under the clouds and the column was moving. The soldier helped him up. "You okay now, buddy?"

"Sure."

"What was so bloody funny?"

"Nothing."

"You can get killed, laughing that way."

"I know. I know that."

"You got to stay calm, buddy." The soldier handed him his rifle. "Half the battle, just staying calm. You'll get better at it," he said. "Come on, now."

He turned away and Private First Class Paul Berlin hurried after him. He

250     was still shivering.

He would do better once he reached the sea, he thought, still smiling a little. A funny war story that he would tell to his father, how Billy Boy Watkins was scared to death. A good joke. But even when he smelled salt and heard the sea, he could not stop being afraid. ✍

*Chopper Lift-Out* (1967), Ken McFadyen. Oil on canvas on hardboard, 30.6 cm × 48.2 cm.
© The Australian War Memorial Collection.

**ⓘ SEQUENCE**
What information has been communicated to the reader in this **flashback?** Explain, citing details from the text.

**COMMON CORE RL 4**
**Language Coach**
**Idioms** An **idiom** is an expression whose meaning differs from the literal meaning of the words, taken together, in the expression. In a war story, a military idiom can be confusing. What does *half the battle* mean literally? What do you think it means in lines 247–248?

**③ Targeted Passage**

## Analyze Visuals

**Activity** Ask students how *Chopper Lift-Out* helps them understand the difficulty of airlifting Billy Boy's body. *Possible answer: The painting depicts the turbulence produced by the moving helicopter. It communicates the rapid and chaotic nature of helicopter landings and take-offs.*

**About the Art** Australian artist Ken McFadyen (1939–1997) was assigned to cover Australia's involvement in the Vietnam War for seven months, starting in mid-August 1967. He was expected to function as a combat soldier, if needed, and had to carry full combat equipment, along with his art materials.

**READING SKILL**                        COMMON CORE
**ⓘ SEQUENCE**                                  RL 5
*Possible answer: The final flashback explains Billy Boy's death and describes its horrendous aftermath. This information further explains Paul's state of mind.*

## SELECTION WRAP–UP

**READ WITH A PURPOSE** Now that students have finished reading the selection, have them describe Paul's fear. Do they think he faced it? Did he overcome it? *Possible answer: Paul's fear is a mixture of many things: fear of death, of war, of disappointing his father and himself. He did not overcome his fear, but he learned to control it.*

★ **CRITIQUE** Have students evaluate O'Brien's description of a soldier's mixed feelings and reactions to fear. Do his descriptions ring true? Why, or why not?

### INDEPENDENT READING

Students who want to read more of Tim O'Brien's stories might enjoy *The Things They Carried*, which describes the physical and emotional burdens carried by U.S. soldiers in Vietnam.

---

### FOR STRUGGLING READERS

**③ Targeted Passage** [Lines 240–254]

This passage concludes the story with a kind of "resolution" of Paul's inner conflict.

• What does Paul hope will happen when he reaches the sea? (line 251)

• How does Paul imagine he will tell his father about the death of Billy Boy? (lines 251–253)

• How does Paul feel when he reaches the sea? Why? (lines 253–254)

• What is O'Brien saying about war? (lines 240–254)

### FOR ENGLISH LANGUAGE LEARNERS

**Language Coach**          COMMON CORE
                                       RL 4
**Idioms** *Possible answer:* Half the battle *literally means "half of a big fight between armed forces." In lines 247–248,* half the battle *is an idiom meaning "an important step toward a goal."* Ask students to identify and look up the meanings of other idioms using a dictionary or a reliable online source. Ask them to report to the class on three idioms they find especially interesting or colorful.

## Interview

After students have read the interview, ask them if they agree with O'Brien's unromantic presentation of war. Give reasons for your answers. *Answers will vary, but students should thoughtfully refer to both the interview and the story to support their answers.*

### TIERED DISCUSSION PROMPTS

Use these prompts to help students connect to O'Brien's attitudes as expressed in this interview:

**Connect** What kinds of memories make you feel nostalgia, or a longing for the past? *Students may mention childhood memories or past triumphs, such as winning a sports event.*

**Analyze** O'Brien notes that some veterans wish he had presented a more nostalgic view of the war. What does he mean? *Possible answer: A more romantic view would have focused on the fellowship among soldiers, fighting for the honor of one's country, and the gallantry of risking one's life. Instead, O'Brien focused on doing what one is forced to do and just surviving.*

---

## Interview

In this revealing interview, Tim O'Brien talks about two kinds of bravery and discusses the courage it took to make one frightening choice.

# Tim O'Brien: **The Naked Soldier**

Douglas Novielli, Christopher Connal, and Jackson Ellis, Verbicide *Magazine*

**Verbicide** Do you think you would have pursued writing if you hadn't gone to Vietnam?

**O'Brien** Probably. It probably would've been something different. If I'd gone to Canada I'd be writing about that. Life provides you plenty of material, with girlfriends or whatever.

**V** Do you think you romanticize Vietnam at all?

**O** No. I think a lot of veterans think I haven't done that enough, but I refuse to do it.

**V** Is there a reason they think it should be romanticized?

**O** Yeah, they look back on it as more heroic, and with nostalgia, and they talk about the fellowship or fraternity among men, and there's some truth to that. But it's an artificial one; it's borne of necessity. Even if you don't like someone, you've got to trust them at night when they're on guard and you're sleeping. And you learn who to trust and who not to trust, and you bond that way. But I never found it very heroic, I just found it stone-man, gotta stay alive stuff. And that's all there was to it.

**V** Are soldiers heroes?

**O** In some ways. It's heroic just not to stop. Physically, there are always alternatives, I mean, just stop walking. What can they do? Court martial you, but they're not gonna kill you. It looks pretty attractive, especially in bad days when guys have been dropping like flies. . . .

You just keep humping. There's a weird heroism in that. Unglamorous kind of valor to just keep going, knowing you might die with every step, and just keep walking.

**V** Is the heroism there in your books to be interpreted if the reader wants it, or is it directly implied?

**O** I remember one part in *The Things They Carried* when I was talking about humping and just taking one step after the next, and at one point I called it a kind of courage, which it is, just to keep your legs moving. I'm kind of explicit about that kind of courage, but there are other kinds of courage just like there are kinds of truth. It took a lot of guts, for example, to go to Canada. Your whole hometown is going to think of you as a sissy or a coward, even though it's totally conscientious. So I admire the heroism and courage it took. I didn't have the guts to do it, to cross over the border.

**V** Do you still regret that?

**O** Yeah, you can't live your life over, but it would have been the right thing to do. I mean, think how hard it would be, even now it would be hard and I'm grown up. It was the thing that was worse than anything about the war, just going to it. Once you're in the war, it's pretty much what you'd expect. But, boy, making that decision, because you're in control of things. You can go in the army, or you can go to Canada. I never actually made that drive and went to the Rainy River.[1] That's invented. But it did happen in my head all summer long. I thought about driving to Canada.

---

1. **Rainy River:** a river on the U.S.–Canadian border. In O'Brien's short story "On the Rainy River," the main character drives to the river and considers whether he should cross the border into Canada and dodge the draft.

## Comprehension

1. **Recall** According to Doc Peret, what causes the death of Billy Boy Watkins?

2. **Clarify** Why does Toby want to keep Paul quiet?

3. **Summarize** How does the story end?

## Text Analysis

4. **Draw Conclusions** Describe how Paul Berlin tries to combat his fear in this story. How successful is he? Cite evidence to support your conclusion.

5. **Identify Conflict** Is the main conflict in this story **internal** or **external?** Explain, citing details from the text to support your answer.

● 6. **Analyze Sequence** Review the chart you made as you read, and think about the **flashback** in lines 183–196, in which Paul recalls the death of Billy Boy Watkins in vivid detail. Why might O'Brien have used the flashback at this point in the story? What did it help you, the reader, understand?

● 7. **Analyze Realism** Find examples in the text that illustrate each element of **style** shown on the chart. Use your completed chart to explain how O'Brien's use of realism contributes to the reader's perceptions of Paul and his situation.

| Element of Style | Examples from Text |
|---|---|
| Realistic dialogue | |
| Description featuring sensory details | |
| Passages made up of both long and short sentences | |
| Use of flashback | |

8. **Synthesize** In "The Naked Soldier" on page 836, O'Brien talks about two different kinds of courage—the courage it took to serve in Vietnam and the courage it took to defy the draft and flee to Canada. In your opinion, which act was more courageous? Use evidence from both the story and the interview to support your opinion.

## Text Criticism

9. **Author's Style** In describing what he strives for when creating stories, O'Brien states, "You aim for tension and suspense, a sense of drama, displaying in concrete terms the actions and reactions of human beings contesting problems of the heart." How successfully does O'Brien fulfill the above criteria in this story? Cite evidence from the story to support your opinion.

### Is FEAR our worst enemy?

How are some reactions to fear negative? How are some positive?

**COMMON CORE**

**RL 4** Determine the figurative meaning of words and phrases and analyze the impact of specific word choices on meaning and tone. **RL 5** Analyze how an author's choices concerning how to order events and manipulate time create mystery, tension, or surprise. **L 3** Apply knowledge of language to understand how language functions in different contexts and to comprehend more fully.

# Practice and Apply

For preliminary support of post-reading questions, use these copy masters:

**R RESOURCE MANAGER—Copy Masters**
Reading Check p. 28
Realism p. 21
Question Support p. 29

Additional selection questions are provided for teachers on page 15.

## ANSWERS

## Comprehension

1. *According to Doc Peret, Billy Boy died of a heart attack brought on by fear.*

2. *Paul's laughter might give away their position to the enemy.*

3. *Paul recovers from his hysterical laughing fit. Paul thinks his fear will lessen when they reach the sea, but it does not.*

## Text Analysis

COMMON CORE **RL 4, RL 5, L 3**

*Possible answers:*

4. *Paul pretends he is not at war (lines 12–13), fantasizes about what will happen when it is over, and imagines it will be better when he reaches the sea (lines 45–47, 85–88). He is not successful; the last line reveals that Paul "could not stop being afraid."*

5. *The main conflict is internal, between Paul and his fear. Students should cite a few passages that deal with Paul's terror.*

6. ■ COMMON CORE FOCUS *Analyze Sequence He uses the flashback toward the end to help the reader understand Paul's strange reaction—a fit of uncontrollable giggles—to Billy Boy's death. Paul's giggling helps him deal with that horrifying death and his own terror of dying.*

7. ● COMMON CORE FOCUS *Analyze Realism Realistic dialogue: Students could cite any of Paul and Toby's conversations. Sensory details: "He would tell his mother how it smelled . . . (lines 41–44). Long and short sentences: "In the afternoon . . . not to think" (lines 58–64). Flashback: Students should cite Paul's flashback to Billy's death. All of these techniques make Paul seem like a real person and lend a sense of immediacy to his terrifying situation.*

8. *Answers will vary. Students should support their answers with references to the story and the interview.*

## Text Criticism

9. *Responses will vary. If students say that O'Brien accomplished this goal, they may cite tense, suspenseful scenes like the one in which Toby tries to make Paul stop giggling. They might discuss Paul's "problem of the heart," his terrible fear, and argue that O'Brien did a good job of depicting Paul's emotional response to that fear.*

### Is FEAR our worst enemy?
*Possible answer: Fear can paralyze our ability to act and think, but it can also sharpen our reactions and speed up our responses.*

## ANSWERS

# Vocabulary in Context

▲ VOCABULARY PRACTICE

1. *stealth*

2. *fecund*

3. *diffuse*

4. *inertia*

 **RESOURCE MANAGER—Copy Master**
Vocabulary Practice p. 26

### ACADEMIC VOCABULARY IN SPEAKING

**Possible answer:** *One attribute of a hero is taking care of other people when they need help. A hero risks his or her life for the sake of others. However, a hero doesn't have to be a hero in everything he or she does.*

### VOCABULARY STRATEGY: WORDS THAT START WITH *in-*

**COMMON CORE L 4c**

For each item, have students look up in an unabridged dictionary the root word without the prefix. Some of these "roots" do not exist. In those cases, students should list the *in-* word in the first column.

**Possible answers:**

*(words marked with asterisks have no positive form)*

1. incorrigible: *not correctable*

2. inclement: *harsh*

3. insomnia*: *prolonged inability to sleep*

4. indolent*: *lazy*

5. insuperable: *unable to be overcome*

6. insipid*: *dull*

7. incognito*: *with one's true identity disguised*

8. incongruous: *seemingly unreasonable or unsuitable*

 **RESOURCE MANAGER—Copy Master**
Vocabulary Strategy p. 27

**Interactive Vocabulary** **THINK central**

Keywords direct students to a **WordSharp** tutorial on **thinkcentral.com** or to other types of vocabulary practice and review.

# Vocabulary in Context

▲ **VOCABULARY PRACTICE**

Write the word from the Word List that best completes each sentence.

1. The soldiers moved with _____ across the countryside so that they would not be spotted by the enemy.

2. In spite of all the bombing it had suffered, the land they traveled through was still _____.

3. In their nervousness, it was hard to bring their _____ thoughts back into clear focus.

4. They relied on _____ and force of habit to keep them on the path.

**WORD LIST**
diffuse
fecund
inertia
stealth

### ACADEMIC VOCABULARY IN SPEAKING

• appreciate • attribute • indicate • unique • vary

What are the **attributes** of a hero? Prepare a brief instructional presentation in which you **indicate** what makes someone a hero and describe what tasks a regular person can accomplish to become an "everyday hero" (for example, helping to solve problems in the community). Be sure to solicit questions from your audience and provide thoughtful answers, and use at least one Academic Vocabulary word in your presentation.

### VOCABULARY STRATEGY: WORDS THAT START WITH *in-*

The forms of certain words beginning with *in-* can sometimes cause confusion. When you see a word like *inertia*, for example, in which *in-* means "unable to" or "not," you might make the assumption that you can remove the prefix to form a word with an opposite, "positive" meaning. However, there is no such English word as *ertia*. To avoid writing incorrect antonyms for words with *in-*, you can look up the word's definition and etymology, or origin, in a dictionary and also check whether the word exists without the prefix.

**PRACTICE** Create a two-column chart with these headings: "No Positive Form" and "Positive Form Not Often Used." Use a dictionary to place each word in the correct column. Then write a brief definition of each word.

1. incorrigible
2. inclement
3. insomnia
4. indolent

5. insuperable
6. insipid
7. incognito
8. incongruous

**COMMON CORE**

**L 4c** Consult reference materials to determine a word's meaning or etymology.

Interactive Vocabulary **THINK central**

Go to **thinkcentral.com**.
KEYWORD: HML9-838

---

## DIFFERENTIATED INSTRUCTION

### FOR ENGLISH LANGUAGE LEARNERS

**Vocabulary: Home Language Equivalents for Word with *in-*** Have students write home-language equivalents of the words in the two columns. Encourage them to write down additional words beginning with *in-*. Ask whether these words have English equivalents. If necessary, have them check them in a bilingual dictionary and report the results. List all the English words beginning with *in-* that the students generate.

### FOR ADVANCED LEARNERS/PRE–AP

**Vocabulary in Writing** Ask students to use at least four of the *in-* words in a paragraph describing another soldier's experience in Paul Berlin's platoon.

# Language

◆ **GRAMMAR AND STYLE: Add Supporting Details**

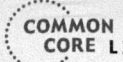
**COMMON CORE**

**L 3** Apply knowledge of language to make effective choices for meaning or style.

Review the **Grammar and Style** note on page 831. O'Brien depicts Paul as a frightened and inexperienced soldier by using details to provide a window into Paul's mental state. The **repetition** that marks Paul's thoughts reflects his continuing fear, anxiety, and denial. Here is an example from the story. Note that O'Brien repeats the verb *pretending*:

> *He was pretending he was not in the war, pretending he had not watched Billy Boy Watkins die of a heart attack that afternoon. He was pretending he was a boy again, camping with his father in the midnight summer along the Des Moines River.* (lines 12–16)

Study the student model. Notice how the revisions in blue use repetition to reflect Paul's feelings of denial and anxiety. Revise your response to the prompt below by using similar techniques.

> **STUDENT MODEL**
>
> I'm exhausted and hungry, but I'm not afraid. Don't worry about me,
> —*I don't worry about me*
> Dad, I know I'll be home soon. *I'll be home sooner than you think*

## READING-WRITING CONNECTION

**YOUR TURN**

Demonstrate your knowledge of "Where Have You Gone, Charming Billy?" by responding to this prompt. Then use the **revising tip** to improve your writing.

| WRITING PROMPT | REVISING TIP |
|---|---|
| **Short Constructed Response: Letter** Think about Paul Berlin's deep desire to please his father and the fear he grapples with in this story. Using details from the text, pretend you are Paul and handwrite a **one- or two-paragraph letter** home. Describe your experiences as a soldier, and be sure to write the letter legibly so that it can be easily read and understood. | Review your letter. Does it sound realistic? It should seem as if it were written by Paul, on the basis of the traits he exhibits in the story. Add some instances of repetition to emphasize Paul's feelings of anxiety—and his desire to hide them. Handwrite the letter again to include your revisions. |

**Interactive Revision**
**THINK**central
Go to **thinkcentral.com**.
KEYWORD: HML9-839

---

## FOR STRUGGLING WRITERS

- Direct students to list three events Paul might describe to his father.
- Suggest that students describe these events in chronological order in the letter.
- Remind students that Paul does not want to reveal his fear to his father.

---

# Language

**COMMON CORE L 3**

◆ **GRAMMAR AND STYLE**

After students examine the lines from the story and the student model, write these lines on the board. Have students add repetition to accentuate feelings.

*We walked for miles and miles—so many miles my soles wore thin. We passed through a rice paddy that smelled like mud and clay. I was looking forward to getting to the sea, really looking forward to it. Later we went through a village and then through another paddy. I was a little tired—to be honest, more than a little tired.*

**R** **RESOURCE MANAGER—Copy Master**
Add Supporting Details p. 30

**READING-WRITING CONNECTION**

Suggest students reread some of Paul's thoughts involving his father (lines 14–21, 56–58, 69–73, 120–122, 235–237, 252–253). Encourage students to recreate Paul's ambivalence toward his fear and toward war.

> **Writing Online**
> **THINK**central
>
> The following tools are available online at **thinkcentral.com** and on **Write*Smart* CD-ROM:**
> - **Interactive Graphic Organizers**
> - **Interactive Student Models**
> - **Interactive Revision Lessons**
> For additional grammar instruction, see **GrammarNotes** on **thinkcentral.com**.

# Assess and Reteach

## Assess

**DIAGNOSTIC AND SELECTION TESTS**
Selection Test A pp. 219–220
Selection Test B/C pp. 221–222

**Interactive Selection Test** on **thinkcentral.com**

## Reteach

**Level Up Online Tutorials** on **thinkcentral.com**

**Reteaching Worksheets** on **thinkcentral.com**
Literature Lesson 46, Reading Lesson 6, Vocabulary Lesson 1

# Practice and Apply

........ COMMON CORE FOCUS

**RL 7** Analyze the representation of a subject in two different artistic mediums.

## Recruitment Poster

Have students think about "Where Have You Gone, Charming Billy?" and the interview with Tim O'Brien. Ask them to look at this poster and discuss its tone and look. Does the recruiting poster send a different message from, or contradict, the short story and interview? If so, in what ways? **Possible answer:** *Yes; the poster sends a romanticized message about what it means to be a soldier in a war, while the story and interview are very realistic.*

---

**ANALYZE VISUALS** — COMMON CORE — RL 7

### 1. DRAW CONCLUSIONS

**Possible answer:** *The poster is trying to recruit women to join the Marines in non-combat roles. A new female recruit— during a time when the U.S. military was all male—could "be a Marine" by performing non-combat duties, which would otherwise be performed by men. Performing these duties would thus "free a Marine to fight."*

---

**ANALYZE VISUALS** — COMMON CORE — RL 7

### 2. ANALYZE DETAILS

**Possible answer:** *The Marine's expression is serious and focused. She is standing up very straight, and her uniform, hair, and makeup are neat and tidy. She looks competent, professional, and honorable—desired traits for a Marine of either gender.*

---

**ANALYZE VISUALS** — COMMON CORE — RL 7

### 3. INFER

**Possible answer:** *I think they were somewhat effective, based on the fact that support for the war effort was strong, but they probably played a much smaller role than other factors. People probably supported U.S. involvement in the war because they viewed it as necessary.*

---

## Recruitment Poster

The short story and the interview you just read both deal with the Vietnam War—a long and bloody conflict that divided the American people. While some Americans thought the United States should participate in the war, others opposed U.S. involvement and protested for peace. The poster below was designed to recruit new Marines during World War II. Even though far more Americans lost their lives in World War II than in Vietnam, the war effort was widely supported on the home front.

COMMON CORE

**RL 7** Analyze the representation of a subject in two different artistic mediums.

### Recruitment Poster

1. **DRAW CONCLUSIONS**
   Consider the image of the Marine on the poster. Whom is this poster intended to recruit? How could a new recruit both "be a Marine" and "free a Marine to fight"?

2. **ANALYZE DETAILS**
   Study the Marine's facial expression, posture, and overall appearance. How would you describe her?

3. **INFER**
   During World War II, posters like this one urged Americans to support the war in various ways. How effective do you think the posters were? What else might have accounted for public support for the war? Explain your thoughts.

## Assessment Practice: Short Constructed Response

### LITERARY TEXT: "WHERE HAVE YOU GONE, CHARMING BILLY?"

Analyzing characters by making comparisons can help you better understand a literary text. Practice this skill by answering the **short constructed response** question below.

> How are the characters Paul Berlin and Billy Boy Watkins in "Where Have You Gone, Charming Billy?" similar? Support your answer with evidence from the story.

◀ **STRATEGIES IN ACTION**

1. Reread the text, looking closely at the descriptions of Paul Berlin and Billy Boy Watkins.
2. Note how the characters are similar in appearance, personality, or actions.
3. In your answer, share the specific **evidence** you find.

### NONFICTION TEXT: "TIM O'BRIEN: THE NAKED SOLDIER"

To demonstrate your understanding of a nonfiction text, you may need to move beyond the text itself and make judgments about how it relates to something else. Practice this skill by answering the **short constructed response** question below.

> What insight into O'Brien's fictional works might a reader gain from "Tim O'Brien: The Naked Soldier"? Support your answer with evidence from the interview.

◀ **STRATEGIES IN ACTION**

1. Reread the interview, paying attention to what O'Brien says about both his life and his writing.
2. Your response to this prompt should be based on the information in the interview, not necessarily the short story. Include a **direct quotation, paraphrase,** or **specific synopsis** from the interview as evidence.

### COMPARING LITERARY AND NONFICTION TEXTS

Practice making connections between literary and nonfiction texts by applying the following **short constructed response** question to "Where Have You Gone, Charming Billy?" and "Tim O'Brien: The Naked Soldier."

> How does Tim O'Brien define heroism in the interview? How is this definition evident in his short story "Where Have You Gone, Charming Billy?" Support your answer with evidence from both texts.

◀ **STRATEGIES IN ACTION**

1. Note that this question has **two parts.** For the first part, skim the interview to find O'Brien's definition of heroism. State this definition in your answer.
2. For the second part, scan the short story to find a specific example of heroism. Use the example as evidence to support the definition.

WHERE HAVE YOU GONE, . . . / TIM O'BRIEN: THE NAKED SOLDIER / BE A MARINE **841**

---

## Assessment Practice: Short Constructed Response

*LITERARY TEXT: "WHERE HAVE YOU GONE, CHARMING BILLY?"* **Possible answer:** Students may say both Paul Berlin and Billy Boy Watkins are afraid of dying and show their fear in peculiar ways. For example, after stepping on a mine and losing his foot, Billy Boy Watkins thought he was going to die. In fact, he was so afraid of dying that he couldn't stop crying and literally scared himself to death by having a heart attack. Paul Berlin is also scared of dying, but he shows his fear by laughing uncontrollably at Billy Boy Watkins's death.

*NONFICTION TEXT: "TIM O'BRIEN: THE NAKED SOLDIER"* **Possible answer:** Students may respond that O'Brien's writing style is realistic. For example, when asked if he romanticizes the Vietnam War in his works, he responds that he does not and won't do it. For him, the relationships between soldiers were less about being heroic and more about staying alive.

*COMPARING LITERARY AND NONFICTION TEXTS* **Possible answer:** Students may say that one way O'Brien defines heroism is as an "Unglamorous kind of valor to just keep going, knowing you might die with every step." His definition of heroism is evident in the short story through the character of Paul Berlin. Berlin is extremely frightened on his first day as a soldier, but he keeps moving, following the other soldiers as they march to the sea.

---

## DIFFERENTIATED INSTRUCTION

### FOR STRUGGLING WRITERS

**Support Answers with Text Evidence** Point out that all three sample questions on this page ask writers to support their answers with evidence from the text. To model this skill, tell students that in order to state in their answer that both soldiers were fearful, they will need to find statements in the story that prove this idea. Have them scan lines 36–47 to find evidence that Paul Berlin was afraid. *(Line 38 says he was afraid.)* Then, have them scan lines 191–196 to find evidence that Billy Watkins was also afraid. *(Line 193 says that Billy was scared because he thought he was going to die.)*

## The Princess and the Tin Box
Fable by James Thurber

## COMMON CORE FOCUS

**RL 4** Analyze the impact of specific word choices on meaning. **RL 5** Analyze how an author's choices concerning how to structure a text create surprise. **L 5a** Interpret figures of speech and analyze their role in the text.

### SUMMARY

"Once upon a time," Thurber begins, a king had a beautiful daughter whom he spoiled with costly possessions. He offered her in marriage to the prince whose gift she liked best. Four rich princes bestowed lavish gifts, including a platinum jewel box. A fifth, handsome but poor, gave her a tin box. The princess chose the jewel box, since it was expensive and would hold many jewels.

## Are **DIAMONDS**
### really a girl's best friend?

Ask the question, and explain to students that "Diamonds Are a Girl's Best Friend" is the title of a song from the movie *Gentlemen Prefer Blondes*, starring Marilyn Monroe. Then ask students if they agree that people who care about things like diamonds and clothes are superficial. Extend the discussion by having students complete the *PRESENT* activity.

# Are **DIAMONDS**
## really a girl's best friend?

## COMMON CORE

**RL 4** Analyze the impact of specific word choices on meaning. **RL 5** Analyze how an author's choices concerning how to structure a text create surprise. **L 5a** Interpret figures of speech and analyze their role in the text.

For that matter, do clothes really make the man? We all know people who are superficial or shallow, concerned only with appearance rather than substance. In this takeoff on a fairy tale, James Thurber presents just such a person: a rich, spoiled princess.

*PRESENT* With a partner, create a "portrait" of a superficial person, using both words and images. Make your portrait as serious or as comically exaggerated as you like, but be sure to communicate how your subject thinks and acts. You can even outfit him or her in whatever clothes and accessories you think appropriate. After you've finished, pair up with another group and take turns presenting your portraits.

842

See resources on the **Teacher One Stop DVD-ROM** and on **thinkcentral.com**.

**R RESOURCE MANAGER UNIT 8**
Plan and Teach, pp. 35–42
Summary pp. 43–44†‡*
Text Analysis and Reading
    Skill, pp. 45–48†*

**DIAGNOSTIC AND SELECTION TESTS**
Selection Tests, pp. 223–226

**TECHNOLOGY**
- Teacher One Stop DVD-ROM
- Student One Stop DVD-ROM
- Audio Anthology CD
- GrammarNotes DVD-ROM
- ExamView Test Generator on the **Teacher One Stop**

\* Resources for Differentiation          † Also in Spanish          ‡ In Haitian Creole and Vietnamese

## TEXT ANALYSIS: PARODY

Humorist James Thurber is known for his sly, skillful way of making fun of society. "The Princess and the Tin Box" begins in a very familiar way:

*Once upon a time, in a far country, there lived a king whose daughter was the prettiest princess in the world.*

With that opening sentence, readers immediately recognize that they have been whisked into a fairy tale. This particular tale, however, is a **parody**—a literary work that imitates another piece of literature in order to poke fun at it. To analyze this imitation fairy tale, be on the lookout for the following stylistic techniques:

- **Word Choice:** Notice how Thurber imitates the language used in fairy tales, as in the opening lines above.
- **Exaggeration:** Look for characters or situations exaggerated by the author for comic effect.
- **Irony:** Identify ironic plot twists, or moments when Thurber structures events in a surprising way, allowing them to unfold very differently from the way you would expect.

As you read, look for evidence of these techniques. Think about the ways in which this parody resembles a traditional fairy tale and the ways in which it does not.

## READING STRATEGY: PREDICT

Fairy tales are usually pretty predictable. As you read this selection, jot down your impressions of the princess. Use these notes about the princess's character to make **predictions** about what will happen next in the story. After the last events have unfolded, ask yourself whether this is the "happily ever after" you anticipated.

 Complete the activities in your **Reader/Writer Notebook**.

## James Thurber
### 1894–1961

**Early Years**
One of the great humorists of American literature, James Thurber made a career out of poking fun at society. Despite a childhood eye injury that left him with lifelong vision problems, Thurber attended college and got early jobs as a clerk and then as a journalist. In 1927, the *New Yorker*, a literary magazine, published one of his stories. He would write for the magazine for the rest of his life.

**The *New Yorker* Years**
The *New Yorker* gave Thurber his fame, and he gave the magazine much of the sophisticated style it has today. Thurber often provided his own illustrations to accompany his writing. Although he did not consider himself an artist, his cartoons had a distinctive style and became as popular as his stories. Readers loved him for being so funny, but Thurber took humor seriously. "I write humor the way a surgeon operates," he said, "because it is a livelihood, because I have a great urge to do it, because many interesting challenges are set up, and because I have the hope it may do some good."

**Last Years**
By the age of 57, Thurber's childhood eye injury had degenerated to almost total blindness. When his vision began to fail completely, Thurber started dictating stories to his secretary. His memory was so sharp that he could easily compose a 2,000-word story in his mind, remember it overnight, and dictate it to his secretary the next day. His friend and fellow-writer E. B. White described him this way: "During his happiest years, Thurber did not write the way a surgeon operates, he wrote the way a child skips rope, the way a mouse waltzes."

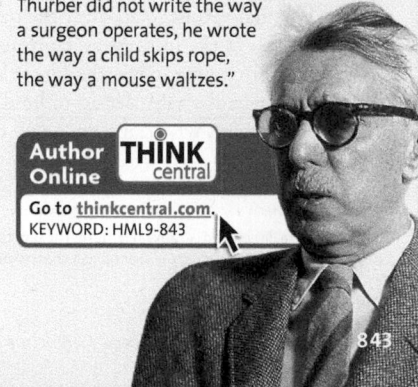

**Author Online**
THINK central
Go to thinkcentral.com.
KEYWORD: HML9-843

843

## DIFFERENTIATED INSTRUCTION

### FOR STRUGGLING READERS

**Concept Support** Initiate a discussion of parody by having students cite fairy tales or folktales they know. Then, explain that parodies combine language and ideas from the original work with exaggeration. Use this example:

Small Bunyan and his blue mouse, Blip, cleared the mighty weeds on the anthill.

Challenge students to parody a few lines from a familiar fairy tale or folktale.

### FOR ENGLISH LANGUAGE LEARNERS

**Language: Skill Words** Give these examples of exaggeration and irony:

- Her eyes got as big as dinner plates.
- After complaining about his meal, Julio cleaned his plate.

Discuss the effect of each, pointing out that eyes never get as big as plates, and after complaining about the meal, Julio's action is unexpected. Help students arrive at definitions of *exaggeration* and *irony*.

TEXT ANALYSIS                    COMMON CORE
RL 4, RL 5

### Model the Skill: PARODY

For instructional support, read aloud this example:

"Then I'll huff and I'll puff and I'll . . . you know," said the wheezing wolf. But the pig, whose house was built of reinforced concrete, merely yawned.

Tell students that the subject of the parody is "The Three Little Pigs" and explain that one indicator of this is the phrase "I'll huff and I'll puff and I'll." Then have them identify other words that echo the story. **Possible answer:** "wolf," "pig," "house"

**GUIDED PRACTICE** Ask students to explain how exaggeration and irony contribute to the parody in the example.

READING STRATEGY                 COMMON CORE
RL 5

### Model the Skill: PREDICT

To support instruction, read aloud this example:

In a story, a man in a dark hat and coat hides in an alley as an unsuspecting man walks up the sidewalk toward him.

Tell students that you can predict that the man in the dark hat may jump out and rob the second man. The reason is that readers expect someone hiding in an alley, dressed in dark clothes, to be planning something sinister.

**GUIDED PRACTICE** Elicit that predicting combines prior knowledge with text clues.

**R** **RESOURCE MANAGER—Copy Master** Predict p. 47 (for student use while reading the selection)

THE PRINCESS AND THE TIN BOX **843**

# THE *Princess* AND THE *Tin Box*

## JAMES THURBER

**Analyze Visuals ▶**

Thurber often sketched childlike line drawings like this one to accompany his stories. What basic ideas about love or courtship does he present in this sketch?

Once upon a time, in a far country, there lived a king whose daughter was the prettiest princess in the world. Her eyes were like the cornflower, her hair was sweeter than the hyacinth, and her throat made the swan look dusty.

From the time she was a year old, the princess had been showered with presents. Her nursery looked like Cartier's window.[1] Her toys were all made of gold or platinum or diamonds or emeralds. She was not permitted to have wooden blocks or china dolls or rubber dogs or linen books, because such materials were considered cheap for the daughter of a king.

When she was seven, she was allowed to attend the wedding of her brother
10 and throw real pearls at the bride instead of rice. Only the nightingale, with his lyre of gold, was permitted to sing for the princess. The common blackbird, with his boxwood flute,[2] was kept out of the palace grounds. She walked in silver-and-samite slippers to a sapphire-and-topaz bathroom and slept in an ivory bed inlaid with rubies. **A**

On the day the princess was eighteen, the king sent a royal ambassador to the courts of five neighboring kingdoms to announce that he would give his daughter's hand in marriage to the prince who brought her the gift she liked the most.

The first prince to arrive at the palace rode a swift white stallion and laid
20 at the feet of the princess an enormous apple made of solid gold which he had taken from a dragon who had guarded it for a thousand years. It was placed on a long ebony table set up to hold the gifts of the princess's suitors. The second prince, who came on a gray charger,[3] brought her a nightingale made

**A** **PARODY**
Reread lines 1–14 and identify at least two examples of **exaggeration**. What is the effect of this stylistic technique? Explain your answer.

**① Targeted Passage**

---

1. **Cartier's** (kär-tyāz′) **window:** the show window of a well-known jewelry store.

2. **lyre** (līr) **of gold . . . boxwood flute:** The nightingale's voice is likened to a golden harp; the blackbird's voice is likened to a cheap wooden flute.

3. **charger:** warhorse.

---

## DIFFERENTIATED INSTRUCTION

**FOR ENGLISH LANGUAGE LEARNERS**

**Reading: Background** Ask students if they have read other stories about princes and princesses. Ask what type of person always marries the princess in these stories.

**Options for Reading** Have students read the tale aloud, taking turns with a partner.

**FOR STRUGGLING READERS**

In combination with the *Audio Anthology CD,* use one or more Targeted Passages (pp. 844, 846) to ensure that students focus on key events, concepts, and skills. Targeted Passages are also good for English learners.

## BACKGROUND

**Fables and Fairy Tales** "The Princess and the Tin Box" combines elements of fairy tales and fables. Fairy tales are a type of folktale—a traditional story that has been passed down from generation to generation by word of mouth. Fairy tales feature magical events and mainly one-dimensional human characters who are usually all good or all bad. While fables are also a type of folktale and also feature one-dimensional characters, these characters are usually animals rather than humans. A fable also offers a moral, or lesson about life, such as "It is dangerous to gossip" or "It is important to plan for the future."

## REVISIT THE BIG QUESTION

### Are **DIAMONDS**
### really a girl's best friend?

**Discuss** Has the princess been raised to be superficial? Explain your answer, giving evidence from the story. *Possible answer: Yes; the princess has been raised to be superficial. She has been taught to prize wealth and appearances. Less exceptional things, such as the common blackbird (lines 11–12), are kept from her.*

## Analyze Visuals

*Possible answer: Thurber offers a stock image of romance and courtship: the prince kneels at the princess's feet, offering her a gift and his love. The viewer gets the feeling that Thurber is making fun of these romantic conventions.*

**About the Art** James Thurber's childlike style cloaks a talent for conveying much information in a simple sketch. Robert Morsberger, Thurber's biographer, believes Thurber's illustrations for his fables represent the peak of his talent.

**①** **Targeted Passage** [Lines 15–22]

This passage introduces the plot and further characterizes the king and the princess.

- What action does the king take that sets the plot in motion? (lines 15–18)
- What does the king's plan reveal about him and the princess? (lines 15–22)
- Based on the action of the first prince, what do you predict will happen next? (lines 19–22)

**FOR ADVANCED LEARNERS/PRE–AP**

Provide these independent projects to extend the lesson:

- Adapt the story for a dramatic reading.
- Create a comic strip based on the story.
- Create a computer animation sequence for the story.

For further details on these projects, see

**R** RESOURCE MANAGER
Ideas for Extension pp. 40–41

**B PARODY**

*Possible answers:* **Plot:** *a marriage contest for the hand of the princess; the princes arrive on horseback, bearing gifts.* **Setting:** *"Once upon a time, in a far country (line 1).* **Characters:** *The poor prince is "the strongest and handsomest" (line 30).*

READING STRATEGY

**C** *Model the Skill:* **PREDICT**

Explain that good readers check their predictions as they read. Suggest that students use a Two-Column Chart to keep track of their predictions and what happens.

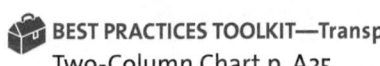 BEST PRACTICES TOOLKIT—Transparency Two-Column Chart p. A25

*Possible answer: Students may predict that, as in a typical fairy tale, virtue will win out and the princess will choose the poor but handsome prince.*

TEXT ANALYSIS

**D PARODY**

*Possible answer: The princess could not change her nature; she was vain and superficial and to expect her to be something else is naive.*

Have students list the sarcasm that is used in the moral to make Thurber's point. Write these examples on the board.

**SELECTION WRAP–UP**

**READ WITH A PURPOSE** Now that students have finished reading the selection, have them discuss the message the tale communicates about human nature. *Possible answer: People don't change; it's romantic, sentimental ,and naive to expect people to do the right thing if it's not who they really are.*

★ **CRITIQUE** Ask students whether they find Thurber's moral satisfying, even if they do not find it morally uplifting. Why or why not?

---

of a thousand diamonds, and it was placed beside the golden apple. The third prince, riding on a black horse, carried a great jewel box made of platinum and sapphires, and it was placed next to the diamond nightingale. The fourth prince, astride a fiery yellow horse, gave the princess a gigantic heart made of rubies and pierced by an emerald arrow. It was placed next to the platinum-and-sapphire jewel box.

30　　Now the fifth prince was the strongest and handsomest of all the five suitors, but he was the son of a poor king whose realm had been overrun by mice and locusts and wizards and mining engineers so that there was nothing much of value left in it. He came plodding up to the palace of the princess on a plow horse and he brought her a small tin box filled with mica and feldspar and hornblende[4] which he had picked up on the way. **B**

The other princes roared with disdainful laughter when they saw the tawdry[5] gift the fifth prince had brought to the princess. But she examined it with great interest and squealed with delight, for all her life she had been glutted with precious stones and priceless metals, but she had never seen tin
40　before or mica or feldspar or hornblende. The tin box was placed next to the ruby heart pierced with an emerald arrow. **C**

"Now," the king said to his daughter, "you must select the gift you like best and marry the prince that brought it."

The princess smiled and walked up to the table and picked up the present she liked the most. It was the platinum-and-sapphire jewel box, the gift of the third prince.

"The way I figure it," she said, "is this. It is a very large and expensive box, and when I am married, I will meet many admirers who will give me precious gems with which to fill it to the top. Therefore, it is the most valuable of all the
50　gifts my suitors have brought me and I like it the best."

The princess married the third prince that very day in the midst of great merriment and high revelry.[6] More than a hundred thousand pearls were thrown at her and she loved it.

*Moral: All those who thought the princess was going to select the tin box filled with worthless stones instead of one of the other gifts will kindly stay after class and write one hundred times on the blackboard "I would rather have a hunk of aluminum silicate[7] than a diamond necklace."*  **D**

 **B PARODY**
Think about the typical plot, setting, and characters of a fairy tale. Find three places where Thurber mimics these conventions in this story.

**C PREDICT**
Consider your impression of the princess and her reactions to her suitors' gifts. Do you think she will choose to marry the poor but handsome prince or one of the rich, snobby ones? Give reasons for your prediction.

**❷ Targeted Passage**

 **D PARODY**
**Sarcasm** is a kind of particularly cutting verbal irony that, though sometimes humorous, can be used to insult or chastise. In this moral, Thurber playfully chastises readers who foresaw a different ending, but he does so to make a point. What point about human nature does the moral suggest? Explain.

---

4. **mica** (mī′kə) **and feldspar and hornblende** (hôrn′blĕnd′): three common minerals.
5. **tawdry** (tô′drē): flashy but cheap.
6. **revelry** (rĕv′əl-rē): noisy celebrating.
7. **aluminum silicate** (sĭl′ĭ-kāt′): a basically worthless chemical compound; refers to the mica, feldspar, and hornblende in the prince's box.

---

## DIFFERENTIATED INSTRUCTION

**FOR STRUGGLING READERS**

**❷ Targeted Passage [Lines 42–58]**

This passage concludes the story with a twist that pokes fun at fables—and romantics.

• What does the king's statement (lines 42–43) lead you to expect will happen?

• How does the princess explain her choice (lines 47–50)? Is it a romantic choice? Why or why not?

• What punishment does the moral dole out for those who predicted the tin box? (lines 54–58)

**Develop Reading Fluency**

Model for readers how to express emotion when reading dialogue by reading aloud the narration and dialogue in lines 42–50. Try to communicate the affection in the king's voice and the calculatedness in the princess's. Then have pairs of students practice reading the dialogue, each taking a role.

## Comprehension

1. **Recall** What does the king do on his daughter's 18th birthday?

2. **Paraphrase** Restate the moral of the story in your own words.

## Text Analysis

3. **Interpret Irony** Reread lines 54–58. How does the end of this story play against the reader's normal expectations of a fairy tale? Explain how the ending is ironic, citing evidence from the text.

4. **Analyze Parody** In a chart like the one shown, record examples of the **stylistic techniques** Thurber uses to parody a fairy tale. Use your completed chart to explain what human trait or quality Thurber is poking fun at in this story.

| Stylistic Technique | Examples from the Text |
|---|---|
| Imitation of standard fairy tale language | |
| Exaggeration | |
| Irony | |

5. **Evaluate Predictions** How accurately did you predict what would happen at the end of the story? Explain whether or not you think Thurber intended to take his readers by surprise, and why.

6. **Make Judgments** A **parody** is an imitation of a writer's style, a type of literature, or a specific work, and is usually designed to make fun of something. In your opinion, is humor an effective tool for social criticism? Can making a joke or commenting on something in a comic way ever help bring about change? Explain your answer.

### READING-WRITING CONNECTION

| WRITING PROMPT | REVISING TIP |
|---|---|
| **Short Constructed Response: New Ending** What would have happened if the princess had made a different choice? How else could this story have ended? In **one or two paragraphs,** imagine an alternate ending to the story and create a new moral to go with it. Try to mimic Thurber's dry, comic style. | Does your response convey what the princess's new choice is and why she made it? Is your response humorous? If not, revise your ending. Be sure to include a moral in a style similar to Thurber's. |

### Are **DIAMONDS** really a girl's best friend?

What do you value more than material possessions?

### COMMON CORE

**RL 4** Analyze the impact of specific word choices on meaning. **RL 5** Analyze how an author's choices concerning how to structure a text create surprise.

---

# Practice and Apply

For preliminary support of post-reading questions, use these copy masters:

**R** RESOURCE MANAGER—Copy Masters
Reading Check p. 49
Parody p. 45
Question Support p. 50

Additional selection questions are provided for teachers on page 39.

## ANSWERS

## Comprehension

1. *The king announces that his daughter will wed the prince who gives her the gift she likes best.*

2. *Everyone who predicted the princess would choose the tin box should be punished for their naïveté.*

## Text Analysis

COMMON CORE **RL 4, RL 5**

*Possible answers:*

3. *Readers expect love or virtue to triumph in fairy tales, but this ending ironically confounds our expectations by showing greed winning out.*

4. ● **COMMON CORE FOCUS** *Analyze Parody* **Imitation of standard fairy tale language:** "Once upon a time..." (lines 1–2). **Exaggeration:** "Her nursery looked like Cartier's window. Her toys were all made of gold or platinum or diamonds or emeralds" (lines 5–6). **Irony:** "The princess... picked up the present she liked the most. It was the... jewel box..." (lines 44–46). Thurber is making fun of superficiality and materialism.

---

# Assess and Reteach

## Assess

**DIAGNOSTIC AND SELECTION TESTS**
Selection Test A pp. 223–224
Selection Test B/C pp. 225–226

**Interactive Selection Test** on **thinkcentral.com**

## Reteach

**Level Up Online Tutorials** on **thinkcentral.com**

**Reteaching Worksheets** on **thinkcentral.com**
Literature Lesson 39: Parody and Satire
Reading Lesson 1: Predicting

---

5. ● **COMMON CORE FOCUS** *Evaluate Predictions* **Predictions will vary.** Thurber intended to surprise readers—that's why his parody is effective.

6. *Some students may say that humor can be an effective tool for social change. For example, some stand-up comics use pointed jokes about racism or sexism to spark conversations about these important topics. Others may say that only serious work can really drive social change.*

### READING-WRITING CONNECTION

Encourage students to reread lines 42–58 to review the ending and Thurber's dry wit. Remind them to write an ironic ending.

### Are **DIAMONDS** really a girl's best friend? *Possible answer:* Many students will cite family, friends, and other nonmaterial elements.

### COMMON CORE FOCUS

**W 1b** Develop claims, supplying evidence for each. **SL 1a** Come to discussions prepared, having read material under study; explicitly draw on that preparation by referring to evidence from texts. **SL 2** Integrate multiple sources of information from diverse media or formats. **SL 4** Present supporting evidence clearly and logically such that listeners can follow the line of reasoning.

### SUMMARY

This clip from *The Birds* opens from a bird's point of view high above a California town as fire spreads through the town's center. More and more birds cross the screen and begin to attack people rushing from a restaurant. The film's heroine, Melanie, seeks shelter in a phone booth, and from there, trapped and powerless, watches chaos and terror unfold around her. Two birds break the glass before a man finally pulls Melanie back to the safety of the restaurant.

### What makes a director a master of STYLE?

Read the question. Ask students what they know about Hitchcock's films, such as *Rebecca, Rear Window, Spellbound, Vertigo,* or *North by Northwest.* Then, broaden the discussion to more recent scary movies. Point out that Hitchcock invented many of the techniques that later directors used to create suspense.

### BACKGROUND

Alfred Hitchcock is among the most widely known and influential directors in film history. From 1927 onward, he made cameo appearances in all of his movies, taking such roles as a man getting on a bus. Hitchcock's movie *Rebecca* received the Academy Award for Best Picture in 1940, though Hitchcock never received an Academy Award as Best Director. For his tombstone, Hitchcock suggested the words "This is what we do to bad little boys." His tombstone ultimately read "I'm in on a plot."

---

**Media Study**

*from* **The Birds**
Film Clip on **Media** 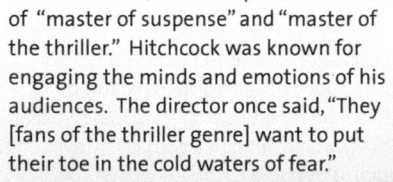 **Smart** DVD-ROM

# What makes a director a master of STYLE?

### COMMON CORE

**SL 1a** Come to discussions prepared, having read material under study; explicitly draw on that preparation by referring to evidence from texts.

Long before there was a Steven Spielberg or a Peter Jackson, there was a world-class director known for creating spellbinding films. By viewing a clip from one of Alfred Hitchcock's most famous movies, you'll experience the stylistic touches that made this director a movie legend.

## Background

**Fear Factor** Born in England in 1899, Alfred Hitchcock learned moviemaking from the ground up, beginning in the 1920s. In 1939, as a full-fledged director, he moved to the United States. Over the next three decades, the director crafted movies, and later produced two TV series, that earned him the titles of "master of suspense" and "master of the thriller." Hitchcock was known for engaging the minds and emotions of his audiences. The director once said, "They [fans of the thriller genre] want to put their toe in the cold waters of fear."

*The Birds* (1963)—considered Hitchcock's last great movie—portrays a California coastal town in which the bird population suddenly turns vicious. The movie is loosely based on the short story by suspense writer Daphne du Maurier.

848

## Media Study Resources

 **RESOURCE MANAGER UNIT 8**
Plan and Teach pp. 51–54
Summary pp. 55†*, 56‡*
Viewing Guide p. 57
Close Viewing p. 58
Media Activity p. 59
Produce Your Own Media p. 60

**TECHNOLOGY**
⊘ **Teacher One Stop DVD-ROM**
⊘ **Student One Stop DVD-ROM**
⊘ **Media*Smart* DVD-ROM**
**MediaScope** on <u>thinkcentral.com</u>

*See resources on the* **Teacher One Stop DVD-ROM** *and on* <u>thinkcentral.com</u>.

\* Resources for Differentiation  † Also in Spanish  ‡ In Haitian Creole and Vietnamese

## Media Literacy: Style in Movies

A writer conveys his or her style primarily through carefully crafted words. A filmmaker achieves style through carefully selected images that can create specific meanings and trigger specific emotions. Director Alfred Hitchcock was often asked for insights into his craft. He once said, "Self-plagiarism is style." By this he meant that directors who consistently use and refine certain techniques from movie to movie can develop features recognizable as their own. To explore Hitchcock's style, it helps to have a sense of a director's basic techniques.

| ELEMENTS OF STYLE | STRATEGIES FOR VIEWING | |
|---|---|---|
| **Expressing Themes** A director's stylistic techniques can be used to express particular themes or viewpoints that are characteristic of the director's work. | Become familiar with some common characteristics of Hitchcock's works. <br>• Presentation of misfortune or evil as a fact of life <br>• Ordinary, innocent people caught up in frightening circumstances <br>• Threat of danger from unlikely settings, such as in a public place in full daylight <br>• Fast-paced scenes in which tension builds <br>• Probing exploration of a character's emotional or psychological state <br>• Strong suspense mixed with humorous touches | *North by Northwest*  <br> *The Birds*  |
| **Creating Atmosphere** Just as a writer's unique style depends on word choice, tone, and other elements, a director can become known for trademark film techniques that convey meaning and create an atmosphere. | Discover a few of Hitchcock's unique visual filming techniques. <br>• Interpret **point of view** (POV) **shots,** which show what a character sees, and **reaction shots,** which show a character's response to whatever he or she faces. Hitchcock's POV shots allow viewers to slip into the role of a character and to identify with the character's predicament. <br>• Watch for **camera placement.** For example, a camera placed at odd angles might portray a very confined setting or a confused state of mind. <br>• Think about what the director is trying to achieve through the **pace** of the **editing.** Hitchcock was known for using **long takes** to promote reflection and **quick cuts** to increase tension. | *Rear Window*  <br> *Vertigo*  |

MEDIA STUDY **849**

---

## MEDIA STUDY: TEACHING OPTIONS

**Teaching Option 1: The Basics (1–2 Days)**

1. Begin the Media Study using the material provided on pages 848–849.
2. Show the Introduction on Media*Smart.* Then show the First Viewing. As they watch, have students use the Viewing Guide on page 850, along with the corresponding copy master on page 57 of the Resource Manager. Discuss their responses.
3. Return to the pupil book for the extension activities on page 851.

**Teaching Option 2: In-Depth Study (2–3 Days)**

1. Begin the Media Study using pages 848–849.
2. Show the Introduction and First Viewing from Media*Smart.* Then continue on Media*Smart* with the Media Lessons, using the teacher notes available in the Resources section.
3. Show the Guided Analysis presentation. Have students record their observations on the Student Viewing Guide available in the Resources section from Media*Smart.*
4. Return to the pupil book, page 851.

---

## Media Literacy  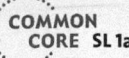 COMMON CORE SL 1a

Ask students to define *style.* Students should recognize that *style* refers to the distinctive way in which someone does something. Ask students what might contribute to style in a movie. On the board, list answers students give, such as music, sound effects, and lighting. Make sure *camera shots, shot selection, pacing,* and *editing* are included in the list. Then discuss the chart on this page.

• **Expressing Themes** To reinforce how themes can become part of a director's style, read aloud this synopsis of part of Hitchcock's *North by Northwest.* Ask students to identify which characteristic Hitchcock themes from the chart are found in the synopsis.

*Advertising executive Roger O. Thornhill stands up from lunch just as a "George Kaplan" is being paged. Three men seize him and take him to the mansion of enemy spy Philip Vandamm. Thornhill denies he is Kaplan and cannot answer Vandamm's questions. Next he is drugged and sent in a car down a treacherous mountain road, barely escaping death. Thornhill can't persuade the police or even his mother that his harrowing stories are true. The police cannot find Vandamm, and his mansion apparently belongs to United Nations ambassador Lester Townsend. Thornhill finds Townsend, who is soon knifed to death. Thornhill holds the knife!*

• **Creating Atmosphere** Ask students to imagine they are directing this movie scene: A character is stood up by his girlfriend. The goal is to invite sympathy for the character and create an atmosphere of sorrow and disappointment. Ask students: How could point of view shots provide information? How could reaction shots generate sympathy for the character? How could camera angles help suggest disappointment and sadness? What pacing and editing suits such a scene?

# Practice and Apply

## VIEWING GUIDE

1. Before students view the movie clip, tell them they will be asked to identify techniques Hitchcock uses to create an atmosphere of fear and helplessness. Ask them to watch for these elements:

   - **point of view shots** and **reaction shots** that show what Melanie sees and how she feels, especially inside the phone booth

   - **camera placement** that begins from above, then switches to Melanie's point of view, changing the mood and atmosphere of the clip

   - **shot selection, pacing, editing,** and **quick cuts** that generate increasing tension, such as the rapid sequence of different birds hitting the booth

2. Some students may not be able to link the techniques with what they see in the clip. Help these students connect the labels to specific examples in the clip.

   **R** RESOURCE MANAGER—Copy Masters
   Viewing Guide p. 57
   Close Viewing p. 58
   Media Activity p. 59

Use this resource with the Viewing Guide:

**MediaSmart DVD**

**MediaScope** on **thinkcentral.com**

## ANSWERS

### *FIRST VIEWING:* Comprehension

1. *The birds attack the phone booth more aggressively. Finally, a man brings Melanie to a restaurant for safety.*

2. *Melaine is inside a phone booth.*

### *CLOSE VIEWING:* Media Literacy

*Possible answers:*

3. *She becomes progressively more panicked, wondering how she can escape from the attacking birds. She is also aghast at the scene outside the booth.*

4. *Hitchcock starts with an overhead shot of the entire scene and then uses medium and tight close-ups. He conveys increasing tension with quick edits.*

---

850

---

## *Viewing Guide for*
# The Birds

Just before the start of the clip, main character Melanie Daniels is in a restaurant, overhearing anxious townspeople discussing the increasing threat of bird attacks. Then, through the windows, Melanie spots another attack in progress, which leads to a fiery explosion at a gasoline station.

   View the clip several times, and take as much time as you need to observe the events that take place. Keep the following questions in mind as you view.

### NOW VIEW

#### *FIRST VIEWING:* Comprehension

1. **Summarize** What happens from the point at which the man crashes his car until the end of the clip?

2. **Recall** Where is Melanie in most of this scene?

#### *CLOSE VIEWING:* Media Literacy

3. **Make Inferences** Describe what you think are Melanie's thoughts and feelings as she witnesses the unfolding events.

4. **Analyze Techniques** What types of shots does Hitchcock use to convey the tense nature of Melanie's situation?

5. **Analyze Mood** In terms of mood and atmosphere, how is the very beginning of the clip different from the ending?

6. **Draw Conclusions** In folklore and other works of literature, the sighting of a bird often signals the coming of chaos. Why do you think a familiar device like the sighting of a bird would appeal to a director known for suspenseful thrillers?

7. **Evaluate Style** A **set piece** is a scene staged so skillfully that it serves as a textbook example of a filmmaking technique or style. The phone booth scene you've viewed is a famous set piece. Review the details about Hitchcock's work on page 849. Explain what examples of Hitchcock's style you think are effectively represented in this scene.

---

5. *The mood at the beginning is almost calm. There's very little sound, and the camera shot is a long, wide overhead shot of the town. By the end, the camera shots are edited in quick succession, and the raging fire and attacking bird sound effects are quite loud.*

6. *Birds are usually viewed as benevolent, so their use as an omen of chaos probably appealed to Hitchcock, who liked to present threats that come from unlikely places.*

7. *Ordinary people are caught up in frightening circumstances; danger threatens a normally peaceful setting; point of view shots, reaction shots, and close-ups build tension and take viewers inside characters' panic and fear; shot selection and pacing get faster as the action gets more intense.*

## Write or Discuss

**Analyzing Hitchcock's Style** Here are more quotes from Alfred Hitchcock about his approach to moviemaking. Choose one that you think comes closest to the stylistic techniques used in the scene. Support your opinion with evidence.

- "Give them [the audience] pleasure—the same pleasure they have when they wake up from a nightmare."
- "If it's a good movie, the sound could go off and the audience would still have a perfectly clear idea of what was going on."
- "Always make the audience suffer as much as possible."

## Produce Your Own Media

**Create a Production Still** Imagine you're part of a team promoting a new, Hitchcock-styled version of a fairy tale or folktale. Create a production still for the movie in the style of Hitchcock. A **production** or **promotional still** is a photograph taken during the making of a film. Sometimes a still shows an actual scene from the movie or an image that represents the highlights.

*HERE'S HOW* Here are a few suggestions for making the production still:

- Choose a familiar tale on which to base the production still. Note how words are used in the tale to present events and communicate information.
- To add Hitchcock-flavored twists, think about how to take any familiar element of the tale to a thrilling extreme visually. Draw a sketch of a daytime setting that is ordinarily a safe public place. Then draw a sketch that includes elements of danger in the same setting.

**PROFESSIONAL MODELS**

These images are production stills from *North by Northwest*.

**COMMON CORE**

**W 1b** Develop claims, supplying evidence for each. **SL 2** Integrate multiple sources of information from diverse media or formats. **SL 4** Present supporting evidence clearly and logically such that listeners can follow the line of reasoning.

**Media Tools** — **THINK**central

Go to **thinkcentral.com**.
KEYWORD: HML9-851

**Tech Tip**

Search the Internet for more images of Hitchcock's threatening settings.

MEDIA STUDY **851**

## Produce Your Own Media

**Rubric: Create a Production Still** The production still should show a scene that

- represents a highlight from the story
- reflects a familiar tale but also includes a Hitchcock-type twist
- is dramatic
- encourages viewers to see the movie

**R** RESOURCE MANAGER—Copy Master
Produce Your Own Media p. 60

---

## Write or Discuss

**COMMON CORE** W 1b, SL 2, SL 4

**Analyzing Hitchcock's Style** Students should cite specific elements from the clip to support their opinions. For example, for the second statement, students might point out that there is almost no sound in the clip. The quick cuts from inside the phone booth to horrific events outside would be enough to explain the situation and frighten the audience. For the last statement, students might point out how claustrophobic the phone booth is and the way in which point of view shots and reaction shots make the viewer suffer along with the main character. Encourage students to include their own personal reactions to the clip as support.

### MEDIA STUDY WRAP–UP

Have students summarize what they have learned about creating a style in movies. Encourage them to use terms such as *theme, atmosphere, point of view shots, reaction shots, camera placement, shot selection, pacing, editing,* and *quick cuts* in their explanations.

### RETEACH

For students who are unable to apply the Media Study skills, select from these reteaching options:

- **Background Music** Have students choose a scene from a movie they are familiar with and describe for a partner the background music. Ask them to critique the music's effectiveness: what the music added to the scene, how the scene might have been less effective without it, and other types of music that might also have been effective.
- **Close-up and Long-Range** Ask students to prepare a list of effects that a director can achieve by using close-up and long-range camera shots. Start with these suggestions: *In a close-up a director can achieve intensity by showing an actor's facial expressions, or even beads of sweat. In a long-range shot, an actor is placed in context, such as a large open field or a big crowd on a city street.*

**Media Tools** — **THINK**central

Media study keywords point to **MediaScope,** a Web site that helps students strengthen media analysis and production skills.

## COMMON CORE FOCUS

**RI 2** Determine a central idea of a text and analyze its development, including how it emerges and is shaped; provide an objective summary. **RI 4** Analyze the impact of specific word choices on meaning and tone. **RI 6** Analyze how an author uses rhetoric to advance a point of view or purpose. **L 4b** Identify patterns of word changes that indicate different meanings. **L 4c** Consult reference materials to determine a word's etymology. **L 5b** Analyze nuances in the meaning of words with similar denotations.

## SUMMARY

"Going to Japan" is an amusing and thought-provoking essay in which Barbara Kingsolver describes a trip she took to Japan. She relates her experiences trying to fit into an unfamiliar culture and explains how she learned an important lesson about the value of forgiveness.

## Have you ever felt OUT OF PLACE?

Ask the question. After students have read the first paragraph, discuss situations in which a person might feel out of place. Have students complete the *QUICKWRITE.* Then encourage volunteers to share their paragraphs with the class.

---

## Going to Japan
Essay by Barbara Kingsolver

# Have you ever felt OUT OF PLACE?

### COMMON CORE

**RI 2** Determine a central idea of a text and analyze its development, including how it emerges and is shaped; provide an objective summary. **RI 4** Analyze the impact of specific word choices on meaning and tone. **RI 6** Analyze how an author uses rhetoric to advance a point of view or purpose. **L 4b** Identify patterns of word changes that indicate different meanings. **L 4c** Consult reference materials to determine a word's etymology.

You know the feeling—that sinking sense of not quite fitting in. Pretty much everybody feels out of place at some point, whether it's at a party where you don't know anyone or on your first day at a new school in a new town. In "Going to Japan," Barbara Kingsolver describes a time when she felt totally out of her element. She relates the blunders she made as she tried to blend in.

*QUICKWRITE* In a paragraph, describe a situation in which you felt out of place. Include all the details you can remember—even the embarrassing ones! What about the situation made you feel self-conscious? Did you eventually relax and feel better, or were you uncomfortable the whole time?

---

See resources on the **Teacher One Stop DVD-ROM** *and on* **thinkcentral.com**.

**RESOURCE MANAGER UNIT 8**
Plan and Teach, pp. 61–68
Summary pp. 69–70*†‡
Text Analysis and Reading
  Skill, pp. pp. 71–74*†
Vocabulary, pp. 75–77*

**DIAGNOSTIC AND SELECTION TESTS**
Selection Tests, pp. 227–230

**BEST PRACTICES TOOLKIT**
Word Squares, p. E10

**TECHNOLOGY**
- Teacher One Stop DVD-ROM
- Student One Stop DVD-ROM
- Audio Anthology CD
- GrammarNotes DVD-ROM
- ExamView Test Generator
  on the **Teacher One Stop**

\* Resources for Differentiation      † Also in Spanish      ‡ In Haitian Creole and Vietnamese

## TEXT ANALYSIS: HUMOR

Have you ever used a joke to get your point across? Writers often use **humor** to convey a point of view on a topic and to create surprise and amusement. The following rhetorical techniques are common devices of humor:

- **Hyperbole:** exaggeration of the truth
- **Irony:** a contrast between what you expect to happen and what actually happens
- **Wordplay:** verbal wit—playing with word choices and word sounds

In this essay, Kingsolver mixes facts with personal, often humorous examples to describe her experiences in Japan. While she explains certain elements of Japanese culture, she also presents an exaggerated account of how she felt out of place. "When I stepped on a streetcar," she writes, "a full head taller than all the other passengers, I became an awkward giant." As you read, note passages that you find humorous.

## READING SKILL: SUMMARIZE

When you **summarize,** you use your own words to restate the central idea, main points, and important details of what you've read, without including your own opinions. As you read, use a chart like the one shown to record the important details presented in each of the essay's three parts. In your own words, sum up the main point of each part, and then determine the essay's central idea.

| Part | Details Included | Main Point |
|---|---|---|
| Part I: lines 1–15 | | |
| Part II: lines 16–59 | | |
| Part III: lines 60–91 | | |

## ▲ VOCABULARY IN CONTEXT

Write sentences showing the meaning of each boldfaced word as you understand it.

1. showed defiance by speaking **brazenly**
2. felt **mortified** when her father sang in public
3. **cede** control to the new student council president
4. accepted his **abject** apology
5. a **baleful** and frightening threat

 Complete the activities in your **Reader/Writer Notebook.**

## Barbara Kingsolver

born 1955

### A Scientific Leaning

Though Barbara Kingsolver began writing stories and essays as a child, she never dreamed she'd someday become a professional author. The writers she read, she explains, "were mostly old, dead men from England. It was inconceivable that I might grow up to be one of those myself." Kingsolver majored in biology in college, but also took one creative writing class—and found she loved it.

### Writing for Change

Kingsolver wrote her first novel holed up in a closet, typing while her husband slept. Her dedication paid off, and *The Bean Trees* was a critical and popular success. Kingsolver is now an award-winning author of essays, novels, and short stories. She believes that literature can be a force for social change. "I'm extremely interested in cultural difference," Kingsolver says, "in social and political history, and [in] the sparks that fly when people with different ways of looking at the world come together."

### BACKGROUND TO THE ESSAY

**Hiroshima**

On August 6, 1945, at a crucial moment in World War II, the U.S. dropped the first atomic bomb on the Japanese city of Hiroshima. The bomb destroyed the city and killed 80,000 people almost instantly; thousands more died later from radiation illness and other injuries. The city of Hiroshima has been rebuilt and is now at the center of a movement to abolish atomic weapons. Ground Zero, where the bomb fell, is now home to Peace Memorial Park.

**Author Online**

**THINK central**

Go to **thinkcentral.com.**
KEYWORD: HML9-853

853

---

### TEXT ANALYSIS
**COMMON CORE**
RI 4, RI 6

#### ● *Model the Skill:* HUMOR

To support instruction, read aloud this example:

> Eric was the kind of kid everyone referred to as a "brainiac." He was amazingly smart—*annoyingly* smart. I'm sure that as a toddler, he could fish the letters out of his alphabet soup and spell Latin phrases.

The writer uses humor to convey an idea. Explain that the writer uses hyperbole to suggest how smart Eric is by exaggerating his ability.

**GUIDED PRACTICE** Have students suggest examples of hyperbole, irony, and word play.

### READING SKILL
**COMMON CORE**
RI 2

#### ■ *Model the Skill:* SUMMARIZE

Use the paragraph under **A Scientific Leaning** to model summarizing: *Barbara Kingsolver never expected to become a professional author. In fact, she majored in biology in college.*

**GUIDED PRACTICE** Have students summarize **Writing for Change.**

**R** RESOURCE MANAGER—Copy Master Summarize p. 73 (for student use while reading the selection)

---

### VOCABULARY SKILL
**COMMON CORE**
L 4

## ▲ VOCABULARY IN CONTEXT

**DIAGNOSE WORD KNOWLEDGE** Have all students complete Vocabulary in Context. Check their words and phrases against the following:

**abject** (ăb′-jĕkt′) *adj.* exceedingly humble
**baleful** (bāl′fəl) *adj.* evil; destructive
**brazenly** (brā′zən-lē) *adv.* boldly and without shame
**cede** (sēd) *v.* to give up; give way

**mortified** (môr′tə-fīd′) *adj.* very embarrassed; humiliated **mortify** *v.*

**PRETEACH VOCABULARY** Use the following copy master to help students predict the meaning of each boldfaced word.

**R** RESOURCE MANAGER—Copy Master Vocabulary Study p. 75

1. Read item 1 aloud, emphasizing *brazenly*.

2. Point out the phrase "Although she meant to be polite." Elicit possible meanings for *brazenly*, such as "utterly."

3. Repeat the procedure for items 2–5.

---

**TEXT ANALYSIS**    COMMON CORE

**Ⓐ Model the Skill: HUMOR**    RI 4, RI 6

Point out the list of items that Aunt Zelda took with her to Japan. Explain that this list is not a real list of items that Zelda took with her to Japan, and is meant to be humorous.

**Possible answer:** *Kingsolver's breezy, informal tone suggests that this will be a humorous essay, as do the references to the "Aunt Zelda" game, with its silly lists of items (lines 1–2, 14–15).*

---

# Going to Japan

## Barbara Kingsolver

My great-aunt Zelda went to Japan and took an abacus, a bathysphere, a conundrum, a diatribe, an eggplant. That was a game we used to play. All you had to do was remember everything in alphabetical order. Right up to Aunt Zelda.

Then I grew up and was actually invited to go to Japan, not with the fantastic Aunt Zelda but as myself. As such, I had no idea what to take. I knew what I planned to be doing: researching a story about the memorial at Hiroshima;[1] visiting friends; trying not to get lost in a place where I couldn't even read the street signs. Times being what they were—*any* times—I intended to do my
10  very best to respect the cultural differences, avoid sensitive topics I might not comprehend, and, in short, be anything but an Ugly American. When I travel, I like to try to blend in. I've generally found it helps to be prepared. So I asked around, and was warned to expect a surprisingly modern place.

My great-aunt Zelda went to Japan and took Appliances, Battery packs, Cellular technology. . . . That seemed to be the idea. **Ⓐ**

And so it came to pass that I arrived in Kyoto[2] an utter foreigner, unprepared. It's true that there are electric streetcars there, and space-age gas stations with uniformed attendants who rush to help you from all directions at once. There are also golden pagodas[3] on shimmering lakes, and Shinto shrines[4]

---

**Analyze Visuals ▶**

Examine the collage on page 855. Name three elements that contribute to how out of place the photograph on top looks against the background images.

**❶ Targeted Passage**

**Ⓐ HUMOR**
What clues in lines 1–15 hint that this will be a humorous essay? Explain your answer, citing evidence.

---

1. **the memorial at Hiroshima** (hĭ-rō'shə-mə): The Hiroshima Peace Memorial Park commemorates the deaths and destruction caused by the U.S. bombing of Hiroshima near the end of World War II.
2. **Kyoto** (kē-ō'tō): A Japanese city rich in history and culture, Kyoto was the nation's capital from 794 until 1868.
3. **pagodas** (pə-gō'dəz): sacred buildings of the Buddhist religion, typically towers with many levels.
4. **Shinto shrines**: shrines from the Shinto religion, one of the main religions of Japan.

---

## DIFFERENTIATED INSTRUCTION

**FOR ENGLISH LANGUAGE LEARNERS**

**Vocabulary Support** Use Word Squares to teach these words: *topics* (line 10), *guidelines* (line 21), *infinite* (line 42), *approximately* (line 44), *presumption* (line 61).

🧰 **BEST PRACTICES TOOLKIT—Transparency** Word Squares p. E10

**FOR STRUGGLING READERS**

In combination with the *Audio Anthology CD*, use one or more Targeted Passages (pp. 854, 856, 857) to ensure that students focus on key events, concepts, and skills. Targeted Passages are also good for English learners.

**❶ Targeted Passage [Lines 1–15]**

This passage explains the reason for Kingsolver's trip, reveals her feelings about it, and introduces the "Aunt Zelda" game.

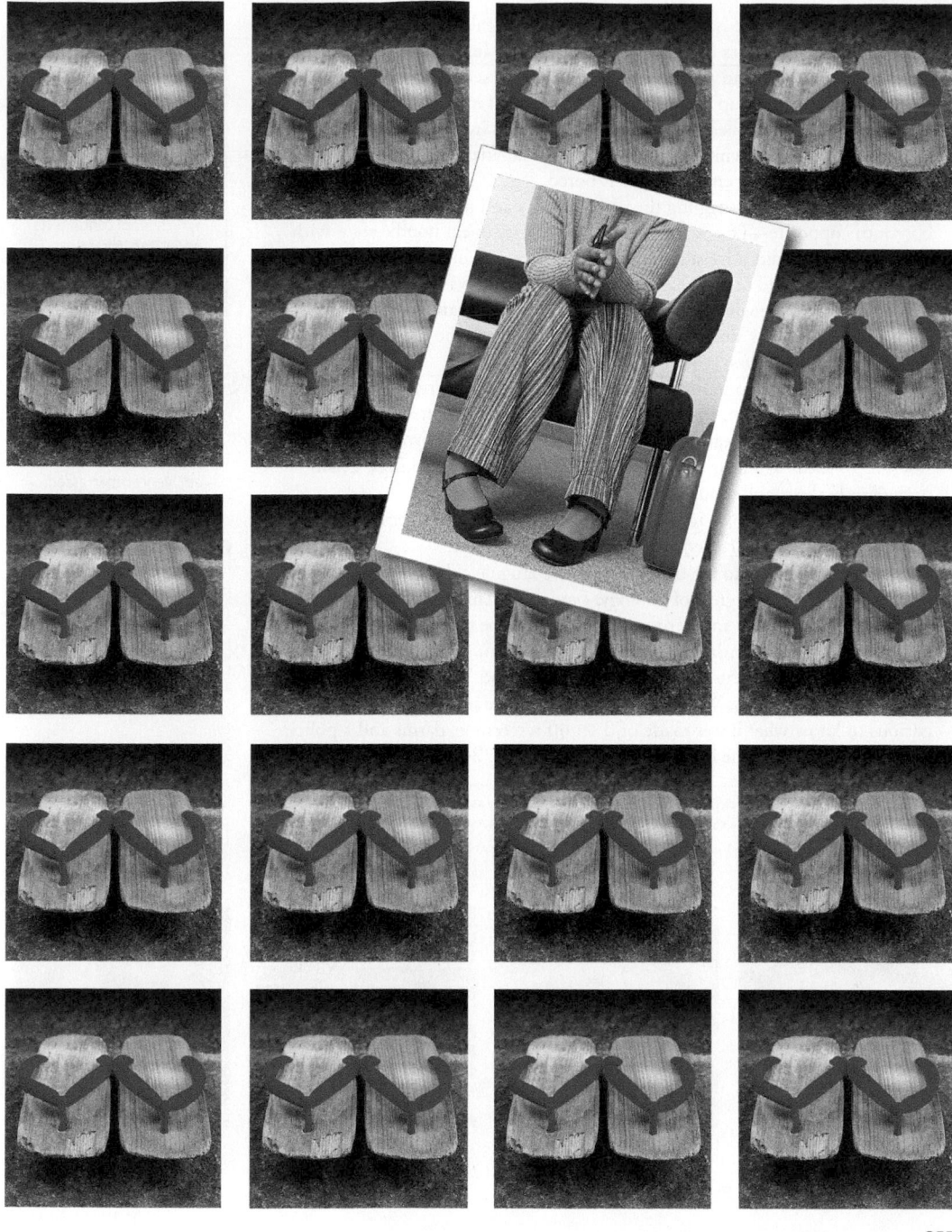

**The Ugly American** The term "Ugly American" (line 11) refers to an obnoxious, thoughtless American in a foreign country whose behavior offends the local people. The term comes from the 1958 bestseller *The Ugly American*, by Eugene Burdick and William Lederer. A collection of linked short stories set in Southeast Asia during the 1950s, the book was an attack on U.S. foreign policy and cultural arrogance in the period leading up to the Vietnam War. Ironically, the title character is a physically ugly American engineer who is in fact culturally sensitive—the very opposite of the type of American the book criticizes and the term has come to signify.

## Analyze Visuals

*Possible answer: The top photograph shows a woman seated on a bench, while the background photographs are close-ups of shoes, with no person in sight. The woman in the top photograph is wearing Western-style clothing, while the shoes in the background photographs are traditional Japanese sandals. The top photo is set at an angle, and the woman's legs are slanting inward. The background photos are all aligned vertically, and the sandals themselves are vertical rather than slanting.*

**REVISIT THE BIG QUESTION**

Have you ever felt

# OUT OF PLACE?

**Discuss** Have students reread lines 9–11. Point out that Kingsolver is determined to "respect the cultural differences" of Japan and not be an "Ugly American." How might being perceived as an Ugly American make an American visitor to a foreign country feel out of place? *Possible answer: An American visitor to a foreign country who was perceived as an Ugly American would not be welcomed by the local people and consequently might feel out of place—if that Ugly American were even aware of how he or she was perceived.*

---

- Why is the author going to Japan? (lines 6–7)
- What challenges does Kingsolver expect to face in Japan? (lines 8–9)
- How does the author feel about visiting a different culture? (lines 9–13)
- How are lines 1–2 and lines 14–15 similar? How are they different?

**FOR ADVANCED LEARNERS/PRE–AP**

**Researching Japan** Allow students to become experts or members of expert groups by researching and sharing additional information about one of these topics. Suggest that they include pictures.

- the city of Kyoto, Japan
- Hiroshima, before, during, and after World War II
- Japanese customs and traditions

**TIERED DISCUSSION PROMPTS**

Refer students to lines 20–38 and use these prompts to help students understand how Kingsolver feels in Japan:

**Connect** Think of a time when you were not sure what to do or say because you did not understand the "invisible guidelines" (line 21). How did you feel? *Students may mention experiences traveling or trying to fit in with a social group.*

**Evaluate** Do you think that Kingsolver could have avoided some of the embarrassment that she experienced? Explain your answer. *Possible answer: Yes; if she had prepared better for her trip, learning more about Japanese ways and expectations, she might have been able to avoid potentially embarrassing situations.*

---

<table>
<tr><td>TEXT ANALYSIS</td><td>COMMON CORE</td></tr>
</table>

**Ⓑ HUMOR**

RI 4,
RI 6

*Possible answer:* Kingsolver changes the alphabetical list to fit with whatever anecdotes she is telling at that point in the essay. She chooses amusing items to include in the lists, such as "Altitude"—referring to her height—and "Bare-naked legs."

---

<table>
<tr><td>VOCABULARY</td><td>COMMON CORE</td></tr>
<tr><td></td><td>L 4</td></tr>
</table>

**OWN THE WORD**

- **brazenly:** Tell students that a synonym for *brazenly* is "shamelessly," and that common antonyms are "decorously" and "well-mannered." Have students use both *brazenly* and one of the antonyms in a sentence showing an understanding of the meanings of both words.

- **mortified:** Tell students that the Latin prefix *mort-* means death. Then, have them explain the relationship between the Latin prefix and the meaning of *mortified.*

---

20 in the forests. There are bamboo groves and nightingales. And finally there are more invisible guidelines for politeness than I could fathom. When I stepped on a streetcar, a full head taller than all the other passengers, I became an awkward giant. I took up too much space. I blended in like Igor would blend in with the corps de ballet in *Swan Lake.*[5] I bumped into people. I crossed my arms when I listened, which turns out to be, in Japanese body language, the sign for indicating **brazenly** that one is bored.

But I wasn't! I was struggling through my days and nights in the grip of boredom's opposite—i.e., panic. I didn't know how to eat noodle soup with chopsticks, and I did it most picturesquely *wrong.* I didn't know how to order, 30 so I politely deferred to my hosts and more than once was served a cuisine with heads, including eyeballs. I managed to wrestle these creatures to my lips with chopsticks, but it was already too late by the time I got the message that *one does not spit out anything.*

I undertook this trip in high summer, when it is surprisingly humid and warm in southern Japan. I never imagined that in such sweltering heat women would be expected to wear stockings, but every woman in Kyoto wore nylon stockings. Coeds in shorts *on the tennis court* wore nylon stockings. I had packed only skirts and sandals; people averted their eyes.

When I went to Japan I took my Altitude, my Bare-naked legs, my Callous 40 foreign ways. I was **mortified.** Ⓑ

My hosts explained to me that the Japanese language does not accommodate insults, only infinite degrees of apology. I quickly memorized an urgent one, *"Sumimasen,"* and another for especially extreme cases, *"Moshi wake gozaimasen."*[6] This translates approximately to mean, "If you please, my transgression is so inexcusable that I wish I were dead."

I needed these words. When I touched the outside surface of a palace wall, curious to know what it was made of, I set off screeching alarms and a police car came scooting up the lawn's discreet gravel path. *"Moshi wake gozaimasen,*

---

5. **Igor . . . corps de ballet** (kôr′də bǎ-lā′) **in** *Swan Lake:* Igor is the clumsy assistant in many Frankenstein movies. *Swan Lake* is a Russian ballet composed by Peter Ilich Tchaikovsky (chī-kôf′skē).

6. *Sumimasen* (soo̅-mē-mä-sĕn′) . . . *Moshi wake gozaimasen* (mō-shē wä-kĕ gō-zī-mä-sĕn).

---

<table>
<tr><td></td><td>COMMON CORE L 4b</td></tr>
</table>

**Language Coach**

**Antonyms** Many words with prefixes such as *a-, dis-, in-,* and *un-* contain their own **antonyms,** or opposites. Reread line 21. Which word contains its opposite? What does each word mean?

**brazenly**
(brā′zən-lē′) *adv.* boldly and without shame

② **Targeted Passage**

**mortified** (môr′tə-fīd′) *adj.* very embarrassed; humiliated **mortify** *v.*

Ⓑ **HUMOR**
Kingsolver repeats this alphabetical **word play** throughout the essay. How does this contribute to the humor of the piece? Explain your answer.

---

**DIFFERENTIATED INSTRUCTION**

**FOR STRUGGLING READERS**

② **Targeted Passage** [Lines 21–33]
In this passage, Kingsolver describes some of the experiences that made her feel out of place during her visit.

- What experiences caused the author to feel out of place in Japan? (lines 21–26)

- Kingsolver's account is amusing, but do you think she found her experiences funny at the time? Explain (lines 27–28).

**FOR ENGLISH LANGUAGE LEARNERS**

**Language Coach**

COMMON CORE L 4b

**Antonyms** *Possible answer:* disembarked *contains* embarked. *The first means "got off (a ship, plane, etc)"; the second means "boarded (a ship, plane, etc)."* Ask students to name antonyms for the following words: "awkward" (line 23), "politely" (line 30), "sweltering" (line 35), "approximately" (line 44).

Officer! Wish I were dead!" And in the public bath, try as I might, I couldn't
50  get the hang of showering with a hand-held nozzle while sitting fourteen inches
from a stranger. I sprayed my elderly neighbor with cold water. In the face.

"*Moshi wake gozaimasen,*" I declared, with feeling.

She merely stared, dismayed by the foreign menace. **C**

I visited a Japanese friend, and in her small, perfect house I spewed out
my misery. "Everything I do is wrong!" I wailed like a child. "I'm a blight
on your country."

"Oh, no," she said calmly. "To forgive, for us, is the highest satisfaction.
To forgive a foreigner, ah! Even better." She smiled. "You have probably made
many people happy here."

60  To stomp about the world ignoring cultural differences is arrogant, to
be sure, but perhaps there is another kind of arrogance in the presumption
that we may ever really build a faultless bridge from one shore to another,
or even know where the mist has **ceded** to landfall. When I finally arrived
at Ground Zero in Hiroshima, I stood speechless. What I found there was
a vast and exquisitely silent monument to forgiveness. I was moved beyond
words, even beyond tears, to think of all that can be lost or gained in the gulf
between any act of will and its consequences. In the course of every failure of
understanding, we have so much to learn.

I remembered my Japanese friend's insistence on forgiveness as the highest
70  satisfaction, and I understood it really for the first time: What a rich wisdom
it would be, and how much more bountiful a harvest, to gain pleasure not
from achieving personal perfection but from understanding the inevitability
of imperfection and pardoning those who also fall short of it. **D**

I have walked among men and made mistakes without number. When I
went to Japan I took my **Abject** goodwill, my **Baleful** excuses, my Cringing
remorse. I couldn't remember everything, could not even recite the proper
alphabet. So I gave myself away instead, evidently as a kind of public service.
I prepared to return home feeling empty-handed.

At the Osaka[7] Airport I sat in my plane on the runway, waiting to leave for
80  terra cognita,[8] as the aircraft's steel walls were buffeted by the sleet and winds
of a typhoon. We waited for an hour, then longer, with no official word from
the cockpit, and then suddenly our flight was canceled. Air traffic control in
Tokyo had been struck by lightning; no flights possible until the following day.

"We are so sorry," the pilot told us. "You will be taken to a hotel, fed, and
brought back here for your flight tomorrow." **A**

As we passengers rose slowly and disembarked, we were met by an airline
official who had been posted in the exit port for the sole purpose of saying
to each and every one of us, "Terrible, terrible. *Sumimasen.*" Other travelers
nodded indifferently, but not me. I took the startled gentleman by the hands
90  and practically kissed him.

"You have no idea," I told him, "how thoroughly I forgive you." ❧

---

7. **Osaka** (ō-sä′kə).
8. **terra cognita** (tĕr′ə  kŏg-nē′tə): Latin for "a familiar land or country."

GOING TO JAPAN  **857**

---

## Side column (center)

**C** HUMOR
Reread lines 49–53.
Do you think that
accidentally splashing
someone is grounds for
being labeled a "foreign
menace"? Identify the
humorous technique
Kingsolver uses here.

**cede** (sēd) *v.* to give up;
give way

❸ **Targeted Passage**

**D** SUMMARIZE
What is Kingsolver's
main point in lines
69–73? Summarize the
feelings she expresses
about forgiveness in
this passage.

**abject** (ăb′-jĕkt′) *adj.*
exceedingly humble

**baleful** (bāl′fəl) *adj.*
evil; destructive

**COMMON CORE L 4c**

**A** FOREIGN WORDS
The phrase *terra cognita*
is a Latin phrase that
means "a familiar land
or country." You might
recognize the word *terra*
as a root in words such
as *terrestrial.* Can you
think of any other English
words that have the Latin
word *terra* as a root?
Consult a dictionary if
necessary.

---

## Right column

**TEXT ANALYSIS**  **COMMON CORE**  **RI 4, RI 6**

**C** HUMOR

***Possible answer:*** *No; Kingsolver is using
hyperbole to make the anecdote amusing.*

**READING SKILL**  **COMMON CORE**  **RI 2**

**D** *Model the Skill:* **SUMMARIZE**

Point out the phrase "inevitability of imperfection" in lines 72–73. Ask students to
demonstrate their understanding of summarizing by asking the following question:
"How does this phrase sum up the author's
realization about human error?"

***Possible answer:*** *People can derive far more
satisfaction from accepting and forgiving
human error than they can from striving to
be perfect.*

**VOCABULARY**  **COMMON CORE**  **L 4c**

**A** *Model The Skill:* **FOREIGN
WORDS**

***Possible answers:*** *terrier, territory, terrace*

Tell students that they are going to work in
small groups to define the words they thought
of. Ask for volunteers to share their words.

**VOCABULARY**  **COMMON CORE**  **L 4**

**OWN THE WORD**

- **cede:** Tell students that the connotation
  of *cede* is to yield or grant. Have students
  write a pair of sentences that show an
  understanding of the meaning of *cede.*

- **abject:** Review the definition of *abject*
  with students; have them list antonyms.

- **baleful:** Tell students to list things that
  could be described as *baleful.* ***Possible
  answers:*** baleful *looks,* baleful *statement*

**SELECTION WRAP–UP**

**READ WITH A PURPOSE** Have students explain
what benefits Kingsolver has gained from being "out of place."

⭐ **CRITIQUE** Ask students what aspect of
Kingsolver's essay they enjoyed the most.

---

## Bottom section

**FOR STRUGGLING READERS**

❸ **Targeted Passage** [Lines 63–73]

In this passage, Kingsolver describes her reaction to Ground Zero and summarizes what
she learned as a result of visiting the site.

- What was the author's reaction to Ground
  Zero in Hiroshima? (line 64)

- What did she come to understand about
  perfection and forgiveness as a result of her
  visit? (lines 69–73)

**FOR ENGLISH LANGUAGE LEARNERS**

**Develop Reading Fluency** Point out the combination of simple and complex sentences in
lines 74–78. Have students notice the different sentence lengths. Explain that the commas within each type of sentence are guides
both to meaning and to reading fluency. Read
the sentences aloud as a demonstration of
fluency and meaning for students. Then, ask
students to take turns with a partner reading
lines 74–78 aloud at least twice, emphasizing
expression and accuracy with each reading.

# Practice and Apply

For preliminary support of post-reading questions, use these copy masters:

**R** RESOURCE MANAGER—Copy Masters
Reading Check p. 79
Humor p. 71
Question Support p. 78

Additional selection questions are provided for teachers on page 65.

## ANSWERS

## Comprehension

1. *Kingsolver went to Japan to research a story about the memorial at Hiroshima and to visit friends.*

2. *Kingsolver was "a full head taller" than most Japanese people, "took up too much space," and "bumped into people" (lines 22–24); she "didn't know how to eat noodle soup with chopsticks" (lines 28–29); Japanese women wore stockings despite the heat, but Kingsolver did not (lines 35–38); Kingsolver "couldn't get the hang of showering with a hand-held nozzle" (lines 49–51).*

## Text Analysis

 COMMON CORE RI 2, RI 4, RI 6

*Possible answers:*

3. *Kingsolver has just had a revelation about forgiveness (people gain far more from forgiving human error than from striving to be perfect), so when the official apologizes to her, she is touched and wants him to know "how thoroughly" she forgives him.*

4. *The essay's central irony is that Kingsolver is determined to blend in and "be anything but an Ugly American" (lines 11–12), yet she ends up making cultural blunders and feeling like a foreigner. For example, she is eager to please, but when she crosses her arms, she unintentionally signals boredom (lines 24–26). Ironically, Kingsolver makes people happy by doing things wrong, because in Japan "to forgive . . . is the highest satisfaction" (line 57). Another irony is that after begging others to forgive her, at the end of the essay, she is the one who is gratefully forgiving an airline official (lines 89–91).*

5. **● COMMON CORE FOCUS** *Summarize We all make mistakes, even when trying our best not to. We can derive far more benefit from accepting and forgiving inevitable human error than from striving to be perfect.*

---

## Comprehension

1. **Recall** Why did the author go to Japan?

2. **Recall** List three examples Kingsolver gives to illustrate her inability to blend in on her trip to Japan.

## Text Analysis

3. **Draw Conclusions** Why did Kingsolver react so strongly to the airline official's apology while her fellow travelers simply "nodded indifferently"? Explain, citing evidence from the text to support your conclusion.

4. **Identify Irony** This essay is filled with examples of **situational irony,** the contrast between what a reader or character expects and what actually exists or happens. Identify three examples of situational irony and explain what is ironic about each.

5. **Summarize** Review the chart you filled in as you read. Taken together, what do the details you recorded reveal about Kingsolver's overall message? Summarize the author's **central idea** in your own words.

6. **Analyze Tone** How would you describe Kingsolver's tone in this essay? Use a graphic like the one shown to record striking or unusual words and phrases from the essay. Then describe the tone Kingsolver's **word choice** helps create.

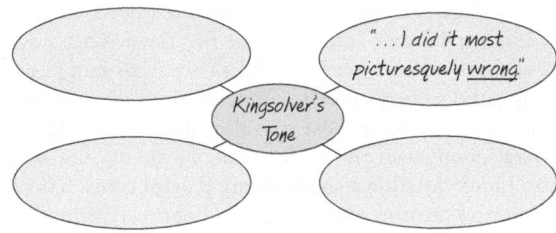

7. **Evaluate Humor** Review the bulleted list of humorous techniques on page 853, and think about how Kingsolver uses humor to communicate her perspective. In your opinion, which technique best helps Kingsolver to convey her thoughts and feelings in a funny way? Give examples from the essay to support your answer.

## Text Criticism

8. **Different Perspectives** Kingsolver is a writer who has long been fascinated by cultural differences and who works to make others see these differences as unique and positive. Would someone less attuned to cultural differences have felt as out of place as Kingsolver did? Explain, citing evidence from "Going to Japan" to support your opinion.

### Have you ever felt OUT OF PLACE?

What can you learn from being in unfamiliar territory?

**COMMON CORE**

RI 2 Determine a central idea of a text and analyze its development, including how it emerges and is shaped; provide an objective summary of a text. RI 4 Analyze the impact of specific word choices on meaning and tone. RI 6 Analyze how an author uses rhetoric to advance a point of view or purpose.

---

6. *The following phrases create a humorous, self-mocking tone: "I blended in like Igor . . ." (line 23); "I got the message that one does not spit out anything" (lines 32–33); "'I'm a blight on your country'" (lines 55–56).*

7. **● COMMON CORE FOCUS** *Evaluate Humor Students should support their opinions with examples from the text.*

## Text Criticism

8. *Some students might respond that Japanese culture is so different from American culture that almost any American would feel out of place. Others may say that Kingsolver was too sensitive and that most people would have been less troubled than she by gaffes such as eating noodle soup incorrectly.*

**Have you ever felt OUT OF PLACE?** *Possible answer: You can gain new insight into life.*

## Vocabulary in Context

**WORD LIST**
abject
baleful
brazenly
cede
mortified

### ▲ VOCABULARY PRACTICE

Decide whether these statements are true or false. If you need to reread the definitions of the boldfaced vocabulary words, consult the Glossary of Vocabulary on page R123.

1. You might be **mortified** if you get the lowest test score in the class.
2. Hearing a **baleful** speech is likely to frighten or anger many people.
3. If you speak **brazenly,** your parents will probably compliment you on your politeness.
4. Mornings usually **cede** to afternoons.
5. **Abject** flattery has to do with praising someone's choice of clothing.

### ACADEMIC VOCABULARY IN WRITING

· appreciate   · attribute   · indicate   · unique   · vary

Is it important for us to learn to **appreciate** the **unique** characteristics of other cultures? Write a paragraph explaining why it is or is not important. Use at least one Academic Vocabulary word in your response.

### VOCABULARY STRATEGY: APPROPRIATE WORD CHOICE

To communicate effectively, you should consider several factors when choosing your words. One is a word's **denotation**—its surface meaning or definition. The other is the word's **connotation,** or the overtone of meaning it carries beyond its surface definition. Saying "Jake spoke *brazenly,*" for example, has a stronger negative connotation than saying that he spoke *boldly.* Another factor to consider is the formality of the situation. A word like *cede* is rather formal and might sound inappropriate in casual speech or writing.

**PRACTICE** Choose the word or phrase that is more appropriate in each situation.

1. In a negative review of a singer: Her voice was (shrill, high-pitched).
2. In a letter to a friend: We were (taken in by a con artist, duped by a charlatan).
3. In a formal report: Dr. White was (uptight, apprehensive) about the decision.
4. In a letter of recommendation: He has a (reserved, tight-lipped) but friendly manner.

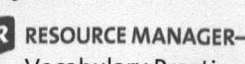

**COMMON CORE**

**L 5b** Analyze nuances in the meaning of words with similar denotations.

**Interactive Vocabulary**

**THINK** central

Go to **thinkcentral.com.**
KEYWORD: HML9-859

---

## *DIFFERENTIATED INSTRUCTION*

### FOR STRUGGLING READERS

**Concept Support: Connotation** To build understanding of the implied meanings of words, explore the differences between pairs of synonyms, such as *determined* and *stubborn, crowd* and *mob, meal* and *feast, skinny* and *slender.* Have students use the words in pairs of sentences and then compare their shades of meaning.

### FOR ADVANCED LEARNERS/PRE–AP

**Vocabulary in Writing** Have students use at least four vocabulary words in a paragraph suggesting how not to feel out of place in new situations.

---

## ANSWERS

## Vocabulary in Context

### ▲ VOCABULARY PRACTICE

1. *true*                 4. *true*
2. *true*                 5. *false*
3. *false*

  **RESOURCE MANAGER**—Copy Master
Vocabulary Practice p. 76

### ACADEMIC VOCABULARY IN WRITING

***Possible answer:*** *We should learn to* appreciate *and understand what is different about other cultures. There is much to be learned from other cultures and how customs* vary.

### VOCABULARY STRATEGY:
### APPROPRIATE WORD CHOICE
*(also an EL language objective)*

**COMMON CORE L 5b**

Discuss with students how an author's word choice can affect tone.

***Answers:***

1. *shrill*
2. *taken in by a con artist*
3. *apprehensive*
4. *reserved*

  **RESOURCE MANAGER**—Copy Master
Vocabulary Strategy p. 77

**THINK** central

**Interactive Vocabulary**

Keywords direct students to a **WordSharp** tutorial on **thinkcentral.com** or to other types of vocabulary practice and review.

## *Assess and Reteach*

### *Assess*

**DIAGNOSTIC AND SELECTION TESTS**
Selection Test A pp. 227–228
Selection Test B/C pp. 229–230

**Interactive Selection Test** on **thinkcentral.com**

### *Reteach*

**Level Up Online Tutorials** on **thinkcentral.com**

**Reteaching Worksheets** on **thinkcentral.com**
Literature Lesson 38, Research and Study Skills Lesson 13, Vocabulary Lesson 17

# Focus and Motivate

## COMMON CORE FOCUS

**RI 4** Analyze the impact of specific word choices on meaning and tone. **RI 10** Read and comprehend literary nonfiction. **W 1a-b** Introduce and develop claims, supplying evidence. **L 3** Apply knowledge of language to understand how language functions in different contexts and to make effective choices for meaning or style. **L 4a, c** Use context as a clue to the meaning of a word; consult reference materials to determine a word's meaning.

## SUMMARY

In, "A Few Words" Mary Oliver declares that, despite what many people think, nothing in nature is "cute." Oliver asserts that humans should stop viewing themselves as powerful masters of nature and instead see themselves as one part of a greater natural whole.

## Is **"CUTE"** a compliment?

After students read the first paragraph, discuss how people use *cute.* For example, is the word applied to adults or just children? Is it applied equally to both genders? Which animals are described as *cute?* Have students complete the *DEBATE* activity. Then discuss which team won, and why.

## Selection Resources

---

*Essential Course of Study* **ECOS**

## A Few Words
### Essay by Mary Oliver

# Is **"CUTE"** a compliment?

**COMMON CORE**

**RI 4** Analyze the impact of specific word choices on meaning and tone. **RI 10** Read and comprehend literary nonfiction. **L 4a** Use context as a clue to the meaning of a word.

Before you answer, think about it: What does *cute* really mean? Can you be cute and still be taken seriously? still be strong? still be respected? In this essay, Mary Oliver has a few words to say about what happens when we label something *cute.*

*DEBATE* With a group of classmates, jot down what comes to mind when you think of something cute. Would you want to be described this way? Form two teams and square off to settle the question of whether or not *cute* is a compliment.

860

---

See resources on the **Teacher One Stop DVD-ROM** and on **thinkcentral.com**.

**R RESOURCE MANAGER UNIT 8**
Plan and Teach, pp. 81–88
Summary pp. 89–90†‡*
Text Analysis and Reading
Skill, pp. 91–94†*
Vocabulary, pp. 95–97*

**DIAGNOSTIC AND SELECTION TESTS**
Selection Tests, pp. 231–234

**INTERACTIVE READER**

**ADAPTED INTERACTIVE READER**

**ELL ADAPTED INTERACTIVE READER**

**TECHNOLOGY**
- Teacher One Stop DVD-ROM
- Student One Stop DVD-ROM
- PowerNotes DVD-ROM
- Audio Anthology CD
- GrammarNotes DVD-ROM
- Audio Tutor CD
- ExamView Test Generator on the **Teacher One Stop**

**Find it Online!** THINK central

Features on **thinkcentral.com** that support the selection include
- **PowerNotes** presentation
- **ThinkAloud** models to enhance comprehension
- **WordSharp** vocabulary tutorials
- interactive writing and grammar instruction

---

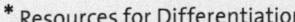

* Resources for Differentiation   † Also in Spanish   ‡ In Haitian Creole and Vietnamese

## ● TEXT ANALYSIS: TONE

A writer's **tone,** or attitude toward a subject, can subtly sneak up on you as you read or boldly hit you over the head in the first paragraph. By noticing a writer's choice of words and details, you can detect and analyze his or her tone. Mary Oliver begins this essay by declaring, "Nothing in the forest is charming." Her blunt statement immediately challenges a common perception of the forest and establishes her tone. As you read "A Few Words," note striking words, details, and images that Oliver uses, and consider the tone they convey.

## ■ READING SKILL: PARAPHRASE

To understand difficult passages or sentences, it is sometimes helpful to **paraphrase,** or restate the writer's ideas in your own words. When you paraphrase, be sure to

- restate both the main idea and any important details
- use your own words, which may be simpler than those in the original text

As you read, paraphrase this essay's difficult passages in a chart like the one shown.

| Passage | My Paraphrase |
|---|---|
| "Gardens are charming, and man-made grottos, and there is a tranquility about some scenes of husbandry and agriculture that is charming—orderly rows of vegetation, or lazy herds, or the stalks of harvest lashed and leaning together." (lines 1–4) | Man-made elements of nature, like gardens and grottos, are pleasant. Some farm scenes, like orderly rows of crops, tame animals, and harvested produce, look peaceful and calm. |

## ▲ VOCABULARY IN CONTEXT

Mary Oliver uses these words to make her case about the perils of cuteness. To see how many you already know, choose the word that makes sense in each phrase.

| WORD LIST | deftness | stalk |
|---|---|---|
| | diminutive | valorous |

1. a _____ of wheat standing tall in the field
2. the _____ of a quarterback eluding tacklers
3. a _____ teddy bear among larger toys
4. _____ action in the face of danger

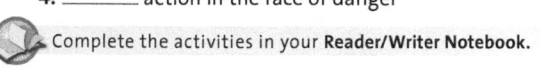 Complete the activities in your **Reader/Writer Notebook.**

---

## Meet the Author

## Mary Oliver
born 1935

### A Natural Writer
Mary Oliver has been mesmerized by the natural world ever since she was a child growing up in Ohio. She has also always been enthralled by poetry. "I decided very early that I wanted to write," she says. "It was the most exciting thing, the most powerful thing, the most wonderful thing to do with my life." So she did it. Many years and countless awards later, Oliver still loves writing. "I feel writing is work, and I feel it's also play—bound together," she explains.

### Perfecting a Gift
Oliver has been described as an "indefatigable guide to the natural world." An ardent observer of nature, she writes about the mysteries and wisdom that it reveals to us. For inspiration, she takes solitary walks in the fields and woods, which she calls part of her writing process. "Walks work for me," she explains. Critics and readers agree with her: Oliver is the winner of numerous awards, including the Pulitzer Prize and a National Book Award. Despite her success, Oliver confesses, "I never have felt yet that I've done it right. This is the marvelous thing about language. It can always be done better."

**Authors Online**
Go to **thinkcentral.com**. KEYWORD: HML9-861

THINK central

861

---

## Teach

TEXT ANALYSIS — COMMON CORE RI 4

## ● *Model the Skill:* TONE

Read aloud the following example. Tell students that you think the tone is light but annoyed.

> Many people think that squirrels are cute. I am *not* one of those people. I have a bird feeder in my yard, and no matter what I do to keep the bushy-tailed bandits away, they treat the feeder as their own private snack bar.

Now ask students what words and images help to create this tone. ***Possible answer:*** *"Bushy-tailed bandits" and "private snack bar" set the tone.*

**GUIDED PRACTICE** Ask students what words or phrases the writer might have used to convey a more serious tone.

READING STRATEGY — COMMON CORE RI 10

## ■ *Model the Skill:* PARAPHRASE

Use the first two sentences under **A Natural Writer** to model paraphrasing for students: *Mary Oliver has always been fascinated by nature and excited by poetry.*

**GUIDED PRACTICE** Have students paraphrase **Perfecting a Gift.**

 RESOURCE MANAGER—Copy Master Paraphrase p. 93 (for student use while reading the selection)

---

## VOCABULARY SKILL

COMMON CORE L 4

## ▲ VOCABULARY IN CONTEXT

**DIAGNOSE WORD KNOWLEDGE** Have all students complete Vocabulary in Context. Check their words and phrases against the following:

**deftness** (dĕft'nĭs) *n.* the quality of quickness and skillfulness
**diminutive** (dĭ-mĭn'yə-tĭv) *adj.* very small
**stalk** (stôk) *n.* a stem or main axis of a plant
**valorous** (văl'ər-əs) *adj.* brave

**PRETEACH VOCABULARY** Use the following copy master to help students predict meanings for each boldfaced word.

R RESOURCE MANAGER—Copy Master Vocabulary Study p. 95

1. Read the first item in Part A aloud, emphasizing *deftness.*
2. Point out the phrase "quickly and accurately." Elicit possible meanings for *deftness,* such as "skill."

3. Repeat the procedure for the other items. Encourage students to use each word in a sentence.

## READ WITH A PURPOSE

*Help students set a purpose for reading. Tell them to look for ways Mary Oliver communicates her attitudes about animals and nature as they read the essay.*

## REVISIT THE BIG QUESTION

### Is **"CUTE"** a compliment?

**Discuss** In lines 6–9, Oliver describes a fox "carrying the soiled wing of a gull" as other foxes "grab onto it and pull." How does this image support her point that foxes "are not adorable, or charming, or cute"? *Possible answer: Oliver is making clear that foxes are wild animals that kill other animals to survive. There is nothing "cute" about such behavior.*

---

**TEXT ANALYSIS**   **COMMON CORE** RI 4

### A Model the Skill: TONE

Point out the first sentence and explain that the strong image it presents sets a determined tone.

*Possible answer: Oliver's tone can be described as direct, brisk, and forceful. She creates this tone through the strong and repeated use of the negative, as in "nothing in the forest is cute. The dog fox is not cute, nor the little foxes" (lines 5–6). She also uses strong, sometimes disturbing images, such as "carrying the soiled wing of a gull . . . small teeth snapping" (lines 6–8). Oliver also uses many short, declarative sentences, as in "Toys are cute. But animals are not toys" (line 13).*

---

**VOCABULARY**   **COMMON CORE** L 4

### OWN THE WORD

- **stalk:** Introduce the word by asking students to name vegetables, such as celery and carrots, that have *stalks*. How many vegetables can students name?
- **diminutive:** Read the sentence with *diminutive* aloud to students. Then have them name animals or insects that might be described as *diminutive*. *Possible answers: ants, bees, gnats, pygmy goats, miniature horses and donkeys*

---

# A Few Words

### Mary Oliver

Nothing in the forest is charming. Gardens are charming, and man-made grottos,[1] and there is a tranquility about some scenes of husbandry[2] and agriculture that is charming—orderly rows of vegetation, or lazy herds, or the **stalks** of harvest lashed and leaning together.

And nothing in the forest is cute. The dog fox is not cute, nor the little foxes. I watch them as they run up and down the dune. One is carrying the soiled wing of a gull; the others grab onto it and pull. They fly in and out of the blond grasses, their small teeth snapping. They are not adorable, or charming, or cute.

10 The owl is not cute. The milk snake is not cute, nor the spider in its web, nor the striped bass. Neither is the skunk cute, and its name is not "Flower." Nor is there a rabbit in the forest whose name is "Thumper," who is cute.

Toys are cute. But animals are not toys. Neither are trees, rivers, oceans, swamps, the Alps, the mockingbird singing all night in the bowers of thorn, the snapping turtle, or the purple-fleshed mushroom. **A**

Such words—"cute," "charming," "adorable"—miss the mark, for what is perceived of in this way is stripped of dignity, and authority. What is cute is entertainment, and replaceable. The words lead us and we follow: what is cute is **diminutive,** it is powerless, it is capturable, it is trainable, it is ours. It is all a

20 mistake. At our feet are the ferns—savage and resolute they rose, when the race of man was *nowhere* and altogether unlikely ever to be at all, in the terrifying shallows of the first unnamed and unnameable oceans. We find them pretty, delicate, and charming, and carry them home to our gardens.

Thus we manage to put ourselves in the masterly way—if nature is full of a hundred thousand things adorable and charming, diminutive and powerless, then who is in the position of power? We are! We are the parents, and the

---

1. **man-made grottos** (grŏt′ōz): artificial caves created for coolness and pleasure.
2. **husbandry** (hŭz′bən-drē): farming.

---

**1 Targeted Passage**

**stalk** (stôk) *n.* a stem or main axis of a plant

**COMMON CORE** L 4a

**Language Coach**

**Denotation/Connotation**
A word's explicit, literal definition is its **denotation**. Reread lines 1–9. What are the denotations of *adorable*, *charming*, and *cute*?

**A TONE**
Reread lines 1–15. How would you describe Oliver's tone? Identify the words and images the author uses to create this tone.

**diminutive**
(dĭ-mĭn′yə-tĭv) *adj.* very small

---

 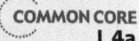
## FOR ENGLISH LANGUAGE LEARNERS

**Language Coach**  **COMMON CORE** L 4a

**Denotation/Connotation**
*Possible answers:* Adorable *is colloquial for "delightful" or "charming."* Charming *means "delightful" or "attractive."* Cute *means "wholesomely pretty or attractive." The words are more or less synonymous.* Have students think of other words that have differing denotations and connotations.

## FOR STRUGGLING READERS

In combination with the *Audio Anthology* CD, use one or more Targeted Passages (pp. 862, 864) to ensure that students focus on key events, concepts, and skills. Targeted Passages are also good for English learners.

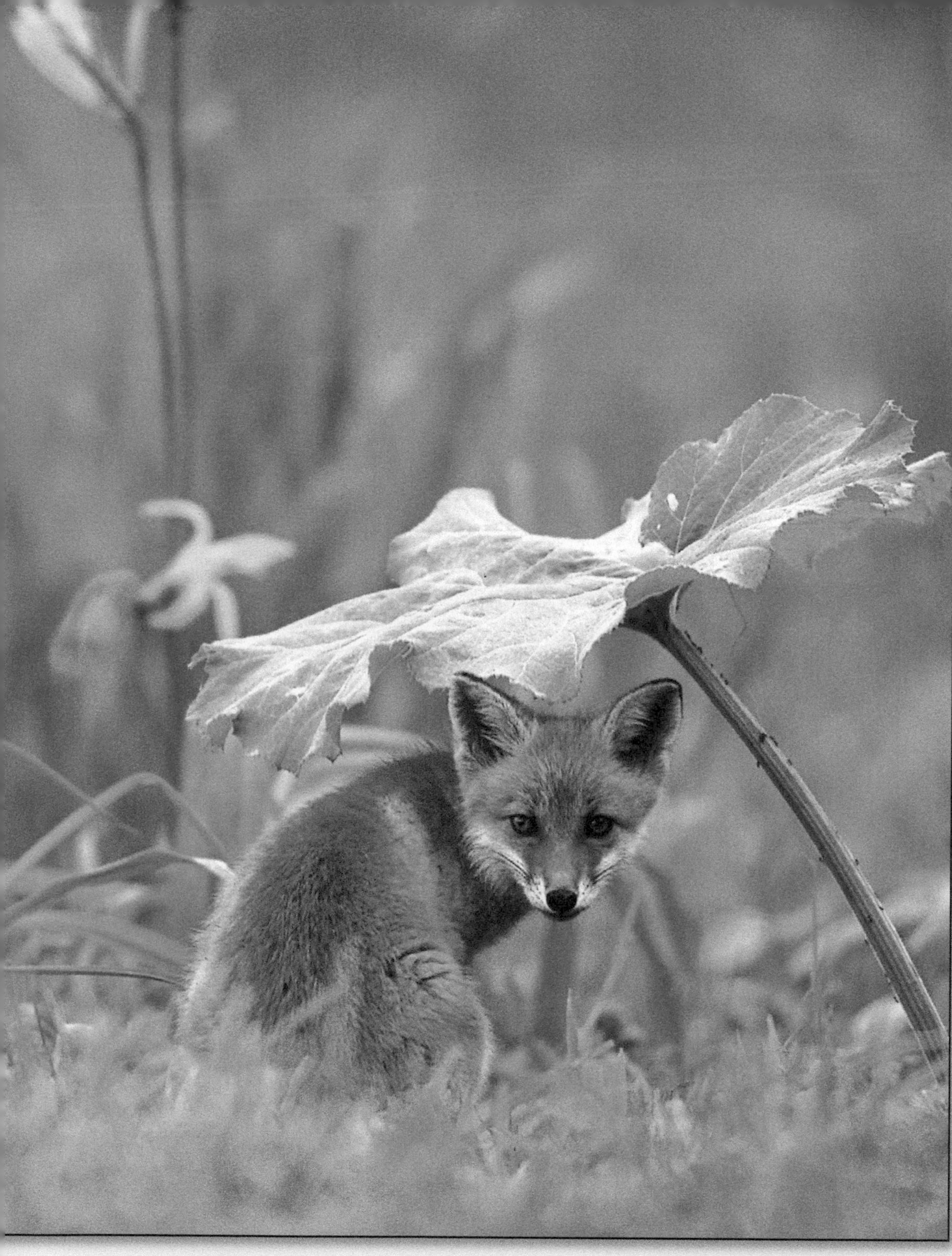

## Reading Support

THINK central

This selection on thinkcentral.com includes embedded **ThinkAloud** models–students "thinking aloud" about the story to model the kinds of questions a good reader would ask about a selection.

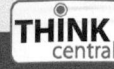

## BACKGROUND

**Cute** Ironically, like nature, *cute* is a word that has been tamed over centuries of its usage. *Cute* is a shortened version of *acute*, a word that dates back to the Middle Ages when it described a brief but severe disease. By the 1500s, *acute* meant penetrating or sharp-witted, and by the 1700s, someone who was cute was thought to be clever, even devious or sly. Our modern sense of cute as pleasing or attractive was first used as slang by American students in 1834.

**Cultural Connection** Unlike the callous observer that Oliver criticizes, many cultures do not consider nature as something that can be controlled or described as something distinct from ourselves. In traditional Japanese culture, there was no separate word for nature, because every living thing is inter-related. Native peoples in Australia speak of "feeling" the land. Many Native Americans believe that they possess the spirit of the land within them, and the land is a conscious, living being. Invite students to share traditional beliefs and values they may have learned about nature.

### ① Targeted Passage [Lines 1–20]

This passage introduces one of Oliver's main points: nothing in nature is "cute."

- What does Oliver consider to be "charming"? (lines 1–4)
- According to Oliver, what is and is not "cute"? (lines 5–15)
- According to Oliver, what is the problem with using the word *cute?* (lines 16–20)

### FOR ADVANCED LEARNERS/PRE–AP

**Research Wildlife** Provide independent learning opportunities for students to research examples of wildlife. Invite students to share information as they respond to Oliver's essay. For further details on this project, see

RESOURCE MANAGER
Ideas for Extension pp. 86–87

governors. The notion facilitates a view of the world as playground and laboratory, which is a meager view surely. And it is disingenuous, for it seems so harmless, so responsible. But it is neither. **B**

30    For it makes impossible the other view of nature, which is of a realm both sacred and intricate, as well as powerful, of which we are no more than a single part. Nature, the total of all of us, is the wheel that drives our world; those who ride it willingly might yet catch a glimpse of a dazzling, even a spiritual restfulness, while those who are unwilling simply to hang on, who insist that the world must be piloted by man for his own benefit, will be dragged around and around all the same, gathering dust but no joy. **C**

Humans or tigers, tigers or tiger lilies—note their differences and still how alike they are! Don't we all, a few summers, stand here, and face the sea and, with whatever physical and intellectual **deftness** we can muster, improve our

40    state—and then, silently, fall back into the grass, death's green cloud? What is cute or charming as it rises, as it swoons? Life is Niagara, or nothing. I would not be the overlord of a single blade of grass, that I might be its sister. I put my face close to the lily, where it stands just above the grass, and give it a good greeting from the stem of my heart. We live, I am sure of this, in the same country, in the same household, and our burning comes from the same lamp. We are all wild, **valorous,** amazing. We are, none of us, cute. ❧

## Comprehension

1. **Recall** How does Oliver describe the foxes at the beginning of the essay?

2. **Recall** List three other animals or plants the author discusses.

3. **Clarify** In Oliver's view, if we see nature as made up of cute, powerless animals, then who is in a position of power?

COMMON CORE

RI 4 Analyze the impact of specific word choices on meaning and tone. RI 10 Read and comprehend literary nonfiction.

## Text Analysis

4. **Draw Conclusions** Reread the essay's last line on page 864. Has "A Few Words" changed your opinion about what it means to label something *cute*? Do you think *cute* can ever be a compliment? Explain, citing lines from the essay you agree or disagree with.

● 5. **Analyze Tone** Describe Oliver's overall tone in this essay. As a reader, what can you tell about her attitude toward nature? Explain, citing evidence from the essay to support your analysis.

● 6. **Paraphrase** Review the paraphrasing chart you created as you read. Using your chart, summarize the central idea of this essay in your own words.

7. **Examine Author's Style** Oliver is most widely known for her poetry. In what way might this selection be described as poetic? In a chart like the one shown, record examples of the poetic elements Oliver uses in this essay. Use your completed chart to explain whether you think "A Few Words" is more like poetry or more like prose.

| Poetic Element | Examples from the Text |
|---|---|
| Alliteration | • "At our feet are the ferns..." (line 20) <br>• <br>• |
| Metaphor | |
| Imagery | |
| Repetition | |

## Text Criticism

8. **Critical Interpretations** Critics have praised Oliver's quest to, in the words of Holly Prado of the *L.A. Times Book Review*, "understand both the wonder and pain of nature." In your opinion, how well does Oliver explain both the beautiful and the not-so-beautiful aspects of the natural world? Support your answer with evidence from the selection.

### Is "CUTE" a compliment?

Is being "cute" respectable? Is being called "cute" offensive?

---

a gull" while other foxes "grab onto it and pull ..., their small teeth snapping" (lines 6–8); "the purple-fleshed mushroom" (line 15). **Repetition:** "Nothing in the forest is charming .... And nothing in the forest is cute" (lines 1, 5); "Humans or tigers, tigers or tiger lilies" (line 37). Students should cite evidence to support their view of Oliver's style.

## Text Criticism

8. Students may respond that Oliver does a good job of explaining both. She portrays

the beautiful side of nature in her lyrical last paragraph, and she portrays its not-so-beautiful side in her description of the fox with a gull in its mouth (lines 6–8).

### Is "CUTE" a compliment?
**Possible answer:** Students' opinions will vary; some may argue that its use is demeaning and it is not really a compliment.

---

## Practice and Apply

For preliminary support of post-reading questions, use these copy masters:

**R** RESOURCE MANAGER—Copy Masters
Reading Check p. 98
Tone p. 91
Question Support p. 100

Additional selection questions are provided for teachers on page 85.

### ANSWERS

## Comprehension

1. *Oliver says that the "dog fox is not cute" and describes one fox with "the soiled wing of a gull" in its mouth as other foxes grab at it, "their small teeth snapping" (lines 5–8).*

2. *Possible answer: Oliver mentions the owl, the milk snake, and ferns.*

3. *We (humans) are.*

## Text Analysis

COMMON CORE RI 4, RI 10

*Possible answers:*

4. *Students should explain their reasoning and cite relevant lines from the essay.*

5. ● **COMMON CORE FOCUS** *Tone Oliver's overall tone can be described as direct, brisk, impassioned, and forceful, sometimes sounding almost angry, as in lines 10–13. When Oliver talks about nature, her tone turns admiring, even reverent: "a realm both sacred and intricate, as well as powerful, of which we are no more than a single part" (lines 30–32). Her tone reveals that she has great respect for nature, which she views as stunning and powerful, not something to be controlled, exploited, or undervalued.*

6. ● **COMMON CORE FOCUS** *Paraphrase Nothing in nature is cute or adorable. We should stop viewing nature as entertainment and stop trying to control it. Humans, animals, and plants are interconnected natural beings, wondrous entities that deserve respect.*

7. *Alliteration: "down the dune" (line 6); "At our feet are the ferns" (line 20); "position of power" (line 26); "Niagara, or nothing" (line 41); "above the grass, and give it a good greeting" (lines 43–44). Metaphor: Oliver refers to the grass as "death's green cloud" (line 40) and nature as "the wheel that drives our world" (line 32). Imagery: Oliver's images portray nature as both violent and beautiful: a fox "carrying the soiled wing of*

## ANSWERS
## Vocabulary in Context

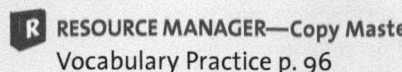

1. *a*          3. *b*

2. *b*          4. *b*

**R** **RESOURCE MANAGER—Copy Master**
Vocabulary Practice p. 96

### ACADEMIC VOCABULARY IN WRITING

Help students focus their responses. Direct them to state Oliver's viewpoint clearly before they explain why they do or do not agree with it. Remind students to support their ideas with clear reasons and evidence from the essay.

**Possible answer:** *As Mary Oliver says, nature is wild, but the man-made can be cute and charming. The natural environment can't be controlled, but the man-made environment is both controlled and constructed by people. We can* appreciate *both the natural and the man-made, but it is important to see their differences.*

### VOCABULARY STRATEGY: HOMONYMS

COMMON CORE **L 4c**

*(also an EL language objective)*

Point out that homonyms are often, but not always, different parts of speech. To extend the activity, have students identify the parts of speech of each pair of homonyms. Then have them use each homonym in a sentence of their own.

**Answers:**

1. *row*          4. *hide*

2. *grave*        5. *mean*

3. *kind*         6. *mine*

**R** **RESOURCE MANAGER—Copy Master**
Vocabulary Strategy p. 97

**Interactive Vocabulary**          THINK central

Keywords direct students to a **WordSharp** tutorial on **thinkcentral.com** or to other types of vocabulary practice and review.

---

## Vocabulary in Context

### ▲ VOCABULARY PRACTICE

WORD LIST
deftness
diminutive
stalk
valorous

In which situation might you use each vocabulary word?

1. **diminutive:** (a) describing a miniature poodle, (b) listing the pros and cons of a school committee's proposal, (c) explaining how to draw trees

2. **stalk:** (a) explaining how to apply paint, (b) describing a field of corn, (c) listing the reasons you like bungee jumping

3. **valorous:** (a) telling about a peaceful day in the country, (b) describing how the hero of a movie saved the day, (c) detailing how to lay a brick sidewalk

4. **deftness:** (a) watching leaves fall in a windstorm, (b) describing how a runner broke away from the pack to win, (c) choosing a birthday card for your brother

### ACADEMIC VOCABULARY IN WRITING

• appreciate   • attribute   • indicate   • unique   • vary

According to Mary Oliver, how does Nature in its natural environment **vary** from nature in a man-made environment? Write a paragraph or two comparing and contrasting those two environments. Use at least one Academic Vocabulary word in your response.

### VOCABULARY STRATEGY: HOMONYMS

**Homonyms** are words that have the same pronunciation and often the same spelling but different meanings. For example, the vocabulary word *stalk*, which means "a stem or main axis of a plant," looks and sounds just like the word *stalk*, meaning "to move threateningly or menacingly." Because they are pronounced and spelled the same way, homonyms can be confusing. The context of the sentence or passage can usually help you determine which of a set of homonyms is being used. However, sometimes it's difficult to figure out the meaning of a homonym from its context. In such cases, check a dictionary.

**PRACTICE** Identify the homonyms described by each pair of definitions. If you're stumped, figure out which word just one of the definitions describes. Then use a dictionary to find out if that word has any homonyms.

1. to move a boat forward with oars/a line of people or objects

2. place where a dead person is buried/very serious or solemn

3. a type of something/friendly and considerate

4. the skin of an animal/to conceal or keep secret

5. to intend to do something/unkind

6. belonging to me/an underground cavern from which gold is extracted

COMMON CORE

L 4c Consult reference materials to determine a word's meaning.

**Interactive Vocabulary**          THINK central

Go to **thinkcentral.com**.
KEYWORD: HML9-866

---

## DIFFERENTIATED INSTRUCTION

### FOR ENGLISH LANGUAGE LEARNERS

**Vocabulary: Homonyms** Have same-language pairs or small groups list homonyms in their home languages. For languages where this is not possible, have students identify other English homonym pairs.

### FOR ADVANCED LEARNERS/PRE—AP

**Vocabulary in Writing** Challenge students to use at least three vocabulary words in a paragraph written in Mary Oliver's style on the topic of nature's wonders.

# Language

◆ **GRAMMAR AND STYLE:** Vary Sentence Types

Reread the **Grammar and Style** note on page 864. Oliver believes that some people have a very condescending view of nature. To express her outrage at this perception, she uses a variety of sentence types that allow her emotions to shine through. Here, Oliver enlists **imperative, interrogative,** and **declarative sentences** to get her point across:

> *Humans or tigers, tigers or tiger lilies—note their differences and still how alike they are! Don't we all, a few summers, stand here, and face the sea and, with whatever physical and intellectual deftness we can muster, improve our state— and then, silently, fall back into the grass, death's green cloud? What is cute or charming as it rises, as it swoons? Life is Niagara, or nothing.* (lines 37–41)

Notice how the revisions in blue employ sentence types that more accurately reflect the emotions of the writer, making the statements more powerful. Revise your response to the prompt below by varying your sentence types.

---

**STUDENT MODEL**

I don't ~~think we should~~ refer to people as "cute." It belittles them~~and it doesn't~~ *Why not* take into account their achievements. ~~I think~~ we should give people credit for something more worthwhile, like hard work!

---

**READING-WRITING CONNECTION**

YOUR TURN

Increase your understanding of "A Few Words" by responding to this prompt. Then use the **revising tip** to improve your writing.

| WRITING PROMPT | REVISING TIP |
|---|---|
| **Extended Constructed Response: Opinion** <br> Oliver makes the case that we do nature a disservice when we label it *cute*. Can this apply to calling a person *cute*, as well? Write a **three-to-five-paragraph response** explaining whether or not you think this label can be harmful to humans. Use evidence from the text to support your opinion. | Review your explanation. Were you able to use a variety of sentence types to express your feelings about the topic? If not, revise your response. |

> **Interactive Revision**
> THINKcentral
> Go to thinkcentral.com.
> KEYWORD: HML9-867

COMMON CORE

L 3 Apply knowledge of language to understand how language functions in different contexts and to make effective choices for meaning or style.
W 1a-b Introduce and develop claims, supplying evidence.

---

**FOR ENGLISH LANGUAGE LEARNERS**

Suggest that students imagine they are conversing with Mary Oliver. Help them reflect on these questions: Would Oliver's tone put them off? Would they think she was coming on too strong? Would a softer, friendlier tone be more likely to win agreement, or does her forceful style inspire them?

---

# Language

COMMON CORE W 1a-b, L 3

◆ **GRAMMAR AND STYLE**

- After students examine the model, ask how the revisions strengthen the statements.
- Point out that Oliver sometimes poses a rhetorical question—a question with an obvious answer—and then answers it with an exclamatory sentence (lines 24–26).
- Tell students to make this passage stronger by using a variety of sentence types:

> *"~~I don't think it's appropriate for you to call me cute,~~ Don't call me cute!" said Ms. Davis. "~~Please notice that I never~~ Do I ever call you cute~~.~~? I am a grown woman~~, so~~. ~~I think I should be~~ Please treated me with more respect~~.~~!"*

**READING-WRITING CONNECTION**

Encourage students to consider the significance of *who* is using the word *cute*. For example, one teen describing another as *cute* is very different from an employer calling an employee *cute*.

---

> **Writing Online**
> THINKcentral
>
> The following tools are available online at **thinkcentral.com** and on **Write*Smart* CD-ROM:**
> - **Interactive Graphic Organizers**
> - **Interactive Student Models**
> - **Interactive Revision Lessons**
> For additional grammar instruction, see **GrammarNotes** on **thinkcentral.com**.

---

# Assess and Reteach

## Assess

**DIAGNOSTIC AND SELECTION TESTS**
Selection Test A, B/C pp. 231–232, 233–234

**Interactive Selection Test** on **thinkcentral.com**

## Reteach

**Level Up Online Tutorials** on **thinkcentral.com**

**Reteaching Worksheets** on **thinkcentral.com**
Literature Lesson 45, Research and Study Skills Lesson 12

# Focus and Motivate

## COMMON CORE FOCUS

**RL 4** Determine the figurative meaning of words and phrases. **RL 10** Read and comprehend poems. **L 4** Clarify the meaning of multiple-meaning phrases. **L 5** Demonstrate understanding of figurative language.

## SUMMARIES

Dickinson uses descriptive and figurative language to depict the appearance and movements of a snake in "A narrow Fellow in the Grass." In a striking metaphor at the end of the poem, the speaker expresses fear at the sight of this "narrow Fellow." In "'Hope' is the thing with feathers—," Dickinson compares the abstract concept of hope with the concrete object of a bird through the use of extended metaphor. The speaker suggests that the bird's song, which "never stops," is the strongest reminder that hope is alive.

## What is a poet's JOB?

Introduce the question, and have students read the introductory paragraph. Discuss with the class some examples of how poets can communicate insights about people, society, nature, or any other topic. In other words, what jobs do modern poets perform? Have students keep these examples in mind as they write want ads for the *PRESENT* activity.

## Selection Resources

---

## A narrow Fellow in the Grass
## "Hope" is the thing with feathers—
Poems by Emily Dickinson

# What is a poet's JOB?

## COMMON CORE

**RL 4** Determine the figurative meaning of words and phrases. **RL 10** Read and comprehend poems. **L 4** Clarify the meaning of multiple-meaning phrases. **L 5** Demonstrate understanding of figurative language.

Have you ever tried to describe something important, only to find yourself at a total loss for words? Some things are hard to explain, but certain people seem able to explain them anyway. Poets use their skill with language to communicate insights, or perceptive comments, about everything from emotions and adventure to animals and art.

*PRESENT* Write a want ad seeking a poet to communicate an insight you think is worth sharing. Include a description of what you want explained, the skills your poet should possess, and the kind of poetry you're looking for. Then pair up with a classmate and take turns presenting your ads.

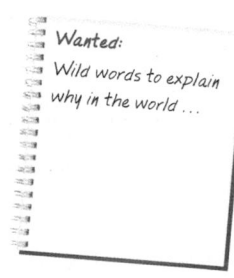

*Wanted:*
*Wild words to explain*
*why in the world ...*

868

---

*See resources on the* **Teacher One Stop DVD-ROM** *and on* **thinkcentral.com**.

**RESOURCE MANAGER UNIT 8**
Plan and Teach, pp. 101–108
Text Analysis and Reading
Skill, pp. 109–112†*

**DIAGNOSTIC AND SELECTION TESTS**
Selection Tests, pp. 235–238

**TECHNOLOGY**
- **Teacher One Stop DVD-ROM**
- **Student One Stop DVD-ROM**
- **Audio Anthology CD**
- **GrammarNotes DVD-ROM**
- **ExamView Test Generator** on the **Teacher One Stop**

---

* Resources for Differentiation      † Also in Spanish      ‡ In Haitian Creole and Vietnamese

## TEXT ANALYSIS: DICKINSON'S STYLE

Emily Dickinson's style is unmistakable. One of the originators of modern American poetry, she broke with tradition, creating a unique style all her own. Dickinson's poems are usually short—no more than 20 lines—but they often convey stunning insights in spite of their brevity. Distinct elements of Dickinson's style include

- dense stanzas that echo the **rhythms** of church hymns
- **slant rhymes,** or words that do not rhyme exactly
- unconventional capitalization that adds emphasis to certain words or phrases
- frequent use of dashes to highlight important words and break up the singsong rhythm of her poems
- original **figurative language,** including similes, metaphors, and personification

As you read, notice the poet's use of these elements, and consider the insights she communicates by using them.

## READING STRATEGY: READING POETRY

The following suggestions can help you increase both your understanding and your enjoyment of Dickinson's poetry:

- Look for unique **diction,** or word choice, and consider how it affects Dickinson's style.
- Read the poems aloud to appreciate Dickinson's unique rhythm and **imagery.**
- Pay close attention to words that are capitalized for emphasis.
- Analyze the poet's use of figurative language.
- Pause when you encounter dashes, just as you would for a comma or a period in a more conventional poem.

 Complete the activities in your **Reader/Writer Notebook.**

## Meet the Author

# Emily Dickinson
1830–1886

**Close to Home**
Except for a year she spent away at school, Emily Dickinson lived her entire life in the small community of Amherst, Massachusetts, with her family. She was very close to her older brother and younger sister. Though she adored her stern and principled father, she had a complicated relationship with her mother. By her 40s, Dickinson began to dress only in white and refused to leave her family's house. Except for the many letters she wrote and received, she withdrew from the world, living in isolation until her death.

**A Private Poet**
After Dickinson's death, her sister Lavinia carried out the poet's wishes, burning all of her letters from family and friends. However, Lavinia rescued a little box filled with poems. Since her late teens or early 20s, Emily Dickinson had been writing poetry. She'd jot down her thoughts during the day—on scraps of paper, old recipes, and the backs of envelopes—and write all night by candlelight. Though she wrote 1,775 poems, Dickinson published only 7, anonymously, during her lifetime. The private poet left the world pondering her untold secrets.

**A Rich Life**
The first volume of Emily Dickinson's poetry was published in 1890, four years after her death. Today, she is known as one of the most popular and influential U.S. poets. Even though Dickinson lived in isolation, her poems, according to 20th-century poet Allen Tate, reveal a life that was "one of the richest and deepest ever lived on this continent."

**Author Online**
**THINK central**
Go to thinkcentral.com.
KEYWORD: HML9-869

869

# Teach

TEXT ANALYSIS    COMMON CORE    RL 4, L 5

### ● *Model the Skill:* DICKINSON'S STYLE

To illustrate Dickinson's style, write these lines from "A narrow Fellow in the Grass" on the board:

> The Grass divides as with a Comb—
> A spotted shaft is seen—

Tell students that one aspect of the poet's style, present in the example, is the use of dashes at the end of each line. Have them point to other aspects of Dickinson's style, as shown in the example. *Possible answer: the lines' regular, hymnlike rhythm; unconventional capitalization ("Grass," "Comb"); figurative language (the grass is likened to a head of hair being divided by a comb)*

**GUIDED PRACTICE** What stylistic element common to Dickinson's poetry is not present in these lines?

READING STRATEGY    COMMON CORE    RL 10

### ■ *Model the Skill:* READING POETRY

Return to the lines written on the board. Model for students how to read poetry. For example, read the lines aloud, emphasizing their rhythm and pausing at the dash. Then, ask students what the figurative language in those lines suggests about the speaker's relationship with nature. *Possible answer: The use of personification suggests that nature is something that the speaker is familiar with, and even close to.*

**GUIDED PRACTICE** Invite several volunteers to practice reading the lines aloud.

---

## DIFFERENTIATED INSTRUCTION

### FOR STRUGGLING READERS

**Concept Support** Help students understand the stylistic elements covered in the **TEXT ANALYSIS** discussion.

- Point out that the hymnlike rhythm that Dickinson often uses consists of an alternating pattern of weak and strong beats. She frequently uses a four-beat line followed by a three-beat line.

- Explain that some slant rhymes include similar vowel sounds but different consonant sounds (*moon/goose*). Others include similar consonant sounds but different vowel sounds (*blade/blood*).

- Remind students that figurative language is language that uses one or more figures of speech to make an imaginative comparison between two things that are unlike yet have something in common.

## READ WITH A PURPOSE

*Help students set a purpose for reading. Tell them to look for ways the two poems are similar.*

---

**TEXT ANALYSIS**

COMMON CORE
RL 4,
L 5

### Ⓐ DICKINSON'S STYLE

***Possible answer:*** *The "narrow Fellow" Dickinson describes is a snake. Capitalizing certain words is a way of emphasizing them.*

---

**TEXT ANALYSIS**

COMMON CORE
RL 4,
L 5

### Ⓑ *Model the Skill:* DICKINSON'S STYLE

Read aloud lines 9–16, pausing at each dash and emphasizing the rhythm of the stanza. Discuss with students how the dashes and capitalization help separate ideas in this stanza.

***Possible answer:*** *Examples of slant rhyme are found at the ends of lines 10 and 12 ("Corn"/"Noon") and lines 14 and 16 ("Sun"/"gone"). Distinctive features of Dickinson's style include the use of dashes at the ends of lines (as in line 2); figurative language (as in line 5); unconventional capitalization (as in line 1); and a hymnlike rhythm.*

---

## REVISIT THE BIG QUESTION
## What is a poet's **JOB**?

**Discuss** What insights has the speaker gained from experience with snakes, according to lines 5–24? ***Possible answer:*** *The speaker realizes that despite being familiar with "Several of Nature's People" (line 17), snakes inspire fear, possibly originating from the childhood experience described in lines 10–16.*

---

# A narrow
# Fellow IN THE Grass
### EMILY DICKINSON

A narrow Fellow in the Grass
Occasionally rides—
You may have met Him—did you not
His notice sudden is—

5  The Grass divides as with a Comb—
A spotted shaft is seen—
And then it closes at your feet
And opens further on— Ⓐ

He likes a Boggy Acre
10  A Floor too cool for Corn—
Yet when a Boy, and Barefoot—
I more than once at Noon
Have passed, I thought, a Whip lash
Unbraiding in the Sun
15  When stopping to secure it
It wrinkled, and was gone— Ⓑ

Several of Nature's People
I know, and they know me—
I feel for them a transport
20  Of cordiality—[1]

But never met this Fellow
Attended, or alone
Without a tighter breathing
And Zero at the Bone—

---

1. **a transport of cordiality:** a very strong feeling of warmth and friendliness.

---

**COMMON CORE L 4**

### Language Coach

**Multiple Meanings** As a verb, *notice* means "take note of." As a noun, it can mean "announcement or warning." Which meaning seems to fit best in line 4?

Ⓐ **DICKINSON'S STYLE** What is the "narrow Fellow" Dickinson describes? Explain why you think the poet chose to capitalize certain words in the first two stanzas.

Ⓑ **DICKINSON'S STYLE** Identify one example of **slant rhyme** in this stanza. What other distinctive features of Dickinson's style can you see in this poem? Support your answer with evidence.

---

## DIFFERENTIATED INSTRUCTION

### FOR ENGLISH LANGUAGE LEARNERS

**Language Coach**  COMMON CORE L 4

**Multiple Meanings** ***Possible answer:*** *A noun would fit best here; "warning" seems to make the most sense.* Ask students to find other words in the poem that have multiple meanings. ***Possible answers:*** *whip, lash, secure*

### FOR STRUGGLING READERS
**Develop Reading Fluency**

Read aloud "A narrow Fellow in the Grass" and discuss with students the sound of the poem. Point out that certain aspects of Dickinson's style, particularly the rhythm, rhyme, and pauses, create this sound. Encourage students to explore the sound of Dickinson's style by working in small groups to perform a choral reading of the poem.

# "Hope" is the thing with feathers—

### EMILY DICKINSON

"Hope" is the thing with feathers—
That perches in the soul—
And sings the tune without the words—
And never stops—at all— **C**

5 And sweetest—in the Gale—is heard—
And sore[1] must be the storm—
That could abash[2] the little Bird
That kept so many warm—

I've heard it in the chillest land—
10 And on the strangest Sea—
Yet, never, in Extremity,[3]
It asked a crumb—of Me. **D**

**C** DICKINSON'S STYLE
What **metaphor** does Dickinson present in the first stanza? Explain your answer.

**D** READING POETRY
Reread lines 11–12 aloud. What is the effect of Dickinson's unusual punctuation and capitalization in these lines?

---

1. **sore:** severe
2. **abash:** cause to be upset or embarrassed.
3. **Extremity:** greatest need or danger.

---

## FOR STRUGGLING READERS

**Syntax** Explain that poets often rearrange the usual order of words to achieve a certain effect. For example, in "A narrow Fellow in the Grass," line 4 reverses the usual word order: "His notice sudden is" instead of "His notice is sudden." This inversion places "is" at the end of the line, creating a slant rhyme with "rides" in line 2. Suggest that students rearrange such lines for comprehension but then reread the poem as it is written to appreciate the effects of the inverted syntax.

## FOR ADVANCED LEARNERS/PRE–AP

**Evaluate Dickinson's Style** [small-group option] Ask students to evaluate the unique stylistic elements that Dickinson employs in both poems. Students should first identify these stylistic elements and discuss their effects on reading and on comprehension. Then, have students critique the style, explaining their opinions of what does and does not enhance their reading experience and why.

---

Prereading for this poem is found on page 868.

## REVISIT THE BIG QUESTION
## What is a poet's JOB?

**Discuss** What insight does Dickinson communicate in lines 1–10? **Possible answer:** Hope can be found everywhere.

### TEXT ANALYSIS
### **C** DICKINSON'S STYLE

COMMON CORE
RL 4, L 5

**Possible answer:** The metaphor is "'Hope' is the thing with feathers" (line 1). The metaphor compares hope with a bird and is extended throughout the stanza with such words as "perches" (line 2) and "sings the tune" (line 3).

### READING STRATEGY
### **D** Model the Skill: READING POETRY

COMMON CORE
RL 10

Point out line 4 and tell students that the dash before "at all" adds emphasis to the idea of the bird's tune never stopping by breaking the rhythm of the line.

**Possible answer:** The effect of Dickinson's unusual punctuation and capitalization is to establish breaks or pauses and to emphasize certain words or ideas. For example, capitalizing "Extremity" draws attention to the word, and placing a dash before "of Me" adds emphasis to the idea by breaking the rhythm of the final line.

## SELECTION WRAP–UP

**READ WITH A PURPOSE** Now that students have finished reading the selection, ask them to identify similarities between the two poems. **Possible answer:** Both poems use figurative language, slant rhymes, a regular rhythm, unconventional capitalization, and dashes.

⭐ **CRITIQUE** Have students discuss which element of Dickinson's style they found most interesting or effective, and why.

## INDEPENDENT READING

For students interested in learning more about Emily Dickinson, recommend *The Life of Emily Dickinson* by Richard B. Sewall.

**JOURNAL ARTICLE** Intrigued by the mysterious Ms. Dickinson? Read on to learn why some scholars think the poet was anything but solitary.

## TIERED DISCUSSION PROMPTS

Use these prompts to help students make connections between Emily Dickinson's life and her poetry:

**Connect** Recall a time in your life when you felt that someone had the wrong idea about you. How did the experience make you feel? *Students might say that they felt frustrated or embarrassed.*

**Analyze** What details did the writer include to provide a wider perspective on Dickinson's personality? *Possible answer: Details include her extensive correspondence, her popularity at parties, her visitors (including her mentor Higginson), her large library, and her busy work routine.*

**Synthesize** What kind of person do you think Emily Dickinson was? Based on the insights expressed in the two poems as well as the article you have just read, how would you answer the question presented in the article's final paragraph? Explain your interpretation. *Possible answer: Based on these two poems, Dickinson seems more of a fulfilled, although solitary, soul than a shy, troubled woman. This interpretation is supported by the playfulness of the first poem and the positive message of hope presented in the second poem.*

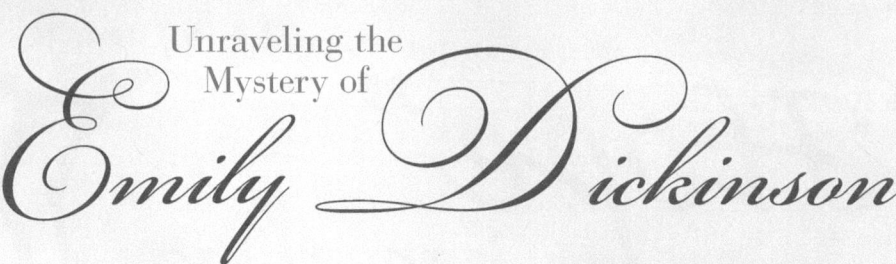

Unraveling the Mystery of **Emily Dickinson**

> "I'm Nobody! Who are you?
> Are you—Nobody—too?"

These lines come from one of Emily Dickinson's famous poems. Imagine that a friend sent those words to you. Would you think your friend was feeling witty? contemplative? sad? Like the faceless e-mail and text messages sent between friends today, Dickinson's letters and poetry could be interpreted numerous ways by her friends. Scholars still debate Dickinson's mysterious words and life.

Many theories exist about her reasons for withdrawing from the world and her seclusion at the family home for the last 20 years of her life. Some say that it was an opportunity to concentrate her energies on her writing. Others believe it was a case of agoraphobia (fear of crowds). No one can prove which, if any, is correct, but the best available evidence is found in her correspondence. Some people even believe her letters indicate her life was far from antisocial. They suggest that it was her editors, who hoped to persuade the public that Dickinson was an upstanding single lady in accordance with her time, who perpetuated the notion of Dickinson as a recluse.

The sheer volume of her writing indicates she often wrote a few letters or poems each day, keeping in frequent touch with family and friends. Scholars also note the Dickinson house was an active gathering place, so Dickinson did not have to leave to socialize. Her best friend, Susan, lived next door for 30 years. Famous writers of Dickinson's time came to visit, as did some of her mentors. In addition, the household library contained nearly 1,000 books, and the grounds offered gardens and woods—some of her favorite spots to spend time when she wasn't helping with the household, working on her writing, or caring for her brother's children.

Although popularly characterized as a shy adult, as a child Dickinson was known for her sense of humor. An account of her meeting with literary critic Thomas Wentworth Higginson in 1870 shows her to be a talkative woman— Higginson found her draining. Of course, it could be that she was simply so excited to finally meet the famous mentor she had corresponded with for eight years. One friend commented that Dickinson was so surrounded by friends at a party that she couldn't even talk to her.

Despite their long correspondence—over 20 years—Higginson didn't know what to make of the mysterious poet. "She was much too enigmatical a being for me to solve in an hour's interview," he wrote in an article for the *Atlantic* after her death.

Was Emily Dickinson a shy, troubled woman; a fulfilled, solitary soul; or someone in between? Study her writing closely, and perhaps you will discover a clue.

## Comprehension

1. **Recall** What are two places where the "narrow Fellow" can be found?

2. **Recall** List three ways Dickinson compares hope to a bird.

## Text Analysis

3. **Interpret Theme in Poetry** In one or two sentences, state the theme of each poem. Then explain which poem you think offers a more interesting or perceptive insight.

4. **Analyze Mood** Reread lines 17–24 of "A narrow Fellow in the Grass." How does the mood of the fourth stanza differ from that of the fifth? Explain which words or phrases contribute to the change in mood.

5. **Identify Symbol** A symbol is something that stands for more than itself. In "'Hope' is the thing with feathers—" what do "the Gale," "the chillest land," and "the strangest Sea" represent? Cite evidence to support your answer.

6. **Analyze Extended Metaphor** An extended metaphor compares two things at some length and in several ways. In "'Hope' is the thing with feathers—" Dickinson compares hope to a bird. How does she develop this metaphor throughout the poem? Use a graphic like the one shown to help organize your evidence.

> Hope is a bird.
>
> stanza 1:
>
> stanza 2:
>
> stanza 3:

● 7. **Examine Emily Dickinson's Style** Review the bulleted list of Dickinson's stylistic hallmarks on page 869. Pick two elements of the poet's style and find examples of them in "A narrow Fellow in the Grass" and "'Hope' is the thing with feathers—." Then explain the effect created by each example.

## Text Criticism

● 8. **Author's Style** Dickinson's first volume of poetry, and each collection after that until 1955, consisted of "corrected" versions of her poems. In other words, editors "fixed" Dickinson's punctuation and capitalization. Acting as a 19th-century editor, rewrite one of Dickinson's poems using standard punctuation and capitalization. Read your finished product. Is there something missing? Do you prefer the poem Dickinson's way? Explain your answer.

### What is a poet's JOB?

How can you tell when a poet has done his or her job well?

**COMMON CORE**

**RL 4** Determine the figurative meaning of words and phrases. **RL 10** Read and comprehend poems. **L 5** Demonstrate understanding of figurative language.

---

# Practice and Apply

For preliminary support of post-reading questions, use these copy masters:

**R** RESOURCE MANAGER—Copy Masters
Dickinson's Style p. 109
Question Support p. 113

Additional selection questions are provided for teachers on page 105.

## ANSWERS

## Comprehension

1. *The "narrow Fellow" can be found in a "Boggy Acre" or "A Floor too cool for Corn."*

2. *Like a bird, hope has "feathers," it "perches," and it "sings" sweetly.*

## Text Analysis

COMMON CORE **RL 4, RL 10, L 5**

*Possible answers:*

3. *"A narrow Fellow . . .": Nature can be both familiar and fascinating, but it may scare us. "'Hope' . . . ": Like a bird that sings through the harshest weather, hope is always there and asks nothing of us in return. Students should support their choices for the more insightful poem.*

4. *The mood of the fourth stanza is light, but in the fifth stanza, the mood turns anxious as the speaker describes her fear. The phrases "tighter breathing" and "Zero at the Bone" contribute to that change.*

5. *They represent difficult times in one's life. The song is "sweetest" when heard in a "Gale" (line 5), suggesting that hope is most appreciated during difficult times.*

6. *Stanza 1: Hope is called "the thing with feathers" that "perches," or rests, in the soul. Stanza 2: The speaker likens the sound*

---

of birdsong during a storm to the hope that one feels during a difficult time in life. *Stanza 3:* The speaker explains that wherever she goes, the singing of birds is still present.

7. ● **COMMON CORE FOCUS** *Dickinson's Style* The poet uses unusual capitalization that emphasizes key words ("Fellow," "Zero," "Me"); dashes that break up the rhythm; slant rhymes that create an off-kilter sound unity ("soul"/"all"); and figurative language that presents imaginative comparisons ("Zero at the Bone").

## Text Criticism

8. ● **COMMON CORE FOCUS** *Author's Style* Students might say that the "edited" version lacks the unique appeal of Dickinson's work.

### What is a poet's JOB? *Answers will vary, but students should support their answers with examples from the poems.*

---

# Assess and Reteach

## Assess

**DIAGNOSTIC AND SELECTION TESTS**
Selection Test A, B/C pp. 235–236, 237–238

**Interactive Selection Test** on **thinkcentral.com**

## Reteach

**Level Up Online Tutorials** on **thinkcentral.com**

**Reteaching Worksheets** on **thinkcentral.com**
Literature Lesson 46: Style and Syntax
Reading Lesson 2: Monitoring

# Focus and Motivate

## COMMON CORE FOCUS

**RL 2** Determine a theme of a text and analyze its development, including how it emerges and is shaped. **RL 4** Analyze the impact of specific word choices on meaning and tone.

### SUMMARIES

In "Luxury," Giovanni considers the luxury of material wealth and technological advances and concludes that the ultimate luxury is the love of another person. Giovanni expresses her desire to capture her beloved in poetry, as she playfully manages to do just that in "Kidnap Poem."

## What would win your **HEART?**

Introduce the question, and have students read the first paragraph. Then discuss whether love poems are preferable to the other suggestions for the purpose of winning students' hearts. Extend the discussion by having students complete the *QUICKWRITE* activity. Discuss how students' responses could be written as love poems.

## Selection Resources

---

## Luxury

## Kidnap Poem
Poems by Nikki Giovanni

# What would win your **HEART?**

**COMMON CORE**

**RL 2** Determine a theme of a text and analyze its development, including how it emerges and is shaped. **RL 4** Analyze the impact of specific word choices on meaning and tone.

What would it take to win you over? Candy and flowers? A pretty face? A sense of humor? What about love poems—could they ever help someone win your heart? The following poems are so passionate that if you answered no, you might change your mind after reading them.

*QUICKWRITE* What is the one thing someone could do to make you totally fall for him or her? In a paragraph, describe the act or gesture—be it grand and thrilling or small and ordinary—that would win your heart.

874

---

*See resources on the* **Teacher One Stop DVD-ROM** *and on* <u>thinkcentral.com</u>.

 **RESOURCE MANAGER UNIT 8**
   Plan and Teach, pp. 115–122
   Text Analysis and Reading
      Skill, pp. 123–126†*

**DIAGNOSTIC AND SELECTION
   TESTS**
   Selection Tests, pp. 239–242

**BEST PRACTICES TOOLKIT**
   Cluster Diagram, p. B18

**TECHNOLOGY**
   🔘 **Teacher One Stop DVD-ROM**
   🔘 **Student One Stop DVD-ROM**
   🔘 **Audio Anthology CD**
   🔘 **GrammarNotes DVD-ROM**
   🔘 **ExamView Test Generator**
      on the **Teacher One Stop**

---

\* Resources for Differentiation      † Also in Spanish      ‡ In Haitian Creole and Vietnamese

## TEXT ANALYSIS: GIOVANNI'S STYLE

Nikki Giovanni is a poet who goes by her own rules. "I want my writing to sound like I talk," she says. To that end, Giovanni employs a conversational style that breaks with convention. Most of her work consists of lyric poetry written in **free verse,** which lacks a regular rhyme and meter and often sounds like natural speech. Giovanni's unique style also includes

- a deliberate lack of punctuation and capitalization
- stanzas and lines of varying length
- simple language and clear metaphors
- the use of sound devices such as **alliteration** and **repetition** to create a distinct rhythm

As you read, look for evidence of these techniques, and think about how Giovanni's diction and style help her communicate her message.

## READING SKILL: INTERPRET IDEAS IN POETRY

The key to understanding and interpreting poetry is often digesting little chunks at a time. Working through a poem slowly can help you identify its **theme,** or underlying message about life or human nature. As you read "Luxury" and "Kidnap Poem," write down interesting stanzas and unusual phrases. Then record what you think each means. Finally, use the meanings you have identified to help you determine each poem's theme.

| Phrase or Stanza | Meaning |
|---|---|
| i suppose living in a materialistic society luxury to some would be having more than what you need ("Luxury," lines 1–5) | People in money-centered societies think excess equals luxury. |

 Complete the activities in your **Reader/Writer Notebook.**

---

## Meet the Author

# Nikki Giovanni
### born 1943

**Family Ties**
Yolande Cornelia Giovanni Jr. was nicknamed Nikki by her older sister. Giovanni's close-knit family moved from Tennessee to Ohio just after she was born, but they often returned to visit her dynamic, outspoken grandmother, who was a huge influence on the poet. Giovanni says her grandmother, a great storyteller, was also "the only person I know for sure whose love I did not have to earn."

**Young and Driven**
Giovanni always suspected she'd be famous one day. Her drive led her to Fisk University, but her independent spirit got her kicked out after just one semester. Giovanni eventually returned to Fisk, where she became active in the civil rights movement. A year after graduating with honors, Giovanni published *Black Feeling, Black Talk,* her first book of poetry. The book was inspired both by the death of her grandmother and by the poet's increasing outrage at the way African Americans were treated in the United States. Giovanni was determined to change society through her poetry. Writing, according to Giovanni, is the easy part. "Then," she says, "comes the hard part: you have to find someone to read it."

**The Journey**
Much of Giovanni's early work consisted of militant calls to action and angry demands for racial equality. While she hasn't lost her political edge, Giovanni's later poetry also explores more personal territory, delving into family, love, and loneliness. Giovanni battled cancer in the 1990s, but after successful surgery, she resumed her work. Writing poetry, Giovanni says, "is a journey without end."

**Author Online**
THINK central
Go to **thinkcentral.com.**
KEYWORD: HML9-875

875

---

## DIFFERENTIATED INSTRUCTION

### FOR STRUGGLING READERS
Review with students that a metaphor is a figure of speech that compares two dissimilar things without using *like* or *as.* Write these examples on the board:

- the curtain of night
- a blanket of love
- kidnap your heart

Discuss the meaning of each metaphor. Make sure students understand the two things that are being compared.

### FOR ADVANCED LEARNERS/PRE–AP
**Analyze a Quotation** Tell students that Nikki Giovanni has called love "the only true adventure." Have students write a brief essay analyzing Giovanni's view of love and explain whether they agree or disagree with her statement. Have students share their essays with a partner.

---

**TEXT ANALYSIS**  COMMON CORE
RL 4

## ● Model the Skill: GIOVANNI'S STYLE

To illustrate Giovanni's style, write these lines from "Luxury" on the board:

> i have thought if only
> i could become rich and famous
>   i would
> live luxuriously in new york

Tell students that one aspect of the poet's style, present in the example, is the lack of capitalization and punctuation. Have them point to other aspects of Giovanni's style, as shown in the example. ***Possible answer:*** *lines of varying length; simple language; alliteration and repetition ("live luxuriously," the repetition of "i" throughout the stanza)*

**GUIDED PRACTICE** Ask students how elements of Giovanni's style help create the sound of natural speech. RL 1

---

**READING SKILL**  COMMON CORE
RL 2

## ■ Model the Skill: INTERPRET IDEAS IN POETRY

Point out that, particularly in free verse, poets pay close attention to where they break their lines, since they do not have to follow a meter or rhyme scheme. Line breaks create chunks of meaning by setting off key words or phrases. Point out to students the varying line lengths in the example. Then, ask them how the line lengths help convey meaning. ***Possible answer:*** *The varying line lengths convey a sense of incompleteness, as if the speaker can only experience fulfillment in something yet to occur in her life.*

**GUIDED PRACTICE** Ask students how the poem's underlying message would be different if Giovanni divided her lines into complete sentences.

**R RESOURCE MANAGER—Copy Master** Interpret Ideas in Poetry p. 125 (for student use while reading the selections)

## READ WITH A PURPOSE

*Help students set a purpose for reading. Tell them to compare and contrast the messages of the two poems about love.*

**TEXT ANALYSIS**

COMMON CORE
RL 4

### Ⓐ *Model the Skill:* GIOVANNI'S STYLE

Point out the first line and note that *i* is not capitalized.

*Possible answer:* Elements of Giovanni's style include the lack of punctuation and capitalization; lines and stanzas of varying lengths (lines 1–14); informal language ("nth degree," line 9); and repetition ("living" in lines 1 and 6, "having" in lines 4 and 12).

**IF STUDENTS NEED HELP . . .** Have them reread page 875 and see which stylistic elements they can find in the first two stanzas.

**READING SKILL**

COMMON CORE
RL 2

### Ⓑ *Model the Skill:* INTERPRET IDEAS IN POETRY

Tell students that the first and second stanzas espouse the idea that one form of luxury is materialistic wealth. Tell students to keep this in mind as they read the last two stanzas. Remind students to use their Reading Skill charts.

*Possible answer:* The idea here is similar to that in previous stanzas: what is luxury? But the idea of luxury to the poet now is not about material things, but rather, love.

# Luxury

### Nikki Giovanni

> i suppose living
> in a materialistic society
> luxury
> to some would be having
> 5  more than what you need
>
> living in an electronic age seeing
> the whole world by
>     pushing a button
> the *nth* degree[1] might
> 10     perhaps be
> adequately represented
>     by having
> someone there to push
> the buttons for you Ⓐ
>
> 15 i have thought if only
> i could become rich and famous
>     i would
> live luxuriously in new york
>     knowing
> 20 famous people eating
> in expensive restaurants calling
> long distance anytime i want
>
> but you held me
> one evening and now i know
> 25 the ultimate luxury
> of your love Ⓑ

---

1. **the *nth* degree:** the ultimate degree of something; as much or as far as possible.

**Analyze Visuals ▶**

Does this painting seem **luxurious** to you? Consider its colors, shapes, and textures, as well as the figures it depicts. Explain your opinion, citing details.

**Ⓐ GIOVANNI'S STYLE**
What elements of Giovanni's distinctive style are apparent so far in this poem? Explain your answer, referring to specific lines for evidence.

**Ⓑ INTERPRET IDEAS IN POETRY**
Reread lines 23–26. How does the idea expressed in this stanza compare with the ideas in previous stanzas of the poem?

*Tumbling Flowers* (1954), Hyacinth Manning-Carner. © Hyacinth Manning-Carner/SuperStock.

## DIFFERENTIATED INSTRUCTION

### FOR ENGLISH LANGUAGE LEARNERS

**Language: Punctuation and Print Cues**  The lack of punctuation and capitalization in this poem may confuse English learners. Read through each stanza with students, pointing out missing punctuation and capital letters. After reviewing the poem, have students paraphrase each stanza, using conventional punctuation and capitalization.

### FOR STRUGGLING READERS

**Options for Reading**  Read the poem aloud for enjoyment and to capture its style. Tell students to listen for the poem's simple, conversational language.

Use these prompts to explore the contrast that the speaker sets up in lines 1–14 between conventional ideas of luxury and her own interpretation:

**Connect** What is your definition of *luxury*? Give some examples of specific things that you consider luxuries. *Students may define luxury as something expensive and perhaps unnecessary. They may mention the latest technological equipment, expensive cars or SUVs, trendy clothing, and fancy jewelry.*

**Evaluate** Do you think that the speaker has a valid insight about our technology-driven society, or is she off the mark? Explain. *Students who feel that she is off the mark may cite the popularity of interactive video games as evidence that people still want to "push the buttons." Other students may feel that she is using exaggeration to make a valid point.*

## Analyze Visuals

*Possible answer: Yes; the painting is luxurious. The figures look as if they are resting in each other's arms. They seem to glow, like a couple in love. The golden arch that surrounds them; the flowers that cascade around them; and the rich, jewel-toned colors and patterns of their clothing all create a sense of luxury.*

**About the Art** In *Tumbling Flowers* and *Sleeping Couple I* (page 878), Hyacinth Manning-Carner uses lush, sunny colors and ethnic patterns that reflect her culture.

**REVISIT THE BIG QUESTION**

## What would win your **HEART?**

**Discuss** How can love be considered the "ultimate luxury"? Do you agree with the idea expressed in lines 23–26 of this love poem? Why, or why not? *Possible answer: Love is more valuable than any material possession, so it is the "ultimate luxury" in the sense that it is the most valuable thing in the world. Students who disagree with this idea may say that love is not a luxury because it is a necessity—something people can't live without.*

**FOR STRUGGLING READERS**

**Develop Reading Fluency**

Read "Luxury" aloud and discuss with students the rhythm and pauses that affect its reading. Have students work in pairs to perform a choral reading of the poem.

**R** RESOURCE MANAGER—Copy Master
Reading Fluency p. 128

**FOR ADVANCED LEARNERS/PRE–AP**

**Writing Poetry** Encourage students to write a poem using Giovanni's conversational, free verse style, on any emotion they are comfortable exploring. After students have written their poems, discuss the ways in which free verse affected how they were able to express their ideas. How would their poems have been different in content or tone if they had used a more structured style? Ask volunteers to read their poems to the class.

Prereading for this poem is found on page 874.

## Analyze Visuals

**Activity** In what ways does this painting reflect the imagery and theme of the poem? *Possible answer: The speaker says that she wants to wrap her beloved in colors (line 16), and in the painting, the two figures are wrapped in a colorful blanket. Their physical closeness suggests a loving relationship that matches the theme of love in the poem.*

---

TEXT ANALYSIS  COMMON CORE RL 4

###  GIOVANNI'S STYLE

*Possible answer: The short phrases help create a driving rhythm, which adds to the intensity of the feelings the speaker expresses.*

**IF STUDENTS NEED HELP . . .** Have them read the poem aloud with a partner, listening for its rhythm, and then discuss how the poem's rhythm supports the speaker's feelings about her subject.

---

## SELECTION WRAP–UP

**READ WITH A PURPOSE** Now that students have finished reading the selection, ask them to compare and contrast the message about love in the two poems. *Possible answer: In the first poem, love is a kind of sanctuary from the world, while in the second it is a part of everything the poet thinks is fun and lively.*

⭐ **CRITIQUE** Have students evaluate each poem by rating it from 1 (did not like) to 5 (liked a lot). Then ask them to support their evaluations.

## INDEPENDENT READING

For students interested in reading more poetry about love, suggest *Great Love Poems*, a treasury of English and American classic love poems edited by Shane Weller.

---

# Kidnap POEM

## Nikki Giovanni

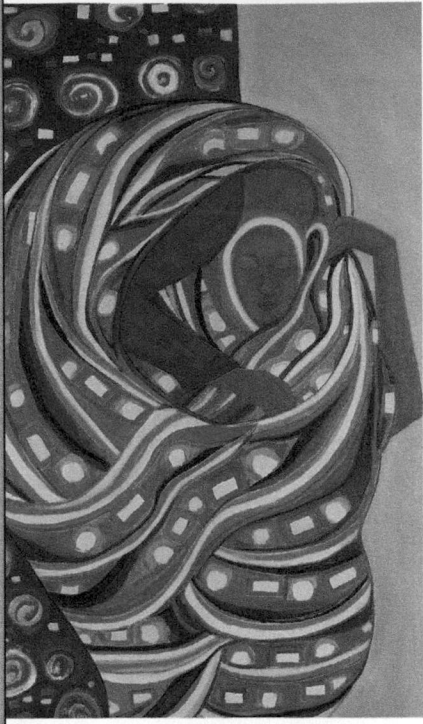

*Sleeping Couple I* (2000), Hyacinth Manning-Carner.
© Hyacinth Manning-Carner/SuperStock.

ever been kidnapped
by a poet
if i were a poet
i'd kidnap you
5　put you in my phrases and meter
you to jones beach
or maybe coney island[1]
or maybe just to my house
lyric you in lilacs
10　dash you in the rain
blend into the beach
to complement my see[2]
play the lyre[3] for you
ode you with my love song
15　anything to win you
wrap you in the red Black green
show you off to mama
yeah if i were a poet i'd kid
nap you

---

1. **jones beach . . . coney island:** beach and amusement areas on the outskirts of New York City.
2. **complement my see:** complete or perfect my kingdom.
3. **lyre** (līr): stringed instrument like a small, U-shaped harp.

---

COMMON CORE RL 4

### Language Coach

**Informal Language** This kind of language is more free with grammar and punctuation rules than formal language is. How could you ask the question in lines 1–2 in a more formal way?

###  GIOVANNI'S STYLE

Read lines 9–12 aloud. Describe the **rhythm** created by Giovanni's use of short phrases like "lyric you in lilacs" and "dash you in the rain." How does the **rhythm** help communicate her ideas in this poem?

---

## DIFFERENTIATED INSTRUCTION

### FOR ENGLISH LANGUAGE LEARNERS

### Language Coach
COMMON CORE RL 4

**Informal Language** *Answer: Have you ever been kidnapped by a poet?* Have students find other informal phrases and sentences and restate them more formally. *Possible answers: (line 5) I'd put you in my phrases; (line 15) I'd do anything to win you.*

### FOR STRUGGLING READERS

**Comprehension Support** Reread the poem with students and help them complete a Cluster Diagram showing the ways the speaker plans to express her love.

 **BEST PRACTICES TOOLKIT—Transparency** Cluster Diagram p. B18

## Comprehension

1. **Recall** What is the "ultimate luxury" described toward the end of the first poem?

2. **Recall** List three things the speaker of "Kidnap Poem" says she would do if she were a poet.

## Text Analysis

● 3. **Interpret Ideas in Poetry** Review the chart you filled in as you read. Using the interpretations you recorded, summarize the main message, or **theme,** of each poem.

4. **Analyze Voice** Voice refers to a writer's unique use of language that allows you to "hear" a personality in his or her writing. How would you characterize the voice of the speaker in "Luxury"? Consider the point of view from which the poem is told and the language it uses, as well as the poem's rhythm and message.

5. **Analyze Word Choice** Reread lines 5–14 of "Kidnap Poem." Consider Giovanni's unconventional use of words like *meter, lyric,* and *ode.* How does Giovanni's unusual word usage help her communicate her message about the power of poetry? Support your answer with evidence from the poem.

● 6. **Examine Giovanni's Style** Think about the poet's description of her own writing on page 875, and review the bulleted list of Giovanni's trademarks. Which stylistic elements help create Giovanni's loose, conversational style in "Kidnap Poem"? Explain your answer, citing evidence.

7. **Compare and Contrast** In terms of **style,** how are "Luxury" and "Kidnap Poem" similar? In what ways do they differ? Think about the form and rhythm of each poem, as well as the language Giovanni uses in each. Cite specific examples from both poems to support your comparison.

## Text Criticism

8. **Critical Interpretations** Rapper, singer, and actress Queen Latifah discovered Giovanni's poetry at age 14. "Nikki's poems struck me," Latifah explains. "I could feel her. I liked how some of the things she wrote were so clever and cool. I liked how she threw a little bit of rhythm around. All her poetry seemed to be real and to have love in it." After reading "Luxury" and "Kidnap Poem," do you agree or disagree with this description? Explain, citing evidence from both poems.

### What would win your HEART?

Are you easily won over?

---

**COMMON CORE**

**RL 2** Determine a theme of a text and analyze its development, including how it emerges and is shaped. **RL 4** Analyze the impact of specific word choices on meaning and tone.

---

# Practice and Apply

For preliminary support of post-reading questions, use these copy masters:

**R** RESOURCE MANAGER—Copy Masters
Giovanni's Style p. 123
Question Support p. 127

Additional selection questions are provided for teachers on page 119.

## ANSWERS

## Comprehension

1. *love*

2. *Possible answer:* "kidnap you," "lyric you in lilacs," "dash you in the rain"

## Text Analysis

COMMON CORE **RL 2, RL 4**

*Possible answers:*

3. ● **COMMON CORE FOCUS** *Interpret Ideas in Poetry "Luxury":* Love, not material wealth, is what makes our lives rich. *"Kidnap Poem":* Love can make us want to do extraordinary things for the one we love; poetry, like love, has the power to sweep us off our feet.

4. *Her voice is intense, wise, and street-smart.*

5. *By using nouns as verbs (meter, lyric, and ode), Giovanni makes poetry seem powerful and surprising. By using them in the context of wooing someone, she also makes these academic poetic terms—and thus poetry itself—seem passionate and enticing.*

6. ● **COMMON CORE FOCUS** *Giovanni's Style* Students should cite examples of simple language and irregular line lengths that create a loose, fluid, conversational style.

---

7. *Both poems lack capitalization and punctuation and contain simple language and lines of varying length. However, "Luxury" has four stanzas, while "Kidnap Poem" is one long stanza. "Kidnap Poem" also uses more unusual diction (nouns as verbs) than "Luxury." Students should find examples of each style similarity and difference.*

*Giovanni "thr[ows] a little bit of rhythm around." They may say that Giovanni's simple, everyday language makes her poems sound "real," and they may point out that both poems are about love.*

### What would win your HEART?
*Answers will vary, but students should support their answers with reasons.*

## Text Criticism

8. *Answers will vary. Students may cite the driving rhythm of "Kidnap Poem" to support Queen Latifah's assertion that*

---

# Assess and Reteach

## Assess

**DIAGNOSTIC AND SELECTION TESTS**
Selection Test A pp. 239–240
Selection Test B/C pp. 241–242

**Interactive Selection Test** on **thinkcentral.com**

## Reteach

**Level Up Online Tutorials** on **thinkcentral.com**

**Reteaching Worksheets** on **thinkcentral.com**
Literature Lesson 46: Style and Syntax

Reading Lesson 2: Monitoring

Reading Lesson 8: Making Inferences

# Focus and Motivate

## COMMON CORE FOCUS

**RL 10** Read and comprehend dramas.

### SUMMARY

In "The Sneeze," Cherdyakov, a clerk in the Ministry of Public Parks, is seated at a play behind the head of the Ministry, General Brassilhov. Because the clerk wants to impress his boss, he is mortified when he sneezes on him. Cherdyakov apologizes profusely, but he cannot forget the incident. Twice he visits the General to apologize, only irritating him. When Cherdyakov sneezes on his boss again, the General hurls abuse at him. A devastated Cherdyakov returns home and dies.

## Who makes you LAUGH?

Introduce the question, and have students read the introductory paragraph. Then discuss the various ways—sight gags, word plays, silly voices—in which people make us laugh. Continue the exploration by having students complete the *QUICKWRITE* activity and compare their lists.

# Selection Resources

---

**Essential Course of Study** ECOS

# The Sneeze
Drama by Neil Simon
Based on a story by Anton Chekhov

**VIDEO TRAILER** THINK central  KEYWORD: HML9-880

# Who makes you LAUGH?

**COMMON CORE**

**RL 10** Read and comprehend dramas.

Whether it's your best friend or a professional comedian, who makes you laugh—*really* laugh? What does this person do that you find so funny? If you get a kick out of ridiculous characters bumbling into trouble because of their out-of-control bodily functions, you'll love "The Sneeze."

*QUICKWRITE* Think about the last time you succumbed to helpless laughter—the kind that makes you gasp for breath and clutch your stomach. What set you off? Create your own top-ten list describing the things and the people you find funniest.

880

---

See resources on the **Teacher One Stop DVD-ROM** and on **thinkcentral.com**.

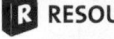 **RESOURCE MANAGER UNIT 8**
  Plan and Teach, pp. 129–136
  Summary pp. 137–138†‡*
  Text Analysis and Reading
   Skill, pp. 139–142†*

**DIAGNOSTIC AND SELECTION TESTS**
  Selection Tests, pp. 243–246

 **BEST PRACTICES TOOLKIT**
  Word Questioning, p. E9
  Jigsaw Reading, p. A1
  T Chart, p. A25

**INTERACTIVE READER**

**ADAPTED INTERACTIVE READER**

**ELL ADAPTED INTERACTIVE READER**

**TECHNOLOGY**

- **Teacher One Stop DVD-ROM**
- **Student One Stop DVD-ROM**
- **PowerNotes DVD-ROM**
- **Audio Anthology CD**
- **GrammarNotes DVD-ROM**
- **Audio Tutor CD**
- **ExamView Test Generator** on the **Teacher One Stop**

### Video Trailer
 THINK central

Go to **thinkcentral.com** to preview the **Video Trailer** introducing this selection. Other features that support the selection include

- **PowerNotes** presentation
- **ThinkAloud** models to enhance comprehension
- **WordSharp** vocabulary tutorials
- interactive writing and grammar instruction

---

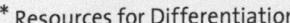 * Resources for Differentiation   † Also in Spanish   ‡ In Haitian Creole and Vietnamese

## TEXT ANALYSIS: FARCE

A **farce** is a humorous play that prompts laughter by presenting ridiculous situations, comic dialogue, and physical humor—in this case, an enormous sneeze. Often, the purpose of a farce is simply to keep the audience laughing. However, sometimes the writer of a farce has the goal of poking fun at someone or something in particular. To spot a farce, look for

- absurd plots driven by humorous conflicts
- exaggerated behavior and language
- characters who often exhibit just one comic trait or quality
- clever wordplay, word choices that include puns and double meanings
- physical comedy

As you read "The Sneeze," think about how it exhibits these conventions. Note situations or characters that you find especially funny.

## READING STRATEGY: VISUALIZE

When you **visualize,** you use details, description, and dialogue to create mental images of what you read. Visualizing this play can help you monitor your understanding of it and enjoy its humor. Try the following:

- Read the stage directions to get a mental picture of the setting and actions taking place.
- Pay attention to the narrator's description of the other characters. Do you get an image of how they might look and behave?
- To help you picture the characters, try mentally casting your favorite comedic actor in the lead role.
- Use your own imagination and sense of humor.

As you read, keep track of the details that help you visualize different aspects of the play.

| Details from the Text | My Visualization |
|---|---|
| "He is in his mid-thirties, mild-mannered and unassuming." (lines 4–5) | I picture a timid-looking, boring man with a pale, slightly anxious face. |

 Complete the activities in your **Reader/Writer Notebook.**

## Neil Simon
**born 1927**

**Popular Playwright**
Neil Simon, one of America's most popular dramatists, was born on the 4th of July in New York City. He began writing comedy sketches for radio during the 1940s, then migrated to television and finally to the theater. Most of Simon's plays are set in his hometown of New York City and deal with the domestic problems of middle-class Americans.

## Anton Chekhov
**1860–1904**

**Russian Master**
One of his country's greatest authors, Anton Chekhov was born to a poor family in Russia. He enrolled in medical school as a young man, but his family needed his financial support, so he began writing comical sketches and selling them to magazines. Writing, not medicine, became his career. Chekhov wrote short stories and one-act farces before turning to the full-length plays that made him a legend.

### BACKGROUND TO THE DRAMA
**A Team . . . Sort of**
Neil Simon's *The Good Doctor* is a series of dramatic sketches based on Chekhov's stories. The sketches are tied together through the character of the Writer, who reveals his ideas for stories to the audience. "The Sneeze" is one of those sketches. Simon has jokingly referred to Chekhov as "my non-consenting collaborator."

 **Authors Online**
Go to thinkcentral.com. KEYWORD: HML9-881

**881**

TEXT ANALYSIS **COMMON CORE** RL 10

● *Model the Skill:* **FARCE**

Tell students you are going to read aloud a short episode of farce, which features the element of physical comedy, an important element of farce.

> Carlton stepped up to the next rung on the ladder, carefully holding the paint can so as not to spill a drop.
>
> "Why can't we hire a professional?" his wife called from inside the house.
>
> "Stop worrying. I know what I'm do—." Just then, he slipped down three rungs and dumped blue paint all over himself.

Now have students describe the physical comedy, as well as other elements of farce in the episode. *Possible answer: The main farcical element is physical comedy—the husband falling off the ladder and spilling paint all over himself. The husband also seems to be a comic character who exhibits overconfidence despite his own incompetence.*

**GUIDED PRACTICE** Elicit other examples of farcical humor from stories, movies, and television shows.

READING STRATEGY **COMMON CORE** RL 10

■ *Model the Skill:* **VISUALIZE**

To support instruction, read aloud this sentence:

> Melinda was about 20, with curly hair and inquiring eyes.

Then, ask students either to draw a sketch or to write a description of Melinda. Compare and discuss students' visualizations of Melinda.

**GUIDED PRACTICE** Ask students to explain what clues help them visualize characters in works of fiction.

 **RESOURCE MANAGER—Copy Master**
Visualize p. 141 (for student use while reading the selection)

## DIFFERENTIATED INSTRUCTION

### FOR STRUGGLING READERS
**Concept Support** After students have read the instruction about visualizing, stress that the strategy relies on information gathered by all the senses, not just the sense of sight. For example, the description of Cherdyakov as "mild-mannered and unassuming" (line 5) could suggest that he speaks softly, a trait perceived by the sense of hearing. Urge students to use all their senses in visualizing.

**Concept Support** Clarify the meaning of these terms related to farce:
- *exaggerated:* overdone or overstated, beyond what is believable
- *puns:* plays on words based on different meanings of the same word or two different words that sound alike
- *physical humor* or *physical comedy:* humor that depends on physical actions, such as when a character slips on a banana peel or is hit in the face with a pie

### READ WITH A PURPOSE

*Help students set a purpose for reading. Tell them to determine which character, Cherdyakov or the General, they have more sympathy for.*

READING STRATEGY

COMMON CORE RL 10

### ■ *Model the Skill:* VISUALIZE

Point out lines 1–32. Tell students that unlike many plays, "The Sneeze" has no introductory description of characters or setting. Then, explain that one way Simon helps readers visualize the characters is by using the Writer as a narrator. Refer students to lines 1–3 as an example. Ask them to find other examples of Simon helping the reader visualize other characters, along with the setting and the actions, in lines 1–32. Tell students to add these details to their Reading Skill charts. **Possible answer:** *Simon's Writer acts as a narrator. In lines 1–3, 12–18, and 20–23, the Writer introduces Cherdyakov and the General and describes the setting— "the very best section of the theater for the opening night performance" (lines 16–17). In addition, Simon uses stage directions to describe Cherdyakov, the setting, and the actions of the characters, as in lines 3–12, 18–20, 24–26, and 31–32.*

# THE SNEEZE

NEIL SIMON

**FROM *THE GOOD DOCTOR***

**BASED ON A STORY BY ANTON CHEKHOV**

**Writer.** If Ivan Ilyitch Cherdyakov,[1] a civil servant, a clerk in the Ministry of Public Parks, had any passion in life at all, it was the theater. (*Enter* Ivan Cherdyakov *and his* Wife. *He is in his mid-thirties, mild-mannered and unassuming. He and his* Wife *are dressed in their best, but are certainly no match for the grandeur around them. They are clearly out of their element here. They move into their seats.*
10 *As his* Wife *peruses her program,* Cherdyakov *is beaming with happiness as he looks around and in back at the theater and its esteemed audience. He is a happy man tonight.*) He certainly had hopes and ambitions for higher office and had dedicated his life to hard work, zeal and patience. Still, he would not deny himself his one great pleasure. So he purchased two tickets in the very best section of the theater for the opening night performance of Rostov's *The Bearded Countess.*[2] (*A splendidly uniformed* General *and his* Wife *enter, looking for*
20 *their seats.*) As fortune would have it, into the theater that night came His Respected Superior, General Mikhail Brassilhov,[3] the Minister of Public Parks himself.

(*The* General *and his* Wife *take their seats in the first row, the* General *directly in front of* Cherdyakov.)

**Cherdyakov** (*leans over to the* General). Good evening, General.

**General** (*turns, looks at* Cherdyakov *coldly*).
30 Hmm? . . . What? Oh, yes. Yes. Good evening.

(*The* General *turns front again, looks at his program.*)

**Cherdyakov.** Permit me, sir. I am Cherdyakov . . . Ivan Ilyitch. This is a great honor for me, sir.

**General** (*turns; coldly*). Yes.

**Cherdyakov.** Like yourself, dear General, I too serve the Ministry of Public Parks . . . That is to say, I serve *you*, who is indeed *himself* the Minister of Public Parks. I am the Assistant Chief Clerk in
40 the Department of Trees and Bushes.

**General.** Ahh, yes. Keep up the good work . . . Lovely trees and bushes this year. Very nice.

**①** **Targeted Passage**

---

1. **Ivan Ilyitch Cherdyakov** (ē-vän′ ĭl-yēch′ chĕrd′yə-kəv).
2. **Rostov's *The Bearded Countess:*** a made-up author and play.
3. **Mikhail Brassilhov** (mē′kä-ēl′ bräs′ĭl-əv).

## DIFFERENTIATED INSTRUCTION

### FOR ENGLISH LANGUAGE LEARNERS

**Vocabulary Support** Use Word Questioning to teach these words: *element* (line 8), *assistant* (line 39), *proportion* (line 128), *motivation* (line 231), *committed* (line 236).

🧰 **BEST PRACTICES TOOLKIT—Transparency** Word Questioning p. E9

### FOR STRUGGLING READERS

In combination with the *Audio Anthology CD*, use one or more Targeted Passages (pp. 882, 885, 888) to ensure that students focus on key events, concepts, and skills. Targeted Passages are also good for English learners.

**①** **Targeted Passage [Lines 1–23]**

This passage introduces the play's setting and describes the characters.

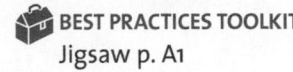

## Who makes you
# LAUGH?

**Discuss** Point out lines 80–110. What aspects of Simon's description of the sneeze are likely to make people laugh? *Possible answer: Simon uses exaggeration and figurative language to describe the event, saying it came "like a bolt from a gray thundering sky" (lines 81–82) and calling it "monstrous" (line 86). He emphasizes the General's "completely bald head" (line 88) and creates a humorous image with "Your complete head is splattered" (lines 108–109).*

## TIERED DISCUSSION PROMPTS

Use these prompts to help students understand the interaction between Cherdyakov and the General in lines 84–116:

**Connect** Have you ever accidentally sneezed or spilled something on someone? How did you feel? *Responses should show a grasp of such embarrassing situations.*

**Analyze** Why does Cherdyakov make so much of the sneeze? *Possible answer: Cherdyakov had hoped to establish a more personal relationship with his boss, making a favorable impression on him, and now he is mortified by what he has done.*

**Evaluate** Do you think that Cherdyakov's apologies and actions after the sneeze make matters better or worse? Explain your answer. *Possible answer: The clerk's actions make matters worse. The General repeatedly tries to put the incident behind him and is getting irritated by Cherdyakov's focus on it.*

---

(*The* General *turns back.* Cherdyakov *sits back, happy, grinning like a cat. The* General's Wife *whispers to him and he shrugs back. Suddenly the unseen curtain rises on the play and they all applaud.* Cherdyakov *leans forward again.*)

**Cherdyakov.** My wife would like very much to say hello, General. This is she. My wife, Madame
50 Cherdyakov.

**Wife** (*smiles*). How do you do?

**General.** My pleasure.

**Wife.** *My* pleasure, General.

**General.** How do you do?

(*He turns front, flustered.* Cherdyakov *beams at his* Wife; *then*)

**Cherdyakov** (*to the* General's Wife). Madame Brassilhov—my wife, Madame Cherdyakov.

**Wife.** How do you do, Madame Brassilhov?

60 **Madame Brassilhov** (*coldly*). How do you do?

**Wife.** I just had the pleasure of meeting your husband.

**Cherdyakov** (*to* Madame Brassilhov). And I am my wife's husband. How do you do, Madame Brassilhov?

(*The* Writer *"shushes" them.*)

**General** (*to the* Writer). Sorry. Terribly sorry.

(*The* General *tries to control his anger as they all go back to watching the play.*)

70 **Cherdyakov.** I hope you enjoy the play, sir.

**General.** I will if I can watch it.

(*He is getting hot under the collar. They all go back to watching the performance.*)

**Writer.** Feeling quite pleased with himself for having made the most of this golden opportunity, Ivan Ilyitch Cherdyakov sat back to enjoy *The Bearded Countess.* He was no longer a stranger to the Minister of Public Parks. They had become, if one wanted to be generous about the matter,

---

80 familiar with each other . . . And then, quite suddenly, without any warning, like a bolt from a gray thundering sky, Ivan Ilyitch Cherdyakov reared his head back, and—

**Cherdyakov.** AHHHHHHHHH—CHOOOOOOOOO!!! (Cherdyakov *unleashes a monstrous sneeze, his head snapping forward. The main blow of the sneeze discharges on the back of the* General's *completely bald head. The* General *winces and his hand immediately goes to his now-*
90 *dampened head.*) Ohhh, my goodness, I'm *sorry,* your Excellency! I'm so terribly sorry!

(*The* General *takes out his handkerchief and wipes his head.*)

**General.** Never mind. It's all right.

**Cherdyakov.** *All right?* . . . It certainly is *not* all right! It's unpardonable. It was monstrous of me—

**General.** You make too much of the matter. Let it rest.

100 (*He puts away his handkerchief.*)

**Cherdyakov** (*quickly takes out his own handkerchief*). How can I let it rest? It was inexcusable. Permit me to wipe your neck, General. It's the least I can do.

(*He starts to wipe the* General's *head. The* General *pushes his hand away.*)

**General.** Leave it be! It's all right, I say.

**Cherdyakov.** But I splattered you, sir. Your complete head is splattered. It was an accident,
110 I assure you—but it's *disgusting!*

**Writer.** Shhhh!

**General.** I'm sorry. My apologies.

**Cherdyakov.** The thing is, your Excellency, it came completely without warning. It was out of my nose before I could stifle it.

**Madame Brassilhov.** Shhh!

---

## DIFFERENTIATED INSTRUCTION

### FOR ENGLISH LANGUAGE LEARNERS
**Vocabulary: Idioms** Use a Jigsaw strategy by dividing students into home groups of five and assigning one of these idioms to a student in each group: *golden opportunity* (line 75), "excellent chance"; *make too much of* (line 98), "give too much importance to"; *Let it rest* (line 99), "forget about it"; *Leave it be* (line 107), "leave it alone."

Then have students reassemble into expert groups, and have each expert group determine its idiom's meaning. Have experts return to their home groups, whose students should then work together to create definitions and example sentences for the five idioms. Have groups share and compare their definitions and sentences.

**BEST PRACTICES TOOLKIT**
Jigsaw p. A1

**Cherdyakov.** Shhh, yes, certainly. I'm sorry . . . (*He sits back, nervously. He blows his nose with his handkerchief. Then* Cherdyakov *leans forward.*) It's
120 not a cold, if that's what you were worrying about, sir. Probably a particle of dust in the nostril—

**General.** Shhh! ② **Targeted Passage**

(*They watch the play in silence, and* Cherdyakov *sits back, unhappy with himself.*)

**Writer.** But try as he might, Cherdyakov could not put the incident out of his mind. The sneeze, no more than an innocent anatomical accident,[4] grew out of all proportion in his mind, until it resembled the angry roar of a cannon aimed
130 squarely at the enemy camp. He played the incident back in his mind, slowing the procedure down so he could view again in horror the infamous deed.

(Cherdyakov, *in slow motion, repeats the sneeze again, but slowed down so that it appears to us as one frame at a time. It also seems to be three times as great in intensity as the original sneeze. The* General, *also in slow motion, reacts as though he has just taken a fifty-pound hammer blow at the*
140 *base of his skull.*) *They all go with the slow motion of the "sneeze" until it is completed, when the unseen curtain falls and they applaud. They all rise and begin to file out of the theater, chattering about the lovely evening they have just spent.*)

**General.** Charming . . . Charming.

**Madame Brassilhov.** Yes, charming.

**General.** Charming . . . Simply charming. Wasn't it charming, my dear?

**Madame Brassilhov.** I found it utterly charming.

150 (Cherdyakov *stands behind them tapping the* General.)

**Writer.** I was completely charmed by it.

---

4. **innocent anatomical accident:** A biological act over which Cherdyakov had no control.

THE SNEEZE **885**

**Cherdyakov** (*still tapping away at the* General). Excuse me, Excellency—

**General.** Who's tapping? Somebody's tapping me. Who's that tapping?

**Cherdyakov.** I'm tapping, sir. I'm the tapper . . . Cherdyakov.

**Madame Brassilhov** (*quickly pulls the* General
160 *back*). Stand back, dear, it's the sneezer.

**Cherdyakov.** No, no, it's all right. I'm all sneezed out . . . I was just concerned about your going out into the night air with a damp head.

**General.** Oh, that. It was a trifle. A mere faux pas. Forget it, young man. Amusing play, don't you think? Did you find it amusing?

**Cherdyakov.** Amusing? Oh, my goodness, yes. Ha, ha. So true. Ha, ha. I haven't laughed as much in years. Ha, ha, ha . . .

170 **General.** Which part interested you the most?

**Cherdyakov.** The sneeze. When I sneezed on you. It was unforgivable, sir.

**General.** Forget it, young man. Come, my dear. It looks like rain. I don't want to get my head wet again.

**Madame Brassilhov.** You shouldn't let people sneeze on you, dear. You're not to be sneezed at.

(*They are gone.*)

**Cherdyakov.** I'm ruined! Ruined! He'll have
180 me fired from Trees and Bushes. They'll send me down to Branches and Twigs.

**Wife.** Come, Ivan.

**Cherdyakov.** What?

**Wife.** You mustn't let it concern you. It was just a harmless little sneeze. The General's probably forgotten it already.

**Cherdyakov.** Do you really think so?

**Wife.** No! I'm scared, Ivan.

## ● *Model the Skill:* FARCE

Point out the phrase "been blown away" in line 193. Explain that this is a pun referring to the sneeze. Then ask students to list other examples on this page of where the dialogue combines word play and exaggeration to create humor. ***Possible answer: Word play:*** *Cherdyakov reminds the General that they met under "'explosive' circumstances" (lines 222–223), pun on the sneeze. Cherdyakov refers to the General as "your kindship" (line 238), an unintentional play on the words* kindness *and* worship. ***Exaggeration:*** *Cherdyakov exaggerates when he tells his wife that people of their own class "love sneezing on each other" (lines 196–197). Cherdyakov's apology is nonstop exaggeration. For example, he insists that "there was no political or antisocial motivation" behind his sneeze (lines 230–231) and that it was merely "a nonpartisan, nonviolent act of God" (line 232). Referring to his nose, he proclaims, "I curse the day the protuberance formed itself on my face" (lines 232–233). Cherdyakov continues to overdo his apology when he sputters, "I worship the chair you sit on and the uniform you wear that sits on the chair that I worship" (lines 257–259).*

### REVISIT THE BIG QUESTION

## Who makes you
# LAUGH?

**Discuss** Why is Cherdyakov's response to the General in lines 229–238 likely to make people laugh? ***Possible answer:*** *Cherdyakov's response is highly exaggerated. He refers to the sneeze as "a nonpartisan, nonviolent act of God" and calls his nose "hateful." Then he grabs it and tells the General to exile his nose, "but absolve the innocent body behind it."*

**Writer.** And so they walked home in despair.

190 **Cherdyakov.** Perhaps I should send him a nice gift. Maybe some Turkish towels.

**Writer.** Cherdyakov's once-promising career had literally been blown away.

**Cherdyakov** (*as they arrive home*). Why did this happen to me? Why did I go to the theater at all? Why didn't I sit in the balcony with people of our own class? They love sneezing on each other.

**Wife.** Come to bed, Ivan.

**Cherdyakov.** Perhaps if I were to call on the
200 General and explain matters again, but in such a charming, honest and self-effacing manner, he would have no choice but to forgive me . . .

**Wife.** Maybe it's best not to remind him, Ivan.

**Cherdyakov.** No, no. If I ever expect to become a gentleman, I must behave like one.

**Writer.** And so the morning came. It so happened this was the day the General listened to petitions, and since there were fifty or sixty petitions ahead of Cherdyakov, he waited from morning till late,
210 late afternoon . . .

(Cherdyakov *moves into the office set.*)

**General.** Next! . . . NEXT!

**Cherdyakov.** I'm not next, your Excellency . . . I'm last.

**General.** Very well, then . . . Last!

**Cherdyakov.** That's me, sir.

**General.** Well, what is your petition?

**Cherdyakov.** I have no petition, sir. I'm not a petitioner.

220 **General.** Then you waste my time.

**Cherdyakov.** Do you not recognize me, sir? We met last night under rather "explosive" circumstances . . . I am the splatterer.

---

5. **Gesundheit** (gə-zŏŏnt′hīt′): German for "good health," this term is often used after someone sneezes.

**General.** The what?

**Cherdyakov.** The sneezer. The one who sneezed. The sneezing splatterer.

**General.** Indeed? And what is it you want now? A *Gesundheit?*[5]

**Cherdyakov.** No, Excellency . . . Your forgiveness.
230 I just wanted to point out there was no political or antisocial motivation behind my sneeze. It was a nonpartisan, nonviolent act of God. I curse the day the protuberance formed itself on my face. It's a hateful nose, sir, and I am not responsible for its indiscretions . . . (*grabbing his own nose*) Punish that which committed the crime, but absolve the innocent body behind it. Exile my nose, but forgive me, your kindship. Forgive me.

**General.** My dear young man, I'm not angry with
240 your nose. I'm too busy to have time for your nasal problems. I suggest you go home and take a hot bath—or a cold one—take *something,* but don't bother me with this silly business again . . . Gibber, gibber gibber, that's all I've heard all day. (*going offstage*) Gibber, gibber, gibber, gibber . . . (Cherdyakov *stands alone in the office sobbing.*)

**Cherdyakov.** Thank you, sir. God bless you and your wife and your household. May your days be sweet and may your nights be better than your days.

250 **Writer.** The feeling of relief that came over Cherdyakov was enormous . . .

**Cherdyakov.** May the birds sing in the morning at your window and may the coffee in your cup be strong and hot . . .

**Writer.** The weight of the burden that was lifted was inestimable . . .

**Cherdyakov.** I worship the chair you sit on and the uniform you wear that sits on the chair that I worship . . .

260 **Writer.** He walked home, singing and whistling like a lark. Life was surely a marvel, a joy, a heavenly paradise . . .

---

## DIFFERENTIATED INSTRUCTION

### FOR ENGLISH LANGUAGE LEARNERS

**Vocabulary: Suffixes** Direct students' attention to the words *tapper* (line 157), *sneezer* (line 225), and *splatterer* (line 226). Elicit the definition of each word ("someone who taps," "someone who sneezes," and "someone who splatters"). Call attention to the suffix *-er,* and explain that it means "one who does an action." Then divide students into small groups, and have groups list other "doer" words ending in *-er, -or* (such as *actor*), or *-ar* (such as *liar*). Challenge groups to create a T Chart listing the action verbs on the left and the nouns naming those who do these actions on the right. The group that can list the most correct entries within a set time limit wins.

**BEST PRACTICES TOOLKIT—Transparency** T Chart p. A25

**Cherdyakov.** Oh, God, I am happy!

**Writer.** And yet—

**Cherdyakov.** And yet—

**Writer.** When he arrived home, he began to think . . .

**Cherdyakov.** Have I been the butt of a cruel and thoughtless joke?

270 **Writer.** Had the Minister toyed with him?

**Cherdyakov.** If he had no intention of punishing me, why did he torment me so unmercifully?

**Writer.** If the sneeze meant so little to the Minister, why did he deliberately cause Cherdyakov to writhe in his bed?

**Cherdyakov.** . . . to twist in agony the entire night?

**Writer.** Cherdyakov was furious!

**Cherdyakov.** I AM FURIOUS!

280 **Writer.** He foamed and fumed and paced the night through, and in the morning he called out to his wife, "SONYA!"

**Cherdyakov.** SONYA! (*She rushes in.*) I have been humiliated.

**Wife.** *You,* Ivan? Who would humiliate *you?* You're such a kind and generous person.

**Cherdyakov.** Who? I'll tell you who! General Brassilhov, the Minister of Public Parks.

**Wife.** What did he do?

290 **Cherdyakov.** The swine! I was humiliated in such subtle fashion, it was almost indiscernible. The man's cunning is equal only to his cruelty. He practically forced me to come to his office to grovel and beg on my knees. I was reduced to a gibbering idiot.

**Wife.** You were that reduced?

---

6. **humiliated by *I* . . . humiliate *he*:** Cherdyakov uses an incorrect pronoun, and the Writer mimics him.

**Cherdyakov.** I must go back and tell him what I think of him. The lower classes must speak up . . . (*He is at the door.*) The world must be made

300 safe so that men of all nations and creeds, regardless of color or religion, will be free to sneeze on their superiors! It is *he* who will be humiliated by *I!*

**Writer.** And so, the next morning, Cherdyakov came to humiliate *he.*[6]

(*Lights up on the* General *at his desk.*)

**General.** Last! (Cherdyakov *goes to the* General's *desk. He stands there glaring down at the* General *with a faint trace of a smile on his lips. The* General *looks up.*) Well?

310 **Cherdyakov** (*smiles*). Well? Well, you say? . . . Do you not recognize me, your Excellency? Look at my face . . . Yes. You're quite correct. It is I once again.

**General** (*looks at him, puzzled*). It is you once again who?

**Cherdyakov** (*confidentially*). Cherdyakov, Excellency. I have returned, having taken neither a hot bath nor a cold one.

**General.** Who let this filthy man in? What is it?

320 **Cherdyakov** (*on top of the situation now*). What is it? . . . What is it, you ask? You sit there behind your desk and ask, What is it? You sit there in your lofty position as General and Minister of Public Parks, a member in high standing among the upper class and ask me, a lowly civil servant, What is it? You sit there with full knowledge that there is no equality in this life, that there are those of us who serve and those that are served, those of us that obey and those that are obeyed, those of us who bow and those that

330 are bowed to, that in this life certain events take place that cause some of us to be humiliated and those that are the cause of that humiliation . . . and still you ask, "WHAT IS IT?"!

**General** (*angrily*). *What is it?* Don't stand there gibbering like an idiot! What is it you want?

THE SNEEZE **887**

Refer students to lines 263–315.

## TIERED DISCUSSION PROMPTS

Refer students to lines 263–315. Use these prompts to help students understand why Cherdyakov goes to see the General again:

**Connect** Have you ever reacted one way to something a person said or did but then reacted altogether differently later on? Why did your reaction change? Which proved more accurate: your initial feelings or your subsequent reaction? *Responses should reflect an understanding of such situations.*

**Analyze** Cherdyakov's mood turns from "happy" (line 263) to "furious" (line 278) in no time at all. Explain why. *Possible answer: As Cherdyakov reflects on recent events, he decides that the General has humiliated and "toyed with" (line 270) him. Cherdyakov attributes his self-inflicted mental anguish to the General's behavior rather than to his own obsessiveness.*

**Evaluate** Do you think there is any truth to Cherdyakov's conclusion that the General meant to humiliate him in "subtle fashion"? Support your answer. *Possible answer: Nothing in the play suggests that the General meant to humiliate Cherdyakov. The General did not even remember Cherdyakov when he came to his office on the morning after the sneeze. He tells Cherdyakov that he is not angry—much as he had at the theater the night before—and that Cherdyakov should not bother him again. Even when Cherdyakov returns the second time, the General still does not understand who he is or why he has come.*

## FOR RELUCTANT READERS

Have students work in small groups and tell them to pick a section of dialogue from the play that includes at least three of the characters. Explain that they are going to rewrite the dialogue using contemporary language. Encourage students to rewrite the word play and exaggeration with modern language and slang.

## FOR STRUGGLING READERS

### Develop Reading Fluency

Model for students how to read words in all capital letters (lines 279, 282, 283, 333) and italics (lines 285, 302, 304, 334) when they appear in dialogue. Point out that the special print appearance on the page is a way for the writer to tell actors and readers to emphasize these words.

## Who makes you LAUGH?

**Discuss** How does the final exchange between Cherdyakov and the General in lines 336–352 show how people make us laugh? *Possible answer: Instead of telling off the General, as the reader anticipates, Cherdyakov apologizes yet again. The General's abusive tirade (lines 340–344) is also humorous. The comical climax occurs when Cherdyakov sneezes again—right in the General's face (line 345). Then the General starts calling him comically inventive, insect-derived names, such as "son-in-law of a bed bug" (line 350).*

**TEXT ANALYSIS**

COMMON CORE
RL 10

● **FARCE**

How does the ending of the play in lines 345–366 illustrate the qualities of farce? *Possible answer: The ending reflects exaggeration to the point of absurdity.*

**Extend the Discussion** How else might Simon have ended the play?

## SELECTION WRAP–UP

**READ WITH A PURPOSE** Now that students have finished reading the selection, have them explain which character they have more sympathy for, Cherdyakov or the General. *Possible answer: Choices will vary; have students justify their choices with evidence from the play.*

★ **CRITIQUE** Ask students if they enjoyed the farcical elements of "The Sneeze," and to explain why or why not. Urge students to give specific reasons for their opinions.

## INDEPENDENT READING

Students may wish to read other plays by Neil Simon. Suggest *The Collected Plays of Neil Simon.*

**Cherdyakov.** *I'll tell you what I want!* . . . I wanted to apologize again for sneezing on you . . . I wasn't sure I made it clear. It was an accident, an accident, I assure you . . .

340 **General** (*stands and screams out*). *Out! Out, you idiot!* Fool! Imbecile! Get out of my sight! I never want to see you again. If you ever cross my line of vision I'll have you exiled forever . . . WHAT'S YOUR NAME?

**Cherdyakov.** Ch—Cherdyakov!

(*It comes out as a sneeze in the* General's *face.*)

**General** (*wiping himself*). You germ spreader! You maggot! You insect! You are lower than an insect. You are the second cousin to a cockroach! The 350 son-in-law of a bed bug! You are the nephew of a *ringworm!* You are nothing, nothing, do you hear me? . . . *NOTHING!*

(Cherdyakov *backs away, and returns home.*)

**Writer.** At that moment, something broke loose inside of Cherdyakov . . . Something so deep and vital, so organic, that the damage that was done seemed irreparable . . . Something drained from him that can only be described as the very life force itself . . . (Cherdyakov *takes off his coat. He* 360 *sits on the sofa, head in hands.*) The matter was over, for once, for all, forever. What happened next was quite simple . . . (Cherdyakov *lies back on the sofa.*) Ivan Ilyitch Cherdyakov arrived at home . . . removed his coat . . . lay down on the sofa—and died! (Cherdyakov's *head drops and his hand falls to the floor.*)

*Blackout*

③ **Targeted Passage**

## *DIFFERENTIATED INSTRUCTION*

### FOR STRUGGLING READERS

③ **Targeted Passage** [Lines 345–366]

This passage concludes the play, as Cherdyakov's second sneeze causes the General to explode, which in turn leads to Cherdyakov's absurd death.

- Why does the General lose his temper and yell at Cherdyakov? (line 346)
- How does Cherdyakov react to the General's outburst? (lines 354–366)

### FOR ADVANCED LEARNERS/PRE–AP

**Updating the Play** Simon's 1973 play is based on a Chekhov story set in 19th-century Russia. Ask students to write a paragraph or two suggesting how Simon might have set "The Sneeze" in contemporary America. If students are familiar with Simon's plays, encourage them to consider how Simon might have adapted "The Sneeze" to reflect his own cultural background and literary themes.

## Comprehension

1. **Recall** Where does the opening scene of the play take place?

2. **Summarize** How does the General react when Cherdyakov sneezes?

3. **Recall** Why does Cherdyakov go to see the General in his office the next morning?

4. **Clarify** How does the play end?

COMMON CORE

RL 10 Read and comprehend dramas.

## Text Analysis

5. **Visualize** Review the chart you filled in as you read. Which scene or situation in the play were you able to picture most vividly? Write a short paragraph describing the details. If you'd like, create a sketch to accompany your paragraph.

6. **Draw Conclusions** What is the role of the Writer in "The Sneeze"? Explain the function he performs, citing evidence to support your answer.

7. **Analyze Farce** Using a chart like the one shown, record examples of ridiculous situations, exaggerated behavior or language, and physical comedy that appear in "The Sneeze." Neil Simon uses these conventions of a farce to make fun of something. What in particular does he seem to be mocking?

| Ridiculous Situations | Exaggerated Behavior/Language | Physical Comedy |
|---|---|---|
| • | • | • |
| • | • | • |

8. **Identify Dramatic Irony** Dramatic irony occurs when the audience (or the reader) knows more information about a character or a situation than the characters themselves know. Find an example of dramatic irony in the play, and explain what makes it ironic.

## Text Criticism

9. **Author's Style** Neil Simon has said, "My idea of the ultimate achievement in a comedy is to make a whole audience fall onto the floor, writhing and laughing so hard that some of them pass out." Did he accomplish this goal with "The Sneeze"? Cite evidence from the play to support your opinion.

### Who makes you LAUGH?

What did you find funniest about "The Sneeze"?

---

**Exaggerated Behavior/Language:** Cherdyakov and his wife's overly polite introduction at the theater (lines 33–71); the description of the first sneeze (lines 80–90); the General's abusive tirade (lines 340–352). Physical Comedy: the first sneeze; Cherdyakov's slow-motion reenactment of the sneeze; the second sneeze (line 345). Simon mocks the human tendencies to blow events out of proportion and to misinterpret other people.

8. Cherdyakov thinks the General has intentionally humiliated him, but the situation is ironic because the audience realizes the General doesn't even remember Cherdyakov, who is humiliating himself.

### Text Criticism

9. Students may cite any of the farcical elements listed for answer 7.

### What makes you LAUGH?

Answers will vary, but should be supported by the text.

---

# Practice and Apply

For preliminary support of post-reading questions, use these copy masters:

**R** **RESOURCE MANAGER**—Copy Masters
Reading Check p. 143
Farce p. 139
Question Support p. 144

Additional selection questions are provided for teachers on page 133.

## ANSWERS

## Comprehension

1. *The opening scene occurs at the theater.*

2. *He is understanding but gets irritated as Cherdyakov keeps frantically apologizing.*

3. *Cherdyakov visits the General to apologize for the sneeze so that he won't fire him.*

4. *Cherdyakov sneezes on the General again, the General screams insults at him, and Cherdyakov goes home and dies.*

## Text Analysis

COMMON CORE RL 10

**Possible answers:**

5. ◼ **COMMON CORE FOCUS** *Visualize* *Students should cite details from the play.*

6. *The Writer serves as the narrator, giving background (lines 74–83), making humorous comments (lines 192–193), and occasionally joining in the dialogue (line 111).*

7. ● **COMMON CORE FOCUS** *Farce Ridiculous Situations:* *Cherdyakov's excessive apologies (lines 90–121, 221–238); his slow-motion reenactment of the sneeze (lines 125–144); his abrupt death (lines 363–366).*

---

# Assess and Reteach

## Assess

**DIAGNOSTIC AND SELECTION TESTS**
Selection Test A pp. 243–244
Selection Test B/C pp. 245–246

**Interactive Selection Test** on **thinkcentral.com**

## Reteach

**Level Up Online Tutorials** on **thinkcentral.com**

**Reteaching Worksheets** on **thinkcentral.com**
Literature Lesson 38: Verbal and Dramatic Irony
Literature Lesson 25: Elements of Drama

# Focus and Motivate

## COMMON CORE FOCUS

**W 2a-f** Write informative/explanatory texts to examine complex ideas clearly and accurately through effective selection, organization, and analysis of content. **W 4** Produce clear and coherent writing. **W 5** Develop and strengthen writing as needed by planning, revising, editing, rewriting, or trying a new approach. **W 10** Write routinely over shorter time frames for a range of tasks, purposes, and audiences. **L 1** Demonstrate command of the conventions of standard English grammar and usage when writing. **L 1b** Use various types of clauses to convey specific meanings and add variety and interest. **L 2** Demonstrate command of the conventions of standard English capitalization, punctuation, and spelling.

## WRITE WITH A PURPOSE

To help students understand the purpose, create a pie diagram on the board. Divide the pie into slices. Write the following terms on individual slices: *word choice, sentence structure, tone, figurative language,* and *imagery.* Explain that an author makes choices in each of these areas when composing a piece in order to impact the reader. These choices affect the outcome.

## COMMON CORE TRAITS

Review the *COMMON CORE TRAITS* with students, focusing primarily on development of ideas and organization of ideas. Compare the list of traits with the rubric on page 898.

## ADDITIONAL TASKS

**Write About Media** Write an analysis of the style in a work of journalism. Keep in mind the medium's purpose and audience.
**Possible subjects:** a report by a news anchor or a regular newspaper editorial column

**Write About Food** Write an analysis of the style of a good meal you enjoyed recently. Keep in mind that the meal should be distinctive in its taste and preparation.
**Possible subjects:** a meal you enjoyed in a restaurant or a home-cooked meal

### Writing Online   THINK central

The following tools are available online at **thinkcentral.com** and on **Write*Smart* CD-ROM:**
• **Interactive Graphic Organizers**
• **Interactive Student Models**
• **Interactive Revision Lessons**

---

## Writing Workshop
**INFORMATIVE TEXT**

# Analysis of an Author's Style

The *way* a writer relates an experience enhances meaning. In this workshop, you will write an analysis of an author's style to gain a deeper understanding of his or her message.

 **Essential Course of Study ECOS**

Complete the workshop activities in your **Reader/Writer Notebook.**

### WRITE WITH A PURPOSE

**WRITING TASK**

Choose a piece of literature and write an **analysis of the author's style.** Your analysis should help the audience understand important elements of the author's style, such as word choice, sentence structure, tone, figurative language, or imagery. Then, explain the effect, or impact, that those elements of style have on readers.

**Idea Starters**
• the effects of Tim O'Brien's use of realism in "Where Have You Gone, Charming Billy?"
• the effects of James Thurber's use of parody in "The Princess and the Tin Box"
• the effects of the lack of punctuation in Nikki Giovanni's poetry

**THE ESSENTIALS**

Here are some common purposes, audiences, and formats for literary analysis.

| PURPOSES | AUDIENCES | FORMATS |
|---|---|---|
| • to examine parts in an effort to discover their nature, function, and relationships <br> • to understand a whole based on an understanding of its parts | • classmates and teacher <br> • author <br> • student literary magazine or newspaper readers | • essay for class <br> • podcast <br> • student literary magazine or newspaper review |

**Writing Online**  THINK central
Go to **thinkcentral.com.**
KEYWORD: HML9N-890

### COMMON CORE TRAITS

**1. DEVELOPMENT OF IDEAS**
• presents an **engaging introduction**
• develops a **controlling idea** that offers an **analysis** of the author's style
• supports main points of analysis with **relevant details** and **quotations from the text**
• concludes with a **summary of main points** and **insights**

**2. ORGANIZATION OF IDEAS**
• **organizes** ideas in a logical way
• uses varied **transitions** to create **cohesion** and **connect ideas**

**3. LANGUAGE FACILITY AND CONVENTIONS**
• establishes and maintains a **formal style** and **objective tone**
• uses **precise language,** including **domain-specific vocabulary**
• varies sentence structure with **compound and compound-complex sentences**
• employs correct **grammar, mechanics,** and **spelling**

---

## Writing Workshop Resources

**R RESOURCE MANAGER UNIT 8**
Plan and Teach pp. 145–148
Prewriting–Editing pp. 149–153
Writing Rubric p. 154
Technology p. 155
Writing Support p. 156*

**BEST PRACTICES TOOLKIT**
Writing Template: Literary Analysis
Analysis Frame: Author's Craft p. D24

**TECHNOLOGY**
💿 **Teacher One Stop DVD-ROM**
💿 **Student One Stop DVD-ROM**
💿 **Write*Smart* CD-ROM**
💿 **GrammarNotes DVD-ROM**

**Writing Center on thinkcentral.com**

*See resources on the **Teacher One Stop DVD-ROM** and on **thinkcentral.com.***

\* Resources for Differentiation

## Planning/Prewriting

 **COMMON CORE** **W 2a-f** Write informative/explanatory texts to examine complex ideas through the effective selection, organization, and analysis of content. **W 5** Develop and strengthen writing by planning.

### Getting Started

**CHOOSE A SUBJECT FOR ANALYSIS**

For your analysis, choose a work that has sufficient **elements of style** to examine. Keep a reader's log, listing elements of style in the work that catch your attention. Also, note questions and comments. Indicate in your log how your understanding of the work develops or changes through multiple readings.

▶ **WHAT DOES IT LOOK LIKE?**

| Details about Nikki Giovanni's "Kidnap Poem" | Comments |
|---|---|
| no punctuation | makes poem hard to read at first; had to mentally insert punctuation |
| "if i were a poet" | but Giovanni is a poet—is she making a joke? |
| "ode you with my love song" | uses poetic terms in unusual ways |

**THINK ABOUT AUDIENCE AND PURPOSE**

Your **purpose** is to respond to elements of style that shape the literary work's meaning and to share your insights with your **audience.** Your audience is likely to include people who have read the work and have their own ideas about its meaning.

▶ **ASK YOURSELF:**

- Who is my audience? Why might they be interested in this analysis?
- What ideas might my audience already have about this work?
- What **domain-specific,** or specialized, vocabulary will my audience need to know to understand my analysis?

**IDENTIFY KEY ELEMENTS OF STYLE**

Use a graphic organizer to list **elements of style** along with **quotations** and **concrete details** from the literary work.

▶ **WHAT DOES IT LOOK LIKE?**

| Elements of Style | "Kidnap Poem" |
|---|---|
| Conventions | no punctuation or capitalization, "kidnap" is broken between two lines with no hyphen |
| Point of View | first person, talking directly to a loved one |
| Word Choice | fun, teasing, "lyric you in lilacs" |

**DEVELOP A CONTROLLING IDEA**

Your **controlling idea,** or thesis statement, should identify the main idea you want to share in your analysis. Identify the main points of your analysis in the introduction, along with the title and author of the work. Continue modifying or reworking the controlling idea as you draft.

▶ **WHAT DOES IT LOOK LIKE?**

*Nikki Giovanni's "Kidnap Poem" is about love. It uses a relaxed, fun style to convey the author's message.*

WRITING WORKSHOP **891**

---

## DIFFERENTIATED INSTRUCTION

**FOR ENGLISH LANGUAGE LEARNERS**

**Language: Reinforce Analytical Terms** Write these terms on the board and review them with students:

- *literary terms:* words that describe a literary genre or style, such as *informal* or *tone*
- *voice:* a writer's (narrator's or speaker's) unique style of expression, which reveals his or her personality, beliefs, and attitudes
- *controlling idea:* one or two sentences stating the main idea of an essay. In an

analysis of an author's style, the controlling idea names the most important elements of the author's style and tells how they affect the work. Share this example:

*The poet uses an informal style to create a sense of intimacy in conveying the message that love is more important than anything else.*

---

# Teach

## Planning/ Prewriting

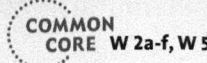 **COMMON CORE** **W 2a-f, W 5**

▶ **CHOOSE A SUBJECT FOR ANALYSIS** Tell students to read and reread their literary works several times. Suggest that they leave space between entries in their readers' logs. This way, they can add comments during each reading.

▶ **THINK ABOUT AUDIENCE AND PURPOSE** Encourage students to use idea webs as they brainstorm what their audiences probably already know about their literary works. Then, have students use different idea webs to brainstorm the ideas they have to share with their audiences.

▶ **IDENTIFY KEY ELEMENTS OF STYLE** Make sure that students understand the distinction between the two charts. In the first chart, students note the reader's reactions to the work. In the second chart, students note the effect of elements of style on the literary work. Make sure that students understand that their analyses will be based primarily on the second chart. The function of the first chart is to help students get ready to create the second chart.

▶ **DEVELOP A CONTROLLING IDEA** Point out to students that a controlling idea may be formed using one or two sentences. However, if possible, students should try to formulate their controlling ideas in single sentences. For example, *Nikki Giovanni's "Kidnap Poem" uses a relaxed, fun style to convey the author's message about love.*

**R** **RESOURCE MANAGER—Copy Masters**
Planning/Prewriting p. 149
Drafting p. 150
Revising and Editing pp. 151–152
Ask a Peer Reader p. 153
Rubric p. 154
Writing Support p. 156

## Planning/Prewriting *continued*

▸ **ORGANIZE YOUR IDEAS** Suggest that students identify the three most important elements of style noted in their charts. Then, tell students to number these three in order of importance. Recommend that students present these elements in reverse order in their essays, ending with the most important element. Remind students that they are trying to convince their readers that their controlling idea is true. Therefore, it's a good idea to end with one's strongest point.

▸ **BACK UP EACH STATEMENT WITH EXAMPLES** For each element of style that students plan to discuss, tell them to identify at least one quotation from the literary work. Remind students that they will also need to explain why each quotation supports the controlling idea.

**YOUR TURN** As students work to analyze elements of style, remind them to pose questions. For example, *Why does Giovanni convert nouns to verbs? What effect does this language trick have on the poem?* Asking such questions will help emphasize the idea that literary works are the products of their authors' choices.

For interactive graphic organizers, see

 **Write*Smart* CD-ROM**

**Writing Center** on **thinkcentral.com**

---

## Planning/Prewriting *continued*

### Getting Started

**ORGANIZE YOUR IDEAS**

Think about how you can organize and convey your ideas to make your analysis clear to the audience. You will want to organize your ideas in a **logical** and **cohesive** way. For example, you can discuss elements of style by **order of importance.**

▸ **WHAT DOES IT LOOK LIKE?**

> *Order of Importance (Least to Most)*
> 1. *Tone*
>    - *mostly simple language*
>    - *straight to the point*
> 2. *Point of View*
>    - *first person*
>    - *extremely personal*
> 3. *Word Choice*
>    - *playful, creative*
>    - *shows poetry as active*

**BACK UP EACH STATEMENT WITH EXAMPLES**

Every point you make about an element of an author's style must be supported with **concrete details** and **quotations.** Make sure to explain exactly how and why each detail or quotation supports your analysis. Then, explain what **effect** each element of style has on readers of the literary work.

▸ **WHAT DOES IT LOOK LIKE?**

> *Shows Poetry as Active*
>
> *Evidence: Giovanni uses nouns related to poetry as verbs: "meter / you to jones beach" and "lyric you in lilacs."*
>
> *Effect: The speaker seems to say that she will use her poetry to capture the one she loves.*

 **PEER REVIEW** Describe to a peer the purpose and audience of your analysis. Then, ask: What are the main points of my analysis? Which points need to be supported with more concrete details or quotations?

**YOUR TURN** In your *Reader/Writer Notebook*, develop your writing plan. Create charts and outlines such as those on page 891 to list and analyze style elements. Consider the following tips as you analyze elements of the author's style:

- Consider the writer's **diction,** or choice of words.
- Identify **imagery,** such as sensory description or figurative language.
- Think about **point of view**—the angle or perspective from which the information is told.
- Examine **sentence structure,** or the type and length of sentences.
- Reflect on **tone**—the narrator's attitude toward the subject.

---

## DIFFERENTIATED INSTRUCTION

### FOR ENGLISH LANGUAGE LEARNERS

**Controlling Ideas** Have students use these sentence starters to help them develop their controlling ideas and support:

- My subject is _____ by _____.
- The three elements of the author's style I will discuss are _____, _____ and _____.
- The author's style affects the author's work _____ because _____.

After students have completed these frames, help them remove references to the first person and recast the sentences.

### FOR STRUGGLING WRITERS

**Organization** Have students follow this frame to plan their analyses. Explain that it features order of importance as a method of organization.

**Introduction**

- Name the title of the work and the author.
- State your controlling idea.

**Body**

- Name the third most important element of style, present a supporting quotation, and explain why the quotation supports the controlling idea. (Repeat this structure for the second most and most important elements of style.)

**Concluding Section**

- Summarize your analysis.
- Include an overall insight about the author's style.

# Drafting

The following chart shows a structure for organizing a clear and coherent literary analysis.

**COMMON CORE**

**W 4** Produce clear and coherent writing.
**L 1** Demonstrate command of the conventions of standard English grammar and usage when writing.

## Organizing Your Analysis

### INTRODUCTION

- Begin with a **question** or a **comment** to help the audience connect to the topic of the analysis.
- Identify the **author** and **title** of the literary work.
- Provide a **controlling idea** that describes the overall effect of the stylistic elements used by the author.
- In the introduction, identify the **main points** of the analysis for your **audience**.

▼

### BODY

- Organize main points by **order of importance,** and use **precise language** to explain your analysis.
- Offer **quotations** and **concrete details** that illustrate each main point. If necessary, define any **domain-specific vocabulary,** such as literary terms.
- Explain the **effect** of each **element of style** on readers of the work and provide supporting examples.
- Use effective **transitions** to create cohesion and connect the relationships between ideas.
- Maintain a **formal style** and **objective tone** by avoiding contractions and using clear, unbiased language.

▼

### CONCLUDING SECTION

- Summarize the **main points** of your analysis.
- Offer an overall **insight** about the author's style and its effects on readers.

## GRAMMAR IN CONTEXT: RUN-ON SENTENCES

A run-on sentence occurs when two independent clauses are combined incorrectly. Writers sometimes mistakenly join the clauses with only a comma. This type of error is called a *comma splice.* To fix a run-on sentence, create a compound sentence or a complex sentence.

**Run-on sentence:** Giovanni *is* a poet, the speaker's repeated comment "if I were a poet" shows a teasing and flirtatious attitude.

| Type of Correction | Example |
|---|---|
| Add a coordinating conjunction to make a compound sentence. | ▶ Giovanni *is* a poet, **so** the speaker's repeated comment "if I were a poet" shows a teasing and flirtatious attitude. |
| Add a semicolon to make a compound sentence. | ▶ Giovanni *is* a poet; the speaker's repeated comment "if I were a poet" shows a teasing and flirtatious attitude. |
| Add a subordinating conjunction to make a complex sentence. | ▶ **Because** Giovanni *is* a poet, the speaker's repeated comment "if I were a poet" shows a teasing and flirtatious attitude. |

**YOUR TURN** Develop a draft of your analysis, following the structure outlined in the *Organizing Your Analysis* chart. As you write, pay attention to your sentence structure in order to avoid run-on sentences.

---

## FOR ENGLISH LANGUAGE LEARNERS

**Using Domain-Specific Vocabulary** To provide students with practice in using domain-specific vocabulary such as literary terms, ask them to write about their favorite selection in this unit. Tell students to use the following sentence frames as the starting point for their writing:

- The poem (story, play) is _____.
- _____ suggests that _____.
- In the story (poem, play), _____.

- The style is _____, and (but) _____.
- For example, _____.

## FOR STRUGGLING WRITERS

**Complex Sentences** To encourage students to write complex sentences, tell them to combine two related sentences using a subordinating conjunction from a word bank: *after, although, because, before, if, since, so, unless, until, where, whether, while*

---

# Practice and Apply

## Drafting

**COMMON CORE W 4, L 1**

▶ *INTRODUCTION* Remind students to make their introductions engaging. Students may begin by making startling statements, telling anecdotes, or asking unusual questions. These strategies will help writers interest readers in reading their analyses.

▶ *BODY* Remind students that a good analysis clearly explains the thoughts or reasoning the writer uses to reach conclusions. Tell students to introduce each element of style, provide a supporting example, and then explain why or how the style element makes the controlling idea true.

▶ *CONCLUDING SECTION* Remind students to end with a strong conclusion. Because the concluding section comes last, it is the first thing readers will remember. Tell students to take this opportunity to summarize their strongest examples and leave readers with final insights that readers may continue thinking about once they've put away the essays.

## GRAMMAR IN CONTEXT: RUN-ON SENTENCES

For additional practice, have students correct the following sentence using each of the types of correction listed in the chart.

- The poem is free verse, Giovanni's informal tone creates a sense of closeness and familiarity. *(The poem is free verse, and Giovanni's informal tone creates a sense of closeness and familiarity. The poem is free verse; consequently, Giovanni's informal tone creates a sense of closeness and familiarity. Because the poem is free verse, Giovanni's informal tone creates a sense of closeness and familiarity.)*

**YOUR TURN** Ask students to complete the **Your Turn** activity independently. Remind students to avoid comma splices and run-on sentences by forming compound and complex sentences. Suggest that students write their drafts double-spaced so that they can make revisions easily later.

For an analytical writing template, see

💿 **Write*Smart* CD-ROM**

**Writing Center** at 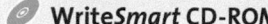 **thinkcentral.com**

## Revising

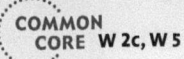

COMMON CORE W 2c, W 5

**Model the Skill** Using a draft analytical essay on a transparency or electronic white-board, model how to use the questions, tips, and strategies suggested in the chart to evaluate and revise. You might use the analysis of a student from another class or from a previous year. Make sure to remove the student's name from the analysis so that the writer remains anonymous.

**YOUR TURN** During peer review, remind students to use the proper tools and to establish a respectful working environment. Students should clear their desks so that they can focus on the task of review. They should use colored pens for comments so that the compliments and suggestions are clearly visible for the writers. However, caution students against using red pen; it looks too much like the peer reviewer is playing teacher. Tell students to sit close together so they are not distracted by classroom noise.

For interactive revision tools, see

**Write*Smart* CD-ROM**

**Writing Center** on **thinkcentral.com**

---

## Revising

As you revise, determine whether you've achieved your purpose and effectively communicated your ideas to the intended audience. Use the chart below to revise, rewrite, and improve your draft.

### ANALYSIS OF AN AUTHOR'S STYLE

| Ask Yourself | Tips | Revision Strategies |
|---|---|---|
| 1. Does the introduction contain a question or comment that will interest readers? Does it list the author and title? | **Underline** the opening question or comment and **circle** the title and author. | **Add** a question or comment about the subject of the literary work to engage the audience. **Add** the work's title and/or author. |
| 2. Does the controlling idea make an overall point about the effects of stylistic elements on readers? | **Put check marks** above the stylistic elements and by descriptions of the effects of these elements on readers. | **Rewrite** the controlling idea to summarize the effect of the author's use of stylistic elements. |
| 3. Are each of your main points presented in order of importance with appropriate and varied transitions between related ideas? | **Label** each paragraph for the strength of its point. Use a **plus sign** for the most important point, a **check mark** for the second most important point, and a **minus sign** for the least important point. **Circle** transitional words that connect ideas. | **Rearrange** body paragraphs as needed to explain points from least to most important, and add transitions to connect related ideas as needed. |
| 4. Is each point illustrated with a quotation? | **Place a star** next to each quotation from the literary work. | **Add** quotations as necessary so that you have at least one quotation for each main point. |
| 5. Do I maintain a formal style throughout the analysis? | **Bracket** contractions, casual slang, or informal language. | **Reword** text to avoid contractions. **Replace** informal language with precise, formal words. |
| 6. Does the concluding section summarize the analysis and give insight into the author's style? | **Place** a check mark above the summarizing statement in the concluding section and **circle** the insight. | **Revise** the concluding section to state the connection between style and meaning in the poem. |

**YOUR TURN** **PEER REVIEW** Exchange your analysis with a classmate, or read your analysis aloud to your partner. Focus on quotations and explanations. Discuss whether the writer effectively supports his or her controlling idea, or whether a new approach is needed.

---

## DIFFERENTIATED INSTRUCTION

### FOR ADVANCED LEARNERS/PRE–AP

**Research** Challenge students to locate and read some professional or collegiate literary analysis essays or reviews that have been written about the same literary works about which students are writing. Ask students to think about which points of analysis are similar to and different than their own. Tell students to consider how such essays affect their understandings of the works. Suggest that students incorporate quotations from these essays into their analyses, agreeing or disagreeing with the writers' ideas.

## ANALYZE A STUDENT DRAFT

Read this draft; notice the comments on its strengths as well as suggestions for improvement.

COMMON CORE  **W 2c** Use appropriate and varied transitions to link the major sections of the text. **W 5** Strengthen writing by revising, editing, rewriting, or trying a new approach.

### Nikki Giovanni's Notable Style
by Leslie Wu, Reagan High School

**1**     Have you ever been kidnapped by a poet? Nikki Giovanni asks this surprising question in "Kidnap Poem." Giovanni uses an informal, personal, playful style of writing to explore the importance of love.

**2**     Giovanni's informal tone creates a sense of closeness and familiarity. The poem is in free verse rather than a more structured style, with line breaks in the middle of thoughts or even in the middle of a word ("i'd kid / nap you"). There is no punctuation except for contractions, which makes the writing sound more like spoken language, and no capitalization. Simple, direct language adds to the conversational tone. Words and phrases such as "maybe coney island / or maybe just to my house" are straightforward and fairly easy to understand. The poem's loosely structured, casual style makes sense because the speaker is addressing a loved one. "Kidnap Poem" is a love poem, or maybe even a love song.

**3**     Giovanni uses the first-person point of view. The speaker addresses the loved one as "you" rather than using a name or giving any details about the person. This technique makes the poem sound like a close, personal conversation. "Kidnap Poem" makes the reader feel as if he or she is eavesdropping on two people who know each other very well. It is an extremely personal poem about love and relationships.

> Leslie's **introduction** includes an intriguing question and identifies the author and the literary work. The **controlling idea** presents the elements of the author's style to be analyzed.

> Leslie supports a main point about the author's style with **quotations** from the poem. She elaborates on each quotation by explaining its **effect** on readers.

> Leslie uses **precise language** in her analysis such as "first-person point of view." However, her analysis would be more compelling if she provided **transitions** between paragraphs.

**LEARN HOW** Use Transitions   A **transition** is a word or a phrase that moves the audience logically from one paragraph to the next. Transitions create cohesion by showing how ideas are connected. Without transitions, the audience may not see the connections among the writer's points.

---

**LESLIE'S REVISION TO PARAGRAPH 3**

*Another important aspect of this poet's style involves point of view.*
Giovanni uses the first-person point of view. The speaker addresses the loved one as "you" rather than using a name or giving any details about the person. This technique makes the poem sound like a close, personal conversation. . . .

---

## ANALYZE A STUDENT DRAFT

Explain that the Student Draft on this page is the first half of an analytical essay. Model reading the draft and the annotations in blue, explaining that the yellow highlighting illustrates the student's language choices. Explain that the following *Learn How* mini-lessons provide helpful information about ways to improve this student draft as well as students' own drafts.

**LEARN HOW**   Use Transitions

- Suggest that students highlight transitional words and phrases that signal new topics in their drafts.
- If they have few to no highlights, tell them to add transitions to clarify how ideas are connected.
- If students find that their analyses are overloaded with transitions, they may need to explore a more logical order of ideas.
- Also, have students check highlighted text to ensure that they have used varied and appropriate transitions to link ideas and create cohesion.

---

### FOR ENGLISH LANGUAGE LEARNERS

**Transitions**   To help familiarize students with transitions, write these sentences on the board and underline the transitional words and phrases:

- **Both** stanzas have a playful tone. (comparison that shows a similarity)
- **For example,** "Fly" is about a bee. (introduces an example)
- **When** the speaker says, "I buzz it," it means "I understand." (introduces an example)
- **The second** line also uses imagery. (shows order)
- **Although** the poem is humorous, it has a serious message. (contrast that shows a difference)

Now, ask student pairs to provide additional examples using the same transitional words and phrases.

### FOR STRUGGLING WRITERS

**Transitional Story**   Post a bank of transitional words and phrases. Offer a narrative sentence to the class such as "When Jimmy stepped outside his front door, he saw the military truck moving slowly up the street." Ask a student to choose a transition word or phrase from the bank and add a sentence to your story. Continue this process until all students have contributed to the story, making use of transitional words and phrases.

## ANALYZE A STUDENT DRAFT *continued*

Explain that the Student Draft is continued and completed on this page. Read the draft and annotations aloud and discuss. Ask students to comment on the student writer's inferences.

❹     A third stylistic device the poem uses is playful word choice. For example, Giovanni uses poetic terms as actions she would take: "put you in my phrases and meter / you to jones beach," "lyric you in lilacs / dash you in the rain," "ode you with my love song."

Leslie's **voice** is straightforward and confident as she analyzes imagery and meaning.

❺     The speaker seems to be saying that she will bring to life in her actions all the techniques that poets have perfected throughout the centuries. The speaker does this mainly by using nouns as verbs in creative and startling ways. The speaker also says "if i were a poet" twice. Giovanni *is* a poet. The speaker's repeated comment conveys a teasing and flirtatious attitude.

Leslie provides **relevant information** and **valid inferences** to support her points. However, she could improve the flow of her analysis by eliminating wordiness.

❻     An author's style helps to bring out the meaning of the work. By analyzing the different elements of Nikki Giovanni's style, a reader can better understand why she constructs her poems in this way and what meaning she conveys to her audience. In "Kidnap Poem," Nikki Giovanni uses tone, point of view, and imagery to deliver her message that love is poetic.

Leslie concludes with an **insightful summary** of the author's style.

### LEARN HOW   Eliminate Wordiness

Provide students with the following tips for eliminating wordiness.

- Rewrite sentences to delete meaningless phrases at the beginnings of sentences: *it is, there is, this is,* and so on.
- Delete *which* and *that* phrases.
- Replace *to be* verbs with strong verbs.
- Replace the passive voice with the active voice.
- Combine short sentences.

**LEARN HOW   Eliminate Wordiness** Because the task of analyzing an author's style is complex, writers sometimes over-explain a point, resulting in wordiness. Too many words can leave the audience feeling confused. As Leslie edits her essay, she finds a place where she can reduce the number of words to make her point clear.

**LESLIE'S REVISION TO PARAGRAPH ❺**

The speaker ~~seems to be saying~~ that she will bring to life ~~in her actions all the techniques that poets have perfected throughout the centuries. The speaker does this mainly~~ by using nouns as verbs in creative ~~and startling~~ ways.
*(suggests)* ... *(poetic techniques, and does so in the poem)*

YOUR TURN   Use the feedback from your peers and teacher as well as the two "Learn How" lessons to revise your essay. Evaluate how well you have analyzed the author's style and addressed the audience by examining your controlling idea, supporting points, quotations, and explanations.

YOUR TURN   Ask students to complete the **Your Turn** activity independently. Remind students to eliminate wordiness to make their writing concise.

For interactive revision tools, see

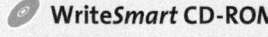 **Write*Smart* CD-ROM**

**Writing Center** on <u>thinkcentral.com</u>

## DIFFERENTIATED INSTRUCTION

### FOR ENGLISH LANGUAGE LEARNERS

**Wordiness** Write the following sentence on the board: *What I am saying is that the main message of the poem "Luxury" is that love is more important than other things such as power and wealth.*

Work with students to apply the tips listed above to eliminate wordiness from this sentence.

### FOR STRUGGLING WRITERS

**Word Bank** Provide students with a bank of words and phrases that can often be eliminated from writing. Have students add suggestions to the bank.

| | |
|---|---|
| actually | mostly |
| basically | really |
| essentially | sort of |
| generally | truly |
| kind of | ultimately |
| mainly | very |

# Editing and Publishing

In the editing stage, it is important to review your essay to make sure that it is free of errors that might distract your audience.

**COMMON CORE**

**W 5** Strengthen writing by editing. **L 1b** Use various types of clauses to convey specific meanings and add variety and interest. **L 2** Demonstrate command of the conventions of standard English capitalization, punctuation, and spelling.

## GRAMMAR IN CONTEXT: COMPOUND-COMPLEX SENTENCES

Authors vary sentence structure to combine or clarify related ideas and to keep the audience interested. Examine these sentences:

> 1. The speaker also says "if i were a poet" twice.
> 2. Giovanni **is** a poet.
> 3. The speaker's repeated comment conveys a teasing and flirtatious attitude.

Leslie notices that these sentences sound choppy and repetitive. They all concern the same point, so they can be combined into one sentence with three **clauses**—chunks of meaning containing a subject and a verb. When combining clauses in one sentence, a writer can keep some clauses **independent,** or able to stand alone as a sentence, and make others **subordinate,** or unable to stand alone.

To join clauses, use punctuation and conjunctions. Independent clauses are joined by a semicolon or by a comma and a coordinating conjunction. A subordinate clause may be added using a comma and a subordinating conjunction.

| Coordinating Conjunctions | Subordinating Conjunctions |
|---|---|
| for, and, nor, but, or, yet, so | after, although, as, because, before, if, since, than, though, unless, until, when, whether, while |

A **compound-complex sentence** adds both an independent clause and a subordinate clause to a simple sentence. Clauses in a compound-complex sentence are united by a common idea. Leslie combines her simple sentences into one compound-complex sentence:

> The speaker also says "if I were a poet" twice; because Giovanni is a poet,
> the speaker's repeated comment conveys a teasing and flirtatious attitude.

### PUBLISH YOUR WRITING

Consider these tips for sharing your analysis with an audience:
- Submit your essay as part of an application to an academic program.
- Send your essay to a magazine or newspaper that publishes literary reviews.
- Create a podcast to share with fans of the author.

**YOUR TURN** Proofread your essay and correct any errors you find. Use compound-complex sentences to add variety to your sentences, but remember to use them sparingly. Then, publish your essay for your audience.

# Editing and Publishing

**COMMON CORE** W 5, L 1b, L 2

## GRAMMAR IN CONTEXT: COMPOUND-COMPLEX SENTENCES

Review compound sentences and complex sentences with students.

- A compound sentence contains two independent clauses joined by a coordinating conjunction, a semicolon, or a conjunctive adverb. For example, *Mary loves soccer, and John loves basketball*.

- A complex sentence contains one subordinate clause and one independent clause. For example, *Because John loves basketball, he joins a team*.

- A compound-complex sentence occurs when these two types of sentences are combined. For example, *Because John loves basketball, he joins a team, and the coach is delighted with John's attitude*.

### PUBLISH YOUR WRITING

Brainstorm with students additional ways to publish their analytical essays.

**YOUR TURN** Allow students time to proofread their drafts. Remind them to add sentence variety by using a few compound-complex sentences.

---

### FOR ENGLISH LANGUAGE LEARNERS

**Sentence Combining** Write these sentences on the board:

- John went to practice.
- Bill stayed home.
- Bill had a cold.

Model for students how to create a compound-complex sentence: *John went to practice, but Bill stayed home because he had a cold.*

Provide student pairs with additional sentence sets and have them work to create compound-complex sentences.

### FOR STRUGGLING WRITERS

**Sentence Identification** Have each student make a series of three signs that read "Compound Sentence," "Complex Sentence" and "Compound-Complex Sentence." On transparency, display a variety of compound, complex, and compound-complex sentences—one at a time. Tell students to raise the correct signs for identifying each sentence. Stop to discuss any discrepancies in students' responses. When there is consensus, have students take turns explaining the reasoning behind the correct response.

## Scoring Rubric

Tell students that the best way to understand a scoring rubric is to use it to score actual writing. Have students work with partners to evaluate each other's essays. Using the language of the rubric, tell students to write their partners letters that explain the reasoning behind the assigned scores. For example, a student might write the following comment in his or her letter in support of a score of 3: *Your controlling idea identifies the points of analysis, but your point is obvious rather than insightful.* The purpose of a rubric is to eliminate subjectivity from the scoring process.

For Rubric Bank, see

 **Write*Smart* CD-ROM**

**Writing Center** on <u>thinkcentral.com</u>

## Assess and Reteach

### Assess

 **R** RESOURCE MANAGER—Copy Masters
Rubric for Evaluation p. 154

**Online Essay Scoring** at <u>thinkcentral.com</u>

### Reteach

**Level Up Online Tutorials** at <u>thinkcentral.com</u>

**Reteaching Worksheets** on <u>thinkcentral.com</u>

  Writing Lesson 5: Combining Sentences and Sentence Parts

  Writing Lesson 24: Elaborate with Incidents, Examples, and Quotations

---

## Scoring Rubric

Use the rubric below to evaluate your analysis from the Writing Workshop or your response to the on-demand task on the next page.

### ANALYSIS OF AN AUTHOR'S STYLE

| SCORE | COMMON CORE TRAITS |
|---|---|
| **6** | • **Development** Has an engaging introduction; includes a controlling idea with an insightful analysis of the author's style; supports main points with quotations; ends powerfully<br>• **Organization** Arranges ideas in an effective, logical order; uses varied transitions to create cohesion and link ideas<br>• **Language** Consistently maintains a formal style; uses precise language; shows a strong command of conventions |
| **5** | • **Development** Has an effective introduction; provides a controlling idea that offers an original analysis of the author's style; adequately supports main points with quotations; has a strong concluding section<br>• **Organization** Arranges ideas logically; uses transitions to link ideas<br>• **Language** Maintains a formal style; uses precise language; has a few errors in conventions |
| **4** | • **Development** Has an introduction that could be more engaging; includes a controlling idea that states an analysis of the author's style; could use some more quotations; has an adequate concluding section<br>• **Organization** Arranges ideas logically; could vary transitions more<br>• **Language** Mostly maintains a formal style; needs more precise language at times; has a few distracting errors in conventions |
| **3** | • **Development** Has an adequate, though not memorable, introduction; has a controlling idea that makes an obvious statement about the author's style; lacks sufficient support and quotations; has a routine concluding section<br>• **Organization** Reflects some flaws in organization; needs more transitions to link related ideas<br>• **Language** Frequently lapses into an informal style; uses some vague word choices; has some significant errors in conventions |
| **2** | • **Development** Has a weak introduction and a controlling idea that does not relate to the writing task; lacks specific details or quotations; has a weak concluding section<br>• **Organization** Has organizational flaws; lacks transitions throughout<br>• **Language** Uses an informal style and vague language; has many distracting errors |
| **1** | • **Development** Has no introduction or controlling idea; offers unrelated quotations as evidence or no evidence at all; ends abruptly<br>• **Organization** Includes a string of disconnected ideas with no overall organization<br>• **Language** Uses an inappropriate style and vague, tired language; has major problems with grammar, mechanics, and spelling |

# Preparing for Timed Writing

COMMON CORE

**W 10** Write routinely over shorter time frames for a range of tasks, purposes, and audiences.

## 1. ANALYZE THE TASK — 5 MIN

Read the task carefully. Then, read it again, noting the words in the task that tell the type of writing, the topic, the audience, and the purpose.

**WRITING TASK**

Style is the particular way someone does something. Choose a person you know and write an ⮜ *Type of writing* ⮜ *Topic* analysis of his or her distinctive style. Explain how this style communicates the ⮜ *Purpose* individual's personality, values, or traits. Plan on giving your analysis to this person ⮜ *Audience* as a gift.

## 2. PLAN YOUR RESPONSE — 10 MIN

Identify the key elements of this person's style. Consider physical appearance, speech patterns, body language, facial expressions, mannerisms, and so on. Then, list an example of each element. Finally, record what this style element and example tell people about the person's personality, values, or traits.

| Style Element | Example | Personality, Values, or Traits |
|---|---|---|
| 1. | | |
| 2. | | |
| 3. | | |

## 3. RESPOND TO THE TASK — 20 MIN

Begin drafting your analysis. Start with a sensory description of this person's style. As you write, keep the following points in mind.

- In the introduction, introduce the person, and include a controlling idea, or thesis statement, that cites your main points.
- In the body, present each main point, concrete details about each point, and an explanation of what is revealed about the person.
- In the concluding section, summarize the main points, and provide an insightful comment regarding the connection between style and inner character traits.

## 4. IMPROVE YOUR RESPONSE — 5–10 MIN

**Revising** Compare your draft with the writing task. Does it analyze a person's style? Does it explain how a person's style is reflective of personality, values, or traits? Does it end with an insightful comment?

**Proofreading** Find and correct any errors in grammar, usage, or mechanics. Make sure that your analysis and any edits are neatly written and legible.

**Checking Your Final Copy** Before you submit your analysis, examine it once more to make sure that you are presenting your best work.

---

## DIFFERENTIATED INSTRUCTION

### FOR ENGLISH LANGUAGE LEARNERS

**Prewriting** Suggest that students begin by sketching pictures of their subjects that include specific physical details. Tell students to label each detail. Then, have students write lists of words that describe these people under their drawings. Recommend that students draw lines between related descriptive words and style elements. Model this strategy for students. Then, tell students to use these sketches to help them complete the graphic organizer in Step 2.

### FOR STRUGGLING WRITERS

**Using Transitions** Point out to students that the scoring rubric emphasizes the use of varied transitions to create cohesion and link ideas. Suggest that students examine their essays for possible overuse of common transitions such as *then* and *next*. Guide them in identifying alternative transition words and phrases as needed.

---

## Preparing for Timed Writing

COMMON CORE W 10

1. **Analyze the Task** Before students begin writing, encourage them to answer the following questions:
   - What is my time limit?
   - What are the key skills assessed in the scoring rubric?
   - Who is my audience?
   - What are my topic and purpose?

2. **Plan Your Response** Point out to students that the scoring rubric emphasizes supporting main points. Explain that while quotations provide relevant support in a literary analysis, students will need to provide concrete details of another type for this writing task. Model for students how to complete a row in the chart to meet this criterion. For example, **Style Element:** hats; **Example:** wears department store hats made of brightly colored felt and decorated with rhinestones, netting, and feathers to church every Sunday; **Personality, Values, or Traits:** Shows an attempt to elevate life from its ordinariness.

3. **Respond to the Task** Remind students to include sensory details in their essays. They are writing about people whom the reader does not know. Therefore, they must use their words to create pictures for readers of these individuals and their mannerisms.

4. **Improve Your Response** Point out that the scoring rubric emphasizes an engaging introduction and a powerful concluding section. Tell writers to ensure that their introductions grab the attention of readers through action or dialogue. Instruct writers to conclude with insightful comments regarding the links between exterior style and interior traits.

## Assess

Use the Scoring Rubric on p. 898 to assess students' analytical essays.

# Focus and Motivate

**W 6** Use technology to produce and publish individual writing products, taking advantage of technology's capacity to display information flexibly and dynamically. **SL 5** Make strategic use of digital media to enhance understanding of findings, reasoning, and evidence and to add interest.

## PRODUCE WITH A PURPOSE

Help students identify their purpose and audience by downloading and listening to a variety of podcasts. Have students brainstorm lists of purposes and techniques that appeal to Internet audiences. Record students' ideas on the board.

## COMMON CORE TRAITS

As students prepare their podcasts, remind them to keep in mind the **COMMON CORE TRAITS** of a strong podcast.

# Practice and Apply

## Planning the Podcast

When writing a script for their podcasts, students should consider the following ideas:

- Keep the text short for a media format. Because we live in an age of sound bites and rapid exchange of ideas, listeners expect to get information speedily.

- Organize the text into short, focused segments that are supported by strategic use of digital media such as sound effects and music.

- Maintain a lighthearted tone to encourage people to listen to your podcast. If you're having fun, listeners will join you.

**R** RESOURCE MANAGER—Copy Master Technology p. 155

---

**Technology Workshop**

# Creating a Podcast

*Essential Course of Study*  **ECOS**

Now that you've written an analytical essay about an author's style, consider sharing it with other fans of that author via the Internet. Transform your essay into a **podcast**—a digital file that others can download from the Web and play.

Complete the workshop activities in your **Reader/Writer Notebook.**

| PRODUCE WITH A PURPOSE | COMMON CORE TRAITS |
|---|---|
| **TASK** <br><br> Adapt your analysis of an author's style to create a **podcast.** Then, upload the podcast to the Internet for other fans of the author to enjoy. | **A STRONG PODCAST . . .** <br><br> • contains an engaging and informative audio track <br> • conveys a distinctive tone and point of view <br> • appeals to a specific audience |

## Planning the Podcast

You will need to adapt your analysis to make it easy for a listening audience to understand. One way is to consider when you can use informal language, when you should use formal language, and when you should explain domain-specific vocabulary, such as literary terms. Then follow these suggestions to translate your analysis into an effective podcast.

- **Decide on the Details** Review your essay and identify key points, examples, and explanations. Think about how strategic use of digital media can enhance your ideas.

- **Craft Your Script** Your script should indicate what you will say about the author's style in a recorded audio track. Then, describe the music and sound effects that will match your narration and convey the tone of the essay.

| Audio Narration | Interpretive Reading | Music/Sound Effects |
|---|---|---|
| Giovanni uses the first-person point of view. The speaker addresses her loved one as "you," making the poem sound like an intimate conversation. The effect of this point of view is that the reader feels as if he or she is eavesdropping. | Interpretive reading of lines: "ode you with my love song." | Romantic, instrumental background music. |
| Giovanni also employs playful imagery. For example, Giovanni uses poetic terms in unusual ways: "put you in my phrases and meter / you to jones beach." The speaker suggests that she will use poetic techniques to capture her love in a song. | Interpretive reading of lines: "lyric you in lilacs / dash you in the rain." | Romantic, instrumental background music; ocean sounds; rain. |

**Media Tools** **THINK**central

Go to **thinkcentral.com**.
KEYWORD: HML9-900

---

## DIFFERENTIATED INSTRUCTION

**FOR ENGLISH LANGUAGE LEARNERS**

**Language: Reinforce Technology Terms**
Review key terms used in this Workshop:

- *podcast:* recorded program of talk, music, and so on made available over the Internet as a file that can be downloaded to a computer or portable device

- *sound effects:* sounds produced artificially or by recording to supply sounds called for

in the script of a radio, stage, film, or TV production

- *software:* the programs, routines, and so on for a computer or computer system

- *upload:* to transfer a file or program from a personal computer to another computer via the Internet

## Creating and Uploading

### CREATING THE PODCAST

Use sound to convey your distinctive point of view and to appeal to your specific audience.

- **Produce the Segment** Using podcasting software, assemble the parts of your presentation. (Check with your school's media specialist to make sure you have the equipment you need.) With your script as a guide, record your audio narration and experiment with sounds to present the information clearly, concisely, and logically.

- **Respect Copyright Laws** Use only audio elements for which you have permission. To add music to your track, you can search the Internet for royalty-free audio clips.

- **Use Your Voice** Speak slowly and enunciate words so the audience can follow your line of reasoning. Use intonations in your voice to add humor, emotion, and passion to your podcast. Be sure to use appropriate volume and maintain a formal tone.

- **Add Another Voice** Add depth and diversity to your podcast by adding another voice and another perspective through a co-host, an interview with an expert, or words from the author.

- **Edit Your Work** Did you make a mistake in your recording? Do you need to include more audio elements to appeal to your audience? Add the finishing touches to your track.

- **Upload the Final Product** With access to a free podcasting subscription service, you can share your analysis with a worldwide audience.

 Consult the following sources for ideas, tips, and additional help: Internet, knowledgeable peers, or a computer or audio/visual teacher. Listen carefully to any instructions you get that will help you produce an engaging podcast and solve potential problems. Then, create and post your podcast for your audience.

901

### FOR STRUGGLING STUDENTS

**Segment Structure** Provide students with a possible segment structure for planning their audio recordings and podcasts.

- **I.** Introduction/Welcome
- **II.** Announcements regarding book signings or publications, poetry slams or readings, and so on
- **III.** Poem Introduction
- **IV.** Style Point #1
- **V.** Interview
- **VI.** Style Point #2
- **VII.** Style Point #3
- **VIII.** Final Words

### Creating the Podcast

Tell students that they need to take advantage of technology to develop introductions that create a context for the information that follows. For example, students might include the date, the topic, introductions of themselves, introductions of any co-hosts or guests, statements of purpose, and so on. If students create regular podcasts, they may also need to include issue or volume numbers.

 You might also suggest that students new to this process work with partners who are familiar with the process.

## Assess and Reteach

### Assess

Use the **COMMON CORE TRAITS** to assess students' podcasts.

A strong podcast
- contains an engaging and informative audio track
- conveys a distinctive tone and point of view
- appeals to a specific audience

### Reteach

Make sure that students understand that there are two tasks here: a written task and a technological task. If students struggle to understand their dual tasks, present them with checklists for each task and monitor the completion of each step.

**Speaking and Listening Online**
- Public speaking tips
- Strategies for effective listening

# Assessment Practice

## COMMON CORE FOCUS

**RL 1** Cite textual evidence to support analysis of what the text says explicitly as well as inferences drawn from the text. **RL 2** Determine a theme of a text. **RI 1** Cite textual evidence to support analysis of what the text says explicitly as well as inferences drawn from text. **RI 2** Determine a central idea of a text. **W 5** Strengthen writing by revising and editing to ensure that it demonstrates the conventions of standard English grammar, usage, and punctuation. **L 4b** Identify patterns of word changes that indicate different meanings.

## CHECK READINESS

Read aloud the paragraph under **ASSESS** and stress to students that this is not the full Unit Test, but a way for them to check their readiness for it. Then have students examine the standards listed under **REVIEW** and look back in the unit or in the **Student Resource Bank** for any skills they need to review.

## READ THE TEXTS

Remind students to keep unit goals in mind as they read each passage, paying particular attention to these literary and reading skills:

- visualize and predict
- summarize and paraphrase
- analyze elements of style
- analyze humor, parody, and farce

To help students focus on elements of style while reading, encourage them to ask questions such as

- What sensory details and figurative language does the author use?
- What stylistic elements add humor to the selection?

## ANSWER THE QUESTIONS

Direct students to page R93–R101 of the **Handbook** to review test-taking strategies.

- As students prepare to answer multiple-choice questions, remind them to first read through all the choices, eliminate any that are clearly wrong, and then choose the *best* answer.

---

**COMMON CORE**

# Assessment Practice

### ASSESS
Taking this practice test will help you assess your knowledge of these skills and determine your readiness for the Unit Test.

### REVIEW
After you take the practice test, your teacher can help you identify any standards you need to review.

### COMMON CORE

**RL 1** Cite textual evidence to support analysis of what the text says explicitly as well as inferences drawn from the text. **RL 2** Determine a theme of a text. **RI 1** Cite textual evidence to support analysis of what the text says explicitly as well as inferences drawn from text. **RI 2** Determine a central idea of a text. **W 5** Strengthen writing by revising and editing to ensure that it demonstrates the conventions of standard English grammar, usage, and punctuation. **L 4b** Identify patterns of word changes that indicate different meanings.

**Practice Test**
THINK central
Take it at thinkcentral.com.
KEYWORD: HML9N-902

**DIRECTIONS** Read the two texts and the poster. Then, answer the questions that follow.

# Jimmy Hayes and Muriel
*by O. Henry*

### I

1   Supper was over, and there had fallen upon the camp a silence. The water hole shone from the dark earth like a patch of fallen sky. Coyotes yelped. Dull thumps indicated the rocking-horse movements of the hobbled ponies as they moved to fresh grass. A half-troop of the Frontier Battalion of Texas Rangers were distributed about the fire.

2   A well-known sound—the fluttering and scraping of chaparral[1] against wooden stirrups—came from the thick brush above the camp. The rangers listened cautiously. They heard a loud and cheerful voice call out reassuringly:

3   "Brace up, Muriel, old girl, we're 'most there now! Been a long ride for ye, ain't it, ye old antediluvian[2] handful of animated carpet-tacks? Hey, now, quit a tryin' to kiss me! Don't hold on to my neck so tight—this here paint hoss ain't any too shore-footed, let me tell ye. He's liable to dump us both off if we don't watch out."

4   Two minutes of waiting brought a tired "paint" pony single-footing into camp. A gangling youth of twenty lolled in the saddle. Of the "Muriel" whom he had been addressing, nothing was to be seen.

5   "Hi, fellows!" shouted the rider cheerfully. "This here's a letter fer Lieutenant Manning."

6   He dismounted, unsaddled, dropped the coils of his stake-rope, and got his hobbles[3] from the saddle-horn. While Lieutenant Manning, in command, was reading the letter, the newcomer rubbed solicitously at some dried mud in the loops of the hobbles, showing a consideration for the forelegs of his mount.

7   "Boys," said the lieutenant, waving his hand to the rangers, "this is Mr. James Hayes. He's a new member of the company. Captain McLean sends him down from El Paso. The boys will see that you have some supper, Hayes, as soon as you get your pony hobbled."

8   The recruit was received cordially by the rangers. Still, they observed him shrewdly and with suspended judgment. Picking a comrade on the border is done with ten times the care and discretion with which a girl chooses a

---

1. **chaparral** (shăp'ə-răl') *n.:* a dense thicket of shrubs or trees.
2. **antediluvian** (ăn'tĭ-də-lōō'vē-ən) *n.:* so old as to belong to an earlier period.
3. **hobbles** (hŏb'əlz) *n.:* a rope or strap used to fasten together the legs of a horse to prevent straying.

---

## DIFFERENTIATED INSTRUCTION

### FOR ENGLISH LANGUAGE LEARNERS
**Assessment Practice: Work Backward**
Prepare students by having them read the questions *before* reading the passages. Have pairs find unfamiliar words in test directions and questions and follow these steps:

1. Write each word on an index card and divide the cards among pairs of students. Tell students that they are going to define these words.

2. Instruct students to work individually to make an initial determination of each word's meaning. Then have students confer with their partners and check their work by using a dictionary.

3. Have students then share the words and definitions with the entire class, who can confirm the definitions or suggest others.

sweetheart. On your "side-kicker's" nerve, loyalty, aim, and coolness your own life may depend many times.

9   After a hearty supper Hayes joined the smokers about the fire. His appearance did not settle all the questions in the minds of his brother rangers. They saw simply a loose, lank youth with tow-coloured, sun-burned hair and a berry-brown, ingenuous face that wore a quizzical, good-natured smile.

10   "Fellows," said the new ranger, "I'm goin' to interduce to you a lady friend of mine. Ain't ever heard anybody call her a beauty, but you'll all admit she's got some fine points about her. Come along, Muriel!"

11   He held open the front of his blue flannel shirt. Out of it crawled a horned frog. A bright red ribbon was tied jauntily around its spiky neck. It crawled to its owner's knee and sat there, motionless.

12   "This here Muriel," said Hayes, with an oratorical wave of his hand, "has got qualities. She never talks back, she always stays at home, and she's satisfied with one red dress for every day and Sunday, too."

13   "Look at that blame insect!" said one of the rangers with a grin. "I've seen plenty of them frogs, but I never knew anybody to have one for a side-partner. Does the blame thing know you from anybody else?"

14   "Take it over there and see," said Hayes.

15   The stumpy little lizard known as the horned frog is harmless. He has the hideousness of the prehistoric monsters whose reduced descendant he is, but he is gentler than the dove.

16   The ranger took Muriel from Hayes's knee and went back to his seat on a roll of blankets. The captive twisted and clawed and struggled vigorously in his hand. After holding it for a moment or two, the ranger set it upon the ground. Awkwardly, but swiftly the frog worked its four oddly moving legs until it stopped close by Hayes's foot.

17   "Well, dang my hide!" said the other ranger. "The little cuss knows you. Never thought them insects had that much sense!"

## II

18   Jimmy Hayes became a favorite in the ranger camp. He had an endless store of good-nature, and a mild, perennial quality of humor that is well adapted to camp life. He was never without his horned frog. In the bosom of his shirt during rides, on his knee or shoulder in camp, under his blankets at night, the ugly little beast never left him.

19   Jimmy was a humorist of a type that prevails in the rural South and West. Unskilled in originating methods of amusing or in witty conceptions, he had hit upon a comical idea and clung to it reverently. It had seemed to Jimmy a

**GO ON** ➡

## ITEM ANALYSIS

| COMPREHENSION AND WRITTEN RESPONSE | ITEMS | UNIT PAGES |
|---|---|---|
| Elements of Style | 1, 2, 11, 12, 18, 22, 24, 25 | 820–825 |
| Writers' Styles | 19, 20, 24 | 820–825 |
| Humor, Parody, and Farce | 6, 15 | 843 |
| Reading Strategies | 3, 7, 14, 21 | 843 |
| Sequence | 8, 9, 13, 15, 16 | 827 |
| Summarize and Paraphrase | 4, 5, 6, 9, 10, 17, 23 | 853 |
| Word Parts | 3, 7, 14 | 838, 856 |

| WRITING AND GRAMMAR | ITEMS | UNIT PAGES |
|---|---|---|
| Support Main Points with Relevant Examples from the Text | 1 | 890–898 |
| Use a Variety of Sentence Types | 2, 3, 4, 5, 6 | 820–825 |

**Practice Test**

On **thinkcentral.com** students can complete an interactive version of this practice test *and* receive remediation for the skills they have not yet mastered.

very funny thing to have about his person, with which to amuse his friends, a tame horned frog with a red ribbon around its neck. As it was a happy idea, why not perpetuate it?

20   The sentiments existing between Jimmy and the frog cannot be exactly determined. The capability of the horned frog for lasting affection is a subject upon which we have had no symposiums.[4] It is easier to guess Jimmy's feelings. Muriel was his chef d'oeuvre of wit, and as such he cherished her. He caught flies for her, and shielded her from sudden northers.[5] Yet his care was half selfish, and when the time came she repaid him a thousand fold. Other Muriels have thus overbalanced the light attentions of other Jimmies.

21   Not at once did Jimmy Hayes attain full brotherhood with his comrades. They loved him for his simplicity and drollness, but there hung above him a great sword of suspended judgment. To make merry in camp is not all of a ranger's life. There are horse-thieves to trail, desperate criminals to run down, bravos to battle with, bandits to rout out of the chaparral, peace and order to be compelled at the muzzle of a six-shooter. Jimmy had been "most generally a cow-puncher," he said; he was inexperienced in ranger methods of warfare. Therefore the rangers speculated apart and solemnly as to how he would stand fire. For, let it be known, the honor and pride of each ranger company is the individual bravery of its members.

22   For two months the border was quiet. The rangers lolled, listless, in camp. And then—bringing joy to the rusting guardians of the frontier—Sebastiano Saldar, an eminent Mexican desperado and cattle-thief, crossed the Rio Grande with his gang and began to lay waste the Texas side. There were indications that Jimmy Hayes would soon have the opportunity to show his mettle. The rangers patrolled with alacrity, but Saldar's men were mounted like Lochinvar,[6] and were hard to catch.

23   One evening, about sundown, the rangers halted for supper after a long ride. Their horses stood panting, with their saddles on. The men were frying bacon and boiling coffee. Suddenly, out of the brush, Sebastiano Saldar and his gang dashed upon them with blazing six-shooters and high-voiced yells. It was a neat surprise. The rangers swore in annoyed tones, and got their Winchesters[7] busy; but the attack was only a spectacular dash of the purest Mexican type. After the florid demonstration the raiders galloped away, yelling, down the river. The rangers mounted and pursued; but in less than two miles the ponies labored so that Lieutenant Manning gave the word to abandon the chase and return to the camp.

---

4. **symposiums** (sĭm-pō'zē-əmz) *n.*: meetings or conferences to discuss a subject.
5. **northers** (nôr'thərz) *n.*: sudden, cold winds from the north.
6. **Lochinvar** (lok-in-vahr) *n.*: the hero of a narrative poem by Sir Walter Scott.
7. **Winchesters** (wĭn'chĕs'tərz) *n.*: a type of rifle.

904

## DIFFERENTIATED INSTRUCTION

### FOR STRUGGLING READERS

**Build Comprehension** Tell students that O. Henry is known for writing stories with surprise endings. "Jimmy Hayes and Muriel" contains many elements of a tall tale: a humorous protagonist, an amusing horned frog, and a wilderness setting. However, its ending is serious and thoughtful. Discuss these questions:

• What does Jimmy's behavior reveal about his character?

• Do you think the group is correct to doubt him?

• Why might people use humor in awkward situations?

**Language Support** Point out to students the phrase "there hung above him a great sword of suspended judgment" (paragraph 21). The phrase is an allusion to "The Sword of Damocles," a story from classical mythology. In the myth, Damocles wants rank and power. His king, Dionysius, favors him by treating him to a banquet. However, the king suspends a sword above Damocles' head that is supported by a single hair. A "Sword of Damocles," then, represents an ever-present danger.

24    Then it was discovered that Jimmy Hayes was missing. Someone remembered having seen him run for his pony when the attack began, but no one had set eyes on him since. Morning came, but no Jimmy. They searched the country around, on the theory that he had been killed or wounded, but without success. Then they followed after Saldar's gang, but it seemed to have disappeared. Manning concluded that the wily Mexican had recrossed the river after his theatric farewell. And, indeed, no further depredations[8] from him were reported.

25    This gave the rangers time to nurse a soreness they had. As has been said, the pride and honor of the company is the individual bravery of its members. And now they believed that Jimmy Hayes had turned coward at the whiz of Mexican bullets. There was no other deduction. Buck Davis pointed out that not a shot was fired by Saldar's gang after Jimmy was seen running for his horse. There was no way for him to have been shot. No, he had fled from his first fight, and afterward he would not return, aware that the scorn of his comrades would be a worse thing to face than the muzzles of many rifles.

26    So Manning's detachment of McLean's company, Frontier Battalion, was gloomy. It was the first blot on its escutcheon.[9] Never before in the history of the service had a ranger shown the white feather. All of them had liked Jimmy Hayes, and that made it worse.

27    Days, weeks, and months went by, and still that little cloud of unforgotten cowardice hung above the camp.

### III

28    Nearly a year afterward—after many camping grounds and many hundreds of miles guarded and defended—Lieutenant Manning, with almost the same detachment of men, was sent to a point only a few miles below their old camp on the river to look after some smuggling there. One afternoon, while they were riding through a dense mesquite flat, they came upon a patch of open hog-wallow prairie. There they rode upon the scene of an unwritten tragedy.

29    In a big hog-wallow lay the skeletons of three Mexicans. Their clothing alone served to identify them. The largest of the figures had once been Sebastiano Saldar. His great, costly sombrero, heavy with gold ornamentation—a hat famous all along the Rio Grande—lay there pierced by three bullets. Along the ridge of the hog-wallow rested the rusting Winchesters of the Mexicans—all pointing in the same direction.

30    The rangers rode in that direction for fifty yards. There, in a little depression of the ground, with his rifle still bearing upon the three, lay

---

8. **depredations** (dĕp'rĭ-dā'shənz) *n.*: attacks, raids, or acts of robbery.
9. **blot on its escutcheon** (ĭ-skŭch'ən) *n.*: a stain on one's reputation.

GO ON

**FOR ENGLISH LANGUAGE LEARNERS**

**Vocabulary: Idioms** Point out to language learners the phrase "shown the white feather" in paragraph 26 and have them use the context to figure out the meaning of the idiom. Then review with student how "to show the white feather" means to exhibit cowardly behavior.

**FOR ADVANCED LEARNERS/PRE–AP**

Have students learn about the border geography discussed in the story. Have them locate on maps the border between the United States and Mexico where rangers would have encountered bandits, and find out more about that region's landscape, which includes plants and animals such as horned frogs, chaparral, and mesquite.

another skeleton. It had been a battle of extermination. There was nothing to identify the solitary defender. His clothing—such as the elements had left distinguishable—seemed to be of the kind that any ranchman or cowboy might have worn.

31    "Some cow-puncher," said Manning, "that they caught out alone. Good boy! He put up a dandy scrap before they got him. So that's why we didn't hear from Don Sebastiano any more!"

32    And then, from beneath the weather-beaten rags of the dead man, there wriggled out a horned frog with a faded red ribbon around its neck, and sat upon the shoulder of its long quiet master. Mutely it told the story of the untried youth and the swift "paint" pony—how they had outstripped all their comrades that day in the pursuit of the Mexican raiders, and how the boy had gone down upholding the honor of the company.

33    The ranger troop herded close, and a simultaneous wild yell arose from their lips. The outburst was at once a dirge, an apology, an epitaph, and a paean of triumph. A strange requiem, you may say, over the body of a fallen comrade; but if Jimmy Hayes could have heard it he would have understood.

# *from* Taming the Nueces Strip:
# The Story of McNelly's Rangers

*by George Durham as told to Clyde Wantland*

1    We ate in the grub shanty. Only it wasn't a shanty—it was a hall with four tables seating maybe a hundred. We filed by and filled our mess kits and got a cup of coffee. A woman and a young girl gave us refills whenever we needed them. I soon found out that by emptying my coffee cup this girl would come up, reach across my shoulder, and say "Could I pour you some more?" I would have drunk cup after cup of coyote poison if she'd have refilled for me. Three times I said, "If you don't mind, ma'm," and three times I said, "Thank you, ma'm."

2    Whenever she walked up it seemed like somebody had dumped over the lilac water. I reckon I'd have sat there and drunk coffee till it ran out of my ears, but she seemed to catch on after awhile and didn't come back to me.

3    I struck up a little talk with one of the stock hands and found that the girl's name was the only name under the sun it could have been—Caroline. Somehow I knew it had to be Caroline. And she was a niece of Captain King's wife. She was Caroline Chamberlain.

906

4  I bedded down out in the open saddle shed, but I didn't go to sleep. That coffee was biling[1] me from foot to head—and my head was spinning like a squirrel cage, but not only from the coffee. I decided not to leave this place. I'd pull out from Captain McNelly and hire on here as a ranch hand. I'd work hard till I got to be a foreman; then I'd ask Caroline to marry me. Only a country boy could have had such crazy ideas. Maybe the three-quarter moon also had something to do with it.

5  I finally dozed off around daylight, and was shaken to my feet by Corporal Rudd. Our nags were gone and the pen was full of some real saddle horses. The others were picking out their mounts, dropping a loop on them easylike and hauling them in.

6  I had a lariat rope, all right, but I don't know what for. I had aimed to practice when I got the chance, but right then I couldn't have looped a post. And Caroline was right down there in the corral, as much at home as she'd been in the mess hall! What to do I didn't know, but I sure did give up any idea of trying to go to work as a ranch hand.

7  Captain King then proved he could read men better than he could read the back of his hand. He spoke to one of his vaqueros,[2] who dropped a rope on a good, rangy sorrel gelding[3] and brought him up. Captain King said, friendlylike, "Where you from, son?" I told him Georgia. Then he asked, "How come you to hire on with Captain McNelly?"

8  I told him my father had worked for Captain during the war. He nodded, again friendlylike. He examined my old saddle. The cotton cords in the cinch were worn thin and one was all but gone. It had no skirt—and the stirrups were the thin, wooden kind, and well worn. It was a cheap farm saddle to begin with, and it had begun many years ago.

9  He told his vaquero to give me another saddle and a rifle scabbard. I never forgot that.

10  I reckon he looked just once at me and knew I never could rope me a mount. Looking back through the years I see how crazy a country boy could get—planning to leave the Rangers and go to work for Captain King as a ranch hand. In the first place, of course, if I had left Captain McNelly there, Captain King wouldn't have let me stay all night on the ranch. I never had a crazier idea—or was it? I finally worked it out, all right. I got to be a foreman, and—but that all comes later. I didn't quit Captain McNelly until he was in his grave.

11  At that time I must have been the shabbiest looker in the outfit. None of the others were dudes, but they wore good hats and boots. Their clothes were

---

1. **biling** (bīˈlǐng) *v.:* making one feel queasy.

2. **vaqueros** (vä-kârˈōz) *n.:* cowboys or ranch hands.

3. **rangy sorrel gelding** (rānˈjē  sôrˈəl  gĕlˈdǐng) *n.:* long-limbed, light brown male horse.

**GO ON** ➤

---

## FOR ENGLISH LANGUAGE LEARNERS

**Vocabulary: Idioms**  Point out the idiom in this passage in paragraph 7: *Captain King proved he "could read men better than he could read the back of his hand."* Elicit responses from students that explain the literal meaning of the idiom "to read someone like the back of his hand." Then have students explain whether the idiom means that Captain King can "read men" well or badly.

**Culture: Connect**  George Durham describes how he felt as a poor, young man from the country when Captain King is kind to him. The captain first spares him the embarrassment of having to show his poor roping skills in front of the woman he likes. He then gives him a good saddle with a rifle scabbard, an act that Durham "never forgot." Ask students to connect with George's feelings in the passage by describing acts of generosity that they have witnessed. Have students discuss why they think people act in generous ways, even at the expense of their time or their money.

worn, but mine were worn and shabby to start with. My hat was skimpy and limber. In fact, it had served my dad for a good many years—and was a cheap farm hat to start with. My britches were homespun jeans, patched in the seat, and I had long ago outgrown them. My boots were farmer's boots—square-toed, with some of the hair still on them. But I was healthy and husky, and willing to learn. And I was dead set to make good with Captain, to go where he sent me and do what he told me to.

12    When I cinched the saddle on that sorrel gelding he made a picture, and I had to step back and look him over. Back home, he and that saddle would have been worth [at] least two hundred dollars. The horse had a good, roomy chest, open flanks, wide nostrils. He had some good breeding. But I was just looking.

13    "You like him, son?" I turned and saw Captain King right behind me, smiling. I could only nod my head for "yes."

14    "How much is a horse like that worth, Captain?"

15    He gave me a little smile and said, "Don't let that bother you, son. Wherever Captain McNelly sends you that horse will take you. He's a good, solid animal. Plenty of stay, and enough speed." I was a happy youngun.

16    Most of the other hands were now saddled, but Captain McNelly had not picked his horse. His eye was roving over the milling pen. You could tell he was following a big bay, a standout even in that pen.

17    "That's Segal. You want him?" Captain King asked, again proving he seemed to see everything and to savvy men.

18    Captain McNelly nodded his head slowly. "That's a five-hundred-dollar horse. What a piece of horse flesh! I couldn't ask you for that animal. Texas would never pay you for him."

19    Then Captain King said the same thing Old Sol had said back in Corpus: "I'd rather give him to you than have those bandits come and take him. Most of those rascals are mounted on my stock, and I at least want to do as good by you, Captain."

20    As we pulled away from Santa Gertrudis we were a lot different outfit from the motley crew that Captain had flung together only a week ago back at Burton. We were forted[4] and ready for anything.

21    For myself, I felt mighty chesty. For the first time in my life I had a prime bit of horse flesh between my knees, and that always does something to a man. We all had good rifles, good pistols, and we were behind a leader who didn't bobble or look back—a leader who had done nothing but win, a leader that the governor was betting on to bring law to the Nueces Strip.

---

4. **forted** (fort' id) v.: equipped.

908

## DIFFERENTIATED INSTRUCTION

**FOR STRUGGLING READERS**

**Vocabulary Support** Have students point out terms related to horses in the selection: *nags* (paragraph 5), *sorrel gelding* (paragraph 12), *open flanks* (paragraph 12), *big bay* (paragraph 16). Have students use context clues to guess the color and condition of the horses described by the terms. Students may use a dictionary to check their guesses, if needed.

**Concept Support** Point out to students that Captain King is outfitting Captain McNelly's band of men who will patrol the area called the Nueces Strip. Review with students that these young men were the first lawmen in this newly settled region of Texas, and people in the region counted on them to provide the rule of law and a measure of security.

**RUSTLE UP A GOOD TIME**

**COWBOY MUSEUM OF THE SOUTHWEST!**

This three-acre museum complex features interactive exhibits that tell the true story of the iconic Southwestern cowboy—from the earliest Spanish *vaqueros* to the hard-working ranchers of today. Attractions at the museum are sure to interest both schoolchildren and adults alike and include the following:

- The **Cowboy Art Gallery,** an exploration of the cowboy in fine art and popular culture

- The **Hall of Heroes,** a tribute to famous Southwestern lawmen of the past

- Live **roping demonstrations**

- A **mechanical bull** ride (and mechanical calf for our junior cowboys and cowgirls)

**... and lots more!**

909

**FOR ENGLISH LANGUAGE LEARNERS**

**Descriptive Language** Point out to students that the visual is an advertisement intended to attract visitors to the Cowboy Museum. Review descriptive words and terms that may be unfamiliar to students, such as *rustle up, interactive exhibits, iconic, roping demonstration,* and *mechanical bull.* Confirm understanding by asking questions about the advertisement such as *Which exhibit might include rangers such as Jimmy Hayes or George Durham? Which attraction might be about the cowboy shown in the photograph?*

# Reading Comprehension

Model a thinking process for answering multiple-choice questions.

1. **C is correct.** The Rangers did not recognize Jimmy's bravery or loyalty at the time of the attack. A is incorrect because the Rangers were in agreement that Jimmy had deserted them. B is incorrect because the Rangers did have knowledge of their own history. D is incorrect because the Rangers do not discuss the reasons for Jimmy's perceived cowardice.

2. **B is correct.** The limited point of view highlights the Rangers' shared values and camaraderie. A is incorrect because readers have access to Jimmy's thoughts as well as to the other Rangers' thoughts. C is incorrect because a third-person limited point of view does not explain every character's thoughts and emotions. D is incorrect because the author's point of view includes more than just one character.

3. **C is correct.** "[E]arlier period" suggests events occurring before. A is incorrect because it is an antonym. B is incorrect because "earlier period" does not suggest a contrast implied by "against." D is incorrect because "for" does not distinguish when the time period occurred.

4. **A is correct.** Jimmy does not want his horse's legs to be scratched by the hard mud on the hobbles. B is incorrect because a ranger living outdoors would have to be comfortable with dirt. C is incorrect because the hobbles are placed on his saddlehorn, not in his saddlebag. D is incorrect because Jimmy rubs off the mud without Lieutenant Manning telling him to.

5. **D is correct.** The men in the troop rely on one another in dangerous situations. A is incorrect because Rangers pursue thieves, so they would probably avoid joining the force. B is incorrect because the Rangers depend on one another for much more than riding. C is incorrect because the Ranger's dependence is serious, not humorous.

6. **D is correct.** Jimmy does not know of other ways to be funny, so he keeps the frog because he thinks he can amuse people with it. A is incorrect because Jimmy's mother is not mentioned. B is incorrect because

## Reading Comprehension

> **Use "Jimmy Hayes and Muriel"**
> **(pp. 902–906) to answer questions 1–9.**

1. One theme of "Jimmy Hayes and Muriel" is —
   A. Conflict results from misunderstanding.
   B. People should know the history of the Rangers.
   C. Bravery and loyalty can be difficult to recognize.
   D. Fear leads to cowardice.

2. The author wrote the story in third-person limited point of view so that readers —
   A. could understand Jimmy's thoughts and emotions
   B. could understand the ranger troop's thoughts and emotions
   C. could understand everyone's thoughts and emotions
   D. could focus on only one character's point of view

3. Since *antediluvian* means "so old as to belong to an earlier period," the prefix *ante-* probably means —
   A. after
   B. against
   C. before
   D. for

4. In paragraph 6, Jimmy rubs mud off of the loops of his hobbles —
   A. so that the dried mud doesn't rub against his horse's legs
   B. because he doesn't like anything dirty
   C. so the hobbles can be packed into his saddlebag
   D. because Lieutenant Manning tells him to do it

5. The Rangers choose comrades carefully because —
   A. they don't want to have thieves in their group
   B. they have to ride very well as a team
   C. they want to make sure that new members have a sense of humor
   D. their lives can depend on a comrade's loyalty, nerve, and aim

6. Jimmy keeps Muriel because —
   A. his mother had given her to him
   B. he is lonely
   C. he had rescued it from a hawk
   D. he thinks it is funny

7. The Latin word *alacritas* means "liveliness." The word *alacrity* in paragraph 22 probably means —
   A. eager readiness
   B. on high alert
   C. total devastation
   D. prominent

8. Immediately after the attack, the Rangers think that Jimmy —
   A. fought bravely
   B. was killed
   C. ran away in fear
   D. killed several cattle-thieves

9. The Rangers yell when they see Muriel because —
   A. they want to scare her away
   B. they miss her
   C. they realize that Saldar is dead
   D. they realize that they were wrong about Jimmy

Jimmy seems friendly, not lonely. C is incorrect because Jimmy does not explain how he found Muriel.

7. **A is correct.** Alacrity *implies lively action.* B is incorrect because liveliness does not imply caution or alertness. C is incorrect because liveliness has a positive connotation, not a negative one such as "devastation." D is incorrect because the thing that is lively does not have to be especially noticeable.

8. **C is correct.** The Rangers think Jimmy has shown the "white feather" of cowardice. A is incorrect because it is the opposite of the Rangers' thoughts. B is incorrect because the Rangers do not discover Jimmy's death until much time has passed. D is incorrect because the Rangers do not suspect that Jimmy has participated in the fight.

9. **D is correct.** The ribbon around Muriel's neck tells the Rangers that the man who fought the bandits was Jimmy. A is incorrect because the Rangers do not try to get Muriel to leave. B is incorrect because the soldiers have not mentioned the loss of Muriel. C is incorrect because the Rangers see Saldar's skeleton before they see Muriel.

10. In "Taming the Nueces Strip" George is —
    A. meeting his girlfriend
    B. being equipped as a ranger
    C. showing off his cowboy skills
    D. riding after cattle-thieves

11. The excerpt is written in —
    A. first-person point of view
    B. second-person point of view
    C. third-person omniscient point of view
    D. third-person limited point of view

12. In paragraph 1, the "grub shanty" is —
    A. a little hut
    B. a large dining hall
    C. a place to grow grubs for fishing bait
    D. a place to change grubby clothes

13. The first night, George decides to quit the Rangers and —
    A. go back to Georgia so he can marry Caroline
    B. become a preacher so he can marry Caroline
    C. become a Captain so he can marry Caroline
    D. become a ranch hand so he can marry Caroline

14. The word *foreman* in paragraph 4 contains the prefix *fore-*, which means "before or first in rank." What does *foreman* mean in that paragraph?
    A. Cowboy
    B. Head ranch hand
    C. Married man
    D. Ranch owner

15. When George gets to the corral, he realizes that —
    A. Captain McNelly is paying for his horse
    B. his old horse is still there
    C. he doesn't know enough to be a ranch hand
    D. he is good with a lariat

16. George signs on with Captain McNelly —
    A. to make money for school
    B. because his father had worked for the Captain
    C. to make money to get married
    D. because the Captain was family

17. Captain King wants to give Segal to Captain McNelly because —
    A. Texas will pay him back
    B. Captain McNelly once saved Captain King's life
    C. they are family
    D. the bandits will steal the horse

18. In paragraph 21, George feels *mighty chesty,* or proud, because —
    A. Caroline agrees to marry him
    B. he has a good horse and a good leader
    C. he learns to rope
    D. the Captain says he will be promoted soon

GO ON

10. **B is correct.** George receives the horse and saddle he will need as a Ranger. A is incorrect because the story does not state that Caroline becomes George's girlfriend. C is incorrect because George's cowboy skills are poor. D is incorrect because the Rangers do not chase cattle thieves in the selection.

11. **A is correct.** George tells the story from his personal point of view, using the pronouns I and me. B is incorrect because second-person point of view would tell the story using the pronoun you. C is incorrect because the excerpt is told from George's viewpoint, not the view of an all-knowing narrator. D is incorrect because although the story is limited to George's point of view, it is told in first person.

12. **B is correct.** The "grub shanty" is where the author eats. A is incorrect because the "grub shanty" is large, not small. C is incorrect because "grub" refers to food, not insects. D is incorrect because the building is a place to eat, not change clothes.

13. **D is correct.** George falls in love and sees becoming a ranch hand as a way to be near Caroline. A is incorrect because George never mentions returning to Georgia. B is incorrect because George wants to be a Ranger, not a preacher. C is incorrect because George never aspires to be a Captain, only a Ranger.

14. **B is correct.** The foreman leads or manages the other workers on the ranch. A is incorrect because "cowboy" does not imply the leadership position of a foreman. C is incorrect because a foreman could be either married or single. D is incorrect because a foreman would work for a ranch owner.

15. **C is correct.** George does not know how to rope a horse, which would be an essential skill for a ranch hand. A is incorrect because the state of Texas will pay Captain King for George's horse. B is incorrect because the old horses are taken away. D is incorrect because George does not know how to use a lariat.

16. **B is correct.** George's father had worked for the Captain during the war. A is incorrect because George does not mention attending school. C is incorrect because George works for the Captain before he becomes interested in getting married. D is incorrect because he is not related to the Captain.

17. **D is correct.** Captain King knows that bandits will want to steal such a good-quality horse. A is incorrect because Texas could not afford to buy such an expensive horse. B is incorrect because the relationship between Captain King and Captain McNelly is not described. C is incorrect because the two captains are not said to be related.

18. **B is correct.** George is proud to be working in the position he is in. A is incorrect because Caroline does not agree to marry George in the selection. C is incorrect because George does not learn cowboy skills in the selection. D is incorrect because the Captain does not mention promotions for his men.

## ANSWERS

**19. C is correct.** *Jimmy is a better horseman than George, who comes from a farm. A is incorrect because neither of the men have girlfriends in the stories. B is incorrect because neither of the characters mentions his military background. D is incorrect because both characters are described as young.*

**20. A is correct.** *In both stories, the troops of men work together to help one another. B is incorrect because George has not yet become friends with his new troop members. C is incorrect because George is just getting ready to do his job in the selection. D is incorrect because the stories emphasize the men's duty to one another, not their organization.*

**21. C is correct.** *The photo shows the movement and excitement of a live roping demonstration in hopes of attracting people to view it. A is incorrect because the photo is focused on action rather than on the cowboy's clothing. B is incorrect because the photo doesn't provide information about lawmen using ropes or fast horses. D is incorrect because the photo doesn't provide information about interactive exhibits.*

**22. B is correct.** *The word* tribute *indicates that the exhibit is intended to show gratitude and praise to the lawmen. A is incorrect because tribute is not given for untrue stories. C is incorrect because in this context a tribute is not a bribe. D is incorrect because there is no information to support the idea in advertisment.*

## SHORT CONSTRUCTED RESPONSE

**Possible responses:**

**23.** *Jimmy was a good ranger because he didn't run away from the fight. Instead, he chased and killed the cattle-thieves.*

**24.** *Captain King recognizes both George's inexperience with horses and Captain McNelly's interest in the horse Segal.*

**25.** *Although George and Jimmy have different temperaments, both are eager to learn. At first they don't look as if they can do the job, but they grow into their work.*

---

> **Use "Jimmy Hayes and Muriel" and "Taming the Nueces Strip" to answer questions 19–20.**

**19.** One difference between Jimmy and George is —
   **A.** George has a girlfriend, but Jimmy does not
   **B.** Jimmy has a military background, but George does not
   **C.** Jimmy has experience as a cow-puncher, but George does not
   **D.** George is young, but Jimmy is middle-aged

**20.** One message in both "Jimmy Hayes and Muriel" and "Taming the Nueces Strip" is the importance to Rangers of —
   **A.** teamwork
   **B.** friendship
   **C.** hard work
   **D.** being organized

> **Use the poster on page 909 to answer questions 21–22.**

**21.** The photo of the cowboy most likely is meant to show that —
   **A.** cowboys wore clothing suited to the work they performed
   **B.** lawmen used ropes and fast horses to capture cattle rustlers
   **C.** the museum's live roping demonstrations will excite viewers of all ages
   **D.** interactive exhibits are located throughout the three-acre complex

**22.** The use of *tribute* in the phrase "tribute to famous Southwestern lawmen" suggests that —
   **A.** stories about Western lawmen are generally untrue
   **B.** the museum respects and honors the lawmen of history
   **C.** lawmen sometimes demanded bribes from the people they protected
   **D.** money from the Hall of Heroes will go to the families of lawmen

## SHORT CONSTRUCTED RESPONSE
**Write a short response to each question, using text evidence to support your response.**

**23.** Do you think Jimmy was a good Ranger? Support your response with evidence from the text.

**24.** Why does George say that Captain King is *savvy*, or understanding, about men? Support your response with evidence from the text.

**Write a short response to the following question, using evidence from both texts to support your response.**

**25.** What is one characteristic that Jimmy and George share? Support your response with evidence from **both** texts.

# Revising and Editing

DIRECTIONS  Read this passage, and answer the questions that follow.

> (1) I saw trees ripping from the ground and people displaced from their homes. (2) I wasn't prepared for the massive destruction of Hurricane Ivan. (3) What began as a tropical depression eventually caused billions of dollars in damage and the deaths of 130 people. (4) The hurricane swept across the Caribbean, slamming into St. Vincent, Barbados, and Jamaica! (5) Another hard-hit place was my country, Grenada. (6) By the time it reached the capital St. George's, Ivan was traveling at 140 miles per hour. (7) Virtually every major building in St. George's suffered structural damage. (8) People wonder how they can avoid this kind of destruction. (9) The best thing to do is never find yourself in the path of a hurricane.

1. What is the most effective way to improve the organization of the paragraph?
   A. Move sentence 1 to follow sentence 6.
   B. Move sentence 2 to follow sentence 8.
   C. Move sentence 3 to follow sentence 4.
   D. Move sentence 8 to follow sentence 4.

2. What change, if any, should be made in sentence 1?
   A. Insert a comma after **ground**.
   B. Change **ripping** to **ripped**.
   C. Change **displaced** to **displace**.
   D. Make no change.

3. What transition could be added to the beginning of sentence 3?
   A. Consequently,
   B. However,
   C. Naturally,
   D. Therefore,

4. What change, if any, should be made in sentence 4?
   A. Insert a comma after **hurricane**.
   B. Delete the comma after **St. Vincent**.
   C. Change the exclamation point to a period.
   D. Make no change.

5. What change, if any, should be made in sentence 6?
   A. Change **was traveling** to **had traveled**.
   B. Delete the comma after **St. George's**.
   C. Add a comma before **St. George's**.
   D. Make no change.

6. What is the most effective way to revise sentence 9 to make it imperative?
   A. Never find yourself in the path of a hurricane.
   B. I recommend that you never find yourself in the path of a hurricane!
   C. Have you ever found yourself in the path of a hurricane?
   D. Finding yourself in the path of a hurricane is never the best thing to do.

913

---

---

## ANSWERS
## Revising and Editing

1. **A *is correct.*** *Sentence 2 should be the first sentence of the paragraph; sentence 1 should be moved to the section of the passage describing the hurricane's damage because it gives an example of the hurricane's destruction. B is incorrect because sentence 2 contains introductory information and should be first. C and D are incorrect because they do not address the passage's main organizational problem, that sentence 2 should be the opening sentence.*

2. **B *is correct.*** Ripping *should be changed to* ripped *in order to have the correct form of the adjective. A is incorrect because a comma is not needed for a compound object. C is incorrect because* displace *is not an adjective. D is incorrect because there is an error in the sentence.*

3. **B *is correct.*** However *emphasizes that even though the speaker was not prepared, Hurricane Ivan's damage was extensive. A, C and D are incorrect because* Consequently, Naturally, *and* Therefore *imply that the damage occurred specifically because the speaker was not prepared.*

4. **C *is correct.*** *The sentence is a statement of fact and should not have an exclamation point. A is incorrect because a comma would separate the subject from the verb. B is incorrect because the comma is required for a list. D is incorrect because there is an error in the sentence.*

5. **C *is correct.*** *A comma is required before an appositive. A is incorrect because* was traveling *is the correct tense to describe the current speed of the hurricane. B is incorrect because an inserted comma would separate the subject from the verb. D is incorrect because there is an error in the sentence.*

6. **A *is correct.*** *A is the only sentence that gives a command; furthermore, its subject is understood to be* you. *B is incorrect because it is exclamatory. C is incorrect because it is interrogative. D is incorrect because it is declarative, not imperative.*

### INTRODUCE *GREAT READS*

In Unit 8, students have discussed a number of big questions. Invite students to tell which question they found most intriguing and why, and then focus attention on the three that appear on this page. Discuss the recommended books and their summaries, pointing out how each connects to the related question. Encourage students to choose one or more of these "great reads" to read independently.

---

## UNIT 8
# Great Reads

## Ideas for Independent Reading

Highly individualistic writing styles are apparent in the following works.

### *Is fear our worst enemy?*

**One Day in the Life of Ivan Denisovich**
*by Alexandr Solzhenitsyn*

The author's indictment of the Soviet gulags, in which he was once a prisoner, shows that hunger, cold, and humiliation are just as powerful as fear.

**Things Fall Apart**
*by Chinua Achebe*

Okonkwo, the main character in Achebe's novel of the effects of colonialism on Nigeria, fears the dissolution of his world and his own powerlessness to resist it.

**Ethan Frome**
*by Edith Wharton*

Ethan Frome is locked into a sterile marriage that keeps him from finding love with Mattie. This famous novel suggests that isolation and loneliness are the enemies of human fulfillment.

### *Have you ever felt out of place?*

**All Creatures Great and Small**
*by James Herriot*

In the well-known veterinarian's first collection, he lands a position in the Yorkshire Dales. He can't understand the dialect, the farmers think he's crazy, and he makes a mess of the first dates with his eventual wife. But his patients love him.

**Brave New World**
*by Aldous Huxley*

In this classic novel's vision of the future, Bernard Marx feels out of place in the World State, in which everything—feelings, childbirth, human experience—is artificial. Can he escape?

**Red Scarf Girl: A Memoir of the Cultural Revolution**
*by Ji-li Jiang*

The author's world was turned upside down during China's Cultural Revolution. At first she accepted the spying, humiliation, and fear. Then, as dangerous as it was, she determined that she would think for herself.

### *Who makes you laugh?*

**I'm a Stranger Here Myself**
*by Bill Bryson*

After living in Britain for 20 years, Bryson returned to the United States with a fresh eye for the absurdities of U.S. life.

**Funny Letters from Famous People**
*by Charles Osgood*

Popular broadcaster Charles Osgood offers us the witty remarks of notable people from Abraham Lincoln to Andy Rooney.

**The Wit and Wisdom of Mark Twain**
*edited by Alex Ayres*

This anthology compiles the most humorous excerpts of Twain's fiction, speeches, and letters.

**Get Novel Wise** **THINK** central

Go to **thinkcentral.com**.
KEYWORD: HML9-914

**914**

---

**THINK** central

**NovelWise**

The keyword on this page points to **NovelWise,** a Web site that helps students choose a novel or other book-length work to read. **NovelWise** also provides
- study guides
- reading strategies and literary elements instruction
- presentations to introduce classic novels
- project ideas

# Putting It in Context

## HISTORY, CULTURE, AND THE AUTHOR

- In Nonfiction
- In Fiction
- In Poetry

915

**About the Art** Louise Freshman Brown created the collage *Jazz Player III* in 1991. For more information, see page 993.

## INTRODUCE THE UNIT

People sometimes ask, "What is the context?" The answer often depends on what you are talking about. For example, the context of a conversation often refers to the circumstances that brought the people together to talk. The context of a story includes the time and place in which it is set, and the characters' background. The context of a painting includes the artist's biography and his or her motivation for creating the art. The context of a political argument includes the issues of the day and the personal views of the people involved. In each case, a reader, viewer, or listener can understand ideas more clearly by putting them in context.

Invite students to consider how the painting and the photograph on this page relate to the matter of context. To elicit ideas, ask:

- How are the painting and the photograph similar?
- What can you tell about the setting of each image? How might the differences affect your thoughts about the musicians in the images?
- What other questions might you ask to put each image in context?

Tell students that in this unit, they will read works of nonfiction, fiction, and poetry. They will consider the context of each selection's **history, culture,** and **author.**

For help in planning this unit, see

**R** **RESOURCE MANAGER UNIT 9**
pp. 1–10

# UNIT 9

## COMMON CORE STRAND

| STRAND | Text Analysis Workshop: History, Culture, and the Author pp. 918–923 | from Angela's Ashes Memoir pp. 924–939 Lexile: 1140 | Revisiting Sacred Ground Essay pp. 940–949 Lexile: 930 Fry: 10 Dale-Chall: 6.6 | Blues Ain't No Mockin Bird Short Story pp. 950–961 Lexile: 960 Fry: 7 Dale-Chall: 6.7 | American History Short Story pp. 962–975 Lexile: 1010 |
|---|---|---|---|---|---|
| **Reading Literature** | Context Within the Work pp. 918–919 RL 4 Context Outside the Work pp. 920–921 RL 4, RL 6 Analyze the Text p. 922 | | | Voice and Dialect pp. 951, 952, 956, 958, 960 RL 4 Draw Conclusions pp. 951, 954, 957, 960 RL 1 Similes p. 959 RL 1, RL 4 | Influence of Author's Background pp. 963, 964, 969, 973, 974 RL 3, RL 10 Character pp. 967, 974 RL 3 Connect pp. 963, 966, 970, 972, 974 RL 10 |
| **Reading Informational Text** | Context Within the Work pp. 918–919 RI 4 Context Outside the Work pp. 920–921 RI 4 Analyze the Text p. 923 | Memoir pp. 925, 926, 928, 930–933, 937 RI 6 Use Allusions to Make Inferences pp. 925, 931, 935, 937 RI 1, RI 6 Language Coach p. 934 RI 4 | Cultural Symbol pp. 941, 944, 945, 947, 948 RI 6 Monitor pp. 941, 942, 946, 948 RI 10 | | |
| **Writing** | | Quickwrite p. 924 Writing Prompt p. 939 | Quickwrite p. 940 | Writing Prompt p. 961 W 2b | |
| **Speaking and Listening** | | | | Discuss p. 950 SL 1 | What's the Connection p. 962 SL 1 |
| **Language** | | Language Coach p. 929 Write Concisely pp. 931, 939 L 1b Latin Root *fid* p. 938 L 4c | Language Coach p. 944 L 4 Greek Root *cosm* p. 949 L 4c | Choose Effective Words pp. 957, 961 L 3 Language Coach p. 959 | Language Coach p. 970 L 4a Idioms p. 975 L 5a |

ECOS

| Comparing Texts<br><br>**Special Report/President Killed**<br>Magazine Article/Photograph<br>pp. 976–981<br><br>Lexile: 830/890/930/N/A<br>Fry: 12/7/10/N/A<br>Dale-Chall: 7.3/5.7/6.6/N/A | **The Tropics in New York/Theme for English B**<br>Poems<br>pp. 982–989 | **Haiku/Haiku/Honku**<br>Haiku<br>pp. 990–995 | **Writing Workshop:**<br>Informative Text:<br>Online Feature Article<br>pp. 996–1003<br><br>**Technology Workshop:**<br>Updating an Online Feature Article pp. 1004–1005<br>ECOS |
| --- | --- | --- | --- |
| Photograph p. 980  **RL 7** | Harlem Renaissance Literature pp. 983, 986, 989  **RL 6**<br>Reading Poetry pp. 983, 984, 987, 989  **RL 4, RL 10** | Haiku pp. 991, 995  **RL 10**<br>Historical and Cultural Context pp. 991–995  **RL 6**<br>Irony p. 993  **RL 4**<br>Interpret Imagery pp. 991, 992, 995  **RL 4** | |
| Controlling Idea pp. 976–979  **RI 2, RI 5, RI 7**<br>Photograph p. 980  **RI 7** | Magazine Article p. 988 | | |
| Writing Prompt p. 979  **W 9b**<br>(RI 6) | Quickwrite p. 982 | Quickwrite p. 990 | Writing an Online Feature Article pp. 996–1003  **W 2a–f, W 4, W 5, W 6, W 7, W 9b (RI 1)**<br>Updating an Online Feature Article pp. 1004–1105  **W 6** |
| | | | Revising pp. 1000–1002  **SL 5**<br>Updating an Online Feature Article pp. 1004–1005  **SL 5** |
| Foreign Phrases p. 978  **L 4**<br>Language Coach p. 978  **L 4** | Language Coach pp. 984, 986  **L 4** | | Drafting p. 999  **L 3a**<br>Editing and Publishing p. 1003  **L 1b, L 2** |

ECOS
To see the complete Essential Course of Study, see pp. T23–T28.

For additional lesson planning help, see **Teacher One Stop DVD.**

# Instructional Support

**Resource Manager Unit 9**

**UNIT SUPPORT**

Academic Vocabulary, p. 3

Additional Academic Vocabulary, p. 4

Grammar Focus p. 5

Text Analysis Workshop pp. 9–10

Writing Workshop: Informative Text:
Online Feature Article p. 135

**SELECTION SUPPORT\***

**Plan and Teach**

Lesson planning pages

Additional leveled selection questions

Extension activities

**Student Copy Masters**

Selection summaries in four languages

Skills copy masters in English and Spanish

Vocabulary preteaching and support

Reading Check and Question Support

Reading Fluency

\*Available for all selections

† Available on **thinkcentral.com**.

**Language Handbook**

**Vocabulary Practice**

**Best Practices Toolkit†**

**PowerNotes** DVD-ROM†

**Connections: Nonfiction for
Common Core** CD-ROM†

**Teacher One Stop** DVD-ROM

**Student One Stop** DVD-ROM

**Write*Smart*** CD-ROM†

**GrammarNotes** DVD-ROM†

**WordSharp** CD-ROM†

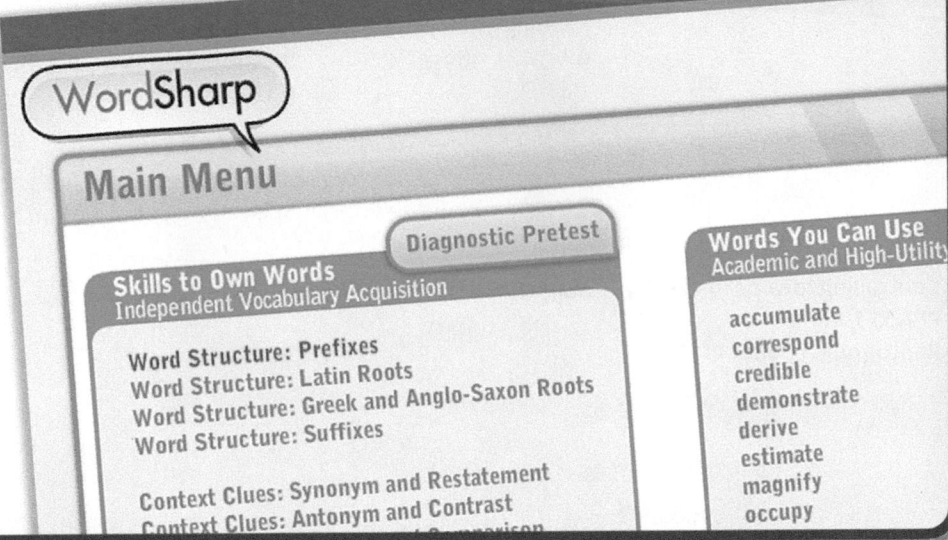

# Differentiated Instruction

| STRUGGLING READERS AND WRITERS | ENGLISH LANGUAGE LEARNERS | ADVANCED LEARNERS |
|---|---|---|
| **Resource Manager Unit 9** | **Resource Manager Unit 9** | **Resource Manager Unit 9** |
| Additional Selection Questions | Selection Summaries in English, Spanish, Vietnamese and Haitian Creole | Additional Selection Questions |
| Question Support | | Ideas for Extension |
| Reading Fluency | Skills Copymasters in Spanish | **Diagnostic and Selection Tests** |
| **Interactive Reader** | **English Language Learner Adapted Interactive Reader Teacher's Guide** | Selection Tests B/C |
| **Adapted Interactive Reader** | | |
| **Level Up Online Tutorials** | **ELL Adapted Interactive Reader** | |
| **Audio Anthology** | **Audio Tutor** | |
| (with Audio summaries) | **Guide to English for Newcomers** | |
| **Diagnostic and Selection Tests** | **Audio Anthology** | |
| Selection Tests A/B | **Audio Summaries in Multiple Languages** (on **thinkcentral.com**) | |

## Assessment and Reteaching

**Diagnostic and Selection Tests**

**Unit and Benchmark Tests**

**ThinkCentral Online Assessment:**

• All program assessments

• Level Up Online Tutorials

**ExamView Test Generator** on the Teacher One Stop DVD-ROM

**Online Essay Scoring** on **thinkcentral.com**

**ThinkCentral Online Reteaching:**

• Level Up Online Tutorials

• Reteaching Worksheets

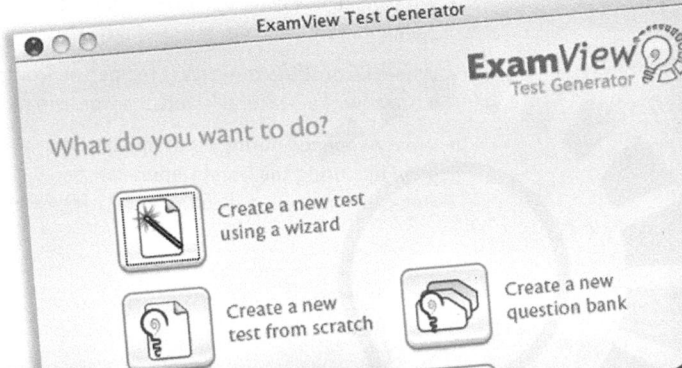

ExamView Test Generator

**ExamView** Test Generator

What do you want to do?

Create a new test using a wizard

Create a new test from scratch

Create a new question bank

## Professional Development

**Video Center** Based on interviews with program consultants and other educational experts, these videos feature classroom-ready teaching strategies.

**Teacher Toolkit** Includes a Teacher Handbook as well as a range of articles and handouts by program consultants and other educators.

Janet Allen

Jim Burke

Kylene Beers

Carol Jago

**THINK** central **at a Glance**

**One Location, Endless Resources**

**Find Resources** Browse all *Holt McDougal Literature* components for the ones that meet your students' needs and match your teaching style.

**Assess Progress and Reteach** Assign electronic versions of program assessments to measure your students' mastery of the Common Core State Standards. On thinkcentral.com, some tests deliver online remediation tutorials to students who have not mastered skills.

### Interactive Whiteboard Lessons

Prepare your students for college and careers by teaching relevant, real-world skills through dynamic, interactive instruction. Go to **thinkcentral.com** to browse through all whiteboard lessons, including the following:

• Historical and Cultural Context

• Author's Purpose and Perspective

• Word Choice and Tone

**HISTORY**

Together Holt McDougal and HISTORY® are revolutionizing the study of English/language arts with video that helps students relive and re-imagine the people, places, and events they are discovering through reading. Look for selections with the HISTORY® icon.

915D

# What **SHAPES**
## who you are?

Introduce the page by reading the question aloud. As students read the opening paragraph, encourage them to take a few notes in which they apply the factors to themselves. If you are comfortable doing so, share an example from your own life or the life of someone you know.

*ACTIVITY* Suggest several possibilities to get students started, such as the historical figures Pocahontas and Dr. Martin Luther King, Jr. and the film character Indiana Jones. Using one of these examples, model the *ACTIVITY* by writing on the board the answers to the questions. After students answer the questions for their own choice following your example, invite volunteers to share their insights with the class.

**CHECK UNDERSTANDING** Have students summarize the reasons that context helps readers understand the experiences of an individual.

# What **SHAPES**
## who you are?

What helped make you the individual you are today? Your family, friends, and personal experiences probably played key roles. But broader factors—like the neighborhood you grew up in and the decade you were born into—have also influenced who you are.

*ACTIVITY* Think of someone who has made a strong impression on you—either a historical figure, a fictional character, or someone you know. Consider how the following factors may have shaped that person:

- **When he or she grew up.** How would his or her daily life have been different from our lives today?

- **Where he or she is from.** Was the person from a bustling city or a tiny town? a peaceful island or a war-torn nation?

- **What happened during his or her lifetime.** Maybe the person grew up during the Great Depression, fled Europe during the Holocaust, or turned 18 in the midst of the Vietnam War.

**Find It Online!** THINK central

Go to thinkcentral.com for the interactive version of this unit.

916

## Unit Resources

See resources on the **Teacher One Stop DVD-ROM** *and on* thinkcentral.com.

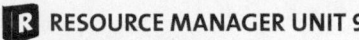 **RESOURCE MANAGER UNIT 9**

**UNIT AND BENCHMARK TESTS**

 **BEST PRACTICES TOOLKIT**

**INTERACTIVE READER**

**ADAPTED INTERACTIVE READER**

**ELL ADAPTED INTERACTIVE READER**

**LANGUAGE HANDBOOK**

**VOCABULARY PRACTICE**

**TECHNOLOGY**

- Teacher One Stop DVD-ROM
- Student One Stop DVD-ROM
- PowerNotes DVD-ROM
- Write*Smart* CD-ROM
- Media*Smart* DVD-ROM
- GrammarNotes DVD-ROM
- Audio Anthology CD
- Audio Tutor CD

**Find It Online!**  THINK central

The interactive version of this unit on thinkcentral.com includes

- video and **PowerNotes** introductions to key selections
- audio support—listen or download
- **ThinkAloud** models
- **WordSharp** vocabulary tutorials
- interactive review and remediation

## Preview Unit Goals

| TEXT ANALYSIS | • Analyze influence of author's background<br>• Analyze influence of historical and cultural context<br>• Recognize how time periods and cultural experiences are represented in texts<br>• Identify and interpret cultural symbols<br>• Identify and analyze allusions, voice, dialect, and figurative language |
|---|---|
| READING | • Make inferences and draw conclusions; cite evidence<br>• Monitor comprehension<br>• Identify controlling idea and supporting details |
| WRITING AND LANGUAGE | • Write an informative text (online feature article)<br>• Understand and use verbals and verbal phrases to add variety and interest to writing<br>• Use vivid verbs |
| SPEAKING AND LISTENING | • Participate in a virtual dicussion |
| VOCABULARY | • Use knowledge of word roots to determine or clarify word meanings<br>• Use context clues to interpret idioms |
| ACADEMIC VOCABULARY | • contrast      • environment<br>• factor       • incorporate<br>• predominant |
| MEDIA AND VIEWING | • Analyze representations in different mediums<br>• Update an online article |

917

Included in this unit: **RL 1-4, RL 6-7, RL 10, RI 1-2, RI 4-7, RI 10, W 2a-f, W 4-7, W 9b (RI 1, 6), SL 1, SL 5, L 1b, L 2, L 3, L 3a, L 4, L 4a, L 4c, L 5, L 5a, L 6**

Complete text of the Common Core State Standards is found in the correlation on p. T10. Standards covered in this unit are found in the standards overview (pp. 915A–915B) and on the lesson pages where they are taught.

## Preview Unit Goals

Explain that the goals listed on this page reflect the main skills focus of Unit 9. To prepare for the unit, have students familiarize themselves with the list and set some goals for themselves. Draw their attention to the color that designates each skill set here and throughout the unit.

Point out the Academic Vocabulary. Invite students to write the list in their **Reader/Writer Notebooks** along with a definition for each term. Urge students to return to and refine the definitions as they read, discuss, and write about the selections in Unit 9.

## DIFFERENTIATED INSTRUCTION

### FOR ENGLISH LANGUAGE LEARNERS

**Academic Vocabulary** Provide students with definitions of each Academic Vocabulary word.

**contrast** (kən trast′) v. to show differences
**environment** (en vī′rən mənt) n. surroundings; the land, water, climate, plants and animals of an area
**factor** (fak′tər) n. elements or conditions that make something what it is or create a result

**incorporate** (in kôr′pə rāt) v. to join or combine into a single whole
**predominant** (prē däm′ə nənt) adj. the most frequent or the most important

Use the copy master to help students learn academic words they will use in this unit and on the Assessment Practice.

🅡 RESOURCE MANAGER—Copy Masters
    Academic Vocabulary p. 3
    Additional Academic Vocabulary p. 4

# Focus and Motivate

## COMMON CORE FOCUS

**RL 4** Determine the figurative meaning of phrases as they are used in a text; analyze the cumulative impact of specific word choices on meaning and tone. **RL 6** Analyze a particular point of view or cultural experience reflected in a work of world literature. **RI 4** Analyze the cumulative impact of specific word choices on meaning and tone. **RI 6** Determine an author's point of view or purpose in a text.

# Teach

## Part 1: Context Within the Work

**Context** Explain that context provides a way for authors to create worlds that differ from readers' worlds. Use this activity to clarify:

- Write on the board a familiar title from students' lists. Then ask students to identify differences between the story context and their own lives in each of these areas: physical environment, clothing, work, education, pastimes, values/dreams, challenges/dangers. Record students' ideas on the board.

- Discuss how the differences in context add to students' reading experiences and their understanding of the literature. Create an Understanding Context word web like this one:

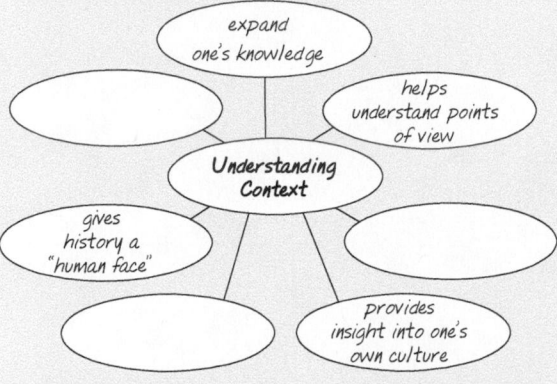

expand one's knowledge

helps understand points of view

Understanding Context

gives history a "human face"

provides insight into one's own culture

## COMMON CORE

Included in this workshop:
**RL 4** Determine the figurative meaning of phrases as they are used in a text; analyze the cumulative impact of specific word choices on meaning and tone. **RL 6** Analyze a particular point of view or cultural experience reflected in a work of world literature. **RI 4** Analyze the cumulative impact of specific word choices on meaning and tone. **RI 6** Determine an author's point of view or purpose in a text.

# History, Culture, and the Author

You are a product of your time. In other words, who you are depends on the year you were born, the places you've lived, and the people—both family and friends—who surround you. Similarly, writers are influenced by the experiences and events they themselves live through. By examining clues within the texts you read, you can learn about a culture or time period, or about how both may have affected the writer. Armed with more knowledge, such as information about the events that inspired a story, you can often see the work in a new light.

## Part 1: Context Within the Work

Think about stories that have introduced you to other times and places, such as Harper Lee's *To Kill a Mockingbird,* set in the South in the 1930s. Unless you had researched small Southern towns in the early 20th century, you probably would have little understanding of that time and place. Yet by analyzing details in the novel, you can learn about the world the writer created.

In nonfiction, writers often provide these details directly. Fiction writers, however, use details of setting and plot and vivid, often figurative language to acquaint you with the times and places they describe. Notice how Bret Harte brings the Old West to life in his short story "The Outcasts of Poker Flat."

### "THE OUTCASTS OF POKER FLAT"

> From this single sentence, you begin to get a sense of a small Western town in the 1850s and can start to question the values of the time. (Is gambling a common pastime?)

As Mr. John Oakhurst, gambler, stepped into the main street of Poker Flat on the morning of the twenty-third of November, 1850, he was conscious of a change in its moral atmosphere. . . .

> The dialect lets you hear how people in Poker Flat sounded.

"It's agin justice," said Jim Wheeler, "to let this yer young man from Roaring Camp—an entire stranger—carry away our money."

> Imagery helps you imagine what the Old West was like at this time.

The road . . . lay over a steep mountain range. It was distant a day's severe travel. In that advanced season, the party soon passed out of the moist, temperate regions of the foot-hills into the dry, cold, bracing air of the Sierras.

918

---

## DIFFERENTIATED INSTRUCTION

### FOR STRUGGLING READERS

**Note Taking** For students who need help with note taking, hand out the note-taking copy master before discussing this page. As volunteers read aloud each section, discuss the main points, and have students record them on the copy master.

**Analysis Support: Context** Point out what these details about period and culture in "The Outcasts of Poker Flat" reveal:

- the town names Poker Flat and Roaring Camp (*importance of gambling; rugged life*)
- Jim Wheeler's dialect and statement (*little education; unsophisticated sense of justice*)

**R** RESOURCE MANAGER—Copy Master
Note Taking p. 9

## MODEL 1: READING NONFICTION

As you read this excerpt, notice the writer's descriptions of people and places, as well as details about historical events and cultural traditions.

*from* THE NAMES
## *of Women*

Biographical essay by **Louise Erdrich**

*Ikwe* is the word for woman in the language of the Anishinabe, my mother's people, whose descendants, mixed with and married to French trappers and farmers, are the Michifs of the Turtle Mountain reservation in North Dakota. Every Anishinabe *Ikwe,* every mixed-blood descendant like me, who can trace

5   her way back a generation or two, is the daughter of a mystery. The history of the woodland Anishinabe—decimated by disease, fighting Plains Indian tribes to the west and squeezed by European settlers to the east—is much like most other Native American stories, a confusion of loss, a tale of absences, of a culture that was blown apart and changed so radically in such a short time that

10  only the names survive.

### Close Read

1. Review the boxed text. What does this historical information tell you about what life was like for the Anishinabe people?

2. What does the writer's choice of words (such as *decimated* and *loss*) reveal about her personal feelings toward her subject?

## MODEL 2: READING FICTION

As you read this excerpt, ask yourself: What do the details tell me about the time and place? What can I infer about the characters' values?

*from*
## The Son from AMERICA

Short story by **Isaac Bashevis Singer**

The village of Lentshin was tiny—a sandy marketplace where the peasants of the area met once a week. It was surrounded by little huts with thatched roofs or shingles green with moss. The chimneys looked like pots. Between the huts there were fields, where the owners planted vegetables or pastured their goats.

5   In the smallest of these huts lived old Berl, a man in his eighties, and his wife, who was called Berlcha (wife of Berl). Old Berl was one of the Jews who had been driven from their villages in Russia and had settled in Poland. In Lentshin, they mocked the mistakes he made while praying aloud. He spoke with a sharp "r." He was short, broad-shouldered, and had a small white beard,

10  and summer and winter he wore a sheepskin hat, a padded cotton jacket, and stout boots. He walked slowly, shuffling his feet. He had a half acre of field, a cow, a goat, and chickens.

The couple had a son, Samuel, who had gone to America forty years ago.

### Close Read

1. What does the simile "The chimneys looked like pots," along with the other details about Lentshin, suggest about this story's time period? Explain.

2. What does the description of old Berl tell you about the people of Lentshin and their culture?

3. The boxed text is a clue to the historical period. Many Jews left Russia following persecution in the 1880s. Find another clue that helps identify the time.

---

## MODEL 1: READING NONFICTION

**Close Read**

1. **Possible answer:** *Life was extremely difficult for the Anishinabe. They suffered from disease, hostile neighboring tribes, and encroaching European settlers (lines 6–7). Their culture was "blown apart" (line 9) so that now "only the names survive" (line 10).*

2. **Possible answer:** *The author's use of the word* decimated *(line 6), which has connotations of merciless brutality, suggests anger. The word* squeezed *(line 7) also indicates anger. Her use of* loss *(line 8) suggests deep sadness and regret. It also reveals why the surviving names are important to her.*

## MODEL 2: READING FICTION

**Close Read**

1. **Possible answer:** *These details suggest that the village of Lentshin is a poor, rural community. The old-fashioned style of chimney and lack of paved roads suggest that the story is set well before the modern era.*

2. **Possible answers:** *The description of old Berl reveals that religious traditions were very important to the culture of Lentshin. When Berl did not follow the traditions correctly, the people made fun of him (line 8). The mention of Berl's accent (lines 8–9) suggests that the small community of Lentshin viewed newcomers as outsiders.*

3. **Possible answer:** *Line 13 provides a clue that identifies the time period: "The couple had a son ... who had gone to America forty years ago." As many Jews left Russia in the 1880s, the story is probably set in the 1920s.*

---

## FOR ENGLISH LANGUAGE LEARNERS

**Comprehension: Transitions** Tell students that Singer uses spatial words to help readers picture the layout of the village. Point out the word *surrounded* in line 2. Give its meaning, and ask a volunteer to sketch on the board a map of the location of the huts relative to the marketplace. Then have students find the signal words in lines 3–5 that help to locate the fields (*Between,* line 3), gardens and pastures (*where,* line 4), and Berl himself (*In,* line 5). Ask a volunteer to revise the map, adding the fields and gardens between the huts and marking the smallest hut as Berl's. Have students describe what the map shows, using the words *surrounded, between, where,* and *in.* Finally, have students repeat the process with Model 1.

### Online Remediation

THINK central

Are your students struggling with text analysis skills? Consider assigning them one or more **Level Up Online Tutorials** as remediation before beginning this unit. Log in to **thinkcentral.com** to view a list of the skills addressed by **Level Up.**

## Part 2: Context Outside the Work

**Historical and Cultural Influences** After students read the section, copy these charts on the board, omitting the examples shown in lightface:

| Historical Influences | |
|---|---|
| **Political** | **Social** |
| U.S. internment of Japanese citizens | the women's movement |
| **Economic** | **Environmental** |
| the Great Depression | the effects of pollution |

| Cultural Influences | |
|---|---|
| **Ethnicity** | **Values/Beliefs** |
| struggles to fit in while maintaining identity | the writer's religion |
| **Technology** | **Arts/Entertainment** |
| world-altering inventions, such as the railroad or computers | popular culture such as rock 'n' roll and baseball |

Make these concepts concrete. Help students generate examples of factors that have influenced the writers of familiar literature. Note their examples in the squares, or use the examples provided to prompt ideas. Ask students to identify examples that reflect **The Writer's Background** and discuss how these specific factors might influence a particular writer.

## CHECK UNDERSTANDING

Have students suggest historical and cultural influences that might affect their own writing.

## Part 2: Context Outside the Work

Writers are often influenced by the literature of earlier times, by classic works that include recurring themes or enduring characters. Even more so, however, writers are products of their own time and place. With a little background on the writer's environment, you can uncover new levels of meaning in a text.

### HISTORICAL AND CULTURAL INFLUENCES

Writers respond to the world around them: events, such as the first moon landing; places, such as the battlefield at Gettysburg; and social conditions, such as racial discrimination. For this reason, it can be helpful to think about a work's **historical** and **cultural contexts**—that is, the social and cultural conditions that may have influenced the work. For instance, consider Dr. Martin Luther King's "I have a dream" speech, which he delivered to a crowd of around 250,000 at the March on Washington on August 28, 1963. King's **purpose**—to deliver a message of peace and hope—becomes more impressive when you discover that he spoke just months after the assassination of another civil rights leader.

| CONTEXT | THE WORK |
|---|---|
| Two months before the March on Washington, the civil rights leader Medgar Evers was assassinated. Concerned about violence, President John F. Kennedy considered canceling the march. | 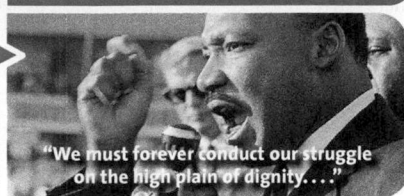 "We must forever conduct our struggle on the high plain of dignity...." |

As you read any text, ask

- What significant events were taking place at the time this text was written?
- What were the predominant values in the society of the time?

### THE WRITER'S BACKGROUND

Personal factors can also affect a writer's work. A writer who grew up poor in the rural South will have been influenced by his or her experiences, as will a writer who spent years working on a nature preserve in Africa. Gender, ethnicity, national identity, family—all these factors help shape a writer's view of the world.

### CONSIDERING A WRITER'S BACKGROUND

| **First analyze the clues within the text.** Ask | **Then consider how a writer's background may be mirrored in his or her work.** Ask |
|---|---|
| • What values are conveyed by the author's words? (Look for direct commentary as well as characters' actions.)<br>• What is the **tone**? (Notice characters and ideas that are respected or criticized.) | • What do I know about the writer's personal history?<br>• How does this information shed light on my reading? |

## DIFFERENTIATED INSTRUCTION

### FOR STRUGGLING READERS

**Note Taking** For students who need help, hand out the note-taking copy master for this page. As students read and discuss the main points, have them record these on the copy master. Provide assistance as needed.

**R** RESOURCE MANAGER—Copy Master
Note Taking p. 10

**Comprehension: Syntax** To help students understand the syntax of "The Butterfly," have them work in pairs and take turns reading it aloud two or three times. Note that the first four lines do not contain complete sentences. Remind students that commas, line breaks, and stanza breaks signal pauses.

## MODEL 1: INTERPRETING POETRY

As you read this poem, look at details such as setting, imagery, and figurative language to help you interpret its meaning.

The Butterfly        Poem by **Pavel Friedmann**

The last, the very last,
So richly, brightly, dazzlingly yellow.
    Perhaps if the sun's tears would sing
    against a white stone . . .

5   Such, such a yellow
Is carried lightly 'way up high.
It went away I'm sure because it wished to
    kiss the world goodbye.

For seven weeks I've lived in here,
10  Penned up inside this ghetto
But I have found my people here.
The dandelions call to me
And the white chestnut candles in the court.
Only I never saw another butterfly.

15  That butterfly was the last one.
Butterflies don't live in here,
    In the ghetto.

**Close Read**

1.  Look at the boxed text. How does it help you understand the speaker's description of the butterfly in lines 1–8?

2.  What might the butterfly symbolize in the poem?

## MODEL 2: UNDERSTANDING THE CONTEXT

To better understand the speaker's perspective, now read this background information about the era in which "The Butterfly" was written.

**BACKGROUND**  Beginning in 1941 when the Holocaust was sweeping across Europe, Adolf Hitler rounded up Jews from Czechoslovakia and many other countries and moved them to the small Czech town of Terezin—the "ghetto" Pavel Friedmann describes in his poem. Originally home to about 7,000
5  people, Terezin eventually held more than 550,000 Jews at one time. Under such conditions, thousands died from starvation and disease. Thousands more were shipped to the Auschwitz death camp. Friedmann was 21 years old when he arrived in the town of Terezin. He died two years later at Auschwitz.

**Close Read**

1.  How does this information change your interpretation of the poem?

2.  What is the theme of the poem? Support your answer with information from the background as well as details from the poem.

## MODEL 1: INTERPRETING POETRY

**Close Read**

1.  *Possible answer: The boxed text clarifies that the speaker's confinement in the ghetto magnifies his appreciation for the butterfly's beauty and freedom. It also helps the reader understand the sadness in the images "the sun's tears" (line 3) and "it wished to kiss the world goodbye" (lines 7–8).*

2.  *Possible answer: The butterfly might symbolize lost freedom, hope, the spirit, or the continuity of life.*

## MODEL 2: UNDERSTANDING THE CONTEXT

**Close Read**

1.  *Possible answer: The background gives readers a more explicit understanding of the specific ghetto from which Friedmann writes. This understanding of the speaker's perspective adds meaning to the repeated word "last" (lines 1 and 15), which suggests that the speaker anticipates his own death.*

2.  *Possible answer: The poem's theme is the fragility of freedom, as symbolized by the butterfly. There is life and beauty in the ghetto—people, dandelions, white chestnut candles (lines 11–13), but not freedom; freedom flutters lightly away (lines 6–8). The butterfly is the last one because "Butterflies don't live in here, / In the ghetto" (lines 16–17). This theme reflects the historical context of the poem: for the Jews at Terezin, freedom had ended suddenly and permanently.*

## DIFFERENTIATED INSTRUCTION

### FOR STRUGGLING READERS

**Comprehension: Interpreting Symbols**  Before students read Model 1, remind them that a symbol is an object that stands for an idea. Explain that a symbol works well when its qualities call to mind the idea. As they read, have students list qualities of the butterfly.

| Qualities | Behavior |
|---|---|
| beautiful | leaves the ghetto |
| light | never returns |
| can fly | |

**Comprehension: Interpreting Theme**  Before students answer question 2 for Model 2, remind them that a theme in a work of literature is a message or idea about life or human nature that the work as a whole imparts. Ask students to name some common themes in literature, movies, or TV shows. *(the triumph of good over evil, the tragedy of war, the power of love, the wonder or power of nature)*

# Practice and Apply

## Part 3: Analyze the Text

**Close Read**

1. **Possible answer:** *Lines 29–32 in the Background on page 923 clarify the imagery and figurative language in the boxed lines by describing the memorial in more literal terms.*

2. **Possible answer:** *According to the Background, the names on the wall were placed in the order in which the soldiers died as a way of "highlighting the individual sacrifices that made up the war" (lines 32–36). The effect of this arrangement on the speaker of the poem is to make him imagine the endless series of individual, agonizing deaths, a vision so disturbing that he starts to leave: "They are in the order of dying, / An alphabet of—somewhere— screaming. / I start to walk out" (lines 24–26).*

## Part 3: Analyze the Text

From the title of this poem, you know it is about the "Vietnam Wall." Think about what you may already know about the wall and read through the poem a first time. Then read the background information on the next page. How does the background information change or enhance your understanding of the poem? Read the poem again before answering the **Close Read** questions.

# THE VIETNAM WALL

Poem by **Alberto Ríos**

I
Have seen it
And I like it: The magic,
The way like cutting onions
5   It brings water out of nowhere.
Invisible from one side, a scar
Into the skin of the ground
From the other, a black winding
Appendix line.
10       A dig.
An archaeologist can explain.
The walk is slow at first
Easy, a little black marble wall
Of a dollhouse,
15   A smoothness, a shine
The boys in the street want to give.
One name. And then more
Names, long lines, lines of names until
They are the shape of the U.N. building
20   Taller than I am: I have walked
Into a grave.
And everything I expect has been taken away, like that, quick:
        The names are not alphabetized.
        They are in the order of dying,
25       An alphabet of—somewhere—screaming.
I start to walk out. I almost leave
But stop to look up names of friends,
My own name. There is somebody
Severiano Ríos.
30   Little kids do not make the same noise
Here, junior high school boys don't run
Or hold each other in headlocks.

No rules, something just persists
Like pinching on St. Patrick's Day
35   Every year for no green.
        No one knows why.
Flowers are forced
Into the cracks
Between sections.
40   Men have cried
At this wall.
I have
Seen them.

## DIFFERENTIATED INSTRUCTION

### FOR STRUGGLING READERS

**Comprehension: Imagery** Imagery contributes to historical and cultural context. Help students understand these images from the poem:

- "like cutting onions / It brings water out of nowhere" (lines 4–5) (*It makes one suddenly weep.*)

- "a black winding / Appendix line" (lines 8–9) (*refers to a scar left by an appendectomy*)

- "a shine / The boys in the street want to give" (lines 15–16) (*refers to boys who earn money by shining shoes*)

- "Like pinching on St. Patrick's Day / Every year for no green" (lines 34–35) (*refers to a schoolchildren's tradition of pinching anyone who does not wear green on St. Patrick's Day*)

## BACKGROUND

# Vietnam: THE WAR AND THE WALL

The Vietnam War was one of the most controversial and divisive wars in U.S. history. During the major years of combat, 1964–1972, more than 58,000 Americans were killed or missing in action. The United States spent about $200 billion to support the South Vietnamese government against soldiers from both North and South Vietnam fighting to unite the country under Communist rule. Two years after the withdrawal of U.S. troops, North Vietnamese forces overran the south and united the country. Many in the United States questioned the worth of our involvement in the war.

In 1979, a group was organized to create the Vietnam Veterans Memorial to honor the U.S. soldiers who died in the war. Some hoped that the construction of a memorial would help to heal the wounds at home caused by the war.

A young Yale University student named Maya Ying Lin won a nationwide competition to design the memorial. Lin's abstract design consisted of two walls of polished black granite plunging on a slant into the ground to meet at a 125° angle. The names of the soldiers were carved into the granite in the order that they died, highlighting the individual sacrifices that made up the war. A walkway running the length of each 246-foot wall allows visitors not only to read the names but to touch them and leave messages and other mementos.

When U.S. involvement in the Vietnam War ended in 1973, the poet Alberto Ríos was 21 years old—the same age as the young Severiano Ríos whose name the speaker notices on the wall. Corporal Ríos died from small-arms fire on April 2, 1970, in Tay Ninh, South Vietnam.

### Close Read

1. Reread the boxed lines of the poem. What information in the background helped you to understand the imagery and figurative language in these lines?

2. According to the background, why were soldiers' names placed in their particular order on the wall? Explain the effect their arrangement has on the speaker of the poem.

3. Why might the speaker of the poem be moved by the sight of the name Severiano Ríos on the wall?

4. According to the background, what was the purpose of the Vietnam Veterans Memorial? After reading Ríos's poem, do you think the wall accomplishes that purpose? Support your answer.

### Close Read

3. **Possible answer:** *The speaker of the poem might be moved by the name Severiano Ríos on the wall (lines 28–29) because Ríos is his own last name. According to the Background, the poet was 21 years old when the war ended (lines 41–43). Perhaps seeing his name intensifies his awareness that he himself could have fought and died in the war.*

4. **Possible answer:** *According to the Background, the purpose of the memorial was "to honor the U.S. soldiers who died in the war" and to help "heal the wounds at home" caused by divided feelings over the war (lines 20–24). Ríos's poem seems to suggest that the wall has accomplished this purpose. Rather than mentioning the political controversy generated by the war, he focuses on the dignity of the long columns of names (line 18), the respect the wall inspires among visitors (lines 30–36), and the sanctuary it provides for personal memorializing (lines 37–39) and emotional catharsis (lines 40–43).*

## Assess and Reteach

### Assess

Ask students to describe the historical context of the poem and explain how that context was important to fully understanding the poem.

### Reteach

For students who are unable to apply the workshop skills to the poem and background selection, use these reteaching activities:

1. Have students review their note-taking copy masters for pages 918 and 920. Ask them to define the terms *historical context* and *cultural context* and to explain why these are important to readers.

2. Return briefly to the two excerpts on page 919 and the poems on pages 921 and 922. Ask students what knowledge of history and of the writer's background deepened their own understanding of each work.

---

### FOR STRUGGLING READERS

**Comprehension: Paragraph Structure** Remind students that paragraphs in informative writing usually contain one main idea and supporting details. Have students reread the first paragraph in the Background and state the main idea. (*The Vietnam War was controversial.*) Ask how the writer supports this idea. (*The writer gives reasons—the enormous cost in lives and money and the war's eventual failure.*)

### FOR ADVANCED LEARNERS/PRE–AP

**Research Context** Have students read the workshop independently. Ask them to choose a work of literature they have read and to do research into the historical context or the author's background. Have them explain what insights they gained about the literature from this new information.

# Focus and Motivate

## COMMON CORE FOCUS

**RI 1** Cite textual evidence to support analysis of what a text says explicitly as well as inferences drawn from the text. **RI 4** Analyze the cumulative impact of an author's specific word choices on tone. **RI 6** Determine an author's point of view in a text and analyze how an author uses rhetoric to advance that point of view. **L 1b** Use various types of phrases to convey specific meanings and add variety and interest to writing. **L 4c** Consult references materials to determine or clarify a word's meaning or etymology.

## SUMMARY

Frank McCourt recalls a hospital stay when he was ten and recovering from typhoid. Despite the disapproval of nurses and nuns, Frank becomes friends with a girl in the next room and with the janitor, Seamus.

## How does FRIENDSHIP begin?

Ask students the Big Question. Have students read the paragraph and complete the *QUICKWRITE*. Then have them compare how their various friendships began.

---

## Selection Resources

---

*Essential Course of Study* **ECOS** *from* **Angela's Ashes**
Memoir by Frank McCourt

 Video link at thinkcentral.com

**VIDEO TRAILER** THINK central KEYWORD: HML9-924

# How does FRIENDSHIP begin?

**COMMON CORE**

**RI 1** Cite textual evidence to support analysis of what a text says explicitly as well as inferences drawn from the text. **RI 4** Analyze the cumulative impact of an author's specific word choices on tone. **RI 6** Determine an author's point of view in a text and analyze how an author uses rhetoric to advance that point of view.

Old friends, new friends, close friends, best friends—what makes two people connect? Whether it's a simple act of kindness or the discovery of a shared interest, something special happens to turn a mere acquaintance into a friend. In his memoir *Angela's Ashes*, writer Frank McCourt describes two friendships that develop under unusual circumstances.

*QUICKWRITE* Have you ever formed an unlikely friendship? Perhaps it was with someone much older or much younger than you—or simply with someone very different from you. Write a paragraph about the circumstances under which your friendship formed.

924

---

*See resources on the* **Teacher One Stop DVD-ROM** *and on* <u>thinkcentral.com</u>.

 **RESOURCE MANAGER UNIT 9**
Plan and Teach, pp. 11–18
Summary pp. 19–20†‡*
Text Analysis and Reading
  Skill, pp. 21–24†*
Vocabulary, pp. 25–27*
Grammar and Style, p. 30

**DIAGNOSTIC AND SELECTION TESTS**
Selection Tests, pp. 247–250

**BEST PRACTICES TOOLKIT**
Spider Map, p. B22
Word Squares, p. E10
T Chart, p. A25

**INTERACTIVE READER**

**ADAPTED INTERACTIVE READER**

**ELL ADAPTED INTERACTIVE READER**

**TECHNOLOGY**
 Video link at thinkcentral.com

- **Teacher One Stop DVD-ROM**
- **Student One Stop DVD-ROM**
- **PowerNotes DVD-ROM**
- **Audio Anthology CD**
- **GrammarNotes DVD-ROM**
- **Audio Tutor CD**
- **ExamView Test Generator** on the **Teacher One Stop**

**Video Trailer**

Go to <u>thinkcentral.com</u> to preview the **Video Trailer** introducing this selection. Other features that support the selection include
- **PowerNotes** presentation
- **ThinkAloud** models to enhance comprehension
- **WordSharp** vocabulary tutorials
- interactive writing and grammar instruction

---

\* Resources for Differentiation    † Also in Spanish    ‡ In Haitian Creole and Vietnamese

## TEXT ANALYSIS: MEMOIR

Frank McCourt was born in New York, but he grew up in Limerick, Ireland, as he describes in his memoir *Angela's Ashes*. A **memoir** is a form of autobiographical writing in which a writer shares his or her personal experiences and perspective on significant events and people. Memoirs usually give readers insights into the influence of history on people's lives.

In this excerpt, McCourt recalls being hospitalized with typhoid, a highly infectious, life-threatening illness. As you read, think about the impact of this event on his life. In addition, note what you learn about Irish history and culture, especially the influence of the Roman Catholic Church.

## READING SKILL: USE ALLUSIONS TO MAKE INFERENCES

One way Frank McCourt adds meaning to his writing is through allusions. An **allusion** is a reference to a well-known person, place, event, or literary work. For example, a writer might refer to a character as having the strength of Samson (a biblical figure granted great strength by God) or Hercules (a Greek hero famous for his strength). Writers use allusions

- to help characterize people or situations
- to evoke ideas or feelings in the reader's mind
- to clarify or highlight important ideas, including the theme

As you read, look for allusions. What can you infer from them? Develop a chart like the one shown.

| Allusion | Significance | Inference |
|---|---|---|
| ...I don't care because it's Shakespeare and it's like having jewels in my mouth when I say the words. (lines 159–160)" | Refers to William Shakespeare, revered English poet and playwright of the Elizabethan era. | Frank loves language and poetry. |

***Review:*** Draw Conclusions

## ▲ VOCABULARY IN CONTEXT

Use context clues to figure out the meanings of the words in bold.

1. The **relapse** of his illness put him back in the hospital.
2. Her persuasive speech **induced** me to support her cause.
3. **Torrents** of rain caused the roads to flood.
4. The officer's **perfidy** led him to be charged with treason.

 Complete the activities in your **Reader/Writer Notebook**.

## Meet the Author

# Frank McCourt
### 1930–2009

**A Spellbinding Storyteller**
Frank McCourt worked as a messenger, a barkeeper, a laborer, and an actor, but it was as a high school writing teacher that he gained his reputation as a consummate storyteller. Columnist Dennis Dugan noted that McCourt "has a way of finding incredible humor in the worst situations"—a trait that has helped him throughout his life. McCourt's advice to students to "write what you know" eventually led him to tell his own story.

**Late-Blooming Writer**
Frank McCourt was 60 years old when he completed his first book, the Pulitzer Prize–winning *Angela's Ashes*. He waited so long to write this memoir of childhood because he needed time to come to terms with his early, poverty-stricken years with an alcoholic father. "I had attitudes and these attitudes had to be softened. I had to get rid of them, I had to become, as it says in the Bible, as a child. The child started to speak in this book. And that was the only way to do it, without judging." The success of *Angela's Ashes* led him to continue his memoir in *'Tis*.

**BACKGROUND TO THE MEMOIR**
**Catholic Ireland in the Mid-1900s**
When Frank McCourt was growing up in Ireland, the Roman Catholic Church held a firm grip on Irish society. Recognized by Ireland's constitution as the "guardian of the faith," the church operated the schools and hospitals; it had such pervasive influence on society that Irish law did not permit divorce, and censorship of books and films was common.

**Author Online**
**THINK** central
Go to **thinkcentral.com**.
KEYWORD: HML9-925

925

---

# Teach

## ● Model the Skill: MEMOIR

Ask students to reread **Text Analysis: Memoir** and *Meet the Author* with these questions in mind: What kind of attitude do you expect McCourt to show in his memoir? Why would his experiences make for a rich memoir? How might time affect memory? Help students recognize that McCourt might be reflective. His childhood probably had many challenges. Time can give a writer perspective.

**GUIDED PRACTICE** Ask students to name incidents that they might include in memoirs of their lives, and why.

## ■ Model the Skill: USE ALLUSIONS TO MAKE INFERENCES

Write this sentence on the board.

> Joe must have had Mercury's wings the day he won the race.

Explain the allusion: Mercury was a Roman god who had wings on his feet. The allusion suggests that Joe ran exceptionally fast.

**GUIDED PRACTICE** Have students create sentences using mythology allusions.

**R** RESOURCE MANAGER—Copy Master
Use Allusions to Make Inferences p. 23 (for student use while reading the selection)

---

## ▲ VOCABULARY IN CONTEXT

**DIAGNOSE WORD KNOWLEDGE** Have all students complete Vocabulary in Context. Check their definitions against the following:

**induced** (ĭn-do͞ost′) *adj.* led on; persuaded
  **induce** *v.*
**perfidy** (pûr′fĭ-dē) *n.* treachery; betrayal of trust
**relapse** (rē′lăps) *n.* a worsening of an illness after a partial recovery

**torrent** (tôr′ənt) *n.* a heavy, uncontrolled outpouring

**PRETEACH VOCABULARY** Use the Vocabulary Study copy master to help students determine word meaning using context clues.

**R** RESOURCE MANAGER—Copy Master
Vocabulary Study p. 25

1. Read item 1 aloud, emphasizing *induced*.
2. Point out the phrase "led her to talk." Elicit possible meanings for *induced*.

3. Have students fill in the chart.
4. Repeat the procedure for items 2–4.

### READ WITH A PURPOSE

*Help students set a purpose for reading. Remind them that a memoir is a person's reflections on important events in his or her life. Have students read to understand why the events described in this excerpt were so important to McCourt.*

**TEXT ANALYSIS**

**COMMON CORE**

**RI 6**

Ⓐ **Model the Skill: MEMOIR**

Reread the lines with students and have them help you list clues in a Spider Map on the board.

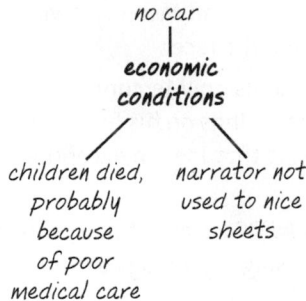

no car

*economic conditions*

*children died, probably because of poor medical care*

*narrator not used to nice sheets*

**Possible answer:** *Readers can infer that economic conditions were harsh. The narrator and Mam go to the hospital in the doctor's car, indicating they have no car. Mam cries, "am I to lose the whole family?" (lines 3–4), suggesting the family has lost other members because it cannot afford good medical care. The narrator remarks on "cool white sheets" (line 6), indicating they are very different from what he has at home.*

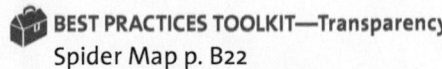  **BEST PRACTICES TOOLKIT—Transparency** Spider Map p. B22

**Extend the Discussion** What other information about economic conditions does the class photograph give you?

# Angela's Ashes

### Frank McCourt

**Analyze Visuals ▶**

What does this class photograph tell you about the time period and subject of this memoir?

Mam comes with Dr. Troy. He feels my forehead, rolls up my eyelids, turns me over to see my back, picks me up and runs to his motor car. Mam runs after him and he tells her I have typhoid fever. Mam cries, . . . am I to lose the whole family? Will it ever end? She gets into the car, holds me in her lap and moans all the way to the Fever Hospital at the City Home.[1]

The bed has cool white sheets. The nurses have clean white uniforms and the nun, Sister Rita, is all in white. Dr. Humphrey and Dr. Campbell have white coats and things hanging from their necks which they stick against my chest and all over. I sleep and sleep but I'm awake when they bring in jars of
10 bright red stuff that hang from tall poles above my bed and they stick tubes into my ankles and the back of my right hand. Sister Rita says, You're getting blood, Francis. Soldier's blood from the Sarsfield Barracks.

Mam is sitting by the bed and the nurse is saying, You know, missus, this is very unusual. No one is ever allowed into the Fever Hospital for fear they'd catch something but they made an exception for you with his crisis coming. If he gets over this he'll surely recover. Ⓐ

I fall asleep. Mam is gone when I wake but there's movement in the room and it's the priest, Father Gorey, from the Confraternity[2] saying Mass at a table in the corner. I drift off again and now they're waking me and pulling down the
20 bedclothes. Father Gorey is touching me with oil and praying in Latin. I know it's Extreme Unction[3] and that means I'm going to die and I don't care. They wake me again to receive Communion. I don't want it, I'm afraid I might get sick. I keep the wafer on my tongue and fall asleep and when I wake up again it's gone.

It's dark and Dr. Campbell is sitting by my bed. He's holding my wrist and looking at his watch. He has red hair and glasses and he always smiles when he talks to me. He sits now and hums and looks out the window. His eyes close and he snores a little. . . .

Ⓐ **MEMOIR**
Reread lines 1–16. What **inferences** can you make about economic conditions in Ireland at this time?

① **Targeted Passage**

Frank McCourt (right front) in the playground of Leamy's school in Limerick, Ireland, about 1938.

---

1. **Mam cries, . . . City Home:** The Fever Hospital was a special section of the Limerick City Home Hospital where patients who had fever-related illnesses like typhoid were treated. The McCourt family had already lost a baby daughter and twin boys to childhood disease.

2. **Confraternity** (kŏn′frə-tûr′nĭ-tē): a religious society or association.

3. **Extreme Unction** (ŭngk′shən): a Roman Catholic sacrament given to a person thought to be near death.

---

**DIFFERENTIATED INSTRUCTION**

**FOR ENGLISH LANGUAGE LEARNERS**

**Vocabulary Support** Use Word Squares to teach these words: *recover* (line 16), *internal* (line 112), *job* (line 118), *circumstances* (line 155), *collapsed* (line 256), *concentrate* (line 290).

**BEST PRACTICES TOOLKIT—Transparency** Word Squares p. E10

**FOR STRUGGLING READERS**

In combination with the *Audio Anthology CD*, use one or more Targeted Passages (pp. 926, 931, 932, 934, 935) to ensure that students focus on key story events, concepts, and skills. Targeted Passages are also good for English learners.

① **Targeted Passage [Lines 17–23]**

This passage provides the first suggestion of the important role Catholicism plays in Frank's life.

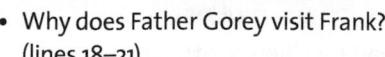

**Reading Support** THINK central

This selection on **thinkcentral.com** includes embedded **ThinkAloud** models—students "thinking aloud" about the story to model the kinds of questions a good reader would ask about a selection.

## BACKGROUND

**Anglo-Irish Relations** In the 1500s, the king of England became king of Ireland. He and later rulers tried to force Protestantism on the largely Catholic population. They gave Irish lands to English and Protestant settlers. The conflicts became religious as Protestants gained property and political rights that Catholics lost. During the potato famine in the 1840s, England did little to help the starving Irish. In 1921, rising up against British rule, Ireland was divided into two parts. Ulster, in the north, remained part of Britain. The rest became the Irish Free State, which gained self-government in the British Empire and full independence by 1949.

## Analyze Visuals

*Possible answer: The photograph suggests that the memoir's time period is the first half of the 20th century and that its subject is childhood events. Support includes the photograph being black and white, creased with age, and showing only boys dressed in old-fashioned clothes.*

- Why does Father Gorey visit Frank? (lines 18–21)
- How does Frank react to receiving Extreme Unction? (lines 20–21)
- How does Frank react when Father Gorey makes him receive Communion? (lines 22–23)
- What can you tell from this passage about the role of Catholicism in Frank's life? (lines 17–23)

**FOR ADVANCED LEARNERS/PRE–AP**

**Expert Groups** Allow individuals or pairs of students to research and then choose a way to share information about one of these topics:

- typhus and diphtheria
- social conditions in Ireland in the 1940s
- Irish patriotic songs and poems
- the Irish potato famine

**S**ister Rita's white habit is bright in the sun that comes in the window. She's holding my wrist, looking at her watch, smiling. Oh, she says, we're awake, are we? Well, Francis, I think we've come through the worst. Our prayers are answered and all the prayers of those hundreds of little boys at the Confraternity. Can you imagine that? Hundreds of boys saying the rosary[4] for you and offering up their communion. **B**

My ankles and the back of my hand are throbbing from the tubes bringing in the blood and I don't care about boys praying for me. I can hear the swish of Sister Rita's habit and the click of her rosary beads when she leaves the room. I fall asleep and when I wake it's dark and Dad is sitting by the bed with his hand on mine.

Son, are you awake?

I try to talk but I'm dry, nothing will come out and I point to my mouth. He holds a glass of water to my lips and it's sweet and cool. He presses my hand and says I'm a great old soldier and why wouldn't I? Don't I have the soldier's blood in me?

The tubes are not in me anymore and the glass jars are gone.

Sister Rita comes in and tells Dad he has to go. I don't want him to go because he looks sad. When he looks sad it's the worst thing in the world and I start crying. Now what's this? says Sister Rita. Crying with all that soldier blood in you? There's a big surprise for you tomorrow, Francis. You'll never guess. Well, I'll tell you, we're bringing you a nice biscuit[5] with your tea in the morning. Isn't that a treat? And your father will be back in a day or two, won't you, Mr. McCourt?

Dad nods and puts his hand on mine again. He looks at me, steps away, stops, comes back, kisses me on the forehead for the first time in my life and I'm so happy I feel like floating out of the bed. **C**

The other two beds in my room are empty. The nurse says I'm the only typhoid patient and I'm a miracle for getting over the crisis.

The room next to me is empty till one morning a girl's voice says, Yoo hoo, who's there?

I'm not sure if she's talking to me or someone in the room beyond.

Yoo hoo, boy with the typhoid, are you awake?

I am.

Are you better?

I am.

Well, why are you here?

I don't know. I'm still in the bed. They stick needles in me and give me medicine.

What do you look like?

I wonder, What kind of a question is that? I don't know what to tell her.

---

4. **rosary** (rō′zə-rē): a series of prayers repeated by Roman Catholics as a form of devotion to the Virgin Mary—usually counted off on a string of beads as they are said.

5. **biscuit:** cookie.

## DIFFERENTIATED INSTRUCTION

### FOR ENGLISH LANGUAGE LEARNERS

**Culture: Clarify** McCourt introduces many elements of Irish Catholicism in the mid-1900s. Ask students to work in small groups to list elements under the categories *Key People* and *Rituals/Objects* on a T Chart. After comparing charts, ask students to add to them as they read the rest of the selection.

 **BEST PRACTICES TOOLKIT—Transparency** T Chart p. A25

### FOR STRUGGLING READERS

**Develop Reading Fluency** Students will notice that the author does not use quotation marks. Discuss lines 58–69. As in ordinary dialogue, each new speaker gets a new paragraph. However, the dialogue is interspersed with comments to the reader. Have students determine which lines are spoken dialogue and who speaks each line. Ask for three volunteers to perform a reading of the passage.

**R RESOURCE MANAGER—Copy Master** Reading Fluency p. 31

70 Yoo hoo, are you there, typhoid boy?

I am.

What's your name?

Frank.

That's a good name. My name is Patricia Madigan. How old are you?

Ten.

Oh. She sounds disappointed.

But I'll be eleven in August, next month.

Well, that's better than ten. I'll be fourteen in September. Do you want to know why I'm in the Fever Hospital?

80 I do.

I have diphtheria[6] and something else.

What's something else?

They don't know. They think I have a disease from foreign parts because my father used to be in Africa. I nearly died. Are you going to tell me what you look like?

I have black hair.

You and millions.

I have brown eyes with bits of green that's called hazel.

You and thousands.

90 I have stitches on the back of my right hand and my two feet where they put in the soldier's blood.

Oh, . . . did they?

They did.

You won't be able to stop marching and saluting.

There's a swish of habit and click of beads and then Sister Rita's voice. Now, now, what's this? There's to be no talking between two rooms especially when it's a boy and a girl. Do you hear me, Patricia?

I do, Sister.

Do you hear me, Francis?

100 I do, Sister.

You could be giving thanks for your two remarkable recoveries. You could be saying the rosary. You could be reading *The Little Messenger of the Sacred Heart*[7] that's beside your beds. Don't let me come back and find you talking. She comes into my room and wags her finger at me. Especially you, Francis, after thousands of boys prayed for you at the Confraternity. Give thanks, Francis, give thanks. She leaves and there's silence for awhile. Then Patricia whispers, Give thanks, Francis, give thanks, and say your rosary, Francis, and I laugh so hard a nurse runs in to see if I'm all right. She's a very stern nurse from the County Kerry[8] and she frightens me. What's this, Francis? Laughing? What is there to laugh about? Are you and that Madigan girl talking? I'll report you to

---

6. **diphtheria** (dĭf-thĭr′ē-ə): a highly infectious disease caused by the bacterium *Corynebacterium diphtheriae*. It is spread by infected secretions from the nose and throat and can create toxins that destroy the heart and nervous system.

7. **The Little . . . Heart:** a Roman Catholic magazine.

8. **County Kerry:** a largely rural county to the west of Limerick.

A Limerick hospital in the early part of the 20th century

## Analyze Visuals

**Activity** Ask students how this photograph helps them visualize Frank's experience in the hospital. ***Possible answer:*** *The photograph shows a very plain and somewhat run-down hospital in Limerick in the early 1900s. This is probably much like the hospital that Frank stays in when he is ill.*

Sister Rita. There's to be no laughing for you could be doing serious damage to your internal apparatus.[9]

She plods out and Patricia whispers again in a heavy Kerry accent, No laughing, Francis, you could be doin' serious damage to your internal apparatus. Say your rosary, Francis, and pray for your internal apparatus.

Mam visits me on Thursdays, I'd like to see my father, too, but I'm out of danger, crisis time is over, and I'm allowed only one visitor. Besides, she says, he's back at work at Rank's Flour Mills and please God this job will last a while with the war on and the English desperate for flour. She brings me a chocolate
120 bar and that proves Dad is working. She could never afford it on the dole.[10] He sends me notes. He tells me my brothers are all praying for me, that I should be a good boy, obey the doctors, the nuns, the nurses, and don't forget to say my prayers. He's sure St. Jude pulled me through the crisis because he's the patron saint of desperate cases and I was indeed a desperate case.

Patricia says she has two books by her bed. One is a poetry book and that's the one she loves. The other is a short history of England and do I want it? She gives it to Seamus,[11] the man who mops the floors every day, and he brings it to me. He says, I'm not supposed to be bringing anything from a diphtheria room to a typhoid room with all the germs flying around and hiding between
130 the pages and if you ever catch diphtheria on top of the typhoid they'll know and I'll lose my good job and be out on the street singing patriotic songs with a tin cup in my hand, which I could easily do because there isn't a song ever written about Ireland's sufferings I don't know. . . .

Oh, yes, he knows Roddy McCorley.[12] He'll sing it for me right enough but he's barely into the first verse when the Kerry nurse rushes in. What's this,

---

9. **internal apparatus:** the internal organs of the body.
10. **on the dole:** living on government unemployment payments.
11. **Seamus** (shā′məs).
12. **Roddy McCorley:** a song about Roddy McCorley, a local leader during an Irish uprising. McCorley was hanged by the English in 1798.

## TEXT ANALYSIS

**COMMON CORE**
RI 6

### Ⓓ MEMOIR

***Possible answer:*** *Mam praying to God that Dad will hold on to his job, and Dad's message that people are praying for him, that he should obey the nuns and say his prayers, and that St. Jude has pulled him through show that the family is religious (lines 117–124).*

### Ⓓ MEMOIR
Reread lines 116–124. What details describe Frank's family and the role of religion in their lives?

---

**REVISIT THE BIG QUESTION**

How does

# FRIENDSHIP
begin?

**Discuss** In lines 125–133, how does the friendship with Patricia develop? How does the friendship with Seamus begin? Do these friendships follow ordinary patterns? Explain.
***Possible answer:*** *The friendship with Patricia develops through sharing books (lines 125–126). Friendship often develops when people share interests. The friendship with Seamus begins because he helps the children communicate with each other (lines 126–128). Helping someone is often the basis for the beginning of a friendship.*

---

## DIFFERENTIATED INSTRUCTION

### FOR ENGLISH LANGUAGE LEARNERS

**Language: Conversational English Patterns**
Point out that Irish speech patterns can differ from American English patterns. Show students these examples and help them paraphrase the sentences containing them into American English: "There's to be no" (line 111); "right enough" (line 134); "Isn't it a great pity" (line 148); "to be had" (line 150); "'twould" (line 228); "'twas" (line 235); "'Tis" (line 237).

### FOR ADVANCED LEARNERS/PRE–AP

**Analyze Social Context** Ask students to locate and share the words to the song "Roddy McCorley." Have students work in groups to summarize the song's story. Then have students discuss what this song and its popularity show about the Ireland of the 1940s. Have groups share their conclusions with one another and with the class.

Seamus? Singing? Of all the people in this hospital you should know the rules against singing. I have a good mind to report you to Sister Rita.

Ah, . . . don't do that, nurse.

Very well, Seamus. I'll let it go this one time. You know the singing could
140 lead to a **relapse** in these patients.

When she leaves he whispers he'll teach me a few songs because singing is good for passing the time when you're by yourself in a typhoid room. He **E** says Patricia is a lovely girl the way she often gives him sweets from the parcel her mother sends every fortnight.[13] He stops mopping the floor and calls to Patricia in the next room, I was telling Frankie you're a lovely girl, Patricia, and she says, You're a lovely man, Seamus. He smiles because he's an old man of forty and he never had children but the ones he can talk to here in the Fever Hospital. He says, Here's the book, Frankie. Isn't it a great pity you have to be reading all about England after all they did to us, that there isn't a history of
150 Ireland to be had in this hospital. **F**

The book tells me all about King Alfred and William the Conqueror and all the kings and queens down to Edward, who had to wait forever for his mother, Victoria, to die before he could be king. The book has the first bit of Shakespeare I ever read.

*I do believe, **induced** by potent circumstances*
*That thou art mine enemy.*

The history writer says this is what Catherine, who is a wife of Henry the Eighth, says to Cardinal Wolsey, who is trying to have her head cut off. I don't know what it means and I don't care because it's Shakespeare and it's like
160 having jewels in my mouth when I say the words. If I had a whole book of Shakespeare they could keep me in the hospital for a year. **G**

> Patricia says she doesn't know what induced means or potent circumstances and she doesn't care about Shakespeare, she has her poetry book and she reads to me from beyond the wall a poem about an owl and a pussycat that went to sea in a green boat with honey and money[14] and it makes no sense and when I say that Patricia gets huffy and says that's the last poem she'll ever read to me. She says I'm always reciting the lines from Shakespeare and they make no sense either. Seamus stops mopping again and tells us we shouldn't be fighting over poetry because we'll have enough to fight about when we grow up and
170 get married. Patricia says she's sorry and I'm sorry too so she reads me part of another poem which I have to remember so I can say it back to her early in the morning or late at night when there are no nuns or nurses about,

*The wind was a **torrent** of darkness among the gusty trees,*
*The moon was a ghostly galleon tossed upon cloudy seas,*
*The road was a ribbon of moonlight over the purple moor,*

---

13. **fortnight:** two weeks.
14. **a poem . . . money:** "The Owl and the Pussycat," a humorous poem by the 19th-century British poet and artist Edward Lear.

---

**relapse** (rĕ'lăps) *n.* a worsening of an illness after a partial recovery

**E GRAMMAR AND STYLE**
Reread lines 139–142. Notice McCourt's use of the **gerund** *singing.* A gerund is a verb form that ends in *–ing* and is used as a noun.

**F ALLUSIONS**
Here Seamus refers to the troubled relationship between England and Ireland. What does this reveal about him? about Irish culture?

**induced** (ĭn-dōōst') *adj.* led on; persuaded **induce** *v.*

**G MEMOIR**
What does this first encounter with Shakespeare reveal about Frank?

2 **Targeted Passage**

**torrent** (tôr'ənt) *n.* a heavy, uncontrolled outpouring

---

**E GRAMMAR AND STYLE**                    COMMON CORE **L 1b**

**Recognize Gerunds**  Without exception, all gerunds end in *-ing.*  However, all present participles also end in *-ing.*  Gerunds can be subjects, objects, or subject complements, while present participles act as modifiers or complete progressive verbs.  Note that using gerunds in writing helps bring variety to it.  Have students locate other gerunds in the selection.

---

**READING SKILL**                    COMMON CORE **RI 1, RI 6**

**F ALLUSIONS**

*Possible answer:  Seamus knows history well and loves his country (lines 148–150). This suggests that ordinary Irish people are politically active and passionately patriotic.*

---

**TEXT ANALYSIS**                    COMMON CORE **RI 6**

**G MEMOIR**

*Possible answer:  Frank's first encounter with Shakespeare reveals his love of language and poetry.  Shakespeare's words are like "jewels in [his] mouth" (line 160).*

---

**VOCABULARY**                    COMMON CORE **L 4**

**OWN THE WORD**

- **relapse:** Tell students that *relapse* comes from the Latin *relabi*, which means "to slide back."

- **induced:** Explain that someone who is *induced* is influenced, perhaps against his or her will.  Ask students for examples of *inducement* they may encounter.

- **torrent:** Tell students that an antonym for *torrent* is *drizzle.*  Ask them to write a sentence using both words.

---

**FOR STRUGGLING READERS**

2 **Targeted Passage** [Lines 162–172]

This passage gives more information about Patricia and describes what the relationship between the two children is like.

- How do Frank and Patricia make up after an argument?  Is it hard?  Explain. (lines 168–170)

- What interests do the children share? (lines 166–168)

- Based on their interactions, why do you think the children like each other? (lines 168–172)

**FOR ENGLISH LANGUAGE LEARNERS**

**Culture: Clarify**  Read full versions of both "The Owl and the Pussycat" and "The Highwayman" to students, or have English speakers do so. As an alternative, you might bring sound recordings or picture books with the poems to class for students.  Have students discuss and summarize the stories in both poems.

And the highwayman came riding  
*Riding riding*  
*The highwayman came riding, up to the old inn-door.*  
*He'd a French cocked-hat on his forehead,*  
180   *a bunch of lace at his chin,*  
*A coat of the claret velvet, and breeches of brown doe-skin,*  
*They fitted with never a wrinkle, his boots were up to the thigh.*  
*And he rode with a jeweled twinkle,*  
*His pistol butts a-twinkle,*  
*His rapier hilt a-twinkle, under the jeweled sky.*[15]

Every day I can't wait for the doctors and nurses to leave me alone so I can learn a new verse from Patricia and find out what's happening to the highwayman and the landlord's red-lipped daughter. I love the poem because it's exciting and almost as good as my two lines of Shakespeare. The redcoats
190 are after the highwayman because they know he told her, I'll come to thee by moonlight. . . .

I'd love to do that myself, come by moonlight for Patricia in the next room. . . . She's ready to read the last few verses when in comes the nurse from Kerry shouting at her, shouting at me, I told ye there was to be no talking between rooms. Diphtheria is never allowed to talk to typhoid and visa versa. I warned ye. And she calls out, Seamus, take this one. Take the by.[16] Sister Rita said one more word out of him and upstairs with him. We gave ye a warning to stop the blathering but ye wouldn't. Take the by, Seamus, take him.
Ah, now, nurse, sure isn't he harmless. 'Tis only a bit o' poetry.
200   Take that by, Seamus, take him at once. ❶

He bends over me and whispers, Ah, . . . I'm sorry, Frankie. Here's your English history book. He slips the book under my shirt and lifts me from the bed. He whispers that I'm a feather. I try to see Patricia when we pass through her room but all I can make out is a blur of dark head on a pillow.

Sister Rita stops us in the hall to tell me I'm a great disappointment to her, that she expected me to be a good boy after what God had done for me, after all the prayers said by hundreds of boys at the Confraternity, after all the care from the nuns and nurses of the Fever Hospital, after the way they let my mother and father in to see me, a thing rarely allowed, and this is how I
210 repaid them lying in the bed reciting silly poetry back and forth with Patricia Madigan knowing very well there was a ban on all talk between typhoid and diphtheria. She says I'll have plenty of time to reflect on my sins in the big ward upstairs and I should beg forgiveness for my disobedience reciting a pagan English poem about a thief on a horse and a maiden with red lips who commits a terrible sin when I could have been praying or reading the life of a saint. She made it her business to read that poem so she did and I'd be well advised to tell the priest in confession.

---

15. **The wind … jeweled sky:** the opening lines of "The Highwayman," a romantic, action-packed narrative poem by the 20th-century British writer Alfred Noyes.

16. **by:** boy (spelled to indicate the nurse's dialectal pronunciation).

---

❶ **MEMOIR**
In what ways is Frank and Patricia's situation like that of the characters in "The Highwayman"?

❸ **Targeted Passage**

❶ **MEMOIR**
Reread lines 193–200. McCourt uses **dialect** to provide a realistic portrayal of the nurse. How does this influence your reaction to her?

---

**REVIST THE BIG QUESTION**

How does

# FRIENDSHIP
### begin?

How do Seamus and Sister Rita differ in their understanding of the friendship between Frank and Patricia? What does this difference show about who they are as people? ***Possible answer:*** *Seamus, who appreciates poetry, understands the romance between the two. Sister Rita sees the friendship as a problem, a constant infraction of the rules. Seamus is a kind-hearted romantic. Sister Rita, while dedicated, values rules and discipline.*

---

## DIFFERENTIATED INSTRUCTION

**FOR STRUGGLING READERS**

❸ **Targeted Passage** [Lines 192–200]
This passage describes how Frank and Patricia are separated.

- Why does the nurse make Frank move? (lines 195–198)
- How does Seamus react when he's asked to move Frank? (line 199)
- What kind of attitude does the nurse show toward the children? (lines 194–200)

**FOR ADVANCED LEARNERS/PRE–AP**

**Analyze Character** Ask students to analyze what Sister Rita finds objectionable in "The Highwayman." Have student pairs read "The Highwayman," then discuss these questions: What makes "The Highwayman" a "pagan English poem"? What about the poem makes Sister Rita think Frank must confess he has read it?

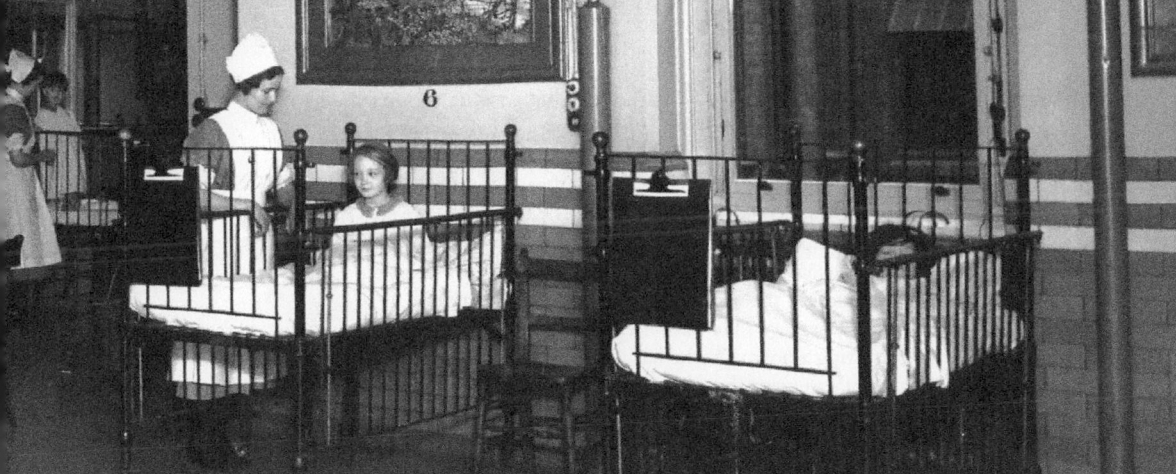
A children's ward typical of British and Irish hospitals in the 1940s

Analyze Visuals

**Activity** Ask students what the photograph suggests about how children in England and Ireland were viewed by adults in the 1940s.
*Possible answer: The placement of an older child in a crib suggests that children were treated as babies long after leaving infancy. The lack of curtains or screens suggests that adults felt children did not need privacy.*

The Kerry nurse follows us upstairs gasping and holding on to the banister. She tells me I better not get the notion she'll be running up to this part of the
220 world every time I have a little pain or a twinge.

There are twenty beds in the ward, all white, all empty. The nurse tells Seamus put me at the far end of the ward against the wall to make sure I don't talk to anyone who might be passing the door, which is very unlikely since there isn't another soul on this whole floor. She tells Seamus this was the fever ward during the Great Famine[17] long ago and only God knows how many died here brought in too late for anything but a wash before they were buried and there are stories of cries and moans in the far reaches of the night. She says 'twould break your heart to think of what the English did to us, that if they didn't put the blight[18] on the potato they didn't do much to take it off.
230 No pity. No feeling at all for the people that died in this very ward, children suffering and dying here while the English feasted on roast beef and guzzled the best of wine in their big houses, little children with their mouths all green from trying to eat the grass in the fields beyond, God bless us and save us and guard us from future famines. ●

Seamus says 'twas a terrible thing indeed and he wouldn't want to be walking these halls in the dark with all the little green mouths gaping at him. The nurse takes my temperature, 'Tis up a bit, have a good sleep for yourself now that you're away from the chatter with Patricia Madigan below who will never know a gray hair.[19]
240 She shakes her head at Seamus and he gives her a sad shake back.

---

17. **Great Famine** (fămʹĭn): a devastating food shortage in Ireland in the late 1840s, caused by a failure of the potato crop. Over a million Irish people died of starvation during the famine, and about 1.5 million emigrated, mainly to the United States.

18. **blight:** a plant disease—in this case, the one that destroyed the Irish potato crop.

19. **never know a gray hair:** won't live to be old.

● **MEMOIR**
Reread lines 221–234. What insights do you get about the sufferings the Irish endured during the famine and its lasting effect on their culture?

**TEXT ANALYSIS**

**COMMON CORE**
RI 6

● **MEMOIR**

*Possible answer: The nurse's remarks indicate there was great suffering during the Great Famine. The memory of that suffering and England's lack of help continued to haunt Ireland in the 1940s.*

**IF STUDENTS NEED HELP . . .**
- Direct them to footnotes 17 and 18 for additional background about the Great Famine.
- Reread lines 221–234 with students, highlighting details that refer to the Great Famine. Discuss what images these create of the Irish experience at that time and how such an experience would make people feel.

**Extend the Discussion** What is ironic about the nurse's criticism of the attitude of the English toward Irish children?

**FOR ADVANCED LEARNERS/PRE–AP**

**Secret Note** Imagine that Frank could have slipped a note to Patricia. Perhaps Seamus might have delivered it. How might Frank have described his surroundings? his feelings for Patricia? Have students write a note that Frank might have written. Have them read their notes aloud to the class.

**FOR RELUCTANT READERS**

Discuss the scene (lines 237–246) in which the nurse remarks that Patricia "will never know a gray hair" but expects Frank not to realize what this means. Ask students if adults have ever made remarks that they were not expected to understand but that they did understand. What were the circumstances? Did they let the adult know they understood? Why or why not? Students can describe their experiences in small groups or write short paragraphs.

Use these prompts to help students understand Frank's feelings toward the nurses and nuns and his reactions to the idea that Patricia might die in lines 237–246:

**Recall** What does the nurse tell Seamus about Patricia? How does Frank respond to this news? *Possible answer: The nurse tells Seamus that Patricia is dying. Frank is upset by this but hides it from the adults.*

**Analyze** Why does Frank feel he can't "cry over this girl"? *Possible answer: The adults think Frank won't realize that Patricia is dying. Also, they believe they have ended an inappropriate friendship by moving Frank. Frank worries that crying over Patricia will reveal that he still cares about her and that he will be scolded for this (lines 241–246).*

**Synthesize** How do these lines help you to understand what Patricia really means to Frank? *Possible answer: Patricia brought romance and beauty into Frank's lonely and isolated world.*

**VOCABULARY**

COMMON CORE
L 4

**OWN THE WORD**

**perfidy:** Have students reread the sentence with *perfidy* and the sentence that follows. Have them identify the context clue that can help determine the meaning of *perfidy*. Ask if they have ever been the victims of *perfidy*. *Possible answer: context clue: terrible; I was the victim of perfidy when one of my friends turned out not to be a friend at all and betrayed me.*

Nurses and nuns never think you know what they're talking about. If you're ten going on eleven you're supposed to be simple like my uncle Pat Sheehan who was dropped on his head. You can't ask questions. You can't show you understand what the nurse said about Patricia Madigan, that she's going to die, and you can't show you want to cry over this girl who taught you a lovely poem which the nun says is bad.

The nurse tells Seamus she has to go and he's to sweep the lint from under 250 my bed and mop up a bit around the ward. Seamus tells me . . . that you can't catch a disease from a poem. . . . He never heard the likes of it, a little fella shifted upstairs for saying a poem and he has a good mind to go to the *Limerick Leader*[20] and tell them print the whole thing except he has this job and he'd lose it if ever Sister Rita found out. Anyway, Frankie, you'll be outa here one of these fine days and you can read all the poetry you want though I don't know about Patricia below, I don't know about Patricia. . . .

He knows about Patricia in two days because she got out of the bed to go to the lavatory when she was supposed to use a bedpan and collapsed and died in the lavatory. Seamus is mopping the floor and there are tears on his cheeks and he's saying, 'Tis a dirty rotten thing to die in a lavatory when you're lovely in yourself. She told me she was sorry she had you reciting that poem and getting 260 you shifted from the room, Frankie. She said 'twas all her fault.

It wasn't, Seamus.

I know and didn't I tell her that.

**Targeted Passage** ④

Patricia is gone and I'll never know what happened to the highwayman and Bess, the landlord's daughter. I ask Seamus but he doesn't know any poetry at all especially English poetry. He knew an Irish poem once but it was about fairies and had no sign of a highwayman in it. Still he'll ask the men in his local pub where there's always someone reciting something and he'll bring it back to me. Won't I be busy meanwhile reading my short history of England 270 and finding out all about their **perfidy.** That's what Seamus says, perfidy, and I don't know what it means and he doesn't know what it means but if it's something the English do it must be terrible.

He comes three times a week to mop the floor and the nurse is there every morning to take my temperature and pulse. The doctor listens to my chest with the thing hanging from his neck. They all say, And how's our little soldier today? A girl with a blue dress brings meals three times a day and never talks to me. Seamus says she's not right in the head so don't say a word to her.

The July days are long and I fear the dark. There are only two ceiling lights in the ward and they're switched off when the tea tray is taken away 280 and the nurse gives me pills. The nurse tells me go to sleep but I can't because I see people in the nineteen beds in the ward all dying and green around their mouths where they tried to eat grass and moaning for soup

COMMON CORE RI 4

**Language Coach**

**Informal Language**
This kind of language differs from the formal tone of school writing. In lines 249–252, the expressions *the likes of* ("anything like") and *fella* ("fellow") re-create the sound of Seamus's informal, Irish-accented speech. Find examples of informal language in lines 252–254 and 258–260.

**perfidy** (pûr´fĭ-dē) *n.* treachery; betrayal of trust

---

20. *Limerick Leader:* a newspaper published in Limerick.

**DIFFERENTIATED INSTRUCTION**

**FOR STRUGGLING READERS**

④ **Targeted Passage [Lines 255–261]**
This passage describes Patricia's death and Seamus's reaction to it.

- How does Patricia die? (lines 255–257)
- How does Seamus react to her death? (lines 257–259)
- What does Patricia tell Seamus before she dies? (lines 259–260)

**FOR ENGLISH LANGUAGE LEARNERS**

**Language Coach**   COMMON CORE RI 4
**Informal Language** *Possible answer:* outa, *meaning "out of";* 'tis, *meaning "it is,"* and 'twas, *meaning "it was"* Read Seamus's dialogue aloud so the class can hear how the use of informal language reflects natural speech and hints at the Irish accent. Formal language is the language the nurse uses to establish authority over Seamus. His use of informal language, which is conversational and reveals his Irish origins, deflects the nurse's more formal, institutional speech.

Protestant soup[21] any soup and I cover my face with the pillow hoping they won't come and stand around the bed clawing at me and howling for bits of the chocolate bar my mother brought last week. **K**

No, she didn't bring it. She had to send it in because I can't have any more visitors. Sister Rita tells me a visit to the Fever Hospital is a privilege and after my bad behavior with Patricia Madigan and that poem I can't have the privilege anymore. She says I'll be going home in a few weeks and my job is
290 to concentrate on getting better and learn to walk again after being in bed for six weeks and I can get out of bed tomorrow after breakfast. I don't know why she says I have to learn how to walk when I've been walking since I was a baby but when the nurse stands me by the side of the bed I fall to the floor and the nurse laughs, See, you're a baby again.

I practice walking from bed to bed back and forth back and forth. I don't want to be a baby. I don't want to be in this empty ward with no Patricia and no highwayman and no red-lipped landlord's daughter. I don't want the ghosts of children with green mouths pointing bony fingers at me and clamoring for bits of my chocolate bar.

300 Seamus says a man in his pub knew all the verses of the highwayman poem and it has a very sad end. Would I like him to say it because he never learned how to read and he had to carry the poem in his head? He stands in the middle of the ward leaning on his mop and recites,

> *Tlot-tlot, in the frosty silence! Tlot-tlot in the echoing night!*
> *Nearer he came and nearer! Her face was like a light!*
> *Her eyes grew wide for a moment, she drew one last deep breath,*
> *Then her finger moved in the moonlight,*
> *Her musket shattered the moonlight,*
> *Shattered her breast in the moonlight and warned him—with her death.*

310 He hears the shot and escapes but when he learns at dawn how Bess died he goes into a rage and returns for revenge only to be shot down by the redcoats.

> *Blood-red were his spurs in the golden noon; wine-red was his velvet coat,*
> *When they shot him down on the highway,*
> *Down like a dog on the highway,*
> *And he lay in his blood on the highway, with a bunch of lace at his throat.*

Seamus wipes his sleeve across his face and sniffles. He says, There was no call at all to shift you up here away from Patricia when you didn't even know what happened to the highwayman and Bess. 'Tis a very sad story and when I said it to my wife she wouldn't stop crying the whole night till we went to bed.
320 She said there was no call for them redcoats to shoot that highwayman, they are responsible for half the troubles of the world and they never had any pity on the Irish, either. Now if you want to know any more poems, Frankie, tell me and I'll get them from the pub and bring 'em back in my head. ∾

---

21. **Protestant soup:** soup provided by the English to the starving Irish during the famine, often in return for renouncing Catholicism and joining the Protestant faith.

**(5) Targeted Passage**

ANGELA'S ASHES **935**

**K ALLUSIONS**
Reread lines 280–285 and identify the allusions McCourt makes to tragic events that occurred during the Great Famine. Why do you think McCourt includes these references?

**K Model the Skill: ALLUSIONS**

Guide students back to the nurse's explanation of what happened in that ward during the Great Famine (lines 224–234) and to the footnote explaining Protestant soup. Have students enter the phrases "green around their mouths" and "Protestant soup" into the Allusion charts they began. Then ask students how they would feel if, like Frank, they were alone in a large hospital room at night.

*Possible answer: The broad allusion to "people in the nineteen beds . . ." (line 281) and the specific allusion to "Protestant soup" (line 283) both refer to hunger and illness during the Great Famine. The allusions show that these events haunt young Frank.*

## SELECTION WRAP-UP

**READ WITH A PURPOSE** Now that students have read the selection, ask them why they think this phase of McCourt's life became an important part of his memoir. *Possible answers: He nearly died; he was exposed for the first time to Shakespeare and other poetry, which influenced his eventual profession; the injustice of his separation from Patricia was deeply painful.*

★ **CRITIQUE** Have students share which episodes within the selection they found the most memorable and explain why.

## INDEPENDENT READING

Suggest that students read *Angela's Ashes* by Frank McCourt, the first in a trilogy of memoirs by the same author, including '*Tis* and *Teacher Man: A Memoir.*

---

**FOR STRUGGLING READERS**

**(5) Targeted Passage [Lines 300–323]**

This passage concludes the selection with the end of the poem "The Highwayman" and Seamus's reactions to it.

- What happens to Bess and the highwayman at the end of the poem? (lines 308–311)

- How does Seamus feel about Patricia not being able to read the end of the poem to Frank? (lines 316–318)

- What sad events are summed up in the final paragraph? (lines 316–322)

**FOR ENGLISH LANGUAGE LEARNERS**

**Compare and Contrast Context** Have students think about the two friendships Frank develops in the hospital. How are they similar? different? What does he take from and give to each one? Have students break into small groups to discuss these questions and then share their conclusions with the class.

# Practice and Apply

## TIERED DISCUSSION PROMPTS

Use these prompts to help students understand why McCourt wrote *Angela's Ashes*:

**Connect** Do you ever feel frustrated when you try to write? Are you sometimes afraid that you just won't get it right? Describe your feelings about writing. *Answers will vary. Encourage students to cite specific situations in their responses.*

**Analyze** What were the most important ideas about writing that McCourt passed on to his students? What were the most important ideas McCourt gained from his students? *Possible answer: Students learned that everyone has a story to tell, to write about things they know, to find their own voices, and to dig deep. They gained inspiration and courage. McCourt recognized that his students were doing what he should be doing and was inspired by their courage. He learned to follow his own advice.*

**Evaluate** McCourt learned from his students just as they learned from him. In your view, who gained more, McCourt or his students? *Possible answer: McCourt may have gained more from his students than they did from him because he gained perspective from reading their work, recognized the many good stories he had to tell as he shared them with his classes, and gained courage by seeing his students challenge themselves.*

---

**MAGAZINE ARTICLE** As a high school teacher, Frank McCourt encouraged his students to write from their experiences. Years later, he recalled the honesty and bravery of their writing and found the inspiration to write his own memoir.

# THE EDUCATION of
## Frank McCourt
### By Barbara Sande Dimmitt

The bell rang in the faculty lounge at Stuyvesant High School in Manhattan. When McCourt began teaching at the prestigious public high school in 1972, he joked that he'd finally made it to paradise. . . .

The bits and pieces that bubbled into his consciousness enlivened the stories he told in class. "Everyone has a story to tell," he said. "Write about what you know with conviction, from the heart. Dig deep," he urged. "Find your own voice and dance your own dance!"

On Fridays the students read their compositions aloud. To draw them out, McCourt would read excerpts from his duffel bag full of notebooks. "You had such an interesting childhood, Mr. McCourt," they said. "Why don't you write a book?" They threw his own words back at him: "It sounds like there's more to that story; dig deeper . . ."

McCourt was past 50 and painfully aware of the passage of time. But despite his growing frustration at his [own memoir begun six years earlier], he never tired of his students' work.

Over the years some talented writers passed through McCourt's popular classes. Laurie Gwen Shapiro was one of them. He decided she was coasting along on her technical skills. "You're capable of much more," McCourt told her. "Try writing something that's meaningful to you for a change."

Near the end of the semester, McCourt laid an essay—graded 100—on Laurie's desk. "If Laurie is willing to read her essay," he announced to the class, "I think we'll all benefit."

Laurie began to read a portrait of love clouded by anger and shame. She told of her father, partially paralyzed, and of resenting his inability to play with her or help her ride a bicycle. The paper shook in her trembling hands, and McCourt understood all too well what it cost her to continue. She also admitted she was embarrassed by her father's limp. The words, McCourt knew, were torn straight from her soul.

When Laurie finished, with tears streaming down her face, the students broke into applause. McCourt looked around the room, his own vision blurred.

*These young people have been giving you lessons in courage, he thought. When will you dare as mightily as they?*

It was October 1994. Frank McCourt, now retired, sat down and read his book's new opening, which he had written a few days before and still found satisfying. But many blank pages lay before him. *What if I never get it right?* he wondered grimly.

He stared at the logs glowing in the fireplace and could almost hear students' voices from years past, some angry, some defeated, others confused and seeking guidance. "It's no good, Mr. McCourt. I don't have what it takes."

Then Frank McCourt, author, heard the steadying tones of Frank McCourt, teacher: *Of course you do. Dig deeper. Find your own voice and dance your own dance.*

He scribbled a few lines. "I'm in a playground on Classon Avenue in Brooklyn with my brother Malachy. He's two, I'm three. We're on the seesaw." In the innocent voice of an unprotected child who could neither comprehend nor control the world around him, Frank McCourt told his tale of poverty and abandonment.

## Comprehension

1. **Recall** Why is Frank in the hospital?

2. **Recall** What rules does Frank break?

3. **Clarify** What happens to Patricia Madigan?

4. **Clarify** According to "The Education of Frank McCourt," who or what finally prompted McCourt to complete *Angela's Ashes*?

## Text Analysis

● 5. **Understand Memoir** Frank develops two friendships in the hospital. What is the basis for each friendship? Give reasons to support your response.

6. **Draw Conclusions About Character** What kind of a man is Seamus? Support your answer with examples of his actions and his words.

7. **Analyze Character Motives** What motivates Sister Rita to forbid Frank to talk to Patricia? Considering Patricia's fate, were Sister Rita's actions justified? Cite details to support your response.

■ 8. **Use Allusions to Make Inferences** Review the allusions and inferences you recorded in your chart as you read. What would your reading experience have been like if McCourt had not included these allusions?

9. **Identify Author's Perspective** On the basis of the numerous **allusions** to Catholic clergy, rituals, practices, and beliefs in this text, what do you think is McCourt's view of the Catholic Church and its influence on Irish culture and society in the 1940s? Explain your answer.

10. **Evaluate Voice** A writer's unique style of expression is called voice. In *Angela's Ashes*, McCourt writes in the "innocent voice of an unprotected child." How effective is this voice in relating not only events from McCourt's childhood but also his adult feelings about these events?

## Text Criticism

11. **Critical Interpretations** One critic has said that while reading *Angela's Ashes* "you never know whether to weep or roar—and find yourself doing both at once." Did you think any of the incidents described in this excerpt were at the same time sad and humorous? Cite examples to support your answer.

### How does **FRIENDSHIP** begin?

How does friendship end?

COMMON CORE

**RI 1** Cite textual evidence to support analysis of what a text says explicitly as well as inferences drawn from the text. **RI 6** Determine an author's point of view in a text and analyze how an author uses rhetoric to advance that point of view.

10. *The use of the "innocent voice" is very effective, but also deceptive. We are reading a child's voice, but one crafted by an adult with the experience of a lifetime. For example, McCourt shapes his image of discovering poetry with adult perspectives (lines 158–161).*

## Text Criticism

**Possible answer:**

11. *Serious and humorous moments include Frank and Patricia's matter-of-fact discussion of their illnesses during which Patricia calls Frank "typhoid boy" (line 70) and Seamus's comments about getting fired and singing patriotic songs on the street (lines 131–133).*

### How does **FRIENDSHIP**
begin? *Answers will vary, but students may recognize that many friendships end when people are separated by circumstance.*

# Practice and Apply

For preliminary support of post-reading questions, use these copy masters:

**R** RESOURCE MANAGER—Copy Masters
Reading Check p. 28
Memoir p. 21
Question Support p. 29

Additional selection questions are provided for teachers on page 15.

### ANSWERS

## Comprehension

1. *Frank is in the hospital with typhoid.*

2. *Frank breaks the rules about talking between rooms and talking with a girl.*

3. *Patricia dies.*

4. *McCourt's students' courage prompted him to complete the book. He decided to follow the same advice he gave students.*

## Text Analysis

COMMON CORE  RI 1, RI 6

**Possible answers:**

5. ● **COMMON CORE FOCUS** *Understand Memoir The friendship with Patricia is based on a shared experience of being sick in a hospital (lines 58–85) and shared feelings about poetry (lines 125–126). The friendship with Seamus is based on a love of poetry and song (lines 132–135), Seamus's love for children, and his role as intermediary between the children (lines 126–128).*

6. *Seamus is kindhearted and loves children. Examples: He brings books to Frank, feels sad over Patricia's death (lines 255–260), and memorizes the end of "The Highwayman" to recite for Frank (lines 300–303).*

7. *Sister Rita is motivated by the idea that talking, laughing, and singing are bad for the health (lines 111–112) and by the desire to exert authority. Sister Rita's actions may have contributed to Patricia's death, as she would have stayed in bed if talking to Frank.*

8. ■ **COMMON CORE FOCUS** *Use Allusions to Make Inferences Students should note that allusions help establish the significance of the Church and the impact of English oppression on Irish culture.*

9. *McCourt implies that people are both nourished and confined by the Church, especially by the authoritative nuns.*

## ANSWERS

## Vocabulary in Context

 VOCABULARY PRACTICE

| | |
|---|---|
| 1. *a* | 3. *b* |
| 2. *b* | 4. *a* |

 **RESOURCE MANAGER—Copy Master**
Vocabulary Practice p. 26

### ACADEMIC VOCABULARY IN WRITING

*Possible answer: In the first room, McCourt is initially very ill, but he is generally happy. In* **contrast**, *in the second room his* **predominant** *mood is sadness even though he regains his health there.*

### VOCABULARY STRATEGY: THE LATIN ROOT *fid*

COMMON CORE **L 4c**

- Encourage students to look for other word parts they know, such as the prefix *in-,* meaning "not," in *infidel.*

- Suggest that students use dictionaries for any word meanings they cannot figure out.

**Possible answers:**

| | |
|---|---|
| 1. *fidelity* | 4. *fiduciary* |
| 2. *confidant* | 5. *infidel* |
| 3. *affidavit* | |

 **RESOURCE MANAGER—Copy Master**
Vocabulary Strategy p. 27

### Interactive Vocabulary

**THINK** central

Keywords direct students to a **WordSharp** tutorial on **thinkcentral.com** or to other types of vocabulary practice and review.

---

## Vocabulary in Context

▲ **VOCABULARY PRACTICE**

Write the letter of the phrase that best clarifies the meaning of the boldfaced word.

1. Experiencing a **relapse** of the flu usually means that (a) one will be sick for a little longer, (b) it is time for a flu shot, (c) it is time to go back to school or work.

2. A **torrent** of water could most likely be produced by (a) a leaky hose, (b) a large rain cloud, (c) a spray bottle.

3. Experiencing an act of **perfidy** might make you (a) get interested in mountain climbing, (b) feel angry and betrayed, (c) decide to read historical fiction.

4. If you have **induced** a friend to join you on a boring errand, you are probably good at (a) persuading others, (b) staying on schedule, (c) working alone.

**WORD LIST**
induced
perfidy
relapse
torrent

### ACADEMIC VOCABULARY IN WRITING

- contrast   - environment   - factor   - incorporate   - predominant

In a brief essay, **contrast** McCourt's experience in the first hospital room with his experience after he is moved upstairs. **Incorporate** information about his surroundings as well as his thoughts and feelings. Use at least one Academic Vocabulary word in your response.

**COMMON CORE**

**L 4c** Consult reference materials to determine or clarify a word's meaning or etymology.

### VOCABULARY STRATEGY: THE LATIN ROOT *fid*

The word *perfidy* contains the Latin root *fid,* which means "faith; trust; belief." This root is found in a number of English words. To understand the meaning of words with *fid,* use context clues as well as your knowledge of the root.

*PRACTICE* Write the word from the word web that best completes each sentence. Use context clues to help you or, if necessary, consult a dictionary.

1. The _____ of the sound from those speakers is amazing; the music sounds like a live concert.

2. Everyone needs a trusted _____, someone to rely on.

3. A (An) _____ is usually sworn to in front of a public official.

4. In a (an) _____ agreement, one party holds money or property in trust for another.

5. You shouldn't call Leo a (an) _____ just because he doesn't believe in your religion.

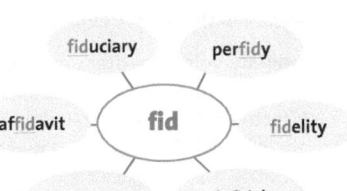

**Interactive Vocabulary**
**THINK** central

Go to **thinkcentral.com.**
KEYWORD: HML9-938

---

## DIFFERENTIATED INSTRUCTION

### FOR ENGLISH LANGUAGE LEARNERS

**Vocabulary: Cognates** Point out that the Spanish cognates *fidelidad* and *perfidia* are similar to the English words *fidelity* and *perfidy.* Invite students who speak Latin-based languages to look for and explain additional words in the selection that are similar to those in their languages. Have students teach the non-English versions of these words to the class.

### FOR ADVANCED LEARNERS/PRE–AP

**Vocabulary in Writing** Ask students to use the words containing the root *fid* in a short paragraph. Challenge them to find and include additional words based on this root.

# Language

◆ **GRAMMAR AND STYLE: Write Concisely**

Review the **Grammar and Style** note on page 931. A gerund is a verb form that ends in *-ing* and acts as a noun. A **gerund phrase** consists of a gerund plus its modifiers and complements. Because gerunds can be used to replace entire groups of words, they often help to make writing more concise.

Here are two examples of McCourt's use of gerund phrases:

> *I practice walking from bed to bed back and forth back and forth.*
> (line 295)

> *He stops mopping the floor and calls to Patricia. . . .* (lines 144–145)

Notice how the revisions in blue insert gerunds and a gerund phrase to make the writing more concise. Revise your response to the prompt below by employing similar techniques.

> **STUDENT MODEL**
>
> *reciting poetry is good for*
> Seamus thinks that Patricia and Frank should be able to recite
>
> poetry to each other while Sister Rita believes that patients
> *refrain from talking or laughing.*
> shouldn't talk with each other or laugh with each other.

## READING-WRITING CONNECTION

 **YOUR TURN** Increase your understanding of the people portrayed in *Angela's Ashes* by responding to this prompt. Then use the **revising tip** to improve your writing.

| WRITING PROMPT | REVISING TIP |
|---|---|
| **Short Constructed Response: Argument** Sister Rita is in charge of patient care, while Seamus takes care of the building. Who is the more caring person? Write **one or two paragraphs** in which you explain why Sister Rita or Seamus is the more compassionate person. | Review your argument. Have you used gerund phrases to make your writing more concise? If not, revise your response. |

**Interactive Revision** THINK central

Go to **thinkcentral.com**.
KEYWORD: HML9-939

ANGELA'S ASHES **939**

---

**COMMON CORE**

**L 1b** Use various types of phrases to convey specific meanings and add variety and interest to writing.

---

# Language

 COMMON CORE **L 1b**

◆ **GRAMMAR AND STYLE**

- After students review page 931, elicit and list examples of gerunds.
- Write these lines on the board. Have students rewrite them using gerunds.

*Sister Rita believes that ~~the most important thing is to talk to the children about being good Catholics.~~ talking to the children about being good Catholics is the most important thing. Seamus believes ~~that the children should be allowed to enjoy each other.~~ in allowing the children to enjoy each other.*

**R** **RESOURCE MANAGER—Copy Master** Write Concisely p. 30

◆ **READING-WRITING CONNECTION**

Suggest students reread some of the passages involving Sister Rita (lines 95–106, 205–217) and Seamus (lines 126–150, 247–272, 300–323). Students might use a Two-Column Chart to list Sister Rita's and Seamus's actions and ideas.

 **BEST PRACTICES TOOLKIT—Transparency** Two-Column Chart p. A25

**Writing Online** THINK central

The following tools are available online at **thinkcentral.com** and on **Write*Smart* CD-ROM:**
- **Interactive Graphic Organizers**
- **Interactive Student Models**
- **Interactive Revision Lessons**
For additional grammar instruction, see **GrammarNotes** on **thinkcentral.com**.

---

## FOR STRUGGLING WRITERS

Suggest students organize their argument this way:

1. Begin by stating which person is more compassionate.
2. Describe three ways in which this person is compassionate.
3. Describe three ways in which the second person is not compassionate.

---

# Assess and Reteach

## Assess

**DIAGNOSTIC AND SELECTION TESTS**
Selection Test A, B/C pp. 247–248, 249–250

**Interactive Selection Test** on **thinkcentral.com**

## Reteach

**Level Up Online Tutorials** on **thinkcentral.com**

**Reteaching Worksheets** on **thinkcentral.com**
Literature Lessons 35, 47
Reading Lesson 8

ANGELA'S ASHES **939**

# Focus and Motivate

## COMMON CORE FOCUS

**RI 6** Determine an author's point of view in a text and analyze how an author uses rhetoric to advance that point of view. **RI 10** Read and comprehend literary nonfiction. **L 4** Determine or clarify the meaning of unknown words. **L 4c** Consult reference materials to determine or clarify a word's meaning or etymology.

## SUMMARY

Accompanied by his friend Chuck, author N. Scott Momaday follows the migration route of his Kiowa ancestors from Montana to Oklahoma. They head to the Medicine Wheel, a sacred site in the Bighorn Mountains. On a forest road they meet Jurg, who is also seeking the ring of stones. Later, Momaday and Chuck journey to Devil's Tower, a monolith also sacred to the Kiowa.

## What makes something SACRED?

Introduce the question. Ask students to identify sacred objects or places they have visited or know about. Extend the discussion by having students complete the *QUICKWRITE*.

## Selection Resources

---

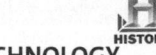

## Revisiting Sacred Ground
Essay by N. Scott Momaday

Video link at thinkcentral.com

# What makes something SACRED?

### COMMON CORE

**RI 6** Determine an author's point of view in a text and analyze how an author uses rhetoric to advance that point of view. **RI 10** Read and comprehend literary nonfiction. **L 4** Determine or clarify the meaning of unknown words.

The word *sacred* means "holy" or "associated with divine power." Different religions and cultures hold different objects and places sacred. In "Revisiting Sacred Ground," Native American author N. Scott Momaday describes a journey to a sacred place that has spiritual significance for his people, the Kiowa.

*QUICKWRITE* Imagine that you have been invited into a sacred place. What do you need to know? How should you behave? List your ideas on how to act in this special location.

*Being in a Sacred Place*
1. Be silent, or speak softly, to allow people to think or to absorb the feeling of the place.
2.
3.

940

---

See resources on the **Teacher One Stop DVD-ROM** and on **thinkcentral.com**.

**R RESOURCE MANAGER UNIT 9**
Plan and Teach, pp. 33–40
Summary pp. 41–42†‡*
Text Analysis and Reading
   Skill, pp. 43–46†*
Vocabulary, pp. 47–49*

**DIAGNOSTIC AND SELECTION TESTS**
Selection Tests, pp. 251–254

**BEST PRACTICES TOOLKIT**
New Word Analysis, p. E8
Think-Pair-Share, p. A18

Video link at thinkcentral.com

**TECHNOLOGY**
- Teacher One Stop DVD-ROM
- Student One Stop DVD-ROM
- Audio Anthology CD
- GrammarNotes DVD-ROM
- ExamView Test Generator on the Teacher One Stop

\* Resources for Differentiation          † Also in Spanish          ‡ In Haitian Creole and Vietnamese

## TEXT ANALYSIS: CULTURAL SYMBOL

You already know that a symbol is an object, a place, or a person that has meaning beyond itself. A **cultural symbol** is one that has shared meaning for an entire culture. In "Revisiting Sacred Ground," N. Scott Momaday incorporates many cultural symbols that are important to the Kiowa and other Plains tribes. These cultural symbols include

- places, such as the Black Hills and the Bighorn Mountains
- animals, such as the deer and the coyote
- concepts, such as the four directions
- objects, such as prayer bundles

As you read, note the significance of these cultural symbols. What do these symbols tell you about Momaday's heritage and the way he feels about it?

## READING STRATEGY: MONITOR

When you read, you can increase your comprehension by pausing occasionally to check, or **monitor,** how well you understand the text. To monitor your comprehension, try

- rereading difficult passages
- writing down questions you may have about the content

Make a chart like the one shown to record your questions, and answer them, when possible, from information found in the text.

| Questions | Answers |
|---|---|
| Why is the Medicine Wheel significant to the author? | |

## VOCABULARY IN CONTEXT

Restate each phrase, using a different word or words for the boldfaced term.

1. ill will and **alienation** within the family
2. suggest **cosmetic** changes to the plan
3. **sauntering** lazily through the park
4. a fender-bender causing **negligible** damage
5. visited an ancient **petrified** forest
6. the **inherent** sweetness of honey
7. a **monolith** standing alone in the desert
8. **engender** goodwill by his kindness

Complete the activities in your **Reader/Writer Notebook.**

---

## Meet the Author

# N. Scott Momaday
born 1934

**Poet with a Native Voice**
N. Scott Momaday was born in Oklahoma and raised on Southwestern Indian reservations. His mother was a teacher and writer of children's stories, and his father was an art teacher. Even though Momaday won a Pulitzer Prize for his novel *House Made of Dawn,* he thinks of himself primarily as a poet—and as a Native American.

**Harmony with Nature**
Momaday's Kiowa heritage inspires both his poetry and his prose, which often portray the Native American view that people need to live in harmony with nature. "I believe that the Indian has a [unique] understanding of the physical world and of the earth as a spiritual entity," says Momaday. "The whole world view of the Indian is predicated upon the principle of harmony in the universe."

**BACKGROUND TO THE ESSAY**
**The Nomadic Kiowa**
As of the 1600s, the Kiowa were living as nomadic hunters in what is now western Montana. Around 1700, they moved to the Black Hills of present-day eastern Wyoming and southwestern South Dakota and then migrated to the southern Great Plains. When the U.S. government moved Native Americans onto reservations by the late 1800s, the Kiowa settled in reservations in Oklahoma. However, many sites in their former homelands, where traditions originated or important tribal events occurred, still have spiritual significance to the Kiowa.

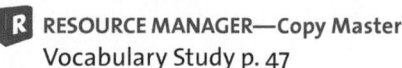

**Author Online**
Go to **thinkcentral.com.**
KEYWORD: HML9-941

941

---

## Teach

TEXT ANALYSIS

COMMON CORE
RI 6

### Model the Skill: CULTURAL SYMBOL

Read aloud this example:

> The Washington Monument's white stone cut into the blue sky. As the old man gazed at the peak of the obelisk, a tingle traveled along the skin of his arms.

Explain that all cultures have important symbols. Ask students to note the meaning of the cultural symbol above. ***Possible answer:*** *The Washington Monument symbolizes our first president, and thus, our nation's origin.*

**GUIDED PRACTICE** Elicit other widely known symbols of the nation.

READING STRATEGY

COMMON CORE
RI 10

### Model the Skill: MONITOR

Read aloud the ***About the Author*** text. Guide students in asking themselves questions about the text, such as: *Why is it helpful for us to know that Momaday's culture is important to him? What does Momaday mean by "harmony in the universe"?*

**GUIDED PRACTICE** Have students read the ***Background*** and write questions to monitor their understanding.

**R** RESOURCE MANAGER—Copy Master Monitor p. 45 (for student use while reading the selection)

---

## VOCABULARY SKILL

COMMON CORE
L 4

### VOCABULARY IN CONTEXT

**DIAGNOSE WORD KNOWLEDGE** Have all students complete Vocabulary in Context. Check their restatements against the following definitions:

**alienation** (āl′yə-nā′shən) *n.* a feeling of separation or isolation

**cosmetic** (kŏz-mĕt′ĭk) *adj.* decorative rather than functional

**engender** (ĕn-jĕn′dər) *v.* to bring into existence

**inherent** (ĭn-hîr′ənt) *adj.* forming part of the essential nature of something; built-in

**monolith** (mŏn′ə-lĭth′) *n.* something, such as a monument, made from a single large stone

**negligible** (nĕg′lĭ-jə-bəl) *adj.* not large or important enough to merit attention

**petrified** (pĕt′rə-fīd′) *adj.* turned into stone **petrify** *v.*

**saunter** (sôn′tər) *v.* to walk in a slow, relaxed manner

**PRETEACH VOCABULARY** Help students predict meanings for each boldfaced word:

**R** RESOURCE MANAGER—Copy Master Vocabulary Study p. 47

1. Read the first sentence in Part A aloud.
2. Point out the phrases "lived easily in its environment" and "no alienation from its wild surroundings." Then elicit possible meanings for *alienation*.
3. Repeat the approach for the other items.

## READ WITH A PURPOSE

*Help students set a purpose for reading. Ask them what sacred means to them. Then have them read to find out what sacred means to the author.*

---

**READING STRATEGY**

COMMON CORE
RI 10

### A Model the Skill: MONITOR

Remind students that their questions should come from what they learned in the text and their own knowledge, and that answering the questions should help them better understand the text. For example, you know that the journey has to do with the writer's ancestry. You want to understand the connection between the two. Have students write their questions in the Reading Strategy charts they began.

**Possible answers:** *What does Momaday's Kiowa ancestry mean to him? How does he know about his ancestors' journey? Why does he feel a need to see what his ancestors saw on their journey?*

**Extend the Discussion** Why may people want to visit places where their ancestors lived?

---

## Revisiting SACRED GROUND

### N. Scott Momaday

There is great good in returning to a landscape that had extraordinary meaning in one's life. It happens that we return to such places in our minds irresistibly. There are certain villages and towns, mountains and plains that, having seen them, walked in them, lived in them, even for a day, we keep forever in the mind's eye. They become indispensable to our well-being; they define us, and we say, I am who I am because I have been there, or there. There is good, too, in actual, physical return.

Some years ago I made a pilgrimage into the heart of North America. I began the journey proper in western Montana. From there I traveled across the high plains of Wyoming into the Black Hills, then southward to the southern plains, to a cemetery at Rainy Mountain, in Oklahoma. It was a journey made by my Kiowa[1] ancestors long before. In the course of their migration they became the people of the Great Plains, and theirs was the last culture to evolve in North America. They had been for untold generations a mountain tribe of hunters. Their ancient nomadism, which had determined their way of life even before they set foot on this continent, perhaps thirty thousand years ago, was raised to its highest level of expression when they entered upon the Great Plains and acquired horses. Their migration brought them to a golden age. At the beginning of their journey they were a people of hard circumstances, often hungry and cold, fighting always for sheer survival. At its end, and for a hundred years, they were the lords of the land, a daring race of centaurs[2] and buffalo hunters whose love of freedom and space was profound.

Recently I returned to the old migration route of the Kiowas. I had in me a need to behold again some of the principle landmarks of that long, prehistoric quest, to descend again from the mountain to the plain. A

With my close friend Chuck I drove north to the Montana-Wyoming border. I wanted to intersect the Kiowa migration route at the Bighorn Medicine Wheel, high in the Bighorn Mountains. We gradually ascended

---

**Analyze Visuals ▶**

How would you describe the landscape of the Bighorn Mountains in this photo? What might it **symbolize** to you?

① **Targeted Passage**

A **MONITOR**
After reading lines 8–25, **question** yourself about what the writer's journey may represent to him.

---

1. **Kiowa** (kī'ə-wō').
2. **centaurs** (sĕn'tôrz'): in Greek mythology, creatures that were half man and half horse.

---

## DIFFERENTIATED INSTRUCTION

### FOR ENGLISH LANGUAGE LEARNERS

**Vocabulary Support** Use New Word Analysis to teach these words: *migration* (line 12), *evolve* (line 13), *design* (line 64), *equation* (line 66), *conformation* (line 130).

🧰 **BEST PRACTICES TOOLKIT—Transparency** New Word Analysis p. E8

### FOR STRUGGLING READERS

In combination with the *Audio Anthology CD*, use one or more Targeted Passages (pp. 942, 944, 947) to ensure that students focus on key events, concepts, and skills. Targeted Passages are also good for English learners.

① **Targeted Passage [Lines 1–7]**

In this passage, the writer explains that the places people love contribute to who they are and what is important to them.

## B CULTURAL SYMBOL

*Possible answer:* The deer could be an indication that they are doing the right thing, that they are on the right track, or that nature (the divine) approves of their quest.

**IF STUDENTS NEED HELP . . .** Ask them what words in lines 38–43 have positive connotations?

## TIERED DISCUSSION PROMPTS

Use these prompts to help students understand the author's experiences on his journey in lines 44–69:

**Connect** Imagine the sudden calm and silence after the bitter wind. How might you feel if this happened to you in a special place? *Students' answers should reflect an understanding of the author's sensitivity to the setting.*

**Analyze** How does Momaday's language change when he begins to describe weather changes at the Medicine Wheel? *Possible answer: Once at the Medicine Wheel, Momaday's factual description of the meeting with Jurg and the wheel itself becomes more atmospheric with phrases such as "a profound silence" (line 69).*

**Evaluate** Momaday uses heightened language to describe certain events and conditions in this passage. Is this language effective in helping you visualize the experience? Cite examples. *Students' answers should include examples from the passage.*

## OWN THE WORD

- **alienation:** Explain that the root of *alienation* is *alien*, meaning someone from a foreign country or different world. Have students write sentences that show understanding of *alien* and *alienation*.

- **cosmetic:** Ask students what *cosmetic* changes could improve the bus in the story's appearance. *Possible answers: washing, painting, cleaning the interior*

---

30 to eight thousand feet on a well-maintained but winding highway. Then we climbed sharply, bearing upon timberline. It was early October, and although the plain below had been comfortable, even warm at midday, the mountain air was cold, and much of the ground was covered with snow. We turned off the pavement, on a dirt road that led three miles to the Medicine Wheel. The road was forbidding; it was narrow and winding, and the grades were steep and slippery; here and there the shoulders fell away into deep ravines. But at the same time something wonderful happened: we crossed the line between civilization and wilderness. Suddenly the earth persisted in its original being. Directly in front of us a huge white-tailed buck crossed our path, ambling without haste into a thicket of pines. As we drove over his tracks we saw four 40 does above on the opposite bank, looking down at us, their great black eyes bright and benign, curious. There seemed no wariness, nothing of fear or **alienation.** Their presence was a good omen, we thought; somehow in their attitude they bade us welcome to their sphere of wilderness. **B**

There was a fork in the road, and we took the wrong branch. At a steep, hairpin curve we got out of the car and climbed to the top of a peak. An icy wind whipped at us; we were among the bald summits of the Bighorns. Great flumes of sunlit snow erupted on the ridges and dissolved in spangles on the sky. Across a deep saddle we caught sight of the Medicine Wheel. It was perhaps two miles away.

50 When we returned to the car we saw another vehicle approaching. It was a very old Volkswagen bus, in much need of repair, **cosmetic** repair at least. Out stepped a thin, bearded young man in thick glasses. He wore a wool cap, a down parka, and well-worn hiking boots. "I am looking for the Medicine Wheel," he said, having nodded to us. He spoke softly, with a pronounced accent. His name was Jurg, and he was from Switzerland; he had been traveling for some months in Canada and the United States. Chuck and I shook his hand and told him to follow us, and we drove down into the saddle. From there we climbed on foot to the Medicine Wheel.

The Medicine Wheel is a ring of stones, some fifty feet in diameter. Stone 60 spokes radiate from the center to the circumference. Cairns[3] are placed at certain points on the circumference, one in the center, and one just outside the ring to the southwest. We do not know as a matter of fact who made the wheel or to what purpose. It had been proposed that it is an astronomical observatory, a solar calendar, and the ground design of a Kiowa Sun Dance lodge.[4] What we know without doubt is that it is a sacred expression, an equation of man's relation to the cosmos.

There was a great calm upon that place. The hard, snow-bearing wind that had burned our eyes and skin only minutes before had died away altogether. The sun was warm and bright, and there was a profound silence. On the wire

---

3. **cairns** (kârnz): mounds of rough stones built as memorials or landmarks.

4. **Kiowa Sun Dance lodge:** For the annual Sun Dance ceremony, the most important Kiowa religious rite through much of the 19th century, Kiowa members built a sweat lodge for their purification and self-renewal.

**alienation** (ăl′yə-nā′shən) *n.* a feeling of separation or isolation

**B CULTURAL SYMBOL**
Native Americans believe animals are representatives of higher powers who impart wisdom to humans. What might the appearance of the deer represent to the author in this setting?

**cosmetic** (kŏz-mĕt′ĭk) *adj.* decorative rather than functional

**2 Targeted Passage**

### Language Coach

**Roots and Affixes** A **prefix** is an affix at the beginning of a word. The Greek prefix *dia-* means "through." The Latin prefix *circum-* means "around." How do these word parts help you understand the meaning of the mathematical terms *diameter* and *circumference* (lines 59–60)?

---

## DIFFERENTIATED INSTRUCTION

### FOR STRUGGLING READERS

**2 Targeted Passage** [Lines 44–58]
In this passage, Momaday relates events that precede his arrival at the Medicine Wheel.

- How does Momaday describe the summits of the Bighorns? (lines 45–47)

- How does he make the setting sound beautiful? (lines 46–48)

- Who do the two men meet on the trail? (lines 52–55)

- How do they help the stranger? (lines 53–57)

### FOR ENGLISH LANGUAGE LEARNERS

**Language Coach**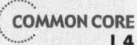

**Roots and Affixes**
*Possible answer: Since the writer is talking about a circle, and* meter *means "measure,"* diameter *must mean "measure through," or the distance across the center of the circle.* Circumference *might mean the distance around the circle.* Have students check their ideas using a dictionary or a math book.

Reaching 80 feet across, the Medicine Wheel sits atop a ridge of Medicine Mountain in north-central Wyoming.

70 fence which had been erected to enclose and protect the wheel were fixed offerings, small prayer bundles. Chuck and Jurg and I walked about slowly, standing for long moments here and there, looking into the wheel or out across the great distances. We did not say much; there was little to be said. But we were deeply moved by the spirit of that place. The silence was such that it must be observed. To the north we could see down to timberline, to the snowfields and draws that marked the black planes of forest among the peaks of the Bighorns. To the south and west the mountains fell abruptly to the plains. We could see thousands of feet down and a hundred miles across the dim expanse.

80     When we were about to leave, I took from my pocket an eagle-bone whistle that my father had given me, and I blew it in the four directions. The sound was very high and shrill, and it did not break the essential silence. As we were walking down we saw far below, crossing our path, a coyote **sauntering** across the snow into a wall of trees. It was just there, a wild being to catch sight of, and then it was gone. The wilderness, which had admitted us with benediction let us go. **C**

**saunter** (sôn′tər)
*v.* to walk in a slow, relaxed manner

**C CULTURAL SYMBOL**
Many ceremonies of the Plains Indians begin with a call to the four directions, which represent different powers or ways of perceiving. Why does the narrator call to the four directions?

REVISITING SACRED GROUND   **945**

---

**Analyze Visuals**

**Activity** Have students study the photograph and then draw parallels to other similar sacred places from other cultures throughout history. *Students may draw parallels to places such as Stonehenge or Easter Island.*

**TEXT ANALYSIS**     COMMON CORE   RI 6

**C** *Model the Skill:* **CULTURAL SYMBOL**

Point out that this calling is usually done at the beginning of a ceremony. Explain that, although the narrator is not about to begin a ceremony, he does want to mark this moment in a special way. Have students explain why the moment is special to the narrator.

*Possible answer: By blowing the whistle in the four directions, he is marking this moment as a sacred one and asking to be endowed with the four powers or ways of perceiving.*

**VOCABULARY**     COMMON CORE   L 4

**OWN THE WORD**

**saunter:** Ask students if they have ever seen people *saunter* at a shopping mall or at school. How did they walk? *Possible answers: at a leisurely pace, strolling, not rushing*

---

**FOR ENGLISH LANGUAGE LEARNERS**
**Vocabulary: Phrasal Verbs** Point out these passive-voice phrasal verbs: "had been proposed" (line 63) and "had been erected" (line 70). Explain that passive voice removes the action-doer. Using Think-Pair-Share, have students write five passive-voice sentences, exchange them, and read each other's sentences aloud.

BEST PRACTICES TOOLKIT—Transparency
Think-Pair-Share p. A18

**FOR ADVANCED LEARNERS/PRE–AP**
**Analyze Tone** Have students analyze the tone of lines 67–86, using these questions:
- How does Momaday's diction affect tone?
- How does the tone of this passage support the author's message?
- How does the tone affect the mood?

When we came within a stone's throw of the highway, Chuck and I said goodbye to Jurg, but not before he had got out his camp stove and boiled water for tea. There in the dusk we enjoyed a small ceremonial feast of tea and crackers. The three of us had become friends. Only later did I begin to understand the extraordinary character of that friendship. It was the friendship of those who come together in recognition of the sacred. If we never meet again, I thought, we shall not forget this day.

On the plains the fences and roads and windmills and houses seemed almost **negligible,** all but overwhelmed by the earth and sky. It is a landscape of great clarity; its vastness is that of the ocean. It is the near revelation of infinity. Antelope were everywhere in the grassy folds, grazing side by side with horses and cattle. Hawks sailed above, and crows scattered before us. The place names were American—Tensleep, Buffalo, Dull Knife, Crazy Woman, Spotted Horse.

The Black Hills are an isolated group of mountains in South Dakota and Wyoming. They lie very close to both the geographic center of the United States, if you include Alaska and Hawaii, and the geographic center of the North American continent. They form an island, an elliptical area of nearly six thousand square miles, in the vast sea of grasses that is the northern Great Plains. The Black Hills are a calendar of geologic time[5] that is truly remarkable. Their foundation rocks are much older than the sedimentary layers[6] of which the Americas are primarily formed. An analysis of this foundation, made in 1964, indicates an age of between two and three billion years.

A documented record of exploration in this region is found in the Lewis and Clark journals, 1804–1806. The first white party known definitely to have entered the Black Hills proper was led by Jedidiah Smith in 1823. The diary of this expedition, kept by one James Clyman, is notable. Clyman reports a confrontation between Jedidiah Smith and a grizzly bear, in which Smith lost one of his ears. There is also reported the discovery of a **petrified** ("putrified," as Clyman has it) forest in which petrified birds sing petrified songs.

The Lakotas, or Teton Sioux, called these mountains *Paha Sapa,* "hills that are black." Other tribes, beside the Kiowas and the Sioux, thought of the Black Hills as sacred ground, a place that is crucial in their past. The Arapahos[7] lived here. So did the Cheyennes. Bear Butte, near Sturgis, South Dakota, on the northeast edge of the Black Hills, is the Cheyennes' sacred mountain. It remains, like the Medicine Wheel, a place of the greatest spiritual intensity. So great was thought to be the power **inherent** in the Black Hills that the Indians did not camp there. It was a place of rendezvous, a hunting ground, but above all an inviolate, sacred ground. It was a place of thunder and lightning, a dwelling place of the gods.

On the edge of the Black Hills nearest the Bighorn Mountain is Devil's Tower, the first of our national monuments. The Lakotas called it *Mateo*

negligible (nĕg'lĭ-jə-bəl) *adj.* not large or important enough to merit attention

 MONITOR Reread lines 94–99 and note how the writer describes man-made objects in relation to nature.

petrified (pĕt'rə-fīd') *adj.* turned into stone petrify *v.*

inherent (ĭn-hîr'ənt) *adj.* forming part of the essential nature of something; built-in

5. **geologic time:** the period of time defined by the formation and development of the earth.
6. **sedimentary layers:** layers of earth and stone deposited by wind, water, and ice.
7. **Arapahos** (ə-răp'ə-hōz').

**946** UNIT 9: HISTORY, CULTURE, AND THE AUTHOR

## READING STRATEGY

 **MONITOR**

Discuss how Momaday conveys the vastness of the land relative to the negligible human-made objects.

## TIERED DISCUSSION PROMPTS

Use these prompts to help students appreciate how Momaday feels about the Black Hills in lines 100–125:

**Connect** Think of a place that impresses you in some way. How would you describe it? *Accept descriptions that point out the remarkable attributes of a place.*

**Analyze** How does Momaday make the Black Hills seem special? Cite details. *Possible answer: He cites impressive facts, such as the Black Hills' 2-billion-year age; he uses vivid language, like "an island . . . in the vast sea of grasses" (lines 103–104); and he tells of their sacredness to tribes.*

**Evaluate** How does the author's ancestry influence the purpose of each paragraph? *Possible answer: Because of his ancestry, Momaday feels a special kinship with the land. In lines 100–108, he tries to give the hills an epic stature. In lines 109–115, he aims to show the triviality of the explorers' visits to the hills. In lines 116–125, he tries to show how Native Americans revered the hills.*

## VOCABULARY

### OWN THE WORD

- **negligible:** Explain that the Latin root of *negligible* is *neglegere,* which means "to neglect." Have students write sentences showing the meaning of *negligible.*

- **petrified:** Tell students that the Greek root of *petrified* is *petra,* which means "rock."

- **inherent:** Tell students that common synonyms for *inherent* include *essential* and *intrinsic.* Have them name other synonyms. *Possible answers: built-in, innate, fundamental*

## DIFFERENTIATED INSTRUCTION

### FOR ENGLISH LANGUAGE LEARNERS

**Vocabulary: Idioms** Offer practice with idioms such as "as a matter of fact" (line 62), "stone's throw" (line 87), and "on our minds" (line 156). Choose three other idioms, and write each, with its line number, on the back of an index card. Divide the cards among small groups. Have each group write two sentences using their idioms on the front of each of their cards. Have groups exchange cards and write sentences until all groups have practiced each idiom.

### FOR STRUGGLING READERS

**Develop Reading Fluency** Explain that the story of the Devil's Tower on page 947 is a Kiowa legend. Its heightened language conveys its importance as a sacred story. Read the legend aloud. Then assign small groups to practice reading it, giving each student two or three sentences. After students have practiced, they can perform their readings for the class.

**946** UNIT 9

*Tepee*, "Grizzly Bear Lodge." The Kiowas called it *Tsoai*, "Rock Tree." Devil's Tower is a great **monolith** that rises high above the timber of the Black Hills.

130 In conformation it closely resembles the stump of a tree. It is a cluster of rock columns of phonolite porphyry[8] 1,000 feet across at the base and 275 feet across at the top. It rises 865 feet above the high ground upon which it stands and 1,280 feet above the Belle Fourch River, which runs in the valley below.

It has to be seen to be believed. "There are things in nature that **engender** an awful quiet in the heart of man; Devil's Tower is one of them." I wrote these words almost twenty years ago. They remain true to my experience. Each time I behold this *Tsoai* anew I am more than ever in awe of it.

Two hundred years ago, more or less, the Kiowas came upon this place. They were moved to tell a story about it:

140 *Eight children were there at play, seven sisters and their brother. Suddenly the boy was struck dumb; he trembled and began to run upon his hands and feet. His fingers became claws, and his body was covered with fur. Directly there was a bear where the boy had been. The sisters were terrified; they ran, and the bear after them. They came to the stump of a great tree, and the tree spoke to them. It bade them climb upon it, and as they did so it began to rise into the air. The bear came to kill them, but they were just beyond its reach. It reared against the tree and scored the bark all around with its claws. The seven sisters were borne into the sky, and they became the stars of the Big Dipper.* **E**

This story, which I have known from the time I could first understand
150 language, exemplifies the sacred for me. The storyteller, that anonymous man who told the story for the first time, succeeded in raising the human condition to the level of universal significance. Not only did he account for the existence of the rock tree, but in the process he related his people to the stars.

When Chuck and I had journeyed over this ground together, when we were about to go our separate ways, I reminded him of our friend Jurg, knowing well enough that I needn't have; Jurg was on our minds. I can't account for it. He had touched us deeply with his trust, not unlike that of the wild animals we had seen, and with his generosity of spirit, his concern to see beneath the surface of things, his attitude of free, clear, direct, disinterested kindness.
160 "Did he tell us what he does?" I asked. "Does he have a profession?"
"I don't think he said." Chuck replied. "I think he's a pilgrim."
"Yes."
"Yes." ❧

**3** Targeted Passage

monolith (mŏn'ə-lĭth') *n.* something, such as a monument, made from a single large stone

engender (ĕn-jĕn'dər) *v.* to bring into existence

**E** CULTURAL SYMBOL
How does the story of the origin of *Tsoai* reflect the Kiowa belief in people's kinship with nature?

---

8. **phonolite porphyry** (fō'nə-līt' pôr'fə-rē): a type of hard volcanic rock with fairly large crystals, set in a fine-grained groundmass.

---

**FOR STRUGGLING READERS**

**3** Targeted Passage [Lines 154–163]

In this passage, the writer expresses how he and Chuck feel about Jurg.

- How does Momaday know that Chuck is thinking about Jurg? (lines 155–156)

- What did Momaday and Chuck admire about Jurg? (lines 157–159)

- What may have caused the men to become so close so quickly? (lines 155–159)

- What do the men mean by "pilgrim"? (lines 160–161)

**FOR ADVANCED LEARNERS/PRE–AP**

**Analyze Symbolic Meaning** Have students read lines 126–153 closely and analyze the symbolic significance of Devil's Tower to the author's thematic message. Why does Momaday choose to retell this story within his essay? Within the story, what might the tower represent? the boy and girls? In retelling the tale, how does Momaday "[relate] his people to the stars" (line 153)?

## What makes something SACRED?

**Discuss** What ideas in the Kiowa story in lines 140–153 does Momaday see as sacred, and what do they share with stories in other cultures?
*Possible answer: Momaday sees explaining the wondrous and linking people to the heavens as sacred. Trying to understand how things came into existence is a theme that appears in the stories of many cultures and religions.*

**TEXT ANALYSIS**

COMMON CORE
RI 6

**E** CULTURAL SYMBOL

*Possible answer: The story reflects the Kiowa belief in kinship with nature in that the people are transformed into natural entities.*

**VOCABULARY**

COMMON CORE
L 4

**OWN THE WORD**

- **monolith:** Tell students that the prefix *mono-* comes from the Greek *monos*, which means "single." Have them list other words with the prefix *mono-* and explain their meanings. *Possible answers: monopoly: exclusive control or ownership*

- **engender:** Write *engender* and the definition "to bring into existence" in a circle. Have students add synonyms in outer circles to complete a semantic map.

**SELECTION WRAP–UP**

**READ WITH A PURPOSE** Now that students have read the story, ask them what they think *sacred* means to the author. *Possible answer: connected with his ancestry and with nature*

⭐ **CRITIQUE** Have students evaluate Momaday's explanation of why and how he views places as sacred. Do you agree or disagree with his view of what is sacred?

**INDEPENDENT READING**

Students might read more Kiowa native American stories in *The Way to Rainy Mountain* by N. Scott Momaday and Al Momaday (illustrator).

# Practice and Apply

For preliminary support of post-reading questions, use these copy masters:

**R** RESOURCE MANAGER—Copy Masters
Reading Check p. 50
Cultural Symbol p. 43
Question Support p. 51

Additional selection questions are provided for teachers on page 37.

## ANSWERS

## Comprehension

1. *He describes his own pilgrimage to the Bighorn Medicine Wheel.*

2. *He wants to make the same journey his Kiowa ancestors made.*

3. *They meet a fellow pilgrim named Jurg.*

4. *They all seek a sacred place and experience.*

## Text Analysis

COMMON CORE RI 6, RI 10

*Possible answers:*

5. ■ **COMMON CORE FOCUS** *Monitor Students should make mention of reading closely to find answers to their questions.*

6. ● **COMMON CORE FOCUS** *Interpret Cultural Symbols journey: respect for Kiowa traditions ("They become indispensable to our well-being" [line 5]); deer: nature's welcome ("bade us welcome" [line 43]); Medicine Wheel: "man's relation to cosmos" (line 66); coyote: spirit (wilderness letting the men go [lines 83–86]); Devil's Tower: the Kiowa's relation to the stars (Tsoai story [lines 140–148]).*

7. *Momaday sees the deer as nature's welcome and the coyote as its farewell blessing.*

8. *On his journey, Momaday honors ancestors, practices the Kiowa's relation to nature by noting the omens of the white-tailed deer and the coyote, pays respect to a sacred place, and recalls the story of the Tsoai.*

9. *Momaday's perspective on the relationship between people and nature is defined by the Kiowa tradition. (Many passages support this.)*

10. *Chuck means Jurg is traveling in search of the sacred. The description is apt, since Jurg did not talk of the material world and had an unspoken bond with his fellow pilgrims.*

---

## Comprehension

1. **Recall** What journey does Momaday describe?

2. **Recall** Why does he want to make this journey?

3. **Recall** Whom do Momaday and Chuck meet at the Medicine Wheel?

4. **Clarify** Why is the friendship between the three men significant to Momaday?

## Text Analysis

5. **Monitor** Review the questions and answers you listed as you read. How many questions were you able to answer from further reading in the text? For questions without answers, how would you go about finding the answers?

6. **Interpret Cultural Symbols** Momaday mentions a number of places, animals, and objects that are considered sacred to the Kiowa. Explain what these symbols represent to Momaday's heritage. Cite evidence from the text.

7. **Draw Conclusions** Momaday describes seeing deer upon entering the site of the Medicine Wheel and a coyote upon leaving. Why is the appearance of the animals meaningful to Momaday at those particular points in his journey?

8. **Analyze Cultural Context** In many Native American traditions, quests helped people define their relationship with the world around them. How does Momaday's journey fit within this tradition?

9. **Analyze Author's Perspective** An author's perspective is the unique combination of ideas, values, and beliefs that influences the way he or she looks at a topic. After reading this essay, how would you define Momaday's perspective on the relationship between people and the natural world? Cite evidence from the text to support your answers.

10. **Evaluate Word Choice** At the end of the selection, Chuck says he thinks Jurg is a "pilgrim." What does he mean by this? Why is this description appropriate?

## Text Criticism

11. **Different Perspectives** Momaday describes the land and its creatures as being responsive to him. For example, he says the "wilderness, which had admitted us with benediction let us go" and the deer "bade us welcome." How does this viewpoint differ from the typical Anglo-American perspective?

> ### What makes something SACRED?
>
> What objects or places do you consider sacred? Why are they sacred to you?

COMMON CORE

RI 6 Determine an author's point of view in a text and analyze how an author uses rhetoric to advance that point of view.
RI 10 Read and comprehend literary nonfiction.

---

## Text Criticism

*Possible answer:*

11. *The typical Anglo-American does not view animals as having this sort of intentional, intelligent, or thinking relationship with humans.*

> What makes something
> **SACRED?** *Students' responses will vary but should include explanations.*

# Vocabulary in Context

## ▲ VOCABULARY PRACTICE

Determine whether these statements are true or false. If you need to reread the definitions of the boldfaced vocabulary words, consult the Glossary of Vocabulary on page R123.

1. If I'm experiencing **alienation** from a friend, it's likely I'm not getting along with him.
2. A woman who **saunters** down the street is probably in a hurry.
3. A large car is a good example of a **monolith.**
4. An **inherent** quality of granite is its hardness.
5. If a committee submits a **cosmetic** reform proposal, it is suggesting major changes.
6. One small critical comment on a long essay would be considered **negligible.**
7. If I **engender** something, I build it with brick and mortar.
8. You would not expect a **petrified** bird to fly.

**WORD LIST**

alienation
cosmetic
engender
inherent
monolith
negligible
petrified
saunter

## ACADEMIC VOCABULARY IN WRITING

- contrast   - environment   - factor   - incorporate   - predominant

In their migration, the Kiowa Indians went from the high mountains of Montana and Wyoming to the Great Plains. In a paragraph or two, identify at least three or four ways in which that change in **environment** would have changed their lives. Use at least one Academic Vocabulary word in your response.

> **COMMON CORE**
>
> **L 4c** Consult reference materials to determine or clarify a word's meaning or etymology.

## VOCABULARY STRATEGY: THE GREEK WORD ROOT *cosm*

The vocabulary word *cosmetic* stems from the Greek word root *cosm,* from the Greek word *kosmos,* meaning "order." You may have encountered words with this root in readings for your science class—the root is found in a number of English words and in a variety of contexts. To understand the meaning of words with *cosm,* use context clues as well as your knowledge of the root.

cosmic   cosmos

cosmopolitan   **cosm**   cosmetology

cosmonaut

*PRACTICE* Write the word from the word web that best completes each sentence. Use word structure and context clues to help you. If necessary, consult a dictionary.

1. Astronomers make an academic study of the _____.
2. After leaving the space station, the _____ had to spend several weeks being reconditioned for life on Earth.
3. My cousin wants to study _____ and become a hairstylist.
4. New York is a very _____ city; people come there from all over the world.
5. _____ dust covered the ground near the fallen meteorite.

> **Interactive Vocabulary**   **THINK** central
>
> Go to **thinkcentral.com**.
> KEYWORD: HML9-949

---

# Vocabulary in Context

## ▲ VOCABULARY PRACTICE

| | |
|---|---|
| 1. *true* | 5. *false* |
| 2. *false* | 6. *true* |
| 3. *true* | 7. *false* |
| 4. *true* | 8. *true* |

 **RESOURCE MANAGER—Copy Master**
Vocabulary Practice p. 48

## ACADEMIC VOCABULARY IN WRITING

*Possible response: The new conditions allowed the Kiowa to grow food, which meant they could settle down in one place. Another* **factor** *was the discovery of horses, which let the Kiowa hunt buffalo.*

**VOCABULARY STRATEGY:**   COMMON CORE **L 4c**
**THE GREEK WORD ROOT** *cosm*

- Have students use context to find each word's part of speech.

**Possible answers:**

| | |
|---|---|
| 1. *cosmos* | 4. *cosmopolitan* |
| 2. *cosmonaut* | 5. *Cosmic* |
| 3. *cosmetology* | |

 **RESOURCE MANAGER—Copy Master**
Vocabulary Strategy p. 49

> **Interactive Vocabulary**   **THINK** central
>
> Keywords direct students to a **WordSharp** tutorial on **thinkcentral.com** or to other types of vocabulary practice and review.

# Assess and Reteach

## Assess

**DIAGNOSTIC AND SELECTION TESTS**
   Selection Test A, B/C pp. 251–252, 253–254

**Interactive Selection Test** on **thinkcentral.com**

## Reteach

**Level Up Online Tutorials** on **thinkcentral.com**

**Reteaching Worksheets** on **thinkcentral.com**
   Literature Lessons 31, 47
   Reading Lesson 2
   Vocabulary Lesson 6

---

# Focus and Motivate

## SUMMARY

Granny is not happy when a reporter and cameraman come filming her property without asking. Granddaddy Cain arrives with a dead hawk. After dispatching the hawk's furious mate, Granddaddy Cain calmly takes the camera, exposes the film, and then politely asks the men to step out of Granny's garden.

### How important is
# SELF-RESPECT?

Introduce the question. Have students demonstrate understanding by giving examples of actions that show self-respect. Begin the *DISCUSS* activity as a group by drawing a word web on the board. Have students complete the web independently.

## Selection Resources

---

## Blues Ain't No Mockin Bird
Short Story by Toni Cade Bambara

# How important is
# SELF-RESPECT?

When you treat someone with respect, you treat him or her with regard and esteem. When you have self-respect, you treat yourself with regard and esteem, and you can often gain others' respect in return. In "Blues Ain't No Mockin Bird," Toni Cade Bambara explores how an African-American family respond with self-respect when their privacy is invaded.

*DISCUSS* Think of a situation you have seen or read about in which someone showed self-respect in the face of ridicule or embarrassment. What did that person do? With a small group of classmates, discuss the situation and the way the person behaved. Then generate a word web detailing actions or behaviors that show self-respect. What is gained by displaying these behaviors?

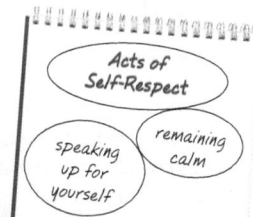

Acts of Self-Respect

speaking up for yourself

remaining calm

The **3** Pillars of Self-Esteem
Suraiya Nathani

BELIEVE IN YOU
A Guide to Self Re...

The Power of YOU
by Erik Koelle

J.D. H...

THE SELF-ESTEEM HANDBOOK
The Power of Self-Esteem

I'm Terrific
'Learning Self-Respect
Kurt Devlaeminck

950

---

## TEXT ANALYSIS: VOICE AND DIALECT

When you pick up the telephone, you probably recognize the voice of your best friend immediately; no one else sounds exactly like him or her. Similarly, writers have a distinct voice in their writing. **Voice** is a writer's unique style of expression.

In "Blues Ain't No Mockin Bird," the narrator seems to be talking personally to the reader. Bambara creates the narrator's voice through the use of **dialect**—a form of language as it is spoken in a particular geographic area or by a particular social or ethnic group. In writing, dialect can be reflected in specific word choices, pronunciations, figurative language, idioms or expressions, and grammatical constructions.

For example, in "Blues Ain't No Mockin Bird," Bambara captures the cadence, or rhythm, of rural Southern black speech in the 1960s.

*. . . and Granny was onto the steps, the screen door bammin soft and scratchy against her palms.*

As you read the story, notice how the author uses dialect to give the narrator an authentic voice for her time and place. By doing so, Bambara creates a believable and engaging character.

## READING SKILL: DRAW CONCLUSIONS

Many of Bambara's stories feature strong African-American female characters and reflect social issues of concern to African Americans. This story was published in 1971—a time when issues of racial equality and civil rights influenced many writers.

As you read "Blues Ain't No Mockin Bird," record details that give you clues about social issues. Then use those details to help you draw conclusions about the writer's beliefs regarding the issues she presents. Ask yourself the following questions:

- Who are the characters? Do they represent stereotypes, real people, or the writer's ideals?
- What do the characters say to each other? What types of issues are at the heart of their dialogue?
- What is the conflict? Does the conflict reflect a social issue unique to the time when the writer lived?

 Complete the activities in your **Reader/Writer Notebook.**

## Meet the Author

# Toni Cade Bambara
**1939–1995**

**Wide-Ranging Career**
Toni Cade Bambara's lifework spanned many arenas. As a social activist, she became a respected leader in the civil rights and feminist movements of the 1960s and 1970s. She was a social worker, teacher, theater director, and filmmaker as well as a writer of short stories, novels, and scripts. Her writing reflects the wide range of her experiences as well as her deep commitment to the welfare of African Americans. In 1981, she won the American Book Award for her novel *The Salt Eaters.*

**Supportive Parenting**
Born Miltona Mirkin Cade in 1939, Toni Cade Bambara adopted the African name Bambara in 1970. She was raised by her mother in New York City, and after attending Queens College there, she studied in Europe and lived in the Harlem and Brooklyn sections of New York. Bambara credited her mother as her main inspiration in life.

**BACKGROUND TO THE STORY**
**Racism in the South**
The civil rights movement of the 1950s and 1960s sought to end decades of racial discrimination against African Americans in the South. This discrimination took many forms, including segregation in education, housing, and public places. Although laws and court rulings from the 1940s through the 1960s made such discrimination illegal, African Americans still faced prejudice, restrictions, and physical and verbal intimidation.

 **Author Online**
Go to **thinkcentral.com.**
KEYWORD: HML9-951

951

## Teach

● *Model the Skill:* **VOICE AND DIALECT**

Read aloud this sample of text from the story:

> Runnin fer the porch ain't goin to stop them bees. They lookin fer your hide and won't take no for an answer.

Identify the evidence of dialect and the details that convey the writer's voice. Dialect is conveyed by *Runnin, fer, ain't, goin, them, They, lookin,* and *hide.* Together, these word choices convey the author's voice.

**GUIDED PRACTICE** Ask students to identify their own local dialect.

■ *Model the Skill:* **DRAW CONCLUSIONS**

Have students read the first sentence under **Supportive Parenting.** Tell them that the main idea of the sentence is that the author gave herself an African last name. Then explain that from this fact they can conclude that the author feels connected to her African heritage.

**GUIDED PRACTICE** Ask students to name clues in the sentences that helped them draw their conclusions.

**R** RESOURCE MANAGER—Copy Master Draw Conclusions p. 65 (for student use while reading the selection)

## DIFFERENTIATED INSTRUCTION

### FOR STRUGGLING READERS
**Concept Support:s Dialect** Explain that the best way to understand dialect is to read it aloud slowly. Readers should also look at context to try to identify unusual word forms and define unfamiliar words. Model this process with the italicized text under Text Analysis, above. Help students paraphrase the text. *(Possible answer: Granny stomped up the steps, pushing the scratchy screen door and letting it bang behind her.)*

### FOR ENGLISH LANGUAGE LEARNERS
**Concept Support: Draw Conclusions** Be sure students know the importance of the racial conflicts that the author coped with in the 1960s and 1970s. Read *Background* with them and answer questions they may have about racial conflicts in America during this time period.

### READ WITH A PURPOSE

*Ask students to set a purpose for reading. Have them examine the title of the story and discuss what they know about the terms* blues *and* mockin (mocking) bird. *You may wish to have students look up both terms. Then ask them to read the story to determine what the title means.*

**Ⓐ Model the Skill: VOICE AND DIALECT**

Reread each sentence slowly. Ask the students to raise their hands each time they hear words that depart from standard English. Then work with students to help them paraphrase the meaning of each sentence.

**Possible answer:** *Student responses should include some of these examples: g dropped off -ing endings ("stompin" "swingin," "waitin," "tap-dancin"); "making the cakes drunk," referring to soaking cakes in rum; "ain't"; "Me and Cathy" rather than "Cathy and I"; "station wagon'd been roamin" for "station wagon had been roaming"; and "lassoed to his shoulder."*

# BLUES AIN'T NO MOCKIN BIRD

## Toni Cade Bambara

The puddle had frozen over, and me and Cathy went stompin in it. The twins from next door, Tyrone and Terry, were swingin so high out of sight we forgot we were waitin our turn on the tire. Cathy jumped up and came down hard on her heels and started tap-dancin. And the frozen patch splintered every which way underneath kinda spooky. "Looks like a plastic spider web," she said. "A sort of weird spider, I guess, with many mental problems." But really it looked like the crystal paperweight Granny kept in the parlor. She was on the back porch, Granny was, making the cakes drunk. The old ladle dripping rum into the Christmas tins, like it used to drip maple syrup into the pails when we

10 lived in the Judson's woods, like it poured cider into the vats when we were on the Cooper place, like it used to scoop buttermilk and soft cheese when we lived at the dairy.

"Go tell that man we ain't a bunch of trees."

"Ma'am?"

"I said to tell that man to get away from here with that camera." Me and Cathy look over toward the meadow where the men with the station wagon'd been roamin around all mornin. The tall man with a huge camera lassoed to his shoulder was buzzin our way. Ⓐ

"They're makin movie pictures," yelled Tyrone, stiffenin his legs and twistin

20 so the tire'd come down slow so they could see.

"They're makin movie pictures," sang out Terry.

"That boy don't never have anything original to say," say Cathy grown-up.

By the time the man with the camera had cut across our neighbor's yard, the twins were out of the trees swingin low and Granny was onto the steps, the screen door bammin soft and scratchy against her palms. "We thought we'd get a shot or two of the house and everything and then—"

*Analyze Visuals* ▶

Consider the **setting** depicted in this painting, as well as the subject's posture and expression. What feelings do these elements convey? Explain.

❶ **Targeted Passage**

Ⓐ **VOICE AND DIALECT** Reread lines 1–18. Identify the distinctive vocabulary and grammar that characterize the narrator's dialect.

Detail of *Cotton Choppers* (1965), Benny Andrews. Oil on canvas, 25″ × 35″. Courtesy of Michael Rosenfeld Gallery, LLC, New York. © Benny Andrews/ACA Galleries, New York. © Estate of Benny Andrews/Licensed by VAGA, New York.

## DIFFERENTIATED INSTRUCTION

### FOR ENGLISH LANGUAGE LEARNERS

**Vocabulary Support** Use Definition Mapping to teach these words: *mental* (line 6), *plus* (line 103), *invisible* (line 131).

🧰 BEST PRACTICES TOOLKIT—Transparency Definition Mapping p. E6

### FOR STRUGGLING READERS

In combination with the *Audio Anthology CD*, use one or more Targeted Passages (pp. 952, 957, 959) to ensure that students focus on key ideas, concepts, and skills. Targeted Passages are also good for English learners.

❶ **Targeted Passage [Lines 1–12]**

This passage introduces the characters, the time period, and the season of the year.

• Who are Cathy, Tyrone, and Terry? How do they feel about one another? (lines 1–4)

**The Food Stamp Program** Granny is offended by the reporter's suggestion that her home could be part of the promotion of the Food Stamp Program, but many benefited from its services. The first Food Stamp Program began in the 1930s under the policies of President Roosevelt's New Deal as a way of helping the very poor. The program ended in 1943, but was reopened during the 1960s and 1970s.

**Cultural Connection** Many nations have no organized food relief program for their citizens. Organizations such as the International Federation of Red Cross and Red Crescent Societies work around the world to bring food relief to victims of drought, earthquakes, and other disasters that emphasize poverty. Since the 1970s, the Red Cross has brought food relief to countries all over the world. Ask students to share any knowledge they might have about food relief services overseas.

## Analyze Visuals

*Possible answer: The setting is a red-hot afternoon, probably in a Southern cotton field. The man's stooped posture and his loose hold on the hoe suggests that he is tired and perhaps discouraged. Yet his calm, intent expression as he pauses in his labor to study the cotton flower also conveys a feeling of self-respect and centeredness.*

**About the Art** The second of ten children, Benny Andrews (b. 1930) grew up in rural Georgia in a family of sharecroppers. After serving in the Korean War and receiving a B.F.A. at the Art Institute of Chicago, Andrews moved to New York City where he became recognized as both an influential artist and educator. The imagery in Andrews's work is often drawn from memories of his family and childhood in Georgia.

- What time of year does the story take place? How can you tell? (lines 1–9)
- Where has the family lived before living in their current house? What can you tell about the family from the places they have lived? (lines 9–12)

**FOR ADVANCED LEARNERS/PRE–AP**

**Expand** A small group of students can research and give a presentation on the practice of sharecropping. Topics they should explore include:

- How, why, and where the practice started
- Who sharecroppers were
- How the system was supposed to work
- Advantages and disadvantages of this system over others
- How and why the practice became less common, and whether it still takes place in the United States

**B** *Model the Skill:* **DRAW CONCLUSIONS**

Explain to students that the smiling man may have intended to end his sentence with "to give people food stamps." Then review with students the evidence in lines 50–57.

*Possible answer: The men want to show poor people growing their own vegetables as a way to show that food stamps are not really necessary. Evidence: He says he is from the county, that his film is for the food stamp campaign. He notes that Granny grows her own vegetables, and says "If more folks did that, see, there'd be no need—" (lines 56–57). The implied end to his statement is "to give them food stamps to help them buy food."*

**REVISIT THE BIG QUESTION**

How important is
# SELF-RESPECT?

**Discuss** How does Granny show her feeling of self-respect to the smiling man in lines 27–57? How does the man react? *Possible answer: The smiling man calls Granny "aunty," which she considers disrespectful, rather than "ma'am" or another respectful term. Granny shows her self-respect when she tells him she is not related to him. Then, when he asks for a statement, she does not reply. The smiling man does not understand her reactions and continues to disrespect Granny.*

---

"Good mornin," Granny cut him off. And smiled that smile.

"Good mornin," he said, head all down the way Bingo does when you yell at him about the bones on the kitchen floor. "Nice place you got here, aunty.
30 We thought we'd take a—"

"Did you?" said Granny with her eyebrows. Cathy pulled up her socks and giggled.

"Nice things here," said the man, buzzin his camera over the yard. The pecan barrels, the sled, me and Cathy, the flowers, the printed stones along the driveway, the trees, the twins, the toolshed.

"I don't know about the thing, the it, and the stuff," said Granny, still talkin with her eyebrows. "Just people here is what I tend to consider."

Camera man stopped buzzin. Cathy giggled into her collar.

"Mornin, ladies," a new man said. He had come up behind us when we
40 weren't lookin. "And gents," discoverin the twins givin him a nasty look. "We're filmin for the county," he said with a smile. "Mind if we shoot a bit around here?"

"I do indeed," said Granny with no smile. Smilin man was smiling up a storm. So was Cathy. But he didn't seem to have another word to say, so he and the camera man backed on out the yard, but you could hear the camera buzzin still. "Suppose you just shut that machine off," said Granny real low through her teeth, and took a step down off the porch and then another.

"Now, aunty,"[1] Camera said, pointin the thing straight at her.

"Your mama and I are not related."

50 Smilin man got his notebook out and a chewed-up pencil. "Listen," he said movin back into our yard, "we'd like to have a statement from you . . . for the film. We're filmin for the county, see. Part of the food stamp campaign. You know about the food stamps?"

Granny said nuthin.

"Maybe there's somethin you want to say for the film. I see you grow your own vegetables," he smiled real nice. "If more folks did that, see, there'd be no need—" **B**

Granny wasn't sayin nuthin. So they backed on out, buzzin at our clothesline and the twins' bicycles, then back on down to the meadow. The
60 twins were danglin in the tire, lookin at Granny. Me and Cathy were waitin, too, cause Granny always got somethin to say. She teaches steady with no let-up. "I was on this bridge one time," she started off. "Was a crowd cause this man was goin to jump, you understand. And a minister was there and the police and some other folks. His woman was there, too."

"What was they doin?" asked Tyrone.

"Tryin to talk him out of it was what they was doin. The minister talkin about how it was a mortal sin,[2] suicide. His woman takin bites out of her own hand and not even knowin it, so nervous and cryin and talkin fast."

---

1. **aunty:** a derogatory term of address once commonly used for black women in the South.
2. **mortal sin:** in many religions, an extremely serious offense against the laws of God.

**B** DRAW CONCLUSIONS
What is the men's purpose for making the film? What evidence in the text helped you draw that conclusion?

---

## DIFFERENTIATED INSTRUCTION

**FOR ENGLISH LANGUAGE LEARNERS**
Show students how Cluster Diagrams can be a strategy to help them learn words such as *head* (line 28), *grow* (line 55), and *stalks* (line 124).

**FOR RELUCTANT READERS**
**Relate to the Text** Have students discuss Granny's methods and motivations for denying the county permission to film. Point out that the men took for granted their right to film. Then ask students if they have ever been in or witnessed a situation in which someone felt their rights were being violated. Have students compare and contrast the situation with Granny's. Or, have them explain whether they think Granny dealt with the men appropriately and what, if anything, they would have done differently.

*Brothers* (1934), Malvin Gray Johnson. Smithsonian American Art Museum, Washington, D.C. Photo © Smithsonian American Art Museum, Washington, D.C./Art Resource, New York.

◀ **Analyze Visuals**

Look at the way the artist mixes colors in this painting—for example, on the boys' sleeves and overalls, as well as on the fence. What effect does this create? How well, in your opinion, does this technique fit the subject matter of the painting? Explain.

"So what happened?" asked Tyrone.

70 "So here comes . . . this person . . . with a camera, takin pictures of the man and the minister and the woman. Takin pictures of the man in his misery about to jump, cause life so bad and people been messin with him so bad. This person takin up the whole roll of film practically. But savin a few, of course."

"Of course," said Cathy, hatin the person. Me standin there wonderin how Cathy knew it was "of course" when I didn't know and it was *my* grandmother.

After a while Tyrone said, "Did he jump?"

"Yeh, did he jump?" say Terry all eager.

---

**Analyze Visuals**

*Possible answer:* *The mix of colors makes the clothing and fence look dirty and worn rather than clean or freshly painted. Since the farm boys look like they work close to the earth, the technique fits the subject matter.*

**About the Art**  Malvin Gray Johnson (1896–1934) painted *Brothers* in 1934. It was painted from sights Johnson saw on a journey through rural Virginia. Johnson's trip was funded by the Public Works of Art project and helped him show one rural African-American community. The oil painting shows two young boys sharing a cane bench, though the younger boy has only half a seat.

---

**FOR STRUGGLING READERS**

**Comprehension Support**  Have students read lines 62–75, in which Granny tells a story about how a cameraman invaded the privacy of a suicidal man. Lead students in a group to figure out what Granny is teaching by the story. Have them decide what the ending of that story might be.

**FOR ADVANCED LEARNERS/PRE–AP**

**Analyze Tone**  Ask students to identify the tone of this story. Then have them break up into groups and have them discuss how that tone contributed to their appreciation of the setting, characters, and subject matter of the story.

 **VOICE AND DIALECT**

*Possible answer:* *"With rocks all in his jaw" suggests that Granddaddy Cain is clenching his jaw in anger.*

**IF STUDENTS NEED HELP . . .** Ask these questions to help them clarify the idiom:

• What might rocks in one's jaw look like?

• What is happening in Granddaddy Cain's face to make it look like it has rocks in it?

• What emotion does Granddaddy Cain feel when he has "rocks all in his jaw?"

## TIERED DISCUSSION PROMPTS

Use these prompts to help students understand some of the events in Granny's life mentioned in lines 78–91:

**Connect** Have you ever been offended by someone even though you knew that person was trying to be nice? *Accept all reasonable responses.*

**Analyze** What do people do for Granny that makes her mad? Explain. *Students should recognize that a gift of old clothes and raggedy magazines and Mrs. Cooper's compliments about cleanliness made Granny mad. They make her feel pitied.*

**Evaluate** What might Granny do instead of moving out of her house when she gets mad? *Possible answer: Granny feels such anger that she fears she will kill someone if she does not move. Instead of moving, she could control her anger and swallow the disrespect she feels. She could resolve to show the well-intentioned landlords that she does not deserve their disrespect.*

---

And Granny just stared at the twins till their faces swallow up the eager and they don't even care any more about the man jumpin. Then she goes back
80 onto the porch and lets the screen door go for itself. I'm lookin to Cathy to finish the story cause she knows Granny's whole story before me even. Like she knew about how come we move so much and Cathy ain't nothin but a third cousin we picked up on the way last Thanksgivin visitin. But she knew it was on account of people drivin Granny crazy till she'd get up in the night and start packin. Mumblin and packin and wakin everybody up sayin, "Let's get on away from here before I kill me somebody." Like people wouldn't pay her for things like they said they would. Or Mr. Judson bringin us boxes of old clothes and raggedy magazines. Or Mrs. Cooper comin in our kitchen and touchin everything and sayin how clean it all was. Granny goin crazy, and Granddaddy
90 Cain pullin her off people sayin, "Now, now, Cora." But next day loadin up the truck, with rocks all in his jaw, madder than Granny in the first place.

"I read a story once," said Cathy soundin like Granny teacher. "About this lady Goldilocks who barged into a house that wasn't even hers. And not invited, you understand. Messed over the people's groceries and broke up the people's furniture. Had the nerve to sleep in the folks' bed."

"Then what happened?" asked Tyrone. "What they do, the folks, when they come in to all this mess?"

"Did they make her pay for it?" asked Terry, makin a fist. "I'd've made her pay me."
100 I didn't even ask. I could see Cathy actress was very likely to just walk away and leave us in mystery about this story which I heard was about some bears.

"Did they throw her out?" asked Tyrone, like his father sounds when he's bein extra nasty-plus to the washin-machine man.

"Woulda," said Terry. "I woulda gone upside her head with my fist and—"

"You woulda done whatcha always do—go cry to Mama, you big baby," said Tyrone. So naturally Terry starts hittin on Tyrone, and next thing you know they tumblin out the tire and rollin on the ground. But Granny didn'y say a thing or send the twins home or step out on the steps to tell us about how we can't afford to be fightin amongst ourselves. She didn't say nuthin. So I get into
110 the tire to take my turn. And I could see her leanin up against the pantry table, starin at the cakes she was puttin up for the Christmas sale, mumblin real low and grumpy and holdin her forehead like it wanted to fall off and mess up the rum cakes.

Behind me I hear before I can see Granddaddy Cain comin through the woods in his field boots. Then I twist around to see the shiny black oilskin cuttin through what little left there was of yellows, reds, and oranges. His great white head not quite round cause of this bloody thing high on his shoulder, like he was wearin a cap on sideways. He takes the shortcut through the pecan grove, and the sound of twigs snapping overhead and underfoot travels clear
120 and cold all the way up to us. And here comes Smilin and Camera up behind

---

## DIFFERENTIATED INSTRUCTION

**FOR STRUGGLING READERS**

**Comprehension Support: Characterization**
Point out that the author calls Cathy "Cathy grown-up" (line 22), "soundin like Granny teacher" (line 92), "Cathy actress" (line 100), and "Cathy dreamer" (line 206). Ask students to discuss why the author uses this treatment to characterize Cathy. Explain that these all refer to the same person. Discuss what it tells readers about Cathy.

**FOR ENGLISH LANGUAGE LEARNERS**

**Vocabulary: Idioms** Have small groups use Word Squares to learn these idioms: *smiling up a storm* (lines 43–44), *talk him out of it* (line 66), *messin with him* (line 72), *in the first place* (line 91), *Had the nerve to* (line 95), *throw her out* (line 102), *can't afford to* (line 109), *go for him* (line 121), *every which way* (line 140).

 **BEST PRACTICES TOOLKIT—Transparency**
Word Squares p. E10

him like they was goin to do somethin. Folks like to go for him sometimes. Cathy say it's because he's so tall and quiet and like a king. And people just can't stand it. But Smilin and Camera don't hit him in the head or nuthin. **D** They just buzz on him as he stalks by with the chicken hawk slung over his shoulder, squawkin, drippin red down the back of the oilskin. He passes the porch and stops a second for Granny to see he's caught the hawk at last, but she's just starin and mumblin, and not at the hawk. So he nails the bird to the toolshed door, the hammerin crackin through the eardrums. And the bird flappin himself to death and droolin down the door to paint the gravel in the
130 driveway red, then brown, then black. And the two men movin up on tiptoe like they was invisible or we were blind, one. **E**

"Get them persons out of my flower bed, Mister Cain," say Granny moanin real low like at a funeral.

"How come your grandmother calls her husband 'Mister Cain' all the time?" Tyrone whispers loud and noisy and from the city and don't know no better. Like his mama, Miss Myrtle, tell us never mind the formality as if we had no better breeding than to call her Myrtle, plain. And then this awful thing—a giant hawk—come wailin up over the meadow, flyin low and tilted and screamin, zigzaggin through the pecan grove, breakin branches and hollerin,
140 snappin past the clothesline, flyin every which way, flyin into things reckless with crazy.

*Woodshed* (1944), Andrew Wyeth. Collection of the Brandywine River Museum. Bequest of C. Porter Schutt, 1995. © Andrew Wyeth.

**2 Targeted Passage**

**D DRAW CONCLUSIONS**
The narrator says that people like to "go for" her grandfather because he is "tall and quiet and like a king" and the "people just can't stand it." What "people" does she mean, and why do they resent the man's regal appearance?

**E GRAMMAR AND STYLE**
Reread lines 124–125. Notice how Bambara chooses imaginative, **vivid verbs,** such as "buzz" and "stalks," to enhance the image of Granddaddy carrying the chicken hawk.

**READING SKILL** COMMON CORE RL 1

**D DRAW CONCLUSIONS**
*Possible answer: She is referring to outsiders, perhaps specifically white people, who might expect that Granddaddy Cain would behave with a deferential or inferior attitude, since they feel superior to him.*

**E GRAMMAR AND STYLE** COMMON CORE L3

**Vivid Verbs** Point out that some of the vivid verbs are effective because they sound like what they mean, such as *buzz* (line 124), *mumblin* (line 127), and *wailin* (line 138). Ask students how this style improves the writing. To extend the activity, have students list vivid verbs used throughout the story.

### Analyze Visuals

**Activity** Ask students what part of the story the painting depicts and how it helps them understand the story. *Possible answer: The painting shows how Granddaddy Cain hammered the hawk on the tool shed. This helps readers picture how this is done.*

**About the Art** *Woodshed* by Andrew Wyeth (born 1917) was painted in 1944, near the end of World War II. It shows a sense of anxiety and death that people of this time period often experienced.

**REVISIT THE BIG QUESTION**

## How important is SELF-RESPECT?

**Discuss** How does Granny show respect to Granddaddy Cain in lines 134–137? How can you tell that Tyrone's family does not share the same values about self-respect? *Possible answer: Granny calls Granddaddy Cain "Mister Cain." Tyrone's mother allows the narrator to call her "Myrtle" instead of "Miss Myrtle."*

**FOR STRUGGLING READERS**

**2 Targeted Passage [Lines 121–133]**
This passage introduces the character of Granddaddy Cain.

- What does Granddaddy Cain look like? How is he different from other people? (lines 121–122)

- What does Granddaddy Cain bring with him from the field? What does he do with it? (lines 124–130)

- What does Granny ask Granddaddy Cain to do? (line 132)

**FOR ENGLISH LANGUAGE LEARNERS**

**Language: English Conversational Patterns**
Point out that these phrases are not standard English. With a Whip Around strategy, read each phrase in context and have a student change it to standard English: *we ain't a bunch of trees* (line 13), *Granny gonna bust through that screen* (lines 157–158), *all around these parts* (line 182).

**BEST PRACTICES TOOLKIT**
Whip Around p. B1

"He's come to claim his mate," say Cathy fast, and ducks down. We all fall quick and flat on the gravel driveway, stones scrapin my face. I squinch my eyes open again at the hawk on the door, tryin to fly up out of her death like it was just a sack flown into by mistake. Her body holdin her there on that nail, though. The mate beatin the air overhead and clutchin for hair, for heads, for landin space.

The camera man duckin and bendin and runnin and fallin, jigglin the camera and scared. And Smilin jumpin up and down swipin at the huge bird, tryin to bring the hawk down with just his raggedy ole cap. Granddaddy Cain straight up and silent, watchin the circles of the hawk, then aimin the hammer off his wrist. The giant bird fallin, silent and slow. Then here comes Camera and Smilin all big and bad now that the awful screechin thing is on its back and broken, here they come. And Granddaddy Cain looks up at them like it was the first time noticin, but not payin them too much mind[3] cause he's listenin, we all listening, to that low groanin music comin from the porch. And we figure any minute, somethin in my back tells me any minute now, Granny gonna bust through that screen with somethin in her hand and murder on her mind. So Granddaddy say above the buzzin, but quiet, "Good day, gentlemen." Just like that. Like he'd invited them in to play cards and they'd stayed too long and all the sandwiches were gone and Reverend Webb was droppin by and it was time to go. Ⓕ

They didn't know what to do. But like Cathy say, folks can't stand Granddaddy tall and silent and like a king. They can't neither. The smile the men smilin is pullin the mouth back and showin the teeth. Lookin like the wolf man, both of them. Then Granddaddy holds his hand out—this huge hand I used to sit in when I was a baby and he'd carry me through the house to my mother like I was a gift on a tray. Like he used to on the trains. They called the other men just waiters. But they spoke of Granddaddy separate and said, The Waiter. And said he had engines in his feet and motors in his hands and couldn't no train throw him off and couldn't nobody turn him around. They were big enough for motors, his hands were. He held that one hand out all still and it gettin to be not at all a hand but a person in itself.

"He wants you to hand him the camera," Smilin whispers to Camera, tiltin his head to talk secret like they was in the jungle or somethin and come upon a native that don't speak the language. The men start untyin the straps, and they put the camera into that great hand speckled with the hawk's blood all black and crackly now. And the hand don't even drop with the weight, just the fingers move, curl up around the machine. But Granddaddy lookin straight at the men. They lookin at each other and everywhere but at Granddaddy's face.

"We filmin for the county, see," say Smilin. "We puttin together a movie for the food stamp program . . . filmin all around these parts. Uhh, filmin for the county."

---

3. **not payin them too much mind:** barely noticing them; ignoring them.

Ⓕ **VOICE AND DIALECT**
Reread lines 160–162. Notice the grammatical construction of this sentence. What effect does the use of a long chain of clauses have on the voice of the narrator?

Ⓕ **VOICE AND DIALECT**

*Possible answer: The run-on sentence makes the writing sound like casual spoken language rather than written language.*

**REVISIT THE BIG QUESTION**

## How important is SELF-RESPECT?

**Discuss** How does Granddaddy Cain show self-respect in dealing with the reporter and the cameraman in lines 164–180? *Possible answer: Granddaddy Cain shows self-respect by demanding respect from the two men. He looks straight at them and confidently holds his large hand out for the camera, knowing that he deserves their compliance.*

---

## DIFFERENTIATED INSTRUCTION

**FOR ENGLISH LANGUAGE LEARNERS**
**Develop Reading Fluency** Use some or all of lines 148–173 to help students practice reading dialect. Remind students that many of the words ending with -in (also commonly written as -in') end in -ing in standard English. Present a reading, by yourself or with help from a fluent student. Then divide students into small groups and assign each student a part of the reading. (You may wish to give each group one paragraph.) Have them practice their readings together, giving one another feedback. Then have the groups perform their readings for the class.

**FOR ADVANCED LEARNERS/PRE–AP**
**Analyze Alternative Perspectives** Have students consider the events of the story from the point of view of the reporter. Then, have them write the narration that the reporter would have written to accompany his documentary's scene at the Cains' house. Ask volunteers to share their narration.

"Can I have my camera back?" say the tall man with no machine on his shoulder, but still keepin it high like the camera was still there or needed to be. "Please, sir."

Then Granddaddy's other hand flies up like a sudden and gentle bird, slaps down fast on top of the camera and lifts off half like it was a calabash[4] cut for sharing. **G**

190 "Hey," Camera jumps forward. He gathers up the parts into his chest and everything unrollin and fallin all over. "Whata tryin to do? You'll ruin the film." He looks down into his chest of metal reels and things like he's protectin a kitten from the cold.

"You standin in the misses' flower bed," say Granddaddy. "This is our own place."

The two men look at him, then at each other, then back at the mess in the camera man's chest, and they just back off. One sayin over and over all the way down to the meadow, "Watch it, Bruno. Keep ya fingers off the film." Then Granddaddy picks up the hammer and jams it into the oilskin pocket, scrapes his boots, and goes into the house. And you can hear the squish of his boots 200 headin through the house. And you can see the funny shadow he throws from the parlor window onto the ground by the string-bean patch. The hammer draggin the pocket of the oilskin out so Granddaddy looked even wider. Granny was hummin now—high, not low and grumbly. And she was doin the cakes again, you could smell the molasses from the rum.

"There's this story I'm goin to write one day," say Cathy dreamer. "About the proper use of the hammer."

"Can I be in it?" Tyrone say with his hand up like it was a matter of first come, first served.

210 "Perhaps," say Cathy, climbin onto the tire to pump us up. "If you there and ready."

---

4. **calabash** (kăl′ə-băsh′): a fruit whose dried shell is used to make things like bottles, bowls, and rattles.

---

COMMON CORE RL 1, RL 4

**G DRAW CONCLUSIONS**
**Similes**—expressions that use *like, as,* or *resembles* to compare seemingly unlike things—are a common form of figurative language. Identify the two similes that the narrator uses in lines 187–189. What do these similes suggest about the narrator's historical and cultural setting?

## ❸ Targeted Passage

### Language Coach

**Word Origins** The word *parlor* comes from the French word *parler,* "to speak." In line 202, *parlor* means "living room." It can also refer to a shop or business (*funeral parlor, beauty parlor*). Why do you think these usages of *parlor* derived from *parler*?

---

READING SKILL

**G DRAW CONCLUSIONS**

COMMON CORE RL 1, RL 4

*Possible answer: These similes suggest that birds and calabashes were common in the lives of the narrator and her family, common enough for these interesting comparisons to come to mind for the narrator.*

Have students write two similes about their culture that would help someone draw a conclusion about that aspect of their culture. Ask for volunteers to share their similes.

## SELECTION WRAP-UP

**READ WITH A PURPOSE** Now that students have read the selection, ask them: Is the story's title explained? What do you think it means? *Possible answer: It is not explained. It may mean that someone's difficult life should not be exploited for someone else's purposes, as a mockingbird uses other birds' voices for its own purpose.*

⭐ **CRITIQUE** Have students decide if Granny and Granddaddy Cain handled the situation with the reporter and cameraman well. Ask them to suggest alternative approaches.

## INDEPENDENT READING

Students may enjoy *American Street*, a collection of stories about American cultural neighborhoods. Authors include Toni Cade Bambara and Gary Soto.

---

## FOR STRUGGLING READERS

**❸ Targeted Passage** [Lines 187–205]

This passage includes the climax of the story in which Granddaddy Cain breaks the camera.

- What does Granddaddy Cain do to the movie camera? (lines 187–189)
- How does the cameraman react? (lines 190–193)
- How does Granny feel after the camera is broken? (lines 204–205)

## FOR ENGLISH LANGUAGE LEARNERS

### Language Coach

**Word Origins** *Possible answer: Parlors, in the sense of living rooms, are places where people talk, especially when company visits. Funeral and beauty parlors are also places where people sit and talk.* Have students name synonyms for *parlor* or *living room* that they know. *Possible answers: den, family room, salon* Discuss the different connotations of each term.

# Practice and Apply

For preliminary support of post-reading questions, use these copy masters:

**R** RESOURCE MANAGER—Copy Masters
Reading Check p. 67
Voice and Dialect p. 63
Question Support p. 68

Additional selection questions are provided for teachers on page 57.

## ANSWERS

## Comprehension

1. *Smilin man and Camera man are from the county and are making a film for the food stamp campaign.*

2. *They film Granny's yard even though she tells them not to, they call her "aunty," and they are patronizing and disrespectful.*

3. *He takes it from them, pulls it into two pieces, and exposes the film.*

## Text Analysis

COMMON CORE RL1, RL4

**Possible answers:**

4. *If he hadn't come home, the men probably would have continued to film.*

5. *The anecdote and the Goldilocks story are inspired by the county men: the first is about people taking pictures to satisfy their own needs before those of the subject; the second is about nosy strangers who meddle.*

6. *Cathy is going to write about using a hammer to punish disrespectful people for meddling or to keep them away.*

7. ● **COMMON CORE FOCUS** *Analyze Voice and Dialect Student charts will vary. Their analyses should note that the narrator's voice is informal, conversational, and energetic; reflects an African-American dialect; and contains idioms and figurative images that create vivid mental pictures.*

8. ■ **COMMON CORE FOCUS** *Draw Conclusions About Values and Beliefs Bambara is concerned about racism and class discrimination. Her respectful (even admiring) use of dialect and the depiction of strong African-American characters suggest that she values the rural African-American culture.*

9. *Granny speaks her mind and is not intimidated by the visitors' patronizing; she has no use for people who refuse to pay for services or otherwise disrespect the family (lines 85–91). Granddaddy carries himself*

---

## Comprehension

1. **Recall** Who are Smilin man and Camera man?

2. **Recall** What do they do that offends Granny?

3. **Recall** What does Granddaddy Cain do to their camera?

## Text Analysis

4. **Predict** What might have happened if Granddaddy Cain had not come home when he did?

5. **Interpret Text** Reread lines 62–95. How do the anecdotes about the suicide attempt and Goldilocks relate to the events in the story?

6. **Make Inferences** What does Cathy mean at the end when she says she is going to write a story about "the proper use of the hammer"?

● 7. **Analyze Voice and Dialect** Create a chart with examples of the distinctive vocabulary, pronunciation, grammar, and idioms that characterize the narrator by shaping her dialect. How would you describe the narrator's voice?

| Distinctive Characteristics of Narrator's Dialect | | | |
|---|---|---|---|
| Vocabulary | Pronunciation | Grammar | Idioms |
| bammin | stompin | me and Cathy went | smiling up a storm |
| | kinda | | |

■ 8. **Draw Conclusions About Values and Beliefs** Review the conclusions you drew about social issues presented in the story. What conclusions can you draw about Bambara's values and beliefs concerning those social issues? Cite evidence from the story to support your conclusions.

9. **Evaluate Characters** How do Granny and Granddaddy Cain demonstrate their self-respect? Cite evidence from the text to support your response.

## Text Criticism

10. **Critical Interpretations** One critic stated that Bambara "presents black culture as embattled but unbowed" in her stories. How does that comment apply to this story? Support your interpretation with evidence from the text.

> **How important is SELF-RESPECT?**
> How can you demonstrate your own self-respect?

**COMMON CORE**

**RL1** Cite textual evidence to support analysis of what the text says explicitly as well as inferences drawn from the text.
**RL4** Determine the figurative meaning of phrases as they are used in a text; analyze the cumulative impact of specific word choices on meaning.

---

*"tall and quiet and like a king" (line 122). He deals with the unwelcome visitors with quiet but fierce strength, demanding their camera, pulling it in two, explaining briefly but clearly what they are doing wrong, and showing them that they are unwelcome.*

## Text Criticism

10. *The black characters in this story are embattled because they have experience dealing with people who disrespect them, including the visitors in the story, those*

*who refuse to pay for services, and people who offer charity in a patronizing manner. However, they continue to face such people with quiet strength and self-assurance.*

> **How important is SELF-RESPECT?** Responses will vary but students should distinguish self-respect from putting others down.

# Language

◆ **GRAMMAR AND STYLE: Choose Effective Words**

Review the **Grammar and Style** note on page 957. Bambara brings life to her story by peppering it with a series of **vivid verbs.** Follow Bambara's example by choosing words that add liveliness and depth to your writing; avoid words that are too bland or generic. Both you and your reader will find the end result far more satisfying. Here is another example of how Bambara effectively uses vivid verbs in her descriptions:

> Then Granddaddy's other hand *flies* up like a sudden and gentle bird, *slaps* down fast on top of the camera and *lifts* off half like it was a calabash cut for sharing. (lines 187–189)

Notice how the revisions in blue enhance the description in this first draft. Revise your response to the prompt below by similarly incorporating vivid verbs.

> **STUDENT MODEL**
>
> Granny seems like a grumpy person. She ~~talks under her breath~~ *mumbles* all the time
>
> and refuses to smile. She doesn't hide her dislike for the two men who come
>
> to film them and ~~tells~~ *commands* Granddaddy to get them out of her flower bed.

## READING-WRITING CONNECTION

 **YOUR TURN** Demonstrate your understanding of the characters portrayed in "Blues Ain't No Mockin Bird" by responding to the prompt below. Then use the **revising tip** to improve your writing.

| **WRITING PROMPT** | **REVISING TIP** |
|---|---|
| **Extended Constructed Response: Description** How would you describe Granny's attitude and behavior? Identify two of her character traits in a **three-to-five-paragraph response.** Be sure to include examples from the story to support your characterization. | Review your response. Did you include descriptive language that accurately conveys Granny's personality? Adding vivid verbs to your draft will help you express the subtleties of Granny's character. |

**Interactive Revision**  THINK central
Go to **thinkcentral.com.**
KEYWORD: HML9-961

---

## DIFFERENTIATED INSTRUCTION

### FOR STRUGGLING WRITERS

- Limit the length of the essay to three paragraphs, with students identifying just one of Granny's characteristics.

- Have students work in small groups to determine Granny's strongest characteristics and evidence to support each one.

- Help students craft a closing paragraph that summarizes the information covered in the essay.

---

# Language

COMMON CORE L3, W 2b

◆ **GRAMMAR AND STYLE**

- Explain that vivid verbs can energize writing and allow readers to visualize the scene. Point out that the scene where the hawk attacked the farm is easy to visualize because the author effectively uses vivid verbs.

- After discussing the model, write these sentences on the board. Have students replace common verbs with vivid verbs.

> The men ~~stepped~~ *bumbled* onto the flower bed, ~~breaking~~ *smashing* petals and ~~bumping into~~ *crushing* stalks. Their heels ~~dug into~~ *gouged* the soil leaving deep holes among the flowers.

**R** **RESOURCE MANAGER—Copy Master** Choose Effective Words p. 69

**READING-WRITING CONNECTION**

Have students write one paragraph to focus on each trait they choose. Explain that the introduction and the conclusion should summarize the qualities mentioned in the paragraphs and should synthesize Granny's character.

> **Writing Online** THINK central
>
> The following tools are available online at **thinkcentral.com** and on **WriteSmart** CD-ROM:
> - **Interactive Graphic Organizers**
> - **Interactive Student Models**
> - **Interactive Revision Lessons**
>
> For additional grammar instruction, see **GrammarNotes** on **thinkcentral.com.**

---

# Assess and Reteach

## Assess

**DIAGNOSTIC AND SELECTION TESTS**
Selection Test A, B/C pp. 255–256, 257–258

**Interactive Selection Test** on **thinkcentral.com**

## Reteach

**Level Up Online Tutorials** on **thinkcentral.com**

**Reteaching Worksheets** on **thinkcentral.com**
Literature Lessons 43, 47
Reading Lesson 9
Writing Lesson 28

### COMMON CORE FOCUS

**RL 3** Analyze how complex characters develop over the course of a text and interact with other characters. **RL 7** Analyze the representation of a subject in different artistic mediums. **RL 10** Read and comprehend stories. **L 4a** Use context as a clue to the meaning of a word. **L 5a** Interpret figures of speech in context and analyze their role in the text.

### SUMMARIES

**"American History"** On the day that President Kennedy is assassinated, fourteen-year-old Elena goes to her friend Eugene's house to study, but is turned away by his mother.

**"Special Report"** This magazine article describes Kennedy's continuing influence.

**"President Killed"** This photograph shows how Americans responded to Kennedy's death.

### When do WORLD EVENTS hit home?

Introduce the question. Discuss the kinds of world events that cause people to feel a personal connection, and why.

### What's the Connection?

Ask students whether they can think of any event in their own lifetimes that affected the American people in a similar way.

---

**Comparing Texts**

**American History**  Video link at thinkcentral.com
Short Story by Judith Ortiz Cofer

*Essential Course of Study* **ECOS**

**Special Report**
Magazine Article from *U.S. News & World Report*

**President Killed**
Photograph

VIDEO TRAILER **THINK**central KEYWORD: HML9-962

# When do WORLD EVENTS hit home?

**COMMON CORE**

**RL 3** Analyze how complex characters develop over the course of a text and interact with other characters. **RL 7** Analyze the representation of a subject in different artistic mediums. **RL 10** Read and comprehend stories. **L 4a** Use context as a clue to the meaning of a word.

Once in a while, large numbers of people feel such a connection to a news event that they stop everything. The short story you are about to read takes place on November 22, 1963, when the assassination of President John F. Kennedy stunned and distressed an entire nation.

### What's the Connection?

President Kennedy's untimely death had a profound and lasting effect on the people of the United States. After "American History," you'll read a magazine article that explores the country's enduring fascination with its 35th president. Then you'll view a photograph that reveals the shock and grief individual people experienced on that tragic November day.

962

---

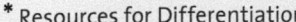

## TEXT ANALYSIS: INFLUENCE OF AUTHOR'S BACKGROUND

An **author's background**—that is, the writer's life experiences and cultural heritage—shapes his or her perspective on the world and inevitably influences what he or she writes, whether it is fiction or nonfiction. For example, Judith Ortiz Cofer was born in Puerto Rico but moved at a young age to Paterson, New Jersey. She sets many of her stories in Paterson, featuring Puerto Rican–born Americans.

Before you read "American History," learn more about Cofer from the biography on this page. Then, as you read the story, look for the following:

- references to places you know Cofer has lived or visited
- realistic, complex characters whose beliefs, values, or heritage echo Cofer's
- events and circumstances that are similar to Cofer's own

*Review:* **Character**

## READING STRATEGY: CONNECT

Good readers **connect** what they know about a person, place, or situation to what they are reading in order to understand it better. As you read "American History," connect your own life experiences to what you find in the story—the characters' circumstances, actions, and feelings. Record your connections on a chart such as the one begun here.

| Detail from Story | Connection | Better Understanding |
|---|---|---|
| tenement | I read about tenements in social studies—large, rundown apartment buildings with poor tenants. | El Building must be big and rundown. |

## ▲ VOCABULARY IN CONTEXT

Try to guess the meaning of each boldfaced word from its context.

1. soft music and **muted** conversation
2. **hierarchy** of command
3. **maneuvering** the car
4. **infatuated** and in love
5. **vigilant** protection
6. **enthralled** by the movie
7. **distraught** at losing her job
8. **resigned** to failing
9. a **dilapidated** shack
10. seeking **solace** in prayer

Complete the activities in your **Reader/Writer Notebook.**

---

## Meet the Author

## Judith Ortiz Cofer
born 1952

**A Child of Two Cultures**
It's no wonder that Judith Ortiz Cofer writes about what it's like to be a Puerto Rican girl growing up in a mainland U.S. city. "I write about the things I have known," she says. Cofer was born in Puerto Rico but moved at a young age to Paterson, New Jersey, where she lived in a large apartment building known by its residents as *El Building.* Whenever her father, a navy man, was on active duty, however, her mother would take the family back to Puerto Rico to live with their grandmother. Her father pushed her to adopt American ways, while her mother counseled her to hold on to Puerto Rican customs.

**The Power of Words**
Cofer first became aware of the power of storytelling during visits with her grandmother, who Cofer says "could silence an entire room when she said 'Tengo un cuento' ('I have a story to tell')." Cofer especially loves writing poetry, because in a poem "every word weighs a ton."

**BACKGROUND TO THE STORY**
**A Great Loss**
"American History" takes place on the day of President John F. Kennedy's assassination. The president's death deeply saddened the Puerto Rican–American community because, as Cofer points out, "President Kennedy was a saint to these people." Not only was he a charming young father and husband, but his goals were their dreams. He pledged to fight racial discrimination in the United States, raise the standard of living, and wipe out communism in Latin American countries.

**Author Online**
Go to **thinkcentral.com.**
KEYWORD: HML9-963

963

---

## Teach

**TEXT ANALYSIS**   COMMON CORE   RL 3, RL 10

### ● *Model the Skill:* INFLUENCE OF AUTHOR'S BACKGROUND

Read aloud this example:

> Carl frowned at his image in the mirror. If only he had the money to buy decent clothes, maybe the kids would accept him.

Ask how the writer's background may have influenced his portrayal of Carl. ***Possible answer:*** *The writer may have once been poor.*

**GUIDED PRACTICE** Elicit other examples of experiences that can affect an author's portrayal of a realistic, complex character.

**READING STRATEGY**   COMMON CORE   RL 10

### ■ *Model the Skill:* CONNECT

Use the text in **The Power of Words** to model the concept of connecting. Say:

> I think about someone who can silence an entire room with a story. With this person in mind, I can better understand how Cofer might be influenced by observing her grandmother.

**GUIDED PRACTICE** Ask students how finding similarities between characters and actual people can help them understand the characters.

**R** RESOURCE MANAGER—Copy Master Connect p. 83 (for student use while reading the selection)

---

**VOCABULARY SKILL**   COMMON CORE   L 4

## ▲ VOCABULARY IN CONTEXT

**DIAGNOSE WORD KNOWLEDGE** Have all students complete Vocabulary in Context. Check their definitions against the following:

**dilapidated** (dĭ-lăp'ĭ-dā'tĭd) *adj.* broken down and shabby
**distraught** (dĭ-strôt') *adj.* deeply upset
**enthralled** (ĕn-thrôld') *adj.* charmed greatly
  **enthrall** *v.*
**infatuated** (ĭn-făch'ōō-ā'tĭd) *adj.* possessed by an unreasoning love or attraction

**hierarchy** (hī'ə-rär'kē) *n.* a body of persons having authority
**maneuvering** (mə-nōō'vər-ĭng) *n.* an action skillfully designed to achieve a goal
  **maneuver** *v.*
**muted** (myōō'tĭd) *adj.* softened or muffled
**resigned** (rĭ-zīnd') *adj.* marked by acceptance of a condition or action as unavoidable
**solace** (sŏl'ĭs) *n.* comfort from sorrow or misfortune
**vigilant** (vĭj'ə-lənt) *adj.* on the alert; watchful

**PRETEACH VOCABULARY** Use the copy master to help students predict meanings.

**R** RESOURCE MANAGER—Copy Master Vocabulary Study p. 85

1. Read item 1 aloud, emphasizing *dilapidated.*
2. Point out *clean and well cared for, old,* and *unlike.* Elicit possible meanings for *dilapidated.*
3. Have students record their predictions.
4. Repeat the procedure for items 2–10.

# Practice and Apply

## READ WITH A PURPOSE

*Help students set a purpose for reading. Point out that although the story is fictional it is entitled "American History." Ask students to observe how the story is connected with American history.*

# American History
## JUDITH ORTIZ COFER

**Targeted Passage**

> I once read in a "Ripley's Believe It or Not" column that Paterson, New Jersey, is the place where the Straight and Narrow (streets) intersect. The Puerto Rican tenement known as *El Building* was one block up from Straight. It was, in fact, the corner of Straight and Market; not "at" the corner, but *the* corner. At almost any hour of the day, El Building was like a monstrous jukebox, blasting out *salsas*[1] from open windows as the residents, mostly new immigrants just up from the island,[2] tried to drown out whatever they were currently enduring with loud music. But the day President Kennedy was shot there was a profound silence in El Building; even the abusive tongues of viragoes,[3] the
> 10  cursing of the unemployed, and the screeching of small children had been somehow **muted**. President Kennedy was a saint to these people. In fact, soon his photograph would be hung alongside the Sacred Heart and over the spiritist altars[4] that many women kept in their apartments. He would become part of the **hierarchy** of martyrs they prayed to for favors that only one who had died for a cause would understand. Ⓐ

On the day that President Kennedy was shot, my ninth grade class had been out in the fenced playground of Public School Number 13. We had been given "free" exercise time and had been ordered by our P.E. teacher, Mr. DePalma, to "keep moving." That meant that the girls should jump rope and the boys
20  toss basketballs through a hoop at the far end of the yard. He in the meantime would "keep an eye" on us from just inside the building.

---

1. *salsas* (säl'säs): Latin-American dance tunes.
2. **the island:** Puerto Rico.
3. **abusive tongues of viragoes** (və-rä'gōz): hurtful comments of noisy, scolding women.
4. **alongside the Sacred Heart ... spiritist altars:** The Sacred Heart, an image showing the physical heart of Jesus Christ, symbolizes Christ's love to some Roman Catholics. Spiritist altars are places of worship set up to observe spiritism, a set of religious beliefs based on the idea that spirits of the dead communicate with the living.

Background, top, center © Corbis;
bottom © Bettmann/Corbis

### Analyze Visuals ▶

Consider the images on page 965. Why might the artist have chosen to place the photographs on a filmstrip background? Describe the effect created by this technique.

**muted** (myōō'tĭd) *adj.* softened or muffled

**hierarchy** (hī'ə-rär'kē) *n.* a body of persons having authority

**Ⓐ AUTHOR'S BACKGROUND**
Reread lines 1–15. What story elements appear to come from the author's background? Explain.

---

**Reading Support**

This selection on **thinkcentral.com** includes embedded **ThinkAloud** models—students "thinking aloud" about the story to model the kinds of questions a good reader would ask about a selection.

## BACKGROUND

**A Tragic Loss** John Fitzgerald Kennedy (1917–1963) was the youngest person ever to be elected President. He was shot to death by an assassin (Lee Harvey Oswald), on November 22, 1963, after less than three years in office. Many Americans who were alive at the time can still recall where they were and what they were doing when they learned of the president's assassination.

### REVISIT THE BIG QUESTION

## When do
# WORLD EVENTS
## hit home?

**Discuss** What do the details that Cofer provides in lines 8–15 suggest about the connection people felt with Kennedy? Explain. *Possible answer: People felt a very strong connection with Kennedy. His death shocked the community into silence, and people displayed his photograph with religious reverence.*

## Analyze Visuals

*Possible answer: The images depict the last moments of President John F. Kennedy's life before his assassination in Dallas, Texas on November 22, 1963. Setting the images on a filmstrip background gives viewers a sense of immediacy, as if they are seeing a moment-by-moment replay of history.*

---

- What is El Building? Where is it located? (lines 2–4)
- Who are the main occupants of El Building? (lines 2–7)
- When does the story take place? (lines 8–9)
- How did Kennedy's assassination affect the people of El Building? (lines 9–13)

**FOR ADVANCED LEARNERS/PRE–AP**

**Research** Encourage interested students to research and present oral reports about one of the following topics:

- Kennedy's appeal to different American groups (Latinos, African Americans, young people)
- the time line of the Kennedy assassination and its immediate aftermath
- the effects of Kennedy's death on American history and policies

**B** *Model the Skill:* **CONNECT**

Model using the chart introduced on page 963. Write "Elena gets teased" in the first column. Ask students how it feels to be teased. Remind students that Elena is in PE class and has no place to escape to even if she wanted. Have students help you complete the second and third columns of the chart.

***Possible answer:*** *The narrator probably continued to turn the jump rope because she was already being taunted by the other girls and did not want to draw any more attention to herself.*

## TIERED DISCUSSION PROMPTS

Use these prompts to help students understand the narrator and how her situation makes her feel in lines 22–40:

**Connect** Think about a time when you found it hard to fit into a social situation. How did the experience affect you? *Answers should demonstrate an understanding of the frustrations involved in trying to fit into certain social situations.*

**Analyze** How does the narrator feel about her life in Paterson? Explain. ***Possible answer:*** *For the most part, she is very unhappy there. She "hated the city, especially in winter," and she hates her school (lines 34–35). She appears to be having a difficult time fitting in with the other girls. Her "one source of beauty and light" (line 38) is seeing Eugene, a boy she likes.*

**Evaluate** Do you think the narrator is a "typical" teenager? Give reasons for your answer. ***Possible answer:*** *The narrator does seem like a typical teenager in several ways. Like so many other teens, she is very concerned about how she appears to her peers. She also appears to have a crush on a boy. However, she may be atypical in that she doesn't seem to have any close friends.*

---

It was a cold gray day in Paterson. The kind that warns of early snow. I was miserable, since I had forgotten my gloves, and my knuckles were turning red and raw from the jump rope. I was also taking a lot of abuse from the black girls for not turning the rope hard and fast enough for them.

"Hey, Skinny Bones, pump it, girl. Ain't you got no energy today?" Gail, the biggest of the black girls had the other end of the rope, yelled, "Didn't you eat your rice and beans and pork chops for breakfast today?"

The other girls picked up the "pork chop" and made it into a refrain: "pork
30 chop, pork chop, did you eat your pork chop?" They entered the double ropes in pairs and exited without tripping or missing a beat. I felt a burning on my cheeks and then my glasses fogged up so that I could not manage to coordinate the jump rope with Gail. The chill was doing to me what it always did; entering my bones, making me cry, humiliating me. I hated the city, especially in winter. I hated Public School Number 13. I hated my skinny flat-chested body, and I envied the black girls who could jump rope so fast that their legs became a blur. They always seemed to be warm while I froze. **B**

There was only one source of beauty and light for me that school year. The only thing I had anticipated at the start of the semester. That was seeing
40 Eugene. In August, Eugene and his family had moved into the only house on the block that had a yard and trees. I could see his place from my window in El Building. In fact, if I sat on the fire escape I was literally suspended above Eugene's backyard. It was my favorite spot to read my library books in the summer. Until that August the house had been occupied by an old Jewish couple. Over the years I had become part of their family, without their knowing it, of course. I had a view of their kitchen and their backyard, and though I could not hear what they said, I knew when they were arguing, when one of them was sick, and many other things. I knew all this by watching them at mealtimes. I could see their kitchen table, the sink, and the stove. During
50 good times, he sat at the table and read his newspapers while she fixed the meals. If they argued, he would leave and the old woman would sit and stare at nothing for a long time. When one of them was sick, the other would come and get things from the kitchen and carry them out on a tray. The old man had died in June. The last week of school I had not seen him at the table at all. Then one day I saw that there was a crowd in the kitchen. The old woman had finally emerged from the house on the arm of a stocky, middle-aged woman, whom I had seen there a few times before, maybe her daughter. Then a man had carried out suitcases. The house had stood empty for weeks. I had had to resist the temptation to climb down into the yard and water the flowers the old
60 lady had taken such good care of.

By the time Eugene's family moved in, the yard was a tangled mass of weeds. The father had spent several days mowing, and when he finished, from where I sat, I didn't see the red, yellow, and purple clusters that meant flowers to me. I didn't see this family sit down at the kitchen table together. It was just the mother, a red-headed tall woman who wore a white uniform—a nurse's,

**B** CONNECT
Think about a time when you continued to do something even though you were miserable doing it. Why might the narrator continue to turn the jump rope?

---

## DIFFERENTIATED INSTRUCTION

**FOR ENGLISH LANGUAGE LEARNERS**

**Culture: Connect** Ask students whether children jump rope or do a similar activity in their home culture. If so, ask what kinds of rhymes the children say or sing. Have students explore such rhymes with other speakers of the same home language.

**Vocabulary Support** Use Definition Mapping to teach these words: *source* (line 38), *suspended* (line 42), *couple* (line 45), *apparent* (line 207), *logic* (line 207), *restraint* (line 247).

 **BEST PRACTICES TOOLKIT—Transparency** Definition Mapping p. E6

I guessed it was; the father was gone before I got up in the morning and was never there at dinner time. I only saw him on weekends when they sometimes sat on lawn chairs under the oak tree, each hidden behind a section of the newspaper; and there was Eugene. He was tall and blond, and he wore glasses.

70 I liked him right away because he sat at the kitchen table and read books for hours. That summer, before we had even spoken one word to each other, I kept him company on my fire escape.

Once school started I looked for him in all my classes, but P.S. 13 was a huge, overpopulated place and it took me days and many discreet questions to discover that Eugene was in honors classes for all his subjects; classes that were not open to me because English was not my first language, though I was a straight A student. After much **maneuvering,** I managed "to run into him" in the hallway where his locker was—on the other side of the building from mine—and in study hall at the library where he first seemed to notice me, but

80 did not speak; and finally, on the way home after school one day when I decided to approach him directly, though my stomach was doing somersaults. **C**

I was ready for rejection, snobbery, the worst. But when I came up to him, practically panting in my nervousness, and blurted out: "You're Eugene. Right?" he smiled, pushed his glasses up on his nose, and nodded. I saw then that he was blushing deeply. Eugene liked me, but he was shy. I did most of the talking that day. He nodded and smiled a lot. In the weeks that followed, we walked home together. He would linger at the corner of El Building for a few minutes then walk down to his two-story house. It was not until Eugene moved into that house that I noticed that El Building blocked most of the sun, and that the only

90 spot that got a little sunlight during the day was the tiny square of earth the old woman had planted with flowers.

I did not tell Eugene that I could see inside his kitchen from my bedroom. I felt dishonest, but I liked my secret sharing of his evenings, especially now that I knew what he was reading since we chose our books together at the school library.

One day my mother came into my room as I was sitting on the window-sill staring out. In her abrupt way she said: "Elena, you are acting 'moony.'" *Enamorada*[5] was what she really said, that is—like a girl stupidly **infatuated.** Since I had turned fourteen . . . , my mother had been more **vigilant** than

100 ever. She acted as if I was going to go crazy or explode or something if she didn't watch me and nag me all the time about being a *señorita*[6] now. She kept talking about virtue, morality, and other subjects that did not interest me in the least. My mother was unhappy in Paterson, but my father had a good job at the bluejeans factory in Passaic[7] and soon, he kept assuring us, we would be moving to our own house there. Every Sunday we drove out to the suburbs of Paterson, Clifton, and Passaic, out to where people mowed grass on Sundays

---

5. *enamorada* (ĕ-nä′mô-rä′dä) *Spanish:* in love.
6. *señorita* (sĕ′nyô-rē′tä) *Spanish:* young lady.
7. **Passaic** (pə-sā′ĭk).

---

**maneuvering**
(mə-nōō′vər-ĭng) *n.* an action skillfully designed to achieve a goal
**maneuver** *v.*

**C CHARACTER**
In what ways are the narrator and Eugene similar? In what ways do they differ? Explain.

**2 Targeted Passage**

**infatuated**
(ĭn-făch′ōō-ā′tĭd) *adj.* possessed by an unreasoning love or attraction

**vigilant** (vĭj′ə-lənt) *adj.* on the alert; watchful

---

**TEXT ANALYSIS** *Review* —  COMMON CORE RL 3

**C CHARACTER**

*Possible answer: Elena and Eugene are both good students (lines 75–77) and both enjoy reading books (lines 43, 70–71). However, Eugene's first language is English, while Elena's is Spanish (line 76). Students might also note that Eugene's family seems to have more money than Elena's, since "Eugene and his family had moved into the only house on the block that had a yard and trees" (lines 40–41), while Elena lives in El Building, a tenement.*

**VOCABULARY** — COMMON CORE L 4

**OWN THE WORD**

- **maneuvering:** Have students explain how the narrator *maneuvered* in order to run into Eugene at school. Then ask if they have ever *maneuvered* so that they could run into friends during the day.

- **infatuated:** Tell students that *infatuation* describes an intense type of attraction. Ask them to compare a person who is *infatuated* with a person who has a crush. What is the difference?

- **vigilant:** Point out that the narrator's mother is *vigilant* about her daughter. Ask students to list three situations in which people are especially *vigilant*.

---

**FOR STRUGGLING READERS**

**2 Targeted Passage** [Lines 77–101]

In this passage, Elena initiates a relationship with Eugene.

- How did Elena think Eugene might react when she approached him? (line 82)

- Did Eugene react as Elena had expected? Explain your answer. (lines 82–85)

- Do you agree with Elena's mother that her daughter is *"enamorada"*? Why or why not? (lines 96–98)

**FOR ENGLISH LANGUAGE LEARNERS**

**Vocabulary: Idioms** Use New Word Analysis to teach these idioms from the story: *run into* (line 77), "meet"; *my stomach was doing somersaults* (line 81), "I was feeling very nervous"; *moony* (line 97), "dreamy"; *Most of all* (line 123), "especially"; *get close to* (line 233), "develop a relationship with."

🧰 **BEST PRACTICES TOOLKIT—Transparency** New Word Analysis p. E8

## Analyze Visuals

*Possible answer:* *The foreground is dominated by books on a table or desk. Like Elena, the protagonist in the story, the girl in the painting is studious; Elena enjoys getting books to read at the library and is a straight-A student.*

*About the Art* French artist Jean Puy (1876–1960) was considered a member of the short-lived Fauve (literally "wild beast") school, which shocked the art establishment in 1905 with its rejection of the impressionist color palette in favor of strong color and line and simplified forms. Other members of this group included Puy's good friends Matisse and Derain.

◄ **Analyze Visuals**

What images dominate the foreground in this painting? What qualities does the girl share with the protagonist in the story? Explain.

Detail of *Study, or the Schoolgirl* (1933–1934), Jean Puy. Oil on canvas, 61 cm × 72 cm. Photo © Musée National d'Art Moderne, Centre Pompidou, Paris /Giraudon/Bridgeman Art Library. © 2010 Artists Rights Society (ARS), New York/ ADAGP, Paris.

**968** UNIT 9: HISTORY, CULTURE, AND THE AUTHOR

## DIFFERENTIATED INSTRUCTION

**FOR ENGLISH LANGUAGE LEARNERS**
**Culture: Connect** After students have read lines 128–135 on page 969, ask what similarities there may be between Eugene's family and Elena's. Elicit or explain that both families have come from another place and are trying to adjust to new surroundings. Discuss the idea that although many immigrants are happy to be living in a new country and feel that their lives have improved, they may still miss their homeland intensely and have difficulty adjusting to their new home.

in the summer, and where children made snowmen in the winter from pure white snow, not like the gray slush of Paterson which seemed to fall from the sky in that hue. I had learned to listen to my parents' dreams, which were
110 spoken in Spanish, as fairy tales, like the stories about life in the island paradise of Puerto Rico before I was born. I had been to the island once as a little girl, to grandmother's funeral, and all I remembered was wailing women in black, my mother becoming hysterical and being given a pill that made her sleep two days, and me feeling lost in a crowd of strangers all claiming to be my aunts, uncles, and cousins. I had actually been glad to return to the city. We had not been back there since then, though my parents talked constantly about buying a house on the beach someday, retiring on the island—that was a common topic among the residents of El Building. As for me, I was going to go to college and become a teacher. **D**

120 But after meeting Eugene I began to think of the present more than of the future. What I wanted now was to enter that house I had watched for so many years. I wanted to see the other rooms where the old people had lived, and where the boy spent his time. Most of all, I wanted to sit at the kitchen table with Eugene like two adults, like the old man and his wife had done, maybe drink some coffee and talk about books. I had started reading *Gone with the Wind*.[8] I was **enthralled** by it, with the daring and the passion of the beautiful girl living in a mansion, and with her devoted parents and the slaves who did everything for them. I didn't believe such a world had ever really existed, and I wanted to ask Eugene some questions since he and his parents, he had told me,
130 had come up from Georgia, the same place where the novel was set. His father worked for a company that had transferred him to Paterson. His mother was very unhappy, Eugene said, in his beautiful voice that rose and fell over words in a strange, lilting way. The kids at school called him "the hick" and made fun of the way he talked. I knew I was his only friend so far, and I liked that, though I felt sad for him sometimes. "Skinny Bones" and the "Hick" was what they called us at school when we were seen together.

The day Mr. DePalma came out into the cold and asked us to line up in front of him was the day that President Kennedy was shot. Mr. DePalma, a short, muscular man with slicked-down black hair, was the science teacher, P.E.
140 coach, and disciplinarian at P.S. 13. He was the teacher to whose homeroom you got assigned if you were a troublemaker, and the man called out to break up playground fights, and to escort violently angry teen-agers to the office. And Mr. DePalma was the man who called your parents in for "a conference."

That day, he stood in front of two rows of mostly black and Puerto Rican kids, brittle from their efforts to "keep moving" on a November day that was turning bitter cold. Mr. DePalma, to our complete shock, was crying. Not just silent adult tears, but really sobbing. There were a few titters from the back of the line where I stood shivering.

---

8. ***Gone with the Wind:*** a 1936 novel, written by Margaret Mitchell and set in the South during and immediately after the Civil War.

**D AUTHOR'S BACKGROUND**
Reread lines 103–119. Think back to what you learned about Cofer in the biography on page 963. What experiences and circumstances from Cofer's life are echoed in Elena's life? Explain.

**enthralled** (ĕn-thrôld′) *adj.* charmed greatly **enthrall** *v.*

 **Targeted Passage**

---

**D** *Model the Skill:* **AUTHOR'S BACKGROUND**

- Have students reread **A Child of Two Cultures** (page 963).
- Help them to list key ideas and details from page 963 that describe Cofer but could also apply to Elena's life.
- Students may also benefit from completing and comparing Cluster Diagrams for Cofer and Elena to help them see similarities.

*Possible answer:* Like Cofer, Elena is "a Puerto Rican girl growing up in a mainland U.S. city," having "moved at a young age to Paterson, New Jersey, where she lived in a large apartment building known . . . as El Building" (**A Child of Two Cultures,** p. 963). Cofer's mother continued to feel a strong pull to Puerto Rico and Puerto Rican customs, while her father "pushed her to adopt American ways." This is perhaps echoed in the story by Elena's father's repeated assurances that the family would be moving into their own house in the suburbs (lines 104–105).

**Extend the Discussion** What differences can you find between Cofer's life and family and Elena's?

**BEST PRACTICES TOOLKIT—Transparency** Cluster Diagram p. B18

---

**FOR STRUGGLING READERS**

**3 Targeted Passage [Lines 125–136]**

This passage provides background information about Eugene and his family.

- Where are Eugene and his family from? (line 130)
- Why did they move to Paterson? (lines 130–131)
- Why does it sound to Elena that Eugene speaks "in a strange, lilting way"? (lines 132–134)
- Why do you think the kids call Eugene the "Hick"? (lines 130–134)

**FOR ADVANCED LEARNERS/PRE-AP**

**Analyze Theme** One of the underlying themes of "American History" is the idea of people having hopes and dreams. Have students write a brief essay analyzing this theme in the story. Encourage them to consider the hopes and dreams of Elena and her mother and father as well as those of all of the American people in relation to President Kennedy. Then have them read their essays aloud in class.

---

**OWN THE WORD**

**enthralled:** Have students reread the passage with *enthralled.* Then have them name books or movies that have *enthralled* them. Have students identify the scenes that they found most *enthralling* and explain their reasoning.

## E CONNECT

*Possible answer:* The students are probably reacting this way because they feel uncomfortable seeing a teacher cry and they don't know how else to react.

## TIERED DISCUSSION PROMPTS

Use these prompts to help students understand Elena's feelings in lines 175–197:

**Connect** Think about a time when you had conflicting feelings. How does your experience help you understand the way that Elena feels? *Answers should demonstrate an understanding of how conflicting feelings can pull a person in different directions.*

**Analyze** How does Cofer use descriptive details about Eugene's house to capture the sense of conflict in this scene? *Possible answer: El Building overshadows Eugene's house, casting it in darkness. This foreshadows the resentment or prejudice that Eugene's family may feel toward El Building's occupants.*

**Synthesize** Why do you think Elena is surprised by her mother's reaction? *Possible answer: Elena is caught up in her own teenage world, unaware of the gravity of the events unfolding around her.*

---

"Listen," Mr. DePalma raised his arms over his head as if he were about 150 to conduct an orchestra. His voice broke, and he covered his face with his hands. His barrel chest was heaving. Someone giggled behind me.

"Listen," he repeated, "something awful has happened." A strange gurgling came from his throat, and he turned around and spat on the cement behind him.

"Gross," someone said, and there was a lot of laughter. E

"The President is dead, you idiots. I should have known that wouldn't mean anything to a bunch of losers like you kids. Go home." He was shrieking now. No one moved for a minute or two, but then a big girl let out a "Yeah!" and ran to get her books piled up with the others against the brick wall of the 160 school building. The others followed in a mad scramble to get to their things before somebody caught on. It was still an hour to the dismissal bell.

A little scared, I headed for El Building. There was an eerie feeling on the streets. I looked into Mario's drugstore, a favorite hangout for the high school crowd, but there were only a couple of old Jewish men at the soda-bar talking with the short order cook in tones that sounded almost angry, but they were keeping their voices low. Even the traffic on one of the busiest intersections in Paterson—Straight Street and Park Avenue—seemed to be moving slower. There were no horns blasting that day. At El Building, the usual little group of unemployed men were not hanging out on the front stoop making it difficult 170 for women to enter the front door. No music spilled out from open doors in the hallway. When I walked into our apartment, I found my mother sitting in front of the grainy picture of the television set.

She looked up at me with a tear-streaked face and just said: "*Dios mio,*"[9] turning back to the set as if it were pulling at her eyes. I went into my room.

Though I wanted to feel the right thing about President Kennedy's death, I could not fight the feeling of elation that stirred in my chest. Today was the day I was to visit Eugene in his house. He had asked me to come over after school to study for an American history test with him. We had also planned to walk to the public library together. I looked down into his yard. The oak tree 180 was bare of leaves and the ground looked gray with ice. The light through the large kitchen window of his house told me that El Building blocked the sun to such an extent that they had to turn lights on in the middle of the day. I felt ashamed about it. But the white kitchen table with the lamp hanging just above it looked cozy and inviting. I would soon sit there, across from Eugene, and I would tell him about my perch just above his house. Maybe I should.

In the next thirty minutes I changed clothes, put on a little pink lipstick, and got my books together. Then I went in to tell my mother that I was going to a friend's house to study. I did not expect her reaction.

"You are going out *today?*" The way she said "today" sounded as if a storm 190 warning had been issued. It was said in utter disbelief. Before I could answer, she came toward me and held my elbows as I clutched my books.

---

9. ***Dios mio*** (dyôs mē′ô) *Spanish:* my God.

## E CONNECT

Reread lines 144–155 and think about how different people receive bad news. Why do you think the students are reacting this way to Mr. DePalma?

---

COMMON CORE L 4a

**Language Coach**

**Word Origins** *Elation* comes from a Latin word meaning "to lift up." How can this clue help you figure out the meaning of *elation* in line 176? What additional clue does the first part of the sentence provide?

---

## DIFFERENTIATED INSTRUCTION

### FOR STRUGGLING READERS

**Vocabulary Support** Point out the following terms in the story and explain their meanings: *eerie* (line 162), "strange or mysterious"; *short order cook* (line 165), "a cook who prepares food quickly."

### FOR ENGLISH LANGUAGE LEARNERS

**Language Coach**

COMMON CORE
L 4a

**Word Origins**

*Possible answer: In the first part of the sentence, the narrator says she is not feeling the way she should about Kennedy's death—that is, grief-stricken. Elation must mean a feeling of being uplifted, very happy. Explain that when one feels elation (n.) one is elated (adj.).*

*Rag in Window* (1959), Alice Neel. 33″ × 24″. Gift of the Estate of Arthur M. Bullowa. Courtesy of the Philadelphia Museum of Art. © Estate of Alice Neel. Courtesy Robert Miller Gallery, New York.

"*Hija,*[10] the President has been killed. We must show respect. He was a great man. Come to church with me tonight."

She tried to embrace me, but my books were in the way. My first impulse was to comfort her, she seemed so **distraught,** but I had to meet Eugene in fifteen minutes.

"I have a test to study for, Mama. I will be home by eight."

**distraught** (dĭ-strôt′) *adj.* deeply upset

---

10. *hija* (ē′hä) *Spanish:* daughter.

AMERICAN HISTORY   **971**

## Analyze Visuals

**Activity**  Ask students in what ways the painting reminds them of the setting of "American History."  *Possible answer: The bleak view brings to mind the tenement in the story, and the snow in the painting suggests the "cold gray day" (line 22) that Elena describes.*

**About the Art**  Although American artist Alice Neel (1900–1984) is best known for her portraits, she also painted street scenes and still lifes.  Her realistic style is evident in *Rag in Window,* which shows the cheerless view from her apartment in Spanish Harlem, a view that perhaps suggests what life was like for many of the residents of El Building in the story.

VOCABULARY  COMMON CORE

L 4

## OWN THE WORD

**distraught:** Have students create a semantic map for *distraught.*  Write the word and the definition "deeply upset" in a circle.  Have students draw spider legs from the circle and add synonyms to complete the map.  *Possible answers: agitated, anxious, frantic*

## FOR ENGLISH LANGUAGE LEARNERS

**Vocabulary: Compound Words**  Point out some of the compound words in the story, such as *homeroom* (line 140), *troublemaker* (line 141), *playground* (line 142), *drugstore* (line 163), *hangout* (line 163), *soda-bar* (line 164), and *streetlight* (line 253).  Ask students to find others.  Then have students in home-language groups list examples of similar words in their language and share their meanings with the class.

**Culture: Clarify**  Ask Spanish-speaking students to pronounce and explain the meaning of Spanish words in the story, such as *Enamorada* (line 98), *Hija* (line 192), *Niña* (line 198), *Verde-Esperanza* (line 213), and *luto* (line 247).

AMERICAN HISTORY   **971**

# When do WORLD EVENTS hit home?

**Discuss** What does Elena's mother mean in lines 198–203 when she says, "You are forgetting who you are, *Niña*"? Why do you think her tone is "resigned"? ***Possible answer:*** *Elena's mother is aware of the discrimination that her daughter will face. However, she knows that Elena is young and must learn of it herself.*

---

**READING STRATEGY**

COMMON CORE
RL 10

### CONNECT

***Possible answer:*** *Elena is shocked to hear what Eugene's mother is saying to her "in such a honey-drenched voice" (line 236). Elena no doubt finds it hard to reconcile the harsh substance of the words with their sweet sound—"a little song" (line 237). This confrontation is probably unlike any Elena has ever had, and she gets caught up in the mother's voice until the anger behind it finally snaps her out of her "trance."*

---

**VOCABULARY**

COMMON CORE
L 4

### OWN THE WORD

- **resigned:** Tell students that the mother's *resigned* tone means "accepting, acquiescent." Another meaning, for the verb form *resign*, is "to quit," as when a person *resigns* from a job. Have students write pairs of sentences showing both meanings of the word.

- **dilapidated:** Have students reread the sentence with *dilapidated*. Then have them cite context clues that can help them determine the meaning of the word. ***Possible answer:*** *the opposite of "neat"*

---

"You are forgetting who you are, *Niña*.[11] I have seen you staring down at that boy's house. You are heading for humiliation and pain." My mother said 200 this in Spanish and in a **resigned** tone that surprised me, as if she had no intention of stopping me from "heading for humiliation and pain." I started for the door. She sat in front of the TV holding a white handkerchief to her face.

I walked out to the street and around the chainlink fence that separated El Building from Eugene's house. The yard was neatly edged around the little walk that led to the door. It always amazed me how Paterson, the inner core of the city, had no apparent logic to its architecture. Small, neat, single residences like this one could be found right next to huge, **dilapidated** apartment buildings like El Building. My guess was that the little houses had been there 210 first, then the immigrants had come in droves, and the monstrosities had been raised for them—the Italians, the Irish, the Jews, and now us, the Puerto Ricans and the blacks. The door was painted a deep green: *verde,* the color of hope, I had heard my mother say it: *Verde-Esperanza.* I knocked softly. A few suspenseful moments later the door opened just a crack. The red, swollen face of a woman appeared. She had a halo of red hair floating over a delicate ivory face—the face of a doll—with freckles on the nose. Her smudged eye make-up made her look unreal to me, like a mannequin seen through a warped store window.

"What do you want?" Her voice was tiny and sweet-sounding, like a little 220 girl's, but her tone was not friendly.

"I'm Eugene's friend. He asked me over. To study." I thrust out my books, a silly gesture that embarrassed me almost immediately.

"You live there?" She pointed up to El Building, which looked particularly ugly, like a gray prison with its many dirty windows and rusty fire escapes. The woman had stepped halfway out and I could see that she wore a white nurse's uniform with St. Joseph's Hospital on the name tag.

"Yes. I do."

She looked intently at me for a couple of heartbeats, then said as if to herself, "I don't know how you people do it." Then directly to me: "Listen. 230 Honey. Eugene doesn't want to study with you. He is a smart boy. Doesn't need help. You understand me. I am truly sorry if he told you you could come over. He cannot study with you. It's nothing personal. You understand? We won't be in this place much longer, no need for him to get close to people— it'll just make it harder for him later. Run back home now."

I couldn't move. I just stood there in shock at hearing these things said to me in such a honey-drenched voice. I had never heard an accent like hers, except for Eugene's softer version. It was as if she were singing me a little song.

"What's wrong? Didn't you hear what I said?" She seemed very angry, and I finally snapped out of my trance. I turned away from the green door, and 240 heard her close it gently.

---

11. *Niña* (nē'nyä) *Spanish:* little girl.

---

**resigned** (rĭ-zīnd') *adj.* marked by acceptance of a condition or action as unavoidable

**dilapidated** (dĭ-lăp'ĭ-dā'tĭd) *adj.* broken down and shabby

### CONNECT
Reread lines 228–240. Think about how you and people you know react to confrontation. Why does Elena become so entranced with Eugene's mother's voice?

---

## DIFFERENTIATED INSTRUCTION

**FOR ENGLISH LANGUAGE LEARNERS**

**Vocabulary: Phrasal Verbs** Have students create Cluster Diagrams with a main verb in the center circle of each cluster and as many phrasal verbs as they can identify in the surrounding circles. Use these phrasal verbs from the story to get students started: *break up* (lines 141–142), *let out* (line 158), *heading for* (line 199), and *come over* (lines 231–232).

**BEST PRACTICES TOOLKIT—Transparency** Cluster Diagram p. B18

**FOR STRUGGLING READERS**

**Develop Reading Fluency** Have students reread lines 219–240. Point out and discuss the descriptions of Eugene's mother's voice and tone. Have students discuss in pairs how her lines of dialogue should sound, given those contradictory descriptors. Then have them practice reading the dialogue between her and Elena. Volunteers can present their readings to the class. You may also wish to present your own reading with a fluent student before or after the volunteers.

Detail of *Loneliness* (1970), Alice Neel. Oil on canvas, 80" × 38". Gift of Arthur M. Bullowa, in honor of the 50th Anniversary of the National Gallery of Art. Photo by Lyle Peterzell. Image © 2005 Board of Trustees, National Gallery of Art, Washington, D.C. © Estate of Alice Neel. Courtesy Robert Miller Gallery, New York.

Our apartment was empty when I got home. My mother was in someone else's kitchen, seeking the **solace** she needed. Father would come in from his late shift at midnight. I would hear them talking softly in the kitchen for hours that night. They would not discuss their dreams for the future, or life in Puerto Rico, as they often did; that night they would talk sadly about the young widow and her two children, as if they were family. For the next few days, we would observe *luto* in our apartment; that is, we would practice restraint and silence—no loud music or laughter. Some of the women of El Building would wear black for weeks. **G**

250    That night, I lay in my bed trying to feel the right thing for our dead President. But the tears that came up from a deep source inside me were strictly for me. When my mother came to the door, I pretended to be sleeping. Sometime during the night, I saw from my bed the streetlight come on. It had a pink halo around it. I went to my window and pressed my face to the cool glass. Looking up at the light I could see the white snow falling like a lace veil over its face. I did not look down to see it turning gray as it touched the ground below. ❧

**solace** (sŏl′ĭs) *n.* comfort from sorrow or misfortune

**G  AUTHOR'S BACKGROUND**
What **inferences** can you make about Puerto Rican culture from the description of mourning in lines 241–249?

**④ Targeted Passage**

AMERICAN HISTORY    **973**

---

## FOR STRUGGLING READERS

**④ Targeted Passage** [Lines 250–257]

This passage concludes the story with Elena in tears, not because of Kennedy's death but as a result of her encounter with Eugene's mother.

- What does Elena mean when she says that she was "trying to feel the right thing for our dead President"? (lines 250–252)

- Explain what Elena means when she says that her tears "were strictly for [herself]." (lines 251–252)

## FOR ADVANCED LEARNERS/PRE–AP

**Analyze Symbolism** Compare lines 105–109 with lines 254–257. Have students discuss the symbolic significance of snow in the story. Ask why Cofer includes in line 256 the specific detail that Elena "did not look down."

---

## Analyze Visuals

**Activity** Ask students how the mood of the painting matches the mood of the story at the end. *Possible answer: Elena is miserable because of her encounter with Eugene's mother. The sadness and loneliness that she feels match the emptiness of the scene depicted in the painting.*

**About the Art** *Loneliness* is another still life by American artist Alice Neel (see page 971).

**VOCABULARY**   COMMON CORE   L 4

### OWN THE WORD

**solace:** Ask students to list other actions or items that could provide *solace* to a needy person. *Possible answers: hug, kind word, a warm blanket*

**TEXT ANALYSIS**   COMMON CORE   RL 3, RL 10

### G AUTHOR'S BACKGROUND

*Possible answer: Readers can infer that the Puerto Rican culture treats a person's death with great seriousness and respect. They avoid music, laughter, and merriment for a period of time, and some wear black to symbolize mourning.*

## SELECTION WRAP–UP

**READ WITH A PURPOSE** Now that students have read the selection, ask them how the story relates to "American History." *Possible answers: Elena plans to study American History with Eugene; instead, an important event in American history (Kennedy's assassination) interferes. In addition, the author may be reflecting on the American history of discrimination which Elena experiences firsthand.*

★ **CRITIQUE** Have students evaluate the ending of the story. Discuss whether the plot was or was not resolved in an effective way.

## INDEPENDENT READING

Students might enjoy *Silent Dancing: A Partial Remembrance of a Puerto Rican Childhood,* a collection of essays and poems by Judith Ortiz Cofer.

# Practice and Apply

For preliminary support of post-reading
questions, use these copy masters:

**R** **RESOURCE MANAGER—Copy Masters**
Reading Check p. 89
Influence of Author's Background p. 81
Question Support p. 90

Additional selection questions are provided for the teacher on page 75.

## ANSWERS

## Comprehension

1. *Elena is attracted to Eugene because he likes to read books, as she does. When Elena approaches him, Eugene smiles and blushes; he likes her, but he is shy.*

2. *President Kennedy is assassinated.*

3. *Elena's greatest concern on this day is her study date with Eugene at his house.*

## Text Analysis

COMMON CORE RL 3, RL 7, RL 10

**Possible answers:**

4. *Eugene's mother looks down on Elena as an immigrant who lives in a dilapidated tenement. She points with disdain at El Building, then says "I don't know how you people do it" (line 229). Aside from the fact that Elena is in a lower socioeconomic class, Eugene's mother may be rejecting her because she is Puerto Rican.*

5.

| WHO | Is Separated HOW | From WHOM |
|-----|------------------|-----------|
| Elena | • She can't turn rope fast enough.<br>• They call her names. | the black girls |
| | • English is not her first language. | honors classes |
| | • He lives in a house; she lives in a tenement.<br>• His mother rejects her. | Eugene |

6. ● **COMMON CORE FOCUS** *Analyze the Influence of the Author's Background* Descriptive passages might include lines 1–15, 162–171, 206–212.

7. ■ **COMMON CORE FOCUS** *Connect Literature to Life Experiences* Students' answers should reflect their understanding of how making personal connections aids understanding of characters and situations.

---

## Comprehension

1. **Recall** What attracts Elena to Eugene? How does he respond to her?

2. **Recall** What world event happens on November 22, 1963?

3. **Summarize** What is Elena's greatest personal concern on this day?

## Text Analysis

4. **Draw Conclusions** What do you think is the real reason that Eugene's mother turns Elena away? Explain why you think as you do.

5. **Understand a Character's Social Context** Elena's interactions with other characters are affected by the social barriers she faces. What are these barriers and how are they demonstrated or enforced? Record your answers in a chart like the one shown.

| WHO | Is Separated HOW | from WHOM |
|-----|------------------|-----------|
| Elena | •<br>•<br>• | the black girls |

● 6. **Analyze the Influence of the Author's Background** Reread Cofer's biography and Background on page 963. Identify three descriptive passages in the story that refer to events or circumstances that actually occurred in Cofer's life.

■ 7. **Connect Literature to Life Experiences** Refer to the chart you created as you read. Did the connections you made while reading improve your understanding of Elena and her situation? Explain.

8. **Make Judgments** Elena is far more preoccupied with her private loss than with the loss affecting the entire nation. Do you think this is reasonable? Explain why or why not.

## Text Criticism

9. **Historical Context** When President Kennedy died, many Americans felt that their chance to realize the dreams and hopes he had championed, such as racial equality, died with him. Why might Cofer have chosen to set Elena's story on the day of the president's assassination?

> ## When do WORLD EVENTS hit home?
>
> What world events, either tragic or transformational, do you remember best?

COMMON CORE

RL 3 Analyze how complex characters develop over the course of a text and interact with other characters. RL 7 Analyze the representation of a subject in different artistic mediums. RL 10 Read and comprehend stories.

---

8. *Students may feel Elena's response is reasonable, because most fourteen-year-olds tend to be self-centered and not involved with current events. Others may feel that Elena's response is not reasonable, because even a fourteen-year-old should react more strongly to an event of such obvious magnitude.*

## Text Criticism

9. *Possible answer: Cofer might have chosen to set the story on the day of the assassination to draw a parallel between America's loss of hopes and dreams and Elena's loss. This parallel is reinforced by Kennedy's association with racial equality and Eugene's mother's likely rejection of Elena at least in part because of her race.*

> When do **WORLD EVENTS** hit home? *Answers will vary but students should explain why the events are memorable.*

# Vocabulary in Context

▲ **VOCABULARY PRACTICE**

Write the letter of the word that is most different in meaning from the others.

1. (a) spellbound, (b) enthralled, (c) considerate, (d) thrilled
2. (a) cowardly, (b) watchful, (c) observant, (d) vigilant
3. (a) muted, (b) noisy, (c) deafening, (d) boisterous
4. (a) consolation, (b) solace, (c) depression, (d) sympathy
5. (a) rejecting, (b) jockeying, (c) maneuvering, (d) strategizing
6. (a) hierarchy, (b) order, (c) religion, (d) classification
7. (a) perplexed, (b) infatuated, (c) surprised, (d) confounded
8. (a) fired, (b) accepting, (c) resigned, (d) submissive
9. (a) enlivened, (b) entertained, (c) amused, (d) distraught
10. (a) dilapidated, (b) antique, (c) decaying, (d) neglected

**WORD LIST**

dilapidated
distraught
enthralled
hierarchy
infatuated
maneuvering
muted
resigned
solace
vigilant

## ACADEMIC VOCABULARY IN SPEAKING

- contrast • environment • factor • incorporate • predominant

With a partner, compare Elena's feelings and thoughts on the day of Kennedy's assassination with those of her mother. What are their **predominant** concerns? What **factors** lead them to react differently to the events of the day? Use at least one Academic Vocabulary word in your discussion.

## VOCABULARY STRATEGY: IDIOMS

An idiom is a phrase whose overall meaning is different from the grammatical or logical, literal meaning of its individual parts. For example, the narrator of this story says, "That summer, . . . I kept him company on my fire escape." "Kept him company" is an idiomatic expression.

If you run into an unfamiliar idiom, you can often use context clues to figure out its meaning. Otherwise, consult a dictionary. Many dictionaries list idioms at the end of the entry for the main word in the idiom. So *kept him company* would be explained under *keep*, as part of a list like this:

—*idioms:* **for keeps** To hold indefinitely: *He gave me the book for keeps.* **keep an eye on** To watch over attentively. **keep (someone) company** To accompany or stay with.

**PRACTICE** Identify the idiom in each sentence and write a definition of it. Use context clues or a dictionary.

1. Your advice flies in the face of good sense.
2. Her shoe fell off, so she finished her dance routine on a wing and a prayer.
3. No one will follow those rules unless you put some teeth into them.
4. Winning this contract will really put him on the map in our community.

**COMMON CORE**

**L 5a** Interpret figures of speech in context and analyze their role in the text.

**Interactive Vocabulary** THINK central
Go to **thinkcentral.com**.
KEYWORD: HML9-975

AMERICAN HISTORY **975**

---

---

## DIFFERENTIATED INSTRUCTION

### FOR STRUGGLING READERS

**Vocabulary Practice** To build students' comprehension, elicit or explain the meaning of each correct word choice (that is, the word most different in meaning from the others), and then have students use the word in a sentence. Expand the activity by exploring how synonyms in the practice set have similar, but not identical, meanings.

### FOR ADVANCED LEARNERS/PRE–AP

**Vocabulary in Writing** Challenge students to use at least four vocabulary words in a paragraph written about Elena from Eugene's point of view.

# Focus and Motivate

## COMMON CORE FOCUS

**RI 2** Determine a central idea of a text and analyze its development over the course of the text. **RI 5** Analyze in detail how an author's ideas are developed and refined. **RI 7** Analyze various accounts of a subject told in different mediums. **W 9b (RI 6)** Draw evidence from informational texts; determine an author's purpose in a text and analyze how an author uses rhetoric to advance that purpose. **L 4** Determine or clarify the meaning of unknown words and phrases.

## SUMMARY

The article "Special Report" reflects on the nation's reaction to President Kennedy's death and our continuing fascination with him forty years after that event.

## What's the Connection?

Use a KWL chart to prepare students for the selection. In the first column, have students note what they know (K) about John F. Kennedy and his assassination. In the second column, have them write questions about what they want to know (W). After reading, have students use the third column to record what they have learned (L).

**BEST PRACTICES TOOLKIT—Transparency** KWL p. A21

# Teach

## Standards Focus: Identify Controlling Idea

Point out that the controlling idea is the central idea, or most important point that the author wants to support with his or her writing. Explain that a well-written informative or explanatory text always has a controlling idea so that the piece remains focused and meets the author's purpose for writing it. Remind students that they should look for the controlling idea of each paragraph to help them determine the overall controlling idea of the article.

**R** RESOURCE MANAGER—Copy Master Controlling Idea p. 99

---

## Special Report

*Essential Course of Study*

Magazine Article, page 977
Political Cartoon, page 978

**COMMON CORE**

**RI 2** Determine a central idea of a text and analyze its development over the course of the text. **RI 5** Analyze in detail how an author's ideas are developed and refined. **RI 7** Analyze various accounts of a subject told in different mediums. **L 4** Determine or clarify the meaning of unknown words and phrases.

## What's the Connection?

"American History" takes place on the day that President John F. Kennedy was killed. The magazine article you are about to read will add to your sense of how that tragic event affected the nation and how and why Kennedy's short presidency remains significant today.

## Standards Focus: Identify Controlling Idea

In a sense, the controlling idea of an informative or explanatory text "controls" the writer's development of the text—it suggests which important details the writer should include to accomplish his or her purpose and how he or she should organize those details. Since the controlling idea shapes the writer's work, it should also leave an impression on you, the reader. From the reader's perspective, the **controlling idea** is the **central idea,** or most important point, that a text conveys.

Here are some tips to help you determine the controlling idea of a magazine article:

- Preview the first paragraph or two of the article. Sometimes the controlling idea will be stated outright at the beginning. More often, however, you'll have to infer the controlling idea.
- As you read, distinguish between the most important and the less important details in each paragraph. Try to state the key idea of each paragraph in your own words. Taken together, these key ideas should suggest the controlling idea of the entire article.

You can keep track of important details and key ideas in a chart like the one started below.

| Paragraph | Important Details | Key Idea |
|---|---|---|
| 1 | After 9/11, many Americans visited the JFK Library and Museum . . . | Kennedy was a strong and skillful leader during trying times. |
| 2 | | |
| | | |
| Article's Controlling Idea: | | |

---

## Selection Resources

See resources on the **Teacher One Stop DVD-ROM** and on **thinkcentral.com**.

**R** **RESOURCE MANAGER UNIT 9**
  Lesson Support, pp. 91–106

**DIAGNOSTIC AND SELECTION TESTS**
  Selection Tests, pp. 263–266

**INTERACTIVE READER**

**ADAPTED INTERACTIVE READER**

**ELL ADAPTED INTERACTIVE READER**

**TECHNOLOGY**

- **Teacher One Stop DVD-ROM**
- **Student One Stop DVD-ROM**
- **PowerNotes DVD-ROM**
- **Audio Anthology CD**
- **Audio Tutor CD**
- **ExamView Generator** on the **Teacher One Stop**

\* Resources for Differentiation

## Special Report

BY KENNETH T. WALSH  **A**

**NOVEMBER 24, 2003**

In the days immediately after 9/11, Americans in large numbers showed up at the John F. Kennedy Library and Museum in Boston, apparently looking for strength and hope at a time of national peril and sorrow. They were drawn in particular to a film recounting the Cuban missile crisis, when Kennedy guided the nation
10 through a confrontation with the Soviet Union that could easily have led to nuclear war. Many visitors seemed comforted by the idea that prudent leadership and common sense could make all the difference, even in the worst of times.

The fact that Kennedy still has such a hold on America's imagination comes as no surprise to historians and other
20 observers of popular culture. This connection will become even more apparent in the coming weeks as the nation marks the 40th anniversary of his assassination, on Nov. 22, 1963.

Yet the reasons for his mystique are less clear. The fact that he was assassinated in the prime of life goes only so far in explaining it. President William McKinley, another popular
30 leader, was murdered in 1901, but his death generated no vast outpouring of emotion and no enduring sense of a lost legacy. In contrast, millions of Americans still recall where they were when they heard that Kennedy had

been shot. (I was attending history class at St. Rose High School in Belmar, N.J., when the principal came on the public-address system and,
40 choking back tears, told us what had happened. Everyone marched to our nearby church, and we spent the next few hours praying for the president's survival and, a bit later, his soul.) **B**

We all seem to have vivid memories of his funeral, carried on live television, with those unforgettable images of his grieving widow and his young son saluting smartly when his father's
50 cortege passed by.

"Kennedy is frozen in our memory at age 46," says historian Robert Dallek, author of *An Unfinished Life: John F. Kennedy 1917–1963*. "People don't realize that this past May 29 he would have been 86 years of age."

Some deft PR by the White House helped to create his charismatic aura in the first place. He and his advisers
60 quickly grasped the power of the new medium of television, and the handsome, eloquent young leader quickly mastered it and went on to convey an image of optimism and charm that still surrounds him today. His performances at live press conferences are remembered as tours de force. His speeches are used as brilliant examples of political
70 communication. And if his legislative

**A** CONTROLLING IDEA
On the 40th anniversary of Kennedy's assassination, *U.S. News & World Report* featured this special report. As you read, consider what this detail suggests about Kennedy and his tragic death.

**B** CONTROLLING IDEA
Reread the first sentence of the third paragraph. What does this **topic sentence** suggest about the **controlling idea** of this article? Turn that sentence into a question and read on to find an answer.

---

INFORMATIONAL ANALYSIS   COMMON CORE   RI 2, RI 5

## **A** CONTROLLING IDEA

After students have read the article, ask how the passage of time enables Walsh to offer new insights into Kennedy's time in office and into his legacy. *Possible answer: Walsh can see Kennedy from a historical perspective. He recognizes, for example, that "Kennedy governed prior to the age of cynicism" that followed his presidency (lines 111–116).*

INFORMATIONAL ANALYSIS   COMMON CORE   RI 2, RI 5

## **B** CONTROLLING IDEA

*Possible answer: The sentence suggests that Walsh will focus on exploring the reasons for the Kennedy "mystique." The sentence might be posed as this question: Why did a mystique develop around John F. Kennedy?*

---

## DIFFERENTIATED INSTRUCTION

### FOR STRUGGLING READERS

**Vocabulary Support**  Have students use a Think-Pair-Share activity to explore the meaning of these words and phrases using context clues and, as needed, a dictionary: *confrontation* (line 10), *prudent* (line 13), *mystique* (line 25), *prime of life* (line 27), *legacy* (line 33), *cortege* (line 50), *deft* (line 57), *charismatic aura* (line 58), *eloquent* (line 62), *tours de force* (lines 67–68).

**BEST PRACTICES TOOLKIT—Transparency** Think-Pair-Share p. A18

### FOR ADVANCED LEARNERS/PRE-AP

**Analyze a Symbol** [small-group option] In the first paragraph of this article, Walsh presents the Cuban missile crisis as a symbol of national stress and presidential leadership. Have students research the Cuban missile crisis, which occurred when the United States learned in 1962 that the Soviet Union planned to install ballistic missiles in Cuba. Ask students to report on the crisis and its resolution and to offer insights on the symbolic importance of the event.

record fell short, his ideas about ending the Cold War and achieving racial equality at home, at least under the law, eventually took root and became reality. ⚠

Further, his glamorous wife, Jacqueline, reinforced the exciting image of Camelot, especially in contrast to his solid but dull 80 predecessor, Dwight Eisenhower. Ike had been the oldest man to serve as president up until that time; Kennedy was the youngest ever elected to the office. The White House never let anyone forget it.

"One of the things President Kennedy did was instill in the American people the idea they could make a difference," says Deborah Leff, 90 director of the Kennedy Library and Museum. ". . . It was a time when you saw America striving to be its best."

For his part, Kennedy said in one of his famous speeches, at American University on June 10, 1963: "No problem of human destiny is beyond human beings. Man's reason and spirit have often solved the seemingly unsolvable—and we believe they can 100 do it again."

The tragic Kennedy mythology was reinforced when his brother Robert was assassinated in 1968 and, later, when his son, John F. Kennedy Jr., died in a plane crash in 1999. All of this perpetuated the idea that the Kennedys, despite all their advantages, were not immune from life's calamities. This deepened their connection to the 110 rest of us.

Yet Kennedy governed prior to the age of cynicism brought on by the Vietnam War, the Watergate scandal,

and the wrenching social changes of the past four decades (including, of course, his own assassination). Perhaps not even Kennedy could have emerged from this era unscathed had he lived and remained in public life.

120 "The sudden end to Kennedy's life and presidency has left us with tantalizing 'might have beens,'" Dallek writes. "Yet even setting these aside and acknowledging some missed opportunities and false steps, it must be acknowledged that the Kennedy thousand days spoke to the country's better angels, inspired visions of a less divisive nation and world, and 130 demonstrated that America was still the last best hope of mankind." It is a legacy any president would be proud of.

**D**

© 1963 Bill Mauldin. Reprinted with special permission from the Chicago Sun-Times, Inc. 2004.

**DIFFERENTIATED INSTRUCTION**

**FOR STRUGGLING READERS**

**Vocabulary Support** Have students work in small groups to define these words and phrases and then use them in sentences: *predecessor* (line 80), *instill* (line 87), *perpetuated* (line 106), *calamities* (line 108), *cynicism* (line 112), *unscathed* (line 118), *tantalizing* (line 122), *"might have beens"* (line 122), *false steps* (line 125), *better angels* (line 128).

**FOR ENGLISH LANGUAGE LEARNERS**

**Language Coach** COMMON CORE L 4
**Word Origins** *Possible answer: teasing by offering something, then withdrawing it* Have students name synonyms for *tantalize*. *Possible answers: tease, tempt, entice, lure, fascinate, taunt, intrigue*

## Comprehension

1. **Recall** What facts did you learn from the article "Special Report" that you did not learn from the short story "American History"?

2. **Summarize** What were Kenneth Walsh's personal experiences on the day of President Kennedy's assassination?

3. **Recall** According to the article, in addition to Kennedy's assassination, what other tragedies befell the Kennedy family?

## Text Analysis

4. **Synthesize** What does the political cartoon add to your understanding of how Kennedy's loss affected the nation? Explain.

5. **Analyze Controlling Idea** Review the chart you filled out as you read. Then state the controlling idea of "Special Report" in your own words.

## Read for Information: Analyze Author's Style and Purpose

**WRITING PROMPT**

Notice how the author of "Special Report" uses several quotations in the article. How does this use of quotations advance the author's purpose?

To answer this prompt, you will need to determine the author's purpose and then analyze how quotations help the author accomplish that purpose. Following these steps can help:

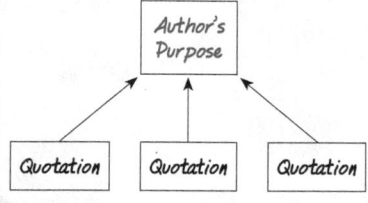

1. Record important quotations that you find in the article.

2. In determining the controlling idea, you've already answered the question "What point is the author trying to make?" Now answer the question "Why is he making that point?" The answer is the author's purpose.

3. Finally, consider how the quotations you recorded support, either individually or collectively, the purpose you identified.

---

---

# Practice and Apply

For preliminary support of post-reading questions, use these copy masters:

**R RESOURCE MANAGER—Copy Masters**
Reading Check p. 103
Question Support p. 104
Identify Controlling Idea p. 99

Additional selection questions are provided for the teacher on page 94.

## ANSWERS

## Comprehension

1. *The reader learns where and how the assassination occurred and that Governor Connally also was shot.*

2. *He learned the news over his school's PA system and then went with classmates to the nearby church to pray.*

3. *His brother Robert was also assassinated; his son John died in a plane crash.*

## Text Analysis

*Possible answers:*   **COMMON CORE RI 2, RI 5, RI 7**

4. *The cartoon suggests that the assassination was not only a historic event but also a symbolic one—an event that united Americans but that did so through tragedy.*

5. ■ **COMMON CORE FOCUS** *Analyze Controlling Idea* Kennedy continues to attract us because he represents America's promise.

## Read for Information

**Writing Prompt** *Possible answer:*   **COMMON CORE W 9b (RI 6)**

*The author's purpose is to explain how Kennedy captivated the American people and why he remains an important figure today. The author advances this purpose by using many direct quotations.*

# Assess and Reteach

## Assess

**DIAGNOSTIC AND SELECTION TESTS**
Selection Tests A, B/C pp. 263–264, 265–266

**Interactive Selection Test** on **thinkcentral.com**

## Reteach

**Level Up Online Tutorials** on **thinkcentral.com**

**Reteaching Worksheets** on **thinkcentral.com**
Reading Lesson 14
Study Skills Lesson 13

---

**FOR STRUGGLING WRITERS**
**Read for Information**

- Encourage students to start by summarizing the emotional impact in a clearly written topic sentence. Explain that they can revise their sentences as they develop their responses, but writing the topic sentence first will help them focus on relevant information as they review the selections.

- Remind students to support their topic sentences with evidence from the selections.

**FOR ADVANCED LEARNERS/PRE–AP**

**Read for Information** Have students integrate information from at least one additional outside source in their written responses to the writing prompt. As volunteers share their work with the class, have them describe the additional source and explain how it added to their understanding.

# Practice and Apply

## Photograph

Have students observe the store sign and newspaper headline. Note that the store is closed. The writer of the sign is both sad and angry. The woman is clearly interested in the newspaper's contents. *Possible answer: The picture shows how unavoidable the fact of the assassination was, but that people continued to look for more information.*

### ANALYZE VISUALS

### 1. ANALYZE DETAILS

*Possible answer: The photo is black-and-white, so it probably isn't recent. The woman's hairstyle and clothes further suggest that the photo was taken in the 1960s. Since the woman is reading a newspaper article announcing Kennedy's death, the photo was likely taken the day after the assassination—November 23, 1963.*

### ANALYZE VISUALS

### 2. INFER

*Possible answer: The creator of the sign was likely appalled by the assassination. Not only is the store closed, but the specific words on the sign suggest the magnitude of the sign creator's reaction. "National disgrace," for instance, is a much stronger way to describe Kennedy's death than, say, "terrible occurrence" or even "tragedy."*

### ANALYZE VISUALS

### 3. INTERPRET

*Possible answer: The photograph conveys that Kennedy's assassination was hugely significant and shocked the entire nation. Businesses closed, and people were transfixed by the news of Kennedy's death.*

---

## Reading for Information

### Photograph

The short story and magazine article you've just read describe people's reactions to President Kennedy's assassination. You've most likely heard the expression "A picture is worth a thousand words." Study the photograph below and consider what it adds to your understanding of Kennedy's death and his legacy.

1. **ANALYZE DETAILS**
   What characteristics of this photograph suggest when it was taken? Explain.

2. **INFER**
   What inferences can you make about the person who created the sign in the background? Focus on the sign creator's word choice.

3. **INTERPRET**
   Consider the composition of the photograph—how the shot is framed and how the foreground and background images work together. What message does this photograph convey to you?

## Assessment Practice: Short Constructed Response

### LITERARY TEXT: "AMERICAN HISTORY"

On assessments, you'll have to analyze the literary techniques authors use in their written works. Analyze foreshadowing by answering the **short constructed response** question below.

> In "American History," what event foreshadows the prejudice Eugene's mother shows toward Elena? Support your answer with evidence from the story.

◀ **STRATEGIES IN ACTION**

1. Reread the text up to Elena's encounter with Eugene's mother.
2. Look for **hints** suggesting that Elena will experience prejudice.
3. Discuss one hint in your answer, supporting it with evidence in the form of a direct quotation, a paraphrase, or a specific synopsis.

### NONFICTION TEXT: "SPECIAL REPORT"

Demonstrate that you can recognize and analyze an author's perspective in a nonfiction text by answering the **short constructed response** question below.

> In "Special Report," what is the author's attitude toward President John F. Kennedy? Support your answer with evidence from the article.

◀ **STRATEGIES IN ACTION**

1. Reread the text, noting the **details** the author includes about Kennedy.
2. State what these particular details reveal about the author's **attitude,** or feelings, about Kennedy.
3. Use evidence from the text to support your statement.

### COMPARING LITERARY AND NONFICTION TEXTS

Some assessment questions ask you to synthesize information from multiple texts. Practice this skill by applying the following **short constructed response** question to "American History" and "Special Report."

> Based on the details in "American History" and "Special Report," how do you think the majority of Americans reacted to the news of President Kennedy's death? Support your answer with evidence from both texts.

◀ **STRATEGIES IN ACTION**

1. Look for details that describe people's reactions to Kennedy's death in both texts. Make a **generalization** about how most people reacted.
2. Use the details that helped you form your generalization as evidence.

## Assessment Practice: Short Constructed Response

*LITERARY TEXT: "AMERICAN HISTORY"*
*Answers will vary, but students may say that one event that foreshadows the prejudice Elena will face is the conversation Elena has with her mother before going to Eugene's house to study. In that conversation, Elena's mother tells her by going to Eugene's house she is "heading for humiliation and pain."*

*NONFICTION TEXT: "SPECIAL REPORT"*
**Possible answer:** *Students may respond that the author's attitude toward Kennedy is one of respect. Evidence to support the claim include the specific examples and direct quotations the author provides that relate to Kennedy's accomplishments.*

*COMPARING LITERARY AND NONFICTION TEXTS* **Possible answer:** *Students may say that many Americans reacted with intense grief upon hearing the news of Kennedy's death, citing examples such as Mr. DePalma's reaction in the short story and the principal's reaction in the report as evidence.*

## DIFFERENTIATED INSTRUCTION

### FOR STRUGGLING WRITERS
**Analyze the Nonfiction Text Question**
Explain to students that an author's perspective is not often directly stated; it must be inferred. In fact, an author may not intend to reveal his or her perspective when the purpose of the article is to convey factual information rather than opinions. In this piece, the author is sharing others' perspectives about Kennedy. To understand the author's own perspective, students should ask themselves what attitude towards President Kennedy is shown by the quoted statements, and whether the author seems to agree or disagree with that attitude.

# Focus and Motivate

## COMMON CORE FOCUS

**RL 4** Analyze the cumulative impact of specific word choices on meaning and tone. **RL 6** Analyze a particular point of view or cultural experience reflected in a work of world literature. **RL 10** Read and comprehend poems. **L 4** Determine or clarify the meaning of unknown and multiple-meaning words.

## SUMMARIES

The speaker of **"The Tropics in New York"** describes a display of fruits and other tropical goods in a New York store window. These sights inspire vivid memories of another place and make the speaker long for home.

In **"Theme for English B,"** the speaker explores a writing assignment given by a college professor. By pondering self-identity and the idea of truth, the speaker reveals intimate details of what his life is like as an African American in the early 1900s.

## How does **HERITAGE** shape identity?

Introduce the question. Then, discuss with students some of the things that comprise one's heritage, such as one's ethnicity, family traditions, religious practices, and belief systems. Encourage them to consider these aspects of their own heritages as they complete the *QUICKWRITE.*

## Selection Resources

---

*Before Reading*

### The Tropics in New York
Poem by Claude McKay

### Theme for English B
Poem by Langston Hughes

# How does **HERITAGE** shape identity?

### COMMON CORE

**RL 4** Analyze the cumulative impact of specific word choices on meaning and tone. **RL 6** Analyze a particular point of view or cultural experience reflected in a work of world literature. **RL 10** Read and comprehend poems. **L 4** Determine or clarify the meaning of unknown and multiple-meaning words.

Your identity is certainly shaped by your personal experiences, but your heritage also has something to do with it. No matter who you are, your family and the culture in which you grew up shaped the person you are today, as well as the person you will be in the future. In the poems "The Tropics in New York" and "Theme for English B," two African-American writers explore and celebrate the importance of their heritage.

*QUICKWRITE* What is your heritage, and how important has it been in shaping your identity? Jot down your thoughts, and then write a paragraph describing how your heritage has influenced who you are.

982

---

*See resources on the **Teacher One Stop DVD-ROM** and on **thinkcentral.com**.*

 **RESOURCE MANAGER UNIT 9**
  Plan and Teach, pp. 107–114
  Text Analysis and Reading
    Skill, pp. 115–118†*

**DIAGNOSTIC AND SELECTION
  TESTS**
  Selection Tests, pp. 267–270

**BEST PRACTICES TOOLKIT**
  Read Aloud, p. A34
  Analysis Frame: Poetic Form
    and Structure, p. D21, D40

**TECHNOLOGY**
  ⊘ **Teacher One Stop DVD-ROM**
  ⊘ **Student One Stop DVD-ROM**
  ⊘ **Audio Anthology CD**
  ⊘ **ExamView Test Generator**
    on the **Teacher One Stop**

---

* Resources for Differentiation          † Also in Spanish          ‡ Also in Haitian Creole, Vietnamese

## TEXT ANALYSIS: HARLEM RENAISSANCE LITERATURE

In the early 1920s, a literary movement known as the **Harlem Renaissance** took root in the New York City neighborhood known as Harlem. African-American writers, artists, and musicians created works that expressed their own heritage, style, and voice rather than mimicking the style and voice of white culture.

Claude McKay and Langston Hughes were key writers in this movement. Both poets were concerned with the social issues facing African Americans. McKay, who grew up on the tropical island of Jamaica, wrote poetry that reflected the lush landscape and the rhythms of life on the island. Langston Hughes experimented with bringing the rhythms of blues and jazz music into his poetry. As you read these poems, note the following:

- images that are unique to the cultural background of the writer
- ideas or cultural experiences that are expressed through the speaker
- words or cultural ideas that are unique to the time period

## READING STRATEGY: READING POETRY

As you've learned, poets are careful and deliberate about their diction—the words they use in their poems. For example, rhythm and melody play an important role in most poetry, including the poetry of the Harlem Renaissance. In fact, you can find in these poems sounds and rhythms that continue to occur in contemporary African-American poetic forms. After reading each poem silently, read the poems aloud. Notice the rhythms created by the words as well as the sounds of the words in combination. Jot down examples of **sound devices,** such as alliteration, assonance, repetition, and rhyme.

| "The Tropics in New York" | |
|---|---|
| Example | Type of Sound Device |
| "dewy dawns" | alliteration |

 Complete the activities in your **Reader/Writer Notebook.**

## Meet the Authors

## Claude McKay
### 1889–1948

**From Rural Jamaican to World Traveler**
The 11th child of peasant farmers, Claude McKay was born and raised in Jamaica. By the time he came to the United States in 1912 to attend college, he had published two volumes of verse in Jamaican dialect. He moved to New York in 1914, and by the early 1920s he had emerged as one of the first inspirational voices of the Harlem Renaissance movement. McKay lived and traveled widely as a poet, novelist, and journalist.

## Langston Hughes
### 1902–1967

**Spokesman for the Common People**
Born in Joplin, Missouri, Langston Hughes moved often during his youth and grew up in various Midwestern cities. Like Claude McKay, Hughes became a world traveler, but he lived in New York's Harlem neighborhood at several points in his life. He was deeply influenced by the sights and sounds of Harlem and played a key role in the Harlem Renaissance. Hughes's poetry focuses on the experiences of ordinary black people in America and reflects his love of blues and jazz music.

**Authors Online**
Go to thinkcentral.com. KEYWORD: HML9-983

**THINK**central

983

## Teach

### TEXT ANALYSIS
COMMON CORE
RL 6

● *Model the Skill:* **HARLEM RENAISSANCE LITERATURE**

After students read the page, discuss what the common elements are in Claude McKay's and Langston Hughes's lives. Ask how these elements relate to Harlem Renaissance literature. *Possible answer: Both men are African American. Both men lived in Harlem, New York, at some time in their lives. Harlem is where the largely African-American Harlem Renaissance movement began.*

**GUIDED PRACTICE** What ideas about culture do you expect to read in the poems of McKay and Hughes?

### READING STRATEGY
COMMON CORE
RL 4, RL 10

■ *Model the Skill:* **READING POETRY**

Write these lines on the board:

Before we leave, we'll feast with ease.
Feasting on fat fishes,
Splayed on Grandma's special dishes.

Read the lines aloud, emphasizing rhythm, rhyme, and other sound devices. Then, ask students to work with you to identify the sound devices in the lines. *Possible answer: Alliteration—Feasting/fat/fishes; Assonance—we/leave/feast/ease; Rhyme—fishes/dishes*

**GUIDED PRACTICE** Invite several volunteers to read the lines aloud.

**R RESOURCE MANAGER—Copy Master** Reading Poetry p. 117 (for student use while reading the selections)

## DIFFERENTIATED INSTRUCTION

### FOR STRUGGLING READERS

**Concept Support** Review the meanings of the skill words discussed under **Reading Poetry.** Explain that *alliteration* refers to repeated use of a similar consonant sound. *Assonance* refers to repeated use of a similar vowel sound. Confirm that students can recognize rhyme when they hear it.

## READ WITH A PURPOSE

*Help students set a purpose for reading. Remind them that both poets were participants in the Harlem Renaissance. Ask students to read to draw conclusions about the goals of members of this movement.*

## BACKGROUND

Claude McKay immigrated to the United States from Jamaica, an island nation in the West Indies section of the Caribbean Sea. The island population features a majority of people descended from enslaved Africans brought by European traders. In addition, people of Spanish, French, and English descent live on Jamaica. Once colonized by Great Britain, Jamaica gained independence in 1962. This colonial heritage leaves most Jamaicans speaking English. Many also speak Creole—a blend of French, Spanish, and West African languages. The culture blends these several influences.

### READING STRATEGY

COMMON CORE
RL 4,
RL 10

**A** *Model the Skill:* **READING POETRY**

Read the first stanza aloud for students, using your voice to emphasize the word *and*. Repeat, having students read aloud with you. Have students record their observations in their Reading Strategy charts.

*Possible answer: The word* and *is repeated in a way that emphasizes the rhythm of the poem.*

## REVISIT THE BIG QUESTION
# How does **HERITAGE** shape identity?

**Discuss** What aspects of the speaker's **heritage** does he reveal in the poem? How do you know that these things reflect his heritage?
*Possible answer: The speaker reveals physical characteristics of his homeland in the poem. He uses the word* memories *to illustrate that the poem's images are not something that he is currently experiencing. He continues to explain that these memories make him "hungry for the old, familiar ways" (line 11), a phrase that further suggests one's heritage.*

**984** UNIT 9

---

# The Tropics in New York

### CLAUDE MCKAY

Bananas ripe and green, and ginger-root,
　　Cocoa in pods and alligator pears,
And tangerines and mangoes and grape fruit,
　　Fit for the highest prize at parish fairs, **A**

5 Set in the window, bringing memories
　　Of fruit-trees laden by low-singing rills,
And dewy dawns, and mystical blue skies
　　In benediction over nun-like hills.

My eyes grow dim, and I could no more gaze;
10　　A wave of longing through my body swept,
And, hungry for the old, familiar ways,
　　I turned aside and bowed my head and wept.

**A** **READING POETRY**
Reread lines 1–4 aloud. What word is repeated in a way that emphasizes the rhythm?

COMMON CORE L 4

**Language Coach**

**Roots and Affixes** The root *bene* means "good," and the root *dic* means "speak." Reread line 8. What do you think *benediction* means?

**984** UNIT 9: HISTORY, CULTURE, AND THE AUTHOR

---

## DIFFERENTIATED INSTRUCTION

### FOR ENGLISH LANGUAGE LEARNERS

**Language Coach** COMMON CORE L 4

**Roots and Affixes**
*Possible answer:* good + speaking = blessing Ask students to think of other words with the prefix *bene-* or the root *dic.* *Possible answers:* benefit, benefactor, benevolent; dictation, dictionary

### FOR STRUGGLING READERS

**Options for Reading** Read aloud "The Tropics in New York," vocally emphasizing the poem's rhythm and melody. Then, draw students' attention to the end rhymes in the first stanza. Point out that such repetitive rhymes help to establish a strong rhythm in a poem. Using the Read Aloud strategy, guide students in performing an echo reading of the poem.

 BEST PRACTICES TOOLKIT—Transparency Read Aloud p. A34

985

## Analyze Visuals

**Activity** Ask students to identify elements of the art that reflect their ideas about "the tropics." *Possible answer: The bold colors in the painting reflect the vivid colors associated with places like the Caribbean Islands, where jewel-toned waters meet sandy, white beaches peppered with lush, green trees. The bright colors also lend the idea of ripeness to the illustrated fruits.*

**About the Art** *Tropical Fruit* was created by Barbara Maslen and features fruits often found in the tropics: citrus, kiwi, and papaya.

## TIERED DISCUSSION PROMPTS

Use these prompts to help students connect their experiences to those described in the poem:

**Connect** What ideas, images, sights, or smells do you associate with your hometown? What might you see or experience in another place that would remind you of the place you live now? *Students' answers will vary.*

**Analyze** What kind of memories might the fruit be calling up for the speaker? *Possible answer: The fruit most likely reminds the speaker of his homeland and "old, familiar ways" (line 11).*

**Evaluate** In the beginning of the poem, the speaker is looking at fruit in a store window. At the end, he is weeping. Is it plausible that such a reaction would occur in real life, or has it been dramatized for literary purposes? *Possible answer: A person's reaction to an object that brings back strong memories could be very intense. It is entirely possible that the sight of a banana could bring a person to tears if it recalled a happier time.*

---

### FOR STRUGGLING READERS

**Vocabulary Support** Explain the following terms from the poem:

- *parish fairs* (line 4), fairs or festivals, held by a religious community to help raise money for its church.
- *laden* (line 6), loaded with a heavy burden
- *rills* (line 6), small streams or creeks
- *mystical* (line 7), spiritual; magical

### FOR ADVANCED LEARNERS

**Write a Poem** Have students write a poem about their own city in a style similar to "The Tropics in New York." Remind students to think of what might have motivated McKay when he wrote this poem. Ask for volunteers to share their poems.

Prereading for this poem is found on page 982.

**REVISIT THE BIG QUESTION**

## How does **HERITAGE** shape identity?

**Discuss** What aspects of the speaker's heritage does he reveal in lines 1–20 and 25–28? How does the speaker feel about his heritage? *Possible answer: The speaker shares that he is an African American and that he was born in North Carolina. He also reveals that living in Harlem (specifically) and New York (in general) has been influential for him. At some points in the poem, the speaker seems to have a matter-of-fact attitude about his heritage; at other points, he seems to express pride in it.*

---

**TEXT ANALYSIS**

COMMON CORE

RL 6

**B** *Model the Skill:* **HARLEM RENAISSANCE**

Reread the lines. As you do so, write key words and phrases you encounter on the board, such as *twenty-two, colored, Winston-Salem, Durham, college on the hill above Harlem,* and *the Harlem Branch Y.* Then discuss what the poet's connection is to each term.

*Possible answer: In lines 6–15, we learn that the speaker is 22 years old, African American, and was born in Winston-Salem, North Carolina. We also learn that the speaker went to school in Winston-Salem, then in Durham, North Carolina, and then at Columbia University in New York City. The speaker is the only African-American student in the class. The speaker lives at the Harlem Branch YMCA.*

---

# Theme for ENGLISH B

### Langston Hughes

The instructor said,

    Go home and write
    a page tonight.
    And let that page come out of you—
5    Then, it will be true.

    I wonder if it's that simple?
    I am twenty-two, colored, born in Winston-Salem.
    I went to school there, then Durham,[1] then here
    to this college on the hill above Harlem.[2]
10 I am the only colored student in my class.
    The steps from the hill lead down into Harlem,
    through a park, then I cross St. Nicholas,
    Eighth Avenue, Seventh, and I come to the Y,
    the Harlem Branch Y, where I take the elevator
15 up to my room, sit down, and write this page: **B**

    It's not easy to know what is true for you or me
    at twenty-two, my age. But I guess I'm what
    I feel and see and hear. Harlem, I hear you:
    hear you, hear me—we two—you, me talk on this page.
20 (I hear New York, too.) Me—who?

---

1.  **Winston-Salem . . . Durham:** cities in North Carolina.
2.  **this college on the hill above Harlem:** Columbia University in New York City.

**986**   UNIT 9: HISTORY, CULTURE, AND THE AUTHOR

---

COMMON CORE L 4

**Language Coach**

**Multiple Meanings** The word *colored* typically means "having color" or "influenced by." In an old-fashioned usage of the term, it meant "African American" (the preferred term today). Which sense of the word is used in line 7?

**B** **HARLEM RENAISSANCE**
Reread lines 6–15. What do you learn about the speaker in these lines?

---

**DIFFERENTIATED INSTRUCTION**

**FOR ENGLISH LANGUAGE LEARNERS**

**Language Coach**    COMMON CORE L 4

**Multiple Meanings** *Possible answer: African American* Help students find other uses of "colored" in the poem and discuss what the word means in each instance. *(In lines 10 and 25 he uses it to mean "African American." In line 27 the meaning includes both "African American" and "having color.")*

**FOR ADVANCED LEARNERS/PRE–AP**

**Analyze Poetic Structure** Ask students to analyze the structure of "Theme for English B," using the Poetic Form and Structure analysis frame. They should focus on the arrangement and length of words and lines, and how these elements affect readers. Ask students to consider why Hughes chose to change form and structure during the poem.

 **BEST PRACTICES TOOLKIT—Transparency** Analysis Frame: Poetic Form and Structure pp. D21, D40

*Young Man Studying* (Portrait of Langston Hughes) (1932), Hilda Wilkinson Brown. Oil on canvas.
Photo by Gregory R. Staley © Lilian T. Burwell/Howard University.

Well, I like to eat, sleep, drink, and be in love.
I like to work, read, learn, and understand life.
I like a pipe for a Christmas present,
or records—Bessie, bop, or Bach.[3]
25 I guess being colored doesn't make me not like
the same things other folks like who are other races.
So will my page be colored that I write?
Being me, it will not be white.
But it will be
30 a part of you, instructor.
You are white—
yet a part of me, as I am a part of you.
That's American.
Sometimes perhaps you don't want to be a part of me.
35 Nor do I often want to be a part of you.
But we are, that's true!
As I learn from you,
I guess you learn from me—
although you're older—and white—
40 and somewhat more free.

This is my page for English B.

---

3. **Bessie, bop, or Bach:** Bessie Smith was a leading jazz and blues singer of the
  1920s and early 1930s. Bop is a style of jazz that became popular in the 1940s.
  Johann Sebastian Bach was an 18th-century German composer.

**C  READING POETRY**
Reread lines 16–28.
What sound devices
do you recognize
in these lines?

THEME FOR ENGLISH B **987**

## TIERED DISCUSSION PROMPTS

Use these prompts to help students make connections between the Harlem Renaissance and the poems by McKay and Hughes:

**Connect** Recall a time in your life when you felt part of a community, or simply that you "belonged." In your opinion, what makes people feel this way? *Students might say that people feel like they "belong" when they are surrounded by people with similar interests, experiences, and beliefs.*

**Analyze** Why might McKay and Hughes have felt that they "belonged" in Harlem at the time of the Harlem Renaissance? *Possible answer: In Harlem at that time, McKay and Hughes found themselves surrounded by other African Americans who celebrated their ethnicity and culture.*

**Evaluate** How might McKay's and Hughes's work be different if the Harlem Renaissance had not taken place? *Answers will vary but should include an awareness of the far-reaching cultural influences of the Harlem Renaissance and the important role of a supportive community in the creative process.*

---

**MAGAZINE ARTICLE** This article sheds further light on the Harlem Renaissance and its groundbreaking influence.

### THE HARLEM RENAISSANCE:

# A Cultural Explosion

From the "stompin'" jazz performances at the Savoy Ballroom to the lavish, racially-integrated literary events at the Dark Tower, 1920s Harlem in New York City hosted a vibrant cultural scene known as the Harlem Renaissance.

Scholars disagree about the exact dates of the Harlem Renaissance but generally place this cultural revolution between 1919 and the mid-1930s. The Harlem Renaissance represented a movement that was occurring throughout the country, as African Americans explored artistic, political, and social acts to raise race consciousness. Black people experiencing poverty and racial tension, particularly in the rural South, flocked to Harlem in the hopes of creating a more unified, self-determined community.

Harlem's population quickly exploded, despite high rents there. The "city within a city" drew residents from as far as Africa and the West Indies, as its influence spread throughout the world. The result was a strong community of African-American businesses, churches, schools, and civic and entertainment centers. Although Harlemites had problems and differences, residents drew together to enjoy "strolling" (a pastime that involved dressing up to walk the neighborhood and meet neighbors), parades (which could occur a few times in one day and involve the whole crowd), and rent parties (hosted by tenants hoping to earn enough money from a cover charge to pay the month's rent).

During the Harlem Renaissance, African Americans from all walks of life, as well as other audiences, developed greater appreciation for both the folk and more sophisticated aspects of black culture. Musical forms such as jazz and the blues swelled in popularity. Plays by African Americans appeared on Broadway, black artists gained prominence, and black writers published more books than during any previous era.

Some of the Harlem Renaissance's most prominent figures, such as poet Langston Hughes, drew inspiration from "the low-down folks," a term he used to describe the masses. Hughes, who experimented with dialect and music in his writing, believed African Americans needed to be proud of their individuality and blackness. Others, such as the scholar W. E. B. DuBois, felt that African-American art should serve the political purpose of portraying its people in the best possible light, in order to show equality with whites and to defy stereotypes. Despite these differences, writers of the movement found enough in common to support one another.

The Harlem Renaissance suffered when the stock market crashed in 1929 and wealthy white patrons from New York City's uptown neighborhoods no longer frequented Harlem's clubs. Other factors, such as race riots, the repeal of Prohibition, and growing dissent affected the movement as well. Today the Harlem Renaissance remains a powerful influence among artists such as Nobel Prize winner Toni Morrison, Pulitzer Prize winner Alice Walker, Poet Laureate Rita Dove, and many others.

## Comprehension

1. **Recall** In "The Tropics in New York," what do the fruits in the window remind the speaker of?

2. **Recall** What causes him to weep?

3. **Recall** In "Theme for English B," what instructions are given to the speaker?

4. **Summarize** What aspect of his identity does he discuss?

## Text Analysis

5. **Examine Title** Consider the title of "The Tropics in New York." How does it affect your understanding of the poem?

6. **Draw Conclusions** In "Theme for English B," the speaker says that he and the instructor are part of each other. What does he mean? Explain.

7. **Analyze Theme** In your own words, explain the theme of the poem "Theme for English B." What is the message the poet wants to convey? Support your answer with evidence from the text.

8. **Identify Tone** A poet's choice of words and details conveys a certain tone, or attitude toward the subject. Identify the tone of each poem by completing a chart like the one shown.

| "The Tropics in New York" | |
|---|---|
| Tone of Poem | Words/Details That Convey Tone |
| sad, nostalgic | |

9. **Understand Sound in Poetry** Review the sound devices you recorded as you read the two poems. How does noticing these sound devices affect the way you perceive these poems?

10. **Interpret Harlem Renaissance Literature** What does the article "The Harlem Renaissance: A Cultural Explosion" add to your understanding of these two poems?

## Text Criticism

11. **Biographical Context** Claude McKay grew up in a Jamaican town populated mainly by blacks. When he went to work in the city of Kingston, with a greater proportion of whites, he was shocked by the racism he encountered. He later went to the United States with great optimism about the opportunity he might find "even for a Negro," but he was quickly disillusioned about the conditions for black Americans: "It was the first time I had ever come face to face with such manifest, implacable hate of my race." What does this knowledge about his life add to your perception of the homesickness described in "The Tropics in New York"? Explain.

### How does **HERITAGE** shape identity?

How important is your heritage to you? Explain.

**COMMON CORE**

**RL 4** Analyze the cumulative impact of specific word choices on meaning and tone. **RL 6** Analyze a particular point of view or cultural experience reflected in a work of world literature. **RL 10** Read and comprehend poems.

# Practice and Apply

For preliminary support of post-reading questions, use these copy masters:

**R** **RESOURCE MANAGER—Copy Masters**
Harlem Renaissance Literature p. 115
Question Support p. 119

Additional selection questions are provided for teachers on page 111.

## ANSWERS

## Comprehension

1. *The fruits remind the speaker of home: of fruit trees, dawns, blue skies, and hills.*

2. *The speaker weeps because he longs for "the old, familiar ways" and misses home.*

3. *The speaker is told to write a page from his heart, a page that is "true."*

4. *The speaker discusses several aspects of his identity, but especially his racial identity.*

## Text Analysis

COMMON CORE **RL 4, RL 6, RL 10**

*Possible answers:*

5. *The title notes the poem's New York setting, far from the speaker's home in the tropics. It explains the speaker's longing.*

6. *The speaker likely means that both are American, so share aspects of culture.*

7. *The message is that the instructor and student—a white American and a black American—are connected. Students should cite lines 31–40 as evidence.*

8. *"The Tropics in New York": Words/Details: "dewy dawns"; "mystical blue skies"; "eyes grow dim"; "wave of longing"; "hungry for the old, familiar ways"; "bowed my head and wept." "Theme for English B": Tone:*

*calm, serious; **Words/Details**: speaker's life details, likes and interests*

9. ■ **COMMON CORE FOCUS** *Understand Sound in Poetry In "The Tropics in New York," the sound devices recall a spiritual song or prayer. "Theme for English B" sounds more like a conversation, except in lines 18–20, where the rhythm of repetition is briefly musical.*

10. ● **COMMON CORE FOCUS** *Interpret Harlem Renaissance Literature The article places the poems in a cultural time frame beyond the poets' personal experiences.*

## Text Criticism

11. *Students might say that McKay's disappointment at finding racism in America sharpens the poignancy of the homesickness expressed in the poem.*

### How does **HERITAGE** shape identity? *Students' responses should include explanations.*

# Assess and Reteach

## Assess

**DIAGNOSTIC AND SELECTION TESTS**
Selection Test A pp. 267–268
Selection Test B/C pp. 269–270

**Interactive Selection Test** on **thinkcentral.com**

## Reteach

**Level Up Online Tutorials** on **thinkcentral.com**

**Reteaching Worksheets** on **thinkcentral.com**
Literature Lesson 47: Author's Perspective

# Focus and Motivate

## Haiku
Poems by Matsuo Bashō

## Haiku
Poems by Richard Wright

## Honku
Poems by Aaron Naparstek

## COMMON CORE FOCUS

**RL 4** Analyze the cumulative impact of specific word choices on meaning. **RL 6** Analyze a particular point of view or cultural experience reflected in a work of world literature. **RL 10** Read and comprehend poems.

### SUMMARIES

**"Haiku" by Matsuo Bashō** In these three haiku, Bashō connects images from nature to the human experience.

**"Haiku" by Richard Wright** Wright uses the haiku form to explore the sensory experiences of urban living.

**"Honku" by Aaron Naparstek** Naparstek uses a modified haiku form to comment on the effects of technology.

## How many **WORDS**
### do you need?

Ask the question. Once students have read the first paragraph, have a volunteer define the word concise. Ask students to give examples of other times writers must be concise—for example, a photo caption or news headline. Have students practice their ability to be concise by completing the *QUICKWRITE*.

# How many **WORDS**
## do you need?

**COMMON CORE**

**RL 4** Analyze the cumulative impact of specific word choices on meaning. **RL 6** Analyze a particular point of view or cultural experience reflected in a work of world literature. **RL 10** Read and comprehend poems.

Sometimes a few words can leave a big impression. Even three short lines can contain a thoughtful observation about life. Poets of haiku are masters of being concise in this way. In this lesson, you'll read the works of three poets from very different places and time periods who use the tiny three-line haiku to create unforgettable images and express powerful ideas.

*QUICKWRITE* Can you create a vivid or unusual image from only three or four words? Choose a few of the words pictured here, and arrange them to create a striking image or idea.

990

## Selection Resources

See resources on the **Teacher One Stop DVD-ROM** and on **thinkcentral.com**.

 **RESOURCE MANAGER UNIT 9**
Plan and Teach, pp. 121–128
Text Analysis and Reading
Skill, pp. 129–132†*

**DIAGNOSTIC AND SELECTION TESTS**
Selection Tests, pp. 271–274

**BEST PRACTICES TOOLKIT**
Read Aloud/Think Aloud, p. A34
Comparison Matrix, p. A24

**TECHNOLOGY**
- Teacher One Stop DVD-ROM
- Student One Stop DVD-ROM
- Audio Anthology CD
- ExamView Test Generator on the **Teacher One Stop**

\* Resources for Differentiation      † Also in Spanish      ‡ In Haitian Creole and Vietnamese

## POETIC FORM: HAIKU

**Haiku** originated in Japan hundreds of years ago and has since inspired poets in many cultures to use and adapt the form. But the haiku still presents a challenge with its strict rules about form and content. It requires

- three unrhymed lines of five, seven, and five syllables
- two common images, usually from nature, that are juxtaposed to suggest a greater meaning
- an allusion to a season, as in the phrase "Heat waves shimmering," which suggests summer

## TEXT ANALYSIS: HISTORICAL AND CULTURAL CONTEXT

The poets Matsuo Bashō and Richard Wright lived in vastly different times and places, and Aaron Naparstek's world is vastly different from theirs. The varied social conditions that inspired these poets to write their poems is the **historical** or **cultural context** of their work.

Before you read each group of poems, read about the author for historical and cultural details that will help you interpret the poetry. Then read the poems, focusing on their figurative language, imagery, symbolism, diction, and themes. Notice how these elements reflect the poet's life, times, and culture.

## READING SKILL: INTERPRET IMAGERY

**Imagery** consists of words and phrases that appeal to a reader's sense of sight, hearing, touch, smell, or taste. In haiku, the imagery has added weight because the form is so brief; each word and phrase is critical to the meaning. As you read, follow these steps to find deeper meaning in each poem.

1. Record the images in the poem.
2. Identify the mood, idea, or feeling the images evoke.
3. Explain the meaning of the images.

Record details in a chart as shown.

| First Haiku by Bashō: "Harvest Moon" | | |
|---|---|---|
| Imagery | Mood, Idea, or Feeling | Meaning |
| the moon walking around the pond all night | mood—quiet or serene; idea—moon stays all night | Nature is abundant and constant. |

 Complete the activities in your **Reader/Writer Notebook**.

## Meet the Authors

### Matsuo Bashō
**1644–1694**

**Japanese Haiku Master**
A samurai before he was a poet, Matsuo Bashō elevated haiku from a popular social pastime into a literary art form. Bashō brought the gentle spirit of Zen Buddhism to both his writing and his life. He spent his later life writing poetry as he journeyed through Japan.

### Richard Wright
**1908–1960**

**African-American Novelist**
Considered one of the most important black authors of the 1900s, Richard Wright is best known for his novel *Native Son* and his autobiography *Black Boy*. He also wrote short stories, essays, and poetry about life in Northern ghettos and racial oppression of blacks.

### Aaron Naparstek
**born 1970**

**Activism Meets Poetry**
Fed up with the noise created by motorists in his Brooklyn neighborhood, Aaron Naparstek began writing "honku"—haiku about honking cars—and taping them to lampposts. Others began posting their own honkus, and a movement was born. In 2003 Naparstek published *Honku: The Zen Antidote to Road Rage*.

**Authors Online**
 **THINK** central
Go to **thinkcentral.com**. KEYWORD: HML9-991

991

## Teach

### TEXT ANALYSIS  COMMON CORE RL 6

● *Model the Skill:* **HISTORICAL AND CULTURAL CONTEXT**

Write these lines on the board:

> And in this deep chill,
> the warmth of the Midwest soul
> welcomes me back home.

Tell students that they can hypothesize that the poem's speaker probably lived in the Midwest and then moved away for a while. He or she finds comfort in the region and is happy to be back home.

**GUIDED PRACTICE** Ask students to identify details in the poem that support this hypothesis about context.

### READING SKILL  COMMON CORE RL 4

■ *Model the Skill:* **INTERPRET IMAGERY**

Focus students' attention once more on the haiku written on the board. Work with them to identify the imagery in the poem and to explain which sense it mostly appeals to. *Possible answer: The image of a cold winter day is presented. This imagery appeals to the sense of touch or feeling. It may also appeal secondarily to the sense of sight.*

**GUIDED PRACTICE** Discuss with students the deeper meaning implied by the juxtaposition of the words *chill* and *warmth*.

**R** RESOURCE MANAGER—Copy Master Interpret Imagery p. 131 (for student use while reading the selections)

## DIFFERENTIATED INSTRUCTION

### FOR STRUGGLING READERS
Review the terms discussed in the haiku instruction. Confirm that students can identify syllables and recognize rhyme. Explain that *juxtaposed* means "to place two things together to highlight a similarity or contrast." Remind students that an allusion is a reference to knowledge the writer thinks readers will have. For example, a poem may allude to a specific mountain and assume that readers know its legends or history.

# Practice and Apply

## READ WITH A PURPOSE

*Help students set a purpose for reading. Remind them of the features that all haiku have in common. Then have them read to discover what else, if anything, all three sets of haiku share.*

## Analyze Visuals

**Activity** Ask students how the artwork and Bashō's haiku are similar. ***Possible answer:*** *The artwork reflects images present in the haiku. The moon is shown peeking through the clouds. The plants are brown and look dead. The brown and yellow tones convey a feeling of autumn.*

**About the Art** Point out to students that this six-fold screen—painted with ink, color, and gold leaf—is one of a pair. It was created during the same time period in which Bashō lived. The painter is unknown.

---

**TEXT ANALYSIS**     **COMMON CORE**    **RL 6**

###  HISTORICAL AND CULTURAL CONTEXT

How does Bashō use nature to express his own feelings at any given moment? ***Possible answer:*** *Bashō presents images from nature that might reflect or provoke the feelings that he is trying to express. For example, an autumnal full moon reflecting off the surface of a pond might inspire a feeling of loneliness or restlessness.*

---

**READING SKILL**     **COMMON CORE**    **RL 4**

###  *Model the Skill:* INTERPRET IMAGERY

Guide students in using the Reading Skill charts they began to record imagery from Bashō's second haiku and express their thoughts about each image.

***Possible answer:*** *Imagery: dry, shimmering heat; dead grass;* ***Mood:*** *exhaustion, stillness;* ***Meaning:*** *Nature can be harsh and beautiful at the same time.*

---

*Millet Fields with the Sun and the Moon* (1600s), Anonymous. Japanese. Pair of six-fold screens. Ink, colors and gold leaf on paper, 150.5 cm. × 348.8 cm. (59.25" x 37.3"). Restricted gift of the Rice Foundation, 1989.625 b: overall. Reproduction, The Art Institute of Chicago. Photo © The Art Institute of Chicago.

# H A I K U
## Matsuo Bashō

Harvest moon—
walking around the pond
   all night long.

     Heat waves shimmering
one or two inches
   above the dead grass.

    You could turn this way,
I'm also lonely
   this autumn evening.

**A HISTORICAL AND CULTURAL CONTEXT**
**Author:** Matsuo Bashō
**Time:** mid- to late 1600s
**Place:** Japan
**Development of haiku:** Bashō established the tradition of focusing the content of haiku on nature. The haiku on this page do not reflect the five-seven-five syllable pattern because they are translations from Japanese.

**992**    UNIT 9: HISTORY, CULTURE, AND THE AUTHOR

---

## DIFFERENTIATED INSTRUCTION

### FOR ENGLISH LANGUAGE LEARNERS

**Read Aloud** Read the haiku aloud. Pause after each stanza to discuss it with the class. Ask students to relate what they think each stanza is about. After discussing all of the stanzas, ask students what the haiku is about.

### FOR STRUGGLING READERS

**Develop Reading Fluency**

Read the poems aloud to convey their moods to students. Then have students work in pairs to read the Bashō and Wright haikus in alternating lines. Next, have students work in groups of three to read each complete haiku aloud. Have groups discuss how the poems should be read and what each means. Students may also listen to the selections on the *Audio Anthology CD* as a reading guide.

 **BEST PRACTICES TOOLKIT—Transparency**
Read Aloud/Think Aloud p. A34

*Jazz Player III* (1991), Louise Freshman Brown. Collage. © SuperStock

# Haiku

## RICHARD WRIGHT

From a tenement,
The blue jazz of a trumpet
Weaving autumn mists. **B**

Twisting violently,
A lost kite seeks its freedom
From telegraph wires.

Standing in the crowd
In a cold drizzling rain,—
How lonely it is. **C**

**B** HISTORICAL AND CULTURAL CONTEXT
**Author:** Richard Wright
**Time:** mid-1900s
**Place:** United States
**Evolution of haiku:** Wright uses the traditional form but adapts the content to reflect on urban life rather than nature.

COMMON CORE RL 4

**C** IRONY
The fact that Wright uses the word *lonely* even though the speaker is standing in a crowd is an example of **irony**, a contrast between expectation and reality. What meaning does this instance of irony help the poet convey to the reader?

---

Prereading for these poems is found on page 990.

## Analyze Visuals

**Activity** Which Wright haiku connects most immediately to the artwork? Explain.
*Possible answer: The first haiku. The background suggests the jazz player is playing "from a tenement." The painting's blue colors evoke the image: "The blue jazz of a trumpet."*

**About the Art** A painter and mixed-medium artist, Louise Freshman Brown has work featured in numerous U.S. and European museums and galleries. Currently, she is a professor of art at the University of North Florida, Jacksonville.

TEXT ANALYSIS — COMMON CORE RL 6

**B** HISTORICAL AND CULTURAL CONTEXT

How does Wright use the urban environment to describe a sense of loneliness?
*Possible answer: In the second haiku, Wright presents the image of a lone kite struggling against telegraph wires, an image that suggests modern technology in an urban environment. In the third haiku, the speaker seems to get lost "in the crowd."*

TEXT ANALYSIS — COMMON CORE RL 4

**C** IRONY

*Possible answer: This instance of irony conveys to the reader that even though surrounded by a crowd it is possible to feel lonely, be it because of the rain, because of being African American, etc.*

Have students list other ironies they are familiar with. Make a list of these on the board and discuss what makes each ironic.

**REVISIT THE BIG QUESTION**
## How many **WORDS** do you need?

**Discuss** What is the main idea conveyed in the third haiku? How does the concise haiku form help the speaker to reinforce this idea?
*Possible answer: The speaker appears to feel alone and insignificant in a crowd. Because the haiku is concise, the feeling is highlighted instead of buried amidst a lot of text.*

---

**FOR ADVANCED LEARNERS/PRE–AP**
**Compare and Contrast Theme** Ask students to work independently to identify and analyze the theme (or themes) conveyed by each of the three haiku by each of the three poets. Then, ask students to use a Comparison Matrix to evaluate which poet used imagery most effectively to convey those themes to readers. Have students summarize their conclusions in a one- to two-page literary analysis. Then, have students share their ideas with one another and discuss the similarities and differences in their analyses.

📋 **BEST PRACTICES TOOLKIT—Transparency** Comparison Matrix p. A24

Prereading for these poems is found on page 990.

## Analyze Visuals

**Activity** How do the two images relate to Naparstek's haiku? *Possible answer: The traffic and crowds of people both reflect images in the three haiku. They illustrate the crowded and noisy images Naparstek conveys.*

---

**TEXT ANALYSIS**

COMMON CORE

RL 6

###  Model the Skill: HISTORICAL AND CULTURAL CONTEXT

What are the poet's concerns about modern life and technology, and how do his modifications of form help express these concerns? Have students reread the information on the student page, then discuss what the changes in punctuation and capitalization say about contemporary life. *Possible answer: Whereas traditional haiku connect nature to an observation on the human condition, Naparstek adds another layer to the form by connecting modern technology to nature, which in turn offers a comment on human experience. By eliminating much of the form's capitalization and punctuation, Naparstek seems to reflect the hurried lifestyles that many 21st-century people lead.*

---

## SELECTION WRAP-UP

**READ WITH A PURPOSE** Now that students have read the haiku, have them discuss what all three have in common. *Possible answer: In addition to sharing the same line format and being about nature, they all convey the author's feelings, which include a sense of discord or unhappiness.*

⭐ **CRITIQUE** Ask students which poet's haiku they respond to more readily. Why?

### INDEPENDENT READING

For students interested in haiku, recommend *The Essential Haiku: Versions of Bashō, Buson, and Issa*, edited by Robert Hass.

---

# Honku   Aaron Naparstek

clinton street autos
honk, guzzle and burn away
our crisp, clean spring days ◉

Morning commuters
follow measured lines, honking—
    how like geese we are

When the light turns green
like a leaf on a spring wind
    the horn blows quickly

◉ **HISTORICAL AND CULTURAL CONTEXT**
**Author:** Aaron Naparstek
**Time:** early 2000s
**Place:** New York City
**Evolution of haiku:** Naparstek modifies the form by eliminating end punctuation and, sometimes, capitalization and adapts the haiku's contents to reflect concerns about modern life and technology.

---

## DIFFERENTIATED INSTRUCTION

### FOR STRUGGLING READERS

**Options for Reading** Read aloud the three "honku" by Aaron Naparstek, and discuss with students how the lack of punctuation affects the reading. Suggest that each haiku is like a poetic sentence that conveys a single thought. Then, have students practice reading the poems independently, and ask volunteers to read them aloud.

**Vocabulary Support** Discuss with students the different meanings these words can convey depending on their part of speech:

- *street*—noun; slang adjective
- *clean*—verb; adjective
- *spring*—noun; verb; adjective
- *like*—verb; conjunction

Help students use a dictionary to understand the differences in meaning.

## Comprehension

1. **Recall** What subject is common to all three of the "honku" by Aaron Naparstek?

2. **Recall** What kind of music is mentioned in the first haiku by Richard Wright?

3. **Clarify** What season is suggested in the first poem by Matsuo Bashō?

**COMMON CORE**

**RL 4** Analyze the cumulative impact of specific word choices on meaning. **RL 6** Analyze a particular point of view or cultural experience reflected in a work of world literature. **RL 10** Read and comprehend poems.

## Text Analysis

4. **Interpret Imagery** Review the chart in which you analyzed the imagery in the haiku. How do the three poets differ in the kinds of imagery they use and the moods they create?

5. **Compare and Contrast Word Choice** Notice the use of verbs in all three sets of poems. Which two sets are the most similar? different? How do the verbs affect the messages of the poems? Explain your answer.

6. **Evaluate Figurative Language** In **personification,** an animal, object, or idea is given human attributes. Identify three examples of personification in these poems, and explain how each strengthens or weakens the writer's message.

7. **Recognize Cultural and Historical Context** For each poet, write a brief summary of how his cultural and historical background may have influenced the images and themes in the haiku.

8. **Analyze Poetic Form** In **haiku,** the image presented is often symbolic of a greater truth or meaning. In the second haiku by Richard Wright, what does the kite trapped in the wires symbolize? Explain your answer, citing evidence from the text.

9. **Interpret Ambiguity** When a situation can be interpreted in more than one way, it has the quality of ambiguity. In the first haiku by Bashō, note the ambiguity in the first two lines. Who is walking around the pond—the moon, the speaker, or both? Explain your answer.

10. **Evaluate** Matsuo Bashō wrote his haiku in the 1600s. Do the poems seem dated, or are they timeless? Explain your answer.

## Text Criticism

11. **Critical Interpretations** Author Aaron Naparstek says that "haiku poems are sort of the perfect little sound bytes. They fit our culture." Using what you know about the haiku and about American culture, explain what Naparstek might mean by that statement. How do the characteristics of the haiku seem well suited to contemporary American culture?

> **How many WORDS do you need?**
>
> Is it possible to express oneself thoroughly without being wordy? Explain.

7. ● **COMMON CORE FOCUS** *Recognize Cultural and Historical Context* Bashō's poems reflect a stillness that might be inspired by his practice of Zen Buddhism. Wright's poems reflect life in the urban setting in which he lived. Naparstek wrote his poems in response to the frustrations of urban living.

8. ● **COMMON CORE FOCUS** *Analyze Poetic Form* The kite symbolizes the desire to escape from the modern world.

9. *Students should support answers with words from the poem.*

10. *Students' answers will vary.*

## Text Criticism

*Possible answer:*

11. *Naparstek is referring to our modern attention span: we only have patience to digest short messages. Like sound bytes, the "honku" are simple and to the point.*

> **How many WORDS do you need?** Make sure students explain their reasoning.

# Practice and Apply

For preliminary support of post-reading questions, use these copy masters:

**R** **RESOURCE MANAGER**—Copy Masters
Historical and Cultural Context p. 129
Question Support p. 133

Additional selection questions are provided for teachers on page 125.

## ANSWERS

## Comprehension

1. *The three "honku" are all about cars honking in city traffic.*

2. *Wright mentions jazz in the first haiku.*

3. *Autumn is suggested in Bashō's first poem.*

## Text Analysis

**COMMON CORE** RL 4, RL 6, RL 10

*Possible answers:*

4. ■ **COMMON CORE FOCUS** *Interpret Imagery* *Bashō uses natural imagery to create a wistful, solitary mood. Wright uses urban and natural imagery to create a similar mood. Naparstek uses noisy urban imagery to create a wistful mood.*

5. *The verbs in Bashō's and Wright's poems are more similar. They end in -ing and describe movement in nature. Both reflect the poems' messages of solitude. Naparstek's poems use harsh verbs that convey a distaste for aspects of urban life.*

6. *Bashō describes the moon "walking" all night, which adds to the sense of loneliness. Wright's kite seeking freedom suggests human desire to escape technology. The "behavior" of Naparstek's cars reinforces modernization's negative aspects.*

# Assess and Reteach

## Assess

**DIAGNOSTIC AND SELECTION TESTS**
Selection Test A, B/C pp. 271–272, 273–274

**Interactive Selection Test** on **thinkcentral.com**

## Reteach

**Level Up Online Tutorials** on **thinkcentral.com**

**Reteaching Worksheets** on **thinkcentral.com**
Literature Lessons 13, 28

# Focus and Motivate

....... COMMON CORE FOCUS

**W 2a–f** Write informative/explanatory texts to convey complex information. **W 4** Produce clear and coherent writing. **W 5** Develop and strengthen writing by revising, rewriting, or trying a new approach. **W 6** Use technology to produce and publish individual writing products. **W 7** Conduct short research projects to answer a question. **W 8** Follow a standard format for citation. **W 9b (RI 1)** Draw evidence from informative texts to support analysis. **SL 5** Make strategic use of digital media to enhance understanding and add interest. **L 1b** Use various types of phrases and clauses to convey specific meanings. **L 2** Demonstrate command of the conventions of standard English capitalization, punctuation, and spelling. **L 3a** Conform to guidelines in a style manual.

## WRITE WITH A PURPOSE

To help students understand the purpose, have them brainstorm reasons that people read articles online. Reinforce the idea that their purpose is to provide information about an interesting topic.

## COMMON CORE TRAITS

Review the three **COMMON CORE TRAITS** with students, focusing on the development of ideas. Compare the list of traits with the rubric on page 1003.

## ADDITIONAL TASKS

**Write About a Career** Write an online feature article that explores training for a career that interests you.
**Possible topics:** music, health care, technology

**Write About Geography** Write an online feature article about a dream vacation destination. Learn all you can about the people and geography of the area.
**Possible topics:** cycling through Europe; climbing Mount Kilimanjaro

### Writing Online  THINK central

The following tools are available online at **thinkcentral.com** and on **WriteSmart CD-ROM:**
• Interactive Graphic Organizers
• Interactive Student Models
• Interactive Revision Lessons

---

## Writing Workshop
**INFORMATIVE TEXT**

# Online Feature Article

In this unit, you learned about author Frank McCourt, the Harlem Renaissance, and the impact of President John F. Kennedy's assassination. If you wanted to find out more about these topics, you might turn to the World Wide Web to access a vast network of information. Now, you will add to this network by creating an **online feature article**—an informative piece of writing on an interesting topic or trend.

Complete the workshop activities in your **Reader/Writer Notebook.**

### WRITE WITH A PURPOSE

**WRITING TASK**

Write an **online feature article** that informs your audience about a topic that interests you.

**Idea Starters**
• What are the effects of global warming?
• How can someone research family heritage?
• What was the role of music in the Harlem Renaissance?
• What does it take to earn a black belt in karate?
• What is the history of haiku poetry?

**THE ESSENTIALS**

Here are some common purposes, audiences, and formats for informative/explanatory writing.

| PURPOSES | AUDIENCES | FORMATS |
|---|---|---|
| • to increase readers' knowledge of a subject<br>• to help readers understand a procedure or process<br>• to develop and maintain an online readership | • classmates and teacher<br>• community members<br>• friends on a social networking site<br>• online communities with an interest in your subject | • wiki article<br>• podcast<br>• news report<br>• magazine article<br>• how-to article<br>• encyclopedia entry |

### COMMON CORE TRAITS

**1. DEVELOPMENT OF IDEAS**
• introduces a topic in a compelling way and states a **controlling idea**
• develops the topic and supports it with **evidence,** such as **relevant facts, details,** and **quotations**
• provides a **concluding section** that supports the information

**2. ORGANIZATION OF IDEAS**
• **logically organizes** complex ideas, concepts, and information
• includes **formatting, links, graphics,** and **multimedia** to support the information
• uses **varied transitions** to create cohesion and connect ideas
• **cites and links to sources**

**3. LANGUAGE FACILITY AND CONVENTIONS**
• uses **precise language** and **domain-specific vocabulary**
• maintains a **formal style** and **objective tone**
• reflects **correct grammar, mechanics,** and **spelling**

**Writing Online**

 Go to **thinkcentral.com.**
KEYWORD: HML9N-996

---

## Writing Workshop Resources

**R RESOURCE MANAGER UNIT 9**
Plan and Teach pp. 135–138
Prewriting–Editing pp. 139–143
Technology p. 144
Writing Support p. 145*

**TECHNOLOGY**
🖫 **Teacher One Stop DVD-ROM**
🖫 **Student One Stop DVD-ROM**
🖫 **WriteSmart CD-ROM**
🖫 **GrammarNotes DVD-ROM**

**Writing Center on thinkcentral.com**
*Print resources are on the **Teacher One Stop DVD-ROM** and on **thinkcentral.com.***

\* Resources for Differentiation

## Planning/Prewriting

 **COMMON CORE** **W 2a-f** Write informative/explanatory texts to convey complex information. **W 6** Use technology to produce and publish individual writing products. **W 7** Conduct short research projects to answer a question.

### Getting Started

#### CHOOSE A TOPIC

Your article should be about something that interests you and that you think will interest others. With a small group of classmates, brainstorm possible topics. Try to frame each topic as a **research question** that could guide your search. (See the Idea Starters on the previous page for samples.) When you think you have a good topic idea, do a preliminary search online to see if you can find enough information about it. Make sure your topic isn't so broad that you can't cover it well in a short article.

▶ **TIPS FOR GENERATING TOPIC IDEAS:**

- Look for topics in the news.
- Review your class notes for topics that touch on an interest you have.
- Consider interests, sports, or hobbies you pursue outside of school.
- Visit blogs and wikis your teacher recommends to see what other students are writing about.

#### THINK ABOUT AUDIENCE AND PURPOSE

As you begin to research your topic, think about your **purpose** and **audience**. Understanding your audience will help you to consider what information to include in your article, as well as where to post your final product. Consider online forums that are popular with your audience and that your teacher approves of.

▶ **ASK YOURSELF:**

- Who would be most interested in my topic?
- What does my audience probably already know (or think they know) about my topic?
- What background information will they need?
- What **domain-specific,** or specialized, terms may be unfamiliar to them?
- What site could host my article?

#### FIND SOURCES

With your research question as your guide, look for sources in your school and local libraries and on the Web. Since you will post your article online, try to find Web sources with photos, audio, or video that you might link to or obtain permission to include. (Remember that you may not publish someone else's copyrighted material without permission.)

Keep track of each source, recording the title, author, and page number or Web address. Add notes to help you remember what kind of information the source includes.

**See pages 1292–1335** for more information on locating and evaluating potential sources.

▶ **WHAT DOES IT LOOK LIKE?**

| Sources | Comments |
|---|---|
| Book: <u>Black Music in the Harlem Renaissance</u> by Samuel A. Floyd | includes 10 essays |
| Web site: PBS.org http://www.pbs.org/jazz-z/index.htm | good background information and lots of musician biographies (see Ellington, Gillespie, and Holiday) includes audio clips |
| Web site: Library of Congress http://memory.loc.gov/ammem/wghtml/wghome.html | has some great images of musicians |

---

## DIFFERENTIATED INSTRUCTION

### FOR ENGLISH LANGUAGE LEARNERS

**Language: Reinforce Terms** Write these terms on the board and review them with students:

- *research:* careful study and investigation in a topic to find information
- *sources:* works that supply information, such as books and Web sites
- *link:* highlighted or underlined words or phrases on a Web page that connect to a new Web page or different Web site

- *storyboard:* a drawing that shows how text features, words, and images will be organized in an online feature article
- *navigate:* to move from one section of an online feature article to another
- *multimedia:* different forms of media, such as video, photographs, and music, used together to communicate information

---

## Teach

### Planning/ Prewriting

**COMMON CORE W 2a-f, W 6, W 7**

▶ **CHOOSE A TOPIC** To help students develop a research question, ask them to answer these questions:

- What is my topic?
- What do I hope to learn about my topic?
- What is my research question?

Tell students they should not be able to answer their research questions with a single word. Their questions should require investigation.

▶ **THINK ABOUT AUDIENCE AND PURPOSE** Emphasize that readers of online feature articles want to read about a writer's original and interesting ideas and the sources that support them. Point out that their audience's needs may require students to cover certain additional aspects of their topic before discussing others. For example, if students write about a current trend in music, their readers may need to know about earlier trends that contributed to its development.

▶ **FIND SOURCES** Encourage students to link to both primary and secondary sources in their articles. Remind them that primary sources, such as letters, diaries, and videos, contain original firsthand information. Secondary sources provide other people's interpretation of primary material. Examples include news articles, documentaries, and biographies.

**R** RESOURCE MANAGER—Copy Masters
Planning/Prewriting p. 139
Drafting p. 140
Revising and Editing pp. 141–142
Ask a Peer Reader p. 143
Writing Support p. 145

## Planning/Prewriting continued

▶ **COLLECT AND SYNTHESIZE INFORMATION**
Encourage students to follow these steps to synthesize their sources:

1. Find the main idea of each source.

2. Look for supporting evidence in each source. A relevant source should include statistics, example, anecdotes, or quotations.

3. Compare and contrast the ideas in each source.

4. Make connections between the ideas in each source and to what you already know.

▶ **DRAFT A CONTROLLING IDEA** Point out to students that there are many possible thesis statements for the same topic and that their controlling idea may change as they complete their research. Encourage students to revisit and rework their controlling ideas as they organize and begin to draft their online articles.

▶ **GENERATE A STORYBOARD** Encourage students to produce several versions of their storyboards. Have them consult with a partner to decide which storyboard is most effective. Tell students that, just like their controlling ideas, their storyboards may evolve as they begin to draft their online articles.

**YOUR TURN** Direct students to pause periodically to critique their progress and to refocus their storyboards. Tell them that they may discover that they need additional sources or evidence for a particular point.

For interactive graphic organizers, see

⊘ **Write*Smart* CD-ROM**

**Writing Center on thinkcentral.com**

---

## Planning/Prewriting *continued*

### Getting Started

**COLLECT AND SYNTHESIZE INFORMATION**

Use a graphic organizer to record evidence—facts, details, quotations, examples, and multimedia—that is **relevant** (related) to your research question. As you take notes, look for opportunities to synthesize information. When you **synthesize,** you make connections using a variety of sources and prior knowledge in order to draw original conclusions about your topic.

▶ **WHAT DOES IT LOOK LIKE?**

| "It seems unlikely that any other musical début has carried such hope of repairing divisions: between jazz and classical, between black and white." *Black, Brown, and Beige* | Gillespie refused to replace his white pianist with a black one to comply with a segregation law. Musicians' contracts soon included a clause to protect them from losing money in such situations. *To Be, or Not...To Bop* |

↓

Seems like the music of this time helped unify blacks and whites despite discrimination.

**DRAFT A CONTROLLING IDEA**

Craft a **controlling idea,** or thesis statement, as an answer to your research question. Your controlling idea should identify what you want your audience to understand about your topic. Modify or refine the idea as you draft.

**WHAT DOES IT LOOK LIKE?**

During the Harlem Renaissance, jazz music helped erode the segregation line. Three musicians, Duke Ellington, Dizzy Gillespie, and Billie Holiday, were at the forefront of this shift.

**GENERATE A STORYBOARD**

Create a storyboard to outline your information.
- Use **text features,** such as a title, headings, and links, to break up the writing and make it easier to read and navigate.
- Decide where to include multimedia.
- Avoid overcrowding your screens.

**WHAT DOES IT LOOK LIKE?**

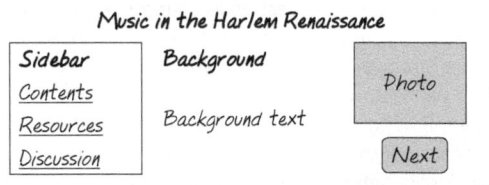

**PEER REVIEW** Exchange storyboards with a classmate. Review controlling ideas and ask: What related questions do you expect my article to answer? Does the information seem easy to navigate?

**YOUR TURN** List possible research questions in your *Reader/Writer Notebook*. Focus on the question that interests you most and that you can find information about. Gather your sources and research. Synthesize the information and draft a controlling idea. Create a storyboard to plan your article.

---

## DIFFERENTIATED INSTRUCTION

### FOR ENGLISH LANGUAGE LEARNERS

**Writing: Controlling Ideas** Have students use these sentence starters to help them develop their controlling ideas and support:

- The topic of my article is _____.

- My article will explain _____, _____, and _____ about my topic.

- I want readers to understand _____ when they read my article.

### FOR STRUGGLING WRITERS

**Storyboards** Bring in printed copies of an online feature article. Have students work with partners to study the structure, organization, and navigation of the article. If possible, use the computers in your classroom or school computer lab to have students view live online feature articles. Encourage students to model their storyboards after the online article they found most effective.

# Drafting

**COMMON CORE**

**W 4** Produce clear and coherent writing. **W 8** Follow a standard format for citation. **W 9b (RI 1)** Draw evidence from informative texts to support ideas. **L 3a** Conform to guidelines in a style manual.

The following chart shows a structure for organizing a **coherent,** or easy to follow, online feature article.

## Organizing Your Online Feature Article

### INTRODUCTION

- Grab your audience's attention with a **compelling quotation** or **question.**
- Supply enough **background** for readers to understand the topic.
- Include a clear **controlling idea,** or thesis statement.
- Establish a **formal style** by using an **objective tone,** or attitude, and **precise language.**

### BODY

- Clearly state your **main ideas,** making sure each idea relates to your controlling idea.
- Include **well-organized facts, details, quotations,** and **multimedia** to support your ideas.
- Document the **source** of each idea. See pages 1314–1335 for information on citations.
- Use varied **transitions** to logically group ideas.
- Rely on **text features,** such as headings and links, to help readers navigate the information.

### CONCLUDING SECTION

- Restate your **controlling idea,** and describe the significance of your topic.

## GRAMMAR IN CONTEXT: INCORPORATING QUOTATIONS

When you quote someone else's work, make sure to cite your source, both in the running text of your article and in the Works Cited section. Use these guidelines to help you.

- Place opening and closing quotation marks around someone else's direct words.
- Integrate short quotations into your own sentences.
- Use ellipses in place of words you want to omit from the quotation.
- Put the author's last name and the page number of the quote in parentheses at the end of the sentence. If you mention the author, include only the page number, as shown here.
- Link your in-text citation to your Works Cited section.

> Though Gillespie struggled against segregation, he recognized that "most of the people who come to see me perform are white. . . . I'll never turn my back on my brothers, but neither will I turn my back on my livelihood and the people who dig my music" (446).

See pages 1334–1335 for Modern Language Association guidelines for creating a Works Cited list.

**YOUR TURN**

Develop a draft of your article in a word-processing document. Integrate and punctuate your quotations. Using your storyboard as a guide, input text into the online forum you chose. Add multimedia and links as appropriate.

---

# Practice and Apply

## Drafting

**COMMON CORE W 4, W 8, W 9b (RI1), L3a**

▶ **INTRODUCTION** Tell students to think about why they chose their topics in the first place. What questions prompted them to choose the topic? What did they already know that made them want to learn more? Encourage students to use their own motivations as a starting point for their introductions.

▶ **BODY** Remind students to use their storyboards as they draft their article. Students need to produce drafts for each Web screen noted on their storyboards.

▶ **CONCLUDING SECTION** Remind students that their concluding sections must include a Works Cited list for all of the sources, print and nonprint, that they credit in their articles.

### GRAMMAR IN CONTEXT: INCORPORATING QUOTATIONS

Give students these additional guidelines for incorporating quotations:

- Set quotations shorter than four lines within your own sentence, using quotation marks.
- Longer quotations should be introduced in your own words, followed by a colon. Set the quotation after the colon in block form: an indented paragraph without quotation marks.

**YOUR TURN**

Ask students to complete the **Your Turn** activity independently. Suggest that students write their drafts double-spaced so that they can make revisions easily later.

For interactive revision tools, see

 **Write*Smart* CD-ROM**

**Writing Center on thinkcentral.com**

---

### FOR ENGLISH LANGUAGE LEARNERS

**Writing: Quotations** Students may benefit from seeing more examples of quotations set within sentences or in block form. Provide students with examples taken from print or online articles or interviews. Have students work in pairs to read the articles or interviews and to identify the quotations and how they are used. Tell students to use their marked copies of the articles as models when they incorporate quotations in their own articles.

### FOR STRUGGLING WRITERS

**Integrate Quotations** Place a variety of quotations from informational works on note cards. Have each student take turns drawing one quotation from a box. Tell students to asses the length of their quotations to determine how they should be incorporated into text. Then, have students incorporate their quotations into their own writing, using quotation marks, ellipses, or indentations as appropriate. Check students' work for accuracy.

## Revising

**COMMON CORE** W 2a, W 5, SL 5

***Model the Skill*** Using a draft feature article on a transparency or electronic whiteboard, model how to use the questions, tips, and strategies suggested in the chart to evaluate and revise. Consider using a feature article written by a student from a different class or from a previous year. Be sure to remove the writer's name from the article so that the writer remains anonymous.

**YOUR TURN** Remind peer reviewers to offer constructive comments to their partners. Suggest that as students read each other's drafts, they jot down several "What if . . .?" questions. For example, students might ask "What if your last sentence in this paragraph became your first?" or "What if you added a quotation to support your point?"

For interactive revision tools, see

💿 **Write*Smart* CD-ROM**

**Writing Center on** thinkcentral.com

## Revising

As you revise the content, organization, and style of your article, make sure that all the information you included supports your controlling idea. The following chart will help you revise and and rewrite the parts of your draft that need reworking.

### ONLINE FEATURE ARTICLE

| Ask Yourself | Tips | Revision Strategies |
|---|---|---|
| 1. Do my opening lines grab the reader's attention? | ▶ **Underline** the opening lines. | ▶ **Add** a compelling quotation or a question to engage the audience. |
| 2. Is my controlling idea clear and appropriate to my audience and purpose? | ▶ **Underline** the controlling idea. | ▶ **Add** a controlling idea if one is missing. **Rework** the existing one to clearly state the main idea of your article. |
| 3. Is my organization logical, effective, and easy to navigate? | ▶ **Circle** headings, links, and menu options. | ▶ **Group** related paragraphs under boldfaced headings. **Add** more links to your menu to allow users to jump to different sections of your article. |
| 4. Did I include relevant evidence to support my controlling idea? | ▶ **Highlight** text or multimedia that doesn't support your controlling idea. | ▶ **Delete** extraneous information. **Add** details for any ideas that are not supported. |
| 5. Are all my sources documented correctly? See pages 1314–1335 for additional support with documenting sources. | ▶ **Underline** each piece of evidence. **Place a check mark** next to each corresponding citation and Works Cited entry. | ▶ **Add** in-text citations and/or Works Cited entries for supporting evidence that lacks check marks. |
| 6. Does my concluding section follow from and support the information I presented? | ▶ **Put a check mark** next to the section that summarizes what you learned about your controlling idea. | ▶ **Insert** sentences that describe the importance of the topic. |

**YOUR TURN** **PEER REVIEW** Have a peer use this chart to evaluate your online article. Ask the following: Do I have a clear, well-supported controlling idea? What questions do you still have about my topic? Is my use of multimedia effective or distracting? Is my article easy to navigate?

---

## DIFFERENTIATED INSTRUCTION

### FOR ENGLISH LANGUAGE LEARNERS

**Writing: Concluding Section** Provide students with sentence frames such as these to help them develop insights they can share in their conclusions:

- In my article about _____, I have shown that _____.

- The topic of _____ is important to me because _____.

- I learned _____ about my topic.

### FOR ADVANCED LEARNERS/PRE–AP

**Analyze Concluding Sections** Have students read the concluding sections of each source (or selected sources) that they are using in their feature articles. Then challenge them to write a brief description of the strategies that each writer used. Suggest that students use the descriptions as a source of ideas when they write their own concluding paragraphs. Work with students to prepare a format for sharing the strategies with the class.

## ANALYZE A STUDENT DRAFT

Read this draft; notice the comments on its strengths as well as suggestions for improvement.

COMMON CORE

**W 2a** Include formatting, graphics, and multimedia to aid comprehension. **W 5** Develop and strengthen writing by revising, rewriting, or trying a new approach. **SL 5** Make strategic use of digital media to enhance understanding and add interest.

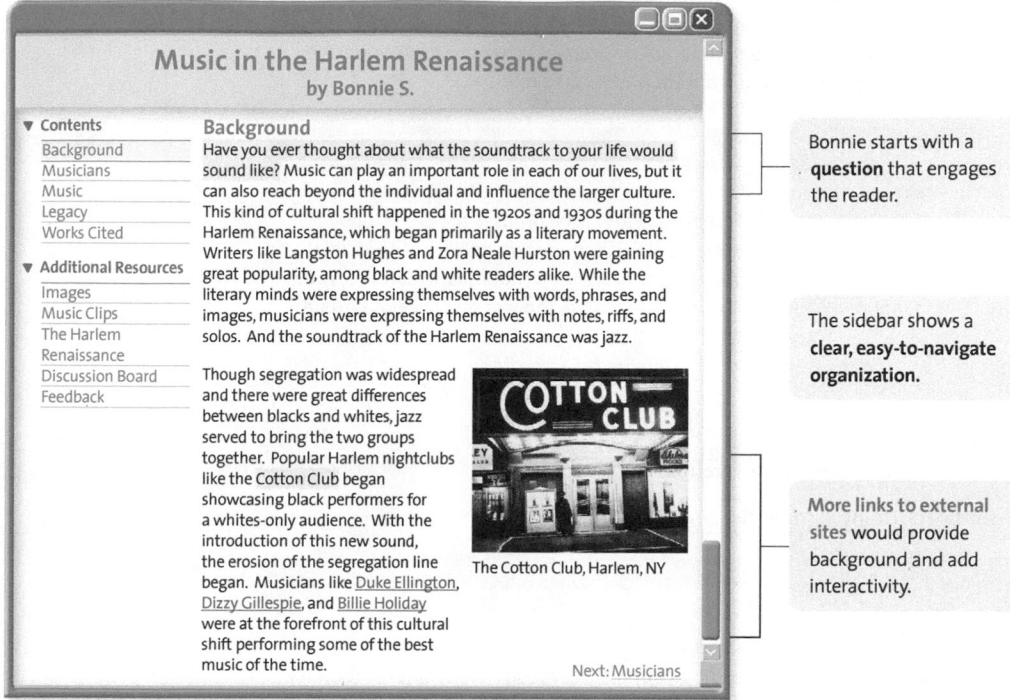

### Music in the Harlem Renaissance
by Bonnie S.

▼ Contents
Background
Musicians
Music
Legacy
Works Cited

▼ Additional Resources
Images
Music Clips
The Harlem Renaissance
Discussion Board
Feedback

**Background**

Have you ever thought about what the soundtrack to your life would sound like? Music can play an important role in each of our lives, but it can also reach beyond the individual and influence the larger culture. This kind of cultural shift happened in the 1920s and 1930s during the Harlem Renaissance, which began primarily as a literary movement. Writers like Langston Hughes and Zora Neale Hurston were gaining great popularity, among black and white readers alike. While the literary minds were expressing themselves with words, phrases, and images, musicians were expressing themselves with notes, riffs, and solos. And the soundtrack of the Harlem Renaissance was jazz.

Though segregation was widespread and there were great differences between blacks and whites, jazz served to bring the two groups together. Popular Harlem nightclubs like the Cotton Club began showcasing black performers for a whites-only audience. With the introduction of this new sound, the erosion of the segregation line began. Musicians like Duke Ellington, Dizzy Gillespie, and Billie Holiday were at the forefront of this cultural shift performing some of the best music of the time.

The Cotton Club, Harlem, NY

Next: Musicians

Bonnie starts with a **question** that engages the reader.

The sidebar shows a **clear, easy-to-navigate organization.**

More links to external sites would provide background and add interactivity.

**LEARN HOW** Link to External Web Sites  Bonnie mentions terms, people, and places that may not be familiar to her audience.  She can strengthen her writing by linking to **reliable,** or trustworthy, external sites to provide extended definitions and background information.

---

**BONNIE'S REVISION TO** *BACKGROUND*

Popular Harlem nightclubs like the Cotton Club began showcasing black performers for a whites-only audience. . . .
*link to online encyclopedia entry for Cotton Club*

---

 **YOUR TURN**  Use the feedback you received as well as the "Learn How" lesson to revise your article.  Evaluate your use of multimedia and online text features.  Consider trying a new approach if something is simply not working.

---

## FOR ENGLISH LANGUAGE LEARNERS

**Links to External Web Sites**  To make sure students understand how a link in an online article works, use the computers in your classroom or school computer lab to have students view live online feature articles. Explain that writers sometimes link to other pages or sections within the article. At other times they may link to completely different, or external, Web sites.

Read through an online article with students, pausing to click on links as you encounter them. Lead them in a discussion of what each link adds to that particular point in the article. Finally,  have students work with a partner to determine the best places to include external links within their own articles.

---

## ANALYZE A STUDENT DRAFT

Explain that the Student Draft on this page is the first screen of an online feature article. Model reading the draft and the annotations in blue, explaining that the yellow highlighting illustrates the student's language choices. Explain that the *Learn How* mini-lesson has helpful information about a way to improve the student draft as well as their own.

**LEARN HOW**  Link to External Web Sites

- Tell students that links to external Web sites can add richness to their articles by providing additional information and by adding interactivity.

- Have students read through their drafts, looking for places that could benefit from links to external Web sites.

- Remind students to link only to reliable and relevant Web sites. Suggest they look through their source material and Works Cited lists for possible links.

 **YOUR TURN**  Have students complete the **Your Turn** independently. Tell students to review their drafts to make sure they have provided enough background information about their topic and have incorporated quotations appropriately. Tell students to place asterisks in the margins next to places that could be improved by a link to an external Web site.

For interactive revision tools, see

**Write*Smart* CD-ROM**

**Writing Center on <u>thinkcentral.com</u>**

## Editing and Publishing

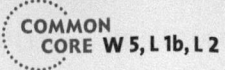 COMMON CORE W 5, L 1b, L 2

### GRAMMAR IN CONTEXT: PARTICIPIAL PHRASES

For practice, have students identify the misplaced participial phrases in the sentences below. Then, have students revise the sentences.

1. The boys were looking for squirrels <u>searching the trees</u>. *(The boys were searching the trees looking for squirrels.)*

2. <u>Buried inside her backpack</u>, Connie tried to find the trail map. *(Connie tried to find the trail map buried inside her backpack.)*

3. Raul found a wallet <u>walking to school</u>. *(Walking to school, Raul found a wallet.)*

### PUBLISH YOUR WRITING

Brainstorm with students about additional ways to publish their online feature articles.

 **YOUR TURN** Allow time for students to proofread their drafts. Remind them to check for misplaced participial phrases.

---

## Editing and Publishing

 COMMON CORE

**W 5** Strengthen writing by editing.
**L 1b** Use various types of phrases and clauses to convey specific meanings.
**L 2** Demonstrate command of the conventions of standard English capitalization, punctuation, and spelling.

In the editing stage, you proofread your article to eliminate grammar, spelling, and punctuation errors. These errors might distract readers from understanding and appreciating your ideas. You also need to make sure all your online features work correctly. Before you launch your article, check your links and make sure all multimedia elements function properly. Consider whether the fonts you have chosen are appropriate for your content and easy to read.

### GRAMMAR IN CONTEXT: PARTICIPIAL PHRASES

A **participle** is a verb form that functions as an adjective. Like adjectives, participles modify nouns and pronouns. **Participial phrases** are participles with all their modifiers and complements. It's important to keep a participial phrase as close as possible to the noun or pronoun it modifies; otherwise, your intended meaning may not be clear. For example, the last sentence of Bonnie's Background section is confusing. The sentence makes it sound like the cultural shift was performing music. Here is Bonnie's revision of the sentence.

> Musicians like <u>Duke Ellington</u>, <u>Dizzy Gillespie</u>, and <u>Billie Holiday</u>, were at the forefront of this cultural shift performing some of the best music of the time.

### PUBLISH YOUR WRITING

After you have finished proofreading your article, you are ready to post it online. In addition, consider these ideas:

- Send an e-mail notifying your audience that your article is ready for viewing.
- Update your status on any social networking sites you participate on to include a link to your article.
- Create a class menu of feature articles on the site that's hosting your work. Group related articles under boldfaced headings, and include links to everyone's article.

 **YOUR TURN** Correct any errors in your article. Make sure to correctly place participial phrases. After you've applied these finishing touches, publish your online feature article for your audience.

---

## DIFFERENTIATED INSTRUCTION

### FOR ENGLISH LANGUAGE LEARNERS

**Language: Participles** Students may need practice in identifying and using participles. First, list the verbs *jump, howl, march, polish, iron,* and *trust* on the board. Ask student to add -ing to the first three verbs and -ed to the last three verbs. Then, have students use these newly formed participles to modify nouns of their choosing. *(**Possible responses:** jumping frogs, howling dogs, marching band, polished floor, ironed shirt, trusted friend)*

### FOR STRUGGLING WRITERS

**Punctuate Participial Phrases** Review with students the punctuation rules concerning participial phrases.

- A participial phrase at the beginning of a sentence is always followed by a comma. *(**Example:** Barking loudly, the dogs approached the door.)*

- When the participial phrase is in the middle of the sentence and is essential to the meaning of the sentence, no commas are

# Scoring Rubric

Use this rubric to evaluate your online feature article.

## ONLINE FEATURE ARTICLE

| SCORE | COMMON CORE TRAITS |
|---|---|
| **6** | • **Development** Effectively introduces a topic; states a well-researched controlling idea; develops the topic with relevant, varied evidence; ends powerfully<br>• **Organization** Logically organizes information; includes formatting and multimedia that enhances the information; uses varied transitions; correctly cites sources<br>• **Language** Ably uses precise words; maintains a formal style and objective tone; shows a strong command of conventions |
| **5** | • **Development** Competently introduces a topic; states a controlling idea; offers relevant evidence; has a strong concluding section<br>• **Organization** Is logically organized; includes formatting and multimedia; uses transitions; correctly cites sources<br>• **Language** Uses precise words; generally maintains a formal style and neutral tone; has a few errors in conventions |
| **4** | • **Development** Sufficiently introduces a topic; states a controlling idea; offers mostly relevant evidence; has an adequate concluding section<br>• **Organization** Is mostly logically organized; could use some more formatting and multimedia; needs a few more transitions; cites most sources<br>• **Language** Uses vague words in some places; mostly maintains a formal style and objective tone; includes a few distracting errors in conventions |
| **3** | • **Development** States a controlling idea, but the introduction could be more compelling; lacks enough evidence; has a somewhat weak concluding section<br>• **Organization** Has some flaws in organization; doesn't include enough formatting and multimedia; lacks many transitions; does not cite all sources<br>• **Language** Needs more precise words; has frequent lapses in style and tone; has some critical errors in conventions |
| **2** | • **Development** Has a weak controlling idea; does not support most ideas; ends abruptly<br>• **Organization** Has organizational flaws; lacks formatting and multimedia; lacks transitions throughout; neglects to cite many sources<br>• **Language** Lacks precise words or uses them incorrectly; uses an informal style and tone; has many distracting errors in conventions |
| **1** | • **Development** Lacks a controlling idea; offers little, if any, development; has no ending<br>• **Organization** Has no organization, formatting, or multimedia; plagiarizes or does not credit sources<br>• **Language** Uses vague words; has an inappropriate style and tone; has major problems in conventions |

## Scoring Rubric

Tell students that the best way to understand a scoring rubric is to use it to evaluate an actual piece of writing. Provide students with a model online feature article. Tell students to evaluate the article using the rubric. Then have them write a brief paragraph using the language of the rubric to explain the reasons for their score.

For Rubric Bank, see

 **Write*Smart* CD-ROM**

**Writing Center** on <u>thinkcentral.com</u>

---

needed. (***Example:*** *The books stored in the attic were my grandfather's.*)

• When the participial phrase is in the middle of the sentence and it is not essential to the meaning of the sentence, it is set off by commas. (***Example:*** *Uncle Bob, whistling a tune, just left for work.*)

# Focus and Motivate

## COMMON CORE FOCUS

**W 6** Use technology to update individual writing products, link to other information, and display information flexibly and dynamically. **SL 1c** Pose and respond to questions. **SL 5** Make strategic use of digital media in presentations.

## PRODUCE WITH A PURPOSE

Encourage students to review their online feature articles regularly in order to keep them fresh and updated. Remind students that online articles are a work-in-progress. Poor links and navigation errors can affect the credibility of their work. Have students test all the links in their articles to ensure their relevancy.

## COMMON CORE TRAITS

As students update their online feature articles, have them keep in mind the *COMMON CORE TRAITS* of a successful online article.

# Practice and Apply

## Maintaining Your Article

### Model the Skill: RESPOND TO FEEDBACK

Students may struggle to maintain objectivity when reading comments posted to their online feature articles. Help students distinguish between strong criticisms and inappropriate comments. Advise students to make prompt and respectful replies to feedback as needed. Replies to some questions or comments may require research. If so, direct students to let the reader know they have read the comment and will make a complete reply as soon as possible.

**GUIDED PRACTICE** Have students write a comment about a partner's article. Then, have his or her partner draft a sample response. Call on volunteers to share their comments and responses.

**R** RESOURCE MANAGER—Copy Master
Technology p. 144

---

## Technology Workshop

**Essential Course of Study ECOS**

# Updating an Online Feature Article

The World Wide Web is constantly changing; every second, content is added, updated, reorganized, or removed to accommodate new information and ideas. As the author of an online feature article, you are responsible for maintaining your published work in the same way. If you want readers to view your article as a reliable source, you need to make sure it isn't outdated. In this workshop, you will learn how to effectively update, improve, and enhance your online article.

 Complete the workshop activities in your **Reader/Writer Notebook**.

| PRODUCE WITH A PURPOSE | COMMON CORE TRAITS |
| --- | --- |
| **TASK**<br><br>**Update your online feature article** to provide new information on your topic, address issues of design and navigation, and replace dead (broken) links. | **A SUCCESSFUL UPDATE . . .**<br><br>• replaces dead links and out-of-date information<br>• responds promptly and respectfully to readers' comments and feedback<br>• adds or revises content to address new information about the topic<br>• modifies design or navigation when appropriate<br>• increases readership by seeking new audiences and drawing return visitors |

## COMMON CORE

**W 6** Use technology to update individual writing products, link to other information, and display information flexibly and dynamically. **SL 1c** Pose and respond to questions. **SL 5** Make strategic use of digital media in presentations.

## Maintaining Your Article

After publishing your article online, visit the site frequently and spend a few minutes maintaining it. Use these guidelines to help you:

- **Update Your Links** The creators of the external Web sources you linked to may update the information and structure of their sites. For this reason, you should check each link to make sure the Web address, or URL, you used is still functional and connects to the information you intended. If you find any incorrect or dead links, update them to reflect the correct URL, find suitable replacements, or remove the links from the article.

- **Respond to Comments** If you have provided a way for readers to give feedback on your article, make sure to read everything that's posted. Address any comments or requests for information with respectful responses. Be on the lookout for inappropriate comments and remove them as quickly as possible.

- **Add a *Last Updated* Date** Include a line of text that provides the date you last updated the article. This lets your readers know how recent the information is and that you are committed to keeping it current.

**Media Tools**

**THINK central**

Go to thinkcentral.com.
KEYWORD: HML9N-1004

---

## DIFFERENTIATED INSTRUCTION

### FOR ENGLISH LANGUAGE LEARNERS

**Language: Reinforce Technology Terms**
Write these terms on the board and review them with students:

- *World Wide Web:* a system of linked documents that people access through the Internet

- *link:* highlighted or underlined words or phrases on a Web page that connect to a new Web page or different Web site

- *dead link:* highlighted words or phrases or images on a Web page that do not connect to anything

- *forum:* discussion site on the World Wide Web

- *URL:* universal resource locator, or the address of a Web site

## Modifying and Improving Your Article

Part of updating an online article is modifying or improving it as you receive feedback and learn more about your topic. Making improvements can add dimension to your article, attract new readers, and encourage readers to return.

You might modify your article for a variety of reasons, such as:

- **To Add Content** The information you included may be outdated, or new material may be available. Incorporate new content by revising the article or adding new links. If you have chosen a topic about something that changes frequently (such as the latest music technologies), you might consider adding a Recent News or Updates section. Subscribing to a Web feed is a good way to stay current on your topic.

- **To Address User Feedback** Readers may offer feedback about a range of things, such as the accuracy of your facts, the design of your site, or the navigational features you incorporate. Be willing to revise your work, or even try a new approach, to address valid reader feedback.

- **To Redesign Your Article** Trying a new design approach can give your article a contemporary look and keep it visually interesting. You might reorganize the menu or navigational features, add new images or multimedia, or try new fonts and backgrounds. Any changes you make should be purposeful; the goal is to make your article look dynamic and engaging without detracting from what you want to communicate.

- **To Increase Your Readership** Anytime you make changes to your article, consider posting a status update on your social networking site. Send e-mail updates to your target audience or post a link to your article on any related sites. This way, you can attract new readers and entice readers to return.

>
> Collins813 (reader) said...
>
> This is a good article! But I noticed you didn't mention the Hot Feet revue (later renamed Connie's Hot Chocolates), which was the first NY nightclub act that was created entirely by black artists. Did you research that at all? Might be interesting....
>
> May 20, 6:25 PM
>
> ──────────────────
>
> BonnieS (Site Administrator) said...
>
> Thanks for your comment. I haven't researched the Hot Feet revue, but I will now! Be on the lookout for updates.
>
> May 21, 10:30 AM

---

**NEWS FEED**

 BonnieS Hey jazz lovers, check out my feature article about music in the Harlem Renaissance. Recent updates include info about Connie's Hot Chocolates!

---

**YOUR TURN**

Visit your online feature article often. Check all links to make sure they still work and update or replace ones that don't. In a respectful manner, address any comments or feedback you've received. Keep your information current and consider trying new approaches to engage your readers.

---

**FOR STRUGGLING STUDENTS**

**Responding to Feedback** Direct students to work in small groups to come up with suitable responses to reader feedback. Provide them with a list of questions to ask for each item of feedback:

- What kind of feedback is this: comment, question, or critique?

- Is this comment appropriate?

- Does this comment require a response?

- What kind of response, if any, is required?

Encourage students to help one another in forming responses to valid reader feedback. Have them suggest updates to articles that might address reader feedback.

---

## Modifying and Improving Your Article

### Model the Skill: UPDATE INFORMATION

Show various Web articles and point out the information on the pages that can be used to determine if the article is current, such as a last updated note or an Updates section. Let them know that it is their job to sift through Web feeds and other sources that might contain new information. As they read, suggest to students that they copy and paste a list of links or a list of headlines to help them determine what additional information is required to ensure that their article remains current.

**GUIDED PRACTICE** Have pairs work together to verify the currency of Web articles for which you provide the links or URLs.

**YOUR TURN** Have pairs of students access each other's online articles. Ask them to identify areas that need to be updated or could be improved by a modification, such as new headings.

## Assess and Reteach

### Assess

Use the *COMMON CORE TRAITS* to assess students' updates.

A strong update
- repairs dead (broken) links
- removes outdated information
- adds new content from current and reliable sources
- responds promptly and politely to reader questions, comments, and feedback
- improves viewing and navigation

### Reteach

Organize students into pairs, making sure that one partner is tech savvy. Then have them perform one or two updating tasks on each of their articles as you circulate around the room, checking their progress.

**THINK central**

**Media Tools**

Keywords for using technology direct students to **MediaScope,** a Web site that helps them strengthen media analysis and production skills.

**RL 1** Cite textual evidence to support analysis of what the text says explicitly as well as inferences drawn from the text. **RL 2** Determine a theme of a text. **RI 1** Cite textual evidence to support analysis of what the text says explicitly as well as inferences drawn from the text. **RI 2** Determine a central idea of a text. **RI 4** Analyze the cumulative impact of specific word choices on meaning and tone. **RI 6** Determine an author's point of view in a text. **W 5** Strengthen writing by revising and editing to ensure that it demonstrates the conventions of standard English grammar, usage, and capitalization. **L 1b** Use various types of phrases to add variety to writing. **L 6** Acquire general academic words and phrases; demonstrate independence in gathering vocabulary knowledge.

### CHECK READINESS

Read aloud the paragraph under **ASSESS** and stress to students that this is not the full Unit Test, but a way for them to check their readiness for it. Then have students examine the standards listed under **REVIEW** and look back in the unit or in the **Student Resource Bank** for any skills they need to review.

### READ THE TEXTS

Remind students to keep unit goals in mind as they read each passage, paying particular attention to these literary and reading skills:

- analyze historical and cultural context
- analyze allusions, voice, dialect, and figurative language
- identify controlling idea and supporting details

To help students focus on history and culture while reading, encourage them to ask:

- What historic period is represented?
- How does the author's background shape the literary work?

### ANSWER THE QUESTIONS

Direct students to page R93–R101 of the **Handbook** to review test-taking strategies.

- Remind students not to choose the first good answer. Instead, they should read all choices, eliminate any that are clearly wrong, and then choose the *best* answer.

---

**ASSESS**
Taking this practice test will help you assess your knowledge of these skills and determine your readiness for the Unit Test.

**REVIEW**
After you take the practice test, your teacher can help you identify any standards you need to review.

COMMON CORE

**RL 1** Cite textual evidence to support analysis of what the text says explicitly as well as inferences drawn from the text. **RL 2** Determine a theme of a text. **RI 1** Cite textual evidence to support analysis of what the text says explicitly as well as inferences drawn from the text. **RI 2** Determine a central idea of a text. **RI 4** Analyze the cumulative impact of specific word choices on meaning and tone. **RI 6** Determine an author's point of view in a text. **W 5** Strengthen writing by revising and editing to ensure that it demonstrates the conventions of standard English grammar, usage, and capitalization. **L 1b** Use various types of phrases to add variety to writing. **L 6** Acquire general academic words and phrases; demonstrate independence in gathering vocabulary knowledge.

Practice Test — THINK central
Take it at **thinkcentral.com**.
KEYWORD: HML9N-1006

**DIRECTIONS** Read the two texts and the photograph. Then, answer the questions that follow.

# Slim  *by Carol Cullar*

**Shamrock, Texas**
**August 1937**

1   *The rolling prairie stretched from the Rockies to the Ozarks across a thousand miles of gently rolling hills cut by dry river beds and small farms plowed higgledy-piggledy and sown with acres of wheat—millions of acres of wheat planted to answer the government's cry during World War I. Slow to convert, some of the farmers were switching to cotton and corn, but too few had gone to modern agricultural methods. Spirits reeled from the War, the Influenza of 1918–19, the Crash. When the market collapsed, they lost money, then equipment, their farms, and heart. As if unsatisfied with the havoc wreaked, Nature unleashed The Drought and aimed it like some great magnifying lens focused incessantly on the western farmland of Oklahoma. Fickle rains fell, only to be sucked away by the burning air. Elsewhere, entire sections flash-flooded away for want of contour plowing. The atmosphere became a destructive engine powering itself on heated updrafts, pulling erosive ground-winds into its maw, along with the topsoil, then the subsoil, and the hopes of all those tied to the land. Thousands quit when the dust storms began to rage; some went insane as the dust-laden, ionized wind scoured every crevice and left nowhere to hide, nowhere to run except away—to California, to South Texas, to sanity—away from the burning eye of the sun. But some stayed.*

2   Bessie Mae stepped to the screen door with the battered tin dipper in her hand and with a deft flick of the wrist splashed what was left of her drink over the top portion of the flour sack stitched there. The cascading droplets wet the thin fabric, and a breeze blew the cooler air over her. She closed her eyes and breathed.

3   "Hey!" The startled voice was deep and unfamiliar and came from the glaring haze on the other side of the screen.

4   "Oh! I'm so sorry! Let me get a towel!" Bessie pushed the screen past its buffer catch and opened it wide. A hobo stood on the stoop, his cap in hand; he mopped his forehead with a red bandanna.

5   "You didn't get me very wet!" After his first quick glance upward, he fixed his gaze respectfully on the yellow tom that came to swish about her ankles.

6   Bessie searched the high-buttoned front of his faded work shirt and saw only a few droplets. Clasping the latch in her hand, she looked higher at the averted

---

## DIFFERENTIATED INSTRUCTION

### FOR ENGLISH LANGUAGE LEARNERS

**Assessment Practice: Work Backward**
Prepare students by having them read the questions *before* reading the passages. Have pairs find unfamiliar words in test directions and questions and follow these steps:

1. Write each word on an index card and divide the cards among pairs of students. Tell students that they are going to define these words.

2. Instruct students to work individually to make an initial determination of each

word's meaning. Then have students confer with their partners and check their work by using a dictionary.

3. Have students then share the words and definitions with the entire class, who can confirm the definitions or suggest others.

**Test-Taking Strategies: Frame the Story**
Suggest that as students read "Slim," they take rough notes on setting, plot, conflict, character, and theme. Framing the story in this way will help students focus their reading, comprehend what they read, and answer questions

head, flushed with heat. When she realized he intended to say nothing, she asked: "Can I help you, Mister?"

7    "Just gettin' ready to knock . . ." the stranger darted a quick look at her face, his hands betrayed a sudden nervousness. "Could . . . could. Do you reckon I could have a drink?" He finished in a rush and looked up again.

8    "Oh! Of course, just a moment." Bessie let the screen door close and stepped to the stone lip of the cistern where the water bucket stood. Taking the hobo dipper from its nail on the closet wall, she scooped it brim full and carried it back to the door.

9    The drifter had replaced his cap and tied his bandanna about his neck. His bony wrists dangled from the too-short sleeves and frayed cuffs of his shirt. Bess continued to watch him as he gulped from the tilted dipper, his head thrown back, adam's apple bobbing. He lifted his cap and poured the last drips on his head, then swiped across his forehead with his sleeve before resettling the battered tweed. He returned the dipper with great deference.

10    "Thank you, ma'am . . . mind if I sit in the shade over there and have my lunch?"

11    "That would be fine, Mister." Bessie looked him up and down. "Where's your lunch?"

12    He blushed. "Ah . . . here. I got me some crackers." He patted his breast pocket.

13    "Hump! Wait right here." She disappeared. In a moment she was back with a glossy red tomato and a large green onion. "These go well with crackers."

14    "Thank you, ma'am!" He bobbed his head and touched his cap. His faded blue eyes shown. "Yes, sir-e-e, thank you!" He turned and strode away, loose in his gait.

15    Bessie let the screen door close with a snap, hooking it behind her to keep the baby from wandering out. In the kitchen she stirred the black-eyed peas on the back burner, checked the cornbread in the oven, then set Jabe's place at the head of the table after giving the worn yellow oil-cloth a final swipe. The hobo was just in sight out the east window, seated, resting his back against the black locust at the margin of the road.

16    "Shoo, Tom!" She toed the persistent mouser-turned-bum out of her path and peeked around the corner of the dining room door to check on Baby Lester. She always thought of him as Baby Lester and was assured to see that he still sat in the middle of the turkey carpet with his nesting cups scattered about. He was chewing one and banging another against the rug.

17    "Bessie! Bessie, you got the screen locked!" Jabe was back from the gin! She clapped her hands for the baby and scooped him up to hurry to the back porch. **GO ON** ▶

## ITEM ANALYSIS

| COMPREHENSION AND WRITTEN RESPONSE | ITEMS | UNIT PAGES |
|---|---|---|
| Historical and Cultural Context | 10, 14, 23 | 918–923 |
| Representation of Cultures and Time Periods in Literature | 9, 19 | 983 |
| Cultural Symbols | 3 | 941 |
| Allusions, Voice, Dialect, and Figurative Language | 2, 4, 6, 11, 12, 22 | 951 |
| Make Inferences and Draw Conclusions | 1, 3, 5, 7, 8, 13, 18, 21, 22 | 951 |
| Controlling Idea and Supporting Details | 13, 15, 16, 17, 20 | 976 |
| Latin Roots | 4, 6, 11 | 938 |

| WRITING AND GRAMMAR | ITEMS | UNIT PAGES |
|---|---|---|
| Verbals, Including Gerunds and Infinitives | 1, 2, 3, 4, 5, 6 | 939 |

### Practice Test

On **thinkcentral.com** students can complete an interactive version of this practice test *and* receive remediation for the skills they have not yet mastered.

about it. Students should note the main idea and author's purpose in the article following "Slim," as well.

### FOR STRUGGLING READERS

**Assessment Support** Consider these options for completing the Assessment Practice:

- Have students "work backward" to review the test questions before reading the passages.

- Select random questions in the Assessment and have students demonstrate *how* and *where* to look for answers.

- Ask students to locate unfamiliar vocabulary words in the Assessment. Elicit the words' meanings from the class.

- Have students record useful testing words and definitions in their journal for later reference.

- Read the selections or parts of them aloud to aid in student comprehension.

18    She smoothed the sides of her simple bun and wiped her nose and forehead with the back of her left hand to erase the stray flour. Jabe was prone to tease if he caught her with flour on her nose. An unconscious smile lit her coffee-brown eyes as she undid the latch and stood to one side.

19    "Here! He's too heavy for you! Come to papa, Lester! Has he been all right today?" Jabe lifted the slack form of the three year old into the crook of his arm and hooked the other about Bess' petite shoulder. His blunt fingers plucked at her left earlobe.

20    "Oh, yes, he's fine. Very happy today. Your lunch is ready to put on the table." She tightened her apron and hastened toward the kitchen.

21    Jabe set the baby down and splashed a dipper full of water into the granite wash basin. Lester toddled on unsteady legs, clinging to his father's tan work pants as Jabe scooped a fragment of lye soap out of the dish and began to scrub. When he had finished he sloshed the dirty water about in the pan, then lifted the lid of the slop crock by the door, reminding himself to take it out to the pigs when he had finished his meal. He smoothed his thinning hair in the tiny mirror, then hoisted the baby back onto his hip for the few steps to the kitchen. Ten steps more than Baby Lester could have made on his own, more than he might ever take. Jabe settled him into the high chair and put the tray down. Lester began to pat the smooth wooden tray.

22    "What chores did you give the hobo fixin' the gate to the chicken pen?" He seated himself at the head of the table and reached from the brimming goblet of buttermilk at the head of his place.

23    Bessie Mae straightened from the oven, her face reddened by the heat. "Oh! I didn't! He came askin' for water, then went to set under the black locust just a few minutes ago!"

24    "Well, he's found himself a job without having to be told. Did you give him any food?" Jabe tucked into the black-eyed peas as she shoveled a huge slab of hot cornbread onto the side of his plate.

25    . . . She busied herself at the sink and spoke over her shoulder. "I gave him a tomato and an onion. He said he had some crackers, but I doubt it." Jabe's chair squeaked back as he left the table.

26    "Mister! Ho! Could you come over here?" Jabe waited until the stranger hung the hammer back on the wall of the garage and made his way to the stoop. "Come on in here and wash up. We was just settin' down to eat."

27    "Well, sir, I ate just a bit ago, but don't mind I do!" He followed Jabe up the steps, went to the wash basin and scrubbed his hands, but wiped their wetness on his pants rather than dirty the pretty towel on the nail. He stepped to the kitchen door. "Ma'am, thank you kindly for the tomato and onion. They was right tasty."

1008

## DIFFERENTIATED INSTRUCTION

### FOR STRUGGLING READERS

**Build Comprehension** Point out to students clues in the text that Baby Lester may be developmentally challenged:

- The baby has a "slack form" (paragraph 19).
- Lester is three years old, yet he "toddled on unsteady legs" (paragraph 21).
- The distance from the door to the kitchen is "ten steps more than Baby Lester could have made on his own, more than he might ever take" (paragraph 21).

Discuss these details from the text and ask students to make predictions about the importance of Lester's condition to the story.

**Language Support** The dialogue in the selection reflects the speech of country people at the time the story is set, 1937. Point out examples of regional speech and make sure students understand the meaning of the idiomatic and colloquial words and phrases:

- "settin' down to eat," (paragraph 26), *sitting down to eat.*

- "I ken tell" (paragraph 37), *I can tell.*

- "A mite slow to walk," (paragraph 39), *A little slow to walk.*

- "botherin' nary a soul," (paragraph 39), *not bothering anyone*

- "if you've a mind to stay," (paragraph 48), *if you want to stay*

28    Jabe pulled out the white wooden chair across the corner from his own place, "Here, set."

29    Bessie filled a plate at the stove, topping it with a slab of cornbread and set it before the gaunt-faced man. "For this bread we take, for our way we make, thank You. Amen!" The stranger ducked his head and began to shovel the peas in with an economy of motion that spoke volumes of the days it had been since his last meal.

30    "Amen! Amen!" Lester chimed in from his place on the other side of the table, banging his tray with more fervor. "Peas! Peas!" he chanted as his mother placed a saucer of cooled black-eyes before him, then went to fill her own plate.

31    "You were fixin' the chicken fence when I came up. . . ."

32    "Yes, sir. Gate was saggin'." He spoke around a mouth full of cornbread.

33    Lester chose this moment to begin whacking the tray of his high chair again. "Nilk . . . nilk!"

34    Bessie moved to the blue Indianhead pitcher on the far end of the table, lifted the cup towel from its top and poured a small mug of buttermilk, placing it on Baby Lester's tray.

35    "That's a fine boy, there." The stranger spoke as he neatly polished the last of the pea juice from his plate. He smiled at the child, who chose for once to return the favor.

36    Jabe continued to eat, his head down toward his food. He spoke finally without raising his head. "He's slow, Mister, real slow."

37    "Yes, sir, I ken tell. . . ."

38    But Jabe went on, as if the hobo hadn't spoken.

39    "A mite slow to walk, he was, and last spring he followed Nettie, she's our middle girl, out to the clothes line. He was playin' in the dirt, botherin' nary a soul, and when she went back with the second basket to hang up, there he was . . . covered with red ants! She brushed them off and ran screamin' for her mother, but when they got his diaper off and got 'em all off him, he was bad stung. Bad stung. Like he never had a chance. Nearly lost him, we did. Had a terrible fever for days! Since then he seems slower. Won't walk, or nothin'." Jabe's midnight blue eyes turned to the stranger, daring him to condemn.

40    The hobo's adam's apple convulsed. "I seen he was slow . . . like me, I reckon. 'Like to like' my grannie used to say. . . . They gave up on me. Sent me away when my momma didn't want me. Been on a farm ever since. Them folks was nice, patient with me, you know?" He forced himself to continue, afraid that the father beside him was going to give up on this child. "Slow folks just take some extra patience. This is a fine boy here." He blushed at his temerity and stammered, "Well . . . I'll get back out there and have that gate hung proper in a jiffy! Much obliged, Ma'am, for that fine meal!"

41    Jabe's eyes glanced over Bessie Mae's tear-filled ones. He nodded his thanks for the meal and followed the hobo out the door.

**GO ON →**

---

**FOR ENGLISH LANGUAGE LEARNERS**

**Comprehension: Contrast** Point out to language learners Slim's statement that "I seen he was slow . . . like me" (paragraph 40). Review with students the types of challenges that both Lester and Slim face, and the difference Lester's supportive family could make to his development and improvement.

**FOR ADVANCED LEARNERS/PRE–AP**

Have students review the introduction to the selection, which describes the economic and cultural challenges facing farmers in 1937. Ask students to discuss how people can react to challenges in a positive way. Ask students to answer the question: *How can people be generous in economic hard times?*

42 "The farm you left burn out?"

43 "Well, yes and no. The Tollivers was real old and when this drought hit, it seemed to dry them up along with the wheat. They both died within two months of one another, and their own son sent me on my way. . . . Didn't want no dummie around, he said. . . . Reckon I'll walk out to Californy and get me a job pickin' cotton." He set his cap, hitched his pants and wiped his hands down the seat of them. "I was just about to finish hangin' that gate when you called me in to eat; reckon I'll get back to that, if it's all right with you?" He looked at Jabe on the step behind him.

44 "What's your name, Mister?" Jabe's hand was extended.

45 "Slim . . . just Slim." The hobo shook Jabe's hand and met his smiling eyes before glancing quickly away.

46 "You got family in California?" Jabe searched the face bent before him.

47 "No family . . . nowhere. On my own." He kicked a dusty clod toward the ragged pale petunias beside the stoop, the ones that got the water that was too dirty for the hogs.

48 "I could use a hand around the place here; there's a cot in the garage over there, if you've a mind to stay. This here drought can't last forever, and we're gonna have a mite of cotton make it through the summer. . . . 'Less you particularly wanted to go to California?"

49 Slim looked up, his face wreathed in joy, "No, sir-e-e! I've a mind to stay!"

50 *And stay he did. For twenty years he shelled peas, hoed cotton, and ate watermelon on the back porch with the family until late one November night in 1956, when a semi, bowling out of Oklahoma City on its way to California, knocked him like a stray pin off the highway on his way back from the domino parlor. In his meager effects Jabe found the address of a prominent physician in Monroe, Louisiana, but when he telegraphed them of the death of their brother, there was no response, so Jabe and Bessie buried him in the family plot on a barren, windy hill south by southwest of Shamrock.*

---

## DIFFERENTIATED INSTRUCTION

**FOR STRUGGING READERS**

**Language Support** Review with students the simile used in paragraph 50: ". . . a semi, <u>bowling</u> out of Oklahoma City on its way to California, <u>knocked him like a stray pin</u> off the highway . . ." Have students identify the comparison made between Slim and a bowling pin, and discuss what the comparison reveals about his vulnerable, fragile position.

**Concept Support** After students read paragraph 48, discuss why Jabe decides to offer Slim a job and a home. Remind them that Jabe is generous even though he has little to offer. Ask students why they think Jabe is moved to be generous, and ask them to connect with the story by giving examples of generous acts they have witnessed.

# "Good Samaritan" Saves Crying Woman's Foreclosed Home

1   (CNN) — Tracy Orr sat in the back of the room and prepared to watch her foreclosed home go up for auction this past Saturday. That's when a pesky stranger sat down beside her and struck up a conversation.

2   "Are you here to buy a house?" Marilyn Mock said.

3   Orr couldn't hold it in. The tears flowed. She pointed to the auction brochure at a home that didn't have a picture. "That's my house," she said.

4   Within moments, the four-bedroom, two-bath home in Pottsboro, Texas, went up for sale. People up front began casting their bids. The home that Orr purchased in September 2004 was slipping away.

5   She stood and moved toward the crowd. Behind her, Mock got into the action.

6   "She didn't know I was doing it," Mock says. "I just kept asking her if [her home] was worth it, and she just kept crying. She probably thought I was crazy, 'Why does this woman keep asking me that?'"

7   Mock says she bought the home for about $30,000. That's when Mock did what most bidders at a foreclosure auction never do.

8   "She said, 'I did this for you. I'm doing this for you,'" Orr says. "When it was all done, I was just in shock."

9   "I thought maybe her and her husband do these types of things to buy them and turn them. She said, 'No, you just look like you needed a friend.'"

10  "All this happened within like 5 minutes. She never even asked me my name. She didn't ask me my financial situation. She had no idea what [the house] looked like. She just did it out of the graciousness of her heart, just a 'Good Samaritan,'" Orr says. "It's amazing."

11  Orr says she had taken out a mortgage of $80,000 in 2004 when she first bought the home. At the time, she says she worked for the U.S. Postal Service. But she lost her job a month after taking out the loan. . . .

12  Without a job, she fell behind on her home payments. She sold some property in 2006 for $12,000 and paid it to the mortgage company, thinking she had done enough to save herself from foreclosure—but to no avail, she says.

13  "It's just been a bad deal," says Orr, who now works at a church camp and conference center.

14  With the foreclosure auction approaching, she planned to make the nearly 80-mile drive to Dallas this past Saturday with an investor friend. But she says he ditched her at the last-minute. She went to the auction with her family, and suddenly found herself in the back with Mock.

**GO ON** ➤

1011

---

## FOR ENGLISH LANGUAGE LEARNERS

**Culture: Clarify** Review with English learners why Tracy Orr and Marilyn Mock meet at an auction. Explain that Tracy Orr borrowed money from a lender to buy her house, and she cannot repay the money. The lender is selling her house to get its money back. Tell students that lenders sometimes give people more time to repay their loans.

## FOR STRUGGLING READERS

**Vocabulary Support** Help students recognize words that are specific to borrowing money. Review the following words and their concepts: *auction* (type of sale); *bid* (offer to buy); *foreclosure* (legal means for a creditor to take back property); *mortgage* (type of loan); *collateral* (property offered to secure a loan).

15    "I always talk to everyone around me," Mock says. "I mean you can always find out all kinds of interesting things when you talk to people around you. So I just asked her, 'Are you here to buy a house?'"

16    Mock, who is known as the "Rock Lady" for her small business selling flagstone and other rocks in Rockwall, Texas, says she went to the auction with her 27-year-old son to help him buy his first home. He bought his home, and soon afterward Mock came across Orr.

17    Mock says she's using one of her business dump trucks as collateral for the $30,000 sale price. "I can't afford to just give [the house] to her," she says.

18    As for Orr's payments, Mock says, "We'll just figure out however much she can pay on it. That way, she can have her house back."

19    Why be so generous?

20    "She was just so sad. You put yourself in their situation and you realize you just got to do something," says Mock, who says she has trouble walking by homeless people on the street and not helping them out.

21    "If it was you, you'd want somebody to stop and help you."

22    When she told her husband of 30 years that she'd just bought a home for a stranger, she says his reaction was: "Whatever."

23    "He's used to it," she says with a booming laugh.

24    Mock says she's excited for another reason too. Orr's house is located near a Texas fishing hot-spot. "She says I can come up there and fish, and I love to fish!"

25    Orr, who nearly lost her home, says her newfound friend has "given me back faith and hope to keep going and hold my head up."

26    "Things happen for a reason," Orr says.

---

## DIFFERENTIATED INSTRUCTION

**FOR STRUGGING READERS**

**Comprehension Support** Events in the story do not occur in chronological order. Explain that before the auction, these things happened to Tracy Orr: 1) she bought a house; 2) she lost her job; 3) she could not make her home payments; and 4) her house was offered for sale at auction. Ask students to list in order the events that occur at the auction after Marilyn Mock meets Tracy Orr. *1) Marilyn learns that Tracy has lost her house; 2) Marilyn buys Tracy's house; 3) Marilyn lets Tracy buy the house from her.*

**Concept Support** Discuss with students the issue of home foreclosure. Explain that banks and lending institutions hold foreclosure sales to try to get back the money that they originally loaned to buy the house. Many people attend foreclosure sales hoping to buy a low-priced, "bargain" home. Point out that each "bargain" home represents some family's tragedy and displacement. Mention that Tracy Orr may have been crying because she did not know where she would live after her home was foreclosed upon.

WORK-IS-WHAT-I
WANT-AND-NOT-CHARITY
WHO-WILL-HELP-ME-
GET-A-JOB-7 Years-
IN-DETROIT. NO-MONEY
SENT-AWAY-FURNISH-
BEST-OF-REFERENCES
PHONE RANDOLPH 8381 Room
#59.

1013

## FOR ENGLISH LANGUAGE LEARNERS

**Comprehension: Problem/Solution** Help English learners to identify key concepts in the sign pictured in the illustration. Important concepts might include *work, charity, job, money.* Help students to identify the problem/solution relationship illustrated by the man and his sign by completing these sentence stems: *The man's problem is that___* (he is out of work and needs money). *The solution to the man's problem is ___* (he finds a job).

**Culture: Clarify** Clarify for language learners the elements of the photograph that indicate its historic period. Explain that the automobiles, the man's clothing, and lettering on the sign indicate that the picture was taken during the Great Depression of the 1930s. The man's plight and his response to his joblessness would have been typical during that time of extreme economic difficulty.

# ANSWERS

## Reading Comprehension

Model a thinking process for answering multiple-choice questions.

1. **D is correct.** As Jabe helps Slim, Slim can help the family with Lester and be able to encourage him. A is incorrect because Bessie Mae's family is not rich. B is incorrect because the story shows that neither Slim nor Lester deserve his condition. C is incorrect because Slim does good work, but he does not represent all homeless people.

2. **A is correct.** The omniscient narrator gives readers access to the thoughts and feelings of all the characters. B is incorrect because the perspective is not limited to that of a single character. C is incorrect because the narrator does not use the pronouns of a first-person point of view. D is incorrect because the narrator does not tell the story using the pronoun you.

3. **C is correct.** Bessie Mae accidentally splashes Slim with water just before the family offers him a job and new life. A is incorrect because water indicates an end to deprivation. B is incorrect because the "free life" does not include ready access to water. D is incorrect because the region in the story is experiencing a drought.

4. **B is correct.** Sanity is the condition of having a healthy mind. A is incorrect because a cavity is a hole or chamber. C is incorrect because a sane person does not have to be holy. D is incorrect because "burned out" is not a healthy condition.

5. **D is correct.** Before air conditioning, people used water to keep cool. A is incorrect because Bessie Mae does not see Slim when she flicks the water. B is incorrect because Bessie Mae is not wasting water. C is incorrect because she flicks drinking water, not dirty water.

6. **C is correct.** A cistern is a collection place for rainwater. A is incorrect because Bessie Mae gets water, not seeds, from the cistern. B is incorrect because Bessie Mae could not get water from Lester's crib. D is incorrect because water would not be stored in an oven.

7. **D is correct.** Lester's inability to walk indicates that he is not merely sleepy or inactive. A is incorrect because chewing on nesting cups is a normal behavior for small children. B is incorrect because repeating "Amen" is a normal response. C is incorrect because Jabe describes Lester's behavior after the narrator explains that Lester cannot walk well.

8. **A is correct.** By fixing the chicken pen, Slim indicates that he is skilled and ready to work. B is incorrect because Slim never asks for work. C and D are incorrect because neither indicates a willingness to work.

9. **B is correct.** Jabe tells Slim he can work and live on the farm. A is incorrect because Slim stays at the farm. C is incorrect because the story does not revisit Lester's condition. D is incorrect because Slim knows the location of his brother is in Louisiana but does not contact him.

---

## Reading Comprehension

> Use "Slim" (pp. 1006–1010) to answer questions 1–9.

1. One theme of "Slim" is that —
   - **A.** you have to be rich to help others
   - **B.** people deserve everything that happens to them
   - **C.** all homeless people do good work
   - **D.** you often help yourself when you help others

2. The author wrote the story in —
   - **A.** third-person omniscient point of view
   - **B.** third-person limited point of view
   - **C.** first-person point of view
   - **D.** second-person point of view

3. The author uses water as a symbol for —
   - **A.** deprivation
   - **B.** the free life of the hobo
   - **C.** life
   - **D.** farming

4. The Latin word *sanus* means "healthy." The word *sanity* in paragraph 1 probably means
   - **A.** sinus cavities in the nose
   - **B.** soundness of mind
   - **C.** saintly, or holy, living
   - **D.** burned out, like the dry ground

5. In paragraph 2, Bessie Mae flicks water on the flour sack curtain because —
   - **A.** she wants to get Slim wet
   - **B.** it doesn't matter if she wastes water
   - **C.** it was dirty water
   - **D.** air going through wet fabric is cooler

6. The word *cistern* in paragraph 8 comes from the Latin word *cista*, which means "box." A *cistern* is —
   - **A.** a seed box
   - **B.** Lester's crib
   - **C.** a stone receptacle for water
   - **D.** part of the oven

7. We **first** know that something is wrong with Lester when we read —
   - **A.** that Lester is chewing on his nesting cups
   - **B.** that Lester repeats "Amen!"
   - **C.** that Jabe says that Lester is "slow, Mister, real slow"
   - **D.** that Lester might never take ten steps by himself

8. Jabe and Bessie Mae know that Slim wants to work because Slim —
   - **A.** fixes the chicken pen without being asked
   - **B.** tells them he wants to work
   - **C.** grew up on a farm
   - **D.** isn't afraid to talk about Lester

9. At the end of the story —
   - **A.** Slim goes to California
   - **B.** Jabe offers Slim a job as a farmhand
   - **C.** Baby Lester gets better
   - **D.** Slim finds his family

Use "'Good Samaritan' Saves Crying Woman's Foreclosed Home" (pp. 1011–1012) to answer questions 10–16.

**10.** One message of the article is that —

**A.** you don't have to be rich to help others

**B.** it's important to make sure your help will be appreciated

**C.** you should help only people that you know

**D.** going to auctions is a good way to meet interesting people

**11.** *Foreclose* combines the Latin words *foris*, meaning "outside," and *claudere*, meaning "to close or shut out." To *foreclose* means —

**A.** to shut before something else happens

**B.** to shut someone out for not making payments

**C.** to get dressed properly before going outside

**D.** to close something four times

**12.** "Good Samaritan" is a Biblical reference that has become a common phrase for someone who —

**A.** faces a great need

**B.** loses a home

**C.** is a good person

**D.** helps a stranger

**13.** The author's description of Marilyn Mock as a "pesky stranger" is ironic because —

**A.** Mock is not a stranger

**B.** Mock is not merely pesky but hurtful

**C.** Mock turned out to be a helper, not a pest

**D.** Mock had been a family friend

**14.** Mock goes to the sale because she —

**A.** wants to buy a house for herself

**B.** wants to help her son buy a house

**C.** wants to help Orr buy a house

**D.** is looking for a house to "turn"

**15.** Mock decides to help Orr because she —

**A.** imagines how she would feel in that circumstance

**B.** expects to make money on the deal

**C.** has a lot of money to give away

**D.** is trying out for a reality TV show

**16.** What is Mock's husband's reaction to her helping Orr?

**A.** He is angry and yells.

**B.** He suggests giving more help.

**C.** She does not tell him.

**D.** He accepts it without question.

Use "Slim" and "'Good Samaritan' Saves Crying Woman's Foreclosed Home" to answer questions 17–18.

**17.** Both the story and the article emphasize that —

**A.** you should help people that you know

**B.** sometimes good people have bad luck

**C.** homeless people don't want to work

**D.** it's best to never trust anyone

**18.** What do Slim and Tracy Orr have in common?

**A.** Both have recently lost their home.

**B.** Neither have family that claims them.

**C.** Both have their lives improved by caring strangers.

**D.** Neither wants to work toward a better life.

**GO ON**

1015

**10. A *is correct.*** *Marilyn Mock was not rich, but she helped a stranger keep her home. B is incorrect because Mock did not require that her help be appreciated. C is incorrect because Mock helps a stranger. D is incorrect because the message is about helping people, not meeting people.*

**11. B *is correct.*** *When a house is foreclosed, its former owner is forced to leave it. A and D are incorrect because they do not have the connotation of being forced to leave a place. C is incorrect because foreclose is not related to clothing.*

**12. D *is correct.*** *The Biblical "Good Samaritan" helps a traveler who has been injured. A is incorrect because the "Good Samaritan" is not the person in need of aid. B is incorrect because "Good Samaritan" is a general description of a person who helps a stranger. C is incorrect because the motivation for the "Good Samaritan's" help is unknown.*

**13. C *is correct.*** *Even though Mock initially appeared to be annoying, she bought a home for a stranger. A is incorrect because Mock was a stranger who did not know Tracy Orr. B is incorrect because Mock was helpful, not hurtful. D is incorrect because Mock had not met Tracy Orr.*

**14. B *is correct.*** *Mock's son buys a house at the auction. A is incorrect because Mock does not buy her own house. C is incorrect because Mock does not know Orr before the auction. D is incorrect because Mock does not want to invest in a house.*

**15. A *is correct.*** *Mock is sympathetic and knows that she would not want to lose her house. B is incorrect because Mock does not anticipate making a profit. C is incorrect because Mock says she cannot afford to give Orr the house. D is incorrect because no television program is mentioned.*

**16. D *is correct.*** *Mock's husband does not question her decision. A and B are incorrect because Mock's husband shows no emotion, just says "Whatever." C is incorrect because Mock tells her husband what she did.*

**17. B *is correct.*** *The selections show that people like Slim and Tracy Orr face challenging circumstances. A is incorrect because in both selections strangers help people who are in need. C is incorrect because Slim wants to work. D is incorrect because Jabe and Marilyn Mock trust people they do not know.*

**18. C *is correct.*** *Both are helped by people they do not know. A is incorrect because Slim did not own a home. B is incorrect because Tracy Orr's family went to the auction with her. D is incorrect because both are willing to work.*

**19. A** *is correct.* The man is letting potential employers know that he would like a job. B and D are incorrect because the man is not offering to sell or promote anything. C is incorrect because the man is not protesting his unemployment.

**20. D** *is correct.* The man needs money and wants to work for it. A is incorrect because he specifically rejects charity. B is incorrect because the man's sign does not mention his rights. C is incorrect because the man offers nothing for sale.

## SHORT CONSTRUCTED RESPONSES

*Possible response:*

**21.** Slim had developmental problems, and he does not want the father to abandon the child as Slim had been abandoned. He wants the father to know that "slow folks just take some extra patience" (paragraph 40).

**22.** Marilyn Mock is trying to decide how important the house is to Orr and whether she should buy it for her (paragraph 6).

**23.** Slim never owned his own house; he only lived on a farm after his family "sent me away" ("slim," paragraph 40). Because he was "slow," Slim was never in a position, like Tracy Orr, to take "out a mortgage of $80,000" to buy his own home ("'Good Samaritan' Saves Crying Woman's Foreclosed Home," paragraph 11).

---

> Use the photograph on page 1013 to answer questions 19–20.

**19.** The man is advertising for —
A. himself
B. a new restaurant
C. nothing, he is protesting
D. a Broadway show

**20.** He wants —
A. charitable donations
B. his civil rights respected
C. to sell his car
D. help finding a job

**SHORT CONSTRUCTED RESPONSE**
Write a short response to each question, using text evidence to support your response.

**21.** Why does Slim tell the man that Lester is a fine boy? Support your response with evidence from the text.

**22.** What does Marilyn Mock mean when she asks Tracy Orr if her house is "worth it"? Support your response with evidence from the text.

Write a short response to answer the following question, using evidence from both texts.

**23.** How are Slim's experiences different from Tracy Orr's? Support your response with evidence from **both** texts.

## DIFFERENTIATED INSTRUCTION

**FOR ENGLISH LANGUAGE LEARNERS**
**Assessment Vocabulary** To help students understand the Comprehension questions, teach or review these key vocabulary words:

• Item 1: *theme*—"broad idea or message"

• Item 3: *symbol*—"something that stands for something else"

• Item 13: *ironic*—"contrary to plan or expectation"

• Item 16: *reaction*—"response"

# Revising and Editing

**DIRECTIONS** Read this passage, and answer the questions that follow.

> (1) Wars are fought and won not just on the battlefield but on the home front as well. (2) In addition to requiring military forces, wars need to be financed and need supplies. (3) So it was with the entry of the United States into world war I. (4) In addition, many family's took steps to cut out expensive purchases and planted "victory gardens." (5) The government decided to sell Liberty Bonds as a good way to raise money. (6) Throughout cities and towns, colorful posters asked citizens to contribute to the war effort. (7) Many people took the opportunity to become involved. (8) Young men enlisted and women knit socks for soldiers. (9) Children collected tin and paper.

1. What is the most effective way to improve the organization of the paragraph?
   A. Move sentence 1 to follow sentence 6
   B. Move sentence 4 to follow sentence 9
   C. Move sentence 3 to follow sentence 4
   D. Move sentence 7 to follow sentence 9

2. Which sentence should be added between sentences 1 and 2?
   A. Of course, everyone knows that.
   B. This key point is often overlooked.
   C. Any soldier can tell how important battlefield strategy is.
   D. You will be surprised to learn this.

3. What change, if any, should be made to sentence 3?
   A. Insert a comma after *was*
   B. Change *entry* to **entrance**
   C. Change *world war* to **World War**
   D. Make no change

4. What change, if any, should be made to sentence 4?
   A. Insert a comma after *purchases*
   B. Change *expensive* to **expansive**
   C. Change *family's* to **families**
   D. Make no change

5. What is the most effective way to rewrite sentence 5 to include a gerund phrase?
   A. Finally, the government decided to sell Liberty Bonds to raise money.
   B. The government decided that a good way to raise money would be to sell Liberty Bonds.
   C. Because the government needed to raise money, it decided to sell Liberty Bonds.
   D. The government decided that selling Liberty Bonds was a good way to raise money.

6. Which transitional word or phrase should be added to sentence 8?
   A. For example,
   B. However,
   C. In other words,
   D. Similarly,

STOP

1017

---

---

# ANSWERS

## Revising and Editing

1. **B is correct.** *Sentence 4 contains an example of an action taken by families during wartime, and it should be moved to the end of the list of examples.* A *is incorrect because sentence 1 is the topic sentence and should be the passage's first sentence.* C *is incorrect because then there would be two consecutive sentences beginning with "In addition."* D *is incorrect because sentence 7 explains sentence 6; therefore, it should not move.*

2. **B is correct.** *Sentence B highlights that the "home front" is as important as the battlefield.* A *is incorrect because the information about the "home front" is not well known and obvious.* C *is incorrect because the emphasis of the passage is on the "home front," not on the battlefield.* D *is incorrect because the tone of this sentence does not fit with the passage.*

3. **C is correct.** *Proper nouns, like World War I, need to be capitalized.* A *is incorrect because no comma is needed before a prepositional phrase.* B *is incorrect because* entry *and* entrance *are synonyms.* D *is incorrect because the sentence contains an error in capitalization.*

4. **C is correct.** *The plural form should be used instead of the possessive.* A *is incorrect because a comma should not be inserted between the compound verbs.* B *is incorrect because* expansive *changes the meaning of the sentence.* D *is incorrect because there is an error in the sentence.*

5. **D is correct.** *Selling is a gerund because it is in the subject position.* A, B, *and* C *are incorrect because they do not include a gerund.*

6. **A is correct.** *Sentence 8 provides an example of how people became involved in the war effort.* B *is incorrect because* However *indicates a contrast with sentence 7.* C *is incorrect because* In other words *indicates a restatement, not a listing of examples.* D *is incorrect because* Similarly *is used to introduce a comparison, not examples.*

# COMMON CORE FOCUS

**RL 10** Read and comprehend literature. **RI 10** Read and comprehend literary nonfiction.

## INTRODUCE *GREAT READS*

In Unit 9, students have discussed a number of big questions. Invite students to tell which question they found most intriguing and why, and then focus attention on the three that appear on this page. Discuss the recommended books and their summaries, pointing out how each connects to the related question. Encourage students to choose one or more of these "great reads" to read independently.

## Ideas for Independent Reading

Which of the questions in Unit 9 intrigued you the most? Continue exploring them with these additional works.

**COMMON CORE**

**RL 10** Read and comprehend literature. **RI 10** Read and comprehend literary nonfiction.

### How does friendship begin?

**Watership Down**
*by Richard Adams*

Adams's unusual novel describes how rabbits Fiver, Hazel, and Bigwig form a friendship in the face of danger. They must flee human encroachment and warlike rabbits to find a new and safe homeland.

**A Separate Peace**
*by John Knowles*

A New England boarding school is the setting for the developing friendship between studious Gene and athletic Phineas. This is a novel of personal growth and the loss of innocence.

**The Beekeeper's Apprentice**
*by Laurie R. King*

Mary, a 15-year-old orphan, stumbles across Sherlock Holmes as he is watching bees. They become friends, and she helps the famous detective solve mysteries.

### When do world events hit home?

**Refuge: An Unnatural History of Family and Place**
*by Terry Tempest Williams*

Williams chronicles the seasons around the Great Salt Lake near her Utah home. She also sees a connection between the high number of family members with cancer—herself included— and their proximity to 1950s atom bomb testing.

**Small Wonder**
*by Barbara Kingsolver*

In the wake of the events of September 11, 2001, the author writes about reasons to have hope. She considers children, conservation projects, gardening, and a new definition of the word *patriotism*.

**A World of Hurt: Between Innocence and Arrogance in Vietnam**
*by Mary Reynolds Powell*

The author, an army nurse in Vietnam, recalls the steps that led her to becoming an anti-war activist. She describes several friends who were with her in Vietnam and who have taken the same journey.

### How does heritage shape identity?

**Dust Tracks on a Road: An Autobiography**
*by Zora Neale Hurston*

Hurston, a writer born in poverty in the American South, wrote during the Harlem Renaissance. She helped preserve African-American heritage as a novelist, a folklorist, and an anthropologist.

**The Names: A Memoir**
*by N. Scott Momaday*

Momaday, a Kiowa Indian, comes from a family of storytellers. His memoir extols the value of words and the voice of the speaker. He writes in many voices to tell of his childhood and youth.

**Lest Innocent Blood be Shed**
*by Philip Hallie*

The people of Le Chambon, France, were descended from Huguenots. They had suffered persecution themselves and during World War II chose to protect the Jews in their midst. They saved over 4,500 people from the Nazi concentration camps.

Get Novel Wise

**Go to thinkcentral.com.**
KEYWORD: HML9-1018

1018

## NovelWise

The keyword on this page points to **NovelWise**, a Web site that helps students choose a novel or other book-length work to read. **NovelWise** also provides

• study guides
• reading strategies and literary elements instruction
• presentations to introduce classic novels
• project ideas

# Shakespearean Drama

## THE TRAGEDY OF ROMEO AND JULIET

- In Drama
- In Media
- In Poetry

1019

**About the Art** French artist Adolphe-William Bouguereau (1825–1905) created *The Proposal* in 1872. During some showings, the painting has been called *Faust and Marguerite*, the lovers from Goethe's famous poem *Faust*. However, Bouguereau did not identify the lovers, and the association with Faust is speculative.

## INTRODUCE THE UNIT

What an immense literary range William Shakespeare had! His works include broad comedy, gripping tragedy, academic history, ardent love poetry, and poignant social criticism. Invite students to name some of Shakespeare's plays; as they do, note that most of his plays are instantly known by title and have been performed around the world countless times. Indeed, Shakespearean references have become part of our cultural vocabulary.

Explain that both the photograph and the painting portray a young couple in love. The photograph on the right shows Romeo and Juliet, perhaps Shakespeare's most famous—and most tragic—young couple. Use these questions to get students thinking about the drama that the images suggest:

- How would you describe the facial expressions visible in each couple?
- What other details in both images suggest the drama of love?
- Can you guess the famous Shakespearean scene that the image on the right depicts?

Tell students that in this unit, they will read the **Shakespearean drama** *The Tragedy of Romeo and Juliet*. They will also read an ancient poem that helped inspire the drama and a critical review of a filmed version of the play.

For help in planning this unit, see

**R** RESOURCE MANAGER UNIT 10
pp. 1–10

# UNIT 10

| STRAND | Shakespeare's World Article pp. 1022–1025 | ECOS Text Analysis Workshop: Shakespearean Drama pp. 1026–1033 | ECOS The Tragedy of Romeo and Juliet, Act One Drama pp. 1034–1063 | ECOS The Tragedy of Romeo and Juliet, Act Two Drama pp. 1064–1087 | ECOS The Tragedy of Romeo and Juliet, Act Three Drama pp. 1088–1113 | ECOS The Tragedy of Romeo and Juliet, Act Four Drama pp. 1114–1129 |
|---|---|---|---|---|---|---|
| **Reading Literature** | | Shakespearean Tragedy pp. 1026–1027 RL 2, RL 3 Shakespearean Language pp. 1028–1029 RL 9 Reading Shakespeare pp. 1030–1031 RL 2, RL 10 Analyze the Text pp. 1032–1033 | Shakespearean Drama pp. 1042, 1051 RL 3 Character Foils p. 1057 RL 3 Reading Shakespearean Drama pp. 1035, 1063 RL 2, RL 3, RL 10 Summarize p. 1037 RL 2, RL 3 | Shakespearean Drama pp. 1069, 1071, 1076, 1087 RL 3, RL 4 Cultural Setting p. 1072 RL 6 Paradox p. 1086 RL 4 Reading Shakespearean Drama p. 1087 RL 2, RL 3, RL 10 Summarize p. 1064 RL 2, RL 3 | Shakespearean Drama pp. 1090, 1092, 1096, 1112, 1113 RL 3, RL 6, RL 9 Reading Shakespearean Drama p. 1113 RL 3 Predict p. 1088 | Shakespearean Drama pp. 1114, 1119, 1122, 1129 RL 3 Reading Shakespearean Drama p. 1129 RL 2, RL 3, RL 10 Review p. 1114 RL 2, RL 3 |
| **Reading Informational Text** | Read Nonfiction pp. 1022–1025 RI 10 | | | | | |
| **Writing** | | | | | | |
| **Speaking and Listening** | Integrate Multiple Sources of Information pp. 1022–1025 SL 2 | | Debate p. 1034 Behind the Curtain pp. 1036, 1045, 1055 SL 2 | Behind the Curtain p. 1081 SL 2 | Behind the Curtain p. 1105 SL 2 | Behind the Curtain p. 1121 SL 2 |
| **Language** | | Shakespearean Tragedy pp. 1026–1027 L 6 Shakespearean Language pp. 1028–1029 L 3 | Shakespearean Drama pp. 1035, 1040, 1047, 1053, 1054, 1059, 1063 L 3 Sarcasm p. 1040 L 5a Language Coach p. 1062 L 4a | Shakespearean Drama pp. 1067, 1083, 1086, 1087 L 3, L 5a Language Coach pp. 1073, 1084 L 4, L 5a Parallelism p. 1066 L 1a-b | Shakespearean Drama p. 1090, 1092, 1094, 1095, 1097, 1103, 1104 L 3 Language Coach pp. 1095, 1102, 1107 L 4a, L 4c | Language Coach p. 1117 L 4a Language Coach p. 1125 L 4b Text Analysis: Shakespearean Drama p. 1119, 1120, 1127, 1129 L 3, L 5a |

| The Tragedy of Romeo and Juliet, Act Five<br>Drama<br>pp. 1130–1147 | Linked Selections | | Pyramus and Thisbe<br>Myth<br>pp. 1158–1165 | Writing Workshop:<br>Argument:<br>Critical Review pp. 1166–1175<br><br>Speaking and Listening Workshop: Evaluating a Critical Review pp. 1176–1177 |
| | Media Study: from Romeo and Juliet<br>Film Clip<br>pp. 1148–1151 | Great Movies: Romeo and Juliet<br>Critical Review<br>pp. 1152–1157 | | |
| | | Lexile: 1282<br>Fry: College<br>Dale-Chall: 8.8 | | |
| Shakespearean Drama pp. 1132, 1137, 1146 RL 2, RL 3, RL 10<br>Reading Shakespearean Drama p. 1146 RL 2, RL 3, RL 10 | | | Myth pp. 1159, 1160, 1163–1165 RL 6, RL 9, RL 10<br>Sequence pp. 1159, 1162, 1163, 1165 RL 5 | |
| | | Analyze a Critical Review pp. 1152, 1153, 1155–1157 RI 2, RI 3, RI 8 | | |
| Writing Prompt p. 1147 | Write or Discuss p. 1151 W 9 (RL 7) | Writing Prompt p. 1157 W 9b (RI 8) | Writing Prompt p. 1165 W 9a (RL 9) | Writing a Critical Review pp. 1166–1175 W 1a–e, W 4, W 5, W 9a (RL 7, 9), W 10 |
| Behind the Curtain p. 1135 SL 2 | Media Literacy pp. 1149–1150<br>Write or Discuss p. 1151 SL 1a, SL 2<br>Visual Treatment p. 1151 | | Discuss p. 1158 SL 1 | Evaluating a Critical Review pp. 1176–1177 SL 3 |
| Shakespearean Drama pp. 1130, 1134, 1136, 1144, 1146 L 3<br>Language Coach pp. 1139, 1143 L 4<br>Create Rhythm p. 1147 L 1a–b | | Language Coach p. 1154 L 4a | Language Coach p. 1164 L 4a, d | Drafting p. 1169 L 1b<br>Editing and Publishing p. 1173 L 1, L 2a |

To see the complete Essential Course of Study, see pp. T23–T28.

For additional lesson planning help, see **Teacher One Stop DVD.**

# Instructional Support

**Resource Manager Unit 10**

**UNIT SUPPORT**

Academic Vocabulary, p. 3

Additional Academic Vocabulary, p. 4

Grammar Focus p. 5

Text Analysis Workshop pp. 9–10

Writing Workshop: Argument: Critical Review p. 117

**SELECTION SUPPORT\***

**Plan and Teach**

Lesson planning pages

Additional leveled selection questions

Extension activities

**Student Copy Masters**

Selection summaries in four languages

Skills copy masters in English and Spanish

Vocabulary preteaching and support

Reading Check and Question Support

Reading Fluency

\*Available for all selections

† Available on **thinkcentral.com**.

**Language Handbook**

**Vocabulary Practice**

**Best Practices Toolkit†**

**PowerNotes** DVD-ROM†

**Connections: Nonfiction for Common Core** CD-ROM†

**Teacher One Stop** DVD-ROM

**Student One Stop** DVD-ROM

**Media*Smart*** DVD-ROM *from* Romeo and Juliet

**Write*Smart*** CD-ROM†

**GrammarNotes** DVD-ROM†

**WordSharp** CD-ROM†

Media Smart

## Media Studies

The Lord of the Rings

The Cask of Amontillado

Coal Miner Rescue News Reports

Boys & Girls Clubs/Peace Corps

The Birds

# Differentiated Instruction

### STRUGGLING READERS AND WRITERS

Resource Manager Unit 10

Additional Selection Questions

Question Support

Reading Fluency

**Interactive Reader**

**Adapted Interactive Reader**

**Level Up Online Tutorials**

**Audio Anthology**
(with Audio summaries)

**Diagnostic and Selection Tests**

Selection Tests A/B

### ENGLISH LANGUAGE LEARNERS

Resource Manager Unit 10

Selection Summaries in English, Spanish, Vietnamese and Haitian Creole

Skills Copymasters in Spanish

**English Language Learner Adapted Interactive Reader Teacher's Guide**

**ELL Adapted Interactive Reader**

**Audio Tutor**

**Guide to English for Newcomers**

**Audio Anthology**

**Audio Summaries in Multiple Languages**
(on **thinkcentral.com**)

### ADVANCED LEARNERS

Resource Manager Unit 10

Additional Selection Questions

Ideas for Extension

**Diagnostic and Selection Tests**

Selection Tests B/C

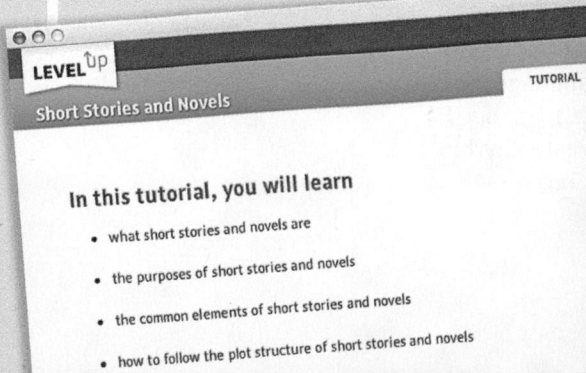

LEVEL up

TUTORIAL

Short Stories and Novels

In this tutorial, you will learn

• what short stories and novels are

• the purposes of short stories and novels

• the common elements of short stories and novels

• how to follow the plot structure of short stories and novels

## Assessment and Reteaching

**Diagnostic and Selection Tests**

**Unit and Benchmark Tests**

**ThinkCentral Online Assessment:**

• All program assessments

• Level Up Online Tutorials

**ExamView Test Generator** on the Teacher One Stop DVD-ROM

**Online Essay Scoring** on **thinkcentral.com**

**ThinkCentral Online Reteaching:**

• Level Up Online Tutorials

• Reteaching Worksheets

Holt McDougal Online Essay Scoring

Welcome to Holt McDougal Online Essay Scoring!

This site is designed to help you improve your writing skills and prepare for standardized writing tests. When you write and submit a response to one of the writing prompts on this site, the computerized scoring system will immediately score and deliver feedback on your essay. Other resources on this site will help you prepare, develop, and revise your essay.

**STUDENTS**
Get started by entering the **Writing Zone** →

## Professional Development

**Video Center** Based on interviews with program consultants and other educational experts, these videos feature classroom-ready teaching strategies.

**Teacher Toolkit** Includes a Teacher Handbook as well as a range of articles and handouts by program consultants and other educators.

**Janet Allen**

**Kylene Beers**

**Jim Burke**

**Carol Jago**

# THINK central at a Glance

## One Location, Endless Resources

**Find Resources** Browse all *Holt McDougal Literature* components for the ones that meet your students' needs and match your teaching style.

**Assess Progress and Reteach** Assign electronic versions of program assessments to measure your students' mastery of the Common Core State Standards. On thinkcentral.com, some tests deliver online remediation tutorials to students who have not mastered skills.

 *Interactive Whiteboard Lessons*

Prepare your students for college and careers by teaching relevant, real-world skills through dynamic, interactive instruction. Go to **thinkcentral.com** to browse through all whiteboard lessons, including the following:

• Character Development and Motivation

• Using Parallel Structure

• Writing Effective Arguments

**HISTORY**

Together Holt McDougal and HISTORY® are revolutionizing the study of English/language arts with video that helps students relive and re-imagine the people, places, and events they are discovering through reading. Look for selections with the HISTORY® icon.

## What is the ultimate
# LOVE STORY?

Introduce the page by reading aloud the question and the opening paragraph. Point out that couples and their love stories appear throughout the world's poetry, folklore, song lyrics, history, and even cartoons, as in these examples:

Cinderella and Prince Charming

Orpheus and Eurydice

Beauty and the Beast

John and Abigail Adams

Sarah and Abraham

Using these examples, explain that some couples fall in love at first sight. Some have a long, loving friendship; others have a turbulent love that is complicated by a variety of differences. Invite student comments and additional examples.

*ACTIVITY* Before partners make their choices about the ultimate love story, have them consider their criteria. For example, does the ultimate love story have the happiest ending? the greatest compatibility between the lovers? the greatest ability to overcome hardship? the greatest potential for marriage? Invite students to share and compare their choices.

**CHECK UNDERSTANDING** As you review the question at the top of the page, elicit that the love stories that students chose need not be famous, only memorable.

## Unit Resources

## What is the ultimate
# LOVE STORY?

From cynics to sentimentalists, almost everyone can appreciate a good love story. These stories are everywhere, from great literary masterpieces to last week's made-for-TV movie. One of the most famous love stories ever written is William Shakespeare's *Romeo and Juliet*, the tale of two reckless teenagers who fall in love at first sight. It is a story that has captivated readers and audiences for over 400 years.

*ACTIVITY* With a partner, think of a few love stories you remember reading or watching. Whether it's an old-fashioned fairy tale or a modern romantic comedy, a tear-jerker novel or a film featuring the couple you love to hate, which story do you remember most vividly? Working together, make a list of titles and then settle on the tale *you* consider the ultimate love story.

**Find It Online!** **THINK** central
Go to thinkcentral.com for the interactive version of this unit.

1020

---

See resources on the **Teacher One Stop DVD-ROM** and on **thinkcentral.com**.

**R** RESOURCE MANAGER UNIT 10

UNIT AND BENCHMARK TESTS

**📁** BEST PRACTICES TOOLKIT

INTERACTIVE READER

ADAPTED INTERACTIVE READER

ELL ADAPTED INTERACTIVE READER

LANGUAGE HANDBOOK

VOCABULARY PRACTICE

TECHNOLOGY

⊘ Teacher One Stop DVD-ROM

⊘ Student One Stop DVD-ROM

⊘ PowerNotes DVD-ROM

⊘ Write*Smart* CD-ROM

⊘ Media*Smart* DVD-ROM

⊘ GrammarNotes DVD-ROM

⊘ Audio Anthology CD

⊘ Audio Tutor CD

**THINK** central

**Find It Online!**

The interactive version of this unit on **thinkcentral.com** includes

• video and **PowerNotes** introductions to key selections

• audio support—listen or download

• **ThinkAloud** models

• **WordSharp** vocabulary tutorials

• interactive review and remediation

COMMON
CORE

## Preview Unit Goals

| | |
|---|---|
| **TEXT ANALYSIS** | • Understand the conventions of Shakespearean drama and tragedy<br>• Analyze Shakespearean language, including word play and blank verse<br>• Analyze characters, including character foils and the tragic hero<br>• Identify and analyze soliloquies, asides, and allusions<br>• Analyze cultural experiences reflected in works of world literature<br>• Determine a theme and analyze its development |
| **READING** | • Read and comprehend Shakespearean drama<br>• Paraphrase passages as an aid to comprehension<br>• Analyze a critical review and provide an objective summary<br>• Compare and contrast a critical review with your own response |
| **WRITING AND LANGUAGE** | • Write a critical review<br>• Understand and use parallel structure |
| **SPEAKING AND LISTENING** | • Evaluate a critical review<br>• Integrate information presented in diverse media and formats |
| **MEDIA AND VIEWING** | • Identify, analyze, and evaluate mise en scène<br>• Create a visual treatment |

## Media Smart DVD-ROM

### Shakespeare Goes to Hollywood

Discover how the director Franco Zeffirelli captures the rapture of first love in this classic film version. Page 1148

1021

COMMON CORE **UNIT GOALS**

Included in this unit: RL 1-6, RL 9-10, RI 2-3, RI 8, RI 10, W 1a-e, W 4-5, W 9 (RL 7), W 9a (RL 7, 9), W 9b (RI 8), W 10, SL 1, SL 1a, SL 2, SL 3, L 1, L 1a, L 1b, L 2a, L 3, L 4, L 4a-d, L 5a, L 6
Complete text of the Common Core State Standards is found in the correlation on p. T10. Standards covered in this unit are found in the standards overview (pp. 1019A–1019B) and on the lesson pages where they are taught.

## Preview Unit Goals

Point out to students that these goals reflect the main skills and strategies taught in Unit 10. Have students read through the list and consider what they already may know about each goal. Review the color-coding of the skill strands, reminding students that this coding will reappear throughout the unit.

# Shakespeare's World

## Shakespeare's World

### COMMON CORE FOCUS

**RI 10** Read and comprehend literary nonfiction.
**SL 2** Integrate multiple sources of information presented in diverse formats.

---

**READING STRATEGY**

### ■ PREVIEW

Have students preview the article by examining it quickly. Suggest that they look at the illustrations and read the heads and subheads. Discuss their initial impressions of the article. After students have read the article, have them compare and contrast their first impressions with what they learned from reading it in detail.

---

**READING SKILL**

### ■ MAKE GENERALIZATIONS

Have students make a general assessment of the era in which Shakespeare wrote.
*Possible answer: The era in which Shakespeare wrote was a period of relative political stability under Queen Elizabeth I and intense intellectual and cultural activity.*

---

## England in Shakespeare's Day

**COMMON CORE**

**RI 10** Read and comprehend literary nonfiction. **SL 2** Integrate multiple sources of information presented in diverse formats.

**Renaissance Man**
William Shakespeare is widely considered to be the greatest writer in the English language and the greatest playwright of all time. His plays have been produced more often and in more countries than those of any other author. Shakespeare lived in England during the flowering of intellectual activity known as the Renaissance. The European Renaissance was marked by a renewed interest in science, commerce, philosophy, and the arts. Basic to Renaissance thinking was a new emphasis on the individual and on freedom of choice. The Renaissance movement began in 14th-century Italy and gradually moved north and west toward England, where it reached its peak during the reign of Queen Elizabeth I. Shakespeare started his literary career during Elizabeth's reign, a period that lasted from 1558 to 1603 and is often called the Elizabethan Age.

**William Shakespeare**
**1564–1616**

**All Hail the Queen** Elizabeth was the last member of England's royal house of Tudor. Her grandfather, King Henry VII, brought stability and prosperity to his kingdom, and it was during his reign that Renaissance ideas began taking hold in England. However, political and religious problems surfaced during the reign of Elizabeth's father, Henry VIII, and continued into the early years of Elizabeth's own reign. Luckily, Elizabeth proved to be a strong monarch, able to guide England along a more moderate and prosperous course. It was a course that most Elizabethans, including Shakespeare, seem to have appreciated.

Like her grandfather and father before her, Elizabeth I was a strong supporter of English culture. As a result, artists of all types—including playwrights, poets, painters, sculptors, musicians, and architects—were held in high esteem. Taking the cue from their monarch, members of England's upper class often became patrons, or financial sponsors, of the arts. In the early 1590s, Shakespeare began acting in and writing plays for a theater company sponsored by two men who had both held the office of lord chamberlain, a high-ranking position in Elizabeth's court. The company was called the Lord Chamberlain's Men, and Elizabeth herself attended some of its productions.

**Queen Elizabeth I**
**1533–1603**

## Theater in Shakespeare's Day

**A Writer for All Time** Though acting companies toured throughout England, London was the center of the Elizabethan stage. In 1576, well before Shakespeare became affiliated with the Lord Chamberlain's Men, the company built England's first theater in the suburbs of London; by the end of the 1590s, London boasted more theaters than any other European capital. One reason the London theaters did so well was that they attracted an audience of rich and poor alike. In fact, the Elizabethan theater was one of the few forms of entertainment available to working-class people of the day, and one of the few places where the working class and the educated upper class could mix. Shakespeare appealed to English audience members of all classes by including a great deal of variety in his plays: poetic speeches, exciting action, fast-paced humor, vivid character portrayals, and wise observations about human nature. Thus, while he was respected by the rich and powerful people of his day, he also became very popular with the common people.

**Around the Globe** In 1599, Shakespeare and the other shareholders of the Lord Chamberlain's Men became joint owners of the company's new home, the Globe Theatre. The Globe was a three-story wooden structure with an open-air courtyard in the center. Actors performed on a raised platform stage. The theater could hold 3,000 spectators, many of whom stood in the part of the courtyard near the stage, known as the pit. These customers paid the lowest admission charge, usually just a penny. Richer theatergoers paid more and sat in the inner balconies, which surrounded most of the courtyard. The illustration below shows the different sections of the theater. Audiences became emotionally involved in performances, openly showing their pleasure or their disappointment. They cheered, booed, hissed, and even threw rotten vegetables. They applauded agile sword fighting and dramatic sound effects, such as blares of trumpets, drum rolls, and claps of thunder.

### THE GLOBE

This illustration shows what scholars believe the Globe Theatre looked like.

1. raised platform stage
2. pit
3. courtyard
4. inner balconies

1023

### ◼ MAKE INFERENCES

Ask students how knowing that a mixed audience—that is, both the upper class and the working class—would be watching his plays might have affected Shakespeare as he wrote his plays. ***Possible answer:*** *Shakespeare probably would not have been afraid to include allusions to literature, which at least some members of the upper class would have the education to understand. At the same time, he would have wanted to include comic elements that would have appealed to the common people. Ultimately, Shakespeare probably would have been aware that an interest in good, fast-paced drama and excitement crossed the boundary between rich and poor, as did an enthusiasm for humor of all kinds.*

## Analyze Visuals

**Activity** How do the numerals in red circles help you understand this illustration? *Possible answer: The numerals in red circles label important elements in the illustration. The key, which appears in the upper left-hand corner, explains what each numeral shows.*

## ■ COMPARE AND CONTRAST

After students have read the section **Theater in Shakespeare's Day** (pp. 1023–1024), ask them how theater in Shakespeare's time differed from theater today. *Possible answer: In Shakespeare's time, many of the spectators stood near the stage instead of sitting in orderly rows. The staging was rather simple, with little scenery and no artificial lighting. Furthermore, women's roles were played by young men. Just the same, audience members identified so strongly with what was happening on the stage that they cheered, booed, hissed, and sometimes even threw things at the actors.*

## ■ IDENTIFY MAIN IDEAS

Ask students to identify the main idea of the section **Impact on Language.** *Possible answer: Shakespeare greatly enriched the English language by including in his plays both the language of his day and words and expressions that he coined himself.*

## Analyze Visuals

**Activity** Which elements of the cartoon evoke a Shakespearean play? Which element does not? Explain. *Possible answer: The castle-like setting and the Elizabethan costumes evoke a Shakespearean play. The caption does not, because it uses contemporary slang rather than Shakespearean language.*

---

Elizabethan theater relied heavily on the audience's imagination. Most theaters had no curtains, no artificial lighting, and very little scenery. Instead, props, sound effects, and sometimes lines of dialogue let the audience know when and where a scene took place. However, while the staging was simple, it was hardly dull. Swords, shields, brightly colored banners, and elegant costumes often added to the spectacle. The costumes also helped audiences imagine that women were playing the female roles, which in fact were played by young male actors. In Shakespeare's day, no women belonged to English acting companies—it was considered improper for women to appear on stage. The boys who played female roles underwent rigorous training in acting, singing, and dancing. Before one could play a role such as Juliet in a first-rate company, he had to learn to move gracefully and speak convincingly.

**HIS WORDS LIVE ON**
Shakespeare continues to influence modern culture, as the following images demonstrate.

Actors from a popular 1993 film based on Shakespeare's *Much Ado About Nothing*

## Impact on Language

**Word Master** Shakespeare's plays have influenced literary works for hundreds of years, and modern retellings of his stories are common. Additionally, Shakespeare was a master of dramatic language and a great experimenter with spoken English. He cleverly played with words and their meanings, creating novel metaphors and striking images that, once heard or read, are rarely forgotten.

Shakespeare contributed more words, phrases, and expressions to the English language than any other writer. Some of these words were his own invention, including *assassination, bump,* and *lonely.* Other expressions might have been part of the everyday speech of Elizabethan England, but Shakespeare was the first to use them in writing.

Many of these phrases and expressions have become so common that people use them without realizing that they are quoting Shakespeare. In fact, the expressions have become "household words"— a term first used in Shakespeare's historical play *Henry V.* Other expressions that have become part of the language include the now common simile "dead as a doornail" (*Henry VI, Part 2*), "laughingstock" (*The Merry Wives of Windsor*), and "for goodness' sake" (*Henry VIII*). Shakespeare's fine ear for the English language prompted the British writer George Orwell to call him a "word musician."

*"He's, like, 'To be or not to be,' and I'm, like, 'Get a life.'"*

A cartoon from the *New Yorker* magazine does a takeoff on *Hamlet.*

## More About the Man

**The Bard of Avon** Although Shakespeare is probably the most famous writer who ever lived, it is largely through his plays and poetry that we know him. The known facts about his personal life are surprisingly few. We know that he came from Stratford-on-Avon, a small town on the river Avon about 90 miles northwest of London. His father was a glove maker who later became the town's mayor; his mother was a distant relative of a wealthy family who lived just outside town. Church records indicate that Shakespeare was baptized on April 26, 1564, which suggests that he was born a few days earlier. He probably went to the local grammar school, although school records no longer exist. There he would have studied Latin and read works by ancient Roman writers, such as Virgil and Seneca.

**Making His Way** At 18, Shakespeare married Anne Hathaway, a local farmer's daughter. The couple had a daughter named Susanna in 1583 and boy and girl twins named Hamnet and Judith two years later. There are no records of what Shakespeare did in the next seven years, which some scholars call the "lost years" of his life. During that time he apparently left his family back in Stratford, where they could live comfortably, and made his way to London, center of the theater world. He probably joined a theater company and traveled with it as an actor. When next we hear of Shakespeare, it is as a successful playwright and sometime actor in London. His earliest plays include *Richard III* and *The Comedy of Errors;* he also was writing lyric and narrative poetry. In 1593 he published his long poem *Venus and Adonis,* apparently written during the 1592–1593 season, when London's theaters were shut because of an outbreak of the plague.

**Fame and Fortune** By 1596, the year *Romeo and Juliet* was probably first performed, ten of Shakespeare's plays had already been produced in London, and he was a shareholder in the Lord Chamberlain's Men. Shakespeare's plays helped make the theater company the most successful of its day. In 1599, he became part owner of London's popular new Globe Theatre. In 1603, when James I succeeded Elizabeth I on the throne of England, the new king himself became the patron of Shakespeare's theater company, which became known as the King's Men. Shakespeare's business interests and revenues from plays brought him a good deal of money, enough to purchase a beautiful home for his family in Stratford. He also may have purchased a coat of arms for his father, an important symbol that allowed his father to move officially into the ranks of gentlemen.

**The End** In 1609, Shakespeare took advantage of his fame by publishing his sonnets, a series of poems about love and friendship that most scholars feel he wrote in the 1590s. Shakespeare also began spending more time in Stratford, retiring there permanently in 1613. He wrote no plays after that year; his last complete plays are believed to be *Cymbeline, The Tempest, The Winter's Tale,* and *Henry VIII.* While there are no documentary records of the date of his death, the monument that marks his grave indicates that he died on April 23, 1616.

**Authors Online**
Go to **thinkcentral.com**. KEYWORD: HML9-1025
THINK central

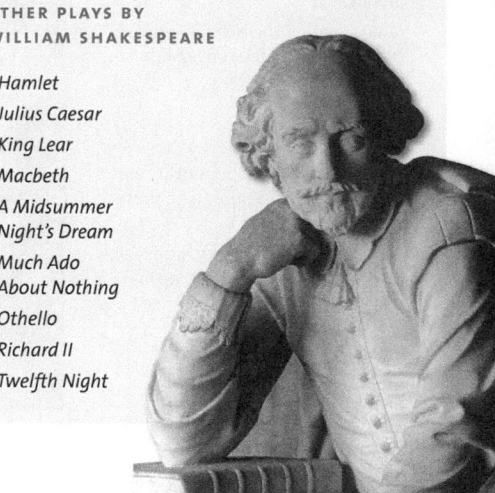

OTHER PLAYS BY WILLIAM SHAKESPEARE

- *Hamlet*
- *Julius Caesar*
- *King Lear*
- *Macbeth*
- *A Midsummer Night's Dream*
- *Much Ado About Nothing*
- *Othello*
- *Richard II*
- *Twelfth Night*

# Focus and Motivate

## COMMON CORE FOCUS

**RL 2** Provide an objective summary of the text.
**RL 3** Analyze how complex characters develop over the course of a text, interact with other characters, and advance the plot or develop the theme. **RL 9** Analyze how an author draws on and transforms source material in a specific work. **RL 10** Read and comprehend dramas. **L 3** Apply knowledge of language to understand how language functions in different contexts, to make effective choices for meaning or style, and to comprehend more fully when reading or listening. **L 6** Acquire and use accurately domain-specific words and phrases.

# Teach

## Part 1: Characteristics of Shakespearean Tragedy

**Characters** Remind students that drama develops plot and characters through dialogue and action. Students learn about characters by what they say and do. A protagonist and antagonist create the conflict that drives the plot. Note that Shakespeare's plays often have many minor characters as well as major ones. Often, a foil is a minor character.

Tell students that one way to keep track of characters is by listing them and their qualities in two-column charts. Students might underline names of main characters and make more detailed notes about them.

| Character | Traits and Qualities |
|-----------|---------------------|
|           |                     |

 **BEST PRACTICES TOOLKIT—Transparency**
Two-Column Chart p. A25

**Dramatic Conventions** Use this activity to help students understand the dramatic conventions that are described:

- Suggest scenarios for a soliloquy and an aside and ask volunteers to improvise dialogue for them. For example, tell students that a character is feeling hopeful about the future. What might the character say?

- Ask students to give examples of dramatic irony or comic relief from television shows or films.

- Discuss what each convention adds to the drama.

**BEST PRACTICES TOOLKIT—Transparency**
Core Analysis Frame: Drama pp. D21, D42

---

# Shakespearean Drama

*Essential Course of Study* ECOS

"If we wish to know the force of human genius," the writer William Hazlitt once proclaimed, "we should read Shakespeare." Though he wrote them over 400 years ago, Shakespeare's 37 plays are arguably as popular today as they were in Elizabethan times; they still draw avid fans to packed theaters. Shakespeare's comedies and histories remain crowd-pleasing classics, but his tragedies are perhaps his most powerful plays. One of Shakespeare's most famous tragedies is *The Tragedy of Romeo and Juliet,* the story of two lovestruck teenagers from feuding families.

## COMMON CORE

Included in this workshop:
**RL 3** Analyze how complex characters develop over the course of a text, interact with other characters, and advance the plot or develop the theme. **RL 9** Analyze how an author draws on and transforms source material in a specific work. **RL 10** Read and comprehend dramas. **L 3** Apply knowledge of language to understand how language functions in different contexts, to make effective choices for meaning or style, and to comprehend more fully when reading or listening. **L 6** Acquire and use accurately domain-specific words and phrases.

## Part 1: Characteristics of Shakespearean Tragedy

A **tragedy** is a drama that ends in catastrophe—most often death—for the main characters. Shakespearean tragedies, however, offer more than just despair; they also include comic moments that counter the overall seriousness of the plot. Familiarize yourself with the characters and dramatic conventions of Shakespearean tragedy before you begin reading *Romeo and Juliet.*

### CHARACTERS

**Tragic Hero**
- is the **protagonist**, or central character—the one with whom audiences identify
- usually fails or dies because of a character flaw or a cruel twist of fate
- often has a high rank or status; shows strength while facing his or her destiny

**Antagonist**
- is the force working against the protagonist
- can be another character, a group of characters, or something nonhuman, such as nature or society

**Foil**
- is a character whose personality and attitude contrast sharply with those of another character
- highlights both characters' traits—for example, a timid character can make a talkative one seem even chattier

### DRAMATIC CONVENTIONS

**Soliloquy**
- is a speech given by a character alone on stage
- lets the audience know what the character is thinking or feeling

**Aside**
- is a character's remark, either to the audience or to another character, that others on stage do not hear
- reveals the character's private thoughts

**Dramatic Irony**
- is when the audience knows more than the characters—for example, the audience is aware of Romeo and Juliet's tragic demise long before the characters themselves face it
- helps build suspense

**Comic Relief**
- is a humorous scene or speech intended to lighten the mood
- serves to heighten the seriousness of the main action by contrast

---

## DIFFERENTIATED INSTRUCTION

### FOR STRUGGLING READERS

**Note Taking** To help students develop their reading comprehension, focus on note-taking skills. Tell students to use the heads on this page to organize their notes; to summarize the main idea of each section; and to include only details that are important.

## MODEL 1: CHARACTER IN TRAGEDY

In this excerpt, Romeo—the young protagonist of the play and a member of the Montague family—complains to his cousin, Benvolio, about a problem that is plaguing him. What do you learn about Romeo's personality?

**COMMON CORE**

**RL 2** Provide an objective summary of a text. **RL 3** Analyze how complex characters develop over the course of a text, interact with other characters, and advance the plot or develop the theme.

### *from* Act One, SCENE I

Lines 153–161

**Benvolio.** Good morrow, cousin.
**Romeo.**                          Is the day so young?
**Benvolio.** But new struck nine.
**Romeo.**                          Ay me! sad hours seem long.
155 Was that my father that went hence so fast?
**Benvolio.** It was. What sadness lengthens Romeo's hours?
**Romeo.** Not having that which having makes them short.
**Benvolio.** In love?
**Romeo.** Out—
160 **Benvolio.** Of love?
**Romeo.** Out of her favor where I am in love.

**Close Read**

1. What is Romeo experiencing that most readers could relate to?

2. What possible weakness or flaw does Romeo's attitude hint at?

## MODEL 2: SOLILOQUY

Through this soliloquy, readers gain access to the thoughts and feelings of Juliet, a Capulet and therefore a hated enemy of any Montague.

### *from* Act Three, SCENE 2

Lines 20–31

20 **Juliet.** . . . Come, gentle night; come, loving, black-browed night;
Give me my Romeo; and, when he shall die,
Take him and cut him out in little stars,
And he will make the face of heaven so fine
That all the world will be in love with night
25 And pay no worship to the garish sun.
O, I have bought the mansion of a love,
But not possessed it; and though I am sold,
Not yet enjoyed. So tedious is this day
As is the night before some festival
30 To an impatient child that hath new robes
And may not wear them. . . .

**Close Read**

1. What does the imagery in lines 20–25 reveal about Juliet's feelings for Romeo?

2. Reread the boxed text. What is Juliet's mood as she waits for Romeo? Point out specific words and details that reveal her state of mind.

---

## MODEL 1: CHARACTER IN TRAGEDY
**Close Read**

1. *Possible answer: Romeo is feeling sad that the girl he loves does not love him. He refers to sadness in line 154 and gives the reason in line 161, when he says, "Out of her favor where I am in love."*

2. *Answers will vary, but students may suggest that Romeo is impatient or that he overdramatizes the ups and downs of his love life.*

## MODEL 2: SOLILOQUY
**Close Read**

1. *Possible answer: The imagery shows Juliet's high regard for Romeo. She envisions that even after death he would make night so wonderful that "all the world" would love him as much as she does.*

2. *Possible answer: Juliet is in an impatient mood. Her use of the word "tedious" to describe the day and her simile comparing herself to "an impatient child" reveal her own state of mind as she waits for night to bring Romeo to her.*

---

### FOR ENGLISH LANGUAGE LEARNERS
**Language: Skill Words** On the board, list and define the literary terms shown in italics. Then give the examples in random order and have students match them to the vocabulary.

- *imagery:* the sky was black velvet
- *character:* Romeo, Juliet, Benvolio
- *dialogue:* Oh, I cannot wait much longer!
- *stage directions:* Midnight in the church-yard. A bell chimes softly.

### FOR ADVANCED LEARNERS/PRE–AP
**Evaluate Characters** Have students discuss which character is more sympathetic, Romeo or Juliet. Have students consider both of the characters' attitudes and words. Tell students to give reasons for their responses and to support their evaluations with evidence from the models.

**Online Remediation**

Are your students struggling with text analysis skills? Consider assigning them one or more **Level Up Online Tutorials** as remediation before beginning this unit. Log in to **thinkcentral.com** to view a list of the skills addressed by **Level Up**.

# Teach

## Part 2: The Language of Shakespeare

**Blank Verse** To help students understand the concept of stressed and unstressed syllables in iambic pentameter, read the two italicized lines aloud again. Tap a pencil or ruler at every stressed syllable. Have students count aloud the taps in each line.

**Allusion and Word Play** To illustrate the concept of an allusion, point out that the character of Romeo has now become an allusion. People often refer to a man in love as a Romeo. Write *allusion* and *illusion* on the board, noting the difference in the spelling and meaning; an illusion is a false perception.

Write this pun on the board:

> Time flies like an arrow. Fruit flies like a banana.

Ask which words have more than one meaning (*flies, like*). Then discuss how the knowledge of the two meanings creates the humorous surprise.

## CHECK UNDERSTANDING

Have students sum up what they have learned about the characteristics of Shakespearean drama and the language of Shakespeare.

---

## Part 2: The Language of Shakespeare

Shakespeare's plays deal with experiences and emotions that are easy to relate to, but his language can be challenging for modern readers to decipher. However, once you get past the play's unfamiliar language, learn the rhythm of its poetry, and discover how to decode Shakespeare's allusions and puns, you will come to appreciate the romance, drama, and humor that await you.

### BLANK VERSE

Shakespeare wrote his plays primarily in **blank verse,** the form of poetry that most resembles natural speech. Blank verse is made up of unrhymed lines of **iambic pentameter,** a type of meter that has five unstressed syllables (˘), each followed by a stressed syllable (ˊ). Read the following lines aloud, making sure to emphasize each stressed syllable:

> *Yet tell me not, for I have heard it all.*
>
> *Here's much to do with hate but more with love.*

While this pattern is the general rule, it is often broken. Variations in the rhythm prevent the play from sounding monotonous. Breaks in the pattern also help to emphasize important ideas or dramatic moments. As you read, pay close attention to places where characters speak in rhyming poetry instead of unrhymed prose.

### ALLUSION AND WORD PLAY

An **allusion** is a reference, within a work, to something that the audience is expected to know. Shakespeare's audience was familiar with Greek and Roman mythology as well as the Bible, so he sprinkled references to these works throughout his plays. In this romantic tragedy, Shakespeare included allusions to Venus, the Roman goddess of love.

Shakespeare was also a master of clever **puns,** or jokes that result from multiple word meanings or rhyming sounds. In Act One, a depressed Romeo puns on two meanings of the word *light* when he offers to carry a torch: "Being but heavy, I will bear the light."

---

### ELIZABETHAN WORDS TO KNOW

Chances are you don't need an Elizabethan glossary to figure out that *dost* means "does." Other words and expressions, however, can prove more of a challenge. Here is a list of words that you should expect to encounter often as you read:

**'a:** he.

**an, and:** if.

**anon:** soon; right away.

**aught:** anything.

**coz:** short for *cousin;* used to refer to relatives or close friends.

**ere:** before.

**e'er:** ever.

**god-den:** good evening.

**God gi' go-den:** God give you a good evening.

**hence:** from here.

**hie:** hurry.

**hither:** here.

**marry:** a short form of "by the Virgin Mary" and so a mild exclamation.

**morrow:** morning.

**naught:** nothing.

**o'er:** over.

**prithee:** pray thee, or please.

**sirrah:** a term used to address a servant.

**soft:** be still; quiet; wait a minute.

**thither:** there.

**whence:** where.

**wherefore:** why.

**wot:** know.

**yond, yonder:** over there.

---

## DIFFERENTIATED INSTRUCTION

### FOR ENGLISH LANGUAGE LEARNERS

**Language: Punctuation** Direct students' attention to the apostrophe in the second line of the italicized example and in the list of **Elizabethan Words to Know.** Point out that an apostrophe can signal ownership or missing letters, such as the missing *i* in *Here's.* Have students find examples of each use on these pages (*e'er, o'er, Cupid's*).

**Culture: Clarify** Draw attention to line 6 in Model 1 on page 1029. Point out that the language is English that contains word forms no longer used, such as *thou* and *art.* Urge student pairs to use context to define these words. Have pairs find other examples of outdated English. Help the class create a master list and decode the meanings of the examples.

## MODEL 1: BLANK VERSE

The fact that Shakespeare wrote in verse should not intimidate you. Since iambic pentameter is fairly close to English speech patterns, it can be spoken naturally, without much awkwardness. Read the following excerpt aloud to get a feel for its rhythm.

---

### *from* Act Two, SCENE 2

Lines 2–6

But soft! What light through yonder window breaks?
It is the East, and Juliet is the sun!
Arise, fair sun, and kill the envious moon,
5  Who is already sick and pale with grief
That thou her maid art far more fair than she.

---

**Close Read**

1. Reread the excerpt, tapping your foot at each stressed syllable. How many stressed syllables are in each line?

2. Point out a place where the pattern breaks. One example has been boxed. What ideas are emphasized by these variations in rhythm?

## MODEL 2: ALLUSION AND WORD PLAY

For a tragedy, *Romeo and Juliet* contains quite a bit of humor. In the first two acts, much of the comedy comes courtesy of Mercutio, who clowns around, trying to make his friend Romeo laugh. Look for several puns and an allusion in this comic conversation.

---

### *from* Act One, SCENE 4

Lines 13–22

**Mercutio.** Nay, gentle Romeo, we must have you dance.
**Romeo.** Not I, believe me. You have dancing shoes
15  With nimble soles; I have a soul of lead
So stakes me to the ground I cannot move.
**Mercutio.** You are a lover. Borrow Cupid's wings
And soar with them above a common bound.
**Romeo.** I am too sore enpiercèd with his shaft
20  To soar with his light feathers, and so bound
I cannot bound a pitch above dull woe.
Under love's heavy burden do I sink.

---

**Close Read**

1. Identify the allusion in this excerpt, and describe the mental image it conjures up for you. Why do you think Shakespeare included this reference?

2. One example of a pun has been boxed. Find one other example and explain the play on words.

## MODEL 1: BLANK VERSE
**Close Read**
1. *Possible answer: There are five stressed syllables in each line.*

2. *Possible answer: The pattern also breaks at the word "envious" in line 4. These breaks add variety to the rhythm. They also help to emphasize Juliet's beauty, which is equated with sun and daylight and which makes even the moon envious.*

## MODEL 2: ALLUSION AND WORD PLAY
**Close Read**
1. *Possible answer: Mercutio alludes to Cupid, the winged Roman god of love, when he suggests that Romeo soar on the wings of love. Students may say the allusion conjures up a mental image of a flying Cupid, piercing hearts with his arrows and making people fall in love. Shakespeare probably included this reference because the play is a tragedy about love.*

2. *Possible answer: Romeo makes the pun that he is too sore to soar. Students should also recognize that bound is used in different ways, although they may not know the three meanings: a common bound, which means "leaping upright"; so bound, meaning "to be tied down"; and bound a pitch, which means "leap the height a falcon reaches when it soars."*

**IF STUDENTS NEED HELP . . .** Explain that they do not need to catch every break in rhythm, every allusion, or every pun to understand a scene. Encourage students to take turns paraphrasing the dialogue in Model 2. Point out that most people enjoy allusions and word play only after they have grasped the meaning of a particular scene or excerpt.

---

**FOR ENGLISH LANGUAGE LEARNERS**

**Culture: Allusions** Students from other cultures will likely struggle with allusions. Identify the allusion to Cupid in line 17 of Model 2, explaining that Cupid was the god of love in ancient Roman myths. Discuss why he might be mentioned in a play about love.

**Language: Conversational English Patterns**
Point out that Shakespeare often changes the usual order of words in sentences. Using Model 1, line 1 as an example, note that today, people would say, "What light breaks through that window?" Have students find another example of a verb placed at the end of a sentence (Model 2, line 22).

# Teach

## Part 3: Reading Shakespearean Drama

**Reading Drama** As you discuss such features as the cast of characters and stage directions, display actual elements from additional plays that students have read or will read. Point out that stage directions may contain important information about how a character appears or speaks, as well as details about the setting. Remind students that most dramas—not only Shakespearean plays—contain these elements.

**Reading Shakespearean Tragedy** Point out to students that Shakespearean tragedies have five acts and that the plot stages are divided among the acts. The exposition and rising action, for example, usually occur in Act One. Suggest that students use a Plot Diagram to track the plot throughout the play.

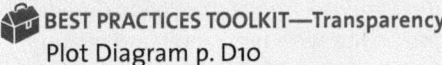 **BEST PRACTICES TOOLKIT—Transparency**
Plot Diagram p. D10

**Reading Shakespeare's Language** Point out that students will not read plays the same way they read novels. For example, suggest that they pause to look at the marginal notes on each page *before* reading the page. This way, they will have some idea of the meanings of certain terms or speeches before reading them in context. Students should use a similar pre-reading strategy with paraphrasing, reading a group of lines completely before attempting to paraphrase its parts in order to get help from context. Remind students that personal opinions should not be included when paraphrasing or summarizing.

---

## Part 3: Reading Shakespearean Drama

As you read *Romeo and Juliet,* you will encounter tools and strategies on every page. The following tips will show you how to make the most of them:

### READING DRAMA

- Study the opening **cast of characters** to see who's in the play.
- Read the **stage directions** to find out where a scene takes place as well as who's on stage and what they're doing. Stage directions in *Romeo and Juliet* are minimal, so you'll sometimes have to infer what's happening from the dialogue.
- Visualize the setting and the action by noting key details in the stage directions and the **synopsis** at the beginning of every scene.

### READING SHAKESPEAREAN TRAGEDY

- Keep track of the characters' relationships, such as whether they are friends, relatives, or enemies. Also think about what role a character has—tragic hero, antagonist, foil, or comic relief. This will help you interpret his or her speech and actions.
- Note important character traits revealed through **dialogue, soliloquies,** and **asides** as well as the action. Consider whether the characters exhibit any flaws or weaknesses.
- Look for cause-and-effect relationships between events, especially those events that lead to the tragic outcome. Track them in a graphic like the one shown.

### READING SHAKESPEARE'S LANGUAGE

- Use the **marginal notes** to help you figure out unfamiliar words and unusual sentence structures. In a chart like this one, record difficult lines and then rephrase them to read like modern speech.
- To help clarify their meaning, **paraphrase** passages and **summarize** events, ideas, and themes. Use your own words to retell what is happening and what it means, without including your own opinions.
- Just as when you read poetry, don't automatically stop reading when you come to the end of a line. Look carefully at each line's punctuation and consider the meaning of the complete sentence or phrase.

**STRATEGIES IN ACTION**

> **KEY DETAILS IN A SYNOPSIS**
>
> ### Act One
>
> SCENE 1 *A public square in Verona.*
> *As the scene opens, two young Capulet servants swagger across the stage, joking and bragging. When they happen to meet servants from the rival house of Montague, a quarrel begins that grows into an ugly street fight.*

| Cause | Effect |
|-------|--------|
| As part of a plan to cheer up Romeo, Benvolio and other Montagues bring him to a party that the Capulets are throwing. | At the party, Romeo sees Juliet for the first time and falls madly in love. |

| Text | What It Really Says | What It Means |
|------|---------------------|---------------|
| "O Romeo, Romeo! wherefore art thou Romeo?" Juliet, Act Two, Scene 2, line 33 | "Why are you Romeo?" | Why do you have to be a Montague, an enemy of my family? |

---

## DIFFERENTIATED INSTRUCTION

### FOR STRUGGLING READERS

**Note Taking** For students who need help with note taking, hand out the second note-taking copy master before discussing this page. Clarify that this copy master addresses strategies for reading Shakespearean plays. Explain that it lists steps that readers should take. As they read this page, they should pay attention to how the steps can help them.

**R** RESOURCE MANAGER—Copy Master
Note Taking p. 10

### FOR ADVANCED LEARNERS/PRE–AP

**Analyze Drama** Have students choose a soliloquy or other monologue from this or another Shakespearean tragedy and read it carefully to clarify its meaning. Challenge students to develop a reading that makes the meaning clear to an audience. Allow practice time, then invite students to perform dramatic readings for the class.

## MODEL: READING SHAKESPEAREAN DRAMA

This fight scene takes place in a public square in Verona, the city in which the play is set. Sampson and Gregory, servants of the Capulets, have gotten into a heated argument with Abram and Balthasar, servants of the Montagues. Use the strategies you learned on the preceding page and what you already know about tragedy to analyze this episode.

*from*

# ACT ONE, SCENE I

Lines 51–67

[*Enter* Benvolio, *nephew of Montague and first cousin of Romeo.*]

**Gregory** [*aside to* Sampson]. Say "better." Here comes one of my master's kinsmen.

**Sampson.** Yes, better, sir.

**Abram.** You lie.

55 **Sampson.** Draw, if you be men. Gregory, remember thy swashing blow.

[*They fight.*]

**Benvolio.** Part, fools! [*beats down their swords*] Put up your swords. You know not what you do.

[*Enter* Tybalt, *hot-headed nephew of Lady Capulet and first cousin of Juliet.*]

**Tybalt.** What, art thou drawn among these heartless hinds?

60 Turn thee, Benvolio! look upon thy death.

**Benvolio.** I do but keep the peace. Put up thy sword, Or manage it to part these men with me.

**Tybalt.** What, drawn, and talk of peace? I hate the word

As I hate hell, all Montagues, and thee.

65 Have at thee, coward!

[*They fight.*]

[*Enter several of both houses, who join the fray; then enter* Citizens *and* Peace Officers, *with clubs.*]

**Officer.** Clubs, bills, and partisans! Strike! beat them down!

**Citizens.** Down with the Capulets! Down with the Montagues!

**51–52** Gregory notices that Tybalt, a Capulet, is arriving.

**59–65** Tybalt does not understand that Benvolio is trying to stop the fight. He challenges Benvolio.

**59 heartless hinds:** cowardly servants.

**63 drawn:** with your sword out.

**65 Have at thee:** Defend yourself.

**66 bills, and partisans:** spears.

### Close Read

1. First, read through this excerpt. Then describe the setting, characters, and action you visualized as you read. Cite details from the dialogue and stage directions that helped you form a mental image.

2. What is Benvolio trying to do when Tybalt enters? Support your answer.

3. Using the marginal notes as necessary, paraphrase Tybalt's speech in the boxed lines. Why does Tybalt hate Benvolio so much?

4. How would you characterize Tybalt on the basis of this excerpt? In what way is he different from Benvolio? Cite details from the text to support your answer.

## MODEL: READING SHAKESPEAREAN DRAMA

**Close Read**

1. *Answers will vary, but students should describe a public square in a city. These details are in the synopsis on page 1030 and the text on page 1031. A small conflict between servants escalates into a heated fight between Benvolio and Tybalt, who is described as "hot-headed" in the stage directions following line 58. His challenge to Benvolio backs up this description. Then additional people enter, according to the stage directions following line 65.*

2. **Possible answer:** *Benvolio is trying to stop a fight between the Montagues' and Capulets' servants. He tells the servants to "part" and he beats down their swords, telling them to put them away. He probably draws his own sword from its scabbard to accomplish this, because Tybalt mentions the drawn sword.*

3. **Possible answer:** *A paraphrased version might read, "What, you wave a sword and talk of peace? I hate peace, just as I hate hell, all Montagues, and you. Get ready to fight, coward!" Tybalt hates all Montagues, so when he sees Benvolio with his drawn sword, he assumes the worst.*

4. **Possible answer:** *Tybalt is described as "hot-headed," and his actions and speech support this. He quickly picks a fight with Benvolio and does not listen when Benvolio asks him to put away his sword or use it to help him maintain peace. Benvolio seems like a reasonable person who wants to maintain peace.*

**IF STUDENTS NEED HELP . . .** Break the page down into these separate parts: the servants enter and fight, Benvolio tries to stop them, Tybalt enters and goads Benvolio into a fight, others join in and criticize both families.

---

## DIFFERENTIATED INSTRUCTION

### FOR ENGLISH LANGUAGE LEARNERS

**Culture: Clarify** List *thou, thee, thy, thine,* and *thyself* on the board. Explain that these are older forms of the pronoun *you* and were usually used between people who were friends or relatives. Write a second list next to the first: *you* (subject), *you* (object), *your, yours, yourself.* Have students create oral sentences using a form of *you* and then restating the sentence using the appropriate form of *thou.*

### FOR ENGLISH LANGUAGE LEARNERS

**Language: Punctuation** Remind students that punctuation helps show how something is said. As an example, read Benvolio's outburst in line 57. Remind students that exclamation marks show strong feeling. Follow a similar procedure with question marks.

## Part 4: Analyze the Text

### Close Read

1. *Answers will vary depending on the chosen passage. Examples include:* **Capulet, lines 13–24:** *"Welcome, gentlemen. Ladies who are able will dance with you. Ah ha, ladies! Which of you refuse to dance? We'll just assume that anyone who shies away from dancing has corns. Can I come near you now? Welcome, gentlemen! Long gone are the days since I wore a mask and courted the ladies. But you are welcome to dance . . . . Come on, ladies, hit the dance floor!"* **Romeo, lines 42–51:** *"She is so beautiful that the torches can learn to shine from her. She is like a rich, sparkling jewel. She is too beautiful for Earth! She stands out from others like a white dove traveling with crows. Since the dance is done, I'll watch where she goes. By touching her hand, my own will be blessed. I didn't know what love was until this moment. Before tonight, I never saw true beauty!"* **Tybalt, lines 52–57:** *"I can tell by Romeo's voice that he's a Montague. Get my sword, boy! How dare he come here, hiding behind a mask, to mock our party! It won't be a sin if I kill him, because I have to defend the honor of my people."*

2. **Possible answer:** *Capulet seems like a jovial and outgoing man. He goes out of his way to make his guests feel welcome, and he tries hard to get the party going. You see these qualities when he teases the ladies, calls for the musicians to play, and jokes about his past exploits. At the same time, he seems a bit bossy, barking orders to the servants.*

## Part 4: Analyze the Text

Apply the skills you've learned in this workshop as you analyze a longer excerpt from the beginning of the tragedy. This scene takes place at a costume party hosted by the Capulets. Disguised by their masks, Romeo and other Montagues have crashed the party. The important moment that follows—when Romeo notices Juliet from across the room and falls in love at first sight—sets the course of tragic events in motion.

*from*

# Act One, Scene 5

Lines 14–62

[Maskers *appear with* Capulet, Lady Capulet, Juliet, *all the* Guests, *and* Servants.]

**Capulet.** Welcome, gentlemen! Ladies that have their toes
15 Unplagued with corns will have a bout with you.
Ah ha, my mistresses! which of you all
Will now deny to dance? She that makes dainty,
She I'll swear hath corns. Am I come near ye now?
Welcome, gentlemen! I have seen the day
20 That I have worn a visor and could tell
A whispering tale in a fair lady's ear,
Such as would please. 'Tis gone, 'tis gone, 'tis gone!
You are welcome, gentlemen! Come, musicians, play.
A hall, a hall! give room! and foot it, girls.

[*Music plays and they dance.*]

25 More light, you knaves! and turn the tables up,
And quench the fire, the room is grown too hot.
Ah, sirrah, this unlooked-for sport comes well.
Nay, sit, nay, sit, good cousin Capulet,
For you and I are past our dancing days.
30 How long is't now since last yourself and I
Were in a mask?

**Second Capulet.** By'r Lady, thirty years.

**Capulet.** What, man? 'Tis not so much, 'tis not so much!

**14–27** Capulet welcomes his guests and invites them all to dance. At the same time, like a good host, he is trying to get the party going. He alternates talking with his guests and telling the servants what to do.

**17–18 She that . . . corns:** Any woman too shy to dance will be assumed to have corns, ugly and painful growths on the toes.

**20 visor:** mask.

**28–38** Capulet and his relative watch the dancing as they talk of days gone by.

### Close Read

1. Choose a passage with several unfamiliar or Elizabethan words. Paraphrase the passage, using the marginal notes and the word list on page 1024 as necessary.

2. Consider Capulet's behavior toward his guests and his treatment of his servants. How would you describe Capulet? Support your answer with details from the text.

## DIFFERENTIATED INSTRUCTION

### FOR STRUGGLING READERS

**Analysis Support: Marginal Notes** Point out that marginal notes often provide a very brief summary of a scene or speech. Have students read all the marginal notes on page 1032 before reading the dialogue. Discuss what students learned from the notes. After they read the dialogue, have them match up lines from the play with details mentioned in the notes.

**Analysis Support: Comic Relief** Remind students that even tragedies have comic relief, or humorous moments. Ask students to identify the comic relief in Capulet's speech (the reference to corns) and contrast it with the fury that Tybalt expresses later in the scene. Have students compare such banter with jokes that appear in action or adventure films.

'Tis since the nuptial of Lucentio,
Come Pentecost as quickly as it will,
35  Some five-and-twenty years, and then we masked.
   **Second Capulet.** 'Tis more, 'tis more! His son is elder,
      sir;
   His son is thirty.
   **Capulet.**        Will you tell me that?
   His son was but a ward two years ago.
   **Romeo** [*to a* Servingman]. What lady's that, which
      doth enrich the hand
40  Of yonder knight?
   **Servant.** I know not, sir.

   **Romeo.** O, she doth teach the torches to burn
      bright!
   It seems she hangs upon the cheek of night
   Like a rich jewel in an Ethiop's ear—
45  Beauty too rich for use, for earth too dear!
   So shows a snowy dove trooping with crows
   As yonder lady o'er her fellows shows.
   The measure done, I'll watch her place of stand
   And, touching hers, make blessed my rude hand.
50  Did my heart love till now? Forswear it, sight!
   For I ne'er saw true beauty till this night.

   **Tybalt.** This, by his voice, should be a Montague.
   Fetch me my rapier, boy. What, dares the slave
   Come hither, covered with an antic face,
55  To fleer and scorn at our solemnity?
   Now, by the stock and honor of my kin,
   To strike him dead I hold it not a sin.
   **Capulet.** Why, how now, kinsman? Wherefore storm
      you so?
   **Tybalt.** Uncle, this is a Montague, our foe;
60  A villain, that is hither come in spite,
   To scorn at our solemnity this night.
   **Capulet.** Young Romeo is it?
   **Tybalt.**                    'Tis he, that villain Romeo.

**33 nuptial:** marriage.

**39–40** Romeo has spotted Juliet across the dance floor and is immediately entranced by her beauty.

**44–45 Ethiop's ear:** the ear of an Ethiopian (African); **for earth too dear:** too precious for this world.

**52–57** Tybalt recognizes Romeo's voice and tells his servant to get his sword (**rapier**). He thinks Romeo has come to make fun of (**fleer**) their party.

**Close Read**

3. Reread the boxed text. How is the pattern of Romeo's smitten speech different from the pattern of earlier lines in this scene?

4. Reread lines 52–57. What does Tybalt want to do to Romeo? Explain what has made Tybalt so enraged.

5. Tybalt is just one of many antagonists working against Romeo and Juliet. Cite details that reveal Tybalt's searing hatred of Romeo.

6. Given what you know about the characters' personalities, what do you think might happen next between Romeo and Tybalt? Support your prediction with evidence.

**Close Read**

3. **Possible answer:** *Unlike earlier lines, Romeo's speech is written in rhymed couplets, or pairs, of iambic pentameter. This change emphasizes the shift from typical party banter to Romeo's realization that he has fallen in love at first sight.*

4. **Possible answer:** *Tybalt wants to kill Romeo. He is furious, because he thinks that Romeo has come disguised by a mask to mock Capulet's party.*

5. **Possible answer:** *Details that reveal Tybalt's hatred include his asking for his sword, his assumption that Romeo has come only to make fun of them, his assertion that killing Romeo would be no sin, and Capulet's line "Wherefore storm you so?" (lines 58–59)*

6. *Predictions will vary, but students will probably predict some type of conflict between Romeo and Tybalt because Tybalt is so hot-headed and angry and because he has mentioned killing Romeo.*

## Assess and Reteach

### Assess

Ask students to briefly summarize what they have read of the play and to tell how they learned the information: through stage directions, dialogue, or marginal notes.

### Reteach

For students who are unable to apply the workshop skills to the excerpts from *Romeo and Juliet*, review with them the note-taking copy masters for this lesson:

- Ask students to look at the text and identify examples of a protagonist, antagonist, soliloquy, stage direction, marginal note, and synopsis.

- Discuss what steps students might follow when starting to read a Shakespearean tragedy.

**FOR ENGLISH LANGUAGE LEARNERS**
**Vocabulary: Multiple-Meaning Words** Write these words from the play on the board:

- Act 1, Scene 1: "drawn" (line 63). Explain that *drawn* is a form of *draw*.

- Act 1, Scene 5: "swear" (line 18), "play" (line 23), "storm" (line 58)

Have student pairs find these words in dictionaries and choose the best meaning for the context in the play. Ask volunteers

to read the meaning they chose. Invite the class to consider and decide if that meaning is correct.

# Focus and Motivate

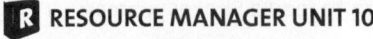

## COMMON CORE FOCUS

**RL 2** Determine a theme of a text. **RL 3** Analyze how complex characters develop over the course of a text, interact with other characters, and advance the plot or develop the theme. **RL 4** Determine the figurative meaning of words and phrases. **RL 5** Analyze how an author's choices concerning how to manipulate time create tension. **RL 6** Analyze a particular point of view or cultural experience reflected in a work of world literature. **RL 9** Analyze how an author draws on source material in a specific work. **RL 10** Read and comprehend dramas. **SL 2** Integrate multiple sources of information presented in diverse formats. **L 1a-b** Use parallel structure and various types of phrases and clauses. **L 3** Apply knowledge of language to understand how language functions in different contexts and to comprehend more fully when reading or listening. **L 4a-c** Determine the meaning of words and phrases using context; identify patterns of words changes; consult reference materials. **L 5a** Interpret figures of speech and analyze their role in the text.

## SUMMARY

Two teenagers fall in love despite the feud between their families. They are married in secret by a friar who hopes that the union will end the feud. His goal is met, but through bitter irony: Believing that Juliet has died, Romeo kills himself; finding Romeo dead, Juliet kills herself. The families reconcile in grief.

## Is LOVE stronger than HATE?

Ask students for responses to the scenario of love and hate in the paragraph. As groups prepare for the *DEBATE* activity, encourage them to support their arguments.

## Selection Resources

---

*Essential Course of Study* **ECOS** ✓

# The Tragedy of Romeo and Juliet
### Drama by William Shakespeare

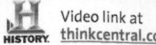 Video link at thinkcentral.com

**VIDEO TRAILER** THINK central | KEYWORD: HML9-1034

# Is **LOVE** stronger than **HATE?**

### COMMON CORE

**RL 2** Determine a theme of a text. **RL 3** Analyze how complex characters develop over the course of a text, interact with other characters, and advance the plot or develop the theme. **RL 9** Analyze how an author draws on source material in a specific work. **RL 10** Read and comprehend dramas. **L 3** Apply knowledge of language to understand how language functions in different contexts and to comprehend more fully when reading or listening.

It sounds like a story ripped from the tabloids. Two teenagers fall in love at a party. Then they learn that their parents hate each other. The teenagers' love is forbidden, so not surprisingly, they cling to each other even more tightly. Murder and suffering ensue, and by the end, a whole town is in mourning. What love can—and cannot—overcome is at the heart of *Romeo and Juliet*, considered by many to be the greatest love story of all time.

**DEBATE** People say that love conquers all. Is this statement true, or is it just a cliché? How powerful *is* love? Discuss this topic in a small group. Talk about instances in which love has brought people together as well as times when hate has driven them apart. Then form two teams and debate the age-old question, Is love stronger than hate?

1034

---

## TEXT ANALYSIS: SHAKESPEAREAN DRAMA

You can probably guess that a **tragedy** isn't going to end with the words "and they all lived happily ever after." Shakespearean tragedies are dramas that end in disaster—most often death—for the main characters. The conflicts in a tragedy are usually set in motion by the main characters' actions, but fate can also play a part in the catastrophic course of events. As you read *Romeo and Juliet*, pay attention to specific characteristics of Shakespearean drama.

- Notice how **soliloquies** and **asides** enhance your understanding of the drama. These conventions allow characters to "think out loud"—often revealing information about their private thoughts.
- Watch for and analyze **allusions.** Once you decode them, they add an extra layer of meaning to certain passages.
- Consider Shakespeare's use of **comic relief** to ease the tension of certain scenes. Think of the comic episodes as brief breaks that allow you to absorb earlier events in the plot and get ready for new developments.
- Pay attention to the rhythm of each line. Shakespeare wrote his plays in **blank verse,** a poetic form that resembles the rhythm of natural speech.

## READING STRATEGY: READING SHAKESPEAREAN DRAMA

Though his plays can sweep you away, Shakespeare's English is sometimes hard for modern readers to understand. These strategies can help:

- Read the synopsis, or summary, of each scene to get an idea of what happens in that part of the play.
- Use the marginal notes to figure out the meanings of unfamiliar words, unusual grammatical structures, and allusions.
- Keep track of events to make the plot easier to follow. All the events in *Romeo and Juliet* take place in six days. As you read, use a chart to record plot developments and interactions between characters.

| Sunday | Monday | Tuesday | Wednesday | Thursday | Friday |
|--------|--------|---------|-----------|----------|--------|
| street brawl | | | | | |

After you complete your chart, use its information to help you determine the play's **theme,** or central message about life or human nature.

## Overview

### Act One
We meet the Montagues and the Capulets, two long-feuding families in the Italian city of Verona. At the beginning of the play, Romeo, a Montague, is in love with Rosaline. Juliet, a Capulet, is asked by her parents to consider marrying Paris. Romeo and Juliet meet at a masked ball and fall in love, each later realizing that the other is from the enemy family.

### Act Two
Forced to meet in secret, Romeo and Juliet declare their love to each other and decide to get married. Romeo visits Friar Laurence, a priest, and asks him to perform the wedding. Aided by Juliet's nurse, Romeo and Juliet meet and marry in secret.

### Act Three
During a street fight, Juliet's cousin Tybalt kills Romeo's friend Mercutio. Romeo loses his temper and kills Tybalt; he then flees, realizing with horror what he has done. Romeo is banished from Verona under pain of death. Juliet grieves the double loss of her cousin and her husband. With the help of Friar Laurence and the nurse, Romeo and Juliet make plans to flee to Mantua, another city. Her parents, not knowing she is already married to Romeo, order her to marry Paris.

### Act Four
A distraught Juliet visits Friar Laurence for help and threatens to kill herself. He gives her a potion that will not kill her but put her into a deathlike sleep for two days, with the plan that Romeo will rescue her from the family tomb when she awakens. Friar Laurence sends a letter to Romeo in Mantua, describing this plan. Juliet takes the potion. Her family finds her and prepares her burial, believing her dead.

### Act Five
Romeo does not get Friar Laurence's letter before he hears of Juliet's death and believes it is real. Grief stricken, he returns to Verona. He finds Juliet in her deathlike sleep, takes real poison, and dies. Juliet awakens and, finding Romeo dead, kills herself with his dagger. When the families realize what has happened, Lord Capulet and Lord Montague agree to end their feud.

## Teach

**COMMON CORE**
L 3

### ● *Model the Skill:* SHAKESPEAREAN DRAMA

Define characteristics as needed. Then read aloud this excerpt from *Romeo and Juliet*, Act Two, Scene 2. Explain that Romeo is speaking to himself when he sees Juliet appear on her balcony.

> But soft! What light through yonder window breaks?
> It is the East, and Juliet is the sun!

Ask students which characteristics of Shakespearean drama the lines illustrate. If necessary, point out that Romeo is, in effect, thinking out loud. ***Possible answer: The lines are a soliloquy spoken in blank verse.***

**GUIDED PRACTICE** Ask students to name other characteristics of Shakespearean drama.

**COMMON CORE**
RL 2, RL 3

### ■ *Model the Skill:* READING SHAKESPEAREAN DRAMA

Explain that the Prologue (p. 1037) serves as a synopsis of the play as a whole; then point out the synopsis of Act One, Scene 1 (page 1038). Use the Prologue to model the use of marginal notes. Read the note for line 6. Think out loud, saying, "The text says the lovers are star-crossed and that people took astrology seriously. Does that mean the lovers were not responsible for their actions? Let's see." Elicit that much of what is said in the Prologue probably would be recorded in the last day or days in the chart.

**GUIDED PRACTICE** Have students explain the three strategies in their own words. Invite volunteers to share how they have used these strategies in the past.

**R** RESOURCE MANAGER—Copy Master Reading Shakespearean Drama p. 21 (for student use while reading the selection)

## DIFFERENTIATED INSTRUCTION

### FOR STRUGGLING READERS
**Preview** Point out that *Romeo and Juliet* is such a famous play that most productions assume that audience members already know some of its key plot events, especially the ending. Have students work with partners to read the *Overview* and check each other's understanding of the summaries before they begin reading the play itself.

### FOR ENGLISH LANGUAGE LEARNERS
**Concept Support** Remind students of some terms that are used in the reading of dramatic works, including *cast, prologue, chorus, act, scene, stage, stage directions,* and *curtain.* Help students define each term. Point out that stage directions for this play appear in brackets and italics (except for names of characters).

■ *Model the Skill:* **MONITOR**

Suggest that students place a bookmark at this page, which lists the play's cast of characters. Doing so will help them refer to the list easily if they become uncertain about who a character is or to which side of the feud he or she belongs. In addition, urge students to make use of the Tracking the Characters copy master as they read.

**R** RESOURCE MANAGER—Copy Masters
Keeping Track of the Characters p. 15

## GO BEHIND THE CURTAIN

**COMMON CORE SL 2**

As students read and discuss the sidebar, explain that *stagecraft* refers to theatrical devices and techniques. Then have students turn to page 1045, the first appearance of the **Behind the Curtain** feature, and tell what the photographs show. *Possible answer: The photographs show different actors who have been cast as Romeo and Juliet.* Point out that casting is just one of the many elements of stagecraft.

## BACKGROUND

The story of Romeo and Juliet had been told by several writers by the time William Shakespeare produced his play between 1594 and 1596. *The Tragicall Historye of Romeus and Juliet*, for example, was written by a now nearly forgotten English poet named Arthur Brooke and was published in 1562. Shakespeare used virtually all of Brooke's major characters and kept the setting of Verona in the 1300s, but added his own unique artistry to the characters and the story.

---

# THE TRAGEDY OF
# *Romeo & Juliet*

## WILLIAM SHAKESPEARE

 **COMMON CORE SL 2**

### GO BEHIND THE CURTAIN

**One Play, Many Productions**
The images at the top of page 1037 capture five different interpretations of *Romeo and Juliet*. Though the productions were staged at different times in different countries, each director had the same goal: to thrill audiences with Shakespeare's timeless tale of two reckless, lovesick teenagers. As you read the play, you will discover many more images from a variety of productions. You'll also encounter **Behind the Curtain** feature pages that will help you explore the stagecraft used to create moving theatrical productions of this famous play.

**TIME**
The 14th century

**CAST**

**THE MONTAGUES**

**Lord Montague** (mŏn'tə-gyōō')

**Lady Montague**

**Romeo,** son of Montague

**Benvolio** (bĕn-vō'lē-ō), nephew of Montague and friend of Romeo

**Balthasar** (băl'thə-sär'), servant to Romeo

**Abram,** servant to Montague

**THE CAPULETS**

**Lord Capulet** (kăp'yōō-lĕt')

**Lady Capulet**

**Juliet,** daughter of Capulet

**Tybalt** (tĭb'əlt), nephew of Lady Capulet

**Nurse** to Juliet

**Peter,** servant to Juliet's nurse

**Sampson,** servant to Capulet

**Gregory,** servant to Capulet

**An Old Man** of the Capulet family

**PLACE**
Verona (və-rō'nə) and Mantua (măn'chōō-ə) in northern Italy

**OTHERS**

**Prince Escalus** (ĕs'kə-ləs), ruler of Verona

**Mercutio** (mĕr-kyōō'shē-ō), kinsman of the prince and friend of Romeo

**Friar Laurence,** a Franciscan priest

**Friar John,** another Franciscan priest

**Count Paris,** a young nobleman, kinsman of the prince

**Apothecary** (ə-pŏth'ĭ-kĕr'ē)

**Page** to Paris

**Chief Watchman**

**Three Musicians**

**An Officer**

**Chorus**

**Citizens** of Verona, **Gentlemen** and **Gentlewomen** of both houses, **Maskers, Torchbearers, Pages, Guards, Watchmen, Servants,** and **Attendants**

---

## DIFFERENTIATED INSTRUCTION

### FOR STRUGGLING READERS
**Read Aloud** Have students take turns reading aloud the cast list to gain an oral familiarity with the names. Remind students that *Montague* and *Capulet* are family names and that each family dislikes the other intensely. Emphasize that keeping track of family alliances will be important to understanding Shakespeare's plot.

### FOR ENGLISH LANGUAGE LEARNERS
**Vocabulary: Outdated Forms** Have students begin a language journal for their reading of *Romeo and Juliet*. Point out that some words and expressions in this play are not used in modern English. Still, they are important to understanding the play, and their modern equivalents are worth knowing. Model a journal entry using *Apothecary* from the cast list. Have students look up the definition and add it to their journals.

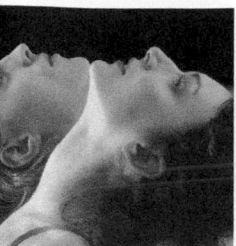

## Prologue

*The Chorus is one actor who serves as a narrator. He enters from the back of the stage to introduce and explain the theme of the play. His job is to "hook" the audience's interest by telling them just enough to quiet them down and make them eager for more. In this prologue, or preview, the narrator explains that the play will be about a feud between two families (the Capulets and the Montagues). In addition, the narrator says that the feud will end in tragedy. As you read the prologue, determine what the tragedy will be.*

[*Enter* Chorus.]

**Chorus.** Two households, both alike in dignity,
In fair Verona, where we lay our scene,
From ancient grudge break to new mutiny,
Where civil blood makes civil hands unclean.
5 From forth the fatal loins of these two foes,
A pair of star-crossed lovers take their life,
Whose misadventured piteous overthrows
Doth with their death bury their parents' strife.
The fearful passage of their death-marked love,
10 And the continuance of their parents' rage,
Which, but their children's end, naught could remove,
Is now the two hours' traffic of our stage,
The which if you with patient ears attend,
What here shall miss, our toil shall strive to mend.

[*Exit.*]

**3–4 ancient ... unclean:** A new outbreak of fighting (**mutiny**) between families has caused the citizens of Verona to have one another's blood on their hands.

**6 star-crossed:** doomed. The position of the stars when the lovers were born was not favorable. In Shakespeare's day, people took astrology very seriously.

**7 misadventured:** unlucky.

**11 but:** except for; **naught:** nothing.

**12 the two hours' ... stage:** what will be shown on the stage in the next two hours.

**14 what ... mend:** The play will fill in the details not mentioned in the prologue.

## Get Into the Act

### SUMMARY

Act One opens with a street brawl between the feuding Capulets and Montagues. Then Romeo enters, pining with unrequited love for Rosaline. In the meantime, Capulet and his wife are considering a marriage between their daughter Juliet and Count Paris. The Capulets give a party that evening, and Romeo attends, uninvited. There he meets and instantly falls in love with Juliet, as does she with him. Only later does each learn that the other comes from the rival family.

### Analyze Visuals

**Activity** What can you predict about the play's events from these photographs?
*Possible answer: You can predict love between Romeo and Juliet, violence, poisoning, and death.*

---

**READING STRATEGY**

COMMON CORE
RL 2,
RL 3

### ■ SUMMARIZE

After allowing time for review of the marginal notes, ask students to summarize what the Chorus explains. ***Possible answer: The Chorus explains that the play will show how a family feud causes the death of two lovers.***

---

## Resources for Act One

*See resources on the **Teacher One Stop DVD-ROM** and on **thinkcentral.com**.*

**R RESOURCE MANAGER UNIT 10**
Plan and Teach, pp. 11–16
Summary pp. 17–18†‡*
Text Analysis and Reading
Skill, pp. 19–22†*

**DIAGNOSTIC AND SELECTION TESTS**
Selection Tests, pp. 275–278

**BEST PRACTICES TOOLKIT**
Cluster Diagram, p. B18
Venn Diagram, p. A26
Character Analysis Chart,
p. D5

**INTERACTIVE READER**

**ADAPTED INTERACTIVE READER**

**ELL ADAPTED INTERACTIVE READER**

**TECHNOLOGY**
⊘ **Teacher One Stop DVD-ROM**
⊘ **Student One Stop DVD-ROM**
⊘ **PowerNotes DVD-ROM**
⊘ **Audio Anthology CD**
⊘ **Audio Tutor CD**
⊘ **ExamView Test Generator** on the **Teacher One Stop**

**Video Trailer**  THINKcentral

Go to **thinkcentral.com** to preview the **Video Trailer** introducing this selection. Other features that support the selection include
• **PowerNotes** presentation
• **ThinkAloud** models to enhance comprehension

**\*** Resources for Differentiation    **†** Also in Spanish    **‡** In Haitian Creole and Vietnamese

**READ WITH A PURPOSE**

*Help students set a purpose for reading. Tell them to look for clues to what kinds of people Romeo and Juliet are.*

# Act One

## SCENE 1 *A public square in Verona.*

*As the scene opens, two young Capulet servants swagger across the stage, joking and bragging. When they happen to meet servants from the rival house of Montague, a quarrel begins that grows into an ugly street fight. Finally the ruler of Verona, Prince Escalus, appears. He is angry about the violence in his city and warns that the next offenders will receive the death penalty. The crowd fades away, and the stage is set for the entrance of Romeo, heir of the Montague family. Romeo, infatuated and miserable, can talk of nothing but his love for Rosaline and her cruelty in refusing to love him back.*

[*Enter* Sampson *and* Gregory, *servants of the house of Capulet, armed with swords and bucklers (shields).*]

**Sampson.** Gregory, on my word, we'll not carry coals.

**Gregory.** No, for then we should be colliers.

**Sampson.** I mean, an we be in choler, we'll draw.

**Gregory.** Ay, while you live, draw your neck out of collar.

5 **Sampson.** I strike quickly, being moved.

**Gregory.** But thou art not quickly moved to strike.

**Sampson.** A dog of that house of Montague moves me.

**Gregory.** To move is to stir, and to be valiant is to stand. Therefore, if thou art moved, thou runnest away.

10 **Sampson.** A dog of that house shall move me to stand. I will take the wall of any man or maid of Montague's.

**Gregory.** That shows thee a weak slave, for the weakest goes to the wall.

**Sampson.** 'Tis true; and therefore women, being the weaker
15 vessels, are ever thrust to the wall. Therefore push I will Montague's men from the wall and thrust his maids to the wall.

**Gregory.** The quarrel is between our masters and us their men.

**Sampson.** 'Tis all one. I will show myself a tyrant. When I have fought with the men, I will be cruel with the maids: I will cut
20 off their heads.

**Gregory.** The heads of the maids?

**Sampson.** Ay, the heads of the maids, or their maidenheads. Take it in what sense thou wilt.

**Gregory.** They must take it in sense that feel it.

**1–2 we'll not carry coals:** we won't stand to be insulted. **Colliers,** those involved in the dirty work of hauling coal, were often the butt of jokes.

**3–4 in choler:** angry; **collar:** a hangman's noose.

**① Targeted Passage**

**11 take the wall:** walk nearest to the wall. People of higher rank had the privilege of walking closer to the wall, to avoid any water or garbage in the street. *What claim is Sampson making about himself and anyone from the rival house of Montague?*

**14–24** Sampson's tough talk includes boasts about his ability to overpower women.

Romeo and Juliet in the Anželika Cholina Dance Theatre's 2003 production

---

## DIFFERENTIATED INSTRUCTION

**FOR ENGLISH LANGUAGE LEARNERS**

**Task Support** Call attention to the question in the marginal note for line 11. Briefly discuss the explanation for the expression "take the wall." **Possible answer:** *Sampson is claiming that no Montague can force him to the nasty side of the walk, for he is superior to anyone from the Montague clan.*

**FOR STRUGGLING READERS**

**Preview** Read through the italicized scene synopsis to give students an overview of Scene 1. Help them create a sequence chain to organize the plot events.

| Capulet and Montague servants fight. |
| --- |
| ↓ |
| Prince Escalus breaks up the fight. |
| ↓ |
| Romeo enters, upset about being jilted. |

**FOR STRUGGLING READERS**

In combination with the *Audio Anthology CD*, use one or more Targeted Passages (pp. 1038, 1047, 1059, 1062) to ensure that students focus on key story events, concepts, and skills. Targeted Passages are also good for English learners.

**① Targeted Passage [Lines 7–16]**

This passage sets up the family feud by showing how even the Capulet servants express ill

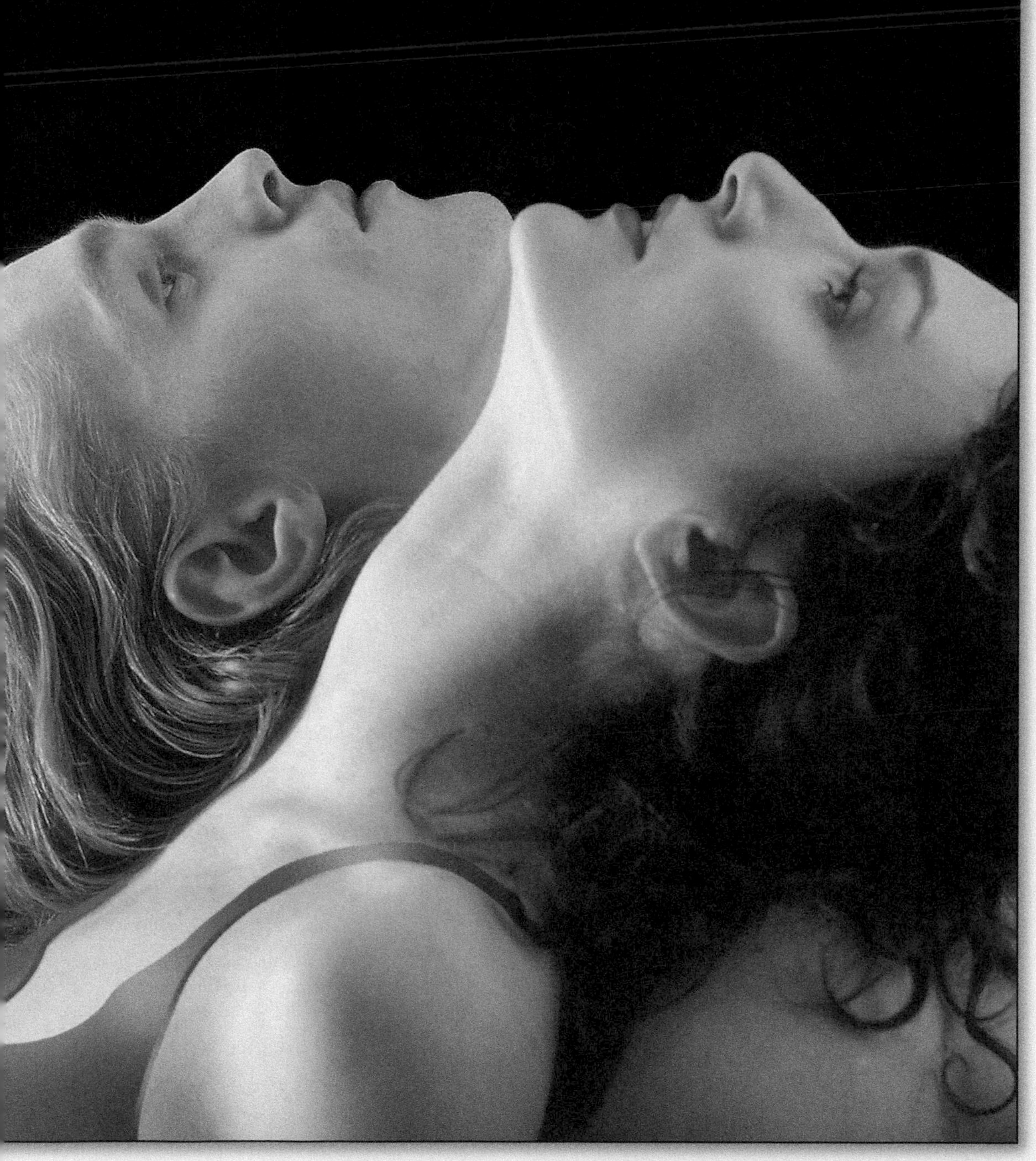

will toward the Montagues.

- Who owns the dog that moves Sampson to stand? (line 7)
- Which members of the Montague clan will Sampson oppose? What would he like to do to them? (line 11)
- Does Gregory agree with Sampson? How can you tell? (lines 11–16)

**FOR ADVANCED LEARNERS/PRE–AP**

Have students research Elizabethan England to find out more about Shakespeare's time and how it reflected the Verona of *Romeo and Juliet.* Ask students to share their findings with the class.

**Reading Support** THINK central

This selection on thinkcentral.com includes embedded **ThinkAloud** models–students "thinking aloud" about the story to model the kinds of questions a good reader would ask about a selection.

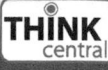

## Analyze Visuals

**Activity** How does the photograph capture the relationship between Romeo and Juliet? ***Possible answer:*** *The characters are looking up, as if they aspire to a happy dream. Their bodies, however, face in opposite directions, symbolizing the feud between their families. Their faces seem to meet and blend, perhaps illustrating the commitment of love that the two share.*

## BACKGROUND

***Romeo and Juliet* in Its Time** Although *Romeo and Juliet* is set in Verona in the 1300s, it is important to remember that Shakespeare wasn't primarily interested in accurately portraying life in Italy in the Middle Ages. He was more interested in presenting a play that his English audience of the 1590s could relate to. He was aware that his audience could understand the characters and events of his play—feuding families, arranged marriages, secretive friars, shady apothecaries, duels, and fate—only through their own knowledge and experience. Like feud-torn Verona, England at that time was a place of strife, suspicion, and revenge. After the defeat of the Spanish Armada in 1588, a Spanish reprisal seemed imminent. Many suspected that Roman Catholic sympathizers were plotting to overthrow the Protestant Queen Elizabeth. Moreover, plague and repeated crop failure had led to economic depression, widespread unemployment, vagrancy, crime, and social conditions similar to those Shakespeare describes toward the end of the play. As students read, have them pay attention to the details Shakespeare weaves into his play to make its tragic tale of "star-crossed" love realistic and relevant.

## TEXT ANALYSIS
COMMON CORE L5a

### Ⓐ SARCASM

***Possible answer:*** *Most students will say yes, feeling that sarcasm is common in their everyday speech.*

Ask students how different this scene would be if it did not include sarcasm.

## TEXT ANALYSIS
COMMON CORE L3

### Ⓑ ASIDE

***Possible answer:*** *When Sampson and Gregory speak openly, their words are bold and rash. In contrast, the words that they speak in asides are cautious and rather timid. The contrast reveals that these characters are not as brave as they claim to be.*

**IF STUDENTS NEED HELP . . .** Have three volunteers (taking the roles of Sampson, Gregory, and Abram) read aloud the dialogue in lines 35–56, with lowered voices for the asides. Discuss how the volume and tone suggest the Capulet servants' public and private emotions.

**REVISIT THE BIG QUESTION**

## Is LOVE stronger than HATE?

**Discuss** Have students reread lines 55–58. How does Benvolio show that he may not be as obsessed with hate as are the other characters in this scene? ***Possible answer:*** *Instead of drawing his sword and fighting alongside Abram and Balthasar against Sampson and Gregory, Benvolio urges them to stop, and he physically beats down their swords.*

**Sampson.** Me they shall feel while I am able to stand;
and 'tis known I am a pretty piece of flesh.

**Gregory.** 'Tis well thou art not fish; if thou hadst, thou hadst been poor-John. Draw thy tool! Here comes two of the house of Montagues.

[*Enter* Abram *and* Balthasar, *servants to the Montagues.*]

**Sampson.** My naked weapon is out. Quarrel! I will back thee.

**Gregory.** How? turn thy back and run?

**Sampson.** Fear me not.

**Gregory.** No, marry. I fear thee!

**Sampson.** Let us take the law of our sides; let them begin.

**Gregory.** I will frown as I pass by, and let them take it as they list.

**Sampson.** Nay, as they dare. I will bite my thumb at them;
which is disgrace to them, if they bear it.

**Abram.** Do you bite your thumb at us, sir?

**Sampson.** I do bite my thumb, sir.

**Abram.** Do you bite your thumb at us, sir?

**Sampson** [*aside to* Gregory]. Is the law of our side if I say ay?

**Gregory** [*aside to* Sampson]. No.

**Sampson.** No, sir, I do not bite my thumb at you, sir; but I bite my thumb, sir. Ⓐ

**Gregory.** Do you quarrel, sir?

**Abram.** Quarrel, sir? No, sir.

**Sampson.** But if you do, sir, I am for you. I serve as good a man as you.

**Abram.** No better.

**Sampson.** Well, sir.

[*Enter* Benvolio, *nephew of Montague and first cousin of Romeo.*]

**Gregory** [*aside to* Sampson]. Say "better." Here comes one of my master's kinsmen.

**Sampson.** Yes, better, sir.

**Abram.** You lie.

**Sampson.** Draw, if you be men. Gregory, remember thy swashing blow. Ⓑ

[*They fight.*]

**Benvolio.** Part, fools! [*beats down their swords*]
Put up your swords. You know not what you do.

**28 poor-John:** a salted fish, considered fit only for poor people to eat.

**33 marry:** a short form of "by the Virgin Mary" and so a mild exclamation.

**34–44** Gregory and Sampson decide to pick a fight by insulting the Montague servants with a rude gesture (**bite my thumb**).

COMMON CORE L5a

**Ⓐ SARCASM**
**Sarcasm** is an ironic remark often used to convey an insult. In this instance, Sampson is being sarcastic by telling Abram and Balthasar he is not quarreling, or starting a fight, when he is clearly doing just that. Does including sarcasm in this scene make the dialogue more realistic? Explain.

**51–52** Gregory notices that Tybalt, a Capulet, is arriving. *Why do you think Gregory and Sampson behave more aggressively as soon as they realize that Tybalt is approaching?*

**Ⓑ ASIDE**
Contrast what the servants say openly in lines 35–56 with what they say in **asides,** or whispers to each other. What does this contrast reveal about Sampson and Gregory?



## DIFFERENTIATED INSTRUCTION

### FOR ENGLISH LANGUAGE LEARNERS

**Vocabulary: Outdated Forms** Remind students that Shakespearean English contains terms that are not used today. Provide these terms and their definitions. Then have students reread the lines noted and substitute the definitions for the words.

- *'tis* (line 26), "it is"
- *thee* (line 30), "you"
- *Put up* (line 58), "put away"
- *art thou* (line 59), "are you"

**Task Support** Have students read the question in the marginal note for lines 51–64. Elicit that "one of my master's kinsmen" (lines 51–52) refers to Tybalt, not Benvolio (who has just entered the scene). ***Possible answer:*** *Gregory and Sampson are outnumbered—three Montagues to two Capulets. Tybalt's arrival gives the Capulets a better chance at winning the fight that they have provoked.*

[*Enter* Tybalt, *hot-headed nephew of Lady Capulet and first cousin of Juliet.*]

**Tybalt.** What, art thou drawn among these heartless hinds?
60 Turn thee, Benvolio! look upon thy death.

**Benvolio.** I do but keep the peace. Put up thy sword,
Or manage it to part these men with me.

**Tybalt.** What, drawn, and talk of peace? I hate the word
As I hate hell, all Montagues, and thee.
65 Have at thee, coward!

[*They fight.*]

[*Enter several of both houses, who join the fray; then enter* Citizens *and* Peace Officers, *with clubs.*]

**Officer.** Clubs, bills, and partisans! Strike! beat them down!

**Citizens.** Down with the Capulets! Down with the Montagues!

[*Enter old* Capulet *and* Lady Capulet.]

**Capulet.** What noise is this? Give me my long sword, ho!

**Lady Capulet.** A crutch, a crutch! Why call you for a sword?
70 **Capulet.** My sword, I say! Old Montague is come
And flourishes his blade in spite of me.

[*Enter old* Montague *and* Lady Montague.]

**Montague.** Thou villain Capulet!—Hold me not, let me go.

**Lady Montague.** Thou shalt not stir one foot to seek a foe.

[*Enter Prince Escalus, with attendants. At first no one hears him.*]

**Prince.** Rebellious subjects, enemies to peace,
75 Profaners of this neighbor-stained steel—
Will they not hear? What, ho! you men, you beasts,
That quench the fire of your pernicious rage
With purple fountains issuing from your veins!
On pain of torture, from those bloody hands
80 Throw your mistempered weapons to the ground
And hear the sentence of your moved prince.
Three civil brawls, bred of an airy word
By thee, old Capulet, and Montague,
Have thrice disturbed the quiet of our streets
85 And made Verona's ancient citizens
Cast by their grave beseeming ornaments
To wield old partisans, in hands as old,
Cankered with peace, to part your cankered hate.
If ever you disturb our streets again,
90 Your lives shall pay the forfeit of the peace.

**59–65** Tybalt does not understand that Benvolio is trying to stop the fight. He challenges Benvolio.

**59 heartless hinds:** cowardly servants.

**63 drawn:** with your sword out.

**65 Have at thee:** Defend yourself.

**66 bills, and partisans:** spears.

**69 A crutch ... sword:** You need a crutch more than a sword.

**74–81** The prince is furious about the street fighting caused by the feud. He orders the men to drop their weapons and pay attention.

**77 pernicious:** destructive.

**82–90 Three ... peace:** The prince holds Capulet and Montague responsible for three recent street fights, each probably started by an offhand remark or insult (**airy word**). He warns that they will be put to death if any more fights occur.

ROMEO AND JULIET: ACT ONE, SCENE 1   **1041**

---

**FOR STRUGGLING READERS**

**Paraphrasing Shakespeare** Have students re-read the marginal note for lines 74–81. Model a paraphrase of lines 76–78: *Can't they hear me? Hey! Listen, you animals, whose fiery anger will not be satisfied until you have shed blood!* Then invite volunteers to paraphrase lines 79–81. *Possible answer: Unless you want to be tortured, drop your weapons and listen to my decision.*

**FOR ENGLISH LANGUAGE LEARNERS**

**Vocabulary Support** Define and discuss these phrases from the prince's speech:

• *neighbor-stained steel* (line 75), "sword with a fellow-citizen's blood on it"

• *purple fountains* (line 78), "spurts of blood"

• *wield old partisans* (line 87), "handle old weapons with a broad blade and long shaft"

• *cankered hate* (line 88), "feud" (literally, "diseased hate")

---

**REVIST THE BIG QUESTION**

# Is **LOVE** stronger than **HATE?**

**Discuss** Refer students to lines 66–73. In what sense does love win over hate in this scene between the heads of the Montague and the Capulet families? *Possible answer: Love wins over hate in the sense that the love that Lady Capulet and Lady Montague have for their husbands is able to stop the hatred between the two men from erupting into more violence.*

## TIERED DISCUSSION PROMPTS

Use these prompts, referring to lines 74–90, to help students explore the role of Prince Escalus:

**Connect** What kinds of officials in American society today would serve the same functions as Prince Escalus? *Possible answer: The same functions would be served by a mayor (Prince Escalus is the head of the city's government), a police chief (he also has the power to enforce the law and to take offenders into custody), and a judge (he has the power to declare offenders guilty and even sentence them to death).*

**Analyze** Why is Prince Escalus upset about what has just happened? Cite evidence from his speech. *Possible answer: Prince Escalus is upset for several reasons: It is just the most recent episode in a series of violent fights (line 82–84); the violence has upset the citizens of Verona, especially the older ones (lines 84–88); and both parties have demonstrated that they will not be bound by his laws (lines 74–76).*

**Synthesize** How might Prince Escalus's threat in line 90 hint at a price that neither party could understand at this moment? *Possible answer: By threatening that Montague and Capulet will pay with their lives, the Prince is foreshadowing not their death but the death of their children. The two enemies will instead pay with their grief.*

For this time all the rest depart away.
You, Capulet, shall go along with me;
And, Montague, come you this afternoon,
To know our farther pleasure in this case,
95 To old Freetown, our common judgment place.
Once more, on pain of death, all men depart.

[*Exeunt all but* Montague, Lady Montague, *and* Benvolio.]

**Montague.** Who set this ancient quarrel new abroach?
Speak, nephew, were you by when it began?

**Benvolio.** Here were the servants of your adversary
100 And yours, close fighting ere I did approach.
I drew to part them. In the instant came
The fiery Tybalt, with his sword prepared;
Which, as he breathed defiance to my ears,
He swung about his head and cut the winds,
105 Who, nothing hurt withal, hissed him in scorn. **C**
While we were interchanging thrusts and blows,
Came more and more, and fought on part and part,
Till the Prince came, who parted either part.

**Lady Montague.** O, where is Romeo? Saw you him today?
110 Right glad I am he was not at this fray.

**Benvolio.** Madam, an hour before the worshiped sun
Peered forth the golden window of the East,
A troubled mind drave me to walk abroad,
Where, underneath the grove of sycamore
115 That westward rooteth from the city's side,
So early walking did I see your son.
Towards him I made, but he was ware of me
And stole into the covert of the wood.
I—measuring his affections by my own,
120 Which then most sought where most might not be found,
Being one too many by my weary self—
Pursued my humor, not pursuing his,
And gladly shunned who gladly fled from me.

**Montague.** Many a morning hath he there been seen,
125 With tears augmenting the fresh morning's dew,
Adding to clouds more clouds with his deep sighs;
But all so soon as the all-cheering sun
Should in the farthest East begin to draw
The shady curtains from Aurora's bed,
130 Away from light steals home my heavy son
And private in his chamber pens himself,
Shuts up his windows, locks fair daylight out,

**exeunt:** the plural form of *exit*, indicating that more than one person is leaving the stage.

**97 Who . . . abroach:** Who reopened this old argument?

**99 adversary:** enemy.

**100 ere:** before.

**C** CHARACTER
According to Benvolio, what kind of person is Tybalt? **Predict** how Tybalt might act if he runs into Benvolio—or any other Montague—again.

**107 on part and part:** some on one side, some on the other.

**110 fray:** fight.

**113 drave:** drove.

**115 rooteth:** grows.

**117–123 made:** moved; **covert:** covering. Romeo saw Benvolio coming and hid in the woods. Since Benvolio himself was seeking solitude, he decided to respect Romeo's privacy and did not go after him. *What does this action tell you about Benvolio?*

**124–135** Romeo has been seen wandering through the woods at night, crying. At dawn he returns home and locks himself in his darkened room. Montague feels that this behavior is a bad sign and that his son needs guidance.

**129 Aurora's bed:** Aurora was the goddess of the dawn.

---

TEXT ANALYSIS  COMMON CORE
RL 3

**C** *Model the Skill:* CHARACTER

Point out the word "fiery" in line 102. Explain that this word indicates that Tybalt is easily angered.

***Possible answer:*** *Benvolio says that Tybalt entered with sword at the ready and that he quickly began to fight. If Tybalt runs into Benvolio or another Montague again, he probably will try to fight again, despite the decree of Prince Escalus.*

---

## DIFFERENTIATED INSTRUCTION

### FOR STRUGGLING READERS

**Inverted Word Order** Explain that Shakespeare often inverted the word order of sentences, stating the verb before the subject. (This was not the pattern of everyday Elizabethan speech.) Encourage students to "translate" such sentences by restating them with the subject first. Model these examples:

• *come you this afternoon* (line 93), "you come this afternoon"

• *Here were the servants of your adversary* (line 99), "the servants of your adversary were here"

Then ask pairs of students to restate these lines for the class:

• "Saw you him today?" (line 109) ***Possible answer:*** *You saw him today?*

• "And private in his chamber pens himself" (line 131) ***Possible answer:*** *and pens himself in his private chamber*

### FOR STRUGGLING READERS

**Develop Reading Fluency** Point out the question in the marginal note for lines 117–123. Ask students to imagine themselves in Benvolio's place, saying these words. Model for students reading the speech. Then have students practice reading the words. Finally, ask them to speculate about the feelings behind the words. ***Possible answer:*** *The action suggests that Benvolio is considerate.*

**R** RESOURCE MANAGER—Copy Master
Reading Fluency p. 25

And makes himself an artificial night.
Black and portentous must this humor prove
135 Unless good counsel may the cause remove.

**Benvolio.** My noble uncle, do you know the cause?

**Montague.** I neither know it nor can learn of him.

**Benvollo.** Have you importuned him by any means?

**Montague.** Both by myself and many other friends;
140 But he, his own affections' counselor,
Is to himself—I will not say how true—
But to himself so secret and so close,
So far from sounding and discovery,
As is the bud bit with an envious worm
145 Ere he can spread his sweet leaves to the air
Or dedicate his beauty to the sun.
Could we but learn from whence his sorrows grow,
We would as willingly give cure as know.

[*Enter* Romeo *lost in thought.*]

**Benvolio.** See, where he comes. So please you step aside,
150 I'll know his grievance, or be much denied.

**Montague.** I would thou wert so happy by thy stay
To hear true shrift. Come, madam, let's away.

[*Exeunt* Montague *and* Lady.]

**Benvolio.** Good morrow, cousin.

**Romeo.**                     Is the day so young?

**Benvolio.** But new struck nine.

**Romeo.**                     Ay me! sad hours seem long.
155 Was that my father that went hence so fast?

**Benvolio.** It was. What sadness lengthens Romeo's hours?

**Romeo.** Not having that which having makes them short.

**Benvolio.** In love?

**Romeo.** Out—

160 **Benvolio.** Of love?

**Romeo.** Out of her favor where I am in love.

**Benvolio.** Alas that love, so gentle in his view,
Should be so tyrannous and rough in proof!

**Romeo.** Alas that love, whose view is muffled still,
165 Should without eyes see pathways to his will!
Where shall we dine?—O me! What fray was here?—
Yet tell me not, for I have heard it all.

**134 portentous:** indicating evil to come; threatening.

**138 importuned:** asked in an urgent way.

**140 his own affections' counselor:** Romeo keeps to himself.

**143–148 so far from . . . know:** Finding out what Romeo is thinking is almost impossible. Montague compares his son to a young bud destroyed by the bite of a worm before it has a chance to open its leaves. Montague wants to find out what is bothering Romeo so he can help him.

**152 shrift:** confession.

**153 cousin:** any relative or close friend. The informal version is *coz*.

**157–163** *Why has Romeo been so depressed?*

**162–164 love:** references to Cupid, the god of love, typically pictured as a blind boy with wings and a bow and arrow. Anyone hit by one of his arrows falls in love instantly. Cupid looks sweet and gentle, but in reality he can be a harsh master.

## Is **LOVE** stronger than **HATE?**

**Discuss** What is Romeo's opinion of love? Cite evidence in lines 168–188. ***Possible answer:*** *Romeo's opinion is that love is a violent, contradictory thing. For example, he refers to love as "Misshapen chaos of well-seeming forms" (line 172) and as "A madness most discreet" (line 186). Romeo does not feel that love is necessarily good, for he calls it both "A choking gall, and a preserving sweet" (line 187). His negative view is perhaps best summed up in his statement that "Love is a smoke raised with the fume of sighs" (line 183).*

Here's much to do with hate, but more with love.
Why then, O brawling love! O loving hate!
170 O anything, of nothing first create!
O heavy lightness! serious vanity!
Misshapen chaos of well-seeming forms!
Feather of lead, bright smoke, cold fire, sick health!
Still-waking sleep, that is not what it is!
175 This love feel I, that feel no love in this.
Dost thou not laugh?

**Benvolio.**                    No, coz, I rather weep.

**Romeo.** Good heart, at what?

**Benvolio.**                    At thy good heart's oppression.

**Romeo.** Why, such is love's transgression.
Griefs of mine own lie heavy in my breast,
180 Which thou wilt propagate, to have it prest
With more of thine. This love that thou hast shown
Doth add more grief to too much of mine own.
Love is a smoke raised with the fume of sighs;
Being purged, a fire sparkling in lovers' eyes;
185 Being vexed, a sea nourished with lovers' tears.
What is it else? A madness most discreet,
A choking gall, and a preserving sweet.
Farewell, my coz.

**Benvolio.**         Soft! I will go along.
An if you leave me so, you do me wrong.

190 **Romeo.** Tut! I have lost myself; I am not here:
This is not Romeo, he's some other where.

**Benvolio.** Tell me in sadness, who is that you love?

**Romeo.** What, shall I groan and tell thee?

**Benvolio.**                              Groan? Why, no;
But sadly tell me who.

195 **Romeo.** Bid a sick man in sadness make his will.
Ah, word ill urged to one that is so ill!
In sadness, cousin, I do love a woman.

**Benvolio.** I aimed so near when I supposed you loved.

**Romeo.** A right good markman! And she's fair I love.

200 **Benvolio.** A right fair mark, fair coz, is soonest hit.

**Romeo.** Well, in that hit you miss. She'll not be hit
With Cupid's arrow. She hath Dian's wit,
And, in strong proof of chastity well armed,
From Love's weak childish bow she lives unharmed.

**168–176** Romeo, confused and upset, tries to describe his feelings about love. He uses phrases like "loving hate" and other contradictory expressions.

**176–182** Benvolio expresses his sympathy for Romeo. Romeo replies that this is one more problem caused by love. He now feels worse than before because he must carry the weight of Benvolio's sympathy along with his own grief.

**184 purged:** cleansed (of the smoke).
**185 vexed:** troubled.

**187 gall:** something causing bitterness or hate.

**188 Soft:** Wait a minute.

**192 sadness:** seriousness.

**201–204 She'll…unharmed:** The girl isn't interested in falling in love. She is like Diana, the goddess of chastity, who fended off Cupid's arrows.

## DIFFERENTIATED INSTRUCTION

**FOR ENGLISH LANGUAGE LEARNERS**
**Vocabulary Support** Have students reread the marginal note for lines 168–176. Emphasize that speaking in opposites shows Romeo's confusion over the fact that love, which should make him happy, has made him miserable. Model the restatement of *heavy lightness* (line 171) as "what should feel light feels heavy." Then guide students to restate these other opposites.

- *serious vanity* (line 171), "What should be unimportant is serious"
- *Feather of lead* (line 173), "A lightweight feather feels as heavy as lead"
- *bright smoke* (line 173), "Dark smoke is actually bright"
- *cold fire* (line 173), "Fire, which should be hot, is now cold"

## Behind the Curtain

### Casting

Even plays as timeless as Shakespearean dramas need powerful performances to bring them to life. Examine these photographs, and think about the choices the directors made when **casting**, or selecting, the pairs of actors for the roles of Juliet and Romeo. If you were in charge of casting a production of *Romeo and Juliet*, which pair would you choose, and why?

The Royal Shakespeare Company's 1992 production

A 2004 coproduction of the Chicago Shakespeare Theater and Second City

The Cottesloe Theatre's 2000 production

---

## BEHIND THE CURTAIN

COMMON CORE SL 2

**Casting** Point out to students that the choice of an actor to play a role is often partly determined by the actor's age, race, and physical features, such as height and overall build. Casting is a particular challenge in *Romeo and Juliet*, as the characters are described as young teenagers. Casting directors must decide whether or not they wish to give the lead roles to youthful actors, or if older actors might present certain dramatic possibilities. For example, the Romeo in the Chicago Shakespeare Theater and Second City coproduction has strong facial features and a shaved head; this couple seems older than the couples in the other photographs. By making distinctive casting choices, a director imposes a personal interpretation upon Shakespeare's text. *Accept any answer that is reasonably supported by details from the photographs. For example, casting an interracial couple in the roles might symbolize and emphasize the differences between the feuding families, and casting the smiling, somewhat animated couple might emphasize the youthful enthusiasm of Romeo and Juliet and the play's touches of humor.*

---

### FOR ADVANCED LEARNERS/PRE–AP

**Make Judgments** Have students do an Internet search to locate photographs from various professional, community, and college productions of *Romeo and Juliet*. As they did for the photographs on this page, ask students to think about the choices that the directors of their researched productions made when casting the play. Have students meet in small groups to share their opinions about the casting choices.

## Is **LOVE** stronger than **HATE?**

**Discuss** We already know that Romeo will kill himself over his love for Juliet. In what sense does Romeo's state of mind in this scene, especially in lines 210–217, foreshadow his death? *Possible answer: We can see from this scene that Romeo is driven by his emotions. These qualities foreshadow his suicide. He is depressed over Rosaline's refusal to accept him. He later will kill himself rather than face life without Juliet.*

## BACKGROUND

**Families** Wealthy Renaissance families relied upon clearly defined roles as well as carefully arranged alliances for stability and power. Families were usually ruled by strong fathers who arranged marriages for their children, sometimes with the fathers of other wealthy families, or else, in the case of his daughters, with an adult male who possessed wealth or political power. A father was also expected to provide a dowry, a gift of money or valuables to the groom. Wives were expected to produce children, preferably male ones, in order to secure an heir to the family's fortunes. They were also expected to support their husbands in their choice of potential spouses for the children. Children were expected to obey their parents without question.

---

205 She will not stay the siege of loving terms,
Nor bide the encounter of assailing eyes,
Nor ope her lap to saint-seducing gold.
O, she is rich in beauty; only poor
That, when she dies, with beauty dies her store.

210 **Benvolio.** Then she hath sworn that she will still live chaste?

**Romeo.** She hath, and in that sparing makes huge waste;
For beauty, starved with her severity,
Cuts beauty off from all posterity.
She is too fair, too wise, wisely too fair,
215 To merit bliss by making me despair.
She hath forsworn to love, and in that vow
Do I live dead that live to tell it now.

**Benvolio.** Be ruled by me: forget to think of her.

**Romeo.** O, teach me how I should forget to think!

220 **Benvolio.** By giving liberty unto thine eyes:
Examine other beauties.

**Romeo.**                          'Tis the way
To call hers (exquisite) in question more.
These happy masks that kiss fair ladies' brows,
Being black, puts us in mind they hide the fair.
225 He that is strucken blind cannot forget
The precious treasure of his eyesight lost.
Show me a mistress that is passing fair,
What doth her beauty serve but as a note
Where I may read who passed that passing fair?
230 Farewell. Thou canst not teach me to forget.

**Benvolio.** I'll pay that doctrine, or else die in debt.

[*Exeunt.*]

## SCENE 2 *A street near the Capulet house.*

*This scene opens with Count Paris, a young nobleman, asking Capulet for permission to marry his daughter, Juliet. Capulet says that Juliet is too young but gives Paris permission to court her and try to win her heart. He also invites Paris to a party he is giving that night.*

*Romeo finds out about the party and discovers that Rosaline, the girl who rejected him, will be present. Benvolio urges Romeo to go to the party to see how Rosaline compares with the other women.*

[*Enter Capulet with Paris, a kinsman of the Prince, and Servant.*]

**Capulet.** But Montague is bound as well as I,
In penalty alike; and 'tis not hard, I think,
For men so old as we to keep the peace.

**205–207 She will not . . . saint-seducing gold:** She is not swayed by Romeo's declaration of love, his adoring looks, or his wealth.

**212–213 For beauty . . . posterity:** By denying herself love and marriage, she wastes her beauty, which will not be passed on to future generations.

**215–216 to merit . . . despair:** The girl will reach heaven (**bliss**) by being so virtuous, which causes Romeo to feel hopelessness or despair; **forsworn to:** sworn not to.

**220–221** *What is Benvolio's advice?*

**221–222 'Tis . . . more:** That would only make me appreciate my own love's beauty more.

**223** Masks were worn by Elizabethan women to protect their complexions from the sun.

**227–229 Show me . . . that passing fair:** A woman who is exceedingly (**passing**) beautiful will only remind me of my love, who is even prettier.

**231 I'll pay . . . debt:** I'll convince you you're wrong, or die trying.

**1 bound:** obligated.

---

## DIFFERENTIATED INSTRUCTION

**FOR STRUGGLING READERS**

**Preview** Model creating a cartoon to record key details in the synopsis for Scene 2.

**Count Paris:**
May I marry Juliet?

**Capulet:**
No. She's too young. You may court her, though. Come to our party tonight.

Invite students to create a cartoon to synthesize the rest of the synopsis.

**FOR ENGLISH LANGUAGE LEARNERS**

**Task Support** As students consider the marginal question for lines 220–221, clarify that Benvolio is responding to Romeo's request in line 219. Help students paraphrase Benvolio's reply. *Possible answer: You can forget Rosaline if you let your eyes look beyond her. Consider the other beautiful girls around here.*

**Paris.** Of honorable reckoning are you both,
5 And pity 'tis you lived at odds so long.
But now, my lord, what say you to my suit?

**Capulet.** But saying o'er what I have said before:
My child is yet a stranger in the world,
She hath not seen the change of fourteen years;
10 Let two more summers wither in their pride
Ere we may think her ripe to be a bride.

**Paris.** Younger than she are happy mothers made.

**Capulet.** And too soon marred are those so early made.
The earth hath swallowed all my hopes but she;
15 She is the hopeful lady of my earth.
But woo her, gentle Paris, get her heart;
My will to her consent is but a part.
An she agree, within her scope of choice
Lies my consent and fair according voice.

20 This night I hold an old accustomed feast,
Whereto I have invited many a guest,
Such as I love, and you among the store,
One more, most welcome, makes my number more.
At my poor house look to behold this night
25 Earth-treading stars that make dark heaven light.
Such comfort as do lusty young men feel
When well-appareled April on the heel
Of limping Winter treads, even such delight
Among fresh female buds shall you this night
30 Inherit at my house. Hear all, all see,
And like her most whose merit most shall be;
Which, on more view of many, mine, being one,
May stand in number, though in reck'ning none.
Come, go with me. [*to* Servant, *giving him a paper*]
          Go, sirrah, trudge about
35 Through fair Verona; find those persons out
Whose names are written there, and to them say,
My house and welcome on their pleasure stay.

[*Exeunt* Capulet *and* Paris.]

**Servant.** Find them out whose names are written here! It is
written that the shoemaker should meddle with his yard and the
40 tailor with his last, the fisher with his pencil and the painter
with his nets; but I am sent to find those persons whose names
are here writ, and can never find what names the writing person
hath here writ. I must to the learned. In good time!

---

**4 reckoning:** reputation.

**6 what say . . . suit:** Paris is asking for Capulet's response to his proposal to marry Juliet.

**10 let two more summers . . . pride:** let two more years pass.

### ② Targeted Passage

**14 The earth . . . she:** All my children are dead except Juliet.

**16 woo her:** try to win her heart.

**18–19 An . . . voice:** I will give my approval to the one she chooses.

**20 old accustomed feast:** a traditional or annual party.

**Ⓓ BLANK VERSE**
Reread lines 16–19 aloud, tapping your foot at each stressed syllable. How many stressed syllables are in each line?

**29–33 among . . . none:** Tonight at the party you will witness the loveliest young girls in Verona, including Juliet. When you see all of them together, your opinion of Juliet may change.

**34 sirrah:** a term used to address a servant.

**38–43** The servant cannot seek out the people on the list because he cannot read. In his remarks he confuses the craftsmen and their tools, tapping a typical source of humor for Elizabethan comic characters.

**43 In good time:** What luck (a reference to the arrival of Romeo and Benvolio, who will be able to help the servant read the list).

ROMEO AND JULIET: ACT ONE, SCENE 2   **1047**

---

## Is **LOVE** stronger than **HATE?**

**Discuss** To what does Benvolio compare love in lines 48–49? How do his words apply to Romeo's thoughts about Rosaline? *Possible answer: Benvolio compares love to an infection and a poison. He says that a love that is going badly can be driven out by introducing a new love. The application is clear: Rosaline is the source of Romeo's pain, but finding another person to love will make that pain go away.*

[*Enter* Benvolio *and* Romeo.]

**Benvolio.** Tut, man, one fire burns out another's burning;
45 One pain is lessened by another's anguish;
Turn giddy, and be holp by backward turning;
One desperate grief cures with another's languish.
Take thou some new infection to thy eye,
And the rank poison of the old will die.

50 **Romeo.** Your plantain leaf is excellent for that.

**Benvolio.** For what, I pray thee?

**Romeo.**                              For your broken shin.

**Benvolio.** Why, Romeo, art thou mad?

**Romeo.** Not mad, but bound more than a madman is;
Shut up in prison, kept without my food,
55 Whipped and tormented and—God-den, good fellow.

**Servant.** God gi' go-den. I pray, sir, can you read?

**Romeo.** Ay, mine own fortune in my misery.

**Servant.** Perhaps you have learned it without book. But
I pray, can you read anything you see?

60 **Romeo.** Ay, if I know the letters and the language.

**Servant.** Ye say honestly. Rest you merry!

[Romeo's *joking goes over the clown's head. He concludes that* Romeo *cannot read and prepares to seek someone who can.*]

**Romeo.** Stay, fellow; I can read. [*He reads.*]
"Signior Martino and his wife and daughters;
County Anselmo and his beauteous sisters;
65 The lady widow of Vitruvio;
Signior Placentio and his lovely nieces;
Mercutio and his brother Valentine;
Mine uncle Capulet, his wife, and daughters;
My fair niece Rosaline and Livia;
70 Signior Valentio and his cousin Tybalt;
Lucio and the lively Helena."
[*gives back the paper*]
A fair assembly. Whither should they come?

**Servant.** Up.

**Romeo.** Whither?

75 **Servant.** To supper, to our house.

**Romeo.** Whose house?

**Servant.** My master's.

**Romeo.** Indeed I should have asked you that before.

**44–49 Tut, man ... die:** Romeo and Benvolio are still discussing Romeo's love problems. Benvolio says Romeo should find a new love—that a "new infection" will cure the old one.

**55 god-den:** good evening. Romeo interrupts his lament to talk to the servant.

**56 God gi' go-den:** God give you a good evening.

**69 Rosaline:** This is the woman that Romeo is in love with. Mercutio, a friend of both Romeo and the Capulets, is also invited to the party.

**72 whither:** where.

## DIFFERENTIATED INSTRUCTION

### FOR ENGLISH LANGUAGE LEARNERS
**Vocabulary: Outdated Forms** Discuss these examples of Shakespearean terms that have passed from use: *thy* (line 48), "your"; *pray* (line 51), "ask," "beg"; *Ay* (line 57), "yes"; *Ye* (line 61), "you"; *Stay* (line 62), "wait"; *Whither* (line 74), "where."

### FOR ADVANCED LEARNERS/PRE–AP
**Analyze Character and Plot** The reference passes by almost too quickly to register, but lines 68–69 reveal that Romeo's beloved Rosaline is a Capulet—a member of the rival clan. Have students comment about how this information (1) sheds light on Romeo's character (and possibly Rosaline's feelings toward him) and (2) helps set up Romeo's reaction to the news (revealed at the end of Act One) that Juliet is a Capulet.

**Servant.** Now I'll tell you without asking. My master is the great
80 rich Capulet; and if you be not of the house of Montagues, I
pray come and crush a cup of wine. Rest you merry!
[*Exit.*]

*81* **crush a cup of wine:** slang for "drink some wine."

**Benvolio.** At this same ancient feast of Capulet's
Sups the fair Rosaline whom thou so lovest,
With all the admired beauties of Verona.
85 Go thither, and with unattainted eye
Compare her face with some that I shall show,
And I will make thee think thy swan a crow.

*85* **unattainted:** unbiased; unprejudiced.

**Romeo.** When the devout religion of mine eye
Maintains such falsehood, then turn tears to fires;
90 And these, who, often drowned, could never die,
Transparent heretics, be burnt for liars!
One fairer than my love? The all-seeing sun
Ne'er saw her match since first the world begun.

*88–91* **When … liars:** If the love I have for Rosaline, which is like a religion, changes because of such a lie (that others may be more beautiful), let my tears be turned to fire and my eyes be burned.

**Benvolio.** Tut! you saw her fair, none else being by,
95 Herself poised with herself in either eye;
But in that crystal scales let there be weighed
Your lady's love against some other maid
That I will show you shining at this feast,
And she shall scant show well that now shows best.

*94–99* **Tut … best:** You've seen Rosaline alone; now compare her with some other women. *How does Benvolio think Rosaline will measure up against the other girls?*

100 **Romeo.** I'll go along, no such sight to be shown,
But to rejoice in splendor of mine own.
[*Exeunt.*]

*100–101* Romeo agrees to go to the party, but only to see Rosaline.

# SCENE 3  *Capulet's house.*

*In this scene, you will meet Juliet, her mother, and her nurse. The nurse, a merry and slightly crude servant, has been in charge of Juliet since her birth. Once she starts talking, she can't stop. Just before the party, Juliet's mother asks if Juliet has thought about getting married. Lady Capulet is matchmaking, trying to convince her daughter that Paris would make a good husband. Juliet responds just as you might if your parents set up a blind date for you—without much enthusiasm.*

[*Enter* Lady Capulet *and* Nurse.]

**Lady Capulet.** Nurse, where's my daughter? Call her forth to me.

**Nurse.** Now, by my maidenhead at twelve year old,
I bade her come. What, lamb! what, ladybird!
God forbid! Where's this girl? What, Juliet!
[*Enter* Juliet.]

*3–4* **what:** a call like "Hey, where are you?"

5 **Juliet.** How now? Who calls?

## BACKGROUND

**Nurses** Most wealthy families employed nurses for their children. Nurses were usually taken from the poorer classes and were often hired because a child of their own had recently died, as was the case with Juliet's nurse's daughter, Susan (lines 19–20). Nurses sometimes stayed on with the family to raise the child, and often developed strong emotional bonds. Notice that it is the nurse, not Lady Capulet, who recounts a story from Juliet's childhood, described in lines 37–49. While the nurse at times seems silly, even coarse, she is devoted to Juliet. Later in the play, she will stand up to Lord Capulet in defense of her charge, an act for which her employer could have had her imprisoned, put to hard labor, and beaten severely.

---

**FOR STRUGGLING READERS**

**Preview** As you read through the Scene 3 synopsis, use a Cluster Diagram to help students identify the women characters.

BEST PRACTICES TOOLKIT—Transparency
Cluster Diagram p. B18

**FOR ENGLISH LANGUAGE LEARNERS**

**Task Support** Point out the question in the marginal note for lines 94–99. Have students reread that note, reread lines 94–99, and review Benvolio's comment in lines 86–87. Help students paraphrase Benvolio's words.
*Possible answer: Benvolio thinks that Rosaline will not measure up; in fact, he thinks that she will go unnoticed next to the beauty of the other girls at the feast.*

**Activity** What can you infer from the photograph about the relationship between Juliet and her nurse? *Possible answer: Juliet shows her love for the nurse through her hug. The nurse shows her affection for Juliet in her dreamy smile; she shows her protective feelings for Juliet in her act of placing her hands over Juliet's.*

**Nurse.** Your mother.

**Juliet.** Madam, I am here. What is your will?

**Lady Capulet.** This is the matter—Nurse, give leave awhile,
We must talk in secret. Nurse, come back again;
10 I have remembered me, thou's hear our counsel.
Thou knowest my daughter's of a pretty age.

**Nurse.** Faith, I can tell her age unto an hour.

**Lady Capulet.** She's not fourteen.

**Nurse.**                   I'll lay fourteen of my teeth—
And yet, to my teen be it spoken, I have but four—
15 She's not fourteen. How long is it now
To Lammastide?

**Lady Capulet.**       A fortnight and odd days.

**8–11 give leave . . . counsel:** Lady Capulet seems flustered or nervous, not sure whether she wants the nurse to stay or leave; **of a pretty age:** of an attractive age, ready for marriage.

**14 teen:** sorrow.

**16 Lammastide:** August 1, a religious feast day. It is two weeks (**a fortnight**) away.

Juliet and her nurse in the 1994 production of the Shakespeare Theatre in Washington, D.C.

## DIFFERENTIATED INSTRUCTION

**FOR ENGLISH LANGUAGE LEARNERS**
**Vocabulary: Outdated Forms** Encourage students to add these outdated terms to their language journals. (See the **For English Language Learners** activity on page 1036.) Then have them reread the lines noted and substitute the definitions for the words.

- *give leave* (line 8), "leave [us] alone"
- *thou's* (line 10), "you should"
- *Thou knowest* (line 11), "you know"
- *Faith* (line 12), "believe me"

- *Yea* (line 42), "indeed"
- *quoth* (line 42), "said"
- *wit* (line 43), "sense"
- *Wilt thou not* (line 44), "won't you"
- *I warrant, an I should live* (line 47), "I swear [promise], if I should live"
- *hold thy peace* (line 50), "stop," "be quiet"
- *when thou comest to age* (line 57), "when you're grown up"

**Nurse.** Even or odd, of all days in the year,
Come Lammas Eve at night shall she be fourteen.
Susan and she (God rest all Christian souls!)
20 Were of an age. Well, Susan is with God;
She was too good for me. But, as I said,
On Lammas Eve at night shall she be fourteen;
That shall she, marry; I remember it well.
'Tis since the earthquake now eleven years;
25 And she was weaned (I never shall forget it),
Of all the days of the year, upon that day.
For I had then laid wormwood to my dug,
Sitting in the sun under the dovehouse wall.
My lord and you were then at Mantua—
30 Nay, I do bear a brain—But, as I said,
When it did taste the wormwood on the nipple
Of my dug and felt it bitter, pretty fool,
To see it tetchy and fall out with the dug!
Shake, quoth the dovehouse! 'Twas no need, I trow,
35 To bid me trudge.
And since that time it is eleven years,
For then she could stand alone; nay, by the rood,
She could have run and waddled all about;
For even the day before, she broke her brow;
40 And then my husband (God be with his soul!
'A was a merry man) took up the child.
"Yea," quoth he, "dost thou fall upon thy face?
Thou wilt fall backward when thou has more wit,
Wilt thou not, Jule?" And, by my holidam,
45 The pretty wretch left crying, and said "Ay."
To see now how a jest shall come about!
I warrant, an I should live a thousand years,
I never should forget it. "Wilt thou not, Jule?" quoth he,
And, pretty fool, it stinted, and said "Ay."
50 **Lady Capulet.** Enough of this. I pray thee hold thy peace.
   **Nurse.** Yes, madam. Yet I cannot choose but laugh
To think it should leave crying and say "Ay."
And yet, I warrant, it had upon its brow
A bump as big as a young cock'rel's stone;
55 A perilous knock; and it cried bitterly.
"Yea," quoth my husband, "fall'st upon thy face?
Thou wilt fall backward when thou comest to age,
Wilt thou not, Jule?" It stinted, and said "Ay."

---

**17–49** The nurse begins to babble about various memories of Juliet's childhood. She talks of her own dead daughter, Susan, who was the same age as Juliet. Susan probably died in infancy, leaving the nurse available to become a wet nurse to (that is, breastfeed) Juliet. She remembers an earthquake that happened on the day she stopped breast-feeding Juliet (**she was weaned**).

**27 laid wormwood to my dug:** applied wormwood, a plant with a bitter taste, to her breast in order to discourage the child from breastfeeding.

**33 tetchy:** touchy; cranky.

**34–35 Shake . . . trudge:** When the dove house shook, I knew enough to leave.

**37 by the rood:** by the cross of Christ (a mild oath).

**39 broke her brow:** cut her forehead.

**42–49 "Yea" . . . "Ay":** To quiet Juliet after her fall, the nurse's husband made a crude joke, asking the baby whether she'd fall the other way (on her back) when she was older. Although at three Juliet didn't understand the question, she stopped crying (**stinted**) and innocently answered "Yes." The nurse finds the story so funny that she can't stop retelling it.

**E CHARACTER**
So far, how would you describe the nurse? List three **traits** this character exhibits.

**55 perilous:** hazardous; dangerous.

---

TEXT ANALYSIS    COMMON CORE
RL 3

**E CHARACTER**

*Possible answer: The nurse is religious, as suggested by her references to God in lines 19, 20, and 40. She also acts very familiarly toward Lady Capulet, even though she is the woman's servant. Most notably, she has a crude sense of humor, revealed in her great enjoyment of the suggestive story that she tells in lines 37–46 and mentions again in lines 47–49 and lines 51–58. Her earthiness makes her a foil to the formal, refined Lady Capulet and to the less mature but mannerly Juliet.*

**IF STUDENTS NEED HELP . . .** Use a Character Analysis Chart to help students note what they know about the nurse. Discuss how she is similar to and different from other characters that students have met thus far in Act One.

**BEST PRACTICES TOOLKIT—Transparency** Character Analysis Chart p. D5

**BACKGROUND**

**Dating the Play** Some scholars believe that the nurse's mention of an earthquake in lines 24 and 34–36 is a clue as to when Shakespeare wrote *Romeo and Juliet*. On April 6, 1580, an earthquake frightened Londoners badly. The nurse's references to the 11 years that have passed since that event—an event that the audience would have remembered—suggest a date of 1591 for *Romeo and Juliet*.

---

**FOR STRUGGLING READERS**

**Inverted Word Order** Point out the repetition of "shall she" in the nurse's speech (lines 18, 22, and 23). Explain that in each case, the words seem like a question to the modern ear, but that, in fact, they are statements. Have a volunteer read the lines aloud, changing *shall she* to *she shall.*

**FOR ENGLISH LANGUAGE LEARNERS**

**Concept Support** Explain that at the time that this play takes place, most European upper-class marriages were arranged by families for social and economic reasons. Because life spans were shorter than they are today, people married younger, and parents often made marriage plans for their children long before the wedding occurred. Romantic love was not seen as a requirement for a sound marriage.

## TIERED DISCUSSION PROMPTS

Use these prompts to help students analyze Lady Capulet's speech about Paris in lines 80–95:

**Connect** Has a parent or family member ever tried to persuade you to do something that you did not want to do? How might that experience help you understand Lady Capulet's speech to Juliet? *Most students will recall such a persuasive speech. The experience might help them understand that Lady Capulet is trying to get her own way without starting an argument with Juliet.*

**Analyze** What features of Paris does Lady Capulet emphasize? *Possible answer: Lady Capulet emphasizes Paris's good looks and, to a lesser extent, his wealth.* What do you suppose is Lady Capulet's real motivation at this moment? *Possible answer: Although Lady Capulet probably wants Juliet to be happy, she also wants Juliet to marry someone who is socially acceptable and who can provide for her (lines 94–95).*

**Evaluate** Do you think that Lady Capulet provides a strong and effective argument in favor of Paris? Why or why not? *Students may suggest that his handsomeness would be persuasive to a young teenager. They may say that this approach is likely to be more successful than an outright demand from Lady Capulet would be.*

### REVIST THE BIG QUESTION

## Is **LOVE** stronger than **HATE?**

**Discuss** In lines 82–87, Lady Capulet describes Paris's looks to persuade Juliet to take an interest in him. What do her words have in common with what Romeo has said about love in Scenes 1 and 2? *Possible answer: Both characters' words have indicated a belief that love springs from physical attractiveness.*

---

**Juliet.** And stint thou too, I pray thee, nurse, say I.

60 **Nurse.** Peace, I have done. God mark thee to his grace!
Thou wast the prettiest babe that e'er I nursed.
An I might live to see thee married once,
I have my wish.

**Lady Capulet.** Marry, that "marry" is the very theme
65 I came to talk of. Tell me, daughter Juliet,
How stands your disposition to be married?

**Juliet.** It is an honor that I dream not of.

**Nurse.** An honor? Were not I thine only nurse,
I would say thou hadst sucked wisdom from thy teat.

70 **Lady Capulet.** Well, think of marriage now. Younger than you,
Here in Verona, ladies of esteem,
Are made already mothers. By my count,
I was your mother much upon these years
That you are now a maid. Thus then in brief:
75 The valiant Paris seeks you for his love.

**Nurse.** A man, young lady! lady, such a man
As all the world—why he's a man of wax.

**Lady Capulet.** Verona's summer hath not such a flower.

**Nurse.** Nay, he's a flower, in faith—a very flower.

80 **Lady Capulet.** What say you? Can you love the gentleman?
This night you shall behold him at our feast.
Read o'er the volume of young Paris' face,
And find delight writ there with beauty's pen;
Examine every several lineament,
85 And see how one another lends content;
And what obscured in this fair volume lies
Find written in the margent of his eyes.
This precious book of love, this unbound lover,
To beautify him only lacks a cover.
90 The fish lives in the sea, and 'tis much pride
For fair without the fair within to hide.
That book in many's eyes doth share the glory,
That in gold clasps locks in the golden story;
So shall you share all that he doth possess,
95 By having him making yourself no less.

**Nurse.** No less? Nay, bigger! Women grow by men.

**Lady Capulet.** Speak briefly, can you like of Paris' love?

**Juliet.** I'll look to like, if looking liking move;
But no more deep will I endart mine eye

**64 Marry..."marry":** two different usages of the same word—the first meaning "by the Virgin Mary" and the second meaning "to wed."

**73–74 I was...maid:** I was your mother at about your age, yet you are still unmarried.

**77 a man of wax:** a man so perfect he could be a wax statue, of the type sculptors once used as models for their works.

**82–89 Read...cover:** Lady Capulet uses an extended metaphor that compares Paris to a book that Juliet should read.

**84 every several lineament:** each separate feature (of Paris' face).

**87 margent...eyes:** She compares Paris' eyes to the margin of a page, where notes are written to explain the content.

**88–91 This...hide:** This beautiful book (Paris) needs only a cover (wife) to become even better. He may be hiding even more wonderful qualities inside.

**96** The nurse can't resist commenting that women get bigger (pregnant) when they marry.

**98 I'll look...move:** I'll look at him with the intention of liking him, if simply looking can make me like him.

**99 endart:** look deeply, as if penetrating with a dart.

**1052** UNIT 10: SHAKESPEAREAN DRAMA

---

## DIFFERENTIATED INSTRUCTION

### FOR STRUGGLING READERS

**Compare and Contrast** Ask students to reread Capulet's conversation with Paris on page 1047. Use a Venn Diagram to help students compare how Capulet and his wife are alike and how they differ on the subject of Juliet's marriage.

**BEST PRACTICES TOOLKIT—Transparency**
Venn Diagram p. A26

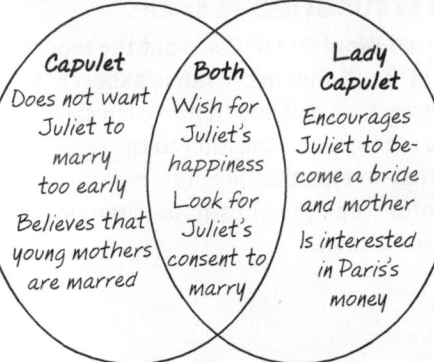

Capulet: Does not want Juliet to marry too early; Believes that young mothers are marred

Both: Wish for Juliet's happiness; Look for Juliet's consent to marry

Lady Capulet: Encourages Juliet to become a bride and mother; Is interested in Paris's money

100 Than your consent gives strength to make it fly. **F**

[*Enter a* Servingman.]

**Servingman.** Madam, the guests are come, supper served up, you
called, my young lady asked for, the nurse cursed in the pantry,
and everything in extremity. I must hence to wait. I beseech you
follow straight.

105 **Lady Capulet.** We follow thee. [*Exit* Servingman.] Juliet, the County
stays.

**Nurse.** Go, girl, seek happy nights to happy days.

[*Exeunt.*]

# SCENE 4   *A street near the Capulet house.*

*It is the evening of the Capulet masque, or costume ball. Imagine the guests
proceeding through the darkened streets with torches to light the way.*

*Romeo and his friends Mercutio and Benvolio join the procession. Their masks
will prevent Romeo's and Benvolio's being recognized as Montagues. Mercutio
and Benvolio are in a playful, partying mood, but Romeo is still depressed by
his unanswered love for Rosaline. Romeo has also had a dream that warned
him of the harmful consequences of this party. He senses trouble.*

[*Enter* Romeo, Mercutio, Benvolio, *with five or six other* Maskers;
Torchbearers.]

**Romeo.** What, shall this speech be spoke for our excuse?
Or shall we on without apology?

**Benvolio.** The date is out of such prolixity.
We'll have no Cupid hoodwinked with a scarf,
5 Bearing a Tartar's painted bow of lath,
Scaring the ladies like a crowkeeper;
Nor no without-book prologue, faintly spoke
After the prompter, for our entrance;
But let them measure us by what they will,
10 We'll measure them a measure, and be gone.

**Romeo.** Give me a torch. I am not for this ambling;
Being but heavy, I will bear the light.

**Mercutio.** Nay, gentle Romeo, we must have you dance.

**Romeo.** Not I, believe me. You have dancing shoes
15 With nimble soles; I have a soul of lead
So stakes me to the ground I cannot move.

**Mercutio.** You are a lover. Borrow Cupid's wings
And soar with them above a common bound.

**Romeo.** I am too sore enpiercèd with his shaft
20 To soar with his light feathers, and so bound

---

**F TRAGEDY**
How might Lady Capulet's desire for
Juliet to marry Paris lead to **conflict**
later in the play? Explain your
answer.

**103–104 extremity:** great confusion;
**straight:** immediately.

**105 the County stays:** Count Paris is
waiting for you.

**1–10 What, shall this . . . be gone:**
Romeo asks whether they should send
a messenger announcing their arrival
at the party. Benvolio replies that this
custom is out of date. He says that they'll
dance one dance with the partygoers
(**measure them a measure**) and
then leave.

**12 heavy:** sad. Romeo makes a joke based
on the meanings of *heavy* and *light.*

**14–32** Romeo continues to talk about his
sadness, while Mercutio jokingly makes
fun of him to try to cheer him up.

---

TEXT ANALYSIS                                    COMMON
                                                        CORE
                                                          L3

**F TRAGEDY**

*Possible answer:  We already know that
Juliet will fall in love with Romeo.  If her
parents want her to marry another man,
there will surely be a conflict.*

**IF STUDENTS NEED HELP . . .** Ask students
how they would respond to this announcement from a parent: "Dear, I have found
a wonderful person for you to marry!"
Discuss possible conflicts that might result
from such an announcement.

---

**FOR STRUGGLING READERS**

**Preview** Have students read the Scene 4 synopsis. Help them fill out a Says Who? chart
with notes about who speaks, and what is
actually being said, in this scene.

| SAYS WHO? | | |
|---|---|---|
| **Romeo** | **Mercutio** | **Benvolio** |
| I am too sad to have a good time. | Have some fun, Romeo! | We'll sneak into the party, dance a little, and then leave. |
| I dreamed that something bad will happen because of this party. | The queen of the fairies is playing with your dreams. | |

##  PUN

**Possible answer:** *In line 12, Romeo makes a pun by using the word heavy to mean both "sad" and "of great weight" and the word light to mean "luminous" and "of little weight." In line 15, Romeo's pun comes from pairing the words soul and soles when explaining his unhappiness. In lines 19–20, Romeo puns on the words sore ("in pain") and soar ("fly"). The effect of the puns is to lighten the mood. Although Romeo is sad, his puns show that he can nevertheless joke with his friends.*

**IF STUDENTS NEED HELP . . .** Read lines 11–22 aloud, emphasizing the words in the puns. Point out that the first pun is based on two different multiple-meaning words: *heavy* and *light.* Then explain that both the second and third puns are based on homophones, or words that sound alike but are spelled differently and have different meanings: *soles* and *soul* and *sore* and *soar.*

---

I cannot bound a pitch above dull woe.
Under love's heavy burden do I sink. **G**

**Mercutio.** And, to sink in it, should you burden love—
Too great oppression for a tender thing.

25 **Romeo.** Is love a tender thing? It is too rough,
Too rude, too boist'rous, and it pricks like thorn.

**Mercutio.** If love be rough with you, be rough with love.
Prick love for pricking, and you beat love down.
Give me a case to put my visage in.

30 A visor for a visor! What care I
What curious eye doth quote deformities?
Here are the beetle brows shall blush for me.

**Benvolio.** Come, knock and enter, and no sooner in
But every man betake him to his legs.

35 **Romeo.** A torch for me! Let wantons light of heart
Tickle the senseless rushes with their heels;
For I am proverbed with a grandsire phrase,
I'll be a candle-holder and look on;
The game was ne'er so fair, and I am done.

40 **Mercutio.** Tut, dun's the mouse, the constable's own word!
If thou art Dun, we'll draw thee from the mire
Of, save your reverence, love, wherein thou stickst
Up to the ears. Come, we burn daylight, ho!

**Romeo.** Nay, that's not so.

**Mercutio.**                    I mean, sir, in delay
45 We waste our lights in vain, like lamps by day.
Take our good meaning, for our judgment sits
Five times in that ere once in our five wits.

**Romeo.** And we mean well in going to this masque;
But 'tis no wit to go.

**Mercutio.**                    Why, may one ask?

50 **Romeo.** I dreamt a dream tonight.

**Mercutio.**                              And so did I.

**Romeo.** Well, what was yours?

**Mercutio.**                         That dreamers often lie.

**Romeo.** In bed asleep, while they do dream things true.

**Mercutio.** O, then I see Queen Mab hath been with you.
She is the fairies' midwife, and she comes
55 In shape no bigger than an agate stone
On the forefinger of an alderman,
Drawn with a team of little atomies

---

**G** PUN
Identify two puns in lines 11–22. What effect do they have on the **mood** of this scene?

**29–32 Give . . . for me:** Give me a mask for an ugly face. I don't care if people notice my appearance. Here, look at my bushy eyebrows.

**34 betake . . . legs:** dance.

**35–38 Let . . . look on:** Let playful people tickle the grass (**rushes**) on the floor with their dancing. I'll follow the old saying (**grandsire phrase**) and just be a spectator.

**40–43 Tut . . . daylight:** Mercutio jokes, using various meanings of the word *dun*, which sounds like Romeo's last word, *done*. He concludes by saying they should not waste time (**burn daylight**).

**53–95** This famous speech is yet one more attempt by Mercutio to cheer up Romeo. He talks of Mab, queen of the fairies, a folktale character well-known to Shakespeare's audience. His language includes vivid descriptions, puns, and satires of people; and ultimately he gets caught up in his own wild imaginings. It is not necessary to understand everything Mercutio says to recognize the beauty of this born storyteller's tale.

**55 agate stone:** jewel for a ring.

**57 atomies:** tiny creatures.

---

## DIFFERENTIATED INSTRUCTION

### FOR STRUGGLING READERS

**Paraphrasing Shakespeare** Draw students' attention to the marginal note that summarizes lines 53–95. Help students paraphrase lines 53–58 to read something like this: *I see that Queen Mab has visited you. She is the helper of fairies and is smaller than the stone on a ring. She rides a tiny carriage pulled by tiny creatures, bringing sweet dreams to sleeping people.*

### FOR RELUCTANT READERS

Invite students to make personal connections with the text through visual images.

- Point out that Mercutio's description of Queen Mab that begins at line 53 contains visual images.

- Ask students to use the details in Mercutio's speech to draw pictures of Queen Mab.

- Suggest that students use the tone of Mercutio's speech to help them choose colors for their drawings.

- Students may also enjoy enhancing their drawings with images or words from their own dreams or from Mercutio's speech.

- Ask students to share their drawings with the class. Create a Queen Mab art gallery to display students' works.

# Behind the Curtain

## Costume Design

Classic dramas such as *Romeo and Juliet* can be staged in many different ways. **Costumes** are one means of making a production distinctive. Think about the interpretations of the play pictured here. (Note: The middle shot is of Romeo and Juliet in the midst of the famous balcony scene, coming up in Act Two—and the ladder serves as the balcony!) How are the different costume choices in these photographs appropriate for the different productions?

Romeo and Juliet in the Globe Theatre's 2004 production

Romeo and Juliet in the Globe Theatre's 2000 production

Romeo and Juliet in the Royal Ballet's 2003 production

---

## BEHIND THE CURTAIN

**COMMON CORE SL 2**

**Costume Design** Point out that costumes can reflect such time periods as, for example, the Renaissance, the Roaring Twenties, or the Old West. Costumes can reflect geographical settings such as a Chinese village, a Caribbean island, or an American high school. Costumes may suggest the attitudes of the characters or a director's unique interpretation of a play. Elicit that the costumes in the Globe Theatre's 2004 production are from the Renaissance era and that the Royal Ballet production uses traditional ballet costuming. Note that the costuming in the Globe Theatre's 2000 production shows a more modern interpretation, with all-white costumes and unusual makeup and headgear. *Possible answer: In each case, the costumes are appropriate for the production. For the Royal Ballet, the costumes reflect and allow for flowing ballet movements. The costuming in the Globe Theatre's 2000 production reflects an alternative interpretation of Shakespeare's text. The costumes in the Globe Theatre's 2004 production aim for a more historical interpretation of the play.*

---

**FOR ADVANCED LEARNERS/PRE–AP**

**Reinterpret the Play** Remind students that costumes play a very visible role in a production's interpretation of a play. Then ask students to reinterpret *Romeo and Juliet* by designing costumes that reflect a specific era or geographical setting. After allowing time for research, have students draw their costuming ideas or write a detailed description. Invite students to share their costuming ideas with the class.

**TIERED DISCUSSION PROMPTS**

Use these prompts to help students analyze Mercutio's famous speech in lines 53–95:

**Recall** What is Mercutio's explanation for where dreams come from? *Possible answer: Mercutio's explanation is that dreams come from Queen Mab, the queen of the fairies, who visits people while they are sleeping, riding her wagon made from "an empty hazelnut" (line 67). The content of a person's dreams is determined by which part of the body she gallops over or through, or perhaps which body part she tickles.*

**Analyze** What do Mercutio's comments about Queen Mab reveal about his character? *Possible answer: Mercutio's comments reveal that he is very imaginative, that he is playful, and perhaps that he loves to hear himself talk (for Romeo finally has to tell him to stop talking).*

**Evaluate** In your opinion, does this passage help the play? Why or why not? *Possible answers: Yes. It reveals the dreamy, imaginative character of Mercutio and lightens Romeo's dark mood. No. It slows down the play's action.*

---

Athwart men's noses as they lie asleep;
Her wagon spokes made of long spinners' legs,
60 The cover, of the wings of grasshoppers;
Her traces, of the smallest spider's web;
Her collars, of the moonshine's wat'ry beams;
Her whip, of cricket's bone; the lash, of film;
Her wagoner, a small grey-coated gnat,
65 Not half so big as a round little worm
Pricked from the lazy finger of a maid;
Her chariot is an empty hazelnut,
Made by the joiner squirrel or old grub,
Time out o' mind the fairies' coachmakers.
70 And in this state she gallops night by night
Through lovers' brains, and then they dream of love;
O'er courtiers' knees, that dream on curtsies straight;
O'er lawyers' fingers, who straight dream on fees;
O'er ladies' lips, who straight on kisses dream,
75 Which oft the angry Mab with blisters plagues,
Because their breaths with sweetmeats tainted are.
Sometime she gallops o'er a courtier's nose,
And then dreams he of smelling out a suit,
And sometime comes she with a tithe-pig's tail
80 Tickling a parson's nose as 'a lies asleep,
Then dreams he of another benefice.
Sometime she driveth o'er a soldier's neck,
And then dreams he of cutting foreign throats,
Of breaches, ambuscadoes, Spanish blades,
85 Of healths five fathom deep; and then anon
Drums in his ear, at which he starts and wakes,
And being thus frighted, swears a prayer or two
And sleeps again. This is that very Mab
That plaits the manes of horses in the night
90 And bakes the elflocks in foul sluttish hairs,
Which once untangled much misfortune bodes.
This is the hag, when maids lie on their backs,
That presses them and learns them first to bear,
Making them women of good carriage.
95 This is she—

**Romeo.**　　　　Peace, peace, Mercutio, peace!
Thou talkst of nothing.

**Mercutio.**　　　　　　True, I talk of dreams;
Which are the children of an idle brain,
Begot of nothing but vain fantasy;
Which is as thin of substance as the air,
100 And more inconstant than the wind, who woos

59 **spinners' legs:** spiders' legs.

61 **traces:** harness.

68 **joiner:** carpenter.

77–78 **Sometimes she ... suit:** Sometimes Mab makes a member of the king's court dream of receiving special favors.

81 **benefice:** a well-paying position for a clergyman.

84 **ambuscadoes:** ambushes; **Spanish blades:** high-quality Spanish swords.

89 **plaits:** braids.

96–103 **True ... South:** Mercutio is trying to keep Romeo from taking his dreams too seriously.

---

## DIFFERENTIATED INSTRUCTION

**FOR ENGLISH LANGUAGE LEARNERS**

**Concept Support** Point out that according to Mercutio, Queen Mab brings dreams to many types of people. Model several of the pairings in lines 70–88, as shown.

- Through lovers' brains: they dream of love (line 71).
- Over lawyers' fingers: they dream of fees, the money they charge (line 73).
- Over ladies' lips: they dream of kisses (line 74).

- Tickling a parson's (minister's) nose: he dreams of receiving more money in exchange for his work (lines 79–81).

Have students similarly identify the dream of a soldier and two dreams of a courtier. *Possible answer: A soldier dreams of killing foreigners and of adventures at sea (lines 82–88). One courtier dreams of being able to make a proper curtsy (line 72); another, of receiving a royal favor (lines 77–78).*

Even now the frozen bosom of the North
And, being angered, puffs away from thence,
Turning his face to the dew-dropping South.

**Benvolio.** This wind you talk of blows us from ourselves.
105 Supper is done, and we shall come too late.

**Romeo.** I fear, too early; for my mind misgives
Some consequence, yet hanging in the stars,
Shall bitterly begin his fearful date
With this night's revels and expire the term
110 Of a despised life, closed in my breast,
By some vile forfeit of untimely death. Ⓗ
But he that hath the steerage of my course
Direct my sail! On, lusty gentlemen!

**Benvolio.** Strike, drum.

[*Exeunt.*]

## SCENE 5  *A hall in Capulet's house; the scene of the party.*

*This is the scene of the party at which Romeo and Juliet finally meet.
Romeo and his friends, disguised in their masks, arrive as uninvited guests.
As he watches the dancers, Romeo suddenly sees Juliet and falls in love at first
sight. At the same time, Tybalt recognizes Romeo's voice and knows he is a
Montague. Tybalt alerts Capulet and threatens to kill Romeo. Capulet, however, insists that Tybalt behave himself and act like a gentleman. Promising
revenge, Tybalt leaves. Romeo and Juliet meet and kiss in the middle of the
dance floor. Only after they part do they learn each other's identity.*

[*Servingmen come forth with napkins.*]

**First Servingman.** Where's Potpan, that he helps not to take
away? He shift a trencher! he scrape a trencher!

**Second Servingman.** When good manners shall lie all in one or
two men's hands, and they unwashed too, 'tis a foul thing.

5 **First Servingman.** Away with the joint-stools, remove the court-
cupboard, look to the plate. Good thou, save me a piece of
marchpane and, as thou lovest me, let the porter let in Susan
Grindstone and Nell. Anthony, and Potpan!

**Second Servingman.** Ay, boy, ready.

10 **First Servingman.** You are looked for and called for, asked for
and sought for, in the great chamber.

**Third Servingman.** We cannot be here and there too. Cheerly,
boys! Be brisk awhile, and the longer liver take all.

[*Exeunt.*]

**106–111** Romeo, still depressed, fears that some terrible event caused by the stars will begin at the party. Remember the phrase "star-crossed lovers" from the prologue on page 1037.

COMMON CORE RL 3

Ⓗ **CHARACTER FOILS**
A **character foil** is a secondary character that acts as a contrast to a main character. This contrast helps to highlight the main character's qualities. Here, Mercutio's playfulness and high spirits contrast with Romeo's lovesick melancholy. What does Romeo's difference from and response to Mercutio in this scene tell you about Romeo?

**1–13** These opening lines are a comic conversation among three servants as they work.

**2 trencher:** wooden plate.

**6–7 plate:** silverware and silver plates; **marchpane:** marzipan, a sweet made from almond paste.

---

TEXT ANALYSIS  COMMON CORE RL 3

Ⓗ **CHARACTER FOILS**

*Possible answer:  He is still melancholy and tends to brood; it also shows that he may believe in fate and that he has bad feelings about what might be in store for him.*

Have students note other instances in the play of characters used as foils. Tell students to keep their findings and share them with the class when they are finished reading the play.

**REVISIT THE BIG QUESTION**
## Is **LOVE** stronger than **HATE?**

**Discuss**  Do you believe that it is possible to fall in love with a person at first sight? Why or why not? *Students may suggest that a person who falls in love at first sight is imagining qualities about the other person that he or she may not actually possess. It may be possible to desire a relationship at first sight, but it is not possible to form a long-term love without shar-ing information and experiences.*

---

**FOR STRUGGLING READERS**

**Preview**  Read through the italicized scene synopsis to give students an overview of Scene 5. Help them create a cause-and-effect diagram to record the actions of Romeo, Tybalt, and Capulet.

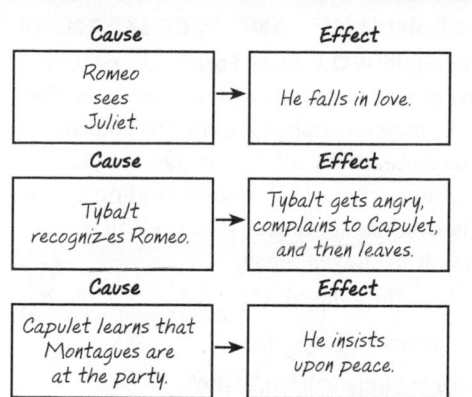

| Cause | | Effect |
|---|---|---|
| Romeo sees Juliet. | → | He falls in love. |

| Cause | | Effect |
|---|---|---|
| Tybalt recognizes Romeo. | → | Tybalt gets angry, complains to Capulet, and then leaves. |

| Cause | | Effect |
|---|---|---|
| Capulet learns that Montagues are at the party. | → | He insists upon peace. |

**Activity** Look closely at the costumes. What do they indicate to you about this production of *Romeo and Juliet*? **Possible answer:** *The costumes indicate that the masked ball was not done as a full masquerade, but with simple masks. The production was done in somewhat stylized period dress, adapted to the needs of ballet dancers.*

[Maskers *appear with* Capulet, Lady Capulet, Juliet, *all the* Guests, *and* Servants.]

**Capulet.** Welcome, gentlemen! Ladies that have their toes
15 Unplagued with corns will have a bout with you.
Ah ha, my mistresses! which of you all
Will now deny to dance? She that makes dainty,
She I'll swear hath corns. Am I come near ye now?
Welcome, gentlemen! I have seen the day
20 That I have worn a visor and could tell
A whispering tale in a fair lady's ear,
Such as would please. 'Tis gone, 'tis gone, 'tis gone!
You are welcome, gentlemen! Come, musicians, play.
A hall, a hall! give room! and foot it, girls.

[*Music plays and they dance.*]

25 More light, you knaves! and turn the tables up,
And quench the fire, the room is grown too hot.
Ah, sirrah, this unlooked-for sport comes well.
Nay, sit, nay, sit, good cousin Capulet,
For you and I are past our dancing days.
30 How long is't now since last yourself and I
Were in a mask?

**Second Capulet.** By'r Lady, thirty years.

**Capulet.** What, man? 'Tis not so much, 'tis not so much!

**14–27** Capulet welcomes his guests and invites them all to dance. At the same time, like a good host, he is trying to get the party going. He alternates talking with his guests and telling the servants what to do.

**17–18 She that . . . corns:** Any woman too shy to dance will be assumed to have corns, ugly and painful growths on the toes.

**20 visor:** mask.

**28–38** Capulet and his relative watch the dancing as they talk of days gone by.

Guests dance at the Capulets' ball in the Royal Ballet's 1996 production.

## DIFFERENTIATED INSTRUCTION

**FOR ENGLISH LANGUAGE LEARNERS**
**Vocabulary: Outdated Forms** Urge students to continue adding outdated terms to their language journals. (See the **For English Language Learners** activity on page 1036.) Have students check their understanding by creating original sentences that use the terms in a way that makes sense.

- *hath* (line 18), "has"
- *knaves* (line 25), "fools"
- *sirrah* (line 27), "sir," "sire"
- *is't* (line 30), "is it"
- *By'r Lady* (line 32), "By Our Lady" (a reference to the Virgin Mary)
- *ward* (line 38), "young person who is still under a guardian's care"
- *Forswear* (line 50), "Deny"
- *hither* (line 54), "here"
- *kin* (line 56), "relatives"
- *hold* (line 57), "consider"

'Tis since the nuptial of Lucentio,
Come Pentecost as quickly as it will,
35 Some five-and-twenty years, and then we masked.

**Second Capulet.** 'Tis more, 'tis more! His son is elder, sir;
His son is thirty.

**Capulet.**                    Will you tell me that?
His son was but a ward two years ago.

**Romeo** [*to a* Servingman]. What lady's that, which doth enrich
    the hand
40 Of yonder knight?

**Servant.** I know not, sir.

> **Romeo.** O, she doth teach the torches to burn bright!
> It seems she hangs upon the cheek of night
> Like a rich jewel in an Ethiop's ear—
> 45 Beauty too rich for use, for earth too dear!
> So shows a snowy dove trooping with crows
> As yonder lady o'er her fellows shows.
> The measure done, I'll watch her place of stand
> And, touching hers, make blessed my rude hand.
> 50 Did my heart love till now? Forswear it, sight!
> For I ne'er saw true beauty till this night. ❶

**Tybalt.** This, by his voice, should be a Montague.
Fetch me my rapier, boy. What, dares the slave
Come hither, covered with an antic face,
55 To fleer and scorn at our solemnity?
Now, by the stock and honor of my kin,
To strike him dead I hold it not a sin.

**Capulet.** Why, how now, kinsman? Wherefore storm you so?

**Tybalt.** Uncle, this is a Montague, our foe;
60 A villain, that is hither come in spite
To scorn at our solemnity this night.

**Capulet.** Young Romeo is it?

**Tybalt.**                         'Tis he, that villain Romeo.

**Capulet.** Content thee, gentle coz, let him alone.
'A bears him like a portly gentleman,
65 And, to say truth, Verona brags of him
To be a virtuous and well-governed youth.
I would not for the wealth of all this town
Here in my house do him disparagement.
Therefore be patient, take no note of him.
70 It is my will; the which if thou respect,

**33 nuptial:** marriage.

**39–40** Romeo has spotted Juliet across the dance floor and is immediately entranced by her beauty.

❸ **Targeted Passage**

**44–45 Ethiop's ear:** the ear of an Ethiopian (African); **for earth too dear:** too precious for this world.

❶ **BLANK VERSE**
Romeo's awestruck speech is in rhymed couplets, not blank verse. Why do you think Shakespeare chose to use rhymed verse here? Explain your answer.

**52–57** Tybalt recognizes Romeo's voice and tells his servant to get his sword (**rapier**). He thinks Romeo has come to make fun of (**fleer**) their party. *What does Tybalt want to do to Romeo?*

**64 portly:** dignified.

**68 do him disparagement:** speak critically or insultingly to him.

---

**TEXT ANALYSIS**     **COMMON CORE**     **L 3**

❶ **BLANK VERSE**

***Possible answer:** Shakespeare chose to use rhymed verse because he wanted to draw attention to this moment in the play. The change in poetic style underscores two facts: (1) Romeo's depression suddenly has been replaced with adoration; and (2) This moment is a turning point in Romeo's life. Furthermore, the rhymed verse seems more romantic because it is sweet and easy to listen to.*

**IF STUDENTS NEED HELP . . .** Have students point out the word that ends each line in lines 42–51. Call on volunteers to say each rhyming pair ("bright"/"night," "ear"/"dear," and so on) aloud. Invite another volunteer to read the entire passage aloud.

**REVISIT THE BIG QUESTION**
Is **LOVE** stronger than
**HATE?**

**Discuss** Why does Capulet refuse to let Tybalt act upon his hate for Romeo in lines 59–68?
***Possible answer:** Capulet says that Romeo is behaving himself (line 64) and that he does not want to cause a scene at his own party by confronting Romeo (lines 67–68).*

---

**FOR STRUGGLING READERS**

❸ **Targeted Passage** [Lines 42–51]

In this passage, Romeo first sees Juliet and declares his sudden love, even though he has not yet met her.

- To what objects does Romeo compare Juliet? How are these objects similar? (lines 42–46)

- What does Romeo imagine will happen when he touches Juliet's hand? (line 49)

- How does Romeo feel about Rosaline now? How can you tell? (lines 50–51)

**FOR ENGLISH LANGUAGE LEARNERS**

**Task Support** Call attention to the question in the marginal note for lines 52–57. Point out the definition of *rapier;* then have students reread what Tybalt says immediately after sending his servant to get the rapier. ***Possible answer:** Tybalt wants to use his sword to kill Romeo.*

Use these prompts to help students analyze the first encounter between Romeo and Juliet in lines 91–107:

**Connect** Recall your first meeting with someone who later became close to you. How were your words different from the words spoken in Romeo and Juliet's first meeting? *Students should identify the usual awkwardness of first meetings and should contrast that way of talking with the gentle poetry of Romeo and Juliet's first meeting.*

**Analyze** What are the religious references in the dialogue? What is meant by them? *Possible answer: Romeo calls Juliet a holy shrine (line 92) and a saint (line 101). He says that his lips are pilgrims (line 93). Juliet calls Romeo a pilgrim (line 95). Romeo says that his sin is purged by Juliet's kiss (line 105). The references show that even though these teenagers have just met, they already idolize each other.*

**Synthesize** What do you think each lover has learned about the other in this brief scene? *Possible answer: Each lover has learned that the other has a similar sense of humor and religious intensity. They both sense a mutual physical attraction and emotional intensity as well.*

---

Show a fair presence and put off these frowns,
An ill-beseeming semblance for a feast.

**Tybalt.** It fits when such a villain is a guest.
I'll not endure him.

**Capulet.**                         He shall be endured.
75 What, goodman boy? I say he shall. Go to!
Am I the master here, or you? Go to!
You'll not endure him? God shall mend my soul!
You'll make a mutiny among my guests!
You will set cock-a-hoop! You'll be the man.

80 **Tybalt.** Why, uncle, 'tis a shame.

**Capulet.**                         Go to, go to!
You are a saucy boy. Is't so, indeed?
This trick may chance to scathe you. I know what.
You must contrary me! Marry, 'tis time.—
Well said, my hearts!—You are a princox—go!
85 Be quiet, or—More light, more light!—For shame!
I'll make you quiet; what!—Cheerly, my hearts!

**Tybalt.** Patience perforce with willful choler meeting
Makes my flesh tremble in their different greeting.
I will withdraw; but this intrusion shall,
90 Now seeming sweet, convert to bitter gall.

[*Exit.*]

**Romeo.** If I profane with my unworthiest hand
This holy shrine, the gentle fine is this:
My lips, two blushing pilgrims, ready stand
To smooth that rough touch with a tender kiss.

95 **Juliet.** Good pilgrim, you do wrong your hand too much,
Which mannerly devotion shows in this;
For saints have hands that pilgrims' hands do touch,
And palm to palm is holy palmers' kiss.

**Romeo.** Have not saints lips, and holy palmers too?

100 **Juliet.** Ay, pilgrim, lips that they must use in prayer.

**Romeo.** O, then, dear saint, let lips do what hands do!
They pray; grant thou, lest faith turn to despair.

**Juliet.** Saints do not move, though grant for prayers' sake.

**Romeo.** Then move not while my prayer's effect I take.
105 Thus from my lips, by thine my sin is purged.

[*kisses her*]

**Juliet.** Then have my lips the sin that they have took.

**72 semblance:** outward appearance.

**75 goodman boy:** a term used to address an inferior; **Go to:** Stop, that's enough!

**79 set cock-a-hoop:** cause everything to be upset.

**82–83 scathe:** harm; **I know . . . contrary me:** I know what I'm doing! Don't you dare challenge my authority.

**84–86** Capulet intersperses his angry speech to Tybalt with comments to his guests and servants.

**87–90 Patience . . . gall:** Tybalt says he will restrain himself, but his suppressed anger (**choler**) makes his body shake. *What do you think he will do about his anger?*

**91–108** Romeo and Juliet are in the middle of the dance floor, with eyes only for each other. They touch the palms of their hands together. Their conversation revolves around Romeo's comparison of his lips to pilgrims who have traveled to a holy shrine. Juliet goes along with the comparison.

**105 purged:** washed away.

---

### FOR STRUGGLING READERS

**Paraphrasing Shakespeare** Have students re-read the marginal note for lines 84–86. Then model a paraphrase of Capulet's mix of angry and friendly words, as shown:

• *Well said, friends!—You are a conceited fighter—Dance! (line 84)*

• *Keep quiet or I will . . . —Let's turn up the lights!—Shame on you! (line 85)*

• *I'll force you to be quiet!—Enjoy the party, my darlings! (line 86)*

### FOR ENGLISH LANGUAGE LEARNERS

**Task Support** Have students read the marginal note and question for lines 87–90. Remind students that when they met Tybalt in Scene 1, they saw him refuse to let Benvolio talk him out of a fight. *Possible answer: He will suppress his anger for the moment and will leave the party, but he will not let the anger go. It will boil over at another place and time.*

Romeo and Juliet in the Shakespeare & Company's 2004 Spring Tour Production

**Romeo.** Sin from my lips? O trespass sweetly urged!
Give me my sin again.

[*kisses her*]

**Juliet.**                    You kiss by the book.

**Nurse.** Madam, your mother craves a word with you.

110 **Romeo.** What is her mother?

**Nurse.**                    Marry, bachelor,
Her mother is the lady of the house.
And a good lady, and a wise and virtuous.
I nursed her daughter that you talked withal.
I tell you, he that can lay hold of her
115 Shall have the chinks.

**Romeo.**              Is she a Capulet?
O dear account! my life is my foe's debt.

**108 kiss by the book:** Juliet could mean "You kiss like an expert, someone who has studied and practiced." Or she could be teasing Romeo, meaning "You kiss coldly, as though you had learned how by reading a book."

**109** At the nurse's message, Juliet walks to her mother.

**115 shall have the chinks:** shall become rich.

**116 my life...debt:** my life belongs to my enemy.

**Activity** Do the actors in this photograph match your vision of Romeo and Juliet? Explain why or why not. *Students should provide reasonable support for their opinions.* What physical features would you look for if you were casting the play? *Students should name physical qualities that would influence their decision, such as youth and innocence.*

## FOR ENGLISH LANGUAGE LEARNERS

**Media and Language** Use a video of *Romeo and Juliet* to build and reinforce the meaning of the language in lines 91–116 of this well-known scene. After students watch and listen to the video, have them form into small groups to discuss the following questions: What words would they use to describe this meeting of Romeo and Juliet? Why have they chosen these descriptive words? Students can then share their descriptive words and explanations with the class.

## FOR ADVANCED LEARNERS/PRE–AP

**Analyze a Motif** Review Romeo's comment about hands in lines 48–49. Have students write a paragraph in which they relate that comment to his first words to Juliet in line 91 and to what both Romeo and Juliet say about hands in their brief conversation (including their pun about "holy palmers" in lines 98–99). Have students share their analyses of this motif in small groups.

## Is **LOVE** stronger than **HATE?**

**Discuss** What great irony has Juliet just begun to grasp about love and hate in lines 136–139?
***Possible answer:*** *Juliet has just begun to grasp the great irony that it is possible—and, indeed, her fate—to love someone whom you have been taught to hate.*

## ACT ONE WRAP-UP

**READ WITH A PURPOSE** Now that students have finished reading the selection, have them list traits of the two main characters as they know them so far. ***Possible answers:*** *Romeo is emotional, dreamy, maybe immature, while Juliet is also emotional. Both are clever with words, and both are very aware of their responsibilities in the community and to their families.*

**PREDICT** Have students make predictions about what may happen if Capulet and Montague learn that Romeo and Juliet have fallen in love. ***Possible answer:*** *They will forbid the lovers to meet. They may well be angry that the two do not understand the impossibility of their love.*

⭐ **CRITIQUE** Ask students to consult their sequence charts for Act I and recall the events so far. Ask them what events they consider the most memorable or important. Then ask them to explain their choices.

---

**Benvolio.** Away, be gone, the sport is at the best.

**Romeo.** Ay, so I fear; the more is my unrest.

**Capulet.** Nay, gentlemen, prepare not to be gone;
120 We have a trifling foolish banquet towards.
[*They whisper in his ear.*]
Is it e'en so? Why then, I thank you all.
I thank you, honest gentlemen. Good night.
More torches here! [*Exeunt* Maskers.] Come on then, let's to bed.
Ah, sirrah, by my fay, it waxes late;
125 I'll to my rest.
[*Exeunt all but* Juliet *and* Nurse.]

**Juliet.** Come hither, nurse. What is yond gentleman?

**Nurse.** The son and heir of old Tiberio.

**Juliet.** What's he that now is going out of door?

**Nurse.** Marry, that, I think, be young Petruchio.

130 **Juliet.** What's he that follows there, that would not dance?

**Nurse.** I know not.

**Juliet.** Go ask his name.—If he be married,
My grave is like to be my wedding bed.

**Nurse.** His name is Romeo, and a Montague,
135 The only son of your great enemy.

**Juliet.** My only love, sprung from my only hate!
Too early seen unknown, and known too late!
Prodigious birth of love it is to me
That I must love a loathed enemy.

140 **Nurse.** What's this? what's this?

**Juliet.**                    A rhyme I learnt even now
Of one I danced withal.
[*One calls within, "Juliet."*]

**Nurse.**              Anon, anon!
Come, let's away; the strangers all are gone.

[*Exeunt.*]

**120** towards: coming up.

**126–130** Juliet asks the nurse to identify various guests as they leave. *What does she really want to know?*

④ **Targeted Passage**

**137–138** Too early...too late: I fell in love with him before I learned who he is; **prodigious:** abnormal; unlucky. *How does Juliet feel about the fact that she's fallen in love with the son of her father's enemy?*

 COMMON CORE L 4a

**Language Coach**

**Word Definitions** Suppose that the Nurse is calling "Anon, anon!" (line 141) in response to the voice offstage calling Juliet. What do you think *anon* means here?

---

## DIFFERENTIATED INSTRUCTION

### FOR STRUGGLING READERS

④ **Targeted Passage** [Lines 134–144]

In this passage, Juliet's thrill over her first meeting with Romeo is challenged by the realization that Romeo is a Montague.

- What is wrong with Juliet's new love? How do you think that her feelings about him have changed? (lines 136–137)

- How can you tell that Juliet is worried about the future? (lines 138–139)

### FOR ENGLISH LANGUAGE LEARNERS

**Task Support** As you call attention to the question in the marginal note for lines 126–130, elicit that Juliet may be trying to distract her nurse by first expressing interest in two other party guests. ***Possible answer:*** *Juliet really wants to know the identity of the young man with whom she has just exchanged words of love (Romeo).*

**Task Support** Have students read the question in the marginal note for lines 137–138. Read aloud the explanation for the lines, especially the meaning of *prodigious*. ***Possible answer:*** *Juliet feels unhappy that she did not learn Romeo's identity until after she had fallen in love with him.*

**Language Coach** COMMON CORE L 4a

**Word Definitions**

***Possible answer:*** *It probably means "Just a minute!" or "Coming soon!"* Have students replace "Anon, anon!" with their definitions and then describe what impact it has on the Nurse's dialogue.

## Comprehension

1. **Recall** What warning does Prince Escalus give the Capulets and the Montagues?

2. **Recall** What agreement do Paris and Lord Capulet reach?

3. **Recall** Why does Romeo go to the Capulets' party?

4. **Clarify** What is the chief obstacle to Romeo and Juliet's love?

## Text Analysis

● 5. **Reading Shakespearean Drama** Review the chart you created. Which events in Act One seem most important in setting up **conflicts** in the plot? Which events seem to suggest a possible theme?

6. **Identify Character Foils** A foil is a character who highlights, through sharp contrast, the qualities of another character. As mentioned on page 1057, Mercutio is a comic foil to Romeo. Identify two other characters in Act One who are foils for each other. What do you learn about the characters by seeing them in contrast to one another?

7. **Analyze Foreshadowing** Examine the examples of foreshadowing listed in the chart. To clarify your understanding of the examples, try paraphrasing them. Then explain what event each ominous passage foreshadows.

| Foreshadowing | Paraphrase | What It Hints At |
|---|---|---|
| I fear, too early; for my mind misgives<br>Some consequence, yet hanging in the stars,<br>Shall bitterly begin his fearful date<br>With this night's revels and expire the term<br>Of a despised life, closed in my breast,<br>By some vile forfeit of untimely death.<br>- Romeo (Act One, Scene 4, lines 106–111) | | |
| My grave is like to be my wedding bed.<br>- Juliet (Act One, Scene 5, line 133) | | |

● 8. **Evaluate Blank Verse** Find and copy a group of four lines of blank verse in Act One, marking the unstressed (˘) and the stressed (´) syllables in each line. Then explain whether the lines show the typical **iambic pentameter** pattern or contain rhythmic variations. In your opinion, does the passage accurately capture the sound of spoken English? Explain.

## Text Criticism

9. **Critical Interpretations** Works of great acclaim sometimes fail to live up to expectations. According to critic Robert Graves, the "remarkable thing about Shakespeare is that he is really very good—in spite of all the people who say he is very good." Is *Romeo and Juliet* living up to your expectations? Explain.

COMMON CORE

**RL 2** Determine a theme of a text. **RL 3** Analyze how complex characters develop over the course of a text, interact with other characters, and advance the plot or develop the theme. **RL 10** Read and comprehend dramas. **L 3** Apply knowledge of language to understand how language functions in different contexts and to comprehend more fully when reading or listening.

# Practice and Apply

For preliminary support of post-reading questions, use these copy masters:

**R** RESOURCE MANAGER—Copy Masters
Reading Check p. 23
Shakespearean Drama p. 21
Question Support p. 24

Additional selection questions are provided for teachers on page 13.

## ANSWERS

## Comprehension

1. *The prince warns that if there is another violent outburst, the head of each family will be executed as punishment.*

2. *They agree that Paris may woo Juliet but will wait two years before marrying her.*

3. *Romeo goes in hopes of seeing Rosaline.*

4. *The chief obstacle is their families' feud.*

## Text Analysis

COMMON CORE **RL 2, RL 3, RL 10, L 3**

**Possible answers:**

5. ■ COMMON CORE FOCUS *Reading Shakespearean Drama* *The opening brawl between the Capulets and Montagues is the key event in setting up conflicts, because it reveals the hatred that threatens Romeo and Juliet's love. Talk of a match between Juliet and Paris and the first meeting of Romeo and Juliet are other conflict-producing events. These events suggest a theme related to the unintended consequences of hatred.*

6. *Tybalt and Benvolio, Lady Capulet and the nurse, and Mercutio and Romeo are foils. Benvolio's peaceful nature highlights Tybalt's eagerness to fight. Lady Capulet's*

*dignity and short, direct statements contrast with the nurse's light, crude chatter. Mercutio's high spirits and playfulness contrast with Romeo's lovesick melancholy.*

7. *Paraphrases will vary. The first passage hints at Romeo's death, the ultimate result of his seeing and meeting Juliet at that night's party. The second passage hints at Juliet's death, which comes soon after her marriage.*

8. ● COMMON CORE FOCUS *Evaluate Blank Verse* *Students should use scansion marks to mark the stressed and unstressed*

*syllables and should note variations in the meter. Students may feel that iambic pentameter sounds stylized yet is still more like spoken English than other meters.*

## Text Criticism

9. *Students should offer a clear opinion about why the play is or is not living up to their expectations. They may suggest it is too soon to tell, since at the end of Act One, Romeo and Juliet have just met.*

# Assess and Reteach

## Assess

**DIAGNOSTIC AND SELECTION TESTS**
Selection Test A pp. 275–276
Selection Test B/C pp. 277–278

**Interactive Selection Test** on **thinkcentral.com**

## Reteach

**Level Up Online Tutorials** on **thinkcentral.com**

**Reteaching Worksheets** on **thinkcentral.com**
Literature Lessons 25, 26, 35, 38

# Practice and Apply

## READ WITH A PURPOSE

*Help students set a purpose for reading. Tell them to look for evidence to help them predict whether Romeo and Juliet's relationship has a solid foundation.*

## Get Into the Act

### SUMMARY

A Prologue summarizes Act One; then Act Two begins. After the party, Romeo comes to Capulet's garden. He sees Juliet at her balcony, and the two declare their love. Juliet promises to marry Romeo if he can arrange the ceremony. Romeo enlists the help of Friar Laurence, who sees in the marriage a way to end the Montague-Capulet feud. Later, Romeo reveals his plan to Juliet's nurse. The lovers meet and marry at Friar Laurence's cell.

---

**READING STRATEGY** | **COMMON CORE** RL 2, RL 3

### ◼ *Model the Skill:* SUMMARY

Have several students share in reading the Prologue aloud. Then summarize the main action of Act Two like this: *Romeo has found a new love in Juliet. There are challenges to their love, but their passion drives them to find a way to be together.* Then ask students to summarize the main action of Act One and remind them to add this to their Reading Strategy charts. ***Possible answer:*** *Romeo and Juliet, children of Verona's leading, but feuding, families, meet and fall in love without knowing who the other is.*

---

## Resources for Act Two

---

# Prologue

*In a sonnet the Chorus summarizes what has happened so far in the play. He reviews how Romeo and Juliet have fallen in love and suggests both the problems and the delights they now face. He also includes hints about what will result from the events of Act One.*

[*Enter* Chorus.]

**Chorus.** Now old desire doth in his deathbed lie,
And young affection gapes to be his heir.
That fair for which love groaned for and would die,
With tender Juliet matched, is now not fair.
5 Now Romeo is beloved, and loves again,
Alike bewitched by the charm of looks;
But to his foe supposed he must complain,
And she steal love's sweet bait from fearful hooks.
Being held a foe, he may not have access
10 To breathe such vows as lovers use to swear,
And she as much in love, her means much less
To meet her new beloved anywhere;
But passion lends them power, time means, to meet,
Temp'ring extremities with extreme sweet.

[*Exit.*]

**1–4 Now . . . fair:** Romeo's love for Rosaline (**old desire**) is now dead. His new love (**young affection**) replaces the old. Compared to Juliet, Rosaline no longer seems so beautiful.

**6** *What attracted Romeo and Juliet to each other?*

**7 but . . . complain:** Juliet, a Capulet, is Romeo's supposed enemy, yet she is the one to whom he must plead (**complain**) his love.

**14 temp'ring . . . sweet:** moderating great difficulties with extreme delights.

# Act Two

## SCENE 1    *A lane by the wall of Capulet's orchard.*

*Later in the evening of the party, Romeo returns alone to the Capulet home, hoping for another glimpse of Juliet. He climbs the wall and hides outside, in the orchard. Meanwhile, Benvolio and Mercutio come looking for him, but he remains hidden behind the wall. Mercutio makes fun of Romeo and his lovesick condition. Keep in mind that Mercutio and Benvolio think Romeo is still in love with Rosaline, since they know nothing about his meeting with Juliet.*

[*Enter* Romeo *alone.*]

**Romeo.** Can I go forward when my heart is here?
Turn back, dull earth, and find thy center out.

[*climbs the wall and leaps down within it*]

[*Enter* Benvolio *with* Mercutio.]

**Benvolio.** Romeo! my cousin Romeo! Romeo!

**1–2 Can . . . out:** How can I leave when Juliet is still here? My body (**dull earth**) has to find its heart (**center**).

Balcony scene from the Globe Theatre's 2004 production

---

*See resources on the **Teacher One Stop DVD-ROM** and on **thinkcentral.com**.*

**R RESOURCE MANAGER UNIT 10**
Plan and Teach, pp. 27–30
Summary pp. 31–32†‡*
Text Analysis and Reading
  Skill, pp. 33–36†*

**DIAGNOSTIC AND SELECTION TESTS**
Selection Tests, pp. 279–282

**💼 BEST PRACTICES TOOLKIT**
Making Inferences, p. A13
Character Analysis Chart,
  p. D5
Sequence Chain, p. B21

**INTERACTIVE READER**

**ADAPTED INTERACTIVE READER**

**ELL ADAPTED INTERACTIVE READER**

**TECHNOLOGY**
- 💿 **Teacher One Stop DVD-ROM**
- 💿 **Student One Stop DVD-ROM**
- 💿 **PowerNotes DVD-ROM**
- 💿 **Audio Anthology CD**
- 💿 **Audio Tutor CD**
- 💿 **ExamView Test Generator** on the **Teacher One Stop**

**Video Trailer**  THINK central

Go to **thinkcentral.com** to preview the **Video Trailer** introducing this selection. Other features that support the selection include
- **PowerNotes** presentation
- **ThinkAloud** models to enhance comprehension

---

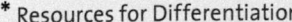

*\* Resources for Differentiation     † Also in Spanish     ‡ In Haitian Creole and Vietnamese*

**Activity** What can you infer from this photograph about the characters and setting of *Romeo and Juliet*? *Possible answer: The reader can identify the Elizabethan setting from the style of the costumes and the richness of the set. The actors' poses suggest their love for one another.*

## Scene Synopsis
## TIERED DISCUSSION PROMPTS

Use these prompts to help students understand why Romeo disappears without telling his friends:

**Connect** Have you ever felt like avoiding your friends? How does that feeling help you understand Romeo as this scene opens? *Students should identify with Romeo's desire for privacy.*

**Analyze** Consider Romeo's plans as Act Two opens. Why do you think Romeo does not want to talk to Mercutio and Benvolio at this time? *Possible answer: He probably doesn't want to face their questions, their teasing, and perhaps their attempts to keep him from seeing Juliet again.*

**Evaluate** In your opinion, is hiding from his friends a wise thing for Romeo to do? Defend your answer. *Possible answers: Yes. Romeo's friends probably would keep him away from Juliet. No. Romeo is acting upon a moment's passion, and his friends probably could help him look at the situation more realistically.*

## DIFFERENTIATED INSTRUCTION

### FOR ENGLISH LANGUAGE LEARNERS

**Task Support** Point out the marginal question for line 6 of the Prologue. Make sure students understand that in the first part of the sonnet, the Chorus is referring to Romeo's previous love: Rosaline. *Possible answer: Romeo and Juliet were attracted by each other's physical appearance ("the charm of looks").*

### FOR STRUGGLING READERS

In combination with the *Audio Anthology CD,* use one or more Targeted Passages (pp. 1067, 1071, 1082, 1086) to ensure that students focus on key story events, concepts, and skills. Targeted Passages are also good for English learners.

**Preview** Have students use a chart like this to organize the Scene 1 synopsis:

|  | Want(s) … | Will … |
|---|---|---|
| Romeo | to see Juliet again | hide in Capulet's orchard |
| Benvolio & Mercutio | to find Romeo | look for him near Capulet's home |

**Mercutio.** He is wise,
And, on my life, hath stol'n him home to bed.

5 **Benvolio.** He ran this way, and leapt this orchard wall.
Call, good Mercutio.

**Mercutio.** Nay, I'll conjure too.
Romeo! humors! madman! passion! lover!
Appear thou in the likeness of a sigh;
Speak but one rhyme, and I am satisfied!
10 Cry but "Ay me!" pronounce but "love" and "dove";
Speak to my gossip Venus one fair word, Ⓐ
One nickname for her purblind son and heir,
Young Adam Cupid, he that shot so trim
When King Cophetua loved the beggar maid!
15 He heareth not, he stirreth not, he moveth not;
The ape is dead, and I must conjure him.
I conjure thee by Rosaline's bright eyes,
By her high forehead and her scarlet lip,
By her fine foot, straight leg, and quivering thigh,
20 And the demesnes that there adjacent lie,
That in thy likeness thou appear to us!

**Benvolio.** An if he hear thee, thou wilt anger him.

**Mercutio.** This cannot anger him. 'Twould anger him
To raise a spirit in his mistress' circle
25 Of some strange nature, letting it there stand
Till she had laid it and conjured it down.
That were some spite; my invocation
Is fair and honest and in his mistress' name
I conjure only but to raise up him.

30 **Benvolio.** Come, he hath hid himself among these trees
To be consorted with the humorous night.
Blind is his love, and best befits the dark.

**Mercutio.** If love be blind, love cannot hit the mark.
Now will he sit under a medlar tree
35 And wish his mistress were that kind of fruit
As maids call medlars when they laugh alone.
Oh, Romeo, that she were, O, that she were
An open et cetera, thou a pop'rin pear!
Romeo, good night. I'll to my truckle bed;
40 This field-bed is too cold for me to sleep.
Come, shall we go?

**Benvolio.** Go then, for 'tis in vain
To seek him here that means not to be found.

[*Exeunt.*]

**6 conjure:** use magic to call him.

**8–21 Appear . . . us:** Mercutio jokes about Romeo's lovesickness. He tries to make Romeo appear by suggestively naming parts of Rosaline's body.

Ⓐ **GRAMMAR AND STYLE**
In lines 8–11, Shakespeare creates rhythm through **parallelism,** or the use of similar grammatical structures to express related ideas. Notice how each of these lines begins with a verb in the imperative mood.

**20 demesnes:** areas; **adjacent:** next to.

**23–29 'Twould . . . raise up him:** It would anger him if I called a stranger to join his beloved (**mistress**), but I'm only calling Romeo to join her.

**31 to be . . . night:** to keep company with the night, which is as gloomy as Romeo is.

**34 medlar:** a fruit that looks like a small brown apple.

**39 truckle bed:** trundle bed, a small bed that fits in beneath a bigger one.

---

Ⓐ **GRAMMAR AND STYLE** COMMON CORE L 1a-b

**Parallelism** Explain that writers use parallelism not only to create rhythm, but also to connect related ideas or details. Elicit that "Speak," "Cry," "pronounce," and "Speak" are the imperative-mood verbs in lines 9–11 and that each refers to a form of verbal communication. Then have students identify two other examples of parallelism in this speech by Mercutio and discuss the way in which each uses the rhythm it creates. *Possible answer: Two other examples of parallelism are line 15 and lines 17–19. The rhythm of the first example emphasizes the verbs ("heareth," "stirreth," "moveth"). The rhythm of the second example emphasizes Rosaline's physical features ("bright eyes," "high forehead," "scarlet lip," "fine foot," "straight leg," "quivering thigh").*

---

## DIFFERENTIATED INSTRUCTION

### FOR STRUGGLING READERS

**Paraphrasing Shakespeare** Draw students' attention to Mercutio's "Romeo, good night" in line 39 and to his declared intention of going to bed. Help students paraphrase Benvolio's closing comment in lines 42–43 to read something like this: *Yes, let's go home. It's no use to keep looking for Romeo if he intends to hide from us.*

**Preview** Read through the italicized scene synopsis with students to provide an overview of Scene 2. Check their understanding of the events mentioned by listing these events in random order and having students put them into the correct order (the order shown here).

Romeo hides in Capulet's garden.
↓
Juliet comes to her balcony and speaks her thoughts about Romeo's being a Montague.
↓
Romeo reveals his presence and declares his love for Juliet.
↓
Juliet declares that she loves him too.
↓
Romeo leaves to arrange their wedding.

# SCENE 2 *Capulet's orchard.*

*The following is one of the most famous scenes in all literature. The speeches contain some of the most beautiful poetry Shakespeare ever wrote.*

    *Juliet appears on the balcony outside her room. She cannot see Romeo, who stands in the garden just below. At the beginning of the scene, both characters are speaking private thoughts to themselves. Romeo, however, can hear Juliet as she expresses her love for him despite his family name. Eventually, he speaks directly to her, and they declare their love for each other. Just before dawn Romeo leaves to make plans for their wedding.*

[*Enter* Romeo.]

**Romeo.** He jests at scars that never felt a wound.

[*Enter* Juliet *above at a window.*]

> But soft! What light through yonder window breaks?
> It is the East, and Juliet is the sun!
> Arise, fair sun, and kill the envious moon,
> 5 Who is already sick and pale with grief
> That thou her maid art far more fair than she.
> Be not her maid, since she is envious;
> Her vestal livery is but sick and green,
> And none but fools do wear it; cast it off.
> 10 It is my lady; O, it is my love!
> O that she knew she were!
> She speaks, yet she says nothing. What of that?
> Her eye discourses; I will answer it.
> I am too bold; 'tis not to me she speaks.
> 15 Two of the fairest stars in all the heaven,
> Having some business, do entreat her eyes
> To twinkle in their spheres till they return.
> What if her eyes were there, they in her head?
> The brightness of her cheek would shame those stars
> 20 As daylight doth a lamp; her eyes in heaven
> Would through the airy region stream so bright
> That birds would sing and think it were not night.
> See how she leans her cheek upon her hand!
> O that I were a glove upon that hand,
> 25 That I might touch that cheek! **B**

**Juliet.**                  Ay me!

**Romeo.**                       She speaks.
O, speak again, bright angel! for thou art
As glorious to this night, being o'er my head,
As is a winged messenger of heaven

**1 He jests . . . wound:** Romeo has overheard Mercutio and comments that Mercutio makes fun of love because he has never been wounded by it.

**2–9 But soft . . . cast it off:** Romeo sees Juliet at the window. For a moment he is speechless (**soft:** be still), but then he describes her beauty in glowing images.

**① Targeted Passage**

**13–14 Her eye . . . speaks:** Romeo shifts back and forth between wanting to speak to Juliet and being afraid.

**15–22 Two of . . . not night:** Romeo compares Juliet's eyes to stars in the sky.

**B SOLILOQUY**
To whom is Romeo speaking in lines 2–25? Explain what this soliloquy tells you about Romeo's thoughts.

**25** Juliet begins to speak, not knowing that Romeo is nearby.

**26–32 thou art . . . of the air:** He compares Juliet to an angel (**winged messenger of heaven**) who stands on (**bestrides**) the clouds.

ROMEO AND JULIET: ACT TWO, SCENE 2   **1067**

**Discuss** Near the end of Scene 1 (lines 30–34), Benvolio and Mercutio both spoke about Romeo's "blind" love. How does Romeo's description of Juliet at the beginning of Scene 2 suggest that Benvolio and Mercutio might be right? ***Possible answer:*** *Romeo's description is dominated by exaggeration. For example, he says that the moon is jealous of Juliet's beauty (lines 4–6), that Juliet speaks with the stars (lines 14–17), and that her eyes could light up the sky (lines 20–22). Romeo's love is "blind" in the sense that Romeo is not seeing Juliet realistically.*

**TEXT ANALYSIS**    COMMON CORE  L 3

### B *Model the Skill:* SOLILOQUY

Have a student look up and share the definition of *soliloquy.* Explain that Romeo has not yet made his presence known to Juliet, the only other person in this scene. Then guide students through a Making Inferences chart to relate Romeo's comments to his likely thoughts.

***Possible answer:*** *Romeo is speaking to himself, giving voice to his thoughts. The soliloquy reveals that Romeo is enraptured by Juliet's beauty, that he idealizes her, that he is uncertain about how to communicate with her, and that he wants to touch her.*

 **BEST PRACTICES TOOLKIT—Transparency** Making Inferences p. A13

---

## FOR STRUGGLING READERS

**① Targeted Passage [Lines 2–25]**

The figurative language in this classic soliloquy emphasizes the poetic nature of Romeo's love.

- Who is the "fair sun" (line 4)? Why, according to Romeo, does this sun make the moon envious?

- With whom does Romeo imagine that Juliet is speaking? about what topic? (lines 14–17)

- As he finishes his speech, why does Romeo wish that he were a glove on Juliet's hand? (lines 23–25)

## FOR ADVANCED LEARNERS/PRE–AP

**Compare and Contrast Criticism** [paired-activity option] It is not surprising that one of the most famous scenes in literature has had much literary criticism written about it. Challenge students to locate two critics' writings about this scene. After they have read the criticisms, have students compare and contrast the authors' views and arguments, either in an essay or as part of a larger oral presentation.

## TIERED DISCUSSION PROMPTS

Use these prompts to explore Juliet's philosophical musing about names and Romeo's response to it in lines 33–51:

**Connect** How strongly do you identify with your family name? Why might you give it up? *Some students may say that their family name is very important and that they would never give it up, even in marriage. Others might be willing to give it up if doing so would achieve something important.*

**Analyze** How does Juliet feel about Romeo's name? about names in general? ***Possible answer:*** *Juliet feels that Romeo's name is hateful, since the Montagues are enemies of the Capulets, but that Romeo himself is not an enemy (lines 38–39). She feels that names are artificial labels that do not indicate the true nature of the things to which they are applied (lines 40–47). Does Romeo agree with her? How can you tell?* ***Possible answer:*** *Romeo agrees, for he offers to give up his name (lines 49–51).*

**Synthesize** Since some Capulets can identify Romeo by sight (Act One, Scene 5), it is doubtful that a name change would improve Romeo's situation. Why, then, do you think that Shakespeare included this speech? ***Possible answer:*** *Shakespeare included this speech to show that the young lovers are above their families' feud and want to try to separate themselves from it.*

---

Unto the white-upturned wond'ring eyes
30 Of mortals that fall back to gaze on him
When he bestrides the lazy-pacing clouds
And sails upon the bosom of the air.

**Juliet.** O Romeo, Romeo! wherefore art thou Romeo?
Deny thy father and refuse thy name!
35 Or, if thou wilt not, be but sworn my love,
And I'll no longer be a Capulet.

**Romeo** [*aside*]. Shall I hear more, or shall I speak at this?

**Juliet.** 'Tis but thy name that is my enemy.
Thou art thyself, though not a Montague.
40 What's Montague? It is nor hand, nor foot,
Nor arm, nor face, nor any other part
Belonging to a man. O, be some other name!
What's in a name? That which we call a rose
By any other name would smell as sweet.
45 So Romeo would, were he not Romeo called,
Retain that dear perfection which he owes
Without that title. Romeo, doff thy name;
And for that name, which is no part of thee,
Take all myself.

**Romeo.**            I take thee at thy word.
50 Call me but love, and I'll be new baptized;
Henceforth I never will be Romeo.

**Juliet.** What man art thou that, thus bescreened in night,
So stumblest on my counsel?

**Romeo.**                    By a name
I know not how to tell thee who I am.
55 My name, dear saint, is hateful to myself,
Because it is an enemy to thee.
Had I it written, I would tear the word.

**Juliet.** My ears have yet not drunk a hundred words
Of that tongue's utterance, yet I know the sound.
60 Art thou not Romeo, and a Montague?

**Romeo.** Neither, fair saint, if either thee dislike.

**Juliet.** How camest thou hither, tell me, and wherefore?
The orchard walls are high and hard to climb,
And the place death, considering who thou art,
65 If any of my kinsmen find thee here.

**33 wherefore:** why. Juliet asks why Romeo is who he is—someone from her enemy's family. *What does Juliet ask Romeo to do? What does she promise to do?*

**43–47** Juliet tries to convince herself that a name is just a meaningless word that has nothing to do with the person. She asks Romeo to get rid of (**doff**) his name.

**52–53** Juliet is startled that someone hiding (**bescreened**) nearby hears her private thoughts (**counsel**).

**63–65** *What warning does Juliet give Romeo?*

---

## DIFFERENTIATED INSTRUCTION

**FOR ENGLISH LANGUAGE LEARNERS**

**Task Support** Direct students to the question in the marginal note for line 33. Have a volunteer read lines 34–36 aloud. ***Possible answer:*** *Juliet asks Romeo to separate from his family and give up the Montague name. If he will not, she says, she will swear her love to him and turn against her family.*

**Task Support** As you have students read the marginal question for lines 63–65, ask them to consider the identity of the "kinsmen" to whom Juliet refers in line 65. ***Possible answer:*** *Juliet warns that her Capulet relatives will kill Romeo, the Montague, if they find him in Capulet's garden.*

**Romeo.** With love's light wings did I o'erperch these walls;
For stony limits cannot hold love out,
And what love can do, that dares love attempt.
Therefore thy kinsmen are no let to me.

70 **Juliet.** If they do see thee, they will murder thee.

**Romeo.** Alack, there lies more peril in thine eye
Than twenty of their swords! Look thou but sweet,
And I am proof against their enmity.

**Juliet.** I would not for the world they saw thee here.

75 **Romeo.** I have night's cloak to hide me from their sight;
And but thou love me, let them find me here.
My life were better ended by their hate
Than death prorogued, wanting of thy love. **C**

**Juliet.** By whose direction foundst thou out this place?

80 **Romeo.** By love, that first did prompt me to enquire.
He lent me counsel, and I lent him eyes.
I am no pilot, yet, wert thou as far
As that vast shore washed with the farthest sea,
I would adventure for such merchandise.

85 **Juliet.** Thou knowest the mask of night is on my face;
Else would a maiden blush bepaint my cheek
For that which thou hast heard me speak tonight.
Fain would I dwell on form—fain, fain deny
What I have spoke; but farewell compliment!

90 Dost thou love me? I know thou wilt say "Ay";
And I will take thy word. Yet, if thou swearst,
Thou mayst prove false. At lovers' perjuries,
They say Jove laughs. O gentle Romeo,
If thou dost love, pronounce it faithfully.

95 Or if thou thinkst I am too quickly won,
I'll frown, and be perverse, and say thee nay,
So thou wilt woo; but else, not for the world.
In truth, fair Montague, I am too fond,
And therefore thou mayst think my 'havior light;

100 But trust me, gentleman, I'll prove more true
Than those that have more cunning to be strange.
I should have been more strange, I must confess,
But that thou overheardst, ere I was ware,
My true love's passion. Therefore pardon me,

105 And not impute this yielding to light love,
Which the dark night hath so discovered.

**66–69 With . . . me:** Love helped me climb (**o'erperch**) the walls. Neither walls nor your relatives are a hindrance (**let**) to me.

**72–73 Look . . . enmity:** Smile on me, and I will be defended against my enemies' hatred (**enmity**).

**78 than death . . . love:** than my death postponed (**prorogued**) if you don't love me.

**C CHARACTER**
Reread lines 75–78, and explain what Romeo means. Do you think he is seriously thinking of death here, or is he just exaggerating because he's head over heels in love? Explain.

**85–89 Thou . . . compliment:** Had I known you were listening, I would have gladly (**fain**) behaved more properly, but now it's too late for good manners (**farewell compliment**). *Why is Juliet embarrassed that Romeo overheard her?*

**92–93 At . . . laughs:** Jove, the king of the gods, laughs at lovers who lie to each other.

**95–101 Or if . . . strange:** You might think I've fallen in love too easily and that I'm too outspoken. But I'll be truer to you than those who play games to hide their real feelings (**be strange**).

## Analyze Visuals

**Activity** What features of the photograph make this famous scene recognizable?
*Possible answer: A man has climbed a balcony to speak with a young woman. The two seem to be fascinated with each other. These features combine to identify the balcony scene of Romeo and Juliet.*

**IF STUDENTS NEED HELP . . .** Ask leading questions, such as "Who is in the photograph?" "How are they dressed?" and "What emotions do their faces reveal?"

**Romeo.** Lady, by yonder blessed moon I swear,
That tips with silver all these fruit-tree tops—

**Juliet.** O, swear not by the moon, the inconstant moon,
110 That monthly changes in her circled orb,
Lest that thy love prove likewise variable.

**Romeo.** What shall I swear by?

**Juliet.**                              Do not swear at all;
Or if thou wilt, swear by thy gracious self,
Which is the god of my idolatry,
115 And I'll believe thee.

*109–111 Why doesn't Juliet want Romeo to swear by the moon?*

Balcony scene from the Seattle Repertory Theatre's 2003 production

## DIFFERENTIATED INSTRUCTION

**FOR STRUGGLING READERS**
**Inverted Word Order** In lines 108 and 147, Shakespeare adds interest and emphasis to sentences by placing the phrase that names a direct object in an unusual position. Call on volunteers to "translate" these lines. *Possible answer: That tips all these fruit-tree tops with silver; And I'll lay all my fortunes at thy foot.*

**FOR ENGLISH LANGUAGE LEARNERS**
**Task Support** Read aloud the marginal question for lines 109–111. Discuss the meanings of "inconstant", "changes", and "variable", then elicit that the moon's appearance changes as it passes through its monthly phases. *Possible answer: Juliet doesn't want Romeo to swear by the moon because the moon constantly changes. If his love is similar to the moon, it will be variable and therefore untrustworthy.*

**Romeo.**                    If my heart's dear love—

**Juliet.** Well, do not swear. Although I joy in thee,
I have no joy of this contract tonight.
It is too rash, too unadvised, too sudden;
Too like the lightning, which doth cease to be
120 Ere one can say "It lightens." Sweet, good night!
This bud of love, by summer's ripening breath,
May prove a beauteous flow'r when next we meet.
Good night, good night! As sweet repose and rest
Come to thy heart as that within my breast!

125 **Romeo.** O, wilt thou leave me so unsatisfied?

**Juliet.** What satisfaction canst thou have tonight?

**Romeo.** The exchange of thy love's faithful vow for mine.

**Juliet.** I gave thee mine before thou didst request it;
And yet I would it were to give again.

130 **Romeo.** Wouldst thou withdraw it? For what purpose, love?

**Juliet.** But to be frank and give it thee again.
And yet I wish but for the thing I have.
My bounty is as boundless as the sea,
My love as deep; the more I give to thee,
135 The more I have, for both are infinite.
I hear some noise within. Dear love, adieu!

[*Nurse* calls within.]

Anon, good nurse! Sweet Montague, be true.
Stay but a little, I will come again.

[*Exit.*]

**Romeo.** O blessed, blessed night! I am afeard,
140 Being in night, all this is but a dream,
Too flattering-sweet to be substantial.

[*Re-enter* Juliet, *above.*]

**Juliet.** Three words, dear Romeo, and good night indeed.
If that thy bent of love be honorable,
Thy purpose marriage, send me word tomorrow,
145 By one that I'll procure to come to thee,
Where and what time thou wilt perform the rite;
And all my fortunes at thy foot I'll lay
And follow thee my lord throughout the world.

**Nurse** [*within*]. Madam!

150 **Juliet.** I come, anon.—But if thou meanst not well,
I do beseech thee—

117 **I have . . . contract:** I am concerned about this declaration of love (**contract**).

**D** CHARACTER
Reread lines 116–124, and describe Juliet's attitude at this point. How does she feel about Romeo? Why does she seem uneasy about their relationship?

137–138 **anon:** right away. Juliet calls to her nurse but asks Romeo to wait, as she will come back soon.

143–146 **If that . . . rite:** I'll send a messenger to you tomorrow. If your intention is to marry me, tell the messenger where and when the ceremony will be.

**2** **Targeted Passage**

150–151 **But if . . . thee:** Juliet is still worried that Romeo is not serious.

**FOR STRUGGLING READERS**

**2** **Targeted Passage** [Lines 142–148]

This passage advances the plot by revealing a plan for the lovers' next meeting.

- What kind of message may Romeo send to Juliet the next day? How will Juliet receive that message? (lines 143–144)

- What specific information will Romeo send to Juliet? (line 146)

- What is Juliet willing to do when she receives that message? Why? (lines 147–148)

**FOR ENGLISH LANGUAGE LEARNERS**

**Vocabulary Support** Explain to students that some of Shakespeare's words are similar to modern English but are changed to fit the meter of the lines. Illustrate with these examples from Scene 2: "'havior" (line 99), "flow'r" (line 122), "falc'ner's" (line 158), and "Rememb'ring" (line 174).

## E CULTURAL SETTING

*Answers will vary; some students may feel it distances them from the story, while others may argue that historical accuracy helps them understand the context in which the play was written.*

Ask students to name some contemporary metaphors they could use in a play to reflect their current historical and cultural setting.

**REVISIT THE BIG QUESTION**

## Is **LOVE** stronger than **HATE?**

**Discuss** Have students look again at lines 165–170. By nine o'clock the next morning, wedding plans for these young lovers may be in place. Do you think that a marriage between Romeo and Juliet is possible, given the fact that their families hate each other? *Possible answer: The lovers plan to wed in secret, which is the only possible way for the marriage to happen. When the news becomes public, the families' hate may lead both sides to become very angry.*

---

**Nurse** [*within*].      Madam!

**Juliet.**      By-and-by I come.—
To cease thy suit and leave me to my grief.
Tomorrow will I send.

**Romeo.**      So thrive my soul—

**Juliet.** A thousand times good night! [*Exit.*]

155 **Romeo.** A thousand times the worse, to want thy light!
Love goes toward love as schoolboys from their books;
But love from love, towards school with heavy looks.

[*Enter* Juliet *again, above.*]

**Juliet.** Hist! Romeo, hist! O for a falc'ner's voice
To lure this tassel-gentle back again!

160 Bondage is hoarse and may not speak aloud;
Else would I tear the cave where Echo lies,
And make her airy tongue more hoarse than mine
With repetition of my Romeo's name.
Romeo!

165 **Romeo.** It is my soul that calls upon my name.
How silver-sweet sound lovers' tongues by night,
Like softest music to attending ears!

**Juliet.** Romeo!

**Romeo.**      My sweet?

**Juliet.**      What o'clock tomorrow
Shall I send to thee?

**Romeo.**      By the hour of nine.

170 **Juliet.** I will not fail. 'Tis twenty years till then.
I have forgot why I did call thee back.

**Romeo.** Let me stand here till thou remember it.

**Juliet.** I shall forget, to have thee still stand there,
Rememb'ring how I love thy company.

175 **Romeo.** And I'll still stay, to have thee still forget,
Forgetting any other home but this.

**Juliet.** 'Tis almost morning. I would have thee gone—
And yet no farther than a wanton's bird,
That lets it hop a little from her hand,

180 Like a poor prisoner in his twisted gyves,
And with a silk thread plucks it back again,
So loving-jealous of his liberty.

**Romeo.** I would I were thy bird.

---

**156–157 Love...looks:** The simile means that lovers meet as eagerly as schoolboys leave their books; lovers separate with the sadness of boys going to school.

**COMMON CORE** RL 6

## E CULTURAL SETTING

In lines 158–159, Juliet is using a metaphor to describe how desperately she wants to call out Romeo's name. Much of Shakespeare's **figurative language** reflects the historical and cultural setting in which he wrote; this figurative language reflects the popularity of falconry in Elizabethan times. Does language that reflects a historical setting help draw you into the play? Explain.

**158–163 Hist...name:** Listen, Romeo, I wish I could speak your name as loudly as a falconer calls his falcon (**tassel-gentle**), but because of my parents I must whisper. **Echo** was a nymph in Greek mythology whose unreturned love for Narcissus caused her to waste away till only her voice was left.

**177–182 I would...liberty:** I know you must go, but I want you close to me like a pet bird that a thoughtless child (**wanton**) keeps on a string.

---

## *DIFFERENTIATED INSTRUCTION*

### FOR ENGLISH LANGUAGE LEARNERS

**Concept Support** Romeo and Juliet plan to run away to marry without parental knowledge or consent. Discuss Romeo and Juliet's rationale for this action. Then invite students to share their thoughts about how various cultures might view the wisdom of this decision.

### FOR ADVANCED LEARNERS/PRE–AP

**Analyze a Speech** Ask students to reread Juliet's final words in Scene 2. Then have students write a brief analysis of her speech, focusing on (1) Juliet's repeated fear of killing Romeo with love (line 184, but see also lines 63–65) and (2) the meaning and importance of the oxymoron "sweet sorrow" (line 185). Invite students to compare their analyses to see if their interpretations agree.

**Juliet.**                    Sweet, so would I.
Yet I should kill thee with much cherishing.
185 Good night, good night! Parting is such sweet sorrow,
That I shall say good night till it be morrow.

[*Exit.*]

**Romeo.** Sleep dwell upon thine eyes, peace in thy breast!
Would I were sleep and peace, so sweet to rest!
Hence will I to my ghostly father's cell,
190 His help to crave and my dear hap to tell.

[*Exit.*]

# SCENE 3 *Friar Laurence's cell in the monastery.*

*Romeo goes from Capulet's garden to the monastery where Friar Laurence lives.
The friar knows Romeo well and often gives him advice. As the scene begins, Friar
Laurence is gathering herbs in the early morning. He talks of good and bad uses
for herbs. Keep this in mind, since Friar Laurence's skill at mixing herbs becomes
important later in the play. Romeo tells the friar that he loves Juliet and wants to
marry her. The friar is amazed that Romeo has forgotten about Rosaline so easily
and suggests that Romeo might be acting in haste. Eventually, however, he agrees to
marry Romeo and Juliet, hoping that the marriage will end the feud between their
families.*

[*Enter* Friar Laurence *alone, with a basket.*]

**Friar Laurence.** The grey-eyed morn smiles on the frowning night,
Chequ'ring the Eastern clouds with streaks of light;
And flecked darkness like a drunkard reels
From forth day's path and Titan's fiery wheels.
5 Now, ere the sun advance his burning eye
The day to cheer and night's dank dew to dry,
I must upfill this osier cage of ours
With baleful weeds and precious-juiced flowers.
The earth that's nature's mother is her tomb,
10 What is her burying grave, that is her womb;
And from her womb children of divers kind
We sucking on her natural bosom find;
Many for many virtues excellent,
None but for some, and yet all different.
15 O, mickle is the powerful grace that lies
In plants, herbs, stones, and their true qualities;
For naught so vile that on the earth doth live
But to the earth some special good doth give;

ROMEO AND JULIET: ACT TWO, SCENE 3   **1073**

---

**COMMON CORE** L 5a

## Language Coach

**Etymology** *Cherish* comes from the Latin root *carus*, meaning "dear; valued." What does *cherishing* mean in line 184? How can someone kill by cherishing?

**189–190 ghostly father:** spiritual adviser or priest; **dear hap:** good fortune.

**1–30** Friar Laurence begins his speech by describing how night changes into day. He then speaks of the herbs he is collecting. The friar is particularly fascinated with the idea that in herbs as well as man both good and evil can exist.

**4 Titan** is the god whose chariot pulls the sun into the sky each morning.

**7 osier cage:** willow basket.

**9–12 The earth . . . find:** The same earth that acts as a tomb is also the womb, or birthplace, of various useful plants that people can harvest.

**15–18 mickle:** great. The friar says that nothing from the earth is so evil that it doesn't do some good.

---

## BACKGROUND

**Friars** Friar Laurence is a Franciscan friar, a member of a Roman Catholic religious order of men, founded by Saint Francis of Assisi (mentioned in line 65) in 1209. Friars typically renounced material possessions and lived in simple rooms or cells, located within monasteries, sometimes called friaries. Friar Laurence's presence in *Romeo and Juliet* is controversial. By 1535, after the spread of Reformation ideas in England, monks and friars were banned. By the 1590s, Roman Catholic priests were thought to be agents of the Spanish and risked execution for treason if they practiced their religion on English soil. Students should notice how Friar Laurence practices a secular occupation, herbalism, in public, but administers the sacraments in private.

## CULTURAL CONNECTION

**Herbalism** Herbalism was practiced by the ancient Greeks and Romans, and even earlier by the ancient Egyptians, Chinese, Native Americans, and various other peoples. During the Middle Ages, members of religious orders (like Friar Laurence) continued to study ancient Greek writings on the subject and to cultivate herbal gardens. In addition, Arabic scholars studied the ancient works and added their own research to them. After the invention of the printing press, information about herbal medicines spread, often in the form of books known as "herbals." This information continues to be used today. As students will see, such information will play a key role in *Romeo and Juliet*.

---

## FOR ENGLISH LANGUAGE LEARNERS

### Language Coach   COMMON CORE L 5a

**Etymology** *Possible answers:*
Cherishing *means "loving, taking care of."* Remind students of the common expression "killing with kindness."

## FOR STRUGGLING READERS

**Preview** Ask a volunteer to read the italicized scene synopsis aloud for the class. Help students create a cause-and-effect diagram to record key events in Scene 3.

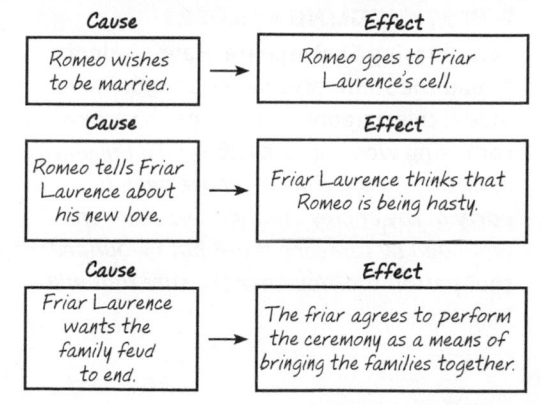

| Cause | Effect |
|---|---|
| Romeo wishes to be married. → | Romeo goes to Friar Laurence's cell. |
| Romeo tells Friar Laurence about his new love. → | Friar Laurence thinks that Romeo is being hasty. |
| Friar Laurence wants the family feud to end. → | The friar agrees to perform the ceremony as a means of bringing the families together. |

Use these prompts to discuss Romeo's visit with Friar Laurence in lines 31–64:

**Connect** Think of a confidant—someone you can go to when you need to talk. How is Friar Laurence like that person? *Students may feel that both are caring, wise people.*

**Analyze** Why is Friar Laurence a particularly good character to counsel Romeo? *Possible answer: Friar Laurence is perceptive. He notices immediately that Romeo is "distempered" (line 33), or upset. He also demands that Romeo be "plain" (line 55), or honest, with him. It seems clear that the friar's manner has won Romeo's respect, affection, and trust.*

**Synthesize** By acting as a counselor and performing the marriage of these young lovers, what risk does Friar Laurence take? *Possible answer: Friar Laurence risks angering both powerful families. As a result, there may be greater violence instead of peace in Verona—and some of that violence might be directed at him.*

---

Nor aught so good but, strained from that fair use,
20 Revolts from true birth, stumbling on abuse.
Virtue itself turns vice, being misapplied,
And vice sometime's by action dignified.
Within the infant rind of this small flower
Poison hath residence, and medicine power;
25 For this, being smelt, with that part cheers each part;
Being tasted, slays all senses with the heart.
Two such opposed kings encamp them still
In man as well as herbs—grace and rude will;
And where the worser is predominant,
30 Full soon the canker death eats up that plant.

[*Enter* Romeo.]

**Romeo.** Good morrow, father.

**Friar Laurence.**                     Benedicite!
What early tongue so sweet saluteth me?
Young son, it argues a distempered head
So soon to bid good morrow to thy bed.
35 Care keeps his watch in every old man's eye,
And where care lodges sleep will never lie;
But where unbruised youth with unstuffed brain
Doth couch his limbs, there golden sleep doth reign.
Therefore thy earliness doth me assure
40 Thou art uproused with some distemp'rature;
Or if not so, then here I hit it right—
Our Romeo hath not been in bed tonight.

**Romeo.** That last is true, the sweeter rest was mine.

**Friar Laurence.** God pardon sin! Wast thou with Rosaline?

45 **Romeo.** With Rosaline, my ghostly father? No.
I have forgot that name, and that name's woe.

**Friar Laurence.** That's my good son! But where hast thou been then?

**Romeo.** I'll tell thee ere thou ask it me again.
I have been feasting with mine enemy,
50 Where on a sudden one hath wounded me
That's by me wounded. Both our remedies
Within thy help and holy physic lies.
I bear no hatred, blessed man, for, lo,
My intercession likewise steads my foe.

55 **Friar Laurence.** Be plain, good son, and homely in thy drift.
Riddling confession finds but riddling shrift.

---

**23–26 Within . . . heart:** He holds a flower that can be used either as a poison or as a medicine. If the flower is smelled, its fragrance can improve health in each part of the body; if it is eaten, it causes death.

**28 grace and rude will:** good and evil. Both exist in people as well as in plants.

**31 Benedicite** (bĕ′nĕ-dī′sĭ-tē′): God bless you.

**33–42 it argues . . . tonight:** Only a disturbed (**distempered**) mind could make you get up so early. Old people may have trouble sleeping, but it is not normal for someone as young as you. Or were you up all night?

**44 God . . . Rosaline:** The friar is shocked that Romeo has not been to bed yet. *Where does he think Romeo has been?*

**49–56** Romeo tries to explain the situation, asking for help both for himself and his "foe" (Juliet). The friar does not understand Romeo's convoluted language and asks him to speak clearly so that he can help.

---

## DIFFERENTIATED INSTRUCTION

### FOR STRUGGLING READERS

**Paraphrasing Shakespeare** Have students reread the summary of lines 49–56. Then model this paraphrase of Romeo's somewhat confusing words in lines 48–52: *I'll tell you before you ask me again: I have been to a party at my enemy's home. I was suddenly wounded by someone there, but I wounded that person too. You have the cure that will help both of us.*

### FOR ENGLISH LANGUAGE LEARNERS

**Task Support** Have students read the marginal note and question for line 44. Point out Romeo's comment about "sweeter rest" (line 43), and explain that Friar Laurence probably hears many people confess their sins. *Possible answer: Friar Laurence thinks that Romeo has spent the night in a romantic encounter with Rosaline.*

**Romeo.** Then plainly know my heart's dear love is set
On the fair daughter of rich Capulet;
As mine on hers, so hers is set on mine,
60 And all combined, save what thou must combine
By holy marriage. When, and where, and how
We met, we wooed, and made exchange of vow,
I'll tell thee as we pass; but this I pray,
That thou consent to marry us today.

65 **Friar Laurence.** Holy Saint Francis! What a change is here!
Is Rosaline, that thou didst love so dear,
So soon forsaken? Young men's love then lies
Not truly in their hearts, but in their eyes.

**66–68** *What is Friar Laurence saying in these lines?*

Friar Laurence counsels Romeo in the University of Victoria's 1998 production.

**Analyze Visuals**

**Activity** What assumptions can you make about Friar Laurence from details in this photograph? Explain your assumptions.
*Possible answer:* The reader can assume that Friar Laurence is interested in plants, for he is holding a plant and has a drawing of a plant on his easel. From his robe and his cross necklace, the reader can assume that he belongs to a Christian religious order. His pose suggests that he is an instructor or counselor to Romeo.

---

**FOR STRUGGLING READERS**

**Explore Characters** Have pairs or small groups of students read Friar Laurence's lines carefully. Then have them work together to fill out a Character Analysis Chart about him. Students can add notes and explore this character further as he reappears in later scenes.

 **BEST PRACTICES TOOLKIT—Transparency** Character Analysis Chart p. D5

**FOR ENGLISH LANGUAGE LEARNERS**

**Task Support** Draw attention to the marginal question for lines 66–68. Ask a volunteer to read the lines aloud for the class. *Possible answer: Friar Laurence is saying that he is surprised that Romeo has so quickly forgotten about his former love. From this event he concludes that love is a function of a young man's attraction, not of his heart.*

Jesu Maria! What a deal of brine

70 Hath washed thy sallow cheeks for Rosaline!
How much salt water thrown away in waste,
To season love, that of it doth not taste!
The sun not yet thy sighs from heaven clears,
Thy old groans ring yet in mine ancient ears.

75 Lo, here upon thy cheek the stain doth sit
Of an old tear that is not washed off yet.
If e'er thou wast thyself, and these woes thine,
Thou and these woes were all for Rosaline.
And art thou changed? Pronounce this sentence then:

80 Women may fall when there's no strength in men.

**Romeo.** Thou chidst me oft for loving Rosaline.

**Friar Laurence.** For doting, not for loving, pupil mine.

**Romeo.** And badest me bury love.

**Friar Laurence.**                    Not in a grave
To lay one in, another ought to have.

85 **Romeo.** I pray thee chide not. She whom I love now
Doth grace for grace and love for love allow.
The other did not so.

**Friar Laurence.**          O, she knew well
Thy love did read by rote, that could not spell.
But come, young waverer, come go with me.

90 In one respect I'll thy assistant be;
For this alliance may so happy prove
To turn your households' rancor to pure love. **F**

**Romeo.** O, let us hence! I stand on sudden haste.

**Friar Laurence.** Wisely, and slow. They stumble that run fast.

[*Exeunt.*]

**69 brine:** salt water—that is, the tears that Romeo has been shedding for Rosaline.

**80 Women . . . men:** If men are so weak, women may be forgiven for sinning.

**81–82 chidst:** scolded. The friar replies that he scolded Romeo for being lovesick, not for loving.

**85–88 She whom . . . spell:** Romeo says that the woman he loves feels the same way about him. That wasn't true of Rosaline. The friar replies that Rosaline knew that he didn't know what real love is.

**91–92 For this . . . prove:** this marriage may work out so well; **rancor:** bitter hate.

**F CHARACTER**
Why does Friar Laurence agree to help Romeo marry Juliet, despite his worry that Romeo falls in love too easily? Explain the friar's **motives**.

## SCENE 4 *A street.*

*Several hours after his meeting with Friar Laurence, Romeo meets Benvolio and Mercutio in the street. He is excited and happy; his mood is key to the comic nature of this scene, which includes much talk of swordplay and many suggestive jokes. Mercutio makes fun of Tybalt and teases Romeo. The nurse comes to carry a message from Romeo to Juliet. Romeo tells her that Juliet should meet him at Friar Laurence's cell for their secret marriage ceremony.*

[*Enter* Benvolio *and* Mercutio.]

**Mercutio.** Where the devil should this Romeo be?
Came he not home tonight?

---

**F CHARACTER**

*Possible answer:* *Friar Laurence agrees to help Romeo because he is motivated to help end the feud between the Capulet and Montague families.*

**IF STUDENTS NEED HELP . . .** Discuss these questions:

- What does Friar Laurence mean when he says that Rosaline "knew well / Thy love did read by rote, that could not spell" (lines 87–88)? *Possible answer: He means that Rosaline understood that Romeo's love was immature or not the real thing.*

- What do you think is the friar's tone of voice when he calls Romeo "young waverer" (line 89)? *Possible answer: His tone probably is kindly, especially as the words are part of an invitation.*

- According to Friar Laurence, why might Romeo's marriage to Juliet be a happy thing? *Possible answer: The marriage might turn the "rancor" (bitterness) between the families into love.*

---

## DIFFERENTIATED INSTRUCTION

### FOR STRUGGLING READERS

**Preview** Ask a volunteer to read aloud the italicized scene synopsis. Help students organize the events of Scene 4 into a Sequence Chain.

 **BEST PRACTICES TOOLKIT—Transparency** Sequence Chain p. B21

| Romeo meets friends to talk and joke. |
| :---: |
| ↓ |
| Juliet's nurse arrives to speak to Romeo. |
| ↓ |
| Romeo tells the nurse of his plan to marry Juliet secretly at Friar Laurence's cell. |

**Benvolio.** Not to his father's. I spoke with his man.

**Mercutio.** Why, that same pale hard-hearted wench, that Rosaline,
5 Torments him so that he will sure run mad.

**Benvolio.** Tybalt, the kinsman to old Capulet,
Hath sent a letter to his father's house.

**Mercutio.** A challenge, on my life.

**Benvolio.** Romeo will answer it.

10 **Mercutio.** Any man that can write may answer a letter.

**Benvolio.** Nay, he will answer the letter's master, how he dares,
being dared.

**Mercutio.** Alas, poor Romeo, he is already dead! stabbed with a
white wench's black eye; shot through the ear with a love song;
15 the very pin of his heart cleft with the blind bow-boy's butt-shaft;
and is he a man to encounter Tybalt?

**Benvolio.** Why, what is Tybalt?

**Mercutio.** More than Prince of Cats, I can tell you. O, he's the
courageous captain of compliments. He fights as you sing
20 pricksong—keeps time, distance, and proportion; rests me his
minim rest, one, two, and the third in your bosom! the very
butcher of a silk button, a duelist, a duelist! a gentleman of the
very first house, of the first and second cause. Ah, the immortal
*passado!* the *punto reverso!* the *hay!*

25 **Benvolio.** The what?

**Mercutio.** The pox of such antic, lisping, affecting fantasticoes—
these new tuners of accent! "By Jesu, a very good blade! a very
tall man! a very good whore!" Why, is not this a lamentable thing,
grandsire, that we should be thus afflicted with these strange flies,
30 these fashion-mongers, these perdona-mi's, who stand so much
on the new form that they cannot sit at ease on the old bench?
O, their bones, their bones!

[*Enter Romeo, no longer moody.*]

**Benvolio.** Here comes Romeo! here comes Romeo!

**Mercutio.** Without his roe, like a dried herring. O, flesh, flesh,
35 how art thou fishified! Now is he for the numbers that Petrarch
flowed in. Laura, to his lady, was but a kitchen wench (marry,
she had a better love to berhyme her), Dido a dowdy, Cleopatra
a gypsy, Helen and Hero hildings and harlots, Thisbe a grey eye

---

**3 man:** servant.

**6–12 Tybalt . . . dared:** Tybalt, still angry about Romeo's crashing the Capulet party, has sent a letter challenging Romeo to a duel. Benvolio says that Romeo will do more than answer the letter; he will accept Tybalt's challenge and fight him.

**15 blind bow-boy's butt-shaft:** Cupid's dull practice arrow. Mercutio suggests that Romeo fell in love with very little work on Cupid's part.

**18–24 More than . . . hay:** Mercutio mocks Tybalt's name. **Prince of Cats** refers to a cat in a fable, named Tybalt, who was known for his slyness. Then Mercutio makes fun of Tybalt's fancy new style of dueling, comparing it to precision singing (**pricksong**). **Passado, punto reverso,** and **hay** were terms used in the new dueling style.

**26–32 The pox . . . their bones:** Mercutio continues to make fun of people who embrace new styles and new manners of speaking.

**34–39 without his roe:** only part of himself (Mercutio makes fun of Romeo's name and his lovesickness); **numbers:** verses. Mercutio mentions Petrarch, who wrote sonnets to his love, Laura. According to Mercutio, Romeo's feelings for Rosaline are so intense that great loves in literature—Laura, Dido, and others—could never measure up.

---

## TIERED DISCUSSION PROMPTS

Refer students to lines 18–32. Use these discussion prompts to help students understand Mercutio's perception of Tybalt:

**Recall** Why did Tybalt send a letter challenging Romeo to a duel? *Because Romeo showed up uninvited at the Capulets' party, an intrusion that was considered disrespectful.*

**Analyze** According to Mercutio, why is Tybalt particularly dangerous? *Possible answer: Tybalt is a master duelist and knows the calculated moves needed to destroy an opponent. "A gentleman of the very first house" (lines 22–23), Tybalt is also a "butcher of a silk button" (line 22), a skilled swordsman, and a dangerous man.*

**Evaluate** Does Mercutio's assessment of Tybalt seem like an objective assessment? *Possible answer: Mercutio is objective enough to be wary of Tybalt's skill as a duelist, but he also harbors a personal resentment of Tybalt and his fancy dueling style.*

---

## FOR ENGLISH LANGUAGE LEARNERS

**Concept Support** To help students understand that another fight is brewing, organize students into pairs. Ask one student in the pair to look for the lines at the beginning of Scene 4 that refer to the challenge (lines 6–12). Ask the other student to look for the lines that involve swordplay (lines 13–24). Have students work together to rephrase or otherwise work out the meaning of the lines.

## FOR ADVANCED LEARNERS/PRE–AP

**Analyze Allusions** [small-group option] Have students reread Mercutio's speech in lines 34–39 and the marginal note about it. Then ask them to do more research about the allusions that Mercutio makes in these lines—to Laura, Dido, Cleopatra, Helen, Hero, and Thisbe. Invite students to give a brief oral report on their findings and to share a few comments about the point that Mercutio is making by using these allusions.

## Is **LOVE** stronger than **HATE?**

**Discuss** After Scenes 2 and 3, which focus on words of romance and plans for a marriage, Scene 4 opens with witty talk and comedy. In what sense, however, is there still a focus upon love? How does the dialogue in lines 42–61 reveal this focus? *Possible answer: There is still a focus on love, but for the moment it is the love between friends rather than romantic love. The dialogue between Romeo and Mercutio is full of jokes and funny threats (line 61). These characters could not jest with each other so personally if they were not friends who love each other.*

---

or so, but not to the purpose. Signior Romeo, *bon jour!* There's
40 a French salutation to your French slop. You gave us the
counterfeit fairly last night.

**Romeo.** Good morrow to you both. What counterfeit did I give you?

**Mercutio.** The slip, sir, the slip. Can you not conceive?

45 **Romeo.** Pardon, good Mercutio. My business was great, and in such a case as mine a man may strain courtesy.

**Mercutio.** That's as much as to say, such a case as yours constrains a man to bow in the hams.

**Romeo.** Meaning, to curtsy.

50 **Mercutio.** Thou hast most kindly hit it.

**Romeo.** A most courteous exposition.

**Mercutio.** Nay, I am the very pink of courtesy.

**Romeo.** Pink for flower.

**Mercutio.** Right.

55 **Romeo.** Why, then is my pump well-flowered.

**Mercutio.** Well said! Follow me this jest now till thou hast worn out thy pump, that, when the single sole of it is worn, the jest may remain, after the wearing, solely singular.

**Romeo.** Oh, single-soled jest, solely singular for the singleness!

60 **Mercutio.** Come between us, good Benvolio! My wits faint.

**Romeo.** Switch and spurs, switch and spurs! or I'll cry a match.

**Mercutio.** Nay, if our wits run the wild-goose chase, I am done; for thou hast more of the wild goose in one of thy wits than, I am sure, I have in my whole five. Was I with you there for the
65 goose?

**Romeo.** Thou wast never with me for anything when thou wast not there for the goose.

**Mercutio.** I will bite thee by the ear for that jest.

**Romeo.** Nay, good goose, bite not!

70 **Mercutio.** Thy wit is a very bitter sweeting; it is a most sharp sauce.

**Romeo.** And is it not, then, well served in to a sweet goose?

**Mercutio.** O, here's a wit of cheveril, that stretches from an inch narrow to an ell broad!

**39–44** *bon jour:* "Good day" in French; **There's . . . last night:** Here's a greeting to match your fancy French trousers (**slop**). You did a good job of getting away from us last night. (A piece of counterfeit money was called a **slip**.)

**44–81** In these lines, Romeo and Mercutio have a battle of wits. They keep trying to top each other with funnier comments and cleverer puns.

**55 pump:** shoe; **well-flowered:** Shoes were "pinked," or punched out in flowerlike designs.

**61 Switch . . . match:** Keep going, or I'll claim victory.

**64–65 Was . . . goose:** Have I proved that you are a foolish person?

**73 cheveril:** kidskin, which is flexible. Mercutio means that a little wit stretches a long way.

---

## DIFFERENTIATED INSTRUCTION

**FOR ENGLISH LANGUAGE LEARNERS**
**Vocabulary Support** Point out the complicated word play in this scene. In lines 46–52, the friends enjoy some word play using the related words *courtesy* (lines 46 and 52), *curtsy* (line 49), and *courteous* (line 51). In lines 57–59, the friends repeat the words *single* and *sole* in five different variations. Help students find other examples of word play in this scene.

**FOR ADVANCED LEARNERS/PRE–AP**
**Evaluate a Scene** Remind students that according to the summary on page 1035, Mercutio will soon die at the hand of Tybalt. Have pairs of students discuss Act Two, Scene 4, focusing on Mercutio, and then write a joint evaluation of its importance to the plot of the play. After students have read Act Three, ask the same pairs of students to reread and refine their evaluations.

75 **Romeo.** I stretch it out for that word "broad," which, added to the goose, proves thee far and wide a broad goose.

**Mercutio.** Why, is not this better now than groaning for love? Now art thou sociable, now art thou Romeo; now art thou what thou art, by art as well as by nature. For this driveling love is like
80 a great natural that runs lolling up and down to hide his bauble in a hole.

**Benvolio.** Stop there, stop there!

**Mercutio.** Thou desirest me to stop in my tale against the hair.

**Benvolio.** Thou wouldst else have made thy tale large.

85 **Mercutio.** O, thou art deceived! I would have made it short; for I was come to the whole depth of my tale, and meant indeed to occupy the argument no longer.

[*Enter* Nurse *and* Peter, *her servant. He is carrying a large fan.*]

**Romeo.** Here's goodly gear!

**Mercutio.** A sail, a sail!

90 **Benvolio.** Two, two! a shirt and a smock.

**Nurse.** Peter!

**Peter.** Anon.

**Nurse.** My fan, Peter.

**Mercutio.** Good Peter, to hide her face; for her fan's the fairer of
95 the two.

**Nurse.** God ye good morrow, gentlemen.

**Mercutio.** God ye good-den, fair gentlewoman.

**Nurse.** Is it good-den?

**Mercutio.** 'Tis no less, I tell ye, for the bawdy hand of the dial is
100 now upon the prick of noon.

**Nurse.** Out upon you! What a man are you!

**Romeo.** One, gentlewoman, that God hath made himself to mar.

**Nurse.** By my troth, it is well said. "For himself to mar," quoth'a? Gentlemen, can any of you tell me where I may find the young
105 Romeo?

**Romeo.** I can tell you; but young Romeo will be older when you have found him than he was when you sought him. I am the youngest of that name, for fault of a worse.

80–81 **great natural:** an idiot, like a jester or clown who carries a fool's stick (**bauble**).

88–89 **goodly gear:** something fine to joke about; **a sail:** Mercutio likens the nurse in all her petticoats to a huge ship coming toward them.

93 Fans were usually carried only by fine ladies. The nurse is trying to pretend that she is more than a servant.

ROMEO AND JULIET: ACT TWO, SCENE 4   **1079**

**REVISIT THE BIG QUESTION**
## Is **LOVE** stronger than **HATE?**

**Discuss** In lines 77–81, Mercutio expresses his relief that Romeo seems to be himself again. What is Mercutio's opinion about people who brood over love? Why do you think that he feels this way? ***Possible answer:*** *Mercutio's opinion is best shown in his reference to "driveling love" (line 79), which indicates that he found Romeo's moodiness over love ridiculous and irritating. (Students may also remember that Mercutio has already ridiculed Romeo's pining for Rosaline.) Mercutio may feel this way because he has never been in love and, therefore, has not experienced the passions that Romeo feels.*

**FOR ADVANCED LEARNERS/PRE–AP**
**Mercutio and Friar Laurence** Even though they possess very different personalities, Mercutio and Friar Laurence share a close-ness to Romeo. After students have finished reading Scene 4, challenge them to reread Scene 3, as well as Mercutio's speech in lines 53–95 in Scene 4 of Act One. Then ask them to write two to three paragraphs comparing and contrasting the approaches that Friar Laurence and Mercutio take in responding to Romeo's moods and offer an assessment as to why each is important in Romeo's life.

Use these prompts to explore the way in which the young men treat Juliet's nurse in lines 88–126:

**Connect** When have you seen someone treated with disrespect? How does that memory help you understand this scene? *Students may recall a time when they saw one person make fun of another. Students should recognize the verbal abuse that Mercutio, in particular, directs at the nurse.*

**Analyze** What can you tell about Mercutio and Benvolio, who ridicule the nurse? Who treats her worse? Why do you think they are so unkind? *Possible answer: Mercutio and Benvolio's behavior shows that they are playful and bawdy. It also reveals them to be class conscious, for they ridicule the low standing of the nurse. Mercutio says more and so is the worse of the two. They are probably being unkind as a way of showing off in front of each other.*

**Synthesize** Romeo is not nearly as unkind as are his friends. In fact, once his friends leave, he is respectful to the nurse and even offers her an apology of sorts (lines 129–130). How do you explain his behavior? *Possible answer: Romeo's behavior is better because he knows why the nurse has come, whereas his friends do not. He probably does not want the nurse to take a bad report back to Juliet; besides, when Mercutio isn't around to egg him on, Romeo seems to display a pleasant personality.*

**Nurse.** You say well.

110 **Mercutio.** Yea, is the worst well? Very well took, i' faith! wisely, wisely.

**Nurse.** If you be he, sir, I desire some confidence with you.

**Benvolio.** She will endite him to some supper.

**Mercutio.** A bawd, a bawd, a bawd! So ho!

115 **Romeo.** What hast thou found?

**Mercutio.** No hare, sir; unless a hare, sir, in a lenten pie, that is something stale and hoar ere it be spent.

[*sings*]

    "An old hare hoar,
    And an old hare hoar,
120    Is very good meat in Lent.
    But a hare that is hoar,
    Is too much for a score
    When it hoars ere it be spent."

Romeo, will you come to your father's? We'll to dinner thither.

125 **Romeo.** I will follow you.

**Mercutio.** Farewell, ancient lady. Farewell, [*sings*] lady, lady, lady. [*Exeunt* Mercutio *and* Benvolio.]

**Nurse.** Marry, farewell! I pray you, sir, what saucy merchant was this that was so full of his ropery?

**Romeo.** A gentleman, nurse, that loves to hear himself talk and 130 will speak more in a minute than he will stand to in a month.

**Nurse.** An 'a speak anything against me, I'll take him down, an 'a were lustier than he is, and twenty such Jacks; and if I cannot, I'll find those that shall. Scurvy knave! I am none of his flirt-gills; I am none of his skainsmates. [*turning to* Peter] And thou must 135 stand by too, and suffer every knave to use me at his pleasure?

**Peter.** I saw no man use you at his pleasure. If I had, my weapon should quickly have been out, I warrant you. I dare draw as soon as another man, if I see occasion in a good quarrel, and the law on my side.

**112–113 confidence:** The nurse means *conference;* she uses big words without understanding their meaning; **endite:** Benvolio makes fun of the nurse by using this word rather than *invite.*

**114–124** Mercutio calls the nurse a **bawd,** or woman who runs a house of prostitution. His song uses the insulting puns **hare,** a rabbit or prostitute, and **hoar,** old.

**128 ropery:** roguery, or jokes.

**133–134** The nurse is angry that Mercutio treated her like one of his loose women (**flirt-gills**) or his gangsterlike friends (**skainsmates**).

## DIFFERENTIATED INSTRUCTION

### FOR STRUGGLING READERS

**Paraphrasing Shakespeare** Have students reread the marginal note for lines 133–134. Model a paraphrase of lines 131–133: *And if he insults me, I'll fight and defeat him, for I am stronger [lustier] than he and twenty of his friends, put together, are; and if I can't defeat him, I'll find someone who will.* Then call on volunteers to paraphrase the nurse's words to Peter (lines 134–135) and Peter's reply (lines 136–139).

*Possible answer:*

**Nurse.** *And is it right for you to stand around and do nothing, letting every rascal treat me as he wishes?*

**Peter.** *I didn't see anyone treat you as he wished. If I had seen that, I guarantee that I would have drawn my weapon [to defend you]. I am as willing to fight as anyone, if the right argument presents itself, and I am acting within the law.*

## Behind the Curtain

The Orlando-UCF Shakespeare Festival's 1992 production

### Set Design

Often, set designers recreate the world of *Romeo and Juliet* in strikingly unique ways. Designers of the productions pictured here created radically different **sets** for the balcony scene. List three adjectives you would use to describe each set. What factors might make a designer choose to create one of these particular set styles?

The Royal Shakespeare Company's 1992 production

The University of South Carolina's 1999 production

1081

**Set Design** Explain that sets are the platforms, walls, and building structures that help create the world within a play. Point out that it is not unusual for set designers to avoid a completely realistic "look." To illustrate this point, draw students' attention to the photographs of the Royal Shakespeare Company's 1992 production and the University of South Carolina's 1999 production. In both cases, the sets require the audience to use its imagination to fill in details. The Orlando-UCF Shakespeare Festival's 1992 production, however, has a much more realistic set, including a real balcony. ***Possible answer:*** *The Orlando-UCF Shakespeare Festival's set is realistic, romantic, and rich; the Royal Shakespeare Company's set is modern, abstract, and geometric; the University of South Carolina's set is stark, bare, otherworldly. In determining a set style, a set designer might consider the actual setting of the work, any interpretation that the director wants to give it, and the production's budget.*

### FOR ADVANCED LEARNERS/PRE–AP

**Create a Set Design** Have groups of students choose a scene they have read and design a creative but appropriate set. Have students use graph paper for an overhead view, as well as drawings that show how the set will look from the front. Encourage students to add details such as colors, fabrics, and foliage that would be part of the set. Display the set designs and compare designs created for the same scene.

## REVISIT THE BIG QUESTION

### Is **LOVE** stronger than **HATE**?

**Discuss** How is Nurse's love for Juliet shown in her response to Romeo in lines 140–147? *Possible answer: She is protective and honest about her feelings. The nurse reminds Romeo that Juliet is young, and should he "deal double" (line 146) with her, it would show him up as "weak" and of poor character. Nurse is of a lower social class than Romeo, so she cannot legitimately threaten him. Still, she is brutally honest in telling him that leading Juliet into a "fool's paradise" (line 144)—that is, a false promise—would be a "very gross kind of behavior" (lines 144–145).*

---

140 **Nurse.** Now, afore God, I am so vexed that every part about me
quivers. Scurvy knave! Pray you, sir, a word; and as I told you,
my young lady bade me enquire you out. What she bid me say,
I will keep to myself; but first let me tell ye, if ye should lead her
into a fool's paradise, as they say, it were a very gross kind of
145 behavior, as they say; for the gentlewoman is young; and
therefore, if you should deal double with her, truly it were an ill
thing to be offered to any gentlewoman, and very weak dealing.

**Romeo.** Nurse, commend me to thy lady and mistress. I protest
unto thee—

150 **Nurse.** Good heart, and i' faith I will tell her as much. Lord,
Lord! she will be a joyful woman.

**Romeo.** What wilt thou tell her, nurse? Thou dost not mark me.

**Nurse.** I will tell her, sir, that you do protest, which, as I take it,
is a gentlemanlike offer.

155 **Romeo.** Bid her devise
Some means to come to shrift this afternoon;
And there she shall at Friar Laurence' cell
Be shrived and married. Here is for thy pains.

**Nurse.** No, truly, sir; not a penny.

160 **Romeo.** Go to! I say you shall.

**Nurse.** This afternoon, sir? Well, she shall be there.

**Romeo.** And stay, good nurse, behind the abbey wall.
Within this hour my man shall be with thee
And bring thee cords made like a tackled stair,
165 Which to the high topgallant of my joy
Must be my convoy in the secret night.
Farewell. Be trusty, and I'll quit thy pains.
Farewell. Commend me to thy mistress.

**Nurse.** Now God in heaven bless thee! Hark you, sir.

170 **Romeo.** What sayst thou, my dear nurse?

**Nurse.** Is your man secret? Did you ne'er hear say,
Two may keep counsel, putting one away?

**Romeo.** I warrant thee my man's as true as steel.

**Nurse.** Well, sir, my mistress is the sweetest lady. Lord, Lord!
175 when 'twas a little prating thing—O, there is a nobleman in
town, one Paris, that would fain lay knife aboard; but she, good
soul, had as lief see a toad, a very toad, as see him. I anger her

**142–147** The nurse warns Romeo that he'd better mean what he said about marrying Juliet. She holds back her news while she tries to decide if Romeo's love is genuine.

**148 commend me:** give my respectful greetings.

**155–159** Romeo tells the nurse to have Juliet come to Friar Laurence's cell this afternoon, using the excuse that she is going to confess her sins (**shrift**). There she will receive forgiveness for her sins (**be shrived**) and be married.

**❸ Targeted Passage**

**164–165 tackled stair:** rope ladder; **topgallant:** highest point.

**167–172 quit thy pains:** reward you. The nurse then asks Romeo if his servant can be trusted, then quotes the saying that two can keep a secret but not three.

**174–177** The nurse begins to babble about Paris' proposal but says that Juliet would rather look at a toad than at Paris.

---

## DIFFERENTIATED INSTRUCTION

### FOR STRUGGLING READERS

**❸ Targeted Passage [Lines 155–168]**

This passage lays out the specifics of Romeo's plan for marrying Juliet.

- To whom is Romeo speaking? Why does he tell his plan to this person? (lines 155–159)
- When and where does Romeo want Juliet to meet him? (lines 156–157)
- What will he send to the nurse first? Why do you think it will be needed? (line 164)

**Infer Action** Explain that Shakespeare uses relatively few stage directions and that readers sometimes must infer action from his dialogue. In lines 158–160, for example, the dialogue implies that Romeo is putting a coin into the nurse's hand to thank her for her help, that she may shake her head and try to give it back, and that Romeo may then use a gesture to underscore his insistence upon her keeping the gift.

sometimes, and tell her that Paris is the properer man; but I'll warrant you, when I say so, she looks as pale as any clout in the
180 versal world. Doth not rosemary and Romeo begin both with a letter?

**Romeo.** Ay, nurse, what of that? Both with an R.

**Nurse.** Ah, mocker! that's the dog's name. R is for the—No; I know it begins with some other letter; and she hath the prettiest
185 sententious of it, of you and rosemary, that it would do you good to hear it.

**Romeo.** Commend me to thy lady.

**Nurse.** Ay, a thousand times. [*Exit* Romeo.] Peter!

**Peter.** Anon.

190 **Nurse.** Peter, take my fan, and go before, and apace.
[*Exeunt.*]

**179–186 clout:** old cloth; **the versal world:** the entire world; **Doth not . . . hear it:** The nurse tries to recall a clever saying that Juliet made up about Romeo and rosemary, the herb for remembrance, but cannot remember it. She is sure that the two words couldn't begin with *R* because this letter sounds like a snarling dog; **sententious:** The nurse means *sentences*.

**190 apace:** quickly.

# SCENE 5  *Capulet's orchard.*

*Juliet is a nervous wreck, having waited for more than three hours for the nurse to return. When the nurse does arrive, she simply won't come to the point. Juliet gets more and more upset, until the nurse finally reveals the wedding arrangements.*

[*Enter* Juliet.]

**Juliet.** The clock struck nine when I did send the nurse;
In half an hour she promised to return.
Perchance she cannot meet him. That's not so.
O, she is lame! Love's heralds should be thoughts,
5 Which ten times faster glide than the sun's beams
Driving back shadows over lowering hills.
Therefore do nimble-pinioned doves draw Love,
And therefore hath the wind-swift Cupid wings. **G**
Now is the sun upon the highmost hill
10 Of this day's journey, and from nine till twelve
Is three long hours; yet she is not come.
Had she affections and warm youthful blood,
She would be as swift in motion as a ball;
My words would bandy her to my sweet love,
15 And his to me.
But old folks, many feign as they were dead—
Unwieldy, slow, heavy, and pale as lead.
[*Enter* Nurse *and* Peter.] O God, she comes! O honey nurse, what news?

**4–6 Love's . . . hills:** Love's messengers should be thoughts, which travel ten times faster than sunbeams.

**7 nimble-pinioned . . . Love:** Swift-winged doves pull the chariot of Venus, goddess of love.

**G ALLUSION**
What do Juliet's allusions to Venus and to Cupid emphasize about her state of mind as she waits for the nurse to return?

**14 bandy:** toss.

**16 feign as:** act as if.

ROMEO AND JULIET: ACT TWO, SCENE 5  **1083**

---

---

**FOR STRUGGLING READERS**

**Preview** As you read through the Scene 5 synopsis, use an Open Mind diagram to help students identify Juliet's emotions.

 **BEST PRACTICES TOOLKIT—Transparency**
Open Mind p. D9

nervous waiting for nurse
excited/anxious about wedding arrangements
happy to see nurse
frustrated with nurse's stalling
impatient to hear news

Use these prompts to provide insight into the relationship between Juliet and her nurse, as revealed in lines 21–77:

**Connect** How do people often feel about asking someone to do them a big favor? How do you think Juliet feels toward her nurse? *Students should understand that asking a big favor leads to feelings of gratitude. Juliet feels grateful to her nurse for meeting with Romeo, but she also becomes frustrated with the nurse for withholding Romeo's news.*

**Analyze** What reason might the nurse have for teasing Juliet by not telling her the news right away? *Possible answer: The nurse might be teasing Juliet because she enjoys the power that withholding the news gives her. By not revealing the information, she forces Juliet to beg her for it.*

**Evaluate** Who do you think is the wiser counselor—Friar Laurence or the nurse? Explain. *Possible answer: Both characters are confidants of the lovers, and both are in favor of the marriage. Friar Laurence may be the wiser counselor, however: he is educated, he is not an employee of one of the families involved, and he is able to see beyond the wedding itself to a greater good that might come from the marriage.*

---

Hast thou met with him? Send thy man away.

20 **Nurse.** Peter, stay at the gate.

[*Exit* Peter.]

**Juliet.** Now, good sweet nurse—O Lord, why lookst thou sad?
Though news be sad, yet tell them merrily;
If good, thou shamest the music of sweet news
By playing it to me with so sour a face.

25 **Nurse.** I am aweary, give me leave awhile.
Fie, how my bones ache! What a jaunce have I had!

**Juliet.** I would thou hadst my bones, and I thy news.
Nay, come, I pray thee speak. Good, good nurse, speak.

**Nurse.** Jesu, what haste! Can you not stay awhile?
30 Do you not see that I am out of breath?

**Juliet.** How art thou out of breath when thou hast breath
To say to me that thou art out of breath?
The excuse that thou dost make in this delay
Is longer than the tale thou dost excuse.
35 Is thy news good or bad? Answer to that.
Say either, and I'll stay the circumstance.
Let me be satisfied, is't good or bad?

**Nurse.** Well, you have made a simple choice; you know not how
to choose a man. Romeo? No, not he. Though his face be better
40 than any man's, yet his leg excels all men's; and for a hand and a
foot, and a body, though they be not to be talked on, yet they are
past compare. He is not the flower of courtesy, but, I'll warrant
him, as gentle as a lamb. Go thy ways, wench; serve God. What,
have you dined at home?

45 **Juliet.** No, no. But all this did I know before.
What say he of our marriage? What of that?

**Nurse.** Lord, how my head aches! What a head have I!
It beats as it would fall in twenty pieces.
My back o' t'other side—ah, my back, my back!
50 Beshrew your heart for sending me about
To catch my death with jauncing up and down!

**Juliet.** I' faith, I am sorry that thou art not well.
Sweet, sweet, sweet nurse, tell me, what says my love?

---

**21–22** The nurse teases Juliet by putting on a sad face as if the news were bad.

**25–26 give me . . . I had:** Leave me alone for a while. I ache all over because of the running back and forth I've been doing.

**COMMON CORE L 4**

**Language Coach**

**Multiple Meanings** The word *stay* has something other than its usual meaning in line 29. What do you think it means? (Hint: The expression "What haste!" means "What a hurry you're in!")

**36 I'll . . . circumstance:** I'll wait for the details.

**38 simple:** foolish.

**50–51 Beshrew . . . down:** Curse you for making me endanger my health by running around. *Considering the nurse's feelings for Juliet, do you think this is really an angry curse? Explain.*

---

**DIFFERENTIATED INSTRUCTION**

**FOR ENGLISH LANGUAGE LEARNERS**

**Task Support** Have students read the marginal note and question for lines 50–51. Urge students to think of the tone of the characters' conversation thus far. *Possible answer: No, this curse is not sincerely angry. The nurse is thrilled to bring Juliet the message, but at the moment, she is having a bit of fun by making Juliet wait.*

**Vocabulary Support** Shakespeare often uses elliptical language. Work with students to add the "missing" words to these lines. *See boldfacing in each possible answer.*

- *Line 23, **Possible answer:** If **the news be good**, . . .*

- *Line 27, **Possible answer:** . . . and I **had** thy news.*

- *Line 71, **Possible answer:** . . . I must **hie [go]** another way.*

**Language Coach** **COMMON CORE L 4**

**Multiple Meanings** *Possible answer: Stay means "wait."* Point out that the nurse is teasing Juliet and may not really be so out of breath she cannot give the news. Juliet suspects as much (lines 31–34) .

**Nurse.** Your love says, like an honest gentleman, and a courteous,
55 and a kind, and a handsome, and, I warrant, a virtuous—Where
is your mother?

**Juliet.** Where is my mother? Why, she is within.
Where should she be? How oddly thou repliest!
"Your love says, like an honest gentleman,
60 'Where is your mother?'"

**Nurse.**                  O God's Lady dear!
Are you so hot? Marry come up, I trow.
Is this the poultice for my aching bones?
Hence forward do your messages yourself.

**Juliet.** Here's such a coil! Come, what says Romeo?

65 **Nurse.** Have you got leave to go to shrift today?

**Juliet.** I have.

**Nurse.** Then hie you hence to Friar Laurence' cell;
There stays a husband to make you a wife.
Now comes the wanton blood up in your cheeks:
70 They'll be in scarlet straight at any news.
Hie you to church; I must another way,
To fetch a ladder, by the which your love
Must climb a bird's nest soon when it is dark.
I am the drudge, and toil in your delight;
75 But you shall bear the burden soon at night.
Go; I'll to dinner; hie you to the cell.

**Juliet.** Hie to high fortune! Honest nurse, farewell.

[*Exeunt.*]

## SCENE 6   *Friar Laurence's cell.*

*Friar Laurence cautions Romeo to be more sensible in his love for Juliet. When
she arrives, the two confess their love to each other and prepare to be married
by Friar Laurence.*

[*Enter* Friar Laurence *and* Romeo.]

**Friar Laurence.** So smile the heavens upon this holy act
That after-hours with sorrow chide us not!

**Romeo.** Amen, amen! But come what sorrow can,
It cannot countervail the exchange of joy
5 That one short minute gives me in her sight.
Do thou but close our hands with holy words,
Then love-devouring death do what he dare—
It is enough I may but call her mine.

**61–62 Marry . . . bones:** Control yourself!
Is this the treatment I get for my pain?

**64 coil:** fuss.

**67–68 Then hie . . . a wife:** Then go
quickly to Friar Laurence's cell, where
Romeo is waiting to marry you.

**71–73** The nurse will get the ladder that
Romeo will use to climb to Juliet's room
after they are married.

**1–2 So smile . . . us not:** May heaven
so bless this act that we won't regret
it in the future (**after-hours**).

**4 countervail:** outweigh.

---

**REVISIT THE BIG QUESTION**
## Is **LOVE** stronger than **HATE?**

**Discuss** How will Scene 6 use love to advance
the plot of the play? *Students may suggest that
as Romeo and Juliet exchange vows of love and
are married, they take the story to the next level.
Once they are joined by the Church, it seems (for
now) that the families will have to settle their
feud.*

### TIERED DISCUSSION PROMPTS

Use these prompts to help students see how,
in lines 1–9, Shakespeare infuses a joyful moment with foreshadowing about the play's
ending:

**Connect** Have you ever worried about the
wisdom of a decision? Why, then, do you
think that Friar Laurence sounds worried?
*Students may recall worrying about an
impulsive decision. Friar Laurence is probably
concerned that his agreement to marry the
couple may not work out positively.*

**Analyze** What words or phrases in Romeo's
speech suggest a tragic future? *Possible
answer: "sorrow" (line 3), "one short minute"
(line 5), and "love-devouring death" (line 7)*

**Evaluate** Do you think Friar Laurence understands that the marriage could lead to tragedy? Does Romeo understand? Explain your
answers. *Possible answers: Friar Laurence
is wise enough to realize that the marriage
could lead to great sorrow (line 2). Romeo
does not have enough life experience to give
serious consideration to tragedy; in fact, he
dares death to attack his marriage (line 7).*

---

### FOR STRUGGLING READERS

**Preview** Call on a volunteer to read aloud
the Scene 6 synopsis. Have students use a
three-column chart to record a statement
that each character might say to summarize
his or her role in this scene.

| Friar Laurence | Romeo | Juliet |
|---|---|---|
| Romeo should be more moderate in his love. | I am passionately in love with Juliet. | I want to marry Romeo. |

##  TRAGEDY

*Possible answer:* *Romeo will not take the friar's advice. Shakespearean tragedies end in death for the main characters, so if moderation is the key to a long love (line 14), Romeo will not be moderate.*

---

**Friar Laurence.** These violent delights have violent ends
10 And in their triumph die, like fire and powder,
Which, as they kiss, consume. The sweetest honey
Is loathsome in his own deliciousness
And in the taste confounds the appetite.
Therefore love moderately: long love doth so;
15 Too swift arrives as tardy as too slow.
[*Enter* Juliet.]
Here comes the lady. O, so light a foot
Will ne'er wear out the everlasting flint.
A lover may bestride the gossamer
That idles in the wanton summer air,
20 And yet not fall; so light is vanity.
**Juliet.** Good even to my ghostly confessor.
**Friar Laurence.** Romeo shall thank thee, daughter, for us both.
**Juliet.** As much to him, else is his thanks too much.

> **Romeo.** Ah, Juliet, if the measure of thy joy
> 25 Be heaped like mine, and that thy skill be more
> To blazon it, then sweeten with thy breath
> This neighbor air, and let rich music's tongue
> Unfold the imagined happiness that both
> Receive in either by this dear encounter.
> 30 **Juliet.** Conceit, more rich in matter than in words,
> Brags of his substance, not of ornament.
> They are but beggars that can count their worth;
> But my true love is grown to such excess
> I cannot sum up sum of half my wealth.
> 35 **Friar Laurence.** Come, come with me, and we will make short work;
> For, by your leaves, you shall not stay alone
> Till Holy Church incorporate two in one.

[*Exeunt.*]

**9–15 These … slow:** The friar compares Romeo's passion to gunpowder and the fire that ignites it—both are destroyed—then to honey, whose sweetness can destroy the appetite. He reminds Romeo to practice moderation in love.

 **TRAGEDY**
Consider what you know about Shakespearean tragedy. Do you think Romeo will take the advice Friar Laurence gives him in lines 9–15? Explain.

**18–20 A lover … vanity:** A lover can walk across a spider's web (**gossamer**) without falling.

**23 as much to him:** I give the same greeting to Romeo that he offers to me.

**24–29 if the measure … encounter:** If you are as happy as I am and have more skill to proclaim it, then sweeten the air by singing of our happiness to the world.

**30–31 Conceit … ornament:** True understanding (**conceit**) needs no words.

④ **Targeted Passage**

COMMON CORE RL 4

 **PARADOX**
A **paradox** is a seemingly contradictory statement that nevertheless expresses a truth. How is the thought expressed by Friar Laurence in line 37 a paradox? Be sure to explain the truth that his statement reveals.

---

##  PARADOX

*Possible answer:* *Although two people are joined in marriage, they become like one person. A married couple, although they are two separate people, usually act together and share most things.*

Have students discuss why a paradox might be a useful tool when conveying information to readers. Suggest that students think about the contradiction it highlights.

---

## ACT TWO WRAP–UP

**READ WITH A PURPOSE** Now that students have finished reading the selection, have them discuss the foundations of the lovers' relationship: is it strong enough to withstand setbacks? *Possible answer: No; they are too young and immature to survive the problems they will face.*

⭐ **CRITIQUE** Ask students what aspects of the play they have found to be the most realistic and why. Then ask them what aspects of the play they have found the most difficult to believe or imagine. Have them provide examples to explain their responses.

---

## DIFFERENTIATED INSTRUCTION

### FOR STRUGGLING READERS

④ **Targeted Passage [Lines 24–37]**
This passage presents the moment before the wedding (which takes place offstage).

- How does Romeo want Juliet to express her joy? (lines 26–29)

- What does Juliet say she cannot "sum up"? Why? (lines 33–34)

- According to Friar Laurence, what power will join Romeo and Juliet? Why is this an important statement? (line 37)

## Comprehension

1. **Recall** Who challenges Romeo to a duel, and why?

2. **Recall** What important message from Romeo does the nurse bring to Juliet?

3. **Clarify** Why does Friar Laurence agree to marry Romeo and Juliet despite his reservations? Explain what he hopes this marriage will accomplish.

## Text Analysis

4. **Reading Shakespearean Drama** Examine the events you recorded in your chart as you read Act Two. Which events seem most crucial in escalating the **conflicts** in the plot? What **theme** seems to be emerging? Explain your answers.

5. **Make Inferences About Character Motives** Why do Romeo and Juliet rush to get married after declaring their love? Support your inference with evidence from the text. Then explain whether you think the young lovers get married too soon, and why or why not.

6. **Analyze Soliloquy and Aside** Identify at least one soliloquy and one aside in Act Two and record them in a chart like the one shown. Complete the chart by explaining what each example reveals about the character speaking.

| Scene and Lines | Character Who Speaks | Soliloquy or Aside? | What Is Revealed? |
|---|---|---|---|
| Scene 2, lines 1–25 | Romeo | | |

7. **Analyze Character Development** Compare Romeo's behavior before he meets Juliet with his behavior after they declare their love for each other. What do you learn about Romeo from the change in his behavior?

## Text Criticism

8. **Author's Style** Shakespeare is often praised for his masterly use of **figurative language,** or language that communicates ideas beyond the ordinary, literal meaning of the words. Find two examples of particularly striking figurative language in Act Two and discuss what makes each example effective.

COMMON CORE

**RL 2** Determine a theme of a text. **RL 3** Analyze how complex characters develop over the course of a text, interact with other characters, and advance the plot or develop the theme. **RL 4** Determine the figurative meaning of words and phrases. **RL 10** Read and comprehend dramas. **L 5a** Interpret figures of speech and analyze their role in the text.

# Practice and Apply

For preliminary support of post-reading questions, use these copy masters:

**R RESOURCE MANAGER—Copy Masters**
Reading Check p. 37
Shakespearean Drama p. 35
Question Support p. 38

Additional selection questions are provided for teachers on page 29.

## ANSWERS

### Comprehension

1. *Tybalt challenges Romeo to a duel because he is angry that Romeo came to Capulet's party.*

2. *Juliet will meet Romeo at Friar Laurence's cell, where they will marry.*

3. *Friar Laurence hopes that the marriage will mend the feud between the families.*

### Text Analysis

COMMON CORE RL 2, RL 3, RL 4, RL 10, L 5a

*Possible answers:*

4. **COMMON CORE FOCUS** *Reading Shakespearean Drama Romeo and Juliet secretly marry, making the situation more tense. Tybalt challenges Romeo; their conflict escalates into a possible fight. An emerging theme is that love can conquer all.*

5. *Students might say that the lovers rush to marry because they are swept away by love, that their families' feud prevents them from courting in the usual manner, or that they fear being discovered by their parents. Students may offer varying responses to the second part of the question.*

6. **COMMON CORE FOCUS** *Analyze Soliloquy and Aside Scene 2, lines 1–25 is a soliloquy in which Romeo reveals his love for Juliet. Scene 2, line 37 is an aside in which Romeo wonders whether he should speak to Juliet or hear more of her private thoughts.*

7. *Before Romeo meets Juliet, he is moody, pessimistic, and passive. After declaring his love, he is joyful and positive, and he takes action. This change in behavior suggests that Romeo is easily moved by his emotions and is quick to change his mind.*

### Text Criticism

*Possible answer:*

8. *In Scene 2, line 121, Juliet compares her love for Romeo to a flower bud. It is an effective comparison because their love is new and full of hope, just as a bud is new growth that holds out hope of a beautiful flower. In Scene 5, line 43, the nurse says that Romeo is gentle as a lamb. It is an effective comparison because it means more than it intends: like a sacrificial lamb, Romeo ultimately will lose his life.*

# Assess and Reteach

### Assess

**DIAGNOSTIC AND SELECTION TESTS**
Selection Test A pp. 279–280
Selection Test B/C pp. 281–282

**Interactive Selection Test** on **thinkcentral.com**

### Reteach

**Level Up Online Tutorials** on **thinkcentral.com**

**Reteaching Worksheets** on **thinkcentral.com**
Literature Lessons 25, 26, 35, 38

# Practice and Apply

## READ WITH A PURPOSE

*Help students set a purpose for reading. Tell them to look for ways other characters' attitudes toward Juliet change during the act.*

## Get Into the Act

### SUMMARY

As Act Three begins, Capulets and Montagues clash again. Tybalt kills Mercutio; enraged, Romeo kills Tybalt. Prince Escalus banishes Romeo, but Friar Laurence promises that he will try to make things right and bring Romeo home again. Meanwhile, the Capulets grieve for Tybalt, and Capulet promises Count Paris that Juliet will marry him in three days. When Juliet refuses, he threatens to disown her.

### READING STRATEGY

■ *Model the Skill:* **PREDICT**

Point out to students that authors, including playwrights, often vary the types of scenes that follow each other; a serious scene followed by a comic one, for example. Review the fact that Act Two ended with a scene of love and happiness. Ask students to make a prediction about the type of scene to which Shakespeare will take us next. ***Possible answer:*** *Shakespeare will introduce a contrasting scene—something that reminds us of the family feud and the challenges that the newlyweds face.*

## Resources for Act Three

---

# Act Three

## SCENE 1 *A public place.*

*Act Two ends with the joyful Romeo and Juliet secretly married. Their happiness, however, is about to end abruptly. In this scene, Mercutio, Benvolio, and Romeo meet Tybalt on the street. Tybalt insults Romeo, but Romeo, who has just returned from his wedding, remains calm. Mercutio, on the other hand, is furious with Tybalt, and they begin to fight. As Romeo tries to separate them, Tybalt stabs Mercutio, who later dies. Romeo then challenges Tybalt, kills him, and flees. The prince arrives and demands an explanation. He announces that Romeo will be killed if he does not leave Verona immediately.*

[*Enter* Mercutio, Benvolio, Page, *and* Servants.]

**Benvolio.** I pray thee, good Mercutio, let's retire.
The day is hot, the Capulets abroad,
And if we meet, we shall not scape a brawl,
For now, these hot days, is the mad blood stirring.

5 **Mercutio.** Thou art like one of those fellows that, when he enters the confines of a tavern, claps me his sword upon the table and says "God send me no need of thee!" and by the operation of the second cup draws him on the drawer, when indeed there is no need.

10 **Benvolio.** Am I like such a fellow?

**Mercutio.** Come, come, thou art as hot a Jack in thy mood as any in Italy; and as soon moved to be moody, and as soon moody to be moved.

**Benvolio.** And what to?

15 **Mercutio.** Nay an there were two such, we should have none shortly, for one would kill the other. Thou! why, thou wilt quarrel with a man that hath a hair more or a hair less in his beard than thou hast. Thou wilt quarrel with a man for cracking nuts, having no other reason but because thou hast hazel eyes. 20 What eye but such an eye would spy out such a quarrel? Thy head is as full of quarrels as an egg is full of meat; and yet thy head hath been beaten as addle as an egg for quarreling. Thou hast quarreled with a man for coughing in the street, because he hath wakened thy dog that hath lain asleep in the sun. Didst 25 thou not fall out with a tailor for wearing his new doublet before Easter? with another for tying his new shoes with old riband? And yet thou wilt tutor me from quarreling!

**3–4 we shall ... stirring:** We shall not avoid a fight, since the heat makes people ill-tempered.

**7–8 by the ... drawer:** feeling the effects of a second drink, is ready to fight (**draw on**) the waiter who's pouring the drinks (**drawer**).

**12–13 as soon moved ... to be moved:** as likely to get angry and start a fight.

**15–27** Mercutio teases his friend by insisting that Benvolio is quick to pick a fight, though everyone knows that Benvolio is gentle and peace loving.

**25 doublet:** jacket.
**26 riband:** ribbon or laces.

Mercutio and Tybalt duel in the 2004 coproduction of the Chicago Shakespeare Theater and Second City.

---

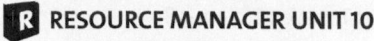

See resources on the **Teacher One Stop DVD-ROM** *and on* **thinkcentral.com**.

**R** **RESOURCE MANAGER UNIT 10**
Plan and Teach, pp. 39–42
Summary pp. 43–44†‡*
Text Analysis and Reading
  Skill, pp. 45–48†*

**DIAGNOSTIC AND SELECTION TESTS**
Selection Tests, pp. 283–286

**BEST PRACTICES TOOLKIT**
Plot Diagram, p. D10
Problem and Solution Charts,
  p. B20

**INTERACTIVE READER**

**ADAPTED INTERACTIVE READER**

**ELL ADAPTED INTERACTIVE READER**

**TECHNOLOGY**
- **Teacher One Stop DVD-ROM**
- **Student One Stop DVD-ROM**
- **PowerNotes DVD-ROM**
- **Audio Anthology CD**
- **Audio Tutor CD**
- **ExamView Test Generator** on the **Teacher One Stop**

### Video Trailer

**THINK**central

Go to **thinkcentral.com** to preview the **Video Trailer** introducing this selection. Other features that support the selection include
- **PowerNotes** presentation
- **ThinkAloud** models to enhance comprehension

---

* Resources for Differentiation  † Also in Spanish  ‡ In Haitian Creole and Vietnamese

## Analyze Visuals

**Activity** What elements of this production's stagecraft reveal that the audience is intended to realize that this duel is meant to be a grim moment in the play? *Possible answer: The literal darkness of both the set and the costumes suggests that this is a dark moment, figuratively speaking, in the plot of Shakespeare's narrative.*

**REVISIT THE BIG QUESTION**

## Is LOVE stronger than HATE?

**Discuss** Based on lines 1–4, what will be the focus of Scene 1: love or hate? Explain your answer. *Possible answer: Hate will probably be the focus of Scene 1. Benvolio speaks of a possible brawl with the Capulets (lines 2–3) and comments upon the "mad blood stirring" on this day (line 4).*

## BACKGROUND

**Shakespeare and Duels** The weapon used most often for duels in Shakespeare's time was the rapier, as shown in the photograph. A rapier's pointed tip frequently meant a fatal outcome in duels. Nevertheless, Elizabethans believed that justice could be determined by the outcome of a duel and that rejecting a challenge to a duel was shameful. In Scene 1, Tybalt's challenge addresses the wrong that he felt took place when the Montagues came, uninvited, to the Capulet party. By rejecting the challenge, Romeo shames his family and friends—a fact that helps to explain why Mercutio rises to Tybalt's challenge.

**TRAGEDY**

*Possible answer: Tybalt is largely responsible: He makes the initial challenge, and he calls Romeo a villain (line 56). Mercutio is largely responsible: He goads Tybalt (lines 35–50); and after Romeo tries to avoid a fight, Mercutio draws his sword first (line 70).*

 *Model the Skill:* **CHARACTER**

Review the cast of characters (page 1036). Explain that both Juliet and Tybalt are Capulets and that they are cousins. Remind students, too, that Romeo married Juliet at the end of Act Two.

*Possible answer: Romeo's motive for not wanting to fight Tybalt is that he has married Juliet, Tybalt's cousin. He does not want conflict with the Capulets, to whom he is now related. Juliet, the nurse, and Friar Laurence are the only other characters who know this reason.*

---

**Benvolio.** An I were so apt to quarrel as thou art, any man should buy the fee simple of my life for an hour and a quarter.

30 **Mercutio.** The fee simple? O simple!

[*Enter* Tybalt *and others.*]

**Benvolio.** By my head, here come the Capulets. **Ⓐ**

**Mercutio.** By my heel, I care not.

**Tybalt.** Follow me close, for I will speak to them. Gentlemen, good den. A word with one of you.

35 **Mercutio.** And but one word with one of us? Couple it with something; make it a word and a blow.

**Tybalt.** You shall find me apt enough to that, sir, an you will give me occasion.

**Mercutio.** Could you not take some occasion without giving?

40 **Tybalt.** Mercutio, thou consortest with Romeo.

**Mercutio.** Consort? What, dost thou make us minstrels? An thou make minstrels of us, look to hear nothing but discords. Here's my fiddlestick; here's that shall make you dance. Zounds, consort!

45 **Benvolio.** We talk here in the public haunt of men.
Either withdraw unto some private place
And reason coldly of your grievances,
Or else depart. Here all eyes gaze on us.

**Mercutio.** Men's eyes were made to look, and let them gaze.
50 I will not budge for no man's pleasure, I.

[*Enter* Romeo.]

**Tybalt.** Well, peace be with you, sir. Here comes my man.

**Mercutio.** But I'll be hanged, sir, if he wear your livery.
Marry, go before to field, he'll be your follower!
Your worship in that sense may call him man.

55 **Tybalt.** Romeo, the love I bear thee can afford
No better term than this: thou art a villain.

**Romeo.** Tybalt, the reason that I have to love thee
Doth much excuse the appertaining rage
To such a greeting. Villain am I none.
60 Therefore farewell. I see thou knowst me not. **Ⓑ**

**Tybalt.** Boy, this shall not excuse the injuries
That thou hast done me; therefore turn and draw.

**Romeo.** I do protest I never injured thee,
But love thee better than thou canst devise

---

**28–29 An I...quarter:** If I picked fights as quickly as you do, anybody could own me for the smallest amount of money.

**Ⓐ TRAGEDY**
As you read lines 31–79, think about the play's mounting **conflict.** Ask yourself: Who is responsible for starting this sword fight? Cite evidence to support your viewpoint.

**40–44 consortest:** keep company with. Tybalt means "You are friends with Romeo." Mercutio pretends to misunderstand him, assuming that Tybalt is insulting him by calling Romeo and him a **consort,** a group of traveling musicians. He then refers to his sword as his **fiddlestick,** the bow for a fiddle.

**45–48** *What does Benvolio want Tybalt and Mercutio to do?*

**51–54** When Romeo enters, Mercutio again pretends to misunderstand Tybalt. By **my man,** Tybalt means "the man I'm looking for." Mercutio takes it to mean "my servant." (**Livery** is a servant's uniform.) He assures Tybalt that the only place Romeo would follow him is to the dueling field.

**57–59** I forgive your anger because I have reason to love you.

**Ⓑ CHARACTER**
What **motive** does Romeo have for not wanting to fight Tybalt? Who else knows about this motive?

**61 boy:** an insulting term of address.

---

## DIFFERENTIATED INSTRUCTION

### FOR STRUGGLING READERS
**Inverted Word Order** Explain that in some lines, Shakespeare places the negative word at the end of the sentence. To illustrate, have students read lines 32 and 59–60 and locate the words "not" and "none". Call on volunteers to restate the lines, moving the negative to a more traditional place. *Possible answer: By my heel, I don't care (line 32); I am no villain. / Therefore farewell. I see you do not know me (lines 59–60).*

### FOR ENGLISH LANGUAGE LEARNERS
**Task Support** Point out the marginal question for lines 45–48. Remind students that Benvolio showed himself to be a peacemaker in the play's opening scene. *Possible answer: Benvolio wants Tybalt and Mercutio either to go and settle their quarrel privately, without violence, or to go their separate ways.*

65 Till thou shalt know the reason of my love;
And so, good Capulet, which name I tender
As dearly as mine own, be satisfied.

**Mercutio.** O calm, dishonorable, vile submission!
*Alla stoccata* carries it away.

[*draws*]

70 Tybalt, you ratcatcher, will you walk?

**Tybalt.** What wouldst thou have with me?

**Mercutio.** Good King of Cats, nothing but one of your nine lives.
That I mean to make bold withal, and, as you shall use me
hereafter, dry-beat the rest of the eight. Will you pluck your

75 sword out of his pilcher by the ears? Make haste, lest mine be
about your ears ere it be out.

**Tybalt.** I am for you.

[*draws*]

**Romeo.** Gentle Mercutio, put thy rapier up.

**Mercutio.** Come, sir, your *passado!*

[*They fight.*]

80 **Romeo.** Draw, Benvolio; beat down their weapons.
Gentlemen, for shame! forbear this outrage!
Tybalt, Mercutio, the Prince expressly hath
Forbid this bandying in Verona streets.
Hold, Tybalt! Good Mercutio!

[Tybalt, *under Romeo's arm, thrusts* Mercutio *in, and flies with
his* Men.]

**Mercutio.** I am hurt.

85 A plague o' both your houses! I am sped.
Is he gone and hath nothing?

**Benvolio.** What, art thou hurt?

**Mercutio.** Ay, ay, a scratch, a scratch. Marry, 'tis enough.
Where is my page? Go, villain, fetch a surgeon.

[*Exit* Page.]

**Romeo.** Courage, man. The hurt cannot be much.

90 **Mercutio.** No, 'tis not so deep as a well, nor so wide as a church
door; but 'tis enough, 'twill serve. Ask for me tomorrow, and you
shall find me a grave man. I am peppered, I warrant, for this
world. A plague o' both your houses! Zounds, a dog, a rat, a
mouse, a cat, to scratch a man to death! A braggart, a rogue, a

**66 tender:** cherish.

**68–70** Mercutio assumes that Romeo is afraid to fight. *Alla stoccata* is a move used in sword fighting; Mercutio is suggesting that Tybalt has won the battle of words with Romeo. Mercutio then dares Tybalt to step aside and fight (**walk**).

**72–74 nothing but ... eight:** I intend to take one of your nine lives (as a cat supposedly has) and give a beating to the other eight.

① **Targeted Passage**

**79 passado:** a sword-fighting maneuver.

**80–84** Romeo wants Benvolio to help him stop the fight. They are able to hold back Mercutio.

**83 bandying:** fighting.

**85 A plague ... sped:** I curse both the Montagues and the Capulets. I am destroyed.

**90–96** Even as he lies dying, Mercutio continues to joke and make nasty remarks about Tybalt. He makes a pun on the word *grave*.

95  villain, that fights by the book of arithmetic! Why the devil came
    you between us? I was hurt under your arm.

  **Romeo.** I thought all for the best.

  **Mercutio.** Help me into some house, Benvolio,
    Or I shall faint. A plague o' both your houses! **C**
100 They have made worms' meat of me. I have it,
    And soundly too. Your houses!

  [*Exit, supported by* Benvolio.]

  **Romeo.** This gentleman, the Prince's near ally,
    My very friend, hath got this mortal hurt
    In my behalf—my reputation stained
105 With Tybalt's slander—Tybalt, that an hour
    Hath been my kinsman, O sweet Juliet,
    Thy beauty hath made me effeminate
    And in my temper softened valor's steel!

  [*Reenter* Benvolio.]

  **Benvolio.** O Romeo, Romeo, brave Mercutio's dead!
110 That gallant spirit hath aspired the clouds,
    Which too untimely here did scorn the earth.

  **Romeo.** This day's black fate on mo days doth depend;
    This but begins the woe others must end.

  [*Reenter* Tybalt.]

  **Benvolio.** Here comes the furious Tybalt back again.

115 **Romeo.** Alive in triumph, and Mercutio slain?
    Away to heaven respective lenity,
    And fire-eyed fury be my conduct now!
    Now, Tybalt, take the "villain" back again
    That late thou gavest me, for Mercutio's soul
120 Is but a little way above our heads,
    Staying for thine to keep him company.
    Either thou or I, or both, must go with him. **D**

  **Tybalt.** Thou, wretched boy, that didst consort him here,
    Shalt with him hence.

  **Romeo.**                    This shall determine that.

  [*They fight.* Tybalt *falls.*]

125 **Benvolio.** Romeo, away, be gone!
    The citizens are up, and Tybalt slain.
    Stand not amazed. The Prince will doom thee death
    If thou art taken. Hence, be gone, away!

## DIFFERENTIATED INSTRUCTION

**Romeo.** O, I am fortune's fool!

**Benvolio.** Why dost thou stay?

[*Exit* Romeo.]

[*Enter* Citizens.]

130 **Citizen.** Which way ran he that killed Mercutio?
Tybalt, that murderer, which way ran he?

**Benvolio.** There lies that Tybalt.

**Citizen.** Up, sir, go with me.
I charge thee in the Prince's name obey.

[*Enter* Prince *with his* Attendants, Montague, Capulet, *their* Wives, *and others.*]

**Prince.** Where are the vile beginners of this fray?

135 **Benvolio.** O noble Prince, I can discover all
The unlucky manage of this fatal brawl.
There lies the man, slain by young Romeo,
That slew thy kinsman, brave Mercutio.

**Lady Capulet.** Tybalt, my cousin! O my brother's child!

140 O Prince! O cousin! O husband! O, the blood is spilled
Of my dear kinsman! Prince, as thou art true,
For blood of ours shed blood of Montague.
O cousin, cousin!

**Prince.** Benvolio, who began this bloody fray?

145 **Benvolio.** Tybalt, here slain, whom Romeo's hand did slay.
Romeo, that spoke him fair, bid him bethink
How nice the quarrel was, and urged withal
Your high displeasure. All this—uttered
With gentle breath, calm look, knees humbly bowed—

150 Could not take truce with the unruly spleen
Of Tybalt deaf to peace, but that he tilts
With piercing steel at bold Mercutio's breast;
Who, all as hot, turns deadly point to point,
And, with a martial scorn, with one hand beats

155 Cold death aside and with the other sends
It back to Tybalt, whose dexterity
Retorts it. Romeo he cries aloud,
"Hold, friends! friends, part!" and swifter than his tongue,
His agile arm beats down their fatal points,

160 And 'twixt them rushes; underneath whose arm
An envious thrust from Tybalt hit the life

---

**129 I am fortune's fool:** Fate has made a fool of me.

**135–136** Benvolio says he can tell (**discover**) what happened.

**141–142 as thou ... Montague:** If your word is good, you will sentence Romeo to death for killing a Capulet.

**146–147 Romeo, that ... was:** Romeo talked calmly (**fair**) and told Tybalt to think how trivial (**nice**) the argument was.

**150–151 could ... peace:** could not quiet the anger of Tybalt, who would not listen to pleas for peace.

**156–157 whose dexterity retorts it:** whose skill returns it.

**159–160 his agile ... rushes:** He rushed between them and pushed down their swords.

---

---

**REVISIT THE BIG QUESTION**

## Is **LOVE** stronger than **HATE?**

**Discuss** According to Benvolio's story, in lines 145–168, in what sense did hate prove stronger than love in the encounter with Tybalt? *Possible answer: Romeo and Benvolio, as peacemakers, tried to stop Tybalt. However, Tybalt's hate and Mercutio's goading enflamed the conflict between the families and caused the death of Mercutio. Only then was Romeo's love for peace overcome by hate for Tybalt.*

## BACKGROUND

**The "Unruly Spleen"** Why does Benvolio blame Tybalt's spleen for his refusal to listen to an appeal for peace (lines 150–151)? Elizabethans considered the spleen an important part of the body. Drawing upon ideas from classical medicine, they believed that the spleen contained and controlled "black bile," a fluid (called a humor) that caused bad temper and violent outbursts. If the spleen was not working properly—if it was "unruly," as Benvolio says—black bile could control a person's behavior. Although these beliefs would not have excused Tybalt's actions, they would have helped to explain them.

---

**FOR STRUGGLING READERS**

**Explore Motivation** Students will grasp this scene better if you help them connect each character's emotions with the events that inspired them. For example, Lady Capulet is very sad about Tybalt's death and is angry with Romeo. Benvolio is very sad about Mercutio's death, but he tries to be honest in his account of the events. Prince Escalus is very angry about the violence in the city and the violation of his decree.

**Ⓔ TRAGEDY**

*Possible answer: Lady Capulet thinks that Benvolio is lying because she cannot imagine that one Montague would endanger another by telling the truth. Her accusation (lines 169–170) can be paraphrased in this way: "Benvolio is related to the Montagues. His love for his family makes him tell lies about what happened." Lady Capulet begs the Prince to execute Romeo for killing Tybalt (line 174).*

## Analyze Visuals

**Activity** What do the opulent scarlet costumes worn by Lady Capulet and Tybalt indicate about the Capulet family? Why do you think the director of the production made this costuming choice? *Possible answer: The costumes indicate the Capulet family's high social status and wealth. The director probably wanted costumes that immediately let the audience know that the Capulets were important, influential people in Verona.*

Of stout Mercutio, and then Tybalt fled,
But by-and-by comes back to Romeo,
Who had but newly entertained revenge,
165 And to't they go like lightning; for, ere I
Could draw to part them, was stout Tybalt slain;
And, as he fell, did Romeo turn and fly.
This is the truth, or let Benvolio die.

**Lady Capulet.** He is a kinsman to the Montague;
170 Affection makes him false, he speaks not true.
Some twenty of them fought in this black strife,
And all those twenty could but kill one life.
I beg for justice, which thou, Prince, must give.
Romeo slew Tybalt; Romeo must not live. Ⓔ

175 **Prince.** Romeo slew him; he slew Mercutio.
Who now the price of his dear blood doth owe?

**Montague.** Not Romeo, Prince; he was Mercutio's friend;
His fault concludes but what the law should end,
The life of Tybalt.

**164** entertained: thought of.

**Ⓔ TRAGEDY**
Why does Lady Capulet think Benvolio is lying? **Paraphrase** the accusation she makes, and explain what she begs the prince to do.

**178–179** Romeo is guilty only of avenging Mercutio's death, which the law would have done anyway.

Lady Capulet mourns Tybalt in the Royal Shakespeare Company's 2004 production.

## DIFFERENTIATED INSTRUCTION

**FOR STRUGGLING READERS**
**Inverted Word Order** Point out lines 166, 167, and 176, in which Shakespeare alters the placement of the verb in the sentence. Have students read the lines aloud, changing the order to suit a modern ear. *Possible answer: stout Tybalt was slain; Romeo did turn and fly; Who now owes the price of his dear blood?*

**FOR ENGLISH LANGUAGE LEARNERS**
**Concept Support** Help students compare the families' attempts to sway Prince Escalus. Discuss how Lady Capulet appeals to his sense of honor (lines 142–143) and stretches the truth (lines 171–172) as she cries for the death of Romeo, whereas Montague tries to justify Romeo's actions by arguing that he merely carried out the sentence that the prince himself would have decreed against Tybalt (lines 178–179).

**Prince.**  And for that offense

180 Immediately we do exile him hence.
I have an interest in your hate's proceeding,
My blood for your rude brawls doth lie a-bleeding;
But I'll amerce you with so strong a fine
That you shall all repent the loss of mine.

185 I will be deaf to pleading and excuses;
Nor tears nor prayers shall purchase out abuses.
Therefore use none. Let Romeo hence in haste,
Else, when he is found, that hour is his last.
Bear hence this body, and attend our will.

190 Mercy but murders, pardoning those that kill.

[*Exeunt.*]

## SCENE 2   *Capulet's orchard.*

*The scene begins with Juliet impatiently waiting for night to come so that Romeo can climb to her bedroom on the rope ladder. Suddenly the nurse enters with the terrible news of Tybalt's death and Romeo's banishment. Juliet mourns for the loss of her cousin and her husband and threatens to kill herself. To calm her, the nurse promises to find Romeo and bring him to Juliet before he leaves Verona.*

[*Enter* Juliet *alone.*]

**Juliet.** Gallop apace, you fiery-footed steeds,
Toward Phoebus' lodging! Such a wagoner
As Phaëton would whip you to the West,
And bring in cloudy night immediately.

5 Spread thy close curtain, love-performing night,
That runaways' eyes may wink, and Romeo
Leap to these arms, untalked of and unseen. **F**
Lovers can see to do their amorous rites
By their own beauties; or, if love be blind,

10 It best agrees with night. Come, civil night,
Thou sober-suited matron, all in black,
And learn me how to lose a winning match,
Played for a pair of stainless maidenhoods.
Hood my unmanned blood bating in my cheeks

15 With thy black mantle; till strange love, grown bold,
Think true love acted simple modesty.
Come, night; come, Romeo, come; thou day in night;
For thou wilt lie upon the wings of night
Whiter than new snow on a raven's back.

20 Come, gentle night; come, loving, black-browed night;
Give me my Romeo; and, when he shall die,
Take him and cut him out in little stars,

---

**179–190** The prince banishes Romeo from Verona. He angrily points out that one of his own relatives is dead because of the feud and declares that Romeo will be put to death unless he flees immediately.

**COMMON CORE** L 4c

### Language Coach

**Etymology** The word *amerce* (line 183), meaning "punish," is rare today. It comes from the Old French phrase *a merci,* which means "completely in the power of." What common English word in line 190 is also related to this French expression? Use a dictionary to check your answer.

**2–3 Phoebus:** Apollo, the god of the sun; **Phaëton:** a mortal who lost control of the sun's chariot when he drove it too fast.

**F ALLUSION**
Paraphrase lines 1–7. Why does Juliet allude to Phoebus and Phaëton in this **soliloquy?**

**14–16 Hood . . . modesty:** Juliet asks that the darkness hide her blushing cheeks on her wedding night.

ROMEO AND JULIET: ACT THREE, SCENE 2   **1095**

---

**REVISIT THE BIG QUESTION**

## Is **LOVE** stronger than **HATE**?

**Discuss** How do love and hate play a role in the prince's decision to banish Romeo in lines 179–184? ***Possible answer:*** *The prince's love of his cousin Mercutio demands he take action against those involved, hence his interest in allowing "hate's proceeding" (line 181). Still, the prince hates violence, and so does not call for Romeo's execution, as others have urged him to do.*

**TEXT ANALYSIS**          COMMON CORE L 3

### F ALLUSION

***Possible answer:*** *Paraphrase of lines 1–7: "Ride quickly, you fast horses, to the house of Phoebus. If only Phaëton were driving, you would be faster, and night would come sooner. Bring darkness for love, so that Romeo can come to me without having anyone see him." By alluding to Phoebus and Phaëton, Juliet is implying that divine powers should be on the lovers' side.*

**IF STUDENTS NEED HELP . . .** Help them paraphrase the passage, one line at a time. Review the marginal note, which points out that both Phoebus and Phaëton are godlike. Then ask the Text Analysis question.

---

**FOR STRUGGLING READERS**
**Preview** Call on a volunteer to read aloud the italicized scene synopsis for the class. Help students complete a Plot Diagram to track the events in Scene 2.

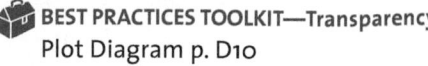 **BEST PRACTICES TOOLKIT—Transparency** Plot Diagram p. D10

**FOR ENGLISH LANGUAGE LEARNERS**

### Language Coach          COMMON CORE L 4c
**Etymology**
Provide support as needed for students to locate information about word history in the dictionary.
***Possible answer:*** *mercy* Ask students who speak French what the word *merci* means in that language today? ***Answer:*** *thank you*

And he will make the face of heaven so fine
That all the world will be in love with night
25 And pay no worship to the garish sun.
 O, I have bought the mansion of a love,
 But not possessed it; and though I am sold,
 Not yet enjoyed. So tedious is this day
 As is the night before some festival
30 To an impatient child that hath new robes
 And may not wear them. Oh, here comes my nurse,

[*Enter* Nurse, *wringing her hands, with the ladder of cords in her lap.*]

 And she brings news; and every tongue that speaks
 But Romeo's name speaks heavenly eloquence.
 Now, nurse, what news? What hast thou there? the cords
35 That Romeo bid thee fetch?

**Nurse.**                                 Ay, ay, the cords.

**Juliet.** Ay me! what news? Why dost thou wring thy hands?

**Nurse.** Ah, well-a-day! he's dead, he's dead, he's dead!
 We are undone, lady, we are undone!
 Alack the day! he's gone, he's killed, he's dead!

40 **Juliet.** Can heaven be so envious?

**Nurse.**                                 Romeo can,
 Though heaven cannot. O Romeo, Romeo!
 Who ever would have thought it? Romeo!

**Juliet.** What devil art thou that dost torment me thus?
 This torture should be roared in dismal hell.
45 Hath Romeo slain himself? Say thou but "I,"
 And that bare vowel "I" shall poison more
 Than the death-darting eye of a cockatrice.
 I am not I, if there be such an "I,"
 Or those eyes shut, that make thee answer "I."
50 If he be slain, say "I," or if not, "no."
 Brief sounds determine of my weal or woe.

**Nurse.** I saw the wound, I saw it with mine eyes,
 (God save the mark!) here on his manly breast.
 A piteous corse, a bloody piteous corse;
55 Pale, pale as ashes, all bedaubed in blood,
 All in gore blood. I swounded at the sight.

**Juliet.** O, break, my heart! poor bankrout, break at once!
 To prison, eyes; ne'er look on liberty!
 Vile earth, to earth resign; end motion here,
60 And thou and Romeo press one heavy bier!

**26–27 I have . . . possessed it:** Juliet protests that she has gone through the wedding ceremony (**bought the mansion**) but is still waiting to enjoy the rewards of marriage.

**34 the cords:** the rope ladder.

**37–42 well-a-day:** an expression used when someone has bad news. The nurse wails and moans without clearly explaining what has happened, leading Juliet to assume that Romeo is dead.

**G DRAMATIC IRONY**
How is Juliet's belief that her new husband is dead an example of dramatic irony?

**45–50** Juliet's "I" means "aye," or "yes." A **cockatrice** is a mythological beast whose glance kills its victims.

**51 my weal or woe:** my happiness or sorrow.

**53–56 God . . . mark:** an expression meant to scare off evil powers, similar to "Knock on wood"; **corse:** corpse; **swounded:** fainted.

**57–60** Juliet say her heart is broken and bankrupt (**bankrout**). She wants to be buried with Romeo, sharing his burial platform (**bier**).

---

**TEXT ANALYSIS**                          COMMON CORE   RL 10

**G DRAMATIC IRONY**

*Possible answer:* *Juliet's belief that her new husband is dead is an example of dramatic irony because although he is not yet dead, he will be by the end of the play. It is also ironic because in this scene, Juliet mistakenly thinks that Romeo is dead. Later, it will be Romeo who mistakenly thinks that Juliet is dead.*

**IF STUDENTS NEED HELP . . .** Define the term *dramatic irony.* Refer students to the Prologue that opens the play and to what it says about the play's outcome. Discuss what students know about death in this story that Juliet herself does not yet know.

---

**DIFFERENTIATED INSTRUCTION**

**FOR ENGLISH LANGUAGE LEARNERS**
**Vocabulary Support** Direct students' attention to lines 45–50, in which Shakespeare uses homophones: the pronoun *I*, the word *eye*, and the implied word *aye*. Point out that this is not humorous word play; rather, Shakespeare mixes the words to indicate Juliet's confusion. Go through lines 45–50 especially slowly, paraphrasing to clear up any misunderstandings.

**Nurse.** O Tybalt, Tybalt, the best friend I had!
O courteous Tybalt! honest gentleman!
That ever I should live to see thee dead!

**Juliet.** What storm is this that blows so contrary?
65 Is Romeo slaughtered, and is Tybalt dead?
My dear-loved cousin, and my dearer lord?
Then, dreadful trumpet, sound the general doom!
For who is living, if those two are gone?

**Nurse.** Tybalt is gone, and Romeo banished;
70 Romeo that killed him, he is banished.

**Juliet.** O God! Did Romeo's hand shed Tybalt's blood?

**Nurse.** It did! it did! alas the day, it did!

**Juliet.** O serpent heart, hid with a flow'ring face!
Did ever dragon keep so fair a cave?
75 Beautiful tyrant! fiend angelical!
Dove-feathered raven! wolvish-ravening lamb!
Despisèd substance of divinest show!
Just opposite to what thou justly seem'st,
A damnèd saint, an honorable villain!
80 O nature, what hadst thou to do in hell
When thou didst bower the spirit of a fiend
In mortal paradise of such sweet flesh?
Was ever book containing such vile matter
So fairly bound? O, that deceit should dwell
85 In such a gorgeous palace!

**Nurse.**                    There's no trust,
No faith, no honesty in men; all perjured,
All forsworn, all naught, all dissemblers.
Ah, where's my man? Give me some aqua vitae.
These griefs, these woes, these sorrows make me old.
90 Shame come to Romeo!

**Juliet.**                    Blistered be thy tongue
For such a wish! He was not born to shame.
Upon his brow shame is ashamed to sit;
For 'tis a throne where honor may be crowned
Sole monarch of the universal earth.
95 O, what a beast was I to chide at him! ⒣

**Nurse.** Will you speak well of him that killed your cousin?

**Juliet.** Shall I speak ill of him that is my husband?
Ah, poor my lord, what tongue shall smooth thy name
When I, thy three-hours' wife, have mangled it?
100 But wherefore, villain, didst thou kill my cousin?
That villain cousin would have killed my husband.

**73–85** Juliet's contradictory phrases here show her conflicting feelings about the events the nurse has described. *What is Juliet's first reaction to the news that Romeo has killed Tybalt?*

**81 bower...fiend:** give a home to the spirit of a demon.

**87 all...dissemblers:** All are liars and pretenders.

**88 aqua vitae:** brandy.

⒣ **TRAGEDY**
Compare Juliet's initial reaction to the news of Tybalt's death with her response to the nurse in lines 90–95. What **internal conflict** is Juliet wrestling with in this scene?

Use these prompts to help students understand Juliet's conflicted grief in lines 100–114:

**Connect** Think of some unexpected news that made you or someone you know very sad. How does that experience help you understand Juliet's reaction to the news of Tybalt's death and Romeo's banishment? *Students should express some empathy for Juliet's shock and grief.*

**Analyze** Why is Juliet happy? Why is she sad? *Possible answer: Juliet is happy that Romeo is not dead. She is sad about the violence, sad about Tybalt's death, and especially sad about the fact that Romeo has been banished from Verona.*

**Synthesize** By this point in the scene, what decision has Juliet made about her loyalty? How does her decision threaten her relationship with her nurse? *Possible answer: By this point, Juliet has decided to be loyal to her husband, even though they have been married for only a few hours. To this point, the nurse has mourned Tybalt and condemned Romeo; if she does not support Romeo, she will be at odds with Juliet and will lose Juliet's trust.*

---

Back, foolish tears, back to your native spring!
Your tributary drops belong to woe,
Which you, mistaking, offer up to joy.
105 My husband lives, that Tybalt would have slain;
And Tybalt's dead, that would have slain my husband.
All this is comfort; wherefore weep I then?
Some word there was, worser than Tybalt's death,
That murdered me. I would forget it fain;
110 But O, it presses to my memory
Like damned guilty deeds to sinners' minds!
"Tybalt is dead, and Romeo—banished."
That "banished," that one word "banished,"
Hath slain ten thousand Tybalts. Tybalt's death
115 Was woe enough, if it had ended there;
Or, if sour woe delights in fellowship
And needly will be ranked with other griefs,
Why followed not, when she said "Tybalt's dead,"
Thy father, or thy mother, nay, or both,
120 Which modern lamentation might have moved?
But with a rearward following Tybalt's death,
"Romeo is banished"—to speak that word
Is father, mother, Tybalt, Romeo, Juliet,
All slain, all dead. "Romeo is banished"—
125 There is no end, no limit, measure, bound,
In that word's death; no words can that woe sound.
Where is my father and my mother, nurse?

**Nurse.** Weeping and wailing over Tybalt's corse.
Will you go to them? I will bring you thither.

130 **Juliet.** Wash they his wounds with tears? Mine shall be spent,
When theirs are dry, for Romeo's banishment.
Take up those cords. Poor ropes, you are beguiled,
Both you and I, for Romeo is exiled.
He made you for a highway to my bed;
135 But I, a maid, die maiden-widowed.
Come, cords; come, nurse. I'll to my wedding bed;
And death, not Romeo, take my maidenhead!

**Nurse.** Hie to your chamber. I'll find Romeo
To comfort you. I wot well where he is.
140 Hark ye, your Romeo will be here at night.
I'll to him; he is hid at Laurence' cell.

**Juliet.** O, find him! give this ring to my true knight
And bid him come to take his last farewell.

[*Exeunt.*]

**102–106** Juliet is uncertain whether her tears should be of joy or of sorrow.

**114–127** Juliet says that if the news of Tybalt's death had been followed by the news of her parents' deaths, she would have felt normal (**modern**), or expected, grief. To follow the story of Tybalt's death with the terrible news of Romeo's banishment creates a sorrow so deep it cannot be expressed in words.

**132 beguiled:** cheated.

**135–137 I...maidenhead:** I will die a widow without ever really having been a wife. Death, not Romeo, will be my husband.

**139 wot:** know.

**② Targeted Passage**

---

## DIFFERENTIATED INSTRUCTION

### FOR STRUGGLING READERS

**② Targeted Passage [Lines 138–143]**

In this passage, Juliet and the nurse make a plan to bring the lovers together.

- Where is Romeo hiding? (line 141)
- What is the nurse going to do and say after she leaves Juliet? (lines 140–141)
- Why does Juliet call the coming night Romeo's "last farewell" (line 143)? (lines 138–141)

### FOR ENGLISH LANGUAGE LEARNERS

**Vocabulary: Outdated Forms** Urge students to continue adding outdated terms to their language journal. (See the **For English Language Learners** activity on p. 1036.) Provide these terms and their definitions. Then have students reread the lines noted and substitute the definitions for the words.

- *would have slain* (lines 105 and 106), "wanted to kill"

- *fain* (line 109), "happily"
- *needly will be* (line 117), "must be"
- *corse* (line 128), "corpse"
- *thither* (line 129), "there"
- *hark ye* (line 140), "listen" (a command)

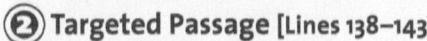

# SCENE 3 *Friar Laurence's cell.*

*Friar Laurence tells Romeo of his banishment, and Romeo collapses in grief. When he learns from the nurse that Juliet, too, is in despair, he threatens to stab himself. The friar reacts by suggesting a plan. Romeo is to spend a few hours with Juliet and then escape to Mantua. While he is away, the friar will announce the wedding and try to get a pardon from the prince.*

[*Enter* Friar Laurence.]

**Friar Laurence.** Romeo, come forth; come forth, thou fearful man.
Affliction is enamored of thy parts,
And thou art wedded to calamity.

[*Enter* Romeo.]

**Romeo.** Father, what news? What is the Prince's doom?
5 What sorrow craves acquaintance at my hand
That I yet know not?

**Friar Laurence.**          Too familiar
Is my dear son with such sour company.
I bring thee tidings of the Prince's doom.

**Romeo.** What less than doomsday is the Prince's doom?

10 **Friar Laurence.** A gentler judgment vanished from his lips—
Not body's death, but body's banishment.

**Romeo.** Ha, banishment? Be merciful, say "death";
For exile hath more terror in his look,
Much more than death. Do not say "banishment."

15 **Friar Laurence.** Hence from Verona art thou banished.
Be patient, for the world is broad and wide.

**Romeo.** There is no world without Verona walls,
But purgatory, torture, hell itself.
Hence banished is banish'd from the world,
20 And world's exile is death. Then "banishment,"
Is death misterm'd. Calling death "banishment,"
Thou cuttst my head off with a golden axe
And smilest upon the stroke that murders me.

**Friar Laurence.** O deadly sin! O rude unthankfulness!
25 Thy fault our law calls death; but the kind Prince,
Taking thy part, hath rushed aside the law,
And turned that black word death to banishment.
This is dear mercy, and thou seest it not.

**Romeo.** 'Tis torture, and not mercy. Heaven is here,
30 Where Juliet lives; and every cat and dog
And little mouse, every unworthy thing,
Live here in heaven and may look on her;
But Romeo may not. More validity,

---

2 **affliction . . . parts:** Trouble loves you.

4 **doom:** sentence.

9 **doomsday:** death.

10 **vanished:** came.

17–23 **There is . . . murders me:** Being exiled outside Verona's walls is as bad as being dead. And yet you smile at my misfortune.

24–28 The angry friar reminds Romeo that by law he should have gotten the death penalty. The prince has shown Romeo mercy.

---

---

## TIERED DISCUSSION PROMPTS

Use these prompts to help students understand Friar Laurence's attempts to console Romeo in lines 53–70:

**Connect** Have you or anyone you know ever tried to calm someone who was particularly upset? How does that experience help you understand the role of Friar Laurence in this scene? *Students may describe the difficulty in getting a person to move beyond his or her emotions and be rational.*

**Analyze** How does the friar attempt to help Romeo deal with his grief about being banished? Is he successful? *Possible answer: Friar Laurence attempts to console Romeo with philosophy, possibly to encourage Romeo to think rationally about his situation.*

**Evaluate** Do Romeo and Friar Laurence seem as close in this scene as they have been? Explain. *Possible answer: Students may note that the closeness is strained, as the friar's attempts to console Romeo are well meaning but intellectual, and Romeo alludes to this when he says that the friar shouldn't comment on feelings he doesn't understand (line 64).*

---

More honorable state, more courtship lives
35 In carrion flies than Romeo. They may seize
On the white wonder of dear Juliet's hand
And steal immortal blessing from her lips,
Who, even in pure and vestal modesty,
Still blush, as thinking their own kisses sin;
40 But Romeo may not—he is banished.
This may flies do, when I from this must fly;
They are free men, but I am banished.
And sayst thou yet that exile is not death?
Hadst thou no poison mixed, no sharp-ground knife,
45 No sudden mean of death, though ne'er so mean,
But "banished" to kill me—"banished"?
O friar, the damned use that word in hell;
Howling attends it! How hast thou the heart,
Being a divine, a ghostly confessor,
50 A sin-absolver, and my friend professed,
To mangle me with that word "banished"?

**Friar Laurence.** Thou fond mad man, hear me a little speak.

**Romeo.** O, thou wilt speak again of banishment.

**Friar Laurence.** I'll give thee armor to keep off that word;
55 Adversity's sweet milk, philosophy,
To comfort thee, though thou art banished.

**Romeo.** Yet "banished"? Hang up philosophy!
Unless philosophy can make a Juliet,
Displant a town, reverse a prince's doom,
60 It helps not, it prevails not. Talk no more.

**Friar Laurence.** O, then I see that madmen have no ears.

**Romeo.** How should they, when that wise men have no eyes?

**Friar Laurence.** Let me dispute with thee of thy estate.

**Romeo.** Thou canst not speak of that thou dost not feel.
65 Wert thou as young as I, Juliet thy love,
An hour but married, Tybalt murdered,
Doting like me, and like me banished,
Then mightst thou speak, then mightst thou tear thy hair,
And fall upon the ground, as I do now,
70 Taking the measure of an unmade grave.

[Nurse *knocks within.*]

**Friar Laurence.** Arise; one knocks. Good Romeo, hide thyself.

**Romeo.** Not I; unless the breath of heartsick groans
Mist-like infold me from the search of eyes.

[*knock*]

**33–35 More validity…than Romeo:** Even flies that live off the dead (**carrion**) will be able to get closer to Juliet than Romeo will.

**44–46 Hadst…to kill me:** Couldn't you have killed me with poison or a knife instead of with that awful word *banished*? *Why does Romeo think banishment is a worse punishment than death?*

**52 fond:** foolish.

**54–56** The friar offers philosophical comfort and counseling (**adversity's sweet milk**) as a way to overcome hardship.

**63 dispute:** discuss; **estate:** situation.

**72–73** Romeo will hide only if his sighs create a mist and shield him from sight.

---

## DIFFERENTIATED INSTRUCTION

### FOR ENGLISH LANGUAGE LEARNERS

**Task Support** As students consider the blue marginal question for lines 44–46, remind them that *banishment* means forcing a person to leave a place, never to return. *Possible answer: Romeo thinks that banishment is worse than death because he must live with the knowledge that Juliet is alive but that he cannot be with her. He believes that if he were dead, he would not have the pain of longing for Juliet.*

### FOR STRUGGLING READERS

**Develop Reading Fluency** Model for students an effective way to read the conversation between Romeo and Friar Laurence in lines 52–70 to emphasize the friar's philosophical tone and Romeo's emotional responses. You might ask for a volunteer to read the dialogue of one character while you read the other. Then have pairs of students practice reading the dialogue aloud together.

**Friar Laurence.** Hark, how they knock! Who's there? Romeo, arise;

75 Thou wilt be taken.—Stay awhile!—Stand up;

[*knock*]

Run to my study.—By-and-by!—God's will,
What simpleness is this.—I come, I come!

[*knock*]

Who knocks so hard? Whence come you? What's your will?

**Nurse** [*within*]. Let me come in, and you shall know my errand.

80 I come from Lady Juliet.

**Friar Laurence.**          Welcome then.

[*Enter* Nurse.]

**Nurse.** O holy friar, O, tell me, holy friar,
Where is my lady's lord, where's Romeo?

**Friar Laurence.** There on the ground, with his own tears made
   drunk.

**Nurse.** O, he is even in my mistress' case,

85 Just in her case! O woeful sympathy!
Piteous predicament! Even so lies she,
Blubb'ring and weeping, weeping and blubbering.
Stand up, stand up! Stand, an you be a man.
For Juliet's sake, for her sake, rise and stand!

90 Why should you fall into so deep an O?

**Romeo** [*rises*]. Nurse—

**Nurse.** Ah sir! ah sir! Well, death's the end of all.

**Romeo.** Spakest thou of Juliet? How is it with her?
Doth not she think me an old murderer,

95 Now I have stained the childhood of our joy
With blood removed but little from her own?
Where is she? and how doth she? and what says
My concealed lady to our canceled love?

**Nurse.** O, she says nothing, sir, but weeps and weeps;

100 And now falls on her bed, and then starts up,
And Tybalt calls; and then on Romeo cries,
And then down falls again.

**Romeo.**          As if that name,
Shot from the deadly level of a gun,
Did murder her; as that name's cursed hand

105 Murdered her kinsman. O tell me, friar, tell me,
In what vile part of this anatomy
Doth my name lodge? Tell me, that I may sack
The hateful mansion.

[*draws his dagger*]

**84–85 he is even . . . her case:** He is acting the same way that Juliet is.

**90 into so deep an O:** into such deep grief.

**96 blood . . . from her own:** the blood of a close relative of hers.

**98 concealed lady:** secret bride.

**102 that name:** the name Romeo.

**106–108 in what vile part . . . mansion:** Romeo asks where in his body (**anatomy**) his name can be found so that he can cut the name out. *What is Romeo about to do?*

## BACKGROUND

**Guns** Romeo's statement that the mention of his name to Juliet was like a "Shot from the deadly level of a gun" (line 103) alludes to technological advances in firearms made around the time of the play's production. The "hand gonne," used in the 15th century, resembled a small cannon and was difficult and dangerous to use. By the 1570s, however, smaller muskets such as the snaphaunce used a trigger to strike a flint against a metal surface, igniting a spark, lighting the gunpowder, and firing the projectile, thereby assuring a deadlier aim. While firearms are never used in *Romeo and Juliet*, they are referred to as a figurative way of describing the explosive nature of passions and emotions (see line 132).

**FOR ENGLISH LANGUAGE LEARNERS**

**Task Support** Point out the question in the marginal note for lines 106–108. Have students reread that note, reread lines 106–108, read the stage direction that follows line 108 (*draws his dagger*), and then answer the question. **Answer:** *Romeo is about to stab himself with his dagger.*

**FOR ADVANCED LEARNERS/PRE–AP**

**Evaluate Meter** [paired-activity option] Remind students that in previous scenes, the nurse's speeches have been written in prose. In lines 84–90, however, she speaks in blank verse. Have students evaluate her lines and share their ideas about (1) why Shakespeare might have changed her speech pattern and (2) whether Shakespeare is being inconsistent in portraying her character.

## Is **LOVE** stronger than **HATE?**

**Discuss** According to Friar Laurence in lines 128–134, why should Romeo's marriage—his commitment to a lifelong love—prevent him from killing himself? *Possible answer: By taking marriage vows, Romeo has promised to cherish his love for Juliet. Friar Laurence argues that Romeo should not kill that love through suicide. If he kills himself, the friar says, he will also destroy the thing for which he cares the most.*

**Friar Laurence.**          Hold thy desperate hand.
Art thou a man? Thy form cries out thou art;
110 Thy tears are womanish, thy wild acts denote
The unreasonable fury of a beast.
Unseemly woman in a seeming man!
Or ill-beseeming beast in seeming both!
Thou hast amazed me. By my holy order,
115 I thought thy disposition better tempered.
Hast thou slain Tybalt? Wilt thou slay thyself?
And slay thy lady too that lives in thee,
By doing damned hate upon thyself?
Why railst thou on thy birth, the heaven, and earth?
120 Since birth and heaven and earth, all three do meet
In thee at once; which thou at once wouldst lose.
Fie, fie, thou shamest thy shape, thy love, thy wit,
Which, like a usurer, aboundst in all,
And usest none in that true use indeed
125 Which should bedeck thy shape, thy love, thy wit.
Thy noble shape is but a form of wax,
Digressing from the valor of a man;
Thy dear love sworn but hollow perjury,
Killing that love which thou hast vowed to cherish;
130 Thy wit, that ornament to shape and love,
Misshapen in the conduct of them both,
Like powder in a skilless soldier's flask,
Is set afire by thine own ignorance,
And thou dismembered with thine own defense.
135 What, rouse thee, man! Thy Juliet is alive,
For whose dear sake thou wast but lately dead.
There art thou happy. Tybalt would kill thee,
But thou slewest Tybalt. There art thou happy.
The law, that threatened death, becomes thy friend
140 And turns it to exile. There art thou happy.
A pack of blessings light upon thy back;
Happiness courts thee in her best array;
But, like a misbehaved and sullen wench,
Thou poutst upon thy fortune and thy love.
145 Take heed, take heed, for such die miserable.

**Targeted Passage ③**

Go get thee to thy love, as was decreed,
Ascend her chamber, hence and comfort her.
But look thou stay not till the watch be set,
For then thou canst not pass to Mantua,
150 Where thou shalt live till we can find a time
To blaze your marriage, reconcile your friends,
Beg pardon of the Prince, and call thee back
With twenty hundred thousand times more joy

**108–125 Hold thy . . . bedeck thy shape, thy love, thy wit:** You're not acting like a man. Would you send your soul to hell by committing suicide (**doing damned hate upon thyself**)? Why do you curse your birth, heaven, and earth? You are refusing to make good use of your advantages, just as a miser refuses to spend his money.

**126–134** The friar explains how by acting as he is, Romeo is misusing his shape (his outer form or body), his love, and his wit (his mind or intellect).

**135–140** The friar tells Romeo to count his blessings instead of feeling sorry for himself. He lists the things Romeo has to be thankful for. *What three blessings does the friar mention?*

**COMMON CORE L 4a**
**Language Coach**
**Multiple Meanings** The words *court* and *array* (line 142) both have multiple meanings. Here, *courts* means "woos"; try to figure out the meaning here of *array*.

**148–149 look . . . Mantua:** Leave before the guards take their places at the city gates; otherwise you will not be able to escape to Mantua.

**151 blaze . . . friends:** announce your marriage and get the families (**friends**) to stop feuding.

## DIFFERENTIATED INSTRUCTION

### FOR STRUGGLING READERS

③ **Targeted Passage [Lines 146–152]**
This passage presents Friar Laurence's solution to Romeo's problem.

- According to Friar Laurence's plan, where will Romeo go after seeing Juliet? When will he leave? (lines 148–149)
- What will Friar Laurence do while Romeo is in Mantua? (lines 150–152)
- Whose help will the friar seek? Why? (lines 151–152)

### FOR ENGLISH LANGUAGE LEARNERS

**Language Coach** **COMMON CORE L 4a**
**Multiple Meanings** *Possible answer: clothing, dress* Point out to students that using words with multiple meanings is a common poetic technique. Ask them to speculate on why poets choose words with more than one meaning. *Possible answer: More layers of meaning enrich the language and help make the characters' speeches more intriguing.*

Than thou wentst forth in lamentation.
155 Go before, nurse. Commend me to thy lady,
And bid her hasten all the house to bed,
Which heavy sorrow makes them apt unto.
Romeo is coming.

**Nurse.** O Lord, I could have stayed here all the night
160 To hear good counsel. O, what learning is!
My lord, I'll tell my lady you will come.

**Romeo.** Do so, and bid my sweet prepare to chide.

[Nurse *offers to go and turns again.*]

**Nurse.** Here is a ring she bid me give you, sir.
Hie you, make haste, for it grows very late.

[*Exit.*]

165 **Romeo.** How well my comfort is revived by this!

**Friar Laurence.** Go hence; good night; and here stands all your
    state:
Either be gone before the watch be set,
Or by the break of day disguised from hence.
Sojourn in Mantua. I'll find out your man,
170 And he shall signify from time to time
Every good hap to you that chances here.
Give me thy hand. 'Tis late. Farewell; good night.

**Romeo.** But that a joy past joy calls out on me,
It were a grief so brief to part with thee.
175 Farewell. ❶

[*Exeunt.*]

# SCENE 4 *Capulet's house.*

*In this scene, Paris visits the Capulets, who are mourning the death of Tybalt.*
*He says he realizes that this is no time to talk of marriage. Capulet, however,*
*disagrees; he decides that Juliet should marry Paris on Thursday, three days*
*away. He tells Lady Capulet to inform Juliet immediately.*

[*Enter* Capulet, Lady Capulet, *and* Paris.]

**Capulet.** Things have fall'n out, sir, so unluckily
That we have had no time to move our daughter.
Look you, she loved her kinsman Tybalt dearly,
And so did I. Well, we were born to die.
5 'Tis very late; she'll not come down tonight.

**162 bid . . . chide:** Tell Juliet to get ready
to scold me for the way I've behaved.

**166–171 and here . . . here:** This is what
your fate depends on: either leave before the
night watchmen go on duty, or get
out at dawn in a disguise. Stay awhile in
Mantua. I'll find out your servant and send
messages to you about what good things
are happening here.

❶ **TRAGEDY**
Despite Romeo and Juliet's
anguish, their problem at this point
seems solvable. **Summarize** the
plan that has been made to resolve
their dilemma.

**1–2 Things have . . . our daughter:** Such
terrible things have happened that we
haven't had time to persuade (**move**)
Juliet to think about your marriage
proposal.

ROMEO AND JULIET: ACT THREE, SCENE 4 **1103**

---

*Making the Plan Work*

*Romeo's Jobs*

*comfort Juliet*
*(lines 146–147)*

*go to Mantua*
*(lines 148–150*
*and 167–169)*

*await messages*
*from*
*Friar Laurence*
*(lines 148–150*
*and 167–169)*
*and the call to*
*return to Verona*
*(lines 152–154)*

*Friar Laurence's*
*Jobs*

*announce the*
*marriage and*
*reconcile the*
*families*
*(lines 150–151)*

*try to get Prince*
*Escalus to*
*pardon Romeo*
*(lines 152–154)*

*keep Romeo*
*informed and*
*eventually bring*
*him back to*
*Verona*
*(lines 152 and*
*169–171)*

---

## Is **LOVE** stronger than **HATE?**

**Discuss** How does Capulet understand the role of love when he offers Juliet in marriage to Count Paris in lines 12–14? *Possible answer: Capulet assumes that Juliet's love is something he is free to offer to whomever he wishes. What seems more important is obedience. Capulet has every confidence that Juliet will "be ruled" (line 13) by him and agree to the marriage.*

---

**TEXT ANALYSIS**

**COMMON CORE**
L 3

### ❶ TRAGEDY

*Possible answer: Juliet will probably react to the news with anger. This turn of events may increase the conflict by forcing Juliet to reveal her secret marriage or to escape her family in some way to avoid marrying Paris.*

---

I promise you, but for your company,
I would have been abed an hour ago.

**Paris.** These times of woe afford no time to woo.
Madam, good night. Commend me to your daughter.

10 **Lady Capulet.** I will, and know her mind early tomorrow;
Tonight she's mewed up to her heaviness.

[Paris *offers to go and* Capulet *calls him again.*]

**Capulet.** Sir Paris, I will make a desperate tender
Of my child's love. I think she will be ruled
In all respects by me; nay more, I doubt it not.

15 Wife, go you to her ere you go to bed;
Acquaint her here of my son Paris' love
And bid her (mark you me?) on Wednesday next—
But, soft! what day is this?

**Paris.**                                    Monday, my lord.

**Capulet.** Monday! ha, ha! Well, Wednesday is too soon.
20 A Thursday let it be—a Thursday, tell her,
She shall be married to this noble earl.
Will you be ready? Do you like this haste?
We'll keep no great ado—a friend or two;
For hark you, Tybalt being slain so late,
25 It may be thought we held him carelessly,
Being our kinsman, if we revel much.
Therefore we'll have some half a dozen friends,
And there an end. But what say you to Thursday?

**Paris.** My lord, I would that Thursday were tomorrow.

30 **Capulet.** Well, get you gone. A Thursday be it then. ❶
Go you to Juliet ere you go to bed;
Prepare her, wife, against this wedding day.
Farewell, my lord.—Light to my chamber, ho!
Afore me, it is so very very late
35 That we may call it early by-and-by.
Good night.

[*Exeunt.*]

---

**8** Sad times are not good times for talking of marriage.

**11** Tonight she is locked up with her sorrow. *What do Juliet's parents think is causing this sorrow?*

**12 desperate tender:** bold offer.

**16** Capulet is so sure that Juliet will accept Paris that he calls Paris "son" already.

**23 no great ado:** no big festivity.

### ❶ TRAGEDY

Predict how Juliet will react to the news that her parents have promised her to Paris. How might this turn of events add to the play's mounting **conflict?**

**34–35 it is . . . by-and-by:** It's so late at night that soon we'll be calling it early in the morning.

---

## DIFFERENTIATED INSTRUCTION

**FOR ENGLISH LANGUAGE LEARNERS**

**Task Support** Draw students' attention to the question in the marginal note about line 11. Ask students to review Juliet's emotional speeches in Scene 2. *Possible answer: Juliet's parents think that Juliet's sorrow is due to Tybalt's death.*

**FOR ENGLISH LANGUAGE LEARNERS**

**Vocabulary: Outdated Forms** Discuss these examples of Shakespearean terms that have passed from use:

- *abed* (line 7), *"in bed"*
- *ere* (line 15), "before" (at an earlier time)
- *mark you* (line 17), "pay attention [to]"
- *we held him carelessly* (line 25), "we cared little about him"
- *get you gone* (line 30), "leave"
- *afore* (line 34), "before" (in front of)

The Clarence Brown Theatre's 2003 production

The Seattle Repertory Theatre's 2003 production

The Bolshoi Ballet's 2004 production

## Behind the Curtain

## Stage Combat

A character's movements can convey as much as his or her words. In fight scenes, **blocking** is used to decide exactly how the actors will move. From a stylistic point of view, how are the movements captured in these photographs different? Which fight looks most realistic, and why?

### BEHIND THE CURTAIN    COMMON CORE SL 2

***Possible answer:*** *From a stylistic point of view, the movements in the Seattle Repertory Theatre's production appear fierce. In contrast, the movements in the Clarence Brown Theatre's production are more disciplined. The movements in the Bolshoi Ballet's production seem carefully choreographed and elegant. The most realistic fight is in the photograph from the Seattle Repertory Theatre because the movements are the most aggressive and the actors' faces portray the most emotion.*

**Stage Combat** The object of stage combat is to portray physical fighting among characters. It can be difficult to stage fights effectively, because the audience realizes that the actors will not really be hurt and therefore will not be easily convinced by the fight. For this reason, some productions, such as that of the Bolshoi Ballet, stage the combat without fierce aggression, allowing the audience to imagine the ferocity of the fight. In the other two images, the scene has been blocked to create excitement and tension, yet with few characters on the stage, to ensure the actors' safety.

**FOR ADVANCED LEARNERS/PRE–AP**

**Research Stage Combat** [small-group option] Have students research and prepare an oral presentation about creating realistic stage combat. Topics might include information on props such as trick daggers or swords made of blunted plastic, theatrical punches and tumbles, choreographing movement, and schools that teach classes in stage combat.

## Is **LOVE** stronger than **HATE?**

**Discuss** Refer students to lines 17–25 and ask them to think about the proverb *Love is blind.* How does Romeo's love blind him and put him in danger? ***Possible answer:** Romeo is "blinded" by love in the sense that he is willing to be captured and killed if staying means pleasing Juliet.*

# SCENE 5   *Capulet's orchard.*

*Romeo and Juliet have spent the night together, but before daylight, Romeo leaves for Mantua. As soon as he leaves, Lady Capulet comes in to tell Juliet of her father's decision—that she will marry Count Paris on Thursday. Juliet is very upset and refuses to go along with the plan. Juliet's father goes into a rage at her disobedience and tells her that she will marry Paris or he will disown her.*

*The nurse advises Juliet to wed Paris, since her marriage to Romeo is over and Paris is a better man anyway. Juliet, now angry with the nurse, decides to go to Friar Laurence for help.*

[*Enter* Romeo *and* Juliet *above, at the window.*]

**Juliet.** Wilt thou be gone? It is not yet near day.
It was the nightingale, and not the lark,
That pierced the fearful hollow of thine ear.
Nightly she sings on yond pomegranate tree.
5 Believe me, love, it was the nightingale.

**Romeo.** It was the lark, the herald of the morn;
No nightingale. Look, love, what envious streaks
Do lace the severing clouds in yonder East.
Night's candles are burnt out, and jocund day
10 Stands tiptoe on the misty mountain tops.
I must be gone and live, or stay and die.

**Juliet.** Yond light is not daylight; I know it, I.
It is some meteor that the sun exhales
To be to thee this night a torchbearer
15 And light thee on thy way to Mantua.
Therefore stay yet; thou needst not to be gone.

**Romeo.** Let me be ta'en, let me be put to death.
I am content, so thou wilt have it so.
I'll say yon grey is not the morning's eye,
20 'Tis but the pale reflex of Cynthia's brow;
Nor that is not the lark whose notes do beat
The vaulty heaven so high above our heads.
I have more care to stay than will to go.
Come, death, and welcome! Juliet wills it so.
25 How is't, my soul? Let's talk; it is not day.

**Juliet.** It is, it is! Hie hence, be gone, away!
It is the lark that sings so out of tune,
Straining harsh discords and unpleasing sharps.
Some say the lark makes sweet division;
30 This doth not so, for she divideth us.
Some say the lark and loathed toad changed eyes;
O, now I would they had changed voices too,

**2 It was . . . lark:** The nightingale sings at night; the lark sings in the morning. *What is Juliet trying to get Romeo to believe?*

**9 night's candles:** stars.

**12–25** Juliet continues to pretend it is night to keep Romeo from leaving. Romeo gives in and says he'll stay if Juliet wishes it, even if staying means death.

**20 reflex of Cynthia's brow:** reflection of the moon. Cynthia is another name for Diana, the Roman goddess of the moon. She was often pictured with a crescent moon on her forehead.

**26** Romeo's mention of death frightens Juliet, and she urges him to leave quickly.

**29 division:** melody.

**31–34** I wish the lark had the voice of the hated (**loathed**) toad, since its voice is frightening us apart and acting as a morning song for hunters (**hunt's-up**).

## DIFFERENTIATED INSTRUCTION

### FOR STRUGGLING READERS

**Preview** Have students read the italicized scene synopsis aloud. Then have them fill in a Cluster Diagram in which they note the opinion that each character takes as it relates to Juliet's future.

**BEST PRACTICES TOOLKIT—Transparency**
Cluster Diagram p. B18

Nurse: Juliet should give up on Romeo and marry Paris.

Lady Capulet: Juliet must marry Paris.

Juliet's Future

Capulet: Juliet must marry Paris or be disowned.

Juliet: I refuse to marry Paris. I'll ask Friar Laurence for help.

### FOR ENGLISH LANGUAGE LEARNERS

**Task Support** As students read the marginal note and question about line 2, remind them that Romeo and Juliet have just spent their wedding night together. ***Possible answer:** Juliet is trying to get Romeo to believe that it is still night and, therefore, that he does not have to leave her yet.*

Since arm from arm that voice doth us affray,
Hunting thee hence with hunt's-up to the day!
35 O, now be gone! More light and light it grows.

**Romeo.** More light and light—more dark and dark our woes!

[*Enter Nurse, hastily.*]

**Nurse.** Madam!

**Juliet.** Nurse?

**Nurse.** Your lady mother is coming to your chamber.
40 The day is broke; be wary, look about.

[*Exit.*]

**Juliet.** Then, window, let day in, and let life out.

**Romeo.** Farewell, farewell! One kiss, and I'll descend.

[*He starts down the ladder.*]

**Juliet.** Art thou gone so, my lord, my love, my friend?
I must hear from thee every day in the hour,
45 For in a minute there are many days.
O, by this count I shall be much in years
Ere I again behold my Romeo!

**Romeo.** Farewell!
I will omit no opportunity
50 That may convey my greetings, love, to thee.

**Juliet.** O, thinkst thou we shall ever meet again?

**Romeo.** I doubt it not; and all these woes shall serve
For sweet discourses in our time to come.

**Juliet.** O God, I have an ill-divining soul!
55 Methinks I see thee, now thou art below,
As one dead in the bottom of a tomb.
Either my eyesight fails, or thou lookst pale.

**Romeo.** And trust me, love, in my eye so do you.
Dry sorrow drinks our blood. Adieu! adieu!

[*Exit.*]

60 **Juliet.** O Fortune, Fortune! all men call thee fickle.
If thou art fickle, what dost thou with him
That is renowned for faith? Be fickle, Fortune,
For then I hope thou wilt not keep him long
But send him back.

**Lady Capulet** [*within*]. Ho, daughter! are you up?

65 **Juliet.** Who is't that calls? It is my lady mother.
Is she not down so late, or up so early?
What unaccustomed cause procures her hither?

**Language Coach**

Etymology A word's **etymology** is its history. The word *affray* (line 33) is an archaic (outdated) verb that comes from the Middle English word *affraien*, meaning "to frighten." What common English adjective comes from this same Middle English word? Use a dictionary to check your answer.

46 **much in years:** very old.

54–56 **I have . . . tomb:** Juliet sees an evil vision of the future. *What is her vision?*

59 **Dry . . . blood:** People believed that sorrow drained the blood from the heart, causing a sad person to look pale.

60–62 **fickle:** changeable in loyalty or affection. Juliet asks fickle Fortune why it has anything to do with Romeo, who is the opposite of fickle.

67 **What . . . hither:** What unusual reason brings her here?

## BACKGROUND

**Fickle Fortune** When Juliet speaks of "Fortune" (lines 60–62), she is not referring to wealth. Instead, she is appealing to a personified cosmic force that greatly influenced Elizabethan thinking. Although Elizabethans believed that God had ordered the universe, they also believed that God used Fortune to raise and lower (as if on a wheel) the circumstances of individuals. In this speech, Juliet recognizes the role of Fortune in bringing her and Romeo into difficulty. She then prays that Fortune will soon raise their circumstances and grant them a happy outcome.

**FOR ENGLISH LANGUAGE LEARNERS**

**Task Support** Point out the question in the marginal note for lines 54–56. Call on a volunteer to read lines 54–56 aloud, then have students focus on line 56. *Possible answer: Juliet's vision is of Romeo as a corpse in a tomb.*

**Language Coach**   COMMON CORE L 4c

**Etymology**

Guide students as needed to locate word history in a dictionary.

*Possible answer: afraid* Ask students to look up the etymology of other words they find interesting that appear in this act in an etymological dictionary and share their findings with the class.

## Is **LOVE** stronger than **HATE?**

**Discuss** How can Juliet's words to her mother in lines 81–102 be words of hate and words of love at the same time? Cite evidence. *Possible answer: Juliet's words, carefully chosen, sound to her mother like words of hatred toward Romeo. We, the audience, know more about the situation than Lady Capulet does, however. We realize that Juliet is voicing the desires of her heart—namely, that she wishes that she could touch Romeo (lines 85–86), that she could see him (line 94), that she could go to him (lines 99–100), and that she could give him her love (line 101–102).*

---

[*Enter* Lady Capulet.]

**Lady Capulet.** Why, how now, Juliet?

**Juliet.**                                    Madam, I am not well.

**Lady Capulet.** Evermore weeping for your cousin's death?
70 What, wilt thou wash him from his grave with tears?
An if thou couldst, thou couldst not make him live.
Therefore have done. Some grief shows much of love;
But much of grief shows still some want of wit.

**Juliet.** Yet let me weep for such a feeling loss.

75 **Lady Capulet.** So shall you feel the loss, but not the friend
Which you weep for.

**Juliet.**                      Feeling so the loss,
I cannot choose but ever weep the friend.

**Lady Capulet.** Well, girl, thou weepst not so much for his death
As that the villain lives which slaughtered him.

80 **Juliet.** What villain, madam?

**Lady Capulet.**                          That same villain Romeo.

**Juliet** [*aside*]. Villain and he be many miles asunder.—
God pardon him! I do, with all my heart;
And yet no man like he doth grieve my heart.

**Lady Capulet.** That is because the traitor murderer lives.

85 **Juliet.** Ay, madam, from the reach of these my hands.
Would none but I might venge my cousin's death!

**Lady Capulet.** We will have vengeance for it, fear thou not.
Then weep no more. I'll send to one in Mantua,
Where that same banished runagate doth live,
90 Shall give him such an unaccustomed dram
That he shall soon keep Tybalt company;
And then I hope thou wilt be satisfied.

**Juliet.** Indeed I never shall be satisfied
With Romeo till I behold him—dead—
95 Is my poor heart so for a kinsman vexed.
Madam, if you could find out but a man
To bear a poison, I would temper it;
That Romeo should, upon receipt thereof,
Soon sleep in quiet. O, how my heart abhors
100 To hear him named and cannot come to him,
To wreak the love I bore my cousin Tybalt
Upon his body that hath slaughtered him!

**Lady Capulet.** Find thou the means, and I'll find such a man.
But now I'll tell thee joyful tidings, girl.

**69–70** *What does Lady Capulet think Juliet is crying about?*

**72–73 have…wit:** Stop crying (**have done**). A little grief is evidence of love, while too much grief shows a lack of good sense (**want of wit**).

**81–102** In these lines Juliet's words have double meanings. To avoid lying to her mother, she chooses her words carefully. They can mean what her mother wants to hear—or what Juliet really has on her mind.

**89 runagate:** runaway.
**90 unaccustomed dram:** poison.

**93–102 Dead** could refer either to Romeo or to Juliet's heart. Juliet says that if her mother could find someone to carry a poison to Romeo, she would mix (**temper**) it herself.

## DIFFERENTIATED INSTRUCTION

### FOR STRUGGLING READERS

**Paraphrasing Shakespeare** Have students paraphrase Juliet's aside in lines 81–83, which reveals her real emotions. *Possible answer: Romeo is far from being a villain. May God forgive him, as I do with all my heart. Still, no man makes me more unhappy (by being away from me).* Then ask students to paraphrase Lady Capulet's words in lines 88–91. Elicit that she plans to send an assassin to Mantua to poison Romeo.

### FOR ENGLISH LANGUAGE LEARNERS

**Task Support** As students read the marginal question about lines 69–70, point out that this is the first time that Lady Capulet has spoken to Juliet since Juliet learned of Tybalt's death, from the nurse, in Scene 2. *Possible answer: Lady Capulet thinks that Juliet is crying about the death of Tybalt, her cousin.*

**105** **Juliet.** And joy comes well in such a needy time.
What are they, I beseech your ladyship?

**Lady Capulet.** Well, well, thou hast a careful father, child;
One who, to put thee from thy heaviness,
Hath sorted out a sudden day of joy
**110** That thou expects not nor I looked not for.

**Juliet.** Madam, in happy time! What day is that?

**Lady Capulet.** Marry, my child, early next Thursday morn
The gallant, young, and noble gentleman,
The County Paris, at Saint Peter's Church,
**115** Shall happily make thee there a joyful bride.

**Juliet.** Now by Saint Peter's Church, and Peter too,
He shall not make me there a joyful bride!
I wonder at this haste, that I must wed
Ere he that should be husband comes to woo.
**120** I pray you tell my lord and father, madam,
I will not marry yet; and when I do, I swear
It shall be Romeo, whom you know I hate,
Rather than Paris. These are news indeed!

**Lady Capulet.** Here comes your father. Tell him so yourself,
**125** And see how he will take it at your hands.

[*Enter* Capulet *and* Nurse.]

**Capulet.** When the sun sets the air doth drizzle dew,
But for the sunset of my brother's son
It rains downright.
How now? a conduit, girl? What, still in tears?
**130** Evermore show'ring? In one little body
Thou counterfeitst a bark, a sea, a wind:
For still thy eyes, which I may call the sea,
Do ebb and flow with tears; the bark thy body is,
Sailing in this salt flood; the winds, thy sighs,
**135** Who, raging with thy tears and they with them,
Without a sudden calm will overset
Thy tempest-tossed body. How now, wife?
Have you delivered to her our decree?

**Lady Capulet.** Ay, sir; but she will none, she gives you thanks.
**140** I would the fool were married to her grave!

**Capulet.** Soft! take me with you, take me with you, wife.
How? Will she none? Doth she not give us thanks?
Is she not proud? Doth she not count her blest,
Unworthy as she is, that we have wrought
**145** So worthy a gentleman to be her bridegroom?

**121–123** Juliet mentions Romeo to show her mother how strongly opposed she is to marrying Paris, yet what she really means is that she loves Romeo.

**127 the sunset . . . son:** the death of Tybalt.

**129–137 conduit:** fountain. Capulet compares Juliet to a boat (**bark**), an ocean, and the wind because of her excessive crying.

**141 take me with you:** let me understand you.

## Is **LOVE** stronger than **HATE?**

**Discuss** What has Juliet done to cause her father's anger in lines 149–168? Is Capulet's hate well founded? *Possible answer: Juliet has caused her father's anger by rejecting his choice for her husband. His disappointment or confusion might be well founded, for choosing a husband for her is part of his traditional role as her father. His hatred, however, goes too far, and it is a dramatic change from his loving, doting demeanor seen earlier in the play. Capulet's anger seems to be founded on the realization that Juliet refuses to be ruled by him. Capulet does not realize that Juliet's response does not express a rejection of his authority as much as it expresses fear of her own unhappiness and betrayal of her secret marriage.*

**Juliet.** Not proud you have, but thankful that you have.
Proud can I never be of what I hate,
But thankful even for hate that is meant love.

**Capulet.** How, how, how, how, choplogic? What is this?
150 "Proud"—and "I thank you"—and "I thank you not"—
And yet "not proud"? Mistress minion you,
Thank me no thankings, nor proud me no prouds,
But fettle your fine joints 'gainst Thursday next
To go with Paris to Saint Peter's Church,
155 Or I will drag thee on a hurdle thither.
Out, you green-sickness carrion! out, you baggage!
You tallow-face!

**Lady Capulet.**     Fie, fie; what, are you mad?

**Juliet.** Good father, I beseech you on my knees,

[*She kneels down.*]

Hear me with patience but to speak a word.

160 **Capulet.** Hang thee, young baggage! disobedient wretch!
I tell thee what—get thee to church a Thursday
Or never after look me in the face.
Speak not, reply not, do not answer me!
My fingers itch. Wife, we scarce thought us blest
165 That God had lent us but this only child;
But now I see this one is one too much,
And that we have a curse in having her.
Out on her, hilding!

**Nurse.**          God in heaven bless her!
You are to blame, my lord, to rate her so.

170 **Capulet.** And why, my Lady Wisdom? Hold your tongue,
Good Prudence. Smatter with your gossips, go!

**Nurse.** I speak no treason.

**Capulet.**               O, God-i-god-en!

**Nurse.** May not one speak?

**Capulet.**               Peace, you mumbling fool!
Utter your gravity o'er a gossip's bowl,
175 For here we need it not.

**Lady Capulet.**          You are too hot.

**Capulet.** God's bread! it makes me mad. Day, night, late, early,
At home, abroad, alone, in company,
Waking or sleeping, still my care hath been
To have her matched; and having now provided
180 A gentleman of princely parentage,

**146–148 Not proud … meant love:** I'm not pleased, but I am grateful for your intentions.

**149–157** In his rage, Capulet calls Juliet a person who argues unnecessarily over fine points (**choplogic**) and says she is a spoiled child (**minion**). He tells her to prepare herself (**fettle your fine joints**) for the wedding or he'll haul her there in a cart for criminals (**hurdle**). He calls her an anemic piece of dead flesh (**green-sickness carrion**) and a coward (**tallow-face**).

**164 My fingers itch:** I feel like hitting you.

**168 hilding:** a good-for-nothing person.

**171 smatter:** chatter.

**174 Utter … bowl:** Save your words of wisdom for a gathering of gossips.

**179 matched:** married.

---

## DIFFERENTIATED INSTRUCTION

**FOR STRUGGLING READERS**

**Explore Character** Students may be surprised to hear Lady Capulet's cruel statement, "I have done with thee" (line 204). Guide students through her earlier statements (lines 124–125, 139–140, 157, and 175). Discuss how she goes from frustration with Juliet's stubbornness to attempts to calm her husband to a realization that she cannot support both Juliet and her husband, and finally, to a decision to stand by her husband.

**FOR ENGLISH LANGUAGE LEARNERS**

**Concept Support** Have students reread the nurse's words and Capulet's reaction to them. Point out that although the nurse has been part of the Capulet household since Juliet was a baby, if not longer, she is still a household servant. Capulet does not hesitate to insult her when she rises to Juliet's defense and speaks to him as an equal.

Of fair demesnes, youthful, and nobly trained,
Stuffed, as they say, with honorable parts,
Proportioned as one's thought would wish a man—
And then to have a wretched puling fool,
185 A whining mammet, in her fortunes tender,
To answer "I'll not wed, I cannot love;
I am too young, I pray you pardon me"!
But, an you will not wed, I'll pardon you.
Graze where you will, you shall not house with me.
190 Look to't, think on't; I do not use to jest.
Thursday is near; lay hand on heart, advise:
An you be mine, I'll give you to my friend;
An you be not, hang, beg, starve, die in the streets,
For, by my soul, I'll ne'er acknowledge thee,
195 Nor what is mine shall never do thee good.
Trust to't. Bethink you. I'll not be forsworn.

[*Exit.*]

**Juliet.** Is there no pity sitting in the clouds
That sees into the bottom of my grief?
O sweet my mother, cast me not away!
200 Delay this marriage for a month, a week;
Or if you do not, make the bridal bed
In that dim monument where Tybalt lies.

**Lady Capulet.** Talk not to me, for I'll not speak a word.
Do as thou wilt, for I have done with thee.

[*Exit.*]

205 **Juliet.** O God!—O nurse, how shall this be prevented?
My husband is on earth, my faith in heaven.
How shall that faith return again to earth
Unless that husband send it me from heaven
By leaving earth? Comfort me, counsel me.
210 Alack, alack, that heaven should practice stratagems
Upon so soft a subject as myself!
What sayst thou? Hast thou not a word of joy?
Some comfort, nurse.

**Nurse.**              Faith, here it is.
Romeo is banish'd; and all the world to nothing
215 That he dares ne'er come back to challenge you;
Or if he do, it needs must be by stealth.
Then, since the case so stands as now it doth,
I think it best you married with the County.
O, he's a lovely gentleman!
220 Romeo's a dishclout to him. An eagle, madam,

184 **puling:** crying.
185 **mammet:** doll.

189–195 Capulet swears that he'll kick Juliet out and cut her off financially if she refuses to marry.

196 **I'll not be forsworn:** I will not break my promise to Paris.

207–211 Juliet is worried about the sin of being married to two men. She asks how heaven can play such tricks (**practice stratagems**) on her.

213–222 The nurse gives Juliet advice. She says that since Romeo is banished, he's no good to her; Juliet should marry Paris. Romeo is a dishcloth (**dishclout**) compared to Paris.

④ **Targeted Passage**

---

Use these prompts to discuss Capulet's harsh words to his daughter in lines 176–196:

**Recall** What good qualities about Paris does Capulet name? ***Possible answer***: *Paris is of a good family (line 180), owns good land ("fair demesnes," line 181), and is handsome, young, and well educated (lines 181–183).*

**Analyze** How do you think Juliet feels when her father demands that she marry Paris? *Students may suggest that Juliet feels desperate and powerless against her father's demand.*

**Synthesize** Paris is a kinsman of Prince Escalus. What effect might that relationship have upon Capulet's anger toward Juliet? ***Possible answer:*** *By marrying Juliet to Paris, Capulet may feel that he will gain favor with the prince, especially when it comes to the feud with the Montagues. If this is indeed his plan, he is probably furious that Juliet is thwarting it by refusing to marry Paris.*

**BACKGROUND**

**Bigamy** Juliet's nurse counsels her to marry Count Paris, even though she is legally married to Romeo. Elizabethan England frowned upon divorce. Many people in unhappy marriages, especially those who were, like the nurse, among the poorer classes, abandoned their spouses and married again. Notice that the nurse urges Juliet to consider Romeo ("your first") dead (line 225). Fraudulent claims of death were common when justifying remarriage.

---

**FOR STRUGGLING READERS**

④ **Targeted Passage** [Lines 213–219]

In this passage, the nurse begins her attempt to change Juliet's mind.

- According to the nurse, what is the status of Juliet's marriage with Romeo? (lines 215–219)

- What specific action does the nurse suggest that Juliet take? (line 218)

- What is the nurse's opinion of Paris? (line 219)

**Inverted Word Order** Remind students that Shakespeare sometimes inverts word order to maintain poetic meter. Point out line 199, in which Juliet pleads with her mother. As written, the line is an example of iambic pentameter. Have students reorder the words so that the line sounds more natural. ***Possible answer:*** *O my sweet mother, [do] not cast me away!* Point out that the new line does not follow the poetic meter.

Hath not so green, so quick, so fair an eye
As Paris hath. Beshrew my very heart,
I think you are happy in this second match,
For it excels your first; or if it did not,
225 Your first is dead—or 'twere as good he were
As living here and you no use of him.

**Juliet.** Speakst thou this from thy heart?

**Nurse.** And from my soul too; else beshrew them both.

**Juliet.** Amen!

230 **Nurse.** What?

**Juliet.** Well, thou hast comforted me marvelous much.
Go in; and tell my lady I am gone,
Having displeased my father, to Laurence' cell,
To make confession and to be absolved.

235 **Nurse.** Marry, I will; and this is wisely done.

[*Exit.*]

**Juliet.** Ancient damnation! O most wicked fiend!
Is it more sin to wish me thus forsworn,
Or to dispraise my lord with that same tongue
Which she hath praised him with above compare
240 So many thousand times? Go, counselor!
Thou and my bosom henceforth shall be twain.
I'll to the friar to know his remedy.
If all else fail, myself have power to die.

[*Exit.*]

222 **beshrew:** curse.

223–225 This new marriage will be better than the first, which is as good as over.

229 **Amen:** I agree—that is, curse your heart and soul.

236–238 **ancient damnation:** old devil; **dispraise:** criticize.

241 **Thou . . . twain:** I'll no longer tell you my secrets.

**Ⓚ CHARACTER**
How has Juliet's relationship with the nurse changed? Citing details from their **interactions,** explain the main reason for the change.

# Comprehension

1. **Recall** How is Romeo accidentally responsible for Mercutio's death?

2. **Recall** Why does Prince Escalus banish Romeo from Verona?

3. **Recall** What promise does Lord Capulet make to Paris?

4. **Clarify** Why does Lord Capulet become so enraged with Juliet?

# Text Analysis

5. **Reading Shakespearean Drama** Review your list detailing the events in Act Three. What event in this act causes the most problems for Romeo and Juliet? Cite evidence to support your answer.

6. **Analyze Character Motivation** What is Romeo's motivation for killing Tybalt? What are the consequences of this action? Citing evidence, explain whether you think Romeo's behavior is justified revenge or a disastrous mistake.

7. **Interpret Allusions** Find two allusions in Act Three, and record them in a chart like the one shown. Complete the chart by describing what each allusion is a reference to and explaining what each means.

| Scene and Lines | Allusion | Meaning |
|---|---|---|
| Scene 1, lines 70–72 | **Mercutio.** . . . Tybalt, you ratcatcher, will you walk? **Tybalt.** What wouldst thou have with me? **Mercutio.** Good King of Cats, nothing but one of your nine lives. | In Act Two, Scene 4, there was an allusion to a cat named Tybalt in a common story of the time. Mercutio alludes to this story again here to taunt Tybalt and make him want to fight. |

8. **Evaluate Characters** Compare and contrast the behaviors of the nurse and Friar Laurence in Act Three. On the basis of their actions and interactions with other characters, which of the two would you trust more if you were Romeo or Juliet? Explain, citing evidence from the play.

# Text Criticism

9. **Philosophical Context** In the first three acts of *Romeo and Juliet*, both the Chorus and the characters make frequent references to the role of fate in life. How does this notion of fate differ from contemporary views? Do people still think this way today? Explain your answer.

## COMMON CORE

**RL 3** Analyze how complex characters develop over the course of a text, interact with other characters, and advance the plot or develop the theme. **RL 6** Analyze a particular point of view or cultural experience reflected in a work of world literature. **RL 9** Analyze how an author draws on source material in a specific work.

ROMEO AND JULIET: ACT THREE **1113**

---

# Practice and Apply

For preliminary support of post-reading questions, use these copy masters:

**R** **RESOURCE MANAGER—Copy Masters**
Reading Check p. 49
Shakespearean Drama p. 47
Question Support p. 50

Additional selection questions are provided for teachers on page 41.

## ANSWERS

## Comprehension

1. *When Romeo comes between Mercutio and Tybalt, trying to stop the fight, Tybalt is able to fatally wound Mercutio.*

2. *as punishment for killing Tybalt*

3. *that Juliet will marry Paris on Thursday*

4. *Juliet refuses to marry Paris.*

## Text Analysis

COMMON CORE **RL 3, RL 6, RL 9**

**Possible answers:**

5. ■ **COMMON CORE FOCUS** *Reading Shakespearean Drama Romeo's slaying of Tybalt is the most problematic event, for it sends Romeo into exile.*

6. *Romeo's motivation is his desire to avenge Mercutio's death. The consequences are Romeo's banishment and separation from Juliet. Romeo's behavior is a disastrous mistake: had he not sought revenge, the law would have put Tybalt to death, and Romeo would not have been banished.*

7. ● **COMMON CORE FOCUS** *Interpret Allusions Scene and Lines: Scene 5, line 20; Allusion: Romeo—'Tis but the pale reflex of*

---

*Cynthia's brow; Meaning: "Cynthia" is the Roman goddess of the moon. The distancing effect of the allusion anticipates the lovers' separation. Scene and Lines: Scene 5, lines 60–64; Allusion: Juliet—O Fortune, Fortune! . . . send him back; Meaning: Fortune was believed to be fickle. Playing on this word, which means "liable to change affections," and on the image of Fortune as a woman who has taken her love, Juliet expresses hope that Fortune will soon tire of Romeo and return him to her.*

8. *Friar Laurence does not waver in his views, but the nurse is easily manipulated. Students may choose Friar Laurence as the more trustworthy confidant because he seems to have more integrity.*

## Text Criticism

9. *Students may suggest that most people today have a different view: they believe that they can shape their "fate" through hard work, honesty, and proper behavior.*

---

# Assess and Reteach

## Assess

**DIAGNOSTIC AND SELECTION TESTS**
Selection Test A pp. 283–284
Selection Test B/C pp. 285–286

**Interactive Selection Test** on **thinkcentral.com**

## Reteach

**Level Up Online Tutorials** on **thinkcentral.com**

**Reteaching Worksheets** on **thinkcentral.com**
Literature Lessons 25, 26, 35, 38

# Practice and Apply

## READ WITH A PURPOSE

*Help students set a purpose for reading. Tell them to read to find out what terrible discovery the Capulets make and how it happened.*

## Get Into the Act

### SUMMARY

Act Four opens with Juliet's plea for Friar Laurence's help. He offers her a drug that will make her appear dead for 42 hours, after which Romeo will take her to Mantua. Juliet returns home and apologizes to her father; delighted, he advances the wedding date. Juliet drinks the drug that night and is discovered the next morning, apparently dead. Despite some comic relief, Act Four ends with lamentation.

TEXT ANALYSIS | COMMON CORE RL 3

### Ⓐ CHARACTER

**Possible answer:** *The friar's real motive is his concern over the fact that Juliet is already married. He needs time to plan.*

READING STRATEGY | COMMON CORE RL 2, RL 3

### ■ *Model the Skill:* REVIEW

Remind students that one way to maintain understanding while reading Shakespeare is to review events in the previous act. Ask a volunteer to recall the situation at the end of Act Three. Start him or her by saying, "Romeo has been banished to..."

## *Resources for Act Four*

---

# Act Four

## SCENE 1 *Friar Laurence's cell.*

*When Juliet arrives at Friar Laurence's cell, she is upset to find Paris there making arrangements for their wedding. When Paris leaves, the panicked Juliet tells the friar that if he has no solution to her problem, she will kill herself. The friar explains his plan. Juliet will drink a potion he has made from his herbs, which will put her in a deathlike coma. When she wakes up two days later in the family tomb, Romeo will be waiting for her, and they will escape to Mantua together.*

[*Enter* Friar Laurence *and* Paris.]

**Friar Laurence.** On Thursday, sir? The time is very short.

**Paris.** My father Capulet will have it so,
And I am nothing slow to slack his haste.

**Friar Laurence.** You say you do not know the lady's mind.

5 Uneven is the course; I like it not. Ⓐ

**Paris.** Immoderately she weeps for Tybalt's death,
And therefore have I little talked of love;
For Venus smiles not in a house of tears.
Now, sir, her father counts it dangerous

10 That she do give her sorrow so much sway,
And in his wisdom hastes our marriage
To stop the inundation of her tears,
Which, too much minded by herself alone,
May be put from her by society.

15 Now do you know the reason of this haste.

**Friar Laurence** [*aside*]. I would I knew not why it should be
slowed.—
Look, sir, here comes the lady toward my cell.

[*Enter* Juliet.]

**Paris.** Happily met, my lady and my wife!

**Juliet.** That may be, sir, when I may be a wife.

20 **Paris.** That may be must be, love, on Thursday next.

**Juliet.** What must be shall be.

**Friar Laurence.**                          That's a certain text.

**Paris.** Come you to make confession to this father?

**Juliet.** To answer that, I should confess to you.

**2–3 My...haste:** Capulet is eager to have the wedding on Thursday and so am I.

**4–5 You...course:** You don't know how Juliet feels about this. It's a very uncertain (**uneven**) plan.

Ⓐ **CHARACTER**
What is the friar's real **motive** for wanting to slow down the wedding preparations?

**13–14 which...society:** which, thought about too much by her in privacy, may be put from her mind if she is forced to be with others. *According to Paris, why does Capulet want Juliet to marry so quickly?*

**19–28** Juliet once again chooses her words carefully to avoid lying and to avoid telling her secret.

Friar Laurence mixes a potion in the Royal Shakespeare Company's 1995 production.

---

*See resources on the* **Teacher One Stop DVD-ROM** *and on* **thinkcentral.com**.

 **RESOURCE MANAGER UNIT 10**
Plan and Teach, pp. 51–54
Summary pp. 55–56†‡*
Text Analysis and Reading
Skill, pp. 57–60†*

**DIAGNOSTIC AND SELECTION TESTS**
Selection Tests, pp. 287–290

 **BEST PRACTICES TOOLKIT**
Two-Column Chart, p. A25
Sequence Chain, p. B21

**INTERACTIVE READER**

**ADAPTED INTERACTIVE READER**

**ELL ADAPTED INTERACTIVE READER**

**TECHNOLOGY**
- **Teacher One Stop DVD-ROM**
- **Student One Stop DVD-ROM**
- **PowerNotes DVD-ROM**
- **Audio Anthology CD**
- **Audio Tutor CD**
- **ExamView Test Generator on the Teacher One Stop**

### Video Trailer

Go to **thinkcentral.com** to preview the **Video Trailer** introducing this selection. Other features that support the selection include
- **PowerNotes** presentation
- **ThinkAloud** models to enhance comprehension

\* Resources for Differentiation     † Also in Spanish     ‡ In Haitian Creole and Vietnamese

## BACKGROUND

**Sleeping Potions** While the sleeping potion that the friar proposes is never described specifically, Elizabethan audiences might well have surmised that it involved a medicinal plant known as mandragora, or mandrake. As Juliet remarks in lines 47–48 of Scene 3, it was popularly believed that the mandrake screamed when uprooted, and anyone who heard the sound perished or went insane. Popular belief held that mandrake could only be uprooted when pulled by a black dog attached to it by a cord. Once freed from the earth, mandrake was often mixed with opium or hemlock and served as a popular and powerful anesthetic. The friar, being an herbalist, would have had access to all of these ingredients.

## Analyze Visuals

**Activity** What details in the photograph reveal the seriousness of Friar Laurence's business? *Possible answer: The friar's expression shows that he is concentrating. The lighting is dramatic, suggesting an ominous event.*

## DIFFERENTIATED INSTRUCTION

### FOR STRUGGLING READERS

In combination with the *Audio Anthology CD*, use one or more Targeted Passages (pp. 1116, 1119, 1122, 1127) to ensure that students focus on key story events, concepts, and skills.

**Preview** Have students use a Two-Column Chart to organize the Scene 1 synopsis.

| Character | Action |
|-----------|--------|
| Paris | plans wedding with Juliet |
| Juliet | threatens suicide and begs the friar for help |
| Friar | explains plan for reuniting Juliet with Romeo |

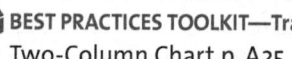 **BEST PRACTICES TOOLKIT—Transparency** Two-Column Chart p. A25

### FOR ENGLISH LANGUAGE LEARNERS

**Task Support** Point out the question in the marginal note for lines 13–14. Ask students to remember how Juliet was acting just before Lady Capulet announced the wedding plans in Act Three, Scene 5. *Possible answer: Paris believes that Capulet wants Juliet to marry so that she will be distracted from her grief over Tybalt.*

**Paris.** Do not deny to him that you love me.

25 **Juliet.** I will confess to you that I love him.

*25 Whom does "him" refer to in this line?*

**Paris.** So will ye, I am sure, that you love me.

**Juliet.** If I do so, it will be of more price,
Being spoke behind your back, than to your face.

**Paris.** Poor soul, thy face is much abused with tears.

30 **Juliet.** The tears have got small victory by that,
For it was bad enough before their spite.

*30–31 The tears . . . spite: The tears haven't ruined my face; it wasn't all that beautiful before they did their damage.*

**Paris.** Thou wrongst it more than tears with that report.

**Juliet.** That is no slander, sir, which is a truth;
And what I spake, I spake it to my face.

35 **Paris.** Thy face is mine, and thou hast slandered it.

*35 Paris says he owns Juliet's face (since she will soon marry him). Insulting her face, he says, insults him, its owner.*

**Juliet.** It may be so, for it is not mine own.
Are you at leisure, holy father, now,
Or shall I come to you at evening mass?

**Friar Laurence.** My leisure serves me, pensive daughter, now.
40 My lord, we must entreat the time alone.

**Paris.** God shield I should disturb devotion!
Juliet, on Thursday early will I rouse ye.
Till then, adieu, and keep this holy kiss.

[*Exit.*]

**Juliet.** O, shut the door! and when thou hast done so,
45 Come weep with me—past hope, past cure, past help!

**Friar Laurence.** Ah, Juliet, I already know thy grief;
It strains me past the compass of my wits.
I hear thou must, and nothing may prorogue it,
On Thursday next be married to this County.

*47–48 compass: limit; prorogue: postpone.*

50 **Juliet.** Tell me not, friar, that thou hearst of this,
Unless thou tell me how I may prevent it.
If in thy wisdom thou canst give no help,
Do thou but call my resolution wise
And with this knife I'll help it presently.
55 God joined my heart and Romeo's, thou our hands;
And ere this hand, by thee to Romeo's sealed,
Shall be the label to another deed,
Or my true heart with treacherous revolt
Turn to another, this shall slay them both.
60 Therefore, out of thy long-experienced time,

 **Targeted Passage**

*52–53 If in . . . wise: If you can't find a way to help me, at least agree that my plan is wise.*

*56–67 And ere this hand . . . of remedy: Before I sign another wedding agreement (deed), I will use this knife to kill myself. If you, with your years of experience (long-experienced time), can't help me, I'll end my sufferings (extremes) and solve the problem myself.*

## DIFFERENTIATED INSTRUCTION

**FOR STRUGGLING READERS**

**① Targeted Passage** [Lines 50–59]

This passage reveals Juliet's fragile state of mind as she asks for Friar Laurence's help.

• Why is Juliet so upset? (lines 50–51)

• What help does Juliet want from Friar Laurence? (line 51)

• What is Juliet prepared to do if Friar Laurence does not help her? How does she want him to feel about her decision? (lines 54–55)

**FOR ENGLISH LANGUAGE LEARNERS**

**Task Support** Direct students to the marginal question about line 25. Help students understand the scene by having two students read lines 22–28 aloud. Remind students that Juliet is choosing her words carefully so that she can speak the truth without giving away her secret. *Possible answer: Juliet uses "him" to refer to Romeo, but Paris thinks that "him" refers to Friar Laurence.*

---

## Is **LOVE** stronger than **HATE?**

**Discuss** How does Paris's expression of love in lines 24–43 compare to Romeo's expression of love when he first met Juliet? *Possible answer: Like Romeo, Paris praises Juliet's beauty (lines 29 and 32). However, unlike Romeo, Paris's expression of love is much less emotional. He does not use poetry or show his complete idolatry of Juliet as Romeo did. Paris also discusses his ownership and control of Juliet, which Romeo did not do.*

Give me some present counsel; or, behold,
'Twixt my extremes and me this bloody knife
Shall play the umpire, arbitrating that
Which the commission of thy years and art
65 Could to no issue of true honor bring.
Be not so long to speak. I long to die
If what thou speakst speak not of remedy.

**Friar Laurence.** Hold, daughter, I do spy a kind of hope,
Which craves as desperate an execution
70 As that is desperate which we would prevent.
If, rather than to marry County Paris,
Thou hast the strength of will to slay thyself,
Then is it likely thou wilt undertake
A thing like death to chide away this shame,
75 That copest with death himself to scape from it;
And, if thou darest, I'll give thee remedy.

**Juliet.** O, bid me leap, rather than marry Paris,
From off the battlements of yonder tower,
Or walk in thievish ways, or bid me lurk
80 Where serpents are; chain me with roaring bears,
Or shut me nightly in a charnel house,
O'ercovered quite with dead men's rattling bones,
With reeky shanks and yellow chapless skulls;
Or bid me go into a new-made grave
85 And hide me with a dead man in his shroud—
Things that, to hear them told, have made me tremble—
And I will do it without fear or doubt,
To live an unstained wife to my sweet love.

**Friar Laurence.** Hold, then. Go home, be merry, give consent
90 To marry Paris. Wednesday is tomorrow.
Tomorrow night look that thou lie alone:
Let not the nurse lie with thee in thy chamber.
Take thou this vial, being then in bed,
And this distilled liquor drink thou off;
95 When presently through all thy veins shall run
A cold and drowsy humor; for no pulse
Shall keep his native progress, but surcease;
No warmth, no breath, shall testify thou livest;
The roses in thy lips and cheeks shall fade
100 To paly ashes, thy eyes' windows fall

---

○ **COMMON CORE** L 4a

**Language Coach**

**Commonly Confused Words** The words *council* and *counsel* are easy to confuse. One means "advice" or "to advise"; the other refers to a group of people who advise, administrate, or govern. Which is which? What does *counsel* mean in line 61?

**71–76 If, rather than . . . remedy:** If you are desperate enough to kill yourself, then you'll be daring enough to try the deathlike solution that I propose.

**77–88** Juliet gives a lengthy list of things she would do rather than marry Paris. **charnel house:** a storehouse for bones from old graves; **reeky shanks:** stinking bones; **chapless:** without jaws. The description in lines 84–88 comes closer to Juliet's future than she knows.

**89–120** The friar explains his plan.

**93 vial:** small bottle.

**96–106 humor:** liquid; **no pulse . . . pleasant sleep:** Your pulse will stop (**surcease**), and you will turn cold, pale, and stiff, as if you were dead; this condition will last for 42 hours.

---

## TIERED DISCUSSION PROMPTS

Use these prompts to explore the depths of Juliet's desperation as revealed in lines 77–88:

**Connect** Think of a time when you had to do something that you did not want to do. How does that memory help you understand how Juliet feels about marrying Paris? *Students may identify with Juliet's gloom and rising panic, especially as she lists terrible preferences to the marriage.*

**Analyze** How would the actions in Juliet's list get her out of the marriage with Paris? *Possible answer: Leaping from the tower's battlements (lines 77–78) would kill her; she might also die by going near serpents or bears (lines 79–80). Becoming a thief (line 79) would either cause Paris to reject her or would require her to live in hiding. Going into a charnel house or a new grave (lines 81–85) would make her seem insane, probably causing Paris to reject her.*

**Evaluate** Why is Juliet so dramatically upset? Does she really dislike Paris so intensely, or does she simply want to avoid the shame of betraying her husband? *Possible answer: In lines 87–88, Juliet says that she would do these things so that she could "live an unstained wife." From this line, it appears that she does not hate Paris; rather, she does not want to betray Romeo. The play indicates Juliet's feelings about what Paris represents, but it offers little to suggest her feelings about Paris as an individual.*

---

## FOR STRUGGLING READERS

**Comprehension Support** [lines 90–91] To make sure that students understand this part of the friar's plan, discuss why he doesn't suggest that Juliet take the sleeping potion that same night. Elicit that he needs time to get a message to Romeo and get Romeo back to Verona before the effects wear off. Refer to this point about timing again when Capulet moves the wedding to Wednesday (Scene 2, line 24).

## FOR ENGLISH LANGUAGE LEARNERS

**Language Coach** ○ **COMMON CORE** L 4a

**Commonly Confused Words**
*Possible answer:* advice Ask students to use the word *council* in a sentence.
*Possible answer: The student* council *decided to sell sweatshirts at the basketball game.*

## TIERED DISCUSSION PROMPTS

Use these prompts to discuss Juliet's apology to her father in Scene 2, lines 17–22:

**Recall** What reason does Juliet give for offering an apology to her father? *Possible answer: She says that she has learned from Friar Laurence that she should repent of her disobedience to him.*

**Analyze** What is the real reason for Juliet's apology? *Possible answer: The real reason is to fool her father so that she may be left in peace to follow through with Friar Laurence's plan.*

**Evaluate** By making an apology, Juliet regains her father's favor. Why do you think Capulet is so quickly convinced? *Possible answer: Capulet is convinced because he hears what he longs to hear—namely, the words "Henceforward I am ever ruled by you" (line 22).*

---

Like death when he shuts up the day of life;
Each part, deprived of supple government,
Shall, stiff and stark and cold, appear like death;
And in this borrowed likeness of shrunk death
105 Thou shalt continue two-and-forty hours,
And then awake as from a pleasant sleep.
Now, when the bridegroom in the morning comes
To rouse thee from thy bed, there art thou dead.
Then, as the manner of our country is,
110 In thy best robes uncovered on the bier
Thou shalt be borne to that same ancient vault
Where all the kindred of the Capulets lie.
In the meantime, against thou shalt awake,
Shall Romeo by my letters know our drift;
115 And hither shall he come; and he and I
Will watch thy waking, and that very night
Shall Romeo bear thee hence to Mantua.
And this shall free thee from this present shame,
If no inconstant toy nor womanish fear
120 Abate thy valor in the acting it.

**Juliet.** Give me, give me! O, tell me not of fear!

**Friar Laurence.** Hold! Get you gone, be strong and prosperous
In this resolve. I'll send a friar with speed
To Mantua, with my letters to thy lord.

125 **Juliet.** Love give me strength! and strength shall help afford.
Farewell, dear father.

[*Exeunt.*]

# SCENE 2  *Capulet's house.*

*Capulet is making plans for the wedding on Thursday. Juliet arrives and apologizes to him, saying that she will marry Paris. Capulet is so relieved that he reschedules the wedding for the next day, Wednesday.*

[*Enter* Capulet, Lady Capulet, Nurse, *and* Servingmen.]

**Capulet.** So many guests invite as here are writ.

[*Exit a* Servingman.]

Sirrah, go hire me twenty cunning cooks.

**Servingman.** You shall have none ill, sir; for I'll try if they can lick their fingers.

**107–112** *According to the friar's plan, what will happen when Paris comes to wake Juliet?*

**111–112 same ancient vault . . . lie:** same ancient tomb where all members of the Capulet family are buried.

**114 drift:** plan.

**119–120 inconstant toy:** foolish whim; **abate thy valor:** weaken your courage.

**1–8** Capulet is having a cheerful conversation with his servants about the wedding preparations. One servant assures him that he will test (**try**) the cooks he hires by making them taste their own food (**lick their fingers**).

---

## DIFFERENTIATED INSTRUCTION

### FOR STRUGGLING READERS

**Preview** Call on a volunteer to read aloud the italicized scene synopsis. Help students create a Sequence Chain like this to organize the events in Scene 2:

BEST PRACTICES TOOLKIT—Transparency
Sequence Chain p. B21

Capulet is planning the wedding.
↓
Juliet arrives and apologizes.
↓
Juliet agrees to marry Paris.
↓
Capulet reschedules the wedding for Wednesday—the next day.

### FOR ENGLISH LANGUAGE LEARNERS

**Task Support** As you direct students to the marginal question for lines 107–112, make sure that they understand the words "bridegroom", "bier", "borne", and "vault". *Possible answer: When Paris arrives in the morning, he will find Juliet seemingly dead. Then her body will be carried to the Capulet family vault.*

**Capulet.** How canst thou try them so?

**Servingman.** Marry, sir, 'tis an ill cook that cannot lick his own fingers. Therefore he that cannot lick his fingers goes not with me. **B**

**Capulet.** Go, begone.

[*Exit* Servingman.]

10  We shall be much unfurnished for this time.
    What, is my daughter gone to Friar Laurence?

**Nurse.** Ay, forsooth.

**Capulet.** Well, he may chance to do some good on her.
    A peevish self-willed harlotry it is.

[*Enter* Juliet.]

15  **Nurse.** See where she comes from shrift with merry look.

**Capulet.** How now, my headstrong? Where have you been gadding?

**Juliet.** Where I have learnt me to repent the sin
    Of disobedient opposition
    To you and your behests, and am enjoined
20  By holy Laurence to fall prostrate here
    To beg your pardon. Pardon, I beseech you!
    Henceforward I am ever ruled by you.

**Capulet.** Send for the County. Go tell him of this.
    I'll have this knot knit up tomorrow morning.

25  **Juliet.** I met the youthful lord at Laurence' cell
    And gave him what becomed love I might,
    Not stepping o'er the bounds of modesty.

**Capulet.** Why, I am glad on't. This is well. Stand up.
    This is as't should be. Let me see the County.
30  Ay, marry, go, I say, and fetch him hither.
    Now, afore God, this reverend holy friar,
    All our whole city is much bound to him. **C**

**Juliet.** Nurse, will you go with me into my closet
    To help me sort such needful ornaments
35  As you think fit to furnish me tomorrow?

**Lady Capulet.** No, not till Thursday. There is time enough.

**Capulet.** Go, nurse, go with her. We'll to church tomorrow.

[*Exeunt* Juliet *and* Nurse.]

---

**B COMIC RELIEF**
Think about the purpose that comic relief serves. Why might Shakespeare have chosen to begin this scene with a light, humorous conversation?

10 **unfurnished:** unprepared.

14  A silly, stubborn girl she is.

19 **behests:** orders; **enjoined:** commanded.

24  I'll have this wedding scheduled for tomorrow morning.

**② Targeted Passage**

**C DRAMATIC IRONY**
What is ironic about Capulet's praise of Friar Laurence?

36–39  Lady Capulet urges her husband to wait until Thursday as originally planned. She needs time to get food (**provision**) ready for the wedding party.

---

**TEXT ANALYSIS**                                    COMMON CORE  L 3

**B COMIC RELIEF**

*Possible answer:* *Shakespeare might have chosen to begin the scene with humor to break away from the heavy, dark ending to Scene 1. Light conversation is also appropriate for planning a party, the focus of the scene.*

**TEXT ANALYSIS**                                    COMMON CORE  RL 10

**C DRAMATIC IRONY**

*Possible answer:* *Capulet's praise of Friar Laurence is ironic because the friar has taken many secret actions for which Capulet would condemn him, if only he knew of them. The friar has married Juliet to Romeo, is scheming to overturn Romeo's sentence of banishment, and is conspiring with Juliet to trick Capulet into believing that she is dead.*

**IF STUDENTS NEED HELP . . .** Have them use Main Idea and Details notes to record the actions that Friar Laurence has taken up to this point in the play. After they have reviewed the details, help them craft a main idea statement that expresses what Capulet would think if he knew of these actions.

**BEST PRACTICES TOOLKIT—Transparency**
Main Idea and Details p. B6

---

**FOR STRUGGLING READERS**

**② Targeted Passage [Lines 23–37]**

By presenting Capulet's response to Juliet's apology, this passage introduces a further complication to the story.

- How does Capulet react to the apology? Which words show his feelings? (lines 28–29)

- When will the wedding take place? Was this the original plan? How does Juliet's mother feel about Capulet's decision? (lines 24, 36–37)

- Who will help Juliet prepare for the wedding? Does Capulet approve? (lines 33–35, 37)

**FOR ENGLISH LANGUAGE LEARNERS**

**Vocabulary: Outdated Forms** Urge students to continue adding outdated terms to their language journals. (See the **For English Language Learners** activity on page 1036.) Provide these terms and their definitions. Then have students reread the lines noted and substitute the definitions for the words.

- *writ* (line 1), "written"

- Sirrah (line 2), "hey, you" (a call to someone inferior)

- *try* (lines 3 and 5), "test"

- *Ay, forsooth* (line 12), "Yes, it's true"

- *gadding* (line 16), "wandering"

- *learnt* (line 17), "learned"

- *prostrate* (line 20), "face down" (showing humility and reverence)

- *Henceforward* (line 22), "from now on"

- *becomed* (line 26), "appropriate"

**D** *Model the Skill:* **TRAGEDY**

Explain that Mantua is almost 40 miles from Verona. Discuss how long students think it would take for a message to travel that distance in Shakespeare's time.

**Possible answer:** *Moving the wedding up by one day threatens to undermine Friar Laurence's plan. Juliet will not be able to wait until Wednesday night to take the sleeping potion. Furthermore, it will be very difficult, perhaps impossible, for Friar Laurence to get word to Romeo about Juliet's feigned death and his plan to have Romeo come and take her to Mantua.*

---

**Lady Capulet.** We shall be short in our provision.
'Tis now near night.

**Capulet.** Tush, I will stir about,
40 And all things shall be well, I warrant thee, wife.
Go thou to Juliet, help to deck up her.
I'll not to bed tonight; let me alone.
I'll play the housewife for this once. What, ho!
They are all forth; well, I will walk myself
45 To County Paris, to prepare him up
Against tomorrow. My heart is wondrous light,
Since this same wayward girl is so reclaimed. **D**

[*Exeunt.*]

**39–46** Capulet is so set on Wednesday that he promises to make the arrangements himself.

**D TRAGEDY**
Think about how the **plot** of this tragedy is unfolding. What does moving the wedding up by one day do to Friar Laurence's plan?

## SCENE 3 *Juliet's bedroom.*

*Juliet sends her mother and the nurse away and prepares to take the drug the friar has given her. She is confused and frightened but finally puts the vial to her lips and drinks.*

[*Enter* Juliet *and* Nurse.]

**Juliet.** Ay, those attires are best; but, gentle nurse,
I pray thee leave me to myself tonight;
For I have need of many orisons
To move the heavens to smile upon my state,
5 Which, well thou knowest, is cross and full of sin.

[*Enter* Lady Capulet.]

**Lady Capulet.** What, are you busy, ho? Need you my help?

**Juliet.** No madam; we have culled such necessaries
As are behooveful for our state tomorrow.
So please you, let me now be left alone,
10 And let the nurse this night sit up with you;
For I am sure you have your hands full all
In this so sudden business.

**Lady Capulet.** Good night.
Get thee to bed and rest, for thou hast need.

[*Exeunt* Lady Capulet *and* Nurse.]

**Juliet.** Farewell! God knows when we shall meet again.
15 I have a faint cold fear thrills through my veins
That almost freezes up the heat of life.
I'll call them back again to comfort me.
Nurse!—What should she do here?
My dismal scene I needs must act alone.

**3 orisons:** prayers.

**7–8 we have ... tomorrow:** We have picked out (**culled**) everything appropriate for the wedding tomorrow.

**17–19** In her fear, Juliet starts to call the nurse back but realizes that she must be alone to drink the poison.

---

## DIFFERENTIATED INSTRUCTION

### FOR STRUGGLING READERS

**Paraphrasing Shakespeare** Draw students' attention to the marginal note for lines 39–46, which explains how Capulet takes over the preparations for the wedding. Help students paraphrase his comments in lines 39–41 to read something like this: *Nonsense! I will get busy, and everything will be fine. I guarantee it, wife. You go to Juliet and help her choose her finest clothes [for the wedding].*

**Preview** As you read through the Scene 3 synopsis, use an Open Mind diagram to help students identify Juliet's actions and emotions.

🧰 **BEST PRACTICES TOOLKIT—Transparency**
Open Mind p. D9

*Juliet's actions*
sends mother and nurse away
prepares to take Friar Laurence's drug
drinks the potion

*Juliet's emotions*
confusion
fear
determination

## Behind the Curtain

The Seattle Repertory Theatre, 2003

WILLIAM SHAKESPEARE
ROMEO & JULIET

LOVE CONQUERS EVERYTHING.
EXCEPT STAB WOUNDS AND POISONING.

Romeo + Juliet
by William Shakespeare

The Arkansas Repertory Theatre, 2004

The National Theater of Poland, 1996

TEATR NARODOWY
Warszawa

SIERGIEJ PROKOFIEW
ROMEO I JULIA
Choreografia Emil Wesolowski

### Promotion

Imagine that you knew nothing about the story of the star-crossed lovers. What clues about the play do each of these **promotional** posters provide? Which poster would most make you want to see the play? Explain your answers.

1121

**Promotion** Discuss the fact that effective promotional materials must give enough information about a play to entice an audience to attend the performance but not so much information that they give away the whole story. Ask how the promotional pieces shown here contain messages that are clear only to people who are familiar with the play. *Possible answer: The Arkansas Repertory Theatre's poster uses the rose motif, an important image in Juliet's famous soliloquy (Act Two, Scene 2) about the importance of names: "A rose by any other name . . . ." The Seattle Repertory Theatre's poster offers a witty caption, compelling lettering, and images of weapons, suggesting the violence in the tale. The National Theater of Poland's poster contains a mysterious image of the lovers unfolding from a flower. It reveals little information about the plot of the play. Answers will vary, but students should identify the features that make their chosen poster appealing.*

### FOR ADVANCED LEARNERS/PRE–AP

**Contrast and Evaluate** [small-group option] Ask students to research print and Internet sources to find more than one poster that advertises the same play or movie. Have them contrast these promotional materials, determine the message of each one, and decide which one is the most effective. To extend the activity, challenge students to create a poster that they think does an even better job of promoting the play or movie.

**Ⓔ CHARACTER**

*Possible answer: Juliet suspects that Friar Laurence, motivated by fear of being dishonored for his role in the plot, has given her a potion that really will kill her. She probably does not really believe this: In lines 28–29, she reminds herself that the friar is a holy man and can be trusted.*

## TIERED DISCUSSION PROMPTS

Use these prompts to discuss Juliet's internal conflict before she takes the sleeping potion, as revealed in lines 30–58:

**Recall** What is Juliet afraid of as she prepares to drink the potion? *Possible answer: She is afraid that she will wake up before Romeo arrives. If she does, she fears that she will suffocate or that she will go crazy at the sight of the corpses and kill herself with the bone of a nearby corpse.*

**Analyze** What emotions does Juliet display when she overcomes her fear and drinks the potion? *Possible answer: She shows courage, bravery, love for Romeo, and devotion to her marriage.*

**Evaluate** Are the fears that Juliet expresses in lines 45–54 justified? Explain. *Some students may feel that waking up in a family cemetery would stir up the imagination and fears of most people. Others might find that lines such as 49–52 express fears that go beyond what is reasonable.*

---

20 Come, vial.
What if this mixture do not work at all?
Shall I be married then tomorrow morning?
No, no! This shall forbid it. Lie thou there.
[*lays down a dagger*]
What if it be a poison which the friar
25 Subtly hath ministered to have me dead,
Lest in this marriage he should be dishonored
Because he married me before to Romeo?
I fear it is; and yet methinks it should not,
For he hath still been tried a holy man. **Ⓔ**
30 How if, when I am laid into the tomb,
I wake before the time that Romeo
Come to redeem me? There's a fearful point!
Shall I not then be stifled in the vault,
To whose foul mouth no healthsome air breathes in,
35 And there die strangled ere my Romeo comes?
Or, if I live, is it not very like
The horrible conceit of death and night,
Together with the terror of the place—
As in a vault, an ancient receptacle
40 Where for this many hundred years the bones
Of all my buried ancestors are packed;
Where bloody Tybalt, yet but green in earth,
Lies fest'ring in his shroud; where, as they say,
At some hours in the night spirits resort—
45 Alack, alack, is it not like that I,
So early waking—what with loathsome smells,
And shrieks like mandrakes torn out of the earth,
That living mortals, hearing them, run mad—
O, if I wake, shall I not be distraught,
50 Environed with all these hideous fears,
And madly play with my forefathers' joints,
And pluck the mangled Tybalt from his shroud,
And, in this rage, with some great kinsman's bone
As with a club dash out my desp'rate brains?
55 O, look! methinks I see my cousin's ghost
Seeking out Romeo, that did spit his body
Upon a rapier's point. Stay, Tybalt, stay!
Romeo, I come! this do I drink to thee.
[*She drinks and falls upon her bed within the curtains.*]

**23 This shall forbid it:** A dagger will be her alternative means of keeping from marrying Paris.

**24–57** Juliet lists her various doubts and fears about what she is about to do.

**Ⓔ CHARACTER**
In her anxious state, what does Juliet suspect about Friar Laurence's **motives** for giving her the potion? Do you think she really believes this to be true? Explain.

**36–43** Juliet fears the vision (**conceit**) she might have on waking in the family tomb and seeing the rotting body of Tybalt.

**45–54** She fears that the smells together with the sounds of ghosts screaming might make her lose her mind and commit bizarre acts. Mandrake root was thought to look like the human form and to scream when pulled from the ground.

 **Targeted Passage**
**57 stay:** stop.

---

## DIFFERENTIATED INSTRUCTION

### FOR STRUGGLING READERS

**③ Targeted Passage [Lines 55–58]**

In this passage, Juliet musters her courage and drinks Friar Laurence's potion.

• Who is the ghost that Juliet imagines she sees? What is it doing, and why?

• What does Juliet mean when she says, "I come!"?

• What fateful action does Juliet take as Scene 3 concludes?

### FOR ENGLISH LANGUAGE LEARNERS

**Develop Reading Fluency** Model for students how to read a section of Juliet's soliloquy expressing the different emotions she feels as she contemplates drinking the poison. After you have read several sections, have pairs of students practice reading the lines aloud together. While one reads, ask the other to listen and offer suggestions on how to improve the reading. Then have them switch roles.

# SCENE 4 *Capulet's house.*

*It is now the next morning, nearly time for the wedding. The household is happy and excited as everyone makes final preparations.*

[*Enter* Lady Capulet *and* Nurse.]

**Lady Capulet.** Hold, take these keys and fetch more spices, nurse.

**Nurse.** They call for dates and quinces in the pastry.

[*Enter* Capulet.]

**Capulet.** Come, stir, stir, stir! The second cock hath crowed,
The curfew bell hath rung, 'tis three o'clock.

5 Look to the baked meats, good Angelica;
Spare not for cost.

**Nurse.** Go, you cot-quean, go,
Get you to bed! Faith, you'll be sick tomorrow
For this night's watching.

**Capulet.** No, not a whit. What, I have watched ere now
10 All night for lesser cause, and ne'er been sick.

**Lady Capulet.** Ay, you have been a mouse-hunt in your time;
But I will watch you from such watching now.

[*Exeunt* Lady Capulet *and* Nurse.]

**Capulet.** A jealous hood, a jealous hood!

[*Enter three or four* Servants, *with spits and logs and baskets.*]
Now, fellow,
What is there?

15 **First Servant.** Things for the cook, sir; but I know not what.

**Capulet.** Make haste, make haste. [*Exit* Servant.] Sirrah, fetch
drier logs.
Call Peter; he will show thee where they are.

**Second Servant.** I have a head, sir, that will find out logs
And never trouble Peter for the matter.

20 **Capulet.** Mass, and well said, merry whoreson, ha!
Thou shalt be loggerhead. [*Exit* Servant.] Good faith, 'tis day.
The County will be here with music straight,
For so he said he would. [*music within*] I hear him near.
Nurse! Wife! What, ho! What, nurse, I say!

**2 pastry:** the room where baking is done.

**5 good Angelica:** In his happy mood, Capulet even calls the nurse by her name.

**6 cot-quean:** The nurse playfully refers to Capulet as a "cottage quean," or housewife. This is a joke about his doing women's work (arranging the party).

**11–13** Lord and Lady Capulet joke about his being a woman chaser (**mouse-hunt**) as a young man. He makes fun of her jealousy (**jealous hood**).

**20–23** The joking between Capulet and his servants includes the mild oath **Mass,** short for "by the Mass," and **loggerhead,** a word for a stupid person as well as a pun, since the servant is searching for drier logs. **straight:** right away.

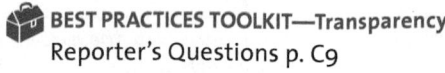

## Is **LOVE** stronger than **HATE?**

**Discuss** Refer students to lines 12–20. Once they realize that Juliet is dead (or so they think), how do the nurse and Lady Capulet express their love for Juliet? *Possible answer: With Juliet gone, the nurse wishes that she herself had never been born (line 15). Lady Capulet wishes that she could die along with her daughter (line 20).*

---

[*Reenter* Nurse.]

25  Go waken Juliet; go and trim her up.
    I'll go and chat with Paris. Hie, make haste,
    Make haste! The bridegroom he is come already:
    Make haste, I say.

[*Exeunt.*]

## SCENE 5   *Juliet's bedroom.*

*The joyous preparations suddenly change into plans for a funeral when the nurse discovers Juliet on her bed, apparently dead. Lord and Lady Capulet, Paris, and the nurse are overcome with grief. Friar Laurence tries to comfort them and instructs them to bring Juliet's body to the Capulet family tomb. The scene abruptly switches to humor, in a foolish conversation between the servant Peter and the musicians hired to play at the wedding.*

[*Enter* Nurse.]

**Nurse.** Mistress! what, mistress! Juliet! Fast, I warrant her, she.
Why, lamb! why, lady! Fie, you slugabed!
Why, love, I say! madam! sweetheart! Why, bride!
What, not a word? You take your pennyworths now,
5  Sleep for a week; for the next night, I warrant,
The County Paris hath set up his rest
That you shall rest but little. God forgive me,
Marry and amen, how sound is she asleep!
I needs must wake her. Madam, madam, madam!
10  Aye, let the County take you in your bed,
He'll fright you up, i' faith. Will it not be?

[*opens the curtains*]

What, dressed and in your clothes and down again?
I must needs wake you. Lady! lady! lady!
Alas, alas! Help, help! my lady's dead!
15  O well-a-day that ever I was born!
Some aqua vitae, ho! My lord! my lady!

[*Enter* Lady Capulet.]

**Lady Capulet.** What noise is here?

**Nurse.**                   O lamentable day!

**Lady Capulet.** What is the matter?

**Nurse.**                 Look, look! O heavy day!

**Lady Capulet.** O me, O me! My child, my only life!
20  Revive, look up, or I will die with thee!
Help! help! Call help.

**1–11** The nurse chatters as she bustles around the room. She calls Juliet a **slugabed,** or sleepyhead, who is trying to get her **pennyworths,** or small portions, of rest now, since after the wedding Paris won't let her get much sleep. When Juliet doesn't answer, the nurse opens the curtains that enclose the bed.

**17 lamentable:** filled with grief.

---

## DIFFERENTIATED INSTRUCTION

### FOR STRUGGLING READERS

**Preview** Read the Scene 5 synopsis aloud to the class. Have students use a Sequence Chain to familiarize themselves with the events of Scene 5.

 **BEST PRACTICES TOOLKIT—Transparency** Sequence Chain p. B21

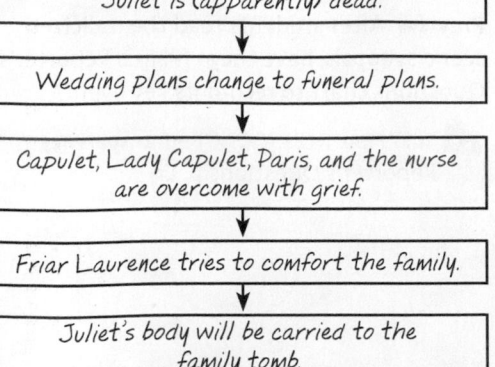

Juliet is (apparently) dead.

↓

Wedding plans change to funeral plans.

↓

Capulet, Lady Capulet, Paris, and the nurse are overcome with grief.

↓

Friar Laurence tries to comfort the family.

↓

Juliet's body will be carried to the family tomb.

[*Enter* Capulet.]

**Capulet.** For shame, bring Juliet forth; her lord is come.

**Nurse.** She's dead, deceased; she's dead! Alack the day!

**Lady Capulet.** Alack the day, she's dead, she's dead, she's dead!

25 **Capulet.** Ha! let me see her. Out alas! she's cold,
Her blood is settled, and her joints are stiff;
Life and these lips have long been separated.
Death lies on her like an untimely frost
Upon the sweetest flower of all the field.

30 **Nurse.** O lamentable day!

**Lady Capulet.**                O woeful time!

**Capulet.** Death, that hath ta'en her hence to make me wail,
Ties up my tongue and will not let me speak.

[*Enter* Friar Laurence *and* Paris, *with* Musicians.]

**Friar Laurence.** Come, is the bride ready to go to church?

*28–29 What simile does Capulet use to describe what has happened to Juliet?*

**COMMON CORE L 4b**

**Language Coach**

**Derivations** Words formed from another word or base are **derivations.** The word *lamentable* (line 30) is derived from the base word *lament*, "to grieve." What does *lamentable* mean? What other words are derived from this same word?

Friar Laurence and the Capulets mourn for Juliet in the University of Victoria's 1998 production.

## Analyze Visuals

**Activity** What details about the costumes and the poses of the actors in the photograph convey a solemn mood? *Possible answer: The actors are dressed in dark clothing (except for Juliet, whose light clothing provides a contrast) and have grim looks on their faces. Almost everyone is huddled around the bed in which Juliet lies; the exception is the nurse, who sits apart, her head in her hands. All of these details help convey the solemnity and grief caused by Juliet's apparent death.*

**FOR ENGLISH LANGUAGE LEARNERS**

**Task Support** Point out the marginal question for lines 28–29. Remind students that a simile is a comparison that uses the words *like* or *as;* then have students reread lines 28–29 to find one of those words and the descriptions that it connects. ***Possible answer:*** *Capulet compares Juliet's death to an unexpected frost that kills the sweetest flower in a field.*

**Language Coach**    **COMMON CORE L 4b**

**Derivations** *Possible answers: very sad, heartbreaking; lamentation* Have students name derivations from these words that appear in this scene: *faith* (line 11), *revive* (line 20), *shame* (line 22), *speak* (line 33).

## TIERED DISCUSSION PROMPTS

Use these prompts to explore Friar Laurence's words to the Capulets in lines 65–83:

**Connect** Have you ever heard someone offering words of comfort about a person's death? Do you find Friar Laurence's words comforting? Why or why not? *Students should cite specific phrases from the text to support their answers.*

**Analyze** According to Friar Laurence, what is the highest form of human advancement? *Possible answer: The highest form of human advancement is to live in heaven (lines 73–74).*

**Synthesize** How might Friar Laurence's advice to the family be different if he did not know that Juliet was alive? *Possible answers: Friar Laurence might not encourage the family to take Juliet's body to the tomb quickly. He might express greater regret and loss. He might sympathize more with the grief-stricken family.*

**Capulet.** Ready to go, but never to return.
35 O son, the night before thy wedding day
Hath death lain with thy wife. See, there she lies,
Flower as she was, deflowered by him.
Death is my son-in-law, Death is my heir;
My daughter he hath wedded. I will die
40 And leave him all. Life, living, all is Death's.
    **Paris.** Have I thought long to see this morning's face,
And doth it give me such a sight as this?
    **Lady Capulet.** Accursed, unhappy, wretched, hateful day!
Most miserable hour that e'er time saw
45 In lasting labor of his pilgrimage!
But one, poor one, one poor and loving child,
But one thing to rejoice and solace in,
And cruel Death hath catched it from my sight!
    **Nurse.** O woe! O woeful, woeful, woeful day!
50 Most lamentable day, most woeful day
That ever, ever I did yet behold!
O day! O day! O day! O hateful day!
Never was seen so black a day as this.
O woeful day! O woeful day!
55   **Paris.** Beguiled, divorced, wronged, spited, slain!
Most detestable Death, by thee beguiled,
By cruel, cruel thee quite overthrown!
O love! O life! not life, but love in death!
    **Capulet.** Despised, distressed, hated, martyred, killed!
60 Uncomfortable time, why camest thou now
To murder, murder our solemnity?
O child! O child! my soul, and not my child!
Dead art thou, dead! alack, my child is dead,
And with my child my joys are buried!
65 **Friar Laurence.** Peace, ho, for shame! Confusion's cure lives not
In these confusions. Heaven and yourself
Had part in this fair maid! now heaven hath all,
And all the better is it for the maid.
Your part in her you could not keep from death,
70 But heaven keeps his part in eternal life.
The most you sought was her promotion,
For 'twas your heaven she should be advanced;
And weep ye now, seeing she is advanced
Above the clouds, as high as heaven itself?
75 O, in this love, you love your child so ill

**40 Life...Death's:** My life, my possessions, and everything else of mine belongs to Death.

**44–48 Most miserable...my sight:** This is the most miserable hour that time ever saw on its long journey. I had only one child to make me happy, and Death has taken (**catched**) her from me.

**55 beguiled:** tricked.

**60–61 why...solemnity:** Why did Death have to come to murder our celebration?

**65–78** The friar comforts the family. He says that the cure for disaster (**confusion**) cannot be found in cries of grief. Juliet's family and heaven once shared her; now heaven has all of her. All the family ever wanted was the best for her; now she's in heaven—what could be better than that? It is best to die young, when the soul is still pure, without sin.

## DIFFERENTIATED INSTRUCTION

**FOR ENGLISH LANGUAGE LEARNERS**

**Concept Support** Have students review the mourning in this scene by writing a one-sentence summary of each character's speech. Begin with these examples:

- Capulet says that his daughter is now the bride of Death (lines 34–40).
- Paris complains that he has waited for this wedding morning and now sees this terrible sight (lines 41–42).

**FOR ADVANCED LEARNERS/PRE–AP**

**Inverted Word Order** Shakespeare inverts word order for effect, for emphasis, and to better fit with his poetic meter. Discuss his reason for doing so in lines 56, 60, 63, 65, and 73. *Possible answer: The inversions in lines 56 and 65 conform to meter. The inversion in line 60 creates a dramatic effect. The inversion in line 63 creates emphasis (on* dead*). The inversion in line 73 creates emphasis (on* weep *and* now*).*

That you run mad, seeing that she is well.
She's not well married that lives married long,
But she's best married that dies married young.
Dry up your tears and stick your rosemary
80 On this fair corse, and, as the custom is,
In all her best array bear her to church;
For though fond nature bids us all lament,
Yet nature's tears are reason's merriment.

**Capulet.** All things that we ordained festival
85 Turn from their office to black funeral—
Our instruments to melancholy bells,
Our wedding cheer to a sad burial feast;
Our solemn hymns to sullen dirges change;
Our bridal flowers serve for a buried corse;
90 And all things change them to the contrary.

**Friar Laurence.** Sir, go you in; and, madam, go with him;
And go, Sir Paris. Every one prepare
To follow this fair corse unto her grave.
The heavens do lower upon you for some ill;
95 Move them no more by crossing their high will.

[*Exeunt* Capulet, Lady Capulet, Paris, *and* Friar.]

**First Musician.** Faith, we may put up our pipes, and be gone.

**Nurse.** Honest good fellows, ah, put up, put up,
For well you know this is a pitiful case.

[*Exit.*]

**Second Musician.** Aye, by my troth, the case may be amended. **F**

[*Enter* Peter.]

100 **Peter.** Musicians, oh, musicians, "Heart's ease, heart's ease." Oh,
an you will have me live, play "Heart's ease."

**First Musician.** Why "Heart's ease"?

**Peter.** Oh, musicians, because my heart itself plays "My heart is
full of woe." Oh, play me some merry dump, to comfort me.

105 **First Musician.** Not a dump we, 'tis no time to play now.

**Peter.** You will not, then?

**First Musician.** No.

**Peter.** I will then give it you soundly.

**79–80 stick ... corse:** Put rosemary, an herb, on her corpse.

**82–83 though ... merriment:** Though it's natural to cry, common sense tells us we should rejoice for the dead.

**84 ordained festival:** intended for the wedding.

**88 sullen dirges:** sad, mournful tunes.

④ **Targeted Passage**

**94–95 The heavens ... will:** The fates (**heavens**) frown on you for some wrong you have done. Don't tempt them by refusing to accept their will (Juliet's death).

**F PUN**
Reread lines 96–99. The musician is talking about the case for his instrument. What "case" is the nurse referring to?

**100–138** After the tragedy of Juliet's "death," Shakespeare injects a light and witty conversation between Peter and the musicians. Peter asks them to play "Heart's Ease," a popular song of the time, or a **dump,** a slow dance melody. They refuse to play, and insults and puns are traded. Peter says that instead of money he'll give them a jeering speech (**gleek**), and he insults them by calling them minstrels. In return they call him a servant. Then both make puns on notes of the musical scale, re and fa.

**F PUN**

***Possible answer:*** *The "case" is the situation of Juliet's apparent death.*

**IF STUDENTS NEED HELP ...** Give students this example of a pun: "How these bugs are flying around my ears! If only I weren't so bugged." Explain that here the word play doesn't reveal itself until the second appearance of the word *bug.* The same is true in lines 96–99: There is no humor in the nurse's use of the word *case,* but when the second musician uses the same word in a different way the pun becomes apparent.

**FOR STRUGGLING READERS**
**Paraphrasing Shakespeare** Draw students' attention to the words of consolation from Friar Laurence in lines 65–78. Elicit that an effective paraphrase of his words in lines 77–78 might read something like this: *A woman who dies after having been married for a short time is better off than a woman who lives as a wife for a long time.*

④ **Targeted Passage [Lines 84–95]**

In this passage, Capulet and Friar Laurence conclude this scene's grieving mood.

• What does Friar Laurence say should be done with Juliet? (lines 92–93)

• What things for Juliet's wedding will now be used for her funeral? (lines 86–89)

• How does Friar Laurence suggest that Juliet's "death" may be her family's fault? Do you think that he means it? (lines 94–95)

**READ WITH A PURPOSE** Now that students have finished reading the selection, have them describe the Capulets' terrible discovery. Ask them how Friar Laurence's plan is—and is not—going as anticipated. *Possible answer: The discovery is of Juliet's body before she is to be married to Paris. Despite moving up the plan a day, the friar's plan is going as he anticipated.*

⭐ **CRITIQUE** Ask students whether the risks that Juliet has taken are justified in her desperate attempt to avoid marriage with Paris. Could Juliet have gotten out of the situation any other way? Encourage students to cite details from Act Three, Act Four, or both to support their opinions.

---

**First Musician.** What will you give us?

110 **Peter.** No money, on my faith, but the gleek. I will give you the minstrel.

**First Musician.** Then will I give you the serving creature.

**Peter.** Then will I lay the serving creature's dagger on your pate. I will carry no crotchets. I'll re you, I'll fa you, do you note me?

115 **First Musician.** An you re us and fa us, you note us.

**Second Musician.** Pray you put up your dagger, and put out your wit.

**Peter.** Then have at you with my wit! I will drybeat you with an iron wit, and put up my iron dagger. Answer me like men:

120     "When griping grief the heart doth wound
        And doleful dumps the mind oppress,
        Then music with her silver sound—"

Why "silver sound"? Why "music with her silver sound"?—What say you, Simon Catling?

125 **First Musician.** Marry, sir, because silver hath a sweet sound.

**Peter.** Pretty! What say you, Hugh Rebeck?

**Second Musician.** I say "silver sound" because musicians sound for silver.

**Peter.** Pretty too! What say you, James Soundpost?

130 **Third Musician.** Faith, I know not what to say.

**Peter.** Oh, I cry you mercy, you are the singer. I will say for you. It is "music with her silver sound" because musicians have no gold for sounding.

        "Then music with her silver sound
135     With speedy help doth lend redress."

[*Exit.*]

**First Musician.** What a pestilent knave is this same!

**Second Musician.** Hang him, Jack! Come, we'll in here. Tarry for the mourners, and stay dinner.

[*Exeunt.*]

113 **pate:** top of the head.

136 **pestilent:** bothersome; irritating.

---

## DIFFERENTIATED INSTRUCTION

**FOR ENGLISH LANGUAGE LEARNERS**
**Vocabulary Support** Help students decipher the word play in the comic ending to Act Four by defining these terms:

- *gleek* (line 110), "insult"
- *pate* (line 113), "top of the head"
- *crochets* (line 114), "stubborn ideas"
- *doleful* (line 121), "sad"
- *redress* (line 135), "correction"
- *Tarry* (line 137), "wait"

## Comprehension

1. **Recall** What reason does Paris give for Lord Capulet's decision to move up the wedding?

2. **Recall** At first, what does Juliet believe is the only solution to her problem?

3. **Summarize** What plan does Friar Laurence devise for Juliet, and what reservations does Juliet have about this plan?

## Text Analysis

4. **Reading Shakespearean Drama** Review the events you recorded as you read Act Four, and think about how the characters' interactions drive the plot forward. If the nurse had accompanied Juliet to Friar Laurence's cell, do you think Juliet would have made a different decision? Explain.

5. **Make Judgments** Do you feel sympathy for the Capulets, the nurse, and Paris when they express grief over Juliet's death? Why or why not?

6. **Identify Dramatic Irony** Dramatic irony exists when the reader or viewer knows something that one or more of the characters do not. Find three examples of dramatic irony in Act Four and record them in a chart like the one shown. Then explain how these ironic moments contribute to the building tension in the play.

| Scene and Lines | Dramatic Irony |
|---|---|
| Scene 1, lines 24–28 | Paris asks Juliet to confess to Friar Laurence that she loves him, and Juliet carefully avoids denying it. We know that Juliet loves Romeo, not Paris. |

7. **Recognize Protagonist and Antagonist** If Romeo and Juliet are the protagonists of this play, who or what is the antagonist? Keep in mind that an antagonist can be a character, a group of characters, a set of circumstances, or even society as a whole. Use details from the play to support your answer.

8. **Evaluate Comic Relief** The humorous exchange between Peter and the musicians at the end of Act Four is an example of comic relief. It lightens the mood after the grief-filled speeches that follow the discovery of Juliet's body. If you were producing a stage or film version of *Romeo and Juliet,* would you cut this passage, or do you think it serves an important purpose? Explain.

## Text Criticism

9. **Different Perspectives** How might older and younger audiences differ in their assessment of Romeo's and Juliet's actions? Explain your opinion, citing specific actions and interactions in the play.

**COMMON CORE**

RL 3 Analyze how complex characters develop over the course of a text, interact with other characters, and advance the plot or develop the theme. RL 10 Read and comprehend dramas. L 3 Apply knowledge of language to understand how language functions in different contexts and to comprehend more fully when reading or listening. L 5a Interpret figures of speech and analyze their role in the text.

---

and Scene 3, lines 1–13. The irony builds tension because readers sense that the unfolding tragedy is unavoidable.

7. *Students might say that the lovers' parents, the family feud, or Fortune itself is the antagonist. Be sure they support their answers.*

8. ● **COMMON CORE FOCUS** *Evaluate Comic Relief Students should offer a reasonable defense for their views—either that the scene needs this moment of comic relief or that the humor is too distracting.*

## Text Criticism

9. *Students may feel that a younger audience may identify with the strong passion of the lovers, whereas an older audience may feel frustrated that the lovers cannot find a more moderate course of action.*

---

# Practice and Apply

For preliminary support of post-reading questions, use these copy masters:

**R** **RESOURCE MANAGER—Copy Masters**
Reading Check p. 61
Shakespearean Drama p. 59
Question Support p. 62

Additional selection questions are provided for teachers on page 53.

### ANSWERS

## Comprehension

1. *Paris says that Capulet acts out of concern over Juliet's grief for Tybalt.*

2. *suicide*

3. *Friar Laurence gives Juliet a sleeping potion that will make her appear dead; when she awakens, Romeo will take her to Mantua. Juliet fears that Romeo will not arrive in time.*

## Text Analysis

COMMON CORE **RL 3, RL 10, L 3, L 5a**

*Possible answers:*

4. ● **COMMON CORE FOCUS** *Reading Shakespearean Drama Juliet might not have shared her feelings; Friar Laurence might not have suggested such a drastic plan.*

5. *Accept all reasonable responses. Some students may suggest that they have more sympathy for the nurse and for Paris than for Juliet's parents.*

6. *Examples should follow this pattern:* **Scene and Line:** *Scene 1, line 6;* **Dramatic Irony:** *Paris thinks that Juliet grieves for Tybalt. We know that she cries for Romeo. Other examples include Scene 2, lines 17–22,*

---

# Assess and Reteach

### Assess

**DIAGNOSTIC AND SELECTION TESTS**
Selection Test A, B/C pp. 287–288, 289–290

**Interactive Selection Test** on **thinkcentral.com**

### Reteach

**Level Up Online Tutorials** on **thinkcentral.com**

**Reteaching Worksheets** on **thinkcentral.com**
Literature Lessons 25, 26, 35, 38

# Practice and Apply

## READ WITH A PURPOSE

*Help students set a purpose for reading. Tell them to read to find out what role love and hate play in this final act of the play.*

## Get Into the Act

### SUMMARY

As Act Five opens, Romeo learns that Juliet has died, and he returns to Verona. Meanwhile, Friar Laurence learns that his message to Romeo was not delivered. Determined to join Juliet, Romeo kills Paris at the tomb, drinks poison, and dies beside Juliet. Friar Laurence arrives just as Juliet awakens but flees when he hears people coming. After he leaves, Juliet kills herself with Romeo's dagger. Finally, the prince determines what has happened, and Capulet and Montague make peace.

**TEXT ANALYSIS**    **COMMON CORE** L3

### Ⓐ Model the Skill: TRAGEDY

Paraphrase for students lines 17–23, allowing them to ask questions. Then have volunteers take turns paraphrasing lines 1–11, a sentence at a time.

***Possible answer:*** *Lines 1–11 may be paraphrased like this: "If dreams can be trusted, I will learn happy news. Today I feel cheerful. I dreamed that Juliet found me dead (how strange!) and kissed me awake, and I found myself an emperor. How sweet is love!" The part of the dream in which Juliet kisses Romeo's corpse foreshadows the tragedy.*

## Resources for Act Five

---

# Act Five

## SCENE 1    *A street in Mantua.*

*Balthasar, Romeo's servant, comes from Verona to tell him that Juliet is dead and lies in the Capulets' tomb. Since Romeo has not yet received any word from the friar, he believes Balthasar. He immediately decides to return to Verona in order to die next to Juliet. He sends Balthasar away and sets out to find a pharmacist who will sell him poison.*

[*Enter* Romeo.]

**Romeo.** If I may trust the flattering truth of sleep,
My dreams presage some joyful news at hand.
My bosom's lord sits lightly in his throne,
And all this day an unaccustomed spirit
5 Lifts me above the ground with cheerful thoughts.
I dreamt my lady came and found me dead
(Strange dream that gives a dead man leave to think!)
And breathed such life with kisses in my lips
That I revived and was an emperor.
10 Ah me! how sweet is love itself possessed,
When but love's shadows are so rich in joy! Ⓐ

[*Enter Romeo's servant,* Balthasar, *booted.*]

News from Verona! How now, Balthasar?
Dost thou not bring me letters from the friar?
How doth my lady? Is my father well?
15 How fares my Juliet? That I ask again,
For nothing can be ill if she be well.

**Balthasar.** Then she is well, and nothing can be ill.
Her body sleeps in Capels' monument,
And her immortal part with angels lives.
20 I saw her laid low in her kindred's vault
And presently took post to tell it you.
O, pardon me for bringing these ill news,
Since you did leave it for my office, sir.

**Romeo.** Is it e'en so? Then I defy you, stars!
25 Thou knowst my lodging. Get me ink and paper
And hire posthorses. I will hence tonight.

**Balthasar.** I do beseech you, sir, have patience.
Your looks are pale and wild and do import
Some misadventure.

---

**1–5 If I may … cheerful thoughts:** If I can trust my dreams, something joyful is about to happen. My heart (**bosom's lord**) is happy and I am content.

Ⓐ **TRAGEDY**
**Paraphrase** lines 1–11. What part of Romeo's seemingly happy dream **foreshadows** the tragic events to come?

**① Targeted Passage**

**17–19** Balthasar replies that Juliet is well, since although her body lies in the Capulets' (**Capels'**) burial vault, her soul (**her immortal part**) is with the angels.

**21 presently took post:** immediately rode (to Mantua).

**23 you did … office:** you gave me the duty of reporting important news to you.

**24 I … stars:** Romeo angrily challenges fate, which has caused him so much grief.

**28–29 import some misadventure:** suggest that something bad will happen.

Romeo and Juliet in the 1994 production of the Shakespeare Theatre in Washington, D.C.

**1130**    UNIT 10: SHAKESPEAREAN DRAMA

---

*See resources on the* **Teacher One Stop DVD-ROM** *and on* **thinkcentral.com**.

**Ⓡ RESOURCE MANAGER UNIT 10**

Plan and Teach, pp. 63–66
Summary pp. 67–68†‡*
Text Analysis and Reading
  Skill, pp. 69–72†*
Grammar and Style, p. 75

**DIAGNOSTIC AND SELECTION TESTS**

Selection Tests, pp. 291–294

**BEST PRACTICES TOOLKIT**

Sequence Chain, p. B21
Problem and Solution Charts, p. B20
Classification Chart, p. B17

**INTERACTIVE READER**

**ADAPTED INTERACTIVE READER**

**ELL ADAPTED INTERACTIVE READER**

**TECHNOLOGY**

- **Teacher One Stop DVD-ROM**
- **Student One Stop DVD-ROM**
- **PowerNotes DVD-ROM**
- **Audio Anthology CD**
- **GrammarNotes DVD-ROM**
- **ExamView Test Generator** on the Teacher One Stop

**Video Trailer**    **THINK central**

Go to **thinkcentral.com** to preview the **Video Trailer** introducing this selection. Other features that support the selection include

- **PowerNotes** presentation
- **ThinkAloud** models to enhance comprehension
- **WordSharp** vocabulary tutorials
- interactive writing and grammar instruction

---

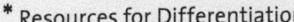
***** Resources for Differentiation    † Also in Spanish    ‡ In Haitian Creole and Vietnamese

## Analyze Visuals

**Activity** How does the photograph capture both the harshness and the tenderness of Romeo's and Juliet's deaths? ***Possible answer:*** *The harshness of death is seen in Juliet's awkward pose, with head lolling back and arms splayed. This harshness is tempered by the tenderness of Romeo's embrace and the scattered roses.*

---

## DIFFERENTIATED INSTRUCTION

### FOR STRUGGLING READERS

In combination with the *Audio Anthology CD*, use one or more Targeted Passages (pp. 1130, 1138, 1145) to ensure that students focus on key story events, concepts, and skills.

**Preview** Have students use a chart like this to organize the Scene 1 synopsis:

| ROMEO ... |
| --- |
| _Hears_ the report of Juliet's death |
| _Does not hear_ Friar Laurence's message |
| _Believes_ Balthasar's report |
| _Decides_ to go to Verona and kill himself |
| _Looks for_ a pharmacist to sell him poison |

### ① Targeted Passage [Lines 17–23]

This passage uses Balthasar's news to set the tragic conclusion of the play in motion.

- What information has Balthasar brought? How does he know it? (lines 18–20)

- Why does Balthasar bring the news to Romeo? Why does he ask forgiveness for doing so? (lines 22–23)

## B CHARACTER

*Possible answer:* Romeo means that he will go to where Juliet is buried and kill himself beside her. As is consistent with his character, Romeo plunges into action without thinking of options (such as consulting Friar Laurence) or the consequences of returning to Verona.

**IF STUDENTS NEED HELP . . .** Discuss whether Romeo was impulsive or thoughtful when he followed Juliet to her balcony, married Juliet, and sought revenge for Mercutio's death. Connect those impulsive events to the impulsiveness that Romeo now shows.

## BACKGROUND

**Apothecaries** In Shakespeare's time, apothecaries were the lowest level of medical practitioners, below physicians and surgeons. Apothecaries were sometimes known as a physician's cook, because they prepared and dispensed the drugs prescribed by a physician. Others, however, dispensed fraudulent prescriptions to those who could barely afford them. The apothecary in *Romeo and Juliet* is clearly one beset by poverty but not necessarily dishonesty. His shop is shabby but contains legitimate ingredients used in prescriptions. Romeo notices "old cakes of roses" (line 47), which would have been used to treat ailments of the head.

---

**Romeo.**          Tush, thou art deceived.
30 Leave me and do the thing I bid thee do.
Hast thou no letters to me from the friar?

**Balthasar.** No, my good lord.

**Romeo.**          No matter. Get thee gone
And hire those horses. I'll be with thee straight.

[*Exit* Balthasar.]

Well, Juliet, I will lie with thee tonight. B
35 Let's see for means. O mischief, thou art swift
To enter in the thoughts of desperate men!
I do remember an apothecary,
And hereabouts he dwells, which late I noted
In tattered weeds, with overwhelming brows,
40 Culling of simples. Meager were his looks,
Sharp misery had worn him to the bones;
And in his needy shop a tortoise hung,
An alligator stuffed, and other skins
Of ill-shaped fishes; and about his shelves
45 A beggarly account of empty boxes,
Green earthen pots, bladders, and musty seeds,
Remnants of packthread, and old cakes of roses
Were thinly scattered, to make up a show.
Noting this penury, to myself I said,
50 "An if a man did need a poison now
Whose sale is present death in Mantua,
Here lives a caitiff wretch would sell it him."
O, this same thought did but forerun my need,
And this same needy man must sell it me.
55 As I remember, this should be the house.
Being holiday, the beggar's shop is shut.
What, ho! apothecary!

[*Enter* Apothecary.]

**Apothecary.**        Who calls so loud?

**Romeo.** Come hither, man. I see that thou art poor.
Hold, there is forty ducats. Let me have
60 A dram of poison, such soon-speeding gear
As will disperse itself through all the veins
That the life-weary taker may fall dead,
And that the trunk may be discharged of breath
As violently as hasty powder fired
65 Doth hurry from the fatal cannon's womb.

**Apothecary.** Such mortal drugs I have; but Mantua's law
Is death to any he that utters them.

---

### B CHARACTER

What does Romeo mean in line 34? Explain whether he thoughtfully considers his options or plunges immediately into action.

**35–40 Let's . . . means:** Let me find a way (to join Juliet in death); **apothecary:** pharmacist; **tattered weeds:** ragged clothes; **culling of simples:** selecting herbs.

**47 cakes of roses:** rose petals pressed together to create a perfume.

**49 penury:** poverty.

**50–52 "An if a man . . . sell it him":** Though it is a crime to sell poison in Mantua, the apothecary is such a miserable (**caitiff**) wretch that he would probably do it for the money.

**59 ducats:** gold coins.

**60–65** Romeo wants fast-acting (**soon-speeding**) poison that will work as quickly as gunpowder exploding in a cannon.

**67 any . . . them:** any person who dispenses or sells them.

---

## DIFFERENTIATED INSTRUCTION

**FOR ENGLISH LANGUAGE LEARNERS**
**Concept Support** As students read Romeo's description of the apothecary (lines 37–54), help them locate and discuss these expressions that indicate his poverty:

- *tattered weeds* (line 39), "ragged clothes"

- *Meager were his looks* (line 40), "he looked puny and thin"

- *worn him to the bones* (line 41), "made him thin through hardship"

- *needy* (line 42), "poorly stocked and ugly"

- *beggarly account* (line 45), "kind of inventory that a penniless person would have"

- *penury* (line 49), "poverty"

- *this same needy man* (line 54), "this man who needs money"

**Romeo.** Art thou so bare and full of wretchedness
And fearest to die? Famine is in thy cheeks,
70  Need and oppression starveth in thine eyes,
Contempt and beggary hangs upon thy back:
The world is not thy friend, nor the world's law;
The world affords no law to make thee rich;
Then be not poor, but break it and take this.

75  **Apothecary.** My poverty but not my will consents.

**Romeo.** I pay thy poverty and not thy will.

**Apothecary.** Put this in any liquid thing you will
And drink it off, and if you had the strength
Of twenty men, it would dispatch you straight.

80  **Romeo.** There is thy gold —worse poison to men's souls,
Doing more murder in this loathsome world,
Than these poor compounds that thou mayst not sell.
I sell thee poison; thou hast sold me none.
Farewell. Buy food and get thyself in flesh.
85  Come, cordial and not poison, go with me
To Juliet's grave; for there must I use thee.

[*Exeunt.*]

**72–74** Romeo urges the apothecary to improve his situation by breaking the law and selling him the poison.

**75** I'm doing this for the money, not because I think it's right.

**79 dispatch you straight:** kill you instantly.

**85** Romeo refers to the poison as a **cordial**, a drink believed to be good for the heart. *Why does he refer to it in this way?*

# SCENE 2  *Friar Laurence's cell in Verona.*

*Friar Laurence's messenger arrives, saying that he was unable to deliver the letter to Romeo. Friar Laurence, his plans ruined, rushes to the Capulet vault before Juliet awakes. He intends to hide her in his room until Romeo can come to take her away.*

[*Enter* Friar John.]

**Friar John.** Holy Franciscan friar, brother, ho!

[*Enter* Friar Laurence.]

**Friar Laurence.** This same should be the voice of Friar John.
Welcome from Mantua. What says Romeo?
Or, if his mind be writ, give me his letter.

5  **Friar John.** Going to find a barefoot brother out,
One of our order to associate me,
Here in this city visiting the sick,
And finding him, the searchers of the town,
Suspecting that we both were in a house
10  Where the infectious pestilence did reign,
Sealed up the doors, and would not let us forth,
So that my speed to Mantua there was stayed.

**5–12** Friar John explains why he did not go to Mantua. He had asked another friar (**barefoot brother**), who had been caring for the sick, to go with him. The health officials of the town, believing that the friars had come into contact with a deadly plague (**infectious pestilence**), locked them up to keep them from infecting others.

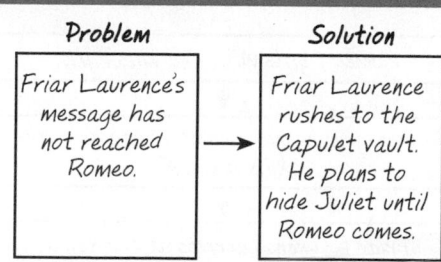

**Friar Laurence.** Who bare my letter, then, to Romeo?

**Friar John.** I could not send it—here it is again—
15 Nor get a messenger to bring it thee,
   So fearful were they of infection.

**Friar Laurence.** Unhappy fortune! By my brotherhood,
   The letter was not nice, but full of charge,
   Of dear import, and the neglecting it
20 May do much danger. Friar John, go hence,
   Get me an iron crow and bring it straight
   Unto my cell.

**Friar John.**          Brother, I'll go and bring it thee.

[*Exit.*]

**Friar Laurence.** Now must I to the monument alone.
   Within this three hours will fair Juliet wake.
25 She will beshrew me much that Romeo
   Hath had no notice of these accidents;
   But I will write again to Mantua,
   And keep her at my cell till Romeo come—
   Poor living corse, closed in a dead man's tomb! **C**

[*Exit.*]

**13 bare:** carried (bore).

**18–20** The letter wasn't trivial (**nice**) but contained a message of great importance (**dear import**). The fact that it wasn't sent (**neglecting it**) may cause great harm.

**21 iron crow:** crowbar.

**25–26 She...accidents:** She will be furious with me when she learns that Romeo doesn't know what has happened.

**C SOLILOQUY**
Explain what you learn about the friar's new plan in this soliloquy. Why is it essential that the friar reach Juliet before Romeo does?

---

# SCENE 3   *The cemetery that contains the Capulets' tomb.*

*In the dark of night Paris comes to the cemetery to put flowers on Juliet's grave. At the same time Romeo arrives, and Paris hides. Paris assumes that Romeo is going to harm the bodies. He challenges Romeo, they fight, and Romeo kills Paris. When Romeo recognizes the dead Paris, he lays his body inside the tomb as Paris requested. Romeo declares his love for Juliet, drinks the poison, and dies. Shortly after, Friar Laurence arrives and discovers both bodies. When Juliet wakes up, the friar urges her to leave with him before the guard comes. Juliet refuses, and when the friar leaves, she kills herself with Romeo's dagger. The guards and the prince arrive, followed by the Capulets and Lord Montague, whose wife has just died of grief because of Romeo's exile. Friar Laurence explains what has happened. Capulet and Montague finally end their feud and promise to erect statues honoring Romeo and Juliet.*

[*Enter* Paris *and his* Page *with flowers and a torch.*]

**Paris.** Give me thy torch, boy. Hence, and stand aloof.
   Yet put it out, for I would not be seen.
   Under yond yew tree lay thee all along,
   Holding thine ear close to the hollow ground.

**1 aloof:** some distance away.

---

---

## DIFFERENTIATED INSTRUCTION

**FOR STRUGGLING READERS**

**Preview** Have students read the scene synopsis carefully. Track the many events of Scene 3 using a Sequence Chain.

> Paris brings flowers to Juliet's grave.
> ↓
> Romeo arrives at the cemetery.
> ↓

> Romeo fights with and kills Paris.
> ↓
> Romeo grieves over Juliet's body and then kills himself.
> ↓
> Friar Laurence arrives at the tomb.
> ↓
> Juliet awakens but refuses to leave.
> ↓

> When Friar Laurence leaves, Juliet stabs herself with Romeo's dagger.
> ↓
> The families and Prince Escalus arrive, and Friar Laurence reveals the truth.
> ↓
> The Capulets and Montagues end their feud.

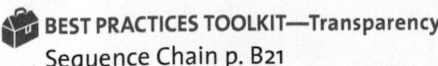 **BEST PRACTICES TOOLKIT—Transparency**
Sequence Chain p. B21

## Behind the Curtain

### Lighting

Directors use a variety of techniques to make a play's **lighting** effective. For example, spotlights can illuminate one character while leaving others in semi-darkness, and effects such as candles or prominent shadows can help create specific moods. What is distinctive about the lighting in each of these shots? Explain the effect each technique produces.

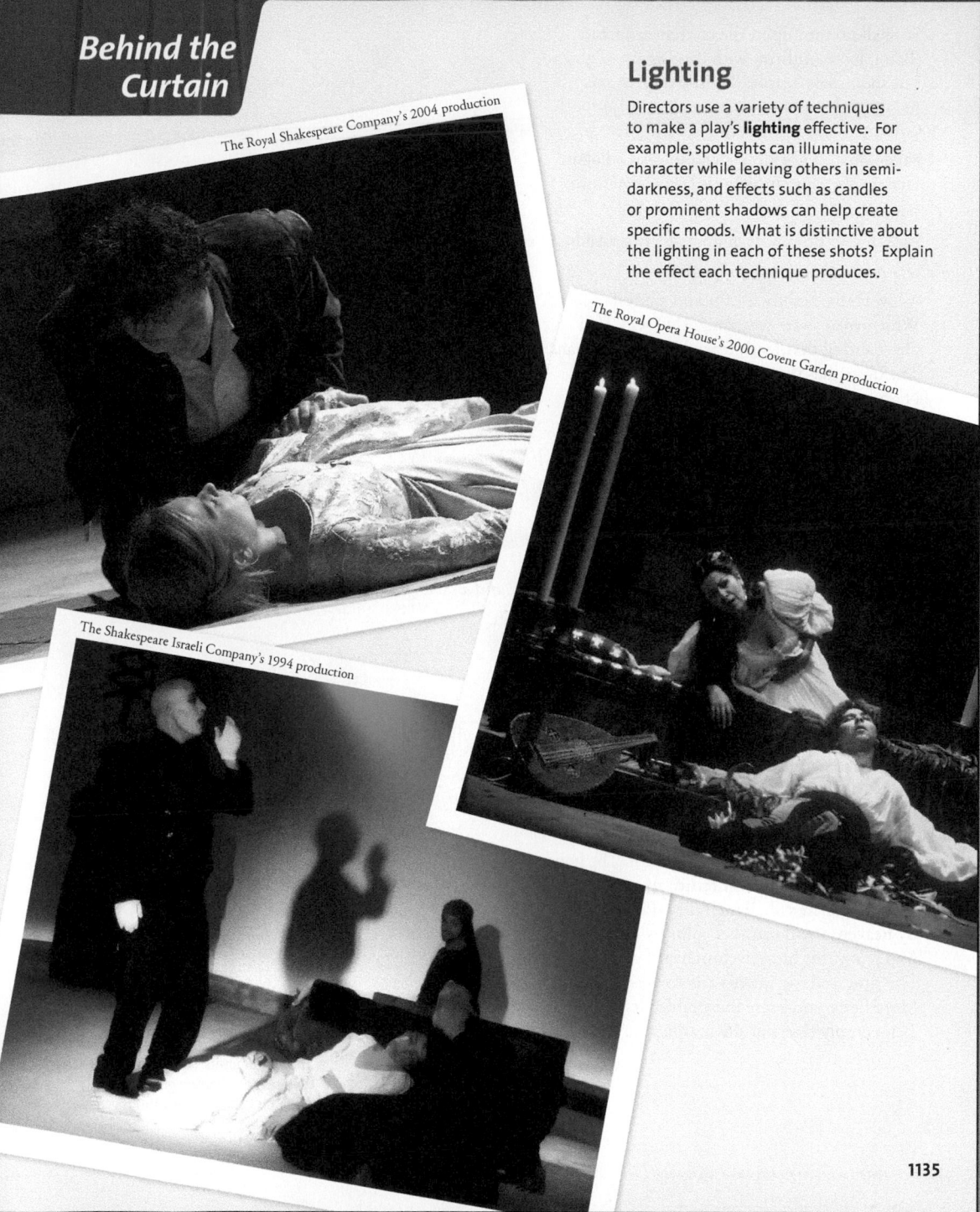

The Royal Shakespeare Company's 2004 production

The Royal Opera House's 2000 Covent Garden production

The Shakespeare Israeli Company's 1994 production

1135

**BEHIND THE CURTAIN**   COMMON CORE SL 2

**Lighting** Explain that because the theaters of Shakespeare's time had no artificial lighting, plays were usually performed outside, during the day. In a modern theater, the ideal situation is a stage that is utterly dark when all lights are off. This setup allows a director to plan the position, color, movement, and effect of every light on the set. For example, for a tomb scene, such as is shown in the Royal Opera House's production, the lights are tinted with a blue filter. The Royal Shakespeare Company's production shows the use of a spotlight to illuminate one important actor or scene, leaving the rest of the stage dark. The position of lights is particularly important for creating dramatic lighting effects, as seen in the image from the Shakespeare Israeli Company's production. ***Possible answer:*** *The dim blue lighting in the Royal Opera House photograph gives the stage an otherworldly feeling of a tomb at night. The dramatic shadows in the Shakespeare Israeli Company create a powerful, bleak feeling around the dead lovers. The spotlight on Juliet in the Royal Shakespeare Company's production draws attention to her, making her body the focal point of the scene.*

**FOR ADVANCED LEARNERS/PRE–AP**

**Research Stage Lighting** [small-group option]  Have students research and prepare a brochure or oral presentation about theater lights and their uses. Topics might include the different types of lights and their advantages in various situations, special-effects lighting, and the use of a light board to control the lighting.

## Is **LOVE** stronger than **HATE?**

**Discuss** How do lines 12–17 indicate that Paris indeed has love for Juliet? *Possible answer: Paris indicates his love by bringing flowers to the tomb and promising to continue to do so (even though he is not obligated to do so).*

---

5  So shall no foot upon the churchyard tread
  (Being loose, unfirm, with digging up of graves)
  But thou shalt hear it. Whistle then to me,
  As signal that thou hearst something approach.
  Give me those flowers. Do as I bid thee, go.

10  **Page** [*aside*]. I am almost afraid to stand alone
  Here in the churchyard; yet I will adventure.

[*withdraws*]

**Paris.** Sweet flower, with flowers thy bridal bed I strew

[*He strews the tomb with flowers.*]

  (O woe! thy canopy is dust and stones)
  Which with sweet water nightly I will dew;

15  Or, wanting that, with tears distilled by moans.
  The obsequies that I for thee will keep
  Nightly shall be to strew thy grave and weep.

[*The* Page *whistles.*]

  The boy gives warning something doth approach.
  What cursed foot wanders this way tonight

20  To cross my obsequies and true love's rite?
  What, with a torch? Muffle me, night, awhile.

[*withdraws*]

[*Enter* Romeo *and* Balthasar *with a torch, a mattock, and a crow of iron.*]

**Romeo.** Give me that mattock and the wrenching iron.
  Hold, take this letter. Early in the morning
  See thou deliver it to my lord and father.

25  Give me the light. Upon thy life I charge thee,
  Whate'er thou hearest or seest, stand all aloof
  And do not interrupt me in my course.
  Why I descend into this bed of death
  Is partly to behold my lady's face,

30  But chiefly to take thence from her dead finger
  A precious ring—a ring that I must use
  In dear employment. Therefore hence, be gone.
  But if thou, jealous, dost return to pry
  In what I farther shall intend to do,

35  By heaven, I will tear thee joint by joint
  And strew this hungry churchyard with thy limbs.
  The time and my intents are savage-wild,
  More fierce and more inexorable far
  Than empty tigers or the roaring sea.

**12–17** Paris promises to decorate Juliet's grave with flowers, as he does now, and sprinkle it with either perfume (**sweet water**) or his tears. He will perform these honoring rites (**obsequies**) every night.

**20 cross:** interfere with.

**21 muffle:** hide.

**mattock … iron:** an ax and a crowbar.

**32 in dear employment:** for an important purpose.

**33 jealous:** curious.

**37–39** Romeo's intention is more unstoppable (**inexorable**) than hungry (**empty**) tigers or the waves of an ocean.

**TRAGEDY**
Reread lines 25–39 and think about how tragedies usually end for the main characters. Paraphrase the two reasons Romeo gives for going into the tomb. What third reason does he hint at?

---

**TEXT ANALYSIS**

COMMON CORE
L3

### **TRAGEDY**

*Possible answer: Tragedies usually end with the death of the main characters. Romeo gives Balthasar two reasons for going into the tomb: he wants to see Juliet's face (line 29) and he wants to take a ring from her finger (lines 30–32). In lines 34 and 37, he hints at a third reason, which he stated in Scene 1: to kill himself with poison and die beside Juliet's dead body.*

**Extend the Discussion** Ask students what they think will happen to Romeo. On what do they base their prediction?

---

## DIFFERENTIATED INSTRUCTION

### FOR STRUGGLING READERS

**Paraphrasing Shakespeare** Have students paraphrase lines 12–15, in which Paris reveals his feelings for Juliet. *Possible answer: You are my sweet flower, and I will place flowers where you lie. (How sad it is that your bed is made of dust and stones!) Each night I will bring water to the flowers, or I will water the flowers with my tears.*

### FOR ADVANCED LEARNERS/PRE–AP

**Hypothesize** In Scene 1, Balthasar left Romeo in Mantua after he delivered his news but before Romeo bought the poison. Ask students to imagine that Balthasar knows about the poison, after all. Have them meet in small groups to discuss what Balthasar might say and do—and whether it would make a difference in the story's outcome. Have groups compare responses and come to a consensus.

40 **Balthasar.** I will be gone, sir, and not trouble you.

**Romeo.** So shalt thou show me friendship. Take thou that.
Live, and be prosperous; and farewell, good fellow.

**Balthasar** [*aside*]. For all this same, I'll hide me hereabout.
His looks I fear, and his intents I doubt.
[*withdraws*]

45 **Romeo.** Thou detestable maw, thou womb of death,
Gorged with the dearest morsel of the earth,
Thus I enforce thy rotten jaws to open,
And in despite I'll cram thee with more food.
[Romeo *opens the tomb.*]

**Paris.** This is that banish'd haughty Montague
50 That murdered my love's cousin—with which grief
It is supposed the fair creature died—
And here is come to do some villainous shame
To the dead bodies. I will apprehend him.
Stop thy unhallowed toil, vile Montague!
55 Can vengeance be pursued further than death?
Condemned villain, I do apprehend thee.
Obey, and go with me; for thou must die.

**Romeo.** I must indeed; and therefore came I hither.
Good gentle youth, tempt not a desp'rate man.
60 Fly hence and leave me. Think upon these gone;
Let them affright thee. I beseech thee, youth,
Put not another sin upon my head
By urging me to fury. O, be gone!
By heaven, I love thee better than myself.
65 For I come hither armed against myself.
Stay not, be gone. Live, and hereafter say
A madman's mercy bid thee run away.

**Paris.** I do defy thy conjuration
And apprehend thee for a felon here.

70 **Romeo.** Wilt thou provoke me? Then have at thee, boy! **E**
[*They fight.*]

---

**43** *Who else besides Balthasar is hiding in the cemetery at this point?*

**45–49** Romeo addresses the tomb as though it were devouring people. He calls it a hateful stomach (**detestable maw**) that is filled (**gorged**) with Juliet, the **dearest morsel of the earth.** He uses his crowbar to open its **rotten jaws** and moves to enter the tomb.

**49–53** Recognizing Romeo, Paris speaks these first few lines to himself. He is angry with Romeo, believing that Romeo's killing Tybalt caused Juliet to die of grief.

**58–67** Romeo rejects Paris' challenge. He tells Paris to think of those already killed and to leave before Romeo is forced to kill him too. Romeo swears that he has come to harm himself, not Paris.

**68** I reject your appeal.

**E** CHARACTER
Consider what you know about Romeo's **traits** and **flaws.** Is Romeo at fault for fighting Paris? Why or why not?

ROMEO AND JULIET: ACT FIVE, SCENE 3   **1137**

---

---

**FOR ENGLISH LANGUAGE LEARNERS**

**Task Support** After students read the marginal question for line 43, elicit what Paris says to his page before Romeo and Balthasar arrive on the scene. ***Possible answer:*** *Besides Balthasar, Paris and his page are hiding in the cemetery.*

**Concept Support** Make sure students understand that in lines 49–57, Paris identifies with the Capulets. He refers to Romeo with a family insult (line 49), believes the Capulets' story about why Juliet died (lines 50–51), assumes that Romeo has come to desecrate the tomb (lines 52–53), and assumes the responsibility of defending the family's honor by taking Romeo into custody (lines 56–57).

Use these prompts to discuss Romeo's state of mind at this moment in the play (lines 88–120):

**Connect** Have you ever been surprised by decisions that you or someone you know made under great stress? What conditions at this point in the story might weaken Romeo's judgment? *Students may suggest that the late hour, worry, and grief probably cause Romeo great stress and compromise his judgment.*

**Analyze** What features of Juliet's face, mentioned by Romeo, should lead Romeo to doubt his intent to commit suicide? *Possible answer: Romeo notices that Juliet's cheeks and lips are red and that she does not look dead at all (lines 94–96).*

**Synthesize** What does Romeo hope to accomplish by killing himself? *Possible answer: Romeo says that by killing himself he will repay Tybalt for murdering him and will be able to protect Juliet from becoming Death's lover (lines 97–107).*

---

**Page.** O Lord, they fight! I will go call the watch.
[*Exit.*]

**Paris.** O, I am slain! [*falls*] If thou be merciful,
Open the tomb, lay me with Juliet.
[*dies*]

**Romeo.** In faith, I will. Let me peruse this face.
75 Mercutio's kinsman, noble County Paris!
What said my man when my betossed soul
Did not attend him as we rode? I think
He told me Paris should have married Juliet.
Said he not so? or did I dream it so?
80 Or am I mad, hearing him talk of Juliet,
To think it was so? O, give me thy hand,
One writ with me in sour misfortune's book!
I'll bury thee in a triumphant grave.
A grave? O, no, a lantern, slaughtered youth,
85 For here lies Juliet, and her beauty makes
This vault a feasting presence full of light.
Death, lie thou there, by a dead man interred.

[*lays* Paris *in the tomb*]

How oft when men are at the point of death
Have they been merry! which their keepers call
90 A lightning before death. O, how may I
Call this a lightning? O my love! my wife!
Death, that hath sucked the honey of thy breath,
Hath had no power yet upon thy beauty.
Thou art not conquered. Beauty's ensign yet
95 Is crimson in thy lips and in thy cheeks,
And death's pale flag is not advanced there.
Tybalt, liest thou there in thy bloody sheet?
O, what more favor can I do to thee
Than with that hand that cut thy youth in twain
100 To sunder his that was thine enemy?
Forgive me, cousin! Ah, dear Juliet,
Why art thou yet so fair? Shall I believe
That unsubstantial Death is amorous,
And that the lean abhorred monster keeps
105 Thee here in dark to be his paramour?
For fear of that I still will stay with thee
And never from this palace of dim night

**74–78** Romeo discovers that the man he has just killed is Paris, who he vaguely remembers being told was supposed to marry Juliet.

 **Targeted Passage**

**82** Romeo notes that, like himself, Paris has been a victim of bad luck.

**84–87** Romeo will bury Paris with Juliet, whose beauty fills the tomb with light. Paris' corpse (**Death**) is being buried (**interred**) by a dead man in that Romeo expects to be dead soon.

**94 ensign:** sign.

**98–100 O, what . . . enemy:** I can best repay you (Tybalt) by killing your enemy (myself) with the same hand that cut your youth in two (**twain**).

**102–105** Romeo can't get over how beautiful Juliet still looks. He asks whether Death is loving (**amorous**) and whether it has taken Juliet as its lover (**paramour**).

---

## DIFFERENTIATED INSTRUCTION

**FOR STRUGGLING READERS**

**② Targeted Passage** [Lines 71–87]

In this passage, Romeo removes one more obstacle between himself and Juliet: Paris.

- Who wins the fight between Paris and Romeo? (lines 72–73)

- When does Romeo figure out who Paris is? How did he find out that Paris was going to marry Juliet? (lines 74–79)

- What does Romeo do and say after killing Paris? (lines 81–87)

**FOR ADVANCED LEARNERS/PRE-AP**

**Analyze Staging** Explain that the original staging of this scene is unclear. A trap door in the stage may have opened into the (unseen) tomb beneath; in that case, Romeo would have given his final speech before disappearing below stage, and Juliet then would have risen through the trap door. There are many other possibilities. Have students write and share a paragraph or two describing how they would stage this scene.

Depart again. Here, here will I remain
With worms that are thy chambermaids. O, here
110 Will I set up my everlasting rest
And shake the yoke of inauspicious stars
From this world-wearied flesh. Eyes, look your last!
Arms, take your last embrace! and, lips, O you
The doors of breath, seal with a righteous kiss
115 A dateless bargain to engrossing death!
Come, bitter conduct; come, unsavory guide!
Thou desperate pilot, now at once run on
The dashing rocks thy seasick weary bark!
Here's to my love! [*drinks*] O true apothecary!
120 Thy drugs are quick. Thus with a kiss I die.
  [*falls*]
  [*Enter* Friar Laurence, *with lantern, crow, and spade.*]
**Friar Laurence.** Saint Francis be my speed! how oft tonight
Have my old feet stumbled at graves! Who's there?
**Balthasar.** Here's one, a friend, and one that knows you well.
**Friar Laurence.** Bliss be upon you! Tell me, good my friend,
125 What torch is yond that vainly lends his light
To grubs and eyeless skulls? As I discern,
It burneth in the Capels' monument.
**Balthasar.** It doth so, holy sir; and there's my master,
One that you love.
**Friar Laurence.**       Who is it?
**Balthasar.**                 Romeo.
130 **Friar Laurence.** How long hath he been there?
**Balthasar.**                             Full half an hour.
**Friar Laurence.** Go with me to the vault.
**Balthasar.**                       I dare not, sir.
My master knows not but I am gone hence,
And fearfully did menace me with death
If I did stay to look on his intents.
135 **Friar Laurence.** Stay then; I'll go alone. Fear comes upon me.
O, much I fear some ill unthrifty thing.

**111–112 shake...flesh:** rid myself of the burden of an unhappy fate (**inauspicious stars**). *On what does Romeo blame his imminent death?*

**115 dateless:** eternal; never-ending. Romeo means that what he is about to do can never be undone.

**117–118** Romeo compares himself to the pilot of a ship (**bark**) who is going to crash on the rocks because he is so weary and sick.

**132–134 My master...intents:** My master told me to go away and threatened me with death if I watched what he did.

**136 unthrifty:** unlucky.

**Balthasar.** As I did sleep under this yew tree here,
I dreamt my master and another fought,
And that my master slew him.

**Friar Laurence.**                        Romeo!

*[stoops and looks on the blood and weapons]*

140 Alack, alack, what blood is this which stains
The stony entrance of this sepulcher?
What mean these masterless and gory swords
To lie discolored by this place of peace?

*[enters the tomb]*

Romeo! O, pale! Who else? What, Paris too?
145 And steeped in blood? Ah, what an unkind hour
Is guilty of this lamentable chance!
The lady stirs.

[Juliet *rises.*]

**Juliet.** O comfortable friar! where is my lord?
I do remember well where I should be,
150 And there I am. Where is my Romeo?

**Friar Laurence.** I hear some noise. Lady, come from that nest

**140–143 Alack . . . place of peace?** Why are these bloody swords lying here at the tomb (**sepulcher**), a place that should be peaceful? (The swords are also **masterless**, or without their owners.)

**148 comfortable:** comforting.

Romeo and Juliet in the 2004 production of the Globe Theatre

## DIFFERENTIATED INSTRUCTION

### FOR STRUGGLING READERS

**Summarize Plot** Help students develop this list of characters whose deaths are a part of Scene 3:

- **Lady Montague:** dead of grief over Romeo's banishment
- **Paris:** killed in a duel with Romeo
- **Romeo:** poisoned by his own hand in grief for Juliet
- **Juliet:** self-inflicted stab wound after realizing that Romeo is dead

Of death, contagion, and unnatural sleep.
A greater power than we can contradict
Hath thwarted our intents. Come, come away.
155 Thy husband in thy bosom there lies dead;
And Paris too. Come, I'll dispose of thee
Among a sisterhood of holy nuns.
Stay not to question, for the watch is coming.
Come, go, good Juliet. I dare no longer stay.

160 **Juliet.** Go, get thee hence, for I will not away.

[*Exit* Friar Laurence.]

What's here? A cup, closed in my true love's hand?
Poison, I see, hath been his timeless end.
O churl! drunk all, and left no friendly drop
To help me after? I will kiss thy lips.
165 Haply some poison yet doth hang on them
To make me die with a restorative.

[*kisses him*]

Thy lips are warm!

**Chief Watchman** [*within*]. Lead, boy. Which way?

**Juliet.** Yea, noise? Then I'll be brief. O happy dagger!

[*snatches Romeo's dagger*]

170 This is thy sheath; there rust, and let me die.

[*She stabs herself and falls.*]

[*Enter* Watchmen *with the* Page *of Paris.*]

**Page.** This is the place. There, where the torch doth burn.

**Chief Watchman.** The ground is bloody. Search about the
churchyard.
Go, some of you; whoe'er you find attach.

[*Exeunt some of the* Watch.]

Pitiful sight! here lies the County slain;
175 And Juliet bleeding, warm, and newly dead,
Who here hath lain this two days buried.
Go, tell the Prince; run to the Capulets;
Raise up the Montagues; some others search.

[*Exeunt others of the* Watch.]

We see the ground whereon these woes do lie,
180 But the true ground of all these piteous woes
We cannot without circumstance descry.

[*Reenter some of the* Watch, *with* Balthasar.]

**153–154 A greater . . . intents:** A greater force than we can fight (**contradict**) has ruined our plans (**thwarted our intents**).

**156–157 I'll dispose . . . nuns:** I'll find a place for you in a convent of nuns.

**158–159** *Why is the friar so anxious to leave?*

**162 timeless:** happening before its proper time.

**163 churl:** miser.

**165 haply:** perhaps.

**173 attach:** arrest.

**178 raise up:** awaken.

**179–181 We see . . . descry:** We see the earth (**ground**) these bodies lie on. But the real cause (**true ground**) of these deaths is yet for us to discover (**descry**).

## TIERED DISCUSSION PROMPTS

Use these prompts to explore the role of Friar Laurence in lines 151–160:

**Recall** What does Friar Laurence propose to do with Juliet? Why? *Possible answer: He wants to send her to a convent of nuns where she can be protected. He fears the approach of the guard who will hand her over to her father, and her father's severe reaction.*

**Analyze** Why does Friar Laurence flee the scene so hastily? *Possible answer: Friar Laurence has broken the law by helping Romeo return from exile. It seems possible that he might be held partially responsible for the death of Paris, if not others. He is also responsible for the secret marriage and the pretended death of Juliet, and so severe punishment almost certainly awaits him.*

**Evaluate** Do Friar Laurence's actions in this scene negate his earlier role as counselor and confidant to Juliet? Explain. *Some students may answer no, as the friar tries to protect Juliet in his offer to place her in a convent. By fleeing, he saved himself and could continue to work on her behalf. Other students may answer yes. If he really cared about Juliet, the friar would have stayed to console her over the death of Romeo and continue to beg for her safety, even after the guards apprehended her.*

## FOR ENGLISH LANGUAGE LEARNERS

**Task Support** After students read the marginal question about lines 158–159, have them review line 71, in which the page runs from the fight between Romeo and Paris to call the watch. *Possible answer: Friar Laurence is afraid that the watch will find him in the vault. He probably doesn't want to have to explain the bodies or be implicated in their deaths.*

## FOR ADVANCED LEARNERS/PRE–AP

**Analyze Character** Critics have remarked that Friar Laurence serves as a kind of surrogate parent to both Romeo and Juliet. After students have finished reading the play, challenge them to write two to three paragraphs expressing their views on the role of Friar Laurence and the degree to which he was or wasn't a positive presence in the lives of Romeo and Juliet.

## Is **LOVE** stronger than **HATE?**

**Discuss** Refer students to lines 194–201. Prince Escalus refers to "this foul murder" (line 198), and the chief watchman says that Romeo has been "slaughtered" (line 199). Both the prince and the watchman seem to interpret the scene as one of hate. In what ironic sense is it actually a scene of love? ***Possible answer:*** *Romeo has killed Paris, reluctantly, in order to be with his beloved Juliet. He then has killed himself rather than live without Juliet's love, and Juliet has killed herself rather than live without Romeo's love.*

---

**Second Watchman.** Here's Romeo's man. We found him in the churchyard.

**Chief Watchman.** Hold him in safety till the Prince come hither.

[*Reenter* Friar Laurence *and another* Watchman.]

**Third Watchman.** Here is a friar that trembles, sighs, and weeps.
185 We took this mattock and this spade from him
As he was coming from this churchyard side.

**Chief Watchman.** A great suspicion! Stay the friar too.

[*Enter the* Prince *and* Attendants.]

**Prince.** What misadventure is so early up,
That calls our person from our morning rest?

[*Enter* Capulet, Lady Capulet, *and others.*]

190 **Capulet.** What should it be, that they so shriek abroad?

**Lady Capulet.** The people in the street cry "Romeo,"
Some "Juliet," and some "Paris"; and all run,
With open outcry, toward our monument.

**Prince.** What fear is this which startles in our ears?

195 **Chief Watchman.** Sovereign, here lies the County Paris slain;
And Romeo dead, and Juliet, dead before,
Warm and new killed.

**Prince.** Search, seek, and know how this foul murder comes.

**Chief Watchman.** Here is a friar, and slaughtered Romeo's man,
200 With instruments upon them fit to open
These dead men's tombs.

**Capulet.** O heavens! O wife, look how our daughter bleeds!
This dagger hath mista'en, for, lo, his house
Is empty on the back of Montague,
205 And it missheathed in my daughter's bosom!

**Lady Capulet.** O me! this sight of death is as a bell
That warns my old age to a sepulcher.

[*Enter* Montague *and others.*]

**Prince.** Come, Montague; for thou art early up
To see thy son and heir now early down.

210 **Montague.** Alas, my liege, my wife is dead tonight!
Grief of my son's exile hath stopped her breath.
What further woe conspires against mine age?

**Prince.** Look, and thou shalt see.

**Montague.** O thou untaught! what manners is in this,
215 To press before thy father to a grave?

**182–187** The guards arrest Balthasar and Friar Laurence as suspicious characters.

**194 startles:** causes alarm.

**203–205 This dagger . . . in my daughter's bosom:** This dagger has missed its target. It should rest in the sheath (**house**) that Romeo wears. Instead it is in Juliet's chest.

**210 liege:** lord.

**214–215 what manners . . . grave:** What kind of behavior is this, for a son to die before his father?

---

## DIFFERENTIATED INSTRUCTION

### FOR ADVANCED LEARNERS/PRE–AP

**Evaluate Resolution (Part 1)** Have students skim these last pages and determine that of the play's main characters, only the nurse and Benvolio appear to be absent from the resolution. What distinguishes these two is that each is the best friend of one of the lovers. Ask students either to defend Shakespeare's omission of these characters or to explain how the two could have been incorporated into the conclusion.

**Prince.** Seal up the mouth of outrage for a while,
Till we can clear these ambiguities
And know their spring, their head, their true descent;
And then will I be general of your woes
220 And lead you even to death. Meantime forbear,
And let mischance be slave to patience.
Bring forth the parties of suspicion.

**Friar Laurence.** I am the greatest, able to do least,
Yet most suspected, as the time and place
225 Doth make against me, of this direful murder;
And here I stand, both to impeach and purge
Myself condemned and myself excused.

**Prince.** Then say at once what thou dost know in this.

**Friar Laurence.** I will be brief, for my short date of breath
230 Is not so long as is a tedious tale.
Romeo, there dead, was husband to that Juliet;
And she, there dead, that Romeo's faithful wife.
I married them; and their stol'n marriage day
Was Tybalt's doomsday, whose untimely death
235 Banish'd the new-made bridegroom from this city;
For whom, and not for Tybalt, Juliet pined.
You, to remove that siege of grief from her,
Betrothed and would have married her perforce
To County Paris. Then comes she to me
240 And with wild looks bid me devise some mean
To rid her from this second marriage,
Or in my cell there would she kill herself.
Then gave I her (so tutored by my art)
A sleeping potion; which so took effect
245 As I intended, for it wrought on her
The form of death. Meantime I writ to Romeo
That he should hither come as this dire night
To help to take her from her borrowed grave,
Being the time the potion's force should cease.
250 But he which bore my letter, Friar John,
Was stayed by accident, and yesternight
Returned my letter back. Then all alone
At the prefixed hour of her waking
Came I to take her from her kindred's vault;
255 Meaning to keep her closely at my cell
Till I conveniently could send to Romeo.
But when I came, some minute ere the time
Of her awaking, here untimely lay
The noble Paris and true Romeo dead.
260 She wakes; and I entreated her come forth

**216–221 Seal . . . patience:** Stop your emotional outbursts until we can find out the source (**spring**) of these confusing events (**ambiguities**). Wait (**forbear**) and be patient, and let's find out what happened.

**223–227** Friar Laurence confesses that he is most responsible for these events. He will both accuse (**impeach**) himself and clear (**purge**) himself of guilt.

**COMMON CORE L 4**

### Language Coach

**Multiple Meanings** The word *date* means something other than "day of the month" in line 229; it means "the length of time something lasts." What does Friar Laurence mean by "my short date of breath"?

**236** It was Romeo's banishment, not Tybalt's death, that made Juliet so sad.

**248 borrowed:** temporary.

**254 kindred's:** family's.

## TIERED DISCUSSION PROMPTS

Use these prompts to explore Friar Laurence's defense before Prince Escalus in lines 223–269:

**Summarize** Summarize Friar Laurence's explanation of the deaths of Romeo, Juliet, and Paris. *Possible answer: Friar Laurence retells the tale of Romeo's marriage to Juliet, his banishment, Juliet's plea for help, and their fateful deaths.*

**Analyze** Why is it appropriate that Friar Laurence be the one to explain the events that led to the three deaths? *Possible answer: Friar Laurence is an appropriate source because he has been involved in many of the steps of the lovers' relationship and has taken great risks to get them together. The fact that he is neither a Capulet nor a Montague means that he can relate the events objectively.*

**Evaluate** Does Friar Laurence think he has done anything wrong? Should he think so? *Possible answer: Friar Laurence thinks that he has done wrong but that his actions are excusable (lines 226–227). Since the lovers followed his plans, Friar Laurence is probably more culpable than he allows in this speech.*

## FOR ENGLISH LANGUAGE LEARNERS

**Vocabulary: Outdated Forms** Have students add these words to their language journals. (See the **For English Language Learners** activity on page 1036.) After they record each term and its definition, have them reread the lines and substitute the definitions for the words.

- *perforce* (line 238), "by necessity"
- *wrought* (line 245), "worked" (made happen)
- *writ* (line 246), "wrote"
- *prefixed* (line 253), "prearranged"

### Language Coach    COMMON CORE L 4

**Multiple Meanings** *Possible answer: the short amount of time he has left to live* Ask students to identify another meaning of the word *date*. *Possible answer: when two people meet to do something together*

And bear this work of heaven with patience;
But then a noise did scare me from the tomb,
And she, too desperate, would not go with me,
But, as it seems, did violence on herself.
265 All this I know, and to the marriage
Her nurse is privy; and if aught in this
Miscarried by my fault, let my old life
Be sacrificed, some hour before his time,
Unto the rigor of severest law.

270 **Prince.** We still have known thee for a holy man.
Where's Romeo's man? What can he say in this?

**Balthasar.** I brought my master news of Juliet's death;
And then in post he came from Mantua
To this same place, to this same monument.
275 This letter he early bid me give his father,
And threatened me with death, going in the vault,
If I departed not and left him there.

**Prince.** Give me the letter. I will look on it.
Where is the County's page that raised the watch?
280 Sirrah, what made your master in this place?

**Page.** He came with flowers to strew his lady's grave;
And bid me stand aloof, and so I did.
Anon comes one with light to ope the tomb;
And by-and-by my master drew on him;
285 And then I ran away to call the watch.

**Prince.** This letter doth make good the friar's words,
Their course of love, the tidings of her death;
And here he writes that he did buy a poison
Of a poor 'pothecary, and therewithal
290 Came to this vault to die and lie with Juliet.
Where be these enemies? Capulet, Montague,
See what a scourge is laid upon your hate,
That heaven finds means to kill your joys with love!
And I, for winking at your discords too,
295 Have lost a brace of kinsmen. All are punished. **F**

**Capulet.** O brother Montague, give me thy hand.
This is my daughter's jointure, for no more
Can I demand.

265–269 **and to . . . law:** Her nurse can bear witness to this secret marriage. If I am responsible for any of this, let the law punish me with death.

270 *How does the Prince respond to the friar's acceptance of blame?*

273 **in post:** at full speed.

279–280 The Prince asks for Paris' servant, who notified the guards (**raised the watch**). Then he asks the servant why Paris was at the cemetery.

283–285 **Anon . . . call the watch:** Soon (**anon**) someone with a light came and opened the tomb. Paris drew his sword, and I ran to call the guards.

292–295 **See what . . . punished:** Look at the punishment your hatred has brought on you. Heaven has killed your children (**joys**) with love. For shutting my eyes to your arguments (**discords**), I have lost two relatives. We have all been punished.

**F** TRAGEDY
Reread lines 291–295. On what does the prince blame all the deaths? What **theme,** or message, might this passage suggest?

297–298 **jointure:** dowry, the payment a bride's father traditionally made to the groom. Capulet means that no one could demand more of a bride's father than he has already paid.

---

## TEXT ANALYSIS

**F** TRAGEDY

*Possible answer: The prince blames the deaths on the enmity between the Capulets and Montagues. The theme may be that hatred hurts the person who hates as well as the person who is hated, or that hatred will be punished by the destruction of joy.*

**IF STUDENTS NEED HELP . . .** Discuss these questions:

• What "joys" does the prince refer to in line 293?

• What does the prince mean when he says that these "joys" have been killed with love?

• What scourge, or punishment, does the prince describe?

• Why and how has the prince also been punished in these events?

---

## DIFFERENTIATED INSTRUCTION

**FOR ENGLISH LANGUAGE LEARNERS**

**Task Support** Have students read the marginal question for line 270 and then reread line 270 itself. Explain that a person in a religious order was thought to answer to the laws of heaven even more than to human laws. ***Possible answer:*** *The prince dismisses the friar's acceptance of blame. Since the friar is a holy man, the prince implies, his character is above reproach.*

**Concept Support** Have students carefully read these last two pages of the play and the marginal notes. Then have them work in pairs to write a speech-by-speech summary of the ending. Use these sentences to start:

• The prince forgives the friar.

• Balthasar says that he has a letter from Romeo to his father.

• The prince takes the letter and asks why Paris was at the cemetery.

**Montague.** But I can give thee more;
For I will raise her statue in pure gold,
300 That whiles Verona by that name is known,
There shall no figure at such rate be set
As that of true and faithful Juliet.
**Capulet.** As rich shall Romeo's by his lady's lie—
Poor sacrifices of our enmity!
305 **Prince.** A glooming peace this morning with it brings.
The sun for sorrow will not show his head.
Go hence, to have more talk of these sad things;
Some shall be pardoned, and some punished;
For never was a story of more woe
310 Than this of Juliet and her Romeo.
[*Exeunt.*]

**③ Targeted Passage**

**301 at such rate be set:** be valued so highly.

**303–304** Capulet promises to do for Romeo what Montague will do for Juliet. Their children have become sacrifices to their hatred (**enmity**).

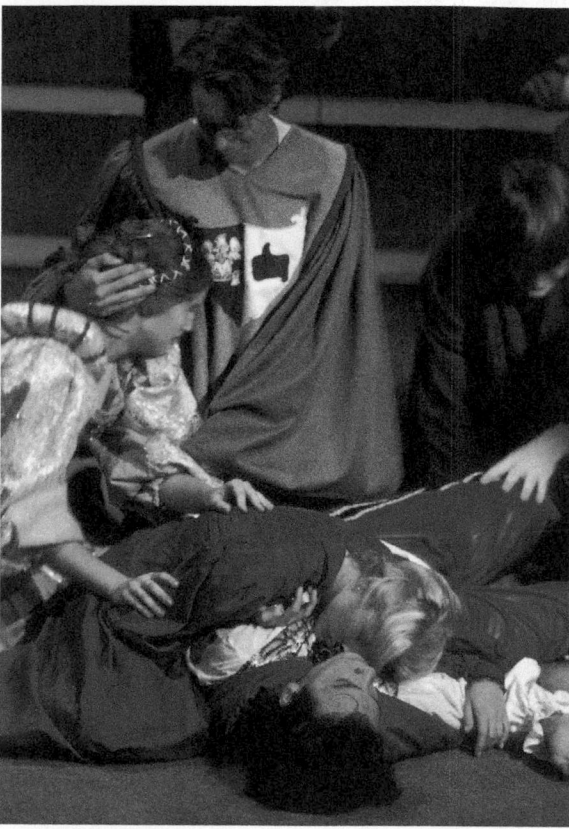

The Capulets and Lord Montague mourn their children's deaths in an Austin, Texas, high school production.

## Analyze Visuals

**Activity** What elements of stagecraft contribute to the mood and energy of the closing scene in this production? ***Possible answer:*** *The costumes show that the play has a traditional Elizabethan setting. The vivid colors and opulent fabrics convey the high social standing of the characters. The bodies of Romeo and Juliet are spotlighted, making them the focus of the scene.*

## ACT FIVE WRAP–UP

**READ WITH A PURPOSE** Ask students to comment on how love and hate play a role in the events of Act Five. Ask them which of the two they believed in the end to be stronger and why. ***Possible answer:*** *The theme of love and hate has its climax in Act Five; some students may feel that love conquers hate, because the families are finally reconciled, while others may point to the many deaths that result from the families' hatred.*

⭐ **CRITIQUE** Have students discuss the reasons that Romeo and Juliet have become symbols of great love. Encourage students to share why they think this drama has retained its power over the centuries.

## INDEPENDENT READING

Students might want to read the comedy *As You Like It* by Shakespeare.

---

**FOR STRUGGLING READERS**

**③ Targeted Passage** [Lines 298–310]

The families settle their feud and make plans to honor Romeo and Juliet.

- What will Montague do to honor Juliet? What will Capulet do to honor Romeo? (lines 299–304)
- How will their actions settle the feud? (line 304)
- How will Prince Escalus follow up on what has happened? (line 308)

**FOR ADVANCED LEARNERS/PRE–AP**

**Evaluate Resolution (Part 2)** Is this feud really over? Point out that both Capulet and Montague speak out of sudden grief and in the presence of the condemning Prince Escalus. In some productions of the play, the actors' body language suggests that the reconciliation is reluctant or even temporary. Ask students to write a paragraph about why it matters that the reconciliation be genuine and lasting; then have them compare responses in small groups.

# Practice and Apply

For preliminary support of post-reading questions, use these copy masters:

**RESOURCE MANAGER—Copy Masters**
Reading Check p. 73
Shakespearean Drama p. 71
Question Support p. 74

Additional selection questions are provided for teachers on page 65.

**ANSWERS**

## Comprehension

1. *A plague quarantines John in Verona.*
2. *Paris thinks that Romeo is an enemy of the Capulets and has come to desecrate the tomb.*
3. *Paris challenges and is killed by Romeo, who places Paris's body in the tomb. Romeo poisons himself in the tomb, thinking that Juliet is dead. Juliet stabs herself in the tomb when she realizes that Romeo is dead.*

## Text Analysis

COMMON CORE RL 2, RL 3, RL 10

***Possible answers:***

4. ■ **COMMON CORE FOCUS** ***Reading Shakespearean Drama*** *The death of Romeo, Juliet, and Paris and the families' reconciliation make up the resolution of the play. There is satisfaction in the fact that the feuding seems to end and the families finally seem to realize how wrong they have been. On the other hand, their reconciliation has only begun, and it may not be strong enough to make up for the death and loss in the play.*
5. *Students may suggest that they would find Friar Laurence worthy of punishment, even though Prince Escalus pardoned him. Students may also identify a punishment for Capulet and Montague, noting that their feud resulted in many deaths.*
6. ● **COMMON CORE FOCUS** ***Identify Soliloquy*** *Answers will vary. In Scene 1, lines 1–11, Romeo describes his happy dream. The soliloquy shows his deep love for Juliet; it also increases the sense of irony, for the audience knows that some of his comments have meanings that are yet to be revealed.*
7. *Some students may feel that rashness is their chief flaw. Others may mention the couple's overly romantic attitudes or their disobedience of social expectations.*
8. ***Family ties:*** *are strong, but romantic love is stronger.* ***Friendship:*** *Hate can ruin everything, even the best of friendships.* ***Love:*** *doesn't care who your family is; anyone, even sworn enemies, can fall in love. Relevance will depend upon students' interpretations of the themes.*

## Text Criticism

***Possible answer:***

9. *Some students may agree that love overshadows hate, for the reasons listed. These students may cite as evidence any of the scenes in which the lovers speak to each other. Other students may argue that since the lovers were destroyed by family hatred, hate is stronger than love.*

**Is LOVE stronger than HATE?**
Answers will vary, but students should be able to explain them and support them with reasons.

---

## After Reading

### Comprehension

COMMON CORE

**RL 2** Determine a theme of a text. **RL 3** Analyze how complex characters advance the plot or develop the theme. **RL 10** Read and comprehend dramas.

1. **Recall** What prevents Friar John from delivering the letter to Romeo?
2. **Recall** Why does Paris attack Romeo at the Capulets' tomb?
3. **Summarize** How do the bodies of Paris, Romeo, and Juliet all end up in the Capulets' tomb? Explain how each character loses his or her life.

### Text Analysis

4. ■ **Reading Shakespearean Drama** In Shakespearean drama, the **resolution,** or final plot stage, occurs in the last act. Look back at the chart you completed as you read. Describe the events that make up the resolution of this tragedy. Do you think this sequence of events brings the play to a satisfying conclusion? Explain.
5. **Make Judgments** In the play's final speech, Prince Escalus declares, "Some shall be pardoned, and some punished." If you were the ruler of Verona, whom would you pardon, and whom would you punish? Explain.
6. ● **Identify Soliloquy** Identify a soliloquy in Act Five. Citing specific lines of the play, explain what you learn about the character who is speaking.
7. **Analyze Tragedy** In a tragedy, the hero or heroine usually has a character flaw that leads to his or her downfall. Is this true of Romeo and Juliet? Cite evidence from the tragedy to support your explanation.
8. **Examine Theme** Many of the themes in *Romeo and Juliet* are universal, meaning they are still relevant today. Examine the values and experiences shown, and think about how each is presented in *Romeo and Juliet.* Complete the chart by stating how each topic is conveyed as a theme in the play.

| *Value or Experience* | *Statement of Theme* |
|---|---|
| Fate | There are forces in life over which people have no control. |
| Family ties | |
| Friendship | |
| Love | |

### Text Criticism

9. **Critical Interpretations** About *Romeo and Juliet,* the critic F. M. Dickey maintains, "love overshadows [hate] dramatically, since it is the passion of the protagonists and since Shakespeare has lavished his most moving poetry upon the love scenes." Do you agree? Support your conclusion with evidence.

**Is LOVE stronger than HATE?**
What consequences can arise from hating someone?

# Language

◆ **GRAMMAR AND STYLE: Create Rhythm**

Review the **Grammar and Style** note on page 1066. **Parallelism** is the repetition of grammatical structures—phrases or clauses, for example. Shakespeare's use of parallelism creates **cadence**, or a balanced, rhythmic flow. Here are two examples from the play. The first contains a series of four past-tense verbs, each followed by the word *for*. In the second, Shakespeare uses the three parallel adjectives *stiff*, *stark*, and *cold*. Think about how these passages might sound without the parallelism.

**COMMON CORE**

**L 1a–b** Use parallel structure and various types of phrases and clauses.

> **First Servingman.** *You are looked for and called for, asked for and sought for, in the great chamber.* (Act One, Scene 5, lines 10–11)
>
> **Friar Laurence.** *. . . Each part, deprived of supple government,*
> *Shall, stiff and stark and cold, appear like death;* (Act Four, Scene 1, lines 102–103)

Now consider how the revision in blue makes use of parallelism to improve the rhythm of this first draft. Revise your response to the prompt below by using parallelism whenever possible.

---

**STUDENT MODEL**

Goodbye my love, I am going to die.
*Farewell my love*
~~Take care my dear~~, I leave you forever.

---

## READING-WRITING CONNECTION

**YOUR TURN**
Increase your understanding of *The Tragedy of Romeo and Juliet* by responding to this prompt. Then use the **revising tip** to improve your writing.

| WRITING PROMPT | REVISING TIP |
|---|---|
| **Short Constructed Response: Blank Verse Poem** What if Romeo had taken slower-acting poison? Imagine that Juliet wakes before the poison kills Romeo, so that he is able to utter his last words of love to her. Write **six to eight lines of a short blank verse poem** in which Romeo says goodbye to Juliet before dying. | Review your poem. Does your poem have a balanced, rhythmic flow? If not, consider using parallelism to create cadence. |

**Interactive Revision** **THINK** central

Go to **thinkcentral.com**.
KEYWORD: HML9-1147

---

## DIFFERENTIATED INSTRUCTION

### FOR STRUGGLING WRITERS

1. Suggest that students write a first draft, in prose, and then manipulate their language by substituting words and phrases that fit the meter.

2. Remind students that they need not be concerned about creating rhymes.

3. Remind students that they can shorten words or invert word order, as Shakespeare often did, to fit the meter.

---

# Language

**COMMON CORE L 1a, b**

◆ **GRAMMAR AND STYLE**

1. Since the elements in each example are phrased in the same way, they create an ear-pleasing cadence.

2. Have students identify the cadence in the student model. ***Possible answer:*** *The cadence comes from "Goodbye my love" and "Farewell my love."*

3. Then have students rewrite this sentence, using parallelism to improve its cadence:

   Romeo intended to enter the cemetery, where he would find Juliet; then he would drink the poison. ***Possible answer:*** *Romeo intended to enter the cemetery, find Juliet, and drink the poison.*

**R** **RESOURCE MANAGER—Copy Master**
Create Rhythm p. 75

**READING-WRITING CONNECTION**
Students might begin by making lists of key words and figurative phrases (for example, *you are like . . .* or *our love is like . . .*) that could be used in their stanzas.

**BEST PRACTICES TOOLKIT—Transparency**
Classification Chart p. B17

**Writing Online**  **THINK** central

The following tools are available online at **thinkcentral.com** and on **WriteSmart CD-ROM:**
• **Interactive Graphic Organizers**
• **Interactive Student Models**
• **Interactive Revision Lessons**
For additional grammar instruction, see **GrammarNotes** on **thinkcentral.com**.

---

# Assess and Reteach

## Assess

**DIAGNOSTIC AND SELECTION TESTS**
Selection Tests A, B/C pp. 291–294

**Interactive Selection Test** on **thinkcentral.com**

## Reteach

**Level Up Online Tutorials** on **thinkcentral.com**

**Reteaching Worksheets** on **thinkcentral.com**
Literature Lessons 25, 26, 35, 38

### COMMON CORE FOCUS

**W 9 (RL 7)** Draw evidence to support an analysis of the representation of a key scene in two different artistic mediums, including what is emphasized or absent in each. **SL 1a** Come to discussions prepared, having read material under study. **SL 2** Integrate multiple sources of information presented in diverse media or formats.

### SUMMARY

This clip from *Romeo and Juliet* shows the famous balcony scene. Romeo is beneath Juliet's window when she appears on the balcony. Juliet despairs that the two are separated because of their names. Romeo responds, and the two confess their love. Juliet says she will send someone the next day at nine to see if Romeo intends to marry her. They restate their love, and Romeo leaves to find Father Laurence to help him.

## Why does HOLLYWOOD love Shakespeare?

Ask students what elements Hollywood producers look for in scripts. List ideas on the board, such as action, intrigue, high drama, love, and hate. Ask students which of these elements appear in Shakespeare's plays.

### BACKGROUND

More than 250 films based on Shakespeare and his plays have been produced. Between 1907 and 2000, 61 film adaptations and 21 TV adaptations were made of *Hamlet* alone. Other versions of *Romeo and Juliet* include those by George Cukor (1935), Renato Castellani (1954), Armando Acosta (1990), and Baz Luhrmann (1996). More than 13 notable films based on Shakespeare's work were made in the 1990s. Zeffirelli's 1967 version of *The Taming of the Shrew* followed the original play closely, while the 1999 film *10 Things I Hate About You* reset the story in a contemporary high school.

---

**Media Study**

*from* **Romeo and Juliet**
Film Clip on **Media Smart** DVD-ROM

# Why does HOLLYWOOD love Shakespeare?

### COMMON CORE

**W 9 (RL 7)** Draw evidence to support an analysis of the representation of a key scene in two different artistic mediums, including what is emphasized or absent in each. **SL 1a** Come to discussions prepared, having read material under study. **SL 2** Integrate multiple sources of information presented in diverse media or formats.

Shakespeare's *Tragedy of Romeo and Juliet* has all the ingredients for a successful Hollywood adaptation: timeless, universal themes; vibrant characters; an exotic setting; and a string of misunderstandings that ultimately lead to tragedy. Now that you have read the play version of *Romeo and Juliet*, notice the choices the film director makes in bringing this play to the screen.

## Background

**Love at First Sight** Some would argue that the true mark of a great movie is its ability to leave a long-lasting impression on its audience. When viewers and critics were first introduced to Franco Zeffirelli's *Romeo and Juliet* in 1968, the reaction was unanimous praise. Everything about the film—from the romantic setting to the playful yet sometimes somber music—captivated audiences. In addition, Zeffirelli did what no other director had done before. He cast as his leads two young, unknown actors who were 16 and 17 years old when filming began. By taking a risk on these young actors, Zeffirelli created an interpretation filled with innocence, liveliness, and passion.

1148

---

## Media Study Resources

**R RESOURCE MANAGER UNIT 10**

Plan and Teach pp. 77–80
Summary pp. 81†*, 82‡*
Viewing Guide p. 83
Close Viewing p. 84
Media Activity p. 85
Produce Your Own Media p. 86

**TECHNOLOGY**

 **Teacher One Stop DVD-ROM**
**Student One Stop DVD-ROM**
**Media*Smart* DVD-ROM**
**MediaScope** on **thinkcentral.com**

*See resources on the* **Teacher One Stop DVD-ROM** *and on* **thinkcentral.com**.

\* Resources for Differentiation  † Also in Spanish  ‡ In Haitian Creole and Vietnamese

## Media Literacy: Shakespearean Drama in Movies

Long before a director can call out, "Lights, camera, action!" he or she must have a vision for the film. Together with a filmmaking crew, a director plans every detail of a movie, including the lighting, setting, props, costumes, and action. The arrangement and use of these filmmaking elements is known as **mise en scène** (mēz' än sĕn'), a term originally associated with French theater. Notice how the following elements of mise en scène in the film clip shape our understanding of Shakespearean drama.

### ELEMENTS OF MISE EN SCÈNE

❶ **Lighting** can be used to create a mood or a dramatic effect. It can also make a scene look realistic and can draw viewers' attention to an important object or person.

❷ The **setting** and **props** build certain expectations in viewers' minds and establish a location. For example, an exotic setting can help create an atmosphere of romance or love.

❸ A character's **facial expressions, body language,** and **actions** convey what he or she is thinking or feeling.

❹ A director deliberately positions characters within a **frame** to indicate the nature of the characters' relationship. For example, characters who don't trust each other may be placed at opposite ends of the frame.

❺ In a Shakespearean movie, **costumes** may provide clues about characters' social status and may also indicate a specific time period. A director can also experiment with costumes to reflect a character's personality.

MEDIA STUDY   **1149**

---

## MEDIA STUDY: TEACHING OPTIONS

### Teaching Option 1: The Basics (1–2 Days)
1. Begin the Media Study using the material provided on pages 1148–1149.
2. Show the Introduction on Media*Smart*. Then show the First Viewing. As they watch, have students use the Viewing Guide on page 1150, along with the corresponding copy master on page 83 of the Resource Manager. Discuss their responses.
3. Return to the pupil book for the extension activities on page 1151.

### Teaching Option 2: In-Depth Study (2–3 Days)
1. Begin the Media Study using pages 1148–1149.
2. Show the Introduction and First Viewing from Media*Smart*. Then continue on Media*Smart* with the Media Lessons, using the teacher notes available in the Resources section.
3. Show the Guided Analysis presentation. Have students record their observations on the Student Viewing Guide available in the Resources section from Media*Smart*.
4. Return to the pupil book, page 1151.

---

# *Teach*

## Media Literacy

Review with students the definition of *mise en scène.* Students should recognize that directors seek a certain look to their films and hope to convey particular ideas or emotions. Ask students what specific elements directors use to create their unique visions. On the board, list students' answers, which may include such elements as lighting and sets. Make sure setting, props, facial expressions, body language, actions, frame, and costumes are included in the list. Then discuss the chart on page 1149.

- **Lighting** To reinforce the impact of lighting, ask students to imagine an empty room first brightly lit and then dark and shadowy. What different moods do the two kinds of lighting convey? Suppose a boy enters the room. What difference would it make if the director directed light on the boy or left the boy in shadow?

- **Setting and Props** Have students imagine a beach on a clear summer day and then a school cafeteria. What differences in the kind of story they will expect do they immediately recognize?

- **Facial Expressions, Body Language, and Actions** Have volunteers describe likely reactions to the sudden appearance of a gorilla and identify actions people might take in response. Discuss how facial expressions, body language, and actions convey such a situation.

- **Frame** Have volunteers draw these movie scenes: (1) teacher and student, (2) close friends, (3) captains of rival football teams. Have other students imagine the scene being portrayed and provide a brief description of the pivotal moment that the frame captures.

- **Costumes** Have students think about costumes they have seen in movies. Ask them to describe costumes they would expect in movies about: (1) an international high school in 2080, (2) a factory outside of London in 1890, (3) a sailing expedition in 2006. Discuss how the costumes reflect the time period and setting.

MEDIA STUDY   **1149**

# Practice and Apply

## VIEWING GUIDE

1. Before students view the movie clip, tell them they will be asked to identify techniques that create the director's vision. Have them watch for these elements:

   - **camera shots** that establish the scene and develop Romeo's and Juliet's emotions and reactions

   - **lighting and sound** that establish the romantic mood between the lovers

   - **music** that stirs the viewers' emotions about the young lovers

2. Some students may struggle to isolate the director's techniques. Help these students focus on the camera shots and lighting by playing the clip without sound. Then help them isolate the use of sound and music by listening to the soundtrack only.

**R** RESOURCE MANAGER—Copy Masters
   Viewing Guide p. 83
   Close Viewing p. 84
   Viewing Activity p. 85

Use this resource with the Viewing Guide:

💿 **Media*Smart* DVD-ROM**

**MediaScope** on **thinkcentral.com**

## ANSWERS

### FIRST VIEWING: Comprehension

*Possible answers:*

1. *The setting is the back of Juliet's house, a stone villa with a wide balcony above an orchard. The action takes place on the balcony or in the orchard.*

2. *The director begins with a long wide shot of the orchard. In a second long wide shot, we see Romeo in the orchard. We then see a medium-angle shot of Romeo's view. Next we see close-ups of Romeo, interspersed with panning shots of Juliet's house. This follows Romeo's view as he moves through the orchard. Romeo is finally able to see Juliet on the balcony.*

### CLOSE VIEWING: Media Literacy

*Possible answers:*

3. *The moonlight effect through the orchard trees creates an intimate, romantic mood.*

4. *The setting in the clip is lush and heavily forested. The balcony is longer and wider and allows for greater movement than the one in the text. Answers will vary.*

---

**Media🎬Smart DVD-ROM**
- **Film Clip:** *Romeo and Juliet*
- **Director:** Franco Zeffirelli
- **Rating:** PG
- **Genre:** Drama
- **Running Time:** 11 minutes

---

## Viewing Guide for
# Romeo and Juliet

The scene you're about to view is perhaps the most well-known one in all of Shakespeare's plays—the balcony scene.

Because of the length of the clip, you may wish to view the scene once for the story. During any additional viewings, concentrate on such elements as mise en scène, camera shots, and sound. Keep the following questions in mind as you view.

### NOW VIEW

**FIRST VIEWING: Comprehension**

1. **Summarize** Describe the setting of the clip in your own words.

2. **Clarify** What types of **shots** does the director use in the beginning of the clip to establish the scene?

**CLOSE VIEWING: Media Literacy**

3. **Interpret Mood** What kind of mood do you think the **lighting** creates?

4. **Analyze Setting** How does the setting compare with what you envisioned? Do you feel the balcony scene is presented better visually or on-page? Explain.

5. **Analyze Director's Techniques** How does the director show that time has passed from the beginning to the end of this scene? Consider how the director uses **lighting** and **sounds** to show the passing of time.

6. **Evaluate Music** Zeffirelli uses music throughout the movie to stir viewers' emotions. When is music used, and how effectively is it used, in this scene?

---

5. *The scene begins under moonlight with very few natural ambient sound effects. By the end of the scene, the sky is lighter, implying the sun is rising, and you can hear a rooster's crow and birds chirping.*

6. *Quiet music plays as a backdrop as first Romeo and then Juliet speak alone. The music fades out when the two see and begin talking to each other. Low, gentle music begins again with Romeo's vow of love, then swells with Juliet's declaration and the lovers' embrace. Then frivolous, lighthearted music plays as the nurse calls Juliet away and Romeo happily swings from a branch. The*  *music becomes flowing with the lovers' next embrace, and the scene ends with a mournful swelling at the lovers' parting. Zeffirelli effectively uses music to make viewers alternately feel passion, joy, and sadness.*

## Write or Discuss

**Evaluate Mise en Scène** In your opinion, is Zeffirelli's film version of the balcony scene appealing, believable, and complete? Why or why not? Cite specific examples from the clip to support your view. Think about

- the actors' physical appearance, actions, and movements
- the details of the setting, costumes, and props
- the camera shots of the scene

## Produce Your Own Media

**Create a Visual Treatment** Imagine you're filming a modern adaptation of *The Tragedy of Romeo and Juliet*. Before you begin filming, you'll want to create a **visual treatment,** a series of images that visually represent key scenes from the play. With a small group, determine who will be the costume designer, the set designer, and the cast of characters. Then choose six key scenes from the play that you want to photograph.

*HERE'S HOW* Use the professional model and the following tips to help you visualize the elements of **mise en scène:**

- **Characters:** What is the relationship between the characters, and how will you position them within the frame?
- **Setting:** What elements of the setting will convey a specific time or place?
- **Costumes:** What clues do the costumes reveal about the characters?
- **Lighting:** How does the lighting create a mood?

**Media Tools** THINK central
Go to **thinkcentral.com**.
KEYWORD: HML9-1151

**Tech Tip**

If you have access to photo-editing software, use it to edit your pictures after the photo shoot.

PROFESSIONAL MODEL

MEDIA STUDY **1151**

## Produce Your Own Media

**Rubric: Create a Visual Treatment** A strong visual treatment should include images that

- convey a clear description of each key scene
- position characters within frames in ways that show their relationships
- use elements of setting to establish time and place
- use costumes to give information about characters
- use lighting to establish mood

**R** RESOURCE MANAGER—Copy Master
Produce Your Own Media p. 86

---

## Write or Discuss

**Evaluate Mise en Scène** In their opinion statements, students should be prepared to cite specific examples from the clip that support their views. For example, if students find the scene appealing, believable, and complete, they might point out that the actors are close to the ages of Romeo and Juliet in the play and that both actors are very attractive. They might point to the wealthy appearance of the villa and its orchard and to the period costumes as elements that make the scene believable and complete. They might point to the panning shot in the opening to reveal Juliet as something making the scene appealing.

### MEDIA STUDY WRAP–UP

Have students summarize what they have learned about using elements of mise en scène to create a vision on film. Encourage them to use terms such as *lighting, setting, props, facial expressions, body language, actions, framing,* and *costumes* in their explanations.

### RETEACH

For students who are unable to apply the Media Study skills, select from these reteaching options:

- **Stage Design** Ask students to choose a scene from the play and make a drawing of how they would stage it. Remind them to consider the backdrop, props and scenery, and the positions and locations of each character. Have them present their drawing to the class and explain their choices.
- **Background Music** Have students choose a scene from the play and select background music for it. They should decide how long the music will play and how loud it should be. Then have students make a short presentation to the class in which they read the lines of the chosen scene, with the music in the background. Discuss with the class the effectiveness of the music selection.

**Media Tools** THINK central

Media study keywords point to **MediaScope,** a Web site that helps students strengthen media analysis and production skills.

# Focus and Motivate

## COMMON CORE FOCUS

**RI 2** Determine a central idea of a text and analyze its development. **RI 3** Analyze how the author unfolds an analysis or series of ideas, including the connections drawn between them. **RI 8** Delineate and evaluate the argument and claims in a text. **W 9b (RI 8)** Draw evidence from informational texts to delineate and evaluate the argument and specific claims of a text. **L 4a** Use context as a clue to the meaning of a phrase.

## SUMMARY

In this critical review, Roger Ebert argues that Franco Zeffirelli's 1968 *Romeo and Juliet* will long endure as a great movie. He compares it to other film versions of the play and discusses the success of its stagecraft.

## What's the Connection?

Use an Anticipation Guide to prepare students for the selection. Have students respond to these statements before and after reading:

- Only experienced actors can convey the language of Shakespeare effectively.

- A good reason to cast unknown actors is so that you can pay them less money.

- Zeffirelli needed more experience before directing *Romeo and Juliet*.

 **BEST PRACTICES TOOLKIT—Transparency** Anticipation Guide p. A14

# Teach

## Standards Focus: Analyze a Critical Review

Elicit that like other kinds of persuasive writing, the purpose of a critical review is to encourage the reader to agree with the writer's central idea. In this case, Roger Ebert will use several techniques to persuade readers to agree with his evaluation of a famous film treatment of *Romeo and Juliet*.

**R** **RESOURCE MANAGER—Copy Master** Analyze a Critical Review p. 95

---

Use with *Romeo and Juliet*, page 1036.

### COMMON CORE

**RI 2** Determine a central idea of a text and analyze its development. **RI 3** Analyze how the author unfolds an analysis or series of ideas, including the connections drawn between them. **RI 8** Delineate and evaluate the argument and claims in a text. **L 4a** Use context as a clue to the meaning of a phrase.

# Great Movies: *Romeo and Juliet*
Critical Review by Roger Ebert    *Essential Course of Study*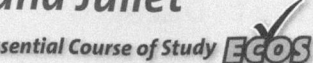

## What's the Connection?

You've just discovered why filmmakers love Shakespeare: plays like *Romeo and Juliet* present directors with terrific material to work with. You've also explored the choices one director, Franco Zeffirelli, made to transform Shakespeare's classic drama into a big-screen blockbuster. How do critics think Zeffirelli's movie measures up? Read to find out one movie reviewer's opinion.

## Standards Focus: Analyze a Critical Review

A **critical review** is an essay in which the writer gives his or her opinions about a movie, a play, a book, a TV show, or another work. A critical review typically includes these elements:

- the name of the work and its creator

- a description of the work, often including some background information and summary of the plot

- a clearly stated central idea, the reviewer's opinion of the work

- reasons that support the opinion

- examples or details that illustrate the reasons

A critical review may include other elements as well, but the heart of a review is the writer's opinion and the reasons and examples he or she uses to back it up. Opinions that are **substantiated,** or supported, in a critical review are more persuasive than those that are simply stated without appropriate support.

As you read this critical review, use a chart like the one shown to record Roger Ebert's opinion and the main reasons he gives to support it. Keep track of the examples and details from the movie that Ebert uses to illustrate each reason.

| Ebert's Opinion: ↓ | |
|---|---|
| Reason | Examples or Details |
| Reason 1: | |
| Reason 2: | |

---

## Selection Resources

*See resources on the* **Teacher One Stop DVD-ROM** *and on* <u>thinkcentral.com</u>.

**R** **RESOURCE MANAGER UNIT 10**
    Lesson Support,* pp. 87–100

**DIAGNOSTIC AND SELECTION TESTS**
    Selection Tests, pp. 295–298

**INTERACTIVE READER**

**ADAPTED INTERACTIVE READER**

**ELL ADAPTED INTERACTIVE READER**

**TECHNOLOGY**

- **Teacher One Stop DVD-ROM**
- **Student One Stop DVD-ROM**
- **PowerNotes DVD-ROM**
- **Audio Tutor CD**
- **ExamView Test Generator** on the **Teacher One Stop**

\* Resources for Differentiation

SECTION 5

### GREAT MOVIES

# Romeo and Juliet

**BY ROGER EBERT**

"Romeo and Juliet" is always said to be the first romantic tragedy ever written, but it isn't really a tragedy at all. It's a tragic misunderstanding, scarcely fitting the ancient requirement of tragedy that the mighty fall through their own flaws. Romeo and Juliet have no flaws, and aren't old enough to be blamed if they did. They die because of the pigheaded
10 quarrel of their families, the Montagues and the Capulets. By writing the play, Shakespeare began the shaping of modern drama, in which the fates of ordinary people are as crucial as those of the great. The great tragedies of his time, including his own, involved kings, emperors, generals. Here, near the dawn of his career, perhaps remembering a sweet early romance before his forced marriage
20 to Anne Hathaway, he writes about teenagers in love. **A**

"Romeo and Juliet" has been filmed many times in many ways; Norma Shearer and Leslie Howard starred in the beloved 1936 Hollywood version, and modern transformations include Robert Wise's "West Side Story" (1961), which applies the plot to Manhattan gang warfare; Abel Ferrara's
30 "China Girl" (1987), about a forbidden romance between a girl of Chinatown and a boy of Little Italy; and Baz Luhrmann's "William Shakespeare's Romeo & Juliet" (1996), with California punk gangs on Verona Beach. But the favorite film version is likely to re-

**Zeffirelli cast two young, unknown actors instead of more experienced stars in his 1968 film.**

main, for many years, Franco Zeffirelli's 1968 production. **B**

His crucial decision, in a film where
40 almost everything went well, was to cast actors who were about the right age to play the characters (as Howard and Shearer were obviously not). As the play opens, Juliet "hath not seen the change of 14 years," and Romeo is little older. This is first love for Juliet, and Romeo's crush on the unseen Rosalind is forgotten the moment he sees **C**

**A** **CRITICAL REVIEW**
In lines 1–21, Ebert introduces the play, mentioning a key element of the plot as well as the context in which Shakespeare wrote the play. In your own words, summarize the information in this paragraph.

**B** **CRITICAL REVIEW**
In lines 22–38, Ebert provides information about other film versions of the play. What opinion about Zeffirelli's film does Ebert state in lines 35–38?

**C** **CRITICAL REVIEW**
What was Zeffirelli's "crucial decision"? Paraphrase the first reason Ebert gives to support his opinion of the movie.

READING FOR INFORMATION **1153**

---

---

## DIFFERENTIATED INSTRUCTION

### FOR STRUGGLING READERS

**Build Comprehension** To check their understanding—and to complete the chart on page 1152—have students first read the selection independently. Next, ask them to meet in pairs to share their understanding of Ebert's ideas and arguments. Finally, have partners work together to list Ebert's reasons and to explain how he supports each one.

### FOR ENGLISH LANGUAGE LEARNERS

**Culture: Connect** In lines 22–35, Ebert gives examples of how Shakespeare's story has been translated into various cultural settings. Invite students to draw upon their own cultural background and suggest how they might adapt *Romeo and Juliet* to an audience with strong ties to that background.

## TIERED DISCUSSION PROMPTS

Refer students to lines 69–77. Use these prompts to discuss the altering of an original script when creating the film version of a play:

**Connect** Have you ever watched a movie that seemed to drag on and on? What are some reasons that a director might choose to make a movie or play shorter? *Accept any reasonable answers. Students should recognize the drawbacks not only of tedious scenes but also of unnecessary scenes.*

**Analyze** Do you agree with Ebert's argument that Shakespeare "might have understood" cutting the verbal description of Juliet's funeral (lines 69–77)? Why or why not? *Possible answer: There is no evidence that reveals Shakespeare's opinion about cutting his plays, but as Ebert says, Shakespeare "took such wholesale liberties with his own sources" (lines 76–77). Also, film is a visual medium. It seems reasonable to cut the verbal description of a scene that might be more powerful if shown rather than merely described.*

**Evaluate** How much can a director change about a play before it is no longer an interpretation and, instead, becomes a different story? Can scenes be rearranged? Can characters be combined or omitted? Can the storyline remain the same without the original dialogue? *Possible answers: Yes. Shakespeare's plays are so timeless that nearly any interpretation of them can reflect the spirit of the play. No. If the original script is not followed, the performance is no longer what Shakespeare intended.*

Olivia Hussey as Juliet proclaims her love in the balcony scene.

COMMON CORE L 4a

**Language Coach**

**Roots and Affixes** A word's **root** is the base part of the word and generally the origin of the word and its related forms. The root of *flourish* is the Latin verb *florere,* "to flower." Reread lines 60–69. What are "rhetorical flourishes," and what does it mean to "prune" them? How can you tell?

Juliet at the masked ball: "I ne'er saw 50 true beauty until this night." After a well-publicized international search, Zeffirelli cast Olivia Hussey, a 16-year-old from Argentina, and Leonard Whiting, a British 17-year-old.

They didn't merely look their parts, they embodied them in the freshness of

---

## Hussey and Whiting were so good because they didn't know any better.

---

their personalities, and although neither was a trained actor, they were fully equal to Shakespeare's dialogue for 60 them; Anthony Holden's new book *William Shakespeare: The Man Behind the Genius* contrasts "the beautiful simplicity with which the lovers speak at their moments of uncomplicated happiness," with "the ornate rhetorical

flourishes which fuel so much else in the play"—flourishes that Zeffirelli severely pruned, trimming about half the play. He was roundly criticized for his 70 edits, but much that needs describing on the stage can simply be shown on-screen, as when Benvolio is shown witnessing Juliet's funeral and thus does not need to evoke it in a description to the exiled Romeo. Shakespeare, who took such wholesale liberties with his own sources, might have understood.

What is left is what people love the play for—the purity of the young lovers' 80 passion, the earthiness of Juliet's nurse, the well-intentioned plans of Friar Laurence, the hot-blooded feud between the young men of the families, the cruel irony of the double deaths. And there is time, too, for many of the great speeches, including Mercutio's poetic evocation of Mab, the queen of dreams.

Hussey and Whiting were so good because they didn't know any better. 90 Another year or two of experience, perhaps, and they would have been too intimidated to play the roles. It was my good fortune to visit the film

## DIFFERENTIATED INSTRUCTION

### FOR STRUGGLING READERS

**Explore Parallelism** Have students reread the paragraph that begins at line 78. Then discuss how Ebert uses parallelism to make his list of characteristics of *Romeo and Juliet* both clear and pleasant to read. Provide these first two items in the list:

- *the purity of the young lovers' passion*
- *the earthiness of Juliet's nurse*

As students list the other items, discuss the cadence and consistency of the parallelism.

### FOR ENGLISH LANGUAGE LEARNERS

**Language Coach** COMMON CORE L 4a

**Roots and Affixes** *Possible answer: "flowery or showy language"; "To prune" must mean "to cut or reduce the language," since "trimming half the play" explains how Zefirelli "pruned" Romeo and Juliet.* Have students name other kinds of flourishes.

set, in a small hill town an hour or so outside Rome, on the night when the balcony scene was filmed. I remember Hussey and Whiting upstairs in the old hillside villa, waiting for their call, unaffected, uncomplicated. And when 100 the balcony scene was shot, I remember the heedless energy that Hussey threw into it, take after take, hurling herself almost off the balcony for hungry kisses. (Whiting, balanced in a tree, needed to watch his footing.) **D**

Between shots, in the overgrown garden, Zeffirelli strolled with the composer Nino Rota, who had written the music for most of Fellini's films 110 and now simply hummed the film's central theme, as the director nodded. Pasqualino De Santis, who was to win an Oscar for his cinematography, directed his crew quietly, urgently, trying to be ready for the freshness of the actors instead of making them wait for technical quibbles. At dawn, drinking strong coffee as cars pulled around to take his actors back to Rome, Zeffirelli 120 said what was obvious: That the whole

movie depended on the balcony and the crypt scenes, and he felt now that his casting decision had proven itself, and that the film would succeed.

It did, beyond any precedent for a film based on Shakespeare, even though Shakespeare is the most filmed writer in history. The movie opened in the tumultuous year of 1968, a 130 time of political upheaval around the world, and somehow the story of the star-crossed lovers caught the mood of rebellious young people who had wearied of their elders' wars. "This of all works of literature eternizes the ardor of young love and youth's aggressive spirit," wrote Anthony Burgess. **E**

Zeffirelli, born in Florence in 1923, came early to the English language 140 through prewar experiences hinted at in the loosely autobiographical "Tea with Mussolini" (1999). His crucial early artistic influence was Laurence Olivier's "Henry V" (1945), which inspired him to go into the theater; he has had parallel careers directing plays, films and operas. Before the great

**D** CRITICAL REVIEW
Reread lines 88–105. Why does Ebert think Hussey and Whiting were so successful at bringing the star-crossed lovers to life? How does Ebert substantiate his opinion?

**E** CRITICAL REVIEW
Why does Ebert think audiences—particularly young people—were so taken with the movie when it premiered in 1968?

Leonard Whiting as Romeo gazes adoringly at his Juliet.

---

INFORMATIONAL ANALYSIS    COMMON CORE    RI 2, RI 3, RI 8

**D** CRITICAL REVIEW

*Possible answer:* *Hussey and Whiting were successful because their youthfulness and their lack of experience gave them great energy for playing their parts and kept them from being intimidated by the very famous roles. To substantiate his opinion, Ebert offers examples of the actors' energy and enthusiasm, such as Hussey nearly throwing herself off the balcony take after take.*

INFORMATIONAL ANALYSIS    COMMON CORE    RI 2, RI 3, RI 8

**E** CRITICAL REVIEW

*Possible answer:* *Ebert thinks that the movie attracted young people because it opened at a time when they were interested in seeing a story about young people who rebel against the values of their parents.*

**IF STUDENTS NEED HELP . . .** Explain that during the 1960s and 1970s, the United States was embroiled in a controversial war in Vietnam, which was heatedly protested by thousands of young people.

---

**FOR ADVANCED LEARNERS/PRE–AP**
**Make Judgments** Zeffirelli believes that the success of his movie depends on the balcony and crypt scenes (lines 120–122). Is this statement true of *Romeo and Juliet* as a play? Have two teams of students choose opposing sides of the question; prepare appropriate arguments, with evidence from the play as support; and debate the issue.

**FOR RELUCTANT READERS**
Lead a discussion with students about the love story that is the basis of the movie. Ask them if they believe the story is timeless or not. If they believe that the story is not always relevant, ask them to describe what they would change about it to make it always relevant. Encourage students to reflect on their own experiences with love.

## F CRITICAL REVIEW

**Possible answer:** *Ebert praises the costuming. He argues that the costumes are essential because they allow bright color to enter the film, adding life to scenes that otherwise would be filled with dark, neutral colors and earth tones (lines 172–175).*

**IF STUDENTS NEED HELP . . .** Urge them not to focus too much on the names of the characters and actors mentioned in these lines. Explain that Ebert includes these details to support the main idea, then use the description of Juliet's costumes (lines 180–183) to model the thinking involved in realizing that Ebert names the characters so that he can classify their costumes.

---

F **CRITICAL REVIEW**
Reread lines 168–186. What aspect of the film does Ebert praise in this paragraph? Explain why he found this element essential to the movie's success.

success of "Romeo and Juliet," he first visited Shakespeare for the shaky but 150 high-spirited "Taming of the Shrew" (1967), with Burton and Taylor. Later he directed Placido Domingo in "Otello" (1986), Verdi's opera, and directed Mel Gibson in "Hamlet" (1990).

---

### Something fundamental has changed in films about and for young people.

---

"Romeo and Juliet" remains the magical high point of his career. To see it again is to luxuriate. It is intriguing that Zeffirelli in 1968 focused on love, while Baz Luhrmann's popular version 160 of 1996 focused on violence; something fundamental has changed in films about and for young people, and recent audiences seem shy of sex and love but eager for conflict and action. I wonder if a modern Friday night audience would snicker at the heart-baring sincerity of the lovers. . . .

The costumes by Danilo Donati won another Oscar for the film (it was 170 also nominated for best picture and director), and they are crucial to its success; they are the avenue for color and richness to enter the frame, which is otherwise filled with gray and ochre stones and the colors of nature. The nurse (Pat Heywood) seems enveloped in a dry goods' sale of heavy fabrics, and Mercutio (John McEnery) comes flying a handkerchief that he uses as a

180 banner, disguise and shroud. Hussey's dresses, with low bodices and simple patterns, set off her creamy skin and long hair; Whiting is able to inhabit his breeches, blouse and codpiece with the conviction that it is everyday clothing, not a costume. F

The costumes and everything else in the film—the photography, the music, above all Shakespeare's language—is so 190 voluptuous, so sensuous. The stagecraft of the twinned death scenes is of course all contrivance; the friar's potion works with timing that is precisely wrong, and yet we forgive the manipulation because Shakespeare has been able to provide us with what is theoretically impossible, the experience of two young lovers each grieving the other's death. When the play was first staged in London, Holden 200 writes, Shakespeare had the satisfaction "of seeing the groundlings moved to emotions far beyond anything before known in the theater." Why? Because of craft and art, yes, but also because Romeo and Juliet were not distant and august figures, not Caesars, Othellos or Macbeths, but a couple of kids in love, as everyone in the theater had known, and everyone in the theater had been.

**Whiting and Hussey in Donati's sumptuous costumes**

---

## DIFFERENTIATED INSTRUCTION

**FOR ENGLISH LANGUAGE LEARNERS**

**Culture: Clarify** Some terms in Ebert's description of the characters' Elizabethan costumes may need clarification. Define these words that relate to clothing of that era:

- *shroud* (line 180), "something that conceals, protects, or screens"

- *bodices* (line 181), "fitted parts of dresses that extend from the waist to the shoulder"

- *breeches* (line 184), "trousers extending to the knee"

- *blouse* (line 184), "a loose-fitting garment resembling a long shirt"

# Comprehension

1. **Recall** What is Ebert's opinion of Franco Zeffirelli's film adaptation of *Romeo and Juliet*?

2. **Paraphrase** Reread lines 198–209. According to Ebert, why have audiences been so moved by the story of *Romeo and Juliet* ever since it was first staged?

# Text Analysis

3. **Analyze a Critical Review** Look at the chart you filled in as you read. What are the main reasons that Ebert gives to substantiate his opinion of the film? Describe at least two examples or details that Ebert uses to illustrate each reason.

4. **Analyze Author's Purpose** How would Ebert's review have been different if his main purpose were to summarize the movie rather than to critique it? Explain.

5. **Evaluate an Opinion** Do you agree with Ebert that "Romeo and Juliet have no flaws" and that they die only "because of the pigheaded quarrel of their families"? Explain your answer.

**COMMON CORE**

**RI 3** Analyze how the author unfolds an analysis or series of ideas, including the connections drawn between them. **RI 8** Delineate and evaluate the argument and claims in a text. **W 9b (RI 8)** Draw evidence from informational texts to delineate and evaluate the argument and specific claims of a text.

## Read for Information: Compare and Contrast

### WRITING PROMPT

What did you think about the casting of Olivia Hussey and Leonard Whiting in Zeffirelli's film version of *Romeo and Juliet*, and how would you rate their performances in the balcony scene? How are your opinions similar to and different from Ebert's?

To answer this prompt, you will have to **compare and contrast,** or explain similarities and differences. To explore the similarities and differences between your views and those expressed by Ebert, follow these steps:

1. Consider your reactions to the movie's two main characters and their acting in the balcony scene. Sum up your opinion, and identify details from the scene that support it.

2. Review Ebert's main points and the evidence he gives to back them up. In your response, you can either examine Ebert's points in order and agree or disagree with each, or you can examine the points you agree with first and then move on to those that you disagree with.

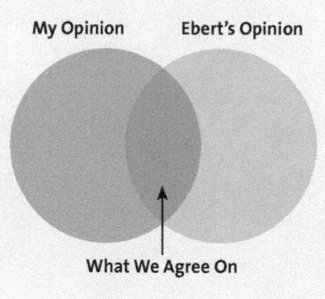

My Opinion    Ebert's Opinion

What We Agree On

## FOR STRUGGLING WRITERS

**Read for Information** Have students answer these questions to compare their reactions to the balcony scene with Ebert's reaction:

- Did the actors seem at ease with Shakespeare's dialogue?

- How would you describe each actor's energy in this scene?

- Can you identify with the actors as teenagers in love?

## FOR ADVANCED LEARNERS/PRE–AP

**Read for Information** Have students extend their essay to discuss their opinion not just of the acting but also of the costuming and other elements of stagecraft in the balcony scene. Ask students to compare their opinions of these elements with what Ebert says about them, as well.

# Practice and Apply

For preliminary support of post-reading questions, use these copy masters:

**R** RESOURCE MANAGER—Copy Masters
Reading Check p. 99
Question Support p. 100
Analyze a Critical Review p. 95

Additional selection questions are provided for teachers on page 90.

## ANSWERS

## Comprehension

1. *Ebert thinks that Zeffirelli's film will remain a favorite for many years.*

2. *Audiences identify with Romeo and Juliet.*

## Text Analysis

COMMON CORE RI 3, RI 8

*Possible answers:*

3. ● **COMMON CORE FOCUS** *Analyze a Critical Review See Skill Focus: Analyze a Critical Review on page 1152.*

4. *If Ebert's main purpose had been to summarize, he would have revealed much more of the movie's plot and not included nearly as many of his own personal opinions.*

5. *Yes. Romeo and Juliet's love would not have been fatal but for the feud. No. Romeo is impulsive, Juliet is stubborn, and both base their love on physical attraction.*

## Read for Information: Compare and Contrast

COMMON CORE W 9 (RI 8)

**Writing Prompt** *Possible answer: Hussey and Whiting are energetic and natural. However, they are so young that it is hard for a modern audience to accept their feelings as real. Ebert feels that the actors' youth was an asset.*

# Assess and Reteach

## Assess

**DIAGNOSTIC AND SELECTION TESTS**
Selection Test A, B/C pp. 295–296, 297–298

**Interactive Selection Test** on **thinkcentral.com**

## Reteach

**Level Up Online Tutorials** on **thinkcentral.com**

**Reteaching Worksheets** on **thinkcentral.com**
Informational Texts Lesson 17

Reading Lesson 12

# Focus and Motivate

## COMMON CORE FOCUS

**RL 5** Analyze how an author's choices concerning how to structure a text and order events within it create such effects as mystery, tension, or surprise. **RL 6** Analyze a particular point of view or cultural experience reflected in a work of world literature. **RL 9** Analyze how an author draws on and transforms source material. **RL 10** Read and comprehend literature. **W 9a (RL 9)** Draw evidence from literary texts to support analysis of how an author draws on and transforms source material in a specific work. **L 4a, d** Use context as a clue to the meaning of a word and verify the preliminary determination of the word's meaning.

## SUMMARY

This myth, told in a narrative poem, is set in ancient Babylon. There, the love between Pyramus and Thisbe is forbidden by their parents. Still, the lovers make a plan to meet by speaking through a crack in a shared wall. Thisbe arrives first and drops her shawl as she runs from a lioness, who tears it apart. Pyramus arrives and finds the bloody, shredded shawl. Believing Thisbe to be dead, he stabs himself. Thisbe returns, grieves his death, and then stabs herself.

## What makes a CLASSIC STORY?

Have students suggest various definitions of *classic* before they complete the *DISCUSS* activity. Ask groups to share their lists of characteristics of classic stories.

## Selection Resources

---

# Pyramus and Thisbe

Myth Retold by Ovid

# What makes a CLASSIC STORY?

### COMMON CORE

**RL 5** Analyze how an author's choices concerning how to structure a text and order events within it create such effects as mystery, tension, or surprise. **RL 6** Analyze a particular point of view or cultural experience reflected in a work of world literature. **RL 9** Analyze how an author draws on and transforms source material. **RL 10** Read and comprehend literature. **L 4a, d** Use context as a clue to the meaning of a word and verify the preliminary determination of the word's meaning.

Two teenagers fall madly in love, but their parents forbid them to see each other. Defying their families, they plan to run away together, but a series of misunderstandings leads to their disastrous demise. Sound familiar? Some stories are so universally appealing that they appear over and over, in everything from ancient myths to Shakespearean drama to modern soap operas. "Pyramus and Thisbe" is one of these classic stories.

*DISCUSS* What are some other examples of classic stories? In a small group, talk about situations that are replayed in fairy tales and bedtime stories, in movies and books, and on TV shows and Broadway stages. What do these stories share? Thrilling plots? Insurmountable conflicts? Happy endings? With your group, come up with a list detailing five characteristics of a classic story.

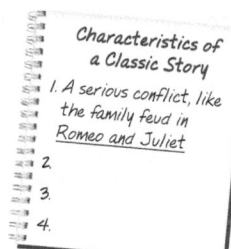

Characteristics of a Classic Story
1. A serious conflict, like the family feud in *Romeo and Juliet*
2.
3.
4.

1158

---

*See resources on the* **Teacher One Stop DVD-ROM** *and on* **thinkcentral.com**.

 **RESOURCE MANAGER UNIT 10**
Plan and Teach, pp. 101–108
Summary pp. 109–110†‡*
Text Analysis and Reading
Skill, pp. 111–114†*

**DIAGNOSTIC AND SELECTION TESTS**
Selection Tests, pp. 299–302

**BEST PRACTICES TOOLKIT**
Character Traits and Textual
Evidence p. D6
Plot Diagram p. D10
Venn Diagram p. A26

**TECHNOLOGY**
⊘ **Teacher One Stop DVD-ROM**
⊘ **Student One Stop DVD-ROM**
⊘ **Audio Anthology CD**
⊘ **GrammarNotes DVD-ROM**
⊘ **ExamView Test Generator**
   **on the Teacher One Stop**

\* Resources for Differentiation    † Also in Spanish    ‡ In Haitian Creole and Vietnamese

## TEXT ANALYSIS: MYTH

Why does the sun rise in the east every morning? What makes thunderstorms strike so violently? Why do the seasons change? Different cultures throughout time have attempted to answer similar questions about the world. Frequently, these questions became the bases of myths. A **myth** is a traditional story usually created to explain why the world is the way it is or why things in nature happen as they do. Myths are also a form of entertainment that people have enjoyed since ancient times. The stories myths tell are filled with colorful characters, suspenseful plots, and daring adventures. Most myths share these basic characteristics:

- They explain how things connected with nature or humans came to be.
- They tell about supernatural beings or events.
- They present lessons or morals.

"Pyramus and Thisbe" is a classic myth, here retold in the form of a **narrative poem,** or a poem that tells a story. Myths with enduring messages are often retold; many are even updated in more modern forms such as novels and films. As you read this myth, notice what it attempts to explain and consider the lesson it teaches about the value of love. Then consider how the story might be retold to better suit the tastes of a modern audience.

*Review:* **Narrative Poem**

## READING SKILL: SEQUENCE

Timing is everything—especially when it comes to myths. The tragic action in "Pyramus and Thisbe" all takes place in two days. As you read this myth, look for signal words, such as *later, then,* and *after,* that make the order of events clear. Record the myth's main events in a sequence chain like this one.

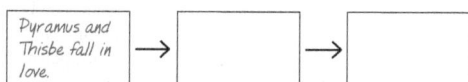

Pyramus and Thisbe fall in love. → [ ] → [ ]

After you have finished your chart, review the myth's order of events. Note how that order helps create and maintain the myth's tense, mysterious, and tragic atmosphere.

Complete the activities in your **Reader/Writer Notebook.**

---

## Meet the Author

## Ovid
43 B.C.–A.D. 17

### A Bright Start
Ovid is considered to be one of the greatest poets of antiquity. But if Ovid's father had had his way, his son would have followed a very different career path. Ovid's father was determined to see his son become a public official in the Roman Empire. He sent Ovid to Rome to study rhetoric and law under the best teachers. Instead of studying, Ovid followed his natural inclinations and focused on writing poetry. Luckily, he achieved success with his first work, the *Amores,* a series of short, witty poems about a love affair. The poet quickly became popular in fashionable Roman society.

### A Lasting Legacy
"Pyramus and Thisbe" is taken from the *Metamorphoses,* Ovid's masterpiece. A long narrative poem, the *Metamorphoses* retells many of the most important myths from ancient Greece and Rome. Ovid breathed new life into the old stories, shaping them in imaginative ways and strengthening their structure. Ovid's retellings have inspired writers for centuries—including Shakespeare.

### A Grim End
Before Ovid was able to publish the *Metamorphoses,* disaster struck. In A.D. 8, the emperor Augustus banished him from Rome and sent him to live in exile in Tomis, a desolate fishing village on the edge of the Roman Empire. The exact reason for this cruel punishment is unknown, but in many of the poems Ovid wrote while in exile, he begs for permission to return to Rome. His pleas fell on deaf ears. Ovid died in exile in A.D. 17.

**Author Online**
**THINK** central
Go to **thinkcentral.com.**
KEYWORD: HML9-1159

1159

---

# Teach

TEXT ANALYSIS — COMMON CORE — RL 6, RL 9

## ● Model the Skill: MYTH

Point out the mythical elements in this summary of a classic myth:

> Arachne was so proud of her weaving that she challenged the goddess Athena to a weaving contest. When Arachne wove a design that showed the gods' follies, the angry Athena punished her by turning her into the first spider.

Make sure students understand the following mythical elements: *how spiders came to be, a super-natural creature (Athena), and a lesson about vanity.*

**GUIDED PRACTICE** Now have students identify mythical elements from other myths they know.

READING SKILL — COMMON CORE — RL 5

## ■ Model the Skill: SEQUENCE

Have students create a sequence chart from the details about Ovid in **A Bright Start.** Fill in the first event listed below to get students started. If necessary, show students where you found the details to begin filling in the chart. *Possible main events: Ovid's father sent him to Rome to study. Ovid wrote poetry instead. Ovid achieved success with* Amores. *Ovid became fashionable.*

**GUIDED PRACTICE** Have students create a sequence chart from details in **A Grim End.**

**R RESOURCE MANAGER—Copy Master** Sequence p. 113 (for student use while reading the selection)

---

## DIFFERENTIATED INSTRUCTION

### FOR STRUGGLING READERS

**Concept Support** Point out to students that many characters from ancient Greek and Roman myths are already familiar, partly because many names in astronomy come from mythical characters. List these names on the board and ask students to tell what they know about any of them.

| | | |
|---|---|---|
| Amazon | Cyclops | Pegasus |
| Atlas | Hercules | Phoenix |
| Cupid | Jupiter | Venus |

**Research a Connection** Shakespeare was not the only Renaissance writer to borrow from Ovid's *Metamorphoses,* nor was "Pyramus and Thisbe" the only story that he borrowed. Ask a group of students to do some research on Shakespeare's use of Ovid. Have them prepare and present to the class a visual aid that shows the connection and that explains why the *Metamorphoses* was such a popular resource.

### READ WITH A PURPOSE

*Help students set a purpose for reading. Tell them to look for ways the concept of fate might influence love.*

---

# Pyramus and Thisbe

### Ovid

The house of Pyramus[1] and that of Thisbe[2]
stood side by side within the mighty city
ringed by the tall brick walls Semíramis
had built[3]—so we are told. If you searched all
5  the East, you'd find no girl with greater charm
than Thisbe; and no boy in Babylon
was handsomer than Pyramus. They owed
their first encounters to their living close
beside each other—but with time, love grows.
10 Theirs did—indeed they wanted to be wed,
but marriage was forbidden by their parents:
yet there's one thing that parents can't prevent:
the flame of love that burned in both of them.
They had no confidant—and so used signs:
15 with these each lover read the other's mind:
when covered, fire acquires still more force.

The wall their houses shared had one thin crack,
which formed when they were built and then was left;
in all these years, no one had seen that cleft;
20 but lovers will discover every thing:
you were the first to find it, and you made
that cleft a passageway which speech could take. **Ⓐ**
For there the least of whispers was kept safe:
it crossed that cleft with words of tenderness.
25 And Pyramus and Thisbe often stood,
he on this side and she on that; and when
each heard the other sigh, the lovers said:
"O jealous wall, why do you block our path?
Oh wouldn't it be better if you let
30 our bodies join each other fully or,
if that is asking for too much, just stretched
your fissure wide enough to let us kiss!

---

1. **Pyramus** (pǐr′ə-məs).
2. **Thisbe** (thǐz′bē).
3. **the mighty city . . . had built:** the walled city of Babylon (băb′ə-lən), the ruins of which are south of Baghdad, Iraq. In Greek mythology, it was founded by Semíramis (sə-mǐr′ə-məs), a powerful Assyrian queen.

*Analyze Visuals ▶*

Explain how this painting conveys a sense of Pyramus and Thisbe's separation and their longing to be together. Consider the painter's use of light and color, as well as Thisbe's expression and Pyramus' absence.

**Ⓐ MYTH**
What is keeping Pyramus and Thisbe apart, and what do they do to overcome these barriers? From what you've read so far, decide what lesson about love this myth might teach.

*Thisbe*, John William Waterhouse. Whitford and Hughes, London. © Bridgeman Art Library.

---

### TEXT ANALYSIS

**COMMON CORE**
RL 6, RL 9

**Ⓐ** *Model the Skill:* **MYTH**

Read line 11 to find what is keeping the lovers apart. Then read lines 12–22 to identify what they do to overcome the barriers. Then ask students to suggest possible lessons about love the myth may teach.

*Possible answer: The lovers' parents are keeping them apart and have forbidden their marriage (line 11). Pyramus and Thisbe overcome these barriers by communicating through a crack in a shared wall (lines 17–22). Based on the text so far, the story may teach a lesson about the enduring power of love.*

**IF STUDENTS NEED HELP . . .** Have them work in pairs to paraphrase the six sentences in the story so far. Offer assistance with defining difficult words and sorting through complicated phrasing.

---

## DIFFERENTIATED INSTRUCTION

### FOR ENGLISH LANGUAGE LEARNERS

**Language: Pronoun Referents** Students may find this myth less challenging if they can identify pronoun referents. Draw students' attention to each of these pronouns and ask students to name its referent:

- *that* (line 1), "house"
- *Theirs* (line 10), "Pyramus and Thisbe's love"
- *that* (line 26), "side"
- *each* (line 27), "lover"

### FOR STRUGGLING READERS

**Develop Reading Fluency** Read the first stanza of the poem aloud to give students an idea of the rhythm of its language. Have volunteers take turns reading several more lines of the poem. Lead students to see that this translation of "Pyramus and Thisbe" (like *Romeo and Juliet*) is presented in blank verse (unrhymed iambic pentameter) to suggest a storyteller's natural speech.

## BACKGROUND

**Ovid and Shakespeare** The myth of Pyramus and Thisbe helped inspire Shakespeare's *Romeo and Juliet.* However, Shakespeare also wrote a spoof of Ovid's tale for *A Midsummer Night's Dream,* with comic characters playing Pyramus, Thisbe, the lion, the moon, and the wall through which the lovers speak. Evidence suggests that *A Midsummer Night's Dream* was first performed just one season after *Romeo and Juliet,* so Shakespeare may have written the comic scene while he was working on or just after he finished *Romeo and Juliet.*

## Analyze Visuals

*Possible answer: The artist conveys a sense of separation by using a dark background and a light foreground and by presenting Thisbe alone. The lovers' longing to be together is suggested in Thisbe's intense, concerned expression as she presses against the crack.*

**About the Art** John William Waterhouse (1849–1917), who was born in Rome but spent most of his life in England, painted *Thisbe* (1909). Waterhouse's art reveals his interest in classic literature. He had a particular interest in femme fatales, women who led their men into tragedy. He featured such women in several paintings, including *Echo and Narcissus, Circe Offering the Cup to Ulysses,* and *Cleopatra.*

### REVISIT THE BIG QUESTION

## What makes a
# CLASSIC STORY?

**Discuss** "Pyramus and Thisbe" is set in ancient Babylon. What does this fact suggest about the universal appeal of classic stories? *Possible answer: This fact suggests that the universal appeal of a classic story is based on elements other than the story's setting.*

**FOR ADVANCED LEARNERS/PRE–AP**

**Evaluate Tone** Direct students to the comments that the speaker makes about love in lines 12–13 and 16. Elicit that these comments inject a somewhat "teachy" tone into the storytelling. As students read on, ask them to decide how strong this tone is in the myth as a whole. When they have finished reading, invite students to share their thoughts about how this tone adds to or detracts from the telling of the story.

And we are not ungrateful: we admit
our words reach loving ears." And having talked
35 in vain, the lovers still remained apart.
Just so, one night, they wished each other well,
and each delivered kisses to the wall—
although those kisses could not reach their goal.
But on the morning after, when firstlight
40 had banished night's bright star-fires from the sky
and sun had left the brine-soaked[4] meadows dry,
again they took their places at the cleft.
Then, in low whispers—after their laments—
those two devised this plan: they'd circumvent
45 their guardians' watchful eyes[5] and, cloaked by night,
in silence, slip out from their homes and reach
a site outside the city. Lest each lose
the other as they wandered separately
across the open fields, they were to meet
50 at Ninus' tomb[6] and hide beneath a tree
in darkness; for beside that tomb there stood
a tall mulberry[7] close to a cool spring,
a tree well weighted down with snow-white berries. **B**
Delighted with their plan—impatiently—
55 they waited for the close of day. At last
the sun plunged down into the waves, and night
emerged from those same waves.

                    Now Thisbe takes
great care, that none detect her as she makes
her way out from the house amid the dark;
60 her face is veiled; she finds the tomb; she sits
beneath the tree they'd chosen for their tryst.
Love made her bold. But now a lioness
just done with killing oxen—blood dripped down
her jaws, her mouth was frothing—comes to slake
65 her thirst at a cool spring close to the tree.
By moonlight, Thisbe sees the savage beast;
with trembling feet, the girl is quick to seek
a shadowed cave; but even as she flees,
her shawl slips from her shoulders. Thirst appeased,
70 the lioness is heading for the woods
when she, by chance, spies the abandoned shawl

---

4. **brine-soaked:** dew-covered.
5. **they'd circumvent . . . eyes:** They would sneak past their parents.
6. **Ninus' (nī'nəs) tomb:** According to Greek legend, King Ninus was Semiramis' husband. When he died, she marked his burial place with a tall monument outside the walls of Babylon.
7. **mulberry:** a type of tree that produces small, sweet berries, which are usually deep red or purple in color.

**1162**   UNIT 10: SHAKESPEAREAN DRAMA

**B** SEQUENCE
Explain the steps in the lovers' plan. Where and when do they decide to meet?

---

**READING SKILL**  COMMON CORE RL 5

**B** *Model the Skill:* **SEQUENCE**

Point out the word "Then" in line 43. Remind students that this word signals a series of events is about to be detailed. Have students add these events to their Sequence charts.

*Possible answer: Pyramus and Thisbe plan to sneak out that night (line 46) and then meet at Ninus's tomb (line 50).*

## TIERED DISCUSSION PROMPTS

Use these prompts to explore the lovers' thinking as they devise their plan in lines 43–57:

**Connect** How might you feel if you were forbidden to see someone who was close to you? In what way do Pyramus and Thisbe show such feelings? *Students should recognize the lovers' desire to be together and their rebellious thoughts and decision.*

**Analyze** Why do the lovers decide to meet at Ninus's tomb? How does this location foreshadow later story events? *Possible answer: The lovers plan to meet at Ninus's tomb because it is outside the city and because they can hide under a tree there. The location foreshadows the fact that both lovers will die there.*

**Evaluate** Do you think that Pyramus and Thisbe would be as interested in one another if their love were not forbidden? Explain. *Possible answer: Pyramus and Thisbe probably would be interested in each other, but the fact that their love is forbidden may add to the attraction. The lovers seem to enjoy the planning of the secret meeting and are impatient to carry out the plan (line 54).*

---

## DIFFERENTIATED INSTRUCTION

### FOR STRUGGLING READERS

**Explore Narrative Poetry** Help students get a better grasp of the nature of narrative poetry by discussing ways in which "Pyramus and Thisbe" is both like a poem and like a prose story. Help them list characteristics of poetry (such as stanza form and poetic meter) and of prose fiction (such as conflict and a sequence of plot events) that they recognize as they read.

### FOR ENGLISH LANGUAGE LEARNERS

**Language: Verb Tenses** Most stories are told with past-tense verbs; in "Pyramus and Thisbe," however, the tense switches between past and present. Have students follow along as you point out these changes in lines 58, 73, 107, and 128. Explain that the use of the present tense, although unusual, heightens the dramatic energy in the parts of the story in which it appears.

upon the ground and, with her bloodstained jaws,
tears it to tatters.

           Pyramus had left
a little later than his Thisbe had,
75 and he could see what surely were the tracks
of a wild beast left clearly on deep dust.
His face grew ashen. And when he had found
the bloodstained shawl, he cried: "Now this same night
will see two lovers lose their lives: she was
80 the one more worthy of long life: it's I
who bear the guilt for this. O my poor girl,
it's I who led you to your death; I said
you were to reach this fearful place by night;
I let you be the first who would arrive.
85 O all you lions with your lairs beneath
this cliff, come now, and with your fierce jaws feast
upon my wretched guts! But cowards talk **C**
as I do—longing for their death but not
prepared to act." At this he gathered up
90 the bloody tatters of his Thisbe's shawl
and set them underneath the shady tree
where he and she had planned to meet. He wept
and cried out as he held that dear shawl fast:
"Now drink from my blood, too!" And then he drew
95 his dagger from his belt and thrust it hard
into his guts. And as he died, he wrenched
the dagger from his gushing wound. He fell,
supine, along the ground. The blood leaped high;
it spouted like a broken leaden pipe
100 that, through a slender hole where it is worn,
sends out a long and hissing stream as jets
of water cleave the air. And that tree's fruits,
snow-white before, are bloodstained now; the roots
are also drenched with Pyramus' dark blood,
105 and from those roots the hanging berries draw
a darker, purple color. **D**

           Now the girl
again seeks out the tree: though trembling still,
she would not fail his tryst;[8] with eyes and soul
she looks for Pyramus; she wants to tell
110 her lover how she had escaped such perils. **E**
She finds the place—the tree's familiar shape;
but seeing all the berries' color changed,

---

8. **fail his tryst:** neglect to meet him.

**C SEQUENCE**
Reread lines 73–87. What does Pyramus think has happened to Thisbe? Explain why Pyramus blames himself for this disaster.

**D MYTH**
Reread lines 96–106. Which events in this section seem supernatural?

**E NARRATIVE POEM**
Like fiction, narrative poetry often includes statements about the main characters. Describe the key traits of Pyramus and Thisbe, using specific words and phrases from the poem.

**READING SKILL**        COMMON CORE  RL 5

**C SEQUENCE**

*Possible answer: Pyramus thinks that the lioness has killed Thisbe. He blames himself because he had helped devise the plan that brought her to this place and because it was he that Thisbe had come to this place to meet.*

**TEXT ANALYSIS**      COMMON CORE  RL 6, RL 9

**D MYTH**

*Possible answer: The leaping of blood from Pyramus's wound (line 98) and the color change of the mulberries (lines 102–106) seem supernatural.*

**IF STUDENTS NEED HELP...** Define difficult words in the passage, such as "wrenched" (line 96), "supine" (line 98), and "cleave" (line 102).

**TEXT ANALYSIS:** *Review*

**E NARRATIVE POEM**

*Possible answer: Pyramus is tender with Thisbe when he speaks through the crack (line 24); he is grief-stricken when he finds her shawl (lines 92–93). Thisbe's love makes her bold (line 62), but she trembles when she sees the lioness (line 67); and although she is still trembling from that encounter, she is brave enough to return to the meeting place (lines 106–108).*

**IF STUDENTS NEED HELP...** Use a Character Traits and Textual Evidence diagram to help students explore these characters' traits.

 **BEST PRACTICES TOOLKIT—Transparency** Character Traits and Textual Evidence p. D6

---

**FOR STRUGGLING READERS**

**Comprehension Support** To clarify the rising action in lines 66–77, write these statements on the board:

    Thisbe runs away → the lioness rips her shawl apart → Pyramus finds the shawl

Help students express the statements in a sentence or two. *Possible answer: After Thisbe runs away, the lioness rips her shawl apart. Then Pyramus finds the shawl.*

**FOR ENGLISH LANGUAGE LEARNERS**

**Comprehension: Transitions** Remind students that certain signal terms can help them track story events. Point out words and phrases that establish a setting (such as "one night" in line 36 and "At last" in line 55), that show that one event follows another (such as "But now" in line 62 and "And then" in line 94), and that indicate that some events are happening at the same time (such as "even as" in line 68 and "as" in line 96).

## What makes a
# CLASSIC STORY?

**Discuss** How can "Pyramus and Thisbe" be considered one of the world's classic stories? *Possible answer: The story is classic because it has a universal appeal. Readers from a wide range of cultures and eras can sympathize with the lovers' desire to be together and can feel sorry that things go so terribly wrong for them.*

---

**TEXT ANALYSIS**

COMMON CORE
RL 6,
RL 9

### F MYTH

*Possible answer: The mulberry tree, stained with the lovers' blood, will continue to produce purple instead of white berries to signify the lovers' sad end and to help people remember their deaths (lines 144–146).*

---

## SELECTION WRAP–UP

**READ WITH A PURPOSE** Now that students have finished reading the selection, ask them how this myth made them feel about the concept of fate and the power of love. *Possible answers: Love can always be affected by fate; while fate is powerful and can place barriers to love, true love can overcome fate, even if tragedy is the result.*

⭐ **CRITIQUE** Ask students to find a purpose in this myth beyond explaining why the mulberry tree has purple berries. Have them state in their own words what they think is the moral of "Pyramus and Thisbe."

## INDEPENDENT READING

If students enjoyed this poem, suggest they read Ovid's *Metamorphoses*.

---

she is not sure. And as she hesitates,
she sights the writhing body on the ground—
115 the bloody limbs—and, paler than boxwood,[9]
retreats; she trembles—even as the sea
when light wind stirs its surface. She is quick
to recognize her lover; with loud blows
she beats her arms—though they do not deserve
120 such punishment. She tears her hair, enfolds
her love's dear form; she fills his wounds with tears
that mingle with his blood; and while she plants
her kisses on his cold face, she laments:
"What struck you, Pyramus? Why have I lost
125 my love? It is your Thisbe—I—who call
your name! Respond! Lift up your fallen head!"
He heard her name; and lifting up his eyes
weighed down by death, he saw her face—and then
he closed his eyes again.

            She recognized
130 her own shawl and his dagger's ivory sheath.
She cried: "Dear boy, you died by your own hand:
your love has killed you. But I, too, command
the force to face at least this task: I can
claim love, and it will give me strength enough
135 to strike myself. I'll follow you in death;
and men will say that I—unfortunate—
was both the cause and comrade of your fate.
Nothing but death could sever you from me;
but now death has no power to prevent
140 my joining you. I call upon his parents
and mine; I plead for him and me—do not
deny to us—united by true love,
who share this fatal moment—one same tomb.
And may you, mulberry, whose boughs now shade
145 one wretched body and will soon shade two,
forever bear these darkly colored fruits
as signs of our sad end, that men remember
the death we met together." With these words, **F**
she placed the dagger's point beneath her breast,
150 then leaned against the blade still warm with her
dear lover's blood. The gods and parents heard
her prayer, and they were stirred. Her wish was granted.

*Translated by Allen Mandelbaum*

---

9. **boxwood:** a white or light yellow type of wood.

**1164** UNIT 10: SHAKESPEAREAN DRAMA

---

### Language Coach

**Roots and Affixes** A word's **root** often contains clues to the word's meaning. Linguists believe that the ancient Indo-European root *wer*, meaning "to twist," led to many words that begin with *wr-*, including *write, wrist, wrench,* and *wrestle.* What do you think *writhing* (line 114) means? Use a dictionary to check your answer.

---

**F MYTH**
Why does the mulberry tree produce deep red berries?

---

## DIFFERENTIATED INSTRUCTION

### FOR ENGLISH LANGUAGE LEARNERS

### Language Coach
COMMON CORE
L 4a, d

**Roots and Affixes** *Possible answer: twisting in pain;* Have students define the other words listed and confirm their responses by checking a dictionary.

### FOR STRUGGLING READERS

**Review the Plot** Have students review the plot of this narrative poem by completing a Plot Diagram.

 **BEST PRACTICES TOOLKIT—Transparency**

Plot Diagram p. D10

| |
|---|
| **Background:** Pyramus and Thisbe, forbidden lovers, make secret plans to meet. |
| **Rising Action:** Thisbe hides from a lioness and drops her shawl, which the lioness shreds. |
| **Climax:** Pyramus finds the shawl, thinks that Thisbe is dead, and kills himself. |
| **Falling Action:** Thisbe finds the dying Pyramus and kills herself. |
| **Resolution:** Mulberry bushes have purple berries in memory of the lovers' deaths. |

## Comprehension

1. **Recall** Describe how Pyramus and Thisbe communicate with each other at the beginning of the myth. Why can't they just talk face to face?

2. **Summarize** What secret plan do Pyramus and Thisbe make?

3. **Clarify** What happens to ruin the lovers' plan?

## Text Analysis

● 4. **Analyze Sequence** Review the sequence chain you created as you read. How might the myth's ending have been different if Pyramus had left for the rendezvous at the same time Thisbe did? Cite evidence to support your answer.

● 5. **Analyze Myth** Use a chart like the following to explain how each characteristic of myth appears in "Pyramus and Thisbe."

| Characteristic of Myth | In "Pyramus and Thisbe" |
|---|---|
| Explains how something connected to humans or nature came to be | |
| Tells about supernatural beings or events | |
| Presents a lesson or moral | |

6. **Evaluate Theme** "Pyramus and Thisbe" is an ancient myth, passed down orally and in writing for generations before Ovid recorded it some 2,000 years ago in the form of a narrative poem. Explain whether you think the theme, or message, of this classic story is still relevant to contemporary audiences.

### READING-WRITING CONNECTION

| WRITING PROMPT | REVISING TIP |
|---|---|
| **Extended Constructed Response: Comparison** Many great writers have looked to myths for inspiration. "Pyramus and Thisbe" was retold by Ovid long before Shakespeare wrote *Romeo and Juliet*, and Ovid was one of Shakespeare's favorite authors. Compare and contrast *Romeo and Juliet* with "Pyramus and Thisbe" in terms of plot, conflict, characters, and theme. Consider how the genre of each text affects these elements. | Review your response. Did your comparison clearly present the selections' similarities and differences, including the effects of genre? If not, revise your response accordingly. |

### What makes a **CLASSIC STORY?**

How do classic stories influence modern literature?

**COMMON CORE**

**RL 5** Analyze how an author's choices concerning how to structure a text and order events within it create such effects as mystery, tension, or surprise. **RL 6** Analyze a particular point of view or cultural experience reflected in a work of world literature. **RL 9** Analyze how an author draws on and transforms source material. **RL 10** Read and comprehend literature. **W 9a (RL 9)** Draw evidence from literary texts to support analysis of how an author draws on and transforms source material in a specific work.

# Practice and Apply

For preliminary support of post-reading questions, use these copy masters:

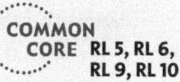 **RESOURCE MANAGER—Copy Masters**
Reading Check p. 115
Myth p. 111
Question Support p. 116

Additional selection questions are provided for teachers on page 105.

## ANSWERS

## Comprehension

1. *Pyramus and Thisbe communicate by whispering through a crack in a shared wall. They cannot talk face to face because their parents have forbidden their love.*

2. *Pyramus and Thisbe make a plan to meet at night outside of the city.*

3. *A lioness scares Thisbe away from the meeting place, and Pyramus assumes that she is dead when he finds her shawl, which the lioness has shredded.*

## Text Analysis

COMMON CORE RL 5, RL 6, RL 9, RL 10

*Possible answers:*

4. ● **COMMON CORE FOCUS** *Analyze Sequence If the lovers had left at the same time, they might have met happily and married. On the other hand, both of them might have been killed by the lioness.*

5. ● **COMMON CORE FOCUS** *Analyze Myth* **Something connected to humans or nature:** *why mulberries are purple in color;* **Supernatural being or event:** *The mulberries darkened after Pyramus's blood spilled on them;* **Lesson or moral:** *Passion can be so strong that it destroys those who feel it.*

---

6. *The myth remains a classic story because people today can relate to the great power of love and because they still feel great sadness when young love is destroyed by tragedy.*

## Reading-Writing Connection

COMMON CORE W 9a (RL 9)

### WRITING PROMPT

Encourage students to use a Venn Diagram as they compare the selections and gather evidence. Offer two methods of organization:

(1) discussing one selection and then going on to discuss the second or (2) comparing both works, point by point, at the same time.

 BEST PRACTICES TOOLKIT—Transparency
Venn Diagram p. A26

### What makes a **CLASSIC STORY?**
Answers will vary; many students may identify timeless themes, appealing characters, and universal situations as part of classic literature's influence.

# Assess and Reteach

## Assess

**DIAGNOSTIC AND SELECTION TESTS**
Selection Test A, B/C pp. 299–300, 301–302

**Interactive Selection Test** on **thinkcentral.com**

## Reteach

**Level Up Online Tutorials** on **thinkcentral.com**

**Reteaching Worksheets** on **thinkcentral.com**
Literature Lesson 18
Reading Lesson 6

# Focus and Motivate

**W 1a–e** Write arguments to support claims using valid reasoning and relevant evidence; develop claims and counterclaims fairly, supplying evidence for each. **W 4** Produce clear and coherent writing appropriate to task, purpose, and audience. **W 5** Strengthen writing by planning revising, editing, rewriting, or trying a new approach. **W 9a (RL 7, 9)** Draw evidence from literary texts; analyze a scene in two mediums; analyze how an author transforms source material. **W 10** Write routinely over shorter time frames for a range of tasks, purposes, and audiences. **L1** Demonstrate command of the conventions of standard English grammar and usage. **L 1b** Use clauses to convey specific meaning. **L 2a** Use semicolons to link independent clauses.

## WRITE WITH A PURPOSE

Encourage students to choose a scene that they find particularly exciting or meaningful. Have them think about why they like the scene and what they would want to see in a good adaptation of that scene.

## COMMON CORE TRAITS

Review the *COMMON CORE TRAITS* with students, focusing on the writing. Compare the list of traits with the rubric on page 1174.

## ADDITIONAL TASKS

**Write About a Current Event/Issue** Find two different news reports (from newspaper, TV, magazine, or Internet) on the same topic. Decide which report is best and explain why. **Possible topics:** an election, environment, education, foreign policy, law, crime

**Write About School** Write about an issue that affects your school. Take a stand on the issue and argue your position in an essay. **Possible topics:** bullying, testing, homework, pressure to achieve, over-scheduling

### Writing Online

The following tools are available online at **thinkcentral.com** and on Write*Smart* CD-ROM:
- **Interactive Graphic Organizers**
- **Interactive Student Models**
- **Interactive Revision Lessons**

---

## Writing Workshop
### ARGUMENT

# Critical Review

**Essential Course of Study**

Through the centuries, Shakespeare's plays have graced both stage and screen. Each adaptation differs, shaped by the director's unique vision. In this workshop, you will write a critical review of an adaptation of a scene from the play *The Tragedy of Romeo and Juliet*. You'll support your **claim,** or position, with evidence from both the text and the production you choose.

Complete the workshop activities in your **Reader/Writer Notebook.**

### WRITE WITH A PURPOSE

**WRITING TASK**

Write a **critical review** of a key scene in a theater or movie adaptation of *The Tragedy of Romeo and Juliet*. Assert a claim, supported by evidence, that states whether the adaptation does justice to the original play.

**Idea Starters**
- Act One, Scene 4 (between Romeo and Mercutio)
- Act Two, Scene 2 (the balcony scene)
- Act Three, Scene 1 (the swordfight)
- Act Five, Scene 3 (the death scene)

**THE ESSENTIALS**

Here are some common purposes, audiences, and formats for writing a critical review.

| PURPOSES | AUDIENCES | FORMATS |
|---|---|---|
| • to convince others to agree with your claim <br> • to evaluate the success of the adaptation | • classmates and teacher <br> • fans of movies, theater, and Shakespeare <br> • newspaper and magazine readers <br> • Web users | • essay for class <br> • film or theater review in school or local newspaper <br> • speech <br> • podcast <br> • blog |

### COMMON CORE TRAITS

**1. DEVELOPMENT OF IDEAS**
- includes an engaging **introduction** that states a **precise claim**
- provides **valid reasons** and **evidence** to support the claim
- acknowledges **opposing claims** and refutes them with **counterclaims**
- offers a **concluding section** that supports the argument presented

**2. ORGANIZATION OF IDEAS**
- **organizes** reasons and evidence in a **logical way**
- uses **transitions** to create cohesion and clarify the relationships among ideas

**3. LANGUAGE FACILITY AND CONVENTIONS**
- maintains a **formal style** and **objective tone**
- uses **semicolons** effectively
- employs correct **grammar, mechanics,** and **spelling**

**Writing Online** THINKcentral

Go to **thinkcentral.com.**
KEYWORD: HML9N-1166

---

## Writing Workshop Resources

 **RESOURCE MANAGER UNIT 10**
Plan and Teach pp. 117–120
Prewriting–Editing pp. 121–125
Speaking and Listening p. 127
Writing Support p. 128*

**BEST PRACTICES TOOLKIT**
Analysis Frame: Persuasion
pp. D46–D47

**TECHNOLOGY**
- **Teacher One Stop DVD-ROM**
- **Student One Stop DVD-ROM**
- **Write*Smart* CD-ROM**
- **GrammarNotes DVD-ROM**

**Writing Center on thinkcentral.com**

*See resources on the **Teacher One Stop** DVD-ROM and on **thinkcentral.com**.*

\* Resources for Differentiation

## Planning/Prewriting

**COMMON CORE**
**W 1a–e** Write arguments to support claims using valid reasoning and relevant evidence. **W 5** Strengthen writing by planning. **W 9a (RL 7, 9)** Draw evidence from literary texts; analyze a scene in two mediums; analyze how an author transforms source material.

### Getting Started

#### CHOOSE A SCENE

Decide which film version or theatrical production of *Romeo and Juliet* you will use as the basis for your critical review. Then list scenes from the play that made an impression on you. Skim the text of the play, or consult the Idea Starters on page 1166 for possibilities. Choose one scene that contributes significantly to the development of the plot or of a particular character. Jot down notes about how the scene is the same as or different from the original. Include ideas about the film techniques, soundtrack, casting, and other elements that reveal the influence of the director.

#### ▶ WHAT DOES IT LOOK LIKE?

*the balcony scene in Zeffirelli's* Romeo and Juliet

| Similarities/Differences |
|---|
| • Some dialogue is eliminated. (different) |
| • Setting is a high balcony with lots of trees surrounding it. (same) |
| • Romeo climbs a tree to the balcony. (same) |

| Film Techniques |
|---|
| • Soft music; heightens the emotion of the scene. |
| • Long camera shots show the setting; close-ups capture the characters' emotions. |

| Casting |
|---|
| • Zeffirelli casts inexperienced teen actors. |

#### THINK ABOUT AUDIENCE AND PURPOSE

To write an effective critical review, you must first identify your **purpose**—to convince your **audience** to agree with your position on the adaptation. To be successful, you need to consider your audience's grasp of the play and of the adaptation. You also need to anticipate opinions that audience members may already have. Then you can choose the reasons and evidence that will be most convincing for them.

#### ▶ ASK YOURSELF:

• Who is my audience?
• What background information about the original play and the adaptation will my audience need to understand my argument?
• What reasons will be most convincing to my audience?
• What views might my audience already have on the adaptation? How will that affect my choice of reasons?

#### STATE YOUR CLAIM AND REASONS

State your **claim,** using precise language. Make sure you can support your claim with **valid reasons** that tell why you believe what you do. If you discover that you can't sufficiently support your claim, then you should rework it or try a new approach, such as considering a different scene.

#### ▶ WHAT DOES IT LOOK LIKE?

**Claim:** *The balcony scene in Franco Zeffirelli's* Romeo and Juliet *is powerfully re-created, emphasizing the characters' emotions.*

| Reason 1 | Reason 2 |
|---|---|
| The set design and camera techniques work together to reveal the setting and characters' emotions. | The casting is faithful to Shakespeare's vision of Romeo and Juliet. |

---

### DIFFERENTIATED INSTRUCTION

#### FOR ENGLISH LANGUAGE LEARNERS

**Language: Reinforce Critical Review Terms**
Write these terms on the board and review them with students:

• *argument:* a stated opinion or point of view

• *claim:* a statement of an idea or belief that may be true

• *counterclaim:* a response to one claim, or statement, with another claim

• *evidence:* facts or information that shows something to be true

• *scene:* a short part of a play or movie

• *relevant:* important

• *anecdote:* story

---

## *Teach*

### Planning/Prewriting

**COMMON CORE** W 1a–e, W 5, W 9a (RL 7, 9)

▶ *CHOOSE A SCENE* To choose a scene, students might ask themselves:

• What is one scene that moves the action of the story forward or emphasizes an important theme?

• Who is my favorite character in the play? What scene reveals a great deal about this character?

In analyzing the adaptation of the scene, students should notice:

• any changes to dialogue or order of events
• music and sound effects
• set design and props
• actors and acting styles
• lighting
• camera shots (close ups, wide shots)

▶ *THINK ABOUT AUDIENCE AND PURPOSE*
Remind students that they need to understand and show readers how a scene fits with the play as a whole. They cannot assume that the reader has the same memory or understanding of the play that they do. Have students compose introductory information that puts the scene in context. Explain that understanding and sharing this information will help them to focus on a purpose and connect to their audience.

▶ *STATE YOUR CLAIM AND REASONS*
Encourage each student to state a claim that will be the basis for his or her critical review. Then have students work in pairs to discuss their claims and reasons and to give each other feedback. Students should keep the following questions in mind:

• Is the argument clear and interesting?

• Can the writer support his/her claims with solid reasons?

**R** RESOURCE MANAGER—Copy Masters
Planning/Prewriting p. 121
Drafting p. 122
Revising and Editing pp. 123–124
Rubric p. 126
Writing Support p. 128

## Planning/Prewriting *continued*

▶ **GATHER EVIDENCE** Encourage students to follow these steps to gather evidence:

1. Write your claim at the top of the page.

2. Below the claim, write two or three reasons that support your claim.

3. For each reason, locate and write down evidence in the form of direct quotations, descriptions, examples, and details.

4. Share your information with a partner. Discuss which reasons have the most solid and convincing evidence. Keep an open mind, and be willing to rethink your position if evidence leads you in a new direction.

▶ **ANTICIPATE OPPOSING CLAIMS** Form the class into small groups. Have students take turns sharing their claims and reasons in their groups. Then ask the other group members to suggest possible counterclaims. Students should write down the counterclaims and try to respond to them by coming up with additional reasons and evidence.

▶ **PLAN YOUR CONCLUDING SECTION** Have students consider the following elements for their concluding sections:

• a restatement of their claim

• a summary of supporting reasons.

• convincing evidence, such as a meaningful quotation or detail from the play

• an insight that emphasizes the main idea of the piece

Have students experiment by creating outlines of two or more possible endings and sharing them in pairs or small groups.

 **YOUR TURN** Direct students to use a chart or graphic organizer to compare and contrast the original play and the adaptation. Remind them to focus on a key scene that moves the plot forward, emphasizes theme, or helps readers to understand characters and their relationships.

For interactive graphic organizers, see

 **Write*Smart* CD-ROM**

**Writing Center on thinkcentral.com**

---

## Planning/Prewriting *continued*

### Getting Started

#### GATHER EVIDENCE

To craft a convincing argument, you need to provide **relevant evidence** that directly supports each reason. Evidence includes direct quotations, descriptions, and examples from both the adaptation and the play.

▶ **TIPS**

• Create a graphic organizer, to track the evidence that you collect in support of each reason. Then, choose the reasons for which you have the most evidence.

• If you find that the evidence you collect suggests an alternative view of the scene, reconsider your claim and try a new approach.

#### ANTICIPATE OPPOSING CLAIMS

Some people may disagree with your evaluation of the adaptation. For your critical review to be convincing, you need to acknowledge **alternate** or **opposing claims** and point out their limitations. Brainstorm a list of opposing claims that viewers might have. For each opposing claim, list a **counterclaim** that refutes the opposition and explains why your viewpoint is more valid.

▶ **WHAT DOES IT LOOK LIKE?**

> *Opposing Claim:* The director takes too many liberties with the dialogue in this scene, leaving out significant segments.
>
> *Counterclaim:* The omissions, mostly extended metaphors or similes, create a flowing and natural exchange between the two actors.

#### PLAN YOUR CONCLUDING SECTION

End your argument with a persuasive concluding section in which you restate your claim and briefly summarize your reasons. You might also leave your audience with a thought-provoking quotation or an insight to keep them thinking about the ideas you have presented. Jot down a brief, informal outline of the details you want to include in this part of your essay.

▶ **WHAT DOES IT LOOK LIKE?**

> *restatement:* Zeffirelli's balcony scene is unmatchable.
>
> *summary of reasons:* His design, camera techniques, and casting bring out the full impact of Shakespeare's words.
>
> *insight:* This scene makes us think about <u>The Tragedy of Romeo and Juliet</u> a little differently. At least they experienced great love once in their lives.

**PEER REVIEW** Share with a peer your claim, reasons, and evidence. Then ask: Are my reasons valid? What other evidence could I include?

 **YOUR TURN** In your *Reader/Writer Notebook*, brainstorm memorable scenes from an adaptation of *Romeo and Juliet*. Then, choose a scene for evaluation. Write a precise claim that captures your opinion of the scene. Then use a graphic organizer to identify valid reasons, relevant evidence, and possible opposing claims.

---

## DIFFERENTIATED INSTRUCTION

### FOR ENGLISH LANGUAGE LEARNERS

**Writing: Gather Support** Have students use the following sentence frames to create a claim and identify reasons that support the claim:

• The topic of my critical review is _____.

• One reason for my claim is _____.

• Some facts of support are _____.

• A second reason for my claim is _____.

• Some facts of support are _____.

### FOR STRUGGLING WRITERS

**Find Supporting Evidence** Explain that an essay will be more effective if it includes different types of supporting evidence, such as examples, ideas, quotations, anecdotes, and facts. Write sentences on the board and ask students to identify what type of evidence each one contains. For example:

• There are many differences. The main character in the movie is small and speaks with a quiet voice, while the book describes this same character as tall and forceful. *(example)*

## Drafting

**COMMON CORE** W 4 Produce clear and coherent writing appropriate to task, purpose, and audience. W 9a (RL 7, 9) Draw evidence from literary texts; analyze a scene in two mediums; analyze how an author transforms source material. L 1b Use clauses to convey specific meaning.

The following chart shows how to organize your draft to create a coherent critical review.

### Organizing Your Critical Review

**INTRODUCTION**

- Grab the attention of the audience with a **challenging question, compelling quotation,** or **relevant anecdote.**
- Introduce the **play,** the **author,** and the **adaptation.** Provide any **background** about your chosen scene that the audience may need to understand your review.
- State your opinion in a **precise claim.**

▼

**BODY**

- Present your reasons in a **logical order,** such as order of importance.
- Support each reason with **direct quotations, examples, descriptive details,** and other types of **evidence** from the text and adaptation.
- Acknowledge **opposing claims** fairly. Provide **counterclaims** to emphasize the validity of your claim and the limitations of other viewpoints.
- Use **transitions**—such as *although, in addition,* or *so that*—to create **cohesion.**
- Maintain a **formal style** by avoiding overly casual language and using an **objective tone** that shows respect for opposing views.

▼

**CONCLUDING SECTION**

- Restate your **claim.**
- End with a **thought-provoking question** or **statement.**

### GRAMMAR IN CONTEXT: USING ADVERBIAL CLAUSES

An **adverbial clause** is a subordinate clause that modifies a verb, an adjective, or another adverb. Like an adverb, an adverbial clause answers the questions *When? Where? Why? How?* or *To what extent?* Adverbial clauses are introduced by subordinating conjunctions, such as *if, although, because,* and *until.* You can use adverbial clauses to clarify meaning and add detail to your writing.

**Examples**

> *Before he meets Juliet,* Romeo thinks he is in love with Rosalind.
>
> Romeo refuses to leave the balcony *until Juliet vows her love for him.*

**YOUR TURN** Develop a draft of your critical review by following the plan outlined in the chart above. As you write, include at least one adverbial clause to convey more specific meaning.

---

**FOR ENGLISH LANGUAGE LEARNERS**

**Language: Adverbial Clauses** Students may benefit from seeing more examples of adverbial clauses. Remind them that they are sentence parts that answer the questions *when, where, why, how,* and *to what extent.* Write the following examples on the board:

**After class,** we went to the library. (when)

They ate **in the cafeteria.** (where)

The kids enjoyed the play **because it was funny.** (why)

**FOR STRUGGLING WRITERS**

**Grammar in Context: Adding Adverbial Clauses** Give students additional practice revising sentences using adverbial clauses. Write the following examples on the board. Have students add additional information to each sentence using an adverbial clause.

1. We liked the play.
2. Romeo visited Juliet.
3. They fell in love.
4. Juliet spoke.

Have students create more sentences with adverbial clauses from their own writing.

---

# Practice and Apply

## Drafting

**COMMON CORE** W 4, W 9a (RL 7, 9) L 1b

▸ **INTRODUCTION** Remind students that the introduction should provide any necessary background information to put the scene in context and state the claim the author will support throughout the essay. Tell students that the introduction should also capture the readers' attention and interest. Discuss ways they might open their essays, such as with a direct quotation or with a vivid description.

▸ **BODY** Encourage students to experiment with different ways of organizing their essays. Explain that sometimes it makes sense to organize the information chronologically—the order in which events occurred. In other cases, they might organize information in order of importance. Have them brainstorm with a partner to figure out which organization makes the most sense for each essay.

▸ **CONCLUDING SECTION** Remind students that the main ideas of the essay should come together in the conclusion and make a strong impression on the reader. Encourage students to experiment with different endings before settling on the best one.

### GRAMMAR IN CONTEXT: USING ADVERBIAL CLAUSES

Tell students that adverbial clauses can add variety to their sentence structure and make their writing less choppy.

**Example**

Romeo went to the ball at the Capulet house. He met Juliet.

*When Romeo went to the ball at the Capulet house,* he met Juliet.

Have students write three statements for their own essays using adverbial clauses.

**YOUR TURN** Ask students to complete the **Your Turn** activity independently. Encourage them to use adverbial clauses to add variety to their sentence structure. Suggest that students write their drafts double-spaced so that they can make revisions easily later.

For interactive revision tools, see

🔘 **Write*Smart* CD-ROM**

**Writing Center on thinkcentral.com**

## Revising

**Model the Skill** Using a critical review on a transparency or electronic whiteboard, model how to use the questions, tips, and strategies suggested in the chart to evaluate and revise. Consider using a critical review written by a student from a different class or from a previous year. Be sure to remove the writer's name from the article so that the writer remains anonymous.

**YOUR TURN** Before students meet in pairs, suggest that they make a list of questions they would like to ask their peer reviewers. For example, a student might want to know if there is enough supporting evidence or background information, or if the introduction is interesting. Remind students to offer each other constructive criticism and to look at each other and listen carefully as they discuss each piece.

For interactive revision tools, see

✐ **Write***Smart* **CD-ROM**

**Writing Center on thinkcentral.com**

---

## Revising

When you revise, you evaluate the development, organization, and style of your draft. Be sure to check that you have met the writing task, achieved your purpose, and provided enough evidence to convince your audience of the merits of your argument. Use the chart shown to help you revise and rewrite where necessary.

### CRITICAL REVIEW

| Ask Yourself | Tips | Revision Strategies |
|---|---|---|
| 1. Do I capture the audience's attention in my introduction? | **Bracket** interesting statements or thought-provoking questions. | **Add** an attention-getting statement or quotation. |
| 2. Does my introduction identify the play, author, and adaptation? Do I state a precise claim about one scene? | **Draw boxes** around the titles of the play and adaptation, as well as the name of the author. **Underline** your claim. | **Add** a sentence that identifies the play, author, and adaptation. **Revise** your claim to more precisely describe your opinion of a key scene. |
| 3. Do I include at least two valid reasons to support my claim? Does relevant evidence support each reason? | **Highlight** the reasons that support your claim. **Circle** the evidence that supports each reason. **Draw an arrow** from the evidence to the reason. | If necessary, **add** valid reasons to lend more support to your claim. **Add** examples, quotations, or descriptive details to bolster unsupported reasons. |
| 4. Do I use transitions to clarify the relationships among my claim, counterclaim, reasons, and evidence? | **Draw a star** next to each transition. | **Reread** the parts that lack stars. **Add** appropriate transitions to link related ideas. |
| 5. Do I address opposing claims fairly and present my counterclaims in response? | **Draw a wavy line** under the opposing claims and your responses to them. | If necessary, **add** a counterclaim that points out the merits of your opinion and the limitations of opposing claims. |
| 6. Does the concluding section restate my claim? Does it leave my audience with something significant to think about? | **Put a check mark** next to the restatement. **Underline** the sentence that leaves the reader with an important insight or observation. | **Add** a restatement of the claim if it is missing. **Insert** a thought-provoking question or statement about the adaptation of the play. |

**YOUR TURN** **PEER REVIEW** Working with a peer, review your drafts. Answer each question in the chart to identify which parts of your drafts need reworking or a new approach.

---

## DIFFERENTIATED INSTRUCTION

### FOR ENGLISH LANGUAGE LEARNERS

**Writing: Concluding Section** Provide students with sentence frames such as these to help them develop insights they can share in their concluding sections:

• In my critical review about _____, I claim that _____.

• Here are two reasons that support my claim: _____
_____

• I would like readers to remember _____ about the adaptation of the play.

### FOR ADVANCED LEARNERS/PRE–AP

**Analyze Argument** Distribute copies of the Analysis Frame: Persuasion. Have students first perform a self-evaluation, completing the sections labeled "Basic Analysis" and "Evaluate and Critique." Then have them exchange essays and carry out the same analysis of their partner's work. Students should compare evaluations to help them determine what to focus on when revising their essays.

**BEST PRACTICES TOOLKIT—Copy Master**
Analysis Frame: Persuasion pp. D46–D47

**ANALYZE A STUDENT DRAFT**

Read this student's draft and the comments about it as a model for revising your own critical review.

COMMON CORE  W 5 Strengthen writing by revising, editing, rewriting, or trying a new approach.

## Shakespeare Would Be Pleased

by Justine Rogers, Jefferson High School

**1** "Parting is such sweet sorrow, / That I shall say good night till it be morrow." Even those who haven't read Shakespeare's *The Tragedy of Romeo and Juliet* are familiar with those words from the balcony scene. It may be the most famous scene in theatrical history. Yet nowhere has it been re-created so brilliantly as in Franco Zeffirelli's film *Romeo and Juliet*. Every decision Zeffirelli makes, from the set design to the camera techniques to the casting, emphasizes the passion between the two doomed lovers in a way that makes it seem he was truly collaborating with Shakespeare.

**2** Zefferelli's set design and camera shots convey the romance of this pivotal scene. Symbolically, he sets Juliet's balcony high above the ground and difficult to reach. The property is surrounded by dense foliage and overhanging trees. These elements visually remind the audience of how sheltered Juliet's life has been. Romeo climbs the wall, literally and figuratively, scaling a tree to reach her. The camera then zooms in to capture subtle expressions, such as Romeo's awe at his good fortune and Juliet's embarrassment when she admits shyly, "I should have been more strange, I must confess." These understated camera shots create a powerful scene.

**3** And I just love Olivia Hussey and Leonard Whiting, the actors. She is really talented. He is cute too.

> Justine opens with a familiar **quotation** to capture the readers' attention.

> Justine's **claim** is stated clearly.

> Justine supports her point about the importance of set design by including **details** from the adaptation.

> In her third paragraph, Justine fails to use **valid reasoning**. She presents a series of personal opinions and unsubstantiated statements.

**LEARN HOW** Use Valid Reasoning In the third paragraph, Justine introduces a new reason, but it is not relevant to her claim. To strengthen her argument, she rewrote the paragraph, presenting a valid reason and supporting it with evidence.

**JUSTINE'S REVISION TO PARAGRAPH ❸**

~~And I just love Olivia Hussey and Leonard Whiting, the actors. She is really talented. He is cute too.~~ *This scene would not have been as effective were it not for the casting. Much has been made of Zeffirelli's decision to choose two young inexperienced actors. Olivia Hussey's movements, gestures, and expressions are extremely natural. A seasoned actor may not have appeared as natural and genuine. As for Whiting, he expresses himself with true style. The action of swinging from a limb would have been ridiculous with an older actor, but Whiting makes it look like a youthful burst of high spirits.*

WRITING WORKSHOP **1171**

---

**ANALYZE A STUDENT DRAFT**

Explain that the Student Draft on this page is the first half of a critical review. Model reading the draft and the annotations in blue that explain the student's language choices. Explain that the *Learn How* mini-lesson has helpful information about a way to improve the student draft as well as their own.

**LEARN HOW** Use Valid Reasoning

- Explain that in order for a critical review to be interesting and meaningful, every statement of opinion needs to be supported with a valid reason. Read aloud the original draft of Justine's paragraph. Then read the revised version. Discuss with students the differences between the two versions. Ask them to explain why adding reasons to support opinions strengthens the paragraph and makes it more interesting.

- Suggest that students return to their own critical reviews and review their statements of opinion. They should ask themselves: Is each opinion supported by a valid reason? Is the reason relevant to my claim? Is it accurate and meaningful?

---

**FOR ENGLISH LANGUAGE LEARNERS**

**Writing: Valid Reasoning** Emphsize the importance of supporting statements of opinion with valid reasoning. Explain why the following statements would be ineffective in a critical review. Work together to write valid reasons that could be added to support the statements.

1. The acting in the play was terrible. *(The actors forgot their lines and seemed uncomfortable on stage.)*

2. The movie was exciting. *(The escape scene, in which the main character had to climb up the side of a building, is typical of the exciting moments in this movie.)*

**FOR STRUGGLING WRITERS**

**Writing: Use Valid Reasoning** Have students in small groups practice using valid reasoning to strengthen their reviews. Have students take turns reading their claims aloud and then stating reasons that support their claims. Students can help each other brainstorm effective ways of phrasing their reasons.

**Explain** that the Student Draft is continued and completed on this page. Read the draft and annotations aloud and discuss. Talk about what the writer does to end her essay in a strong and effective way.

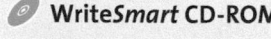 **LEARN HOW** Strengthen Your Counterclaim

- Remind students that they need to anticipate valid opposing arguments and to prepare strong counterclaims.

- Read aloud Justine's original paragraph and then her revised paragraph. Ask students to explain why the revision does a better job of supporting Justine's counterclaim.

- Have students review their own critical reviews. Encourage them to find places where they have included statements of opinion and possible opposing claims. Have pairs decide if these statements are sufficiently strong and logical to refute any opposing viewpoints.

**YOUR TURN** Have students complete the **Your Turn** independently. Tell students to review their drafts to make sure they've supported their opinions with reasons, solid evidence, and valid counterclaims. Encourage students to mark places in their draft that might need additional work, and then have them discuss possible changes with a peer reviewer.

For interactive revision tools, see

*WriteSmart* CD-ROM

**Writing Center on thinkcentral.com**

---

**4**      It is true that the dialogue is not completely faithful to the play. Zeffirelli makes some cuts. He eliminates many of the lines that develop extended metaphors and similes, such as Juliet's comparison of Romeo to a "wanton's bird, / That lets it hop a little from her hand, / Like a poor prisoner in his twisted gyves, / And with a silk thread plucks it back again."

**5**      Zeffirelli's balcony scene is unmatchable. He does not clutter his interpretation with fussy props, unusual special effects, or distracting costumes. Rather, he lets the power of Shakespeare's words speak for themselves. He simply provides the perfect medium for the actors to bring those words to life. This scene also makes the audience feel more deeply the tragedy of what is to come. It leads them to think that perhaps, as another great poet once expressed, it is "better to have loved and lost than never to have loved at all."

> Although Justine acknowledges a significant **opposing claim,** she needs to strengthen her counterclaim. She offers no support for why the opposing claim is less valid than her viewpoint.

> Justine ends with a **thought-provoking quotation,** presenting a slightly different perspective on the tragedy.

 **LEARN HOW** Strengthen Your Counterclaim Justine acknowledges a valid opposing claim, but she does not present the limitations of this position or offer a counterclaim. As a result, her argument is not as strong as it could be. She rewrote this part of her essay, presenting and supporting her counterclaim.

**JUSTINE'S REVISION TO PARAGRAPH 4**

It is true that the dialogue is not completely faithful to the play. Zeffirelli makes
*significant*
some cuts. He eliminates many of the lines that develop extended metaphors
and similes, such as Juliet's comparison of Romeo to a "wanton's bird, / That lets
it hop a little from her hand, / Like a poor prisoner in his twisted gyves, / And
with a silk thread plucks it back again." *These omissions are unnoticeable. In fact, they
are wisely done. The additional lines would have been distracting and would have sounded
fake. As a result of Zeffirelli's deletions, the pacing is effective.*

 **YOUR TURN** Use feedback from your peers and teacher as well as the two "Learn How" lessons to revise your critical review. Evaluate how well you convince your audience to adopt your claim through valid reasoning, strong evidence, legitimate opposing claims, and convincing counterclaims.

---

## DIFFERENTIATED INSTRUCTION

### FOR ENGLISH LANGUAGE LEARNERS

**Opposing Claim and Counterclaim** To help students understand the terminology *opposing claim* and *counterclaim,* ask volunteers to state simple opinions about school, music, television, or current events. Present an opposing claim. Then ask them to respond with a counterclaim.

***Example:***

**Claim:** The school day should be shorter.

**Opposing Claim:** If the school day were shorter, students wouldn't learn everything they need to know each year.

**Counterclaim:** Students could still use that time for learning. We could do more reading and explore hobbies.

Repeat this activity using claims from their critical review papers.

### STRUGGLING WRITERS

**Strengthen Your Counterclaim** Form small groups. Have one person in each group present the claim stated in the introduction of his or her critical review. Then have other group members present opposing claims. The student presenter must then defend his or her claim with counterclaims. Each student should have a turn presenting and defending his or her claim.

# Editing and Publishing

**COMMON CORE** W 1b Develop claims and counterclaims fairly. W 5 Strengthen writing by revising and editing. L 1 Demonstrate command of the conventions of standard English grammar and usage. L 2a Use semicolons to link independent clauses.

In the editing stage, you proofread your essay to make sure it is free of grammar, spelling, and punctuation errors. You don't want mistakes to detract from your critical review and prevent your audience from accepting the validity of your argument.

## GRAMMAR IN CONTEXT: USING SEMICOLONS CORRECTLY

Interesting ideas can lose their impact if they are lost in monotonous writing. While a period interrupts the flow and distances the connection between sentences, a **semicolon** provides a brief break and shows a close relationship between two related sentences. For example:

| Original | Revised |
|---|---|
| The music provides a subtle accompaniment to the scene. It enhances rather than distracts. | The music provides a subtle accompaniment to the scene; it enhances rather than distracts. |

As Justine edited her critical review, she realized she could improve her work by joining some related sentences with semicolons instead of separating them with periods.

> This scene also makes the audience feel more deeply the tragedy of what is to come. It leads them to think that perhaps, as another great poet once expressed, it is "better to have loved and lost than never to have loved at all."

## PUBLISH YOUR WRITING

Share your critical review with an audience.

- Make copies of your writing and distribute them to your classmates.
- Submit your work for publication in your school or local newspaper, or in a literary magazine.
- Share your critical review in a speech or discussion.
- Post your review on a blog and invite other classmates to submit their feedback and comments. Elicit others' opinions on the adaptation and your claim.

**YOUR TURN** Correct any errors in your review by carefully proofreading it. Remember not to rely on your computer's spell-checking program, but to check for spelling errors yourself. Also look for places where you might strengthen the connection between your ideas by inserting semicolons. Then publish your review where it is most likely to reach your intended audience.

---

# Editing and Publishing

**COMMON CORE** W 1b, W 5, L 1, L 2a

## GRAMMAR IN CONTEXT: USING SEMICOLONS CORRECTLY

Have students read the paragraph below and identify a place where two related independent clauses could be joined by semicolons.

*The director of the play experimented with lighting. In one key scene, the main character appeared to be hiding in the shadows as he gave a quiet speech. The darkness was revealing. It helped us understand the character's feelings.* (The darkness was revealing; it helped us understand the character's feelings.)

Have students look through their own reviews to find appropriate places to connect related clauses.

## PUBLISH YOUR WRITING

Brainstorm with students about additional ways to publish their critical reviews.

**YOUR TURN** Allow time for students to proofread their drafts. Remind them to check for any spelling and punctuation errors. They should also look for places where semicolons would improve the flow of their writing.

---

## FOR ENGLISH LANGUAGE LEARNERS

**Language: Semicolons** To give students additional practice using semicolons, ask them to join the sentences below with a semicolon. Then help them to write four sentences that include semicolons.

We brought our umbrellas this morning. We brought umbrellas because we heard a storm was coming. (*We brought our umbrellas this morning; we heard a storm was coming.*)

## FOR STRUGGLING WRITERS

**Using Semicolons** Review the purpose of semicolons and when it is appropriate to use them. Then have students work in pairs to revise their drafts and discuss where semicolons could be added to combine related ideas. Encourage students to include semicolons in at least two sentences in their drafts. Invite students to share these revisions with the rest of the group.

## Scoring Rubric

Tell students that the best way to understand a scoring rubric is to use it to evaluate an actual piece of writing. Provide students with a model critical review. Tell them to evaluate the review using the rubric. Then have them write a brief paragraph using the language of the rubric to explain the reasons for their score.

For Rubric Bank, see

💿 **Write*Smart* CD-ROM**

**Writing Center on thinkcentral.com**

## Scoring Rubric

Use the rubric below to evaluate your critical review from the Writing Workshop or your response to the on-demand writing task on the next page.

**CRITICAL REVIEW**

| SCORE | COMMON CORE TRAITS |
|---|---|
| **6** | • **Development** Persuasively asserts a precise claim; supports the claim with valid reasons and relevant, sufficient evidence; ably counters opposing claims with counterclaims; has a powerful concluding section<br>• **Organization** Arranges reasons and evidence in a persuasive, logical order; effectively uses transitions to create cohesion and show relationships among the claim, reasons, and evidence<br>• **Language** Consistently maintains a formal style and objective tone; shows a strong command of conventions |
| **5** | • **Development** Presents a precise claim; supports the claim with valid reasons and relevant evidence; counters opposing claims with counterclaims; has a strong concluding section<br>• **Organization** Logically organizes reasons and evidence; uses transitions to show the relationships among the claim, reasons, and evidence<br>• **Language** Maintains a formal style and objective tone; has a few errors in conventions |
| **4** | • **Development** States a claim; offers mostly valid reasons and evidence; needs to more thoroughly address opposing claims; has an adequate concluding section<br>• **Organization** Arranges the reason and evidence logically with some exceptions; needs more transitions<br>• **Language** Mostly maintains a formal style and tone; includes a few distracting errors in conventions |
| **3** | • **Development** States a claim that could be more precise; provides some relevant support but not enough to be sufficient; unfairly dismisses other viewpoints; has a concluding section that repeats ideas<br>• **Organization** Arranges reasons and evidence in a somewhat confusing way; needs more transitions to show how ideas are linked<br>• **Language** Often lapses into an informal style or inappropriate tone; has several errors in conventions |
| **2** | • **Development** Has a weak claim; offers some unclear reasons and needs more evidence; fails to acknowledge other viewpoints; has a weak concluding section<br>• **Organization** Arranges reasons and evidence in a confusing way; uses few transitions<br>• **Language** Uses an informal style and defensive tone; has many errors in conventions |
| **1** | • **Development** Lacks a claim; has no support; ignores opposing claims; ends abruptly<br>• **Organization** Has no organization and transitions<br>• **Language** Uses an inappropriate style and tone; has major problems with grammar, mechanics, and spelling |

## Preparing for Timed Writing

COMMON CORE

**W 10** Write routinely over shorter time frames for a range of tasks, purposes, and audiences.

**Writing Workshop**

### 1. ANALYZE THE TASK — 5 MIN

Read the writing task carefully. Then read it again, underlining words that tell the topic, the audience, and the purpose. Circle the type of writing you are being asked to do.

> **WRITING TASK**
>
> *Audience*
> Your school newspaper wants you to write about *a movie you've seen recently that was* *Topic*
> adapted from a book. Write a (critical review) in which you evaluate whether the movie *Type of Writing*
> does justice to the book. *Purpose*

### 2. PLAN YOUR RESPONSE — 10 MIN

First, jot down titles of movies you have seen recently that are based on books. After choosing one, identify the ways in which the movie is similar to or different from the book. Then use what you have listed to assert your claim and major reasons. Support each reason with evidence, including examples, description, or dialogue. Also identify an opposing claim and respond to it.

| Claim: | |
|---|---|
| Reason 1: | Evidence: |
| Reason 2: | Evidence: |

Possible Opposing Claim:

My Counterclaim:

### 3. RESPOND TO THE TASK — 20 MIN

After identifying your reasons, evidence, opposing claim, and counterclaim, draft your critical review. As you write, keep these guidelines in mind:

- In the introduction, grab your audience's attention, and clearly state your claim.
- In each body paragraph, provide a reason and the evidence that supports it.
- Address an opposing claim and refute it with an effective counterclaim.
- Conclude by restating your claim and sharing a relevant observation or insight.

### 4. IMPROVE YOUR RESPONSE — 5–10 MIN

**Revising** Review key aspects of your critical review. Do you state a precise claim? Do you include valid reasons, relevant evidence, possible opposing claims, and counterclaims? Do you end with a powerful concluding section?
**Proofreading** Neatly correct any errors in grammar, spelling, and mechanics.
**Checking Your Final Copy** Before you turn in your critical review, read it again to catch any errors you may have missed and to apply any finishing touches.

---

## Preparing for Timed Writing

COMMON CORE W 10

1. **Analyze the Task** Before students begin writing, encourage them to answer the following questions:
   - What is my time limit?
   - What are the core skills assessed in the scoring rubric?
   - Who is my audience?
   - What are my topic and purpose?

2. **Plan Your Response** Remind students that the critical review rubric emphasizes the importance of presenting a strong claim and then supporting the claim with valid reasons and relevant evidence.

3. **Respond to the Task** Remind students that they should mention possible opposing claims and then present strong evidence to support a counterclaim.

4. **Improve Your Response:** Point out that the rubric stresses the importance of arranging reasons and evidence capably and effectively using transitions to link ideas and create cohesion.

## Assess

Use the Scoring Rubric on page 1174 to assess students' essays.

---

## DIFFERENTIATED INSTRUCTION

### FOR ENGLISH LANGUAGE LEARNERS

**Writing: Plan a Response** Demonstrate how to use a Venn diagram to analyze the similarities and differences between a book and its movie adaptation. Help students use the details they record to make a claim about whether or not the movie does the book justice. Then ask them to write down two reasons to support their claim. Work with students to locate facts, details, or examples, to support each reason.

### FOR STRUGGLING WRITERS

**Organize Ideas** Have students use this outline to record details for their essays:

**Introduction**

- question, quotation, or anecdote to grab a reader's attention: _____
- Claim: _____

**Body**
*First paragraph*
- First reason: _____
  Supporting evidence: _____

*Second paragraph*
- Second reason: _____
  Supporting evidence: _____
  Opposing claim: _____
  Counterclaim: _____

**Concluding Section**

- Restatement of claim: _____
- Final insight or quotation: _____

# Focus and Motivate

## COMMON CORE FOCUS

**SL 3** Evaluate a speaker's point of view, reasoning, and use of evidence and rhetoric, identifying any fallacious reasoning or exaggerated or distorted evidence.

### SPEAK WITH A PURPOSE

Remind students that they cannot listen passively as they evaluate a speaker. They should formulate questions as they listen, such as "Does the speaker's claim make sense?" "Does the speaker present solid reasons?" "Does anything sound false or exaggerated?"

### COMMON CORE TRAITS

As students prepare to deliver and evaluate oral critical reviews, remind them to keep in mind the *COMMON CORE TRAITS* of a strong oral critical review.

# Practice and Apply

## Evaluating the Speaker's Claim

### Model the Skill: THINK ABOUT REASONS AND EVIDENCE

Model for students how to evaluate a review using both critical thinking skills and an open mind. Remind students of the student model on pages 1171–1172. Tell students: "I don't know why Franco Zeffirelli uses such young actors for the roles of Romeo and Juliet. Adults could never relate to these young characters!" Then read aloud the revised third paragraph, in which the speaker explains her opinion of the casting of young actors. Tell students that although you were firm in your opinion earlier, you can now understand another point of view because the speaker presented a well-supported argument.

**GUIDED PRACTICE** Form small groups. Give students general topics to argue such as dress codes, homework, or curfews. Have the students try to present valid reasons and evidence to support both sides of the issue.

**R** RESOURCE MANAGER—Copy Master
Speaking and Listening p. 127

---

*Speaking & Listening Workshop*

# Evaluating a Critical Review  *Essential Course of Study* ECOS

In your daily life, you are regularly exposed to arguments in which speakers try to convince you to accept their claims. Some of this persuasion takes the form of critical reviews—of movies, restaurants, and new products. Before you accept the arguments, it is important to evaluate the validity of the claim, reasons, and evidence presented.

Complete the workshop activities in your **Reader/Writer Notebook**.

| SPEAK WITH A PURPOSE | COMMON CORE TRAITS |
|---|---|
| **TASK**<br><br>Actively listen to and **evaluate another speaker's oral review** of a scene from an adaptation of a Shakespearean play. | **A STRONG EVALUATION . . .**<br><br>• analyzes the validity of the speaker's claim, or point of view<br><br>• assesses the strength and relevance of the reasoning<br><br>• judges the accuracy of the evidence<br><br>• identifies fallacious, or flawed, reasoning and evidence, including any that is exaggerated or distorted |

## COMMON CORE

**SL 3** Evaluate a speaker's point of view, reasoning, and use of evidence and rhetoric, identifying any fallacious reasoning or exaggerated or distorted evidence.

## Evaluating the Speaker's Claim

Before you evaluate a speaker's argument, you must know exactly what he or she is asserting. Use these strategies to evaluate the claim:

- **Restate the claim in your own words.** Make sure you understand the speaker's position on the adaptation.

- **Assess the validity of the claim.** Do you agree with the claim? Does it make sense? Suppose a speaker asserts that an adaptation is ineffective because the director is not faithful to Shakespeare's text. You probably know that many directors take liberties in adapting Shakespeare's works, re-imagining the settings or the characters in fresh, surprising ways. For that reason, you might decide that the speaker's claim is not logical.

- **Think about the reasons and evidence that might persuade you to agree with the speaker.** For example, if the speaker includes statements and quotations from critics you respect, you might be willing to reconsider your own point of view.

**Speaking &
Listening Online**

THINK central

Go to thinkcentral.com.
KEYWORD: HML9N-1176

---

## DIFFERENTIATED INSTRUCTION

### FOR ENGLISH LANGUAGE LEARNERS

**Language: Reinforce Critical Review Terms**
Review with students the following terms:

- *persuasion:* the act of trying to convince someone to believe something or do something

- *evaluate:* examine and judge the qualities of something

- *counterclaim:* a response to one claim or statement with another claim

- *fallacy:* something that is untrue or misleading

- *circular reasoning:* supporting a statement by repeating it in different words

- *overgeneralization:* a generalization that is too broad, signaled by everyone, no one, all

## Examining Reasons and Evidence

Once you have evaluated the speaker's point of view, you must assess the reasons and evidence he or she offers in support of the claim.

### EVALUATE REASONING

Reasons must be relevant to the claim and make sense to you. They should also be presented in a logical order. To help you recognize fallacious reasoning, examine the chart below:

| Fallacy | Example |
|---------|---------|
| **Circular reasoning**—supporting a statement by repeating it in different words | It is not a successful adaptation because the changes the director makes don't work. |
| **Either/or fallacy**—a statement that suggests that there are only two choices when, in fact, there are many options | An adaptation of a famous scene can be either good or bad; this one is bad. |
| **Overgeneralization**—a generalization that is too broad, often signaled by words such as *everyone, no one,* or *all* | Clearly Zeffirelli's adaptation is brilliant. Everyone loves it. |
| **False cause and effect**—the assumption that because one event occurred after another event in time, the first event caused the second one to occur | My dad fell asleep during that scene, which proves it was too dull. |

### EVALUATE EVIDENCE

Ask yourself these questions to help you weigh the evidence presented:

- Is the evidence relevant and thorough? Each fact or detail should relate to the reason it supports. Sufficient evidence should be presented to fully explain each reason.
- Are the quotations, examples, or other details accurate? Check to see if the supporting evidence can be traced to a credible source.
- Is the evidence exaggerated? Look for words such as *all, always,* or *never.*
- Does the speaker include distorted evidence to suit his or her purpose? The speaker might present evidence for only one side of the argument or describe that evidence using **loaded language,** words with strong connotations.

**As a Speaker** Do a self-evaluation of your critical review before reading it aloud. Assess your claim, reasoning, and evidence. Then present your critical review to a peer, incorporating feedback to improve your argument.

**As a Listener** Evaluate the speaker's point of view, reasoning, and evidence. Jot down notes on points of disagreement, fallacious reasoning, or exaggerated or distorted evidence. Address these weaknesses in your response.

SPEAKING AND LISTENING WORKSHOP **1177**

---

**FOR STRUGGLING WRITERS**

**Prepare to Give and Evaluate a Presentation**
Have students in small groups develop their own checklists to help them prepare their own oral reviews and evaluate the reviews of others. Encourage students to help each other remember what they should be looking for, such as:

- a strong claim
- solid evidence
- valid reasons

Their checklists should include a place to jot notes as they listen and discuss reviews.

Have students read their reviews aloud in their groups, pausing frequently to discuss any issues they or other students notice.

---

### Examining Reasons and Evidence

*Model the Skill:* **EVALUATE REASONING**

Model for students how to identify an instance of fallacious reasoning. Tell them that one reason for not liking a particular adaptation is that actors were terrible because they were not quality performers. Point out that this is an example of circular reasoning.

**GUIDED PRACTICE** Have students come up with examples for each type of fallacy. Have them work in pairs to revise the statements so they are no longer fallacious.

**YOUR TURN** Give students time to read aloud their critical reviews. Students should take turns both reading and critiquing.

## Assess and Reteach

### Assess

Use the *COMMON CORE TRAITS* to assess students' evaluation skills.

A strong evaluation...
- analyzes the validity of the speaker's claim
- assesses the supporting reasons
- evaluates the accuracy of the evidence
- identifies fallacies and flawed evidence

### Reteach

Have students work with a partner to evaluate their oral reviews. Have students debate each claim, trying to use strong examples and avoid faulty reasoning.

**Speaking and Listening Online** | **THINK** central
- Public speaking tips
- Strategies for effective listening

# Assessment Practice

**COMMON CORE**

## COMMON CORE FOCUS

**RL 1** Cite evidence to support analysis of what the text says explicitly as well as inferences drawn from the text. **RL 3** Analyze how complex characters develop over the course of a text, interact with other characters, and advance the plot. **RL 4** Determine the figurative meaning of words and phrases as they are used in a text. **RL 10** Read and comprehend dramas. **W 5** Strengthen writing by editing to ensure that writing demonstrates conventions of standard English grammar. **L 1a** Use parallel structure. **L 3** Apply knowledge of language to understand how language functions in different contexts and to comprehend more fully when reading.

## CHECK READINESS

Read aloud the paragraph under **ASSESS** and stress to students that this is not the full Unit Test, but a way for them to check their readiness for it. Then have students examine the standards listed under **REVIEW** and look back in the unit or in the **Student Resource Bank** for any skills they need to review.

## READ THE TEXTS

Remind students to keep unit goals in mind as they read each passage, paying particular attention to these literary and reading skills:

- characteristics of tragedy
- conflict
- character motivation
- character foil
- tragic hero

To help students focus on characteristics of tragedy while reading, encourage them to ask questions like these:

- Why does Romeo react so strongly to being banished? Is he right to be so upset?
- What is the conflict between Romeo and the friar?

## ANSWER THE QUESTIONS

Direct students to pages R93–R101 of the **Handbook** to review test-taking strategies.

- Remind students not to choose the first alternative that seems to fit. Instead, they should read through all the choices, eliminate any that are clearly wrong, and then choose the *best* answer.

---

**COMMON CORE**

### ASSESS
Taking this practice test will help you assess your knowledge of these skills and determine your readiness for the Unit Test.

### REVIEW
After you take the practice test, your teacher can help you identify any standards you need to review.

**COMMON CORE**

**RL 1** Cite evidence to support analysis of what the text says explicitly as well as inferences drawn from the text. **RL 3** Analyze how complex characters develop over the course of a text, interact with other characters, and advance the plot. **RL 4** Determine the figurative meaning of words and phrases as they are used in a text. **RL 10** Read and comprehend dramas. **W 5** Strengthen writing by editing to ensure that writing demonstrates conventions of standard English grammar. **L 1a** Use parallel structure. **L 3** Apply knowledge of language to understand how language functions in different contexts and to comprehend more fully when reading.

**Practice Test**
**THINK** central
Take it at thinkcentral.com.
KEYWORD: HML9N-1178

## Assessment Practice

**DIRECTIONS** Read the following excerpt, and then answer the questions.

### *from* The Tragedy of Romeo and Juliet  *by William Shakespeare*

*Friar Laurence's cell.*
*In Act Three, Scene 3, Friar Laurence tells Romeo of his banishment for the murder of Tybalt, and Romeo collapses in grief. Then he learns from the nurse that Juliet, too, is in despair.*

[*Enter* Friar Laurence.]

**Friar Laurence.** Romeo, come forth; come forth, thou fearful man.
Affliction is enamored of thy parts,
And thou art wedded to calamity.

[*Enter* Romeo.]

**Romeo.** Father, what news? What is the Prince's doom?
5 What sorrow craves acquaintance at my hand
That I yet know not?

**Friar Laurence.**        Too familiar
Is my dear son with such sour company.
I bring thee tidings of the Prince's doom.

**Romeo.** What less than doomsday is the Prince's doom?

10 **Friar Laurence.** A gentler judgment vanished from his lips—
Not body's death, but body's banishment.

**Romeo.** Ha, banishment? Be merciful, say "death";
For exile hath more terror in his look,
Much more than death. Do not say "banishment."

15 **Friar Laurence.** Hence from Verona art thou banished.
Be patient, for the world is broad and wide.

**Romeo.** There is no world without Verona walls,
But purgatory, torture, hell itself.
Hence banished is banish'd from the world,
20 And world's exile is death. Then "banishment,"
Is death misterm'd. Calling death "banishment,"
Thou cuttst my head off with a golden axe
And smilest upon the stroke that murders me.

---

## DIFFERENTIATED INSTRUCTION

### FOR ENGLISH LANGUAGE LEARNERS

**Assessment Practice: Work Backward**
Prepare students by having them read the questions *before* reading the passages. Have pairs find unfamiliar words in test directions and questions and follow these steps:

1. Write each word on an index card and divide the cards among pairs of students. Tell students that they are going to define these words.

2. Instruct students to work individually to make an initial determination of each word's meaning. Then have students confer with their partners and check their work by using a dictionary.

3. Have students then share the words and definitions with the entire class, who can confirm the definitions or suggest others.

**Friar Laurence.** O deadly sin! O rude unthankfulness!
25  Thy fault our law calls death; but the kind Prince,
    Taking thy part, hath rushed aside the law,
    And turned that black word death to banishment.
    This is dear mercy, and thou seest it not.
**Romeo.** 'Tis torture, and not mercy. Heaven is here,
30  Where Juliet lives; and every cat and dog
    And little mouse, every unworthy thing,
    Live here in heaven and may look on her;
    But Romeo may not. More validity,
    More honorable state, more courtship lives
35  In carrion flies than Romeo. They may seize
    On the white wonder of dear Juliet's hand
    And steal immortal blessing from her lips,
    Who, even in pure and vestal modesty,
    Still blush, as thinking their own kisses sin;
40  But Romeo may not—he is banished.
    This may flies do, when I from this must fly;
    They are free men, but I am banished.
    And sayst thou yet that exile is not death?
    Hadst thou no poison mixed, no sharp-ground knife,
45  No sudden mean of death, though ne'er so mean,
    But "banished" to kill me—"banished"?
    O friar, the damned use that word in hell;
    Howling attends it! How hast thou the heart,
    Being a divine, a ghostly confessor,
50  A sin-absolver, and my friend professed,
    To mangle me with that word "banished"?
**Friar Laurence.** Thou fond mad man, hear me a little speak.
**Romeo.** O, thou wilt speak again of banishment.
**Friar Laurence.** I'll give thee armor to keep off that word;
55  Adversity's sweet milk, philosophy,
    To comfort thee, though thou art banished.
**Romeo.** Yet "banished"? Hang up philosophy!
    Unless philosophy can make a Juliet,
    Displant a town, reverse a prince's doom,
60  It helps not, it prevails not. Talk no more.
**Friar Laurence.** O, then I see that madmen have no ears.

**GO ON** ➡

## ITEM ANALYSIS

| COMPREHENSION AND WRITTEN RESPONSE | ITEMS | UNIT PAGES |
|---|---|---|
| Characteristics of Tragedy: | | 1026–1033 |
| Conflict | 3, 4, 10 | |
| Character Motivation | 13 | |
| Character Foil | 9 | |
| Tragic Hero | 8, 12 | |
| Shakespearean Language: | | 1026–1033 |
| Blank Verse | 5 | |
| Word Play | 1, 6 | |
| Figurative Language | 6, 15 | 1026–1033 |
| Paraphrase | 2, 7, 11 | 1035 |

| WRITING AND GRAMMAR | ITEMS | UNIT PAGES |
|---|---|---|
| Parallelism | 1, 2, 3, 4, 5 | 1147 |

### Practice Test

On **thinkcentral.com** students can complete an interactive version of this practice test *and* receive remediation for the skills they have not yet mastered.

---

**FOR STRUGGLING READERS**

**Assessment Support** Consider these options for completing the Assessment Practice:

- Have students "work backward" to review the test questions *before* reading the passages.

- Select random questions in the Assessment and have students demonstrate how and where to look for answers.

- Ask students to locate unfamiliar vocabulary words in the Assessment. Elicit the words' meanings from the class.

- Have students record useful testing words and definitions in their journals for later reference.

- Read the selection or parts of it aloud to aid in student comprehension.

**Romeo.** How should they, when that wise men have no eyes?

**Friar Laurence.** Let me dispute with thee of thy estate.

**Romeo.** Thou canst not speak of that thou dost not feel.
65 Wert thou as young as I, Juliet thy love,
An hour but married, Tybalt murdered,
Doting like me, and like me banished,
Then mightst thou speak, then mightst thou tear thy hair,
And fall upon the ground, as I do now,
70 Taking the measure of an unmade grave.

[Nurse *knocks within*.]

**Friar Laurence.** Arise; one knocks. Good Romeo, hide thyself.

**Romeo.** Not I; unless the breath of heartsick groans
Mist-like infold me from the search of eyes.

[*knock*]

**Friar Laurence.** Hark, how they knock! Who's there? Romeo, arise;
75 Thou wilt be taken.—Stay awhile!—Stand up;

[*knock*]

Run to my study.—By-and-by!—God's will,
What simpleness is this.—I come, I come!

[*knock*]

Who knocks so hard? Whence come you? What's your will?

**Nurse** [*within*]. Let me come in, and you shall know my errand.
80 I come from Lady Juliet.

**Friar Laurence.**　　　　Welcome then.

[*Enter* Nurse.]

**Nurse.** O holy friar, O, tell me, holy friar,
Where is my lady's lord, where's Romeo?

**Friar Laurence.** There on the ground, with his own tears made
　　drunk.

**Nurse.** O, he is even in my mistress' case,
85 Just in her case! O woeful sympathy!
Piteous predicament! Even so lies she,
Blubb'ring and weeping, weeping and blubbering.
Stand up, stand up! Stand, an you be a man.
For Juliet's sake, for her sake, rise and stand!
90 Why should you fall into so deep an O?[1]

**Romeo** [*rises*]. Nurse—

---

1. **Into so deep an O:** into such deep grief.

**FOR ENGLISH LANGUAGE LEARNERS**

**Assessment Vocabulary** To help students understand questions on pages 1181–1182, teach or review these assessment vocabulary words:

- Item 3: *conflict*, "state of opposition between people or ideas"

- Item 5: *phrase*, "a group of words that lacks a subject or a verb"

- Item 8: *excerpt*, "part of a story, passage"

- Item 11: *paraphrase*, "state main ideas and supporting details in your own words"

**Nurse.** Ah sir! ah sir! Well, death's the end of all.

**Romeo.** Spakest thou of Juliet? How is it with her?
Doth not she think me an old murderer,
95 Now I have stained the childhood of our joy
With blood removed but little from her own?
Where is she? and how doth she? and what says
My concealed lady to our canceled love?

**Nurse.** O, she says nothing, sir, but weeps and weeps;
100 And now falls on her bed, and then starts up,
And Tybalt calls; and then on Romeo cries,
And then down falls again.

## Reading Comprehension

> **Use the excerpt from *Romeo and Juliet*
> (pp. 1178–1181) to answer questions 1–13.**

1. Which of the following lines contains a play
   on words?
   A. *What less than doomsday is the Prince's
      doom?* (line 9)
   B. *There is no world without Verona walls,*
      (line 17)
   C. *This is dear mercy, and thou seest it not.*
      (line 28)
   D. *O, she says nothing, sir, but weeps and
      weeps;* (line 99)

2. In line 25, when Friar Laurence says "Thy
   fault our law calls death" he means —
   A. the law says the punishment for Romeo's
      crime is death
   B. according to the law, death is a fault, not
      a crime
   C. Romeo's death would be Friar Laurence's
      fault
   D. the law mistakenly calls for Romeo's death

3. The conflict in lines 17–28 presents two
   views of —
   A. banishment       C. murder
   B. jealousy         D. the law

4. Friar Laurence disagrees with Romeo in lines
   24–28 because —
   A. he hopes to keep Romeo from acting
      rashly or causing more harm
   B. he blames Romeo for all that has gone
      wrong and wants to punish him
   C. he thinks Romeo is ignorant of the law
      and needs to learn the facts
   D. he thinks that Juliet deserves a better
      husband than Romeo

5. In lines 29–36, which phrase breaks the
   pattern of blank verse?
   A. *But Romeo may not.*
   B. *And little mouse, every unworthy thing,*
   C. *Where Juliet lives;*
   D. *On the white wonder of dear Juliet's hand*

**GO ON** ➡

1181

## ANSWERS

## Comprehension

Model a thinking process for answering
multiple-choice questions.

1. **A *is correct.*** *Romeo's play on words involves
   the prince's doom, or final decision, and
   Romeo's doomsday, or death. B is incorrect
   because it states his grief at banishment
   without additional word play. C is incorrect because the friar reprimands Romeo
   without including a play on words. D is
   incorrect because the nurse simply reports
   Juliet's actions.*

2. **A *is correct.*** *The friar explains that Romeo's
   crime demands the death penalty. B is
   incorrect because it misstates the friar's
   meaning. C is incorrect because the friar
   knows that Romeo killed Tybalt. D is incorrect because Romeo has been banished
   rather than sentenced to death.*

3. **A *is correct.*** *Romeo sees banishment as
   more frightening than death, while Friar
   Laurence believes that Romeo should feel
   lucky he was saved from death. B and
   C are incorrect because the men are not
   discussing jealousy or murder. D is a weaker
   answer because Romeo has clearly broken
   the law. It is his punishment that causes
   the conflict.*

4. **A *is correct.*** *The friar's role here is that of
   mediator. He points out that the Prince has
   been kind to Romeo by choosing banishment rather than death. B is incorrect
   because the friar assigns no blame. He
   thinks Romeo should be thrilled that he has
   escaped death. C is incorrect because the
   friar spends most of his time explaining the
   positive aspects of banishment. D is incorrect because Juliet is not mentioned.*

5. **D *is correct.*** *The word* white *and the first
   syllable of the word* wonder *are two stressed
   syllables that follow each other, varying from
   the usual rhythm of iambic pentameter.*

## FOR ENGLISH LANGUAGE LEARNERS

**Review Assessment Vocabulary** On the
board, list the assessment vocabulary shown
in italics. Then provide examples in random
order for students to classify.

- *play on words* (item 1): "If love be rough
  with you, be rough with love;/Prick love for
  pricking and you beat love down."

- *conflict* (item 3): the Montagues versus the
  Capulets

- *blank verse* (item 5): "But soft! What light
  through yonder window breaks?"

- *pun* (item 6): the argument in the opening scene of the play between the servants
  Sampson and Gregory (collier/choler)

- *foil* (item 9): Benvolio (calm and sensible)
  and Romeo (moody, emotional)

- *character flaw* (item 12): Romeo's idealism
  and defiance of fate

## ANSWERS

**6. D is correct.** *Romeo plays on the words fly (the insect) and fly, meaning "to go through the air." He implies that flies are better off than he is, since they may land on Juliet's hand. A is incorrect because Romeo specifically compares flies to his own condition, not Juliet's. B is the weaker answer because it is more general. C is incorrect because Romeo, not Juliet, is the object of comparison.*

**7. A is correct.** *Unable or unwilling to listen to advice, Romeo is acting irrationally. B is incorrect because while madness causes Romeo's "deafness," deafness is not a sign of madness. C is incorrect because the friar is not angry. D is incorrect because Friar Laurence is not saying Romeo is going mad.*

**8. D is correct.** *Romeo is absorbed in his own problems and emotions. A is incorrect because Romeo is heated with emotion in this scene and not at all cold. B and C are incorrect because Romeo shows no dignity or generosity.*

**9. B is correct.** *The friar is trying to reason with an irrational Romeo. A is incorrect because Laurence is not cynical; rather he is trying to highlight positive aspects of banishment. C and D are incorrect because Romeo and the friar do not exhibit these traits in the scene.*

**10. C is correct.** *Romeo is concerned with what Juliet will think of him and how his act of murder had caused her pain. A and D are incorrect because Romeo is concerned with Juliet, not Friar Laurence or the Prince. B is incorrect because Romeo is torn over defending his honor and being worthy of Juliet, not impressing Juliet and hating Juliet's family.*

## SHORT CONSTRUCTED RESPONSE

### Possible responses:

**11.** *Friar Laurence tells Romeo that the work of great thinkers can help him cope with his forced exile. Like a coat of armor, philosophy will shield him. Like a sweet drink, it can remove exile's bitterness.*

---

**6.** The author's pun in lines 41–42 contrasts —
  **A.** flies and Juliet
  **B.** flies and free men
  **C.** Juliet and Romeo
  **D.** Romeo and flies

**7.** In line 61, when Friar Laurence says "madmen have no ears" he means that —
  **A.** an irrational person won't listen to advice
  **B.** deafness in a person is a sign of madness
  **C.** Friar Laurence is angry at someone who doesn't listen
  **D.** Romeo's anger is a sign of madness

**8.** In this excerpt, Romeo most strongly exhibits the trait of —
  **A.** coldness      **C.** generosity
  **B.** dignity       **D.** self-absorption

**9.** Which statement best describes Friar Laurence's role as a foil to Romeo in this excerpt?
  **A.** Laurence is cynical; Romeo is hopeful.
  **B.** Laurence is reasonable; Romeo is emotional.
  **C.** Laurence is fearful; Romeo acts bravely.
  **D.** Laurence is comic; Romeo is tragic.

**10.** Romeo's sorrow over killing Tybalt intensifies his conflict between —
  **A.** remaining loyal to Friar Laurence and upholding family responsibilities
  **B.** wanting to impress Juliet and hating her family
  **C.** defending his personal honor and being worthy of Juliet
  **D.** performing religious duties and keeping his obligations to the Prince

**SHORT CONSTRUCTED RESPONSE**
Write three or four sentences to answer each question.

**11.** Paraphrase lines 54–56, and identify which character is speaking.

**12.** What character flaw of Romeo's does the nurse call attention to in lines 84–90? Support your answer with details from the excerpt.

**Write two to three paragraphs to answer this question.**

**13.** Why does Romeo disagree with Friar Laurence's advice in line 16? Discuss Romeo's motivation for rejecting this advice, and support your answer with details from the excerpt.

1182

---

**12.** *The nurse scolds Romeo for being too emotional. She implies that his response is weak by telling him, "Stand, an you be a man" (line 88). She compares his display of grief to Juliet's and seems to be frustrated or annoyed with the behavior. She refers to their "Blubb'ring and weeping, weeping and blubbering" (line 87) as if they were children.*

**13.** *Friar Laurence suggests that Romeo's situation is not that bad; Romeo's life has been spared, and he can go anywhere to let time heal his grief. Romeo, however, can't imagine life away from Verona and Juliet (lines 29–30). As a result, he equates banishment with death (lines 43–46).*

# Revising and Editing

**DIRECTIONS** Read this passage, and answer the questions that follow.

> (1) The musical *West Side Story* is based on Shakespeare's play Romeo and Juliet. (2) Unlike the play, however, both *West Side Story's* Broadway production and its Hollywood adaptation set the 14th-century tale of Italian lovers in 20th-century New York. (3) *Romeo and Juliet* features two wealthy and prominent families, while the depiction of working-class people is the focus of *West Side Story*. (4) In the musical, Romeo becomes "Tony," and filling the shoes of Juliet is "Maria." (5) Many aspects of Romeo and Juliet are updated in *West Side Story*. (6) An opulent house becomes a crowded apartment building. (7) A duel becomes a street fight. (8) Maria uses a fire escape instead of a balcony. (9) West Side Story represents a modern urban tragedy.

1. What change, if any, should be made in sentence 1?
   A. Insert a comma after *West Side Story*
   B. Change **Shakespeare** to **his**
   C. Change **Romeo and Juliet** to *Romeo and Juliet*
   D. Make no change

2. What is the best way to rewrite sentence 3 so that its elements are parallel?
   A. *Romeo and Juliet* features wealthier and more prominent families, while working-class people are the focus of *West Side Story*.
   B. *Romeo and Juliet* features two families that are wealthy and prominent, while working- class people are focused on in *West Side Story*.
   C. *Romeo and Juliet* features two wealthy and prominent families, while *West Side Story* focuses on working-class people.
   D. *Romeo and Juliet* features two wealthy and prominent families; working-class people are the focus of *West Side Story*.

3. What is the most effective way to rewrite sentence 4 so that its elements are parallel?
   A. In the musical, Romeo becomes "Tony," while "Maria" is busy filling the shoes of Juliet.
   B. In the musical, Romeo becomes "Tony," and Juliet becomes "Maria."
   C. In the musical, Romeo becomes "Tony," with "Maria" trying to fill the shoes of Juliet.
   D. In the musical, Romeo becomes "Tony," and "Maria" and Juliet are each other.

4. What word could be substituted for "opulent" in sentence 6 without changing the meaning of the sentence?
   A. cold
   B. elegant
   C. pretty
   D. unseemly

5. Which transition should be added to the beginning of sentence 9?
   A. Meanwhile,
   B. However,
   C. And also,
   D. In this way,

STOP

1183

**ANSWERS**
# Revising and Editing

1. **C is correct.** The title of the play should be italicized. A is incorrect because a comma would separate the sentence's subject and verb. B is incorrect because Shakespeare has not yet been identified as the play's author. D is incorrect because the play's title is not correctly formatted.

2. **C is correct.** The sentence has parallel subjects: Romeo and Juliet, West Side Story; parallel verbs: features, focuses; and parallel objects: families, people. A is incorrect; the first part of the sentence is active, while the second part is passive. B is incorrect; because Romeo and Juliet *is the subject of the first part of the sentence, and* West Side Story *is the object of the second part.* D is incorrect because it substitutes a semicolon for a comma and conjunction (while).

3. **B is correct.** The order of both parts of the sentence is subject/verb/object. Two independent clauses are joined with a coordinating conjunction. A is incorrect because the clause "while 'Maria' is busy filling the shoes of Juliet" is in subject/verb/modifier order. C is incorrect because two independent clauses become one independent and one dependent. D is incorrect because the second part of the sentence does not make sense.

4. **B is correct.** Elegant, *or "tasteful," could be exchanged for* opulent, *or "lavish."* A is incorrect because a rich, or opulent, house would not be considered cold. C is a weaker answer because pretty *does not have the weight or intensity of* opulent. D is incorrect because it does not have the positive connotation of opulent.

5. **D is correct.** In this way *provides a concluding statement for the passage's final sentence.* A is incorrect because Meanwhile *implies a chronological order not present in the passage.* B is incorrect because However *implies a contrast rather than a summation.* C is incorrect because And also *implies that additional examples will follow, rather than a concluding statement.*

---

## DIFFERENTIATED INSTRUCTION

### FOR ENGLISH LANGUAGE LEARNERS
**Assessment Support: Parallelism** Define parallelism as a similarity of grammatical form in two or more elements of a compound sentence. Post this sentence:

Wherever *ideas are connected* with coordinating or correlative conjunctions, wherever *elements are compared*, and wherever *items are arranged* in a list, the elements should match each other in structure.

Use the underlined and italicized text to clarify parallelism. Then give students sentences like this one:

Romeo matures as a result of his love for Juliet and he was involved in the feud.

Ask a volunteer to revise for parallelism.

***Possible answer:*** *Romeo matures as a result of his love for Juliet and his involvement in the feud.*

## INTRODUCE *GREAT READS*

In Unit 10, students have discussed the power of love. Discuss the recommended books and their summaries, pointing out how each connects to the theme of love. Encourage students to choose one or more of these "great reads" to read independently.

---

# UNIT 10
## Great Reads

## Ideas for Independent Reading

Find out who inspired Shakespeare and who Shakespeare inspired, and read more of his classic plays.

**COMMON CORE**

**RL 10** Read and comprehend literature. **RI 10** Read and comprehend literary nonfiction.

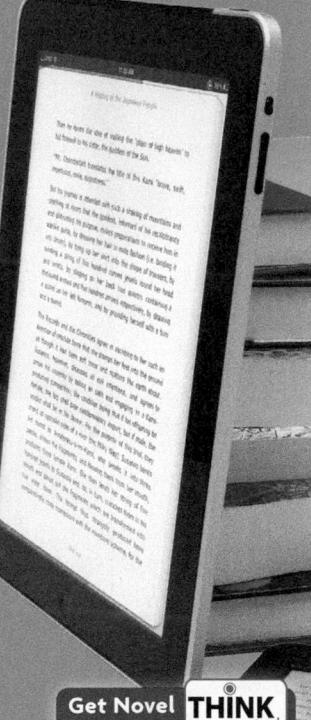

### West Side Story
*by Leonard Bernstein, Irving Schulman, and Stephen Sondheim*

Sondheim, Schulman, and Bernstein move the story of *Romeo and Juliet* to 1950s New York City, where gang warfare dominates the West Side. Tony and Maria meet at a school dance and instantly fall in love. At first their happiness erases all else from their minds, but the harsh realities of their lives cannot be kept at bay. In some parts of the play, the authors are faithful to Shakespeare's plot; in others, they take greater liberty. In either case, the power of true love remains a resonant theme.

### Metamorphoses
*by Ovid*

*Metamorphoses* is a collection of stories in which love causes physical transformation. One tale of thwarted love, "Pyramus and Thisbe," was an inspiration for *Romeo and Juliet*. The characters in the myths are sometimes brought closer together by their transformations, but sometimes they are pushed apart or separated forever. Ovid's tone, like Shakespeare's, changes suddenly from humorous to tragic and back again, allowing him to constantly surprise and entertain his readers.

### A Midsummer Night's Dream
*by William Shakespeare*

In this play, Shakespeare takes a comic and magical approach to forbidden love. Four young people have run away from the Athenian court to escape an impending forced marriage. Far from their homes, they fall asleep in the forest on a summer evening. There they are visited by Puck, a devilish spirit who will use magic to change their passions and their lives. While their passions are as forceful as those of Romeo and Juliet, the results are both funnier and more hopeful.

### Othello
*by William Shakespeare*

The mastermind in this Shakespearean tragedy is not Fate but a jilted assistant in the army. Othello, a military general, is choosing a new lieutenant; he passes over Iago in favor of another man in his battalion. Iago vows revenge on both of them. He tells Othello that the new lieutenant is romantically involved with Othello's beloved wife, Desdemona. Though both protest to the contrary, Othello's jealously blinds him to reason and reality, with devastating consequences.

### The Wings of the Dove
*by Henry James*

Kate Croy is desperately in love with Merton Densher. Kate's family claims that Merton is too poor and will keep Kate from rising in the world, but the two have promised each other that they will somehow marry. When a wealthy, gravely ill young woman befriends Kate and falls in love with Merton, Kate plans to use the woman's feelings and friendship to meet her own needs. In *Romeo and Juliet,* overt tragedy and political strife change the lives of lovers. In *The Wings of the Dove,* subtle and intimate personal interactions cause love itself to change.

### A Natural History of Love
*by Diane Ackerman*

In this book, Ackerman studies and explores the ways in which love has been portrayed through the ages. *A Natural History of Love* discusses the lessons that can be taken from tales of love throughout history, both from historical romances and from such fictional romances as Romeo and Juliet's, and examines how love has been treated throughout history. Both a poet and a journalist, Ackerman uses poetic language in writing this detailed and thorough history of a subject that has significance for every reader.

**Get Novel Wise**

**THINK** central

Go to **thinkcentral.com**.
KEYWORD: HML9-1184

1184

---

**THINK** central

### NovelWise

The keyword on this page points to **NovelWise,** a Web site that helps students choose a novel or other book-length work to read. **NovelWise** also provides

- study guides
- reading strategies and literary elements instruction
- presentations to introduce classic novels
- project ideas

# Epic Poetry

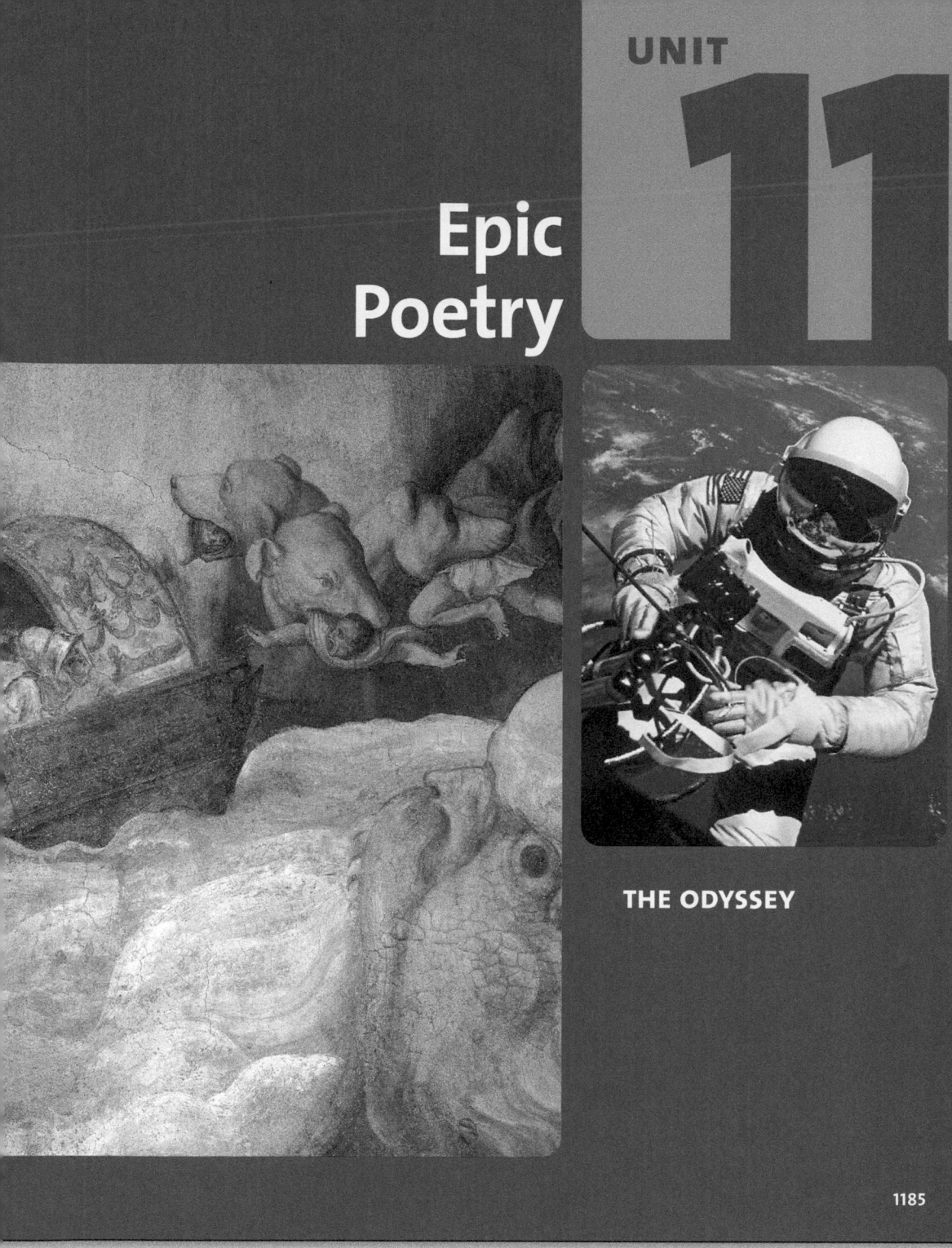

**THE ODYSSEY**

1185

## INTRODUCE THE UNIT

What do we mean when we describe a story or an event as "epic"? Broadly speaking, epics reveal powerful qualities, such as heroism, majesty, and bravery. They tell stories of great horror, great tragedy, great triumph, or any combination of the three. More specifically, narrative poems such as Homer's *Iliad* and *Odyssey*, Milton's *Paradise Lost*, and Dante's *Divine Comedy* are considered epics because they share a dignified style and a subject that is important to a large group of readers. Epic characteristics can appear in modern-day events, too. For example, the exploration of space has been called an epic journey because of its heroic nature and the way that it represents the aspirations of humanity as a whole.

Invite students to consider how the pictures on this page illustrate the meaning of the word *epic*. Ask:

- What is happening in each picture?
- The people shown are travelers. What qualities might they share?
- What danger or potential for tragedy can you see in each scene? What courage or potential for triumph can you see?

Tell students that as they read the *Odyssey* in this unit, they will consider the importance of the story to the ancient Greeks. They also will explore its epic qualities and think about why it has become perhaps the most famous of all epic tales.

For help in planning this unit, see

**R** RESOURCE MANAGER UNIT 11
pp. 1–10

**About the Art** Alessandro Allori (1535–1607) painted this fresco of Odysseus' journey around 1580. For more information, see page 1237.

# UNIT 11

## COMMON CORE

**STRAND**

| | **Homer's World**<br>Informational Article<br>pp. 1188–1193 | **Text Analysis Workshop: The Epic**<br>pp. 1194–1201 | **The Wanderings of Odysseus**<br>*from the* **Odyssey**<br>Epic Poem<br>pp. 1202–1239 |
|---|---|---|---|
| **Reading Literature** | Examining the Homeric Epics<br>p. 1188–1189  **RL 6**<br>Homer: The Epic Poet p. 1190  **RL 9**<br>People and Places of the *Odyssey* p. 1192<br>The *Odyssey* in Art pp. 1193–1194  **RL 7** | Characteristics of the Epic<br>pp. 1194–1195  **RL 5**<br>Language of Homer pp. 1196–1197  **RL 4,**<br>**RL 10**<br>Reading the Epic pp. 1198–1199  **RL 4,**<br>**RL 6**<br>Analyze the Text pp. 1200–1201 | Epic Hero pp. 1203, 1204, 1208,<br>1210, 1216, 1218, 1220, 1221, 1223,<br>1229, 1233–1235, 1238  **RL 5, RL 6**<br>Reading an Epic Poem pp. 1203, 1211,<br>1225, 1227, 1231, 1238  **RL 4, RL 10**<br>Language Coach p. 1235  **RL 4** |
| **Reading Informational Text** | | | |
| **Writing** | | | |
| **Speaking and Listening** | | | Discuss p. 1202  **SL 1** |
| **Language** | | | Language Coach pp. 1209, 1212, 1217,<br>1222, 1227, 1232  **L 4a–c**<br>Words with the Prefix *fore-* p. 1239  **L 4d** |

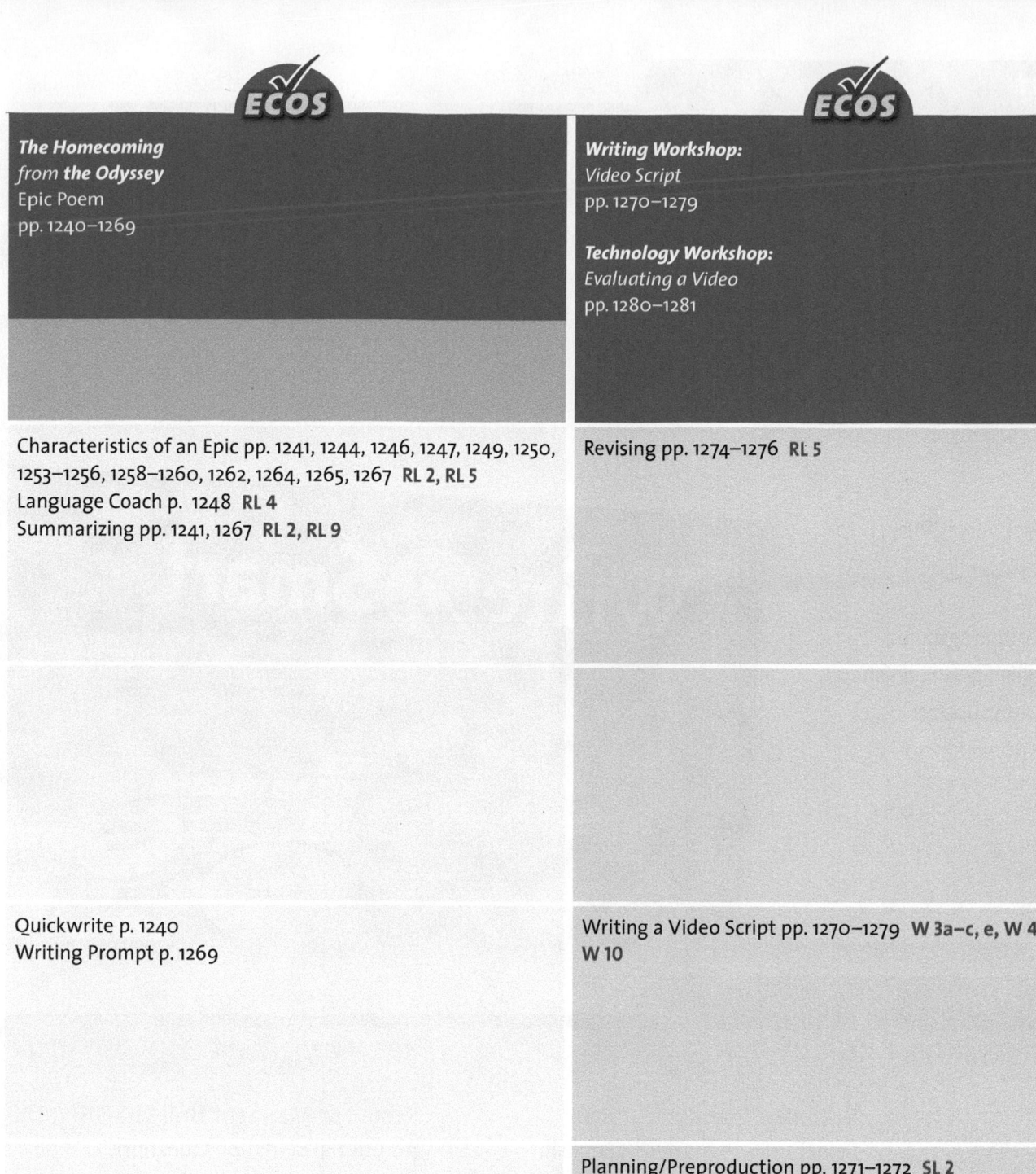

ECOS

**The Homecoming**
*from the Odyssey*
Epic Poem
pp. 1240–1269

**Writing Workshop:**
*Video Script*
pp. 1270–1279

**Technology Workshop:**
*Evaluating a Video*
pp. 1280–1281

Characteristics of an Epic pp. 1241, 1244, 1246, 1247, 1249, 1250, 1253–1256, 1258–1260, 1262, 1264, 1265, 1267 **RL 2, RL 5**
Language Coach p. 1248 **RL 4**
Summarizing pp. 1241, 1267 **RL 2, RL 9**

Revising pp. 1274–1276 **RL 5**

Quickwrite p. 1240
Writing Prompt p. 1269

Writing a Video Script pp. 1270–1279 **W 3a–c, e, W 4, W 5, W 6, W 10**

Planning/Preproduction pp. 1271–1272 **SL 2**
Production p. 1273 **SL 5**
Revising pp. 1274–1276 **SL 5**
Editing and Publishing p. 1277 **SL 5**
Evaluating a Video pp. 1280–1281 **SL 1a, c**

Descriptive Details pp. 1256, 1269 **L 3**
Language Coach pp. 1245, 1252, 1259, 1264 **L 4**
Latin Word Root *solus* p. 1268 **L 4c**

ECOS

To see the complete Essential Course of Study, see pp. T23–T28.

For additional lesson planning help, see **Teacher One Stop DVD.**

# Instructional Support

**Resource Manager Unit 11**

**UNIT SUPPORT**

Academic Vocabulary, p. 3

Additional Academic Vocabulary, p. 4

Grammar Focus pp. 5–6

Text Analysis Workshop pp. 9–10

Writing Workshop: Video Script p. 55

**SELECTION SUPPORT***

**Plan and Teach**

Lesson planning pages

Additional leveled selection questions

Extension activities

**Student Copy Masters**

Selection summaries in four languages

Skills copy masters in English and Spanish

Vocabulary preteaching and support

Reading Check and Question Support

Reading Fluency

*Available for all selections

† Available on **thinkcentral.com**.

**Language Handbook**

**Vocabulary Practice**

**Best Practices Toolkit**†

**PowerNotes** DVD-ROM†

**Connections: Nonfiction for Common Core** CD-ROM†

**Teacher One Stop** DVD-ROM

**Student One Stop** DVD-ROM

**WriteSmart** CD-ROM†

**GrammarNotes** DVD-ROM†

**WordSharp** CD-ROM†

# Differentiated Instruction

| STRUGGLING READERS AND WRITERS | ENGLISH LANGUAGE LEARNERS | ADVANCED LEARNERS |
|---|---|---|
| **Resource Manager Unit 11** | **Resource Manager Unit 11** | **Resource Manager Unit 11** |
| Additional Selection Questions | Selection Summaries in English, Spanish, Vietnamese and Haitian Creole | Additional Selection Questions |
| Question Support | Skills Copymasters in Spanish | Ideas for Extension |
| Reading Fluency | **English Language Learner Adapted Interactive Reader Teacher's Guide** | **Diagnostic and Selection Tests** |
| **Interactive Reader** | | Selection Tests B/C |
| **Adapted Interactive Reader** | **ELL Adapted Interactive Reader** | |
| **Level Up Online Tutorials** | **Audio Tutor** | |
| **Audio Anthology** (with Audio summaries) | **Guide to English for Newcomers** | |
| **Diagnostic and Selection Tests** | **Audio Anthology** | |
| Selection Tests A/B | **Audio Summaries in Multiple Languages** (on **thinkcentral.com**) | |

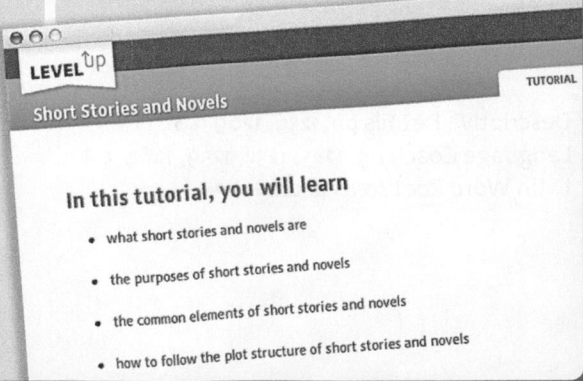

## Assessment and Reteaching

**Diagnostic and Selection Tests**

**Unit and Benchmark Tests**

**ThinkCentral Online Assessment:**
- All program assessments
- Level Up Online Tutorials

**ExamView Test Generator** on the Teacher One Stop DVD-ROM

**Online Essay Scoring** on **thinkcentral.com**

**ThinkCentral Online Reteaching:**
- Level Up Online Tutorials
- Reteaching Worksheets

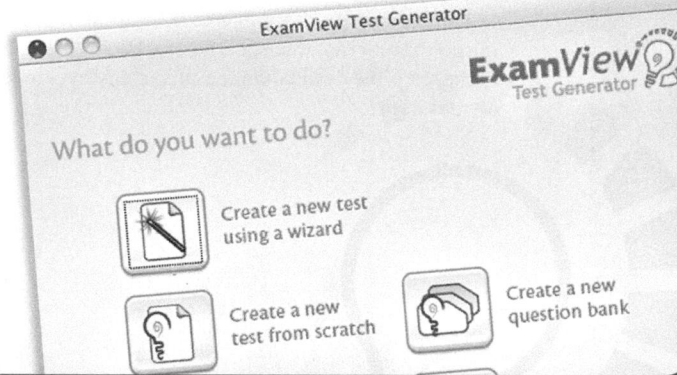

ExamView Test Generator

ExamView
Test Generator

What do you want to do?

Create a new test using a wizard

Create a new test from scratch

Create a new question bank

## Professional Development

**Video Center** Based on interviews with program consultants and other educational experts, these videos feature classroom-ready teaching strategies.

**Teacher Toolkit** Includes a Teacher Handbook as well as a range of articles and handouts by program consultants and other educators.

**Janet Allen**

**Jim Burke**

**Kylene Beers**

**Carol Jago**

---

## THINK central at a Glance

### One Location, Endless Resources

**Find Resources** Browse all *Holt McDougal Literature* components for the ones that meet your students' needs and match your teaching style.

**Assess Progress and Reteach** Assign electronic versions of program assessments to measure your students' mastery of the Common Core State Standards. On thinkcentral.com, some tests deliver online remediation tutorials to students who have not mastered skills.

 **Interactive Whiteboard Lessons**

Prepare your students for college and careers by teaching relevant, real-world skills through dynamic, interactive instruction. Go to **thinkcentral.com** to browse through all whiteboard lessons, including the following:

- Narrative Techniques
- Figurative Language and Imagery
- Summarizing Text

 Together Holt McDougal and HISTORY® are revolutionizing the study of English/language arts with video that helps students relive and re-imagine the people, places, and events they are discovering through reading. Look for selections with the HISTORY® icon.

## Is it the JOURNEY or the DESTINATION?

To introduce the page, read the question and then restate it as "Which is more important: the goal itself, or the things that you learn as you work toward the goal?" As students read the opening paragraph, discuss examples of high-school moments that students have come to appreciate or that they think they will appreciate even more in the future. Then relate the paragraph to the photograph by discussing what the climber might have learned during his journey to the top of the mountain.

*ACTIVITY* Model the activity, using a familiar story that involves a journey. (The *Lord of the Rings* trilogy is a good choice: the destination is Mount Doom and the goal, the destruction of the One Ring; but the journey teaches lessons about teamwork, courage, selflessness, perseverance, and more.) After students have completed the activity, call on volunteers to share their responses.

**CHECK UNDERSTANDING** Confirm that students understand the metaphor of a journey in this context. Have them explain why the journey can be even more important than the destination.

# Is it the JOURNEY or the DESTINATION?

If attending high school is a journey, then the ultimate destination is graduation. As you strive to cross that finish line, you'll face new experiences, build friendships, and even run into some frustrating roadblocks. As you consider this journey, what do you think is more important—reaching your goal and clutching that diploma in your hand, or taking time to appreciate the many moments (both good and bad) that will lead up to graduation day?

*ACTIVITY* With a classmate, think of books, movies, or TV shows that depict a journey of some sort—whether it's a quest to find a long-lost family member, a struggle to make it safely back home, or a mission to fulfill an important dream. Which seems more important to the story, the destination the character strives to reach or the journey itself?

**Find It Online!**

Go to **thinkcentral.com** for the interactive version of this unit.

## Unit Resources

See resources on the **Teacher One Stop DVD-ROM** *and on* **thinkcentral.com**.

**R** RESOURCE MANAGER UNIT 11

UNIT AND BENCHMARK TESTS

BEST PRACTICES TOOLKIT

INTERACTIVE READER

ADAPTED INTERACTIVE READER

ELL ADAPTED INTERACTIVE READER

LANGUAGE HANDBOOK

VOCABULARY PRACTICE

**TECHNOLOGY**

- Teacher One Stop DVD-ROM
- Student One Stop DVD-ROM
- PowerNotes DVD-ROM
- Write*Smart* CD-ROM
- Media*Smart* DVD-ROM
- GrammarNotes DVD-ROM
- Audio Anthology CD
- Audio Tutor CD

**Find It Online!**

The interactive version of this unit on **thinkcentral.com** includes
- video and **PowerNotes** introductions to key selections
- audio support—listen or download
- **ThinkAloud** models
- **WordSharp** vocabulary tutorials
- interactive review and remediation

## Preview Unit Goals

| | |
|---|---|
| **TEXT ANALYSIS** | • Identify and evaluate characteristics of an epic, including the cultural perspective reflected by the work<br>• Identify and analyze epic hero and archetypes<br>• Identify and analyze epic similes, epithets, and allusions<br>• Identify and analyze plot, setting, and theme in an epic |
| **READING** | • Use strategies for reading an epic<br>• Objectively summarize plot |
| **WRITING AND LANGUAGE** | • Write a narrative script for a video<br>• Use figurative language to add descriptive detail |
| **SPEAKING AND LISTENING** | • Evaluate a speaker's presentation |
| **VOCABULARY** | • Use prefixes and word roots to help determine or clarify the meanings of unfamiliar words |
| **ACADEMIC VOCABULARY** | • demonstrate    • emphasis<br>• ideology      • monitor<br>• undertake |
| **MEDIA AND VIEWING** | • Produce a video<br>• Analyze media techniques<br>• Evaluate media content |

1187

Complete text of the Common Core State Standards is found in the correlation on p. T10. Standards covered in this unit are found in the standards overview (pp. 1185A–1185B) and on the lesson pages where they are taught.

## Preview Unit Goals

The main skills and strategies taught in Unit 11 are presented on this page. Have a volunteer read the goals aloud while students read along silently and consider what they already know about each skill and term. Remind students about the color-coding of the skills strands, as well.

Model the strategy of copying the Academic Vocabulary and writing a preliminary definition for each term. Suggest that students use their **Reader/Writer Notebooks** for this purpose. Encourage them to use the terms in discussions and in writing. Also urge students to revisit each term throughout the unit and to refine its meaning.

---

## *DIFFERENTIATED INSTRUCTION*

### FOR ENGLISH LANGUAGE LEARNERS

**Academic Vocabulary** Provide students with definitions of each Academic Vocabulary word.

**demonstrate** (dĕm′ən-strāt) *v.* to show clearly and purposefully

**emphasis** (em′fə sis) *n.* special stress on something—a word, phrase, idea, etc.—to make it stand out

**ideology** (ī-dē-′ä-lə-jē) *n.* the beliefs or way of thinking—especially political, economic, or social beliefs and ways of thinking—of an individual or group of people

**monitor** (män′i tər) *v.* to check in on, watch, regulate

**undertake** (un-dər-′tāk′) *v.* to take on a task or assume a responsibility

Use the copy master to help students learn academic words they will use in this unit and on the Assessment Practice.

**R** RESOURCE MANAGER—Copy Masters
    Academic Vocabulary p. 3
    Additional Academic Vocabulary p. 4

# Homer's World

## COMMON CORE FOCUS

**RL 6** Analyze a particular point of view or cultural experience reflected in a work of world literature. **RL 7** Analyze the representation of a subject or key scene in two different artistic mediums. **RL 9** Analyze how an author draws on and transforms source materials in a specific work.

### READING STRATEGY

#### ◼ SET A PURPOSE FOR READING

Point out to students that their reason for reading "Homer's World" is to enable them to read the *Odyssey* with increased understanding and enjoyment. Ask students to look over the article quickly, and suggest how it might prepare them for reading the *Odyssey*. List their ideas on the board. After reading, encourage them to add to this list.

## BACKGROUND

**Ancient Troy** Troy, also known as Ilium, was an ancient seaport on the Aegean Sea in present-day Turkey. In the 1870s and 1880s, Heinrich Schliemann, a wealthy German businessman, excavated the site of ancient Troy. His findings suggest that the story of the Trojan War may be based on fact.

### READING SKILL

#### ◼ MAKE INFERENCES

Ask students what they can infer about Odysseus' character from information in the section **The Trojan War**. *Possible answer: Odysseus was a clever, intelligent leader, skilled at outwitting his enemies.*

# HOMER'S WORLD

The acropolis of Athens, Greece, was the high point of the city and a place to worship the goddess Athena, the city's patroness.

**COMMON CORE** **RL 6** Analyze a particular point of view or cultural experience reflected in a work of world literature. **RL 7** Analyze the representation of a subject or key scene in two different artistic mediums. **RL 9** Analyze how an author draws on and transforms source material in a specific work.

## Examining the Homeric Epics

Composed in Greece around 750–725 B.C., the *Iliad* and the *Odyssey* are perhaps the greatest masterpieces of the epic form, narrative poetry about a hero's adventures. Both stories were first told orally, perhaps even sung, and it may not have been until several generations later that these traditional stories were set down in writing. The poems are traditionally credited to a blind poet named Homer. Although there have been many translations of the poems into English, Robert Fitzgerald's verse renderings are considered among the best at capturing the poems' high drama and intense emotions. Three important elements of the plot of each epic are the Trojan War, the heroism of Odysseus, and the interference of the gods.

**The Trojan War** This legendary war seems to have occurred sometime around 1200 B.C. The earliest literary accounts of it, found in the *Iliad* and the *Odyssey,* are elaborated in later classical literature.

According to legend, the Trojan War began after Paris, a Trojan prince, kidnapped the beautiful Helen from her husband, Menelaus (mĕn´ə-lā´əs), the king of Sparta. Menelaus recruited kings and soldiers from all over Greece to help him avenge his honor and recover his wife. The Greeks held Troy under siege for ten years.

The *Iliad* takes place during the tenth year of this war. It tells the story of the Greek warrior Achilles and his quarrel with Menelaus' brother Agamemnon, ending with the death and funeral of Paris' brother Hector.

After Hector's death, the Greeks brought the war to an end thanks to the cleverness of Odysseus, ruler of the island of Ithaca. To break the ten-year stalemate, Odysseus thought of a scheme to make the Trojans think that the Greeks had finally given up. He ordered a giant wooden horse to be built and left at the gates of Troy. The Trojans, waking to find it there—without a Greek in sight—assumed that the enemy had fled and left them a peace offering. They took the horse inside the city, only to discover, too late, that it was filled with Greek soldiers and that Troy was doomed.

Giovanni Domenico Tiepolo's *The Procession of the Trojan Horse into Troy*, painted in 1773

**The Heroic Story of Odysseus** The *Odyssey* deals with Odysseus' adventures as he makes his way home from Troy and with events that take place on Ithaca just before and after his return. The first excerpts that you will read depict some of the wanderings of Odysseus after his departure from Troy with a fleet of 12 ships carrying about 720 men. This time his opponents are not military ones. Instead, he encounters various monsters who try to devour him and enchanting women who try to keep him from his wife, Penelope. The final excerpts describe Odysseus' homecoming and his reunion with Penelope and his son, Telemachus. In addition to great strength and courage, what sets Odysseus apart from others is a special quality that has been called his craft or guile: the ingenious tricks he uses to get himself out of difficult situations.

**The Intervention of the Gods and Goddesses**
Adding another dimension to the human struggles recounted in Homer's epics are the mythic elements—the conflicts among the gods and goddesses on Mount Olympus (ə-lĭm′pəs). In Homer's time, most Greeks believed that their gods not only took an active interest in human affairs but also behaved in recognizably human ways, often engaging in their own trivial quarrels and petty jealousies. For example, Athena, the goddess of war and practical wisdom, supported the Greek cause in the Trojan War and championed Odysseus, while Aphrodite (ăf′rə-dī′tē), the goddess of love, sided with Paris and his fellow Trojans. The story of Odysseus' return from Troy contains some notable instances of divine interference. Odysseus has Athena on his side, but he has displeased the gods who were on the side of Troy. Furthermore, as you will see, he angers another god during one of his first adventures and still another later on. As a result, he is forced to suffer many hardships before he manages to return home.

To Homer's audience, the *Odyssey,* with its interfering gods and goddesses and its strange lands and creatures, must have seemed as full of mystery and danger as science fiction and fantasy adventures seem to people today. Just as we can imagine aliens in the next galaxy or creatures created in a laboratory, the ancient Greeks could imagine monsters living just beyond the boundaries of their known world. It was not necessary for them to believe that creatures such as one-eyed giants did exist, but only that they might.

| **Eros** | **Aphrodite** | **Apollo** | **Athena** | **Muses** |
|---|---|---|---|---|
| God of love (also known as Cupid) | Goddess of love and mother of Eros | God of music, poetry, and prophecy | Goddess of war, wisdom, and cleverness | Daughters of Zeus (three shown here), often viewed as sources of divine inspiration |

Detail of a frieze representing a procession of mythological divinities. Oil on plaster. Chateux de Malmaison et Bois-Preau, Rueil-Malmaison, France. Photo © Gerard Blot/Art Resource, New York.

## Homer: The Epic Poet

**Shadowy Figure** Although the ancient Greeks credited a man named Homer with composing the *Iliad* and the *Odyssey,* scholars have long debated whether Homer really existed. There are many theories about who Homer may have been and when and where he may have lived. According to ancient accounts, he lived sometime between 900 and 700 B.C., possibly on the island of Chios in the eastern Aegean Sea, and he was blind. Most modern scholars agree that the Homeric poems are the work of one or two exceptionally talented bards—singers who made up their verses as they sang.

**Oral History** Homer's epics are all that remains of a series of poems that told the whole story of the Trojan War. In later centuries, the *Iliad* and the *Odyssey* were memorized by professional reciters, who performed them at religious festivals throughout Greece. They were also the first works read by Greek schoolchildren. By 300 B.C. many slightly different versions of the poems existed, and scholars began to work at restoring them to their original form.

**Models for the Ages** Homer's epics became models for many later writers, including the Roman poet Virgil, who wrote his own epic in Latin. Poets throughout English literature, from Chaucer in the Middle Ages to Shakespeare in the Renaissance to Keats in the Romantic era, have found inspiration in Homer's epics. Moreover, by helping to shape classical Greek culture, the epics contributed to the development of many later Western ideas and values.

**A Living Tradition** Artists of all kinds continue to draw on Homer's work. In 1922, the Irish writer James Joyce published his groundbreaking novel *Ulysses* ("Ulysses" is a Latin form of Odysseus' name), in which he turned a day in the life of an ordinary man into an Odyssean journey. In 2000, the Coen brothers' film *O Brother, Where Art Thou?* told the story of a Depression-era Ulysses, an escaped convict returning home to prevent his wife from marrying another man. The 2004 movie *Troy* is a more straightforward adaptation of Homer's *Iliad.*

**Author Online**

Go to **thinkcentral.com**. KEYWORD: HML9-1190

THINK central

A scene from the 2004 movie *Troy;* a bust of Homer

## People and Places of the *Odyssey*

You will find it helpful to become familiar with important people and places in the *Odyssey* before you begin reading. The map identifies real places mentioned in the poem, such as Troy, Sparta, and Ithaca. It also shows where later readers have thought that some of the imaginary lands visited by Odysseus could have been located, after applying Mediterranean geography to Homer's descriptions. Following is a list of important characters. All Greek names used in Robert Fitzgerald's translation have been changed from their original spelling to a more familiar, Latinized spelling.

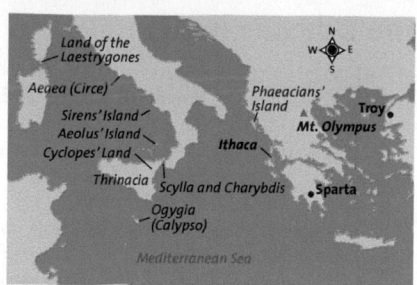

### IMPORTANT CHARACTERS IN THE *ODYSSEY* (in order of mention)

**BOOK 1**

**Helios** (hē′lē-ŏs′)—the sun god, who raises his cattle on the island of Thrinacia (thrĭ-nā′shə)

**Zeus** (zo͞os)—the ruler of the Greek gods and goddesses; father of Athena and Apollo

**Telemachus** (tə-lĕm′ə-kəs)—Odysseus' son

**Penelope** (pə-nĕl′ə-pē)—Odysseus' wife

**BOOK 5**

**Hermes** (hûr′mēz)—the god of invention, commerce, and cunning; messenger of the gods

**Calypso** (kə-lĭp′sō)—a sea goddess who lives on the island of Ogygia (ō-gĭj′yə)

**Laertes** (lā-ûr′tēz)—Odysseus' father

**BOOK 9**

**Alcinous** (ăl-sĭn′ō-əs)—the king of the Phaeacians (fē-ā′shənz)

**Circe** (sûr′sē)—a goddess and enchantress who lives on the island of Aeaea (ē-ē′ə)

**Cicones** (sĭ-kō′nēz)—allies of the Trojans, who live at Ismarus (ĭs-mär′əs)

**Lotus Eaters**—inhabitants of a land Odysseus visits

**Cyclopes** (sī-klō′pēz)—a race of one-eyed giants; an individual member of the race is a Cyclops (sī′klŏps)

**Apollo** (ə-pŏl′ō)—the god of music, poetry, prophecy, and medicine

**Poseidon** (pō-sīd′n)—the god of the seas, earthquakes, and horses; father of the Cyclops who battles Odysseus

**BOOK 10**

**Aeolus** (ē′ə-ləs)—the guardian of the winds

**Laestrygones** (lĕs′trĭ-gō′nēz)—cannibal inhabitants of a distant land

**Eurylochus** (yo͝o-rĭl′ə-kəs)—a trusted officer of Odysseus'

**Persephone** (pər-sĕf′ə-nē)—the wife of Hades, ruler of the underworld

**Tiresias** (tī-rē′sē-əs) of Thebes (thēbz)—a blind prophet whose spirit Odysseus visits in the underworld

**BOOK 11**

**Elpenor** (ĕl-pē′nôr)—one of Odysseus' crew, killed in an accident

**BOOK 12**

**Sirens** (sī′rənz)—creatures, part woman and part bird, whose songs lure sailors to their death

**Scylla** (sĭl′ə)—a six-headed sea monster who devours sailors

**Charybdis** (kə-rĭb′dĭs)—a dangerous whirlpool personified as a female sea monster

**BOOK 16**

**Athena** (ə-thē′nə)—the goddess of war, wisdom, and cleverness; goddess of crafts

**Eumaeus** (yo͞o-mē′əs)—a servant in Odysseus' household

**BOOK 17**

**Argos** (är′gŏs)—Odysseus' dog

**BOOKS 21—23**

**Antinous** (ăn-tĭn′ō-əs)—a suitor of Penelope's

**Eurymachus** (yo͝o-rĭm′ə-kəs)—a suitor of Penelope's

**Philoetius** (fĭ-lē′shəs)—a servant in Odysseus' household

**Amphinomus** (ăm-fĭn′ə-məs)—a suitor of Penelope's

**Eurynome** (yo͝o-rĭn′ə-mē)—a female servant in Odysseus' household

**Eurycleia** (yo͝or′ĭ-klē′ə)—an old female servant, still loyal to Odysseus

## Analyze Visuals

Ask students what information the map shows that is not in the text under **People and Places of the *Odyssey*? Possible answer:** *The map shows that the seas around Greece are dotted with islands and that Greece is close to Troy. The map also helps the reader to understand why the sea profoundly influenced life in Greece.*

### READING STATEGY

■ **MONITOR READING**

Suggest that students bookmark **Important Characters in the *Odyssey*** to use as a reference as they read.

## ALTERED SPELLINGS

The following is a list of altered spellings of characters' names taken from Fitzgerald's *Odyssey* and used in this selection:

| Original | Altered |
|---|---|
| Antiklos | Anticlus |
| Deïphobos | Deiphobus |
| Andraimon | Andraemon |
| Thoas | <no change> |
| Olympos | Olympus |
| Meneláos | Menelaus |
| Agamémnon | Agamemnon |
| Akhaians | Achaeans |
| Ithaka | Ithaca |
| Thrinákia | Thrinacia |
| Mount Neion | <no change> |
| Doulíkhion | Dulichium |
| Samê | Same |
| Zakynthos | Zacynthus |
| Aiaia | Aeaea |
| Malea | <no change> |
| Kythera | Cythera |

*(List continues on page 1192.)*

## ● MAKE INFERENCES

Why did the two artists use seascapes in their depictions of the *Odyssey*? **Possible answer:** *A seascape offers an opportunity to explore color and light; moreover, the sea is central to the plot and setting of the epic.*

## ALTERED SPELLINGS LIST *(cont.)*:

| Original | Altered |
|----------|---------|
| Euanthês | Euanthes |
| Maron | <no change> |
| Ísmaros | Ismarus |
| Kronos | Cronus |
| Erebos | Erebus |
| Amphitritê | Amphitrite |
| Phaêthousa | Phaethusa |
| Lampetía | Lampetia |
| Neaira | Neaera |
| Perimêdês | Perimedes |
| Politês | Polites |
| Pylos | <no change> |
| Hêlios | Helios |
| Telémakhos | Telemachus |
| Penélopê | Penelope |
| Hermês | Hermes |
| Kalypso | Calypso |
| Laërtês | Laertes |
| Alkínoös | Alcinous |
| Kirkê | Circe |
| Kikonês | Cicones |
| Lotos Eaters | Lotus Eaters |

*(List continues on page 1205.)*

## ● MAIN IDEA

What is the main idea of the section **The *Odyssey* in Art?** *Possible answer: The Odyssey has inspired artists from the seventh century B.C. through modern times.*

# The *Odyssey* in Art

Artists have been representing images and events from the *Odyssey* since the seventh century B.C., when Greek artists painted Odyssean images and scenes as decoration on ceramic urns and vases. Since then, artists have continued to tell Odysseus' story in painting, sculpture, and other media.

Throughout the unit, you will see how numerous artists have interpreted this epic in a range of styles and forms. As you look at the art illustrating each episode, ask yourself what the artists were trying to show about each part of the story and what their own attitudes toward characters and events may have been.

**Looking at Art** You've seen how understanding a writer's craft can help you appreciate the beauty and meaning of a literary text. In the same way, knowing about artists' techniques can help you understand and appreciate their work. The following list of terms and related questions may help you identify and think about the choices each artist made. Consider how these choices have contributed to the meaning and beauty of each piece.

| Term | Questions |
|------|-----------|
| composition | What shape or space is emphasized? |
| material | Has the artist used paint, clay, pencil, ink, or some other material? |
| function | Is the piece useful, decorative, or both? |
| color | Does the piece have a broad palette (range of colors) or a limited one? |
| line | Are the lines clean, simple, rough, ornate, or jagged? |
| shape | Does the piece have large, bold shapes or smaller, more complex ones? Are they geometric or organic (free-form)? |
| texture | In painting, are the brush strokes distinct or smooth looking? In sculpture or ceramics, is the surface polished or rough? |
| scale | Does the piece show large things or small ones? |
| representation | Are the images realistic, stylized, or abstract? |

**Landscapes** When you look at a Homeric landscape, ask questions like the ones that follow. See if the answers help you understand each artist's purpose.

- Which of the following two landscapes is more **realistic?** How so?
- What **material** has each artist used? Which do you prefer, and why?
- Look at the **composition** of each piece. What part of the scene is emphasized in the painting? What is emphasized in the collage?
- Describe the **mood** and **tone** of each piece. Which is more lush, and which is more spare? Consider the techniques that created these differences.

**200s:** *Ulysses and the Sirens*, Roman. Mosaic, 130 cm x 344 cm. Musée du Bardo, Tunis, Tunisia. © Bridgeman Art Library.

**About 1650:** *Ulysses Returns Chryseis to Her Father,* Claude Lorrain. Oil painting.

**Portraiture** As you look at a portrait, ask yourself what the image suggests about the character or characters being depicted. Try to identify the techniques that helped the artist create that impression.

- What does the **position** of the characters tell you about the scene rendered in terra cotta?
- Consider the difference in **dimension** between the two pieces; one is flat, while the other is in **relief.** How does that difference affect the feel of each piece?
- The pastel drawing is a highly **abstract** figure, as opposed to a realistic one. What do you think of it? Why might an artist choose such an abstract style?

**About 460–450 B.C.:** Terra cotta plaque showing the return of Odysseus

**1931–1932:** *Ulysses,* Georges Braque. Pastel drawing.

**Narrative Art** Most of the artwork in this selection tells a story in one way or another. Consider how the artist's choices of what to include and emphasize affect your sense of the events portrayed in each work. Compare and contrast how these events are presented in visual form with how they are presented in the text.

- One of the following pieces is a decorative scene painted on a useful object, and the other is a book illustration. How does each piece's **function** affect its **style?**
- Compare the **backgrounds** on which the two scenes are painted. How does each background affect the way you view and understand the scene?
- Which scene makes more sense to you? Explain.

**About 450–440 B.C.:** Clay urn showing Odysseus slaying Penelope's suitors

**About 1915:** Illustration from *Tales of the Gods and Heroes* by Sir G. W. Cox, Innes Fripp. Hermes, messenger of Zeus, urges the nymph Calypso to release Odysseus.

## Analyze Visuals

Ask students to choose which artistic rendering best illustrates the characters from the *Odyssey. Students' answers will vary but should cite specific elements from the piece.*

---

**READING SKILL**

### ■ MAKE INFERENCES

What can you learn about ancient Greece by studying the plaque and urn from that period? *Possible answer: The plaque and urn reveal information about the clothing, hairstyles, and tools of the ancient Greeks. They also demonstrate the high level of skill in different art forms.*

---

**READING STRATEGY**

### ■ SET A PURPOSE FOR READING

Ask students how "Homer's World" helped them accomplish their purpose of getting ready to read the *Odyssey. Possible answer: Students may say that "Homer's World" provided historical and geographical background, that it gave them an overview of the characters, that it provided images that will help them visualize events and characters, and that it stimulated their interest in reading the story.*

# Focus and Motivate

⌜······⌝
## COMMON CORE FOCUS

**RL 4** Determine the figurative meanings of words and phrases as they are used in a text; analyze the cumulative impact of specific word choices on meaning and tone. **RL 5** Analyze how an author's choices concerning how to structure a text create such effects as mystery, tension, or surprise. **RL 6** Analyze a particular point of view or cultural experience reflected in a work of world literature. **RL 10** Read and comprehend stories and poems.

# Teach

## Part 1: Characteristics of the Epic

**Epic Hero and Plot** Explain that an epic is more than a good adventure story; an epic has an outcome that affects an entire nation or even the world. Its scale is vast, covering many countries or worlds. The hero may have super-human abilities but still has human flaws. Such flaws make the hero more appealing than a perfect character, because the audience can identify with him.

- Brainstorm a list of stories from literature or film that might fit this description.

- Draw a web on the board and test each example against the qualities of an epic:

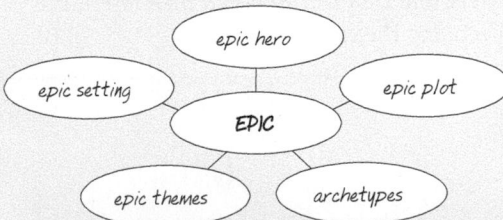

**Epic Archetypes and Themes** Ask students why they enjoy films, television shows, and stories about heroes who overcome great odds. Point out that people enjoyed such stories long before films, televisions, or even novels existed.

- Identify additional archetypes, such as the warrior princess or the traitorous friend.

- Discuss how archetypes, which are quickly recognizable, yield stories with wide appeal.

- Point out that themes of universal concern also generate stories with wide appeal.

---

## UNIT 11

### Text Analysis Workshop

⌜·····⌝
**COMMON CORE**

Included in this workshop:
**RL 4** Determine the figurative meanings of words and phrases as they are used in a text; analyze the cumulative impact of specific word choices on meaning and tone. **RL 5** Analyze how an author's choices concerning how to structure a text create such effects as mystery, tension, or surprise. **RL 6** Analyze a particular point of view or cultural experience reflected in a work of world literature. **RL 10** Read and comprehend stories and poems.

## The Epic

*Essential Course of Study*

Extraordinary heroes and hideous monsters. Brutal battles and dangerous voyages. Spectacular triumphs and crushing defeats. The epic tradition, still very much alive in today's movies and novels, began thousands of years ago with the orally told epic poem. In ancient Greece, listeners crowded around poet-storytellers to hear about the daring exploits of a hero named Odysseus. With its storm-tossed seas, powerful evildoers, and narrow escapes, it's no wonder that Homer's *Odyssey* remains one of the most famous epics in Western literature. It captivates us because it is a compelling narrative and a window into a time and place different from our own.

### Part 1: Characteristics of the Epic

In literature, an **epic** is a long narrative poem. It recounts the adventures of an **epic hero,** a larger-than-life figure who undertakes great journeys and performs deeds requiring remarkable strength and cunning. As *you* journey through many episodes from the *Odyssey*, expect to encounter the following elements.

#### THE EPIC AT A GLANCE

**EPIC HERO**
- Possesses superhuman strength, craftiness, and confidence
- Is helped and harmed by interfering gods
- Embodies ideals and values that a culture considers admirable
- Emerges victorious from perilous situations

**EPIC PLOT**
Involves a long journey, full of complications, such as
- strange creatures
- large-scale events
- divine intervention
- treacherous weather

**EPIC SETTING**
- Includes fantastic or exotic lands
- Involves more than one nation

**ARCHETYPES**
All epics include **archetypes**—characters, situations, and images that are recognizable in many times and cultures:
- sea monster
- buried treasure
- epic hero
- wicked temptress
- suitors' contest
- loyal servant

**EPIC THEMES**
Reflect such universal concerns as
- courage
- a homecoming
- loyalty
- the fate of a nation
- beauty
- life and death

---

## DIFFERENTIATED INSTRUCTION

### FOR STRUGGLING READERS

**Note Taking** For students who need help with note taking, hand out the note-taking copy master before discussing the instructions in Part 1. Then have students read the first para-graph. Review the meaning of *narrative* and explain that an epic poem is a very specific kind of narrative poem; it has a number of distinguishing elements. As you discuss the elements identified in the chart, have stu-dents record notes on their copy masters.

 **RESOURCE MANAGER—Copy Master**
Note Taking p. 9

### FOR STRUGGLING READERS

**Comprehension: Point of View and Pro-nouns** Make sure students understand the pronoun referents in the model. Reread the first line of the instructional text to clarify who is speaking in the model. Then ask a volunteer to read the first line of the model aloud. Ask who is referenced with the pro-noun *I*. Repeat with other pronouns in the model: *he* (line 5), *we* (line 6), *you* (line 8), *it* (line 12), *his* (line 21), and *he* (line 23).

## MODEL: CHARACTERISTICS OF THE EPIC

Here, the Greek (Achaean) king Menelaus is speaking to his wife, Helen. He recalls the moment when he and Odysseus hid with their fellow soldiers inside a giant wooden horse, waiting to attack the Trojans. Formerly a Trojan herself, Helen stood outside the horse and called to the soldiers inside, mimicking the voices of their wives. As you read, notice the characteristics of an epic that are revealed.

### from BOOK 4: *The Red-Haired King and His Lady*

"In my life I have met, in many countries,
foresight and wit in many first rate men,
but never have I seen one like Odysseus
for steadiness and a stout heart. Here, for instance,

5   is what he did—had the cold nerve to do—
inside the hollow horse, where we were waiting,
picked men all of us, for the Trojan slaughter,
when all of a sudden, you came by—I dare say
drawn by some superhuman

10  power that planned an exploit for the Trojans;
and Deiphobus, that handsome man, came with you.
Three times you walked around it, patting it everywhere,
and called by name the flower of our fighters,
making your voice sound like their wives, calling.

15  Diomedes and I crouched in the center
along with Odysseus; we could hear you plainly;
and listening, we two were swept
by waves of longing—to reply, or go.
Odysseus fought us down, despite our craving,

20  and all the Achaeans kept their lips shut tight,
all but Anticlus. Desire moved his throat
to hail you, but Odysseus' great hands clamped
over his jaws, and held. So he saved us all,
till Pallas Athena led you away at last."

### Close Read

1. King Menelaus mentions several heroic traits that Odysseus exhibited while carrying out his plan to defeat the Trojans. One trait has been boxed. Identify two more.

2. What archetype does Helen represent? Explain your answer.

3. Reread lines 8–10 and 23–24. Explain how the gods interfered in the episode that Menelaus is describing.

---

## MODEL: CHARACTERISTICS OF THE EPIC
### Close Read

1. **Possible answers:** *Other heroic traits mentioned by Menelaus in his description of Odysseus include "foresight and wit" (line 2), "steadiness and a stout heart" (line 4), and the strength to fight down everyone, including Anticlus (lines 19–24).*

   **IF STUDENTS NEED HELP . . .** Explain that a hero's traits are shown in many different ways: through actions, words, and other people's descriptions. Ask what specific qualities Menelaus mentions in lines 2 and 4. Point out too that in line 23 Menelaus credits Odysseus with saving them all.

2. **Possible answer:** *Helen represents the beautiful temptress whom no man— except Odysseus—can resist. This is evident when she walks around the horse, mimics their wives' voices, and creates "waves of longing" (lines 12–18).*

3. **Possible answer:** *The gods interfered at two points. First, some god or goddess on the side of the Trojans seemed to have influence over Helen's behavior, as evidenced by the words "drawn by some superhuman power that planned an exploit for the Trojans" (lines 9–10). Then later, the goddess Athena led Helen away at last from the men who were hiding (lines 23–24).*

---

## FOR ADVANCED LEARNERS/PRE–AP

**Evaluate Genre** Explain that historically, epics were presented orally. Have students work in small groups to identify features that make this passage especially suitable for oral presentation, such as the way descriptions lend themselves to visualization and the rhythm and sounds of the words. Afterward, have students take turns identifying and giving examples of features that enhance oral presentations.

### Online Remediation

**THINK** central

Are your students struggling with text analysis skills? Consider assigning them one or more **Level Up Online Tutorials** as remediation before beginning this unit. Log in to **thinkcentral.com** to view a list of the skills addressed by **Level Up.**

## Part 2: The Language of Homer

**Translations** Tell students that all the model passages are from the 1961 Robert Fitzgerald translation.

**Poetic Elements** Explain that *epithet* has another meaning: it can mean "an abusive or nasty phrase." In addition, because students may confuse *allusion* with *illusion*, write both words on the board and clarify the difference.

Point out that authors use similes, epithets, and allusions as different means for expressing ideas indirectly. For example, a writer might compare a robe to a butterfly's wings or to the skin of a poisonous snake. Discuss how each comparison would affect listeners.

Ask students to make up epithets that they would like used to describe themselves, such as "Kim, builder of friendships" or "Duane, singer of songs." Encourage them to be playful but accurate. Ask how epithets might help others form opinions about each student.

To illustrate what an allusion might add, ask students what allusion they would use to refer to the *Odyssey*. Would they call it the *Star Wars* of its day, for example, or something else? Ask how the choice of allusion might affect someone's views of the *Odyssey*.

## Part 2: The Language of Homer

Because the language of Homer was ancient Greek, what you will read is an English translation. The *Odyssey* has been translated many times, and each translator has interpreted it differently. Read these two versions of the opening of Book 2. The first is written in verse and has a more formal **tone** and **diction**—closer to the original—while the second is written in prose and is less formal.

| TRANSLATION 1 | TRANSLATION 2 |
|---|---|
| When primal Dawn spread on the eastern sky her fingers of pink light, Odysseus' true son stood up, drew on his tunic and his mantle, slung on a sword-belt and a new-edged sword, tied his smooth feet into good rawhide sandals, and left his room, a god's brilliance upon him.<br><br>—translated by Robert Fitzgerald (1961) | Dawn came, showing her rosy fingers through the early mists, and Telemachus leapt out of bed. He dressed himself, slung a sharp sword over his shoulder, strapt a stout pair of boots on his lissom feet, and came forth from his chamber like a young god.<br><br>—translated by W. H. D. Rouse (1937) |

The Greeks who first experienced the *Odyssey* did not read a written version; they heard it as a live performance. Singing or reciting, a poet kept the audience enthralled with **epic similes, epithets,** and **allusions.**

- A **simile** is a comparison between two unlike things, using the word *like* or *as*. Homer often develops a simile at great length, so that it goes on for several lines. This is known as an **epic simile.** In this passage from Book 20, an angry Odysseus is compared to a sausage being roasted over a fire.

> His rage
> held hard in leash, submitted to his mind,
> while he himself rocked, rolling from side to side,
> as a cook turns a sausage, big with blood
> and fat, at a scorching blaze, without a pause,
> to broil it quick: so he rolled left and right, . . .

- An **epithet** is a brief descriptive phrase used to characterize a particular person or thing. When a poet needed to fill out a line, he'd add an epithet with the right meter and number of syllables. Odysseus is known by various epithets, including "son of Laertes" and "raider of cities."

- An **allusion** is a reference to a famous person, place, or event. To help his audience picture what he described, a poet might have made an allusion to something they already knew. For instance, when Odysseus' son first sees the palace of Menelaus, he says, "This is the way the court of Zeus must be." Every Greek would have understood this allusion to the ruler of the gods.

## DIFFERENTIATED INSTRUCTION

### FOR STRUGGLING READERS

**Note Taking** For students who need help with note taking, hand out the note-taking copy master before beginning the instruction on this page. Point out that the copy master is to be used for Parts 2 and 3 of this workshop. As you discuss the terms and ideas in both parts, have students record notes on their copy masters.

**R** RESOURCE MANAGER—Copy Master
Note Taking p. 10

### FOR ENGLISH LANGUAGE LEARNERS

**Culture: Allusions** Students from other cultures may have particular difficulty recognizing certain allusions. As they read, have students jot down the names of people, places, or events with which they are unfamiliar. Afterward, they can meet in small groups to compare their notes and to learn more about the names they recorded.

## MODEL 1: EPIC SIMILE

In this excerpt, Odysseus is watching the performance of a bard (a poet like Homer himself). Suddenly he finds himself listening to the story of the fall of Troy and of his own part in it. Notice the epic simile that is developed over this entire passage.

### *from* BOOK 8: *The Songs of the Harper*

> And Odysseus
> let the bright molten tears run down his cheeks,
> weeping [like] the way a wife mourns for her lord
> on the lost field where he has gone down fighting
> 5  the day of wrath that came upon his children.
> At sight of the man panting and dying there,
> she slips down to enfold him, crying out;
> then feels the spears, prodding her back and shoulders,
> and goes bound into slavery and grief.
> 10  Piteous weeping wears away her cheeks:
> but no more piteous than Odysseus' tears,
> cloaked as they were, now, from the company.

**Close Read**

1. What two things are being compared in this epic simile?

2. In the boxed lines, the wife cries first for her dying husband, then for herself. Consider what this might suggest about Odysseus' feelings. What might the epic hero be crying about?

## MODEL 2: EPITHET

Here, the goddess Athena speaks to her father, Zeus, on behalf of Odysseus. Reminding Zeus of sacrifices made to him during the Trojan War, she begs him to let Odysseus return home. Athena has told Zeus that Odysseus is so homesick that he "longs to die."

### *from* BOOK 1: *A Goddess Intervenes*

> "Are you not moved by this, Lord of Olympus?
> Had you no pleasure from Odysseus' offerings
> beside the Argive ships, on Troy's wide seaboard?
> O Zeus, what do you hold against him now?"
>
> 5  To this the summoner of cloud replied:
>
> "My child, what strange remarks you let escape you.
> Could I forget that kingly man, Odysseus?
> There is no mortal half so wise; no mortal
> gave so much to the lords of open sky."

**Close Read**

1. One epithet of Zeus is boxed. Find another.

2. What epithet does Zeus use to refer to Odysseus?

---

## MODEL 1: EPIC SIMILE
### Close Read

1. *Possible answer: A weeping Odysseus is being compared to a wife who first weeps for her husband, who has died on the battlefield.*

2. *Possible answer: The comparison emphasizes Odysseus' deep love for whomever he cries for. He is probably crying for his comrades who died in the Trojan War and perhaps for his family.*

## MODEL 2: EPITHET
### Close Read

1. *Possible answer: Another epithet used to describe Zeus is "the summoner of cloud" (line 5).*

2. *Possible answer: Zeus refers to Odysseus as "that kingly man" (line 7).*

---

## FOR ENGLISH LANGUAGE LEARNERS

**Language: Punctuation** Draw attention to *Odysseus'* in line 11 of Model 1. Note that the apostrophe shows possession. Usually a singular noun takes an apostrophe plus s to show possession. However, multi-syllabic Greek names that end in s are exceptions to this rule. Have students find additional examples of an apostrophe alone signaling ownership (*Odysseus'*, Model 2, line 2; *Telemachus'*, Model, page 1199, before line 10).

# Practice and Apply

## Part 3: Reading the Epic

Use a Cluster Diagram to show students how an epic can be read in different ways. Draw a circle on the board and write *Odyssey* in the center. Add a section for narrative as you discuss how an epic can be read as narrative. Then add sections as you discuss other ways an epic can be read.

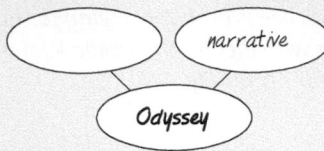

**BEST PRACTICES TOOLKIT—Transparency**
Cluster Diagram p. B18

**Reading the Epic as Narrative** Point out to students that an epic is a bit like a soap opera: a cast of characters appears in numerous episodes that address narrow plot issues yet each are part of a larger story. Ask students for examples of television shows that have one basic premise—such as a character trying to solve one basic problem—which inspires the plots of the separate episodes.

**Reading the Epic as Poetry** Remind students that in figurative language, words are not always used in their literal sense but may instead be used to symbolize ideas and to evoke emotions in listeners. Ask why imagery would be so useful in a poem that was spoken aloud to a group of people.

**Reading the Epic as a Reflection of its Time** Ask students to identify modern heroes, fictional or real-life. Then ask what these heroes show about our culture's values. Encourage students to choose heroes that reflect a variety of values, such as respect for intelligence, strength, leadership, and money.

## CHECK UNDERSTANDING

Have students summarize the characteristics of the epic and describe what poetic elements are found in the *Odyssey*.

---

## Part 3: Reading the Epic

Reading the *Odyssey* is a complex experience. On one level, the poem is an action-packed, tension-filled narrative that makes readers eagerly anticipate the hero's homecoming. On another level, it's a work of art to be appreciated and analyzed. Use the following strategies to help you make the most of your journey through the epic.

### READING THE EPIC AS NARRATIVE

- Note the changing narrators. Who is telling the story at any given point? Consider how the different narrators deepen your understanding of characters and events.
- **Visualize** the action and the settings by using details in the text.
- Track the events and conflicts and try to **predict** the outcomes.
- Use a chart like the one shown to keep track of the characters, including gods and goddesses and Odysseus' friends and foes. What does each do to either help or harm him?

### READING THE EPIC AS POETRY

- Try reading the lines aloud, as the epic was originally performed.
- Read the lines for their sense, just as you would read prose. Follow the punctuation, and remember that the end of a line does not always mean the end of a thought.
- Listen for sound devices such as **alliteration, assonance, consonance,** and **rhyme** and notice how they reinforce meaning. (Although the sound devices in English aren't the same as those in the original Greek, they do reflect the translator's attempt to capture the spirit and technique of Homer's verse.)
- Consider how the **imagery** and **figurative language**—especially the **epic similes**—help you understand characters and events.

### READING THE EPIC AS A REFLECTION OF ITS TIME

- Pay attention to the **character traits** of Odysseus, the epic hero, by looking closely at how he behaves and how he is described. What do these traits tell you about the values of the time?
- Think about what you've learned of Greek history and culture. What events may have influenced Homer?
- Remember that in Homer's time most Greeks believed that the gods took an active interest in human affairs and themselves behaved much like humans. How are these religious beliefs apparent in the epic?

### STRATEGIES IN ACTION

| Characters Who Help Odysseus | Characters Who Harm Odysseus |
|---|---|
| Athena (goddess)<br>• pleads with Zeus to help Odysseus escape Calypso's island | Poseidon (god)<br>• stirs up nasty weather to create problems for Odysseus |

*from* BOOK 4: *The Red-Haired King and His Lady*

but never have I seen one like Odysseus for steadiness and a stout heart. . . .

*Alliteration:* The repeated "s" sound emphasizes the strength of the epic hero.

| Odysseus' Traits | Evidence |
|---|---|
| strong, skilled, and swift | frequently referred to as "master mariner and soldier" |
| quick-witted; thinks on his feet | described as "strategist" when he responds to a difficult question posed by Calypso (Book 5) |

---

## DIFFERENTIATED INSTRUCTION

### FOR ENGLISH LANGUAGE LEARNERS

**Language: Skill Words** On the board, list the literary terms shown in italics. Then give the examples in random order and have students match them to the vocabulary.

- *alliteration:* sailing the seven seas
- *assonance:* eight were taken away
- *consonance:* the tick of a clock
- *rhyme:* better letter

- *imagery:* the sea exploded onto the rocky shore
- *figurative language:* jewels sparkled like stars in a velvety night sky
- *character trait:* bravery, intelligence, thoughtfulness, loyalty

## MODEL: READING THE EPIC

Odysseus has been gone from his homeland for years, and all except his family believe him dead. Young men make themselves at home in Odysseus' castle while vying to marry his "widow," Penelope. Odysseus' son, Telemachus, calls an assembly to discuss the situation. The following excerpt is an exchange between Telemachus and one of Penelope's suitors.

### *from* BOOK 2: *A Hero's Son Awakens*

*Telemachus addresses the crowd, complaining of the suitors' behavior.*

"No; these men spend their days around our house
killing our beeves and sheep and fatted goats,
carousing, soaking up our good dark wine,
not caring what they do. They squander everything.
5    We have no strong Odysseus to defend us,
and as to putting up a fight ourselves—
we'd only show our incompetence in arms.
Expel them, yes, if I only had the power;
the whole thing's out of hand, insufferable."

*A suitor responds to Telemachus' heated accusation.*

10    "You want to shame us, and humiliate us,
but you should know the suitors are not to blame—
it is your own dear, incomparably cunning mother.
For three years now—and it will soon be four—
she has been breaking the hearts of the Achaeans,
15    holding out hope to all, and sending promises
to each man privately—but thinking otherwise.

Here is an instance of her trickery:
she had her great loom standing in the hall
and the fine warp of some vast fabric on it;
20    we were attending her, and she said to us:
'Young men, my suitors, now my lord is dead,
let me finish my weaving before I marry,
or else my thread will have been spun in vain.
It is a shroud I weave for Lord Laertes,
25    when cold death comes to lay him on his bier.
The country wives would hold me in dishonor
if he, with all his fortune, lay unshrouded.'
We have men's hearts; she touched them; we agreed.
So every day she wove on the great loom—
30    but every night by torchlight she unwove it;
and so for three years she deceived the Achaeans."

**Close Read**

1. Try to visualize the suitors at Odysseus' home by using details in lines 1–9. Describe the image that the lines conjured up in your mind.

2. Note the two speakers. What does Telemachus accuse the suitors of doing? How does one suitor defend his and the other suitors' actions?

3. Identify two examples of sound devices in the boxed text.

4. What do the accusations made in this excerpt tell you about Greek values?

5. How would you describe Penelope? Cite details that help you to understand the traits Greeks prized in a woman.

## MODEL: READING THE EPIC
### Close Read

1. ***Possible answer:*** *Although answers will vary, students should describe the suitors as lazy and wasteful. According to Telemachus, they lie around the house all day, eating, drinking, and "not caring what they do."*

2. ***Possible answer:*** *Telemachus accuses the suitors of being wasteful and taking advantage of the situation. The suitor defends his and others' actions by pointing out that the length of their stay is Penelope's fault. The suitor claims that she is leading them on, saying that she will marry again once she has finished weaving a shroud for Laertes. However, every night she unweaves what she wove during the day.*

3. ***Possible answer:*** *Two examples of sound devices include the assonance (repetition of the long o sound) and alliteration (repetition of the h sound) in "holding" and "hope," and the consonance (repetition of the s sound) in "sending promises."*

4. ***Possible answer:*** *The accusations suggest that Greeks condemned laziness or living off of others. The suitor's description of Penelope's actions suggests that deception was not viewed favorably but that loyalty to a spouse was an admired value.*

5. ***Possible answer:*** *Penelope is an honorable, loyal wife. She refuses to let her husband's father lie "unshrouded," and she does not want other women to hold her in dishonor. However, Penelope is also shrewd and clever. She does not want to anger her suitors, so she stalls for time by destroying her weaving, which means that the shroud is never completed.*

**IF STUDENTS NEED HELP . . .** Briefly summarize each section before students read it.

## DIFFERENTIATED INSTRUCTION

### FOR STRUGGLING READERS

**Comprehension: Characters** Draw attention to the title of the model. Clarify that Telemachus is the son of Odysseus. Then draw attention to the italic notes in the model, asking volunteers to read them aloud. Before students read independently, have them describe the situation and identify who is speaking which lines.

### FOR ENGLISH LANGUAGE LEARNERS

**Vocabulary: Multiple-Meaning Words** Identify these multiple-meaning words: *addresses* (first italic line), *arms* (line 7), and *touched* (line 28). In groups of three, have students look up the meanings of the words. Then have them create a sentence for at least two meanings of each word. One sentence should use the meaning that is used in the model.

# Practice and Apply

## Part 4: Analyze the Text

**Close Read**

1. *Possible answer: Through his actions, Odysseus shows extreme cunning and a lack of trust. He creates an elaborate ruse simply to test someone's loyalty. The ruse also shows that Odysseus is creative.*

2. *Possible answer: The imagery in the boxed lines serves to emphasize how frigid and wintry the weather is. The use of "black" and "white," coupled with the use of the words "wintry," "sleet," "frost," and "ice," all create a feeling of cold desolation.*

3. *Possible answer: The "soldier," who is actually Odysseus pretending, uses the epithets "Son of Laertes and the gods of old" (line 28) and "master mariner and soldier" (line 29) to address Odysseus.*

**IF STUDENTS NEED HELP...** Remind them that Odysseus is pretending to be an anonymous soldier, so he has invented an entirely new person. As a result, there are actually two Odysseuses in this model—the new person and the Odysseus who is described by that person.

## Part 4: Analyze the Text

Here, Odysseus returns to his homeland at last, disguised as an old beggar. The first person he approaches is Eumaeus, his head swineherd. Welcoming the unknown beggar in the name of his missing lord, Eumaeus gives him a hot meal, a drink, and a place to sleep. To test the faithful swineherd and to try to keep warm in the frigid cold, the disguised Odysseus devises a story. Through the story, he hopes to encourage Eumaeus to give him—a supposed stranger—the cloak off his back. As you read this excerpt, use what you've learned to make sense of the episode.

### *from* BOOK 14: *Hospitality in the Forest*

"Listen," he said,

"Eumaeus, and you others, here's a wishful
tale that I shall tell. The wine's behind it,
vaporing wine, that makes a serious man
5    break down and sing, kick up his heels and clown,
or tell some story that were best untold.
But now I'm launched, I can't stop now.

                                    Would god I felt

the hot blood in me that I had at Troy!
Laying an ambush near the walls one time,
10    Odysseus and Menelaus were commanders
and I ranked third. I went at their request.
We worked in toward the bluffs and battlements
and, circling the town, got into canebrakes,
thick and high, a marsh where we took cover,
15    hunched under arms.

                The northwind dropped, and night
came black and wintry. A fine sleet descending
whitened the cane like hoarfrost, and clear ice
grew dense upon our shields. The other men,
all wrapt in blanket cloaks as well as tunics,
20    rested well, in shields up to their shoulders,
but I had left my cloak with friends in camp,
foolhardy as I was. No chance of freezing hard,
I thought, so I wore kilts and a shield only.
But in the small hours of the third watch, when stars
25    that rise at evening go down to their setting,
I nudged Odysseus, who lay close beside me;
he was alert then, listening, and I said:

'Son of Laertes and the gods of old,
Odysseus, master mariner and soldier,
30    I cannot hold on long among the living.

**Close Read**

1. Think about why Odysseus is telling Eumaeus this elaborate story. Through his plan of action, what traits does he display? Explain.

2. Reread the boxed text and visualize the imagery used to describe the setting. What does the imagery serve to emphasize?

3. What epithets does the soldier use to address Odysseus in the story?

---

## DIFFERENTIATED INSTRUCTION

### FOR STRUGGLING READERS

**Analysis Support: Details** Help students recognize the various speakers in this model. Point out that in the first eight lines, Odysseus sets his trap and explains why he is telling this story. Then, in lines 9–11, he identifies himself as third in command. It is this character who tells the rest of the story. Later, in line 51, the speaker switches to Eumaeus. Have students identify the lines that he says.

Afterward, discuss with students whether they think such a charade would actually work. Encourage them to give reasons for their responses.

The cold is making a corpse of me. Some god
inveigled me to come without a cloak.
No help for it now; too late.'

                                    Next thing I knew

he had a scheme all ready in his mind—
35  and what a man he was for schemes and battles!
Speaking under his breath to me, he murmured:

'Quiet; none of the rest should hear you.'

                                    Then,

propping his head on his forearm, he said:

'Listen, lads, I had an ominous dream,
40  the point being how far forward from our ships
and lines we've come. Someone should volunteer
to tell the corps commander, Agamemnon;
he may reinforce us from the base.'

                                    At this,

Thoas jumped up, the young son of Andraemon,
45  put down his crimson cloak and headed off,
running shoreward.
                        Wrapped in that man's cloak
how gratefully I lay in the bitter dark
until the dawn came stitched in gold! I wish
I had that sap and fiber in me now!"

50  Then—O my swineherd!—you replied, Eumaeus:

"That was a fine story, and well told,
not a word out of place, not a pointless word.
No, you'll not sleep cold for lack of cover,
or any other comfort one should give
55  to a needy guest. However, in the morning,
you must go flapping in the same old clothes.
Shirts and cloaks are few here; every man
has one change only. When our prince arrives,
the son of Odysseus, he will make you gifts—
60  cloak, tunic, everything—and grant you passage
wherever you care to go."

                                    On this he rose

and placed the bed of balsam near the fire,
strewing sheepskins on top, and skins of goats.
Odysseus lay down. His host threw over him
65  a heavy blanket cloak, his own reserve
against the winter wind when it came wild.

### Close Read

4. What quality does Odysseus attribute to himself in telling this tale? Cite specific details to support your answer.

5. Reread lines 31–33 and 39–46. What do you learn about how the ancient Greeks perceived their gods and ominous dreams?

6. Think about where else you have encountered a character like Eumaeus. What archetype does he represent? Explain.

---

**FOR ADVANCED LEARNERS/PRE–AP**

**Evaluate** On the basis of the models they have read, have students discuss whether the *Odyssey* would make a good adventure film. Have them first develop criteria for a good adventure film and then rate the *Odyssey* based on those criteria. Remind students that films sometimes make changes in language, setting, and plot details, while trying to maintain the overall sense of the original.

---

### Close Read

4. **Possible answer:** *In lines 33–35, the "soldier" describes Odysseus as clever and quick-thinking in difficult situations. He says that Odysseus "had a scheme all ready in his mind."*

5. **Possible answer:** *Lines 31–33 suggest that Greeks felt the gods were responsible for some human actions. The soldier says that some god tricked him into coming without his cloak. In lines 39–46, Odysseus describes an "ominous dream" about the course they are on. He urges a volunteer to warn Agamemnon. That Thoas volunteered so eagerly suggests that he believed that such dreams were real warnings that should be heeded.*

6. **Possible answer:** *Eumaeus represents the archetype of the faithful servant or sidekick. Students may recall television shows, films, or novels in which they have encountered such an archetype.*

## Assess and Reteach

### Assess

Have students identify epic elements in Book 14 of the *Odyssey*.

### Reteach

For students who are unable to apply the workshop skills to the excerpts from the *Odyssey*, select from these reteaching options:

1. Display one blank note-taking copy master for this lesson.

   • Ask students which parts were hard to complete. Focus instruction on only those parts.

   • Have students work in teams to take turns identifying details for sections on the copy masters. Tell one group to suggest details. Then have another group either confirm the choice or offer an alternative.

   • Follow a similar procedure with the second copy master.

2. Review with students the main elements of an epic poem, including the language used by Homer. Help students identify these elements in the models.

# Focus and Motivate

## SUMMARY

**Books 1–12** After the Greek victory over Troy, Odysseus sails for home with his warriors. They wander for many years. All are killed except Odysseus, who is held captive by the goddess Calypso. Then he sails to the island of King Alcinous, whom he tells of his adventures.

## What is a **HERO?**

Ask students to suggest situations in which someone may prove to be a hero. Do those situations require strength, courage, or other qualities? Continue the exchange by having students complete the *DISCUSS* activity.

---

## Selection Resources

---

**Essential Course of Study ECOS**

## The Wanderings of Odysseus
### *from the* Odyssey

Epic Poem by Homer
Translated by Robert Fitzgerald

 Video link at thinkcentral.com

**VIDEO TRAILER** THINK central KEYWORD: HML9-1202

# What is a **HERO?**

When you hear the word *hero*, who comes to mind? Do you think of someone with unusual physical strength? great courage? a rare talent? In Homer's *Odyssey*, you'll meet one of the classic heroes of Western literature—Odysseus, a man with many heroic traits as well as human faults.

**DISCUSS** Work with a small group to make a list of people—male and female—who are generally considered heroes. Discuss the heroic qualities of each person. Which qualities seem essential to every hero?

1202

---

## TEXT ANALYSIS: EPIC HERO

Common to myths, the **epic hero** is a larger-than-life character, traditionally a man, who pursues long and dangerous adventures. Alternately aided and blocked by the gods, he carries the fate of his people on his shoulders. The epic hero is an **archetypal** character—one found in works across time and cultures. Odysseus, one of the most famous heroes in Western culture, has shaped our ideas about the traits that a hero should have.

- extraordinary strength and courage
- cleverness and deceit, also known as guile
- extreme confidence and a tendency to dismiss warnings

Every epic hero embodies the values of his culture. As you read the *Odyssey,* consider how Odysseus faces various conflicts. What does this tell you about his character? What do his character traits tell you about what the ancient Greeks found admirable?

## READING STRATEGY: READING AN EPIC POEM

The strategies for reading an epic are very similar to those for reading any narrative poem.

- Keep track of the events.
- Visualize the **imagery.**
- Notice how **figurative language,** including **epic similes,** makes the story vivid and interesting.
- Read difficult passages more than once. Use the side notes for help in comprehension.
- Read the poem aloud, as it was originally conveyed.

## ▲ VOCABULARY IN CONTEXT

Place each of the following words in the appropriate column.

| WORD LIST | | | |
|---|---|---|---|
| | abominably | assuage | meditation |
| | adversary | beguiling | ponderous |
| | appalled | foreboding | profusion |
| | ardor | harried | travail |

| Know Well | Think I Know | Don't Know |
|---|---|---|
| | | |

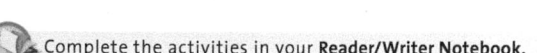 Complete the activities in your **Reader/Writer Notebook.**

---

## Overview

**Book 1: A Goddess Intervenes**
The poet introduces Odysseus, a successful warrior who, after conquering the city of Troy, has wandered the seas for many years. Now he wants only to return safely to his home and family.

**Book 5: Calypso, the Sweet Nymph**
Odysseus has been held captive for many years by the goddess Calypso on her island. Zeus sends the god Hermes to order her to release Odysseus; she offers her advice and helps him build a raft on which he can sail to Scheria, his next destination.

**Book 9: New Coasts and Poseidon's Son**
Odysseus has met King Alcinous and begins telling him of his adventures since leaving Troy. He relates the tale of the Lotus Eaters and his encounter with the brutal Cyclops, a son of the sea-god Poseidon. Odysseus continues his tales in Books 10–12.

**Book 10: Circe, the Grace of the Witch**
Eventually, Odysseus and his men arrive at the island home of Circe, a goddess and enchantress. She detains the men for a year, allowing them to go home only if they will visit the land of the dead and hear a prophecy from the ghost of Tiresias.

**Book 11: The Land of the Dead**
Odysseus and his crew travel to the underworld, where Tiresias warns Odysseus against stealing the cattle of Helios, god of the sun. According to the prophecy, if Odysseus raids the cattle, he will lose his ship and crew and return home only after many years alone at sea.

**Book 12: The Sirens; Scylla and Charybdis**
Odysseus and his men return to Circe's island, where she advises him on how to get past the bewitching Sirens and the horrible sea monsters Scylla and Charybdis. He successfully evades the Sirens but does not escape the monsters without losing some of his men.

---

## Teach

### ● Model the Skill: EPIC HERO

Direct students to the *Overview.* Have a volunteer read the summary of Book 1. Ask students what traits Odysseus shows by his resolve to return home. Point out that his resolve might indicate toughness, steadfastness, determination.

**GUIDED PRACTICE** Continue this process with the other book summaries in the overview.

### ■ Model the Skill: READING AN EPIC POEM

Have students make a timeline of each book to track events and monitor their comprehension. To illustrate how to do so, draw a timeline on the board showing the major events from Books 1–12 as summarized in the overview.

**GUIDED PRACTICE** Ask students to use the overview to identify "obstacles" and "helpers" of Odysseus.

**R** RESOURCE MANAGER—Copy Master Reading an Epic Poem p. 25 (for student use while reading the selection)

---

## ▲ VOCABULARY IN CONTEXT

**DIAGNOSE WORD KNOWLEDGE** Have all students complete Vocabulary in Context. Check their words against the following:

**abominably** (ə-bŏm′ə-nə-blē) *adv.* in a hateful way; horribly

**adversary** (ăd′vər-sĕr′ē) *n.* an opponent; enemy

**appalled** (ə-pôld′) *adj.* filled with dismay; horrified **appall** *v.*

**ardor** (är′dər) *n.* passion

**assuage** (ə-swāj′) *v.* to calm or pacify

**beguiling** (bĭ-gī′lĭng) *adj.* charming; pleasing **beguile** *v.*

**foreboding** (fôr-bō′dĭng) *n.* a sense of approaching evil

**harried** (hăr′ēd) *adj.* tormented; harassed **harry** *v.*

**meditation** (mĕd′ĭ-tā′shən) *n.* the act of being in serious, reflective thought

**ponderous** (pŏn′dər-əs) *adj.* heavy in a clumsy way; bulky

**profusion** (prə-fyōō′zhən) *n.* abundance

**travail** (trə-vāl′) *n.* painful effort

**R** RESOURCE MANAGER—Copy Master Vocabulary Study p. 27

# Practice and Apply

## READ WITH A PURPOSE

*Help students set a purpose for reading. Have them keep a list of character traits of an epic hero as they read the story of Odysseus.*

## Get Into the Book
### SUMMARY

Book 1 introduces Odysseus, gives a brief overview of his epic struggle to return home, and tells the reader what has been happening at home during Odysseus' long absence.

**TEXT ANALYSIS** · **COMMON CORE** · **RL 6**

###  Model the Skill: EPIC HERO

Draw a Character Traits and Textual Evidence chart on the board. Point out that Odysseus is described as "skilled in all ways of contending" (line 2). As you write the phrase in the chart, explain that it means Odysseus is skilled, or talented. Have students continue to find and interpret phrases that describe the character of Odysseus. Write each phrase and explanation in the chart.

**Possible answer:** *Odysseus is shown to have toughness, aggressiveness, bravery, talent, and determination. He is a survivor.*

 **BEST PRACTICES TOOLKIT—** Transparency Character Traits and Textual Evidence p. D6

**VOCABULARY** · **COMMON CORE** · **L 4**

### OWN THE WORD

**harried:** Tell students that common synonyms for *harried* include "attacked," "tormented," and "harassed." Antonyms include "comforted," "consoled," and "soothed."

---

# BOOK 1:
## *A Goddess Intervenes*

Sing in me, Muse, and through me tell the story
of that man skilled in all ways of contending,
the wanderer, **harried** for years on end,
after he plundered the stronghold
5 on the proud height of Troy.
                                        He saw the townlands
and learned the minds of many distant men,
and weathered many bitter nights and days
in his deep heart at sea, while he fought only
to save his life, to bring his shipmates home.
10 But not by will nor valor could he save them,
for their own recklessness destroyed them all—
children and fools, they killed and feasted on
the cattle of Lord Helios, the Sun,
and he who moves all day through heaven
15 took from their eyes the dawn of their return. ⓐ

Of these adventures, Muse, daughter of Zeus,
tell us in our time, lift the great song again. . . .

*The story of Odysseus begins with the goddess Athena's appealing to Zeus to help Odysseus, who has been wandering for ten years on the seas, to find his way home to his family on Ithaca. While Odysseus has been gone, his son, Telemachus, has grown to manhood and his wife, Penelope, has been besieged by suitors wishing to marry her and gain Odysseus' wealth. The suitors have taken up residence in her home and are constantly feasting on the family's cattle, sheep, and goats. They dishonor Odysseus and his family. Taking Athena's advice, Telemachus travels to Pylos for word of his father. Meanwhile, on Ithaca, the evil suitors plot to kill Telemachus when he returns.*

**1 Muse:** a daughter of Zeus, credited with divine inspiration.

**harried** (hăr′ēd) *adj.* tormented; harassed **harry** *v.*

**11–13 their own recklessness . . . the Sun:** a reference to an event occurring later in the poem—an event that causes the death of Odysseus' entire crew.

ⓐ **EPIC HERO**
This invocation (lines 1–15) introduces us to Odysseus, "that man skilled in all ways of contending." What **traits** is he shown to have?

### Analyze Visuals ▶

This 1930s print, *The Ship of Odysseus,* is part of an *Odyssey* series by Francois-Louis Schmied. What qualities of this ship has Schmied emphasized with his use of color and shape? Explain.

*The Ship of Odysseus,* Francois-Louis Schmied. From *Homer, the Odyssey,* published Paris (1930–1933). Color lithograph. Private collection, The Stapleton Collection. © 2007 Artists Rights Society (ARS), New York/ADAGP, Paris. © Bridgeman Art Library.

---

## *DIFFERENTIATED INSTRUCTION*

### FOR ENGLISH LANGUAGE LEARNERS
**Task Support** Review with students all side-column notes, especially those that paraphrase the text.

### FOR STRUGGLING READERS
**Preview** Read aloud the Book 1 synopsis at the bottom of the page. To give students a clear idea of the plot, help them list the events in a Sequence Chain.

 **BEST PRACTICES TOOLKIT—Transparency** Sequence Chain p. B21

This selection on **thinkcentral.com** includes embedded **ThinkAloud** models—students "thinking aloud" about the story to model the kinds of questions a good reader would ask about a selection.

## Analyze Visuals

*Possible answer:* *The shape of the ship implies strength and seaworthiness; the black hull suggests power; the gold implies royalty.*

**About the Art** Swiss artist Francois-Louis Schmied (1873–1941) was a prominent illustrator of printed books in the Art Deco style. Art Deco was a luxury style, often aimed at wealthy connoisseurs.

### ALTERED SPELLINGS LIST *(cont.)*:

| Original | Altered |
|---|---|
| Kyklopês | Cyclopes |
| Kyklops | Cyclops |
| Polyphêmos | Polyphemus |
| Apollo | <no change> |
| Poseidon | <no change> |
| Aiolos | Aeolus |
| Laistrygonês | Laestrygones |
| Eurylokhos | Eurylochus |
| Perséphonê | Persephone |
| Teirêsias | Tiresias |

*(List concludes on page 1206.)*

**READING STRATEGY**

### ▶ PREDICT

Remind students that making and revising predictions can help them concentrate on details and follow the sequence of events. Ask them to predict what will happen to Odysseus' shipmates. *Possible answer: They will be killed or die of other causes because of their recklessness in feasting on the cattle of Helios.*

**FOR STRUGGLING READERS**
**Minor Characters** Remind students to refer back to the list **Important Characters in the Odyssey** on page 1191 during reading. Ask them where the ancient Greeks believed Helios (line 13) pastured his cattle. (*the island of Thrinacia*)

**FOR ADVANCED LEARNERS/PRE-AP**
**The Odyssey Today** Have students find an example of 20th or 21st century literature, film, or other art that is based on the story of the *Odyssey*. Ask students to create a poster showing the parallels between the stories.

| Original | Altered |
|----------|---------|
| Elpênor | Elpenor |
| Seirênês | Sirens |
| Skylla | Scylla |
| Kharybdis | Charybdis |
| Athena | <no change> |
| Eumaios | Eumaeus |
| Argos | <no change> |
| Philoítios | Philoetius |
| Antínoös | Antinous |
| Eurymakhos | Eurymachus |
| Amphínomos | Amphinomus |
| Eurynomê | Eurynome |
| Eurykleia | Eurycleia |
| Télemos | Telemus |
| Eurymos | Eurymus |
| Antikleía | Anticlea |
| Autólykos | Autolycus |
| Parnassos | Parnassus |
| Kroníon | Cronion |
| Hephaistos | Hephaestus |
| Aktoris | Actoris |

## TEXT ANALYSIS

### ⓑ EPIC SIMILE

***Possible answer:*** *The simile compares the flight of a seagull, fishing in the waves, to Hermes' trip to Calypso. The comparison conveys Hermes' dexterity, speed, and supreme confidence as messenger of the gods.*

**IF STUDENTS NEED HELP . . .** Point out that a gull is a sea bird. Ask students to visualize a seagull flying between waves and dipping into the water to catch a fish.

# BOOK 5:
## *Calypso, the Sweet Nymph*

*For seven of the ten years Odysseus has spent wandering the Mediterranean Sea, he has been held captive by the goddess Calypso on her island. As Book 5 begins, Zeus sends the god Hermes to tell Calypso to release Odysseus. However, she is only to help him build a raft. He must sail for 20 days before landing on the island of Scheria, where he will be helped in his effort to return home.*

No words were lost on Hermes the Wayfinder,
who bent to tie his beautiful sandals on,
ambrosial, golden, that carry him over water
or over endless land in a swish of the wind,
5 and took the wand with which he charms asleep—
or when he wills, awake—the eyes of men.
So wand in hand he paced into the air,
shot from Pieria down, down to sea level,
and veered to skim the swell. A gull patrolling
10 between the wave crests of the desolate sea
will dip to catch a fish, and douse his wings;
no higher above the whitecaps Hermes flew ⓑ
until the distant island lay ahead,
then rising shoreward from the violet ocean
15 he stepped up to the cave. Divine Calypso,
the mistress of the isle, was now at home.
Upon her hearthstone a great fire blazing
scented the farthest shores with cedar smoke
and smoke of thyme, and singing high and low
20 in her sweet voice, before her loom a-weaving,
she passed her golden shuttle to and fro.
A deep wood grew outside, with summer leaves
of alder and black poplar, pungent cypress.
Ornate birds here rested their stretched wings—
25 horned owls, falcons, cormorants—long-tongued
beachcombing birds, and followers of the sea.
Around the smoothwalled cave a crooking vine
held purple clusters under ply of green;
and four springs, bubbling up near one another
30 shallow and clear, took channels here and there
through beds of violets and tender parsley.

**1–6 Hermes** (hûr′mēz): the messenger of the gods, also known for his cleverness and trickery.

**8 Pieria** (pī-îr′ē-ə): an area next to Mount Olympus, home of the gods.

ⓑ **EPIC SIMILE**
Identify the epic simile in lines 9–12. What does this comparison tell you about Hermes?

① **Targeted Passage**

**Analyze Visuals ▶**

How has the painter characterized Calypso in this 1906 portrait? Consider any relationship between her white dress and the white clouds.

**28 purple clusters:** grapes.

*Calypso* (c. 1906), George Hitchcock. Oil on canvas, 111 cm × 89 cm. © Indianapolis Museum of Art, Indianapolis, Indiana/Bridgeman Art Library.

## DIFFERENTIATED INSTRUCTION

**FOR STRUGGLING READERS**
In combination with the *Audio Anthology CD*, use one or more Targeted Passages (pp. 1206, 1213, 1218, 1223, 1230, and 1236) to ensure that students focus on key events, concepts, and skills. Targeted Passages are also good for English learners.

① **Targeted Passage [Lines 15–31]**
This passage describes the home of Calypso, who has held Odysseus captive for the past seven years.

- In what kind of dwelling does Calypso live? (line 15)
- What relationship does she appear to have with nature? (lines 17–31)
- What do you know about Calypso from this first description? (lines 15–31)

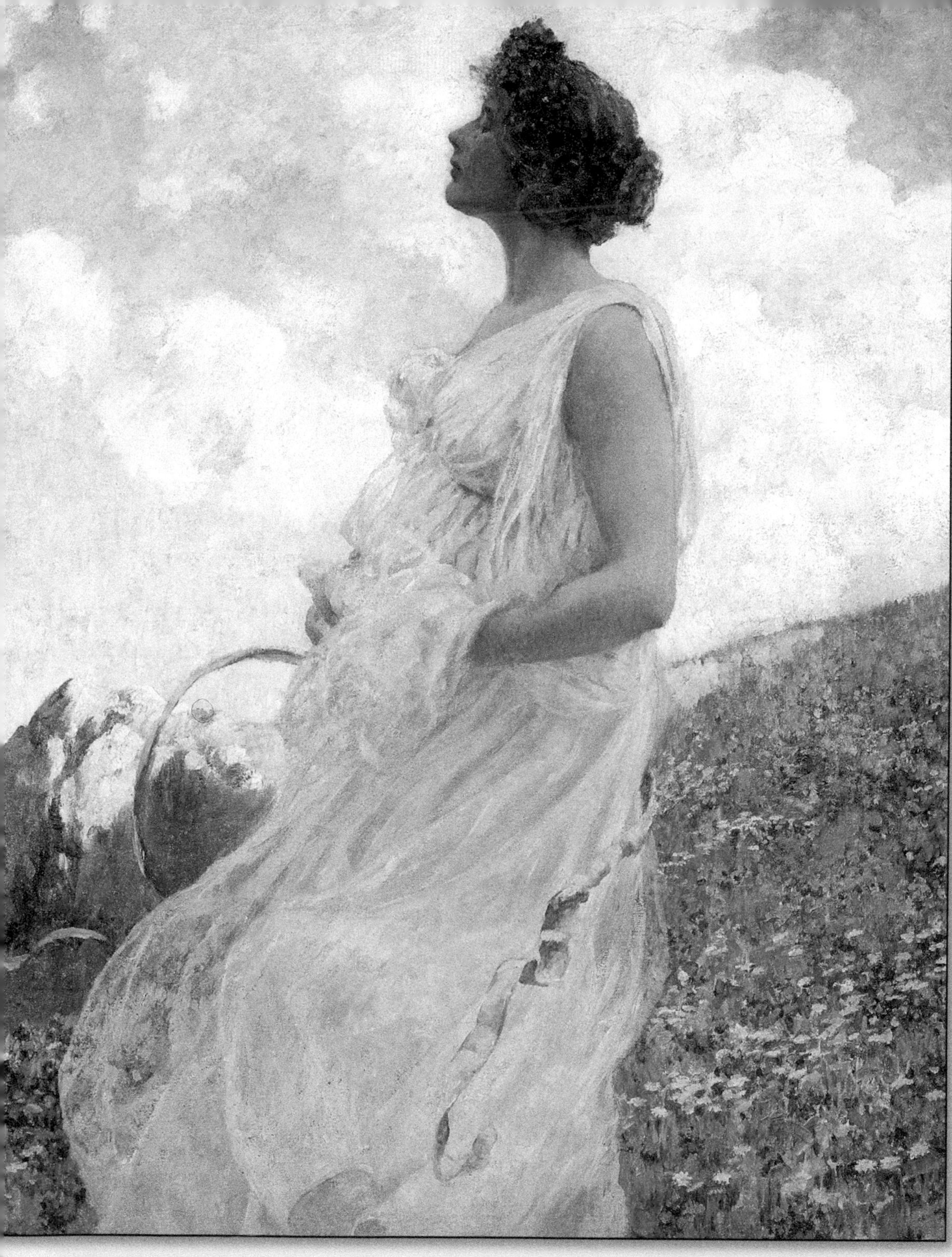

## Get Into the Book

### SUMMARY

Book 5 explains that Odysseus has been a captive on Calypso's island for seven years. Zeus orders Calypso, through his messenger Hermes, to release Odysseus. She offers Odysseus a meal, advice, and a raft before sending him on his way.

### Analyze Visuals

**Possible answer:** *The painter has characterized Calypso as a vibrant free spirit, at ease in nature. The wispy white fabric of her dress suggests a connection with the clouds—boundless, beautiful, and uncontained, like Calypso herself.*

**About the Art** Lawyer-turned-artist George Hitchcock (1850–1913) left the United States to study art in Paris. In the early 1880s, he settled in Egmond, the Netherlands. His paintings of Dutch life and scenery won him acclaim. Later, he employed a decorative, impressionist style in his paintings, as he did in this 1906 portrait of Calypso in a meadow.

READING STRATEGY

### VISUALIZE IMAGERY

Reread lines 22–31 aloud to students. Tell them to picture details of Calypso's island as you read. Afterward, challenge them to recall specific trees, birds, and plants. (*alder, poplar, cypress; owls, falcons, cormorants; grapes, violets, parsley*) How do the sensory details of the island reflect the character traits of Calypso? ***Possible answer:*** *The island is a beautiful place where even gods stare in awe. This is a reflection of Calypso's immense beauty.*

### FOR ENGLISH LANGUAGE LEARNERS

**Vocabulary Support** Point out that the poem's descriptions contain numerous contrasts. Using a T Chart, have students contrast words and phrases from lines 3–27. Provide models as well as definitions of unfamiliar words.

**BEST PRACTICES TOOLKIT—Transparency** T Chart p. A25

| Term 1 | Term 2 |
|---|---|
| over water | over endless land (lines 3–4) |
| asleep | awake (lines 5–6) |
| shoreward | the violet ocean (line 14) |
| singing high | [singing] low (line 19) |
| to | fro (line 21) |

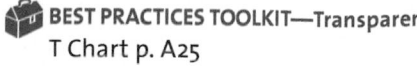

Even a god who found this place
would gaze, and feel his heart beat with delight:
so Hermes did; but when he had gazed his fill
35 he entered the wide cave. Now face to face
the magical Calypso recognized him,
as all immortal gods know one another
on sight—though seeming strangers, far from home.
But he saw nothing of the great Odysseus,
40 who sat apart, as a thousand times before,
and racked his own heart groaning, with eyes wet
scanning the bare horizon of the sea. . . .

*Calypso invites Hermes to her table for food and drink, asking why he has come.*
*Hermes explains that he has brought with an order from Zeus that Calypso must*
*not detain Odysseus any longer but send him on his way home. She reluctantly*
*obeys, agreeing to offer Odysseus her advice about how to get home.*

The strong god glittering left her as he spoke,
and now her ladyship, having given heed
45 to Zeus's mandate, went to find Odysseus
in his stone seat to seaward—tear on tear
brimming in his eyes. The sweet days of his life time
were running out in anguish over his exile,
for long ago the nymph had ceased to please.
50 Though he fought shy of her and her desire,
he lay with her each night, for she compelled him.
But when day came he sat on the rocky shore
and broke his own heart groaning, with eyes wet
scanning the bare horizon of the sea.
55 Now she stood near him in her beauty, saying:

"O forlorn man, be still.
Here you need grieve no more; you need not feel
your life consumed here; I have pondered it,
and I shall help you go. . . ."

60 Swiftly she turned and led him to her cave,
and they went in, the mortal and immortal.
He took the chair left empty now by Hermes,
where the divine Calypso placed before him
victuals and drink of men; then she sat down
65 facing Odysseus, while her serving maids
brought nectar and ambrosia to her side.
Then each one's hands went out on each one's feast
until they had their pleasure; and she said:

** EPIC HERO**
Reread lines 43–54. Which
of Odysseus' qualities is
emphasized here?

---

## TEXT ANALYSIS

COMMON CORE
RL 6

###  EPIC HERO

Read lines 43–54 aloud. Point out that
Odysseus is crying in lines 45–46, which
shows that he is very sad because he
misses home. Read each sentence and ask
students what Odysseus is feeling. Then
discuss what the poem shows about Odysseus's character.

**Possible answer:** *These lines emphasize*
*Odysseus' loyalty and determination.*
*Although he is the captive of the beautiful*
*Calypso, he still longs for home and looks*
*to the horizon.*

**IF STUDENTS NEED HELP . . .** Ask them who
would have the advantage in a contest: a
goddess with magical powers or a human?
What would it take for the human to win?

---

## DIFFERENTIATED INSTRUCTION

**FOR ENGLISH LANGUAGE LEARNERS**

**Vocabulary Support** Point out to students
examples of words and phrases that are now
used infrequently and that evoke a time long
past. Encourage them to use context to determine their meaning. Examples include:

- *had gazed his fill* (line 34), "had looked long
enough"

- *her ladyship* (line 44), "a woman of high
rank"

- *having given heed* (line 44), "having paid
attention to"

- *victuals* (line 64), "food"

- *nectar and ambrosia* (line 66), "the drink
and food of the gods"

- *pine* (line 76), "long"

- *hearthfires* (line 87), "fires in fireplaces"

"Son of Laertes, versatile Odysseus,
70  after these years with me, you still desire
    your old home? Even so, I wish you well.
    If you could see it all, before you go—
    all the adversity you face at sea—
    you would stay here, and guard this house, and be
75  immortal—though you wanted her forever,
    that bride for whom you pine each day.
    Can I be less desirable than she is?
    Less interesting? Less beautiful? Can mortals
    compare with goddesses in grace and form?"

80  To this the strategist Odysseus answered:

    "My lady goddess, here is no cause for anger.
    My quiet Penelope—how well I know—
    would seem a shade before your majesty,
    death and old age being unknown to you,
85  while she must die. Yet, it is true, each day
    I long for home, long for the sight of home. . . ." **D**

*With Calypso's help, Odysseus builds a raft and sets out to sea. For 17 days he sails
until he is in sight of Scheria. For 3 more days he is pummeled by storms and finally
swims for the island. He makes it safely ashore and crawls to rest under some bushes.*

    A man in a distant field, no hearthfires near,
    will hide a fresh brand in his bed of embers
    to keep a spark alive for the next day;
90  so in the leaves Odysseus hid himself,
    while over him Athena showered sleep
    that his distress should end, and soon, soon.
    In quiet sleep she sealed his cherished eyes.

THE WANDERINGS OF ODYSSEUS: BOOK 5  **1209**

---

**COMMON CORE L 4**

**Language Coach**

**Roots and Affixes** A word's root often suggests the word's meaning. The Latin root *versare*, from which *versatile* (line 69) is derived, means "to turn often." What do you think *versatile* means?

**D EPITHET**
Reread Odysseus' answer to Calypso in lines 81–86. Why do you think he is referred to in line 80 as "the strategist Odysseus"? Explain.

---

**TEXT ANALYSIS**

**D EPITHET**
Remind students that an epithet is a descriptive term or phrase used like a title to characterize a person. *Possible answer: He is referred to as "the strategist Odysseus" because of his shrewd, diplomatic way of handling people and situations. In lines 81–86, Odysseus cleverly flatters Calypso, allaying her jealousy and anger, while he remains loyal to Penelope. The epithet also supports Calypso's reference to him as "versatile Odysseus" (line 69).*

**TIERED DISCUSSION PROMPTS**

Direct students to lines 69–79. Use these prompts to help students understand Calypso's final attempt to convince Odysseus to stay with her:

**Connect** Are you influenced by flattery when someone is trying to persuade you to do something? *Students may acknowledge the power of flattery.*

**Analyze** In addition to flattery, what strategies does Calypso use to try to convince Odysseus to stay with her? *Possible answer: She tries to frighten him about the dangers he will face, to bribe him with immortality, and to instill guilt in him about insulting her.*

**Synthesize** What do these lines reveal about Odysseus and Calypso? *Possible answer: They reveal how hard Calypso worked to win Odysseus' heart and how Odysseus needed great willpower to resist her. The lines show that the two were well-matched competitors: willful, clever, and tough.*

---

**FOR RELUCTANT READERS**

To help students make a connection with Odysseus and the challenges he meets on his journey home from Troy, have students name favorite or familiar superheroes or action heroes, such as Spiderman, Batman, and Indiana Jones. Discuss the character traits and experiences of the heroes students name. Tell students to make a list of the various heroes' qualities. Then, as they read the selection, have students make a list of Odysseus' quali-

ties. Have students compare and contrast the qualities of their favorite superheroes with the qualities of Odysseus after they finish reading. Ask students which of their favorite superheroes have the most in common with Odysseus.

**FOR ENGLISH LANGUAGE LEARNERS**

**Language Coach**  COMMON CORE L 4

**Roots and Affixes**
*Possible answer: capable of doing many things well* Point out that the word *immortal* (line 75) comes from the Latin word *mortalis*, which means "mortal, or subject to death," and the prefix *im-*, which means "the opposite of." Ask students what *immortality* means. *Possible answer: able to live forever*

Book 9 begins with Odysseus telling of his raid on the Cicones and his loss of 72 men. Then he explains how he avoided disaster in the Land of the Lotus Eaters. Finally, he describes their exploration of the land of the Cyclopes—giant, one-eyed monsters—where they are trapped in a cave by the Cyclops Polyphemus, who eats two men at every meal. Odysseus blinds the monster and works out a clever escape from the cave. Sailing away, Odysseus calls back and taunts Polyphemus, who prays to his father, the sea god Poseidon, to take revenge on Odysseus.

---

### Ⓔ Model the Skill: EPIC HERO

Show students how to approach this question by paraphrasing Odysseus' question (lines 24–25) in this way:

*Where can a man find anything as appealing as his home and family?*

Then call on a volunteer to paraphrase his answer (lines 25–26). (*Not even a house of gold is as appealing as home and family.*)

**Possible answer:** *He values his family and home above all else.*

---

# BOOK 9:
## New Coasts and Poseidon's Son

*In Books 6–8, Odysseus is welcomed by King Alcinous, who gives a banquet in his honor. That night the king begs Odysseus to tell who he is and what has happened to him. In Books 9–12, Odysseus relates to the king his adventures.*

"I AM LAERTES' SON"

                             "What shall I
say first? What shall I keep until the end?
The gods have tried me in a thousand ways.
But first my name: let that be known to you,
5  and if I pull away from pitiless death,
friendship will bind us, though my land lies far.

I am Laertes' son, Odysseus.

                          Men hold me
formidable for guile in peace and war:
this fame has gone abroad to the sky's rim.
10  My home is on the peaked sea-mark of Ithaca
under Mount Neion's wind-blown robe of leaves,
in sight of other islands—Dulichium,
Same, wooded Zacynthus—Ithaca
being most lofty in that coastal sea,
15  and northwest, while the rest lie east and south.
A rocky isle, but good for a boy's training;
I shall not see on earth a place more dear,
though I have been detained long by Calypso,
loveliest among goddesses, who held me
20  in her smooth caves, to be her heart's delight,
as Circe of Aeaea, the enchantress,
desired me, and detained me in her hall.
But in my heart I never gave consent.
Where shall a man find sweetness to surpass
25  his own home and his parents? In far lands
he shall not, though he find a house of gold. Ⓔ

**Analyze Visuals ▶**

How would you describe the expression on Odysseus' face in this sculpture?

**7–8 hold me formidable for guile:** consider me impressive for my cunning and craftiness.

**11–13 Mount Neion's** (nē'ŏnz'); **Dulichium** (dōō-lĭk'ē-əm); **Same** (sā'mē); **Zacynthus** (zə-sĭn'thəs).

**18–26** Odysseus refers to two beautiful goddesses, Calypso and Circe, who have delayed him on their islands. (Details about Circe appear in Book 10.) At the same time, he seems nostalgic for his family and homeland, from which he has been separated for 18 years—10 of them spent fighting in Troy.

Ⓔ **EPIC HERO**
Reread lines 24–26. What does Odysseus value most highly?

Detail of *Ulysses* from the *Polyphemos* group (second century B.C.), Hagesandros, Polydoros, and Athenodoros. Sperlonga, Italy. © Araldo de Luca/Corbis.

---

## DIFFERENTIATED INSTRUCTION

### FOR STRUGGLING READERS

**Preview** Read line by line through the italicized synopsis of Books 6–12 at the top of page 1210 to give students a clear idea of the plot of this part of the *Odyssey*. Help them organize the events in a simple Sequence Chain.

**BEST PRACTICES TOOLKIT—Transparency**
Sequence Chain p. B21

| |
|---|
| King Alcinous welcomes Odysseus. |

↓

| |
|---|
| The king begs Odysseus to share his adventures. |

↓

| |
|---|
| Odysseus tells his story. |

## Analyze Visuals

*Possible answer:* *Odysseus' expression reflects his epic struggle: he appears beleaguered but brave; careworn but hopeful; defiant and unbowed.*

**About the Art** In 1957, a huge deposit of marble fragments was uncovered in a cave at Sperlonga, south of Rome on the west coast of Italy. The Roman emperor Tiberius once had a villa on this site (from 14–37 A.D.). The fragments, including this bust of Odysseus, were remains of sculpture groups that once depicted scenes from Odysseus' return home.

READING STRATEGY     COMMON CORE     RL 4, RL 10

### ● *Model the Skill:* READING AN EPIC POEM

Remind students that the *Odyssey* is meant to be read orally, as it was in ancient Greece. In Books 9–12, Odysseus relates his adventures. Point out that Odysseus would speak like a strong leader. His voice would probably be deep, clear, confident, loud, and strong. Ask students to brainstorm how Odysseus would present himself to his audience. Mention that he would enjoy being the center of attention and would be able to keep his audience's interest through his dramatic presentation of the story.

## CULTURAL CONNECTION

Outside of Greece, oral poetry has existed in many cultures. Between the 9th and 13th centuries, Icelandic poets developed a form of oral poetry called Skaldic, which praised leaders, memorialized the dead, and retold history and lineage. In Africa, the priests of the Yoruba tribe must memorize poems exactly to pass down the wisdom and history the poems contain. Invite students to share examples of festivals or contests where poets must recite their work from memory.

## FOR ADVANCED LEARNERS/PRE–AP

**Narrative** The book opens as Odysseus begins to tell his tale to King Alcinous. Write a narrative describing Odysseus' arrival at the king's court. Describe Odysseus from Alcinous' point of view. How might the king have told of Odysseus' arrival, his appearance, and what prompted him to tell his story?

## TIERED DISCUSSION PROMPTS

Direct students to lines 29–55. Use these prompts to help students understand the challenge presented by the Lotus Eaters to Odysseus and his men:

**Connect** Think of a situation that turned out to be different from what it seemed at first. How does this help you understand the reaction of Odysseus' men to the Lotus Eaters? *Responses should demonstrate an understanding that appearances can be deceptive and connect to Odysseus' experience with the Lotus Eaters.*

**Analyze** Odysseus devotes only about 25 lines to the Lotus Eaters. Why do you think he didn't extend his description of this adventure? *Possible answer: The Lotus Eaters were not aggressive, evil, or a powerful foe, and Odysseus was not called upon to use his guile or demonstrate his prowess in battle or as a leader of his men. It was just one more adventure among many and so he told the story quickly and efficiently.*

**Evaluate** Do you think Odysseus handled the situation with the Lotus Eaters effectively? Was he too lenient or too harsh? *Possible answer: Odysseus neutralized the situation quickly. He did not overreact, and nobody was hurt. He showed strong leadership.*

What of my sailing, then, from Troy?
                                What of those years
of rough adventure, weathered under Zeus? . . ."

*Odysseus explains that soon after leaving Troy, he and his crew land near Ismarus, the city of the Cicones. The Cicones are allies of the Trojans and therefore enemies of Odysseus. Odysseus and his crew raid the Cicones, robbing and killing them, until the Ciconian army kills 72 of Odysseus' men and drives the rest out to sea. Delayed by a storm for two days, Odysseus and his remaining companions then continued their journey.*

### THE LOTUS EATERS

"I might have made it safely home, that time,
30 but as I came round Malea the current
took me out to sea, and from the north
a fresh gale drove me on, past Cythera.
Nine days I drifted on the teeming sea
before dangerous high winds. Upon the tenth
35 we came to the coastline of the Lotus Eaters,
who live upon that flower. We landed there
to take on water. All ships' companies
mustered alongside for the mid-day meal.
Then I sent out two picked men and a runner
40 to learn what race of men that land sustained.
They fell in, soon enough, with Lotus Eaters,
who showed no will to do us harm, only
offering the sweet Lotus to our friends—
but those who ate this honeyed plant, the Lotus,
45 never cared to report, nor to return:
they longed to stay forever, browsing on
that native bloom, forgetful of their homeland.
I drove them, all three wailing, to the ships,
tied them down under their rowing benches,
50 and called the rest: 'All hands aboard;
come, clear the beach and no one taste
the Lotus, or you lose your hope of home.'
Filing in to their places by the rowlocks
my oarsmen dipped their long oars in the surf,
55 and we moved out again on our sea faring.

### THE CYCLOPS

In the next land we found were Cyclopes,
giants, louts, without a law to bless them.
In ignorance leaving the fruitage of the earth in mystery
to the immortal gods, they neither plow

**30 Malea** (mä-lē'ä).

**32 Cythera** (sĭ-thîr'ə).

**38 mustered:** assembled; gathered.

○ COMMON CORE L 4c

**Language Coach**

**Synonyms** Words with the same meaning are called **synonyms**. Reread line 40. Another way to say this line is "to learn what race of people lived there." What synonym could you substitute for *sustained* in line 40? Refer to a thesaurus if you need help.

**44–52 those who ate . . . hope of home.** *How do the Lotus Eaters pose a threat to Odysseus and his men?*

**56 Cyclopes** (sī-klŏ'pēz): refers to the creatures in plural; *Cyclops* is singular.

---

## DIFFERENTIATED INSTRUCTION

### FOR ENGLISH LANGUAGE LEARNERS

**Text Digest** Read aloud the two italicized text digests to ensure that students understand the intervening plot. After reading the first digest (after line 28), ask them what they can infer about Odysseus as a warrior. *Possible answer: He is aggressive, harsh, and without pity.*

**Task Support** Direct students' attention to the side note for lines 44–52. *Possible answer: The lotuses that they eat cause the sailors to forget their intentions.*

**Language Coach**   ○ COMMON CORE L 4c

**Synonyms** *Possible answer: supported;* Have students reread lines 44–48. Ask students to name synonyms for the following words: *honeyed* (line 44), *browsing* (line 46), and *wailing* (line 48).

60 nor sow by hand, nor till the ground, though grain—
wild wheat and barley—grows untended, and
wine-grapes, in clusters, ripen in heaven's rain.
Cyclopes have no muster and no meeting,
no consultation or old tribal ways,
65 but each one dwells in his own mountain cave
dealing out rough justice to wife and child,
indifferent to what the others do. . . ."

**58–67** *Why doesn't Odysseus respect the Cyclopes?*

*Across the bay from the land of the Cyclopes was a lush, deserted island. Odysseus and his crew landed on the island in a dense fog and spent days feasting on wine and wild goats and observing the mainland, where the Cyclopes lived. On the third day, Odysseus and his company of men set out to learn if the Cyclopes were friends or foes.*

"When the young Dawn with finger tips of rose **F**
came in the east, I called my men together
70 and made a speech to them:

                    'Old shipmates, friends,
the rest of you stand by; I'll make the crossing
in my own ship, with my own company,
and find out what the mainland natives are—
for they may be wild savages, and lawless,
75 or hospitable and god fearing men.'

At this I went aboard, and gave the word
to cast off by the stern. My oarsmen followed,
filing in to their benches by the rowlocks,
and all in line dipped oars in the gray sea.

**F** EPITHET
Notice the descriptive phrase used to characterize the dawn in line 68. What does this description tell you about the dawn?

**77 stern:** the rear end of a ship.

---

80 As we rowed on, and nearer to the mainland,
at one end of the bay, we saw a cavern
yawning above the water, screened with laurel,
and many rams and goats about the place
inside a sheepfold—made from slabs of stone
85 earthfast between tall trunks of pine and rugged
towering oak trees.
                    A prodigious man
slept in this cave alone, and took his flocks
to graze afield—remote from all companions,
knowing none but savage ways, a brute
90 so huge, he seemed no man at all of those
who eat good wheaten bread; but he seemed rather
a shaggy mountain reared in solitude.
We beached there, and I told the crew

**82 screened with laurel:** partially hidden by laurel trees.

**2** **Targeted Passage**

**91–92** *What does Odysseus' metaphor imply about the Cyclops?*

THE WANDERINGS OF ODYSSEUS: BOOK 9   **1213**

---

**TEXT ANALYSIS**

**F** EPITHET

***Possible answer:*** *The description tells us that it was the start of dawn ("young Dawn"); the dawn was colorful, with reddish rays brightening the horizon.*

**BACKGROUND**

**Sailing** The ancient Greeks used two kinds of ship: the galley and the sailboat, or cargo boat. The galley, which was propelled by tiers of rowers, was used primarily in battles. As shown in the image on page 1205, galleys were painted black with pitch and had no raised decks. They were propelled by a sail attached to a large mast at the center of the ship or by rowers who sat on benches (line 78) and rowed with oars fastened with leather oarlocks. Sailboats, like the one Odysseus builds on page 1209, depended solely on the wind and so were used less often.

---

**FOR STRUGGLING READERS**

**2** **Targeted Passage [Lines 80–92]**

This passage introduces the setting of Odysseus' next adventure and foreshadows his great conflict with the Cyclops.

- What did Odysseus see as they approached land? (lines 81–86)
- What words does Odysseus use to describe the Cyclops? (lines 87–92)

**FOR ENGLISH LANGUAGE LEARNERS**

**Text Digest** After reading the text digest (after line 67), ask them why Odysseus waited three days before he set out to learn about the Cyclops. ***Possible answer:*** *He bided his time to plan his moves and perhaps to rest his men.*

**Task Support** Direct students' attention to the side note for lines 58–67. ***Possible answer:*** *The Cyclopes are lawless creatures with no sense of community and no drive to cultivate the land.*

**Task Support** Direct students' attention to the side note for lines 91–92. ***Possible answer:*** *The Cyclops is as large as a mountain.*

## What is a **HERO?**

**Discuss** Odysseus has been referred to as "the Strategist." Based on lines 96–115, how does he reveal that trait in this passage? *Possible answer: He plans for potential conflict with the Cyclops: he leaves guards with his ship, and he brings along Maron's irresistible drink as a possible weapon to use against the giants.* What other qualities does Odysseus reveal in this passage? *Possible answer: He shows that he can be kind and gracious to a friend like Maron (lines 99–100).*

## BACKGROUND

**Food and Drink** The soil in many parts of ancient Greece was poor for growing most crops. However, the Greek farmers could grow wheat, barley, grapes, and olive trees. Olives and olive oil were a major part of the Greek diet. Grapes were used to make wine, which could be served at any meal. In addition, the ancient Greeks kept goats for milk and cheese, and kept chickens for meat and eggs. Many kinds of seafood were also eaten on a regular basis. Food and drink were also used as gifts, tribute to conquerors, and offerings to deities. Notice how a rare wine is given as tribute to Odysseus (lines 96–111) for sparing a family during his conquest of Ismarus, and Odysseus in turn uses the wine in his attempts to win over the Cyclops. Later, Odysseus and his men burn an offering (line 133) that was most likely food.

---

to stand by and keep watch over the ship;
95  as for myself I took my twelve best fighters
and went ahead. I had a goatskin full
of that sweet liquor that Euanthes' son,
Maron, had given me. He kept Apollo's
holy grove at Ismarus; for kindness
100  we showed him there, and showed his wife and child,
he gave me seven shining golden talents
perfectly formed, a solid silver winebowl,
and then this liquor—twelve two-handled jars
of brandy, pure and fiery. Not a slave
105  in Maron's household knew this drink; only
he, his wife and the storeroom mistress knew;
and they would put one cupful—ruby-colored,
honey-smooth—in twenty more of water,
but still the sweet scent hovered like a fume
110  over the winebowl. No man turned away
when cups of this came round.

                              A wineskin full
I brought along, and victuals in a bag,
for in my bones I knew some towering brute
would be upon us soon—all outward power,
115  a wild man, ignorant of civility.

We climbed, then, briskly to the cave. But Cyclops
had gone afield, to pasture his fat sheep,
so we looked round at everything inside:
a drying rack that sagged with cheeses, pens
120  crowded with lambs and kids, each in its class:
firstlings apart from middlings, and the 'dewdrops,'
or newborn lambkins, penned apart from both.
And vessels full of whey were brimming there—
bowls of earthenware and pails for milking.
125  My men came pressing round me, pleading:

                                  'Why not
take these cheeses, get them stowed, come back,
throw open all the pens, and make a run for it?
We'll drive the kids and lambs aboard. We say
put out again on good salt water!'

                              Ah,
130  how sound that was! Yet I refused. I wished
to see the caveman, what he had to offer—
no pretty sight, it turned out, for my friends.

**97–98 Euanthes** (yōō-ăn′thēz); **Maron** (mär′ŏn′).

**101 talents:** bars of gold or silver of a specified weight, used as money in ancient Greece.

**112 victuals** (vĭt′lz): food.

**121–122** The Cyclops has separated his lambs into three age groups.

**123 whey:** the watery part of milk, which separates from the curds, or solid part, during the making of cheese.

**129 good salt water:** the open sea.

**130–132** *Why does Odysseus refuse his men's "sound" request?*

---

## DIFFERENTIATED INSTRUCTION

### FOR ENGLISH LANGUAGE LEARNERS

**Task Support** Direct students' attention to the side note for lines 130–132. Explain that one trait of an epic hero is a tendency to dismiss warnings. *Possible answer: Odysseus' curiosity about "the caveman" caused him to refuse his men's "sound" request. Also, Odysseus may have been intrigued by the challenge of confronting this prodigious brute in a battle of brains against brawn.*

### FOR STRUGGLING READERS

**Develop Reading Fluency** Model for students an effective way to read the poem. Begin at line 87 and read through line 111. When finished, ask students what they noticed about the phrasing of the poem, pointing out that while you read you paused at commas, periods, and dashes. Then have pairs of students practice reading stanzas of the poem together.

**R** RESOURCE MANAGER—Copy Master
Reading Fluency p. 32

We lit a fire, burnt an offering,
and took some cheese to eat; then sat in silence
135 around the embers, waiting. When he came
he had a load of dry boughs on his shoulder
to stoke his fire at suppertime. He dumped it
with a great crash into that hollow cave,
and we all scattered fast to the far wall.
140 Then over the broad cavern floor he ushered
the ewes he meant to milk. He left his rams
and he-goats in the yard outside, and swung
high overhead a slab of solid rock
to close the cave. Two dozen four-wheeled wagons,
145 with heaving wagon teams, could not have stirred
the tonnage of that rock from where he wedged it
over the doorsill. Next he took his seat
and milked his bleating ewes. A practiced job
he made of it, giving each ewe her suckling;
150 thickened his milk, then, into curds and whey,
sieved out the curds to drip in withy baskets,
and poured the whey to stand in bowls
cooling until he drank it for his supper.
When all these chores were done, he poked the fire,
155 heaping on brushwood. In the glare he saw us.

'Strangers,' he said, 'who are you? And where from?
What brings you here by sea ways—a fair traffic?
Or are you wandering rogues, who cast your lives
like dice, and ravage other folk by sea?'

160 We felt a pressure on our hearts, in dread
of that deep rumble and that mighty man.
But all the same I spoke up in reply:

'We are from Troy, Achaeans, blown off course
by shifting gales on the Great South Sea;
165 homeward bound, but taking routes and ways
uncommon; so the will of Zeus would have it.
We served under Agamemnon, son of Atreus—
the whole world knows what city
he laid waste, what armies he destroyed. **G**
170 It was our luck to come here; here we stand,
beholden for your help, or any gifts
you give—as custom is to honor strangers.
We would entreat you, great Sir, have a care
for the gods' courtesy; Zeus will avenge
175 the unoffending guest.'

**133 burnt an offering:** burned a portion of the food as an offering to secure the gods' goodwill. (Such offerings were frequently performed by Greek sailors during difficult journeys.)

**151 withy baskets:** baskets made from twigs.

**157 fair traffic:** honest trading.

**G ALLUSION**
Reread lines 163–169. Agamemnon was the Greek king who led the war against the Trojans. Consider what Odysseus says about Agamemnon; what point is he making about himself by claiming this association?

**172–175** It was a sacred Greek custom to honor strangers with food and gifts. Odysseus is reminding the Cyclops that Zeus will punish anyone who mistreats a guest.

THE WANDERINGS OF ODYSSEUS: BOOK 9 **1215**

**TEXT ANALYSIS**

**G ALLUSION**

*Possible answer: By associating himself with Agamemnon, Odysseus is laying claim to the Greeks' great victory at Troy. Odysseus is also suggesting that he is a warrior to be reckoned with.*

**IF STUDENTS NEED HELP . . .** Point out to students that the Greeks considered war a noble undertaking. Men achieved honor through their deeds of valor at war. The Greeks craved honor—and the public esteem that accompanied it.

**Activity** Ask students whether they think the painting depicts the pitiless cannibal of Homer's *Odyssey*. ***Possible answer:*** *The painting shows a subdued Cyclops in a whimsical presentation; it is much different from the brutish savage of Homer's tale.*

**About the Art** Odilon Redon (1840–1916) was one of the foremost symbolist painters of his period. This painting is a detail of *The Cyclops*. The full illustration shows Polyphemus looking down on the sleeping Galatea. In Greek myth, the Cyclops falls hopelessly in love with this charming sea nymph, who mocks him.

---

###  EPIC HERO

***Possible answer:*** *Odysseus now knows with certainty that the Cyclops has no qualms about mistreating his guests or their property; he lies to protect the ship.*

---

###  EPITHET

***Possible answer:*** *The epithet of "young Dawn with fingertips of rose" is repeated in lines 211–212.*

---

#### OWN THE WORD

- **appalled:** Have students name times when they have been *appalled*. What foods would they consider *appalling* that others might consider a delicacy?
- **ponderous:** Have students reread the lines around the line with *ponderous* and have them identify context clues that can help determine the meaning of the word. ***Possible answers:*** *"could never move"; "slab"*

---

He answered this from his brute chest, unmoved:

'You are a ninny,
or else you come from the other end of nowhere,
telling me, mind the gods! We Cyclopes
care not a whistle for your thundering Zeus
180 or all the gods in bliss; we have more force by far.
I would not let you go for fear of Zeus—
you or your friends—unless I had a whim to.
Tell me, where was it, now, you left your ship—
around the point, or down the shore, I wonder?'

185 He thought he'd find out, but I saw through this,
and answered with a ready lie:

'My ship?

Poseidon Lord, who sets the earth a-tremble,
broke it up on the rocks at your land's end.
A wind from seaward served him, drove us there.
190 We are survivors, these good men and I.'

Neither reply nor pity came from him,
but in one stride he clutched at my companions
and caught two in his hands like squirming puppies
to beat their brains out, spattering the floor.
195 Then he dismembered them and made his meal,
gaping and crunching like a mountain lion—
everything: innards, flesh, and marrow bones.
We cried aloud, lifting our hands to Zeus,
powerless, looking on at this, **appalled;**
200 but Cyclops went on filling up his belly
with manflesh and great gulps of whey,
then lay down like a mast among his sheep.
My heart beat high now at the chance of action,
and drawing the sharp sword from my hip I went
205 along his flank to stab him where the midriff
holds the liver. I had touched the spot
when sudden fear stayed me: if I killed him
we perished there as well, for we could never
move his **ponderous** doorway slab aside.
210 So we were left to groan and wait for morning.

When the young Dawn with fingertips of rose
lit up the world, the Cyclops built a fire
and milked his handsome ewes, all in due order,

---

*The Cyclops* (c. 1914), Odilon Redon. Oil on canvas. Kroller-Muller Museum, Otterlo, Netherlands. © Peter Will/SuperStock.

**178–182** *What is the Cyclopes' attitude toward the gods?*

 **EPIC HERO**
Reread lines 185–190. Why does Odysseus lie to the Cyclops about his ship?

**appalled** (ə-pôld') *adj.* filled with dismay; horrified **appall** *v.*

**ponderous** (pŏn'dər-əs) *adj.* heavy in a clumsy way; bulky

**207–210** *Why doesn't Odysseus kill the Cyclops right now?*

 **EPITHET**
What **epithet** is repeated in lines 211–212? Look for more repetitions like this one.

---

## DIFFERENTIATED INSTRUCTION

### FOR ENGLISH LANGUAGE LEARNERS

**Task Support** Direct students to the question in the side note for lines 178–182. ***Possible answer:*** *The Cyclopes' attitude toward the gods is disrespectful. The Cyclops has no regard for, or fear of, the Olympians.* Point out that the Cyclops' arrogance foreshadows trouble: the gods will likely punish such disrespect.

**Task Support** Direct students to the question for lines 207–210. ***Possible answer:*** *Odysseus doesn't kill the Cyclops because only*

*Polyphemus is strong enough to move the slab that blocks the mouth of the cave.*

### FOR ADVANCED LEARNERS/PRE–AP

**Analyze Repetition** Remind students that poets often use repetition. Ask them to discuss the effect of the repetition of the dawn epithet. Then have students create an original epithet for the passage of time.

putting the sucklings to the mothers. Then,
215 his chores being all dispatched, he caught
another brace of men to make his breakfast,
and whisked away his great door slab
to let his sheep go through—but he, behind,
reset the stone as one would cap a quiver.
220 There was a din of whistling as the Cyclops
rounded his flock to higher ground, then stillness.
And now I pondered how to hurt him worst,
if but Athena granted what I prayed for.
Here are the means I thought would serve my turn:

225 a club, or staff, lay there along the fold—
an olive tree, felled green and left to season
for Cyclops' hand. And it was like a mast
a lugger of twenty oars, broad in the beam—
a deep-sea-going craft—might carry:
230 so long, so big around, it seemed. Now I
chopped out a six foot section of this pole
and set it down before my men, who scraped it;
and when they had it smooth, I hewed again
to make a stake with pointed end. I held this
235 in the fire's heart and turned it, toughening it,
then hid it, well back in the cavern, under
one of the dung piles in **profusion** there.
Now came the time to toss for it: who ventured
along with me? whose hand could bear to thrust
240 and grind that spike in Cyclops' eye, when mild
sleep had mastered him? As luck would have it,
the men I would have chosen won the toss—
four strong men, and I made five as captain.

At evening came the shepherd with his flock,
245 his woolly flock. The rams as well, this time,
entered the cave: by some sheep-herding whim—
or a god's bidding—none were left outside.
He hefted his great boulder into place
and sat him down to milk the bleating ewes
250 in proper order, put the lambs to suck,
and swiftly ran through all his evening chores.
Then he caught two more men and feasted on them.
My moment was at hand, and I went forward
holding an ivy bowl of my dark drink,
255 looking up, saying:

216 **brace:** pair.

218–219 The Cyclops reseals the cave with the massive rock as easily as an ordinary human places the cap on a container of arrows.

226 **left to season:** left to dry out and harden.

228 **lugger:** a small, wide sailing ship.

**profusion** (prə-fyōō′zhən) *n.* abundance

238–243 *What does Odysseus plan to do to the Cyclops?*

THE WANDERINGS OF ODYSSEUS: BOOK 9 **1217**

---

### Language Coach

**Word Definitions** The use of words whose sounds echo their meanings, such as *buzz* and *croak*, is called **onomatopoeia**. What word in line 249 is an example of onomatopoeia?

---

## TIERED DISCUSSION PROMPTS

Ask students to reread lines 225–247. Use these prompts to help students understand how a combination of careful planning and good luck is pushing the momentum toward Odysseus' advantage:

**Recall** What three things happened that showed luck was on Odysseus' side? *Possible answer: First: Odysseus found the olive tree in the cave. Second: The four men Odysseus would have chosen to help him all won the toss. Third: The Cyclops brought all the rams into the cave, not just the youngest.*

**Analyze** How does Odysseus take advantage of his good luck? What do his reactions reflect about his character? *Possible answer: Odysseus quickly formulates a plan based on the tools he has available, namely, the olive tree and the rams. His actions reflect his intelligence.*

**Evaluate** Which do you think will be most important to the outcome of Odysseus' conflict with the Cyclops: careful planning or good luck? *Possible answer: Both good luck and good planning will contribute to the outcome.*

---

**VOCABULARY**  COMMON CORE
**L 4**

### OWN THE WORD

**profusion:** Write the word *profusion* on the board, and draw lines between the prefix *pro-*, the root *fus-*, and the suffix *-ion*. Explain that *pro-* means "forth," *fus-* means "pour," and *-ion* means "the result of." Use these word parts to define *profusion* as "the result of pouring forth," in other words, "abundance." Then ask students to name things that might be found in *profusion* and where. *Possible answers: flowers in a field, dirty dishes in a sink, leaves under trees, litter in the street*

---

## FOR ENGLISH LANGUAGE LEARNERS

**Task Support** Call attention to the question in the side note for lines 238–243. Make sure students understand that Odysseus has made a six-foot-long stake with a pointed end (lines 230–234) from the olive tree that the Cyclops left in the cave. *Possible answer: Odysseus plans to push the stake into the Cyclops' single eye after he falls asleep.*

### Language Coach

**Word Definitions**
*Possible answer: bleating.* Have students read lines 278–281 on page 1218. Ask students to identify what word or words in those lines are examples of onomatopoeia.

'Cyclops, try some wine.
Here's liquor to wash down your scraps of men.
Taste it, and see the kind of drink we carried
under our planks. I meant it for an offering
if you would help us home. But you are mad,
260  unbearable, a bloody monster! After this,
will any other traveller come to see you?'

He seized and drained the bowl, and it went down
so fiery and smooth he called for more:

255–261 *Why does Odysseus offer the Cyclops the liquor he brought from the ship?*

'Give me another, thank you kindly. Tell me,
265  how are you called? I'll make a gift will please you.
Even Cyclopes know the wine-grapes grow
out of grassland and loam in heaven's rain,
but here's a bit of nectar and ambrosia!'

Three bowls I brought him, and he poured them down.
270  I saw the fuddle and flush come over him,
then I sang out in cordial tones:

                           'Cyclops,
you ask my honorable name? Remember
the gift you promised me, and I shall tell you.
My name is Nohbdy: mother, father, and friends,
275  everyone calls me Nohbdy.'

                            And he said:
'Nohbdy's my meat, then, after I eat his friends.
Others come first. There's a noble gift, now.' ❶

Even as he spoke, he reeled and tumbled backward,
his great head lolling to one side: and sleep
280  took him like any creature. Drunk, hiccupping,
he dribbled streams of liquor and bits of men.

Now, by the gods, I drove my big hand spike
deep in the embers, charring it again,
and cheered my men along with battle talk
285  to keep their courage up: no quitting now.
The pike of olive, green though it had been,
reddened and glowed as if about to catch.
I drew it from the coals and my four fellows
gave me a hand, lugging it near the Cyclops
290  as more than natural force nerved them; straight
forward they sprinted, lifted it, and rammed it

268 **nectar** (nĕk'tər) **and ambrosia** (ăm-brō'zhə): the drink and food of the gods.

270 **fuddle and flush:** the state of confusion and redness of the face caused by drinking alcohol.

**❸ Targeted Passage**

**❶ EPIC HERO**
Say the name *Nohbdy* out loud and listen to what it sounds like. What might Odysseus be planning? Consider what this tells you about his **character.**

286 **the pike:** the pointed stake.

---

**TEXT ANALYSIS**

COMMON CORE
RL 6

**❶ EPIC HERO**

***Possible answer:*** *The name* Nohbdy *sounds like "nobody." Odysseus is concealing his identity, which tells us that he is planning ahead, possibly setting some trap for the Cyclops. Odysseus didn't mention the name* Nohbdy *until after the Cyclops' wits had been dulled by three drinks. These moves show that Odysseus is both clever and careful in his planning.*

---

## DIFFERENTIATED INSTRUCTION

### FOR STRUGGLING READERS

**❸ Targeted Passage** [Lines 264–281]

This passage illustrates how Odysseus' plan depends on the Cyclops' carelessness.

- How many bowls of wine did the Cyclops drink? (line 269)
- Why didn't Odysseus tell Cyclops his name as soon as he asked? (lines 270–272)
- Why did the Cyclops believe that Odysseus' name was Nohbdy? (lines 278–281)

- Why did the Cyclops trust Odysseus, drink his wine, and ask for more? (lines 264–268)

### FOR ENGLISH LANGUAGE LEARNERS

**Task Support** Point out the question in the side note for lines 255–261. ***Possible answer:*** *He offers the wine, knowing that Cyclops won't be able to resist and counting on its sleep-inducing effect.*

deep in his crater eye, and I leaned on it
turning it as a shipwright turns a drill
in planking, having men below to swing

295 the two-handled strap that spins it in the groove.
So with our brand we bored that great eye socket
while blood ran out around the red hot bar.
Eyelid and lash were seared; the pierced ball
hissed broiling, and the roots popped.

                                    In a smithy

300 one sees a white-hot axehead or an adze
plunged and wrung in a cold tub, screeching steam—
the way they make soft iron hale and hard—:
just so that eyeball hissed around the spike. **K**
The Cyclops bellowed and the rock roared round him,

305 and we fell back in fear. Clawing his face
he tugged the bloody spike out of his eye,
threw it away, and his wild hands went groping;
then he set up a howl for Cyclopes
who lived in caves on windy peaks nearby.

310 Some heard him; and they came by divers ways
to clump around outside and call:

                                    'What ails you,

Polyphemus? Why do you cry so sore
in the starry night? You will not let us sleep.
Sure no man's driving off your flock? No man

315 has tricked you, ruined you?'

                                    Out of the cave

the mammoth Polyphemus roared in answer:

'Nohbdy, Nohbdy's tricked me, Nohbdy's ruined me!'

To this rough shout they made a sage reply:

'Ah well, if nobody has played you foul

320 there in your lonely bed, we are no use in pain
given by great Zeus. Let it be your father,
Poseidon Lord, to whom you pray.' **L**

                                    So saying

they trailed away. And I was filled with laughter
to see how like a charm the name deceived them.

325 Now Cyclops, wheezing as the pain came on him,
fumbled to wrench away the great doorstone

---

**299  smithy:** blacksmith's shop.

**300  adze** (ădz): an axlike tool with
a curved blade.

**K  EPIC SIMILE**
Find the epic similes in lines 292–297
and lines 299–303. What two
things are being compared in each
case? What are the effects of this
**figurative language?**

**310  divers:** various.

**312  Polyphemus** (pŏl′ə-fē′məs):
the name of the Cyclops.

**318  sage:** wise.

**319–322**  Odysseus' lie about his
name has paid off. *What do the other
Cyclopes assume to be the source of
Polyphemus' pain?*

**L  ALLUSION**
What do you learn about
Polyphemus from the allusion
in lines 321–322?

---

**TEXT ANALYSIS**

**K  EPIC SIMILE**

*Possible answer:  In lines 292–297, Odysseus
compares pushing and turning the spike in
the Cyclops' eye socket to a ship carpenter
turning a drill in a plank on a ship's deck.  In
lines 299–303, he compares the hissing of
the Cyclops' eye to the steam given off by a
white-hot axehead that is dipped in a cold
tub of water.*

**REVISIT THE BIG QUESTION**
## What is a HERO?

**Discuss**  What leadership qualities does
Odysseus, the hero, display in lines 292–299?
Remind students that Greek warriors won
honor through noble deeds, and that honor,
they believed, was the greatest good. *Possible
answer: Odysseus joins his men in the maneuver, leaning on the spike himself, rather than
removing himself from harm's way.  In displaying such bravery and confidence, he acts as an
inspiring role model for his men.*

**TEXT ANALYSIS**

**L  ALLUSION**

*Possible answer:  The reader learns that the
Cyclops is the son of Poseidon.*

Point out that during the Trojan War, the
Greeks had incurred the anger of Poseidon;
the god of the sea was responsible for
Odysseus' long journey and suffering.

---

**FOR ENGLISH LANGUAGE LEARNERS**

**Task Support**  Draw students' attention to the
question in the side note for lines 319–322.
Reread Cyclops' response ("Nohbdy, Nohbdy's
tricked me, Nohbdy's ruined me!"). *Possible
answer: The other Cyclopes assume that no
one is hurting Polyphemus.  They think it must
be some injury or sickness imposed by Zeus.*

**FOR ADVANCED LEARNERS/PRE–AP**

**Compare and Contrast**  Point out that
Polyphemus and Odysseus are not entirely
dissimilar.  Have students work in pairs and
create a Comparison Matrix that shows the
similarities and differences between the
two.  Tell them to consider personal as well
as physical features.  Have pairs discuss their
findings and share their results with the class.

**BEST PRACTICES TOOLKIT—Transparency**
**Comparison Matrix p. A24**

330  But I kept thinking how to win the game:
death sat there huge; how could we slip away?
I drew on all my wits, and ran through tactics,
reasoning as a man will for dear life,
until a trick came—and it pleased me well.
335  The Cyclops' rams were handsome, fat, with heavy
fleeces, a dark violet.

Three abreast

I tied them silently together, twining
cords of willow from the ogre's bed;
then slung a man under each middle one
340  to ride there safely, shielded left and right.
So three sheep could convey each man. I took
the woolliest ram, the choicest of the flock,
and hung myself under his kinky belly,
pulled up tight, with fingers twisted deep
345  in sheepskin ringlets for an iron grip.
So, breathing hard, we waited until morning.

When Dawn spread out her finger tips of rose
the rams began to stir, moving for pasture,
and peals of bleating echoed round the pens
350  where dams with udders full called for a milking.
Blinded, and sick with pain from his head wound,
the master stroked each ram, then let it pass,
but my men riding on the pectoral fleece
the giant's blind hands blundering never found.
355  Last of them all my ram, the leader, came,
weighted by wool and me with my **meditations.**
The Cyclops patted him, and then he said:

'Sweet cousin ram, why lag behind the rest
in the night cave? You never linger so,
360  but graze before them all, and go afar
to crop sweet grass, and take your stately way
leading along the streams, until at evening
you run to be the first one in the fold.
Why, now, so far behind? Can you be grieving
365  over your Master's eye? That carrion rogue
and his accurst companions burnt it out
when he had conquered all my wits with wine.
Nohbdy will not get out alive, I swear.

### 327 breach: opening.

**EPIC HERO**
Notice Odysseus' great mental
struggle in lines 330–336. As you
read on, note the clever plan he
has managed to come up with
on the spot.

**353 pectoral fleece:** the wool covering
a sheep's chest.

**meditation** (mĕd′ĭ-tā′shən)
*n.* the act of being in serious,
reflective thought

This 1910 color print depicts Odysseus taunting
Polyphemus as he and his men make their escape.

Detail of *Odysseus and Polyphem* (1910), after L. du Bois-
Reymond. Color print. From *Sagen des klasseschen Altertums* by
Karl Becker, Berlin. © akg-images.

---

## TEXT ANALYSIS — COMMON CORE RL 6

### Ⓜ EPIC HERO

Remind students that Odysseus was the
mastermind behind the Trojan horse,
which broke the stalemate and won the
war for Greece. Ask them how this situation, and the plan that he devises, is similar. **Possible answer: *Odysseus and his men
are at a kind of stalemate with the Cyclops.
They have neutralized but not defeated
him. Odysseus again thinks of a trick, this
time to deceive the Cyclops. Once again, his
clever planning will fool a formidable foe.***

## Analyze Visuals

**Activity** Compare this depiction of the Cyclops
with the one on page 1216. How do they
differ? Which do you think better illustrates
Polyphemus? *Possible answer: The expression
of the Cyclops in the painting on page 1216
and the soft colors make the creature seem
harmless. The Cyclops on page 1220, however,
is depicted as strong and threatening, using
bold colors to highlight his strong physique.
Students' opinions on which painting is more
effective will vary.*

## VOCABULARY — COMMON CORE L 4

### OWN THE WORD

**meditation:** Tell students that when they
are *meditating*, they are contemplating, or thinking about a particular thing.
Then remind them that in Buddhism and
Hinduism, *meditation* means clearing the
mind and that there are specific steps
that one takes to learn *meditation*.

## DIFFERENTIATED INSTRUCTION

### FOR ENGLISH LANGUAGE LEARNERS

**Vocabulary: Outdated Forms** Call attention to these words and phrases (on pages
1220–1221) that are now rarely used and that
suggest a bygone time. Work with students
to use context clues to determine their
meaning:

- *so* (line 359), "this way"
- *afar* (line 360), "far away"
- *carrion rogue* (line 365), "rotten, dishonest
person"

- *accurst* (line 366), "damned"
- *I should have rest* (lines 372–373), "I would
be free"

Oh, had you brain and voice to tell
370 where he may be now, dodging all my fury!
Bashed by this hand and bashed on this rock wall
his brains would strew the floor, and I should have
rest from the outrage Nohbdy worked upon me.'

He sent us into the open, then. Close by,
375 I dropped and rolled clear of the ram's belly,
going this way and that to untie the men.
With many glances back, we rounded up
his fat, stiff-legged sheep to take aboard,
and drove them down to where the good ship lay. **N**
380 We saw, as we came near, our fellows' faces
shining; then we saw them turn to grief
tallying those who had not fled from death.
I hushed them, jerking head and eyebrows up,
and in a low voice told them: 'Load this herd;
385 move fast, and put the ship's head toward the breakers.'
They all pitched in at loading, then embarked
and struck their oars into the sea. Far out,
as far off shore as shouted words would carry,
I sent a few back to the **adversary**:

390 'O Cyclops! Would you feast on my companions?
Puny, am I, in a Caveman's hands?
How do you like the beating that we gave you,
you damned cannibal? Eater of guests
under your roof! Zeus and the gods have paid you!'

395 The blind thing in his doubled fury broke
a hilltop in his hands and heaved it after us.
Ahead of our black prow it struck and sank
whelmed in a spuming geyser, a giant wave
that washed the ship stern foremost back to shore.
400 I got the longest boathook out and stood
fending us off, with furious nods to all
to put their backs into a racing stroke—
row, row, or perish. So the long oars bent
kicking the foam sternward, making head
405 until we drew away, and twice as far.
Now when I cupped my hands I heard the crew
in low voices protesting:

                    'Godsake, Captain!
Why bait the beast again? Let him alone!'

**N EPIC HERO**
What **character traits** has Odysseus demonstrated in his dealings with Polyphemus?

**385 put . . . the breakers:** turn the ship around so that it is heading toward the open sea.

**adversary** (ăd'vər-sĕr'ē)
*n.* an opponent; enemy

**390–394** Odysseus assumes that the gods are on his side.

**395–403** The hilltop thrown by Polyphemus lands in front of the ship, causing a huge wave that carries the ship back to the shore. Odysseus uses a long pole to push the boat away from the land.

**406 cupped my hands:** put his hands on either side of his mouth in order to magnify his voice.

**N EPIC HERO**
***Possible answer:*** *Odysseus has demonstrated leadership, bravery, and cunning in his dealings with Polyphemus. His actions also reveal his curiosity and his tendency to be rash and even foolhardy.*

**OWN THE WORD**
**adversary:** Review the definition provided for the term. Then ask students these questions: Who is Odysseus' *adversary* here? ***Possible answer:*** *the Cyclops* Who is the Cyclops' *adversary*? ***Possible answer:*** *Odysseus*

**FOR STRUGGLING READERS**
**Paraphrasing Homer** Have students reread the summaries of lines 390–394 and lines 395–403. Then model how to paraphrase lines 390–394: *You were going to eat up all my friends and take me in your hands. So, how do you like having us beat you? The gods have punished you for mistreating your guests.*

Invite volunteers to paraphrase lines 395–403: *The blind Cyclops tore off the top of a hill and threw it at us. It landed in front of our ship and sent up a geyser; a wave washed us back to shore. I pushed us away with a pole and ordered my men to row for their lives.*

'That tidal wave he made on the first throw
410 all but beached us.'

                                        'All but stove us in!'

'Give him our bearing with your trumpeting,
he'll get the range and lob a boulder.'

                                                'Aye

He'll smash our timbers and our heads together!'

I would not heed them in my glorying spirit,
415 but let my anger flare and yelled:

                                        'Cyclops,

if ever mortal man inquire
how you were put to shame and blinded, tell him
Odysseus, raider of cities, took your eye:
Laertes' son, whose home's on Ithaca!' ⊙

420 At this he gave a mighty sob and rumbled:

'Now comes the weird upon me, spoken of old.
A wizard, grand and wondrous, lived here—Telemus,
a son of Eurymus; great length of days
he had in wizardry among the Cyclopes,
425 and these things he foretold for time to come:
my great eye lost, and at Odysseus' hands.
Always I had in mind some giant, armed
in giant force, would come against me here.
But this, but you—small, pitiful and twiggy—
430 you put me down with wine, you blinded me.
Come back, Odysseus, and I'll treat you well,
praying the god of earthquake to befriend you—
his son I am, for he by his avowal
fathered me, and, if he will, he may
435 heal me of this black wound—he and no other
of all the happy gods or mortal men.'

Few words I shouted in reply to him:
'If I could take your life I would and take
your time away, and hurl you down to hell!
440 The god of earthquake could not heal you there!'

At this he stretched his hands out in his darkness
toward the sky of stars, and prayed Poseidon:

**1222** UNIT 11: THE ODYSSEY

## Language Coach

**Multiple Meanings** The word *stove* has multiple meanings. It can mean "a mechanism used for heating or cooking," or it can mean "smashed" (as the past tense of *stave*). Which meaning applies in line 410? How can you tell?

## ⊙ EPITHET

Notice that Odysseus uses the warlike **epithet** "raider of cities" in his second boast to the Cyclops. What **trait** does he display in revealing so much about himself?

**421 Now comes . . . of old:** Now I recall the destiny predicted long ago.

**421–430 Now comes . . . you blinded me:** Polyphemus tells of a prophecy made long ago by Telemus, a prophet who predicted that Polyphemus would lose his eye at the hands of Odysseus. *How have the actual events turned out differently from what Polyphemus expected?*

**432 the god of earthquake:** Poseidon.
**433 avowal:** honest admission.

---

## ⊙ EPITHET

**Possible answer:** *In revealing this information, Odysseus displays his pride. It is a rash, foolhardy action: the Cyclops may use this information to cause Odysseus trouble with his father, Poseidon, who is already angry with the Greek.*

## REVISIT THE BIG QUESTION
# What is a HERO?

**Discuss** Odysseus was a great hero. Based on lines 437–440, are his faults of heroic proportions? Or are they failings that you would expect most people to share? **Possible answer:** *Odysseus' faults are not shared by most ordinary people. His fatal flaw is his excessive pride, as well as his tendency to act at times without thinking of consequences. Both traits bring him bad luck. Thus, Odysseus is responsible for much of the misfortune he suffers.*

---

## DIFFERENTIATED INSTRUCTION

### FOR ENGLISH LANGUAGE LEARNERS
**Task Support** Direct students' attention to the side note for lines 421–430. Help them answer the question. **Possible answer:** *Polyphemus expected Odysseus to be a "giant, armed in giant force" and not a frail human.*

### Language Coach
**Multiple Meanings** **Possible answer:** *Only* smashed *makes sense when substituted for* stove *in line 410.* Have students identify other words on this page and the facing page that have multiple meanings, using a dictionary if necessary.

'O hear me, lord, blue girdler of the islands,
      if I am thine indeed, and thou art father:
445   grant that Odysseus, raider of cities, never
      see his home: Laertes' son, I mean,
      who kept his hall on Ithaca. Should destiny
      intend that he shall see his roof again
      among his family in his father land,
450   far be that day, and dark the years between.
      Let him lose all companions, and return
      under strange sail to bitter days at home.'

**EPIC HERO**
Reread lines 437–452. Paraphrase
Polyphemus' curse. How has
Odysseus brought this curse upon
himself?

      In these words he prayed, and the god heard him.
      Now he laid hands upon a bigger stone
455   and wheeled around, titanic for the cast,
      to let it fly in the black-prowed vessel's track.
      But it fell short, just aft the steering oar,
      and whelming seas rose giant above the stone
      to bear us onward toward the island.

**455 titanic for the cast:** drawing on all his
enormous strength in preparing to throw.

**457 aft:** behind.

                                                    There
460   as we ran in we saw the squadron waiting,
      the trim ships drawn up side by side, and all
      our troubled friends who waited, looking seaward.
      We beached her, grinding keel in the soft sand,
      and waded in, ourselves, on the sandy beach.

**459 the island:** the deserted island where
most of Odysseus' men had stayed behind.

④ **Targeted Passage**

465   Then we unloaded all the Cyclops' flock
      to make division, share and share alike,
      only my fighters voted that my ram,
      the prize of all, should go to me. I slew him
      by the sea side and burnt his long thighbones
470   to Zeus beyond the stormcloud, Cronus' son,
      who rules the world. But Zeus disdained my offering;
      destruction for my ships he had in store
      and death for those who sailed them, my companions.

**470 Cronus' son:** Zeus' father, Cronus,
was a Titan, one of an earlier race of gods.

      Now all day long until the sun went down
475   we made our feast on mutton and sweet wine,
      till after sunset in the gathering dark
      we went to sleep above the wash of ripples.

      When the young Dawn with finger tips of rose
      touched the world, I roused the men, gave orders
480   to man the ships, cast off the mooring lines;
      and filing in to sit beside the rowlocks
      oarsmen in line dipped oars in the gray sea.
      So we moved out, sad in the vast offing,
      having our precious lives, but not our friends."

**483 offing:** the part of the deep sea
visible from the shore.

THE WANDERINGS OF ODYSSEUS: BOOK 9    **1223**

**TEXT ANALYSIS**

**COMMON CORE**
RL 6

P **EPIC HERO**

*Possible answer: Paraphrase: May Odysseus the son of Laertes and conqueror of cities never again see Ithaca, his home. And if the fates decree that he does return home, may that day be far from now, may the time between be troubled with the loss of his companions. May his homecoming be by strange passage, and upon his arrival, may he find chaos. Odysseus has brought this curse on himself by provoking Polyphemus with his boasting—not once but three times, despite the warnings of his men (lines 390–394 and lines 415–419)—his anger, and his taunts (lines 437–440). Odysseus' pride will cost him dearly.*

**FOR STRUGGLING READERS**

④ **Targeted Passage** [Lines 453–473]

This passage shows the resolution of
Odysseus' great conflict with Polyphemus.

- What did the Cyclops do after cursing
  Odysseus? (lines 454–456)

- What happened to Odysseus' ship?
  (lines 457–459)

- What did Odysseus and his crew do after
  they landed? (lines 465–471)

**FOR ADVANCED LEARNERS/PRE–AP**

**Foreshadowing** Have students list all the
prophecies mentioned in Book 9. Then have
them talk about these questions: What effect
does the knowledge that Odysseus' men
are doomed have on the story? Why do you
think Homer may have given this information
rather than keeping his audience in the dark?

**Activity** Ask students what qualities of Circe are captured in this painting. *Possible answer: The painting reveals her beauty and charm. There is mischief in her eyes, suggesting that danger lurks beneath the lovely surface.*

**About the Art** German painter Franz von Struck (1863–1928) used myth and imagination in his Art Nouveau works. A painter, sculptor, and designer, von Struck influenced a generation of important painters, including Albers, Kandinsky, and Klee.

---

**TEXT ANALYSIS**

## EPIC SIMILE

*Possible answer: The simile compares the drugged wolves and mountain lions, shaking their tails and looking up at Odysseus' men, to tame dogs that wag their tails and fawn on their masters when fed at the table. The point of the comparison is to show the power of Circe's magic, which can turn vicious predators into pets. This description inspires awe and fear of Circe and her great hall.*

---

**VOCABULARY**

COMMON CORE
L 4

### OWN THE WORD

**beguiling:** Review the definition of *beguiling* with students. Then have students name people, including actors and actresses, who have *beguiling* voices.

---

# BOOK 10:
## *Circe, the Grace of the Witch*

Detail of *Tilla Durieux as Circe* (c. 1912–1913), Franz von Struck. Oil on paper, 53.5 cm × 46.5 cm. Private collection. © akg-images.

*Odysseus and his men next land on the island of Aeolus, the wind king, and stay with him a month. To extend his hospitality, Aeolus gives Odysseus two parting gifts: a fair west wind that will blow the fleet of ships toward Ithaca, and a great bag holding all the unfavorable, stormy winds. Within sight of home, and while Odysseus is sleeping, the men open the bag, thinking it contains gold and silver. The bad winds thus escape and blow the ships back to Aeolus' island. The king refuses to help them again, believing now that their voyage has been cursed by the gods.*

*The discouraged mariners next stop briefly in the land of the Laestrygones, fierce cannibals who bombard the fleet of ships with boulders. Only Odysseus, his ship, and its crew of 45 survive the shower of boulders. The lone ship then sails to Aeaea, home of the goddess Circe, who is considered by many to be a witch. There, Odysseus divides his men into two groups. Eurylochus leads one platoon to explore the island, while Odysseus stays behind on the ship with the remaining crew.*

"In the wild wood they found an open glade,
around a smooth stone house—the hall of Circe—
and wolves and mountain lions lay there, mild
in her soft spell, fed on her drug of evil.
5 None would attack—oh, it was strange, I tell you—
but switching their long tails they faced our men
like hounds, who look up when their master comes
with tidbits for them—as he will—from table.
Humbly those wolves and lions with mighty paws
10 fawned on our men—who met their yellow eyes
and feared them.
                    In the entrance way they stayed
to listen there: inside her quiet house
they heard the goddess Circe.
                                        Low she sang

in her **beguiling** voice, while on her loom
15 she wove ambrosial fabric sheer and bright,

---

**10 fawned on:** showed affection for.

## EPIC SIMILE
In lines 6–11, notice the simile involving Circe's wolves and mountain lions. What is the point of this comparison? How does it affect your impression of Circe's hall?

**beguiling** (bĭ-gī'lĭng) *adj.* charming; pleasing **beguile** *v.*

**15 ambrosial:** fit for the gods.

**1224** UNIT 11: THE ODYSSEY

---

## DIFFERENTIATED INSTRUCTION

### FOR STRUGGLING READERS

**Preview** Read aloud the italicized synopsis that begins Book 10, and help students create a Story Map of the characters and events. They can complete the organizer as they read.

**Characters:** Odysseus, Aeolus, the Laestrygones, Circe, Eurylochus

**Events:**

1. Odysseus and crew stay with Aeolus.
2. Aeolus gives Odysseus two parting gifts.

3. The men open a bag with bad winds.
4. The winds blow them back to Aeolus.
5. The Laestrygones destroy all the ships but one.
6. The ship sails to Circe's home, Aeaea.
7. Eurylochus explores the island with some men.

**BEST PRACTICES TOOLKIT—Transparency** Story Map p. D14

by that craft known to the goddesses of heaven.
No one would speak, until Polites—most
faithful and likable of my officers, said:

'Dear friends, no need for stealth: here's a young weaver
20 singing a pretty song to set the air
a-tingle on these lawns and paven courts.
Goddess she is, or lady. Shall we greet her?'

So reassured, they all cried out together,
and she came swiftly to the shining doors
25 to call them in. All but Eurylochus—
who feared a snare—the innocents went after her.
On thrones she seated them, and lounging chairs,
while she prepared a meal of cheese and barley
and amber honey mixed with Pramnian wine,
30 adding her own vile pinch, to make them lose
desire or thought of our dear father land.
Scarce had they drunk when she flew after them
with her long stick and shut them in a pigsty—
bodies, voices, heads, and bristles, all
35 swinish now, though minds were still unchanged.
So, squealing, in they went. And Circe tossed them
acorns, mast, and cornel berries—fodder
for hogs who rut and slumber on the earth.

Down to the ship Eurylochus came running
40 to cry alarm, foul magic doomed his men!
But working with dry lips to speak a word
he could not, being so shaken; blinding tears
welled in his eyes; **foreboding** filled his heart.
When we were frantic questioning him, at last
45 we heard the tale: our friends were gone. . . ."

*Eurylochus tells Odysseus what has happened and begs him to sail away from
Circe's island. Against this advice, however, Odysseus rushes to save his men from
the enchantress. On the way, he meets the god Hermes, who gives him a magical
plant called moly to protect him from Circe's power. Still, Hermes warns Odysseus
that he must make the goddess swear she will play no "witches' tricks." Armed with
the moly and Hermes' warning, Odysseus arrives at Circe's palace.*

*Circe gives Odysseus a magic drink, but it does not affect him and he threatens
to kill her with his sword. Circe turns the pigs back into men but puts them all
into a trance. They stay for one year, until Odysseus finally begs her to let them
go home. She replies that they must first visit the land of the dead and hear a
prophecy from the ghost of Tiresias.*

**17 Polites** (pə-lī′tēz).

**23–26** *If you were among this group,
whom would you follow—Polites or
Eurylochus? Why?*

**27–36** *What happens to the men after
they drink Circe's magic potion?*

**foreboding** (fôr-bō′dĭng) *n.* a sense
of approaching evil

---

## SUMMARY

Book 10 recounts how Odysseus and his crew
visit the wind king, Aeolus. He sends them off
with a fair wind and a bag of violent winds.
One night, close to home, the men open the
bag. The winds blow the ship back to Aeolus,
who refuses to help them again. Next, the
Laestrygones destroy all their ships but one.
Odysseus sails his last ship to Aeaea, home of
Circe. Circe offers them food and drink, which
turns them into pigs. Eurylochus tells Odysseus, who hurries to save his men. A magical
plant from Hermes protects him from Circe.
She releases his crew but exacts a price: they
must visit the ghost of Tiresias in the land of
the dead to hear a prophecy.

### READING STRATEGY
COMMON CORE
RL 4,
RL 10

■ *Model the Skill:* **READING AN
EPIC POEM**

Remind students that an important strategy for reading any narrative poem is keeping track of events. Refer students to the
Story Map they created on page 1224. Using
the map, summarize Book 10 as follows:

*Odysseus and his men receive a gift from
Aeolus, but greed leads Odysseus' men to
open the bad winds, blowing them away
from home. Laestrygones destroy all the
ships except Odysseus', which then sails to
Circe's island. Circe traps the men for a year
until they visit the land of the dead to hear
a prophecy.*

Have students read pages 1224–1225 and
then revise the summary as needed.

### VOCABULARY
COMMON CORE
L 4

### OWN THE WORD

**foreboding:** Have students create a
semantic map for *foreboding*. Write
the word in a center circle and then add
the definition given, "a sense of approaching evil." Draw spider legs from
the center circle and have students add
synonyms to complete the map. ***Possible
answers:*** *dread, misgiving, apprehension,
premonition*

---

**FOR ENGLISH LANGUAGE LEARNERS**

**Task Support** Point out the question in the
side note for lines 23–26. *Some students may
acknowledge Circe's magic; others may suggest that they would have learned from their
experience with the Lotus Eaters not to trust
strangers.*

**Task Support** Draw students' attention to
the side-note question for lines 27–36.
***Possible answer:*** *They turn into swine; then
Circe forces them into a pigsty and feeds them
food fit for hogs.*

**Text Digests** Read line by line through the
italicized text digest at the end of page 1225
to make sure students understand the plot of
the rest of Book 10.

## Get Into the Book

### SUMMARY

Book 11 describes how Odysseus and his crew travel to the underworld to meet with the blind sage Tiresias, as Circe has demanded. Odysseus meets Elpenor, a shipmate who had died in an accident, and promises to give him a proper burial. Then Tiresias tells him that his crew will return to Ithaca only if they avoid stealing from Helios' herd. Odysseus speaks with many other spirits, including his mother, who had died of a broken heart.

---

### TEXT ANALYSIS

#### Ⓡ ALLUSION

**Possible answer:** *The reference to the myth of Hades and Persephone reminds us that Hades is determined, ruthless, and self-centered. It helps to create the impression of the underworld as a gloomy, dark, and frightening place. It also reinforces the sense of foreboding.*

---

### BACKGROUND

**Death and the Underworld** The land of the dead was ruled by the god Hades, who was also the god of earth's fertility. His kingdom was also called Hades, and it was divided into two regions. The first region, called Erebus, was where a person's spirit (or psyche) passed at death. The second region was called Tartarus. It was separated from the land of the living by the river Styx. An old boatman named Charon transported the dead across the river to Hades. The land of the dead was also guarded by a three-headed, dragon-tailed dog named Cerberus.

---

### VOCABULARY

#### OWN THE WORD

**assuage:** Give students these examples: The mother was able to calm the child and *assuage* his nighttime fears about monsters. Despite his reassurances, the college counselor did little to *assuage* my concerns about getting into college.

---

# BOOK 11:
## *The Land of the Dead*

*Odysseus and his crew set out for the land of the dead. They arrive and find the place to which Circe has directed them.*

"Then I addressed the blurred and breathless dead,
vowing to slaughter my best heifer for them
before she calved, at home in Ithaca,
and burn the choice bits on the altar fire;
5   as for Tiresias, I swore to sacrifice
a black lamb, handsomest of all our flock.
Thus to **assuage** the nations of the dead
I pledged these rites, then slashed the lamb and ewe,
letting their black blood stream into the wellpit.
10  Now the souls gathered, stirring out of Erebus,
brides and young men, and men grown old in pain,
and tender girls whose hearts were new to grief;
many were there, too, torn by brazen lanceheads,
battle-slain, bearing still their bloody gear.
15  From every side they came and sought the pit
with rustling cries; and I grew sick with fear.
But presently I gave command to my officers
to flay those sheep the bronze cut down, and make
burnt offerings of flesh to the gods below—
20  to sovereign Death, to pale Persephone. Ⓡ
Meanwhile I crouched with my drawn sword to keep
the surging phantoms from the bloody pit
till I should know the presence of Tiresias.

One shade came first—Elpenor, of our company,
25  who lay unburied still on the wide earth
as we had left him—dead in Circe's hall,
untouched, unmourned, when other cares compelled us.
Now when I saw him there I wept for pity
and called out to him:

**assuage** (ə-swāj′) *v.* to calm or pacify

**10 Erebus** (ĕr′ə-bəs): a region of the land of the dead, also known as the underworld or Hades. Hades is also the name of the god of the underworld.

**18 flay:** to strip off the outer skin of.

#### Ⓡ ALLUSION

In lines 17–20, Odysseus makes a sacrifice to "sovereign Death," or Hades, and "pale Persephone" (pər-sĕf′ə-nē), his bride, who was kidnapped and forced to live with him for six months of every year. Her mother, goddess of the harvest, grieves during that time, causing winter to fall. What does this background information tell you about Hades? Consider how this information affects your impression of the underworld.

---

## DIFFERENTIATED INSTRUCTION

### FOR STRUGGLING READERS

**Preview** Read aloud the italicized synopsis of Book 11 at the top of page 1226 to give students a clear idea of the plot from the end of Book 10 to Odysseus' descent to the underworld. Ask students to recall what task Circe had set for Odysseus to perform in the land of the dead. (*to hear a prophecy from the ghost of Tiresias*)

*Ulysses Descending into the Underworld* (16th century), Giovanni Stradano. Fresco. Palazzo Vecchio, Florence. Photo © Scala/Art Resource, New York.

'How is this, Elpenor,
30 how could you journey to the western gloom
swifter afoot than I in the black lugger?'

He sighed, and answered:

'Son of great Laertes,
Odysseus, master mariner and soldier,
bad luck shadowed me, and no kindly power;
35 ignoble death I drank with so much wine.
I slept on Circe's roof, then could not see
the long steep backward ladder, coming down,
and fell that height. My neck bone, buckled under,
snapped, and my spirit found this well of dark.
40 Now hear the grace I pray for, in the name
of those back in the world, not here—your wife
and father, he who gave you bread in childhood,
and your own child, your only son, Telemachus,
long ago left at home.

▲ **Analyze Visuals**

This 16th-century painting illustrates the descent of Ulysses (Odysseus) into the underworld. How has the artist distinguished between Ulysses and the dead, also known as shades?

---

COMMON CORE **L 4b**

**Language Coach**

**Roots and Affixes** The prefix *in-* ("not") changes form depending on the first letter of the word to which it affixes. (That is, the letter *n* changes to a different letter.) What word in line 35 contains a form of the prefix *in-*? What does the word mean?

---

*Possible answer:* The shades are literally featureless shadows. By contrast, Odysseus is dressed in full regalia; his clothing and weapons are presented in detail. His body, face, and limbs are well-defined and solid.

**About the Art** Giovanni Stradano (1523–1605) painted *Ulysses Descending into the Underworld* in a Mannerist style. Mannerism developed during the late Renaissance. Using the masters of the Renaissance, such as Michelangelo and Raphael, for inspiration, Mannerist artists created idealized and highly refined work.

---

READING STRATEGY    COMMON CORE    RL 4, RL 10

■ *Model the Skill:* **READING AN EPIC POEM**

Point out to students that visualizing the imagery will help them understand and remember the opening of Book 11. Ask them what words or images appeal to the senses in lines 10–16. Point out that the main image is of a crowd of many souls, coming "from every side": brides, young men, old men, tender girls "new to grief," wounded warriors with "their bloody gear." The sound of the shadows' "rustling cries" and Odysseus' admission that he "grew sick with fear" also draw on the senses. Ask students what mood these words and images create. *Possible answer: The accumulation of words and ghastly images helps to create a mood of fear and foreboding.*

---

**FOR ADVANCED LEARNERS/PRE–AP**

**Analyze** Ask students to reflect on the similarities and differences between Persephone's forced abduction and Odysseus' reluctant descent into the underworld. Encourage students to investigate details of the Hades-Persephone-Demeter myth to include in their analysis.

**FOR ENGLISH LANGUAGE LEARNERS**

**Language Coach**    COMMON CORE **L 4b**
**Roots and Affixes**
*Possible answer: ignoble = ig- (in-) + noble, meaning "not noble; dishonorable."* The prefix *un-* also means "not" or "the opposite of." Have students reread lines 24–27. Have them use their knowledge of the prefix *un-* and the root words to define *unburied, untouched,* and *unmourned,* using a dictionary if needed.

**TIERED DISCUSSION PROMPTS**

Refer to lines 44–67 and use these prompts to help students understand the mix of emotions Odysseus would have felt as he waited in the underworld for Tiresias:

**Connect** Have you or anyone you know during a moment of crisis or tension bumped into an old friend or a family member? *Responses should demonstrate an understanding that the bad timing and bad location might cause discomfort, worry, and even pain.*

**Analyze** What does the reader learn about Odysseus from his encounters with Elpenor and Anticlea? *Possible answer: The reader learns that Odysseus commanded the respect of his crew and in turn felt responsibility for them. We learn from his response to Elpenor that he is a dutiful and gracious leader and from his grief over his mother that he is a devoted son.*

**Evaluate** How well do you think Odysseus handled his meetings with Elpenor and Anticlea? *Possible answer: Odysseus handled these trying situations with patience, respect, and grace. It must have been a shock to see his lost crewmate and to learn of his mother's death. Nevertheless, he maintained control, operating calmly in the midst of personal loss and the horrors of the underworld.*

When you make sail
45 and put these lodgings of dim Death behind,
you will moor ship, I know, upon Aeaea Island;
there, O my lord, remember me, I pray,
do not abandon me unwept, unburied,
to tempt the gods' wrath, while you sail for home;
50 but fire my corpse, and all the gear I had,
and build a cairn for me above the breakers—
an unknown sailor's mark for men to come.
Heap up the mound there, and implant upon it
the oar I pulled in life with my companions.'

**50–51 fire my corpse . . . cairn:** Elpenor wants Odysseus to hold a funeral for him.

55 He ceased, and I replied:

'Unhappy spirit,
I promise you the barrow and the burial.'

So we conversed, and grimly, at a distance,
with my long sword between, guarding the blood,
while the faint image of the lad spoke on.
60 Now came the soul of Anticlea, dead,
my mother, daughter of Autolycus,
dead now, though living still when I took ship
for holy Troy. Seeing this ghost I grieved,
but held her off, through pang on pang of tears,
65 till I should know the presence of Tiresias.
Soon from the dark that prince of Thebes came forward
bearing a golden staff; and he addressed me:

**58 with my long sword . . . blood:** the ghosts are attracted to the blood of the sacrifice; Odysseus must hold them at bay with his sword.

**66 prince of Thebes:** Tiresias, the blind seer, comes from the city of Thebes (thēbz).

'Son of Laertes and the gods of old,
Odysseus, master of land ways and sea ways,
70 why leave the blazing sun, O man of woe,
to see the cold dead and the joyless region?
Stand clear, put up your sword;
let me but taste of blood, I shall speak true.'

At this I stepped aside, and in the scabbard
75 let my long sword ring home to the pommel silver,
as he bent down to the sombre blood. Then spoke
the prince of those with gift of speech:

'Great captain,
a fair wind and the honey lights of home
are all you seek. But anguish lies ahead;
80 the god who thunders on the land prepares it,
not to be shaken from your track, implacable,

**DIFFERENTIATED INSTRUCTION**

**FOR ENGLISH LANGUAGE LEARNERS**

**Paraphrase** Make sure that students understand Tiresias' prophecy. Have small groups paraphrase sections of the prophecy: lines 77–90, lines 91–104, and lines 105–116. Invite them to create cartoon frames to illustrate each part of the prophecy. Circulate to check comprehension and to make sure each group has identified the key elements. Students can draw the international "No" symbol (x) between frames to indicate what Tiresias tells Odysseus that he and his men should not do and the word *or* between frames to show what will happen if they do.

in rancor for the son whose eye you blinded.
One narrow strait may take you through his blows:
denial of yourself, restraint of shipmates.
85 When you make landfall on Thrinacia first
and quit the violet sea, dark on the land
you'll find the grazing herds of Helios
by whom all things are seen, all speech is known.
Avoid those kine, hold fast to your intent,
90 and hard seafaring brings you all to Ithaca.
But if you raid the beeves, I see destruction
for ship and crew. Though you survive alone,
bereft of all companions, lost for years,
under strange sail shall you come home, to find
95 your own house filled with trouble: insolent men
eating your livestock as they court your lady.
Aye, you shall make those men atone in blood!
But after you have dealt out death—in open
combat or by stealth—to all the suitors,
100 go overland on foot, and take an oar,
until one day you come where men have lived
with meat unsalted, never known the sea,
nor seen seagoing ships, with crimson bows
and oars that fledge light hulls for dipping flight.
105 The spot will soon be plain to you, and I
can tell you how: some passerby will say,
"What winnowing fan is that upon your shoulder?"
Halt, and implant your smooth oar in the turf
and make fair sacrifice to Lord Poseidon:
110 a ram, a bull, a great buck boar; turn back,
and carry out pure hekatombs at home
to all wide heaven's lords, the undying gods,
to each in order. Then a seaborne death
soft as this hand of mist will come upon you
115 when you are wearied out with rich old age,
your country folk in blessed peace around you.
And all this shall be just as I foretell.' . . ." **S**

*Odysseus speaks to the shade of his mother. She tells him that Penelope
and Telemachus are still grieving for him and that his father, Laertes,
has moved to the country, where he, too, mourns his son. Odysseus'
mother explains that she died from a broken heart. Odysseus also speaks
with the spirits of many great ladies and men who died, as well as those
who were being punished for their earthly sins. Filled with horror,
Odysseus and his crew set sail.*

**89–91 kine; beeves:** two words for cattle.

**101–102 where men have lived with meat
unsalted:** refers to an inland location
where men do not eat salted (preserved)
meat as sailors do aboard a ship.

COMMON CORE RL 5

**S** **EPIC HERO**
An epic hero's fate is often a matter
of great importance to the gods
and to the hero's homeland. In lines
77–117, Odysseus' fate is the subject
of a prophecy by Tiresias, a blind seer
who now dwells among the dead.
A prophecy such as this can serve as
**foreshadowing,** a plot device in
which future evens are hinted at to
increase tension. Do you think that
Odysseus' fate will unfold exactly as
Tiresias foretells it? Explain why you
think as you do.

## ADDITIONAL TEACHING OPPORTUNITY: ETYMOLOGY

Remind students that etymology is the study
of the origins and historical development of
words. Explain that there are many word
variations that have become obsolete. For example, *kine* (line 89) is a Middle English plural
of cow, and *beeves* (line 91) is the plural of *beef*.

**TEXT ANALYSIS**

COMMON CORE RL 5

**S** **EPIC HERO**

***Possible answer:*** *In the* Odyssey, *the predictions of wise men carry great weight. Tiresias' predictions are likely to come to pass.*
Lead a discussion with students about how
foreshadowing can increase tension in a
story. Make sure to discuss how the story
would be different if foreshadowing was
not used. Then have students keep track
of further instances of foreshadowing and
their predictions for how the events will
turn out.

## FOR STRUGGLING READERS

**Text Digests** Read aloud the italicized text digest at the bottom of page 1229. Ask students
to summarize what Odysseus learned about
his family during his visit to the underworld.
***Possible answer:*** *Odysseus learned that this
wife, his son, and his father were still alive but
that his mother had died of a broken heart. He
learned that his home is under assault by rude
suitors. He also learned that he will ultimately
see his family again and prevail over those
who wish him harm.*

## SUMMARY

Book 12 narrates how Circe advises Odysseus on what he must do to survive the Sirens and Scylla and Charybdis. Odysseus orders his men to put beeswax in their ears, so they can avoid the Sirens' tantalizing song. He listens, tied to the mast. Then Odysseus navigates past Scylla to avoid Charybdis, sacrificing six men. Finally, they come to Thrinacia, where Odysseus' starving men steal Helios' cattle, despite Circe's warning. As a result, all but Odysseus are lost at sea. He drifts to Calypso's island.

## REVISIT THE BIG QUESTION

# What is a **HERO?**

**Discuss** Odysseus learns from Circe about the terrible danger that the Sirens present to any sailor who hears their song. Have students reread lines 4–12. Ask them what they have learned about Odysseus that suggests he will listen to the Sirens' song. **Possible answer:** *Odysseus' great curiosity often leads him to accept unnecessary challenges. Just as he chose to meet the Cyclops, so he will choose to hear the Sirens' song.*

# BOOK 12:
## *The Sirens; Scylla and Charybdis*

*Odysseus and his men return to Circe's island. While the men sleep, Circe takes Odysseus aside to hear about the underworld and to offer advice.*

> "Then said the Lady Circe:
> 'So: all those trials are over.
>
> Listen with care
> to this, now, and a god will arm your mind.
> Square in your ship's path are Sirens, crying
> 5  beauty to bewitch men coasting by;
> woe to the innocent who hears that sound!
> He will not see his lady nor his children
> in joy, crowding about him, home from sea;
> the Sirens will sing his mind away
> 10  on their sweet meadow lolling. There are bones
> of dead men rotting in a pile beside them
> and flayed skins shrivel around the spot.
>
> Steer wide;
> keep well to seaward; plug your oarsmen's ears
> with beeswax kneaded soft; none of the rest
> 15  should hear that song.
>
> But if you wish to listen,
> let the men tie you in the lugger, hand
> and foot, back to the mast, lashed to the mast,
> so you may hear those harpies' thrilling voices;
> shout as you will, begging to be untied;
> 20  your crew must only twist more line around you
> and keep their stroke up, till the singers fade.
> What then? One of two courses you may take,
> and you yourself must weigh them. I shall not
> plan the whole action for you now, but only
> 25  tell you of both.

**1230**  UNIT 11: THE ODYSSEY

**Analyze Visuals ▶**

This detail from a 19th-century painting shows Odysseus tied to the mast of his ship to protect him from the Sirens' tempting song. Notice that his men have all covered their ears. How does the artist's depiction of the Sirens affect your understanding of the story? Explain.

**2–3** In Circe, Odysseus has found a valuable ally. In the next hundred lines, she describes in detail each danger that he and his men will meet on their way home.

**⑤ Targeted Passage**

**14 kneaded** (nē′dĭd): squeezed and pressed.

**18 those harpies' thrilling voices:** the delightful voices of those horrible female creatures.

Detail of *Ulysses and the Sirens* (1891), John William Waterhouse. Oil on canvas, 100 cm × 201.7 cm. National Gallery of Victoria, Melbourne, Australia. Photo © Bridgeman Art Library.

## DIFFERENTIATED INSTRUCTION

### FOR STRUGGLING READERS

**Review** Read the italicized introduction to Book 12 at the top of page 1230. Ask students to recall how Circe had treated Odysseus and his men during their previous stay on her island. **Possible answer:** *Circe had turned a platoon of Odysseus' men into swine and attempted to do the same to Odysseus. After that, she held them in a trance for a year. Then she forced Odysseus to go to the underworld to hear Tiresias' prophecy.*

### FOR ADVANCED LEARNERS/PRE–AP

**Debate** Present this topic for discussion: Did the Greeks believe in free will or in predestination? Ask students to base their conclusions on evidence from the *Odyssey*.

## Analyze Visuals

*Possible answer:* The depiction of the Sirens as huge birds of prey with women's faces conveys incongruent qualities: beauty and horror, delicacy and strength, allure and repulsiveness. It provides a strong visual image for understanding the power and intensity of their song. Bound to the mast, even the strong-willed Odysseus seems to bend to their will.

**About the Art** British artist John William Waterhouse (1849–1917) was the son of a painter. He had a lifelong interest in classical, historical, and literary subjects, including the *Odyssey*. Like other Pre-Raphaelite artists, Waterhouse was fascinated by tragic or powerful *femmes fatales*—"dangerous women"—as evidenced by the painting *Ulysses and the Sirens*.

**READING STRATEGY**                    COMMON CORE

**■** *Model the Skill:* **READING AN**    RL 4,
   **EPIC POEM**                          RL 10

Remind students to read all side notes to improve their comprehension. Demonstrate how the side notes can be used to answer the following questions: In what way is Circe a valuable ally? (side note lines 2–3) (*She warns Odysseus of the dangers he and his men will meet on the way.*) How can Odysseus soften the beeswax? (side note line 14) (*by kneading it*) What is another name for the Sirens? (side note line 18) (*harpies*)

**⑤ Targeted Passage** [Lines 4–21]

This passage explains the danger of the Sirens and how Odysseus can avoid that danger and listen to their song.

- What happens to sailors who hear the Sirens? (lines 7–10)

- How can Odysseus protect his men from this danger? (lines 12–21)

- How can he listen to their song and survive? (lines 10–15)

## TIERED DISCUSSION PROMPTS

Refer to lines 26–70 and use these prompts to help students understand the choices that Odysseus must make in order to pass Scylla and Charybdis without disaster:

**Connect** What is it like to be faced with a "no-win proposition"—where you lose something important no matter what decision you make? *Responses should reflect an understanding that a no-win proposition is unpleasant, stressful, and difficult: nobody likes being faced with a decision that will lead inevitably to loss.*

**Analyze** Are all the "courses" Circe suggests equal? *Possible answer: No one can pass the Prowling Rocks or Charybdis. Though Scylla will eat some of Odysseus' men, their ship can pass by her.*

**Evaluate** What course should Odysseus choose? Give your reasons. *Possible answer: Odysseus should pass by Scylla. In a sense, he has no other choice; passing by her is the only way he can continue homeward.*

---

**VOCABULARY**

**COMMON CORE**
**L 4**

### OWN THE WORD

**abominably:** Review the definition of *abominably* with students. Then have them name terms that are similar in meaning, but carry less intensity. *Possible answers: badly, poorly, incorrectly, unsatisfactorily*

---

                                              Ahead are beetling rocks
and dark blue glancing Amphitrite, surging,
roars around them. Prowling Rocks, or Drifters,
the gods in bliss have named them—named them well.
Not even birds can pass them by. . . .

30                                    A second course
lies between headlands. One is a sharp mountain
piercing the sky, with stormcloud round the peak
dissolving never, not in the brightest summer,
to show heaven's azure there, nor in the fall.
35 No mortal man could scale it, nor so much
as land there, not with twenty hands and feet,
so sheer the cliffs are—as of polished stone.
Midway that height, a cavern full of mist
opens toward Erebus and evening. Skirting
40 this in the lugger, great Odysseus,
your master bowman, shooting from the deck,
would come short of the cavemouth with his shaft;
but that is the den of Scylla, where she yaps
**abominably**, a newborn whelp's cry,
45 though she is huge and monstrous. God or man,
no one could look on her in joy. Her legs—
and there are twelve—are like great tentacles,
unjointed, and upon her serpent necks
are borne six heads like nightmares of ferocity,
50 with triple serried rows of fangs and deep
gullets of black death. Half her length, she sways
her heads in air, outside her horrid cleft,
hunting the sea around that promontory
for dolphins, dogfish, or what bigger game
55 thundering Amphitrite feeds in thousands.
And no ship's company can claim
to have passed her without loss and grief; she takes,
from every ship, one man for every gullet.

The opposite point seems more a tongue of land
60 you'd touch with a good bowshot, at the narrows.
A great wild fig, a shaggy mass of leaves,
grows on it, and Charybdis lurks below
to swallow down the dark sea tide. Three times
from dawn to dusk she spews it up
65 and sucks it down again three times, a whirling
maelstrom; if you come upon her then
the god who makes earth tremble could not save you.

**1232** UNIT 11: THE ODYSSEY

---

**25 beetling:** jutting or overhanging.

**26 glancing Amphitrite** (ăm′fĭ-trī′tē): sparkling seawater. (Amphitrite is the goddess of the sea and the wife of Poseidon. Here, Circe uses the name to refer to the sea itself.)

**31 headlands:** points of land jutting out into the sea; promontories.

**34 heaven's azure** (ăzh′ər): the blue sky.

**abominably** (ə-bŏm′ə-nə-blē) *adv.* in a hateful way; horribly

**COMMON CORE L 4c**

### Language Coach

**Homophones** Words that sound alike but have different meanings, and often different spellings, are called **homophones**. What verb in line 49 is a homophone of *born*? What is the present tense form of this verb? Refer to a dictionary if you need help.

**43–55** Circe presents a very unpleasant image of Scylla. *To get a better idea of what Odysseus and his crew will be up against, try using this detailed description to either visualize or draw a picture of Scylla.*

**66 maelstrom** (māl′strəm): a large, violent whirlpool.

---

## DIFFERENTIATED INSTRUCTION

### FOR ENGLISH LANGUAGE LEARNERS

**Task Support** Help students break down and categorize the description of Scylla: *Sound:* horrible yaps, like those of a newborn animal (lines 43–44); *size:* huge and monstrous (line 45); *appearance:* 12 huge, unjointed legs, like tentacles (lines 46–48), six necks that look like a serpent's (lines 48–49), sharp fangs in triple rows (line 50), deep black throats (lines 50–51); *food:* dolphins, dogfish, or bigger game (lines 54–55).

### Language Coach
**COMMON CORE**
**L 4c**

**Homophones** *Possible answer: borne*; bear; Have students identify what word in line 53 has a homophone. *Possible answer: sea*

No, hug the cliff of Scylla, take your ship
through on a racing stroke. Better to mourn
70 six men than lose them all, and the ship, too.'

So her advice ran; but I faced her, saying:

'Only instruct me, goddess, if you will,
how, if possible, can I pass Charybdis,
or fight off Scylla when she raids my crew?'

75 Swiftly that loveliest goddess answered me:

'Must you have battle in your heart forever?
The bloody toil of combat? Old contender,
will you not yield to the immortal gods?
That nightmare cannot die, being eternal
80 evil itself—horror, and pain, and chaos;
there is no fighting her, no power can fight her,
all that avails is flight.

              Lose headway there
along that rockface while you break out arms,
and she'll swoop over you, I fear, once more,
85 taking one man again for every gullet. **T**
No, no, put all your backs into it, row on;
invoke Blind Force, that bore this scourge of men,
to keep her from a second strike against you.

Then you will coast Thrinacia, the island
90 where Helios' cattle graze, fine herds, and flocks
of goodly sheep. The herds and flocks are seven,
with fifty beasts in each.

                No lambs are dropped,
or calves, and these fat cattle never die.
Immortal, too, their cowherds are—their shepherds—
95 Phaethusa and Lampetia, sweetly braided
nymphs that divine Neaera bore
to the overlord of high noon, Helios.
These nymphs their gentle mother bred and placed
upon Thrinacia, the distant land,
100 in care of flocks and cattle for their father.

Now give those kine a wide berth, keep your thoughts
intent upon your course for home,
and hard seafaring brings you all to Ithaca.
But if you raid the beeves, I see destruction
105 for ship and crew.

**82 all ... flight:** all you can do is flee.

**T EPIC HERO**
Summarize the exchange between Odysseus and Circe in lines 68–85. What is Circe's advice to Odysseus? Do you think he will follow her advice? Explain.

**87 invoke ... men:** pray to the goddess Blind Force, who gave birth to Scylla.

**89 coast:** sail along the coast of.

**95–96 Phaethusa** (fā'ə-thōō'sə); **Lampetia** (lăm-pē'shə); **Neaera** (nē-ē'rə).

**101–105** Circe warns Odysseus not to steal Helios' fine cattle because Helios will take revenge.

THE WANDERINGS OF ODYSSEUS: BOOK 12    **1233**

**TEXT ANALYSIS**

**COMMON CORE**

**T EPIC HERO**

RL 6

**Possible answer:** *Circe advises Odysseus to pass by Scylla and accept the loss of six men. She points out that trying to fight the monster will only cost him more men. Odysseus will pass Scylla, but he will not heed her warning about avoiding a fight. In the past, he has turned his back on such sound warnings.*

**FOR STRUGGLING READERS**
**Paraphrasing Homer** Have students reread the summary of lines 101–105 in the side column. Then model how to paraphrase lines 101–102: *Stay away from those cattle, and think only about your journey.* Invite volunteers to paraphrase lines 103–105: *And then you will all get back to Ithaca. But if you steal the beef, your ship and crew will be destroyed.*

**FOR ENGLISH LANGUAGE LEARNERS**
**Task Support** Help students to paraphrase lines 76–88 in preparation for answering the text analysis question: *Stop thinking about fighting, because you cannot kill that nightmarish monster. Instead, flee by rowing quickly so she cannot strike again.*

 *Model the Skill:* EPIC HERO

Tell students to think carefully about what has occurred in the story thus far. Remind students that both Circe and Tiresias offered Odysseus the same warning about Helios: His men and ship will be destroyed if they steal his cattle, and only Odysseus will return to Ithaca. Consider the importance of prophecies and fate in epic stories while formulating an answer.

**Possible answer:** *Odysseus has some limited power to steer his fate. He can heed the advice himself and can try to influence his men, but he cannot control their actions.*

VOCABULARY                    COMMON CORE    L 4

## OWN THE WORD

**ardor:** Tell students that *ardor* comes from the Latin word *ardor,* which means "burning heat."

---

Rough years then lie between
you and your homecoming, alone and old,
the one survivor, all companions lost.' . . ." Ⓤ

*At dawn, Odysseus and his men continue their journey. Odysseus decides to tell the men only of Circe's warnings about the Sirens, whom they will soon encounter. He is fairly sure that they can survive this peril if he keeps their spirits up. Suddenly, the wind stops.*

     "The crew were on their feet
briskly, to furl the sail, and stow it; then,
110 each in place, they poised the smooth oar blades
and sent the white foam scudding by. I carved
a massive cake of beeswax into bits
and rolled them in my hands until they softened—
no long task, for a burning heat came down
115 from Helios, lord of high noon. Going forward
I carried wax along the line, and laid it
thick on their ears. They tied me up, then, plumb
amidships, back to the mast, lashed to the mast,
and took themselves again to rowing. Soon,
120 as we came smartly within hailing distance,
the two Sirens, noting our fast ship
off their point, made ready, and they sang. . . .

  The lovely voices in **ardor** appealing over the water
made me crave to listen, and I tried to say
125 'Untie me!' to the crew, jerking my brows;
but they bent steady to the oars. Then Perimedes
got to his feet, he and Eurylochus,
and passed more line about, to hold me still.
So all rowed on, until the Sirens
130 dropped under the sea rim, and their singing
dwindled away.
     My faithful company
rested on their oars now, peeling off
the wax that I had laid thick on their ears;
then set me free.
     But scarcely had that island
135 faded in blue air than I saw smoke
and white water, with sound of waves in tumult—
a sound the men heard, and it terrified them.
Oars flew from their hands; the blades went knocking
wild alongside till the ship lost way,
140 with no oarblades to drive her through the water.

Ⓤ **EPIC HERO**
Reread lines 104–107, and reconsider your thoughts about Tiresias' prophecy. Do you think Odysseus has the power to steer his fate? Explain.

**117–118 plumb amidships:** exactly in the center of the ship.

**ardor** (är′dər) *n.* passion

**126 Perimedes** (pĕr′ĭ-mē′dēz).

**134–139** The men panic when they hear the thundering surf.

---

## DIFFERENTIATED INSTRUCTION

**FOR STRUGGLING READERS**

**Text Digest** Have a volunteer read aloud the italicized text at the top of page 1234. Ask students why Odysseus told his men only of Circe's warnings about the Sirens. **Possible answer:** *He wanted them to concentrate on getting past the Sirens, not to worry about anything else.*

**FOR RELUCTANT READERS**

To elicit a response to this episode, tell students to imagine that they have been invited to participate in creating a film that dramatizes the famous struggle of Odysseus and his crew against the Sirens, Scylla, and Charybdis. Form small groups, and have students discuss the following topics for their film adaptation: setting, music, visuals, costumes, design of sirens, Scylla and Charybdis, and the possibility of metaphors. Encourage students to pick out music and sketch character designs, setting, staging, and costumes.

Well, I walked up and down from bow to stern,
trying to put heart into them, standing over
every oarsman, saying gently,

                                        'Friends,

have we never been in danger before this?
145 More fearsome, is it now, than when the Cyclops
penned us in his cave? What power he had!
Did I not keep my nerve, and use my wits
to find a way out for us?

                                Now I say

by hook or crook this peril too shall be
150 something that we remember.

                                Heads up, lads!

We must obey the orders as I give them.
Get the oarshafts in your hands, and lay back
hard on your benches; hit these breaking seas.
Zeus help us pull away before we founder.
155 You at the tiller, listen, and take in
all that I say—the rudders are your duty;
keep her out of the combers and the smoke;
steer for that headland; watch the drift, or we
fetch up in the smother, and you drown us.'

160 That was all, and it brought them round to action.
But as I sent them on toward Scylla, I
told them nothing, as they could do nothing.
They would have dropped their oars again, in panic,
to roll for cover under the decking. Circe's
165 bidding against arms had slipped my mind,
so I tied on my cuirass and took up
two heavy spears, then made my way along
to the foredeck—thinking to see her first from there,
the monster of the gray rock, harboring
170 torment for my friends. I strained my eyes
upon that cliffside veiled in cloud, but nowhere
could I catch sight of her.

                                And all this time,

in **travail**, sobbing, gaining on the current,
we rowed into the strait—Scylla to port
175 and on our starboard beam Charybdis, dire
gorge of the salt sea tide. By heaven! when she
vomited, all the sea was like a cauldron
seething over intense fire, when the mixture
suddenly heaves and rises. Ⓥ

---

**154 founder:** sink.

**157 combers:** breaking waves.

**158–159 watch . . . smother:** keep the ship on course, or it will be crushed in the rough water.

**travail** (trə-vāl′) *n.* painful effort

**176 gorge:** throat; gullet.

---

**TIERED DISCUSSION PROMPTS**

Use these prompts to help students understand how Odysseus leads his crew out of danger in lines 141–164:

**Connect** Have you ever been in a situation where it was important to do everything exactly as you were told? How does that help you understand the importance of the crew's obeying Odysseus? *Students' responses should reflect an understanding of the importance of following orders in order to get through a task.*

**Analyze** On the basis of their actions, do you think the crew trusts Odysseus? *Possible answers: Yes, the crew falls into action as soon as Odysseus explains their orders. No, Odysseus must withhold the truth from them in order to keep them from hiding in fear.*

**Evaluate** Does Odysseus lead effectively by withholding the truth? *Possible answers: Yes, he tells his men only what they must know in order to save the ship and most of the crew. No, Odysseus should have told them of their fate and trusted their actions.*

**VOCABULARY**  **COMMON CORE L 4**

**OWN THE WORD**

**travail:** Ask students to explain why rowing would be described as *travail*. *Possible answer: It is hard work, requiring strenuous, painful effort.*

**TEXT ANALYSIS** **COMMON CORE RL 6**

Ⓥ **EPIC HERO**

*Possible answer: Odysseus is an excellent leader. When the men falter in turbulent waters, Odysseus keeps his head and cajoles them into going back to their duties. He uses Circe's information judiciously. He tells them what they need to know but holds back unhelpful, disturbing information.*

---

**FOR ADVANCED LEARNERS/PRE–AP**

**Characterization** Only a few of Odysseus' shipmates are identified by name. In Book 12, Odysseus mentions Perimedes and Eurylochus (lines 126–127). Ask students to recall what we know about these men. Discuss why the narrative rarely focuses on Odysseus' shipmates. Ask students to rewrite one adventure from Book 12 from the point of view of Eurylochus.

**FOR ENGLISH LANGUAGE LEARNERS**

**Language Coach** **COMMON CORE RL 4**

**Idioms** *Possible answer: It seems to mean "by any means necessary." This makes sense given the etymology of the expression.* Have students identify the idiomatic expression in line 147 ("keep my nerve"). Ask students what it means in this context. *Possible answer: be courageous*

## What is a **HERO**?

As Odysseus' ship nears Scylla, he forgets Circe's warning and takes up spears and ties on his cuirass (lines 166–167). Ask students, based on lines 185–203, why Odysseus does not attempt to stop the monster when they finally pass Scylla. **Possible answer:** *Odysseus must have realized that Circe was right: any effort to fight Scylla would have cost him more men.*

                                    The shot spume
180 soared to the landside heights, and fell like rain.

But when she swallowed the sea water down
we saw the funnel of the maelstrom, heard
the rock bellowing all around, and dark
sand raged on the bottom far below.
185 My men all blanched against the gloom, our eyes
were fixed upon that yawning mouth in fear
of being devoured.
                        Then Scylla made her strike,
whisking six of my best men from the ship.
I happened to glance aft at ship and oarsmen
190 and caught sight of their arms and legs, dangling
high overhead. Voices came down to me
in anguish, calling my name for the last time.

A man surfcasting on a point of rock
for bass or mackerel, whipping his long rod
195 to drop the sinker and the bait far out,
will hook a fish and rip it from the surface
to dangle wriggling through the air:
                                    so these
were borne aloft in spasms toward the cliff.

She ate them as they shrieked there, in her den,
200 in the dire grapple, reaching still for me—
and deathly pity ran me through
at that sight—far the worst I ever suffered,
questing the passes of the strange sea.
                                    We rowed on.
The Rocks were now behind; Charybdis, too,
205 and Scylla dropped astern. . . ."

*Odysseus tries to persuade his men to bypass Thrinacia, the island of the sun god, Helios, but they insist on landing. Driven by hunger, they ignore Odysseus' warning not to feast on Helios' cattle. This disobedience angers the sun god, who threatens to stop shining if payment is not made for the loss of his cattle. To appease Helios, Zeus sends down a thunderbolt to sink Odysseus' ship. Odysseus alone survives. He eventually drifts to Ogygia, the home of Calypso, who keeps him on her island for seven years. With this episode, Odysseus ends the telling of his tale to King Alcinous.*

**179 shot spume:** flying foam.

**185 blanched:** became pale.

**189 aft:** toward the rear of the ship.

**6** **Targeted Passage**

**198 borne aloft in spasms:** lifted high while struggling violently.

**200 grapple:** grasp.

### Analyze Visuals ▶

Apart from depicting a different narrative moment, how does this 16th-century painting differ from the one on page 1231? Be specific in describing the differences in style and mood.

---

## DIFFERENTIATED INSTRUCTION

### FOR STRUGGLING READERS

**6** **Targeted Passage [Lines 193–198]**
In this passage, a simile illustrates the powerlessness of the men caught in Scylla's grasp.

- To what does Homer compare the men hanging in the air? (lines 193–198)

- How does the image express their hopelessness? (lines 193–198)

- Fishing is an ordinary activity. How does this add to the horror of the simile? (lines 193–198)

**Text Digests** Read aloud the italicized text digest at the bottom of page 1236. Ask students to explain what happened to Odysseus after leaving Scylla and Charybdis behind. **Possible answer:** *Odysseus' starving men feasted on Helios' cattle. As punishment, Zeus sank their ship. Only Odysseus lived, drifting to Calypso's island.*

*Scylla and Charybdis* from the *Ulysses Cycle* (1580), Alessandro Allori. Fresco. Banca Toscana (Palazzo Salviati), Florence. Photo © Erich Lessing/Art Resource, New York.

## Analyze Visuals

*Possible answer:* This painting is not as "realistic" as Waterhouse's *Ulysses and the Sirens*. Waterhouse portrayed two sides of these female monsters—both their beauty and their horror. By contrast, the painting of Scylla is concerned only with the monster's horror. Also, Waterhouse's painting is rich in detail, whereas Allori's fresco lacks the specific details of the clothing, the ship, and the expressions of the subjects.

**About the Art**  Alessandro Allori (1535–1607) painted this fresco in about 1580, near the end of the Renaissance. It is in the style known as Mannerism. Remind students that Mannerist artists tended to create works that were idealized and refined. Their paintings were often made for rich patrons.

## SELECTION WRAP–UP

**READ WITH A PURPOSE**  Now that students have finished reading the selection, discuss Odysseus and his character. How does his character reflect the characteristics of an epic hero? *Possible answer: Odysseus is cunning, brave, strong, and very confident.*

⭐ **CRITIQUE**  Ask students if they think Odysseus is a believable character. Have them give specific examples to support their opinions.

# Practice and Apply

For preliminary support of post-reading questions, use these copy masters:

**R** RESOURCE MANAGER—Copy Masters
Reading Check p. 30
Epic Hero p. 23
Question Support p. 31

Additional selection questions are provided for teachers on page 15.

## ANSWERS

## Comprehension

1. *Odysseus longs for his home and family.*

2. *Odysseus and his men blind Polyphemus and escape by hiding under his sheep.*

3. *They turn into pigs.*

4. *Tiresias predicts that Odysseus will lose his crew and ship.*

5. *Odysseus survives the Sirens by blocking his men's ears with beeswax; he avoids Charybdis and sacrifices six men to pass Scylla.*

## Text Analysis

COMMON CORE RL 4, RL 6, RL 10

*Possible answers:*

6. ● **COMMON CORE FOCUS** *Analyze Epic Hero* Strengths: guile, determination, bravery, leadership, self-sacrifice; weaknesses: pride, stubbornness, unwillingness to listen to advice. Odysseus' traits seem fitting for an epic hero of his culture: his weaknesses represent his strengths taken too far.

7. *"that man skilled in all ways of contending" (Book 1, line 2), aggressive, brave; "the wanderer" (Book 1, line 3), curiosity; "son of Laertes, versatile Odysseus" (Book 5, line 69), multitalented, family pride; "the strategist" (Book 5, line 80), clever; "raider of cities" (Book 9, line 418), ruthless, warlike; "master mariner and soldier" (Book 11, line 33), multitalented; "master of land ways and sea ways" (Book 11, line 69), multitalented*

8. *Odysseus' pride and anger cause him to taunt Polyphemus. He cares because Polyphemus killed his men and insulted him. The consequences: the continued wrath of Poseidon.*

9. ■ **COMMON CORE FOCUS** *Interpret Epic Simile The two items being compared are the hooking of a fish by a fisherman and the capturing of Odysseus' trapped men by Scylla. The comparison emphasizes the size*

---

## Comprehension

1. **Recall** Why does Odysseus want to leave Calypso and her island?

2. **Recall** How does Odysseus escape from Polyphemus?

3. **Recall** What happens to Eurylochus' men after they drink Circe's wine?

4. **Recall** What does Tiresias predict will happen if Odysseus raids the herds of Helios?

5. **Summarize** How does Odysseus survive the dangers posed by the Sirens, Scylla, and Charybdis?

## Text Analysis

6. **Analyze Epic Hero** Create a two-column chart to analyze Odysseus' strengths and weaknesses. Considering the cultural values that Odysseus reflects, to what extent do the traits in each column seem fitting for an epic hero? Explain.

| Strengths | Weaknesses |
|---|---|
| shows loyalty in his desire to reach home | pride |

7. **Analyze Epithets** Identify at least five epithets used to describe Odysseus in Part 1. For each epithet, explain what it tells you about his **character**.

8. **Understand Character Motivation** After Odysseus escapes from Polyphemus, he makes sure that Polyphemus knows who outwitted him. Why does he care? What are the consequences of Odysseus' behavior?

9. **Interpret Epic Simile** Reread the **epic simile** on page 1236, lines 193–198, which describes the men being caught by Scylla. Explain what two items are being compared. What does the comparison help to emphasize?

10. **Interpret Allusions** In the opening lines of Book 1, the poet calls upon Muse, a daughter of Zeus often credited with inspiration. Why would he open the epic in this way? What does this allusion tell you about him as a poet?

11. **Examine Theme** One theme in Part 1 is that a hero must rely on clever deceit, or guile, to survive. Explain how this theme is conveyed.

## Text Criticism

12. **Critical Interpretations** In discussing Homer's use of epic similes, the critic Eva Brann contends that "similes do much the same work in Homeric epic as do the gods, who also beautify and magnify human existence." Think about how the gods interact with humans in the *Odyssey*. Do you agree that they "beautify and magnify" human existence? Then consider the epic similes you have encountered so far; how might they be seen to do the same? Explain.

### What is a HERO?

What heroes like Odysseus have you encountered in modern texts?

COMMON CORE

RL 4 Determine the figurative meaning of phrases as they are used in a text. RL 6 Analyze a particular point of view or cultural experience reflected in a work of world literature. RL 10 Read and comprehend stories and poems.

---

*and strength of Scylla, the powerlessness of the men, and the men's hopelessness.*

10. *Calling upon Muse emphasizes the seriousness of the task. The allusion also tells us that Homer is respectful of the gods.*

11. *Odysseus uses guile in his encounters with the Cyclops, Circe, and the Sirens. Other themes: be careful of whom you trust; treat guests honorably; do not enrage the gods.*

## Text Criticism

*Possible answer:*

12. *The comparison is apt: the concern and involvement of the gods adds significance to the trials and actions of Odysseus. So, too, the similes uplift the deeds and trials of the mortals and make them resonate.*

**What is a HERO?** Students should name other heroes they have read about that have the characteristics of an epic hero, such as bravery, determination, self-sacrifice, leadership, and so on.

## Vocabulary in Context

### ▲ VOCABULARY PRACTICE

Decide whether the words in each pair are synonyms or antonyms.

1. harried/calmed
2. appalled/dismayed
3. profusion/shortage
4. ardor/indifference
5. assuage/soothe
6. adversary/friend
7. ponderous/awkward
8. travail/relaxation
9. beguiling/entrancing
10. foreboding/prediction
11. abominably/atrociously
12. meditation/contemplation

**WORD LIST**
abominably
adversary
appalled
ardor
assuage
beguiling
foreboding
harried
meditation
ponderous
profusion
travail

### ACADEMIC VOCABULARY IN WRITING

- demonstrate   - emphasis   - ideology   - monitor   - undertake

Why is it taking Odysseus so long to get back to Ithaca? **Demonstrate** your understanding by writing a short description of Odysseus' journey so far. Explain Homer's **emphasis** on the trials Odysseus faces. Use at least one Academic Vocabulary word in your response.

### VOCABULARY STRATEGY: WORDS WITH THE PREFIX *fore-*

Recognizing prefixes can help you determine the meanings of unfamiliar words, whether in literature or nonfiction readings. The prefix *fore-*, which comes from Old English and means "earlier," "in front of," or "beforehand," is used in forming numerous English words. In *foreboding*, it is combined with the verb *bode*, "to give signs of something." *Fore-* is also combined with many common words, as in *forehead* and *foretell*.

**COMMON CORE**

**L 4d** Verify the preliminary determination of the meaning of a word.

**PRACTICE** Choose a word from the box to complete each sentence. Use a dictionary to check your answers.

1. Our _____ came to this land looking for freedom.
2. Diandra tried to _____ Jack before he walked right into the trap.
3. In the _____ of the painting was a large house; behind the house was a barn.
4. Casual comments early in a story often _____ coming events.
5. The tennis star's strong _____ made her a formidable opponent.
6. To _____ a quick vote on the issue, the committee voted to study it further.
7. In what way was the horse and buggy the _____ of the automobile?

**WORDS WITH fore-**
forefathers
foreground
forehand
forerunner
foreshadow
forestall
forewarn

Interactive Vocabulary

Go to **thinkcentral.com**.
KEYWORD: HML9-1239

---

## Vocabulary in Context

### ▲ VOCABULARY PRACTICE

1. *antonyms*
2. *synonyms*
3. *antonyms*
4. *antonyms*
5. *synonyms*
6. *antonyms*
7. *synonyms*
8. *antonyms*
9. *synonyms*
10. *synonyms*
11. *synonyms*
12. *synonyms*

**R** RESOURCE MANAGER—Copy Master
Vocabulary Practice p. 28

### ACADEMIC VOCABULARY IN WRITING

**Possible answer:** *After the Trojan War, Odysseus spends many years away before he is able to* **undertake** *the journey to Ithaca. Homer probably wanted to make this an exciting story.*

### VOCABULARY STRATEGY: WORDS WITH THE PREFIX *fore-*

**COMMON CORE L 4d**

**Possible answers:**

1. *forefathers*
2. *forewarn*
3. *foreground*
4. *foreshadow*
5. *forehand*
6. *forestall*
7. *forerunner*

**R** RESOURCE MANAGER—Copy Master
Vocabulary Strategy p. 29

**Interactive Vocabulary**

Keywords direct students to a **WordSharp** tutorial on **thinkcentral.com** or to other types of vocabulary practice and review.

---

## DIFFERENTIATED INSTRUCTION

### FOR ENGLISH LANGUAGE LEARNERS

**Vocabulary** Have partners write sentences with six words from the word list. Then call out each word and ask volunteers to read their sentences.

### FOR ADVANCED LEARNERS/PRE–AP

**Vocabulary Practice Challenge** Have students write a description of one of Odysseus' adversaries, using as many of the words from the word list as possible.

---

## Assess and Reteach

### Assess

**DIAGNOSTIC AND SELECTION TESTS**
Selection Test A, B/C pp. 303–306

**Interactive Selection Test** on **thinkcentral.com**

### Reteach

**Level Up Online Tutorials** on **thinkcentral.com**

**Reteaching Worksheets** on **thinkcentral.com**
Vocabulary Lesson 2

# Focus and Motivate

## COMMON CORE FOCUS

**RL 2** Determine a theme of a text; provide an objective summary of the text. **RL 4** Determine the connotative meaning of words as they are used in a text. **RL 5** Analyze how an author's choices concerning how to structure a text create tension. **RL 9** Analyze how an author draws on and transforms source material in a specific text. **L 3** Apply knowledge of language to make effective choices for meaning or style. **L 4** Determine or clarify the meaning of unknown and multiple-meaning words. **L 4c** Consult general and specialized reference materials.

## SUMMARY

**Books 16–23** When Odysseus returns home, Penelope proposes to marry the winner of an archery contest. Odysseus, in disguise, wins the contest but must prove his identity to Penelope.

### How does it feel to come **HOME** again?

Read the question and have students look at the picture on page 1240. What details convey the intensity of the moment? What emotions do the people project? How can you tell this is a homecoming? Then have students complete the *QUICKWRITE*.

---

**Essential Course of Study ECOS**

## The Homecoming
### *from the* Odyssey

Epic Poem by Homer
Translated by Robert Fitzgerald

**VIDEO TRAILER** THINK central KEYWORD: HML9-1240

# How does it feel to come **HOME** again?

### COMMON CORE

**RL 2** Determine a theme of a text; provide an objective summary of the text. **RL 4** Determine the connotative meaning of words as they are used in a text. **RL 5** Analyze how an author's choices concerning how to structure a text create tension. **L 4** Determine or clarify the meaning of unknown and multiple-meaning words.

If you spend enough time at any airport or bus station, you're bound to witness an emotional scene. A long-awaited homecoming can touch us more deeply than almost anything. Imagine a traveler who's been away for years, whose family thought he might never return. What kind of scene might you expect at his homecoming?

*QUICKWRITE* Recall a time when you or someone you know returned home after some time away. Write a brief description of the scene, and explain the emotions that went along with it.

1240

---

# Selection Resources

## TEXT ANALYSIS: CHARACTERISTICS OF AN EPIC

In the simplest terms, an epic is a long adventure story. An epic **plot** spans many years and involves a long journey. Often, the fate of an entire nation is at stake. An epic **setting** spans great distances and foreign lands. Epic **themes**—the underlying messages in an epic—reflect timeless concerns, such as courage, honor, life, and death.

Epics also contain **archetypes,** or patterns found in works across different cultures and time periods. As explained in Part 1, the epic hero is an archetype. So is the notion of a heroic journey. Other archetypes found in the *Odyssey* include intervention by gods, floods and storms, descent into the underworld, and heroic battles against monsters. As you read the second part of the epic, look for these and other archetypes. Consider where else you might have encountered them in literature, art, or film.

## READING STRATEGY: SUMMARIZING

Writing a **plot summary**—a brief retelling of a story—is a good way to make sure you're following the events of a narrative. An epic consists of many episodes, each with its own set of characters, conflicts, and resolution. As you read, record information that will help you summarize each episode. Remember that a summary should be **objective.** It should include only what happens in the text, not your personal opinions.

| **Episode:** *Father and Son* | |
|---|---|
| **Characters:** *Odysseus, Eumaeus* | **Setting:** *Ithaca, Odysseus' homeland* |
| **Conflict:** | **Resolution:** |

## ▲ VOCABULARY IN CONTEXT

Replace the words in bold with synonyms from the word list.

| WORD LIST | | | |
|---|---|---|---|
| | adversity | desolation | revulsion |
| | aloof | implacable | tremulous |
| | commandeer | restitution | |
| | contemptible | revelry | |

1. It's **disgusting** to be **shaky** in the face of **hardship.**
2. He felt an **unforgiving hatred** for his captors.
3. Don't act **distant;** forget **sorrow** and join the **celebration!**
4. He could **seize** enemy ships as **repayment** for wrongs.

 Complete the activities in your **Reader/Writer Notebook.**

### Book 16: Father and Son
Sent safely on his way by King Alcinous, Odysseus reaches Ithaca. The goddess Athena disguises him as an old man so that he may surprise the evil suitors who are courting his wife, Penelope. Odysseus greets Eumaeus, his faithful swineherd, and Telemachus, his own son, returned home after many years abroad.

### Book 17: The Beggar and the Manor
Disguised as a beggar, Odysseus returns to his home.

### Book 21: The Test of the Bow
Not recognizing the beggar as her husband, and weary from grief and waiting, Penelope proposes an archery contest to the suitors, with marriage to her as the prize. Still disguised as an old man, Odysseus beats them all in the contest.

### Book 22: Death in the Great Hall
With Telemachus and Eumaeus at his side, Odysseus sheds his disguise and does battle with the suitors, showing them no mercy.

### Book 23: The Trunk of the Olive Tree
Hardened by years of waiting, Penelope is not convinced that this man is really her husband. She tests him, playing a trick that only Odysseus would recognize. Odysseus passes the test, and husband and wife are reunited.

Penelope weaving at her loom.

THE HOMECOMING **1241**

TEXT ANALYSIS — COMMON CORE — RL 2

● *Model the Skill:*
### CHARACTERISTICS OF AN EPIC

Point out the following examples of archetypes from Part 1:

- Interventions by gods: Athena and Zeus help Odysseus; Poseidon against him;
- Descent into the underworld: Odysseus and his men go see Tiresias;
- Heroic battles against monsters: Cyclops, Sirens, Scylla

**GUIDED PRACTICE** Have students list examples of archetypes from literature, art, or film.

READING STRATEGY — COMMON CORE — RL 2

■ *Model the Skill:* **SUMMARIZING**

Refer students to lines 130–190 in Book 9 as you copy a chart like the one on the student page to the board. Then work with students to fill it out starting with the episode where Odysseus and his men meet the Cyclops.

**GUIDED PRACTICE** Have students summarize the *Overview* on this page in three or four sentences. Remind them to avoid including opinions in their summaries.

**R** RESOURCE MANAGER—Copy Master Summarizing p. 47 (for student use while reading the selection)

---

VOCABULARY SKILL — COMMON CORE — L 4

## ▲ VOCABULARY IN CONTEXT

**DIAGNOSE WORD KNOWLEDGE** Have all students complete Vocabulary in Context. Check their definitions against the following:

**adversity** (ăd-vûr'sĭ-tē) *n.* hardship; misfortune

**aloof** (ə-lōōf') *adj.* distant; remote; standoffish

**commandeer** (kŏm'ən-dîr') *v.* to take control of by force

**contemptible** (kən-tĕmp'tə-bəl) *adj.* deserving of scorn; despicable

**desolation** (dĕs'ə-lā'shən) *n.* lonely grief; misery

**implacable** (ĭm-plăk'ə-bəl) *adj.* impossible to soothe; unforgiving

**restitution** (rĕs'tĭ-tōō'shən) *n.* a making good for loss or damage; repayment

**revelry** (rĕv'əl-rē) *n.* noisy merrymaking; festivity

**revulsion** (rĭ-vŭl'shən) *n.* a sudden feeling of disgust or loathing

**tremulous** (trĕm'yə-ləs) *adj.* marked by trembling or shaking

**PRETEACH VOCABULARY** Use the copy master to help students predict meanings for each boldfaced word.

1. Read item 1 aloud, emphasizing *adversity*.
2. Point out that "survive" and "so much hardship" give clues to the word's meaning.
3. Have students try to figure out what the word means.
4. Repeat the procedure for items 2–10.

**R** RESOURCE MANAGER—Copy Master Vocabulary Study p. 49

### READ WITH A PURPOSE

*Help students set a purpose for reading by telling them to keep track of the events leading up to Odysseus's reunion with his wife.*

## BOOK 16:
*Father and Son*

### Get Into the Book
#### SUMMARY

Book 16 begins when Odysseus comes to the mountain hut of his swineherd, Eumaeus. Telemachus arrives and they share a meal. After the swineherd leaves to tell Penelope that her son is safe, Odysseus reveals his identity to Telemachus. A tearful reunion ensues.

#### REVISIT THE BIG QUESTION

### How does it feel to come **HOME** again?

**Discuss** Point out that Odysseus has been gone from his home for 20 years. Based on lines 10–14, what changes does Odysseus find on his homecoming? *Possible answer: All of the people from his former life have grown older. His son is now a tall man. Furthermore, Ithaca has changed to the extent that Odysseus does not even recognize his island (text digest).*

*In Books 13–15, King Alcinous and his friends send Odysseus on his way home. Odysseus sleeps while the rowers bring him to Ithaca. When he awakens, he fails to recognize his homeland until Athena appears and tells him that he is indeed home. She disguises him as an old man, so that he can surprise the suitors, and then urges him to visit his faithful swineherd, Eumaeus. The swineherd welcomes the disguised Odysseus and tells him about what has been happening in Odysseus' home. Athena goes to Telemachus and tells him to return home. She warns him of the suitors' plot to kill him and advises him to stay with the swineherd for a night. Telemachus does as she bids.*

But there were two men in the mountain hut—
Odysseus and the swineherd. At first light
blowing their fire up, they cooked their breakfast
and sent their lads out, driving herds to root
5  in the tall timber.

                 When Telemachus came,
the wolvish troop of watchdogs only fawned on him
as he advanced. Odysseus heard them go
and heard the light crunch of a man's footfall—
at which he turned quickly to say:

                        "Eumaeus,
10  here is one of your crew come back, or maybe
another friend: the dogs are out there snuffling
belly down; not one has even growled.
I can hear footsteps—"

                    But before he finished
his tall son stood at the door.

### Analyze Visuals ▶

Review the information given in the summary at the top of this page. What do you think Marc Chagall wanted to capture in this painting?

*Athene and Telemach,* from *Odyssey II* (1975), Marc Chagall. Lithograph on Arches paper. 16.9″ × 13″. Photograph by Gregory R. Staley. Courtesy of the Georgetown Frame Shoppe. © 2007 Artists Rights Society (ARS), New York/ADAGP, Paris.

## DIFFERENTIATED INSTRUCTION

### FOR ENGLISH LANGUAGE LEARNERS

**Preview** Point out that the italicized synopsis of Books 13–15 at the top of the page contain strong verbs that help readers get a sense of the action in the story. Have students list all the verbs contained in the synopsis. Then have them write their own summaries of the synopsis, using at least five of the verbs.

## BACKGROUND

**Home and Family** A palace like the one belonging to Odysseus was known as a *megaron* and stood in the center of town. The chief held court in a large chamber with a circular hearth, and retainers slept in a vestibule outside. Husbands and wives often lived in separate chambers within the home and engaged in separate activities. For example, a husband might arrange a party for his male friends from which wives and daughters were excluded. Children stayed in the women's chambers with their mothers. At an appropriate age, boys moved out of the women's chambers. They attended school while girls stayed home to learn how to cook, to weave, and to care for children.

The swineherd

15 rose in surprise, letting a bowl and jug
tumble from his fingers. Going forward,
he kissed the young man's head, his shining eyes
and both hands, while his own tears brimmed and fell.
Think of a man whose dear and only son,
20 born to him in exile, reared with labor,
has lived ten years abroad and now returns:
how would that man embrace his son! Just so
the herdsman clapped his arms around Telemachus
and covered him with kisses—for he knew
25 the lad had got away from death. He said:

"Light of my days, Telemachus,
you made it back! When you took ship for Pylos
I never thought to see you here again.
Come in, dear child, and let me feast my eyes;
30 here you are, home from distant places!
How rarely anyway, you visit us,
your own men, and your own woods and pastures!
Always in the town, a man would think
you loved the suitors' company, those dogs!"

35 Telemachus with his clear candor said:

"I am with you, Uncle. See now, I have come
because I wanted to see you first, to hear from you
if Mother stayed at home—or is she married
off to someone and Odysseus' bed
40 left empty for some gloomy spider's weaving?"

Gently the forester replied to this:

"At home indeed your mother is, poor lady,
still in the women's hall. Her nights and days
are wearied out with grieving."

                              Stepping back
45 he took the bronze-shod lance, and the young prince
entered the cabin over the worn door stone.
Odysseus moved aside, yielding his couch,
but from across the room Telemachus checked him:

"Friend, sit down; we'll find another chair
50 in our own hut. Here is the man to make one!"

---

## TEXT ANALYSIS

### Ⓐ EPIC

COMMON CORE — RL 2

**Possible answer:** *The simile compares Eumaeus' reunion with Telemachus to a father meeting with his only son after ten years' absence. The simile explains Eumaeus' relationship with Telemachus: he had been like a father to the boy. It develops the theme that family relationships are deep and enduring. It also prepares us for Odysseus' reunion with his son.*

## TEXT ANALYSIS

### Ⓑ EPIC

COMMON CORE — RL 2

**Possible answer:** *These lines indicate a journey to strange and distant lands—an epic setting. They suggest that Telemachus has been engaged in his own epic voyage during his father's absence and that he shares the heroic traits of his father.*

**Extend the Discussion** What do these lines suggest about Telemachus' character?

---

Ⓐ **EPIC**
Reread lines 19–23. What **theme** is being developed in this **epic simile**?

**27 when you took ship for Pylos:** Ten years earlier, Telemachus went to Pylos (pī'läs') in search of knowledge about Odysseus' whereabouts.

Ⓑ **EPIC**
Reread lines 26–30. How do these lines indicate an epic **setting**?

① **Targeted Passage**

---

## DIFFERENTIATED INSTRUCTION

### FOR STRUGGLING READERS

In combination with the *Audio Anthology CD*, use one or more Targeted Passages (pp. 1244, 1250, 1258, 1262, 1265) to ensure that students focus on key story events, concepts, and skills. Targeted Passages are also good for English.

① **Targeted Passage** [Lines 26–50]

This passage introduces Telemachus and develops the character of Eumaeus.

- What words does the narrator use to describe Telemachus? (lines 26–50)

- How does Telemachus treat Eumaeus? How does he treat Odysseus? What does this tell us about him? (lines 35–50)

- Why might Odysseus and Penelope have chosen a swineherd to help raise their son? (lines 26–46)

The swineherd, when the quiet man sank down,
built a new pile of evergreens and fleeces—
a couch for the dear son of great Odysseus—
then gave them trenchers of good meat, left over
55 from the roast pork of yesterday, and heaped up
willow baskets full of bread, and mixed
an ivy bowl of honey-hearted wine.
Then he in turn sat down, facing Odysseus,
their hands went out upon the meat and drink
60 as they fell to, ridding themselves of hunger. . . .

*Telemachus sends the swineherd to let his mother know he has returned safely.
Athena appears and urges Odysseus to let Telemachus know who he really is.*

                                    Saying no more,
she tipped her golden wand upon the man,
making his cloak pure white and the knit tunic
fresh around him. Lithe and young she made him,
65 ruddy with sun, his jawline clean, the beard
no longer grew upon his chin. And she
withdrew when she had done.

**C EPIC**

*Possible answer: Athena transforms Odysseus into a young, clean-shaven man in fresh clothing.*

**IF STUDENTS NEED HELP . . .** Have them list details and changes described in lines 61–67.

## Analyze Visuals

**About the Art** The mosaic of Odysseus and Telemachus is from first-century A.D. Rome. Romans used mosaics to decorate their walls and floors. Roman artists often copied the subject matter and techniques of painting in their mosaics. *Possible answer: The tiles are clustered in similar ways for the two men, highlighting similarities in facial features, coloring, and size. The images are flat and not realistic, but the placement and appearance of the figures make them look like father and son.*

---

Then Lord Odysseus **C**
reappeared—and his son was thunderstruck.
Fear in his eyes, he looked down and away
70 as though it were a god, and whispered:

"Stranger,
you are no longer what you were just now!
Your cloak is new; even your skin! You are
one of the gods who rule the sweep of heaven!
Be kind to us, we'll make you fair oblation
75 and gifts of hammered gold. Have mercy on us!"

The noble and enduring man replied:

"No god. Why take me for a god? No, no.
I am that father whom your boyhood lacked
and suffered pain for lack of. I am he."

80 Held back too long, the tears ran down his cheeks
as he embraced his son.

**C EPIC**
What supernatural event is described in lines 61–67?

**74 oblation:** sacrifice

**▼ Analyze Visuals**

This detail of an ancient Roman mosaic shows Odysseus (Ulysses) and Telemachus. How does the technique of clustering colored tiles together affect the kind of image that can be created? Be specific.

*Ulysses and His Son Telemachus* (A.D. first century). Mosaic, 31.5 cm. Kunsthistorisches Museum, Vienna. © Erich Lessing/Art Resource, New York.

---

## DIFFERENTIATED INSTRUCTION

**FOR ADVANCED LEARNERS/PRE–AP**
**Analyze** Ask students how Odysseus shows himself to be "noble and enduring" (line 76) in his first conversation with Telemachus. How is your understanding of his character deepened by this interaction?

**FOR STRUGGLING READERS**
**Concept Support** Help students recall these terms related to the elements of plot: *conflict,* "a struggle between opposing forces, either internal or external"; *resolution,* "the final outcome of events and conflicts and tying up of loose ends."

Only Telemachus,

uncomprehending, wild
with incredulity, cried out:

"You cannot

be my father Odysseus! Meddling spirits
85  conceived this trick to twist the knife in me!
No man of woman born could work these wonders
by his own craft, unless a god came into it
with ease to turn him young or old at will.
I swear you were in rags and old,
90  and here you stand like one of the immortals!"

Odysseus brought his ranging mind to bear
and said:

"This is not princely, to be swept

away by wonder at your father's presence.
No other Odysseus will ever come,
95  for he and I are one, the same; his bitter
fortune and his wanderings are mine.
Twenty years gone, and I am back again
on my own island. . . ."

Then, throwing

100  his arms around this marvel of a father
Telemachus began to weep. Salt tears
rose from the wells of longing in both men,
and cries burst from both as keen and fluttering
as those of the great taloned hawk,
105  whose nestlings farmers take before they fly.
So helplessly they cried, pouring out tears,
and might have gone on weeping so till sundown. . . .

*Telemachus lets Odysseus know that they face more than 100 suitors. Odysseus
tells Telemachus to return home. He will follow—still disguised as an old man—
and Telemachus must pretend not to know him. He must also lock away
Odysseus' weapons and armor.*

---

**D EPIC**
Reread lines 61–90. What central **conflict** is beginning to find resolution in this scene? What elements indicate the importance of this moment?

**91 brought his ranging mind to bear:** took control of his wandering thoughts.

**E EPIC**
Reread lines 99–107. What striking **character trait** is emphasized in both Odysseus and Telemachus? Why is this unusual?

THE HOMECOMING: BOOK 16  **1247**

---

---

In Book 17 Odysseus, still disguised as a beggar, arrives with Telemachus at his home. Eumaeus follows. Seeing his dog, Argos, now old and mistreated, saddens Odysseus. When he enters his home, the suitors ridicule him.

### REVISIT THE BIG QUESTION

## How does it feel to come **HOME** again?

**Discuss** Based on lines 18–27, how did Odysseus feel about seeing his old dog? Why didn't he let Eumaeus know? *Possible answer: Odysseus felt sad and nostalgic seeing this once vibrant puppy, now so old and badly treated. He couldn't tell Eumaeus because he feared that the swineherd might give away his secret, intentionally or inadvertently.*

# BOOK 17:
## *The Beggar at the Manor*

*Telemachus returns home, and Odysseus and the swineherd soon follow. Odysseus is still diguised as a beggar.*

                                                While he spoke
an old hound, lying near, pricked up his ears
and lifted up his muzzle. This was Argos,
trained as a puppy by Odysseus,
5  but never taken on a hunt before
his master sailed for Troy. The young men, afterward,
hunted wild goats with him, and hare, and deer,
but he had grown old in his master's absence.
Treated as rubbish now, he lay at last
10  upon a mass of dung before the gates—
manure of mules and cows, piled there until
fieldhands could spread it on the king's estate.
Abandoned there, and half destroyed with flies,
old Argos lay.
                                  But when he knew he heard
15  Odysseus' voice nearby, he did his best
to wag his tail, nose down, with flattened ears,
having no strength to move nearer his master.
And the man looked away,
wiping a salt tear from his cheek; but he
20  hid this from Eumaeus. Then he said:

"I marvel that they leave this hound to lie
here on the dung pile;
he would have been a fine dog, from the look of him,
though I can't say as to his power and speed
25  when he was young. You find the same good build
in house dogs, table dogs landowners keep
all for style."
                                  And you replied, Eumaeus:

"A hunter owned him—but the man is dead
in some far place. If this old hound could show

**Analyze Visuals ▶**

This illustration of Odysseus and his dog comes from the late 19th or early 20th century. Compare it with the scene depicted on the clay urn shown on page 1193. What elements do the two pieces have in common?

**COMMON CORE** RL 4

**Language Coach**

**Denotation/Connotation** A word's context can usually help you distinguish its **connotation,** the feelings associated with the word, from its **denotation,** or dictionary meaning. *Marvel* denotatively means "to be amazed or filled with admiration." Reread lines 1–27. How does the connotation of *marvel* in line 21 differ from the word's denotation?

1248  UNIT 11: THE ODYSSEY

---

## DIFFERENTIATED INSTRUCTION

### FOR STRUGGLING READERS

**Preview** Read aloud the italicized synopsis at the top of the page to give students a clear idea of the intervening plot. To check their comprehension, ask them where Telemachus, Odysseus, and Eumaeus are at the start of Book 17. **Possible answer:** *back at Odysseus' home in Ithaca*

### FOR ENGLISH LANGUAGE LEARNERS

**Language Coach**    COMMON CORE RL 4

**Denotation/Connotation:**
*Possible answer: In line 21,* marvel *connotes that Odysseus is shocked and angry by how his dog has been treated; here, the word does not have the positive connotations that it often does.* Have students write a paragraph about an event in their own lives, using *marvel* or another verb in a way which has a connotation different from its denotation.

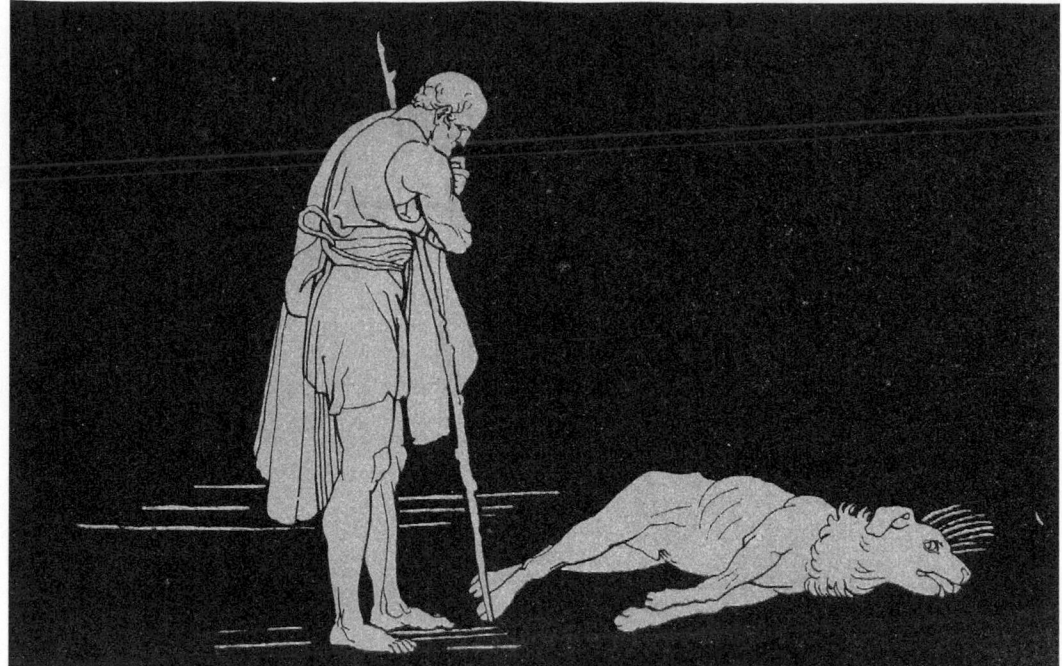

*Ulysses and His Dog* (c. 1900). © Bettman/Corbis.

30 the form he had when Lord Odysseus left him,
   going to Troy, you'd see him swift and strong.
   He never shrank from any savage thing
   he'd brought to bay in the deep woods; on the scent
   no other dog kept up with him. Now misery
35 has him in leash. His owner died abroad,
   and here the women slaves will take no care of him.
   You know how servants are: without a master
   they have no will to labor, or excel.
   For Zeus who views the wide world takes away
40 half the manhood of a man, that day
   he goes into captivity and slavery." **F**

   Eumaeus crossed the court and went straight forward
   into the mégaron among the suitors;
   but death and darkness in that instant closed
45 the eyes of Argos, who had seen his master,
   Odysseus, after twenty years. . . .

*Odysseus enters his home as a beggar, and the suitors mock and abuse him.*
*Penelope asks to speak with the beggar, but Odysseus puts her off until nightfall.*

---

**COMMON CORE** RL 5

**F EPIC**

Reread lines 28–41. Eumaeus still does not know that he is speaking to Odysseus in disguise. This is known as **dramatic irony**—a plot device in which the reader knows more than the character knows. Dramatic irony can create **suspense** (a feeling of tension or excitement) as the reader anticipates what might happen. What event does this speech cause you to anticipate?

**43 mégaron:** the main hall of a palace or house

---

**TEXT ANALYSIS**   COMMON CORE RL 5

**F EPIC**

*Possible answer:* *The reader knows that Odysseus is not only alive but also walking and talking to Eumaeus, who believes him to be dead. The fact that neither Eumaeus nor Telemachus had seen through Odysseus' disguise sets up the possibility that it will also fool Penelope and her suitors. Eumaeus' speech causes us to anticipate this meeting.*

In small groups, have students discuss other examples of dramatic irony. Remind students to think of movies where viewers often know more than characters do to build suspense or humor.

---

**FOR STRUGGLING READERS**

**Text Digest** Read aloud the italicized text digest at the end of page 1249 to make sure students understand what happens right after Odysseus enters his home. Ask them what we learn about the suitors from the way they treat Odysseus. *Possible answer: The suitors are crude bullies. They assume that Odysseus is helpless because he appears to be a poor beggar, and they have no sympathy for him.*

**FOR ADVANCED LEARNERS/PRE–AP**

**Point of View** In the scene where Odysseus sees his old dog, the narrator switches point of view several times (lines 1–41). Have students discuss how the changing point of view increases the poignancy of the scene.

## Get Into the Book

### SUMMARY

Book 21 tells how Penelope sobs when she takes out Odysseus' bow for a contest to win her hand in marriage. While the suitors try to string the bow, Odysseus enlists the help of Eumaeus and Philoetius. Despite the suitors' protests, which are followed by their jeers, Odysseus gets the bow. He strings it and carries out Penelope's task. Then, with his son by his side, Odysseus faces his enemies.

### Ⓖ ARCHETYPE

**Possible answer:** *The image of a bull bellowing in a field is an archetypal male image. The bull suggests strength, anger, power. Its bellowing indicates both a warning and a challenge. The bull represents Odysseus and reminds us that he is preparing to defend his home and family.*

---

# BOOK 21:
## *The Test of the Bow*

*In Books 18–20, Odysseus observes the suitors and finds that two in particular, Antinous and Eurymachus, are rude and demanding. Penelope asks Odysseus the beggar for news of her husband. He says he has heard that Odysseus is on his way home. Penelope, however, has given up hope for Odysseus' return. She proposes an archery contest to the suitors, with marriage to her as the prize. She enters the storeroom and takes down the heavy bow that Odysseus left behind.*

> Now the queen reached the storeroom door and halted.
> Here was an oaken sill, cut long ago
> and sanded clean and bedded true. Foursquare
> the doorjambs and the shining doors were set
> 5  by the careful builder. Penelope untied the strap
> around the curving handle, pushed her hook
> into the slit, aimed at the bolts inside
> and shot them back. Then came a rasping sound
> as those bright doors the key had sprung gave way—
> 10  a bellow like a bull's vaunt in a meadow— Ⓖ
> followed by her light footfall entering
> over the plank floor. Herb-scented robes
> lay there in chests, but the lady's milkwhite arms
> went up to lift the bow down from a peg
> 15  in its own polished bowcase.
>                         Now Penelope
> sank down, holding the weapon on her knees,
> and drew her husband's great bow out, and sobbed
> and bit her lip and let the salt tears flow.
> Then back she went to face the crowded hall,
> 20  tremendous bow in hand, and on her shoulder hung
> the quiver spiked with coughing death. Behind her
> maids bore a basket full of axeheads, bronze
> and iron implements for the master's game.
> Thus in her beauty she approached the suitors,
> 25  and near a pillar of the solid roof

**Analyze Visuals** ▶

This is a detail from an 18th-century portrait of Penelope. What qualities are emphasized in this portrait, and how do they compare with qualities emphasized in the text on this page? Explain.

❷  **Targeted Passage**

Ⓖ **ARCHETYPE**
Reread lines 8–10. What archetypal image do you recognize in these lines? Explain how this image helps to build **suspense**.

**15–18** Notice that Penelope still grieves for Odysseus, even after 20 years.

**21 quiver** (kwĭv´ər): a case in which arrows are carried. *What is meant by "the quiver spiked with coughing death"?*

**22–23 axeheads … game:** metal heads of axes (without handles) that Odysseus employs in a display of archery skill.

Detail of *Penelope Weeping Over the Bow of Ulysses* (c. 1779), Angelica Kauffmann. Wolverhampton Art Gallery (OP 531), Wolverhampton, United Kingdom.

---

## DIFFERENTIATED INSTRUCTION

### FOR STRUGGLING READERS

❷ **Targeted Passage** [Lines 5–25]
This passage introduces Penelope and illustrates her conflict:

- What words are used to describe Penelope? (lines 11–25)

- How can you tell that she is physically strong? (lines 5–10)

- Why is she carrying the bow? (lines 15–23)

- How can you tell that she still loves Odysseus? (lines 15–18)

### FOR ENGLISH LANGUAGE LEARNERS

**Task Support**  Direct students' attention to the question in the side note for line 21.
**Possible answer:** *A quiver holds arrows; these weapons have the potential for killing, especially in Odysseus' hands. They foreshadow his revenge. "Coughing death" suggests that an arrow may pierce someone's lungs.*

## Analyze Visuals

*Possible answer:* *The painting emphasizes Penelope's purity, her sturdiness, her sadness, and her grief. The text, too, emphasizes her strength, as she lifts the heavy bow in its bow-case (lines 14–15), as well as her sadness, as she sinks down and sobs (line 18).*

**About the Art** Swiss-born artist Angelica Kauffmann (1741–1807) studied in Italy and settled in Britain. One of the few 18th-century women to achieve distinction as an artist, she was part of Sir Joshua Reynolds's circle. Even so, she suffered discrimination: Kauffmann was not allowed to take life classes or attend meetings of the Royal Academy, although she was a founding member.

**READING STRATEGY**

### ■ VISUALIZE IMAGERY

Have students pay attention to the words and images used to describe Odysseus' storeroom as you reread lines 1–15. Challenge them to recall specific visual details of the doorway and storeroom. What other senses does the scene appeal to? Explain. ***Possible answer:*** *It appeals to the senses of hearing and smell: sound of bolts, rasping sound of the doors, Penelope's light footfall; the smell of herb-scented robes.*

**FOR ADVANCED LEARNERS/PRE–AP**

**Women Characters** Have students compare and contrast the different types of women in the *Odyssey*: Penelope, the archetype of loyalty and patience, and the *femme fatales*—Circe, Calypso, and the Sirens.

## TIERED DISCUSSION PROMPTS

Refer to lines 28–40 and use these prompts to help students understand Penelope's long ordeal and her decision to hold the contest:

**Recall** What has Penelope decided to do? *She has decided to take Odysseus' heavy bow and see which of the suitors is able to string it and accurately make a difficult shot.*

**Analyze** What is Penelope's attitude toward the suitors? Why is she having this contest? *Possible answer: She seems to feel some resentment for the way they took over her home. She has reached a point of desperation, needing to resolve the situation.*

**Evaluate** Do you think Penelope's contest is a good way to resolve her ordeal? *Possible answer: She seems to have little choice but to take some action, having no one to protect her and knowing that her son is at risk. She may hope that none of the suitors can manage her husband's bow.*

### REVISIT THE BIG QUESTION

## How does it feel to come **HOME** again?

**Discuss** Based on lines 41–56, how might Odysseus assess his chances at the end of his encounter with Eumaeus and Philoetius? *Possible answer: Odysseus knows that he is greatly outnumbered. However, he has the support of trusty servants and of his son. He also knows that the suitors are struggling with his bow. Moreover, he holds the advantage of surprise, everyone believing him dead. The element of surprise has worked well for him in the past.*

### VOCABULARY

### OWN THE WORD

**commandeer:** Tell students that the root of *commandeer* is *command,* "to give orders to." Have students write a pair of sentences that show an understanding of both *command* and *commandeer.* *Possible answer: The ship captain was forced to give up* command *of the ship when the pirates* commandeered *the ship and its crew.*

---

she paused, her shining veil across her cheeks,
her maids on either hand and still,
then spoke to the banqueters:

> "My lords, hear me:
> suitors indeed, you **commandeered** this house
> 30   to feast and drink in, day and night, my husband
> being long gone, long out of mind. You found
> no justification for yourselves—none
> except your lust to marry me. Stand up, then:
> we now declare a contest for that prize.
> 35   Here is my lord Odysseus' hunting bow.
> Bend and string it if you can. Who sends an arrow
> through iron axe-helve sockets, twelve in line?
> I join my life with his, and leave this place, my home,
> my rich and beautiful bridal house, forever
> 40   to be remembered, though I dream it only." . . .

*Despite heating and greasing the bow, the lesser suitors prove unable to string it. The most able suitors, Antinous and Eurymachus, hold off. While the suitors are busy with the bow, Odysseus—still disguised as an old beggar—goes to enlist the aid of two of his trusted servants, Eumaeus, the swineherd, and Philoetius, the cowherd.*

> Two men had meanwhile left the hall:
> swineherd and cowherd, in companionship,
> one downcast as the other. But Odysseus
> followed them outdoors, outside the court,
> 45   and coming up said gently:

> "You, herdsman,
> and you, too, swineherd, I could say a thing to you,
> or should I keep it dark?
>                                      No, no; speak,
> my heart tells me. Would you be men enough
> to stand by Odysseus if he came back?
> 50   Suppose he dropped out of a clear sky, as I did?
> Suppose some god should bring him?
> Would you bear arms for him, or for the suitors?"

> The cowherd said:

>                                      "Ah, let the master come!
> Father Zeus, grant our old wish! Some courier
> 55   guide him back! Then judge what stuff is in me
> and how I manage arms!"

**commandeer** (kŏm′ən-dîr′) *v.* to take control of by force

**35–37** Note that the contest has two parts: first the suitor must bend the heavy bow and string it—a task that requires immense strength and skill—and then he must shoot an arrow straight through the holes in 12 axe heads set up in a row.

### COMMON CORE L 4

### Language Coach

**Etymology** A word's **etymology** is its history. You can usually guess the etymology of compound words like *downcast* (line 43): The word *down* became attached to the word *cast,* meaning "thrown." Do you think the two herders have literally been "thrown down"? Explain.

---

## DIFFERENTIATED INSTRUCTION

### FOR STRUGGLING READERS

**Text Digest** Read the italicized text digest after line 40 to make sure students understand the intervening plot. Then ask them why Odysseus chooses this moment to test the allegiance of Eumaeus and Philoetius. *Possible answer: The suitors are occupied with the bow and not paying attention to the beggar or his cohorts.*

### FOR ENGLISH LANGUAGE LEARNERS

### Language Coach

**Etymology:**
*Possible answer: The herders have not been literally thrown down; instead, they feel down or beaten.* Ask students to explain the etymology of *outdoors* (line 44).

Likewise Eumaeus
fell to praying all heaven for his return,
so that Odysseus, sure at least of these,
told them:

"I am at home, for I am he.
60 I bore **adversities,** but in the twentieth year
I am ashore in my own land. I find
the two of you, alone among my people,
longed for my coming. Prayers I never heard
except your own that I might come again.
65 So now what is in store for you I'll tell you:
If Zeus brings down the suitors by my hand
I promise marriages to both, and cattle,
and houses built near mine. And you shall be
brothers-in-arms of my Telemachus. **H**
70 Here, let me show you something else, a sign
that I am he, that you can trust me, look:
this old scar from the tusk wound that I got
boar hunting on Parnassus. . . ."

Shifting his rags
75 he bared the long gash. Both men looked, and knew,
and threw their arms around the old soldier, weeping,
kissing his head and shoulders. He as well
took each man's head and hands to kiss, then said—
to cut it short, else they might weep till dark—

80 "Break off, no more of this.
Anyone at the door could see and tell them.
Drift back in, but separately at intervals
after me.

Now listen to your orders:
when the time comes, those gentlemen, to a man,
85 will be dead against giving me bow or quiver.
Defy them. Eumaeus, bring the bow
and put it in my hands there at the door.
Tell the women to lock their own door tight.
Tell them if someone hears the shock of arms
90 or groans of men, in hall or court, not one
must show her face, but keep still at her weaving.
Philoetius, run to the outer gate and lock it.
Throw the cross bar and lash it."... **I**

---

adversity (ăd-vûr′sĭ-tē) *n.* hardship;
misfortune

**H** ARCHETYPE
Identify the **trait** that Odysseus
values so highly in these two
servants. Where else in film or
literature have you encountered
these archetypal characters?

**73 Parnassus** (păr-năs′əs): a mountain
in central Greece.

**I** EPIC
Identify the **plot stage** in lines
84–93. What do you think is about
to happen?

---

TEXT ANALYSIS                    COMMON CORE
                                          RL 2

**H** ARCHETYPE

***Possible answer:*** *Both Eumaeus and Philoetius possess loyalty, a trait that Odysseus values highly. The archetypal loyal servant or friend appears frequently in literature and in film. Shakespeare developed this archetype in his tragedies; for example, Anthony is the loyal friend and the foil of the assassins in* Julius Caesar. *Many American Westerns use this archetype; examples are the movies featuring Doc Holliday and Wyatt Earp.*

TEXT ANALYSIS                    COMMON CORE
                                          RL 2

**I** EPIC

***Possible answer:*** *The conflict between Odysseus and the suitors is coming to a climax; the action is rising. Odysseus is preparing to face the suitors with his loyal servants and his son by his side.*

VOCABULARY                       COMMON CORE
                                          L 4

**OWN THE WORD**

**adversity:** Ask students to give specific examples of an *adversity* that sailors might face at sea. ***Possible answers:*** *storms, sharks, lack of food or water, capsizing*

---

**FOR ENGLISH LANGUAGE LEARNERS**
**Vocabulary Support** Point out these idiomatic phrases to students:

• *dropped out of a clear [blue] sky* (line 50), "appeared suddenly, without warning"

• *what is in store for you* (line 65), "what your future will be"

• *to cut it short* (line 79), "to conclude what otherwise might continue"

• *to a man* (line 84), "every one"

• *dead [set] against* (line 85), "completely opposed to the idea of"

Have partners write original sentences using these idioms. Invite volunteers to share their work.

## Analyze Visuals

*Possible answer: Odysseus, aiming at the iron axes, takes center stage. The suitors, by comparison, seem small, even childlike, crowded together in the shadows. They all face the courtyard, riveted on the ax heads through which Odysseus must shoot his arrow. The sky and courtyard are luminous and colorful, suggesting a favorable outcome.*

**About the Art** Newell Convers Wyeth (1882–1945) was a prolific American illustrator and painter. His works were paired with dozens of famous classics, including many works of Robert Louis Stevenson. In 1929, he illustrated the *Odyssey*. Wyeth has been heralded as one of the greatest painters of American outdoor life and among the top illustrators of his day.

TEXT ANALYSIS · COMMON CORE · RL 2

 **EPIC**

*Possible answer: The primary conflict in lines 94–104 is between Odysseus, who hopes to reclaim his home and family, and the rude suitors who want to displace him and kill his son.*

---

*Odysseus the beggar asks the suitors if he might try the bow. Worried that the old man may show them up, they refuse, but Penelope urges them to let Odysseus try. At Telemachus' request, Penelope leaves the men to settle the question of the bow among themselves. Two trusted servants lock the doors of the room, and Telemachus orders the bow be given to Odysseus.*

◀ **Analyze Visuals**

How does 20th-century-artist N. C. Wyeth show suspense in this detail from the painting *The Trial of the Bow*? Be specific.

Detail of *The Trial of the Bow* (1929), N. C. Wyeth. Illustration from *The Odyssey of Homer*, translated by George Herbert Palmer. © 1929 by Houghton Mifflin Company.

    And Odysseus took his time,
95  turning the bow, tapping it, every inch,
    for borings that termites might have made
    while the master of the weapon was abroad.
    The suitors were now watching him, and some
    jested among themselves:

                    "A bow lover!"

100 "Dealer in old bows!"

                        "Maybe he has one like it
    at home!"

            "Or has an itch to make one for himself."

    "See how he handles it, the sly old buzzard!"

    And one disdainful suitor added this:

    "May his fortune grow an inch for every inch he bends it!"

**1254**  UNIT 11: THE ODYSSEY

 **EPIC**
What is is the primary **conflict** in lines 94–104?

---

## DIFFERENTIATED INSTRUCTION

### FOR STRUGGLING READERS

**Text Digest** Read the italicized text digest at the top of page 1254 to make sure students understand the intervening plot. Ask them why the servants locked the doors of the room. *Possible answer: to make sure that the suitors cannot escape when Odysseus exacts his revenge.*

### FOR ADVANCED LEARNERS/PRE–AP

**Present a Poem** Have students read a poem based on the *Odyssey* and then present it to the class, analyzing the poem's connection to characters, scenes, or themes in Homer's epic. Suggest that students present one of these poems: "Ulysses," by Alfred, Lord Tennyson; "Ithaka," by C. P. Cavafy; "An Ancient Gesture," by Edna St. Vincent Millay; "Odysseus to Telemachus," by Joseph Brodsky; "Circe's Power," by Louise Glück; or "Odysseus," by W.S. Merwin.

105 But the man skilled in all ways of contending,
   satisfied by the great bow's look and heft,
   like a musician, like a harper, when
   with quiet hand upon his instrument
   he draws between his thumb and forefinger
110 a sweet new string upon a peg: so effortlessly
   Odysseus in one motion strung the bow.
   Then slid his right hand down the cord and plucked it,
   so the taut gut vibrating hummed and sang
   a swallow's note.

                              In the hushed hall it smote the suitors
115 and all their faces changed. Then Zeus thundered
   overhead, one loud crack for a sign.
   And Odysseus laughed within him that the son
   of crooked-minded Cronus had flung that omen down.
   He picked one ready arrow from his table
120 where it lay bare: the rest were waiting still
   in the quiver for the young men's turn to come.
   He nocked it, let it rest across the handgrip,
   and drew the string and grooved butt of the arrow,
   aiming from where he sat upon the stool.

                                        Now flashed
125 arrow from twanging bow clean as a whistle
   through every socket ring, and grazed not one,
   to thud with heavy brazen head beyond.

                                    Then quietly
   Odysseus said:

                        "Telemachus, the stranger
   you welcomed in your hall has not disgraced you.
130 I did not miss, neither did I take all day
   stringing the bow. My hand and eye are sound,
   not so **contemptible** as the young men say.
   The hour has come to cook their lordships' mutton—
   supper by daylight. Other amusements later,
135 with song and harping that adorn a feast."

   He dropped his eyes and nodded, and the prince
   Telemachus, true son of King Odysseus,
   belted his sword on, clapped hand to his spear,
   and with a clink and glitter of keen bronze
140 stood by his chair, in the forefront near his father. Ⓚ

---

106 **heft:** weight.

107–111 In this epic simile, Odysseus' stringing of the bow is compared to the stringing of a harp. *What qualities of Odysseus does this comparison emphasize?*

114 **smote:** struck; affected sharply.

115–116 The thunder, a sign from Zeus, indicates that the gods are on Odysseus' side.

118 **Cronus** (krō′nəs): Zeus' father.

122 **nocked it:** placed the arrow's feathered end against the bowstring.

127 **brazen:** made of brass.

**contemptible** (kən-tĕmp′tə-bəl) *adj.* deserving of scorn; despicable

Ⓚ **EPIC**
Book 21 ends with the image of father and son standing side by side facing more than 100 enemies. How can this be considered an epic moment?

THE HOMECOMING: BOOK 21    **1255**

---

REVISIT THE BIG QUESTION
## How does it feel to come **HOME** again?

**Discuss** What details does the narrator use in lines 94–97 and lines 115–132 to suggest that Odysseus is relishing this part of his homecoming? *Possible answer: He takes his time inspecting the bow; he laughs at the crack of thunder; after completing both tasks with the bow, he speaks quietly to his son.*

**TEXT ANALYSIS**     COMMON CORE RL 2

Ⓚ *Model the Skill:* **EPIC**
Remind students that the epic hero is an archetype who is courageous, strong, cunning, determined, and loyal. In this passage, father and son display these characteristics as they stand ready to engage in a heroic battle against an enemy that outnumbers them.

*Possible answer: This is an epic moment because Odysseus is making a heroic stand against an enemy that greatly outnumbers him in order to defend home, hearth, and honor against those who have scorned and abused him and his family. He must bring to bear all of his heroic traits—bravery, strength, determination, and cunning—in order to vanquish the enemy.*

**VOCABULARY**     COMMON CORE L 4

## OWN THE WORD

**contemptible:** Tell students that the root of *contemptible* is *contempt*, meaning "scorn, disdain." Give students extra practice by having them write a pair of sentences that show an understanding of the meaning of both words. *Possible answer: His betrayal of his friend was a contemptible action. Although we used to be friends, I have nothing but contempt for him after his rude behavior to my family.*

---

### FOR ENGLISH LANGUAGE LEARNERS

**Task Support** Direct students' attention to the question in the side note for lines 107–111. *Possible answer: Odysseus shows himself to be a true "master of the weapon" (line 97). Self-assured, strong, and athletic, with a virtuoso's touch, he makes the task look easy, though many suitors had failed.*

### FOR STRUGGLING READERS

**Develop Reading Fluency** Model for students an effective way to read Odysseus' words on lines 128–135. Be sure to emphasize that Odysseus spoke quietly. Then have pairs of students find the words of other characters in this book and practice reading them aloud together.

# BOOK 22:
## *Death in the Great Hall*

Now shrugging off his rags the wiliest fighter of the islands
leapt and stood on the broad door sill, his own bow in his hand.
He poured out at his feet a rain of arrows from the quiver **L**
and spoke to the crowd:

"So much for that. Your clean-cut game is over.
5 Now watch me hit a target that no man has hit before,
if I can make this shot. Help me, Apollo." **M**

He drew to his fist the cruel head of an arrow for Antinous
just as the young man leaned to lift his beautiful drinking cup,
embossed, two-handled, golden: the cup was in his fingers:
10 the wine was even at his lips: and did he dream of death?
How could he? In that **revelry** amid his throng of friends
who would imagine a single foe—though a strong foe indeed—
could dare to bring death's pain on him and darkness on his
    eyes?
Odysseus' arrow hit him under the chin
15 and punched up to the feathers through his throat.

Backward and down he went, letting the winecup fall
from his shocked hand. Like pipes his nostrils jetted
crimson runnels, a river of mortal red,
and one last kick upset his table
20 knocking the bread and meat to soak in dusty blood.

Now as they craned to see their champion where he lay
the suitors jostled in uproar down the hall,
everyone on his feet. Wildly they turned and scanned
the walls in the long room for arms; but not a shield,
25 not a good ashen spear was there for a man to take and throw.
All they could do was yell in outrage at Odysseus:

*The Slaughter of the Suitors* (1929), N. C. Wyeth. Illustration from *The Odyssey of Homer,* translated by George Herbert Palmer. © 1929 by Houghton Mifflin Company.

**Epithets** Have students identify the epithets used to characterize Odysseus during the homecoming part of the *Odyssey*. How do they compare with those used during his wanderings? To what extent do these epithets help to foreshadow important scenes?

## Get Into the Book
### SUMMARY

Book 22 begins when Odysseus kills Antinous as Antinous carouses with the other suitors. Eurymachus tries to placate and bargain with Odysseus, to no avail. Odysseus, backed by Telemachus, Eumaeus, and Philoetius, slaughters the suitors, with some help from Athena.

### Analyze Visuals

*Possible answer: Odysseus, in the foreground, appears godlike and heroic, overshadowing the other men. The background is an impressionistic cauldron of hot colors—fiery reds, "white-hot" whites, and yellows—that suggest the hellish perdition to which the godlike Odysseus is sending the evil suitors.*

**About the Art** *The Slaughter of the Suitors*, like *The Trial of the Bow* (page 1254), is one of N. C. Wyeth's 1929 illustrations for the *Odyssey*.

### BACKGROUND

**Arms and Armor** The battle equipment gathered up by Telemachus in lines 110 and following is typical of the lightweight, effective armaments used during the Greek Bronze Age. Warriors went into battle protected by helmets that were fronted by nasal guards and cheek pieces, and topped by horsetails. Greaves covered the legs, and body armor or corselets covered the upper body. All were made of thin sheets of bronze that could bend to fit. Warriors also wore bucklers, or leather shields, strapped to their arm and carried bronze-tipped ash-wood spears that could be thrown from a distance. Broadswords needed to be held with both hands, but nobles carried shorter, single-handed swords for easier use. Bows like the one Odysseus used were made of wood covered with strips of goat-horn.

## TEXT ANALYSIS

### EPIC

COMMON CORE — RL 2

**Possible answer:** *Odysseus says that the suitors are cowards who stole his goods and tried to take his wife, because they believed he was dead. He tells them they are going to die, because they showed no regard for what was right and thereby dishonored him and themselves.*

## TEXT ANALYSIS

### EPIC

COMMON CORE — RL 2

**Possible answer:** *Eurymachus' motivation is the wish to save himself and his friends. He tries to mollify Odysseus by saying that his reasons for being angry are correct, but that only Antinous, as ringleader, was to blame, and Antinous is dead. He reminds Odysseus that despite their errors, he and the other suitors are of Ithaca, Odysseus' own people. He also promises that the suitors will pay him for everything they consumed and an additional 20 oxen each, as well as bronze and gold.*

## VOCABULARY

COMMON CORE — L 4

### OWN THE WORD

**restitution:** Tell students that *restitution*, compensation for loss, is usually paid in money. Ask students what form *restitution* takes in this scene. **Possible answers:** *wine, meat, oxen, gifts of bronze and gold*

---

"Foul! to shoot at a man! That was your last shot!"

"Your own throat will be slit for this!"

"Our finest lad is down!
You killed the best on Ithaca."

"Buzzards will tear your eyes out!"

**③ Targeted Passage**

30   For they imagined as they wished—that it was a wild shot,
an unintended killing—fools, not to comprehend
they were already in the grip of death.
But glaring under his brows Odysseus answered:

"You yellow dogs, you thought I'd never make it
35   home from the land of Troy. You took my house to plunder,
twisted my maids to serve your beds. You dared
bid for my wife while I was still alive.
Contempt was all you had for the gods who rule wide heaven,
contempt for what men say of you hereafter.
40   Your last hour has come. You die in blood."

As they all took this in, sickly green fear
pulled at their entrails, and their eyes flickered
looking for some hatch or hideaway from death.
Eurymachus alone could speak. He said:

45   "If you are Odysseus of Ithaca come back,
all that you say these men have done is true.
Rash actions, many here, more in the countryside.
But here he lies, the man who caused them all.
Antinous was the ringleader; he whipped us on
50   to do these things. He cared less for a marriage
than for the power Cronion has denied him
as king of Ithaca. For that
he tried to trap your son and would have killed him.
He is dead now and has his portion. Spare
55   your own people. As for ourselves, we'll make
**restitution** of wine and meat consumed,
and add, each one, a tithe of twenty oxen
with gifts of bronze and gold to warm your heart.
Meanwhile we cannot blame you for your anger."

60   Odysseus glowered under his black brows
and said:

**N EPIC**
Paraphrase Odysseus' speech in lines 34–40. What reasons does he give for killing the suitors?

**42 entrails:** internal organs.

**47 rash:** foolish; thoughtless.

**51 Cronion** (krō'nē-ŏn'): Zeus, the son of Cronus.

**restitution** (rĕs'tĭ-tōō'shən) *n.* a making good for loss or damage; repayment
**57 tithe:** payment.

**O EPIC**
What is Eurymachus' **motivation** in lines 45–59? What is his strategy for achieving his goal?

---

## DIFFERENTIATED INSTRUCTION

### FOR STRUGGLING READERS

**③ Targeted Passage [Lines 27–33]**

This passage illustrates how Odysseus' plan counts on the element of surprise.

- Why did the suitors think Odysseus' killing of Antinous was "a wild shot"? (lines 30–31)

- Why does the narrator call them "fools"? (lines 30–32)

**Paraphrasing Homer** To help students paraphrase Odysseus' speech in lines 34–40, model how to paraphrase lines 34–37: *You cowards believed I was dead, so you stole from my home and tried to marry my wife.* Invite volunteers to paraphrase lines 38–40: *You didn't care that what you did was wrong; now you are going to die.*

"Not for the whole treasure of your fathers,
all you enjoy, lands, flocks, or any gold
put up by others, would I hold my hand.
There will be killing till the score is paid.
65 You forced yourselves upon this house. Fight your way out,
or run for it, if you think you'll escape death.
I doubt one man of you skins by."

They felt their knees fail, and their hearts—but heard
Eurymachus for the last time rallying them.

70 "Friends," he said, "the man is **implacable.**
Now that he's got his hands on bow and quiver
he'll shoot from the big door stone there
until he kills us to the last man.

Fight, I say,
let's remember the joy of it. Swords out!
75 Hold up your tables to deflect his arrows.
After me, everyone: rush him where he stands.
If we can budge him from the door, if we can pass
into the town, we'll call out men to chase him.
This fellow with his bow will shoot no more."

80 He drew his own sword as he spoke, a broadsword of fine
bronze,
honed like a razor on either edge. Then crying hoarse and loud
he hurled himself at Odysseus. But the kingly man let fly
an arrow at that instant, and the quivering feathered butt
sprang to the nipple of his breast as the barb stuck in his liver.
85 The bright broadsword clanged down. He lurched and fell
aside,
pitching across his table. His cup, his bread and meat,
were spilt and scattered far and wide, and his head slammed
on the ground.
**Revulsion,** anguish in his heart, with both feet kicking out,
he downed his chair, while the shrouding wave of mist closed
on his eyes.

90 Amphinomus now came running at Odysseus,
broadsword naked in his hand. He thought to make
the great soldier give way at the door.
But with a spear throw from behind Telemachus hit him
between the shoulders, and the lancehead drove
95 clear through his chest. He left his feet and fell
forward, thudding, forehead against the ground. ⓟ

61–67 Why do you think Odysseus rejects Eurymachus' explanation and offer of restitution?

**67 skins by:** sneaks away.

**implacable** (ĭm-plăk′ə-bəl) *adj.* impossible to soothe; unforgiving

COMMON CORE L 4

**Language Coach**

**Roots and Affixes** A word's root often suggests its meaning. The Latin root *flect* (no relation to the Spanish *flecha*, "arrow") means "to bend." What do you think *deflect* means in line 75? What mental image can help you remember its meaning?

**revulsion** (rĭ-vŭl′shən) *n.* a sudden feeling of disgust or loathing

**88–89** Eurymachus' death is physically painful, but he also has "revulsion, anguish in his heart." *What do you think causes this emotional pain?*

**90 Amphinomus** (ăm-fĭn′ə-məs): one of the suitors.

**93–100** Telemachus proves to be a valuable help to his father.

ⓟ **EPIC**
How has the battle with the suitors taken on epic proportions?

THE HOMECOMING: BOOK 22   **1259**

---

**TIERED DISCUSSION PROMPTS**
Direct students to lines 70–84. Use these prompts to help students understand that Eurymachus has heroic qualities that make him a formidable enemy:

**Analyze** What heroic qualities does Eurymachus possess? *Possible answer: He is strong and brave, thinks on his feet, and enjoys a good fight, which are heroic qualities.*

**Evaluate** Do you think that Eurymachus is a good leader? Explain your opinion. *Possible answer: Yes, he is a good leader. He keeps his head, effectively cajoles the other men to act, and is a model of bravery and confidence.*

**TEXT ANALYSIS**                 COMMON CORE RL 2

ⓟ *Model the Skill:* **EPIC**

Point out to students that to answer this question, they need to review the characteristics of an epic, such as intervention by the gods, a descent into the underworld, heroic battles, and a hero who is brave, honorable, strong, and determined.

*Possible answer:* **Eurymachus has rallied nearly 100 suitors. Odysseus, his son, and the two servants face terrifying odds. Odysseus' heroic traits must now come into play. The gods have already shown signs that they are on Odysseus' side, in Zeus' thunderbolt (Book 21, lines 115–118) and Apollo's apparent response to his plea for help (Book 22, lines 5–6). The interest of the gods heightens the epic proportions of the battle.**

---

**FOR ENGLISH LANGUAGE LEARNERS**
**Task Support** Direct students' attention to the question in the side note for lines 61–67. *Possible answer: Odysseus probably doesn't believe that Antinous caused all the trouble. His anger is too deep to accept restitution for the dishonor they caused him.* Also point out the question in the side note for lines 88–89. *Possible answer: Eurymachus realizes that he had brought this disaster on himself by disregarding what was right.*

**Language Coach**         COMMON CORE L 4
**Roots and Affixes** *Possible answer: "to bend away from;" Knowing* flecha *means "arrow," I can imagine a shield "deflecting* la flecha*" to remember* deflect's *meaning.* Point out the word *comprehend* on line 31. Tell students the Latin word *prehendere* means to grasp or understand. What must *comprehend* mean?

**VOCABULARY**         COMMON CORE L 4

**OWN THE WORD**
- **implacable:** Remind students that the Latin prefix *im-* means "not" and the Latin word *placare* means "to placate." So someone who is *implacable* cannot be soothed or placated.
- **revulsion:** Review the definition of *revulsion* with students. Then have them name terms that are similar in meaning, but carry less intensity. *Possible answers: disgust, distaste, dislike, disdain*

*Possible answer: The mood is somber, sad, dark, and oppressive. The black lines and colors heighten this mood. The black lines suggest death and set into relief the blood red and fading yellow. These colors signify the ebbing of blood and of life from the victims.*

**About the Art** One of England's greatest sculptors, Henry Spencer Moore (1898–1986) drew *Death of the Suitors: The Odyssey.* Moore's most famous sculptures are massive reclining figures that swoop and swirl like the hills and valleys of a landscape. Moore periodically turned to drawing. The piece on page 1261 was among a number of works completed during World War II, when the Germans were blitzing London.

---

**TEXT ANALYSIS**

COMMON CORE

RL 2

**❸ EPIC**

**Possible answer:** *Telemachus shows that he is the son of Odysseus in character and action as well as in blood. He is brave, able, and quick of foot and mind.*

---

Telemachus swerved around him, leaving the long dark spear
planted in Amphinomus. If he paused to yank it out
someone might jump him from behind or cut him down with
    a sword
100 at the moment he bent over. So he ran—ran from the tables
to his father's side and halted, panting, saying:

"Father let me bring you a shield and spear,
a pair of spears, a helmet.
I can arm on the run myself; I'll give
105 outfits to Eumaeus and this cowherd.
Better to have equipment."

               Said Odysseus:

"Run then, while I hold them off with arrows
as long as the arrows last. When all are gone
if I'm alone they can dislodge me."

              Quick
110 upon his father's word Telemachus
ran to the room where spears and armor lay.
He caught up four light shields, four pairs of spears,
four helms of war high-plumed with flowing manes,
and ran back, loaded down, to his father's side.
115 He was the first to pull a helmet on
and slide his bare arm in a buckler strap.
The servants armed themselves, and all three took their stand
beside the master of battle. **❸**

             While he had arrows
he aimed and shot, and every shot brought down
120 one of his huddling enemies.
But when all barbs had flown from the bowman's fist,
he leaned his bow in the bright entry way
beside the door, and armed: a four-ply shield
hard on his shoulder, and a crested helm,
125 horsetailed, nodding stormy upon his head,
then took his tough and bronze-shod spears. . . .

*The suitors make various unsuccessful attempts to expel Odysseus from his post at the door. Athena urges Odysseus on to battle, yet holds back her fullest aid, waiting for Odysseus and Telemachus to prove themselves. Six of the suitors attempt an attack on Odysseus, but Athena deflects their arrows. Odysseus and his men seize this opportunity to launch their own attack, and the suitors begin to fall. At last Athena's presence becomes known to all, as the shape of her shield becomes visible*

**Analyze Visuals ▶**

Describe the **mood** of this 1944 chalk and ink drawing. How has the artist's use of color and black line contributed to this mood?

113 **helms:** helmets.

**❸ EPIC**
How does Telemachus conduct himself in this **conflict** with the suitors?

---

**DIFFERENTIATED INSTRUCTION**

**FOR ENGLISH LANGUAGE LEARNERS**
**Vocabulary Support** Point out phrasal verbs on page 1260: *yank (it) out* (line 98), "pull (the arrow) out"; *jump (him) from behind* (line 99), "come from behind to attack (him)"; *cut (him) down* (line 99), "kill (him)"; *hold (them) off* (line 107), "keep (them) at bay"; *brought down* (line 119), "shot down; struck down."

*above the hall. The suitors, recognizing the intervention of the gods on Odysseus' behalf, are frantic to escape but to no avail. Odysseus and his men are compared to falcons who show no mercy to the flocks of birds they pursue and capture. Soon the room is reeking with blood. Thus the battle with the suitors comes to an end, and Odysseus prepares himself to meet Penelope.*

*Death of the Suitors: The Odyssey* (1944), Henry Spencer Moore. Black chalk, wash and ink on paper, 13.3 × 28.8 cm. Cecil Higgins Art Gallery, Bedford, Bedfordshire, United Kingdom. © The Henry Moore Foundation. Photo © Bridgeman Art Library.

**REVISIT THE BIG QUESTION**

## How does it feel to come HOME again?

**Discuss** Direct students to the text digest. How is the role of Athena crucial to Odysseus' homecoming? *Possible answer: Athena has been performing supernatural feats to disguise and protect Odysseus. She finally challenges Odysseus to prove himself and act on his own behalf, thus realizing his own physical and emotional strength. She then rewards him by displaying her shield and frightening the suitors.*

**FOR STRUGGLING READERS**

**Text Digest** Read aloud the italicized text digest that follows line 126 to make sure students understand the intervening plot. Then ask them why Athena might have aided Odysseus when the six suitors tried to attack him. *Possible answer: At six to one, the fight had become unfair, so Athena decided to even the odds for Odysseus.*

# BOOK 23:
## *The Trunk of the Olive Tree*

## Get Into the Book
### SUMMARY

In Book 23 Odysseus bathes and, with Athena's help, dresses to meet Penelope. Instead of embracing him, however, Penelope holds back, testing him one last time. Odysseus proves his identity with information to which no one else was privy: nobody could have moved their bed, because one post was built from the trunk of an olive tree, still rooted in the ground.

---

### TEXT ANALYSIS
**COMMON CORE**
RL 2

**Ⓡ EPIC**

*Possible answer: Penelope is being cautious and deliberate. She has spent many years fending off unwanted suitors who treated her family badly. She may still fear for Telemachus' life. She may also figure that if this man really is Odysseus, he will understand her caution and reserve. What's more, she may not want to get her hopes up and be disappointed if he proves to be another fraud.*

---

### VOCABULARY
**COMMON CORE**
L 4

### OWN THE WORD

**aloof:** Ask students to describe how an aloof person might act. *Possible answers: unfriendly, cold, snobbish, indifferent*

---

Greathearted Odysseus, home at last,
was being bathed now by Eurynome
and rubbed with golden oil, and clothed again
in a fresh tunic and a cloak. Athena
5 lent him beauty, head to foot. She made him
taller, and massive, too, with crisping hair
in curls like petals of wild hyacinth
but all red-golden. Think of gold infused
on silver by a craftsman, whose fine art
10 Hephaestus taught him, or Athena: one
whose work moves to delight: just so she lavished
beauty over Odysseus' head and shoulders.
He sat then in the same chair by the pillar,
facing his silent wife, and said:

"Strange woman,
15 the immortals of Olympus made you hard,
harder than any. Who else in the world
would keep **aloof** as you do from her husband
if he returned to her from years of trouble,
cast on his own land in the twentieth year?

20 Nurse, make up a bed for me to sleep on.
Her heart is iron in her breast."

Penelope

spoke to Odysseus now. She said:

"Strange man,

if man you are . . . This is no pride on my part
nor scorn for you—not even wonder, merely.
25 I know so well how you—how he—appeared
boarding the ship for Troy. But all the same . . . Ⓡ

**Analyze Visuals ▶**

This terracotta plaque from ancient Greece depicts Odysseus pleading with his wife. What can you tell about this moment in the story from looking at this image? Explain.

**2 Eurynome** (yōō-rĭn′ə-mē): a female servant.

 **Targeted Passage**

**10 Hephaestus** (hĭ-fĕs′təs): the god of metalworking.

**11 lavished:** showered.

**15 immortals of Olympus:** the gods, who live on Mount Olympus.

**aloof** (ə-lōōf′) *adj.* distant; remote; standoffish

**Ⓡ EPIC**
Reread lines 22–26. What do you think is the **motivation** for Penelope's skepticism about this man who claims to be the husband she hasn't seen in 20 years? Consider her experiences in his absence.

Plaque with the return of Odysseus (c. 460–450 B.C.). Classical Greek. Melian. Terracotta, height 7 ³/₈″. The Metropolitan Museum of Art, Fletcher Fund, 1930. (30.11.9) © 1982 The Metropolitan Museum of Art/Art Resource, New York.

---

## DIFFERENTIATED INSTRUCTION

### FOR STRUGGLING READERS
 **Targeted Passage** [Lines 1–16]
This passage sets up the scene for Odysseus' meeting with Penelope.

- What did Athena do to get Odysseus ready to meet his wife? (lines 4–12)

- Why did the goddess go to such lengths to make Odysseus handsome? (lines 4–12)

- Why does Odysseus need the help of a goddess now? (lines 13–16)

- Do you think Odysseus' beauty will melt Penelope's heart? Give your reasons. (lines 1–16)

**Confirm Understanding** Help students to answer the Text Analysis question as fully as possible. On the board, list their ideas about Penelope's motivation. Then direct their attention to pages 1264–1265, lines 58–67. Ask them to discuss how their explanations compare with Penelope's.

**Analyze Visuals**

*Possible answer: The image suggests that Penelope is unhappy and that Odysseus is try-ing to comfort or reassure her. He gazes directly at her, but she looks down and away from him, reflecting her uncertainty and caution.*

**About the Art** This detail from a fifth-century B.C. Greek plaque shows Penelope seated as Odysseus approaches her. In the full image, other faithful members of Odysseus' house-hold, including Laertes, Telemachus, and Eumaeus, stand behind Penelope.

**READING STRATEGY**

## ● CONFLICT

Encourage students to discuss the new conflict that Odysseus faces at the be-ginning of Book 23. How is this conflict different from his other struggles in the homecoming section of the *Odyssey*? How is it ironic? *Possible answer: This conflict involves proving his identity to his wife. The conflict is not a physical struggle but an emotional one between Odysseus and Penelope. It is ironic that he must prove himself to his wife after struggling all these years to get back to her. Penelope is a for-midable adversary, possessing many of the heroic traits of her husband—determina-tion, persistence, loyalty, bravery, and guile. Odysseus' happiness depends upon the outcome of this final conflict, a "battle of the sexes." His preparations in the opening of this book show how seriously he takes the encounter.*

## How does it feel to come **HOME** again?

**Discuss** How are Penelope's actions similar to those of Athena at Odysseus' homecoming? How are they different? *Possible answer: Penelope's actions are similar in that like Athena, Penelope tests Odysseus by making him prove himself. They are different in that Penelope acts out of the insecurity of a mortal, being not at all sure of the identity of the man in front of her. Athena acts out of the power and privilege of a goddess.*

---

Make up his bed for him, Eurycleia.
Place it outside the bedchamber my lord
built with his own hands. Pile the big bed
30  with fleeces, rugs, and sheets of purest linen."

With this she tried him to the breaking point,
and he turned on her in a flash raging:

"Woman, by heaven you've stung me now!
Who dared to move my bed?
35  No builder had the skill for that—unless
a god came down to turn the trick. No mortal
in his best days could budge it with a crowbar.
There is our pact and pledge, our secret sign,
built into that bed—my handiwork
40  and no one else's!

                     An old trunk of olive
grew like a pillar on the building plot,
and I laid out our bedroom round that tree,
lined up the stone walls, built the walls and roof,
gave it a doorway and smooth-fitting doors.
45  Then I lopped off the silvery leaves and branches,
hewed and shaped that stump from the roots up
into a bedpost, drilled it, let it serve
as model for the rest. I planed them all,
inlaid them all with silver, gold and ivory,
50  and stretched a bed between—a pliant web
of oxhide thongs dyed crimson.
                       There's our sign!
I know no more. Could someone else's hand
have sawn that trunk and dragged the frame away?"

Their secret! as she heard it told, her knees
55  grew **tremulous** and weak, her heart failed her.
With eyes brimming tears she ran to him,
throwing her arms around his neck, and kissed him, **⑤**
murmuring:

               "Do not rage at me, Odysseus!
No one ever matched your caution! Think
60  what difficulty the gods gave: they denied us
life together in our prime and flowering years,
kept us from crossing into age together.
Forgive me, don't be angry. I could not
welcome you with love on sight! I armed myself

---

**27–30** The bed, built from the trunk of an olive tree still rooted in the ground, is actually unmovable.

### Language Coach

**Synonyms** Words with the same or similar meanings are **synonyms.** Sometimes writers use two synonyms when one word would be sufficient. What synonyms appear in lines 38–40? What do the words mean? Why do you think the poet/translator uses both words?

**50–51 a pliant web ... crimson:** a network of ox-hide straps, dyed red, stretched between the sides of the bed to form a springy base for the bedding.

**tremulous** (trĕm'yə-ləs) *adj.* marked by trembling or shaking

**⑤ ARCHETYPE**
How has Penelope tricked Odysseus into proving his identity? What do her actions suggest about archetypal characters?

---

### ⑤ ARCHETYPE

*Possible answer: Penelope wanted to check Odysseus' reaction when she told her servant to move his bed and make it up; this would be impossible, because Odysseus had made one bedpost from an olive tree still rooted in the ground. Only he would have known this. Penelope's actions show caution and guile, traits expected of archetypal heroic characters.*

### OWN THE WORD

**tremulous:** Tell students that *tremulous* comes from the noun *tremor*, which means "shaking or trembling." Have students explain how both people and the ground can be *tremulous.* **Possible answers:** *When people are nervous or afraid, they may become* tremulous *like Penelope. During an earthquake, the ground shakes.*

---

## DIFFERENTIATED INSTRUCTION

### FOR ADVANCED LEARNERS/PRE–AP

**Debate** Have students discuss whether Penelope is a fitting match for Odysseus. Elaborate on characteristics such as caution, bravery, cleverness, and patience, finding examples in the selection for both characters.

### FOR ENGLISH LANGUAGE LEARNERS

### Language Coach    COMMON CORE L 4

**Synonyms** *Possible answer:* pact *and* pledge; *both mean "solemn promise or oath"; for emphasis, rhythm, or for both reasons;* Have students reread lines 34–51. Ask students to name synonyms for "skill," "trick," and "shaped."

65 long ago against the frauds of men,
   impostors who might come—and all those many
   whose underhanded ways bring evil on!
   Helen of Argos, daughter of Zeus and Leda,
   would she have joined the stranger, lain with him,
70 if she had known her destiny? known the Achaeans
   in arms would bring her back to her own country?
   Surely a goddess moved her to adultery,
   her blood unchilled by war and evil coming,
   the years, the **desolation**; ours, too.

75 But here and now, what sign could be so clear
   as this of our own bed?
   No other man has ever laid eyes on it—
   only my own slave, Actoris, that my father
   sent with me as a gift—she kept our door.
80 You make my stiff heart know that I am yours." **T**

   Now from his breast into his eyes the ache
   of longing mounted, and he wept at last,
   his dear wife, clear and faithful, in his arms,
   longed for
             as the sunwarmed earth is longed for by a swimmer
85 spent in rough water where his ship went down
   under Poseidon's blows, gale winds and tons of sea.
   Few men can keep alive through a big surf
   to crawl, clotted with brine, on kindly beaches
   in joy, in joy, knowing the abyss behind:
90 and so she too rejoiced, her gaze upon her husband,
   her white arms round him pressed as though forever. . . . **U**

*Odysseus and Penelope tell each other about all that happened to them while Odysseus was away. Then Odysseus visits his father, Laertes, to give him the good news of his safe return. Meanwhile, the townspeople, angry about the deaths of the young suitors, gather to fight Odysseus. In the end, Athena steps in and makes peace among them all.*

68 **Argos** (är'gŏs); **Leda** (lē'də).

**desolation** (dĕs'ə-lā'shən) *n.* lonely grief; misery

78 **Actoris** (ăk-tôr'ĭs).

**T** EPIC
Reread lines 58–80. What **traits** of Penelope's does this speech reveal?

**⑤ Targeted Passage**

**U** EPIC SIMILE
What is Penelope compared to in these final lines?

---

**FOR STRUGGLING READERS**

**⑤ Targeted Passage** [Lines 75–91]

This passage concludes the epic with Odysseus' and Penelope's reunion.

- What does Penelope mean by her "stiff heart"? (line 80)

- How is Penelope different from Helen of Argos? (lines 68–79)

- What worries do Odysseus and Penelope still have to face? (lines 75–91)

**Text Digest** Read the italicized text digest that follows line 91 to make sure students understand how loose threads of the *Odyssey* are wrapped up.

---

**TEXT ANALYSIS**    COMMON CORE   RL 2

**T EPIC**

***Possible answer:*** *This speech reveals Penelope's thoughtfulness, her self-awareness, her loyalty, her strength, and her underlying tenderness.*

**TEXT ANALYSIS**

**U EPIC SIMILE**

***Possible answer:*** *Penelope is compared to a safe shore, where a tired, shipwrecked swimmer comes to rest after a monumental struggle for survival in tumultuous seas.*

**VOCABULARY**    COMMON CORE   L 4

**OWN THE WORD**

**desolation:** Tell students that the adjective form of *desolation* is *desolate,* meaning "deserted" or "dismal." Have students describe landscapes that could be described as *desolate.* Then have them write a sentence that shows an understanding of the meaning of *desolation.* ***Possible answers:*** *a deserted, rugged coastline; the barren desert; an empty city street with boarded up store fronts*

**SELECTION WRAP-UP**

**READ WITH A PURPOSE** Ask students what Odysseus had to do once he was back in Ithaca before he could reunite with Penelope. ***Possible answer:*** *Odysseus greets his faithful swineherd Eumaeus and his son Telmachus; he then returns to his home disguised as a beggar; beats all of Penelope's suitors in an archery contest; sheds his disguise and kills Penelope's suitors; and finally convinces Penelope he is truly her husband.*

**★ CRITIQUE** Have students rate the *Odyssey* as an adventure story, with 1 being the least adventurous and 5 being the most exciting.

**INDEPENDENT READING**

For students who enjoyed this epic, recommend Edith Hamilton's *Mythology.*

*Connect: Poem*

Dorothy Parker, an American writer of the early 20th century, wrote many poems offering a woman's perspective on life. In "Penelope," Parker imagines what Odysseus' wife might have thought about his journeys.

PENELOPE

DOROTHY PARKER

In the pathway of the sun,
   In the footsteps of a breeze,
Where the world and sky are one,
   He shall ride the silver seas,
5     He shall cut the glittering wave.
I shall sit at home, and rock;
Rise, to heed a neighbor's knock;
Brew my tea, and snip my thread;
Bleach the linen for my bed.
10     They will call him brave.

## Comprehension

1. **Recall** Why is Telemachus fearful when his father first reveals his identity?

2. **Recall** How does Odysseus react when Argos recognizes him?

3. **Recall** Who helps Odysseus fight the suitors?

4. **Clarify** Why does Penelope test Odysseus?

## Text Analysis

● 5. **Summarize the Plot** Review the chart you created as you read these episodes about Odysseus' homecoming. Use the chart to write an objective **plot summary** of Part 2; feel free to use the overview on page 1241 as a starter.

6. **Analyze Character** Why do you think Penelope devises the contest with the bow? What does this contest reveal about her character?

7. **Examine Archetypes** Think about other contests you have encountered in literature or film. Would you say that the contest of the bow is archetypal? Explain why or why not.

8. **Analyze Universal Theme** The *Odyssey* has themes reflecting timeless and universal concerns, such as courage and honor, good and evil, life and death, and the importance of home. Choose one of these topics. What message about this topic does Homer convey? Give evidence from the text to support your answer.

● 9. **Evaluate Epic Characteristics** One thing that all epics have in common is tremendous **scale.** Everything about an epic is big: an extended and complicated plot, a long journey over great distances, powerful gods and horrible monsters, and major universal themes. Identify one aspect each of epic **plot, setting, character,** and **theme** in the *Odyssey*. Which do you consider most impressive? Give reasons for your choice.

10. **Compare and Contrast Texts** In Dorothy Parker's poem "Penelope," is the attitude toward Odysseus similar to or different from Penelope's attitude in the *Odyssey* excerpts you have just read? Cite evidence to support your answer.

## Text Criticism

11. **Social Context** Assume that Odysseus represents the ancient Greeks' ideal of a man and that Penelope represents their ideal of a woman. In what ways are the characters similar to and different from the ideal man and woman of today?

> ### How does it feel to come HOME again?
> In what ways is home more than just a place?

that is central to Parker's poem. In Book 21, Penelope weeps when she pulls Odysseus' bow from its case (lines 5–18). In Book 23, when she realizes it is indeed Odysseus, she weeps and kisses him (lines 54–67).

## Text Criticism
**Possible answer:**

11. **Similar:** The ideal man and the ideal woman, then and now, are strong, brave, intelligent, and admired. **Different:** The Greeks' ideal woman spent her time in domestic pursuits. The ideal man went out into the world. Today, the ideal man and the ideal woman share a balance of domestic and worldly pursuits.

> **How does it feel to come HOME again?** Students should reflect on Odysseus' joy at being back in Ithaca, and why he felt so joyous.

---

# Practice and Apply

For preliminary support of post-reading questions, use these copy masters:

**R** RESOURCE MANAGER—Copy Masters
Reading Check p. 52
Characteristics of an Epic p. 45
Question Support p. 53

Additional selection questions are provided for teachers on page 37.

### ANSWERS

## Comprehension

1. *He fears that the transformed Odysseus is a god who might harm him.*

2. *Odysseus wipes a tear from his cheek but hides his emotions from Eumaeus.*

3. *Telemachus, Eumaeus, and Philoetius fight beside him; Athena intervenes.*

4. *She tests Odysseus to check his identity.*

## Text Analysis

**COMMON CORE RL 2, RL 9**

**Possible answers:**

5. ■ COMMON CORE FOCUS **Summarize the Plot** *Athena disguises Odysseus as a beggar. Penelope has promised to marry the winner of an archery contest. Odysseus reveals his identity to Telemachus. Then he goes home, wins the contest, and kills the suitors. Penelope tests Odysseus to prove his identity.*

6. *She devises the test to get rid of the suitors, believing that none will pass the test. She is crafty and not easily deceived.*

7. *The contest is archetypal, pitting a worthy underdog (Odysseus) against bullies who underestimate him.*

8. *Homer conveys the message that good will win out over evil. (See answer to **7.**)*

9. ● COMMON CORE FOCUS **Evaluate Epic Characteristics Plot:** *Odysseus travels 20 years to return home.* **Setting:** *the known world and beyond* **Character:** *Odysseus— heroic in strength, bravery, cunning* **Theme:** *People have little control over life or death.* **Most impressive:** *theme, made memorable by powerful characters, setting, and plot*

10. *In the* Odyssey, *Penelope loves Odysseus without the obvious bitterness or irony*

## ANSWERS

## Vocabulary in Context

▲ VOCABULARY PRACTICE

1. *false*       6. *false*
2. *false*       7. *false*
3. *true*        8. *true*
4. *true*        9. *true*
5. *false*       10. *false*

**R** RESOURCE MANAGER—Copy Master
Vocabulary Practice p. 50

### ACADEMIC VOCABULARY IN SPEAKING

*Answers will vary.* **Possible answer:** *Athena* **demonstrates** *her concern for Odysseus' success and safety when she helps him. The* **ideology** *of the ancient Greeks included the intervention of their gods and goddesses in the lives of humans.*

### VOCABULARY STRATEGY:
### THE LATIN WORD ROOT
*solus*

COMMON CORE L 4c

Review the words in the word web. Have students use what they know about each word to come up with a working definition. Possibilities include *soliloquy,* "a monologue; speaking to oneself"; *desolation,* "loneliness; misery"; *sole,* "only; one and only"; *solitude,* "space to oneself; time alone"; *solitaire,* "a card game played by oneself"; *solo,* "alone; on one's own."

**Answers:**

1. *solo*          4. *sole*
2. *solitaire*     5. *soliloquy*
3. *solitude*

**R** RESOURCE MANAGER—Copy Master
Vocabulary Strategy p. 51

**Interactive Vocabulary**     THINK central

Keywords direct students to a **WordSharp** tutorial on **thinkcentral.com** or to other types of vocabulary practice and review.

---

## Vocabulary in Context

▲ **VOCABULARY PRACTICE**

Decide whether each item is true or false. If you need to reread the definitions of the boldfaced vocabulary words, consult the Glossary of Vocabulary on page R123.

1. A person making **restitution** is trying to get revenge.
2. If I **commandeer** your boat, I have asked your permission before taking it.
3. A person who acts **aloof** often is unwilling to make friends.
4. One might feel **desolation** at the death of a close relative.
5. If I feel **revulsion** for you, I enjoy spending time with you.
6. **Adversity** is a serious skin condition.
7. A **tremulous** person tends to have very steady hands.
8. If my anger is **implacable,** I am not going to get over it soon.
9. New Year's Eve is a common night for **revelry.**
10. Being kind to a pet is **contemptible** behavior.

**WORD LIST**

adversity
aloof
commandeer
contemptible
desolation
implacable
restitution
revelry
revulsion
tremulous

### ACADEMIC VOCABULARY IN SPEAKING

- demonstrate  - emphasis  - ideology  - monitor  - undertake

The goddess Athena **monitors** Odysseus' journey and attempts to help him return home. With a partner, discuss why Athena **undertakes** this responsibility. What is her motivation? What does it tell us about the ancient Greeks and their religion? Use at least one Academic Vocabulary word in your discussion.

**COMMON CORE**

L 4c Consult reference materials to determine or clarify a word's meaning or etymology.

### VOCABULARY STRATEGY: THE LATIN WORD ROOT *solus*

The vocabulary word *desolation* contains a form of the Latin root *solus,* which means "alone." This root is found in numerous other English words used in everyday language as well as a variety of academic disciplines. To understand the meaning of words formed from *solus,* use context clues as well as your knowledge of the root.

soliloquy   desolation
                          sole
      **solus**
solo
                      solitude
        solitaire

**PRACTICE** Insert the word from the word web that best completes each sentence. Use context clues to help you or, if necessary, consult a dictionary.

1. After months of training with an instructor, he was ready for his first _____ flight.
2. Jeannette often plays a game of _____ on her computer.
3. Rupert lived on a desert island because he wanted _____.
4. The _____ requirement for joining the club is that you are 13 or older.
5. An actor delivering a _____ generally stands on the stage alone.

**Interactive Vocabulary**   THINK central

Go to **thinkcentral.com.**
KEYWORD: HML9-1268

---

## DIFFERENTIATED INSTRUCTION

### FOR ENGLISH LANGUAGE LEARNERS

**Vocabulary: Latin Word Root *solus*** After students complete the vocabulary practice with the Latin root *solus,* have them work in home-language groups. Ask them to create word webs with the same root word in those languages, including as many words as possible. Encourage them to then write the English equivalent for each word. Invite volunteers to present their webs to the class.

### FOR ADVANCED LEARNERS/PRE–AP

**Vocabulary Practice Challenge** Have students write a note that Penelope might have written to a relative, describing the situation in her home before Odysseus' return. Tell them to use as many of the words from the word list as possible.

# Language

◆ **GRAMMAR AND STYLE: Add Descriptive Details**

Review the **Grammar and Style** note on page 1256. In line 3, Homer uses an interesting metaphor to describe the image of a Greek warrior. Similes and metaphors are types of **figurative language**—they communicate ideas beyond their literal meaning. A **simile** is a comparison that uses the **prepositions** *like* or *as*. A **metaphor** directly compares two things by saying or suggesting that one thing *is* another. Using figurative language can make your readers see things in a new way. Here are two more examples.

> *"Like pipes his nostrils jetted*
> *crimson runnels, a river of mortal red. . . ."* (simile, Book 22, lines 17–18)

> *"'Her heart is iron in her breast.'"* (metaphor, Book 23, line 21)

Notice how the revisions in blue use figurative language to add interesting descriptive details to this first draft. Similarly, you can revise your response to the writing prompt below by incorporating different types of figurative language.

---

**STUDENT MODEL**

We have missed one another for many years.

*Like two pieces of the same puzzle,*
∧We have been separated

and then joined again.

---

## READING-WRITING CONNECTION

Engage with the main characters in the *Odyssey* by responding to the prompt below. Then use the **revising tip** to improve your writing.

| WRITING PROMPT | REVISING TIP |
|---|---|
| **Short Constructed Response: Monologue** What do you think Penelope's hopes for the future might be after Odysseus' **homecoming?** Write a **stanza** (at least ten lines) in the style of the *Odyssey* in which Penelope expresses her dreams for her future years with Odysseus. | Review your response. Did you mimic the style of Homer's writing? Does your stanza include figurative language? Revise your response by adding another interesting simile or metaphor. |

Interactive Revision

**THINK** central

Go to **thinkcentral.com**.
KEYWORD: HML9-1269

---

## FOR STRUGGLING WRITERS

- Help students list some dreams Penelope might have about her and Odysseus, their home, their son, their grandchildren.

- Help students write one line of a stanza.

- Suggest that students begin with one of the models, changing it slightly.

- Limit the length of the stanza to five lines.

---

# Language

◆ **GRAMMAR AND STYLE**

- After students review the student model, ask them to identify the type of figurative language used there. (*a simile*) Ask them to revise the same model by turning the simile into a metaphor. (*We are two puzzle pieces, long separated, now joined.*)

- Write this model on the board. Have students complete it by comparing the future to a hearth fire; encourage them to use the comparison as a simile and then as a metaphor.

I dream of a future together that is as bright and warm *as the fire in our hearth.*

*Our future is a hearth fire that fills me with warmth and happiness.*

**R** RESOURCE MANAGER—Copy Master
Add Descriptive Details p. 54

**READING-WRITING CONNECTION**
Encourage students to reread Penelope's speech to Odysseus in Book 23, lines 58–80, to help them get a feel for the style of Homer's writing and the rhythms of Penelope's speech.

---

**Writing Online**

**THINK** central

The following tools are available online at **thinkcentral.com** and on **Write***Smart* CD-ROM:
- **Interactive Graphic Organizers**
- **Interactive Student Models**
- **Interactive Revision Lessons**
For additional grammar instruction, see **GrammarNotes** on **thinkcentral.com**.

---

# Assess and Reteach

## Assess

**DIAGNOSTIC AND SELECTION TESTS**
Selection Test A, B/C pp. 307–310

**Interactive Selection Test** on **thinkcentral.com**

## Reteach

**Level Up Online Tutorials** on **thinkcentral.com**

**Reteaching Worksheets** on **thinkcentral.com**:
Literature Lessons 2, 12, 17, 29, 32
Vocabulary Lessons 7, 8

# Focus and Motivate

## COMMON CORE FOCUS

**RL 5** Analyze how an author's choices concerning how to manipulate time (e.g., pacing) create such effects as mystery, tension, or surprise. **W 3a, b, c, e** Write narratives to develop real experiences. **W 4** Produce clear and coherent writing appropriate to the task, purpose, and audience. **W 5** Develop and strengthen writing as needed by planning, revising, editing, rewriting, or trying a new approach, addressing what is most significant for a specific purpose and audience. **W 6** Use technology to produce, publish, and update writing products. **W 10** Write routinely over shorter time frames for a range of tasks, purposes, and audiences. **SL 2** Integrate multiple sources of information. **SL 5** Make strategic use of digital media in presentations.

## PRODUCE WITH A PURPOSE

To help students understand the purpose, ask them to complete the following sentence frame: Life is like a journey because _____. Record students' responses on the board. Make sure that students understand that because all people journey through life, stories about individual journeys capture the attention of audiences who hope to learn lessons they can apply to their own journeys.

## COMMON CORE TRAITS

Review the *COMMON CORE TRAITS* with students, focusing primarily on development of ideas and organization of ideas.

## ADDITIONAL TASKS

**Produce a Visual Parody** Develop a visual product that parodies a well-known work and utilizes graphics, images, and sound.
**Possible subjects:** *Romeo and Juliet* or the *Odyssey*

**Produce a Music Video** Use technology to develop a product that complements a particular song. Make sure to use music that is part of the public domain and not copyrighted. Include graphics, images, and sound.
**Possible subjects:** Teenage relationships or feeling like an outsider

### Writing Online

The following tools are available online at **thinkcentral.com** and on **Write*Smart* CD-ROM:**
• Interactive Graphic Organizers
• Interactive Student Models
• Interactive Revision Lessons

---

**Writing Workshop**

**NARRATIVE**

# Video Script

**Essential Course of Study** **ECOS**

Many popular movies tell the story of an odyssey or journey. The hero leaves the comforts of his or her home with a sidekick or two, battles through a series of obstacles, and returns home a wiser, more mature individual with something to share with the community. The visual medium lends itself to this plot structure because graphics, images, and sound combine to involve viewers in the journey. In this workshop, you will produce a **video script** to tell the story of your own journey.

 Complete the workshop activities in your **Reader/Writer Notebook.**

## PRODUCE WITH A PURPOSE

### TASK

Produce a **video** that uses graphics, images, and sound to tell the story of a journey that you have taken.

### Idea Starters
• a journey from one place to another
• a journey toward a goal
• a journey of a change in understanding or thinking

### THE ESSENTIALS

Here are some common purposes, audiences, and formats for video scripts.

| PURPOSES | AUDIENCES | FORMATS |
|---|---|---|
| • to entertain<br>• to express a theme, observation, or point of view | • classmates and teacher<br>• audio/visual program members<br>• Internet video viewers<br>• community or business leaders | • screening for classmates or younger students<br>• online video or podcast<br>• presentation for a class, club, or business or community organization |

## COMMON CORE TRAITS

**1. DEVELOPMENT OF IDEAS**
• conveys a **real experience** and develops it with **well-chosen details**
• uses narrative techniques such as **dialogue** and **pacing**, and **audio** and **visual elements** to develop the experience
• establishes and reflects on the **significance of the experience**

**2. ORGANIZATION OF IDEAS**
• presents a smooth **progression of events** that build to create a **coherent whole**
• uses effective **pacing** to advance the narrative

**3. LANGUAGE FACILITY AND CONVENTIONS**
• establishes and maintains a consistent **point of view**
• uses **verb tenses** correctly
• employs correct **grammar, mechanics,** and **spelling**

Writing Online THINK central
Go to **thinkcentral.com.**
KEYWORD: HML9N-1270

---

# Writing Workshop Resources

 **RESOURCE MANAGER UNIT 11**
Plan and Teach pp. 55–58
Planning–Editing pp. 59–63
Writing Rubric p. 64
Speaking and Listening p. 65
Writing Support p. 66*

**BEST PRACTICES TOOLKIT**
Analysis Frame: Plot p. D28

**TECHNOLOGY**
⊘ **Teacher One Stop DVD-ROM**
⊘ **Student One Stop DVD-ROM**
⊘ **Write*Smart* CD-ROM**
⊘ **GrammarNotes DVD-ROM**

**Writing Center on thinkcentral.com**

*See resources on the **Teacher One Stop DVD-ROM** and on **thinkcentral.com**.*

* Resources for Differentiation

# Planning/Preproduction

COMMON CORE | W 3a, b, c, e  Write narratives to develop real experiences. **W 5** Develop and strengthen writing as needed by planning. **SL 2** Integrate multiple sources of information; evaluate the credibility and accuracy of each source.

## Getting Started

**CHOOSE A JOURNEY**

Choose a significant personal journey for this project. It need not be a journey from place to place but may be a journey toward a goal.

▶ **WHAT DOES IT LOOK LIKE?**

* moving from Monterrey to Houston
* overcoming shyness by entering talent show
* becoming starting goalie

**GATHER STORY RESOURCES**

Consider the potential **story resources** you have on hand, including existing photographs and video footage. Decide whether these resources can tell your story in a credible and accurate way. Think about integrating other sources by listing people and places that are accessible for video or photography shoots.

▶ **WHAT DOES IT LOOK LIKE?**

* maps
* photographs of move from Monterrey, Mexico, to Houston, Texas
* photographs of friends/family members
* video footage of Abuela and other family members
* video footage of roadway, of car, and of Houston

**GATHER TECHNOLOGICAL TOOLS**

Producing a video script depends on **technological resources.** Look for these resources at school and at home. Without access to video cameras, you will be limited to photos.

▶ **ASK YOURSELF:**

Do I have access to the following equipment?
• digital camera and photo-editing software
• scanner
• video camera and video-editing software

**CHOOSE YOUR VISUAL FORMAT**

Think about which **visual format** best lends itself to your story line and available resources.

▶ **TIP**

Use the chart below to choose an appropriate format.

| Visual Format | Definition | Choose If . . . |
|---|---|---|
| documentary | film or video that analyzes or chronicles an event without fictional elements | you have photographs and video footage of the journey |
| docudrama | film or video of a fictional reenactment of an event | you have resources to reenact the journey |
| theatrical production | film or video version of a stage production | you can use actors and imagined locations to convey the journey |

## DIFFERENTIATED INSTRUCTION

### FOR ENGLISH LANGUAGE LEARNERS

**Language: Reinforce Technology Production Terms** Write these terms on the board and review them with students:

• *graphics:* visual artistic representations such as paintings, drawings, photographs, and so on

• *images:* representations of people or things that have been drawn, painted, or photographed

• *photo-editing software:* computer program that allows users to edit or manipulate digital photographs

• *scanner:* machine used to capture images from hard copies and transfer them to a computer

• *video-editing software:* computer program that allows users to edit or manipulate digital video

# Teach

## Planning/Preproduction

COMMON CORE | W 3a, b, c, e, W 5, SL 2

▶ **CHOOSE A JOURNEY** Suggest that students create autobiographical timelines of important events. Then, tell students to consider each event carefully. What were the circumstances surrounding each event? Were there obstacles that students had to overcome before each event? Was the event the realization of a goal? This reflection will help students select appropriate journeys for this project.

▶ **GATHER STORY RESOURCES** Because students must integrate multiple forms of information for this project, they should carefully evaluate the available story resources to be sure they will support the project credibly and accurately. Although a student may have a particular story to tell, he or she may have to select another story if the story resources are not available. Help students decide which stories from their timelines can best be supported by available resources.

▶ **GATHER TECHNOLOGICAL TOOLS** Remind students that the final products that are based on their video scripts are dependent on available technological resources. Before beginning this project, consult with computer or audio/visual staff members to learn about available resources. Use this information to guide students in planning their video scripts.

▶ **CHOOSE YOUR VISUAL FORMAT** Provide students with video examples of each of the visual formats. Lead students to discuss further pros and cons for each format. Help students select the formats that complement their topics, story resources, and technological resources.

**R** RESOURCE MANAGER—Copy Masters
Planning/Preproduction p. 59
Production p. 60
Revising and Editing pp. 61–62
Ask a Peer Reader p. 63
Rubric p. 64
Writing Support p. 66

## Planning/Preproduction *continued*

▶ **DEVELOP AN OUTLINE** Remind students that a smooth progression of events or experiences will usually follow the basic structure of a narrative:

• Introduce the people, setting, and conflict.

• Describe the rising action.

• Pinpoint a climax.

• Describe the falling action.

• Provide a resolution for the conflict.

Students can use this structure to help them complete their outlines.

▶ **CREATE A STORYBOARD** Provide students with storyboard templates to help them complete their storyboards. Remind them that their choices about what to include—and what to exclude—impact the pacing of the narrative and can be used to create mystery or surprise.

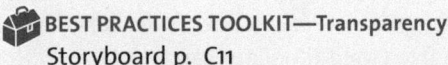 BEST PRACTICES TOOLKIT—Transparency
Storyboard p. C11

▶ **WRITE A SCRIPT** As students work on their scripts, suggest that they read portions aloud to get a sense of how the words will sound. Recommend that students revise any passages that are difficult to read or that sound too formal or stilted.

**YOUR TURN** Explain to students that their storyboards and scripts will contain many notes about how they want to produce their videos. Suggest that students enclose these notes in brackets. They may also highlight them or use a different color of pen or font. These strategies will help to distinguish production notes from narration or dialogue.

For interactive graphic organizers, see

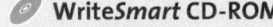 **WriteSmart CD-ROM**

**Writing Center on <u>thinkcentral.com</u>**

---

## Planning/Preproduction *continued*

### DEVELOP AN OUTLINE

Write a brief **synopsis** or summary of your journey. Consider the choices you can make to tell the story of your journey. Is there a detail you might reveal at the end to create mystery or a surprise? Then, create a **story outline** that shows a smooth progression of events that build on one another.

▶ **WHAT DOES IT LOOK LIKE?**

> *Synopsis:* When my family moved from Monterrey, Mexico, to Houston, Texas, I felt as if I'd lost my home.
>
> I. **Introduction**
> * News about move; feelings about move
>
> II. **Journey**
> * Problems on the road; feelings and thoughts
>
> III. **Conclusion**
> * Arrival in Houston

### CREATE A STORYBOARD

Use the choices you made in your outline to create a **storyboard**—a visual script that includes descriptions of images, camera shots, sounds, and graphics. A well-done storyboard can provide a "snapshot" that will help you order events to improve the **pacing** of your story and keep the action moving. Refer to the Student Draft on pages 1275–1276 for examples of completed storyboard scenes.

▶ **WHAT DOES IT LOOK LIKE?**

> *Images:* Map of route from Monterrey to Houston > Zoom in on map of Monterrey > Photos of neighborhood, street, home > Photo of happy narrator inside home with family
>
> *Sounds:* Nostalgic background music; laughter; muted voices of happy family members
>
> *Graphics:* Call to Texas

### WRITE A SCRIPT

Use your storyboard to create a **script.** The script will contain the **narration** or **dialogue** that the **audience** will hear. If you use voiceover narration, convey a clear **point of view.** Is the narrator involved in the action or watching it from a distance?

▶ **WHAT DOES IT LOOK LIKE?**

> *Voiceover Narration:* When I was 11, my parents told me we were moving from Monterrey, Mexico, to Houston, Texas. I was overwhelmed with feelings of worry and loss. In a way, my parents were going "home" to family, but I was leaving the only home I'd ever known.

 **PEER REVIEW** Describe to a peer the purpose and audience of your video script. Then, ask: Do my images, graphics, and sounds complement my narration or dialogue effectively?

**YOUR TURN** In your *Reader/Writer Notebook,* develop your production plan. Create an outline, storyboard, and script. Follow these tips:

• When writing narration, make sure to maintain a consistent point of view and a natural speaking style.

• If you use an interview, note in your script the person's name and the topic.

• Insert hand-drawn sketches in your storyboard to show your plans for shots.

---

## DIFFERENTIATED INSTRUCTION

### FOR ENGLISH LANGUAGE LEARNERS

**Storyboards** Students may also cut images from magazines or use copies of photographs to create images for their storyboards. Recommend that students use arrows to show movement. Students may also develop additional icons to indicate other production elements such as camera angles and shots.

### FOR ADVANCED LEARNERS/PRE–AP

**Camera Shots and Angles** Encourage students to research how cinematographers use camera shots and angles to tell stories. Provide students with the following key terms:

• wide and close-up shots

• point-of-view, two, over-the-shoulder, and reverse angle shots

• cutting between shots

• horizontal and vertical angles

• line of action

• composition

• camera moves: pan, tilt, zoom, and dolly

## Production

The following chart explains the technological steps involved in producing a video script.

 **COMMON CORE** W 4 Produce clear and coherent writing appropriate to task, purpose, and audience. **W 6** Use technology to produce, publish, and update writing products. **SL 5** Make strategic use of digital media in presentations.

### Producing Your Video Script

**SHOOT, SCAN, AND IMPORT IMAGES**
- If you plan to create new photographs or video, shoot in a **well-lit location.**
- Try to capture natural-looking **images.**
- Finally, **scan** or **import all images**—old and new—into your **editing software.**

▼

**RECORD AUDIO**
- Choose a **quiet space** in which to record your narration or dialogue.
- To project sound via speakers, adjust the computer's **input and output sound settings.**
- Follow **software instructions** for recording sound.
- Perform a **sound check** and adjust the volume as necessary.
- Record the **narration** or **dialogue** in parts. Then, stop, save, and play each part. Re-record if needed.
- Record the silent room for about 30 seconds. You will use this **"room tone"** to fill silent moments.

▼

**EDIT VIDEO**
- Use the **time line** in your editing software to place images and sound.
- Put compatible **image** and **sound files** together on the time line as you work through the story.
- Don't forget to insert the **"room tone"** file wherever there are gaps in sound.
- As you work, edit images and sound for **timing** and **pacing** by replaying segments.

▼

**ADD TRANSITIONS AND EFFECTS**
- The moment when one image ends and another begins is called a **cut.**
- Use **transitional techniques** between images such as a fade, a dissolve, a wipe, or a spin.
- Make sure that each **transition** continues the flow of the story without interrupting it.
- Experiment with other **visual effects** such as panning or zooming when using still images.

▼

**ADD MUSIC AND GRAPHICS**
- Make strategic use of digital media by adding **music** to create **mood.** You can collect music files through Web sites that offer royalty-free music or by recording an original live performance.
- Add on-screen **graphics** such as **titles, headings, captions,** or **credits** to provide clarity.

▼

**EXPORT YOUR VIDEO**
- When this process is complete, save your video **file.**

 **YOUR TURN** Use the movie-making program available to you to produce a rough cut (similar to a rough draft) of your video following the steps above. As you work, follow the instructions of a media specialist or tech-savvy friend to solve any production problems you might encounter.

---

# Practice and Apply

## Production

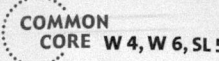 **COMMON CORE W 4, W 6, SL 5**

▶ **SHOOT, SCAN, AND IMPORT IMAGES** If students are shooting video, tell them to make sure that their microphones are near their subjects—no more than four to seven feet away.

▶ **RECORD AUDIO** Recommend that students use one project folder for storing their files. They can create subfolders for each element—narration or dialogue, images, sound effects, and graphics.

▶ **EDIT VIDEO** Make sure that students understand that they will drag and drop their audio and visual files into digital time lines that will help them assemble the elements into a final product.

▶ **ADD TRANSITIONS AND EFFECTS** Make sure that students understand that transitional techniques can be used to add action to a series of still images. They can also use effects to highlight a particular portion of a photograph.

▶ **ADD MUSIC AND GRAPHICS** Tell students that they can drag and drop musical files into their time lines in the same way that they added audio and visual files.

▶ **EXPORT YOUR VIDEO** Tell students to save their videos in a common format, such as QuickTime files.

 **YOUR TURN** Ask students to complete the **Your Turn** activity independently.

For a video script template, see

💿 **WriteSmart CD-ROM**

**Writing Center on <u>thinkcentral.com</u>**

---

### FOR ENGLISH LANGUAGE LEARNERS

**Graphics** Have students work with partners to develop titles, headings, captions, and credits for their videos. Work with each pair to correct errors in grammar, spelling, or usage. Use this opportunity to teach English conventions in context. When students add these graphics to their videos, remind them to choose colors that contrast with images on the screen.

### FOR STRUGGLING WRITERS

**Edit Video** Make sure that students understand that there should be a sound file for every video segment on their time lines. If students do not have a dialogue, narration, or music file to use, they must insert the room tone file.

## Revising

**Model the Skill** Using a sample rough cut, model how to use the questions and strategies suggested in the chart to evaluate and revise. You might use the rough cut of a student from another class or from a previous year. Make sure to remove the student's name from the rough cut so that the producer remains anonymous.

**YOUR TURN** Before students view each rough cut, tell each producer to state for his or her partner the theme or message of the video. This statement will help the partner determine whether or not this theme is being successfully conveyed. It will also help the partner offer suggestions about how to make the theme clear for audiences.

For interactive revision tools, see

💿 Write*Smart* CD-ROM

**Writing Center on thinkcentral.com**

---

## Revising

As you edit your rough cut, consider how successfully you have combined words, images, sound, and graphics to convey your story. The goal is to determine whether you've achieved your purpose and effectively communicated your ideas to the intended audience. Take notes as you consider the questions in the following chart. Then, use these notes to help you edit your rough cut.

**VIDEO**

| Ask Yourself | Revision Strategies |
|---|---|
| 1. Is the narrative point of view clear and consistent throughout? | ▶ **Revise** language to convey a distinct perspective. Check that verb tenses are used correctly throughout. |
| 2. Is the pacing effective? Do I use narration and dialogue to engage viewers and help them follow the story? | ▶ **Delete** narration or dialogue that is irrelevant or unnecessarily slows the pace. **Add** narration that provides needed background information to orient viewers or creates an element of mystery or surprise. |
| 3. Do the images make clear the events and emotions of the journey? | ▶ **Replace** static images with images that better develop characters or convey action. |
| 4. Does the sound support the story without creating distractions? | ▶ **Delete** sounds that might draw viewer attention away from the main point or story. **Add** sound files that support the main point or story. |
| 5. Do the graphics support the story without creating distractions? | ▶ **Delete** graphics that might draw viewer attention away from the main point or story. **Add** graphics that support the main point or story. |
| 6. Does the video hold the attention of the audience? | ▶ **Delete** any content that does not build effectively toward your conclusion. |

 **YOUR TURN** **PEER REVIEW** View your rough cut with a partner. As you view and discuss each other's videos, make sure to focus on images, sound, and graphics. Address how well each producer makes strategic use of these digital elements to complement narration or dialogue. If your video is not clear or easy to follow, use the revision strategies in the chart to clarify your script or try a new approach.

---

## DIFFERENTIATED INSTRUCTION

### FOR STRUGGLING WRITERS

**Note-Taking** Provide students with a frame for taking notes during peer review.

**Changes to Language:**
Add _____
Delete _____

**Changes to Narration or Dialogue:**
Add _____
Delete _____

**Changes to Images:**
Add _____
Delete _____

**Changes to Sounds:**
Add _____
Delete _____

**Changes to Graphics:**
Add _____
Delete _____

## ANALYZE A STUDENT DRAFT

Read this **excerpt** from a draft of a storyboard; notice the comments on its strengths as well as suggestions for improvement.

COMMON CORE

**RL 5** Analyze how an author's choices (e.g., pacing) create mystery, tension, or surprise. **W 5** Develop and strengthen writing by revising, editing, rewriting, or trying a new approach. **SL 5** Make strategic use of digital media in presentations.

### Documentary Storyboard

**Title:** Crossing the Border: A Hero's Journey
**Producer:** Daniel Marquez, Calhoun High School
**Media Resources:** School audio and video equipment; maps; family photographs; family interviews/video clips; sound clips from family members; scene titles

> The storyboard contains a listing of **story** and **technological resources** for this project.

#### SCENE 1

**Description:**

- **Images:** Map of route from Monterrey to Houston > Zoom in on map of Monterrey > Photos of neighborhood, street, home > Photo of happy narrator inside home with family
- **Graphics:** Call to Texas
- **Sounds:** Background music; laughter; happy family members' voices
- **Purpose:** Set up theme of leaving home, moving

> Daniel describes **images, sounds,** and **graphics** for the first scene.

**Scene 1 Narration:** Call to Texas

When I was 11, my parents told me we were moving from Monterrey, Mexico, to Houston, Texas. I was overwhelmed with feelings of worry and loss. In a way, my parents were going "home" to family, but I was leaving the only home I'd ever known.

> Daniel includes the **narration** that the audience will hear as they view the images and graphics. However, the narration will be more effective if Daniel includes more background information.

**LEARN HOW** Provide Sufficient Background Information Background information includes details to help the audience understand a story. The audience should know how or why a situation began and who is involved. However, too much background information can distract viewers.

#### DANIEL'S REVISION TO THE NARRATION

When I was 11, my parents told me we were moving from Monterrey, Mexico, to Houston, Texas. I was overwhelmed with feelings of worry and loss. . . . *where we had family living. My parents said they would find good jobs, and said that my siblings and I would attend good schools. However,*

---

## ANALYZE A STUDENT DRAFT

Explain that the Student Draft on this page is an excerpt from a storyboard. Model reading the draft and the annotations in blue, explaining that the yellow highlighting illustrates the student's plans. Explain that the following *Learn How* mini-lessons provide helpful information about ways to improve this storyboard as well as students' own storyboards.

**LEARN HOW** Provide Sufficient Background Information

Make sure that students understand that it is the job of a script writer to give the audience information that occurs before the point at which the story begins so that the audience is not left wondering about the origin of the journey. Encourage students to think about the progression of events that led up to the beginnings of their journeys. Are any of those events essential to the audience's understanding? This information should be included as background.

---

### FOR ENGLISH LANGUAGE LEARNERS

**Ask Questions to Elicit Background** Have students meet with partners to discuss the following questions with regard to their journeys. Tell students to take notes during their discussions. Then, help students use their notes to make sure that this information is clear in their videos.

- Who is involved in the journey?
- Where does the journey take you?
- When does the journey begin?
- Why does the journey begin?
- How does the journey begin?

### FOR STRUGGLING WRITERS

**Time Lines** Have students construct time lines of the events leading up to their journeys. Then, have students meet with partners to discuss these time lines. Have partners provide students with feedback regarding which information is essential to their stories. Students can circle this information on their time lines and then work to incorporate it into their videos.

## ANALYZE A STUDENT DRAFT *continued*

Explain that the Student Draft is continued and completed on this page. Read the draft and annotations aloud and discuss. Ask students to comment on how the student writer establishes appropriate pacing.

---

> **SCENE 6**
>
> **Description:**
> - **Images:** Footage of new home; interviews with Texas family; photos of new school, coaches, teachers fading to photos of family, home, school, coaches, teachers in Monterrey
> - **Graphics:** The End of the Road
> - **Sounds:** Background music that suggests theme of home; muted voices of family/friends
> - **Purpose:** Establish narrator's return "home" as a wiser individual with a message to share
>
> **Narration:** The End of the Road
> Finally, we arrived in Houston, where I met and got to know my new family members. I also met new friends, coaches, and teachers. I stayed in touch with my Monterrey "family" through telephone calls, letters, and e-mails.

Daniel ensures that each scene fulfills a **purpose** in telling the story of his journey. This step helps Daniel maintain appropriate **pacing**.

First person pronouns such as *we*, *I*, and *my* establish a first-person narrative **point of view**.

The arrival in Houston signals the end of Daniel's journey. However, the concluding section will be more effective if Daniel explains the significance of his journey.

---

**LEARN HOW** Explain the Significance

Explain that the concluding section of the narrative is an opportunity to reflect on the experience students have shared, and to clarify why it was significant. Suggest that students think about what they learned as a result of their journeys. Tell them to add or highlight this information in the concluding section.

**LEARN HOW** Explain the Significance Out of all the journeys Daniel has experienced, he chose to tell about one in particular. Perhaps he learned something about himself or about life in general. Telling why this journey was significant to him will leave the audience with something to reflect on and perhaps apply to their own lives.

---

**DANIEL'S REVISION TO THE NARRATION**

Finally, we arrived in Houston, where I met and got to know my new family members. I also met new friends, coaches, and teachers. I stayed in touch with my Monterrey "family" through telephone calls, letters, and e-mails.

*I came to understand that home can be more than one place. Home exists anywhere one feels connected. Me? I now had two homes.*

---

 **YOUR TURN**

Ask students to complete the **Your Turn** activity independently. Remind students to ensure that their videos explain the significance of their experience to their audience.

For interactive revision tools, see

💿 **Write*Smart* CD-ROM**

**Writing Center on thinkcentral.com**

**YOUR TURN** Use the feedback from your peers and teacher as well as the two "Learn How" lessons to revise the rough cut of your video. Evaluate how well you have used narration, images, sounds, graphics, and point of view to communicate your journey to a specific audience.

---

## DIFFERENTIATED INSTRUCTION

### FOR ENGLISH LANGUAGE LEARNERS

**Statements of Significance** Provide students with a sentence frame to help them think about the significance of their experience.

- As a result of my journey, I learned that _____. This was important to me because _____.

Encourage students to find places in their concluding sections where they can add these statements.

### FOR STRUGGLING WRITERS

**Explore Significance** Encourage students to use cluster diagrams to brainstorm ideas about the significance of their journeys. In the center circle, tell students to write, "As a result of my journey, I learned that . . . ." Have students fill the radiating circles with possible endings for this statement. Then, have students choose the most important ideas or combination of ideas to formulate statements that explain why the experience was important to them.

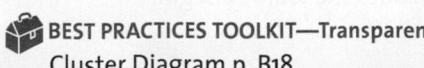 **BEST PRACTICES TOOLKIT—Transparency** Cluster Diagram p. B18

## Editing and Publishing

 **COMMON CORE** **W 5** Strengthen writing by revising, editing, rewriting, or trying a new approach. **SL 5** Make strategic use of digital media.

In the editing stage, you check your narration to make sure that it is free of grammar and usage errors. These kinds of mistakes distract your audience from focusing on the meaningful experience of your journey.

### GRAMMAR IN CONTEXT: CONSISTENT VERB TENSE

Close your eyes and listen carefully to your narration. You may have slipped into present tense when talking about specific images ("Here I am saying goodbye to my grandmother."). Make sure to use past tense for the main part of the narrative and past perfect tense for events that happened before the events of the narrative. You may choose to end your journey in the present tense: "Home exists anywhere one feels connected."

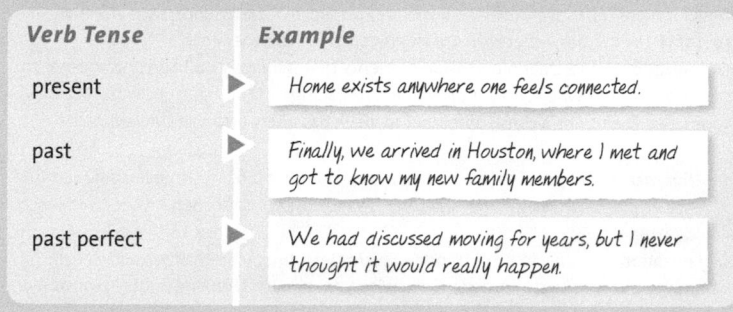

| Verb Tense | Example |
|---|---|
| present | Home exists anywhere one feels connected. |
| past | Finally, we arrived in Houston, where I met and got to know my new family members. |
| past perfect | We had discussed moving for years, but I never thought it would really happen. |

### PUBLISH YOUR VIDEO

It's time to hold a screening. Consider one of these ideas:
- Host a classroom screening of your video and evaluate it during a small-group discussion.
- Host a home screening of your video for family and friends.
- Upload your video to the Internet.

 **YOUR TURN** Correct any errors in your narration. Pay particular attention to any shifts of verb tense that might confuse your viewers about what happened when. Then, publish your video script for your audience.

---

## Editing and Publishing

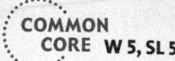 **COMMON CORE W 5, SL 5**

### GRAMMAR IN CONTEXT: CONSISTENT VERB TENSE

Explain to students that they should choose one verb tense for the bulk of their narratives, such as simple present or simple past. Although students should stick with this choice for the most part, there may be instances within their narratives where students may need to change tenses in order to make the time relationship between events clear for viewers. Students should note, however, that unnecessary shifts in verb tense serve only to confuse their audiences.

### PUBLISH YOUR VIDEO

Brainstorm with students additional ways to publish their video scripts.

 **YOUR TURN** Allow students time to edit their rough cuts. Remind them to check their narratives for consistent verb tense.

---

### FOR ENGLISH LANGUAGE LEARNERS

**Perfect Tenses** Tell students that the use of the following time words and phrases is a good sign that students may need to employ perfect tense verbs:
- *after*
- *before*
- *by the time*

### FOR STRUGGLING WRITERS

**Tense Tips** Provide students with these tips regarding verb tense:

**Use the past tense for . . .**
- narrative
- history

**Use the present tense for . . .**
- facts
- continuing action
- ideas
- references to artistic works
- narrative

## Scoring Rubric

Tell students that the best way to understand a scoring rubric is to use it to score an actual video. Have students work as a class to score a video. You may use a video from another class, but make sure to remove the student's name to maintain anonymity. Encourage students to use the language of the rubric to support their assessments of the video. Make sure that the class comes to a consensus regarding the score. The purpose of a rubric is to eliminate subjectivity from the scoring process.

For Rubric Bank, see

 **Write*Smart* CD-ROM**

**Writing Center on <u>thinkcentral.com</u>**

---

# Assess and Reteach

## Assess

 **RESOURCE MANAGER—Copy Masters**
Rubric for Evaluation p. 64

**Online Essay Scoring at <u>thinkcentral.com</u>**

## Reteach

**Level Up Online Tutorials at <u>thinkcentral.com</u>**

**Reteaching Worksheets on <u>thinkcentral.com</u>**

    Writing Lesson 3: Thinking About Purpose, Audience, and Form

    Grammar Lesson 18: Common Errors in Verb Form

---

## Scoring Rubric

Use the rubric below to evaluate and revise your video script.

| VIDEO SCORE | COMMON CORE TRAITS |
|---|---|
|  6 | • **Development** Skillfully conveys a real experience with well-chosen details; effectively uses narrative techniques; reflects on the significance of the experience<br>• **Organization** Has a smooth progression of events that build on one another to create a coherent whole; uses effective pacing<br>• **Language** Selects an appropriate narrative point of view and maintains it consistently; shows a strong command of conventions |
|  5 | • **Development** Effectively conveys a well-developed, real experience; uses effective narrative techniques; reflects on the significance of the experience<br>• **Organization** Has a clear progression of events that generally build on one another to create a coherent whole; uses mostly effective pacing<br>• **Language** Maintains a consistent point of view; has a few errors in conventions |
|  4 | • **Development** Conveys a real experience; uses some well-chosen details; could use more dialogue or more effective audio or visual elements; reflection on the experience could be more powerful<br>• **Organization** Includes some extraneous events, resulting in ineffective pacing<br>• **Language** Has inconsistencies in point of view; has a few distracting errors in conventions |
|  3 | • **Development** Conveys a real experience, but needs more development; includes narrative techniques intermittently; offers limited reflection<br>• **Organization** Has a confusing progression and includes extraneous events; has a lagging pace at times<br>• **Language** Includes confusing variations in point of view; has some significant errors in conventions |
|  2 | • **Development** Conveys a real experience but lacks development, narrative techniques, and reflection on the significance of the experience<br>• **Organization** Includes too many events that distract from the experience; has choppy pacing<br>• **Language** Lacks a clear point of view; has many distracting errors in conventions |
|  1 | • **Development** Has no identifiable experience and lacks development and narrative techniques<br>• **Organization** Has no apparent organization<br>• **Language** Lacks a specific point of view; has major problems with conventions |

# Preparing for Timed Writing

COMMON CORE

**W 10** Write routinely over shorter time frames for a range of tasks, purposes, and audiences.

## 1. ANALYZE THE TASK  5 MIN

Read the task carefully. Then, read it again, noting the words that tell the type of writing, the topic, the audience, and the purpose.

> **WRITING TASK**  ↙ *Topic*  ↗ *Type of writing*
>
> Think about <u>a place that holds special meaning for you</u>. What sights, sounds, smells, and other sensations make this place live in your memory? Write a <u>description</u> using figurative language and sensory details. Your description will be published in a <u>review guide at a local travel agency</u> intended to <u>entertain people who like to travel</u>. ← *Purpose*
> ↙ *Audience*

## 2. PLAN YOUR RESPONSE  10 MIN

First, choose the place you want to describe. Make sure to select a place you know well and focus on a specific experience there. Then, use a graphic organizer to list sensory details. Think about how you might describe some of these details figuratively, using metaphor, simile, personification, or onomatopoeia.

| Sense | Details |
|-------|---------|
| Sight | |
| Sound | |
| Smell | |
| Touch | |
| Taste | |

## 3. RESPOND TO THE TASK  20 MIN

Begin drafting your description. Start with a description of prominent sights, sounds, or smells to introduce the place to review readers. Then, move on to a detailed description using sensory language. Organize your information according to space (top to bottom, side to side) or importance. As you write, keep the following points in mind.
- In the introduction, use sensory language to present your dominant impression of the place.
- In the body, use transitions to help readers visualize the place you are describing.
- In the concluding section, make clear why the place is significant to you.

## 4. IMPROVE YOUR RESPONSE  5–10 MIN

**Revising** Compare your draft with the task. Does your draft provide sensory language to describe the place? Does your description make clear why the place matters to you?

**Proofreading** Find and correct any errors in grammar, usage, or mechanics. Make sure that your description and any edits are neatly written and legible.

**Checking Your Final Copy** Before you submit your description, examine it once more to make sure that you are presenting your best work.

## DIFFERENTIATED INSTRUCTION

### FOR ENGLISH LANGUAGE LEARNERS

**Draw to Write** Encourage students to draw quick sketches of their places before beginning to write. Students may also generate word banks for their essays by labeling sensory details in their drawings. Remind students to choose words that convey the right moods and tones for their places. Then, students may work to describe their drawings in their essays, focusing on moving readers through the spaces—side to side, top to bottom, or bottom to top.

### FOR STRUGGLING WRITERS

**Figurative Language** Remind students that personification occurs when a writer uses human characteristics to describe a nonhuman thing. For example, "the clouds race across the sky." Clouds do not race, people do. Ask students to think about ways that particular aspects of their places are like people. Then, tell students to use human characteristics to describe these particular aspects. It may help students to use a sentence frame:

- _____ is like a person because _____.

---

# Preparing for Timed Writing

COMMON CORE W 10

1. **Analyze the Task** Before students begin writing, encourage them to answer the following questions:
   - What is my time limit?
   - What are the key skills assessed in the scoring rubric?
   - Who is my audience?
   - What are my topic and purpose?

2. **Plan Your Response** Point out to students that the task emphasizes the use of figurative language and sensory details. Explain that while these types of details are important, the task also requires them to tell why a place has special meaning. Remind students to include details about special events or memories related to the place to help readers understand its significance.

3. **Respond to the Task** Remind students to utilize spatial transitions effectively to help readers mentally "move" about the space writers are describing.
   - *To the right (left), At the top (bottom), Outside (inside) the gate,* and so on

4. **Improve Your Response** Point out that the task requires the writer to reflect on why the topic— in this case, a special place—is significant to him or her. Tell students that they should express their emotional connections with these places rather than present themselves as objective observers.

## Assess

A successful description should include
- precise words, phrases, and telling details about the place
- sensory language that presents a dominant impression of the place
- transitions that help readers visualize the place
- a concluding section that explains the significance of the place.

## COMMON CORE FOCUS

**SL 1a, c** Come to discussions prepared and draw on that preparation to stimulate a thoughtful exchange of ideas; propel conversations by posing and responding to questions that relate the discussion to broader themes or larger ideas.

### VIEW WITH A PURPOSE

Explain that an evaluation offers a positive or negative judgment of a product and supports this judgment with evidence. Tell students that gathering this evidence during the viewing will prepare them to discuss the video thoughtfully.

### COMMON CORE TRAITS

As students prepare their evaluations, remind them to keep in mind the **COMMON CORE TRAITS** of a strong evaluation.

# Practice and Apply

## Analyze Content and Organization

### Model the Skill: ANALYZE CONTENT AND ORGANIZATION

Tell students that to prepare for a thoughtful exchange of ideas, they will need to analyze the parts of the video and how they are organized to create to its overall message, or theme. Point out that main ideas, sequencing, background information, and transitions are just some of the parts that they might choose to analyze. Prompt students to consider broader themes that might be suggested by the video, such as what is meant by *home* or the impact of major life changes for adolescents.

**GUIDED PRACTICE** As students analyze content and organization, remind them to note evidence as well as their assessments. For example, how effectively did the producer present his or her main ideas?

**R** RESOURCE MANAGER—Copy Master
Speaking and Listening p. 65

---

## Speaking & Listening Workshop

# Evaluating a Video

"How was the movie?" a parent asks. "The story was good, but the acting was terrible!" you reply. When you **evaluate a video** in a conversation like this, you combine comprehension with sensory observation. In this workshop, you'll prepare to discuss and evaluate a video by analyzing it to determine its effectiveness.

 Complete the workshop activities in your **Reader/Writer Notebook**.

| VIEW WITH A PURPOSE | COMMON CORE TRAITS |
|---|---|
| **TASK**<br>Analyze the content, organization, and delivery of a video. Then, draw on your analysis to **discuss** and **evaluate the effectiveness of the video.** | **A STRONG EVALUATION . . .**<br>• notes main ideas and themes<br>• analyzes organization and assesses its effectiveness<br>• analyzes the delivery, including narration or dialogue, images, sounds, and graphics |

### COMMON CORE

**SL 1a, c** Come to discussions prepared and draw on that preparation to stimulate a thoughtful exchange of ideas; propel conversations by posing and responding to questions that relate the discussion to broader themes or larger ideas.

## Analyze Content and Organization

Choose one video that engages you. Then, prepare to discuss it by analyzing its content and organization. Complete a graphic organizer such as the one below to note evidence you can present during a thoughtful exchange of ideas. Think about the effectiveness of the video, and plan to give instructions that might help the producer solve any problems you notice.

| Elements for Analysis | Notes for Discussion |
|---|---|
| Summary of Main Ideas and the Video's Theme | *The speaker moves to Texas. He feels as if he is losing his home. The theme is that home can be anyplace. A broader theme might be that home is more a feeling than a place.* |
| Questions that I Have | *How does the idea of having two homes change the narrator's view?* |
| Sequence of Events or Information | *chronological sequence* |
| Background Information | *explains history behind the move; describes differences between Monterrey and Houston* |
| Transitions Between Events or Ideas | *narrator uses sequence transitions to connect scenes* |
| Concluding Section | *narrator reflects on the significance of the move* |

**Speaking & Listening Online**

**THINK** central

Go to **thinkcentral.com**.
KEYWORD: HML9-1280

---

## DIFFERENTIATED INSTRUCTION

### FOR ENGLISH LANGUAGE LEARNERS

**Language: Reinforce Evaluative Terms**
Explain to students that evaluating a video involves some of the same tasks as producing such a product—making choices and judging their effectiveness in telling a particular story. Review key terms used in the Workshop:

• *evaluate:* to find the value of something or to judge or determine the worth or quality of something

• *analyze:* to separate a thing into its parts so as to find out their function and interrelationships

• *content:* all that is dealt with in a work of art; essential meaning or substance

• *organization:* the manner of arrangement

• *delivery:* act or manner of presenting something

## Analyze Delivery

The delivery of a video helps to convey the story by combining verbal and sensory elements. Producers use narration, dialogue, images, sounds, and graphics to communicate basic ideas as well as broader themes. Use a graphic organizer such as the one below to take notes in preparation for a discussion.

| Elements of Delivery | Notes |
|---|---|
| **NARRATION/DIALOGUE**<br>• Does narration or dialogue add to the information or overall impression?<br>• Are speakers easy to understand? | *Rate:* not too fast or too slow<br>*Volume:* too low at times<br>*Enunciation:* a few words not clear<br>*Point of View:* first-person<br>*Tone/Mood:* shifts from anger and sadness to acceptance |
| **IMAGES**<br>• Do the images help tell the story?<br>• Do the images convey emotions or enhance the overall impression of the topic? | combination of still photographs and action footage maintains viewer interest in story and engages emotions |
| **SOUNDS**<br>• Do the sounds complement the story?<br>• Do the sounds reinforce the mood and tone? | background music adds to a sad tone early on and then a happier tone at end |
| **GRAPHICS**<br>• Do the graphics add to or detract from the story? | titles clarify each scene change |
| **EDITING**<br>• Is it clear how each segment relates to those before and after it?<br>• Does the placement of scenes, images, or ideas add to the presentation's impact? | flashback interrupts sequence for added impact |
| **TONE/PURPOSE**<br>• Is the tone appropriate for the story?<br>• Do any shifts in tone help achieve the producer's purpose? | sudden shift to informal, comic tone breaks tension of story; narrator successfully conveys theme of journey |

**YOUR TURN**

**Discuss Your Evaluation** Discuss the content, organization, and delivery of the video with a small group. Try to bring everyone into the discussion by posing and responding to questions related to your analysis. Be willing to challenge the ideas and conclusions of others, supporting your ideas with evidence from the video. Then, write a short evaluation describing the effectiveness and quality of the video.

1281

---

---

## Analyze Delivery

### Model the Skill: ANALYZE DELIVERY

Make sure that students understand the differences among content, organization, and delivery. Explain that content is what the video is about; organization is how the video is structured or put together; and delivery is how the content is communicated to audiences. Each of these aspects of video production may be further subdivided into the particular elements that students see noted in the text. Model for students how to identify examples of delivery and evaluate these examples for effectiveness.

**GUIDED PRACTICE** After students complete their analyses, tell them to survey their notes to determine overall impressions of their videos. Lead a discussion in which students draw on their preparation to support their impressions with evidence. Encourage them to clarify, verify, or challenge one another's ideas. Students can use these general impressions to develop controlling ideas for their written evaluations.

**YOUR TURN** Have students use their notes to write evaluations that assess the effectiveness and quality of their videos.

## Assess and Reteach

### Assess

Use the **COMMON CORE TRAITS** to assess students' evaluations.

A strong evaluation
• notes main ideas and themes
• analyzes organization and its effectiveness
• analyzes the delivery, including narration or dialogue, images, sounds, and graphics

### Reteach

If students struggle with evaluation, provide them with Critical Review templates.

 **BEST PRACTICES TOOLKIT—Transparency** Critical Review p. C25

**Speaking and Listening Online**
• Public speaking tips
• Strategies for effective listening

# Assessment Practice

## COMMON CORE FOCUS

**RL 1** Cite textual evidence to support analysis of what the text says explicitly as well as inferences drawn from the text. **RL 2** Determine a theme of a text and analyze its development over the course of the text; provide an objective summary of the text. **RL 10** Read and comprehend stories and poems. **W 5** Strengthen writing by revising and editing to ensure that it demonstrates the conventions of standard English punctuation and spelling. **L 2c** Spell correctly. **L 4a** Use context as a clue to the meaning of a word. **L 6** Acquire general academic words; demonstrate independence in gathering vocabulary knowledge.

## CHECK READINESS

Read aloud the paragraph under **ASSESS** and stress to students that this is not the full Unit Test, but a way for them to check their readiness for it. Then have students examine the standards listed under **REVIEW** and look back in the unit or in the **Student Resource Bank** for any skills they need to review.

## READ THE TEXTS

Remind students to keep unit goals in mind as they read each passage, paying particular attention to these literary and reading skills:

- characteristics of an epic: setting, conflict, theme
- epic hero
- summarize

To help students focus on the epic hero, encourage them to consider these questions:

- What details in this selection show Odysseus' words and actions?
- What character traits do those details reveal?

## ANSWER THE QUESTIONS

Direct students to page R93–R101 of the **Handbook** to review test-taking strategies.

- As students prepare to answer multiple-choice questions, remind them not to choose the first alternative that seems to fit. Instead, they should read through all the choices, eliminate any that are clearly wrong, and then choose the *best* answer—the one that is the most accurate and complete.

---

**COMMON CORE**

**ASSESS**
Taking this practice test will help you assess your knowledge of these skills and determine your readiness for the Unit Test.

**REVIEW**
After you take the practice test, your teacher can help you identify any standards you need to review.

### COMMON CORE

**RL 1** Cite textual evidence to support analysis of what the text says explicitly as well as inferences drawn from the text. **RL 2** Determine a theme of a text and analyze its development over the course of the text; provide an objective summary of the text. **RL 10** Read and comprehend stories and poems. **W 5** Strengthen writing by revising and editing to ensure that it demonstrates the conventions of standard English punctuation and spelling. **L 2c** Spell correctly. **L 4a** Use context as a clue to the meaning of a word. **L 6** Acquire general academic words; demonstrate independence in gathering vocabulary knowledge.

**Practice Test** THINK central

Take it at thinkcentral.com.
KEYWORD: HML9N-1282

---

# Assessment Practice

**DIRECTIONS** Read the following excerpt, and then answer the questions.

## *from the* Odyssey    *by Homer*

Blinded, and sick with pain from his head wound,
the master stroked each ram, then let it pass,
but my men riding on the pectoral fleece
the giant's blind hands blundering never found.
5 Last of them all my ram, the leader, came,
weighted by wool and me with my meditations.
The Cyclops patted him, and then he said:

'Sweet cousin ram, why lag behind the rest
in the night cave? You never linger so,
10 but graze before them all, and go afar
to crop sweet grass, and take your stately way
leading along the streams, until at evening
you run to be the first one in the fold.
Why, now, so far behind? Can you be grieving
15 over your Master's eye? That carrion rogue
and his accurst companions burnt it out
when he had conquered all my wits with wine.
Nohbdy will not get out alive, I swear.
Oh, had you brain and voice to tell
20 where he may be now, dodging all my fury!
Bashed by this hand and bashed on this rock wall
his brains would strew the floor, and I should have
rest from the outrage Nohbdy worked upon me.'

He sent us into the open, then. Close by,
25 I dropped and rolled clear of the ram's belly,
going this way and that to untie the men.
With many glances back, we rounded up
his fat, stiff-legged sheep to take aboard,
and drove them down to where the good ship lay.
30 We saw, as we came near, our fellows' faces
shining; then we saw them turn to grief
tallying those who had not fled from death.
I hushed them, jerking head and eyebrows up,
and in a low voice told them: 'Load this herd;

---

## DIFFERENTIATED INSTRUCTION

### FOR ENGLISH LANGUAGE LEARNERS

**Assessment Practice: Work Backward**
Prepare students by having them read the questions *before* reading the passages. Have pairs find unfamiliar words in test directions and questions and follow these steps:

1. Write each word on an index card and divide the cards among pairs of students. Tell students that they are going to define these words.

2. Instruct students to work individually to make an initial determination of each word's meaning. Then have students confer with their partners and check their work by using a dictionary.

3. Have students then share the words and definitions with the entire class, who can confirm the definitions or suggest others.

35     move fast, and put the ship's head toward the breakers.'
    They all pitched in at loading, then embarked
    and struck their oars into the sea. Far out,
    as far off shore as shouted words would carry,
    I sent a few back to the adversary:
40     'O Cyclops! Would you feast on my companions?
    Puny, am I, in a Caveman's hands?
    How do you like the beating that we gave you,
    you damned cannibal? Eater of guests
    under your roof! Zeus and the gods have paid you!'

45     The blind thing in his doubled fury broke
    a hilltop in his hands and heaved it after us.
    Ahead of our black prow it struck and sank
    whelmed in a spuming geyser, a giant wave
    that washed the ship stern foremost back to shore.
50     I got the longest boathook out and stood
    fending us off, with furious nods to all
    to put their backs into a racing stroke—
    row, row, or perish. So the long oars bent
    kicking the foam sternward, making head
55     until we drew away, and twice as far.
    Now when I cupped my hands I heard the crew
    in low voices protesting:
                         'Godsake, Captain!
    Why bait the beast again? Let him alone!'

    'That tidal wave he made on the first throw
60     all but beached us.'
                         'All but stove us in!'
    'Give him our bearing with your trumpeting,
    he'll get the range and lob a boulder.'
                         'Aye
    He'll smash our timbers and our heads together!'
    I would not heed them in my glorying spirit,
65     but let my anger flare and yelled:
                        'Cyclops,
    if ever mortal man inquire
    how you were put to shame and blinded, tell him

**GO ON** ➡

## ITEM ANALYSIS

| COMPREHENSION AND WRITTEN RESPONSE | ITEMS | UNIT PAGES |
|---|---|---|
| Characteristics of an Epic | 1, 3, 5, 7, 8, 9 | 1194–1201 |
|     Setting | 1, 9 | 1194–1201 |
|     Conflict | 5, 8 | 1194–1201 |
|     Theme | 7 | 1194–1201 |
| Epic Hero | 3, 6, 7 | 1194–1201 |
| Summarize | 2, 4, 8 | 1241 |

| VOCABULARY | ITEMS | UNIT PAGES |
|---|---|---|
| Prefixes | 1, 2, 3, 4 | 1239 |
| Word Roots | 5, 6, 7, 8 | 1268 |

| WRITING AND GRAMMAR | ITEMS | UNIT PAGES |
|---|---|---|
| Figurative Language | 1, 2, 3, 4, 5 | 1269 |

### Practice Test

On **thinkcentral.com** students can complete an interactive version of this practice test *and* receive remediation for the skills they have not yet mastered.

## FOR STRUGGLING READERS

**Assessment Support** Consider these options for completing the Assessment Practice:

- Have students "work backward" to review the test questions *before* reading the poem.
- Select random questions in the Assessment and have students demonstrate how and where to look for answers.

- Ask students to locate unfamiliar vocabulary words in the Assessment. Elicit the words' meanings from the class.
- Have students record useful testing words and definitions in their journal for later reference.
- Read the selection or parts of it aloud to aid in student comprehension.

Odysseus, raider of cities, took your eye:
Laertes' son, whose home's on Ithaca!'

70    At this he gave a mighty sob and rumbled:

'Now comes the weird upon me, spoken of old.
A wizard, grand and wondrous, lived here—Telemus,
a son of Eurymus; great length of days
he had in wizardry among the Cyclopes,
75    and these things he foretold for time to come:
my great eye lost, and at Odysseus' hands.
Always I had in mind some giant, armed
in giant force, would come against me here.
But this, but you—small, pitiful and twiggy—
80    you put me down with wine, you blinded me.
Come back, Odysseus, and I'll treat you well,
praying the god of earthquake to befriend you—
his son I am, for he by his avowal
fathered me, and, if he will, he may
85    heal me of this black wound—he and no other
of all the happy gods or mortal men.'

Few words I shouted in reply to him:
'If I could take your life I would and take
your time away, and hurl you down to hell!

90    The god of earthquake could not heal you there!'

At this he stretched his hands out in his darkness
toward the sky of stars, and prayed Poseidon:

'O hear me, lord, blue girdler of the islands,
if I am thine indeed, and thou art father:
95    grant that Odysseus, raider of cities, never
see his home: Laertes' son, I mean,
who kept his hall on Ithaca. Should destiny
intend that he shall see his roof again
among his family in his father land,
100    far be that day, and dark the years between.

Let him lose all companions, and return
under strange sail to bitter days at home.'

1284

## Reading Comprehension

> **Use the excerpt from the *Odyssey*
> (pp. 1282–1284) to answer questions 1–9.**

1. The cave mentioned in line 9 is an epic
   setting because it is —
   **A.** home to a fantastic, archetypal creature
   **B.** a beautiful, hidden location
   **C.** a rugged, barren land formation
   **D.** an imaginary but believable place

2. Which statement best summarizes the escape
   plan for Odysseus and his men?
   **A.** They beg Poseidon to make the Cyclops
   free them.
   **B.** They blind the Cyclops and then sneak
   away during the night.
   **C.** They hide in the rams' wool and let the
   rams carry them past the Cyclops.
   **D.** They roll boulders down a hill to distract
   the Cyclops, and then run.

3. The quality of an epic hero Odysseus displays
   in lines 24–35 is —
   **A.** strength in pursuit of adventure
   **B.** honesty in the face of conflict
   **C.** dependence on the gods
   **D.** cleverness in the face of danger

4. Which statement summarizes Odysseus'
   heroic actions in lines 45–55?
   **A.** He blinds the Cyclops with a boathook.
   **B.** He throws a boulder that causes a wave
   to flood the ship.
   **C.** He single-handedly pushes the ship out
   to sea while urging his men to row.
   **D.** He taunts the Cyclops from the shore.

5. What conflict develops between Odysseus and
   his men in lines 56–69?
   **A.** They disagree about where to hide from
   the Cyclops.
   **B.** The men beg Odysseus to stop taunting
   the Cyclops, but he continues.
   **C.** They disagree about whether or not to kill
   the Cyclops.
   **D.** The men want to steal the Cyclops' sheep
   without telling Odysseus.

6. Which character trait causes Odysseus to
   reveal his name to the Cyclops in lines 66–69?
   **A.** Cowardice
   **B.** Dishonesty
   **C.** Pride
   **D.** Vengefulness

7. The Cyclops' speech in lines 75–80 expresses
   the theme of —
   **A.** the rescue of a nation from invaders
   **B.** a hero's loyalty to his friends
   **C.** the victorious homecoming of a hero
   **D.** a hero's triumph over a powerful opponent

### SHORT CONSTRUCTED RESPONSE
**Write three or four sentences to answer this
question.**

8. Briefly summarize the conflict between
   Odysseus and the Cyclops. Support your
   answer with details from the excerpt.

**Write two to three paragraphs to answer this
question.**

9. In what ways are the sea and the role of
   Poseidon important in this excerpt? Support
   your answer with details from the excerpt.

**GO ON**

1285

---

## SHORT CONSTRUCTED RESPONSE

### *Possible responses:*

**8.** *This conflict pits human brains against
monstrous brawn. The Cyclops traps Odysseus and his men in a cave, but Odysseus
enables his men to escape by hiding them
among Cyclops' rams (lines 1–4). When
Odysseus taunts the monster (lines 40–45),
the Cyclops prays that Poseidon will end the
conflict (lines 91–102).*

**9.** *The sea is a key element in this excerpt
because it is both a means of escape and*
*a danger. The Cyclops tries to use the sea
against the escaping prisoners (lines 45–49,
91–102.) Poseidon is a key player in this
scene because he is the god of the sea and
the Cyclops' father. As such, Poseidon may
desire to fulfill the prayer of his son, whom
Odysseus has harmed; Poseidon has the
means to fulfill the Cyclops' wish that Odysseus be kept from his home (lines 95–96) or
that he return home only after many years
(lines 97–102).*

---

## Reading Comprehension
Model a thinking process for answering
multiple-choice questions.

1. **A *is correct.*** *The cave is home to a monster,
   and one characteristic of an epic poem is its
   inclusion of monsters and other supernatural beings.* B, C, and D *are incorrect because
   these settings are not specific to epics.*

2. **C *is correct.*** *The prisoners' escape plan—
   clinging to the underside of the rams—is
   described at the start of the passage.* A *is
   incorrect because it is the Cyclops who calls
   upon Poseidon (lines 91–102).* B *is incorrect
   because the escape is made in the daytime
   (lines 8–12).* D *is incorrect because the prisoners are never said to roll boulders.*

3. **D *is correct.*** *In this passage Odysseus
   shows cunning in overseeing the theft of
   the Cyclops' sheep.* A *is incorrect because
   Odysseus does not rely much on physical
   strength, nor is he seeking adventure.* B *is
   incorrect because stealing the sheep is an
   act of dishonesty.* C *is incorrect because
   Odysseus does not ask the gods for help.*

4. **C *is correct.*** *Odysseus' actions are described
   in lines 50–52.* A *is incorrect because Odysseus blinds the Cyclops earlier.* B *is incorrect
   because the Cyclops tries to flood the ship
   (lines 45–49).* D *is incorrect because Odysseus taunts the Cyclops from the sea.*

5. **B *is correct.*** *The men's begging words are
   presented in lines 57–63.* A and C *are incorrect because the men do not disagree about
   where to hide from the Cyclops or whether
   or not to kill it.* D *is incorrect because the
   sheep are not discussed in this passage.*

6. **C *is correct.*** *In line 64, Odysseus says that
   his "glorying spirit" led him to declare his
   name.* A *is incorrect because revealing his
   name is unwise, but it is bold.* B *is incorrect
   because Odysseus is honest in revealing his
   true name.* D *is incorrect because Odysseus
   avenges nothing by revealing his name.*

7. **D *is correct.*** *The fact that the Cyclops
   expected to be defeated by a giant emphasizes Odysseus' greatness.* A *is incorrect because the Cyclops has not invaded Odysseus'
   nation.* B *is incorrect because these lines
   do not mention that trait.* C *is incorrect because the scene concerns Odysseus' escape.*

## Vocabulary

**1. B is correct.** Untying reverses the action of tying; in line 26, untie refers to freeing the men from their ropes. A is incorrect because it describes the prefix re-, not un-. C is incorrect because untie refers to an action, not to an object. D is incorrect because untie does not involve going against something.

**2. D is correct.** The context of line 36—loading a ship and rowing away—verifies the meaning. A is incorrect because the men are leaving, not staying. B is incorrect because they are rowing away from land rather than toward it. C is incorrect because it suggests that embarked relates to the sound of barking, but that meaning is not supported in this context.

**3. D is correct.** In line 82, the Cyclops falsely tells Odysseus that he will get Poseidon to help—become friendly to—Odysseus. A is incorrect because it suggests the opposite of befriend. B is incorrect because be- does not imply begging. C is a weaker answer because be- implies finding a friend, not just looking for one.

**4. A is correct.** The context discusses Odysseus' returning again to go back home. B is incorrect because it implies that return means "different turn." C is incorrect because it implies that return means "more turn." D is incorrect because the context does not imply any meaning of regarding.

**5. A is correct.** The context describes a huge wave overwhelming the ship, and such a wave would be foaming with bubbles. B is incorrect because it describes a wave's force, but not the wave's foam. C and D are incorrect because they describe the wave's action, but not the wave's appearance.

**6. B is correct.** The context contrasts mortal humans with gods, and the chief difference is that humans die but gods do not. A is a weaker choice, since all people are subject to death whether their lives are long or short. C is incorrect because it does not make sense in the context, even though it has the same root as mortal. D is incorrect because it is not implied by the context, even though it reflects the meaning of the root.

## Vocabulary

| Use context clues and your knowledge of prefixes to answer the following questions. |
| --- |

1. The prefix *un-* in the word *untie* in line 26 most likely means —
   - **A.** performs an action over again
   - **B.** reverses a specified action
   - **C.** removes a specific thing
   - **D.** goes against something

2. The prefix *em-* means "to put onto." In line 36 the word *embarked* means —
   - **A.** stayed on shore
   - **B.** rowed toward land
   - **C.** made a loud noise
   - **D.** got onto a ship

3. The prefix *be-* means "to make." The word *befriend* in line 82 means to —
   - **A.** form a rivalry
   - **B.** beg for companionship
   - **C.** look for friendship
   - **D.** become friends with

4. The prefix *re-* in the word *return* in line 101 most likely means —
   - **A.** back
   - **B.** different
   - **C.** more
   - **D.** regarding

| Use context clues and your knowledge of Latin words and roots to answer the following questions. |
| --- |

5. The Latin word *spuma* means "foam." In line 48 the word *spuming* means —
   - **A.** bubbling
   - **B.** raging
   - **C.** rising
   - **D.** shooting

6. *Mortal* comes from the Latin root *-mors-*, which means "to die." In line 86 the word *mortal* means —
   - **A.** short-lived
   - **B.** subject to death
   - **C.** morbid
   - **D.** deadly

7. The Latin root *-civ-* means "citizen." Which word most likely comes from that root?
   - **A.** Carrion (line 15)
   - **B.** Cities (line 95)
   - **C.** Companions (line 16)
   - **D.** Crew (line 56)

8. The Latin word *destinare* means "to determine." In line 97 the word *destiny* means —
   - **A.** fate
   - **B.** misfortune
   - **C.** privilege
   - **D.** shame

**7. B is correct.** Dwellers in cities often are called "citizens." A is incorrect because carrion, or decaying flesh, has nothing to do with citizens. C is incorrect because citizenship and companionship are not closely related concepts. D is incorrect because citizenship has to do with cities and nations, not the crew of a boat.

**8. A is correct.** Fate determines whether Odysseus "shall see his roof again" (line 98). B is a weaker answer because misfortune suggests bad luck, a weaker concept than determination. C and D are incorrect because neither shame nor privilege will determine whether Odysseus returns home safely.

# Revising and Editing

**DIRECTIONS** Read this passage, and answer the questions that follow.

> (1) Ithaca, an island west of the Greek mainland was the home of Odysseus. (2) Today, the island's rugged terrain and other phisical features still mirror those described in the *Odyssey*. (3) Ancient ruins lie south of the narrow isthmus that gives Ithaca its distinctive shape. (4) On a hilltop in Pilikáta, you may view the three seas and mountains that Odysseus saw from his palace. (5) The Fountain of Arethusa, mentioned in the *Odyssey*, is a spring located beneath a towering sea cliff. (6) You may visit this spring by hiking along steep mountain paths. (7) The word "spring" has several meanings, including a small stream. (8) Visiting these sites allows a person to trace the ancient travels of Odysseus.

**1.** What change, if any, should be made to sentence 1?

  **A.** Change *west* to **West**

  **B.** Delete the comma after *Ithaca*

  **C.** Insert a comma after *mainland*

  **D.** Make no change

**2.** What change, if any, should be made to sentence 2?

  **A.** Change *rugged* to **ruged**

  **B.** Change *phisical* to **physical**

  **C.** Change *mirror* to **miror**

  **D.** Make no change

**3.** What is the best way to revise sentence 3 to include a simile?

  **A.** Ancient ruins lie south of the isthmus that gives Ithaca an hourglass shape.

  **B.** Ancient ruins lie south of the narrow isthmus that separates Ithaca in two.

  **C.** Ancient ruins lie south of the narrow isthmus that divides Ithaca like the neck of an hourglass.

  **D.** Ancient ruins lie south of the narrow isthmus that separates Ithaca into north and south.

**4.** What is the best way to revise sentence 4 to include a metaphor?

  **A.** A Pilikáta hilltop view offers a scenic landscape of the three seas and mountains that Odysseus saw from his palace.

  **B.** On a hilltop in Pilikáta, the view is a landscape painting of the three seas and mountains that Odysseus saw from his palace.

  **C.** In Pilikáta, the hilltop view is like the view of the three seas and mountains that Odysseus saw from his palace.

  **D.** On a hilltop in Pilikáta, the view features the three raging seas and towering mountains that Odysseus saw from his palace.

**5.** What is the most effective way to improve the organization of this paragraph?

  **A.** Delete sentence 7

  **B.** Switch sentences 6 and 7

  **C.** Delete sentence 8

  **D.** Switch sentences 7 and 8

1287

## ANSWERS
## Revising and Editing

**1. C** *is correct.* *The appositive phrase "an island west of the Greek mainland" should be set off with commas.* A *is incorrect because* west *is not a proper noun.* B *is incorrect because the comma is needed for the appositive phrase.* D *is incorrect because a comma is needed to set off the appositive.*

**2. B** *is correct.* Physical *is the correct spelling.* A *is incorrect because* rugged *is spelled correctly.* C *is incorrect because* mirror *is spelled correctly.* D *is incorrect because the spelling of* physical *is incorrect in the sentence.*

**3. C** *is correct.* *Like the neck of an hourglass is a simile for the shape of the isthmus.* A *is incorrect because* hourglass shape *is a metaphor, not a simile.* B *and* D *are incorrect because they contain no figurative comparisons.*

**4. B** *is correct.* *The phrase* the view is a landscape painting *is a comparison that does not use signal words, and so is a metaphor.* A *and* D *are incorrect because they are literal descriptions that do not use figurative comparisons.* C *is incorrect because it is phrased as a simile and offers a literal, rather than a figurative, comparison.*

**5. A** *is correct.* *The information about the meanings of* spring *do not relate to the passage about Ithaca.* B *is incorrect because* spring *in sentence 7 refers to* spring *in sentence 6.* C *is incorrect because sentence 8 contains relevant information about Ithaca.* D *is incorrect because sentence 8 contains a concluding statement and should remain at the end of the passage.*

## COMMON CORE FOCUS

**RL 10** Read and comprehend literature. **RI 10** Read and comprehend literary nonfiction.

## INTRODUCE *GREAT READS*

In Unit 11, students have discussed two big questions. Invite students to tell which question they found more intriguing and why, and then focus attention on this page. Discuss the recommended books and their summaries, pointing out how each connects to the related question. Encourage students to choose one or more of these "great reads" to read independently.

## Ideas for Independent Reading

Read more epic tales, and see how Homer's masterpiece has inspired contemporary writers.

**COMMON CORE**

**RL 10** Read and comprehend literature. **RI 10** Read and comprehend literary nonfiction.

Get Novel Wise
**THINK** central
Go to **thinkcentral.com**.
KEYWORD: HML9-1288

### The Iliad
*by Homer*

In the *Iliad,* Homer writes of the events that preceded the *Odyssey*—the actual battles and conflicts during the Trojan War. Menelaus and his brother, Agamemnon, struggle for power; Agamemnon fights with his greatest warrior, Achilles; Achilles shows loyalty to his closest friend, Patroclos; Odysseus commands his powerful army. The *Iliad* shows what the men in the *Odyssey* have left behind them, depicting the greater and smaller aspects of ancient war.

### The Aeneid
*by Virgil*

Odysseus had tremendous difficulty returning home. What was the experience of the Trojans, who no longer had a home? Defeated in the Trojan War, Aeneas and his companions set sail at the instruction of the gods on Mount Olympus. The goddess Venus, Aeneas' mother, has told them they must found a new city. That city will eventually become the center of a new and majestic power—the Roman Empire. However, they are waylaid by storms, the wrath and vengefulness of the goddess Juno, and Aeneas' affection for Dido, the queen of Carthage in northern Africa.

### The Epic of Gilgamesh
*translated by Stephen Mitchell*

*The Epic of Gilgamesh* is the oldest known piece of writing in the world. Experts believe it preceded the *Odyssey* by at least a thousand years; it was found written on broken clay tablets in the ruined city of Nineveh. Gilgamesh, the great but selfish king of Uruk (modern-day Iraq), has his life transformed by his friendship with Enkidu. Together, the two bring peace to his city, battle monsters similar to those encountered in Homer's work, and go on a quest for immortality.

### Omeros
*by Derek Walcott*

Walcott, a Caribbean-American poet and playwright, resets the *Odyssey* in contemporary St. Lucia. This book-length poem follows contemporary characters—fishermen, a household servant, a seer—who share traits and names with those in Homer's work, as they travel through the Caribbean Islands, Europe, and the United States. Throughout the book, the poet himself addresses Omeros (Greek for "Homer") as a source of inspiration. Like Odysseus' traveling companions, all the characters are, in one way or another, searching for a home.

### Cold Mountain
*by Charles Frazier*

This novel has been called "an American *Odyssey.*" Inman, a Confederate soldier in the Civil War, has been severely wounded and leaves the army, walking home to Ada, whom he loved before going to war. The journey is difficult, and Inman is consistently waylaid by others in the South who have been affected by the war. Like Odysseus, Inman must use all the cunning and determination he has to make it home. Like Penelope, Ada must figure out how to live without the love she had relied upon, knowing he might never return to her.

### The Hero with a Thousand Faces
*by Joseph Campbell*

What makes a hero? Do all heroes embody the same ideals, even in different social contexts? Joseph Campbell examines heroes, looking at sources that range from Greek mythology to fairy tales and Eastern philosophy, and claims that the hero is timeless. No matter how the story changes, Campbell says the hero is a constant figure; his attributes are similar and equally significant through time.

1288

**THINK** central
**NovelWise**

The keyword on this page points to **NovelWise,** a Web site that helps students choose a novel or other book-length work to read. **NovelWise** also provides
• study guides
• reading strategies and literary elements instruction
• presentations to introduce classic novels
• project ideas

# The Power of Research

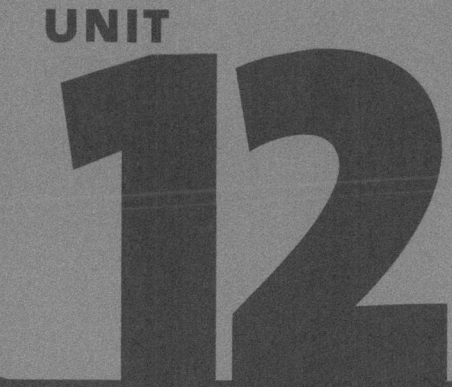

## RESEARCH WORKSHOPS

- **Research Strategies**
- **Writing Research Papers**

1289

## INTRODUCE THE UNIT

This unit is divided into two parts. The **Research Strategies Workshop,** pages 1292–1313, introduces students to strategies they can use to do both academic and everyday research. Students learn about selecting and using various electronic and print resources. As they learn, they also apply the information in hands-on activities designed to help them gain proficiency in using these various research tools and strategies.

The **Writing Workshop,** pages 1314–1337, provides a framework for students to apply the strategies they have learned to an academic writing assignment: a research paper. After analyzing a student model, students are guided through a step-by-step process in writing their own research papers.

For help in planning this unit, see

**R** RESOURCE MANAGER UNIT 12
pp. 1–34

**COMMON CORE**

**STRAND**

| | |
|---|---|
| **Reading Literature** | |
| **Reading Informational Text** | |
| **Writing** | Quickwrite p. 1292<br>Planning Your Research pp. 1293–1294  **W 7**<br>Using the Internet pp. 1295–1297<br>Using the Library or Media Center pp. 1298–1304  **W 8, W 9**<br>Evaluating Information pp. 1305–1309  **W 8**<br>Research Tips and Strategies pp. 1312–1313  **W 8** |
| **Speaking and Listening** | Collecting Your Own Data pp. 1310–1311  **SL 1a, c** |
| **Language** | Terms for the Internet p. 1295<br>Terms for the Library p. 1298 |

| | |
|---|---|
| **COMMON CORE**<br><br>**STRAND** | *Writing Workshop:* Research Paper<br>pp. 1314–1335<br><br>*Technology Workshop:* Creating a Wiki<br>pp. 1336–1337 |
| **Reading Literature** | |
| **Reading Informational Text** | |
| **Writing** | Research Paper pp. 1314–1335  **W 2a-f, W 4, W 5, W 7, W 8, W 9** |
| **Speaking and Listening** | Creating a Wiki pp. 1336–1337  **SL 1b, SL 2, SL 5** |
| **Language** | Drafting pp. 1322–1323  **L 2, L 3a**<br>Editing and Publishing p. 1332  **L 2b, L 3a**<br>Review MLA Guidelines pp. 1334–1335  **L 3a** |

To see the complete Essential Course of Study, see pp. T23–T28.

For additional lesson planning help, see **Teacher One Stop DVD.**

**1289B**

# Instructional Support

**Resource Manager Unit 12**

**UNIT SUPPORT**

Academic Vocabulary, p. 2

Additional Academic Vocabulary, p. 3

Writing Workshop: Research Paper
   pp. 5–34

**SELECTION SUPPORT***

**Plan and Teach**

**Student Copy Masters**

*Available for all selections

† Available on **thinkcentral.com**.

**Language Handbook**

**Best Practices Toolkit**†

**Teacher One Stop** DVD-ROM

**Student One Stop** DVD-ROM

**Write*Smart*** CD-ROM†

**GrammarNotes** DVD-ROM†

# Differentiated Instruction

## STRUGGLING READERS AND WRITERS

**Level Up Online Tutorials**

## ENGLISH LANGUAGE LEARNERS

**English Language Learner Adapted Interactive Reader Teacher's Guide**

**Guide to English for Newcomers**

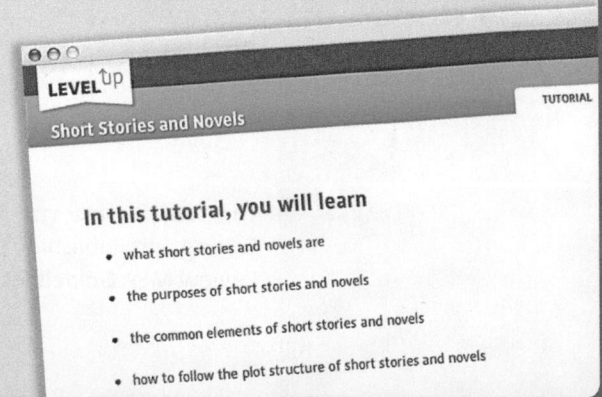

## Assessment and Reteaching

**Unit and Benchmark Tests**

**ThinkCentral Online Assessment:**
• All program assessments
• Level Up Online Tutorials

**ExamView Test Generator** on the Teacher One Stop DVD-ROM

**ThinkCentral Online Reteaching:**
• Level Up Online Tutorials
• Reteaching Worksheets

Holt McDougal **Online Essay Scoring**

Welcome to Holt McDougal Online Essay Scoring!

This site is designed to help you improve your writing skills and prepare for standardized writing tests. When you write and submit a response to one of the writing prompts on this site, the computerized scoring system will immediately score and deliver feedback on your essay. Other resources on this site will help you prepare, develop, and revise your essay.

**STUDENTS**
Get started by entering the
**Writing Zone** →

## Professional Development

**Video Center** Based on interviews with program consultants and other educational experts, these videos feature classroom-ready teaching strategies.

**Teacher Toolkit** Includes a Teacher Handbook as well as a range of articles and handouts by program consultants and other educators.

**Janet Allen**

**Kylene Beers**

**Jim Burke**

**Carol Jago**

 **at a Glance**

**One Location, Endless Resources**

**Find Resources** Browse all *Holt McDougal Literature* components for the ones that meet your students' needs and match your teaching style.

**Assess Progress and Reteach** Assign electronic versions of program assessments to measure your students' mastery of the Common Core State Standards. On thinkcentral.com, some tests deliver online remediation tutorials to students who have not mastered skills.

 *Interactive Whiteboard Lessons*

Prepare your students for college and careers by teaching relevant, real-world skills through dynamic, interactive instruction. Go to **thinkcentral.com** to browse through all whiteboard lessons, including the following:

• Conducting Research on the Web
• Evaluating Sources
• Synthesizing Information
• Writing Informative Text

 Together Holt McDougal and HISTORY® are revolutionizing the study of English/language arts with video that helps students relive and re-imagine the people, places, and events they are discovering through reading. Look for selections with the HISTORY® icon.

## Why do RESEARCH?

Read the question. Then read and discuss the introductory paragraph, emphasizing the ways in which research is part of daily life. Elicit or explain that even such minor questions as "What time does the movie start?" and "How long should this food cook in the microwave?" require research of some sort. Invite students to suggest additional examples of everyday research questions.

*ACTIVITY* Encourage students to recall different places they have gone—the mall, the supermarket, sports events, and so on—and explore links between these places and doing research. For example, discuss what kind of research students might do when shopping for clothing. Have students make some notes about how they go about getting answers to their questions.

**CHECK UNDERSTANDING** Ask students how doing research is important for success not only in school but also in their daily lives.

## Why do **RESEARCH?**

When you look up movie reviews, gather information for a report, or explore careers in computer animation, you are doing research to answer questions you have. No matter what your questions are, there are resources available to help you find the answers. You just need to know how to access those resources.

*ACTIVITY* Make a list of the research challenges or problems you have had over the past week. Next to each question, write the answer and how you found it. Think about topics in the following areas:

- school assignments
- local and national news
- consumer products and services
- movies and television programs

**Find It Online!**
Go to **thinkcentral.com** for the interactive version of this unit.

1290

---

## Unit Resources

*See resources on the* **Teacher One Stop DVD-ROM** *and on* **thinkcentral.com**.

 **RESOURCE MANAGER UNIT 12**

 **BEST PRACTICES TOOLKIT**

**LANGUAGE HANDBOOK**

**VOCABULARY WORKSHOP**

**READER/WRITER NOTEBOOK**

**TECHNOLOGY**

- **Teacher One Stop DVD-ROM**
- **Student One Stop DVD-ROM**
- **Write***Smart* **CD-ROM**
- **GrammarNotes DVD-ROM**

**Writing and Research in a Digital Age** on **thinkcentral.com**.

**Find It Online!**

The interactive version of this unit on **thinkcentral.com** includes
- **Writing and Research in a Digital Age**
- Citation Guide

## Preview Unit Goals

| | |
|---|---|
| **DEVELOPING RESEARCH SKILLS** | • Plan research<br>• Organize information<br>• Use library and media center resources<br>• Distinguish between primary and secondary sources<br>• Use parts of a book to locate information<br>• Evaluate information and sources, including nonfiction books, newspaper articles, and Web sites<br>• Collect your own data |
| **WRITING AND LANGUAGE** | • Write a research paper<br>• Formulate a research question and narrow or broaden a research inquiry<br>• Develop a research plan and locate sources, assessing their usefulness<br>• Make a source list or source cards<br>• Take notes<br>• Summarize, paraphrase, and quote directly<br>• Integrate information selectively, avoiding plagiarism<br>• Document sources correctly, using a standard format for citations<br>• Punctuate titles correctly<br>• Format your paper |
| **SPEAKING AND LISTENING** | • Follow instructions to post your research findings |
| **ACADEMIC VOCABULARY** | • accurate          • cite          • investigate<br>• source            • synthesize |
| **MEDIA AND VIEWING** | • Create a wiki |

# Writing and Research in a Digital Age

**THINK** central

KEYWORD: HML9-1291

From online news feeds and electronic archives to podcasts and digital notebooks, technology tools can help you tackle any research project. Find out how.

1291

---

Complete text of the Common Core State Standards is found in the correlation on p. T10. Standards covered in this unit are found in the standards overview (pp. 1289A–1289B) and on the lesson pages where they are taught.

## Preview Unit Goals

An overview of the main skills and strategies discussed in Unit 12 appears on this page. Remind students that previewing will help them get more from their reading. As students skim the list to preview the skills that this unit will cover, urge them to apply two or three of the skills to the *Activity* on the preceding page. Note that in this unit, too, color-coding marks the skills strands.

Model for students the strategy of copying the Academic Vocabulary and writing a preliminary definition for each term. Suggest that students use their **Reader/Writer Notebooks** for this purpose. Encourage students to use the terms in discussions and in writing. Also urge students to review the terms throughout the unit, revising their preliminary definitions as needed.

---

## DIFFERENTIATED INSTRUCTION

### FOR ENGLISH LANGUAGE LEARNERS

**Academic Vocabulary** Provide students with definitions of each Academic Vocabulary word.

**accurate** (ăk´yər-ĭt) *adj.* correct; free from errors

**cite** (sīt) *v.* to refer to as example or proof

**investigate** (ĭn-vĕs´tĭ-gāt´) *v.* to search carefully, as to acquire or verify facts

**source** (sôrs) *n.* a book, document, person, etc., that supplies information

**synthesize** (sĭn´thĭ-sīz´) *v.* to combine separate elements into a whole

Use the copy master to help students learn academic words they will use in this unit and on the Assessment Practice.

**R** **RESOURCE MANAGER—Copy Masters**
Academic Vocabulary pp. 2–3

# How can I **FIND** what I need?

*Essential Course of Study* ECOS

### ⦿ COMMON CORE FOCUS

**W 7** Conduct sustained research projects to answer a question or solve a problem; narrow or broaden a research inquiry; synthesize multiple sources on a research subject. **W 8** Gather relevant information from multiple authoritative print and digital sources; use advanced searches effectively; assess the usefulness of each source. **W 9** Draw evidence from informational texts to support research. **SL 1a** Come to discussions prepared, having researched material under study. **SL 1c** Propel conversations by posing and responding to questions that relate the discussion to broader themes or larger ideas.

Tell students that this unit presents strategies that will help them with all kinds of research, not just research for school assignments. Explain that the unit is divided into two parts:

- the **Research Strategies Workshop,** in which students will learn to select and use print and electronic resources, as well as find activities that will strengthen their ability to use reference sources and tools

- the **Writing Workshop,** in which students will apply the strategies to write a research paper

## How can I **FIND** what I need?

Elicit or explain that an effective, efficient researcher can find *useful* information in a reasonable amount of time. Extend the discussion by having students complete the *QUICKWRITE* and inviting volunteers to share a few of their subjects.

## Research Workshop Resources

### ⦿ COMMON CORE

Included in this workshop:
**W 7** Conduct sustained research projects to answer a question or solve a problem; narrow or broaden a research inquiry; synthesize multiple sources on a research subject. **W 8** Gather relevant information from multiple authoritative print and digital sources; use advanced searches effectively; assess the usefulness of each source. **W 9** Draw evidence from informational texts to support research.

Finding the information you need can be a challenge. For example, typing a single word or phrase into an Internet search engine could yield tens of thousands of pages to look at. You need to find a way to do research efficiently and effectively.

*QUICKWRITE* Knowing how to do research can help you in many situations. For example, the student handbook pages shown here illustrate a situation requiring research. The skills you will learn in this unit will help you do almost any kind of research. Right now, make a list of subjects that intrigue you. Then choose one or two of them to investigate as you learn research skills.

**Graduation Requirement**

COMMUNITY SERVICE

All students must complete at least ten hours of community service work by the end of each school year. Service must be completed for

28 STUDENT HANDBOOK

a nonprofit organization within 15 miles of the school. Students must submit a written description of what service they plan to perform, what agency or organization will benefit, and why performing this service would help the community.

STUDENT HANDBOOK 29

1292

---

*See resources on the* **Teacher One Stop DVD-ROM** *and on* <u>thinkcentral.com</u>.

 **RESOURCE MANAGER UNIT 12**
Lesson at a Glance and Note-Taking, pp. 5–10

 **BEST PRACTICES TOOLKIT**
Mapping Main Ideas and Details p. C6

Question and Answer Note-Taking p. B7

Interactive Notes p. B4

Reflection Chart p. B8

Jigsaw p. A1

Y Chart p. A27

T Chart p. A25

New Word Analysis p. E8

Comparison Matrix p. A24

Cluster Diagram p. B18

**TECHNOLOGY**

🎧 **Teacher One Stop DVD-ROM**
🎧 **Student One Stop DVD-ROM**
🎧 **Write*Smart* CD-ROM**
🎧 **GrammarNotes DVD-ROM**

**ThinkCentral student and teacher access at** <u>thinkcentral.com</u>.

# Planning Your Research

You have a general idea of what you want to accomplish, but you're not sure where to begin. What are the first steps to take?

## Getting Started

Just as how having prepared for a trip or studied for a test leads to a better experience, you will have a better research experience if you make a plan and carry out each step as completely as you can.

### CLARIFY YOUR GOAL

What do you want your research to achieve? Your first step is to list your general and specific goals.

> **GENERAL GOAL:** find volunteer work with a nonprofit organization
>
> **SPECIFIC NEEDS:**
>
> **Time:** Saturday afternoons are best.
>
> **Preferences:** working with animals, working outdoors
>
> **Limitations:** Where can 15-year-olds volunteer? Check age requirements. Also, I'll have to walk or bike.
>
> **SPECIFIC GOAL:** I want to do volunteer work on weekends, either with animals or in the outdoors, for a nonprofit organization that is near my home.

### GET AN OVERVIEW

Now that you have a goal, the next step is to get a broad overview of your subject.

- **Talk to people.** To explore volunteering, for example, you might talk to students who have already volunteered or to a school counselor.

- **Try the Internet.** Choose **keywords**—specific words and phrases from your goal statement that are related to your subject. For example, you might use the word *volunteer* and the name of your city or town. Plug them into search engines and explore related Web sites.

- **Visit your school's media center or the local public library.** Share your goal with the research librarian.

- **Think creatively.** Does the phone book list places you might call for information? Is there a local business that you might visit?

As you explore your subject, you may decide to change the focus of your research. For instance, Web sites of local volunteer organizations may list opportunities to work with special-needs children, an option you may not have considered.

**Research Tools**

Go to **thinkcentral.com**.
KEYWORD: HML9-1293

RESEARCH STRATEGIES WORKSHOP **1293**

---

---

## Teach

### Planning Your Research
### Getting Started

COMMON CORE **W 7**

### CLARIFY YOUR GOAL

- Point out that the examples in this unit relate to the community service scenario introduced on page 1292.

- Illustrate the difference between general goals and specific goals by presenting several general goals and having the class (or small groups) refine them into specific goals. Examples of general goals might include *tutor students* and *improve the neighborhood;* related specific goals might include *tutor elementary students in math* and *start a litter patrol in my neighborhood.*

### GET AN OVERVIEW

- Discuss the kinds of information students might expect to collect from people, from the Internet, and from the media center or public library.

- Point out that each source of information has advantages and disadvantages. For example, talking to someone might provide first-hand information, but the facts might be mixed with statements of opinion. Students will learn more about evaluating sources on pages 1305–1309.

- Have students preview the content of the Research Strategies Workshop by skimming the heads and graphics on pages 1294–1313.

**Research Tools**

Research keywords for **thinkcentral.com** connect students to the Web site, **Writing and Research in a Digital Age.** This resource contains presentations covering all aspects of the research process, including research planning and selecting sources.

## Focusing Your Research

### NARROW OR BROADEN YOUR RESEARCH INQUIRY

- Model the use of Reporter's Questions to brainstorm this starter list of questions:

  **Who** would have the best information?

  **What** are the requirements?

  **Where** would I be working?

  **Why** is this service needed?

  **When** would I be working?

  **How** can I apply for the position?

 BEST PRACTICES TOOLKIT—Transparency
    Reporter's Questions p. C9

- Have students refine the list, making the questions as specific as possible.

- Help students look for key terms in the new questions. Compare these terms, which signal specific facts that they will want to find, to keywords in an Internet search.

### CHOOSE A NOTE-TAKING METHOD

Discuss the note-taking methods in the text.

**Note Cards** Preview the note cards on page 1319.

**Category Chart** Explain that this chart also helps students to retrieve facts quickly.

**Pro-Con Chart** Compare this chart to the thought process that students go through when they make decisions.

**Additional Note-Taking Methods** Point out some other note-taking methods. For example, students also might take notes using a Mapping Main Ideas and Details or Question and Answer Note Taking.

 BEST PRACTICES TOOLKIT—Transparencies
    Mapping Main Ideas and Details p. C6
    Question and Answer Note Taking p. B7

**Reteaching Workshops** on **thinkcentral.com**
    Research and Study Skills Lesson 1:
        Research Questions and Topic

    Research and Study Skills Lesson 8:
        Source Cards and Notecards

**R** RESOURCE MANAGER—Copy Master
    Develop Research Questions p. 11

## Focusing Your Research

Now that you have a better sense of what you want to find out, you can direct your research in more specific ways.

### NARROW OR BROADEN YOUR RESEARCH INQUIRY

To focus your research—and avoid wasting time—narrow or broaden your inquiry. Develop a set of specific questions that you would like answered, and use those questions to guide your inquiry.

> - Which nonprofit organizations in my area help stray animals or do animal rescue?
> - Which of these organizations are looking for volunteers?
> - What requirements do volunteers have to meet? Are there age limitations or time requirements?

### CHOOSE A NOTE-TAKING METHOD

To avoid drowning in a sea of facts, figures, and details, record information from multiple sources in a way that matches your purpose. Here are some examples:

- If you are doing research for a formal report, you should probably use **electronic** or **written note cards**. See page 1318 to learn more.

- Use a **category chart** to help you compare details.

| Name of Animal Shelter | Age Requirements | Hours per Week Required | Other Details |
|---|---|---|---|
| CARE Shelter for Animals | 16+ | No minimum | closer to my house |
| Humane Society | 14+ | 2 hr/week | Saturdays OK |

- Consider a **pro-con chart** if you want to examine two options.

| Volunteering at CARE Shelter for Animals | |
|---|---|
| Advantages: | Disadvantages: |
| • can get there on my bike | • must be at least 16 years old, so I'd have to wait until my birthday in January |
| • no minimum number of hours | • dogs and cats only; no exotic animals |

| Volunteering at Humane Society | |
|---|---|
| Advantages: | Disadvantages: |
| • has a wide range of positions | • need a ride there |
| • lets 14-year-olds volunteer | • charges a volunteer orientation fee |

## DIFFERENTIATED INSTRUCTION

### FOR ADVANCED LEARNERS/PRE–AP

**Demonstrate Note-Taking Methods** Assign each of several groups of students a specific note-taking method not already discussed, such as Interactive Notes or a Reflection Chart. Have each group prepare and present a class demonstration that explains the method and why it might be used and gives clear examples of how the method might be used with specific topics.

 BEST PRACTICES TOOLKIT—Transparencies
    Interactive Notes p. B4
    Reflection Chart p. B8

# Using the Internet

The Internet is a great place to find a vast amount of information quickly. How can you target your search so that you don't get lost?

## Understanding the Web

You probably know that the World Wide Web is accessible through the Internet, a vast system of linked computers. The Web includes literally hundreds of millions of Web sites and billions of Web pages.

Each type of Web site has its own purpose. One clue to the purpose is the URL, or "address," of a Web page. Each Web address includes an abbreviation that often will tell you what type of site the page is in.

**TERMS FOR THE INTERNET**
- World Wide Web
- Web site
- URL (uniform resource locator, also called Web address)
- search engine
- keyword search
- menu
- hyperlink or link
- icon

### WEB ABBREVIATIONS AND MEANINGS

**.COM** commercial organization—product information and sales; some personal sites; some combinations of products and information, such as World Book Online

**.EDU** education—information about schools, courses, campus life, and research projects; may also include students' personal sites

**.GOV** U.S. government—official sites of the White House, the CIA, and many other government agencies

**.MIL** U.S. military—official sites of the armed forces, the Department of Defense, and related agencies

**.NET** network—product information and sales

**.ORG** organization—charities, libraries, and other nonprofit organizations; political parties; also includes some commercial organizations and personal sites

### SEARCH THE WEB

**Keyword Search** Start with a **search engine,** a Web site that allows you to look for information by using a phrase or term related to your subject. This kind of search is called a **keyword search.** Here are some search tips:

- Be as specific as possible. Instead of *volunteering,* try *volunteer programs in Austin.* Look at your research questions for ideas.

- Some search engines allow you to replace letters at the end of a word with an asterisk. For example, a search for the keyword *volunt** will find sites that contain *volunteer, voluntary,* and *volunteerism.*

- Enclose an exact phrase in quotation marks. For example, a search for *"volunteer with animals"* will find sites that include those three words in that order.

**TIP** Search engines often have "Advanced Search" or "Search Tips" links that you can click for more information.

---

# Using the Internet
## Understanding the Web

### TERMS FOR THE INTERNET
Write the terms on the board. Elicit preliminary definitions, but urge students to refine those definitions as they meet the terms on pages 1295–1297.

### WEB ABBREVIATIONS AND MEANINGS
- Have students read the abbreviations and meanings. Note that this is a partial listing.
- Have small groups of students work at classroom computers to find an example of each type of site. (Groups might begin with www.cnn.com, www.health.harvard.edu, and www.irs.gov.) Ask groups to share a piece of information found at each site.

### SEARCH THE WEB
**Keyword Searches** Brainstorm a list of familiar search engines, such as Google, Yahoo!, and ASK Jeeves. After pointing out the **TIP**, have students use each search engine to try the searches described in the text. Compare their findings. Then challenge students to conduct searches using key terms from the specific research questions that they developed for page 1294. Again, ask students to use various search engines and compare results.

**Reteaching Workshops** on <u>thinkcentral.com</u>
Research and Study Skills Lesson 4: Using a Web site for Research

---

**FOR STRUGGLING READERS**

**Comprehension Support** Use a Jigsaw strategy by dividing the class into "home groups" of five students each and assigning one or two Web abbreviations to a student in each group. Then have students reassemble into "expert groups," each group working at classroom computers to find examples of their Web type(s). Have "experts" return to their home groups and share their favorite examples.

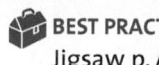 **BEST PRACTICES TOOLKIT**
Jigsaw p. A1

**FOR ENGLISH LANGUAGE LEARNERS**

**Oral Language** Explain to students that in spoken English, the suffixes of the Web site addresses presented on this page are pronounced "dot com," "dot e-d-u," "dot guv," "dot mil," "dot net," and "dot org."

## ADDITIONAL TEACHING OPPORTUNITY

**Getting a Home Page** Students can make their favorite search engine their home page—the page that opens when they access the Internet. To make Google their home page, for example, they can go to www.google.com and click on "Make Google Your Homepage!" Then have them follow the instructions provided.

To check understanding, ask

- Once you have input your preferences for your home page, what must you do to save them? *Possible answer: click OK*

- After you have saved your changes, how can you go directly to your new home page? *Possible answer: by clicking the Home button on the browser toolbar*

**Boolean Searches** To conduct Boolean searches, have students use the key terms they developed for the research questions on page 1294. Point out the  about metasearch engines.

## ASSESS AND SELECT RELEVANT SITES

Review the meaning of *URL*.

 **YOUR TURN** **Close Read**

*Possible answers:*

1. *The words used were* volunteer, Austin, *and* animals. *The combination effectively specifies the type of volunteer activities (animals) and the location (Austin).*

2. *The total number of sites found was 1,550,000. This is too large a number to open and read every item.*

3. *All four sites are relevant. Each site provides information about volunteering.*

**R** RESOURCE MANAGER—Copy Master
Select Relevant Web Sites p. 12

---

**Boolean Search** A Boolean search allows you to specify the relationships between keywords and phrases.

- **AND search:** The AND tells the search engine to find all documents that contain every word (*volunteer* AND *animals*). Some search engines use a plus sign instead (*+volunteer +animals*).

- **OR search:** The OR broadens the search to include all documents that contain either word (*cats* OR *dogs*).

- **NOT search:** A NOT excludes unwanted terms from the search (*pets* NOT *breeders*). Some search engines use a minus sign (*+pets –breeders*).

**TIP** Use a metasearch engine to scan multiple search engines simultaneously. See page 1312 for more information.

### ASSESS AND SELECT RELEVANT SITES

Your search may result in a list that puts what the search engine considers the most relevant sites at the top of the page. Most search engines base relevance on how often your search terms appear on a particular page and on whether any or all of your search terms appear in the page's URL. However, just because a site is at the top of a list doesn't mean it's the most relevant site for you. Read the full entries in the list, looking for words that are related to your needs.

**YOUR TURN** **Look at Search Engine Results**

A search for volunteer opportunities in one community resulted in a number of possibilities. Which ones would you choose to explore?

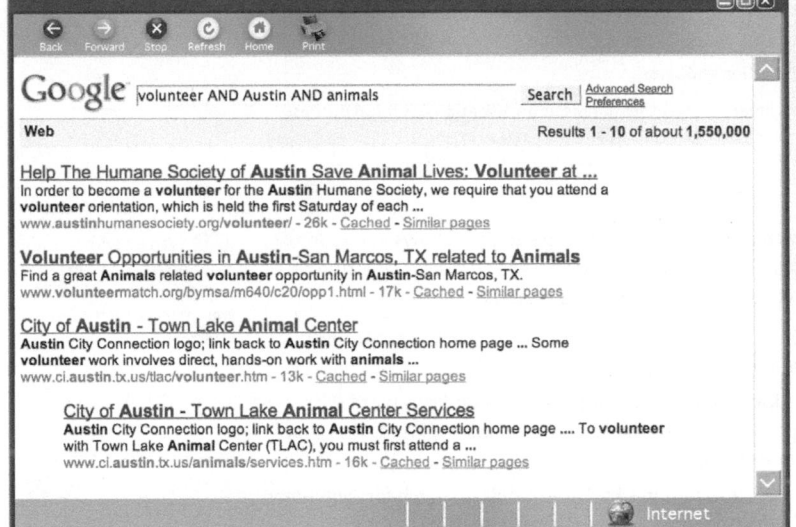

**Close Read**

1. Which three words were used in this Boolean search? What makes them an effective combination?

2. What was the total number of sites found? Is this a manageable number of sites to open and read? Why or why not?

3. Of the sites shown, which seem relevant to volunteer work with animals in Austin? Explain your answer.

---

## DIFFERENTIATED INSTRUCTION

### FOR STRUGGLING READERS

**Concept Support** Assess and reinforce students' understanding of keyword searches and Boolean searches by having them work in small groups to create a chart summarizing what they have learned and making clear the differences between the two kinds of searches. Encourage students to include specific examples of searches. Have groups exchange and compare their finished charts.

**Task Support** Reinforce the application of Boolean search techniques by working with students to conduct searches of increasing specificity. For example, search first for *volunteers* AND *animals,* then for *volunteers* AND *cats* OR *dogs,* and then for *volunteers* AND *cats* OR *dogs* NOT *puppies.* Have students record the number of "hits" for each search and observe how the total decreases as the search becomes more specific.

## EXPLORE WEB SITES

Once you have chosen a site to look at, you have to know how to read it and how to use the special features it contains. Most Web pages have features that aren't used in books.

- **Hyperlinks,** or links, are usually underlined or highlighted words. Clicking on a link leads you to related information on another page on the site or on a different site.
- **Icons** are pictures that can be clicked on to take you to another page.
- Most Web pages include at least one **menu,** or list of choices. These are often on one side of the page, at the top, or at the bottom.

**TIP** To evaluate the usefulness and accuracy of the information on a Web site, use the evaluation guidelines on page 1306.

**YOUR TURN**

### Read a Web Site

Let's say you choose to visit the first site that the search engine listed. Take a close look at the volunteering section of the site and see what information you can find.

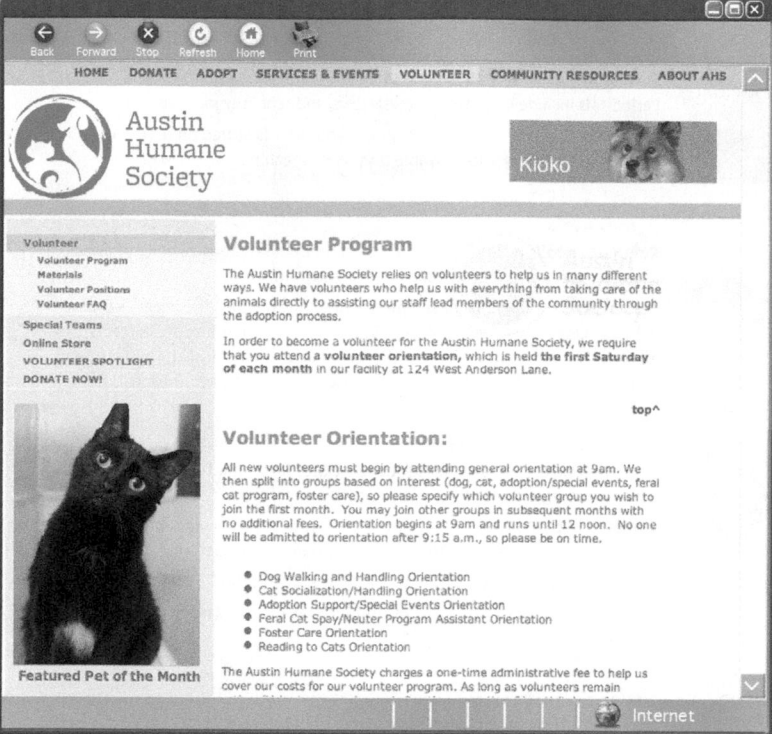

**Close Read**

1. Is this site a useful one for someone looking for volunteer work with animals? Give reasons for your answer.

2. Where would you click to learn more about this organization's objectives and goals?

3. This site has menus on the left side of the page and at the top. Which link would you click to find out about specific volunteer opportunities?

---

### EXPLORE WEB SITES

If classroom computers are available, have students go to the actual Web site displayed on page 1297: www.austinhumanesociety.org. Mention the **TIP** and encourage students to evaluate these features as you discuss them:

**Hyperlinks** Explain that hyperlinks provide fast connections to information that visitors to a site often want to find. For example, clicking on "Events" (in the top bar) takes you to a page with information about upcoming events. Have students identify hyperlinks on the google.com site shown on page 1296.

**Icons** Explain that icons serve the same purpose as hyperlinks. For example, clicking on the photograph of the dog and cat takes you to a page with information about donating to the shelter.

**Menus** Point out the menus along the top of this site. Explain that each menu item is a hyperlink.

**YOUR TURN**

### Close Read

*Possible answers:*

1. *The site is a good match, because there is a lot of information for anyone who wants to volunteer.*

2. *To learn more about the organization, you would click on the link "About AHS."*

3. *You would click on the link "Volunteer" (at the top) to learn about such opportunities.*

**R** RESOURCE MANAGER—Copy Master
Navigate Relevant Web Sites p. 13

---

### FOR STRUGGLING READERS

**Comprehension Support** Direct groups to input a Web address, such as www.un.org/english, www.nytimes.com, or www.archives.gov. Then have students create an oversize mock-up of the home page on poster paper. Ask them to label features of the page, using the terms and information presented on page 1297. Create a classroom display of the groups' finished posters and invite student discussion.

### FOR ADVANCED LEARNERS/PRE–AP

**Create a Home Page** Have students design the home page of a personal Web site. Encourage them to be creative, including graphics as well as text. The page should contain at least one menu, several hyperlinks and icons, a description of the site, the identity of the creator, and any other features that the student wants to include. Call on volunteers to present and explain their home page to the class.

# Using the Library or Media Center

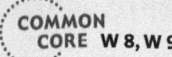

COMMON CORE W 8, W 9

## TERMS FOR THE LIBRARY

Read the terms aloud; then invite volunteers to share situations in which they have found these resources helpful when using school or community libraries. Elicit preliminary definitions that can be refined as students read and discuss the page.

## Understanding Today's Library

### LIBRARY AND MEDIA CENTER RESOURCES

Display or demonstrate the use of each library resource on this page. Explain that students will learn more about each type of information on the next several pages.

**Books** Explain that nonfiction books focus on factual explanations and real-life stories. Nonfiction books are usually more reliable resources than fiction books, due to the imaginative nature of fiction.

**Newspapers and Periodicals** Have students name newsmagazines and subject-area magazines that they might use for a research project. Invite students who have used microfilm or microfiche in past projects to comment on those resources.

**Reference Sources** Discuss the different kinds of information presented in the references listed. Point out the organization of information in each resource.

**Electronic Resources** Ask students to suggest research topics for which some of these resources might be appropriate.

**Other Resources** Urge students to consult with a librarian about the use and usefulness of some of these resources for the topic they have chosen. For example, students might use audio resources to research a famous speech.

**R** RESOURCE MANAGER—Copy Master
Use Library and Media Center Sources p. 14

---

## TERMS FOR THE LIBRARY
- reference sources
- abstract
- catalog
- database
- table of contents
- bibliography
- index

# Using the Library or Media Center

Let's say you find information on animal shelters and begin to volunteer at one. You meet veterinarians and veterinary technicians, and you begin to wonder about a career in veterinary medicine. Now you have a new topic—one that requires in-depth research.

## Understanding Today's Library

Libraries and media centers today are information supersources. They offer access to print, audio-visual, electronic, and human resources. Here is a quick look at the many types of information libraries have to offer.

### LIBRARY AND MEDIA CENTER RESOURCES

**BOOKS**
**Nonfiction books** are organized by subject. See "Library Sleuth" on page 1312 to learn about the two systems for classifying nonfiction books.
**Fiction books** are organized alphabetically by the authors' last names.

**NEWSPAPERS AND PERIODICALS**
**Periodicals** include magazines, newsletters, and scholarly journals.
**Microforms** are periodicals, newspapers, and reports stored on film (microfilm) or cards (microfiche) and viewable on special machines.

**REFERENCE SOURCES**
**Reference books** include dictionaries, encyclopedias, atlases, and almanacs. These usually cannot be checked out of the library.
**Search tools** include databases, directories, indexes, and the library's online catalog. One search tool that can save you time is an index of abstracts. An **abstract** is a short summary of a journal article. By looking at abstracts, you can determine which articles are most closely related to your topic.

**ELECTRONIC RESOURCES**
**DVDs and videos** of documentaries and other films and television shows are available at most libraries for free or for a small fee.
**E-books** are books available in electronic form. They are readable on a personal computer or on various hand-held electronic devices.
**Audio resources** include books, music, and speeches on CDs or in MP3 files.
**CD-ROMs** of encyclopedias, maps, and other resources are available at many libraries.

**OTHER RESOURCES**
Your library may have a careers section, a college search section, maps, music scores, genealogy resources, and many other items. Most libraries have special sections for both young adults and children.

---

## DIFFERENTIATED INSTRUCTION

### FOR STRUGGLING READERS

**Understanding Today's Library** Arrange one or more visits to the school library or media center. Before students visit, help them create a list of questions to be answered. Then ask a librarian or center director to conduct a tour and explain resources available for student use. Answer questions not covered during the tour. Invite each student to share something that he or she learned about research resources during this activity.

### FOR ADVANCED LEARNERS/PRE–AP

**Present Terms** Assign groups of students two or three words from the Terms for the Library list. Instruct each group to use the information in the text, their own knowledge, and additional resources to teach the term to the class. Encourage groups to illustrate the meaning of each term through examples, illustrations, or additional facts.

# Finding What You Need

All the different departments and resources in your local library can seem overwhelming. Where should you start? Ask a librarian, or consult the library's online resources.

## THE RESEARCH LIBRARIAN

Librarians are experts in finding information. These experts can help you

- define what you need to know
- locate print, electronic, and audio-visual sources of information
- use the library's resources and operate equipment
- use interlibrary catalogs to expand your research to other libraries

## THE LIBRARY'S CATALOG

The catalog is your road map to the library's vast resources. There are four ways to search for a source:

- author    • title    • subject    • keyword

In addition to a source's author, title, and publication date, the catalog entry may include a brief summary of its content and the subject categories it addresses. The entry will also indicate where it is shelved and whether it is available.

**YOUR TURN** | **Search a Library Catalog**
This example of a catalog entry shows information about a specific book.

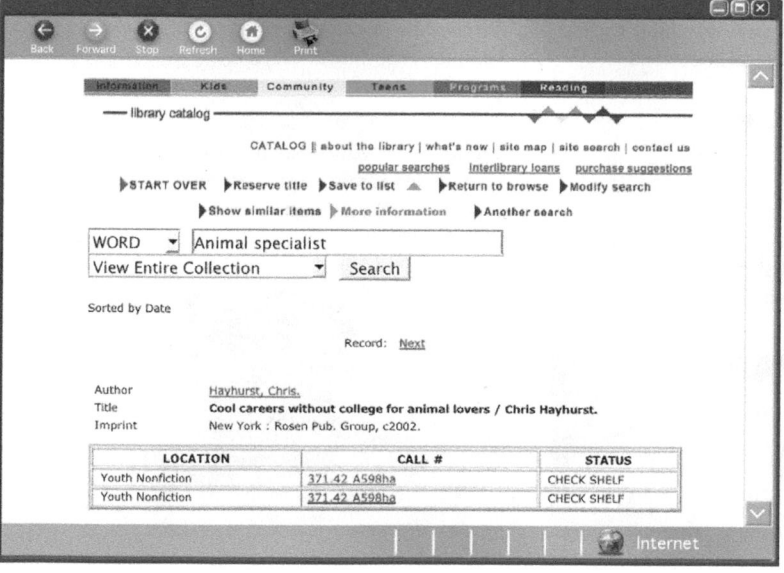

**Close Read**

1. What search term did this student use? List some other search terms that might produce similar results.

2. Is the book *Cool Careers* available at this library? How can you tell?

3. When was this book published? How do you know?

---

## FOR ENGLISH LANGUAGE LEARNERS

**Vocabulary Support** Write these terms on the board. Ask groups of students to define each term, using context clues, prior knowledge, and a dictionary. Have groups share and compare their definitions.

- *online:* connected to or available through a computer system
- *catalog:* listing of books and other resources
- *interlibrary:* between or shared by libraries

## FOR ADVANCED LEARNERS/PRE–AP

**Map Out the Library** Have students visit the school or public library to explore and take note of its layout and facilities. Then have students work individually or in pairs to create a detailed map of the library and the various resources that it offers. Encourage students to make the map as clear and precise as possible. Work with students to create a format for sharing the completed maps.

---

# Finding What You Need

## THE RESEARCH LIBRARIAN

Brainstorm questions to ask a research librarian—for example, "Where can I find a news article published 50 years ago?" or "What should I do if my library does not have the book I need?"

## THE LIBRARY'S CATALOG

Make these points as you discuss the different kinds of online searches:

**Author** Searching by an author's last name will produce a list of works by that author. Use an author's full name, because some authors have the same last name, such as Charlotte Brontë and Emily Brontë. Some search engines may require the author's last name first (Twain, Mark), while others require the first name first (Mark Twain).

**Title** Searching by title will produce a list of books and other materials with that title. Use the full title, because many works have similar titles. Point out that titles are listed alphabetically, but not by the articles *a* and *the* that appear at the beginning of some titles.

**Subject** Searching by subject may produce a long list of entries. The more specific the subject, the more relevant the list will be.

**Keyword** Searching for a combination of two or three keywords will produce results in much the same way that Internet searches do. For example, searching on "Austen Prejudice" will produce not only Jane Austen's novel *Pride and Prejudice,* but also books about the novel, audiobooks, films of the novel, and so on.

**YOUR TURN** | **Close Read**

*Possible answers:*

1. *The student used the search term "animal specialist." Other search terms might be "veterinarian" or "veterinary technician."*

2. *The book is available; the status line says "CHECK SHELF." If the book were not available, the status line would say, "CHECKED OUT" and might give the date it is due.*

3. *The book was published in 2002, as indicated in the "Imprint" line.*

**Reteaching Workshops** on **thinkcentral.com**
Research and Study Skills Lesson 2

# Choosing Sources

## PRIMARY AND SECONDARY SOURCES

Point out that the terms *primary source* and *secondary source* usually apply only to non-fiction sources.

**Primary Sources** Primary sources can provide vivid details and personal accounts of an event. For example, reading the words of an earthquake victim enables a researcher to see the event through the victim's eyes and understand better the impact of the event.

**Secondary Sources** Secondary sources can help a researcher put an event in context. For example, a soldier in a war (primary source) can only tell about his or her experiences. However, a history book (secondary source) can address the war on a larger scale and place it in a historical context.

**Comparing Sources** Point out that evaluating and comparing sources can help students judge a source's accuracy and bias. Distinguishing the type of resource and the source of information can help students find reliable information. For example, an encyclopedia entry on World War I might be more objective and reliable than an interview with an American protester of the war.

To check understanding, direct students to identify both a primary source and a secondary source that relate to the same subject. Use a Y Chart to note students' comments and comparisons about the information that the two sources would be likely to provide.

 BEST PRACTICES TOOLKIT—Transparency Y Chart p. A27

**Reteaching Worksheets** on **thinkcentral.com** Research and Study Skills Lesson 5: Using Primary and Secondary Sources

R RESOURCE MANAGER—Copy Master Determine Primary and Secondary Sources p. 15

---

# Choosing Sources

You have arrived at the library and looked at the online catalog. You're amazed at the amount of information available on your subject. How can you find which sources best fit your needs?

## PRIMARY AND SECONDARY SOURCES

One of the first steps in choosing a source is to determine whether it is a primary or a secondary source. This chart explains the differences.

| PRIMARY SOURCES | SECONDARY SOURCES |
|---|---|
| **Definition:** materials written or created by people who were present at events, either as participants or as observers | **Definition:** records of events that were written or created after the events occurred by people who were not directly involved in the events |
| **Advantages:** firsthand information; can help the researcher understand the attitudes and beliefs of a particular time period; may contain very specific information | **Advantages:** sometimes include excerpts from many primary sources; often have a broad perspective and many viewpoints; good for getting an overview of a topic |
| **Disadvantages:** limited perspective; may need interpretation; may be biased | **Disadvantages:** only as reliable as the sources used; may be biased |
| **Often used when researching:** current events, biographical information | **Often used when researching:** complex or technical subjects, ancient history |
| **Examples:** letters, diaries, speeches, travelogues, photographs, autobiographies, interviews, e-mails, public documents such as census data, first-person newspaper and magazine articles | **Examples:** encyclopedias, textbooks, biographies, some newspaper and magazine articles, documentaries and other films |

---

## DIFFERENTIATED INSTRUCTION

### FOR STRUGGLING READERS

**Concept Support** Distribute a primary source and a secondary source—for example, an eyewitness account of an event and a news article describing the same event—to small groups of students. Have each group use a T Chart to compare the two and make observations about the differences.

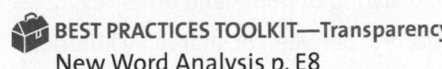 BEST PRACTICES TOOLKIT—Transparency T Chart p. A25

### FOR ENGLISH LANGUAGE LEARNERS

**Vocabulary: Cognates** Note the similarity between the English words *primary, secondary,* and *reference* and the Spanish words *primario, secundario,* and *referencia.* Then have pairs of students apply New Word Analysis to help them define these terms: *primary source, secondary source,* and *reference work.* Encourage students to use context clues.

BEST PRACTICES TOOLKIT—Transparency New Word Analysis p. E8

## REFERENCE SOURCES

A good first step in finding primary and secondary sources is to examine the library's reference collection. Reference works can give you a good overview of a topic and help you identify people, dates, and publications associated with your topic. They can also help you focus your topic and develop research questions. Many types of reference works are available on CD-ROMs and online. Ask a research librarian for help.

| REFERENCE SOURCES | EXAMPLES |
|---|---|
| **ENCYCLOPEDIAS**<br>**General:** Detailed articles on many topics<br><br>**Specialized:** Articles on topics in a specific field, such as medicine, art, or careers | *Encyclopaedia Britannica*<br>*The World Book Encyclopedia*<br><br>*Encyclopedia of Careers and Vocational Guidance* |
| **DICTIONARIES**<br>**General:** Word meanings, origins, spellings, pronunciations, and usage<br><br>**Specialized:** Terms used in a specific field, such as medicine or music | *The American Heritage Student Dictionary*<br><br>*Delmar's Veterinary Technician Dictionary* |
| **ALMANACS AND YEARBOOKS**<br>Facts and statistics | *The World Almanac and Book of Facts* |
| **THESAURI**<br>Synonyms and antonyms | *Webster's New World Thesaurus*<br>*Roget's II: The New Thesaurus* |
| **BIOGRAPHICAL REFERENCES**<br>Detailed information on the lives and careers of noteworthy people | *Native American Women* |
| **ATLASES**<br>Maps and geographic information | *Rand McNally Classroom Atlas* |
| **DIRECTORIES**<br>Names, addresses, and phone numbers of people and organizations | Telephone books; lists of business organizations, agencies, and publications |
| **INDEXES**<br>Alphabetical lists of information, usually subjects, authors, and titles | *Readers' Guide to Periodical Literature*<br>*New York Times Index* |

## REFERENCE SOURCES

Elicit or provide examples of research tasks for which each reference source might be helpful. Use examples such as these to fill in a T Chart that associates each reference source with appropriate tasks:

**Encyclopedias:** find biographical information about a famous person; gather background information for a research paper

**Dictionaries:** check spelling and pronunciation of a technical term

**Almanacs and Yearbooks:** gather economic data about foreign nations; find statistics for past U.S. national elections

**Thesauri:** identify synonyms to add variety to a piece of writing

**Biographical References:** learn more about a historical person; read about a favorite author

**Atlases:** locate an unfamiliar country; determine distance between cities

**Directories:** find contact information for a local business; identify agencies or publications serving a particular need

**Indexes:** identify magazine or journal articles about a particular subject; find a book review

BEST PRACTICES TOOLKIT—Transparency T Chart p. A25

**Reteaching Workshops** on **thinkcentral.com**
Research and Study Skills Lesson 3: Using Reference and Search Tools

Vocabulary Lesson 24: Using Vocabulary Reference Sources

---

### FOR STRUGGLING READERS

**Comprehension Support** Ask pairs or small groups to review the chart on this page. Then have each pair or group create an outline that places each type of reference source in at least one of these categories:

- Facts About People
- Facts About Places
- Facts About Events
- Facts About Words

Have students present and discuss the results.

### FOR ADVANCED LEARNERS/PRE-AP

**Demonstrate Reference Sources** Have students work in pairs. Assign each pair one or two reference sources; then instruct pairs to prepare and present a class demonstration of each reference source. Presentations should describe the key features of each source and demonstrate how to use the source effectively.

## DATABASES

Have students read the description of databases. Then elicit or provide examples of research activities for which databases would be helpful. For example, students might use a database for tasks such as these:

- To find education-related articles, using a Department of Education database (www.eric.ed.gov)

- To gather health-related information, using a National Institutes of Health database (www.nlm.nih.gov/medlineplus)

- To find articles about genetic research, using a database of scientific information (www.scirus.com/srsapp)

**YOUR TURN**

### Close Read

*Possible answers:*

1. *The first or third match might be most useful. The first is the most recent; the third is older but may be more relevant. Similarly, the second match or the last match may be least useful. The second may be too narrowly focused; the last may be too out of date.*

**IF STUDENTS NEED HELP . . .** Have them ask

- How relevant is each source to the keywords used for the search?

- How recent is each source?

- How broad or limited in scope is each source likely to be?

2. *The information is organized by date, in descending order. This organization makes spotting the most current source easy, but it also may cause a researcher to overlook an older but more useful source.*

3. *You would click on "Limit search."*

---

**DATABASES**

**What Are They?** A database is a collection of information arranged so that it is easy to search. You may be familiar with some free online databases, such as the Internet Movie Database. Other databases require a subscription, but your local library may have access to them. For instance, InfoTrac is a database of articles from newspapers, magazines, and journals. America's Newspapers contains articles from about 270 American newspapers. The Veterinary Medical Database is a collection of case histories of individual animals that have been given veterinary care.

**Why Are They Useful?** One advantage to using databases rather than search engines is that database searches are more targeted. Unlike search engines, databases have no advertisements. Also, most databases are collections of specific types of material—only newspaper articles, only scientific papers, and so on.

**When Do I Use Them?** Use databases when you have narrowed your topic considerably and have a good idea of what information you are seeking. Ask a librarian which databases are available to you.

**YOUR TURN**

### Examine a Database

A search of InfoTrac brought up the following information about veterinary technicians.

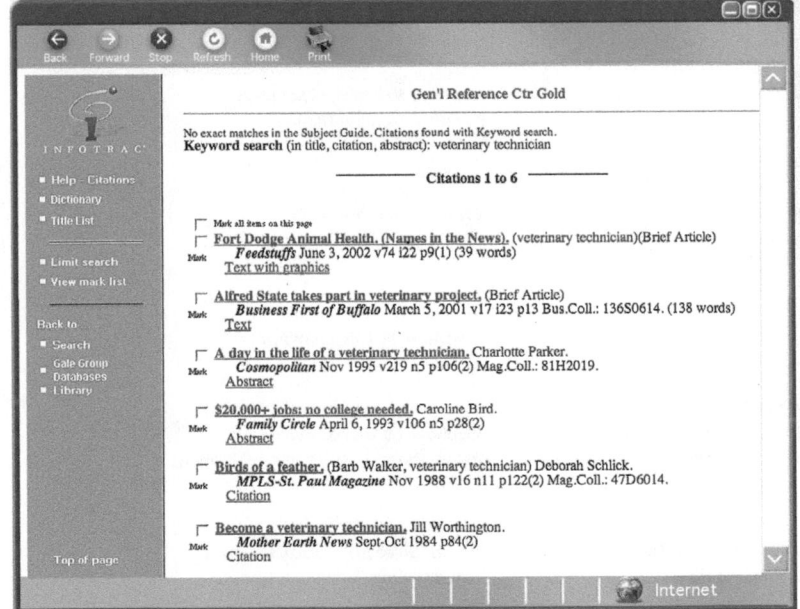

### Close Read

1. InfoTrac found six matches for the keywords. Which of these matches might be most useful? least useful? Why?

2. Is the information organized alphabetically or by date? What are the advantages or disadvantages of this organization?

3. Which menu item on the left would you click on to make your search more specific?

---

## DIFFERENTIATED INSTRUCTION

### FOR STRUGGLING READERS

**Explore Databases** If classroom computers are available, guide students as they go to an online database, such as the Internet Movie Database (www.imdb.com), for firsthand experience. Call students' attention to the on-screen menus, hyperlinks, and icons; have students review the functions of each. Invite students to perform and comment on some sample searches.

### FOR ADVANCED LEARNERS/PRE–AP

**Analyze Databases** [paired-activity option] Have students investigate several databases and report their findings and observations to the class. Students should consider each database's range of information, ease of use, and special features.

## NEWSPAPERS AND PERIODICALS

**Newspapers** are publications that contain news and advertising and that are published daily, weekly, or very frequently. Publications that are issued at regular intervals of more than one day are **periodicals.** Magazines and journals are examples of periodicals.

| TYPES OF SOURCES | EXAMPLES |
|---|---|
| **MAGAZINE**<br>**General:** For most readers<br>**Specialized:** Articles on specific topics | *Time, Newsweek, Parade*<br>*Horse Illustrated*<br>*Popular Mechanics*  |
| **NEWSPAPERS**<br>**General:** For most readers in a particular geographic area<br>**Specialized:** For readers interested in a particular topic, such as finance | *Fort Worth Star-Telegram*<br>*Los Angeles Times*<br>*Wall Street Journal*  |
| **JOURNALS**<br>Journals present specialized information and are designed for experts. Journals are usually more formal than magazines and have fewer advertisements. | *American Journal of Veterinary Research*<br>*Journal of Interactive Media in Education*  |

Here are tips to help you find an article on your topic:

- Ask the research librarian about specialized magazines or journals that may contain articles on your topic.
- Use databases of articles, such as InfoTrac, to help you find information on your topic in newspapers and magazines. If the database doesn't provide the full articles, you can ask at the periodicals desk for the specific issues you want to see.

### DOCUMENTARIES AND OTHER FILMS

Your list of possible sources may include some titles on DVD or videocassette. How can you quickly assess whether these sources are worth watching?

- Is the source **fiction** or **nonfiction?** To identify a nonfiction film, read the library's online catalog description. Look for the word *documentary* or *interview*. A fictional film probably would not have enough factual information to serve as a reliable source.
- Does the film contain the kind of **information** you need? Check the online catalog description and the front and back covers of the DVD or videocassette. Does the film include **primary sources,** such as interviews or speeches?

## NEWSPAPERS AND PERIODICALS

If possible, bring in an assortment of newspapers and periodicals for students to examine or have students list newspapers and magazines with which they are familiar. Divide the class into small groups, asking each group to answer these questions about each periodical as specifically as possible:

- What is the purpose of the periodical?
- How frequently is the periodical published?
- Who are the intended readers?
- What does the advertising in the periodical suggest about the periodical's readers?
- Does the periodical present facts, opinions, or a mix of both?
- What are the periodical's most notable features? For example, are there striking photographs? interesting first-person articles? well-researched statistical tables?

Follow up with a class discussion that encourages students to compare their findings and suggest specific research tasks for which various periodicals would be useful.

## DOCUMENTARIES AND OTHER FILMS

- Explain that a documentary is a factual film that dramatically presents or analyzes key events, people's lives, or social conditions, for example. Point out that documentaries often are good sources of information but that they may reflect the bias of the filmmaker.
- Note that some films are "based on" facts but may contain fictionalized elements, as well. Such films are not reliable sources.
- Elicit or provide examples of documentaries and other films. Discuss why each documentary would or would not be a useful reference.

### FOR ADVANCED LEARNERS/PRE–AP

**Compare and Contrast Films** [small-group option] Have students compare fiction and nonfiction films about particular subjects. For example, students might compare *Jaws* with a documentary about sharks or compare a war movie with a documentary about the same war. Have students summarize their findings in an oral report to the class, making clear why one film would make a more reliable source than the other. Encourage

students to use a graphic organizer, such as a Comparison Matrix, in their presentations. Comparisons should include references to factual content and should point out instances of distortion and bias.

📁 **BEST PRACTICES TOOLKIT—Transparency** Comparison Matrix p. A24

## NONFICTION BOOKS

In addition to using the illustrations on this page, have individual students or pairs of students refer to a nonfiction book as you lead a discussion of the book parts described. Direct students to find the corresponding parts in their books as you discuss these questions:

- What can you learn from examining the book's title, chapter titles, and headings?

- What is the copyright date? Point out that some books have revision dates.

- What information can you get from the table of contents and the index?

- How can a bibliography or list of recommended readings help?

- How can a glossary help? What types of books are likely to have glossaries?

**YOUR TURN** **Close Read**

***Possible answers:***

1. *The subtitle makes clear that the book focuses on certain types of careers that involve working with animals.*

2. *This book was published in 2006. Because it is relatively recent, it is likely to be a useful source.*

3. *The book probably includes interviews, as suggested by the inclusion of "Meet a _____" features in the table of contents.*

4. *The book includes such information. The index lists "jobs in" under the heading "Animal shelters." Since there is only a single page reference, however, the book probably contains only a little information.*

**R** **RESOURCE MANAGER—Copy Master**
Use Parts of a Book to Locate Information
p. 17

## NONFICTION BOOKS

Your library search may result in a list of book titles and call numbers. How can you quickly determine which books have the information you're seeking?

- Read each book's **title** (and **subtitle**, if there is one) and skim chapter titles and headings to get an idea of the general subject matter.

- Check the **copyright page** for the date of publication. If you need up-to-the-minute information, don't depend on a book that is several years old.

- Examine the **table of contents** at the front of the book and the **index** at the back for terms related to your subject. Is there sufficient information on your subject or very little?

- Many books also have **bibliographies** or lists of **recommended readings**. These can give you ideas for other sources to consult.

- If the book contains difficult technical terms, look for a **glossary** at the back. This section lists specialized terms and their definitions.

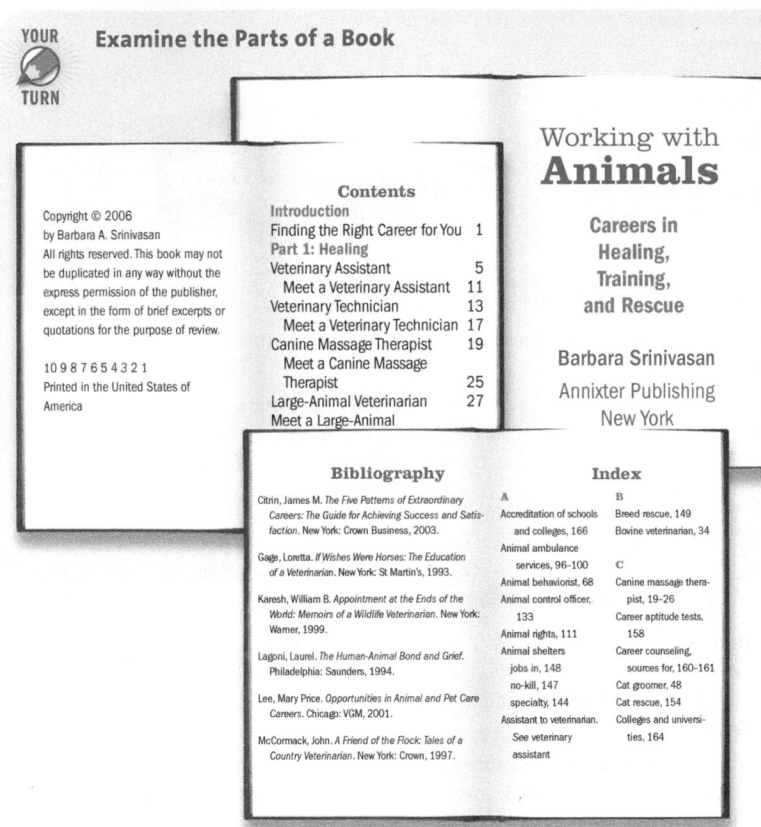

**YOUR TURN** **Examine the Parts of a Book**

**Close Read**

1. How does the subtitle of this book help you understand its content?

2. When was this book published? Is it recent enough to be a useful source?

3. Does this book include interviews with people employed in certain jobs? How do you know?

4. Does this book include information on jobs in animal shelters? How do you know?

**1304** UNIT 12: THE POWER OF RESEARCH

---

## DIFFERENTIATED INSTRUCTION

### FOR STRUGGLING READERS

**Comprehension Support** To check students' grasp of the book parts, supplement the Close Read with these questions:

1. Who wrote the book? ***Answer:*** *Barbara A. Srinivasan*

2. What kind of warning appears on the copyright page? ***Answer:*** *a warning about how the book may and may not be duplicated*

3. How long is the chapter about the work of a veterinary technician? ***Answer:*** *six pages (pages 13–18)*

4. Which book in the bibliography would probably be least helpful when it comes to up-to-date information? Explain. ***Possible answer:*** *The book by Loretta Gage might have the least up-to-date information; its copyright is 13 years earlier than that of Srinivasan's book.*

### FOR ADVANCED LEARNERS/PRE–AP

**Evaluate Book Parts** Divide students into small groups; then have each group locate three nonfiction books about the same subject. Ask students to compare the books and reach a consensus about the most useful source for a research paper. Invite each group to share its evaluation, supporting the evaluation with specific reasons.

# Evaluating Information

Now that you have found a number of useful sources, how can you figure out which ones can be trusted?

## Applying General Evaluation Guidelines

No matter what kind of source you have chosen—in print or online—or where you have found it, you need to look at it critically before deciding whether the information is **authoritative** and **reliable**, or trustworthy.

**Evaluating Sources**
Go to **thinkcentral.com**.
KEYWORD: HML9-1305

### EVALUATING SOURCES

| | |
|---|---|
| *Is the information still valid and up-to-date?* | Look for a copyright date or a "last updated" reference. Recent information is critical in some fields, such as science, medicine, and sports. Older publications can be helpful for historical topics. |
| *Is the information accurate?* | Can the facts be verified by more than one source? Most print and online encyclopedias, dictionaries, directories, and almanacs are considered reliable because they are updated regularly and go through a rigorous review process. |
| *What are the author's credentials?* | Does the author have a position or job title that qualifies him or her as an expert on the topic? In other words, is he or she an **authority** on this topic? |
| *What kinds of materials does the publisher produce?* | University presses usually publish information that is carefully researched. Magazines that publish trendy articles and gossip are not as reliable as newsmagazines or science magazines. |
| *Is the source objective or biased?* | Why does the source exist? Does the author mention his or her goals in a foreword, preface, or introduction? Is the author's purpose to inform, to persuade, to entertain, or some combination of these? Does the author use loaded language, such as "Millions of people are joining the fight against this unforgivable injustice"? |
| *How much information does the source cover?* | Does the source give an overview or detailed information? Does the material support other information you have read or add new information? Start by looking at the table of contents, menu, or index. |
| *Is the source relevant?* | Does the source cover aspects of the topic that interest you? Is it written at a level you can understand? |

---

## FOR STRUGGLING READERS

**Vocabulary Support** Elicit or provide the meanings of these terms:

- *credentials:* knowledge, skill, or experience that qualifies a person as an expert
- *loaded language:* language with positive or negative connotations, designed to stir people's feelings

## FOR ADVANCED LEARNERS/PRE–AP

**Analyze Fact, Opinion, and Bias** [paired-activity option] Instruct students to read a magazine article or newspaper editorial and analyze its mix of factual information and opinion. Have students use a T Chart to list facts and opinions and to comment on signs of subtle bias in the piece. Work with students to create a format for sharing their findings.

**BEST PRACTICES TOOLKIT**
T Chart p. A25

---

# Evaluating Information

 COMMON CORE **W 8**

## Applying General Evaluation Guidelines

### EVALUATING SOURCES

Discuss the chart, providing clarification and additional instruction as needed. Consider including these comments and activities:

**Up-to-date Information** Ask students why a five-year-old publication would be an acceptable source of information about Abraham Lincoln but not about a current president. *Possible answer: Lincoln lived so long ago that the facts about him are well established, but a current president's story is not yet complete. Elicit additional examples of topics that would or would not require current information.*

**Accuracy** Stress the importance of distinguishing fact from opinion when evaluating accuracy. Also urge students to find a second, authoritative confirming source for any questionable material. Note that accuracy and reliability are particular concerns when doing Internet research because anyone can post a Web site. (Guidelines for evaluating Web sites appear on page 1306.)

**Bias** Explain that bias may be obvious or subtle. For instance, the writer of an article about popular music may express a distaste for rap music (1) by saying so directly, (2) by discussing several kinds of music in detail but giving just a few lines to rap music at the end of the article, or (3) by using words with negative connotations to describe rap music or its performers.

**Reteaching Workshops** on **thinkcentral.com**
    Reading Lesson 5: Distinguishing Fact from Opinion
    Reading Lesson 17: Author's Credibility

**R** RESOURCE MANAGER—Copy Master
Identify Bias p. 16

 **THINK**central

**Evaluating Sources**

Go to **thinkcentral.com** to preview instructional presentations on evaluating sources—part of the **Writing and Research in a Digital Age Web site.**

## Evaluating Specific Sources

### EVALUATE WEB SITES

Discuss the information about evaluating Web sites, providing clarification as needed. If possible, have students visit various *.com*, *.net*, and *.org* Web sites and examine actual examples.

**Commercial Web Sites** Explain that commercial Web sites can be informative at some times but misleading at others. For example, some commercial sites mix facts with product claims or sales pitches, or they make unsubstantiated or exaggerated statements; other sites, such as those of some organizations, may present facts primarily as part of persuasive arguments to influence your thinking. Call students' attention to the **TIP** about knowing who created a site. Also encourage students to question any content that seems questionable and to check it against a second, trustworthy source.

**Personal Web Sites** As you discuss the **TIP** regarding personal Web sites, point out that obtaining information from a personal Web site is like getting information from an individual—that is, the person may or may not be an authoritative, reliable source. (See pages 1310–1311.) Urge students not to accept as fact any statement made by an unknown source unless they can verify the information elsewhere.

**Reteaching Workshops** on **thinkcentral.com**
> Research and Study Skills Lesson 7:
> Evaluating Electronic Sources

**R** RESOURCE MANAGER—Copy Master
Evaluate Web Sites p. 18

---

## Evaluating Specific Sources

The evaluation guidelines on the previous page apply to every source you use. The questions and tips on these pages will help you evaluate specific types of sources.

### EVALUATE WEB SITES

Web sites are often a mix of helpful information and attempts to promote points of view or to sell products or services.

**Commercial Web Sites** As you learned on page 1295, sites with URLs containing *.com* or *.net* are sometimes for-profit sites. When you look at a commercial site, ask yourself these questions:

- **Who is the author?** Look for a menu link called "About This Site" or "Contact Us."
- **Why was the site created?** If the site was designed to sell you something, the site creators may have omitted any negative information about the product.

> **TIP** Knowing who created a site can help you figure out why the site exists and whether it is appropriate to use in your research.

**Organization (.org) Web Sites** Although many of these sites are nonprofit organizations, such as the Red Cross, *anyone* can create a *.org* site. If you think you have pulled up a nonprofit page but are not sure, ask yourself these questions:

- **Who created the site, and when was it last updated?** Look for a link titled "About Us" or "Mission Statement." If there is no way to identify the creator of the site, then you should be cautious about the content.
- **Are statements of fact supported by examples and evidence?** Look for links to supporting evidence from respected institutions or publications.

**Personal Web Sites** Because anyone can post anything on the World Wide Web, there are millions of personal Web sites. Some have misleading URLs. For example, students and faculty members can set up personal Web sites on a university's server, and their Web addresses will contain the university's URL. However, these sites might not be reviewed, evaluated, or in any way sanctioned by the institution.

> **TIP** Not all personal Web sites are unreliable, but be cautious.

- **How can I tell if a site is personal when its address contains the name of an institution?** Look for a forward slash and tilde (/~) and a name or initials following *.edu* in the URL.
- **What does the lack of an official institution logo tell me?** Don't expect the information to have been reviewed or approved by the institution.
- **What does it mean if links in the site don't work or are mostly links to other items by the same author?** The author may be careless, or he or she may lack outside support.

---

## DIFFERENTIATED INSTRUCTION

### FOR ENGLISH LANGUAGE LEARNERS

**Task Support** Have students compare two Web sites on the same topic, one in English and one in their home language. Suggest that they study aspects such as differences in structure and the way information is presented. Help them with any Internet-related terms that they may not be familiar with.

### FOR ADVANCED LEARNERS/PRE–AP

**Evaluate a Web Site** Have pairs of students use the criteria in the text to create a Web site evaluation checklist. Ask students to identify a Web site related to a topic that interests them. Then have them use their checklist to evaluate the Web site, refining the checklist as they do so. Invite students to combine their individual checklists into a master checklist that they can share with the class.

## YOUR TURN

**Examine Web Sites**

Examine this Web site. What does it offer a visitor?

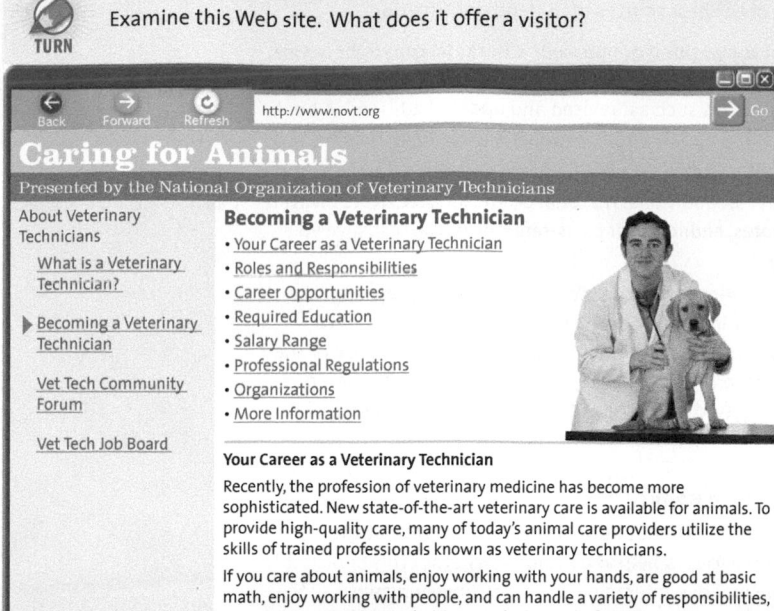

**Close Read**

1. Who created this site?
2. What is the purpose of the site?
3. Who is the intended audience?
4. What clues tell you that it is a nonprofit site?

 **TIP** To get to a site's home page from a page with a long URL, simply delete everything after the domain name (such as *www.novt.org*) and press Enter. The home page will come up.

Here is an example of a personal Web site. What does it offer?

**Close Read**

1. How reliable are the statistics about homeless animals? Give reasons for your answer.
2. Does Dunston Community College support the efforts of the site's creator? How can you tell?

---

As you present the **TIP**, refer students to the URL abbreviations on page 1295.

## YOUR TURN

**Close Read**

*Possible answers:*

1. *The National Organization of Veterinary Technicians (NOVT) created the site.*
2. *The main purpose of this screen of the Web site is to provide information about a career as a veterinary technician.*
3. *The intended audience of this screen of the Web site is anyone wanting career information about becoming a veterinary technician.*
4. *The URL is .org, which generally is associated with nonprofit sites. Furthermore, no products or services are being advertised on this screen.*

**If students need help . . .** ask

- What is the URL? What Web sites usually have such a URL? *Possible answer: The URL is www.novt.org. Nonprofit organizations usually have such a URL.*
- What is one way to recognize a for-profit site? *Possible answer: the presence of advertising*

## YOUR TURN

**Close Read**

*Possible answers:*

1. *The statistics are not very reliable or useful. The first point is vague and general, with no factual support. The second point refers to a study, but the conductors of the study are not identified. Moreover, a 1990 study on this topic would be out of date today.*
2. *The site displays no official logo of Dunston Community College, so there is no reason to believe that it has been reviewed or approved by the college.*

---

**FOR ADVANCED LEARNERS/PRE–AP**

**Create a Site Guide** Have students work in small groups to develop a guide to interesting Web sites that pertain to the subjects that they are studying this year. The guide should explain the features of each site, describe the kind of information that it offers, and evaluate the site's usefulness and reliability. Groups can add the guides to the classroom library as a permanent reference.

For a challenge, invite groups to create a Web site that presents the information and includes a link to each site listed.

## EVALUATE NONFICTION BOOKS

As you lead a class discussion of this page, ask students about the various sources that they use to write their papers and reports. For example, what kinds of nonfiction books would they be likely to use for learning about a person's life? *Possible answer: a biography, autobiography, encyclopedia, or biographical reference book*

**Copyright** Ask students why a book that has been updated many times over a period of years is likely to be reliable. *Possible answer: The author has had multiple opportunities to correct errors and update information.*

**Author's Qualifications** Remind students to consider an author's knowledge, skill, and experience. Ask students how these factors can help shape the content and tone of a book. *Possible answer: An author who is strong in one or more of these qualities is likely to provide deeper insight into a subject than is a writer who has done only book research.*

**Close Read**

*Possible answers:*

1. *The book is about career options in the veterinary field.*

2. *The author has been a veterinarian for eight years and has been a veterinary assistant.*

3. *The book was published recently; the back cover proclaims that it is the 7th Edition, "Revised and updated for 2010."*

4. *Examine the table of contents, the index, and perhaps the preface.*

**R** RESOURCE MANAGER—Copy Master
Evaluate Nonfiction Books p. 19

---

## EVALUATE NONFICTION BOOKS

Nonfiction books are one of the best sources of in-depth information.

- **When was the book last copyrighted or updated?** Check the **copyright notice,** which is usually on the back of the title page. Also look on the copyright page or on the cover for a statement such as "revised and updated edition." A book that has gone through many updates and printings is likely to be reliable.

- **What sources did the writer use?** Look for a **bibliography.** Some books include an **appendix**—a collection of additional material on the subject. Notes within the book, such as **footnotes, endnotes,** or **cross-references,** can also give you clues about sources.

- **What are the author's qualifications?** Look for an author's biography on the book jacket or at the beginning or end of the book. The author may have written a **preface,** a short introductory essay that explores the purpose of the book, the intended audience, and the research on which the book is based. If the source is a biography, find out if the author is related to the person he or she has written about.

 **Examine a Nonfiction Book**

Use what you have learned about nonfiction books and about the parts of a book (page 1304) to help you evaluate whether this book is a relevant source for someone interested in a career involving work with animals.

**Close Read**

1. What is this book about?

2. What qualifies the author to write a book on this topic?

3. Was this book published recently? How do you know?

4. What other parts of the book should you examine to determine if it is a worthwhile source? (Hint: See page 1304.)

---

## DIFFERENTIATED INSTRUCTION

### FOR STRUGGLING READERS

**Comprehension Support** To check students' understanding about an author's use of sources, distribute several nonfiction books to pairs of students. Ask students to identify examples of bibliographies, appendices, footnotes, and endnotes. Then have students write four statements, each one summarizing the type of information that one of these features contains. Have pairs of students exchange and compare their summary statements.

### FOR ADVANCED LEARNERS/PRE–AP

**Evaluating Usefulness** [paired-activity option] Ask students to brainstorm questions that they can ask themselves to decide whether or not a particular book will be useful. Offer these examples: *When was the book written? Does the book have an index so that I can locate information quickly? Is the book clearly written? Does the book have helpful illustrations?* Have students choose their best questions to create a "Ten Questions" chart.

## EVALUATE NEWSPAPERS AND PERIODICALS

Newspapers and periodicals can be good sources of up-to-the-minute, easy-to-read information. Different publications are available in a print edition, online, or on microfilm or microfiche. Evaluating an article can be tricky, because you need to assess the publication, the author of the specific article, and the content. Here are some basic questions to ask:

- **Is the source well-known and respected?** Most large-circulation newspapers and national magazines are reliable sources. Beware of sensationalist publications such as the *National Enquirer*, however.

- **When was it published?** Old is not necessarily bad. Out-of-date newspaper and magazine articles can provide rich information on historical events.

- **Who is the author?** You can usually assume that articles by staff writers or contributing editors are as reliable as the source they're published in.

- **Was the article reprinted from another source?** If so, make sure the original source—for example, *Scientific American* or a news service such as the Associated Press (AP)—is reliable.

- **Can the facts in the article be verified?** Always consult multiple sources.

**TIP** Even the most reliable publications may contain errors. Whenever possible, check facts in more than one source.

 **YOUR TURN**

**Examine a Newspaper Article**
Use what you have learned to evaluate this article.

*from* The Dallas Morning News

# Animal ER

## For injured pets, 'round-the-clock clinics provide a haven and hope

BY ALINE MCKENZIE, STAFF WRITER

It's an ordinary night. One of life-and-death situations, tears and relief, small miracles. Meals eaten on the fly, calm during lulls.

Animals don't time their ills and injuries to convenient office hours.

So when regular veterinarians are off duty, the after-hours emergency animal clinics take over. From kennel cough to surgery, every night brings a different mix.

"It's just something I've always wanted to do, just as a kid," says Dr. Michelle

Hazlewood, 32. "I've always loved animals."

"Neither of us could go back into a regular day practice," says Dr. Kathleen Bowe, 38. The variety and the excitement beat the ordinary well-animal care of a day job, she says.

The two are the vets on duty this night at the Emergency Animal Clinic of Collin County in Plano, one of a

**See ANIMALS, page B2**

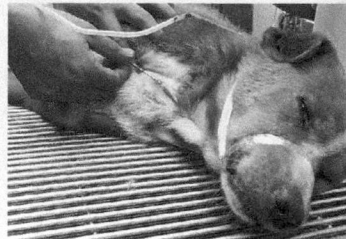
*Buster the dog donates blood.*

### Close Read

1. What kind of veterinary clinic is the focus of this article?

2. Knowing that Dallas is a large city and that the *Dallas Morning News* is its major newspaper, would you expect this to be a reliable source of information?

3. How could a reader verify the facts in an article like this?

4. At the end of the article, there is an e-mail address that allows readers to contact the newspaper. Why is this important?

1309

# Collecting Your Own Data

## Using People as Primary Sources

### FIELD RESEARCH AND OBSERVATION

Ask students what skills they need to carry out field research and observation. ***Possible answer:*** *listening skills, note-taking skills, attention to detail, interpersonal skills*

Have students read through the sample field notes. Then discuss these questions:

- What kinds of information did the observer record? ***Possible answer:*** *number of people working at the shelter, number of animals there and what kinds, who's in charge*

- What conclusion can you draw from the field notes? ***Possible answer:*** *The CARE Shelter is a busy place, with many people taking care of 50–70 dogs and cats—and with a need for volunteers.*

### INTERVIEWS

Elicit examples of various kinds of research projects, such as finding a part-time job or writing a research paper about a foreign country. For each project, ask students to identify people whom they might interview. Draw a simple Cluster Diagram of possible interview subjects for each project.

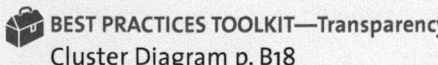 **BEST PRACTICES TOOLKIT—Transparency** Cluster Diagram p. B18

---

# Collecting Your Own Data

Sometimes the answers to your questions cannot be found on a Web site or in a library. How can you collect original data?

## Using People as Primary Sources

For some topics, your own observations and data will be your best source of information. The following techniques can turn you into your own search engine.

### FIELD RESEARCH AND OBSERVATION

Any focused, purposeful observations you make can be considered field research. For instance, you might visit an animal shelter or a veterinarian's office to learn about careers in veterinary medicine, or you might listen to a **lecture** at school about veterinary careers. If you wish to make a visit, be sure to call ahead to ask permission and to make an appointment. For some research projects, you may want to set up a **field study** in which you make observations and collect specific types of data.

> *Notes on Visit to CARE Shelter for Animals, 10/21/2010*
>
> - *staff: 4 full-time employees plus 8 to 12 part-time volunteers*
> - *provides medical care for 20 to 30 dogs plus 30 to 40 cats; no rabbits, rodents, wild animals, or exotic animals*
> - *Dogs are in individual cages, but most cats are 3 or 4 to a cage.*
> - *"no-kill" shelter, which means that animals stay until they are adopted*
> - *Jackie Kirchner coordinates all the volunteers. The shelter needs people to clean cages and to feed and exercise the animals.*
> - *Ms. Kirchner says that Kyle Faris, their veterinary technician, would probably agree to an interview.*

### INTERVIEWS

Try talking with people who have experience in what you are researching. For example, you could interview a veterinary assistant, a veterinary technician, and a veterinarian about their jobs. You might interview someone in person, over the telephone, or by e-mail. First, ask if the person is willing to talk with you, and then set a date and time for the interview. Prepare a list of clear, open-ended questions that must be answered with specific information, not just yes or no. Take thorough notes during the interview. Here are some sample interview questions.

---

## DIFFERENTIATED INSTRUCTION

### FOR STRUGGLING READERS

**Concept Support** Invite a reporter from the school newspaper or a community newspaper to come to class and speak to students about interview techniques, note taking, and listening skills. Have students get ready for the visit by preparing a list of questions to ask the reporter. Follow up with a discussion in which students share what they have learned from the talk.

### FOR ADVANCED LEARNERS/PRE–AP

**Do a Field Study** Ask students to choose a community activity or exhibit that they would like to research. For example, students might investigate a community gardening project or the public library's new art exhibit. Ask students to visit the activity or exhibit to make observations and collect information. Have them use their field research to write a report. Then work with students to create a format for sharing the reports in class.

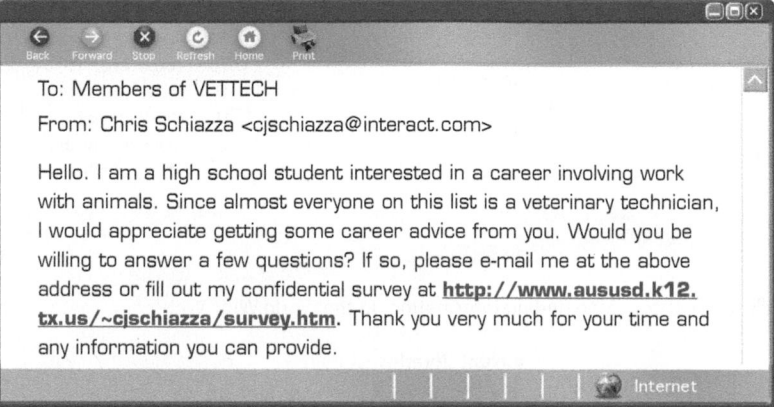

*Questions for Kyle Faris*

1. How long have you been a veterinary technician?
2. What is the best part of the job? Why?
3. What is the worst part of the job? Why?
4. What kind of education and work experience would I need to become a veterinary technician?

See pages R81–R82: Interview

If you are able to identify an expert, you may wish to send a politely worded, specific question by e-mail or letter. You can gain an inside track to a group of experts by joining a relevant Internet discussion group, also called a list server. For instance, VETTECH is a discussion group for veterinary technicians.

To: Members of VETTECH

From: Chris Schiazza <cjschiazza@interact.com>

Hello. I am a high school student interested in a career involving work with animals. Since almost everyone on this list is a veterinary technician, I would appreciate getting some career advice from you. Would you be willing to answer a few questions? If so, please e-mail me at the above address or fill out my confidential survey at **http://www.aususd.k12. tx.us/~cjschiazza/survey.htm**. Thank you very much for your time and any information you can provide.

### SURVEYS AND QUESTIONNAIRES

You can collect survey and questionnaire information by telephone, by mail, by e-mail, through a Web site, or in person. Keep the names of participants confidential to protect their privacy.

**TIP** Stay safe—give only an e-mail address for people to use in responding to your survey. Do not give your home address or telephone number.

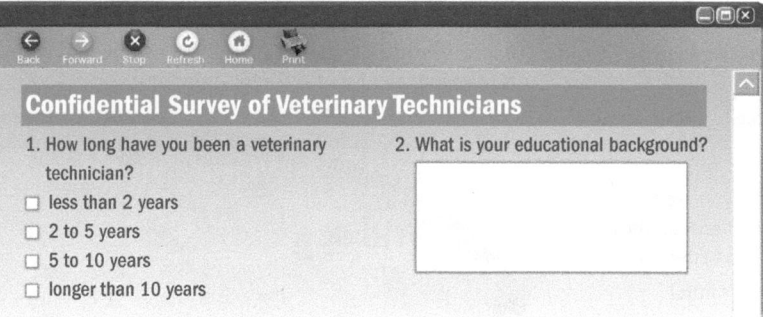

**Confidential Survey of Veterinary Technicians**

1. How long have you been a veterinary technician?
   - [ ] less than 2 years
   - [ ] 2 to 5 years
   - [ ] 5 to 10 years
   - [ ] longer than 10 years

2. What is your educational background?

---

Share these interviewing tips with students:

- Do research ahead of time about the person whom you are interviewing and the topics that you plan to discuss. Ask students why such preparation is important. **Possible answer:** *Knowledge about the person and the topic leads to better questions and shows that the interviewer is serious.*

- Write each question on an index card, allowing space to record the response. Alternatively, ask permission in advance to audiotape or videotape the interview. Be flexible about the order in which you ask questions, however, and be ready to ask follow-up questions as you listen to what the person says. Ask students why such flexibility is important. **Possible answer:** *Interesting information and insights might result if the person is allowed to volunteer additional ideas.*

- If you are not taping the interview, save some time at the end of the interview to summarize and confirm important points. Also, consider asking the person to suggest sources of additional information.

- If you conduct an interview by e-mail or letter, use formal language, proper grammar, and correct capitalization and punctuation.

- Always remember to thank people whom you interview. Sending a polite thank-you note after the interview is appropriate, too.

## SURVEYS AND QUESTIONNAIRES

Explain to students that surveys should contain specific questions and should not be overly long or complicated. Brief, straightforward surveys are most likely to get a response. Call students' attention to the **TIP** regarding survey safety.

---

## DIFFERENTIATED INSTRUCTION

### FOR STRUGGLING READERS

**Develop Interview Skills** Brainstorm with students for questions that an interviewer might ask a teenager about his or her interests or plans for the future. Instruct students to list the questions on paper or on index cards. Then have pairs of students interview each other, drawing their questions from the brainstormed list. Afterward, discuss with students what they have learned about the interview process from conducting these interviews.

# Research Tips and Strategies

## Library Sleuth

Share with the class examples of nonfiction books as they are classified under the Dewey decimal system and under the Library of Congress system. Make sure that students know which system is used (1) in the school library and (2) in the community public library system.

**Reteaching Workshops** on **thinkcentral.com**
Research and Study Skills Lesson 3: Using Reference and Search Tools

## Web Watch

Discuss the search tool options, using one or more of these activities. Make sure that students understand the differences between search engines, metasearch engines, and directories.

- Have pairs of students use and compare some of the sources listed. For example, ask students to conduct an identical keyword search using Google, Dogpile, and About.com. Have them compare results, noting similarities and differences.

- As a class, have students share and compare their observations about various tools and sites that they have used. Ask students which tools and sites they found most helpful, and why.

- Invite students to explore the Internet Public Library (www.ipl.org). Discuss the sources of information available at the site and the types of research projects for which this site would prove most useful.

---

# Research Tips and Strategies

## Library Sleuth

Two basic systems are used to classify nonfiction books. Most high school and public libraries use the Dewey decimal system; university and research libraries generally use the Library of Congress system.

| DEWEY DECIMAL SYSTEM | |
|---|---|
| 000–099 | General works |
| 100–199 | Philosophy and psychology |
| 200–299 | Religion |
| 300–399 | Social sciences |
| 400–499 | Language |
| 500–599 | Natural sciences and mathematics |
| 600–699 | Technology (applied sciences) |
| 700–799 | Arts and recreation |
| 800–899 | Literature and rhetoric |
| 900–999 | Geography and history |

| LIBRARY OF CONGRESS SYSTEM | | | |
|---|---|---|---|
| A | General works | L | Education |
| B | Philosophy, psychology, religion | M | Music |
| C | History | N | Fine arts |
| D | General and Old World history | P | Language and literature |
| E–F | American history | Q | Science |
| G | Geography, anthropology, recreation | R | Medicine |
| H | Social sciences | S | Agriculture |
| J | Political science | T | Technology |
| K | Law | U | Military science |
| | | V | Naval science |
| | | Z | Bibliography and library science |

## Web Watch

Knowing what search tools to use is crucial to finding information on the World Wide Web.

### Search Engines

Search engines differ in speed, size of database, method of searching, and other variables. Never use only one search engine.

- Google  • Yahoo!  • Ask.com

### Metasearch Engines

A metasearch tool can save you time by sending a search to multiple search engines simultaneously.

- TheInfo.com  • Dogpile  • Metacrawler

### Directories

Directories are useful when you are researching a general topic, because they arrange resources into subject categories.

- AOL  • About.com  • Yahoo!

### Virtual Libraries

At a virtual library, you can look up information in encyclopedias, directories, and indexes.
You can even e-mail a question to a librarian.

- Internet Public Library
- Librarians' Index to the Internet

### Other Web Resources

Library catalogs: Library of Congress
Encyclopedias: Encyclopaedia Britannica Online
Newspaper archives: New York Times Index
Specialized databases: Medline

**Writing and Research in a Digital Age**
THINK central
KEYWORD: HML9-1312
Discover a wealth of Web search tools and resources.

---

## DIFFERENTIATED INSTRUCTION

### FOR STRUGGLING READERS

**Concept Support** Invite an experienced librarian to speak to students about the Dewey decimal system and the Library of Congress system. Also ask the librarian to discuss with students how the advent of the Internet has changed the librarian's job and expanded the research capabilities of library users.

### FOR ADVANCED LEARNERS/PRE–AP

**Create a Search Tools Bulletin Board** Have students work together to create a bulletin-board display of search tools for finding information on the World Wide Web and tips for using them. Information should be based on the content on this page as well as preceding content in the Research Strategies Workshop. Students should include specific examples to illustrate the key points in the display.

## Checklist for Evaluating Sources

☑ The information is relevant to the topic you are researching.

☑ The information is **valid** and up-to-date. (This point is especially important when researching time-sensitive fields such as science, medicine, and sports.)

☑ The information is from someone who is an **authority** on this topic.

☑ The information is from a trusted, **reliable** source that is updated or reviewed regularly.

☑ The author's or institution's purpose for writing is clear, so you can determine whether the source is **objective** or biased.

☑ The information is written at the right level for your needs. For example, a children's book is probably too simplistic, while a scientific paper may be too complex.

☑ The information has the level of detail you need—neither too general nor too specific.

☑ The facts are **accurate** and can be verified in more than one source.

## Sharing Your Research

At last you have established your research goal, located sources of information, evaluated the materials, and taken notes on what you learned. Now you have a chance to share the results with the people in your world—and even beyond. Here are some options:

- Use presentation software to create a power presentation for your classmates, friends, or family.
- Publish your research findings on a wiki.
- Develop a newsletter or brochure summarizing your information.
- Explain what you learned in an oral presentation to your classmates or to people in your community.
- Write up your research in a formal research paper.
  **See the following pages.** ▶

See pages 1336–1337: Creating a Wiki

## Checklist for Evaluating Sources

COMMON CORE **W 8**

Review with students the checklist items, which summarize what students have learned. Have students explain the importance of each item on the list, giving examples as appropriate.

## Sharing Your Research

Discuss the options for sharing research. Create a master list by adding to that list other possible options that students suggest—for example:

- Create a manual or introductory guide to your topic. If you speak more than one language, consider making it a bilingual publication.
- Prepare a presentation that makes your research accessible to children.
- Find a classmate who chose a related topic. Collaborate on an oral presentation that links your research.
- Use your research to support a cause that matters to you. Write an editorial or persuasive speech that includes that research.

Have students consider the pros and cons of each option on the master list. For example, which one(s) would communicate information to the greatest number of people? Which one(s) would allow for the most creativity? Then ask students to pick and rank their top three options and to explain their choices.

**Reteaching Workshops** on thinkcentral.com

   Research and Study Skills Lesson 6:
      Evaluating Print Sources

   Research and Study Skills Lesson 7:
      Evaluating Electronic Sources

**FOR STRUGGLING READERS**

**Comprehension Support** Assess and reinforce students' understanding of the Research Strategies Workshop by having them work in small groups to create a graphic/visual summary of what they have learned about planning and carrying out research. Have groups share their graphic displays with the class.

# Focus and Motivate

**W 2a–f** Write informative/explanatory texts to examine and convey complex ideas, concepts and information. **W 4** Produce clear and coherent writing. **W 5** Develop and strengthen writing as needed by planning, revising, editing, rewriting, or trying a new approach, focusing on addressing what is most significant for a specific purpose or audience. **W 7** Conduct sustained research projects to answer a question or to solve a problem. **W 8** Gather relevant research from multiple sources, using advanced searches effectively; assess the usefulness of each source. **W 9** Draw evidence from literary or informational texts to support research. **L 2** Demonstrate command of the conventions of standard English punctuation and capitalization. **L 2b** Use a colon to introduce a list or a quotation. **L 3a** Write and edit work so that it conforms to the guidelines in a style manual.

## WRITE WITH A PURPOSE

To help students understand the purpose, lead them to brainstorm reasons that people conduct research. Make sure students understand that conducting research is one way that writers collect evidence to support their ideas.

## COMMON CORE TRAITS

Review the *COMMON CORE TRAITS* with students, focusing primarily on the development of ideas and the organization of ideas. Compare the list of traits with the rubric on page 1333.

## ADDITIONAL TASKS

**Write About the Workforce** Write a research paper that investigates a career opportunity in a particular field. Include information about training, duties, hours, salary, and related work aspects.
**Possible subjects:** graphic design or medicine

### Writing Online

The following tools are available online at **thinkcentral.com** and on **Write***Smart* CD-ROM:
- **Interactive Graphic Organizers**
- **Interactive Student Models**
- **Interactive Revision Lessons**

---

# Research Paper
**Essential Course of Study**

Now that you have thoroughly explored a variety of research strategies, you are ready for your next challenge: the formal research paper. Perhaps you will have the opportunity to learn more about people, places, or events in history, science, or art. To start your investigation, refer to the information below.

 Complete the workshop activities in your **Reader/Writer Notebook**.

## WRITE WITH A PURPOSE

### WRITING TASK

Write a **research paper** that investigates a question that interests you.

### Idea Starters
- How has the Internet changed the music industry?
- To what extent are settings and events in the *Odyssey* based on fact?
- How has an author or artist of the past influenced today's pop culture?

### THE ESSENTIALS

Here are some common purposes, audiences, and formats for research-based writing.

| PURPOSES | AUDIENCES | FORMATS |
|---|---|---|
| • to inform or enlighten others with an interest in your subject | • classmates and teacher | • essay for class |
| | • community members | • encyclopedia article |
| • to offer a unique perspective on a subject | • Web users | • oral report |
| | | • power presentation |
| • to learn more about a subject | | • documentary |

## COMMON CORE TRAITS

### 1. DEVELOPMENT OF IDEAS
- clearly introduces a topic and states a **controlling idea** that answers the **research question**
- supports the topic with **sufficient, well-chosen evidence**
- draws information from **multiple authoritative sources**
- provides a **concluding section** that supports the information

### 2. ORGANIZATION OF IDEAS
- **logically organizes** ideas, concepts, and information
- includes **formatting** and **graphics**, when useful
- uses **appropriate and varied transitions** to create cohesion

### 3. LANGUAGE FACILITY AND CONVENTIONS
- uses **precise language** and **domain-specific vocabulary**
- maintains a **formal style** and **objective tone**
- uses standard **format** for quoting or citing sources
- reflects **correct grammar, mechanics, and spelling**

**Writing Online**

Go to **thinkcentral.com**.
KEYWORD: HML9N-174

---

# Writing Workshop Resources

 **RESOURCE MANAGER UNIT 12**
Plan and Teach pp. 5–10
Prewriting–Editing pp. 22–31
Writing Rubric p. 32
Technology p. 33
Writing Support p. 34*

**BEST PRACTICES TOOLKIT**
Writing Template: Informative Essay
Analysis Frame: Informational
    Nonfiction p. D46

**TECHNOLOGY**

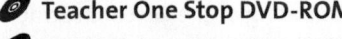 **Teacher One Stop DVD-ROM**
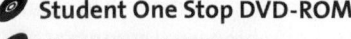 **Student One Stop DVD-ROM**
**Write***Smart* CD-ROM
**GrammarNotes DVD-ROM**

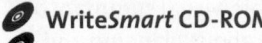 **Writing Center on thinkcentral.com**

*See resources on the **Teacher One Stop DVD-ROM** and on **thinkcentral.com**.*

\* Resources for Differentiation

## Planning/Prewriting

### Getting Started

#### SELECT A TOPIC

With so many topics to research, where should you start? Because you'll spend considerable time and energy on this assignment, the topic of your paper should be something that interests you and will also interest others. With your classmates, you might brainstorm a list of possible topics before you decide on one.

#### NARROW YOUR FOCUS

Your topic should be broad enough to support a full-length paper, but not so broad that it could fill a book. Use a graphic organizer to narrow your topic and decide on an aspect to research. Consult with your teacher, a school librarian, or an expert on your topic to make sure your focus is compelling and complex enough for a detailed paper.

**TIP** Check the catalogs in your school and local libraries and databases such as InfoTrac to see how much information is available on your topic. If there's too little, broaden your focus; if there's too much, you may need to limit it.

#### THINK ABOUT AUDIENCE AND PURPOSE

Before you do any further planning, make sure you identify your **purpose** and **audience;** these two considerations will guide you throughout the research process.

▶ **TIPS FOR GENERATING TOPIC IDEAS**
- Look for topics in the news—for example, new legislation affecting teens or scientific breakthroughs.
- Consider hobbies, sports, types of music, or other personal interests you want to learn more about.
- Think about historical or literary figures you have studied.

▶ **WHAT DOES IT LOOK LIKE?**

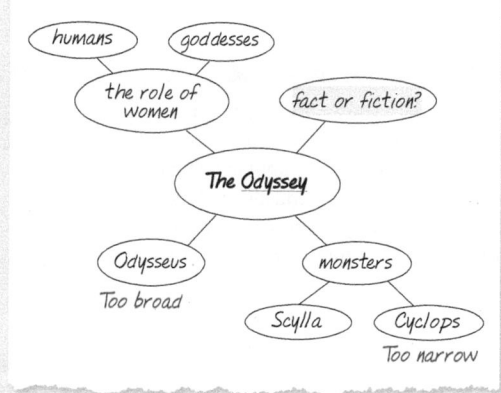

▶ **ASK YOURSELF:**
- Who would be most interested in my topic?
- What does this audience probably already know (or think they know) about my topic?
- What background information will they need?

---

## Teach

### Planning/ Prewriting

▶ **SELECT A TOPIC** Point out that a research paper is an opportunity to explore a topic in depth and to analyze perspectives and opinions related to it. Encourage students to consider topics that will yield original ideas rather than topics where students will simply go back to learn about the ideas of others.

▶ **NARROW YOUR FOCUS** Encourage students to include as many topics as they can without being concerned yet about which topic will work best. Then, direct them to evaluate each possibility, eliminating choices that are unacceptable, unworkable, or simply less desirable. In this way, students gradually will zero in on viable topics that interest them. Also invite students to try the tip and report on the results to the class.

▶ **THINK ABOUT AUDIENCE AND PURPOSE** Tell students that when the audience already knows a great deal about a topic, there is increased pressure on the researcher to say something new or to present a new perspective.

**R** **RESOURCE MANAGER—Copy Masters**
Planning/Prewriting p. 22
Drafting pp. 23–29
Ask a Peer Reader p. 30
Proofreading and Editing p. 31
Rubric p. 32
Writing Support p. 34

---

## DIFFERENTIATED INSTRUCTION

### FOR ENGLISH LANGUAGE LEARNERS

**Language: Reinforce Research Terms** Write these terms on the board and review them with students:

- *research:* careful study and investigation in some field of knowledge for the purpose of answering a question or solving a problem
- *sources:* works that supply information, such as books, encyclopedias, Web sites, and so on

- *Works Cited:* a list of sources for a research paper
- *document:* to provide supporting information
- *paraphrase:* to state an idea in one's own words
- *summarize:* to state main ideas and important supporting details in one's own words
- *plagiarism:* act of representing another's work as one's own

## Planning/Prewriting *continued*

▶ **FORMULATE A RESEARCH QUESTION** Use the Reporter's Questions graphic organizer to help students get started. Remind students that they need not come up with a question for every question word—and that some question words may generate more than one question. Also point out that some questions may be useful even if they do not fit neatly into the Reporter's Questions format, such as the text example, *Have historians tried to retrace Odysseus' journey?*

 **BEST PRACTICES TOOLKIT—Transparency**
Reporter's Questions p. C9

▶ **DEVELOP A RESEARCH PLAN** Emphasize the importance of planning and focus during the research process. Because students will need to synthesize information from many sources, it will be easy for them to lose track of their purposes and research questions.

**R** **RESOURCE MANAGER—Copy Masters**
Narrowing a Research Topic p. 21
Prewriting p. 22

**YOUR TURN** As students work to narrow their topics, reiterate the importance of asking good questions. All useful and insightful research begins with a genuine question (or two) on the part of the researcher.

For interactive graphic organizers, see

🖉 **Write*Smart* CD-ROM**

**Writing Center on thinkcentral.com**

---

## Planning/Prewriting *continued*

### Getting Started

#### FORMULATE A RESEARCH QUESTION

Transform your focused topic into a major question that you want to answer in your paper. This question will keep you on track as you find sources and gather information. Make sure your research question is open-ended and cannot be answered in a single word; it should require investigation.

Consider generating additional related, focused questions for further research and investigation. Such questions will help you find the specific evidence you will need for your paper.

▶ **WHAT DOES IT LOOK LIKE?**

*Topic:* Settings and events in the Odyssey

*Major Research Question:* To what degree are settings and events in the Odyssey based on fact?

*Related Questions:*

- If any of the events are real, where did they take place?
- If events or settings were made up, what were they based on?
- Have historians tried to retrace Odysseus' journey? If so, what have they learned?
- To what extent do historians disagree on which aspects of the Odyssey are real?

#### DEVELOP A RESEARCH PLAN

Create a plan that outlines your purpose, audience, major research question, potential sources you might investigate, and schedule. It's a good idea to have your teacher review and approve your plan before you embark on your research.

▶ **TEMPLATE FOR A RESEARCH PLAN**

Student Name:_____
Purpose:_____
Audience:_____
Major Research Question:_____
_____

Potential Sources:_____

**Schedule**
Research Due:_____
First Draft Due:_____
Final Draft Due:_____

Teacher Approval:_____

**PEER REVIEW** Exchange research plans with a classmate. Review each other's major research questions, and ask: What related questions would you expect to be answered in my paper? What potential sources do you think I should investigate?

 **YOUR TURN** List four or five topic ideas in your *Reader/Writer Notebook*, and evaluate which one would be best for your essay. Then, narrow your topic and develop a major question to guide your research. With your purpose and audience in mind, formulate a research plan using a template like the one above.

---

## DIFFERENTIATED INSTRUCTION

### FOR STRUGGLING WRITERS

**Brainstorm Possible Topics** After students have read the planning and prewriting pages, help them visualize topics for themselves by using Cluster Diagrams. Work with students to follow these steps:

- Write a possible topic inside a circle.
- Make a list of ideas related to the topic.
- Group these ideas into related clusters. Choose a key term that identifies each.
- Write the key terms in smaller circles around the topic circle. Draw lines connecting each circle to the topic circle.
- Write words relating to the key terms around the smaller circles. Circle these words, too, and draw lines connecting them to the key term circles.
- If students find that their topics are not working, have them repeat the process with different topics.

🛠 **BEST PRACTICES TOOLKIT—Transparency**
Cluster Diagram p. B18

# Researching

**COMMON CORE**

**W 8** Gather relevant research from multiple sources, using advanced research searches effectively; assess the usefulness of each source. **W 9** Draw evidence from literary or informational texts to support research.

## Following Your Research Plan

### LOCATE SOURCES

To find answers to your research question, gather information from a range of primary and secondary sources. **Primary sources** contain original, firsthand information that is usually unedited, such as letters, diaries, autobiographies, and eyewitness accounts. **Secondary sources** provide other people's versions of primary materials in encyclopedia entries, newspaper articles, biographies, and textbooks.

Begin your search for sources at the library and on the World Wide Web. Use advanced search features to find things quickly. Add a minus sign (–) before a word that should not appear in your results. Try using an asterisk (*) in place of unknown words. List the name and location of each potential source, adding comments that will help you decide whether the source will be useful.

**See pages 1298–1304** for more information about research tools available to you.

### ASSESS EACH SOURCE

A key step in the research process involves assessing your sources. A source is **credible,** or reliable and trustworthy, if it is:

• **relevant**—covers the aspect of the topic you are researching
• **accurate**—contains information that can be verified by more than one **authoritative** source
• **objective**—presents multiple viewpoints on the topic and is not **biased,** or showing favor to one view of the topic

### ▶ WHAT DOES IT LOOK LIKE?

| Sources | Comments |
|---|---|
| **World Wide Web (bookmarked)** | |
| "Map of Odysseus' Journey" | go to "Background" |
| "In the Wake of Odysseus: Localiz-ation of the Mythological Journey" | solid info |
| "Synesthesia and Homer's World" | far-out theory |
| "Homer's Odyssey Resources on the Web." | guide to other sources |
| **School Library** | |
| "Homeric Legend." *Britannica Student Encyclopedia* CD-ROM | study "Analysis" section |
| *The Odyssey of Homer: A Modern Translation.* Trans. Richmond Lattimore (883 HOM) | easy reading |
| **Public Library** | |
| *The Odyssey of Homer.* Trans. Robert Fagles (883.01 Homer) | great introduction by B. Knox |
| *Tales from the Odyssey.* Mary Pope Osborne | retelling of Odyssey |
| "Was Troy a Metropolis? Homer Isn't Talking." *New York Times* | scientific evidence |

### ▶ ASK YOURSELF:

• Is this a primary or secondary source? In what ways will it be useful in answering my research question?
• Is the information up-to-date?
• Are the facts accurate? How can I verify them?
• What qualifies the author to be writing about this topic? Is he or she an authority in this field?
• What, if any, biases can I detect?

## FOR STRUGGLING WRITERS

**Assess Sources** For each source or category of sources in the sample list, lead students to consider these questions.

• Does this source contain reliable information? What about the author's background helps me make this decision?

• Who is the intended audience for this information? Is the information presented at a level that is appropriate for my audience?

• Is the source biased? How can I tell?

• Is the information useful and related directly to my specific topic?

• Is the information up-to-date? How do I know?

• Is this a primary source or a secondary source?

• If I were to keep this source, how might I use it in my paper?

# *Practice and Apply*

## Researching

**COMMON CORE  W 8, W 9**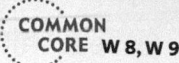

▶ **LOCATE SOURCES** Point out to students that the initial goal is to look for sources that are not just interesting, but also informative and relevant for their research questions. Lead students to discuss why it is a wise idea to identify multiple sources. Make sure that students understand that a variety of sources will provide different kinds of information and reflect different authors' viewpoints. Consulting different sources allows a researcher to compare and verify data.

Suggest that students review pages 1295–1296 before conducting an Internet search. Point out that the suggestions for advanced searches can help them to set more specific search parameters. Explain that this will result in better information because many unwanted Web sites will be filtered out.

▶ **ASSESS EACH SOURCE** Divide the class into four groups. Have each group prepare and present a brief summary of one part of the guidelines for evaluating sources presented on pages 1305–1313. That is, assign one group to cover each of these topics:

• general evaluation guidelines
• evaluation of Web sites
• evaluation of nonfiction books
• evaluation of periodicals

Encourage students to include visual aids, such as reference charts, in their presentations. As needed, emphasize that a key aspect of assessing any type of source is determining its usefulness in addressing the research question. Lead students to understand that while information may be accurate, it is not useful if it is not relevant for the topic.

**R RESOURCE MANAGER—Copy Masters**
Sources pp. 14–15, 23

## Researching *continued*

▶ **PREPARE A SOURCE LIST** Explain that a source card is a record of the bibliographic data about a particular source. Note that students will need this information if they need to double-check their facts while writing or revising and when they prepare their Works Cited lists.

Call students' attention to the sample source cards in the text. Point out the numbers in the top line of each card. Explain that numbering source cards makes it easy to use them in conjunction with note cards; that is, when taking research notes, students should write the number of each source card on the corresponding note card. Then, they can quickly determine which information came from which source.

For each type of source listed, call on volunteers to identify where the pieces of information listed in the text appear on the sample source card. For additional practice, have pairs of students refer to the models as they work together to create their own source cards for a Web site, a book, and a periodical article.

## Researching *continued*

**PREPARE A SOURCE LIST**

Once you have sorted through your initial list of sources, record information about the "keepers" in an electronic file or on index cards. Another option is to use special note-taking software designed to guide you through the research process. Check with your school librarian or media specialist to see if this option is available to you.

Include the following details, making sure to number each source. The information you compile now will help you build your Works Cited list later on.

### World Wide Web source
- author's name (if given)
- title of Web page or article
- name of sponsoring organization or institution
- date of publication
- medium of publication (Web)
- date of access

### Book
- author or editor
- title
- location and publisher
- year of publication
- medium of publication (Print)

### Newspaper or magazine article
- author
- title of article
- name of newspaper or magazine
- day, month, and year of publication
- edition and section information (for newspaper articles)
- beginning page number
- medium of publication (Print)

▶ **WHAT DOES IT LOOK LIKE?**

**World Wide Web source**

> **Source #:** 3
> **Type:** Article on Web site
>
> ---
>
> Burgess, Jonathan S. "In the Wake of Odysseus: Localization of the Mythological Journey." University of Toronto. 2004. Web. 9 Mar. 2011.

**Book**

> **Source #:** 6
> **Type:** Book
>
> ---
>
> Severin, Tim. *The Ulysses Voyage: Sea Search for the Odyssey.* London: Hutchinson, 1987. Print.

**Newspaper or magazine article**

> **Source #:** 4
> **Type:** Newspaper article
>
> ---
>
> Wilford, John Noble. "Was Troy a Metropolis? Homer Isn't Talking." *New York Times* 22 Oct. 2002: D1+. Print.

## DIFFERENTIATED INSTRUCTION

### ENGLISH LANGUAGE LEARNERS

**Language: Skill Words** Review these terms with students.

- *Web page:* a page or screen displayed at an Internet site on the World Wide Web

- *URL (uniform resource locator):* the address of a document or Web site on the Internet

- *call number:* a combination of letters, numbers, or both assigned to a library book to indicate its location in the library

- *CD-ROM:* an optical disk containing recorded data

## Following Your Research Plan

### TAKE NOTES

As you skim your sources, look for information that addresses your major research question as well as for relevant facts, extended definitions, concrete details, and quotations and examples. Your notes should focus on details that respond directly to your research question, or suggest new areas for your research. You can record each piece of information in an electronic file (for each source), on a separate index card, or using special note-taking software. Consult with your teacher to determine the option you should use.

For each entry, include

- a heading that tells the main idea
- the number of the source (from your source list)
- a page number, section name, or other way of locating the information

Unless you are directly quoting material from the source, be sure to restate it in your own words. There are two ways to do this: in a paraphrase or in a summary.

**Paraphrase**—captures all the ideas of the original and is about the same length

**Summary**—presents the main idea of the original; may include key facts and statistics but is shorter because it omits unnecessary details

*TIP*  Consider adding comments or questions that you have. For example, note whether the information supports what you already know or if there's a debate within the field you are researching.

### ▶ WHAT DOES IT LOOK LIKE?

**Original Source**

> The vividly fictional characteristics of the story have not prevented critics, past and present, from seeking to place it in a specific geographic context. Hesiod, who wrote later than Homer, believed that Odysseus and his ships sailed around in the general area of Italy and Sicily, to the west of . . .
>
> *"Homeric Legend." Britannica Student Encyclopedia CD-ROM*

**Paraphrase**

> **Source #:** 1
> **Early Ideas—Italy and Sicily**
>
> Although the *Odyssey* includes many fantastic creatures and events, people throughout history have tried to identify a real setting for the tale. Hesiod, a writer who came after Homer, thought that Odysseus' journey took him around Italy and Sicily. (Section: "Analysis of the *Odyssey*")
>
> **Comments/Questions:** Who was Hesiod? Look him up.

**Summary**

> **Source #:** 1
> **Early Ideas—Italy and Sicily**
>
> The early writer Hesiod believed that the *Odyssey* took place near Italy and Sicily. (Section: "Analysis of the *Odyssey*")
>
> **Comments/Questions:** Modern explorer Tim Severin agrees.

## Researching *continued*

▶ *TAKE NOTES*  Be sure that students understand the difference between note cards and source cards—whether recorded on an electronic file or on separate index cards—and that they grasp how the two work together. Ask students to identify the source of the information on the note cards on this page and to explain how they are able to do so. Students may say that the number 1 on the first line of the note cards indicates that the information comes from source 1.

Remind students that if they need to check their information again later, they can do so by referring to the source cards. To pinpoint the location of the facts and examples that students use, they should include on each note card the page number of the printed work or the section title of a nonprint work on which the information appears.

Explain that when students record ideas, details, and examples on note cards, they do not always have to write complete sentences, even when summarizing. Short phrases are often sufficient, as in these examples:

- Smith born 1947—London, England
- Age 6—came to the U.S.

Emphasize that comments on note cards are meant to help students organize information or write the paper. Discuss how comments that connect or compare information from various sources can prove especially helpful.

Point out that taking notes is also a means of condensing a large volume of information into a more manageable form. For that reason, notes should focus on details that are most relevant to the research topic or question. For example, in the models shown, the writer has focused on possible settings for the *Odyssey* but has not taken notes about its themes or character development.

> **R** RESOURCE MANAGER—Copy Masters
> Summarize and Paraphrase pp. 24–25

### FOR STRUGGLING WRITERS

**Take Notes**  Choose a paragraph from a nonfiction book. Divide the class into two groups. Have one group paraphrase the paragraph and the other group summarize it. After groups share the results, discuss the differences among direct quotations, paraphrases, and summaries. Repeat, using another paragraph, but switch the tasks. After results have been shared, extend the discussion by asking students to identify situations when they would choose to quote, paraphrase, and summarize.

### FOR ADVANCED LEARNERS/PRE–AP

**Create Note-taking Guides**  Invite groups of students to draw upon this text, other research-skills resources, and their own experiences to write clear, engaging "how-to" guides for novice note takers. The guide should include tips about recognizing helpful information, as well as instructions and examples regarding paraphrasing and summarizing. Invite groups to present their guides and then add them to the classroom library as permanent references.

## Researching *continued*

▶ **QUOTE WELL-STATED IDEAS DIRECTLY**
Review the difference between a direct quotation and a paraphrase. Remind students that when a direct quotation appears in a paper, it is enclosed in quotation marks unless it is a long quotation; in that case, it gets extra indentation.

Make sure that students understand why "ancient geographer" appears in brackets in the example. Using the same example, model for students how to omit part of the quotation and replace it with ellipses: "During the time of [ancient geographer] Eratosthenes, speculation about the truth . . . of Odysseus [and his journey] was rampant."

▶ *AVOID PLAGIARISM* Stress that plagiarism is unacceptable because it is the theft of someone else's words or ideas. Define *common knowledge* as "facts that can be found rather easily in numerous sources and that are likely to be known by many people." Point out that plagiarism can occur as a part of the note-taking process or when incorporating research into the paper itself. Remind students to document facts that are not common knowledge and authors' ideas that interpret or draw conclusions from the facts.

**R** RESOURCE MANAGER—Copy Masters
Avoid Plagiarism pp. 26–27

---

## Researching *continued*

### Following Your Research Plan

**QUOTE WELL-STATED IDEAS DIRECTLY** ▶
Sometimes, information in a source is expressed so powerfully that you want to use the author's own words. In recording direct quotations, be sure to type or write the material exactly as it appears in the original.

**TIP** If you are quoting an online source, save some time by copying and pasting the quotation directly into your electronic notes.

**AVOID PLAGIARISM**
*Plagiarism*, or the unauthorized use of others' words or ideas, is not honest. To avoid plagiarism, you must document the sources of any ideas that aren't common knowledge. You must do this whether you are paraphrasing, summarizing, or directly quoting the material.

**TIP** Remember that quoting word-for-word several sentences or more without documenting the source is not the only type of plagiarism. When you include others' phrases within your paraphrase or summary and do not use quotation marks, you are plagiarizing.

**GUIDELINES FOR RECORDING QUOTATIONS:**

- Make sure to enclose all original material in quotation marks.
- If you want to leave out phrases or sentences, insert ellipses (. . .) in place of the omitted material.
- If you need to add a word or phrase to clarify an idea, enclose it in brackets [ ].

*EXAMPLE:* "During the time of [ancient geographer] Eratosthenes, speculation about the truth of the tale of Odysseus was rampant."

▶ **WHAT DOES IT LOOK LIKE?**
**Original Source**

> Odysseus' wanderings in the west have inspired many attempts to plot his course and identify his ports of call. This wild-goose chase had begun already in the ancient world, as we know from . . . the great Alexandrian geographer Eratosthenes, who said that you would be able to chart the course of Odysseus' wanderings when you found the cobbler who sewed the bag in which Aeolus confined the winds.
> *Knox, Bernard. Introduction. The Odyssey of Homer. Trans. Robert Fagles*

**Plagiarized**

> The great Alexandrian geographer Eratosthenes said that trying to identify Odysseus' ports of call would be a wild-goose chase.

**Correctly Documented**

> The third-century-B.C. geographer Eratosthenes, for example, thought that Homer's story was totally imaginary (Knox 25).

---

## DIFFERENTIATED INSTRUCTION

**FOR ADVANCED LEARNERS/PRE–AP**
**Quote Ideas Directly** Ask small groups of students to prepare instructional presentations regarding punctuation guidelines for quotations. Students should cover the rules regarding the placement of quotation marks in conjunction with periods, commas, semicolons, question marks, and exclamation points. Presentations should also cover the punctuation of lengthy quotations and the use of ellipses and brackets. Direct students to include charts that display simple, specific examples. You also may wish to have students choose their examples from nonfiction selections in this textbook that students have read in the past few months. During the presentations, help listeners practice their note-taking skills as they record key points.

## Following Your Research Plan

### CRAFT A CONTROLLING IDEA

Review the material you've gathered from your sources. What answer does it suggest to your original research question? Write a controlling idea that states this question and describes the main idea of your report. You may also want to provide hints in your controlling idea about the answers you've found.

**TIP** You may discover that the information you've compiled answers a different question than the one you initially asked. Just make sure to modify your question and then draft a controlling idea that accurately captures the information you plan to present.

### CREATE AN OUTLINE

Read through your files or cards and group them by similar headings or main ideas. Organize the main ideas into an order in which you will present the information in your paper. Choose the method or methods that best fit your topic:

**Chronological order** presents events in the order in which they happened.

**Logical order** groups related ideas together— explaining the parts of a whole or comparing two subjects, for instance.

**Order of importance** places the least important ideas first and moves to the most important (or vice versa).

Then, develop an outline in which each main idea is listed as a Roman numeral. Supporting details, facts, and examples should be identified as sublevels of your outline. As you draft, you will use this outline to guide your writing.

 **YOUR TURN** Locate and evaluate sources, jotting notes about their credibility, usefulness, and accuracy in your *Reader/Writer Notebook*. Then, prepare a source list and compile a variety of quotations, paraphrases, and summaries. Use this information to write a controlling idea and develop an outline. Periodically critique your research, and refocus your plan as needed.

### ▶ A CONTROLLING IDEA SHOULD . . .

- tell the subject of your paper
- state your major research question
- be a statement that can be supported with evidence
- reveal your point of view on the topic, rather than simply state a fact

### ▶ WHAT DOES IT LOOK LIKE?

The Mystery of the *Odyssey*

I. Introduction
  A. Based on real places?
  B. Investigate to understand *Odyssey*
II. Early theories
  A. Imaginary
  B. Real
    1. Italy and Sicily
    2. Other Mediterranean sites; the Atlantic
    3. Schliemann proved Troy real
III. Modern ideas
  A. All over the map
  B. Mediterranean (Severin)
    1. Re-created Odysseus' voyage
    2. Identified some sites, not others
IV. Conclusion
  A. Homer's era a time of exploration
  B. Unsolved mystery

## Researching *continued*

▶ **CRAFT A CONTROLLING IDEA** Remind students that an effective controlling idea is clear and specific, is interesting, encourages the reader to read on, and links to the research question.

Model for students how to draft a controlling idea: *Scholars may never know for certain how much of the* Odyssey *is real and how much is made up, but doing some investigating can help readers understand the tale better.*

Remind students that they may modify their controlling ideas as necessary during the drafting and revising processes.

▶ **CREATE AN OUTLINE** As you discuss the sample outline, explain that outlining is a flexible process. Students may also outline their material by using graphic organizers or by grouping ideas into questions and answers. Regardless of the approach, however, students should identify main ideas and have sufficient information to support these ideas.

**R** RESOURCE MANAGER—Copy Masters
Write a Controlling Idea p. 28

**YOUR TURN** As students conduct research, remind them to review the instructions in the textbook frequently in order to avoid mistakes that will cost them time later.

## FOR STRUGGLING WRITERS

**Organize and Outline Your Material** Have students use the Microtheme organizer to help them plan their research papers. For the introduction, suggest that students think of two or three different approaches to writing their controlling ideas. Remind students that the points they make in the bodies of their papers must support their controlling ideas.

**BEST PRACTICES TOOLKIT**
Microtheme p. C13

## FOR ADVANCED LEARNERS/PRE–AP

**Demonstrate an Outline at Work** Have students illustrate the value of an outline by applying the outline on this page to the Student Draft. Ask students to copy the outline and then, next to each point, note the line numbers of the Student Draft that correspond with the point. Invite students to exchange and compare annotated outlines.

# Practice and Apply

## Drafting

COMMON CORE  W 4, L 2, L 3a

▶ **INTRODUCTION** Remind students to include details that will interest readers, such as monsters, gods, bloody battles, or raging storms. Tell students to consider what they can safely assume that readers already know about their topics and what background information readers will need as they read students' papers. Finally, students should place their controlling ideas near the end of their introductory paragraphs. Remind students that a formal style and objective tone are most appropriate for a research paper.

▶ **BODY** Emphasize the fact that if students have done adequate research and created good working outlines, the actual drafting should proceed smoothly. This is a point worth stressing because students often think—mistakenly—that they can save time by eliminating steps in the process.

▶ **CONCLUDING SECTION** Encourage students to think carefully about the research information that they have gathered. What personal observations can they make? What connections can they find? What conclusions can they draw? Stress that what makes one research paper different from another is not just the information presented, but also the personal insight that the writer incorporates into the paper.

▶ **WORKS CITED LIST** Point out that a Works Cited list is similar, but not identical, to a bibliography. A bibliography would include *all* of the sources that a writer used, including sources used just to verify facts or gather background information.

For a research writing template, see

 **Write*Smart* CD-ROM**

**Writing Center** on [thinkcentral.com](thinkcentral.com)

 **RESOURCE MANAGER**—Copy Masters
Use Quotations Effectively p. 29

## Drafting

The following chart gives a framework for drafting a research paper.

### Organizing a Research Paper

**INTRODUCTION**

- Grab your audience's attention with a **compelling quotation,** an **anecdote,** or a **question.**
- Supply enough **background information** for readers to understand the topic.
- Include a clear **controlling idea** that introduces your major research question.
- Establish a **formal style** by avoiding contractions and choosing precise language. Maintain an **objective tone** by avoiding words with strong positive or negative connotations.

▼

**BODY**

- Incorporate the **main ideas** from your outline into the body of your paper. Make sure each idea directly relates to your controlling idea.
- Support your ideas with **sufficient and well-chosen evidence.** Introduce quotations using phrases like or *According to Severin, . . .* In addition, try inserting phrases or words into your sentences—for example, *The story is "a cunning weave" . . . .*
- Arrange main ideas and evidence in a **logical order.** Use varied **transitions** to link ideas.
- Synthesize ideas from **multiple sources.** Compare and contrast them and add your own **interpretations, observations,** and **conclusions.**
- Define **domain-specific,** or specialized, terms that may be unfamiliar to readers.
- Document the **source** of each idea in parentheses at the end of each sentence. Consult the "Learn How" lesson on the next page for help.
- Consider using boldfaced **subheadings** to divide the text into manageable sections and help your audience track main ideas.
- Look for opportunities to include **graphics**—photographs, maps, time lines, and charts—to illustrate your points.

▼

**CONCLUDING SECTION**

- Sum up the **answer** you have found to your research question.
- Leave your audience with something to think about, such as the overall **importance** of your topic, unanswered **questions,** or **ideas** for new research.

▼

**WORKS CITED LIST**

- Include a **Works Cited list** as a separate page at the end of your draft.
- Use a **style manual,** such as the *MLA Handbook for Writers of Research Papers* or the *Chicago Manual of Style,* to ensure that you are correctly documenting your sources according to your teacher's preference. Refer to the MLA Citation Guidelines on pages 1334–1335.
- List sources in **alphabetical order** by the authors' last names (or by the title for a work with no author listed).
- Begin each entry on a **separate line,** aligned with the left margin; additional lines should be indented one-half inch.

### DIFFERENTIATED INSTRUCTION

**FOR ENGLISH LANGUAGE LEARNERS**

**Prepare a Works Cited List** Give students practice in alphabetizing entries for a Works Cited list, reminding them to use work titles when no author is named. For example, present these partial entries in mixed order and have students arrange them alphabetically as shown.

- *Greek Literature: An Overview*

- Heubeck, Alfred, Stephanie West, and J.B. Hainsworth. *A Commentary on Homer's Odyssey.*

- "Homer." *The World Book Encyclopedia.*
- Severin, Tim. "The Quest for Ulysses."
- Steiner, George, and Robert Fagles, eds. *Homer: A Collection of Critical Essays.*
- Struck, Peter. "Map of Odysseus's Journey."

**LEARN HOW** Document Your Sources Credit the source of each paraphrase, summary, or quotation as a parenthetical citation at the end of the sentence. This will avoid the serious academic offense of plagiarism. If the same information can be found in most sources on your topic, it is considered common knowledge and does not need to be documented. Use these guidelines to format parenthetical citations. When you finish your draft, highlight each citation. Then, use this information to help you compile your Works Cited list.

**COMMON CORE**

**W 4** Produce clear and coherent writing. **L 2** Demonstrate command of the conventions of standard English. **L 3a** Write and edit work so that it conforms to the guidelines in a style manual.

### Guidelines for Citing Sources Within a Research Paper

| | |
|---|---|
| **Source with one author** | ▶ Author's last name, page number (if any) of the work cited: (Severin 22) |
| **Author unknown** | ▶ Shortened title of the work, page number (if any): ("Homeric Legend") |
| **Multiple authors** | ▶ Last names of all authors, page number (if any): (Steiner and Fagles 12). For more than three authors, use the first author's last name and *et al.*: (Greene et al. 45). |
| **More than one work by an author** | ▶ Author's last name, title of work, page number (if any): (Jones, <u>Readings</u> 39). |
| **More than one source supporting an idea** | ▶ First author's last name, page number (if any); second author's last name, page number; and so on: (Knox 5; Nardo 20; Wilford D1) |
| **Author already mentioned in the sentence** | ▶ Page number only: (22) |

### GRAMMAR IN CONTEXT: PUNCTUATING TITLES

Use the following chart to help you correctly punctuate any titles you include in your text, parenthetical citations, or Works Cited list.

| Rule | Example |
|---|---|
| **Underline** or **italicize** titles of books, encyclopedias, epic poems, plays, films, magazines, newspapers, journals, CDs, works of art, TV and radio programs, and Web sites. | ▶ The <u>Odyssey</u> is full of fantastic creatures, gods, and events . . . |
| **Use quotation marks** for newspaper, encyclopedia, and magazine articles; short poems; short stories; essays and chapters in books; songs; TV episodes; radio segments; and Web pages. | ▶ Burgess, Jonathan S. "In the Wake of Odysseus: Localization of the Mythological Journey." University of Toronto. 2004. Web. 9 Mar. 2011. |

 **YOUR TURN** Using your outline and the chart on the preceding page, develop a first draft of your research paper. Remember to credit all sources using parenthetical citations and use correct punctuation for any titles.

---

## Drafting *continued*

**LEARN HOW** Document Your Sources
Provide students with the following examples. Have students explain the format of each parenthetical citation.

- According to the literary expert George Steiner, the story seems to take place in the waters surrounding Greece, Italy, and Egypt, though he admits, "The geography of the tale is a riddle" (9). (*author mentioned in sentence*)

- For example, in Book Four of the *Odyssey*, Menelaus describes the island of Pharos as "as far out as the distance a hollow ship can make in a whole day's sailing" (Homer 74). (*basic documentation—author and page number*)

- One explanation is that the *Odyssey* actually describes two separate voyages and that the adventures after line 135 of Book Ten are based on the stories of another Greek hero, Jason, and his Argonauts. ("Homeric Legend") (*no page number in source*)

### GRAMMAR IN CONTEXT: PUNCTUATING TITLES

For additional practice, have students correctly punctuate the following titles:

- book: The Odyssey of Homer: A Modern Translation (*underline or italicize*)

- encyclopedia: Britannica Student Encyclopedia (*underline or italicize*)

- newspaper article: Was Troy a Metropolis? Homer Isn't Talking (*quotation marks*)

- Web page: In the Wake of Odysseus: Localization of the Mythological Journey (*quotation marks*)

 **YOUR TURN** As students begin drafting their research papers, suggest that they recall what made their topic compelling to them and to incorporate that interest into their writing. Remind them to credit their sources and to correctly punctuate titles.

---

### FOR ENGLISH LANGUAGE LEARNERS

**Punctuating Titles** Point out that whole works are underlined (or italicized when written with a computer) and that parts of works are enclosed in quotation marks. For example, show students the front page of a newspaper on a transparency and underline the title of the newspaper because it is the title of the whole publication. Choose the title of one article to enclose in quotation marks because the article is part of the whole publication.

### FOR STRUGGLING WRITERS

**Documenting Sources** Discuss the correct use of periods, commas, semicolons, and quotation marks. Have students correct the following examples:

- (Knox, 25, "Homeric Legend."). (*Knox 25; "Homeric Legend"*).

- (Knox, 5, Nardo, 20; Wilford, D1). (*Knox 5; Nardo 20; Wilford D1*).

## Revising

**COMMON CORE W 5**

***Model the Skill*** Using a draft research paper on a transparency or electronic whiteboard, model how to use the questions, tips, and strategies suggested in the chart to evaluate and revise. You might use the research paper of a student from another class or from a previous year. Make sure to remove the student's name from the research paper so that the writer remains anonymous.

**YOUR TURN** Tell students that writers make sense of their own writing when they hear it read aloud, which is why it's a good idea to read one's writing aloud to a peer during review time. In this way, the writer will recognize problems, points of inconsistency, and gaps in logic.

Recommend that peer listeners jot down phrases or words the writer uses that grab their attention. The listeners may also write down "What if . . . ?" suggestions, such as "What if your last sentence became your lead?"

For interactive revision tools, see

💿 **Write*Smart* CD-ROM**

**Writing Center on <u>thinkcentral.com</u>**

## Revising

At this point, you should evaluate the content, structure, and style of your paper with your purpose and audience in mind. Use this chart to help you revise.

**RESEARCH PAPER**

| Ask Yourself | Tips | Revision Strategies |
|---|---|---|
| 1. Does the controlling idea clearly state the major research question? | ▶ **Underline** the controlling idea. **Draw a box** around the part that states the major research question. | ▶ **Add** to or clarify your controlling idea so that it more clearly answers your research question. |
| 2. What concrete and credible evidence is given to support each main point? | ▶ **Label** each main point in the margin. Then, **label** each piece of evidence the same way. | ▶ **Add** additional evidence for any main points that have too little support. |
| 3. Is the organization clear and logical? Do subheads and transitions help readers to link ideas? | ▶ **Circle** subheads and transitions. | ▶ **Rearrange** information not in the same paragraph as its main point. **Add** a subhead and/or transition at the beginning of each main point. |
| 4. Are direct quotations smoothly integrated? Are all sources given proper credit within the paper? | ▶ **Draw an arrow** from each direct quotation to the words that introduce the quotation. **Place check marks** by parenthetical citations. | ▶ **Reword** the text around quotations so that the flow of ideas is not disrupted. **Add** parenthetical citations for direct quotations, paraphrases, or summaries that lack check marks. |
| 5. Does the concluding section sum up the answer to the research question and leave readers with something more to think about? | ▶ **Circle** the part of the concluding section that answers the research question. **Draw a wavy line** under the sentences that give readers an interesting thought, idea, or question to contemplate. | ▶ **Add** an answer to the research question. **Insert** sentences that describe the importance of the topic, raise unanswered questions, or recommend additional research. |
| 6. Does a Works Cited list correctly document all sources? | ▶ Put a **check mark** next to each source used in your paper and in your Works Cited list. | ▶ **Add** an entry to the Works Cited list for each source mentioned in your paper. **Delete** entries that are not mentioned in your paper. |

**YOUR TURN** **PEER REVIEW** Have a peer evaluate and suggest improvements to your paper using the chart on this page. Ask him or her the following: Do I answer the major research question I set out to address? If not, what additional evidence do I need to include? How can I modify my controlling idea to more accurately reflect my points? Identify which parts of your draft, if any, need reworking or a new approach.

**1324** UNIT 12: THE POWER OF RESEARCH

## DIFFERENTIATED INSTRUCTION

### FOR ADVANCED LEARNERS/PRE–AP

**Graphics** Suggest that students incorporate graphs, pie charts, or diagrams into their research papers to illustrate statistical information. Recommend that students follow the instructions in a software program to help them convert statistics into graphs or pie charts as appropriate.

## ANALYZE A STUDENT DRAFT

Read this draft; notice the comments on its strengths and weaknesses as well as suggestions for improvement.

 **COMMON CORE** **W 5** Strengthen writing by revising, editing, rewriting, or trying a new approach, focusing on addressing what is most significant for a specific purpose or audience.

Bergstrom 1

Ilona Bergstrom
Mr. Grant
English 9
10 May 2011

### The Mystery of the *Odyssey*

❶ The *Odyssey* by Homer is a real adventure story. For modern readers, though, it's also a mystery. Did the place Homer described really exist? This is a question which has fascinated readers for centuries, with no definitive answer; even so, investigating the events and geography of Odysseus' wanderings can lead to a better understanding of this great literary work.

❷ As readers begin the *Odyssey*, they are swept into a journey that is so exciting that they suffer along with Odysseus (or Ulysses, as he is known in Latin) and rejoice when he finally returns home. Only after closing the book do readers step back to consider these earlier questions.

> Ilona includes a clear **controlling idea** that introduces her major research question. However, her introduction is dull and unlikely to grab her readers' attention.

**LEARN HOW** Craft an Effective Introduction Ilona begins her essay with a bland general statement that's not likely to make her audience want to continue reading. To captivate her readers, she instead might open with a **thought-provoking question,** a **powerful quotation,** or a **vivid image.** Notice how the revision in blue improves Ilona's introduction. Why might this opening be more interesting to readers?

**ILONA'S REVISION TO PARAGRAPH ❶**

*Everybody loves a great adventure story, especially one that has a compelling hero, horrible monsters, bloody battles, raging storms, and a happy ending.*

The *Odyssey* by Homer is ~~a real~~ *that kind of* adventure story. For modern readers, though, it's also a mystery.

---

## ANALYZE A STUDENT DRAFT

Explain that the Student Draft on this page is the beginning of a research paper. Model reading the draft and the annotations in blue, explaining that the yellow highlighting illustrates the student's language choices. Explain that the following *Learn How* mini-lessons provide helpful information about ways to improve this student draft as well as students' own drafts.

**LEARN HOW** Craft an Effective Introduction

- Many students mistakenly believe that academic writing is boring. This belief leads students to rely on bland, general statements.

- Explain that for readers who enjoyed the *Odyssey*, reading this Student Draft should be an exciting and insightful experience.

- Remind students that one purpose of an introduction is to grab the attention of readers. The same techniques that writers use in fiction can also be applied here. The writer may begin with action, a quotation, or a provocative thought or question.

- Encourage students to write more than one introduction for their research papers. Then, students should choose the introductions that are most likely to get the attention of readers.

- **Controlling Idea** Point out that the controlling idea often appears in the first paragraph but that it usually is not the opening sentence. Discuss the characteristics of an effective controlling idea. Elicit or explain that the revision of the controlling idea in the Student Draft makes it clear, specific, and interesting enough to encourage readers to keep reading.

---

## FOR ENGLISH LANGUAGE LEARNERS

**Introduction Word Banks** Provide students with banks of active verbs, words to replace *said,* and reflective verbs. Encourage students to add words to these banks as they work. Tell students to use these word banks to develop their introductions.

**Active Verbs:** *abduct, blast, collapse, diagnose, escape,* and so on

**Words to Replace** *said: accused, barked, cried, denied, exclaimed,* and so on

**Reflective Verbs:** *believe, consider, imagine, reflect, think,* and so on

## FOR STRUGGLING WRITERS

**Introduction Experiment** Provide small groups of students with the following phrases:

- *compelling hero, horrible monsters, bloody battles, raging storms,* and *tragic situation*

Tell students to use these phrases to write three introductions for the Student Draft— one that begins with action, one that begins with dialogue or a quotation, and one that begins with an insightful thought. Invite groups to present their introductions to the class. Lead students to discuss the pros and cons of several introductions.

Explain that the Student Draft is continued on this page. Read the draft and annotations aloud and discuss. Ask students to comment on how the student writer synthesizes information from multiple sources.

- **Paraphrasing** Point out that paraphrasing information from research sources is an alternative to quoting directly and that it is an often-used method of supporting main ideas in nonfiction writing.

Have students identify the credited sources of the paraphrased details. Explain that the Works Cited page will give complete information about these sources.

- **Organizational Pattern** Make sure that students understand that subheadings are helpful because they serve as guideposts for the reader, indicating what content will follow.

Point out that subheadings should be specific enough to convey, or at least suggest, major ideas. To reinforce this concept, ask students why subheadings such as "So Many Theories" or "A Puzzling Situation" would not have been as effective as the one that appears on this page. Make sure that students understand that these subheadings are too general. The first would leave readers wondering, "Many Theories about what?" The second is vague and gives no indication regarding the content that follows.

---

Bergstrom 2

**❸** The *Odyssey* is full of fantastic events, such as Odysseus' battle with the Cyclops, that seem too amazing to be true. The third-century-B.C. geographer Eratosthenes, for example, thought that Homer's story was totally imaginary (Knox 25; "Homeric Legend"). Many people throughout history have tried to identify a real setting for the tale, though. The Greek poet Hesiod, who lived in the eighth century B.C., probably not long after the *Odyssey* was written, thought that Odysseus' wanderings took him around Italy and Sicily. Other historians throughout the ages have thought he traveled to other places in the Mediterranean Sea or even the Atlantic Ocean ("Homeric Legend").

**❹** The debate has continued into modern times. About the only thing people seem to agree on is that Troy existed where Homer said it was and that the Trojan War took place sometime between 1300 and 1200 B.C. (Knox 5; Nardo 20; Wilford D1). The reason they agree is that archaeologists have found proof. Heinrich Schliemann first excavated the ruins of Troy in the 1870s, and other layers of the site have been identified since then (Nardo 16). It is what happened after Odysseus left Troy—and where it happened—that remains a mystery.

**Many Theories About *Odyssey* Locations**

**❺** To try to solve this mystery, people have to assume that the events reported in the *Odyssey* actually happened. Unfortunately, though, many of Homer's descriptions of places are vague or confusing. Unlike the events of the Trojan War, which took place on land, Odysseus' sea voyage left no traces (Severin 17; Struck). Therefore, all of the ideas historians have come up with about where the events occurred are just guesses.

She **supports** her point with a specific detail **paraphrased** from one of her sources.

She **synthesizes** information from **multiple sources** and uses correct parenthetical citation **format**.

Ilona uses **subheadings** to help readers see at a glance the main points in her paper.

Bergstrom 3

**❻** Interestingly, guesses have ranged from the North to the South Pole and from Norway to South Africa (Knox 25). One look at a map would reveal the impossibility. One sea captain claims that he identified every location described in the *Odyssey* along the coast of the Adriatic Sea (Severin 22).

> This paragraph lacks cohesion. The **absence of transitions** makes it hard to understand the relationship between ideas.

**Focus on the Mediterranean**

**❼** Other historians have looked for the location of the *Odyssey* closer to Homer's own Mediterranean home. According to the literary expert George Steiner, the story seems to take place in the waters surrounding Greece, Italy, and Egypt. Even so, Steiner admits, "The geography of the tale is a riddle" (9). For example, in Book Four of the *Odyssey*, Menelaus describes the island of Pharos as "as far out as the distance a hollow ship can make in a whole day's sailing" (Homer 74). However, Pharos is now no longer an island but connected to the mainland of Egypt.

> **Direct quotations** are seamlessly integrated into this paragraph.

**LEARN HOW** Maintain Cohesion  Often, research papers are long and packed with an overwhelming amount of information for readers to digest. To help your audience follow your points, create cohesion—a logical connectedness—across sentences and paragraphs. If you reread Ilona's fifth paragraph, for instance, you'll notice that it's difficult to understand the relationship between the ideas in each sentence. To connect her ideas and create a smooth flow, Ilona added **transitions** and **references to ideas in previous paragraphs,** shown in blue.

---

**ILONA'S REVISION TO PARAGRAPH ❻**

Interestingly, *those* guesses have ranged from the North to the South Pole and from Norway to South Africa (Knox 25). One look at a map would reveal *of such far-ranging travels at the time. However, one modern-day* the impossibility. One sea captain claims that he has identified every location described in the *Odyssey* along the coast of the Adriatic Sea (Severin 22).

---

---

## ANALYZE A STUDENT DRAFT *continued*

Explain that the Student Draft is continued on this page. Read the draft and annotations aloud and discuss. Ask students to comment on the student writer's use of quotations.

- **Quotations**  Remind students that direct quotations are an alternative to paraphrasing. To illustrate the difference, have students paraphrase the quotation about Ulysses's vessel in paragraph 8, restating the meaning in their own words. For example, *Ulysses's ship could not have moved around the Mediterranean Sea in exactly the way Homer described. Land masses would have blocked Ulysses's route, and the ship could not have traveled at such a fast speed.* Lead students to compare and contrast the quotation and a paraphrase. Which rendition best serves the purpose of the Student Draft and why?

**LEARN HOW** Maintain Cohesion

Explain that transitional words and phrases, such as *however* and *on the other hand,* may appear at the beginning, in the middle, or at the end of a sentence and can serve a variety of purposes. For example, they can add information (*in addition, also*), give an example (*for instance*), show sequence (*first, next*), offer a comparison (*similarly*), or introduce a conclusion (*therefore*). Ask students to identify transitions in the Student Draft and to state purposes for each.

---

## DIFFERENTIATED INSTRUCTION

**FOR ENGLISH LANGUAGE LEARNERS**

**Comprehension: Transitions**  List on the board transitional words and phrases that are often used in research papers, such as *for example, for instance, such as, another, for this reason, as a result, however,* and *although.*

Call students' attention to contextual examples used in the Student Draft. Then, work with students to use transitional words and phrases from the list in original sentences such as these.

- The author of the *Odyssey* is called Homer; _____, the work's true authorship is debatable. (*however*)
- There are many stories about Homer. _____, it is said that he was born in Smyrna and that he was blind. (*for instance*)

Explain that the Student Draft is continued on this page. Read the draft and annotations aloud and discuss. Ask students to comment on the background information that the student writer supplies.

- **Background Information** Lead students to discuss why the student writer chooses to explain Severin's research techniques to readers. Is this information necessary for reader understanding? Why or why not?

Bergstrom 4

**8** The explorer Tim Severin compared many theories of Odysseus' route with nautical maps and concluded that "Ulysses' vessel jumps up and down the length of the Mediterranean like the knight on a chessboard. It skips over inconvenient land masses, skids around capes, travels at speeds that would do credit to a modern cruise liner . . ." (22). Between lines 134 and 135 in Book Ten (Homer 155), for example, Odysseus somehow manages to get from one side of the island of Ithaca to the other without stopping off there, "as though he had sailed right by his homeland" (Severin 240). One explanation is that the *Odyssey* actually describes two separate voyages and that the adventures after line 135 of Book Ten were based on the stories of another Greek hero, Jason, and his Argonauts ("Homeric Legend").

> This lively quotation from one source **supports** a main idea and adds interest to the report.

**Retracing Odysseus' Route**

**9** Since none of the theories Severin examined came from sailors, he thought the best way to discover the route taken by Odysseus was to retrace it. Using a replica of a Bronze Age ship he had built, Severin set sail from Troy. He took the most direct route to the present-day island of Ithaca, assuming that's what Odysseus would have done in his hurry to return home after the Trojan War (Burgess; Severin 22–23). He used both landmarks and local folk tales to help him trace the places and events in Homer's story.

> Ilona supplies **background information** to help readers understand one source's research.

**10** Severin did locate many places and things mentioned in the *Odyssey*, such as Scylla and Charybdis, described in Book Twelve: "On one side was Scylla, and on the other side was shining Charybdis, who made her terrible ebb and flow of the sea's water. When she vomited it up, like a cauldron over a strong fire, the whole sea would boil up in turbulence" (Homer 191).

Bergstrom 5

⓫     Cape Scylla still exists, and Severin found the cave of the monster that ate six of Odysseus' men. According to Homer, Charybdis was just across a narrow channel. Today, however, the channel is too wide to create the violent whirlpools that Homer described. Severin did locate a narrow channel a little south of Cape Scylla that may have caused whirlpools in ancient times, though (199). I believe that Homer could have figured out the whole idea of Charybdis from this spot. Then he just made a bigger deal out of its powers to make the story more exciting. We all know that a larger-than-life hero needs larger-than-life problems to struggle with, right?

> Though Ilona offers her own **interpretation,** she lapses into an informal style that isn't appropriate for a serious paper.

**LEARN HOW**   Use a Formal Style   Any writer sharing unique ideas and interpretations with an audience wants to be taken seriously. That's why it's important to use formal language throughout your paper. Avoid first-person pronouns (*I, me, my, we, us, ours*), contractions, and slang. In the eleventh paragraph of her paper, Ilona uses words and phrases that seem more appropriate for an informal conversation with a friend than an academic paper. Review the revisions Ilona made to maintain a formal style.

**ILONA'S REVISION TO PARAGRAPH ⓫**

*It's possible*
~~I believe~~ that Homer ~~could have figured out the whole idea of~~ Charybdis, *used this place as the basis for*

~~from this spot. Then he just made a bigger deal out of its powers~~ to make *exaggerating its power*

the story more exciting. ~~We all know that~~ a larger-than-life hero needs *After all,*

larger-than-life problems to struggle with, right?

---

**ANALYZE A STUDENT DRAFT** *continued*

Explain that the Student Draft is continued on this page. Read the draft and annotations aloud and discuss. Ask students to comment on how the student writer offers her own interpretation.

- **Interpretation**   Discuss how the student writer has woven a personal interpretation into the paper. Ask students what original ideas the writer has added and what facts serve as the basis for those ideas. Students may note that the writer explains that Severin found a channel near Cape Scylla that long ago might have caused whirlpools. She suggests that Homer may have based the whirlpool Charybdis on this channel, exaggerating its power in order to make the story more exciting. The writer further suggests that Homer may have wanted his "larger-than-life hero" to contend with a "larger-than-life" problem.

**LEARN HOW**   Use a Formal Style

Remind students that a writer's style reflects the choices he or she makes regarding word choice, sentence structure, tone, figurative language, and imagery. Explain that the use of a formal style in a research paper reflects the writer's efforts to show that he or she considers the topic important and worthy of respect. Have students identify and compare and contrast the student writer's style in the original version of paragraph 11 and the revised version. Which style is more appropriate for academic writing and why?

---

## DIFFERENTIATED INSTRUCTION

**FOR ENGLISH LANGUAGE LEARNERS**

**Word Choice and Style**   Make sure that students understand that one way style is conveyed is through word choice. For example, write the following items on the board:

1. *hero, man, superman, champion, conqueror, idol, star*

2. *problems, difficulties, troubles, crises, dilemmas, predicaments*

- After all, a larger-than-life 1. _____ needs larger-than-life 2. _____.

Have students complete the sentences using different combinations of words from the two lists. Lead students to discuss how the tone and style changes in each example.

**FOR STRUGGLING WRITERS**

**Adjust Tone**   Remind students that to achieve a formal style in their research papers, a serious, thoughtful tone is appropriate. As you urge students to use this tone consistently throughout the paper, discuss some of the ways in which students can keep their language lively without changing

tone—for example, concrete nouns, vivid verbs and adjectives, active instead of passive verbs, and a variety of sentence structures.

## ANALYZE A STUDENT DRAFT continued

Explain that the Student Draft is continued on this page. Read the draft and annotations aloud and discuss. Ask students to comment on the student writer's concluding section.

- **Concluding Section** Explain that the concluding section to a research paper usually summarizes or reinforces the paper's most important ideas. In addition, a strong concluding section encourages readers to think about what they have read. Point out that in these respects the concluding section to a research paper is similar to the concluding section that students would write for any essay.

Lead students to discuss whether the student writer should have paraphrased instead of quoting directly in her concluding section, and why or why not. What effects does the quotation have on the concluding section and on readers' acceptance of the writer's controlling idea? What effect would a paraphrase have had?

⑫     Odysseus's first stop, the land of the Lotus-Eaters, also turned out to be where other people had thought it was—past the island of Cythera in Tunisia (Burgess). Severin used Homer's mention of "wild goats beyond number" in Book Nine (Homer 140) to locate Odysseus' next stop, the island of Cyclopes on present-day Crete. The savage people described by Homer were nothing like the civilized Cyclopes of folklore, however (Severin 86). On the other hand, Severin failed to find anything like Calypso's island, Ogygia. For this reason, he agreed with other scholars that Homer may have created it and Odysseus' imprisonment there to help explain why the hero had been wandering for so long (Severin 243).

**Transitions** show how ideas are related.

⑬     In the end, Severin was unable to trace Odysseus' journey exactly and found many parts of Homer's tale puzzling. He concluded that:

    The geographies of folklore and navigation overlapped. (245) Although he didn't set out to prove whether the *Odyssey* was real or imagined, his findings suggest that it was a mixture of both.

Ilona **summarizes** one source's research and relates it to her **controlling idea.**

### An Unsolved Mystery

⑭     What conclusions can modern readers draw from these confusing ideas about the *Odyssey*? Robert Fagles, a well-known translator and scholar of Homer, gives probably the best summary of the possibilities and of the *Odyssey*'s lasting influence and interest:

    I think it's altogether likely that, however "mythological" the Greek experience may seem, it nevertheless stems from experience. Was that experience actual or imagined, or a combination of the two? I don't think we'll ever know. . . . Homer's period in history was in fact a time of exploration and new settlements, and these events survive in the [*Odyssey*], strikingly dramatized by Homer's incorporation of the fabulous, the Cyclops, the witches, and the other monsters and seductresses. All of it is stranger than fiction, as we'd say, and even more compelling than fact.

An insightful, well-stated **quotation** from a reputable source serves as a satisfying concluding section.

Bergstrom 7

## Works Cited

❶ Burgess, Jonathan S. "In the Wake of Odysseus: Localization of the Mythological Journey." University of Toronto. 2004. Web. 9 Mar. 2011.

❷ Fagles, Robert. Reply to query of Terry J. Keely. *Online News Hour*. Public Broadcasting Service. 13 Mar. 1997.

❸ Homer. *The Odyssey of Homer: A Modern Translation*. Trans. Richmond Lattimore. New York: Harper, 1967. Print.

❹ "Homeric Legend." *Britannica Student Encyclopedia*. 2004 ed. Chicago: Encyclopaedia Britannica, 2004. CD-ROM.

❺ Knox, Bernard. Introduction. *The Odyssey of Homer*. Trans. Robert Fagles. New York: Penguin, 1996. 3–64. Print.

❻ Nardo, Don, ed. *Readings on Homer*. San Diego: Greenhaven, 1998. Print.

❼ Severin, Tim. *The Ulysses Voyage: Sea Search for the Odyssey*. London: Hutchinson, 1987. Print.

❽ Steiner, George, and Robert Fagles, eds. *Homer: A Collection of Critical Essays*. Englewood Cliffs: Prentice, 1962. Print.

❾ Struck, Peter. Map of Odysseus' Journey. *Mythology*. Course pages. Dept. of Classical Studies, U of Pennsylvania. 2004. Web. 9 Mar. 2011.

❿ Wilford, John Noble. "Was Troy a Metropolis? Homer Isn't Talking." *New York Times* 22 Oct. 2002: D1+

**ILONA'S REVISION TO ENTRIES ❷ AND ❿**

Fagles, Robert. Reply to query of Terry J. Keely. *Online News Hour*. Public Broadcasting Service. 13 Mar. 1997. Web. 10 Apr. 2008.

Wilford, John Noble. "Was Troy a Metropolis? Homer Isn't Talking." *New York Times* 22 Oct. 2002: D1+. Print.

 **YOUR TURN** Use the feedback from your peers and teacher as well as the four "Learn How" lessons to revise or rewrite parts of your essay.

Ilona makes a few common errors in her source citations.

**LEARN HOW** Format a Works Cited List Correctly When writing a research paper, it's critical that you not only give credit where credit is due but also cite *all* your sources according to the guidelines your teacher gives you. In developing a first draft of her Works Cited list using MLA guidelines, Ilona did not adhere to the following guidelines:

- End each entry with a period.

- Indent the second and subsequent lines of entries one-half inch (or five spaces).

- Include the date of access for online sources.

- Include medium of publication for all entries.

Ilona revised her Works Cited list, making the corrections in blue.

---

**ANALYZE A STUDENT DRAFT** *continued*

Explain that the Student Draft is continued and completed on this page. Read the draft and annotations aloud and discuss. Ask students to comment on the student writer's source citations.

 **LEARN HOW** Format a Works Cited List Correctly

Explain to students that the term *Works Cited* refers to a list of all the works that a writer quotes from, or directly refers to, in a research paper. Point out that the list includes both print and nonprint sources.

Also, explain that *Works Cited* is a term based on MLA style guidelines for documentation; that MLA stands for Modern Language Association; and that MLA is widely used by schools as well as by many magazines, journals, and newsletters.

Review with students how the works that are listed are referred to parenthetically in the research paper. Point out that a parenthetical citation usually includes the name of the author and the page number on which the information or quotation appears.

Have students study this Works Cited list and identify print and nonprint sources, sources *not* listed by an author's last name, and the organizational structure (alphabetization).

 **YOUR TURN** Ask students to complete the **Your Turn** activity independently. Remind students to craft effective introductions, maintain cohesion, use a formal style, and format their Works Cited pages correctly.

For interactive revision tools, see

**WriteSmart CD-ROM**

**Writing Center** on **thinkcentral.com**

---

## DIFFERENTIATED INSTRUCTION

**FOR ENGLISH LANGUAGE LEARNERS**

**Language: Skill Words** Write these terms from this page on the board and review them to ensure students' understanding:

- *online source:* an informational resource published on the Internet—for example, the Web site of a company or organization or the online edition of an encyclopedia

- *periodical:* a publication that is issued on a regular basis (such as daily or monthly)—for example, a magazine or newspaper

**FOR STRUGGLING WRITERS**

**Comprehension Support** To check students' grasp of the items on the Works Cited list, ask

1. In which city was Tim Severin's book published? (*London*)

2. What kind of CD-ROM does the student writer cite? (*CD-ROM of the* Britannica Student Encyclopedia)

3. What kind of work did John Noble Wilford write, and when and where was it published? (*a newspaper article, published in 2002 in the* New York Times)

4. Which Homeric scholar appears on the list three times? (*Robert Fagles*) For which source did he serve as a translator? as an editor? (The Odyssey of Homer *and* Homer: A Collection of Critical Essays, *respectively*)

## Editing and Publishing

COMMON CORE W 5, L 2, L 2b, L 3a

### GRAMMAR IN CONTEXT: INTEGRATING QUOTATIONS

Encourage students to use the HELP function of their word processing software to learn how to carry out tasks that can help them write, revise, and edit their work. For example, students can consult HELP to get directions for finding and replacing, cutting and pasting, and formatting text.

Divide the class into small groups and assign each group a particular word processing function, including formatting long quotations. Remind students that in addition to indenting a quotation of longer than four lines, they must introduce the quotation with their own words followed by a colon. Have groups consult HELP to learn how to perform the functions. Then, have them demonstrate for the class what they have learned, explaining why the functions are useful.

 **RESOURCE MANAGER—Copy Masters**
Ask a Peer Reader p. 30
Proofreading and Editing p. 31

### PUBLISHING

Brainstorm with students additional ways to publish their research papers.

 **YOUR TURN** Allow students time to proofread their drafts. Remind them to integrate both short and long quotations artfully and correctly.

---

## Editing and Publishing

COMMON CORE

**W 5** Strengthen writing by editing. **L 2** Demonstrate command of the conventions of standard English punctuation. **L 2b** Use a colon to introduce a list or quotation. **L 3a** Write and edit work so that it conforms to the guidelines in a style manual.

In the editing stage, you find and correct errors in grammar, spelling, and mechanics—errors that could prevent your audience from following and appreciating your ideas. You should also format your paper according to the following guidelines:

- Leave one-inch margins at the top, bottom, and sides of each page (except for page numbers).
- On separate lines, type your name, your teacher's name, the class, and the date at the top left of the first page.
- On each page, type your last name and the page number one-half inch from the top, aligned at the right corner.
- Double-space all text, including quotations and the Works Cited list.
- Indent the first line of paragraphs one-half inch from the left margin. Indent set-off quotations one inch from the left margin.

### GRAMMAR IN CONTEXT: INTEGRATING QUOTATIONS

Place quotations shorter than four lines within your own sentences, and use quotation marks. For quotations longer than four lines, introduce the quotation in your own words, followed by a colon. Indent the entire quotation, and do not use quotation marks.

As Ilona proofread her draft, she realized that she had incorrectly formatted a short quotation. Her revision in blue shows how she fixed the problem.

> **13** In the end, Severin was unable to trace Odysseus' journey exactly and found many parts of Homer's tale puzzling. He concluded that "The geographies of folklore and navigation overlapped" (245). Although he didn't set out to prove whether the Odyssey was real or imagined, his findings suggest that it was a mixture of both (Homer 191).

### PUBLISHING

Here are some suggestions for sharing your research with an audience:

- Locate a group or organization that would have an interest in your research. See if the group would like to publish your paper in a newsletter or on its Web site.
- Transform your paper into a collaborative **wiki,** a series of Web pages on which you and other classmates add and edit information about your topic.
- Deliver an oral report to classmates or interested community members.

 **YOUR TURN** Proofread your draft for errors. Be sure to correctly integrate quotations. Then, publish your research using one of the options on this page.

---

## DIFFERENTIATED INSTRUCTION

### FOR ENGLISH LANGUAGE LEARNERS

**Language: Skill Words** Write these terms on the board and review them to ensure students' understanding:

- *quotation:* an author's words, repeated exactly from a book or other source, enclosed in quotation marks or indented without quotation marks

- *transitions:* words and phrases that connect a quotation to the writer's ideas and guide the reader from one thought to the next

### FOR STRUGGLING WRITERS

**Integrate Quotations** Place a variety of quotations from nonfiction works on note cards. Have students take turns drawing one quotation each from a box. Tell students to assess the length of their quotations to determine how they should be integrated into sentences. Then, have students incorporate their quotations into original sentences, using quotation marks or indentations as appropriate. Check students' work for accuracy.

# Scoring Rubric

Use the following rubric to evaluate and revise your research paper.

## RESEARCH PAPER

| SCORE | COMMON CORE TRAITS |
|---|---|
| **6** | • **Development** Effectively introduces a topic; states an insightful, well-researched controlling idea; develops the topic with sufficient and relevant evidence; ends powerfully<br>• **Organization** Logically organizes information; effectively incorporates formatting or graphics to enhance the information; effectively uses varied transitions<br>• **Language** Ably uses precise words; maintains a formal style and objective tone; shows a strong command of conventions; correctly cites all sources |
| **5** | • **Development** Competently introduces a topic; states a well-researched and clear controlling idea; offers sufficient and relevant evidence; has a strong concluding section<br>• **Organization** Is logically organized; includes formatting and graphics that aid comprehension; effectively uses transitions<br>• **Language** Uses precise words; generally maintains a formal style and objective tone; has a few errors in conventions; correctly cites sources |
| **4** | • **Development** Adequately introduces a topic; states a clear controlling idea; offers mostly relevant evidence; has an adequate concluding section<br>• **Organization** Is mostly logically organized; could use some more formatting or graphics; needs more transitions<br>• **Language** Uses some vague words; mostly maintains a formal style and objective tone; includes a few distracting errors in conventions; correctly formats most source citations |
| **3** | • **Development** States a controlling idea, but the introduction could be more engaging; lacks enough evidence; has a somewhat weak concluding section<br>• **Organization** Has some flaws in organization; doesn't include enough formatting or graphics; lacks transitions<br>• **Language** Needs more precise words; has frequent lapses in style or tone; has some critical errors in conventions; incorrectly formats some source citations |
| **2** | • **Development** Has a weak and/or unoriginal introduction and controlling idea; does not support most ideas; ends abruptly<br>• **Organization** Has organizational flaws; lacks formatting or graphics; lacks transitions throughout<br>• **Language** Lacks precise words or uses them incorrectly; uses an informal style or biased tone; has many errors in conventions; does not cite all sources and cites many incorrectly |
| **1** | • **Development** Lacks a controlling idea; offers little, if any, development; has no concluding section<br>• **Organization** Has no organization, formatting or graphics, or transitions<br>• **Language** Uses vague words; has an inappropriate style or tone; has major problems in conventions; plagiarizes or does not credit sources |

## Scoring Rubric

Tell students that the best way to understand a scoring rubric is to use it to score actual writing. Have students work as a class to evaluate a research paper. Students may assess a paper from another class with the student's name removed or a paper from an online state education Web site. Encourage students to use the language of the rubric as they score the paper. Work until the class reaches a consensus regarding a final score. The purpose of a rubric is to eliminate subjectivity from the scoring process.

For Rubric Bank, see

**WriteSmart CD-ROM**

**Writing Center on thinkcentral.com**

## Assess and Reteach

### Assess

**R** RESOURCE MANAGER—Copy Master
Rubric for Evaluation p. 32

**Online Essay Scoring at thinkcentral.com**

### Reteach

**Level Up Online Tutorial at thinkcentral.com**

**Reteaching Worksheets on thinkcentral.com**

Writing Lesson 2: Limiting or Expanding a Topic

Writing Lesson 15: Writing a Controlling Idea

## Review MLA Guidelines   COMMON CORE L3a

Direct students to consider these points:

**BOOKS**

- When a book by two or three authors or editors is cited, only the first person is listed with the last name first; the others are listed with their first names first.

- When listing an author and a translator or editor, give the author's name before the book's title and the other name or names after the title.

**PARTS OF BOOKS**

- Short works, such as poems and short stories, are designated by quotation marks, not underlining or italics.

## MLA Citation Guidelines

Today, you can find free Web sites that generate ready-made citations for research papers, using the information you provide. Such sites have some time-saving advantages when you're developing a Works Cited list. However, you should always check your citations carefully before you turn in your final paper. If you are following MLA style, use these guidelines to evaluate and finalize your work.

### BOOKS

**One author**
Severin, Tim. *The Ulysses Voyage: Sea Search for the Odyssey.* London: Hutchinson, 1987. Print.

**Two authors or editors**
Steiner, George, and Robert Fagles, eds. Homer: *A Collection of Critical Essays.* Englewood Cliffs: Prentice, 1962. Print.

**Three authors**
Heubeck, Alfred, Stephanie West, and J. B. Hainsworth. *A Commentary on Homer's Odyssey.* New York: Oxford UP, 1988. Print.

**Four or more authors**
*The abbreviation* et al. *means "and others." Use* et al. *instead of listing all the authors.*
Melick, Peter, et al. *The Odyssey Explained.* New York: Garden UP, 1997. Print.

**No author given**
*Greek Literature: An Overview.* New York: Sunrise, 1993. Print.

**An author and a translator**
Homer. *The Odyssey of Homer: A Modern Translation.* Trans. Richmond Lattimore. New York: Harper, 1967. Print.

**An author, a translator, and an editor**
La Fontaine, Jean de. *Selected Fables.* Trans. Christopher Wood. Ed. Maya Slater. New York: Oxford UP, 1995. Print.

### PARTS OF BOOKS

**An introduction, a preface, a foreword, or an afterword written by someone other than the author(s) of a work**
Knox, Bernard. Introduction. *The Odyssey of Homer.* Trans. Robert Fagles. New York: Penguin, 1996. 3–64. Print.

**A poem, a short story, an essay, or a chapter in a collection of works by one author**
Sappho. "He Is More Than a Hero." *The Works of Sappho.* Trans. Edward Osmond. New York: Garden UP, 1990. 53. Print.

## DIFFERENTIATED INSTRUCTION

**FOR ENGLISH LANGUAGE LEARNERS**
**Vocabulary Support** Write these terms on the board. Elicit or provide the meaning of each:

- *preface:* the introduction to a book or other work, usually written by the author to explain his or her purpose for writing

- *foreword:* the introduction to a book or other work, often written by someone other than the author

- *afterword:* a section that sometimes follows the main body of a book or other work, often containing comments written by someone other than the author

- *anthology:* a collection of literary pieces or passages within a single book

**A poem, a short story, an essay, or a chapter in an anthology of works by several authors**
Solonos, Costa. "Journeys." Trans. Carl Foreman. *Greek Voices*. Ed. Katharine Greene and Gerald Spencer. London: Greenwood, 1985. 83–85. Print.

**A novel or a play in a collection**
Sophocles. *Antigone. The Three Theban Plays*. Trans. Robert Fagles. New York: Penguin, 1984. Print.

## MAGAZINES, NEWSPAPERS, AND ENCYCLOPEDIAS

**An article in a newspaper**
Wilford, John Noble. "Was Troy a Metropolis? Homer Isn't Talking." *New York Times* 22 Oct. 2002: D1+. Print.

**An article in a magazine**
Severin, Tim. "The Quest for Ulysses." *National Geographic* Aug. 1986: 194–225. Print.

**An article in an encyclopedia**
"Homer." *The World Book Encyclopedia*. 2000 ed. Print.

## MISCELLANEOUS NONPRINT SOURCES

**An interview**
Baldwin, Richard. Personal interview. 13 Mar. 2011.

**A video recording**
*The Odyssey of Troy*. A&E Home Video, 1994. DVD.

## ELECTRONIC PUBLICATIONS

**A CD-ROM**
"Homeric Legend." *Britannica Student Encyclopedia*. 2004 ed. Chicago: Encyclopaedia Britannica, 2004. CD-ROM.

**A document from an Internet site**
*Entries for online sources should contain as much of the information shown as available.*

Author or compiler | Title or description of document | Title of Website
Fagles, Robert. | Reply to query of Terry J. Keely. | Online NewsHour.

Site sponsor | Date of document | Medium of publication
Public Broadcasting Service. | 13 Mar. 1997. | Web.

Date of access
10 Apr. 2011.

Struck, Peter. "Map of Odysseus' Journey." Mythology. Course pages. Dept. of Classical Studies, U of Pennsylvania. 2004. Web. 9 Mar. 2011.

## MAGAZINES, NEWSPAPERS, AND ENCYCLOPEDIAS

- The names of newspapers and magazines are underlined (or italicized), but titles of articles appear within quotation marks.

- When citing a periodical article, include the page numbers on which the article appears.

## MISCELLANEOUS NONPRINT SOURCES

- Lead students to brainstorm other examples of nonprint sources (*a radio talk show, a movie, a speech*).

## ELECTRONIC PUBLICATIONS

- Have students explain how the listing for the *Britannica Student Encyclopedia CD-ROM* differs from the listing for the *World Book Encyclopedia* article. (*The* Britannica *listing identifies the source as a CD-ROM and includes the location and publisher.*)

- Suggest that students take the time to study the examples regarding the documentation of online sources, as such listings can be confusing. Point out to students that the MLA no longer recommends citing URLs, or Web addresses, because of their instability and length. However, there are two instances when URLs may be cited: when source information cannot be located without URLs, or when you require your students to include URLs. If URLs are included in the list of Works Cited, they are always set within angled brackets.

- Have pairs of students work together to practice documenting several online sources.

## FOR ENGLISH LANGUAGE LEARNERS

**Vocabulary Support** Write these terms on the board. Elicit or provide the meaning of each:

- *compiler:* a person who gathers materials, such as documents or statistics, from one or more sources

- *site sponsor:* the person or organization responsible for a Web site

- *angle brackets:* marks (< >) that enclose words or characters in certain situations— in this case, when citing a Web site

# Focus and Motivate

## PRODUCE WITH A PURPOSE

Help students identify their purposes for production by brainstorming reasons that Internet users might be interested in learning of their research findings. Record students' ideas on the board.

## *COMMON CORE TRAITS*

As students prepare their wikis, remind them to keep in mind the *COMMON CORE TRAITS* of a wiki.

# Practice and Apply

## Planning the Wiki

Remind students to begin their project by establishing rules for discussion and decision-making within the group. Point out that setting these rules early in the process may help them to avoid disagreements later.

Encourage students to use Classification Charts, or other graphic organizers, to help them plan their Web sites. Suggest that students experiment with different page arrangements to see what works best.

 **BEST PRACTICES TOOLKIT—Transparency** Classification Chart p. B17

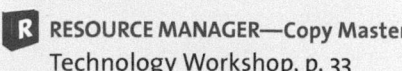 **RESOURCE MANAGER—Copy Master** Technology Workshop, p. 33

---

# Creating a Wiki  *Essential Course of Study*  ECOS

Producing a **wiki**, or a group Web site, can add interactivity and dimension to any research project. Not only does a wiki foster collaboration and creativity, but it also allows you to share information with others who are interested in your topic.

Complete the workshop activities in your **Reader/Writer Notebook**.

| PRODUCE WITH A PURPOSE | COMMON CORE TRAITS |
|---|---|
| **TASK** Create a **wiki** that uses text, graphics, and links to present information on a topic. With a team of classmates, use the wiki to collaborate on the project and post your research findings. | **A STRONG WIKI . . .** • focuses on a compelling topic • includes group planning documents, such as a project schedule and description of roles • shows evidence of collaboration, including rules for discussion and decision-making, peer editing, and discussion threads • has an inviting design that suits the topic, purpose, and audience • presents information effectively, using text, graphics, and links |

## Planning the Wiki

Before creating your wiki, formulate a research topic and some related questions that you want to answer. Group projects require team members to collaborate effectively to make decisions and reach consensus, so work with your team to choose a new research topic or to find a topic that allows members to incorporate research they have already done. Then, use these tips to get your wiki up and running:

- **Launch Your Project** In your group, set rules for managing your discussions and a process—such as taking a vote—for decision-making. Then, decide what kinds of information will appear on each page of your wiki. Each team member should create a page about a different aspect of the topic. For example, in a wiki on Homer's *Odyssey*, one page might analyze the epic's locations, while another might focus on the role of women.

- **Choose a Moderator** A moderator or administrator can manage pages and invite others to view and comment on your research. All other team members should have writing and editing rights.

- **Establish a Schedule** As a team, use your agreed-upon decision-making process to create a project plan that gives deadlines for the researching, writing, and editing stages.

- **Build Your Wiki** With the help of your school technology coordinator, choose a free Web site to host your wiki. Pay close attention to his or her instructions for building your wiki. Then, create the basic structure of your site, including a title and planning documents.

 **Media Tools** THINK central

Go to **thinkcentral.com**. KEYWORD: HML9-1336

---

## DIFFERENTIATED INSTRUCTION

**FOR ENGLISH LANGUAGE LEARNERS**

**Language: Reinforce Technology Terms** Review key terms used in this Workshop:

- *Web site:* location on the World Wide Web

- *discussion thread:* series of messages that have been posted on the Web in response to one another

- *Web page:* document on the World Wide Web identified by a URL

- *link:* connection in one Web document that redirects the user to another Web document

- *home page:* first page of a Web site that contains navigation information

## Developing the Wiki

Now you're ready to research your topic and develop your pages. Follow these steps to make your wiki worth visiting.

- **Conduct Research** Consult Web sites, books, and other sources to find information that's **relevant,** or related to, the aspect of the topic you're researching. Be sure the information you find is **credible** and **accurate** by using respected and authoritative sources. See pages 1305–1309 for guidelines for evaluating sources.

- **"Check in" With Your Team** Use the wiki's communication tools, such as **discussion threads**—chains of related messages. Using the same rules you set for live discussions, report on your progress, ask a question, or elicit feedback from your team.

- **Create Your Pages** Present the information you found on a page or pages in your wiki. Consider formatting your findings as an easy-to-read bulleted list. Don't forget to cite all your sources, just as you would in a traditional research paper.

- **Add Links** The power of a wiki is in its interactivity. Look for opportunities to link to appropriate Web sites with additional information or to other pages within your wiki.

- **Create Visual Interest** You may want to include graphics, such as photographs or maps, and multimedia to clarify and emphasize the information on your pages. Use copyright-free images readily available on the Web.

- **Review and Revise** "Exchange" pages with another team member and give feedback on each other's work. Then, make final changes to the pages you wrote. If you run into problems, ask an expert to explain ways to solve them.

- **Design Your Home Page** As a group, create a visually appealing home page. Include a catchy statement summarizing the contents of your group's wiki, a splashy title, and graphics.

- **Invite Your Teacher and Classmates to Explore** Once you've put the finishing touches on your wiki, send an e-mail inviting others to read your research and participate in discussion threads about it.

 **YOUR TURN** Plan and produce a wiki using the guidelines on these pages. Visit your wiki often, even after you've launched it. Make an effort to respond to comments from other visitors. You also may consider updating your wiki if new information about your topic becomes available.

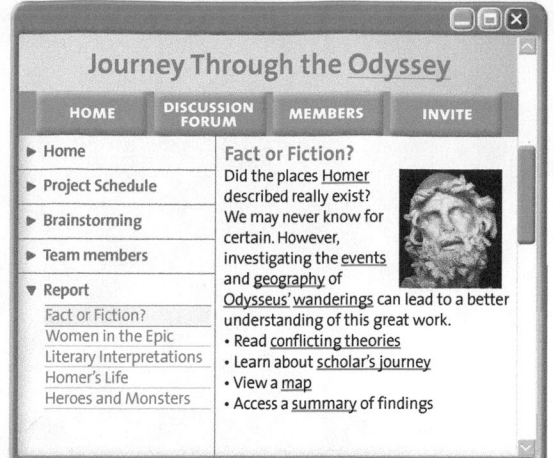

Journey Through the Odyssey

HOME | DISCUSSION FORUM | MEMBERS | INVITE

▶ Home
▶ Project Schedule
▶ Brainstorming
▶ Team members
▼ Report
  Fact or Fiction?
  Women in the Epic
  Literary Interpretations
  Homer's Life
  Heroes and Monsters

**Fact or Fiction?**
Did the places Homer described really exist? We may never know for certain. However, investigating the events and geography of Odysseus' wanderings can lead to a better understanding of this great work.
- Read conflicting theories
- Learn about scholar's journey
- View a map
- Access a summary of findings

---

---

## Teach

### Developing the Wiki

**Conduct Research** Remind students that in addition to looking for relevant information, they must also confirm the credibility and accuracy of each source they use.

**Create Visual Interest** Direct students' attention to the warning about copyright-free images. Explain that it is not always clear what material is copyrighted, who the copyright holder is, or under what conditions material may be used. When in doubt, students should check with a teacher before adding materials to their project files.

- Encourage students to experiment with different fonts and color combinations to see which ones are most effective.

- Direct students' attention to the sample home page. Ask what they might do differently if they were presenting the same material.

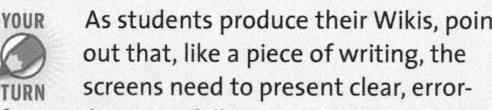 **YOUR TURN** As students produce their Wikis, point out that, like a piece of writing, the screens need to present clear, error-free, and easy-to-follow text. With screens, however, students also need to evaluate the effectiveness of visuals and the accuracy and effectiveness of links.

## Assess and Reteach

### Assess

Use the **COMMON CORE TRAITS** to assess students' wikis.

A strong wiki
- includes group planning documents
- shows evidence of collaboration
- has an inviting design that suits the topic, purpose, and audience
- presents information effectively

### Reteach

Some students may have trouble planning their wikis. Suggest that students use storyboards to develop sequences of pages.

 **BEST PRACTICES TOOLKIT—Transparency** Storyboard p. C11

**Media Tools** **THINK** central

Keywords for using technology direct students to **MediaScope,** a Web site that helps them strengthen media analysis and production skills.

# Student Resource Bank

# COMMON CORE FOCUS

**RL 2** Determine a theme or central idea of a text and analyze in detail its development over the course of the text, including how it emerges and is shaped and refined by specific details; provide an objective summary of the text. **RL 3** Analyze how complex characters develop over the course of a text, interact with other characters, and advance the plot or develop the theme. **RL 4** Determine the meaning of words and phrases as they are used in the text, including figurative and connotative meanings; analyze the cumulative impact of specific word choices on meaning and tone. **RI 2** Determine a central idea of a text and analyze its development over the course of the text; provide an objective summary of the text. **RI 3** Analyze how the author unfolds an analysis or series of ideas or events, including the order in which the points are made, how they are introduced and developed, and the connections that are drawn between them. **RI 4** Determine the meaning of words and phrases as they are used in a text, including figurative, connotative, and technical meanings; analyze the cumulative impact of specific word choices on meaning and tone. **RI 5** Analyze in detail how an author's ideas or claims are developed and refined by particular sentences, paragraphs or larger portions of a text. **RI 8** Delineate and evaluate the argument and specific claims in a text, assessing whether the reasoning is valid and the evidence is relevant and sufficient; identify false statements and fallacious reasoning.

Reading any text—short story, poem, magazine article, newspaper, Web page—requires the use of special strategies. For example, you might plot events in a short story on a diagram, while you may need to use text features to spot main ideas in a magazine article. You also need to identify patterns of organization in the text. Using such strategies can help you read different texts with ease and also help you understand what you're reading.

**COMMON CORE**
Included in this handbook:
RL 2–4, RI 2–5, RI 8

## 1 Reading Literary and Nonfiction Texts

**Literary and nonfiction texts** include short stories, novels, poems, dramas, and nonfiction biographies, autobiographies, and essays. To appreciate and analyze literary and nonfiction texts, you will need to understand the characteristics of each type of text.

### 1.1 READING A SHORT STORY
*Strategies for Reading*

- Read the title. As you read the story, you may notice that the title has a special meaning.
- Keep track of events as they happen. Plot the events on a diagram like this one.

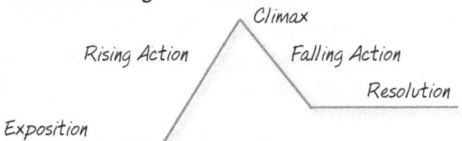

- From the details the writer provides, **visualize** the characters. **Predict** what they might do next.
- Look for specific adjectives that help you visualize the **setting**—the time and place in which events occur.
- Use the story's **details** to help you determine its **theme** or **central idea.**

### 1.2 READING A POEM
*Strategies for Reading*

- Notice the **form** of the poem, or the number of its lines and their arrangement on the page.
- Read the poem aloud a few times. Listen for **rhymes** and **rhythms.**
- **Visualize** the images and comparisons.
- Determine the meaning of the poem's **figurative language.**
- Create a word web or another **graphic organizer** to record your reactions and questions.
- Use the poem's **details** to help you determine its **theme** or **central idea.**

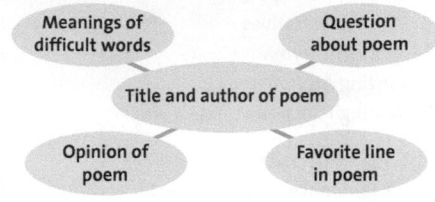

### 1.3 READING A PLAY
*Strategies for Reading*

- Read the stage directions to help you **visualize** the setting and characters.
- **Question** what the title means and why the playwright chose it.
- Identify the main conflict (struggle or problem) in the play. To **clarify** the conflict, make a chart that shows what the conflict is and how it is resolved.
- **Evaluate** the characters. What do they want? How do they change during the play? You may want to make a chart that lists each character's name, appearance, and traits.

### 1.4 READING NONFICTION TEXTS
*Strategies for Reading*

- If you are reading a biography, an autobiography, or another type of biographical writing, such as a diary or memoir, use a family tree or word web to keep track of the people mentioned.
- When reading an essay, **evaluate** the writer's ideas and reasoning. Does the writer present his or her perspective in a thesis statement? identify the main points? support opinions with facts?

# 2 Reading Informational Texts: Text Features

An **informational text** is writing that provides factual information. Informational materials, such as chapters in textbooks and articles in magazines, encyclopedias, and newspapers, usually contain elements that help the reader recognize their purposes, organizations, and key ideas. These elements are known as **text features.**

## 2.1 UNDERSTANDING TEXT FEATURES

**Text features** are design elements of a text that indicate its organizational structure or otherwise make its key ideas and information understandable. Text features include titles, headings, subheadings, boldface type, bulleted and numbered lists, and graphic aids, such as charts, graphs, illustrations, and photographs. Notice how the text features help you find key information on the textbook page shown.

Ⓐ The **title** identifies the topic.

Ⓑ A **subheading** indicates the start of a new topic or section and identifies its focus.

Ⓒ **Boldface type** is used to make key terms obvious.

Ⓓ A **bulleted list** shows items of equal importance.

Ⓔ **Graphic aids,** such as graphs, illustrations, photographs, charts, diagrams, maps, and timelines, often present data and clarify ideas in the text.

Ⓕ A **caption,** or the text that accompanies a graphic aid, gives information about the graphic aid that isn't necessarily obvious from the image itself.

### PRACTICE AND APPLY

1. What are the subheadings on the textbook page shown?

2. What are the key terms on the page? How do you know?

3. What does the illustration tell you about shield volcanoes? Can you find this information elsewhere on the page?

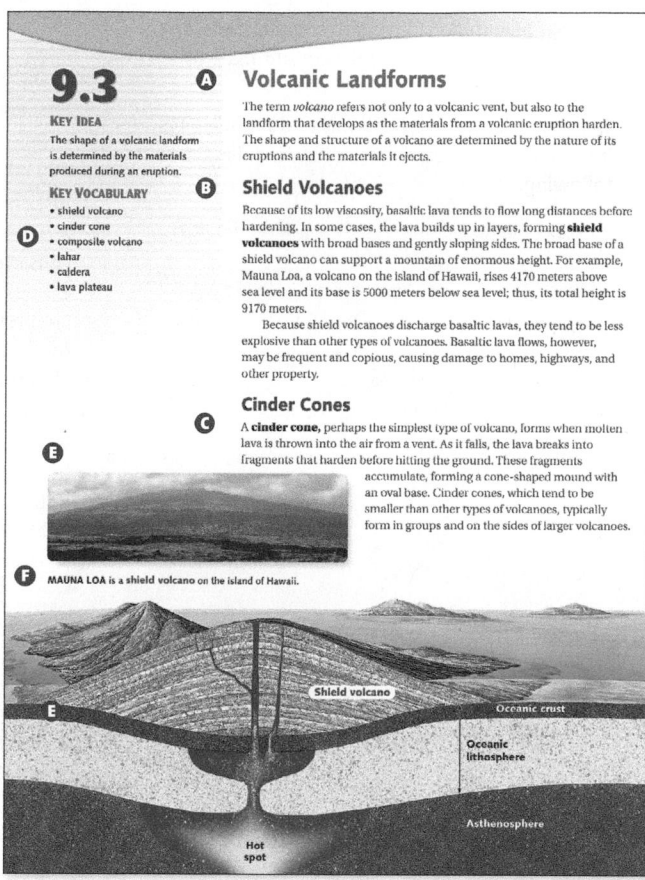

## 9.3

Ⓐ **Volcanic Landforms**

**KEY IDEA**
The shape of a volcanic landform is determined by the materials produced during an eruption.

**KEY VOCABULARY**
Ⓓ
• shield volcano
• cinder cone
• composite volcano
• lahar
• caldera
• lava plateau

The term *volcano* refers not only to a volcanic vent, but also to the landform that develops as the materials from a volcanic eruption harden. The shape and structure of a volcano are determined by the nature of its eruptions and the materials it ejects.

Ⓑ **Shield Volcanoes**

Because of its low viscosity, basaltic lava tends to flow long distances before hardening. In some cases, the lava builds up in layers, forming **shield volcanoes** with broad bases and gently sloping sides. The broad base of a shield volcano can support a mountain of enormous height. For example, Mauna Loa, a volcano on the island of Hawaii, rises 4170 meters above sea level and its base is 5000 meters below sea level; thus, its total height is 9170 meters.

Because shield volcanoes discharge basaltic lavas, they tend to be less explosive than other types of volcanoes. Basaltic lava flows, however, may be frequent and copious, causing damage to homes, highways, and other property.

Ⓒ **Cinder Cones**

A **cinder cone,** perhaps the simplest type of volcano, forms when molten lava is thrown into the air from a vent. As it falls, the lava breaks into fragments that harden before hitting the ground. These fragments accumulate, forming a cone-shaped mound with an oval base. Cinder cones, which tend to be smaller than other types of volcanoes, typically form in groups and on the sides of larger volcanoes.

Ⓕ **MAUNA LOA is a shield volcano on the island of Hawaii.**

Shield volcano
Oceanic crust
Oceanic lithosphere
Asthenosphere
Hot spot

READING HANDBOOK   **R3**

## PRACTICE AND APPLY

## ANSWERS

1. *Shield Volcanoes, Cinder Cones*

2. *The key terms,* shield volcanoes *and* cinder cone, *are in boldface type.*

3. ***Possible answer:*** *The illustration shows how shield volcanoes form. This information can also be found in the section subtitled "Shield Volcanoes."*

## PRACTICE AND APPLY

### ANSWERS

Students' outlines will vary. They should follow the format on page R4 and include a main idea for each roman numeral entry, a subheading for each capital letter entry, and one or more details for each numbered entry. The following is an example of a partial outline:

**I.** *A new life*
  **A.** *Fargo, North Dakota*
  **B.** *Lost Boys of Sudan*
    **1.** *Civil war*
    **2.** *Exodus from Sudan*
    **3.** *Kakuma Refugee Camp*
  **C.** *Agreement between United Nations and United States*
    **1.** *Lost Boys sent to America*
    **2.** *Foster care and school*
    **3.** *Citizenship*
**II.** *Nighttime in America*
  **A.** *Meeting the social worker*
  **B.** *New home*
    **1.** *Fargo's south side*
    **2.** *Donations*
    **3.** *Food*
**III.** *Living on Leaves and Berries*
  **A.** *Family is killed*
  **B.** *Ethiopia*

### 2.2 USING TEXT FEATURES

You can use text features to locate information, to help you understand it, and to categorize it. Just use the following strategies when you encounter informational text.

#### Strategies for Reading

- Scan the title, headings, and subheadings to get an idea of the main concepts and the way the text is organized.

- Before you begin reading the text more thoroughly, read any questions that appear at the end of a lesson or chapter. Doing this will help you set a purpose for your reading.

- Turn subheadings into questions. Then use the text below the subheadings to answer the questions. Your answers will be a summary of the text.

- Take notes by turning headings and subheadings into main ideas. You might use a chart like the following.

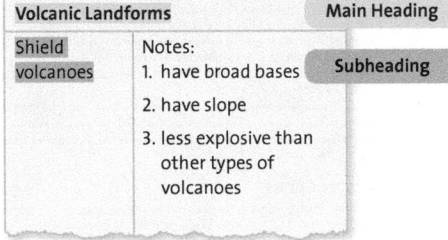

### 2.3 TURNING TEXT HEADINGS INTO OUTLINE ENTRIES

You can also use text features to take notes in outline form. The following outline shows how one student used text headings from the sample page on page R3. Study the outline and use the strategies that follow to create an outline based on text features.

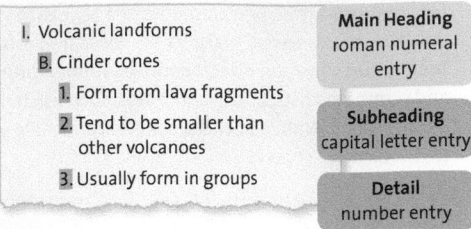

#### Strategies for Using Text Headings

- Preview the headings and subheadings in the text to get an idea of what different kinds there are and what their positions might be in an outline.

- Be consistent. Note that subheadings that are the same size and color should be used consistently in Roman-numeral or capital-letter entries in the outline. If you decide that a chapter heading should appear with a Roman numeral, then that's the level at which all other chapter headings should appear.

- Write the headings and subheadings that you will use as your Roman-numeral and capital-letter entries first. As you read, fill in numbered details from the text under the headings and subheadings in your outline.

**PRACTICE AND APPLY**

Reread *The Lost Boys*, pages 592–597. Use text features in the selection to take notes in outline form.

Preview the subheadings in the text to get an idea of the different kinds. Write the headings and subheadings you are using as your Roman-numeral and capital-letter entries first. Then fill in the details.

## 2.4 GRAPHIC AIDS

Information is communicated not only with words but also with graphic aids. **Graphic aids** are visual representations of verbal statements. They can be charts, webs, diagrams, graphs, photographs, or other visual representations of information. Graphic aids usually make complex information, such as technical or quantitative data, easier to understand. For that reason, graphic aids are often used to organize, simplify, and summarize information for easy reference.

### Graphs

Graphs are used to illustrate statistical information. A **graph** is a drawing that shows the relative values of numerical quantities. Different kinds of graphs are used to show different numerical relationships.

### *Strategies for Reading*

**A** Read the title.

**B** Find out what is being represented or measured.

**C** In a circle graph, compare the sizes of the parts.

**D** In a line graph, study the slant of the line. The steeper the line, the faster the rate of change.

**E** In a bar graph, compare the lengths of the bars.

A **circle graph,** or **pie graph,** shows the relationships of parts to a whole. The entire circle equals 100 percent. The parts of the circle represent percentages of the whole.

MODEL: CIRCLE GRAPH

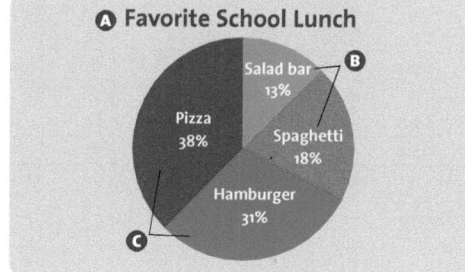

Line graphs show changes in numerical quantities over time and are effective in presenting trends such as attendance at a drama fair from 2003 to 2007. A line graph is made on a grid. Here, the vertical axis indicates quantity, and the horizontal axis shows years. Points on the graph indicate data. The line that connects the points highlights a trend or pattern.

MODEL: LINE GRAPH

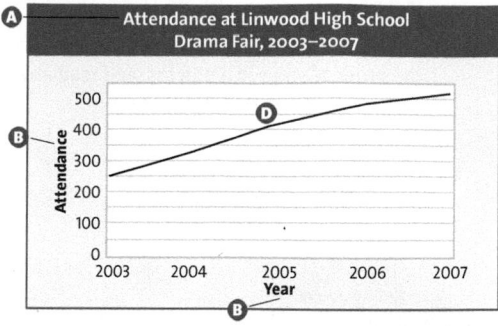

In a **bar graph,** vertical or horizontal bars are used to show or compare categories of information, such as the gestation periods of certain mammals. The lengths of the bars indicate the quantities.

MODEL: BAR GRAPH

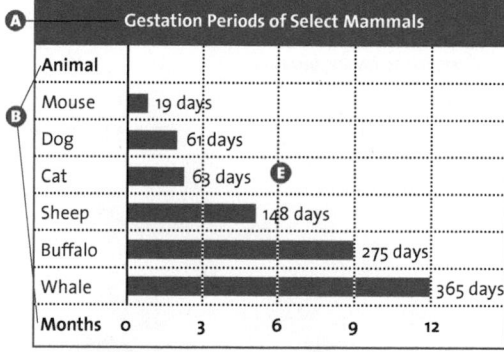

**WATCH OUT!** Evaluate carefully the information presented in graphs. For example, circle graphs show major factors and differences well but tend to minimize smaller factors and differences.

## Diagrams

A **diagram** is a drawing that shows how something works or how its parts relate to one another.

A **picture diagram** is a picture or drawing of the subject being discussed.

### Strategies for Reading

Ⓐ Read the title.

Ⓑ Read each label and look at the part it identifies.

Ⓒ Follow any arrows or numbers that show the order of steps in a process, and read any captions.

**MODEL: PICTURE DIAGRAM**

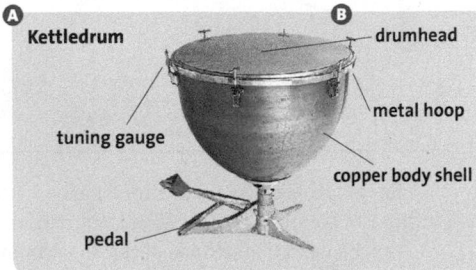

In a **schematic diagram,** lines, symbols, and words are used to help readers visualize processes or objects they wouldn't normally be able to see.

**MODEL: SCHEMATIC DIAGRAM**

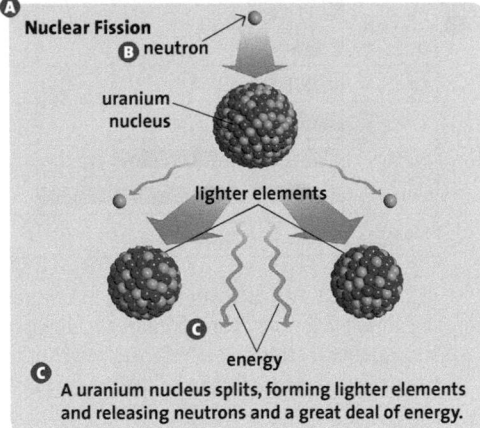

Ⓒ A uranium nucleus splits, forming lighter elements and releasing neutrons and a great deal of energy.

## Charts and Tables

A **chart** presents information, shows a process, or makes comparisons, usually in rows or columns. A **table** is a specific type of chart that presents a collection of facts in rows and columns and shows how the facts relate to one another.

### Strategies for Reading

Ⓐ Read the title to learn what information the chart or table covers.

Ⓑ Study column headings and row labels to determine the categories of information presented.

Ⓒ Look down columns and across rows to find specific information.

**MODEL: CHART**

| Ⓐ Sounds in Poetry | |
| --- | --- |
| Ⓑ **Technique** | **Example** |
| Onomatopoeia | the slow **clip clop** of the ox Ⓒ |
| Alliteration | rough reaches of ranch and sky |
| Assonance | the **costly tossing** of **lost** dreams |
| Consonance | his meager nuggets of begrudging praise |
| Rhyme | A truth that's told with bad **intent** Beats all the lies you can **invent.** |

**MODEL: TABLE**

| Ⓐ Bus Route 333: Grand Avenue | | | | Weekday Mornings— EASTBOUND | |
| --- | --- | --- | --- | --- | --- |
| Ⓑ Lawrence Station | Chestnut St. Mall | Grand & Lincoln | Memorial Hospital | Grand & Delaware | Three Rivers Station |
| 4:57 A.M. | 5:03 A.M. | 5:06 A.M. | 5:10 A.M. | 5:16 A.M. | 5:19 A.M. |
| 5:38 | 5:44 | 5:48 | 5:53 | 5:59 | 6:02 |
| 5:55 | 6:02 | 6:06 | 6:11 | 6:18 | 6:22 |
| 6:15 | 6:22 | 6:26 | 6:31 | 6:38 | 6:42 |
| 6:35 | 6:42 | 6:46 | 6:51 | 6:58 | 7:02 |
| 7:00 | 7:08 | 7:13 | 7:19 | 7:28 | 7:33 |
| 7:15 | 7:23 | 7:28 | 7:34 | 7:43 | 7:48 |

## Maps

A **map** visually represents a geographic region, such as a state or country. It provides information about areas through lines, colors, shapes, and symbols. There are different kinds of maps.

- **Political maps** show political features, such as national borders.

- **Physical maps** show the landforms in areas.

- **Road or travel maps** show roads and highways.

- **Thematic maps** show information on a specific topic, such as climate, weather, or natural resources.

### Strategies for Reading

Ⓐ Read the title to find out what kind of map it is.

Ⓑ Read the labels to get an overall sense of what the map shows.

Ⓒ Look at the **key** or **legend** to find out what the symbols and colors on the map stand for.

MODEL: WEATHER MAP

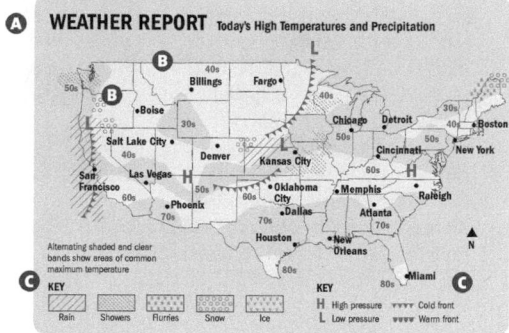

MODEL: POLITICAL MAP

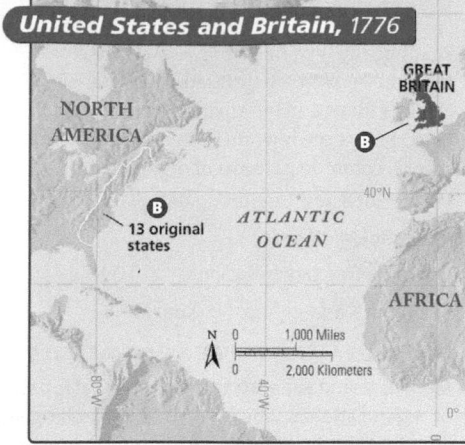

### PRACTICE AND APPLY

Use the graphic aids shown on pages R5–R7 to answer the following questions:

1. What was the approximate attendance at the Linwood High School Drama Fair in 2005?

2. Is there more than one tuning gauge on a kettledrum?

3. What is the least favorite lunch according to the circle graph?

4. Write a definition of *alliteration*, using the information in the chart.

5. Use the bus schedule to figure how long your trip would be if you boarded the bus at Lawrence Station at 7:15 A.M. and got off the bus at Memorial Hospital.

6. According to the weather map, which states have temperatures in the 80s?

7. Using the scale on the political map, find the approximate number of miles from the 13 original states across the Atlantic Ocean to Great Britain.

## PRACTICE AND APPLY

### ANSWERS

1. *Approximately 400*

2. *Yes*

3. *Salad bar*

4. ***Possible answer:*** *Alliteration is the repetition of the same sound or letter at the beginning of words.*

5. *19 minutes*

6. *Texas and Florida*

7. *Approximately 3,000 miles*

## 3 Reading Informational Texts: Patterns of Organization

Reading any type of writing is easier once you recognize how it is organized. Writers usually arrange ideas and information in ways that best help readers see how they are related. There are several common patterns of organization:

- main idea and supporting details
- chronological order
- cause-effect organization
- compare-and-contrast organization

### 3.1 MAIN IDEA AND SUPPORTING DETAILS

**Main idea and supporting details** is a basic pattern of organization in which a central, controlling idea about a topic is supported by details. The **main** or **central idea** is the most important idea about a topic that a particular text or paragraph conveys. **Supporting details** are words, phrases, or sentences that tell more about the main idea. The main idea may be directly stated at the beginning and then followed by supporting details or may be merely implied by the supporting details. It may also be stated after it has been implied by supporting details.

### Strategies for Reading

- To find a stated main idea in a paragraph, identify the paragraph's topic. The topic is what the paragraph is about and can usually be summed up in one or two words. The word, or synonyms of it, will usually appear throughout the paragraph. Headings and subheadings are also clues to the topics of paragraphs.

- Ask: What is the topic sentence? The topic sentence states the most important idea, message, or information the paragraph conveys about this topic.

- To find an implied main idea, ask yourself: Whom or what did I just read about? What do the details suggest about the topic?

- Formulate a sentence stating this idea and add it to the paragraph. Does your sentence convey the main idea?

Notice how the main idea is expressed in each of the following models.

**MODEL: MAIN IDEA STATED IN THE BEGINNING**

Some of the most impressive of all human achievements took place during the prehistoric period called the Stone Age. **[Main idea]** These accomplishments included the invention of tools and pottery, as well as the development of farming. Stone chopping tools date from the early Stone Age—2.5 million to 8000 B.C. Polished tools, pottery, and agriculture were developed during the late Stone Age— 8000 to 3000 B.C. **[Supporting details]**

**MODEL: MAIN IDEA IMPLIED BY SUPPORTING DETAILS**

Imagine that the 102-story Empire State Building represents the history of the earth. Each story is the equivalent of about 40 million years. The earth was formed at the ground floor. Not until floor 30 or so did the first single-celled organism appear. The first dinosaurs arose at the base of the radio antenna. Mammals appeared on earth about three-quarters of the way up the antenna. The ancestors of modern humans did not appear until the tip of the antenna—about 40,000 years ago. **[Supporting details]**

**[Implied main idea: Humans have existed for only a small percentage of the history of the planet.]**

**MODEL: MAIN IDEA STATED AFTER IT HAS BEEN IMPLIED BY SUPPORTING DETAILS**

Scientists believe that Cro-Magnons planned their hunts carefully. Cro-Magnons studied animals' habits. They also developed advanced language skills, which improved their ability to cooperate and plan. **[Supporting details]** These survival skills helped the Cro-Magnon population to grow and thrive. **[Main idea]**

Read each paragraph, and then do the following:

1. Identify the main idea in the paragraph, using one of the strategies discussed on the previous page.

2. Identify whether the main idea is stated or implied in the paragraph.

> It was deeply unnerving. It took us over two hours to cover six-tenths of a mile of trail. By the time we reached solid ground at a place called Bearpen Gap, the snow was four or five inches deep and accumulating fast. The whole world was white, filled with dime-sized snowflakes that fell at a slant before being caught by the wind and hurled in a variety of directions. We couldn't see more than fifteen or twenty feet ahead, often not even that.
>
> —Bill Bryson, *A Walk in the Woods*

> For many people with Parkinson's managing their disease is a full-time job. It is a constant balancing act. Too little medicine causes tremors and stiffness. Too much medicine produces uncontrollable movement and slurring. And far too often, Parkinson's patients wait and wait for the medicines to "kick-in."
>
> —Michael J. Fox, testimony before the Senate

## 3.2 CHRONOLOGICAL ORDER

**Chronological order** is the arrangement of events in their order of occurrence. This type of organization is used in fictional narratives, historical writing, biographies, and autobiographies. Sometimes fiction writers will manipulate time by breaking from strictly linear plot development with flashbacks and flash forwards, but the general pattern may still be chronological. To indicate the order of events, writers use words such as *before, after, next,* and *later* and words and phrases that identify specific times of day, days of the week, and dates, such as *the next morning, Tuesday,* and *on July 4, 1776.*

## Strategies for Reading

- Look in the text for headings and subheadings that may indicate a chronological pattern of organization.

- Look for words and phrases that identify times, such as *in a year, three hours earlier, in 202 B.C.,* and *the next day.*

- Look for words that signal order, such as *first, afterward, then, during,* and *finally,* to see how events or steps are related.

- Note that a paragraph or passage in which ideas and information are arranged chronologically will have several words or phrases that indicate time order, not just one.

- Ask yourself: Are the events in the paragraph or passage presented in time order?

Notice the words and phrases that signal time order in the first two paragraphs of the following model.

> **MODEL**
>
> **Dynasties of China from 202 B.C. to A.D. 1279**
>
> The Han dynasty ruled China from 202 B.C. to A.D. 220. (A dynasty is a series of rulers from a single family.) For more than 350 years after the Han dynasty collapsed, no emperor was able to unite northern and southern China. Then, in 589, Emperor Sui Wendi created a strong central government and laid the foundation for a golden age of China under the Tang and Song dynasties. Literature, poetry, architecture, sculpture, painting, and dance all flourished during this period.
>
> The Tang dynasty ruled China for almost 300 years, from 618 to 907. The first important Tang emperor, Tang Taizong, held the throne from 626 until 649. During his reign, China regained its northern and western lands. After 660 or so, the real power in China was Empress Wu Zhao, although a series of weak emperors actually sat on the throne. Under her leadership, Chinese armies

Events

Time words and phrases

Order words and phrases

## PRACTICE AND APPLY

### ANSWERS

1. *Possible answers: Paragraph 1: The blizzard obscured the trail and made hiking in the woods dangerous. Paragraph 2: For many people with Parkinson's, managing their disease is a full-time job.*

2. *In the first paragraph, the main idea is implied. In the second paragraph, the main idea is stated.*

overran Korea before 668. By 690, Wu Zhao had become emperor in her own right, the only woman to hold that title.

By the mid-700s, the Tang emperors had begun losing control over their huge empire. Arab armies defeated the Chinese on their far western frontier in 751. For the next 150 years, China suffered attacks on its borders and internal rebellions. Then, in 907, Chinese rebels burned the capital city of Ch'ang-an and murdered the child emperor, ending the Tang dynasty.

Much of China was reunited in 960 under the first Song emperor, Song Taizu. However, in the early 1100s, the Song lost all of northern China to the Jurchen people. The Song established a new capital in the coastal city of Hangzhou, where they continued to rule from 1127 to 1279. During this century and a half, southern China became a prosperous trading center.

The 600 years of Song and Tang rule were years of great growth. Copper coins and paper money came into regular circulation. High-quality schools were established to train government workers. Standard editions of great works of literature were published. Although both dynasties included periods of turmoil, their cultural and economic accomplishments are still impressive today.

---

**PRACTICE AND APPLY**

Refer to the last three paragraphs of the preceding model to do the following:

1. List at least eight words in the paragraphs that indicate time or order.

2. Plot the events in the paragraphs on a timeline, using the dates mentioned. Some events may overlap.

3. A writer may use more than one pattern of organization in a text. In the last paragraph of the model, what pattern of organization does the writer use? How does this pattern contribute to your understanding of the passage?

---

## PRACTICE AND APPLY

### ANSWERS

1. *Possible answers:* "By the mid-700s"; "in 751"; "For the next 150 years"; "Then, in 907"; "in 960"; "in the early 1100s"; "from 1127 to 1279"; "During this century and a half"; "The 600 years of Song and Tang rule"

2. To help students create a timeline, show them one or two examples. Students should include the following events in their timelines: *751: Arab armies defeat China on the western frontier; 907: Chinese rebels burn the capital city of Ch'ang-an and murder the child emperor; 960: China reunited under the first Song emperor, Song Taizu; 960–1279: Song Dynasty; Early 1100s: Song loses all of northern China to the Jurchen people; 1127: New capital established at Hangzhou*

3. *Possible answer:* The writer organizes the paragraph using a main idea and supporting details. This pattern conveys the cultural and economic significance of the Song and Tang dynasties.

---

### 3.3 CAUSE-EFFECT ORGANIZATION

**Cause-effect organization** is a pattern of organization that establishes causal relationships between events, ideas, and trends. Cause-effect relationships may be directly stated or merely implied by the order in which the information is presented. Writers often use the cause-effect pattern in historical and scientific analyses. Cause-effect relationships may take several forms.

**One cause with one effect**

**One cause with multiple effects**

**Multiple causes with a single effect**

**A chain of causes and effects**

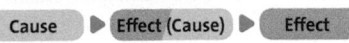

#### Strategies for Reading

- Look for headings and subheadings that indicate a cause-effect pattern of organization, such as "Effects of Population Density."

- To find the effect or effects, read to answer the question, What happened?

- To find the cause or causes, read to answer the question, Why did it happen?

- Look for words and phrases that help you identify specific relationships between events, such as *because, since, had the effect of, led to, as a result, resulted in, for that reason, due to, therefore, if . . . then,* and *consequently.*

- Evaluate each cause-effect relationship. Do not assume that because one event happened before another, the first event caused the second event.

- Use graphic organizers like the diagrams shown to record cause-effect relationships as you read.

Notice the words that signal causes and effects in the following model.

**MODEL**

### The Lasting Effects of the Krakatau Eruption

In 1883, the massive explosion of a volcano called Krakatau resulted in tens of thousands of deaths as well as long-term changes in climate conditions.

Krakatau, also called Krakatoa, takes up much of a small island called Rakata. Part of the country of Indonesia, Rakata lies between the islands of Java and Sumatra in the Indian Ocean. Until 1883, Krakatau was a huge volcano, with a height of about 6,000 feet above sea level.

At 10:00 A.M. on August 27, 1883, a huge eruption destroyed most of Krakatau. As a result of the explosion, volcanic ash spewed into the air as high as 50 miles above the volcano.

The effects of the explosion were deadly. The blast caused nearly five cubic miles of rock fragments to be released into the air. In the region of the blast, the sun was not visible for the next two and a half days. Burning ash and rocks killed thousands. Tsunamis, underwater earthquakes, struck Java and Sumatra causing waves up to 120 feet. Because of the ash, rocks, and waves, about 36,000 people lost their lives.

The destruction at Krakatau had effects around the world. People in Australia, more than 2,000 miles away, heard the boom. Weather forecasters all over the planet detected sudden increases in atmospheric pressure. A series of tsunamis resulting from the blast reached as far as Hawaii and South America. Some scientists believe that dust from Krakatau may have been the reason the world experienced unseasonably cool weather for months after the eruption.

Causes
Signal words
Effects

**PRACTICE AND APPLY**

Refer to the preceding model to do the following.

1. Use the pattern of one cause with multiple effects illustrated on page R10 to make a graphic organizer showing the main cause described in the text and at least three effects of that cause.

2. List at least four words and phrases that the writer uses to signal causes and effects in the last two paragraphs.

### 3.4 COMPARE-AND-CONTRAST ORGANIZATION

**Compare-and-contrast organization** is a pattern of organization that serves as a framework for an analysis of similarities and differences in two or more subjects. A writer may use this pattern of organization to analyze two or more subjects, such as characters or movies, in terms of their important points or characteristics. These points or characteristics are called points of comparison. The compare-and-contrast pattern of organization may be developed in either of two ways:

**Point-by-point organization**—The writer discusses one point of comparison for both subjects, then goes on to the next point.

**Subject-by-subject organization**—The writer covers all points of comparison for one subject and then all points of comparison for the next subject.

*Strategies for Reading*

• Look in the text for headings, subheadings, and sentences that may suggest a compare-and-contrast pattern of organization, such as "Plants Share Many Characteristics." These will help you identify where similarities and differences are addressed.

• To find similarities, look for words and phrases such as *like, similarly, both, also,* and *in the same way.*

• To find differences, look for words and phrases such as *unlike, but, on the other hand, in contrast,* and *however.*

**PRACTICE AND APPLY**

**ANSWERS**

1. *Possible answers (on graphic organizer):* Cause: In 1883, Krakatau, a volcano on an island in Indonesia, erupted in a massive explosion. Effects: volcanic ash spewed as high as 50 miles into the air; blast released nearly five cubic miles of rock fragments into the air; sun was not visible for two and a half days; tsunamis struck Sumatra, Java, Hawaii, and South America; about 36,000 people lost their lives; atmospheric pressure over the entire planet suddenly increased

2. *Possible answers:* effects; caused; Because of; had effects; resulting from; may have been the reason

- Use a graphic organizer, such as a Venn diagram or a compare-and-contrast chart, to record points of comparison and similarities and differences.

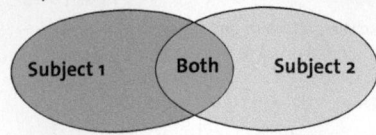

|  | Subject 1 | Subject 2 |
|---|---|---|
| Point 1 | | |
| Point 2 | | |
| Point 3 | | |

Read the following models. As you read, use the signal words and phrases to identify the similarities and differences between the subjects and how the details are organized in each text.

**MODEL 1**

### Pyramids in Egypt and the Americas

The pyramid is perhaps the most well-known accomplishment of ancient peoples. When most people think of these amazing structures, they think of Egypt. However, Egypt was not the only place where pyramids were built. Pyramids were also constructed in the Americas, mainly in Central America and South America.

> **Subjects**

Most pyramid construction in Egypt took place between 2686 and 2345 B.C. In contrast, most Central American and South American pyramids were built much later. So far, only one pyramid of the Americas has been found to be similar in age to the Egyptian pyramids. A pyramid in Caral, Peru, has been dated to 2627 B.C.

> **Contrast words and phrases**

> **Comparison words and phrases**

The Pyramid of the Sun at Teotihuacán, Mexico, and the Great Pyramid at Giza, Egypt, measure nearly the same at their base. Egyptian pyramids are taller, however. The Great Pyramid originally reached a height of 481 feet, while the tallest pyramid in the Americas is 216 feet high. Even the pyramid at Caral is only one-eighth the height of the Great Pyramid.

Pyramids in Egypt and the Americas have major structural differences as well. Pyramids in the Americas have receding steps that resemble the layers of a cake. Egyptian pyramids, on the other hand, have smooth sides that connect in a point at the top.

Egyptian pyramids were always part of larger groups of buildings, including temples and houses. Similarly, American pyramids were built in the middle of cities. However, pyramids in the Americas typically served as temples and were the sites of human and animal sacrifices. In contrast, all Egyptian pyramids were built to be royal burial chambers.

Modern scientists are amazed at the size and durability of these structures. Many pyramids took as long as 20 years to build, requiring millions of stone blocks and thousands of laborers. Pyramids in Egypt and in the Americas were both outstanding accomplishments of the civilizations that created them.

**MODEL 2**

## The Governments of Rome and the United States

After fighting the Revolutionary War, Americans were faced with the task of creating a new government. The vision of the new nation as a republic—a government in which citizens rule through their elected representatives—was based on the republic of ancient Rome. The republican governments of Rome and the United States have both similarities and differences.

The guiding principles of the government of Rome were recorded in the Twelve Tables, a list of legal rules. Only adult male landowners could be citizens, and only they could vote. The government was divided into three branches—executive, legislative, and judicial. The executive branch was made up of two consuls, or leaders, chosen by the legislative assembly to serve one-year terms. The legislative branch was divided into three houses: a 300-member Senate chosen from the aristocracy, a Centuriate Assembly of citizen-soldiers, and a Tribal Assembly of general citizens. All assembly members served life terms. The judicial branch consisted of eight judges chosen by the Centuriate Assembly for one-year terms.

Like the republic of Rome, the government of the United States is based on a code of laws, the U.S. Constitution, which gives its citizens the right to select their leaders. However, U.S. citizens now include all native-born and naturalized persons, not just adult male landowners as in Rome. The U.S. government also consists of an executive, a legislative, and a judicial branch. In contrast to the Roman consuls, the U.S. executive is one person—a president elected by citizens for a four-year term. The legislative branch includes only two houses rather than Rome's three—

**Subjects**

**Comparison words and phrases**

**Contrast words and phrases**

a Senate, whose 100 members are elected by the people for six-year terms, and a House of Representatives whose members are elected for two-year terms. These legislators all serve shorter terms than their Roman counterparts. However, the federal judges in the U.S. judicial branch are appointed by the president to life terms, in contrast to the Roman judges' single-year appointments.

### PRACTICE AND APPLY

Refer to the preceding models to answer the following questions:

1. Which model is organized by subject? Which model is organized by points of comparison?

2. Identify at least two words or phrases in each model that signal a compare-and-contrast pattern of organization. Do not choose words or phrases that have already been highlighted.

3. List at least three points that the writer of each model compares and contrasts.

4. Use a Venn diagram or a compare-and-contrast chart to identify at least two points of comparison and their similarities and differences in model 2.

## PRACTICE AND APPLY

## ANSWERS

1. *Model 2 is organized by subject. Model 1 is organized by points of comparison.*

2. *Possible answers:* **Model 1:** *only, nearly the same, while, differences, as well, on the other hand, and Similarly.* **Model 2:** *both, Only, All, rather than, and than*

3. *Possible answers:* Model 1: *construction of the pyramids in Egypt and South America; height and measurement of the pyramids; structural differences of the pyramids; cultural purpose and function of the pyramids.* Model 2: *guiding principles of Roman and U.S. governments; citizenship; branches of government*

4. Students should create a Venn diagram or a compare-and-contrast chart like the ones shown on page R12. *Possible answers:* **Roman Government:** *only adult male landowners could be citizens and could vote; executive branch consisted of two consuls; consuls were chosen by the legislative assembly; consuls served for one year; legislative branch was divided into three houses; all assembly members served life terms; judges were chosen by the Centuriate Assembly; judges served for one year.* **U.S. Government:** *all native-born and naturalized citizens can vote; president is elected by citizens and serves a four-year term; legislative branch includes two houses; senators serve a six-year term; representatives serve a two-year term; federal judges are appointed by the president and serve a life term.* **Similarities:** *only citizens elect their officials; government was divided into three branches: executive, legislative, and judicial; government is based on a code of law.*

## 4 Reading Informational Texts: Forms

Magazines, newspapers, Web pages, and consumer, public, and workplace documents are all examples of informational materials. To understand and analyze informational texts, pay attention to text features and patterns of organization.

### 4.1 READING A MAGAZINE ARTICLE

Because people often skim magazines, magazine publishers use devices to attract attention to articles.

*Strategies for Reading*

**Ⓐ** Notice whether **graphic aids** or **quotations** attract your attention. Sometimes a publisher pulls a quotation out of the text and displays it to get your attention. Such quotations are called **pull quotes.**

**Ⓑ** Once you decide that you're interested in the article, read the title and other headings to find out more about its topic and organization.

**Ⓒ** Notice whether the article has a **byline,** a line naming the author.

**Ⓓ** Sometimes an article will be accompanied by a **sidebar,** a short article that presents additional information. This sidebar also has a **title.** Is your understanding of the main article enhanced by the information in the sidebar?

**Ⓑ** ## Is "youth sports rage" on the rise?

### Parents become violent and abusive during kids' games

**Ⓒ** by Belinda Liu

The news stories are frightening. In Virginia, the mother of a soccer player assaults a 14-year-old referee and is fined. In Pennsylvania, a "midget league" football game results in a brawl involving about 100 players and spectators. Accounts of "youth sports rage" are reported in Britain, Canada, Australia, and New Zealand.

Are spectators at youth sports becoming more violent? Some observers believe they are.

"There have always been problem parents in kids' sports," explains soccer coach Larry Fiore. "But the vast majority of parents, coaches, and athletes act appropriately."

However, some factors are making the problem worse, believes sports psychologist Theresa Mathelier. "Sports are getting more expensive for parents in terms of equipment, traveling, and coaching," she explains. "The tendency now is to start kids in organized sports earlier and to get them to specialize in one sport."

As a result, Mathelier says, "a few parents get unrealistic ideas about college scholarships and professional careers in sports. They start to live through their kids, and if something goes wrong, they blow up."

**Ⓐ** *"Parents should be role models."*

Fiore and Mathelier both say that it is rarely the athletes who cause the problems. Serena Terell, a 15-year-old soccer player, agrees. "It's so embarrassing when the parents yell and curse," Serena explains, adding that her parents always behave themselves. "Their kids just want them to stop. After all, it's only a game, and parents should be role models."

**Ⓓ** **STOPPING SPORTS RAGE: STEPS YOU CAN TAKE**

Here are steps that some groups have taken to prevent youth sports rage.

• The National Youth Sports Safety Foundation has created a Sport Parent Code of Conduct. Penalties range from a verbal warning to a season suspension for parents.

• Some soccer leagues designate one day as "Silent Sunday." Spectators are not allowed to cheer or even talk until the game is over.

• Some coaches choose one parent to be in charge of crowd control. This parent patrols the bleachers or sidelines, making sure that fans of his or her team behave.

---

**PRACTICE AND APPLY**

1. Which graphic aids in the article attracted your attention?

2. What heading other than the title tells you what the article is about?

3. From what part of the article is the pull quote taken?

---

## PRACTICE AND APPLY

## ANSWERS

1. *Possible answers:* the angry faces at the top of the page; the image of the football players

2. *The subtitle states, "Parents become violent and abusive during kids' games"*

3. *The pull quote is taken from the last paragraph in the article.*

## 4.2 READING A TEXTBOOK

Each textbook that you use has its own system of organization based on the content in the book. Often an introductory unit will explain the book's organization and special features. If your textbook has such a unit, read it first.

### Strategies for Reading

**ⓐ** Before you begin reading the lesson or chapter, read any **questions** that appear at the end of it. Then use the questions to set your purpose for reading.

**ⓑ** **Read slowly and carefully** to better understand and remember the ideas presented in the text. When you come to an unfamiliar word, first try to figure out its meaning from **context clues.** If necessary, find the meaning of the word in a **glossary** in the textbook or in a dictionary.

For more information, see the **Vocabulary and Spelling Handbook,** pages R68 and R72.

**ⓒ** Use the book's graphic aids, such as illustrations, diagrams, and captions, to clarify your understanding of the text.

**ⓓ** Take notes as you read. Use text features such as **subheadings** and boldfaced terms to help you organize your notes. Use graphic organizers, such as cause-effect charts, to help you clarify relationships among ideas.

---

#### PRACTICE AND APPLY

1. How would you find the definition of *pyroclastic*?

2. Where on the page can you find out the names of different composite volcanoes?

3. Use the text to answer the second question in the Section Review.

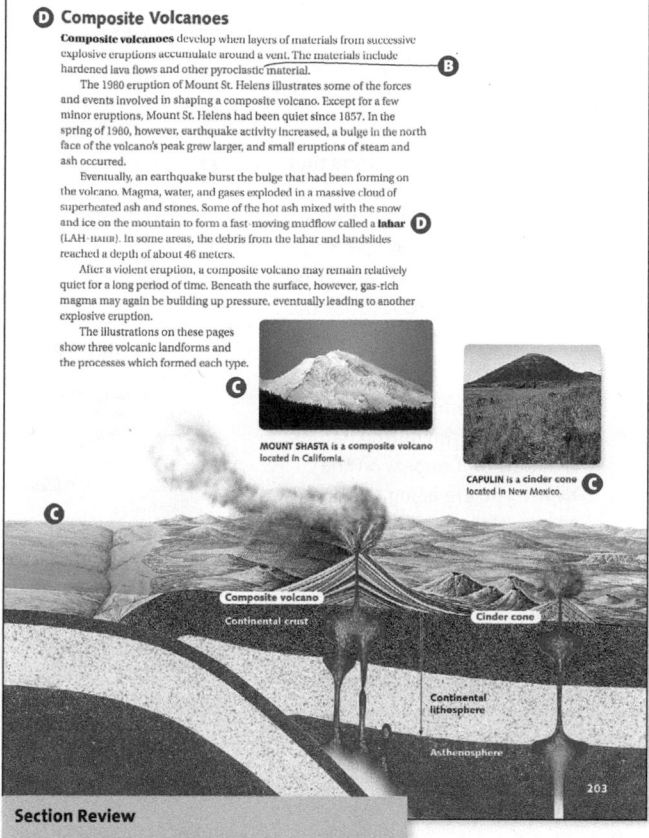

**ⓓ** **Composite Volcanoes**

**Composite volcanoes** develop when layers of materials from successive explosive eruptions accumulate around a vent. The materials include hardened lava flows and other pyroclastic material. **ⓑ**

The 1980 eruption of Mount St. Helens illustrates some of the forces and events involved in shaping a composite volcano. Except for a few minor eruptions, Mount St. Helens had been quiet since 1857. In the spring of 1980, however, earthquake activity increased, a bulge in the north face of the volcano's peak grew larger, and small eruptions of steam and ash occurred.

Eventually, an earthquake burst the bulge that had been forming on the volcano. Magma, water, and gases exploded in a massive cloud of superheated ash and stones. Some of the hot ash mixed with the snow and ice on the mountain to form a fast-moving mudflow called a **lahar** **ⓓ** (LAH-HAHR). In some areas, the debris from the lahar and landslides reached a depth of about 46 meters.

After a violent eruption, a composite volcano may remain relatively quiet for a long period of time. Beneath the surface, however, gas-rich magma may again be building up pressure, eventually leading to another explosive eruption.

The illustrations on these pages show three volcanic landforms and the processes which formed each type. **ⓒ**

**MOUNT SHASTA** is a composite volcano located in California.

**CAPULIN** is a cinder cone located in New Mexico. **ⓒ**

Composite volcano
Continental crust
Cinder cone
Continental lithosphere
Asthenosphere

203

**ⓐ** **Section Review**

• Compare and contrast the ways in which shield volcanoes and cinder cones are formed.

• **Critical Thinking** Describe the formation of a composite volcano.

• **Writing** The eruption of Mount Rainier, a composite volcano, could pose a serious threat to local residents. Write a description of the potential hazards that people living near Mount Rainier might face.

---

## PRACTICE AND APPLY

### ANSWERS

1. *Possible answers: using context clues; looking up the word in a glossary of the textbook; looking for the word in a dictionary*

2. *Possible answers: in the main text of the section titled "Composite Volcanoes"; in the captions on the graphic aids; in the Section Review*

3. *Possible answer: Gas-rich magma builds up pressure, eventually causing an explosive eruption. Material from that eruption, such as hardened lava flows and other pyroclastic material, accumulates around the vent at the top of the volcano to form layers.*

### 4.3 READING A CONSUMER DOCUMENT

**Consumer documents** are printed materials that accompany products and services. They usually provide information about the use, care, operation, or assembly of the products they accompany. Some common consumer documents are contracts, warranties, manuals, instructions, and schedules. Two examples of consumer documents follow.

#### Strategies for Reading

**Ⓐ** Read the **subheadings** to learn what process each section of the instructions explains.

**Ⓑ** Look for **numbers** or **letters** that indicate the order in which the steps should be followed. If you do not find letters or numbers, look for signal words such as *first*, *next*, *then*, and *finally* to see the order in which the steps should be followed.

**Ⓒ** Words that appear in **all capital letters** are often button names or labels that appear on the device you are being shown how to use. If there is an illustration or diagram, try to match the capitalized words in the instructions to words or symbols in the graphic aid.

**Ⓓ** Look for **verbs that describe actions** you should take, such as *press*, *select*, *set*, and *turn*.

**Ⓔ** Pay attention to **warnings** or **notes** that describe potential problems.

---

**INSTRUCTIONS FOR OPERATING A TELEVISION REMOTE CONTROL**

**Ⓐ** **SETTING THE SLEEP TIMER**

**Ⓑ** 1. Press the MENU key. The Setup menu will appear on your television.

**Ⓒ** 2. Select the Timer Setup on your screen by using the UP/DOWN arrows on your remote control.

3. Now press the RIGHT or LEFT arrow. A menu of the Timer Setup will appear on the screen.

4. Sleep Timer: Use the RIGHT/LEFT arrows to program the length of time until the TV shuts down. You can select any time from ten minutes to four hours. Press ENTER to return to TV viewing.

**Ⓐ** **SETTING THE ON/OFF TIMER**

5. Follow steps 1–3 above to get to the Timer Setup menu. Using the UP/DOWN arrows on the remote control, select On Time on your screen.

**Ⓒ** 6. Press the RIGHT or LEFT arrow to adjust the time your television will turn on automatically.

**Ⓓ** 7. Press the TIMER button to choose either A.M. or P.M.

8. Repeat steps 5–7 to set Off Time. Use the UP/DOWN arrows to select the On/Off Timer, and activate the timer by pressing a RIGHT/LEFT arrow.

**Ⓔ** **WARNING:** The On/Off Timer will not work until the clock on your television has been set.

---

**PRACTICE AND APPLY**

Reread the page from the manual for a television remote control and then answer the following questions:

1. What do these instructions explain how to do?

2. According to the instructions, what happens when the Enter button is pressed?

3. What button allows the user to select A.M. or P.M.?

---

## PRACTICE AND APPLY

### ANSWERS

1. *The instructions show how to set the sleep timer and how to set the on/off timer using a television remote control.*

2. *When the ENTER button is pressed, the remote allows you to exit the menu and return to TV viewing.*

3. *the TIMER button*

The instructions on this page are from a manual for operating a graphing calculator.

### Strategies for Reading

**Ⓐ** Read the **heading** to learn the kind of operation this section of the manual explains.

**Ⓑ** Look at any **introductory text** to get an overview of what the numbered steps will cover.

**Ⓒ** Look for **numbers** that indicate the order in which the steps should be followed.

**Ⓓ** Look for **verbs that describe actions** you should take, such as *press, position,* and *select.*

**Ⓔ** Examine **graphic aids** that illustrate steps. If you have trouble completing the process, the graphic aids can help you pinpoint what you are doing wrong.

---

**INSTRUCTIONS FOR OPERATING A GRAPHING CALCULATOR**

**Ⓐ** Zooming on the Graph

**Ⓑ** You can magnify the viewing WINDOW around a specific location by using the ZOOM instructions, thus making it easier to help identify maximums, minimums, roots, and intersections of functions.

1. Press ZOOM to display the ZOOM menu.

   This menu is typical of TI-82 menus. To select an item, you may either press the number to the left of the item, or you may press ▼ until the item number is highlighted and then press ENTER.

   **Ⓔ**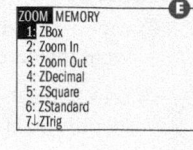

   ```
   ZOOM MEMORY
   1: ZBox
   2: Zoom In
   3: Zoom Out
   4: ZDecimal
   5: ZSquare
   6: ZStandard
   7↓ZTrig
   ```

**Ⓒ** 2. To zoom in, press 2. The graph is displayed again. The cursor has changed to indicate that you are using a ZOOM instruction.

   X=37.234043     Y=411290.32

**Ⓓ** 3. Use ◀, ▲, ▶, and ▼ to position the cursor near the maximum value of the function and press ENTER.

   The new viewing WINDOW is displayed. It has been adjusted in both the X and Y directions by factors of 4, the values for ZOOM factors.

   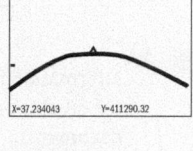

   X=37.234043     Y=411290.32

4. Press WINDOW to display the new WINDOW settings.

   ```
   WINDOW FORMAT
   Xmin=-24.734042...
   Xmax=49.734042...
   Xscl=10
   Ymin=-348790.32...
   Ymax=473790.32...
   Yscl=100000
   ```

---

### PRACTICE AND APPLY

Reread the page from the manual and then answer the following questions:

1. What does this page explain how to do?

2. According to the instructions, how do you select a menu item?

3. What key should you press to zoom in?

4. What key should you press to display new window settings?

Refer to the documents on pages R16–R17 to answer the following questions.

5. Compare the document on page R16 with the document on this page. In terms of text features and organization, are they more alike or more different? Support your answer.

6. Do you think the directions for the remote control would be clearer if the steps below "Setting the On/Off Timer" were also numbered 1–4? Why or why not?

---

## PRACTICE AND APPLY

### ANSWERS

1. *This page gives instructions that explain how to use a graphing calculator to zoom in on a graph.*

2. *Press the number of the item; press the down arrow to highlight the item, then press ENTER.*

3. *Press the "2" key.*

4. *Press the WINDOW key.*

5. *Possible answers: The documents are more different than they are alike. While both documents provide numbers to show the steps involved, the graphing calculator document appears more organized and easier to follow. For example, in the graphing calculator document, each step is accompanied by a visual representation that helps the reader see what is actually happening. The graphing calculator document also uses less text than the television remote document to explain each step. Finally, whereas the visuals on the calculator document are well-organized and help the reader understand each step, the image of the remote control is not very useful.*

6. *Possible answer: Yes, if the steps were numbered 1–4, readers would recognize the two sets of directions as two separate functions.*

**Public documents** are documents that are written for the public to provide information that is of public interest or concern. These documents are often free. They can be federal, state, or local government documents. They can be speeches or historical documents. They may even be laws, posted warnings, signs, or rules and regulations. The following is one type of public document.

*Strategies for Reading*

**A** Look at the **title** to determine what the document is about.

**B** Look for **subheadings** to identify main ideas and topics and to determine how the document is organized.

**C** Read the body of the document and examine any **illustrations** or other **graphic aids.** Think about how the text and the images are related.

**D** Check the document to find information on how to contact the creator or source of the document.

**A Rules of the Road for Cyclists**
Follow these rules when you are bicycling in our area.

**B** Be Visible

Don't Ride Against Traffic: Motorists may not see you on the wrong side of the road.

Use Hand Signals: These let drivers know what you plan to do. Be polite—and be safer, too!

Protect Yourself: Local laws require you to wear a helmet while cycling. If you are riding at night, your bike must have a headlight and a rear reflector.

**B** Ride Defensively

Watch for Vehicles: Cars and trucks may pull out suddenly.

Obey Traffic Signs and Signals: They apply to you as well as to drivers. For example, don't go straight in a lane marked "Right Turn Only."

Don't Weave Between Parked Cars: Drivers may not see you as you move back into traffic.

Thank you for being a courteous cyclist!
**D** Buena Vista County Parks Department (602) 555-6367 www.buenavistacounty.az.gov/parksdept
Para los hispanohablantes, llame por favor a (602) 555-6388.

**PRACTICE AND APPLY**

Refer to the document shown to answer the following questions.

1. Into what two subtopics is the information organized? What are the central ideas covered within each subtopic?

2. What appears to be the purpose of this document?

3. Many people may find the rules of the road for cyclists easier to follow than the directions for operating a TV remote control on page R16 or those for operating a graphing calculator on page R17. How do the text features used in "Rules of the Road for Cyclists" make it effective in accomplishing its objective of communicating safety information? In your answer, be sure to address each of the following features:
   - graphic aids
   - subheadings
   - use of color
   - arrangement of words and visuals on the page

*For more information, see Reading Informational Texts: Text Features, pages R3–R7.*

## PRACTICE AND APPLY

## ANSWERS

1. *The two subtopics are "Be Visible" and "Ride Defensively." The central ideas covered in the first subtopic include riding against traffic, using hand signals, and protecting oneself. In the second subtopic, the central ideas include watching for vehicles, obeying traffic signs and signals, and weaving between cars.*

2. *The purpose of the document is to explain the rules of riding bicycles on the road.*

3. *Possible answers: The illustrations are simple but help illustrate the point of each rule. The subheadings divide the rules into two categories. The use of color makes it easier to skim the subheadings and main ideas. The arrangement of words and visuals makes it easier to visualize and understand each rule.*

## 4.5 READING A WORKPLACE DOCUMENT

**Workplace documents** are materials that are produced or used within a workplace, usually to aid in the functioning of a business. These may be documents generated by a business to monitor itself, such as minutes of a meeting or a sales report. These documents may also explain company policies, organizational structures, and operating procedures. Workplace documents include memos, business letters, job applications, and résumés.

### Strategies for Reading

**Ⓐ** Read a workplace document slowly and carefully, as it may contain **details** that should not be overlooked.

**Ⓑ** Notice how to contact the creator of the document. You will need this information to clear up anything that you don't understand.

**Ⓒ** **Take notes** to help you remember times, dates, deadlines, and actions required. In particular, note whether you are expected to respond to the document, whether there is a deadline for your response, and to whom you should address your reply.

### PRACTICE AND APPLY

Refer to both workplace documents to answer the following questions:

1. Why might the letter from Fred Fenton be classified as a workplace document?

2. According to the details in Fenton's letter, what actions should the yearbook staff take?

3. How does the author of the memo use text features, such as graphics and headings, to get his message across clearly and quickly?

4. What actions is the recipient of the memo expected to take?

LETTER

**Ⓑ Famous Fred's Bike Store**
7451 East Trenton Boulevard
Asheville, NC 28804
voice (408) 555-BIKE
fax (408) 555-3658
info@famousfreds.net

January 14, 2010  **Ⓐ**

Yearbook Staff
James Madison High School
300 Elmwood Avenue
Asheville, NC 28804

Dear Yearbook Staff:

**Ⓒ** I would like to buy an advertisement in your upcoming yearbook. Would you call me at the above number to discuss the layout and cost of the ad? I also need to know whether you require camera-ready copy **Ⓐ** and art, plus the total measurement, in inches or picas, of a full-page ad. I look forward to hearing from you.  **Ⓒ**

Yours truly,

*Fred Fenton*

Fred Fenton

MEMO

**To:** Rayna Jordan
**Ⓑ From:** Mr. Jeff Kniffen, Yearbook Adviser
**Re:** Customer Letter
**Date:** January 21, 2010

**Ⓒ** Rayna, please call Mr. Fenton with the prices for the ads for the yearbook. The chart below shows the price breakdown.

| Size of ad | Price |
|---|---|
| 1/4 page (3 1/2" W x 5" H) | $75.00 |
| 1/2 page (7 1/2" W x 5" H) | $125.00 |
| 1 full page (7 1/2" W x 10" H) | $200.00 |

Also, let him know that we do need camera-ready copy and art. Don't forget to tell him what the deadlines are for submitting the ad and paying for it.  **Ⓐ**

Thanks.

READING HANDBOOK  **R19**

## PRACTICE AND APPLY

### ANSWERS

1. **Possible answer:** The letter can be classified as a workplace document because it is written in the form of a business letter, including a business address, date, greeting, body, and closing.

2. The letter asks the yearbook staff to call Mr. Fenton with the price of a full-page ad, the requirements for the copy and art, and the measurements of a full-page ad.

3. **Possible answer:** The author uses a graphic aid to organize important information and to make it stand out from the rest of the text. The headings help the reader scan for information that pertains to the price and measurement of each ad.

4. **Possible answer:** The recipient is expected to call Mr. Fenton with the price of each ad, inform him about camera-ready copy and art, and mention the deadline and payment schedule for submitting ads.

1. *http://www.nasa.gov/home/index.html*

2. *The menu bar on the top left side of the Web page provides information for different audiences.*

3. *Click the hyperlink "View Article" under "World Book @ NASA Feature Topic."*

## 4.6 READING ELECTRONIC TEXT

**Electronic text** is any text that is in a form that a computer can store and display on a screen. Electronic text can be part of Web pages, CD-ROMs, search engines, and documents that you create with your computer software. Like books, Web pages often provide aids for finding information. However, each Web page is designed differently, and information is not in the same location on each page. It is important to know the functions of different parts of a Web page so that you can easily find the information you want.

### Strategies for Reading

**A** Look at the **title** of a page to determine what topics it covers.

**B** For an online source, such as a Web page or search engine, note the **Web address,** known as a **URL** (Uniform Resource Locator). You may want to make a note of it if you need to return to that page.

**C** Look for a **menu bar** along the top, bottom, or side of a Web page. Clicking on an item in a menu bar will take you to another part of the Web site.

**D** Notice any hyperlinks to related pages. **Hyperlinks** are often underlined or highlighted in a contrasting color. You can click on a hyperlink to get to another page—one that may or may not have been created by the same person or organization.

**E** For information that you want to keep for future reference, save documents on your computer or print them. For online sources, you can pull down the **Favorites** or **Bookmarks** menu and bookmark pages so that you can easily return to them or print the information you need. Printing the pages will allow you to highlight key ideas on a hard copy.

### PRACTICE AND APPLY

1. What is the URL of the Web page shown?

2. How do you know that the Web site has information for different audiences?

3. What would you do to view an article about astronauts?

# 5 Reading Persuasive Texts

## 5.1 ANALYZING AN ARGUMENT

An **argument** expresses a position on an issue or problem and supports it with reasons and evidence. Being able to analyze and evaluate arguments will help you distinguish between claims you should accept and those you should not. A sound argument should appeal strictly to reason. However, arguments are often used in texts that also contain other types of persuasive devices. An argument includes the following elements:

- A **claim** (or **thesis** or **controlling idea**) is the writer's position on an issue or problem.

- **Support** is any material that serves to prove a claim. In an argument, support usually consists of reasons and evidence.

- **Reasons** are declarations made to justify an action, decision, or belief—for example, "My reason for thinking we will be late is that we can't make it to the appointment in five minutes."

- **Evidence** is the specific references, quotations, facts, examples, and opinions that support a claim. Evidence may also consist of statistics, reports of personal experience, or the views of experts.

- **Counterarguments** and **counterclaims** are arguments made to oppose other arguments. A good argument anticipates opposing counterclaims by providing counterarguments to answer them.

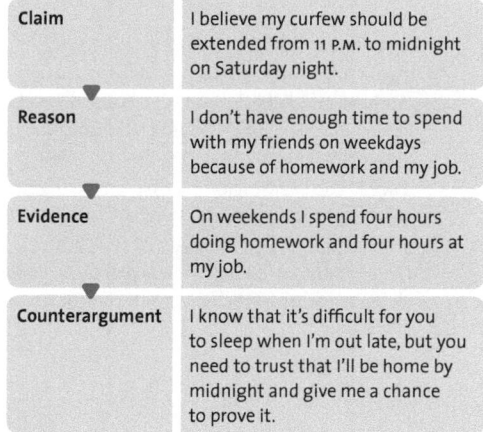

| Claim | I believe my curfew should be extended from 11 P.M. to midnight on Saturday night. |
| --- | --- |
| Reason | I don't have enough time to spend with my friends on weekdays because of homework and my job. |
| Evidence | On weekends I spend four hours doing homework and four hours at my job. |
| Counterargument | I know that it's difficult for you to sleep when I'm out late, but you need to trust that I'll be home by midnight and give me a chance to prove it. |

Read the following editorial and use a chart like the one shown to identify the claim, reason, evidence, and counterargument.

On the second Monday in October, Americans celebrate Columbus Day. We honor the Italian explorer who has been credited with discovering the Americas in 1492. Some people, however, think that we need to look more closely at what Christopher Columbus actually did and at his place in our history. I am one of those people.

First of all, although we honor Columbus as the first European to set foot in the Americas, he may not have been the first. Archaeologists have found Norse ruins in Greenland and what is now Newfoundland, dating from around A.D. 1000. This evidence seems to prove that Vikings actually reached the North American continent nearly 500 years before Columbus ever left the shores of Spain.

Second, although Columbus did reach the Americas, he did not discover them. Millions of people were already living here when he arrived.

Defenders of Columbus argue that, in a way, he did discover the Americas. Even if he wasn't the first person, or even the first European, to set foot on the land, his voyages made the rest of the world aware of the Americas. In the years following Columbus' voyages, Europeans came to establish colonies and to explore the land.

I argue that this spread of culture brought great harm as well as great good to the Americas. The Europeans who came to the Americas brought deadly diseases with them. The native people had no immunity to such diseases as mumps, measles, smallpox, and typhus. As a result, hundreds of thousands of them died.

In conclusion, I don't suggest that people should boycott their local Columbus Day parades. I do think, though, that we should create a more balanced picture of the man we're honoring.

## PRACTICE AND APPLY
## ANSWERS

*Students should create a chart like the one on page R21. The chart should include details similar to the ones below.*

*Claim: We need to look more closely at what Christopher Columbus actually did and his place in our history.*

*Reason: We honor Columbus as the first European to set foot in the Americas when he may not have been the first.*

*Evidence: Archaeologists found Norse ruins in Greenland and in what is now Newfoundland, dating from A.D. 1000. This evidence seems to prove that Vikings reached North America almost 500 years before Columbus.*

*Evidence: Although Columbus did reach the Americas, he did not discover them. Millions of people were already living here when he arrived.*

*Counterargument: Even though he may not have been the first European to set foot on American soil, Columbus' voyages made the rest of the world aware of the Americas.*

## PRACTICE AND APPLY

### ANSWERS

**Appeals by Association:** *snob appeal; appeal to loyalty; testimonial*

**Emotional Appeals:** *appeal to vanity, appeal to patriotism*

**Word Choice:** *glittering generality*

---

### 5.2 RECOGNIZING PERSUASIVE TECHNIQUES

Argumentative texts typically rely on more than just the logical appeal of an argument to be convincing. They also rely on **persuasive techniques**—devices that can sway you to adopt a position or take an action. Persuasive techniques are used in advertising, political speeches, films, and fundraisers. The chart shown here explains several ways a writer may attempt to sway you to adopt his or her position. Learn to recognize these techniques, and you will be less likely to be influenced by them.

| Persuasive Technique | Example |
|---|---|
| **Appeals by Association** | |
| **Bandwagon appeal** Uses the argument that a person should believe or do something because "everyone else" does | More and more people are making the switch to Discountline long-distance service. |
| **Testimonial** Relies on endorsements from well-known people or satisfied customers | Pierre DuPont, world-class rock climber, would be left hanging without DuraTwine rope. |
| **Snob appeal** Taps into people's desire to be special or part of an elite group | Treat yourself to Tropical Paradise because, after all, you deserve the best under the sun. |
| **Transfer** Connects a product, candidate, or cause with a positive emotion or idea | Freedom . . . you can feel it the instant you put your hands on the wheel of a Farnsworth 4 × 4 SL. |
| **Appeal to loyalty** Relies on people's affiliation with a particular group | This car is made in America by Americans. |
| **Emotional Appeals** | |
| **Appeals to pity, fear, or vanity** Use strong feelings, rather than facts, to persuade | Without more police, we'll be at the mercy of thieves. |
| **Word Choice** | |
| **Glittering generality** Makes a generalization that includes a word or phrase with positive connotations to promote a product or idea. | A vote for Evan Smith is a vote for democracy. |

Identify the persuasive techniques used in the model.

#### Indiana and Issun Boshi— Building Another Great Team

Indiana is basketball country. Names like Bobby Knight, Larry Bird, and Isiah Thomas have added greatness to the game for over a quarter century.

That's why Issun Boshi, Japan's leading automobile company, chose Indiana as its U.S. teammate. The new plant will produce 150,000 new vehicles a year, built by 25,000 hard-working Hoosiers just like you. In addition, many of those workers will be driving the cars they make at a special discount—that's only fair; that's the American way. It's how we play the game.

Just ask Indiana sportscaster Wally Elliot, who says, "Issun Boshi and Hoosier pride—now that's what I call an expansion team."

### 5.3 ANALYZING LOGIC AND REASONING

When you evaluate an argument, you need to look closely at the writer's logic and reasoning. To do this, it is helpful to identify the type of reasoning the writer is using.

#### The Inductive Mode of Reasoning

When a writer leads from specific evidence to a general principle or generalization, that writer is using **inductive reasoning.** Here is an example of inductive reasoning.

##### SPECIFIC FACTS

**Fact 1** The American Society of Composers, Authors, and Publishers (ASCAP) was formed on Friday, February 13, 1914, to collect royalties on copyrighted music.

**Fact 2** The licensing of the first female flight instructor took place on Friday, October 13, 1939.

**Fact 3** On Friday, February 13, 1948, Orville Wright announced that he was giving the famous flying machine *Kitty Hawk* to the Smithsonian Institution.

##### GENERALIZATION

Good things can happen on Friday the 13th.

## Strategies for Evaluating Inductive Arguments

Ask yourself the following questions to evaluate an inductive argument:

- **Is the evidence credible and of sufficient quality to support the conclusion?** Inaccurate facts lead to inaccurate conclusions.

- **Does the conclusion follow logically from the evidence?** From the facts listed in the previous example, the conclusion that good things happen only on Friday the 13th would be too broad a generalization.

- **Is the evidence drawn from a large enough sample?** Even though there are only three facts listed above, the sample is large enough to support the claim. If you wanted to support the conclusion that only good things happen on Friday the 13th, the sample is not large enough.

### *The Deductive Mode of Reasoning*

When a writer arrives at a conclusion by applying a general principle to a specific situation, the writer is using **deductive reasoning.** Here's an example.

| Journalism that stretches the truth is deceptive. | General principle or premise |
|---|---|

| *Hollywood Snoop Magazine* stretches the truth. | Specific situation |
|---|---|

| *Hollywood Snoop Magazine* practices deceptive journalism. | Specific conclusion |
|---|---|

## Strategies for Evaluating Deductive Arguments

Ask yourself the following questions to evaluate a deductive argument:

- **Is the general principle actually stated, or is it implied?** Note that writers often use deductive reasoning in an argument without stating the general principle. They just assume that readers will recognize and agree with the principle. So you may want to identify the general principle for yourself.

- **Is the general principle sound?** Don't just assume the general principle is sound. Ask yourself whether it is really true.

- **Is the conclusion valid?** To be valid, a conclusion in a deductive argument must follow logically from the general principle and the specific situation.

The following chart shows two conclusions drawn from the same general principle.

| All team members wore school colors on Friday. | |
|---|---|
| **Accurate Deduction** | **Inaccurate Deduction** |
| Mara is on the volleyball team; therefore, Mara wore school colors on Friday. | Jaime wore school colors on Friday; therefore, Jaime is on a school team. |

Jaime could have worn school colors in support of a team without being a member.

### PRACTICE AND APPLY

Identify the mode of reasoning used in the following paragraph.

> . . . America has digitized, and there's no going back. Worldwide there are almost 200 million people on the Internet. In the United States alone, 80 million. . . . A third of wired Americans now do at least some of their shopping on the Net, and some are already consulting doctors on the Net, listening to radio on the Net, making investments on the Net, getting mortgages on the Net. . . . Each of these activities is impressive, but the aggregate effect is a different kind of life.
> —*Newsweek,* September 20, 1999

## PRACTICE AND APPLY

### ANSWER

*Deductive reasoning*

## Identifying Faulty Reasoning

Sometimes an argument at first appears to make sense but isn't valid because it is **fallacious,** or based on a fallacy. A **fallacy** is an error in logic. Learn to recognize these common fallacies.

| TYPE OF FALLACY | DEFINITION | EXAMPLE |
|---|---|---|
| Circular reasoning | Supporting a statement by simply repeating it in different words | Teenagers should avoid fad diets, because it is important for **adolescents to stay away from popular weight-loss plans.** |
| Either/or fallacy | A statement that suggests that there are only two choices available in a situation that really offers more than two options | **Either** students should be allowed to leave school to have lunch at nearby fast-food restaurants, **or** they should be allowed to choose the cafeteria menu. |
| Oversimplification | An explanation of a complex situation or problem as if it were much simpler than it is | Making the team depends on **whether the coach likes you.** |
| Overgeneralization | A generalization that is too broad. You can often recognize overgeneralizations by the use of words such as *all, everyone, every time, anything, no one,* and *none.* | **No one** cares that there is not enough parking downtown. |
| Stereotyping | A dangerous type of overgeneralization. Stereotypes are broad statements about people on the basis of their gender, ethnicity, race, or political, social, professional, or religious group. | The only thing **the members of that political party** care about is big business. |
| Attacking the person or name-calling | An attempt to discredit an idea by attacking the person or group associated with it. Candidates often engage in name-calling during political campaigns. | **My opponent is not smart enough** to be mayor. |
| Evading the issue | Refuting an objection with arguments and evidence that do not address its central point | Yes, I broke my campaign promise not to raise taxes, **but higher taxes have led to increases in police patrols, paved highways, and smaller class size in schools.** |
| Non sequitur | A statement that uses irrelevant "proof" to support a claim. A non sequitur is sometimes used to win an argument by diverting the reader's attention to proof that can't be challenged. | I know I'll pass math. **Mr. Gray is my math teacher and my football coach.** |
| False cause | The mistake of assuming that because one event occurred after another event in time, the first event caused the second one to occur | The mayor declared a get-tough crime policy, and sure enough, **crime rates dropped.** |
| False analogy | A comparison that doesn't hold up because of a critical difference between the two subjects | She walks to the store and back every day, **so surely she can walk in the 10K race.** |
| Hasty generalization | A conclusion drawn from too little evidence or from evidence that is biased | That corner must be dangerous. **There were two car accidents there last week.** |

Look for examples of logical fallacies in the following argument. Identify each one and explain why you identified it as such.

> Watching television causes a child's grades to drop. What other conclusion can be drawn? Money-hungry media moguls produce horrible programming just to sell advertising time. These programs interfere with children's thinking. If you say television isn't bad for children, you would probably say the earth is flat. Parents who care should at least limit their children's viewing. The most responsible parents should turn off the TV—permanently. They can either unplug the TV or expect their children to become uneducated slugs.

## 5.4 EVALUATING PERSUASIVE TEXTS

Learning how to evaluate a text's arguments and identify bias will help you become more selective when doing research and also help you improve your own reasoning and arguing skills. **Bias** is an inclination for or against a particular opinion or viewpoint. A writer may reveal a strongly positive or negative opinion on an issue by presenting only one way of looking at it or by heavily weighting the evidence on one side of the argument. Additionally, the presence of either of the following is often a sign that a writer is biased:

**Loaded language** consists of words with strongly positive or negative connotations that are intended to influence a reader's attitude.

EXAMPLE: *The safety of our children depends on our driving the savage criminals out of this horrible neighborhood.* (*Savage* and *horrible* have very negative connotations.)

**Propaganda** is any form of communication that is so distorted that it conveys false or misleading information. Some politicians create and distribute propaganda. Logical fallacies are often used in propaganda. For instance, the following example shows an oversimplification. The writer uses one fact to support a particular point of view but does not reveal another fact that does not support that viewpoint.

EXAMPLE: *Since the new park opened, vandalism in the area has increased by 10 percent. Clearly, the park has had a negative impact on the area.* (The writer does not include the fact that the vandalism was caused by people who were not drawn into the area by the park.)

*For more information, see* **Identifying Faulty Reasoning,** *page R24.*

### Strategies for Evaluating Evidence

It is important to have a set of standards by which you can evaluate persuasive texts. Use the questions below to help you critically assess facts and opinions that are presented as evidence to support or oppose an argument.

- **Are the facts presented credible and thus verifiable?** Facts can be proved by eyewitness accounts, authoritative sources such as encyclopedias and almanacs, experts, or research.

- **Are the opinions presented well substantiated?** Any opinions offered should be supported by facts, be based on research or eyewitness accounts, or be the opinions of experts on the topic.

- **Is the evidence relevant and sufficient?** Relevant evidence applies to the conclusion, and sufficient evidence leaves no reasonable questions unanswered. If a choice is offered, background for making the choice should be provided. If taking a side is called for, all sides of the issue should be presented.

- **Is the evidence biased?** Be alert to evidence that contains loaded language or other signs of bias.

- **Is the evidence authoritative?** The people, groups, or organizations that provided the evidence should have credentials that support their authority.

- **Is it important that the evidence be current?** Where timeliness is crucial, as in the areas of medicine and technology, the evidence should reflect the latest developments in the areas.

## PRACTICE AND APPLY ANSWERS

*Possible answers:*

1. *Oversimplification:* "Watching television causes a child's grades to drop." **Explanation:** *The explanation for the problem, a drop in children's grades, is oversimplified. Not all children's grades drop.*

2. **Attacking the Person or Name-Calling:** "Money-hungry media moguls produce horrible programming." **Explanation:** *The writer is attempting to discredit media moguls by attacking them and using harsh language.*

3. *False Analogy:* "If you say television isn't bad for children, you would probably say the earth is flat." **Explanation:** *The writer compares two subjects that have nothing in common.*

4. *Either/Or Fallacy and Stereotyping:* "They can either unplug the TV or expect their children to become uneducated slugs." **Explanation:** *The either/or fallacy suggests that there is only one alternative to watching television (unplugging the TV). The term uneducated slug is a stereotype of children who watch television.*

## PRACTICE AND APPLY

### ANSWERS

*Possible answers:*

*Facts: A study by economists William Landes and Lewis Solomon found little evidence to show that compulsory attendance laws increase attendance rates.*

*Opinions: Kids who are forced to be in school because of attendance laws are to blame for the reduced quality of instruction in school. Poor attenders are almost always failing. The ability to expel students contributes to a positive climate in schools.*

*Elements of bias: "Why are students who show up late for tests, fill in answers randomly, and then snooze for the rest of the period allowed to jeopardize school test scores and reduce the quality of instruction for motivated kids?" "Why not tell poor attenders . . . 'You're done. You don't belong here.'"*

## PRACTICE AND APPLY

### ANSWERS

*Students' responses will vary, but they should evaluate the strength of the claim, the evidence supporting the claim, and the counterclaims:*

*Possible answers: Overall, the editorial does not illustrate a very strong argument. The claim—that animal testing is unnecessary and cruel and that it must be stopped—reveals a heavily biased opinion. The writer uses words and phrases with a negative connotation and emotional or biased tone (for example, "unnecessary, cruel," and "must be stopped"). In addition, many of the statements presented as facts are inappropriate and not supported by sufficient evidence. Finally, the author does not adequately refute opposing claims with logical arguments or evidence. Instead, the writer engages in name-calling and faulty reasoning.*

---

Read the argument below. Identify the facts, opinion, and elements of bias.

> Why are students who show up late for tests, fill in answers randomly, and then snooze for the rest of the period allowed to jeopardize school test scores and reduce the quality of instruction for motivated kids? The answer is simple—compulsory attendance laws. These laws say that kids must be in school. But a study by economists William Landes and Lewis Solomon found little evidence that such laws increase attendance rates at all. Why not tell poor attenders, who are almost always failing too, "You're done. You don't belong here." Private schools do it, and the ability to expel students contributes to a positive climate.

### Strategies for Determining a Strong Argument

Make sure that all or most of the following statements are true:

- The argument presents a claim or controlling idea.
- The claim is connected to its support by a general principle that most readers would readily agree with. Valid general principle: *It is the job of a school to provide a well-rounded physical education program.* Invalid general principle: *It is the job of a school to produce healthy, physically fit people.*
- The reasons make sense.
- The reasons are presented in a logical and effective order.
- The claim and all reasons are adequately supported by sound evidence.
- The evidence is sufficient, credible, and relevant.
- The logic is sound. There are no instances of faulty reasoning.
- The argument adequately anticipates and addresses reader concerns and counterclaims with counterarguments.

---

Use the preceding criteria to evaluate the strength of the following editorial.

> According to veterinarian and animal-rights advocate Dr. Michael W. Fox, more than 100 million animals are used each year in laboratory tests. These animals are used to study such things as the causes and effects of illnesses and to test drugs. This unnecessary and cruel animal testing must be stopped.
>
> The most important reason to stop this testing is that it's wrong to make living creatures suffer. Even though they can't talk or use tools as people do, animals have feelings. Zoologist Ann Speirs says that animals may suffer even more than people do, because they can't understand what's happening to them.
>
> People who favor animal research argue that the medical advances gained justify animal experimentation. They also say that the suffering experienced by the animals is minor. People like that are dumber than any guinea pig or rat.
>
> Another important reason to stop this testing is that everybody knows it isn't reliable. Many drugs that help animals are harmful to people. One example is the drug thalidomide. After it was tested in animals in the 1950s and early 1960s, it was given to pregnant women. More than 10,000 of these women gave birth to handicapped babies. The process works the other way, too. Many drugs that help people kill animals. Two common examples are penicillin and aspirin.
>
> Animal testing also affects the environment. The Animal Protection Service says that a quarter of a million chimpanzees, monkeys, and baboons are taken from their natural homes and used in laboratory experiments every year. Those animals will never be able to reproduce, and whole species may become extinct.
>
> A final reason for not using animals in experiments is that there are other research methods available. Two examples are using bits of animal tissue and cells and using computer models.
>
> In conclusion, animal testing has to stop because it just can't go on.

---

# 6 Adjusting Reading Rate to Purpose

You may need to change the way you read certain texts in order to understand what you read. To properly adjust the way you read, you need to be aware of what you want to get out of what you are reading. Once you know your purpose for reading, you can adjust the speed at which you read in response to your purpose and the difficulty of the material.

## Determine Your Purpose for Reading

You read different types of materials for different purposes. You may read a novel for enjoyment. You may read a textbook unit to learn a new concept or to master the content for a test. When you read for enjoyment, you naturally read at a pace that is comfortable for you. When you read for information, you need to read material more slowly and thoroughly. When you are being tested on material, you may think you have to read fast, especially if the test is being timed. However, you can actually increase your understanding of the material if you slow down.

## Determine Your Reading Rate

The rate at which you read most comfortably is called your **independent reading level.** It is the rate that you use to read materials that you enjoy. To learn to adjust your reading rate to read materials for other purposes, you need to be aware of your independent reading level. You can figure out your reading level by following these steps:

1. Select a passage from a book or story you enjoy.
2. Have a friend or classmate time you as you begin reading the passage silently.
3. Read at the rate that is most comfortable for you.
4. Stop when your friend or classmate tells you one minute has passed.
5. Determine the number of words you read in that minute and write down the number.
6. Repeat the process at least two more times, using different passages.
7. Add the numbers and divide the sum by the number of times your friend timed you.

## Reading Techniques for Informational Material

Use the following techniques to adapt your reading for informational texts, to prepare for tests, and to better understand what you read:

- **Skimming** is reading quickly to get the general idea of a text. To skim, read only the title, headings, graphic aids, highlighted words, and first sentence of each paragraph. In addition, read any introduction, conclusion, or summary. Skimming can be especially useful when taking a test. Before reading a passage, you can skim questions that follow it in order to find out what is expected and better focus on the important ideas in the text.

  When researching a topic, skimming can help you determine whether a source has information that is pertinent to your topic.

- **Scanning** is reading quickly to find a specific piece of information, such as a fact or a definition. When you scan, your eyes sweep across a page, looking for key words that may lead you to the information you want. Use scanning to review for tests and to find answers to questions.

- **Changing pace** is speeding up or slowing down the rate at which you read parts of a particular text. When you come across familiar concepts, you might be able to speed up without misunderstanding them. When you encounter unfamiliar concepts or material presented in an unpredictable way, however, you may need to slow down to process and absorb the information better.

**WATCH OUT!** Reading too slowly can affect your ability to comprehend what you read. Make sure you aren't just reading one word at a time. Practice reading phrases.

### PRACTICE AND APPLY

Find an article in a magazine or textbook. Skim the article. Then answer the following questions:

1. What did you notice about the organization of the article from skimming it?

2. What is the central idea of the article?

## PRACTICE AND APPLY ANSWERS

*Accept answers that provide an accurate description of the article, its central ideas, and its organization.*

# COMMON CORE FOCUS

**W 1a-e** Write arguments to support claims in an analysis of substantive topics or texts, using valid reasoning and relevant and sufficient evidence. **W 2a-f** Write informative/explanatory texts to examine and convey complex ideas, concepts, and information clearly and accurately through the effective selection, organization, and analysis of content. **W 3a-e** Write narratives to develop real or imagined experiences or events using effective technique, well-chosen details, and well-structured event sequences. **W 4** Produce clear and coherent writing in which the development, organization, and style are appropriate to task, purpose, and audience. **W 5** Develop and strengthen writing as needed by planning, revising, editing, rewriting, or trying a new approach, focusing on addressing what is most significant for a specific purpose and audience. **W 6** Use technology, including the Internet, to produce, publish, and update individual or shared writing products taking advantage of technology's capacity to link to other information and to display information flexibly and dynamically.

*Writing is a process, a journey of discovery in which you can explore your thoughts, experiment with ideas, and search for connections. Through writing, you can explore and record your thoughts, feelings, and ideas for yourself alone or you can communicate them to an audience.*

**COMMON CORE**

Included in this handbook:
W 1a–e, W 2a–f, W 3a–e, W 4,
W 5, W 6

## 1 The Writing Process

The writing process consists of the following stages: prewriting, drafting, revising and editing, proofreading, and publishing. These are not stages that you must complete in a set order. Rather, you may return to an earlier stage at any time to improve your writing.

### 1.1 PREWRITING

In the prewriting stage, you explore what you want to write about, what your purpose for writing is, whom you are writing for, and what form you will use to express your ideas. Ask yourself the following questions to get started.

| Topic | • Is my topic assigned, or can I choose it?<br>• What would I be interested in writing about? |
|---|---|
| Purpose | • Am I writing to entertain, to inform, or to persuade—or some combination of these?<br>• What effect do I want to have on my readers? |
| Audience | • Who is the audience?<br>• What might the audience members already know about my topic?<br>• What about the topic might interest them? |
| Format | • What format will work best? Essay? Poem? Speech? Short story? Article? Research paper? |

### Find Ideas for Writing

- Browse through magazines, newspapers, and Web sites.

- Start a file of articles you want to save for future reference.

- With a group, brainstorm as many ideas as you can. Compile your ideas into a list.

- Interview someone who is an expert on a particular topic.

- Write down anything that comes into your head.

- Use a cluster map to explore subordinate ideas that relate to a general topic.

### Organize Ideas

Once you've chosen a topic, you will need to compile and organize your ideas. If you are writing a description, you may need to gather sensory details. Or you may need to record information from different sources for an essay or a research paper. To record notes from sources you read or view, use any or all of these methods:

- **Summarize:** Briefly retell the central ideas of a piece of writing in your own words.

- **Paraphrase:** Restate all or almost all of the information in your own words.

- **Quote:** Record the author's exact words.

Depending on what form your writing takes, you may also need to arrange your ideas in a certain pattern.

*For more information, see the* **Writing Handbook***, pages R34–R41.*

### 1.2 DRAFTING

In the drafting stage, you put your ideas on paper and allow them to develop and change as you write. You don't need to worry about correct grammar and spelling at this stage. There are two ways that you can draft:

**Discovery drafting** is a good approach when you are not quite sure what you think about your subject. You just start writing and let your feelings and ideas lead you in developing the topic.

**Planned drafting** may work better if you know that your ideas have to be arranged in a certain way, as in a research paper. Try making a writing plan or an informal outline before you begin drafting.

Always remember that your drafts represent an early stage of your work. During drafting you may

discover that you need to start over by trying a new approach to your topic.

### 1.3 REVISING AND EDITING

The revising and editing stage allows you to polish your draft and make changes in its content, organization, and style. Use the questions that follow to assess problems and determine what changes would improve your work:

- Does my writing have a **controlling idea** or central focus? Is my point clear?

- Have I used **precise** nouns, verbs, and modifiers?

- Have I incorporated **adequate detail** and **evidence?** Where might I include a telling detail, a revealing statistic, or a vivid example?

- Is my writing **unified?** Do all ideas and supporting details pertain to my controlling idea or advance my thesis?

- Is my writing clear and **coherent?** Is the flow of sentences and paragraphs smooth and logical?

- Have I used a consistent **point of view?**

- Do I need to add **transitional words, phrases,** or **sentences** to create cohesion and clarify and connect relationships among ideas?

- Have I used a **variety of sentence types?** Are they well constructed? What sentences might I combine to improve the rhythm of my writing?

- Have I used a **tone** appropriate for my purpose, audience, and genre?

### 1.4 PROOFREADING

When you are satisfied with your revision, proofread your paper for mistakes in grammar, usage, and mechanics. You may want to do this several times, looking for a different type of mistake each time. Use the following questions to help you correct errors:

- Have I corrected any errors in **subject-verb agreement** and **pronoun-antecedent agreement?**

- Have I double-checked for errors in **confusing word pairs,** such as *it's/its, than/then,* and *too/to?*

- Have I corrected any **run-on sentences** and **sentence fragments?**

- Have I followed rules for **correct capitalization?**

- Have I used **punctuation marks** correctly?

- Have I checked the **spellings of all unfamiliar words** in the dictionary?

**TIP** If possible, don't begin proofreading just after you've finished writing. Put your work away for at least a few hours. When you return to it, it will be easier for you to identify and correct mistakes.

*For more information, see the **Grammar Handbook** and the **Vocabulary and Spelling Handbook**, pages R46–R75.*

Use the proofreading symbols in the chart to mark changes on your draft.

| Proofreading Symbols | |
| --- | --- |
| ∧ Add letters or words. | / Make a capital letter lowercase. |
| ⊙ Add a period. | ¶ Begin a new paragraph. |
| ≡ Capitalize a letter. | ⌇ Delete letters or words. |
| ⊂ Close up space. | ∾ Switch the positions of letters or words. |
| ∧ Add a comma. | |

### 1.5 PUBLISHING AND REFLECTING

Always consider sharing your finished writing with a wider audience. Reflecting on your writing is another good way to finish a project.

**Publishing Ideas**

- Post your writing on a Weblog.

- Create a multimedia presentation and share it with classmates.

- Publish your writing in a school newspaper, local newspaper, or literary magazine.

- Present your work orally in a report, speech, reading, or dramatic performance.

**Reflecting on Your Writing**

Think about your writing process and whether you would like to add what you have written to your writing portfolio. You might attach a note in which you answer questions like these:

- Which parts of the process did I find easiest? Which parts were more difficult?

- What was the biggest problem I faced during the writing process? How did I solve the problem?

- What changes have occurred in my writing style?

- Have I noticed any features in the writing of

published authors or my peers that I can apply to my own work?

### 1.6 PEER RESPONSE

Peer response consists of the suggestions and comments you make about the writing of your peers and also the comments and suggestions they make about your writing. You can ask a peer reader for help at any time in the writing process.

#### Using Peer Response as a Writer

- Indicate whether you are more interested in feedback about your ideas or about your presentation of them.

- Ask questions that will help you get specific information about your writing. Open-ended questions that require more than yes-or-no answers are more likely to give you information you can use as you revise.

- Encourage your readers to be honest.

#### Being a Peer Reader

- Respect the writer's feelings.

- Offer positive reactions first.

- Make sure you understand what kind of feedback the writer is looking for, and then respond accordingly.

*For more information on the writing process, see the* **Introductory Unit,** *pages 20–23.*

## 2 Building Blocks of Good Writing

Whatever your purpose in writing, you need to capture your reader's interest and organize your thoughts clearly.

### 2.1 INTRODUCTIONS

An introduction should present a controlling idea or thesis statement and capture your reader's attention.

#### Kinds of Introductions

There are a number of ways to write an introduction. The one you choose depends on who the audience is and on your purpose for writing.

**Make a Surprising Statement** Beginning with a startling statement or an interesting fact can arouse your reader's curiosity about a subject, as in the following model.

> **MODEL**
>
> W. H. Auden is one of the major poets of the 20th century. Until he was 14 years old, however, Auden's greatest interests were machinery and mining. He intended to become a mining engineer.

**Provide a Description** A vivid description sets a mood and brings a scene to life for your reader.

Here, details about heating the air for a hot-air balloon set the tone for a narrative about a balloon ride.

> **MODEL**
>
> Whoosh! The red and yellow flame shot up into the great nylon cone. The warm air filled the balloon so that the cooler air below held the apparatus aloft. A soft breeze helped to push the balloon and basket along. The four passengers hardly noticed the noise or the heat as they stared in awe at the hilly farmland and meandering streams below.

**Pose a Question** Beginning with a question can make your reader want to read on to find out the answer. The following introduction asks a question about the breadth of a popular author's imagination.

> **MODEL**
>
> Between 1915 and 1973, Agatha Christie wrote 184 works of crime fiction. How was it possible for her to create so many clever plots that depend on intricate puzzles, clues, and solutions?

**Relate an Anecdote** Beginning with an anecdote, or brief story, can hook your reader and help you make a point in a dramatic way. The following anecdote introduces a firsthand account of a rescue from a burning apartment building.

**MODEL**

A red light began blinking. A siren started up slowly but built to a screeching pitch. Twenty-five sleepy faces appeared a few at a time in the hallway. As I recall, each of us looked to left and right almost in unison, as if watching an imaginary tennis match that would give some clue to the source of this midnight disturbance.

**Address the Reader** Speaking directly to your reader establishes a friendly, informal tone and involves the reader in your topic.

**MODEL**

Find out how to maintain your cardiovascular system while enjoying yourself. Come to a free demonstration of Fit for Life at the community center, Friday night at 7:00 P.M.

**Begin with a Controlling Idea** A statement expressing a controlling idea, the main idea you intend your composition to convey, may be woven into both the beginning and the end of a piece of nonfiction writing. The following statement introduces a literary analysis.

**MODEL**

In "The Great Taos Bank Robbery," Tony Hillerman presents eccentric characters in loving detail. It is clear that he has affection for the hapless criminals as well as for the fascinated, easygoing townspeople.

**TIP** To write the best introduction for your paper, you may want to try more than one of the methods and then decide which is the most effective for your purpose and audience.

## 2.2 PARAGRAPHS

A paragraph is made up of sentences that work together to develop an idea or accomplish a purpose. Whether or not it contains a topic sentence stating the central idea, a good paragraph must have unity and coherence.

### Unity

A paragraph has unity when all the sentences support and develop one stated or implied idea. Use the following techniques to create unity in your paragraphs:

**Write a Topic Sentence** A topic sentence states the main, or central, idea of the paragraph; all other sentences in the paragraph provide supporting details. A topic sentence is often the first sentence in a paragraph. However, it may also appear later in a paragraph or at the end, to summarize or reinforce the main idea, as shown in the model that follows.

**MODEL**

Tomás lifted the skimmer baskets and emptied the collection of bugs and leaves. Then he filled the small vials with water and carefully measured four different solutions to test the pH, chlorine, total alkalinity, and acid demand. Next, he got out the equipment for vacuuming. Tomás had not realized that taking care of a swimming pool would require so much time and effort.

**Relate All Sentences to an Implied Main Idea** A paragraph can be unified without a topic sentence as long as every sentence supports an implied, or unstated, main idea. In the model, all the sentences work together to create a unified impression of baking an apple pie.

**MODEL**

The chef carefully poured in the mixture of freshly sliced apples, sugar, flour, salt, cinnamon, and nutmeg. Then she floured her hands again before adding strips of pastry in crisscrosses over the top. She dotted some butter all around the top and sprinkled on a little more sugar and cinnamon. Finally she placed the masterpiece in the oven.

### Coherence

A paragraph is coherent when all its sentences are related to one another and each flows logically to the next. The following techniques will help you achieve coherence in paragraphs:

- Present your ideas in the most logical order.
- Use pronouns, synonyms, and repeated words to connect ideas.
- Use transitional devices to show relationships among ideas.

In the model shown here, the writer used some of these techniques to create a unified paragraph.

> **MODEL**
>
> Just the name "alligator snapping turtle" brings to mind a ferocious, frightening creature. The alligator snapping turtle can grow to more than 200 pounds. In fact, whereas common snapping turtles rarely weigh 30 pounds, alligator snappers have been recorded with weights up to 300 pounds.

## 2.3 TRANSITIONS

Transitions are words and phrases that show connections between details. Clear transitions help show how your ideas relate to one another.

### Kinds of Transitions

The types of transitions you choose depend on the ideas you want to convey.

**Time or Sequence** Some transitions help to clarify the sequence of events over time. When you are telling a story or describing a process, you can connect ideas with such transitional words as *first, second, always, then, next, later, soon, before, finally, after, earlier, afterward,* and *tomorrow.*

> **MODEL**
>
> The orchestra members were seated. At first, the sounds conflicted with one another as the players tuned and tested their instruments. Then, the concertmaster stood and played one note on her violin. Next, all the instruments tuned to that tone, so that one great sound on the same pitch filled the auditorium.

**Spatial Relationships** Transitional words and phrases such as *in front, behind, next to, along, nearest, lowest, above, below, underneath, on the left,* and *in the middle* can help your reader visualize a scene.

> **MODEL**
>
> Gardeners have kept the tall-grass maze in perfect order. They have mowed the paths that weave in and out within the 15-foot diameter of the maze. On the left, a clearly marked entrance invites walkers to try the maze. At the center, a small clump of clover signals to the careful observer that the path winds toward the exit on the right.

**Degree of Importance** Transitional words and phrases such as *mainly, strongest, weakest, first, second, most important, least important, worst,* and *best* may be used to rank ideas or to show degrees of importance.

> **MODEL**
>
> Nathan has several qualifications that make him a good candidate for class representative; his greatest strength is his tolerance of more than one point of view.

**Compare and Contrast** Words and phrases such as *similarly, likewise, also, like, as, neither . . . nor,* and *either . . . or* show similarity between details. *However, by contrast, yet, but, unlike, instead, whereas,* and *while* show difference. Note the use of both types of transitions in the model.

> **MODEL**
>
> Like dogs, cats are wonderful pets. Dogs give unconditional affection and have a great desire to please. You will find out, however, that there is no substitute for the comfort of a cat's purr.

**TIP** Both *but* and *however* can be used to join two independent clauses. When *but* is used as a coordinating conjunction, it is preceded by a comma. When *however* is used as a conjunctive adverb, it is preceded by a semicolon and followed by a comma.

**Cause and Effect** When you are writing about a cause-effect relationship, use transitional words and phrases such as *since, because, thus, therefore, so, due to, for this reason,* and *as a result* to help clarify that relationship and make your writing coherent.

**MODEL**

Because a tree fell across the electric wires Monday night, we lost our electricity for four hours.

## 2.4 CONCLUSIONS

A conclusion should follow from, reflect on, or support the body of your writing, leaving readers with a strong final impression.

### Kinds of Conclusions

Good conclusions sum up ideas in a variety of ways. Here are some techniques you might try.

**Restate Your Controlling Idea** A good way to conclude an essay is by restating your controlling idea in different words. The following conclusion restates the idea introduced on page R31.

**MODEL**

The kind humor with which Hillerman portrays the would-be bank robbers as well as the curious townspeople in "The Great Taos Bank Robbery" shows his affection for all his characters.

**Ask a Question** Try asking a question that sums up what you have said and gives your reader something new to think about. This question concludes a request to consider a visit to a place of educational entertainment.

**MODEL**

If you enjoy science experiments and you like puzzles, shouldn't you plan to visit the Magic House soon?

**Make a Recommendation** When you are persuading your audience to take a position on an issue, you can conclude by recommending a specific course of action.

**MODEL**

Today's youth are at risk of damaging their hearing by listening to very loud music. Consider turning down the bass and turning down the volume on your headphones.

**Make a Prediction** Readers are concerned about matters that may affect them and therefore are moved by a conclusion that predicts the future.

**MODEL**

If this state continues to permit landowners to drain wetlands, we will see a tremendous decline in the numbers and variety of wildlife.

**Summarize Your Information** Summarizing reinforces your main idea, leaving a strong, lasting impression. The model concludes with a statement that summarizes a literary analysis of the works of Agatha Christie.

**MODEL**

Although there are a few examples of unrealistic situations in Agatha Christie's novels, for the most part each story is well crafted, providing an excellent plot and entertaining reading.

## 2.5 ELABORATION

Elaboration is the process of developing an idea by providing specific supporting details that are relevant and appropriate to the purpose and form of your writing.

**Facts and Statistics** A fact is a statement that can be verified, and a statistic is a fact expressed as a number. Make sure the facts and statistics you supply are from reliable, up-to-date sources.

**MODEL**

Female cicadas cut little slits in the bark of twigs and lay their eggs inside the slits. The eggs hatch after 6 to 10 weeks. When the eggs hatch, the nymphs drop from the trees.

**Sensory Details** Precise details that show how something looks, sounds, tastes, smells, or feels can enliven a description, making readers feel they are actually experiencing what you are describing.

**MODEL**

About 4:00 in the afternoon, the racket would begin in earnest. The cicadas must have dozed all day, but they seemed to awake in the heat of the afternoon to begin their persistent mating screeches. In lush suburban areas with large trees, the din was almost deafening.

**Incidents** From our earliest years, we are interested in hearing "stories." One way to illustrate a point powerfully is to relate an incident or tell a story, as shown in the example.

**MODEL**

The pavement was slippery from the rain, but I was going to miss the bus if I didn't run. As I rushed toward the bus stop, I tripped and fell on the sidewalk close to the curb. Now I had dirt on my skirt. As I got up from the pavement, the bus roared past me, splashing muddy water on my skirt and shoes.

**Examples** An example can help make an abstract idea concrete or can serve to clarify a complex point for your reader.

**MODEL**

Many fiction writers use real locations for their settings. For example, Tony Hillerman uses cities and towns in New Mexico and Arizona for his mystery novels.

**Quotations** Choose quotations that clearly support your points, and be sure that you copy each quotation word for word. Remember always to credit the source.

**MODEL**

The sky looks blue because air is not completely transparent. In *The Cosmological Milkshake,* Robert Ehrlich explains that "a fraction of sunlight is scattered by the molecules of the atmosphere, with blue light scattered the most." Even without smog and other forms of pollution, the sky would still look blue.

# 3 Writing Description

Descriptive writing allows you to paint word pictures about anything, from events of global importance to the most personal feelings. It is an essential part of almost every piece of writing.

> **RUBRIC: Standards for Writing**
>
> **Successful descriptive writing should**
> - have a clear focus and sense of purpose
> - use sensory details and precise words to create a vivid image, establish a mood, or express emotion
> - present details in a logical order

### 3.1 KEY TECHNIQUES

**Consider Your Goals** What do you want to accomplish with your description? Do you want to show why something is important to you? Do you want to make a person or scene more memorable? Do you want to explain an event?

**Identify Your Audience** Who will read your description? How familiar are they with your subject? What background information will they need? Which details will they find most interesting?

**Think Figuratively** What figures of speech might help make your description vivid and interesting? What simile or metaphor comes to mind? What imaginative comparisons can you make? What living thing does an inanimate object remind you of?

**Gather Sensory Details** Which sights, smells, tastes, sounds, and textures make your subject come alive? Which details stick in your mind when you observe or recall your subject? Which senses does it most strongly affect?

You might want to use a chart like the one shown here to collect sensory details about your subject.

| Sights | Sounds | Textures | Smells | Tastes |
|--------|--------|----------|--------|--------|
|        |        |          |        |        |

**Create a Mood** What feelings do you want to evoke in your readers? Do you want to soothe them with comforting images? Do you want to build tension with ominous details? Do you want to evoke sadness or joy?

## 3.2 OPTIONS FOR ORGANIZATION

**Option 1: Spatial Order** Choose one of these options to show the spatial order of elements in a scene you are describing.

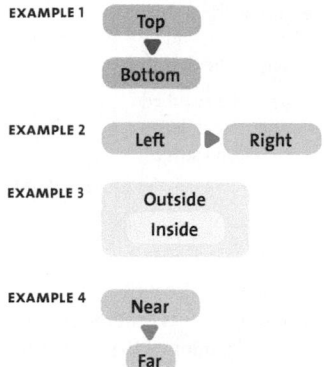

EXAMPLE 1 Top ▼ Bottom

EXAMPLE 2 Left ▶ Right

EXAMPLE 3 Outside Inside

EXAMPLE 4 Near ▼ Far

**MODEL**

The tour group squeezed through the door and into the long, narrow entryway. The leader began describing what they would see when it was their turn to enter the great center room. Some in the group tried to steal a glimpse of the enormous spectacle just ahead of them. At the end of the hall, a light illuminated a magnificent marble sculpture.

*For more information, see **Transitions**, page R32.*

**Option 2: Order of Impression** Order of impression is the order in which you notice details.

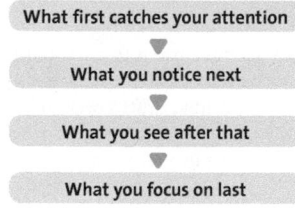

What first catches your attention ▼ What you notice next ▼ What you see after that ▼ What you focus on last

**MODEL**

When I first looked at the painting, I saw a brightly illuminated, sophisticated face looking toward me and well-manicured hands turning the pages of a book. The longer I looked at the painting, the more I saw. I noticed that a letter seems to have just been opened, read, and set down. Before long my eyes fastened on bits of paper or maybe flower petals that might have come with the letter. At this point, I studied the expression on the young man's face. He seems very serious, maybe sad or worried. Suddenly, I really wanted to know more about this subject. I stared at the painting a long time.

**TIP** Use transitions that help readers understand the order of the impressions you are describing. Some useful transitions are *after, next, during, first, before, finally,* and *then.*

**Option 3: Order of Importance** You can use order of importance as the organizing structure for a description.

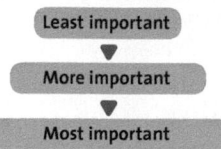

Least important ▼ More important ▼ Most important

**MODEL**

Annaliese tried to dredge up from her memory everything about the accident. She remembered unimportant details, like the song that was playing on her radio before the truck loomed up ahead. She remembered her panic as she steered into the guardrail. Gradually she recalled more important information—her conservative speed, the fact that the truck was coming toward her on the wrong side of the road, the driver's long beard. Finally, when she closed her eyes and really concentrated, she could remember the license-plate number at eye level as the truck zoomed by.

*For more information, see **Transitions**, page R32.*

# 4 Writing Narratives

Narrative writing tells a story. If you write a story from your imagination, it is a fictional narrative. A true story about actual events is a nonfictional narrative. Narrative writing can be found in short stories, novels, news articles, personal narratives, and biographies.

## RUBRIC: Standards for Writing

**A successful narrative should**

- hook the reader's attention with a strong introduction
- use precise words and phrases
- include descriptive details and dialogue to develop the characters, setting, and plot
- have a clear beginning, middle, and end
- have a logical organization, with clues and transitions that help the reader understand the order of events
- maintain a consistent tone and point of view
- use language that is appropriate to the audience
- demonstrate the significance of events or ideas

*For more information, see* **Writing Workshop: Personal Narrative,** *pages 174–183, and* **Writing Workshop: Short Story,** *pages 412–421.*

### 4.1 KEY TECHNIQUES

**Identify the Main Events** What are the most important events in your narrative? Is each event needed to tell the story?

**Describe the Setting** When do the events occur? Where do they take place? How can you use setting to create mood and to set the stage for the characters and their actions?

**Depict Characters Vividly** What do your characters look like? What do they think and say? How do they act? What details can show what they are like?

**TIP** Dialogue is an effective way of developing characters in a narrative. As you write dialogue, choose words that express your characters' personalities and that show how the characters feel about one another and about the events in the plot.

### 4.2 OPTIONS FOR ORGANIZATION

**Option 1: Chronological Order** One way to organize a piece of narrative writing is to arrange the events in chronological order, as shown in the following example.

**EXAMPLE**

Kid Turner is missing from the ranch. Fearing that he is hurt, Jake and Edna Mae set out to search for him.

> **Introduction**
> *Characters and setting*
> ▼

As a thunderstorm approaches, they find his horse and backtrack up a dry wash.

> **Event 1**
> ▼

They find Turner just as the storm breaks. He has a broken leg, and he can't drag himself out of the dry wash.

> **Event 2**
> ▼

They carry him out of the riverbed and find shelter under a rock ledge. As they watch, a flash flood surges over the riverbed where Turner had been lying.

> **End**
> *Perhaps showing the significance of the events*

**Option 2: Flashback** In narrative writing, it is also possible to introduce events that happened sometime before the beginning of the story. You can use a flashback to show how past events led up to the present situation or to provide background about a character or event. Use clue words such as *last summer, as a young girl, the previous school year,* and *his earliest memories* to let your reader know that you are interrupting the main action to describe earlier events.

Notice how the flashback interrupts the action in the model.

**MODEL**

At the trials for the first big meet of the school year, Shayna was anxious to prove to the coach that she could be a leader on the track team. During warm-ups, her mind drifted back to her disastrous showing in the final meet last year, when she had dropped a baton in a relay race.

**Option 3: Focus on Conflict** When a fictional narrative focuses on a central conflict, the story's plot may be organized as shown in the following example.

**EXAMPLE**

Before a championship basketball game, two players arrive at the school gym an hour before the rest of the team. The players are identical twins, but their personalities couldn't be more different. Mark is outgoing and impulsive, while Matt is thoughtful and shy.

> **Describe main characters and setting.**

As they prepare for the game, Matt notices a man enter the locker room and give Mark a wad of cash. In the first quarter of the game, Matt notices that his brother is missing shots on purpose. He realizes that Mark has taken cash to lose the game.

> **Present conflict.**

- Matt has a chance at a basketball scholarship if they win the championship.
- Mark needs money to buy a car.
- Matt and Mark have always supported each other's goals.

> **Relate events that make conflict complex and cause characters to change.**

During halftime, Matt reminds Mark of a family story in which their grandfather chose honor and integrity over easy money. When the game resumes, Mark plays to win.

> **Present resolution or outcome of conflict.**

## 5 Writing Informative Texts

Informative and explanatory writing informs and explains. You can use it to evaluate the effects of a new law, to compare two movies, to analyze a piece of literature, or to examine the problem of greenhouse gases in the atmosphere. There are many types of informative writing. Think about your topic and select the type that presents the information most clearly.

### 5.1 COMPARISON AND CONTRAST

Compare-and-contrast writing analyzes the similarities and differences between two or more subjects. You might, for example, compare and contrast two short stories, the main characters in a novel, or two movies.

> **RUBRIC: Standards for Writing**
>
> **Successful compare-and-contrast writing should**
> - hook the reader's attention with a strong introduction
> - clearly identify the subjects that are being compared and contrasted
> - include specific, relevant details
> - follow a clear plan of organization
> - use language and details appropriate to the audience
> - use transitional words and phrases to clarify similarities and differences
> - use a formal style and objective tone

### Options for Organization

Compare-and-contrast writing can be organized in different ways. The examples that follow demonstrate point-by-point organization and subject-by-subject organization.

#### Option 1: Point-by-Point Organization

**EXAMPLE**

I. Both women want something that they cannot afford.

**Point 1**

**Subject A** Mathilde in "The Necklace": new dress and fancy jewelry to go to a ball

**Subject B** Della in "The Gift of the Magi": special Christmas present for her husband

II. Both make sacrifices that turn out to be ironic.

**Point 2**

**Subject A** Mathilde: works for years to replace a necklace that turns out to be a cheap imitation

**Subject B** Della: sells her hair to buy a chain for a watch that her husband has sold

## Option 2: Subject-by-Subject Organization

**EXAMPLE**

I. Mathilde in "The Necklace"  **Subject A**

   **Point 1/Wish:** new dress and fancy jewelry to go to a ball

   **Point 2/Ironic Sacrifice:** works for years to replace a necklace that turns out to be a cheap imitation

II. Della in "The Gift of the Magi"  **Subject B**

   **Point 1/Wish:** special Christmas present for her husband

   **Point 2/Ironic Sacrifice:** sells her hair to buy a chain for a watch that her husband has sold

*For more information, see **Writing Workshop: Analysis of Literary Nonfiction**, pages 524–533, and **Writing Workshop: Online Feature Article**, pages 996–1003.*

### 5.2 CAUSE AND EFFECT

Cause-effect writing explains why something happened, why certain conditions exist, or what resulted from an action or a condition. You might use cause-effect writing to explain a character's actions, the progress of a disease, or the outcome of a war.

> **RUBRIC: Standards for Writing**
>
> **Successful cause-effect writing should**
>
> - hook the reader's attention with a strong introduction
> - clearly state the cause-and-effect relationship
> - show clear connections between causes and effects
> - present causes and effects in a logical order and use transitions effectively
> - use facts, examples, and other details to illustrate each cause and effect
> - use language and details appropriate to the audience
> - use a formal style and objective tone

### Options for Organization

Your organization will depend on your topic and your purpose for writing.

**Option 1: Effect-to-Cause Organization**  If you want to explain the causes of an event, such as the closing of a factory, you might first state the effect and then examine its causes.

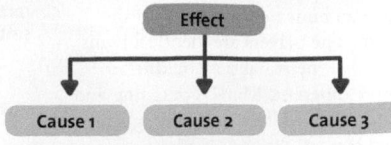

**Option 2: Cause-to-Effect Organization**  If your focus is on explaining the effects of an event, such as the passage of a law, you might first state the cause and then explain the effects.

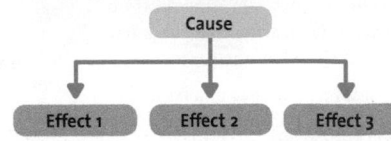

**Option 3: Cause-Effect Chain Organization**

Sometimes you'll want to describe a chain of cause-effect relationships to explore a topic, such as the disappearance of tropical rain forests or the development of home computers.

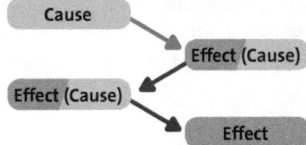

**TIP**  Don't assume that a cause-effect relationship exists just because one event follows another. Look for evidence that the later event could not have happened if the first event had not caused it.

## 5.3 PROBLEM-SOLUTION

Problem-solution writing clearly states a problem, analyzes the problem, and proposes a solution to the problem. It can be used to identify and solve a conflict between characters, investigate global warming, or tell why the home team keeps losing.

> **RUBRIC: Standards for Writing**
>
> **Successful problem-solution writing should**
> - hook the reader's attention with a strong introduction
> - identify the problem and help the reader understand the issues involved
> - analyze the causes and effects of the problem
> - include quotations, facts, and statistics
> - explore possible solutions to the problem and recommend the best one(s)
> - use language and details appropriate to the audience
> - use a formal style and objective tone

### Options for Organization

Your organization will depend on the goal of your problem-solution piece, your intended audience, and the specific problem you have chosen to address. The organizational methods that follow are effective for different kinds of problem-solution writing.

### Option 1: Simple Problem-Solution

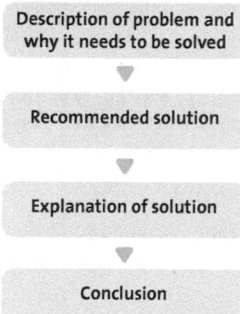

### Option 2: Deciding Between Solutions

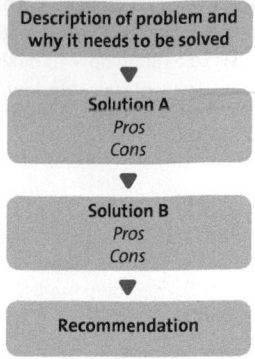

## 5.4 ANALYSIS

In writing an analysis, you explain how something works, how it is defined, or what its parts are.

> **RUBRIC: Standards for Writing**
>
> **A successful analysis should**
> - hook the reader's attention with a strong introduction
> - clearly define the subject and its parts
> - use a specific organizing structure to provide a logical flow of information
> - show connections among facts and ideas through transitional words and phrases
> - use language and details appropriate for the audience
> - use a formal style and objective tone

### Options for Organization

Organize your details in a logical order appropriate to the kind of analysis you're writing. Use one of the following options:

**Option 1: Process Analysis** A process analysis is usually organized chronologically, with steps or stages in the order they occur. You might use a process analysis to explain how to bake a pie, prepare for a test, or replace a windowpane.

EXAMPLE

Repairing a window is easy.    **Introduce process.**

You will need to measure the frame and purchase a new pane. You will also need to buy glazing compound and glazier's points.    **Give background.**

Step 1: Remove broken glass and clean frame.    **Explain steps.**

Step 2: Put glazing compound in frame; set new glass.

Step 3: Push in glazier's points to secure glass.

Step 4: Apply glazing compound to space where glass meets frame.

**Option 2: Extended Definition** or **Definition Analysis** You can organize the details of an extended definition in order of importance or impression. Use an extended definition to explain a quality (such as proficiency), the distinguishing features of a sonnet, or the features of a lever.

EXAMPLE

A lever is a simple machine that allows a person to move heavy loads with less effort.    **Introduce term and definition.**

Feature 1: Force

Feature 2: Fulcrum (pivot point)    **Explain features.**

Feature 3: Load

**Option 3: Parts Analysis** The following parts analysis explains the parts of the intestinal tract.

EXAMPLE

The intestinal tract breaks food into particles the body can use.    **Introduce subject.**

Part 1: Mouth, esophagus, stomach

Part 2: Small intestine    **Explain parts.**

Part 3: Large intestine, appendix, rectum

*For more information, see **Writing Workshop: Analysis of an Author's Style**, pages 890–899.*

## 6 Writing Arguments

Argumentative writing allows you to use the power of language to inform and influence others. It includes speeches, persuasive essays, newspaper editorials, advertisements, and critical reviews.

**RUBRIC: Standards for Writing**

**Successful argumentative writing should**

- hook the reader's attention with a strong introduction
- state the issue and the writer's claim
- give claims and support them with facts or reasons
- rely on a formal style and objective tone
- answer opposing views
- use sound logic and effective language
- conclude by summing up reasons or calling for action

*For more information, see **Writing Workshop: Persuasive Essay**, pages 712–721, and **Writing Workshop: Critical Review**, pages 1166–1175.*

### 6.1 KEY TECHNIQUES

**Clarify Your Claim** What do you believe about the issue? How can you express your opinion most clearly?

**Know Your Audience** Who will read your writing? What do they already know and believe about the issue? What objections to your position might they have? What additional information might they need? What approach would be most effective?

**Support Your Opinion** Why do you feel the way you do about the issue? What facts, statistics, examples, quotations, anecdotes, or expert opinions support your view? What reasons will convince your readers? What evidence can answer their objections?

| Ways to Support Your Argument | |
|---|---|
| **Statistics** | facts that are stated in numbers |
| **Examples** | specific instances that explain points |
| **Observations** | events or situations you yourself have seen |
| **Anecdotes** | brief stories that illustrate points |
| **Quotations** | direct statements from authorities |

*For more information, see* **Identifying Faulty Reasoning,** *page R24.*

**Begin and End with a Bang** How can you hook your readers and make a lasting impression? What memorable quotation, anecdote, or statistic will catch their attention at the beginning or stick in their minds at the end? What strong summary or call to action can you conclude with?

---

**MODEL**

**Beginning**

If you want to spend an evening with your neighbors, seeing a live performance or shopping for homemade crafts, will you come to the community center? Probably not. It's too hot!

**End**

Many people put hours and weeks into providing our town with entertainment. Often only a few people attend these events at the community center because the building is too hot on summer evenings. One "cool" solution would be to purchase an air-conditioning system.

---

## 6.2 OPTIONS FOR ORGANIZATION

In a two-sided persuasive essay, you want to show the weaknesses of other opinions as you explain the strengths of your own.

**Option 1: Reasons for Your Opinion**

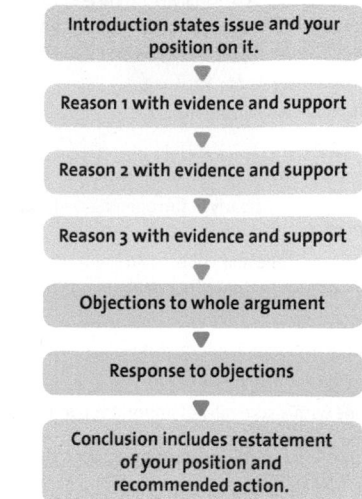

**Option 2: Point-by-Point Basis**

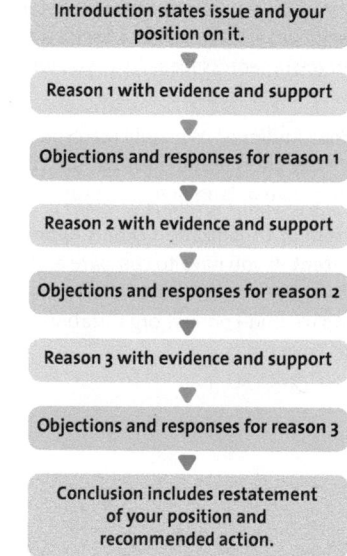

## 7 Writing Functional Texts

A common use of functional texts is in business writing. Business writing is writing done in a workplace to support the work of a company or business. Several types of formats, such as memos, letters, e-mails, applications, and bylaws, have been developed to make communication easier.

> ### RUBRIC: Standards for Writing
> **Successful business writing should**
> - be courteous
> - use language that is geared to its audience
> - state the purpose clearly in the opening sentences or paragraph
> - have a formal tone and not contain slang, contractions, or sentence fragments
> - use precise words
> - present only essential information
> - present details in a logical order
> - conclude with a summary of important points

### 7.1 KEY TECHNIQUES

**Think About Your Purpose** Why are you doing this writing? Do you want to promote yourself to a college admissions committee or a job interviewer? Do you want to order or complain about a product? Do you want to set up a meeting or respond to someone's ideas? Are you writing bylaws for an organization?

**Identify Your Audience** Who will read your writing? What background information will they need? What tone or language is appropriate?

**Use a Pattern of Organization That Is Appropriate to the Content** If you have to compare and contrast two products in a memo, you can use the same compare-and-contrast organization that you would use in an essay.

**Support Your Points** What specific details might clarify your ideas? What reasons do you have for your statements?

**Finish Strongly** How can you best sum up your statements? What is your main point? What action do you want the recipients to take?

**Revise and Proofread Your Writing** Just as you are graded on the quality of an essay you write for a class, you will be judged on the quality of your writing in the workplace.

### 7.2 MATCHING THE FORMAT TO THE OCCASION

E-mail messages, memos, and letters have similar purposes but are used in different situations. The chart shows how each format can be used.

| Format | Occasion |
|--------|----------|
| Memo | Use to send correspondence **inside** the workplace only. |
| E-mail message | Use to send correspondence **inside or outside** the company. |
| Letter | Use to send correspondence **outside** the company. |

**TIP** Remember that e-mail messages in the workplace require formal language and standard spelling, capitalization, and punctuation.

> ### PRACTICE AND APPLY
>
> Refer to the documents on page R43 to complete the following:
>
> 1. Draft a response to the letter. Then revise your letter as necessary according to the rubric at the beginning of this section. Make sure you have included the necessary information and have written in an appropriate tone. Proofread your letter for grammatical errors and spelling mistakes. Follow the format of the model and use appropriate spacing between elements.
>
> 2. Write a memo in response to the memo. Tell the recipient what actions you have taken. Follow the format of the model.

## PRACTICE AND APPLY

## ANSWERS

1. *Students' letters should include a heading, inside address, salutation, body, and closing. Students should thank Mr. Geraci for submitting the letter and application. They should also schedule an interview with the applicant.*

2. *Students should model the memo on page R43. In their replies, students should indicate that they have sent out a brochure to Kerry Takata and have contacted the Pennsylvania alumni group regarding Tom Martinez.*

## 7.3 FORMATS

Business letters usually have a formal tone and a specific format as shown below. The keys to writing a business letter are to get to the point as quickly as possible and to present your information clearly.

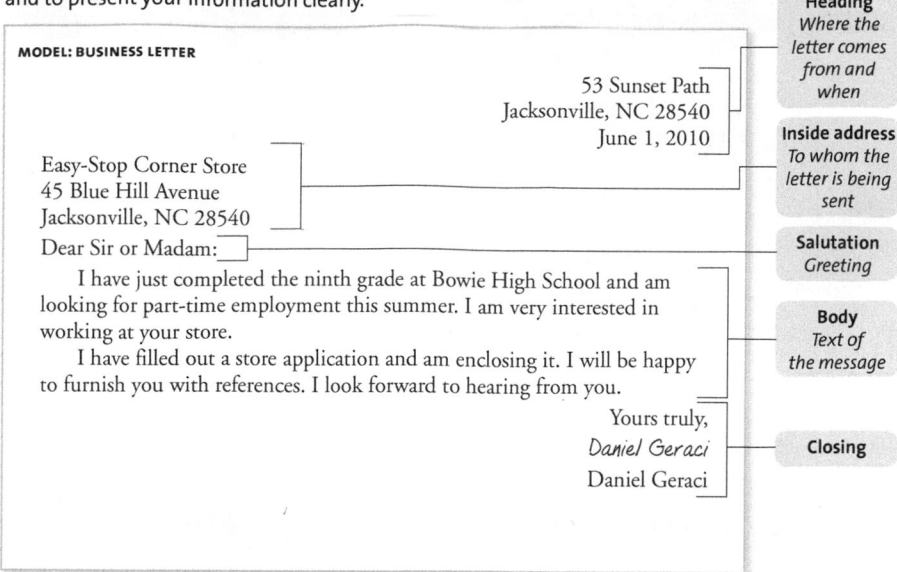

**MODEL: BUSINESS LETTER**

53 Sunset Path
Jacksonville, NC 28540
June 1, 2010

Easy-Stop Corner Store
45 Blue Hill Avenue
Jacksonville, NC 28540

Dear Sir or Madam:

    I have just completed the ninth grade at Bowie High School and am looking for part-time employment this summer. I am very interested in working at your store.
    I have filled out a store application and am enclosing it. I will be happy to furnish you with references. I look forward to hearing from you.

Yours truly,
*Daniel Geraci*
Daniel Geraci

**Heading**
*Where the letter comes from and when*

**Inside address**
*To whom the letter is being sent*

**Salutation**
*Greeting*

**Body**
*Text of the message*

**Closing**

Memos are often used in workplaces as a way of conveying information in a direct and concise manner. They can be used to announce or summarize meetings and to request actions or specific information.

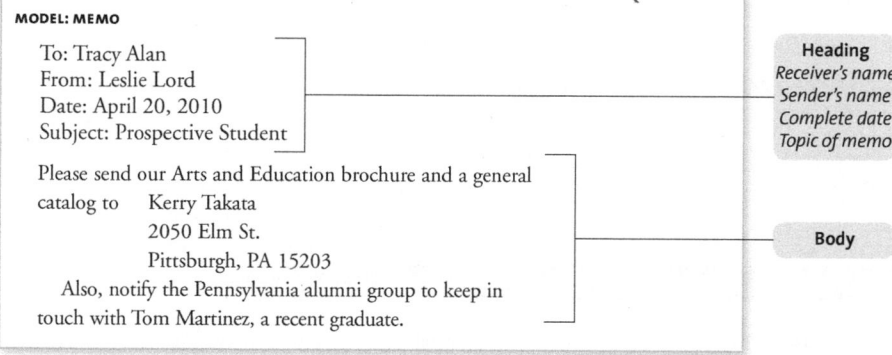

**MODEL: MEMO**

To: Tracy Alan
From: Leslie Lord
Date: April 20, 2010
Subject: Prospective Student

Please send our Arts and Education brochure and a general catalog to   Kerry Takata
        2050 Elm St.
        Pittsburgh, PA 15203
  Also, notify the Pennsylvania alumni group to keep in touch with Tom Martinez, a recent graduate.

**Heading**
*Receiver's name*
*Sender's name*
*Complete date*
*Topic of memo*

**Body**

**TIP** Don't forget to write the topic of your memo in the subject line. This will help the receiver determine the importance of your memo.

When you apply for a job, you may be asked to fill out an application form. Application forms vary, but most of them ask for similar kinds of information. (If you are mailing your application, you may want to include a brief letter.)

---

**MODEL: JOB APPLICATION**

EASY-STOP CORNER STORE
EMPLOYMENT APPLICATION

Date  _June 1, 2010_

Name  _Daniel_          _Allen_          _Geraci_
      FIRST           MIDDLE           LAST

Address  _53 Sunset Path_     _Jacksonville_     _NC_     _28540_
         STREET              CITY              STATE    ZIP

Phone  _214-555-9447_          Social Security Number  _535-89-7779_

Date of Birth  _June 3, 1995_          Place of Birth  _Dallas, Texas_

Have you been employed here before?  ____ Yes  _x_ No

AVAILABILITY
Date You Can Start  _June 30, 2010_     Full Time ____     Part Time _x_     Summer _x_

Total Hours Available per Week  _20_

If hired, and you are under 16, can you furnish proof of age and/or a work permit?

_x_ Yes  ____ No

EDUCATION
Highest Grade Completed (circle one)

Middle 6 7 8     High (9) 10 11 12     College 13 14 15 16

College  _N/A_          From _N/A_ To _N/A_

High School  _James Bowie_          From _2009_ To _2010_

Middle School  _Fulmore Middle School_     From _2006_ To _2009_

REFERENCES

1  _____

---

Refer to the documents on pages R44 and R45 to complete the following:

1. Visit a business and request an employment application for a job you would like to have. Make sure you understand what each question is asking before you begin to write. Fill out the application as neatly and completely as possible.

2. Write a set of bylaws for an organization that you already belong to or one that you would like to form. Follow the format of the document on page R45.

**PRACTICE AND APPLY**

**ANSWERS**

1. *Have students fill out the application. Encourage them to verify that the information is correct before turning in their applications.*

2. *Students' bylaws should include a mission statement, a description of activities, membership requirements, election laws, rules for meetings, and other pertinent information.*

Sometimes you may have to write technical documents, such as a list of procedures for conducting a meeting, a manual on rules of behavior, or the minutes of a meeting. These documents contain written descriptions of rules, regulations, and meetings and enable organizations and businesses to run smoothly.

These bylaws for a drama club include a description of the organization and detailed information about how the club operates. The writer began each section with a heading, so that readers could easily find information. The writer was also very specific, so that readers would not misunderstand the rules.

---

**MODEL: BYLAWS DOCUMENT**

### Central High School Drama Club Bylaws

We, the current members of the Central High School Drama Club, create the following laws for our organization. Our members include actors, scenery designers, makeup artists, costume designers, lighting and sound specialists, stagehands, and stage managers.

**MISSION STATEMENT:** To provide an organization through which members of the dramatic arts program at Central High School heighten awareness of theater in the school and provide entertainment for the community

**ACTIVITIES**
- Biweekly meetings to talk about concerns and programming
- Publicity for upcoming school productions
- Performances, including two major drama productions

**MEMBERSHIP REQUIREMENTS**

To qualify for membership in the Drama Club, a candidate must
- be enrolled as a student at Central High School
- complete ten hours of participation in a school or community production

To remain a member of the Drama Club, an individual must
- actively contribute to the goals of the club
- complete a minimum of five hours of production participation each year

**OFFICER ELECTION LAWS**

Each year the members will vote for a president, a vice-president, a treasurer, and a secretary.
1. Each individual running for office must be nominated by another Drama Club member.
2. To be elected, a nominee must receive a majority of the votes.

**RULES OF ORDER FOR MEETINGS**
1. All meetings will be conducted according to *Robert's Rules of Order.*
2. A quorum of five members must be present for discussion of business items and voting.
3. The president will call the meeting to order.
4. The secretary will record, distribute, and manage meeting minutes.

**Writing Online**

Go to thinkcentral.com.
KEYWORD: HML9N-R45

WRITING HANDBOOK **R45**

---

**Writing Online**

The keyword on this page directs students to interactive models, revision lessons, and other resources designed to support the writing process.

# COMMON CORE FOCUS

**L 1a-b** Demonstrate command of the conventions of standard English grammar and usage when writing or speaking; use parallel structure; use various types of phrases and clauses to convey specific meanings and add variety and interest to writing or presentations. **L 2a-b** Demonstrate command of the conventions of standard English capitalization, punctuation, and spelling when writing; use a semicolon to link two or more closely related independent clauses; use a colon to introduce a list or quotation.

*Writing that has a lot of mistakes can confuse or even annoy a reader. A business letter with a punctuation error might lead to a miscommunication and delay a reply. Or a sentence fragment might lower your grade on an essay. Paying attention to grammar, punctuation, and capitalization rules can make your writing clearer and easier to read.*

**COMMON CORE**
Included in this handbook:
L 1a–b, L 2a–b

# Quick Reference: Parts of Speech

| PART OF SPEECH | FUNCTION | EXAMPLES |
|---|---|---|
| Noun | names a person, a place, a thing, an idea, a quality, or an action | |
| Common | serves as a general name, or a name common to an entire group | poet, novel, love, journey |
| Proper | names a specific, one-of-a-kind person, place, or thing | Lewis, Jackson, Pleasant Street, Stanley Cup |
| Singular | refers to a single person, place, thing, or idea | child, park, flower, truth |
| Plural | refers to more than one person, place, thing, or idea | children, parks, flowers, truths |
| Concrete | names something that can be perceived by the senses | roof, flash, Dublin, battle |
| Abstract | names something that cannot be perceived by the senses | intelligence, fear, joy, loneliness |
| Compound | expresses a single idea through a combination of two or more words | haircut, father-in-law, Christmas Eve |
| Collective | refers to a group of people or things | army, flock, class, species |
| Possessive | shows who or what owns something | Strafford's, Bess's, children's, witnesses' |
| Pronoun | takes the place of a noun or another pronoun | |
| Personal | refers to the person making a statement, the person(s) being addressed, or the person(s) or thing(s) the statement is about | I, me, my, mine, we, us, our, ours, you, your, yours, she, he, it, her, him, hers, his, its, they, them, their, theirs |
| Reflexive | follows a verb or preposition and refers to a preceding noun or pronoun | myself, yourself, herself, himself, itself, ourselves, yourselves, themselves |
| Intensive | emphasizes a noun or another pronoun | (same as reflexives) |
| Demonstrative | points to one or more specific persons or things | this, that, these, those |
| Interrogative | signals a question | who, whom, whose, which, what |
| Indefinite | refers to one or more persons or things not specifically mentioned | both, all, most, many, anyone, everybody, several, none, some |
| Relative | introduces an adjective clause by relating it to a word in the clause | who, whom, whose, which, that |
| Reciprocal | refers to individual parts of a plural antecedent | each other, one another |

| PART OF SPEECH | FUNCTION | EXAMPLES |
|---|---|---|
| Verb | expresses an action, a condition, or a state of being | |
| Action | tells what the subject does or did, physically or mentally | run, reaches, listened, consider, decides, dreamed |
| Linking | connects the subject to something that identifies or describes it | am, is, are, was, were, sound, taste, appear, feel, become, remain, seem |
| Auxiliary | precedes the main verb in a verb phrase | be, have, do, can, could, will, would, may, might |
| Transitive | directs the action toward someone or something; always has an object | The storm **sank** the ship. |
| Intransitive | does not direct the action toward someone or something; does not have an object | The ship **sank.** |
| Adjective | modifies a noun or pronoun | **strong** women, **two** epics, **enough** time |
| Adverb | modifies a verb, an adjective, or another adverb | walked **out, really** funny, **far** away |
| Preposition | relates one word to another word | at, by, for, from, in, of, on, to, with |
| Conjunction | joins words or word groups | |
| Coordinating | joins words or word groups used the same way | and, but, or, for, so, yet, nor |
| Correlative | used as a pair to join words or word groups used the same way | both . . . and, either . . . or, neither . . . nor |
| Subordinating | introduces a clause that cannot stand by itself as a complete sentence | although, after, as, before, because, when, if, unless |
| Interjection | expresses emotion | wow, ouch, hurrah |

# Quick Reference: The Sentence and Its Parts

The diagrams that follow will give you a brief review of the essentials of a sentence and some of its parts.

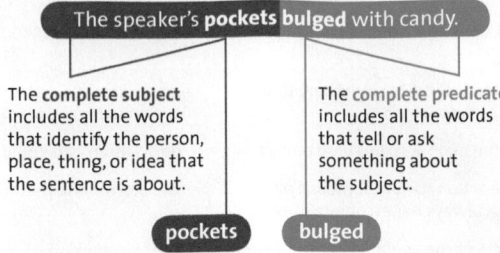

The speaker's **pockets bulged** with candy.

The **complete subject** includes all the words that identify the person, place, thing, or idea that the sentence is about.

The complete predicate includes all the words that tell or ask something about the subject.

**pockets**

The **simple subject** tells exactly whom or what the sentence is about. It may be one word or a group of words, but it does not include modifiers.

**bulged**

The simple predicate, or verb, tells what the subject does or is. It may be one word or several, but it does not include modifiers.

Every word in a sentence is part of a complete subject or a complete predicate.

**At the drugstore**, an understanding clerk **had given** the speaker a chocolate bar.

A **prepositional phrase** consists of a preposition, its object, and any modifiers of the object. In this phrase, *at* is the preposition and *drugstore* is its object.

subject

Verbs often have more than one part. A verb may be made up of a main verb, like *given*, and one or more auxiliary, or helping, verbs, like *had*.

A **direct object** is a word or group of words that tells who or what receives the action of the verb.

An **indirect object** is a word or group of words that tells to whom or for whom or to what or for what the verb's action is performed. A sentence can have an indirect object only if it has a direct object. The indirect object always comes before the direct object.

# Quick Reference: Punctuation

| MARK | FUNCTION | EXAMPLES |
|---|---|---|
| **End Marks** period, question mark, exclamation point | ends a sentence | We can start now. When would you like to leave? What a fantastic hit! |
| period | follows an initial or abbreviation | Mrs. Dorothy Parker, C. P. Cavafy, p.m., a.d., lb., oz., Blvd., Dr. |
| | **Exception:** postal abbreviations of states | NE (Nebraska), NV (Nevada) |
| period | follows a number or letter in an outline | I. Volcanoes   A. Central-vent     1. Shield |
| **Comma** | separates part of a compound sentence | I had never disliked poetry, but now I really love it. |
| | separates items in a series | She is brave, loyal, and kind. |
| | separates adjectives of equal rank that modify the same noun | The slow, easy route is best. |
| | sets off a term of address | Maria, how can I help you? You must do something, soldier. |
| | sets off a parenthetical expression | Hard workers, as you know, don't quit. I'm not a quitter, believe me. |
| | sets off an introductory word, phrase, or dependent clause | Yes, I forgot my key. At the beginning of the day, I feel fresh. While she was out, I was here. Having finished my chores, I went out. |
| | sets off a nonrestrictive, or nonessential, phrase or clause | Ed Pawn, the captain of the chess team, won. Ed Pawn, who is the captain, won. The two leading runners, sprinting toward the finish line, finished in a tie. |
| | sets off parts of dates and addresses | Mail it by May 14, 2010, to the Hauptman Company, 321 Market Street, Memphis, Tennessee. |
| | follows the salutation and closing of a letter | Dear Jim, Sincerely yours, |
| | separates words to avoid confusion | By noon, time had run out. What the minister does, does matter. While cooking, Jim burned his hand. |
| **Semicolon** | separates items that contain commas in a series | We spent the first week of summer vacation in Chicago, Illinois; the second week in St. Louis, Missouri; and the third week in Albany, New York. |
| | separates parts of a compound sentence that are not joined by a coordinating conjunction | The last shall be first; the first shall be last. I read the Bible; however, I have not memorized it. |
| | separates parts of a compound sentence when the parts contain commas | After I ran out of money, I called my parents; but only my sister was home, unfortunately. |

| MARK | FUNCTION | EXAMPLES |
|---|---|---|
| Colon | introduces a list | Those we wrote were the following: Dana, John, and Will. |
| | introduces a long quotation | Abraham Lincoln wrote: "Four score and seven years ago, our fathers brought forth on this continent a new nation...." |
| | follows the salutation of a business letter | To Whom It May Concern: Dear Leonard Atole: |
| | separates certain numbers | 1:28 P.M., Genesis 2:5 |
| Dash | emphasizes parenthetical information or indicates an abrupt break in thought | I was thinking of my mother—who is arriving tomorrow—just as you walked in. |
| Parentheses | enclose less important material | It was so unlike him (John is always on time) that I began to worry. The last World Series game (did you see it?) was fun. |
| Hyphen | joins parts of a compound adjective before a noun | The not-so-rich taxpayer won't stand for this! |
| | joins part of a compound with *all-*, *ex-*, *self-*, or *-elect* | The ex-firefighter helped rescue him. Our president-elect is self-conscious. |
| | joins part of a compound number (to ninety-nine) | Today, I turned twenty-one. |
| | joins part of a fraction | My cup is one-third full. |
| | joins a prefix to a word beginning with a capital letter | Which Pre-Raphaelite painter do you like best? It snowed in mid-October. |
| | indicates that a word is divided at the end of a line | How could you have any reasonable expect- ations of getting a new computer? |
| Apostrophe | used with *s* to form the possessive of a noun or an indefinite pronoun | my friend's book, my friends' books, anyone's guess, somebody else's problem |
| | replaces one or more omitted letters in a contraction or numbers in a date | don't (omitted *o*), he'd (omitted *woul*), the class of '99 (omitted *19*) |
| | used with *s* to form the plural of a letter | I had two A's on my report card. |
| Quotation Marks | set off a speaker's exact words | Sara said, "I'm finally ready." "I'm ready," Sara said, "finally." Did Sara say, "I'm ready"? Sara said, "I'm ready!" |
| | set off the title of a story, article, short poem, essay, song, or chapter | I liked McLean's "Marine Corps Issue" and Roethke's "My Papa's Waltz." I like Joplin's "Me and Bobby McGee." |
| | indicate sarcasm or irony | Chris is a real "friend." He always shows up when he needs help but never when I do. |
| Ellipses | replace material omitted from a quotation | "When in the course of human events ... and to assume among the powers of the earth. ..." |
| Italics | indicate the title of a book, play, magazine, long poem, opera, film, or TV series, or the name of a ship | *The House on Mango Street, Hamlet, Newsweek, the Odyssey, Madama Butterfly, Gone with the Wind, Seinfeld,* USS *Constitution* |

# Quick Reference: Capitalization

| CATEGORY | EXAMPLES |
|---|---|
| **People and Titles** | |
| Names and initials of people | Amy Tan, W. H. Auden |
| Titles used before names | Professor Holmes, Senator Long |
| Deities and members of religious groups | Jesus, Allah, Buddha, Zeus, Baptists, Roman Catholics |
| Names of ethnic and national groups | Hispanics, Jews, African Americans |
| **Geographical Names** | |
| Cities, states, countries, continents | Philadelphia, Kansas, Japan, Europe |
| Regions, bodies of water, mountains | the South, Lake Baikal, Mount Everest |
| Geographic features, parks | Great Basin, Yellowstone National Park |
| Streets and roads, planets | 318 East Sutton Drive, Charles Court, Jupiter, Neptune |
| **Organizations, Events, Etc.** | |
| Companies, organizations, teams | Ford Motor Company, Boy Scouts of America, St. Louis Cardinals |
| Buildings, bridges, monuments | Empire State Building, Eads Bridge, Washington Monument |
| Documents, awards | Declaration of Independence, Stanley Cup |
| Special named events | Mardi Gras, World Series |
| Government bodies, historical periods and events | U.S. Senate, House of Representatives, Middle Ages, Vietnam War |
| Days and months, holidays | Thursday, March, Thanksgiving, Labor Day |
| Specific cars, boats, trains, planes | Porsche, *Mississippi Queen, Stourbridge Lion,* Concorde |
| **Proper Adjectives** | |
| Adjectives formed from proper nouns | French cooking, Freudian psychology, Edwardian age, Midwestern university |
| **First Words and the Pronoun *I*** | |
| First word in a sentence or quotation | This is it. He said, "Let's go." |
| First word of sentence in parentheses that is not within another sentence | The spelling rules are covered in another section. (Consult that section for more information.) |
| First words in the salutation and closing of a letter | Dear Madam, Very truly yours, |
| First word in each line of most poetry / Personal pronoun *I* | Then am I / A happy fly / If I live / Or if I die. |
| First word, last word, and all important words in a title | *A Tale of Two Cities,* "The World Is Too Much with Us" |

# 1 Nouns

A **noun** is a word used to name a person, a place, a thing, an idea, a quality, or an action. Nouns can be classified in several ways.

*For more information on different types of nouns, see* **Quick Reference: Parts of Speech,** *page R46.*

## 1.1 COMMON NOUNS

**Common nouns** are general names, common to entire groups.

## 1.2 PROPER NOUNS

**Proper nouns** name specific, one-of-a-kind people, places, and things.

| Common | Proper |
|---|---|
| guitarist, museum, lake, month | B. B. King, Rock and Roll Hall of Fame, Lake Pontchartrain, February |

*For more information, see* **Quick Reference: Capitalization,** *page R51.*

## 1.3 SINGULAR AND PLURAL NOUNS

A noun may take a singular form (*city, foot*) or a plural form (*cities, feet*), depending on whether it names a single person, place, thing, or idea or more than one. Be sure to spell plural forms correctly.

*For more information, see* **Forming Plural Nouns,** *page R74.*

## 1.4 POSSESSIVE NOUNS

A **possessive noun** shows who or what owns something.

*For more information, see* **Forming Possessives,** *page R74.*

# 2 Pronouns

A **pronoun** is a word that is used in place of a noun or another pronoun. The word or word group to which the pronoun refers is called its **antecedent.**

## 2.1 PERSONAL PRONOUNS

**Personal pronouns** change their form to express person, number, gender, and case. The forms of these pronouns are shown in the following chart.

|  | Nominative | Objective | Possessive |
|---|---|---|---|
| **Singular** | | | |
| First person | I | me | my, mine |
| Second person | you | you | your, yours |
| Third person | she, he, it | her, him, it | her, hers, his, its |
| **Plural** | | | |
| First person | we | us | our, ours |
| Second person | you | you | your, yours |
| Third person | they | them | their, theirs |

## 2.2 AGREEMENT WITH ANTECEDENT

Pronouns should agree with their antecedents in number, gender, and person.

If an antecedent is singular, use a singular pronoun.

> **EXAMPLE:** *I lost my new* **cell phone.** *I may have left it on the bus.*

If an antecedent is plural, use a plural pronoun.

> **EXAMPLES:** *Take the* **snacks** *out of the grocery bag and put them in the pantry.*
>
> ***Delores and Arnetta*** *rode their bikes to the park.*

The gender of a pronoun must be the same as the gender of its antecedent.

> **EXAMPLE:** *The* **man** *thought he left his hat in the* **room.** *He ran back to it to look for the hat.*

The person (first, etc.) of the pronoun must be the same as the person of its antecedent.

> **EXAMPLE:** *You folks will have to go to the stadium to buy your tickets for the concert.*

### GRAMMAR PRACTICE

Rewrite each sentence so that the underlined pronoun agrees with its antecedent.

1. The story "A Sound of Thunder" tells about a man who travels back in time and <u>its</u> adventures.

2. Eckels is warned, "If you disobey instructions, there will be a stiff penalty upon <u>our</u> return."

3. Eckels panics at the size of the dinosaur and <u>his</u> enormous teeth.

4. Travis looks at Eckels's shoes and notices dirt on <u>it</u>.

5. Travis feels <u>they</u> has to kill Eckels, so he shoots him.

---

## GRAMMAR PRACTICE

### ANSWERS

1. *The story "A Sound of Thunder" tells about a man who travels back in time and <u>his</u> adventures.*

2. *Eckels is warned, "If you disobey instructions, there will be a stiff penalty upon <u>your</u> return."*

3. *Eckels panics at the size of the dinosaur and <u>its</u> enormous teeth.*

4. *Travis looks at Eckels's shoes and notices dirt on <u>them</u>.*

5. *Travis feels <u>he</u> has to kill Eckels, so he shoots him.*

## 2.3 PRONOUN CASE

Personal pronouns change form to show how they function in sentences. Different functions are shown by different **cases: nominative, objective,** and **possessive.** For examples, see Section 2.1.

A **nominative pronoun** is used as a subject or a predicate nominative in a sentence.

An **objective pronoun** is used as a direct object, an indirect object, or the object of a preposition.

SUBJECT   OBJECT

*He will lead them to us.*

OBJECT OF PREPOSITION

A **possessive pronoun** shows ownership. The pronouns *mine, yours, hers, his, its, ours,* and *theirs* can be used in place of nouns.

EXAMPLE: *This horse is mine.*

The pronouns *my, your, her, his, its, our,* and *their* are used before nouns.

EXAMPLE: *This is my horse.*

WATCH OUT! Many spelling errors can be avoided if you watch out for *its* and *their.* Don't confuse the possessive pronouns *its* and *their* with the contractions *it's* and *they're.*

TIP To decide which pronoun to use in a comparison, such as "He likes it more than (I *or* me)," fill in the missing word(s): *He likes it more than I do.*

### GRAMMAR PRACTICE

Replace the underlined words with an appropriate pronoun and identify the pronoun's case.

1. In "The Necklace," <u>Mme. Loisel</u> was not happy about her life.

2. Mme. Loisel married a clerk but wished <u>the couple</u> could be wealthy.

3. She hated <u>the apartment's</u> dirty walls.

4. One evening <u>Mme. Loisel's</u> husband said, "I have something for you."

5. Mme. Loisel's reaction to the party invitation was puzzling to <u>M. Loisel.</u>

## 2.4 REFLEXIVE AND INTENSIVE PRONOUNS

These pronouns are formed by adding *-self* or *-selves* to certain personal pronouns. Their forms are the same, and they differ only in how they are used.

A **reflexive pronoun** follows a verb or preposition and reflects back on an earlier noun or pronoun.

EXAMPLES: *He likes himself too much.*

*She is now herself again.*

**Intensive pronouns** intensify or emphasize the nouns or pronouns to which they refer.

EXAMPLES: *They themselves will educate their children.*

*You did it yourself.*

WATCH OUT! Avoid using *hisself* or *theirselves.* Standard English does not include these forms.

NONSTANDARD: *The sniper kept hisself hidden behind a chimney.*

STANDARD: *The sniper kept himself hidden behind a chimney.*

## 2.5 RECIPROCAL PRONOUNS

The **reciprocal pronouns** *each other* and *one another* refer to the individual members of a plural antecedent. These pronouns express mutual actions or relationships between the members they represent. Reciprocal pronouns can also take the possessive forms *each other's* and *one another's.*

EXAMPLES: *The ducks on the pond quacked at one another.*

*John and Pedro borrowed each other's favorite book.*

TIP Some authorities hold that *each other* should be used in reference to two things or people and that *one another* should be used in reference to more than two. Following traditional usage guidelines such as this can give your writing a more formal tone.

## GRAMMAR PRACTICE
### ANSWERS

1. *she; nominative*
2. *they; nominative*
3. *its; possessive*
4. *her; possessive*
5. *him; objective*

## 2.6 DEMONSTRATIVE PRONOUNS

**Demonstrative pronouns** point out things and persons near and far.

|  | Singular | Plural |
|---|---|---|
| Near | this | these |
| Far | that | those |

## 2.7 INDEFINITE PRONOUNS

**Indefinite pronouns** do not refer to specific persons or things and usually have no antecedents. The chart shows some commonly used indefinite pronouns.

| Singular | Plural | Singular or Plural | |
|---|---|---|---|
| another | both | all | most |
| anybody | few | any | none |
| no one | many | more | some |
| neither | several | | |

**TIP** Indefinite pronouns that end in *one, body,* or *thing* are always singular.

> INCORRECT: *Did everybody play their part well?*
> CORRECT: *Did everybody play his or her part well?*

If the indefinite pronoun might denote either a male or a female, *his or her* may be used to refer to it, or the sentence may be recast.

> EXAMPLES: *Did everybody play his or her part well?*
> *Did all the students play their parts well?*

## 2.8 INTERROGATIVE PRONOUNS

An **interrogative pronoun** tells a reader or listener that a question is coming. The interrogative pronouns are *who, whom, whose, which,* and *what.*

> EXAMPLES: *Who is going to rehearse with you?*
> *From whom did you receive the script?*

**TIP** *Who* is used as a subject; *whom,* as an object. To find out which pronoun you need to use in a question, change the question to a statement.

> QUESTION: *(Who/Whom) did you meet there?*
> STATEMENT: *You met (?) there.*

Since the verb has a subject (*you*), the needed word must be the object form, *whom.*

> EXAMPLE: *Whom did you meet there?*

**WATCH OUT!** A special problem arises when you use an interrupter, such as *do you think,* within a question.

> EXAMPLE: *(Who/Whom) do you think will win?*

If you eliminate the interrupter, it is clear that the word you need is *who.*

## 2.9 RELATIVE PRONOUNS

**Relative pronouns** relate, or connect, adjective clauses to the words they modify in sentences. The noun or pronoun that a relative clause modifies is the antecedent of the relative pronoun. Here are the relative pronouns and their uses.

|  | Subject | Object | Possessive |
|---|---|---|---|
| Person | who | whom | whose |
| Thing | which | which | whose |
| Thing/Person | that | that | whose |

Often short sentences with related ideas can be combined by using a relative pronoun to create a more effective sentence.

> SHORT SENTENCE: *Poe wrote "The Raven."*
> RELATED SENTENCE: *"The Raven" is one of the most famous poems in American literature.*
> COMBINED SENTENCE: *Poe wrote "The Raven," which is one of the most famous poems in American literature.*

### GRAMMAR PRACTICE

Write the correct form of each incorrect pronoun.

1. Whom has read "The Gift of the Magi"?
2. Jim needs money for a present for Della, so he takes his watch to the pawnshop hisself.
3. Would anybody else sell their watch to buy a Christmas present?
4. He chooses a beautiful pair of them jeweled combs for Della's hair.
5. Della sells her long hair to buy a watch chain for himself.

## GRAMMAR PRACTICE

## ANSWERS

1. *Who has read "The Gift of the Magi"?*
2. *Jim needs money for a present for Della, so he takes his watch to the pawnshop himself.*
3. *Would anybody else sell his or her watch to buy a Christmas present?*
4. *He chooses a beautiful pair of those jeweled combs for Della's hair.*
5. *Della sells her long hair to buy a watch chain for him.*

## 2.10 PRONOUN REFERENCE PROBLEMS

The referent of a pronoun should always be clear. Avoid problems by rewriting sentences.

An **indefinite reference** occurs when the pronoun *it, you,* or *they* does not clearly refer to a specific antecedent.

UNCLEAR: *In the new production of* Romeo and Juliet, *you have more experienced actors.*

CLEAR: *The new production of* Romeo and Juliet *has more experienced actors.*

A **general reference** occurs when the pronoun *it, this, that, which,* or *such* is used to refer to a general idea rather than a specific antecedent.

UNCLEAR: *Jenna takes acting lessons. This has improved her chances of getting a part in the school play.*

CLEAR: *Jenna takes acting lessons. The lessons have improved her chances of getting a part in the school play.*

*Ambiguous* means "having more than one possible meaning." An **ambiguous reference** occurs when a pronoun could refer to two or more antecedents.

UNCLEAR: *Odysseus escaped from Cyclops, and he blinded him.*

CLEAR: *Odysseus escaped from Cyclops, and he blinded Cyclops.*

### GRAMMAR PRACTICE

Rewrite the following sentences to correct indefinite, ambiguous, and general pronoun references.

1. In Miss Lottie's yard you don't have any grass.
2. Miss Lottie plants marigolds. This makes her barren yard look strange.
3. Lizabeth and her brother throw stones at the marigolds, which ends Miss Lottie's planting.
4. Miss Lottie stares at Lizabeth as if she is strange.

## 3  Verbs

A **verb** is a word that expresses an action, a condition, or a state of being.

*For more information, see **Quick Reference: Parts of Speech**, page R47.*

### 3.1 ACTION VERBS

**Action verbs** express mental or physical activity.

EXAMPLE: *Mr. Cho slept with the window open.*

### 3.2 LINKING VERBS

**Linking verbs** join subjects with words or phrases that rename or describe them.

EXAMPLE: *When he awoke the next morning, his bed was wet from the rain.*

### 3.3 PRINCIPAL PARTS

Action and linking verbs typically have four principal parts, which are used to form verb tenses. The principal parts are the **present,** the **present participle,** the **past,** and the **past participle.**

Action verbs and some linking verbs also fall into two categories: regular and irregular. A **regular verb** is a verb that forms its past and past participle by adding *-ed* or *-d* to the present form.

| Present | Present Participle | Past | Past Participle |
|---------|-------------------|------|-----------------|
| risk | (is) risking | risked | (has) risked |
| solve | (is) solving | solved | (has) solved |
| drop | (is) dropping | dropped | (has) dropped |
| carry | (is) carrying | carried | (has) carried |

An **irregular verb** is a verb that forms its past and past participle in some other way than by adding *-ed* or *-d* to the present form.

| Present | Present Participle | Past | Past Participle |
|---------|-------------------|------|-----------------|
| begin | (is) beginning | began | (has) begun |
| break | (is) breaking | broke | (has) broken |
| go | (is) going | went | (has) gone |

### 3.4 VERB TENSE

The **tense** of a verb indicates the time of the action or state of being. An action or state of being can occur in the present, the past, or the future. There are six tenses, each expressing a different range of time.

## GRAMMAR PRACTICE

### ANSWERS

1. *Miss Lottie's yard doesn't have any grass.*

2. *Possible answer: Miss Lottie plants marigolds. The marigolds make her barren yard look strange.*

3. *Possible answer: Lizabeth and her brother throw stones at Miss Lottie's marigolds. Miss Lottie stops planting marigolds.*

4. *Miss Lottie stares at Lizabeth as if Lizabeth is strange.*

The **present tense** expresses an action or state that is happening at the present time, occurs regularly, or is constant or generally true. Use the present part.

> NOW: *That snow looks deep.*
> REGULAR: *It snows every day.*
> GENERAL: *Snow falls.*

The **past tense** expresses an action that began and ended in the past. Use the past part.

> EXAMPLE: *The storyteller finished his tale.*

The **future tense** expresses an action or state that will occur. Use *shall* or *will* with the present part.

> EXAMPLE: *They will attend the next festival.*

The **present perfect tense** expresses an action or state that (1) was completed at an indefinite time in the past or (2) began in the past and continues into the present. Use *have* or *has* with the past participle.

> EXAMPLE: *Poetry has inspired many readers.*

The **past perfect tense** expresses an action in the past that came before another action in the past. Use *had* with the past participle.

> EXAMPLE: *He had built a fire before the dog ran away.*

The **future perfect tense** expresses an action in the future that will be completed before another action in the future. Use *shall have* or *will have* with the past participle.

> EXAMPLE: *They will have read the novel before they see the movie version of the tale.*

An auxiliary verb is not used with a past-tense irregular verb, but it is always used with a past-participle irregular verb.

> INCORRECT: *I have saw her before.* (*Saw* is the past tense form and shouldn't be used with *have*.)
> CORRECT: *I have seen her somewhere before.*
> INCORRECT: *I seen her before.* (*Seen* is the past participle form of an irregular verb and shouldn't be used without an auxiliary verb.)

### 3.5 PROGRESSIVE FORMS

The progressive forms of the six tenses show ongoing actions. Use forms of *be* with the present participles of verbs.

PRESENT PROGRESSIVE: *She is rehearsing her lines.*
PAST PROGRESSIVE: *She was rehearsing her lines.*
FUTURE PROGRESSIVE: *She will be rehearsing her lines.*
PRESENT PERFECT PROGRESSIVE: *She has been rehearsing her lines.*
PAST PERFECT PROGRESSIVE: *She had been rehearsing her lines.*
FUTURE PERFECT PROGRESSIVE: *She will have been rehearsing her lines.*

**WATCH OUT!** Do not shift from tense to tense needlessly. Watch out for these special cases.

- In most compound sentences and in sentences with compound predicates, keep the tenses the same.

> INCORRECT: *His boots freeze, and he shook with cold.*
> CORRECT: *His boots freeze, and he shakes with cold.*

- If one past action happens before another, do shift tenses.

> INCORRECT: *They wished they started earlier.*
> CORRECT: *They wished they had started earlier.*

#### GRAMMAR PRACTICE

Rewrite each sentence, using a form of the verb in parentheses. Identify each form that you use.

1. Many people (benefit) from the civil rights movement.
2. Martin Luther King Jr. (remain) a towering figure in the history of nonviolent protest.
3. King (become) the leader of the Montgomery bus boycott.
4. When he (speak) to the crowds in Washington, D.C., more than 200,000 people heard his words.
5. Our class (read) his speech "I Have a Dream."

Rewrite each sentence to correct an error in tense.

6. It is a chilly morning as Rosa Parks went to work.
7. She leaves her job early and was preparing to go out of town.
8. She boarded the bus and is taking a seat in the "colored" section.
9. After several more stops, there are no more seats in the front of the bus.
10. Rosa Parks refused to give up her seat and is arrested.

## GRAMMAR PRACTICE

### ANSWERS

1. *Many people benefited from the civil rights movement. (past tense)*

2. *Martin Luther King Jr. remains a towering figure in the history of nonviolent protest. (present tense)*

3. *King became the leader of the Montgomery bus boycott. (past tense)*

4. *When he spoke to the crowds in Washington, D.C., more than 200,000 people heard his words. (past tense)*

5. *Our class read his speech "I Have a Dream." (past tense)* **Alternate answer:** *Our class is reading his speech "I Have a Dream." (present progressive)*

6. *It was a chilly morning as Rosa Parks went to work.*

7. *She left her job early and prepared to go out of town.*

8. *She boarded the bus and took a seat in the "colored" section.*

9. *After several more stops, there were no more seats at the front of the bus.*

10. *Rosa Parks refused to give up her seat and was arrested.*

## 3.6 ACTIVE AND PASSIVE VOICE

The voice of a verb tells whether its subject performs or receives the action expressed by the verb. When the subject performs the action, the verb is in the **active voice.** When the subject is the receiver of the action, the verb is in the **passive voice.**

Compare these two sentences:

ACTIVE: *Richard Wilbur wrote "The Writer."*

PASSIVE: *"The Writer" was written by Richard Wilbur.*

To form the passive voice, use a form of *be* with the past participle of the verb.

**WATCH OUT!** Use the passive voice sparingly. It can make writing awkward and less direct.

AWKWARD: *"The Writer" is a poem that was written by Richard Wilbur.*

BETTER: *Richard Wilbur wrote the poem "The Writer."*

There are occasions when you will choose to use the passive voice because

- you want to emphasize the receiver: *The king was shot.*

- the doer is unknown: *My books were stolen.*

- the doer is unimportant: *French is spoken here.*

## 4 Modifiers

Modifiers are words or groups of words that change or limit the meanings of other words. Adjectives and adverbs are common modifiers.

### 4.1 ADJECTIVES

**Adjectives** modify nouns and pronouns by telling which one, what kind, how many, or how much.

WHICH ONE: *this, that, these, those*
EXAMPLE: *That bird is a scarlet ibis.*

WHAT KIND: *small, sick, courageous, black*
EXAMPLE: *The sick bird sways on the branch.*

HOW MANY: *some, few, ten, none, both, each*
EXAMPLE: *Both brothers stared at the bird.*

HOW MUCH: *more, less, enough, fast*
EXAMPLE: *The bird did not have enough strength to remain perched.*

### 4.2 PREDICATE ADJECTIVES

Most adjectives come before the nouns they modify, as in the examples above. A **predicate adjective,** however, follows a linking verb and describes the subject.

EXAMPLE: *My friends are very intelligent.*

Be especially careful to use adjectives (not adverbs) after such linking verbs as *look, feel, grow, taste,* and *smell.*

EXAMPLE: *The bread smells wonderful.*

### 4.3 ADVERBS

**Adverbs** modify verbs, adjectives, and other adverbs by telling where, when, how, or to what extent.

WHERE: *The children played outside.*

WHEN: *The author spoke yesterday.*

HOW: *We walked slowly behind the leader.*

TO WHAT EXTENT: *He worked very hard.*

Adverbs may occur in many places in sentences, both before and after the words they modify.

EXAMPLES: *Suddenly the wind shifted.*

*The wind suddenly shifted.*

*The wind shifted suddenly.*

### 4.4 ADJECTIVE OR ADVERB?

Many adverbs are formed by adding *-ly* to adjectives.

EXAMPLES: *sweet, sweetly; gentle, gently*

However, *-ly* added to a noun will usually yield an adjective.

EXAMPLES: *friend, friendly; woman, womanly*

### 4.5 COMPARISON OF MODIFIERS

Modifiers can be used to compare two or more things. The form of a modifier shows the degree of comparison. Both adjectives and adverbs have **comparative** and **superlative** forms.

The **comparative form** is used to compare two things, groups, or actions.

EXAMPLES: *His father's hands were stronger than his own.*

*His father was more courageous than the other man.*

The **superlative form** is used to compare more than two things, groups, or actions.

> EXAMPLES: *His father's hands were the strongest in the family.*
>
> *His father was the most courageous of them all.*

### 4.6 REGULAR COMPARISONS

Most one-syllable and some two-syllable adjectives and adverbs have comparatives and superlatives formed by adding *-er* and *-est*. All three-syllable and most two-syllable modifiers have comparatives and superlatives formed with *more* or *most*.

| Modifier | Comparative | Superlative |
|----------|-------------|-------------|
| small | smaller | smallest |
| thin | thinner | thinnest |
| sleepy | sleepier | sleepiest |
| useless | more useless | most useless |
| precisely | more precisely | most precisely |

**WATCH OUT!** Note that spelling changes must sometimes be made to form the comparatives and superlatives of modifiers.

> EXAMPLES: *friendly, friendlier* (Change *y* to *i* and add the ending.)
>
> *sad, sadder* (Double the final consonant and add the ending.)

### 4.7 IRREGULAR COMPARISONS

Some commonly used modifiers have irregular comparative and superlative forms. They are listed in the following chart. You may wish to memorize them.

| Modifier | Comparative | Superlative |
|----------|-------------|-------------|
| good | better | best |
| bad | worse | worst |
| far | farther *or* further | farthest *or* furthest |
| little | less *or* lesser | least |
| many | more | most |
| well | better | best |
| much | more | most |

### 4.8 PROBLEMS WITH MODIFIERS

Study the tips that follow to avoid common mistakes:

**Farther and Further** Use *farther* for distances; use *further* for everything else.

**Double Comparisons** Make a comparison by using *-er/-est* or by using *more/most*. Using *-er* with *more* or using *-est* with *most* is incorrect.

> INCORRECT: *I like her more better than she likes me.*
>
> CORRECT: *I like her better than she likes me.*

**Illogical Comparisons** An illogical or confusing comparison results when two unrelated things are compared or when something is compared with itself. The word *other* or the word *else* should be used when comparing an individual member to the rest of a group.

> ILLOGICAL: *The narrator was more curious about the war than any student in his class.* (implies that the narrator isn't a student in the class)
>
> LOGICAL: *The narrator was more curious about the war than any other student in his class.* (identifies that the narrator is a student)

**Bad vs. Badly** *Bad,* always an adjective, is used before a noun or after a linking verb. *Badly,* always an adverb, never modifies a noun. Be sure to use the right form after a linking verb.

> INCORRECT: *Ed felt badly after his team lost.*
>
> CORRECT: *Ed felt bad after his team lost.*

**Good vs. Well** *Good* is always an adjective. It is used before a noun or after a linking verb. *Well* is often an adverb meaning "expertly" or "properly." *Well* can also be used as an adjective after a linking verb when it means "in good health."

> INCORRECT: *Helen writes very good.*
>
> CORRECT: *Helen writes very well.*
>
> CORRECT: *Yesterday I felt bad; today I feel well.*

**Double Negatives** If you add a negative word to a sentence that is already negative, the result will be an error known as a double negative. When using *not* or *-n't* with a verb, use *any-* words, such as

*anybody* or *anything*, rather than *no-* words, such as *nobody* or *nothing*, later in the sentence.

INCORRECT: *We haven't seen nobody.*

CORRECT: *We haven't seen anybody.*

Using *hardly, barely,* or *scarcely* after a negative word is also incorrect.

INCORRECT: *They couldn't barely see two feet ahead.*

CORRECT: *They could barely see two feet ahead.*

**Misplaced Modifiers** Sometimes a modifier is placed so far away from the word it modifies that the intended meaning of the sentence is unclear. Prepositional phrases and participial phrases are often misplaced. Place modifiers as close as possible to the words they modify.

MISPLACED: *We found the dog in the park that was missing.* (The dog was missing, not the park.)

CLEARER: *We found the dog that was missing in the park.*

**Dangling Modifiers** Sometimes a modifier doesn't appear to modify any word in a sentence. Most dangling modifiers are participial phrases or infinitive phrases.

DANGLING: *Looking out the window, his brother was seen driving by.*

CLEARER: *Looking out the window, Josh saw his brother driving by.*

**GRAMMAR PRACTICE**

Choose the correct word or words from each pair in parentheses.

1. *The House on Mango Street* gives (better, more better) insight into Mexican-American culture than any other book I've read.

2. Sandra Cisneros's family moved so often that she hardly had (any, no) friends.

3. She felt (bad, badly) that she didn't live in a perfect house like the ones she saw on TV.

4. At one time Cisneros didn't think (nothing, anything) was positive about belonging to a different culture.

**GRAMMAR PRACTICE**

Rewrite each sentence that contains a misplaced or dangling modifier. Write "correct" if the sentence is written correctly.

1. The house on Loomis Street belongs to Esperanza's family with the broken water pipes.

2. Esperanza has to carry water from the house in empty milk jugs.

3. A nun asks Esperanza where she lived.

4. Feeling bad about the nun's reaction, the house is no longer good enough for Esperanza.

## 5 The Sentence and Its Parts

A **sentence** is a group of words used to express a complete thought. A complete sentence has a subject and a predicate.

*For more information, see* **Quick Reference: The Sentence and Its Parts,** *page R48.*

### 5.1 KINDS OF SENTENCES

There are four basic types of sentences.

| Type | Definition | Example |
|---|---|---|
| Declarative | states a fact, a wish, an intent, or a feeling | Joan Bauer understands youths. |
| Interrogative | asks a question | Did you read "Pancakes"? |
| Imperative | gives a command or direction | Read the story. |
| Exclamatory | expresses strong feeling or excitement | The story is funny! |

### 5.2 COMPOUND SUBJECTS AND PREDICATES

A compound subject consists of two or more subjects that share the same verb. They are typically joined by the coordinating conjunction *and* or *or.*

EXAMPLE: *A short story or novel will keep you engaged.*

A compound predicate consists of two or more predicates that share the same subject. They too are typically joined by a coordinating conjunction, usually *and, but,* or *or.*

## GRAMMAR PRACTICE

### ANSWERS

1. *better*
2. *any*
3. *bad*
4. *anything*

## GRAMMAR PRACTICE

### ANSWERS

1. *The house with the broken water pipes on Loomis Street belongs to Esperanza's family.*
2. *correct*
3. *A nun asks Esperanza where she lives.*
4. *Feeling bad about the nun's reaction, Esperanza no longer thinks the house is good enough.*

**EXAMPLE:** *The class finished all the poetry but did not read the short stories.*

### 5.3 COMPLEMENTS

A **complement** is a word or group of words that completes the meaning of the sentence. Some sentences contain only a subject and a verb. Most sentences, however, require additional words placed after the verb to complete the meaning of the sentence. There are three kinds of complements: direct objects, indirect objects, and subject complements.

**Direct objects** are words or word groups that receive the action of action verbs. A direct object answers the question *what* or *whom*.

> **EXAMPLES:** *The students asked many questions.* (Asked what?)
> *The teacher quickly answered the students.* (Answered whom?)

**Indirect objects** tell to whom or what or for whom or what the actions of verbs are performed. Indirect objects come before direct objects. In the examples that follow, the indirect objects are highlighted.

> **EXAMPLES:** *My sister usually gave her friends good advice.* (Gave to whom?)
> *Her brother sent the store a heavy package.* (Sent to what?)

**Subject complements** come after linking verbs and identify or describe the subjects. A subject complement that names or identifies a subject is called a **predicate nominative.** Predicate nominatives include **predicate nouns** and **predicate pronouns.**

> **EXAMPLES:** *My friends are very hard workers.*
> *The best writer in the class is she.*

A subject complement that describes a subject is called a **predicate adjective.**

> **EXAMPLE:** *The pianist appeared very energetic.*

### 6 Phrases

A **phrase** is a group of related words that does not contain a subject and a predicate but functions in a sentence as a single part of speech.

### 6.1 PREPOSITIONAL PHRASES

A **prepositional phrase** is a phrase that consists of a preposition, its object, and any modifiers of the object. Prepositional phrases that modify nouns or pronouns are called **adjective phrases.** Prepositional phrases that modify verbs, adjectives, or adverbs are **adverb phrases.**

> **ADJECTIVE PHRASE:** *The central character of the story is a villain.*
> **ADVERB PHRASE:** *He reveals his nature in the first scene.*

### 6.2 APPPOSITIVES AND APPOSITIVE PHRASES

An **appositive** is a noun or pronoun that identifies or renames another noun or pronoun. An **appositive phrase** includes an appositive and modifiers of it.

An appositive can be either **essential** or **nonessential.** An **essential appositive** provides information that is needed to identify what is referred to by the preceding noun or pronoun.

> **EXAMPLE:** *The book is about the author Richard Wright.*

A **nonessential appositive** adds extra information about a noun or pronoun whose meaning is already clear. Nonessential appositives and appositive phrases are set off with commas.

> **EXAMPLE:** *The book, an autobiography, tells how he began writing.*

### 7 Verbals and Verbal Phrases

A **verbal** is a verb form that is used as a noun, an adjective, or an adverb. A **verbal phrase** consists of a verbal along with its modifiers and complements. There are three kinds of verbals: **infinitives, participles,** and **gerunds.**

## 7.1 INFINITIVES AND INFINITIVE PHRASES

An **infinitive** is a verb form that usually begins with *to* and functions as a noun, an adjective, or an adverb. An **infinitive phrase** consists of an infinitive plus its modifiers and complements. The examples that follow show several uses of infinitive phrases.

NOUN: *To know her is my only desire.* (subject)
*I'm planning to walk with you.* (direct object)
*Her goal was to promote women's rights.* (predicate nominative)

ADJECTIVE: *We saw his need to be loved.* (adjective modifying *need*)

ADVERB: *She wrote to voice her opinions.* (adverb modifying *wrote*)

Because *to,* the sign of the infinitive, precedes infinitives, it is usually easy to recognize them. However, sometimes *to* may be omitted.

EXAMPLE: *Let no one dare [to] enter this shrine.*

## 7.2 PARTICIPLES AND PARTICIPIAL PHRASES

A **participle** is a verb form that functions as an adjective. Like adjectives, participles modify nouns and pronouns. Most participles are present-participle forms, ending in *-ing,* or past-participle forms ending in *-ed* or *-en.* In the examples below, the participles are highlighted.

MODIFYING A NOUN: *The dying man had a smile on his face.*

MODIFYING A PRONOUN: *Frustrated, everyone abandoned the cause.*

**Participial phrases** are participles with all their modifiers and complements.

MODIFYING A NOUN: *The dogs searching for survivors are well trained.*

MODIFYING A PRONOUN: *Having approved your proposal, we are ready to act.*

## 7.3 DANGLING AND MISPLACED PARTICIPLES

A participle or participial phrase should be placed as close as possible to the word that it modifies. Otherwise the meaning of the sentence may not be clear.

MISPLACED: *The boys were looking for squirrels searching the trees.*

CLEARER: *The boys searching the trees were looking for squirrels.*

A participle or participial phrase that does not clearly modify anything in a sentence is called a **dangling participle.** A dangling participle causes confusion because it appears to modify a word that it cannot sensibly modify. Correct a dangling participle by providing a word for the participle to modify.

DANGLING: *Running like the wind, my hat fell off.* (The hat wasn't running.)

CLEARER: *Running like the wind, I lost my hat.*

## 7.4 GERUNDS AND GERUND PHRASES

A **gerund** is a verb form ending in *-ing* that functions as a noun. Gerunds may perform any function nouns perform.

SUBJECT: *Running is my favorite pastime.*

DIRECT OBJECT: *I truly love running.*

INDIRECT OBJECT: *You should give running a try.*

SUBJECT COMPLEMENT: *My deepest passion is running.*

OBJECT OF PREPOSITION: *Her love of running keeps her strong.*

**Gerund phrases** are gerunds with all their modifiers and complements.

SUBJECT: *Wishing on a star never got me far.*

OBJECT OF PREPOSITION: *I will finish before leaving the office.*

APPOSITIVE: *Her avocation, flying airplanes, finally led to full-time employment.*

## GRAMMAR PRACTICE

### ANSWERS

1. *"Daughter of Invention," a short story, was written by Julia Alvarez.*

2. *The narrator loves writing to record her experiences.*

3. *She will appear at an assembly to give a speech.*

4. *Working feverishly for hours, she finally finishes her speech.*

5. *Feeling proud, she reads her speech to her parents.*

## 8 Clauses

A **clause** is a group of words that contains a subject and a predicate. There are two kinds of clauses: independent clauses and subordinate clauses.

### 8.1 INDEPENDENT AND SUBORDINATE CLAUSES

An **independent clause** can stand alone as a sentence, as the word *independent* suggests.

> INDEPENDENT CLAUSE: *Taos is famous for its Great Bank Robbery.*

A sentence may contain more than one independent clause.

> EXAMPLE: *Many people remember the robbery, and they will tell you all about it.*

In the preceding example, the coordinating conjunction *and* joins two independent clauses.

*For more information, see Coordinating Conjunction, page R47.*

A **subordinate clause** cannot stand alone as a sentence. It is subordinate to, or dependent on, an independent clause.

> EXAMPLE: *Although the two men needed cash, they didn't get it from the bank.*

The highlighted clause cannot stand by itself.

### 8.2 ADJECTIVE CLAUSES

An **adjective clause** is a subordinate clause used as an adjective. It usually follows the noun or pronoun it modifies.

> EXAMPLE: *Tony Hillerman is someone whom millions know as a mystery writer.*

Adjective clauses are typically introduced by the relative pronoun *who, whom, whose, which,* or *that.*

*For more information, see **Relative Pronouns**, page R54.*

> EXAMPLES: *A person who needs money should get a job.*
> *The robbers, whose names were Gomez and Smith, had guns.*

An adjective clause can be either essential or nonessential. An **essential adjective clause** provides information that is necessary to identify the preceding noun or pronoun.

> EXAMPLE: *One robber wore a disguise that was meant to fool Taos's residents.*

A **nonessential adjective clause** adds additional information about a noun or pronoun whose meaning is already clear. Nonessential clauses are set off with commas.

> EXAMPLE: *The suspects, who drove away in a pickup truck, sideswiped a car driven by a minister.*

**TIP** The relative pronouns *whom, which,* and *that* may sometimes be omitted when they are objects in adjective clauses.

> EXAMPLE: *Hillerman is a writer [whom] millions enjoy.*

### 8.3 ADVERB CLAUSES

An **adverb clause** is a subordinate clause that is used to modify a verb, an adjective, or an adverb. It is introduced by a subordinating conjunction.

*For examples of subordinating conjunctions, see **Noun Clauses**, page R63.*

Adverb clauses typically occur at the beginning or end of sentences.

> MODIFYING A VERB: *When we need you, we will call.*
> MODIFYING AN ADVERB: *I'll stay here where there is shelter from the rain.*
> MODIFYING AN ADJECTIVE: *Roman felt as good as he had ever felt.*

## 8.4 NOUN CLAUSES

A **noun clause** is a subordinate clause that is used as a noun. A noun clause may be used as a subject, a direct object, an indirect object, a predicate nominative, or the object of a preposition. Noun clauses are introduced either by pronouns, such as *that, what, who, whoever, which,* and *whose,* or by subordinating conjunctions, such as *how, when, where, why,* and *whether.*

*For more information, see* **Quick Reference: Parts of Speech,** *page R47.*

**TIP** Because the same words may introduce adjective and noun clauses, you need to consider how a clause functions within its sentence. To determine if a clause is a noun clause, try substituting *something* or *someone* for the clause. If you can do it, it is probably a noun clause.

> EXAMPLES: *I know whose woods these are.*
> ("I know *something*." The clause is a noun clause, direct object of the verb *know*.)
> *Give a copy to whoever wants one.* ("Give a copy to *someone*." The clause is a noun clause, object of the preposition *to*.)

### GRAMMAR PRACTICE

Add descriptive details to each sentence by writing the type of clause indicated in parentheses.

1. My aunt has an interesting hobby. (adjective clause)
2. She works on her craft at night. (adverb clause)
3. She writes. (noun clause)
4. She has written several books. (adjective clause)
5. I asked her to write a story about me. (adverb clause)

## 9 The Structure of Sentences

When classified by their structure, there are four kinds of sentences: simple, compound, complex, and compound-complex.

### 9.1 SIMPLE SENTENCES

A **simple sentence** is a sentence that has one independent clause and no subordinate clauses.

The fact that such a sentence is called simple does not mean that it is uncomplicated. Various parts of simple sentences may be compound, and simple sentences may contain grammatical structures such as appositive and verbal phrases.

> EXAMPLES: *Ray Bradbury, a science fiction writer, has written short stories and novels.* (appositive and compound direct object)
> *The narrator, recalling the years of his childhood, tells his story.* (participial phrase)

### 9.2 COMPOUND SENTENCES

A **compound sentence** consists of two or more independent clauses. The clauses in compound sentences are joined with commas and coordinating conjunctions (*and, but, or, nor, yet, for, so*) or with semicolons. Like simple sentences, compound sentences do not contain any subordinate clauses.

> EXAMPLES: *I enjoyed Bradbury's story "The Utterly Perfect Murder," and I want to read more of his stories.*
> *The narrator has lived a normal, complete life; however, he decides to kill his childhood playmate.*

**WATCH OUT!** Do not confuse compound sentences with simple sentences that have compound parts.

> EXAMPLE: *A subcommittee drafted a document and immediately presented it to the entire group.* (Here *and* joins parts of a compound predicate, not a compound sentence.)

### 9.3 COMPLEX SENTENCES

A **complex sentence** consists of one independent clause and one or more subordinate clauses. Each subordinate clause can be used as a noun or as a modifier. If it is used as a modifier, a subordinate clause usually modifies a word in the independent clause, and the independent clause can stand alone. However, when a subordinate clause is a noun clause, it is a part of the independent clause; the two cannot be separated.

## GRAMMAR PRACTICE
## ANSWERS

*Possible answers:*

1. *My aunt, who lives in Baltimore, has an interesting hobby.*
2. *She works on her craft at night when she can't sleep.*
3. *She writes what she knows.*
4. *She has written several books that have become bestsellers.*
5. *When I visited my aunt last summer, I asked her to write a story about me.*

MODIFIER: *One should not complain unless one has a better solution.*

NOUN CLAUSE: *We sketched pictures of whomever we wished.* (The noun clause is the object of the preposition *of* and cannot be separated from the rest of the sentence.)

### 9.4 COMPOUND-COMPLEX SENTENCES

A **compound-complex sentence** contains two or more independent clauses and one or more subordinate clauses. Compound-complex sentences are, simply, both compound and complex. If you start with a compound sentence, all you need to do to form a compound-complex sentence is add a subordinate clause.

COMPOUND: *All the students knew the answer, yet they were too shy to volunteer.*

COMPOUND-COMPLEX: *All the students knew the answer that their teacher expected, yet they were too shy to volunteer.*

### 9.5 PARALLEL STRUCTURE

When you write sentences, make sure that coordinate parts are equivalent, or **parallel,** in structure.

NOT PARALLEL: *Erin loved basketball and to play hockey.* (*Basketball* is a noun; *to play hockey* is a phrase.)

PARALLEL: *Erin loved basketball and hockey.* (*Basketball* and *hockey* are both nouns.)

NOT PARALLEL: *He wanted to rent an apartment, a new car, and traveling around the country.* (*To rent* is an infinitive, *car* is a noun, and *traveling* is a gerund.)

PARALLEL: *He wanted to rent an apartment, to drive a new car, and to travel around the country.* (*To rent, to drive,* and *to travel* are all infinitives.)

## 🔟 Writing Complete Sentences

Remember, a sentence is a group of words that expresses a complete thought. In writing that you wish to share with a reader, try to avoid both sentence fragments and run-on sentences.

### 10.1 CORRECTING FRAGMENTS

A **sentence fragment** is a group of words that is only part of a sentence. It does not express a complete thought and may be confusing to a reader or listener. A sentence fragment may be lacking a subject, a predicate, or both.

FRAGMENT: *Waited for the boat to arrive.* (no subject)

CORRECTED: *We waited for the boat to arrive.*

FRAGMENT: *People of various races, ages, and creeds.* (no predicate)

CORRECTED: *People of various races, ages, and creeds gathered together.*

FRAGMENT: *Near the old cottage.* (neither subject nor predicate)

CORRECTED: *The burial ground is near the old cottage.*

In your writing, fragments may be a result of haste or incorrect punctuation. Sometimes fixing a fragment will be a matter of attaching it to a preceding or following sentence.

FRAGMENT: *We saw the two girls. Waiting for the bus to arrive.*

CORRECTED: *We saw the two girls waiting for the bus to arrive.*

### 10.2 CORRECTING RUN-ON SENTENCES

A **run-on sentence** is made up of two or more sentences written as though they were one. Some run-ons have no punctuation within them. Others may have only commas where conjunctions or stronger punctuation marks are necessary. Use your judgment in correcting run-on sentences, as you have choices. You can make a run-on two sentences if the thoughts are not closely connected. If the thoughts are closely related, you can keep the run-on as one sentence by adding a semicolon or a conjunction.

RUN-ON: *We found a place for the picnic by a small pond it was three miles from the village.*

MAKE TWO SENTENCES: *We found a place for the picnic by a small pond. It was three miles from the village.*

**RUN-ON:** *We found a place for the picnic by a small pond it was perfect.*

**USE A SEMICOLON:** *We found a place for the picnic by a small pond; it was perfect.*

**ADD A CONJUNCTION:** *We found a place for the picnic by a small pond, and it was perfect.*

**WATCH OUT!** When you form compound sentences, make sure you use appropriate punctuation: a comma before a coordinating conjunction, a semicolon when there is no coordinating conjunction. A very common mistake is to use a comma alone instead of a comma and a conjunction. This error is called a **comma splice.**

> **INCORRECT:** *He finished the apprenticeship, he left the village.*
>
> **CORRECT:** *He finished the apprenticeship, and he left the village.*

## 11 Subject-Verb Agreement

The subject and verb in a clause must agree in number. Agreement means that if the subject is singular, the verb is also singular, and if the subject is plural, the verb is also plural.

### 11.1 BASIC AGREEMENT

Fortunately, agreement between subjects and verbs in English is simple. Most verbs show the difference between singular and plural only in the third person of the present tense. In the present tense, the third-person singular form ends in *-s.*

| Present-Tense Verb Forms | |
|---|---|
| **Singular** | **Plural** |
| I sleep | we sleep |
| you sleep | you sleep |
| she, he, it sleeps | they sleep |

### 11.2 AGREEMENT WITH *BE*

The verb *be* presents special problems in agreement, because this verb does not follow the usual verb patterns.

| Forms of *Be* | | | |
|---|---|---|---|
| **Present Tense** | | **Past Tense** | |
| **Singular** | **Plural** | **Singular** | **Plural** |
| I am | we are | I was | we were |
| you are | you are | you were | you were |
| she, he, it is | they are | she, he, it was | they were |

### 11.3 WORDS BETWEEN SUBJECT AND VERB

A verb agrees only with its subject. When words come between a subject and a verb, ignore them when considering proper agreement. Identify the subject, and make sure the verb agrees with it.

> **EXAMPLES:** *A story in the newspapers tells about the 1890s.*
>
> *Dad as well as Mom reads the paper daily.*

### 11.4 AGREEMENT WITH COMPOUND SUBJECTS

Use plural verbs with most compound subjects joined by the word *and.*

> **EXAMPLE:** *My father and his friends read the paper daily.*

To confirm that you need a plural verb, you could substitute the plural pronoun *they* for *my father and his friends.*

If a compound subject is thought of as a unit, use a singular verb. Test this by substituting the singular pronoun *it.*

> **EXAMPLE:** *Peanut butter and jelly [it] is my brother's favorite sandwich.*

Use a singular verb with a compound subject that is preceded by *each, every,* or *many a.*

> **EXAMPLE:** *Each novel and short story seems grounded in personal experience.*

When the parts of a compound subject are joined by *or, nor,* or the correlative conjunctions *either . . . or* or *neither . . . nor,* make the verb agree with the noun or pronoun nearest the verb.

> **EXAMPLES:** *Cookies or ice cream is my favorite dessert.*
>
> *Either Cheryl or her friends are being invited.*
>
> *Neither ice storms nor snow is predicted today.*

### 11.5 PERSONAL PRONOUNS AS SUBJECTS

When using a personal pronoun as a subject, make sure to match it with the correct form of the verb *be*. (See the chart in Section 11.2.) Note especially that the pronoun *you* takes the forms *are* and *were*, regardless of whether it is singular or plural.

**WATCH OUT!** *You is* and *you was* are nonstandard forms and should be avoided in writing and speaking. *We was* and *they was* are also forms to be avoided.

INCORRECT: *You was a good student.*
CORRECT: *You were a good student.*
INCORRECT: *They was starting a new school.*
CORRECT: *They were starting a new school.*

### 11.6 INDEFINITE PRONOUNS AS SUBJECTS

Some indefinite pronouns are always singular; some are always plural.

| Singular Indefinite Pronouns | | | |
|---|---|---|---|
| another | either | neither | one |
| anybody | everybody | nobody | somebody |
| anyone | everyone | no one | someone |
| anything | everything | nothing | something |
| each | much | | |

EXAMPLES: *Each of the writers was given an award.*
*Somebody in the room upstairs is sleeping.*

| Plural Indefinite Pronouns | | | |
|---|---|---|---|
| both | few | many | several |

EXAMPLES: *Many of the books in our library are not in circulation.*
*Few have been returned recently.*

Still other indefinite pronouns may be either singular or plural.

| Singular or Plural Indefinite Pronouns | | |
|---|---|---|
| all | more | none |
| any | most | some |

The number of the indefinite pronoun *any* or *none* often depends on the intended meaning.

EXAMPLES: *Any of these topics has potential for a good article.* (any one topic)
*Any of these topics have potential for good articles.* (all of the many topics)

The indefinite pronouns *all, some, more, most,* and *none* are singular when they refer to quantities or parts of things. They are plural when they refer to numbers of individual things. Context will usually give a clue.

EXAMPLES: *All of the flour is gone.* (referring to a quantity)
*All of the flowers are gone.* (referring to individual items)

### 11.7 INVERTED SENTENCES

Problems in agreement often occur in inverted sentences beginning with *here* or *there*; in questions beginning with *how, when, why, where,* or *what*; and in inverted sentences beginning with phrases. Identify the subject—wherever it is—before deciding on the verb.

EXAMPLES: *There clearly are far too many cooks in this kitchen.*
*What is the correct ingredient for this stew?*
*Far from the embroiled cooks stands the master chef.*

## GRAMMAR PRACTICE

Locate the subject of each verb in parentheses in the sentences below. Then choose the correct verb form.

1. Many Greeks sail home from Troy, but few (struggles, struggle) as hard as Odysseus to get there.

2. Neither Odysseus nor his men (know, knows) what dangers lie ahead.

3. There (is, are) more dangers awaiting him than there (is, are) gods to save him.

4. Everybody who has read about Odysseus' trials (knows, know) what he endured.

5. There (is, are) few friends who can help him during his ten-year odyssey.

6. The herds of the Cyclops Polyphemus (gives, give) Odysseus an idea for escape.

7. Does anyone (escapes, escape) the spell of Circe?

8. Standing before the hogs that are his friends (is, are) Odysseus.

9. Some of the winds (blows, blow) favorably, but many (blows, blow) ill.

10. Penelope, Telemachus, and the suitors (awaits, await) Odysseus upon his return.

## 11.8 SENTENCES WITH PREDICATE NOMINATIVES

When a predicate nominative serves as a complement in a sentence, use a verb that agrees with the subject, not the complement.

**EXAMPLES:** *The speeches of Martin Luther King Jr. are a landmark in American civil rights history.* (*Speeches* is the subject—not *landmark*—and it takes the plural verb *are*.)

*One landmark in American civil rights history is the speeches of Martin Luther King Jr.* (The subject is *landmark*—not *speeches*—and it takes the singular verb *is*.)

## 11.9 *DON'T* AND *DOESN'T* AS AUXILIARY VERBS

The auxiliary verb *doesn't* is used with singular subjects and with the personal pronouns *she, he,* and *it*. The auxiliary verb *don't* is used with plural subjects and with the personal pronouns *I, we, you,* and *they*.

**SINGULAR:** *She doesn't know Martin Luther King's famous "I Have a Dream" speech.*

*Doesn't the young woman read very much?*

**PLURAL:** *We don't have the speech memorized.*

*Don't speakers usually memorize their speeches?*

## 11.10 COLLECTIVE NOUNS AS SUBJECTS

**Collective nouns** are singular nouns that name groups of persons or things. *Team,* for example, is the collective name of a group of individuals. A collective noun takes a singular verb when the group acts as a single unit. It takes a plural verb when the members of the group act separately.

**EXAMPLES:** *Our team usually wins.* (The team as a whole wins.)

*Our team vote differently on most issues.* (The individual members vote.)

## 11.11 RELATIVE PRONOUNS AS SUBJECTS

When the relative pronoun *who, which,* or *that* is used as a subject in an adjective clause, the verb in the clause must agree in number with the antecedent of the pronoun.

**SINGULAR:** *I didn't read the **poem** about fireworks that was assigned.*

The antecedent of the relative pronoun *that* is the singular *poem;* therefore, *that* is singular and must take the singular verb *was.*

**PLURAL:** ***William Blake and Amy Lowell,** who are very different from each other, are both outstanding poets.*

The antecedent of the relative pronoun *who* is the plural compound subject *William Blake and Amy Lowell.* Therefore *who* is plural, and it takes the plural verb *are.*

## GRAMMAR PRACTICE
## ANSWERS

1. *struggle*
2. *know*
3. *are; are*
4. *knows*
5. *are*
6. *give*
7. *escape*
8. *is*
9. *blow; blow*
10. *await*

# COMMON CORE FOCUS

**RL 4** Determine the meaning of words and phrases as they are used in the text, including figurative and connotative meanings; analyze the cumulative impact of specific word choices on meaning and tone. **RI 4** Determine the meaning of words and phrases as they are used in a text, including figurative, connotative, and technical meanings; analyze the cumulative impact of specific word choices on meaning and tone. **L 2c** Spell correctly. **L 3** Apply knowledge of language to understand how language functions in different contexts, to make effective choices for meaning or style, and to comprehend more fully when reading or listening. **L 4a-d** Determine or clarify the meaning of unknown and multiple-meaning words and phrases, choosing flexibly from a range of strategies. **L 6** Acquire and use accurately general academic and domain-specific words and phrases.

## 1.3 IDIOMS, SLANG, AND FIGURATIVE LANGUAGE

Use this opportunity to have students identify and use figurative meanings of words. For each word in the list below, have students first identify the literal meaning and then use the same word in a figurative sense:

dirt

fire

water

snake

gold

---

The key to becoming an independent reader is to develop a toolkit of vocabulary strategies. By learning and practicing the strategies, you'll know what to do when you encounter unfamiliar words while reading. You'll also know how to refine the words you use for different situations—personal, school, and work.

Being a good speller is important when communicating your ideas in writing. Learning basic spelling rules and checking your spelling in a dictionary will help you spell words that you may not use frequently.

**COMMON CORE**
Included in this handbook:
RL 4, RI 4, L 2c, L 3, L 4a–d, L 6

## 1 Using Context Clues

The context of a word is made up of the punctuation marks, words, sentences, and paragraphs that surround it. A word's context can give you important clues about its meaning, including both its denotation and connotation.

*For more information, see Denotation and Connotation, page R71.*

### 1.1 GENERAL CONTEXT

Sometimes you need to infer the meaning of a word by reading all the information in a passage.

> *After twelve hours without food, I was so ravenous that I ate seven slices of pizza.*

You can figure out from the context that *ravenous* means "extremely hungry."

### 1.2 SPECIFIC CONTEXT CLUES

Sometimes writers help you understand the meanings of words by providing specific clues such as those shown in the chart.

### 1.3 IDIOMS, SLANG, AND FIGURATIVE LANGUAGE

An **idiom** is an expression whose overall meaning is different from the meaning of the individual words. **Slang** is informal language in which made-up words and ordinary words are used to mean something different from their meanings in formal English. **Figurative language** is language that communicates meaning beyond the literal meaning of the words. Use context clues to figure out the meanings of idioms, slang, and figurative language.

> *The mosquitoes drove us crazy on our hike through the woods. (idiom; means "bothered")*

> *That's a really cool backpack that you're wearing. (slang; means "excellent" or "first-rate")*

> *I was angry. Heat rose under my skin until I felt as if searing flames were threatening to engulf my whole body. (figurative language; hot skin and flames symbolize anger)*

| Specific Context Clues | | |
|---|---|---|
| **Type of Clue** | **Key Words/ Phrases** | **Example** |
| **Definition or restatement** of the meaning of the word | or, which is, that is, in other words, also known as, also called | His first conjecture, **or guess,** was correct. |
| **Example** following an unfamiliar word | such as, like, as if, for example, especially, including | She loved macabre stories, **such as those by Edgar Allan Poe and Stephen King.** |
| **Comparison** with a more familiar word or concept | as, like, also, similar to, in the same way, likewise | Despite his physical suffering, his mind was as **lucid** as any **rational** person's. |
| **Contrast** with a familiar word or experience | unlike, but, however, although, on the other hand, on the contrary | Unlike her **clumsy** partner, she was an **agile** dancer. |
| **Cause-and-effect** relationship in which one term is familiar | because, since, when, consequently, as a result, therefore | **Because** this perfume has such a sharp scent, **I will buy** the one with a subtle fragrance. |

*For more information, see Vocabulary Strategy: Using Context Clues, pages 399 and 491.*

# 2 Analyzing Word Structure

Many words can be broken into smaller parts. These word parts include base words, roots, prefixes, and suffixes.

## 2.1 BASE WORDS

A **base word** is a word part that by itself is also a word. Other words or word parts can be added to base words to form new words.

## 2.2 ROOTS

A **root** is a word part that contains the core meaning of the word. Many English words contain roots that come from older languages such as Greek, Latin, Old English (Anglo-Saxon), and Norse. Knowing the meaning of the word's root can help you determine the word's meaning.

| Root | Meaning | Examples |
|---|---|---|
| *bi* (Greek) | life | biography |
| *gramm* (Greek) | letter, something written | grammar |
| *grad* (Latin) | step, degree | graduate |
| *man* (Latin) | hand | manual |
| *hēadfod* (Old English) | head, top | headfirst |

*For more information, see **Vocabulary Strategy: Word Roots**, pages 53, 220, 368, 576, and 599.*

## 2.3 PREFIXES

A **prefix** is a word part attached to the beginning of a word. Most prefixes come from Greek, Latin, or Old English.

| Prefix | Meaning | Examples |
|---|---|---|
| pre- | before | preschool |
| ex- | out, from | extend |
| re- | again, back | return |

*For more information, see **Vocabulary Strategy: Prefixes**, pages 98, 838, and 1239.*

## 2.4 SUFFIXES

A **suffix** is a word part that appears at the end of a root or base word to form a new word. Some suffixes do not change word meaning. These suffixes are

- added to nouns to change the number of persons or objects
- added to verbs to change the tense
- added to modifiers to change the degree of comparison

| Suffix | Meaning | Examples |
|---|---|---|
| -s, -es | to change the number of a noun | snack + s = snacks |
| -d, -ed, -ing | to change verb tense | walk + ed = walked |
| -er, -est | to change the degree of comparison in modifiers | wild + er = wilder<br>fast + est = fastest |

Other suffixes can be added to a root or base to change the word's meaning. These suffixes can also determine a word's part of speech.

| Suffix | Meaning | Examples |
|---|---|---|
| -age | action or process | pilgrimage |
| -able | ability | enjoyable |
| -ize | to make | criticize |

*For more information, see **Vocabulary Strategy: Suffixes**, page 453.*

### Strategies for Understanding Unfamiliar Words

- Look for any prefixes or suffixes. Remove them to isolate the base word or the root.

- See if you recognize any elements—prefix, suffix, root, or base—of the word. You may be able to guess its meaning by analyzing one or two elements.

- Consider the way the word is used in the sentence. Use the context and the word parts to make a logical guess about the word's meaning.

- Consult a dictionary to see whether you are correct.

## 3.1 ETYMOLOGIES

Have students research the etymology of these words:

audience

butterfly

chronic

despot

inquire

pretty

imperial

cosmology

speak

qualm

## 3.3 WORDS FROM CLASSICAL MYTHOLOGY

Have students look up the etymology of each word and locate the myth associated with it. Use the information from the myth to explain the origin and meaning of each word.

# 3 Understanding Word Origins

### 3.1 ETYMOLOGIES

**Etymologies** show the origin and historical development of a word. When you study a word's history and origin, you can find out when, where, and how the word came to be.

**dra•ma** (drä′mə) *n.* **1.** A work that is meant to be performed by actors. **2.** Theatrical works of a certain type or period in history. [Late Latin *drāma, drāmat-,* from Greek *drān,* to do or perform.]

**for•mi•car•y** (fôr′mĭ-kĕr′ē) *n., pl.* **-ies** A nest of ants; an anthill. [Medieval Latin *formīcārium,* from Latin *formīca,* ant.]

**lock**[2] (lŏk) *n.* **1a.** A length or curl of hair; a tress. **b.** The hair of the head. Often used in the plural. **2.** A small wisp or tuft, as of wool or cotton. [Middle English, from Old English *locc.*]

*For more information, see **Vocabulary Strategy: Etymologies,** pages 300 and 522.*

### 3.2 WORD FAMILIES

Words that have the same root make up a word family and have related meanings. The chart shows a common Greek and a common Latin root. Notice how the meanings of the example words are related to the meanings of their roots.

| Latin Root | *vid, vis:* "see" |
|---|---|
| English | **vision** eyesight |
| | **video** visual portion of a televised broadcast |
| | **visible** possible to see |
| **Greek Root** | *phonē:* "sound" |
| English | **homophone** word that sounds like another word |
| | **phonetics** the study of speech sounds |
| | **telephone** a device that converts voice into a form that can be transmitted as sound waves |

*For more information, see **Vocabulary Strategy: Word Family,** pages 137 and 382.*

### 3.3 WORDS FROM CLASSICAL MYTHOLOGY

The English language includes many words from classical mythology. You can use your knowledge of Greek, Roman, and Norse myths to understand the origins and meanings of these words. For example, *herculean task* refers to the strongman Hercules. Thus *herculean task* probably means "a job that is large or difficult." The chart shows a few common words from mythology.

| Greek | Roman | Norse |
|---|---|---|
| Achilles' heel | cereal | Thursday |
| aegis | volcano | berserk |
| muse | cupid | rune |
| Midas touch | floral | valkyrie |

### 3.4 FOREIGN WORDS

The English language has grown to include words from diverse languages such as French, Dutch, Spanish, Italian, Portuguese, and Chinese. Many of these words stayed the way they were in their original languages.

| French | Dutch | Spanish | Italian |
|---|---|---|---|
| ballet | boss | canyon | diva |
| beret | caboose | rodeo | carnival |
| mirage | dock | salsa | spaghetti |

# 4 Synonyms and Antonyms

### 4.1 SYNONYMS

A **synonym** is a word with a meaning similar to that of another word. You can find synonyms in a thesaurus or a dictionary. In a dictionary, synonyms are often given as part of the definition of the word. The following word pairs are synonyms:

happy/joyful    sad/unhappy

angry/mad    beautiful/lovely

## 4.2 ANTONYMS

An **antonym** is a word with a meaning opposite that of another word. The following word pairs are antonyms:

best/worst  well/ill

light/dark  happy/sad

# 5 Denotation and Connotation

## 5.1 DENOTATION

A word's dictionary meaning is called its **denotation.** For example, the denotation of the word *rascal* is "an unethical, dishonest person."

## 5.2 CONNOTATION

The images or feelings you connect to a word add a finer shade of meaning, called **connotation.** The connation of a word goes beyond its basic dictionary definition. Writers use connotations of words to communicate positive or negative feelings.

| Positive | Neutral | Negative |
|----------|---------|----------|
| gaze | look | glare |
| slender | thin | scrawny |
| playful | active | rowdy |

Make sure you understand the denotation and connotation of a word when you read it or use it in your writing.

*For more information, see* **Vocabulary Strategy: Denotation and Connotation,** *pages 82, 352, and 478.*

# 6 Analogies

An **analogy** is a comparison between two things that are similar in some way. Analogies are sometimes used in writing when unfamiliar objects or ideas are described or explained in terms of familiar ones. Analogies often appear on tests as well, usually in a format like this:

bird : fly ::  A) boat : water
              B) bear : cave
              C) fish : scales
              D) fish : swim
              E) sparrow : wings

Follow these steps to determine the correct answer:

- Read the first half of the analogy as *"bird* is to *fly* as...."
- Read the answer choices as *"boat* is to *water," "bear* is to *cave,"* and so on.
- Ask yourself how the words *bird* and *fly* are related. (A bird can fly.)
- Ask yourself which of the choices shows the same relationship. (A boat can't water and a bear can't cave, but a fish can swim. Therefore, the answer is D.)

# 7 Homonyms and Homophones

## 7.1 HOMONYMS

**Homonyms** are words that have the same spelling and sound but have different meanings.

*The girl had to stoop to find her ball under the stoop.*

*Stoop* can mean "a small porch," but an identically spelled word means "to bend down." Because the words have different meanings, each word has its own dictionary entry.

*The lawyer argued the case of the missing jewelry case.*

*Case* can mean "evidence in support of a claim." However, another identically spelled word means "container." Each word has a different meaning and its own dictionary entry.

Sometimes only one of the meanings of a homonym may be familiar to you. Use context clues to help you figure out the meaning of an unfamiliar word.

## 7.2 HOMOPHONES

**Homophones** are words that sound alike but have different meanings and spellings. The following homophones are frequently misused:

it's/its  they're/their/there

to/too/two  stationary/stationery

Many misused homophones are pronouns and contractions. Whenever you are unsure whether to write *your* or *you're* and *who's* or *whose*, ask yourself if you mean *you are* or *who is/has*. If you do, write the contraction. For other homophones, such as *fair* and *fare*, use the meaning of the word to help you decide which one to use.

## 8 Words with Multiple Meanings

Some words have acquired additional meanings over time that are based on the original meaning.

*Thinking of the horror movie made my skin creep.*
*I saw my little brother creep around the corner.*

These two uses of *creep* have different meanings, but both of them have the same origin. You will find all the meanings of *creep* listed in one entry in the dictionary.

*For more information, see* **Vocabulary Strategy: Multiple-Meaning Words,** *page 266.*

## 9 Specialized Vocabulary

**Specialized vocabulary** is special terms suited to a particular field, or domain, of study or work. For example, science, mathematics, and history all have their own domain-specific technical or specialized vocabularies. To figure out specialized terms, you can use context clues; your knowledge of Latin, Greek, and Old English roots and affixes; and reference sources, such as dictionaries on specific subjects, atlases, or manuals.

*For more information, see* **Vocabulary Strategy: Specialized Vocabulary,** *pages 281, 589, and 692.*

## 10 Using Reference Sources

### 10.1 DICTIONARIES

A **general dictionary** will tell you not only a word's definitions but also its pronunciation, parts of speech, and history and origin. A **specialized dictionary** focuses on terms related to a particular field of study or work. Use a dictionary to check the spelling of any word you are unsure of in your English class and for other subjects as well.

### 10.2 THESAURI

A **thesaurus** (plural, thesauri) is a dictionary of synonyms. A thesaurus can be especially helpful when you find yourself using the same modifiers over and over again.

### 10.3 SYNONYM FINDERS

A **synonym finder** is often included in word-processing software. It enables you to highlight a word and be shown a display of its synonyms.

### 10.4 GLOSSARIES

A **glossary** is a list of specialized terms and their definitions. It is often found in the back of a book and sometimes includes pronunciations. Many textbooks contain glossaries. In fact, this textbook has four glossaries: the **Glossary of Literary and Nonfiction Terms,** the **Glossary of Reading and Informational Terms,** the **Glossary of Academic Vocabulary in English & Spanish,** and the **Glossary of Vocabulary in English & Spanish.** Use these glossaries to help you understand how terms are used in this textbook.

## 11 Spelling Rules

### 11.1 WORDS ENDING IN A SILENT *E*

Before adding a suffix beginning with a vowel or *y* to a word ending in a silent *e*, drop the *e* (with some exceptions).

> **amaze + -ing = amazing**
> **love + -able = lovable**
> **create + -ed = created**
> **nerve + -ous = nervous**

**Exceptions:** *change + -able = changeable; courage + -ous = courageous*

When adding a suffix beginning with a consonant to a word ending in a silent *e*, keep the *e* (with some exceptions).

> **late + -ly = lately**
> **spite + -ful = spiteful**
> **noise + -less = noiseless**
> **state + -ment = statement**

**Exceptions:** *truly, argument, ninth, wholly, awful,* and others.

When a suffix beginning with *a* or *o* is added to a word with a final silent *e,* the final *e* is usually retained if it is preceded by a soft *c* or a soft *g.*

bridge + -able = bridgeable
peace + -able = peaceable
outrage + -ous = outrageous
advantage + -ous = advantageous

When a suffix beginning with a vowel is added to words ending in *ee* or *oe,* the final silent *e* is retained.

agree + -ing = agreeing    free + -ing = freeing
hoe + -ing = hoeing    see + -ing = seeing

## 11.2 WORDS ENDING IN Y

Before adding most suffixes to a word that ends in *y* preceded by a consonant, change the *y* to *i.*

easy + -est = easiest
crazy + -est = craziest
silly + -ness = silliness
marry + -age = marriage

**Exceptions:** *dryness, shyness,* and *slyness.*

However, when you add *-ing,* the *y* does not change.

empty + -ed = emptied   but
empty + -ing = emptying

When adding a suffix to a word that ends in *y* preceded by a vowel, the *y* usually does not change.

play + -er = player
employ + -ed = employed
coy + -ness = coyness
pay + -able = payable

## 11.3 WORDS ENDING IN A CONSONANT

In one-syllable words that end in one consonant preceded by one short vowel, double the final consonant before adding a suffix beginning with a vowel, such as *-ed* or *-ing.* These are sometimes called 1+1+1 words.

dip + -ed = dipped    set + -ing = setting
slim + -est = slimmest    fit + -er = fitter

The rule does not apply to words of one syllable that end in a consonant preceded by two vowels.

feel + -ing = feeling    peel + -ed = peeled
reap + -ed = reaped    loot + -ed = looted

In words of more than one syllable, double the final consonant when (1) the word ends with one consonant preceded by one vowel and (2) the word is accented on the last syllable.

be•gin´ per•mit´    re•fer´

In the following examples, note that in the new words formed with suffixes, the accent remains on the same syllable:

be•gin´ + -ing = be•gin´ning = beginning
per•mit´ + -ed = per•mit´ted = permitted

**Exceptions:** In some words with more than one syllable, though the accent remains on the same syllable when a suffix is added, the final consonant is nevertheless not doubled, as in the following examples:

tra´vel + er = tra´vel•er = traveler
mar´ket + er = mar´ket•er = marketer

In the following examples, the accent does not remain on the same syllable; thus, the final consonant is not doubled:

re•fer´ + -ence = ref´er•ence = reference
con•fer´ + -ence = con´fer•ence = conference

## 11.4 PREFIXES AND SUFFIXES

When adding a prefix to a word, do not change the spelling of the base word. When a prefix creates a double letter, keep both letters.

dis- + approve = disapprove
re- + build = rebuild
ir- + regular = irregular
mis- + spell = misspell
anti- + trust = antitrust
il- + logical = illogical

When adding *-ly* to a word ending in *l,* keep both *l*'s. When adding *-ness* to a word ending in *n,* keep both *n*'s.

careful + -ly = carefully
sudden + -ness = suddenness
final + -ly = finally
thin + -ness = thinness

## 11.5 FORMING PLURAL NOUNS

To form the plural of most nouns, just add -s.

prizes   dreams   circles   stations

For most singular nouns ending in o, add -s.

solos   halos   studios   photos   pianos

For a few nouns ending in o, add -es.

heroes   tomatoes   potatoes   echoes

When the singular noun ends in s, sh, ch, x, or z, add -es.

waitresses   brushes   ditches
axes   buzzes

When a singular noun ends in y with a consonant before it, change the y to i and add -es.

army—armies       candy—candies
baby—babies       diary—diaries
ferry—ferries     conspiracy—conspiracies

When a vowel (a, e, i, o, u) comes before the y, just add -s.

boy—boys          way—ways
array—arrays      alloy—alloys
weekday—weekdays  jockey—jockeys

For most nouns ending in f or fe, change the f to v and add -es or -s.

life—lives    calf—calves   knife—knives
thief—thieves shelf—shelves loaf—loaves

For some nouns ending in f, add -s to make the plural.

roofs   chiefs   reefs   beliefs

Some nouns have the same form for both singular and plural.

deer   sheep   moose   salmon   trout

For some nouns, the plural is formed in a special way.

man—men        goose—geese
ox—oxen        woman—women
mouse—mice     child—children

For a compound noun written as one word, form the plural by changing the last word in the compound to its plural form.

stepchild—stepchildren       firefly—fireflies

If a compound noun is written as a hyphenated word or as two separate words, change the most important word to the plural form.

brother-in-law—brothers-in-law
life jacket—life jackets

## 11.6 FORMING POSSESSIVES

If a noun is singular, add 's.

mother—my mother's car       Ross—Ross's desk

**Exception:** The s after the apostrophe is dropped after *Jesus', Moses',* and certain names in classical mythology *(Zeus').* These possessive forms can thus be pronounced easily.

If a noun is plural and ends with s, just add an apostrophe.

parents—my parents' car
the Santinis—the Santinis' house

If a noun is plural but does not end in s, add 's.

people—the people's choice
women—the women's coats

## 11.7 SPECIAL SPELLING PROBLEMS

Only one English word ends in -sede: supersede. Three words end in -ceed: exceed, proceed, and succeed. All other verbs ending in the sound "seed" are spelled with -cede.

concede   precede   recede   secede

In words with ie or ei, when the sound is long e (as in she), the word is spelled ie except after c (with some exceptions).

| i before e | thief | relieve | field |
| --- | --- | --- | --- |
| | piece | grieve | pier |
| except after c | conceit | perceive | ceiling |
| | receive | receipt | |
| Exceptions: | either | neither | weird |
| | leisure | seize | |

## 12 Commonly Confused Words

| WORDS | DEFINITIONS | EXAMPLES |
|---|---|---|
| accept/except | The verb *accept* means "to receive or believe"; *except* is usually a preposition meaning "excluding." | **Except** for some of the more extraordinary events, I can **accept** that the *Odyssey* recounts a real journey. |
| advice/advise | *Advise* is a verb; *advice* is a noun naming that which an *adviser* gives. | I **advise** you to take that job. <br> Whom should I ask for **advice?** |
| affect/effect | As a verb, *affect* means "to influence." *Effect* as a verb means "to cause." If you want a noun, you will almost always want *effect*. | Did Circe's wine **affect** Odysseus' mind? It did **effect** a change in Odysseus' men. In fact, it had an **effect** on everyone else who drank it. |
| all ready/already | *All ready* is an adjective meaning "fully ready." *Already* is an adverb meaning "before or by this time." | He was **all ready** to go at noon. <br> I have **already** seen that movie. |
| allusion/illusion | An *allusion* is an indirect reference to something. An *illusion* is a false picture or idea. | There are many **allusions** to the works of Homer in English literature. <br> The world's apparent flatness is an **illusion**. |
| among/between | *Between* is used when you are speaking of only two things. *Among* is used for three or more. | **Between** *Hamlet* and *King Lear*, I prefer the latter. <br> Emily Dickinson is **among** my favorite poets. |
| bring/take | *Bring* is used to denote motion toward a speaker or place. *Take* is used to denote motion away from such a person or place. | **Bring** the books over here, and I will **take** them to the library. |
| fewer/less | *Fewer* refers to the number of separate, countable units. *Less* refers to bulk quantity. | We have **less** literature and **fewer** selections in this year's curriculum. |
| leave/let | *Leave* means "to allow something to remain behind." *Let* means "to permit." | The librarian will **leave** some books on display but will not **let** us borrow any. |
| lie/lay | To *lie* is "to rest or recline." It does not take an object. *Lay* always takes an object. | Rover loves to **lie** in the sun. <br> We always **lay** some bones next to him. |
| loose/lose | *Loose* (lo͞os) means "free, not restrained"; *lose* (lo͞oz) means "to misplace or fail to find." | Who turned the horses **loose?** <br> I hope we won't **lose** any of them. |
| precede/proceed | *Precede* means "to go or come before." Use *proceed* for other meanings. | Emily Dickinson's poetry **precedes** that of Alice Walker. <br> You may **proceed** to the next section of the test. |
| than/then | Use *than* in making comparisons; use *then* on all other occasions. | Who can say whether Amy Lowell is a better poet **than** Denise Levertov? I will read Lowell first, and **then** I will read Levertov. |
| their/there/they're | *Their* means "belonging to them." *There* means "in that place." *They're* is the contraction for "they are." | **There** is a movie playing at 9 P.M. **They're** going to see it with me. Sakara and Erin drove away in **their** car after the movie. |
| two/too/to | *Two* is the number. *Too* is an adverb meaning "also" or "very." Use *to* before a verb or as a preposition. | Meg had **to** go **to** town, **too.** We had **too** much reading **to** do. **Two** chapters is **too** many. |

**Interactive Vocabulary**

Go to thinkcentral.com. <br> KEYWORD: HML9-R75

**Interactive Vocabulary**

The keyword on this page directs students to **WordSharp** tutorials on key vocabulary strategies.

**COMMON CORE**

Included in this handbook:
SL 1a–d, SL 3, SL 4

## COMMON CORE FOCUS

**SL 1a–d** Initiate and participate effectively in a range of collaborative discussions, building on others' ideas and expressing their own clearly and persuasively. **SL 3** Evaluate a speaker's point of view, reasoning, and use of evidence and rhetoric, identifying any fallacious reasoning or exaggerated or distorted evidence. **SL 4** Present information, findings, and supporting evidence clearly, concisely, and logically such that listeners can follow the line of reasoning and the organization, development, substance, and style are appropriate to purpose, audience, and task.

# 1 Speech

In school, in business, and in community life, a speech is one of the most effective means of communicating.

## 1.1 AUDIENCE, PURPOSE, AND OCCASION

When developing and delivering a speech, your goal is to deliver a focused, coherent presentation that conveys your ideas clearly and relates to the background of your audience. By understanding your audience, you can tailor your speech to them appropriately and effectively.

- **Know Your Audience** What kind of group are you presenting to? Fellow classmates? A group of teachers? What are their interests and backgrounds? Understanding their different points of view can help you organize the information so that they understand and are interested in it.

- **Understand Your Purpose** Keep in mind your purpose for speaking. Are you trying to convince the audience to do something? Perhaps you simply want to entertain them by sharing a story or experience. Your reason for giving the speech will guide you in organizing your thoughts and deciding on how to deliver it.

- **Know the Occasion** Are you speaking at a special event? Is it formal? Will others be giving speeches besides you? Knowing what the occasion is will help you tailor the language and the length for the event.

## 1.2 PREPARING YOUR SPEECH

There are several approaches to preparing a speech. Your teacher may tell you which one to use.

| | |
|---|---|
| **Manuscript** | Prepare a complete script of the speech in advance and use it to deliver the speech. Use for formal occasions, such as graduation speeches and political addresses, and to present technical or complicated information. |
| **Memory** | Prepare a written text in advance and then memorize it in order to deliver the speech word for word. Use for short speeches, as when introducing another speaker or accepting an award. |
| **Extemporaneous** | Prepare the speech and deliver it using an outline or notes. Use for informal situations, for persuasive messages, and to make a more personal connection with the audience. |

## 1.3 DRAFTING YOUR SPEECH

If you are writing your speech beforehand, rather than working from notes, use the following guidelines to help you:

- **Create a Unified Speech** Do this first by organizing your speech into paragraphs, each of which develops a single central idea. Then make sure that just as all the sentences in a paragraph support the central idea of the paragraph, all the paragraphs in your speech support the controlling idea of the speech.

- **Use Appropriate Language** The subject of your speech—and the way you choose to present it—should match your audience, your purpose, and the occasion. You can use informal language, such as slang, to share a story with your classmates. For a persuasive or argumentative speech in front of a school assembly, use formal, standard American English. If you are giving an

informative or explanatory presentation, be sure to explain any technical terms that the audience may not be familiar with.

- **Provide Evidence** Include relevant facts, statistics, and incidents; quote experts to support your ideas and opinions. Elaborate—provide specific details, perhaps with visual or media displays—to clarify what you are saying.

- **Emphasize Important Points** To help your audience follow the main ideas and concepts of your speech, be sure to draw attention to important points. You can use rhyme, repetition, and other rhetorical devices.

- **Use Precise Language** Use precise language to convey your ideas, and vary the structure and length of your sentences. You can keep the audience's attention with a word that elicits strong emotion. You can use a question or interjection to make a personal connection with the audience.

- **Start Strong, Finish Strong** As you begin your speech, consider using a "hook"—an interesting question or statement meant to capture your audience's attention. At the end of the speech, restate your central ideas simply and clearly. Perhaps conclude with a powerful example or anecdote to reinforce your message.

- **Revise Your Speech** After you write your speech, revise, edit, and proofread it as you would a written report. Use a variety of sentence structures to achieve a natural rhythm. Check for correct subject-verb agreement and consistent verb tense. Correct run-on sentences and sentence fragments. Use parallel structure to emphasize ideas. Make sure you use complete sentences and correct punctuation and capitalization, even if no one else will see it. Your written speech should be clear and error-free. If you notice an error in your notes during the speech, you may not remember what you actually wanted to say.

## 1.4 DELIVERING YOUR SPEECH

Confidence is the key to a successful presentation. Use these techniques to help you prepare and present your speech:

### Prepare

- **Review Your Information** Reread your notes and review any background research. You'll feel more confident during your speech.

- **Organize Your Notes** Some people prefer to include only key points. Others prefer the entire script. Write each main point, or each paragraph, of your speech on a separate numbered index card. Be sure to include your most important evidence and examples.

- **Plan Your Visual Aids** If you are planning on using visual aids, such as slides, posters, charts, graphs, video clips, overhead transparencies, or computer projections, now is the time to design them and decide how to work them into your speech.

### Practice

- **Rehearse** Rehearse your speech several times, possibly in front of a practice audience. Maintain good posture by standing with your shoulders back and your head up. If you are using visual aids, practice handling them. Adapt your rate of speaking, pitch, and tone of voice to your audience and setting. Glance at your notes to refresh your memory, but avoid reading them word for word. Your style of performance should express the purpose of your speech. Use the following chart to help you.

| Purpose | Pace | Pitch | Tone |
|---|---|---|---|
| To convince or present a claim | fast but clear | even | urgent |
| To inform | using plenty of pauses | even | authoritative |
| To entertain | usually building to a "punch" | varied to create characters or drama | funny or dramatic |

- **Use Audience Feedback** If you had a practice audience, ask them specific questions about your delivery: Did I use enough eye contact? Was my voice at the right volume? Did I stand straight, or did I slouch? Use the audience's comments to evaluate the effectiveness of your delivery and to set goals for future rehearsals.

- **Evaluate Your Performance** When you have finished each rehearsal, evaluate your performance. Did you pause to let an important point sink in or use gestures for emphasis? Make a list of the aspects of your presentation that you will try to improve for your next rehearsal.

### Present

- **Begin Your Speech** Try to look relaxed and smile.

- **Make Eye Contact** Try to make eye contact with as many audience members as possible. This will establish personal contact and help you determine if the audience understands your speech.

- **Remember to Pause** A slight pause after important points will provide emphasis and give your audience time to think about what you're saying.

- **Speak Clearly** Speak loud enough to be heard clearly, but not so loud that your voice is overwhelming. Use a conversational tone.

- **Maintain Good Posture** Stand up straight and avoid nervous movements that may distract the audience's attention from what you are saying.

- **Use Expressive Body Language** Use facial expressions to show your feelings toward your topic. Lean forward when you make an important point; move your hands and arms for emphasis. Use your body language to show your own style and reflect your personality.

- **Watch the Audience for Responses** If they start fidgeting or yawning, speak a little louder or get to your conclusion a little sooner. Use what you learn to evaluate the effectiveness of your speech and to decide what areas need improvement for future presentations.

### Respond to Questions

Depending on the content of your speech, your audience may have questions. Follow these steps to make sure that you answer questions in an appropriate manner:

- Think about what your audience may ask and prepare answers before your speech.

- Before you begin, set the rules: tell your audience that you will take questions only after you finish speaking. This helps avoid audience interruptions that may make your speech hard to follow.

- Call on audience members in the order in which they raise their hands.

- Repeat each question before you answer it to ensure that everyone has heard it. This step also gives you time to prepare your answer.

## 2 Different Types of Oral Presentations

### 2.1 INFORMATIVE SPEECH

When you deliver an informative or explanatory speech, you give the audience new information, provide a better understanding of information, or enable the audience to use the information in a new way. An informative speech is presented in an objective way. Some informative speeches are of an instructional nature.

*For more information, see **Oral Instructions,** page R72.*

Use the following questions to evaluate the presentation of a peer or a public figure, or your own presentation.

**Evaluate an Informative Speech**

- Did the speaker have a specific, clearly focused topic?
- Did the speaker take the audience's previous knowledge into consideration?
- Did the speaker cite sources for the information?
- Did the speaker communicate the information logically and objectively?
- Did the speaker explain technical terms?
- Did the speaker use visual aids effectively?
- Did the speaker anticipate and address any audience concerns or misunderstandings?

## 2.2 PERSUASIVE SPEECH

When you deliver a persuasive or argumentative speech, you offer a thesis or clear statement on a subject, provide relevant evidence to support your position, and attempt to convince the audience to accept your point of view.

Use the following questions to evaluate the presentation of a peer or a public figure, or your own presentation.

### Evaluate a Persuasive Speech

- Did the speaker present a clear thesis or argumentative claim?
- Did the speaker anticipate and address audience concerns, biases, and counterarguments?
- Did the speaker use sound logic and reasoning in developing the argument, avoiding the use of fallacious reasoning?
- Did the speaker support the argument with valid evidence, examples, facts, expert opinions, and quotations, avoiding the use of exaggerated or distorted evidence?
- Did the speaker use rhetorical devices, such as emotional appeals, to support assertions?
- Did the speaker hold the audience's interest with an effective voice, facial expressions, and gestures?
- Is your reaction to the speech similar to other audience members'?

## 2.3 DEBATE AN ISSUE

A debate is a balanced argument covering both sides of an issue. In a debate, two teams compete to win the support of the audience. In a formal debate, two teams, each with two members, present their arguments on a given proposition or policy statement. One team argues for the proposition or statement and the other argues against it. Each debater must consider the proposition closely and must research both sides of it. To argue convincingly either for or against a proposition, a debater must be familiar with both sides of the issue.

*For more information, see* **Speaking and Listening Workshop: Debating an Issue,** *pages 722–723.*

Use the following guidelines to evaluate a debate.

### Evaluate a Team in a Debate

- Did the team prove that a significant problem does or does not exist? How thorough was the analysis?
- How did the team convince you that the proposition is or is not the best solution to the problem?
- How effectively did the team present reasons and evidence supporting the case?
- How effectively did the team rebut arguments made by the opposing team?
- Did the speakers maintain eye contact and speak at an appropriate rate and volume?
- Did the speakers observe proper debate etiquette?

### PRACTICE AND APPLY

View a political debate for a local, state, or national election. Use the preceding criteria to evaluate it.

## 2.4 NARRATIVE SPEECH

When you deliver a narrative speech, you tell a story or present a subject using a story-type format. A good narrative keeps an audience informed and entertained. It also allows you to deliver a message in a creative way.

*For more information, see* **Speaking and Listening Workshop: Presenting an Informal Speech,** *pages 184–185.*

Use the following questions to evaluate a speaker or your own presentation.

### Evaluate a Narrative Speech

- Did the speaker choose a context that makes sense and contributes to a believable narrative?
- Did the speaker locate scenes and incidents in specific places?
- Does the plot flow well?
- Did the speaker use words that convey the appropriate mood and tone?
- Did the speaker use sensory details that allow the audience to experience the sights, sounds, and smells of a scene and the specific actions, gestures, and thoughts of the characters?
- Did the speaker use a range of narrative devices to keep the audience interested?
- Is your reaction to the presentation similar to other audience members'?

### 2.5 DESCRIPTIVE SPEECH

Description is part of most presentations. In a descriptive speech, you describe a subject that you are personally involved with. A good description will enable your listeners to tell how you feel toward your subject through the images you provide.

Use the following questions to evaluate a speaker or your own presentation.

#### Evaluate a Descriptive Speech

- Did the speaker make clear his or her point of view toward the subject being described?
- Did the speaker use sensory details, figurative language, and factual details?
- Did the speaker use tone and pitch to emphasize important details?
- Did the speaker use facial expressions to emphasize his or her feelings toward the subject?
- Did the speaker change vantage points to help the audience see the subject from another position?
- Did the speaker change perspectives to show how someone else might feel toward the subject or place?

### 2.6 ORAL INTERPRETATION

When you perform an oral reading, you use appropriate vocal intonations, facial expressions, and gestures to bring a literature selection to life.

Use the following questions to evaluate an artistic performance by a peer or a public presenter, a media presentation, or your own performance.

#### Evaluate an Oral Interpretation

- Did the speaker speak clearly, enunciating each word carefully?
- Did the speaker maintain eye contact with the audience?
- Did the speaker control his or her volume, projecting without shouting?
- Did the speaker vary the rate of speech appropriately to express emotion, mood, and action?
- Did the speaker use a different voice for the character(s)?
- Did the speaker stress important words or phrases?
- Did the speaker use voice, tone, and gestures to enhance meaning?
- Did the speaker's presentation allow you to identify and appreciate elements of the text such as character development, rhyme, imagery, and language?

#### PRACTICE AND APPLY

Listen to an oral reading by a classmate or view a dramatic performance in a theater or on television. Use the preceding criteria to evaluate it.

### 2.7 LITERARY ANALYSIS / ORAL RESPONSE TO LITERATURE

A literary analysis explores aspects of a writer's story, novel, poem, or drama. It demonstrates to an audience a solid and comprehensive understanding of a select element or elements of a text.

*For more information, see **Speaking and Listening Workshop: Presenting a Literary Analysis,** pages 808–809.*

Use the following questions to evaluate a speaker or your own presentation.

**Evaluate a Literary Analysis / Oral Response to Literature**

- Did the speaker choose an interesting piece that he or she understands and feels strongly about?
- Did the speaker demonstrate an understanding of significant ideas from the text?
- Did the speaker direct the audience to specific parts of the piece that support his or her idea?
- Did the speaker identify and analyze appropriate elements such as imagery, figurative language, and character development?
- Did the speaker explain any ambiguous or difficult passages?

**PRACTICE AND APPLY**

Listen as a classmate delivers a literary analysis of a text you have read. Use the preceding criteria to evaluate the presentation.

## 3 Other Types of Communication

### 3.1 CONVERSATION

Conversations are informal, but they are important means of communicating. When two or more people exchange messages, it is equally important that each person contribute and actively listen.

### 3.2 GROUP DISCUSSION

In successful collaborative discussions, groups assign a role to each member. These roles distribute responsibility among the members and help keep discussions focused.

**Leader or Chairperson**

- Introduces topic
- Explains goal or purpose
- Participates in discussion and helps propel conversation by posing and responding to questions
- Helps resolve conflicts
- Helps group reach goal

**Recorder**

- Takes notes on discussion
- Reports on suggestions and decisions

- Organizes and writes up notes
- Participates in discussion

**Participants**

- Contribute relevant facts or ideas to discussion
- Respond thoughtfully to one another's ideas
- Reach agreement or vote on final decision

*Guidelines for Discussion*

- Set rules for how your group will make decisions, and develop a plan to build a consensus among group members.
- Come to discussions prepared.
- Participate in the discussion.
- Ask questions and respond appropriately to questions.
- Don't talk while someone else is talking.
- Support statements and opinions with facts and examples.
- Listen attentively; be courteous and respectful of others' viewpoints.

*For more information, see **Speaking and Listening Workshop: Participating in a Discussion**, pages 312–313, and **Speaking and Listening Workshop: Participating in a Panel Discussion**, pages 534–535.*

### 3.3 INTERVIEW

An **interview** is a formal type of conversation with a definite purpose and goal. To conduct a successful interview, use the following guidelines:

*Prepare for the Interview*

- Select your interviewee carefully. Identify who has the kind of knowledge and experience you are looking for.
- Set a time, a date, and a place. Ask permission to record the interview.
- Learn all you can about the person you will interview or the topic you want information on.
- Prepare a list of questions. Create questions that encourage detailed responses instead of yes-or-no answers. Arrange your questions in order from most important to least important.
- Arrive on time with everything you need.

SPEAKING AND LISTENING HANDBOOK **R81**

### Conduct the Interview

- Ask your questions clearly and listen to the responses carefully. Give the person whom you are interviewing plenty of time to answer.
- Be flexible; follow up on any responses you find interesting.
- Avoid arguments; be tactful and polite.
- Even if you record an interview, take notes.
- Thank the person for the interview, and ask if you can call with any follow-up questions.

### Follow Up on the Interview

- Summarize your notes or make a written copy of the recording as soon as possible.
- If any points are unclear or if information is missing, call and ask more questions.
- Select the most appropriate quotations to support your ideas.
- If possible, have the person you interviewed review your work to make sure you haven't misrepresented what he or she said.
- Send a thank-you note to the person in appreciation of his or her time and effort.

> **Evaluate an Interview**
>
> You can determine how effective your interview was by asking yourself these questions:
> - Did you get the type of information you needed?
> - Were your most important questions answered?
> - Did your interviewee stay focused on the subject?

### 3.4 ORAL INSTRUCTIONS

You may be called upon to follow or give oral instructions to perform specific tasks, answer questions, solve problems, and complete processes.

> **Evaluate Oral Instructions**
>
> Ask yourself these questions after **listening** to oral instructions:
> - Did you **restate** each step in your own words?
> - Did you **consider** how each step fits into the process or problem as a whole?
> - Did you **ask** for clarification if necessary?

> Ask yourself these questions after **giving** oral instructions:
> - Did you **plan** your instructions carefully?
> - Did you **speak slowly** so your audience could follow each step?
> - Did you **repeat** important details as necessary?
> - Did you provide **diagrams** or **visual aids** to illustrate your instructions?

## 4 Active Listening

**Active listening** is the process of receiving, interpreting, evaluating, and responding to a message. Whether you listen to a class discussion or a formal speech, use the following strategies to get as much as you can from the message.

### Before Listening

- Learn what the topic is beforehand. You may need to read background information about the topic or learn technical terms in order to interpret the speaker's message.
- Think about what you know or want to know.
- Be prepared to take notes.
- Establish a purpose for listening.

### While Listening

- Focus your attention on the speaker. Your facial expressions and body language should demonstrate your interest in hearing the topic.
- Listen for the speaker's purpose (usually stated at the beginning), which alerts you to main ideas.
- To help you interpret the speaker's message, listen for words or phrases that signal important points, such as *to begin with, in addition, most important, finally,* and *in conclusion.*
- Listen carefully for explanations of technical terms. Use these terms to help you understand the speaker's message.
- Listen for ideas that are repeated for emphasis.
- Take notes. Write down only the most important points.
- If possible, use an outline or list format to organize main ideas and supporting points.

- Note comparisons and contrasts, causes and effects, or problems and solutions.

- As you take notes, use phrases, abbreviations, and symbols to keep up with the speaker.

- To aid your comprehension, note how the speaker uses word choice, voice pitch, posture, and gestures to convey meaning.

### After Listening

- Ask relevant questions to clarify anything that was unclear or confusing.

- Review your notes right away to make sure you understand what was said.

- Summarize and paraphrase the speaker's ideas.

- You may also wish to compare your interpretation of the speech with the interpretations of others who listened to it.

### 4.1 CRITICAL LISTENING

**Critical listening** involves interpreting and analyzing a spoken message to judge its accuracy and reliability. You can use the following strategies as you listen to messages from advertisers, politicians, lecturers, and others:

- **Determine the Speaker's Purpose** Think about the background, viewpoint, and possible motives of the speaker. Separate facts from opinions. Listen carefully to details and evidence that a speaker uses to support the message.

- **Listen for the Central Idea** Figure out the speaker's main message before allowing yourself to be distracted by seemingly convincing facts and details.

- **Recognize the Use of Persuasive Techniques** Pay attention to a speaker's choice of words. Speakers may slant information to persuade you to buy a product or accept an idea. Persuasive devices such as inaccurate generalizations, either/or reasoning, and bandwagon or snob appeal may represent faulty reasoning and provide misleading information.

*For more information, see **Persuasive Techniques**, pages 656 and R22.*

- **Observe Nonverbal Messages** A speaker's gestures, facial expressions, and tone of voice should reinforce the message. If they don't, you should doubt the speaker's sincerity and his or her message's reliability.

- **Give Appropriate Feedback** An effective speaker looks for verbal and nonverbal cues from you, the listener, to gauge how the message is being received. For example, if you understand or agree with the message, you might nod your head. If possible, during or after a presentation, ask questions to clarify understanding.

### 4.2 VERBAL FEEDBACK

At times you will be asked to give direct feedback to a speaker. You may be asked to evaluate the way the speaker delivers the presentation as well as the content of the presentation.

---

**Evaluate Delivery**

- Did the speaker articulate words clearly and distinctly?
- Did the speaker pronounce words correctly?
- Did the speaker vary his or her rate?
- Did the speaker's voice sound natural and not strained?
- Was the speaker's voice loud enough?

---

**Evaluate Content**

Here's how to give constructive suggestions for improvement:

**Be Specific** Don't make statements like "Your charts need work." Offer concrete suggestions, such as "Please make the type bigger so we can read the poster from the back of the room."

**Discuss Only the Most Important Points** Don't overload the speaker with too much feedback about too many details. Focus on important points, such as:

- Is the topic too advanced for the audience?
- Are the supporting details well organized?
- Is the conclusion weak?

**Give Balanced Feedback** Tell the speaker not only what didn't work but also what did work: "Consider dropping the last two slides, since you covered those points earlier. The first two slides got my attention."

Every day you are exposed to hundreds of images and messages from television, radio, movies, newspapers, and the Internet. What is the effect of all this media? What do you need to know to be a smart media consumer? Being media literate means that you have the ability to think critically about media messages. It means that you are able to analyze and evaluate media messages and how they influence you and your world. To become media literate, you'll need the tools to study media messages.

# COMMON CORE FOCUS

**SL 3** Evaluate a speaker's point of view, reasoning, and use of evidence and rhetoric, identifying any fallacious reasoning or exaggerated or distorted evidence.

## 1 Five Core Concepts in Media Literacy

*from* The Center for Media Literacy

The five concepts of media literacy provide you with the basic questions you can consider when examining media messages.

**All media messages are "constructed."** All media messages are made by someone. In fact, they are carefully thought out and researched and have attitudes and values built into them. Much of the information that you use to make sense of the world comes from the media. Therefore, it is important to know how a medium is put together so you can better understand the message it conveys.

**Media messages are constructed using a creative language with its own rules.** Each means of communication—whether it is film, television, newspapers, magazines, radio, or the Internet—has its own language and design. Therefore, the contents of a message must use the language and design of the medium that conveys the message. Thus, the medium actually shapes the message. For example, a horror film may use music to heighten suspense, or a newspaper may use a big headline to signal the significance of a story. Understanding the language of each medium can increase your enjoyment of it as well as alert you to obvious and subtle influences.

**Different people experience the same media messages differently.** Personal factors such as age, education, and experience will affect the way a person responds to a media message. How many times has your interpretation of a film or book differed from that of a friend? Everyone interprets media messages through his or her own lens.

**Media have embedded values and points of view.** Media messages carry underlying values, which are purposely built into them by the creators of the message. For example, a commercial's main purpose may be to persuade you to buy something, but it also conveys the value of a particular lifestyle. Understanding both the core message and the embedded point of view will help you decide whether to accept or reject the message.

**Most media messages are constructed to gain profit and/or power.** The creators of media messages often provide a commodity, such as information or entertainment, in order to make money. The bigger the audience, the higher the cost of advertising. Consequently, media outlets want to build large audiences in order to bring in more revenue from advertising. For example, a television network will create programming to appeal to the largest audience possible, in the hope that the viewer ratings will attract more advertising dollars.

## 2 Media Basics

### 2.1 MESSAGE

When a film or TV show is created, it becomes a media product. Each media product is created to send a **message,** or an expression of belief or opinion, that serves a specific purpose. In order to understand the message, you will need to deconstruct it.

**Deconstruction** is the process of analyzing a media presentation. To analyze a media presentation you will need to look at its content, its purpose, the audience it's aimed at, and the techniques and elements that are used to create certain effects.

### 2.2 AUDIENCE

A **target audience** is a specific group of people that a product or presentation is aimed at. The members of a target audience usually share certain characteristics, such as age, gender, ethnic background, values, or lifestyle. For example, a target audience may be males, ages 15 to 20, who live in urban areas and engage in sports.

**Demographics** are the characteristics of a population, including age, gender, profession, income, education, ethnicity, and geographical location. Media decision makers use demographics to shape their content to suit the needs and tastes of a target audience.

**Nielsen ratings** are the system used to track TV audiences and their viewing preferences. Nielsen Media Research, the company that provides this system, monitors TV viewing in a random sample of 5,000 U.S. households selected to represent the population as a whole.

### 2.3 PURPOSE

The **purpose,** or intent, of a media presentation is the reason it was made. Most media have more than one purpose. However, every media message has a **core purpose.** To discover that purpose, think about why its creator paid for and produced the message. For example, an ad might entertain you with humor, but its core purpose is to persuade you to buy something.

### 2.4 TYPES AND GENRES OF MEDIA

The term *media* refers to television, newspapers, magazines, radio, movies, and the Internet. Each

is a **medium,** or means, for carrying information, entertainment, and advertisements to an audience.

Each type of media has different characteristics, strengths, and weaknesses. Understanding how different types of media work and the role they play will help you become more informed about the choices you make in response to the media. For example, you're likely to encounter the same news event covered in various media. If you are familiar with each medium, you'll be better equipped to compare, contrast, and synthesize the different portrayals.

*For more information, see **Types of Media**, page 10.*

### 2.5 PRODUCERS AND CREATORS

People who control the media are known as **gatekeepers.** Gatekeepers decide what information to share with the public and the ways it will be presented. The following diagram gives examples.

**Who Controls the Media?**

**Media Owners**
TV networks
Recording companies
Publishing companies

**Media Products**
Television
Radio
Magazines
Movies
Newspapers
Internet

**Media Creators**
Actors
Writers
Directors
Webmasters

**Media Sponsors**
Clothing manufacturers
Fast-food restaurants
Department stores

Some forms of media are independently owned, while others are part of a corporate family. Some corporate families might own several different kinds of media. For example, a company may own three radio stations, five newspapers, and a small television station. Often a corporate "parent" decides the content for all of its holdings.

**Media Tools**

Go to thinkcentral.com.
KEYWORD: HML9-R85

**Media Tools**  THINK central

The keyword on this page points to **MediaScope,** a Web site that helps students strengthen media analysis and production skills.

### 2.6 LAWS GOVERNING MEDIA

Four main laws and policies affect the content, delivery, and use of mass media.

**The First Amendment** to the Constitution forbids Congress to limit speech or the press.

**Copyright law** protects the rights of authors and other media creators against the unauthorized publishing, reproduction, and selling of their works.

Laws prohibit **censorship,** any attempt to suppress or control people's access to media messages.

Laws prohibit **libel,** the publication of false statements that damage a person's reputation.

### 2.7 INFLUENCE OF MEDIA

By sheer volume alone, media influences our very existence, values, opinions, and beliefs. Our environment is saturated with media messages from television, billboards, radio, newspapers, magazines, video games, and so on. Each of these media products is selling one message and conveying another—a message about values—in the subtext. For example, a car ad is meant to sell a car, but if you look closer, you will see that it is using a set of values, such as a luxurious lifestyle, to make the car attractive to the target audience. One message of the ad is that if you buy the car, you'll have the luxurious lifestyle. The other message is that the luxurious lifestyle is good and desirable. TV shows, movies, and news programs also convey subtexts of values and beliefs.

Media can also shape your opinions about the world. For example, news about crime shapes our understanding about how much and what type of crime is prevalent in the world around us. TV news items, talk show interviews, and commercials may shape our perception of a political candidate, a celebrity, an ethnic group, a country, or a regional area. As a consequence, our knowledge of someone or someplace may be completely based on the information we receive from the television.

## 3 Film and TV

Films and television programs come in a variety of types. Films include comedies, dramas, documentaries, and animated features. Televison programs cover an even wider array, including dramas, sitcoms, talk shows, reality shows, newscasts, and so on. Producers of films and producers of television programs rely on many of the same elements to convey their messages. Among these elements are scripts, visual and sound elements, special effects, and editing.

### 3.1 SCRIPT AND WRITTEN ELEMENTS

The writer and editor craft a story for television or film using a script and storyboard. A **script** is the text or words of a film or television show. A **storyboard** is a device often used to plan the shooting of a film and to help the director envision and convey what the finished product will look like. It consists of a sequence of sketches showing what will appear in the film's shots, often with explanatory notes and dialogue written beside or underneath them, as shown in the example.

*For more information, see **Media Study: Produce Your Own Media,** page 115.*

*Shot type: LS (long shot)*
*Action: Black Rider races dangerously fast.*
*Audio: Horse screeches. Silence.*

*Shot type: MS (medium shot)*
*Action: Camera zooms in to show image of Black Rider. Audio: Music plays to indicate danger.*

## 3.2 VISUAL ELEMENTS

Visual elements in film and television include camera shots, angles, and movements, as well as film components such as mise en scène, set design, props, and visual special effects.

A **camera shot** is a single, continuous view taken by a camera. **Camera angle** is the angle at which the camera is positioned during the recording of a shot or image. Each angle is carefully planned to create an effect. The chart shows what different shots are used for.

| Camera Shot/Angle | Effect |
|---|---|
| **Establishing shot** introduces viewers to the location of a scene, usually by presenting a wide view of an area | establishes the setting of a film |
| **Close-up shot** shows a detailed view of a person or object | helps to create emotion and make viewers feel as if they know the character |
| **Medium shot** shows a view wider than a close-up but narrower than an establishing or long shot | shows part of an object or a character from the knees or waist up |
| **Long shot** is a wide view of a scene, showing the full figure(s) of a person or group and their surroundings | allows the viewer to see the "big picture" and shows the relationship between characters and the environment |
| **Reaction shot** shows someone reacting to something that occurred in a previous shot | allows the viewer to see how the subject feels in order to create empathy in the viewer |
| **Low-angle shot** looks up at an object or person | makes a character, object, or scene appear more important or threatening |
| **High-angle shot** looks down on an object or person | makes a character, object, or scene seem vulnerable or insignificant |
| **Point-of-view (POV) shot** shows a part of the story through a character's eyes | helps viewers identify with that character |

**Camera movement** can create energy, reveal information, or establish a mood. The following chart shows some of the ways filmmakers move the camera to create an effect.

| Camera Movement | Effect |
|---|---|
| **Pan**–a shot in which the camera scans a location from right to left or left to right | reveals information by showing a sweeping view of an area |
| **Tracking shot**–a shot in which the camera moves with the subject | establishes tension or creates a sense of drama |
| **Zoom**–the movement of the camera as it closes in or moves farther away from the subject | captures action or draws the viewer's attention to detail |

*Mise en scène* is a French term that refers to the arrangement of actors, props, and action on a film set. It is used to describe everything that can be seen in a frame, including the setting, lighting, visual composition, costumes, and action.

**Framing** is capturing people and objects within the "frame" of a screen or image. Framing is what the camera sees.

**Composition** is the arrangement of objects, characters, shapes, and colors within a frame and the relationship of the objects to one another.

## 3.3 SOUND ELEMENTS

**Sound elements** in film and television include music, voice-over, and sound effects.

**Music** may be used to set the mood and atmosphere in a scene. Music can have a powerful effect on the way viewers feel about a story. For example, fast-paced music helps viewers feel excited during an action scene.

**Voice-over** is the voice of the unseen commentator or narrator of a film, TV program, or commercial.

**Sound effects** are the sounds added to films, TV programs, and commercials during the editing process. Sound effects, such as laugh tracks or the sounds of punches in a fight scene, can create humor, emphasize a point, or contribute to the mood.

### 3.4 SPECIAL EFFECTS

**Special effects** include computer-generated animation, manipulated video images, and fast- or slow-motion sequences in films, TV programs, and commercials.

**Animation** on film involves the frame-by-frame photography of a series of drawings or objects. When these frames are projected—at a rate of 24 per second—the illusion of movement is achieved.

A **split screen** is a special-effects shot in which two or more separate images are shown in the same frame. One example is when two people, actually a distance apart, are shown talking to each other.

### 3.5 EDITING

**Editing** is the process of selecting and arranging shots in a sequence. The editor decides which scenes or shots to use, as well as the length of each shot, the number of shots, and their sequence. Editing establishes pace, mood, and a coherent story.

**Cut** is the transition from one shot to another. To create excitement, editors often use quick cuts, which are a series of short shots strung together.

**Dissolve** is a transitional device in which one scene fades into another.

**Fade-in** is a transitional device in which a white or black shot fades in to reveal the beginning of a new scene.

**Fade-out** is a transitional device in which a shot fades to darkness to end a scene.

**Jump cut** is an abrupt and jarring change from one shot to another. A jump cut shows a break in time or continuity.

**Pace** is the length of time each shot stays on the screen and the rhythm that is created by the transitions between shots. Short, quick cuts create a fast pace in a story. Long cuts slow down a story.

## 4 News

The **news** is information on events, people, and places in your community, your region, the nation, and the world. The news can be categorized by type, as shown in the chart.

| Type | Description | Examples |
| --- | --- | --- |
| **Hard news** | fact-based accounts of current events | local newspapers, newscasts, online wire services |
| **Soft news** | human-interest stories and other accounts that are less current or urgent than hard news | magazines and tabloid TV shows such as *Sports Illustrated, Access Hollywood* |
| **News features** | stories that elaborate on news reports | documentaries such as history reports on PBS |
| **Commentary and opinion** | essays and perspectives by experts, professionals, and media personalities | editorial pages, personal Web pages |

### 4.1 CHOOSING THE NEWS

**Newsworthiness** is the significance of an event or action that makes it worthy of media reporting. Journalists and their editors usually weigh the following criteria in determining which stories should make the news:

**Timeliness** is the quality of being very current. Timely events usually take priority over previously reported events. For example, a car accident with fatalities will be timely on the day it occurs. Because of its timeliness it may be on the front page of a newspaper or may be the lead story on a newscast.

**Widespread impact** refers to the importance of an event and the number of people it could affect. The more widespread the impact of an event, the more likely it is to be newsworthy.

**Proximity** gauges the nearness of an event to a particular city, region, or country. People tend to be more interested in stories that take place locally and affect them directly.

**Human interest** is a quality of stories that cause readers or listeners to feel emotions such as happiness, anger, or sadness. People are interested in reading stories about other people.

**Uniqueness** refers to uncommon events or circumstances that are likely to be interesting to an audience.

**Compelling video** and **photographs** grab people's attention and stay in their minds.

### 4.2 REPORTING THE NEWS

While developing a news story, a journalist makes a variety of decisions about how to construct the story, such as what information to include and how to organize it. The following elements are commonly used in news stories:

**5 *W*'s and *H*** are the six questions reporters answer when writing news stories—*who, what, when, where, why,* and *how.* It is a journalist's job to answer these questions in any type of news report. These questions also serve as a structure for writing and editing a story.

**Inverted pyramid** is the means of organizing information according to importance. In the inverted-pyramid diagram below, the most important information (the answers to the 5 *W*'s and *H*) appears at the top of the pyramid. The less important details appear at the bottom. Not all stories are reported using the inverted-pyramid form. The form remains popular, however, because it enables a reader to get the essential information without reading the entire story. Notice the following example.

Marcus Albright, star guard for the Streaking Impalas, scored the winning basket in an 87–86 come-from-behind victory over the Rovers.

The Impalas had trailed by as many as 15 points with just over four minutes left in the game.

Albright dominated the last three minutes with four three-pointers.

**Angle or slant** is the point of view from which a story is written. Even an objective report must have an angle.

Consider the different focus and tone of these two headlines that describe the same house fire.

Family Heirlooms Destroyed in Fire

Firefighters Slow to Respond to Fire

The first headline focuses on facts about the family's loss and has a human-interest angle. The second headline focuses on an opinion about the firefighters' response time and has a negative slant.

### Standards for News Reporting

The ideal of journalism is to present news in a way that is objective, accurate, and thorough. The best news stories contain the following elements:

- **Objectivity** The story takes a balanced point of view on the issues; it is not biased, nor does it reflect a specific attitude or opinion.

- **Accuracy** The story presents factual information that can be verified.

- **Thoroughness** The story presents all sides of an issue; it includes background information, telling *who, what, when, where, why,* and *how.*

### Balanced Versus Biased Reporting

Objectivity in news reporting can be measured by how balanced or biased the story is.

**Balanced reporting** means that all sides of an issue are represented equally and fairly.

A balanced news story

- represents people and subjects in a neutral light

- treats all sides of an issue equally

- does not include inappropriate questions, such as "Will you seek counseling after this terrible tragedy?"

- does not show stereotypes or prejudice toward people of a particular race, gender, age, religion, or other group

- does not leave out important background information that is needed to establish a context or perspective

**Biased reporting** is reporting in which one side is favored over another or in which the subject is unfairly represented. Biased reporting may show an overly negative view of a subject, or it may encourage racial, gender, or other stereotypes and prejudices. Sometimes biased reporting is apparent in the journalist's choice of sources.

**Sources** are the people interviewed for the news report and also any written materials and documents the journalist used for background information. From each source, the journalist gets a different point of view. To decide whether news reporting is balanced or biased, you will need to pay attention to the sources. For a news story on a new medicinal drug, for instance, if the journalist's only source is a representative from the company that made the drug, the report may be biased. But if the journalist also includes the perspective of someone neutral, such as a scientist who is objectively studying the effects of drugs, the report may be more balanced. The following chart shows which sources are credible.

| Sources for News Stories | |
|---|---|
| **Credible Sources** | **Weak Sources** |
| • experts in a field<br>• people directly affected by the reported event (eyewitnesses)<br>• published reports that are specifically mentioned or shown | • unnamed or anonymous sources<br>• people who are not involved in the reported event (for example, people who heard about a story from a friend)<br>• research, data, or reports that are not specifically named or are referred to only in vague terms (for example, "Research shows that …") |

## 5 Advertising

**Advertising** is a sponsor's paid use of various media to promote products, services, or ideas. Some common forms of advertising are shown in the chart.

| Type of Ad | Characteristic |
|---|---|
| **Billboard** | large outdoor advertising sign |
| **Print ad** | typically appears in magazines and newspapers; uses eye-catching graphics and persuasive copy |
| **Flyer** | print ad that is circulated by hand or mail |
| **Infomercial** | an extended ad on TV that usually includes detailed product information, demonstrations, and testimonials |
| **Public service announcement** | a message aired on radio or TV to promote ideas that are considered to be in the public interest |
| **Political ad** | broadcast on radio or TV to promote political candidates |
| **Trailer** | a short film promoting an upcoming movie, TV show, or video game |

**Marketing** is the process of transferring products and services from producer to consumer. It involves determining the packaging and pricing of a product, how it will be promoted and advertised, and where it will be sold. One way companies market their product is by becoming media sponsors.

**Sponsors** pay for their products to be advertised. These companies hire advertising agencies to create and produce specific campaigns for their products. They then buy television or radio airtime or magazine, newspaper, or billboard space to feature ads where the target audience is sure to see them. Because selling time and space to advertisers generates much of the income the media need to function, the media need advertisers just as much as advertisers need the media.

**Product placement** is the intentional and identifiable featuring of brand-name products in movies, television shows, video games, and other media. The intention is to have viewers feel positive about a product because they see a favorite character using it. Another purpose may be to promote product recognition.

### 5.1 PERSUASIVE TECHNIQUES

**Persuasive techniques** are the methods used to convince an audience to buy a product or adopt an idea. Advertisers use a combination of visuals, sound, special effects, and words to persuade their target audience. Recognizing the following techniques can help you evaluate persuasive media messages and identify misleading information:

**Emotional appeals** use strong feelings rather than factual evidence to persuade consumers. An example of any emotional appeal is, "Is your home safe? ProAlarm systems will make sure it is."

**Bandwagon appeals** use the argument that a person should believe or do something because "everyone else" does. These appeals take advantage of people's desire to be socially accepted by other people. Purchasing a popular product seems less risky to those concerned about making a mistake. An example of a bandwagon appeal is "More and more people are making the switch to Discountline long-distance service."

**Slogans** are memorable phrases used in advertising campaigns. Slogans substitute catchy phrases for factual information.

**Logical appeals** rely on logic and facts, appealing to a consumer's reason and his or her respect for authority. Two examples of logical appeals are expert opinions and product comparison.

**Celebrity ads** use one of the following two categories of spokesperson:

- **Celebrity authorities** are experts in a particular field. Advertisers hope that audiences will transfer the respect or admiration they have for the person to the product. For example, a famous chef may endorse a particular brand of cookware. The manufacturers of the cookware want you to think that it is a good product because a cooking expert wouldn't endorse pots and pans that didn't work.

- **Celebrity spokespeople** are famous people who endorse a product. Advertisers hope that audiences will associate the product with the celebrity.

**Product comparison** is comparing a product and its competition. Often mentioned by name, the competing product is portrayed as inferior. The intended effect is for people to question the quality of the competing product and to believe the featured product is superior.

## 6 Elements of Design

The design of a media message is just as important as the words are in conveying the message. Like words, visuals are used to persuade, inform, and entertain.

Graphics and images, such as charts, diagrams, maps, timelines, photographs, illustrations, and symbols, present information that can be quickly and easily understood. The following basic elements are used to give meaning to visuals:

**Color** can be used to highlight important elements such as headlines and subheads. It can also create mood, because many colors have strong emotional or psychological impacts on the reader or viewer. For example, warm colors more readily draw the eye and are often associated with happiness and comfort. Cool colors are often associated with feelings of peace and contentment or sometimes with sadness.

**Lines**—strokes or marks—can be thick or thin, long or short, and smooth or jagged. They can focus attention and create a feeling of depth. They can frame an object. They can also direct a viewer's eye or create a sense of motion.

**Texture** is the surface quality or appearance of an object. For example, an object's texture can be glossy, rough, wet, or shiny. Texture can be used to create contrast. It can also be used to make an object look "real." For example, a pattern on

wrapping paper can create a feeling of depth even though the texture is only visual and cannot be felt.

**Shape** is the external outline of an object. Shapes can be used to symbolize living things or geometric objects. They can emphasize visual elements and add interest. Shapes can symbolize ideas.

Notice how this movie poster uses design elements:

- **Lines** The reader's eyes are led downward to the cityscape and film's title by the vertical line or ray of light.
- **Shape** The spacecraft's shape immediately suggests a flying saucer. It may also symbolize a friendly or unfriendly visitor.
- **Color** Deep blues and purples lend an air of mystery and also make the central ray of light stand out.

## 7 Evaluating Media Messages

Being able to respond critically to media images and messages will help you evaluate the reliability of the content and make informed decisions. Here are six questions to ask about any media message:

**Who made—and who sponsored—this message, and for what purpose?** The source of the message is a clue to its purpose. If the source of the message is a private company, that company may be trying to sell you a product. If the source is a government agency, that agency may be trying to promote a program or philosophy. To discover the purpose, think about why its creator paid for and produced the message.

**Who is the target audience and how is the message specifically tailored to it?** Think about the age group, ethnic group, gender, and/or profession the message is targeting. Decide how it relates to you.

**What are the different techniques used to inform, persuade, entertain, and attract attention?** Analyze the elements, such as rhetorical devices, humor, sound effects, and graphics, that have been used to create the message. Think about how the formality and tone of these elements support the purpose behind the message.

**What messages are communicated (and/or implied) about certain people, places, events, behaviors, lifestyles, and so forth?** The media try to influence who we are, what we believe in, how we view things, and what values we hold. Look or listen closely to determine whether certain types of behavior are being depicted and if judgments or values are communicated through those behaviors. What are the biases in the message?

**How current, accurate, and credible is the information in this message?** Think about the reputation of the source. Note the broadcast or publication date of the message and whether the message might change quickly. If a report or account is not supported by facts, authoritative sources, or eyewitness accounts, you should question the credibility of the message.

**What is left out of this message that might be important to know?** Think about what the message is asking you to believe. Also think about what questions come to mind as you watch, read, or listen to the message.

# Strategies and Practice for the SAT, ACT, and Other Standardized Tests

*The test items in this section are modeled after test formats that are used on the SAT. The strategies presented here will help you prepare for that test and others. This section offers general test-taking strategies and tips for answering multiple-choice items, as well as short-response and extended-response questions in critical reading and writing. It also includes guidelines and samples for impromptu writing and essay writing. For each test, read the tips in the margin. Then apply the tips to the practice items. You can also apply the tips to Assessment Practice Tests in this book.*

## 1 General Test-Taking Strategies

- Arrive on time and be prepared. Be sure to bring either sharpened pencils with erasers or pens—whichever you are told to bring.

- If you have any questions, ask them before the test begins. Make sure you understand the test procedures, the timing, and the rules.

- Read the test directions carefully. Look at the passages and questions to get an overview of what is expected.

- Tackle the questions one at a time rather than thinking about the whole test.

- Refer back to the reading passages as needed. For example, if a question asks about an author's attitude, you might have to reread a passage for clues.

- If you are not sure of your answer, make a logical guess. You can often arrive at the correct answer by reasoning and eliminating wrong answers.

- As you fill in answers on your answer sheet, make sure you match the number of each test item to the numbered space on the answer sheet.

- Don't look for patterns in the positions of correct choices.

- Only change an answer if you are sure your original choice is incorrect. If you do change an answer, erase your original choice neatly and thoroughly.

- Look for central or main ideas as you read passages. They are often stated at the beginning or the end of a paragraph. Sometimes the central idea is implied.

- Check your answers and reread your essay.

## 2 Critical Reading

Most tests contain a critical reading section that measures your ability to read, understand, and interpret passages. The passages may be either fiction or nonfiction, and they can be 100 words or 500 to 800 words. They are drawn from literature, humanities, social studies, and natural sciences.

**Directions:** Read the following passage. Base your answers to questions 1 and 2 on what is stated or implied in the passage.

> **PASSAGE**
>
> By global or historical standards, much of what Americans consider poverty is luxury. A rural Russian is not considered poor if he cannot afford a car and his home has no central heating; a rural American is. Most impoverished people in the world would be dazzled by the apartments, telephones, television sets, running water, clothing, and other amenities that surround the poor in America. But that does not mean that the poor are not poor, or that those on the edge of poverty are not truly on the edge of a cliff.
>
> —David Shipler, *The Working Poor*

**❶** stem

1. The (main) idea of this paragraph is that ❷
   - (A) the definition of poverty can differ from one country to another
   - (B) no one in America is really poor
   - **❸** choices (C) many people in Russia are very poor
   - (D) being poor is like falling off a cliff
   - (E) running water and central heating are basic amenities

2. What does the author mean when he says that those on the edge of poverty are standing on the edge of a cliff? ❺
   - (A) Poor people sometimes feel suicidal.
   - (B) For poor people, life can be risky and uncertain.
   - (C) Being poor is like looking down into a black hole. ❹
   - (D) Many poor people are homeless.
   - (E) It is hard to pull yourself up out of poverty.

**Directions:** Base your answers to questions 1 through 3 on the two passages below.

### PASSAGE 1

Contemporary students now sample the once-exotic sounds of African pennywhistle, Tuvian throat singing, or Scandinavian mandolin as casually as they choose between tacos, pizza, and sushi. . . . Madonna's *Ray of Light,* for example, borrowed from bhangra, an Indian-inflected dance music. . . . Some fear that globalization will destroy cultural diversity, resulting in a world ruled by American exports. Yet the world-music scene suggests an alternative, where global popular culture enters our marketplace with help from American youth.

—Henry Jenkins, "Culture Goes Global"

### PASSAGE 2

As the unrivaled global superpower, America exports its culture on an unprecedented scale. From music to media, film to fast food, language to literature and sport, the American idea is spreading inexorably, not unlike the influence of empires that preceded it. The difference is that today's technology flings culture to every corner of the globe with blinding speed. Sometimes, U.S. ideals get transmitted—such as individual rights, freedom of speech, and respect for women—and local cultures are enriched. At other times, materialism or worse becomes the message and local traditions get crushed.

—"In 2,000 Years, Will the World Remember Disney or Plato?"
*The Christian Science Monitor*

1. Which statement best describes the attitudes of the authors of Passages 1 and 2 toward the spread of U.S. culture to other countries?
   (A) Only the author of Passage 1 sees this trend as positive.
   (B) Only the author of Passage 2 sees this trend as positive.
   (C) Neither author sees this trend as positive.
   (D) Both authors see this trend as positive.
   (E) Both authors see positive and negative aspects of this trend.

2. The author of Passage 1 claims that
   (A) globalization will destroy cultural diversity
   (B) students and musicians are influenced by music from other cultures
   (C) non-Westerners prefer American culture to their own
   (D) American ideals are spreading around the world
   (E) pop musicians fear globalization

3. The author of Passage 2 believes that
   (A) freedom of speech will have a negative effect on local traditions
   (B) international music is a problem for American culture
   (C) local traditions can be crushed by American culture
   (D) other cultures have no interest in American culture
   (E) American influence abroad has been uniformly negative

## Tips: Two Passages

Questions are sometimes based on a pair of related passages. Sometimes the passages have completely different views. At other times, the passages describe different aspects of the same subject.

❶ Before reading the passages, skim the questions to see what information you will need.

❷ Look for topic sentences in each passage. Ask yourself whether the passage supports or refutes its topic sentence. Passage 1 refutes its topic sentence, while Passage 2 supports its topic sentence.

❸ Focus on key words, especially ones that are used in both passages (though possibly in different forms). You can figure out that *globe* is the root word of *global* and *globalization*. If *globe* refers to the earth, then *global* means "worldwide," and *globalization* means "the process of making worldwide."

❹ Look for clues about an author's attitude toward a subject in the author's choice of words and examples. In Passage 2, the author's use of the word *flings* suggests that he has some negative feelings about the spread of American culture.

**Answers: 1.** (E), **2.** (B), **3.** (C)

**Directions:** Read the following passage. Base your answers to questions 1 through 3 on what is stated or implied in the passage. Then base your answer to question 4 on your knowledge of types of writing.

*In the following passage, the narrator recalls her childhood growing up in Puerto Rico.*

**PASSAGE**

**❶**—I had not meant to start a contest of wills between my parents when I mentioned my dreams of playing the piano to Papi. My hands seemed to yearn for action, moving constantly as I talked, seeking textures when I sat reading a book, digging fearlessly into holes on walls, dipping into containers, drawers, boxes with lids that didn't quite close. Since I loved music, learning to play piano seemed like a good choice, even though I'd never actually seen a piano, let alone had any idea of what it took to play one.

**❷** When I mentioned it to Papi, he was excited. The idea of a concert career for me appealed to his vision of himself as a poet and of me as more than a spunky tomboy. He took it upon himself to find me a teacher and **❷**—came up with the principal at my new school, an elderly gentleman with thinning hair and a thick mustache that seemed pasted on his delicate features. We wouldn't have to pay anything, Papi said, because "he's willing to give you lessons in exchange for some carpentry on his porch."

On Sunday afternoon I set off with Papi for my first piano lesson. I had never seen a teacher outside of school, and as we neared Don Luis's house, I was scared and dug my thumbnail into the other nails to scrape out any dirt that might have escaped the scratchy bristles of Mami's vegetable brush.

"Buenas!" he greeted us. I held on to Papi's hand as to a lifeline, not **❸** trusting my knocking knees to hold me up. But Don Luis's warm smile soon melted my fear into awe at finding myself in his house, away from the unpleasant implications of a student face-to-face with the school principal.

His house was detached from those around it, surrounded by flowers that bloomed in splendid colors and overwhelming fragrances. The inside **❹** was small but as ornate as the yard, with lace curtains, glass-topped tables, invitingly curvy furniture, and, dominating the back wall, an enormous reddish-brown piano, lustrous and dust free, majestic against a fabric-covered wall. I looked at Papi, who winked at me and smiled. We shared the joy of being in this room, in the home of an artist, a person whose life was gracious and carefree, whose furnishings and decorations were as impractical as ours were utilitarian.

—Esmeralda Santiago, *When I Was Puerto Rican*

## Tips: Reading Text

**❶** Identify the narrator's point of view. In the first-person point of view, the narrator is a character in the story and describes people and events as he or she experiences them, using the pronouns *I* and *me*. In the third-person point of view, the narrator is outside of the story and uses pronouns such as *he*, *she*, and *they*.

**❷** Notice the characters who are presented in a passage. The characters in this passage are the narrator, Papi, and the principal. Look for details about personality such as appearance, feelings, actions, and things that a character owns.

**❸** Find words that contribute to the mood or atmosphere of a passage. When the narrator says she held onto Papi's hand "as to a lifeline," she conveys her fear.

**❹** Look at details that describe the setting of a narrative passage. The details in this passage take the reader inside the piano teacher's home.

**Answers: 1.** (C), **2.** (E), **3.** (A), **4.** (B)

1. What was Papi's vision of his daughter?
   (A) He envisioned her as a poet.
   (B) He saw her as nothing more than a tomboy.
   (C) He believed she could have a musical career.
   (D) He wanted her to become a teacher.
   (E) He thought she was spoiled.

2. How would you describe the narrator's feelings before her first piano lesson?
   (A) She felt that the piano lessons were a mistake.
   (B) She felt humble because her family didn't own a piano.
   (C) She was embarassed because she had never seen a piano.
   (D) She felt proud because her father was able to arrange free lessons.
   (E) She was scared because the piano teacher was the principal of her school.

3. The narrator wanted to play piano
   (A) to find an outlet for her nervous energy
   (B) to impress her father
   (C) to test her will against her parents' will
   (D) to develop discipline by practicing an instrument
   (E) to prove she was not a tomboy

4. The last paragraph of the passage is an example of what kind of writing?
   (A) persuasive
   (B) descriptive
   (C) expository
   (D) dramatic
   (E) analytic

The critical reading section may also feature sentence-completion questions that test your knowledge of vocabulary. They may also measure your ability to figure out how different parts of a sentence logically fit together.

**Directions:** Choose the word or set of words that, when inserted, best fits the meaning of each of the following sentences.

1. The personal computer, which was a _____ tool just 30 years ago, has had a _____ impact on our lives since then. ❶
   - (A) forgotten . . profound
   - (B) fledgling . . huge
   - (C) whimsical . . significant ❷
   - (D) negligible . . munificent
   - (E) practical . . healthy

2. Today there is _____ evidence that the earth orbits the sun, (but) before the telescope was invented, facts to back that claim were _____. ❸
   - (A) mammoth . . tenuous
   - (B) ample . . unstinting
   - (C) dynamic . . credible
   - (D) circumstantial . . incalculable
   - (E) copious . . scant

3. The island of Alcatraz was once the _____ of an _____ federal prison.
   - (A) topography . . idyllic
   - (B) portal . . impromptu
   - (C) locale . . eclectic
   - (D) site . . infamous ❹
   - (E) milieu . . illicit

4. The woman left food every day for a colony of _____ cats that lived behind her barn, but they shied away from her nonetheless.
   - (A) feral ❺
   - (B) affectionate
   - (C) fierce
   - (D) indoor
   - (E) docile

## Tips: Sentence Completion

❶ When you are completing sentences with two words missing, look at both blanks and think about what kinds of words will fill them.

❷ If one of the words in an answer choice is wrong, you can eliminate that whole set of words from consideration. In sentence 1, *significant* makes sense, but *whimsical* does not.

❸ Look for key words or phrases that link the ideas in a sentence. The word *but* signals that the two parts of the sentence express contrasting ideas.

❹ A prefix can change the meaning of a word. Someone becomes famous for doing something positive but infamous for doing something negative. An artist might be famous; a criminal would be infamous.

❺ If you don't know the exact meaning of a word, you can look for clues in the sentence. For sentence 4, you can ask yourself: What kind of cat lives outdoors and shies away from people? *Feral* means "untamed" and is the best answer to that question.

**Answers: 1.** (B), **2.** (E), **3.** (D), **4.** (A)

# 3 Writing

To measure your ability to express ideas clearly and correctly, tests ask you to identify errors in grammar and usage and to improve sentences and paragraphs.

> **Directions:** Select the one underlined part that must be changed to make the following sentence correct. There is no more than one error in the sentence. If the sentence is correct as written, select answer choice E.

1. Since the first dinosaur bones <u>collected</u> in 19th-century England,
   ❷      (A)
   dinosaur remains—<u>ranging from bone fragments to nearly complete skeletons</u>— ❶
   ❸            ❹ (B)
   have been <u>unearthed</u> on every continent <u>except</u> Antarctica. No error
   (C)            (D)        (E)

> **Directions:** Determine whether the underlined section of the following sentence needs improvement. If it does, select the best change presented in the choices below the sentence. Note that Choice A repeats the original phrase.

2. The author of a definitive work on Abraham Lincoln, Carl Sandburg is renowned as a biographer <u>as well as for his poetry</u>. ❻

   (A) as well as for his poetry ❺

   (B) as well as a poet

   (C) as well as for being a poet

   (D) and for being a poet

   (E) and also for poetry

> **Directions:** Read the passage below and select the best answer to the question that follows the passage.

> (1) Scott Joplin was an African-American pianist and composer. (2) He is regarded as the father of ragtime, a form of popular music. (3) Joplin wanted to establish his name with more serious music. (4) His opera titled *Treemonisha* received the Pulitzer Prize for music in 1976, 59 years after the composer's death. (5) It is considered the first truly American opera.

3. What is the best way to combine sentences 2 and 3?
   (A) He is regarded as the father of ragtime, a form of popular music, so Joplin wanted to establish his name with more serious music.
   (B) He is regarded as the father of ragtime, a form of popular music; Joplin wanted to establish his name with more serious music.
   (C) He is regarded as the father of ragtime, a form of popular music, but Joplin wanted to establish his name with more serious music. ❼
   (D) Rather than being regarded as the father of ragtime, a form of popular music, Joplin wanted to establish his name with more serious music.
   (E) He is regarded as the father of ragtime, a form of popular music, and Joplin wanted to establish his name with more serious music.

## Tips: Grammar and Style

❶ Read the entire sentence or passage to grasp its overall meaning. Pay particular attention to any underlined portions.

❷ Parenthetical thoughts can be inserted between dashes to interrupt the main flow of a sentence.

❸ Use prefixes to help you understand unfamiliar words. In test item 1, *un-*, for example, means "a reverse action." To unearth is to dig up.

❹ Don't confuse words that look or sound alike. *Except* means "other than"; *accept* means "to receive willingly."

❺ In choosing a revision, read through all of the choices before you and decide which one is best. Choose this answer (A) only if the sentence is correct as it appears originally.

❻ Parallelism is an important part of sentence structure. In test item 2, *biographer* and *poet* are both nouns and both descriptions of Sandburg.

❼ Know the meanings of conjunctions.

**Answers: 1.** (A), **2.** (B), **3.** (C)

Some tests may measure your understanding of a passage by asking you to write a response.

> **Directions:** Read the passage. Then answer the questions that follow.

> When I was a boy my grandfather died, and he was a sculptor. He was also a very kind man who had a lot of love to give the world, and he helped clean up the slum in our town; and he made toys for us and he did a million things in his lifetime; he was always busy with his hands. . . .
>
> Everyone must leave something behind when he dies, my grandfather said. A child or a book or a painting or a house or a wall built or a pair of shoes made. Or a garden planted. Something your hand touched some way so your soul has somewhere to go when you die, and when people look at that tree or that flower you planted, you're there. It doesn't matter what you do, he said, so long as you change something from the way it was before you touched it into something that's like you after you take your hands away. The difference between the man who just cuts lawns and a real gardener is in the touching, he said. The lawn-cutter might just as well not have been there at all; the gardener will be there a lifetime.
>
> —Ray Bradbury, *Fahrenheit 451*

## SHORT RESPONSE

What things does the grandfather say we can create that will live after we die? Write a sentence that names two of those things.

> **SAMPLE SHORT RESPONSE**
>
> The grandfather says we can live on in a book we write or a house we build. **❶**

## EXTENDED RESPONSE

What does the grandfather mean when he says, "Everyone must leave something behind when he dies"? Write one or two paragraphs to answer this question.

> **SAMPLE EXTENDED RESPONSE**
>
> The grandfather in this passage believes that people should create things that they will be remembered for. The things we create, whether they are **❸** works of art or the children we raise, express our individuality. Just as we leave fingerprints when we touch something, we leave a part of ourselves in the things we create. A person who creates something of worth or **❷** beauty will be remembered for generations to come. For that reason, the grandfather is urging his grandchild to make a difference with his life.

**❶** Short-response prompts are often fact based rather than interpretive. Get right to the point in your answer, and stick to the facts.

**❷** Make sure that you write about the assigned topic. Support your answer with details from the passage, such as a quotation, a paraphrase, or an example.

**❸** When you are writing an extended response, build your paragraphs around clear topic sentences that will pull your ideas together.

**❹** If you are asked to interpret a passage, don't just copy the author's words. Try to express the ideas in your own words. Express your ideas clearly, so that the reader understands your viewpoint.

**❺** Proofread your response for errors in capitalization, punctuation, spelling, or grammar.

# 4 Essay

To determine how well you can develop and support your thoughts, many tests ask you to write an essay in response to an assignment, or prompt. The essay will represent a first draft and will be scored based on the following:

- **Focus** Establish a point of view in the opening paragraph.
- **Organization** Maintain a logical progression of ideas.
- **Support for ideas** Use details and examples to develop an argument.
- **Style/word choice** Use words accurately and vary sentences.
- **Grammar** Use standard English and proofread for errors.

Think carefully about the issue presented in these quotations and the assignment that follows.

> No slogan of democracy; no battle cry of freedom is more stirring than the American parent's simple statement which all of you have heard so many times: 'I want my child to go to college.' —Lyndon Baines Johnson
>
> Everybody can be great. Because anybody can serve. You don't have to have a college degree to serve. —Dr. Martin Luther King Jr.

**Assignment:** What is your view on the idea that a college education is needed to be successful in our society? Plan and write an essay in which you develop your point of view on this issue. Support your position with examples from your reading, your experience, or current events.

---

**SAMPLE ESSAY**

Some people believe that everyone needs a college degree. Education is important, but I don't think a four-year university education is needed to be ❶ successful in our society.

Electricians, plumbers, and carpenters go through specialized training in their fields. They don't need to be college graduates to do their work. Blue-collar workers are the backbone of our society. Where would we be if no one took vocational training? Who would repair our cars and unclog our sinks? The college-educated professional won't do it. Unskilled work is important, too. Dishwashers and taxi drivers may not have even a high school education, but many people rely on the services they provide. ❸

On the other hand, a practical education combined with some college ❷ courses in business administration might mean the difference between being an electrician and owning a successful electrical contracting business. Bill Gates is a good example. He started building computers from kits when he was in high school. He went to Harvard for a while, but he dropped out so that he could pursue his own idea of creating an operating system for personal ❸ computers. He invented DOS (disk operating system) and founded Microsoft.

In conclusion, people should have a chance to receive the highest level of education that their potential and effort allow. It's great to have some college experience, because it exposes you to new people and new ideas, but it is not ❹ necessary for everyone to receive a four-year university education.

---

## Tips: Writing an Essay

The SAT test allows only 25 minutes for you to write an essay. So before you begin writing, take a few minutes to gather your thoughts. Write down the main points you want to make. Allow time to reread your essay before you hand it in. Make sure your handwriting is legible.

❶ When you're writing a persuasive essay, state your point of view in the introduction.

❷ Take the opposing point of view into consideration and respond to it.

❸ Use examples in the body of your essay to clarify your points and strengthen your arguments.

❹ Make sure your essay has a conclusion, even if it's just a single sentence. A conclusion pulls your ideas together and lets the reader know you've finished.

❺ Allow enough time to reread what you have written. If you have to make a correction, do so neatly and legibly.

**Act** An act is a major division within a play, similar to a chapter in a book. Each act may be further divided into smaller sections, called scenes. Plays can have as many as five acts, as in Shakespeare's *Romeo and Juliet*. Neil Simon's *The Sneeze* is a one-act play.

**Allegory** An allegory is a work with two levels of meaning—a literal one and a symbolic one. In such a work, most of the characters, objects, settings, and events represent abstract qualities. Personification is often used in traditional allegories. As in a fable or a parable, the purpose of an allegory may be to convey truths about life, to teach religious or moral lessons, or to criticize social institutions.

**Alliteration** Alliteration is the repetition of consonant sounds at the beginning of words. Note the repetition of the *d* sound in these lines.

> Deep into that darkness peering, long I stood there
>     wondering, fearing,
> Doubting, dreaming dreams no mortal ever dared to
>     dream before
>                     —Edgar Allan Poe, "The Raven"

*See pages 145, 742, 875.*
*See also* **Consonance.**

**Allusion** An allusion is an indirect reference to a famous person, place, event, or literary work. The title of Maya Angelou's autobiography *I Know Why the Caged Bird Sings* is an allusion to the poem "Sympathy" by Paul Laurence Dunbar.
*See pages 265, 668, 925, 1029, 1196.*

**Analogy** An analogy is a point-by-point comparison between two things that are alike in some respect. Often, writers use analogies in nonfiction to explain unfamiliar subjects or ideas in terms of familiar ones.
*See also* **Extended Metaphor; Metaphor; Simile.**

**Antagonist** An antagonist is a principal character or force in opposition to a **protagonist,** or main character. The antagonist is usually another character but sometimes can be a force of nature, a set of circumstances, some aspect of society, or a force within the protagonist. In "The Most Dangerous Game," General Zaroff is the antagonist.
*See pages 398, 1026.*

**Archetype** An archetype is a pattern in literature that is found in a variety of works from different cultures throughout the ages. An archetype can be a plot, a character, an image, or a setting. For example, the association of death

and rebirth with winter and spring is an archetype common to many cultures.

**Argumentative Essay** *See* **Essay.**

**Aside** In drama, an aside is a short speech directed to the audience, or another character, that is not heard by the other characters on stage. In Act Four, Scene 1, of *Romeo and Juliet*, Paris is urging that his marriage to Juliet take place soon. Friar Laurence expresses his uneasiness in an aside.

> Friar Laurence [*aside*]. I would I knew not why it
>     should be slowed.—
> Look, sir, here comes the lady toward my cell.
>                     —William Shakespeare, *Romeo and Juliet*

*See pages 1035, 1114.*
*See also* **Soliloquy.**

**Assonance** Assonance is the repetition of vowel sounds within nonrhyming words. An example of assonance is the repetition of the *u* sound in the following line.

> Only their usual maneuvers, dear
>                     —W. H. Auden, "O What Is That Sound"

**Author's Perspective** An author's perspective, or point of view, is a unique combination of ideas, values, feelings, and beliefs that influences the way the writer looks at a topic. **Tone,** or attitude, often reveals an author's perspective. Julia Alvarez in "Daughter of Invention" writes from a perspective that reflects her feelings about being an immigrant in America.
*See pages 389, 493, 554, 613.*
*See also* **Author's Purpose; Tone.**

**Author's Purpose** A writer usually writes for one or more of these purposes: to express thoughts or feelings, to inform or explain, to persuade, to entertain. For example, Pat Mora's purposes for writing "A Voice" are to express her feelings and to explain.
*See pages 127, 552, 591, 605.*
*See also* **Author's Perspective.**

**Autobiography** An autobiography is a writer's account of his or her own life. In almost every case, it is told from the first-person point of view. Generally, an autobiography focuses on the most significant events and people in the writer's life over a period of time. Richard Wright's *Black Boy* is an autobiography. Shorter autobiographical narratives include **journals, diaries,** and **letters.** An **autobiographical**

**essay,** another type of short autobiographical work, focuses on a single person or event in the writer's life.

*See pages 9, 117, 255.*

*See also* **Memoir.**

**Ballad** A ballad is a type of narrative poem that tells a story and was originally meant to be sung or recited. Because it tells a story, a ballad has a setting, a plot, and characters. **Traditional ballads** are written in four-line stanzas with regular rhythm and rhyme. **Folk ballads** were composed orally and handed down by word of mouth. These ballads usually tell about ordinary people who have unusual adventures or perform daring deeds. A **literary ballad** is a poem written by a poet in imitation of the form and content of a folk ballad. "O What Is That Sound" is an example of a literary ballad.

**Biography** A biography is the true account of a person's life, written by another person. As such, a biography is usually told from a third-person point of view. The writer of a biography usually researches his or her subject in order to present accurate information. The best biographers strive for honesty and balance in their accounts of their subjects' lives.

**Blank Verse** Blank verse is unrhymed poetry written in **iambic pentameter.** That is, each line of blank verse has five pairs of syllables. In most pairs, an unstressed syllable is followed by a stressed syllable. The most versatile of poetic forms, blank verse imitates the natural rhythms of English speech. Much of Shakespeare's drama is in blank verse.

> But soft! What light through yonder window breaks?
> It is the East, and Juliet is the sun!
> —William Shakespeare, *Romeo and Juliet*

*See also* **Iambic Pentameter.**

**Cast of Characters** In the script of a play, a cast of characters is a list of all the characters in the play, usually in order of appearance. It may include a brief description of each character.

**Central Idea** *See* **Theme.**

**Character** Characters are the individuals who participate in the action of a literary work. Like real people, characters display certain qualities, or **character traits;** they develop and change over time; and they usually have **motivations,** or reasons, for their behaviors. Complex characters can have multiple or conflicting motivations.

> **Main characters:** Main characters are the most important characters in literary works. Generally, the

plot of a short story focuses on one main character, but a novel may have several main characters.

> **Minor characters:** The less prominent characters in a literary work are known as minor characters. Minor characters support the plot. The story is not centered on them, but they help carry out the action of the story and help the reader learn more about the main character.

> **Dynamic character:** A dynamic character is one who undergoes important changes as a plot unfolds. The changes occur because of his or her actions and experiences in the story. The change is usually internal and may be good or bad. Main characters are usually, though not always, dynamic.

> **Static character:** A static character is one who remains the same throughout a story. The character may experience events and have interactions with other characters, but he or she is not changed because of them.

> **Round character:** A round character is one who is complex and highly developed, having a variety of traits and different sides to his or her personality. Some of the traits may create conflict in the character. Round characters tend to display strengths, weaknesses, and a full range of emotions. The writer provides enough detail for the reader to understand their feelings and emotions.

> **Flat character:** A flat character is one who is not highly developed. A flat character is a one-sided character: he or she usually has one outstanding trait, characteristic, or role. Flat characters exist mainly to advance the plot, and they display only the traits needed for their limited roles. Minor characters are usually flat characters.

*See pages 85, 202, 223, 251.*

*See also* **Characterization.**

**Characterization** The way a writer creates and develops characters' personalities is known as characterization. There are four basic methods of characterization:

- The writer may make direct comments about a character's personality or nature through the voice of the narrator.
- The writer may describe the character's physical appearance.
- The writer may present the character's own thoughts, speech, and actions.
- The writer may present pertinent thoughts, speech, and actions of other characters.

*See pages 204, 255, 293.*

*See also* **Character.**

**Chorus** In early Greek tragedy, the chorus commented on the actions of the characters in a drama. In some Elizabethan plays, such as Shakespeare's *Romeo and Juliet,*

the role of the chorus is taken by a single actor who serves as a narrator and speaks the lines in the **prologue** (and sometimes in an **epilogue**). The chorus serves to foreshadow or summarize events.

**Climax** In a plot, the climax is the point of maximum interest or tension. Usually the climax is a turning point in the story, which occurs after the reader has understood the **conflict** and become emotionally involved with the characters. The climax sometimes, but not always, points to the **resolution** of the conflict. In "American History" by Judith Ortiz Cofer, the climax occurs when Elena encounters Eugene's mother at the door of Eugene's house.
*See pages 452, 964.*
*See also* **Plot.**

**Comedy** A comedy is a dramatic work that is light and often humorous in tone, usually ending happily with a peaceful resolution of the main conflict. A comedy differs from a farce by having a more believable plot, more realistic characters, and less boisterous behavior.

**Comic Relief** Comic relief consists of humorous scenes, incidents, or speeches that are included in a serious drama to provide a reduction in emotional intensity. Because comic relief breaks the tension, it allows an audience to prepare emotionally for events to come. Shakespeare often uses this device in his tragedies.
*Example:* In many of Shakespeare's plays, a scene involving a fool, or bawdy interplay among common folks or between a servant and his or her master, provides comic relief. Comic relief in *Romeo and Juliet* is provided by the nurse in Act Two, Scene 5, when she returns to Juliet after learning the wedding plans from Romeo. Although Juliet is anxious to hear of the plans, which the audience already knows, the nurse deliberately withholds the information until the end of the scene.

**Complex Character** *See* **Character.**

**Complication** A complication is an additional factor or problem introduced into the rising action of a story to make the conflict more difficult. Often, a plot complication makes it seem as though the main character is getting farther away from the thing he or she wants.

**Conflict** A conflict is a struggle between opposing forces. Almost every story has a main conflict—a conflict that is the story's focus. An **external conflict** involves a character pitted against an outside force, such as nature, a physical obstacle, or another character. An **internal conflict** is one that occurs within a character.
*Examples:* In "The Most Dangerous Game" by Richard Connell, Rainsford is in conflict with General Zaroff. In Doris

Lessing's "Through the Tunnel," Jerry is torn between the safety of familiar beach surroundings and the challenge of swimming through the tunnel.
*See pages 28, 59, 60, 356, 837.*
*See also* **Plot.**

**Connotation** A connotation is an attitude or a feeling associated with a word, in contrast to the word's **denotation,** which is its literal, or dictionary, meaning. The connotations of a word may be positive or negative. For example, *enthusiastic* has positive associations, while *rowdy* has negative ones. Connotations of words can have an important influence on style and meaning and are particularly important in poetry.

**Consonance** Consonance is the repetition of consonant sounds within and at the end of words, as in "lonely afternoon." Consonance is unlike rhyme in that the vowel sounds preceding or following the repeated consonant sounds differ. Consonance is often used together with **alliteration, assonance,** and **rhyme** to create a musical quality, to emphasize certain words, or to unify a poem.
*See also* **Alliteration.**

**Couplet** A couplet is a rhymed pair of lines. A couplet may be written in any rhythmic pattern.

> From what I've tasted of desire
> I hold with those who favor fire.
> —Robert Frost, "Fire and Ice"

*See also* **Stanza.**

**Critical Essay** *See* **Essay.**

**Denotation** *See* **Connotation.**

**Dénouement** *See* **Falling Action.**

**Dialect** A dialect is a form of language that is spoken in a particular geographic area or by a particular social or ethnic group. A group's dialect is reflected in its pronunciations, vocabulary, expressions, and grammatical structures. Writers use dialects to capture the flavors of locales and to bring characters to life, re-creating the way they actually speak. In "Two Kinds" by Amy Tan, the narrator's mother uses grammatical constructions that are not common in English and therefore speaks a kind of dialect.

> "Who ask you be genius?" she shouted. "Only ask you be your best. For your sake. You think I want you be genius?"
> —Amy Tan, "Two Kinds"

**Dialogue** Dialogue is written conversation between two or more characters. Writers use dialogue to bring characters to life and to give readers insights into the characters' qualities, traits, and reactions to other characters. Realistic, well-paced dialogue also advances the plot of a narrative. In fiction, dialogue is usually set off with quotation marks. In drama, stories are told primarily through dialogue. Playwrights use stage directions to indicate how they intend the dialogue to be interpreted by actors.

**Diary** A diary is a daily record of a writer's thoughts, experiences, and feelings. As such, it is a type of autobiographical writing. The terms *diary* and *journal* are often used synonymously.

**Diction** A writer's or speaker's choice of words and way of arranging the words in sentences is called diction. Diction can be broadly characterized as formal or informal. It can also be described as technical or common, abstract or concrete, and literal or figurative. A writer for *Scientific American* would use a more formal, more technical, and possibly more abstract diction than would a writer for the science section of a local newspaper.

*See pages 559, 757.*
*See also* **Style.**

**Drama** Drama is literature in which plots and characters are developed through dialogue and action; in other words, it is literature in play form. Drama is meant to be performed. Stage plays, radio plays, movies, and television programs are types of drama. Most plays are divided into acts, with each act having an emotional peak, or climax. Certain modern plays, such as *The Sneeze*, have only one act. Most plays contain stage directions, which describe settings, lighting, sound effects, the movements and emotions of actors, and the ways in which dialogue should be spoken.

**Dramatic Irony** *See* **Irony.**

**Dramatic Monologue** A dramatic monologue is a lyric poem in which a speaker addresses a silent or absent listener in a moment of high intensity or deep emotion, as if engaged in private conversation. The speaker proceeds without interruption or argument, and the effect on the reader is that of hearing just one side of a conversation. This technique allows the poet to focus on the feelings, personality, and motivations of the speaker. The poem known as "The Seven Ages of Man," spoken by Jaques, a character in Shakespeare's play *As You Like It,* is a dramatic monologue.

*See page 792.*
*See also* **Lyric Poetry; Soliloquy.**

**Dynamic Character** *See* **Character.**

**Elegy** An elegy is an extended meditative poem in which the speaker reflects on death—often in tribute to a person who has died recently—or on an equally serious subject. Most elegies are written in formal, dignified language and are serious in tone.

**Epic** An epic is a long narrative poem on a serious subject, presented in an elevated or formal style. It traces the adventures of a great hero whose actions reflect the ideals and values of a nation or race. Epics address universal concerns, such as good and evil, life and death, and sin and redemption. The *Odyssey* is an epic.

**Epic Hero** An epic hero is a larger-than-life figure who embodies the ideals of a nation or race. Epic heroes take part in dangerous adventures and accomplish great deeds. Many undertake long, difficult journeys and display great courage and superhuman strength.

*See page 1194.*

**Epic Simile** An epic simile (also called a Homeric simile) is a long, elaborate comparison that often continues for a number of lines.

> Just as a farmer's hunger grows, behind
> the bolted plow and share, all day afield,
> drawn by his team of winedark oxen: sundown
> is benison for him, sending him homeward
> stiff in the knees from weariness, to dine;
> just so the light on the sea rim gladdened
> Odysseus.
>
> —Homer, *Odyssey*

*See page 1196.*
*See also* **Simile.**

**Epilogue** An epilogue is a short addition at the end of a literary work, often dealing with the future of the characters. The concluding speech by Prince Escalus in *Romeo and Juliet* serves as an epilogue.

**Epithet** An epithet is a brief phrase that points out traits associated with a particular person or thing. In the *Odyssey*, Odysseus is often called " the master strategist."
*See page 1196.*

**Essay** An essay is a short work of nonfiction that deals with a single subject. Some essays are **formal**—that is, tightly structured and written in an impersonal style. Others are **informal,** with a looser structure and a more personal style.

Generally, an **informative** or **expository essay** presents or explains information and ideas. A **personal essay** is typically an informal essay in which the writer expresses his or her thoughts and feelings about a subject, focusing on the meaning of events and issues in his or her own life. In a **reflective essay,** the author makes a connection between a personal observation or experience and a universal idea, such as love, courage, or freedom. A **critical essay** evaluates a situation, a course of action, or a work of art. In an **argumentative** or **persuasive essay,** the author attempts to convince readers to adopt a certain viewpoint or to take a particular stand.

*See pages 8, 492, 558, 568, 854, 860.*

**Exposition** Exposition is the first stage of a plot in a typical story. The exposition provides important background information and introduces the setting and the important characters. The conflict the characters face may also be introduced in the exposition, or it may be introduced later, in the rising action.

*See page 28.*

*See also* **Plot.**

**Expository Essay** *See* **Essay.**

**Extended Metaphor** An extended metaphor is a figure of speech that compares two essentially unlike things at some length and in several ways. It does not contain the word *like* or *as.* For example, in "The Seven Ages of Man" by William Shakespeare, an extended metaphor compares the world to a stage.

> All the world's a stage,
> And all the men and women merely players
> —William Shakespeare, *As You Like It*

*See also* **Metaphor.**

**External Conflict** *See* **Conflict.**

**Fable** A fable is a brief tale told to illustrate a moral or teach a lesson. Often the moral of a fable appears in a distinct and memorable statement near the tale's beginning or end. "The Princess and the Tin Box" by James Thurber is a humorous fable.

*See also* **Moral.**

**Falling Action** In a plot, the falling action follows the climax and shows the results of the important action that happened at the climax. Tension eases as the falling action begins; however, the final outcome of the story is not yet fully worked out at this stage. Events in the falling action

lead to the **resolution,** or **dénouement,** of the plot. In "American History" by Judith Ortiz Cofer, the falling action begins when the narrator turns away from the door of Eugene's house.

*See page 28.*

*See also* **Climax; Plot.**

**Fantasy** Fantasy is a type of fiction that is highly imaginative and portrays events, settings, or characters that are unrealistic. The setting might be a nonexistent world, the plot might involve magic or the supernatural, and the characters might employ superhuman powers.

**Farce** Farce is a type of exaggerated comedy that features an absurd plot, ridiculous situations, and humorous dialogue. The main purpose of a farce is to keep an audience laughing. The characters are usually stereotypes, or simplified examples of individual traits or qualities. Comic devices typically used in farces include mistaken identity, deception, physical comedy, wordplay—such as puns and double meanings—and exaggeration.

**Fiction** Fiction is prose writing that consists of imaginary elements. Although fiction can be inspired by actual events and real people, it usually springs from writers' imaginations. The basic elements of fiction are plot, character, setting, and theme. The novel and short story are forms of fiction.

*See also* **Character; Novel; Plot; Setting; Short Story; Theme.**

**Figurative Language** Figurative language is language that communicates meanings beyond the literal meanings of words. In figurative language, words are often used to symbolize ideas and concepts they would not otherwise be associated with. Writers use figurative language to create effects, to emphasize ideas, and to evoke emotions. Simile, metaphor, extended metaphor, hyperbole, and personification are examples of figurative language.

*See pages 775, 869, 1087.*

*See also* **Hyperbole; Metaphor; Onomatopoeia; Personification; Simile.**

**First-Person Point of View** *See* **Point of View.**

**Flashback** A flashback is an account of a conversation, an episode, or an event that happened before the beginning of a story. Often, a flashback interrupts the chronological flow of a story to give the reader information needed to understand a character's present situation. Flashbacks also help create such effects as mystery, tension, or surprise.

*Example:* In "Where Have You Gone, Charming Billy?" Tim O'Brien uses flashbacks to help capture the thought process

of the main character as he copes with the realities of his wartime experience, increasing the story's level of tension.

**Foil** A foil is a character who provides a striking contrast to another character. By using a foil, a writer can call attention to certain traits possessed by a main character or simply enhance a character by contrast. In Shakespeare's *Romeo and Juliet,* Mercutio serves as a foil to Romeo.

**Foreshadowing** Foreshadowing is a writer's use of hints or clues to suggest events that will occur later in a story. The hints and clues might be included in a character's dialogue or behavior, or they might be included in details of description. Foreshadowing creates suspense, mystery, and surprise, and makes readers eager to find out what will happen. For example, in Stephen King's teleplay *Sorry, Right Number,* the opening camera close-up and the first line of dialogue seem to hint that the telephone and Bill's health will be important in the play.

**Form** *Form* refers to the principles of arrangement in a poem—the ways in which lines are organized. Form in poetry includes the following elements: the length of lines, the placement of lines, and the grouping of lines into stanzas.
*See also* **Stanza.**

**Free Verse** Free verse is poetry that does not contain regular patterns of rhythm or rhyme. The lines in free verse often flow more naturally than do rhymed, metrical lines and thus achieve a rhythm more like that of everyday speech. Although free verse lacks conventional meter, it may contain various rhythmic and sound effects, such as repetitions of syllables or words. Free verse can be used for a variety of subjects. Billy Collins's poem "Today" is an example of free verse.
*See pages 741, 875.*
*See also* **Meter; Rhyme.**

**Genre** The term *genre* refers to a category in which a work of literature is classified. The major genres in literature are fiction, nonfiction, poetry, and drama.

**Haiku** Haiku is a form of Japanese poetry in which 17 syllables are arranged in three lines of 5, 7, and 5 syllables. The rules of haiku are strict. In addition to the syllabic count, the poet must create a clear picture that will evoke a strong emotional response in the reader. Nature is a particularly important source of inspiration for Japanese haiku poets, and details from nature are often the subjects of their poems.

> Harvest moon—
> walking around the pond
> all night long.
>
> —Bashō

**Hero** A hero is a main character or protagonist in a story. In older literary works, heroes tend to be better than ordinary humans. They are typically courageous, strong, honorable, and intelligent. They are protectors of society who hold back the forces of evil and fight to make the world a better place. In modern literature, a hero may simply be the most important character in a story. Such a hero is often an ordinary person with ordinary problems.

**Historical Fiction** A short story or novel can be classified as historical fiction when the settings and details of the plot include real places and real events of historical importance. Historical figures may appear as major or minor characters, as Napoleon does in Leo Tolstoy's classic novel *War and Peace.* In historical fiction, the setting generally influences the plot in important ways.

**Horror Fiction** Horror fiction contains strange, mysterious, violent, and often supernatural events that create suspense and terror in the reader. Edgar Allan Poe and Stephen King are famous authors of horror fiction.

**Humor** In literature, there are three basic types of humor, all of which may involve exaggeration or irony. **Humor of situation** arises out of the plot of a work. It usually involves exaggerated events or situational irony, which arises when something happens that is different from what was expected. **Humor of character** is often based on exaggerated personalities or on characters' failure to recognize their own flaws, a form of dramatic irony. **Humor of language** may include sarcasm, exaggeration, puns, or verbal irony, in which what is said is not what is meant.
*See page 853.*
*See also* **Irony.**

**Hyperbole** Hyperbole is a figure of speech in which the truth is exaggerated for emphasis or humorous effect.

**Iambic Pentameter** Iambic pentameter is a metrical pattern of five feet, or units, each of which is made up of two syllables, the first unstressed and the second stressed. Iambic pentameter is the most common meter used in English poetry; it is the meter used in blank verse and in the sonnet. The following lines are examples of iambic pentameter.

> My lips, two blushing pilgrims, ready stand
> —William Shakespeare, *Romeo and Juliet*

*See pages 797, 1028.*
*See also* **Blank Verse; Sonnet.**

**Idiom** An idiom is a common figure of speech whose meaning is different from the literal meaning of its words. For example, the phrase "raining cats and dogs" does not literally mean that cats and dogs are falling from the sky; the expression means "raining heavily."

**Imagery** Imagery consists of descriptive words and phrases that re-create sensory experiences for the reader. Imagery usually appeals to one or more of the five senses—sight, hearing, smell, taste, and touch—to help the reader imagine exactly what is being described. The imagery in the poem "Incident in a Rose Garden" by Donald Justice helps the reader to see Death, who wears a black coat, black gloves, and a black hat. Truman Capote uses vivid imagery appealing to multiple senses in order to re-create the childhood of the narrator in "A Christmas Memory."
*See pages 151, 291, 332, 337, 407, 749.*

**Informative Essay** *See* **Essay.**

**Internal Conflict** *See* **Conflict.**

**Interview** An interview is a conversation conducted by a writer or reporter, in which facts or statements are elicited from another person, recorded, and then broadcast or published. "Tim O'Brien: The Naked Soldier" is an example of an interview.
*See page 836.*

**Irony** Irony is a special kind of contrast between appearance and reality—usually one in which reality is the opposite of what it seems. One type of irony is **situational irony,** a contrast between what a reader or character expects and what actually exists or happens. The unexpected twist in the outcome of "The Gift of the Magi" by O. Henry is an example of situational irony. Another type of irony is **dramatic irony,** where the reader or viewer knows something that a character does not know. **Verbal irony** exists when someone knowingly exaggerates or says one thing and means another.
*See pages 101, 858, 889.*

**Journal** *See* **Diary.**

**Limited Point of View** *See* **Point of View.**

**Line** The line is the core unit of a poem. In poetry, line length is an essential element of the poem's meaning and rhythm. **Line breaks,** where a line of poetry ends, may coincide with grammatical units. However, a line break may also occur in the middle of a grammatical or syntactical unit, creating a meaningful pause or emphasis. Poets use a variety of line breaks to play with sense, grammar, and syntax and thereby create a wide range of effects.

**Literary Criticism** *See* **Text Criticism.**

**Literary Nonfiction** Literary nonfiction is nonfiction that is recognized as being of artistic value or that is about literature. Autobiographies, biographies, essays, and eloquent speeches typically fall into this category.

**Lyric Poetry** A lyric poem is a short poem in which a single speaker expresses personal thoughts and feelings. Most poems other than dramatic and narrative poems are lyric poems. In ancient Greece, lyric poetry was meant to be sung. Modern lyrics are usually not intended for singing, but they are characterized by strong melodic rhythms. Lyric poetry has a variety of forms and covers many subjects, from love and death to everyday experiences. Langston Hughes's "Theme for English B" and Pat Mora's "A Voice" are examples of lyric poems.

**Memoir** A memoir is a form of autobiographical writing in which a writer shares his or her personal experiences and observations of significant events or people. Often informal or even intimate in tone, memoirs usually give readers insight into the impact of historical events on people's lives. *Angela's Ashes* by Frank McCourt is a memoir.
*See pages 171, 925.*
*See also* **Autobiography.**

**Metaphor** A metaphor is a figure of speech that makes a comparison between two things that are basically unlike but have something in common. Unlike similes, metaphors do not contain the word *like* or *as*. In "Ode to My Socks," Pablo Neruda uses metaphors to compare his socks to multiple objects, including "two long sharks of lapis blue."
*See also* **Extended Metaphor; Figurative Language; Simile.**

**Meter** Meter is a regular pattern of stressed and unstressed syllables in a poem. The meter of a poem emphasizes the musical quality of the language. Each unit of meter, known as a **foot,** consists of one stressed syllable and one or two unstressed syllables. In representations of meter, a stressed syllable is indicated by the symbol ´; an unstressed syllable, by the symbol ˘. The four basic types of metrical feet are the **iamb,** an unstressed syllable followed by a stressed syllable (˘´); the **trochee,** a stressed syllable

followed by an unstressed syllable (`˘`); the **anapest,** two unstressed syllables followed by a stressed syllable (`˘˘´`); and the **dactyl,** a stressed syllable followed by two unstressed syllables (`´˘˘`).

*See pages 743, 793.*

*See also* **Rhythm.**

**Mise en Scène** *Mise en scène* is a term from the French that refers to the various physical aspects of a dramatic presentation, such as lighting, costumes, scenery, makeup, and props.

**Mood** In a literary work, mood is the feeling or atmosphere that a writer creates for the reader. Descriptive words, imagery, and figurative language contribute to the mood of a work, as do the sound and rhythm of the language used. In "The Cask of Amontillado," Edgar Allan Poe creates a mood of dread and horror.

*See pages 332, 371, 389.*

*See also* **Tone.**

**Moral** A moral is a lesson taught in a literary work, such as a fable. For example, the moral "Do not count your chickens before they are hatched" teaches that one should not count on one's fortunes or blessings until they appear. In James Thurber's "The Princess and the Tin Box," the moral, like the fable itself, is satirical.

*See also* **Fable.**

**Motivation** *See* **Character.**

**Myth** A myth is a traditional story, usually concerning some superhuman being or unlikely event, that was once widely believed to be true. Frequently, myths were attempts to explain natural phenomena, such as solar and lunar eclipses or the cycle of the seasons. For some peoples, myths were both a kind of science and a religion. In addition, myths served as literature and entertainment, just as they do for modern-day audiences.

    Greek mythology forms much of the background in Homer's *Odyssey*. For example, the myth of the judgment of Paris describes events that led to the Trojan War. The goddesses Athena, Hera, and Aphrodite asked a mortal—Paris—to decide which of them was the most beautiful. Paris chose Aphrodite and was rewarded by her with Helen, wife of the Greek king Menelaus.

**Narrative Nonfiction** Narrative nonfiction is writing that reads much like fiction, except that the characters, setting, and plot are real rather than imaginary. Its purpose is usually to entertain or to express opinions or feelings. Narrative nonfiction includes, but is not limited to, autobiographies, biographies, memoirs, diaries, and journals. *Seabiscuit* by Laura Hillenbrand is an example of narrative nonfiction.

*See page 128.*

**Narrative Poetry** Narrative poetry tells a story or recounts events. Like a short story or a novel, a narrative poem has the following elements: plot, characters, setting, and theme. "The Raven" by Edgar Allan Poe is a narrative poem.

**Narrator** The narrator of a story is the character or voice that relates the story's events to the reader.

*See also* **Persona; Point of View.**

**Nonfiction** Nonfiction is writing that tells about real people, places, and events. Unlike fiction, nonfiction is mainly written to convey factual information, although writers of nonfiction shape information in accordance with their own purposes and attitudes. Nonfiction can be a good source of information, but readers frequently have to examine it carefully in order to detect biases, notice gaps in the information provided, and identify errors in logic. Nonfiction includes a diverse range of writing—newspaper articles, letters, essays, biographies, movie reviews, speeches, true-life adventure stories, advertising, and more.

**Novel** A novel is an extended work of fiction. Like a short story, a novel is essentially the product of a writer's imagination. Because a novel is considerably longer than a short story, a novelist can develop a wider range of characters and a more complex plot.

*Example:* In John Knowles's novel *A Separate Peace,* Gene's character develops as he struggles with guilt that resulted from the "accident" that crippled Phineas.

**Novella** A novella is a work of fiction that is longer than a short story but shorter than a novel. A novella differs from a novel in that it concentrates on a limited cast of characters, a relatively short time span, and a single chain of events. The novella is an attempt to combine the compression of the short story with the development of the novel.

**Ode** An ode is a complex lyric poem that develops a serious and dignified theme. Odes appeal to both the imagination and the intellect, and many commemorate events or praise people or elements of nature.

**Omniscient Point of View** *See* **Point of View.**

**Onomatopoeia** Onomatopoeia is the use of words whose sounds echo their meanings, such as *buzz, whisper, gargle,* and *murmur.* Onomatopoeia as a literary technique goes

beyond the use of simple echoic words, however. Skilled writers, especially poets, choose words whose sounds intensify images and suggest meanings.

**Oxymoron** An oxymoron is a special kind of concise paradox that brings together two contradictory terms. In *Romeo and Juliet*, each of the phrases "brawling love," "loving hate," "bright smoke," and "feather of lead" is an oxymoron.

**Paradox** A paradox is a seemingly contradictory or absurd statement that may nonetheless suggest an important truth.

**Parallelism** Parallelism is the use of similar grammatical constructions to express ideas that are related or equal in importance.

> Go back to Mississippi. Go back to Alabama. Go back to South Carolina. Go back to Georgia. Go back to Louisiana. Go back to the slums and ghettos of our Northern cities. . . .
> —Martin Luther King Jr., "I Have a Dream"

**Parallel Plot** A parallel plot is a particular type of plot in which two stories of equal importance are told simultaneously. The story moves back and forth between the two plots.

**Parody** A parody is an imitation of another work, a type of literature, or a writer's style, usually for the purpose of poking fun. It may serve as an element of a larger work or be a complete work in itself. The purpose of parody may be to ridicule through broad humor, deploying such techniques as exaggeration or the use of inappropriate subject matter. Such techniques may even provide insights into the original work. "The Princess and the Tin Box" by James Thurber is a parody of the typical moralistic fairy tale.

**Persona** A persona is a voice that a writer assumes in a particular work. A persona is like a mask worn by the writer, separating his or her identity from that of the speaker or the narrator. It is the persona's voice—not the writer's voice—that narrates a story or speaks in a poem.
*See also* **Narrator; Speaker.**

**Personal Essay** *See* **Essay.**

**Personification** Personification is a figure of speech in which human qualities are given to an object, animal, or idea. In "Incident in a Rose Garden" by Donald Justice, death is personified as someone who wears black and grins. In the following line by Shakespeare, morning and night are personified.

> The grey-eyed morn smiles on the frowning night
> —William Shakespeare, *Romeo and Juliet*

*See pages 744, 775.*
*See also* **Figurative Language.**

**Persuasive Essay** *See* **Essay.**

**Play** *See* **Drama.**

**Plot** The sequence of events in a story is called the plot. A plot focuses on a central **conflict** or problem faced by the main character. The actions that the characters take to resolve the conflict build toward a climax. In general, it is not long after this point that the conflict is resolved and the story ends. A plot typically develops in five stages: exposition, rising action, climax, falling action, and resolution.
*See pages 28, 85.*
*See also* **Climax; Exposition; Falling Action; Rising Action.**

**Poetry** Poetry is a type of literature in which words are carefully chosen and arranged to create certain effects. Poets use a variety of sound devices, imagery, and figurative language to express emotions and ideas.
*See also* **Alliteration; Assonance; Ballad; Free Verse; Imagery; Meter; Rhyme; Rhythm; Stanza.**

**Point of View** *Point of view* refers to the method of narration used in a short story, novel, narrative poem, or work of nonfiction. In a work told from a **first-person** point of view, the narrator is a character in the story, as in "The Cask of Amontillado" by Edgar Allan Poe. In a work told from a **third-person** point of view, the narrative voice is outside the action, not one of the characters. If a story is told from a **third-person omniscient,** or all-knowing, point of view, as in "The Gift of the Magi" by O. Henry, the narrator sees into the minds of all the characters. If events are related from a **third-person limited** point of view, as in Doris Lessing's "Through the Tunnel," the narrator tells what only one character thinks, feels, and observes.
*See pages 202, 209.*
*See also* **Narrator.**

**Prologue** A prologue is an introductory scene in a drama. Some Elizabethan plays include prologues that comment on the theme or moral point that will be revealed in the play. The prologue is a feature of all Greek drama.

**Prop** The word *prop*, originally an abbreviation of the word *property*, refers to any physical object that is used in a drama. In the teleplay *Sorry, Right Number*, a telephone is an important prop.

**Prose** Generally, *prose* refers to all forms of written or spoken expression that are not in verse. The term, therefore, may be used to describe very different forms of writing— short stories as well as essays, for example.

**Protagonist** A protagonist is the main character in a work of literature—the character who is involved in the central conflict of the story. Usually, the protagonist changes after the central conflict reaches a climax. He or she may be a hero and is usually the one with whom the audience tends to identify. In Judith Ortiz Cofer's "American History," Elena is the protagonist as well as the narrator.

**Pun** A pun is a joke that comes from a play on words. It can make use of a word's multiple meanings or of a word's sound. In *Romeo and Juliet*, when Mercutio is fatally wounded, he says, "Ask for me tomorrow, and you shall find me a grave man," with a pun on the word *grave*, meaning both "solemn" and "a tomb."

**Quatrain** A quatrain is a four-line stanza, or group of lines, in poetry. The most common stanza in English poetry, the quatrain can have a variety of meters and rhyme schemes.

**Realistic Fiction** Realistic fiction is fiction that is a truthful imitation of ordinary life. "Through the Tunnel" by Doris Lessing and "A Christmas Memory" by Truman Capote are examples of realistic fiction.

**Recurring Theme** *See* **Theme.**

**Reflective Essay** *See* **Essay.**

**Refrain** A refrain is one or more lines repeated in each stanza of a poem.
*See also* **Stanza.**

**Repetition** Repetition is a technique in which a sound, word, phrase, or line is repeated for emphasis or unity. Repetition often helps to reinforce meaning and create an appealing rhythm. The term includes specific devices associated with both prose and poetry, such as alliteration and parallelism.
*See pages 742, 787.*
*See also* **Alliteration; Parallelism; Sound Devices.**

**Resolution** *See* **Falling Action.**

**Rhetorical Devices** Rhetorical devices are techniques writers use to enhance their arguments and communicate more effectively. Rhetorical devices include **analogy, parallelism, rhetorical questions,** and **repetition.**
*See also* **Analogy; Repetition; Rhetorical Questions,** *Glossary of Reading and Informational Terms, page R119.*

**Rhyme** Rhyme is the occurrence of similar or identical sounds at the end of two or more words, such as *suite, heat,* and *complete.* Rhyme that occurs within a single line of poetry is **internal rhyme.** Rhyme that occurs at the ends of lines of poetry is called **end rhyme.** End rhyme that is not exact but approximate is called **slant rhyme,** or **off rhyme.** Notice the following example of slant rhyme involving the words *care* and *dear.*

O haven't they stopped for the doctor's <u>care</u>,
   Haven't they reined their horses, their horses?
Why, they are none of them wounded, <u>dear</u>.
   None of these forces.
         —W. H. Auden, "O What Is That Sound"

*See pages 742, 788, 869.*

**Rhyme Scheme** A rhyme scheme is a pattern of end rhymes in a poem. A rhyme scheme is noted by assigning a letter of the alphabet, beginning with *a*, to each line. Lines that rhyme are given the same letter. Notice the rhyme scheme of the first stanza of this famous poem.

| | |
|---|---|
| Two roads diverged in a yellow wood, | *a* |
| And sorry I could not travel both | *b* |
| And be one traveler, long I stood | *a* |
| And looked down one as far as I could | *a* |
| To where it bent in the undergrowth | *b* |
| —Robert Frost, "The Road Not Taken" | |

*See page 742.*

**Rhythm** Rhythm is a pattern of stressed and unstressed syllables in a line of poetry. Poets use rhythm to bring out the musical quality of language, to emphasize ideas, to create moods, to unify works, and to heighten emotional responses. Devices such as alliteration, rhyme, assonance, consonance, and parallelism often contribute to creating rhythm.
*See pages 742, 869.*
*See also* **Meter.**

**Rising Action** Rising action is the stage in a plot in which the conflict develops and story events build toward a climax. During this stage, complications arise that make the conflict more intense. Tension grows as the characters struggle to resolve the conflict.

*See page 28.*

*See also* **Plot.**

**Sarcasm** Sarcasm is a kind of particularly cutting irony. Generally, sarcasm is the taunting use of praise to mean its opposite—that is, to insult someone or something.

**Satire** Satire is a literary technique in which ideas, customs, behaviors, or institutions are ridiculed for the purpose of improving society. Satire may be gently witty, mildly abrasive, or bitterly critical, and it often involves the use of irony and exaggeration to force readers to see something in a critical light.

**Scansion** Scansion is the notation of stressed and unstressed syllables in poetry. A stressed syllable is indicated by the symbol ´; an unstressed syllable, by the symbol ˇ. Using scansion can help you determine the rhythm and meter of a poem.

*See page 742.*

*See also* **Meter.**

**Scene** In drama, the action is often divided into acts and scenes. Each scene presents an episode of the play's plot and typically occurs at a single place and time.

*See also* **Act.**

**Scenery** Scenery is a painted backdrop or other structures used to create the setting for a play.

**Science Fiction** Science fiction is fiction in which a writer explores unexpected possibilities of the past or the future, using known scientific data and theories as well as his or her creative imagination. Most science fiction writers create believable worlds, although some create fantasy worlds that have familiar elements. Ray Bradbury, the author of "A Sound of Thunder," is a famous writer of science fiction.

*See also* **Fantasy.**

**Screenplay** A screenplay is a play written for film.

**Script** The text of a play, film, or broadcast is called a script.

**Sensory Details** Sensory details are words and phrases that appeal to the reader's senses of sight, hearing, touch, smell, and taste. For example, the sensory detail "a fine film of rain" appeals to the senses of sight and touch. Sensory details stimulate the reader to create images in his or her mind.

*See also* **Imagery.**

**Setting** Setting is the time and place of the action of a story. Some stories, such as "The Open Window" by Saki, have only minimal descriptions of setting. In other works, such as Eugenia Collier's "Marigolds" and Edgar Allan Poe's "The Cask of Amontillado," settings are described in detail and become major contributors to the stories' overall effect.

*See pages 330, 337, 389.*

*See also* **Fiction.**

**Short Story** A short story is a work of fiction that centers on a single idea and can be read in one sitting. Generally, a short story has one main conflict that involves the characters, keeps the story moving, and stimulates readers' interest.

*See also* **Fiction.**

> I am offering this poem to you,
> since I have nothing else to give.
> Keep it <u>like a warm coat</u>
> When winter comes to cover you
> —Jimmy Santiago Baca, "I Am Offering This Poem"

**Simile** A simile is a figure of speech that makes a comparison between two unlike things, using the word *like* or *as*.

*See pages 744, 775.*

*See also* **Epic Simile; Figurative Language; Metaphor.**

**Situational Irony** See **Irony.**

**Soliloquy** In drama, a soliloquy is a speech in which a character speaks his or her thoughts aloud. Generally, the character is on the stage alone, not speaking to other characters and perhaps not even consciously addressing an audience. At the beginning of Act Two, Scene 3, of *Romeo and Juliet*, Friar Laurence has a long soliloquy. Shakespeare makes use of soliloquies in many of his plays.

*See also* **Aside; Dramatic Monologue.**

**Sonnet** A sonnet is a lyric poem of 14 lines, commonly written in **iambic pentameter.** Sonnets are often classified as Petrarchan or Shakespearean. The Shakespearean, or Elizabethan, sonnet consists of three quatrains, or four-line units, and a final couplet. The typical rhyme scheme is *abab cdcd efef gg*.

*See also* **Iambic Pentameter; Rhyme Scheme.**

**Sound Devices** Sound devices, or uses of words for their auditory effect, can convey meaning and mood or unify a work. Some common sound devices are **alliteration, assonance, consonance, meter, onomatopoeia, repetition, rhyme,** and **rhythm.** The following lines contain alliteration, repetition, assonance, consonance, rhyme, and rhythm, all of which combine to help convey both meaning and mood.

> O what is that sound which so thrills the ear
> 　　Down in the valley drumming, drumming:
> Only the scarlet soldiers, dear,
> 　　The soldiers coming.
> 　　　　　　—W. H. Auden, "O What Is That Sound"

*See pages 145, 787.*

*See also* **Alliteration; Assonance; Consonance; Meter; Onomatopoeia; Repetition; Rhyme; Rhythm.**

**Speaker** In poetry the speaker is the voice that "talks" to the reader, similar to the narrator in fiction. The speaker is not necessarily the poet. For example, in Pat Mora's "A Voice," the experiences related may or may not have happened to the poet.

*See pages 287, 745, 787.*

*See also* **Persona.**

**Speech** A speech is a talk or public address. The purpose of a speech may be to entertain, to explain, to present a claim, to inspire, or any combination of these aims. "I Have a Dream" by Martin Luther King Jr. was written and delivered in order to inspire an audience.

*See pages 660, 670.*

**Stage Directions** A play typically includes instructions called stage directions, which are usually printed in italic type. They serve as a guide to directors, set and lighting designers, performers, and readers. When stage directions appear within passages of dialogue, parentheses are usually used to set them off from the words spoken by characters.

> Jeff *gets up, walks to the window, and looks out into the dark. He's really upset.* Dennis *and* Connie, *in the grand tradition of older brothers and sisters, are delighted to see it.*
> 　　　　　　—Stephen King, *Sorry, Right Number*

*See pages 7, 156, 1030.*

**Stanza** A stanza is a group of two or more lines that form a unit in a poem. A stanza is comparable to a paragraph in prose. Each stanza may have the same number of lines, or the number of lines may vary. "The Road Not Taken" by Robert Frost is divided into four stanzas.

*See also* **Couplet; Form; Poetry; Quatrain.**

**Static Character** *See* **Character.**

**Stereotype** In literature, a simplified or stock character who conforms to a fixed pattern or is defined by a single trait is known as a stereotype. Such a character does not usually demonstrate the complexity of a real person. Familiar stereotypes in popular literature include the absent-minded professor and the busybody.

**Stream of Consciousness** Stream of consciousness is a literary technique developed by modern writers, in which thoughts, feelings, moods, perceptions, and memories are presented as they randomly flow through a character's mind.

**Structure** Structure is the way in which the parts of a work of literature are put together. In poetry, structure involves the arrangement of words and lines to produce a desired effect. A common structural unit in poetry is the stanza, of which there are numerous types. In prose, structure is the arrangement of larger units or parts of a work. Paragraphs, for example, are basic units in prose, as are chapters in novels and acts in plays. The structure of a poem, short story, novel, play, or nonfictional work usually emphasizes certain important aspects of content.

*See also* **Act; Stanza.**

**Style** Style is the particular way in which a work of literature is written—not *what* is said but *how* it is said. It is the writer's unique way of communicating ideas. Many elements contribute to style, including word choice, sentence structure and length, tone, figurative language, and point of view. A literary style may be described in a variety of ways, such as formal, informal, journalistic, conversational, wordy, ornate, poetic, or dynamic.

**Surprise Ending** A surprise ending is an unexpected plot twist at the end of a story. The surprise may be a sudden turn in the action or a piece of information that gives a different perspective to the entire story. O. Henry is famous for using this device, as exemplified in his story "The Gift of the Magi."

*See pages 102, 152.*

**Suspense** Suspense is the excitement or tension that readers feel as they wait to find out how a story ends or a conflict is resolved. Writers create suspense by raising questions in readers' minds about what might happen next. The use of **foreshadowing** and **flashback** are two ways in which writers create suspense.

*See page 113.*

*See also* **Foreshadowing; Flashback.**

**Symbol** A symbol is a person, a place, an object, or an activity that stands for something beyond itself. For example, a flag is a colored piece of cloth that stands for a country. A white dove is a bird that represents peace.

**Example:** In "Through the Tunnel" by Doris Lessing, the rocky bay represents challenge, danger, and adulthood; the beach represents safety and Jerry's childhood.

*See pages 351, 355, 434, 461, 941.*

**Tall Tale** A tall tale is a humorously exaggerated story about impossible events, often involving the supernatural abilities of the main character. Stories about folk heroes such as Pecos Bill and Paul Bunyan are typical tall tales.

**Teleplay** A teleplay is a play written for television. In a teleplay, scenes can change quickly and dramatically. The camera can focus the viewer's attention on specific actions. The camera directions in teleplays are much like the stage directions in stage plays.

*See page 155.*

**Text Criticism** Text criticism is writing in which literary works, including their various elements, are analyzed, interpreted, evaluated, or compared.

**Theme** A theme, or central idea, is an underlying message about life or human nature that a writer wants the reader to understand. It is a perception about life or human nature that the writer shares with the reader. In most cases, themes are not stated directly but must be inferred. A theme may imply how a person should live but should not be confused with a **moral.** The theme of "The Scarlet Ibis" by James Hurst might be expressed as "Pride, love, and cruelty are often intermingled in human relationships."

    **Recurring themes** are themes found in a variety of works. For example, authors from varying backgrounds might convey similar themes having to do with the importance of family values. **Universal themes** are themes that are found throughout the literature of all time periods. For example, the *Odyssey* and *The Lord of the Rings* both contain a universal theme relating to the hero's search for truth, goodness, and honor.

*See pages 113, 434, 501.*
*See also* **Moral.**

**Third-Person Point of View** *See* **Point of View.**

**Tone** Tone is the attitude a writer takes takes toward a subject. Unlike mood, which is intended to shape the reader's emotional response, tone reflects the feelings of the writer. A writer communicates tone through choice of words and details. Tone may often be described by a single word, such as *serious, humorous, formal, informal, somber, sarcastic, playful, ironic, bitter,* or *objective.* For example, the tone of "Grape Sherbet" by Rita Dove might be described as tender and loving, whereas the tone of Mary Oliver's essay "A Few Words" might be described as persistent and somewhat angry.

*See pages 569, 605, 822, 860.*
*See also* **Author's Perspective; Mood.**

**Tragedy** A tragedy is a dramatic work that presents the downfall of a dignified character (**tragic hero**) or characters who are involved in historically or socially significant events. The events in a tragic plot are set in motion by a decision that is often an error in judgment (**tragic flaw**) on the part of the hero. Succeeding events are linked in a cause-and-effect relationship and lead inevitably to a disastrous conclusion, usually death. Shakespeare's *Romeo and Juliet* is a tragedy.

**Tragic Flaw** *See* **Tragedy.**

**Tragic Hero** *See* **Tragedy.**

**Traits** *See* **Character.**

**Turning Point** *See* **Climax.**

**Understatement** Understatement is a technique of creating emphasis by saying less than is actually or literally true. It is the opposite of **hyperbole,** or exaggeration. One of the primary devices of irony, understatement can be used to develop a humorous effect, to create satire, or to achieve a restrained tone.

*See also* **Hyperbole; Irony.**

**Universal Theme** *See* **Theme.**

**Verbal Irony** *See* **Irony.**

**Voice** Voice is a writer's unique use of language that allows a reader to "hear" a human personality in the writer's work. Elements of style that contribute to a writer's voice include sentence structure, **diction,** and **tone.** Voice can reveal much about the author's personality, beliefs, and attitudes.

*See pages 879, 951.*

**Word Choice** *See* **Diction.**

**Almanac** *See* **Reference Works.**

**Analogy** *See Glossary of Literary and Nonfiction Terms, page R102.*

**Argument** An argument is speech or writing that presents a claim about an issue or problem and supports it with reasons and evidence. An argument often takes into account other points of view, anticipating and answering objections that opponents of the position might raise.
*See also* **Claim; Counterargument; Evidence.**

**Assumption** An assumption is an opinion or belief that is taken for granted. It can be about a specific situation, a person, or the world in general. Assumptions are often unstated.

**Author's Message** An author's message is the main idea or theme of a particular work.
*See also* **Main Idea; Theme,** *Glossary of Literary and Nonfiction Terms, page R114.*

**Author's Perspective** *See Glossary of Literary and Nonfiction Terms, page R102.*

**Author's Position** An author's position is his or her opinion on an issue or topic.
*See also* **Claim.**

**Author's Purpose** *See Glossary of Literary and Nonfiction Terms, page R102.*

**Autobiography** *See Glossary of Literary and Nonfiction Terms, page R102.*

**Bias** Bias is an inclination toward a particular judgment on a topic or issue. A writer often reveals a strongly positive or strongly negative opinion by presenting only one way of looking at an issue or by heavily weighting the evidence. Words with intensely positive or negative connotations are often a signal of a writer's bias.

**Bibliography** A bibliography is a list of books and other materials related to the topic of a text. Bibliographies can be good sources of works for further study on a subject.
*See also* **Works Consulted.**

**Biography** *See Glossary of Literary and Nonfiction Terms, page R103.*

**Business Correspondence** Business correspondence includes all written business communications, such as business letters, e-mails, and memos. In general, business correspondence is brief, to the point, clear, courteous, and professional.

**Cause and Effect** A **cause** is an event or action that directly results in another event or action. An **effect** is the direct or logical outcome of an event or action. Basic **cause-and-effect relationships** include a single cause with a single effect, one cause with multiple effects, multiple causes with a single effect, and a chain of causes and effects. The concept of cause and effect also provides a way of organizing a piece of writing. It helps a writer show the relationships between events or ideas.
*See also* **False Cause,** *Reading Handbook, page R24.*

**Central Idea** *See* **Main Idea.**

**Chronological Order** Chronological order is the arrangement of events in their order of occurrence. This type of organization is used in both fictional narratives and in historical writing, biography, and autobiography.

**Claim** In an argument, a claim is the writer's position on an issue or problem. Although an argument focuses on supporting one claim, a writer may make more than one claim in a work.
*See also* **Argument; Thesis Statement.**

**Clarify** Clarifying is a reading strategy that helps a reader to understand or make clear what he or she is reading. Readers usually clarify by rereading, reading aloud, or discussing.

**Classification** Classification is a pattern of organization in which objects, ideas, or information is presented in groups, or classes, based on common characteristics.

**Cliché** A cliché is an overused expression. "Better late than never" and "hard as nails" are common examples. Good writers generally avoid clichés unless they are using them in dialogue to indicate something about characters' personalities.

**Compare and Contrast** To compare and contrast is to identify similarities and differences in two or more subjects. Compare-and-contrast organization can be used to structure a piece of writing, serving as a framework for analyzing the similarities and differences in two or more subjects.

**Conclusion** A conclusion is a statement of belief based on evidence, experience, and reasoning. A **valid conclusion** is a conclusion that logically follows from the facts or statements upon which it is based. A **deductive conclusion** is one that follows from a particular generalization or premise. An **inductive conclusion** is a broad conclusion or generalization that is reached by arguing from specific facts and examples.

**Connect** Connecting is a reader's process of relating the content of a text to his or her own knowledge and experience.

**Consumer Documents** Consumer documents are printed materials that accompany products and services. They are intended for the buyers or users of the products or services and usually provide information about use, care, operation, or assembly. Some common consumer documents are applications, contracts, warranties, manuals, instructions, package inserts, labels, brochures, and schedules.

**Context Clues** When you encounter an unfamiliar word, you can often use context clues as aids for understanding. Context clues are the words and phrases surrounding the word that provide hints about the word's meaning.

**Controlling Idea** *See* **Main Idea.**

**Counterargument** A counterargument is an argument made to answer an opposing argument, or counterclaim. A good argument anticipates opposing viewpoints and provides counterarguments to refute (disprove) or answer them.

**Counterclaim** *See* **Counterargument.**

**Credibility** *Credibility* refers to the believability or trustworthiness of a source and the information it contains.

**Critical Review** A critical review is an evaluation or critique by a reviewer or critic. Different types of reviews include film reviews, book reviews, music reviews, and art-show reviews.

**Database** A database is a collection of information that can be quickly and easily accessed and searched and from which information can be easily retrieved. It is frequently presented in an electronic format.

**Debate** A debate is basically an argument—but a very structured one that requires a good deal of preparation. In academic settings, *debate* usually refers to a formal argumentation contest in which two opposing teams defend and attack a proposition.
*See also* **Argument.**

**Deductive Reasoning** Deductive reasoning is a way of thinking that begins with a generalization, presents a specific situation, and then advances with facts and evidence to a logical conclusion. The following passage has a deductive argument imbedded in it: "All students in the drama class must attend the play on Thursday. Since Ava is in the class, she had better show up." This deductive argument can be broken down as follows: generalization—all students in the drama class must attend the play on Thursday; specific situation—Ava is a student in the drama class; conclusion—Ava must attend the play.
*See also* **Analyzing Logic and Reasoning,** *Reading Handbook, pages R22–R23.*

**Dictionary** *See* **Reference Works.**

**Draw Conclusions** To draw a conclusion is to make a judgment or arrive at a belief based on evidence, experience, and reasoning.

**Editorial** An editorial is an opinion piece that usually appears on the editorial page of a newspaper or as part of a news broadcast. The editorial section of a newspaper presents opinions rather than objective news reports.
*See also* **Op-Ed Piece.**

**Either/Or Fallacy** An either/or fallacy is a statement that suggests that there are only two possible ways to view a situation or only two options to choose from. In other words, it is a statement that falsely frames a dilemma, giving the impression that no options exist but the two presented—for example, "Either we stop the construction of a new airport, or the surrounding suburbs will become ghost towns."
*See also* **Identifying Faulty Reasoning,** *Reading Handbook, page R24.*

**Emotional Appeals** Emotional appeals are messages that evoke strong feelings—such as fear, pity, or vanity—in order to persuade instead of using facts and evidence to make a point. An **appeal to fear** is a message that taps into people's fear of losing their safety or security. An **appeal to pity** is a message that taps into people's sympathy and compassion for others to build support for an idea, a cause, or a proposed action. An **appeal to vanity** is a message that attempts to persuade by tapping into people's desire to feel good about themselves.
*See also* **Recognizing Persuasive Techniques,** *Reading Handbook, page R22.*

**Encyclopedia** *See* **Reference Works.**

**Essay** *See Glossary of Literary and Nonfiction Terms, page R105.*

**Evaluate** To evaluate is to examine something carefully and judge its value or worth. Evaluating is an important skill for gaining insight into what you read. A reader can evaluate the actions of a particular character, for example, or can form an opinion about the value of an entire work.

**Evidence** Evidence is the specific pieces of information that support a claim. Evidence can take the form of facts, quotations, examples, statistics, or personal experiences, among others.

**Expository Essay** *See* **Essay,** *Glossary of Literary and Nonfiction Terms, page R105.*

**Fact versus Opinion** A **fact** is a statement that can be proved or verified. An **opinion**, on the other hand, is a statement that cannot be proved because it expresses a person's beliefs, feelings, or thoughts.
*See also* **Inference; Generalization.**

**Fallacy** A fallacy is an error in reasoning. Typically, a fallacy is based on an incorrect inference or a misuse of evidence. Some common logical fallacies are **circular reasoning, either/or fallacy, oversimplification, overgeneralization,** and **stereotyping.**
*See also* **Either/Or Fallacy, Logical Appeal, Overgeneralization; Identifying Faulty Reasoning,** *Reading Handbook, page R24.*

**Faulty Reasoning** *See* **Fallacy.**

**Feature Article** A feature article is a main article in a newspaper or a cover story in a magazine. A feature article is focused more on entertaining than informing. Features are lighter or more general than hard news and tend to be about human interest or lifestyles.

**Functional Documents** *See* **Consumer Documents; Public Documents; Workplace Documents.**

**Generalization** A generalization is a broad statement about a class or category of people, ideas, or things, based on a study of only some of its members.
*See also* **Overgeneralization.**

**Government Publications** Government publications are documents produced by government organizations. Pamphlets, brochures, and reports are just some of the many forms these publications may take. Government publications can be good resources for a wide variety of topics.

**Graphic Aid** A graphic aid is a visual tool that is printed, handwritten, or drawn. Charts, diagrams, graphs, photographs, and maps can all be graphic aids.
*See also* **Graphic Aids,** *Reading Handbook, pages R5–R7.*

**Graphic Organizer** A graphic organizer is a "word picture"—that is, a visual illustration of a verbal statement—that helps a reader understand a text. Charts, tables, webs, and diagrams can all be graphic organizers. Graphic organizers and graphic aids can look the same. For example, a table in a science article will not be constructed differently from a table that is a graphic organizer. However, graphic organizers and graphic aids do differ in how they are used. Graphic aids are the visual representations that people encounter when they read informational texts. Graphic organizers are visuals that people construct to help them understand texts or organize information.

**Historical Documents** Historical documents are writings that have played a significant role in human events or are themselves records of such events. The Declaration of Independence, for example, is a historical document.

**How-To Book** A how-to book is a book that is written to explain how to do something—usually an activity, a sport, or a household project.

**Implied Main Idea** *See* **Main Idea.**

**Index** The index of a book is an alphabetized list of important topics and details covered in the book and the page numbers on which they can be found. An index can be used to quickly find specific information about a topic.

**Inductive Reasoning** Inductive reasoning is the process of logically reasoning from specific observations, examples, and facts to arrive at a general conclusion or principle.
*See also* **Analyzing Logic and Reasoning,** *Reading Handbook, pages R22–R23.*

**Inference** An inference is a logical assumption that is based on observed facts and one's own knowledge and experience.

**Informational Nonfiction** Informational nonfiction is writing that provides factual information. It often explains ideas or teaches processes. Examples include news reports, science textbooks, software instructions, and lab reports.

**Internet** The Internet is a global, interconnected system of computer networks that allows for communication through e-mail, listservers, and the World Wide Web. The Internet connects computers and computer users throughout the world.

**Journal** A journal is a periodical publication issued by a legal, medical, or other professional organization. Alternatively, the term may be used to refer to a diary or daily record.

**Loaded Language** Loaded language consists of words with strongly positive or negative connotations intended to influence a reader's or listener's attitude.

**Logical Appeal** A logical appeal relies on logic and facts, appealing to people's reasoning or intellect rather than to their values or emotions. Flawed logical appeals—that is, errors in reasoning—are considered logical fallacies.
*See also* **Fallacy.**

**Logical Argument** A logical argument is an argument in which the logical relationship between the support and the claim is sound.

**Main Idea** A main idea, or controlling idea, is the most important idea or impression about a topic that a writer or speaker conveys. It can be the central idea of an entire work or of just a paragraph. Often, the main idea of a paragraph is expressed in a topic sentence. However, a main idea may just be implied, or suggested, by details. A main idea and supporting details can serve as a basic pattern of organization in a piece of writing, with the central idea about a topic being supported by details.

**Make Inferences** *See* **Inference.**

**Monitor** Monitoring is the strategy of checking your comprehension as you are reading and modifying the strategies you are using to suit your needs. Monitoring may include some or all of the following strategies: **questioning, clarifying, visualizing, predicting, connecting,** and **rereading.**

**Narrative Nonfiction** *See Glossary of Literary and Nonfiction Terms, page R109.*

**News Article** A news article is a piece of writing that reports on a recent event. In newspapers, news articles are usually written concisely and report the latest news, presenting the most important facts first and then more detailed information. In magazines, news articles are usually more elaborate than those in newspapers because they are written to provide both information and analysis. Also, news articles in magazines do not necessarily present the most important facts first.

**Nonfiction** *See Glossary of Literary and Nonfiction Terms, page R109.*

**Op-Ed Piece** An op-ed piece is an opinion piece that usually appears opposite ("op") the editorial page of a newspaper. Unlike editorials, op-ed pieces are written and submitted by named writers.

**Organization** *See* **Pattern of Organization.**

**Overgeneralization** An overgeneralization is a generalization that is too broad. You can often recognize overgeneralizations by the appearance of words and phrases such as *all, everyone, every time, any, anything, no one,* and *none.* Consider, for example, this statement: "None of the sanitation workers in our city really care about keeping the environment clean." In all probability, there are many exceptions; the writer can't possibly know the feelings of every sanitation worker in the city.

*See also* **Identifying Faulty Reasoning,** *Reading Handbook, page R24.*

**Overview** An overview is a short summary of a story, a speech, or an essay. It orients the reader by providing a preview of the text to come.

**Paraphrase** Paraphrasing is the restating of information in one's own words.
*See also* **Summarize.**

**Pattern of Organization** A pattern of organization is a particular arrangement of ideas and information. Such a pattern may be used to organize an entire composition or a single paragraph within a longer work. The following are the most common patterns of organization: **cause-and-effect, chronological order, compare-and-contrast, classification, deductive, inductive, order of importance, problem-solution, sequential,** and **spatial.**
*See also* **Cause and Effect; Chronological Order; Classification; Compare and Contrast; Problem-Solution Order; Sequential Order; Reading Informational Texts: Patterns of Organization,** *Reading Handbook, pages R8–R13.*

**Periodical** A periodical is a publication that is issued at regular intervals of more than one day. For example, a periodical may be a weekly, monthly, or quarterly journal or magazine. Newspapers and other daily publications generally are not classified as periodicals.

**Personal Essay** *See* **Essay,** *Glossary of Literary and Nonfiction Terms, page R105.*

**Persuasion** Persuasion is the art of swaying others' feelings, beliefs, or actions. Persuasion normally appeals to both the intellect and the emotions of readers. **Persuasive techniques** are the methods used to influence others to adopt certain opinions or beliefs or to act in certain ways. Types of persuasive techniques include emotional appeals, logical appeals, and loaded language. When used properly, persuasive techniques can add depth to writing that's meant to persuade. Persuasive techniques can, however, be misused to cloud factual information, disguise poor reasoning, or unfairly exploit people's emotions in order to shape their opinions.
*See also* **Emotional Appeals; Loaded Language; Logical Appeal; Recognizing Persuasive Techniques,** *Reading Handbook, page R22.*

**Predict** Predicting is a reading strategy that involves using text clues to make a reasonable guess about what will happen next in a story.

**Primary Source** *See* **Sources.**

**Prior Knowledge** Prior knowledge is the knowledge a reader already possesses about a topic. This information might come from personal experiences, expert accounts, books, films, or other sources.

**Problem-Solution Order** Problem-solution order is a pattern of organization in which a problem is stated and analyzed and then one or more solutions are proposed and examined. Writers use words and phrases such as *propose, conclude, reason for, problem, answer,* and *solution* to connect ideas and details when writing about problems and solutions.

**Procedural Texts** Procedural texts are functional texts that were created to communicate instructions, rules, processes, or other detailed, step-by-step information. *See also* **Consumer Documents; Public Documents; Workplace Documents.**

**Propaganda** Propaganda is a form of communication that may use distorted, false, or misleading information. It usually refers to manipulative political discourse.

**Public Documents** Public documents are documents that were written for the public to provide information that is of public interest or concern. They include government documents, speeches, signs, and rules and regulations. *See also* **Government Publications.**

**Reference Works** General reference works are sources that contain facts and background information on a wide range of subjects. More specific reference works contain in-depth information on a single subject. Most reference works are good sources of reliable information because they have been reviewed by experts. The following are some common reference works: **encyclopedias, dictionaries, thesauri, almanacs, atlases, chronologies, biographical dictionaries,** and **directories.**

**Review** *See* **Critical Review.**

**Rhetorical Devices** *See Glossary of Literary and Nonfiction Terms, page R111.*

**Rhetorical Questions** Rhetorical questions are those that do not require a reply. Writers use them to suggest that their arguments make the answer obvious or self-evident.

**Scanning** Scanning is the process of searching through writing for a particular fact or piece of information. When you scan, your eyes sweep across a page, looking for key words that may lead you to the information you want.

**Secondary Source** *See* **Sources.**

**Sequential Order** A pattern of organization that shows the order in which events or actions occur is called sequential order. Writers typically use this pattern of organization to explain steps or stages in a process.

**Setting a Purpose** The process of establishing specific reasons for reading a text is called setting a purpose.

**Sidebar** A sidebar is additional information set in a box alongside or within a news or feature article. Popular magazines often make use of sidebar information.

**Signal Words** Signal words are words and phrases that indicate what is to come in a text. Readers can use signal words to discover a text's pattern of organization and to analyze the relationships among the ideas in the text.

**Sources** A source is anything that supplies information. **Primary sources** are materials written by people who were present at events, either as participants or as observers. Letters, diaries, autobiographies, speeches, and photographs are primary sources. **Secondary sources** are records of events that were created sometime after the events occurred; the writers were not directly involved or were not present when the events took place. Encyclopedias, textbooks, biographies, most newspaper and magazine articles, and books and articles that interpret or review research are secondary sources.

**Spatial Order** Spatial order is a pattern of organization that highlights the physical positions or relationships of details or objects. This pattern of organization is typically found in descriptive writing. Writers use words and phrases such as *on the left, to the right, here, over there, above, below, beyond, nearby,* and *in the distance* to indicate the arrangement of details.

**Speech** *See Glossary of Literary and Nonfiction Terms, page R113.*

**Stereotyping** Stereotyping is a type of overgeneralization. Stereotypes are broad statements made about people on the basis of their gender, ethnicity, race, or political, social, professional, or religious group.

**Summarize** To summarize is to briefly retell, or encapsulate, the main ideas of a piece of writing in one's own words. *See also* **Paraphrase.**

**Support** Support is any material that serves to prove a claim. In an argument, support typically consists of reasons and evidence. In persuasive texts and speeches, however, support may include appeals to the needs and values of the audience.

**Supporting Detail** *See* **Main Idea.**

**Synthesize** To synthesize information is to take individual pieces of information and combine them with other pieces of information and with prior knowledge or experience to gain a better understanding of a subject or to create a new product or idea.

**Text Features** Text features are design elements that indicate the organizational structure of a text and help make the key ideas and supporting information understandable. Text features include headings, boldface type, italic type, bulleted or numbered lists, sidebars, and graphic aids such as charts, tables, timelines, illustrations, and photographs.

**Thesaurus** *See* **Reference Works.**

**Thesis Statement** In an argument, a thesis statement is an expression of the claim that the writer or speaker is trying to support. In an essay, a thesis statement is an expression, in one or two sentences, of the main idea or purpose of the piece of writing.
*See also* **Claim.**

**Topic Sentence** The topic sentence of a paragraph states the paragraph's central idea. All other sentences in the paragraph provide supporting details.

**Visualize** Visualizing is the process of forming a mental picture based on written or spoken information.

**Web Site** A Web site is a collection of "pages" on the World Wide Web that is usually devoted to one specific subject. Pages are linked together and are accessed by clicking hyperlinks or menus, which send the user from page to page within the site. Web sites are created by companies, organizations, educational institutions, branches of the government, the military, and individuals.

**Workplace Documents** Workplace documents are materials that are produced or used within a work setting, usually to aid in the functioning of the workplace. They include job applications, office memos, training manuals, job descriptions, and sales reports.

**Works Cited** A list of works cited lists names of all the works a writer has referred to in his or her text. This list often includes not only books and articles but also nonprint sources.

**Works Consulted** A list of works consulted names all the works a writer consulted in order to create his or her text. It is not limited just to those works cited in the text.
*See also* **Bibliography.**

**accurate** (ăk′yər-ĭt) *adj.* correct; free from errors
   **preciso** *adj.* correcto; sin errores

**analyze** (ăn′ə-līz′) *v.* to separate or break into parts and examine
   **analizar** *v.* separar o dividir en partes y examinar

**appreciate** (ə-prē′shē-āt′) *v.* to think highly of; to recognize favorably the quality or value of
   **apreciar** *v.* tener una buena opinión de algo o alguien; reconocer de manera favorable la calidad o el valor de algo o alguien

**aspect** (ăs′pěkt) *n.* a quality, part, or element
   **aspecto** *sust.* cualidad, parte o elemento

**attribute** (ăt′rə-byōōt′) *n.* a quality thought of as a natural part of someone or something
   **atributo** *sust.* cualidad considerada como parte natural de alguien o algo

**circumstance** (sûr′kem-stăns′) *n.* a happening, event, or fact occurring near or in company with another
   **circunstancia** *sust.* suceso, evento o hecho que ocurre cerca a otro o junto a otro

**cite** (sīt) *v.* to refer to as example or proof
   **citar** *v.* hacer referencia a un ejemplo o prueba

**coherent** (kō-hîr′ənt) *adj.* logical, consistent, or connected
   **coherente** *adj.* lógico, constante o relacionado

**complex** (kəm-plěks′) *adj.* made up of two or more parts; hard to understand or analyze
   **complejo** *adj.* compuesto por dos o más partes; difícil de comprender o analizar

**conclude** (kən-kōōd′) *v.* to decide or infer by reasoning
   **concluir** *v.* decidir o inferir por medio del razonamiento

**construct** (kən-strŭkt′) *v.* to systematically create or build
   **construir** *v.* crear o edificar de manera sistemática

**context** (kŏn′těkst′) *n.* the words that surround a particular word or passage and make the meaning of that word or passage clear; the circumstances in which an event occurs
   **contexto** *sust.* palabras que rodean una palabra o un pasaje en particular y aclaran el significado de esa palabra o pasaje; circunstancias en las que ocurre un evento

**contrast** (kən-trăst′) *v.* to show differences
   **contrastar** *v.* mostrar las diferencias

**contribute** (kən-trĭb′yōōt) *v.* to provide or give ideas, knowledge, material goods, etc.
   **contribuir** *v.* dar u ofrecer ideas, conocimientos, bienes materiales, etc.

**demonstrate** (děm′ən-strāt′) *v.* to show clearly and purposefully
   **demostrar** *v.* mostrar en forma clara y con determinación

**device** (dĭ-vīs′) *n.* a thing created; a mechanical invention or creation
   **dispositivo** *sust.* algo creado; invento o creación mecánica

**differentiate** (dĭf′ə-rěn′shē-āt′) *v.* to perceive or create a difference between
   **diferenciar** *v.* percibir o crear una diferencia

**distinct** (dĭ-stĭngkt′) *adj.* separate or different; defined clearly
   **distinto** *adj.* individual o diferente; definido con claridad

**element** (ěl′ə-mənt) *n.* one necessary or basic part of a whole
   **elemento** *sust.* parte necesaria o básica de un todo

**emphasis** (ěm′fə-sĭs) *n.* special stress on something—a word, phrase, idea, etc.— to make it stand out
   **énfasis** *sust.* hincapié que se hace en algo (palabra, frase, idea, etc.) para destacarlo

**environment** (ěn-vī′rən-mənt) *n.* surroundings; the land, water, climate, plants, and animals of an area
   **ambiente** *sust.* entorno; tierra, agua, clima, plantas y animales de un área

**evaluate** (ĭ-văl′yōō-āt′) *v.* to find out the value or worth of something; to judge or examine
   **evaluar** *v.* hallar el valor o el precio; juzgar o examinar

**evident** (ěv′ĭ-dənt) *adj.* obvious, easy to see or understand
   **evidente** *adj.* obvio, fácil de ver o comprender

**factor** (făk′tər) *n.* elements or conditions that make something what it is or create a result
   **factor** *sust.* elementos o condiciones que hacen que algo exista o produzca un resultado

**ideology** (ī′dē-ŏl′ə-jē) *n.* the beliefs or way of thinking—especially political, economic, or social beliefs and ways of thinking—of an individual or group of people
   **ideología** *sust.* creencias o maneras de pensar, especialmente políticas, económicas o sociales, de una persona o un grupo de personas

**implicit** (ĭm-plĭs′ĭt) *adj.* not plainly obvious or exhibited; suggested or implied
   **implícito** *adj.* que no es obvio o se muestra; sugerido o tácito

**incorporate** (ĭn-kôr′pə-rāt′) *v.* to join or combine into a single whole
   **incorporar** *v.* unir o combinar en un todo

**indicate** (ĭn′dĭ-kāt′) *v.* to point out or show
   **indicar** *v.* señalar o mostrar

**infer** (ĭn-fûr′) *v.* to decide based on evidence or knowledge; to draw a conclusion
   **inferir** *v.* decidir a partir de pruebas o del conocimiento; sacar una conclusión

**interact** (ĭn′tər-ăkt′) *v.* to act or work with someone or something; to act with one another
   **interactuar** *v.* actuar o trabajar con alguien o algo; actuar en forma conjunta

**interpret** (ĭn-tûr′prət) *v.* to explain the meaning of or translate
   **interpretar** *v.* explicar el significado o traducir

**investigate** (ĭn-vĕs′tĭ-gāt′) *v.* to search carefully, as to acquire or verify facts
   **investigar** *v.* buscar en detalle para obtener o verificar datos

**monitor** (mŏn′ĭ-tər) *v.* to check in on, watch, regulate
   **supervisar** *v.* controlar, observar, regular

**perceive** (pər-sēv′) *v.* to observe or become aware of
   **percibir** *v.* observar o tomar conciencia de algo

**perspective** (pər-spĕk′tĭv) *n.* point of view or mental view
   **perspectiva** *sust.* punto de vista u opinión

**predominant** (prĭ-dăm′ə-nənt) *adj.* the most frequent or the most important
   **predominante** *adj.* el más frecuente o el más importante

**primary** (prī′mĕr-ē) *adj.* highest in rank or first in importance
   **primario** *adj.* de categoría superior o primero en importancia

**relevant** (rĕl′ə-vənt) *adj.* related or pertinent to the matter at hand
   **relevante** *adj.* relacionado con el tema en cuestión o pertinente

**reveal** (rĭ-vēl′) *v.* to show, make known, or expose
   **revelar** *v.* mostrar, dar a conocer o exponer

**sequence** (sē′kwəns) *n.* the chronological, causal, or logical order in which one thing follows another
   **secuencia** *sust.* orden cronológico, causal o lógico en el que una cosa sigue a otra

**significant** (sĭg-nĭf′ĭ-kənt) *adj.* having meaning; important
   **significativo** *adj.* que tiene sentido; importante

**source** (sôrs) *n.* a book, document, person, etc., that supplies information
   **fuente** *sust.* libro, documento, persona, etc., que proporciona información

**specific** (spĭ-sĭf′ĭk) *adj.* definite; of a special sort
   **específico** *adj.* definitivo; de una clase en especial

**structure** (strŭk′chər) *n.* something constructed or built, such as a building
   **estructura** *sust.* algo que se construye, como un edificio

**synthesize** (sĭn′thĭ-sīz′) *v.* to combine separate elements into a whole
   **sintetizar** *v.* combinar elementos individuales para formar un todo

**technique** (tĕk-nēk′) *n.* a method of procedure or a manner of doing something
   **técnica** *sust.* método para proceder o manera de hacer algo

**tradition** (trə-dĭsh′ən) *n.* a practice passed down from generation to generation
   **tradición** *sust.* práctica que se transmite de generación en generación

**undertake** (ŭn′dər-tāk′) *v.* to take on a task or assume a responsibility
   **asumir** *v.* aceptar una tarea o contraer una responsabilidad

**unique** (yōō-nēk′) *adj.* the only one; having no equal
   **único** *adj.* exclusivo; sin igual

**vary** (vâr′ē) *v.* to modify or alter; to change the characteristics of something
   **variar** *v.* modificar o alterar; cambiar las características de algo

**abject** (ăb-jĕkt') *adj.* exceedingly humble
abyecto *adj.* sumamente pobre

**abominably** (ə-bŏm'ə-nə-blē) *adv.* in a hateful way; horribly
abominablemente *adv.* de manera odiosa u horrible

**abscond** (ăb-skŏnd') *v.* to go away suddenly and secretly
fugarse *v.* huir de repente

**abysmal** (ə-bĭz'məl) *adj.* very bad
pésimo *adj.* desastroso; atroz

**acclimatization** (ə-klī'mə-tĭ-zā'shən) *n.* the act of getting accustomed to a new climate or environment
aclimatación *s.* acción de acostumbrarse a un nuevo clima o ambiente

**adulation** (ăj'ə-lā'shən) *n.* excessive praise or flattery
adulación *s.* halago exagerado

**adversary** (ăd'vər-sĕr'ē) *n.* an opponent; enemy
adversario *s.* opositor; enemigo

**adversity** (ăd-vûr'sĭ-tē) *n.* hardship; misfortune
adversidad *s.* infortunio; desgracia

**advocacy** (ăd'və-kə-sē) *adj.* involving public support for an idea or policy
defensa *s.* apoyo público a una idea o medida

**affiliate** (ə-fĭl'ē-ĭt) *n.* a person or an organization officially connected to a larger body
afiliado *s.* persona u organización conectada oficialmente con una entidad

**aghast** (ə-găst') *adj.* filled with shock or horror
horrorizado *adj.* muy atemorizado

**agile** (ăj'əl) *adj.* able to move quickly and easily
ágil *adj.* capaz de moverse con rapidez y facilidad

**alienation** (āl'yə-nā'shən) *n.* a feeling of separation or isolation
alienación *s.* sensación de separación o aislamiento

**aloof** (ə-lōōf') *adj.* distant; remote; standoffish
distante *adj.* remoto; indiferente

**amenity** (ə-mĕn'ĭ-tē) *n.* something that adds to one's comfort or convenience
comodidad *s.* cosa que aumenta el confort

**analytic** (ăn'ə-lĭt'ĭk) *adj.* using logical reasoning or analysis
analítico *adj.* que usa razonamiento o análisis lógico

**annihilate** (ə-nī'ə-lāt') *v.* to destroy completely
aniquilar *v.* destruir por completo

**anonymity** (ăn'ə-nĭm'ĭ-tē) *n.* the condition of being unknown
anonimato *s.* condición de no ser conocido

**anthem** (ăn'thəm) *n.* an uplifting song or hymn
himno *s.* composición musical solemne

**anthropology** (ăn'thrə-pŏl'ə-jē) *n.* the science or study of human beings, including their physical characteristics and cultures
antropología *s.* ciencia que estudia las características físicas y las culturas de los seres humanos

**aperture** (ăp'ər-chər) *n.* an opening, such as a hole or a gap
abertura *s.* agujero o grieta

**aplomb** (ə-plŏm') *n.* poise; self-assurance
aplomo *s.* serenidad; circunspección

**appalled** (ə-pôld') *adj.* filled with dismay; horrified **appall** *v.*
asombrado *adj.* pasmado; asustado **asombrar** *v.*

**archaic** (är-kā'ĭk) *adj.* very old or unfashionable
arcaico *adj.* muy antiguo o pasado de moda

**ardor** (är'dər) *n.* passion
ardor *s.* pasión

**arduous** (är'jōō-əs) *adj.* requiring much effort; difficult
arduo *adj.* que requiere mucho esfuerzo; difícil

**articulate** (är-tĭk'yə-lĭt) *adj.* able to speak clearly and coherently; well-spoken
elocuente *adj.* que se expresa con claridad y convicción

**artifact** (är'tə-făkt') *n.* something created by humans, usually for a practical purpose
artefacto *s.* objeto creado por los seres humanos, usualmente con propósitos prácticos

**askew** (ə-skyōō') *adj.* crooked; to one side
torcido *adj.* chueco; que se inclina hacia un lado

**assertion** (ə-sûr'shən) *n.* a statement
aseveración *s.* declaración; afirmación

**assuage** (ə-swāj') *v.* to calm or pacify
calmar *v.* tranquilizar o mitigar

**awry** (ə-rī') *adj.* off course; wrong
sesgado *adj.* desviado; torcido

**baleful** (bāl′fəl) *adj.* evil; destructive
  **torvo** *adj.* funesto; siniestro

**banal** (bə-năl′) *adj.* commonplace; trite
  **banal** *adj.* común; trillado

**beguiling** (bĭ-gī′lĭng) *adj.* charming; pleasing  **beguile** *v.*
  **encantador** *adj.* seductor; atrayente  **encantar** *v.*

**benign** (bĭ-nīn′) *adj.* good; kindly
  **benigno** *adj.* bondadoso; amable

**boon** (bōōn) *n.* a benefit; blessing
  **beneficio** *s.* gran ayuda; bendición

**bravado** (brə-vä′dō) *n.* a false show of courage or defiance
  **bravata** *s.* alarde; demostración falsa de valor o valentía

**brazenly** (brā′zən-lē′) *adv.* boldly and without shame
  **descaradamente** *adv.* con descaro y frescura

**browser** (brou′zər) *n.* a program used to navigate the Internet
  **browser** *s.* programa para desplazarse en la Internet

**buffeted** (bŭf′ĭ-tĭd) *adj.* knocked about or struck  **buffet** *v.*
  **golpeado** *adj.* empujado o azotado  **golpear** *v.*

**cadence** (kād′ns) *n.* a balanced, rhythmic flow
  **cadencia** *s.* repetición regular de sonidos o movimientos

**cascade** (kă-skād′) *v.* to fall or flow like a waterfall
  **precipitarse** *v.* caer o deslizarse como una cascada

**cavort** (kə-vôrt′) *v.* to leap or romp about
  **retozar** *v.* saltar; divertirse

**cede** (sēd) *v.* to give up; give way
  **ceder** *v.* conceder; rendirse

**chronicle** (krŏn′ĭ-kəl) *n.* a record of events
  **crónica** *s.* registro de sucesos

**clamor** (klăm′ər) *n.* a noisy outburst; outcry
  **clamor** *s.* conjunto de gritos o ruidos fuertes

**clarity** (klăr′ĭ-tē) *n.* clearness
  **claridad** *s.* transparencia

**commandeer** (kŏm′ən-dîr′) *v.* to take control of by force
  **confiscar** *v.* tomar por la fuerza

**compile** (kəm-pīl′) *v.* to put together by gathering from many sources
  **compilar** *v.* reunir de muchas fuentes

**condescending** (kŏn′dĭ-sĕn′dĭng) *adj.* assuming an air of superiority
  **condescendiente** *adj.* que asume un aire de superioridad

**condiment** (kŏn′də-mənt) *n.* a sauce, relish, or spice used to season food
  **condimento** *s.* salsa o especia para sazonar la comida

**condone** (kən-dōn′) *v.* to forgive or overlook
  **condonar** *v.* perdonar, olvidar o ignorar

**contemptible** (kən-tĕmp′tə-bəl) *adj.* deserving of scorn; despicable
  **despreciable** *adj.* que merece desdén o desprecio; vil

**contrition** (kən-trĭsh′ən) *n.* a feeling of regret for doing wrong
  **contrición** *s.* arrepentimiento por haber actuado mal

**correlate** (kôr′ə-lāt′) *v.* to figure out or create a relationship between two items or events
  **correlacionar** *v.* establecer una relación entre dos puntos o sucesos

**cosmetic** (kŏz-mĕt′ĭk) *adj.* decorative rather than functional
  **cosmético** *adj.* decorativo más que funcional

**coveted** (kŭv′ĭ-tĭd) *adj.* greedily desired or wished for  **covet** *v.*
  **codiciado** *adj.* que se desea con envidia  **codiciar** *v.*

**crass** (krăs) *adj.* crude; unrefined
  **craso** *adj.* burdo; grosero

**crevasse** (krĭ-văs′) *n.* a deep crack or split in a glacier
  **grieta** *s.* hendidura profunda, especialmente en un glaciar

**cultivated** (kŭl′tə-vā′tĭd) *adj.* refined or cultured in manner
  **cultivado** *adj.* refinado o de modales cultos

**daunted** (dôn′tĭd) *adj.* discouraged  **daunt** *v.*
  **amilanado** *adj.* intimidado  **amilanar** *v.*

**debut** (dā-byōō′) *n.* first public performance or showing
  **debut** *s.* estreno; primera presentación

**default** (dĭ-fôlt′) *v.* to fail to keep a promise, especially a promise to repay a loan
  **incumplir** *v.* no cumplir una promesa, especialmente no pagar un préstamo

**deftness** (dĕft′nĭs) *n.* the quality of quickness and skillfullness
  **destreza** *s.* agilidad y habilidad

**degenerate** (dĭ-jĕn′ər-ĭt) *n.* a corrupt or vicious person
  degenerado *s.* persona corrupta o viciosa

**degradation** (dĕg′rə-dā′shən) *n.* condition of being brought to a lower level; humiliation
  degradación *s.* pérdida de status y dignidad; humillación

**demeanor** (dĭ-mē′nər) *n.* a way of behaving; manner
  comportamiento *s.* conducta externa

**derisive** (dĭ-rī′sĭv) *adj.* expressing contempt or ridicule
  desdeñoso *adj.* que expresa burla o ridículo

**desolation** (dĕs′ə-lā′shən) *n.* lonely grief; misery
  desolación *s.* dolor en soledad; desgracia

**dialect** (dī′ə-lĕkt′) *n.* a variety of a standard language unique to a certain region or social group
  dialecto *s.* variedad de una lengua que se habla en una región o que habla un grupo social

**diffuse** (dĭ-fyōōs′) *adj.* unfocused
  difuso *adj.* vago e impreciso

**dilapidated** (dĭ-lăp′ĭ-dā′tĭd) *adj.* broken down and shabby
  dilapilado *adj.* en ruinas

**diminutive** (dĭ-mĭn′yə-tĭv) *adj.* very small
  diminuto *adj.* muy pequeño

**disarming** (dĭs-är′mĭng) *adj.* removing or overcoming suspicion; inspiring confidence
  apaciguador *adj.* tranquilizador; que elimina sospechas; que crea confianza

**disclaimer** (dĭs-klā′mər) *n.* a denial of responsibility or knowledge
  descargo *s.* repudiación de responsabilidad o conocimiento

**disconcerting** (dĭs′kən-sûr′tĭng) *adj.* causing one to feel confused or embarrassed  **disconcert** *v.*
  desconcertante *adj.* que causa confusión, malestar o desconcierto  desconcertar *v.*

**disconsolate** (dĭs-kŏn′sə-lĭt) *adj.* extremely depressed or dejected
  desconsolado *adj.* extremadamente triste

**discordant** (dĭ-skôr′dnt) *adj.* having a disagreeable or clashing sound
  discordante *adj.* disonante; de sonidos desagradables; sin armonía

**dispirited** (dĭ-spĭr′ĭ-tĭd) *adj.* dejected
  desanimado *s.* abatido

**distraught** (dĭ-strôt′) *adj.* deeply upset
  perturbado *adj.* profundamente molesto

**doggedness** (dô′gĭd-nĭs) *n.* persistence; stubbornness
  obstinación *s.* persistencia; tenacidad

**droll** (drōl) *adj.* amusingly odd or comical
  divertido *adj.* gracioso y curioso

**encore** (ŏn′kôr) *n.* a repeated or additional performance
  bis *s.* repetición

**engender** (ĕn-jĕn′dər) *v.* to bring into existence
  engendrar *v.* causar; originar

**enthralled** (ĕn-thrôld′) *adj.* charmed greatly  **enthrall** *v.*
  cautivado *adj.* encantado  **cautivar** *v.*

**eradicate** (ĭ-răd′ĭ-kāt′) *v.* to do away with completely
  erradicar *v.* acabar por completo

**evanesce** (ĕv′ə-nĕs′) *v.* to disappear; vanish
  desvanecerse *v.* desaparecer; disiparse

**exhilarate** (ĭg-zĭl′ə-rāt′) *v.* to make merry or lively
  regocijar *v.* alegrar; levantar el ánimo

**exhortation** (ĕg′zôr-tā′shən) *n.* a communication strongly urging that something be done
  exhortación *s.* palabras que inducen a una acción

**exodus** (ĕk′sə-dəs) *n.* a mass departure
  éxodo *s.* partida en masa

**exotic** (ĭg-zŏt′ĭk) *adj.* excitingly strange
  exótico *adj.* extraño; curioso

**expansive** (ĭk-spăn′sĭv) *adj.* outgoing; showing feelings openly and freely
  expansivo *adj.* comunicativo; que muestra sus sentimientos

**expendable** (ĭk-spĕn′də-bəl) *adj.* not worth keeping; not essential
  prescindible *adj.* que no es esencial

**exuberance** (ĭg-zōō′bər-əns) *n.* condition of unrestrained joy
  exuberancia *s.* euforia; exaltación

**falter** (fôl′tər) v. to hesitate from lack of courage or confidence
  **vacilar** v. titubear por falta de valor o de confianza

**fecund** (fē′kənd) adj. producing much growth; fertile
  **fecundo** adj. fértil; abundante

**fiasco** (fē-ăs′kō) n. a complete failure
  **fiasco** s. fracaso total

**flay** (flā) v. to whip or lash
  **desollar** v. despellejar a latigazos

**foreboding** (fôr-bō′dĭng) n. a sense of approaching evil
  **presentimiento** s. sentimiento de que algo malo sucederá

**fractious** (frăk′shəs) adj. hard to manage or hold together; unruly
  **quisquilloso** adj. cascarrabias; rebelde

**frenetically** (frə-nĕt′ĭk-lē) adv. in a frenzied or frantic way
  **frenéticamente** adv. de modo frenético o desenfrenado

**futile** (fyōōt′l) adj. having no useful result
  **fútil** adj. inútil; sin resultados útiles

**gamut** (găm′ət) n. an entire range or series
  **gama** s. serie; variedades

**genesis** (jĕn′ĭ-sĭs) n. the origin or coming into being (of something)
  **génesis** s. origen o principio de una cosa

**goad** (gōd) v. to drive or urge
  **provocar** v. urgir; instar

**harried** (hăr′ēd) adj. tormented; harassed **harry** v.
  **agobiado** adj. atribulado; acosado **agobiar** v.

**heresy** (hĕr′ĭ-sē) n. an action or opinion contrary to what is generally thought of as right
  **herejía** s. acto u opinión contrario a lo que se considera correcto

**hierarchy** (hī′ə-rär′kē) n. a body of persons having authority
  **jerarquía** s. grupo de personas de autoridad

**homely** (hōm′lē) adj. characteristic of home life; simple; everyday
  **casero** adj. característico de la vida hogareña; sencillo

**hypothesis** (hī-pŏth′ĭ-sĭs) n. an assumption made in order to test its possible consequences
  **hipótesis** s. suposición que se pone a prueba

**illiteracy** (ĭ-lĭt′ər-ə-sē) n. a lack of ability to read and write
  **analfabetismo** s. desconocimiento de la lectura y escritura

**imminent** (ĭm′ə-nənt) adj. about to occur
  **inminente** adj. que está por ocurrir

**immolation** (ĭm′ə-lā′shən) n. death or destruction
  **inmolación** s. muerte o destrucción

**immutable** (ĭ-myōō′tə-bəl) adj. unchanging
  **inmutable** adj. que no cambia

**imperative** (ĭm-pĕr′ə-tĭv) adj. absolutely necessary
  **imperativo** adj. absolutamente necesario

**implacable** (ĭm-plăk′ə-bəl) adj. impossible to soothe; unforgiving
  **implacable** adj. desalmado; despiadado; que no perdona

**impotent** (ĭm′pə-tənt) adj. powerless; lacking strength or vigor
  **impotente** adj. sin poder o capacidad; carente de fuerza o vigor

**impunity** (ĭm-pyōō′nĭ-tē) n. freedom from penalty or harm
  **impunidad** s. falta de castigo, penalidad o daño

**inaudibly** (ĭn-ô′də-blē) adv. in a way that is impossible to hear
  **inaudiblemente** adv. de modo que no se oye

**inaugurate** (ĭn-ô′gyə-rāt′) v. to make a formal beginning of
  **inaugurar** v. dar principio o estrenar

**incessantly** (ĭn-sĕs′ənt-lē) adv. without interruption; continuously
  **incesantemente** adv. continuamente; sin parar

**incredulous** (ĭn-krĕj′ə-ləs) adj. doubtful; disbelieving
  **incrédulo** adj. no creyente

**increment** (ĭn′krə-mənt) n. a small, slight growth or increase
  **incremento** s. pequeño aumento o crecimiento

**induced** (ĭn-dōōst′) adj. led on; persuaded **induce** v.
  **inducido** adj. persuadido; convencido **inducir** v.

**inept** (ĭn-ĕpt′) adj. generally incompetent
  **inepto** adj. incompetente

**inertia** (ĭ-nûr′shə) n. tendency to continue to do what one has been doing
  **inercia** s. tendencia a continuar haciendo lo que se ha estado haciendo

**inevitability** (ĭn-ĕv′ĭ-tə-bĭl′ĭ-tē) *n.* something that is certain to happen
    **inevitabilidad** *s.* lo que no se puede evitar

**inexplicably** (ĭn-ĕk′splĭ-kə-blē) *adv.* in a way that is difficult or impossible to explain
    **inexplicablemente** *adv.* de modo difícil o imposible de explicar

**inextricably** (ĭn-ĕk′strĭ-kə-blē) *adv.* in a way impossible to untangle
    **inextricablemente** *adv.* de manera imposible de descifrar o desenredar

**infallibility** (ĭn-făl′ə-bĭl′ĭ-tē) *n.* an inability to make errors
    **infalibilidad** *s.* incapacidad para cometer errores

**infatuated** (ĭn-făch′ōō-ā′tĭd) *adj.* possessed by an unreasoning love or attraction
    **encaprichado** *adj.* locamente enamorado o atraído irracionalmente hacia una persona

**infinitesimally** (ĭn′fĭn-ĭ-tĕs′ə-mə-lē) *adv.* in amounts so small as to be barely measurable
    **infinitesimalmente** *adv.* en cantidades tan pequeñas que casi no se puede medir

**infuse** (ĭn-fyōōz′) *v.* to fill, as if by pouring
    **infundir** *v.* llenar

**inherent** (ĭn-hîr′ənt) *adj.* forming part of the essential nature of something; built-in
    **inherente** *adj.* que por naturaleza es parte esencial de algo

**inhospitable** (ĭn-hŏs′pĭ-tə-bəl) *adj.* not welcoming; hostile
    **inhóspito** *adj.* hostil; que rechaza

**inquisitive** (ĭn-kwĭz′ĭ-tĭv) *adj.* curious; inquiring
    **inquisitivo** *adj.* curioso; preguntón

**instigate** (ĭn′stĭ-gāt′) *v.* to stir up; provoke
    **instigar** *v.* provocar; incitar

**insubordinate** (ĭn′sə-bôr′dn-ĭt) *adj.* disobedient to a superior
    **insubordinado** *adj.* desobediente a un superior

**insurmountable** (ĭn′sər-moun′tə-bəl) *adj.* impossible to overcome
    **insuperable** *adj.* insalvable; infranqueable

**intuitive** (ĭn-tōō′ĭ-tĭv) *adj.* based on what seems to be true without conscious reasoning; instinctive
    **intuitivo** *adj.* que se conoce sin razonamiento consciente; instintivo

**lament** (lə-mĕnt′) *v.* to express grief or deep regret
    **lamentar** *v.* expresar dolor o profundo arrepentimiento

**lavish** (lăv′ĭsh) *adj.* extravagant; more than is needed
    **espléndido** *adj.* extravagante; despilfarrador

**leer** (lîr) *v.* to give a sly, evil glance
    **mirar de reojo** *v.* lanzar una mirada lasciva o maliciosa

**legitimate** (lə-jĭt′ə-mĭt) *adj.* justifiable; reasonable
    **legítimo** *adj.* justificable; razonable

**malfunctioning** (măl-fŭngk′shə-nĭng) *adj.* not working or operating properly **malfunction** *v.*
    **dañado** *adj.* que no funciona bien **dañar** *v.*

**maneuvering** (mə-nōō′vər-ĭng) *n.* an action skillfully designed to achieve a goal **maneuver** *v.*
    **maniobras** *s.* acciones diseñadas para alcanzar una meta **maniobrar** *v.*

**marauding** (mə-rô′dĭng) *adj.* roaming about in search of plunder **maraud** *v.*
    **saqueador** *adj.* que merodea en busca de botín **saquear** *v.*

**meager** (mē′gər) *adj.* lacking in quantity or quality
    **escaso** *adj.* poco, insuficiente en cantidad y número

**meditation** (mĕd′ĭ-tā′shən) *n.* the act of being in serious, reflective thought
    **meditación** *s.* reflexión atenta y profunda

**mesmerizing** (mĕz′mə-rīz′ĭng) *adj.* holding one's attention in an almost hypnotic manner **mesmerize** *v.*
    **fascinante** *adj.* que capta la atención de forma casi hipnótica **fascinar** *v.*

**militancy** (mĭl′ĭ-tənt-sē) *n.* the act of aggressively supporting a political or social cause
    **militancia** *s.* apoyo enérgico a una causa política o social

**misnomer** (mĭs-nō′mər) *n.* an inaccurate or incorrect name
    **incorrección** *s.* nombre erróneo o incorrecto

**momentous** (mō-mĕn′təs) *adj.* of great importance
    **trascendental** *adj.* de gran importancia

**monolith** (mŏn'ə-lĭth') *n.* something, such as a monument, made from a single large stone
    **monolito** *s.* monumento u objeto tallado de un solo bloque de piedra

**mortified** (môr'tə-fīd') *adj.* very embarrassed; humiliated **mortify** *v.*
    **mortificado** *adj.* avergonzado; apenado **mortificar** *v.*

**muted** (myōō'tĭd) *adj.* softened or muffled
    **apagado** *adj.* débil o suave

**negligible** (nĕg'lĭ-jə-bəl) *adj.* not large or important enough to merit attention
    **insignificante** *adj.* que no merece atención; desdeñable

**neurological** (nŏŏr'ə-lŏj'ĭ-kəl) *adj.* having to do with the nervous system
    **neurológico** *adj.* relacionado con el sistema nervioso

**noncommittal** (nŏn'kə-mĭt'l) *adj.* not committing oneself; not revealing what one thinks
    **indefinido** *adj.* evasivo; que no revela su opinión o propósito

**nonpartisan** (nŏn-pär'tĭ-zən) *adj.* not supporting or controlled by any political group
    **independiente** *adj.* no afiliado a un grupo político

**nostalgia** (nŏ-stăl'jə) *n.* bittersweet longing for things from the past
    **nostalgia** *s.* recuerdo triste del pasado

**optimal** (ŏp'tə-məl) *adj.* most favorable; best
    **óptimo** *adj.* sumamente favorable; lo mejor

**ostensibly** (ŏ-stĕn'sə-blē) *adv.* seemingly; to all outward appearances
    **aparentemente** *adv.* en apariencia

**paradox** (păr'ə-dŏks') *n.* a statement or an event that sounds impossible but seems to be true
    **paradoja** *s.* afirmación o suceso que suena imposible pero parece verdadero

**paramount** (păr'ə-mount') *adj.* of highest importance
    **primordial** *adj.* de suma importancia

**paraphernalia** (păr'ə-fər-nāl'yə) *n.* the articles needed for a particular event or activity
    **parafernalia** *s.* conjunto de artículos necesarios para una actividad

**pauper** (pô'pər) *n.* a poor person, especially one who depends on public charity
    **pobre** *s.* indigente; persona que depende de la caridad pública

**perfidy** (pûr'fĭ-dē) *n.* treachery; betrayal of trust
    **perfidia** *s.* traición; abuso de confianza

**persistence** (pər-sĭs'təns) *n.* the act of refusing to stop or be changed
    **persistencia** *s.* constancia; perseverancia

**pervasive** (pər-vā'sĭv) *adj.* spreading widely through an area or group of people
    **penetrante** *adj.* que todo lo invade; dominante

**perverse** (pər-vûrs') *adj.* stubbornly contrary; wrong; harmful
    **perverso** *adj.* malvado; vil

**petrified** (pĕt'rə-fīd') *adj.* turned into stone **petrify** *v.*
    **petrificado** *adj.* convertido en piedra **petrificar** *v.*

**plagiarized** (plā'jə-rīzd') *adj.* copied from someone else's writings **plagiarize** *v.*
    **plagiado** *adj.* copiado de los escritos de otro **plagiar** *v.*

**poignantly** (poin'yənt-lē) *adv.* in a profoundly moving manner
    **emocionadamente** *adv.* de manera muy conmovedora

**ponderous** (pŏn'dər-əs) *adj.* heavy in a clumsy way; bulky
    **pesado** *adj.* lento y torpe; sin gracia

**posse** (pŏs'ē) *n.* a band
    **banda** *s.* grupo; cuadrilla

**potent** (pōt'nt) *adj.* powerful
    **potente** *adj.* poderoso

**precariously** (prī-kâr'ē-əs-lē) *adv.* insecurely; in a dangerous or unstable way
    **precariamente** *adv.* peligrosamente; de manera incierta o insegura

**preclude** (prĭ-klōōd') *v.* to make impossible, especially by taking action in advance
    **imposibilitar** *v.* impedir mediante un acto realizado con anticipación; prevenir

**presumed** (prĭ-zōōmd') *adj.* thought to be true **presume** *v.*
    **supuesto** *adj.* presunto; que se cree que es verdad **suponer** *v.*

**privation** (prĭ-vā′shən) *n.* the lack of a basic necessity or a comfort of life
    **privación** *s.* carencia de lo básico o de comodidades

**prodigy** (prŏd′ə-jē) *n.* a person who is exceptionally talented or intelligent
    **prodigio** *s.* persona con inteligencia o talento especiales

**profusion** (prə-fyōō′zhən) *n.* abundance
    **profusión** *s.* abundancia

**promontory** (prŏm′ən-tôr′ē) *n.* a high ridge of land or rock jutting out into a body of water
    **promontorio** *s.* altura de tierra que avanza dentro del mar

**prosaic** (prō-zā′ĭk) *adj.* dull; commonplace
    **prosaico** *adj.* vulgar; corriente

**prospects** (prŏs′pĕkts′) *n.* chances or possibilities, especially for financial success
    **perspectivas** *s.* oportunidades o posibilidades, especialmente de éxito o ganancia

**protégé** (prō′tə-zhā′) *n.* a person who is guided or supported by an older or more influential person
    **protegido** *s.* persona guiada o financiada por una persona mayor o de más influencia

**prudence** (prōōd′ns) *n.* the use of good judgment and common sense
    **prudencia** *s.* juicio y sentido común

**quarry** (kwôr′ē) *n.* the object of a hunt; prey
    **presa** *s.* objeto de la cacería

**rabid** (răb′ĭd) *adj.* uncontrollable; fanatical
    **rabioso** *adj.* furibundo; fanático

**rancor** (răng′kər) *n.* bitter and deep ill will
    **rencor** *s.* sentimiento persistente de animosidad o de resentimiento

**ransack** (răn′săk′) *v.* to search or examine vigorously
    **registrar** *v.* buscar por todas partes

**ravage** (răv′ĭj) *n.* serious damage
    **estrago** *s.* daño grave

**reconnoiter** (rē′kə-noi′tər) *v.* to make a preliminary inspection
    **reconocer** *v.* hacer una inspección preliminar del terreno o de una situación

**refute** (rĭ-fyōōt′) *v.* to prove false by argument or evidence
    **refutar** *v.* demostrar una falsedad con argumento o evidencia

**reiterate** (rē-ĭt′ə-rāt′) *v.* to repeat
    **reiterar** *v.* repetir

**relapse** (rē′lăps) *n.* a worsening of an illness after a partial recovery
    **recaída** *s.* empeoramiento de una enfermedad después de una recuperación parcial

**repose** (rĭ-pōz′) *v.* to lie dead or at rest
    **reposar** *v.* yacer muerto o en descanso

**reproach** (rĭ-prōch′) *n.* blame; criticism
    **reproche** *s.* reprimenda; crítica

**resigned** (rĭ-zīnd′) *adj.* marked by acceptance of a condition or action as unavoidable
    **resignado** *adj.* que acepta algo como inevitable

**resilient** (rĭ-zĭl′yənt) *adj.* strong but flexible; able to withstand stress without injury
    **elástico** *adj.* fuerte pero flexible; que tolera presión

**restitution** (rĕs′tĭ-tōō′shən) *n.* a making good for loss or damage; repayment
    **restitución** *s.* reposición que se da por algo perdido o dañado

**retaliate** (rĭ-tăl′ē-āt′) *v.* to pay back an injury in kind
    **tomar represalias** *v.* contraatacar; responder con agresión

**retribution** (rĕt′rə-byōō′shən) *n.* something given in repayment, usually as a punishment
    **castigo** *s.* represalia; merecido

**retrieve** (rĭ-trēv′) *v.* to find and return safely
    **recuperar** *v.* rescatar; salvar

**revelry** (rĕv′əl-rē) *n.* noisy merrymaking; festivity
    **juerga** *s.* jolgorio; festejo alegre y ruidoso

**reverie** (rĕv′ə-rē) *n.* a state of daydreaming
    **ensueño** *s.* sueño despierto; ensoñación

**revulsion** (rĭ-vŭl′shən) *n.* a sudden feeling of disgust or loathing
    **repugnancia** *s.* sentimiento repentino de asco o desprecio

**sacrilegious** (săk′rə-lĭj′əs) *adj.* disrespectful toward a sacred person, place, or thing
    **sacrílego** *adj.* irrespetuoso hacia una persona, lugar o cosa sagrada

**saunter** (sôn′tər) *v.* to walk in a slow, relaxed manner
  **pasear** *v.* caminar de una forma lenta y relajada

**scenario** (sĭ-nâr′ē-ō′) *n.* a description of a possible course of action or events
  **panorama** *s.* descripción de un curso posible de acción

**scruple** (skrōō′pəl) *n.* a feeling of uneasiness that keeps a person from doing something
  **escrúpulo** *s.* malestar provocado por la conciencia o por los principios personales

**serene** (sə-rēn′) *adj.* calm; peaceful
  **sereno** *adj.* calmo; con paz

**sever** (sĕv′ər) *v.* to cut off
  **arrancar** *v.* partir; cortar por completo

**singularity** (sĭng′gyə-lăr′ĭ-tē) *n.* something peculiar or unique
  **singularidad** *s.* rareza; peculiaridad

**solace** (sŏl′ĭs) *n.* comfort from sorrow or misfortune
  **solaz** *s.* consuelo frente al dolor o el infortunio

**solicitously** (sə-lĭs′ĭ-təs-lē) *adv.* in a manner expressing care or concern
  **solícitamente** *adv.* con preocupación e interés

**spartan** (spär′tn) *adj.* simple, plain, and frugal
  **espartano** *adj.* sencillo y frugal

**squalor** (skwŏl′ər) *n.* a filthy, shabby, and wretched condition, as from poverty
  **escualidez** *s.* condición sucia y miserable

**squander** (skwŏn′dər) *v.* to spend or use wastefully
  **despilfarrar** *v.* desperdiciar; gastar o usar algo descuidadamente

**stagnating** (stăg′nā′tĭng) *adj.* becoming foul or rotten from lack of movement  **stagnate** *v.*
  **estancado** *adj.* putrefacto por falta de movimiento  **estancar** *v.*

**stalk** (stôk) *n.* a stem or main axis of a plant
  **tallo** *s.* tronco o eje central de una planta

**stark** (stärk) *adj.* complete or utter; extreme
  **marcado** *adj.* absoluto; extremo

**status quo** (stăt′əs kwō) *n.* the existing state of affairs
  **statu quo** *s.* estado actual

**stealth** (stĕlth) *n.* cautious or secret action or movement
  **secreto** *s.* conducta callada u oculta

**steel** (stēl) *v.* to make hard or strong
  **templar** *v.* endurecer; fortalecer

**stoicism** (stō′ĭ-sĭz′əm) *n.* indifference to pleasure or pain; a lack of visible emotion
  **estoicismo** *s.* indiferencia ante el dolor o placer

**subliminal** (sŭb-lĭm′ə-nəl) *adj.* below the level of consciousness
  **subliminal** *adj.* por debajo de la conciencia

**subside** (səb-sīd′) *v.* to decrease in amount or intensity; settle down
  **calmarse** *v.* tranquilizarse; disminuir

**subsist** (səb-sĭst′) *v.* to support oneself at a minimal level
  **subsistir** *v.* vivir con lo mínimo

**suffuse** (sə-fyōōz′) *v.* to gradually spread through or over
  **envolver** *v.* extenderse gradualmente

**superannuated** (sōō′pər-ăn′yōō-ā′tĭd) *adj.* obsolete with age
  **caduco** *adj.* que se ha vuelto obsoleto con el tiempo

**supplication** (sŭp′lĭ-kā′shən) *n.* a humble request or prayer
  **súplica** *s.* ruego; solicitud o petición humilde; rezo

**surrogate** (sûr′ə-gĭt) *adj.* serving as a substitute
  **suplente** *adj.* que sustituye

**surveillance** (sər-vā′ləns) *adj.* having to do with close observation
  **vigilante** *adj.* que hace una observación detallada

**sustenance** (sŭs′tə-nəns) *n.* food or provisions that sustain life
  **sustento** *s.* alimentos para vivir

**tangible** (tăn′jə-bəl) *adj.* capable of being touched or felt; having actual form and substance
  **tangible** *adj.* que puede tocarse o sentirse; que tiene forma o sustancia real

**taut** (tôt) *adj.* pulled or drawn tight
  **tenso** *adj.* tirante

**termination** (tûr′mə-nā′shən) *n.* an end, limit, or edge
  **terminación** *s.* fin de algo; límite u orilla

**torrent** (tôr′ənt) *n.* a heavy, uncontrolled outpouring
  **torrente** *s.* aguacero fuerte

**transcend** (trăn-sĕnd') *v.* to pass beyond the limits of
transcender *v.* ir más allá de los límites

**travail** (trə-vāl') *n.* painful effort
congoja *s.* esfuerzo doloroso

**tremulous** (trĕm'yə-ləs) *adj.* marked by trembling or shaking
trémulo *adj.* tembloroso

**trepidation** (trĕp'ĭ-dā'shən) *n.* nervous fear
trepidación *s.* incertidumbre; nerviosismo

**uncanny** (ŭn-kăn'ē) *adj.* so remarkable as to seem supernatural
extraordinario *adj.* tan asombroso que parece sobrenatural

**undulate** (ŭn'jə-lāt') *v.* to move in waves or in a smooth, wavelike motion
ondular *v.* moverse en olas

**unequivocal** (ŭn'ĭ-kwĭv'ə-kəl) *adj.* allowing no doubt or misunderstanding
inequívoco *adj.* que no admite duda o malentendido

**unnerving** (ŭn-nûr'vĭng) *adj.* causing loss of courage
unnerve *v.*
desconcertante *adj.* que pone nervioso **desconcertar** *v.*

**valorous** (văl'ər-əs) *adj.* brave
valeroso *adj.* valiente

**veneer** (və-nîr') *v.* to cover with a thin layer of material
enchapar *v.* cubrir con una fina capa de un material fino

**vestibule** (vĕs'tə-byōōl') *n.* a small entryway within a building
vestíbulo *s.* pequeña entrada en un edificio

**vexation** (vĕk-sā'shən) *n.* irritation; annoyance
molestia *s.* irritación o ira

**vigilant** (vĭj'ə-lənt) *adj.* on the alert; watchful
alerta *adj.* atento para evitar un peligro

**wry** (rī) *adj.* dryly humorous, often with a bit of irony
irónico *adj.* de un humor seco; sardónico

**zealous** (zĕl'əs) *adj.* intensely enthusiastic
fervoroso *adj.* intensamente dedicado y entusiasta

# Pronunciation Key

| Symbol | Examples | Symbol | Examples | Symbol | Examples |
|--------|----------|--------|----------|--------|----------|
| ă | at, gas | m | man, seem | v | van, save |
| ā | ape, day | n | night, mitten | w | web, twice |
| ä | father, barn | ng | sing, hanger | y | yard, lawyer |
| âr | fair, dare | ŏ | odd, not | z | zoo, reason |
| b | bell, table | ō | open, road, grow | zh | treasure, garage |
| ch | chin, lunch | ô | awful, bought, horse | ə | awake, even, pencil, |
| d | dig, bored | oi | coin, boy | | pilot, focus |
| ĕ | egg, ten | ŏŏ | look, full | ər | perform, letter |
| ē | evil, see, meal | ōō | root, glue, through | | |
| f | fall, laugh, phrase | ou | out, cow | **Sounds in Foreign Words** | |
| g | gold, big | p | pig, cap | KH | *German* ich, auch; |
| h | hit, inhale | r | rose, star | | *Scottish* loch |
| hw | white, everywhere | s | sit, face | N | *French* entre, bon, fin |
| ĭ | inch, fit | sh | she, mash | œ | *French* feu, cœur; |
| ī | idle, my, tried | t | tap, hopped | | *German* schön |
| îr | dear, here | th | thing, with | ü | *French* utile, rue; |
| j | jar, gem, badge | *th* | then, other | | *German* grün |
| k | keep, cat, luck | ŭ | up, nut | | |
| l | load, rattle | ûr | fur, earn, bird, worm | | |

## Stress Marks

′    This mark indicates that the preceding syllable receives the primary stress. For example, in the word *language*, the first syllable is stressed: lăng′gwĭj.

′    This mark is used only in words in which more than one syllable is stressed. It indicates that the preceding syllable is stressed, but somewhat more weakly than the syllable receiving the primary stress. In the word *literature*, for example, the first syllable receives the primary stress, and the last syllable receives a weaker stress: lĭt′ər-ə-chŏŏr′.

Adapted from *The American Heritage Dictionary of the English Language,* fourth edition. Copyright © 2006 by Houghton Mifflin Harcourt Publishing Company. Used with the permission of Houghton Mifflin Harcourt Publishing Company.

# Index of Skills

## A

Abbreviations
  periods in, R49
  postal, R49
  Web, 1295
Academic vocabulary, 16–19, 27, 53, 110, 201, 220, 329, 382, 433, 478, 491, 551, 576, 589, 599, 653, 669, 678, 692, 819, 838, 859, 866, 917, 938, 975, 1187, 1291, R121–R122
Act (in a play), 7, R102
Active listening, R82–R83
Active voice. *See* Voice.
Adjective clauses, 261, 267, R62
Adjective phrases, 309, R60
Adjectives, 99, 1107, R47, R57
  versus adverbs, 572, R57
  avoiding too many, 221
  commas and, R49
  precise, 212, 221
  predicate, R57, R60
  proper, R51
Adverb clauses, 1169, R62
Adverb phrases, 309, R60
Adverbs, 99, 393, R47, R57
  versus adjectives, 572, R57
  relative, 267
Advertising, 4, 10, 694–697, R90–R91
  audience and cost of, R84
  billboard, R90
  celebrities in, 695–696, R91
  flyer, R90
  infomercial, R90
  marketing, R90
  persuasive techniques in, 656, 695, R22, R91
  political ad, R90
  print ad, R90
  product comparison, R91
  product placement, R91
  promotional posters, 1121
  public service announcement, 694–697, R90
  sponsors, R90
  trailer, R90
  types of, R90–R91
Aesthetics and text criticism. *See* Text criticism.
Affixes. *See* Prefixes; Suffixes.
Agreement
  pronoun-antecedent, R52
  subject-verb agreement, R65–R67
Allegory, R102

Alliteration, 145, 148, 742, 769, 875, 1198, R102. *See also* Sound devices.
Allusions, 109, 668, 925–937, 1028–1029, 1035, 1083, 1095, 1113, 1196, 1215, 1219, 1226, 1238, R102
  author's perspective and, 937
  to make inferences, 925–937
Almanacs, 1301. *See also* References.
Ambiguity, interpreting, 995
Analogy, 480, 489, 628, 658, 659, 661, 668, 714, R71, R102. *See also* Rhetorical devices; Vocabulary skills and strategies.
  false, R24
Analysis of an Author's Style, 890–899
Analysis of a Poem, 798–807
Analysis, literary sources, FM46
Analysis, seminal U.S. documents, FM46
Analysis, writing, 668, R37–R40
  definition, R40
  process, R40
Analyze media, 851
Anapest, R109
Anecdotes, 481, 592, 714, R30–R31
Angle, in news reporting, R89
Anglo-Saxon affix, 1239
Animation, 601, R88
Antagonist, 398, 1026, 1129, R102
Antecedent-pronoun agreement, R52
Antonyms, 124, 279, 856, R71
Apostrophes, R50
Appeals
  by association, 656, R22
  to authority, R91
  bandwagon, 656, R22, R91
  emotional, 656, 671, 677, 695, 697, R22, R91, R116
  ethical, 656
  to fear, 656, R22, R116
  logical, R91, R117
  to loyalty, R22
  to pity, 656, R22, R116
  "plain folks," 656
  to values, 656
  to vanity, R22
Appearance in oral presentations, R77–R78
Applications, job, R44
Appositives, R60
Approaches to literature. *See* Text criticism.
Archetypes, 1194, 1203, 1241, 1250, 1253, 1264, 1267, R102
Argumentative writing
  analysis of, 668, 677, 691, R21, R26
  claim, 654, 661, 668, 1166–1175, R115

  counterarguments, 677, 712, 713, 716, 718, 721, R21, R116
  counterclaims, 712, 713, 1166–1175
  critical review, 1166–1175, 1176–1177
  deductive, R23, R116
  elements of, 654, 655
    by emotion, 656, 671, 677, 695, 697, R22, R91, R116
  ethical, 656
  evidence, 654, R21
  faulty, R24
  general principle, R23
  inductive, 691, R22–R23, R117
  literary criticism, 302–311
  logical, R118
  opposing claim, 302–311, 712–721, 1166–1175
  persuasive essay, 712–721
  persuasive writing, 552, 591
  reasons, 654, 655, 659, 661, 713, 715, 1166–1175, R21, R41
  strategies for determining strong, R26
  strategies for reading, 654, R21
  support, 654, 661, 668, 713, 715, R21, R119
  writing, 693, 939
Arguments, 8, 661–668, 939, R115. *See also* Appeals.
  key techniques, R40–R41
  opinion statement, 867
  options for organizing, R41
  rubric for, 310, 720, 1174, R40
Art. *See* Visuals, analysis of.
Articles (part of speech), 236
Articles (written). *See* Feature articles; Journal articles; Magazine articles; News articles; Newspapers, articles in.
Articulation. *See* Speaking strategies.
Artistic effects. *See* Media; Media elements and techniques; Multimedia presentations.
Aside, 1026, 1030, 1035, 1040, 1087, R102
Assessment practice 186–197, 314–325, 424–429, 536–547, 644–649, 724–735, 810–815, 902–913, 1006–1017, 1178–1183, 1282–1287
Assonance, 742, 787, 788, 791, 983, 1198, R102
Assumption, R115
Atlases, 1301. *See also* References.
Attitudes, comparing, 221, 249
Audience, 302–311, 1129
  media, 695, 696, R85

speaking and listening, R76, R78, R83
target, 695, R85
writing, 695, 712, 717, R34, R41, R42
Authority. *See* Arguments; Sources.
Author's background, 441, 481, 501, 507, 559, 569, 605, 613, 920, 963–974, 1159
Author's intent. *See* Author's purpose.
Author's message, 405, 699–708, R115
Author's perspective, 389–398, 493–498, 554, 566, 613–619, 858, 937, 948, R102
Author's point of view. *See* Author's perspective.
Author's position, R21, R40–R41, R115. *See also* Author's perspective; Author's purpose; Claims.
Author's purpose, 127–136, 186, 405, 550, 552–553, 591–598, 605–610, 979, 1157, R85, R102
Author's stance. *See* Author's perspective; Author's position.
Author's style. *See* Style.
Author's viewpoint. *See* Author's perspective.
Autobiographical essay, R102–R103
Autobiography, 4, 8, 9, 117–123, R102–R103. *See also* Memoirs.
    characterization in, 255–265
    dialogue in, 117, 120
    interpreting, 123
    narrative techniques in, 123

## B

Background, 833, 1275
Ballad, 787–791, R103
Bandwagon appeal, 656, R22, R91
Bar graphs, R5
Base words, R69
Bias, 681–691, R115
    analysis, 691
    in evidence, R25
    recognizing, 681–691, 1305, R25
    in reporting, R90
Bibliography, 1304, 1308, R115. *See also* Works cited.
    MLA citation guidelines, 1334–1335
Biographical context, 265, 291, 351, 989
Biographical essay, 1301
Biographical references, 1301. *See also* References.
Biography, 4, 8, 126, R103
    suspense in, 127–136,
Blank verse, 1028–1029, 1035, 1047, 1059, 1063, 1147, R103
Block-style format, 637
Boldface type, as text feature, 554, R3
Boolean searches, 1296
Brainstorming, 23, 303, 413, 480, 670, 1315
Bulleted list, as text feature, R3
Business and technical writing, 632–641, R42–R45

audience, R42
correspondence, R115
formats for, R43–R45
key techniques, R42
online, 642–643
rubric for, R42
Business letter, 632–641
Bylaws, R45
Bylines, R14

## C

Calculator, graphing, R17
Call to action, 712–721
Camera shots in film and video, 113
    camera movement, R87
    close-up, 115, 385, 386, R87
    establishing, R87
    extreme long, 115
    high-angle, 113, 114, 115, R87
    long, 115, 849, R87
    low-angle, 113, 114, 115, R87
    medium, 115, R87
    pan, R87
    point-of-view, 113, 114, 115, 849, R87
    reaction, 849, R87
    tracking shot, R87
    zoom, R87
Capitalization, 635
    in outlines, 454
    quick reference chart, R51
    in quotations, 707
Captions
    as text features, 554, 579, 580, R3
    in Web news report, 601
Career-related writing. *See* Business and technical writing.
Case, pronoun
    nominative, R53
    objective, R53
    possessive, R53
Casting, 1045
Cast of characters, 1030, R103
Cause-and-effect organization, 117, 280, R10–R11, R38, R115. *See also* Patterns of organization.
    setting and, 392
    in Shakespearean tragedy, 1030
    in writing, R38
Cause-and-effect relationships, reading, 117–123, 280
CD-ROMs, of reference works, 1298
Censorship, R86
Chain of events, 370, R38. *See also* Cause-and-effect organization.
Characterization, 253, 255–265, 577, 961, R103
    in autobiography, 255–265, 937
    in biography, 293–299
    across genres, 293–299

methods of, 204, 205, 253, 255–265, 293–299, 367, 461, 577, 1112, 1149
    in poetry, 293–299
Characters, 412, 416, 420, 967, 1042, 1051, 1069, 1071, 1076, 1092, 1112, 1137, 1151, R103. *See also* Characterization; Character types.
    actions of, 204, 205, 369, 479
    analysis of, 219, 236, 251, 253, 367, 369, 477, 755, 937, 974, 1087, 1113, 1129, 1267
    archetypes, 1203, 1250, 1253, 1264, 1267, R102
    cast of, 1030, R103
    comparing and contrasting, 81, 97, 136, 234, 251
    creating memorable, 200, 413
    creating realistic, 173, 413
    describing, 961
    details in creating, 351
    development, 1087, 1171
    dialogue in revealing, 415, R36
    drawing conclusions about, 351, 514, 519, 928, 937
    evaluating, 960, 1113, R116
    facial expressions, body language, and actions of, 1149
    humor of, R107
    making inferences about, 85–97, 102, 288, 381, 461–477, 613–619, 752, 1087, 1112
    motivation of, 206, 223–234, 265, 575, 937, 1076, 1087, 1090, 1113, 1114, 1122, 1238, 1258, 1262
    in narrative poetry, 151, 1163
    in narrative writing, R36
    physical appearance of, 204, 205
    plot and, 28, 85–97
    point of view and, 202–203, 240–251, 1270–1279, R110
    reactions of other, 204
    relationships between, 367, 461, 755, 1112
    settings in influencing, 330, 331
    social context of, 974, 1267
    study, 269–280
    theme and, 436, 508
    thoughts of, 204, 205
    in tragedy, 1027, 1132, 1136
    traits. *See* Character traits.
    words of, 204, 205
Character study, 269–280
Character traits, 81, 204–205, 209–219, 240, 251, 255–265, 267, 270, 1051, 1137, 1198, 1221, 1247, 1253, R103
    evaluating, 219, 398, 960
Character types
    antagonist, 398, 1026, 1129, R102
    archetypal, 1194, 1203, 1253, 1264, 1267, R102

567, 631, 668, 679, 693, 709, 755, 763, 769, 867, 961, 1165

Extended metaphor, 797, 873, R106

External conflict, 28, 490, 837, R104

Eye contact, 185, R78

## F

Fable, R106

Facts, 681, R116–R117. *See also* Supporting statements.
  in elaboration, R33
  versus opinion, 681–691, R25, R116–R117
  recognizing, 681
  verifying, R25

Fallacy, R24, R117

Falling action, 28, 35, R106. *See also* Plot.

False analogy, R24

False cause, R24

Fantasy, R106

Farce, 4, 881, 889, R106

Faulty reasoning, R24

Fear, appeal to, 656, R22, R116

Feature articles, 4, 8, 282–285, 454–457, R117

Feedback. *See* Peer review.

Fiction, strategies for reading, 11–15, 919. *See also* Reading skills and strategies

Fiction, structure and elements of, 28, 97, 330, 336, 351, R9

Fiction, types of, 4, 5
  fable, R106
  fantasy, R106
  historical, 919, R107
  horror, R107
  novellas, 4, 5, R109
  novels, 4, 5, R109
  realistic, R111
  science, 5, 37, 699, 702–707, R112
  short stories, 4, 5, 13–14, R112
  tall tales, R114

Field research, 1310

Figurative language, 452, 702, 708, 744, 745, 775–784, 869, 995, 1072, 1087, 1198, 1203, 1219, 1269, R68, R106
  in descriptive writing, R34
  epic similes, 1196–1197, 1198, 1203, 1206, 1219, 1224, 1238, 1244, R105
  epithets, 1196–1197, 1209, 1213, 1216, 1222, 1238, R105
  extended metaphor, 797, 873, R106
  hyperbole, 687, 744, 853, R107, R114
  metaphor, 88, 744, 775, 779, 871, 1256, 1269, R108
  paradox, 618, R110
  personification, 123, 774, 775, 782, 784, 995, R110
  in relation to historical and cultural setting, 240, 250, 919, 921, 948, 993, 995
  similes, 775, 778, 959, 1196, 1269, R112

Figure of speech. *See* Figurative language.

Film reviews, 1152–1157

Films, 1303, R86–R88. *See also* Camera shots in film and video; Media elements and techniques.
  atmosphere in, 849
  differences between text and, 387
  documentaries, 1303
  editing of, 113, 114, 849, R88
  feature, 4, 10
  irony in, 385
  mood in, 385, 850, 1150
  point of view in, 849, 1270–1279
  script and written elements, 1270–1279 R86, R112
  setting in, 385, 1150
  sound in, 113, 1150, R87
  storyboard, 115, R86
  strategies for viewing, 849
  style in, 849, 851
  suspense in, 112, 113, 115,
  theme, 849
  visual elements in, 1270, R87

First Amendment, R86

Firsthand and expressive writing. *See* Narrative writing.

First-person narrator. *See* Narrators.

First-person point of view. *See* Point of view.

Fixed expressions, 374, 516, 616, 1245

Flashbacks, 30, 31, 336, 350, 827, 835, 837, R9, R36, R106–R107

Flat characters, 251, R103

Fluency, oral, 131

Fluency in writing, 567

Foils (character), 1026, 1057, 1063, R107

Folk ballads, R103

Folktales. *See* Oral tradition.

Foreground, 833

Foreign words in English, 379, 675, 678, 779, 795, 857, 978, R70

Foreshadowing, 30, 37–52, 58, 69, 127, 172, 477, 1063, 1092, 1130, 1229, R107
  in creating suspense, 30, 37, 41, 81, 127, 172, R107, R113

Formal language, 376, 383, 632, 637, 666, 878, 1329

Formatting
  research paper, 1332
  workplace documents, R42–R44
  works cited, 1334–1335

Form in poetry, 6, 740, 765–769, R107

Forms of writing. *See* Writing skills and strategies.

Fragments. *See* Sentence fragments.

Framing (on screen), 1149, R87

Framing inquiries, 534–535, 642–643, 722–723

Free verse, 740, 741, 875, R107

Freewriting, 21, 23. *See also* Quickwriting.

Functional reading, R3–R20

Functional texts, 8, 620–625, R16–R19, R119. *See also* Consumer documents; Workplace documents.

## G

Generalizations, R117
  hasty, R24
  making, 285
  overgeneralization, 681, R24, R117, R118

General pronoun reference, R55

Genre, 4, R107. *See also* Drama; Fiction; Informational texts; Literary nonfiction; Poetic forms.
  characterization across, 293–299
  comparing across, 292–301, 506–521, 698–709
  theme across, 507–521
  writer's message across, 699

Gerunds and gerund phrases, 719, 931, 939, R61

Gestures, R79

Glittering generality, R22

Glossary, 1304, R15, R72

Government publications, R117

Grammar, R46–R67. *See also specific grammar concepts.*
  and style, 44, 54, 75, 83, 99, 108, 111, 125, 173, 212, 221, 230, 236, 250, 253, 261, 267, 344, 353, 359, 369, 376, 383, 468, 479, 496, 499, 562, 567, 573, 577, 609, 611, 676, 679, 690, 693, 707, 755, 785, 831, 839, 864, 867, 931, 939, 957, 961, 1066, 1147, 1256, 1269

Grammar in Context, 177, 181, 305, 309, 415, 419, 527, 531, 635, 639, 715, 719, 801, 805, 893, 897, 999, 1002, 1169, 1173, 1277, 1323, 1332

Graphic aids 579, R3, R5–R7, R117
  captions, 554, 579, 580, 601, R3
  charts, R6
  in consumer documents, 620–625, R17
  diagrams, 269–280, R6
  graphs, R5
  interpreting, 269–280, 591–598
  maps, 582, 591–598, R7
  photographs, 591–598,
  pie graphs, R5
  in public documents, R18
  tables, R6

Graphical components, 620–625

Graphic organizers, 11, 23, R117
  balance scale, 354
  cause-and-effect, 1030
  charts, 12, 15, 37, 52, 85, 97, 109, 117, 123, 136, 138, 145, 153, 209, 223, 255, 269, 280, 282, 291, 293, 299, 337, 355,

script, 1270, R86, R112
set design, 385, 386, 1081
shape, R92
sound, 113, 114, 1150, 1270, R87
sound bites, 601
sound effects, 113, 385, R87
special effects, R88
storyboard, 115, 1272, 1275–1276, R86
texture, R91–R92
visual, 112–115, 1272, 1275
voice-over narration, 601, R87
Media genres and types, 4, 10, 1271, R85
advertising, 4, 10, R90–R91
feature films, 4, 10
magazines, 10, 1303,
news media, 10, 1303, 1309
news photographs, 980
online information. *See* Internet.
TV newscast, 600–603, R86, R88
TV shows, 10
Web news report, 601
Web sites, 4, 10, 1306–1307, 1336–1337, R120
Wikis, 1336–1337
Media Handbook, R84–R92
Media literacy, 10, 114, 385, 695, 849, 850, 980, 1149, R84
Media messages, R84, R85
evaluating, 56, 695, 1280, R92
viewing strategies for, 601, 602
Media presentations and products.
creating, 1151
planning, 1151
producing, 387, 603, 1151
production design board, 387
production still, 851
promotional posters, 1121
promotional still, 851
storyboard, 115, 1272, 1275–1276, R86
Web site, 1336–1337, R120
Wikis, 1336–1337
Media study, 112–115, 384–387, 600–603, 657, 694–697, 848–851, 980, 1148–1151
Memoirs, 171, 481–490, 925–937, R108. *See also* Autobiography.
Memorandums, R42–R43
formatting, R43
writing, 679
Menus, Web site, 601, 1297, R20
Metaphor, 88, 744, 775, 779, 873, 1256, 1269, R108
extended, 797, 873, R106
Metasearch engines, 1296, 1312
Meter, 742, 743 793–797, R108–R109
anapest, R109
dactyl, R109
foot, 743, R108

iamb, 743, R108
iambic pentameter, 743, 797, 1028, 1063, R103, R107, R112
iambic tetrameter, 797
pentameter, 743
spondee, 743
tetrameter, 743
trimeter, 743
trochee, 743, R108–R109
Microfiche, 1298
Microform, 1298
Minor characters, R103
*Mise en scène,* R87, R109
elements of, 1149, 1151
evaluating, 1151
MLA citation guidelines, 1334–1335
Modifiers, 88, 99, R57. *See also* Adjectives; Adverbs; Commonly confused words.
clauses. *See* Clauses.
comparative and superlative forms of, R57–R58
comparison of, R57–R58
dangling, R59
essential adjective clauses, R62
irregular comparison of, R58
nonessential adjective clauses, R62
phrases. *See* Phrases.
placement of, R59
precise, 221
problems with, R58–R59
regular comparison of, R58
Monitoring, 12, 13, 241–251, 493–498, 583, 584, 941–948, R118
comprehension, 58, 81, 138, 143, 154
Monologue
creating, 383
dramatic, 793–797, R105
writing, 1269
Mood, 146, 332, 462, 477, 788, 873, 1054, 1150, 1260, R109
analysis of, 143, 371–381, 386, 850
in descriptive writing, R35
evaluating, 411
imagery in creating, 332, 407, 408, R35
setting and, 332, 333, 386, 389–398
subjunctive, 125, 717
visuals in conveying, 60, 210
Motivation
of characters, 206, 223–234, 575, 1033, 1076, 1090, 1113, 1114, 1122, 1238, 1258, 1262
making judgments about, 367
understanding, 265
Motives, 125, 265, 575
Movies. *See* Films.
Multimedia presentations. *See* Media presentations and products; Oral presentations.

creating, 901, 1270–1279, 1336–1337
evaluating, 1280–1281
planning, 900, 1271–1272, 1336
podcast, 900–901
producing, 422–423
Multiple-choice questions, R94
Multiple-meaning words, 63, 216, 246, 266, 584, 622, 704, 767, 870, 986, 1084, 1102, 1143, 1222, R72
Multiple-step instructions. *See* Instructions.
Music, 113, 385, 386, 1150, R87
Mythology, words from classical, 252, R70
Myths, 1159–1165, R109
characteristics of, 1165

## N

Name-calling, as logical fallacy, R24
Narrative writing, R36–R37
alternative ending, 125, 847
analysis, 267, 479, 499, 598, 668, 755, 839, 961
anecdotes, 481, R30–R31
blank verse, 1028–1029, 1035, 1059, 1063, 1147
character analysis, 236, 353, 369, 967
characterization, 253, 255–265, 577
conflict organization for, R37
critiques, 693
description, 111, 221, 961
dialogue, 54
diary, 83, R105
interpreting endings, 383
key techniques in, 123, R36
letters, 499, 839
monologues, 383, 1269
options for organization, R36–R37
personal, 174–183
response, 611
rubric for, R36
scene, 99, 353
short stories, 412–421, R112
video script, 1270–1279
Narrative elements. *See* Characters; Conflict; Plot; Point of view; Setting; Themes.
Narrative essay. *See* Essays.
Narrative nonfiction, 388–399, R36–R37, R109. *See also* Literary nonfiction.
Narrative poetry, 4, 145–153, 1163, R109
characters in, 151
conflict in, 151
interpretation of, 153
speakers in, 145–153
surprise endings in, 152
Narrative speeches, 184–185, R79. *See also* Oral presentations.
Narrators, 109, 202, 381, R109
drawing conclusions about, 109
first-person, 202–203, 209–219, 1276

point of view of, 202–203, 209–219, 230, 241–251, R110
third-person, 202–203, 241
third-person limited, 241
third-person omniscient, 219
Negatives, double, R58–R59
News, 10, R88–R90. *See also* Media genres and types.
angle, R89
balance in reporting, R89
bias in reporting, R90
choosing the news, R88
commentary and opinion, R88
editorial, 688–690, R116
five W's and H, 601, R89
human interest, R88
inverted pyramid, R89
newscast, 600–603, R86, R88
newsworthiness, R88
op-ed, R118
proximity, R88
reporting, 600–603, R88–R90
slant, R89
sources for, R90
standards for reporting, R89
timeliness, R88
Web news reports, 601
widespread impact, R88
News articles, 4, 8, 9, R118
News formats, 601–603,
Newspapers, 1303
articles in, 4, 8, 282–285, 454–457, R117
editorials in, 688–690, R116
evaluating, 1309
News reports, 600–603, R88–R90
viewing guide for, 602
Newsworthiness, R88
Nielsen ratings, R85
Nominative pronoun case, R53
Non sequitur, R24
Note cards, 1294, 1318–1322, 1322
Notes. *See also* Graphic aids; Graphic organizers.
in adapting informal speech, 184
marginal, 1030
in reading consumer documents, R16
in reading workplace documents, R19
summarizing, 588
Note taking, 11, 579–588, 1294, 1319, R4
as study skill for writing, 1294, R28
Noun clauses, R63
Nouns, R46, R52
abstract, R46
collective, R46, R67
common, R46, R52
compound, R46
concrete, R46
plural, R46, R52, R74

possessive, 801, R46, R52, R74
predicate, R60
proper, R46, R52
singular, R46, R52
Novellas, 4, 5, R109
Novels, 4, 5, R109

# O

Objections, anticipating, R21, R116
Objective pronoun case, R53
Objectivity
in news reporting, R89
of sources. *See* Sources, evaluating.
Objects
direct, R48, R60
indirect, R48, R60
of prepositions, R60
Observations, 1310
Ode, 775–784, R109
Off rhyme, 790, 869, 870, R111
Online catalog, 1299
Online feature article, 996–1003
updating an, 1004–1005
Online information. *See* Internet.
Online professional profile, 642–643
Onomatopoeia, 929, 1217, R109–R110
Op-ed pieces, R118
Open-ended response. *See* Short constructed response, Assessment practice.
Opinions, 681, R117
evaluating, 1157
expert, 681, R25, R41
expressing, 867
versus facts, 681–691, R25, R116–R117
supporting, 763, 773
Opinion statement. *See* Persuasion.
Oral fluency, 131, 348, 396, 513, 1139
Oral histories, 1190
Oral instructions, 642–643, 838
Oral interpretation, R80
Oral presentations. *See also* Oral instructions; Speaking strategies.
audience feedback, R78, R83
debate, 680, 860, 1034, R79, R116
delivery of, R77–R78
descriptive speech, R80
evaluating, R78, R83
extemporaneous, R76
informative speech, R78
multimedia presentation, 1270–1279
narrative speech, 184–185, R79
oral interpretation, R80
oral response to literature, 808–809, R80–R81
panel discussions, 534–535
persuasive speech, 657, R79, R83
preparing for, 312, R76–R77
props in, R111

responding to questions, 643, R78
visual aids in, R77
Oral tradition
fables, R106
folk ballad, R103
myths, 1159–1165, R109
tall tales, R114
Order of importance, 893, R35
Order of impression, R35
Organizational patterns. *See* Patterns of organization.
Organizing. *See* Graphic organizers; Patterns of organization.
Origin of words, 252, 300, 370, 522, 959, R70. *See also* Word roots.
Outlines, 454–457, 1321
drafting from, 21, 1322
for taking notes, R4
Overgeneralization, 681, R24, R118
Oversimplification, R24, R117
Overstatement, 780
Overview, R118
Oxymoron, R110

# P

Pace, 113, 114, 849, R27, R88
Pacing. *See* Speaking strategies, Writing skills and strategies
Panel discussions, 534–535
Paradox, 298, 618, R110
Paragraphs, R31–R32
coherence of, R31–R32
organizing, R31
topic sentence in, R31, R120
transitions in, R32–R33
unity of, R31
Parallelism, 658, 690, 715, 1066, 1147, R64, R110
as a rhetorical device, 658, 661, 666, 668, 693
Parallel plot, R110
Parallel structure, 715
Paraphrasing, 371–381, 451, 575, 606, 757–763, 861–865, 1030, 1063, 1094, 1130, 1319, 1320, 1326, R118. *See also* Plagiarism.
Parentheses, R50
Parenthetical documentation, 1323–1324
Parodies, 843–847, R110
Participating in group discussions, FM46. *See also* Discussion.
Participles and participial phrases, 415, 609, 755, 1002, R61
dangling, R61
misplaced, R61
past, R55
present, R55
Parts analysis, R40

describing, in narrative writing, R36
details of, 56, 337–351
in epic poetry, 1194, 1241, 1244, 1267
imagery in creating, 332, 333, 918
influence of, 351, 452
mood and, creating, 332, 333, 386, 389–398
in movies, 385
in short story, 330–335
as symbol, 330, 355–367
theme and, 436, 441–452
visualizing, 229, 1198, R120
Setting a purpose for reading, 293, 507–521, 699, R119
Shakespearean drama, 1026–1033, 1146
analysis of, 1035–1146,
in movies, 1149
reading, 1030–1031, 1035–1146
Shakespearean language, 1028–1029, 1030
Shakespearean sonnet, 746, R112
Shakespearean tragedy, 1026–1027, 1030, 1035–1146, 1147
Shakespeare's world, 1022–1025
Short constructed response, Assessment practice, 57, 195, 239, 324, 427, 459, 546, 647, 733, 813, 841, 912, 981, 1016, 1182, 1285
Short stories, 32, 38, 60, 84, 100, 208, 222, 336, 354, 370, 437, 440, 460, 506, 604, 702, 826, 950, 962
reading, 4, 5, 13–14, R112
strategies for reading, R2
writing, 412–421,
Sidebars, 770, R14, R119
Signal words, R9, R119
for cause and effect, R32
for chronological order, 559, R9
for comparison and contrast, 559
for sequence of events, 481, 1159, R32
Similes, 744, 775, 778, 1196, 1269, R112
epic, 1196–1197, 1203, 1206, 1219, 1224, 1238, 1244, R105
Situational irony, 101, 109, 234, 375, 858, R108
Skimming, 627–631, 770, 772, R27
Slang, 142, 173, 416, 833, R68, R76
Slant, in news reporting, R89
Slant rhyme, 869, 870, R111
Slogans, R91
for public service announcements, 695
Snob appeal, R22
Social context, 452, 498, 974, 1267
Social criticism, 699
Software
photo-editing, 697, 1151
presentation, 1313
video-editing, 1270–1279
Soliloquy, 1026, 1027, 1030, 1035, 1067, 1087, 1095, 1134, 1146, R112

Solutions, R119
Sonnets, 4, R112
Petrarchan, 741
Shakespearean, 746, R112
Sound devices, 145, 153, 742–743, 787–791, 983, 987, 989, R112–R113
alliteration, 145, 148, 742, 769, 983, 1198
assonance, 742, 787, 788, 791, 983, 1198, R102
consonance, 742, 1198, R104
onomatopoeia, 784, 929, 1217, R109–R110
repetition, 145, 150, 742, 787, 790, 791, 983, 984, R111
rhyme, 145, 149, 787, 790, 791, 983, 1198, R111
rhyme scheme, 742, 787, 796, R111
slant rhyme, 869, 870, R111
Sound elements. See Media elements and techniques.
Source cards, 1318–1321
MLA citation guidelines, 1334–1335
Sources, analysis of. See Analysis, literary sources.
Sources, documenting, 1317–1321, 1322. See also Parenthetical documentation; Works cited.
Sources, evaluating, 1305–1309, 1317, R116, R119
accuracy, 1305
authority or authorship, 1305
bias, 1305, R25
checklist for, 1313
coverage, 1305
credibility, 1305, R90, R116
currency, 1305
for news stories, R90
relevance, 1305
Sources, types of, R119, R120. See also References.
databases, 1302, R116
electronic, 1298, 1337
field studies, 1310
film, 1303
government publications, R117
Internet, 1293, 1295–1297, R117
interviews, 836, 1310–1311, R81–R82, R108
journals, 1303, R117
linking to external, 1001
magazines, 1303
microforms, 1298
newspapers, 1298, 1303, 1309
observations, 1310
periodicals, 1298, 1303, 1309, R118
primary, 400–405, 1300, 1303, R119
questionnaires, 1311
reference books, 1298, 1301

secondary, 1300, R119
survey, 1311
Spatial order, R32, R35, R119
Speakers, 145, 148, 150, 153, 287–291, 411, 501, 505, 745, 750, 763, 787–791, R113
Speaking. See also Oral presentations; Speaking strategies.
to entertain, R77
to inform, R77
to persuade, R77, R79
Speaking and Listening, FM46, 184–185, 312–313, 534–535, 722–723, 808–809, 1176–1177, 1280–1281, R82–R83
adapting a literary analysis, 808
debating an issue, 722–723
evaluating a critical review, 1176–1177
evaluating a video, 1280–1281
participating in a discussion, FM46, 312–313
participating in a panel discussion, 534–535
presenting an informal speech, 184–185
presenting a literary analysis, 808–809
teamwork in, 131, 534–535, 722–723
Speaking strategies, R76–R78
body language, R78
emphasis, R77
enunciation, 809
eye contact, 185, 809, R78
facial expressions, 185, 809
gestures, 185, 313, 809, R78
interpretation of text, R80
nonverbal, R78
pace, 185, R77
pitch, R77
posture, 185, R78
pronunciation, 131, 348, 396, 513
tone, 185, R77
Special effects. See Media elements and techniques.
Specialized dictionaries, 1301, R72
Specialized vocabulary, 281, 314, 589, R72.
Speech, 4, 8, R76–R78, R113. See also Nonfiction, types of; Oral presentations; Speaking strategies.
Spelling
commonly confused words, 803, 1117, R58, R71–R72, R75
errors in, of pronouns, R53
homonyms and, 866
plural nouns, R74
possessives, R74
prefixes, R73
rules for, R72–R74
special problems, R74
suffixes, R72–R73
using resources for, R72

Tragic flaw, 1146, R114
Tragic hero, 1026, R114
Trailer
    producing a short story, 422–423
Traits. *See* Character traits; Common Core
    Traits.
Transfer, 656, R22
Transitions, 305, 308, 712, 802, 890, 893,
    895, 1314, 1324, 1330, R29, R32–R33
    cause and effect, R32–R33
    commas to set off introductory, R49
    compare and contrast, R32
    create cohesion and connect ideas, to,
        890, 893, 895
    degree of importance, R32
    spatial relationships, R32
    time or sequence, R32
    using, in critical esssay, 305
Transitive verbs, R47
Trochee, 743, R108–R109
Turning point. *See* Climax.

**U**

Understatement, R114
Universal themes, 434, 501–505, 1146,
    1267, R114
URLs, 1295, R20
Usage. *See* Grammar.
U.S. documents. *See* Analysis, seminal U.S.
    documents.

**V**

Valid conclusion, R115
Validity of sources. *See* Sources, evaluating.
Vantage points. *See* Oral presentations.
Venn diagrams, 81, 251, R12
Verb agreement. *See* Subject-verb agreement.
Verbal irony, 101, 375, 820, R108
Verbals and verbal phrases, R60–R62
    gerunds, 931, R61
    infinitives, 785, R61
    participles, 755, R55, R61
Verbs, R47, R48, R55–R57
    action, R47, R55
    auxiliary (helping), R47, R48, R56
    with compound subjects, R65
    in fixed expressions, 374, 516, 1245
    intransitive, R47
    irregular, R55
    linking, R47, R55
    main, R48
    plural, R65
    precise, 108, 111
    principal parts of, R55
    in reading consumer documents, R16, R17
    regular, R55
    singular, R65
    transitive, R47
    vivid, 957, 961

Verb tense, R55–R56
    choosing effective, 353
    consistent, 1277
    errors in, R56
    future, R56
    future perfect, R56
    past, R56
    past perfect, R56
    present, 344, 353, R56
    present perfect, R56
    progressive forms, R56
    shifting, R56
Verifying information, 1309
Verse. *See* Poetic forms.
Video. *See* Media; Technology.
Video-editing software, 1270–1279
Video Script, 1270–1279
Viewing skills and strategies
    analyzing details, 840
    analyzing techniques, 602
    compare and contrast audience, 696
    comparing formats, 387, 602
    core concepts in media literacy, R84
    deconstructing media, R85
    drawing conclusions, 602, 840
    evaluating advertisements, 710
    evaluating a video, 1280–1281
    5 W's and the H questions, 601
    making inferences, 56, 696, 840
    message analysis, 696, 710, R92
    spotting lead, 601
Viewpoint. *See* Author's perspective; Bias.
Virtual libraries, 1312
Visual aids. *See also* Graphic aids.
    in oral presentations, R77
Visual elements
    of advertisements, 56
    of film, 113–115, 384–387, 848–851,
        1148–1151, R87
    of TV, 600–603, R87
Visualizing, 12, 13, 62, 63, 64, 69, 80, 81,
    155, 241, 442, 775, 776, 780, 783,
    881, 889, 1198, R120
Visuals, analysis of, 38, 47, 56, 60, 86, 95,
    102, 118, 128, 133, 134, 146, 210,
    214, 224, 229, 232, 238, 242, 256,
    259, 270, 277, 289, 294, 338, 344,
    356, 360, 372, 377, 390, 408, 442,
    447, 462, 470, 482, 494, 508, 560,
    565, 570, 573, 574, 606, 614, 662,
    665, 673, 701, 702, 710, 750, 758,
    768, 776, 788, 795, 828, 833, 840,
    844, 854, 864, 876, 926, 942, 952,
    955, 964, 968, 980, 1160, 1192–1193,
    1204, 1206, 1210, 1227, 1230, 1236,
    1242, 1246, 1248, 1250, 1254, 1256,
    1260, 1262
Vocabulary. *See also* Vocabulary skills and
    strategies.

assessment practice, 428, 648, 1286
building, FM46, 19
in context, 37, 53, 82, 85, 98, 101, 110,
    117, 124, 127, 137, 209, 220, 223, 235,
    241, 252, 255, 266, 269, 281, 293,
    300, 337, 352, 355, 368, 371, 382,
    389, 399, 441, 453, 461, 478, 481, 491,
    507, 522, 569, 576, 579, 589, 591, 599,
    661, 669, 671, 678, 681, 692, 827,
    838, 853, 859, 861, 925, 938, 941,
    949, 963, 975, 1203, 1239, 1241, 1268
in speaking, 589, 599, 975, 1268
in writing, 82, 98, 220, 252, 266, 281,
    352, 399, 453, 478, 491, 522, 576, 669,
    678, 692, 859, 866, 938, 949, 1239
Vocabulary skills and strategies, 15,
    R68–R75. *See also* Vocabulary.
    analogies, 658, 661, 668, 669, R71, R102
    antonyms, 124, 856, R71
    base words, 393, 445, 572, 581, 1125,
        1154, R69
    clarify definitions, 19
    cognates, 675, 779
    commonly confused words, 1117, R75
    connotation, 82, 149, 227, 352, 478, 859,
        862, 1248, R71, R104
    context clues, 19, 218, 399, 465, 491,
        704, 1248, R68, R116
    denotation, 82, 149, 227, 352, 478, 859,
        862, 1248, R71, R104
    dictionary, 75, 106, 248, 266, 281, 368,
        382, 396, 485, 685, 1232, R72
    foreign words in English, 678, 795, 857,
        978, R70
    glossaries, 19, 266, 859, 1304, R15, R72
    homographs, 402
    homonyms, 866, R71
    homophones, 106, 260, 1232, R71
    idioms, 88, 90, 121, 218, 562, 608, 835,
        956, 975, 1235, R68, R108
    Internet words, 692
    multiple-meaning words, 63, 216, 246,
        266, 584, 622, 704, 767, 870, 986,
        1084, 1102, 1143, 1222, R72
    prefixes, 98, 470, 581, 838, 944, 1227,
        1239, R69
    root words. *See* word roots, *below*.
    slang, 833
    specialized vocabulary, 281, 589, R72
    suffixes, 68, 393, 453, 596, R69
    synonyms, 124, 497, 1212, 1264, R70,
        R72
    word choice, 859
    word families, 137, 382, R70
    word list, 19
    word origins, 75, 248, 252, 300, 448,
        522, 959, 978, 1073, 1095, 1107, 1154,
        1252, R70
    word parts. *See* Word parts.

INDEX OF SKILLS   **R153**

word roots, 53, 110, 137, 220, 235, 296, 382, 576, 599, 938, 949, 959, 984, 1154, 1209, 1259, 1268, R69

words from Greek culture, 252, 978

Voice. *See also* Oral presentations; Speaking strategies; Style.

active, 412, 417, 638, R57

conversational, 185

in literature, 879, 890, 937, 951–960, R114

passive, 638, 684, R57

in writing, 22, 712, 896

Volume. *See* Speaking strategies.

# W

Web address, 1295, R20

Webs (graphics), 58, 110, 220, 235, 254, 368, 413, 492, 500, 576, 599, 858, 938, 950, 1315

Web sites, 4, 10, R120. *See also* Internet; References.

evaluating, 1306–1307

reading, 1297

Wiki, *see also* Media genres and types; Media presentations and products.

developing, 1337

planning, 1336

Word choice, 822, 858, 859, 948, 995, 1139, 1264. *See also* Diction.

in author's perspective, 554

compare and contrast, 995

making effective, 111

in persuasive techniques, 656, R22, R91

precise words, 108, 111, 212, 221, 798–807, 890, 895, 898

tone and, 574, 616, 822, 856, R114

Word derivations, 366, 445, 572, 1125. *See also* Word families; Word parts; Word roots.

Word families, 137, 382, R70. *See also* Word roots.

Word order, 757. *See also* Diction.

Word origins, 75, 248, 252, 300, 448, 522, 959, 978, 1073, 1095, 1107, 1154, 1252, R70. *See also* Word roots.

Word parts, analyzing

base words, 393, 445, 572, 581, 1125, 1154, R69

prefixes, 98, 366, 470, 581, 838, 856, 944, 1227, 1239, R69

roots, 53, 68, 110, 137, 220, 235, 296, 366, 368, 382, 393, 576, 599, 938, 949, 959, 984, 1154, 1209, 1259, 1268, R69

suffixes, 68, 131, 366, 393, 596, R69

Word play, 853, 858, 1028–1029

Word-processing software. *See* Software.

Word roots, 675, 984, 1125, R69

Anglo-Saxon (Old English), 248, 393, 470, R69

Greek, 110, 576, 944, 949, 978, R69

Latin, 53, 98, 137, 220, 235, 296, 366, 368, 382, 448, 596, 599, 675, 938, 944, 1073, 1154, 1209, 1259, 1268, R69

Word structure. *See* Word roots.

Workplace and technical writing, R42–R45. *See also* Business writing.

formats for, R43–R45

key techniques in, R42

matching the organization to the content, R42

rubric for, R42

Workplace documents, 8, R19, R120. *See also* Business writing; Workplace and technical writing.

strategies for reading, R19

Works cited, 1322, 1323, 1331, R120. *See also* Parenthetical documentation.

direct quotations, 1320, 1322

formatting, 1331, 1334–1335

MLA citation guidelines, 1334–1335

preparing list, 1322, 1323

Works consulted, R120

World connections. *See* Cultural contexts; Cultural symbols.

World Wide Web. *See* Internet.

Writer's message, 699–708. *See also* Author's message.

Writing

analysis of author's style, 798–801, 890–899

analysis of literary nonfiction, 524–533

analysis of a poem, 798–801

audience, 20, 302, 525, 695, R34, R41, R42

business letter, 632–641

clarity and coherence, FM46

critical review, 1166–1175

format of, 20

goals in, R34

literary criticism, 302–311

from literature, 798, 890

monologue, 383

online feature article, 996–1003

peer review. *See* Peer Review.

personal narrative, 174–183

persuasive, 712–721

purpose of, 20

research paper, 1314–1335

short story, 412–421

style, R113

prompts. *See* Writing tasks.

across texts, 54, 236

video script, 1270–1279

Writing about literature, 236, 253, 267, 285, 301, 405, 798, 890

Writing for assessment, 301, 523, 711, R100, R101

Writing modes. *See* Argumentative writing; Informative writing; Narrative writing.

Writing process, 20–23, R28–R30

drafting, 21, 177, 305, 415, 523, 527, 635, 715, 801, 893, 999, 1169, 1273, 1322–1323, R28

editing and publishing, 21, 181, 309, 419, 531, 639, 719, 897, 1003, 1173, 1277, 1332, R29

evaluating, 21, R34–R42

peer review 21, 23, 306, 414, 416, 526, 528, 634, 636, 714, 716, 800, 892, 894, 998, 1000, 1168, 1274, 1316, 1324, R30

planning/prewriting, 21, 23, 175–176, 303–304, 413–414, 525–526, 633–634, 713–714, 799–800, 891–892, 997–998, 1167–1168, 1271–1272, 1315–1316, R28

production, 1273

proofreading, 21, 181, 309, 419, 531, 636, 719, 806, 897, 1003, 1173, 1277, 1332, R29

reflecting, R29–R30

researching, 1317–1321

revising, 21, 54, 99, 111, 125, 173, 178, 253, 301, 306, 353, 369, 383, 416, 528, 636, 679, 693, 716, 802, 755, 769, 785, 839, 847, 867, 894, 939, 961, 1000, 1170, 1274, 1324, R29

Writing skills and strategies. *See also* Reading-writing connection.

analogies, 658, 661, 668, R71, R102

anecdotes, R30–R31

cause and effect, R32, R38, R115

characters, analyzing, 302–311

characters, creating, 173, 200, 351, 416

claim, creating a precise, 302–311, 712–721, 1166–1175

coherence, 22, 1327, R31–R32

compare and contrast, 567, 588, 1157, 1165, R32, R115

conciseness, 369, 785, 939

considering audience and purpose, 302–311, 524–533, 632–641, 712–721, 996–1003, 1314–1335

description, 111, 174, 221, R30, R34

details, 174, 178, 179, 417, 895, R33

development of ideas, 22

dialogue, 54, 173, 178, 179, 415, 1270, R36

elaboration, 803, 895, R33–R34

examples, 304, 528, 892, 894, R34

humor, R107

monologue, 383

Page numbers that appear in italics refer to biographical information.

# ACKNOWLEDGMENTS

## INTRODUCTORY UNIT

**Scribner:** Excerpt from *The Old Man and the Sea* by Ernest Hemingway. Copyright © 1952 by Ernest Hemingway, copyright renewed 1980 by Mary Hemingway. Used with the permission of Scribner, an imprint of Simon & Schuster Adult Publishing Group, a Division of Simon & Schuster, Inc.

**Arte Público Press:** "Los Ancianos," from *My Own True Name* by Pat Mora. Copyright © 2000 by Pat Mora. Used by permission of Arte Público Press, University of Houston.

**Flora Roberts:** Excerpt from *The Miracle Worker* by William Gibson. Copyright © 1956, 1957 by William Gibson, copyright © 1959, 1960 by Tamarack Productions, Ltd., and Geroge S. Klein and Leo Garel as trustees under three separate deeds of trust, copyright renewed © 1977 by William Gibson. Used by permission of Flora Roberts, Inc.

**Little, Brown and Company:** Excerpt from *Nisei Daughter* by Monica Sone. Copyright @ 1953 by Monica Sone, renewed © 1981 by Monica Sone. Used by permission of Little, Brown and Co., Inc.

**New York Times:** Excerpt from "Japan Wars on U.S. and Britain; Makes Sudden Attack on Hawaii; Heavy Fighting At Sea Reported" by Frank L. Kluckhohn from the *New York Times,* December 8, 1941. Copyright © 1941 by The New York Times Co. All rights reserved. Used by permission and protected by the Copyright Laws of the United States. The printing, copying, redistribution, or retransmission of the Material without express written permission is prohibited.

**Barbara Hogenson Agency:** Excerpt from "The Secret Life of Walter Mitty," from *My World—And Welcome To It* by James Thurber. Copyright © 1942 by James Thurber, copyright renewed 1970 by Rosemary A. Thurber. Used by arrangement with Rosemary Thurber and The Barbara Hogenson Agency. All rights reserved.

## UNIT 1

**Pollinger Limited:** Excerpt from *The Splendid Outcast: Beryl Markham's African Stories* compiled and introduced by Mary S. Lovell. Copyright ©1987 by the Beryl Markham Estate. Reproduced by permission of Pollinger Limited and the proprietor.

**Eugenia Collier:** "Sweet Potato Pie," by Eugenia Collier from *Black World,* August 1972, pp. 54-62. Copyright © 1969 by Eugenia Collier. Reprinted by permission of the author.

**Scholastic:** "Checkouts" from *A Couple of Kooks and Other Stories* by Cynthia Rylant. Published by Scholastic Inc./Orchard Books. Copyright © 1990 by Cynthia Rylant. All rights reserved. Reprinted by permission.

**Don Congdon Associates:** "A Sound of Thunder" from *R is for Rocket* by Ray Bradbury. Copyright © 1952 by Crowell Collier Publishing Company, renewed 1980 by Ray Bradbury. Reprinted by permission of Don Congdon Associates, Inc.

**Newsweek:** "From Here to There: The Physics of Time Travel," by Brad Stone, from *Newsweek,* March 16, 1998. Copyright © 1998 by Newsweek, Inc. All rights reserved. Used by permission and protected by the Copyright Laws of the United States. The printing, copying, redistribution, or retransmission of the Material without express written permission is prohibited.

**Brandt & Hochman Literary Agents:** "The Most Dangerous Game" by Richard Connell. Copyright © 1924 by Richard Connell. Copyright renewed © 1952 by Louise Fox Connell. Used by permission of Brandt & Hochman Literary Agents, Inc. Any copying or distribution of this text is expressly forbidden.

**Susan Bergholz Literary Services:** "Daughter of Invention," from *How the Garcia Girls Lost Their Accents* by Julia Alvarez. Copyright © 1991 by Julia Alvarez. Published by Plume, an imprint of The Penguin Group (USA) and originally in hardcover by Algonquin Books of Chapel Hill. Reprinted by permission of Susan Bergholz Literary Services, New York, NY and Lamy, NM. All rights reserved.

**HarperCollins Publishers:** Excerpt from "Hunger stole upon me...streets of Memphis" from *Black Boy* by Richard Wright. Copyright 1937, 1942, 1944, 1945 by Richard Wright; renewed © 1973 by Ellen Wright. Reprinted by permission of HarperCollins Publishers Inc.

**Janklow & Nesbit Associates:** Excerpt from Seabiscuit: *An American Legend* by Laura Hillenbrand. Copyright © 2001 by Laura Hillenbrand. Originally published by Random House. Reprinted by permission of the author.

**Laura Hillenbrand:** "Four Good Legs Between Us," from *American Heritage,* July/August 1998, by Laura Hillenbrand. Copyright © 1998 by Laura Hillenbrand. Reprinted by permission of the author.

**WGBH/Boston:** Excerpt from "Timeline: Seabiscuit" from the American Experience Web site located at <u>Http://www.pbs.org/wgbh/ amex/seabiscuit/timeline/timeline2.html.</u> Copyright © 2003 by WGBH/Boston. Reprinted by permission of WGBH Educational Foundation.

**NBC News Archives:** Excerpt from the radio broadcast "Santa Anita Handicap," by Clem McCarthy and Buddy Twist. Copyright © 1937 by NBC News Archives. Reprinted by permission of NBC News Archives.

**Alfred A. Knopf:** "Incident in a Rose Garden" from *Collected Poems of Donald Justice* by Donald Justice. Copyright © 2004 by Donald Justice. Used by permission of Alfred A. Knopf, a division of Random House, Inc.

**Stephen King:** "Sorry, Right Number" by Stephen King. Copyright © 1993 by Stephen King. Reprinted with permission.

**Simon & Shuster:** Excerpt from *On Writing: A Memoir of the Craft* by Stephen King. Copyright © 2000 by Stephen King. All rights reserved. Reprinted with the permission of Scribner, a division of Simon & Shuster, Inc.

**Cecilia Burciaga:** "La Puerta" by José Antonio Burciaga. Copyright © 1992 by José Antonio Burciaga. Reprinted by permission of Cecilia Burciaga.

**Robert D. Ballard:** Excerpt from "Live Your Dreams" by Robert D. Ballard, 89th Commencement, delivered May 20, 2007. Copyright © 2007 Robert D. Ballard. Reprinted by permission of the author.

## UNIT 2

**Random House:** Excerpt from *The Chocolate War* by Robert Cormier. Copyright © 1974 by Robert Cormier. Used by permission of Random House Children's Books, a division of Random House, Inc.

**HarperCollins Publishers:** Excerpt from "Life Without Go-Go Boots," from *High Tide in Tucson: Essays from Now or Never* by Barbara Kingsolver. Copyright © 1995 by Barbara Kingsolver. Reprinted by permission of HarperCollins Publishers.

Excerpt from *To Kill a Mockingbird* by Harper Lee. Copyright © 1960 by Harper Lee. Renewed © 1988 by Harper Lee. Reprinted by permission of HarperCollins Publishers.

**Bancroft Library:** Excerpt from *Picture Bride* by Yoshiko Uchida. Copyright © 1987 by Yoshiko Uchida. Courtesy of the Bancroft Library, University of California, Berkeley.

**Sterling Lord Literistic:** "Pancakes," by Joan Bauer from *Trapped! Cages of Mind and Body* by Lois Duncan. Copyright © 1998 by Joan Bauer. Reprinted by permission of SLL/Sterling Lord Literistic, Inc.

**Houghton Mifflin Harcourt:** "The Necklace" by Guy de Maupassant from *Adventures in Reading,* Laureate Edition, Grade 9. Copyright © 1963 by Harcourt, Inc., and renewed 1991 by Deborah Jean Lodge, Alice Lodge, Jeanne M. Shutes, Jessica Sand, Lydia Winderman, Florence F. Potell, and Mary Rives Bowman. Reprinted by permission of the publisher. This material may not be reproduced in any form or by any means without prior written permission of the publisher.

**Naomi Shihab Nye:** "Hamadi" by Naomi Shihab Nye. Copyright © 1993 by Naomi Shihab Nye. First published in *America Street,* edited by Anne Mazer. Reprinted by permission of the author.

**Random House:** Excerpt from "Sister Flowers," from *I Know Why the Caged Bird Sings* by Maya Angelou. Copyright © 1969 and renewed © 1997 by Maya Angelou. "Sister Flowers" is not the original title. Used by permission of Random House, Inc.

**Random House and Little, Brown Book Group Limited:** "Caged Bird," from Shaker, *Why Don't You Sing?* by Maya Angelou. Copyright © 1983 by Maya Angelou. Used by permission of Random House, Inc. and Little, Brown Book Group Limited.

**Time:** "Blind to Failure" by Karl Taro Greenfeld from *Time,* June 18, 2001. Copyright © 1991 by Time, Inc. Reprinted by permission.

**Anne Stein:** "A Different Level of Competition" by Anne Stein from *Chicago Tribune,* February 24, 2002. Copyright © 2002 by Anne Stein. Reprinted by permission of the author.

**Arte Público Press:** "A Voice," from *Communion* by Pat Mora. Copyright © 1991 by Pat Mora. Reprinted with permission of Arte Público Press, University of Houston.

**Simon J. Ortiz:** "My Father's Song," by Simon J. Ortiz from *Going for the Rain.* Originally published in *Woven Stone,* University of Arizona Press. Copyright © 1976 by Simon J. Ortiz. Used by permission of the author.

**Viking Penguin:** Excerpt from "The Bus Boycott" from *Rosa Parks* by Douglas Brinkley. Copyright © 2000 by Douglas Brinkley. Used by permission of Viking Penguin, a division of Penguin Group (USA) Inc.

**Rita Dove:** "Rosa" from *On the Bus with Rosa Parks* by Rita Dove . Published by W.W. Norton. Copyright © 1999 by Rita Dove. Reprinted by permission of the author.

**Pauline Kaldas:** "Airport" by Pauline Kaldas, from *Dinarzad's Children,* edited by Pauline Kaldas and Khaled Mattawa. Copyright © 2004 by Pauline Kaldas. Reprinted by permission of the author.

**Random House and Little, Brown Book Group Limited:** "New Directions," from *Wouldn't Take Nothing for My Journey Now* by Maya Angelou. Copyright © 1993 by Maya Angelou. Used by permission of Random House, Inc. and Little, Brown Book Group, Ltd.

## UNIT 3

**Houghton Mifflin Harcourt:** Excerpt from *Nineteen Eighty-Four* by George Orwell. Copyright © 1949 by Harcourt, Inc., and renewed 1977 by Sonia Brownell Orwell. Reprinted by permission of the publisher. This material may not be reproduced in any form or by any means without the prior written permission of the publisher.

**Arkham House Publishers:** Excerpt from "The Music of Erich Zann" by H. P. Lovecraft, from *Masterpieces of Terror and the Supernatural,* selected by Marvin Kaye. Copyright © 1925. Used by permission of Arkham House.

**Connie L. Ulibarri:** Excerpt from "My Wonder Horse/Mi caballo mago," from *Tierra Amarilla: Stories of New Mexico* by Sabine R. Ulibarri, translated from the Spanish by Thelma Campbell Nason. Reprinted by permission of the Connie L. Ulibarri.

**Random House:** "A Christmas Memory" by Truman Capote. Copyright © 1956 by Truman Capote. Used by permission of Random House, Inc.

**HarperCollins Publishers and Jonathan Clowes:** "Through the Tunnel," from *The Habit of Loving* by Doris Lessing. Copyright © 1954, 1955 by Doris Lessing, originally appeared in the *New Yorker.* Reprinted by permission of HarperCollins Publishers Inc. and the kind permission of Jonathan Clowes Ltd., London, on behalf of Doris Lessing.

**The Estate of Edward Rowe Snow:** Excerpt from "The Roving Skeleton of Boston Bay" by Edward Rowe Snow, from *Yankee* magazine. Reprinted by permission of Dorothy Snow Bicknell on behalf of the Estate of Edward Rowe Snow.

**Broadway Books, and The Random House Group Ltd.:** Excerpt from *A Walk in the Woods* by Bill Bryson. Copyright © 1997 by Bill Bryson. Used by the permission of Broadway Books, a division of Random House, Inc., and The Random House Group Ltd.

**Doubleday:** "Wilderness Letter" from *The Sound of Mountain Water* by Wallace Stegner. Copyright © 1969 by Wallace Stegner. Used by permission of Doubleday, a division of Random House, Inc.

**New Directions and Pollinger Limited:** "The Sharks," from *Collected Earlier Poems* 1940–1960 by Denise Levertov. Copyright © 1957, 1958, 1959, 1960, 1961, 1979 by Denise Levertov. Reprinted by permission of New Directions Publishing Corp. and Pollinger Limited.

**Counterpoint:** "The Peace of Wild Things," from *The Selected Poems of Wendell Berry* by Wendell Berry. Copyright © 1999 by Wendell Berry. Reprinted by permission of Counterpoint.

**Houghton Mifflin Harcourt:** Excerpt from *The Hobbit* by J.R.R. Tolkien. Copyright © 1937 by George Allen & Unwin Ltd. Copyright © 1966 by J.R.R. Tolkien. Copyright © renewed 1994 by Christopher R. Tolkien, John F.R. Tolkien, and Priscilla M.A.R.

Tolkien. Copyright © restored 1996 by the Estate of J.R.R. Tolkien, assigned 1997 to the J.R.R. Tolkien Copyright Trust. Reprinted by permission of Houghton Mifflin Harcourt Publishing Company. All rights reserved.

## UNIT 4

**PFD:** "The Sniper," from *Spring Sowing* by Liam O'Flaherty. Copyright © 1924 by Liam O'Flaherty. Reproduced by permission of PFD on behalf of the Estate of Liam O'Flaherty.

**Eugenia Collier:** "Marigolds," from *Breeder and Other Stories* by Eugenia Collier. Copyright © 1994 by Eugenia Collier. First published by Black Classic Press, Baltimore. Reprinted by permission of the author.

**Donna Freedman:** "Sowing Change" by Donna Freedman, from *Chicago Tribune*, August 31, 2003. Copyright © 2003 by Donna Freedman. Reprinted by permission of the author.

**James Hurst:** "The Scarlet Ibis" by James Hurst. Copyright © 1960 by the *Atlantic Monthly* and renewed 1988 by James Hurst. Reprinted by permission of James Hurst.

**Naomi Long Madgett:** "Woman With Flower," from *Star By Star* by Naomi Long Madgett. Copyright © 1965, 1970 by Naomi Long Madgett. Reprinted by permission of the author.

**Ruth Cohen, Inc.:** "Math and After Math" by Lensey Namioka from *Going Where I'm Coming From,* edited by Anne Mazer. Copyright © 1994 by Lensey Namioka. Reprinted by permission of Lensey Namioka. All rights are reserved by the author.

**Aragi Inc.:** "The Future in My Arms" by Edwidge Danticat, first published in *Ebony*. Reprinted by permission of Edwidge Danticat and Aragi Inc.

**Thames & Hudson:** "Poem on Returning to Dwell in the Country," from *T'ao the Hermit: Sixty Poems by Tao Chien* by Tao Ch'ien, translated by William Acker. Copyright © 1952 by William Acker. Reprinted by kind permission of Thames & Hudson Ltd., London.

**Beacon Press:** "The Sun," from *New and Selected Poems* by Mary Oliver. Copyright © 1992 by Mary Oliver. Reprinted by permission of Beacon Press, Boston.

**Penguin Group (USA):** "Two Kinds," from *The Joy Luck Club* by Amy Tan. Copyright © 1989 by Amy Tan. Used by permission of G. P. Putnam's and Sons, a division of Penguin Group (USA) Inc.

**Diane Mei Lin Mark:** "Rice and Rose Bowl Blues" by Diane Mei Lin Mark. Copyright © by Diane Mei Lin Mark. Reprinted by permission of the author.

**Don Congdon Associates:** "The Golden Kite, the Silver Wind" by Ray Bradbury. Copyright © 1953 by Epoch Associates; copyright renewed © 1981 by Ray Bradbury. Reprinted by permission of Don Congdon Associates, Inc.

**Albert Einstein Archives:** "The Arms Race," from *Einstein on Peace* by Albert Einstein. Albert Einstein's statement for appearance on *Today with Mrs. Roosevelt,* recorded on February 10, 1950. Reproduced by permission of the Albert Einstein Archives, Hebrew University of Jerusalem.

## UNIT 5

**Joe Bower:** Excerpt from "Web Masters" by Joe Bower, *Audubon,* January-February 2002. Copyright © by Joe Bower 2002. Reprinted by permission of the author, who lives in Michigan and writes on environmental issues.

**Janisse Ray:** Excerpt from "Weaving the World" by Janisse Ray, *Audubon,* January-February 2002. Copyright © 2002 by Janisse Ray. Reprinted by permission of the author.

**Kids Discover:** "Germ Warfare" by *Kids Discover,* October 2003, Volume 13, Issue 10. Copyright © 2003, 2005 by Kids Discover. Reprinted by permission of Kids Discover. All rights reserved.

**Susan Bergholz Literary Services:** Excerpt from "Aha Moment" by Julia Alvarez, first published in *O, The Oprah Magazine* 1, no. 5 (November 2000). Copyright © 2000 by Julia Alvarez. Reprinted by permission of Susan Bergholz Literary Services, New York, NY and Lamy, NM. All rights reserved.

**Chicago Sun-Times:** Excerpt from "Aircraft Built to Shrug Off Lightning Strike" by Tom McNamee, as published in the *Chicago Sun-Times,* May 9, 1996. Copyright © 2005 by Chicago Sun-Times, Inc. Reprinted with permission.

**Farrar, Straus and Giroux:** Excerpt from "Notes and Comments," from *Talk Stories* by Jamaica Kincaid. Copyright © 2001 by Jamaica Kincaid. Used by permission of Farrar, Straus and Giroux, LLC.

"Georgia O'Keeffe," from *The White Album* by Joan Didion. Copyright 1979 by Joan Didion. Used by permission of Farrar, Straus and Giroux, LLC.

**National Geographic Society:** "Who Killed the Iceman?" *National Geographic,* February 2002. Copyright © 2002 by National Geographic Society. Reprinted by permission of the National Geographic Society.

**Little, Brown and Company:** Excerpt from "Skeletal Sculptures" from *The Bone Detectives* by Donna Jackson. Copyright © 1996 by Donna Jackson (text) and Charlie Fellenbaum (photographs). By permission of Little, Brown and Company. All rights reserved.

**Scholastic:** "The Lost Boys," by Sara Corbett, from *The New York Times Upfront* magazine, September 3, 2001. Copyright © 2001 by Scholastic Inc. and The New York Times Company. Reprinted by permission of Scholastic Inc.

**Cable News Network:** "All Nine Pulled Alive from Mine" by Jeff Flock and Jeff Goodell on CNN.com, July 28, 2002. Copyright © 2002 by CNN. Reprinted by permission of Cable News Network.

**Susan Bergholz Literary Services:** "The House on Mango Street," "My Name," and "Mango Says Goodbye Sometimes," from *The House on Mango Street* by Sandra Cisneros. Copyright © 1984 by Sandra Cisneros, published by Vintage Books, a division of Random House, Inc., and in hardcover by Alfred A. Knopf in 1994. Reprinted by permission of Susan Bergholz Literary Services, New York, NY and Lamy, NM. All rights reserved.

**Random House and The Random House Group Ltd.:** "His Name Was Pete," from *Essays, Speeches, Public Letters* by William Faulkner, edited by James B. Meriwether, published by Chatto & Windus. Copyright © 1965 by Random House, Inc. Used by permission of Random House, Inc. and The Random House Group Ltd.

**National Post:** "Dog Proves As Smart As Average Toddler" by Margaret Munro, *National Post,* November 6, 2004. Copyright © 2004 The National Post Company. Used by permission.

## UNIT 6

**Writers House:** "I Have a Dream" speech by Martin Luther King Jr. Copyright © 1963 by Martin Luther King Jr., copyright renewed 1991 by Coretta Scott King. Reprinted by arrangement with the heirs to the Estate of Martin Luther King Jr., c/o Writers House as agent for the proprietor, New York, NY.

**Andrea Rock:** "How Private Is Your Private Life?" by Andrea Rock, *Ladies Home Journal,* October 2000. Copyright © 2000 by Andrea Rock. Reprinted with the permission of the author.

**Arthur M. Ahalt:** "The Privacy Debate – One Size Doesn't Fit All" by Arthur M. Ahalt. Reprinted by permission of the author.

**The Boston Globe:** "Primal Screen" by Ellen Goodman from *The Boston Globe.* Copyright © July 1,1980 by The Boston Globe. All rights reserved. Used by permission and protected by the Copyright Laws of the United States. The printing, copying, redistribution, or retransmission of the Material without express written permission is prohibited.

**Don Congdon Associates, Inc.:** "The Pedestrian" by Ray Bradbury. Copyright © 1951 by The Fortnightly Publishing Company, renewed 1979 by Ray Bradbury. Reprinted by permission of Don Congdon Associates, Inc.

**Houghton Mifflin Harcourt:** "The Happy Man's Shirt," from *Italian Folktales: Selected and Retold* by Italo Calvino, translated by George Martin. Copyright © 1956 by Giulio Einaudi editore, S.p.A; translation copyright © 1980 by Harcourt, Inc. Reprinted by permission of Houghton Mifflin Harcourt Publishing Company.

**The Miami Herald:** "A story full of the stuff of sorrow" by Leonard Pitts, Jr., from *The Miami Herald,* December 5, 2008. Copyright © 2008 by The Miami Herald. Reprinted by permission of The Miami Herald.

## UNIT 7

**Lowenstein-Yost Associates:** "Beware: Do Not Read This Poem," from *Ishmael Reed New and Collected Poems* by Ishmael Reed. Copyright © 1988 by Ishmael Reed. Permission granted by Lowenstein-Yost Associates, Inc.

**Henry Holt and Company:** "Fire and Ice," from *The Poetry of Robert Frost* by Robert Frost, edited by Edward Connery Lathem. Copyright © 1923, 1969 from Henry Holt and Company, copyright 1951 by Robert Frost. Reprinted by permission of Henry Holt and Company, LLC.

**BOA Editions:** "miss rosie," from *Good Woman: Poems and a Memoir 1969–1980* by Lucille Clifton. Copyright © 1987 by Lucille Clifton. Reprinted with the permission of BOA Editions, Ltd.

**The Edna St. Vincent Millay Society:** "Sonnet XI," from *Fatal Interview* by Edna St. Vincent Millay. Copyright © 1931, 1958 by Edna St. Vincent Millay and Norman Millay Ellis. Used by permission of The Edna St. Vincnet Millay Society. All rights reserved.

**New Directions:** "I Am Offering This Poem," from *Immigrants In Our Own Land* by Jimmy Santiago Baca. Copyright © 1979 by Jimmy Santiago Baca. Reprinted by permission of New Directions Publishing Corp.

**Random House and Faber and Faber Ltd.:** "My Papa's Waltz," from *Collected Poems of Theodore Roethke* by Theodore Roethke. Copyright © 1942 by Hearst Magazines, Inc. Used by permission of Doubleday, a division of Random House, Inc. and Faber and Faber Ltd.

**BOA Editions:** "I Ask My Mother to Sing," from *Rose, poems by Li-Young Lee* by Li-Young Lee. Copyright © 1986 by Li-Young Lee. Reprinted by permission of BOA Editions, Ltd.

**Rita Dove:** "Grape Sherbet," by Rita Dove from *Museum* published by Carnegie-Mellon University. Copyright © 1983 by Rita Dove. Reprinted by permission of the author.

**Liveright:** "Spring is like a perhaps hand," from *Complete Poems: 1904–1962* by E. E. Cummings.. Copyright © 1923, 1925, 1951, 1953, © 1991 by the Trustees for the E. E. Cummings Trust. Copyright © 1976 by George James Firmage. Used by permission of Liveright Publishing Corporation.

**Houghton Mifflin Harcourt:** "Elegy for the Giant Tortoises," from *Selected Poems 1965–1975* by Margaret Atwood. Copyright © 1976 by Margaret Atwood. Reprinted by permission of Houghton Mifflin Harcourt Publishing Company. All rights reserved.

**Random House:** "Today," from *Nine Horses* by Billy Collins. Copyright © 2002 by Billy Collins. Used by permission of Random House, Inc.

**W. W. Norton:** "400-Meter Freestyle," from *Selected Poems 1960–1990* by Maxine Kumin. Copyright © 1959 and renewed 1987 by Maxine Kumin. Used by permission of W. W. Norton & Company, Inc.

**Houghton Mifflin Harcourt:** "Bodybuilders' Contest," from *View with a Grain of Sand* by Wislawa Szymborska, English translation by Stanislaw Baranczak and Clare Cavanagh. Copyright © 1993 by Wislawa Szymborska, English translation copyright 1995 by Harcourt, Inc. Reprinted by permission of the publisher. This material may not be reproduced in any form or by any means without the prior written permission of the publisher.

**Scholastic:** "The Night Poetry Rocked the House" by Rachel Shapiro from the *New York Times Upfront,* September 4, 2000. Copyright © 2000 by Scholastic Inc. and The New York Times Company. Reprinted by permission of Scholastic Inc.

**Al Young:** "For Poets" by Al Young. Copyright © 1968, 1992 by Al Young. Reprinted and reproduced with permission of the author.

**University of California Press:** "Ode to My Socks," from *Selected Odes of Pablo Neruda* by Pablo Neruda, translated by Margaret Sayers Peden. Copyright © 1990 by Regents of the University of California and Fundación Pablo Neruda. Reprinted by permission of the University of California Press.

**Agencia Literaria Carmen Balcells:** "Oda a los calcetines," from *Nuevas odas elementales* by Pablo Neruda. Copyright © 1956 by Fundación Pablo Neruda. Reprinted by permission of Agencia Literaria Carmen Balcells, S.A. on behalf of Fundación Pablo Neruda.

**Laurel Winter:** "egg horror poem," by Laurel Winter from *Nebula Awards: Showcase 2001,* edited by Robert Silverberg. Copyright © 2001 by Laurel Winter. Reprinted by permission of the author.

**Random House:** "O What Is That Sound," from *Collected Poems* by W. H. Auden. Copyright © 1937 and renewed 1965 by W. H. Auden. Used by permission of Random House, Inc.

**Alfred A. Knopf:** "To be of Use," from *Circles on the Water* by Marge Piercy. Copyright © 1982 by Marge Piercy. Used by permission of Alfred A. Knopf, a division of Random House, Inc.

## UNIT 8

**Susan Bergholz Literary Services:** Excerpt from "Geraldo No Last Name" from *The House on Mango Street* by Sandra Cisneros. Copyright 1984 by Sandra Cisneros. Published by Vintage Books, a division of Random House, Inc., and in hardcover by Alfred A. Knopf in 1994. Reprinted by permission of Susan Bergholz Literary Services, New York, NY and Lamy, NM. All rights reserved.

**International Creative Management:** Excerpt from "Single Room, Earth View" by Sally Ride from *Air & Space,* April/May 1986. Copyright © 1986 by Sally Ride. Reprinted by permission of International Creative Management, Inc.

**Tim O'Brien:** "Where Have You Gone, Charming Billy?" by Tim O'Brien, from *Redbook,* May 1975. Copyright © 1975 by Tim O'Brien. Reprinted by permission of the author.

**Scissor Press:** Interview with Tim O'Brien by Douglas Novielli, Chris Connal, and Jackson Ellis. From *Verbicide,* Issue 8. Copyright © 2003 by Scissor Press. Reprinted by permission of Scissor Press.

**Barbara Hogenson Agency:** "The Princess and the Tin Box," from *The Beast In Me and Other Animals* by James Thurber. Copyright © 1948 by Rosemary A. Thurber. Reprinted by arrangement with Rosemary A. Thurber and The Barbara Hogenson Agency. All rights reserved.

**HarperCollins Publishers:** "Going to Japan," from *Small Wonder: Essays* by Barbara Kingsolver. Copyright © 2002 by Barbara Kingsolver. Reprinted by permission of HarperCollins Publishers.

**Houghton Mifflin Harcourt:** "A Few Words," from *Blue Pastures* by Mary Oliver. Copyright © 1995, 1992, 1991 by Mary Oliver. Reprinted by permission of Houghton Mifflin Harcourt Publishing Company. This material may not be reproduced in any form or by any means without the prior written permission of the publisher.

**Harvard University Press:** "A Narrow Fellow in the Grass" and "'Hope' Is the Thing with Feathers" from *The Poems of Emily Dickinson* by Emily Dickinson, edited by Thomas H. Johnson, Cambridge, Mass.: The Belknap Press of Harvard University Press. Copyright © 1951, 1955, 1979, 1983 by the President and Fellows of Harvard College. Reprinted by permission of the publishers and the Trustees of Amherst College.

**HarperCollins Publishers:** "Luxury" from *The Women and the Men* by Nikki Giovanni. Copyright © 1970, 1974, 1975 by Nikki Giovanni. Reprinted by permission of HarperCollins Publishers.

"Kidnap Poem" from *The Selected Poems of Nikki Giovanni* by Nikki Giovanni. Compilation copyright © 1996 by Nikki Giovanni. Reprinted by permission of HarperCollins Publishers.

**Gary N. DaSilva:** "The Sneeze" from *The Good Doctor,* by Neil Simon. Copyright © 1974 by Neil Simon, copyright renewed 2004 by Neil Simon. Professionals and amateurs are hereby warned that *The Good Doctor* is fully protected under the Berne Convention and the Universal Copyright Convention and is subject to royalty. All rights, including without limitation professional, amateur, motion picture, television, radio, recitation, lecturing, public reading and foreign translation rights, computer media rights and the right of reproduction, and electronic storage or retrieval, in whole or in part and in any form, are strictly reserved and none of these rights can be exercised or used without written permission from the copyright owner. Inquiries for stock and amateur performances should be addressed to Samuel French, Inc., 45 West 25th Street, New York, NY 10010. All other inquiries should be addressed to Gary N. DaSilva, 111 N. Sepulveda Blvd., Manhattan Beach, CA, 90266-6850.

## UNIT 9

**The Wylie Agency:** Excerpt from "The Names of Women" by Louise Erdrich. Copyright © 1995 by Louise Erdrich. Reprinted with permission of The Wylie Agency LLC.

**Farrar, Straus and Giroux:** Excerpt from "The Son from America," from *A Crown of Feathers and Other Stories* by Isaac Bashevis Singer. Copyright © 1973 by Isaac Bashevis Singer. Reprinted by permission of Farrar, Straus and Giroux, LLC.

**Jewish Museum in Prague:** Excerpt from "The Butterfly," by Pavel Friedmann from ... *I Never Saw Another Butterfly: Children's Drawings and Poems from Terezin Concentration Camp 1942–1944.* Copyright © 1962 by the Jewish Museum in Prague. Reprinted by permission of the Jewish Museum in Prague.

**Alberto Ríos:** "The Vietnam Wall," from *The Lime Orchard Woman* by Alberto Ríos. Copyright © 1988 by Alberto Ríos. Reprinted by permission of the author.

**Scribner:** Excerpt from *Angela's Ashes* by Frank McCourt. Copyright © 1996 by Frank McCourt. All rights reserved. Reprinted with the permission of Scribner, an division of Simon & Schuster, Inc.

**Reader's Digest:** Excerpt from "The Education of Frank McCourt," by Barbara Sande Dimmitt published in *Reader's Digest,* November 1977. Copyright © 1997 by The Reader's Digest Association, Inc. Reprinted with the permission of Reader's Digest.

**N. Scott Momaday:** "Revisiting Sacred Ground," from *The Man Made of Words* by N. Scott Momaday. Copyright © 1997 by N. Scott Momaday. Reprinted by permission of the author.

**Random House:** "Blues Ain't No Mocking Bird," from *Gorilla, My Love* by Toni Cade Bambara. Copyright © 1971 by Toni Cade Bambara. Used by permission of Random House, Inc.

**University of Georgia Press:** "American History," from *The Latin Deli: Prose & Poetry* by Judith Oritz Cofer. Copyright © 1992 by Judith Ortiz Cofer. Reprinted by permission of the University of Georgia Press.

**U.S. News & World Report:** "Dark Day" by Kenneth T. Walsh from *U.S. News & World Report,* November 24, 2003. Copyright © 2003 by U.S. News & World Report L.P. Reprinted with permission of U.S. News & World Report.

**Schomburg Center for Research in Black Culture:** "The Tropics of New York" by Claude McKay. Courtesy of the Literary Representative for the Works of Claude McKay, Schomburg Center for Research in Black Culture, The New York Public Library, Astor, Lenox and Tilden Foundations.

**Alfred A. Knopf and Harold Ober Associates:** "Theme for English B," from *The Collected Poems of Langston Hughes* by Langston Hughes. Copyright © 1994 by The Estate of Langston Hughes. Used by permission of Alfred A. Knopf, a division of Random House, Inc. and Harold Ober Associates Incorporated.

**HarperCollins Publishers:** "Harvest moon—," "Heat waves shimmering," and "You could turn this way," by Matsuo Basho– from *The Essential Haiku: Versions of Basho–, Buson & Issa,* edited and with an introduction by Robert Hass. Introduction and selection copyright © 1994 by Robert Hass. Unless otherwise noted, all translations © 1994 by Robert Hass. Reprinted by permission of HarperCollins Publishers.

**Arcade Publishing:** "From a tenement," "Twisting violently," and "Standing in the crowd," from *Haiku: This Other World* by Richard Wright. Copyright © 1998 by Ellen Wright, published by Arcade Publishing, New York, New York. Reprinted by permission of Arcade Publishing.

**Aaron Naparstek:** "clinton street autos," by Aaron Naparstek from www.honku.org. Copyright © 2003 by Aaron Naparstek. Reprinted by permission of the author.

**Villard Books:** "Morning commuters," and "When the light turns green" from *HONKU* by Aaron Naparstek. Copyright © 2003 by Aaron Naparstek. Reprinted by permission of Villard Books, a division of Random House, Inc.

**Carol Cullar:** "Slim" by Carol Cullar. Copyright © 1997 Carol Cullar. Reprinted by permission of the author.

**Cable Network News:** "Good Samaritan' saves crying woman's foreclosed home" *CNN,* October 30, 2008. Copyright © 2008 by CNN. Courtesy CNN.

## UNIT 10

**Universal Press Syndicate:** Excerpt from "Romeo and Juliet" by Roger Ebert, from the *Chicago Sun-Times,* September 17, 2000. Copyright © 2000 by The Ebert Company. Reprinted with permission. All rights reserved.

**Houghton Mifflin Harcourt:** Excerpt from *The Metamorphoses of Ovid: A New Verse Translation* by Allen Mandelbaum. English translation copyright © 1993 by Allen Mandelbaum. Reprinted by permission of Houghton Mifflin Harcourt Publishing Company. This material may not be reproduced in any form or by any means without the prior written permission of the publisher.

## UNIT 11

**Farrar, Straus and Giroux:** Excerpts from *The Odyssey* by Homer, translated by Robert Fitzgerald. Translation copyright © 1961, 1963 renewed 1989 by Benedict R. C. Fitzgerald on behalf of the Fitzgerald children. This edition © 1998 by Farrar, Straus & Giroux, LLC. Reprinted by permission of Farrar, Straus and Giroux, LLC.

**Viking Penguin:** "Penelope," from *The Portable Dorothy Parker* by Dorothy Parker, edited by Brendan Gill. Copyright © 1928, renewed 1956 by Dorothy Parker. Used by permission of Viking Penguin, a division of Penguin Group (USA) Inc.

## UNIT 12

**Dallas Morning News:** Excerpt from "Animal ER" by Aline McKenzie from the *Dallas Morning News,* January 19, 2005.

Copyright © 2005 by The Dallas Morning News. Reprinted with the permission of *The Dallas Morning News.*

## STUDENT RESOURCE BANK

**Broadway Books and Doubleday Canada:** Excerpt from *A Walk in the Woods* by Bill Bryson. Copyright © 1997 by Bill Bryson. Used by the permission of Broadway Books, a division of Random House, Inc. and Doubleday Canada, a division of Random House of Canada Limited.

**Newsweek:** Excerpt from "e-Life: How the Internet is Changing America" from *Newsweek,* September 20, 1999. Copyright © 1999 by Newsweek, Inc. All rights reserved. Used by permission and protected by the Copyright Laws of the United States. The printing, copying, redistribution, or retransmission of the Material without express written permission is prohibited.

**Center for Media Literacy:** The "Five Core Concepts in Media Literacy" may be found in the *CML MediaLit Kit ™/Part I—Literacy for the 21st Century: An Overview and Orientation to Media Literacy Education.* Copyright © Center for Media Literacy. Reprinted by permission of Center for Media Literacy, whose Web site is located at www.medialit.org.

**Project Look Sharp:** "Six Questions to Ask About Any Media Message," from Project Look Sharp, Ithaca College. Copyright © Project Look Sharp. Reprinted by permission of Project Look Sharp, www.ithaca.edu/looksharp/resources.php.

**Copyright Clearance Center:** Excerpt from "Culture Goes Global," by Henry Jenkins from *Technology* Review, July/August 2001. Copyright © 1991 by Technology Review. Reprinted by permission of the Copyright Clearance Center.

**Random House, Inc.:** Excerpt from *The Working Poor* by David K. Shipler. Copyright © 2004, 2005 by David K. Shipler. Used by permission of Random House, Inc.

**Christian Science Monitor:** Excerpt from "In 2000 Years, Will the World Remember Disney or Plato," from the *Christian Science Monitor,* January 15, 2004. Reprinted by permission of the author.

**Da Capo Press:** Excerpt from *When I was Puerto Rican* by Esmeralda Santiago. Copyright © 1993 by Esmeralda Santiago. Reprinted by permission of the Perseus Group.

**HarperCollins Publishers:** "Harvest moon—," by Matsuo Basho– from *The Essential Haiku: Versions of Basho–, Buson & Issa,* edited and with an introduction by Robert Hass. Introduction and selection copyright © 1994 by Robert Hass. Unless otherwise noted, all translations © 1994 by Robert Hass. Reprinted by permission of HarperCollins Publishers.

**Random House:** "O What Is That Sound," from *Collected Poems* by W. H. Auden. Copyright © 1937 and renewed 1965 by W. H. Auden. Used by permission of Random House, Inc.

**New Directions:** "I Am Offering This Poem," from *Immigrants In Our Own Land* by Jimmy Santiago Baca. Copyright © 1979 by Jimmy Santiago Baca. Reprinted by permission of New Directions Publishing Corp.

**Stephen King:** "Sorry, Right Number" by Stephen King. Copyright © 1993 by Stephen King. Reprinted with permission.

## CONSULTANTS

*Janet Allen* © Duane McCubrey; *Arthur Applebee* © Mark Schmidt; *Kylene Beers* © Sam Dudgeon/Houghton Mifflin Harcourt; *Jim Burke* © Bruce Forrester; *Douglas Carnine* © Houghton Mifflin Harcourt; *Carol Jago* © Maggie's Photography, Pacific Palisades, CA; *Yvette Jackson* © Howard Gollub; *Robert Jimenez* © Tamra Stallings; *Judith Langer* © Mark Schmidt; *Robert Marzano* © Robert J. Marzano; *Donna Ogle* © Houghton Mifflin Harcourt; *Carol Booth Olson* © Dawson & Associates Photography; *Carol Tomlinson* © Gitchell's Studio; *May Lou McClosky* © Michael Romeo; *Lydia Stack* © Monica Ani; *William McBride* © William McBride; *David Considine* © Bill Caldwell; *Larkin Pauluzzi* © Gabriel Pauluzzi; *Lisa Scheffler* © Steven Scheffler.

## TABLE OF CONTENTS

**FM9** © Getty Images; **FM12** *left* © Firefly Productions/Corbis; *right* © Don Carstens/Brand X/Corbis; **FM13** © PunchStock; **FM14** *left* © Bettmann/Corbis; *right* Detail of *Girls from Guadalupita, New Mexico*, Miguel Martinez. Oil pastel on paper, 30" x 40". Michael McCormick Gallery, Taos, New Mexico; **FM15** © PunchStock; **FM16** *left* © Stone/Getty Images; *right* Detail of *Sparkling Sennen*, Ken Howard. Oil on board. Private collection. © Manya Igel Fine Arts, London, United Kingdom /Bridgeman Art Library; **FM17** © PunchStock; **FM18** *left* © Tom Salyer; *right* © Mary Rhodes/Animals Animals; **FM19** © PunchStock; **FM20** *left* Detail of *Brownstones*, Patti Mollica. © Patti Mollica/SuperStock; *right* Detail of *Farm in Haiti*, Roosevelt. Oil on canvas. Private collection. © SuperStock; **FM21** © PunchStock; **FM22** *left* Detail of *A Tempestuous Evening at the Maison de la Culture* (1937), Albert Lafloret. Oil on canvas, 54cm x 81 cm. Private collection. Photo © Bridgeman Art Library; *right* © Robert W. Kelley/Time Life Pictures/Getty Images; **FM23** © PunchStock; **FM24** *left* Detail of *Flower* (1964), Andy Warhol. Screenprint printed on white paper. 23" x 23". Photo © Art Resource, New York. © 2007 Andy Warhol Foundation for the Visual Arts/Artists Rights Society (ARS), New York; *right* From *Wings* by Christopher Myers. © 2000 by Christopher Myers. Reprinted by permission of Scholastic, Inc.; **FM25** © PunchStock; **FM26** *left* Detail of *Tumbling Flowers* (1954), Hyacinth Manning-Carner. © Hyacinth Manning-Carner/SuperStock; *right* Detail of *Infantry* (1997), James E. Faulkner. Oil on canvas. Collection of Nature's Nest Gallery, Golden, Colorado. Courtesy of the artist; **FM27** © PunchStock; **FM28** *left* © Images.com/Corbis; *right* Detail of *Young Man Studying* (Portrait of Langston Hughes) (1932), Hilda Wilkinson Brown. Oil on canvas. Photo by Gregory R. Staley. © Lilian T. Burwell/Howard University; **FM29** © PunchStock; **FM30** *left* © ArenaPal/Topham/The Image Works; *right* © The University of South Carolina Department of Theatre and Dance, Directed by Dennis Krausnick, Scenery by Kim Jennings, Lighting by Jim Hunter, Costumes by Kenneth Wolfe; **FM31** © PunchStock; **FM32** *left* © Araldo de Luca/Corbis; *right* Detail from *Ulysses and the Sirens* (1891), John William Waterhouse. Oil on canvas, 100 cm x 201.7 cm. National Gallery of Victoria, Melbourne, Australia. Photo © Bridgeman Art Library; *right* Detail from *Ulysses and the Sirens* (1891), John William Waterhouse. Oil on canvas, 100 cm x 201.7 cm. National Gallery of Victoria, Melbourne, Australia. Photo © Bridgeman Art Library; **FM33** © PunchStock; **FM34** *left* © PictureNet/Corbis; *right* © Ken Chernus/Stone/Getty Images.

## STUDENT GUIDE TO ACADEMIC SUCCESS

**FM39** © Age Fotostock America, Inc.; **FM40** © PunchStock; **FM 40** © Maggie's Photography, Pacific Palisades, CA; **FM60** © Mau Horng/Shutterstock; **FM62** Courtesy of The Advertising Archives.

## INTRODUCTORY UNIT

**1** *left* From *Wings* by Christopher Myers. © 2000 by Christopher Myers. Reprinted by permission of Scholastic, Inc.; *top right* © MGM/The Kobal Collection; *center right, Healing* (1996), Daniel Nevins. Oil on wood, 7.4" x 9.0". © Daniel Nevins/SuperStock; **2** *left* © ArenaPal/Topham/The Image Works; *right* © Araldo de Luca/Corbis; **3** *left, The Lord of the Rings: The Fellowship of the Ring* © 2001 New Line Productions, Inc. TM The Saul Zaentz Company, d/b/a Tolkien Enterprises under license to New Line Productions, Inc. All rights reserved. Photo appears courtesy of New Line Productions, Inc.; *right* Detail of *Tender Moments* (2000), Francks Deceus. Mixed media. 101.6 cm x 101.6 cm. Haitian. Private Collection. Photo © Bridgeman Art Library; **8** *1, 3* © Bettmann/Corbis; *4* © Peter Turnley/Corbis; *5* Commuter Rail Division of the Regional Transportation Authority, d/b/a/ Metra; **10** *1* © Universal/The Kobal Collection; *2* News footage of *All 9 Coal Miners Brought to Safety* courtesy of NBC News Archives; *3* © NBC/courtesy Everett Collection; *4 bench* © Tony Freeman/PhotoEdit; *inset* Courtesy Kansas Department of Transportation, Bureau Traffic Safety; *5* © Richard Thornton/ShutterStock; **11** © Jaume Gual/Age Fotostock America, Inc.; **15** *top* © Brian Hagiwara/Getty Images ; *bottom* © Thinkstock/Getty Images; **20** *left* © Corbis; *center* © Getty Images; *collage: bottom left* © Time & Life Pictures/Getty Images; *bottom right* Public Domain; **23** *left* © Brian Mcweeney/Getty Images; *center* © Dex Image/Getty Images; *right* © Flying Colours, Ltd./Getty Images.

## UNIT 1

**25** *left* Detail of *Raven* (1994), Jim Dine. Charcoal on wall, 128" x 98 1/2". Kunstverein Ludwigsburg, Germany, destroyed. © 2007 Jim Dine/Artists Rights Society (ARS), New York; *right* © Firefly Productions/Corbis; **26–27** © New Line Cinema/Photofest; **28** © Stockbyte; **36** © Reuters/Corbis; **37** © Bassouls Sophie/Corbis Sygma; **39** © Mary Evans Picture Library; **42** *Orinoco Jungle Life* (1894), A. Goering. Lithograph. © Mary Evans Picture Library; **46–47** Illustration by Steve Kirk/Wildlife Art Ltd. From *A Guide to Dinosaurs* © Weldon Owen Pty Ltd; **50** *Blue Morpho Butterfly* (1864–1865), Martin Johnson Heade. Oil on canvas, 12 1/4" x 10". Anonymous Collection; **55** NASA; **56** *The Time Machine*, 1960. Courtesy Everett Collection; **58** AP/Wide World Photos; **59** The Schlesinger Library, Radcliffe Institute, Harvard University; **61** © Terry Deroy Gruber/Getty Images; **65** *Castle at Noon*, William Low. © William Low; **66** © Earl and Nazima Kowall/Corbis; **71** Detail of *Downtime*, Dale Kennington. © Dale Kennington/SuperStock; **73** *foreground* © Bertrand Demée/Amana America/Getty Images; *background* © Lee Cates/Getty Images; **74** *man* © Keith Goldstein/Amana America Inc./Getty Images; *forest* © Getty Images; **77** *Tree Circle* (1992), Peter Schroth. Oil on paper, 7 1/2" x 8 1/2". © Peter Schroth; **79** © Wieteke Teppema/Getty Images; **84** © Jeff Greenberg/PhotoEdit; **85** AP/Wide World Photos; **87** *Reader with Green Hat* (1909), Henri Charles Manguin. Musée d'Art Moderne de la Ville de Paris, Paris. Photo © Art Resource, New York. © 2007 Artists

Rights Society (ARS), New York/ADAGP, Paris; **91** *La Mere de l'artiste* (1889), Paul Gauguin. Oil on canvas. Staatsgalerie, Stuttgart. Photo © akg-images; **93** *Pedro Mañach* (1901), Pablo Picasso. Oil on linen, 41 1/2" x 27"; framed: 53" x 38 7/8" x 6". National Gallery of Art, Washington, D.C., Chester Dale Collection. Photo © 2004 Board of Trustees of the National Gallery of Art. © 2007 Estate of Pablo Picasso/Artists Rights Society (ARS), New York (1963.10.53); **95** *The Third of May, 1808* (1814), Francisco de Goya y Lucientes. Oil on canvas, 266 cm x 345 cm. Museo del Prado, Madrid. Photo © Erich Lessing/Art Resource, New York; **100** © Michael Newman/PhotoEdit; **101** © Bettmann/Corbis; **103** *The Kiss* (1891), Edouard Vuillard. Oil on paper mounted on board, 23 cm x 16.5 cm. Philadelphia Museum of Art, The Louis E. Stern Collection, 1963. Photo © Philadelphia Museum of Art/Art Resource, New York. © 2007 Artists Rights Society (ARS), New York/ADAGP, Paris (1963-181-76); **104** *Woman Combing Her Hair*, Edgar Degas. Charcoal and pastel. © The Fine Art Society, London/Bridgeman Art Library; **107** © Corbis; **112, 113, 114** *The Lord of the Rings: The Fellowship of the Ring* © 2001 New Line Productions, Inc. TM The Saul Zaentz Company, d/b/a Tolkien Enterprises under license to New Line Productions, Inc. All rights reserved. Photos by Pierre Vinet. Photos appear courtesy of New Line Productions, Inc.; **114** *background* © Stone/Getty Images; **116** © Eric Gaillard/Reuters News Picture Archive; **117** © Corbis; **119** *Alley* (1942), Jacob Lawrence. Gouache on composition board, 27 5/8" x 24". Clark Atlanta University Art Collections. Gift of David Levy. © 2007 Gwendolyn Knight Lawrence/Artists Rights Society (ARS), New York; **120** *Woman Worker* (1951), Charles White. Photo © Walter O. Evans Collection of African American Art/The Charles White Archives; **126** AP/Wide World Photos; **127** © Lauren Chelec; **129** © Bettmann/Corbis; **130** © Keeneland-Cook Association, Inc.; **132–133** © Bettmann/Corbis; **134** © Bettmann/Corbis; **139** © Morgan Collection/Getty Images; **140** *bottom* © Bettmann/Corbis; *top* © Hulton Archive/Getty Images; **141** *right* © Corbis; *left* © Hulton Archive/Getty Images; **144** © Corbis; **145** *bottom* Photo by Nathaniel Justice; *top* © Bettmann/Corbis; **147** *Raven* (1994), Jim Dine. Charcoal on wall, 128" x 98 1/2". Kunstverein Ludwigsburg, Germany, destroyed. © 2007 Jim Dine/Artists Rights Society (ARS), New York; **150** *Red Passion* (1996), Jim Dine. Cardboard relief intaglio. Image size 33 1/8" x 59". Paper size 39 1/2" x 63 7/8". Published by Pace Editions, Inc. Edition of 12. © 2007 Jim Dine/Artists Rights Society (ARS), New York; **151** *The Back of a Man with a Rose*, René Magritte. Private Collection Bloch, Santa Monica, CA. Photo © SuperStock, Inc. © 2007 C. Herscovici, Brussels/Artists Rights Society (ARS), New York; **154** © Aaron Horowitz/Corbis; **155** © Seth Joel/Corbis; **157** © Joel Sartore/Getty Images; **159** © William Whitehurst/Corbis; **160** © Getty Images; **163** © Andrea Pistolesi/Getty Images; **167** © Corbis; **168** © Lorna Clark/Getty Images; **171** AP/Wide World Photos; **174** © Craig Aurness/Corbis; **185** © Mary Kate Denny/PhotoEdit; **192** Courtesy of The Advertising Archives; **198** © Siede Preis/Getty Images.

## UNIT 2

**199** *left* Detail of *Louise Augusta, Queen of Prussia* (1801), Marie Louise Elisabeth Vigée-LeBrun. Pastel, 51 cm x 41 cm. Stiftung PreuSSische Schlösser und Gärten Berlin-Brandenburg. Photo by J.P. Anders; *right* © BananaStock/Punchstock; **200–201** © Pawel Libera/Corbis; **200** *left* Public Domain; *right* © Paul C. Chauncey/Corbis; **209** Photo by Jim Lundquist/Sterling Lord Literistic, Inc., on behalf of Joan Bauer; **211** © Peter M. Fisher/Corbis; **214** © George Diebold Photography/

Iconica/Getty Images; **217** © Ian Kahn/Iconica/Getty Images; **222** © Mauro Panci/Corbis; **223** © Chris Hellier/Corbis; **225** *Louise Augusta, Queen of Prussia* (1801), Marie Louise Elisabeth Vigée-LeBrun. Pastel, 51 cm x 41 cm. Stiftung PreuSSische Schlösser und Gärten Berlin-Brandenburg. Photo by J.P. Anders; **227** *A Paris Street, Rain* (1877), Gustave Caillebotte. Oil on canvas. The Art Institute of Chicago. Photo © Erich Lessing/Art Resource, New York; **229** *The Ball*, Victor Gilbert. Photo © Christie's Images/Corbis; **232** *The Laundress* (1869), Edgar Degas. Pastel, white crayon and charcoal. Musée d'Orsay, Paris, France. Photo © Réunion des Musées Nationaux/Art Resource, New York; **237** © Dave Nagel/Stone/Getty Images; **238** *foreground* © Scott Maxwell/LuMaxArt/ShutterStock; *top left* © Creatas/PunchStock; *top right* © PunchStock; *bottom left, bottom right* © Jupiterimages Corporation; **240** © Andersen Ross/Getty Images; **241** Photo by Madison Nye; **243** *Inspiration* (1994), Daniel Nevins. Oil, acrylic and collage on wood, 6.6" x 9.0". © Private Collection/Daniel Nevins/SuperStock; **246** *Healing* (1996), Daniel Nevins. Oil on wood, 7.4" x 9.0". © Daniel Nevins/SuperStock; **250** *right* Detail of *Healing* (1996), Daniel Nevins. Oil on wood, 7.4" x 9.0". © Daniel Nevins/SuperStock; *left* Detail of *Inspiration* (1994), Daniel Nevins. Oil, acrylic and collage on wood, 6.6" x 9.0". © Private Collection/Daniel Nevins/SuperStock; **254** © Gabe Palmer/Corbis; **255** © Mitchell Gerber/Corbis; **257** *Woman with Umbrella*, Bill Farnsworth. Photo © Images.com/Corbis; **259** *Ancilla with an Orange* (1956), Dod Procter. Oil on canvas. Royal West of England Academy, Bristol, United Kingdom. Photo © Bridgeman Art Library; **262** *Lemonade* (2002), Michele Hausman. © Michele Hausman; **264** © Getty Images; **268** © Peter Turnley/Corbis; **269** © Amy Etra/Time Life Pictures/Getty Images; **271** © Didrik Johnck/Corbis; **273** © Chris Curry/Hedgehoghouse.com; **277** © Didrik Johnck/Corbis; **283** © Adam Pretty/Getty Images; **286** © Jeff Greenberg/Age Fotostock America, Inc.; **287** *top* Courtesy Pat Mora/Photo by Cheron Bayman; *bottom* Photo by David Burkhalter. Reprinted by permission of the University of Arizona Press; **289** *Girls from Guadalupita, New Mexico*, Miguel Martinez. Oil pastel on paper, 30" x 40". Michael McCormick Gallery, Taos, New Mexico; **290** *Navajo Power Plant* (1990). © Shonto Begay/Avery Collection of American Indian Painting; **292** *white gloves* © Getty Images; *Empress Michiko* © Andy Rain-Pool/Getty Images; *man* © Getty Images; *frames* © Image Farm, Inc.; *working gloves* © Rubberball Productions/Getty Images; **293** *top* AP/Wide World Photos; *bottom* © Fred Viebahn/Rita Dove; **295** © Bettmann/Corbis; **298** From *Americans Who Tell The Truth*, Robert Shetterly. Used by permission of Dutton Children's Books, a division of Penguin Young Readers Group, a member of Penguin Group, Inc. 345 Huds on Street, New York, NY 10014. All rights reserved. © Robert Shetterly; **302** © Joseph Sohm/ChromoSohm Inc./Corbis; **313** © Houghton Mifflin Harcourt; **321** Photo © Andrew Yates; Advertisement © St. Edward's University/LatinWorks; **326** © Siede Preis/Getty Images.

## UNIT 3

**327** *left* Burial niches with fresco of Christ Pantocrator. Catacomb of San Callisto, Rome, Italy. Photo © Erich Lessing/Art Resource, New York; *right* © Keith Kapple/SuperStock; **328–329** © Sekai Bunka/Premium/Panoramic Images; **332** © The Kobal Collection; **336** Peanuts: © United Feature Syndicate, Inc.; **337** © Slim Aarons/Getty Images; **339** *Anna Kuerner* (1971), Andrew Wyeth. Tempera on panel. Private collection. Photo © 1995 Andrew Wyeth; *background* © Getty Images; **340** Detail of *Wild Dog Mushroom* (1974), Bob Timberlake. © Bob Timberlake;

343 Detail of *Winter Sun* (1971), Bob Timberlake. © Bob Timberlake;
344 Detail of *Mrs. Dorset's Kitchen* (1973), Bob Timberlake. © Bob
Timberlake; 346 Detail of *Another World* (1974), Bob Timberlake. ©
Bob Timberlake; 349 *Christmas Orange* (1975), Bob Timberlake. © 1975
Bob Timberlake; 354 © Stanley Chou/Getty Images; 355 © Bettmann/
Corbis; 357 *Sparkling Sennen*, Ken Howard. Oil on board. Private
collection. © Manya Igel Fine Arts, London/Bridgeman Art Library;
361 *Reflections* (1970), Ken Danby. Original egg tempera, 38" x 52." ©
Ken Danby/Gallery Moos, Toronto, Canada; 364–365 *Ice Blue* (1981),
Susan Shatter. Oil on canvas, 40" x 90." Private collection. Courtesy of
the Fischbach Gallery, New York; 370 © Photographer's Choice/Getty
Images; 371 © Bettmann/Corbis; 373 © Stone/Getty Images; 377
Burial niches with fresco of Christ Pantocrator. Catacomb of San Callisto,
Rome, Italy. Photo © Erich Lessing/Art Resource, New York; 378 ©
Punchstock/Royalty Free; 380 © Getty Images; 384 © Nik Wheeler/
Corbis; 385 *top, center, bottom* Footage from *Ethan Allen Poe: The Soul
of Terror, The Cask of Amontillado.* Courtesy of Film Odyssey, Inc.; 386
*top, bottom* Footage from *Ethan Allen Poe: The Soul of Terror, The Cask of
Amontillado.* Courtesy of Film Odyssey, Inc.; *background* © Jupiterimages
Corporation; 387 *top center* © Image Farm, Inc.; *bottom left* © Brand X
Pictures/Fotosearch Stock Photography; *all others* © Getty Images; 388
© Paul Katz/Index Stock Imagery/Jupiterimages Corporation; 389 ©
Rick Friedman/Corbis; 391 © Patrik Giardino/Corbis; 392–393 © Ric
Ergenbright/Ric Ergenbright Photography; 397 © Creatas/Jupiterimages
Corporation; 401 © Margaretta K. Mitchell; 404 Public Domain; 406
© SuperStock; 407 *bottom* Courtesy The Land Institute, Prairie Writers
Circle; *top* © Christopher Felver/Corbis; 409 © Kiefner/Premium Stock/
Jupiterimages Corporation; 410 © John Warden/Index Stock Imagery/
Photolibrary; 412 © Daryl Benson/Masterfile; 423 © PhotoDisc/Getty
Images; 430 © Siede Preis/Getty Images.

## UNIT 4

431 *left, Mama's Cradle,* April Harrison. Mixed media collage on
canvas board, 14" x 18". © April Harrison; *right* © Dorothea Lange/
Corbis; 432–433 © Richard Cummins/Corbis; 432 *left* © Corbis; 434
© Kevin Anthony Horgan/Getty Images; 440 © Digital Vision Ltd./
SuperStock; 441 © Olan Mills; 443 Detail of *Full Spittoon* (1974),
Bob Timberlake. Watercolor. Private Collection. © Bob Timberlake;
447 *Field of Hope,* Charly Palmer. Mixed media collage on canvas, 24"
x 18". © Charly Palmer; 450 *New Dreams* (2002), Ernest Crichlow.
Lithograph (Edition 150), 24 3/4" x 16 3/4". Photo by Maureen Turci,
Mojo Portfolio. Courtesy of the Ernest Crichlow Estate; 455 © Jeff
Greenberg/PhotoEdit; 458 *center* © fantasista/ShutterStock; *background*
Photo by Teresa Foote/Houghton Mifflin Harcourt; 460 FOXTROT. ©
1997 Bill Amend. Reprinted with permission of UNIVERSAL PRESS
SYNDICATE. All rights reserved; 461 Courtesy of James Hurst; 463
*Richard at Age Five* (1944), Alice Neel. Oil on canvas, 26" x 14." ©
Estate of Alice Neel. Courtesy Robert Miller Gallery, New York; 465
*Cypress Swamp, Texas* (1940), Florence McClung. Oil on masonite, 24" x
30" . The Ogden Museum of Southern Art. Gift of the Roger H. Ogden
Collection. The Ogden Museum of Southern Art; 469 © Vincent
McIndoe/Images.com/Corbis; 470 *Autumn Embers (Frosted Scarlet Sage)*
(1944), Charles Burchfield. Watercolor on paper, 22 1/2" x 28". ©
Estate of Charles Burchfield. Courtesy DC Moore Gallery, New York;
472 © Mary Rhodes/Animals Animals; 476 © Sam Abell/National
Geographic Image Collection; 480 © Spencer Grant/PhotoEdit; 481
© Richard McNamee; 483 © Keren Su/Corbis; 484 © Images.com/
Corbis; 487 © Dean Conger/Corbis; 492 © Richard T. Nowitz/Corbis;

493 © Getty Images; 495 *Mama's Cradle,* April Harrison. Mixed media
collage on canvas board, 14" x 18". © April Harrison; 497 *Circle of Joy,*
Keith Mallett. © Keith Mallett Studio, Inc./www.keithmallett.com;
500 © Craig C. Sheumaker/PanStock/Jupiterimages Corporation; 501
*top* © ChinaStock; *center* The Granger Collection, New York; *bottom* ©
Barbara Savage Cheresh; 502 *Viewing Plum Blossoms by Moonlight,* Ma
Yuan. Ink and color on silk, 9 7/8" x 10 1/2". Gift of John M. Crawford
Jr. (1986.493.2). Photo by Malcolm Varon. © Metropolitan Museum of
Art, New York/Art Resource, New York; 503 © Bill Binzen/Corbis; 504
© Tom Salyer; 506 © Pete Saloutos/Corbis; 507 *top* © Lawrence Lucier/
Getty Images; *bottom* © Photo by Paul H. Mark; 509 *top* © Corbis;
*left* © Getty Images; *right* © Rykoff Collection/Corbis; 512 *center* ©
Ed Sullivan Show/Photofest; *bottom* © Trinette Reed/Corbis; 515 ©
Richard Cummins/SuperStock; 518 © Catherine Karnow/Corbis;
520 © Anthony-Masterson/Foodpix/Getty Images/Jupiterimages
Corporation; 524 © Richard Sisk/Jupiterimages; 535 © Design Pics,
Inc./Alamy Images; 543 © TiPannell/Corbis Super RF/Alamy Ltd; 548
© Siede Preis/Getty Images.

## UNIT 5

549 *left* Detail of *Cow's Skull: Red, White, and Blue* (1931), Georgia
O'Keeffe. Oil on canvas, 39 7/8" x 35 7/8". The Metropolitan Museum
of Art, Alfred Stieglitz Collection, 1952. Photo © Georgia O'Keeffe/
Metropolitan Museum of Art (52.203). © 2008 Georgia O'Keeffe
Museum/Artists Rights Society (ARS), New York; *right* © Joseph Sohm/
Visions of America/Corbis; 550 *far left* © Creatas Images/Jupiterimages
Corporation; *top center* © Karl Weatherly/Getty Images; *bottom center*
© Time & Life Pictures/Getty Images; *bottom right* Public Domain;
551 © Norbert Rosing/National Geographic Image Collection; 553
© Getty Images; 555 © Matthew Frey/Wood Ronsaville Harlin; 557
© Erik Simonsen/Getty Images; 558 © Bryan and Cherry Alexander;
559 © Taro Yamasaki/Time Life Pictures/Getty Images; 561 Detail of
*Harvest Scene with Twelve People,* R. Mervilus. Oil on canvas. Private
collection. © SuperStock; 563 *Farm in Haiti,* Roosevelt. Oil on canvas.
Private Collection. © SuperStock; 565 *Brownstones,* Patti Mollica.
© Patti Mollica/SuperStock; 568 © Abigail Pope/LuckyPix; 569 ©
Neville Elder/Corbis; 571 Phillips Collection/AP/Wide World Photos;
573 *Cow's Skull: Red, White, and Blue* (1931), Georgia O'Keeffe. Oil on
canvas, 39 7/8" x 35 7/8". The Metropolitan Museum of Art, Alfred
Stieglitz Collection, 1952. Photo © Georgia O'Keeffe/Metropolitan
Museum of Art (52.203). © 2008 Georgia O'Keeffe Museum/Artists
Rights Society (ARS), New York; 574 *Jimson Weed* (1932), Georgia
O'Keeffe. The Georgia O'Keeffe Museum, Santa Fe, New Mexico. ©
2008 Georgia O'Keeffe Museum/Artists Rights Society (ARS), New
York. Photo © Art Resource, New York; 578 © Reuters/Corbis; 579
© Corbis Sygma; 580 *photo* © Hanny Paul/Gamma Press USA, Inc.;
*masthead* © National Geographic Society. Reprinted by permission of
the National Geographic Society; 581 *left* CT-scan of Iceman's thorax.
© Regional Hospital of Bolzano/South Tyrol Museum of Archaeology/
www.iceman.it; *right* © South Tyrol Museum of Archaeology; 582
*bottom* © GeoNova LLC; *right* © South Tyrol Museum of Archaeology;
583 © Hinterleitner Gerhard/Gamma Press USA, Inc.; 584, 585, 586,
587 Photos from *The Bone Detective* © Charles Fellenbaum, Boulder,
Colorado; 590 AP/Wide World Photos; 593 © Jeff Riedel/Creative
Photographers, Inc.; 595 © Hudson Derek/Corbis Sygma; 597 © Jeff
Riedel/Creative Photographers, Inc.; 600 Guy Wathen/AP/Wide World
Photos; 601 *top, center left, center right, bottom right* News footage of *All
9 Coal Miners Brought to Safety* courtesy of NBC News Archives; *bottom*

© by CNN. Reprinted by permission of Cable News Network; *bottom inset* © Getty Images; **602** *top left, bottom left* News footage of *All 9 Coal Miners Brought to Safety* courtesy of NBC News Archives; *bottom* © by CNN. Reprinted by permission of Cable News Network; *bottom inset* © Getty Images; *background* © Larry Lee Photography/Corbis; **603** © IT International Ltd./eStock Photo/Jupiterimages Corporation; **604** © Andrew McKim/Masterfile; **605** The Granger Collection, New York; **606** *Veil of Elegance,* Peter Miller. Private Collection. Photo © Bridgeman Art Library; **612** © Mike Powell/Getty Images; **613** © Gene Blevins/Corbis; **615** Photo by Kerry Vitali; **617** *The Cashier* (2003), Lisa Reinke. Oil on canvas, 5" x 7". © Lisa Reinke; **620** GARFIELD © 2008 Paws, Inc. Reprinted with permission of UNIVERSAL PRESS SYNDICATE. All rights reserved; **621** © Banana Stock/Photolibrary; **626** © ESA-Corvaja; **627** © Jupiterimages Corporation; *inset* © BenC/ShutterStock; **632** © Daryl Benson/Masterfile; **643** © Justin Horrocks/istockphoto.com; **646** © Daily News Leader. All rights reserved. Reproduced with the permission of Gannett Co., Inc. by NewsBank, Inc.; **650** © Siede Preis/Getty Images.

## UNIT 6

**651** *left, A Tempestuous Evening at the Maison de la Culture* (1937), Albert Lafloret. Oil on canvas, 54 cm x 81 cm. Private collection. Photo © Bridgeman Art Library; *right* © Bettmann/Corbis; **652–653** © Spencer Platt/Getty Images; **652** *left* © Leon Zernitsky/Getty Images; **657** © Ad Council/Firewise Communities; **660** © Alex Wong/Getty Images; **661** © Time Life Pictures/Getty Images; **663** © Bettmann/Corbis; **664–665** © Robert W. Kelley/Time Life Pictures/Getty Images; **664** *top left* © Paul Schutzer/Time Life Pictures/Getty Images; **665** *top right* © MPI/Getty Images; **667** AP/Wide World Photos; **670** © Tatsuyuki Tayama/Fujifotos/The Image Works; **671** © Thierry Orban/Corbis Sygma; **673** © Ron Sachs/CNP/Corbis; **674** © Corbis Sygma; **675** © Ron Sachs/CNP/Corbis; **676** © Eurelios/Phototake; **680** © Jeffrey Sylvester/Getty Images; **681** © Mike Baldwin/www.CartoonStock.com; **682** © Peter Ciresa/Index Stock Imagery, Inc.; **684** AP/Wide World Photos; **685** © Reuters/Corbis; **686** © Ed Quinn/Corbis; **689** © The Image Bank/Getty Images; **690** © Mauro Fermariello/Photo Researchers, Inc.; **694** *inset* Courtesy Kansas Department of Transportation, Bureau of Traffic Safety; *background* © Tony Freeman/PhotoEdit; **695** *top, Billy Thomas* Public Service Announcement courtesy of Boys and Girls Clubs of America; *bottom, How Far would You Go?* Public Service Announcement courtesy of Peace Corps of America; **696** *top left, Billy Thomas* Public Service Announcement courtesy of Boys and Girls Clubs of America; *bottom left* © Corbis/Second Line Search; *background* © Layne Kennedy/Corbis; **697** © NCPC; **698** © Nicholas Rigg/Getty Images; **699** *bottom* © Bassouls Sophie/Corbis Sygma; *top* © Washington Post Writers Group; **701** © Chip Simons/Getty Images; **703** Detail of *Tourists Beware: New Buffalo Speed Trap* (1985), Roger Brown. Oil on canvas, 48" x 48". © The School of the Art Institute of Chicago and the Brown family; **704** *Clouds Over Alabama or Midnight in Alabama* (1994), Roger Brown. Oil on canvas, 48" x 72". © The School of the Art Institute of Chicago and the Brown family; **706** Detail of *Tourists Beware: New Buffalo Speed Trap* (1985), Roger Brown. Oil on canvas, 48" x 48". © The School of the Art Institute of Chicago and the Brown family; **710** *top left* Photo by Teresa Foote/Houghton Mifflin Harcourt; *top right, bottom* © SuperStock Inc.; *background* © Cracknell/ShutterStock; **712** © J. David Andrews/Masterfile; **723** © Michelle D. Bridwell/PhotoEdit; **729** © Puzant Apkarian/Age Fotostock; **736** © Siede Preis/Getty Images.

## UNIT 7

**737** *left* From *Wings* by Christopher Myers. © 2000 by Christopher Myers. Reprinted by permission of Scholastic, Inc.; *right* © Pete Turner/Getty Images; **738–739** *right* The Granger Collection, New York; **738** *left* Public Domain; *center, The Cow Jumped Over the Moon* (1885), Randolph Caldecott. From *R. Caldecott's Second Collection of Pictures and Songs*/Mary Evans Picture Library; **748** © Colin Paterson/Getty Images; **749** *top* © Bettmann/Corbis; *center* © 2002 Margaretta Mitchell; *bottom* © Fred Viebahn/Rita Dove; **751** *Tender Moments* (2000), Francks Deceus. Mixed media, 101.6 cm x 101.6 cm. Haitian. Private Collection. Photo © Bridgeman Art Library; **752** *Mother and Child by Grand Canal* (2000), Hung Liu. Oil on canvas, 80" x 80". © Hung Liu/Rena Bransten Gallery; **753** *Ice Cream Dessert* (1959), Andy Warhol. Photo © Andy Warhol Foundation/Corbis © 2008 Andy Warhol Foundation for the Visual Arts/Artists Rights Society (ARS), New York; **756** © Kevin Fleming/Corbis; **757** *top* © Bettmann/Corbis; *center* © Touhig Sion/Corbis Sygma; *bottom* © Christopher Felver/Corbis; **759** Untitled (2001), Laura Owens. Watercolor, color pencil, collage and photo on paper. 14" x 10". LO 185d. Courtesy of Gavin Brown's Enterprise, New York; **760** *Sea Turtle* (1985), Andy Warhol. Synthetic polymer paint and silkscreen ink on canvas, 42" x 50". Photo © Art Resource, New York. © 2007 Andy Warhol Foundation for the Visual Arts/Artists Rights Society (ARS), New York; **761** *Flower* (1964), Andy Warhol. Screenprint printed on white paper. 23" x 23". Photo © Art Resource, New York. © 2007 Andy Warhol Foundation for the Visual Arts/Artists Rights Society (ARS), New York; **762** *top* J. P. Beato III/The Battalion/Texas Agricultural and Military University. © J. P. Beato III; *bottom* AP/Wide World Photos; **764** AP/Wide World Photos; **765** *top* © Nancy Crampton; *bottom* © Wojda/Free/Corbis Sygma; **766–767** © Franco Vogt/Corbis; **768** *Municipal Bonds* (2004), Byron Spicer. Mixed media, 45" x 45". © Byron Spicer; **771** © Bob Daemmrich/PhotoEdit; **772** *photo* © Spencer Platt/Getty Images; *masthead* The New York Times Company; **774** Leslloyd F. Alleyne Jr./Journal Inquirer/AP/Wide World Photos; **775** *top* © Christopher Felver/Corbis; *center* © Getty Images; *bottom* Photo taken by Colin Beltz and used courtesy of the Red Wing Republican Eagle; **777** From *Wings* by Christopher Myers. © 2000 by Christopher Myers. Reprinted by permission of Scholastic, Inc.; **779, 781** Photos by Sharon Hoogstraten; **783** © Corbis; **786** © Corbis; **787** © Harry Redl/Time Life Pictures/Getty Images; **789** *Returning to the Trenches* (1914–15), C. R. W. Nevinson. Oil on canvas, 51 cm x 76 cm. Gift of the Massey Collection of English Painting, 1946. Photo © National Gallery of Canada, Ottawa. © The Nevinson Estate/Bridgeman Art Library; **790** Detail of *Returning to the Trenches* (1914–15), C. R. W. Nevinson. Oil on canvas, 51 cm x 76 cm. Gift of the Massey Collection of English Painting, 1946. Photo © National Gallery of Canada, Ottawa. © The Nevinson Estate/Bridgeman Art Library; **792** © Tobbe/zefa/Corbis; **793** *top* © Pixtal/Age Fotostock America, Inc.; *bottom* National Archives; **795** *The First and the Last Steps,* Emilio Longoni. Private Collection. © Alinari/Art Resource, New York; **796** *In the Beechwoods,* William Samuel Jay. Oil on canvas, 91.4" x 122". Private collection. © Bourne Gallery, Reigate, Surrey/ Bridgeman Art Library; **798** © Jason Ernst/Age Fotostock America, Inc.; **809** © ColorBlind Images/Getty Images; **816** © Siede Preis/Getty Images.

## UNIT 8

**817** *left, Tumbling Flowers* (1954), Hyacinth Manning-Carner. © Hyacinth Manning-Carner/SuperStock; *right* © Brand X Pictures/Getty Images; **818–819** *The Persistence of Memory* (1931), Salvador Dali. Oil on canvas, 9 1/2" x 13". Museum of Modern Art, New York. © 2000 Foundation Gala-Salvador Dali/VEGAP © 2007 Salvador Dali, Gala-Salvador Dali Foundation/Artists Rights Society (ARS), New York; **818** *left* © Jack Launois/Black Star; **822** *left* © Bettmann/Corbis; *right* © Darryl Bush/Getty Images; **826** © Ron Fehling/Masterfile; **827** © Marilyn Knapp Litt; **829** *Infantry* (1997), James E. Faulkner. Oil on canvas. Collection of Nature's Nest Gallery, Golden, Colorado. Courtesy of the artist; **833** *Class of '67* (1987), Charlie Shobe. Oil on canvas. Photo © Michael Tropea/National Vietnam Veterans Art Museum, Chicago; **835** *Chopper Lift-Out* (1967), Ken McFadyen. Oil on canvas on hardboard, 30.6 cm x 48.2 cm. © The Australian War Memorial Collection; **840** © Swim Ink 2, LLC/Corbis; **842** © CinemaPhoto/Corbis; **843** © Berko/Time Life Pictures/Getty Images; **845** *The Princess and the Tin Box* (1948), James Thurber. © renewed 1976 by Rosemary A. Thurber. Reprinted by arrangement with Rosemary A. Thurber and Barbara Hogenson Agency; **848** © akg-images; **849** *top* © MGM/The Kobal Collection; *top center* © Universal/The Kobal Collection; *bottom center, bottom* © Paramount/The Kobal Collection; **850** *top left, bottom left, The Birds* © 1963 Alfred J. Hitchcock Productions, Inc., courtesy of Universal Studios Licensing LLLP; *background* © Joe McDonald/Corbis; **851** *left* © MGM/The Kobal Collection; *right* © MGM/The Kobal Collection; **852** © Lluis Real/Age Fotostock America, Inc.; **853** Photo © Steven Hopp; **855** © Tadashi Miwa/Getty Images; *inset* © Sarma Ozols/Getty Images; **856** *center left* © Anthony Johnson/Getty Images; *left* © ImageState-Pictor/PictureQuest/Jupiterimages Corporation; *center right* © Stone/Getty Images; *right* © Tadashi Miwa/Getty Images; **860** © Tony Anderson/Getty Images; **861** © Barbara Savage Cheresh; **863** © 2003 Aflo Foto Agency; **864** *left* © Tom Lazar/Earth Scenes/Animals Animals; *right* Roy Toft/National Geographic Image Collection; **868** © Susan Meiselas/Magnum Photos; **869** The Granger Collection, New York; **870, 871** Illustrations by Ingrid Hess; **874** © Alamy Images; **875** © Mike Simons/Getty Images; **877** *Tumbling Flowers* (1954), Hyacinth Manning-Carner. © Hyacinth Manning-Carner/SuperStock; **878** *Sleeping Couple I* (2000), Hyacinth Manning-Carner. © Hyacinth Manning-Carner/SuperStock; **880** © Pete Stone/Corbis; **881** *top* © Bettmann/Corbis; *bottom* © Hulton Archive/Getty Images; **883** © Bettmann/Corbis; **884–888** The Granger Collection, New York; **890** © Alain Choisnet/Getty Images; **901** © Rubberball/Punchstock; **909** © Lisa Dearing/Alamy Ltd.; **914** © Siede Preis/Getty Images.

## UNIT 9

**915** *left, Jazz Player III* (1991), Freshman Brown. Collage. © SuperStock; *right* © Frans Lemmens/Iconica Limited/Getty Images; **916–917** *right* © Margo Cohn; **918** © Charles and Josette Lenars/Corbis; **920** © Bettmann/Corbis; **923** © J. Sohm/VOA LLC/Panoramic Images; **924** © The Image Bank/Getty Images; **925** © Michael Brennan/Corbis; **927** © Aaron M. Priest Literary Agency, Inc.; **930** Courtesy of the *Limerick Leader*, Limerick, Ireland; **933** © Hulton Archive/Getty Images; **940** © Chris Rainier/Corbis; **941** © N. Scott Momaday/Courtesy of Royce Carlton, Inc.; **943** © David Muench/Corbis; **945** © Courtney Milne; **951** © The New York Public Library/Art Resource, New York; **953** Detail of *Cotton Choppers* (1965), Benny Andrews. Oil on canvas, 25" x 35." Courtesy of Michael Rosenfeld Gallery, LLC, New York, New York and ACA Galleries, New York. © Estate of Benny Andrews/Licensed by VAGA, New York; **955** *Brothers* (1934), Malvin Gray Johnson. Smithsonian American Art Museum, Washington, D. C. Photo © Smithsonian American Art Museum, Washington, D.C./Art Resource, New York; **957** *The Woodshed* (1944), Andrew Wyeth. Tempera on panel. Collection of the Brandywine River Museum. Bequest of C. Porter Schutt, 1995. © Andrew Wyeth; **962** Photo by Suraiya Nathani; **963** Photo of Judith Ortiz Cofer is reprinted with permission from the publisher Arte Publico Press. © 2005, University of Houston, Houston, Texas; **965** *top, center, background* © Corbis; *bottom* © Bettmann/Corbis; **968** Detail of *Study, or The Schoolgirl* (1933–1934), Jean Puy. Oil on canvas, 61cm x 72 cm. Photo © Musée National d'Art Moderne, Centre Pompidou, Paris/Giraudon/Bridgeman Art Library. © 2010 Artists Rights Society (ARS), New York/ADAGP, Paris; **971** *Rag in Window* (1959), Alice Neel. 33" x 24". Gift of the Estate of Arthur M. Bullowa. Courtesy of the Philadelphia Museum of Art. © Estate of Alice Neel. Courtesy Robert Miller Gallery, New York; **973** Detail of *Loneliness* (1970), Alice Neel. Oil on canvas, 80" x 38". Gift of Arthur M. Bullowa, in honor of the 50th Anniversary of the National Gallery of Art. Photo by Lyle Peterzell. Image © 2005 Board of Trustees, National Gallery of Art, Washington, D.C. © Estate of Alice Neel. Courtesy Robert Miller Gallery, New York; **978** © 1963 Bill Mauldin. Reprinted with special permission from the Chicago Sun-Times, Inc., 2004; **980** © Bettmann/Corbis; **982** © Ed Kashi/Corbis; **983** *top* Yale Collection of American Literature, Beinecke Rare Book and Manuscript Library; *bottom* © Corbis; **985** © Images.com/Corbis; **987** *Young Man Studying* (Portrait of Langston Hughes) (1932), Hilda Wilkinson Brown. Oil on canvas. Photo by Gregory R. Staley. © Lilian T. Burwell/Howard University; **990** © Ryan McVay/Getty Images; **991** *top* © Roger-Viollet/The Image Works, Inc.; *center* © Bettmann/Corbis; *bottom* © Frances M. Roberts/NewsCom; **992** *Millet Fields with the Sun and the Moon* (1600s), Anonymous. Japanese. Pair of six-panel screens. Ink, colors and gold leaf on paper, 150.5 cm x 348.8 cm (59.25" x 37.3"). Restricted gift of the Rice Foundation, 1989.625 b: overall. Reproduction, The Art Institute of Chicago. Photo © The Art Institute of Chicago; **993** *Jazz Player III* (1991), Freshman Brown. Collage. © SuperStock; **994** © Digital Vision Ltd./SuperStock; **996** © Sam Barricklow/Jupiterimages Corporation; **1005** © Bettmann/Corbis; **1013** © Archive Holdings Inc./Getty Images; **1018** © Siede Preis/Getty Images.

## UNIT 10

**1019** *left, The Proposal* (1872), Adolphe-William Bouguereau. Oil on canvas, 64 3/8" x 44". Gift of Mrs. Elliott L. Kamen, in memory of her father, Bernard R. Armour, 1960 (60.122). © The Metropolitan Museum of Art, New York/Art Resource, New York; *right* © ArenaPal/Topham/The Image Works; **1020–1021** *bottom right, Romeo and Juliet,* Claire Danes, 1996 © 20th Century Fox/courtesy Everett Collection; **1020** *top center* The Granger Collection, New York; *center left, Francesca da Rimini* (1837), William Dyce. Oil on canvas, 142 cm x 176 cm. National Gallery of Scotland, Edinburgh. © Bridgeman Art Library; *center right* Clip from *Romeo and Juliet* courtesy of Paramount Pictures; *bottom left, A Bridal Couple,* (about 1470). German. Oil on wood, 62.2 cm x 36.5 cm. © The Cleveland Museum of Art, 2004. Dellia E. and L.E. Holden Funds, 1932.179; **1022** *top, center, right* The Granger Collection, New York; **1023** Illustration by John James/Temple Rogers Artists' Agents; **1024** *left, Much Ado About Nothing*

poster © Samuel Goldwyn Films, Courtesy Everett Collection; *right* © 1995 Lee Lorenz/The New Yorker Collection from cartoonbank.com. All rights reserved; **1025** The Granger Collection, New York; **1026** © Andrea Pistolesi/Getty Images; **1034** © 1993 Jay Ullah/Stern/Black Star; **1037** *left* © Dmitrij Matvejev/Anzelika Cholina Dance Theatre, Lithuania; *center left* © ArenaPal/Topham/The Image Works; *center* Chicago Shakespeare Theater's production of *Romeo and Juliet* toured to 14 communities in the Southeast United States, as part of the National Endowment for the Arts Shakespeare in American Communities initiative. Martin Yurek as Mercutio (left) and Ryan Kitley as Tybalt (right). Photo by: SteveLeonardPhotography.com, courtesy Chicago Shakespeare Theater; *center right* © ArenaPal/Topham/The Image Works; *right* Marin Hinkle as Juliet and Jay Goede as Romeo in The Shakespeare Theatre Company's 1993–1994 production of *Romeo and Juliet,* directed by Barry Kyle. Photo by Richard Anderson; **1039** © Dmitrij Matvejev/Anzelika Cholina Dance Theatre, Lithuania; **1045** *top left* © Robbie Jack/Corbis; *bottom left* ©ArenaPal/Topham /The Image Works, Inc.; *center* Chicago Shakespeare Theater and Second City Theatrical's production of *the Romeo and Juliet Musical, The People vs. Friar Lawrence, The Man Who Killed Romeo and Juliet.* Nicole Parker as Juliet and Keegan-Michael Key as Romeo. Photo by Michael Brosilow, courtesy Chicago Shakespeare Theater; **1050** Jean Stapleton as Nurse and Marin Hinkle as Juliet in The Shakespeare Theatre Company's 1993–1994 production of *Romeo and Juliet,* directed by Barry Kyle. Photo by Richard Anderson; **1055** *top* © Elliott Franks/ Arena Pal/Topham /The Image Works, Inc.; *bottom left* © Reuters/ Corbis; *right* © ArenaPal/Topham/The Image Works; **1058** © Robbie Jack/Corbis; **1061** Katie Atkinson as Juliet and Brian Weaver as Romeo in Shakespeare & Company's 2004 Spring Tour Production of *Romeo and Juliet.* Directed by Kevin Coleman. Photo by Kevin Sprague; **1065** © ArenaPal/Topham/The Image Works; **1070** © Chris Bennion Photography; **1075** © Don Pierce/University of Victoria Photographic Services; **1081** *top left* © Orlando-UCF Shakespeare Festival; *top right* Photo Reg Wilson: © Royal Shakespeare Company; *bottom* © The University of South Carolina Department of Theatre and Dance. Directed by Dennis Krausnick. Scenery by Kim Jennings. Lighting by Jim Hunte. Costumes by Kerith Wolfe; **1089** Chicago Shakespeare Theater's production of *Romeo and Juliet* toured to 14 communities in the Southeast United States, as part of the National Endowment for the Arts Shakespeare in American Communities initiative. Martin Yurek as Mercutio (left) and Ryan Kitley as Tybalt (right). Photo by: SteveLeonardPhotography.com, courtesy Chicago Shakespeare Theater; **1094** Photo by Peter Coombs: © Royal Shakespeare Company; **1105** *top left* © Scot J. Mann/Atlanta Stage Combat Studio; *top right* © Chris Bennion Photography; *bottom* © 2004 Susana Raab; **1115** © ArenaPal/Topham/The Image Works; **1121** *left* © Gary Wayne Golden; *center* The Seattle Repertory Theatre's 2003 *Romeo and Juliet* poster. © Sedgwick Rd.; *right* © Wieslaw Walkuski; **1125** © Don Pierce/ University of Victoria Photographic Services; **1131** Marin Hinkle as Juliet and Jay Goede as Romeo in The Shakespeare Theatre Company's 1993–1994 production of *Romeo and Juliet,* directed by Barry Kyle. Photo by Richard Anderson; **1135** *top left* Photo by Peter Coombs/© Royal Shakespeare Company; *bottom left* © ArenaPal/Topham/The Image Works, Inc.; *right* © Clive Barda/ArenaPal/Topham/The Image Works, Inc.; **1140** © ArenaPal/Topham/The Image Works, Inc.; **1145** © Bob Daemmrich/The Image Works, Inc.; **1148** Clip from *Romeo and Juliet* courtesy of Paramount Pictures; **1149** From *Romeo and Juliet* (1968), Paramount Pictures/Courtesy The Everett Collection; **1150** *top*

*left,* Clip from *Romeo and Juliet* courtesy of Paramount Pictures; *center left* From *Romeo and Juliet* (1968), Paramount Pictures/Courtesy The Everett Collection; *bottom* © Image 100/Alamy Images; *background* © Getty Images; **1151** *top left, top right, Romeo and Juliet,* Leonardo Di Caprio and Claire Danes, 1996. © 20th Century Fox/courtesy Everett Collection; *top center, Romeo and Juliet,* Claire Danes, 1996 © 20th Century Fox/courtesy Everett Collection; *bottom left, bottom center, bottom right* Still from *William Shakespeare's Romeo and Juliet* courtesy of Twentieth Century Fox. All rights reserved; *cork* © Artbeats; *frame* © Image Farm, Inc.; **1153** Courtesy Everett Collection; **1154, 1155** Clips from *Romeo and Juliet* courtesy of Paramount Pictures; **1156** From *Romeo and Juliet* (1968), Paramount Pictures/Courtesy The Everett Collection; **1158** © Digital Stock; **1159** *Ovid* (1500–1503). Fresco. Post-restoration. Duomo, Orvieto, Italy. Photo © Scala/Art Resource, New York; **1161** *Thisbe,* John William Waterhouse. Whitford and Hughes, London. © Bridgeman Art Library; **1166** © Jupiterimages Corporation; **1177** © Houghton Mifflin Harcourt; **1184** © Siede Preis/Getty Images.

## UNIT 11

**1185** *left, Scylla and Charybdis,* from *the Ulysses Cycle* (1580), Alessandro Allori. Fresco. Banca Toscana (Palazzo Salviati), Florence, Italy. Photo © Erich Lessing/Art Resource, New York; *right* © Corbis; **1186–1187** © Don Mason/Corbis; **1188** *top* © Corbis; *bottom, Procession of Trojan Horse into Troy,* G. D. Tiepolo. The Granger Collection, New York; **1189** Detail of a frieze representing a procession of mythological divinites, muses, graces, etc. Oil on plaster. Chateaux de Malmaison et Bois-Preau, Rueil-Malmaison, France. Photo © Gerard Blot/Art Resource, New York; **1190** *left* © 2004 Warner Bros./ Photofest; *right, Homer* (about 150 B.C.). Marble sculpture. Museo Nazionale Archeologico. Photo © akg-images; **1191** © GeoNova LLC; **1192** *bottom, Ulysses Returns Chryseis to Her Father,* Claude Lorrain. Louvre, Paris. Photo © Scala/Art Resource, New York; *top, Ulysses and the Sirens* (200s), Roman. Mosaic, 130 cm x 344 cm. Musée du Bardo, Tunis, Tunisia. © Bridgeman Art Library; **1193** *top left* Plaque with the return of Odysseus (about 460–450 B.C.). Classical Greek. Melian. Terracotta, Height 7 3/8". The Metropolitan Museum of Art, Fletcher Fund, 1930. (30.11.9) © 1982 The Metropolitan Museum of Art/Art Resource, New York; *top right, Odysseus Slaying the Suitors* (400s B.C.), Penelope Painter. Attic red figure painting on kylix. Height 20 cm. Inv F 2588. Antikensammlung, Staatliche Museen zu Berlin, Berlin. Photo by Juergen Liepe. © Bildarchiv Preussischer Kulturbesitz/Art Resource, New York; *bottom left, Ulysses* (1931–1932), Georges Braque. Pastel, 180.5 cm x 73.5 cm. Private Collection . Photo © Visual Arts Library/ Art Resource, New York. © 2007 Artists Rights Society (ARS), New York/ADAGP, Paris; *bottom right* Illustration by Innes Fripp in *Tales of the Gods and Heroes* by Sir G.W. Cox. © Edwin Wallace/Mary Evans Picture Library; **1194** *1* © Araldo de Luca/Corbis; *2* Detail of *Odysseus and Polyphemus* (1896), Arnold Böcklin. Tempera on wood, 65.5 cm x 148.5 cm. Private collection. © akg images; *3* Detail of *Ulysses Returns Chryseis to Her Father,* Claude Lorrain. Louvre, Paris. Photo © Scala/Art Resource, New York; *4* Detail of *Tilla Durieux as Circe* (about 1912–1913), Franz von Struck. Oil on paper, 53.5 cm x 46.5 cm. Private collection. Photo © akg-images; *5* Detail of *The Ship of Odysseus,* Francois-Louis Schmied. From *Homer, the Odyssey,* published Paris (1930–1933). Color lithograph. Private collection, The Stapleton Collection. © 2007 Artists Rights Society (ARS), New York/ADAGP, Paris. Photo © Bridgeman Art Library; **1202** © Liu Jin/AFP/Getty

Images; **1205** *The Ship of Odysseus,* Francois-Louis Schmied. From *Homer, the Odyssey,* published Paris (1930–1933). Color lithograph. Private collection, The Stapleton Collection. © 2007 Artists Rights Society (ARS), New York/ADAGP, Paris. Photo © Bridgeman Art Library; **1207** *Calypso* (about 1906), George Hitchcock. Oil on canvas, 111cm x 89 cm. © Indianapolis Museum of Art, Indianapolis, Indiana/ Bridgeman Art Library; **1211** © Araldo de Luca/Corbis; **1216** *The Cyclops* (about 1914) Odilon Redon. Oil on canvas. Kroller-Muller Museum, Otterlo, Netherlands. © Peter Will/SuperStock; **1220** Detail of *Odysseus and Polyphem* (1910), after L. du Bois-Reymond. Color print. From *Sagen des klasseschen Altertums* by Karl Becker, Berlin. © akg-images; **1224** Detail of *Tilla Durieux as Circe* (about 1912–1913), Franz von Struck. Oil on paper, 53.5 cm x 46.5 cm. Private collection. Photo © akg-images; **1227** *Ulysses Descending into the Underworld* (1500s), Giovanni Stradano. Fresco. Palazzo Vecchio, Florence. Photo © Scala/Art Resource, New York; **231** Detail from *Ulysses and the Sirens* (1891), John William Waterhouse. Oil on canvas, 100 cm x 201.7 cm. National Gallery of Victoria, Melbourne, Australia. © Bridgeman Art Library; **1237** *Scylla and Charybdis,* from the *Ulysses Cycle* (1580), Alessandro Allori. Fresco. Banca Toscana (Palazzo Salviati), Florence. © Erich Lessing/Art Resource, New York; **1240** AP/Wide World Photos; **1241** *Penelope Embroidering* (1903), Mrs. H. de Rudder. Photo © Mary Evans Picture Library; **1243** *Athene and Telemach,* from *Odyssey II* (1975), Marc Chagall. Lithograph on Arches paper. 16.9" x 13". Photograph by Gregory R. Staley. Courtesy the Georgetown Frame Shoppe. © 2007 Artists Rights Society (ARS), New York/ADAGP, Paris; **1245** Detail of *Goddess Athena Disguises Ulysses as Beggar.* Giuseppe Bottani. Civiche Racc d'Arte, Pavia, Italy. Photo © Dagli Orti /The Art Archive; **1246** *Ulysses and his son Telemachus* (A.D. first century). Mosaic, 31.5 cm. Kunsthistorisches Museum, Vienna. © Erich Lessing/Art Resource, New York; **1249** *Ulysses and His Dog* (about 1900). © Bettmann/Corbis; **1251** Detail of *Penelope Weeping over the Bow of Ulysses* (about 1779), Angelica Kauffmann. Wolverhampton Art Gallery (OP 531), Wolverhampton, United Kingdom; **1254** Illustration by N.C. Wyeth from *The Odyssey of Homer,* translated by George Herbert Palmer. © 1929 by N.C. Wyeth. © renewed 1957 by Carolyn Wyeth. Reprinted by permission of Houghton Mifflin Company. All rights reserved; **1257** Illustration by N.C. Wyeth from *The Odyssey of Homer,* translated by George Herbert Palmer. © 1929 by N.C. Wyeth. © renewed 1957 by Carolyn Wyeth. Reprinted by permission of Houghton Mifflin Company. All rights reserved; **1261** *Death of the Suitors: The Odyssey* (1944), Henry Spencer Moore. Black chalk, wash and ink on paper, 13.3 x 28.8 cm. Cecil Higgins Art Gallery, Bedford, Bedfordshire, United Kingdom. Photo © Bridgeman Art Library. © The Henry Moore Foundation. This image may not be reproduced or altered without prior consent from the Henry Moore Foundation; **1263** Plaque with the return of Odysseus (about 460–450 B.C.). Classical Greek. Melian. Terracotta, height 7 3/8". The Metropolitan Museum of Art, Fletcher Fund, 1930. (30.11.9) © 1982 The Metropolitan Museum of Art/Art Resource, New York; **1266** © Lindsay Hebberd/Corbis; **1270** © Neil Emmerson/Getty Images; **1275** *top* © Thinkstock Images/Jupiterimages Corporation; *center* © Jupiterimages Corporation; *bottom* © Suzanne Tucker/Shutterstock; **1288** © Siede Preis/Getty Images.

## UNIT 12

**1289** *left* © Zac Macaulay/Getty Images; *collage: top right* © Brand X Pictures; *top far right* © Rich Phalin/istockphoto.com; *left* © Getty

Images; *binoculars* Courtesy of the National Audubon Society; *bottom center 1* © Altrendo Nature/Altrendo/Getty Images; *bottom center 2* © Brand X Pictures/PunchStock; *bottom center 3, bottom right 3* © Michael and Patricia Fogden/Minden Pictures/Getty Images; *bottom right 1, 2* © Jupiterimages Corporation; **1290–1291** © Digital Vision Ltd./SuperStock; **1292** © Ken Chernus/Stone/Getty Images; **1296** © Google; **1297** Courtesy the Austin Humane Society; **1299** © Skokie Public Library; **1300** *left* © Getty Images; *right* © Brian Hagiwara/ Brand X Pictures; *left background, right background* © 1994 Artbeats; **1301** *top* Cover from *The Concise Geography Encyclopedia.* © Kingfisher Publications Plc 2005. Reprinted by permission of Kingfisher Publications Plc., an imprint of Houghton Mifflin Company. All rights reserved; *top inset* © Ron Watts/Corbis; *2nd from top , 4th from top* © Houghton Mifflin Company. All rights reserved; *2nd top-inset 1* © Larry Brownstein/Getty Images; *2nd top-inset 2* © Digital Vision/Getty Images; *2nd top-inset 3* © Cartesia/Getty Images; *2nd top-inset 4* © Alan & Sandy Carey/Getty Images; *2nd top-inset 5* © C Squared Studios/ Getty Images; *bottom inset* © musicman/ShutterStock; **1302** From Gale. *InfoTrac.* © Gale, a part of Cengage Learning, Inc. Reproduced by permission. www.cengage.com/permissions; **1303** *top* © Time Life Pictures/Getty Images; *center* © Wall Street Journal; *bottom* © American Veterinary Medical Association; **1307** © JupiterImages/Comstock Images/Alamy Ltd.; **1308** *left, center, right* © Getty Images; **1309** *photo* © Reuters/Corbis; *masthead* SOURCE: Dallas Morning News; **1313** © PictureNet/Corbis; **1314** © Jupiterimages Corporation; **1337** *top* © Araldo de Luca/Corbis; *bottom* © Photodisc/PunchStock.

## STUDENT RESOURCE BANK

**R3** *top* © Mike Zens/Corbis; *bottom* Illustration by Gary Hincks; **R6** *top* © Getty Images; *bottom* Illustration by SlimFilms; **R7** *top right* © Mapping Specialists; **R14** *top* © Paul Simcock/Brand X Pictures/ Jupiterimages Corporation; *bottom* © Getty Images; **R15** *top left* © Galen Rowell/Corbis; *right* © David Muench/Corbis; *bottom* Illustration by Gary Hincks; **R20** NASA; **R84** © Digital Vision/Getty Images; **R92** © Coneyl Jay/Getty Images.

## BACK COVER

(tl) © Taro Yamasaki/Time Life Pictures/Getty Images; (c) The Granger Collection, New York; (br) Photo by Mary Altaffer/AP/Wide World Photos; (bl) Detail of Ulysses from the Polyphemos group (second century B.C.), Hagesandroa, Polydoros, and Athenodoros. Sperlonga, Italy. © Araldo de Luca/Corbis.

Houghton Mifflin Harcourt has made every effort to locate the copyright holders of all copyrighted material in this book and to make full acknowledgment for its use. Omissions brought to our attention will be corrected in a subsequent edition.